NAME	WEB ADDRESS
Europa (European Union)	http://europa.eu.int/
Family and Medical Leave Act (FMLA) of 1993	http://www.dol.gov/dol/esa/
Federal Arbitration Act—9 U.S.C. § 1	http://www.law.cornell.edu/uscode/9/ch1.html
Federal Reserve Board Regulations	http://www.bog.frb.fed.us/frregs.htm
Federal Rules of Civil Procedure (1999)	http://www.law.cornell.edu/rules/frcp/overview.htm
Federal Trade Commission (FTC) Act, 15 U.S.C. § 41–58	http://www4.law.cornell.edu/uscode/15/41.html
Federal Trade Commission Act, 15 USC §§ 41–58	http://www4.law.cornell.edu/uscode/15/41.html
FedLaw	http://www.legal.gsa.gov/
Foreign Corrupt Practices Act—15 U.S.C. § 78dd-2	http://www4.law.cornell.edu/uscode/15/78dd-2.html
Franchising Online	http://www.abanet.org/forums/franchising/home.html
FranInfo	http://www.frannet.com/
General Business Forms	http://www.lectlaw.com/formb.htm
"Getting Around Barriers to Non-Compete Pacts"	http://wsgrgate.wsgr.com/library/libFileshtm.asp?file=barriers.htm
Independent Contractor Report	http://www.webcom.com/ic_rep
The Institute for Global Ethics	http://www.globalethics.org/
Internal Revenue Service (IRS)	http://www.irs.ustreas.gov/
International Academy of Mediators	http://www.iamed.org/
International Association of Constitutional Law	http://www.eur.nl/frg/iacl/indexe.htm
International Centre for Commercial Law	http://www.link.org/
International Chamber of Commerce (ICC) World Business Organization	http://www.iccwbo.org/
International Financial Law Review	http://www.lovellwhitedurrant.com
International Trade Law (ITL)	http://www.lexmercatoria.net/
ISO Online	http://www.iso.ch/
Johnson & Kindness	http://www.LawInfo.com/law/WA/christensen
Lanham Act	http://wwwsecure.law.cornell.edu/lanham/lanham.table.html
Law Journal EXTRA! (LJX!)—Corporate Law	http://www.ljx.com/practice/corporate/index.html
Lawyers Weekly	http://www.lawyersweekly.com/
The Legal Information Institute (LII)	http://www.law.cornell.edu/
Legal Information Institute (LII)—Decisions of the U.S. Supreme Court	http://supct.law.cornell.edu/supct/
Legal Information Institute (LII)—Bankruptcy Law Materials	http://www.law.cornell.edu/topics/bankruptcy.html
Legal Information Institute (LII)—Contract Law Materials	http://wwwsecure.law.cornell.edu/topics/contracts.html
Legal Information Institute (LII)—Criminal Law	http://www.law.cornell.edu/topics/criminal.html
Legal Information Institute (LII)—Estate and Gift Tax Law Materials	http://wwwsecure.law.cornell.edu/topics/estate_gift_tax.html
Legal Information Institute (LII)—Estates and Trusts Law Materials	http://wwwsecure.law.cornell.edu/topics/estates_trusts.html
Legal Information Institute (LII)—Land Use Law Materials	http://www.law.cornell.edu/topics/land_use.html
Legal Information Institute (LII)—Negotiable Instruments Law	http://www.law.cornell.edu/topics/negotiable.html
Legal Information Institute (LII)—Tort law	http://www.law.cornell.edu/topics/torts.html

SEVENTH EDITION

BUSINESS LAW

PRINCIPLES AND CASES IN THE LEGAL ENVIRONMENT

DANIEL V. DAVIDSON
Radford University

BRENDA E. KNOWLES
Indiana University South Bend

LYNN M. FORSYTHE
California State University, Fresno

WEST WEST LEGAL STUDIES IN BUSINESS
Thomson Learning™

Australia • Canada • Denmark • Japan • Mexico • New Zealand • Philippines
Puerto Rico • Singapore • South Africa • Spain • United Kingdom • United States

Business Law: Principles and Cases in the Legal Environment, 7th edition, by
Daniel V. Davidson, Brenda E. Knowles, Lynn M. Forsythe

Sr. Acquisitions Editor: Rob Dewey
Acquisitions Editor: Scott D. Person
Developmental Editor: Bob Sandman
Marketing Manager: Michael Worls
Production Manager: Sharon L. Smith
Manufacturing Coordinator: Charlene Taylor
Internal Design: Michael H. Stratton
Cover Design: Michael H. Stratton
Cover Illustration: SIS/Timothy Cook
Production House: The Left Coast Group, Inc.
Compositor: The Left Coast Group, Inc.
Printer: World Color–Versailles, KY

Printed in the United States of America
1 2 3 4 03 02 01 00

For more information contact West Legal Studies in Business, South-Western College
Publishing, 5101 Madison Road, Cincinnati, Ohio, 45227. Or you can visit our Internet site at
http://www.westbuslaw.com
For permission to use material from this text or product contact us by
• telephone: 1-800-730-2214
• fax: 1-800-730-2215
• web: http://www.thomsonrights.com

Library of Congress Cataloging-in-Publication Data

Davidson, Daniel V.
    Business law : principles and cases in the legal environment /
  Daniel V. Davidson, Brenda E. Knowles, Lynn M. Forsythe.—7th ed.
      p. cm.
    Includes bibliographical references and index.
    ISBN 0-324-04080-6 (hardcover)
    1. Commercial law—United States—Cases. I. Knowles, Brenda E. II.
  Forsythe, Lynn M. III. Title.

KF888 .D28 2000
346.7307—dc21   00-027072

To my wife, Dee, and my children, Jaime and Tara, thanks for your help and support! And to our reviewers and adopters, thanks for making it worth the time and the effort.

Daniel V. Davidson

To my mother, Madge L. Knowles, and my aunt, Helen I. McDonald, the two who have known me the longest, loved me anyway, and taught me the most.

Brenda E. Knowles

To Jim and Mike Poptanich for their love and patience, and to my extended family, especially Aileen and Robert Zollweg and Mary Helen and John Poptanich. And to our students, your ideas and suggestions are greatly appreciated.

Lynn M. Forsythe

BRIEF CONTENTS

C O N T E N T S

A BUSINESS-ORIENTED BUSINESS LAW TEXT

Business Law: Principles and Cases in the Legal Environment, Seventh Edition, offers students a business-oriented introduction to the legal and ethical topics that affect business. This perspective may seem obvious. After all, isn't a business law textbook by its very nature oriented toward the practice of business? While it might seem that they should, not all business law textbooks adopt such an orientation. Textbooks that typically teach the law, often clearly and in great detail, can fail to show students how the law will affect their future careers in the business world. Our goal as business law and legal environment instructors is not to train lawyers, but rather to train future businesspeople to anticipate and avoid legal problems. If legal problems arise, it is critical to know how to recognize the nature of these problems and work with a lawyer to achieve solutions. Legal problems, even lawsuits, are business problems that can be managed.

Our strategy in revising this, our seventh, edition is threefold:

- To present, in an accessible style, a current and comprehensive introduction to the legal topics relevant to business
- To demonstrate how these topics apply to the practice of business
- To provide an approach to legal analysis—often termed *critical thinking*—for addressing legal problems encountered in the practice of business

We also support more fully the teaching and learning process associated with using the text. Our association with West Legal Studies in Business allows us to offer a wide array of supplementary materials for instructors and students.

NEW COVERAGE IN THE SEVENTH EDITION

As we mentioned, our first goal is to present, in an accessible style, a current and comprehensive introduction to the legal topics relevant to business. Toward this goal, the book is divided into 10 parts based on traditional topical areas of undergraduate business law. We have made the following content changes and updates to the seventh edition.

Part I Foundations of Law. Part 1 presents an overview of law and the legal system. The seventh edition provides extended coverage of ethics and international law topics. In particular, Chapter 1, "Introduction to Law," provides a more detailed discussion of theories of jurisprudence and a new exhibit outlining these theories. Chapter 2, "Business Ethics," has an increased focus on the application of ethical theories in the practice of business, including the introduction and discussion of some additional ethical theories and a new exhibit comparing a number of these theories.

Part 2 The American Legal System. Part 2 examines the court system and the legal system used in the United States. We have moved the coverage of constitutional regulation of business to this section. This encourages a discussion of fundamental constitutional law principles while maintaining the focus on *business* and the application of the legal system to business problems and concerns. The material on dispute resolution has been reorganized into one chapter for this edition. This chapter combines the materials in two chapters of the previous edition and is designed to show the similarities and the differences in the various types of dispute resolution. We examine a civil trial and then look at a number of Alternative Dispute Resolution (ADR) approaches to the same problem. This section concludes with an examination of torts and business crimes, respectively. The criminal law coverage includes computer crimes. Simply put, the material in Part 2 has been rearranged to improve the flow of topics.

Part 3 Contracts. Part 3 examines the primary importance of contract law to business. The chapters contained here have been substantially updated, and some of the coverage has been relocated among the chapters. Chapter 9 is an introduction to contracts, discussing contract theories and the various areas included in contract law. Chapter 10 covers offer and acceptance, and Chapter 11 discusses consideration. Chapter 12 deals with voidable contract areas, "Contractual Capacity," while Chapter 13, "Legality of Subject Matter and Proper Form of Contracts," examines void agreements and unenforceable contracts, respectively. Chapter 14 discusses the rights of third persons and contract interpretation. The contract section ends with Chapter 15, "Contractual Discharge and Remedies."

Part 4 Sales and Leases. Part 4 introduces the Uniform Commercial Code (UCC) in significant detail and examines the law of sales from an international perspective. Part 4 now offers comparisons of Article 2 contracts with Article 2A contracts and the similarity in treatment between contracts for the sale of goods and contracts for the leasing of goods. Part 4 also provides a detailed examination of the international sale of goods, including increased coverage of the UN Convention on Contracts for the International Sale of Goods (CISG), Incoterms, and ISO 9000. There is also a brief discussion of several proposed United Nations Conventions that may soon be ratified and that will also affect international sales and other international business transactions.

Part 5 Negotiables. Part 5 discusses UCC Articles 3 (Revised), 4 (Revised), 4A, and 7. In addition, it includes a discussion of electronic fund transfers. This new coverage reflects the changes in negotiable instrument law with the revision of Articles 3 and 4 of the UCC.

Part 6 Debtor–Creditor Relations. Part 6 examines secured transactions under Article 9 of the UCC and the federal protections available under the Bankruptcy Reform Act of 1994. A new chapter has been added to this part. Chapter 28, "Other Credit Transactions," discusses various types of consumer debt besides secured transactions and bridges the gap between secured transactions and bankruptcy. In addition, this part includes increased coverage of the Bankruptcy Reform Act of 1994 and looks at the proposed Bankruptcy Reform Act of 1999, which Congress has not yet approved.

Part 7 Agency. Part 7 explains the agency relationship and its importance in conducting a business enterprise. Special emphasis is given to the liability of both the principal and the agent for contracts entered into by the agent and to the liability of both the employer and the employee for torts and crimes committed by the employee. Policy reasons for the rules are addressed. Protection of the employer's confidential information and covenants not to compete are also discussed.

Part 8 Business Organizations. Part 8 treats the various types of business organizations in a unique manner. Rather than have separate chapters dealing with the various organizations, the text treats the organizations in a compare-and-contrast fashion within the chapters. The emphasis is no longer on how the various types of business organizations should be implemented, but rather on why a particular form should be chosen. The coverage includes an examination of the limited liability company (LLC) and the limited liability partnership (LLP), as well as the traditional business organizations: proprietorship, partnership, limited partnership, and corporation. Coverage of the Revised Uniform Partnership Act is increased, since it has been adopted by more states. We also include thorough discussions of franchising in Chapter 37 and securities regulation in Chapter 38.

Part 9 Government Regulation of Business. Part 9 addresses the regulatory issues regularly faced by businesses, including coverage of antitrust law, consumer protection, environmental protection, and labor and fair employment law. Chapter 40, "Consumer Protection," is devoted entirely to consumer law and stresses concepts that relate back to Chapter 28, "Other Credit Transactions," from Part 6. There is also one chapter devoted to environmental law—Chapter 41, "Environmental Protection"—that addresses most of the major environmental statutes. This coverage includes a discussion of some of the policy reasons behind the statutes and the penalties to be faced for violations. The final chapter in this section is "Labor and Fair Employment Practices," a detailed examination of the rights and responsibilities of management and its employees.

Part 10 Property Protection. Part 10 examines real and personal property law and "wealth protection." Part 10 also offers updated coverage on intellectual property law. The first chapter in this part discusses real property, government regulation of real property, and the types of joint ownership. Transfer on death ownership has been added to this edition. The second chapter examines personal property and bailments. The third chapter addresses intellectual property, including a discussion of copyright law and of computers and the law. The part and the text conclude with a consideration of techniques for transferring wealth, including wills, estates, and trusts. Recent changes in transfer tax laws are included.

NEW AND IMPROVED APPLICATIONS

Our second goal for this revision is to demonstrate how the legal topics presented here apply to the practice of business. Toward this goal, *Business Law* offers the following features, many of them unique to this text.

Court Cases

Each chapter contains three court cases primarily in the language of the court. Cases are organized into the following parts:

- Facts—the facts of the case
- Issue(s)—the issues, in the form of questions, on which the decision hinges
- Holding—the court's answer to the issue(s)
- Reasoning—the reasoning the court used in reaching its decision

We have made an effort in this edition to include more judicial language in the cases. Our selection of cases includes both classic, landmark opinions and current, cutting-edge cases. In addition, all of the court cases end with a Business Considerations question and an Ethical Considerations question. These questions illustrate the impact of court cases on business and how business decisions may lead to litigation. Ethical considerations show how ethics constantly affect decision making. Limiting ethical concerns to a cursory examination in an obligatory ethics chapter profits no one; rather, an emphasis on ethics should be an integral part of business decision making.

Call-Image Technology (CIT) Business Application Thread Case

We have included an integrated, continuous business "thread" case, or scenario, throughout the text. This "thread" case profiles the experiences of a hypothetical videophone business, Call-Image Technology (CIT), owned and operated by a "local" family known to the students. Each chapter begins with an Agenda that highlights the major legal issues relevant to CIT. Within each chapter there are three CIT Application Boxes that address particular legal issues and call for students to offer guidance to the firm.

Each application box is categorized by the relevant functional area of business—management, manufacturing, finance and accounting, sales, marketing, and international business. Finally, application boxes include Business Considerations and Ethical Considerations questions, asking the students to go beyond CIT's problem to decide how the type of problem faced might affect other business concerns. See page 2 for an introduction to the CIT business application thread case.

Resources for Business Law Students

Resources for Business Law Students, included in every chapter, highlight World Wide Web sites of particular relevance to the study of business law and legal environment. For convenience, Web sites are listed by their name, the resources of particular interest, and the address.

You Be the Judge Boxes

"You Be the Judge" boxes, included in every chapter, highlight newsworthy scenarios involving legal or ethical problems. They illustrate the real-world legal problems of businesses. Students, using the material in the chapter, are asked to decide the outcome of the scenario. Students have the opportunity to think critically and to discuss these problems in class; also, the problems provide potential writing assignments or team projects for students. Finally, the You Be the Judge boxes include Business Considerations and Ethical Considerations questions, asking the students to go beyond the given scenario and decide how the type of problem faced might affect other business concerns.

Discussion Questions, Case Problems and Writing Assignments

Each chapter concludes with 10 discussion questions, five legal case problems, one business applications case, one ethics applications case, and one critical thinking case. The legal case problems ask students to test their understanding of principles and terms covered in the chapter, and the business applications, ethics applications, and critical thinking problems ask students to apply these concepts to business situations. All the end-of-chapter materials can be used as study tools in reviewing the material, as class or small-group discussion material, or for writing assignments.

SUPPLEMENTAL RESOURCES

The seventh edition of *Business Law* now has a site on the World Wide Web devoted to teaching and learning resources for the text (http://davidson.westbuslaw.com). Come visit to see for yourself.

The following supplemental resources are available with the seventh edition:

- *Study Guide to Accompany Business Law: Principles and Cases in the Legal Environment* (0-324-04294-9).
- *Telecourse Study Guide* (0-324-04297-3)
- *Instructor's Manual* (0-324-04298-1)
- *Test Bank* (0-324-06169-2)
- ExamView testing software (0-324-06170-6)
- Microsoft PowerPoint Lecture Review Slides (download at http://davidson.westbuslaw.com/)
- Telecourse Videos—30 half-hour telecourse videos, developed by INTELECOM in conjunction with the third edition of *Business Law,* provide coverage for key topics in business law. Contact your local Thomson Learning/West Legal Studies Sales Representative for more details.

- *The New York Times Guide to Legal Studies in Business* (ISBN 0-324-04160-8), by Marianne Jennings and Jamie Murphy. More than just a printed collection of articles, this guide gives you access, via password, to an online collection of the most current and relevant *New York Times* articles that are continually posted as news breaks. Also included are articles from *CyberTimes,* the online technology section of the *New York Times* on the Web. Correlation guides for all West/South-Western legal studies in business texts are available on the South-Western/*New York Times* Web site at http://nytimes.swcollege.com.

- InfoTrac College Edition. This online library contains hundreds of scholarly and popular periodicals, including *American Business Law Journal, Journal of International Business Studies, Environmental Law,* and *Ethics.* A package can be created that provides students access to InfoTrac College Edition when they purchase this textbook. Contact your local Thomson Learning/West Legal Studies Sales Representative to learn more.

- Videos. Qualified adopters using this text have access to the entire library of West videos, a vast selection covering most business law issues. There are some restrictions, and if you have questions, please contact your local Thomson Learning/West Legal Studies Sales Representative or visit http://www. westbuslaw.com/video_library.html.

A Note on AACSB Curricular Standards

The AACSB curricular standards relevant to business law and the legal environment of business state that curricula should include ethical and global issues; the influence of political, social, legal and regulatory, environmental, and technology issues; and the impact of demographic diversity on organizations. We believe *Business Law: Principles and Cases in the Legal Environment* uniquely satisfies these standards.

First, global issues are treated in depth in two chapters: Chapter 3, "International Law," and Chapter 20, "International Sales of Goods: CISG" (more than any other current business law text). Also, we have revised Chapter 2, "Business Ethics," to reflect more of the application of ethical theories than the theories themselves. Ethics questions also appear following court cases, You Be the Judge boxes, CIT business application boxes, and at the ends of chapters.

Second, we have revised the text with the intent of creating a book that is intuitive, engaging, and oriented toward providing the legal skills students will need in the business world. Hence, the contents of the book stretch beyond the mere presentation of "legal topics" to encompass the spectrum of "political, social, legal, regulatory, environmental, and technological issues." The pedagogical features are designed to augment this content.

Finally, the attention to applications, evidenced in the Agenda, CIT business application thread case, and the You Be The Judge cases uniquely contributes to a showing of how demographic diversity affects organizations. In the CIT case, the Kochanowskis—founders of a family business—must understand the cultural and political challenges that a larger domestic and international market (and workforce) pose for them. These include issues ranging from employee privacy to labor law, from employee use of CIT computers to sexual harassment. By following the case, students are immersed in these problems and are asked to offer advice as questions arise. This encourages sensitivity and an understanding of other points of view.

On another level, the Kochanowskis (and, vicariously, the students) learn that successful businesses today are often cross-functional. In this case, the Kochanowskis need to recognize how the law applies to marketing, sales, management, finance and accounting, and manufacturing, and they must be able to act on this knowledge. The students, by assuming an advisory role with CIT, have a unique glimpse at the cross-functional nature of many business activities today. *Business Law* supports the current trend toward integrating business disciplines.

ACKNOWLEDGMENTS

Writing a textbook is always an arduous undertaking, even if the text is "merely" a revision of a previous edition. This edition has been no different, and in many ways it has been more difficult. There have been numerous substantive changes in the law since the last edition, and each of these warrented our attention. There are also several areas that are in a state of upheaval as we go into print, and trying to be as up-to-date as possible while meeting a production deadline can be a problem for the entire production team.

This edition of the book would not have been possible without the help, assistance, and guidance of our developmental editor, Bob Sandman. Bob is always there when we need him. His good humor, his patience, and his support have been invaluable to us. Sharon Smith has also been tremendous. She has provided advice when needed and has assisted Bob in helping us put together this book.

Chris Schabow and the staff at The Left Coast Group have done an excellent job. They have been cooperative and supportive throughout the process, and their attention to detail helped to create a professional and integrated text.

Each of the authors owes a hearty "thank you" and a sincere "well done" to the other two authors. Each provided feedback, (positive) criticism, and support to the others during the hectic days of reading copyedited pages and page proofs. Each of us brings a unique personality to the process, and we have learned how and when to merge our talents to produce the best book possible. As authors, we have been a team for quite some time, working together through seven editions of the text. We each write about an equal number of chapters, and we each have input into the chapters written by the other authors. We sincerely believe that our group effort has been successful and that the sum of our contributions is greater than the parts. We hope you enjoy using this book as much as we have enjoyed preparing it.

A special thanks to our families. They put up with the late nights and the short deadlines and provide support and suggestions to help us get through the process every time we revise the text. Without their support and encouragement, we would never be able to accomplish our goal.

Finally, a sincere thank you to the following reviewers, whose suggestions, criticism, questions, observations, and keen and insightful commentaries on our work helped us maintain our focus and write a text that preserves content but is user-friendly, readable, and enjoyable:

Khamis Bilbeisi
Troy State University Dothan

Sue Cunningham
Rowan-Cabarrus Community College

H. Daniel Holt
Southeastern Illinois College

Edward Kissling
Ocean County College

Martha Wright Sartoris
North Hennepin Community College

Edward L. Welsh, Jr.
Mesa Community College

A B O U T   T H E   A U T H O R S

Daniel V. Davidson

Daniel V. Davidson received both his B.S. in Business Administration and his J.D. from Indiana University School of Law, Bloomington. He is an inactive member of the Connecticut Bar Association. He has taught at Central Connecticut State College in New Britain; St. Cloud State University in Minnesota; the University of Arkansas, Fayetteville; and California State University, Fresno. He recently finished serving as the Associate Dean of the College of Business and Economics at Radford University in Virginia and is Professor of Business Law.

Professor Davidson has published numerous articles on business law, the teaching of business law, and business ethics. He was named the Outstanding Teacher of the Year at Central Connecticut State College. In 1979 he received the Outstanding Faculty Award from Beta Alpha Psi, and in 1980 he was named the Razorback Award winner as the Outstanding Business Professor, both at the University of Arkansas. In 1984, Professor Davidson was awarded the Meritorious Performance Award at California State University, Fresno.

Professor Davidson is a member of Alpha Kappa Psi, Beta Gamma Sigma, Sigma Iota Epsilon, and Beta Alpha Psi. He is also a member of the Academy of Legal Studies in Business and its Southern Regional. He has held all of the offices in the Southern Regional, including President, and is currently serving as the Senior Advisory Editor for the *Southern Law Journal* and the *Proceedings* of the region's annual meeting.

Brenda E. Knowles

Brenda E. Knowles received a B.A. *magna cum laude* from the University of Evansville, an M.A. from Miami University, and a J.D. from the Indiana University School of Law, Bloomington. She is Professor of Business Law and Director of the Honors Program at Indiana University South Bend, where she has been the recipient of the Amoco Foundation Excellence in Teaching Award, a systemwide, all-university teaching award. She has received other systemwide and divisional citations for excellent teaching. She also has been active in FACET, the faculty colloquium on excellence in teaching, which is a systemwide, all-university effort to encourage effective teaching and learning in the academic community. In 1995, Professor Knowles was named Director of the Honors Program (a position theretofore always held by liberal arts faculty members). In 1997, the Student Association at Indiana University South Bend chose her as the campus's "Outstanding Educator."

Professor Knowles specializes in research on employment discrimination, pedagogy, and intellectual property law. She publishes her work in professional journals and has won an award for her research. In addition, she has been recognized both nationally and locally for her professional and civic accomplishments, most recently through the W. George Pinnell Award for outstanding service to Indiana University.

Professor Knowles is an active member of the Academy of Legal Studies in Business and of several regionals. More specifically, having held every office, she is a past president of both the ALSB and the Tri-State Regional. Professor Knowles presently serves as the Chairperson of the ALSB's Research and Teaching Mentorship Programs, and, in 1994, she won the ALSB's Master Teacher Award. In 1998, she received the ALSB's Senior Faculty Excellence Award. Moreover, she is a member of Beta Gamma Sigma. She is licensed to practice law in Indiana and is a member of the American, Indiana State, and St. Joseph County Bar Associations.

Lynn M. Forsythe

Lynn M. Forsythe received her B.A. from the Pennsylvania State University and her J.D. from the University of Pittsburgh School of Law. She has passed the bar examination in the states of California and Pennsylvania. She is Professor of Business Law at the Craig School of Business at California State University, Fresno. Professor Forsythe has also held administrative positions, including Director of Graduate Business Programs, Interim Department Chair, and Co-Chair of the AACSB Reaccredidation Committee. She currently is the Assessment Coordinator for the Legal Environment option.

Professor Forsythe is the author of numerous articles on business law and business law pedagogy. She has held the positions of Editor-in-chief, Staff Editor, and Reviewer for *The Journal of Legal Studies Education,* and is currently the Advisory Editor for this journal. She received the 1992 School of Business Faculty Award for Educational Innovation and previously was awarded a university Meritorious Performance Award. She has been an estate and gift tax attorney for the Internal Revenue Service and has taught business law, administrative law, government regulation of business, real estate law, business ethics, estate planning, and business and society.

Professor Forsythe is a member of Beta Gamma Sigma and Alpha Kappa Psi. She has been active in the American Bar Association, for which she chaired subcommittees and panels, including an American Law Institute–American Bar Association advanced program. She is active in the Academy of Legal Studies in Business, for which she served as academic program coordinator for the 1983 meeting, liaison to the National Conference of Commissioners on Uniform State Laws, a member of the Executive Committee, co-chairperson, and chairperson of its Business Ethics Section. She has held all the offices, including President, in the Western Regional Academy of Legal Studies in Business.

FOUNDATIONS OF LAW

Ignorance of the law is no excuse. The basic truth of this old adage seems simple and obvious. However, the simplicity of the truth hides the complexity of the law. Each citizen—and resident—of this country has "constructive notice" of the law. This means that each person is expected to be aware of, and to abide by, all the laws of the land. Yet the enormity of "the law" makes such an expectation futile. No one person can know *all* of the law, but every person is expected to obey it. Thus, a built-in contradiction exists in the system.

Part I of this book will first help you understand what law is, how it operates in the United States, and how it affects business. Next, this part will introduce you to business ethics. Finally, it will introduce the international legal environment in which business operates.

Each part of this book will shed light on and offer insights into aspects of the law. A thorough knowledge of law takes years of specialized study, and this text will not provide it. But it will begin to open the doors of understanding for you, and help remove the "ignorance of the law [that] is no excuse."

P A R T

1

CALL-IMAGE TECHNOLOGY NEEDS YOU!

What Is Call-Image Technology?

To own your own business, to be an entrepreneur, is the dream of many people, and Tom and Anna Kochanowski are living this dream through their own videophone company, Call-Image Technology (CIT). CIT began as a family business, with Tom and Anna's children being its first employees, but it has grown quickly. CIT now designs, produces, manufactures, markets, and sells "Call-Image," its interactive videophone, in the United States and around the world.

While CIT has expanded, it still is a small business at heart, and relies on the services of its family and friends for help. Lately, Tom and Anna have found more and more of their time consumed by legal questions: What laws govern the sales of Call-Image? How can CIT protect its trade secrets? How should CIT handle employee and customer disputes? What elements does CIT need in its contracts? What does CIT need to be aware of when acquiring financing and capital? CIT retains the services of a lawyer, Amy Chen, a family friend, but Tom and Anna realize they cannot seek Amy's advice in every decision CIT makes. For this reason, they need a consultant with training in business law matters to help CIT avoid legal problems before they arise, identify them when they do arise, and then intelligently communicate these legal problems to Amy Chen to find solutions. This consultant is you, and CIT needs your help!

Your Role in Call-Image Technology

Call-Image Technology, of course, is a fictional company, but it does allow you to see how the legal concepts discussed in each chapter apply to the business world. Chapters begin with an "Agenda," which highlights the major issues relevant to a small business. This agenda introduces you to the key concepts in the chapter. Within chapters, particular issues involving CIT require your help. As in the business world, you are asked to give your advice, based on what you have learned, on how to avoid legal problems, how to manage problems should they arise, and how to work with attorneys to solve problems. You are not asked to be a lawyer, but rather you an enlightened consultant on business law issues. You will become an enlightened consultant as you progress through the text. The issues you are asked to help CIT with involve many different functional areas of business—management, manufacturing, finance and accounting, sales and marketing, international business—and even a few personal legal issues. Hence, the text, and this course, will help you understand not only the law but your other business courses as well.

The Product and the People Behind Call-Image Technology

Call-Image   Call-Image is a videophone that allows parties in a conversation to speak and to see each other simultaneously on a 6" × 6" monitor.

Anna Kochanowski   Anna Kochanowski, a founder of CIT with her husband, Tom, is a former engineer for a major fiber optics firm and the primary designer of Call-Image. Anna works full-time for CIT.

Tom Kochanowski   Tom Kochanowski, a founder of CIT with his wife, Anna, is a 25-year veteran of the business world, working primarily in marketing and sales. Tom continues to work part-time in the marketing department of a major telecommunications firm and devotes free time to planning the marketing strategy and managing the various other aspects of CIT.

Amy Chen   Amy Chen, a successful attorney and friend of the Kochanowski family, provides legal advice and performs legal functions for CIT. Amy has a general practice.

Donna Kochanowski   Donna Kochanowski, Anna and Tom's 27-year-old daughter, is a certified public accountant (CPA). Donna offers financial advice and works part-time for CIT.

Julio Rodriguez   Julio Rodriguez, Donna Kochanowski's fiancé, is also a CPA. Julio offers financial advice to CIT, although he is not an employee.

Dan Kochanowski   Dan Kochanowski, Anna and Tom's 23-year-old son, works full-time for CIT. Dan's background is in engineering, but he assists Tom and Anna in all aspects of the business.

John Kochanowski   John Kochanowski, Anna and Tom's 20-year-old son, works part-time for CIT. John is pursuing management/finance studies at a local college.

Lindsay Kochanowski   Lindsay Kochanowski, Anna and Tom's 16-year-old daughter, attends high school. Lindsay works for CIT after school and on weekends.

1

INTRODUCTION TO LAW

A G E N D A

The Kochanowskis need to understand what type(s) of law will influence Call-Image Technology (CIT). Will CIT be subject to federal regulation? To state regulation? To administrative regulation? How will these types of regulations affect CIT? Most of the legal issues in business law involve civil law. Obviously, the family needs to concern itself with numerous civil law topics. Should the family also be concerned with criminal law? How does criminal law influence business?

What happens when a person in a lawsuit asks the court for a particular action as the remedy? Why are lawyers and courts so interested in prior court decisions?

These and other questions need to be addressed as you cover the material in this chapter of the text. Be prepared! You never know when one of the Kochanowskis will need your help or advice.

O U T L I N E

WHAT IS THE RELATIONSHIP AMONG LAW, ORDER, AND JUSTICE?

Law

This book is about understanding the law of business. Before we begin our study, however, we must answer a basic question: What is *law*? Many definitions exist, ranging from the philosophical to the practical. Plato (427–347? B.C.), a Greek philosopher who studied and wrote in the area of philosophical idealism, said law was *social control*. Sir William Blackstone (1723–1780), an English judge and legal commentator, said law was rules specifying what was right and what was wrong. For our purposes, however, we will define law as *rules that must be obeyed*. People who disobey these rules are subject to sanctions that may result in their having to do something they would not voluntarily do such as paying a fine or going to jail. Our society has many kinds of rules, but not all rules can be considered "law." A rule in baseball, for example, says that after three strikes, the batter is out. This rule, however, is not law. All laws are rules, but all rules are not laws. What differentiates a law from a rule? Simply stated, *enforceability* separates laws from rules. People who do not follow the rules in baseball are not arrested or taken to court. They are simply ejected from the game. In contrast, people who break laws can be held accountable for their actions through court-imposed sanctions.

Many different types of legal rules exist. One legal rule defines a specific way to create a legal document, for example, a contract or a will. A second forbids certain kinds of conduct; **criminal law** is an excellent example of this. A third type of legal rule was created to compensate persons who have been injured because someone else breached a duty. For example, when an automobile manufacturer negligently builds a car, and the manufacturer's **negligence** is the direct cause of an injury, the manufacturer may have to pay the injured person monetary damages. Rules about creating legal documents, defining crimes, and specifying legal duties are generally rules about **substantive law**. Finally, rules exist that our legislative bodies and courts establish to take care of their everyday business. For example, all states have a rule concerning the maximum number of days defendants have before they must answer a civil lawsuit; this is an example of **procedural law**. The distinction between substantive law and procedural law is important and will be revisited throughout our discussion of business law.

We will view the law as a body of rules that establish a certain level of social conduct, or of *duties* that members of the society must honor. One way to view these duties is shown in Exhibit 1.1. The party or parties who are injured can seek enforcement of their rights in courts of law. Enforcement consists of one of three legal remedies: the defendant (1) paying money as damages or as a fine, (2) being subject to a court order that directs a person to do or not do something (an **injunction**), or (3) going to jail or prison.

Order

The law usually considers an *order* as a legal command issued by a judge. But we are not concerned with order in that sense. Another definition of *order* is the absence of chaos. *Chaos* is confusion and total disorganization. If the laws of a society were always followed and never broken, perfect order would result. No crime would exist, and everyone would be safe. History, however, tells us that no society with perfect order has ever existed.

Criminal law
The body of law dealing with public wrongs called crimes.

Negligence
Failure to do something a reasonable person would do, or doing something a reasonable and prudent person would not do.

Substantive law
The portion of law that creates and defines legal rights. It is distinct from the law that defines how laws should be enforced in court.

Procedural law
Methods of enforcing rights or obtaining compensation for the violation of rights.

Injunction
A court order prohibiting a person from doing a certain thing or ordering that some particular thing be done.

E X H I B I T   1.1 | **Duties in a Society**

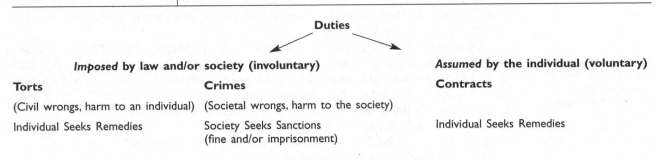

Duties

Imposed by law and/or society (involuntary)

Torts

(Civil wrongs, harm to an individual)

Individual Seeks Remedies

Crimes

(Societal wrongs, harm to the society)

Society Seeks Sanctions
(fine and/or imprisonment)

Assumed by the individual (voluntary)

Contracts

Individual Seeks Remedies

The words *law* and *order* are often linked together. It is natural to link them because, when the law is followed, there will be order. However, precisely because the law is not followed all the time by all the people, perfect order does not exist. Society is always *somewhat* chaotic and disorganized. One of the reasons people do not always obey the law is that they may not be aware of what the law is. However, our legal system *presumes* that everyone *is* aware of the law and what it requires. If a society did not presume that everyone knows the law, it would be more chaotic than it already is. In that case, individuals accused of breaking the law would have an excellent defense: They could argue that they did not know they were breaking the law, and the society would then have to prove the person's knowledge before sanctions could be imposed. The presumption that everyone knows the law, that "ignorance of the law is no excuse," creates an incentive for all citizens to study the law. Our educational system plays an important role in educating us about the law.

Justice

Justice is a difficult term to define. When we speak of *justice*, we normally mean "fairness." Although perfect justice *is* fair, there is more to the concept of justice than merely being fair. Justice, as used in the Anglo-American legal system, refers to both the *process* and the *results* obtained in the process. Courts try to *administer* justice in conformity with the laws of the territory. From a social perspective, justice may be affected as much—or even more—by appearances than by results. Thus, lawyers are required to avoid the *appearance* of impropriety in their dealings. If the public perceives that the system is not just, they will be less likely to accept the results the system provides. This, in turn, might lead to the destruction of the order developed in a society through its laws and their enforcement.

The ultimate goal of any legal system should be attaining justice by continually searching for fairness and equity. Fairness is less abstract than justice, and thus it is easier to address on a practical level. Most people have a basic concept of "fairness" that can be applied to any given situation, even though those same people may not have a similar concept of "justice." For example, when you see a bully pick on a victim, you probably believe that this conduct is not fair. In this type of situation, the conduct is clearly unfair, and it also is clearly unjust. In most situations, however, it is difficult to determine what a fair-and-just result would be. For example, suppose that a wealthy individual is accused of committing a crime. That person hires the best attorneys he or she can find, and—in a very public trial—is found not guilty by the jury. Many people might question whether this result is *fair*. However, the process followed in the legal system assures—at least to some extent—that the result of the trial is *just*.

Different theories of justice exist, causing additional confusion. In Anglo-American law, there are two primary theories of justice: **commutative justice** and **distributive justice.** This distinction originated with Aristotle.[1] In our legal system, each theory is followed in some situations and not followed in others. By using both types of justice, the courts try to mete out a form of justice that is perceived as fair to the public and that allows for some flexibility by the courts. While reading cases in the text, ask yourself which theory of justice is being applied by the courts.

Commutative justice attempts to give every person that which is due to him or her. It does this by placing everyone on an equal footing. Commutative justice ignores personal worth, merit, and social class. In most situations, misdemeanors are punished under the concept of commutative justice. All speeders are treated the same, regardless of factors such as income, profession, type of automobile, and so forth. Much of contract law uses a commutative justice perspective.

Distributive justice attempts to treat each person as that person should be treated, taking into account the differences among people. It does *not* consider all people equally deserving or equally blameworthy. It assigns to a person the rewards he or she deserves based on personal merit or services provided. Different types of distributions may be appropriate in various situations; for example, distribution of salary may be based on contribution to the company, while distribution of food stamps may be based on need. Distributive justice also assigns the punishment that the specific crime deserves. In criminal law, distributive justice is often used in felony cases, especially when the judge has a significant amount of discretion in sentencing. Suppose two people attempt an armed robbery together and get caught, arrested, tried, and convicted. One may be sentenced to a much longer jail term than the other. Why? Perhaps one person planned the crime, and the other person was persuaded to participate. Perhaps one person is a first-time criminal, and the other has been convicted of five prior armed robberies. Distributive justice might also be used as a philosophical basis for affirmative action programs, which attempt to make up for past unconstitutional discrimination. Some ethicists focus their attention on issues of distributive justice.

Commutative justice
The attempt to give all persons identical treatment based on the assumption that equal treatment is appropriate. Individual differences are not considered.

Distributive justice
The attempt to allocate justice in a way that considers individual differences.

The Nexus: Practicability

What we often refer to as "the Law" is really a system consisting of law, order, and justice. Combined, they make up the U.S. legal system. All the elements should balance in perfect equilibrium so that one element does not adversely affect any other. If we had total order, we would have very little justice; if we had total justice, we might have very little order. The *nexus* (link between elements) of the two concepts is the point of *practicability*. For example, to achieve perfect justice with respect to traffic violations, we need jury trials with counsel to ascertain precisely whether a driver did in fact violate the speed limit. However, the costs of such a venture are so prohibitive that no municipality or other local jurisdiction can afford to pay for it. As a result, most traffic courts tend to achieve "assembly line" justice rather than perfect justice.

THE LAW AS AN ARTIFICIAL LANGUAGE SYSTEM

Many terms used in the law are also used in everyday speech, but often they have totally different meanings in the law. This text will define the terms for you in the chapter, in notes in the margins, and/or in the glossary at the back of the book. The list of terms may seem endless: *offer, acceptance, consideration, guaranty, employee,* and so on. How many times do you use the word *consideration* or *employee* without intending the legal meaning? Because terms may have different connotations within the law, be on guard for subtle shifts in meaning. If you are in doubt, read the passage again or check the glossary for a definition.

In addition, it is impossible to discuss the law intelligently without reference to some words that are only defined in the law. Examples of this specialized vocabulary include *estoppel, appellee, assignee, bailee, causa mortis, caveat venditor, quid pro quo,* and *codicil.* You make no assumptions when you study a foreign language; therefore, make none about the law. Remember these three rules about our artificial language system to improve your mastery of this material:

1. Legal terms may appear to be synonymous with everyday words, but they are not.
2. Legal terms may have more than one legal meaning.
3. Some legal terms have no relation to everyday language.

THE ORIGINS OF THE LAW OF BUSINESS

The law of business began as a private system administered outside regular law courts in England. It began as rules observed by businesspeople in their dealings with one another. It was called the **law merchant** because it was administered in courts established in the various merchant guilds, commonly called Merchant Courts. Eventually, it was integrated into the English **common law** court system. It is now recognized and enforced by the courts. We will generally consider the law merchant as part of the common law. Today, the law of business includes contracts, sales, negotiable instruments, secured transactions, agency, partnerships, and corporations, among other topics.

WHY STUDY THE LAW OF BUSINESS?

This textbook may be called a primer in **preventive law.** The focus is how to avoid legal problems and how to resolve them as quickly as possible when they do arise. *Remedial law* is also an important aspect of the law. When a particular problem begins to arise, legislatures or courts may anticipate its future development and attempt to resolve the problem. The lawmakers, however, cannot predict or prevent every potential legal problem.

You should understand the legal implications of what you are doing in your roles as businessperson and consumer. Otherwise, many actions will have unexpected legal consequences. If you understand the issues raised here and can apply your knowledge to particular business situations, you may save yourself great expense later. It is helpful to understand the legal environment in which a business operates. If business executives "scan" their environment, they can often identify trends. Sometimes a business or industry may impact the direction of the change, if it is alert to the changing environment. A business that takes direct action is called

Law merchant
Those rules of trade and commerce used by merchants in England beginning in the Middle Ages.

Common law
Unwritten law, which is based on custom, usage, and court decisions; distinct from statute law, which consists of laws passed by legislatures.

Preventive law
Law designed to prevent harm or wrongdoing before it occurs.

Proactive
Identifying potential problem areas and participating in resolving them.

proactive. For example, industries may decide to self-regulate in order to persuade the legislature that government regulation is unnecessary. The video game industry created a rating system for games to avoid legislative action. In general, business is a very practical subject. As you will see, the law of business is just as practical.

Another reason to study the law of business is that it will help you develop valuable decision-making skills. Legal style of analysis can be used in business decision making. This study will also sensitize you to particular situations in which you may need the assistance of a lawyer. Legal counsel can be helpful in preventive law. For example, in the sale of commercial real estate, you will discover that the buyer or seller needs the assistance of a lawyer *before,* rather than after, an earnest money contract is signed.

1.1 | MANAGEMENT

CALL-IMAGE TECHNOLOGY

HEALTH INSURANCE FOR CIT EMPLOYEES

When the Kochanowskis first began the firm, they gave virtually no consideration to providing health insurance benefits for the employees of CIT. When the employees were family members who were covered under the family's health insurance plan, there was no need to give the matter any consideration. However, as the firm has grown and expanded, it has hired personnel who are not family members. The employees have asked Tom about a benefits package that would include health insurance coverage. They have also asked Tom to see if any health insurance coverage acquired for the employees can be made convertible into private coverage or portable to a new employer if any employee changes jobs. Tom has asked you whether the firm should provide health insurance for the employees, and what the consequences of providing—or not providing—such coverage would be. What advice will you give him?

BUSINESS CONSIDERATIONS Should the Kochanowskis provide health insurance as an employee benefit for their employees? What are the business implications—including taxation—if such coverage is provided? What are the legal implications if such coverage is not provided?

ETHICAL CONSIDERATIONS Would it be ethical for the family to provide coverage for family members but not for other employees? What are the ethical implications of not offering insurance coverage for one's employees merely to increase profits for the firm?

WHAT ARE THE NEEDS OF A LEGAL SYSTEM?

The Need to Be Reasonable

A legal system must be reasonable. It should rely on reasonable conclusions based on facts. Speeding laws are reasonable because one can prove that higher speeds on busy streets are related to higher numbers of accidents.

In addition to being reasonable, laws must be applied in a reasonable manner. A law stating that Juana, a consumer, will have property taken away from her if she does not pay for the property is certainly reasonable. It would be unreasonably applied if Juana stopped paying for the property and, without notice or warning, Ramiro, the seller, removed the property. Juana should first be informed that the money is due and payable and then receive a chance to say why the money could or should not be paid. Then, if the money still was not paid, Ramiro could repossess the property through the legal process.

The Need to Be Definite

The law must be definite, not vague. For example, a law stating that all contracts "for a lot of money" must be in writing would not clearly specify when a contract must be in writing, leading to confusion. The Statute of Frauds, however, states that all contracts for the sale of goods costing $500 or more must be in writing, which is very clear. A contract for $499.99 need not be in writing; a contract for $500.01 must be in writing.

Sometimes the law is unable to state precisely what one must do in all circumstances. In such cases, the law uses the word *reasonable* rather than set precise boundaries. If an automobile hits a pedestrian and causes injury, the pedestrian may sue the driver of the vehicle.

In this situation, the court does not rely solely on the speed of the vehicle in deciding whether to find the driver at fault. If the only information you had was that the speed limit was 55 miles per hour and the car was going 50 miles per hour, would you find the driver at fault? Under these conditions, the law would ask the question: Was the driver's conduct reasonable under the circumstances? If so, it will be written off as an accident without civil liability; if not, the driver will be liable for any injury to the pedestrian. In the final analysis, the law provides an answer. Thus, the law is definite.

The Need to Be Flexible

To say that the law must be both definite and flexible seems like a contradiction in terms. The law needs to be definite in order to establish a standard. In other respects, the law must be flexible so that it can be applied in many different *individual* situations. For example, if a family wage earner is killed by a drunk driver and the family files a **wrongful death** lawsuit, recovery would be based on the future earning capacity of the wage earner. It would not be based on a table of damages. If trees did not bend in the wind, they would break. Our legal system is like those trees: It must bend without breaking. However, because of this flexibility, our legal system loses some of its predictability.

Wrongful death
Unlawful death. It does not necessarily involve a crime.

The Need to Be Practical

Because people depend on the law to guide their actions, the law needs to be practical and oriented to action rather than to thought. However, there are thoughtful ideas supporting the legal system. The law must deal with real issues faced by real people. For example, most courts will only decide real disputes between the parties. They will not decide hypothetical cases. Courts will also avoid cases where the issue is **moot** or where there is no real **case and controversy.**

Moot
Abstract; a point not properly submitted to the court for a resolution. A point not capable of resolution.

Case and controversy
A case brought before the court where the plaintiff and defendant are really opposed to each other on significant issues.

The Need to Be Published

If we had the best set of laws imaginable but no one knew about them, they would be useless. In traffic law, for example, speed limits need to be posted so drivers know how fast they can legally drive. If no speed limits were posted, arbitrary enforcement would be the rule, and drivers would not know how fast they could legally drive. In general, people cannot voluntarily comply with secret laws and rules. Therefore, all laws must be published. Once a law has been published, we can presume that all people know it. Consequently, ignorance of the law is no excuse.

The Need to Be Final

If a controversy exists and the legal system is used to resolve it, one thing is certain: At some point in the future, the matter will be resolved. It may not be resolved to the full satisfaction of the person who "won" the case, but it will be resolved. In this sense, the law is like a political election. On election day, someone wins and someone loses. The outcome is final. In criminal law, if the defendant wins the case in trial court, the matter ends. In many situations, the prosecutor cannot appeal. A defendant who is convicted in trial court, however, can appeal to the highest court in the state system. If the defendant does not gain a reversal, the matter ends unless the U.S. Supreme Court chooses to review the case. Exhibit 1.2 on page 10 outlines the needs of a legal system.

E X H I B I T 1.2 | **The Needs of a Legal System**

Legal System

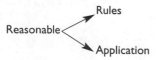

Reasonable < Rules / Application

Definite rules and limits

Flexible standards (to keep up with changes in society and technology)

Practical rules based on reality

Published (communicated)

Final—to put an end to a case at a particular time

Anarchy/Chaos

Unreasonable < Arbitrary and/or unreasonable rules / Uneven and/or biased applications

Vague or unclear rules, no defined standards

Rigid and unbending standards; "Stone-Age" rules in a modern world

Hypothetical or impractical rules based on wishful thinking

Unpublished—"Surprise" rules

Ongoing, continuous—never seeming to end

WHAT ARE THE PURPOSES OF A LEGAL SYSTEM?

Achieving Justice

As previously discussed, justice is basically fairness. Sometimes we achieve it, and sometimes we do not. In the law of business, we deal more with commutative justice—treating each person equally—than with distributive justice. In a contract, for example, commutative justice gives each person what he or she is entitled to under the contract—no more, no less. The rule of caveat emptor (let the buyer beware) is an example of how the law allocates risk in a business transaction. If the buyer does not thoroughly examine the goods before they are bought, the buyer cannot seek redress in the courts if what is bought does not conform to his or her expectations.

A trend exists, however, to introduce elements of distributive justice into the law of business. The legislatures, courts, and administrative agencies are attempting to reallocate the risks of business transactions by taking into account the status of the parties. For example, a number of bills have been introduced in the U.S. Congress to address online computer privacy protection.

Another limit placed on the doctrine of commutative justice is that of **unconscionability**. An eighteenth-century English case provides an excellent working definition: unconscionable contracts are contracts that are so unfair "no man in his senses and not under delusion would make [them] on the one hand, and no honest and fair man would accept [them] on the other."[2] Our legal system must consider that some contracts ought not to be enforced even if they fully comply with all the rules concerning contract formation.

Providing Police Power

Because justice is the ultimate purpose of a legal system, providing police power may be viewed as an intermediate purpose of a legal system. When most students see the term *police power*, they usually envision a uniformed police officer with a badge and gun. That, however, is just one part of what is meant. Police power is

Unconscionability
Condition of being so unreasonably favorable to one party, or so one-sided, as to shock the conscience.

Nuisance
Wrongs that arise from the unreasonable or unlawful use of a person's own property.

Appellate court
A court that has the power to review the decisions of lower courts.

inherent in all governments and allows for the creation and enforcement of laws designed to protect the public's health, safety, and general welfare.[3] Laws and ordinances concerning police, fire, sanitation, and social welfare departments in state and local governments stem from police power.

Maintaining Peace and the Status Quo

Since the days of ancient England, one of the most obvious purposes of the law has been to "keep the King's peace." Most modern torts and crimes can trace their origin to a simple breaching of the King's peace. Today, laws that govern the relationships between private individuals, such as the laws governing assault, battery, trespass, and false imprisonment, are private forms of keeping the peace. Closely associated with keeping the peace is the concept of maintaining the status quo—that is, keeping things the way they are. It is natural for the law to maintain the status quo unless changing things will benefit society. It is possible to obtain a preliminary injunction from a court that will maintain the status quo until the lawsuit is finally resolved. The petitioner must allege and prove irreparable injury to obtain a preliminary injunction.

Providing Answers

On a philosophical level, the law should be just; but on a practical level, it should provide answers. Sometimes the answers the law provides are not satisfactory. If Melanie sues Troy, a neighbor, because Troy is allegedly creating a **nuisance** on his property, and Troy wins the case in the trial court, then Melanie can appeal the decision to the next higher court. In most states, this higher court is called an **appellate court.** If an appellate court rules in favor of Troy, a further appeal may be taken to the state's highest court. In that court, Melanie may win and thereby receive a satisfactory answer. But whether she wins or loses, she and Troy will each be provided with an answer to the matter on completion of the appellate process.

Providing Protection

The law protects all kinds of interests. You have already seen that the law concerns itself with protecting individuals. The tort law of assault and battery is a classic example of protection of the individual. The law also protects persons less conspicuously when it protects their **civil rights.** Civil rights laws are extremely important in modern litigation and have their historical background in the first 10 amendments to the U.S. Constitution. (Refer to the Constitution in

1.2 | MANAGEMENT

CIT SECURITY ISSUES

Dan Kochanowski plans to visit Washington, D.C., next week for a conference on video technology, including a session at the White House. Anna and Tom recognize that this trip is important to CIT, but they are a little concerned because of several violent incidents at the White House over the last few years. For example, two individuals have fired shots at the White House, and one individual apparently tried to crash a plane into the building. White House security and the D.C. police have strengthened security around the White House and have applied strict rules about people carrying weapons and/or acting in a suspicious manner. While Anna and Tom appreciate the extra security, they do not understand why different rules seem to apply to the White House than exist in their hometown. They have asked you to explain how or why this is permitted. What will you tell them?

BUSINESS CONSIDERATIONS Is it reasonable to have different legal rules about carrying weapons near the White House than in other areas? Should the police apply the rules differently in this vicinity? Can a business impose different rules concerning the carrying of weapons on or around the workplace? What factors would cause a business to do so?

ETHICAL CONSIDERATIONS Is it ethical for the government to have different rules near the White House than it has in other places? What are the ethical implications of having special rules in certain specified areas or under certain conditions?

Civil rights
The rights in the first 10 amendments to the U.S. Constitution (the Bill of Rights) and due process and equal protection under the Fourteenth Amendment.

Appendix A at the end of this book; it is worthwhile for you to refresh your memory about its features.) Persons are protected in the free exercise of their speech, are free to choose or not to choose a religion, can peacefully assemble, and may petition their government for a redress of grievances (a rarely used freedom). The U.S. Constitution contains the right to be protected from unreasonable searches and seizures, the right against compulsory self-incrimination of a crime, the right to a grand jury, the right against **double jeopardy,** the right to a jury trial, and the right to bail. Proponents argue that the Constitution provides a right to bear arms, but constitutional experts disagree on whether this is an individual right or a right to form a militia.

The government is also in the business of protecting *itself*. A government's self-protection is an ancient right that goes back to Roman law. It is based on the concept that if the **sovereign** is *truly* sovereign, it cannot be attacked legally. Because the sovereign is, by definition, supreme, it cannot be subject to attack or held liable to its inferiors. Thus, the rule of *sovereign immunity* was developed, shielding the sovereign from lawsuits against it but permitting the sovereign to file lawsuits. This rule still stands, to some extent, although the federal government and many states have passed special statutes permitting individuals to sue them for torts.

Finally, the law is concerned with the protection of property. All property is characterized as either personal or real property. *Personal property* is all property with the exception of real property. In general, if property is movable, it is personal property. *Real property*, on the other hand, is land and whatever is affixed to land, such as a house. However, personal property can have dual meanings in law. In addition to the meaning above, it may also mean property that is owned by individuals, as opposed to public property that is owned by the government or the community. Our legal system has a variety of laws that protect both types of property.

Enforcing Intent

The law of contracts is based on *freedom of contract*. It is this rule that allows each of us to be our own "legislator" to a limited extent. We make our own "laws" of conduct, as long as the contracts into which we enter do not violate the general principles of contract law. For example, you may wish to enter into a contract with a supplier of goods. You may want to make the contract today so that it will immediately bind the other party. Perhaps you have found a good price and do not expect to find a better one. Your problem, however, is that you do not presently have the money to pay for the goods, but you know that you can easily resell them for an immediate cash profit within 10 days after delivery. You should, therefore, seek a provision in the contract stating that the buyer will pay the seller for the goods 11 days after receipt of them. Of course, if you cannot resell the goods within the 10 days as anticipated, you will have a financial problem. This is more a question of business judgment, however, than of law.

Providing Rehabilitation

Both criminal law and civil law are directed toward rehabilitation. Criminal law should, among other things, rehabilitate the criminal. Civil law is also involved in rehabilitation to some extent. Contract law provides rehabilitation for a party harmed by a breach of the contract. Tort law provides for a form of rehabilitation in the assessment of damages for the victim of the tort. The federal bankruptcy law is directed toward the rehabilitation of debtors.

Facilitating Commercial Transactions

One of the major characteristics of the U.S. legal system is that it facilitates commercial transactions. For example, very few automobiles would be sold in the United States if car dealers insisted on cash payment. Our national economy is still very reliant on the automobile industry. The prosperity of the steel, energy, and transportation industries is directly related to that of the automobile. Thus, reducing the number of automobiles sold could be harmful to the national economy. Accordingly, the extension of credit for the purchase of automobiles greatly facilitates trade. The use of checks and credit cards also accelerates commercial transactions. The taking of a **security interest** in goods expedites trade to persons who might otherwise not be in a financial position to make the purchase. The U.S. legal system fosters free and open competition and facilitates trade. This characteristic of the legal system has done much to contribute to the business and financial power of the United States. Exhibit 1.3 outlines the purposes of a legal system.

Security interest
Collateral interest taken in the property of another to secure payment of a debt or contract performance.

JURISPRUDENCE

Jurisprudence is the study of the science or philosophy underlying the law. In Latin, jurisprudence means the "wisdom of the law." However, there are really many different "wisdoms" of the law reflected in a number of different philosophical views; these views vary based on the values inherent in the law, the development of the law, and its proper role in society. The law continues to change, and knowledge of the legal philosophies will improve your ability to understand the law and predict future trends. Here is a brief introduction to some of the philosophical approaches. Note that sometimes there is even disagreement among philosophers who basically subscribe to the same theory. The theories are summarized in Exhibit 1.4 on page 16.

E X H I B I T 1.3 | **The Purposes of a Legal System**

Purpose	Reason
Achieving justice	To provide "justice" so that the needs of the members of society are addressed.
Providing police power	To provide a social structure so that "wronged" individuals do not have to resort to self-help; to give society control of the system.
Maintaining peace and the status quo	To provide each member of society with a feeling of personal security and a structure on which each individual can rely.
Providing answers	To achieve practical justice; lets the members of society know what is expected of them and what they may reasonably expect from others.
Providing protection	To define and establish social guidelines and protect the entire society if any of these guidelines are not followed and obeyed.
Enforcing intent	To provide some method for permitting private agreements and for ensuring that these agreements are honored or enforced.
Providing rehabilitation	To allow a person who violates the guidelines of the society a second chance; recognizes that anyone can make a mistake.
Facilitating commercial transactions	To support freedom of contract and private ownership of property; each of these concepts encourages and promotes business transactions.

Natural Law Theory

The *natural law* theory says that the law should be based on what is correct and moral. It is composed of four concepts:

1. There are certain legal values or value judgments.
2. These values are unchanging because their source is absolute. Natural law theorists disagree about the source, generally saying it is either Nature, God, or Reason.
3. These values can be determined by human reason.
4. Once they are determined, these values supersede any form of human law. Once the natural law is discovered, it nullifies any contradictory law created by humans.

This theory rests on some significant assumptions: The world is perceived as having a rational order with values and purposes built into it; the laws of nature describe how things should be; and humans should use reason to grasp what should be done. Many early Greek philosophers were natural law theorists. In the history of Christian thought, the dominant theory of ethics has been the theory of natural law,[4] best exemplified by St. Thomas Aquinas.[5] Natural law theory is found in the words of the Declaration of Independence: "We hold these truths to be self-evident, that all Men are created equal, that they are endowed by their Creator with certain unalienable Rights . . . " The natural law theory focuses on fairness and justice, even though some disorder will result when individuals decide that the written law is not "natural law." Criticisms of natural law include questions of whose values are to be included in the natural law and who determines whether a man-made law is unjust because it violates natural law.

Legal Positivism

Legal positivism is composed of three theoretical parts. (1) "[T]hat legal validity is ultimately a function of certain kinds of social facts."[6] (2) That social facts give rise to legal validity which is authoritative due to some kind of social convention. (3) There is *no* overlap between notions of law and morality. This last part is in direct opposition to natural law theory. Legal positivists disagree on the correct interpretation of these three theoretical parts. One alternate statement proposed by some positivists includes these primary beliefs: (1) law is the expression of the will of the legislator or sovereign and must be followed; (2) morals are separate from law and should not be considered in making legal decisions—for example, judges should not consider factors outside the legal system such as contemporary community values; and (3) law is a closed system in which correct legal decisions are reached by reference to statutes and court precedents. The *legal positivist* approach believes that the law is the result of lawmaking by a legitimate government. In the United States, this is primarily executive orders, legislation, court opinions, and administrative bodies. Under this theory, legality and morality are separated. The positive law approach promotes stability in the law and the supremacy of written laws. Criticisms of legal positivism include that it is too narrow, too literal-minded, and that its refusal to consider social, ethical, and other factors makes it static and unable to serve society well.

Sociological Theory

Under the *sociological* theory, the role of prior law in the form of **precedents** is minimized. The law's source should be contemporary opinion and customs. In creating statutes or court decisions, the lawmaker should record community interests; become familiar with the community standards and mores; and make a decision conforming to these standards. Community standards change, and thus the law would be changing all the time. In a court decision relying on this theory, the judge may discuss sociological factors and current customs. For example, a court may consider "contemporary community standards" in determining whether a magazine is obscene. One criticism of the sociological theory is that following the theory would make the law too unpredictable.

Precedents
Decided cases that establish legal authority for later cases.

Historical Theory

The *historical* theory says that the law is primarily a system of customs and social traditions that have developed over time. It is very similar to the sociological school, but its focus is more historical than contemporary. Each nation develops its own individual consensus about what the law should be. The law is an evolving system, and precedents have a significant role. Legitimacy is obtained from the historical will of the people of a nation.

Law and Economics Theory

The *law and economics* theory applies classical economic theory and empirical methods to explain legal doctrines and to predict judicial decisions. It argues for using economic analysis as both a description about how courts and legislators behave and a prescription about how they *should* behave. The law and economics theory is closely allied with the University of Chicago, where it originated and is sometimes called The Chicago School. This theory is commonly used in areas such as torts, contracts, and property law. Under the theory, the legal system should be viewed as a system to promote the efficient allocation of resources in society. For example, buyers and sellers in the market exchange goods or services of value. The exchange is maximizing value for both the buyer and seller. Richard A. Posner is currently a leader in law and economics theory. In his words,

> [M]any areas of law, especially the great common law fields of property, torts, crimes, and contracts, bear the stamp of economic reasoning. It is not a refutation [of this theory] that few judicial opinions contain explicit references to economic concepts. Often the true grounds of decision are concealed rather than illuminated by the characteristic **rhetoric** of judicial opinions. Indeed, legal education consists primarily of learning to dig beneath the rhetorical surface to find those grounds, many of which may turn out to have an economic character.[7]

The proper goal of statutory and common law is to promote wealth maximization, which can be accomplished by facilitating the mechanisms of the free market. Also, market transactions reflect **autonomous** judgments about the value of individual preferences. Critics contend that this theory tends to be politically conservative and generally rests on only one type of economic philosophy to the exclusion of others. Another criticism is that the theory could be acceptable as a **descriptive theory** to explain what the law is, but it is not helpful as a **prescriptive theory.**

Rhetoric
The art or science of using words effectively.

Autonomous
The right of the individual to govern him- or herself according to his or her own reason.

Descriptive theory
Theory that describes how things are. It reports what is observed.

Prescriptive theory
Theory that reports what people should do or what should occur.

E X H I B I T 1.4 | **Theories of Jurisprudence**

Theory	Primary Characteristic
Natural law	Source of law is Nature, God, or Reason.
Legal Positivism	Source of law is the legislature.
Sociological	Source of law is contemporary community standards and customs.
Historical	Law evolves over time based on custom and social traditions.
Law and Economics	Classical economic theory should be applied to all areas of the law.
Feminist Legal	Legal system is dominated by the perspective of white males; women's perspectives are ignored and women are victimized.
Critical Legal Studies	Law is a combination of legal and nonlegal beliefs; it must be critiqued to bring social change and political growth.

Feminist Legal Theory

The *feminist legal* theory believes that the law does not treat women equally. The law is structured to promote the interests of white males and to exclude women. As with some of the other theories, there is a wide variety of views under this theory. Many feminist legal theorists are also concerned about persons of color. (There is also a critical race theory that focuses on how people of color are excluded from the legal system.) Followers of feminist legal theory assert that the current legal system is dominated by men, and that women are often victimized and their perspectives ignored. They argue that the male perspective has shaped many areas of law including property, contract, criminal law, constitutional law, and civil rights law. They also contend that the law should consider the female perspective. For example, workplace behavior that may not seem harassing to men may seem harassing to women, and the law should address this accordingly. In the 1991 case of *Ellison* v. *Brady*,[8] federal courts began using the reasonable women standard in cases where women were being sexually harassed.

A 1998 Italian case attracted the attention of feminist legal theorists. The case was heard by Italy's highest criminal appeals court, which determined that an 18-year-old girl was not raped, based in part on the fact that she was wearing jeans. For more details on this case, see Case Problems and Writing Assignment 8 at the end of this chapter. The ruling said that it is "common knowledge that it's nearly impossible to even partially remove jeans from a person without their co-operation, since this operation is already very difficult for the wearer."[9] It also said that "jeans cannot be removed easily and certainly it is impossible to pull them off if the victim is fighting against her attacker with all her force."[10] The case has been sent back for retrial, but Rosa, the victim, says she doesn't think she can go through another trial.[11] The decision sparked protests from Italy to California. On a historical note, rape has been considered a criminal felony in Italy only since 1996. Prior to that time, it was considered a "crime of honor" against the woman's family. A defendant could avoid punishment by agreeing to marry the woman or by proving that she had had many sexual experiences.[12]

The feminist legal theory is criticized for being too narrow in focus and for failing to recognize changes taking place as more women enter the workforce, including the legal profession.

Critical Legal Studies Theory

The *critical legal studie*s (CLS) theory believes that the content of the law in liberal democracies reflects "'ideological struggles among social factions in which competing conceptions of justice, goodness, and social and political life get compromised, truncated, vitiated, and adjusted.' The inevitable outcome of such struggles, [in] this view, is a profound inconsistency permeating the deepest layers of the law."[13] The law is not objective and neutral. The current law reflects a cluster of beliefs that convinces people they are living in a natural hierarchy, while in fact this cluster of beliefs has been created by those in power. The elite use these beliefs to rationalize their power. The elite maintain their power, wealth, and privilege using law, economics, mass communication, and religion. In order to accomplish social and political change, the law must be examined and critiqued. The current law is a combination of legal and nonlegal beliefs that is used to maintain the status quo, especially in the political and economic spheres. This is accomplished by convincing others that those in power should remain in power. The legal system, including legal education, is a deceptive social mechanism for the preservation of power by those who currently have it. People can only free themselves of this perspective by critically examining these beliefs. Generally, people who subscribe to the CLS view wish to overturn the status quo. This theory is criticized as being basically a negative position; it does not have any concrete suggestions about how to change the social, political, and legal systems.

CHANGE IN THE LEGAL SYSTEM

A student of the law should note that people do not always comply with the law. When you observe people in your community repeatedly doing something, you might conclude that this behavior is lawful. This assumption may be unwise. For example, drivers may repeatedly violate posted speed limits. During your study of business law, you should try to distinguish these three distinct questions:

1. What is the law about this topic?
2. How do people and businesses behave?
3. What should the law be on this topic?

Answers to these questions will vary based on the state or region under analysis. The most variance will occur about what the law should be. Individuals will disagree on the answer to this question, based on their views about jurisprudence and their values. Proactive businesspeople may suggest answers that will benefit their particular business enterprise or industry.

WHAT ARE THE SOURCES OF LAW IN THE U.S. LEGAL SYSTEM?

The U.S. legal system is based on the Constitution, treaties, statutes, ordinances, administrative regulations, common law, case law, and equity. Although each of the elements is separate, the elements are interdependent; together they constitute our system. These elements must be thought of as a system; a change in one element should not be considered in isolation. Such a change will affect one or more parts of the system. In a civil rights suit, a person may allege a violation of constitutional

Stare decisis
To abide by, or adhere to, decided cases; policy of courts to stand by decided cases and not to disturb a settled point of law.

Judicial review
The power of the courts to say what the law is.

rights (Fourteenth Amendment), a statutory right (Civil Rights Act of 1964), an administrative regulation (Equal Employment Opportunity Commission guideline), past decisions of the court (*stare decisis*), and equity (if all else fails, the person should win because it is fair). The important thing to remember is that all the parts of the legal system are interconnected and that the whole is more than the sum of the parts.

Constitutions

A *constitution* is the fundamental law of a nation. It may be written or unwritten. The British constitution is said to be unwritten. Clearly, the U.S. Constitution is written. (See Appendix A of this text.) It allocates the powers of government and also sets limits on those powers. Our founding fathers knew that all tyrants had two powers: the power of the purse and the power of the sword. The Constitution places the power of the purse exclusively with Congress and the power of the sword with the executive branch. The judiciary, our third branch of government, has neither the power of the purse nor the power of the sword. However, it has the power to interpret the meaning of the U.S. Constitution and to decide the constitutionality of the laws passed by Congress. In the case of *Marbury* v. *Madison*,[14] the U.S. Supreme Court for the first time applied the doctrine of **judicial review.** That case held that the Supreme Court has the power to decide whether laws passed by Congress comply with the Constitution. If they do not, they are unconstitutional and thus of no force or effect. We will discuss the unique nature of the Constitution further in Chapter 5.

Our states also have constitutions, and they are the fundamental laws of those states. The U.S. Constitution, however, is the supreme legal document in the United States and thus will take precedence over state constitutions.

Treaties

Treaties are formal agreements between two or more nations. The United States enters into treaties for various purposes including providing protection—for example, the North Atlantic Treaty Organization (NATO)—and promoting trade—for example, the North American Free Trade Agreement (NAFTA). Treaties are the only elements of our legal system that do not stem from the Constitution. Treaties are made not with the authority of the Constitution, but under the authority of the United States. This difference is important because the power to make a treaty is a function of sovereignty and not one of a constitution. In most cases, treaties require enabling legislation to be passed by Congress. The case of *Missouri* v. *Holland*[15] established that statutes passed in accordance with a valid treaty cannot be declared unconstitutional. Once made, treaties also become the supreme law of the land.

Statutes

Statutes are the acts of legislative bodies. They prohibit or command the doing of something. The word *statute* is preferred when referring to a legislative act to distinguish it from such other "laws" as ordinances, regulations, common law, and case law. The best example of state statutory law is found in the Uniform Commercial Code (UCC) (see Appendix B). All 50 states, the District of Columbia, and the U.S. Virgin Islands have adopted at least portions of the law. The UCC is very important and, accordingly, is the subject of many of the chapters in this book. The

UCC covers the following subjects: sales, leases, negotiable instruments, bank deposits and collections, fund transfers, letters of credit, bulk transfers, documents of title, investment securities, and secured transactions.

Ordinances

Ordinances are laws passed by municipal bodies. Cities, towns, and villages, if incorporated, have the power to establish laws for the protection of the public's health, safety, and welfare. These entities are to be distinguished from counties, which generally do not have legislative power. Counties usually have the power to enforce state laws within their boundaries.

Administrative Regulations

Administrative regulations are rules promulgated by governmental agencies, which have been created by the legislative branch of government. Examples of agencies include the Federal Trade Commission on the federal level and an insurance commission on the state level. These bodies have unusual powers, which will be discussed in Chapter 5. The rules and regulations of these entities have the full force and effect of law.

Common Law

Common law consists of the unwritten law of a country, based on custom, usage, *and* the decisions of the law courts. The development of the common law is depicted in Exhibit 1.5.

Case Law

Case law derives from the many reported cases being decided by federal and state courts. It is part of the common law previously discussed. Quite often the judges must interpret statutes in order to apply them to actual cases and controversies. These interpretations place what lawyers call a "judicial gloss" on the statute. You will not fully understand a particular statute until you have read both the statute *and* the cases that have interpreted it. *Case law,* then, is the law as pronounced by judges.

The American Law Institute (ALI) is dedicated to promoting clarification of the law, improving the administration of justice, and drafting the *Restatements of the Law Governing Lawyers. Restatements* are not actually part of the law; rather, they are treatises that summarize the law on a subject. When there are conflicting approaches, the *Restatement* "recommends" one of the alternatives. *Restatements* become part of the case law when a court relies on a particular section in reaching its opinion.

E X H I B I T   1.5 | **Common Law**

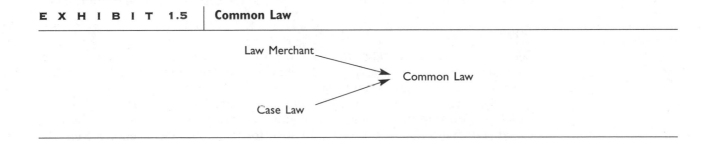

Stare decisis is an ancient doctrine that means the question has been decided. For example, if a particular legal point is well settled in a certain jurisdiction, a future case with substantially the same facts will be decided in accordance with the principle that has already been decided. This is one of the reasons that lawyers do a great deal of legal research. The doctrine of *stare decisis* is also called *precedents.* (Precedents do not play a major role in all legal systems.) Even though a legal matter has been settled, it does not mean the legal system must remain static.

A precedent remains in effect until it is changed. It must be remembered that the legal system evolves. Lawyers and petitioners in court are constantly asking to have precedents changed, and sometimes they are successful. Occasionally, the court will change or modify the precedents. When a court changes the precedents, it will generally support this decision with one of the following three reasons:

1. The prior rule is out of date; it is not appropriate to present-day society.
2. The prior case is distinguishable because the facts are different in one or more significant details.
3. The judge or justice who made the prior ruling was incorrect or wrong.

Judges may be reluctant to state that the prior ruling was in error, especially if they participated in the prior ruling. It is easier to "admit" that someone else made an error. Judges *sometimes* do admit that the rule they fashioned earlier is not the preferred response to a particular legal problem.

When a court follows precedent it is striving to make the law *definite,* satisfying one of the needs of a legal system. However, as times and situations change, courts need to be able to change. The law would not be *flexible,* if precedents could never be changed. Courts have a difficult time balancing these two needs— definiteness and flexibility—in applying the law within the area of precedents. *Brown* v. *Board of Education*[16] is an example of a court overturning precedents. In that case, the U.S. Supreme Court decided, contrary to prior decisions, that providing separate schools for black and white children was unconstitutional.

Dictum is language in a court opinion that is not necessary to the decision before the court. These remarks or asides are not part of the precedents. Dictum can provide valuable clues about how that judge might decide future cases.

An opportunity to "make law," as it is called, occurs when jurisdictions are in conflict over a point of law. For example, many states are divided into various judicial districts, and courts in each of these districts may issue written legal opinions. If two or more districts have published conflicting opinions on a particular point, and the state's supreme court has *not* issued an opinion on the point, the time is ripe for the creation of a new rule, statewide, that will resolve the matter once and for all. Until the statewide rule is created, however, each court creates precedents for itself and for any courts directly under it. When there are no prior court decisions on a point of law, the court may state that the case is one of **first impression.**

Equity

Equity is defined as a body of rules applied to legal controversies when no adequate remedy at law exists. These rules are based on the principles outlined by Justinian during his reign as the Byzantine emperor of Rome (527–565 A.D.): "to live honestly, to harm nobody, [and] to render to every man his due." These rules were developed outside the common law courts in England by an officer of the king called the chancellor. The primary reasons for development of equity were the

Dictum

An observation or remark by a judge that is not necessarily involved in the case or essential to its resolution. An aside written by the judge.

First impression

Case that is presented to the court for an initial decision; the case presents an entirely novel question of law for the court's decision. It is not governed by any existing precedent.

unfair decisions made by law courts and the limited types of remedies available in law courts.

Today, the rules of law and equity are joined into one system of law. The injunction is an equitable remedy, but before U.S. courts will issue an injunction, the person requesting it must show proof that the remedy at law would be inadequate. For example, if your neighbors are burning rubber tires on their property and the prevailing wind carries the obnoxious odor directly across your property, their action will destroy the peaceful use and enjoyment of your land. In general, no amount of monetary damages would be sufficient to allow them to continue to burn rubber tires. In that case, you would not have an adequate remedy at law, and you could request that the court issue an injunction to stop your neighbors from burning those tires. In a larger sense, however, equity may be viewed as a doctrine that results in the legal system's adhering to the principle of fairness. Exhibit 1.6 summarizes some of the differences between law and equity.

E X H I B I T 1.6	Distinctions Between Actions in Law and in Equity[a]	
Characteristic	**In Law**	**In Equity[b]**
Type of relief	Money to compensate plaintiff for his or her losses	Action, either in the form of ordering the defendant to do or not to do something, or in the form of a decree about the status of something[c][d]
Nature of proceeding	More restricted by precedents	More flexible and less restricted by precedents, supposed to create equity (justice)
Time limit for filing lawsuit	Applicable period fixed by the statute of limitations[e]	A reasonable period of time as determined by the judge on a case-by-case basis[f]
Decider of fact	Jury trial, if requested by a party	No jury trial, judge decides the facts[g]
Enforcing a decision	Plaintiff may begin an execution of the judgment[h]	Plaintiff may begin contempt proceedings if the defendant does not perform as directed; defendant may be placed in jail and/or fined[i]

a. Actions at law and those in equity are no longer as distinct as they once were. As a result, many states allow "combined" trials with issues of law and issues of equity being tried together.

b. Traditionally, courts of equity were called courts of chancery, and the judge was called the chancellor.

c. Common equitable remedies include injunction, specific performance of a contract, rescission of a contract, and reformation (correction or rewriting of) a contract.

d. Courts would prefer to award monetary damages. Equitable relief is only granted when the plaintiff can show the court that money would be inadequate.

e. The statute of limitations period will depend on the state and the type of lawsuit. It will be a fixed period.

f. If the plaintiff has waited too long to file suit under the circumstances, the judge will apply the doctrine of laches and the suit will be dismissed.

g. Some states permit the use of an advisory jury.

h. In an execution, the clerk of the court issues a formal document and the sheriff seizes the defendant's money and/or other property. If property is seized, the sheriff will sell it and use the proceeds to pay the plaintiff.

i. The court is authorized to place the defendant in jail until he or she complies (or agrees to comply) with the court decree.

HOW IS THE LAW CLASSIFIED?

Federal Versus State Law

Our legal system is divided into two branches: federal and state. American lawyers must learn not only the law of their states but the law of the federal courts as well. In addition, they should know the majority rule. The *majority rule* is simply the rule that most states have adopted. Quite often, a *minority rule*, which a smaller number of states follow, also exists. Rarely, if ever, do the states agree on all aspects of a law. Exhibit 1.7 outlines the sources of the U.S. legal system. Note that there is some overlap between case law and common law, as illustrated in Exhibit 1.5.

Common Versus Statutory Law

As discussed earlier, the legal system consists of both common and statutory laws. Judges in the United States and England generally have the power to "make law" by interpreting statutes or applying precedents, and those interpretations become "common" law. Judges also apply the statutory law. *Statutory law* refers to legislative enactments, the statutes passed by the legislative bodies of the state. *Common law* is "unwritten" law, law developed over time by judicial action. Common law fills the gaps where other sources of law do not cover a particular topic. Statutory enactments override common law, filling the gap with a statutory provision and eliminating the need for unwritten coverage.

Civil Versus Criminal Law

The U.S. legal system also separates civil and criminal law. *Civil law* is private law wherein one person sues another person. *Criminal law* is public law in which a government entity files charges against a person. For example, if a person becomes

Res judicata
A rule of civil law that states that a person will not be sued more than once by the same party for the same civil wrong.

Pleadings
Statements filed in court specifying the claims of the parties.

E X H I B I T   1.7 | **The Sources of the U.S. Legal System**

Authority	Source	Definition
F, S	Constitution	Supreme law of the land; fundamental basis of domestic law
F	Treaties	Not based on the Constitution; formal agreements between nations; fundamental basis of international law/relations
F, S	Statutes	Acts of the legislature; control of domestic conduct; subject to limits imposed by the Constitution
S	Ordinances	Laws passed by municipal bodies and designed to control purely local problems, subject to any limits imposed by statutes or by the Constitution
F, S	Administrative Regulations	Acts of administrative agencies; control of specific areas of conduct; subject to any limits imposed by statutes or by the Constitution
S	Common Law	Principles and rules that have developed over time and are based on custom and usage; provide rules when statutes and the Constitution do not
F, S	Case Law	Precedents, established interpretations of areas of law in which the courts define what the law is
F, S	Equity	Special rules and relief when "the law" does not provide a proper and/or adequate remedy

Legend: F = federal; S = state

violently abusive and attacks another individual, and thus inflicts bodily harm on the innocent individual, the district attorney, as the representative of a government entity, may prosecute the attacker for assault. If convicted, the attacker may go to jail or prison. In addition, the person who was injured may sue the attacker in court for money damages. The additional suit would not constitute double jeopardy or its civil law equivalent, **res judicata,** since two different theories of action exist: civil and criminal.

Substantive Versus Procedural Law

Substantive law deals with rights and duties given or imposed by the legal system. *Procedural law* is devoted to how those rights and duties are enforced. For example, the law of contracts is substantive law. The law of **pleadings** describes the steps used to enforce those rights or duties. A controversy over the mental ability to form a valid contract is a substantive matter, but how one goes about getting the dispute into a court is a matter of procedure. Where one files the lawsuit, what must be alleged, how one notifies the defendant, and how long the defendant has to answer the allegations are all examples of procedural law. This book is devoted primarily to *substantive* law.

LEGAL SYSTEMS IN OTHER COUNTRIES

Sometimes we assume that all countries have the same or similar legal systems. This ethnocentric view can result in a rude shock when a U.S. citizen traveling in a foreign country continues to act the same as he or she would act at home. The U.S. citizen may find that behavior that is tolerated in the United States constitutes a crime in a foreign country, and that many of the protections he or she expects in the United States do not apply abroad. Other countries have different historical and sociological backgrounds. The values of the citizens and government rules may differ from those of U.S. citizens. For example, life insurance isn't accepted under traditional Muslim law.[17]

With the exception of England, most of Europe, including France, Germany, and Sweden, follows civil law. In this context, *civil law* means that the legal system relies on statutory law. The statutes are grouped into codes, and the codes are administered by judges. Judges, therefore, do not make law to the degree that they do in the United States. The judge relies primarily on the code and secondarily on statutes passed by the legislative bodies.

Until recently, the former Union of Soviet Socialist Republics (U.S.S.R.) followed a unique version of civil law. Owing to its socialist philosophy, private ownership

1.3 | MANAGEMENT

CALL-IMAGE TECHNOLOGY

LOBBYING GOVERNMENT FOR CALL-IMAGING

A number of citizens are concerned that products such as the Call-Image phone will lead to the invasion of privacy for many customers who are merely using the telephone in their own homes. These citizens have lobbied members of the state legislature demanding a statutory approach to guarantee the privacy of people who own Call-Image or similar videophones. Responding to complaints from organized consumer groups and individuals, the state legislature is considering the enactment of a statute that prohibits the marketing of videophones in the state unless they have an on/off switch for the video function. CIT is currently developing such an on/off switch but has not yet perfected it. As a result, the switch is not available for Call-Image phones and may not be available for quite some time. CIT would obviously like to stop the state legislature from enacting this proposed legislation because such a statute would prevent CIT from selling any of its existing phones in the state. CIT and the Kochanowski family members wonder what they can do, and turn to you for advice. What advice can you give them?

BUSINESS CONSIDERATIONS Under these circumstances, what options are available to CIT? What can—or should—a business do when it feels that proposed legislation will have a serious impact on the firm's profitability?

ETHICAL CONSIDERATIONS Would it be ethical for a firm to attempt to influence potential legislation? What ethical considerations would come into play should a firm decide to attempt to influence members of the legislature?

"DO-NOT-CALL LISTS"

Under federal law, telemarketers must keep "do-not-call lists." If you get a call from a telemarketer, and you don't want any more calls, be clear and direct. Ask them to put you on their "do-not-call list." Write down the name of the company and the date. If the company calls again, hang up and file a complaint with the Federal Trade Commission. The company faces fines of up to $10,000 per violation if they continue to call homes on the list. The Direct Marketing Association, an organization of mail-order companies and other direct marketers, also maintains a list of people who do not wish to be called—known as the Telephone Preference Service.[18] In a recent letter to the editor, Charlie Hollomon wrote, "If a telemarketer has a right to call, the citizen has a greater right to know who is calling. Instead of No-Call Lists, there should be OK to Call Lists, which citizens could use to indicate their willingness to receive solicitations. Telemarketers should then be required by law to be sure a citizen's phone is on such a list before calling."[19]

A number of states have passed or are considering statutes to protect consumers. For example, Louisiana is considering a statute permitting consumers to place their names on a "do-not-call list" in the state attorney general's office. The list would be revised quarterly and sold to telemarketing companies. Violators would face a $500 fine and up to six months in jail for the first offense.[20] A proposed statute in Nebraska has not been successful. Telemarketing is a big industry in Nebraska. One of the opponents, State Senator Jon Bruning, said, "Philosophically, it was a big government bill. People can simply not answer the phone or hang up the phone if they don't want to talk. I didn't think we needed government to step in and save us from the free market."[21]

Assume that your state has just enacted a statute providing for a "do-not-call list" with penalties for violators. Three telemarketers have filed a **class action suit.** The case has been brought in *your* court. How will *you* rule?

BUSINESS CONSIDERATIONS What businesses or industries should be concerned about "do-not-call lists"? Do affected businesses have any recourse? Should they be proactive or **reactive**? Why? Are the identified businesses affected by e-commerce and the use of the Internet?

ETHICAL CONSIDERATIONS Do businesses have any right to use phone lines? What rights do homeowners have not to be disturbed? Identify the ethical concerns involved with these statutes.

SOURCES: Asa Aarons, *Daily News* (New York) (23 March 1999), p. 18; Ed Anderson, *The Times-Picayune* (20 May 1999, Orleans Edition), p. A5; Robynn Tysver, *Omaha World-Herald* (8 April 1999, Sunrise Edition), News, p. 11; Charlie Hollomon, *The Atlanta Journal and Constitution* (31 March 1999), p. 17A.

Privatization
The process of going from government ownership of business and other property to private individual ownership.

of property was limited. The primary goal of this legal system was to preserve state ownership of all means of production. Consequently, the Soviet Union's law primarily consisted of public law such as criminal law. The law of property, contracts, and business organizations did not play a role. Many of the former Soviet republics are now beginning to engage in **privatization.** A body of private law is being developed as these countries move toward a more traditional civil law system. The new countries often rely on consultants, like attorneys, from the United States in developing their new system of commercial law.

In addition, the U.S. legal system is based on the law of precedents previously discussed in this chapter. However, there are other countries, such as Mexico, where precedent is not important. Each judge does his or her best to fashion a fair result in the particular case before the court. In civil law systems, precedent is not significant. In the European Union (EU), the role of precedents is increasing. Decisions made by the EU Court of Justice become precedents in all the member countries. Although the EU is primarily a code system, it is moving toward the use of precedents and more of a common law approach.

There are a number of legal systems based on religious teachings. The Hindu legal system is one example. Their system is a personal and religious law system that states that Hindus should act in accordance with this law wherever they live. The Hindu system has been recorded in law books called *smitris*. Most Hindu law applies to family matters. Anglo-Hindu law evolved in most Hindu countries while they were British colonies, where judges were applying a combination of English and Hindu laws. When India gained its independence from England, it replaced Anglo-Hindu law with a civil code primarily based on Hindu law.

Muslims believe in Islamic law or *Shari'a*, which is based on the Koran and other religious writings. Saudi Arabia relies almost exclusively on Islamic law. Other countries apply Islamic law in some areas, such as family law, and supplement it with secular law. In 1998, Pakistani Prime Minister Nawaz Sharif proposed a constitutional amendment to transform their legal system into an Islamic system. (The current legal system is based on British common law.) Their constitution already permits the courts to overturn any statute that is un-Islamic.[22]

A number of other religions also have legal systems, including Catholicism and Judaism. These legal systems generally provide tribunals for resolving disputes.

THE ATTORNEY-CLIENT RELATIONSHIP

Legal issues are critical in all businesses, even though some businesses are subjected to more government regulation than others. Whether the business is faced with litigation or is practicing preventive law and attempting to avoid legal problems, attorneys can be important "partners" in a business. One of the primary purposes of this text is to assist you in speaking intelligently with your attorney and to enable you to more fully understand what he or she says to you.

Hiring an Attorney

Each state has a body of law dealing with the attorney-client relationship. It generally addresses an attorney's obligation to his or her client and the extent of the obligation to keep client confidences. The ALI has written *The Restatement (Third) of the Law Governing Lawyers*,[23] which is expected to be released in 2000.[24]

Attorneys are generally paid a flat fee (a one-time fee), an hourly fee (based on an hourly rate), or a contingent fee (based on a percentage of the settlement or award.) Contingent fees are not permitted in criminal cases; in some states, they may be disallowed for other types of cases, too. The following should be helpful when you need to hire an attorney:

1. Generate a list of potential lawyers by asking personal and/or business contacts. Try to find friends who have had a similar type of legal difficulty. Use *Martindale-Hubbell Law Directory*, West's Legal Directory (online), or

Class action suit
Lawsuit involving a group of plaintiffs or defendants who are substantially in the same position as each other.

Reactive
Permitting others to act first and waiting to see what develops.

directories maintained by your state bar association to discover additional information about the lawyers on your list.

2. Shop around and interview more than one attorney.

3. When interviewing, ask lawyers about their experience in this particular area of the law. Also ask: What are the probable outcomes of your dispute? How long will the legal matter take?

4. Find out how the attorney is going to charge and what services you as the client will receive for the fee. For example, it is common in litigation for a fee to include a trial, but no appellate work. Will a contingent fee be based on the award before or after expenses? If the attorney is going to charge an hourly rate, what is the smallest unit of time that is used for billing? In other words, will you be billed for 10 minutes or 15 minutes for a simple phone call to the lawyer? What is a realistic estimate for the total bill and expenses? You should realize that it is more difficult to make a realistic estimate for some types of cases than others, particularly when the workload may depend on the decisions of the opponent. How often will the attorney send you a bill? Will the attorney put the estimate in writing? Will the attorney enter into a written contract with you?

5. Ask whether the fee will include private investigators, filing fees, expert witnesses, other attorneys, paralegals, photocopies, and so on. Generally, it does not. What other types of fees and expenses does the lawyer anticipate?

6. Find out if you can take steps to reduce the legal fees. For example, you may be able to do some tasks yourself.

7. Ask if the attorney will need additional information from you.

8. Find out the attorney's procedure for handling billing disputes. Will the attorney charge for the additional hours spent on the billing dispute? Will the attorney agree to mandatory arbitration of the fee if the parties cannot resolve the dispute?

9. What are the alternatives to litigation? (See Chapter 6.) Does the attorney recommend any of them for this case? Does the attorney know any mediators or arbitrators who would be appropriate?

10. Try to discern whether client complaints have been filed against this attorney. Often this information is made public and is available from the disciplinary agency for the state. This is generally the state bar association or the state supreme court.

11. Select the approach you plan to take with the case, and choose a lawyer whose style is similar to the approach you selected. Do you want someone who is extremely aggressive or more conciliatory?

12. Do *not* hire an attorney who is unable to communicate effectively with you or is unwilling to answer questions.

Clients are sometimes dissatisfied with the services provided by their attorneys. In 1994, Consumer Union surveyed members regarding their experiences with attorneys from 1991 to 1994 and discovered that of the 30,000 respondents, clients involved in adversarial cases were more likely to be displeased with the legal services they received than those involved in nonadversarial matters. For example, 27 percent of the people who had hired an attorney for an adversarial matter were dissatisfied with the work performed by the lawyer. The survey noted that *some* clients were unhappy with an aspect of their case. Common complaints included the manner in which the attorney expedited the resolution of the matter; kept them informed; charged fees and expenses; protected their rights and financial interests; informed them about costs early in the process; and the attorney's behavior, for example, whether the attorney was polite and considerate.[25]

Resolving Problems with Legal Counsel

If a problem does arise from the attorney-client relationship, you should first try to resolve it with the attorney and/or the law firm. Begin with a clear letter expressing your concern and what you would like the attorney to do. If the problem is not resolved at this stage, you can fire the attorney and hire another. However, it may be costly for the replacement to become familiar with the dispute, and replacing an attorney may postpone the ultimate resolution of the legal matter.

If you believe the attorney breached one of the codes of ethics, you can report him or her to the disciplinary board. The American Bar Association (ABA) has a code of ethics for attorneys; in addition, most states also have their own codes of ethics. Copies are usually available from the library or the state bar association or disciplinary board. Bar associations or disciplinary boards will not provide legal

RESOURCES FOR BUSINESS LAW STUDENTS

NAME	RESOURCES	WEB ADDRESS
The Legal Information Institute (LII)	LII, maintained by the Cornell Law School, provides Supreme Court decisions, opinions of the New York Court of Appeals, a hypertext version of the full U.S. Code and Uniform Commercial Code (UCC), treaties, statutes, and other legal documents.	**http://www.law.cornell.edu/**
Thomas: Legislative Information on the Internet	The U.S. Congress, via Thomas (for Thomas Jefferson), provides news and information on Congress, bills before Congress (text, summary, and status), the **Congressional Record,** and committee information.	**http://thomas.loc.gov/**
FedLaw	FedLaw, maintained by the U.S. General Services Administration (GSA), includes federal laws and regulations, executive orders, and Office of Management and Budget (OMB) circulars and bulletins.	**http://www.legal.gsa.gov/**
StateLaw	StateLaw, maintained by the Washburn School of Law, provides links for state legislative and governmental information—including court cases and statutes—as well as local information.	**http://www.washlaw.edu**
West's Legal Directory	West's Legal Directory, updated daily, offers over 800,000 profiles of lawyers and law firms in the United States and Canada, including international offices.	**http://www.lawoffice.com**

assistance to you, but they may investigate and take punitive action against the attorney, if appropriate. Most states have established a fund for clients who lose money because the attorney takes it from them and uses it inappropriately (e.g., embezzles it). Practicing attorneys in the state are generally required to pay into the fund. As a last resort, you can sue the attorney for malpractice; however, then you will have to hire another attorney and begin a new litigation. In addition, it may be difficult for you to prove your damages, especially if you lost a lawsuit while the first attorney was representing you. Then the defendant will argue that even with another attorney, you still would have lost the suit.

SUMMARY

Law consists of rules that must be observed. These rules must be obeyed because they are enforceable in courts of law. Order is the absence of chaos. Our legal system strives to create and to maintain order. Justice is fairness. Commutative justice seeks to treat each person the same regardless of circumstances. Distributive justice seeks to vary treatment as appropriate in the situation. Our legal system seeks constantly to balance law, order, and justice. Its ultimate goal is to achieve equilibrium.

The law is an artificial language system. It includes everyday words, but they have technical meanings. The law also uses words that are unique to the law. The law of business includes contracts, sales, negotiable instruments, secured transactions, agency, partnerships, and corporations. By studying the law of business, you will learn how to avoid legal problems. If legal problems should develop, however, this knowledge will sensitize you to their ramifications. As a result, you will know when an attorney should be consulted.

A legal system needs to be reasonable, definite, practical, published, and final. A legal system should be directed toward achieving justice. It does so by properly utilizing police power; by keeping the peace or maintaining the status quo when irreparable injury is threatened; by providing answers; by protecting people, property, and government; by enforcing intent; by rehabilitating people; and by facilitating commercial transactions. There are various philosophies about how the law works or how it should work.

Our legal system is like a three-dimensional chess game in which a move in one subsystem can affect other subsystems. The sources of the U.S. legal system are constitutions, treaties, statutes, ordinances, administrative regulations, common law, case law, and equity. The law is a multidimensional system, including common and statutory law, civil and criminal law, and substantive and procedural law. The legal system is also composed of two branches: federal law and state law. A traveler or businessperson should not assume that the foreign law is similar to U.S. law.

DISCUSSION QUESTIONS

1. John Locke stated, "Where there is no law, there is no freedom."[26] What do you think he meant by this statement?

2. Noted legal scholar Roscoe Pound said, "Law must be stable and yet it cannot stand still."[27] What do you think he meant? How does this statement relate to the purposes of the legal system? Explain your answer.

3. What are the risks when a business takes a reactive approach to a potential problem arising in the legal system?

4. What is the jurisprudential approach(es) of the following court opinion discussing whether an obligation to return an engagement ring should be based on fault?

   [T]he fault rule is sexist and archaic, a too-long enduring reminder of the times when even the law discriminated against women.... In ancient Rome the rule was fault. When the woman broke the engagement, however, she was required not only to return the ring, but also its value, as a penalty. No penalty attached when the breach was the man's. In England, women were oppressed by the rigidly stratified social order of the day. They worked as servants or, if not of the servant class, were dependent on their relatives. The fact that men were in short supply, marriage above one's station rare[,] and travel difficult abbreviated betrothal prospects for women. Marriages were arranged. Women's lifetime choices were limited to a marriage or a nunnery.... Men, because it was a man's world, were much more likely than women to break engagements. When one did, he left behind a woman of tainted reputation and ruined prospects. The law ... gave her the engagement ring, as a consolation prize. When the man was jilted, a seldom thing, justice required the ring's return to him. Thus, the rule of life was the rule of law—both saw women as inferiors.[28]

5. Which jurisprudential view do you most closely agree with? Why?

6. John Rawls writes about justice and the elements that are necessary for a just society. He describes the "Bargaining Game," a theoretical community of men and women who get together to bargain for a completely new set of moral rules (laws) that they all must obey in the future. Once the rules are selected, the players must adhere to the them, even if the rules are not in their self-interest in a particular situation. The players choosing the rules do not know their own position in society, talents, or abilities. Rawls calls this the veil of ignorance.[29] Rawls has been interpreted as saying, "In effect, the parties choose principles for the design of society as if their places in it were to be determined by their worst enemies."[30] What rules do you think the players would choose, and why?

7. When does a business need to be familiar with the laws and legal systems of other countries?

8. Jeremy Bentham (1748–1832), an English lawyer, is best known for his utilitarian philosophy that the object of law should be to achieve the "greatest happiness of the greatest number." Discuss the implications of the following statement based on your knowledge of common versus statutory law:

   Do you know how they make [common law]? Just as a man makes laws for his dog. When your dog does anything you want to break him of, you wait until he does it and then beat him. This is the way you make law for your dog, and this is the way judges make laws for you and me. They won't tell a man beforehand.... The French have had enough of this dog-law; they are turning it as fast as they can into statute law, that everybody may have a rule to go by....[31]

9. Explain the role of the *Restatements of Law.*

10. In the United States, the general rule is that each party pays his or her own attorney's fees. There are a few exceptions provided under specific statutes. In Great Britain, the general rule is that the loser pays the winner's attorney's fees. Should the United States adopt the British rule? Why or why not?

CASE PROBLEMS AND WRITING ASSIGNMENTS

1. The Smithsonian Institute has a collection of nude photographs taken of college freshmen from Ivy League and other elite schools. Schools involved include Harvard, Princeton, Swarthmore, Yale, Vassar, and Wellesley. Many of the universities and colleges involved required all freshmen to pose in the nude for a frontal and a profile picture. This practice began in the early 1900s. At first, the pictures were taken as part of physical education classes to study posture; poise and posture were considered important in health. The pictures were then continued as part of a research project by W. H. Sheldon, who believed that there was a relationship between body shape and other traits such as intelligence. (His research is generally dismissed by scientists today.) Schools allowed Sheldon to take pictures of their students from the

1940s through the 1960s. Many of the schools have destroyed their collections. How the Smithsonian received the collection and who is actually pictured in the Smithsonian collection are unclear. Some prominent people were allegedly photographed during this period, including former President George Bush and President Clinton's wife, Hillary Rodham Clinton. A number of people have filed suit seeking an injunction against any displays or other uses of these pictures without permission of the subject in the photograph. What should the Smithsonian or other museums or research institutes do when they receive property of this nature? Why? Should a business have a policy for handling sensitive information about or photographs of its employees or customers? Who should have ownership rights in pictures such as these? What should be the Smithsonian's ethical obligation in regard to these pictures? Would the fact that some prominent people may be included affect this ethical obligation? [See Brigette Greenberg, "Smithsonian Blocks Access to Nude Photos," *The Fresno Bee* (21 January 1995), pp. A1, A12.]

2. The Environmental Defense Fund (EDF) requested an injunction, a form of equitable relief. In 1966, the U.S. Army Corps of Engineers recommended increasing the width of the channel. There was public notice. As early as 1967, EDF knew about the plan to widen the channel. In 1976, EDF filed its complaint, and in 1978 the complaint was changed to include the legal question about lack of authority on the part of the Army Corps. A large amount of money was expended in the intervening time. A prompt hearing was not requested by EDF. Should EDF's lawsuit be barred by *laches* because it waited too long to file the suit? [See *Environmental Defense Fund* v. *Alexander*, 614 F.2d 474 (5th Cir. 1980).]

3. Margaret Beattie was seriously injured in an automobile accident in Delaware. She incurred medical expenses of nearly $300,000 and was a quadriplegic following the accident. She filed suit against her husband for damages, alleging that his negligence was the cause of her injuries. Because the Beatties had substantial liability insurance, Margaret Beattie would have received a large sum in damages if she were able to establish her case. Unfortunately for her, Delaware follows the precedent of not allowing one spouse to sue the other spouse in tort. Should this precedent prevent Margaret from being allowed to sue her husband for damages in this case? [See *Beattie* v. *Beattie*, 630 A.2d 1096 (Del. 1993).]

4. Universal Studios and Walt Disney Productions filed suit against Sony Corporation for copyright infringement, alleging that the sale of videotape recorders, which allow the taping of shows from television, allowed and encouraged the infringement of copyrights. Sony denied that it was responsible for any copyright infringements and denied liability. How should the court resolve this case? What factors should the court consider in reaching its decision? [See *Sony Corporation of America* v. *Universal City Studios*, 464 U.S. 417 (1984).]

5. Connecticut enacted a statute that went into effect 1 October 1993. Under the statute, police are permitted to seize a person's car if he or she patronizes prostitutes from the car. Police may arrest the person hiring the prostitute and impound the car. The person can recover his or her car for use prior to trial by posting a bond equal to the vehicle's book value. If the person is found innocent in court, he or she would be entitled to the return of the car and any bond that has been posted. If someone else owns the car and the owner did not realize the car would be used to solicit prostitutes, the owner is entitled to have the car returned. Is this Connecticut law fair or just? [See "Police Hope to Drive Away Prostitutes by Confiscating Clients' Cars," *The Fresno Bee* (17 October 1993), p. A9.]

6. **BUSINESS APPLICATION CASE** The Italian federal corporate tax system is structured in a manner similar to that of the United States. However, there is a general practice in Italy by which corporations are expected to submit tax returns that understate income by 30 to 70 percent. After the corporate tax returns are filed, the tax authority asks the corporation to "discuss" the tax return. At this discussion, the firm and the tax authority haggle over the amount of tax actually owed, eventually reaching an agreement. A U.S. firm opened a division in Italy and filed its Italian return in the same manner as it would have done in the United States. When asked to "discuss" the return, the firm's manager refused. Instead, he wrote a letter to the tax authority informing it that the return was accurate and that there was nothing to discuss. Following receipt of this letter, the Italian tax authority filed a formal tax assessment in which the firm was told that its tax liability was three times the amount reflected on its return. What should the manager do in this case? Why did you recommend this particular course of action? [See Arthur L. Kelly, *Case Study—Italian Tax Mores*, Case Studies in Business Ethics (Englewood Cliffs, NJ: Prentice-Hall, Inc., 1984).]

7. **ETHICAL APPLICATION CASE** Michael Fay, an American teenager, age 18, was found guilty of spray-painting and throwing eggs at cars and possessing street signs in his room in Singapore. After Fay confessed, he was sentenced to four months in jail, fined $2,215, and subjected to six blows with a cane. This is a standard penalty for this type of behavior. Caning involves blows with a soaked rattan cane that is one-half inch-thick. Prisoners often become unconscious during canings; however, they are revived by a doctor before the flogging continues. Caning causes severe pain and can cause serious bleeding and leave permanent scars. Prior to the caning, President Clinton and the parents (George Fay and Randy Chan) requested clemency from Singapore's president, Ong Teng Cheong. Is Fay's punishment under the Singapore criminal justice system appropriate? Why or why not? Is this a reasonable method to obtain law and order? Should the U.S. president have intervened? Why or why not? [See William Murphy, "Boy's Parents Losing Hope on Flogging," *The Fresno Bee* (15 April 1994), p. A13; Jim Steinberg, "Fresnans Split on Flogging Penalty," *The Fresno Bee* (2 April 1994), pp. B1, B2.]

8. **CRITICAL THINKING CASE** In 1992, Rosa, an 18-year-old woman in Southern Italy went for a driving lesson. Rosa claims that the 45-year-old instructor took her to a remote area and raped her. The instructor argued that the sex was consensual. The all-male panel of judges on the criminal appeals court concluded that Rosa consented after considering that it is difficult to remove jeans without the cooperation of the wearer, that Rosa waited several hours to tell her parents, and that she returned to the driving school later that day for a driving theory lesson. The appeals court also said, "It should be noted that it is instinctive, especially for a young woman, to oppose with all her strength the person who wants to rape her. And it is illogical to say that a young woman would passively submit to a rape . . . for fear of undergoing other hypothetical and no more serious offenses to her physical safety."[32] The case has been returned for retrial. Do you agree with the appeals court decision? Why or why not? Some information is lacking in the English-language press. What additional information is important? [See "Judge Defends Rape-Jeans Ruling: 'We Have Complete Respect for Women,' Says Italian at Centre of Storm," *The Gazette (Montreal)* (13 February 1999), Art & Entertainment, p. D20; Alessandra Stanley, "'Denim Defense': Court Ruling in Italy Rekindles Angry Debate About Rape, Justice//The Judges' Ruling—That a Woman Who Is Wearing Jeans Can't Be the Victim of Rape—Incensed the Nation and Prompted a Protest in Parliament," *Star Tribune* (Minneapolis, MN) (17 February 1999) Source: *New York Times*, p. 11A; and "The Denim Defense," *Sacramento Bee* (19 February 1999), Editorials, p. B6.]

NOTES

1. *Black's Law Dictionary*, 3rd ed. (St. Paul, MN: West Publishing Co., 1933), p. 1050.
2. *Earl of Chesterfield* v. *Janssen*, 28 Eng. Rep. 82, 100 (Ch. 1750).
3. *Drysdale* v. *Prudden*, 143 S.E. 530, 536 (1928).
4. James Rachels, *The Elements of Moral Philosophy*, 2nd ed. (New York: McGraw-Hill, 1993), p. 50.
5. Ibid.
6. "Philosophy of Law," Section I.2, *The Internet Encyclopedia of Philosophy*, James Fiesher, general editor, The University of Tennessee at Martin (1999), http://www.utm.edu/research/iep/.
7. Ibid., Section III.3. Internal quote is from Richard Posner, *Economic Analysis of Law*, 4th ed. (Boston: Little, Brown, and Company, 1992), p. 23. Posner currently serves as the Chief Judge of the U.S. Court of Appeals for the Seventh Circuit.
8. 924 F.2d 872, 878 (9th Cir. 1991).
9. "Judge Defends Rape-Jeans Ruling: 'We Have Complete Respect for Women,' Says Italian at Centre of Storm," *The Gazette* (Montreal) (13 February 1999), Art & Entertainment, p. D20.
10. Alessandra Stanley, "'Denim Defense': Court Ruling in Italy Rekindles Angry Debate About Rape, Justice//The Judges' Ruling—That a Woman Who Is Wearing Jeans Can't Be the Victim of Rape—Incensed the Nation and Prompted a Protest in Parliament," *Star Tribune* (Minneapolis, MN) (17 February 1999). Source: *New York Times*, p. 11A.
11. "Judge Defends Rape-Jeans Ruling," p. D20.
12. "The Denim Defense," *Sacramento Bee* (19 February 1999), Editorials, p. B6.
13. *The Internet Encyclopedia of Philosophy*, Section III.2. Internal quote is from Andrew Altman, "Legal Realism, Critical Legal Studies, and Dworkin," *Philosophy and Public Affairs*, 15, no. 2 (1986), p. 221.
14. 1 Cranch 137, 2 L.Ed. 60 (1803).
15. 252 U.S. 416.
16. 347 U.S. 483 (1954).
17. "American Phoenix Will Provide Reinsurance to Oman Insurer," *Mealey's Litigation Report: Reinsurance* (11 February 1999), vol. 9, no. 19.
18. Asa Aarons, "Getting Your Name on Do-Not-Call List Can Pull the Plug on Telemarketers," *Daily News* (New York) (23 March 1999), p. 18.

19. Charlie Hollomon, "Letters: In My Opinion; Put Limits on Telemarketers," *The Atlanta Journal and Constitution* (31 March 1999), p. 17A.

20. Ed Anderson, "No-Call List May Quiet Phones; Bill Hangs Up on Telemarketers," *The Times-Picayune* (20 May 1999, Orleans Edition), p. A5.

21. Robynn Tysver, "'No Call' Phone List Hung Up a Bill Targeting Unwanted Telemarketing Pitches Fails to Advance to the Next Round," *Omaha World-Herald* (8 April 1999, Sunrise Edition), News, p. 11.

22. "An Islamic Legal System? Pakistan," *The National Law Journal* (14 September 1998), p. A14; Beena Sarwar Lahore, "Rights-Pakistan: Nawaz Sharif's Use of Religion Fools No One," IAC (SM) Newsletter Database (TM), Global Information Network, Inter Press Service (16 September 1998).

23. "ALI Pushes Restatements Along, Hones Lawyer Ethics, Product Liability," *The United States Law Week* (28 May 1996), p. 1177 (64 LW1177).

24. Henry Gottlieb, "Pushing the Envelope on Disclosure Invoking Restatement, Court Expands Fraud Exception to Client-Confidence Rule," *New Jersey Law Journal* (19 April 1999), p. 1.

25. "When You Need a Lawyer," *Consumer Reports* (February 1996), pp. 34–39.

26. John Locke, *Second Treatise of Government,* Section 57, ed. and introduction by Thomas P. Perdon (New York: Liberal Arts Press, 1952).

27. Roscoe Pound, *Interpretations of Legal History* (New York: Macmillan Publishing Co., 1923), p. I.

28. *Lindh* v. *Surman,* 702 A.2d 560 (Pa.Super. 1997), citing *Aronow* v. *Silver,* 538 A.2d 851, 853 (N.J.Super. 1987).

29. John Rawls, *A Theory of Justice* (Cambridge, MA: Belknap Press of Harvard University Press, 1971).

30. Chandran Kukathas and Philip Pettit, *Rawls: A Theory of Justice and Its Critics* (Palo Alto, CA: Stanford University Press, 1990), p. 39.

31. Jeremy Bentham, *The Works of Jeremy Bentham* (New York: Russell and Russell, 1962), p. 231.

32. Alessandra Stanley, "'Denim Defense," p. 11A.

2

BUSINESS ETHICS

A G E N D A

The Kochanowskis need to understand the ethical restrictions under which they will operate Call-Image Technology. Businesses today are expected to act ethically, even if they do not have any formulated ethical theory that provides guidance in this area. A business must also satisfy the social contract it has with society. In addition, the business must weigh decisions, taking into account the potential impact—both beneficial and harmful—on each of its constituents. How can the family measure the ethics of any conduct they undertake for the business? How does a business manager know what the social contract theory demands of the business? Who are the constituents of a business? These and other questions need to be addressed in covering the material in this chapter. Be prepared! You never know when one of the Kochanowskis will need your help or advice.

ETHICS AND MORALITY

It is fairly standard for people to equate ethics with morality and to use the words *ethics* and *morals* interchangeably. In so doing, they find it easier to discuss the topic of ethics. However, such an equation is not altogether accurate. *Ethics* refers to a guiding philosophy—the principles of conduct governing an individual or a group.[1] By contrast, *morals* relate to principles of right and wrong behavior as sanctioned by or operative on one's conscience.[2] From the perspective of an individual, ethics and morals may, and frequently do, have the same meaning. However, from the perspective of a group—including a society—it is more appropriate to speak of ethics. Thus, when we speak of ethics, we are talking about societal values, the accepted conduct within a given society. In contrast, when we speak of morals, we are talking about individual values, the accepted conduct *of* an individual *by* that individual. Different societies may have different ethics, but the morals of any given individual should remain relatively constant no matter which society that person should happen to be in at any point in time. Ethical conduct is conduct that is deemed right—or at least accepted as not wrong—within a societal setting. Moral conduct is conduct that the individual considers right—or at least does not consider as wrong—without regard to the attitude of the society.

To further complicate this already complex issue, societies also have standards that go beyond ethics. The ethical standards of a society reflect what is considered "right" and "wrong" within that society in a general manner. Some wrong behavior may be merely a matter of rude conduct, frowned on within the society, but not of sufficient seriousness or severity to merit more than a social dislike of the conduct. Other "wrong" conduct may be considered much more serious, calling for more than a societal frown; this conduct may be so inappropriate for the society that the person who acts in this "wrongful" manner may be subjected to a fine or even to incarceration. To help ensure that people within a society act in a socially acceptable manner, the society enacts laws and regulations, usually with penalties attached for conduct in violation of the law or regulation in question. These laws enacted by society provide an ethical floor—a minimum standard of behavior that is expected from each member of that society.

Although it is a broad generalization, conduct that violates a law or regulation of a society is generally deemed unethical by that society. This is not to say that all unethical conduct is also illegal; rather, that all illegal conduct is also unethical. Of course, there are examples where some members of a society will act in a manner that violates a law or a regulation in order to force the society to reconsider its official position, with the aim of changing the law, and thereby changing the official social values the law affects. One such example involves Dr. Martin Luther King, Jr., and his encouragement of civil disobedience in the 1950s. His conduct was technically illegal—and thus could be viewed as unethical—at the time. However, the success of the Civil Rights movement ultimately changed the laws regarding equal rights and racial discrimination, thereby changing the social values reflected by the laws governing human rights in this country. Dr. King acted in a *moral* manner, effecting changes that, in turn, made his conduct ethical *in hindsight*.

To take a simple, albeit controversial, example, let us examine the abortion issue in the United States. Since the Supreme Court's opinion in *Roe* v. *Wade*,[3] doctors in the United States have been able to legally, and therefore ethically, perform abortions in this country. Prior to that opinion, abortions were illegal in numerous states, and any doctor who performed an abortion was acting in an unethical—not to mention illegal—manner. The change in the law led to a change in the ethics of the society. In a similar vein, women now may ethically choose to have an abortion when they could not have so chosen prior to the *Roe* v. *Wade* decision. However, the fact that such a decision is ethical (acceptable to society) does not mean that it will be considered moral by everyone. Many women would not consider having an abortion because they view abortions as immoral. For these women, to have an abortion would require them to violate their personal moral values. The fact that *society* considers such a procedure ethical would not affect how these women feel from a *personal* perspective. If these women choose not to have an abortion, they are acting both morally (adhering to their personal values) and ethically (adhering to society's values). In other words, as long as their personal values—their morals—do not involve acting in a manner that calls for action prohibited by society's ethics, there is no problem with their adherence to their values.

If the personal morals of an individual call for conduct prohibited by society's ethics, however, there is a potential problem. For example, suppose a person feels that stealing is moral as long as the victim of the theft is wealthy. This person will encounter problems if he or she acts on the basis of this moral value by stealing from a wealthy victim. In deciding to steal from the wealthy, such a person may be acting morally (adhering to his or her personal values) but will be deemed to have acted unethically by society (violating the society's values). Our society has deemed theft to be an illegal and an unethical act, and the person whose morals conflict with this value will find that society has deemed the conduct both illegal and unethical even though, purely personally, the conduct may have been moral to the individual.

ETHICAL THEORIES

Before the topic of business ethics can be addressed, it is imperative to have at least an introductory exposure to some of the more widely cited ethical theories and principles. This section of the chapter introduces several of these ethical theories and principles and compares them to one another. When we study these ethical theories, it is important to remember that there is no single "best" ethical theory everyone should follow. Each individual and each organization must choose the theory that best suits his, her, or its values and morals. The theory followed can be chosen in any fashion, even if that fashion seems entirely arbitrary. The theory chosen can even be a combination of features from several different theories. For example, some people base their ethical beliefs on the Golden Rule (Do unto others as you would have others do unto you), while others select an "ends" approach (the outcome of the conduct determines its ethical nature). The important point is that a theory has been chosen and is being followed.

The study of ethics and of ethical principles is well known in philosophy, but it is relatively new to business. Business students have long been used to "hard-and-fast" rules and theories in their classes. Some of these rules or theories, such as **caveat emptor** and **laissez–faire** economics, were followed for a while and then discarded as society and its values changed. Others are still followed today. For example, "debits equal credits" is a given in accounting classes, and an accounting student can tell at a glance if the debits and the credits are equal. If they are not equal, that same accounting student knows that a problem exists and will then endeavor to find the problem and to solve it. However, the mere fact that debits do, in fact, equal credits does not guarantee that there is not a problem. An error

Caveat emptor
Let the buyer beware.

Laissez–faire
Let (the people) do as they choose; a doctrine opposing governmental interference in economic affairs beyond the minimum necessary for the maintenance of peace and property rights.

might still exist, but that error may be exactly offset by one or more other errors. Such errors are not as obvious as the one that exists when the debits and the credits do not match, but they are every bit as real, and they are more difficult to find. Business ethics is somewhat similar to this latter example.

Studying ethical theories and principles is not nearly as "hard and fast" as most other business topics, and the problems are not nearly as obvious in an ethical setting as the problems from the examples here. Yet questions of ethics—particularly of business ethics—are among the most important the modern businessperson will face in his or her career. The manager may face a "Hobson's choice" among bad alternatives; or the decision may entail a trade-off between short-term and long-term gains; or the decision may involve short-term gains (or losses) compared to long-term losses (or gains).

While *ethics* can be defined as the system, or code, of morals of a particular person, religion, group, or profession,[4] such a definition does not provide much help in the area of business ethics. Why? Business does not fit neatly into any of the categories mentioned in the definition. Although a business may be recognized as a legal person, the business is not a "particular person," nor does any one individual influence business enough to provide moral or ethical modeling for the firm. Even though it is undoubtedly true that some businesspeople worship "the almighty dollar," business does not qualify as a religion in any realistic sense of the term. Likewise, the "group" to which business belongs is too diverse to have a single system or code of morals.

Similarly, "business" is not a single profession like medicine or law, susceptible to the adoption of a single code of professional conduct, or of ethics. Thus, for most people, the study of business ethics comes down to an analysis of the system or code of morals of a particular person, the specific businessperson whose conduct is being evaluated. Unfortunately, the ethical standard too often applied in this situation is that of the observer rather than the observed. To properly treat the ethical issues of a businessperson, some kind of analysis framework must be established, and some basic understanding of the ethical parameters of business needs to be developed.

Consequential and Nonconsequential Principles

Before a framework for the analysis of business ethics can be developed, some decisions must be made as to what values and standards are being measured, and on what basis the measurement is being made. Two broad categories of ethical theories exist. Ethical theories may be based on either consequential (teleological) principles or on nonconsequential (deontological) principles.

Consequential principles judge the ethics of a particular action by the consequences of that action. Consequential ethics, therefore, determine the "rightness" or the "wrongness" of any action by determining the ratio of good to evil that a given action will produce. A person practicing consequential ethics needs to evaluate each of his or her possible alternative actions, measuring the good (and the evil) that may result from the alternatives. The "right" action is the one that produces the greatest ratio of good to evil of any of the available alternatives. Among the major theories of ethical behavior under the consequential principles are egoism, utilitarianism, and feminism, also known as the *feminist philosophy*. Each of these theories will be examined in more detail later in this section.

Nonconsequential principles tend to focus on the concept of *duty* rather than on any concepts of right and/or wrong. Under the nonconsequential approach, a person acts ethically if that person is faithful to his or her duty, regardless of the consequences that may follow. If a person carries out his or her duties, the greatest good must occur because the duty of the individual was carried out. If each individual carries out his or her duty, society knows what to expect from each individual in any and every given situation. This provides for greater long-term continuity than would arise if each individual based every personal choice on the anticipated consequences of each particular action for that individual. In addition, society imposes duties to maximize the values society wants, and by meeting that duty the individual is furthering the interests of that society. The "categorical imperative" advanced by Immanuel Kant and the "veil of ignorance" advocated by John Rawls are two of the best-known theories in support of the nonconsequential principles of ethics. Both of these theories will be discussed in detail later in this chapter.

Consequential Ethics

Egoism. The doctrine that posits that self-interest is the proper goal of all human action is known as *egoism*.[5] (Do not confuse an *egoist*, a person who follows the ethical theory of egoism, with an *egotist*, a person who has an exaggerated sense of self-importance.) In the doctrine of egoism, each person is expected to act in a manner that will maximize his or her long-term interests. In so doing, society is expected to benefit because when each individual acts in a manner that produces the greatest ratio of good to evil, the sum of all of these individual "good-producing" actions within the society will produce the greatest total good for the society.

One common misconception of egoism is that all egoists are hedonistic seekers of pleasure who desire instant gratification. This concept treats one's pleasure as being equal to one's best interests. In fact, an egoist may well decide to act in a "selfless" manner because doing so will further his or her long-term self-interest more than will any short-term pleasures. Making a personal sacrifice today to receive some benefit in the future is perfectly consistent with the doctrine of egoism. Similarly, an egoist may obtain self-gratification from performing acts that benefit others so that such actions further the individual's long-term interests by increasing his or her satisfaction.

An organization, too, may follow egoism. From an organizational perspective, egoism involves those actions that best promote the long-term interests of the organization. Thus, a corporation may establish a minority hiring program or a college scholarship program and, in so doing, may be acting in a purely egoistic manner. These programs may advance the long-term interests of the corporation by improving its public image, reducing social tensions, or avoiding legal problems that might otherwise have arisen. The short-term expenses incurred in such programs are more than offset by future benefits, so that the programs may appear to be generous and public spirited when in reality they are undertaken for purely "selfish" reasons—as befits the ethical theory of the particular firm.

Utilitarianism. The second major consequential approach to ethics is *utilitarianism*. To a utilitarian, the proper course of conduct to follow in any given setting is the one that will produce the greatest good (or the least harm) for the greatest number.[6] Rather than focusing on the interests of the individual (as an egoist would), the utilitarian focuses on the interests of the society. The ethical course of conduct is the one that best serves the interests of the social group as a whole, regardless of the impact on any individuals or any subgroups of the total social system. In theory, someone who is a utilitarian does not care if the "good" is immediately felt or if it is long term in nature. The only concern is whether the "good" to be derived—whenever it is derived—produces the greatest possible quantity of good available among the alternatives from which the choice was made.

There are two primary types of utilitarianism: act utilitarianism and rule utilitarianism. *Act utilitarianism* is more concerned with individual actions and their effect on the social group as a whole than it is with obeying rules. An act utilitarian expects each person to act in a manner that will produce the greatest net benefit for the social group, even if such actions require the breaking of a social "rule." While it is felt that rules should generally be followed, exceptional situations may compel an act utilitarian to break the rules for the greater good of the society. Thus, to an act utilitarian, telling a "little white lie" may be the most ethical course of conduct in a given situation if doing so would produce more total good than would telling the truth, avoiding the answer, or any other alternative.

A *rule utilitarian* believes that strict adherence to the rules of the society will generally produce the greatest good for the greatest number. A rule utilitarian tends to follow all of the rules of the society without exception. This can lead to a problem in some situations. The rules that are followed can cause the rule utilitarian to become inflexible, especially when he or she faces a unique situation for which the rules were not designed.

Feminism. Feminism, or the feminist philosophy (also called the *ethics of caring*), has gained in popularity recently. This ethical theory emphasizes that particular attention be paid to the effect of decisions on individuals, especially those individuals in a close relationship with the decision maker.[7] This philosophy focuses on character traits such as sympathy, compassion, loyalty, and friendship. While decisions are still based on doing the greatest good, other factors must also be considered— among them social cooperation and the realization of inequities in power or ability. The structure of the society must be protected, but the rights and interests of the less capable person should be protected as well. This philosophy is still developing, but it bears watching in the future.

Nonconsequential Ethics

Kant and the Categorical Imperative. The nonconsequential principles of ethical theory are best exemplified by the categorical imperative developed by the German philosopher Immanuel Kant (1724–1804). Kant felt that certain universal moral standards existed without regard to the circumstances of the moment or the values of any particular society.[8] Under Kant's theory, when people follow these universal moral principles, they are acting morally and ethically. When people do not follow them, they are acting unethically. Individual variations and consequences are irrelevant. The universal moral principles impose a duty on each person, and the performance of that duty is what determines the "rightness" or the "wrongness" of any given action.

Kant also posited perfect duties and imperfect duties. *Perfect duties* are those things a person must always do or refrain from doing, such as the duty of a merchant never to cheat a customer. *Imperfect duties* involve things a person should, but not necessarily must, do. For example, a person should contribute to charities but not necessarily all charities, nor should a person have to contribute to any particular charity every time that charity solicits contributions.

Based on his theories, Kant developed his categorical imperative. Simply stated, it says that each person should act in such a manner that his or her actions could become the universal law. In a perfectly ethical and moral world, each person is expected to act as every person ought to act. The rules to be followed are unconditional, and adherence to them is imperative. If each person carries out his or her duty by following these "universal rules," society will be properly served by each individual.

Kant's approach to ethics is also applicable to organizations. An organization is judged in the same manner as an individual; it is expected to obey the categorical imperative just as is an individual. The organization is to act according to its duty, with its actions judged against the "universal law" standard—would such conduct be proper if all organizations were to act in the same manner? The organization would be expected to act in a manner that discharges its duty to every aspect of society, which would include recognition of the rights of others and the duty owed to others.

Rawls and the Veil of Ignorance. John Rawls took the works of Locke, Rousseau, and Kant as a starting point to develop his own theory of justice.[9] Rawls viewed these earlier works as the foundation for a "contract theory" of justice, and he presented his conception of justice as a higher level of abstraction from the earlier theories. Rawls felt that a truly just society would be one where the rules governing the society were developed behind a *veil of ignorance,* behind which no person would know his or her personal characteristics. Since the people making the rules were doing so while wholly ignorant of their unique combination of race, religion, color, gender, wealth, age, or education, they would enact rules they would be willing to live under regardless of which combination of factors they would have to live under once they stepped out from behind the veil of ignorance.

By creating a situation in which each member of the society is willing to live under the rules developed behind the veil, true justice can be obtained by the society. A proper constitution will be adopted; an appropriate method for legislation based on that constitution will be created; a proper method for dispute resolution will be developed; and, finally, the application of rules to particular cases by judges and administrators, and the following of rules by citizens generally, will be implemented.[10] These theories are summarized and analyzed as they apply in a business setting in Exhibit 2.1 on page 40.

Other Theories

There are other ethical theories that may also influence one's ethical outlook. Two of these will be discussed very briefly.

Relativism. Ethical relativism states that two people or two societies may hold ethical views that are opposed to one another, and yet both may be correct. In other words, ethics and values are relative and may change from one location to another. While it is true that different societies have different values (e.g., the death penalty is a socially acceptable punishment in some societies, but not in others), the individual is more commonly governed by his or her *morals,* and personal morals do not change from one location to another. Relativism seems to be of more importance to sociologists and anthropologists than it is to ethicists.[11]

The Golden Rule. The Golden Rule theory of ethics advises each person to "do onto others as you would have others do unto you." This is a generally accepted principle in Judeo-Christian thought and is an admirable rule for people to follow. However, as an ethical theory it is difficult to measure or to define in terms of one's conduct.

EXHIBIT 2.1 | **A Comparison of Ethical Theories**

Ethical Theory	Positive Aspects in a Business Context	Negative Aspects in a Business Context
Egoism (Consequential theory—an act is ethical when it promotes the best long-term interests of the firm.)	1. Provides a basis for formulating and testing policies. 2. Provides flexibility in ethical decision making for business. 3. Allows a business to tailor codes of conduct to suit the complexity of its particular business dealings.	1. May ignore blatant wrongs. 2. Incompatible with the nature and role of business. 3. Cannot resolve conflicts of egoistic interests. 4. Introduces inconsistency into ethical counsel.[12]
Utilitarianism (Consequential theory—the most ethical decision is the one that produces the greatest good, or the least harm, for the greatest number of people.)	1. Provides a basis for formulating and testing policies. 2. Provides an objective manner for resolving conflicts of self-interest. 3. Recognizes the four constituent groups of a business. 4. Provides the latitude in ethical decision making that business seems to need.	1. Utilitarians ignore conduct which appears to be wrong in-and-of itself. 2. The principle of utility may be in conflict with the principle of justice. 3. It is very difficult to formulate satisfactory rules.[13]
Feminism (Consequential theory—the ethics of caring, it recognizes the importance of personal relationships.)	1. Provides a basis for formulating and testing policies. 2. Provides an objective manner for resolving conflicts of self-interest. 3. Recognizes the four constituent groups of a business. 4. Provides flexibility in ethical decision making for business.	1. Places undue emphasis on those closest to the decision maker. 2. May be more concerned with the "community" than with the business. 3. It is very difficult to formulate satisfactory rules.[14]
Categorical Imperative (Nonconsequential theory—only when we act from a sense of duty do actions have ethical worth.)	1. The categorical imperative takes the guesswork out of ethical decision making in business. 2. Introduces a needed humanistic dimension into business ethics decisions. 3. The concept of duty implies the ethical obligation to act from a respect for rights and the recognition of responsibilities.	1. Provides no clear way to resolve conflicts among duties. 2. There is no compelling reason that the prohibition against certain actions should hold without exception.[15]
Veil of Ignorance (Nonconsequential theory—rational agents, unaware of their personal characteristics or places in society, choose the principles they wish to have govern everyone in society.)	1. The veil of ignorance takes the guesswork out of ethical decision making in business. 2. Introduces a needed humanistic dimension into business ethics decisions. 3. Implies the ethical obligation to act from a respect for rights and the recognition of responsibilities.	1. Uses the better-off members of society to assume the welfare of the worst-off. 2. There is no compelling reason for following universal principles that might be agreed to in theory.[16]

A SYNTHESIS FOR ETHICAL DECISION MAKING

Each of these ethical theories provides a possible framework for evaluating the ethics of a business and the people who operate it. Remember, there is no one universally accepted theory or approach to ethics in general, nor is there an accepted and universal approach to business ethics. Each firm in the business environment can select a theory of ethics to follow in developing its own ethical approach to conducting its business, whether it chooses a consequential theory, a nonconsequential theory, or a composite theory. Before choosing a theory, however, the businessperson should also take into account several other factors. These should include, but not be limited to, the short-term versus the long-term impact of any decisions, the constituent groups that will be affected by the decision being made (constituent groups are discussed later in the chapter), and the way in which the ethical decision fits within the laws and regulations affecting the business in this area.

Perhaps a business would be best advised to seek a synthesis of these different theories, as tempered by the social contract theory, to develop an approach to ethical issues. This approach would provide a structure for evaluating actions and options regardless of the ethical theory that most closely reflects the values of the business. One such synthesis is suggested by the work of Vincent Ruggerio.[17] Ruggerio suggests that there are three common concerns in ethical decision making: obligations, ideals, and effects. From this foundation we can develop a framework for ethical decision making without regard to whether the theory followed is a consequential or a nonconsequential theory. In making a decision, the following factors should be considered:

1. The obligations that arise from organizational relationships
2. The ideals involved in any decisions that are made
3. The effects or consequences of alternative actions

Any actions that honor obligations while simultaneously advancing ideals and benefiting people can be presumed to be moral actions. Any actions that fall short in any respect become suspect.[18] This is not to say that these latter actions are necessarily unethical. However, since they have a negative impact on one or more of the areas of concern, the actions should be very carefully evaluated, and alternatives should be examined to see if a better one has been overlooked.

With this in mind, the firm should follow a two-step process in order to assure that it is making ethical decisions. The first step is to identify the important considerations involved (obligations, ideals, and effects). The second step is to decide where the emphasis should lie among these three considerations. This approach allows the firm to apply its ethical principles to an ethical problem while also taking into account the social contract and the relative positions of each of the four constituent groups of the business.

The following case was decided in the late nineteenth century. Although the case has nothing to do with business, it does provide an opportunity to examine some of the problems that can arise in the study of ethics. Compare the ethical stances of the defendants in this case with the ethical theories discussed earlier. This case illustrates how simple it is for a person to sometimes rationalize conduct that would generally be viewed as reprehensible.

2.1

REGINA V. DUDLEY AND STEPHENS
14 Q.B.D. 273 (1884)

FACTS In July 1884 four British sailors were cast away in a storm 1,600 miles from the Cape of Good Hope in an open lifeboat. The only food the crew found aboard the lifeboat was two one-pound tins of turnips. They were able to catch a turtle on their fourth day at sea, but had no other food beyond the turnips and the turtle through the 20th day. All four of the seamen were suffering from hunger and thirst by this time, and the youngest was delirious from drinking seawater. At that point in time, Dudley proposed that the other three should kill the youngest so that the other three would have food and liquid, and Stephens agreed. The next day, while Brooks was sleeping, Dudley killed the boy. While Brooks did not condone the act, he shared in the "bounty," and for the next four days the three men fed on the body and blood of the boy. They were rescued by a passing ship on the 29th day and taken to England, where they were arrested and charged with murder.

ISSUE Was the killing of the boy an act of murder or an act of self-defense?

HOLDING It was an act of murder.

REASONING The court granted "that if the men had not fed upon the body of the boy they would probably not have survived to be so picked up and rescued, but would within the four days have died of famine." It also agreed "that the boy, being in a much weaker condition, was likely to have died before them . . . [t]hat under these circumstances there appeared to the prisoners every probability that unless they then fed or very soon fed upon the boy or one of themselves they would die of starvation. That there was no appreciable chance of saving life except by killing some one for the others to eat. . . . "

The court addressed the self-defense issue by examining the words of Lord Hale. In the chapter in which he deals with the exemption to murder created by compulsion or necessity, he stated: "If a man be desperately assaulted and in peril of death, and cannot otherwise escape unless, to satisfy his assailant's fury, he will kill an innocent person then present, the fear and actual force will not acquit him of the crime and punishment of murder, for he ought rather to die himself than kill an innocent; but if he cannot otherwise save his own life the law permits him in his own defense to kill the assailant."

The court recognized the stress the sailors faced, and acknowledged that the temptations they faced were powerful, but denied that these things created a "necessity" justifying homicide. "Nor is this to be regretted. Though law and morality are not the same, and many things may be immoral which are not necessarily illegal, yet the absolute divorce of law from morality would be of fatal consequence; and such divorce would follow if the temptation to murder in this case were to be held by law an absolute defense of it. It is not so. To preserve one's life is generally speaking a duty, but it may be the plainest and the highest duty to sacrifice it. . . . It is not needful to point out the awful danger of admitting the principle which has been contended for. Who is to be the judge of this sort of necessity? By what measure is the comparative value of lives to be measured? Is it to be strength, or intellect, or what? It is plain that the principle leaves to him who is to profit by it to determine the necessity which will justify him in deliberately taking another's life to save his own. . . . [I]t is quite plain that such a principle once admitted might be made the legal cloak for unbridled passion and atrocious crime. There is no safe path for judges to tread but to ascertain the law to the best of their ability and to declare it according to their judgment; and if in any case the law appears to be too severe for individuals, to leave it to the Sovereign to exercise that prerogative of mercy which the Constitution has intrusted to the hands fittest to dispense it. . . . It is therefore our duty to declare that the prisoners' act in this case was willful murder, that the facts as stated in the verdict are no legal justification of the homicide; and to say that in our unanimous opinion the prisoners are upon this special verdict guilty of murder."

[The court then proceeded to pass a sentence of death on the prisoners. Queen Victoria subsequently commuted the sentences, setting the punishment to be served by Dudley and Stephens at six months imprisonment.]

BUSINESS CONSIDERATION Assume that a business is facing serious economic problems. While there are several alternatives available, the easiest method of economic recovery for the business is to "cannibalize" (strip away the assets, leaving an empty

2.1

REGINA V. DUDLEY AND STEPHENS, *continued*
14 Q.B.D. 273 (1884)

shell) a subsidiary of the firm. What should the business do?

ETHICAL CONSIDERATIONS Is it possible to make a (superficially) persuasive ethical argument in

support of the defendants on either an egoistic or a utilitarian basis, if one so desires? Can a persuasive argument be made under either the categorical imperative or the veil of ignorance?

THE GAME THEORY OF BUSINESS

Business as an Amoral Institution

Historically, business was viewed by many as an amoral institution. Since any given business was inanimate, and since only animate objects could be expected to possess "morality," it stood to reason that a business was not expected to possess "morality." Because it could not be expected to be moral, it also could not be immoral. Morality and immorality were reserved for animate beings, and inanimate objects were **amoral.** When most businesses were relatively small and local in nature, this did not present much of a problem. The owners and operators of businesses were known in the community, and even though the business was viewed as amoral, the owner or operator was held to community standards. Thus, most businesses were operated in an ethical manner in order to keep the local customers satisfied. However, as businesses grew increasingly larger and more complex, this local flavor was lost. Businesses no longer operated in a restricted geographic market, and no longer had to adhere to community standards. Eventually, society began to demand some minimal ethical standards for businesses. Included among these standards were the expectations of fair play and honesty, and the expectation that a business would seek profits for its investors. If a business did not meet these demands voluntarily, society sought direction from the legislature, which enacted statutes setting minimal business standards of behavior. If the business obeyed these laws, it met the duty of fair play; if the managers did not blatantly lie to the customers, the business met the duty of honesty; if the firm generated profits for its investors, it met this duty.

As an example, look at the court opinion in *Dodge* v. *Ford Motor Company,*[19] a 1919 opinion by the Supreme Court of Michigan. Ford Motor Company was an extremely successful enterprise at the time, and it was paying dividends reflecting that success. Between "ordinary dividends" of 5 percent *per month* and special dividends that had averaged more than *400 percent* per annum over the previous five years, the stockholders were receiving substantial returns on their investments. At that point, Henry Ford and the board of directors announced a change. While Ford would continue to pay regular dividends of 5 percent per month, there would be no more special dividends. Instead, the board announced its intention to reduce the price of new cars and to make substantial investments in socially beneficial programs for the employees and the community. Two of the stockholders, the Dodge brothers, filed suit to prevent this conduct proposed by Mr. Ford. The Michigan Supreme Court ruled that the board of directors of a corporation may *not* place

Amoral
Being neither moral nor immoral; lying outside the sphere to which moral judgments apply.

the interests of the public ahead of the interests of the stockholders, and may *not* divert corporate funds to noncorporate purposes. The board was instructed to continue to maximize profits and to leave any charitable or public-benefit contributions for individuals who chose to make such contributions from personal funds.

Notice what the court said a corporation is expected to do. Would such conduct by a corporation be considered ethical today?

The *Dodge* v. *Ford Motor Company* case is viewed as a landmark opinion, providing guidance for boards of directors in closely held corporations. While this opinion deals directly with the conflict between the desire of the Ford board to provide for the workers, and the challenge by shareholders who want dividends, the basic thrust of the opinion is that the board has a duty to the shareholders to maximize the return on their investments.

Many people have argued that the Dodge opinion, as described above, prohibited any charitable contributions by a corporation, unless such contributions were expressly authorized in the corporation's charter or bylaws. However, courts have generally disagreed with this position, finding an implicit authority to make contributions, if such contributions are in the best long-term interests of the firm. The next case is the landmark opinion on this topic.

Intra vires
Acts within the scope of the power of a corporation.

Ultra vires
Acts beyond the scope of the power of a corporation.

2.2

A.P. SMITH MFG. CO. V. BARLOW
98 A.2D 581 (N.J. 1953)

FACTS The A.P. Smith Manufacturing Company was incorporated in 1896, and is engaged in the manufacture and sale of valves, fire hydrants, and special equipment, mainly for the water and gas industries. The plant is located in East Orange and Bloomfield, New Jersey. Over the years, the firm was a regular contributor to the local community chest, as well as to Upsala College in East Orange and to Newark College (now a part of Rutgers University). In 1951 the board of directors adopted a resolution to join in the Annual Giving to Princeton University, authorizing the payment of $1,500 to the university. The board's resolution stated that the contribution was "in the best interests of the company." Several stockholders questioned the propriety of this contribution, and the corporation instituted a declaratory judgment action in the Chancery Division to determine whether the contribution was **intra vires** (within the powers of the corporation) or **ultra vires** (outside the powers of the corporation).

ISSUE May a corporation legally make charitable contributions from corporate funds, or is such an issue an unlawful "wasting" of corporate assets?

HOLDING Yes. A corporation may—in fact, should—make charitable contributions under certain circumstances.

REASONING The president of the corporation testified that the contribution was a sound investment, that the public expects corporations to aid philanthropic and benevolent institutions, that such contributions create goodwill, and that the overall effect is to create a favorable environment in which to conduct business. He added that such contributions increase the likelihood that the firm will help to create a flow of properly trained personnel for potential future employment. He also asserted that the public "expected" business to contribute to the society, and that a failure to do so was not good business. To strengthen the president's assertions, the state of New Jersey enacted a statute in 1930 expressly authorizing corporations to make charitable contributions in many situations.

The challenges by the stockholders—that the contributions were a waste of corporate assets, and that the statute should not apply to A.P. Smith because it had been incorporated prior to the adoption of the statute—were deemed of lesser weight by the court. The public policy considerations involved,

A.P. SMITH MFG. CO V. BARLOW, *continued*
98 A.2D 581 (N.J. 1953)

the statutory approval, and the size of the contribution all point to a positive effect on the community, without any harm to the corporation. The conduct of the firm was approved.

BUSINESS CONSIDERATION How can charitable contributions by a corporation be justified from a business perspective, presuming that the primary purpose of the business is to generate profits for its stockholders?

ETHICAL CONSIDERATIONS If the court's opinion reflects society's values in this case, what happened to social expectations concerning corporate conduct between the *Dodge* v. *Ford Motor Company* opinion and this opinion? How should this change have affected corporate decision making?

The "Game Theory"

As society and the courts began to recognize the existence of corporate duties, the concept of business as an amoral institution became untenable. If a business had duties, it had some ethical responsibilities. These responsibilities, however, tended to be based on adherence to "rules" and obeying those rules. If a business obeyed the rules and stayed within the law, it was deemed to be acting in an ethical manner. This approach to business ethics led to the development of the "game theory" as a means of judging the ethical stance of the business.[20] Basically, the game theory equates the operation of a business with playing a game, and the rules from various games were applicable to determine the ethics of the business. If a manager of a firm lied to his or her customers, the manager—and consequently, the business—had acted unethically. However, if the manager bluffed his or her customer, the manager—and the firm—may have acted in an ethical manner, presuming that bluffing is an acceptable part of the game being played. Bluffing is, after all, an accepted part of several games, including poker. Of course, one person's bluffing may well be another person's lying, but such conundra were left for others to solve.

There is a basic flaw in the game theory of business ethics. Game theories and game rules are fair and equitable only if all of the participants in the game are aware a game is being played. If any of the participants do not realize a game is being played, they cannot be aware of the rules of that game, and thus will be at a disadvantage. To take advantage of people under such circumstances would not be ethical.

Under the game theory, a number of rules were developed and followed. For example, *caveat emptor* (let the buyer beware) was a rule of the business game for a substantial period in U.S. history. Similarly, laissez–faire economic regulation was a rule of business in the United States. Business and its customers were aware of these rules, and they played the business game accordingly. Eventually, however, business began to industrialize and to gain an increasing ability to produce for larger and larger markets. The game was no longer quite as fair as it had been before, and as the game became more one-sided in favor of business, the other players (the customers) began to seek new rules for the game. When business would

2.1 | MARKETING/ MANAGEMENT

IS BUSINESS A GAME?

A family friend was visiting the Kochanowskis over the weekend, and he seemed excited to learn that the family was starting a business. He pointed out that he too had formed a business, and that he was now doing quite well for himself. He then offered the family some "free advice" for their business. He urged them to set their price high when they first enter the market, because there will be little competition, and the public will pay dearly for Call-Image. He also urged them to use the cheapest components possible, allowing them to maximize their profits early, before any other firms enter the market. As he pointed out, CIT can always increase its quality and lower its prices later. After all, business is "a game, just like Monopoly, only with real money." This advice bothered the Kochanowskis, and they have asked your advice. To what extent is business "just a game"? If business is "just a game," what are the rules (if any)?

BUSINESS CONSIDERATION What business problems might arise for CIT if it adopts an attitude such as this?

ETHICAL CONSIDERATION Can the ethical theory the firm follows help the Kochanowskis in determining whether to listen to the advice of their friend? Explain your reasoning.

not voluntarily change the rules, the customers asked the government to intervene. This led to government regulation of business and eventually an entirely new playing field on which the game of business was to be conducted. This new playing field is the one on which business must operate today.

THE SOCIAL CONTRACT THEORY

Many business executives today argue that U.S. business is too regulated by the government. These people see domestic business drowning in a sea of bureaucratic red tape while less-regulated foreign firms are assuming control of the economy. They want to be unfettered, set free from the "excessive" regulations imposed by the government and allowed to compete freely with foreign producers. Although this attitude can be justified from a simplistic economic position, it fails to take into account two factors: the spillover costs society must pay when a business fails to act in a responsible and ethical manner, and the social contract between business and society. When business became too large for local control, the society sought legislative intervention to force compliance with social demands. This is the gist of the social contract. Business must comply with the demands of the society if it wants to continue to exist and to operate within that society. The social contract defines the permissible scope of business conduct and goes beyond the purely economic issues. If society wants more from business than profits, business must accept this mandate in order to survive in society. To do otherwise is to breach the social contract.

The social contract theory basically posits that business can exist only because society allows it to exist, that business must satisfy the demands of the society if it is to be allowed to continue. If business does not satisfy the demands of society, society will change the "rules of the game" and, in doing so, perhaps revoke the permission that business now has. Today, society expects (and demands) more from business than mere profits. Environmental concerns, consumer safety and protection, and quality of life, among other things, must also be provided for in the production process. If these added demands cause costs to rise, so be it. If business will not meet these demands voluntarily, it will be forced to do so by regulation—or by society's changing the form of business or the rules of doing business. Not only has the "game theory" of business been rejected by society, but the rules by which business is allowed to exist have also been changed by the social contract theory.

In dealing with the social contract theory and evaluating the ethical stance of any given business, it is important to recognize that each business has a number of constituent groups—stakeholders, employees, customers, and the community in which it operates—and that each group of constituents will have different wants, needs, and desires. The business manager must base decisions affecting the business, at least in part, on the impact the decisions will have on the various constituents. Some decisions will affect all of the constituent groups, although not equally. Others will only affect some of the groups. Deciding how each group will be affected, and how much weight to give to each group, is essential in reaching ethical decisions. Exhibit 2.2 shows the constituent groups that a corporation must consider.

Businesses owe duties to each of the constituent groups. Businesses also expect duties from each of the constituent groups.

As an example of how these duties can affect a business in its decision process, consider the following example. A firm has developed a new production method that will lower costs (which will lead to increased profits) while simultaneously making safer products. To adopt this new method will benefit two constituent groups: stakeholders and customers. However, it will require relocating the plant, and it may produce a number of pollutants. Relocating the plant will cause harm to current employees who may be unable or unwilling to relocate, and to the current community, which will suffer economic harm from reduced employment. The possible increase in pollutants will harm the community at the site of the new plant, although this harm will be offset to some extent by the increase in employment and the economic "ripple effect" a new plant will cause. Somehow a balancing of these competing interests must be undertaken in reaching a decision that reflects the best short-term and long-term interests of the firm.

The Changing Social Environment

Over the years, business has changed, and with it the attitudes of society toward business. The early days of commerce featured primarily local trade, with mainly handcrafted goods produced and sold by local merchants and artisans. Under these circumstances, the rule of caveat emptor was followed, and the success of any business was, to a significant extent, dependent on the reputation of its owner/operator.

E X H I B I T   2.2 | **Constituents of a Business**

——— a duty owed to a constituent group by the business
- - - - - a duty owed to the business by the constituent group

Eventually, business began to industrialize and to gain an increased capacity for productivity. As businesses began to produce more, they were able to expand their geographic markets from local to regional. This expansion caused some minor changes, although the buyer still had to beware. No longer could the buyer expect to be personally acquainted with the seller. Although the reputation of the seller remained important, much of the spread of that reputation was now only hearsay. The buyer and the seller were becoming separated by distance.

Industrialization continued to expand, and transportation and communication also grew and developed. The advent of the railroads allowed truly national business operations for the first time. With this opportunity to deal on a national scope, manufacturers became aware of "economies of scale." The age of "bigger is better" had arrived. Now caveat emptor took on more meaning. No longer could a buyer rely on a seller's reputation. Sellers were combining into trusts, and available substitutes for a seller's goods began to decline. Buyers were being thrust into a "take-it or leave-it" position.

For the first time, the public expectation of business made a drastic change. The public began to request government intervention to protect the consumer and the worker from "big business." The government responded with what business must have thought was a vengeance. The Interstate Commerce Commission, the antitrust statutes, the Securities and Exchange Commission, and a myriad of other agencies and acts were passed in relatively rapid succession.

Why did these changes occur? Fundamentally, because business was so busy meeting its own perceived needs that it ignored the expectations and the demands of the public. Was business acting illegally? In most cases, no. Was business acting unethically? From our contemporary perspective, probably; from an historical point of view, probably not. The key point to remember is that, in most cases, business was being conducted in a manner that had been socially and legally acceptable up to that time. However, as society changed and as the demands of society changed, business failed to respond. Then, when business failed to respond, society sought legislative intervention. The end of the nineteenth century saw the birth of the social contract as an essential element of conducting business.

One example of the changing social environment is the area of "employment at will." An at-will employee is one who works for the employer only so long as both parties agree to the employment. There is no fixed term of employment, and either party may terminate the employment relationship at any time merely by giving notice to the other party. Historically, courts upheld the right of the employer to discharge an at-will employee "for good cause, for no cause, or even for cause morally wrong. . . ."[21] The employer's unlimited right to discharge an employee was too often abused by the employer, which led to a reevaluation of the traditional "at-will" doctrine. In *Pierce* v. *Ortho Pharmaceutical Corporation*,[22] the court ruled that, generally speaking, an employer in an employment-at-will arrangement is free to terminate the employment relationship at any time, with or without cause. However, the court also stated that firing an employee for a reason that violates public policy would not be done in good faith and could result in liability for wrongful discharge.

The following case relies to a great extent on the *Pierce* opinion, as described above, in addressing the issue of wrongful discharge. It also involves the issue of whether criminal conduct by an employee provides "cause" for terminating an employment contract. Follow the court's reasoning, and then decide whether you would have reached the same result.

2.3

McGARRY V. ST. ANTHONY OF PADUA
704 A.2D 1353 (N.J.SUPER.A.D. 1998)

FACTS On September 27, 1994, plaintiff entered into a one-year employment contract with Saint Anthony's and began serving as Music Minister/Director of Music in October 1993 [sic]/ St. Anthony's Pastor, Father Robert Lynam, who was authorized to hire and fire employees, signed the contract. The contract contained the following provision for termination:

The parties involved shall give notice of termination of employment at least thirty days in advance of the termination. The termination time must be completed by the employee or if the employer does not wish the termination to be completed the employer shall fulfill all contractual financial agreements.

This litigation arose out of the fact that plaintiff had been receiving shipments of illegal anabolic steroids at St. Anthony's. He was arrested on February 1, 1995 in the parking lot of St. Anthony's for possession of anabolic steroids . . . He admitted he was expecting the package and that he knew it contained anabolic steroids . . . Plaintiff stated he had been taking steroids to assist him with bodybuilding even though he knew they were illegal. He admitted that he had the steroids delivered to him at St. Anthony's on three prior occasions and that he injected himself with the deca durabolin approximately once a week. On February 2, 1995, Father Lynam received word of a newspaper article which reported plaintiff's arrest at St. Anthony's for receiving anabolic steroids. The same day, plaintiff met with Father Lynam and, according to the Pastor, agreed to resign and to turn in his keys. The following morning, plaintiff called Father Lynam's secretary to arrange removal of his belongings . . . On February 5, 1995, Father Lynam found that a microphone was missing and faxed a note to plaintiff asking him to look for it. On February 7, 1995, plaintiff wrote back that he intended to continue his duties at the church unless he was fired. He also wrote that if he was not fired, he would show up for choir rehearsal the next day. Father Lynam immediately replied by fax that it was clear that plaintiff had resigned on February 2, 1995 by virtue of his returning his keys and equipment and not appearing for mass after his resignation. Plaintiff responded by fax that he did not resign and intended to continue unless fired. Father Lynam then sent the following fax: "Let me make it perfectly clear that you are not to come

on Church property, and you are not to cause any disruption with choir or Masses." Plaintiff faxed back a message questioning whether he had been fired. On or prior to February 6, 1995, plaintiff applied to another parish for similar employment, but was rejected when inquiry was made to Father Lynam regarding plaintiff's employment at St. Anthony's and Father Lynam informed the prospective employer of the incident which had occurred . . . On March 30, 1995, plaintiff filed a complaint . . . against St. Anthony's alleging breach of employment contract, wrongful discharge, defamation and interference with a prospective economic advantage . . . Defendant moved for summary judgment. On December 20, 1996, an order was executed dismissing with prejudice plaintiff's . . . claims.

ISSUES Did St. Anthony's breach the employment contract with McGarry? Was McGarry wrongfully discharged? Did St. Anthony's improperly interfere with a prospective economic advantage?

HOLDINGS No to all three issues. St. Anthony's acted in an appropriate manner in this situation.

REASONING The . . . judge dismissed plaintiff's . . . count alleging interference with a prospective economic advantage finding that the plaintiff could not show that "there was an intentional, without justification, interference" with his economic advantage. He reasoned that Father Lynam supplied the information only after it was requested, and the information supplied was of criminal conduct admitted by plaintiff and covered in the newspaper. Additionally, Father Lynam was protected by a qualified privilege for employment references . . . The judge also dismissed the wrongful discharge portion of count one, finding that there was not a factual dispute. The judge, however, perceived that there was a factual dispute concerning whether there was a resignation or a firing, and if there was a resignation, whether it was voluntary . . . After receiving briefs, the judge ruled on December 20, 1996, that the breach of contract count could not survive the dismissal of the wrongful termination court. The court found:

[Plaintiff] used, actually the church address in a scheme to obtain steroids. They were actually mailed

continued

2.3

McGARRY V. ST. ANTHONY OF PADUA, *continued*
704 A.2D 1353 (N.J.SUPER.A.D. 1998)

to the church and he was arrested at the church. How a fact finder could not view that as being in bad faith, is beyond me. And I think I am comfortable finding as a matter of law, that plaintiff breached an inherent constructive condition to comport his conduct to moral norms and standards . . .

We first consider the wrongful termination issue. Terms will be implied into a contract where the parties intended them and the terms are necessary to give business efficacy to the contract as written . . . In every contract, there is an implied covenant of good faith and fair dealing . . . In other words, there is an implied covenant that "neither party shall do anything which will have the effect of destroying or injuring the right of the other party to receive the fruits of the contract[.]". . . Even where, as here, the employee performs the duties contracted for satisfactorily, criminal activity by the employee can justify his discharge for breach of an employment contract . . . It is clear that plaintiff intentionally ordered the anabolic steroids for this personal use and had them shipped to St. Anthony's address. This constituted a breach of the implied conditions of plaintiff's contract of employment. The receipt of anabolic steroids at work indirectly involved St. Anthony's in the commission of a criminal offense and constituted gross misconduct. The criminal offense while not immediately injurious to St. Anthony's, eventually resulted in his arrest on church property and a newspaper report naming St. Anthony's as plaintiff's employer . . . When the duty of good conduct is violated by an employee, the employer has good cause to terminate

a contract and the termination will not support a cause of action for breach of contract . . . We are convinced that plaintiff, having breached the employment contract, and having been rightfully discharged for cause, should not be allowed to recover termination pay under the termination clause of the breached contract . . . This is particularly so where it would have been so strikingly improvident for the pastor to have permitted plaintiff to continue for the thirty day period referred to in the termination clause. We, therefore, affirm the dismissal of count one as it relates to both the wrongful discharge and breach of contract claims. We also affirm as to the dismissal of count four which was not briefed on appeal and was thereby abandoned. Affirmed.

BUSINESS CONSIDERATIONS Should a business include a "morals clause" of some sort in its employment contracts, making the dismissal of employees convicted of criminal conduct easier? How should a business react when one of its employees is convicted of a crime? Should the type of crime matter?

ETHICAL CONSIDERATIONS One of the grounds on which McGarry sued was based on the "bad" recommendation given to a prospective employer. Is it ethical for an employer to give a bad recommendation to a former employee? Should the current or former employer have a policy under which he or she simply refuses to comment unless the comments are positive? What ethical issues would such a policy provide?

Problems with Business Ethics

A basic problem faces any business that seeks to act in an "ethical" manner. There are no fixed guidelines to follow, no formal code of ethics to set the standards under which the business should operate. Numerous professional organizations have their own codes of ethics or conduct. For example, the legal profession has the Code of Professional Responsibility; the medical profession has its Hippocratic Oath; the accounting profession has a code of ethics and also has generally accepted auditing standards (GAAS) and generally accepted accounting principles (GAAP); the real estate industry has a code of conduct; and various other groups or organizations have similar codes. However, business has no code, no "road map" of ethical conduct. The closest thing business has to an ethical guideline is the law. If a business is acting within the law, it is acting legally and is arguably meeting its minimum social requirements. However, this forces business into a reactive posture, always responding to legislative demands. It would seem that a proactive position in which business establishes its own path would be preferable.

Given this overriding problem, what can be done to provide a solution? At the present time, probably nothing can be done in the global sense. But it may be possible for each industry to develop a code of ethics for that particular industry, in much the same manner that the real estate industry has developed a code for its members. If such an industrywide approach does not prove feasible, each individual firm can develop its own personal code of ethics. Although such a micro-approach may not be ideal, at least it gets business to embark on the journey toward formalizing its ethical posture.

The Human Factor. As mentioned earlier, business was frequently viewed as an amoral institution in the past. Workers were expected to leave their personal values at the front gate when they reported to work, and then (presumably) to retrieve them at the close of the working day. At the same time, workers were expected to be loyal agents of the firm. Generally, this was interpreted to mean that if a course of conduct was beneficial to the employer, the employee was to follow that course. If a course of conduct was not beneficial to the employer, the employee was not to follow it. The attitudes and opinions of the employees were ignored.

The "loyal agent" attitude was described—and then rebutted—by Alex C. Micholos in his article "The Loyal Agent's Argument."[23] The loyal agent's argument presumes that the principal follows the ethical theory of egoism, and that the loyal agent must also act egoistically for the principal. The argument runs as follows:

1. As a loyal agent of the principal, I ought to serve his interests as he would serve them himself if he possessed my expertise.
2. The principal will serve his interests in a thoroughly egoistic manner.
3. Therefore, as a loyal agent of this principal, I must operate in a thoroughly egoistic manner on his behalf.

In order to operate in a thoroughly egoistic manner, a person acts in the way that best advances his or her interests, presuming that everyone else is doing the same thing. The gist of the loyal agent's argument is that a truly loyal agent will put the principal first in any decisions between conflicting interests. Thus, the traditional argument posits that a loyal agent is expected to act without regard to ethical considerations as long as the conduct puts the principal first. There is a major flaw in this traditional loyal agent's argument. Too many people feel that a loyal agent, if acting in a truly egoistic manner, has license—if not a duty—to act immorally and

SHOULD CIT ADOPT A CODE OF ETHICS?

John recently took a business ethics seminar at his school, and he feels that CIT should adopt a "Code of Ethics" for the firm to follow. He asserts that such a code will help the company not only to respond to ethical dilemmas as they arise but also to plan ahead in order to avoid ethical problems in the future. Dan argues to the contrary, pointing out that the business is run by the family and that the family is already ethical—so that a code is not necessary. The family is seeking your advice on this matter.

BUSINESS CONSIDERATIONS Why might it be a good idea to adopt a code for the business now, even if it is family owned and operated and the family is already ethical? Why might such a code be a bad idea?

ETHICAL CONSIDERATION If the firm is to adopt a code of ethics, what ethical theory should be selected as the foundation for the code? Explain your reasons.

unethically if doing so will advance the interests of the principal. Micholos argued that the truly loyal agent must exercise due care and skill in the performance of the agency duties and must act in a socially acceptable manner while furthering the interests of the principal. To do otherwise will have a long-term detrimental impact on the principal and will therefore be disloyal.

The Legal Aspect. The U.S. legal system contains numerous ethical components. For example, a person is presumed to be innocent until proven guilty in criminal law. Each person is entitled to due process of the law and to equal protection under the law. Protections exist against compulsory self-incrimination and cruel and unusual punishment. The Constitution provides for free speech, free exercise of religion, and the right to counsel, among other rights and guarantees.

Business law also attempts to reflect the ethical standards of the society and to promote ethical conduct in the realm of business. The law of sales imposes a duty on each party to a sales contract to act in good faith. Bankruptcy is designed to give an honest debtor a fresh start. Agency law imposes the duties of loyalty and good faith on the agent.

The laws that regulate business have developed, to a significant extent, under the social contract theory. Governmental regulations of business were enacted initially, in many cases, in response to a public demand for protection from the abuses and excesses of "big business." Antitrust laws were intended to control business and to protect the ideal of a free-and-competitive economy, while the Federal Trade Commission was established to stop unfair and deceptive trade practices.

The apparent success of the antitrust laws encouraged both the public and the government in the use of statutes to force business to meet the demands of the public. The consumer movement of the 1960s led to a number of protective statutes by both the federal and state governments. The federal government was concerned with protecting consumer credit and consumer product safety. State governments tended to be more concerned with safety and with home solicitations. In either case, government became involved only after a perceived problem was identified, public demands for protection were raised, and the business community failed or refused to adequately meet the demands of the public.

The 1960s and 1970s also saw an increased public awareness of and concern about pollution of the environment. Again, a number of protests and a great deal of public action were ignored by the business community in general, and once again governmental intervention was the tool used to address the problem. Governmental environmental protection statutes were intended to clean up the environment in order to protect the quality of life for our population, for wildlife, and for future generations. Government involvement was triggered once more by the failure of the business community to address environmental issues the public had raised.

Similar steps were followed in other areas such as labor and fair employment. The public expressed a concern over how business was treating a perceived problem. However, the steps business took toward solving the problem were less than the public demanded. Consequently, the legislature was asked to intervene on behalf of the public.

In virtually every circumstance, though, the statutory treatment of the problems adopted by the legislature is relatively rigid and potentially expensive for business. Similar protections could have—and should have—been developed within the business community, with a great deal less rigidity and a great deal less expense, had business been willing to meet the challenge directly. Instead, by

YOU BE THE JUDGE

MAN UNDER "HOUSE ARREST" MAY LOSE HOUSE

A number of realtors in the Atlanta metropolitan area believe that it is easier to sell homes if the homes have a "lived-in" look. This is especially important in upscale neighborhoods with more expensive homes. In line with this philosophy, the Atlanta Showcase of Homes arranges for people with a flair for decorating to rent certain homes for sale. In exchange for their decorating talent and their residence in the homes, these tenants are given very favorable rent and flexible leases.

Samuel Rael, an attorney in Atlanta, rented a very nice home in the Marietta area just outside Atlanta from the Atlanta Showcase of Homes. While living in the house, Rael took in a roommate, his friend Michael Wright. Shortly thereafter, the Atlanta Showcase of Homes began eviction proceedings against Rael and his friend. The reason for the eviction notice was quite simple. Wright is awaiting trial on charges of rape, and he is under "house arrest." He must wear an ankle monitor that prevents him from venturing more than 150 feet from the house.

Rael and Wright are fighting the eviction efforts of the Atlanta Showcase of Homes, alleging that they have done nothing wrong and have not violated the terms of their rental agreement. Atlanta Showcase of Homes alleges that an accused felon living in the house makes any sale unlikely and that Wright's presence in the house violates at least the spirit of the agreement.

This case has been brought in *your* court. How will *you* decide it?[24]

BUSINESS CONSIDERATION Should a realtor who rents houses to people in order to make the houses easier to sell specify conditions in its rental agreements to prevent "unsavory" characters from living in them?

ETHICAL CONSIDERATIONS Is it ethical for a business to discriminate against a person who has been charged but not yet tried for a crime, in a situation such as this? Should the presumption of innocence until a person is proven guilty have any impact on this sort of situation?

SOURCE: *Roanoke Times* (10 March 1999: Associated Press), p. A8.

having waited until the government told it what to do, business now has a much stricter regulatory environment in which to operate.

In each of these areas, and in a number of others, the application of the social contract theory is apparent. Society perceived problems and demanded that certain corrective steps be taken to alleviate them. Business had an opportunity to take the corrective steps in a manner devised by business but failed—or refused—to do so. At that point, the government stepped in to resolve the problem in a rigid, statutory manner when no satisfactory solutions were advanced by business. By failing to respond in a proactive manner, which would have permitted a custom-tailored, microfocused solution by each affected business or industry, the business community was left with a reactive, macro-oriented solution that must, by definition, extend across industry lines and that is intended to control all aspects of the business community with one broad regulation.

MULTINATIONAL ETHICS

There is an old adage that states: "When in Rome, do as the Romans do." This is very appropriate when considering business ethics in a multinational setting. If business ethics tended to be Kantian in nature, with firms throughout the world seeking—and then following—a categorical imperative, there would not be any problem. Since a categorical imperative is a rule for which any and every exception has been developed, businesses would merely have to follow the resulting rules, and their actions would be ethical by definition. Unfortunately, there is no categorical imperative for business, nor are most businesses Kantian in their ethical perspectives. Thus, problems with business ethics exist, and they are compounded in an international environment.

A businessperson tends to follow his or her personal moral and ethical values and to apply these values in judging the ethics of others. While the "loyal agent's" argument stresses that a truly loyal agent will put the interests of the principal ahead of the interests of the agent, that same agent will normally only work for a principal whose interests and values can be reconciled with the interests and the values of the agent. If the demands and requirements of a job consistently conflict with the morals and the ethics of an employee, that employee is likely to give up the job before changing his or her ethical perspective. Similarly, the ethical stance of the firm is likely to be consistent with the ethical values of the society. If the firm does not conform to socially acceptable standards, the "social contract theory" is used to change the permissible scope of the firm's conduct.

Even if a business has a formal stated objective of acting in a socially responsible and ethical manner, problems may occur. What happens when that firm expands its operations into another country? What happens when a truly loyal and ethical agent of the firm is reassigned to a foreign post within the company? Both of these scenarios may have serious ethical implications. The social contract between the new location and its businesses may well be different from the social contract between the firm and its domicile state, calling for a reappraisal of what is acceptable—or even desirable—behavior. For instance, a firm may open a new plant in a nation with very lax environmental protection statutes. This same firm, in its domicile state, has been an environmentally concerned business that has taken many pro-environment steps to reduce pollution in its production. If the firm tries to be as environmentally active in its new location, it will be at a short-term competitive disadvantage. If it seeks to be economically competitive, it will be acting in a manner contrary to its stated company policy of environmental concern and protection. What should the firm do?

Although there is no perfect solution, any firm that is considering expansion into another country needs to make every effort to learn about the cultural differences that exist between the two nations and to take steps to reduce any culture shock or conflict prior to the expansion. The firm may consider hiring citizens of the other nation, or it may consider requiring some form of educational exposure to prepare its employees for the move. The employees should be taught as much as possible about the new country, and they should also be urged to "watch and learn." The firm and its employees should be aware that they are visitors, guests in another nation, and should act as if they were the personal guests at the home of a new friend. Above all, the firm and its employees should avoid being judgmental. New countries and new cultures may seem strange and exotic, or they may merely seem different, but the new country will provide the social values that drive the social contract under which the firm will now be conducting business. Assimilation and acceptance are essential!

A RECOMMENDATION FOR BUSINESS

U.S. businesses need to develop a model or a framework of ethical behavior. It is more than likely that no single model can be developed that will apply equally to every industry within the U.S. economy, but it is possible to suggest a general outline for business. This can then be tailored by each industry to the needs and demands of that particular industry. For example, business should probably lean toward the consequential ethical theories rather than the nonconsequential theories. Consequential theories are more readily understood and more easily accepted by the public than the more esoteric nonconsequential approaches. Additionally, consequential theories are more flexible and thus are more responsive to social and technological changes.

Regardless of the overriding theory, business should adopt a "synthesis" approach of resolving ethical issues. The firm should first identify the important considerations involved (obligations, ideals, effects), and then decide where the emphasis should lie among these three considerations, especially with respect to its four constituents (stakeholders, employees, customers, community). This approach works well with any ethical principle adopted, takes into account the people to whom the firm must answer, and provides a framework for decision making that is comparable to other types of business decisions regularly made by managers.

Business should also consider its public relations image in deciding how to proceed within the consequential area. A utilitarian approach, one that is most concerned with the greatest good for the greatest number, is more acceptable to society than an egoistic approach. Society already tends to view business as egoistic—perhaps excessively so—without formally adopting such a theory as the driving force behind ethical considerations. Also, many people seem incapable of distinguishing between egoistic and egotistic. (Egoists measure their conduct on the basis of self-interest, choosing the course of conduct that will provide the greatest benefit to themselves. Egotists are self-centered, characterized by excessive references to themselves.)

Next, business should avoid rigid rules that force specific actions or reactions, especially with the rapid changes

2.3 | MARKETING/ MANAGEMENT

OPERATING CIT ETHICALLY

Tom and Anna have each seen numerous examples of what they consider unethical conduct when they were working full-time for other firms. Tom knows several salespeople who believe that it is perfectly legitimate to say virtually anything short of an outright lie in order to close a sale with a customer. They frequently "push the envelope" to the edge, grossly exaggerating qualities of the product being marketed, often to the detriment of the purchasers of that product. Anna knew electrical engineers who would not hesitate to claim credit for the work of others, or who would even assert privileges due to seniority in order to gain credit for the work of others. (Of course, both knew even more people who did not act in this manner, but these others did not disturb them.) They feel that such conduct is generally harmful to a business and its reputation, especially with repeat customers. They also know they would like to operate the family business ethically, but they don't know how to verbalize this goal.

ETHICAL CONSIDERATION What might you suggest to Tom and Anna to help them operate CIT in an ethical manner?

BUSINESS CONSIDERATIONS Where might Tom and Anna look for examples of what they should or should not do? As one of the original entrants into this particular field, should CIT attempt to be proactive in establishing an ethical code, or should the firm wait for governmental guidance?

of the modern technological age. This does not mean business should not have rules and standards, but rather that the rules and standards should be flexible enough to change as society and the business environment change. Business should also advocate the loyal agent's argument, while emphasizing that a truly loyal agent will act within the law while keeping the best interests of the principal in mind.

Whenever possible, businesses should learn to work with the government in establishing statutory regulations. By taking a proactive role in regulation, business can not only help protect its own best interests but also show its concern for society and its various constituents.

The development of a comprehensive business ethic will not be easy, nor will it be greeted with open arms by all businesses or business leaders. The alternative, however, is excessive regulation, public distrust, and a general malaise in the business community. Steps can be taken to benefit both business and society, which can ultimately only be better for business.

RESOURCES FOR BUSINESS LAW STUDENTS

NAME	RESOURCES	WEB ADDRESS
DePaul University Institute for Business and Professional Ethics	The DePaul University Institute for Business and Professional Ethics maintains materials on ethics, including articles, professional papers, an online journal, and book reviews.	http://condor.depaul.edu/ethics/
Ethics Connection	Ethics Connection, maintained by the Markkula Center for Applied Ethics at Santa Clara College, provides current and past issues of *Issues in Ethics,* case problems for ethics, and other ethics materials.	http://www.scu.edu/SCU/Centers/Ethics/
Centre for Applied Ethics	The University of British Columbia's Centre for Applied Ethics provides working papers, research projects, and links for applied ethics sites.	http://www.ethics.ubc.ca/
Students for Responsible Business (SRB)	SRB, a network of business students dedicated to integrating social responsibility into business schools, provides a newsletter, media resources, press releases, and association information.	http://www.srbnet.org/
Ethics Update	Ethics Updates provides updates on current ethics literature, both professional and popular.	http://ethics.acusd.edu/index.html
The Institute for Global Ethics	The Institute for Global Ethics, an independent, nonsectarian, and nonpolitical organization, provides general resources on ethics.	http://www.globalethics.org/

SUMMARY

It is important to distinguish ethics from morals. *Ethics* refers to either individual or group (including society) values, whereas *morals* refers to individuals' values and matters of conscience. Throughout this book, we use ethics to refer to group or social values and morals to refer to individual values.

Over the history of this country, the social environment in which business operates has changed drastically. As the social environment has changed, the demands of society on business also have changed. Business, however, has been slow to recognize or to accept these changes.

For a long time, business was judged by the "game theory." This theory does not take into account several factors, including the fact that the customers of a business may not be aware that a game is being played. For a substantial part of the twentieth century, business has been judged by the social contract theory. The social contract theory says that business must respond to the demands of the society, or the society will be permitted to change the "rules of the game" to ensure that business will comply. If business does not act as society demands, society will have the legislature enact rules to force compliance.

Even if businesses (and businesspeople) want to act ethically, it is difficult for them to do so. There are no clear-cut guidelines for most businesses to follow in adopting a code of ethics, and agreements among competing firms within an industry as to what should be done could be challenged as a conspiracy to restrain trade, a violation of antitrust laws. Still, some effort must be made. Business can make this effort by recognizing the human element—the fact that its employees are humans, with human wants, desires, and values. Business needs to recognize that, unless it responds voluntarily, the legislature will often intervene. Business also needs to acknowledge that the courts are beginning to recognize ethical aspects to corporate conduct. Cases such as Pinto and Pennzoil-Texaco will help establish a new line of precedents concerning business ethics and the liability of the firms that fail to toe the ethical line.

Finally, business must make these changes and develop these ethical standards in a more global setting. Multinational trade carries with it multinational responsibilities, including meeting the ethical standards and expectations of other nations. The social contract business must follow will become more confusing and more restrictive as more and more businesses discover the profits of international trade.

DISCUSSION QUESTIONS

1. What is the "social contract theory," and how does it affect the ethical conduct of business within the society in which that business operates? Does the United States follow the social contract theory?

2. What are the advantages and disadvantages for a business that decides to be "proactive" in the area of ethics? What are the advantages and disadvantages for a business that decides to be "reactive" in this area? Based on your response, which option would better serve a business? Explain your reasoning.

3. Assume that a manager for a national business must make a decision between two alternatives. Alternative A would be very profitable for the company in the short term but might have some long-term negative repercussions. Alternative B would have very positive long-term implications but would not be profitable in the short term. Alternative A will make the manager look good immediately, while Alternative B will not enhance the manager's reputation in the near future. The manager's employment contract with the firm will expire in the near future, and she would like to negotiate a new contract for a longer time period. Presuming that this manager is to act as a truly "loyal agent," which alternative should be chosen? Explain.

4. Can the "game theory," which allows—and even encourages—bluffing, be reconciled with the basic social obligations and responsibilities a business is expected to perform? Should business follow the game theory in every situation, only in some situations, or in no situations? Explain and give examples where appropriate.

5. It has been established scientifically and medically that cigarette smoking is a health hazard, not only to the smoker but also to those persons subjected to second-hand smoke. As a result, sales and profits for tobacco companies have declined substantially in the United States. Cigarette smoking is increasing in some parts of the world, especially in Asia, with a steadily growing demand for American-made cigarettes. The sale of American cigarettes to this growing Asian market can generate literally billions of dollars in sales over the next few years. Many of the restrictions the tobacco companies face in the United States do not exist in these Asian nations, nor are there any restrictions on advertising. However, the health hazards posed by consumption of the product are the same as those faced in the United States. From an ethical perspective, what should American cigarette manufacturers do under these circumstances? Justify your answer, and explain the theory under which you reached your conclusions.

6. Steven teaches English to immigrants who are studying English as a prelude to seeking citizenship in the United States. When Steven and his wife, Helen, were expecting their first child, an event they eagerly anticipated, his students were also excited about the pregnancy, even having a baby shower for them after class one evening. Helen gave birth to a healthy baby girl, and Steven shared this news with his students the day after the birth. Much to his surprise, the students did

not share in his enthusiasm. In fact, several members of the class expressed their sorrow over the news. To these students, it was viewed as bad luck for a couple's first child to be female rather than male. Steven would like to explain to these students that such a view is not prevalent in the United States. How should he approach this situation with his students? How does ethical relativism affect this situation?

7. A business has its headquarters in nation A and has plants in nations B and C. The ethical standards in nation A prohibit a certain business practice as illegal. That same practice is considered ethical in nation B, while nation C views it as legal but highly unethical. What position regarding this practice should the business follow? Should it follow a different practice in each of the three nations, or should it adopt one uniform policy? Why?

8. Assume that an employee has strong ethical and philosophical problems with a company's policies and practices. As a result, the employee refuses to carry out certain instructions from his or her supervisor. When questioned about the refusal to follow the instructions, the employee explains why they were not obeyed. What should the company do in this case to protect the integrity of the firm and the values of the employee? What should an employee do in this type of employment relationship?

9. How does the utilitarian theory of ethics compare with the ethical views expressed in the feminist philosophy? Which do you think is more appropriate for a business to follow? Explain your reasoning.

10. John Rawls proposes that universal rules can be developed provided this is done behind a "veil of ignorance." How would this veil enhance or hinder the development of a business code of ethics for an industry?

CASE PROBLEMS AND WRITING ASSIGNMENTS

1. Hennessey was employed as a lead pumper (a supervisory but nonmanagerial position) by Coastal Eagle Point Oil Company. Hennessey's job performance was evaluated as "above average," and it was noted that his work "always got done well." After purchasing the facility from Texaco, Coastal Eagle conducted physical examinations of the employees, including a drug test. More than 19 percent of the employees tested positive for drug use, causing Coastal Eagle to establish a formal, written policy regarding drug use that included provision for subsequent random drug tests of any and all employees. The company also adopted a policy calling for the dismissal of any

employees who failed these random drug tests, and it notified the plant managers of this new policy. (Many of the plant managers did not relay this information to the nonmanagers at the company; Hennessey's supervisor was one of the managers who did not notify his employees.) When Hennessey was randomly selected for testing on 9 June, his drug urinalysis revealed positive results for marijuana and diazepam (the active ingredient in Valium). After verifying the results of the test, Coastal Eagle dismissed Hennessey. Hennessey then filed suit for wrongful discharge, alleging that the random drug test was an unwarranted invasion of his privacy and violated public policy.

The company asserted that the position was "safety-sensitive," so that it had the need to conduct random drug tests, and that it was fully within its rights to dismiss a worker who tested positive for any of various controlled substances. Evaluate each party's arguments from an ethical perspective, and determine which argument is ethically superior. Justify your answer. [See *Hennessey* v. *Coastal Eagle Point Oil Co.*, 609 A.2d 11 (N.J. 1992).]

2. Combs worked for AT&T for 12½ years, from 1979 through 1989, in the Phoenix area. With the exception of a back injury suffered in 1986, she never complained of any health problems due to her job. In 1990, Combs hurt her back again while lifting a heavy mail sack. Thereafter, the AT&T doctors restricted her to lifting no more than 10 to 15 pounds. Despite this restriction, her supervisor insisted that she do the same work as all other employees in the mailroom. Combs refused to lift more than 15 pounds, and her supervisor treated this refusal as a resignation by Combs. Combs was denied unemployment benefits because she had "resigned" her job "voluntarily." Should Combs be entitled to unemployment benefits? Did she resign or was she fired? If she was fired, was the firing proper or improper? [See *Combs* v. *Board of Review*, 636 A.2d 122 (N.J.Super. 1994).]

3. The University of Texas law school is one of the most prestigious in the country, consistently ranking in the top 20 listing of America's top law schools. Admission is extremely competitive, with many applicants being denied each year. In making its admission decision, the law school applied its "Texas Index" (TI), a numerical ranking system based on the applicant's undergraduate grade-point average and Law School Admission Test score, to sort applicants into three categories: "presumptive admit," "presumptive deny," and "discretionary zone." The TI category of each applicant determined how extensive a review would be applied to the application by the admissions office.

Candidates in the "presumptive admit" and the "presumptive deny" categories were subjected to little review, while the students in the "discretionary zone" category were subjected to extensive review. All students in this category except blacks and Mexican Americans were grouped and their files reviewed by a subcommittee from the admissions committee. These subcommittees could vote to extend an admission offer, place the student on the waiting list, or reject the application. Black and Mexican American candidates were reviewed differently. They were given a lower TI for initial classification (189 for blacks and Mexican Americans, 199 for other

candidates in 1992), and had a much higher admission rate "on the margin" than did "nonminority" candidates. This was done, at least in part, to allow the University of Texas to attain its stated target of 10 percent Mexican Americans and 5 percent blacks in each law school class year. In addition, the law school maintained segregated waiting lists, using them to help ensure that the school met its stated targets for minority membership in the class.

Four white applicants were denied admission to the law school in 1992, even though they had higher TI's than a number of black and/or Mexican American candidates who were admitted. These students sued the school, alleging a denial of due process and/or equal protection of the law under the Fourteenth Amendment to the U.S. Constitution. The law school relied on the precedent set in *Regents of the University of California* v. *Bakke*, a 1978 Supreme Court decision upholding this sort of admission program for public universities. Without regard to the legal issues involved, how should this case be resolved ethically? Would the resolution of this case by a utilitarian be different than its resolution under the theories of Kant or Rawls? [See *Hopwood* v. *State of Texas*, 78 F.3d 932 (5th Cir. 1996).]

4. Ibanez is a member of the Florida Bar Association. She is also a Certified Public Accountant (CPA), licensed by the Florida Board of Accountancy, and she is authorized by the Certified Financial Planner Board of Standards to use the designation Certified Financial Planner (CFP). Ibanez referred to these credentials in her advertising and other communications with the public concerning her law practice. She included the designations CPA and CFP on her business cards, her law office stationary, and in her Yellow Pages listing. Despite the fact that she had qualified for each of her designations and that there was no question raised as to the truthfulness of these communications, the Florida Department of Business and Professional Regulation, Board of Accountancy issued a reprimand to Ibanez for "false, deceptive, and misleading" advertising. Ibanez challenged this reprimand on the grounds that her advertising qualifies as "commercial speech," subject to constitutional protections. Commercial speech can be banned or regulated by the state if it is false, deceptive, or misleading. If it is not, the state can only regulate such speech by showing that such regulation directly and materially advances a substantial state interest in a manner no more extensive than is necessary to serve that state interest.

Was the advertising by Ibanez "commercial speech," and therefore entitled to constitutional protections? Was the Florida Department of Professional and Business Regulation acting within its authority by reprimanding her for her advertisements? How far should a business (including a member of a profession) be allowed to go in advertising goods or services before it should be subjected to state regulation affecting the right of the business to advertise? [See *Ibanez* v. *Florida Dep't of Business and Professional Regulation*, 512 U.S. 136 (1994).]

5. Norris was hired as a mechanic by Hawaiian Airlines in 1987. The terms of his employment were governed by a collective bargaining agreement between Hawaiian Airlines and the International Association of Machinists and Aerospace Workers. In 1987, during a routine preflight inspection of an airplane, Norris noticed that one of the tires on the plane was worn. After removing the wheel to replace the tire, he noticed that the axle sleeve was scarred and grooved (it should have been "mirror-smooth"), which could cause the landing gear to fail. He recommended that it be replaced, but his supervisor said that it should just be sanded smooth and returned to the plane. The sleeve was sanded and returned, and the plane flew as scheduled. At the end of the shift, Norris refused to sign the maintenance record indicating that the repairs had been performed satisfactorily and that the plane was fit to fly. He was then suspended by his supervisor pending a termination hearing. Norris immediately went home and reported the problem with the sleeve to the Federal Aviation Administration (FAA). He then invoked the grievance procedure called for by the collective bargaining agreement. Following the grievance hearing, Norris was discharged for insubordination. He then sued the airline in Hawaii's circuit court for wrongful discharge, alleging that his discharge violated both the public policy of the Federal Aviation Act and the Hawaii Whistleblower Protection Act. The airline removed the case to the U.S. district court and asserted that Norris was not entitled to remedies due to the provisions of the Railway Labor Act (which also has covered airlines since 1936), which provides for mandatory arbitration proceedings to resolve such controversies. How should the court resolve this case? What ethical issues are raised by these facts? Would this case be resolved differently under ethical considerations than it would under legal considerations? [See *Hawaiian Airlines, Inc.* v. *Norris*, 512 U.S. 246 (1994).]

6. **BUSINESS APPLICATION CASE** Haworth was the blood bank supervisor at the Deborah Heart and Lung Center within the Deborah Hospital. Part of the responsibility of the blood bank was to collect blood samples from patients and to test those samples. The blood bank also ensured that there was an adequate supply of the proper blood type for the patient when the patient underwent surgery. Following an argument with his supervisor, Haworth destroyed an entire rack of patient blood samples. Following a leave of absence due to "stress," Haworth was offered a less stressful—but lower-level—job. Haworth refused to accept this reassignment, and the hospital discharged him at that time. Haworth claimed the discharge violated the Conscientious Employee Protection Act (CEPA). He alleged that the destruction of the blood samples was a communicative act designed to show his objection to an allegedly defective blood identification system, and that the discharge was an illegal retaliatory act by the hospital. Was Haworth's conduct a communicative act, protected by the CEPA? How should a manager react when an employee takes actions that are contrary to the firm's interests but that may involve a legitimate protest by the employee? What if the manager believes the protest is not legitimate? [See *Haworth* v. *Deborah Heart and Lung Center*, 638 A.2d 1354 (N.J.Super. 1994).]

7. **ETHICAL APPLICATION CASE** Dr. Humberto Alvarez-Machain is a Mexican national. He was charged in connection with the torture/murder of U.S. DEA Special Agent Enrique Camarena-Salazar. An indictment charged 22 people, including Dr. Machain, with crimes in connection with the torture/murder of Camarena. Since Machain resided in Mexico, and since his extradition was not deemed politically possible, the DEA and the Mexican Judicial Police worked out an agreement under which the Mexican police would deliver the doctor to the DEA, in exchange for the DEA's initiation of deportation proceedings against Isaac Naredo Moreno. (Moreno was suspected of the theft of a large sum of money in Mexico prior to his relocation to the United States.) The DEA also agreed to provide $50,000 in reward money for the delivery of Dr. Machain. On 2 April 1990, Dr. Machain was forceably abducted from his office in Guadalajara at gunpoint, allegedly subjected to some corporal abuse, and then flown to El Paso, Texas, where he was turned over to the DEA. On 18 April 1990, the Embassy of Mexico presented a diplomatic note to the U.S. State Department, requesting information concerning the possible abduction of Dr. Machain. In a second diplomatic note on 16 May 1990, the Mexican government demanded that Dr. Machain be returned to Mexico. A third diplomatic note, dated 19 June 1990, requested the arrest and extradition of two DEA agents in conjunction with the abduction in Mexico. Did the abduction and delivery of Dr. Machain to the DEA in El Paso, Texas,

violate the U.S.–Mexico extradition treaty? Was it ethical or appropriate for the DEA to pay the Mexican police for the delivery of a suspect when the DEA could not gain jurisdiction over him in any other manner? What approach should the DEA have taken in order to gain control over Dr. Machain without violating any legal or ethical principles? [See *United States* v. *Caro-Quintero*, 745 F.Supp. 599 (C.D.Cal. 1990).]

8. **CRITICAL THINKING CASE** Charles and Delores Sabino conducted a business as a partnership in the state of New Jersey. In 1985, the partnership made charitable contributions to a number of organizations. Charles Sabino deducted his proportionate share of these contributions made by the partnership on both his federal and his state tax returns. New Jersey income tax law does not permit a separate deduction for charitable contributions by a partnership. Despite this statutory prohibition, Charles Sabino insisted that his proportionate share of the partnership's charitable contributions should be deducted from his partnership income in arriving at his net income for taxation purposes of New Jersey law. The Director of the Division of Taxation and the State Tax Court disagreed, and Charles Sabino appealed. Should a partner be allowed to take his or her proportionate share of charitable contributions made by the partnership as a deduction for state income tax purposes? Should contributions by a partnership be treated differently than comparable contributions by a corporation? What issues are raised by the state tax regulation prohibiting such deductions? [See *Sabino* v. *Director, Div. of Tax.*, 686 A.2d 1197 (N.J.Super.A.D. 1996).]

NOTES

1. *Merriam-Webster's Collegiate Dictionary*, 10th ed. (Springfield, MA: Merriam-Webster, 1993), p. 398.
2. Ibid., p. 756.
3. 410 U.S. 113, 93 S.Ct. 705 (1973).
4. William H. Shaw and Vincent Berry, *Moral Issues in Business*, 4th ed. (Belmont, CA: Wadsworth Publishing, 1989), p. 2.
5. Ibid., p. 51.
6. Ibid., p. 55.
7. Rogene A. Buchholz and Sandra B. Rosenthal, *Business Ethics: The Pragmatic Path Beyond Principles to Process* (Upper Saddle River, NJ: Prentice-Hall, Inc., 1998), pp. 68–69.
8. Shaw and Barry, p. 63.
9. John Rawls, *A Theory of Justice* (Cambridge, MA: Belknap Press of Harvard University Press, 1971).
10. Ibid., pp. 195–201.
11. Hugh LaFollette, "The Truth in Ethical Relativism," *Journal of Social Philosophy* (1991), pp. 146–154.
12. Shaw and Berry, pp. 52–55.
13. Ibid., pp. 58–60.
14. Buchholz and Rosenthal, pp. 68–69.
15. Shaw and Berry, pp. 66–67.
16. Rawls, pp. 195–210.
17. Vincent Ryan Ruggerio, *The Moral Imperative* (Port Washington, NY: Alfred Publishers, 1973).
18. Shaw and Berry, p. 77.
19. 170 N.W. 668 (Mich. 1919).
20. A. Carr, "Is Business Bluffing Ethical?" *Harvard Business Review* (January-February 1968).
21. *Payne* v. *Western & Atl. R.R Co.*, 81 Tenn. 507, 519–20 (Tenn. 1884).
22. 417 A.2d 505 (N.J. 1980).
23. Tom L. Beauchamp and Norman E. Bowie, *Ethical Theory and Business*, 2nd ed. (Englewood Cliffs, NJ: Prentice-Hall, Inc., 1983), p. 247.
24. "Man Won't Leave Posh Digs Without a Fight," *Roanoke Times* (10 March 1999: Associated Press), p. A8.

3

INTERNATIONAL LAW

A G E N D A

The Kochanowskis need to understand how their business will operate in an increasingly global marketplace. CIT will be a regional business initially, so the family has some question as to whether it should even be concerned with international law and international business. What should a local or regional company know about the international business environment? How can international business and international law influence a local or regional business operation? Will the North American Free Trade Agreement affect the operation of CIT? If the firm expands its operations to include international sales, what must it know in order to export its product to other nations?

These and other questions need to be addressed in covering the material in this chapter. Be prepared! You never know when one of the Kochanowskis will need your help or advice.

O U T L I N E

INTRODUCTION

A mere generation ago, any business forecaster who had predicted the end of the Cold War, the political (and economic) collapse of the Soviet Union, the dismantling of apartheid in South Africa, or the possibility that the Czech Republic, Hungary, and Poland would become members in the North Atlantic Treaty Organization (NATO) might have been told to sell the story to the supermarket tabloid newspapers. Many people would also have been very dubious about the prospects for a strong, unified European community. Yet each of these events has taken place over one generation. And these changes represent only some of the massive political and economic shifts that have occurred around the world in recent years. One can add to that list the destruction of the Berlin Wall and the reunification of Germany, the separatist referendum in Quebec, the split of Czechoslovakia into two countries, and the cruel civil wars in such countries as the former Yugoslavia and Somalia. Hong Kong, the Asian economic powerhouse, has reverted to the control of the Chinese government. A number of the economies in Asia have suffered devastating downturns, affecting world trade and international markets. Mexico has been through a recession, and Brazil's economy has faced the threat of collapse. The last quarter of the twentieth century has been a time of unprecedented political and economic change; in such a climate, a businessperson must develop an international—even global—perspective in order to have the greatest chance for success.

Business in a Global Village

Each of these events has created both opportunities and risks for U.S. businesses. For example, the changes in the former Soviet Union have created new opportunities for companies such as Pepsico and McDonald's to develop substantial business activities in these newly independent nations. On the other hand, the war in the former Yugoslavia has caused the destruction of many of the factories and offices of foreign businesses, the killing of employees, and the prevention of goods from entering and leaving the area. Market fluctuations in Asia and South America have caused concern in other markets around the world, including the U.S. market. However, the American markets have remained relatively strong, and the United States has enjoyed an unprecedented period of prosperity and growth. From a long-term perspective, however, opportunities for U.S. businesses to compete in global markets have never been better.

If U.S. businesses have learned one lesson in the past few years, it is, as Marshall McLuhan said, that we all live in a "global village." Companies such as Coca-Cola and General Electric employ global advertising strategies. Other companies, including all of the major U.S. auto companies, have joint manufacturing and marketing agreements with their Japanese competitors. Numerous other firms and industries are also affected by the global market, some for the better and some for the worse. The textile firms of the American Southeast find themselves competing with textiles imported from a number of other nations. Retail outlets across the country carry products manufactured in other nations. State governments are establishing departments to promote international trade by businesses located within the state. "Internationalization" is permeating society at virtually every level.

In 1997, the United States exported $937.6 billion in goods and services and imported $1,047.8 billion. When measured in goods and merchandise alone, U.S. imports have grown from $244 billion in 1980 to $877 billion in 1997. During that same period, U.S. exports have grown from $220.8 billion to $689 billion.[1] In many cases, typically American companies such as McDonald's, General Motors, and Digital Equipment find most of their revenues or profits coming from overseas operations. Foreign investment in the United States doubled between 1985 and 1990. Marshall McLuhan was right: We are so economically interdependent on one another that we do live in a global village. To succeed in the business world of the twenty-first century, every businessperson must be familiar with the basic rules of international business.

"Going Global"

As communications and transportation have improved, buyers and sellers in different markets have been able to find one another more easily, which has made it easier for them to do business together. Technology has opened the global marketplace to businesses of all sizes, allowing them to sell their goods, services, and technology. Future advances in technology will make interactions between buyers and sellers in different markets even easier, increasing the potential for international trade and the likelihood—or even the need—for a business to "go global."

A business has many options once it decides to go global. For example, as it develops its international customer base, the business may decide to change the way it organizes itself. The business may move from simple selling relationships toward direct investments in major foreign markets. Most businesses start their international operations simply by selling to foreign customers. They may exhibit their products at international trade fairs, or an international buyer may visit a potential seller on a buying trip or be referred to the seller by another satisfied international customer. As in any direct selling relationship, the parties govern their rights and obligations using a contract. Many of the concerns a seller or buyer would have in a local transaction will be the same in an international transaction. Others, however, are peculiar to the international transaction.

Suppose that Acme Novelties, Inc., a company based in Arizona, decides to expand its business from national to international. Acme may be selling a variety of items to its traditional buyers in the United States, another variety of items to a Mexican business, and still other items to a buyer in Ireland. Most sales in the United States will be governed by the **Uniform Commercial Code (UCC);** the sale to the Mexican customer will be subjected to the **North American Free Trade Agreement (NAFTA)** and its rules; and the sale to the Irish customer will be influenced by the **European Union (EU)** and its rules. What happens if the tendered goods are rejected by each of these buyers? Whose law will govern the rights and obligations of the parties? The UCC will govern the sales to the U.S. buyers, but it may not govern the international sales. The domestic laws of each buyer may be controlling. Mexican law is likely to be very different from either Irish law or the UCC, which would normally be followed in Arizona. Similarly, Irish law is likely to be different from both Mexican law and the UCC. What is the seller to do?

Historically, experienced international traders would specify in their contracts which law would govern the transaction. Thus, the Arizona seller could have negotiated the contract so that the UCC was controlling in all three transactions from the example. Or the parties could have agreed to have any disputes settled by **arbitration.** International sales contracts would often call for any disputes to be arbitrated, rather than tried, so the parties could avoid using unfamiliar court systems and unfamiliar laws.

Uniform Commercial Code (UCC)
State statutory provisions covering various aspects of commercial law in the United States.

North American Free Trade Agreement (NAFTA)
The North American Free Trade Agreement is a treaty between the United States, Canada, and Mexico designed to create a free-trade zone within North America.

European Union (EU)
The EU, formerly called the Common Market, creates a free-trade zone among the member nations of Europe.

Arbitration
The submission for determination of a disputed matter to private unofficial persons selected in a manner provided by law or agreement, with the substitution of their award or decision for the judgment of a court.

In 1988, the **United Nations Convention on Contracts for the International Sale of Goods (CISG)** went into effect. The CISG provides a law of sales contracts specifically for contracts between businesses in countries that have approved the convention. In the United States, the CISG replaces the Uniform Commercial Code in any sales transactions between a U.S. firm and a business from another CISG country. Fortunately, the CISG is much like Article 2 (the law of sales) of the Uniform Commercial Code and follows many UCC provisions, so it should quickly become familiar to American managers. (Articles 2 and 2A of the UCC are covered in detail in Chapters 16 to 19; the CISG is covered in detail in Chapter 20.)

As of March 1999, 54 countries had ratified the CISG, including the United States and other important trading countries, such as China, France, Germany, and several republics of the former Soviet Union. (The complete list of member nations is shown in Exhibit 20.1.) Over the next several years, the CISG is likely to become the law in even more countries. This should reduce the concerns faced by companies like Acme Novelties in the example above.

United Nations Convention on Contracts for the International Sale of Goods (CISG)
A treaty developed by the United Nations and intended to provide uniform treatment for contracts involving the international sales of goods.

Doing Business in a Global Market

As a business grows, it may decide that it needs a more systematic effort to find customers in foreign markets. Often, it will turn to individuals or businesses in other major markets to act as go-betweens in attracting foreign buyers to the company's products. The business may seek an agent, or it may opt for a distributor. An agent is a person or company that finds buyers on behalf of the seller and usually is paid a commission for the resulting sales. The sales contract is still between the buyer and seller (although in a few cases the agent has the authority to accept orders on the seller's behalf). The buyer gets the goods directly from the seller and looks to the seller to solve any problems with the sale. A distributor, by contrast, buys goods from the seller and resells them directly to customers. The distributor bears the risk that the goods will not sell or that customers will fail to pay for the goods. Generally, customers look to the distributor for service after the sale. Businesses with intellectual property rights—such as patents, copyrights, and trademarks—sometimes find it best to sell to a foreign business the right to make, copy, or market the products covered by those rights. Generally, the buyer of the rights will pay a fee plus a royalty—that is, a percentage of the price or profit—on any products sold.

One very popular method for entering the international business environment is **franchising.** U.S. fast-food businesses have used franchising as the major method of entering foreign markets. In a franchise, a **license** is granted by the franchisor to allow the franchisee to conduct business under the name of the franchisor. This license primarily covers trademarks—for example, brand names such as Big Mac, Whopper, or Century 21. In return for a fee and royalty paid to the franchisor, the franchisee earns the benefit of the reputation of the trademarks, national and international advertising, and a wide customer base. Many U.S.-based franchisors have identified their largest growth opportunities as coming from international franchising. (Franchising is covered in detail in Chapter 37.)

Franchising
Special privileges granted by a corporation that allow the franchisee to conduct business under the corporate name of the franchisor.

License
A permission granted by a competent authority to do some act that, without such authorization, would be illegal or a trespass or a tort.

Another method for entering the international marketplace is through a joint venture. *Black's Law Dictionary* defines a *joint venture* in the United States as "an association of two or more persons to carry out a single business enterprise for profit." In international business, joint ventures are viewed somewhat more broadly than that definition implies. The concept covers businesses such as General Motors

3.1 | INTERNATIONAL BUSINESS

BENEFITS AND COSTS OF "GOING GLOBAL"

Lindsay has been using the Internet in her computer class at school, and she believes that CIT should take an international approach to its operation from the beginning. Dan is convinced that the best approach for the firm is to go slow at the start. He thinks that the firm will be best served by starting out with a regional perspective, with a relatively short-term goal of expanding into a national operation. Since Dan does not believe that CIT will be active in the international market for quite some time, he does not see any reason to adopt an international perspective now. The family agrees with Dan that the firm will initially be operating regionally, but Lindsay's argument intrigues them. While they don't expect to "go global" in the near future, they also don't think that it would hurt the firm if it at least "thinks globally" while it acts regionally. They ask you what the firm should consider from a global perspective, and whether this is in conflict with the basically regional/national thrust of the business at its outset. What will you tell them?

BUSINESS CONSIDERATIONS Should a newly created business operation be concerned with "going global," or should its emphasis be on survival for the short term in its natural regional location? When should a high-tech firm begin to think about global, or at least international, operations? Should a more traditional manufacturing firm approach this issue differently?

ETHICAL CONSIDERATIONS Should the firm take international considerations into account in setting up its business practices and internal code of ethics, or should it leave such considerations for the future? How might such international considerations affect how the firm conducts its business or establishes its code of ethics?

and Toyota, who built a plant together in California to manufacture Chevrolets and Toyotas on the same production lines. It also covers groups of companies that cooperate in research and development activities and even those that jointly market products. The joint venture has proven itself a successful way for companies to enter new markets, because they get the benefit of local expertise from their joint venture partners.

In many instances, a growing international business will decide to incorporate an operation separately in another country. If the business controls the new corporation, then it is the parent, and the new corporation is the subsidiary. A subsidiary may be wholly owned by the parent company, or the parent company may have partial ownership. (In some countries, foreign businesses must involve local owners in the ownership and management of subsidiaries.)

Cross-Cultural Negotiations

The United States is geographically isolated from most of its trading partners. When the U.S. economy was the benchmark for the rest of the world, such isolation was not much of a problem. In those halcyon days, the U.S. international business was frequently able to employ a "take it or leave it" attitude, knowing that the other party had little choice but to "take it," unless the other party was willing to do without. Why? Not many alternative sources existed for many goods beyond the United States.

Such a situation no longer exists. International competition has become heated, and the emergence of alternative sources of goods and services has produced the need for international traders to become aware of cultural differences in dealing with their customers. If a customer can receive satisfactory goods or services from several sources, other factors besides quality or price may enter into the equation. The successful international businessperson needs to learn as much as possible about his or her trading partners and their cultures in order to present his or her goods and services in the best possible light.

While there are no universal characteristics of any given culture, there are certain guidelines that tend to hold true. Among them are the following: national negotiating styles; differences in decision-making techniques; proper protocol in the negotiations; the social aspects of negotiating; time, and how it is viewed by various cultures; the importance of developing personal relationships between the negotiators; and social mores and taboos.[2] For example, the American desire to get things done, and preferably quickly, is at odds with the Chinese approach to proceed more slowly, operating at a pace that is personally satisfying. Americans frequently make decisions based on a cost-benefit analysis, with little consideration given to face-saving. By contrast, the Japanese consider saving face crucial in their social inter-actions. Many gestures are deemed to be acceptable in some cultures but may be considered rude—or even obscene—in others. The ability of a businessperson to successfully navigate through the cultural differences of his or her trading partners is instrumental to success in the international arena.

Differences in language can also have an impact on cross-cultural negotiations and business dealings. When the parties to a contract speak different languages, each may have a significantly different understanding of the contract.

The following case is a classic in the area of international sales. It involves parties from three different nations, and each party used a different language for the formation of the contract. Ironically, the central controversy involved the definition of a seemingly simple term: "chicken."

3.1

FRIGALIMENT IMPORTING CO. V. B.N.S. INT'L SALES CORP.
190 F.SUPP. 116 (S.D.N.Y. 1960)

FACTS Stovicek, a representative of the Czechoslovak government, was in New York at the World Trade Fair, where he met Bauer, the secretary of B.N.S. Several days later, Stovicek contacted Bauer to see if B.N.S. would be interested in exporting chicken to Switzerland. Frigaliment, a . . . Swiss firm represented by Stovicek, offered to purchase "25,000 lbs. of chicken 2½–3 lbs. weight, Cryovac packed, grade A government-inspected, at a price up to 33 cents per pound," and stated an interest in further offerings. B.N.S. accepted the offer, and Frigaliment sent a confirmation the following morning. The cables exchanged by the parties were predominantly in German, although the English word "chicken" was used to avoid confusion. (The German word "huhn" includes both broilers and stewing chickens.) B.N.S. sent a total of 175,000 pounds of chicken to Frigaliment under the two contracts the parties entered. Frigaliment objected to the tendered delivery, alleging that the "heavier" chickens (125,000 pounds of 2½–3 pound chickens) were not young chickens suitable for broiling or frying, but were older, stewing chickens, or "fowl." Frigaliment sued for breach of warranty, alleging that the goods delivered did not correspond to the description of the goods as established by trade usage. B.N.S. denied a breach, asserting that it delivered goods that corresponded to the contract term "chicken."

ISSUE The issue is, what is chicken? Or, more specifically, did the goods tendered by B.N.S. satisfy the description of the term chicken as used in the contract?

HOLDING Yes. Frigaliment failed to persuade the court that the word chicken meant only young chickens suitable for broiling and frying.

REASONING The issue is, what is chicken? Plaintiff says "chicken" means a young chicken, suitable for broiling and frying. Defendant says "chicken" means any bird of that genus that meets contract specifications on weight and quality, including what it calls "stewing chicken" and plaintiff pejoratively terms "fowl." Dictionaries give both meanings, as well as some others not relevant here. To support its claim, plaintiff sends a number of volleys over the net; defendant essays to return them and adds a few serves of its own. Assuming that both parties were acting in good faith, the case nicely illustrates Holmes's remark "that the making of a contract depends not on the agreement of two minds in one intention, but on the agreement of two sets of external signs—not on the parties' having meant the same thing but on their having said the same thing. . . ." I have concluded that the plaintiff has not sustained its burden of persuasion that the contract used "chicken" in the narrow sense.

continued

3.1

FRIGALIMENT IMPORTING CO. V. B.N.S. INT'L SALES CORP., *continued*
190 F.SUPP. 116 (S.D.N.Y. 1960)

The action is for breach of the warranty that goods sold shall correspond to the description. Two contracts are in suit. In the first, dated 2 May 1957, defendant, a New York sales corporation, confirmed the sale to plaintiff, a Swiss corporation, of

US Fresh Frozen Chicken, Grade A, Government Inspected, Eviscerated 2½–3 lbs. and 1½–2 lbs. each

all chicken individually wrapped in Cryovac, packed in secured fiber cartons or wooden boxes, suitable for export

75,000 lbs 2½–3 lbs @ $33.00
25,000 lbs 1½–2 lbs @ $36.50
per 100 lbs FAS New York

Scheduled May 10, 1957, pursuant to instructions from Penson & Co., New York.

The second contract, also dated 2 May 1957, was identical save that only 50,000 lbs. of the heavier "chicken" were called for, the price of the smaller birds was $37 per 100 lbs., and shipment was scheduled for 30 May. The initial shipment under the first contract was short but the balance was shipped on 17 May. When the initial shipment arrived in Switzerland, plaintiff found, on 28 May, that the 2½–3-lb. birds were not young chicken suitable for broiling and frying but stewing chicken or "fowl"; indeed many of the cartons and bags plainly so indicated. Protests ensued. Nevertheless, shipment under the second contract was made on 29 May, the 2½–3-lb. birds again being stewing chicken. Defendant stopped the transportation of these at Rotterdam.

This action followed. Plaintiff says that, notwithstanding that its acceptance was in Switzerland, New York law controls. Defendant does not dispute this, and relies on New York decisions. I shall follow the apparent agreement of the parties as to the applicable law. Since the word "chicken" standing alone is ambiguous, I turn first to see whether the contract itself offers any aid to its interpretation. Plaintiff says that 1½–2-lb. birds necessarily had to be young chickens since the older birds do not come in that size, hence the 2½–3-lb. birds must likewise be young. This is unpersuasive—a contract for "apples" of two different sizes could be filled with different kinds of apples even though only one species came in both

sizes. Defendant notes that the contract called not simply for "chickens" but for "US Fresh Frozen Chicken, Grade A, Government Inspected." It says the contract thereby incorporated by reference the Department of Agriculture's regulations, which favor its interpretation. . . .

When all the evidence is reviewed, it is clear that defendant believed it could comply with the contracts by delivering stewing chicken in the 2½–3-lb. size. Defendant's subjective intent would not be significant if this did not coincide with an objective meaning of "chicken." Here it did coincide with one of the dictionary meanings, with the definition in the Department of Agriculture's regulations to which the contract made at least oblique reference, with at least some usage in the trade, with the realities of the market, and with what plaintiff's spokesman had said. Plaintiff asserts it to be equally plain that plaintiff's own subjective intent was to obtain broilers and fryers; the only evidence against this is the material as to market prices and this may not have been sufficiently brought home. In any event, it is unnecessary to determine that issue. For plaintiff has the burden of showing that "chicken" was used in the narrower rather than in the broader sense, and this it has not sustained.

This opinion constitutes the Court's findings of fact and conclusions of law. Judgment shall be entered dismissing the complaint with costs.

BUSINESS CONSIDERATION One of the potential problems in international trade is the likelihood of misunderstandings when the parties to a contract speak different languages. What should a business do to minimize such risk?

ETHICAL CONSIDERATIONS Is it ethical for a U.S. business to insist that any contracts it enters into with firms from other nations be written in English rather than in the language of the other nation? Should the contract be drafted in both languages to ensure that each party is dealing with a contract written in its native tongue?

EXTRATERRITORIALITY: U.S. LAWS, INTERNATIONAL APPLICATIONS

American businesses are used to operating under the laws of the United States. However, as more and more businesses expand into foreign nations, they will begin to face a dilemma. Obviously, they will have to obey the laws of the nations in which they are operating. But will they also have to continue to obey the laws of the United States? Put another way, do the laws of the United States (or of any other sovereign nation) end at its borders, or do they reach across borders into other nations? This question is of major concern to international businesses. In addition, if domestic law does apply internationally, businesses need to know whether all, or only some, domestic laws apply internationally.

Antitrust Law

The U.S. antitrust laws are intended to ensure that business in the United States is conducted on a level playing field by protecting competition. Various anticompetitive activities are prohibited by these statutes. For example, the Sherman Antitrust Act states in its first section that "every contract, combination . . . or conspiracy in restraint of trade or commerce among the several States, or with foreign nations, is declared to be illegal." Is this statute applicable internationally, or only domestically? While several courts have addressed this issue, the following landmark opinion is probably the best-known answer to this question.

3.2

TIMBERLANE LUMBER CO. V. BANK OF AMERICA N. T. & S. A.

549 F.2D 597 (9TH CIR. 1976)

FACTS Timberlane is a lumber company with a long history in the lumber business. In looking for alternative sources of lumber for delivery to its distribution system on the east coast of the United States, Timberlane decided to expand its operation to Honduras. Accordingly, it formed a local company, acquired tracts of forest land, developed plans for a modern log-processing plant, and acquired equipment to transport to Honduras. Timberlane also learned that a plant once operated by Lima (another lumber company) might be available and began attempts to acquire this plant. According to Timberlane, Lamas and Casanova, both lumber companies, and the Bank of America, which had significant financial interests in Lamas and Casanova, conspired to prevent Timberlane from acquiring the Lima plant. In addition, Timberlane alleged that its operations were crippled and that its employees were harassed, defamed, and falsely imprisoned at various times in an effort to prevent Timberlane from gaining a position in the lumber industry in Honduras. Timberlane alleged that these actions constituted violations of the Sherman Act and the Wilson Tariff Act and sued the alleged conspirators, claiming more than $5 million in damages.

ISSUES Did the alleged conduct constitute a violation of the Sherman Act? Does the Sherman Act have extraterritorial application so that it applied in this case?

HOLDINGS Yes. The conduct alleged would constitute a violation of the Sherman Act. Yes, the Sherman Act has extraterritorial application, although if foreign interests outweigh American interests, the court should not exercise jurisdiction.

REASONING The defendants relied on the act of state doctrine, asserting that U.S. courts had no jurisdiction in this case because "Every sovereign state is bound to respect the independence of every other sovereign state, and the courts of one country will not

continued

3.2

TIMBERLANE LUMBER CO. V. BANK OF AMERICA N. T. & S. A., *continued*
549 F.2D 597 (9TH CIR. 1976)

sit in judgment on the acts of the government of another done within its territory." However, the court rejected this argument, pointing out that "there is no doubt that American antitrust laws extend over some conduct in other nations. . . . That American law covers some conduct beyond the nation's borders does not mean that it embraces all, however. . . . it is evident that at some point the interests of the United States are too weak and the foreign harmony incentive for restraint too strong to justify an extraterritorial assertion of jurisdiction. . . . What that point is or how it is determined is not defined by international law." The court felt the test was whether the alleged restraint affected, or was intended to affect, the foreign commerce of the United States. Timberlane's complaint alleged a direct impact on the foreign commerce of the United States, which placed the case within the jurisdiction of the federal court under the Sherman Act. [The case was then **remanded** for a trial on the issues raised in the complaint.]

BUSINESS CONSIDERATIONS Why would Timberlane decide to form a local company rather than operate the Honduran facility under the Timberlane corporate name? What advantages and disadvantages do you see for operating a foreign location as a separate firm?

ETHICAL CONSIDERATIONS Suppose that a plant located in another nation would be subject to much less stringent regulations than a similar plant located in the United States. From an ethical perspective, should the U.S. firm conform to the local regulations or to the regulations it would face in the United States? Why?

Remanded
Sent back; sending a case back to the court from which it came for purposes of having some action taken on it there.

According to the precedent set in the Timberlane case, the United States does have antitrust laws with extraterritorial application. U.S. courts have not been in full agreement, however, on the meaning of those statutes with respect to international commerce. Among U.S. courts, there is no consensus on how far the jurisdiction should extend. Some courts use the "direct and substantial effect" test; they examine the effect on U.S. foreign commerce as a prerequisite for proper jurisdiction. Other courts have used a test that looks at whether a conspiracy exists that adversely affects American commerce.

In general, however, most courts prefer to evaluate and balance the relevant considerations in each case. The courts determine whether the contacts and interests of the United States are sufficient to support the exercise of extraterritorial jurisdiction. The U.S. Supreme Court even allowed an alleged violation of the Sherman Act to be decided by Japanese arbitration. In that case, *Mitsubishi Motors Corp.* v. *Soler Chrysler-Plymouth, Inc.,*[3] a firm in Puerto Rico entered into a contract with a Swiss firm and a Japanese firm. The contract specified that any disputes were to be resolved by submission of the case to the Japanese Arbitration Association. An antitrust issue arose in the case, and the Puerto Rican firm asserted that antitrust issues could not be resolved by arbitration, despite the contract's terms, but rather had to be settled by a U.S. federal court. The U.S. Supreme Court disagreed and compelled arbitration as provided for in the contract to settle the dispute.

The Foreign Corrupt Practices Act

Many businesses that are new to the international marketplace have some trouble understanding the different values of people from other cultures or the way business may be conducted in foreign nations. The differences may be relatively minor, or they may be substantial. One area that has been particularly troublesome involves payments to officials in other countries. If a business makes a payment to a foreign official, is the business giving that official a gift or a bribe?

In an effort to address this problem and to provide guidelines for U.S. firms doing business in other nations, Congress passed the Foreign Corrupt Practices Act (FCPA) in 1977. This act, an amendment to the Securities Exchange Act of 1934, covers foreign corrupt practices and provides accounting standards that firms must follow in reporting payments made to foreign officials.

The FCPA only applies to firms that have their principal offices in the United States. The act prohibits giving money or anything else of value to foreign officials with the intent to corrupt. This is a very broad standard, but basically the act is intended to prevent the transfer of money or other items of value to any person who is in a position to exercise discretionary authority in order to have that person exercise his or her authority in a manner that gives an advantage to the donor of the "gift."

Interestingly, the act does not prohibit so-called grease payments to foreign officials, although these, too, may look like bribes. A *grease payment* is a payment to a person in order to have him or her perform a task or render a service that is part of the person's normal job. The "grease" is intended to get the person to do the job more quickly or more efficiently than he or she might have otherwise. By contrast, a payment that is made with the intent to corrupt is one that is designed to have the donee do something he or she might not have been obligated to do or to make a favorable choice among options.

Many businesspeople have claimed that the FCPA places American firms at a competitive disadvantage. These people argue that prohibiting American firms from making bribes means they are not able to compete with foreign firms, thus costing the American firms contracts, profits, and jobs. They argue that "everyone else is doing it, so why shouldn't we?" It is apparent that the U.S. Congress does not agree with them; and the FCPA will continue to regulate payments made or gifts given to foreign officials by representatives of American companies for the foreseeable future.

Employment

As pointed out previously, U.S. antitrust law, at least in some cases, has extraterritorial application. Similar reasoning has led the courts to conclude that some U.S. employment laws also apply outside the domestic environment. Of particular concern are the nondiscrimination provisions of domestic employment law. Congress has amended Title VII of the Civil Rights Act of 1964, extending protection against employment discrimination to Americans working for American companies, even when the employee is working in another nation. Thus, the protections of Title VII extend across national boundaries, at least for U.S. workers employed by U.S. firms, regardless of the location to which the worker is assigned.

FREE TRADE ZONES

At one time, it was necessary to know the laws of each of the countries involved in an international transaction. The complexity that followed, as well as the increased number of countries in the world since the end of World War II, impeded international trade. In an effort to alleviate this problem, countries in common

3.2 | INTERNATIONAL BUSINESS

CALL-IMAGE TECHNOLOGY

INTERNATIONAL MARKETS AND FREE TRADE ZONES

Tom is excited about the marketing opportunities presented to CIT by NAFTA. He feels that strong potential markets exist in both Canada and Mexico, as well as the United States, and that CIT will be in an excellent position to exploit all three national markets. Anna would prefer to have CIT plan its eventual international expansion into the European Union, arguing that there is a larger and wealthier market available and that there is more potential for growth and profits by dealing in the EU. They have asked you to prepare a position paper for them that addresses this question. What will you tell them?

BUSINESS CONSIDERATIONS Should the firm be concerned with an "either-or" position in considering international growth and expansion, or should it be more willing to consider planned expansion into both trade zones? Should the firm look only at these two trade zones (NAFTA and EU), or should it be concerned with expanding to any global markets that seem interested in the product?

ETHICAL CONSIDERATIONS In considering expansion into new markets in other countries, what sorts of ethical issues might cause concern? Are there potential privacy and/or cultural issues the firm should consider? Might these potential privacy and/or cultural issues vary from one nation or free trade zone to another?

geographical areas have banded together to form economic unions to facilitate and expedite trade. The two most significant regional groupings are the European Union (EU), comprised of 15 Western European nations, and the North American Free Trade Area, which includes the United States, Canada, and Mexico. Other groups in Asia, Africa, and Latin America are now looking to the examples set by these major regional groups to create a legal foundation for their own free-trade areas.

The European Union

The European Union was created by the Treaty of Rome in 1957. Currently, the member states are Austria, Belgium, Denmark, Finland, France, Germany, Greece, Ireland, Italy, Luxembourg, the Netherlands, Portugal, Spain, Sweden, and the United Kingdom. Several other nations have applied to join the EU, and Switzerland is preparing for a referendum on joining the EU. Several former socialist nations of Eastern Europe and several republics of the former Soviet Union have also indicated their interest in joining the EU. The final composition of the EU will not be known for several more years.

The purpose of the European Union is to establish a common customs tariff for outside nations importing goods into the community and to eliminate tariffs among EU members. In furtherance of this purpose, the EU has its own legislative, executive, and judicial branches. The treaty also covers the free movement of workers, goods, and capital within the community. It is aimed at accomplishing international cooperation. The EU is governed by the Council of Ministers, the European Commission, the European Parliament, and the Court of Justice. Exhibit 3.1 depicts the governing structure of the European Union.

The Council of Ministers. The Council of Ministers is the legislative branch of the EU. Each country sends a cabinet-level official to the council to represent its interests in the EU. While the council includes a permanent representative from each member nation, its actual members change regularly, depending on the issue it is addressing at any given time. For example, when the council is considering agricultural matters, the ministers of agriculture from each country attend. If the matter involves the environment, then the ministers for the environment from each country attend.

The council issues both directives and regulations, depending on the circumstances it faces. Directives are instructions to each member country, generally asking it to bring its laws into harmony with overall EU policy. The EU has issued directives on such topics as insider trading, product liability, and television broadcasting, to name just a few examples. When directives are issued, the member

E X H I B I T 3.1 | **The European Union**

Council of Ministers
Legislative branch of the EU

Issues directives, impelling each member state to put its law into compliance with EU policy

Issues regulations, superior to national laws and that may require national amendments in order to ensure compliance with EU

EUROPEAN COMMUNITY

Austria	Denmark	Finland
Belgium	Germany	France
Greece	Luxembourg	Ireland
Italy	Spain	The Netherlands
Portugal	Sweden	The United Kingdom

European Commission
Advisory body that proposes legislation to the council

Enforces EU law, primarily by means of imposing substantial fines for noncompliance

Creates detailed regulations in the areas of competition and agricultural law (under a delegation from the Council of Ministers)

Assembly
European Parliament

Consults with the council on legislation
Proposes amendments to legislation
Can force the council to resign with a vote of "no confidence"

Court of Justice
Court of last resort within the EU

Court opinions become the domestic law for all member nations of the EU

countries may continue their own way of handling the issues, so long as their laws conform to the overall policy of the EU.

By contrast, council regulations are superior to each nation's law, and each nation must specifically comply with the terms of the regulation. If a nation's laws do not specifically comply with the regulation, that nation has to amend its laws to be in complete compliance with the EU regulation. The EU has a merger-control regulation requiring EU approval of mergers that might tend to restrict competition; this regulation extends to all countries in the EU, and each country's laws must reflect the need for EU approval of mergers that might tend to restrict competition within the EU.

The European Commission. The European Commission is composed of 17 persons, with at least one from each member nation. However, members of the commission do not represent their nations or national interests, as do the members of the Council of Ministers. Rather, they represent the EU as a whole. The commission has two functions in the EU. First, it proposes legislation to the council. (The council members cannot create directives or regulations by themselves, but must act only on matters coming to them from the commission.) Second, the commission enforces EU law. It has the power to impose substantial fines on businesses violating EU law. In the areas of agriculture and competition law (the EU's name for antitrust law), the council has delegated to the commission the powers to create detailed regulations. The commission also has the power to issue exemptions from the competition law (see the discussion of negative clearance later in this section).

The European Parliament. The European Parliament has 518 members elected by voters in the member nations. While it is probably intended to be the European equivalent of the U.S. Congress, the Parliament has not yet found its role as a legislative body. It does have the right to consult with the council on legislation and to propose amendments to legislation. It also approves parts of the EU budget. The Parliament can vote "no confidence" in the council, which would then compel the council as a group to resign.

The Court of Justice of the European Communities. The Court of Justice of the European Communities functions in much the same way the United States Supreme Court does; it is the final arbiter of all disputes within the EU. Once the Court of Justice makes a ruling, that ruling becomes the domestic law of all the member nations. Convincing the member states to agree to this authority on the part of the court was a tremendous achievement. In order to accomplish this feat, all the member nations had to be convinced that it was in their best interests to give up some of their sovereignty in exchange for the uniformity necessary to maintain the union.

The Court of Justice issued an average of nearly 190 rulings per year from 1979 through 1993, and this caseload began to increase in 1991. From 1991 through 1993, the Court of Justice issued more than 200 judgments each year. In an effort to reduce the increasing workload of the Court of Justice and the backlog of cases awaiting argument before the court, the EU created an inferior court, the Court of First Instance (COFI) in 1989. Since its creation, the COFI has handled approximately 300 cases per year, cases that otherwise would have been heard by the Court of Justice. Even though the caseload for each of these courts is substantial, the load that the Court of Justice would have faced alone was truly daunting.

Objectives Within the EU. The Treaty of Rome established four main objectives for the freedom of movement within the EU: the movement of goods, people, services, and capital. Since the treaty, the EU has developed a large body of law designed to achieve these four objectives.

In 1986, the EU adopted the Single European Act, mandating the creation of a unified market by the end of 1992. In 1991, the heads of state of the EU member countries signed the Maastricht Treaty on European Political and Monetary Union, which strengthened the EU institutions and called for the establishment of a common currency, the European Currency Unit (ECU), by the close of the decade.

GOODS. The EU has a customs union that is designed to eliminate customs duties among all member nations. In addition, the union has a common tariff with respect to trade between member nations and nonmember nations. As a result, no burdens are placed on trade between member nations, but a burden is placed on trade with countries outside the EU.

PERSONS. One of the benefits of citizenship in an EU member country is the right to free movement anywhere within the union. EU nationals and their families may reside anywhere in the EU. Students may enroll in vocational programs anywhere in the EU. Workers may work anywhere in the EU without work permits, on the same terms as nationals of that country. One of the more controversial provisions of the Maastricht Treaty allows any EU national to vote in both municipal and European Parliament elections wherever they may live. Thus, an Irish citizen living in Rome could vote in Rome's city elections, as well as voting for Rome's representative to the European Parliament.

SERVICES. As the world moves toward a more service-oriented economy, the free movement of services becomes an increasingly important benefit of EU membership. Banks, insurance companies, and financial-service businesses are now entitled to provide their services equally across the EU. Similarly, many kinds of professionals may now practice their professions anywhere in the EU. For example, doctors, dentists, architects, travel agents, and hairdressers—once they meet minimum requirements—may practice in countries other than their own. The EU also gives people the right to establish businesses anywhere in the EU on the same terms that apply to local entrepreneurs, thus allowing them to operate freely throughout the EU.

CAPITAL. The European Monetary System (EMS) was created in 1979. Its purpose is to allow only limited fluctuations in the currencies of various member nations from preset parity prices. This was to be accomplished through a joint credit facility that would lend support to an EMS currency when it needed an infusion of capital. To further stabilize the currencies of member countries, the EU created the European Currency Unit, or ECU. The ECU was actually a "basket" of currencies, based on the exchange rates of the member countries. In 1992, the Maastricht Treaty called for the creation of the ECU as a real currency, designed to replace the pounds, marks, pesos, and francs used in the various member nations. Not all of the member states were willing to join in the move to the ECU, and the ECU left each member state with its own currency as well as the ECU, creating some potential for confusion. Subsequently, the European Commission decided to take a significantly different approach. It decided to create a new currency to replace both the ECU and the national currencies of the member states.

This new EU currency, the "euro," was introduced effective 1 January 1999. The euro has been approved as the official currency of 11 of the 15 EU member states. The euro replaced the ECU 1 January 1999 at a conversion rate of 1:1. To help effectuate and smooth the transition, the European Commission enacted two Council Regulations. The first of these regulations provided for continuity of contracts, precision in conversion rates, and rounding rules to deal with this new currency.[4] The second regulation addressed the issues of substituting the euro for national currencies, the transition period for the changeover to the euro, the currency itself, and some other related issues or topics. Council Regulations were used because they are applicable directly to the member states without the need for any national implementing legislation, debate, or other concerns.[5]

Competition (Antitrust) Law in the EU. To create a truly common market, the EU needs extensive rules on competition. The Treaty of Rome set up the basic structure of EU competition law, and the Council of Ministers has issued a large body of directives and regulations. Further, the European Commission, as the law's main enforcer, has issued regulations and decisions implementing the law. The main concerns under competition law are covered in Article 85, Article 86, the area of negative clearances, and extraterritoriality.

ARTICLE 85. In a manner similar to U.S. antitrust law, Article 85 of the Treaty of Rome prohibits agreements, contracts, cartels, and joint activities that intend to restrict or distort competition within the EU. For example, price fixing, limiting or

3.3 | MANUFACTURING/ INTERNATIONAL BUSINESS

PRODUCTION AND LICENSE OF CALL-IMAGE INTERNATIONALLY

A European manufacturer has expressed serious interest in Call-Image and its product. This firm would like to manufacture Call-Image videophones at its European plant and sell them within the EU. The manufacturer has suggested a licensing agreement that would designate it as the sole and exclusive distributor of any CIT products or technology for Europe. This manufacturer claims that by so doing, they (the distributor and CIT) can control at least 85 percent of the interactive telephone market in Europe, cornering the market before any other firms develop the technology to provide any serious competition. Tom and Anna are worried about several potential legal issues raised by this proposal. They are especially concerned about the prospect of possibly violating EU competition rules, as well as possible problems with the U.S. government over the exportation of new technology. They have asked for your advice on these matters. What will you tell them?

BUSINESS CONSIDERATIONS What are the potential drawbacks to allowing a firm to have an exclusive distributorship for Europe for the CIT product and other technology? Should the firm seek some other arrangement to better protect and position itself for sales in Europe?

ETHICAL CONSIDERATIONS Assume that the technology used by CIT has substantial national security implications but that an export license can be acquired by the firm. Without regard to profits, should the firm export its products despite the potential for compromising national security? What argument(s) support your response?

allocating markets, tying arrangements, and price discrimination are all prohibited under Article 85. However, the article recognizes that some contracts benefit consumers by improving the production or distribution of goods or by promoting product improvements. The European Commission, therefore, can exempt activities from Article 85, either by issuing an individual exemption for a particular situation or by a block exemption for similarly situated businesses. An example of a block exemption would be the commission guidelines for franchises; these tell potential franchise businesses which contract provisions are acceptable and which will bring commission action.

ARTICLE 86. The second major EU competition law is Article 86 of the Treaty of Rome. It bars one or more companies from using a dominant market position to restrict or distort trade. Prohibited abuses of dominant positions include tying arrangements, price fixing, price discrimination, and other conduct similar to that prohibited under U.S. antitrust law. Either buyers or sellers can have dominant positions. The Commission and the Court of Justice of the European Union have defined dominance by a practical test: a firm or firms having the power to "act without taking into account their competitors, purchasers or suppliers" possesses a dominant position. [See *Europemballage Corp.* v. *Commission*, E.C.R. 215 (1973).] Thus, no specific market share is required; instead, the commission looks at the firm's power to control suppliers and customers and its ability to prevent competition.

NEGATIVE CLEARANCE. A business concerned about its actions violating either Article 85 or Article 86 can apply to the European Commission for permission to engage in activities that appear to violate EU competition laws. This permission is known as a **negative clearance.** If a negative clearance is granted, this means that the commission has reviewed the proposed conduct, and—if the business does what it has indicated—the commission will not prosecute it under either Article 85 or Article 86.

EXTRATERRITORIALITY. The EU position on the reach of its power to regulate competition has expanded considerably over the last 20 years. It now appears that conduct anywhere can be subject to EU competition rules if it is intended to affect and does affect the EU market. The European Court of Justice has ruled that Article 85 has extraterritorial application if the conduct in question is intended to affect parties or businesses located within the European Union.[6] This should serve as a warning to companies that engage in activities lawful in their home country but that also affect the European market.

The North American Free Trade Agreement

One powerful alternative to the EU is the free-trade partnership recently formed in North America under NAFTA. The first piece of NAFTA went into effect in 1989, with the ratification of the Canada–U.S. Free Trade Agreement. As with its counterpart, the EU, one major purpose of the Canada–U.S. Free Trade Agreement was the elimination of tariffs on sales of goods between the two countries. The agreement called for the elimination of all tariffs between the nations by 1998. (As a practical matter, most such tariffs were already gone.) Goods qualify for tariff-free treatment if they are 50 percent North American in content. Also like the EU, the Canada–U.S. Free Trade Agreement made it easier for Canadian and U.S. citizens to work in each other's countries and for investments to flow across the border. Unlike the EU, however, the Free Trade Agreement did not set up a host of new institutions or require the two countries to give up much of their sovereignty. The only new institutions created by the agreement were binational panels of experts to be convened as needed to resolve trade disputes between the two countries. These expert panels replace the court systems for both countries in eligible cases.

In 1993, Mexico joined its Canadian and U.S. counterparts in the North American Free Trade Agreement. NAFTA creates a free trade area encompassing all of North America, a market large enough to compete successfully with Asian and European trade groups. There are still some concerns about NAFTA, but there is no concerted effort by any of the governments involved to rescind the agreement. Free trade with Mexico presents different concerns than it did with Canada. U.S. environmental and labor groups object to Mexico's reputation for having a lax legal environment, and Canadians worry about more jobs moving south. In addition, several South American and Central American nations have expressed interest in joining the agreement, presenting the potential for an even larger and more powerful Western Hemisphere Free Trade Agreement (WHFTA). [n.b. We feel that the American Free Trade Agreement (AFTA) provides a better acronym, but it does not appear to be the name of choice at this point in time.] Already, businesses from several non-American nations, especially Japan, are looking into investment in South or Central America in preparation for the day when WHFTA is implemented.

Other Free Trade Zones

There are a number of other free trades zones around the world, although none of them possesses the economic might of either the European Union or NAFTA. For example, there are at least four free trade zones in Latin America. The Central American Common Market is comprised of Costa Rica, El Salvador, Guatemala, Honduras, Nicaragua, and Panama. The MERCOSUS Common Market is comprised of Argentina, Brazil, Paraguay, and Uruguay. The Andean Common Market is made up of Bolivia, Ecuador, Colombia, and Venezuela. And the Caribbean Community includes Barbados, Belize, Dominica, Jamaica, Trinidad-Tobago, Grenada, St. Kitts-Nevus-Anguilla, St. Lucia, and St. Vincent.

There are at least three African free trade zones as well. These include the Economic Community of West African States, the Economic and Customs Union of Central Africa, and the East African Community. There is also a treaty, the Treaty Establishing the African Economic Community, which has 51 signatories. This treaty is intended to create an African equivalent to the European Union.

Negative clearance Permission given by the EU Commission to a firm(s) to act in a manner that appears to violate EU competition laws.

Each of these free trade zones has the potential to influence international trade within its member states and to help—or hinder—the economic growth and development of the member nations.

THE GENERAL AGREEMENT ON TARIFFS AND TRADE

Following World War II, the Western Allies envisioned an international economic organization that would provide leadership and coordination for international trade in the same manner as the United Nations was to provide in the political environment. A charter was drafted for an International Trade Organization (ITO) in 1948, but the charter was not adopted by enough nations, effectively shelving it.

Prior to the proposed ITO charter, U.S. negotiators proposed a general agreement on tariffs and trades as a stepping-stone to prepare the way for ITO ratification. The Western Allies accepted this American proposal in 1947, creating the first General Agreement on Tariffs and Trade (GATT). When the ITO failed to generate sufficient support for ratification, GATT became the accepted framework for regulating international trade.

The GATT promoted free trade by seeking to reduce tariffs and quotas between nations. It promoted fair trade by defining such trade practices as unfair government subsidies of exports and dumping (selling goods below fair value on a foreign market). It also provided panels to resolve trade disputes. The GATT worked through "rounds" of discussions, during which countries agreed to reduce tariffs for all GATT members. The final round of GATT, known as the Uruguay Round, also raised nongoods-related issues, such as trade-related intellectual property rights, investment protection, services, and agricultural subsidies.

The Uruguay Round was frustrating for many of the participants, and a number of the objectives that were expected were not achieved. One major achievement, however, was the establishment of the World Trade Organization (WTO). The WTO is an international economic organization that is intended to provide leadership and coordination for international trade. Thus, 47 years after the ITO was defeated, the WTO has been created. The GATT did indeed provide an interim stepping-stone to the international organization, albeit for a much longer period than originally expected.

WORLD TRADE ORGANIZATION

The World Trade Organization was created during the Uruguay Round of GATT discussions and was officially established on 1 January 1995. However, the WTO is not merely an extension of GATT. The WTO has a completely different character than did GATT and has a completely different mission. GATT was a multinational agreement, not an organization. There was no institutional foundation for GATT. By contrast, the WTO is an *organization* headquartered in Geneva, Switzerland, with a formal structure, a permanent staff, and a (sizeable) operating budget. As of February 1999, there were 134 member countries in the WTO, with several dozen more nations listed as "observers," most of which had applied for membership.

The highest authority within the WTO is the Ministerial Conference, which is comprised of representatives from each member nation. The Ministerial Conference must meet at least once every two years, and has the authority to make decisions

"YES, WE HAVE *SOME* BANANAS"

The European Union and the United States are locked in a trade dispute involving bananas. The EU has given import preferences to bananas grown in former European colonies, primarily in the Caribbean and in Africa, over bananas grown in Central America. This policy has substantially reduced the quantity of bananas that can be exported to the EU by the Central American growers, including Chiquita and Dole, both U.S. firms. The United States filed a complaint with the WTO, asking the WTO to review the EU policies regarding bananas, quotas, and tariffs. The WTO agreed with the U.S. position and instructed the EU to review and revise its position.

The EU offered several concessions but planned to retain some preferences for the banana trade with their former colonies. In addition, a number of Caribbean producers have appealed to the United States to accept the EU proposal. These nations point out that they depend on banana exports for their economic survival, and that the removal of the preferences would place them in an untenable position, unable to compete with the larger producers from Central America. The United States has rejected these appeals and threatened to impose substantial tariffs against numerous EU goods unless the EU changes its position with regard to the importation of bananas into the EU.

The EU has filed suit against the United States in *your* court seeking an injunction against any U.S. trade retaliation. How will *you* rule in this case?[7]

BUSINESS CONSIDERATIONS Should a company that exports most of its production seek favorable trade treatment from the various trade zones (e.g., the EU, NAFTA), or should it look for new markets that provide more favorable trading regulations? How should an exporter view barriers to trade with a nation or a group of nations?

ETHICAL CONSIDERATIONS Is it ethical for the United States to impose trade barriers against the EU in retaliation for perceived negative treatment of American firms by the EU? Should the economic dependence of the Caribbean nations on a trade advantage in this situation be sufficient to justify a preference over the stronger American producers?

SOURCE: Jim Lobe, *World News* (Inter Press Service, 2 November 1998).

on any matters under any of the multilateral trade agreements recognized by the WTO. While the Ministerial Conference is the highest authority, the day-to-day operations of the WTO are conducted by the General Council. The General Council serves as the Dispute Settlement Body of the WTO and as the Trade Policy Review Body. It also reports to the Ministerial Conference. The General Council delegates a great deal of its responsibility to three other councils—the Council for Trade in Goods, the Council for Trade in Services, and the Council for Trade-Related Aspects of Intellectual Property Rights. Obviously, the WTO has a much wider responsibility than did GATT, covering areas other than international trade in goods.

Dispute resolution under the WTO is considerably quicker than was the case under GATT, and it promises to be much more effective. When controversies arise under the WTO, the dispute is submitted to a panel of trade experts. This panel will then have the authority to rule for one or the other of the complainants.

When the panel rules for one of the nations, that nation will be given permission to retaliate against the other nation unless or until the losing nation changes the trade practice that was the subject of the dispute. In addition, the other member nations are expected to exert pressure on the losing nation to encourage a change in practice in order to ensure compliance. Since the member nations encompass a significant majority of world trade, such pressure and unofficial sanctions should prove to be very effective.

EXPORTS

In order to have truly international trade, some countries must import goods and other countries must export goods. Many students have a simplistic view of importing and exporting, not realizing that there are a significant number of problems to resolve in moving goods from one nation to another. These problems frequently begin with getting goods out of their nation of origin.

All exports leaving the United States must be licensed. For most goods and technology, the licensing process simply involves stamping a general license statement on the export documents. Some goods and technology, however, require validated licenses issued by the Department of Commerce, which maintains a commodity control list that gives the licensing status of thousands of export items. Businesses that export in violation of the export-licensing policy face criminal prosecution and loss of export privileges.

U.S. exports are regulated for three purposes. The first is to protect the nation in times of short supply. For example, Alaskan crude oil may be exported only if it does not adversely affect domestic supply. The second purpose is to protect national security. For example, exporting nuclear material to Iraq is not permitted currently. The third purpose is to further U.S. foreign policy interests. For example, all exports to Libya were banned in 1986 as a response to Libya's support of terrorism.

IMPORTS

Getting the goods out of their home country is only half the battle. Next the goods must be moved into the nation of destination. All goods imported into a country must "pass" customs. Passing customs usually means paying a certain sum of money—known as a tariff or duty—at the port of entry, based on the type and value of the goods. For example, when Subaru imported the Brat motor vehicle into this country, the U.S. Customs Service had to determine whether the Brat was a truck or a sports car. This was an important determination, since the duty to be paid differed depending on the category to which it rightfully belonged. If the Brat was a truck, it would require a larger duty than if it was a sports car. Subaru successfully argued that the Brat—despite the fact that it was a two-seat vehicle with a cargo bed—was a sports car. To further this argument, Subaru sold the Brat with two rear-facing plastic seats bolted into the bed of the cargo deck.

Once the type of import is determined, the analysis turns to its valuation. Is the proper valuation its wholesale value at the point of origin or destination, its retail value at the point of origin or destination, or a combination of these factors? In general, the transaction value of the goods is used. The transaction value is the price the importer paid for the goods, plus certain other necessary and related expenses.

The U.S. Customs Court has exclusive jurisdiction over civil actions challenging administrative decisions of the U.S. Customs Service.

LETTERS OF CREDIT

International traders also face special problems when paying for goods, services, and technology. In a domestic transaction, a seller can easily check the buyer's creditworthiness. If the buyer wrongfully rejects the goods, the seller is probably familiar enough with the market to know how to resell the goods or can have them returned fairly easily. In an international transaction, however, the seller will find it harder to check the buyer's financial status, harder to collect unpaid amounts from a foreign buyer, and more expensive or difficult to resell or reship rejected goods. To solve these problems posed by the international marketplace, buyers and sellers often use letters of credit to pay for goods, services, or technology.

When a letter of credit is used, the contract between buyer and seller will require the buyer to get a letter from its bank. The letter is the bank's promise that it will pay the contract price upon the seller's presentation of documents specified in the contract. To protect itself, the buyer will carefully specify which documents the seller must present to the bank to get payment. If the seller does not want to collect from a foreign bank, the contract can require the buyer to have a bank convenient to the seller that will confirm the letter of credit.

Suppose that Salesco, Inc., in California, contracts with Buyco, in Australia, for the sale of 5,000 electric motors at a total price of U.S. $5,000,000. The sales contract specifies that Buyco will pay by means of a letter of credit issued by First Australia Bank and confirmed by First San Diego Bank. The sales contract also specifies that payment will be made upon presentation of an invoice, packing list, export declaration, and negotiable on-board bill of lading (indicating the goods had been loaded on the ship). Buyco would go to its bank, First Australia, which would—for a fee—issue a letter stating the terms as specified in the contract. The bank would send that letter to First San Diego Bank, which would then write a letter to Salesco confirming the terms of the original letter of credit. Once Salesco obtained all the documents specified in the letter, it would go to its bank, First San Diego, which would compare the documents with the list in the letter of credit. If the documents were in order, First San Diego would pay Salesco, then forward the documents to First Australia, which would get payment from Buyco, and then give Buyco the documents so that it could take delivery of the motors. Exhibit 3.2 on page 82 illustrates how the transaction would work.

As you can see, sellers are pleased to use letters of credit. They are paid for goods even before the buyer receives them, and they are paid even if the goods turn out to be defective. Buyers are less pleased to use letters of credit, but at least they know the goods are present, loaded, and ready for shipment before they pay for them. In order to further protect themselves, buyers can carefully specify which documents are required before the letter is to be paid. In some instances, the buyer will also require a third party to inspect the goods as they are loaded for shipment. Buyers are also protected by the legal obligation that the documents the seller presents must strictly comply with the documents required in the letter of credit before the bank can pay the seller.

The importance of letters of credit is further emphasized by the fact that there is a United Nations Convention dealing with them, the *United Nations Convention*

E X H I B I T   3.2 | **Using a Letter of Credit in an International Sales of Goods**

1. Buyco and Salesco enter a sales agreement, with Buyco agreeing to provide a letter of credit and Salesco agreeing to deliver 5,000 electric motors to Buyco.

2. Buyco goes to its bank, First Australia, to acquire a letter of credit to be paid at First San Diego Bank. The letter of credit specifies that payment is to be made on presentation at First San Diego Bank of an invoice, a packing list, an export declaration, and a negotiable on-board bill of lading.

3. First Australia produces the letter of credit and sends it to First San Diego Bank.

4. First San Diego Bank receives the letter of credit and contacts Salesco confirming the terms of the letter of credit and the documents required in order to receive payment.

5. Salesco arranges for the transportation of the goods, procures the necessary documents, and takes those documents to First San Diego Bank.

6. First San Diego Bank confirms that all required documents are present and in proper order and pays Salesco as per the letter of credit.

7. The paid letter of credit is returned to First Australia, which then pays First San Diego Bank for the letter of credit.

8. First Australia informs Buyco that the letter of credit has been paid and collects the amount of the letter, plus any fees, from Buyco.

---

on Independent Guarantees and Stand-by Letters of Credit, drafted in New York in 1995. This convention had only been signed by seven nations as of March 1999, but it is scheduled to go into effect 1 January 2000. (The United States is the only major trading nation that had signed the convention. Other signatories include Belarus, Ecuador, El Salvador, Kuwait, Panama, and Tunisia.)

INFORMATION AND TECHNOLOGY

Historically, patent, copyright, and trademark protection extended only within the boundaries of each country. An inventor who wanted to protect an invention in any other countries would have to obtain a patent in each country. To complicate matters, some countries did not recognize exclusive patent rights in some kinds of products, such as pharmaceuticals. These countries felt it was more important to deliver lifesaving drugs to their people than to protect the profits of the pharmaceutical companies. Today, although no worldwide intellectual property rights exist, a real trend has grown toward international protection of copyrights, patents, and trademarks. In 1988, for example, the United States became the eightieth member of the Berne Convention for the Protection of Literary and Artistic Works. A copyright holder who publishes a book in the United States will now receive the same protection in other member countries that local authors do.

The area of patent law is also moving toward international protection. The European Patent Convention allows only one filing and one patent examination to obtain protection in 18 countries. Similarly, the Patent Cooperation Treaty also allows only one patent application and examination to serve as a basis for patent filings in up to 47 countries, as of 1991.

Trademark law has also moved toward some international recognition, though not as quickly as the other areas of intellectual property protection. The Madrid Agreement—to which 42 countries (but not the United States) belonged as of 1996—

allows one application to provide protection in all member countries. The EU has moved toward an EU-wide recognition of trademarks but does not yet have uniformity. U.S. businesses have faced serious problems in recent years with counterfeit goods. Levi Strauss, Apple Computer, and other companies have reported large revenues lost due to imports that counterfeit company trademarks or patents. The United States has toughened its enforcement of the laws designed to oppose these counterfeiters. Section 337 of the Tariff Act of 1930 was amended in 1988 to allow any owner of a registered U.S. intellectual property right who believes that an import infringes on that right to apply to the U.S. International Trade Commission for an order banning the goods. This order can also fine the importer up to $100,000 per day or twice the domestic value of the goods. In addition, Congress amended the Trade Act of 1974 with a section called "Special 301," requiring the U.S. trade representative to identify countries that do not protect U.S. intellectual property rights. Once identified, the United States will negotiate improvements with those countries. If no improvements result, the United States must retaliate against those countries. Special 301 has been effective in getting many countries to improve their intellectual property laws.

NATIONALIZATION

Nationalization of privately owned business entities is a risk that exists primarily in developing countries. *Nationalization* is the act of converting privately owned businesses into governmentally owned businesses. In general, international trade can be carried on without fear of nationalization; the exporter merely ensures that payment is guaranteed before shipment of goods. However, international investment is not so simple. To build and operate an aluminum plant or an oil refinery requires a large investment of capital. If, during the time the investment is paying for itself, it is nationalized, the result is usually a loss to the investor. It is for that reason, as well as for others, that international investment decisions usually require a shorter payback period than national investment decisions.

Is nationalization legal? It depends on your perspective. For the most part, from the viewpoint of the country that nationalizes a private property, some act of the legislature or head of state makes it legal within that country. From the viewpoint of international law, however, it may not be legal. If it does not comply with international law, it is termed a *confiscation*, not a nationalization. If it does comply with international law, it is called an *expropriation*. The key element is whether the state had a proper public purpose and, in addition, whether "just compensation" was paid for the property. No matter what it is called, there is little that can be done about it if it occurs. One means of insuring an investment against the risk of loss is by utilizing the facilities of the Overseas Private Investment Corporation (OPIC). OPIC furnishes low-cost insurance against nationalization; confiscation; lack of convertibility of foreign earnings; and general loss due to insurrection, revolution, or war. OPIC currently insures more than 400 projects in 50 countries.

ACT OF STATE DOCTRINE

One reason for the importance of seeking insurance protection for overseas investments is the *act of state doctrine.* The doctrine states that every sovereign state is bound to respect the independence of every other sovereign state, and the courts of one country will not sit in judgment on the acts of the government of another performed within its own borders. The concept of the act of state doctrine is embedded in the notion of sovereign immunity. Certainly each sovereign state recognizes all other states' sovereignty. But the act of state doctrine is not a specific rule of international law. International law does not require that nations follow this rule; and in the United States, the Constitution does not require it. Judicial decisions of the United States, however, have recognized the doctrine. The doctrine is based on the theory that a nation is not qualified to question the actions of other nations taken on their own soil. In fact, denouncing the public decisions of other nations can have a decidedly adverse effect on the conduct of a nation's foreign policy.

But what about a situation in which a U.S. bank held promissory notes issued by a group of Costa Rican banks payable in the United States in U.S. dollars? Would there be a lack of jurisdiction if the Costa Rican government, after the notes were signed, refused to allow the payments in U.S. dollars? Does the act of state doctrine apply? The Second Circuit said an emphatic no when it held that the *situs* (location) of the debt was in the United States and not Costa Rica, and, therefore, the doctrine did not apply. [See *Allied Bank* v. *Banco Credito*, 757 F.2d 516 (2d Cir. 1985).]

SOVEREIGN IMMUNITY

In the traditions of international law, all nations are equal and sovereign. Thus, a nation is immune from suit for its actions, either by individuals or by other countries. To be sued, a nation must agree to give up its sovereign immunity. For example, the United States passed the Federal Tort Claims Act to allow individuals to sue the U.S. government for negligent or wrongful acts. On an international level, the doctrine of sovereign immunity causes businesses some trouble, especially because many governments operate businesses such as airlines, banks, auto companies, and even computer firms. The United States has taken actions to limit the effect of sovereign immunity in its courts. In 1976, Congress enacted the Foreign Sovereign Immunities Act, which declared that U.S. courts would not recognize sovereign immunity when the sovereign engaged in commercial, rather than political, activities. So, for example, a state-owned bank could be subject to suit over its failure to pay a letter of credit. The United States has also negotiated many bilateral investment treaties, containing provisions for other governments to waive the right to claim sovereign immunity.

DISPUTE RESOLUTION

The best method of resolving an international business dispute is by providing a means for handling that contingency at the time the international transaction is created. Three principal options for settling a dispute are available: the International Court of Justice, national courts, and arbitration.

The International Court of Justice

The International Court of Justice (ICJ) has limited value in solving international business disputes. The ICJ is an agency of the United Nations, and its procedures were established in the United Nations Charter. A private person has no standing before the ICJ. Only nations may appear before the court. A private person who has a grievance against a state which is not his or her own must first secure the agreement of his or her own state to present the claim. If his or her state asserts the claim, the issue then becomes whether the other state will allow the matter to appear before the ICJ for resolution. Each state must agree to be bound by the court's decision; if they do not, there is no jurisdiction to hear the claim. Exhibit 3.3 lists the authorities the ICJ uses in reaching its decisions.

National Courts

A private person can usually resort to settlement of a dispute with a foreign nation by seeking redress through the courts of that state. Private persons can sometimes obtain adequate relief in their native state's judicial system. For example, a favorable judgment from a U.S. court may be filed in another country and, under certain conditions, can execute on assets in the foreign country on the basis of the other country's judicial decision. U.S. courts are likely to enforce a judgment obtained in another country following a full and fair trial, before an impartial court, with an opportunity for the defendant to be heard. A biased or corrupt court, or a case that

---

E X H I B I T   3.3 | **The International Court of Justice**

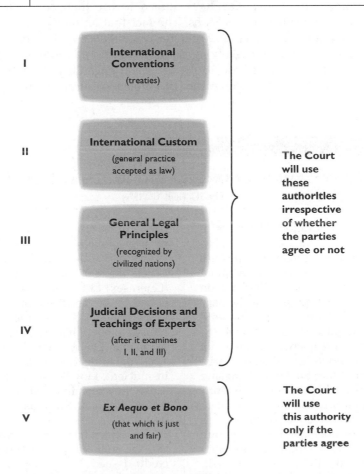

I — International Conventions (treaties)

II — International Custom (general practice accepted as law)

III — General Legal Principles (recognized by civilized nations)

IV — Judicial Decisions and Teachings of Experts (after it examines I, II, and III)

The Court will use these authorities irrespective of whether the parties agree or not

V — Ex Aequo et Bono (that which is just and fair)

The Court will use this authority only if the parties agree

did not give a defendant an adequate chance to defend against the claims of the plaintiff, would probably lead a U.S. court to require a plaintiff to retry the entire claim in a U.S. court, rather than enforce the prior judgment.

The recognition of foreign judgments is not a matter of international law but rather of comity. As the U.S. Supreme Court stated in the landmark case of *Hilton v. Guyot*, 159 U.S. 113 (1895), *comity* is "the recognition which one nation allows within its territory to the . . . acts of another nation, having due regard both to international duty and convenience, and to the rights of its own citizens, or other persons. . . ." Comity is a matter of respect, goodwill, and courtesy that one nation gives to another, at least partly with the hope that the other nation will return the favor.

Arbitration

For a variety of reasons, a particular international dispute may not be appropriate for resolution in the ICJ or national courts. In that case, international arbitration might be the best course of action. Many international commercial contracts include provisions for using arbitration. More than 121 countries, including the United States, have signed the 1958 United Nations Convention on the Recognition and Enforcement of Foreign Arbitral Awards (T.I.A.S. No. 6997). The countries that have signed this convention have agreed to use their court systems to recognize and enforce arbitration decisions. The fact that so many nations have ratified this UN convention provides fairly persuasive evidence that arbitration is becoming the preferred method for resolving disputes in international business.

The following case addresses the applicability of the UN's Convention on the Recognition and Enforcement of Foreign Arbitral Awards, among other issues.

3.3

RILEY V. KINGSLEY UNDERWRITING AGENCIES, LTD.
969 F.2D 953 (10TH CIR. 1992)

FACTS Lloyd's is a British corporation with its principal place of business in London. Lloyd's . . . has functioned as a market for writing insurance policies for some 300 years. Riley was interested in becoming a member of Lloyd's and traveled to England on several occasions to pursue this quest . . . In January 1980, Riley entered into a General Undertaking with Lloyd's and a Members' Agent's Agreement with the Underwriters. Both of these agreements provided that the courts of England would have exclusive jurisdiction over any dispute and that the laws of England would apply. Additionally, the Members' Agent's Agreement provided for arbitration in the event of any dispute. Riley's underwriting began in January 1980. . . . He remained a member of Lloyd's through 1990, and each year increased the amount of premium income underwritten. By 1989, Riley was underwriting premium income in excess of a million pounds. In connection with his underwriting, Riley was required to meet Lloyd's deposit requirements. Riley obtained letters of credit from FirstBank. FirstBank in turn issued letters of credit to First National Bank of Boston (Guernsey) Ltd. as security for a letter of credit to be issued by the London branch of the Guernsey Bank in favor of Lloyd's . . . In the event a member fails or refuses to cover his pro rata share of underwriting liability, then Lloyd's may draw on the letter of credit to cover the obligation. In the event the letter of credit is insufficient, Lloyd's will look to a member's assets to satisfy any remaining underwriting liability. The syndicate in which Riley participated have experienced large losses, resulting in calls in excess of 300,000 pounds. Riley has been notified that, if he does not satisfy the calls, Lloyd's will draw against the letter of credit issued by Guernsey Bank. Guernsey Bank would then draw on the FirstBank letters of credit.

3.3

RILEY V. KINGSLEY UNDERWRITING AGENCIES, LTD., *continued*
969 F.2D 953 (10TH CIR. 1992)

Proceeding apparently on the theory that the best defense is a good offense, Riley filed this action seeking declaratory judgment, rescission and damages against defendants other than FirstBank. Riley claimed that these defendants engaged in the offer and sale of unregistered securities and made untrue statements of material fact and material omissions in connection with the sale of securities, violating the Securities Act of 1933 . . . , the Securities Exchange Act of 1934 . . . , and Rule 10b-5 . . . Riley sought a writ of attachment against Lloyd's and an injunction to prevent Defendants from drawing on the letters of credit . . . Prior to a preliminary injunction hearing [the parties] entered into a court-approved stipulation that the hearing would be limited to the threshold issues of the applicability and effect of the forum selection clause and the arbitration clause discussed above . . .

ISSUES Were the choice of forum and law provisions in Riley's contract with Lloyd's valid and enforceable? Were the arbitration and choice of law provisions in Riley's contract with the Underwriters, requiring arbitration in England and the application of English law, valid and enforceable?

HOLDINGS Yes to both issues. Both the choice of forum and law and the arbitration and choice of law provisions in the two contracts were valid.

REASONING We hold that the parties must abide by their agreement and resolve the disputes in England, either before an English court or arbitrator, as the case may be. Three reasons persuade us: (1) the parties' undertaking is truly international in character, (2) all parties other than Riley and FirstBank are British, and (3) virtually all activities giving rise to the suggested claims occurred in England. . . . Riley concedes, as he must, that "the enforcement of choice of forum and choice of law clauses is consistent with recent U.S. Supreme Court decisions." . . . When an agreement is truly international, as here, and reflects numerous contacts with the foreign forum, the Supreme Court has quite clearly held that the parties' choice of law and forum selection provisions will be given effect . . . In *M/S Bremen,* the Court identified an important rationale for the rule that such provisions should be enforced.

The expansion of American business and industry will hardly be encouraged if, notwithstanding solemn contracts, we insist on a parochial concept that all disputes must be resolved under our laws and in our courts . . . We cannot have trade and commerce in world markets and international waters exclusively on our terms, governed by our laws, and resolved in our courts . . . Thus, in light of present day commercial realities and expanding international trade we conclude that the forum clause should control absent a strong showing that it should be set aside.

Forum selection provisions are "prima facie valid" and a party resisting enforcement carries a heavy burden of showing that the provision itself is invalid due to fraud or overreaching or that enforcement would be unreasonable and unjust under the circumstances . . . Only a showing of inconvenience so serious as to foreclose a remedy, perhaps coupled with a showing of bad faith, overreaching or lack of notice, would be sufficient to defeat a contractual forum selection clause . . . Riley suggests that enforcement of the choice of forum and law provisions is unreasonable because he effectively will be deprived of his day in court. The basis underlying this contention is his perception that recovery will be more difficult under English law than under American law. Riley will not be deprived of his day in court. He may, though, have to structure his case differently than if proceeding in federal district court. The fact that an international transaction may be subject to laws and remedies different or less favorable than those of the United States is not a valid basis to deny enforcement, provided that the law of the chosen forum is not inherently unfair . . . Given the international nature of the insurance underwriting transaction, the parties' forum selection and choice of law provisions contained in the agreement should be given effect . . . Any discussion regarding the efficacy of an agreement to arbitrate in a foreign country between citizens or entities of different countries must begin with a review of the Convention on the Recognition and Enforcement of Foreign Arbitral Awards . . . The Convention was ratified by the United States for differences arising out of commercial legal relationships and it became effective on December 29, 1970. The United Kingdom and the United States are Contracting States to the Convention. Of course, the ratification of the Convention makes it the supreme

continued

3.3

RILEY V. KINGSLEY UNDERWRITING AGENCIES, LTD., *continued*
969 F.2D 953 (10TH CIR. 1992)

law of the land, as enforceable as Congressional enactments . . . Article II of the Convention imposes a mandatory duty on the courts of a Contracting State to recognize, and enforce an agreement to arbitrate unless the agreement is "null and void, inoperative or incapable of being performed." . . . Only if a court finds that the agreement "null and void, inoperative or incapable of being performed," . . . may it act to the contrary . . . Riley argues that the "null and void" exception applies. His argument is that the agreement requiring arbitration should be held void as against public policy because several of his claims are grounded in the 1933 and 1934 securities acts, and the application of English law would result in a waiver of certain provisions of those acts. We disagree . . . Finally, Riley's suggestion that everyone in England will be biased against him has no basis in the record and we will not assume that Riley would get anything other than a full and fair hearing . . .

BUSINESS CONSIDERATIONS Why might a business prefer to submit controversies to arbitration rather than to the courts for resolution? Is the business more or less likely to want to resort to arbitration in a contract with a foreign business entity?

ETHICAL CONSIDERATIONS Is it ethical to seek to avoid arbitration because "everyone" in the foreign country will be biased against you? What does this sort of assertion say about the ethics imputed to the citizens of the foreign nation?

SUMMARY

We live in an interdependent world. Consequently, businesspersons should be aware of the international implications of their business dealings. In addition to being familiar with the laws and customs of the countries where they do business, managers must be aware that competition and employment laws, among others, may reach beyond national borders.

Global trade agreements (such as GATT and the WTO) and regional free-trade zones (such as the EU and NAFTA) are becoming much more important in the world economy. They provide businesses with frameworks for trade and, increasingly, with efficient access to large markets. These organizations have substantially changed the rules of the game in international business recently, and familiarity with them is essential if a businessperson desires success in the international arena. These organizations will serve as models for others all over the world in the years to come.

Changes in international trade, and in the emphasis placed on global development, have led to a number of "new" business concerns. Although imports and exports, labor, and information and technology have been recognized as important aspects of domestic trade for years, it is only recently that they have gained similar recognition in the international arena. Continuing development of regulation in these areas will shape the global market in the near future.

One risk to international business investment is nationalization. Nationalization is the taking of private property by a national government. If the nationalization complies with international law, it is called an expropriation. If it does not, it is called a confiscation. The act of state doctrine is used to justify the position that one country will not stand in judgment of the actions of other countries carried on within their own territories.

RESOURCES FOR BUSINESS LAW STUDENTS

NAME	RESOURCES	WEB ADDRESS
International Trade Law (ITL)	ITL, hosted by the University of Tromsö (Norway), provides international trade conventions and documents.	**http://www.lexmercatoria.net/**
The Multilaterals Project	The Multilaterals Project, maintained by Tufts University, provides texts of multilateral treaties, including GATT and NAFTA.	**http://www.fletcher.tufts.edu/**
Pace University School of Law Institute of International Commercial Law (IICL)	IICL provides the full text of the United Nations Convention on Contracts for the International Sale of Goods (CISG), its legislative history, cases, and commentaries.	**http://www.cisg.law.pace.edu/**
Foreign Corrupt Practices Act—15 U.S.C. § 8dd-2	LII provides a hypertext and searchable version of 15 U.S.C. § 78dd-2, popularly known as the Foreign Corrupt Practices Act.	**http://www.law.cornell.edu/uscode/15/78dd-2.html**
Europa (European Union)	Europa, maintained by the European Commission, provides official documents, press releases, publications, and statistics on the European Union.	**http://europa.eu.int/**
World Trade Organization (WTO)	The WTO provides economic research and analysis, dispute settlement material, international trade policy, and publications.	**http://www.wto.org/**
United Nations (UN)	The UN provides material on the International Court of Justice, the report of the International Law Commission, materials from the UN Commission on International Trade Law (UNCITRAL), and access to the UN treaty database.	**http://www.un.org/law/**

Sovereign immunity is a doctrine of law that a sovereign government cannot be sued unless it allows itself to be sued. International law provides three mechanisms for the resolution of international business disputes. The International Court of Justice (ICJ) is the appropriate forum when one nation sues another, provided that each nation agrees to the suit. Domestic courts are used for the resolution of disputes between citizens of different nations. Lastly, arbitration is used in international as well as domestic business disputes.

DISCUSSION QUESTIONS

1. Which recent agreements and enactments have increased the accuracy of the term *global village* in the area of international business? What, if anything, seems to be operating in a manner contrary to the concept of developing a global village?

2. What arguments support restricting the application of a nation's laws to its territorial limits? What arguments support expanding the application of a nation's laws beyond its territorial limits? Which set of arguments is more persuasive ethically?

3. What is the significance of the Treaty of Rome? How does the Treaty of Rome compare with the North American Free Trade Agreement (NAFTA)?

4. What are the main differences between Article 85 and Article 86 of the Treaty of Rome? Suppose that a business fears that conduct it is proposing may be subject to challenge under either of these articles. How can that business be sure in advance that its activities will not be found to violate either section?

5. Two corporations, one organized in Belgium and the other in Great Britain, seek to merge. They are both in the computer software business. The Belgian corporation has 15 percent of the EU market, and the British corporation has 30 percent. What problems do these facts raise with respect to the Treaty of Rome? If, instead, these two firms were located in the United States, with one in New York and the other in Illinois, would the same problems be raised by their prospective merger?

6. Assume that a letter of credit issued for the sale of goods internationally contains a simple typographical error. Is it more appropriate to penalize the seller or the buyer in such a situation? How substantial should an error be before either of the parties is penalized?

7. An American corporation wishes to export a new computer microchip outside the United States. Do you envision any problems in complying with U.S. law in exporting the microchip? Do you envision any problems in complying with European Union (EU) law in importing it into the European market? Would problems exist in importing the microchip into nations outside the NAFTA or EU nations?

8. How do the United Nations Convention on Contracts for the International Sale of Goods (CISG), the General Agreement on Tariffs and Trade (GATT), and the World Trade Organization (WTO) affect international trade? To which types of international trade contracts do each of these three apply?

9. Three doctrines are often applied to international dealings: comity, act of state, and sovereign immunity. How do each of these doctrines affect international dealings and potential legal controversies?

10. You are a financial adviser to a multinational manufacturing corporation. You have been asked to evaluate a proposal for the firm to invest $500 million in a foreign country. The investment will involve building and staffing a factory in the foreign nation. What factors would influence your decision if the proposed location was in an underdeveloped nation with a relatively unstable government? Would your consideration be different if the proposed investment were to take place in a nation in the EU or in Russia? Why should the location of the investment affect the decision to invest?

CASE PROBLEMS AND WRITING ASSIGNMENTS

1. Moosehead Breweries, a Canadian company, licensed its trademark rights and its secret brewing process to Whitbread, giving Whitbread the exclusive right to make and sell Moosehead beer in the United Kingdom. In exchange, Whitbread agreed not to brew or sell any other Canadian beer in the United Kingdom and also to purchase its brewer's yeast only from Moosehead. Once the agreement was made, the two companies applied to the European Commission for an individual exemption under Article 85. Should the commission grant an exemption under Article 85 in this case? Explain your reasoning. [See *Re the Agreement Between Moosehead Breweries, Ltd. and Whitbread and Co.*, (1990) O.J. L100/32; (1991) 4 C.M.L.R. 391.]

2. Stuth purchases ski boots from Artex, paying for them with a letter of credit issued by Bank One. The letter of credit was for 128,691,300 Italian lira. Sturgeon Bay Bank executed the letter of credit for Stuth. Eventually, the letter of credit was presented to Bank One, and the request for payment was denied by Bank One. When Artex sought to recover from Sturgeon Bay, Sturgeon Bay denied liability. According to Sturgeon Bay, it was only acting as a correspondent bank, so that its only obligations were to Bank One, the issuing bank. Is the fact that Sturgeon Bay served as an "advising bank" to Bank One in the handling of the letter of credit sufficient to make it liable on the dishonored letter? Explain your reasoning. [See *Artex, S.R.L.* v. *Bank One, Milwaukee, National Ass'n*, 801 F.Supp. 228 (E.D.Wis. 1991).]

3. In 1981, Harry Carpenter, chairman and chief executive officer of W.S. Kirkpatrick & Co., learned that the Republic of Nigeria was interested in contracting for the construction and equipment of an aeromedical center at Kaduna Air Force Base in Nigeria. Carpenter made arrangements with Benson Akindele, a Nigerian citizen, under which Akindele agreed to secure the contract for W.S. Kirkpatrick. It was further agreed that, provided Akindele did secure the contract for W.S. Kirkpatrick, a "commission" equal to 20 percent of the total contract price would be paid to two Panamanian entities controlled by Akindele. It was understood that this "commission" would be paid to officials of the Nigerian government as a bribe

once the contract was awarded to W.S. Kirkpatrick. The contract was awarded to W.S. Kirkpatrick, the "commission" was paid to the Panamanian entities, and was then distributed to various Nigerian officials. Environmental Tectronics, one of the unsuccessful bidders for the contract, learned of the arrangement between Carpenter and Akindele and brought the matter to the attention of both the Nigerian Air Force and the U.S. Embassy in Lagos, Nigeria. [All parties agreed that it is a violation of Nigerian law to pay or to receive a bribe in connection with the award of a government contract.] If the allegations made by Environmental Tectronics are proven, should Carpenter, Akindele, and W.S. Kirkpatrick be found guilty for violations of the Foreign Corrupt Practices Act? Should Environmental Tectronics be entitled to any remedies in a civil action against any or all of the parties accused of illegal conduct in this case? Explain your reasoning. [See *W.S. Kirkpatrick & Co.* v. *Environmental Tectronics Corp., Int'l*, 493 U.S. 400 (1990).]

4. Bonny filed suit against Lloyd's, alleging that he was fraudulently and in violation of various federal and state securities laws induced to become a member of Lloyd's and to participate as an underwriter in several insurance syndicates marketed by Lloyd's. The complaint sought damages, rescission of the membership agreement with Lloyd's, and an injunction barring Lloyd's from drawing upon letters of credit issued by Harris Bank that Bonny was required to obtain as a condition to acquiring membership with Lloyd's. Lloyd's objected to the court's jurisdiction. According to Lloyd's, the agreement between Bonny and Lloyd's contained a choice of law clause and a forum selection clause, either of which negated jurisdiction by the U.S. courts. The choice of laws clause specified that all disputes should be decided under English law. The forum selection clause required that all disputes be resolved before an English court or before an English arbitrator. Should the U.S. court deny jurisdiction due to these two clauses, or should the court assert jurisdiction in this case? What arguments support each side to this controversy? Which arguments are more persuasive? [See *Bonny* v. *Society of Lloyd's*, 784 F.Supp. 1350 (N.D.Ill. 1991).]

5. The European Commission charged 41 wood pulp producers with violations of Article 85, accusing them of taking concerted action to fix prices for the wood pulp sold to EU customers. Each of the wood pulp producers was operating outside the EU, although all of them imported products into the EU market. The producers claimed that the EU had no jurisdiction in this case, since all of the alleged price-fixing activity took place outside the EU and was therefore beyond the jurisdiction of the commission or its sanctions. The commission rejected this claim, and fined 36 of the producers. These 36 producers appealed to the Court of Justice of the European Communities. Does Article 85 have extraterritorial application beyond the borders of the EU in a case such as this? Which factors most influenced your decision? [See *Re Wood Pulp Cartel* v. *Commission*, 4 C.M.L.R. 901 (1988).]

6. **BUSINESS APPLICATION CASE** On 3 March 1989, Banque de L'Union Haitienne (Union Bank) issued a letter of credit in favor of its customer, Eleck S.A., in the amount of $1,400,000. On the same day, Union Bank contracted with Manufacturers Hanover to act as advising, confirming, and paying bank in the transaction. The parties all agreed that their relationship would be governed by the Uniform Customs and Practices (UCP) for documentary credit. After several amendments to the original document, the letter of credit was assigned an expiration date of 30 April 1989. The original letter was assigned to North American Trading, which subsequently changed its name to International Basic Economic Company (IBEC). On 19 April 1989, IBEC first presented the documents to Manufacturers Hanover, which rejected the initial request due to its (Manufacturers Hanover's) determination that the documents did not conform to the terms and conditions of the letter of credit. Eleck contacted Union Bank to notify them of the rejection. On 20 April, Union Bank telexed Manufacturers Hanover, inquiring as to the nature of the discrepancies that caused the rejection of the documents. On 21 April, Manufacturers Hanover telexed Union Bank, informing them that IBEC should resubmit the documents on 24 April. This telex did not reach Union Bank until 24 April, and it did not identify any particular discrepancies contained in the original documents submitted by IBEC. IBEC resubmitted its documents to Manufacturers Hanover without success twice, on 21 April and again on 24 April. On the afternoon of 24 April, IBEC finally made a successful presentation of the documents to an employee of Manufacturers Hanover who had not been involved in any of the earlier rejections of the documentation. As a result, Manufacturers Hanover transferred $1,473,189 to IBEC's account with Republic National Bank of Miami. The next day, IBEC wire-transferred the funds overseas, and the principals of IBEC disappeared shortly thereafter. Upon notification of the payment, Union Bank transferred the funds to Manufacturers Hanover. The documents presented to Manufacturers Hanover ultimately proved to be fraudulent, and Union Bank sued Manufacturers Hanover for reimbursement of the

amount transferred under the letter of credit. Did the presentation of the documents satisfy the conditions as set out in the original letter of credit? What could or should Union Bank have done differently in this case in order to maximize its protections and/or to minimize its risks? What, if anything, did Manufacturers Hanover do improperly in paying the questionable documents? [See *Banque de L'Union Haitienne* v. *Manufacturers Hanover International Banking Corp.*, 787 F.Supp. 1416 (S.D.Fla. 1991).]

7. **ETHICAL APPLICATION CASE** Boureslan was a naturalized U.S. citizen who was born in Lebanon. The two defendants were both Delaware corporations. In 1979, Boureslan went to work for Aramco Service Company (ASC), a subsidiary of Arabian American Oil Company (Aramco), in Houston, Texas. [Aramco's principal place of business was Dhahran, Saudi Arabia; ASC's principal place of business was Houston.] In 1980, Boureslan requested, and was granted, a transfer to Saudi Arabia to work for Aramco. He remained in Saudi Arabia until 1984, at which time he was discharged by Aramco. Boureslan filed a complaint of employment discrimination with the Equal Employment Opportunity Commission (EEOC) and also sought relief under both federal and state law, alleging that he was harassed and ultimately discharged because of his race, religion, and national origin in violation of law, including Title VII of the Civil Rights Act of 1964. The respondents filed a motion for summary judgment, alleging that the district court lacked subject matter jurisdiction in the case since Title VII protections do not extend to U.S. citizens working in other nations, even if working for an American company. The district court dismissed the suit, and this decision was upheld by the Fifth Circuit Court of Appeals. Boureslan and the EEOC petitioned for *certiorari*, and the Supreme Court granted their petitions in order to resolve the issue. Did Congress intend for the protections of Title VII to apply to U.S. citizens employed by American employers outside the United States? What are the ethical implica-

tions when a multinational firm provides different protections and benefits to workers in two or more of its locations, based purely on the happenstance of geographic location and inconsistent national laws? What should the firm do in such a situation? [See *Equal Employment Opportunity Commission* v. *Arabian American Oil Co.*, 499 U.S. 244 (1991)].

8. **CRITICAL THINKING CASE** Alberto-Culver, an American manufacturer based in Illinois, purchased from Scherk, a German citizen, three enterprises owned by Scherk and organized under the laws of Germany and Liechtenstein, together with all trademark rights of these enterprises. The sales contract, which was negotiated in the United States, England, and Germany, signed in Austria, and closed in Switzerland, contained express warranties by petitioner that the trademarks were unencumbered. It also contained a clause that provided that "any controversy or claim [that] shall arise out of this agreement or the breach thereof" would be referred to arbitration before the International Chamber of Commerce in Paris, France, and that Illinois laws would govern the agreement and its interpretation and performance. Subsequently, after allegedly discovering that the trademarks were subject to substantial encumbrances, Alberto-Culver offered to rescind the contract. Scherk refused, and Alberto-Culver filed suit for breach of contract and fraud. Scherk moved to dismiss the action or, in the alternative, to stay the proceedings pending arbitration of the dispute before the ICC in Paris. The district court denied the motions by Scherk, ruling that the arbitration clause was unenforceable. The court of appeals affirmed, and Scherk appealed to the U.S. Supreme Court. How should the Supreme Court rule in this case? What reasons can you posit in support of the decision the Supreme Court should reach? If the contract was between two American businesses, would a different result be reached by the courts? [See *Scherk* v. *Alberto-Culver Co.*, 417 U.S. 506 (1974).]

NOTES

1. Report FT900 (97). Bureau of Census, Foreign Trade Division, Final 1997.
2. Paul A. Herbig and Hugh E. Kramer, "Do's and Don't's of Cross-Cultural Negotiations," *Industrial Marketing Management* 21 (1992), p. 287.
3. 473 U.S. 614 (1985).
4. "What Does the Euro Mean to You?" http://www.lovellwhitedurrant.com. (This is an update of an

article originally published in the December 1997 issue of the *International Financial Law Review*.)
5. Ibid.
6. *Re Wood Pulp Cartel et al.* v. *Commission,* 4 C.M.L.R. 901 (1988).
7. Jim Lobe, "Trade: U.S. Renews Banana Battle with EU," *World News* (Inter Press Service, 2 November 1998).

THE AMERICAN LEGAL SYSTEM

To successfully handle (and avoid) legal problems in the workplace, businesspeople need to understand how the U.S. legal system operates. Chapter 4 describes the powers and limitations of the federal government as set forth in the U.S. Constitution. It also describes courts and jurisdiction. Chapter 5 examines the constitutional bases for government regulation of business, paying special attention to the clauses that provide a foundation for government regulation while simultaneously constraining that foundation: the commerce clause, the equal protection clause, the due process clause, and the takings clause.

Chapter 6 examines several methods for dispute resolution in the legal system. This chapter includes the anatomy of a hypothetical civil case, and a discussion of alternative dispute resolution choices. Chapter 7 describes torts and the body of civil law concerned with these "private" wrongs that may arise. In particular, this chapter discusses intentional torts, negligence, and strict liability. Chapter 8 describes crimes and the body of law concerned with "public" wrongs. This chapter focuses on crimes that are more likely to affect business—computer crimes, embezzlement, forgery, and fraud, for example. The chapter discusses the objectives of criminal law, the bases of criminal responsibility, and the nature of the various offenses.

4

THE AMERICAN LEGAL SYSTEM
AND COURT JURISDICTION

The Kochanowskis never realized how important it is for owners and operators of a business to understand the complexities of the U.S. legal system until they began CIT. Now a number of questions have arisen. What, for example, does CIT need to know about state and federal court systems, or about the different types of jurisdiction? Might they be sued—or be forced to sue—in states other than their state of residence? What types of cases might they encounter? For example, Tom and Anna obtained a U.S. patent on Call-Image. However, they are not sure how well this patent will protect the technology behind the videophone. Can CIT test this claim in court before a challenge arises, or will the firm have to wait until the patent is being used without authorization before they can sue? They have also discovered that they will have to use care to distinguish the rules applicable to the federal government and those applicable to the states. Be prepared! You never know when one of the Kochanowskis will need your help or advice.

THE FEDERAL CONSTITUTION

The Constitution of the United States is a unique document for two reasons: it is the oldest written national constitution, and it was the first to include a government based on the concept of a separation of powers. A copy of the Constitution appears as Appendix A of this book. The U.S. Constitution was created in reaction to the tyranny of English rule; it was intended to prevent many of the problems the founding fathers felt were present under the English government. England has an unwritten constitution and a system of government that tends to merge the legislative, executive, and judicial functions. In contrast, our written constitution established a governmental structure that has three separate "divisions" and a series of checks and balances whereby the power of one "compartment" is offset, at least to some extent, by that of the others.

History taught the persons who founded the United States that all tyrants had at least two powers—the power of the purse and the power of the sword. Consequently, they separated these powers by placing the power of the purse (fiscal and monetary control) in the legislative branch of government and the power of the sword (control over armed forces) in the executive branch. The third branch of government, the judicial branch, does not have the formal, written power that exists in the other branches. It does, however, possess what may be the most important power, at least from a constitutional perspective. The judicial branch has the power to decide where and how the other two branches may properly exercise their powers. This power was "created" by the court itself in the landmark case of *Marbury v. Madison*[1] and is called the power of judicial review. We will discuss judicial review in greater detail later in this chapter.

Allocation of Power

Legislative Power. Article I of the Constitution creates a Congress consisting of two houses: the Senate and the House of Representatives. Congress has the power to levy and collect taxes, pay debts, and pass all laws with respect to certain enumerated powers, such as providing for the common defense and general welfare, regulating commerce, borrowing and coining money, establishing post offices and building highways, promoting science and the arts, and creating courts inferior to the U.S. Supreme Court.

Executive Power. Article II of the Constitution creates the executive branch of government by establishing the offices of president and vice president. The president is the commander in chief of the armed forces of the United States. In addition, the president has the power to make treaties and to nominate ambassadors, judges, and other officers of the United States. The Senate must confirm all presidential appointments. Without Senate confirmation, the appointee cannot take office. The vice president is the president of the Senate and also serves for the president when or if the president is unable to serve.

Administrative Agencies, an Additional Executive Power. Administrative agencies also wield power under the executive branch of government, even though they are not discussed in the U.S. Constitution. These agencies are sometimes called a fourth branch of government. They are generally created by statute at the request of the executive branch. The statute that creates the agency is called the *enabling statute,* and it specifies the power and authority of the agency. Most federal agencies have the power, within their authority, to make rules that are similar to statutes and to

Cases and controversies
Claims brought before the court in regular proceedings to protect or enforce rights or to prevent or punish wrongs.

Advisory opinion
A formal opinion by a judge, court, or law officer on a question of law but not presented in an actual case.

Moot case
A case not properly submitted to a court for resolution because it seeks to determine an abstract question that does not arise upon the existing fact pattern.

Standing
Legal involvement; the right to sue.

Political questions
Questions that would encroach on executive or legislative powers, concerning government, the state, or politics.

Assault
A threat to touch someone in an undesired manner.

Battery
Unauthorized touching of another person without legal justification or that person's consent.

District court
Trial court in the federal court system.

Appellee
Party who "defends" the decision of the lower court.

Justiciability
Capable of a court decision; decidable by a court.

decide cases involving these rules and regulations. (These cases take the form of administrative hearings; they are not cases in the literal sense of the word.) The exact authority and the organization of the agencies vary greatly. Administrative agencies exist on the federal, state, and local levels. See Chapter 5 for a more detailed discussion of administrative agencies.

Judicial Power. Article III of the Constitution vests federal judicial power in one Supreme Court and in such other inferior courts as Congress may create. All U.S. federal judges are nominated by the president; moreover, if they are confirmed by the Senate, they are permitted to serve in office for the rest of their lives, as long as their behavior is "good."

The actual wording of Article III limits rather than expands judicial power. Under Section 2 of Article III, generally the federal courts may only hear and decide **cases and controversies.** *Cases and controversies* can be defined as matters that are appropriate for judicial determination. For a matter to be appropriate for judicial determination, it must be "definite and concrete, touching the legal relations of parties having adverse legal interests. It must be a real and substantial controversy admitting of specific relief through a decree of a conclusive character, as distinguished from an opinion advising what the law would be upon a hypothetical state of facts."[2] Constitutional law has evolved through precedents so that, today, the following are not considered to be a case or a controversy:

1. **Advisory opinions**
2. **Moot cases**
3. The litigant lacks **standing**
4. **Political questions**

The doctrine of the separation of powers requires that *federal* courts deal only with judicial matters. An advisory opinion is one in which the executive branch refers a question to the judicial branch for a nonbinding opinion. However, that is not the purpose of the federal judicial system. Accordingly, whenever a member of the executive branch requires an advisory opinion, the question is referred to the Justice Department within the executive branch for an opinion from the Attorney General. Under the U.S. federal system of government, the Attorney General is the appropriate person to issue an advisory opinion. Contrary to the federal rule, some state courts are empowered to give advisory opinions.

The federal courts will only hear cases that are appropriate for a judicial solution. Moot cases are those cases in which the matter has been resolved. Sometimes the "resolution" occurs through the passage of time or a change in circumstances. In the case of *DeFunis* v. *Odegaard,*[3] the Supreme Court stated that the question of whether a student should be admitted to a law school was a moot case because by the time the Court could have issued its opinion, the student would have been on the brink of graduation. The law school informed the Supreme Court that regardless of the outcome of the suit, the law school would award DeFunis a degree if he passed his final quarter of coursework. Accordingly, as an example of judicial efficiency, the Court chose not to write an opinion on the merits of the suit.

Only persons who can demonstrate that they have actually been harmed or injured have standing to sue. Courts will generally define standing as having a direct and immediate personal injury. Courts view standing as part of the Article III limitation of federal judicial power to decide cases and controversies. In addition, statutes may grant standing to sue. For example, if you saw a person punch someone in the nose, you would not have standing to sue the aggressor for **assault** or **battery;** only the person who was hit would have standing to sue because he or she was the one who was injured. The following Supreme Court case addresses the issue of standing under Article III of the Constitution.

4.1

DOC V. UNITED STATES HOUSE OF REPRESENTATIVES

119 S. CT. 765 (1999)

FACTS The Census Bureau (Bureau) . . . announced a plan to use two forms of statistical sampling in the 2000 Decennial Census to address a chronic and . . . growing problem of "undercounting" certain identifiable groups of individuals. Two sets of plaintiffs filed separate suits challenging the legality and constitutionality of the Bureau's plan. We . . . consolidated the cases for oral argument.

. . . For the last few decades, the Census Bureau has sent census forms to every household, which it asked residents to complete and return. The Bureau followed up . . . by sending enumerators to personally visit all households that did not respond by mail. Despite this comprehensive effort . . . , the Bureau has always failed to reach . . . a portion of the population. This shortfall has been labeled the census "undercount." . . . Some identifiable groups—including certain minorities, children, and renters—have historically had substantially higher undercount rates than the population as a whole. . . . [T]he Bureau formulated a plan for the 2000 census that uses statistical sampling to supplement data obtained through traditional census methods. . . . Congress passed the 1998 Departments of Commerce, Justice, and State, the Judiciary, and Related Agencies Appropriations Act . . . which provides that . . . the Bureau's Census 2000 Operational Plan "shall be deemed to constitute final agency action regarding the use of statistical methods in the 2000 decennial census." The Act also permits any person aggrieved by the plan to use statistical sampling in the decennial census to bring a legal action [in **district court**] . . . It further provides for review by appeal directly to this Court.

The publication of the Bureau's plan for the 2000 census occasioned two separate legal challenges. . . . The first suit . . . was filed . . . by four counties . . . and residents of 13 States . . . who claimed that the Bureau's planned use of statistical sampling to apportion Representatives among the States violates the Census Act and the Census Clause of the Constitution. . . . The second challenge was filed by the United States House of Representatives . . .

ISSUE Do the counties, individuals, and the House of Representatives have standing to sue the Census Bureau?

HOLDING Several of the **appellees** have standing.

REASONING Article 1, § 2, cl. 3, of the United States Constitution states that "Representatives . . . shall be apportioned among the several States . . . according to their respective Numbers." . . . § 2 of the Fourteenth Amendment provides that "Representatives shall be apportioned among the several States according to their respective numbers . . . " Pursuant to this constitutional authority . . . Congress enacted the Census Act . . .

[W]e begin our analysis with the threshold issue of **justiciability.** Congress has eliminated any . . . concerns . . . by providing that "any person aggrieved by the use of any statistical method in violation of the Constitution or any provision of law (other than this Act), in connection with the 2000 census or any later decennial census, to determine the population for purposes of the apportionment or redistricting of Members in Congress, may in a civil action obtain declaratory, injunctive, and any other appropriate relief against the use of such method." . . . Thus, the only open justiciability question in this case is whether appellees satisfy the requirements of Article III standing.

We have repeatedly noted that in order to establish Article III standing, "[a] plaintiff must allege personal injury fairly traceable to the defendant's allegedly unlawful conduct and likely to be redressed by the requested relief." . . . [T]he record before us amply supports the conclusion that several of the appellees have met their burden of proof regarding their standing . . . [A]ppellees submitted the affidavit of Dr. Ronald F. Weber, a professor of government at the University of Wisconsin, which demonstrates that Indiana resident Gary A. Hofmeister [one of the individual appellees] has standing to challenge the

continued

4.1

DOC V. UNITED STATES HOUSE OF REPRESENTATIVES, *continued*
119 S. CT. 765 (1999)

proposed census 2000 plan. Utilizing data published by the Bureau, Dr. Weber projected year 2000 populations and net undercount rates for all States under the 1990 method of enumeration and under the Department's proposed plan for the 2000 census. He then determined on the basis of these projections how many Representatives would be apportioned to each State under each method and concluded that "it is a virtual certainty that Indiana will lose a seat . . . under the Department's Plan." . . .

Appellee Hofmeister's expected loss of a Representative to the United States Congress undoubtedly satisfies the injury-in-fact requirement of Article III standing. In the context of apportionment, we have held that voters have standing to challenge an apportionment statute because "they are asserting 'a plain, direct and adequate interest in maintaining the effectiveness of their votes.'" . . . [T]he threat of vote dilution through the use of sampling is "concrete" and "actual or imminent, not 'conjectural' or 'hypothetical.'" . . . [I]t is certainly not necessary for this Court to wait until the census has been conducted to consider the issues presented here, because such a pause would result in extreme—possibly irremediable—hardship. . . . Hofmeister meets the second and third requirements of Article III standing. There is undoubtedly a "traceable" connection between the use of sampling in the decennial census and Indiana's expected loss of a Representative, and there is a substantial likelihood that the requested relief—a permanent injunction against the proposed uses of sampling in the census—will redress the alleged injury.

. . . Dr. Weber indicated . . . that "it is substantially likely that voters in Maricopa County, Arizona, Bergen County, New Jersey, Cumberland County, Pennsylvania, LaSalle County, Illinois, Orange County, California, St. Johns County, Florida, Gallatin County, Montana, Forsyth County, Georgia, and Loudoun County, Virginia, will suffer vote dilution in state and local elections as a result of the [Bureau's] Plan." Several of the appellees reside in these counties, and several of the States in which these counties are located require use of federal decennial census population numbers for their state legislative redistricting. . . . [T]he appellees who live in the aforementioned counties have a strong claim that they will be injured by the Bureau's plan because their votes will be diluted vis-à-vis residents of counties with larger "undercount" rates. . . .

BUSINESS CONSIDERATIONS Is reliance on consultants such as Dr. Weber valid? Will the use of sampling provide more accurate information?

ETHICAL CONSIDERATIONS Do voters have an ethical right to avoid dilution of their vote, even if the use of sampling will provide more accurate information?

Judicial questions
Questions that are proper for a court to decide.

Judicial restraint
A judicial policy of refusing to hear and decide certain types of cases.

In the preceding case, the justices discussed the history of the U.S. Census and legislative apportionment. For example, originally the census required census takers to personally visit each household and obtain information from the head of household.

Even though many political questions in our society involve real controversies, the doctrine of our courts is that courts will not hear them. Why? While a political question may be considered a very real controversy, it is not considered to be a **judicial question.** This rule is based on the concept of **judicial restraint.** For example, if a citizen asserts that a state is not based on a democratic form of government, that claim will not be heard in a U.S. federal court because it is a political question. Similarly, if a citizen thinks that our nation's foreign policy is incorrect, our courts cannot be used to debate the point because foreign policy is a political question. What constitutes a political question, however, is not always clear. For instance, is *legislative apportionment*—the ratio of legislative representation to constituents—a political question? Historically, the courts have said no. The rule is now well established; the issue was not even addressed in *DOC* v. *United States House of Representatives.*

Now that you know the four limits that constrain judicial power, we will consider the one concept that has expanded judicial power. When you read the Constitution, you will not find the specific power of judicial review mentioned. That is because it is a court-created power. In 1803, the Chief Justice of the U.S. Supreme Court, John Marshall, created this doctrine in the landmark case of *Marbury* v. *Madison.*[4] This power is based on an interpretation of the Constitution, which states that our courts may examine the actions of the legislative and executive branches of government to ascertain whether those actions conform to the Constitution. If they do not, the courts have the power to declare those actions unconstitutional and, therefore, unenforceable. Thus, the Supreme Court can declare an act of Congress invalid. This concept of judicial power does not exist in England, where the Parliament is supreme. Therefore, the judicial branch of government, which has neither the power of the purse nor the power of the sword, has significant power because it can determine what action by the other branches is legal. Since 1803, the power of U.S. courts to judicially review all actions of the legislative and executive branches of government has gone unchallenged. It has become the cornerstone of our doctrine of the separation of powers. Furthermore, this power of the Supreme Court to invalidate legislation also extends to all state legislation because of the supremacy clause in the federal Constitution.

The Watergate scandal, remembered by many as a low point in American history, may be viewed as a high point with respect to the doctrine of judicial review. In 1974, President Nixon was ordered to produce the now-famous Watergate tapes for use in a federal prosecution. Nixon claimed executive privilege and refused the order to turn over the tapes to the federal prosecutor. The Supreme Court, in a unanimous opinion, denied Nixon's claim and ordered him to release the tapes. President Nixon complied with the order of the Supreme Court, thus ending a constitutional crisis. Subsequently, Nixon became the first—and, so far, only—U.S. president to resign from office.

Role of Judges. The personalities of individual judges and justices affect their rulings. The jurisprudential views of the judges impact the rulings in particular cases and the precedents being set for a jurisdiction. [For example, there are numerous articles about how Justice Ruth Bader Ginsburg's work experiences and views affect her decisions.[5]] Judges who favor judicial restraint believe that the judge's role is to make

4.2 | MARKETING

HOW TO PROTECT CIT'S PATENT

Tom is very concerned that another firm will "steal" the technology behind Call-Image, produce a copy, and sell it, perhaps even at a price below what CIT can sell its Call-Image. Although CIT holds a patent on Call-Image, Tom knows that patents are not always upheld in court. Consequently, he would like to file a suit with the court to determine if the patent will be upheld before a competitor duplicates it. He asks you how he should proceed. What advice will you give Tom?

BUSINESS CONSIDERATIONS How does uncertainty about the validity of a patent affect a business? What can a business do to reduce the risk? What technique(s) would be most effective?

ETHICAL CONSIDERATIONS Analyze the ethical perspective of any business that would attempt to "steal" CIT's technology. Is commercial or industrial espionage an ethical business technique?

Habeas corpus
The name given to a variety of writs issued to bring a party before a court or judge.

Writ
A writing issued by a court in the form of a letter ordering some designated activity.

Ex post facto law
A law passed after an occurrence or act, which retrospectively changes the legal consequences of such act.

sure that a law is legal and constitutional. If there is something wrong with the legal system, judges should not correct it; this should be left to the legislature. For example, in one of the asbestos liability lawsuits, Justice David H. Souter writes, "[T]his litigation defies customary judicial administration and calls for national legislation."[6] Judges who are activists believe that their role is to encourage social change: it is not necessary to wait for the legislature to act. The impact of the U.S. Supreme Court justices is particularly strong. The current justices on the Supreme Court are Chief Justice William H. Rehnquist, and Justices Stephen Breyer, Ruth Bader Ginsburg, Anthony M. Kennedy, Sandra Day O'Connor, Antonin Scalia, David H. Souter, John Paul Stevens, and Clarence Thomas. President Clinton appointed Justices Ginsburg and Breyer.

Original Constitution

The original Constitution, signed on 17 September 1787, contained a number of rights pertaining to individuals. Among these is the right of *habeas corpus.* The original act is the English statute of 31 Car. II, c.2; it has been amended in England and adopted throughout the United States.[7] In Latin, *habeas corpus* means "You have the body."[8] This right may be used by all persons who have been deprived of their liberty. There are special forms of the **writ;** however, when the words "writ of *habeas corpus*" are used alone, the writ is addressed to the person who detains an individual. The writ commands that person to produce the individual in a court and to comply with any order by the court issuing the writ. This is probably the most common form of the writ.

Another right established by the Constitution is that Congress may pass no bills of attainder. A *bill of attainder* is a "legislative trial" whereby a person is judged a felon or worse by act of the legislature and not by a court of law.

Congress may not enact *ex post facto* **laws.** For example, if a business entered into a perfectly legal transaction in January, Congress cannot declare that transaction illegal in a statute passed after January. As used in the Constitution, the prohibition on *ex post facto* laws only applies to criminal law.[9] This prohibition includes laws that make an act into a crime; make a crime into a more serious crime; change the punishment for a crime; or alter the legal rules of evidence for proving a crime.

These are some of the most notable constitutional rights. However, other individual rights, such as trial by jury in most criminal cases, were also written into the original Constitution.

Amendments to the Constitution

Four years after the U.S. Constitution was signed, the first 10 amendments were passed. These amendments, known as the Bill of Rights, were designed to ensure that certain individual rights were protected. For example, the First Amendment

YOU BE THE JUDGE

BIBLE STORIES IN CLASS

Zachary Hood attended a first-grade class in a public school in Medford, New Jersey. As a reward, his teacher told Zachary that he could read a story of his choice to the class. He selected one of his favorites, the biblical tale of Jacob and Esau. His teacher decided that a Bible story would not be appropriate and would not allow Zachary to read his story out loud. The version that Zachary wanted to read does not mention God or the Bible. It is simply the story of two brothers who quarrel and then resolve their differences. The other students in the class were permitted to read the stories they chose.

"[T]he case underscores the enduring tension between a teacher's right to supervise assignments and a student's right to express individual initiative." The teacher would have allowed Zachary to read the story to her privately. His parents wanted the story read aloud to the class. Eric Treene, an attorney with the Becket Fund for Religious Liberty, is representing the Hoods before the appellate court. He argues, "The government requires the school to be neutral to religion and this is being hostile to religion."

A lawsuit on behalf of Zachary has been brought before *your* appellate court. How will *you* resolve this case?[10]

BUSINESS CONSIDERATIONS How can teachers avoid this type of litigation? Are businesses immune from litigation involving the separation of church and state? Why? When might a businesses become embroiled in this type of controversy? Would any businesses have standing to sue in Zachary's case?

ETHICAL CONSIDERATIONS Is it ethical for groups like the Becket Fund for Religious Liberty, the Americans United for Separation of Church and State, and the American Civil Liberties Union to support litigation and to file **amicus briefs**? Is it ethical for a business to provide financial support to these organizations?

SOURCE: Marjorie Coeyman, *The Christian Science Monitor* (15 June 1999), p. 1.

provides that "Congress shall make no law respecting an establishment of religion, or prohibiting the free exercise thereof; . . ." The First Amendment provides the basis for the separation of church and state. In all, 27 amendments to the Constitution have been passed—see Appendix A. The amendments to the Constitution reflect the citizens' concerns about particular topics and reflect changes in the society. The Constitution itself serves as the supreme law over U.S. society.

Amicus brief
Court brief filed by individual or group who does not have standing in the dispute.

THE COURTS AND JURISDICTION

Jurisdiction, the power of a court to affect legal relationships, is a basic concept with respect to our courts. We will examine four aspects of jurisdiction:

1. **Subject matter jurisdiction**
2. Jurisdiction over the persons or property
3. Concurrent versus exclusive jurisdiction
4. Venue

Subject matter jurisdiction
The power of a court to hear certain kinds of legal questions.

Subject Matter Jurisdiction

In our discussion of the Constitution, we said that the Supreme Court was limited to deciding cases and controversies. In addition, Article III of the Constitution defines the Supreme Court's subject matter jurisdiction as including all cases in law and equity arising under the Constitution, the statutes of the United States, and all treaties. The subject matter jurisdiction granted to the Supreme Court is extensive. A state juvenile court, on the other hand, is limited solely to hearing matters concerning children, provided that the case or controversy arose within that state and under its laws. If an adult were brought before a juvenile court, the court would lack subject matter jurisdiction. Because it may decide only matters concerning people under 18 years of age, a juvenile court is inappropriate for a case involving an adult. Likewise, a federal bankruptcy court may not decide a criminal matter because its jurisdiction is limited to bankruptcy matters. Subject matter jurisdiction determines which court is the "right" court to hear a particular type of case or controversy.

Jurisdiction over the Persons or Property

In addition to the appropriate subject matter jurisdiction, a court must also have jurisdiction over the persons or property whose rights, duties, or obligations it will decide. Basically, three techniques exist for obtaining jurisdiction over persons or property—*in personam, in rem,* and *quasi in rem* (see Exhibit 4.1). First we will discuss **in personam jurisdiction,** the authority of the court over the person.

In Personam *Jurisdiction.* Jurisdictional questions do not arise over the person of the **plaintiff.** The plaintiff chooses to file the suit in a particular court and so implicitly consents to the court's jurisdiction. It is inconsistent to allow the plaintiff to file the suit and then complain that the same court lacks jurisdiction over him or her.

The **defendant,** however, does not choose the court. Often, if the defendant were given a choice, he or she would choose not to have any trial. If a trial *must* take place, he or she might well prefer to have it held elsewhere. The question, then, is how to get jurisdiction over the person of the defendant. The defendant may consent to the court's jurisdiction. Consent can occur by merely responding to a lawsuit that has been filed. It can occur either by express consent or by failure to raise the issue of jurisdiction and, instead, responding to the legal questions. Consent can also be given prior to the lawsuit. This is commonly accomplished by a contract clause or by appointment of an agent to accept **service of process.** A corporation is considered to have given consent when it registers with a state as a **foreign corporation** and asks permission to conduct business in a state. Courts have concluded that a corporation that engages in business as a foreign corporation without the required registration has given implied consent.

A court will also have jurisdiction over a defendant who is physically present in the state when he or she is served with process. This would include a person who is on a trip to the state or even merely passing through the state on his or her way to another destination. Courts will generally decide that there is no jurisdiction over a defendant who is tricked into entering the state by the plaintiff. A corporation is physically present in a state in which it is *doing business.* (Doing business is also used as the basis of implied consent by some states.) For example, a corporation is doing business in a state in which it has stores, offices, warehouses, and regular employees. The courts have decided numerous cases about what

In personam jurisdiction
Authority over a specific person or corporation within the control of the court.

Plaintiff
A person who files a lawsuit; the person who complains to the court.

Defendant
A person who answers a lawsuit; the person whose behavior is the subject of the complaint.

Service of process
Delivery of a notice to the person named to inform that person of the nature of the legal dispute.

Foreign corporation
A corporation that had its articles of incorporation approved in another state.

constitutes doing business and have devised various tests for recognizing doing business. Two of these tests are: (1) whether the corporation's activities were single, isolated transactions or continuous and substantial activities; or (2) whether

E X H I B I T 4.1	Methods to Obtain Jurisdiction over the Defendant		
Type of Jurisdiction	**Type of Judgment**	**Differences Between Individual and Corporate Defendants**	
		Individual	*Corporation*
In personam Authority over a specific person or corporation within the control of the state. Authority may derive from consent, domicile, physical presence, or long-arm statutes.	Affects the person	**Consent** Defendant consents to personal jurisdiction; consent can occur before or after a suit has begun.	**Consent** A corporation consents when it registers as a foreign corporation within the state.[c]
		Domicile Defendant has a residence—usually a home—at which he or she is/has been physically present and intends to remain for the time being; individuals have only one domicile.[a]	**Domicile** A corporation is incorporated (articles of incorporation) and/or has corporate headquarters in the state.
		Physical Presence Defendant is served by hand while he or she is within the geographic boundaries of the state.[b]	**Physical Presence** A corporation is recognized as "doing business" in the state.
In rem Authority over property or status within the control of the state. Settles ownership interests in property or status for all persons.	Affects the property or status	The rules for individuals and corporations are basically the same.	
Quasi in rem Authority obtained through property under the control of the state. Settles issues of ownership, possession, or use of property; or settles personal disputes unrelated to the property.	Affects the rights of specific people to property[d]	The rules for individuals and corporations are basically the same.	

a. Some people are not capable of selecting domiciles for themselves; thus, they have domiciles determined for them by legal rules (e.g., minors).

b. Most states will decline to exercise jurisdiction if the defendant is brought into the state by force or enticed into the state by fraud.

c. If the corporation failed to register, the court may imply consent from the act of doing business in the state. Generally, implied consent is limited to cases arising from the actual doing of business in the state.

d. A successful plaintiff is limited to the value of the property.

the corporation's agents were only soliciting offers in the state or were engaged in additional activities.

In the landmark case of *International Shoe Co.* v. *Washington,* 326 U.S. 310 (1945), the U.S. Supreme Court concluded that before a defendant is required to appear in a state court, he or she must have certain *minimum contacts* with the state. Otherwise, the suit would offend traditional concepts of fair play and substantial justice. This case created a constitutional test for *in personam* jurisdiction. The defendant in this case was a corporation, but the ruling appears to apply to individuals as well.

In personam jurisdiction also exists in the state of domicile. Domicile is a complicated legal doctrine (and most of its complexity is outside the scope of this text). Human beings have one and only one domicile. It may be chosen by the person or assigned by the law. *Domicile* is usually a person's home, the place where he or she is physically present and where he or she intends to remain for the time being. Domicile does *not* require that a person live in a state for a certain minimum period of time. Consequently, domicile contrasts with residency statutes that require, for example, a person to live in a state for a set period of time before voting in the state or being eligible for in-state tuition at its colleges and universities.

Suppose that both the plaintiff and the defendant are domiciliaries of Alaska; Alaska has jurisdiction over them. On the other hand, if the plaintiff is a domiciliary of Alaska but the defendant is a domiciliary of Oregon, Alaska *may* not have proper jurisdiction over the defendant. If the plaintiff wants to sue the defendant in a state court, the plaintiff might need to go to Oregon and sue the defendant there, since a defendant's state of domicile is almost always an appropriate forum. Potential jurisdiction in a federal court will be discussed later in this chapter.

Corporations are domiciled in the state in which they are incorporated. They are also considered to be domiciled in the state where they have their corporate headquarters, if this is a different state. A corporation may be sued where it is domiciled. A corporation is also subject to *in personam* jurisdiction in all states in which the corporation does business because it is physically present there.

Most states have laws called *long-arm statutes.* The purpose of these statutes is to permit the state to exercise *in personam* jurisdiction when ordinarily this would not be possible. A common type of long-arm statute permits a state to exercise authority over a person who drives on its roads. This is also called a nonresident motorist statute. Suppose a resident of Nebraska drives a car on the roads of Kansas and injures a resident of Kansas. Under this statute, the courts of Kansas would have jurisdiction over the person of the resident of Nebraska, because it would be unfair to require the resident of Kansas to go to Nebraska to sue. Other states have enacted much broader long-arm statutes. For example, Illinois enacted a statute that listed certain acts that would confer jurisdiction, if done in Illinois. California and Texas,[11] on the other hand, enacted long-arm statutes that provide for *in personam* jurisdiction whenever it complies with the U.S. Constitution. As with other matters under the control of the states, there is great variation among long-arm statutes.

In rem jurisdiction
Authority over property or status within the control of the court.

Condemnation proceeding
Court proceeding to take property for public use or declare property forfeited.

In Rem *Jurisdiction.* If a state cannot obtain *in personam* jurisdiction on any of these grounds, another approach—called *in rem* **jurisdiction**—can be used. *In rem jurisdiction* allows the state to exercise its authority over something such as land or a marital domicile, within its boundaries. The court's judgment will affect everyone's rights in that "thing." It does not impose a personal obligation on the defendant. For example, if an individual or a corporation has real property in one state but resides in another, the state where the property is located can exercise *in rem* jurisdiction over the property in a **condemnation proceeding.**

Quasi in Rem *Jurisdiction.* In this type of jurisdiction, the court determines the rights of particular persons to specific property. (It is distinct from *in rem* jurisdiction, because a court with *in rem* jurisdiction will determine the rights of all persons in the thing. It differs from *in personam* jurisdiction because there is no authority over the person of the defendant.) The court obtains control of the property in *quasi in rem* jurisdiction through two methods. In one, the property is within the jurisdiction of the court, and the plaintiff wishes to resolve issues of ownership, possession, or use of the property—for example, to foreclose a mortgage. In the second method, the dispute does not concern the property but is personal to the plaintiff, such as a breach of contract or the commission of a tort. Jurisdiction will exist if the plaintiff can locate the defendant's property within the state and bring it before the court by **attachment** or **garnishment.** Limitations exist on when attachment or garnishment is allowed. When the plaintiff's suit is successful, the recovery is limited to the value of the property. Exhibit 4.1 summarizes the techniques for obtaining jurisdiction over the defendant.

Service of Process. In cases of either *in personam, in rem,* or *quasi in rem* jurisdiction, there must be proper service of process on the defendant to inform him or her of the lawsuit. Proper service of process includes *actual notice,* in which one is personally served by an officer of the court; this can also include service by registered mail. If actual notice cannot be obtained after reasonable attempts to do so, notice may be served publicly by a posting on the property or in a newspaper. This is called *constructive service.* Proper notice may also include service at the office of the state's secretary of state. For example, when an out-of-state corporation registers in Delaware, the state may specify that process may be served on Delaware's secretary of state. The following case discusses timing of service of process.

Quasi in rem jurisdiction
Authority obtained through property under the control of the court.

Attachment
Seizure of the defendant's property.

Garnishment
Procedure to obtain possession of the defendant's property when it is in the custody of another person.

Removed
A request to have the case moved to another court.

Diversity of citizenship
The parties are citizens of different states..

Remand
Return the case to the lower court or state court for further hearings.

4.2

MURPHY BROTHERS, INC. V. MICHETTI PIPE STRINGING, INC.

119 S. CT. 1322 (1999)

FACTS On January 26, 1996, . . . Michetti Pipe Stringing, Inc. (Michetti), filed a complaint in Alabama state court seeking damages for an alleged breach of contract and fraud by . . . Murphy Bros., Inc. (Murphy). Michetti did not serve Murphy at that time, but three days later it faxed a "courtesy copy" of the file-stamped complaint to one of Murphy's vice presidents. The parties then engaged in settlement discussions until February 12, 1996, when Michetti officially served Murphy under local law by certified mail.

On March 13, 1996 (30 days after service but 44 days after receiving the faxed copy of the complaint), Murphy **removed** the case under 28 U.S.C. § 1441 to the United States District Court for the Northern District of Alabama. [Murphy invoked the jurisdiction of the Federal District Court under 28 U.S.C. § 1332 based on **diversity of citizenship.** Michetti is a Canadian company with its principal place of business in Alberta, Canada; Murphy is an Illinois corporation with its

principal place of business in that State.] Michetti moved to **remand** the case to the state court . . . Michetti asserted, the removal was untimely under 28 U.S.C. § 1446(b), which provides:

The notice of removal of a civil action or proceeding shall be filed within thirty days after the receipt by the defendant, through service or otherwise, of a copy of the initial pleading setting forth the claim for relief upon which such action or proceeding is based, or within thirty days after the service of summons upon the defendant if such initial pleading has then been filed in court and is not required to be served on the defendant, whichever period is shorter.

. . . Because lower courts have divided on the question whether service of process is a prerequisite for the running of the 30-day removal period under § 1446(b), we granted certiorari.

continued

4.2

MURPHY BROTHERS, INC. V. MICHETTI PIPE STRINGING, INC., continued
119 S. CT. 1322 (1999)

ISSUE . . . [W]hether the . . . defendant must be officially summoned to appear in the action before the time to remove begins to run[?] . . .

HOLDING Yes. The official summons begins the time period.

REASONING . . . An individual or entity named as a defendant is not obliged to engage in litigation unless notified of the action, and brought under a court's authority, by formal process. . . . [W]e hold that a named defendant's time to remove is triggered by simultaneous service of the summons and complaint, or receipt of the complaint, "through service or otherwise," after and apart from service of the summons . . . Service of process, under longstanding tradition in our system of justice, is fundamental to any procedural imposition on a named defendant. . . . In the absence of service of process . . . , a court ordinarily may not exercise power over a party . . . as defendant. . . .

Congress in 1948 enacted the original version of § 1446(b), which provided that "the petition for removal of a civil action or proceeding may be filed within twenty days after commencement of the action or service of process, whichever is later. . . . " Congress soon recognized . . . that § 1446(b), as first framed, did not "give adequate time and operate uniformly" in all States. . . . To ensure that the defendant would have access to the complaint before commencement of the removal period, Congress in 1949 enacted the current version of § 1446(b): "The petition for removal of a civil action or proceeding shall be filed within twenty days [now thirty days] after the receipt by the defendant, through service or otherwise, of a copy of the initial pleading setting forth the claim for relief upon which such action or proceeding is based." The accompanying Senate Report explained:

"In some States suits are begun by the service of a summons or other process without the necessity of filing any pleading until later. As the section now stands, this places the defendant in the position of having to take steps to remove a suit to Federal court before he knows what the suit is about. As said section is herein proposed to be rewritten, a defendant is not required to file his petition for removal until 20 days after he has received (or it has been made available to him) a copy of the initial pleading filed by the plaintiff setting forth the claim upon which the suit is based and the relief prayed for." . . .

. . . Nothing in the legislative history of the 1949 amendment so much as hints that Congress . . . intended to dispense with the historic function of service of process . . . The interpretation of § 1446(b) adopted here adheres to tradition, makes sense of the phrase "or otherwise," and assures defendants adequate time to decide whether to remove an action to federal court. . . . [T]he so-called "receipt rule" . . . could . . . operate with notable unfairness to individuals and entities in foreign nations. Because facsimile machines transmit instantaneously, but formal service abroad may take much longer than 30 days, plaintiffs "would be able to dodge the requirements of international treaties and trap foreign opponents into keeping their suits in state courts." . . .

Chief Justice Rehnquist, with whom Justice Scalia and Justice Thomas join, dissenting.

Respondent faxed petitioner a copy of the file-stamped complaint in its commenced state-court action, and I believe that the receipt of this facsimile triggered the 30-day removal period under the plain language of 28 U.S.C. § 1446(b). The Court does little to explain why the plain language of the statute should not control, opting instead to superimpose a judicially created service of process requirement onto § 1446(b). In so doing, it departs from this Court's practice of strictly construing removal and similar jurisdictional statutes. . . .

BUSINESS CONSIDERATIONS Was it advisable for Michetti to send a facsimile copy to a Murphy vice president? Is a vice president the appropriate recipient of the facsimile copy? Should Murphy have filed for removal based on the facsimile copy? Why? Does this decision encourage parties to negotiate a settlement?

ETHICAL CONSIDERATIONS Was it ethical for Michetti to attempt to sue Murphy in Alabama state court? Is it ethical for Michetti to object to the removal to federal court?

Concurrent Versus Exclusive Jurisdiction

In certain cases, more than one court may exercise jurisdiction. If so, it is called *concurrent jurisdiction*. On the other hand, some subjects can be heard only by a particular court; this is called *exclusive jurisdiction*. Examples of exclusive jurisdiction in the federal courts are suits in which the United States is a party or suits that involve some areas of admiralty law, bankruptcy, copyright, federal crimes, and patent cases. Exhibit 4.2 illustrates the jurisdictional domains of federal and state courts.

Venue

Once a court establishes that it has proper jurisdiction over the subject matter and the person, it must then ascertain whether proper venue exists. *Venue* literally means "neighborhood." In a legal sense, however, it means the proper geographical area or district where a suit can be brought. In state practice, it is usually a question of which county is appropriate. In federal practice, the question of venue is which federal judicial district is the appropriate one. In state practice, if both the plaintiff and the defendant are residents of the same state, *in personam* jurisdiction exists in that state's courts. But which state courts? Venue could be proper in the area where an incident, such as an automobile accident, occurred. The residence of the defendant also may be considered in determining the proper venue. More than one court may have proper venue. The laws of each state spell out in great detail the appropriate courts that would have venue.

Choice of Laws

Choice of laws is the selection of which jurisdiction's laws should be applied to a particular incident; that is, what laws should govern the subject before the court. Although it is also called "conflict of laws," legal scholars argue that "choice of laws" is the more appropriate title. Another complication in this area is that the

EXHIBIT 4.2 | **A Comparison of Federal and State Court Jurisdiction**

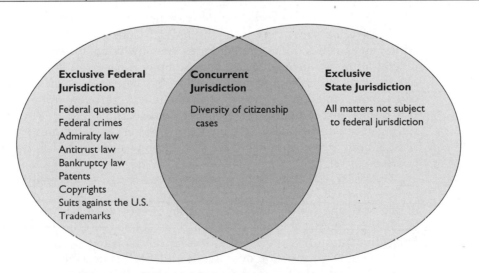

Substantive law
The law that creates, defines, and regulates rights.

Forum
The court conducting the trial.

Procedural law
The methods of enforcing rights or obtaining redress for the violation of rights.

court will use choice of laws rules to determine the **substantive laws** that should be applied to the dispute; however, the **forum** court will use its own **procedural laws.** The following example provides a hint of the difficulties that may arise when a choice of laws case arises.

> *Julia, a domiciliary of Massachusetts, entered into a contract with Karen, a domiciliary of Vermont, while they both were in Connecticut. The contract concerned goods that were located in Maine and were to be shipped to New York. While the goods were in transit, they were stopped and taken by Dawn, a domiciliary of New Hampshire, who was a creditor of Julia. This situation raises many legal questions. What should Karen do to get the goods? In which state should the lawsuit be filed? And, specifically with reference to the choice of laws doctrine: What law should the court apply—the law of Massachusetts, Vermont, Connecticut, Maine, New York, or New Hampshire? It could be that Karen would win if the law of Massachusetts, Connecticut, or New York were applied but would lose if the law of Vermont, Maine, or New Hampshire were applied. Hence, choice of laws issues are quite important.*

Choice of laws issues are sometimes resolved by statutes that indicate which law should be applied. In business transactions, these issues may also be resolved by the parties' specifying which state (or national) law should apply. The courts generally will use the parties' selection as long as there is a reasonable relationship between the state selected and the transaction.

We will not attempt to resolve this example's question in this text because it is clearly too complex for an undergraduate course in the law of business. You need only be aware of the complexity of this matter and the often quite simple solution to the problem—that is, stating in the written contract that if there should be any dispute concerning the contract, the laws of a specified state will apply. This is a form of *preventative law.*

Federal Courts

In addition to the general grounds discussed previously with respect to jurisdiction, two specific grounds exist for federal jurisdiction: (1) federal question and (2) diversity of citizenship *plus* amount in controversy.

Federal question jurisdiction derives directly from Article III of the Constitution. *Federal questions* pertain to the federal Constitution, statutes of the United States, and treaties of the United States. Also included, today, are all regulations of federal administrative agencies. For example, if a person is denied a job because of race, that will raise a federal question, because such discrimination raises concerns about violations of the Constitution, federal statutes, and federal regulations. If a publishing company brings an action asserting that its copyright has been infringed by another publishing company, it raises a federal question, because copyright is both a constitutional and a statutory question. States do not have the right to issue copyrights.

Federal question jurisdiction is not necessary when diversity of citizenship is present and vice versa. *Diversity of citizenship* exists when the plaintiff is a citizen of one state and the defendant is a citizen of another; it also exists when one party is a foreign country and the other is a citizen of a state. The primary reason underlying diversity jurisdiction is that if a citizen of Hawaii must file suit in Iowa in order to obtain jurisdiction over the defendant, it is possible that the court of Iowa might favor its citizen over the citizen of Hawaii. In that case, the plaintiff can file suit in federal court. Exhibit 4.3 depicts the two grounds for federal jurisdiction.

E X H I B I T 4.3 | **The Two Grounds for Federal Jurisdiction**

For Federal Jurisdiction the Case Must Involve

Either	*Or*
Federal Question	**Diversity of Citizenship**
The controlling law involves a federal statute, rule, or regulation; an issue of U.S. constitutional law; or a treaty.	Parties on one side of the controversy are citizens of a different state than the parties on the other side.
The case involves a consul or ambassador as a party.	*and*
The case involves maritime or admiralty law.	**A Minimum Amount in Controversy (Excluding Costs and Interest)**
The United States is a party to the action.	The minimum amount for which the plaintiff must sue currently exceeds $75,000.
The case is between two or more states.	

When federal jurisdiction is based on diversity of citizenship, a further requirement exists: a *minimum amount* in question. Title 28, § 1332(a) of the United States Code requires that the amount in question must exceed $75,000 in diversity cases. In contrast, cases in which the federal courts have exclusive jurisdiction generally do not require a minimum amount. The purpose behind the amount is to prevent federal courts from dealing with trifles and to reduce the caseload in federal courts.

Most federal cases are highly complex, and the precise amount is often unknown when the lawsuit is filed. Accordingly, the courts look to the amount the plaintiff, acting in good faith, has determined to be in dispute. This is called the *plaintiff viewpoint rule.*

Another aspect of diversity jurisdiction is called complete diversity. *Complete diversity* requires that no plaintiff be a citizen of the same state as any of the defendants. This rule, however, poses complex problems when there are multiple plaintiffs and/or defendants. Complete diversity also prohibits having an **alien** plaintiff and an alien defendant in the same suit, even when the aliens are from different countries. In the following case, the Supreme Court addresses issues of personal and subject matter jurisdiction. Note the special treatment of complete diversity when the case involves foreign parties.

Alien
A person or corporation belonging to another country.

4.3

RUHRGAS AG V. MARATHON OIL COMPANY
119 S. CT. 1563 (1999)

FACTS The underlying controversy stems from a venture to produce gas in the Heimdal Field of the Norwegian North Sea. In 1976, respondents Marathon Oil Company and Marathon International Oil Company acquired Marathon Petroleum Company (Norway) (MPCN) and respondent Marathon Petroleum Norge (Norge). [Ruhrgas is a German corporation; Norge is a Norwegian corporation. Marathon Oil Company, an Ohio corporation, and Marathon International Oil Company, a Delaware corporation, [which] moved their principal places of business from Ohio to Texas while the venture [was being formed] . . . Before the acquisition, Norge held a license to produce gas in the Heimdal Field; following the transaction, Norge assigned the license to MPCN. In 1981, MPCN contracted to sell 70% of its share of the Heimdal gas production to a group of European buyers, including petitioner Ruhrgas AG. The parties' agreement was incorporated into the Heimdal Gas Sales

continued

4.3

RUHRGAS AG V. MARATHON OIL COMPANY, *continued*
119 S. CT. 1563 (1999)

Agreement . . . , which is "governed by and construed in accordance with Norwegian Law," disputes thereunder are to be "exclusively and finally . . . settled by arbitration in Stockholm, Sweden, in accordance with" International Chamber of Commerce rules.

Marathon Oil Company, Marathon International Oil Company, and Norge (collectively, Marathon) filed this lawsuit against Ruhrgas in Texas state court on July 6, 1995, asserting state-law claims of fraud, tortious interference with prospective business relations, participation in breach of fiduciary duty, and civil conspiracy. . . . Marathon asserted that Ruhrgas had furthered its plans at three meetings in Houston, Texas, and through a stream of correspondence directed to Marathon in Texas. . . . Ruhrgas removed the case to the District Court for the Southern District of Texas. . . . [A suit between "citizens of a State and citizens or subjects of a foreign state" lies within federal diversity jurisdiction. 28 U.S.C. § 1332(a)(2). Section 1332 has been interpreted to require "complete diversity." The foreign citizenship of defendant Ruhrgas, a German corporation, and plaintiff Norge, a Norwegian corporation, rendered diversity incomplete.] . . .

[T]he District Court dismissed the case for lack of personal jurisdiction. . . . The District Court addressed the constitutional question and concluded that Ruhrgas' contacts with Texas were insufficient to support personal jurisdiction. Finding "no evidence that Ruhrgas engaged in any tortious conduct in Texas," the court determined that Marathon's complaint did not present circumstances adequately affiliating Ruhrgas with Texas. [. . . [T]he District Court concluded that Marathon had not shown that Ruhrgas pursued the alleged pattern of fraud and misrepresentation during the Houston meetings. The court further found that Ruhrgas attended those meetings "due to the [Heimdal Agreement] with MPCN." As the Heimdal Agreement provides for arbitration in Sweden, . . . "Ruhrgas could not have expected to be haled into Texas courts based on these meetings." The court also determined that Ruhrgas did not have "systematic and continuous contacts with Texas" of the kind that would "subject it to general jurisdiction in Texas."] We granted certiorari to resolve a conflict between the Circuits . . .

ISSUE Must a district court resolve issues of subject-matter jurisdiction before issues of personal jurisdiction?

HOLDING No. Issues of personal jurisdiction may be resolved first.

REASONING . . . Jurisdiction to resolve cases on the merits requires both authority over the category of claim in suit (subject-matter jurisdiction) and authority over the parties (personal jurisdiction), so that the court's decision will bind them. . . . We hold that in cases removed from state court to federal court, as in cases originating in federal court, there is no unyielding jurisdictional hierarchy. Customarily, a federal court first resolves doubts about its jurisdiction over the subject matter, but there are circumstances in which a district court appropriately accords priority to a personal jurisdiction inquiry. The proceeding before us is such a case. . . .

Subject-matter limitations on federal jurisdiction serve institutional interests. They keep the federal courts within the bounds the Constitution and Congress have prescribed. . . . [S]ubject-matter delineations must be policed by the courts on their own initiative even at the highest level. . . . Personal jurisdiction . . . "represents a restriction on judicial power . . . as a matter of individual liberty." Therefore, a party may insist that the limitation be observed, or he may forgo that right, effectively consenting to the court's exercise of adjudicatory authority. These distinctions do not mean that subject-matter jurisdiction is ever and always the more "fundamental." Personal jurisdiction, too, is "an essential element of the jurisdiction of a district . . . court," without which the court is "powerless to proceed to an adjudication." In this case, . . . the [proposed] impediment to subject-matter jurisdiction . . . rests on statutory interpretation, not constitutional command. Marathon joined an alien plaintiff (Norge) as well as an alien defendant (Ruhrgas). If the joinder of Norge is legitimate, the complete diversity required by 28 U.S.C. § 1332 . . . is absent. . . .

If a federal court dismisses a removed case for want of personal jurisdiction, that determination may preclude the parties from relitigating the very same personal jurisdiction issue in state court. . . . [O]ur "dualistic . . . system of federal and state courts" allows federal courts to make issue-preclusive rulings about state law in the exercise of supplemental jurisdiction . . . Most essentially, federal and state courts are complementary systems for administering justice in our Nation. Cooperation and comity, not

SJCC CAMPUS STORE

1103 CASH-1   9951 0001 104

290053887808 USED
GUFFEY/BUSINESS EN   MDS 1   56.00
9780130325592 NEW
HORNE/COMPUTERIZED   MDS 1   64.90

            SUBTOTAL   120.90
8.25% SALES TAX   9.97
            TOTAL   130.87
                               130.87

APPROVAL: 022582   REFER. NUM: 1546
NT NUMBER 6011XXXXXXXXXXXX 1100
        Card   FULL REFUND IS SEPT 15

/22/00 11:01 AM

4.3

RUHRGAS AG V. MARATHON OIL COMPANY, *continued*
119 S. CT. 1563 (1999)

competition and conflict, are essential to the federal design. . . . If personal jurisdiction raises "difficult questions of [state] law," and subject-matter jurisdiction is resolved . . . easily . . . , a district court will ordinarily conclude that "federalism concerns tip the scales in favor of initially ruling on the motion to remand." . . . The federal design allows leeway for sensitive judgments of this sort. . . . What the concept does represent is a system in which there is sensitivity to the legitimate interests of both State and National Governments." . . .

BUSINESS CONSIDERATIONS How can a company involved in international transactions protect itself from being drawn into a lawsuit in a foreign county? Would Ruhrgas be surprised by this lawsuit in light of the arbitration agreement?

ETHICAL CONSIDERATION Would it be ethical for Marathon to add Norge as a plaintiff to avoid diversity of citizenship?

Specialized Courts

Congress has, from time to time, created courts of *limited* jurisdiction. At present, these courts include the claims court, the court of military appeals, the court of international trade, and the tax court. Congress has created *federal district courts* in every state. Each state has at least one; some states have many. Rhode Island, for example, has one district court, and Texas has four. The courts contained in each district constitute the general trial courts of the federal system.

All of the district courts are grouped into circuits. Currently there are 13 circuits. Each circuit has a court of appeals that hears appeals from the trial courts. Courts of appeal do not retry the case; rather, they review the record to determine whether the trial court made errors of law. Generally, a panel of three judges from the circuit hears appeals. Decisions of the court of appeals establish precedents for all district courts in the circuit. For the most part, the decisions of these *circuit courts of appeals* are final. In a very few cases, further appeal may be made to the U.S. Supreme Court.

The 13 federal judicial circuits and their seats are: First: Boston, Massachusetts; Second: New York, New York; Third: Philadelphia, Pennsylvania; Fourth: Richmond, Virginia; Fifth: New Orleans, Louisiana; Sixth: Cincinnati, Ohio; Seventh: Chicago, Illinois; Eighth: St. Louis, Missouri; Ninth: San Francisco, California; Tenth: Denver, Colorado; Eleventh: Atlanta, Georgia; Twelfth: District of Columbia, Washington, D.C.; Thirteenth: Federal Circuit, Washington, D.C. For more detail on the these circuits, see Exhibit 4.4 on page 112.

The *Supreme Court* sits at the apex of the U.S. judicial system. It is the only court created by the Constitution. The Constitution does not specify the number of judges on the Supreme Court. It has nine judges, called justices, by tradition. They are nominated by the president and confirmed by the Senate, and they serve for life. All federal judges—except those appointed to serve in the specialized courts—serve for life.

As mentioned previously, certain cases may be appealed to the Supreme Court. However, the court may affirm a case routinely without permitting oral arguments or giving the case formal consideration. The court is more likely to hear a case under the following conditions:

EXHIBIT 4.4 | **The Thirteen Federal Judicial Circuits**

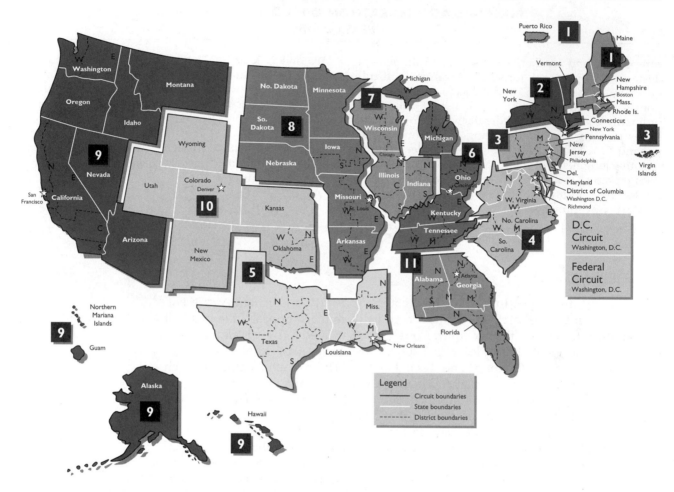

SOURCE: Administrative Office of The United States Courts, January 1983.

1. Whenever the highest state court declares a federal law invalid
2. Whenever the highest state court validates a state law that is challenged based on a federal law
3. Whenever a federal court declares a federal statute unconstitutional and the government was a party to the suit
4. Whenever a federal appellate court declares a state statute invalid on the grounds that it violates federal law
5. Whenever a federal three-judge court has ruled in a civil case involving an equitable remedy

Certiorari

A writ used by a superior court to direct a lower court to send it the records and proceedings in a case for review.

Certiorari, which means "to be more fully informed," is used whenever the Supreme Court desires to hear a particular case even though there is no right of appeal. It is through this technique that state court cases can be heard by the Supreme Court. When the Supreme Court decides to grant *certiorari*, it issues a writ of *certiorari,* which orders the lower court to certify a record of the proceedings and send it to the Supreme Court. A minimum of four justices must agree to hear the case on *certiorari.* Other than that, there are no hard-and-fast rules. Nevertheless, there are certain situations in which the Supreme Court is more likely to grant *certiorari:*

1. Whenever two or more circuit courts of appeals disagree with respect to the same legal issue
2. Whenever the highest state court has decided a question in such a manner that it conflicts with prior decisions of the U.S. Supreme Court
3. Whenever the highest state court has decided a question that has not yet been determined by the U.S. Supreme Court
4. Whenever a circuit court of appeals has decided a state law question that appears to be in conflict with established state law
5. Whenever a circuit court of appeals has decided a federal question that has not yet been decided by the U.S. Supreme Court

The Supreme Court also has original jurisdiction in a number of cases or controversies. When the Supreme Court exercises its original jurisdiction, it serves as a trial court. Article III, Section 2 of the Constitution declares that the "Supreme Court shall have original jurisdiction in all cases affecting ambassadors, other public ministers and consuls, and those in which a state is a party."

Exhibit 4.5 on page 114 describes how the federal courts are related to each other.

State Courts

All states have *inferior trial* courts. These may include municipal courts, juvenile courts, domestic relations courts, traffic courts, small claims courts, probate courts, and justice courts presided over by justices of the peace. (Historically, justices of the peace were not required to be lawyers. Many states have changed their rules and now require new justices of the peace to be lawyers.) For the most part, inferior trial courts are not *courts of record*—that is, there is no record or transcript made of the trial. In cases of appeals from their decisions, there is a *trial de novo,* "a new trial," in a court of general jurisdiction.

The more significant cases involving matters of state law originate in *courts of general jurisdiction* (courts having the judicial power to hear all matters with respect to state law). In some jurisdictions, two courts exist at this level. One court is charged with resolving all questions of law and the other with resolving all matters of equity. An example of a question of law is a suit seeking money damages. Most business law cases fall into this category. Equity suits, on the other hand, are those where the plaintiff is seeking a special remedy, such as an **injunction,** because monetary damages will not make the plaintiff "whole."

4.3 | **MANAGEMENT/ MARKETING**

LAWSUIT AGAINST A SUPPLIER

The Kochanowskis purchased a license for software from MicroSources, a California firm located in Silicon Valley. The software was supposed to be year 2000 compliant (Y2K); unfortunately, it was not. Unaware that the software was defective, CIT installed it in their videophones, which eventually caused them to malfunction. These videophones were sold to customers directly and through retail outlets. Customers have been calling CIT and complaining about the videophones. This situation has also caused an increase in warranty repair work. Assume that CIT is an Ohio corporation. Tom and Anna are concerned about the short- and long-term effects on the company's finances and reputation. They ask what you would advise the company to do. What will you tell them?

BUSINESS CONSIDERATIONS What can a business do to reduce the chance of purchasing defective supplies and software? Can CIT sue the software firm? In what court(s) could the suit be filed? What additional information will be necessary and why? Would filing the suit improve or harm CIT's reputation?
ETHICAL CONSIDERATIONS What should CIT do to protect its reputation? Are there any ethical restrictions on what CIT does to protect its reputation?

Injunction
A writ issued by the court of equity ordering a person to do or not do a specified act.

E X H I B I T 4.5 | **The Federal Judicial System**

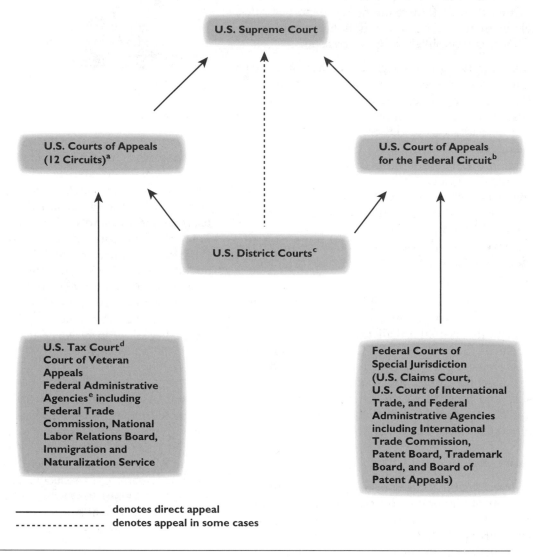

denotes direct appeal
denotes appeal in some cases

a. Includes D.C. Circuit.
b. Takes appeals from some specialized courts.
c. Bankruptcy courts exist as units of the district courts.
d. In some cases, there is Supreme Court review.
e. Administrative agencies perform courtlike functions; however, they are *not* courts.

Each state has at least one *court of appeals.* It is usually called the supreme court. There are exceptions. In New York State, for example, the "supreme court" is a court of general trial jurisdiction, whereas the Court of Appeals is the highest court in the state. Sometimes intermediate courts of appeals also exist, as in the federal system. These appellate courts review the trial court record to determine whether the lower court made any errors of law. Appellate courts do not usually review decisions of facts made by the lower court. Trials *de novo* are exceptions to this general rule.

An example of a case history is *Bennis* v. *Michigan,* 134 L.Ed 2d 68 (1996). It was originally decided by the Wayne County Circuit Court and then appealed (in this order) to the Michigan Court of Appeals, the Michigan Supreme Court, and the U.S. Supreme Court.

Exhibit 4.6 describes a typical state system and its interrelationship with the federal system.

E X H I B I T   4.6 | **The Typical State Judicial System[a]**

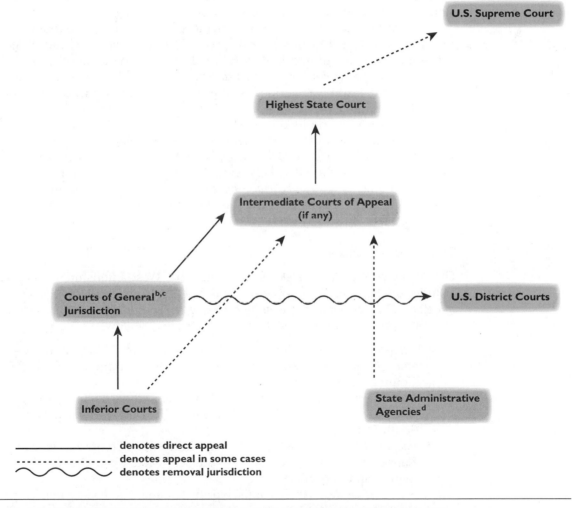

_____ denotes direct appeal
- - - - - - - - - - - - denotes appeal in some cases
〰〰〰〰〰 denotes removal jurisdiction

a. As noted in the text, there is great variation among the states. The titles of the courts vary from state to state.

b. The state trial courts may be divided into divisions, for example, the civil division, the criminal division, family court.

c. Removal jurisdiction generally is exercised when the defendant asks that the case filed in one court be moved to the other court.

d. Administrative agencies perform some courtlike functions; however, they are *not* courts.

How to Find the Law

We have already referred to some legal cases in this and previous chapters. Other cases will be cited in succeeding chapters. If you want to go to the library and read these or other cases in their entirety, you will need to know how to find the law.

Federal Court Cases

If you are looking for the case *Mitsubishi Motors Corporation v. Soler Chrysler-Plymouth, Inc.*, 473 U.S. 614, 87 L.Ed.2d 444, 105 S.Ct. 3346 (1985), for example, you will find it in any one of three sources. First, the U.S. Government Printing Office publishes the official *United States Reports*. The case will be found on page 614 of volume 473. Alternatively, you can find the case on page 444 of volume 87 of *Lawyers Edition, Second*, published by the Lawyers Cooperative Publishing Company. Finally, you can find the case in volume 105 of the *Supreme Court Reporter*, which is published by West Publishing Company, at page 3346.

All reported cases decided by the circuit courts of appeals are found in the *Federal Reporter*. If you are looking for the case of *Johnson Controls v. United Association of Journeymen*, you will find it at 39 F.3d 821 (7th Cir. 1994). In other words, go to volume 39 of the *Federal Reporter, Third Series*, and turn to page 821. The (7th Cir. 1994) means the case was decided by the Seventh Circuit Court of Appeals, which sits in Chicago and hears cases from district courts in Illinois, Indiana, and Wisconsin. The case was decided in 1994.

U.S. district court cases are found in the *Federal Supplement Series*. If you are looking for the case of *Hoeflich v. William S. Merrell Co.*, you will find it at 288 F.Supp. 659 (E.D.Pa. 1968). Following the established format for legal references, look for volume 288 of the *Federal Supplement*; the case will be found on page 659. The (E.D.Pa. 1968) means the case was decided in the U.S. District Court for the Eastern District of Pennsylvania in 1968.

State Court Cases

The *National Reporter System* is published by West Publishing Company and includes the *Supreme Court Reporter*, the *Federal Reporter*, the *Federal Supplement*, *Federal Rules Decisions*, and the *Bankruptcy Reporter*. The reporter system also contains seven regional reporters for state cases. They are as follows:

1. *Atlantic Reporter*—Connecticut, Delaware, Maine, Maryland, New Hampshire, New Jersey, Pennsylvania, Rhode Island, Vermont, and the District of Columbia Municipal Court of Appeals
2. *Northeastern Reporter*—Illinois, Indiana, Massachusetts, New York, and Ohio
3. *Northwestern Reporter*—Iowa, Michigan, Minnesota, Nebraska, North Dakota, South Dakota, and Wisconsin
4. *Pacific Reporter*—Alaska, Arizona, California, Colorado, Hawaii, Idaho, Kansas, Montana, Nevada, New Mexico, Oklahoma, Oregon, Utah, Washington, and Wyoming
5. *Southeastern Reporter*—Georgia, North Carolina, South Carolina, Virginia, and West Virginia
6. *Southwestern Reporter*—Arkansas, Kentucky, Missouri, Tennessee, and Texas
7. *Southern Reporter*—Alabama, Florida, Louisiana, and Mississippi

These reporters contain most of the reported cases at the state supreme court and appellate court levels. Some significant trial court decisions are also included. Decisions of inferior courts are not included. The *National Reporter System* also includes the *Military Justice Reporter* and separate state reporters such as the *New York Supplement,* the *California Reporter,* and *Illinois Decisions.*

States generally also have their own system for publishing cases independent of the *National Reporter System.*

Computerized Legal Research

Legal research has entered the computer age. Two systems devoted to legal research are available—Lexis (part of Lexis/Nexis) and Westlaw. The techniques are similar, although the particular computer commands vary. Both systems allow you to indicate what material you wish to search and to enter key words for search terms. If your search terms are not appropriate or are too broad, you may not locate the desired material. Historical cases may not have been added to the data banks, but recent cases and articles generally are available. Manuals and handbooks specify which material can be retrieved from the system, including the years that are in the database.

There are also a number of sites on the World Wide Web that contain articles on statutory law, court cases, and government activity. A few of these sites are highlighted at the end of each chapter. Web sites can be established without much restriction, and some of the sites change addresses or stop operating. Consequently, the web addresses may become dated. When conducting research on the web, also remember that the information may not be reliable.

RESOURCES FOR BUSINESS LAW STUDENTS

NAME	RESOURCES	WEB ADDRESS
U.S. Constitution	Emory Law School maintains a hypertext and searchable version of the U.S. Constitution.	**http://www.law.emory.edu/FEDERAL/usconst.html**
U.S. Federal Judiciary	The U.S. Federal Judiciary site, maintained by the Administrative Office of the U.S. Courts, provides a clearinghouse for information from and about the judicial branch of the U.S. government.	**http://www.uscourts.gov/**
U.S. Federal Courts Finder	Emory Law School maintains links to recent court decisions from the 13 U.S. circuit courts of appeals and the Supreme Court.	**http://www.law.emory.edu/FEDCTS/**
StateLaw	StateLaw, maintained by the Washburn School of Law, provides links for state and local legislative and governmental information—including court cases and statutes.	**http://lawlib.wuacc.edu/washlaw/uslaw.edu**

SUMMARY

The federal Constitution is unique because it created the doctrine of separation of powers. As a result, our government is divided into three distinct branches: legislative, executive, and judicial. There is also an unofficial "fourth branch" of government: administrative agencies.

Judicial power has limits. For example, federal courts cannot issue advisory opinions or decide moot cases or political questions. In all cases, the plaintiff must have standing to sue. The doctrine of judicial review was created by Chief Justice John Marshall in the landmark case of *Marbury* v. *Madison*. The doctrine represents an expansion of judicial power, because it allows the Supreme Court to determine whether a statute passed by Congress is in compliance with the Constitution or whether the executive branch has acted in accordance with the Constitution.

Our court system is based on the concept of jurisdiction. Jurisdiction means the legal power to decide a case. It can be divided into subject matter jurisdiction, jurisdiction over the dollar amount (which is often considered an aspect of subject matter jurisdiction), and jurisdiction over the persons or property. There are basically three techniques for obtaining jurisdiction over the persons or property—*in personam, in rem,* and *quasi in rem.* The type of jurisdiction will affect the type of judgment the court can award.

Jurisdiction can be concurrent, in which case more than one court can hear and decide a case, or it may be exclusive, in which case only one court can hear the matter. A federal district court's jurisdiction is based on either federal question or diversity of citizenship jurisdiction. In all diversity cases, the jurisdictional amount of over $75,000 must be met. Complete diversity is also required. The federal court system includes specialized courts, district courts, appellate courts, and the Supreme Court.

DISCUSSION QUESTIONS

1. Why is the U.S. Constitution considered unique?
2. Where is the constitutional protection of *habeas corpus* found? What does the term mean?
3. Why is the identity of the individual Supreme Court justices important?
4. The school board for Lindsay Kochanowski's public school is considering posting the Ten Commandments in all schools in the district. Is such a practice legal? Why? Who would have standing to sue in order to challenge this decision by the school board?
5. What is meant by the term *jurisdiction?*
6. Describe long-arm statutes. Do they serve a legitimate state purpose? Do they make it easier to sue businesses? Do they make it easier for businesses to file suit?

7. Why do some state courts have only one court of general jurisdiction, whereas others have two?
8. What are the advantages and disadvantages of specialized courts, such as tax court or family court?
9. Assume that the highest court in a state determines that a state law violates the federal Constitution. Can that decision be reviewed by the U.S. Supreme Court, or is the decision of the state court final?
10. Go to the nearest law library, or Westlaw or Lexis terminal, and determine who were the attorneys for the appellees in *Department of Commerce et al.* v. *United States House of Representatives,* 119 S.Ct. 765 (1999).

CASE PROBLEMS AND WRITING ASSIGNMENTS

1. A federal taxpayer brought suit to prohibit the spending of federal monies to finance instructional materials in parochial schools. The spending was authorized under the Elementary and Secondary Education Act of 1965. The suit was based on the grounds that such expenditures were in violation of the First Amendment provisions guaranteeing freedom of religion. Does a taxpayer have standing to sue? [See *Flast* v. *Cohen*, 392 U.S. 83 (1968).]

2. Does segregation of children in public schools on the basis of race, even though the physical facilities and other "tangible" factors may be equal, deprive the children of the minority group of equal educational opportunities? Discuss this situation with respect to the Fourteenth Amendment. [See *Brown* v. *Board of Education*, 347 U.S. 483 (1954).]

3. A Republican Senate candidate, Michael Huffington, alleges that 17 deceased citizens "voted" in Fresno County in the 1994 election. Les Kimber, an ousted Fresno city council member, also charges that campaign workers for his opponent, Dan Ronquillo, used voter fraud. In one incident, election materials indicate D. Eddie Ronquillo, Dan Ronquillo's son, registered a 2-year-old boy and his 17-year-old mother. Absentee ballots were requested for these two minors. The absentee ballot requests indicated at the bottom "Paid for by the friends of Dan Ronquillo." (These two individuals did not vote, and the absentee ballots were discarded.) The mother contends that she never registered to vote. Norma Logan, Fresno County elections manager, says that part of the problem is allowing political groups to pay a bounty for registering voters or getting the voters to use absentee ballots. She contends that it is an incentive for some people to file fraudulent documents. Logan would like California to ban bounty payments. Consider the practice of paying a bounty for registering voters. What is the likely consequence of this practice? When bounties are paid in business situations, what are they called? What sometimes happens in businesses when "bounties" are offered to workers? Analyze the ethics of individuals registering people who are not eligible to vote (e.g., minors and people who are deceased). Is whether the individuals are motivated by the bounty, or by political reasons, relevant? [See Jim Boren and Angela Valdivia, "Kimber Lawsuit Against Ronquillo Alleges Voter Fraud," *The Fresno Bee* (29 December 1994), pp. A1 and A12; and Jim Boren, "Huffington Says 17 Who Voted Were Dead," *The Fresno Bee* (5 January 1995), pp. A1 and A14.]

4. Producers of chemicals used for pesticides sued the U.S. Administrator of the Environmental Protection Agency challenging Section 3(c)(1)(D) of the Federal Insecticide, Fungicide, and Rodenticide Act (FIFRA), alleging a denial of their rights. The challenged section of the law allowed parties to submit disputes to binding arbitration rather than to the courts for judicial resolution. The producers alleged that the law violated Article III of the U.S. Constitution by removing judicial functions from the court. The district court held that Congress acted unconstitutionally by assigning judicial power to arbitrators. The case was subsequently appealed to the U.S. Supreme Court. How should this case be resolved? [See *Thomas* v. *Union Carbide*, 473 U.S. 568, 105 S.Ct. 3325 (1985).]

5. International Shoe Co. was a Delaware corporation, having its principal place of business in St. Louis, Missouri. The state of Washington sued International Shoe because it wanted the company to contribute to the state's unemployment compensation fund. International Shoe had no office, manufacturing plant, or warehouse in Washington. It had local sales representatives there who created a large volume of business. The sales representatives exhibited their samples and solicited orders from customers. The orders were transmitted to the office in St. Louis, where the company either rejects or accepts them. Was there sufficient contact between International Shoe and the state to justify jurisdiction, or would it offend traditional notions of fair play and substantial justice? [See *International Shoe Co.* v. *Washington*, 326 U.S. 310 (1945).]

6. **BUSINESS APPLICATION CASE** Viking Industries, Inc. (Viking) is an Oregon corporation that manufactures and sells windows to buyers in 30 different states. Viking brought a breach-of-contract action against Sierra Glass & Mirror (Sierra), a Nevada company, when Sierra refused to pay for windows delivered to it. At trial, Sierra claimed that Viking was not entitled to bring this action in a Nevada court because it was a foreign corporation doing business in the state without complying with Nevada law. A Nevada statute precluded foreign corporations doing business in Nevada from commencing an action in Nevada courts if the corporation had not filed qualifying documents with the secretary of state. Viking's total sales amounted to approximately $20 million in the 30 states in which it conducted business, and approximately $3 million stemmed from sales in Nevada. Viking had one sales representative who worked in Nevada, resided in Las Vegas, and spent

two weeks per month calling on customers and visiting sales prospects in Reno and Las Vegas. Viking maintained a listed telephone number in Las Vegas at the representative's home. Nevada customers placed orders through the representative, who then phoned the orders and forwarded the checks to Portland. Viking contended that its contacts with Nevada were purely interstate, and that it was not required to qualify as a foreign corporation. Is Viking correct? Why? [See *Sierra Glass & Mirror* v. *Viking Industries, Inc.*, 808 P.2d 512 (Nev. 1991).]

7. **ETHICAL APPLICATION CASE** The Pasadena Crematorium and other funeral service companies allegedly sold human body parts and organs to a biological supply company. The body parts were allegedly removed without permission from the decedents being prepared for cremations or funerals. In the class action lawsuit, the plaintiffs were suing for negligent infliction of emotional distress. The plaintiffs were relatives and friends of the deceased persons. Who has standing to sue in this situation? Would the alleged behavior of the crematorium and funeral homes be ethical? Why or why not? [See *Christensen* v. *Pasadena Crematorium of Altadena*, 2 Cal.Rptr.2d 79 (1991).]

8. **CRITICAL THINKING CASE** G. Charles Middour manufactures storm windows and doors in Franklin County, Pennsylvania. He does no business in Philadelphia, Pennsylvania. He has been in Philadelphia twice in the past five years. Arthur M. Holten sells Middour's products in Philadelphia. Sidney Smith placed an order with Holten, who in turn contracted with Middour. Smith did not pay. Holten told Middour not to ship the product even though some of the frames had already been constructed. After a number of phone conversations, Holten told Middour that Smith would only pay Holten directly. An appointment was set up for Middour to come to Philadelphia to meet with Holten and Smith. When Middour arrived in Philadelphia, Holten greeted him and then excused himself. A deputy sheriff approached Middour and served him with a summons for a lawsuit, which was a complete surprise to Middour. Is the service of process on Middour valid? Does the court have *in personam* jurisdiction over Middour? [See *Holten* v. *Middour*, 404 Pa. 351 (1961).]

NOTES

1. See 1 Cranch 137, 2 L.Ed. 60 (1803).
2. *Aetna Life Ins. Co.* v. *Haworth*, 300 U.S. 227 (1937).
3. See 416 U.S. 312 (1974).
4. See 1 Cranch 137, 2 L.Ed. 60 (1803).
5. See Sheila M. Smith, "Comment: Justice Ruth Bader Ginsburg and Sexual Harassment Law: Will the Second Female Supreme Court Justice Become the Court's Women's Right Champion?" 63 U. Cin. L. Rev. 1893, Summer 1995.
6. *Ortiz* v. *Fibreboard Corporation*, 1999 U.S. Lexis 4373 (1999).
7. *Black's Law Dictionary*, 7th ed. (St. Paul, MN: The West Group, 1999).
8. Ibid.
9. Ibid.
10. Marjorie Coeyman, "First-Grader Tests Ban on Religion in Class," *The Christian Science Monitor* (15 June 1999), p. 1.
11. Tex. Civ. Prac. & Rem. Code Ann. § 17.042 (1997).

5

CONSTITUTIONAL REGULATION
OF BUSINESS

A   G   E   N   D   A

In its various activities, CIT probably will face fairly substantial regulation at both the state and the federal levels. The Kochanowskis will want to know *why* the government is able to regulate their efforts and *how* these regulations will affect them. Given the use of the Call-Image videophone, its production may raise some freedom of speech questions. If the government does increase its regulation of videophones, several due process issues may result from this heightened regulation of a particular industry. Most of this potential governmental oversight will subject the firm to administrative regulation as well.

These and other issues are likely to arise during your study of this chapter. Be prepared! You never know when one of the Kochanowskis will need your help or advice.

O   U   T   L   I   N   E

A HISTORICAL PERSPECTIVE

In the United States today, government heavily regulates business. Local regulations tell a company where it may conduct business. State regulations cover the selling of securities, loan rates, and highway weight limits. Federal regulations address pollution, the safety of employees, consumer protection, and labor negotiations. And these represent only a few of the regulations that a business faces.

Pervasive governmental regulation of business, however, has not always been the case. As is often mentioned in American history texts, the United States was built on a **laissez–faire** economy. Business owners ran business and politicians ran government, and the two groups left each other alone. Buyers often were ignored, with **caveat emptor** being the rule of the land. Workers remained virtually unprotected. If they did not like their jobs, they could quit. If they did not go to work, they were fired. If they joined a union, they also were fired—and they quite often faced criminal conspiracy charges as well.

The nineteenth century was a great time to be an American entrepreneur, especially a wealthy one. These easy times came to an end, however. The general populace viewed too many "captains of industry" as "robber barons." Many people, moreover, resented the abuse and mistreatment that workers suffered. And, given the lack of land remaining for westward migration, people increasingly clamored for reform. Present-day governmental regulation emerged from these tumultuous times.

Laissez–faire
A term meaning "hands-off"; the belief that business operates best when uninhibited by the government.

Caveat emptor
A term meaning "let the buyer beware"; a reference to the fact that the buyer had very few, if any, remedies for defective products.

SHOULD GOVERNMENT REGULATE BUSINESS?

Yet, over the last few decades, people have been asking the question, "Should government regulate business?" The answer is either *yes* or *no*, depending on which type of business is at issue, what type of regulation is being discussed, and which level of government is involved. The answer also depends to some degree on whether the business involves international trade, domestic trade, or regional/local trade. In general, such a question involves a number of factors, and the answers may vary over time as the circumstances of the business change.

History shows that society needs some regulation—or intervention—by government. Governmental regulation typically takes two forms: social regulation (concern for such issues as workplace safety, equal opportunity, environmental protection, and consumer protection) and economic regulation (the behavior of firms, especially the firms' effects on prices, production, industry conditions for entry or exit, and so on). In 1997, 2,783,704 people worked in federal agencies.[1] Obviously, had they not been working in the federal bureaucracy, presumably they could have worked at jobs producing other goods and services. Clearly, then, one must compare the costs—in terms of administration, compliance, and efficiency—of regulation with its perceived benefits.

Many people today believe this balance has tipped too far toward the over-regulation of business. Indeed, the pervasiveness of the government's reach over business activities has led to cries for deregulation and a lessening of this glut of laws. Given the complexities of business at the advent of the twenty-first century, however, no one realistically believes that these laws magically will disappear.

Business's "social contract" requires that it pay heed to the various social and economic issues mentioned above. Somewhere between the extremes of overregulation and underregulation, a happy medium must exist so as to maximize the well-being of business, society, and government. Yet, as we learned in the preceding chapters, in the absence of this balance, laws can become so burdensome on individuals that such persons can argue that the laws violate the rights guaranteed to individuals by the Constitution. Since the law in many instances views firms as legal, or *juristic*, persons, businesses also can assert various constitutional rights and thus curb what they view as excessive governmental regulation. Hence, just as the Constitution stands as the guardian of individual rights, it in addition represents a significant weapon for businesses to use when they challenge the laws and regulations that affect them.

THE COMMERCE CLAUSE

Perhaps the single most important constitutional provision that affects business is the commerce clause. Article I, Section 8 of the Constitution states that Congress shall have the power "to regulate Commerce with foreign Nations, and among the several States, and with the Indian Tribes." In addition, the article gives Congress the power to levy taxes. The interplay between these two powers forms the basis for much of the federal government's regulation of business.

The history of the commerce clause has been checkered. The Supreme Court initially had interpreted the clause, next expanded these interpretations, later contracted these interpretations, and then expanded them again. In 1824, the Supreme Court had its first occasion to interpret the commerce clause. Chief Justice Marshall's opinion in *Gibbons* v. *Ogden* defined *commerce* as "the commercial intercourse between nations, in all its branches . . . regulated by prescribing rules for carrying on that intercourse."[2] Marshall further noted that the federal government can regulate commerce that *affects* other states, even if that commerce is local in nature.

As a result of this interpretation, for nearly three-quarters of a century, federal power to regulate business was broad. The Interstate Commerce Act of 1887 permitted the Interstate Commerce Commission (ICC) to regulate local railroad rates and local railroad safety because such issues directly affected interstate rates and safety.[3] The federal government also could regulate local grain and livestock exchanges because they, too, involved transactions that affected the rest of the nation.

Not all the court opinions of the period favored regulation by the federal government, however. In the 1873 Supreme Court decision *In re State Freight Tax,* the Court stated that the commerce clause's phrase *among* meant *between*.[4] As a result, this opinion held that the federal government could regulate only **interstate** commerce. By limiting the definition of commerce, the Court similarly contracted the federal power to regulate business. In its 1888 *Kidd* v. *Pearson* decision, the Court ruled that *commerce* meant *transportation*.[5] As a result of these two opinions, federal regulation of business suddenly became restricted to actual interstate **transportation** and did not reach business deals that affected interstate business but that were conducted entirely in one state. Such transactions, defined as **intrastate,** therefore remained beyond the scope of federal regulation.

This new, restricted definition of interstate commerce underlay the passage of the Sherman Act in 1890 (see Chapter 39 for a detailed treatment of this act). Indeed, this new definition of the federal authority to regulate business led the Court to narrower interpretations and, consequently, the Court's invalidation of many subsequent federal enactments.

Interstate
Between two or more states; between a point in one state and a point in another state.

Transportation
Carrying or conveying from one place to another; the removal of goods or persons from one place to another.

Intrastate
Begun, carried on, and completed wholly within the boundaries of a single state.

A shift in the Court's restrictive view of the exercise of federal power did not occur until 1937. In *NLRB* v. *Jones & Laughlin Steel Corp.*, which overturned 50 years of narrow interpretation, Chief Justice Hughes said:

> *When industries organize themselves on a national scale, making their relation to interstate commerce the dominant factor in their activities, how can it be maintained that their industrial relations constitute a forbidden field into which Congress may not enter when it is necessary to protect interstate commerce from the paralyzing consequences of industrial war?*[6]

Thus, the Court had come full circle. As Justice Jackson noted in *United States* v. *Women's Sportswear Manufacturers Association*, a 1949 case involving a Sherman Act challenge to a local price-fixing arrangement, "If it is interstate commerce that feels the pinch, it does not matter how local the operation which applies the squeeze."[7] In upholding the right of the federal government to regulate the conduct in dispute, Justice Jackson provided us with both a picturesque definition of interstate commerce and the one most courts presently would accept as controlling.

This expansive definition of the reach of the federal government under the commerce clause also provided the federal government with a vehicle for ridding society of discrimination and bigotry, as the *Heart of Atlanta Motel, Inc.* v. *U.S.*[8] decision demonstrates. Heart of Atlanta Motel, Inc., had a policy of refusing service to blacks. The federal government challenged this policy as a violation of Title II of the Civil Rights Act of 1964, which prohibits racial, religious, or national origin discrimination by those who offer public accommodations. The government claimed that the motel was involved in interstate commerce and that federal intervention therefore was justifiable. The motel argued that it was a purely intrastate business and hence exempt from federal regulation under Title II. The Supreme Court held that because of its provision of services to interstate travelers, the motel was involved in interstate commerce. In reaching its decision, the Court focused on the following facts: (1) The motel was readily accessible from two interstate highways; (2) it also advertised in national magazines and placed billboards on federal highways; and (3) approximately 75 percent of its guests came from outside the state of Georgia. In the Court's view, allowing such discrimination would discourage travel by the black community. Furthermore, the motel was set up to serve interstate travelers; it drew much of its business from interstate travelers; and it was involved in interstate commerce. Hence, the Court concluded that Title II gave the government authority to prohibit Heart of Atlanta Motel, Inc.'s discriminatory practice of renting rooms only to white people.

The myriad of current state and federal laws has relegated this function of the commerce clause largely to a legal artifact. Nevertheless, you should remain mindful of the significance of the commerce clause in this historical context and its continuing importance as the jurisdictional basis for many federal regulatory schemes.

Exclusive Federal Power

Early on, court constructions viewed three areas as exclusive enclaves of federal regulation: commerce with foreign nations, commercial activities involving Indian tribes (i.e., Native Americans), and commerce between the states (i.e., interstate commerce). Courts generally have recognized that Congress enjoys **plenary** power over foreign commerce or trade. For instance, the state of Washington does not have the authority to sign a treaty regulating tuna-fishing rights with Japan or Canada; only Congress has such power.

Plenary
Full; complete; absolute.

Similarly, owing to the unique status that Native Americans have occupied in U.S. history, only Congress has the power to regulate such commerce. Congress's plenary power in this area stems from the quasi-sovereign status that historically has been accorded to Native American tribes. As such, Native American tribes have virtually complete control over their own reservations and land; the states have little say over reservation affairs. Federal law generally preempts even state or local regulation of off-reservation activities.

As we noted earlier, the phrase "among the several states" has spawned a great deal of litigation concerning when federal power over interstate commerce is plenary. Precedents over the years have established two such areas: (1) Congress's power to regulate the channels and facilities of interstate commerce and (2) Congress's power to regulate activities that originate in a single state but have a national economic effect. Under this first prong, Congress can regulate interstate carriers, roads, television and radio stations, and so on. Congress also has the power to exclude from such interstate channels or facilities the goods, persons, or services designated by Congress as harmful to interstate commerce. Congress, then, under this federal police power, can stop the interstate shipment of stolen vehicles, diseased animals, spoiled meat, fungi-ridden fruit, or defective products. Businesses so affected can do little to challenge this exercise of federal power. Besides the channels or facilities of interstate commerce, Congress has plenary power to regulate all commerce or activity that affects more than one state. Note that even intrastate commerce may be subject to such federal control if the intrastate activity has a "substantial effect" on interstate commerce or if Congress rationally can conclude that the activity in question affects interstate commerce.

As the *Heart of Atlanta Motel, Inc.,* case indicates, it takes very little commercial activity to trigger the application of this federal power over commerce. To illustrate, in *Burbank* v. *Lockheed Air Terminal, Inc.,* the Supreme Court struck down a local ordinance that prohibited jet airplane takeoffs during specified hours (11:00 P.M. to 7:00 A.M. local time).[9] The Court invalidated this ordinance because of the need for national uniformity in airplane flight patterns (having this airport "off-limits" for several hours could create clogs in air traffic) and because federal law, in the form of agencies concerned with aeronautical and environmental matters, preempted such local or state initiatives.

Clearly, though, this federal power is not boundless. For example, in *U.S.* v. *Lopez,* the Supreme Court invalidated a federal law that had made it a federal criminal offense for anyone to possess a firearm in a school zone.[10] The Court held that the act exceeds Congress's authority under the commerce clause. Why? The possession of a gun in a local school zone in no sense constitutes an economic activity that might, through repetition elsewhere, have a substantial effect on interstate commerce. The advocates of the law argued that possession of firearms in a school zone could lead to violent crime, which, in turn, would hurt the national economy by (1) increasing the costs associated with violent crime; (2) reducing people's willingness to travel to areas they deem unsafe; and (3) threatening the learning environment, which would lead to poorly educated citizens. The Court, however, concluded that this argument demonstrated too tenuous a *nexus* (or connection) to interstate commerce for the Court to sustain the law. Although not a business case, this decision may affect business in the future; the decision seems to cut back on 60 years of Supreme Court precedents that had shown broad deference to congressional authority to regulate activities that arguably affect interstate commerce.

Concurrent State Power

In our interdependent domestic economy, virtually all businesses vie for market shares with similar firms in other states. Consequently, Congress's sweeping power to regulate commerce seems practically absolute.

Yet the states enjoy concurrent power with the federal government as to the regulation of commerce within the state. Just as the federal government wishes to promote the welfare of its citizens, so does each state. Hence, state regulation of economic matters is permissible as long as the regulation in question passes muster under a so-called "balancing" test that compares the burdens on interstate commerce caused by the regulation and the importance of the state interest that underlies the regulation.

Therefore, courts generally uphold valid state initiatives in furtherance of local health and safety measures that do not purport merely to protect local economic interests. For example, assume that a state has decided to regulate milk products by testing or certifying the milk. This statutory scheme ordinarily will survive a legal challenge based on the commerce clause unless the state regime discriminates in favor of in-state producers (that is, "local yokels") to the detriment of out-of-state producers. Courts also will invalidate the regulation if the costs of compliance, when compared with the putative benefits of the law, impose an unreasonable, or undue, burden on interstate commerce. In the absence of discrimination against out-of-state firms or the imposition of an undue burden, the states have concurrent power to regulate commerce.

This power ceases, however, if the state regulation conflicts with federal law. As you may remember, the supremacy clause of Article VI of the Constitution invalidates such state legislation. If Congress expressly prohibits state regulation in a given area or if federal law impliedly preempts the regulatory area, federal law supersedes the state's power to regulate as well.

State powers of taxation can pose special problems under the commerce clause because the states' legitimate interest in increasing their revenues by taxing business entities may burden interstate commerce. As we will see later, such discriminatory taxes, in addition to violating the commerce clause, may pose due process and equal protection problems, too. Although Congress, pursuant to the commerce clause, can authorize or prohibit state taxation that affects interstate commerce, in the absence of such federal legislation the states can tax corporations and other business entities.

State tax laws that single out—that is, discriminate against—interstate commerce usually violate the commerce clause. Nondiscriminatory taxation schemes—schemes that impose the same type of tax on local business or commerce as is imposed on interstate entities—require courts to employ a "balancing" test in which they weigh the state's need for additional revenue against the burden imposed on interstate commerce by such taxes. Although entities of interstate commerce do not remain immune from paying state taxes, such businesses need only pay their fair share; taxation that amounts to undue burdens, unfair discrimination, or multiple taxation generally does not survive challenges brought under the commerce clause (and perhaps not under the due process clause, either).

For a state tax to be legal under the commerce clause, it must be applied to an activity that has a substantial nexus with the taxing state; it must be fairly apportioned; it must not discriminate against interstate commerce; and it must be fairly related to the services provided by the state. Many courts then look at whether

E X H I B I T   5.1 | **Commerce Clause Analysis**

I. Areas of Exclusive Federal Regulation

   A. Commerce with foreign nations

   B. Commerce involving Indian tribes (i.e., Native Americans)

   C. Commerce involving the channels and facilities of interstate commerce

   D. Commerce that is interstate in nature or that originates in a single state but that has a "substantial effect" on interstate commerce

   E. Commerce where Congress has prohibited state regulation or where federal law impliedly preempts the regulatory area

II. Areas of Concurrent Federal and State Regulation

   A. "Balancing" test employed: the burdens on interstate commerce compared to the importance of the state interest underlying the state regulation

   B. State initiatives in furtherance of the state's "police power" (i.e., the promotion of the general welfare of the state's citizens) generally permissible unless:

      1. The state regulation imposes an undue, or unreasonable, burden on interstate commerce

      2. The state regulation discriminates in favor of in-state firms and against out-of-state firms

      3. The state regulation conflicts with federal law and thus is invalidated by the supremacy clause

III. Areas of Exclusive State Regulation

   A. Purely local activities with remote effects on other states' commerce

---

certain *minimum contacts* exist between the person, entity, or transaction taxed and the state that is levying the tax. If such state *jurisdiction* seems lacking, a violation of due process may have occurred.

Most of the precedents in this area involve state legislative schemes that tax goods shipped in interstate commerce; taxes imposed on firms doing business in a given state; and highway, airport, sales, and use taxes. As a businessperson, you therefore should recognize the possible legal issues that inhere in such state tax laws.

Exclusive State Power

The state's plenary power to regulate commerce covers purely local activities that only remotely affect other states. Given the interdependent nature of our economy and the Supreme Court precedents we have discussed, the instances in which a state has exclusive power over commerce remain comparatively rare.

Exhibit 5.1 provides a useful framework for understanding the analysis that courts employ during their disposition of a challenge based on the commerce clause.

Using the foregoing principles, analyze *Chemical Waste Management, Inc.* v. *Hunt.*

5.1

CHEMICAL WASTE MANAGEMENT, INC. V. HUNT
504 U.S. 334 (1992)

FACTS Chemical Waste Management, Inc. (CWMI), a Delaware corporation with its principal place of business in Oak Brook, Illinois, owns and operates one of the nation's oldest commercial hazardous waste treatment, storage, and land-disposal facilities, located in Emelle, Alabama. Opened in 1977 and acquired by CWMI in 1978, the Emelle facility operates pursuant to permits issued by the U.S. Environmental Protection Agency (EPA) under the Resource Conservation and Recovery Act of 1976 (RCRA) and the Toxic Substances Control Act and by the state of Alabama. Alabama is one of only 16 states that have commercial hazardous waste landfills, and the Emelle facility is the largest of the 21 landfills of this kind located in these 16 states. The wastes and substances being landfilled at the Emelle facility include substances that are inherently dangerous to human health and safety and to the environment. From 1985 to 1989, the tonnage of hazardous waste received per year more than doubled, increasing from 341,000 tons in 1985 to 788,000 tons by 1989. Of this, up to 90 percent of the tonnage permanently buried each year is shipped in from other states. Against this backdrop, Alabama enacted legislation that, among other provisions, included a cap that generally limits the amount of hazardous wastes or substances that may be disposed of in any one-year period. Moreover, the amount of hazardous waste disposed of during the first year under the act's new fees becomes the permanent ceiling in subsequent years. This cap applies to commercial facilities that dispose of more than 100,000 tons of hazardous wastes or substances per year, but only the Emelle facility meets this description. The act also requires the operator of a facility to pay a base fee of $25.60 per ton on all hazardous wastes and substances to be disposed of at commercial facilities. Finally, the act imposes the additional fee at issue here: "For waste and substances which are generated outside of Alabama and disposed of at a commercial [disposal site] in Alabama, an additional fee shall be levied at the rate of $72.00 per ton." Filing suit in state court, CWMI requested declaratory relief and sought to enjoin the enforcement of the act. In addition to its state law claims, CWMI contended that the act violated the commerce, due process, and equal protection clauses of the U.S. Constitution and was preempted by various federal statutes. The trial court

declared the base fee and the cap provisions of the act valid and constitutional; but, finding the only basis for the additional fee to be the origin of the waste, the trial court declared this latter fee to be in violation of the commerce clause. The Alabama Supreme Court affirmed the rulings concerning the base fee and cap provisions but reversed the decision regarding the additional fee. The court held that the fee at issue advanced legitimate local purposes that could not be adequately served by reasonable nondiscriminatory alternatives and therefore was valid under the commerce clause. The U.S. Supreme Court granted *certiorari* limited to CWMI's commerce clause challenge to the additional fee.

ISSUE Did the Alabama statute that imposed an additional fee on all hazardous waste generated outside of Alabama and disposed of at Alabama facilities violate the commerce clause?

HOLDING Yes. The Alabama statute in question represented economic protectionism that discriminates against out-of-state commerce and violates the commerce clause.

REASONING No state, by raising barriers to the free flow of interstate trade, may attempt to isolate itself from a problem common to several states. The Supreme Court consistently has found parochial legislation of this kind to be constitutionally invalid, whether the ultimate aim of the legislation is, by erecting barriers to allegedly ruinous outside competition, to assure a steady supply of milk; by keeping industry within the state to create jobs; or, by fencing out indigent immigrants, to preserve the state's financial resources from depletion. To this list may be added cases striking down a tax discriminating against interstate commerce, even where such a tax was designed to encourage the use of ethanol and thereby reduce harmful exhaust emissions, or to support inspection of foreign cement to ensure structural integrity. In all these cases, the legislation sought, by the illegitimate means of isolating the state economy, to achieve presumably legitimate goals. The act's additional fee represents **facial** discrimination against hazardous waste generated in states other than Alabama, and the act overall plainly has discouraged the full operation of

5.1

CHEMICAL WASTE MANAGEMENT, INC. V. HUNT, *continued*
504 U.S. 334 (1992)

CWMI's Emelle facility. Such burdensome taxes imposed on interstate commerce alone generally are forbidden, since a state may not tax a transaction or incident more heavily when it crosses state lines than when it occurs entirely within the state. The state, however, argued that the additional fee imposed on out-of-state hazardous waste serves legitimate local purposes related to its citizens' health and safety. At a minimum, such facial discrimination invokes the strictest scrutiny of any purported legitimate local purpose and of the absence of nondiscriminatory alternatives. The state proffered four legitimate local purposes that it argued could not be adequately served by nondiscriminatory alternatives: (1) protection of the health and safety of the citizens of Alabama from toxic substances; (2) conservation of the environment and the state's natural resources; (3) provision for compensatory revenues for the costs and burdens that out-of-state waste generators impose when these firms dump their hazardous waste in Alabama; and (4) reduction of the overall flow of wastes traveling on the state's highways, which traffic creates a great risk to the health and safety of the state's citizens. But, as found by the trial court, "there is absolutely no evidence that waste generated outside Alabama is more dangerous than waste generated in Alabama . . . [T]he only basis for the additional fee [of $72.00 per ton] is the [out-of-state] origin of the waste." Given such findings, invalidity under the commerce clause necessarily follows; for whatever Alabama's ultimate purpose, it may not be accomplished by discriminating against articles of commerce coming from outside the state unless there is some reason, apart from their origin, to treat them differently. In short, the burden is on the state to show that the discrimination demonstrably is justified by a valid factor unrelated to economic protectionism. Less discriminatory alternatives, however, are available to alleviate this concern, not the least of which is a generally applicable per-ton additional fee on all hazardous waste disposed of within Alabama, or a per-mile tax on all vehicles transporting hazardous wastes across Alabama roads, or an even-handed cap on the total tonnage landfilled at Emelle, which limitation would curtail the volume from all sources. In sum, the additional fee clearly is impermissible under the commerce clause of the Constitution. Moreover, Supreme Court decisions regarding quarantine laws do not counsel a different conclusion. While it is true that the Court has not viewed certain quarantine laws as forbidden protectionist measures, even though directed against out-of-state commerce, those laws refrained from discriminating against interstate commerce as such and simply prevented traffic in noxious articles, whatever their origin. In contrast, the hazardous waste at issue in this case is the same regardless of its point of origin. Because no unique threat is posed and because adequate means other than overt discrimination meet Alabama's concerns, the state's legislative scheme is unconstitutional. Accordingly, the decision of the Alabama supreme court is reversed.

BUSINESS CONSIDERATION The problem of hazardous waste has galvanized a lot of states into resisting the storage or disposal of such waste on sites in their states. Other states have vied for the opportunity to engage in the disposal of chemical, atomic, and other hazardous waste. What factors should a state take into account when it makes the decision either to resist this type of business activity or to seek it out?

ETHICAL CONSIDERATION Do firms that engage in the disposal of hazardous wastes have a heightened ethical responsibility to evaluate (through pre-hire disclosures and continuous monitoring [via blood tests, for example]) the health and well-being of every employee? Why or why not?

THE EQUAL PROTECTION CLAUSE

Another constitutional provision that acts as a curb on the government's power to regulate business is the equal protection clause. The Fourteenth Amendment states: "[N]or shall any State . . . deny to any person within its jurisdiction the equal

Facial
Void on its face; totally invalid.

protection of the laws." Supreme Court precedents have determined that in most situations the Fifth Amendment's due process clause provides that the *federal* government must guarantee equal protection to all persons as well. Basically, this guarantee means that when the government classifies people, it must treat similarly situated people similarly. In recent years, courts have used the equal protection clause to protect a broad panoply of individual rights. Yet this provision also limits the types of regulations that government can impose on businesses.

Invidious
Repugnant; discrimination stemming from bigotry or prejudice.

Whether applied to the protection of individuals' civil rights or businesses' rights, the equal protection clause protects individuals and other entities only from **invidious** discrimination. What constitutes invidious discrimination? All governmental statutes and regulations classify (or discriminate) among groups. This kind of discrimination—mere differentiation—does not necessarily implicate the equal protection clause, however. For example, when the government says professionals or businesses must secure licenses, the government is differentiating (discriminating) among people who need such licenses as a prerequisite for doing business and those who do not. But such differentiation per se does not constitute the discrimination banned by the equal protection clause. Only when such differentiation stems from prejudice, bigotry, or stereotyping on racial, ethnic, gender, or similar bases does illegal discrimination result.

The equal protection clause also prohibits only discrimination that derives from governmental (i.e., so-called state) action; it does not reach actions taken by private individuals. Hence, under this clause, one can challenge only those actions taken by federal and state governments (or by any subdivisions or agencies thereof) pursuant to enacted laws or regulations.

Over the years, the Supreme Court has developed various tests for determining the legality of economic regulations challenged under the equal protection clause. As to each of these three possible tests, courts will review the legislative classification at issue with regard to the "fit" that exists between the means the legislative body has used to accomplish a desired end, or objective, and the impact the legislation has on the people affected by the regulation.

Level 1: The "Rational Basis" Test

Under the traditional, or so-called "rational basis" test, the government can distinguish among similarly situated persons if the statutory scheme—or classification—is rationally related to a legitimate state interest (or aim). Courts generally do not second-guess legislators' intent. Courts thus presume that the regulation is valid unless no conceivable justification exists for the law. Simply put, courts allow governmental entities wide latitude when, pursuant to their police power, these regulators enact social and economic regulations; courts only rarely invalidate such measures.

Level 2: The "Compelling State Interest" Test

If a regulatory measure involves *invidious discrimination* (that is, intentional discrimination against certain racial or ethnic groups) or certain fundamental rights, courts initially will presume such regulations are invalid. Courts will apply strict scrutiny to all such legislation and uphold only those measures necessary to accomplish a compelling state interest. In these instances, the regulating body must show that no alternative, less burdensome ways exist to accomplish the state objective or goal. Regulators only occasionally have successfully justified this type of legislation.

Over the years, the Supreme Court has held that laws that impinge on so-called "suspect" classifications and thus burden the rights of African Americans, Hispanics, and Asian Americans must meet this compelling state interest standard. The Court has protected these groups from the application of such laws because these groups represent discrete, **insular** minorities whom other citizens view as unassimilable into American society and whom the government may easily identify because of the groups' immutable physical characteristics.

In order to justify the singling out of such **disenfranchised** groups, the entity enacting the legislation must satisfy the compelling state interest (or level 2) test and the strict scrutiny approach that a court must apply to the law. For example, *Yick Wo* v. *Hopkins* involved a denial of a permit to operate a laundry business.[11] Since all 199 non-Chinese permit seekers had been granted the permit, the egregious denial of the license to Yick Wo, the only Chinese applicant, violated the Fourteenth Amendment. Given the systemic prejudice against Chinese people at the time (1886) because of the widely held view that they were unworthy of citizenship, Yick Wo was a member of a discrete, insular minority who had suffered historical disenfranchisement. His immutable physical characteristics—the shape of his eyes and his skin color, for example—also made him more easily identified and singled out by the government. The city council could not show that its denial of Yick Wo's permit represented the only means of accomplishing the state interest (avoidance of fire hazards) involved here; hence, the city council had failed to show that its treatment of Yick Wo passed muster under the compelling state interest test.

Citing *Yick Wo* v. *Hopkins* and upholding its underlying predicates, the Supreme Court recently—in *Romer* v. *Evans*—held as violative of the equal protection clause a referendum-based amendment to the Colorado state constitution that prohibited all legislative, executive, or judicial action at any level of state or local government designed to protect homosexual persons from discrimination.[12] Finding that the amendment was a status-based enactment divorced from any factual context from which the Court could discern a relationship to a legitimate state interest, the Court concluded that the amendment instead "classifie[d] homosexuals not to further a proper legislative end but to make them unequal to everyone else. This Colorado cannot do. A state [under the equal protection clause] cannot so deem a class of persons a stranger to its laws."[13]

Note that if the facts had been different in the *Yick Wo* v. *Hopkins* case and that if all 199 Chinese had obtained their permits and the lone unsuccessful applicant had been white, he presumably could sue under the Fourteenth Amendment for

5.1 | MANAGEMENT

CALL-IMAGE TECHNOLOGY

CHALLENGING AN APPARENTLY UNCONSTITUTIONAL LAW

The Kochanowskis have recently learned that the federal government has enacted a law requiring all new telecommunication devices to provide auxiliary peripheral devices to users who are disabled. This new law does not apply to any telecommunication devices that were available on the market last year (the year before CIT was established). In order to comply with the law, CIT will need to enhance substantially the audio and visual components, and these changes in turn will significantly increase the cost per unit. The Kochanowskis view this law as unconstitutional and wish to challenge it. If they ask you for your advice in this matter, what will you advise?

BUSINESS CONSIDERATIONS How should a business react to a proposed change in the law that will affect its current business practices? Should the business immediately begin the implementation of methods for complying with the new law, or should it try to take steps to prevent or delay the effective date of the new law?

ETHICAL CONSIDERATIONS Is it ethical for the government to enact laws that apply to all customers so as to provide needed benefits or protections for a small number who require special accommodations in order to utilize the products covered? Would it be more ethical for the government to refrain from requiring such accommodations, thereby leaving some members of society unable to receive benefits otherwise generally available within society?

Insular
Isolated from others.

Disenfranchised
Restricted from enjoying certain constitutional or statutory rights; burdened by systemic prejudice or bigotry.

"reverse discrimination." The Supreme Court since 1989 has said that "benign" racial classifications used by the government for affirmative action purposes (e.g., a city's deciding to award a certain percentage of city contracts to minority-owned businesses because of the city's desire to correct societal discrimination) will be judged under the strict scrutiny/compelling state interest test as well. *Adarand Constructors, Inc.* v. *Peña,* which involved a challenge to a federal program that granted preferential treatment to minority subcontractors, reinforces this 1989 holding.[14]

In *Adarand,* the Supreme Court held that reviewing courts must subject all racial classifications, imposed by whatever federal, state, or local governmental entity, to the strict scrutiny standard.[15] This case makes it clear that federal racial classifications, like those set up by a state, must serve a compelling governmental interest and must be narrowly tailored to further that interest. Under this standard, only affirmative action plans that respond to specific, provable past discrimination and that are narrowly tailored to eliminate such bias would be legal. Although the Court acknowledged that, practically speaking, it will be hard for the government to meet this test, the Court did not view its decision as dealing a fatal blow to the vast network of federal affirmative action programs that presently exist. Many commentators, however, believe this decision will bring on an avalanche of court challenges to governmental minority preference programs and will fuel the growing political backlash against affirmative action efforts.

Just as the equal protection clause prohibits virtually all legislation that burdens a suspect classification, it also subjects to the compelling state interest test any governmental action that penalizes or unduly burdens a *fundamental right* (i.e., rights expressly or impliedly guaranteed in the Constitution). Accordingly, the Supreme Court has struck down laws that forbade a drugstore's selling birth control devices and a doctor's discussing birth control issues with his or her patients. The Court believed that these laws implicate the right of privacy, interpreted by the Court as encompassing the marital relationship and procreation. Similarly, in our earlier example, had Yick Wo been a Presbyterian and the only unsuccessful applicant, he could have argued that the city council's prior, publicly articulated anti-Presbyterian sentiments had led to the penalizing of his First Amendment right of freedom of religion.

Intermediate Level: The "Substantially Important State Interest" Test

In the 1970s, the Supreme Court flirted with the idea of placing gender-based laws under level 2 analysis, particularly if the challenged legislative enactment unduly burdened women. At that time, many commentators argued that, first, women represent a discrete, insular minority owing to their belated receipt of the right to vote, the existence of Married Women's Property Acts that denied women the capacity to contract, and so on. Second, women represent a group of individuals who manifest immutable physical characteristics; in other words, women's secondary sex characteristics ordinarily distinguish women from men and vice versa.

While the Court never accepted these arguments—apparently it believed the discrimination caused by gender-based laws failed to rise to the level of invidiousness found in most level 2 cases—the Court carved out an intermediate tier of analysis for decisionmakers to use in evaluating challenges to gender-based laws. Consequently, although classifications based on gender are not "suspect," they deserve more judicial attention than classifications judged under the level 1, rational basis test. Hence, the Court formulated an intermediate tier of analysis and placed classifications based on gender in this "quasi-suspect" classification.

Statutory schemes that encompass quasi-suspect classifications must be "substantially related to an important state interest." If the enacting body cannot meet this test, courts will invalidate the legislation. Thus, older laws that prohibited women from entering certain occupations (say, becoming a barber) nowadays would be decided under this intermediate tier of analysis. Similarly, if Yick Wo had been a woman and the city council's ordinance had said no woman can obtain a permit, the city council would need to show that its prohibition against women advanced a substantially important governmental objective. Otherwise, the ordinance would violate the equal protection clause. Note that men are protected from burdensome laws as well. In *Craig* v. *Boren*, the Supreme Court invalidated an Oklahoma law that allowed females to drink beer at age 18 but prohibited males from drinking beer until age 21.[16]

Relying on these precedents, the Supreme Court recently held that the exclusion of women by the Virginia Military Institute (VMI) violated the equal protection clause. The Court characterized VMI's argument that the alterations to its "adversarial" method of training that would be necessary to accommodate women would be so drastic as to destroy VMI's program and its mission to produce "citizen-soldiers" as falling well short of the showing necessary to justify the classification as "substantially related to an important state interest." The Court therefore concluded that because neither VMI nor the state of Virginia had proffered an "exceedingly persuasive justification" for categorically excluding all women from VMI's programs, the school's policies were unconstitutional.[17]

THE DUE PROCESS CLAUSE

Besides guaranteeing equal protection, both the Fifth and Fourteenth Amendments protect against deprivations of "life, liberty, or property without due process of law." You probably associate the due process clause with individual rights, and perhaps specifically with the protection of criminals, as mentioned in Chapter 8. Hence, the government cannot deprive us of our lives (e.g., by subjecting us to capital punishment) without according us due process. Similarly, the government cannot deprive us of liberty—interpreted by the Court to include one's freedom from physical restraints imposed without due process and in noncriminal contexts to include such issues as involuntary commitments to mental institutions. In the context of business, the term *liberty* also encompasses the right to contract and to engage in gainful employment.

Still, the life and liberty components of the due process clause fade in importance compared with the property dimension of the provision. The Supreme Court has found few interpretive problems inherent in this third prong of the clause, perhaps because most of us more intuitively understand the concept *property* than we do the intangible concept *liberty*. Thus, the Court not surprisingly has construed the word *property* to include ownership of real estate, personal property, and money; but the Court also has extended the term *property* to entitlements to specific benefits set out under applicable state or federal law. Hence, if state action deprives us of property rights such as public employment, public education, continuing welfare benefits, or continuing public utility services, that deprivation cannot constitutionally occur in the absence of due process. The due process required by notions of fundamental fairness involves two dimensions: procedural protections and substantive considerations.

Procedural Due Process

Before the government can deprive one of life, liberty, or property, one usually must be afforded some kind of hearing. Such hearings generally require notice to the aggrieved party, an opportunity for that person to present his or her side of the story, and an impartial decisionmaker. The government ordinarily can refrain from providing counsel, because counsel usually is not constitutionally required as is the case with indigent criminal defendants. The applicable rules and regulations, however, often allow counsel to be present. The timing of the hearing—whether it must occur before or after the deprivation of a protected interest—and the extent of the procedural safeguards afforded to the affected individual vary.

Courts generally balance the individual interests involved with the governmental interest in fiscal and administrative efficiency. Prior Supreme Court precedents have held that a hearing must precede, for example, the termination of welfare benefits, the government's seizure and forfeiture of real estate allegedly used in connection with the commission of crimes, termination of public employment, and prejudgment garnishment of wages (a concept discussed in Chapter 30). Evidentiary hearings prior to the termination of benefits need not occur in situations involving disability benefits, some terminations of parental rights, and some license suspensions (e.g., failure to take a Breathalyzer test); but postsuspension hearings may be required in such circumstances.

For example, assume a state passes a law saying women can cut only women's hair and men can cut only men's hair. Patrick McCann, who runs a unisex barber shop, flouts the law and continues to cut women's hair. The state licensing board in response notifies him that it plans to revoke his license (state action has occurred), gives him a hearing in which he has an opportunity to present his side of the dispute, and convenes a panel (probably made up of other licensed barbers) that has no apparent biases against McCann. With these procedural steps taken against him, McCann ordinarily will not be able to use the due process clause to challenge the subsequent revocation of his license; the hearing he has received apparently fulfills the requirements of procedural due process.

Substantive Due Process

The substantive aspects of due process, however, may hold more promise for McCann. The *substantive* dimension of due process focuses not on providing fundamentally fair procedures but on the content, or the subject matter, of the law. One deprived of life, liberty, or property under arbitrary, irrational, and capricious social or economic laws may challenge such losses under the due process clause. In short, under substantive due process principles, a regulation is invalid if it fails to advance a legitimate governmental interest or if it constitutes an unreasonable means of advancing a legitimate governmental interest.

Owing to its overuse in the first 30 years of the twentieth century, courts for many years viewed substantive due process as a discredited constitutional doctrine. In that earlier period, judges, by substituting their personal views for those of the legislatures that had enacted the laws, struck down a whole host of social and economic legislation. In the mid-1930s, however, the resurrection of the theory began. Today, courts generally defer to legislators' judgments regarding social and economic matters and thus presume that such laws are valid unless the challenger can persuade the courts that the laws actually are demonstrably arbitrary and irrational. Judicial deference normally leads to the courts' upholding such laws, as occurred in *Pacific Mutual Life Insurance Co.* v. *Haslip,* where the Supreme Court upheld as reasonable a jury award of punitive damages and the state's postverdict procedures for reviewing such awards.[18]

Since the mid-1960s, the Supreme Court has used substantive due process primarily as a vehicle for protecting certain fundamental personal rights that are implied by constitutional wording and phraseology. Hence, beginning in the mid-1960s, the Court has struck down on grounds of irrationality and arbitrariness state laws making the use of contraceptives by anyone, including married persons, illegal. Such laws impermissibly infringe on the so-called zone of marital privacy protected by the Court. In coming to this result, the Court viewed such legislation in a fashion virtually identical to strict scrutiny and applied something very akin to the compelling state interest test. The liberty component of the due process clause also guarantees a competent person, who has clearly made his or her wishes known beforehand, the right to terminate unwanted medical treatment.[19] Laws holding otherwise can be challenged on substantive due process grounds.

As you have studied this section, you probably have noticed the complementary relationship between substantive due process and guarantees of equal protection under the law. Both constitutional guarantees mandate a rational fit between the objectives of the law and the group of people affected thereby. When all persons are subject to a law that deprives them of a life, liberty, or property interest, due process probably applies. When a law classifies certain people for certain purposes, the equal protection doctrine probably becomes the appropriate vehicle for challenging the law.

Under either theory, the Supreme Court since the mid-1930s has required judges to give great deference to legislative prerogatives when judges are called on to review social legislation that does not involve personal fundamental rights. The same is true of economic legislation: Judges should uphold all such legislation unless the challenger can show the absence of any rational relationship to any legitimate governmental aim or interest.

To check your understanding of this section, ask yourself whether Pat McCann, from our earlier example, could challenge his license revocation under substantive due process. Consider, too, whether he could sue under the equal protection clause.

THE TAKINGS CLAUSE

Besides guaranteeing procedural and substantive due process, the Fifth Amendment also provides that "private property [shall not] be taken for public use, without just compensation." This Fifth Amendment restraint on the power of the

5.2 | MANAGEMENT

CHALLENGING LOCAL LAWS

One city in which CIT has opened a retail outlet has announced that a new city ordinance will go into effect in three months. This new ordinance requires all firms selling interactive videophones to have a switch that either party to a conversation can use to turn off the video transmission. CIT is the only firm that is currently selling interactive videophones in that state, and the family members believe that CIT has been singled out for discriminatory treatment by this ordinance. They ask you what they can or should do under these circumstances. What will you tell them?

BUSINESS CONSIDERATION Suppose that a city ordinance makes conducting business in that city too difficult or too expensive for a particular firm. Should the firm move its operation out of the city, or should it seek a variance or exemption from the city?

ETHICAL CONSIDERATIONS Is it ethical for a business to pick and choose where it will operate based on local laws or regulations? What ethical considerations will such a decision raise?

federal government moreover applies to the states through the Fourteenth Amendment's due process clause. Under this "takings" clause, the government must take the property for "public use" and must pay "just compensation" to the property owner involved.

In litigation, the disagreement between the parties often centers on whether a *taking* has occurred, in which case the Constitution obligates the government to pay just compensation, or whether the governmental action amounts only to *regulation* under the exercise of its police power, in which case no compensation is owed. While the Court has set out no clear formula for judging when a taking has occurred, any actual appropriation of property will suffice. For example, if the state through formal procedures condemns a business for the purpose of constructing a parking garage on a state college campus, a taking has occurred; and the state will have to pay just compensation to the owner of the property that was razed owing to the state's exercise of its power of **eminent domain.**

Eminent domain

A state's or municipality's power to take private property for public use.

But less-than-complete appropriations of property may suffice as takings as well. For instance, the Court has held that federal dam construction resulting in the repeated flooding of private property and low, direct flights over private property located contiguous to federal or municipal airports constitute takings if the activities in question destroy the property's present use or unreasonably impair the value of the property and the owners' reasonable expectations regarding it.

As the *Lucas* v. *South Carolina Coastal Council* case discussed in Chapter 43 demonstrates, a land use regulation that fails to advance substantially legitimate state interests or that denies an owner the economically viable use of his or her land is a taking subject to the Fifth Amendment.[20] In the absence of such factors, zoning ordinances—the most common type of land use regulations—ordinarily pass muster under the takings clause even if the regulations restrict the use of the property and cause a reduction in its value, so long as the ordinances substantially advance legitimate state interests and do not extinguish fundamental attributes of ownership.

During the attempted taking, the government must afford the affected property owner procedural due process. However, the just compensation paid by the governmental regulator need reflect only the fair market value of the property; the price paid need not compensate the owner for the sentimental value of the property, the owner's unique need for the property, or the gain that the regulating body realizes by virtue of the taking.

Analyze *Dolan* v. *City of Tigard* in light of the principles just discussed.

5.2

DOLAN V. CITY OF TIGARD
512 U.S. 374 (1994)

FACTS The Tigard, Oregon, City Planning Commission conditioned approval of Florence Dolan's application to expand her plumbing and electric supply store and pave her parking lot on her agreeing to dedicate land (1) for a public greenway so as to minimize the Fanno Creek flooding that would result from the increases in the impervious surfaces associated with her development and (2) for a pedestrian/bicycle pathway intended to relieve traffic congestion in the city's central business district. In appealing the Commission's denial of her request for variances from these standards to the Land Use Board of Appeals (LUBA), Dolan alleged that the land dedication requirements were not related to the proposed development and therefore constituted an uncompensated taking of her property under the Fifth Amendment.

5.2

DOLAN V. CITY OF TIGARD, *continued*

512 U.S. 374 (1994)

The LUBA, the state court of appeals, and the state supreme court affirmed the Commission's decision.

ISSUE Did the land dedication requirements imposed on Dolan constitute an unconstitutional taking of her property under the Fifth Amendment?

HOLDING Yes. The city had not shown that it had made an individualized determination that the required dedications related both in nature and extent to the impact of the proposed settlement. The absence of such a connection therefore rendered the city's actions unlawful under the takings clause of the Fifth Amendment.

REASONING The takings clause of the Fifth Amendment of the U.S. Constitution, made applicable to the states through the Fourteenth Amendment, provides: "[N]or shall private property be taken for public use, without just compensation." One of the principal purposes of the takings clause is "to bar Government from forcing some people alone to bear public burdens which, in all fairness and justice, should be borne by the public as a whole." Without question, had the city simply required Dolan to dedicate a strip of land along Fanno Creek for public use, rather than conditioning the grant of her permit to redevelop her property on such a dedication, a taking would have occurred. Such public access would deprive Dolan of the right to exclude others, "one of the most essential sticks in the bundle of rights that are commonly characterized as property." On the other side of the ledger, the authority of state and local governments to engage in land use planning has been sustained against constitutional challenge since 1926. The Supreme Court consistently has held that a land use regulation does not effect a taking if the regulation "substantially advance[s] legitimate state interests" and refrains from denying "an owner the economically viable use of his [or her] land." The sort of land use regulations discussed in the Supreme Court precedents just cited, however, differ in two relevant particulars from the present case. First, they involved essentially legislative determinations classifying entire areas of the city, whereas here the city has made an adjudicative decision to condition Dolan's application for a building permit on an individual parcel. Second, the conditions imposed were not simply a limitation on the use

Dolan might make of her own parcel, but a requirement that she deed portions of the property to the city. Recent Supreme Court precedents under the Fifth and Fourteenth Amendments circumscribe governmental authority to exact such a condition. Under the well-settled doctrine of unconstitutional conditions, the government lacks the authority to require a person to give up a constitutional right—here, the right to receive just compensation when property is taken for public use—in exchange for a discretionary benefit conferred by the government where the property sought has little or no relationship to the benefit. Apropos of this, Dolan contended that the city has forced her to choose between the building permit and her right under the Fifth Amendment to just compensation for public easements. She argued that the city has failed to identify either any "special benefits" conferred on her or any "special quantifiable burdens" created by her new store that would justify the particular dedications required from her and which are not required from the public at large. In evaluating Dolan's claim, the Court first must determine whether the "essential nexus" exists between the "legitimate state interest" and the permit conditions exacted by the city. If such a nexus exists, the Court then must decide the required degree of connection between the exactions and the projected impact of the proposed developments. The minimization of flooding along Fanno Creek and the reduction of traffic congestion in the central business district qualify as the type of legitimate public purposes upheld by earlier Court decisions. The second part of the analysis requires the Court to determine whether the degree of the exactions demanded by the city's permit conditions bears the required relationship to the projected impact of Dolan's proposed development, since a use restriction may constitute a taking if not reasonably necessary to the effectuation of a substantial government purpose. The states previously have adopted various tests for determining whether the necessary connection between the required dedication and the proposed development suffices for constitutional purposes. But the Court today enunciates a new test: A term such as *rough proportionality* best encapsulates what the Court sees as the requirement of the Fifth Amendment. No precise mathematical calculation is required, but the city must make some sort of

continued

DOLAN V. CITY OF TIGARD, *continued*

512 U.S. 374 (1994)

individualized determination that the required dedication is related both in nature and in extent to the impact of the proposed development. When one applies this test to the city's findings, it becomes apparent that the city's imposition of a permanent recreational easement on Dolan's property that borders Fanno Creek would cause her to lose all her rights to regulate the time in which the public entered onto the city's greenway, regardless of any interference it might impose with regard to her retail store. Her right to exclude would not be regulated; it would be eviscerated. Hence, the findings upon which the city relied do not show the required reasonable relationship between the floodplain easement and Dolan's proposed new building. With respect to the pedestrian/bicycle pathway, the city has not met its burden of demonstrating that the additional number of vehicle and bicycle trips generated by Dolan's development reasonably relates to the city's requirement for a dedication of the pedestrian/bicycle pathway easement. Although no precise mathematical calculation is required, the city must make some effort to quantify its findings in support of

the dedication for the pedestrian/bicycle pathway beyond the conclusory statement that the pathway could offset some of the traffic demand generated. The city's failure to meet its burden of proof therefore mandates the reversal of the judgment the Supreme Court of Oregon previously rendered.

BUSINESS CONSIDERATIONS Was it reasonable for Dolan to expect the city to absorb the adverse effects on the city that arguably would result from Dolan's proposed expansion of her business? How should a business react to a situation in which the business is expected to make a community-benefit "contribution" in exchange for permission to expand or move the business activity?

ETHICAL CONSIDERATIONS If the Court had disposed of this case on ethical—rather than legal—grounds, would its decision have been different? What ethical concerns did this case raise?

Inverse condemnation
An action brought by a property owner against a governmental entity that has the power of eminent domain; the property owner typically seeks just compensation for land taken for public use in situations in which the governmental entity does not intend to initiate eminent domain proceedings.

The Supreme Court recently added to its property rights jurisprudence when it decided *City of Monterey* v. *Del Monte Dunes at Monterey, Ltd.*[21] In this case, a firm sought to develop a condominium project on a parcel of environmentally sensitive land along the California coast. After the planning commission over a period of five years had rejected several plans and had imposed increasingly stringent demands on the developer, the firm filed a lawsuit under § 1983, which creates a duty to refrain from interfering with the federal rights of others and provides money damages and injunctive relief for violations of that duty that are effected under color of state law. In a 5–4 decision, the Court held that the developer was entitled to a jury trial on its regulatory taking claim. In doing so, the Court emphasized the narrowness of its ruling on the availability of jury trials in such cases. Indeed, the Court stressed that it was not setting out the precise demarcation of the respective provinces of judges and juries in determining whether a zoning decision substantially advances governmental interests. Nevertheless, the Court concluded that whether a challenged regulation has deprived a landowner of all the economically viable uses of his or her property is a jury question. The Court conceded that whether a land use decision substantially advances legitimate public interests involves a tougher call probably best understood as a mixed question of fact and law. In this case, however, the Court viewed the protracted sequence of the developer's applications and the city's rejections as sufficiently factbound to make the question of liability appropriate for a jury's consideration. The dissenters, in contrast, viewed such **inverse condemnation** cases as analogous to eminent domain proceedings in which no jury trial ordinarily is available because the measure of compensation required by the Fifth Amendment is the fair market value of the property on the date on which the property is appropriated.

Interestingly, the Court held that the "rough proportionality" standard enunciated in the *Dolan* case applies only in the special context of *exactions*—that is, land use decisions conditioning approval of development on the dedication of the property to public use. According to the Court, the *Dolan* rule considers whether dedications demanded as conditions of development are proportional to the development's anticipated impacts. *Dolan* is not readily applicable to situations like the *Monterey* case, in which a landowner bases his or her challenge on a denial of development rather than excessive exactions. Hence, the Court concluded that *Dolan* would not apply to the regulatory taking context exemplified by the *Monterey* decision.

Although we have emphasized only the due process and takings clauses of the Fifth Amendment, as you have learned from earlier chapters, this provision in the Constitution also prohibits *double jeopardy* (being tried twice for the same criminal offense) and compulsory self-incrimination. Thus, the Fifth Amendment's many facets represent an effective curb on illegitimate governmental action taken against individuals or businesses.

THE FIRST AMENDMENT/ COMMERCIAL SPEECH

The First Amendment, as you remember, protects individual freedom of speech. Businesses, however, as legal (or *juristic*) persons, arguably enjoy protectable First Amendment rights as well. Indeed, commercial speech— speech that involves commercial transactions, particularly the advertising of business products and services—does qualify for First Amendment protection. Although the Supreme Court has had difficulty in defining the term *commercial speech* with precision, one thing is clear: The parameters of this protection are not coextensive with the boundaries of protected individual speech.

Clearly, the government can—and does—regulate private expression. The First Amendment, though a fundamental right, is not an absolute one. In deciding whether to limit speech, the government engages in yet another balancing test in which it compares such factors as the importance of these rights in a democratic society, the nature of the restriction imposed by the law, the type and importance of the governmental interest the law purports to serve, and the narrowness of the means used to effectuate that interest.

Courts ordinarily view laws that, by punishing some speech and favoring other speech, burden the content of individual speech ("content-based" regulations), as

5.3 | MANAGEMENT

CITY OFFICIALS CONFISCATE CALL-IMAGE UNITS

Assume that the proposed ordinance requiring a switch that turns off video transmissions has taken effect. CIT has decided to add such a switch to its units as soon as practicable. In the meantime, the firm has decided to suspend any new sales in that community until the reconfigured units are ready. Anna calls the store manager to inform him of this decision and to have him return all the unsold units in the store to the CIT factory for redistribution to areas where the present units can legally be sold. Anna thereupon learns that the city, citing the units' noncompliance with the city ordinance, has already confiscated all the units in the store. Anna asks you if the city can legally do this. What will you tell her?

BUSINESS CONSIDERATIONS What should a business do to protect itself from takings carried out by the government? What sorts of protections are available for the business?

ETHICAL CONSIDERATIONS Is it ethical for the government to take private property for a public purpose? What alternatives might be available that would allow the government to meet its obligation to the public while protecting the property interests of owners?

presumptively invalid. Hence, such laws must pass the "strict scrutiny/compelling state interest" (i.e., the "least restrictive alternative") test and be narrowly drawn measures designed to achieve such a compelling state interest. Courts in addition can strike down substantially overbroad and vague laws (i.e., those that proscribe protected activity and thus "chill" others into refraining from the exercise of constitutionally protected expression). The government, however, may outlaw defamation, advocacy of unlawful action, obscenity, and "fighting words." The government also can subject lawful speech to time, place, and manner regulation (it can require demonstrators to obtain permits, limit the demonstration to a certain venue, and so on).

Thus, because the government can regulate private expression, it comes as no surprise that the government can regulate commercial speech and even ban such speech that is false and misleading. Although the First Amendment protects commercial speech, the greater potential for deception and confusion posed by commercial speech allows the government to regulate even the content of commercial (as opposed to noncommercial) speech so long as the restriction serves and advances a substantial governmental interest and in a manner no more extensive than necessary (i.e., "sufficiently tailored") to achieve that governmental objective. For example, in 1994, the Supreme Court held in *Turner Broadcasting System, Inc.* v. *Federal Communications Commission (Turner I)* that the provisions of the federal law that required cable television stations to devote a specified portion of their channels to the transmission of local programming (the "must carry" provisions) were not content-based laws.[22] In 1997, after a remand for more fact finding, the Court—in *Turner II*—affirmed this holding.[23] Hence, the Court rejected the argument that these "must carry" provisions must be judged under the strict scrutiny/compelling state interest test and instead upheld the challenged provisions because they were sufficiently tailored to serve the important governmental interest relating to the preservation of local broadcasting. The recent challenges to Congress's attempt to regulate "indecent" content on the Internet (specifically, the Communications Decency Act of 1995, which outlawed the electronic transmission of lewd and indecent materials to anyone under age 18 and subjected to criminal penalties any commercial communication service that allows its system to be used for such transmissions) implicate similar issues. The Supreme Court's invalidation of this law as illegal, content-based, blanket restrictions on speech[24] is a harbinger of the types of issues that promise to provide a fertile field for continuing litigation. Try, therefore, to keep abreast of the Supreme Court's disposition of the legal developments relating to the regulation of telecommunications.

The Supreme Court in *44 Liquormart* v. *Rhode Island* utilizes many of the principles of law just discussed.

5.3

44 LIQUORMART, INC. V. RHODE ISLAND
517 U.S. 484 (1996)

FACTS 44 Liquormart, Inc. (44 Liquormart) and Peoples Super Liquor Stores, Inc. (Peoples) are licensed retailers of alcoholic beverages. 44 Liquormart operates a store in Rhode Island, and Peoples operates several stores in Massachusetts that are patronized by Rhode Island residents. Peoples uses alcohol price advertising extensively in Massachusetts, where such advertising is permitted, but Rhode Island newspapers and other media outlets have refused to accept such ads. In 1991, 44 Liquormart placed an advertise-

5.3

44 LIQUORMART, INC. V. RHODE ISLAND, *continued*
517 U.S. 484 (1996)

ment in a Rhode Island newspaper. The advertisement did not state the price of any alcoholic beverages. Indeed, it noted that "State law prohibits advertising liquor prices." The ad did, however, state the low prices at which peanuts, potato chips, and Schweppes mixers were being offered, identify various brands of packaged liquor, and include the word "WOW" in large letters next to pictures of vodka and rum bottles. Based on the conclusion that the implied reference to bargain prices for liquor violated the statutory ban on price advertising, the Rhode Island Liquor Control Administrator assessed a $400 fine. After paying the fine, 44 Liquormart, joined by Peoples, sought in federal court a declaratory judgment that the two statutes and the administrator's implementing regulations violate the First Amendment and other provisions of federal law. The parties stipulated that the price advertising ban is vigorously enforced, that Rhode Island permits "all advertising of alcoholic beverages excepting references to price outside the licensed premises," and that the proposed ads concern a legal activity and presumably would not be false or misleading. The parties disagreed, however, about the impact of the ban on the promotion of temperance in Rhode Island. The district court concluded that the price advertising ban was unconstitutional because it did not "directly advance" the state's interest in reducing alcohol consumption and was "more extensive than necessary to serve that interest." The district court reasoned that the party seeking to uphold a restriction on commercial speech carries the burden of justifying it and that the Twenty-first Amendment did not shift or diminish that burden. Acknowledging that it might have been reasonable for the state legislature to "assume a correlation between the price advertising ban and reduced consumption," the court held that more than a rational basis was required to justify the speech restriction and that the state had failed to demonstrate a reasonable fit between its policy objectives and its chosen means. The court of appeals reversed. It found inherent merit in the state's submission that competitive price advertising would lower prices and that lower prices would produce more sales. Moreover, it agreed with the reasoning of the Rhode Island Supreme Court that the Twenty-first Amendment gave the statutes an added presumption of validity. The Supreme Court thereafter granted *certiorari*.

ISSUES Did Rhode Island's statutory bans on the advertising of liquor prices except at the place of sale violate the First Amendment? Would the Twenty-first Amendment shield this advertising ban from constitutional scrutiny?

HOLDINGS Yes, as to the first issue. The state had failed to carry its heavy burden of justifying its complete ban on advertising; hence, that ban was invalid under the First Amendment. No, as to the second issue. The Twenty-first Amendment was unavailable as a means of saving Rhode Island's price-advertising ban because that amendment does not qualify the First Amendment's prohibition against laws that abridge freedom of speech.

REASONING After reviewing its numerous precedents concerning advertising, the Court submitted that Rhode Island had erred when it had concluded that all commercial speech regulations are subject to a similar form of constitutional review simply because they target a similar category of expression. The mere fact that messages propose commercial transactions does not in and of itself dictate the constitutional analysis that should apply to decisions to suppress them. According to the Court, when a state regulates commercial messages to protect consumers from misleading, deceptive, or aggressive sales practices, or requires the disclosure of beneficial consumer information, the purpose of its regulation is consistent with the reasons for according constitutional protection to commercial speech and therefore justifies less than strict review. However, when a state entirely prohibits the dissemination of truthful, nonmisleading commercial messages for reasons unrelated to the preservation of a fair bargaining process, there is far less reason to depart from the rigorous review that the First Amendment generally demands. Sound reasons justify reviewing the latter type of commercial speech regulation more carefully. Most obviously, complete speech bans, unlike content-neutral restrictions on the time, place, or manner of expression, are particularly dangerous because they all but foreclose alternative means of disseminating certain information. Supreme Court commercial speech cases have recognized the dangers that attend governmental attempts to single out certain messages for suppression. Hence,

continued

5.3

44 LIQUORMART, INC. V. RHODE ISLAND, *continued*
517 U.S. 484 (1996)

complete bans on truthful, nonmisleading commercial speech cannot be explained away by appeals to the "commonsense distinctions" that exist between commercial and noncommercial speech. It is the state's interest in protecting consumers from "commercial harms" that provides "the typical reason why commercial speech can be subject to greater governmental regulation than noncommercial speech." Yet bans that target truthful, nonmisleading commercial messages rarely protect consumers from such harms. Instead, such bans often serve only to obscure an "underlying governmental policy" that could be implemented without regulating speech. In this way, these commercial speech bans not only hinder consumer choice, but also impede debate over central issues of public policy. Precisely because bans against truthful, nonmisleading commercial speech rarely seek to protect consumers from either deception or overreaching, they usually rest solely on the offensive assumption that the public will respond "irrationally" to the truth. The First Amendment directs everyone to be especially skeptical of regulations that seek to keep people in the dark for what the government perceives to be their own good. That teaching applies equally to state attempts to deprive consumers of accurate information about their chosen products. In this case, Rhode Island's price advertising ban unquestionably constitutes a blanket prohibition against truthful, nonmisleading speech about a lawful product. There is also no question that the ban serves an end unrelated to consumer protection. Accordingly, any court must review the price advertising ban with "special care" and remain mindful that speech prohibitions of this type rarely survive constitutional review. The state argues that the price advertising prohibition nevertheless should be upheld because it directly advances the state's substantial interest in promoting temperance and because it is no more extensive than necessary. Although there is some confusion as to what Rhode Island means by temperance, the state presumably asserts an interest in reducing alcohol consumption. In evaluating the ban's effectiveness in advancing the state's interest, a court may not sustain a commercial speech regulation if it provides only ineffective or remote support for the government's purpose. For that reason, the state bears the burden of showing not merely that its regulation will advance its interest, but also that it will do so "to a

material degree." The need for the state to make such a showing is particularly great given the drastic nature of its chosen means—the wholesale suppression of truthful, nonmisleading information. Accordingly, a court must determine whether the state has shown that the price advertising ban will *significantly* reduce alcohol consumption. And the state has failed to meet its burden in this case. The state also cannot satisfy the requirement that its restriction on speech be no more extensive than necessary. It is perfectly obvious that alternative forms of regulation that would not involve any restriction on speech—for example, the maintenance of higher prices through higher taxation, limitations on per capita purchases, and educational programs that focus on the problems of excessive (or even moderate) drinking—would be more likely to achieve the state's goal of promoting temperance. Furthermore, the Twenty-first Amendment, which repealed the Eighteenth Amendment's prohibitions on liquor and which delegated the power to regulate commerce in alcoholic beverages to the states, does not qualify the constitutional prohibition against laws abridging the freedom of speech embodied in the First Amendment. The Twenty-first Amendment, therefore, cannot save Rhode Island's ban on liquor price advertising. Rhode Island's failure to carry its heavy burden of justifying its complete ban on price advertising means that the statutes in question abridge speech in violation of the First Amendment as made applicable to the states by the Due Process Clause of the Fourteenth Amendment. The judgment of the court of appeals consequently must be reversed.

BUSINESS CONSIDERATIONS Some businesses, such as liquor stores, sell products that are more likely to be subject to public concern and scrutiny than others. Should these businesses expect more stringent regulation than businesses not subjected to such public scrutiny? How can these businesses protect themselves in such situations?

ETHICAL CONSIDERATIONS
Is it ethical to single out certain types of businesses for different types or degrees of regulation? How can such treatment be justified ethically?

YOU BE THE JUDGE

A COLLISION OF LANDLORDS' AND RENTERS' RIGHTS

An Alaskan fair housing statute and a similar Anchorage ordinance bar landlords from discriminating against renters on the basis of marital status. A Christian landlord who objected on religious grounds to renting to unmarried couples and refused to do so challenged the statute on the basis of the free exercise clause of the First Amendment. The landlord also claimed that because the statute authorizes a "physical invasion" of an owner's property, the legislation effects an infringement of a landlord's right under the takings clause of the Fifth Amendment. In addition, the landlord submitted that the law's precluding owners from inquiring about the marital status of prospective tenants infringes on landlords' speech.

If *you* were the judge, how would *you* decide this case?[25]

BUSINESS CONSIDERATIONS Is it advisable for a firm to take into account the values and mores of its customers when it conducts its business? Or are the values and mores of its customers outside the legitimate purview of the business? What benefits may a firm derive from such an approach? What are the drawbacks?

ETHICAL CONSIDERATIONS One of the plaintiffs was an avowed Christian. In refusing to rent to unmarried persons, was the landlord fulfilling the dictates of the Golden Rule? In general, should a business conduct its affairs in a value-neutral fashion? Explain your reasoning.

SOURCE: *Thomas v. Anchorage Equal Rights Comm'n,* 67 U.S.L.W. (2 February 1999), pp. 1439–1440.

ADMINISTRATIVE AGENCIES

Administrative agencies conduct much of the work of regulating business. Most of us are familiar with the three official branches of the federal government—the legislative, executive, and judicial—but we may tend to overlook the unofficial fourth branch. This so-called administrative branch of government has been especially active since the 1930s. The Great Depression and the presidency of Franklin Delano Roosevelt saw a tremendous growth in the use of administrative agencies as a major means of effecting regulation. Because a great deal of government intervention in the business sphere derives from the actions of administrative agencies, some familiarity with administrative law is essential to understanding governmental regulation of business.

Congress sets up administrative agencies, and since it "creates" them, it can terminate them. Hence, they are not an independent branch of government. They have only as much authority as the legislature has **delegated** to them, and as a result they must answer to Congress for their conduct. Congress establishes a basic policy or standard and then authorizes an agency to carry it out.

Once established, the agency will have certain **quasi-legislative** and **quasi-judicial** powers. The agency is allowed to pass rules and regulations within its area of authority and to hold hearings when it believes that violations of its rules and regulations have occurred. In so doing, federal administrative agencies must follow the Administrative Procedures Act (APA), which mandates public participation and sets out the rules and procedures that such agencies must follow as they legislate,

Delegated
Assigned responsibility and/or authority by the person or group normally empowered to exercise the responsibility or authority.

Quasi-legislative
Partly legislative; empowered to enact rules and regulations but not statutes.

Quasi-judicial
Partly judicial; empowered to hold hearings but not trials.

adjudicate, and enforce their regulations. The power of Congress to abolish any agency and the power of the courts to review any agency's conduct are considered sufficient control devices. It is believed that the agency will not exceed its authority or abuse its discretion as long as these two *official* branches of government keep a watchful eye on the agency's conduct.

Some of the constitutional provisions discussed earlier in the chapter limit the power of administrative agencies. Remember that an agency, in order to ensure procedural due process, must provide fairness in its proceedings. A person involved in a proceeding that affects his or her individual rights (i.e., those involving *adjudicative* facts) ordinarily is entitled to a hearing of some sort. Also remember that due process generally includes the right to present witnesses, the right to cross-examine witnesses, the right to an impartial decisionmaker, and possibly other rights as well. Agency proceedings involving only rulemaking or fact finding concerning principles of general application (i.e., those involving *legislative* facts) usually require fewer procedural safeguards. Notice of the time, place, and purpose of the meeting might satisfy procedural due process in this latter context. Moreover, the agency may enact only rules and regulations that bear a rational relationship to the agency's purpose or function. Under substantive due process doctrines, then, litigants may challenge unreasonable, arbitrary, and capricious administrative rules. Such rules also may deny the equal protection of the law to the persons affected.

The respective agencies' enabling statutes ordinarily spell out the methods by which one can seek review of agency decisions. Those dissatisfied with treatment received at the hands of an administrative agency generally may ask a federal district or circuit court of appeals to review the administrative proceedings in question. Judicial review ordinarily focuses on four possible areas of agency error:

RESOURCES FOR BUSINESS LAW STUDENTS

NAME	RESOURCES	WEB ADDRESS
U.S. Constitution	Emory Law School maintains a hypertext and searchable version of the U.S. Constitution.	**http://www.law.emory.edu/FEDERAL/usconst.html**
The Legal Information Institute (LII)—Decisions of the U.S. Supreme Court	LII, maintained by the Cornell Law School, provides recent Supreme Court decisions (1990–present), as well as various historical decisions and background material on the Court.	**http://supct.law.cornell.edu/supct/**
Oyez Oyez Oyez: A Supreme Court Resource	Oyez Oyez Oyez (pronounced "oh-yay"), maintained by Jerry Goldman and Northwestern University, provides digital recordings (via Real Audio technology) of selected Supreme Court cases ranging from 1955 to the present.	**http://oyez.nwu.edu**
International Association of Constitutional Law	International Association of Constitutional Law provides information and constitutions for countries around the world.	**http://www.eur.nl/frg/iacl/indexe.htm**

1. The agency violated procedural due process.
2. The agency violated substantive due process.
3. The agency otherwise violated the Constitution.
4. The agency exceeded its authority.

A court, however, will review the proceedings only from the point of view of their legality. As to *questions of fact* (e.g., what actually transpired), a court must follow the *substantial evidence rule,* which states that the agency's findings of fact must be upheld if such findings are based on substantial evidence. If instead the judicial review involves *questions of law* (e.g., jurisdictional or procedural issues), courts remain free to substitute their judgment for the agencies'; courts need not give deference to the agencies' determinations regarding these issues.

Courts will review *discretionary* acts under the "abuse of discretion" rationale and therefore will invalidate arbitrary, unreasonable, or capricious decisions.

Owing to the restricted nature of judicial review and the pervasive nature of administrative agencies in the business world, this area of regulation has become quite important today. A person who plans to advance very far in business is well advised to study administrative law in further detail.

SUMMARY

Governmental regulation of business is a fact of life in the modern business environment. Whether regulation takes the form of local zoning ordinances, state income taxation, or federal antitrust regulation, businesses today must address it. And the only way to deal with government regulation is to recognize and understand it. Federal regulation of business is based on both the commerce clause of the U.S. Constitution, which authorizes Congress to "regulate commerce among the several states," and Congress's taxing power, also included in the Constitution.

Most regulation derives from the commerce clause. The commerce clause has been interpreted in such a way that federal regulation is permitted only if interstate commerce is involved. To qualify as interstate, the transaction must directly affect citizens of at least two different states or countries. If an interstate connection is present, federal regulation may be applied. The federal government exclusively regulates many aspects of business, but the states have concurrent power to regulate in certain areas. States, however, can exercise exclusive regulatory power over commerce only rarely.

The equal protection clause protects against invidious discrimination. Over the years, the Supreme Court has developed various tests for determining the legality of regulations challenged under this provision of the Constitution.

The Constitution's guarantee of due process has distinct procedural and substantive dimensions. These aspects guarantee fundamental fairness and freedom from the application of irrational, unreasonable, and arbitrary laws whenever the government deprives anyone of life, liberty, or property.

Under the takings clause of the Fifth Amendment, the government can take property for public use so long as the government pays just compensation to the affected property owner. In addition, the Fifth Amendment's prohibitions on double jeopardy and compulsory self-incrimination also serve as curbs on illegitimate governmental action.

The First Amendment protects commercial speech but to a lesser degree than it does individual speech. The government can ban false and misleading commercial speech and can even regulate other types of commercial speech as long as the restriction serves and advances a substantial governmental interest and in a manner no more extensive than necessary to achieve that governmental objective.

Much of the actual regulation of business is effectuated by administrative agencies. Administrative agencies are created by Congress, which then delegates to the agencies the authority to carry out certain duties. Agencies are involved in a large number of regulatory areas. In carrying out their responsibilities, these agencies are required to assure due process of law, and they are subject to judicial review to ensure that they conduct themselves properly.

DISCUSSION QUESTIONS

1. How do you define the phrase *interstate commerce?* Do you accept or reject the Supreme Court's definition of this term? Why?
2. Name and explain the areas of commerce over which the federal government has exclusive jurisdiction. What are the areas of concurrent state and federal regulation? When does the state have exclusive jurisdiction over commerce?
3. Explain in detail the various tests a court must apply when it evaluates a law challenged on equal protection grounds.
4. Discuss the factors that courts must take into account in deciding whether a group is a "suspect classification" for purposes of equal protection analysis.
5. Name and explain the various interests protected under the Fifth Amendment.

6. What does *substantive due process* mean? How does a court determine when a violation of this constitutional right has occurred?
7. How does *procedural due process* differ from substantive due process? What protections must the government provide to individuals and businesses under this aspect of the Fifth and Fourteenth Amendments?
8. What powers does the government enjoy under the takings clause? What rights does an individual or business have under this clause?
9. How does the protection accorded commercial speech differ from the protection granted to individual speech?
10. What powers are possessed by administrative agencies? From what source do administrative agencies derive these powers?

CASE PROBLEMS AND WRITING ASSIGNMENTS

1. In order to establish and maintain orderly marketing conditions and fair prices for agricultural commodities, Congress enacted the Agricultural Marketing Agreement Act of 1937 (AMAA). Pursuant to the AMAA, the secretary of agriculture promulgates marketing orders. Such marketing orders represent a species of economic regulation that has displaced competition in a number of discrete markets. The orders also are expressly exempted from the antitrust laws. Put differently, collective action, rather than the aggregate consequences of independent competitive choices, characterizes these regulated markets. These marketing orders typically provide a uniform price to all producers in a particular market and thereby limit the quality and quantity of any commodity placed on the market. The expenses of administering such orders are paid from assessments collected pursuant to the marketing orders. Among the collective activities authorized under the AMAA are the advertising and marketing promotion of certain products. Wileman Brothers & Elliott, Inc. (Wileman), one such California

producer and handler of California nectarines, peaches, and plums, in 1997 refused to pay the required assessments because the firm believed individualized advertising would be more effective than the generic advertising effected under the marketing orders. Wileman and certain other handlers thereafter challenged the requirement that the producers finance such generic advertising as violative of the First Amendment. Specifically, the plaintiffs claimed that the assessments, by reducing the amount of money available for them to conduct their own advertising, violated the First Amendment's guarantees of freedom of speech. The secretary of agriculture, in contrast, argued that the generic advertising was germane to the marketing orders' purposes and consistent with the overall statutory scheme. The secretary further submitted that the assessments were constitutional under Supreme Court commercial speech precedents because the assessments were not used to fund ideological or political views. In these circumstances, whose arguments were more compelling?

[See *Glickman* v. *Wileman Brothers & Elliott, Inc.*, 521 U.S. 457 (1997).]

2. In 1985, the city of Dallas authorized the licensing of "Class E" dance halls to provide a place where younger teenagers could socialize with one another but not be subject to the potentially detrimental influences of older teenagers and young adults. The ordinance restricted admission to Class E dance halls to persons between the ages of 14 and 18. Parents, guardians, law enforcement, and dance hall personnel were excepted from the ordinance's age restriction. The ordinance also limited the hours of operation of Class E dance halls to between 1 P.M. and midnight daily when school was not in session. Charles M. Stanglin operated the Twilight Skating Rink in Dallas and obtained a license for a Class E dance hall. Using movable plastic cones or pylons, he divided the floor of his roller-skating rink into two sections. On one side of the pylons, persons between the ages of 14 and 18 dance, while on the other side, persons of all ages skate to the same music. No age or hour restrictions applied to the skating rink. Stanglin did not serve alcohol on the premises, and security personnel were present. Stanglin sued in district court to enjoin the enforcement of the age and hour restrictions of the ordinance. He contended that the ordinance violated substantive due process and equal protection under the U.S. and Texas constitutions and that it unconstitutionally infringed the rights of persons between the ages of 14 and 18 to associate with persons outside that age bracket. The trial court, in upholding the ordinance, found that it was rationally related to the city's legitimate interest in ensuring the safety and welfare of children. The Texas court of appeals upheld the ordinance's time restriction, but it struck down the age restriction as violative of minors' First Amendment associational rights. To support a restriction on the fundamental right of "social association," the court said, "the legislative body must show a compelling interest"; and the regulation "must be accomplished by the least restrictive means." The court recognized the city's interest in "protect[ing] minors from detrimental, corrupting influences" but held that the "[c]ity's stated purposes . . . may be achieved in ways that are less intrusive on minors' freedom to associate." The U.S. Supreme Court granted *certiorari*. Did the Dallas ordinance violate any constitutional right of association? Did a rational relationship exist between the ordinance's age restriction and the city's interests? [See *City of Dallas* v. *Stanglin*, 490 U.S. 19 (1989).]

3. Montana's Dangerous Drug Tax Act took effect on 1 October 1987. The act imposes a tax "on the possession and storage of dangerous drugs" and expressly provides that the tax is to be "collected only after any state or federal fines or forfeitures have been satisfied." The tax is either 10 percent of the assessed market value of the drugs as determined by the Montana Department of Revenue (DOR) or a specified amount depending on the drug (e.g., $100 per ounce for marijuana and $250 per ounce for hashish), whichever is greater. The act directs the state treasurer to allocate the tax proceeds to special funds to support "youth evaluation" and "chemical abuse" programs and "to enforce the drug laws." In addition to imposing reporting responsibilities on law enforcement agencies, the act also authorizes the DOR to adopt rules to administer and enforce the tax. Under those rules, taxpayers must file a return within 72 hours of their arrest. These rules also provide that "[a]t the time of arrest, law enforcement personnel shall complete the dangerous drug information report as required by the department and afford the taxpayer an opportunity to sign it." If the taxpayer refuses to do so, the law enforcement officer is required to file the form within 72 hours of the arrest. The taxpayer has no obligation to file a return or to pay any tax unless and until he or she is arrested. About two weeks after the new Drug Tax Act went into effect, Montana law enforcement officers raided the Kurths' ranch; arrested six members of the extended Kurth family; and confiscated all the marijuana plants, materials, and paraphernalia found at the ranch. This raid put an end to the Kurths' marijuana business and gave rise to four separate legal proceedings. In one of those proceedings, the state filed criminal charges against all six and charged each with conspiracy to possess drugs with intent to sell. Second, the county attorney also filed a civil forfeiture action seeking the recovery of cash and equipment used in the marijuana operation. The third proceeding involved the assessment of the new tax on dangerous drugs wherein the DOR ultimately attempted to collect almost $900,000 in taxes on marijuana plants, harvested marijuana, hash tar and hash oil, interest, and penalties. In administrative proceedings, the Kurths contested these assessments. Those proceedings were automatically stayed in September 1988, however, when the Kurths initiated the fourth legal proceeding triggered by the raid on their ranch: a petition for bankruptcy under Chapter 11 of the Bankruptcy Code. In the bankruptcy proceedings, the Kurths objected to the DOR's proof of claim for unpaid drug taxes and challenged the constitutionality

of the Montana tax. The bankruptcy court held that while the assessment of $181,000 on 1,811 ounces of harvested marijuana was authorized by the act, the assessment nonetheless was invalid under the U.S. Constitution as a form of double jeopardy. The court rejected the state's argument that the tax was not a penalty because it was designed to recover law enforcement costs. The district court, holding that the Montana Dangerous Drug Tax Act simply punished the Kurths a second time for the same conduct, affirmed the bankruptcy court's determination. How should the Supreme Court rule in this case? Why? [See *Department of Revenue of Montana* v. *Kurth Ranch*, 511 U.S. 767 (1994).]

4. Feim Azizi illegally entered the United States in early 1986. Soon afterward, the Immigration and Naturalization Service (INS) instituted a deportation proceeding against him, issued an order to show cause, and gave him notice of a hearing. After admitting that he had illegally entered the country, Azizi applied for political asylum. While his application for political asylum was pending, Azizi married Saboet Elmazi, a naturalized U.S. citizen. In January 1987, Mr. Azizi's application for political asylum was denied. The new Mrs. Azizi then filed a petition for an immigrant visa for her husband as an "immediate relative." Under the Immigration Marriage Fraud Amendments, however, an alien who marries a citizen during the pendency of deportation proceedings must reside outside the United States for two years before the INS will consider a petition for an immediate relative visa. In challenging the deportation order of the INS and the denial of the immediate relative visa, the Azizis asserted that they had been denied due process and equal protection. They pointed out that an alien who marries a U.S. citizen while no deportation hearing is pending is given a two-year conditional period to remain in the country; and, if the marriage is still intact at the end of the two years, the conditional status expires. They therefore argued that the deportation order discriminates against people facing deportation hearings in an unfair manner and without any rational basis. Was this rule a denial of due process and equal protection, or was it a legitimate exercise of power by the government? Why? [See *Azizi* v. *Thornburgh*, 908 F.2d 1130 (2nd Cir. 1990).]

5. The Town of Clarkstown, New York (Clarkstown), agreed to allow a private contractor to construct within the town's limits a solid-waste transfer system to separate recyclable from nonrecyclable items and to operate the facility for five years, at which time

Clarkstown would buy it for one dollar. To finance the transfer station's cost, the town guaranteed a minimum waste flow to the facility, for which the contractor could charge the hauler a tipping fee, which, at $81 per ton, exceeded the disposal cost of unsorted solid waste on the private market. In order to meet this waste flow guarantee, Clarkstown adopted a flow control ordinance requiring all nonhazardous solid waste within the town to be deposited at the transfer station. While recyclers like C & A Carbone, Inc. (Carbone) might receive solid waste at its own sorting facilities, the ordinance required such recyclers to bring nonrecyclable residue to the transfer station. The ordinance in effect thus forbade such recyclers to ship such waste themselves and required them to pay the tipping fee on trash that already had been sorted. After discovering that Carbone had shipped nonrecyclable waste to out-of-state destinations, Clarkstown sought a state court injunction requiring that this residue be shipped to the transfer station. Finding the ordinance constitutional, the state court granted summary judgment to Clarkstown, and the appellate division affirmed. On appeal, on what constitutional basis should Carbone focus its arguments? [See *C & A Carbone, Inc.* v. *Town of Clarkstown, New York,* 511 U.S. 383 (1994).]

6. **BUSINESS APPLICATION CASE** In 1978, California enacted its Mobile Home Residency Law. The California legislature found that, because of the high cost of moving mobile homes, the potential for damage resulting therefrom, the requirements relating to the installation of mobile homes, and the cost of landscaping or lot preparation, the owner of mobile homes occupied within mobile home parks needs protection from actual or constructive eviction. Hence, the Mobile Home Residency Law limits the bases upon which a park owner may terminate a mobile home owner's tenancy. These include nonpayment of rent, the mobile home owner's violation of law or park rules, and the park owner's desire to change the use of his or her land. While a rental agreement is in effect, however, the park owner generally may not require the removal of a mobile home when it is sold. The park owner may neither charge a transfer fee for the sale nor disapprove of the purchaser, provided the purchaser has the ability to pay the rent. Consequently, various communities in California adopted mobile home rent control ordinances. In 1988, the voters of Escondido did the same when they approved Proposition K, the rent control ordinance challenged here. This ordinance sets rents back to their 1986 levels and prohibits rent increases without the approval of

the City Council (the council). Park owners may apply to the council for rent increases at any time. In addition, the council must approve any increases it determines to be "just, fair and reasonable."

John and Irene Yee owned the Friendly Hills and Sunset Terrace mobile home parks, both of which were located in the city of Escondido. A few months after the adoption of Escondido's rent control ordinance, they filed a lawsuit in which they alleged that the rent control law represented an illegal taking of their property because the rent control ordinance transferred a discrete interest in land—the right to occupy the land indefinitely at a submarket rent—from the park owner to the mobile home owner. The Yees thus contended that what was transferred from the park owner to the mobile home owner was no less than a right of physical occupation of the park owner's land. Should the Supreme Court agree with the Yees' reasoning? In addition, muster arguments for and against this proposition: The Escondido ordinance represents a valid consumer protection measure for adjusting the relative bargaining power between mobile home owners and mobile home park owners. [See *Yee* v. *City of Escondido, California*, 503 U.S. 519 (1992).]

7. **ETHICAL APPLICATION CASE** In September 1992, the operators of the Women's Health Center (WHC), an abortion clinic in Melbourne, Florida, sought an injunction against certain anti-abortion protestors. At that time, a Florida state court permanently enjoined Madsen and the other protestors from blocking or interfering with public access to the clinic and from physically abusing persons entering or leaving the clinic. Six months later, WHC, complaining that access to the clinic was still impeded by the protestors' activities and that such activities also had discouraged some potential patients from entering the clinic and had had deleterious physical effects on others, sought to broaden the injunction. In issuing this broader injunction, the trial court found that, despite the initial injunction, protestors, by congregating on the paved portion of the street leading up to the clinic and by marching in front of the clinic's driveways, had continued to impede access to the clinic. The trial court found that as vehicles heading toward the clinic slowed to allow the protestors to move out of the way, "sidewalk counselors" would attempt to give the vehicles' occupants anti-abortion literature. The number of people congregating varied from a handful to 400, and the noise varied from singing and chanting to the use of loudspeakers and bullhorns. A clinic doctor testified that as a result of having to run such a gauntlet

to enter the clinic, the patients, owing to heightened anxiety and hypertension, needed a higher level of sedation before they could undergo surgical procedures and thereby faced increased risks from such procedures. The noise caused stress not only for the patients undergoing surgery but also for those recuperating in the recovery rooms. Doctors and clinic workers in turn were not immune even in their homes. The protestors picketed in front of clinic employees' residences, rang the doorbells of neighbors, provided literature identifying the particular clinic employee as a "baby killer," and occasionally confronted the clinic employees' minor children who were home alone. Given this and similar testimony, the state court viewed the original injunction as insufficient "to protect the health, safety and rights of women in Brevard and Seminole County, Florida, and surrounding counties seeking access to [medical and counseling] services." The state court therefore amended its prior order and enjoined a broader array of activities. Although the Florida supreme court had upheld the injunction, the Court of Appeals for the Eleventh Circuit had struck it down. At the U.S. Supreme Court, what constitutional arguments would the parties make? Who should win and why? If you were deciding this case on ethical grounds, with whom would you side—the protestors or the clinic and its personnel? Why? [See *Madsen* v. *Women's Health Center, Inc.*, 512 U.S. 753 (1994), modified at *Schenck* v. *Pro-Choice Network of Western New York*, 519 U.S. 357 (1997).]

8. **CRITICAL THINKING CASE** Wyoming, a major coal-producing state, does not sell coal but does impose a severance tax on those who extract it. From 1981 to 1986, Wyoming provided virtually 100 percent of the coal purchased by four Oklahoma electric utilities, including the Grand River Dam Authority (GRDA), a state agency. After the Oklahoma legislature had passed an act requiring coal-fired electric utilities to burn a mixture containing at least 10 percent Oklahoma-mined coal, however, the utilities reduced their purchases of Wyoming coal in favor of Oklahoma coal. In fact, Wyoming's severance tax revenues had declined by approximately $1.2 million after the passage of the Oklahoma statute. The stipulated facts demonstrated that, from 1981 to 1986, Wyoming provided virtually 100 percent of the coal purchased by Oklahoma utilities. In 1987 and 1988, following the effective date of the act, the utilities purchased Oklahoma coal in amounts ranging from 3.4 to 7.4 percent of their annual needs, with a necessarily corresponding reduction in purchases of Wyoming

coal. When Wyoming sued Oklahoma, Oklahoma first argued that Wyoming had no basis for suing and that the trial court accordingly should dismiss the case. Oklahoma furthermore contended that the Oklahoma legislature's requiring the utilities to supply 10 percent of their needs for fuel from Oklahoma coal, which because of its higher sulfur content cannot be the primary source of supply, permitted Oklahoma thereby to conserve Wyoming's cleaner coal for future use. Wyoming thereupon responded that its reserves of low sulfur, clean-burning, sub-bituminous coal from the Powder River Basin are estimated to be in excess of 110 billion tons, thus, at current rates of extraction, providing Wyoming coal for several hundred years. Oklahoma also submitted that the "saving clause" of the Federal Power Act (§ 824(b)(1))—which reserves to the states the regulation of local retail electric rates, whenever electric power has been transmitted and/or sold in interstate commerce, but leaves all other regulatory issues to the federal government—validates the state act because Oklahoma has deter-

mined that effective and helpful ways of ensuring lower local utility rates include (1) reducing overdependence on a single source of supply or a single fuel transporter and (2) conserving needed low-sulfur coal for the future. In rebuttal, Wyoming maintained that, despite Oklahoma's arguments, nothing in the federal statute or its legislative history would permit even a partial—much less a total—ban or the interpretation that in-state purchasing quotas imposed on utilities in an effort to regulate utility rates are within the "lawful authority" of the states under the federal act. According to Wyoming, Congress merely left standing whatever valid state laws then existed relating to the exportation of hydroelectric energy; that is, by its plain terms, § 824(b) simply saves from preemption under Part II of the Federal Power Act such state authority as was otherwise "lawful." Was Oklahoma correct that the case merited dismissal at the outset? Why or why not? In challenging this law, what argument(s) should Wyoming make? [See *Wyoming v. Oklahoma*, 502 U.S. 437 (1992).]

NOTES

1. *Statistical Abstract of the United States 1998,* 118th ed. (Washington, D.C.: U.S. Department of Commerce), p. 353.
2. 9 Wheat (22 U.S.) 1 (1824).
3. 24 Stat. 379 (1887).
4. 15 Wall. (82 U.S.) 232 (1873).
5. 128 U.S. 1 (1888).
6. 301 U.S. 1 (1937).
7. 336 U.S. 460, 464 (1949).
8. 379 U.S. 241 (1964).
9. 411 U.S. 624 (1973).
10. 514 U.S. 549 (1995).
11. 118 U.S. 356 (1886).
12. 517 U.S. 620 (1996).
13. Ibid. at 635.
14. 515 U.S. 200 (1995).
15. Ibid. at 202.
16. 429 U.S. 190 (1976).
17. *U.S. v. Virginia,* 518 U.S. 515, at 516 and 534 (1996).
18. 499 U.S. 1 (1991).
19. *Cruzan v. Director, Missouri Department of Health,* 497 U.S. 261 (1990).
20. *Lucas v. South Carolina Coastal Council,* 505 U.S. 1003 (1992).
21. 526 U.S. 687 (1999).
22. 512 U.S. 622 (1994).
23. *Turner Broadcasting System, Inc. v. Federal Communication Comm'n,* 520 U.S. 180 (1997).
24. *Reno v. American Civil Liberties Union,* 521 U.S. 844 (1997).
25. "Landlords Win Free Exercise Exemption from Ban on Marital Status Bias in Housing," 67 *U.S.L.W.* (2 February 1999), pp. 1439–1440.

6

DISPUTE RESOLUTION

CALL-IMAGE TECHNOLOGY

A G E N D A

While driving a CIT van, Dan Kochanowski is involved in an accident with another vehicle, causing property damage to both vehicles and physical injuries to the parties inside the other vehicle. Both parties in the other car are planning to file a lawsuit against Dan and the firm. The family will want to know whether CIT is liable for Dan's actions. They will also want to know how CIT should defend itself in this situation. What steps should the Kochanowskis take to minimize their involvement or the involvement of the firm in any future traffic accidents?

The Kochanowskis do not *plan* to be involved in any legal proceedings while conducting their business. They intend to be careful to minimize the chance of a lawsuit. They hope to select clients, customers, employees, and suppliers who will honor their contracts with CIT, so that CIT will not be forced to seek legal relief. The Kochanowskis recognize, however, that inevitably they

and/or the firm are likely to have a legal controversy. From discussions with Amy Chen, and from their experience in the workplace, they realize that lawsuits can be time-consuming and expensive. As a result, they would prefer to be able to settle any disputes or controversies in some alternative manner, if possible. Should they include mandatory arbitration provisions in their contracts with suppliers and retailers? Who should be specified as the arbitrator? Would it be better to include a provision for arbitration or a provision for mediation in their employment contracts? When might the firm want to "rent-a-judge" in settling a controversy? When is it better to negotiate than to litigate?

These and other questions need to be addressed in covering the material in this chapter of the text. Be prepared! You never know when one of the Kochanowskis will ask for your help or advice.

O U T L I N E

Introduction
Costs of Litigation
The Problem
Client's Interview with a Lawyer
Investigation of the Facts
Negotiation of Settlement
A Civil Suit
The Need for Alternatives to a Civil Suit
Negotiation

Mediation
Arbitration
Minitrial
Rent-a-Judge Trial
Small Claims Court
Summary
Discussion Questions
Case Problems and Writing Assignments

INTRODUCTION

People in American society have a great many fears and concerns. Some of these fears may seem irrational—for example, a fear of the dark or a fear of heights. Others are viewed as much more rational to most members of our society—for example, a fear of catching certain diseases or a fear of losing one's job.

One area that causes fear and concern to the average person is involvement in the legal process. For example, someone might fear becoming involved in the legal process as a result of an automobile accident: They may fear either being sued or filing **suit** for the damages.

This chapter explores the stages of a hypothetical case arising from such a situation. While this material may not alleviate your concern or fear, it should help shed some light on *what* is done, *why* it is done, and *how* it all ties together within the workings of our judicial system in a civil suit. Exhibit 6.1 sets out the six stages a **party** is likely to encounter in a civil suit. Each of these stages is examined in more detail as we follow the progress of the suit through the legal system.

COSTS OF LITIGATION

Before pursuing litigation, an individual or business entity should consider the costs involved. There are likely to be direct and obvious costs, and indirect, often hidden, costs. The kinds and amounts of fees will vary depending on the type of litigation. In order to make an informed decision about whether to sue or defend a suit, the parties should consider the probable outcomes of litigation. They should also consider the costs of **alternate dispute resolution (ADR)** and whether it might be effective. Even though some forms of ADR are becoming more formal, time-consuming, and expensive, ADR may still reduce overall costs. There are a number of factors that a potential party should consider before deciding whether to initiate any lawsuit or settle a dispute. Some of the more important ones include:

Suit
Lawsuit; the formal legal proceeding used to resolve a legal dispute.

Party
Plaintiff or defendant in the lawsuit.

Alternate dispute resolution (ADR)
Methods of resolving disputes other than traditional litigation.

E X H I B I T 6.1	**The Six Steps Involved in Most Civil Lawsuits**
Pleadings	The case begins by filing documents identifying the parties (the person suing and the person being sued), explaining what the claim is about, and asking the court to do something—usually to award money.
Service	The person being sued must be formally notified. Service is usually obtained by preparing a summons and then having the summons and a copy of the complaint personally delivered to the defendant.
Discovery	Both sides have to gather facts and information to prepare for trial. Discovery can involve examining documents, records, and other pieces of physical evidence as well as taking the statements of witnesses or the parties themselves.
Pretrial motions	Parties request the court to make procedural decisions or other rulings by filing motions with the court. Motions are often in writing.
Trial	The court hears the evidence offered by both sides and decides issues of both fact and law during this process.
Enforcing the judgment	If a party wins a judgment at trial, he or she still has to collect the money awarded. A judgment can be enforced by putting a lien on property, garnishing wages, or obtaining a court order for the transfer of bank accounts or other property.

- The legal system is unpredictable, and a trial may be very time-consuming.
- It is difficult to determine the likelihood of winning the suit with any degree of certainty.
- The amount of money a party might win (or lose) may determine whether he or she wants to proceed with a trial or seek a settlement.
- The willingness of the opponent to enter into alternate dispute resolution.
- The ability of the other party to pay any judgment might make suing a waste of time and money *or* may make suing seem like the best alternative available.
- The amount that the lawyer(s) would charge, and when they would charge it.
- The amount of court costs, including filing fees.
- The costs that might be incurred in fees, including the fees for preparing exhibits, for medical tests and exams, for **depositions,** for jury consultants, and for expert witnesses (i.e., accountants, economists, and doctors).

> **Deposition**
> The process of asking a potential witness questions under oath before a court reporter.

- The amount of time that the parties, their families and friends, and company employees would spend in preparing for the litigation.
- The manner in which this lawsuit and/or additional publicity would affect the reputations of the parties.
- The effect on the continuing relationship between parties to the suit.
- The stress and emotional toll that the lawsuit will take on those involved.
- Time and effort—for example, employees will be preparing for the litigation in lieu of working on other tasks.
- Distraction from personal and professional goals—for example, employees will be distracted from the goals of the enterprise.

These are some of the primary factors to be considered. In addition, there may be some hidden costs associated with the suit.

THE PROBLEM

Nic Grant, a college sophomore, saved some money earned from a part-time job to take his girlfriend, Nancy Griffin, to dinner at a very expensive and sophisticated restaurant on Mount Washington, overlooking the Point in downtown Pittsburgh. Nic called for Nancy at her apartment in Cranberry Township about six o'clock on June 9 and was driving through Butler County toward the restaurant when his car was struck by a white van with the Call-Image logo on it. The accident happened at the intersection of Route 19 (Perry Highway) and Rowan Road in Cranberry Township, Butler County.

Nic spent the next five days in the hospital. As a result, he did not show up for work and consequently lost his job. He also failed to take his college final examinations and complete his research projects, forcing him to withdraw from college for the semester. Nancy, who did not have a job, also suffered injuries from the impact and sought medical treatment. Nic's roommate, who is taking a course in business law, advised Nic to consult a lawyer.

Dan Kochanowski, a full-time employee of Call-Image Technology, was in Pittsburgh to work at a trade show displaying electronic products. He worked at the booth in the Pittsburgh Convention Center from 8:30 A.M. until 5:30 P.M., with a half-hour lunch break. No one else could leave the Call-Image office for the trade show, so Dan had to work the booth by himself.

Dan packed the sample products in the CIT van and left the Convention Center parking lot at 5:45 P.M. Before heading home, he drove toward Butler, to a restaurant recommended by a friend, Trattoria Restaurant on Main Street. Dan had directions but was unfamiliar with the area. While he was trying to negotiate the streets and follow his friend's instructions, the CIT van hit the car owned and operated by Nic Grant. Call-Image is an Ohio corporation licensed as a foreign corporation doing business in Pennsylvania.

CLIENT'S INTERVIEW WITH A LAWYER

Nic recognized that he needed legal assistance and consulted the local bar association. The local bar association referred him to an attorney, Lyn Carroll. Nic called her and scheduled an initial interview, at which Nic recounted all the facts of that evening, to the best of his recollection. He then mentioned that he had not notified either the driver of the other vehicle or CIT. Ms. Carroll agreed to assist Nic in obtaining compensation and offered to help Nancy as well. Ms. Carroll recognized that it may be a conflict of interest for her to represent both Nic and Nancy, especially if Nic was also negligent in causing the accident. (In order for Lyn Carroll to comply with the ethics rules for attorneys, she sent each prospective client a letter disclosing the possible conflict of interest.) When meeting with Ms. Carroll, Nic asked a number of questions including payment terms and opportunities to negotiate or arbitrate a settlement (i.e., is Ms. Carroll willing to work toward a negotiated settlement?). Will this affect the amount of attorney's fees that will be owed? The three met a few days later to discuss, read, and sign the client-attorney contract. As indicated in the contract, payment will be based on a **contingency fee.** Other possible bases for attorney's fees are not dependent on results: for example, flat rate and hourly rate fees. Whatever the fee arrangement, it is specified in the contract between the client and the attorney. The contract appears as Exhibit 6.2.

Contingency fee
A fee stipulated to be paid to an attorney only if the case is settled or won, or is based on some other contingency or event.

The Kochanowskis decided that it is unwise to ask Amy Chen to defend them in this lawsuit because she is not familiar with personal injury litigation and with the Butler County courts. Instead, the Kochanowskis asked her for a recommendation. She gave them the name of the Pittsburgh law firm of Jones, Murphy, Sabbatino, and Schwartz, which specializes in defending against personal injury suits. The Kochanowskis scheduled an appointment to meet with Jefferson Jones. (Chapter 1 contains additional information about hiring an attorney.)

Even though the accident occurred in Butler County, the defendants can hire an attorney from Pittsburgh, located in Allegheny County. Attorneys are licensed at the state level, not the county level. Once licensed, the attorney can practice law anywhere within the state's jurisdiction. Rules of court and court procedures may vary somewhat from county to county, and the attorney will need to know or learn the rules in Butler County for this trial, as well as knowing the Pennsylvania Rules of Civil Procedure. (Trials in federal court are controlled by the Federal Rules of Civil Procedure.)

INVESTIGATION OF THE FACTS

In the interviews with her clients and in subsequent telephone conversations, Ms. Carroll gathered information concerning the accident. On the basis of this preliminary information, she obtained medical releases from both clients in order to

E X H I B I T 6.2 | **Client-Attorney Contract**

AGREEMENT

THIS CONTRACT entered into, by, and between NIC GRANT and NANCY GRIFFIN, hereinafter referred to as CLIENTS, and LYN CARROLL, hereinafter referred to as ATTORNEY, WITNESSETH:

1. Clients hereby retain and employ attorney to represent them in the prosecution of their claim and cause of action for damages sustained by them as a result of an automobile accident occurring 9 June 2000, on Route 19 and Rowan Road, Butler County, Pennsylvania, resulting in injuries and damages to clients.

2. Clients agree to pay attorney for her services rendered pursuant to this employment contract at the rate of twenty-five percent (25%) if the case is settled prior to trial and at the rate of thirty-three and one-third percent (33⅓%) of the net amount recovered if the case goes to trial.

3. All necessary and reasonable costs, expenses, investigation, preparation for trial, and litigation expenses shall be initially paid for by attorney and then deducted from the amount of any settlement or recovery, and the division between the parties shall be made after deduction of said expenses. Furthermore, clients shall reimburse attorney for all such costs and expenses even if no recovery is made or, in the alternative, if the costs and expenses should exceed the amount of the recovery.

4. Attorney agrees to undertake the representation of clients in the prosecution of the above claims and causes of action, using her highest professional skill to further the interest of said clients in all matters in connection with their claims and causes of action, and to diligently pursue said claims and causes of action.

5. No settlement or other disposition of the matter shall be made by attorney without the written approval of clients.

IN WITNESS WHEREOF, the parties hereto have executed this instrument in triplicate originals this 20th day of June 2000.

CLIENT _____
NIC GRANT

CLIENT _____
NANCY GRIFFIN

ATTORNEY _____
LYN CARROLL

---

review the hospital and medical records. Nic also gave her copies of the hospital bills and the estimate for the car repair. Finally, Ms. Carroll obtained a copy of the police report filed by José Gonzalez, the officer who responded to the accident scene.

After reviewing the file, Ms. Carroll wrote to the university that Nic and Nancy had been attending for proof that they had withdrawn from classes after 9 June 2000. She also wrote to Nic's former employer for information about Nic's wages, normal workweek, and proof that he was fired on 13 June 2000. Once all the material requested was in the file, her preliminary investigation was finished. She concluded that Nic was driving with Nancy in his car on Rowan Road, Cranberry Township, Butler County, when the car was struck by a van operated by Dan Kochanowski. The van was owned by Call-Image Technology and was decorated with permanent signs on both doors advertising Call-Image products. At this point,

Ms. Carroll wrote a letter to an officer of Call-Image. It appears as Exhibit 6.3. It is important that Ms. Carroll determine that there is basis for a suit; attorneys and clients who file frivolous lawsuits may be subject to penalties.

NEGOTIATION OF SETTLEMENT

Upon receipt of the letter of notice, Anna Kochanowski contacted CIT's insurance company to inform them of its contents. The insurance carrier immediately assigned an adjuster to the case. The adjuster contacted Ms. Carroll to ascertain the nature of the injuries. On the basis of this information, the adjuster attempted to

---

E X H I B I T   6.3 | **Letter of Notice**

LYN CARROLL J.D.
Attorney at Law
Suite 654
Butler Savings Building
Butler, Pennsylvania 15205

28 June 2000

Ms. Anna Kochanowski
President
Call-Image Technology
9876 Appian Way
Maineville, OH 44444

Mr. Dan Kochanowski
c/o Call-Image Technology
9876 Appian Way
Maineville, OH 44444   RE: *Nic Grant and Nancy Griffin v. Call-Image Technology*
                                          and Dan Kochanowski

Dear Ms. Anna Kochanowski and Mr. Dan Kochanowski:

I have been retained by Mr. Nic Grant and Ms. Nancy Griffin to represent them in a cause of action arising from your van colliding with the car owned and operated by Mr. Grant on 9 June 2000. Ms. Griffin was a passenger in Mr. Grant's car at that time. My preliminary investigation indicates that the accident was caused by inattention and carelessness by your driver, Mr. Dan Kochanowski, and by improper maintenance of your van.

Should you or your liability carrier wish to discuss this matter with me in order to achieve a just and equitable settlement, please contact me within twelve days from the date of this letter. If I do not hear from you or your representative within that period, I shall file suit against you without further notice.

Sincerely,

Lyn Carroll

LC:rj
cc: Mr. Grant
    Ms. Griffin

negotiate a settlement by offering $17,027 to Mr. Grant and $5,680 to Ms. Griffin. Since the offer covered only out-of-pocket expenses and did not include lost wages and pain and suffering, it was rejected, and Ms. Carroll filed suit on 15 November 2000. (Nic Grant is claiming at least $16,000 and Nancy Griffin at least $8,000 in pain and suffering.) In many situations, the negotiations would be more extensive. Ms. Carroll might have a conference with the insurance adjuster, CIT's attorney, or the insurance company's attorney.

There is some advantage to waiting to initiate suit. Plaintiffs will want to know that their injuries are completely healed and no new injuries are discovered. In this case, waiting might also be an advantage to CIT, since Nic may obtain replacement employment. In general, a plaintiff must be sure to initiate his or her suit by filing the **complaint** before the statute of limitations expires. The suit should also commence before the memories of the parties and witnesses begin to fade. At this time, the attorney should discuss alternatives to litigation.

Complaint
In civil practice, the plaintiff's first pleading. It informs the defendant that he or she is being sued.

A CIVIL SUIT

Filing the Suit

The complaint should be definite and contain sufficient information for the defendant to understand the nature of the litigation and begin his or her defense. Exhibit 6.4 on page 158 shows the plaintiffs' original complaint, which was filed in the **Court of Common Pleas.** After it was filed, the **prothonotary**'s office delivered a copy to the sheriff. (In many states, the clerk of court's office performs the same functions as the prothonotary's office.) The sheriff then serves copies of the complaint on all the defendants. Depending on the type of suit and the state, any responsible adult who is not a party to the suit may be able to serve the complaint. In some states, the complaint is accompanied by a **summons.**

Court of Common Pleas
Title used in some states for trial courts of general jurisdiction.

Prothonotary
Title used in some states to designate the chief clerk of courts.

Since Call-Image is registered as a foreign corporation, its complaint was delivered by mail to Anna at the principal office of the corporation. Many states permit service of process for registered foreign corporations on their own secretary of state. If Call-Image Technology or Dan Kochanowski had planned to claim that the court lacked jurisdiction over them or the lawsuit, they would have done it at this time instead of filing a general answer. (See Chapter 4 for a discussion of jurisdiction.) Call-Image or Dan Kochanowski could ask to have the case removed to federal court under diversity jurisdiction if the jurisdictional amount is met (see Chapter 4).

Summons
A writ requiring the sheriff to notify the person named that he or she must appear in court to answer a complaint.

Sometimes the defendant does not answer the complaint. In these cases, the court will generally enter a *default judgment*, a judgment in default of the defendant's appearance. Since the court is only listening to the plaintiff's side, the judgment generally awards the plaintiff what he or she is requesting. Default judgments are valid in civil cases if the court has proper jurisdiction, including jurisdiction over the defendant, and the defendant has been properly served in the case. Exhibit 6.5 on page 159 displays a copy of the defendants' answer. Most complaints and answers will be more detailed than these examples and must include individual numbered items specifying the details that constitute the legal cause of action.

At this point in the proceedings, the plaintiffs have filed suit against the defendants in a court of law, and the defendants have filed an answer. Before trial, both attorneys may simplify the legal issues, amend their complaints and answers, and attempt to limit the number of expert witnesses, if any. The purpose is to reduce costs and the length of trial.

EXHIBIT 6.4 | Plaintiffs' Original Complaint

Plaintiffs' Original Complaint
COURT OF COMMON PLEAS OF BUTLER COUNTY, PENNSYLVANIA

NIC GRANT	:	A.D. No. 23465
and	:	
NANCY GRIFFIN, Plaintiffs	:	Civil Action Law
	:	
V.	:	A jury trial is demanded.
	:	
CALL-IMAGE TECHNOLOGY[a]	:	
and	:	
DAN KOCHANOWSKI[b], Defendants	:	

NOW COME NIC GRANT and NANCY GRIFFIN, hereinafter called PLAINTIFFS, complaining of CALL-IMAGE TECHNOLOGY, a foreign corporation doing business in the Commonwealth of Pennsylvania, and DAN KOCHANOWSKI, hereinafter call DEFENDANTS, who may be served with citation by service, upon Call-Image's statutory agent and Mr. Kochanowski's place of employment, ANNA KOCHANOWSKI, 9876 Appian Way, Maineville, Ohio, and for cause of action would respectfully show unto the court that:

On or about 9 June 2000, plaintiffs were driving on Rowan Road, Butler County, Pennsylvania. As a result of defendants' negligence, plaintiffs have incurred, and will continue to incur, various medical expenses; they have suffered, and will continue to suffer, pain; Mr. Grant has been unable to work and has already lost wages in the sum of $10,000.00; Mr. Grant's ability to earn wages in the immediate future has been temporarily impaired; and plaintiffs have suffered a loss of tuition incurred in the course of furthering their education by having to leave school and by having to postpone their graduation date by one semester.

WHEREFORE, plaintiffs demand judgment against defendants, individually, jointly, and/or severally in an amount in excess of $50,000.00[c], their costs, and all other proper relief.

LYN CARROLL
Attorney at Law
Suite 654
Butler Savings Building
Butler, PA 15205
(412) 555-0123

---

a. If Call-Image Technology was not a corporation, but was the name under which the Kochanowski family did business, the complaint would name Anna and Tom Kochanowski, d.b.a. Call-Image Technology (d.b.a. is an abbreviation for "doing business as" that is used when people operate a business under another name).

b. Some states, including California, permit a plaintiff to include "John Doe(s)" as defendant(s), if the plaintiff does not know the true names of all the defendants. Then the plaintiff can add the defendant(s) later, if it would be just to do so.

c. Many courts today require compulsory arbitration for smaller cases. For example, in Butler County, cases under $10,000 will be referred to compulsory arbitration. The arbitrators there consist of a panel of three attorneys who have agreed to serve as arbitrators. A party who is not satisfied with this arbitrators' award could appeal to the Court of Common Pleas.

E X H I B I T 6.5 | **Defendants' Answer**

Defendants' Original Answer

COURT OF COMMON PLEAS OF BUTLER COUNTY, PENNSYLVANIA

NIC GRANT	:	A.D. No. 23465
and	:	
NANCY GRIFFIN, Plaintiffs	:	Civil Action Law
	:	
V.	:	
	:	
CALL-IMAGE TECHNOLOGY	:	
and	:	
DAN KOCHANOWSKI, Defendants	:	

NOW COMES CALL-IMAGE TECHNOLOGY and DAN KOCHANOWSKI, defendants in the above styled and numbered cause, and for answer to Plaintiffs' Original Complaint would respectfully show unto the court:

Defendants deny each and every material allegation contained in Plaintiffs' Original Complaint. In addition, defendants allege that it was the negligent driving of Nic Grant that caused plaintiffs' injuries and the injuries of the defendants.

WHEREFORE, having fully answered, defendant prays that the complaint be dismissed, for their costs, and for all other proper relief, including damage to the Call-Image van.

JONES, MURPHY, SABBATINO, and SCHWARTZ
Suite 1010
First National Bank Building
Pittsburgh, PA 15205
(412) 555-0191

By _____

ATTORNEYS FOR DEFENDANTS

ON 14 December 2000 the original of this answer was filed in the Prothonotary's office. A copy of this answer was mailed to Ms. Lyn Carroll, attorney for plaintiffs, Suite 654, Butler Savings Building, Butler, Pennsylvania 15205.

By _____

JEFFERSON JONES

Pretrial Proceedings

At this point, the discovery process begins. *Discovery* is a general term that applies to a group of specific methods used to narrow the issues to be decided by the trial. Lawyers use the process to shorten the actual trial, if there is one, or to eliminate the need for a trial if the case can be settled before trial. If one side sees that there is little hope they can win the suit, it is in their best interests to settle the case. The scope of discovery is very broad. Generally, one can discover all information that is relevant even if it cannot be introduced as evidence during the trial. The test

6.1 | MANAGEMENT

PREPARING TO MEET WITH THE ATTORNEY

Anna and Dan are preparing for their first meeting with Jefferson Jones, and they are understandably nervous. They would like to know what information they should collect and take to the meeting. They would also like to know what they should expect at the meeting. They ask you to make a list of the information that would be legally relevant to this lawsuit. What will you tell them?

BUSINESS CONSIDERATIONS Frequently, a business will have certain items it wishes to treat in a confidential manner, but the business may need to reveal some or all of this information to its attorneys in a legal proceeding. What steps should the law firm take to protect the confidentiality of its clients? What procedures should the business follow to maximize its protection while still being as open and honest as necessary with its counsel? **ETHICAL CONSIDERATIONS** Suppose that the known facts make it relatively obvious that a business is liable for the wrongful conduct of one of its agents. Is it ethical for the business and its attorneys to use expensive and time-consuming delaying tactics in an effort to persuade the injured party to settle out of court? Would it be ethical to seek an alternate form of dispute resolution rather than going to trial?

Impeach
To question the truthfulness of a witness by means of some evidence.

Subpoena duces tecum
A court order to produce evidence at a trial.

is whether the discovery request is reasonably calculated to lead to admissible evidence. Exhibit 6.6 depicts the five common discovery devices.

Depositions. Traditionally, a *deposition* is the reducing to writing of a witness's sworn testimony taken outside of court. The testimony begins with the witness swearing that the testimony will be truthful. If it is not, the witness can be held in contempt as President Clinton was in Paula Jones's case.[1] Increasingly, attorneys also videotape the deposition. This is permitted in a number of jurisdictions, including federal courts (Federal Rules of Civil Procedure § 30[b][2]) and California courts (California Civil Procedure § 2025[p]). If the deposition is later used at trial, the jury will view the film of the deposition instead of having the deposition read to them. Generally, this is more interesting, and the jurors are more likely to pay close attention to the questions and answers. Depositions are used routinely today. They are used to preserve testimony from someone who, for good cause, may not be able to attend the trial. They are also used to **impeach** the witness when the witness does appear at trial and gives evidence that conflicts with what he or she gave at the time the deposition was taken. A deposition may be obtained from *any* party *or* witness.

Interrogatories. *Interrogatories* are written questions from one side to the other. Like depositions, interrogatories produce a written record of answers to questions. However, because both the questions and the answers are written, the answers are not as spontaneous as in a deposition. The answer is made under oath, but the respondent has the time to contemplate and carefully phrase the written answers to the questions posed. Interrogatories may be obtained from any party to the lawsuit but *not* from other witnesses. That is, if a witness is neither a plaintiff nor a defendant, an interrogatory may not be obtained from them.

Production of Documents and Things. In many lawsuits, testimony alone is insufficient to win the case. In Nic and Nancy's case, Ms. Carroll also must introduce the records of the two doctors, the hospital, and the police report. Because of the circumstances, Ms. Carroll may also request that CIT produce records it possesses reflecting when and where the van was bought and any internal CIT communications used in tracking repair records and mechanical difficulties. The legal form used to obtain those documents is called a **subpoena duces tecum.**

Physical or Mental Examination. Whenever the physical or mental condition of a party to the suit is in question, the court may order that party to submit to an examination by a physician. Here, both the present condition of the plaintiffs and their physical condition prior to the accident are in question, so a medical examination is necessary.

EXHIBIT 6.6 | **Discovery**

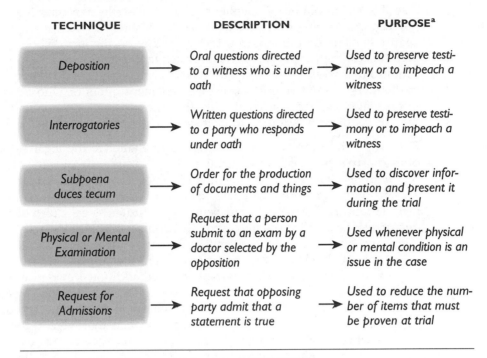

TECHNIQUE	DESCRIPTION	PURPOSE[a]
Deposition	Oral questions directed to a witness who is under oath	Used to preserve testimony or to impeach a witness
Interrogatories	Written questions directed to a party who responds under oath	Used to preserve testimony or to impeach a witness
Subpoena duces tecum	Order for the production of documents and things	Used to discover information and present it during the trial
Physical or Mental Examination	Request that a person submit to an exam by a doctor selected by the opposition	Used whenever physical or mental condition is an issue in the case
Request for Admissions	Request that opposing party admit that a statement is true	Used to reduce the number of items that must be proven at trial

a. One of the purposes of all discovery techniques is to obtain information

Request for Admission. One party can serve on the other party a written request for an *admission*, which takes the form of a question asked by one party to which the answer is either yes or no. If the party who receives the request fails to answer in a stated period of time (usually 30 days), the matter is deemed admitted. For example, Ms. Carroll may request an admission that Dan Kochanowski was driving the van.

The Result of Discovery. As a result of the discovery process, the attorneys for the defendants, CIT and Dan Kochanowski, informed their clients that it appears the accident was primarily caused by Dan's negligence and his unfamiliarity with the streets. Mr. Jones recommended a settlement offer of $23,000, and the Kochanowskis agreed. Ms. Carroll informed her clients of the offer and recommended rejection. A settlement offer is really an offer to negotiate. Nic and Nancy rejected the offer, and the case went to trial.

Pretrial Conferences. Many courts now utilize pretrial conferences to encourage the parties to settle the dispute themselves. Depending on the situation, participation in settlement conferences may be mandatory or voluntary. However, not all judicial systems and judges favor these conferences. Often the pretrial conferences result in a settlement. Even if they do not, they generally succeed in clarifying the legal and factual issues involved in the case.

Businesspeople need to be aware that *many* courts require the parties to participate in pretrial conferences. Some jurisdictions base the requirement on the amount of damages. In Butler County, for example, during pretrial conferences, the attorneys meet with the judge. The parties are requested to be available either outside the courtroom or by telephone. Then, if a settlement offer is made, the attorney can quickly inform his or her client and obtain a prompt response. This procedure is common in many courts. Depending on the jurisdiction and the judge's preferences, the judge *may* take a very active role in attempting to fashion a compromise that would be acceptable to both parties. Some judges may be harsh with parties who do not accept reasonable settlement offers or who do not participate in pretrial conferences in good faith. In some jurisdictions, nonbinding arbitration may be required in addition to or instead of a settlement conference.

Demurrer. The purpose of a demurrer is to challenge the legal sufficiency of the other party's pleading as a pleading. For example, demurrers can be raised to the plaintiff's complaint, the defendant's answer, or the defendant's counterclaim. The grounds for a demurrer are usually limited by statute. Common grounds include failure to state facts sufficient to constitute a legal cause of action (general demurrer); lack of jurisdiction (special demurrer); lack of capacity to sue (special demurrer); and uncertainty or ambiguity (special demurrer).

A general demurrer only challenges defects that appear on the *face* of the pleading. At this point, the parties cannot produce additional evidence or sworn statements. Each jurisdiction has different requirements as to what constitutes a sufficient pleading and the amount of detail required. In deciding whether to grant a demurrer, the court must accept as true all the facts that were in the pleading. The issue is whether, assuming all the facts that are pleaded are true, they would entitle the plaintiff to any judicial relief. If the demurrer is denied, the party requesting the demurrer will be given time to answer. If the demurrer is granted, generally the losing party will be given permission to amend the pleading to make it sufficient.

Demurrers have been abolished before federal courts. In federal courts, a party would use a **motion** to dismiss instead of a general demurrer. Motions to dismiss are discussed in the following section.

Motion to Dismiss. Depending on the jurisdiction, motions to dismiss can be raised on the same grounds as general or special demurrers. A motion to dismiss can be made after different pleadings. When a court considers a motion to dismiss, it *generally* accepts that the material facts alleged in the complaint are true. The pleading is construed in the light most favorable to the party who filed it. The pleading need only state a claim upon which relief can be granted. The purpose of a motion to dismiss is to avoid the expense of unnecessary trials.

If the motion to dismiss is granted, it may be with or without prejudice. If the motion is granted *without prejudice,* the plaintiff can amend and refile the complaint. In some jurisdictions, there is an absolute right to amend once. The judge will often establish a deadline for amending the complaint. If the motion is granted *with prejudice,* the plaintiff cannot revise the complaint and the trial is terminated. A motion to dismiss is a final decision in the case that can be appealed. Many of the cases in this text were decided on a demurrer or a motion to dismiss.

Motion for a Summary Judgment. A *motion for a summary judgment* is a request to have the judge declare one side the winner because there are no material issues of fact. It is a technique for *going beyond the allegations stated in the pleadings* and attacking the basic merits of the opponent's case. Traditionally, it was difficult to obtain

Motion
Request to a judge to take certain action. These requests are often in writing.

summary judgment, because most courts believed that its use violated the non-moving party's right to a trial. Other courts indicated that there was no *right* to a trial when there was no genuine dispute about the facts. The modern view is that there is no right to a trial under these circumstances, and courts today are thus more willing to grant summary judgments.

This technique permits the examination of evidentiary material, such as admissions and depositions, without a full-scale trial. The purpose of a motion for a summary judgment is to avoid the expense of unnecessary trials. Consequently, it is usually decided before trial. Either party can file a motion for summary judgment. The party filing the motion must make an initial showing to justify the court's review. The opposing parties are entitled to have time to present their own materials. The length of time depends on the jurisdiction. The standard for granting a summary judgment is that *no genuine issue or no triable issue exists as to any material fact.* If this standard is satisfied, the moving party is entitled to a judgment as a matter of law. In some jurisdictions, the court will not consider the pleadings in making its decision. The court can grant a partial summary judgment on some issues or claims and not on others. In most courts, summary judgment is procedurally distinct from *judgment as a matter of law* even though they use essentially the same standard. It is also distinct from motions on the pleadings, which only permit the court to review the pleadings and do *not* permit review of evidence.

On Nic and Nancy's behalf, Ms. Carroll introduced a motion for a summary judgment claiming that no material facts appear to be in dispute; rather, the case is merely a matter of applying the law.

The Trial

In Nic and Nancy's case, the judge denied the plaintiffs' pretrial motions; the legal process continues. The actual trial proceeding is governed by technical rules of trial practice. Generally, representation in court is best left to the attorneys. A good plaintiff or defendant, however, takes an active role in assisting the lawyer.

Jury Selection. A legal case can be resolved by a trial before a judge, without a jury. The judge then decides questions of fact *and* questions of law. Such a trial is often less expensive and less time-consuming. Nic Grant and Nancy Griffin agree with their attorney that a jury will generally favor the plaintiffs and their arguments and elect to have a jury trial. A request for a jury trial must be made in a timely manner. This was noted on the plaintiffs' original complaint (Exhibit 6.4).

Members of the jury are referred to as **petit jurors.** Traditionally, civil juries consisted of 12 jurors. Some jurisdictions have reduced this number in civil trials. Generally, 6 to 12 jurors are used. In federal court, a civil jury also consists of 6 to 12 members.[2]

Alternate jurors may also be selected. Alternate jurors sit with the regular jurors and hear the evidence. If a regular juror becomes ill or has to leave the jury for some reason, an alternate "joins" the jury and it continues to function. Without alternate jurors, the judge would have to select a new jury and begin the trial again. An alternate juror can even substitute for a regular juror during deliberations in some jurisdictions: The jury will then start its deliberations from the beginning.

Most states select potential jurors from the voter registration list or the list of licensed drivers or both. The prospective jurors may be required to complete a juror information form. The form elicits information on which the respective attorneys may base their questions to the jury in what is called the *voir dire* examination.

Petit jurors
Ordinary jurors comprising the panel for the trial of a civil or criminal action.

Voir dire
The examination of potential jurors to determine their competence to serve on the jury.

This process is an important part of the trial. Questions need to be asked in the proper manner to obtain helpful, accurate answers, without offending potential jurors. The information offered by the prospective jurors is used by the judge and counsel as the basis for challenging jurors as biased and, thus, ineligible for service. The attorneys for both parties and/or the judge can ask questions. For example, an attorney may request that the judge ask any potentially embarrassing questions so that the attorney can try to maintain good rapport with the potential jurors. Generally, the procedure is that the attorneys submit written questions to the judge prior to voir dire. In some jurisdictions, the judge may control voir dire by asking all the questions of the potential jurors. At the opposite extreme—New York, for example—voir dire is conducted by the attorneys outside the courtroom; the judge is called in only if problems arise. The procedure depends on the rules of court and the judge's preferences in courtroom procedure. In civil disputes in Butler County, the judge usually conducts voir dire of all the prospective jurors at one time. In Nic and Nancy's case, for example, if a potential juror happened to work for CIT, Ms. Carroll would challenge that person and request that the judge excuse the person. On the other hand, if one of the prospective jurors is a member of Nic's fraternity, Mr. Jones would examine the student very carefully to see whether he or she would favor a fellow member.

There are businesses that specialize in assisting parties in selecting sympathetic jurors. These *jury consultants* come from varying backgrounds including psychology, sociology, and marketing. They investigate the backgrounds of potential jurors and collect statistics about the reactions of some socioeconomic groups to trials generally and to issues that are expected to arise in the particular trial on which they are consulting.

Jury consultants sometimes arrange a *shadow jury* consisting of "jurors" with demographic backgrounds similar to the impaneled jurors. The shadow jury sits in the public area of the courtroom, and members report their impressions of the evidence. This can be particularly helpful in highly technical cases, where there is a concern that the jurors may be confused by the details. Through this technique, attorneys can have continuous feedback on how their presentation is being perceived.

Another technique is the *mock jury*—the lawyers practice their case before a group of mock jurors with demographic backgrounds similar to those of the actual jurors.

Two methods exist for dismissing prospective jurors. First, a potential juror can be removed *for cause.* When a juror is removed for cause, generally, an attorney first suggests to the judge that the juror will probably be biased. Challenges for cause occur if (1) the juror has a financial stake in the case or similar litigation; (2) members of the juror's family have such an interest; or (3) there is reason to believe the juror will be partial. The judge then decides whether he or she agrees; if so, that potential juror is dismissed. The judge can also make this decision on his or her own initiative. (When a judge raises an issue on his or her own, we say that the judge does it **sua sponte.**) There is no limit on the number of potential jurors who can be removed for cause.

A second technique is to remove a prospective juror by the use of a *peremptory challenge.* Unlike removal for cause, each side is allotted a limited number of peremptory challenges. The judge decides about the number of peremptory challenges prior to beginning the jury selection process. In federal court, for example, each side receives three peremptory challenges.[3] With peremptory challenges, an attorney does not need to discuss his or her reasons for wanting to remove the

Sua sponte
Voluntarily, without prompting or suggestion, of his or her own will or motion.

juror. The purpose of peremptory challenges is to allow each side to act on hints of bias that may not be provable or even rationally explainable. Some attorneys act on their intuition in deciding who to eliminate from the jury. The attorney intuitively decides which potential jurors he or she trusts and which he or she does not trust. The attorney then uses peremptory challenges to eliminate those potential jurors in whom there is the greatest distrust. The use of these challenges is discretionary with the attorney. Historically, there have been no limits on the use of this discretion. Recent court decisions, however, have determined that one side may not use peremptory challenges to remove jurors of one gender, religion, race, or color from the jury. The U.S. Supreme Court has specifically ruled that peremptory challenges cannot be used to remove prospective jurors on the basis of their gender.[4] The court discusses restrictions on peremptory challenges in the following case.

6.1

WEBER V. STRIPPIT, INC.
1999 U.S. APP. LEXIS 17919 (8TH CIR. 1999)

FACTS . . . In May 1990, Weber was hired by defendant Strippit, Inc. as an international sales manager for various Asian markets. . . . After an initial training period at Strippit's headquarters in Akron, New York, Weber was officed out of his home in Minnesota. On February 2, 1993, Weber, then 54 years old, suffered a major heart attack. . . . About a month later, Weber was again hospitalized. . . . Following his second hospital stay, Weber was placed on strict physical limitations and was advised by his doctor not to work for nearly two months. On numerous occasions in 1993 and 1994, Weber was hospitalized for his heart disease, hypertension, anxiety, and related conditions. Weber continued to perform his job responsibilities throughout this period.

Beginning in October 1993, several months after Weber had returned to work following his second hospitalization, defendants required Weber to complete further training and advised him of the possibility that he would be required to relocate to Akron. In January 1994, Strippit reduced Weber's commissions and informed him that his employment could be terminated at anytime. Weber underwent another angioplasty in early 1994. . . . [D]efendants informed Weber that he must relocate to Akron. Defendants eventually ordered Weber to either relocate to Akron or, if he was unwilling to leave Minnesota, to accept a position as a domestic sales engineer at a much lower salary. Weber told defendants that his doctor advised him to remain in Minnesota for six months for medical reasons prior to relocating. Defendants refused to wait the six months and, by the end of October 1994, Weber was either terminated or abandoned his employment.

. . . After Weber had presented his case at trial, the district court granted judgment as a matter of law for defendants on Weber's actual disability claim under the Americans with Disabilities Act (ADA) and Minnesota Human Rights Act (MHRA). . . . At the conclusion of trial, the jury returned a unanimous verdict for defendants. Weber filed a post-trial motion for judgment as a matter of law or . . . for a new trial, which the district court denied. Weber timely appealed. . . .

During jury selection, defendants exercised all three of their peremptory challenges to remove jurors over the age of fifty. At that time, and again as part of his motion for a new trial, Weber alleged that defendants violated his right to a representative jury through this use of their peremptory challenges. . . .

ISSUE Did the defendants violate Weber's rights by using their peremptory challenges to remove older jurors?

HOLDING No. Excluding jurors on the basis of age is not analogous to excluding jurors on the basis of race or gender, and does not violate the rights of the plaintiff.

REASONING In *Batson*, the Supreme Court held that the equal protection clause forbids prosecutors from striking jurors solely on account of their race. The Court subsequently extended *Batson* to counsel participating in jury selection in civil cases, and to peremptory challenges based on gender. . . . [T]he

continued

6.1

WEBER V. STRIPPIT, INC., *continued*
1999 U.S. APP. LEXIS 17919 (8TH CIR. 1999)

party asserting an equal protection violation must make a *prima facie* showing that the other party exercised a peremptory challenge on the basis of race or gender; the burden then shifts to the challenging party to offer a non-pretextual race or gender-neutral explanation for their strikes.

Neither the Supreme Court nor any other court has extended *Batson* to peremptory challenges based on age. Several circuits, in fact, have expressly considered and rejected the claim that *Batson* applies to age-based challenges, and other circuits have accepted age as a legitimate race or gender-neutral factor for exercising peremptory challenges.

We decline to extend *Batson* to peremptory challenges based on age. . . . "[T]he practice of allowing peremptory challenges may be overridden only for the strongest constitutional reasons." Age, unlike race or gender, is not a suspect classification subject to strict or even heightened scrutiny under the equal protection clause. Thus, an age-based motivation for exercising peremptory challenges does not violate equal protection.

Even if *Batson* were extended to age-based peremptory challenges, the district court assessed the age-neutral reasons for defendants' exercise of their peremptory challenges. . . . Defendants had requested, for instance, that one of the three jurors be excluded because her brother-in-law had made claims of age discrimination against a former employer; when the court declined to strike the juror for cause, defendants exercised a peremptory challenge to exclude the juror. The district court further found that all three jurors' answers during voir dire could support defense counsel's view that the jurors were predisposed to rule against defendants. . . . [T]he district court's findings on discriminatory purpose were not clearly erroneous . . .

BUSINESS CONSIDERATIONS How could Strippit have handled Weber's employment? Should the parties have used ADR instead of a trial? Why? Which type(s) would seem most appropriate?

ETHICAL CONSIDERATIONS Is it ethical to force Weber to move or be fired? Is it ethical to fire an employee who has suffered heart attacks? Was it ethical for Weber to sue when he refused to be transferred?

The decision about whether to exclude a person from the petit jury may be reached after that individual juror is questioned. In the alternative, it may be made after an entire set of jurors is sitting in the jury box. For example, the judge may then ask each attorney in turn if the attorney has any objections to the jury sitting in the box. A judge may discuss eliminating jurors at both points. The techniques used for jury selection will depend on the rules of court and the judge's preferences.

Removal of Judges. California has a unique procedure that allows each party one peremptory challenge against the judge assigned to the case. This peremptory challenge must be filed before any proceedings begin in front of the judge being challenged.[5]

Most jurisdictions do not permit peremptory challenges to a judge; however, they have other procedures to disqualify a judge. A judge is not permitted to preside over any action in which he or she has any bias, has a financial interest, or is related to any of the parties or attorneys; or if there are any facts that would impair the judge's impartiality. For example, if the plaintiffs have appealed the judge's **gag order** to the state supreme court, the judge may be biased. The judge may raise this issue *sua sponte,* or it can be raised by one of the parties.[6]

Gag order
Order by judge to be silent about a pending case.

Opening Statements. After the jury is chosen, each side has an opportunity to tell the jury what it intends to prove during the trial. This serves as an introduction to the party's case and helps the jury integrate the evidence that follows. The attorney for the plaintiff makes an opening statement, followed by the attorney for the defendant.

Direct Examination. An attorney questions his or her witnesses after they have been sworn in. Witnesses who lie can be held in contempt. The plaintiffs' attorney questions his or her witnesses first. The rules of evidence include rules concerning what information an attorney may elicit from the witnesses as well as how an attorney may request information from them. (A detailed discussion of these rules, however, is beyond the scope of this book.)

Trial attorneys are reluctant to ask questions when they do not know how a witness will respond. This is the reason for pretrial preparation of witnesses. Failure to adequately prepare can be disastrous.

Expert Witnesses. An expert witness is a witness possessing special knowledge who offers opinions based on facts that have been produced as evidence. For example, Nic Grant or CIT may call medical experts and accident-reconstruction engineers. Expert witnesses are permitted to testify concerning their opinions. They are allowed to state their own conclusions and to discuss hypothetical situations described by the attorneys. In this way, expert witnesses are distinguished from regular witnesses, who are not permitted to present opinions, conclusions, or respond to hypothetical questions.

Cross-examination. After Ms. Carroll questions each of her witnesses, Mr. Jones has an opportunity to question them. Skillful use of cross-examination by competent counsel is the best means to clarify matters brought up in direct examination. After the cross-examination, the party who called the witness (Ms. Carroll) *may* examine the witness again on redirect, and the opposing party (Mr. Jones) *may* examine the witness on recross.

Courts may accommodate special witnesses, such as experts, by allowing them to testify when it is convenient for the witness's schedule. The process of examination and cross-examination continues until Ms. Carroll has no other witnesses to call. Next, Mr. Jones directly examines his witnesses one at a time, and Ms. Carroll cross-examines each one until the defense has no further witnesses to call. At this point, both sides "rest" their cases.

Motion for a Directed Verdict. A motion for a directed verdict is addressed to the judge. It is usually requested at the close of the opponent's case. The standard used by the judge is whether the plaintiff has made a *prima facie* case on which he or she is entitled to recover. If the plaintiff has *not* presented a *prima facie* case, the

6.2 | MANAGEMENT

SELECTING JURORS

Ms. Carroll and Mr. Jones are conducting the voir dire examination of a prospective juror, Andy Motz. Andy is a 23-year-old business student at the same university as Nic Grant and Nancy Griffin. His father, Ted Motz, is a senior claims supervisor at State-Wide Insurance Company. The Kochanowskis believe that Mr. Jones should exclude this person from the jury. The Kochanowskis ask you what additional questions Mr. Jones should ask Andy before making a decision about possibly removing him from the jury. What additional information would be helpful in making a rational decision? If cause for removal cannot be established, should Mr. Jones use a peremptory challenge to remove this potential juror? What should Mr. Jones do if he disagrees with his clients?

BUSINESS CONSIDERATIONS Should the attorney for a business that sells high-tech, upscale products try to select jurors who have a relatively high income level and a higher-than-average educational level? Would such a firm be better served by waiving their right to a jury trial and letting the judge serve as finder of fact?

ETHICAL CONSIDERATIONS What ethical considerations enter into the jury selection process? Some wealthy parties to lawsuits are able to afford expensive jury consultants and profilers. Does this give them an unethical advantage over people who cannot afford such support?

Prima facie **case**
A case that is obvious on its face. It may be rebutted by evidence to the contrary.

defendant is entitled to a directed verdict. In most jurisdictions, the judge cannot weigh the evidence—the judge must look solely at the evidence produced by the party against whom the motion is sought; accept any reasonable inference from that evidence; and disregard all challenges to the credibility of that evidence. (A minority of jurisdictions permit the weighing of evidence.) If the motion is granted, the court has found that the defendant must win as a matter of law.

If the motion is not granted, the trial will continue. After the presentation of the defendant's evidence, the plaintiff may request a directed verdict on the defendant's cross-complaint and/or the defendant can again request a directed verdict. In some states, a motion for nonsuit is used in a similar manner.

Closing Arguments. After both sides rest, each has an opportunity to persuade the jury by reviewing the testimony, restating the significant facts, and then drawing conclusions from those facts that best support its position. Thus, each attorney takes the same body of evidence and attempts to obtain a favorable decision by emphasizing the evidence favorable to his or her client and minimizing unfavorable evidence. This stage is called *closing arguments* or *summation.*

The Verdict. At the conclusion of closing arguments, the judge discusses the law with the jury and charges them to answer certain questions with respect to the evidence **adduced** at trial. As part of the charge, he or she instructs them in the applicable areas of law and defines any legal concepts. This is called the *charge to the jury* or *jury instructions.* Many states now have published standardized jury instructions so that the judge does not have to write new ones each time.

Adduced
Given as proof.

The jury may be requested to reach a general verdict and/or a special verdict. In a *general verdict,* the jury is asked who should win the lawsuit and how much damage was suffered, if any. In a *special verdict,* the jury is asked specific questions about the relevant factual issues in the case.

After the jury withdraws from the courtroom, they *deliberate* on the evidence in private and attempt to reach a verdict. In many jurisdictions, the jury *may* request that parts of the evidence be "read back" to them during the deliberation process. In a civil case, many rules of court do not require a unanimous decision; some even authorize a decision by a majority vote of the jurors. In Pennsylvania, the verdict is valid if at least five-sixths of the jurors agree to it.[7] In federal court, a civil case must be decided by a unanimous jury unless the parties agree to the contrary.[8] After the petit jurors reach a verdict, it is announced in open court. The verdict is the stated opinion of the jury. If the judge concurs in the verdict, he or she enters a judgment. This is the most common type of verdict.

In our case, the jury deliberated and held for the plaintiffs, Nic Grant and Nancy Griffin, for $21,026 and $5,498, respectively. The judgment is the court's official decision and appears as Exhibit 6.7.

Judgment. In most cases, the judge will agree with the jury's verdict. The judge may disagree with it, however. In these situations, the judge may enter a *judgment notwithstanding the verdict.* Traditionally, this was called a judgment *non obstante veredicto,* hence the abbreviation judgment n.o.v. When a judge declares a judgment n.o.v., he or she substitutes his or her own decision for that of the jury. Either a plaintiff or a defendant may be awarded a judgment n.o.v. A judgment n.o.v. is appropriate only if the jury's verdict is incorrect as a matter of law—that is, if there is no substantial evidence to support the jury verdict. Most courts use the same standard as that used for a directed verdict. The court disregards all conflicts in the

E X H I B I T   6.7 | Court's Judgment

COURT'S JUDGMENT

COURT OF COMMON PLEAS OF BUTLER COUNTY, PENNSYLVANIA

NIC GRANT	:	A.D. No. 23465
and	:	
NANCY GRIFFIN, Plaintiffs	:	Civil Action Law
	:	
V.	:	
	:	
CALL-IMAGE TECHNOLOGY	:	
and	:	
DAN KOCHANOWSKI, Defendants	:	

On the 7th day of November 2001 this cause came to be heard, plaintiffs appearing in person and by their attorney, LYN CARROLL, and defendants appearing in person and by their attorneys, JONES, MURPHY, SABBATINO, and SCHWARTZ. All parties announcing ready for trial, a jury composed of Mae Brown and eleven others of the regular panel of the petit jurors of this court was selected and impaneled and sworn according to law to try the issues of fact arising in this cause. After the introduction of all the evidence, the instructions of the court, and the arguments of counsel, said jury retired to consider its verdict, and after deliberating thereon returned unto court the following verdict:

We, the jury, find in favor of the plaintiffs, Nic Grant and Nancy Griffin, and assess their damages as $21,026 and $5,498, respectively.

_____

MAE BROWN, FOREPERSON

IT IS, THEREFORE, BY THE COURT, CONSIDERED, ORDERED, AND ADJUDGED that the plaintiffs, NIC GRANT and NANCY GRIFFIN, are entitled to recover of and from the defendants, Call-Image Technology and/or Dan Kochanowski, the sums of $21,026 and $5,498, respectively, plus their court costs herein expended. Said judgment shall bear interest from this date until paid at the rate of SIX PERCENT PER ANNUM.[a]

ENTERED this 13th day of November 2001.[b]

_____

JUDGE

APPROVED AS TO FORM:

_____

Attorney for Plaintiffs

_____

Attorneys[c] for Defendants

---

a. The rate of interest allowed depends on the jurisdiction. Butler County allows 6 percent.
b. Notice that this is approximately one year after the lawsuit was initiated.
c. This is plural because the defendants are represented by a law firm—Jones, Murphy, Sabbatino, and Schwartz.

Judgment debtor
A person against whom a judgment has been entered.

De novo
The court will hear the case or issue anew.

evidence, does not consider whether the witnesses are credible, and gives face value to the evidence in favor of the party who received the verdict. The party who won the original verdict will likely appeal the judgment n.o.v.

A party who wins a judgment can attach the **judgment debtor**'s property. In the following case, the court addresses whether the deputy violated the owners' rights when attaching the boat and trailer.

6.2

JOHNSON V. OUTBOARD MARINE CORPORATION

172 F.3D 531 (8TH CIR. 1999)

FACTS . . . Following a default judgment for approximately $650.00 against Starfish Marine, Inc., a Lancaster County court issued a valid writ of execution. The writ instructed the sheriff of Lancaster County to execute, or levy, on "any and all personal property of the judgment debtor located at 1812 W. Arlington, Lincoln, NE." Deputy Pekarek determined that the judgment debtor had been dissolved for nonpayment of taxes. He tried to execute the writ at the above address on September 16, 1996. No one answered the door, so Pekarek left a civil process card with instructions to contact him. . . . Three days later, Deputy Pekarek again attempted to contact the occupants of the W. Arlington address . . . and left another card. He . . . learned from the Secretary of State that Marvin Rumery had been the secretary of Starfish Marine, and Lawrence Johnson had been the president and treasurer. On September 24, Pekarek phoned the Rumery residence and left a message stating that he was attempting to serve the writ, and that he intended to levy on the boat in the driveway. Pekarek . . . received a phone call from an individual claiming to be Rumery's attorney. Pekarek . . . explained his attempts to serve the writ and his intention to levy on the boat.

On September 26, Pekarek failed for a third time to speak with anyone . . . [at] W. Arlington. . . . [H]e received a report that Rumery was cleaning out the boat. Pekarek . . . went to the W. Arlington address and spoke with Rumery. Rumery stated that the boat was actually owned by his father-in-law, Lawrence Johnson, but could not produce any documentation of ownership for either the boat or the trailer. . . . Pekarek . . . spoke with Rumery's attorney on the phone, who told Pekarek that he could not levy on the boat. . . . Pekarek seized the boat and trailer and had them towed away. On October 2, 1996, Rumery and Johnson delivered a Notice of Exemptions to the execution, which was filed with the court. . . . On October 11, the county court ordered the boat and trailer released to Rumery and Johnson.

ISSUE Did the sheriff and deputies violate Rumery and Johnson's rights under the Fourth and Fourteenth Amendments of the Constitution?

HOLDING No. The sheriff and the deputies were acting under a valid writ and did not act in an unreasonable manner in seizing the property.

REASONING We review a grant of summary judgment *de novo,* considering all evidence in a light most favorable to the nonmoving party. A motion for summary judgment should be granted if there is no genuine issue of material fact and the moving party is entitled to judgment as a matter of law. We may uphold a grant of summary judgment for any reason supported by the record, even if different from the reasons given by the district court.

Public servants may be sued under [U.S.C.] section 1983 in either their official capacity, their individual capacity, or both. The amended complaint does not specify in what capacity the law enforcement defendants are being sued. . . . This court has held that, in order to sue a public official in his or her individual capacity, a plaintiff must expressly and unambiguously state so in the pleadings. . . . Absent . . . an express statement, the suit is construed as being against the defendants in their official capacity. A suit against a public employee in his or her official capacity is merely a suit against the public employer. . . . A political subdivision may be held liable for the unconstitutional acts of its officials or employees when those acts implement or execute an unconstitutional policy or custom of the subdivision. . . . Rumery and Johnson have failed to allege facts—or produce evidence—showing that the deprivation of their property was the result of a policy or custom of Lancaster

JOHNSON V. OUTBOARD MARINE CORPORATION, *continued*
172 F.3D 531 (8TH CIR. 1999)

[C]ounty. . . . [T]he plaintiffs have presented nothing that would indicate liability on the part of the county. Thus, summary judgment was proper. . . .

Even assuming . . . the plaintiffs properly named the deputies and the sheriff in their individual capacities, the plaintiffs' case must fail because there are no alleged facts or evidence that suggest a violation of their rights under the Constitution or statutes of the United States, a prerequisite to section 1983 liability. In section 1983 actions against public officials in their individual capacity, a plaintiff must show that the defendant violated "clearly established statutory or constitutional rights of which a reasonable person would have known." . . .

Plaintiffs allege violations of the Fourth and Fourteenth Amendments. The Fourth Amendment prohibits . . . unreasonable searches and seizures by government actors. In the context of the Fourth Amendment, a seizure of property occurs whenever there is "some meaningful interference with an individual's possessory interest in that property." The boat and trailer were undoubtedly "seized." . . . The question is whether there was anything unreasonable about the seizure which would place it among those prohibited by the Fourth Amendment. . . . The deputy was executing a valid writ. . . . Pekarek was informed by a superior that, even if the property was not corporate property, Rumery, as an officer of the dissolved corporation, had no protection from an execution to satisfy the judgment. Rumery was cleaning out the boat, some indication that it was soon to be moved or hidden, and Rumery could not produce any documentation of ownership for either the trailer or the boat. The boat was levied upon in the daylight hours in Rumery's driveway so there were few of the privacy concerns often associated with Fourth Amendment analysis. . . .

The plaintiffs' only argument that the execution was an unreasonable seizure, is that Pekarek was wrong in his belief that he could levy on the boat and trailer, and Rumery's attorney told him so at the time of the levy. This fails for two reasons. . . . [T]he fact that Pekarek was in error does not in itself make the seizure unreasonable. . . . [I]t cannot seriously be suggested that a deputy has an obligation to follow or even believe the legal advice given by a stranger under these facts. Failure to heed the threats or warnings of Rumery's attorney did nothing to make the seizure unreasonable for purposes of the Fourth Amendment. The plaintiffs also claim they were deprived of their property without due process of law in violation of the Fourteenth Amendment. . . . "In general, due process requires that a hearing before an impartial decisionmaker be provided at a meaningful time, and in a meaningful manner." . . . Plaintiffs have not argued that the hearing on October 11 was not meaningful or reasonably prompt. Therefore, . . . due process was satisfied and there was no Fourteenth Amendment violation.

BUSINESS CONSIDERATIONS What could Rumery and his attorney do to prevent the attachment of the property? What type of evidence would have persuaded Pekarek?

ETHICAL CONSIDERATIONS Was it ethical for Pekarek to proceed with the attachment after discussing the matter with Rumery's attorney? Was it ethical for Rumery and Johnson to file this suit?

Post-Trial Proceedings

Motion for a New Trial. A losing party may make a motion for a new trial. This motion is filed with the same judge who originally heard the case, unless that judge is disabled or disqualified. Often the party will request the court to either enter a judgment n.o.v. *or* grant a new trial. The party making the motion is requesting the court to order a new trial. The party must justify the request and explain why a new trial is proper.

Prejudicial
Causing harm, injurious, disadvantageous, or detrimental.

Common grounds for a motion for a new trial include: the judge committed a **prejudicial** error in conducting the trial; irregularities in the jury's behavior; or the evidence was insufficient to support the verdict. In extremely rare cases, a new trial may be granted based on newly discovered evidence. To obtain a new trial on this basis, the moving party must show that the newly discovered evidence pertains to facts in existence at the time of trial; the evidence is material; and the moving party with reasonable diligence could not have obtained the information prior to trial. The latter requirement is to prevent a party from obtaining a new trial when the party was negligent in failing to obtain the evidence for the original trial. A new trial will *not* be granted because a party's attorney in the original trial was incompetent. A new trial *can* be requested by a party who believes that the damage award is excessive *or* too small. When the motion for new trial is based on the amount of damages, a judge may, for example, grant a new trial unless a plaintiff agrees to accept a reduction in the amount of damages. This is called *remittitur.* Some states also permit granting a new trial unless a defendant agrees to accept an increase in the amount of the award. This is called *additur.* Obviously, conducting a new trial is expensive for the parties and the court system.

Appeal. After losing the decision, the attorneys for CIT considered filing a notice of appeal before a higher court. The rules of court specify the time limit for filing a notice of appeal. Appeals, however, are limited to questions of law. In other words, the appellate court will generally not reverse a lower court unless the lower court made an error of law. In this case, the decision is in accordance with the law; consequently, no appeal is filed. CIT now owes the plaintiffs $21,026 and $5,498.

If a case is appealed, the appellate court can *affirm* the decision, which indicates approval, or *reverse* the decision, which indicates an error of law. Appellate courts can affirm some parts of the decision and reverse others. Sometimes the appellate court reverses and *remands* the case because the lower court made a mistake of law, and the case is returned to it for correction. Exhibit 6.8 depicts the stages of a trial.

A Comment on Finality

One of the great virtues of the law is finality. When a cause of action has been litigated and reduced to a judgment and all appeals have been exhausted, the matter comes to an end. At this point, the doctrine of *res judicata* applies. *Res judicata* means that when a court issues a final judgment, the subject matter of that lawsuit is finally decided between the parties to the suit. This doctrine prevents further suits from being brought. In other words, the matter comes to rest. Remember, however, that *res judicata* does not prevent timely appeals, nor does it prevent criminal proceedings based on the same behavior.

THE NEED FOR ALTERNATIVES TO A CIVIL SUIT

Lawsuits are often expensive and time-consuming. A business that is plagued by frequent lawsuits will suffer financially, and the financial burden for businesses facing large class-action lawsuits may be even worse. As a result, many businesses may prefer to seek an alternative form of dispute resolution, such as arbitration. Even the federal government is participating in arbitration. For example, the United States arbitrated the value that was due to the amateur filmmaker Abraham

EXHIBIT 6.8 | **Common Steps of a Trial**

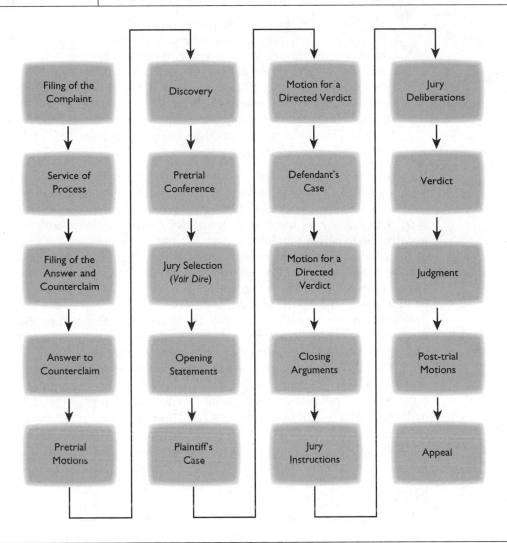

Zapruder for seizing his film of the assassination of President John F. Kennedy.[9] There is normally a significant passage of time between the filing of a lawsuit and the resolution of the case by the court. Even if a plaintiff has what seems to be a good case, there is no guarantee that the plaintiff will prevail at trial. Product liability cases on average have a processing time of 530 days. Moreover, only 40 percent of the plaintiffs in these cases win. For a business defendant, the time spent in preparing for the trial and then having officers attend the pretrial and trial proceedings represents a significant cost factor even if the business wins the case. Many businesses prefer to settle the case—the earlier the better—by paying the plaintiff and saving all the time and trouble that a trial requires. If an alternative means of resolving the dispute were available, those businesses would be likely to use it.

Alternatives to litigation do exist, and these *alternate* forms of *dispute resolution* are becoming increasingly popular. ADR provides a number of benefits:

1. The burden on the court system is reduced.
2. An injured party with a legitimate claim is likely to be compensated sooner. When one considers the time-value of money, this can be a significant factor.
3. Businesses (and other defendants) are less likely to settle specious claims merely for the sake of expediency and/or because the settlement is less expensive than the expenses of a trial.
4. ADR is less adversarial, allowing the parties to reach a more amicable resolution. This, in turn, permits the parties to continue to do business together or to coexist in harmony in the future.

As a result of these—and other—benefits, the use of ADR is becoming more common, especially in the resolution of disputes involving a business. Increasingly, courts are *requiring* parties to attempt alternative methods of dispute resolution first, before allowing them to seek judicial remedies. Because these processes are usually less expensive and faster, they tend to create less tension in the relationship of the parties. This is particularly important in disputes between family members, such as child-custody cases, and in business situations where the parties may wish to continue to do business together. For example, difficulties arose when Whoopi Goldberg was filming the movie *T. Rex*. The parties agreed to use arbitration whenever problems occurred so that they could continue to produce the film.[10] Continuity of relationship is not an issue in Nic Grant and Nancy Griffin's suit against CIT, since the parties do not have an ongoing relationship.

ADR has its limits, and it is not appropriate for resolving every form of legal dispute. ADR cannot be used in criminal matters, for example, and it does not establish legal precedent. In addition, some matters need to be debated in a public forum, which is not provided by ADR. When used within its limits, ADR provides quick and sure resolutions for a number of problems in a manner that is mutually advantageous for all of the parties involved.

NEGOTIATION

Perhaps the earliest, and simplest, form of ADR is *negotiation*. Negotiation involves the discussion and resolution of a controversy between two or more parties by the parties involved. Negotiation is so common that most people do not even consider it a form of ADR. Instead, they think of it as merely a method for settling disputes or controversies. That is the gist of ADR, however—settling a dispute or a controversy without resorting to the courts.

If the parties to the dispute recognize the wisdom in handling the dispute themselves and are willing and able to negotiate a solution acceptable to the parties, negotiation is an excellent method of dispute resolution. If the parties are able to resolve the matter themselves, with or without consulting their attorneys, they can probably save time and money. However, the parties may not *think* of negotiation as a possible solution, or they may not be *willing* to negotiate a settlement. Since negotiation is handled strictly by the parties, all interested parties must be willing to negotiate before it can serve as an effective method for resolving the dispute. Nic and Nancy could try to negotiate a settlement with CIT's insurance company. They may wish to have Ms. Carroll assist them in the negotiation. The insurance adjuster may serve as the representative of the company.

MEDIATION

Mediation is similar to negotiation, although there is a significant difference. Mediation involves the use of an impartial third party, a *mediator,* who attempts to help the parties reach a mutually acceptable resolution to their dispute. Usually, just one mediator is used. The mediator does not act as a decisionmaker; however, he or she facilitates communication. The mediator listens to the parties and assists them in resolving their differences or as many of the aspects of their dispute as possible. There are no formal procedures. The parties may choose to have a lawyer, a family member, or some other adviser present during the mediation. Generally, the mediator should not have any financial or personal interest in the result of the mediation without the written consent of all the parties. A prospective mediator should promptly disclose to the parties any circumstance likely to cause bias or the appearance of bias. The advantages of mediation are that it is less expensive than litigation, it is quicker, and generally the results are perceived as more satisfactory. Participants are typically more satisfied because they agreed to the result. Nic, Nancy, Anna, and Dan could use mediation to attempt to resolve their dispute. The insurance company should also be represented if it is going to be asked for payment. The parties may use a commercial service to locate an appropriate, unbiased mediator. Generally, the mediator does not impose a solution on the parties. Some mediators, however, take a more forceful role in attempting to fashion an agreement; others believe a more passive role is appropriate.

More than one mediation technique can be used in an attempt to resolve the disagreement. One mediation technique is **caucusing.** In this technique, the mediator meets with each party separately. Another mediation technique is **shuttle mediation,** where the mediator physically separates the parties during the mediation session and then runs messages between them. Mediation sessions are private: Usually only the parties, their representatives, and the mediator will be present. Other people generally may only attend with the permission of the parties and the mediator.

In most cases, mediation is successful; however, if it is not, the parties can utilize another ADR technique or submit their dispute for judicial resolution. Consequently, an important principle of mediation is confidentiality; otherwise, the parties will not discuss the issues freely. The parties must be confident that what they say or admit in mediation will not be used against them in court. The parties should agree to maintain the confidentiality of the mediation and not to rely on or introduce into evidence at any arbitration, judicial, or other proceeding the views expressed by a party, suggestions made by a party, admissions made by a party, proposals made by the mediator, views expressed by the mediator, and/or the fact that a party was or was not willing to accept a proposal. The

Caucusing
Mediation technique in which the mediator meets with each party separately.

Shuttle mediation
Mediation technique in which the mediator physically separates the parties during the session and then runs messages between them.

6.3 | MANAGEMENT

SERVING AS A MEDIATOR

Anna Kochanowski has been asked to serve as a mediator in a dispute between two local firms that are each active in telecommunication research. Both firms agreed that their controversy should be resolved without taking the issue to court; both agreed that they needed a person with experience and expertise in the field; and both agreed that Anna possessed the necessary qualifications to mediate their dispute. Anna is concerned about the request, and she has asked you whether she is qualified to serve as a mediator in this situation. What advice will you give her?

BUSINESS CONSIDERATIONS Should a business adopt a policy concerning its officers serving as mediators in disputes? What are the possible drawbacks—or benefits—to having officers mediate disputes between other firms?
ETHICAL CONSIDERATIONS Suppose a businessperson learned about certain new techniques or technical developments while serving as a mediator and this information would be of great use to the businessperson's firm. What ethical considerations would enter into any decision as to whether the information should be used? What legal considerations might enter into this situation?

mediator should not be required to testify or divulge records in any adversarial proceeding. No stenographic record is prepared of the mediation process. An American Arbitration Association (AAA) mediation usually follows these steps:

1. When parties request mediation, a qualified mediator is appointed by the AAA. If the agreement of the parties names a mediator or specifies a method of appointing a mediator, that designation or method is followed.
2. After a mediator has been selected, the first meeting date is arranged.
3. The parties meet with the mediator, who guides their negotiations and helps them to reach a settlement.
4. Private caucuses may be held between the mediator and each party in an attempt to bring disputants closer together.[11]

The proponents of mediator certification believe that standards would encourage the confidence of the courts and the disputing parties. It would also ease civil court backlogs. The opponents to certification feel that it would limit the diversity of mediators at a time when this diversity is in demand. Lawyers, judges, psychotherapists, and ministers have entered the field of mediation. In addition, opponents argue that the profession is still developing and that it is too early for certification; there are no adequate standards for certification. Certification at this time, they say, would be unfair and misleading to the public. In addition, there have been relatively few complaints against mediators.

A mediator should have good problem-solving skills and be fair. Roberta Kerr Parrott, a professional mediator, explains:

The challenge is always, when there's conflict, to create a possibility for both sides, both parties, to win. To make sure that I'm quiet enough long enough to hear what the real issues are so that we're dealing with what people are feeling and thinking at the heart of the issue rather than dealing with the surface.[12]

Knowledge of the law, while important in some cases, is only one possible competency a good mediator needs. Other necessary skills include:

1. Patience, persistence, concentration, and focus toward the goal.
2. The ability to distinguish between stated positions of the disputants and their real interests.
3. The ability to remain positive and constructive, even with difficult parties, while maintaining confidentiality.
4. The ability to remain unbiased in the search for the truth of the situation and the solutions that work best for all concerned under the circumstances.
5. The ability to secure a resolution that is truly satisfactory for the participants: substantively, procedurally, and psychologically.[13]

Standards of Conduct

A model standards of conduct for mediators has been drafted. The standards are nonbinding. The final draft has been available since September 1995 and has been endorsed by the American Bar Association (ABA) section on Dispute Resolution, the ABA section on Litigation, the American Arbitration Association (AAA), and the Society of Professionals in Dispute Resolution.[14] A summary appears as Exhibit 6.9.

The standards do not choose between the conflicting approaches to mediation; instead, they concentrate on the similarities between the approaches. One particularly difficult issue is how active a mediator should be. Some contend that a

E X H I B I T 6.9 | **Model Standards of Conduct for Mediators**

A Mediator shall:

1. Recognize that mediation is based on the principles of self-determination by the parties.

2. Conduct the mediation in an impartial manner.

3. Disclose all actual and potential conflicts of interest reasonably known to the mediator.

4. Mediate only when the mediator has the necessary qualifications to satisfy the reasonable expectations of the parties.

5. Maintain the reasonable expectations of the parties with regard to confidentiality.

6. Conduct the mediation fairly and diligently, and in a manner consistent with the principle of self-determination by the parties.

7. Be truthful in advertising and solicitation for mediation.

8. Fully disclose and explain the basis of compensation, fees, and charges to the parties.

9. Have a duty to improve the practice of the profession.

SOURCE: Reprinted by permission of the American Arbitration Association, New York, NY.

mediator should only *facilitate* the settlement of disputes. Others believe that mediators should *evaluate* the proposals and *comment* on the viability of an approach in court. A number of states—e.g., Florida, Texas, and Indiana—have adopted standards of conduct for mediators.[15]

Compensation

There is no hard-and-fast rule regarding the compensation of mediators. In fact, such compensation can vary widely. Many mediators are volunteers who perform this job through various community organizations. Others are professional mediators who rely on mediation for much of their income. The parties should discuss the compensation issue and how the expenses will be shared before agreeing to submit their situation to mediation. The National Conference of Commissioners on Uniform State Laws (NCCUSL) is drafting the Uniform Mediation Act, which is scheduled to be completed in August of 2000.

ARBITRATION

Arbitration is the process of submitting a dispute to the judgment of a person or group of persons called *arbitrators* for resolution. The final decision of the arbitrator or panel of arbitrators is called an *award.* It is usually binding on the parties. *Advisory arbitration* is similar to traditional arbitration; however, it focuses on specific issues in the dispute, and the award is not binding on the parties.

Arbitration begins with an agreement between the parties to arbitrate, usually in the initial agreement. The parties *can* agree to arbitrate after an actual dispute arises, if they are willing to do so. The terms in an arbitration agreement can vary widely. An agreement to arbitrate is basically a contract or a portion of a contract. Like all contracts, to be valid, it must be based on **mutual assent.** If a party agrees

Mutual assent
The parties agree to be bound by exactly the same terms.

Fraud

When one party enters into a contract due to a false statement of material fact.

Duress

When one party enters into a contract due to a wrongful threat of force.

to an arbitration clause because of **fraud** or **duress,** the agreement will not be valid. (For a detailed discussion of what constitutes a valid contract, see Chapters 9 through 15.) Litigation may ensue if a party feels that the arbitration agreement was invalid. A judge would then determine the legality of the arbitration provision. AAA recommends a standard contract clause such as this one:

> *Any controversy or claim arising out of or relating to this contract, or the breach thereof, shall be settled by arbitration administered by the American Arbitration Association in accordance with its [applicable] rules and judgment on the award rendered by the arbitrator may be entered in any court having jurisdiction thereof.*[16]

Exhibit 6.10 illustrates the steps used in an American Arbitration Association arbitration. The form for submitting a dispute to the AAA appears as Exhibit 6.11.

In arbitration, a hearing is held before an arbitrator or a panel of arbitrators. There are two types of arbitration—binding and nonbinding or advisory. In non-binding arbitration, the parties can consider the decision but do not have to follow it. Generally, a party *cannot* appeal the decision in binding arbitration. There are limited grounds for appeal, including problems of mutual assent in the agreement to arbitrate. Some courts will also consider an appeal if the arbitrator refused to admit evidence that would have been admissible in court.

Many states have statutes that provide for arbitration and the enforcement of the arbitrators' awards in the courts of the state. Statutes in Arizona,[17] California,[18] and Michigan[19] expressly authorize arbitration agreements, as does the Federal Arbitration Act.[20] At one time, the law did not favor arbitration because it was considered an improper means of avoiding the judicial system. Today, that is no longer the case.

Various organizations offer panels of arbitrators. Parties may select their own arbitrator(s), or the arbitrator(s) may be selected by the organization. The AAA, for example, has a specific panel of arbitrators for commercial disputes. It also has

---

E X H I B I T 6.10 | **Steps in an AAA Arbitration**

1. A party files a demand for arbitration with an AAA regional office, and a case administrator is assigned to follow the case through to its conclusion.

2. Other parties named in the demand are notified and replies are requested.

3. The case administrator reviews panel qualifications and lists individuals suitable for the particular case. Information on AAA panelists is maintained on a computer.

4. The list is sent to the parties, each of whom numbers in order of preference the names that it finds acceptable.

5. An arbitrator is selected by the administrator according to the mutual desires of the parties. If the parties are unable to agree, the AAA may appoint an arbitrator.

6. The administrator arranges a hearing date and location convenient to the parties and to the arbitrator.

7. At the hearing, testimony and documents are submitted to the arbitrator, and witnesses are questioned and cross-examined.

8. The arbitrator then issues a binding award, copies of which are sent to the parties by the case administrator.

SOURCE: American Arbitration Association, *Resolving Your Disputes* (November 1995), p. 8. Reprinted with permission of AAA.

E X H I B I T   6.11 | **American Arbitration Association Submission to Dispute Resolution**

American Arbitration Association
SUBMISSION TO DISPUTE RESOLUTION

Date: _____

The named parties hereby submit the following dispute for resolution under the _____
_____ Rules* of the American Arbitration Association.

Procedure Selected: ☐ Arbitration   ☐ Mediation Settlement
                      ☐ Other _____
                                      (Describe.)
FOR INSURANCE CASES ONLY:

_____ _____ to _____ _____
Policy Number   Effective Dates   Applicable Policy Limits

Date of Incident _____   Location _____
Insured: _____   Claim Number: _____

Names of Claimants	**Check if a minor.**	**Amounts Claimed**
_____	☐	_____
_____	☐	_____

Nature of Dispute and/or Injuries Alleged (Attach additional sheets if necessary.):

Place of Hearing: _____

We agree that, if binding arbitration is selected, we will abide by and perform any award rendered hereunder and that a judgment may be entered on the award.

To Be Completed by the Parties

Name of Party _____   Name of Party _____

Address _____   Address _____

City, State, and ZIP Code _____   City, State, and ZIP Code _____
(___)   (___)
        Telephone   Fax   Telephone   Fax

Name of the Party's Attorney or Representative   Name of the Party's Attorney or Representative

Name of Firm (if Applicable) _____   Name of Firm (if Applicable) _____

Address _____   Address _____

City, State, and ZIP Code _____   City, State, and ZIP Code _____
(___)   (___)
        Telephone   Fax   Telephone   Fax

Signed† (may be signed by a representative) Title   Signed† (may be signed by a representative) Title

Please file three copies with the AAA.

* *If you have a question as to which rules apply, please contact the AAA.*
† *Signatures of all parties are required for arbitration.*

Form G1-9/95

SOURCE: Reprinted by permission of the American Arbitration Association, New York, NY.

---

panels for other types of disputes. The parties select their arbitrator from the panel members. Nic, Nancy, Anna, and Dan could contact the AAA to obtain an arbitrator for their dispute.

Arbitrators charge about $400 to $700 a day.[21] Fees vary depending on the region and the type of case. Despite the expense, one finance company reported a 66 percent reduction in legal expenses by using arbitration.[22]

If both parties comply willingly with the arbitration award, no further action is required. If one side does not, court action to "confirm" the decision is necessary.

ARBITRATION AT HOOTERS

Annette Phillips worked as a bartender at a Hooters restaurant in Myrtle Beach, South Carolina, since 1989. She alleges that in June 1996 a Hooters official grabbed and slapped her buttocks. Phillips asked her manager for help and was told to "let it go." She quit her job. Phillips's attorney contacted Hooters claiming that the attack and the restaurant's failure to deal with it violated Phillips's Title VII rights. Hooters responded that Phillips was required to submit her claims to arbitration.

In 1994, Hooters implemented an ADR program. The company conditioned eligibility for raises, transfers, and promotions upon an employee signing an agreement to arbitrate employment-related disputes. Phillips signed the agreement. The agreement said that Hooters and the employee agree to arbitrate all disputes arising out of employment, including "any claim of discrimination, sexual harassment, retaliation, or wrongful discharge, whether arising under federal or state law." It further stated that "the employee and the company agree to resolve any claims pursuant to the company's rules and procedures for alternative resolution of employment-related disputes, as promulgated by the company from time to time. Company will make available or provide a copy of the rules upon written request of the employee." No employee was given a copy of Hooters' arbitration rules and procedures. Hooters sent a copy of the rules to Phillips's attorney.

Under these rules, the employee must provide the company with a notice of her claim at the outset, including the nature of the claim and the specific acts or omissions on which it is based. Hooters does not have to file a response or a list of its defenses. Simultaneously, the employee must provide the company with a list of all fact witnesses and a brief summary of the facts known by each one. The employee's arbitrator and the company do not have to reciprocate. Each party selects an arbitrator, and those two arbitrators select a third arbitrator. The third arbitrator must be selected from a list provided by Hooters. There is no input from the employee in the generation of the list. Hooters is free to make a list consisting solely of managers and people with family and/or financial relationships with Hooters. Nothing in the rules prevents Hooters from retaliating against arbitrators who rule against Hooters. Hooters may expand the scope of the arbitration to any matter, but the employee cannot raise any matter not included in the original notice. Hooters can move for summary dismissal of the employee's claims, but the employee cannot move for summary dismissal of Hooters' claims. Hooters may record the arbitration hearing by audiotaping, videotaping, or verbatim transcription. The employee cannot. Hooters can bring suit to cancel or modify an arbitral award, or Hooters can cancel the agreement to arbitrate upon 30 days notice, but the employee cannot do either. Hooters reserves the right to modify the rules "in whole or in part," whenever it wishes and "without notice" to the employee. Hooters could even modify the rules in the middle of an arbitration.

Hooters filed suit to compel arbitration. Phillips argues that she should not be required to arbitrate. How would *you* rule? Why?[23]

BUSINESS CONSIDERATIONS What factors should a businessperson consider in deciding whether to use ADR rather than going to trial to resolve a controversy? What procedures should a business use when establishing ADR for its disputes with employees?

ETHICAL CONSIDERATIONS Was it ethical for Hooters to require its employees to arbitrate? Are these arbitration provisions equitable? Why or why not?

SOURCE: *Hooters of America, Inc. v. Phillips*, 173 F.3d 933 (4th Cir., 1999).

Controls on Arbitration

The states have developed their own individual approaches and laws to address arbitration issues. Some state statutes are more pro-arbitration than others. Some have attempted to restrict the scope of arbitration. For example, some states (such as Alabama) did not permit arbitration clauses in consumer contracts, although they permitted the use of arbitration and arbitration clauses in other types of contracts.[24] The U.S. Supreme Court addressed this issue in *Allied-Bruce Terminix Companies, Inc. v. Dobson.*[25] (For more on this case, see Case Problem and Writing Assignment 5.) The Alabama Supreme Court, relying on state law, had declared that a consumer did not have to go to arbitration as specified in the arbitration agreement signed by the parties. The U.S. Supreme Court heard the case on writ of *certiorari* to the Alabama Supreme Court and overturned that decision. It ruled that individual states could not regulate or prevent the use of arbitration by their statutes. The Federal Arbitration Act covers all transactions involving interstate commerce. For a more detailed discussion of what constitutes interstate commerce, see Chapters 5 and 39.

The Supreme Court in the following case discusses whether an American with Disabilities Act (ADA) dispute must be arbitrated.

6.3

WRIGHT V. UNIVERSAL MARITIME SERVICE CORPORATION
119 S.CT. 391 (1998)

FACTS . . . Ceasar Wright began working as a longshoreman in Charleston, South Carolina. He was a member of Local 1422 of the International Longshoremen's Association, AFL-CIO (Union), which uses a hiring hall to supply workers to several stevedore companies represented by the South Carolina Stevedores Association (SCSA). Clause 15(B) of the [Collective Bargaining Agreement (CBA)] . . . between the Union and the SCSA provides in part as follows: "Matters under dispute which cannot be promptly settled between the Local and an individual Employer shall, no later than 48 hours after such discussion, be referred in writing covering the entire grievance to a Port Grievance Committee. . . . " If the Port Grievance Committee . . . cannot reach an agreement within five days of receiving the complaint, then the dispute must be referred to a District Grievance Committee. . . . If the District Grievance Committee cannot reach a majority decision . . . , then the committee must employ a professional arbitrator.

. . . [W]hile Wright was working for . . . Stevens Shipping and Terminal Company . . . , he injured his right heel and his back. He sought compensation from Stevens . . . and ultimately settled the claim for $250,000 and $10,000 in attorney's fees. . . . In January 1995 Wright returned to the Union hiring hall and asked to be referred for work. . . . Between January 2 and January 11, Wright worked for four stevedoring companies, none of which complained about his performance. When . . . the stevedoring companies realized that Wright had previously settled a claim for permanent disability, they informed the Union that they would not accept Wright for employment. . . . The Union . . . suggested that the ADA entitled Wright to return to work if he could perform his duties. . . . Wright hired an attorney and . . . filed charges of discrimination with the Equal Employment Opportunity Commission (EEOC) and the South Carolina State Human Affairs Commission, alleging that the stevedoring companies and the SCSA had violated the ADA by refusing him work. . . .

ISSUE . . . [W]hether a general arbitration clause in a . . . CBA requires an employee to use the arbitration procedure for an alleged violation of the . . . ADA?

HOLDING No. The presumption in favor of arbitration is based on disputes involving the collective bargaining agreement. This dispute involves a federal statute, not the CBA, thus negating the presumption in favor of arbitration.

continued

6.3

WRIGHT V. UNIVERSAL MARITIME SERVICE CORPORATION, *continued*
119 S.CT. 391 (1998)

REASONING . . . [W]e find it unnecessary to resolve the question of the validity of a union-negotiated waiver, since it is apparent to us . . . that no such waiver has occurred. . . . In collective bargaining agreements . . . "there is a presumption of arbitrability. . . . " That presumption . . . [is based on] . . . the . . . rationale that . . . arbitrators are in a better position than courts to interpret the terms of a CBA. This rationale finds support in the very text of the [Labor Management Relations Act] LMRA. . . . This case . . . ultimately concerns not the application or interpretation of any CBA, but the meaning of a federal statute. The cause of action . . . arises not out of contract, but out of the ADA, and is distinct from any right conferred by the . . . [CBA]. . . . [Companies] argue that Wright is not qualified for his position as the CBA requires, but even if that were true he would still prevail if the refusal to hire violated the ADA.

Nor is the . . . focus of the claim altered by the fact that Clause 17 of the CBA recites it to be "the intention and purpose of all parties hereto that no provision or part of this Agreement shall be violative of any Federal or State Law." . . . [T]his does not incorporate the ADA by reference. Even if it did so, . . . the ultimate question for the arbitrator would be not what the parties have agreed to, but what federal law requires; and that is not a question which should be presumed to be included within the arbitration requirement. Application of that principle is unaffected by the fact that the CBA in this case . . . does not expressly limit the arbitrator to interpreting and applying the contract. . . . It may well be that ordinary textual analysis of a CBA will show that matters which go beyond the interpretation and application of contract terms are subject to arbitration; but they will not be presumed to be so.

Not only is [Wright's] . . . statutory claim not subject to a presumption of arbitrability; we think any CBA requirement to arbitrate it must be particularly clear. " . . . [T]he waiver must be clear and unmistakable." . . . [T]he right to a federal judicial forum is of sufficient importance to be protected against less-than-explicit union waiver in a CBA. The CBA in this case does not meet that standard. Its arbitration clause is very general, providing for arbitration of "matters under dispute," which could be understood to mean matters in dispute under the contract. And the remainder of the contract contains no explicit incor-

poration of statutory antidiscrimination requirements. . . . [Companies] . . . rely upon Clause 15(F) of the CBA, which states that "this Agreement is intended to cover all matters affecting wages, hours, and other terms and conditions of employment." But even if this could, in isolation, be considered a clear and unmistakable incorporation of employment-discrimination laws . . . , it is surely deprived of that effect by the provision, later in the same paragraph, that "anything not contained in this Agreement shall not be construed as being part of this Agreement." [Companies] . . . also rely upon Clause 17 of the CBA, which states that "it is the intention and purpose of all parties hereto that no provision or part of this Agreement shall be violative of any Federal or State Law." They argue that this requires the arbitrator to "apply legal definitions derived from the ADA" in determining whether Wright is "qualified" for employment within the meaning of the CBA. Perhaps so, but that is not the same as making compliance with the ADA a contractual commitment that would be subject to the arbitration clause. . . . Clause 17 seems to us nothing more than a [statement] . . . that an agreement should be interpreted in such fashion as to preserve, rather than destroy, its validity . . .

Our conclusion that a union waiver of employee rights to a federal judicial forum for employment discrimination claims must be clear and unmistakable means that, absent a clear waiver, it is not "appropriate" . . . to find an agreement to arbitrate. . . . We hold that the collective-bargaining agreement . . . does not contain a clear and unmistakable waiver of the covered employees' rights to a judicial forum for federal claims of employment discrimination. We do not reach the question whether such a waiver would be enforceable. . . .

BUSINESS CONSIDERATIONS Should a business establish an arbitration structure similar to that under the stevedores' CBA? What are the advantages and disadvantages of such a structure?

ETHICAL CONSIDERATIONS Was it ethical for the stevedoring companies to refuse to hire Wright? Was it ethical for Wright to accept the disability payments and then to return to work?

Statutory Coverage

Arbitration is not exclusively applied to state-law issues; it is applicable at the state, national, and international levels. Arbitration is covered at the state level by state statutes, at the national level by federal statute, and at the international level by treaty. The statutory law is clarified by judicial interpretation at all levels. Parties seeking resolution of their disputes through arbitration should ascertain how arbitration is viewed and regulated at the level(s) in which they are involved.

At the state level, the Uniform Arbitration Act has been adopted in 46 states and the District of Columbia, Puerto Rico, and the Virgin Islands. Alabama, Georgia, Mississippi, and West Virginia have not adopted it; they each have their own methods for regulating arbitration.[26] The NCCUSL is drafting a revision of the Uniform Arbitration Act that is scheduled to be completed in 2001.[27]

At the federal level, the Federal Arbitration Act (FAA), originally enacted in 1925, provides some federal guidelines to be followed in arbitration. It also attempts to ensure that arbitration clauses be given the same protection and enforceability as any other contract clauses. Section 2 of the Federal Arbitration Act provides that a "written provision in any maritime transaction or a contract evidencing a transaction involving commerce to settle by arbitration a controversy thereafter arising out of such contract or transaction . . . shall be valid, irrevocable, and enforceable, save upon such grounds as exist at law or in equity for the revocation of any contract."

At the international level, arbitration is most likely to be regulated by the 1958 United Nations Convention on Recognition and Enforcement of Arbitral Awards, an international treaty dealing with arbitration. This convention has been ratified by more than 80 nations.[28] In this hemisphere, international arbitration is also regulated by the Inter-American Convention on International Commercial Arbitration.[29] The International Chamber of Commerce also supports and encourages arbitration, and many firms involved in international business seek to resolve their disputes through its arbitration provisions. The federal statute and the international treaties are designed to increase the acceptance and use of arbitration as an alternative method for resolving disputes.

Organizations

There are a number of organizations that actively support arbitration and provide both the forum in which an arbitration occurs and the arbitrator. Some of these organizations operate exclusively within the United States; others operate internationally. Within the United States, arbitration is supported by the Judicial Arbitration and Mediation Services, Inc. (J.A.M.S.), which employs only former judges as arbitrators, the Federal Mediation and Conciliation Service, as well as the AAA. Internationally, arbitration is supported by the AAA (which operates both domestically and internationally); the International Chamber of Commerce, headquartered in Paris; and the London Court of Arbitration (which is not a court, despite the title of the organization).

The AAA administers more than 60,000 cases in an average year.[30] Its services include arbitration, mediation, minitrial, **fact finding,** education, and training. When the AAA is involved in an arbitration, it can refer a list of potential arbitrators, serve as an *intermediator* between the parties and the arbitrator in negotiating the arbitrator's compensation, and collect a deposit for arbitrator compensation. The AAA administrator handles the administrative details so that the parties do not deal directly with the arbitrator. This helps ensure that the parties will not discuss

Fact finding
A process where an arbitrator investigates a dispute and issues findings of fact and a nonbinding report.

the case privately with the arbitrator prior to the hearing. The AAA requires its arbitrators to issue awards within 30 days after the close of the hearings, unless the contract between the parties specifies another time limit.[31] Except in labor and international cases, the AAA does not encourage arbitrators to write lengthy opinions. Instead, it encourages them to write an itemized award.[32] It promulgates rules for specific types of arbitration, and it also has special procedures for large, complex commercial cases. The slogan of the AAA is "Speed, Economy, and Justice."

MINITRIAL

In ADR, the term *minitrial* describes a process in which the parties' attorneys present an abbreviated form of their case. The parties are permitted to use expert witnesses to support their case. A *neutral,* an unbiased person, chairs the case. Senior executives from the firms involved also attend the presentation. After the presentation, the senior executives meet in an attempt to resolve the dispute. Prior to the presentation, the parties usually specify what will happen if the senior executives are unable to settle the case. For example, if the senior executives are unable to settle the case, the neutral may be empowered to mediate or to provide a nonbinding advisory opinion informing the parties of the probable outcome of litigation. A minitrial would not be appropriate to resolve Nic and Nancy's claims.

Note that in court matters, judges use the term *minitrial* to refer to an abbreviated judicial proceeding on a few issues, for example, a minitrial on damages.

RENT-A-JUDGE TRIAL

A "rent-a-judge" trial is another alternative method of dispute resolution. When the parties elect to use this method, they pay a fee to a "judge" to settle the dispute. "Judges" in these cases are typically retired judges, well trained in presiding over dispute resolution and able to bring the reputation and prestige of their former positions to their current roles. Rent-a-judge "cases" occasionally involve a "jury" of hired experts, particularly in technical cases.

The major advantage of the rent-a-judge option is that it is much faster than regular civil litigation. In addition, the proceedings are relatively private and do not become part of the public record. Many time-consuming trial procedures are eliminated in rent-a-judge trials, providing an additional savings of time and money.[33] These "trials" are significantly less formal and are generally conducted in conference rooms.

It is not uncommon for the parties in a civil case to wait four to five years before they can get their case to trial. With a rent-a-judge, the "trial" can occur in a matter of weeks. As a result, the use of rent-a-judge trials is growing more popular. Because all states accept some form of private resolution of cases, rent-a-judge resolutions are likely to become more common in the future. A number of companies now exist to assist clients in locating a rent-a-judge. One company, Judicate, even has its own private courthouse in Los Angeles. In some jurisdictions, the clerk of court's office maintains a list of retired judges who are willing to serve as rent-a-judges. In some jurisdictions, the decisions of rent-a-judges may be appealed to the public court of appeals.[34] Nic and Nancy might agree to having a retired judge from

RESOURCES FOR BUSINESS LAW STUDENTS

NAME	RESOURCES	WEB ADDRESS
Federal Rules of Civil Procedure (1999)	Legal Information Institute (LII), maintained by the Cornell Law School, provides the Federal Rules of Civil Procedure in a hypertext and searchable format.	**http://www.law.cornell.edu/rules/frcp/overview.htm**
The National Registry of Experts (NRE)	NRE is a professional organization established to provide support, recognition, training, and continuing education to expert witnesses as well as those interested in becoming experts.	**http://www.expert-registry.com/**
Trial Behavior Consulting, Incorporated	Trial Behavior Consulting, Incorporated, provides mock trials, case strategy, **voir dire** questions, community surveys, focus groups, witness preparation, and jury selection, among other services.	**http://www.trialbehavior.com**
American Bar Association's Center for Professional Responsibility	The American Bar Association's Center for Professional Responsibility provides standards and scholarly resources in legal ethics, professional regulation, professionalism, and client protection mechanisms.	**http://www.abanet.org/cpr/home.html**
West's Legal Directory	West's Legal Directory, updated daily, offers more than 800,000 profiles of lawyers and law firms in the United States and Canada, including international offices.	**http://www.lawoffice.com**
American Arbitration Association (AAA)	The American Arbitration Association provides membership information, rules and procedures, education and research, publications, a directory of its members, and information on ADR law.	**http://www.adr.org/**
International Academy of Mediators	The International Academy of Mediators provides membership information and a directory of members, as well as other information on mediation.	**http://www.iamed.org/**
Society of Professionals in Dispute Resolution (SPIDR)	SPIDR provides membership information, publications, and current events in ADR.	**http://www.spidr.org/**
Federal Arbitration Act— 9 U.S.C. § I	LII, maintained by the Cornell Law School, provides a hypertext and searchable version of 9 USC § I, popularly known as the Federal Arbitration Act.	**http://www.law.cornell.edu/uscode/9/ch1.html**
International Chamber of Commerce— Dispute Resolution	The International Chamber of Commerce provides an index of international arbitration and alternative dispute resolution services, including information on the International Court of Arbitration.	**http://www.iccwbo.org/**

Butler County serve as a rent-a-judge. If they are experiencing financial difficulty, the speed of using this approach and the opportunity for a quick payment would be attractive.

SMALL CLAIMS COURT

Another technique to reduce legal expenses is for a party to file the legal dispute in small claims court. Although this is still litigation, it significantly reduces the costs. This option permits a party to effectively represent him- or herself. Generally, the opponent can also appear without a lawyer. Small claims courts do not utilize legalese and standard rules of evidence. Quick resolution of disputes is usually available. The procedures in small claims courts vary from state to state. The jurisdictional amounts also vary—the upper limit may range from $1,000 (Mississippi and parts of Virginia) to $10,000 (parts of Tennessee).[35] In most states, Nic and Nancy's claims would exceed the jurisdictional limits of small claims court.

Some small claims courts publish booklets to assist parties in small claims actions. There may also be government employees who provide free or low-cost legal services to parties who are filing complaints in small claims courts. Participants do not need to be familiar with legal jargon; however, they need to be organized and to bring their witnesses and any physical evidence with them to the hearing. Participants should prepare a brief, coherent presentation of the case. It is also helpful to observe a couple of small claims cases in advance of the hearing date.

If the defendant does not show up on the trial date, the court hears only the plaintiff's side. This is called a *default judgment.* If the plaintiff does not appear on the trial date, the case is dismissed.

Before filing the complaint, consider whether the defendant is likely to be able to pay a judgment. Generally, a successful plaintiff will have to conduct the collection process him- or herself. This is usually accomplished by discovering the defendant's assets and obtaining permission (in a written legal document called a *writ*) from the court to levy on them. The plaintiff then takes the writ to the court in the locality where the assets are located; completes a form requesting execution; pays a fee; and asks a sheriff, marshal, or constable to collect the described assets. Execution is described briefly in Case 6.2, *Johnson* v. *Outboard Marine Corporation.*

SUMMARY

Lawsuits are based on factual circumstances. Therefore, it is the client's responsibility to reveal all the facts to his or her attorney. If all the facts are not known, the attorney might draw the wrong legal conclusion. If the facts warrant a lawsuit, one of the first things the attorney should do is to apprise the potential defendant of liability and seek to settle the case without filing a lawsuit.

Attorney's fees are an important consideration in deciding whether the client should sue. Nic Grant and Nancy Griffin had contingency fee arrangements, whereby if the plaintiffs had lost the case, their attorney would have received no fees. Other bases for attorney's fees also exist, including a flat rate or an hourly rate. In these cases, the attorney receives compensation whether or not the attorney wins the case. The fee arrangement is specified in the oral or written contract that creates the attorney-client relationship.

Before a lawsuit is filed, the attorney has a duty to investigate the facts to determine whether sufficient evidence exists to justify litigation. Before filing suit, an opportunity is usually provided for the parties to settle the matter, either through a settlement conference or arbitration.

After suit is filed, the *discovery* process takes place. Discovery is designed to narrow the legal issues, thus encouraging pretrial settlement or reducing the duration of the actual trial. During *voir dire*, the petit jury is selected for the trial. Potential jurors can be dismissed for cause or by use of a peremptory challenge. Consultants may be hired to assist the attorneys in selecting the jury and/or presenting an effective case before the jury.

The doctrine of *res judicata* means that when a court issues a final judgment, the subject matter of the case cannot be relitigated between the same parties. However, it does not prevent appeals from the final judgment.

The time, trouble, and expense associated with trials have led to an increasing emphasis on ADR methods. There are five major ADR methods outside the judicial system, and one ADR within the judicial system.

Negotiation is probably the oldest and most common form of ADR. The parties discuss their dispute and reach a mutually agreeable solution to the problem. Negotiation is only restricted by the willingness of the parties to compromise.

Mediation is slightly more formal than negotiation. In mediation, the parties turn to a mediator, a third person who helps the parties find a mutually acceptable solution. Mediators do not provide a solution; they provide a procedure for helping the parties reach a solution. The mediator facilitates communication rather than acting as a decisionmaker.

Arbitration involves a third party, the arbitrator, who listens to the arguments of each party and then renders an award to resolve the controversy. The arbitrator is a decisionmaker. Arbitration is commonly *binding*, meaning that the parties agree to abide by the decision prior to actual arbitration.

Minitrials involve a neutral party chairing a presentation of the evidence before the senior executives of the companies. After this presentation, the senior executives meet and attempt to settle the dispute.

Rent-a-judge trials are a variation on arbitration, using a person in the role of "judge" rather than arbitrator to resolve a controversy. Rent-a-judges, often retired judges, preside over informal "trials" in private "courtrooms" to resolve disputes.

Small claims courts provide relatively informal resolution for small civil claims. The rules and the jurisdictional limits of these specialized courts vary widely among the states.

DISCUSSION QUESTIONS

1. Is there any conflict of interest if Lyn Carroll represents both plaintiffs in this case? Why or why not? Is there any conflict of interest if Jefferson Jones represents both defendants in this case? Why or why not?

2. Are contingency fee contracts fair to clients? What are the advantages of contingency fee arrangements for clients? What are the disadvantages for clients?

3. Why are interrogatories limited to a party to a lawsuit while depositions can be taken from any witness?

4. In the case of Nic Grant versus CIT, suppose a jury is made up almost solely of people on public assistance. In your opinion, is this providing the parties with a fair trial? Why?

5. What is *res judicata*? How does the concept of *res judicata* affect lawsuits?

6. What ethical perspective(s) are reflected in the model standards of conduct for mediators?

7. The Los Angeles County Bar Association sued in federal court to obtain more local judges, primarily due to a backlog of cases in the civil courts.[36] What are the primary causes of the backlog in civil courts? What could be done to alleviate it?

8. What are the advantages and disadvantages of including the following clause in an agreement to arbitrate: "Upon the request of a party, the arbitrator's award shall include findings of fact and conclusions of law"?[37]

9. Parties who submit their claims to resolution with a rent-a-judge may be allowed to appeal the result of their "case" to the court of appeals. Will wealthy parties, who can afford to use rent-a-judge trials, lose interest in reforming the legal system if they can use private judging and still appeal to public appellate courts? Is that a concern? Why or why not?

10. Small claims courts are specialized civil courts within the state court system. Why is small claims court more like ADR than it is like a regular civil court? How is small claims court more like a regular civil court than a category of ADR?

CASE PROBLEMS AND WRITING ASSIGNMENTS

1. The Federal Rules of Civil Procedure provide that a motion for summary judgment "shall be served at least ten days before the time fixed for the hearing" on the motion. Suppose that one of the parties to a lawsuit makes an oral motion for summary judgment during the proceedings. Can the trial court grant the motion? Why or why not? [See *Hanson* v. *Polk County Land, Inc.*, 608 F.2d 129 (5th Cir. 1979).]

2. Thaddeus Donald Edmonson, a black man, was employed as a construction worker. He was injured at work and sued Leesville Concrete Company, claiming that the company allowed one of its trucks to roll backwards, pinning him against some construction equipment. During *voir dire*, Leesville used two of its three peremptory challenges to remove potential jurors who were black. Edmonson asked the judge to require Leesville to provide a race-neutral explanation for its use of peremptory challenges. The judge refused the request on the basis that it was a civil trial, not a criminal trial. The jury found for Edmonson; however, it found that he was 80 percent responsible for his own injuries under comparative negligence. Consequently, his recovery was limited to 20 percent. Was the trial judge's decision on peremptory challenges proper? [See *Edmonson* v. *Leesville Concrete Co., Inc.*, 500 U.S. 614 (1991).]

3. Dr. Gerald Zuk brought a suit for copyright infringement against the Eastern Pennsylvania Psychiatric Institute (EPPI). Dr. Zuk was a psychologist on the faculty of EPPI. In the 1970s, he had an EPPI technician film two of his family therapy sessions. As academic demand for the films developed, Zuk had EPPI duplicate the films and make them available for rental through their library. Zuk subsequently wrote a book which, among other things, contained transcripts of the therapy sessions. He registered the book in 1975 with the U.S. Copyright Office. In 1980, EPPI furloughed Zuk. In 1995, Lipman (Zuk's attorney) filed this suit, alleging that EPPI was renting out the films and thereby infringing on Zuk's copyright. The trial court, dismissing the claim, found that the copyright of the book afforded no protection to the films, that EPPI owned the copies of the films in its possession, that their use was not an infringement, and that Zuk's claims were barred by the statute of limitations. Should Lipman be sanctioned for filing this lawsuit? This was Lipman's first copyright infringement case. Was it ethical for him to accept this case when he was unfamiliar with copyright law? As he told the court, a practitioner has to start somewhere. Is it lack of experience or was he merely unprepared? Does it make a difference? [See *Zuk* v. *Eastern Penn. Psychiatric Inst. of the Medical College of Penn.*, 1996 U.S. App. LEXIS 33917 (3d Cir. 1996).]

4. Melinda Kay Broemmer was 21 years old, unmarried, and 16 or 17 weeks pregnant. She was a high school graduate earning less than $100 a week and had no medical benefits. The father-to-be insisted that Broemmer have an abortion, but her parents advised against it. Broemmer said that the time was one of considerable confusion and emotional and physical turmoil for her. Her mother contacted Abortion Services of Phoenix and made an appointment for Broemmer. During their visit to the clinic, Broemmer and her mother expected to receive information and counseling on alternatives to abortion and the nature of the operation. They did not receive that information. Broemmer was escorted into an adjoining room and asked to complete three forms, one of which was an agreement to arbitrate. The agreement to arbitrate included language that "any dispute aris[ing] between the Parties as a result of the fees and/or services" would be settled by binding arbitration and that "any arbitrators appointed by the American Arbitration Association (AAA) shall be licensed medical doctors who specialize in obstetrics/gynecology." Broemmer completed all three forms in less than five minutes and returned them to the front desk. Clinic staff made no attempt to explain the agreement before or after she signed it, and did not provide her with copies of the forms. After she returned the forms to the front desk, she was taken into an examination room where pre-operation procedures were performed. Broemmer returned the following day, and Doctor Otto performed the abortion. As a result of the procedure, she suffered a punctured uterus that required medical treatment. Was the arbitration provision binding on Broemmer? [See *Broemmer v. Abortion Services of Phoenix, Ltd.*, 840 P.2d 1013 (Ariz. 1992).]

5. Steven Gwin bought a lifetime "Termite Protection Plan" (Plan) from the local office of Allied-Bruce Terminix Companies, a franchise of Terminix International Company. In the Plan, Allied-Bruce promised "to protect" Gwin's house "against the attack of subterranean termites," to reinspect periodically, to provide any "further treatment found necessary," and to repair, up to $100,000, damage caused by new termite infestations. The Plan's contract provided in writing that "any controversy or claim . . . arising out of or relating to the interpretation, performance or breach of any provision of this agreement shall be settled exclusively by arbitration." In the spring of 1991, Mr. and Mrs. Gwin wished to sell their house to Mr. and Mrs. Dobson. The Gwins had Allied-Bruce reinspect the house. They obtained a clean bill of health. But, no sooner had they sold the house and transferred the Termite Protection Plan to Mr. and Mrs. Dobson than

the Dobsons found the house swarming with termites. Allied-Bruce attempted to treat and repair the house, but the Dobsons thought that Allied-Bruce's efforts were inadequate. They sued the Gwins, Allied-Bruce, and Terminix. Allied-Bruce and Terminix immediately asked the court for a stay, to allow arbitration to proceed. Was the arbitration clause enforceable against the Dobsons? What is the effect of the Federal Arbitration Act? [See *Allied-Bruce Terminix Companies, Inc.* v. *Dobson*, 513 U.S. 265 (1995).]

6. **BUSINESS APPLICATION CASE** AMF and Brunswick, rivals in the bowling industry, resolved a lawsuit alleging false advertising in 1983. Part of the resolution was an agreement to submit any future disputes concerning advertisements that claimed data-based superiority of one company's bowling products over similar products of the other company to an advisory third party, the National Advertising Division of the Better Business Bureau. In 1985, Brunswick began to advertise the alleged superiority of its new lane surfaces over the lanes surfaced by AMF. AMF asked for data from the research that supposedly supported this claim, but Brunswick refused. AMF then asked that the data be turned over to the National Advertising Division of the Better Business Bureau, as called for in their resolution. Again Brunswick refused. AMF then filed suit, asking the court to compel Brunswick to turn over the data for nonbinding arbitration. How should the court handle this request? Why? [See *AMF, Inc.* v. *Brunswick Corp.*, 621 F.Supp. 456 (1985).]

7. **ETHICAL APPLICATION CASE** Interstate Johnson Lane Corporation (Interstate) hired Gilmer as manager of financial services in 1981. At the time of the hiring, Gilmer signed a "registration agreement" that provided, among other things, that Gilmer agreed to submit any disputes arising between him and Interstate to arbitration. In 1987, Interstate fired Gilmer, who was 62 years old. Gilmer filed suit in the U.S. District Court, alleging that he had been fired due to his age, in violation of the Age Discrimination in Employment Act. Interstate filed a motion asking the court to compel Gilmer to submit his claim to arbitration as specified in the registration agreement. Should the court grant the motion, compelling resolution of the controversy through arbitration, or should it deny the motion, permitting Gilmer to pursue his remedies in a trial? Why? Why might the business prefer arbitration rather than a trial in a situation such as this? What ethical considerations are raised by such a preference? [See *Gilmer* v. *Interstate Johnson Lane Corp.*, 111 S.Ct. 1647 (1991).]

8. **CRITICAL THINKING CASE** On 31 January 1997, Judge Hiroshi Fujisaki instructed jurors in the civil trial of O. J. Simpson that they must "insulate themselves from all news media—watch no TV, listen to no radio and read no newspapers." He told them that he wanted to avoid sequestering the jury. A juror had just been removed from the trial for legal cause during deliberations; he was concerned that she might be giving interviews and did not want the jury tainted.

Jurors were also instructed to "have someone screen their phone calls, mail and faxes." The judge was concerned about reports that two jurors in the Simpson criminal trial were contacting members of the civil jury panel. They were allegedly trying to promote a deal for public appearances after the trial. Brenda Moran and Gina Marie Rosborough, two criminal jurors, announced a book deal shortly after the verdict in the criminal trial. Moran acknowl-

edged writing a letter to the civil jurors recommending Bud Stewart as an agent. Both women stated that it was supposed to be delivered *after* the verdict, not while deliberations were going on. Faxes were sent to news producers offering to arrange interviews with three civil trial jurors in the case. The faxes were signed Bud Stewart, the agent mentioned in the letter from Moran.

Discuss the interrelationships between fair trials, the public's interest in obtaining information, and the media's business interests. It appears that Bud Stewart was attempting to get ahead of other agents. How could he have solicited business and clients without interfering with the legal process? [See Linda Deutsch and Michael Fleeman, "Simpson Juror Replaced; Talks Start Anew," *The Fresno Bee* (1 February 1997), pp. A1, A11; and "Juror Dismissed in Simpson Case," *Merced Sun-Star* (1 February 1997), pp. A1, A8.]

NOTES

1. David A. Lieb, "Clinton Ordered to Pay $90,000 in Penalty Fees in Jones Contempt Case," *The Fresno Bee* (30 July 1999), pp. A1, A22.
2. Federal Rules of Civil Procedure § 48.
3. See 28 U.S.C. § 1870.
4. See *J.E.B.* v. *T.B.*, 114 S.Ct. 1419 (1994).
5. California Code of Civil Procedure § 170.6.
6. See 28 U.S.C. § 455 and California Code of Civil Procedure § 170.
7. See 42 Pa. C.S.A. § 5104.
8. Federal Rules of Civil Procedure § 48.
9. Eric Lichtblau, "Zapruder Film Costs U.S. $16 Million," *The Fresno Bee* (4 August 1999), pp. A1, A5.
10. *Whoop, Inc.* v. *Dyno Productions, Inc.*, 75 Cal.Rptr. 2d 90 (Cal. App. 2 Dist. 1998).
11. American Arbitration Association, *Resolving Your Disputes* (November 1995), pp. 8–9. Reprinted by permission of AAA.
12. Quoted in Teresa V. Carey, "Credentialing for Mediators—To Be or Not To Be?," *University of San Francisco Law Review* 30 (Spring 1996), p. 640.
13. Ibid., p. 641.
14. Richard C. Reuben, "Model Ethics Rules Limit Mediator Role: Despite Controversy, Standards Expected to Improve Respect for Profession," *ABA Journal* (January 1996), p. 25.
15. Ibid.
16. American Arbitration Association, *Drafting Dispute Resolution Clauses—A Practical Guide* (June 1994), p. 5. Reprinted by permission of AAA.
17. A.R.S. §§ 12-1501 to 1518.
18. 9 Cal. Civ. Proc. Code §§ 1280 *et seq.*, at § 1295.
19. Mich. Stat. Ann. §§ 27A.5040–27A.5065.
20. 9 U.S.C. §§ 1 *et. seq.*, at § 2.
21. "When You Need a Lawyer," *Consumer Reports* (February 1996), p. 39.
22. Curtis D. Brown, Esq., "New Law Lets Creditors Cut Court Costs," *Credit World* (July/August 1996), pp. 30–31.
23. *Hooters of America, Inc.* v. *Phillips*, 173 F.3d 933 (4th Cir. 1999).
24. Curtis D. Brown, Esq., "New Law Lets Creditors Cut Court Costs," *Creditor World* (July/August 1996), pp. 30–31.
25. 513 U.S. 265 (1995).
26. Information on the current status of adoptions of Uniform State Laws was provided by Katie Robinson, NCCUSL, in an e-mail on 7 January 2000.
27. NCCUSL web page, http://www.nccusl.org/uniformacts.htm.
28. American Arbitration Association, *Drafting*, p. 37.
29. Ibid.
30. American Arbitration Association, *Resolving*, p. 3.
31. American Arbitration Association, *Why Labor and Management Use the Services of the American Arbitration Association* (November 1993), p. 5.
32. American Arbitration Association, *Drafting*, p. 30.
33. Deborah Shannon, "Rent-a-Judge," *American Way Magazine* (February 1991), pp. 33–36.
34. Ibid., p. 34.
35. "Do-It-Yourself Justice—Small Claims Court," *Consumer Reports* (February 1996), p. 36.
36. Shannon, "Rent-a-Judge," p. 33.
37. American Arbitration Association, *Drafting*, p. 30.

7

TORTS

CALL-IMAGE TECHNOLOGY

A G E N D A

CIT recently has been victimized by some tortious activity. What steps can it legally pursue in the protection of its property interests? CIT also desires to prevent tort commission. A videophone competitor has been advertising the merits of its product in comparison to another videophone that appears to be a Call-Image unit in form if not in performance. Call-Image is not specifically named in the advertisement. Can Tom and Anna successfully sue the competitor to protect CIT's image? If so, on what basis? Also, a group of people have banded together to prevent the use of interactive videophones, and they have threatened to file invasion-of-privacy lawsuits. Should Tom and Anna worry about these legal threats? What legal defenses might be available to them? Huey, a former CIT employee, is applying for new positions; potential employers are calling Anna to inquire about Huey's employment with CIT. What should Anna tell them when they call? What would occur if an employee were negligent in operating a CIT vehicle on "official" business? Who would be liable for any damages? CIT? The employee? Or both? What can the Kochanowskis do to avoid liability?

These and other questions are discussed in this chapter. Be prepared! You never know when one of the Kochanowskis will need your help or advice.

OBJECTIVES OF TORT LAW

Tort law is concerned with a body of "private" wrongs, whereas *criminal law,* which we will study in Chapter 8, is concerned with "public" wrongs. Tort law has evolved over hundreds of years. It supports the protection of an individual's rights with respect to his or her property and person. It is a complicated body of law because of the long period of development and the various exceptions that have evolved in its application. In addition, tort law is based on common law; consequently, the rules vary from state to state. The discussion here, therefore, is fairly general.

Torts provide a mechanism for persons who have been wronged to seek remedies in our court system. In general, the remedy sought is money damages to compensate for the injury. People can avoid committing these wrongs by adhering to various "duties." For example, society recognizes a duty to refrain from physically injuring other persons or their property. Society also recognizes a duty to refrain from injuring the reputation of others.

Because tort law recognizes certain duties, it raises the policy question of exactly which rights society should protect through the imposition of duties. For example, should society recognize as a wrong only behavior intended to be a wrong? Should society also recognize as a wrong an unintended wrong due to someone's negligence? Should society also recognize as a wrong an unintended behavior in which the person is not negligent? These are the questions discussed in this chapter.

Society has developed the body of tort law to resolve social and economic policy questions. The law has to take into consideration a number of factors including: the social usefulness of the conduct of a person; the interests asserted by the plaintiff; the justification (if any) for the defendant's conduct; the economic burden placed on the defendant if liability is imposed; and the question of spreading the cost of liability from one to many persons. The law also has the unique problem of respecting past decisions while maintaining flexibility within the legal system by providing solutions to modern problems. For instance, tort law has to adjust to problems created by technological advances such as defamation and invasion of privacy through the use of the computer.

THEORIES OF TORT LIABILITY

This chapter discusses intentional torts, negligence, and strict liability. Exhibit 7.1 depicts the three theories of tort liability. *Intentional torts* are those wrongs in which the persons being sued acted in a willful or intentional manner; they either wanted the act to occur or knew that the act would probably occur. Suppose that someone said something offensive to you, and you said, "If you don't apologize, I'll punch you in the nose." If that person did not apologize and you then punched him in the nose, the law states that you were wrong. You committed the tort of *battery* on the other person. (Provocation is not an issue here, since generally the law does not recognize the **privilege** of striking someone for making offensive remarks.)

The law of *negligence* is based on a concept of fault in which morality and law have been intermingled. How should society apportion the costs of accidents? Often, society has to make a moral statement when an injury occurs. Suppose a child darts out from behind a parked car an instant before the driver's car reaches that point; the driver immediately brakes in an effort to avoid hitting the child but

Privilege
A particular benefit or advantage beyond the common advantages of other citizens; an exceptional right, power, franchise, or immunity held by a person, class, or company.

E X H I B I T   7.1 | **The Three Theories of Tort Liability**

TORT LIABILITY

Intentional Torts	Negligence	Strict Liability in Tort
The accused acts in a willful or intentional manner.	The conduct of the accused is compared to the "reasonable and prudent" person.	The accused is generally involved in conduct that is deemed abnormally dangerous.
Involves a simple duty to avoid the act or conduct.	Involves a reasonable duty to avoid the act or conduct.	Involves a strict duty to be responsible for harm caused, without regard to care.
There must be a showing of fault.	There must be a showing of fault.	There is no need to show fault.
The harm must be foreseeable.	The harm must be foreseeable.	The harm must be foreseeable.

is unable to stop in time to avoid the accident. In all likelihood, this accident would be considered unavoidable—it occurred without any negligence on the part of the driver. The child, even though injured, would be denied any compensation from the driver for the accident.

On the other hand, if a child is walking across the street in a designated crosswalk and is hit by an automobile because the driver is drunk or driving too fast, then society says that the driver breached a duty to drive the car in a reasonable manner. Accordingly, the driver will have to pay for damages suffered by the child. The amount of injury is not a factor in determining liability: what is relevant is how the injury occurred.

Under *strict liability,* persons are liable even if their conduct was unintentional or nonnegligent, that is, even if the damage was not their fault. Some activities are classified as either ultrahazardous or abnormally dangerous, and if injury results from either of those situations, the actor will be held liable. For example, suppose you have a pet rattlesnake in a sealed glass cage and you place the cage in your backyard with signs on the fence that say "Danger—Poisonous Snake, Beware." If the snake somehow gets out and bites someone, you will be held liable. The law prevents you from trying to prove how careful you were. Instead, if your rattlesnake caused injury, you will simply have to pay. Increasingly, legislatures are creating strict liability for parents when their children intentionally cause injury to others.[1]

Duty

We live in a legal system in which we all have a duty to protect other persons from harm. The question the courts must examine is what degree of duty exists under what specific circumstances. With respect to intentional torts, we all have a simple duty to avoid liability-causing behavior. However, with respect to negligence, we all have a "reasonable" duty to avoid this type of behavior. Generally, the law states that reasonable duty is a standard of ordinary skill and care, based on the facts of each individual case. In order to test for a duty in any particular situation, the law has constructed a person against whom the conduct of the defendant is to be compared. This purely hypothetical person is known as the *reasonable and prudent person*—not perfect, merely reasonable.

Foreseeability

Foreseeability
The knowledge or notice that a result is likely to occur if a certain act occurs.

Both intentional torts and negligence are based on the concept of fault. Strict liability, to the contrary, is not. All theories of liability, however, require **foreseeability.**

Foreseeability addresses the likelihood that something will happen in the future. It is easy to see that if you point a loaded gun at someone and pull the trigger, you will cause that person harm. But suppose you get in your car and drive down a dark street, within the speed limit and with your lights on. A child darts out from behind a parked car, and you hit the child. Were you negligent, or was it merely an unavoidable accident? This is a more difficult question. Foreseeability is determined by what a "reasonable and prudent person" would expect. Thus, the foreseeability of a child darting into the street in front of your car would depend on such factors as the degree of darkness, the lateness of the hour, how densely populated the area was (i.e., rural or urban, residential or business), other children observed in the area, signs regarding children at play, and so forth. Until these factors are considered, there can be no determination of the foreseeability of the child's action and, consequently, of your negligence.

INTENTIONAL TORTS

Assault

Assault is wrongful, intentional conduct that would put a reasonable person or victim in immediate apprehension *or* fear of offensive, nonconsensual touching. Verbal threats alone are not an assault. A verbal threat must be accompanied by some movement toward the person. The threats of harm must be immediate; threats of future harm are not sufficient. The actor must have actual or apparent ability to harm the victim. Pointing an unloaded pistol at a person, for example, is an assault if the victim has no way of knowing whether the pistol is loaded. The victim must feel apprehension; actual fear is not required.

Battery

Some legal authorities have defined *battery* as a consummated assault. It is the wrongful, intentional, offensive, and nonconsensual touching of the victim. Touching an extension of the victim's body, such as a purse or backpack, also constitutes a battery. For example, removing a chair from underneath a person who briefly stood up and began to sit down again is a battery when the person hits the floor. The key element is that the actor intended the natural consequence of removing the chair: falling to the ground. As far as the law is concerned, it is the same as pushing the person to the ground. On the other hand, if the removal of the chair had been unintended, there is no battery.

Defamation

Defamation occurs when an actor intentionally makes an untrue statement concerning a victim that injures the victim's reputation. As with other intentional torts, it is sufficient that the actor made the statement willfully. The defamatory remark must be *published,* which is defined as read or heard by others. Consequently, a negative remark that is made directly to the victim but is not overheard by anyone else is not "published." The statement need not name the victim; however, the statement must be reasonably interpreted as referring to the victim. The statement must reduce the victim's reputation among well-meaning individuals. If the actor curses at the victim, this will not reduce the victim's reputation. It is interpreted more as an indication that the *actor* is extremely angry and may not be controlling his or her temper. Some courts apply the libel-proof plaintiff doctrine when the fact finder decides that the plaintiff's reputation for a trait is so poor that, with regard to that trait, it could not be further damaged by the statement.[2] An interesting development in this area of law presents a potential problem for employers and supervisors. Recently, disgruntled employees, especially those who have been discharged, have been suing their ex-employers for defamation. A number of these suits have been based on remarks made by the employer to coworkers of the employee filing the suit. In addition, a number of former employees have sued for defamation due to comments about the former employee made by the employer or supervisor to potential new employers, often as a result of the potential new employer contacting the former one for a reference or "character check."

Two forms of defamation exist: **slander** and **libel**. The reason for the two forms, each of which has different elements, is that each was developed in a different English court. Slander, which is spoken defamation, developed in the *English church courts* (the ecclesiastical courts that had jurisdiction over spiritual matters). Libel (written defamation) developed in the *Star Chamber* (an English common law court that had jurisdiction over cases in which the ordinary course of justice was so obstructed by one party that no inferior court could have its process obeyed). The tort of defamation is an important limitation on the First Amendment's guarantee of free speech. Accordingly, U.S. courts have modified some of the common law rules.

Slander is spoken communication that causes a person to suffer a loss of reputation. The common law rule distinguished between *slander per se* and *slander per quod*. *Slander per se* occurs when a person says that another person is seriously immoral, seriously criminal, has a social disease, or is unfit as a businessperson or professional. In those cases, there is no need to prove actual damages. *Slander per quod* is any other type of oral defamatory statement.

Libel is written communication that causes a person to suffer a loss of reputation. There are also two kinds of libel. *Libel per se* is libelous without having to resort to the context in which the remark appeared. For example, if a newspaper printed a story that referred to a person as a "known assassin for hire," there is no need to show the context of the statement. On the other hand, *libel per quod* requires proof of the context. For example, suppose a television talk show host says that a particular woman just gave birth to a child. In order to prove that it was libel, the woman must prove that she is not married and that she has not made public knowledge of her cohabiting, but unmarried, private life.

The *New York Times Co.* v. *Sullivan*[3] case is a landmark in U.S. jurisprudence. The U.S. Supreme Court held that when a public official sues for libel, the public official must also prove that the false statement was made with actual malice in addition to the other elements of libel. The Court defined actual malice as knowledge that the statement was false or was made with reckless disregard of whether it was false or not. Some courts actually call it *New York Times malice* instead of actual malice. Since 1964, the Court extended the definition of a *public official* to include candidates for public office as well as incumbents. The Court has also extended the holding to "public figures" as well as public officials. A *public figure* is a person who has a degree of prominence in society. Thus, a person who chooses to become active in society and who not only receives but actually solicits attention in the media will be classified as a public figure.

Slander
Any oral statement that tends to expose a person to public ridicule or injures a person's reputation.

Libel
Any written or printed statement that tends to expose a person to public ridicule or injures a person's reputation.

7.1 | MARKETING

UNFAIR ADVERTISING

Another firm in the interactive videophone industry has been advertising that it has the best available videophone on the market. The firm's ads do not name any competitors, but they do show what appears to be a Call-Image phone next to their product. In the ads, the Call-Image phone has an unclear picture and generally seems to be an inferior product. Dan wants to sue the other company for defamation, or disparagement, or something similar. Tom is not sure that CIT has grounds to sue, but he is concerned about what these ads will do to CIT's image. The family asks you what CIT's rights are in this situation, and what they would need to prove in court if they sue. What will you tell them?

BUSINESS CONSIDERATIONS What practical steps can a business take to bolster its reputation? What could a business do to counteract negative publicity by a competitor?

ETHICAL CONSIDERATIONS Is it ethical to use comparison advertising to create a false impression of a competitor's product? Is it ethical to intentionally create a negative impression of a competitor's product if you believe the impression to be reasonably accurate? What moral obligations do you owe to competitors?

Disparagement

Disparagement occurs when a business product is defamed. Generally it requires that a person make a false statement about a business's products, services, reputation, honesty, or integrity; the speaker publishes the remark to a third party; and the speaker knows the remark is false *or* the speaker makes the statement maliciously and with intent to injure the victim. It is also called *trade libel,* if the statements are written, or *slander of title,* if the statements are oral. It is also sometimes called *product disparagement.*

False Imprisonment

False imprisonment is the unlawful detention of one person by another against the former's will, and without just cause, for an appreciable amount of time. This tort protects a person from the loss of liberty and freedom of movement. For example, if after the end of a college class your professor locks the door and says that no one can leave the room, that action is false imprisonment. Sometimes standing in a doorway and refusing to let a person pass is also false imprisonment. As with other torts, there are defenses. A privilege exists when a retail store's security officer has just cause to suspect a customer of shoplifting. If the security officer detains the customer, the security officer's acts will be privileged as long as the officer uses reasonable means in the detention.

Emotional Distress

A growing body of law concerns situations that, for public policy reasons, are being recognized by courts and legislatures as torts. The law protects an individual from suffering *serious indignity* that causes emotional distress. This right, however, is balanced against the interest of the state in not opening the courts to frivolous and trivial claims. Many states require a physical injury in addition to emotional distress. In this context, an airline was liable when it unreasonably insulted a passenger on an aircraft. Liability has also been found where a mortician displayed a dead body without its having been embalmed. In that case, damages were recovered by near relatives who suffered the emotional distress. Employees are suing former employers for inflicting emotional distress. Most states recognize causes of action for both the intentional infliction and the negligent causing of emotional distress.

Invasion of Privacy

Actionable
Furnishing legal grounds for an action.

Under common law, no tort of invasion of privacy existed. However, our courts have begun to recognize that unwarranted invasions of privacy are **actionable.** *Privacy* refers to an individual's right to be left alone. Originally, this tort began with someone's peering into a home without permission. A person's privacy is invaded if that person becomes subject to unwarranted intrusions into his or her right to be left alone. Such intrusions have led to lawsuits and to the awarding of damages to the person whose privacy was invaded. Liability has been found for the public disclosure of private matters, such as playing a tape of a private citizen's telephone call without permission or a valid search warrant. In most states, simple invasion of privacy has been expanded: It now includes (1) intrusion on physical solitude; (2) unauthorized use of the plaintiff's likeness or life story; (3) presenting the plaintiff in a false light; and (4) appropriation of the plaintiff's name, face, or likeness for commercial purposes. For example, the use of a famous person's name, photograph, voice, song, or image in an advertisement without permission is an invasion of privacy. This version of invasion of privacy is often described as an invasion of the famous person's right of publicity, since he or she is deprived of the opportunity to sell his or her name or likeness to some other company. Publication is not required for invasion of privacy. Unlike in defamation, truth is not a defense. Under the First Amendment, the courts have created a privilege for the media when it is reporting on newsworthy events. Then the media will be protected even when the news report is inaccurate, unless the error was made deliberately or recklessly.

The court in the following case discussed the tort of invasion of privacy.

7.1

SANDERS V. AMERICAN BROADCASTING COMPANIES, INC.
978 P.2D 67 (CA 1999)

FACTS . . . In 1992, . . . Mark Sanders was working as a telepsychic in PMG's Los Angeles office, giving "readings" to customers who telephoned PMG's 900 number (for which they were charged a per-minute fee). The psychics' work area consisted of a large room with rows of cubicles, about 100 total, in which the psychics took their calls. Each cubicle was enclosed on three sides by five-foot-high partitions. The facility also included a separate lunch room and enclosed offices for managers and supervisors.

. . . [T]he door to the PMG facility was unlocked during business hours, but PMG, by internal policy, prohibited access to the office by nonemployees without specific permission. An employee testified the front door was visible from the administration desk and a supervisor greeted any nonemployees who entered.

. . . Stacy Lescht, employed by . . . ABC in an investigation of the telepsychic industry, obtained employment as a psychic in PMG's Los Angeles office. When she first entered the PMG office to apply for a position, she was not stopped at the front door or greeted by anyone until she found and approached the administration desk. Once hired, she sat at a cubicle desk, where she gave telephonic readings to customers. Lescht testified that while sitting at her desk she could easily overhear conversations conducted in surrounding cubicles or in the aisles near her cubicle.

When not on the phone, she talked with some of the other psychics in the phone room. Lescht secretly videotaped these conversations with a "hat cam," i.e., a small camera hidden in her hat; a microphone attached to her brassiere captured sound as well. Among the conversations Lescht videotaped were two with Sanders, the first at Lescht's cubicle, the second at Sanders's.

. . . Sanders pled two causes of action against Lescht and ABC based on the videotaping itself: violation of Penal Code section 632 . . . and the common law tort of invasion of privacy by intrusion. The court ordered trial on these counts . . . [separated] with the section 632 count tried first. . . . [T]he jury found defendants liable on the [second] cause of action for invasion of privacy by intrusion. . . . [T]he jury fixed compensatory damages at $335,000; found defendants had acted with malice, fraud or oppression; and awarded exemplary damages of about $300,000. . . .

ISSUE May a person who lacks a reasonable expectation of complete privacy in a conversation because it could be seen and overheard by coworkers (but not the general public) nevertheless have a claim for invasion of privacy by intrusion based on a television reporter's covert videotaping of that conversation?

continued

7.1

SANDERS V. AMERICAN BROADCASTING COMPANIES, INC., *continued*

978 P.2D 67 (CA 1999)

HOLDING Yes. A person may have a reasonable expectation of privacy from investigative reporters even though his coworkers can hear the conversation.

REASONING . . . In an office or other workplace to which the general public does not have unfettered access, employees may enjoy a limited, but legitimate, expectation that their conversations and other interactions will not be secretly videotaped by undercover television reporters, even though those conversations may not have been completely private from the participants' coworkers. . . . [W]e do not hold or imply that investigative journalists necessarily commit a tort by secretly recording events and conversations in offices, stores or other workplaces. Whether a reasonable expectation of privacy is violated by such recording depends on the exact nature of the conduct and all the surrounding circumstances. In addition, liability under the intrusion tort requires that the invasion be highly offensive to a reasonable person, considering, among other factors, the motive of the alleged intruder. . . . We hold . . . that where the other elements of the intrusion tort are proven, the cause of action is not defeated as a matter of law simply because the events or conversations upon which the defendant allegedly intruded were not completely private from all other eyes and ears. . . .

[W]e adopted the definition of the intrusion tort. . . . The cause of action, we held, has two elements: (1) intrusion into a private place, conversation or matter, (2) in a manner highly offensive to a reasonable person. The first element . . . is not met when the plaintiff has merely been observed, or even photographed or recorded, in a public place. Rather, "the plaintiff must show the defendant penetrated some zone of physical or sensory privacy surrounding, or obtained unwanted access to data about, the plaintiff. The tort is proven only if the plaintiff had an objectively reasonable expectation of seclusion or solitude in the place, conversation or data source."

. . . [M]ass media videotaping may constitute an intrusion even when the events and communications recorded were visible and audible to some limited set of observers at the time they occurred. . . . [A] person may reasonably expect privacy against the electronic recording of a communication, even though he or she had no reasonable expectation as to confidentiality of the communication's contents. " . . . 'Such secret monitoring denies the speaker an important aspect of privacy of communication—the right to control the nature and extent of the firsthand dissemination of his statements.'" . . . [P]rivacy, for purposes of the intrusion tort, is not a binary, all-or-nothing characteristic. There are degrees and nuances to societal recognition of our expectations of privacy. " . . . The mere fact that a person can be seen by someone does not automatically mean that he or she can legally be forced to be subject to being seen by everyone."

. . . "[I]t remains an issue of fact for the jury whether [plaintiff] had an expectation that the interview was not being recorded and whether that expectation was justified under the circumstances." . . . Privacy for purposes of the intrusion tort must be evaluated with respect to the identity of the alleged intruder and the nature of the intrusion. . . . [M]oreover, decisions on the common law and statutory protection of workplace privacy show that the same analysis applies in the workplace as in other settings; consequently, an employee may, under some circumstances, have a reasonable expectation of visual or **aural privacy** against electronic intrusion by a stranger to the workplace, despite the possibility the conversations and interactions at issue could be witnessed by coworkers or the employer. . . . [We do not suggest that the same standards necessarily apply to private intrusions as to government searches, or vice versa. We observe . . . that the United States Supreme Court has recognized, in the Fourth Amendment context, that even employees without personal offices may have a reasonable, but limited, expectation of privacy against intrusions by strangers to the workplace. . . .] As for possible First Amendment defenses, any discussion must await a later case, as no constitutional issue was decided by the lower courts or presented for our review here. . . .

BUSINESS CONSIDERATION What can the media do to reduce the likelihood of lawsuits while still participating in investigative reporting?

ETHICAL CONSIDERATION Was Lescht's behavior ethical? Why or why not?

Trespass

In common law, trespass was one of the most common torts. Today, the general tort of trespass has evolved into some of the specific torts already discussed. The traditional tort of *trespass* remains as the tort used to protect property interests against nonconsensual infringements. There are two types of trespass—trespass to land and trespass to personal property. A person who ventures onto the property of another without permission is a trespasser. The following is an example of trespass to personal property. If you return to the parking lot after class, and someone is sleeping in the back seat of your car, that person is trespassing on your car. The only question is one of damages. Even if the person trespassed through mistake and did no harm, there will be *nominal damages* of, say, five dollars. If, on the other hand, the person trespassed before and had been warned, then higher damages likely would be assessed in order to compensate you for the unwarranted invasion of your car. Of course, the trespasser will be liable for any actual harm.

Conversion

Conversion occurs when a person intentionally exercises exclusive control over the personal property of another without permission. In such a case, the converter is liable for damages. If a person obtains possession of the property lawfully but is then told by the owner to return it yet refuses to do so, that person is also a converter. If the owner seeks the return of the property, the proper action is one for **replevin.** Damages can also be obtained if the owner suffered harm during the conversion. Sometimes the owner does not desire the return of the property, for example, if it is now in damaged condition. In this case, the owner asks for reimbursement for the loss.

Misappropriation of Trade Secrets

Misappropriation of trade secrets occurs when an actor unlawfully acquires and uses the trade secrets of another business enterprise. The victim must prove that a trade secret exists. The owner must have implemented reasonable steps to protect the trade secret. The actor must have acquired it by some unlawful means such as industrial espionage, theft, or bribery. Some states, like Texas, require that the actor acquire the secret as a result of a confidential relationship with the victim.[4] Texas also requires that the actor "use" the trade secret.[5] This tort is also called *theft of trade secrets.* Most states have adopted the Uniform Trade Secrets Act to codify their laws on trade secrets.[6]

CALL-IMAGE TECHNOLOGY

7.2 | MANAGEMENT

INVASION OF PRIVACY

Several people have complained that interactive videophones are overly intrusive and should be prohibited. A number of these people have banded together to form "SLAM" (Stop Looking At Me) and have threatened to file invasion-of-privacy lawsuits against every interactive videophone manufacturer and retailer in the United States. CIT is not yet on solid financial ground, and Tom is concerned that such a lawsuit could bankrupt the firm before it has a chance to succeed. Anna seems less concerned, but she is still worried. She has asked you if Tom's fears are valid. What will you tell her? Why?

BUSINESS CONSIDERATION Suppose that a business is facing the prospect of a number of lawsuits over its product. Should the business be proactive on the issue, or would it be better to wait and react to any suits that are filed?

ETHICAL CONSIDERATIONS Assume that a group is attempting to intimidate manufacturers and retailers in a given industry by threatening to file lawsuits unless the demands of the group are met. Is such behavior ethical? From an ethical perspective, how should the firms in the industry react to such threats?

Aural privacy
A privacy right for normal conversations; the right to privacy from eavesdropping.

Replevin
A personal action brought to recover possession of goods unlawfully taken.

Fraud

Fraud is an extremely complex tort. It concerns the misrepresentation of a material fact made with the intent to deceive. If an innocent person reasonably relies on the misrepresentation and is damaged as a result, the injured person may successfully sue for fraud. There are five elements of fraud:

1. A material fact was involved: An opinion usually will not constitute fraud (fact).
2. The fact was misrepresented (a falsehood).
3. The falsehood was made with the intent to deceive (scienter).
4. The falsehood was one on which another person justifiably relied (reasonable reliance).
5. That person was injured as a result (damage).

For example, if a jeweler sells a rhinestone as a diamond with the knowledge that it is a rhinestone, the action is fraud. If a bank customer knowingly obtains a loan on the basis of a false financial statement, it is fraud. If a corporation solicits persons to buy stock for the purpose of building a new plant when in reality the corporation wants the money to pay off existing liabilities, it is fraud. The list is virtually endless. Exhibit 7.2 summarizes the intentional torts discussed in this chapter.

Civil RICO Violations

The Racketeer Influenced and Corrupt Organizations Act, commonly referred to by the acronym RICO,[7] is discussed in more detail in Chapter 8; however, it also deserves mention here. RICO is directed at a pattern of racketeering activity. A *pattern* means two or more racketeering acts within a 10-year period. Racketeering acts range from violent acts such as murder, to less violent acts such as mail fraud. The RICO statute includes a long list of racketeering acts. Individuals and businesses that are injured can sue those who are violating the statute. For example, on 22 September 1999 the U.S. Justice Department filed a civil RICO lawsuit against the tobacco industry.[8] Successful plaintiffs in a civil action may recover **treble damages,** attorney's fees, and reasonable court costs. A criminal conviction is not a prerequisite to filing a RICO civil suit.

Treble damages
Three times the amount of actual damages.

Defenses to Intentional Torts

As is true with the torts themselves, there is a great deal of variation from state to state in how the defenses are actually defined and what constitutes a defense. Note that a defense can only be used against certain torts. The following sections contain a brief description of some of the common defenses.

Implied consent
A concurrence of wills manifested by signs, actions, or facts, or by inaction or silence, that raises a presumption that agreement has been given.

Consent. Even though a tort has been committed, the law may not compensate the injured party if, in fact, that person consented to the tort. Most cases involve issues of **implied consent.** The law will not infer consent unless it is reasonable under the circumstances. For example, football players obviously batter each other throughout the course of a game. Therefore, even though the tort of battery may have been committed, it is not actionable because the law views each player as having consented to the touching. If a player intentionally exceeds the implied consent, however, he or she may be liable for the tort. For example, a professional boxer consents to being punched; however, most courts would hold that a boxer does not consent to being bitten on the ear during a match.

E X H I B I T   7.2 | **Intentional Torts**

Specific Tort	Definition	Defenses
Assault	Conduct that would put a reasonable person in apprehension of an immediate battery	Conditional privilege Consent Necessity/Justification Self-defense
Battery	Intentional offensive touching	Conditional privilege Consent Necessity/Justification Self-defense
Defamation	Slander (spoken), libel (written) Statements that harm a person's reputation	Truth Absolute privilege (legal or congressional proceeding) Conditional privilege
Disparagement	Defamation of a business product, service, or reputation	
False Imprisonment	The detention of one person by another against his or her will and without just cause	Privilege Consent
Mental Distress	Causing a serious indignity	
Invasion of Privacy	Unwarranted intrusions on the privacy of another	Privilege
Trespass	Subjecting real or personal property to harm or infringement	Privilege Consent Necessity
Conversion	Intentional exercise of exclusive control over the personal property of another without permission	Necessity Consent
Theft of trade secrets	Taking secret business data for unauthorized use	
Fraud	The misrepresentation of a material fact made with the intention to deceive	

Privilege. Permission is given voluntarily, whether it is expressed or implied. The law also recognizes a defense that is not voluntary. Because the law seeks to protect certain social interests more than others, it developed the concept of privilege. Privilege may be recognized in a number of situations including:

1. If someone moves to strike you, you have the ancient privilege of self-defense. Most states also recognize the privilege to defend family members.
2. Retail businesspersons have a privilege to detain persons who they reasonably believe have committed theft.
3. Persons whose property is stolen have the privilege of going onto another person's property in order to retrieve it.
4. Judges and legislators have the privilege of saying things that might be defamation under other circumstances in order to stimulate debate and encourage independence of thought and action.

Necessity. Whenever a person enters another's land for self-protection, the law recognizes that as necessity and disallows the nominal damages ordinarily awarded for trespass. For example, if you are in a boat on a lake and a storm suddenly develops, you may enter a private cove, tie up to a private dock, and find shelter on the land in order to protect yourself. Due to the necessity, no trespass exists. However, the law permits the landowner to collect actual losses if, for example, you use his or her provisions while tied to his or her private dock.

Truth. Truth is one of the best defenses with respect to the tort of defamation. A defendant will win if the defendant can prove that the statement was true. If an individual accuses a businessperson of being a crook and is sued for defamation, the actor will win if it can be proven that the businessperson is a "fence" for stolen property. Exhibit 7.3 summarizes the defenses available against specific intentional torts.

NEGLIGENCE

Negligence exists when four conditions are met. First, the defendant must have owed the plaintiff a duty. Second, the defendant must have breached the duty by acting in a particular manner or failing to act as required. Third, the breach of that duty must be the actual as well as the "legal" cause of the plaintiff's injury. Fourth, that injury must be one that the law recognizes and for which money damages may be recovered.

Duty

The reasonable-and-prudent-person rule has been established in negligence law in order to determine the "degree" of duty. With respect to negligence, everyone has a "reasonable" duty to avoid this type of behavior. This standard is more difficult to define, explain, and apply than is the standard of simple duty. Generally, however, the law states that *reasonable duty* is a standard of ordinary skill and care, based on the facts of each individual case.

If, while you are quietly fishing on the shore of a lake, you see a man fishing who is 100 feet away fall out of his boat and begin to drown, does common law place on you a duty to help him? The answer is no, because you did not create the hazard in the first place. On the other hand, suppose you own a boatyard on the lake and the fisherman rents his boat from you. If the boat springs a leak because it was defective when you rented it, thereby causing the fisherman to drown, you

E X H I B I T 7.3 | **Effective Defenses Against Intentional Torts**

Consent	Privilege	Necessity	Truth
Assault	Assault	Trespass	Defamation
Battery	Battery	Conversion	
False Imprisonment	False Imprisonment		
Trespass	Trespass		
Conversion	Defamation		
Invasion of Privacy	Invasion of Privacy		

have breached your duty to rent safe boats. You created the harm in the second situation but not in the first.

Foreseeability, in negligence, addresses the likelihood that something will happen in the future. It is determined by what a "reasonable and prudent person" would expect.

To test for a duty in any particular situation, the law has constructed a person against whom the conduct of the defendant is to be compared. This purely hypothetical person is known as the *reasonable and prudent person*—not perfect, merely reasonable. Three areas help to define the reasonable and prudent person: knowledge, investigation, and judgment. There are also statutory standards that are applied in certain situations.

Knowledge. As the amount of knowledge existing in the world increases, so does the amount of knowledge that the reasonable and prudent person is expected to possess. In this sense, therefore, the law presumes that everyone has complete knowledge of the law. If we have no knowledge of the law, how can we be expected to obey it?

Investigation. Investigation is closely related to knowledge. It is our obligation to find out. We assume that a reasonable person knows certain information. We also assume that the reasonable person will do research or tests to discover additional information. Before you drive a car, for example, the law presumes that you will have ascertained that the brakes are working properly. If you are a drug manufacturer, the law presumes that you will have discovered if your drug will cause any harmful side effects. If you have failed to do adequate testing, you will have violated the standard of care of a reasonable and prudent person. Note that a harmful side effect does not necessarily mean that the manufacturer is negligent. Some drugs do have harmful side effects for some or many patients; however, the drug is still beneficial for the majority to whom it is administered. In this case, distribution of the drug with proper warnings attached is permitted. The adequacy of the warning was an issue in a recent lawsuit against a manufacturer of the oral polio vaccine, when a father alleged that he contracted polio as a result of his daughter receiving the vaccine.[9]

Judgment. You have heard some people say that one person has "good" judgment or another has "bad" judgment. The law measures both persons against the same standard. In a tort case, the defendant must have acted reasonably or he or she will be found to have breached the duty of reasonable care. We have no hard-and-fast rules here. The outcome always depends on the facts of each case. A missing fact, once supplied, can change the outcome. Therefore, before beginning any activity, the law expects people to ask questions such as: What is the likelihood that this

7.3 | MANAGEMENT

JOB REFERENCES FOR FORMER EMPLOYEES

Recently, CIT expanded by hiring three workers who are not family members. Unfortunately, Tom and Anna have not had much experience in selecting employees. Two of the workers are excellent and fit in well with the business and family members. The third, Huey, was not a good fit. He was fired after the first three weeks. Tom and Anna also suspect Huey of falsifying company reports. Since his dismissal, Huey has been applying for other jobs. Although he did not list CIT as a reference, Huey did list CIT as his last place of employment. Consequently, potential employers have been calling CIT and leaving messages for Anna. They are understandably interested in why Huey's employment lasted only three weeks. Anna knows she cannot avoid the messages from four prospective employers much longer. She calls you to ask what she should do. What should she say and not say when she returns the calls?

BUSINESS CONSIDERATIONS Should a business adopt a policy regarding references for former employees? Is a business less likely to face liability if it only gives oral recommendations, or should it put everything in writing? Why?

ETHICAL CONSIDERATIONS Is it ethical to give a good recommendation for a "bad" employee to help that employee obtain other employment? Is it ethical to give a bad recommendation for a good employee to make his or her leaving more difficult?

particular activity will harm someone else? If harm might occur, what is the likely extent of the harm? What must I give up to avoid risk to others?

Assume that you just got a new rifle and want to test it and adjust the sights (or scope) for maximum accuracy for the deer season. You find an isolated field in the country and set up a target at the base of a bald hill 300 yards away. No one else is present. After firing the first shot, however, you begin to attract a crowd. Assume that with each shot the crowd gets larger. At what point do you stop shooting to avoid injury to an innocent person? The decision to stop involves the exercise of reason. The exercise of reason is *judgment.*

Statutory Standard. In some cases, the law solves the problem of limits, like the ones just raised, by providing a standard contained in a statute. For example, most state traffic laws say that when it begins to get dark, all drivers are required to turn on their headlights. If, while traveling down a road at night without your lights on, you hit and injure a pedestrian, the law will conclude that you breached a standard of reasonableness no matter what your excuse. Most of these statutes provide a criminal penalty, but that penalty is irrelevant in a civil proceeding such as a tort case. In most states, breaching the statutory standard is **negligence per se.** However, the states are not in agreement as to whether this should be treated as a conclusive presumption where evidence to the contrary is not permitted. Some states, such as California,[10] instead treat negligence per se as a rebuttable presumption. The person is allowed to present evidence that, under the circumstances, violating the statutory standard was the most careful behavior.

Negligence per se
Inherent negligence; negligence without a need for further proof.

Breach of Duty

In general, the plaintiff has to prove that the defendant caused injury by not adhering to the reasonable-and-prudent-person standard. In some cases, however, that strict requirement of proof is relaxed because the law has developed the doctrine of *res ipsa loquitur,* which means "the thing speaks for itself." To apply *res ipsa loquitur* in a case, the injury must meet the following three tests: (1) this occurrence would ordinarily not happen in the absence of someone's negligence; (2) it must be caused by a device within the exclusive control of the defendant(s); and (3) the plaintiff in no way has contributed to his or her own injury. For example, if a patient submits to an operation to remove infected tonsils and leaves the operating room with a surgical instrument embedded in her throat, there is no need to require direct testimony on the point. It speaks for itself; someone in the surgery room was negligent. In some states *res ipsa loquitur* creates a presumption of negligence. Its effect is to shift the burden of proof from the plaintiff to the defendant(s). In this situation, the hospital personnel and the surgeons will each need to show that they were careful. In other states the burden of proof remains with the plaintiff. *Res ipsa loquitur* creates an inference of negligence. Then the jury weighs the evidence including the inference of negligence.

Causation

The heart of the law of negligence is causation. Causation has two components: actual cause and "legal" cause, which is also called proximate cause.

Actual Cause. The law determines whether X, an act by one party, is the actual cause of Y, a result affecting the other party. The courts examine whether "but for" the occurrence of act X, result Y would have happened: X is an event, without which

Y would not occur. This is called the *but-for test.* For example, a defendant in an automobile accident case may have failed to signal a turn properly. But if the accident would have happened even if he had signaled properly, the failure to signal is not the actual cause of the accident. It fails the "but-for" test.

Proximate Cause. *After* actual cause has been established, the focus shifts to what the law calls *policy questions.* Some boundary must be established for legal liability for the consequences of any act. What is decided here is whether or not the law should hold the defendant liable. At some point the law will say, "Enough." Beyond this point the defendant will not be held liable. Courts ask if it is unfair or unreasonable to hold the defendant liable. To solve these policy questions, the law has developed a three-pronged test:

1. What is the likelihood that this particular conduct will injure other persons?
2. If injury should occur, what is the degree of seriousness of the injury?
3. What is the interest that the defendant must sacrifice to avoid the risk of causing the injury?

For example, if the defendant is negligent with respect to Tommy, and Bob tries to rescue Tommy and suffers some injury as a result, the defendant will be held liable for Bob's injuries as well as Tommy's because it is foreseeable that people will try to rescue someone in peril.

Harm

If the plaintiff is not injured, the defendant will not be held liable in damages. For example, a driver speeding down a road at 180 miles per hour is clearly breaching the duty to drive in a safe and reasonable manner; but if no one is injured, no one can successfully sue for negligence.

Defenses to Negligence

Assumption of the Risk. Common law developed a doctrine in which the defendant will win if it can be proved that the plaintiff voluntarily assumed a known risk. For example, have you ever examined cigarette packages? They bear various warnings, some of which are "Surgeon General's Warning: Smoking by pregnant women may result in fetal injury, premature birth, and low birthweight," or "Quitting smoking now greatly reduces serious risks to your health," or "Cigarette smoke contains carbon monoxide." Historically, a longtime cigarette smoker who contracted lung cancer and sued the cigarette manufacturer has lost because the manufacturer defended on the basis of the plaintiff's voluntary assumption of the risk. (New scientific evidence is allowing the courts to reexamine tobacco company liability in this area.) Courts will generally apply assumption of the risk to a skier who breaks her leg while skiing on a mountain slope.

Contributory Negligence. Another defense at common law is *contributory negligence.* Suppose Justin wears a black raincoat at night, jaywalks across a busy street, and is hit by a car. If Justin sues and the defendant can assert and prove Justin actually contributed to the injury, Justin will lose in a state that applies contributory negligence because contributory negligence would **bar** recovery.

Bar
In the legal sense, to prevent or to stop.

Comparative Negligence. In a growing number of jurisdictions, the doctrine of contributory negligence has been replaced by the doctrine of *comparative negligence,* which has been adopted by the legislature or through judicial precedents. Here, the fact finder (usually the jury) determines to what degree the plaintiff contributed to his or her own injury. Comparative negligence is generally perceived to be more fair; however, it may be difficult for the trier of fact to determine the relative faults. For example, if Jason is injured to the extent of $100,000 in damages but contributed 35 percent to his injury, he will be awarded $65,000 instead of losing completely, as he would under the doctrine of contributory negligence.

Jurisdictions may select from three variations of comparative negligence. Pure comparative negligence would allow the plaintiff to recover no matter how negligent he or she was. (For example, the California Supreme Court adopted pure comparative negligence in *Li* v. *Yellow Cab Co.*, 119 Cal.Rptr. 858, 532 P.2d 1226 [1975].) However, some jurisdictions feel it would be unfair to allow the plaintiff to recover if he or she was the primary cause of the injury—for example, if the plaintiff was 95 percent responsible for causing the accident. Consequently, two other variations prevent recovery to the party who was mostly to blame. One version only permits recovery if the plaintiff contributed less than 50 percent of the negligence to his or her injury. This is commonly called the "less than" type of comparative negligence. This is probably the most common variety of comparative negligence. Another version allows recovery if the plaintiff contributed 50 percent or less to his or her injury, which is commonly called the "equal to or less than" version. The differences between these two may appear inconsequential, but they are significant to the parties of a lawsuit who may be denied recovery because the jury concluded that they were each 50 percent at fault. The application of comparative negligence becomes difficult when there are more than two parties. States have different ways of handling multiple-party situations. The effect of comparative negligence laws may be minimal in automobile accidents in "no fault" states.

The court in the following case discussed the defense of comparative negligence.

7.2

REED V. UNION PACIFIC RAILROAD COMPANY
1999 U.S. APP. LEXIS 16008 (7TH CIR. 1999)

FACTS ... On September 1, 1994, Ronald Reed was driving his pickup truck on E.L. Harris' Ranch in Murphysboro, Illinois, where he had been working as a farmhand for approximately thirteen years. As he approached a private railroad crossing which had no crossbucks, gates, or warning lights, Reed slowly rolled up to the crossing and checked both right and left for any approaching trains. He did not, however, look directly in front of him. As Reed crossed over the train tracks, his truck hit a replacement rail that had been left uncovered by Union Pacific. The impact caused Reed to be thrown and twisted around the inside of the truck and jerked the steering wheel to the right, causing the truck to become stuck on the rail. After dislodging his truck, Reed brought his co-worker, Ted Vanbuskirk, to the railroad crossing where the accident occurred. They approached the accident scene in the same truck Reed had been

driving at the time of the accident. As they neared the track, Vanbuskirk testified that, although specifically looking for the replacement rail, he could not see it from the truck. Only after stepping out of the truck and walking up to the tracks was he able to see the replacement rail. Harris, Reed's employer, corroborated Reed's story by testifying that he could not see the rail from his truck, and saw it only when he walked up to the tracks to fix a gate.

Later that day, Reed began to feel pain and stiffness in his neck, arm, shoulder, and head. That evening, Reed went to the hospital where he saw Dr. Gregorio F. Macareg. ... A few weeks after the initial emergency room visit, Dr. Macareg performed a CT scan which showed that Reed had a mild degenerative disk disease between C5–C6 levels, and between C6–C7 levels. ... Dr. Macareg opined that the accident on September 1, 1994 aggravated Reed's

7.2

REED V. UNION PACIFIC RAILROAD COMPANY, *continued*

1999 U.S. APP. LEXIS 16008 (7TH CIR. 1999)

pre-existing degenerative disk condition. Dr. Macareg was unsure whether Reed would be able to perform heavy labor in the future as back and neck ailments heal with differing results. . . .

The jury returned a verdict in favor of Reed and determined that he suffered damages totaling $83,022.90. This amount was composed of $41,511.45 for pain and suffering and $41,511.45 for medical expenses. But the jury also found that Reed's own negligence contributed 50% to his injuries, so the total compensation was $41,511.45.

ISSUE Was it proper for the trial court to instruct the jury on comparative negligence?

HOLDING Yes. The jury instruction on comparative negligence was proper.

REASONING . . . When determining whether a new trial is warranted because of improper jury instructions we ask "whether the instructions, when considered in their entirety and not in isolation, were sufficient to inform the jury of the applicable law." Reed argues that the jury should not have been instructed on the issue of comparative negligence because Union Pacific introduced no affirmative evidence showing that Reed failed to exercise the proper degree of care when driving his truck across the train tracks. Union Pacific has the burden of proving that Reed failed to adhere to the proper standard of care, i.e. that Reed, through his own negligence, contributed to his injuries. In order to prevail on this issue, Union Pacific must show by a preponderance of the evidence that Reed was negligent and his negligence was a proximate cause of his injuries.

. . . Union Pacific elicited testimony from Reed that, although he did look to both sides when crossing the railroad tracks, he did not look straight in front of him, where the replacement rail was situated. Reed

also said there was nothing either outside or on the inside of his truck that obstructed his view of the tracks. He further testified that he did not stop prior to crossing over the tracks. Illinois courts have held that it is negligent for an individual to fail to keep a proper lookout while driving because a driver should reasonably anticipate danger at all times. . . . [T]he jury saw numerous photographs of the accident scene, and it could determine whether Reed should have been able to see the replacement rail if exercising the proper duty of care.

. . . [I]t is within the province of the jury to determine damages in a personal injury case. Union Pacific responded in its answer that Reed's injuries were proximately caused by his own negligence and it introduced sufficient evidence to allow the jury to determine if that was true. Given the testimony and visual evidence presented to the jury, there was sufficient evidence to get the question of comparative negligence to the jury. Indeed, the jury found that Reed was 50% negligent. The district court did not abuse its discretion by instructing the jury about comparative fault. . . .

BUSINESS CONSIDERATIONS What could Union Pacific have done to help prevent the accident? Should a business have a policy for its employees to follow when performing maintenance work to help minimize any risk of harm to others from the work? How could Reed have avoided the accident?

ETHICAL CONSIDERATIONS Was it ethical for Union Pacific to deny liability in this case? From an ethical perspective, should the railroad admit that it was negligent and accept liability rather than force the injured party to undertake a lawsuit to collect damages for his injuries?

STRICT LIABILITY

Recall that with respect to intentional torts, everyone has a duty to avoid such behavior. With respect to negligence, we have a duty to use reasonable care. This section examines a situation in which the law states that our duty to reimburse for losses is absolute, regardless of whether we are at fault or not. The law prescribes the situations in which there is strict liability.

Whenever a person undertakes an extremely hazardous activity and it is foreseeable that injury may result, that person can be held "strictly liable" if injury does result whether or not the person was at fault. *Strict liability* is imposed without regard to fault. For example, if you use explosives on your property and by so doing cause windows to be blown out of an adjoining neighbor's house, you will be held liable no matter how careful you were in handling those explosives. Generally, the areas in which we have strict liability are set out in the applicable statutes and court precedents. *Rylands* v. *Fletcher*[11] is credited with creating this legal doctrine.

Through the development of the doctrine of strict liability, U.S. courts have shifted emphasis from ultrahazardous activity to dangerous activity, and the doctrine seems to be expanding in scope. Today, the following activities are considered strict liability activities in most states: the keeping of wild animals, the use of explosives, and dangerous activities. Some states have added strict liability for the owner of a motor vehicle if injury occurs when the driver has the owner's permission.[12] California imposes strict liability on parents for the willful misconduct of their minor children. There is a $10,000 limit on parental liability.[13] Remember, though, strict liability does not automatically arise. Courts can create new precedents; generally, however, courts look to existing precedents and statutory law. This is another area in which the legal system is making policy decisions about who should justly bear the loss.

PRODUCT LIABILITY

Product liability is a growing concern of businesses. Manufacturers *and* distributors of products may be held liable based on these legal theories: (1) fraud in the marketing of the product, (2) express or implied warranties (warranties will not be discussed in this chapter, since they are based on contract theories), (3) negligence, and (4) strict liability. People who are injured by a product may claim and attempt to prove more than one theory of liability; that is, these theories are not mutually exclusive.

Fraud in marketing will follow the general rules of fraud previously discussed in this chapter. Negligence in product liability can include negligence in design, construction, labeling, packaging, and assembly. When an injured person uses the negligence theory for product liability, there must be a close causal connection between the negligence and the injury. The lawsuit will be subject to the usual defenses for negligence, including contributory negligence, comparative negligence, and assumption of the risk.

Strict liability for products is clarified by § 402A of the *Restatement (Second) of Torts*, and has been adopted by most states. *Restatement (Second) of Torts*, a publication of the American Law Institute (ALI), states the preferred version of the common law of torts. It is used by courts as an authoritative reference but is not binding on them. It becomes a precedent in the court only after a judge has relied on a section and referred to it in his or her opinion. Section 402A of the *Restatement (Second) of Torts* has long been considered the seminal document on product liability. However, in spring of 1997, the ALI adopted revisions to the *Restatement (Second) of Torts* in a document entitled *Restatement (Third) of Torts: Product Liability.*[14] This new document will shape product liability law in the future.

Section 402A of the *Restatement (Second) of Torts* establishes the strict liability rule: A seller will be held liable for a product that contains a defect or is unreasonably dangerous to use. (*Unreasonably dangerous* seems vague to both laypersons and lawyers; there have been many court decisions attempting to define and clarify the term.) The defect must be in the product when it leaves the control of the defendant. As with other forms of strict liability, the plaintiff does not need to prove negligence or fraud in order to recover. Generally, the plaintiff must show that strict liability applies to this situation, that the product had a defect when it left the defendant's possession or was unreasonably dangerous, and that the plaintiff was harmed. Since this is a tort cause of action, the seller cannot avoid liability by disclaiming it. Contributory or comparative negligence by the plaintiff cannot be used as a defense. The manufacturer may prove the following defenses depending on the situation—**obviousness of hazard,** product misuse by the plaintiff, and assumption of the risk.

The court in the following product liability case addresses both the negligent and strict liability versions of failure to warn.

Obviousness of hazard
The hazard in the product is obvious, such as a sharp knife.

Lessor
Individual or company owner who rents out property.

Judgment as a matter of law
A decision by the court to remove the issue from the jury because there is only one possible answer to the issue.

7.3

TENBARGE V. AMES TAPING TOOL SYSTEMS, INC.
1999 U.S. APP. LEXIS 15028 (8TH CIR. 1999)

FACTS . . . From 1983 to 1993, [Douglas R.] Tenbarge worked as a drywall installer. His primary duty was to apply drywall compound and tape along the seams of drywall panels with an Ames Auto Taper, known as a Bazooka. The Bazooka is a tube fifty-six inches in length and two and one-fourth inches in diameter used to apply joint compound and tape simultaneously to drywall seams in ceilings and walls. It weighs seven pounds when empty and twenty pounds when filled to capacity with joint compound and a 500-foot roll of tape. The Bazooka is operated by holding it with both hands and applying pressure against the seam as the joint compound and tape are being fed out of the tube. . . . [T]he Bazooka requires repetitive wrist motions and the exertion of considerable pressure to apply the tape and compound. Lacking handholds, "the Bazooka is awkward to support and maneuver, particularly while doing overhead work."

In 1991, after experiencing numbness in his hands and fingers, Tenbarge consulted a physician and was diagnosed with carpal tunnel syndrome (CTS). In December 1992 and January 1993, Tenbarge underwent surgery on both wrists. He returned to work in April 1993, only to sustain an elbow injury. He underwent a third surgery late in 1993.

Tenbarge filed suit in Missouri state court in 1994 against Ames, the manufacturer and **lessor** of the Bazooka. . . . Ames removed the case to federal court . . . [T]he district court granted **judgment as a matter of law** in favor of Ames on Tenbarge's claims

of liability based upon Ames's failure to warn of the danger of injury resulting from the use of the Bazooka. The jury found in favor of Ames on Tenbarge's claims based upon negligence, strict liability for defective condition, and breach of both express and implied warranties. . . .

ISSUE Should the trial court have permitted the jury to consider whether Ames had a duty to warn Tenbarge?

HOLDING Yes. The jury should have been permitted to consider whether Ames had a duty to warn.

REASONING . . . In Missouri, there are five elements of a strict liability failure to warn claim: (1) the defendant sold the product in the course of its business; (2) when used as reasonably anticipated and without knowledge of its characteristics, the product was unreasonably dangerous at the time of sale; (3) the defendant did not give an adequate warning of the danger; (4) the product was used in a reasonably anticipated manner; and (5) the plaintiff was damaged as a direct result of the product being sold without an adequate warning.

It is uncontested that Ames provided the Bazooka in the ordinary course of business and that Tenbarge used the Bazooka in the manner for which it was intended. Tenbarge introduced evidence sufficient to support an inference that the Bazooka was

continued

TENBARGE V. AMES TAPING TOOL SYSTEMS, INC., *continued*
1999 U.S. APP. LEXIS 15028 (8TH CIR. 1999)

unreasonably dangerous by presenting testimony concerning the risk of repetitive trauma injury. The parties agree that Tenbarge was never given any warnings about the use of the Bazooka during his job training. Bazookas shipped by Ames to Tenbarge's employer contained no accompanying literature instructing on their proper use nor any warnings regarding the advisability of limiting their use. Ames admitted that from 1984 to 1995, it did not issue any warnings concerning the possibility of repetitive trauma or repetitive stress injuries as a result of using the Bazooka.

. . . [T]he plaintiff must show that the product caused his injuries and that a warning would have altered his behavior. Tenbarge's treating physician, Dr. Richard Chusak, testified that the Bazooka caused the onset of Tenbarge's CTS . . .

Under Missouri law, a rebuttable presumption that adequate warnings would have been heeded arises if the plaintiff shows that no warning was given. The presumption should be recognized, however, only if there is a "legitimate jury question whether the plaintiff did not already know the danger." "[A] preliminary inquiry before applying the presumption is whether adequate information is available absent a warning." Tenbarge was not told of any risks associated with using the Bazooka when he first began using the tool. No analysis of ergonomic risk factors had been conducted on the Bazooka; thus, no literature was available that could have informed Tenbarge of the risks involved in using the Bazooka. . . . Tenbarge is entitled to the presumption that he would have altered his behavior had he received an adequate warning.

. . . In 1992 and 1993, when Tenbarge underwent surgery on both wrists, his physician told him that his CTS was caused by the use of the Bazooka. Despite this information, Tenbarge returned to work following the operations and used the Bazooka as before. This post-operative behavior, Ames argues, indicates that Tenbarge would not have followed warnings had they been given. Although Tenbarge's return to work following the surgeries is relevant to the question whether he would have heeded warnings, we conclude that it is insufficient to entitle Ames to judgment as a matter of law on this issue in light of the fact that Tenbarge returned to work pursuant to his doctor's instructions rather than in knowing disregard of the health risks associated with using the Bazooka.

. . . To establish . . . a [negligent failure to warn] claim, Tenbarge was required to introduce evidence establishing the existence of the following elements: (1) that Ames designed the Bazooka; (2) that Ames knew or had reason to know that the Bazooka was likely to be unreasonably dangerous; (3) that Ames had no reason to believe that the Bazooka's users would realize the danger in using it; (4) that Ames failed to use ordinary care in warning Tenbarge of the risk of harm; and (5) that the failure to warn directly caused the injury. In addition, the product must malfunction or fail. It is uncontested that Ames designed the Bazooka and offered no warning concerning its use. . . . [T]he company knew of the repetitive motion required to use the Bazooka. Evidence that use of the Bazooka presented ergonomic risk factors was sufficient to show defective condition. The risk of developing CTS by using the Bazooka was not so open and obvious as to allow Ames to assume that users would understand the danger in using it. . . . Tenbarge made a prima facie showing of causation . . . Accordingly, the district court should have submitted Tenbarge's negligent failure to warn claim to the jury. . . .

BUSINESS CONSIDERATIONS What should Ames have done to avoid liability? Should a manufacturer or lessor of equipment be liable when use of the equipment causes injury such as CTS? What types of businesses manufacture products that are likely to cause CTS?

ETHICAL CONSIDERATIONS Who is responsible for providing Tenbarge with a safe place to work and appropriate equipment and breaks? What ethical duty does an employer owe to the employees regarding safety, breaks, and equipment?

YOU BE THE JUDGE

PARENTS OF VICTIMS SUE FOR WRONGFUL DEATH

Parents of the three high school students who were shot and killed in a Paducah, Kentucky, high school in December 1997 have filed a $100 million wrongful death lawsuit. Eighteen computer and video games companies have been named as defendants in the suit. The producers of the film *The Basketball Diaries* are also named as defendants; it is contended that the film and games influenced Michael Carneal. Michael was a devotee of violent games. The complaint directly alleges that Michael was "profoundly influenced" by his exposure to violent media and that "the media's depiction of violence as a means of resolving conflict . . . further condoned his thinking." "In fact, Carneal's sharpshooting may be linked to his video game prowess. He had never shot a pistol before and yet got hits with eight out of nine shots, three of which were kills, according to Mike Breen, lead counsel for the plaintiffs in the case." According to Lt. Col. Dave Grossman, who teaches the psychology of murder for the federal government, "They are murder simulators which over time teach a person how to look another person in the eyes and snuff their life out." The Marine Corps uses the game Doom to train soldiers. (Similar lawsuits may also result from the shooting in Littleton, Colorado. The killers in that school were identified as obsessive players of violent games.)

Game makers made it big in 1998, with revenues of $6.2 million. The action game category accounts for 52 percent of Sony Playstation sales and 36.5 percent of Nintendo 64 sales. The video game industry is keeping a low profile until the heat cools. Doug Lowenstein, president of the Interactive Digital Software Association, is the only spokesman. He indicates that game manufacturers are making an increased effort to promote the ratings system, including working with retailers to enforce age restrictions when the games are sold.

This case has been brought in *your* court. How will *you* rule?[15]

BUSINESS CONSIDERATIONS What should game manufacturers do to protect the public from players' actions? What responsibility does a business have for torts and crimes committed by players or viewers? Does someone who gives a child access to these games commit a tortious and/or criminal act?

ETHICAL CONSIDERATIONS Is a business morally responsible for acts of their customers— for example, if their customers act out scenes from movies, television shows, or video games? Who is responsible when movies, television shows, or games are viewed by people who are too young or immature? Is it ethical for the victim's parents to seek recovery from the game manufacturers?

SOURCE: Deborah Claymon, *The Fresno Bee* (13 June 1999), pp. C1, C2.

TORT LIABILITY OF BUSINESS ENTITIES

Before leaving this introduction to tort law, we should mention that businesses *can* be held liable for the torts of their employees. Initially, courts were reluctant to impose liability in many situations. Today, however, liability is more readily assessed. Liability is generally imposed through the doctrine of *respondeat superior*. *Respondeat superior* means that the superior should answer or pay for the torts of

RESOURCES FOR BUSINESS LAW STUDENTS

NAME	RESOURCES	WEB ADDRESS
Legal Information Institute (LII)—Tort law	LII, maintained by the Cornell Law School, provides an overview of tort law, including the Federal Torts Claim Act (28 U.S.C. § 2671-80), recent Supreme Court tort decisions, and other information.	**http://www.law.cornell.edu/topics/torts.html**
American Bar Association's Tort and Insurance Practice Section (TIPS)	TIPS, a national professional group of plaintiff attorneys, defense attorneys, and insurance company counsel, provides information and links addressing tort law and insurance.	**http://www.abanet.org/tips/home.html**
American Tort Reform Association (ATRA)	ATRA provides information on tort reform issues, press releases, **The Reformer Newsletter,** "horror stories" about tort law abuse, and contact information.	**http://www.atra.org/atra/**

employees that occur in the course and scope of employment. *Respondeat superior* does not excuse the employee: The employee will be held liable in addition to his or her employer. *Respondeat superior* is discussed in detail in Chapter 33.

Summary

Tort law is designed to protect an individual's rights with respect to person and property. To do this, the law uses the concept of "duty." Tort law deals with "private" wrongs, whereas criminal law deals with "public" wrongs.

Three theories of tort liability exist: intentional torts, negligence, and strict liability. Intentional torts are those in which a person acted in a willful or intentional manner. Intentional torts to persons are assault, battery, defamation, disparagement, false imprisonment, emotional distress, and invasion of privacy. Invasion of privacy includes intrusion on physical solitude; unauthorized use of the plaintiff's likeness; presenting the plaintiff in a false light; and appropriation of plaintiff's likeness for commercial purposes. Intentional torts to property are trespass, conversion, and misappropriation of trade secrets. Different torts have various defenses. Common defenses include consent, privilege, necessity, and truth.

Negligence is the unintentional causing of harm that could have been prevented if the defendant had acted as a reasonable and prudent person. Defenses to negligence suits include assumption of the risk, contributory negligence, and comparative negligence. Strict liability is a separate basis of tort liability because it is independent from intent or negligence. Our legal system, through the legislature and/or courts, has declared that if certain activities cause harm, the actor will be found liable.

Central to a discussion of all three theories of liability are the concepts of duty and foreseeability. Duty imposes a certain kind of conduct and therefore is action oriented. Intentional torts establish that one has a duty to avoid committing the tort. Negligence establishes that one has a "reasonable" duty to avoid it. Strict liability, on the other hand, establishes a strict duty so that no matter how reasonable the conduct, there is automatic liability if harm occurs. Foreseeability concerns the thought process. If the hypothetical reasonable and prudent person would have foreseen harm, liability exists.

DISCUSSION QUESTIONS

1. A person decides to go shopping at the XYZ Department Store. While in the sportswear department, the store detective suspects the person of stealing a swimsuit. The detective approaches the person and says, "Excuse me, but would you mind if I asked you a few questions?" The person responds with, "Well, I'm really in quite a rush. I'm on my lunch hour and I have to get back to work." Nevertheless, the person submits to the questioning. The questioning lasts for 20 minutes. Has there been a false imprisonment? Would your answer be any different if the detective had said, "Excuse me, I suspect you of stealing a swimsuit. Would you mind if I asked you a few questions?"

2. A hotel waiter asks a male guest, "Is this woman your wife or your mistress?" Is the hotel liable for the waiter's insult? Would your answer be any different if the waiter had asked, "Is this woman your wife or your daughter?"

3. Someone knocks on your front door; after you have admitted him, he accuses you of being a stalker and a serial killer. Has he committed a tort against you? Would your answer be any different if he said the same things in the presence of another person?

4. When the legislature and the courts make parents civilly liable for their children's acts, what public policy is being advanced? Is this beneficial to society? Why or why not?

5. Why is it that intentional torts, negligence, and strict liability all involve the issue of foreseeability?

6. We all have a duty to protect other persons from harm. How does tort law resolve the question of the extent of that duty?

7. A manufacturer of chemical products markets suntan oil without sufficiently investigating the fact that, under certain circumstances, the vapors of the product become flammable. Suppose a person uses the product, and, as he rubs the oil on his chest, it ignites and burns him. Can he successfully sue the manufacturer for its negligence? Why?

8. It can be scientifically proven that pollution from the smokestacks of a steel plant in Beaumont, Texas, is carried in the clouds over the Gulf of Mexico and deposited on Orlando, Florida. It is also known that the pollutants carry cancer-causing chemicals. On what theory can a person who contracted cancer while living in Orlando successfully sue the steel plant? Discuss your answer with respect to proximate cause.

9. A gorilla escapes from a traveling circus, enters a shopping center, and destroys $347,500 worth of property. The businesses whose property was destroyed decide to sue the circus to recover their damages. The circus can prove that it did not act negligently and that it was not at fault in the escape of the gorilla. Given this situation, will the lawsuit succeed against the circus?

10. Professor Ortiz has established a listserver for her business law class. She posts procedural announcements on the listserver. She also uses it to inform the class about interesting web sites and to discuss journal articles and current events with the class. Students can post information to the listserver. Professor Ortiz also communicates with students individually via e-mail. She will often inform them about their grades and comment on student work.

 One day immediately after grading their second set of papers, she prepared an e-mail note to Nora Williamson. It said, "Nora, your last paper was extremely poorly written. It contained five sentence fragments, incorrect usages of words, and numerous misspelled words. In addition, you seem to have misunderstood the assignment. Consequently, your grade on this assignment is a D−. Sincerely, Professor Ortiz." Professor Ortiz intended to send this message only to Nora; however, she accidentally hit the group reply function on her e-mail and sent the message to the entire class. There are two students named Nora in the class.

 Assume also that some of the students in Professor Ortiz's class begin discussing the dean of students, Dr. Watts, on the listserver. Many of the comments are critical since Dr. Watts has taken a strong stand against alcoholic beverages on campus. In addition, Dr. Watts is dating the president of the university. Some typical comments on the listserver include: "She is such a prude"; "Dr. Watts seems to believe in 'do as I say and not as I do.' "; and "The quality of student services has declined drastically since she was appointed as dean of students." Analyze the potential torts in all of these situations.

CASE PROBLEMS AND WRITING ASSIGNMENTS

1. Todd Johnson has filed a suit demanding more than $2,000 in reimbursement for various items, all of which he previously stole from a couple. He stole their car and its contents at gunpoint outside a movie theater in San Bruno, California. Johnson contends that he should be reimbursed for the items that were still in the car when he was arrested for the carjacking. Todd is currently serving time in prison for the crime. Should Todd be permitted to recover from the police department for the confiscated items? [See "Carjacker Sues for $2,000 for Items Left Behind," *The Fresno Bee* (29 January 1995), p. A4).]

2. Michael Salima occasionally did repair work for Scherwood Country Club, which was operated by Marvin and Ron Hanson. He was not a licensed electrician. One day Salima was at the country club doing other repairs when Marvin asked him to look at a parking lot light that was malfunctioning. The day prior to the accident, a Scherwood employee had examined the light but was unable to determine the cause of the problem. Close to the light there were some electrical wires that were cut during some home construction in the vicinity. The wires had been spliced together and were clearly visible above ground. Salima decided that the problem was probably in some wiring that was on the pole about 18 feet above the ground. He climbed a ladder to investigate, touched the wires, was shocked, and fell to the ground, suffering serious injuries. Salima contended that the country club, through the Hansons, owed him a duty to warn him about a dangerous condition. Did the Hansons violate a duty to Salima? Was Salima contributorily negligent in this situation? If the state where the accident occurred applied comparative negligence, how should the negligence be allocated between the Hansons and Salima? [See *Salima* v. *Scherwood South, Inc.*, 38 F.3d 929 (7th Cir. 1994).]

3. "G.J.D. and Darwin Thebes were involved in an intimate relationship for approximately five years. During that time Thebes took sexually explicit photographs of G.J.D. which he then kept hidden. G.J.D. did not see the photographs until several years later after she had ended her relationship with Thebes. G.J.D. alleged that Thebes distributed photocopies of the photographs throughout the community when he learned she was ending their relationship. The photocopies included G.J.D.'s address and phone number as well as captions which implied that she was a prostitute. The distribution of the photocopies was calculated to ensure that they would be found by G.J.D.'s friends and relatives including her minor children, her mother, her brother, and her employer." Should G.J.D. recover for defamation, intentional infliction of emotional distress, or invasion of privacy? Thebes committed suicide while the lawsuit was pending. Should his estate be liable for actual and punitive damages? [See *G.J.D.* v. *Johnson*, 552 Pa. 169 (Pa. 1998).]

4. Helen Palsgraf was standing on a railroad platform waiting for her train. Another passenger attempted to board a train that was pulling out of the station. A railroad employee standing nearby pushed the passenger to help him board the moving train. In the process, a package the passenger was carrying was dropped onto the tracks and exploded because it contained fireworks. The force of the explosion caused some scales standing at the opposite end of the railroad platform to fall on Palsgraf, causing severe injury. Palsgraf sued the railroad for her injuries, alleging negligence by the employee. Is the railroad liable for the injury to Palsgraf? Explain fully. [See *Palsgraf* v. *Long Island Railroad Co.*, 284 N.Y. 339 (1928).]

5. Frank Ferlito and his wife, Susan, planned to attend a costume party for Halloween. They agreed to dress as "Mary had a little lamb." Frank was to be the lamb. Susan made him a costume from a suit of long underwear with cotton batting glued to it. Susan also made a headpiece with ears, which was also covered in cotton batting. The cotton batting was manufactured by Johnson & Johnson. The package said that the cotton batting was for cleansing, applying medications, and infant care. At the party, Frank tried to light a cigarette with a butane lighter. The flame got close to his costume, setting the cotton batting on fire. Frank suffered serious burns. Should Frank and Susan be able to recover against Johnson & Johnson? Why or why not? [See *Ferlito* v. *Johnson & Johnson Products, Inc.*, 771 F.Supp. 196 (E.D. Mich. 1991).]

6. **BUSINESS APPLICATION CASE** On a rainy day Betty Jane Stewart, a 70-year-old woman, entered a Wendy's restaurant in St. Louis, Missouri. Immediately after entering, Stewart slipped and fell in the entry area. As a result of the fall, she sustained medical injuries. Stewart testified that she didn't see the water before she fell because she wasn't looking down when she entered. Stewart's husband, who entered the restaurant shortly after her fall, testified that he saw an eighth-inch of water on the floor. The Wendy's store manager testified that it was raining

hard during the busy hour right before noon and that no mat was placed inside the door. The manager also testified that the floor was dry right before the fall. However, a wet floor sign had been put out about two hours before the fall due to the rainy conditions. Was Wendy's negligent in the care extended to its business invitees? Was there sufficient evidence of negligence on the part of Wendy's for the jury to deliberate on the issue? In a comparative negligence state, what should be the relative faults of the parties? What should a business do to avoid these types of accidents? [See *Stewart* v. *M.D.F., Inc.*, 83 F.3d 247 (8th Cir. 1996).]

7. **ETHICAL APPLICATION CASE** Rose Cipollone smoked cigarettes from 1942 until 1984, when she died. She smoked cigarette brands made by the defendant until 1968. She claimed that she started smoking because she wanted to imitate the "pretty girls and movie stars" in defendant's advertisements. Rose claims that she believed advertisements which said, "Play Safe, Smoke [Liggett's] Chesterfield" and "Nose, Throat, and Accessory Organs Not Adversely Affected by Smoking Chesterfield." In 1981, Rose was diagnosed with lung cancer. Rose filed suit alleging that her cancer was caused by her use of the defendant's products for a 40-year period. Rose died before trial because of complications from the lung cancer. Thomas Cipollone, her son, continued the suit, individually and as a representative of her estate. The lawsuit requested compensation based on the following legal theories: strict liability, negligence, breach of warranty, intentional tort, and conspiracy. Did the cigarette manufacturers breach a duty to warn? Why or why not? What is the effect of the printed warnings imposed by federal statute on cigarette manufacturers beginning in 1969? [See *Cipollone* v. *Liggett Group, Inc.*, 505 U.S. 504 (1992). Aspects of the case were also considered by the Supreme Court at 502 U.S. 1055 (1992);

502 U.S. 923 (1991); and 499 U.S. 935 (1991). Lower courts considered the case at 893 F.2d 541 (3rd Cir. 1990); 789 F.2d 181 (3rd Cir. 1986); 649 F.Supp. 664 (NJ 1986); and 593 F.Supp. 1146 (NJ 1984).]

8. **CRITICAL THINKING CASE** Teresa Penland and J. Ronnie Jackson were both employed as guards at the Buncombe County jail. A female inmate alleged that she was sexually assaulted by Jackson. Jackson and Penland were on duty the night of the alleged assault. Penland was the matron on the floor. Sheriff Long, who supervised the jail, fired both Jackson and Penland. In his press release and interviews, Sheriff Long implied that both Penland and Jackson were involved in an assault on an inmate. In the press release, Sheriff Long mentioned that allegations had been made by an inmate, an investigation was being conducted, and two employees had been dismissed. WLOS-TV broadcast a story the same day: "Newscaster: Buncombe County Sheriff Charles Long today fired two detention officers at the Buncombe County Detention Center. Long ordered an investigation of Officers Ronnie Jackson and Teresa Penland after a female prisoner accused Jackson of assaulting her. Sheriff Long: 'Anytime we have an assault or anything that might be of an unlawful nature its [sic] a matter of concern . . . we have a high liability in the detention center and we have a lot of worry . . . we don't like for these things to happen.'" Penland and Jackson denied having anything to do with an assault on an inmate. [The investigation of the assault was later dropped when it was discovered that the inmate had a history of mental illness and a history of claiming sexual assault.] Are Penland and/or Jackson "public officials" who would have to show "malice" under *New York Times* v. *Sullivan*? [See *Penland* v. *Long*, 922 F.Supp. 1085 (W.D.N.C. 1996).]

NOTES

1. See California Civil Code, § 1714.1.
2. *Church of Scientology Int'l.* v. *Time Warner, Inc.*, 932 F.Supp. 589 (S.D.N.Y. 1996), at pp. 593–594.
3. 376 U.S. 254 (1964).
4. *Texas Tanks, Inc.* v. *Owens-Corning Fiberglas Corp.*, 99 F.3d 734 (5th Cir. 1996).
5. Ibid.
6. The Uniform Trade Secrets Act with the 1985 amendments has been adopted in Alabama, Arizona, Colorado, Delaware, District of Columbia, Florida, Georgia, Hawaii, Idaho, Iowa, Kansas, Kentucky, Maine, Maryland, Michigan, Minnesota, Mississippi, Montana, Nebraska, Nevada, New Hampshire, New Mexico, North Dakota, Ohio, Oklahoma, Oregon, South Carolina, South Dakota, Utah, Vermont, Virginia, West Virginia, and Wisconsin. The following states have adopted the 1979 act, but not the 1985 amendments: Alaska, Arkansas, California, Connecticut, Illinois, Indiana, Louisiana, Rhode Island, and Washington. See the NCCUSL web site, "A Few Facts About the Uniform Trade Secrets Act," http://www.nccusl.org/uniformact_factsheet/ uniformact-fs.utsa.htm, revised 1 December 1999.
7. See 18 U.S.C., §§ 1961 *et seq.*

8. Susan B. Garland, "Can a Tough-Guy Law Deck Big Tobacco?" *Business Week* (11 October 1999), pp. 158, 160.

9. Michael Riccardi, "Drug Manufacturer Must Warn of Risks," *The Legal Intelligencer* (15 July 1999), p. 4.

10. See Jury Instructions for Negligence Per Se, BAJI 3.45 (1992 Revision), *California Jury Instructions, Civil,* 7th ed. (St. Paul, MN: West Publishing Co., 1992). Drafted by the Committee of Standard Jury Instructions, Civil, of the Superior Court of Los Angeles County and used throughout the state of California.

11. L.R. 3 H.L. 330 (1868).

12. For example, California Vehicle Code, § 17150.

13. California Civil Code, § 1714.1.

14. James L. Peterson, "Product Liability and Tort Reform," *The Indiana Lawyer* (22 July 1998), p. 4.

15. Deborah Claymon, "Game Makers Scramble for Way to Avoid Spotlight over Violence," *The Fresno Bee* (13 June 1999), pp. C1, C2.

8

CRIMES AND BUSINESS

A G E N D A

CIT has recently been victimized by a series of minor crimes, including theft from its warehouses. This has led the family to a general discussion of crimes, and especially of victim's rights when crimes are committed. Throughout this chapter, we consider what CIT and other businesses can do to deter crime and to reduce the likelihood of becoming victims of criminal conduct.

Tom and Anna recognize that Call-Image videophones may be used for purposes other than those they intend. For instance, another business may broadcast deceptive or false advertising or pornography through Call-Image units. What preventative measures should CIT take to avoid responsibility for these illegal activities?

In general, is CIT liable for criminal activity perpetrated by its employees on company time or on company property? For example, must CIT pay traffic tickets issued to its employees while driving company vehicles? What if its employees make unauthorized copies of computer software? Who will be criminally responsible in these situations—the employee, CIT, or both? Try to distinguish criminal law and civil law throughout this chapter.

These and other questions need to be addressed in this chapter. Be prepared! You never know when one of the Kochanowskis will need your help or advice.

O U T L I N E

WHY STUDY CRIMINAL LAW?

Why should a business law textbook contain a chapter on criminal law? The reason is that businesses are constantly confronted with the *effects* of crimes such as embezzlement, forgery, and fraud, to name only a few kinds of crimes we discuss in this chapter. In addition, there are a number of crimes with which a business can be charged. Therefore, to prevent a crime from happening, or to deal effectively with a crime once it has occurred, you need to know what constitutes a crime and its legal ramifications.

The criminal law developed through a long history of precedents. However, most states have codified their criminal laws. As you should expect, the exact rules vary from state to state. Begin by referring to Exhibit 8.1, which summarizes the primary distinctions between civil law and criminal law. Try to distinguish between the two areas throughout this chapter. Remember that one action or series of actions may constitute *both* a civil wrong and a criminal wrong. It will also be helpful to look at Exhibit 8.2, which examines the six steps in a typical criminal proceeding.

OBJECTIVES OF CRIMINAL LAW

The objectives of criminal law are the protection of persons and property, the deterrence of criminal behavior, the punishment of criminal activity, and the rehabilitation of the criminal.

E X H I B I T   8.1 | **Distinctions Between Civil Law and Criminal Law**

Question	Civil Law	Criminal Law
What type of action leads to the lawsuit or case?	Action against a private individual	Action against society
Who initiates the action?	Plaintiff	Government
Who is their attorney?	Private attorney	District Attorney (D.A.) or the U.S. Attorney General
What is the burden of proof in the case?	Preponderance of the evidence	Beyond a reasonable doubt
Who generally has the burden of proof?	Plaintiff	Government
Is there a jury trial?	Yes, except in actions in equity.	Yes, except in cases involving certain infractions and misdemeanors
What jury vote is necessary to win the case?	Jury vote depends on jurisdiction or agreement of the parties. Often a simple majority or two-thirds jury vote is sufficient.	Unanimous jury vote needed for the government to win a conviction
What type(s) of punishment is imposed?	Monetary damages or equitable remedies	Capital punishment, prison, fines, and/or probation

E X H I B I T 8.2	The Six Steps in a Typical Criminal Proceeding

1. **Preliminary Hearing or a Grand Jury Hearing**
   A preliminary hearing is generally a public hearing where a magistrate considers the evidence against the accused and determines if there is probable cause to hold a criminal trial. The prosecutor need not present all the government's evidence at the preliminary hearing, just sufficient evidence to have the case go to trial. A grand jury, on the other hand, hears the evidence in secret: Generally the witnesses appear before the grand jury one at a time. The district attorney appears before the grand jury and may lead the questioning of the witnesses. The grand jury determines if a crime has been committed and, if so, which individuals were involved in the crime. If a grand jury issues an indictment against an individual, there will be a trial.

2. **Arraignment**
   The suspect is informed of the criminal charges before the court and asked how he or she pleads. Generally, the amount of bail is set at this stage.

3. **Discovery**
   Both sides have to gather facts and information to prepare for trial. Discovery can involve examining documents, records, and other pieces of physical evidence as well as taking the depositions (statements) of witnesses or the parties themselves. Discovery is generally more limited in criminal cases. One of the concerns is that if the defendant knows who will testify for the government, the defendant, defendant's relatives, and friends may intimidate the witnesses. Some discovery actually occurs at the preliminary hearing and arraignment.

4. **Pretrial Motions**
   If the parties need the court to make procedural decisions or other rulings as the case moves along toward trial, they do so by filing the appropriate motions with the court. In criminal cases, this may include a motion to suppress evidence that was illegally obtained by the police.

5. **Trial**
   The court hears the evidence offered by both sides and decides issues of both fact and law during the process.

6. **Sentencing**
   If the defendant is found guilty beyond a reasonable doubt, the defendant will be sentenced to jail, probation, parole, and/or a fine.

Protection of Persons and Property

Someone once said that a lock was designed to keep an honest person honest. It is for the same reason that the government declares certain conduct to be illegal. The government believes that all persons and their property should be protected from harm. In Chapter 7, however, you learned that tort law also protects persons and property. What is the difference? The primary difference between tort law and criminal law is that tort law results in money damages being paid by the actor, whereas criminal law may result in loss of freedom by sending the actor to jail or prison. Private interests are served through the awarding of damages. The public interest, on the other hand, is served by punishing criminal activity. If all persons respected everyone else's person and property, there would be very little reason for criminal law.

Deterrence of Criminal Behavior

One method used to reduce criminal behavior is to present a sufficient **deterrent** to antisocial behavior. The presumption inherent in criminal law is that if we make the punishment sufficiently harsh, people and businesses that contemplate criminal behavior will avoid it because they fear punishment. If people fear the punishment, they will not commit a criminal act. If sufficient people fear the

Deterrent
A danger, difficulty, or other consideration that stops or prevents a person from acting.

8.1 | MANAGEMENT

CALL-IMAGE TECHNOLOGY

PROTECTING AGAINST CRIME

The Kochanowskis have become somewhat concerned about crimes in their community and how those crimes may affect the business. They have read that the crime rate is rising in their community and across the country and that crimes against business cause special hardships to family-owned operations. They are also worried because one of the students at Lindsay's high school was killed in a "random shooting" in a municipal park last weekend. The Kochanowskis wonder what they can do to protect their family and the business without violating legal rules. They ask you for advice. What will you suggest to them?

BUSINESS CONSIDERATIONS Suppose that a business decided to take aggressive steps to try to reduce crime in its community, especially crimes that affect the business enterprise. Would this be viewed favorably or unfavorably in the community? Why? From a business perspective, is public perception an important factor in making this decision? Why?

ETHICAL CONSIDERATIONS If a business *did* decide to take aggressive steps to try to reduce crime in its community, its conduct should be practical as well as legal. Is this feasible? Would such a decision be ethical? What ethical considerations should constrain the firm's decision?

Criminal forfeiture
The government confiscates property as a punishment for criminal activity.

Beyond a reasonable doubt
The degree of proof required in a criminal trial, which is proof to a moral certainty; there is no other reasonable interpretation.

punishment, there will be a reduction in that crime. The severity of the punishment is often an issue with corporate defendants. What constitutes a substantial penalty for an individual would be a minimal penalty for a corporation such as General Motors or Merrill Lynch & Co., Inc.

Criminologists have noted that severity alone is not a sufficient deterrent. Individuals considering criminal behavior must also believe that they are likely to be identified and punished. If criminals believe that they will not be identified and tried or that they will not be found guilty in court, the deterrent effect will be reduced.

In our society, the Constitution states that there shall be no cruel and unusual punishment. If our laws allowed the death penalty for even minor offenses, there would probably be fewer minor offenses. But is that just? To many people, the loss of one's life for stealing a loaf of bread seems too high a price to pay for fewer loaves of bread being stolen. Similarly, many feel that caning a teenager for vandalism or graffiti or castrating a rapist is too extreme. The problem, therefore, is to decide how much punishment will deter criminal behavior without being excessive.

Punishment of Criminal Activity

Since we most likely cannot deter all criminal activity, our legal system accepts that a certain level of criminal activity will exist in society. Accordingly, we punish criminal activity for punishment's sake. There is no such thing as a free lunch: If a criminal takes something without paying for it, the criminal law makes that individual pay for it through deprivation of freedom for a period of time. Use of **criminal forfeiture** as a punishment is growing. For example, some jurisdictions confiscate the vehicle when the driver solicits a prostitute from the vehicle.

Rehabilitation of the Criminal

Our criminal justice system does not *end* with imprisonment, probation, or a fine. Our government has designed various programs to educate and train criminals in legitimate occupations during the period of incarceration. Theoretically, then, criminals should have no reason to return to a life of crime. Sometimes a sentence is suspended; that is, it is not put into effect. In such cases, the court supervises the individuals' activities to ensure that they have learned from their mistakes.

BASES OF CRIMINAL RESPONSIBILITIES

Generally, an individual is presumed innocent until proven guilty. The government has the burden of proving that the suspect is guilty **beyond a reasonable doubt.** The government must prove all the parts of the crime.

All crimes consist of two primary elements: a criminal *act* and a corresponding *mental state*. If only one element is present, no crime exists. For example, if you decide to embezzle from your employer and then take no steps to implement your decision, you have not committed a crime. Similarly, if a cigarette you are smoking in a motel ignites the draperies in your room and causes the motel to burn down, you have not committed the crime of arson. In the latter case, you may be liable for negligence, but you have not committed arson.

The Act

The law generally imposes criminal liability only when an individual acts in a manner that is prohibited by law. Ordinarily, the prohibited act must be voluntarily committed by the person before criminal liability will attach. This means that a person who is forced to act illegally against his or her will does not act voluntarily and may not be legally responsible for the act. However, the court *may* decide that the threat used to force the conduct was not sufficient to remove the free will of the actor, and will still impose liability. Also, some situations may *require* an individual to act or respond to the circumstances in a particular way. In these situations, a failure to act may be deemed a criminal "action" sufficient to justify prosecution by the government. This responsibility to act may be imposed by a statute or by judicial precedent.

Mental State

To be held criminally responsible for an illegal act, the actor must intend to do the act. Historically, various terms were used to describe this mental state: *consciously, intentionally, maliciously, unlawfully,* and *willfully.* Today our approach to the problem is more systematic. This current approach involves the use of one of five terms, depending on the particular requirements of the statute; it is more specific of intent than the prior terms. The terms used are as follows:

1. *Purpose*—An actor acts with purpose if it is his or her conscious objective to perform the prohibited act.
2. *Knowledge*—An actor acts with knowledge if he or she is aware of what he or she is doing.
3. *Recklessness*—An actor acts with recklessness if he or she disregards a substantial and unjustifiable risk that criminal harm or injury may result from his or her action.
4. *Negligence*—An actor acts in a criminally negligent manner if he or she should have known that a substantial and unreasonable risk of harm would result from his or her action.
5. *Strict liability*—An actor will be held strictly liable if he or she acts in a manner that our law declares criminal even if none of the above four elements is present. This theory is used primarily for crimes that have a light punishment—for example, violating public health laws with respect to the sale of food. This theory is also used in statutory rape cases simply because our society has a vested interest in protecting our youth.

SERIOUSNESS OF THE OFFENSE

Criminal law classifies all offenses into three categories according to their level of seriousness. These categories are, from least to most serious, misdemeanors, felonies, and treason. Some states have an additional category called infractions or violations.

8.2 | MANAGEMENT

CAN A BUSINESS COMMIT A CRIME?

The Kochanowskis have a large barn on their property. This barn has been vacant for quite some time, and Dan thinks that, with minor renovations, it would make an excellent warehouse from which to ship Call-Image videophones. Anna points out that the property is not zoned for commercial activities, and that such use might be criminal without the proper zoning. Dan counters that it cannot be criminal because CIT cannot *intend* to commit a crime (since businesses are inanimate creatures, they cannot have *any* intent), and criminal intent is an essential element in any criminal conviction. Anna doubts that this analysis is accurate, but she seeks your advice to be sure. What advice will you give her?

BUSINESS CONSIDERATIONS What can a business do to reduce the likelihood that it will commit a crime? Are there certain factors that reduce or increase the likelihood that a business or its agents will commit crimes?

ETHICAL CONSIDERATIONS Is it ethical for a business to knowingly violate a law, such as a zoning law? Would it be ethical for a business to engage in an act that would be criminal for an individual but that is not criminal for a business entity?

Infractions or Violations

Some states have a separate category for petty offenses called *infractions* or *violations*. They are generally punishable only by fines. Some examples include illegal gaming and disturbing the peace.

Misdemeanors

Misdemeanors are minor offenses that are punishable by confinement of up to one year in a city or county jail, a small fine, or both. Public intoxication, speeding, and vandalism are likely to be classified as misdemeanors.

Felonies

Felonies are major offenses punishable by confinement from one year to life in a state or federal prison, a large fine, or both. In some states special capital felony statutes provide for the sentence of death. Murder, arson, rape, burglary, and grand theft are normally classified as felonies.

Treason

Treason is the most serious offense against the government. It consists of waging war against the government or of giving aid and comfort to our enemies in time of war.

CRIMES VERSUS TORTS

It is important to remember that one act can be the legal basis for both a criminal lawsuit and a civil lawsuit. The two separate suits will not be barred by the doctrine of *res judicata,* nor by the rule against double jeopardy. In many situations, a *criminal act* (an act against the rules of society) will also involve an infringement on the social rights and expectations of an individual. If one act is both a crime and a tort, it may be prosecuted by the criminal system, and the harmed individual may be able to seek remedies in the civil system.

SELECTED CRIMES

Currency transaction report (CTR)
A report businesses must file if a customer brings $10,000 or more in cash to the business.

We are unable to list all of the common crimes in this text. We will, however, mention selected crimes that have applications for either detection or prevention in the marketplace. In many situations, the business is the victim, not the perpetrator, of the crime. It is possible for a business to be the perpetrator of a crime, and there are a number of criminal statutes aimed primarily at business activities. Some of the federal statutes directed at business activities are discussed in other chapters of the text. In this chapter, we will discuss the federal Counterfeit Access Device and Computer Fraud and Abuse Act of 1984; the Racketeer Influenced and Corrupt Organization Act (RICO); and the Currency and Foreign Transactions Reporting Act, among others. The Currency and Foreign Transactions Reporting Act is a statute passed to prevent money laundering and requires the filing of **Currency Transaction Reports (CTRs)**.

The court in the following case reviewed the defendant's conviction on conspiring to "launder" money.

Indictment
A written accusation of criminal conduct issued to a court by a grand jury.

U.S.C.
Abbreviation for the United States Code (statutes).

8.1

UNITED STATES OF AMERICA V. TOWNSEND
1999 U.S. APP. LEXIS 13872 (5TH CIR. 1999)

FACTS . . . Braxton Townsend ("Townsend") was charged alone in a five-count **indictment.** Count I charged that . . . Townsend possessed with intent to distribute approximately five grams of cocaine base . . . Count II charged that . . . Townsend possessed with intent to distribute four ounces of cocaine base . . . Count III charged Townsend with carrying a firearm during and in relation to a drug-trafficking crime . . . Count IV charged Townsend with conspiring to commit money laundering with drug trafficking proceeds . . . in violation of 18 **U.S.C.** § 1956(h). Count V charged Townsend with causing a financial institution to fail to file a Currency Transaction Report for a currency transaction in excess of $10,000, in violation of 31 U.S.C. §§ 5313 and 5324(a)(1). . . .

In August of 1993, Townsend began building a home in Lena, Mississippi. Prior to the commencement of the building process, Townsend made arrangements with his cousin, Diane Kincaid . . . , to open two accounts at Deposit Guaranty National Bank. Kincaid opened a checking account and a savings account under her name and the name of Townsend's sister, Willie DuPlasser. . . . The purpose of opening the two bank accounts was to permit Kincaid to write checks for expenses related to the construction of Townsend's home in Lena. At the time that the construction began, Townsend lived in Milwaukee, Wisconsin and Kincaid lived in the Lena, Mississippi area.

The [original] arrangement between Townsend and Kincaid encompassed the following: when Townsend wanted Kincaid to make a deposit, he would travel to Mississippi and bring her the cash in a bank bag. Once Townsend had moved to Mississippi and before the construction of the home was completed, Kincaid would pick up the money from Townsend. Townsend would often give Kincaid money in excess of $10,000. Townsend instructed Kincaid, however, that when making bank deposits she should keep each deposit under $10,000. Townsend also told Kincaid to make

the deposits at different branches of the bank and to vary the deposits between the savings and checking accounts. Due to Townsend's illiteracy, Kincaid handled all of Townsend's legal and financial matters until the completion of his home in September of 1994. [Kincaid was not charged in the crime: She testified for the government.]

During the construction process, Townsend would place money in a safe deposit box to pay for the cost of building his home. The contractor testified at trial that he presented receipts for the building materials to Kincaid, who, in turn, would pay him. The contractor explained that the house measured approximately 8,000 square feet and that Townsend spent approximately $380,000 building it.

The Government produced evidence that Townsend had not filed tax returns for the 1990, 1993 and 1994 tax years. In 1991, Townsend failed to report any income and his wife Lora's reported income was $6,077. In 1992, the Townsends reported an income of $7,000.

An agent with the Internal Revenue Service (IRS) testified that as early as 1989, Townsend had been receiving food stamps and other governmental assistance from Illinois, Wisconsin and Mississippi. The IRS agent stated that it was her professional opinion that the funds used to build the house came from drug activities. The agent explained that in the course of her investigation, she had checked with authorities and determined that there were open investigations on Townsend for criminal activity involving drugs in other states. The agent stated that her investigation allowed her to gather intelligence information that showed that Townsend had been previously involved in drug activities, that he had no legal sources of income, and that he had large sums of money that legitimately could not be accounted for. . . .

Based upon the probable cause resulting from . . . [a controlled drug buy], officers . . . obtained a
continued

8.1

UNITED STATES OF AMERICA V. TOWNSEND, *continued*
1999 U.S. APP. LEXIS 13872 (5TH CIR. 1999)

warrant to search Townsend's property. On the morning of November 17, 1996, the search transpired. In the course of the search, a box containing money was discovered in the downstairs master bedroom closet of Townsend's home. [The agents found over $5,000 in cash during the search of Townsend's home . . .] [A]gents found a total of approximately four ounces of crack cocaine at Townsend's residence. . . . The . . . agents also found forty-one guns. . . . The jury found Townsend guilty on all five counts of the indictment. . . .

ISSUE Did the prosecutor present sufficient evidence at trial to support Townsend's conviction on violation of 18 U.S.C. § 1956(h)?

HOLDING Yes. The evidence was sufficient to support his conviction.

REASONING . . . When the sufficiency of the evidence is challenged on appeal, this Court reviews the evidence and all the reasonable inferences which flow therefrom in the light most favorable to the verdict. The conviction must be affirmed if any rational trier of fact could have found the essential elements of the offense beyond a reasonable doubt. . . . Townsend contends that the evidence at trial was insufficient to support his conviction for conspiracy to launder money under 18 U.S.C. § 1956(h). We do not agree with Townsend's assertion. To establish a violation of section 1956 (a)(1), the Government must prove that Townsend: "(1) knowingly conducted a financial transaction (2) that involved the proceeds of an unlawful activity (3) with the intent to promote or

further that unlawful activity." Section 1956(h) states: "any person who conspires to commit any offense defined in this section or section 1957 shall be subject to the same penalties as those prescribed for the offense . . . which was the object of the conspiracy."

After reviewing the record, the parties' briefs and hearing oral argument, we find that the evidence presented at trial is sufficient to support Townsend's conviction for conspiracy to commit money laundering. The Government showed that Townsend's only legitimate sources of income were food stamps and disability payments. The fact that Townsend routinely provided his cousin with large sums of cash for deposit into bank accounts, that he had purchased a home worth approximately $300,000 without substantial evidence of any legitimate income, that he sold crack cocaine to Jones on November 14, 1996, and that four ounces more of crack cocaine were discovered on his property, is sufficient to support his conviction. . . .

BUSINESS CONSIDERATION What procedures should a bank or other business establish to prevent violating the requirements for Currency Transaction Reports?

ETHICAL CONSIDERATIONS Was it ethical for Townsend to jeopardize Kincaid's welfare by involving her in this scheme? Was it ethical for Kincaid to testify against Townsend during his trial? Did the contractor have an obligation to report Townsend?

Murder/Manslaughter

Homicide is the killing of one human being by another. It is not necessarily a criminal act. It will *not* be a criminal act if the killing was lawful—for example, if there was a justification such as self-defense. *Murder,* however, is the willful, unlawful killing of a human being by another with *malice aforethought* (deliberate purpose or design). *Manslaughter* occurs when the killing is unlawful but without malice. Manslaughter is usually divided into two categories—voluntary (upon a sudden heat of passion) or involuntary (in the commission of an unlawful act or in the commission of a lawful act without due caution). It is common for the state to charge a defendant with both murder and manslaughter and to let the decider of fact determine which crime was actually committed.

Arson

Arson is the intentional or willful burning of property by fire or explosion. Originally, this crime was restricted to the burning of a house. Today, in most states, the crime has been expanded to include the burning of all types of **real property** and many types of **personal property.**

Burglary

Burglary is the breaking and entering of a structure with the intent to commit a felony inside. Originally, this crime was restricted to the breaking and entering of a house at night, but, like arson, it has been expanded to include other structures, such as stores and warehouses. It is no longer limited to nighttime.

Embezzlement

Embezzlement is the taking of money or other property by an employee who has been entrusted with the money or property by his or her employer. Businesses should establish practices and procedures to reduce the likelihood of being victimized by embezzlement.

Forgery

Forgery is the making or altering of a **negotiable instrument** or credit card invoice in order to create or to shift legal liability for the instrument. It generally consists of signing another person's name to a check, promissory note, or credit card invoice or altering an amount on any of those documents. To win any such case, the government must generally prove that the accused acted with the intent to **defraud.** A business entity should use care in maintaining checks and signature stamps: It should also reconcile bank statements to discover potential forgeries.

Credit Card and Check Legislation

Today, customers make extensive use of credit cards, **debit cards,** and checks. This creates a number of difficulties, particularly for mail order, e-commerce, and other businesses. For instance, criminals may steal an individual's credit card, debit card, or card number and use it to make substantial purchases. Card numbers may be obtained by accessing computer files where an owner has charged a purchase to his or her credit card. Carbon copies of credit slips are also used to obtain numbers. There are also small machines that quickly swipe a card and retain the card information. Dishonest employees can obtain this information and then sell it to other criminals. Some states have enacted *separate* legislation making it a crime to use someone else's credit or debit card without permission. Other states treat this as a type of forgery. Businesses can establish procedures to reduce the likelihood of being victimized by criminals with fraudulent account numbers.

Criminals may steal the checks of an individual or business and forge the signature on the checks. A different type of problem arises when the owner of a bank account writes checks when there are insufficient funds in the account. Most states have enacted statutes that make it a crime to write or transfer (make, draw, or deliver) a check when there are insufficient funds in the account. These are commonly called *bad check statutes.* Some states require the *mens rea* (criminal intent) that the suspect intended to defraud the recipient of the check.

Real property
Real estate and property permanently attached to real estate.

Personal property
Property that is not real estate.

Negotiable instrument
Transferable documents used as a substitute for money.

Defraud
To deprive a person of property or of any interest, estate, or right by fraud, deceit, or artifice.

Debit card
Card that transfers funds from customer's bank account to merchant's bank account.

Criminal Fraud

Fraud is a broad term that covers many specific situations. The English courts were very reluctant to criminalize fraudulent behavior, preferring to allow tort law to handle most situations. Over the years, however, legislation was passed in both England and the United States to overcome the historic view of "[we] are not to indict one for making a fool of another."[1] Today, most states have statutes that cover variations of what is generally called *criminal fraud, false pretense,* or *theft by deception.* Most states require proof of the following elements to convict a person of criminal fraud: the speaker (or writer) made a false statement of fact; the statement was material, that is, it would affect the listener's decision; the listener relied on the statement; and the speaker intended to mislead the listener. Note that the fraudulent party can be either the buyer or the seller. For example, suppose that a savings and loan creates the impression that certain real estate assets are worth $100,000 through the distribution of false appraisals in order to induce a person to invest in those assets. In fact, the assets are worth substantially less than the false appraisals show. The savings and loan and its officers could be found guilty of criminal fraud if an investor enters a partnership with the savings and loan in those assets. The court discusses how the district attorney's office investigated the criminal fraud complaint in the following case.

Grand jury

A jury that receives complaints of criminal conduct and returns a bill of indictment if the jury is convinced that a trial should be held.

With prejudice

A dismissal of a lawsuit that also prohibits reinitiating the lawsuit.

8.2

HERB HALLMAN CHEVROLET, INC. V. NASH-HOLMES
169 F.3D 636 (9TH CIR. 1999)

FACTS . . . Rick Wells complained to the Reno Police Department that Hallman Chevrolet [its owner, John Stanko, and employees] appropriated his $600 factory rebate, due on a new car purchase, by forging his signature on a rebate assignment form. Wells recounted his dealings with Hallman Chevrolet to police in a written statement . . . Wells underwent a polygraph examination at the Reno Police Department and the examiner concluded that Wells was speaking truthfully. . . . [T]he county handwriting analyst determined that the signature in question "exhibits the characteristics of a 'simulated forgery.'" . . . [P]olice forwarded their report to the Washoe County District Attorney's Office . . .

. . . District Attorney investigators (D.A. investigators) confronted owner Stanko. . . . Stanko stated that Wells had authorized the dealership to reproduce his signature. In support of his claim, Stanko voluntarily produced two power of attorney forms purportedly signed by Wells and a list of rebates ("Rebate Recap Sheet") credited to the dealership. The D.A. investigators submitted the power of attorney forms to the county handwriting analyst who concluded that there was "no basis for identifying [Wells] as the writer." Investigators discovered that the forms, even if signed by Wells, did not authorize the dealership to repro-

duce his signature on other documents. Investigators returned to the dealership to question Stanko . . . whereupon he angrily refused to cooperate.

D.A. investigators began to contact other customers listed on the Rebate Recap Sheet, including Daniel and Donna Pease . . . The dealership received a $500 rebate from Chevrolet for the Peases' transaction, but the Peases apparently did not receive credit for the rebate. . . . D.A. investigators decided to seek a search warrant because they believed they had probable cause to suspect Hallman Chevrolet of criminal conduct. . . . D.A. investigators executed the warrant and seized 151 transaction files. . . . [O]ne current and two former Hallman Chevrolet employees voluntarily came forward to confirm dealership policies encouraging salesmen to engage in fraudulent and unfair business practices. They stated that it was dealership policy not to tell customers about rebates and to get them unknowingly to assign their rebates to the dealership. . . . [F]ormer employee William Dallman stated that he had observed salesmen forging names on rebate assignment documents and that it was common practice to add the cost of an extended warranty to the purchase price without informing the customer. . . . Another former employee, Bobby Atkerson, stated that he once overheard three salesmen

8.2

HERB HALLMAN CHEVROLET, INC. V. NASH-HOLMES, *continued*
169 F.3D 636 (9TH CIR. 1999)

discussing the forgery of a customer's signature. When the discussion ended, Atkerson entered the room and observed a piece of paper with sixteen versions of customer Rick Wells' signature. . . .

. . . Assistant District Attorney Donald Coppa (A.D.A. Coppa) impaneled a Washoe County **grand jury** on July 8, 1992. Before presenting the evidence, A.D.A. Coppa told the grand jury that they were investigating the "business practices" of Hallman Chevrolet and its employees. . . . [T]he grand jury returned an eighty-one count indictment, the largest in the history of the county, charging seventeen Hallman Chevrolet employees with 409 felony offenses. [The Deputy D.A. dismissed most of the charges, and] . . . Judge Whitehead dismissed the remaining charges [against Hallman] **with prejudice** based on what he found to be egregious prosecutorial misconduct. The Washoe prosecutors appealed the decision to the Nevada Supreme Court, but the newly elected D.A. dismissed that appeal before it was heard. . . . Hallman Chevrolet filed this civil rights action . . .

ISSUE Are the D.A.s liable for violating Hallman's rights in establishing probable cause, seeking search warrants, and convening the grand jury?

HOLDING No. The D.A.s had immunity for their actions.

REASONING . . . A prosecutor may only shield his investigative work with qualified immunity. The qualified immunity question turns on the "objective legal reasonableness" of the action. It is not objectively reasonable for a prosecutor deliberately or recklessly to misstate or omit facts material to the existence of probable cause. Hallman Chevrolet asserts that the Washoe prosecutors misrepresented material facts in affidavits supporting two search warrant applications. . . . Wells made a sworn statement, which the polygraph analyst found to be truthful, that he never received his rebate. Moreover, the county handwriting analyst determined that Wells' signature was a probable forgery. The Washoe prosecutors were also aware that owner Stanko and several Hallman Chevrolet employees had given different versions of the events to Wells, the police and D.A. investigators. . . . Hallman Chevrolet failed to produce any documentary evidence or reliable testimony refuting Wells' version of the events. . . .

To show that an omission is material, "the plaintiff must establish that the remaining information in the affidavit is insufficient to establish probable cause." The standard for determining probable cause under Nevada law is whether there is "slight, even marginal, evidence" to support the charge. Although the Washoe prosecutors did omit facts from their affidavits, none of these facts was material. . . . [A] neutral and detached magistrate would have found probable cause even if the Washoe prosecutors had included these unfavorable facts. . . .

A prosecutor performing an advocate's role is an officer of the court entitled to absolute immunity. A prosecutor's acts in the course of his role as an advocate "include the professional evaluation of the evidence assembled by the police and appropriate preparation for its presentation at trial or before a grand jury after a decision to seek an indictment has been made." The Supreme Court has recognized that "prosecutors are absolutely immune from liability under [U.S.C.] § 1983 for their conduct before grand juries." The Washoe prosecutors functioned as advocates in the grand jury proceedings. . . . The Nevada standard for determining probable cause is whether there is "slight, even marginal, evidence" to support the charge. "The state need only present enough evidence to create a reasonable inference that the accused committed the offense with which he or she is charged." . . . Washoe prosecutors had ample and convincing evidence that Hallman Chevrolet employees had forged customers' signatures, withheld rebates, retained customer down-payments . . . and made material misrepresentations to customers. . . .

BUSINESS CONSIDERATIONS What could a company such as Hallman Chevrolet do to protect its reputation during a criminal investigation and prosecution? What procedures could Chevrolet and Hallman establish to reduce the likelihood of occurrences like these in the future?

ETHICAL CONSIDERATIONS Did Hallman Chevrolet and its employees behave ethically? Was the behavior of the A.D.A.s ethical?

Larceny

Larceny is the wrongful taking and carrying away of the personal property of another without the owner's consent and with the intent to permanently deprive the owner of the property. The most common forms of larceny are shoplifting and pickpocketing. The use of force is not needed. Larceny is a serious problem for retail businesses. Merchandise is often lost through shoplifting. In addition, if customers feel unsafe due to pickpocketing, they will avoid certain stores and shopping centers.

Robbery

Robbery is a form of aggravated theft. It is basically larceny *plus* the threat to use violence or force. To be classified as a robbery, the robber must use either violence or the threat of injury sufficient to place the victim in fear, and the robber then takes and carries away something either in the possession or the immediate presence of the victim. If the same property had been carried away without the use of violence or a threat of injury, the act would be a mere theft.

Espionage

Hacker
An outsider who gains unauthorized access to a computer or computer network.

In 1996, the federal government enacted the Economic Espionage Act to assist in prosecuting **hackers.**[2] Stealing trade secrets is called economic spying or *espionage.* The act makes espionage a federal offense punishable by 25 years in jail or a $25,000 fine for an individual. It also provides for fines of up to $10 million for companies.[3] The "victim," however, must have taken reasonable safety precautions to protect its trade secrets.[4] FBI director Louis Freeh told a Senate panel that 23 countries are engaged in economic spying against U.S. businesses.[5]

Computer Crime

"The only secure computer is one that's turned off, locked in a safe, and buried 20 feet down in a secret location—and I'm not completely confident of that one either" (quote from Bruce Schneier, author of the book *E-mail Security*).[6] The legal aspects of computers will be discussed in detail in Chapter 45. Advances in computer technology have led to the development of new activities, some positive and some negative. Some of these negative behaviors are now recognized as crimes. Companies like the Gap, Hitachi America, PeopleSoft, Playboy Enterprises, and Twentieth Century Fox each attract from 1 to 30 hacker attempts per day.[7]

With our increased dependence on computers, computer criminals can create extensive damage. According to a recent article on computer safety, "The going estimates for financial losses from computer crime reach as high as $10 billion a year. But the truth is that nobody really knows. Almost all attacks go undetected—as many as 95 percent, says the FBI. . . . "[8] In addition to civil liability for improper use, many states now recognize the following activities as crimes:

1. *Unauthorized use of computers or computer-related equipment.* This would include the use of business computers for personal projects, including homework and personal e-mail. It also includes transferring software purchased by a business to a personal computer.

Viruses
Computer programs that destroy, damage, rearrange, or replace computer data.

2. *Destruction of a computer or its records.* Computer **viruses** destroy or alter records, data, and programs. Annually there are numerous virus alerts—some are fakes and some are legitimate. Businesses expend significant resources to protect themselves from viruses and to correct the damage they

cause. This would include a virus that "infects" the computers in a college computer lab and subsequently infects students' disks and home computers.

3. *Alteration of legitimate records.* This would include altering a student's grade record in the registrar's office.

4. *Accessing computer records to transfer funds, stocks, or other property.* This would include entering a bank's computer system and transferring funds without authorization. For example, in 1994 Citibank discovered that Russian hackers made $10 million in illegal transfers. Initially the bank called in a private security firm. When Citibank finally spoke to the FBI and the media, it lost some of its top customers. Competitors lured them away by promising customers that the competitors' computer systems were more secure than those of Citibank.[9]

Congress enacted the federal Counterfeit Access Device and Computer Fraud and Abuse Act of 1984 to strengthen state attempts to deal with computer crime. The act criminalized the unauthorized, knowing use or access of computers in the following ways:

1. To obtain classified military or foreign policy information with the intent to injure the United States or to benefit a foreign country. This would include accessing classified Pentagon files. This constitutes a felony under the act.

2. To collect financial or credit information, which is protected under federal privacy law. This would include accessing credit card accounts to obtain credit card numbers and credit limits.

3. To use, modify, destroy, or disclose computer data and to prevent authorized individuals from using the data. This would include intentionally transferring a virus to a computer.

4. To alter or modify data in financial computers that causes a loss of $1,000 or more. (This would include the unlawful transfer of funds from Citibank.)

5. To modify data that impair an individual's medical treatment.

6. To transfer computer data, including passwords, that could assist individuals in gaining unauthorized access that either affects interstate commerce or allows access to a government computer. This would include the use of a "sniffer" program, which can hide in a computer network and record passwords, and then transferring this information to others.

8.3 | SALES/ MANAGEMENT

CALL-IMAGE TECHNOLOGY

PROTECTING AGAINST CHANGES IN TECHNOLOGY

CIT is involved in a business with rapidly changing technology. Dan noticed an article in a trade journal that Virtual Images, an independent company, has developed the technology to send prerecorded video and audio messages on interactive videophones like those produced by CIT and its competitors. This would effectively enable businesses and individuals to play VCR tapes to people at remote locations. As such, it may be used to play advertisements on the phone lines, to show clients a product, and even to demonstrate its use.

This ability does not disturb CIT. However, the device may be used to defraud people by showing them products that do not exist or features that do not appear on the actual product. For example, people who are selling resort properties can show a false picture and entice someone to invest in the resort. Dan has even heard of companies that plan to send pornographic videos to their clients by way of this device. Dan has asked you what CIT should do about these potential uses of its product line, and also what preventative measures CIT should take to avoid involvement in fraud. What will you tell him?

BUSINESS CONSIDERATION Legally, businesses are not restricted to any "moral minimum." Should a business take a proactive stand in a situation where it fears that its product might be used for an unethical or illegal purpose? (Remember that the law, including criminal law, often lags behind technological developments.)

ETHICAL CONSIDERATION Does a business have any moral responsibility for the manner in which its products are used? Suppose that a business has the opportunity to make a new product that will be very profitable but that is likely to be used in an unethical manner by a number of its customers. From an ethical perspective, what should the firm do?

The first category constitutes a felony, and the remaining five categories constitute misdemeanors.

Computer users may engage in some of these new crimes. In addition, computer technology has enabled some individuals to commit more traditional crimes. For example, Mark Johnson has been investigated for a number of computer-linked activities—computer fraud, computer "stalking" under the computer nickname "Vito," harassing and threatening computer users online, transporting a minor for sexual purposes, and sexual molestation.[10]

Corporate Liability for Crimes

Originally, courts held that a corporation was not answerable for crimes because the corporation was not authorized to commit crimes and, therefore, lacked the power to commit them. However, there is a growing trend in many states to hold corporations criminally responsible when their officers and agents commit criminal actions in the execution of their duties. Corporate directors, officers, and employees are also *personally* liable for crimes they commit while acting for the corporation. This trend is evidenced by court decisions and statutory law and the Model Penal Code.[11] Another specific example is the California Corporate Criminal Liability Act, which enlarged the criminal liability of corporate managers.[12]

Mala prohibita
Wrong because it is prohibited.

Corporate liability is more common when the corporation is accused of violating a statute that is *mala prohibita.* However, when the criminal act is one requiring a specific mental state, such as battery with intent to kill, the courts generally refuse to hold the corporation liable unless the corporation itself participated in the acts or a high-ranking official participated in the acts with the intent to benefit the corporation.

Corporate liability is sometimes limited to *white-collar crime.* Although this term does not have a precise meaning, it generally means crimes committed in a commercial context by professionals and managers. The officers and agents are generally tried separately and convicted for their behavior. When liability is imposed against the corporation, punishment is usually in the form of a fine.

There is an active debate over whether, as a matter of policy, corporations *should* be held criminally liable. The following arguments are generally advanced in support of corporate criminal liability:

1. Financial sanctions against the corporation will reduce dividends for the shareholders. The shareholders will then take a more active role to ensure that the corporation will behave legally; express concern to management when acts or policies appear to be unethical or illegal; and elect directors who will carefully monitor corporate behavior.
2. The shareholders are the ones who benefit when the corporation commits crimes. They receive higher dividends when the crime increases revenue or lowers the cost of doing business. If the corporation is not assessed a fine, the shareholders benefit from the criminal activity. For example, past violation of criminal statutes controlling the disposal of hazardous wastes may have benefited the company and the stockholders by reducing expenses and increasing profits.
3. There are a large number of potential individual suspects in a corporation. Governments lack the resources to build cases against specific individuals; it is less expensive and time-consuming to build a case against the corporation as a whole.

4. Many corporate decisions are committee decisions or are decisions that are approved at a number of managerial levels. The responsibility for making decisions and implementing them is often divided between individuals or divisions. In these cases it is difficult to identify the culpable individuals, so the entire corporation should be held responsible for the decision.

5. When individual wrongdoers can be identified, it is unfair to single them out for punishment. Their actions are probably consistent with the general pattern of conduct throughout the corporation.

6. Corporations are not really harmed by the loss of an individual manager. The manager can take the blame and act as a scapegoat, and the corporation can continue to thrive. The corporation benefits from the illegal act and does not suffer the costs of the crime. The public may forgive the corporation for the crime if an individual wrongdoer is identified and punished.

7. When the sanction is based on a crime of omission (i.e., failure to act), the failure often occurs because the duty to perform was not clearly delegated to any specific person or office. If no specific person is held liable and the corporation is not held liable, there is no incentive to comply with the law.

8. When the government takes action against the corporation, the public then identifies the crime with the corporation. Disclosure of full information about businesses is essential in market-oriented societies. Consumers can then make informed decisions about which firms they want to transact business with. An example of this is Archer Daniels Midland's (ADM) alleged price fixing.[13]

The following arguments are advanced by those opposed to corporate criminal liability:

1. Imposing fines against corporations is a waste of time and effort because the fines are not substantial and do not act as a deterrent. The firm will respond by increasing prices and passing the costs on to consumers. In reality, consumers would be punished and not the corporation.

2. Fines themselves are paid from profits and, therefore, reduce shareholders' dividends. It is unjust to pass the costs on to the shareholders because in most corporations they lack the power to control corporate decision making.

3. Commonly, criminal prosecutions of corporations are not well publicized. Consequently, they do not harm the corporation's public image. Corporations will use their public relations expertise to overcome any negative publicity.

RICO: Racketeer Influenced and Corrupt Organizations Act

The RICO statute[14] became law in 1970. It was included as part of the Organized Crime Control Act. According to the law's legislative history, it was the intent of Congress to remedy a serious problem: the infiltration of criminals into legitimate businesses as both a "cover" for their criminal activity and as a means of "laundering" profits derived from their crimes. RICO makes it a federal crime to obtain or maintain an interest in, use income from, or conduct or participate in the affairs of an enterprise through a pattern of racketeering activity. The federal courts are in the process of interpreting the provisions of RICO.

Criminal prosecutors and plaintiffs' attorneys soon recognized the opportunity to use the statute against commercial enterprises. Plaintiffs' attorneys are involved

YOU BE THE JUDGE

RICO—THE "TRIALS" OF GENERAL MOTORS AND VOLKSWAGEN

José Ignacio Lopez de Arriortua (Lopez) was a high-level General Motors (GM) executive when Volkswagen AG of Germany (VW) hired him as president after a "public and bitter" contest between GM and VW. (VW in this "You Be the Judge" refers to VW of Germany only.) Much of the bidding war for Lopez's services was reported in newspapers like *The Wall Street Journal*. When Lopez eventually left GM for VW, he took other GM managers with him. Subsequently, GM documents were found in "possession" of these executives and in apartments frequented by them in Germany. GM contended that its proprietary information was taken, including designs for "Plant X," a new factory design that was supposed to improve flexibility.

GM accused Lopez and VW of conspiring to steal company secrets when Lopez left GM in 1993. The VW board tried unsuccessfully to extricate itself from this conflict. German prosecutors filed criminal charges of industrial spying against Lopez in December 1996. In addition, U.S. federal judge Nancy Edmonds in Detroit ruled that GM could proceed with a civil suit against Lopez and all of VW's top management.

Lopez resigned his position with VW on 29 November 1996. This occurred shortly after a federal judge decided that GM was permitted to file RICO charges against VW. Consequently, if GM won the lawsuit, they would be eligible for treble damages.[15]

A number of issues have been raised in this case. Among them are the following: Is it likely that VW violated RICO? Is it likely that Lopez and his colleagues who "relocated" to VW violated RICO? What critical evidence must be proven by GM?

Suppose that this case is brought in *your* court. How would *you* resolve the issues presented?[16]

BUSINESS CONSIDERATIONS What should a business do to reduce the risk of losing a key executive and of having that executive "confiscate" confidential information when he or she leaves? If a business *really* wants to hire a key executive away from one of its rivals, how can the hiring firm protect itself from these types of charges by the rival firm?

ETHICAL CONSIDERATIONS Is it ethical for an employee to take material and information to a new position when that material or information has been treated as confidential by the former employer? Suppose that the former employer had decided not to follow through with a planned development (such as "Plant X" in this case). Would that decision influence the ethics of the conduct by the former employer?

SOURCES: Daniel Howes, *The Detroit News* (19 February 1997), p. A1; Daniel Howes and David Shepardson, *The Detroit News* (22 May 1998), p. F1.

because the statute permits individuals whose business or property is injured by a violation of the statute to file a civil action. Successful plaintiffs in a civil action may recover treble damages, attorney's fees, and reasonable court costs. For example, beneficiaries of group health insurance policies used RICO to sue the insurance company.[17] This is an example of the overlap between criminal and civil law systems. A prior conviction in a criminal suit is not required in order to file a civil RICO suit. Some observers contend that this is leading to unfounded lawsuits and out-of-court settlements by intimidated firms. The government can also file civil

RICO actions. When the federal government proceeds with a civil suit, the burden of proof is lower than that for a criminal case. High civil penalties can provide a lucrative law-enforcement technique.

Since 1970, Congress has amended the law, which is incorporated in 18 U.S.C. §§ 1961–1968, and the courts have interpreted a number of its sections. The definitions of terms used in the statute are found in § 1961. Section 1962 lists the activities that are prohibited. Persons employed or associated with any enterprise are prohibited from engaging in a pattern of racketeering activity. A *pattern* constitutes committing at least two racketeering acts in a 10-year period. These racketeering acts are called *predicate acts* under RICO. Racketeering activity has been broadly defined and includes most criminal actions, such as bribery, antitrust violations, securities violations, fraud, acts of violence, and providing illegal goods or services. Michael Milken was convicted under RICO of scheming to manipulate stock prices and of defrauding customers. Racketeering acts also include acts relating to the Currency and Foreign Transactions Reporting Act, which was passed to prevent money laundering and requires the filing of CTRs. RICO violations are added to other criminal charges when there is a pattern of corrupt behavior, such as bribery. Defendants may raise issues of double jeopardy when they are tried for both the predicate acts and the RICO violation. Courts generally determine that the prohibition against double jeopardy is not violated because the predicate acts and the RICO offenses are separate and distinct crimes.[18]

Criminal and civil penalties are described in U.S.C. § 1963, and §§ 1965 to 1968 cover procedural rules. Individuals convicted of criminal RICO violations can be fined up to $25,000 per violation, imprisoned for up to 20 years, or both. RICO also provides for the forfeiture of any property, including business interests obtained through RICO violations. The property will be forfeited even if the property or business is itself legitimate. The defendant's assets can be temporarily seized before the trial begins to prevent further crimes. Some states have enacted their own RICO laws.

Since the federal RICO law is applied to legitimate business activities, it presents a potential concern for all business organizations, public and private. Recently, businesses have been taking the proactive approach of lobbying for legislative amendments to limit the application of RICO.

SELECTED DEFENSES

The four classic defenses to criminal liability are duress, insanity, intoxication, and justification.

Duress

Duress exists when the accused is coerced into criminal conduct by threat or use of force that any person of reasonable firmness could not resist. Not all governments permit this defense. Those governments that recognize it vary with respect to the crimes to which it is applicable. Generally, the three essential elements of this defense are:

1. An immediate threat of death or serious bodily harm
2. A well-grounded fear that the threat will be implemented, *and*
3. No reasonable opportunity to escape the threatened harm

Insanity

Insanity exists when, as a result of a mental disease or defect, the accused either did not know that what he or she was doing was wrong or could not prevent him- or herself from doing what he or she knew to be wrong. The exact definition varies from state to state. This defense has been attacked for a variety of reasons, but chiefly because the definition is still ambiguous. Although it is raised often, the insanity defense is rejected in many of the cases in which it is used.

Intoxication

Intoxication may be either voluntary or involuntary. Voluntary intoxication is not a defense unless it negates the specific intent required by a statute. For example, the crime of rape is said to require a general intent. Intoxication, therefore, would not be a valid defense. On the other hand, assault with the intent to commit rape is said to require specific intent. In that case, intoxication may be a valid defense. Generally, involuntary intoxication is a good defense. *Involuntary* intoxication, for instance, can occur if one is forced to drink an alcoholic beverage against one's will or without one's knowledge. An example of the latter would be if a host offered a guest a soft drink that was spiked with drugs without the guest's knowledge.

The defense of intoxication is summarized in Exhibit 8.3.

Justification

Justification exists when a person believes an act is necessary in order to avoid harm to him- or herself or to another person. The key to this defense is that whatever the person does to avoid harm must be lesser than the harm to be avoided. For

---

E X H I B I T   8.3 | **Intoxication as a Defense**

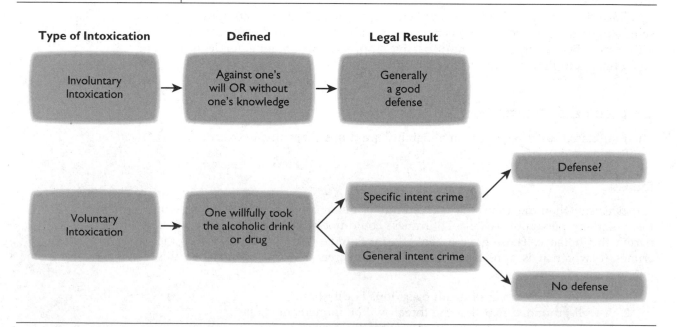

example, sometimes property has to be destroyed to prevent the spread of fire or disease. A rancher's cows may be destroyed to prevent the spread of mad cow disease. A pharmacist may dispense a drug without a prescription if to do so would save a person's life.

THE LAW OF CRIMINAL PROCEDURE

Criminal procedure is the area of law that addresses the judicial process in a criminal case. It is concerned with ensuring criminal justice without unduly infringing on individual rights. The drafters of the U.S. Constitution were determined to avoid the excesses and abuses that had occurred under English rule. There was a desire to protect the rights of the individual to the greatest extent possible without making law enforcement impossible. As a result, the area of criminal procedure was very important.

The Constitution contains numerous criminal procedure provisions and protections, among them the guarantees of **due process** and **equal protection.** The defendant must be informed of the charges against him or her, must be tried before an impartial tribunal, must be permitted to confront witnesses against him or her, and cannot be compelled to testify against him- or herself. The defendant is entitled to a speedy trial, may not be held subject to excessive **bail,** and may not be subjected to cruel and unusual punishment if convicted. No citizen may be subjected to unreasonable searches and seizures, and the only evidence that may be admitted at trial is evidence properly and lawfully obtained. Exhibit 8.4 on page 236 depicts the stages of criminal procedure. Note that a criminal trial is similar to a civil trial in many respects. The stages of a civil trial are discussed in Chapter 6. Many of the motions discussed in Chapter 6 can also be used in criminal trials.

The law presumes that the defendant is innocent until he or she is proven guilty. The burden of proof that must be satisfied in a criminal trial is the heaviest such burden in U.S. jurisprudence. The government must convince the jury of the defendant's guilt beyond a reasonable doubt, or the defendant must be acquitted.

Legal disputes may arise between a suspect and the police who search the suspect's business, home, car, or person. Under the Fourth Amendment to the Constitution, people are protected from unreasonable searches and seizures. When is a search and possible seizure legal? A search will be valid if any *one* of the following occurs:

1. It is properly conducted under a legal search warrant based on probable cause.
2. It is conducted without a warrant by officers acting with probable cause. In some situations, courts use a more reduced standard than probable cause. The most common examples of the reduced standards are when an officer "pats down" a suspect because the officer is concerned that the suspect has a concealed weapon, or the evidence is in a motor vehicle that could be driven away.
3. It is conducted with the permission of the owner of the property or a person with proper possession of the property, such as a tenant who rents an apartment.
4. An emergency or exigent circumstance exists that requires police to enter onto the premises, such as a fire in the building.

Due process
The proper exercise of judicial authority as established by general concepts of law and morality.

Equal protection
The assurance that any person before the court will be treated the same as every other person before the court.

Bail
The posting of money or property for the release of a person charged with a crime while ensuring his or her presence in the court at future hearings.

EXHIBIT 8.4 | **The Common Stages of Criminal Procedures**[a]

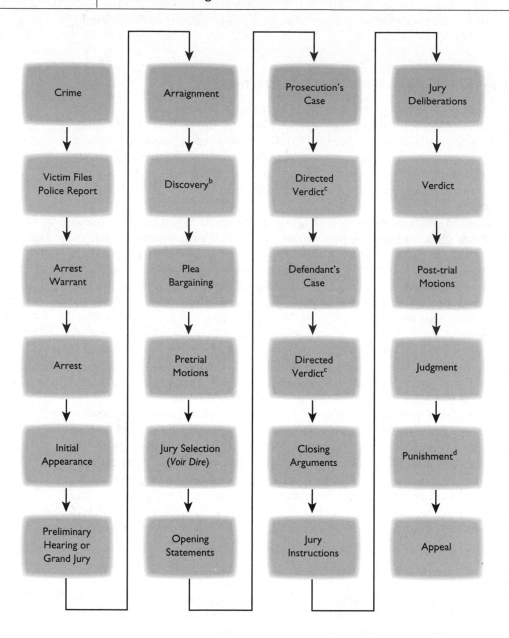

a. The exact order may vary.
b. Discovery is more limited in criminal cases than in civil cases.
c. Directed verdicts are not generally used *against* a criminal defendant.
d. A criminal defendant may be imprisoned beginning at the time of the arrest, if the court
   determines that bail is not appropriate or if the defendant cannot raise the amount of bail.

Once police are legally on the property, they may observe and act on any criminal behavior they see.

In England, police who conduct illegal searches are punished by the police force for violating the rules. In the United States, we generally use a different approach. Evidence obtained through an illegal search may not be used in court; this is called *suppression of evidence.* Many of the disputes involving searches of businesses are based on the validity of searches by the Occupational Safety and Health Administration (OSHA).

A police officer acting with probable cause may arrest and accuse an individual of committing a crime, or the arrest may occur under a warrant issued by a judge. A police officer who has probable cause to believe that a crime has been committed, or is being committed, may take the suspect into custody without obtaining a warrant. If an arrest warrant is used, it must be issued by a judge based on probable cause. The judge *may* find probable cause to believe that a crime has been committed solely on the basis of a sworn, written complaint that names the person to be arrested or adequately describes him or her.

The Supreme Court in the following case discusses whether it is proper to bring the media when serving an arrest warrant.

8.3

WILSON V. LAYNE
119 S.CT. 1692 (1999)

FACTS . . . [T]he Attorney General of the United States approved "Operation Gunsmoke," a special national fugitive apprehension program . . . One of the fugitives identified as a target of "Operation Gunsmoke" was Dominic Wilson, the son of . . . Charles and Geraldine Wilson. Dominic Wilson had violated his probation on previous felony charges . . . The [police] computer . . . listed his address as 909 North StoneStreet Avenue in Rockville, Maryland. Unknown to the police, this was actually the home of . . . Dominic Wilson's parents. . . . [T]he Circuit Court for Montgomery County issued three arrest warrants for Dominic Wilson . . . The warrants made no mention of media presence or assistance.

In the early morning hours of April 16, 1992, a Gunsmoke team of Deputy . . . Marshals and . . . Police officers assembled to execute the Dominic Wilson warrants. The team was accompanied by a reporter and a photographer from the Washington Post, who had been invited by the Marshals to accompany them on their mission as part of a Marshal's Service ride-along policy. At around 6:45 A.M., the officers, with media representatives in tow, entered the dwelling at 909 North StoneStreet Avenue in the Lincoln Park neighborhood of Rockville. . . . Charles and Geraldine Wilson were still in bed when they heard the officers enter the home. . . . Charles

Wilson, dressed only in a pair of briefs, ran into the living room to investigate. Discovering at least five men in street clothes with guns in his living room, he angrily demanded that they state their business, and repeatedly cursed the officers. Believing him to be an angry Dominic Wilson, the officers quickly subdued him on the floor. Geraldine Wilson next entered the living room . . . wearing only a nightgown. She observed her husband being restrained by the . . . officers.

When . . . the officers learned that Dominic Wilson was not in the house . . . they departed. . . . [T]he *Washington Post* photographer took numerous pictures. The print reporter was also apparently in the living room observing the confrontation between the police and Charles Wilson. At no time . . . were the reporters involved in the execution of the arrest warrant. The *Washington Post* never published its photographs of the incident.

. . . [The Wilsons] sued the law enforcement officials in their personal capacities for money damages . . . They contended that the officers' actions in bringing members of the media . . . violated their Fourth Amendment rights. . . . Recognizing a split among the Circuits on this issue, we granted *certiorari* . . .

continued

8.3

WILSON V. LAYNE, *continued*
119 S.CT. 1692 (1999)

ISSUE When police officers invite the media into a private home to observe the execution of a search warrant, do the officers violate the Fourth Amendment?

HOLDING Yes. These officers are entitled to qualified immunity because the law was not clearly established when the officers tried to execute the arrest warrant.

REASONING . . . [G]overnment officials performing discretionary functions generally are granted a qualified immunity and are "shielded from liability for civil damages insofar as their conduct does not violate clearly established statutory or constitutional rights of which a reasonable person would have known." . . . The Fourth Amendment embodies this centuries-old principle of respect for the privacy of the home: "The right of the people to be secure in their persons, houses, papers, and effects, against unreasonable searches and seizures, shall not be violated, and no Warrants shall issue, but upon probable cause, supported by Oath or affirmation, and particularly describing the place to be searched, and the persons or things to be seized." . . . Our decisions have applied these basic principles . . . to situations . . . in which police enter a home under the authority of an arrest warrant . . . Here, of course, the officers had such a warrant, and they were undoubtedly entitled to enter the Wilson home in order to execute the arrest warrant for Dominic Wilson. But it does not necessarily follow that they were entitled to bring a newspaper reporter and a photographer with them. . . . [T]he Fourth Amendment does require that police actions in execution of a warrant be related to the objectives of the authorized intrusion . . .

Certainly the presence of reporters inside the home was not related to the objectives of the authorized intrusion. Respondents concede that the reporters did not engage in the execution of the warrant, and did not assist the police in their task. . . . It may well be that media ride-alongs further the law enforcement objectives of the police in a general sense, but that is not the same as furthering the purposes of the search. . . . Surely the possibility of good public relations for the police is simply not enough, standing alone, to justify the ride-along intrusion into a private home. And even the need for accurate reporting on police issues in general bears no direct relation to the constitutional

justification for the police intrusion into a home in order to execute a felony arrest warrant. . . . While it might be reasonable for police officers to themselves videotape home entries as part of a "quality control" effort to ensure that the rights of homeowners are being respected, or even to preserve evidence . . . [t]he *Washington Post* reporters in the Wilsons' home were working on a story for their own purposes. . . . We hold that it is a violation of the Fourth Amendment for police to bring members of the media or other third parties into a home during the execution of a warrant when the presence of the third parties in the home was not in aid of the execution of the warrant.

. . . [W]e now must decide whether this right was clearly established at the time of the search. . . . In this case, the appropriate question is . . . whether a reasonable officer could have believed that bringing members of the media into a home during the execution of an arrest warrant was lawful, in light of clearly established law and the information the officers possessed. . . . First, the constitutional question presented by this case is by no means open and shut. . . . [I]t is not obvious from the general principles of the Fourth Amendment that the conduct of the officers in this case violated the Amendment. Second, although media ride-alongs of one sort or another had apparently become a common police practice, in 1992 there were no judicial opinions holding that this practice became unlawful when it entered a home. . . . If judges . . . disagree on a constitutional question, it is unfair to subject police to money damages for picking the losing side of the controversy.

BUSINESS CONSIDERATIONS What guidelines should the Marshal's Service include in their ride-along policy? What guidelines should be established by the *Washington Post?* What other enterprises are likely to violate privacy rights?

ETHICAL CONSIDERATIONS Was it ethical for the officers to invite the media into the Wilson home? Was it ethical for the *Washington Post* employees to enter onto private property? What ethical guidelines should the media use in deciding what it may do to obtain a story?

Once arrested and charged with criminal conduct, the accused should be given a preliminary hearing. Preliminary hearings are not required in most jurisdictions if there has been a grand jury hearing. At the preliminary hearing, a magistrate determines whether there is probable cause to proceed to a trial. The charges against the accused will be dropped if the magistrate decides that there is no probable cause, or that there is not enough evidence to proceed to trial, or that there is virtually no chance to obtain a conviction. Then the accused will be released from custody.

A grand jury may also be involved in the pretrial stages of criminal proceedings. A *grand jury* is a panel charged with determining whether there is reason to believe that a person has committed a crime. After hearing the evidence presented by the prosecutor, the grand jury will issue an indictment if it believes that the accused has committed a crime. The government will then proceed to trial on the basis of this indictment, and a preliminary hearing is not required.

Once the grand jury has issued an indictment or the magistrate at a preliminary hearing has determined that probable cause exists, the accused is **arraigned.** At the arraignment, the accused is informed of the charges against him or her, and, if necessary, the court appoints an attorney to represent the defendant.

Arraigned
Called before a court to enter a plea on an indictment or criminal complaint.

A common pretrial motion at this point is a motion for *change of venue.* In criminal cases, change of venue is requested if pretrial publicity was negative to the defendant. The defense counsel argues that the location should be moved to ensure the defendant a fair trial.

The defendant enters a plea to the charges. If the plea that is entered is guilty or **nolo contendere,** the court moves to the sentencing stage. If the plea is not guilty, a trial date is set and bail is determined, if appropriate.

Nolo contendere
A plea in a criminal proceeding that has the same effect as a plea of guilty but that cannot be used as evidence of guilt.

At the trial, the government has the burden of proving its case beyond a reasonable doubt, and it must satisfy this burden within the established rules of evidence. Any violation of the rules of evidence will result in the exclusion of the improper evidence, which often effectively destroys the government's case. When this happens, the defendant will be acquitted.

In criminal cases we still use 12 jurors plus alternates. An alternate replaces a regular juror who is not able to continue on the jury. A jury may be *sequestered.* When this occurs, jurors are not permitted to return home during the evenings and weekends. They are kept separate from the rest of society so that others will not influence their views. Jurors are generally not sequestered in civil cases. For example, in the O. J. Simpson civil trial, Judge Fujisaki rejected the plaintiffs' request that the jury be sequestered, stating that "there was no precedent for sequestering jurors at public expense in a civil trial . . ."[19]

If the jurors are deadlocked and are unable to reach a decision, it is called a *hung jury.* In 1993–94, Erik and Lyle Menendez were tried for the murder of their parents. The Menendez brothers admitted to the killing but defended themselves based on self-defense. In the first trial "twin" juries were used since some evidence was only admissible against Erik and other evidence was only admissible against Lyle. The "twin" juries were unable to reach verdicts. The Los Angeles County D. A. had the brothers retried and obtained convictions against both brothers. This does not violate the prohibition against double jeopardy.

If the defendant is found guilty, the court moves to the sentencing stage. Sentencing is governed by legislative guidelines to some extent, but the guidelines are normally very broad and somewhat vague. A great deal of judicial discretion

RESOURCES FOR BUSINESS LAW STUDENTS

NAME	RESOURCES	WEB ADDRESS
Legal Information Institute (LII)—Criminal Law	The LII, maintained by the Cornell Law School, provides links to federal and state criminal statutes, organizations, journals, and other resources.	**http://www.law.cornell.edu/topics/criminal.html**
U.S. Department of Justice	The U.S. Department of Justice provides links to its agencies, including the Federal Bureau of Investigation and the Bureau of Justice Statistics, as well as to cases and statutes.	**http://www.usdoj.gov/**
U.S. Sentencing Commission	The U.S. Sentencing Commission provides publications and guidelines, statistics, reports to Congress, and links to state sentencing commissions.	**http://www.ussc.gov/**
Racketeer Influenced and Corrupt Organizations (RICO) Act, 18 U.S.C. § 1961	The LII provides a hypertext and searchable version of 18 U.S.C. § 1961, popularly known as the Racketeer Influenced and Corrupt Organizations (RICO) Act.	**http://www4.law.cornell.edu/uscode/18/1961.html**

is usually involved in sentencing. Under current federal law, federal judges have much less discretion in sentencing for federal crimes than most state court judges. Federal judges rely heavily on the federal sentencing guidelines.

SUMMARY

Criminal law is designed to protect persons and property from harm. In addition, it is designed to deter criminal behavior. Of course, the best protection is the absence of criminal activity; however, some criminal activity will always exist. Many believe that the law should punish criminals for their wrongful acts and/or try to rehabilitate them while they are incarcerated.

Criminal responsibility is based on two essential elements—a physical act and a mental state. The physical act must be overt. The mental state actually consists of one of the following: purpose, knowledge, recklessness, negligence, or strict liability. A similarity to civil law exists, but the interests protected are different: Civil law protects private interests, whereas criminal law protects public interests. Accordingly, one can be held liable twice for the same act, once in civil law and once in criminal law. This is not double jeopardy because there are two distinct bases of liability.

Crimes can be classified as infractions, misdemeanors, felonies, or treason. Some states now categorize minor offenses as infractions. These offenses are punished by fines. Misdemeanors constitute less serious crimes; felonies are more serious. Treason, the most serious, involves acts to overthrow the government or provide aid or information to another government.

The selected crimes discussed in the chapter include murder/manslaughter, arson, burglary, embezzlement, forgery, credit card and check crimes, fraud, larceny, robbery, espionage, computer crimes, and violations of the Currency and Foreign Transactions Reporting Act and the RICO statute. Courts may hold a corporation liable for crimes committed on its behalf. A public policy debate is occurring over the appropriateness of this trend. The criminal defenses mentioned are duress, insanity, intoxication, and justification.

The law of criminal procedure is very technical. An individual suspected of committing a crime can be arrested only upon probable cause. Probable cause is initially determined either by the arresting officer or by a judge issuing an arrest warrant. Once arrested, the accused is entitled to a preliminary hearing, which requires finding that there is sufficient evidence to proceed to a trial. Grand jury hearings can also be used. The grand jury may issue an indictment if it believes the accused has committed a crime.

During a criminal trial the government must prove its case beyond a reasonable doubt, and it must abide by numerous constitutional guarantees, such as due process, equal protection, and the rules of evidence. Only after a conviction can an accused person be sentenced to a fine or imprisonment. However, temporary forfeiture is permitted for certain crimes. In addition, a criminal defendant can be imprisoned pending trial because the magistrate determines that bail is not appropriate or the defendant is not able to post bail.

DISCUSSION QUESTIONS

1. A man coated a carousel at Watkins Park in Indianapolis with skin-dissolving chemicals. Eleven children and one adult were sent to the hospital with irritated skin on their faces, hands, and legs.[20] Has the man committed any crimes? If so, which ones?

2. Some states have enacted "Son of Sam" laws, which prevent criminal defendants from receiving financial gain by publishing books about their crimes. These laws are not applicable to attorneys, the victims, or the victims' families. Are these laws just? Why or why not? Should these laws be applied to defendants who wish to use profits from books for their legal defense? Why or why not?

3. A house is on fire during a drought, and there is not enough water available to put out the fire. A volunteer firefighter dynamites the houses immediately surrounding the house that is on fire to prevent the spread of the fire. Will this firefighter face any criminal responsibility? Explain your reasoning.

4. What crimes are associated with increasing computer usage? What steps can a company take to protect itself from falling victim to these crimes?

5. Nazik's business is losing money. She decides to burn down her place of business, collect the proceeds of her insurance, and start over again. The building burns down, but a homeless person sleeping in the building at the time is burned to death. What is Nazik's criminal liability? Is she liable for arson, homicide, criminal fraud? Why?

6. If an individual is observed entering an alleyway next to a retail store at night and carrying a ladder and a bag of tools, can that person be convicted of attempted burglary? Why?

7. Crimes are either *mala in se* (morally wrong) or *mala prohibita* (wrong because the law says they are wrong). To which category do arson, cultivation of marijuana, income tax evasion, and the activities covered under the RICO statute belong? Why?

8. The Model Penal Code is a proposed criminal code that many states have used to revise and modernize their criminal laws. It consolidates larceny, embezzlement, false pretense, extortion, blackmail, fraudulent conversion, receiving stolen property, and all other similar offenses into the one general offense of theft. What advantages and/or disadvantages can you find to this approach?

9. A Justice Department study of 12 cities found that blacks' rate of dissatisfaction with police is more than twice that of whites. For example, in Chicago, 11 percent of the whites and 31 percent of the blacks were dissatisfied with the police.[21] What might explain the difference in satisfaction?

10. Every day people die in police chases. Based on federal studies, about 40 percent of police chases end in crashes.[22] Oftentimes, people are injured or killed. It may be the suspect who is running from the police, or it may be the officer or bystanders who are injured. How can the legal system balance the need to keep the peace and apprehend suspects with the need for public safety?

CASE PROBLEMS AND WRITING ASSIGNMENTS

1. San Pedro criminal defense attorney Barry Post was arrested at the California State Bar Association offices in Los Angeles. Post was there to discuss disciplinary proceedings against him. He faces 13 counts of professional wrongdoing and failing to represent clients properly, including failure to competently perform legal services, return unearned fees, cooperate with the bar's investigation, and collecting an unconscionable fee. One client paid a $5,000 retainer to an attorney in Post's office, Brent Carruth, who had his license to practice law suspended at the time. The sheriff's office received a tip that Post was unhappy with the bar association's investigation. He allegedly solicited a private investigator to contract with someone to kill the prosecutor; the private investigator contacted the authorities. Post wanted his former partner also killed. Has Post committed any crimes? What can a business do to protect itself from disgruntled partners and employees? [See "Attorney Nabbed at State Bar Offices for Soliciting Murders," *California Bar Journal* (April 1999), pp. 25, 30.]

2. The Michigan state treasurer has filed a lawsuit against Jack Kevorkian, the advocate of assisted suicide. In March 1999, Kevorkian was convicted of second-degree murder in the death of Thomas Youk, who had Lou Gehrig's disease. Kevorkian was 71 years old at the time. He was sentenced to 10 to 25 years in prison. The state treasurer wants to charge Kevorkian for the cost of keeping him in prison. The treasurer is asking the court to freeze all of Kevorkian's assets and to appoint the prison warden at the Oaks Correctional Facility as a receiver to control Kevorkian's funds. Does this constitute cruel and unusual punishment? Why? [See "In Brief, Kevorkian Sued by State," *The Fresno Bee* (11 July 1999), p. A4.]

3. Film Recovery Systems, Inc., was engaged in the business of extracting, for resale, silver from used x-ray and photographic film. Metallic Marketing Systems, Inc., operated out of the same premises and owned 50 percent of the stock of Film Recovery. The recovery process involved "chipping" the film product and soaking the granulated pieces in large open bubbling vats containing a solution of water and sodium cyanide. The cyanide solution caused the release of silver contained in the film. A continuous flow system pumped the silver-laden solution into polyurethane tanks that contained electrically charged stainless steel plates to which the separated silver adhered. Workers removed the plates from the tanks to another room where the accumulated silver was scraped off. On the morning of 10 February 1983, shortly after Stefan Golab had disconnected a pump on one of the tanks and had begun to stir the contents of the tank with a rake, he became dizzy and felt faint. He left the production area to rest in the lunchroom area. Golab eventually lost consciousness, and he was pronounced dead on arrival at the hospital. After receiving the toxicological report, the Cook County medical examiner determined that Golab had died from acute cyanide poisoning through the inhalation of cyanide fumes in the plant air. Those who testified as to the working conditions in the plant had established that the firms had not told the employees they were working with cyanide or that the compound put into the vats could be harmful when inhaled. Should Film Recovery and/or its high-ranking officers be criminally liable for Golab's death? Why? [See *People* v. *O'Neil*, 550 N.E.2d 1090 (Ill.App. 1990).]

4. Carolyn Grant-Campbell admitted that she stole more than $220,000 from Light Line United Mission, a homeless shelter founded by her adoptive mother 36 years ago. According to the indictment, Grant-Campbell embezzled and misapplied funds between 4 February 1994 and 10 January 1995, while she was the director of the mission. According to the indictment, she obtained the funds by writing checks to herself from mission bank accounts. Grant-Campbell pled guilty to 10 counts of embezzlement of money given to the mission by the federal government. The mission was receiving funds from the Federal Emergency Management Agency to help homeless and dispossessed families obtain shelter. She has agreed to make restitution of $146,310 and to cooperate with the federal government in the "investigation and prosecution of other individuals." The federal government stopped funding the mission when the thefts were discovered. Now, the mission is falling behind on its payments and owes a number of creditors. Is theft morally wrong? Is some theft worse than others? Is it more wrong when the theft is against those in need? Is it worse to steal from the government (and the

people)? If an officer or employee steals from his or her organization, what is his or her moral perspective? Explain your reasons. [See Jerry Bier, "Shelter's Former Director Admits Embezzling Money," *The Fresno Bee* (5 February 1997), pp. B1, B2.]

5. Robert J. Riggs, a.k.a. Prophet, and Craig Neidorf, a.k.a. Knight Lightning, collaborated on a scheme to defraud Bell South Telephone Company. They agreed to steal Bell South's computer text file containing information on its enhanced 911 emergency calling system. Using his home computer in Decatur, Georgia, Riggs accessed Bell South's computer system, retrieved the file, and concealed his unauthorized access by using account codes of persons with legitimate access. Riggs transferred the file to Neidorf, a university student at the University of Missouri, via a bulletin board system and the interstate computer network. Subsequently, Neidorf altered the file so that people could not identify its source and published it in his Phrack newsletter. Can Riggs and Neidorf be successfully prosecuted for any crimes? If so, which ones? [See *U.S.* v. *Riggs*, 967 F.2d 561 (11th Cir. 1992); *U.S.* v. *Riggs*, 743 F.Supp. 556 (N.Dist.Ill., E.Div. 1990); and *U.S.* v. *Riggs*, 739 F.Supp. 414 (N.Dist.Ill., E.Div. 1990).]

6. **BUSINESS APPLICATION CASE** Michael Lasch has been arrested and charged with theft by deception, criminal attempt, unlawful use of a computer, criminal trespass, and impersonating an employee. Lasch, a plumber in the Philadelphia area, called Bell Atlantic and ordered an "ultra call-forwarding" service for telephones of at least five of his competitors. [Callforwarding can be used to transfer phone calls from one phone number to another and is activated by entering code numbers from any phone.] Through this technique, Lasch was able to intercept calls placed to his competitors. Moreover, Lasch knew most of the plumbers whose calls he intercepted.

One competitor, Lucas Ltd., claimed that Lasch only took the better customers and told others that he would not take their service calls. Lucas says he is getting phone calls from angry customers who were not served. The scheme was discovered when a customer called Lucas to compliment him on work that was done over the Christmas holiday. Lucas told her that his plumbers had not been to her home during the holidays. How would you decide this case?

Why? What could Lasch's competitors have done to protect their telephone calls and customers? Can you suggest any business practices that would have helped the plumbers discover the scheme more quickly? What steps could Bell Atlantic have taken to prevent this from occurring or to discover it more quickly? [See Dinah Wisenberg Brin, "Plumber Flushes His Competitors by Using Call-Forwarding," *The Fresno Bee* (29 January 1995), p. A10.]

7. **ETHICAL APPLICATION CASE** *Fortune* magazine published an article about security on company computers. They hired WheelGroup Corp., a computer security firm, to "break into" the computer system of a *Fortune 500* company. The company agreed to have its security tested as long as its identity was kept secret. A computer expert from Coopers & Lybrand was hired to protect the company, its data, and systems during the experiment. In a companion article, *Fortune* published the steps used by WheelGroup to gain access to the computer system, including the names and functions of software commonly used by hackers to gain access. There are also periodicals, such as *Phrack* and *2600: The Hacker Quarterly*, that specialize in hacker information. Is it ethical to publish detailed information about how to break into others' computers? Why or why not? [See "How We Invaded a Fortune 500 Company," *Fortune* (3 February 1997), pp. 58–61; and Richard Behar, "Who's Reading Your E-mail?" *Fortune* (3 February 1997), pp. 57–70.]

8. **CRITICAL THINKING CASE** At 2:30 A.M., three bounty hunters came to the home of Linda Childs in Kansas City. They were searching for Virgil McCubbins, her son. The bounty hunters had received a tip that morning that Virgil was there, and they had a certified copy of his bond with them, as required by state law. Virgil had apparently "skipped bail." During the search, the bounty hunters broke Childs's front door, hurt her husband, and sprayed her grandsons, ages 5 and 10, with mace. According to Childs, her son had moved out three years ago. The law allows bondsmen and bounty hunters a lot of latitude in capturing people who have skipped bail. Often they have more freedom than police officers do in making arrests. Analyze this situation in terms of the objectives of the criminal justice system. [See Paula Barr, "Old Law Upholds Leeway Given to Bounty Hunters," *The Fresno Bee* (29 January 1995), p. A9.]

NOTES

1. See *Regina* v. *Jones,* 91 Eng.Rep. 330 (1703).
2. "The Enemy Within: Christian Tyler Reports on How Cold War Spy Tactics Are Being Adapted to Big Business," *Financial Times* (London) (12 April 1997), p. 1.
3. Ibid.
4. Richard Behar, "Who's Reading Your E-mail?" *Fortune* (3 February 1997), pp. 57–70, at p. 59.
5. Ibid., at p. 64.
6. Ibid., at pp. 58, 59.
7. Ibid., at p. 70.
8. Ibid., at p. 59.
9. Ibid., at p. 64.
10. Jerry Bier, "Computer Stalker Trial Is Delayed," *The Fresno Bee* (5 June 1996), pp. B1, B3.
11. See Model Penal Code (1985) § 2.07.
12. See California Penal Code § 387.
13. See Mark Whitacre as told to Ronald Henkoff, "My Life as a Corporate Mole for the FBI," *Fortune* (4 September 1995), pp. 52–62.
14. See 18 U.S.C. §§ 1961 *et seq.*
15. On 9 January 1997, GM and VW voluntarily settled their legal differences, thus avoiding costly and highly publicized litigation. Both sides officially apologized. The agreement specified that GM would get $100 million in cash, and VW promised to purchase $1 billion of GM parts over a seven-year period. German prosecutors have dropped the criminal charges. Brian Coleman, "Lopez Case Is Dropped in Germany," *The Wall Street Journal* (28 July 1998), p. A12.
16. Daniel Howes, "Ex-GM Exec Faces Bribery Investigation: Automaker Isn't Included in Justice Department Probe, Source Says," *The Detroit News* (19 February 1997), p. A1; Daniel Howes and David Shepardson, "U.S.: Lopez Probe 'Still Active': Justice Department Vows to Keep Working on Espionage Case Against Ex-GM Official," *The Detroit News* (22 May 1998), p. F1.
17. See *Humana, Inc.* v. *Forsyth,* 119 S.Ct. 710 (1999).
18. See *U.S.* v. *Bellomo,* 1997 U.S.Dist. LEXIS 434 (S.Dist. N.Y. 1997).
19. Linda Deutsch and Michael Fleeman, "Simpson Juror Replaced; Talks Start Anew," *The Fresno Bee* (1 February 1997), pp. A1, A11.
20. "Police Say Chemical Coated on Carousel; National Briefs/Indiana," *The Boston Globe* (21 June 1999), p. A11; Man Charged in Placing Chemical on Carousel," *The Arizona Republic* (21 June 1999), p. A8.
21. "What's News—World-Wide" column, "Blacks' Dissatisfaction with Police Is . . . ," *The Wall Street Journal* (4 June 1999), p. A1.
22. Mike Madden, "It's Your Average Day in the U.S. and Someone Will Die in a Police Chase," *The Fresno Bee* (11 July 1999), p. A7.

Contracts

The law of contracts forms the foundation of business law. Virtually every aspect of business involves contracts, as does much of a person's everyday life. When you rent an apartment, you sign—or orally agree to—a contract known as a lease. When you take a job, you enter into a contract of employment. Any purchase of goods, services, or real estate involves some form of contract. Even marriage is a type of contract.

This part of the book will examine the traditional elements of contract law—the common law of contracts. Later parts will consider various special types of contracts, among them sales, negotiable instruments, and secured transactions. Keep in mind, however, that all of these specialized forms are merely variations on the basic form. Thus, to understand these specialized types of contracts, you first need a thorough understanding of the common law of contracts presented here.

P A R T

3

9

INTRODUCTION TO CONTRACT LAW AND CONTRACT THEORY

A G E N D A

CIT will enter into a large number of contracts as the business develops. It will have contracts with suppliers, customers, and employees. CIT is likely to have contracts with its insurer and may well have to enter into leases for rented space. Tom and Anna Kochanowski will need to know how contract formation occurs, what type of contract is involved, and what rights and liabilities they undertake as a result of contract formation. It is quite likely that they will turn to you for help and assistance at many steps along the way. Be prepared! You never know when one of the Kochanowskis will need your help or advice.

O U T L I N E

THE IMPORTANCE OF CONTRACT LAW

Of all the aspects of law examined in this text, none is as significant or pervasive in our lives as the law of contracts. Virtually every personal or business activity involves contract law: Charging a birthday gift on a credit card, buying and insuring a car, leasing an apartment, writing a check, paying for college, and working at an establishment covered by an employment agreement are some examples. Even filling up our gasoline tanks involves contract law. Not only are we making a contract with the gasoline retailer, but the gasoline companies themselves receive much of their oil as a result of international contracts.

The law of contracts affects our most mundane activities, as well as some rather sensational ones, such as surrogacy contracts (whereby women agree contractually to have babies for infertile couples) and privately forged settlements of international business disputes that courts otherwise would have to resolve. This chapter discusses the broad categories of contracts and contractual situations.

Commercial Law Contracts

When most of us think of the word *contract*, we envision the **mercantile** world. Historically, our system of **free enterprise** has stressed the importance of freedom of contract and a corresponding protection of contractual rights. This was not always so, however. Blackstone's *Commentaries on the Laws of England*, first published in 1756, devoted 380 pages to real property law but only 28 pages to contracts. Thus, the law of contracts apparently constituted a subdivision of the law of property rather than the independent branch of law as we know it today.[1]

The eighteenth century's de-emphasis of contract law stems in part from the historical roots of this substantive area of the law. Although always broadly a part of the common law, mercantile traditions grew out of the law merchant, which represented the accumulation of commercial customs from as early as Phoenician times. The mercantile courts were separate from courts of law, and the merchants (or guilds) administered their own rules and customs. Hence, the evolution of commercial law remained outside the mainstream of legal development until fairly late in English history, the end of the seventeenth century. In the late 1800s, after the assimilation of the law merchant into the common law, several acts of Parliament addressed commercial law subjects.

Influenced by these English precedents, various legal bodies in the United States penned a wide variety of statutes, such as the Uniform Negotiable Instruments Law and the Uniform Sales Act, covering American commercial law. By the 1930s, several such model acts existed. But the effectiveness of these acts was limited: Commercial remedies differed from state to state, and the acts quickly became outmoded and thus not reflective of modern commercial practices. For these reasons, and especially to effect an integration of inconsistent statutes, the American Law Institute (ALI) and the National Conference of Commissioners on Uniform State Laws (NCCUSL) in the 1940s began working on what we today call the Uniform Commercial Code (UCC).[2]

By viewing commercial transactions as a single subject of the law, the UCC revolutionized prior approaches to commercial transactions. The drafters saw, for example, that a sale of **goods** may constitute one facet of such a transaction. They also realized that a buyer may use a check for payment of the purchase price of the goods or that, alternatively, the seller may retain a **security interest** in the goods

Mercantile
Having to do with business, commerce, or trade.

Free enterprise
The carrying on of free, legitimate business for profit.

Goods
Movable, identifiable items of personal property.

Security interest
An interest in personal property or fixtures that secures payment or performance of an obligation.

9.1 | SALES/ MANAGEMENT

WHAT TYPE OF LAW WILL GOVERN CIT'S CONTRACTS?

CIT will sell its interactive videophones directly to a number of its initial customers, and the firm also will install many of the systems purchased. The sale of the product involves the sale of *goods* and thus is governed by the Uniform Commercial Code. However, the installation of the product is a *service* and as such is governed by common law principles. Tom and Anna want to know whether the contracts the firm enters will be governed in part by one type of law (the UCC) and in part by another type of law (the common law of contracts) or whether a court is more likely to determine that one aspect of the transaction "controls," so that the entire contract will be governed by this type of law. What will you tell them?

BUSINESS CONSIDERATIONS If a business provides both goods and services, should it price one higher than the other in order to imply which aspect of law—the UCC or common law—controls? Should the firm specify in the contract which aspect controls? Why?
ETHICAL CONSIDERATION If the seller is a merchant, the sale of goods carries certain *warranties*. Is it ethical to try to designate the contract as being primarily for services in order to avoid giving these warranty protections to the customers?

Negotiable instruments
Checks, drafts, notes, and certificates of deposit; governed by Article 3 of the UCC, negotiable instruments are used for credit and/or as substitutes for money.

to ensure payment of the balance of the debt. The UCC articles on sales, **negotiable instruments,** bank deposits and collections, and **secured transactions** correspond roughly to the scenarios described above. The UCC has fulfilled its original goals of simplifying, clarifying, and modernizing the law governing commercial transactions; permitting the continued expansion of commercial practices through custom, usage, and agreement of the parties; and making uniform the law among the various jurisdictions [§ 1-102(2) and Comment 1]. Most states' commercial statutes, with minor variations, have reproduced the UCC articles in their entirety. Louisiana, while it has incorporated some of the articles of the UCC into its commercial laws, remains unique in that it has not wholly adopted the UCC. The Code appears in the back of the text as Appendix B.

In addition to the UCC, the National Conference of Commissioners on Uniform State Laws has drafted other statutes for possible adoption by the states. Examples include the Uniform Partnership Act and the Uniform Consumer Credit Code. These laws have regularized commercial transactions so that transactions will remain more consistent from state to state. Such uniformity fosters predictability of result without necessarily sacrificing the law's capacity to change when commercial practices dictate such adjustments. You should check whether your state has adopted these uniform acts and codes or whether it instead relies on its own statutes to cover these areas of the law.

Common Law Contracts

The existence of statutes concerned with commercial contract law should not overshadow the importance of common law contracts. Many doctrines regarding modern-day contracts stem from "judge-made" law, or court decisions growing out of contractual disputes from earlier times. Contract disputes decided on a daily basis in jurisdictions around the country significantly add to this body of precedents. The UCC states that common law supplements the UCC in those areas where the Code is silent. It is appropriate, then, that most of the discussion in Chapters 9 through 15 centers on common law contract principles—that is, principles derived from the judgments and decrees of courts.

Definition of a Contract

Many definitions exist for the word *contract*. In general, a contract is a legally binding and legally enforceable promise, or set of promises, between two or more competent parties. Put another way, a contract is "a promise or set of promises for the breach of which the law gives a remedy, or the performance of which the law in some way recognizes as a duty."[3] Most of us intuitively understand what a contract is. Still, situations exist that at first glance may appear to be contracts but are not.

Assume that you are a Rolling Stones fan. The Stones are in the United States for a concert tour. You are extremely eager to attend a concert by these vintage rock-and-rollers. A friend promises you tickets to the show, and you of course are elated. Two days later, your friend calls to tell you he is taking an old flame instead of you. As you hang up, your anger and disappointment cause you to think about suing your friend. After all, you had an agreement, and he has broken a promise to you. You think you deserve to collect money damages for the harm you have suffered.

Does your agreement give rise to a legally enforceable contract? Will a court protect your expectations and award you damages? The short answer is probably no. Most courts will view this situation as a breached social obligation, not a breached contractual promise. You occasionally may read of people suing in small claims courts for the expenses incurred in making plans for dates that never occurred because they were "stood up." If the plaintiffs win these "contract" actions (and sometimes they do), higher courts generally overturn these results on appeal because the more settled rule calls such situations broken social obligations, not breached contracts. Stated differently, you should be aware that a court will not deem all agreements "contracts."

Contrast the earlier situation involving the Rolling Stones with this scenario: You call a ticket outlet, order two tickets for the Rolling Stones concert, and give your credit card number. When you arrive at the box office days before the concert to pick up your tickets, you learn that the outlet has sold them to someone else. Can you successfully sue this time? Perhaps you can, because this situation seems to involve more than a mere social obligation; it seems to have created binding economic obligations on both sides. Thus, to protect your economic expectations, a court may call this a contract and award you damages (i.e., the amount of money it will take to put you back in the position you would have enjoyed had the contract been performed). Hence, the part of the definition that alludes to a "legally enforceable" or "legally binding" agreement takes on significance because it means that not every promise, agreement, or expectation ripens into a contract. In essence, a contract is any agreement between two or more parties that a court will recognize as one that creates legally binding duties and obligations between the parties.

Elements of a Contract

Given the law's emphasis on promises or mutual assent, it is not surprising that the first requirement for a valid contract is an *agreement*. Basically, an agreement consists of an offer and an acceptance of that offer. The law looks at the agreement from the viewpoint of a reasonable person and asks whether such a person would believe that an offer and an acceptance, respectively, actually had occurred. Second, the parties must support their agreement with *consideration*, that is, something bargained for and given in exchange for a promise. Third, the parties must have *capacity*, or the legal ability to contract. Fourth, the contract must reflect the *genuine assent* of each party. If one party has procured the assent of the other person by fraud or duress, for example, courts may set the contract aside owing to the disadvantaged party's lack of genuine assent to the agreement. Fifth, the subject matter of the contract must be *legal*. The legality of the bargain is questionable, for instance, if the parties have agreed to do something that violates a statute or

Secured transactions
Credit arrangements, covered by Article 9 of the UCC, in which the creditor retains a security interest in certain assets of the debtor.

public policy. Sixth, in some cases, the law requires that a contract evince certain *formalities*. Despite the fact that courts ordinarily will enforce oral contracts (even though it is risky to make an oral contract because of the difficulties in trying to prove exactly what each party said), some categories of contracts must be in writing to be legally effective.

In summary, to be valid, a contract must be (1) founded on an agreement (i.e., an offer and an acceptance); (2) supported by consideration; (3) made by parties having the capacity to contract; (4) based on these parties' genuine assent; (5) grounded in a legal undertaking; and (6) expressed in proper form, if applicable. Each of these requirements is discussed in detail in Chapters 9–13. Exhibit 9.1 shows the elements of a contract.

FROM STATUS TO FREEDOM OF CONTRACT AND BACK AGAIN

The development of contract law occurred relatively late in English legal history. Why? In part, because of feudalism. Feudal society set social hierarchies that prevailed throughout Europe between the eleventh and thirteenth centuries. In such a rigid, stratified society, each person occupied a specific social position. Social circumstances thus determined one's rights and the conduct expected of that individual. For example, feudal lords owed few duties to lowly serfs, but serfs owed their lives to their lords.

Imagine the disruptive effect that contract law, which calls for the performance of mutual duties and obligations, would have had on such a social order. It is not surprising, then, that property law assumed foremost importance during these times and that status was more important than contract rights. If a serf was the property of the lord, courts did not need to bother with protecting what the state considered the serf's rather trivial expectations. Accordingly, the development of contract law was unnecessary.

Yet, as England became a commercial center, the law merchant and contracts became more important than status. Furthermore, during the social and political reforms of the late eighteenth and nineteenth centuries, the rise of capitalism brought with it demands for freedom of contract. This political emphasis on the importance of the individual and of private property accelerated the growth of what we now call contract law. To a largely agrarian society dedicated to self-reliance and individualism, protection of expectations and enforcement of obligations took on added importance. The demise of a status-oriented society thus ushered in a contractually oriented social order.

Ironically, as an aftermath of the Industrial Revolution, the twentieth century has witnessed numerous restrictions on the nineteenth century's adoption of virtually unrestricted freedom of contract. Legislatures and courts have curtailed this freedom of contract and have reinstated—to a limited extent—a tilt back toward status. Labor laws, environmental protection statutes, and consumer enactments represent a few examples of how lawmakers lately have restricted freedom of contract. Similarly, through common law decisions, courts, by protecting individuals who have little bargaining power even after these persons have consummated a contract, have hampered the continued development of freedom of contract.

The doctrine of unconscionability, mentioned in Chapter 1 and explored in Chapters 11 and 12, provides a perfect example of this protection. Suppose two

E X H I B I T 9.1 | **The Elements of a Contract**

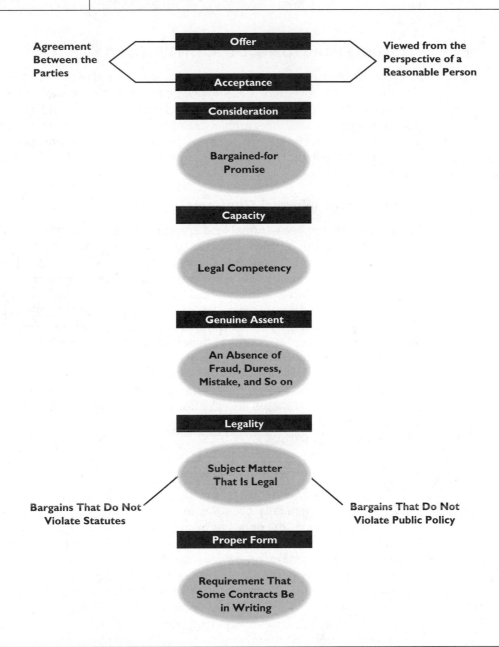

parties have bargained. If, in the court's opinion, one of them (usually a corporation or business entity) had grossly superior bargaining power, or leverage, over the other (especially a consumer), the court sometimes will set such contracts aside on the grounds of unconscionability—that is, because the contract is shockingly oppressive or grossly unfair to one of the parties. (Do not, however, make the mistake of believing you can rely on this remedy to get out of every contract for which you belatedly wish to avoid responsibility!) Such developments have convinced some commentators that this progression shows an interesting circularity, that is, a movement from status to freedom of contract and back to status again.

CLASSIFICATIONS OF CONTRACTS

The law categorizes or distinguishes contracts in various ways. These categories are not always mutually exclusive, so several different terms may apply to the same contract. For example, suppose a restaurant orders produce and meat from its supplier at set prices, and the supplier promises to deliver on a predetermined schedule. The understanding between these parties invokes several categories of contracts simultaneously: In short, this agreement is an informal, bilateral, valid, express contract.

Formal Versus Informal Contracts

The distinction between formal and informal contracts derives from the method used in creating the contract. In early common law times, the contracting parties generally engaged in certain formalities (hence, the term *formal*). To be valid, for example, a contract had to be under seal; that is, the document had to be closed with wax and imprinted with one's insignia, or distinctive mark. Very few contracts are under seal today because most jurisdictions have abolished the need for certain classes of private contracts or instruments to be under seal. This trend toward eliminating sealed, or formal, contracts demonstrates that the need for ceremonies and formalities to ensure validity largely has passed.

Informal (or simple) contracts are a more common category of contracts today. In these, the emphasis is not on the form or mode of expression but instead on giving effect to the promises of the parties. Informal contracts do not require a seal. Such contracts may be either oral or written and, in fact, may even be implied from the conduct of the parties.

Unilateral Versus Bilateral Contracts

Every contract has at least two contracting parties. The person who makes an offer (called the *offeror*) generally promises to do something or to pay a certain amount if the person to whom the offer has been made (called the *offeree*) will comply with the offeror's request. Usually, then, in return for this promise, the offeror demands a certain act or a certain promise of the offeree as acceptance. The form of the acceptance that is demanded determines whether the contract is a *unilateral* contract (a promise on one side only) or a *bilateral* contract (promises on both sides).

If the offeror promises to pay the offeree $50 for raking the offeror's yard, this contract is unilateral. Only one person, the offeror, has promised to do anything. The offeree accepts the offer by performing the requested act (i.e., raking).

The case of *Kuhnhoffer* v. *Naperville Community School District 203*, 758 F.Supp. 468 (N.D.Ill. 1991), illustrates the nature of unilateral contracts. From 1979 to 1988, Larry Kuhnhoffer worked for the Naperville Community School District #203 as a school bus driver. At the end of each school year, Kuhnhoffer received a letter from the school district thanking him for the previous year's work and inviting him to return as a driver in the fall. However, during the summer of 1988, the Naperville police department arrested Kuhnhoffer for driving under the influence of alcohol. This arrest resulted in the suspension of his driving privileges for six months. When

Dr. Michael Kiser, the school district's assistant superintendent, learned of this suspension, Kiser informed Kuhnhoffer that the district could not hire him as a school bus driver in the fall. Consequently, Kuhnhoffer sued for breach of contract. Because of the definition of unilateral contracts, Kuhnhoffer's suit did not succeed. The judge ruled that the school district's offer constituted a unilateral contract offer. Because an offer of a unilateral contract is accepted by performance, no contract could result between Kuhnhoffer and the school district until he commenced performance. Without a valid license, Kuhnhoffer would be unable to perform fully his end of the bargain; hence, no contract ever came into existence.

In contrast, if one party (the promisor) makes a promise and the other party (the promisee) accepts the offer by promising to do the requested act, a bilateral contract results because promises exist on both sides of the agreement. To use the earlier example involving raking , assume the offeror this time promises to pay the offeree $50 if the offeree will promise to rake the offeror's yard. When the offeree accepts by so promising, an exchange of promises has occurred, and a bilateral contract has derived from the parties' bargaining.

The next case addresses these issues. See if you agree with the court's application of these concepts in *Wells Fargo Bank, N.A. v. U.S.*

9.1

WELLS FARGO BANK, N.A. V. U.S.
88 F.3D 1012 (FED. CIR. 1996)

FACTS In 1982, American Gasohol Refiners (American) sought a $20,000,000 loan from Mid-Kansas Federal Savings and Loan Association (Mid-Kansas) to build an ethanol manufacturing plant in rural Kansas. Farmers use ethanol (an alcohol that may be blended with gasoline) as fuel. Ethanol's price fluctuates depending on changes in the prices of corn or the other grains from which it is made and of oil. Mid-Kansas and American applied to the Farmers Home Administration (the Administration) for a guarantee of 90 percent of this loan. According to one Administration official, "the purpose of the lender program is to get banks to make loans that they ordinarily wouldn't make. They are high risk loans." Upon receipt of a request for a loan guarantee, the Administration evaluates the application and determines whether it may guarantee the loan. If so, the Administration provides the lender and the applicant with a Conditional Commitment for Guarantee. This form advises the lender that the approval of any guarantee it has submitted is subject to the completion of all conditions and requirements set forth in the Conditional Commitment, one of which conditions is that the lender certify "that it has no knowledge of any adverse change, financial or otherwise, in the borrower, his business, or any parent, subsidiaries, or affiliates since it requested a loan note guarantee." The Conditional Commitment issued

to Mid-Kansas and American in October 1982 also stated that "when these conditions and requirements are met, Farmers Home Administration will issue a loan note guarantee in the amount of ninety percent." In December 1982, Wells Fargo Bank, N.A. (Wells Fargo) agreed to finance American's construction of the proposed ethanol plant and to extend the 1983 expiration date of the Conditional Commitment issued to Mid-Kansas and American (which had changed its name to High Plains). The ethanol plant was built and began production in 1984; but because Wells Fargo and High Plains determined that an additional $3.5 million was necessary to bring the plant to full production, Wells Fargo, High Plains, the Administration, and several other interested parties in September 1985 extended the Conditional Commitment through June 1986. This agreement also reaffirmed that upon compliance with the conditions of the Conditional Commitment, the Administration would issue the guarantee for the benefit of Mid-Kansas or for Wells Fargo, if Wells Fargo became the lead lender. A new Conditional Commitment naming Wells Fargo as the lead lender was executed in October 1986. However, owing to its apprehensions about the economic viability of alcohol production facilities, the Administration at this time issued a directive under which it
continued

9.1

WELLS FARGO BANK, N.A. V. U.S., *continued*
88 F.3D 1012 (FED. CIR. 1996)

identified 15 areas of deficiency with regard to Wells Fargo. Additional correspondence ensued, some of which documents indicated the Administration's satisfaction with the bank's responses to each point and the Administration's intention to issue the guarantee. Based on these discussions, Wells Fargo agreed to provide an additional $5,000,000 in financing for the project. Nonetheless, in December 1986, the Administration refused to execute a guarantee because of the Administration's belief that the low price of ethanol and the high cost of grain constituted an adverse change in High Plains's financial condition. Wells Fargo thereafter filed a breach of contract suit against the Administration owing to the Administration's failure to honor its commitment to guarantee a construction loan that Wells Fargo had extended pursuant to the federal ethanol loan guaranty program.

ISSUE Was the Conditional Commitment a unilateral contract, under which the Administration's commitment to issue the guarantee became binding when the bank began performance by making the loan to American?

HOLDING Yes. The Conditional Commitment constituted a unilateral contract by which the government had agreed to guarantee the loan upon Wells Fargo's performance of the conditions specified, and Wells Fargo had accepted the contract through beginning performance (i.e., by making the $20,000,000 loan to finance the construction of the ethanol plant).

REASONING To bolster its contention that the Conditional Commitment was not a contract, the Administration first pointed to the regulations that characterize the Conditional Commitment as mere "advice" to the lender. However, the document itself shows that the government is making a binding promise: For example, Conditional Commitments are signed by the Administration's state director, the lender, and the borrower. The document in addition lists 29 separate conditions that the applicant must satisfy before the Administration issues the loan guarantee. No lender and borrower would be willing to undertake such steps (many of which are costly) in reliance on mere "advice" rather than on a firm promise. Moreover, in reliance on the Conditional Commitment, Wells Fargo risked the $20,000,000 it had furnished to High Plains.

That the government's promise to issue the loan guarantee was contingent on High Plains and Wells Fargo's performance of numerous conditions does not make the promise any less binding. Indeed, the essence of a unilateral contract is that one party's promise is conditional on the other party's performance of certain acts; and when the other party performs, the first party is bound. The substitution of Wells Fargo as the lead lender in 1986 does not affect the binding nature of the 1982 Commitment, either. The Administration was aware from the outset that Wells Fargo would provide the $20,000,000 financing for the ethanol facility. Similarly, the 1986 Conditional Commitment that explicitly made Wells Fargo the lead lender stated that the 1982 Conditional Commitment would continue in effect and thus would apply to Wells Fargo. Furthermore, the proffered reason for the Administration's refusal to issue the guarantee did not justify its later failure to do so. Indeed, High Plains's alleged financial problems that resulted from low ethanol prices and high grain prices represented the very kinds of economic risks that inhere in the ethanol manufacturing business and the very risks that underlie the loan guarantee program. Also, any such price fluctuations, was not an "adverse change . . . in the Borrower, [or] his business" within the meaning of the certification clause of the Conditional Commitment. That provision related to changes in High Plains's own internal financial condition, not to changes in the markets in which High Plains operated and did business. Hence, the evidence offered by the Administration failed to support the finding that an adverse change had taken place.

BUSINESS CONSIDERATION Is the government's guaranteeing high-risk loans an advisable public policy? Why or why not?

ETHICAL CONSIDERATIONS Did the Administration have an ethical obligation to refrain from "changing the rules of the game" four years into the parties' relationship? Or did commendable ethics obligate the Administration to be very conservative with regard to guaranteeing high-risk loans, particularly since the taxpayers ultimately would bear the risk of High Plains's default on its loan?

Valid, Voidable, Void, and Unenforceable Contracts

A *valid* contract is one that is legally binding and enforceable. In contrast, a *voidable* contract is one that may be either affirmed or rejected at the option of one or more of the contracting parties. The agreement is nonetheless valid until it is rejected or disaffirmed. For example, if a person buys a car in the belief that it was driven only 50,000 miles when in actuality it was driven 250,000 miles, that agreement may be voidable on the basis of fraud or misrepresentation. However, the contract remains valid and fully enforceable until the buyer disaffirms it.

Void agreements, though they outwardly may appear to be contracts, can never have any legal effect. They are unenforceable and never become contracts because they lack one of the essential elements of a contract. An agreement to murder someone is void; courts will not enforce this agreement because it lacks the element of legality.

On the other hand, it is possible to have a seemingly binding contract that will not be given effect in a court of law. Suppose, for example, that the contract involved is one that must be in writing (such as a contract for a sale of goods priced at $500 or more); if this contract is oral, it will be *unenforceable.* Note that the contract otherwise appears to meet all the criteria of a valid contract.

Express Versus Implied Contracts

An *express contract* is one in which the parties set forth their intentions specifically and definitely, either in writing or orally. Most contracts are of this type.

An implied contract is one that must be discerned or inferred from the actions or conduct of the parties. Even though the parties should have expressed their intentions more clearly, it still is possible to conclude that a true contract exists. These agreements are often called *contracts implied in fact* because, given the facts, it is possible to say that, despite the absence of explicit language to this effect, the parties intended to create a contract.

Assume, for example, that two parties have had a well-known, years-long understanding that grain will be accepted when delivered. If one party takes grain to the elevator and the elevator refuses to accept it, the facts of the parties' prior, long-standing relationship and their previous conduct may allow a court to enforce this agreement as a contract implied in fact. Practically speaking, many agreements have express provisions and also include terms that must be discerned from the actions of the parties. In short, a given contract may not fall neatly into one or the other of these categories, as *Cheloha* v. *Cheloha* illustrates.

9.2

CHELOHA V. CHELOHA
582 N.W.2D 291 (NEB. 1998)

FACTS Alphons Cheloha was a bachelor and retired farmer who lived in rural Nebraska. In late July or August 1988, Alphons was admitted to a nursing home, where he remained until his death on 10 October 1993. Robert Cheloha, Alphons's nephew, lived less than a mile from Alphons's home. During Alphons's lifetime, few people other than Robert paid any attention to Alphons's needs. Robert provided transportation for Alphons's doctor's appointments and grocery shopping, made arrangements for Alphons's medical and nursing home care, and managed Alphons's finances. Robert testified that in April 1986, he had a discussion with Alphons regarding

continued

9.2

CHELOHA V. CHELOHA, *continued*
582 N.W.2D 291 (NEB. 1998)

Robert's desire to be compensated for the services that Robert had been providing to Alphons. As corroborated by Robert's mother, Alphons allegedly responded, "I am so glad that you have been helping me . . . , and I want you to be paid." On 11 August 1988, Alphons executed a durable power of attorney, naming Carl, Robert's father (and Alphons's brother), and Robert as Alphons's attorneys in fact. This instrument did not contain a provision authorizing Robert to compensate himself or to make gifts from Alphons's property. On 20 September 1995, Sophia Cheloha, as the personal representative of the estate of Alphons, filed a petition in equity that sought an accounting from Carl and Robert as to all transactions they had entered into by virtue of the power of attorney. Sophia alleged that the sums expended by Carl and Robert, in their capacities as Alphons's attorneys in fact, were not solely for the benefit of Alphons and were, in fact, paid to his detriment. At the bench trial on the matter, Robert admitted that he had used the power of attorney to convert $33,495.05 in certificates of deposit owned by Alphons to his (Robert's) own use. Robert, however, testified that these monies represented compensation for services rendered by him pursuant to an oral contract with Alphons.

ISSUE Had Alphons entered into an express oral contract or, alternatively, an implied contract with Robert, by which Alphons had agreed to pay Robert $33,495.05 in certificates of deposit as compensation for services rendered?

HOLDING No. Robert had failed to provide any credible evidence of the existence of either type of contract.

REASONING Robert claimed that an express oral contract existed because Alphons had specifically told Robert in the presence of his immediate family that Alphons wanted Robert to be paid for his services. However, a court of equity will not enforce a contract unless it is complete and certain in all its essential elements. The parties themselves must agree on the material and necessary details of the bargain; and if any of these is omitted or left obscure or indefinite so as to leave the intention of the parties uncertain respecting the substantial terms, the case is not one for specific performance (i.e., a situation in which a court will order the parties to fulfill the agreement).

In the instant case, the self-serving testimony of Robert and his mother that Alphons had told Robert that Alphons would pay Robert for his services constituted the only evidence that would support a mutual understanding between Alphons and Robert that Robert's services had not been rendered gratuitously. Even assuming that this conversation had, in fact, taken place and that a contract was formed between the parties, the record contained no evidence of a mutual understanding as to the specific terms of the compensation Alphons would pay Robert. As to the certificates of deposit Alphons had allegedly promised Robert as compensation for services rendered, the record failed to show which certificates of deposit or the amounts to which Robert had been entitled. In short, the record was devoid of any evidence as to the material terms of the purported contract. Moreover, the record revealed that Robert never had reported the income received from the certificates of deposit on his tax returns. This failure to report income thus would support an inference that the certificates of deposit had not represented compensation for services rendered. Mutual assent to an agreement is determined by the objective manifestations of intent by the parties, not by their subjective statements of intent. Therefore, Robert's conversion of Alphons's certificates of deposit to Robert's own use was not pursuant to any enforceable oral contract, but rather represented a substantially gratuitous transaction. Finally, since the power of attorney had not expressly granted Robert the power to make gifts with Alphons's property, the district court was correct in awarding Sophia the sum of $33,495.05 with respect to such certificates of deposit.

BUSINESS CONSIDERATION What could the parties have done differently so as to minimize the chances of subsequent litigation?

ETHICAL CONSIDERATIONS Do you think Robert acted in an ethically admirable fashion? Why or why not? Should relatives provide services to each other without any expectation of payment? Does your decision depend on the particular circumstances involved?

Executory Versus Executed Contracts

An *executory contract* is one in which some condition or promise remains unfulfilled by one or more of the parties. For instance, if a person agrees to buy a king-sized mattress set from Honest John's, the contract is executory: The firm still must deliver the mattresses, and the buyer must pay for the set. If the buyer pays for the mattresses prior to delivery, the contract is also executory, although technically the buyer has executed his or her part of the contract.

An *executed contract* is one in which the parties have fully completed or performed all the conditions or promises set out in the agreement. In the last example, when Honest John's delivers the mattress set, the contract will be executed. Neither party has anything further to do.

Quasi Contracts Versus Contracts Implied in Fact

One type of implied contract deserves special attention. This is a contract implied in law, or a *quasi contract*. Lawsuits alleging quasi contract as the basis for recovery also may be called suits for *unjust enrichment*. Under certain circumstances, the law will create a contract between the parties, despite their wishes and intentions, in order to prevent the unjust enrichment of one party. In these circumstances, even

YOU BE THE JUDGE

WHO'S SINGING A DIFFERENT TUNE NOW?

Bridget Griffin-Amiel, of Nanuet, New York, who wed Michael Amiel last March, had agreed to pay $3,725 for a five-piece orchestra and singers Paul Rich and Gloria Carpenter to perform at her wedding reception. She had selected the two vocalists after auditioning several at a "Wedding Showcase" staged for brides-to-be by the Frank Terris Orchestra. After the signing of the contract but before the wedding, Mr. Rich quit the band, a fact Rocco Terris, the owner of the orchestra, neglected to tell the bride. Instead, he sent Tony Avena to cover for Mr. Rich. After the wedding, the bride, who disliked the "Sinatra-type tunes" belted out by the pinch-hitting Avena, demanded her money back. To Terris's comments that Avena had done a "wonderful job" and that the musicians had played and the singer had sung, the bride responded that Mr. Rich would have been more upbeat and youth oriented. When Terris refunded only $1,000, the bride sued for the remainder.

Should a court grant her this $2,275?[4]

BUSINESS CONSIDERATIONS Interestingly, wedding days spawn a great deal of litigation. Can you think of other wedding-related details that may lead to lawsuits? What should the parties have done to avoid this litigation (and that stemming from other situations)?

ETHICAL CONSIDERATIONS Did Mr. Terris have an ethical duty to inform the bride that he was substituting a different wedding singer? Did the bride behave unethically when she refused to accept the substitute as equivalent to Mr. Rich, or when she refused to accept the $1,000 set-off?

SOURCE: *The National Law Journal* (12 October 1998), p. A23.

9.2 | PERSONAL LAW

COLLECTING DAMAGES FROM A FRIEND

One of Dan's friends recently purchased a car stereo and a set of speakers for his new car. As a favor for his friend, Dan installed the stereo and the speakers. In order to complete the installation, Dan had to purchase some installation hardware and had to cut larger openings in the dash and the rear deck. By the time Dan had obtained the installation hardware, cut the holes, and installed the stereo system, he had spent about four hours working on his friend's car. Once the installation was complete, the friend complained that, because Dan had taken too long to complete the job, the friend had missed an appointment. He also complained about the holes Dan had cut, alleging that they were not needed and that they hurt the aesthetic look of the interior. Dan was offended by this response to his "good deed" and decided that he should be compensated for his efforts. (He also would like an apology but realizes that there *are* limits to his legal options.) He asks you whether he can recover for his time and expenses in either contract law or under quasi contract. What will you tell him?

BUSINESS CONSIDERATIONS If a service business needs to modify or alter the customer's property in order to render the service, should the business obtain permission before making the modification or alteration, or should the business just complete the job? What legal issues might be raised by doing the alteration without prior permission raise?

ETHICAL CONSIDERATIONS Is it ethical for an employee to use his or her employer's tools and equipment to do favors for friends? What ethical issues arise when an employee does so?

though it may be clear that the parties did not actually contract with each other, the law will treat them as if they had.

Like a contract implied in law, a contract implied in fact is also an implied contract. It differs from a contract implied in law in that sufficient facts or evidence of conduct exist for a court to find on equitable grounds that the parties actually meant to contract with each other. Perhaps the language should have been more explicit, but a court can conclude with some certainty that the parties intended to create a binding agreement. Thus, a contract implied in fact is a true contract. On the other hand, a contract implied in law is a fiction engineered by a court so as to effect justice between two parties. Unlike a contract implied in fact, this is not a true contract, hence the name quasi contract.

To clarify further the difference between a contract implied in fact and a contract implied in law, consider this example: Mattie is sitting on her front porch when a painting crew arrives. The painting crew has the wrong address (111 Riverside Drive instead of 1111 Riverside Drive). Mattie nevertheless allows the crew to paint her house and later tries to argue that since she had not asked for the services, she owes zero for them. To prevent Mattie's unjust enrichment at the painters' expense, most courts will force Mattie to pay the painters, on a **restitutionary** basis, for the benefit she has received (a newly painted house) or, put another way, for the detriment suffered by the painters (the cost of their supplies, services, and so on). Mattie will be liable in quasi contract or a contract implied in law only for the reasonable value of the services rendered; the painters cannot "gouge" her by charging, after the fact, an exorbitant price. A contract implied in fact does not exist here because of the lack of any facts suggesting that Mattie and the painting company had dealt with each other before the crew arrived at Mattie's house. Evidence of an intention to contract, however sloppy the execution of the contract, would have made this a true contract, or a contract implied in fact. Given the absence of any such evidence, the court instead creates a contract—a quasi contract or contract implied in law—to prevent Mattie's unjust enrichment.

Do not be misled into believing that every time one person receives a benefit, a quasi-contractual recovery will be possible. Remember that the policy underlying such recoveries is the avoidance of injustice. Mattie has to pay because she knowingly allowed the painters to proceed. Had she not been present, however, the painters probably would be unable to hold Mattie liable because they had conferred the services on her as a result of their negligence or mistake; they had come to the wrong house. In these circumstances, it is not inequitable to allow Mattie to retain the benefits bestowed on her. By the same token, a person who confers a gift (e.g., assume Mattie's brother contracts with a painting company to redo Mattie's dilapidated house as a surprise for her) or one who volunteers a service (a neighbor who decides to paint Mattie's house while Mattie is away for the weekend) will not be able to recover later from Mattie in quasi contract, either. The same result will apply to a person who buys supplies in a mistaken belief that a contract exists or who incurs foreseeable difficulties and later tries to make the recipients of the services pay for these extra costs or services on a quasi-contractual basis. Still, remember that courts can, in a given circumstance, create a contract in order to avoid injustice.

Woods v. *Hobson* addresses several of these issues. Analyze the court's opinion in light of these principles of contract law.

Restitutionary
An equitable basis by which the law restores an injured party to the position he or she would have enjoyed had a loss not occurred.

Counterclaimed
Presented a cause of action in opposition to the plaintiff's.

9.3

WOODS V. HOBSON
980 S.W.2D 614 (MO.APP.S.D. 1998)

FACTS In early 1993, Willis S. and Stephanie A. Hobson, the defendants, moved to the guest house on John R. and Judith A. Woods's property. In June, while the Hobsons were occupying the guest house, Mr. Woods agreed that the defendants would fix up another house on the Woodses' property, the rock house. Mr. Woods testified that he orally agreed, in return for the Hobsons' fixing up the rock house, "to give them a life estate on a small portion of . . . land, perhaps two or three acres, surrounding the rock house." In September, the Hobsons began working on the house so they could eventually occupy it. The defendants had expected to have $30,000 available from the sale of a residence they owned in Florida to use in remodeling the rock house; but, owing to complications stemming from the sale of the Hobsons' Florida home, this figure did not materialize. Mr. Woods eventually loaned the Hobsons this amount so that they could continue the rehabilitation of the rock house. After living in the house and making repairs on it for a year, the Hobsons' marriage broke up; and they left Missouri. When the Woodses sued the Hobsons for breach of contract owing to the Hobsons' failure to repay the $30,000 loan, the Hobsons **counterclaimed** for unjust enrichment.

ISSUE Did the improvements the Hobsons had made on the rock house entitle them to recover on a theory of unjust enrichment?

HOLDING Yes. The Hobsons' labor and the expenditures of their own funds in repairing and remodeling the Woodses' rock house had conferred a benefit on the Woodses; the Woodses had recognized this benefit; and the Woodses had retained this benefit. Hence, the Hobsons had proved all the elements of their counterclaim of unjust enrichment.

REASONING Unjust enrichment occurs where a benefit is conferred upon a person in circumstances in which retention by him or her of that benefit without paying its reasonable value would be unjust. Missouri precedents explain that an action for unjust enrichment is based on a theory of quasi contract, or contract implied in law. Its elements include: (1) a benefit conferred by one party on another; (2) appreciation (or recognition) by the receiving party of the fact that what was conferred was a benefit; and (3) acceptance and retention of the benefit by the receiving party. The Hobsons had presented sufficient evidence from which a court could find they were entitled to recover for unjust enrichment. Testimony indicated that before the Hobsons remodeled the house, its roof was falling in and that "[i]t was a mess." Moreover, after the defendants had moved from the house, the Woodses rented it for $450 per month; the house was occupied continually from 1 November 1994 through the trial date, 28 February 1997; and the Woodses received rental income for that period in the amount of $12,600. Furthermore, the defendants had contributed $19,766.43 in out of pocket expenditures for goods and materials, as well as labor, services, and travel expenses, in the repair and remodeling of the rock house. Indeed, the Hobsons' remodeling of the rock house increased its value by $40,000. In short, sufficient evidence existed to indicate that the Hobsons' labor and the expenditures of their own funds

continued

9.3

WOODS V. HOBSON, *continued*
980 S.W.2D 614 (MO.APP.S.D. 1998)

(in addition to the funds they had secured from the plaintiffs) in repairing and remodeling the rock house on the plaintiffs' property had conferred a benefit on the plaintiffs. The rental of the house by the Woodses was evidence that they had recognized the benefit provided by the defendants' labor and expenditures. Furthermore, the plaintiffs had retained this benefit. Hence, the court affirmed the trial court's granting of the Hobsons' $10,000 counterclaim based on a theory of unjust enrichment.

BUSINESS CONSIDERATION Assume that the Woodses and Hobsons had sought your advice before they entered into the arrangement regarding the rock house. What would you have told them? Why?

ETHICAL CONSIDERATION Assess the Woodses and the Hobsons' conduct from an ethical standpoint. Among other things, discuss who—if anyone—in these circumstances has a rightful claim to the moral high ground.

Exhibit 9.2 shows the different classifications of contracts.

RESOURCES FOR BUSINESS LAW STUDENTS

NAME	RESOURCES	WEB ADDRESS
Uniform Commercial Code (UCC)	The Legal Information Institute (LII), maintained by the Cornell Law School, provides a hypertext and searchable version of Articles 1–9 of the Uniform Commercial Code. LII also maintains links to the UCC as adopted by particular states, as well as proposed revisions.	**http://www.law.cornell.edu/ucc/ucc.table.html**
Legal Information Institute— Contract Law Materials	The LII provides an overview of contract law; links to federal government statutes, treaties, and regulations; federal and state judicial decisions regarding contract law (including Supreme Court decisions); state statutes; and other materials.	**http://wwwsecure.law.cornell.edu/topics/contracts.html**
The American Law Institute	The American Law Institute, publisher of *Restatements of the Law,* Model Codes, and other proposals for law reform, provides press releases, its newsletter, and other publications.	**http://www.ali.org/**
The National Conference of Commissioners on Uniform State Laws	The National Conference of Commissioners on Uniform State Laws (NCCUSL), the drafters of the UCC, provides drafts and revisions of its uniform and model acts.	**http://www.law.upenn.edu/library/ulc/ulc.htm**

E X H I B I T 9.2	**Classification of Contracts**

Type of Contract	Definition	Example
Formal	One created by certain rituals, ceremonies, or formalities.	A contract that requires notarization, such as the transfer of an automobile title to another person.
Informal	One created through oral or written statements or through the parties' conduct; needs no special rituals.	An oral contract to buy a used compact disk player costing $400.
Unilateral	One created by a promise given in exchange for an act.	A contract in which the borrower agrees to pay back the $400 consumer loan obtained from a bank.
Bilateral	One created by a promise given in exchange for another promise.	A contract in which one person promises to sell her dental equipment and another promises to buy the equipment.
Valid	One that manifests all the essential elements of a contract.	A contract to buy a car from a dealership.
Voidable	One that manifests all the essential elements of a contract and is legally binding unless disaffirmed by one or more of the contracting parties.	A contract to sell a termite-ridden house when the seller has knowledge of the extensive termite damage.
Void	One that lacks the essential elements of a contract.	A contract in which a lender charges the borrower a 40 percent rate of interest on a loan.
Unenforceable	One that manifests the essential elements of a contract but will not be given effect by a court of law.	An oral contract to guarantee the payment of another person's debts if that person fails to pay.
Express	One created by the parties' setting out their intentions specifically and definitely.	A contract that lists the price, the terms of the sale, the delivery date, and other details regarding the purchase of a car.
Implied	One discerned or inferred from the actions or conduct of the parties.	A person walking into a hair salon and asking for a haircut without discussing price.
Implied in fact	Despite the absence of explicit language, the parties intended to contract with each other; a true contract.	A contract in which a person has received medical care without discussing the terms. The person will be obligated to pay for the treatment.
Implied in law	Contract created by a court for the parties, despite their wishes and intentions, in order to avoid injustice and/or the unjust enrichment of one party.	A contract to provide landscaping around a home in a development. When the homeowner fails to pay, a court orders the owner of the development to pay the landscaper because of the enhanced value of the development.
Executory	One in which some promise or obligation remains unfulfilled.	A contract to sell a horse, saddle, and bridle. The seller forgets to bring the saddle on the date of delivery.
Executed	One in which all parties have completed their promises or obligations under the terms of the agreement.	A contract to buy a computer for $2,000 with delivery effected by the seller in exchange for the buyer's giving a certified check for $2,000 at the time of delivery.

9.3 | SALES/ MANAGEMENT

CONTRACTUAL CONSIDERATIONS

From your consultation, the Kochanowskis realize that, in any potential contract, CIT must first ascertain whether common law or the Uniform Commercial Code governs the transaction. However, Tom and Anna still have trouble making this distinction. What law—the UCC or common law—will govern CIT's contracts to buy, for instance, the metals and other alloys that it will use in manufacturing the Call-Image units? What law will govern CIT's contracts with trucking firms to deliver manufactured Call-Image units to distributors across the country? Why? If these contracts amount to $10,000 or more, should they be in writing?

From your consultation, Tom and Anna also recognize that they must be aware of the requirements for contract formation under both the UCC and the common law. Again, however, Tom and Anna need your assistance. For example, if a friend of Anna's has helped complete the design for Call-Image, should CIT take care to spell out a formal pay arrangement in advance? Why?

Furthermore, because Call-Image involves intellectual property, should the firm have its employees (yes, even the family members!) sign restrictive covenants to refrain, for a specified time and in a specified geographic area, from competing with CIT? What law will govern this contract? Should this covenant also specify that employees may not divulge trade secrets and other proprietary, confidential information? The family has asked for your advice on these matters. What will you tell them?

BUSINESS CONSIDERATIONS Why is it important for business practitioners to become well versed in contract law? To ensure the general public's understanding of the rudiments of contract law, should high schools make business law a required course?
ETHICAL CONSIDERATION Does a family-owned business face more ethically related issues (e.g., the division of responsibility and/or financial accountability) than a business that is not so structured?

SUMMARY

The law of contracts affects us more often than any other area of law. Commercial law, especially the Uniform Commercial Code's integration of older statutes and common law rules, has become increasingly important in the United States. For the first time, many statutes exist that attempt to harmonize areas of the law that previously varied from state to state. The common law has also spawned numerous contract principles that affect the legal environment of business. Although the word *contract* has many definitions, it commonly means a legally binding and legally enforceable promise or set of promises between two or more competent parties.

Historically, contracts were of minor importance because a feudal society had little interest in protecting the parties' expectations. With the advent of freedom of contract and rising industrialism, by the nineteenth century contract law had outstripped property law in significance. Ironically, today the law appears to be swinging back to a concern with status, as evidenced by protective statutes and recent common law decisions.

Six requirements must be met for a contract to be valid: (1) an agreement (i.e., an offer and an acceptance); (2) supported by consideration; (3) made by parties having the capacity to contract; (4) based on these parties' genuine assent; (5) grounded in a legal undertaking; and (6) expressed in proper form, if applicable. Contracts may be classified as formal or informal; unilateral or bilateral; valid, voidable, void, or unenforceable; express or implied; and executed or executory. These categories are not necessarily mutually exclusive.

A contract implied in fact consists of evidence of sufficient facts or conduct from which a court can conclude that the parties intended to enter into a binding agreement. A contract implied in fact thus is a true contract. A quasi contract, or contract implied in law, is not a true contract. It is a different type of implied contract in which a court creates a contract for the parties, despite their wishes and intentions, in order that justice may be served. Not every situation in which a benefit has been conferred, however, gives rise to this equitable, restitutionary remedy called a quasi contract.

DISCUSSION QUESTIONS

1. Define the term *contract*.
2. Distinguish between a *contractual* obligation and a *social* obligation.
3. Name and define the six requirements for a valid contract.
4. Why do some commentators claim that the history of contract law has swung from status to freedom of contract and back again?
5. Explain the following categories of contracts: (a) formal, (b) informal, (c) unilateral, (d) bilateral, (e) valid, (f) voidable, (g) void, (h) unenforceable, (i) express, (j) implied, (k) executory, and (l) executed.
6. What are the legal requirements for showing a quasi contract?
7. What is the Uniform Commercial Code, and why is it important?
8. Suppose Joan asks the bank for a loan. What kind of a contract will result from the bank's granting her this loan?
9. A contract involving an interest in land (such as a contract for the sale of a house) must be in writing. What is the legal effect of an oral contract in this situation?
10. What is the difference between a contract implied *in fact* and a contract implied *in law*?

CASE PROBLEMS AND WRITING ASSIGNMENTS

1. Dynamic In Situ Geotechnical Testing, Incorporated (Dynamic) submitted a grant proposal to the National Science Foundation (NSF) in April 1993. For all funded grants, the NSF "agrees to support a specified level of effort for a specified period of time" and to cover "the costs of the project to be performed under the provisions of the award instrument," while "[t]he grantee agrees to the performance of the project, to the prudent management of the funds provided by the grant, and to the provisions of the award instrument." The award instrument in turn imposes numerous conditions to which the grantee must agree before the grantee can receive any funds. Acceptance of the grant occurs when the grantee takes action to obtain the grant funds from the government, unless the NSF requires a written acceptance. The NSF can suspend or terminate a grant when "the grantee has materially failed to comply with the terms and conditions of the grant." Finally, the government can, at least in some circumstances, sue to enforce the conditions of a NSF grant agreement. Dynamic's application listed Wanda and Robert Henke (Dynamic's co-owners) as the project's PI and co-PI, respectively, meaning that they were the scientists responsible for carrying out the research. A peer review panel consisting of 12 experts from universities and other government agencies convened in August 1993 to evaluate Dynamic's proposal as well as 36 others. Before this meeting, 4 of the 12 panelists had prepared individual written comments regarding Dynamic's proposal. Based on the panel's negative recommendation, the NSF denied Dynamic's request for funding. Thereafter, the agency, in accordance with its standard practice, notified Wanda Henke and provided her with a summary of the panel discussion and verbatim copies of the 4 written re-

views with the authors' names omitted. Wanda Henke then filed with the NSF a Privacy Act request seeking the names of the 4 peer reviewers who had prepared the written comments as well as the names of the other 8 panel members who had evaluated Dynamic's proposal. In response, the NSF disclosed the names of the 12 panel members but refused to indicate which 4 had authored the written comments. NSF relied on Privacy Act exemption (k)(5), which provides that an agency may promulgate rules to exempt from the Privacy Act's access provisions a system of records that is

> investigatory material compiled solely for the purpose of determining suitability, eligibility, or qualifications for Federal civilian employment, military services, Federal contracts, or access to classified information, but only to the extent that the disclosure of such material would reveal the identity of a source who furnished information to the government under an express promise that the identity of the source would be held in confidence. 5 U.S.C. § 552a(k)(5) (emphasis added).

The NSF construed "Federal contracts" in exemption (k)(5) as encompassing NSF grant agreements. The plaintiffs argued that exemption (k)(5) was inapplicable because the reviewers had provided information in connection with an application for a federal grant, not a federal contract. Did the NSF grant agreement in question include the essential elements of a contract and establish what would commonly be regarded as a contractual relationship between the government and the grantee? [See *Henke v. U.S. Department of Commerce*, 83 F.3d 1445 (D.C. Cir. 1996).]

2. Plaintiff Miguel Angel Gonzalez, a citizen of Mexico, is a highly ranked professional boxer. Defendant Don King is the chief executive officer and sole owner of DKP, a boxing promotional firm. This lawsuit involves two contracts. The first contract, dated 15 February 1996, is an exclusive promotional agreement between Gonzalez and DKP. The second contract, dated 15 January 1998, is a bout agreement for a boxing match with Julio Cesar Chavez held on 7 March 1998. The bout agreement incorporates some of the terms of the promotional agreement and also provides for a purse of $750,000 for the Chavez match. DKP paid this purse, a fact not disputed in this litigation. Paragraph 11 of the bout agreement, the focus of the dispute here, gives DKP the option to promote four of Gonzalez's matches following the Chavez match. The relevant portion of Paragraph 11 then provides:

> In the event FIGHTER loses or draws the BOUT, or any option Bout, FIGHTER'S purse for each bout subsequent to such loss or draw shall be negotiated between PROMOTER and FIGHTER but shall not be less than AS PER PROMOTIONAL AGREEMENT unless a different sum is mutually agreed upon. The foregoing options as well as all other terms set forth in this Agreement are valid and enforceable regardless of the outcome of any bout provided for hereunder, i.e., win, lose or draw.

Moreover, pursuant to the terms of the promotional agreement, Gonzalez and DKP apparently agreed that if Gonzalez won the Chavez match, Gonzalez would receive at least $75,000 for the next fight, unless the parties agreed otherwise. Similarly, if Gonzalez lost the Chavez match, Gonzalez would receive at least $25,000 in subsequent matches, unless the parties agreed otherwise. However, neither the promotional agreement nor the bout agreement explicitly stated the purse for subsequent matches in the event of a draw in the Chavez match. Since the Chavez match ended in a draw, the parties subsequently disputed whether the purse for subsequent matches could be determined with sufficient certainty to enforce the contract. Gonzalez contended that the omission of a purse for fights following a draw rendered the contract so indefinite as to constitute an unenforceable agreement to agree. Should a court accept Gonzalez's contention? Why or why not? [See *Gonzalez v. Don King Productions, Inc.*, 17 F.Supp.2d. 313 (S.D.N.Y. 1998).]

3. Participants in American Airlines' (American's) frequent flyer program challenged American's retroactive changes in the program's terms and conditions that would limit the seats subject to frequent flyer credits and restrict the dates on which one could use such credits. The plaintiffs claimed that the application of these changes to previously accumulated mileage credits violated the Illinois consumer fraud and deceptive business practices act and constituted a breach of contract. American maintained that the Airline Deregulation Act of 1978 (ADA), which prohibits states from enacting or enforcing any law having the force and effect of law relating to airlines' rates, routes, or services, preempted (i.e., precluded) the plaintiffs' claims. The plaintiffs answered that contention by arguing that the terms and conditions offered by airlines and accepted by consumers are privately ordered obligations and therefore do not amount to a state's enforcing any law relating to airlines' rates, routes, or services. Rather, according to the plaintiffs, the common law remedy for a contractual commitment voluntarily undertaken and confined to the contract's terms simply holds parties to their agreements—in this case, to business judgments an airline has made public about its rates and services. Would the ADA permit state-law-based court adjudications of routine breach of contract claims? [See *American Airlines, Inc.* v. *Wolens*, 513 U.S. 219 (1995).]

4. Housewright Lumber Company (Housewright) was the general contractor and Frank Millard & Company, Inc. (Millard) was a mechanical and electrical subcontractor on a project for the Iowa Army Ammunition Plant in Middletown, Iowa. In November 1993, Housewright contacted Millard concerning a bid on the project. The original bid submitted by Millard for $132,000 included the mechanical portion of the contract but did not include the insulation section involved in the present dispute. Housewright thereupon requested that a Millard official provide a quote on that item because Housewright was relying on Millard to do the insulation work. On 1 March 1994, after Millard had already begun work on the mechanical portion of the contract, Housewright mailed Millard a contract including the insulation work and adding an additional $2,000 to the contract price. Millard refused to sign that contract because neither Housewright nor Millard could ascertain the extent of the insulation work until another subcontractor had completed some asbestos abatement work. On 24 March 1994, the parties signed a second contract, which was identical to the 1 March contract, with one exception. On the second contract, Millard's chairman had added a handwritten addendum that provided: "At [the] end of [the] project we will review the cost of duct insulation and responsibility." This

addition occurred prior to either party's signing the contract. After completing its work, Millard sent Housewright an invoice for $12,009.56, an amount representing a $14,009.56 charge for the insulation work less the $2,000 figure added to the original bid. Refusing to pay this charge, Housewright claimed that the written addendum to the contract was without legal significance. In rebuttal, Millard argued that the addendum required Housewright to pay Millard on a time-and-material basis for all the insulation work actually performed. In these circumstances, who had the more persuasive argument? [See *Frank Millard & Co., Inc.* v. *Housewright Lumber Company*, 588 N.W.2d 440 (Iowa 1999).]

5. While serving as a chaplain in the United States Air Force, Timothy Sugrue, a Marist priest, sexually assaulted Kimberly Phillips, then seven or eight years of age. Years later, Phillips sued both Sugrue and the Marist Society of Washington Province (the Society) for the injuries she suffered as a result of Sugrue's intentional, tortious conduct. Phillips obtained a $1.5 million judgment against Sugrue, but the jury did not find the Society liable for negligent supervision. According to Phillips, the Society had entered into an implied contract pursuant to which it would pay all the expenses, debts, and obligations of its priests in return for the priests' pledges to turn over all their income and property to the Society. (As a priest, Sugrue had taken a vow of poverty.) Phillips produced evidence showing that the Society had paid Sugrue's living expenses and that the Society regularly informed creditors of individual priests that the "priests' assets (as well as any debts incurred) are those of the Society." The Society claimed that it never had promised to pay all of Sugrue's debts (however incurred) as long as he remained a member of the Society. Indeed, the Society presented evidence that the head of the Society (or the Society's board) would have to approve the payment of any out-of-the-ordinary expenses. When Phillips subsequently made a demand on the Society for the amount of the judgment against Sugrue, the Society refused to pay. Phillips contended that this refusal constituted a breach of an implied contract between the Society and Sugrue and that in fact she was a third-party beneficiary of this implied contract. Could a reasonable jury find the existence of an implied in fact contract between the Society and Sugrue? Would such a contract obligate the Society to pay a judgment entered against Sugrue for such intentional, tortious conduct as the sexual abuse of a minor? [See *Phillips* v. *Marist Society of Washington Province*, 80 F.3d 274 (8th Cir. 1996).]

6. **BUSINESS APPLICATION CASE** Charles Koehler, the owner of Gateway Exteriors, Inc. (Gateway), claimed that in the spring or summer of 1990 a concrete contractor recommended Gateway to Joseph Knapp, one of Suntide Homes's (Suntide's) employees. According to Koehler, Knapp stopped by Gateway's office and told Koehler about Suntide's Tiffany Square subdivision, for which Suntide anticipated building 60 homes. Knapp said that Suntide had a couple of siding contractors doing its work, but Suntide was not happy with them. Koehler then told Knapp about Gateway's operations, and Knapp said he would give Koehler preliminary plans to bid. Knapp subsequently sent Koehler plans for four different home styles. On 26 July 1990, Gateway gave Knapp a proposal for (and some samples of) Dutch-lap vinyl siding for these four home styles. Knapp said the proposal and prices looked good and asked for cost information for Triple 3 siding. Koehler told him it would be 9 percent more than Dutch-lap, and Knapp indicated that this price would be fine. At that point, Knapp told Koehler that Suntide had not as yet broken the ground for the subdivision. However, Knapp gave Koehler the names of other subdivisions and asked Koehler to examine the siding installation and tell him what Gateway would do differently to avoid some of the problems that had arisen in those subdivisions. Koehler thereafter told Knapp what he (Koehler) had observed and how Gateway would do the job. Knapp later informed Koehler that Suntide still was waiting for the final plans for the Tiffany Square subdivision. In August 1990, after Koehler had met with Knapp about colors and styles, Gateway ordered Triple 3 and Dutch-lap siding for approximately 12 homes at a cost of $32,640.25. Suntide had not yet built any homes in the subdivision. Nor had Knapp asked Koehler to order ahead of time. Nonetheless, Koehler had ordered the materials because he understood that Knapp wanted him to be prepared. Koehler furthermore testified that he had not known how many homeowners would order vinyl siding or what colors, styles, or amounts they would choose. On 5 September 1990, Gateway received what Koehler termed a "start sheet" for lot 44, a display house. This document, entitled "Tiffany Square Color Selection," indicated the outside selections for a display house on lot 44. In October 1990, after Koehler had shown Knapp the siding Koehler had ordered, Koehler submitted a second proposal for Tiffany Square. At the end of October or the beginning of November, Koehler went to the Tiffany Square development, where he noticed display homes had been started and that a siding crew was working on one

house. Koehler testified that Knapp apologized and said that the office mistakenly had sent out the old contractors and that Suntide would let Koehler construct houses in another subdivision. On about 5 November 1990, Gateway received a payment schedule addressed "to whom it may concern" and which showed the payment schedules for six of Suntide's subdivision developments, including Tiffany Square. Ultimately, Gateway never supplied or installed siding on any of the Tiffany Square homes. On 20 January 1991, Gateway filed a breach of contract action against Suntide. Had Koehler provided sufficient evidence of the existence of a valid and enforceable contract with Suntide? [See *Gateway Exteriors, Inc.* v. *Suntide Homes, Inc.*, 882 S.W.2d 275 (Mo.App.E.D. 1994).]

7. **ETHICAL APPLICATION CASE** In July 1997, plaintiff Jason Brody and 10 other rejected medical school applicants sued Finch University of Health Sciences/The Chicago Medical School for breach of contract stemming from the plaintiffs' reliance on certain of the defendant medical school's alleged representations. Specifically, the plaintiffs pointed to statements in the school's catalog to the effect that "[t]hose students who enrolled in defendant's Applied Physiology Program (the Program) and received a grade point average (GPA) of 3.0 or higher would be admitted to the defendant's medical school." The evidence at the trial showed that on 22 July 1996, the first day of orientation, Timothy R. Hansen, the director of the Program, had issued to the plaintiffs a memorandum stating that the medical school "[did] not expect to accept more than 50 students from the 1996–97 Applied Physiology class into the entering class in 1997." The "School of Graduate and Post Doctoral Studies Catalog" for 1995–96 states that the school reserves the right to modify programs. However, it also states that "modification[s] of program requirements will not adversely affect those students already in a program." Eighty students in the 1996–97 Program—including the plaintiffs—achieved a 3.0 GPA or better. On or around 26 June 1997, Michael Booden, general counsel for the defendant, informed the plaintiffs' counsel that the medical school was accepting only the top 50 students from the Program and that the class size of the medical school would consist of approximately 150 students. As of 26 June 1997, 50 applicants from the Program had been offered admission to the medical school. At the 1997 bench trial of the plaintiffs' lawsuit, Theodore Booden, the dean of the medical school, noted that the Program had been built on the premise that some highly qualified students were being rejected by medical schools. Hence, the defendant wanted to give such students an opportunity to prove that they were capable of handling the curriculum in the hopes they would be accepted into a medical school, either the defendant's or another's. In recent years, however, the defendant had received an abundance of qualified applicants applying to the medical school from outside the Program and thus had decided to "raise the bar" and limit acceptance of the Program's graduates to 50 students. At the trial, each of the plaintiffs recounted their communications with the defendant, their employment prior to enrolling in the Program, and their circumstances before and after enrolling in the Program. According to the plaintiffs, the defendant's admissions department routinely informed the plaintiffs that, if they achieved a 3.0 or better GPA, they would have a 90 to 95 percent chance of obtaining admission to the defendant's medical school. Some of the plaintiffs had visited the campus and had spoken with Dr. Hanson and Dean Booden, who also had indicated to those plaintiffs that, historically, a GPA of 3.0 was enough to get accepted into its medical school. With the defendant's encouragement, some plaintiffs even had telephoned former graduates of the Program who subsequently had been admitted to the defendant's medical school. Given the evidence offered at the trial, had the plaintiffs shown the existence of a implied contract in fact that the students who successfully completed the Program would be admitted to the defendant's medical school? Discuss the ethics of both the school and the rejected applicants/plaintiffs. [See *Brody* v. *Finch University of Health Sciences*, 698 N.E.2d 257 (Ill.App. 2 Dist. 1998).]

8. **CRITICAL THINKING CASE** In 1974, Spiro George bought a meat-packing plant site that included a house and approximately 40 acres of land. In 1981, George leased the property to the Heatons, who, in turn, hired Gary Custer, an experienced butcher, who occupied the house as part of his financial arrangements with the Heatons. In 1984, when the Heatons decided to leave the meat-packing business, Custer continued to reside in the house at a rental rate of $400 per month. At this time, George, by offering Custer free rent the first year and a monthly rate of $1,500 the second year, coupled with Custer's continuing to rent the house for $400 a month, encouraged Custer to reopen the meat-packing plant. George and Custer agreed it would take a substantial investment of both time and money to make the plant operational. The parties understood that Custer was to have an option to buy the plant, house, and eight acres of land. But,

during the exchanges relating to this agreement, the parties had not discussed a time frame for exercising the option, a definite purchase price, or either payment or security terms. Custer made improvements on the plant and expended time, labor, and $8,600 in equipment to make the plant operational and to meet certain certification requirements. During this initial three-month period, George indicated to Custer that he would sell Custer the facility for $150,000. Custer eventually decided to bring the plant up to federal standards so that he could sell meat to third parties. The acquisition of the necessary equipment and renovations for this upgrade took place over a period of two years. In June 1987, George informed Custer that the rent was being raised to $2,500 per month. Custer responded that, as he could not afford this rent increase, he would either have to leave or purchase the premises. George indicated that he would now sell the plant to Custer for $300,000. Custer did not attempt to negotiate the price with George and refrained from making any effort to obtain the money to purchase the property until 1988. When George sued Custer for $11,500 owed in back rent, George counterclaimed for the damages allegedly resulting from George's breach of the alleged option agreement to purchase the property. Had George and Custer entered into an option contract? In the absence of a binding contract, could Custer nonetheless sue on a restitutionary (i.e., quasi-contractual) basis as opposed to a contractual one? [See *George* v. *Custer*, 862 P.2d 176 (Alaska 1993).]

NOTES

1. A. G. Guest, *Anson's Law of Contracts,* 26th ed. (Oxford: Clarendon Press, 1984), p. 1.
2. Bradford Stone, *Uniform Commercial Code in a Nutshell,* 2nd ed. (St. Paul, MN: West Publishing Co., 1995), pp. ix–x.
3. *Restatement (Second) of Contracts,* § 1 (St. Paul, MN: American Law Institute Publishers, 1981), p. 5.
4. "Substitute Crooner Hits Sour Note at Wedding," *The National Law Journal* (12 October 1998), p. A23.

10

CONTRACTUAL AGREEMENT: MUTUAL ASSENT

A G E N D A

As the Kochanowskis work to get CIT up and running, they will enter into quite a few contracts. They also will buy goods and services from a number of businesses. They therefore need to know *how* to enter contracts, and they will need to know what legal effect that different types of communications have on the existence—or lack thereof—of contracts. They moreover will want to know whether any advertising they use constitutes a potential contract offer.

These represent just a few of the areas where they may have questions. Be prepared! You never know when one of the Kochanowskis will ask for your help or advice.

O U T L I N E

THE FIRST STEP IN CONTRACT FORMATION

Agreement is the essence of a contract. Once there has been a valid offer by the offeror (the person making the offer) and a valid acceptance by the offeree (the person to whom the offer is made), we are well on our way to having a legally binding contract because, generally, few problems remain concerning capacity, genuine assent, legality, and proper form (the other requirements for a contract). On the other hand, precisely because these two aspects of contract formation (offer and acceptance) are so important, courts closely examine the words and conduct of the parties to determine whether a **bona fide** offer and acceptance indeed are present.

From common law times, numerous rules have developed for checking the authenticity of the offer and the acceptance. Under these rules, the threshold for contract formation remains high because courts require clear-cut statements that the parties are freely and voluntarily entering into a particular agreement. Conversely, under the Uniform Commercial Code (UCC), a court can more easily infer a bona fide offer and acceptance from the conduct of the parties, even if the parties have omitted terms such as price, mode of payment, or mode of delivery. In this chapter, we discuss the reasons for these developments.

Bona fide
In good faith; honest; without deceit; innocent.

MUTUAL ASSENT

The initial phase of contract formation requires the assent of both parties to the agreement. The parties must agree to exactly the same terms. Without this mutual assent, no agreement ever comes into existence.

THE OBJECTIVE THEORY OF CONTRACTS

How do we judge whether the parties have mutually consented to the transaction? If you are in a particularly mischievous mood, you may say to a friend, "Tom, I'll let you buy my mountain bike for $200; that's the offer." Since Tom knows the frame itself sells for $500, he quickly says, "I'll take it." Does this exchange constitute a valid offer and acceptance? Will you have to sell the bike, or will the law permit you to say that you were kidding and did not intend to make an offer?

Common law rules tell us that the offeror has the right to set the terms of the offer (and to control the method by which the offeree accepts the offer). In so doing, the offeror must exhibit a clear and present intent to offer. You fairly straightforwardly enumerated the terms of the offer. But is it apparent from the content of your statement that you were only kidding?

To determine whether a valid offer exists, the law applies an **objective** standard. Under common law, to decide whether an offer has been made, a court or a jury puts itself in the offeree's place (i.e., in Tom's shoes) to ascertain if a reasonable offeree would believe that you, in offering the bike at this price, were serious. Since your words and conduct are judged by an objective (instead of a **subjective**) test, your secret intent (i.e., you were joking and did not really want to sell the bike) cannot be shown. Hence, in this example, a court may find that you have made a valid offer to Tom.

Obviously, this result depends heavily on the facts. If you clearly are jesting, are excited, or are even visibly angry, details supporting the existence of these facts may lead to a different result. Thus, a word to the wise: Beware of making "offers"

Objective
Capable of being observed and verified without being distorted by personal feelings and prejudices.

Subjective
Capable of being observed and verified through individual feelings and emotions.

you do not mean, since both common law and UCC principles may hold you to these statements.

The following case illustrates these important concepts.

10.1

BARBER V. SMH (U.S.), INC.
509 N.W.2D 791 (MICH.APP. 1993)

FACTS In May 1989, SMH (U.S.), Inc. (SMH) employed Jon Barber as a sales representative to sell Tissot watches to independent jewelry stores in certain Midwest states. Barber claimed that during the course of his discussions with company executives, he had negotiated the specific terms and conditions under which the company could terminate him. Barber thus argued that SMH's vice president of sales had promised Barber that "as long as [Barber] was profitable and doing the job for [SMH], [Barber] would be [SMH's] exclusive representative in . . . Michigan, Ohio, and Indiana." Barber likewise maintained that the company's executives had reiterated this promise during his tenure as a sales representative. In 1991, upon SMH's termination of his employment, Barber filed a breach of contract lawsuit based on his contention that this alleged verbal promise had created an employment relationship that SMH could not terminate in the absence of just cause.

ISSUE Had SMH's executives orally promised that Barber's employment could not be terminated in the absence of just cause?

HOLDING No. The application of the "reasonable person"/objective test would lead to the conclusion that Barber's employment was at will and that the company consequently could terminate him even in the absence of just cause.

REASONING The court noted that the law presumes that employment contracts of indefinite duration provide for **employment at will.** However, the court emphasized that one may rebut this presumption if one shows the existence of an express contract, oral or written, forbidding discharge in the absence of just cause. The court moreover stressed that contractual liability is consensual and will not arise unless the parties mutually assent to be bound. Put differently, when analyzing oral statements for contractual implications, a court must determine the meaning that reasonable persons might have attached to the language. In order to determine whether mutual assent to a

contract exists, the court applies an objective test that looks "to the expressed words of the parties and their visible acts." In other words, a court must consider the relevant circumstances surrounding the transaction, including all writings, oral statements, and other conduct by which the parties have manifested their intent. According to the court, the law will recognize oral contracts for just-cause employment only where the circumstances suggest that both parties intended to be bound. In short, to overcome the presumption of employment at will, a court must find that the oral statements relating to job security are clear and unequivocal. Here, the court found an absence of evidence to prove the existence of terminations for just cause only.

As to Barber's assertion that SMH had promised it would employ him "as long as he was profitable and doing the job," the court commented that Barber had not asserted that SMH had made this promise in response to Barber's articulated concerns that he be terminated only for just cause. The court also viewed as dispositive a written document purporting to constitute an agreement between Barber and the company. (Barber acknowledged receiving a copy of this "agreement" but denied signing it.) Specifically, the court construed the language allowing for the termination of the agreement by either party as the only objective evidence presented, indicative in itself of an intent and understanding—at least on the part of SMH—that the relationship between it and Barber was one of employment at will. Accordingly, the court held that the oral statements were insufficient to rise to the level of an agreement for just-cause employment.

BUSINESS CONSIDERATION Although a majority of states follow the employment-at-will doctrine, some states have carved out public policy exceptions to this rule. In other words, courts in some cases will disregard the rule if the courts believe the employer has asked the employee to engage in activities that are detrimental to the welfare and mores of the public.

10.1

BARBER V. SMH (U.S.), INC.,*continued*
509 N.W.2D 791 (MICH.APP. 1993)

(Usually the employee refuses to accede to the employer's wishes, and when fired, subsequently uses the employer's request as a basis for a wrongful discharge suit against the employer.) Give some examples of activities that you believe may constitute such public policy exceptions.

ETHICAL CONSIDERATION Some employment-at-will jurisdictions prohibit firings based on whistle-blowing. Discuss the ethics of whistle-blowing, especially when, how, and why an employee should (or should not) engage in whistle-blowing.

OFFER

Let us look more closely at this first phase of reaching agreement: the offer. An offer involves an indication (by a promise or another commitment) of one's willingness to do or refrain from doing something in the future. An offer implicitly invites another person, in order to seal the bargain, to assent to the promise or commitment.

Clear Intention to Contract and Definiteness of the Offer

To fulfill the common law's requirements, an offer must show a clear intention to contract and be definite in all respects. An agreement to agree at some future time, for example, lacks these prerequisites of a common law offer. Similarly, statements of opinion, statements of intention, and preliminary negotiations do not result in bona fide offers because they lack definiteness. But reasonable people will differ as to what constitutes a clear, definite offer and what instead involves only preliminary negotiations or dickering.

Since these are questions of fact that a judge or jury can later decide, be cautious. If you want to make an offer, be specific in all particulars. Haggling or dickering lacks definiteness regarding the details of the transaction and your intentions; hence, such preliminary negotiations ordinarily are too vague to constitute a valid offer. Winning or losing a lawsuit can turn on such minute distinctions as how a court interprets the words expressed by the parties. For example, are the words "I can send you two trademark logos at $5,000 per logo" identical in intent to "I offer to sell you two trademark logos at $5,000 per logo"? Many people would view these statements as virtually identical, but a strict common law interpretation treats only the second statement as a bona fide offer. The law views the other statement merely as an indication of a willingness to negotiate rather than a bona fide offer.

Despite the common law requirement that an offer be definite in all its material (or essential) terms, you should be aware that the UCC relaxes this common law prerequisite in several significant ways. For instance, UCC § 2-204 states that a contract for sale under the Code will not fail for indefiniteness as long as the parties have intended to form a contract, and as long as a reasonably certain basis for giving an appropriate remedy exists even though one or more of the terms of the agreement may have been left open. In addition, the UCC contains several so-called gap-filling provisions whereby the court can supply the terms—including price, place of delivery, and mode of payment—omitted by the parties.[1] The Code also

Employment at will
An employment relationship in which, owing to the absence of any contractual obligation to remain in the relationship, either party can terminate the relationship at any time and for any reason not prohibited by law.

Output contract
A contract that calls for the buyer to purchase all the seller's production during the term of the contract.

Requirements contract
A contract in which the seller agrees to provide as much of a product or service as the buyer needs during the contract term.

Indemnify
To reimburse a party for a loss suffered by that party for the benefit of another.

validates **output contracts** and **requirements contracts,** both of which would be too indefinite for common law courts to enforce.[2] Because the Code is predicated on the idea that commercial people (particularly merchants) want to deal with each other, it has eliminated some of the ticklish technicalities that impede contract formation under common law. You will learn more about these and other revolutionary changes in common law brought about by the Uniform Commercial Code when you read Chapters 16 through 20.

Advertisements and Auctions

The law in general does not treat advertisements as valid offers because they generally lack sufficient specificity to be defined as such. Instead, the law views advertisements as invitations for persons to come in and make offers for the types of goods and at the prices indicated in the advertisements. Notice that this rule demonstrates yet another "pro-offeror" tilt of the common law. A contrary perspective that advertisements constitute offers would presuppose that a merchant has an unlimited supply of merchandise. Thus, the principle that advertisements ordinarily are not offers protects merchants from the hardships such a contrary rule might produce. On occasion, however, an advertisement, catalog, circular, price list, or price quotation shows sufficient detail for a court to say that a valid offer exists. Such a result, however exceptional, sometimes occurs.

In the following case, the court used many of these common law principles when it determined whether the parties had created a binding contract.

10.2

ABBOTT LABORATORIES V. ALPHA THERAPEUTIC CORPORATION
164 F.3D 385 (7TH CIR. 1999)

FACTS In 1978 Abbott Laboratories (Abbott) had sold its scientific products division to Alpha Therapeutic Corporation (Alpha). The division manufactured and distributed "factor concentrate," a blood product used to treat hemophiliacs. Abbott agreed to **indemnify** Alpha for any losses arising from the inventory transferred. As it turned out, Abbott chose a good time to get out of the blood products business. In the 1980s, a class of hemophiliacs who claimed to be infected with HIV through the use of factor concentrate brought suit against members of the blood products industry, including Alpha. In the negotiations to create an industry-wide class settlement, Alpha brought up the Abbott indemnification issues. On 9 August 1996, after extensive negotiations, Sharon Jones, Abbott's senior counsel, wrote to Edward Colton, Alpha's general counsel. In this "final settlement offer," Jones named the proposed dollar figure and outlined the "essential terms from Abbott's perspective," including a series of releases that Abbott sought in exchange for its settlement payment. Jones also noted that because "it is Abbott's intention to have no further obligation to

Alpha, . . . Abbott will be proposing more precise language in the anticipated settlement agreement in order to accomplish this directive." Finally, in response to a request from Alpha, the letter indicated that Abbott would be willing to defer its payment if the parties could agree on an interest rate. In a 26 August letter, Colton responded, "Alpha has agreed to accept Abbott Laboratories' settlement offer of [the proposed settlement amount]. In general, we agreed with the terms and conditions contained in your 9 August 1996 letter." Colton also requested that the settlement agreement be "resolved with respect to all the terms and conditions and ready for execution before September 13th." He wanted to present the agreement as a "done deal" at Alpha's 13 September board meeting because several executives from Japan who could execute the agreement would be present. Finally, Colton asked Abbott to defer payment until 15 January 1997, and proposed a 7 percent interest rate. In the following months, the parties exchanged and modified several proposed settlement agreements. On 9 December 1996, Jones sent Colton her final version of the settlement

10.2

ABBOTT LABORATORIES V. ALPHA THERAPEUTIC CORPORATION, *continued*
164 F.3D 385 (7TH CIR. 1999)

agreement and asked that the agreement be executed by 11 December. On 6 January 1997, Colton informed Jones that in light of the uncertainty of the blood products class settlement negotiations, Alpha would not be willing to settle unless Abbott significantly increased the settlement amount. Instead, Abbott sued, seeking to enforce an alleged agreement that required Alpha to indemnify Abbott indefinitely into the future for any defense costs and losses related to factor concentrate.

ISSUE Did the exchange of the two letters in August constitute a binding settlement agreement between Abbott and Alpha?

HOLDING No. The letters failed to show the parties' intentions to be bound to the material terms of the proposed settlement. Hence, the parties lacked the mutual assent necessary for a legally binding agreement.

REASONING Under Illinois contract law, a binding agreement requires a meeting of the minds, or mutual assent, as to all the material terms. Whether the parties had a "meeting of the minds" is determined not by their actual subjective intent, but by what they express to each other in their writings. Thus, the parties decide for themselves whether the results of preliminary negotiations bind them, and they do so through their words. Abbott contended that the August letters between Jones and Colton constitute a legally binding offer and acceptance that show the parties' mutual assent to the terms contained in Jones's letter. That letter, according to Abbott, outlined all the material terms: (1) the settlement amount; (2) a global release by Alpha for all hemophiliac claims; (3) indemnification of defense costs for all such claims; (4) a release of all environmental claims arising from any property sold to Alpha; and (5) a release of any other indemnification claims arising from the 1978 asset sale agreement. Abbott further pointed out that Jones had characterized these terms as Abbott's "final settlement offer," thus expressing her belief that Abbott would be bound by the terms of the offer if Alpha had accepted. Lastly, Abbott claimed, Colton accepted the offer on behalf of Alpha in Colton's 26 August letter, when he wrote, "Alpha has agreed to accept Abbott Laboratories' settlement offer of [the proposed amount]." However, despite the superficial

appeal of Abbott's argument that it was unfair for Alpha to pull a "switcheroo" in its position on the proposed settlement amount solely because the class action negotiations were going badly, this argument would break down when one examines the degree to which the parties had decided to bind themselves in August. In this case, the words in the two August letters did not show a clear intent to be bound on behalf of either Abbott or Alpha. Jones wrote in her 9 August letter that she was only reiterating the "general terms" of the proposal currently on the table and attempting to identify the "essential terms from Abbott's perspective," thus leaving the strong implication that Jones expected Alpha to counter with essential terms of its own that would require further negotiation. She also said she would be proposing more precise language regarding the release terms in the "anticipated settlement agreement." As a general rule, anticipation of a more formal future writing would not nullify an otherwise binding agreement. Here, however, the fact that Jones explicitly left the details of the release provisions—i.e., material terms—open for future negotiation called into question Abbott's intent to be bound at that time. Similarly, Colton's 26 August letter did not sufficiently express an intent to be bound to Jones's terms, since Colton noted that Alpha had agreed to the terms in the 9 August letter "in general." He also wrote that he wanted "the Agreement resolved with respect to all terms and conditions and ready for execution before 12 September." All this language strongly implied that Colton did not yet consider the settlement a "done deal." Instead, he understood that the executives would have to hammer out certain terms before the executives signed off on the deal. Abbott claimed that informal writings between the parties can constitute a binding settlement agreement unless the parties decide to expressly condition their deal on the signing of a formal document. True, but such informal writings still must manifest each party's intent to be bound by the material terms proposed. The settlement that Alpha and Abbott were hammering out was a complicated, long-term arrangement involving huge sums of money. Although even a big agreement need not be "signed, sealed, and delivered" to be binding, the magnitude of this deal required careful scrutiny of any claim that informal letters in the course of freewheeling settlement

continued

10.2

ABBOTT LABORATORIES V. ALPHA THERAPEUTIC CORPORATION, *continued*

164 F.3D 385 (7TH CIR. 1999)

negotiations constitute a binding agreement. To be legally binding, such letters must clearly manifest the desire of each party to be bound to the material terms of the proposed deal. Agreement "in general" with a clear contemplation that further negotiations as to material terms will be required would simply not be enough to form ties that bind. Here, no binding settlement agreement existed between Abbott and Alpha.

BUSINESS CONSIDERATIONS Would it have been advisable for the parties to have sought a mediator, or some other objective third party, to help them arrive at a settlement figure? Or are the determinations of such financial matters best left to the internal management of each firm? Support your position fully.

ETHICAL CONSIDERATION Do you agree with Abbott that it was unfair of Alpha to pull a "switcheroo" in Alpha's position on the proposed settlement amount solely because the class action negotiations were going badly? Why or why not?

Normally, courts require a showing that the merchant has placed some limitation on the advertised goods before courts will find that the advertisement constitutes an offer. For example, the merchant may have specified a time limit, such as "for one day only." Or the merchant may have designated a quantity limit, such as "while they last" or "to the first 10 customers," in the advertisement. In such a situation, courts are somewhat more likely to find that the advertisement is an offer and not an invitation to deal or to negotiate. Again, courts utilize as the deciding factor the objective standard of what a reasonable person would have thought.

Auctions are similar to advertisements in that the seller is not actually the offeror, although he or she may appear to be offering the goods for sale through the auctioneer. In reality, the law treats the bidder as the offeror. For a sale to occur, the seller must accept the bid. The seller can even refuse to sell to the highest bidder unless the auction is publicized as "without reserve." In this type of auction, the seller must let the goods go to the highest bidder; he or she cannot withdraw the goods if the price bid is too low. Once the auctioneer lets the hammer fall, the seller has accepted the bid. But until this point, the bidder can withdraw the offer and thus avoid the formation of a contract of sale. Section 2-328 of the UCC covers these points, which are discussed again in Chapter 17.

Communication of the Offer to the Offeree

Another requirement for a bona fide offer is that the offeror (or his or her agent) must communicate the offer to the offeree. At first glance this rule may seem nonsensical. How can a person accept an offer if he or she does not know it exists? Believe it or not, that sometimes happens. For example, assume that two parties have been haggling over the terms of a real estate transaction. After much correspondence, the would-be buyer (offeree) writes, "Okay, you win. I will pay $80,000 for the land," and mails the letter to the offeror. A day later, before the arrival of the mail, the would-be seller (offeror) coincidentally arrives at the same figure, and writes, "This is my final offer. I will sell you the land for $80,000. Take it or leave it," and mails this letter to the offeree. Later, the offeror wants to sell this land to a third person who is interested in purchasing it, but the original offeree claims that he and the offeror now have a contract for $80,000. Despite the claims of the original offeree, the offeror probably can sell the land to the third party because most courts will hold that the original offeree has not validly accepted the offer. This is true because at the time of the would-be buyer's purported acceptance, no offer to sell the land at a price of $80,000 had been communicated to the original offeree. And, you will recall, an offer has no legal effect until the offeror (or his or her agent) communicates it to the offeree. Courts liken the correspondences in this example to identical offers crossing in the mail, each asking for and necessitating an acceptance before any valid contract ensues, and neither receiving the required acceptance. This result once again underscores the common law offeror's iron-fisted control over the terms of the offer (and the method of acceptance).

This requirement of communicating the offer to the offeree sometimes arises in the context of general offers. Although most offers are made by one person to another, offers made to the general public or a similar class of large numbers of persons are perfectly legal. A reward, such as money for the arrest and conviction of the persons who vandalized an office complex, represents the best example of a general offer. Even though some case results to the contrary exist, most courts require that the party who performs the act contemplated by the reward (here, the identification of the vandals so as to lead to their prosecution and conviction) must have known of the reward and must have intended the act as acceptance of that offer. Under this view, in order for a valid acceptance to occur, a general offer must be communicated to the offeree. Under the rule followed in a majority of jurisdictions, then, a person who coincidentally identifies the vandals without knowledge of the reward is ineligible to receive the reward.

Exhibit 10.1 summarizes the initial steps needed for reaching an agreement.

Duration of the Offer

Usually, offers satisfy these common law rules and will be legally effective. The next question that often arises concerns the duration of the offer: that is, how long will it remain open? Four methods for terminating an offer exist: (1) lapse, (2) revocation, (3) rejection, and (4) acceptance.

Sometimes the offeror will state in the offer when it will terminate and thus set the life span for the offer. This brings about the potential **lapse** of the offer. For

Lapse
The expiration or the loss of an opportunity because of the passage of a time limit within which the opportunity had to be exercised.

E X H I B I T   10.1 | **Offer: The First Phase of Reaching an Agreement**

A *bona fide* offer by the offeror must:
- Show a *clear* intention to enter into a contract.
- Be *definite* in all respects.
- Be *communicated* to the offeree or to his or her agent.

Communications by the offeror that do *not* reflect a *bona fide* offer include:
- Any *undisclosed secret* intentions.
- Statements made in *jest* or in *strong excitement.*
- Preliminary negotiations.
- Price quotations, dickering, advertisements, invitations to deal.

instance, an offer may state, among other things, "This offer will remain open for 30 days." If after 30 days the offeree has not responded, the offer automatically lapses. The offeror is under no legal duty to communicate the fact that the offer has lapsed to the offeree. After 30 days, the offeror can, without worrying about facing a lawsuit from the first offeree, make the same offer to anyone else.

In many cases, the offeror neglects to state any time period in the offer. In these situations, how long does the offeree have before he or she must respond? To avoid lapse, the offeree must accept within a reasonable time. Determination of what constitutes a reasonable time becomes a question of fact that a judge or jury decides. The trier of fact will consider such things as industry conditions, customs, and usages of trade. In volatile commodities markets, an offer may lapse in a matter of seconds. On the other hand, given a downturn in the real estate market, a period of days or weeks may constitute a reasonable time if the offer involves a sale of real property. To avoid such uncertainties, the offeror should state specifically when the offer lapses.

Supervening
Coming or happening as something additional or unexpected.

Lapse also may occur by operation of law. That is, regardless of the wishes of the parties, an offer automatically lapses upon the following occurrences: (1) the death or insanity of the offeror or offeree, (2) the **supervening** illegality of the subject matter of the offer, or (3) the destruction of the subject matter involved in the offer. In other words, if Joe Olivetti offers to sell his farm to Joan Hays but dies before she accepts, the offer automatically lapses. Joe's estate does not have to inform Joan of his death. Similarly, if two days after Joe makes the offer, his township passes an ordinance stating that sales of farms without an inspection by the local firefighting unit are illegal, Joe's offer will lapse if such an inspection has not occurred. If lightning strikes the farm and destroys all the outbuildings, the offer also lapses. No communication to Joan is necessary in these last instances, either.

Revocation
The cancellation, rescission, or annulment of something previously done or offered.

Another method of terminating an offer, besides lapse, is **revocation.** Under common law, the offeror possesses virtually unlimited rights to revoke at any time before acceptance. This is true whether or not the offeror uses the word *revoke*, as long as an intention to terminate the offer is clear. In general, revocation does not become effective until it is communicated to (or received by) the offeree. Interestingly, such communication may be effective whether communicated directly or indirectly. Using our earlier example, Joe may state bluntly, "Joan, I revoke my offer to you." Alternatively, Joan may hear that Joe has sold the farm to Len Hill. In either case, an effective revocation has occurred.

Usually, Joe will be dealing only with Joan or, at most, with a few parties. This is not the case with a general offer to the public. If Joe has lost his prize Dalmatian, Jake, and has offered a reward for the return of or information about the dog, Joe need only revoke his offer in the same manner (or medium) in which he made the original offer. Because it is too burdensome to require Joe to communicate with every possible "taker" of his offer, public revocation suffices. It is even effective against a person who has not seen the advertisement and who later comes forward with information about Jake.

Option
A contract to keep an offer open for some agreed-on time period.

Merchant
A person who regularly deals in goods of the kind or has the knowledge or skill peculiar to the practices or goods involved in the transaction.

Methods do exist for taming this seemingly unlimited power of revocation by the Joes of the world. For example, by forcing Joe to promise to keep the offer open for a stated time, Joan can prohibit Joe's power of revocation. The promise itself does not protect Joan from revocation. But if she takes an **option** on the farm, Joe is legally bound to hold the offer open for the agreed-on period of time. Joan will have to pay Joe for the option; but once she does so, he cannot sell the farm to anyone else during the option period without breaching this option contract. Usually,

Joan is under no obligation to exercise the option. If she does not, Joe can keep the money or other consideration paid to him for the option. If Joan does exercise the option, normally the money paid for the option will be subtracted from the purchase price. Depending on the bargaining position of the parties, however, this is not always the case.

Another exception to the rule that an offeror can revoke an offer at any time before acceptance comes from UCC § 2-205, which is also known as the "firm offer" provision:

> *An offer by a* merchant *[emphasis added] to buy or sell goods which by its terms gives assurance that it will be held open is not revocable, for lack of consideration, during the time stated, or if no time is stated, for a reasonable time, but in no event may such period of irrevocability exceed three months.*

The Code demands that merchants, as professionals, keep their word even if they have been given no consideration for their assurances. Simply put, the Code dramatically changes the common law doctrine regarding the offeror's right to revoke when the offeror is a **merchant** and the other provisions of § 2-205 have been met.

Finally, the equitable doctrine of **promissory estoppel** prohibits offerors from revoking their offers. Under this theory, offerors are prevented (estopped) from asserting a defense otherwise available to them (generally that they as common law offerors have the right to revoke the offer). If Joan, the offeree in our earlier example, wishes to assert this doctrine, she must show that (1) Joe, the offeror, promised or represented to her that he would hold the offer open; (2) she relied on these promises or representations; (3) she consequently suffered a detriment (maybe she passed up another farm because she thought she would get Joe's); and (4) injustice can be avoided only by forcing the offeror to leave the offer open. In several cases, successful plaintiffs have used this doctrine to cut off the offeror's power of revocation.

Thus far, we have dwelt on the offeror's power to terminate the offer. Any offeree, of course, can refuse the offer and thereby terminate it. The law calls the offeree's power of termination **rejection.** Like revocations, rejections are not effective until communicated to (or received by) the offeror. Hence, as the offeree, Joan can tell Joe that she is no longer interested in the car and thereby reject Joe's offer.

The usual rule holds that an offer cannot later be accepted after lapse, revocation, or rejection, because after these events the offer has expired. Yet, if the parties nonetheless still are willing to deal, there may be a valid agreement subsequent to one of these events. However, the parties generally are not obligated to continue the transaction unless they find it advantageous to do so.

Exhibit 10.2 summarizes the various methods for terminating an offer.

10.1 | SALES/ MANUFACTURING

CALL-IMAGE TECHNOLOGY

REVOKING AN OFFER

CIT made a written offer to Joe Daily, one of its suppliers, in which the firm offered to buy Joe's entire supply of diagram boards and fiber optics at list price. CIT's letter promised to keep the offer open for four weeks. Two weeks after mailing the letter, CIT received an offer from another firm to sell diagram boards and fiber optics to CIT for 20 percent less than Joe's list price. Tom wants to accept this offer and has asked you whether he can revoke the offer to Joe. What will you tell him?

BUSINESS CONSIDERATIONS What factors should a business consider when it makes a written promise to keep an offer for goods open for a specific time? Would the business consider different factors if the offer were for the purchase of services?

ETHICAL CONSIDERATIONS Is the common law rule that generally permits revocation of an offer at any time prior to acceptance an ethical rule? Is the UCC rule regarding merchants and the sale of goods more ethical?

Promissory estoppel
A doctrine that prohibits a promisor from denying the making of a promise or from escaping the liability for that promise because of the justifiable reliance of the promisee that the promise would be kept.

Rejection
A refusal to accept what is offered.

E X H I B I T 10.2 | **Termination of the Offer**

Method of Terminating the Offer	General Rule	Exceptions to the General Rule
1. Lapse—the termination of an offer through the passage of time or the occurrence of some condition	1. The offer ends at the time stated in the offer if a time is stated. 2. If no time is stated, the offer lapses after a reasonable time has passed. 3. The offeror does not need to communicate to the offeree the fact that the offer has lapsed. 4. Lapse may occur by operation of law upon: (1) the death or insanity of any of the contracting parties; (2) the supervening illegality of the subject matter; or (3) the destruction of the subject matter when neither party is at fault.	
2. Revocation—the termination of an offer by the offeror	1. Under common law, the offeror has a virtually unlimited right to revoke at any time before acceptance.	1. Options—contracts for which a person has paid money and that allow the person to buy or sell property at an agreed-on price or time period—make an offer irrevocable. 2. The "firm offer" provision of the UCC (§2-205) makes an offer irrevocable. 3. Promissory estoppel, whereby an offeror will be prevented from asserting a defense otherwise available to him or her in order to serve justice, can be applied to cut off the power of revocation.
	2. Revocation is not effective until it is communicated to (or received by) the offeree or the offeree's agent (i.e., the mailbox rule is inapplicable to revocations).	1. In public offers, public revocation is effective even against a person who does not know about it. The offeror need not communicate directly with every possible offeree.
3. Rejection—the termination of an offer by the offeree	1. The offeree rejects the offer by indicating directly or indirectly that he or she will not accept the offer. 2. A counteroffer is tantamount to a rejection of the offer.	1. Inquiries, requests, and terms implied by law that avoid making the acceptance conditional are not counteroffers. 2. The original offeror can deal with the new "offeror" on the new terms if he or she so desires.
	3. Rejection is not effective until it is communicated to (or received by) the offeror or the offeror's agent (i.e., the mailbox rule is inapplicable to rejections).	

E X H I B I T 10.2 | **Termination of the Offer, continued**

Method of Terminating the Offer	General Rule	Exceptions to the General Rule
4. Acceptance—the termination of an offer by the offeree's assenting to all the terms of the offer	1. Acceptance must be clear and unconditional.	
	2. Silence generally is not tantamount to acceptance.	1. The prior dealing of the parties may validate acceptance based on silence.
	3. Acceptance must match, term by term, the provisions of the original offer.	1. Inquiries, requests, and terms implied by law that avoid making the acceptance conditional have no effect on the validity of the acceptance. 2. Under UCC § 2-207, an acceptance containing additional or different terms may still constitute a valid acceptance unless acceptance is expressly made conditional on assent to such terms.
	4. Qualified, or conditional, acceptances are counteroffers.	1. The original offeror can accept these new terms if he or she wishes.
	5. Acceptance may be oral, written, or implied.	1. Under the UCC, the conduct of the parties alone may establish a contract (see UCC § 2-207).
	6. Acceptance must be accomplished by the offeree or the offeree's agent.	
	7. Acceptance is not effective until it is communicated to (or received by) the offeror or the offeror's agent.	1. In the absence of a stipulated mode, acceptance is effective upon dispatch to the implied agent in jurisdictions that recognize the mailbox rule. 2. The UCC sanctions acceptances in any manner and by any medium reasonable in the circumstances (UCC § 2-206).

ACCEPTANCE

Acceptance is the usual mode of terminating an offer. This represents a significant moment for the offeror and offeree because they have arrived at an agreement. Barring problems with consideration, capacity, genuineness of assent, legality, or proper form, a binding contract now exists.

Acceptance involves the offeree's assent to all the terms of the offer. Because this is so, the offeree's intention to be bound to the total offer must be clear. Thus, the offeree's uncommunicated mental reservations will not be binding on the offeror. As with offers, courts apply the objective test to see whether the acceptance is valid. That the acceptance is oral, written, or implied (e.g., through an act such as cashing a check) generally does not affect its validity, as long as the offer has been communicated to the offeree (or the offeree's agent), and it is the offeree (or the offeree's agent) who accepts.

10.2 | SALES/ MANAGEMENT

UNDERSTANDING CONTRACT FORMATION

John has been studying contract law in his Legal Environment of Business course. He explains to the family that, based on what he has been told in class, contracts are fairly technical and difficult to create, owing in part to such things as the "mirror-image" rule. He believes that this principle gives CIT a great deal of latitude in discussing its product with potential customers because one can classify much of the conversation as mere "sales talk," and no contract offer will result. Tom is not sure that John has a thorough knowledge of contract law. Tom remembers that service contracts and employment contracts are often technical and that courts are likely to examine them very carefully. However, he also has heard that courts are much more likely to "find" contracts in the area of sales even if the courts discern that the traditional common law requirements are lacking. Tom asks you for your advice. What will you tell him?

BUSINESS CONSIDERATION What can a business do to protect itself from an overly exuberant sales force when the sales representatives are trying to make contracts with customers?

ETHICAL CONSIDERATIONS Suppose a business finds itself with a questionable deal and recognizes a possible escape from that deal owing to a technicality in contract law. Is it ethical for the firm to use this technicality to get out of the deal? Is it ethical to hold another party to a contract that he or she does not realize is being formed?

Mirror-Image Rule

Under common law rules, an acceptance must not only be clear but also unconditional. This concept, called the *mirror-image* or *matching-ribbons* rule of common law, means that the acceptance must match, term by term, the provisions in the offer. Any deviation from these terms, whether by alteration, addition, or omission, makes the acceptance invalid and tantamount to a rejection of the offer originally made. This result follows from the common law offeror's power to set the terms of the offer and the acceptance.

Any deviation from the terms of the offer brings about a qualified acceptance, known as a *counteroffer.* Counteroffers terminate offers unless the original offeror remains willing to accept the terms of the counteroffer. As you have seen in other contexts, such offerors are not obligated to do so unless they still want to deal. Therefore, if you desire to enter into a contract with the offeror, you should pay close attention to the language of the acceptance. Mere inquiries, requests, and terms implied by law, if part of the acceptance, do not invalidate it. Thus, if Joan says, "I'll take the farm at $200,000 as you offered, but I'd like you to throw in the farm machinery," a valid acceptance probably exists (Joan's added statement is a request). Contrast this with Joan's saying, "I accept if you throw in the farm machinery." The latter statement sounds more like a proviso or a condition and may make the purported acceptance legally ineffective unless Joe is prepared to let Joan have the machinery as part of the deal.

By permitting a contract to arise between the parties even if the offeree adds terms or includes different terms in the purported acceptance, Uniform Commercial Code § 2-207 continues its relaxation of common law rules. This provision of the UCC reflects the drafters' knowledge of commercial realities, specifically the fact that buyers and sellers in commercial settings generally exchange their respective forms (e.g., purchase order forms or order acknowledgment forms), which may contain contradictory terms. Rather than hamper commercial dealings by judging the inconsistent terms under the common law rule that any variance in the material terms of the offer and acceptance constitutes a counteroffer and hence a rejection of the original offer, the UCC drafters permit a contract to arise between the parties unless the offeree expressly has indicated that his or her acceptance of the offer is conditioned on the offeror's assent to these additional or different terms.

Section 2-207 of the Code, furthermore, sets out a scheme for determining the operative terms of the contract in these circumstances. For instance, between merchants, the additional terms automatically become part of the contract without the offeror's consent unless the original offer expressly requires the offeree to accept the terms of the offer; the additional terms materially alter the contract (i.e., they would unfairly surprise or be unduly oppressive to the offeror); or the offeror has notified the offeree that he or she will not accept the new terms. This same Code section also states that conduct by both parties that recognizes the existence of a contract is sufficient to establish a contract for sale even though the writings of the parties otherwise do not establish a contract. You will learn more about these concepts in succeeding chapters but, for now, appreciate the alterations of common law rules embodied in the UCC and the underlying rationales for these changes.

Manner and Time of Acceptance

Besides accepting unconditionally, in order to effect a valid acceptance, the offeree must avoid one other pitfall: The offeree must accept in exactly the mode *specified*, or *stipulated*, by the offeror in the offer. Thus, if the offeror says that acceptance must occur by telegram, a letter will not constitute an effective acceptance. Similarly, if the offer says, "Acceptance required by return mail," an acceptance placed in the mail two days later is invalid. Finally, when the offer says, "Acceptance effective only when received at our home office," a contract will not arise until the offeror receives the acceptance.

Although the offeror enjoys the right to set out exactly the terms of acceptance, the offeror may choose not to stipulate the mode necessary for a valid acceptance. In such cases, the offeree can use any *reasonable* medium of communication, as long as he or she acts within a reasonable time. Usually, the offeree will choose the same medium used by the offeror. By implication, this medium is a reasonable and therefore an *authorized* mode of communication. Hence, in the absence of a stipulated method of acceptance, if the offeror makes the offer via the mail, the offeree's mailing of an acceptance represents a reasonable (or authorized) mode of acceptance and thus a valid response. Another medium, such as the telephone, may be reasonable, and therefore authorized as well, if the parties have used this medium in their prior dealings or if local or industry custom sanctions it.

Use of an authorized mode of communication in such circumstances takes on particular significance because, in most states, these acceptances become legally effective *at the time of dispatch* (mailing, wiring, etc.). This is called the *mailbox rule*, or *implied-agency rule*, because the post office or telegraph office is deemed to be the agent of the offeror. To illustrate, assume that the offeror has not stipulated the mode of acceptance for an offer that was mailed to the offeree on 28 September. The offeror subsequently attempts to revoke the offer on 1 October and then learns that the offeree had mailed an acceptance to the offeror on 30 September. A contract exists as of 30 September, and thus there is no "mere offer" that the offeror can revoke. The fact that the offeror had not received the acceptance until after he or she attempted to revoke the offer is irrelevant. The law treats the post office as the offeror's agent and thus concludes that the offeror "received" the acceptance on 30 September, the date the offeree deposited the letter with the post office. Because some letters never arrive, it is advisable, of course, for the offeree to secure postal or telegraphic receipts in order to prove after the fact the date on which he or she actually dispatched the acceptance.

In contrast, where the offeree has used an unauthorized mode of communication, the strict rule states that the acceptance is ineffective until the offeror actually receives it; the mailbox rule is not applicable. Even so, some courts will enforce the

YOU BE THE JUDGE

TIME IS MONEY

The old truism "time is money" still holds sway. Businesspeople across the world have championed facsimile ("fax," or telecopy) machines, electronic mail (e-mail), electronic data interchanges (EDIs), and video-texts as speedier and more efficient modes of communication than those of years past. Given the time and dollar costs associated with "paper," it is no wonder that electronic communications are becoming increasingly popular. EDIs, or communications solely between computers in which computer-generated purchase orders beget computer-generated order acknowledgments, may even bring about the total displacement of the human aspects of contracting. Hence, contract law is moving toward a regime that will be largely faceless as well as paperless. Whereas communication nowadays can occur instantaneously, the evolution of common law in contrast moves at glacial speeds. This contradiction has led to an absence of clear-cut rules as to the applicability of the common law to situations involving the role of these new technologies in contracts. The few courts that have considered some of the situations that involve the intersection of the old and the new have done so in a summary fashion and have come to inconsistent results. Many businesspeople may have blithely assumed that the law will treat faxes, e-mail, and EDIs in the same fashion as it historically has treated paper communications. Hence, the present dearth of precedents may be misleading (and short-lived), once questions over such issues become more public and widespread. Moreover, given this unsettled state of the law, business firms' reluctance to eschew totally the older, slower technologies (mail, telegraph, and delivery services) arguably impedes the further development of the newer technologies and erodes the potential future efficiencies represented by these breakthrough modes of communication.

A transatlantic order for a compact disk (CD) illustrates some of these very concerns. David J. Loundy, a Chicago lawyer, ordered the CD from a web site in Surrey, England. The web page listed the price as the equivalent of $15 in U.S. currency. Loundy received an e-mail acknowledgment of his order. Shortly thereafter, though, another e-mail—this one from Victoria Bowles, the manager of the mail-order house that would supply the CD—informed him that the price on the web site was wrong and inquired whether he still wanted the CD (now priced at $21). Loundy did want the CD but at the listed price. He argued that under American law, a valid contract had been formed. Raising the price, he argued, might constitute false advertising and breach of contract. But under English law, Bowles (who also is a lawyer) countered, no contract existed. The web site price was an "invitation to treat," and Loundy's was the first offer, which the seller could decline or renegotiate. At issue—aside from the $6—was where the transaction had occurred and thus which country would have jurisdiction over the dispute. The parties eventually resolved the dispute amicably (Loundy received the CD free), but this situation represents a cautionary tale, nonetheless, especially for business transactions that involve substantially larger sums than this nominal amount.

Assume that this case has been filed in *your* court asking *you* to rule on when acceptance occurs if the mode of communication is by fax or e-mail. How will *you* rule?[3]

BUSINESS CONSIDERATION Should the mailbox rule apply to electronic means of communication, or should acceptance be effective only when received by the offeror when electronic means are used?

ETHICAL CONSIDERATIONS What ethical issues are raised by the continuing advent of technology in the formation of contracts? What should businesspeople do to protect their interests, both ethically and legally?

SOURCES: *The National Law Journal* (9 September 1996), p. B3; and Wendy R. Leibowitz, *The National Law Journal* (14 June 1999), p. B21.

agreement if the acceptance, even though communicated via an unauthorized mode, is timely, especially if the courts can construe the offeror's language about the proper mode as a suggestion rather than a stipulation or condition. UCC § 2-206(1)(a), by sanctioning acceptances "in any manner and by any medium reasonable in the circumstances," lends credence to such decisions.

As you can see, the time of contract formation is crucial. The mailbox rule allows acceptance, and hence a contract, to occur even before the offeror knows of the acceptance. Such acceptances cut off the offeror's otherwise almost unlimited right to revoke, because in order for an attempted revocation to be effective, it must occur prior to acceptance. Offerors can curtail the effect of the mailbox rule if they stipulate that acceptances will not be effective until received by them. Note, too, that in any event, the mailbox rule applies only to acceptances: Revocations and rejections do not take effect until they are communicated to (i.e., are received by) the offeree and offeror, respectively. Moreover, revocations and rejections do not become legally binding upon dispatch, as acceptances sometimes do.

Silence

As the foregoing discussion implies, some overt act necessarily accompanies acceptance. For this reason, acceptance requires a clear intent to accept. Thus, the settled weight of authority holds that mere silence by the offeree cannot constitute acceptance. However, in some isolated cases, the prior dealings of the parties may permit acceptance based on silence. The following case illustrates many of the concepts that relate to the manner of and the time when acceptance occurs.

10.3

OKOSA V. HALL
718 A.2D 1223 (N.J.SUPER. A.D. 1998)

FACTS Obianuju Okosa was involved in an accident with defendant Tawn D. Hall on 16 March 1994. Hall was uninsured. Accordingly, the plaintiffs, Mr. and Mrs. Okosa, seeking Personal Injury Protection (PIP) benefits, brought an action against Hall and the plaintiffs' insurer, New Jersey Citizens United Reciprocal Exchange. The plaintiffs were insured under an automobile insurance policy that required a quarterly premium payment to be made on 28 February 1994. At the close of business on 28 February 1994, the insurer directed a letter to the Okosas. The letter, which was posted on 1 March 1994, advised the Okosas that they had failed to pay the $347.50 installment then due and that their policy would be automatically canceled at 12:01 A.M. on 16 March 1994, unless they made payment by that date. The letter further advised them:

If we receive payment on or before the cancellation date, *we will continue your policy with no interruption in the protection it affords.* If you've recently mailed your payment, please disregard this notice. *[emphasis added]*

On 15 March 1994, while the policy was still in effect, the plaintiffs mailed, by certified mail, a check for the required payment. The automobile accident with the uninsured defendant occurred the next day. It is not known exactly when the plaintiffs' check was received, but the insurer deposited and cashed the check on 22 March 1994. In response to the Okosas' claims, the insurer subsequently advised them that the company would pay no PIP benefits because of the policy's cancellation prior to the accident. This litigation then ensued.

ISSUE Had the insureds' payment of the premium by certified mail on the day before the expiration of the policy avoided the cancellation of the policy?

HOLDING Yes. The application of the mailbox rule would validate the payment as timely and hence effective in avoiding the cancellation of the policy.

continued

10.3

OKOSA V. HALL, *continued*
718 A.2D 1223 (N.J.SUPER. A.D. 1998)

REASONING The Okosas contended that the so-called "mailbox rule" applies to the facts of this case and that the installment payment mailed on 15 March 1994, constituted a timely payment made prior to 12:01 A.M. on 16 March 1994. Generally speaking, the mailbox rule sanctions the formation or completion of a contractual undertaking upon the act of mailing where the other party has authorized the use of the mail as the medium for response. The rule is succinctly set forth as follows:

> *Where parties are at distance from one another, and an offer is sent by mail, it is universally held in this country that the reply accepting the offer may be sent through the same medium, and, if it is so sent, the contract will be complete when the acceptance is mailed . . . and beyond the acceptor's control; the theory being that, when one makes an offer through the mail, he authorizes the acceptance to be made through the same medium,* and constitutes that medium his agent to receive his acceptance; that the acceptance, when mailed, is then constructively [i.e., legally imputed; having an effect in law if not in fact] communicated to the offeror.

The insurer unquestionably addressed the plaintiffs by mail concerning their tardy payment. Its letter of 28 February 1994, posted 1 March 1994, invited the plaintiffs to respond with payment by mail. In responding, the plaintiffs did so by means of certified mail. The use of certified mail by the plaintiffs was shrewd because it insured proof of mailing, and its use avoided the thorny issue that would have arisen from a fraudulent response by them that post-dated the accident. The record showed that, by authorizing the use of mail as a means of paying premiums, the insurer made the postal authorities its agent. Because the mailbox rule controls the decision in this matter, the entry of summary judgment in favor of the insurer must be reversed.

BUSINESS CONSIDERATIONS The mailbox rule imposes the risk of nondelivery on the offeror. Could the insurer have changed the language of the notice sent to those who had not paid installments on time so as to reduce or eliminate bearing this risk? What might such a provision have stated?

ETHICAL CONSIDERATIONS How can the risk of nondelivery of a reply be allocated in a manner that is fair and equitable to both parties? Is the current rule ethical? Was the Okosas' conduct in waiting until the last minute to mail in the overdue installment ethical? Why or why not?

Bilateral Versus Unilateral Contracts

The last major issue regarding acceptance concerns whether the contract, if formed, will be bilateral or unilateral. The weight of authority holds that an offer that contemplates the making of a *bilateral* contract may be accepted by either a direct communication of a promise to the offeror or a counterpromise inferred from the offeree's conduct or other circumstances.

When the offer instead contemplates the formation of a *unilateral* contract, it usually is unnecessary for the offeree to communicate acceptance. The offeree accepts the offer merely by completing the act called for in the offer. Subsequent notice to the offeror would be redundant because the offeror eventually will learn of the acceptance when the offeree requests payment for the services rendered.

Nevertheless, disputes may arise between the parties as to how much time an offeree has for completing the performance mentioned in the purported unilateral contract. If the offeror says, "I'll pay you $50 to chop firewood for me," and the offeree says, "Okay," the offeree may think chopping wood at any time within the next two months will constitute a binding acceptance. On the other hand, the offeror may get nervous when the firewood is not in the wood rack within two weeks and therefore may make the same offer to someone else who completes the job sooner. In such circumstances, the offeror may not want to pay the first offeree for the wood delivered two months later; enough wood already has been supplied.

Because of such timing problems, courts remain somewhat hostile to unilateral contracts and, if possible, construe such alleged contracts as bilateral. More important, the contracting parties can avoid such timing problems by writing down all the pertinent details (delivery date, price, etc.) in advance, whether the offeror proposes a bilateral or a unilateral contract. Good business planning, even in everyday affairs, helps avoid potential legal difficulties.

Section 2-206(1)(b) of the Uniform Commercial Code, by specifying that unless the parties unambiguously indicate otherwise, "an order or other offer to buy goods for prompt or current shipment shall be construed as inviting acceptance either by a prompt promise to ship or by the prompt or current shipment of conforming or non-conforming goods . . . ," eliminates many of the distinctions made in the common law between bilateral and unilateral contracts. In the first instance, a bilateral contract is formed; in the second, a unilateral contract. Acceptance is effective in either case.

Summary

Agreement represents perhaps the most important aspect of contract formation. To have agreement, there must be an offer and an acceptance. Assent to a contract must be mutual, and the common law offeror can set the terms of both the offer and the acceptance. An offer is an indication (by a promise or another commitment) of one's willingness to do or to refrain from doing something in the future. Courts employ an objective test to assess whether the parties have mutually assented to the terms of the agreement. Such a test asks whether a reasonable offeree would believe that the offeror has made an offer. No secret intent on the offeror's part can be shown.

To be a genuine offer under the common law, the offer must manifest a clear and present intent to contract and be definite in all respects. Statements of opinion, statements of intention, and preliminary negotiations are too indefinite to constitute offers. The same is true of most advertisements: The law usually construes advertisements as invitations for persons to come in and make offers for the types of goods and at the prices indicated in the advertisements. An offer has no legal effect until the offeror communicates it to the offeree. General offers are perfectly legal, but many jurisdictions require that they, too, be communicated to the offeree in order for a valid acceptance to occur.

10.3 | SALES/ MANUFACTURING

CALL-IMAGE TECHNOLOGY

ACCEPTING OFFERS

Unbeknownst to the rest of the family, Dan and John have been negotiating the purchase of a piece of real estate that they believe will represent an ideal distribution center once the firm has secured a loyal customer base. The would-be seller has the contracts ready and has asked Dan and John to stop by and sign the papers. Although they have indicated verbally that they probably will sign the agreements, several weeks have passed without their having done so. John is worried that the would-be seller will bring a breach of contract action against them and the firm. He thus seeks your advice as to whether his fears are unfounded or legitimate. How will you answer his queries?

BUSINESS CONSIDERATIONS Why is it important for a firm to act diligently on all its obligations? What does a firm risk if it does not do so?

ETHICAL CONSIDERATION Do you condone, on ethical grounds, the fashion in which Dan and John are acting in these circumstances? Why or why not?

RESOURCES FOR BUSINESS LAW STUDENTS

NAME	RESOURCES	WEB ADDRESSES
Uniform Commercial Code (UCC)	The Legal Information Institute (LII), maintained by the Cornell Law School, provides a hypertext and searchable version of Articles 1–9 of the UCC.	**http://www.law.cornell.edu/ucc/ucc.table.html**
The American Law Institute	The American Law Institute, publisher of *Restatements of the Law,* Model Codes, and other proposals for law reform, provides press releases, its newsletter, and other publications.	**http://www.ali.org**

The four methods of terminating an offer include (1) lapse, (2) revocation, (3) rejection, and (4) acceptance. Generally, neither a revocation nor a rejection takes legal effect until communicated to or received by the other party. However, if an offeree uses an authorized (or reasonable) mode of communication, an acceptance may be effective on dispatch. The offeror's power of revocation may be limited by options, by the "firm offer" provision of the Code, or by promissory estoppel. All three doctrines have certain elements that the offeree must prove before the offeree can cut off the offeror's right to revoke. Acceptance is the usual mode of terminating an offer. A bona fide offer and acceptance bring about an agreement, which in most cases will be tantamount to a contract. Acceptance involves the offeree's assent to all the terms of the offer. The acceptance must be clear and must be communicated to the offeror. Under the mirror-image rule of common law, an acceptance has to match, term by term, the provisions in the offer. A qualified acceptance—one that deviates from the original terms—is called a counteroffer. A counteroffer terminates the original offer and in effect brings about the rejection of the offer unless the original offeror is willing to deal on the new terms. If the offeror has not stipulated the mode necessary for a valid acceptance, use of any reasonable (or authorized) mode of communication will make the acceptance effective on dispatch. This is called the mailbox rule. If, in contrast, the offeree has used an unauthorized mode, acceptance actually must be received to be effective; the mailbox rule will be inapplicable. The mailbox rule does not apply to revocations or rejections. Silence by the offeree ordinarily does not constitute acceptance.

In bilateral contracts, communication of the acceptance usually is necessary, but this is not true for unilateral contracts. In unilateral contracts, the offeree accepts the offer merely by completing the act called for in the offer. Because of the problems that can arise from disputes concerning how much time the offeree in unilateral contracts has to accept, courts are hostile to this category of contract. The Uniform Commercial Code eliminates many of the common law distinctions between bilateral and unilateral contracts.

DISCUSSION QUESTIONS

1. What does a court mean by "mutual assent"?
2. Explain the phrase "objective theory of contracts."
3. Briefly state the common law rules surrounding a valid offer.
4. Name and define the ways in which an offer can terminate.
5. Is an advertisement a bona fide offer? Why or why not?
6. In what situations will "lapse" occur by operation of law?
7. Discuss the common law rules of revocation.
8. Name and list the elements for each of the methods available for terminating the offeror's power of revocation.
9. What are "counteroffers," and how do they arise?
10. Explain the term *mailbox rule* and its significance.

CASE PROBLEMS AND WRITING ASSIGNMENTS

1. After John Roth made a written offer to buy real property, George E. Malson, the seller, made a written counteroffer on a standard form adopted by the California Association of Realtors. The form had a signature line, entitled "ACCEPTANCE," whereby Roth could accept the counteroffer. Instead of signing the "ACCEPTANCE" portion of the form, however, Roth signed a different portion of the form, entitled "COUNTER TO COUNTER OFFER." In the portion of the form called "CHANGES/AMENDMENTS" Roth also wrote in certain terms of the purchase, although it ultimately turned out that these terms did not vary from the terms of Malson's counteroffer. Roth left the line for the expiration date for the counter-counteroffer blank. Roth conveyed the form to Stromer Realty (Stromer) by the 8 November deadline for the expiration of Malson's counteroffer. However, Malson did not accept Roth's counter-counteroffer. Rather, on 16 November 1995, Malson's attorney advised Stromer that Malson had rejected Roth's counter to Malson's counteroffer and was taking the property off the market. On 17 November 1995, Malson memorialized this conversation in a letter sent to Stromer. Arguing that a contract existed between the parties, Roth later sued Malson for specific performance and breach of contract. Roth contended that his giving an absolute, unqualified acceptance—in substance though not in form—to Malson's counteroffer had formed a binding contract. Should a court agree with Roth's claim? [See *Roth* v. *Malson*, 79 Cal.Rptr. 2d 226 (Cal.App. 3 Dist. 1998).]

2. Gregg Gill, a former employee of B&R International, Inc. (B&R), alleged that B&R had breached an agreement to provide him severance pay. To establish his contention, Gill relied on an unsigned memorandum, dated 22 February 1993, and the response to that memorandum. The memorandum was written by Robbie Reid, B&R's president, chief executive officer, and controlling shareholder. Addressed to Gill and three other employees, the memorandum, which was not written on corporate letterhead, stated: "Attached is a Shareholder's Agreement for your review, and comments. The amounts shown are the final amounts being offered for their respective values. I have reviewed this and feel this agreement to be not only equitable, but very simple. . . . My alternative offer is to give each of you a Promissory Note equal to the dollars I have earlier indicated that would become due and payable upon the sale of the company. If the company [is] never sold, or if you were terminated for cause or left at your own discretion, then there would be no value payment. . . . I would like to have your comments on the Shareholder's Agreement before Wednesday . . . and whether or not you intend to become a shareholder on [the] terms offered." Gill's response stated: "Given my current financial obligations, the appropriate option at this time is the $100,000 promissory note. If the stock option can remain open (Feb. 22 memo), I would like to consider it at a future date." Reid made this handwritten notation on Gill's response: "I *respect* your decision—no problem—It is not fair to leave stock option open for you & not for others—We can discuss stock [at] a future date & a different price—Robbie." No promissory note was ever executed or delivered to Gill by either Reid or B&R. Gill also acknowledged that he was the only B&R employee to accept the lump sum payment option; the other employees elected to buy the stock. Had B&R offered Gill and certain other employees an opportunity either to purchase B&R stock at a favorable price or to receive a lump sum payment of $100,000? Had Gill accepted this offer so as to form an enforceable contract? [See *Gill* v. *B&R International, Inc.*, 507 S.E.2d 477 (Ga.App. 1998).]

3. Greene put up for sale several pieces of antique furniture from her mother's estate. After seeing the furniture, Keener inquired about the price of an antique secretary. Greene actually wished $6,000 and was unsure whether she genuinely wanted to sell it, but in conversation with Keener she agreed to sell it for $4,200. Keener said he was very interested but wanted to be sure it blended with the rest of his furniture.

After some discussion, Greene permitted Keener to take the secretary home to see if it matched. The night after Keener had the secretary taken to his home, Greene called and informed him that she no longer wanted to sell the secretary and asked that he return it. Keener said, "Hold on a minute," and went to speak with his wife, who indicated that she liked the piece. When Keener refused to return the secretary, Greene sued for rescission (cancellation) of the sale. Should she prevail? [See *Greene v. Keener*, 402 S.E.2d 284 (Ga.App. 1991).]

4. Sewell Coal Company (Sewell) operated a coal mining facility in Nicholas County, West Virginia. In early 1982, a severe downturn in the coal market forced Sewell to shut down some of its facilities and to lay off certain of its supervisory and clerical employees. Through March and April 1982, Sewell paid, in conformity with its normal severance plan, such laid-off employees two weeks' severance. In May 1982, when it became apparent that the layoffs would be permanent, the company sent a letter to all laid-off salaried personnel informing them that a special severance procedure would be used for that layoff and would apply retroactively to salaried employees laid off since 1 January 1982. A memorandum attached to the letter explained the special procedure: The laid-off employee would receive one week's severance pay for each year of service, with a minimum of two weeks, not to exceed 20 weeks' severance pay. The letter and accompanying memorandum went only to those salaried employees who were laid off. The company neither distributed these materials to the workforce in general nor posted or circulated them among the remaining workforce. Further layoffs occurred in August and October 1982. On each occasion, the laid-off employee received a letter similar to that of May 1982, which letter set forth the special severance procedure. On each occasion, the company sent the letter and accompanying memorandum only to those salaried employees who were being laid off.

In November 1982, the company promulgated guidelines stating that the special severance procedure henceforth would be discontinued and would not apply to future layoffs. Rather, for future layoffs, employees would receive the normal two weeks' severance pay. The company distributed these guidelines to the managers who were to implement them, but the company did not provide the information to the general workforce to whom the guidelines were inapplicable. The company treated the layoffs that occurred through 1987 according to these written guidelines. Mark Bailey, a salaried employee laid off after the discontinuation of the special severance procedure, sub-

sequently filed suit. He contended that the adoption of the special severance plan constituted an offer that he had accepted by continuing to work for the company and that, as a consequence, upon the termination of his employment, he was entitled to the special severance pay. Should a court agree with Bailey's reasoning? [See *Bailey v. Sewell Coal Co.*, 437 S.E.2d 448 (W.Va. 1993).]

5. Alison H. is a minor female who resides with her parents in Belchertown, Massachusetts. The Belchertown Public School System is responsible for providing special education to students with learning disabilities. Though it began providing special education services to Alison at the beginning of the fifth grade, these were discontinued halfway through the school year. From then on, Alison's parents, the plaintiffs, had a running dispute with the school as to the special education services Alison should receive and where they would be given. No agreement ever could be reached on an appropriate individualized educational plan (IEP) for Alison. On 30 January 1996, the plaintiffs retained attorney Claire Thompson to represent them as to the question of an appropriate IEP for Alison. During the subsequent negotiations, the plaintiffs made clear that they thought that White Oak School was the most appropriate placement for Alison and would meet their IEP demands. White Oak School is a private institution specializing in special education for children with learning disabilities. On 21 August 1996, the attorney for the school system faxed Thompson a letter that indicated the school system's belief that it was unlikely that Thompson or her clients would ever be satisfied with the IEP developed by Belchertown or the educational program provided by it. Therefore, the school officials offered Mr. and Mrs. H. the opportunity for Alison to attend White Oak for the 1996–1997 school year. This letter further stated: "*As a condition of finalizing this agreement, Belchertown would be looking for the withdrawal of the request for hearing, which hearing is scheduled for 11 September 1996, as well as a release of any and all claims arising prior to the execution of the agreement.*" The letter asked for an answer to this offer by 23 August 1996. Within a matter of hours, Thompson replied by fax and accepted Belchertown's offer. The school prepared a new IEP for Alison's attendance at White Oak School; the parents accepted the IEP on 3 September 1996; and the scheduled hearing before the Bureau of Special Education Appeals was canceled. For Alison's attendance at White Oak School for the 1996–97 school year, Belchertown paid a total of $22,295.20 in tuition and transportation costs. By a letter dated 6 November 1996, Thompson asked that Belchertown School pay

her attorney's fees totaling $6,112.40 through 26 August 1996. Taking the position that the plaintiffs had waived any claim for attorney's fees when they had accepted Belchertown's offer to place Alison in White Oak School, the Belchertown school officials rejected the demand for attorney's fees. Had the plaintiffs' acceptance of Belchertown's offer to place Alison in White Oak School subject to the condition that there be "a release of any and all claims arising prior to the execution of the agreement" amounted to a waiver of the plaintiffs' claim for attorney's fees? [See *Alison H. v. Byard*, 163 F.3d 2 (1st Cir. 1998).]

6. **BUSINESS APPLICATION CASE** Rollins Environmental Services (NJ), Inc. (Rollins) operates a waste disposal facility in Bridgeport, New Jersey, where it disposes of hazardous waste materials through incineration and other chemical and biological processes for customers throughout the country. During the 1970s, Polaroid Corporation (Polaroid) and Hooker Chemical Corporation (Hooker) were customers of Rollins, which disposed of their hazardous wastes. Between 1971 and 1976, 13 of the 14 purchase orders issued by Hooker contained an indemnity (reimbursement) clause and instructions that stated, among other things, that Rollins was to return to Hooker the acknowledgment orders containing this language regarding indemnification. Hooker used this language until 6 January 1977, when Rollins objected to the typed indemnity request for the first time. At Rollins's behest, the parties thereafter adopted an indemnification clause that provided indemnification only for negligent acts by Rollins. When the Environmental Protection Agency (EPA) notified Polaroid and Hooker that, as waste generators, they faced possible liability under the Comprehensive Environmental Response Compensation and Liability Act (CERCLA) for cleanup costs incurred by the government in Bridgeport, both companies requested that Rollins indemnify them with regard to the Bridgeport site spills. In refusing these requests, Rollins argued that, by failing to return the acknowledgment copy of the purchase agreement as requested, it had rejected the indemnification language. Polaroid and Hooker dismissed Rollins's failure either to return the acknowledgment or to object to the indemnification clause until 1977 as irrelevant. In their view, Rollins's routinely completing performance under the various purchase orders showed that Rollins had accepted all the purchase orders' terms. Should a court agree with Polaroid and Hooker's reasoning, or could a court use other aspects of contract law to find in favor of Rollins? What should each party have done differently so as to minimize the probability of this litigation occurring? [See

Polaroid Corp. v. *Rollins Environmental Services (NJ), Inc.*, 624 N.E.2d 959 (Mass. 1993).]

7. **ETHICAL APPLICATION CASE** The Denis F. McKenna Co. (McKenna) sought a declaratory judgment against Mary Ann Smith, David Drew, and Drew Holdings, Inc. (Drew). McKenna filed the lawsuit so as to enforce an alleged real estate contract between McKenna and Smith and to obtain a preliminary injunction to prevent Smith from selling the property to Drew. Smith owned residential property that she placed up for sale for $459,000. On 18 November 1997, at approximately 10:30 A.M., Denis McKenna, president of The Denis F. McKenna Co., made an offer to buy the property through Peg Spengler, his real estate agent. The offer, for $435,000, expired at noon that day. When Smith saw the offer at about 11:00 or 11:30 A.M., she told Mary Jane Kraus, her real estate agent, that she wanted to consult with her attorney, Eugene Callahan, and her brother before she entered into a contract. Just before noon, although Smith still wanted to speak with Callahan, she made a counteroffer of $450,000, subject to Callahan's approval. McKenna responded by offering $442,500 and imposed a deadline of 2:00 P.M. that afternoon. Because she wanted to speak with Callahan before making her decision about the offer, Smith requested that McKenna extend the deadline until 3:00 P.M. When informed of Smith's comments, McKenna raised his offer to $450,000. Krause informed Spengler that, while Smith likely would accept McKenna's offer, Smith still wanted to speak with Callahan. Spengler then asked Kraus for permission to deliver the offer to Smith personally. Krause agreed but reiterated that Smith wanted to speak with her attorney before Smith signed any contract. At approximately 1:30 P.M., Spengler took the offer (which expired at 2:00 P.M. and included an attorney approval clause) to Smith's home. While Spengler waited, Smith unsuccessfully continued her attempts to reach Callahan. Callahan's secretary told Smith that as long as the contract included an attorney approval clause, Smith could sign it because Callahan, after reviewing the document, could reject the offer. However, Spengler told Smith that there was "no deal" and McKenna "would walk" if Smith did not sign the contract by 2:00 P.M. As a result, Smith signed the contract even though she had not reached Callahan. Spengler then sent a copy of the contract by facsimile to Callahan's office. The contract, a standardized real estate contract widely used in the Chicago area, included a nonnegotiable attorney approval clause that stated:

This contract is contingent upon the approval hereof as to form by the attorneys for Purchaser and Seller within 5 business days after Seller's acceptance of this contract. . . . [Written] notice of disapproval . . . given within the time period specified [makes] this contract . . . null and void. . . . [The] earnest money shall be returned to Purchasers.

On 18 November 1997, Drew offered to buy Smith's property for $480,000. On 19 November 1997, Callahan sent Spengler written notice that Smith was rejecting the McKenna contract pursuant to the attorney approval clause, and Coldwell Banker returned the $2,000 earnest money check to McKenna. Smith accepted the Drew offer on 25 November 1997. Callahan subsequently stated that the Drew contract was not relevant to his rejection of the McKenna contract. Rather, Callahan specifically objected to paragraph one of the contract, which gave Smith only a maximum of three hours in which to accept the contract. Did Smith's purported acceptance of the contract before her attorney, in accordance with the attorney approval clause, had the opportunity to review the contract constitute a valid acceptance? Had Callahan acted in bad faith in disapproving the contract? Had Callahan materially breached the agreement when he sent the notice of rejection to Spengler, McKenna's agent, rather than to McKenna? Assess the ethics of all the parties here. Does the existence of a standard realty form give an inherent advantage to the seller? If so, does this fact make the use of such forms unethical? Does the arguably excessive verbiage employed in such forms confuse—or enlighten—the would-be purchaser? Would the adoption of a "plain English" approach to the drafting of these forms affect your assessment of the underlying ethical issues? [See *Denis F. McKenna Co. v. Smith*, 704 N.E.2d 826 (Ill.App. 1 Dist. 1998).]

8. **CRITICAL THINKING CASE** Cyberchron Corporation (Cyberchron) produces customized computer hardware for military and civilian use. During 1989 and 1990, Grumman Data Systems Corp. (Grumman) and its subsidiary, Calldata Systems Development, Inc., engaged in extensive negotiations with Cyberchron aimed at producing "ruggedized" computer equipment. Grumman had contracted with the U.S. Marine Corps to build a combat command control system that included a "rugged computer workstation" designed to operate under combat conditions in a command center. Grumman planned to use this "ruggedized" computer equipment—consisting of a video processor, a workstation, and a color monitor—in a Marine Corps defense program known as Advanced Tactical Air Command Central (ATACC). From the outset, the weight of the three units became critical, because the Marine Corps needed lightweight, compact, easily deployable equipment. By 1 March 1990, the parties had agreed on a total price of $1,383,879. But the question of the weight of the units and the penalties (i.e., deductions in the per-unit price) that Grumman would impose for units that exceeded a combined weight of 175 pounds remained unsettled. In a 24 May 1990, letter to Grumman, Cyberchron took exception to both the weight specifications and the penalties set by Grumman. Grumman responded on 15 June 1990 that the weight of the units and the weight penalties were nonnegotiable elements of the order it had given to Cyberchron. On 22 June 1990, Cyberchron answered that it was suspending all its testing and manufacturing activities with regard to this hardware until both companies could arrive at mutually acceptable terms.

Over the next two months, through a series of exchanged memos, the sparring between the two companies continued. Verbally, off the record, Grumman apparently was insisting that Cyberchron perform; but in writing, on the record, Grumman refrained from authorizing the initiation of any work. While orally pressuring Cyberchron to do the work, Grumman assured Cyberchron that, if it did, the negotiation problems could be resolved. Even after the delivery date of 22 August 1990 had passed, Grumman officials pushed Cyberchron to keep performing and told Cyberchron officials to ignore Grumman's written notice that indicated it was considering terminating the order owing to Cyberchron's default. In fact, as late as 7 September 1990, Cyberchron still was proposing a detailed delivery schedule. On 25 September 1990, Grumman terminated its relationship with Cyberchron and, on 26 September 1990, entered into a contract with another company to produce the "ruggedized" equipment. When Grumman refused to pay the $495,207.58 that Cyberchron had billed for its work, Cyberchron sued for breach of contract. Would Cyberchron prevail on this theory? Could Cyberchron argue other theories for imposing liability on Grumman? [See *Cyberchron Corp. v. Calldata Systems Development, Inc.*, 831 F.Supp. 94 (E.D.N.Y. 1993).]

NOTES

1. See Uniform Commercial Code, §§ 2-305, 2-309, and 2-310.
2. Ibid., § 2-306.
3. "Fax Notice by Union Not Enough for Offer," *The National Law Journal* (9 September 1996), p. B3; and Wendy R. Leibowitz, "E-Litigation: Border in Net Space," *The National Law Journal* (14 June 1999), p. B21.

11

CONSIDERATION:
THE BASIS OF THE BARGAIN

A G E N D A

The Kochanowskis want to be certain that CIT is entering into legally binding contracts. One of their concerns centers on whether they are truly giving and/or receiving consideration in their contracts. They also want to avoid illusory promises in all such contracts. They understand that bargaining, promises, and exchanges figure prominently in any assessment of whether consideration exists. Yet they also have heard that in certain situations, courts will enforce agreements despite an absence of consideration.

These and other contractual issues face CIT. Be prepared! You never know when one of the Kochanowskis will ask need your help or advice.

INTRODUCTION

As discussed in Chapter 10, contract law addresses the importance of the parties' reaching an agreement. In addition, the law requires some evidence that the parties' agreement is mutual. One way for the courts to find this "mutuality" is by determining that the parties have made an *exchange* of value. This exchange of value, the quid pro quo of contract formation, is called *consideration*. This chapter concentrates on this third requisite of contract formation.

THE BARGAIN AS A CONTRACT THEORY

Despite the rather checkered history that surrounds its principles, no doctrine of common law is as firmly entrenched today as the concept of consideration. Although the meaning of the concept is shrouded in historical traditions, familiarity with the doctrine's tenets remains fundamental to an understanding of modern contract law.

Remember that early in the history of contracts the parties underwent elaborate rituals, such as sealing their contracts with wax and placing their insignia in the wax, in order to demonstrate their willingness to be bound to the terms embodied in the agreement. Although few contracts are under seal nowadays, the idea that the parties actually ought to bargain and exchange something of value rather than merely make empty promises has lingered. Today, this emphasis is evident in the notion that the presence of consideration indicates the parties' exchange of something of value that results in an agreement between the parties. Thus, consideration shows that some obligation or duty worthy of a court's protection genuinely exists. It also establishes that the parties are acting deliberately and intend to bind themselves to the terms of the agreement.

Because it rids contracts of excessive formality while encouraging exchanges between people, the doctrine of consideration initially appears well suited to commercial and economic activity and hence to the study of business law. Nevertheless, some of the legal results under this doctrine seem quite harsh. For this reason, theories have emerged that permit an agreement to be binding in some cases despite a lack of consideration.

DEFINITION OF CONSIDERATION

Waiver
The voluntary surrender of a legal right; the intentional surrender of a right.

Among the many definitions of the term, one of the most common states that consideration is a **waiver,** or promised waiver, of rights bargained for in exchange for a promise. Consideration always consists of either a benefit to the promisor or a detriment to the promisee, bargained for and given in exchange for a promise. In view of the previous discussion, it is no surprise that the words *bargain, promise,* and *exchange* play such a prominent role in this definition. Consideration usually takes the form of money, but it may consist of an intangible, noneconomic benefit (or detriment) or anything of value to the parties.

Consideration as an Act or a Forbearance to Act

Implicit in this doctrine is the necessity of the parties' bargaining over some present event or object and exchanging something of value so as to bind themselves to do (or to refrain from doing) something. It is important, then, to check the parties' language closely. Words that sound like promises actually may be **illusory** because the parties really have not committed themselves in any manner to the bargain. If one party never actually agrees to do anything (e.g., if someone says, "I will sell you my farm for $80,000 if I feel like it"), the promise is illusory and unenforceable because consideration is absent.

Illusory
Fallacious; nominal as opposed to substantial; of false appearance.

In unilateral contracts, consideration manifests itself in an act or a forbearance to act. In the latter situation, the consideration comes from refraining from engaging in a legal act. For example, suppose your parents promise to send you to Europe for the summer if you will earn straight A's in school. If you do, the agreement is supported by consideration and will be enforceable in a court of law, assuming you live in a state where family members can sue each other if they breach (i.e., fail to perform) this agreement.

Now apply the definition of consideration to see why this agreement is enforceable. You waived your right to unlimited leisure time in exchange for your parents' promise. You and your parents bargained about the straight A's, so the trip is not a gift to you. You must do something (study more than you would like) or refrain from doing something (watching television and engaging in other leisure activities) to earn it. Furthermore, as a result of this bargain, your parents, the **promisors,** received a benefit (the satisfaction of knowing you are an honor student), while you, the **promisee,** suffered a detriment (studying hard all year). Your act of making perfect grades therefore has been given in exchange for your parents' promise to pay for your trip abroad. Note that the benefit they receive has no dollars-and-cents economic value, yet the law views the benefit as sufficient consideration to support their side of the bargain. They will receive what they asked of you.

Promisors
Those who make a promise or commitment.

Promisee
One to whom a promise or commitment has been made.

Think about these principles as you consider the case of *Herremans* v. *Carrera Designs, Inc.*

11.1

HERREMANS V. CARRERA DESIGNS, INC.
157 F.3D 1118 (7TH CIR. 1998)

FACTS Carrera Designs, Inc. (Carrera) employed Timothy Herremans as the manager of one of its plants. The failure of a major customer to pay its bills had caused Herremans's annual bonus in 1995 to be lower than usual. Carrera decided that, since the failure was not Herremans's fault, the company would, though not contractually obligated to do so, pay him the additional bonus that he would have earned but for the customer's default. Carrera promised to pay the additional bonus in three equal annual installments, and Herremans promised to continue working for Carrera. However, Carrera fired Herremans ten months later, in November 1996. Thereupon, Herremans sued Carrera for the unpaid portion of his 1995 and 1996 bonuses. Carrera claimed that because Herremans had intended to work for Carrera until his retirement (which would not have occurred in the next three years), its contract with Herremans lacked consideration.

ISSUE Had Herremans given consideration in exchange for Carrera's promise to pay Herremans's bonus in three additional installments?

HOLDING Yes. As an at-will employee, Herremans was free to quit his employment with Carrera at any time. Hence, his giving up that right in exchange for Carrera's promise of a bonus constituted consideration for that promise.

REASONING Carrera argued that since Herremans had intended to work for Carrera until his retirement, which would not occur within the next three years, Herremans had failed to give up anything of value when he had agreed to continue working. But consideration is a formal rather than a substantive requirement of the law of contracts. A promise is supported by consideration if it is formally conditioned

continued

11.1

HERREMANS V. CARRERA DESIGNS, INC., *continued*
157 F.3D 1118 (7TH CIR. 1998)

on a promise by the promisee, even if the promisor would have carried out the promised undertaking without a reciprocal promise. As Farnsworth's treatise on contracts notes, if X promises to go to work for Y, a successful investment advisor, at a salary of $40,000 a year, Y's reciprocal promise of that salary is enforceable without inquiry into whether X, who let us say is independently wealthy, would have agreed to work for Y without any pay at all, perhaps for the experience or because he likes Y. To allow promisors' motives to be dissected would disserve an important purpose of contract law—to minimize the occasions on which parties to contracts must submit themselves to the whims of juries. If Herremans had been contractually obligated to remain in Carrera's employ, in that event, the promise of the bonus in exchange for his agreeing to stay on would have been a modification of the contract unsupported by consideration and thus unenforceable. However, his contract was one of employment at will; he was free to quit at any time; and his giving up that right in exchange for the promise of a bonus was consideration for that promise, even if, as in the earlier Farnsworth example, he would have stayed on anyway.

BUSINESS CONSIDERATION Assume Carrera Designs, Inc., has asked you to modify its contractual language so that in the future it can avoid litigation of the type it had with Herremans. What additions, deletions, or modifications will you make?

ETHICAL CONSIDERATIONS Ethically speaking, should Carreras have denied Herremans's bonuses? Should Herremans, as a terminated employee (assuming he had deserved to be fired), have accepted them?

Consideration as a Promise to Act or to Forbear

Both the *Herremans* case and the earlier hypothetical bargain evince the formation of a unilateral contract. The analysis will be the same, however, if you *promise* to earn straight A's in exchange for your parents' *promise* to send you to Europe. In this situation, a bilateral contract is created, with the respective promises constituting the consideration to support the agreement, as long as the promises are genuine and not illusory.

Take this example one step further. For instance, if your parents breach this contract and you want to sue them, they may bargain with you about dropping the lawsuit. If they promise to pay you $1,000 in exchange for your promise to forgo legal action, you will have made another enforceable contract. Why? A promise to act or to forbear from a certain action, bargained for and given in exchange for another promise, constitutes consideration. Therefore, you should be able to convince a court to force your parents to pay, should they refuse to do so.

Adequacy of Consideration

Will your parents win in the earlier example if they argue that the $10,000 they will spend on your trip to Europe is too much, or that you really are doing nothing—because becoming an honor student is insufficient to constitute a detriment to you—to secure your side of the bargain? Usually not, because courts generally are unreceptive to such arguments. The classic rule states that courts will not inquire into the adequacy of the consideration. Courts instead will assume that the parties themselves remain the best judges of how much their bargain is worth and whether their performances are substantially equivalent. In other words, courts ordinarily will not second-guess the parties after the fact. *Brooksbank* v. *Anderson* illustrates this important principle.

11.2

BROOKSBANK V. ANDERSON
586 N.W.2D 789 (MINN. APP. 1998)

FACTS In 1984, Harlan Anderson and James Brooksbank formed a corporation, Total Mix Ration, Inc., for the purpose of developing, producing, and marketing a device for mixing feed for farm animals. Each owned one-half of the outstanding shares. The parties signed two shareholder agreements between 1994 and 1996. On 30 April 1996, Anderson and Brooksbank signed a new shareholder agreement that superseded all prior agreements. This 1996 agreement stated that Anderson would personally guarantee the repayment of fifty percent of the amount of the loans ($173,739.90) incurred in connection with the Phase 1 and Phase 2 loans obtained in 1994 and 1995. In the 1996 agreement, Anderson and Brooksbank also promised to contribute equal amounts of loans to the corporation, but neither guaranteed any of these loans. Moreover, the agreement obligated both men to make an additional loan in the amount of $33,000 each should Phase 3 of the development of the corporation occur. The agreement further obligated each to make other loans from time to time as needed. After signing the 1996 agreement, Anderson and Brooksbank issued a loan to the corporation in the amount of $6,000 each. Nothing in the agreement or on the checks indicated the purpose of these loans, but the letter sent with a later shareholder agreement signed only by Brooksbank and mailed to Anderson described the $6,000 amounts as loans for Phase 3. Less than three months after the execution of the 1996 agreement, Brooksbank notified Anderson that he (Brooksbank) was recalling the $173,739.90 note relating to the loans and that Anderson's share under the note was $86,869.95. Two months later, Brooksbank filed a lawsuit to recover the $86,869.95 allegedly owed under Anderson's personal guarantee. Anderson claimed the guarantee was unenforceable because he had given no consideration for the 1996 agreement.

ISSUE Did Brooksbank, by promising in the 1996 agreement to advance an additional $33,000 in unguaranteed loans to the corporation and through his commitment to contribute unguaranteed loans to the corporation in amounts equal to those to be made by Anderson, provide sufficient consideration to make the 1996 agreement unenforceable?

HOLDING No. Nothing in the 1996 agreement created new or different obligations on Brooksbank's part. Because this agreement merely contained obligations set out in the prior agreements, consideration was lacking.

REASONING Determining whether sufficient consideration exists for an agreement is a question of law. Minnesota follows the long-standing contract principle that a court will not examine the adequacy of consideration as long as something of value has passed between the parties. However, one must distinguish the adequacy of consideration from the existence of consideration. The issue of whether consideration truly exists is not one of mere formalism; something of value must be given in return for performance or a promise of performance. Brooksbank argued that the consideration for the 1996 agreement consisted of: (1) his commitment to lend at least $33,000 more to the corporation; (2) the loan of $6,000 at the time of the execution of the 1996 agreement; and (3) his forbearance on the guarantees and notes earlier signed by Anderson. In the 1996 agreement, the parties promised that they each would loan $33,000 to the corporation if they made a decision to proceed to Phase 3. While the 1994 agreement had said each would contribute $32,000, in exchange for stock, should Phase 3 occur, the difference between the amounts to be loaned was irrelevant and insignificant, particularly when one evaluates this issue in light of Brooksbank's decision to terminate the 1996 agreement less than three months after executing it. Second, the 1996 agreement was entirely silent concerning the two $6,000 loans made to the corporation by the shareholders. Brooksbank initially, in a writing sent to Anderson, characterized the $6,000 payment as a Phase 3 expense. He later argued at trial that this payment was consideration for the 1996 agreement. Because the record was devoid of any evidence

continued

11.2

BROOKSBANK V. ANDERSON, *continued*

586 N.W.2D 789 (MINN. APP. 1998)

characterizing the loan, the loan could not constitute consideration. Third, while it is correct that a creditor's agreement to forbear from collecting on a note can constitute consideration for a third party's guarantee, if no time for forbearance is specified, a reasonable period of time is implied. Here, Brooksbank waited less than three months. Considering that at the time of the 1996 agreement, the parties disagreed as to whether a marketable product even existed, the shareholders unquestionably were some significant period of time away from realizing any revenue. Hence, forbearance of less than eighty days was not sufficient to constitute consideration. Finally, the 1996 agreement did not expressly require the parties to make additional loans to the corporation. It stated that the additional funds advanced would be loans; but in the absence of any enforceable promise to make additional loans, no consideration existed. Thus, since Brooksbank gave no consideration for the 1996 agreement, the lower court's decision in his favor warranted reversal.

BUSINESS CONSIDERATIONS Should Brooksbank have given Anderson more time, or was Brooksbank justified in suing a mere 80 days after the execution of the 1996 agreement? Would you need more information before you could answer this question?

ETHICAL CONSIDERATIONS Is it ethical for a corporation to leave itself thinly financed and then rely on the limited liability aspects of this form of business organization to protect its interests if a third party sues it? Do small businesses face greater or lesser ethical challenges than large companies do?

Exceptions to the general rule that courts will not inquire into the adequacy of the consideration do exist, however. If a court finds evidence of fraud, duress, undue influence, mistake, or other similar situations at the time of contract formation, adequacy of consideration becomes a much more significant issue. Courts in these situations may permit one or more of the litigants to back out of the deal. The doctrine of unconscionability under either the common law or the Uniform Commercial Code (see § 2-302 of the UCC, which holds that a court may refuse to enforce a contract if it is shockingly unfair or oppressive) in some circumstances also can form a further basis for overturning bargains when the consideration appears to be grossly inadequate. But remember that courts do not routinely use this rationale to overturn bargaining between parties.

CONSIDERATION IN SPECIAL CONTEXTS

Contracts for the Sale of Goods

As explained in Chapter 9, the "firm offer" provision of the Uniform Commercial Code (§ 2-205) states that an offer to buy or sell goods by a merchant who gives assurance in writing that the offer will be held open may be irrevocable for a period of up to three months even if no consideration has been paid to the offeror. Intended to encourage commercial activity that is free from hagglings about "options," this provision dramatically changes the common law rules concerning consideration. Thus, even in the absence of consideration, courts will enforce a UCC firm offer. The same is true of modifications under the UCC: They too are enforceable without consideration (§ 2-209(1)). In contrast, the common law would require consideration in both situations.

In this context, recall again output and requirements contracts, two types of sales contracts mentioned earlier in Chapter 10. Unless the language of these contracts indicates otherwise, courts ordinarily enforce output and requirements contracts as contracts supported by consideration. These courts reason that consideration is present in the form of the respective detriments suffered by the buyer and seller when they obligate themselves to deal exclusively with the other party in these circumstances. The promises undergirding such contracts, then, are nonillusory and make the bargains enforceable.

Suretyship Contracts

Although the UCC has relaxed the requirement of consideration in some situations, the common law definitely requires consideration in suretyship contracts. Such contracts always involve three parties: a principal debtor, a creditor, and a surety. The surety agrees to be liable to the creditor in the event of the principal debtor's **default.** This occurs in a typical commercial transaction. To illustrate, assume that Chan Wai (the principal debtor) wishes to buy a new car. She may seek financing from a credit union (the creditor), which in turn may require that she bolster her credit (and decrease its risk) by having another person (such as her father or mother) sign the note as a surety. In so doing, the surety agrees to be primarily liable on the debt; the credit union can sue the surety once Chan Wai defaults. The lender does not have to sue Chan Wai first as a prerequisite to seeking payment from the surety.

If the principal debtor and surety simultaneously promise to pay the promissory note, a single consideration (the loan of money to Chan Wai by the credit union) will support these promises. Given the presence of consideration, both promises will be enforceable. If, in contrast, the credit union lends the money for the car to Chan Wai and later asks a surety to promise to pay in the event of her default, this second promise must be supported by new consideration before the surety's promise is legally binding. As will be discussed in the "Past Consideration" section of this chapter, Chan Wai's preexisting obligation to the credit union (because the loan already has been made) does not constitute consideration for enforcing the surety's subsequent promise to pay the credit union.

Liquidated Debts

If one owes a debt to another person, partial payment of that debt is not consideration for full discharge of the debt. For instance, assume Jim Hays has his dentist perform a root canal treatment on him. At the outset, the dentist tells Jim the treatment will cost $190, and Jim agrees that this is a fair price. If Jim pays $150, he cannot successfully argue that this part payment is consideration for full discharge of the debt. Put in legal terms, the dentist will be able to argue that Jim is under a

ACQUIRING FINANCING FOR CIT

The Kochanowskis are considering a number of options to acquire financing for the firm as it grows. Tom recently has discussed acquiring a line of credit for CIT from a local commercial bank. The bank officer with whom Tom has dealt has informed Tom that CIT at this time does not have an adequate history to justify a significant line of credit. The officer does point out, however, that the bank may be willing to grant the firm a line of credit if the firm has a *surety* who is willing to join the firm in its application. Tom remains unsure of exactly what a suretyship arrangement entails. He therefore has asked you what a surety is and whether the firm should seek such an arrangement. What will you tell him?

BUSINESS CONSIDERATIONS When should a business be willing to enter into a suretyship arrangement? When should an officer of a business be willing to serve as a surety for the firm?

ETHICAL CONSIDERATIONS Is it ethical for a lender to require the officers of a small business to serve as sureties for the firm? Would your answer be different if the business were a partnership or proprietorship rather than a corporation? Why?

Default
A failure to do what should be done, especially in the performance of a contractual obligation, without legal excuse or justification for the nonperformance.

Bankruptcy
An area of law designed to give an "honest debtor" a fresh start; the proceedings undertaken against a person or a firm under the bankruptcy laws.

preexisting duty to pay the entire $190. Since neither party has waived any rights nor has either engaged in any bargaining in exchange for this promise to pay $150, there is, by definition, an absence of consideration here. Hence, by the settled rule, Jim is liable for the entire bill, or $190. It is crucial to note that the debt is *liquidated;* that is, the amount owed is not disputed. Jim has agreed to pay $190, and he should not, after the fact, be allowed to escape this obligation. Such a legal result would throw commercial dealings into shambles!

Unliquidated Debts

Now let us assume that the debt is not liquidated. Suppose that Jim initially has agreed to pay $190 for the root canal treatment. However, after the dentist treats him, Jim continues to have soreness around the gums, and the treated tooth still is sensitive to thermal changes. Although Jim wants to live up to his obligation to pay his debt, he does not believe he should pay the dentist the entire amount because he remains dissatisfied with the results of the treatment. At the point Jim expresses these objections to the dentist, the debt is unliquidated; that is, the precise amount owed is in dispute. If Jim in these circumstances sends the dentist a check for $150— particularly if he in some fashion indicates that this amount represents full payment for his entire indebtedness—the dentist should understand that cashing Jim's check permits Jim to argue that he owes her nothing more. Her act of cashing the check shows that she impliedly has agreed to accept $150 as full payment of the debt. Thus, she is subject to the common law rule that payment toward an unliquidated debt that is intended as and accepted as full payment is consideration for full discharge of the debt.

Instead, if the dentist wishes both to collect the entire $190 she alleges Jim owes and to protect her rights fully, she should not cash Jim's check for $150. Rather, she should return it to Jim with a note stating that she is not agreeing to accept the tendered amount as full payment of the debt. If she is strapped for cash, she may be able to cash the check and try to preserve her rights against Jim by endorsing it "with full reservation of all rights." Ideally, to avoid the application of the rule that partial payment of an unliquidated debt that is accepted (expressly or impliedly) as full payment of the debt is consideration for a full discharge of that debt, she should refrain from cashing the check.

Alternatively, Jim and the dentist may negotiate and ultimately agree that $150 is the amount owed. In this case, each receives a benefit—Jim, by paying $40 less than he thought he would have to pay; the dentist, by getting most of the $190; and each suffers a detriment—Jim, by believing $150 is still too much; the dentist, by thinking she has lost $40—as a result of the bargained-for promise to pay. This notion of an exchange of rights is a hallmark of consideration.

One last note is appropriate. When Jim and the dentist agree on the $150 sum, technically there is a compromise (of the unliquidated debt) that subsequently has led to a satisfaction and an accord. A *compromise* is the settlement of a disputed claim by the mutual agreement of the parties. The agreement as to the amount is an *accord,* and the fulfillment of the agreement (the actual payment of the agreed-upon amount) is a *satisfaction.*

Composition Agreements

Unliquidated debt situations form the basis for a court's enforcement of a composition agreement, or an agreement between a debtor and a group of creditors to accept a smaller percentage of the debt owed in full satisfaction of the claim, as consideration for full discharge of the debt. Even though you will not study **bankruptcy** until Chapters 29 and 30, you probably are aware that the bankruptcy of the debtor poses grave financial risks for the creditor, because in bankruptcy proceedings a creditor ordinarily realizes only a few cents on every dollar owed. Consequently, it often is in the creditor's best interest to give the debtor more time to pay (before the creditor forces the debtor into bankruptcy) or to agree with other creditors to accept smaller sums in full cancellation of larger claims through a composition agreement.

For example, suppose Doug (the debtor) owes Ann, Bill, and Cara (the creditors) $6,000, $4,000, and $2,000, respectively. The creditors each may agree to accept 50 percent of the respective debts as full satisfaction of their claims against Doug. Thus, if Doug pays Ann $3,000, Bill $2,000, and Cara $1,000, none of the three will be able to sue for the remaining amount. Courts analogize the result here to a settlement of an unliquidated debt situation, in which the resultant compromise between the debtor and a creditor represents a satisfaction and accord for the debts. Similarly, in composition agreements, those agreed to by the debtor and a group of creditors, payments accepted by the creditors are supported by consideration and thus constitute full discharge of the debts.

Some courts instead will characterize the sums owed to Ann, Bill, and Cara as liquidated debts and will find insufficient consideration in the subsequent agreement to justify full discharge of the debts. Ironically, these same courts in the next breath may sanction such agreements on public policy grounds (the debtor's avoidance of bankruptcy and the creditors' realization of partial payment). Whatever the rationale, courts clearly favor composition agreements and therefore enforce them.

ABSENCE OF CONSIDERATION

Under certain circumstances, courts will find a total absence of consideration and will not enforce the agreement that the parties have shaped.

Illusory Promises

You will recall that promises that do not bind the promisor to a commitment are illusory promises. Such promises can be performed without any benefit to the promisor or without any detriment to the promisee and hence are not supported by consideration. A promise "to order such goods as we may wish" or "as we may want from time to time" is not a genuine promise at all; it only appears to set up

11.2 | FINANCE/ MANAGEMENT

ARRANGING CREDIT TERMS

CIT recently made a large sale to a retail establishment. The purchaser arranged credit terms with CIT and agreed to pay for the purchase over the next 24 months. Shortly after making this purchase, the customer encountered some serious short-term financial difficulties. As a result, it has fallen behind in its payments to CIT and now faces the possibility of being forced into bankruptcy. The customer is convinced that it can weather these problems and shortly can become a profitable and viable business entity again, *if* it can find a way to meet its short-term financial problems without resorting to bankruptcy. The customer has asked CIT to agree to accept smaller monthly payments spread over the next 36 months. The company's president states that his company has proposed similar arrangements with several of its other creditors. The family members ask you what they should do under these circumstances. What will you say? What is the legal significance of agreeing to the customer's proposal?

BUSINESS CONSIDERATIONS Should a business that regularly sells on credit to its customers establish a policy for handling situations in which its customers encounter financial problems, or should a firm handle each case individually as the situation arises? What are the benefits and the drawbacks to each approach?

ETHICAL CONSIDERATIONS Is it ethical for a firm, after granting credit to its customers, to adopt a hard-line approach when any of the customers encounter difficulties? Is it ethical for a credit customer to threaten to resort to bankruptcy relief if the other party (i.e., the creditor) balks at allowing the refinancing of the credit arrangement?

YOU BE THE JUDGE

IS THIS PROMISE ENFORCEABLE?

In 1985, Meril Joseph, an attorney, and Christine Oms, a sales director for a real estate company, began living together as a couple. During the next eight years, the couple jointly acquired assets, including a co-op apartment in Manhattan and property in East Hampton, Long Island. In 1993, Joseph's employer asked her to relocate to Atlanta. Thereupon, the couple discussed an arrangement under which Oms would give up her career as sales director, move with Joseph to Atlanta, and handle the couple's domestic arrangements. In October 1993, Oms memorialized the proposed arrangement in a dictated letter that read: "Because you are leaving your job and moving with me to Atlanta next month, I want to ensure [sic] you that should anything occur between the two of us to split us apart that you and I are to divide our assets 50/50 to reflect the partnership that we share and the life we built together." Joseph later signed this written letter. On moving to Atlanta, the couple purchased a home as joint tenants with rights of survivorship. Two years later, Joseph ended the relationship. Oms then filed a lawsuit seeking the equal division of assets spelled out in the October 1993 letter. In rebuttal, Joseph argued that no enforceable contract existed owing to the absence of any consideration. Put differently, Joseph claimed that Oms already had decided to move to Atlanta and would have relocated for her own reasons, whether or not Joseph would have made the offer memorialized in the letter.

Should a court agree that the letter was unenforceable because it did not obligate Oms to move to Atlanta and instead merely set forth a gratuitous promise by Joseph?[1]

BUSINESS CONSIDERATIONS Same-sex domestic relationships have become more prevalent in recent years. Should the law obligate Joseph's and Oms's employers to offer the two women the same benefit packages (insurance coverage, pension rights, etc.) that the employers would have offered to married heterosexual couples? Would such a result be advisable on public policy grounds? Why or why not?

ETHICAL CONSIDERATIONS Is it ethical to treat same-sex domestic partners differently from married couples? Should attorneys such as Joseph be held to higher ethical standards even when their conduct involves a mixture of personal and business matters? Fully support your views as to both issues.

SOURCE: Bruce Balestier, *The New York Law Journal* (19 May 1999), pp. 1, 7.

a binding commitment. Instead, it actually allows the promisor to order nothing. Such "will, wish, or want contracts," as they often are called, are void because they lack consideration.

Cancellation
Any action shown on the face of a contract that indicates an intent to destroy the obligation of the contract.

Contracts that purport to reserve an immediate right of arbitrary **cancellation** fall into this category of contracts as well. Because of the potential unfairness of allowing one side, by merely giving notice of cancellation, to free itself from an agreement to which the other side considers itself bound, courts are hostile to attempted exercises of a right of arbitrary cancellation. Courts therefore try to find some actual or implied limitations on the purported immediate right of arbitrary cancellation so as to make it a nonillusory, or binding, promise. Since consideration will exist for such promises, the agreement will be enforceable.

Preexisting Duty

If one performs or refrains from performing an act that one has a preexisting obligation to do or to refrain from doing, settled law holds that such a person has suffered no detriment. Consequently, no consideration is present to support the underlying promise or performance.

This principle often manifests itself in cases involving law enforcement officers. Assume you live next door to a policewoman, and she approaches you with this proposition: For $50 she will patrol around your house when you are gone on a trip. Since this sounds like a good deal to you, you agree. But you have second thoughts later and do not pay her. When she sues you in small claims court, she probably will lose because she has a preexisting duty (imposed by law) to try to keep your home free from burglaries. In patrolling around your house, she has suffered no detriment, so consideration to support her promise to you is lacking.

Besides obligations or duties imposed by law, preexisting duties may stem from contractual agreements. Numerous cases address these situations. For example, suppose G & H Painting Service has contracted with you to paint your basement for $900. Halfway through the job, the crew boss tells you he will dismiss the crew unless you agree to pay him $200 more (he has just seen the latest consumer price index and knows inflation is winning against him). Because you are having a party in two days, you grudgingly say yes. On completion of the job, do you have to pay $900 or $1,100? Based on the doctrine of preexisting obligations, you generally will have to pay only $900, since the firm already owes you the duty of finishing the basement. But if you subsequently want G & H to lay a concrete patio for you, your promise to pay $500 in return for G & H's work on the patio is supported by new consideration—G & H has not obligated itself to construct the patio as part of the original agreement—and you must pay $500 more for this additional work.

To return to the earlier example, assume now that in the middle of winter a freakish humid spell causes a paint-resistant fungus to grow in your basement. As a result, G & H has to paint the walls three times to cover them. If this blight arises after the firm begins the work, most courts will characterize it as an unforeseen or unforeseeable difficulty and will order you to pay the higher price. The same will hold true if you and the firm had canceled the original contract and had started anew with different promises and obligations. In both situations, consideration will support the new promises. Under the common law, strikes, inflation in the prices of raw materials, and lack of access to raw materials do not

11.3 | FINANCE/ MANAGEMENT

CANCELLATION PROVISIONS AND PRICE INCREASES

Assume that CIT receives an order acknowledgment form from High-Tech for an order placed by High-Tech over the phone. In checking the order acknowledgment form it has received from High-Tech, CIT discovers that High-Tech has included a number of terms and conditions that the two companies never discussed. One of these additional terms says that High-Tech reserves the right to cancel its resultant contract with CIT for any reason and at any time. What legal problems—if any—does this language potentially present for CIT?

Suppose that one of CIT's subcontractors calls with the news that the price of copper has risen dramatically owing to a strike by copper miners and that it therefore must raise its prices to CIT by $2,000 per ton. If CIT has a contract with the subcontractor for a substantially lower per-ton price, is CIT obligated to pay this higher amount? Why or why not?

BUSINESS CONSIDERATION The order acknowledgment form that High-Tech sent to CIT here included proposed additional terms to the contract between the parties. Very commonly when businesses conduct their negotiations over long distances, they do so by exchanging forms. Should a business have a policy of always reading the forms sent by the other party and of objecting to any terms in the form that are different from the terms the recipient thought the contract included?

ETHICAL CONSIDERATIONS Is it ethical to put new terms in the written confirmation of the contractual agreement? Does it matter if the proposed additional terms favor the party who sent the writing, favor the party to whom the writing was sent, or are neutral?

meet the test of "unforeseen or unforeseeable difficulties." Accordingly, new promises extracted on these bases ordinarily will lack consideration and thus be unenforceable.

Moral Consideration

Remember that harsh outcomes sometimes result from the application of the doctrine of consideration. Promises made from a so-called moral obligation embody one such subcategory of consideration and ordinarily are not enforced. In general, courts adhere strictly to the requirement of consideration in these contexts.

For example, suppose your child has been saved without injury from the jaws of a snarling Doberman pinscher because of the efforts of a passerby. The person who saved your child unfortunately suffers deep cuts that eventually require cosmetic surgery. Faced with such generosity, who among us will not promise this person the world? You are only human, so you offer to pay this Good Samaritan's lost wages while she is in the hospital. As time passes, though, you grow less willing to pay, and finally you cease paying her altogether. If she sues you, you usually will win because a court will conclude that she has bestowed a gift on you—that is, saving your child. Consequently, no consideration was present. Note, too, that prior to the humanitarian gesture, no bargaining in exchange for your promise to pay occurred. You may not think this particular result under this doctrine is harsh. Another disinterested party might, however, and may question your ethics here as well. Therefore, in a few jurisdictions, courts will reject the settled rule and hold that the passerby is entitled to win. Remember, though, that this position is taken by a minority of courts.

Past Consideration

Related to this doctrine of moral consideration is the doctrine of past consideration. This issue typically arises when a person retires and the company offers the former employee a small stipend "in consideration of 25 years of faithful service." Since the old services are executed (completed or finished), they cannot form the basis for a new promise. The same is true of a promise to pay a relative based on the promisor's "love and affection" for the promisee. Notice that, in both cases, neither bargaining nor an exchange of anything of value has occurred. Neither of the promises is supported by consideration, and neither will be enforceable. In short, as traditional legal authority holds, "Past consideration is no consideration."

In disposing of the following case, the court resorted to many of the concepts covered in this chapter.

11.3

CARLISLE V. T&R EXCAVATING, INC.
704 N.E.2D 39 (OHIO APP. 9 DIST. 1997)

FACTS Thomas Carlisle owned and operated T&R Excavating, Inc. (T&R). Janis Carlisle was the owner and director of Wishing Well, Inc. Ms. Carlisle and Mr. Carlisle married in 1988. Shortly afterward, she began doing all the bookkeeping for T&R, including organizing and modernizing its bookkeeping system. Mr. Carlisle allegedly offered to pay her for her work, but she refused to accept any salary. During 1992, Ms. Carlisle decided to build a preschool and kindergarten facility. Mr. Carlisle helped her find a location

11.3

CARLISLE V. T&R EXCAVATING, INC., *continued*
704 N.E.2D 39 (OHIO APP. 9 DIST. 1997)

for the preschool and choose a general contractor for the construction of the preschool. In September 1992, Ms. Carlisle signed a proposal in which T&R agreed to do all the excavation work for the facility at no cost, provided the preschool paid T&R's expenses. In December 1992, in anticipation of a divorce, the Carlisles prepared a document in which, to repay Ms. Carlisle for her secretarial and computer services to T&R, Mr. Carlisle agreed to fulfill the terms of the 1992 proposal. Sometime during early 1993, T&R began performing the excavation and site work for the preschool. According to Mr. Carlisle's testimony, Ms. Carlisle stopped providing bookkeeping or secretarial services to T&R after January 1993. The couple separated during March 1993, but T&R continued working on the project until late May or early June 1993. By that time, Wishing Well, Inc., had paid approximately $35,000 for the materials used by T&R for the excavation and site work. However, Ms. Carlisle ultimately hired other workers to finish the excavation and site work. After the preschool opened for business on 28 August 1993, one week later than originally planned, Ms. Carlisle sued T&R for breach of contract. The lawsuit requested damages equal to the amount it had cost to have others finish the excavation and site work, as well as the amount lost owing to delays allegedly attributable to T&R's failure to work during certain periods prior to T&R's final abandonment of the job. T&R, in turn, claimed that the agreement lacked consideration and that the scope of the work T&R had agreed to do was so uncertain that the meeting of the minds necessary for contract formation had never existed.

ISSUE Was the agreement between the parties supported by consideration?

HOLDING No. The absence of any consideration meant no contract between the parties existed.

REASONING A contract consists of an offer, an acceptance, and consideration. Without consideration, no contract can exist. Under Ohio law, consideration consists of either a benefit to the promisor or a detriment to the promisee. To constitute consideration, the benefit or detriment must be "bargained for." Something is bargained for if it is sought by the promisor in exchange for his or her promise and is given by the

promisee in exchange for that promise. The benefit or detriment does not need to be great. In fact, a benefit need not even be actual, as in the nature of a profit, or be as economically valuable as whatever the promisor promises in exchange for the benefit; it need only be something regarded by the promisor as beneficial enough to induce a promise. Generally, therefore, a court will not inquire into the adequacy of consideration once a court finds that consideration exists. Whether consideration exists at all, however, is a proper question for a court. Gratuitous promises are unenforceable as contracts, because of the absence of consideration. A written gratuitous promise, even if it evinces an intent by the promisor to be bound, is not a contract. Likewise, conditional gratuitous promises, which require the promisee to do something before the promised act or omission will take place, are not enforceable as contracts. Given these longstanding principles of contract law, the evidence in the record showed the absence of any benefit accruing to T&R or any detriment suffered by Ms. Carlisle owing to their agreement. Mr. Carlisle testified that he wanted to help Ms. Carlisle with the preschool and that they both agreed the preschool would be a good retirement benefit for them. However, a desire to help cannot constitute consideration for a contract; rather, it is merely a motive. Moreover, the possibility of sharing in the income from a spouse's business, which would be marital income, cannot be consideration for a contract because one is entitled to share in marital income. No bargaining is necessary to obtain that which one already has. Furthermore, the decision to build the preschool to provide income later was more akin to a joint effort by the Carlisles to obtain a single benefit together, rather than a bargained-for exchange. Ms. Carlisle testified that she understood the agreement to consist of T&R's promise to do excavation and site work for no charge and of her promise to pay T&R's expenses. This promise of reimbursement for out-of-pocket costs, standing alone, was not a benefit or detriment supporting a contract. Money changed hands, but the reimbursement was not a bargained-for benefit to the promisor or a detriment to the promisee. No reasonable interpretation of Ms. Carlisle's testimony could support a conclusion that T&R had promised to provide the free services in order to induce her to promise to reimburse it for

continued

11.3

CARLISLE V. T&R EXCAVATING, INC., *continued*
704 N.E.2D 39 (OHIO APP. 9 DIST. 1997)

materials only. Rather, the testimony suggested a gratuitous promise by T&R to provide free services on the condition that Ms. Carlisle agree to reimburse it for the cost of the materials used in providing those services. Ms. Carlisle's testimony that Mr. Carlisle had told her, after she had refused payment for her bookkeeping services to T&R, that he would help her with her building failed to show any consideration, either. First, Ms. Carlisle did not argue that her secretarial services were consideration for T&R's promise. Second, if Mr. Carlisle made the statement after Ms. Carlisle had done the work for T&R, her services were "past consideration" and could not support a contract. The same would be true of the "separation agreement" signed by Mr. Carlisle and Ms. Carlisle during December 1992. In describing his promise to do the work as "repayment to Jan for her secretarial services and computer programming to T&R Excavating, Inc.," this agreement reflected only a gratuitous promise by Mr. Carlisle. Past consideration cannot be a bargained-for benefit or detriment, since it has already occurred or accrued. Hence, past consideration is not legally sufficient to support a contract. The theory of promissory estoppel, pursuant to which Ms. Carlisle might have tried to argue that she had reasonably relied to her detriment on T&R's promise, similarly was unavailable as a substitute for a showing of consideration. Nothing in the record

suggested that she would have refrained from building the preschool in the absence of the promise of free services by T&R. Moreover, the preschool had cost approximately $800,000 to build; and T&R's fulfilled promise would have saved Ms. Carlisle only about $35,000, or less than five percent of the building's cost. No basis for inferring that Ms. Carlisle had relied to her detriment on T&R's promise therefore existed. Since Ms. Carlisle had failed either to establish consideration for T&R's promise to do free excavation and site work for the preschool or reliance to her detriment on the promise, the promise was not legally enforceable.

BUSINESS CONSIDERATION The parties here, though married, tried to separate their business and marital interests—a laudable objective. In hindsight, what additional steps could they have undertaken to minimize the probability of litigation and thus fulfill their initial objective?

ETHICAL CONSIDERATION Is it ethical for one spouse to expect the other to do work of a business nature for a nominal fee? Fully support whichever position you take.

EXCEPTIONS TO THE BARGAINING THEORY OF CONSIDERATION

As you should now realize, whether or not the parties have bargained with a resulting exchange of value appears crucially important under the common law rules relating to consideration. Still, in the following four situations, courts will enforce agreements despite a lack of consideration: (1) promissory estoppel, (2) charitable subscriptions, (3) promises made after the statute of limitations has expired, and (4) promises to repay debts after a discharge in bankruptcy.

Promissory Estoppel

Promissory estoppel was discussed in Chapter 10 in the context of preventing an offeror's revocation of an offer. To recapitulate, courts apply this equitable doctrine in order to avoid injustice. Essentially, the elements are the same for consideration as for offers. In both, the promisor makes a definite promise that he or she expects, or should reasonably expect, will induce the plaintiff/promisee to act (or refrain from acting) in a manner that may be detrimental to the latter person. Accordingly, the law, to avoid injustice, holds the promisor to his or her promise. Simply put, the promisor is prevented from asserting a defense (here, that no consideration exists) normally available to the promisor.

Though unavailable in the *Carlisle* decision, promissory estoppel might apply in the case of an employer who offered to pay its employee "in consideration of 25 years of faithful service." The employee might use promissory estoppel as a substitute for consideration in order to win. In other words, if the employer in fact has paid the former employee $100 a month for 10 years, and the employee, owing to an expectation of continued stipends, has given up opportunities for part-time employment, some courts will conclude that the employer must continue the payments despite the absence of bargaining or of an exchange of anything of value.

Charitable Subscriptions

Likewise, promissory estoppel may help promisees win in the category of charitable subscriptions, which is another exception to the requirement of consideration. You probably can guess how this legal issue—the written promise to pay a certain sum to a nonprofit charity—arises.

Typically, a generous person wishes to donate a sizable amount to a worthy charity and promises to do so. Later, this humanitarian zeal wanes, and the person no longer wishes to live up to the written agreement. If you are the donor, what do you argue? In all likelihood, you will try to argue that you intended to bestow a gift. Since by definition a gift lacks consideration (there is neither bargaining nor an exchange of value), you will claim that you therefore can avoid liability for this promise.

Ordinarily, though, a would-be donor will have to live up to the agreement because charitable institutions rely on the belief that the amount pledged in written subscriptions will be forthcoming and because people make pledges based on the knowledge that other people will be making similar pledges. Courts, of course, believe that charitable institutions (like universities, hospitals, agencies, or churches) serve noble purposes. Thus, in addition to resorting to promissory estoppel as a substitute for consideration, courts alternatively may enforce the promise on public policy grounds. Again, the would-be donor needs to examine the ethical dimensions of his or her decision to renege on the promised charitable subscription.

Promises Made After the Expiration of the Statute of Limitations

State statutes of limitations set time limits on when creditors can bring suit against debtors for the sums owed to the creditors. Ordinarily, this period is from two to six years, after which the creditor cannot maintain suit against the debtor. Sometimes the debtor wants to repay the debt even if this time limit has passed. As you already have learned, there seems to be no consideration present in such a circumstance; there is an absence of any bargaining, and the debtor's promise arguably represents moral consideration at best.

Yet under most state statutes and decisions, the law will enforce the debtor's new promise to pay if it is in writing. The public policy of encouraging people to pay their debts generally forms the basis for this exception to the bargaining theory of consideration.

Promises to Pay Debts Covered by Bankruptcy Discharges

The same policy applies and the result is similar when a debtor promises to pay a debt covered by a discharge in bankruptcy. Again, no consideration underlies this new promise, but most states will allow the enforcement of the promise, provided that the debtor makes the promise to pay in full compliance with the reaffirmation provisions of the Bankruptcy Act and with a full understanding of the significance of this promise, as required by the Bankruptcy Code. Exhibit 11.1 offers a summary of many of the principles associated with consideration.

SUMMARY

Consideration is a firmly entrenched doctrine in modern law. Consideration consists of any waiver or promised waiver of rights bargained for in exchange for a promise. Consideration exists when there is a benefit to the promisor or a detriment to the promisee bargained for and given in exchange for a promise. In unilateral contracts, consideration may take the form of an act or a forbearance to act. In bilateral contracts, the respective promises constitute consideration. In the absence of fraud, duress, undue influence, or unconscionability, courts generally will not inquire into the adequacy of the consideration. Although no consideration

---

E X H I B I T 11.1 | **Consideration: A Summary**

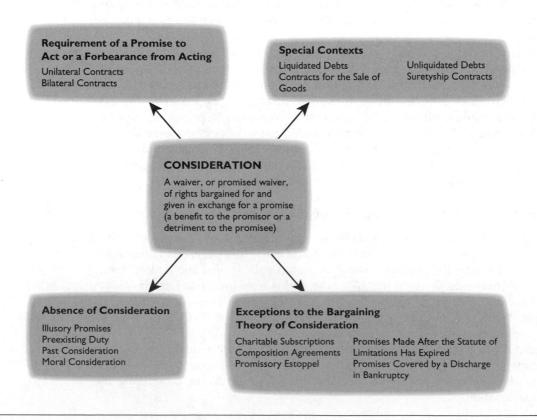

RESOURCES FOR BUSINESS LAW STUDENTS

NAME	RESOURCES	WEB ADDRESS
Legal Information Institute (LII)— Contract Law Materials	The LII provides an overview of contract law; links to federal government statutes, treaties, and regulations; federal and state judicial decisions regarding contract law (including Supreme Court decisions); state statutes; and other materials.	**http://wwwsecure.law.cornell.edu/topics/contracts. html**
The American Law Institute (ALI)	ALI, publisher of *Restatements of the Law*, Model Codes, and other proposals for law reform, provides press releases, its newsletter, and other publications.	**http://www.ali.org**

is necessary under the UCC provisions relating to firm offers and modifications of sales contracts, consideration is necessary to hold a surety liable.

The doctrine of preexisting obligations mandates that one pay a liquidated debt in full; part payment is not consideration for full discharge of the debt. In contrast, part payment of an unliquidated debt, if accepted as full payment, represents a compromise of the debt and is supported by consideration. Such a satisfaction and an accord completely cancel the debt. The same rationale validates composition agreements between the debtor and a group of creditors.

Agreements based on illusory promises or promises grounded in either preexisting legal duties or preexisting contractual relationships lack consideration. The same is true of promises founded on moral obligations and on past consideration. The four exceptions to the bargaining theory of consideration are (1) promissory estoppel, (2) charitable subscriptions, (3) promises to repay made after the statute of limitations has expired, and (4) promises to repay debts covered by discharges in bankruptcy. Courts will give effect to agreements without consideration in these situations.

DISCUSSION QUESTIONS

1. Define *consideration*.
2. Can "doing nothing" ever suffice as consideration to support a promise?
3. Why do courts refuse to inquire into the adequacy of consideration?
4. Why does the UCC dispense with requiring consideration in situations involving "firm offers" and modifications?
5. Explain why part payment of a liquidated debt is not consideration for full discharge of the debt, but part payment accepted as full payment for an unliquidated debt is.

6. Define the following: a *compromise*, an *accord*, and a *satisfaction*.
7. Discuss why an illusory promise can never constitute consideration.
8. Why does it make sense to say that performing a preexisting duty does not constitute consideration?
9. Why does the law generally refuse to recognize moral and past "consideration" as sufficient to support an agreement between two or more parties?
10. Explain the four situations in which courts will enforce agreements despite a lack of bargaining (and hence consideration).

CASE PROBLEMS AND WRITING ASSIGNMENTS

1. Jackie Mohr worked as a secretary for Arachnid, Inc. (Arachnid). On 13 February 1989, Mohr and Arachnid entered into a written agreement for the payment of six months' severance pay if Mohr's employment should cease as a result of a significant change in the ownership of the firm's stock. The agreement was to be effective only if such termination occurred within one year of the date of the agreement. On 24 February 1989, owing to a shareholder buyout, the ownership of the company changed significantly. Mohr consequently was notified on 12 April 1989 that her employment would terminate. At that time, Arachnid paid Mohr two weeks' severance pay. When Mohr sued for breach of contract, Arachnid argued that the agreement was void and unenforceable because Mohr had provided no consideration. Did Mohr's continuing to work for Arachnid constitute consideration sufficient to support an express agreement to pay severance wages? [See *Mohr* v. *Arachnid, Inc.*, 559 N.E.2d 1098 (Ill.App.2 Dist. 1990).]

2. Robert C. Apfel had sold a computerized system of trading municipal securities (the Apfel system) to Prudential-Bache Securities, Inc. (Prudential Bache), an investment bank. The Apfel system permitted bonds to be sold, traded, and held exclusively through computerized "book entries." Under the sale agreement, Apfel conveyed the rights to the techniques involved in the system in exchange for a stipulated rate based on actual usage from October 1982 to January 1988. The contract obligated Prudential-Bache to pay even if the techniques became public knowledge or standard industry practice and even if Apfel's patent and trademark applications were denied. Apfel agreed to keep the techniques, which had been disclosed only to Prudential-Bache, confidential until the information became public. From 1982 until 1985, Prudential-Bache implemented the contract, although the parties disputed whether Prudential-Bache had fully paid the amounts due. Prudential-Bache actively encouraged bond issuers to use the computerized "book entry" system and, for at least the first year, served as the sole underwriter in the industry employing such a system. In 1985, however, following a change in personnel, Prudential-Bache refused to make any further payments because of its belief that the ideas conveyed by Apfel had been in the public domain at the time of the sale agreement and that what Apfel had sold Prudential-Bache never actually had been its to sell. Moreover, by 1990 computerized systems handled 60 percent of the dollar volume of all new issues of municipal securities. Apfel sued, seeking $45 million in damages. As one of its numerous defenses, Prudential-Bache asserted that no contract ever existed between the parties because the sale agreement lacked consideration. Did the agreement lack consideration? [*Apfel* v. *Prudential-Bache Securities, Inc.*, 600 N.Y.S.2d 433 (Ct.App. 1993).]

3. James "Buster" Douglas and his manager, John P. Johnson, signed a boxing promotional agreement with Don King Productions, Inc. (DKP) for $25,000 on 31 December 1988. The agreement provided DKP with the "sole and exclusive right to secure and arrange all professional boxing bouts" for Douglas for the term of the agreement. The promotional agreement also set forth DKP's intention to promote a heavyweight championship bout involving Douglas, and it provided that the three-year term of the agreement automatically would be extended in the event that Douglas was recognized as world champion "to cover the entire period [Douglas was] world champion and a period of two years following." Pursuant to this promotional agreement, Douglas participated in three bouts arranged by DKP during the first year (ending 26 February 1990). The last of these involved the heavyweight championship bout held on 10 February 1990, in Tokyo, Japan, between Douglas and then-heavyweight champion Michael Tyson. Douglas won the bout and became the undisputed heavyweight champion of the world. Relations between Don King and the Douglas camp soured, however, when King, who also was Tyson's promoter, objected to the alleged "long count" that had occurred during the eighth round of the fight. Shortly after this championship bout, Douglas and Johnson executed a contract for Douglas, now the heavyweight champion, to fight two bouts at the Mirage Hotel for a minimum of $50 million. But the Mirage Hotel contracts would not become binding until Douglas and Johnson obtained a release from DKP of its allegedly exclusive promotional rights or, alternatively, a judicial declaration that the promotional and bout agreements (whereby Douglas would receive at least $1 million for each of the three bouts following the Tokyo bout) were void and unenforceable. In filing suit, Douglas and Johnson argued that the contractually specified million-dollar purse represented inadequate consideration because this figure amounted to a "mere token" of Douglas's value as the world heavyweight champion. Should a court accept these arguments in these circumstances? [See *Don King Productions., Inc.* v. *Douglas*, 742 F.Supp. 741 (S.D. N.Y. 1990).]

4. John P. S. Janda, a physician born in India, sued the Madera Community Hospital for the breach of his

employment contract allegedly occasioned by the hospital's decision to close its orthopedic department. Upon the closure of the department, the hospital had awarded an exclusive contract to the only Caucasian orthopedic surgeon on staff. Janda claimed that the closure thus was motivated by a racial animus that contravened the hospital's bylaws, which prohibit the denial of medical staff privileges on the basis of race, color, sex, religion, or national origin. Put differently, Janda argued that the bylaws form a contract between the hospital and its medical staff. In rebuttal, the hospital asserted that the bylaws do not create an enforceable contract because of the absence of a mutual exchange of consideration. Specifically, the hospital submitted that California statutes mandate a hospital's adoption of written bylaws concerning the organization and governance of the hospital and its medical staff and that, by statute, physicians have a legal duty to abide by the written bylaws adopted by the medical staff. Hence, the hospital maintained that because it had a preexisting legal duty to establish the bylaws and Dr. Janda had a preexisting legal duty to comply with them, no legally recognizable consideration ever passed between the parties. Would you agree that no contract existed between the parties? Why? [See *Janda* v. *Madera Community Hospital*, 16 F.Supp.2d 1181 (E.D. Cal. 1998).]

5. In the spring of 1991, Coulter & Smith, Ltd. (Coulter) and Dr. Roger Russell entered into a letter agreement whereby Coulter would develop Russell's property in conjunction with adjacent property it owned. Pursuant to their agreement, Coulter had the option to purchase the lots located on Russell's property after Coulter had completed the initial stages of the development of the subdivision. Among other things, Coulter stated in the letter agreement that it "would proceed posthaste to annex and develop our tracts jointly." The letter agreement, signed by Dr. Russell, gave Coulter a 10-year option to purchase lots. At the time of the execution of the letter agreement, Coulter and Russell also entered into a three-way work exchange agreement in which Coulter promised to make improvements in the master drain system for the benefit of Russell's property. Unfortunately, when the development did not proceed as expeditiously as planned, each party blamed the other for the delays. In 1994, after Russell had taken steps to sell the property to someone else, Coulter filed a lawsuit alleging breach of the option contract contained in the letter agreement. Russell claimed the option contract lacked consideration. Would you agree? [*Coulter & Smith, Ltd.* v. *Russell*, 966 P.2d 852 (Utah 1998).]

6. **BUSINESS APPLICATION CASE** Kenneth W. Morris and Mack S. Love were employees of Milner Airco, Inc. (Milner). After working for the company for several years, both Morris and Love were asked to sign employment contracts that contained a noncompete clause. Morris signed the contract on 21 January 1990, so he could become an account manager "when the economy improved." (Morris actually became an account manager on 1 April 1991, some 15 months later.) Love signed the agreement on 1 May 1991, shortly after he had received a demotion. Indeed, Love was told either to sign the document or leave the company. Milner explained that it was asking the employees to sign the documents so as to increase the employees' job security, to protect the company's investment in job training for its employees, and to prevent future competition from former employees. When Morris and Love began working for a competing company in October 1991, Milner petitioned the court to enforce the covenant not to compete provisions of the two men's employment contracts. Morris and Love argued that no consideration supported their signing of the covenants. How should the court rule in this case? Could the company have taken any steps that would have minimized Morris and Love's chances of prevailing in this litigation? Explain. [See *Milner Airco, Inc.* v. *Morris*, 433 S.E.2d 811 (N.C.App. 1993).]

7. **ETHICAL APPLICATION CASE** Ross-Simons of Warwick, Inc. (Ross-Simons), the plaintiff, is a substantial national retailer of items such as china and crystal. Ross-Simons ordinarily sells at prices below suggested retail prices, with discounts often reaching 50 percent. An important aspect of Ross-Simons's sale strategy is the development of a large bridal registry actively promoted by the firm. Each year the program attracts approximately 15,000 new registrants, business that is important to Ross-Simons because each new registration likely will result in multiple purchases on behalf of the registered couple. Baccarat, Inc. (Baccarat) is the U.S. subsidiary of Companie des Cristalleries de Baccarat and the exclusive U.S. distributor of the world-renowned French lead crystal. Prior to 1992, Baccarat had refused to sell crystal to Ross-Simons because of Baccarat's philosophy that luxury items such as Baccarat crystal were not appropriate for discounting. Furthermore, when Baccarat had become the exclusive distributor of Haviland Limoges china in 1991, it had terminated Ross-Simons's status as an authorized dealer of the china. As a result of Baccarat's decisions, Ross-Simons in 1992 filed an antitrust lawsuit against Baccarat. Prior to a court hearing of the antitrust suit on its merits, the parties entered into an "agreement of compromise

and settlement." The substance of the 1992 agreement was contained in section three, which enumerated the respective obligations of the parties under the settlement. According to these "mutual covenants," Ross-Simons agreed to dismiss its antitrust suit, that such dismissal would be without prejudice (i.e., Ross-Simons had not waived, or given up, its right to sue some time in the future), and that each party would bear its own costs and legal expenses. In exchange for this dismissal, Baccarat accepted several duties. First, Baccarat agreed to reinstate Ross-Simons as an authorized dealer of Haviland Limoges porcelain dinnerware and to appoint Ross-Simons as an authorized dealer of Baccarat crystal. For each line of goods, Baccarat promised that Ross-Simons would be "entitled to purchase and resell such products at such prices and upon such terms as are available to other authorized dealers." Second, Baccarat promised not to "terminate Ross-Simons's status as an authorized dealer, or otherwise discriminate against Ross-Simons in any manner" because of Ross-Simons's discount pricing policies. Baccarat further agreed not to discriminate against Ross-Simons's applications for authorization to sell at additional stores, but would "consider all applications . . . under the same standards generally applied to other authorized dealers." Following the execution of the 1992 agreement, the parties cordially maintained a sizable business relationship. Indeed, during this period, Ross-Simons grossed approximately $1 million annually in Baccarat crystal sales. The dynamics of that relationship changed, however, when Jean-Luc Negre assumed the presidency of Baccarat in 1994. Replacing Francois de Montmorin, the Baccarat president who had executed the 1992 agreement on Baccarat's behalf, Negre told Ross-Simons officials that he viewed discounting as an inappropriate method of selling luxury items like Baccarat crystal.

NOTE

1. Bruce Balestier, "A Letter Promise to Companion to Divide Assets Is Enforceable," *The New York Law Journal* (19 May 1999), pp. 1, 7.

Shortly thereafter, Baccarat refused to grant authorized dealer status to a new Ross-Simons store. A 1995 Baccarat-initiated, proposed agreement containing authorized dealership provisions inimical to Ross-Simons's discount pricing strategies resulted in Ross-Simons's filing a lawsuit alleging Baccarat's breach of the 1992 agreement. Baccarat countered by arguing that the 1992 agreement lacked consideration. To support its claims, Baccarat pointed out that while the agreement required Baccarat to deal with Ross-Simons without regard to the latter's discounting policies, the 1992 settlement had not required that Ross-Simons order any amount of products from Baccarat except that which Ross-Simons had chosen to order. Furthermore, Baccarat viewed Ross-Simons's dismissal of the antitrust suit as inadequate consideration because the parties had agreed that the dismissal would be without prejudice. Should a court agree with Baccarat's contentions? Did Negre behave ethically? Do different nationalities view ethics differently, or are ethics universal in application? [*Ross-Simons of Warwick, Inc.* v. *Baccarat, Inc.*, 182 F.R.D. 386 (D.R.I. 1998).]

8. **CRITICAL THINKING CASE** Assume that the owner of A-1 Motors (A-1) had hired a painter to paint the showroom for an agreed-on rate of $15 per hour plus materials. The painter finished the job and presented A-1 with a bill for $2,000. The owner of A-1 contended that the job was worth only $1,000. After protracted negotiations, the painter agreed to settle for $1,700. The owner then wrote a $1,700 check, on the back of which he wrote "payment in full." The painter cashed the check but subsequently sued A-1 in small claims court for $300. Who would win and why? [Case derived from materials developed for in-class discussions and hypothetical questions.]

12

CONTRACTUAL CAPACITY:
THE ABILITY TO AGREE AND REALITY OF CONSENT

A G E N D A

Tom has heard about "voidable contracts" but is unclear as to what this term means. He definitely wants to refrain from entering into any contracts that are voidable at the option of the other party. Lindsay thinks that a large market for the videophones potentially exists among well-to-do teenagers. She therefore thinks the firm should investigate this market. From both a professional and a legal perspective, Dan does not think the firm should target this youth-oriented market.

The Kochanowskis also will have to decide how to advertise and market the CIT videophones. Should they

use slick advertising that portrays the product as capable of doing more than it actually does? Will adopting this strategy have any effect on the contracts they enter? Can a firm be held responsible for misleading ads that may constitute misrepresentation and fraud? The family members also differ as to how "hard-line" an approach the firm should take in securing a contractual agreement.

These and other questions are likely to surface in this chapter. Be prepared! You never know when one of the Kochanowskis will need your help or advice.

O U T L I N E

LEGAL CAPACITY

Capacity, the fourth requirement for a valid contract, mandates that the parties to the contract have the legal ability to bind themselves to the agreement and to enforce any promises made to them. However, *incapacity,* or the lack of such capacity, is the exception, not the rule. Hence, the burden of proof regarding incapacity falls on the party raising it as a defense to the enforcement of the contract or as a basis for rescission of the contract.

To determine contractual capacity, the law looks at the relative bargaining power of the parties involved. Historically, older persons have taken care of the younger members of society. By allowing children under a certain age to disaffirm (or withdraw from) the contract, the law attempts to protect children, who remain less adept at bargaining, from overreaching by these more experienced bargainers. The same is true of persons who lack mental capacity, such as insane persons: Contracts made by these persons may be absolutely void, voidable (the insane person can disaffirm the contract), or even valid (if, e.g., contract formation occurs during a period of lucidity). Thus, the existence or absence of legal capacity and the consequences of proving incapacity depend heavily on the facts and on a given person's status.

Circumscribe
Limit the range of activity associated with something.

Indeed, the law often uses the status of a person as a basis for making legal distinctions and in fact may **circumscribe** the legal rights of any persons falling within these classifications. For this reason, many jurisdictions limit the contractual rights of minors, insane persons, intoxicated persons, aliens, and convicts. In earlier times, the common law, through statutes called Married Women's Property Acts, curtailed the contractual rights of married women. Most states have eliminated these legislative restrictions, but some vestiges of these acts remain in a few states. The extent of the legal disability placed on such classes of individuals comprises the focus of this section of the chapter.

MINORS

Most jurisdictions no longer follow the earlier common law rule that any person of either sex under 21 years of age is a minor (or an infant). Most states by statute have changed this rule to allow for achievement of majoritarian status (i.e., adult status) as early as age 18 for almost all purposes. (A common exception involves the purchase or consumption of alcoholic beverages.) Some states allow for termination of infancy status upon marriage or **emancipation.**

Emancipation
Freedom from the control or power of another; release from parental care; or the attainment of legal independence.

Disaffirmance/Rescission

To protect minors in their dealings with adults, the law allows minors to disaffirm (or avoid) their contracts with adults except in certain specialized cases, such as contracts involving necessaries (things that directly foster the minor's well-being). When the minor decides not to perform the legal obligations contemplated in the agreement and thus *disaffirms* the contract, this action results in a voidable contract. Stated differently, the minor has the option either of performing the contract or avoiding it. The converse is untrue: The adult who has contracted with a minor ordinarily will not be able to use the infancy of the minor to avoid the contract unless the minor allows the adult to disaffirm the contract. Simply put, do not contract with minors! Or, if you do, realize that the minor's powers in a given instance may be quite pervasive. Practically speaking, besides refusing to deal with minors, you can curtail their powers of avoidance by insisting that a parent or other adult co-sign the contract as well. In this fashion, you effectively will limit the minor's power of *rescission,* the ability to have the contract set aside. This is true because even if the minor disaffirms the contract, the adult cosigner still will remain liable on it.

Note how the court in the following case utilizes many of these principles.

Conservator
A person appointed by a court to manage the affairs of one who is incompetent.

Tortfeasor
One who commits a tort.

12.1

MITCHELL V. MITCHELL
963 S.W.2D 222 (KY.APP. 1998)

FACTS Sherri R. Mitchell sustained injuries on 14 October 1995, while she was a passenger in an automobile owned by her father, Donnie Fee, and operated by her husband, Michael J. Mitchell. On 26 October 1995, Sherri, who was seventeen, executed a release settling her bodily injury claim for $2,500. No **conservator** was appointed at the time of the execution of the release. Sometime later, Sherri filed a lawsuit seeking a determination that the settlement she had signed was null and void owing to her incapacity as a minor.

ISSUE Did Sherri, as a married minor, have the capacity to enter into a settlement agreement covering a personal injury situation?

HOLDING No. Parental emancipation frees the minor from parental control but does not preclude the minor's ability to disaffirm a contract owing to infancy.

REASONING The lower court had held that Sherri's marriage emancipated her, thereby removing any disability she had as a minor, including the capacity to contract. Kentucky statutes define a minor as anyone under the age of eighteen. Ordinarily, contracts executed by minors are enforceable by the minors; but the minors may avoid the contract if it is not affirmed after they reach adulthood. Put differently, although minors have the legal capacity to contract, they have the privilege of avoiding the contract. Although certain exceptions to this general rule exist (e.g., the minor's liability for necessaries), none applied to this case. Moreover, courts have held a settlement agreement and release of a third-party **tortfeasor** to be voidable by the infant. A repudiation of the agreement requires that the minor return the consideration paid pursuant to that agreement. The privilege bestowed on a minor to avoid contracts made during infancy is given for policy reasons. The law presumes

that infants, like the other classes of disabilities, lack sufficient maturity or experience to bargain effectively with those who have attained legal age. Accordingly, courts must scrutinize closely any transaction that may result in a financial loss to infants or in a depletion of their estates. Granted, the marriage of an infant emancipates the minor. But as Kentucky precedents hold, parental emancipation, while it may free the infant from parental control, does not remove all the disabilities of infancy. Emancipation does not, for example, enlarge or affect the minor's capacity or incapacity to contract. To some, it may seem ironic that a minor can drive a car yet not be bound by the contract to purchase that car or be responsible for his or her torts and crimes yet be unable to settle a dispute against a tortfeasor. The distinction hinges on the fact that all too frequently a contract involves negotiation and thought beyond the maturity of most people under the age of eighteen. Hence, Kentucky courts should not adopt a rule that marriage by the minor somehow classifies him or her as more mature and intelligent than his or her unmarried counterpart. Logic and common sense would not encourage such a result, since marriage by a minor often in itself might indicate a lack of wisdom and maturity. Kentucky statutes provide a means by which a court can appoint a conservator so as to protect the financial interests of a married minor. Although the lack of such appointment will not render the contract void, a minor, such as Sherri, remains free to avoid her obligations under the contract.

BUSINESS CONSIDERATIONS What could the insurance company have done differently here? What policies should the company establish as a consequence of this litigation?

continued

12.1

MITCHELL V. MITCHELL, *continued*

963 S.W.2D 222 (KY.APP. 1998)

ETHICAL CONSIDERATIONS Given the fact that she had signed the agreement, was Sherri acting in an ethically admirable fashion when she disaffirmed the release? Did the insurance company, since it was dealing with a minor, have an ethical duty to press for the appointment of a conservator?

Upon disaffirmance, the minor, if possible, must return to the adult the property or other consideration that was the object of the contract. Strong policy reasons exist for this rule, called the *duty of restoration.* It clearly seems unfair to let the minor "have it both ways"—that is, get out of the contract and yet retain the consideration. The law therefore says that if the minor wants to avoid a contract, he or she must *totally* avoid it.

Sometimes, however, the minor cannot return the property or other consideration because it has been damaged or destroyed. For example, Ace Used Cars will be very upset if, 18 months into the agreement, Marcie, the 17-year-old with whom Ace has dealt, asks for the money that she already has paid on the car as well as total release from the contract and in exchange presents Ace with a demolished car. In most states, minors like Marcie will get exactly what they wish because merely giving the car back fulfills the minor's duty of restoration. In some states, however, Ace will be able to set off any payments received from Marcie owing to the damaged condition of the car. Courts in other jurisdictions will impose liability on minors like Marcie for the reasonable value of the benefit the minor received by virtue of Marcie's having use of the car for the period prior to the wreck.

Misrepresentation of Age

What if the minor intentionally misrepresents his or her age? For example, suppose 17-year-old Marcie tells the salesperson at Ace Used Cars that she is 21 and, to "prove it," pulls out a falsified driver's license. If Marcie later tries to avoid the contract with Ace, can Ace argue that this intentional misrepresentation (fraud) prevents rescission? Under the law of most jurisdictions, the minor still can disaffirm the contract. But some states by statute hold that such a misrepresentation completely cuts off the minor's power of disaffirmance. Alternatively, some states allow rescission but force the minor to put the adult back in the position he or she would have been in but for the contract. In other words, in such age-misrepresentation cases, some states will allow Marcie to disaffirm the contract but will either force her to return the car or hold her liable in quasi contract for the reasonable value of the benefit Ace has conferred on her by furnishing her with the car. Also, Marcie probably will have to pay for any damage done to the car while she has had custody of it. Courts may employ some of these alternatives in situations involving minors who have not misrepresented their ages; but when age misrepresentation is present, courts increasingly will hold the minor to a heightened duty of restoration (or even restitution). Given the lack of uniformity among the states, you should check your own jurisdiction's precedents in this regard.

Changing the circumstances of the previous example in which Marcie had not misrepresented her age, assume now that Marcie had traded in another car when she had purchased the now-demolished car from Ace. When she avoids the contract, Ace has to return the trade-in to the minor as well in order to fulfill the adult's corresponding duty of restoration. If Ace already has sold this car to a **bona fide purchaser,** the minor cannot get the car back (as would be the usual result under the common law) but can recover the price paid to Ace by the third party. This result follows from the fact that the UCC (in § 2-403) covers this transaction. Thus, the UCC, by cutting off the minor's power of disaffirmance in some circumstances, has changed the common law.

> **Bona fide purchaser**
> A person who purchases in good faith, for value, and without notice of any defects or defenses affecting the sale or transaction.

When minors like Marcie attempt to disaffirm transactions with adults, the law requires no special words or acts to effect an avoidance. Disaffirmances may be made orally or in writing, formally (by a lawsuit) or informally, directly or indirectly (the minor's conveying the car to someone else when the minor reaches majority age is an avoidance of the contract with Ace Used Cars).

The minor's power of disaffirmance, whether the contract is executory or executed, ordinarily extends through his or her minority and for a reasonable time after achieving majority. How long is reasonable becomes a question of fact for a judge or jury to decide in light of all the circumstances.

Ratification

Ratification means that the minor in some fashion has indicated (1) approval of the contract made while he or she is an infant and (2) an intention to be bound to the provisions of that contract. Ratification, then, represents the opposite of disaffirmance and cuts off any right to disaffirm. Ratification takes two separate forms: express and implied. Even with express ratifications, or those situations in which the minor explicitly and definitely agrees to accept the obligations of the contract, the policy of protecting minors is so strong that many states require express ratifications to be in writing.

The more common type of ratification occurs through indirect means, such as conduct that shows approval of the contract, even though the minor has said nothing specifically about agreeing to be bound to it. To illustrate, failure to make a timely disaffirmance constitutes an implied ratification of an executed contract. Thus, a minor who is not diligent in disaffirming within a reasonable time after attaining majority will have impliedly ratified the contract. Such inaction does not ordinarily bring about the ratification of an executory contract, however. Some courts will hold that, by itself, partial payment of a debt usually is not tantamount to ratification, unless payment is coupled to the minor's express intention to be bound to the contract. In any event, ratification cannot occur until the minor achieves majority status. If ratification were possible beforehand, the law's protection of minors would be meaningless.

Necessaries

Even in the absence of ratification, minors will be liable for transactions whereby an adult has furnished them with "necessaries." *Necessaries* formerly encompassed only food, clothing, and shelter, but the law has broadened the doctrine to cover other things that directly foster the minor's well-being. The basis for the minor's liability is quasi contract, which you learned about in Chapter 9. (Remember that there can be no liability in *contract* law because of a lack of capacity.) If an adult has supplied necessaries to the minor, the law will imply liability for the reasonable value of those necessaries. Often, though, the law will not impose liability on

12.1 | SALES/ MANAGEMENT

CALL-IMAGE TECHNOLOGY

PURCHASES BY MINORS

Lindsay recently joined a music club, purchased seven compact disks (CDs) for $5, and committed herself to purchase another five disks (at an average cost of $14.99 each) over the next two years. When Lindsay received the CDs, she made cassette tape copies and returned the CDs to the music club. She enclosed with the CDs a letter informing the music club that she (Lindsay) was a minor and that she was disaffirming her contract with the club to purchase the seven CDs now and five CDs in the future. She also demanded, with disaffirmance of the agreement, that the music company return her $5 payment. Naturally, Tom and Anna were extremely upset when they learned of Lindsay's actions. They ask you to talk with Lindsay about the legal and ethical implications of her behavior. What would you tell her?

BUSINESS CONSIDERATIONS Why do firms such as the music club involved here continue to woo the teenage market when they know minors can disaffirm such contracts? Does this orientation represent a prudent business strategy?

ETHICAL CONSIDERATIONS Is the law's protection of minors an ethical rule? Do parents have an obligation to act as ethical role models for their children? Does that role diminish in importance once a child reaches a certain age, say 17?

the minor for the cost of necessaries unless the minor's parents are unable to discharge their obligation to support their child and pay for such essentials.

The definition of necessaries depends on the minor's circumstances, or social and economic situation in life. In this sense, the rule is applied somewhat subjectively. Although food, clothing, and shelter are covered, is a fur coat a necessary for which the minor is liable? It may be, depending on the minor's social station. Similarly, loans for medical or dental services or education also may comprise necessaries in some situations. Numerous cases involve cars; and many courts hold that a car, especially if the minor uses it for coming and going to work, is a necessary for which the minor remains liable. The definition of what constitutes a necessary changes as community values and mores change.

Special Statutes

Legislatures in many states have passed special statutes making minors liable in a variety of circumstances. Under such laws, minors may be responsible for educational loans, medical or dental expenses, insurance policies, bank account contracts, transportation by common carrier (e.g., airline tickets), and other expenses. These statutes protect the interests of those persons who deal with minors who, despite their age, exhibit the skills and maturity of adults.

Torts and Crimes

The law similarly protects the interests of adults when an adult has suffered losses owing to a minor's torts and crimes. Minors, therefore, generally cannot disaffirm liability for torts and crimes unless the minor is of *tender years,* or too young to understand the consequences of his or her acts. Minors sometimes may escape liability in these areas if the imposition of tort liability will bring about the enforcement of a contract the minor previously has disaffirmed. Note how, in this latter context, the law once again has chosen to protect minors at the expense of adults.

INSANE PERSONS

Like minors, insane persons may lack the capacity to make a binding contract. However, the law in this area is somewhat more complicated.

To be insane, a person must be so mentally infirm or deranged as to be unable to understand what he or she is agreeing to or the consequences attendant upon that agreement. The causes of such disability—lunacy, mental retardation, senility, or alcohol or drug abuse—are irrelevant.

Effects of Transactions by Insane Persons

The contract of a person whom a court has adjudged insane through court proceedings is absolutely void. Only his or her **guardian** has the legal capacity to contract on the person's behalf. The contracts of other insane persons are voidable, however. To disaffirm a contract, the person using insanity as a defense must prove that he or she actually was insane at the time of contracting. If the person instead was lucid and understood the nature and consequences of the contract, that person is bound by the contract.

This power of an insane person to avoid contracts also extends to the heirs or personal representative of a deceased insane person. A living insane person's guardian possesses similar powers. Upon regaining sanity, a formerly insane person nonetheless may ratify a contract made during the period of insanity.

Determining whether a transaction by an insane person is void, voidable, or enforceable depends heavily on the facts.

Guardian
A person legally responsible for taking care of another who lacks the legal capacity to do so.

Necessaries

By analogy to the rules covering minors, the law makes insane persons liable for necessaries in quasi contract. The categories of goods and services deemed necessaries for minors generally extend to insane persons. In the context of insanity, fewer controversies should arise regarding whether medical or legal services are necessaries—they probably constitute necessaries for which the insane person remains liable.

INTOXICATED PERSONS

If a person is so thoroughly intoxicated that he or she does not understand the nature or consequences of the agreement being made, the person's mental disability approaches that of an insane person. Hence, under certain circumstances, such a person can disaffirm a given agreement. This power of possible disaffirmance depends, however, on the degree of intoxication involved, which in turn involves a question of fact. Slight degrees of intoxication do not constitute cause for the disaffirmance of a contract.

Whether the intoxication was involuntary or voluntary may bear on the result, too. If a plaintiff has plied the defendant with liquor, any resulting intoxication may factor into a court's finding of incapacity, fraud, or overreaching that will release the defendant from the agreement. Even voluntary intoxication sometimes can result in a voidable contract if the facts support this conclusion.

Upon regaining sobriety, the formerly intoxicated person may either avoid or ratify the contract. The rules about acting within a reasonable time apply here as well; if the person does not quickly disaffirm the contract, an implied ratification will result. Courts generally are hostile to avoiding contracts on the basis of intoxication except in unusual circumstances.

ALIENS

An *alien* is a citizen of a foreign country. Most of the disabilities to which the law formerly subjected an alien have been removed, usually through treaties. Thus, a *legal* alien ordinarily can enter into contracts and can pursue gainful employment without legal disabilities, just as any U.S. citizen can. Some states make distinctions based on the alien's right to hold or convey personal property (generally authorized under such statutes) and the right to hold, convey, or inherit real property (some restrictions potentially apply here). *Enemy* aliens, or those who reside in countries with whom we officially are at war, cannot enforce contracts during the period of hostility but sometimes can after the war ends. Given the large number of illegal aliens in the United States, this area of the law, with its attendant ethical questions, promises to be ripe for future developments.

CONVICTS

In many states, conviction of a felony or treason carries with it certain contractual disabilities. For instance, laws may prohibit convicts from conveying property during their periods of incarceration. Such disabilities, if applicable, exist only during imprisonment. Upon release from prison, these persons have full rights to contract.

MARRIED WOMEN

Under early common law, married women's contracts were void. The law viewed women as their husbands' property and as otherwise lacking in capacity to make contracts. This common law disability, reflected in Married Women's Property Acts, has been eliminated by statute or by judicial decision in almost all states.

Exhibit 12.1 summarizes the contractual capacities of minors, insane persons, intoxicated persons, aliens, convicts, and married women.

THE REQUIREMENT OF REALITY (OR GENUINENESS) OF CONSENT

Appearances often are deceptive. The same is true of contract formation; what seems to be a valid agreement in actuality may lack the parties' genuine assent. Put another way, the law has to ascertain whether the consent given by the parties is real or whether the facts actually differ from those to which the parties have outwardly agreed. As a prerequisite for contract formation, the law therefore requires reality (or genuineness) of consent. The existence of fraud, misrepresentation, mistake, duress, undue influence, or unconscionability precludes genuine mutual assent.

FRAUD

Fraud is a word everyone uses fairly loosely, mainly because it lends itself to many definitions. At base, it consists of deception or hoodwinking; and it seems to involve a communication of some sort. But as one ancient case notes, "[a] nod or a wink, or a shake of the head or a smile" will do. [See *Walters* v. *Morgan,* 3 Def., F. & J. 718, 724 (1861).] Sometimes even silence will suffice. The essence of fraud is hard to pin down. One common definition states that fraud is a deliberate misrepresentation of a material fact with the intent to induce another person to enter into a contract that will be injurious to that person.[1] If you break this definition down into smaller components, you can see that fraud consists of six elements.

EXHIBIT 12.1 | **Contractual Capacity**

Class of Person	Classification of Contract	Exceptions
Minors	Voidable (upon return of consideration to seller)	1. Misrepresentation of age, which eliminates power of rescission in some jurisdictions 2. Failure to rescind within a reasonable time after achieving majority (implied ratification) 3. Express ratification after achieving majority (necessity of a writing in some jurisdictions) 4. Necessaries (liability in quasi contract in some cases if parents are unable to pay) 5. Special statutes making minors liable
Insane persons	Those adjudged insane — Void	1. Capacity by guardians to contract on these insane persons' behalf
	Those insane but not adjudged so by a court — Voidable	1. Ratification possible during periods of lucidity 2. Necessaries (liability in quasi contract in some circumstances)
Intoxicated persons	Slightly intoxicated persons — Valid	
	Seriously intoxicated persons — Voidable	1. Subsequent ratification upon regaining sobriety possible 2. Failure to rescind within a reasonable time after achieving sobriety in involuntary intoxication circumstances (implied ratification)
Aliens	Legal aliens — Valid	1. Some restrictions sometimes regarding ownership of real property and workers' compensation claims
	Enemy aliens during hostilities — Void	
	Enemy aliens after hostilities end — Valid	
	Illegal aliens — Valid	
Convicts	Convicts during incarceration — Void	
	Convicts after release — Valid	
Married women	Valid	1. Some anachronistic restrictions remaining in a few states

Elements of Fraud

To constitute fraud, the misrepresentation or misstatement first must concern a fact. A *fact* is something reasonably subject to exact knowledge. Thus, statements about the size of a car engine or the dimensions of a real estate parcel involve facts.

To show this first element of fraud, then, the plaintiff will have to prove that the defendant misstated a fact. Predictions, statements of value, and expressions of opinions generally do not equate with misrepresentations of fact. Neither do misstatements of law.

Actually, in any given situation, it may be difficult to distinguish a fact from an opinion. Suppose a car salesperson says to you, "This little dandy will get you down the road at a pretty good clip. It has a great engine. It's a V-6, and those engines have been very serviceable." The first two remarks probably are opinions, also known as "puffs" or "dealer's talk." The statement about the type of engine probably constitutes a fact. You may be unhappy, for instance, if you find a V-8 engine in the car after you purchase it or if you find out V-6 engines have many problems and the salesperson knows this. You may want to argue that you have been a victim of intentional misrepresentation. On the other hand, courts tend to discount statements of value because of genuine differences in the way people assess things. When Joe says, "That ring is worth a thousand dollars," unless Joe is a jewelry dealer or an expert and the other person is not, most courts will refuse to call Joe's statement a fact. Such nonfactual statements of value ordinarily do not fulfill this first element of a showing of fraud.

The second element of fraud that a plaintiff must prove involves the *materiality* of the fact that the defendant allegedly has misstated. A fact is not material unless the plaintiff, when making the decision to enter the contract, considers it a substantial factor. To use the earlier example, if you do not care if the engine is a V-6, the lack of a V-6 in the car you buy makes the fact immaterial. A court will enforce the bargain despite your protestations. The mileage of the car, the number of previous owners, and the extent of any **warranties** given, however, all ordinarily are material. Misstatements about these facts therefore may lead to liability if you prove the other elements of fraud.

The most distasteful element of fraud, as well as the most difficult to prove, is the defendant's knowledge of the falsity of his or her statements. This sometimes is called **scienter.** In other words, at the time of making the statement, the defendant knew, or should have known, that he or she was misstating an important fact. Outright lies, of course, would meet this third requirement. Interestingly, the defendant also may be liable for reckless use of the truth or for a statement made without verifying its accuracy when verification is possible. To illustrate, assume that a prospective buyer says to the homeowner, "I guess the property line extends to the fence, doesn't it?" The homeowner nods yes, even though the line actually does not extend that far. If the buyer purchases in reliance on this statement, a cause of action in fraud may result.

Closely related to the requirement of knowledge of the falsity of the statement is an *intent to deceive.* As noted earlier, deception is the hallmark of fraud. This element is difficult to disprove if the first three elements have been established, because courts usually can find no satisfactory reason for a defendant's misstatements except as an intent to induce the plaintiff into accepting a "sharp" bargain.

The plaintiff also must prove that he or she *relied* on the deception. Assuming the plaintiff's reliance is reasonable, this showing will not be particularly burdensome. For example, if Tom inspects a lakefront cottage with a front porch that is on the verge of caving into the lake, a court will not allow him to cry "foul" (or "fraud") if the porch crumbles into the water one month after Tom buys the cottage. The same will be true even if the owner has said the cottage is structurally sound. Clearly, Tom should have been aware of such a *patent* (obvious) defect.

Warranties
Representations that become part of the contract and that are made by a seller of goods at the time of the sale and that concern the character, quality, or nature of the goods.

Scienter
Guilty knowledge; specifically, one party's prior knowledge of the cause of a subsequent injury to another person.

Assuming the damage instead derives from a *latent* (hidden/unobservable by the human eye) defect, such as carpenter ant infestation, Tom may win unless the court thinks Tom's refraining from ordering a pest inspection is in itself unreasonable.

The final element of a plaintiff's proof—*injury,* or *detriment*—normally is not difficult to show. In the last example, Tom can argue that his damages amount to the sum needed to rid the cottage of carpenter ants and to repair the substructure of the dwelling. Alternatively, Tom may ask for rescission of the contract. When a court grants rescission, Tom will turn the cottage over to the original owner, and the owner will make restitution of the price Tom has paid for the property.

The following case, *W.D.I.A. Corporation* v. *McGraw-Hill, Inc.,* involves a thought-provoking intersection of contract and constitutional law principles.

Test
A case brought to ascertain an important legal principle or right.

12.2

W.D.I.A. CORPORATION V. McGRAW-HILL, INC.

34 F.SUPP. 2D 612 (S.D. OHIO 1998)

FACTS On or about 1 April 1989, Jeffrey Rothfeder presented to his editors the idea for an article for *Business Week* magazine. The article, entitled "Is Nothing Private?", subsequently was published in the 4 September 1989 *Business Week.* With the prior approval of his supervisors at McGraw-Hill, Inc. (McGraw-Hill) and McGraw-Hill attorneys, Rothfeder executed a **test** of the system used by the credit reporting industry to comply with the federal Fair Credit Reporting Act (FCRA). The test, as devised by Rothfeder and approved by McGraw-Hill, called for Rothfeder to lie deliberately to consumer reporting agencies in order to induce the agencies to grant McGraw-Hill access to sensitive confidential information protected by federal law. The article reported that Rothfeder told at least one fib and successfully acquired consumer credit information on various individuals, including then-Vice President Dan Quayle, from an on-line information reseller. The reseller was not identified in the article. W.D.I.A., an on-line credit bureau, claimed Rothfeder, acting with McGraw-Hill's authorization and on behalf of McGraw-Hill, deliberately, willfully and wantonly lied to W.D.I.A. when he stated that McGraw-Hill had a permissible purpose under the FCRA for obtaining credit reports. (The FCRA permits the acquisition of credit information only for permissible purposes as defined in the FCRA and makes it a criminal offense for any person to acquire such information under false pretenses.) Based on the promises of Rothfeder and McGraw-Hill and after processing the McGraw-Hill application through its FCRA-required procedures, conducting an on-site visit to McGraw-Hill offices, considering Rothfeder's oral and written representations, and making sure that Rothfeder understood the FCRA requirements,

W.D.I.A. agreed to release credit information to McGraw-Hill. Subsequent to McGraw-Hill's successful execution of the Rothfeder test, the Federal Trade Commission (FTC) launched an investigation into W.D.I.A.'s procedures. The McGraw-Hill test also became the focus of congressional hearings as to the effectiveness of the FCRA. W.D.I.A. alleged that the defendants' actions injured the firm by causing W.D.I.A. to engage in damage control efforts with regard to the credit bureaus from whom W.D.I.A. purchases credit information (including a trip to Chicago by W.D.I.A. representatives to avert being cut off from access to the major credit reporting entities) and to expend monies addressing the FTC and congressional concerns that later surfaced. W.D.I.A. therefore sought compensatory damages in excess of $75,000 and $45 million in punitive damages for fraud and breach of contract. McGraw-Hill and Rothfeder countered that the First Amendment's prohibition of actions for reputational injury flowing from the publication of truthful information about matters of public concern barred W.D.I.A.'s claims.

ISSUE Had the defendants engaged in fraud and breach of contract when they had lied to W.D.I.A.?

HOLDING Yes. The defendants had engaged in fraud and thus became liable for W.D.I.A.'s pre-publication compensatory—but not punitive—damages. The other alleged damages resulted from the publication of the truthful article rather than from breach of contract or fraud and therefore could not provide a basis for an award of damages.

continued

12.2

W.D.I.A. CORPORATION V. McGRAW-HILL, INC., *continued*
34 F.SUPP. 2D 612 (S.D. OHIO 1998)

REASONING In order to sustain its fraud count, W.D.I.A. had the burden of proving each of the following elements: (1) a representation or concealment of a fact; (2) which was material to the transaction at hand; (3) made falsely, with knowledge of the falsity, or with such utter disregard and recklessness as to whether it is true or false that knowledge may be inferred; (4) with the intent of misleading another into relying on it; (5) justifiable reliance on the representation or concealment; and (6) a resultant injury proximately (i.e., foreseeably) caused by the reliance. W.D.I.A. was able to demonstrate proximate causation between the acts of the defendants on the one hand and its losses incurred by the trip to Chicago and the costs of collecting on the McGraw-Hill account. Justifiable reliance on the claimed misrepresentation is an essential element of a claim for fraud in Ohio. In determining whether reliance is justifiable with respect to a fraud claim, courts consider the various circumstances involved in the particular transaction, such as the nature of the transaction, the form and materiality of the representation, the relationship of the parties, the respective intelligence, experience, age and mental and physical condition of the parties, and their respective knowledge and means of knowledge. The evidence proved that W.D.I.A. had justifiably relied on Rothfeder's material misrepresentations because he represented entities (McGraw-Hill and *Business Week*) that enjoyed a reputation for truthfulness and fair dealings. W.D.I.A.'s reliance on Rothfeder's representations about his intention to comply with the FCRA thus was justified. The plaintiff moreover had proved that the misrepresentations were material to the transaction. W.D.I.A., but for Rothfeder's misrepresentations, would not have entered into any contract. Hence, W.D.I.A. had proved all the elements of fraud and therefore merited the $7,349.95 in damages it could show with reasonable certainty (the trip to Chicago and the costs of collecting on the McGraw-Hill account). However, the trips to Washington and Arizona for which W.D.I.A. had sought compensation were not proximately caused by the fraud and contract breach committed by the defendants but rather were made for reasons unrelated to these causes of action. These costs derived from the publication of the article, and a court may not hold the defendants liable for the expenses so incurred. Similarly, the defendants' use of a "tester" to determine whether the credit reporting system properly protects the rights of the individuals it purportedly safeguards would not support an award of punitive damage in this case. The defendants' tactics served to inform Congress and the general public about a matter of vital public interest and were undertaken in such a way as to protect the identity of W.D.I.A. and the rights of consumers. Additionally, the court was convinced that the defendants had committed themselves to an enlightened philosophy that would ensure that they never again would engage in similar conduct and would always publish the truth. The need to deter future conduct that lies at the heart of any grant of punitive damages consequently was not present in this case, the court concluded.

BUSINESS CONSIDERATIONS W.D.I.A. took numerous steps before it allowed Rothfeder access to credit information. W.D.I.A. also put a great deal of faith in McGraw-Hill's responses to W.D.I.A.'s concerns. Could W.D.I.A. have done anything else to stave off the situation in which it found itself? Should corporations train their employees to refrain from ever making an exception when a customer requests such? If so, how does a firm do this, what sanctions for violations should it establish, and the like?

ETHICAL CONSIDERATIONS Is the filing of a "test" case ethical? Are the use of hidden cameras or tape recorders and lies on employment applications—all undertaken in the name of "investigatory journalism"—ethical? Do the public interests involved justify the tactics that journalists often use?

Successful proof of a cause of action in fraud usually justifies *rescission*, or the setting aside of the contract. Hence, such contracts are voidable at the injured party's option. As mentioned, an alternative to rescission is the recovery of damages sufficient to restore the injured party to the status quo, or the position he or she would have enjoyed had the facts of the transaction mirrored his or her conception of them at the time of acceptance. The facts of each case normally will dictate which remedy a plaintiff will elect to pursue. The injured party, as plaintiff, faces a final pitfall: He or she must act as quickly as possible or, as will be discussed later in this chapter, possibly waive the cause of action.

Silence

No discussion of fraud is complete without a reference to *silence* and its effect on whether a court will grant relief. The common law steadfastly held that "mere silence is not fraud." This conclusion rests on the belief that fraud necessitates some sort of overt communication. Because, by definition, silence denotes the total absence of any statement, the rule arose that one cannot be liable for fraud unless one had said or done something. (Remember the first element that requires a misstatement or misrepresentation of a fact.)

Many jurisdictions, in order to encourage nonconcealment and honesty in business transactions, now reject this rule and hold, for instance, that the seller must inform the buyer of any defects in a house. Similarly, if the buyer asks a question, the seller must answer truthfully and correct any wrong assumptions that the buyer holds. A seller's silence in such instances today may not prevent legal liability. Still, the strict rule is that there generally is no duty to speak (i.e., to disclose such facts).

Even the common law, however, deemed some situations so fraught with the possibility of injury or detriment that it placed a duty to speak on the party possessing the information. One of these situations, latent defects, already has been examined.

A duty to speak also arises in situations in which the parties owe each other **fiduciary** duties, or duties that arise from a relationship of trust. For example, an investment adviser should inform all clients of her part ownership in ABC Corporation before she suggests that clients purchase ABC stock. Similarly, if you are applying for insurance coverage, you cannot be silent if the insurer asks you questions about your medical history. To avoid fraud, you must, for example, disclose the existence of a heart condition. Finally, a statement made in preliminary negotiations that no longer is true at the time of the execution of the contract must be disclosed in order for one to escape a possible lawsuit based on fraud.

12.2 | SALES/ MARKETING

MARKETING AND SALES STRATEGIES

CIT needs to generate revenues very quickly at the outset of its business life if it hopes to survive. As a result, Dan favors a very aggressive approach to the marketing of the videophones. Tom, in contrast, prefers a more cautious marketing strategy. Tom believes that sales representatives who answer questions honestly and completely will build a loyal customer base and that a few lost sales early on are preferable to a number of lost customers in the future. Dan responds that, in the absence of robust sales early on, the company's financial future will remain so shaky that CIT will have few worries about customer concerns in the future because such a clientele will be nonexistent. Dan and Tom have asked for your advice. What will you tell them?

BUSINESS CONSIDERATIONS What sort of policy should a business adopt regarding the information a sales representative can or should communicate to the customer? What factors will influence the firm's decision?
ETHICAL CONSIDERATION Suppose a sales representative knows that a customer has an erroneous impression of the product, but no legal obligation for the representative to speak exists. From an ethical perspective, what should the sales representative do? Why?

Fiduciary
One who holds a special position of trust or confidence and who thereby is expected to act with the utmost good faith and loyalty.

MISREPRESENTATION

In general, everything previously discussed about the elements of fraud is true of a cause of action involving misrepresentation, with one notable exception: Misrepresentation lacks the elements of *scienter* and *intent to deceive*. Nevertheless, misrepresentation (often called *innocent misrepresentation* to differentiate it from fraud) can lead to the imposition of legal remedies. The property owner's statement about the property boundaries may amount to innocent misrepresentation if the plaintiff cannot prove *scienter*. *Misrepresentation,* or the innocent misstatement of a material fact that is relied on with resultant injury, makes the contract voidable at the option of the injured party. Rescission thus remains a possible (and, in many jurisdictions, the exclusive) remedy. Again, the plaintiff must act in a timely manner so as not to waive the cause of action.

Practically speaking, most plaintiffs allege both fraud and misrepresentation in the same lawsuit. Fraud is harder to prove but more desirable from the plaintiff's point of view; successful proof of fraud brings with it the possibility of recovering damages under the tort of deceit. The elements of deceit are identical to those of fraud. Upon a showing of deceit, a court may award *punitive* damages (damages beyond the actual losses suffered) in addition to the actual (or compensatory) damages normally recoverable for fraud. But even if the plaintiff fails to prove fraud (and its twin, deceit), recovery on grounds of misrepresentation is possible. At the very least, a showing of fraud or misrepresentation will be the basis for rescission.

Exhibit 12.2 describes the elements of misrepresentation and fraud; it shows the analysis a court may follow in determining the presence of either of these elements as a defense to a contract.

MISTAKE

Human nature is such that people often try to unravel transactions because they have made an error about some facet of the deal. Imagine the chaos, however, if courts readily accepted these hindsight arguments. The result would be a decrease in contracts, since people would be wary of dealing with each other. On the other hand, we have repeatedly stressed the importance of mutual assent in contract law. Thus, the law, on policy grounds, wishes to set the contract aside if the error is so great that it has tainted the parties' consent to the agreement.

The legal doctrine of mistake tries to balance these competing interests. *Mistake* occurs when the parties are wrong about the existence or absence of a past or present fact that is material to their transaction. Note that the parties must be wrong about *material* facts. Thus, legal mistake is not synonymous with ignorance, inability, or inaccurate judgments relating to value or quality. Courts will rescind contracts on the ground of mistake only if the error is so fundamental that it cannot be said that the parties' states of mind were in agreement about the essential facts of the transaction. Mistakes as to law, in contrast, oftentimes will not form grounds for rescission of the contract. Two kinds of mistakes exist: unilateral and bilateral (or mutual) mistakes.

Unilateral Mistake

As the term implies, in a unilateral mistake, only one party is mistaken about a material fact. The general rule, with some exceptions, is that the courts will not rescind such contracts.

E X H I B I T   12.2 | The Elements of Fraud and Misrepresentation

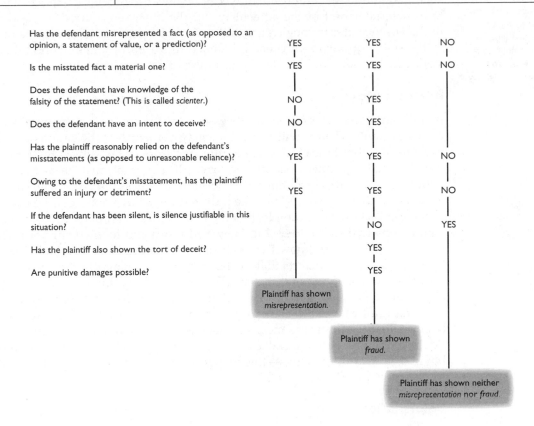

Has the defendant misrepresented a fact (as opposed to an opinion, a statement of value, or a prediction)? — YES / YES / NO

Is the misstated fact a material one? — YES / YES / NO

Does the defendant have knowledge of the falsity of the statement? (This is called *scienter*.) — NO / YES

Does the defendant have an intent to deceive? — NO / YES

Has the plaintiff reasonably relied on the defendant's misstatements (as opposed to unreasonable reliance)? — YES / YES / NO

Owing to the defendant's misstatement, has the plaintiff suffered an injury or detriment? — YES / YES / NO

If the defendant has been silent, is silence justifiable in this situation? — NO / YES

Has the plaintiff also shown the tort of deceit? — YES

Are punitive damages possible? — YES

Plaintiff has shown *misrepresentation*.

Plaintiff has shown *fraud*.

Plaintiff has shown neither *misrepresentation* nor *fraud*.

Unilateral mistakes often occur because of misplaced expectations of value. Let us suppose that Jacques goes to an antique store to look for a Duncan Phyfe table. He finds a table he believes to be a Duncan Phyfe and, without mentioning his belief to the store owner, pays a hefty price for it. Later that evening, a friend informs him that the table is not a Duncan Phyfe. If Jacques tries to avoid the contract, he will not be successful because only he was mistaken about a material fact—that is, that the table was a Duncan Phyfe. He also was mistaken as to value. In such unilateral mistake situations, courts take a hands-off approach and leave the parties with the bargains they have made. Rescission of the contract ordinarily is not granted.

The result here might differ if the store owner knew (or should have known) of Jacques's error or in some other fashion acted fraudulently or unconscionably. But the facts in this example do not support such a conclusion; if they did, courts might allow rescission of the contract, despite the unilateral mistake.

Similarly, in situations in which the mistake is a result of business computations, courts will suspend the general rule of refusing to grant relief for unilateral mistakes. Such situations may arise if a contractor makes an addition error (say $100,000) in computing a bid. The person soliciting the bid generally will choose the lowest bidder. Once the successful contractor/bidder recognizes its mistake, it will wish to rescind the contract. Even though these circumstances involve a unilateral mistake on the bidder's part, it can attempt to show that a court should grant

Reformation
Equitable remedy whereby a court corrects a written instrument in order to remove a mistake and to make the agreement conform to the terms to which the parties originally had agreed.

the equitable remedy of rescission (or **reformation**) because (1) the mistake was of such magnitude that enforcement would be unconscionable, (2) the mistake related to a material aspect of the agreement, (3) the mistake occurred in good faith and in the absence of clear negligence, (4) it would be possible to return the other party to the status quo without causing injury to third parties, and (5) no other circumstances exist that would make the granting of relief inequitable.

Bilateral Mistake

If both parties are in error about the essence of the agreement, bilateral (or mutual) mistake results. Courts will rescind such agreements on the rationale that, owing to a mistake about the existence, identity, or nature of the subject matter of the contract, a valid agreement has not occurred. If a mutual mistake of fact is present, either party may disaffirm this voidable contract unless rescission will cause injuries to innocent third parties. Why? The parties' minds have not met on the salient facts of the transaction. For example, assume an American company contracts with a foreign company (headquartered in New York) for hand-loomed rugs. The firms contract in April, but, unknown to both parties, a warehouse fire had destroyed the rugs in March. The destruction of the subject matter makes the contract voidable on the grounds of bilateral mistake: The parties have made an error regarding a significant fact—that the rugs existed at the time of contract formation.

Ambiguities
Uncertainties regarding the meanings of expressions used in contractual agreements.

Ambiguities constitute another cause of mutual mistake. If the American buyer believes that the term *rugs* means room-sized carpets, but, because of language difficulties, the international seller envisions rugs as smaller—that is, more comparable in size to wall hangings—this ambiguity may constitute mutual mistake. If so, rescission is justifiable.

Reformation

If a court can easily remedy the mistake, a court may *reform* the contract, or rewrite it to reflect the parties' actual intentions. In the ambiguity example, assuming the rugs were obtainable, once the ambiguity comes to light, reformation would permit a court to make room-sized rugs the subject matter of the contract. After the parties resort to a court's equitable powers of reformation, the contract will be fully enforceable. Be aware, though, that large backlogs of court cases form a substantial impediment to the availability of reformation as a practical remedy. Therefore, take pains when making a deal to ascertain exactly what your agreement means: You thereby will avoid a great many frustrations (and expenses).

DURESS

No genuine assent to the terms of an agreement results from a person's assenting while under duress. The person who has so assented, then, can ask for rescission of the contract on the ground of duress.

To assert the defense of *duress* means to allege that the other party has forced one into the contract against one's will. To constitute duress, the coercion must be so extreme that the victim has lost all ability to assent freely and voluntarily to the transaction. Given this definition, courts look for evidence of physical threats or threats that, if carried out, will cause intense mental anguish. Forcing a person to sign a contract at gunpoint, of course, will represent duress. To most courts, so will

IS THIS INSURANCE PRACTICE ILLEGAL?

The long-standing insurance practice of using company-owned law firms to defend policy-holders has recently come under attack in a series of state lawsuits alleging that the practice is fraudulent or an unauthorized practice of law. A case filed recently in Chicago against 16 personal liability carriers—including the two largest, State Farm Fire & Casualty Company and All-state Insurance Company—seeks to ban the use of these outside salaried attorneys, or so-called captive house counsel. The issue arises from the insurance companies' promising to designate a law firm to defend the insured if the insured becomes involved in an automobile accident. While the companies usually promise that they will pay all such litigation costs, typically left unsaid is the fact that the companies ordinarily assign such defense work to a house counsel whose ostensibly "outside"—or independent—law firm actually is on the insurance company's payroll and thus subject to strict spending controls. The insurers respond that the practice allows them to manage litigation costs more effectively and to exercise more direct control over settlements. Yet the plaintiffs' lawyers in the various suits filed across the country counter that common sense leads one to the conclusion that since the house counsel are full-time employees of the insurance company, if a difference of opinion over legal strategies and costs arises, the "boss" (i.e., the insurance company) will always get its way, even if the client suffers as a result.

If such a case surfaces in *your* court, how will *you* rule on the fraud count?[2]

BUSINESS CONSIDERATIONS Does the practice in question here, designed as it is to keep soaring legal expenses and spiraling premiums in check, represent a valid public policy outcome or an abuse of consumers' rights? Does an insurance firm from state Y need to worry about its use of captive house counsel in state X being characterized as the unauthorized practice of law and thus violative of state X's laws?

ETHICAL CONSIDERATIONS Do the conflicts of interest arguably experienced by such captive house counsel—a choice between economics and professionalism, for example—give rise to ethical issues? Will your answer differ once you learn that about 20 states have held that house counsel's provision of insurance defense services to policyholders poses no violation of applicable legal ethics rules? Explain your position.

SOURCE: Darryl Van Duch, *The National Law Journal* (14 December 1998), pp. A1, A15.

a spouse's threat to tell the parties' children that the other spouse has committed adultery: If, as a result of this intimidation, the spouse signs over a disproportionate share of the marital property, courts can rescind this agreement on the basis of duress. Similarly, courts generally view threats to initiate criminal actions (even if a basis for these exists) in order to extract a contractual agreement as duress. Courts, however, ordinarily do not see threats of civil suits as constituting duress.

The discussion to this point has focused on personal duress. Recently, the doctrine of economic duress has arisen. *Economic duress* occurs when one party is forced to agree to a further, wrongful, and coercive demand (usually a price increase) as a consequence of receiving the commodities or services to which he or she is entitled under the original contract. The party alleging economic duress ordinarily must show (1) wrongful acts or threats by the defendant, (2) financial distress caused by these wrongful acts or threats, and (3) the absence of any reasonable alternative to the terms presented by the wrongdoer (i.e., the injured party cannot obtain the goods or services elsewhere). Whether a court will grant a recovery to a plaintiff who alleges economic duress (or business compulsion) depends heavily on the particular facts of a given situation. The earlier example of the hand-loomed rugs illustrates this concept. Assume that the New York–based rug company has the only available hand-loomed rugs, and the American buyer has agreed to pay $2,500 per rug. Economic duress exists if the seller subsequently tells the American buyer (who wants to fill his orders for the rugs) that he can have the rugs only if he is willing to pay $4,000 apiece for them. Basing its decision on the concept of economic duress, a court may force the seller to sell the rugs at the original price of $2,500 or allow the American buyer after the fact to recover any difference in price.

As with most of the reality-of-consent situations discussed in this chapter, contracts made under duress ordinarily are voidable. Hence, rescission may be effected at the option of the injured party *unless* the injured party, by acquiescing in the coercive conduct for an unreasonably long time, ratifies the contract. Sometimes in such cases, however, the conduct exemplifying duress is so extreme that a court will find the contract void. Threats directed at third parties (such as a relative) may give rise to duress of this sort if one party enters into the contract to protect the innocent third party from these threats.

Draw
An arrangement by which an employee receives a predetermined amount each pay period.

The court's use of various of these principles in the next case is instructive.

12.3

GOLDEN V. McDERMOTT, WILL & EMERY
702 N.E.2D 581 (ILL.APP. I DIST. 1998)

FACTS Bruce Golden worked as a securities lawyer for the law firm of McDermott, Will & Emery (MWE) for 21 years. In 1989, eight years after he had become an income partner, a client he had brought to MWE, Avanti Associates (Avanti), and its promoter, Timothy Sasak, found themselves subject to a class action suit for securities violations. The suit named MWE as a defendant as well and sought $120 million from the firm. As a result of the suit, MWE's malpractice insurance carrier, Attorney's Liability Assurance Society, Ltd. (ALAS), had to pay the largest claim it had ever covered for a law firm. Golden alleged that owing to the initiation of the Avanti suit, ALAS was hesitant about renewing MWE's policy and wanted Golden removed from the firm. Golden further claimed that MWE at that time postponed his termination because the firm needed his cooperation in the Avanti litigation. Nonetheless, Golden maintained, from the time of the institution of the Avanti suit until his termination about 18 months later, MWE took various steps to limit his participation in partnership business and to reduce his partnership income. In January 1991, the firm reduced Golden's partnership units—and thus his compensation—by one-third. The day after the settlement of the Avanti litigation, two of MWE's partners

(and who also were the named defendants in the class action) informed Golden the firm was ready to fire him but that he could resign if he wished. The articulated reason for his termination was "lack of production," but Golden asserted that one of the partners later confided that pressure from ALAS was the real reason. Golden ultimately signed a severance agreement that contained a clause releasing the firm from all other claims. In February 1992, Golden accepted the agreed-upon, a one-time payment of $225,000 minus a deduction for the **draw** the firm had paid to Golden during the period in question. Around the time that Golden signed the severance agreement, he also was having personal problems. When Golden sought counseling, the mental health professional reported that the termination had left Golden paranoid, depressed, and dysfunctional. Filing suit in 1995, Golden, among other things, claimed that the release he had signed was voidable because he had executed it under personal and economic duress.

ISSUE Was the release voidable because Golden had signed it under personal, economic, and/or moral duress?

12.3

GOLDEN V. McDERMOTT, WILL & EMERY, *continued*
702 N.E.2D 581 (ILL.APP. 1 DIST. 1998)

HOLDING No. The facts failed to show any type of duress. Moreover, Golden's conduct in retaining the consideration for an unreasonable time before the institution of his lawsuit amounted to a ratification of the release.

REASONING Golden alleged three closely related types of duress. First, he claimed that MWE had coerced him by threatening to fire him. Next, he submitted that the firm had practiced economic duress (also known as "business compulsion") by taking unfair advantage of his financial and personal difficulties. Finally, he alleged moral duress. Illinois precedents define duress as "a condition where one is induced by a wrongful act or threat of another to make a contract under circumstances which deprive him of the exercise of his free will." MWE contended that the pressure it had applied to Golden failed to rise to duress, because the pressure was not wrongful. MWE argued that it had a right to expel Golden without cause and that duress cannot derive from one's threatening to do what it has a legal right to do. But while it is true that to be guilty of duress one must threaten a "wrongful" action, Illinois case law does not limit the meaning of "wrongful" to acts that are criminal, tortious, or in violation of a contractual duty, but extends the term to acts that are wrongful in a moral sense. Thus, even though an employee may be terminable at will, the threat of discharge may constitute duress. On the other hand, it ordinarily is neither wrongful nor does it constitute duress for an employer to offer an employee it is about to fire the option to resign. Given the evidence, the firm's actions thus failed to rise to duress. Golden further alleged economic duress, or business compulsion. Economic duress occurs where "undue or unjust advantage has been taken of a person's economic necessity or distress to coerce him [or her] into making the agreement." These dire circumstances must be such as to overbear the will of the plaintiff. Whether the circumstances did in fact overbear the plaintiff's will is ordinarily a question of fact. However, it is not enough that the plaintiff be in great financial or personal difficulty. For economic duress to exist, the defendant must have been in some way responsible for that difficulty. Consequently, the claim of economic duress lacked this necessary element of the defendants' responsibility for the plaintiff's circumstances. Economic duress therefore had not occurred here. Finally, Golden claimed moral duress. Moral duress resembles economic duress and consists of imposition, oppression, undue influence, or the taking of undue advantage of the business or financial stress or the extreme necessities or weaknesses of another. Courts grant relief in such cases on the rationale that the party benefitting thereby has received money, property, or other advantages that equity and good conscience should not permit the party to retain. Reported Illinois opinions have found moral duress only in extreme circumstances, such as those in which a third party pressured an unwed mother into giving up her child for adoption when she had been told if she failed to agree, she would be unable to keep her other children and when she had not read the document she had signed. In contrast, Golden was a legally sophisticated attorney who had negotiated the severance agreement over the course of several months. Given the dissimilarity of these facts to the applicable precedents, Golden had not established a claim for moral duress. Moreover, even if the severance agreement were voidable because of duress or a breach of fiduciary duty, Golden had ratified the agreement by his subsequent conduct. It is well established that the retention of consideration by one who has knowledge of the facts will amount to a ratification of a release executed by him or her in settlement of a claim, where the retention is for an unreasonable time under the circumstances of the case. His retention of the money for a further five-year period, despite his knowledge that the agreement might be voidable, thus constituted a ratification of the release.

BUSINESS CONSIDERATIONS Was the firm justified in firing Golden because of the securities violations lawsuit? Should the firm inform all potential hires that such situations may lead to termination? Or should it make such decisions on a case-by-case basis?

ETHICAL CONSIDERATIONS Golden had been a member of the firm for 21 years and was a partner. Do partners as well as professional/personal friends owe each other higher standards of ethical behavior? If so, should the parties here have behaved differently? If the firm had actually capitulated to the pressure brought by its insurer—as Golden alleged—was the firm's conduct appropriate, ethically speaking?

12.3 | MARKETING/ MANAGEMENT

A MANUFACTURING DILEMMA

Anna Kochanowski has entered into a contract with Total Fabricator, Inc. (TFI), a manufacturing company, to assemble 2,000 units of Call-Image for $50 per unit. However, with the sudden popularity of videophones, and with it the greater likelihood that Call-Image will succeed, TFI also wants to produce the next 10,000 units at the same price per unit. Consequently, TFI refuses to assemble the first 2,000 Call-Image units for the agreed-on $50 per unit price unless CIT guarantees that TFI will have the subcontract for the next 10,000 units as well. Both Anna and Tom know that, for a larger order, they can negotiate a better per unit price; however, they also know that, to ride the present wave of popularity, they must receive the 2,000 assembled units immediately and therefore must use TFI. Hence, Tom and Anna seek your advice. What legal risks inhere in TFI's refusal? What legal remedy can CIT seek?

BUSINESS CONSIDERATIONS How does a firm gauge when a "hard-line" approach verges on illegality? Should a firm err on the side of caution and always disavow such an approach?

ETHICAL CONSIDERATIONS Is the intersection of law and ethics represented by the Uniform Commercial Code's section on unconscionability advisable? Does this section represent a statutory abrogation of the principles of freedom of contract that goes too far? Why or why not?

Testamentary
Pertaining to a will.

UNDUE INFLUENCE

Closely related to duress is the concept of undue influence. Indeed, many courts view it as a subcategory of duress. Like duress, its existence depends heavily on the facts.

Undue influence is the use of a relationship of trust and confidence to extract contractual advantages. Newspapers are full of examples of such situations. Recall the allegations of undue influence involving nurses who have been named beneficiaries of their patients' sizable estates, or lawyers who have benefited enormously from their clients' **testamentary** dispositions. Since the favored nurse or lawyer by virtue of the relationship enjoyed with the other party has the ability to dominate or overreach the other party, the law often allows the rescission of such contracts. Because of the domination by another, the contracting party actually has not exercised his or her free will in entering into the contract but instead has given effect to the will or wishes of the other party.

The law will presume undue influence in certain circumstances, notably in fiduciary relationships. In the lawyer example just cited, the mere existence of the relationship will require the lawyer to prove that the client made the disposition free from the lawyer's coercion. The law will demand that the lawyer, as a fiduciary, act with utmost good faith in dealing with persons who will be predisposed to follow whatever the lawyer advises. Like lawyers, parents may enjoy fiduciary relationships with their children, doctors with their patients, accountants with their clients, and so on. Sometimes it is difficult for courts to determine when the persuasiveness of the fiduciary has become so intense that the other party has lost all vestiges of free will. But when they are convinced that this has occurred, they permit rescission of the challenged contract.

UNCONSCIONABILITY

You may note similarities between the concept of unconscionability, which we addressed in Chapters 9 and 11, and the ideas we discuss in this chapter. Especially in the context of consumer law, some courts have set contracts aside when these courts have found the bargaining power of the parties so unequal as to be commercially shocking or unreasonably oppressive. (In Chapter 13, you will learn that some courts call such agreements *contracts of adhesion*, meaning that one party to the contract, through overreaching, is able to impose its will on the other party.) The Uniform Commercial Code validates this approach in § 2-302, but not all states have adopted this section of the UCC. Nevertheless, unconscionability may signal a lack of meaningful assent to a contract and may justify a court's subsequent intervention on behalf of the injured party.

RESOURCES FOR BUSINESS LAW STUDENTS

NAME	RESOURCES	WEB ADDRESSES
National Fraud Information Center	The National Fraud Information Center, a project of the National Consumers League, provides a daily report and other information on fraud, as well as the opportunity to report fraud.	**http://www.fraud.org./**
Legal Information Institute (LII), Contract Law Materials	The LII provides an overview of contract law; links to federal statutes, treaties, and regulations; federal and state judicial decisions regarding contract law; state statutes; and other materials.	**http://wwwsecure.law.cornell.edu/topics/contracts.html**
The American Law Institute (ALI)	The ALI publishes *Restatements of Law*, Model Codes, and other proposals for law reform. It also disseminates press releases, a newsletter, and other publications.	**http://www.ali.org.**

SUMMARY

Certain classes of people may lack capacity, or the legal ability to bind themselves to an agreement and to enforce any promises made to them. For example, the contracts of a minor, usually defined as a person under age 18, often are voidable at the option of the minor, even when the minor has misrepresented his or her age. This power of disaffirmance ordinarily extends through the person's minority and for a reasonable time after attaining majority. After reaching majority, however, a minor may ratify, or approve, the contract. Ratification may be express or implied. Even in the absence of ratification, a minor may be liable for necessaries in quasi contract. The definition of necessaries depends on the minor's station in life and the parents' ability to provide for the minor. Sometimes special statutes broaden a minor's areas of liability. A minor almost always will be liable for any tort or crime unless the minor is very young or the imposition of tort liability will bring about the enforcement of a contract previously disaffirmed by the minor.

The contracts of insane persons may be void, voidable, or valid. To be insane, a person must demonstrate sufficient mental derangement to be unable to understand that to which he or she is agreeing or the consequences attendant on that agreement. Such agreements are void, but contracts entered into during periods of lucidity are enforceable. Upon regaining sanity, a person may either ratify the contract or avoid it. Insane persons are liable for necessaries, just as minors are.

Total intoxication may render a person incapable of entering into a binding contract, but slight intoxication will not. Upon regaining sobriety, the person either may disaffirm or ratify the contract. However, courts generally are hostile to avoiding contracts on the basis of intoxication, except in unusual circumstances.

Aliens, or persons who are citizens of foreign countries, may face legal disabilities with regard to contractual capacity. This is particularly true of enemy aliens, that is, residents of countries with whom the United States officially is at war. Convicts and even married women may have limited rights to contract as well. To determine the degree of disability, if any, that exists for these persons, one should consult the relevant state statutes.

To have a valid contract, one also must prove that the assent of the parties is genuine. The existence of fraud, misrepresentation, mistake, duress, undue influence, or unconscionability precludes the reality of consent that serves as the foundation of modern contract law. Fraud is a deliberate misrepresentation of a material fact with the intent to induce another person to enter a contract that will be injurious to that person. Predictions, statements of value, opinions, and misstatements of law do not constitute fraud. Probably the most difficult element to prove is the defendant's knowledge of the falsity of the statement, or scienter. The plaintiff's reliance on the deception must be reasonable, or the plaintiff will be precluded from recovering. Successful proof of fraud makes the contract voidable and justifies rescission. Although the common law held that mere silence is not fraud, exceptions to this doctrine existed even in early common law times. Today, the judicial trend is to force disclosure of material facts if their concealment may injure the other party. Innocent misrepresentation also may result in legal liability. Mistake occurs when the parties are wrong about the existence or absence of a past or present fact that is material to their transactions. Two types of mistakes exist: unilateral (one person is in error) and bilateral/mutual (both parties are in error). Courts generally will not rescind unilateral mistakes unless the other party knows, or should have known, of the mistaken party's error or uses it to take unconscionable advantage of the injured party. In these cases, as in situations involving errors in business computations, courts will allow rescission. If a mutual or bilateral mistake of fact is present, either party can disaffirm the contract. Ambiguity, for example, may lead to rescission. The equitable remedy of reformation allows a court to rewrite a contract to reflect the parties' actual intentions, but courts will not always permit reformation. Duress exists when a person's will has been overridden as a result of another person's threats. Duress may be either personal or economic, the latter occurring when a seller, in order to extract a higher contract price, wrongfully or coercively withholds scarce commodities or services. Undue influence is the use of a relationship of trust and confidence to gain contractual advantages. In certain relationships, the law will presume undue influence. The existence of unconscionability may signal a lack of meaningful assent to a contract and thus constitute grounds for a court's setting aside the contract as well.

DISCUSSION QUESTIONS

1. Why do smart businesspeople say, "Don't deal with minors"? Can minors disaffirm contracts if they have misrepresented their ages at the time of contracting?
2. How long does an infant's power to rescind a contract last?
3. What is *ratification,* and how can it occur?
4. Define *necessaries.*
5. Can an insane or intoxicated person's contracts ever be enforceable? Why or why not?

6. Set out, respectively, the legal requirements of fraud and misrepresentation.
7. How does silence relate to the legal theory of fraud? In what situations does a legal duty to speak arise?
8. Name, define, and explain the remedies for the two types of mistake.
9. Discuss the difference between *duress* and *economic duress.*
10. Define *undue influence.*

CASE PROBLEMS AND WRITING ASSIGNMENTS

1. On 18 May 1991, Larry Moeckel, a district manager for the Parke-Davis Division of Warner-Lambert Company (Warner-Lambert), conducted a products seminar for pharmaceutical representatives and physicians at a resort in Phoenix, Arizona. The seminar included several leisure activities, including a cocktail party. After the seminar concluded, Moeckel was driving home in a company-owned car when he collided with a car driven by Cynthia Emmons. Emmons suffered severe injuries and filed this lawsuit, alleging that Moeckel was negligent and that Warner-Lambert was directly and vicariously liable for her injuries. The case proceeded against Moeckel personally and against Warner-Lambert on the vicarious liability theory. On 20 September 1996, the jury, finding that Moeckel had been acting in the scope of his employment at the time of the accident, returned a $2.5 million compensatory damages verdict against Moeckel. As a consequence, Warner-Lambert would be subjected to the punitive damages phase of the trial, scheduled to begin on 24 September 1996. On 23 September 1996, Warner-Lambert, in a settlement offer, stated: "Warner-Lambert is willing to pay the full verdict of $2,500,000.00 to settle all disputes between the parties. Although . . . there are many appealable issues already in the record, Warner-Lambert would like to resolve the case without further court proceedings. There is every reason to expect that the appellate courts will reverse any award against the defendants or else remand the case for a new trial." Emmons rejected this offer. Later that day, Warner-Lambert faxed to Emmons and her counsel a "final offer of $5,000,000 to settle the case for all parties on all issues." At 4:00 P.M., Emmons accepted the offer and the accompanying confidentiality terms. The judge thereupon dismissed the jury and cancelled the punitive damages portion of the trial. Two days later, the trial court held a telephonic conference with all counsel and advised them that the court clerk had inadvertently marked into evidence a letter to the court from the defense counsel concerning the company's indemnification of Moeckel and had sent the exhibit into the jury room. Believing that this exhibit might have led to a larger jury verdict than otherwise might have occurred, Warner-Lambert filed a motion to set aside the settlement agreement. Finding a mutual mistake of fact (the belief of the parties that the jury had based its verdict on the jurors' consideration of only the admitted evidence), the trial judge granted Warner-Lambert's motion to set aside the settlement agreement. Emmons in turn sought enforcement of the agreement. How should the appellate court dispose of this issue? [See *Emmons* v. *Superior Court of the State of Arizona*, 968 P.2d 582 (Ariz.App. Div. 1 1998).]

2. Kristin Fletcher and John E. Marshall III dated while in high school. When Marshall's parents ejected him from their home shortly after his graduation from high school, he and Fletcher decided to rent an apartment and share the expenses. The parties disputed when Marshall signed the lease: He said he signed it on 29 April 1991, when he was only 17 years old and a minor; Fletcher maintained that, although the apartment complex manager had typed the lease on 29 April 1991, Marshall had signed it on 30 June 1991, the day preceding the commencement of the lease. Everyone agreed that Marshall turned 18 on 30 May 1991. Marshall also admitted that he had paid part of the security deposit (although the date on which he had done so remained unclear) and that he had made rent payments. Marshall moved out of the apartment in August (he said on the second, while Fletcher said the fifteenth) because he and Fletcher were not getting along and because he planned to attend college. When Fletcher sued Marshall for $2,500 in rent, he argued that his lack of capacity permitted him to disaffirm the lease. Fletcher disputed Marshall's statement that he had signed the lease while a minor but argued in the alternative that Marshall had ratified the contract after turning 18. Had Marshall ratified the contract and thereby become liable for his part of the rent? [See *Fletcher* v. *Marshall*, 632 N.E.2d 1105 (Ill.App. 2 Dist. 1994).]

3. O. C. Harden and several other cruise ship passengers who missed two days of a cruise because of flight delays sued the travel agency, the airline, and the cruise operator. On the cruise ticket was a so-called forum selection clause saying that any lawsuit arising out of any matter related to the cruise must be tried in the courts of Hawaii. The litigants, many of whom were from Alabama, challenged the validity of this clause on several grounds, including the fact that two of the plaintiffs were minors. Would the minors' incapacity constitute grounds for their avoiding the contract and thus making the forum selection clause inapplicable to them? Or had the minors, by suing on the contract, given up the ability to disaffirm the contract? (See *Harden* v. *American Airlines*, 178 F.R.D. 583 [M.D.Ala. 1998].)

4. Verna and Joseph Baum agreed to sell a lot to David Burggraff and his wife, Roberta Rubly-Burggraff, in July 1994. Roberta drafted the contract, and the

parties signed it without the advice of counsel. The parties originally became acquainted in April 1993 when the Burggraffs began renting the Baums' house on nearby Patten Point. The couples became close friends, indeed "almost like family." During the summer or fall of 1993, the Burggraffs offered to buy a portion of the Baums' land at Mill Cove. The Burggraffs wanted the lot because it had an ocean view and a potential building site near the water. Negotiations proceeded slowly, however, because the land had been in Verna Baum's family for generations and had sentimental value to her. During this time, the parties discussed in detail their plans for the land, including potential building sites and the importance of limited development so as to preserve the parcel's natural beauty. The Burggraffs planned to build both a primary residence and a cabin on the lot. They wanted the cabin to be located within 75 feet of the water, with the residence in the woods and up the hill from the water. Throughout the negotiations, the parties continued their close relationship and discussed the Burggraffs' building plans frequently. Roberta Rubly-Burggraff, in researching some of the zoning statutes that applied to the land, determined that the general state setback was 100 feet, while the local setback was only 75 feet. Both parties believed, based on her efforts and what they called "common knowledge," that those were the only relevant zoning ordinances applicable to the lot. In April 1995, after the contract was signed, the Burggraffs hired a civil engineer to discuss improving an access road that led to the building site of the primary residence. He then informed the Burggraffs that the land was in the town's Resource Protection District (RPD), which generally extends 250 feet from the water's edge. While the site chosen for the main residence would remain unaffected, the Burggraffs could build neither the access road nor the cabin in the RPD without permits from various local authorities. The Burggraffs thereupon informed the Baums that the lot was in the RPD and asked for a price reduction. After the parties ultimately were unable to come to an agreement, in June 1996, the Burggraffs filed a complaint based on mutual mistake. Would they win this lawsuit? [See *Burggraff* v. *Baum,* 720 A.2d 1167 (Me. 1998).]

5. When Sean T. Power was 17 years old, he bought an automobile insurance policy from Allstate Insurance Company (Allstate). At that time, Power rejected the underinsured motorist portion of the coverage. Three months after the issuance of the policy, Power suffered injuries in an automobile accident. Power thereafter filed a declaratory judgment action in which he sought to repudiate his rejection of Allstate's offer and to add the underinsured motorist coverage to his policy.

Could Power, as an adult, disaffirm a portion of the agreement that he, as a minor, had made with Allstate and ratify the remainder of the contract? [See *Power* v. *Allstate Ins. Co.,* 440 S.E.2d 406 (S.C.App. 1994).]

6. **BUSINESS APPLICATION CASE** In May 1993, Pamela Zivich registered her seven-year-old son, Bryan, for soccer with the Mentor Soccer Club, Inc. (the Club) for the 1993–1994 season. The Club is a nonprofit organization that provides children in the greater Mentor, Ohio, area with the opportunity to learn and play soccer. The Club is primarily composed of parents and other volunteers who provide their time and talents to help fulfill the Club's mission. The Club's registration forms contained an exculpatory clause that released the Club from liability for any claims resulting from the registrant's participation in soccer. On 7 October 1993, Bryan attended soccer practice and participated in an intrasquad scrimmage, which Bryan's team won. Excited about the win, Bryan, unsupervised, jumped on the soccer goal and swung back and forth on it. The goal, which was not anchored down, tipped over on Bryan. As a result, Bryan sustained three broken ribs, a broken collarbone, and severe bruising of the lungs. In 1995, Bryan's parents sued the Club for the injuries Bryan had sustained. The Club argued that the exculpatory agreement executed by Mrs. Zivich on behalf of her minor son released the club from the minor and the parents' claims as a matter of law. The Ziviches, in contrast, maintained that the release was voidable on public policy grounds owing to the general rule that a minor can avoid any contract entered into on his or her behalf until the minor reaches the age of majority and for a reasonable time thereafter. In these circumstances, should public policy concerns favor the Club or the Ziviches? (See *Zivich* v. *Mentor Soccer Club, Inc.,* 696 N.E. 2d 201 [Ohio 1998].)

7. **ETHICAL APPLICATION CASE** On 19 March 1996, Mark, Raelynn, and Milton Ramsden were the high bidders on a dairy farm sold at public auction by Agribank. Farm Credit Services of North Central Wisconsin (FCS), which had financed the prior owners, Triple L Dairy, also financed the Ramsdens' purchase, which closed on 17 April 1996. Thomas Hass, an Agribank employee and an agent of both Agribank and FCS, was the auctioneer and also handled the details of the Ramsdens' purchase from Agribank. While Triple L Dairy owned the property, it had complained to Hass, Agribank, and FCS that its cattle were sick and dying. After an investigation and prior to selling the property to the Ramsdens, Agribank, FCS, and Hass learned that an underground gasoline storage tank on the property was leaking and contaminating

the soil. On 15 June 1995, Hass reported to the Department of Natural Resources that the groundwater on the property was contaminated. Thereafter, that agency directed Agribank to remove the underground storage tank and to remedy the contamination to both the soil and the groundwater. Agribank removed the tank, but it did not remedy the contamination. Notwithstanding their knowledge of the contamination and its effect on dairy cows, Agribank and Hass sought to sell the property as a dairy farm. At the auction, Hass told the Ramsdens, who said they were considering buying the property for a dairy farm, that: (1) Agribank would be responsible for any contamination, cleanup, or problems associated with an underground storage tank that had leaked; (2) the property was suitable for use as a dairy farm; and (3) there was plenty of good, clean water available for the cattle. Hass did not mention the contamination of the groundwater or the deaths of Triple L's cattle. Based on Hass's factual representations and the failure of Hass, Agribank, and FCS to disclose that the groundwater was not fit for consumption and that the prior owner's cattle had died, the Ramsdens bought the property. On 18 April 1996, the Ramsdens moved their cattle onto the property. By 20 April 1996, the cows began to appear depressed, ceased producing milk, and exhibited sunken eyes, general weakness, bellowing, and a lack of appetite. By 23 April 1996, four of the cows had died. Mark Ramsden also became ill. To determine the cause of these problems, the Ramsdens submitted water samples to the University of Wisconsin at Stevens Point. The samples showed benzene contamination from the underground storage tank that had leaked. The Ramsdens also had a local toxicologist perform a necropsy on one of the dead cows. The toxicologist determined that the cow had died of benzene poisoning as well. As a result of the poisoning, the Ramsdens suffered the loss of 186 head of cattle and the loss of profits from the operation of their dairy. Additionally, Mark Ramsden suffered personal injuries, both physical and emotional, owing to benzene poisoning. In 1997, the Ramsdens sued Agribank, FCS, and Hass. Hass moved to dismiss the complaint of fraud filed against him. Among other things, he argued that as an agent, he had no duty to disclose his knowledge of the property to the Ramsdens because any disclosures might have been contrary to the interests of his principal, Agribank. Who should win this case? Should a firm take a "zero-tolerance" stance toward ethical violations by employees, or should it base its decisions on the egregiousness of the conduct? What sanctions should a firm impose for ethical violations? [See *Ramsden* v. *Farm Credit Services*, 590 N.W.2d 1 (Wis.App. 1998).]

8. **CRITICAL THINKING CASE** In 1984, when defendant Andrew M. Kavovit was 12 years of age, he and his parents entered into a contract with Scott Eden Management (Scott Eden) whereby Scott Eden became the exclusive personal manager to supervise and promote Andrew's career in the entertainment industry. This agreement ran from 8 February 1984 to 8 February 1986, with an extension for another three years to 8 February 1989. It entitled Scott Eden to a 15 percent commission on Andrew's gross compensation, including the residuals or royalties from such contracts, notwithstanding any earlier termination of the agreement. In 1986, Andrew signed an agency contract with the Andreadis Agency (Andreadis), a licensed agent selected by Scott Eden pursuant to industry requirements. This agreement involved an additional 10 percent commission. Thereafter, Andrew signed several contracts for his services. The most important contract, from a financial and career point of view, secured a role for Andrew on *As the World Turns*, a long-running television soap opera. Income from this employment contract appears to have commenced on 28 December 1987 and continued through 28 December 1990, with a strong possibility for renewal. One week before the expiration of the contract with Scott Eden, Andrew's attorney notified Scott Eden of Andrew's disaffirmance on the basis of infancy. Until then, the Andreadis Agency had been forwarding Scott Eden its commissions, but by a letter on 4 February 1989, Andrew's father, David Kavovit, advised Andreadis that Andrew's salary should go directly to Andrew and that Andrew would send Andreadis its 10 percent. Because Scott Eden received no additional commissions thereafter, it sued, seeking money damages for the commissions owed it. Would a 15-year-old child actor have the right to disaffirm his contract with his exclusive personal manager? Could Scott Eden have done anything to prevent this litigation? [See *Scott Eden Management* v. *Kavovit*, 563 N.Y.S.2d 1001 (Sup. 1990).]

NOTES

1. A.G. Guest, *Anson's Law of Contracts*, 26th ed. (Oxford: Clarendon Press, 1984), pp. 209–210.

2. Darryl Van Duch, "Insurance Counsel Under Attack," *The National Law Journal* (14 December 1998), pp. A1, A15.

CHAPTER

13

LEGALITY OF SUBJECT MATTER AND PROPER FORM OF CONTRACTS

CALL-IMAGE TECHNOLOGY

AGENDA

Many people have questioned the legality of video-phones. These people assert, among other things, that videophones invade the privacy of the user and thus violate public policy. Should the firm concern itself with such controversies? Could these issues affect the legality of contracts into which the firm enters? What other legal considerations might arise?

The Kochanowskis recognize that CIT will enter into a number of contracts in the near future. They plan to put most of their contracts in writing, but they may

need to know which of their contracts *must* be in writing in order to be enforceable and which contracts merely *should* be in writing but do not have to be. They also will need to know how detailed their writings should be and whether any of CIT's written agreements are subject to amendment or alteration by oral testimony.

They are likely to look to you for help as they work through this area. Be prepared! You never know when one of the Kochanowskis will need your help or advice.

OUTLINE

THE REQUIREMENTS OF LEGALITY OF SUBJECT MATTER AND PROPER FORM

By this time, you undoubtedly have noted the emphasis that U.S. contract law places on bargaining and contract formation through the agreement of the parties. Yet, as with most human activities, the permissible boundaries of such conduct remain limited. Society at large may have a stake in the agreement the parties have forged. An agreement to bribe public officials or to murder someone, for instance, has definite repercussions for society that extend beyond the parties who initiated the bargain. The law, then, imposes a requirement that in order for the bargain to be recognized as a valid contract, the subject matter and purpose of the bargain must be legal. In this sense, the term *illegal contract* is a misnomer; in general, a bargain cannot attain the status of "contract" unless it is legal. Hence, illegal "contracts" are void. A bargain, however innocent it seems, nevertheless may involve a violation of a statute, common law, or public policy and hence is void.

In addition to this last transactional element of contract formation—legality—under the Statute of Frauds, certain categories of contracts must be in proper form—that is, they must be in writing—in order to be enforceable. Such categories include contracts to answer for the debt of another if the debtor defaults, contracts involving interests in land, and several other classifications of contracts. The writing provides evidence that the parties actually entered into the contracts at issue. Once the parties have reduced their contract to writing, application of the parol evidence rule ordinarily means that courts will not admit oral testimony that will alter, add to, or vary the terms of the written agreement. Hence, this chapter will focus on this substantive rule of evidence as well.

Components of Illegality

A widely accepted definition of *illegality*, taken from the *Restatement (First) of Contracts*, § 512, and augmented by the *Restatement (Second) of Contracts*, § 178, states that a bargain is illegal if its performance is criminal, tortious, or otherwise opposed to public policy.[1] Both the subject matter of the bargain and the realization of its objectives must be permissible under state and federal statutes. Sometimes these statutes impose criminal penalties for their violation (e.g., an agreement to engage in arson for money). Other statutes, however, may prohibit certain kinds of bargains (e.g., a contract with an improperly licensed electrician) without imposing criminal penalties on those who violate these statutes.

The desire to protect the public also underlies the prohibition of bargains involving **tortious** conduct (e.g., an agreement between two parties for the purpose of defrauding a third person).

Tortious
Relating to private or civil wrongs or injuries.

Similarly, even in the absence of an agreement that violates a statute or requires the commission of a tort, courts may declare as illegal on *public policy* grounds any bargain that will be detrimental to the public at large. Although the concept of public policy may fluctuate as different courts apply different standards, courts increasingly have used this rationale in a variety of contexts in which there appears to be no other basis for protecting the peace, health, or morals of the community. For instance, a bank may offer a rather one-sided night depository agreement in which it refuses to accept liability for a deposit placed in its after-hours slot, even if the loss stems from the negligence of its own employee and the depositor can prove that he or she actually deposited the amount in question with the bank. The concept of public policy—here, the protection of depositors' expectations that the bank will take proper care of their deposits and the protection of consumers against one-sided agreements—will permit a court to invalidate such agreements on the grounds of illegality.

A court may characterize such agreements as **exculpatory clauses** or **contracts of adhesion** (in these circumstances, depositors may have had no choice but to accept the bank's terms). In general, an illegal bargain is void and hence unenforceable. This ordinarily is true whether the agreement is executory or fully executed. Usually a court merely leaves the parties where it finds them. Neither party, then, can sue the other. Exceptions to the general rule that courts will not give relief to parties who have created an illegal bargain do exist, however.

> **Exculpatory clauses**
> Parts of agreements in which a prospective plaintiff agrees in advance not to seek to hold the prospective defendant liable for certain losses for which the prospective defendant otherwise would be liable.

> **Contracts of adhesion**
> Contracts in which the terms are not open to negotiation; so-called take-it-or-leave-it contracts.

MALA IN SE AND MALA PROHIBITA BARGAINS

Early on, many courts became dissatisfied with the rule that illegal contracts are absolutely void. Some of these courts therefore distinguished between bargains that violate statutes because they are evil *in themselves (mala in se)* and bargains that have been merely *forbidden by statute (mala prohibita)*. The first type (e.g., an agreement to murder someone) fell within the general rule and was void. Some courts, however, depending on the nature and effect of the act prohibited by the statute, were prepared to view bargains included within the second type as voidable rather than void.

To illustrate, one case involved the sale of cattle in violation of a law stating that all cattle sold must be tested for brucellosis (a serious disease in cattle) within the 30-day period preceding the sale. The court clearly could have used this statutory violation as a basis for holding the agreement void. Yet the court concluded that this bargain was *mala prohibita,* rather than *mala in se,* because the contract was neither in bad faith nor contrary to public policy, and therefore enforced the contract.[2]

More recent commentators have criticized the distinction between *mala in se* and *mala prohibita* bargains as invalid because any bargain that violates a statute is absolutely void no matter what underlying rationale the prohibition involves. This conclusion represents the position most widely accepted today. Nevertheless, the continued use of these terms demonstrates the tendency of courts to weigh differences in the degree of evil and accordingly determine the availability of judicial relief.

Courts, however, almost universally recognize two types of agreements as *mala in se* bargains: agreements to commit a crime and agreements to commit a tort. The agreement mentioned earlier involving arson could be called a *mala in se* bargain because the subject matter of the agreement itself, the commission of a crime, is morally unacceptable. The same would be true of an agreement to kill someone, a so-called murder "contract." Neither party can enforce such agreements; they are absolutely void. Likewise, an agreement that involves the commission of a tort is void. Besides fraud, such bargains may include agreements to damage the good name of a competitor, to inflict mental distress on a third party, or to trespass against another's **chattels** or real property in order to cause injury to the property.

> **Chattels**
> Articles of personal (as opposed to real) property.

Determining whether a particular activity violates a statute (assuming the activity is not *mala in se*) is more difficult and requires that courts resort first to the words of the underlying statute. Courts then must assess the legislative intent and, finally, examine the social effects of giving or refusing a remedy in the particular situation.

AGREEMENTS VIOLATIVE OF STATUTES

Courts ordinarily find certain categories of activities in violation of statutes. These include price-fixing agreements, performances of services without a license, Sunday closing laws, and wagering and usury statutes.

Price-Fixing Agreements

The purpose of price-fixing agreements generally is to restrain competition so as to create a **monopoly** or **oligopoly** in order to control price fluctuations. The Sherman Antitrust Act, the Clayton Act, and the Federal Trade Commission Act comprise the major federal legislative enactments that make such bargains illegal. Price-fixing agreements also may violate state statutes, or, alternatively, courts may invalidate these arrangements on public policy grounds.

Performances of Services Without a License

Agreements relating to the performances of services without a license may constitute another type of statutory violation. To protect the public from unqualified persons, state statutes often require (or regulate) the licensing of professions such as law, medicine, and public accountancy and trades such as electrical work, contracting, and plumbing. Before the state grants a license, the would-be practitioner, after achieving the required educational qualifications, usually must demonstrate minimal competency by successfully passing an examination. In such cases, the absence of a license prevents the professional or tradesperson from enforcing these bargains.

In contrast to such a regulatory licensing scheme, some states require licensing primarily as a revenue-producing mechanism rather than as a device for protecting the health and welfare of its citizens. If the primary intent of the licensing requirement is to produce revenue, the lack of a license will not affect the contract between the parties.

It pays to remember that courts have fairly wide discretion in these matters and may take into account such factors as the absence of harm resulting from failure to obtain the license, the extent of the knowledge of the persons involved, and the relative "guilt" of the respective parties. If, for example, a court deems the amount forfeited by the unlicensed professional sufficiently large to constitute a penalty, the professional ordinarily will be able to sue for the fee, despite the lack of a license. As mentioned earlier, even in statutes assigning criminal sanctions, courts will look closely at the legislative intent of the statute as they decide whether to give or to withhold remedies.

Sunday Closing Laws

Sunday closing laws (also called "blue laws") are so named because they prohibit the formation or performance of contracts on Sundays. These laws are troublesome because the terms of such statutes vary widely from state to state. The most common type of statute prohibits the conducting of secular business, or one's "ordinary calling" (such as selling merchandise), on Sunday. You may be familiar with Sunday laws that forbid the sale of certain alcoholic beverages. Exceptions usually involve works of charity or necessity, which one can undertake on Sunday without fear of sanctions.

Monopoly
The power of a firm to carry on a business or a trade to the exclusion of all competitors.

Oligopoly
An economic condition in which a small number of firms dominates a market, but no one firm controls it.

In some jurisdictions, a violation of a Sunday statute voids the contract, unless the party asking for recovery can show, for instance, that he or she had no knowledge that the execution of the contract occurred on Sunday. He or she also can argue that the agreement, though initiated on Sunday, was not accepted until later in the week and thus actually ripened into a contract at that time.

Litigants in some jurisdictions have challenged the constitutionality of such statutes. These laws, by singling out Sunday as a "day of rest" from mercantile activity, may violate the First Amendment's prohibition against a governmentally established religion. State governments' enactments of such laws, therefore, arguably put the interests of one religious group ahead of the interests of others and thus raise constitutional questions.

Wagering Statutes

Wagering contracts and lotteries are illegal in certain states because of statutes prohibiting gambling, betting, and other games of chance. The underlying rationale for these laws focuses on the protection of the public from the crime and familial discord often associated with gambling. To constitute illegal wagering, the activity must involve a person's paying consideration or value in the hope of receiving a prize or other property by chance. Wagering in the legal sense always consists of a scheme involving the artificial creation of risk; hence, insurance contracts or stock transactions in which risk is an inherent feature do not comprise situations that implicate illegal wagering. On the other hand, courts may view raffles as unlawful wagering. For instance, because of the relatively soft demand in the housing market, some enterprising couples in various parts of the country recently have attempted to raffle off their homes. The conduct of these people has violated the wagering statutes of some of these jurisdictions. Note, however, that public lotteries are perfectly legal in many states. Additionally, in the absence of a requirement that the participant give something of value in order to take part in the activity, the activity probably is not a lottery and consequently probably is legal.

Usury Statutes

Acceleration clauses
Clauses in contracts that advance the date for payment based on the occurrence of a condition or the breach of a duty.

Prepayment clauses
Contract clauses that allow the debtor to pay the debt before it is due without penalty.

Conditional sales contracts
Sales contracts in which the transfer of title is subject to a condition, most commonly the payment of the full purchase price by the buyer.

Usurious contracts occur when a lender loans money at a greater profit (or rate of interest) than state law permits. For usury to exist, there must be a loan of money (or an agreement to extend the maturity of a monetary debt) for which the debtor agrees to repay the principal at a rate that exceeds the legal rate of interest. In addition, the lender must intend to violate the usury laws. If these elements are present, the resultant contract is illegal. In most states, a usurious lender will be unable to collect any interest and also may be subject to criminal or other statutory penalties. In some states, courts deny only the amount of excess interest; the lender can recover the remaining interest and principal. In a few states, the agreement is void; the lender receives no interest or principal.

Because such wide variations exist among state usury laws, it is difficult to generalize one set of rules. Loans to corporations may be exempt from a jurisdiction's usury statutes, for example, as may short-term loans, especially if the lender, in making the loans, will incur large risks.

Acceleration clauses and **prepayment clauses** generally are not usurious. The same is true of service fees that reflect the incidental costs of making a loan—filing and recording fees, for example. Sales under revolving charge accounts (open-ended credit accounts) or **conditional sales contracts** ordinarily are not usurious even if the seller charges a higher-than-lawful rate. Two reasons have been forwarded in justification of this position: (1) A bona fide conditional sale on a deferred-payment basis is not a loan of money, and (2) the finance charge is merely a part of an increased purchase price reflective of the seller's risk in giving up possession of personal property (clothes, refrigerators, compact disk players, and the like) that depreciates quickly in value.

Time-price differential sales contracts may or may not be usurious, depending on applicable state law and/or special consumer protection statutes. Time-price differential sales contracts involve an offer to sell at a designated price for cash (say $6,000 for an entertainment center) or at a higher price on credit (say $7,500). Even though the maximum legal rate of interest in this state may be 18 percent, the 25 percent actual rate represented by the credit price does not involve usury as long as the final price reflects the credit nature of the sale rather than an intent to evade the usury laws.

The trend today is to raise the maximum interest rate and to increase the exceptions to the usury laws. Moreover, federally guaranteed loans allow interest rates that otherwise would violate state law. These factors have seriously eroded the original purpose of usury laws—the protection of debtors from excessive rates of interest. But, as mentioned earlier, little uniformity exists in the various states' usury statutes; it is wise, therefore, to consult these statutes if you have doubts about the legality of a particular transaction.

AGREEMENTS VIOLATIVE OF PUBLIC POLICY

Ample precedents indicate that judges more and more frequently resort to public policy as a basis for invalidating agreements. In holding that a contract is void on public policy grounds, a court is deciding the legality of the agreement in light of the public interests involved. Hence, public policy frequently becomes an alternative ground for finding illegality. To illustrate, a court may strike down a contract to fix prices because the agreement violates statutes (for example, the Sherman Act) or will damage the public. However, because *public policy* is such a wide-ranging term, courts, in judging the legality of certain types of bargains, often have to juggle competing interests. Keep this point in mind as you consider the following concepts.

Covenants Not to Compete

Covenants not to compete, also called *restrictive covenants*, are express promises that a seller of a business or an employee who leaves a company will not engage in the same or similar business or occupation for a period of time in a certain geographic area. Such bargains may or may not be legal. If the purpose of these "noncompete

13.1 | FINANCE

MALA PROHIBITA CONTRACT SITUATIONS

CIT has obtained a guaranteed offer to provide a $100,000 line of credit, which will be very helpful in any upcoming expansion or growth for the firm. However, the prospective lender insists on receiving 3 percent simple interest on any balance each month. Tom is concerned that this interest rate amounts to a usurious loan, and he asks your advice. What will you tell him?

BUSINESS CONSIDERATIONS Should lenders gouge their customers who are in desperate need of money by charging these customers the highest possible interest? What factors should a lender (or a borrower) consider when it decides how much interest is appropriate in a credit transaction?

ETHICAL CONSIDERATIONS Is it ethical for a lender to charge the highest interest rate the market will permit? Does such conduct take advantage of the lender's customers? Is it ethical for a borrower to agree to credit terms and then later object because the terms are too high?

Time-price differential sales contracts Contracts with a difference in price based on the date of payment, with one price for an immediate payment and another for a payment at a later date.

clauses" is to protect the recent buyer of a business from the possibility that the seller will set up shop two blocks from the original business establishment or the former employer from the possibility that the ex-employee will sign on with a competitor, the restrictions on the seller or former employee, if *reasonable* in *time* and in *geographic scope*, ordinarily are legal. But, as mentioned earlier, competing policies complicate these situations. It clearly is unfair to shackle unduly the employment opportunities of the seller (or former employee) who must make a living. Similarly, to curtail this person's business or occupational activities in effect insulates the buyer (or former employer) from competition and thereby may result in higher prices. For this reason, when examining these covenants, many courts use public policy considerations.

Usually such covenants are incidental to the sale of a business or to an employment contract and are legal. (Agreements not to compete that have as their sole purpose the curtailing of competition are illegal as restraints on trade—they violate the antitrust laws.) If, however, under the facts and circumstances, a particular covenant not to compete is unreasonably restrictive in time or geographic scope, a court has the power to rewrite the covenant so that it is less restrictive— a process called *blue-penciling*—and hence reasonable. Bargainers should not expect courts to save them from bad or illegal bargains, however. Blue-penciling is relatively rare. In fact, most courts reject this approach and will void the restrictive covenant and construe the agreement without any reference to the covenant not to compete.

The *Standard Register Company* v. *Cleaver* case shows how the question of the legality of a restrictive covenant can become the basis for a lawsuit.

13.1

STANDARD REGISTER COMPANY V. CLEAVER
30 F.SUPP.2D 1084 (N.D.IND. 1998)

FACTS In 1981, Phil Cleaver became an employee at will for UARCO, Inc. (Uarco), a firm engaged in the sales of printed business items. As such, Cleaver signed a non-compete clause that obligated him to refrain from divulging any of the company's trade secrets or confidential information he might learn while in the company's employ. He further promised—in paragraph 9 of the agreement—that

[f]or a period of two years following the termination of his employment for any reason whatsoever . . . , [he would] not contact, with a view towards selling any product competitive with any product sold or proposed to be sold by [the] Company at the time of the termination of [his] employment, or sell any product to, any person, firm, association or corporation: (a) to which [he] sold any product of [the] Company during the year preceding the termination of [his] employment,

(b) which [he] solicited, contacted, or otherwise dealt with on behalf of [the] Company during the year preceding [the] termination of [his] employment.

Cleaver worked for Uarco until 1998, when the company merged with Standard Register Company (Standard). Shortly after the merger, Cleaver went to work for Prograde, Inc. (Prograde), a firm engaged in selling printed business materials similar to those sold by Uarco and Standard. While at Uarco, Cleaver, as was typical in the industry, had worked for many years to develop customer relationships. For example, it had taken him four years to increase the $350,000 in initial sales to HWI, a major Uarco customer, to $1,000,000 at the time of his departure from Standard's employ. In his first four months with Prograde, Cleaver sold over $1,000,000 to HWI and also solicited other Uarco/Standard customers whom he previously had serviced. As a consequence, Standard sued to enforce the restrictive covenant Cleaver had signed.

13.1

STANDARD REGISTER COMPANY V. CLEAVER, *continued*
30 F.SUPP.2D 1084 (N.D.IND. 1998)

ISSUE Were the nondisclosure and nonsolicitation provisions in the restrictive covenant valid and enforceable?

HOLDING Yes. The limitations set out by the provisions coincided perfectly with Standard's protectable interest in its good will (the customers with whom Cleaver had developed a relationship while in Uarco and Standard's employ); hence, the provisions were enforceable.

REASONING Indiana precedents disfavor covenants not to compete as restraints on trade. Courts therefore strictly construe such agreements against the covenantee (here, Standard) and enforce only such covenants as are reasonable ones. The issue of reasonableness is a question of law that rests upon facts gleaned from the totality of the circumstances. Whether a covenant contains reasonable restrictions depends on the legitimate business interests of the employer that the covenant may protect, in conjunction with the duration, the geographic area, and the types of activity proscribed. Standard contended that the business interests at stake here include its good will, trade secrets, and confidential information. It further argued that it first seeks to prevent Cleaver from directly or indirectly communicating or divulging trade secrets or confidential information to others, including Prograde. However, when it comes to the specifics as to what it considers "trade secrets" or "confidential information," Standard retreated to generalities. And while Indiana by statute protects trade secrets, Standard identified little that would qualify as true proprietary information. However, Standard's argument that Cleaver had traded on Standard's good will deserved analysis. "Good will" consists of more than simply the names, addresses, and requirements of customers, or some pricing information; it also includes the advantageous familiarity and personal contact that employees, such as Cleaver, derive from their dealings with the employer's customers. This, of course, was the thrust of the nonsolicitation provision of paragraph 9 of the restrictive covenant. In short, Cleaver's familiarity with customers and their accounts represented a protectable interest for the employer, regardless of whether Cleaver had access to confidential information. The evidence indicated that Cleaver had assiduously courted HWI and had held out to Prograde the relationship he had developed with HWI as a good reason for Prograde's hiring him as a salesperson. Moreover, given his long-standing relationship with HWI, Cleaver had developed some special skill and knowledge as to the operation of that firm. Given that Standard had a protectable property interest in its good will, a court must determine whether paragraphs 9(a) and (b) are overly broad, since these provisions must be no broader than is necessary for the protection of Standard's good will. In imposing the "no-solicitation"restrictions set out in paragraph (a), the covenant did not seek to define a geographic scope; rather, it sought to recognize that if any good will had developed between Cleaver and his customers, it could only have come from Cleaver's personal contacts with them. Thus, while one can limit the scope of a covenant through geographical boundaries, one also can do this by increasing the specificity of the class of persons with whom contact is prohibited. In other words, the covenant must be sufficiently specific in scope so as to cover only the legitimate interests of the employer and to allow the employee a clear understanding of the conduct prohibited by the covenant. Here, the limitation coincided perfectly with what was clearly Standard's protectable interest—the buying customers with whom Cleaver had developed a relationship. Cleaver was in frequent, indeed sometimes weekly, contact with his customers so as to monitor their needs and foster his personal relationship with them. That upon leaving Standard Cleaver was able to switch the business to Prograde with virtually no drop-off in sales derived from the trust and confidence that HWI had reposed in him (and in reality, in Uarco and Standard), an intangible factor that one can obtain only after some considerable period of time. Consequently, the time period stated in paragraph 9(a) was enforceable. Moreover, such a limited restraint as paragraph 9(a) of the agreement sets forth would not be so substantial as to injure Cleaver. The provisions preclude him only from soliciting or contacting former entities to whom he had sold products during the year preceding his termination with Standard. Thus, Cleaver would be entirely free to sell to any other potential customers on behalf of Prograde. The court therefore granted Standard's motion for a preliminary injunction to prohibit Cleaver from working for Prograde.

continued

13.1

STANDARD REGISTER COMPANY V. CLEAVER, *continued*
30 F.SUPP.2D 1084 (N.D.IND. 1998)

BUSINESS CONSIDERATION Assume that you are on a student-consultants' team as part of one of your management courses and that your team has been assigned for the entire semester to the Standard Register Company. Would you expect the firm to ask everyone on the team to sign a nondisclosure clause as well as a non-compete clause? Why or why not?

ETHICAL CONSIDERATIONS Assuming as true the evidence showing that Cleaver had used his relationship with HWI as a good reason for Prograde's hiring him, how would you characterize Prograde's ethics in these circumstances? If Prograde had adhered to the Golden Rule, would the firm have hired Cleaver? Explain.

13.2 | MANAGEMENT

EMPLOYEE AGREEMENTS AND RELEASES

Tom and Anna would like any employees hired by CIT (including family members) to sign a covenant not to compete with the firm anywhere in the United States for at least three years after leaving employment with CIT. Both Lindsay and Dan consider such a covenant an insult and refuse to sign an employment contract unless the clause is removed. Tom and Anna have asked you for your advice. What will you tell them?

BUSINESS CONSIDERATIONS What sort of policy regarding covenants not to compete should a business adopt? When would such a covenant be a good idea? When would such a covenant be inadvisable? Explain.

ETHICAL CONSIDERATIONS Is it ethical for a firm to routinely require employees to sign covenants not to compete, even if the employee would not have access to any confidential business information? What ethical issues are raised by the use of such covenants?

Exculpatory Clauses

Agreements to commit torts are illegal. Indeed, little justification exists for a court to validate an agreement that stipulates an intentional breach of the duty of reasonable care to others. On the other hand, is anything illegal about a bargain in which one party tries in advance to limit its liability in a particular set of circumstances? Unfortunately, no clear-cut answer exists to this question. Courts judge the legality of such *exculpatory clauses*, or bargains in which one person agrees *in advance* to exonerate another person's activities from liability, on a case-by-case basis.

For example, a dry cleaner may always write on his customers' tickets, "Not responsible for elastic and buttons." When customers sign the tickets, the dry cleaner can argue that the customers agree to hold him harmless for any damages to elastic and buttons. Similarly, restaurants that have signs saying "Not responsible for belongings left in booths" attempt to achieve the same end. In general, these and other agreements in which one party promises not to hold the other liable for tortious or wrongful conduct are legal.

In many jurisdictions, statutes covering workers' compensation, innkeepers, and landlord-tenant relationships make the issue of liability for these particular areas moot. In the absence of statutes or clear precedents, however, courts look closely to see whether the party who agrees to assume the risk of tortious conduct without any recovery has done so voluntarily. In other words, the courts consider whether the party who has initiated the exculpatory clause has vastly superior bargaining power (or superior knowledge) over the other person. (Recall the bank deposit example earlier in this chapter.) If so, courts may strike down the exculpatory clause as contrary to public policy.

If the court believes an *adhesion contract* exists—that is, a contract drafted by the stronger party in order to force unfavorable terms on the weaker party—the court probably will find the clause contrary to public policy and thus illegal. This finding is by no means an easy task, though. Courts necessarily will weigh a variety of factors, such as the age of the parties, their respective degrees of expertise, their mental condition at the time they signed the clause (was the injured party drunk when he signed the exculpatory clause just before climbing onto the mechanical bull in Joe's Pub?), and the language of the clause (i.e., whether it was in fine print). After analyzing these and other facts and policies, the court decides the legality of such clauses.

The *Reed* v. *University of North Dakota* case that follows illustrates the disposition of a lawsuit involving exculpatory clause issues.

13.2

REED V. UNIVERSITY OF NORTH DAKOTA
589 N.W.2D 880 (N.D. 1999)

FACTS In 1989, the University of North Dakota (UND) offered Jace Reed, a Minnesota high school student, a scholarship to play hockey at UND. Reed signed a national letter of intent and played hockey at UND for two years. On 15 September 1991, Reed ran in a ten-kilometer charity road race sponsored by the North Dakota Association for the Disabled (NDAD). Before the race, Reed signed a registration form that, among other things, released the NDAD from all liability for injuries or any claims arising from his participation in the race. According to Reed, UND coaches presented the registration form to him before the race; and he had to sign it to run in the race, which was a mandatory part of the UND hockey team's preseason conditioning program. During the race, Reed became severely dehydrated and suffered extensive damage to his kidneys and liver. As a result, Reed required extensive medical care, including one kidney and two liver transplants, and thereby incurred substantial expenses for medical treatment. He subsequently brought a lawsuit challenging the validity of the release he had signed.

ISSUE Was the release a valid exculpatory clause?

HOLDING Yes. The release was supported by consideration; it was unambiguous; and it contravened no public policy. Hence, the release was fully enforceable against Reed.

REASONING Reed first asserted that the release was unenforceable, because it was not supported by consideration. The existence of consideration is a question of law. Consideration consists of any benefit con-

ferred or detriment suffered. The forbearance of a legal right is a legal detriment that constitutes good consideration. NDAD allowed the UND hockey players, as part of their preseason conditioning program, to run on the same course as its road race. When the hockey players, including Reed, signed the registration form, they agreed not to hold the participating sponsors responsible for any claims arising from their participation in the event; and NDAD agreed to let them run on the course during NDAD's road race. Reed's surrender of a legal right in exchange for NDAD's allowing him to run on the course during the race constituted consideration for the release. Reed further claimed that the release was ambiguous because he had neither contemplated the extreme nature of his injuries nor the allegedly improper medical attention he had received after collapsing from dehydration. Specifically, he viewed as vague and ambiguous the language to the effect that he was releasing NDAD from liability for "injuries [he] may incur as a direct or indirect result of [his] participation." The law in general does not favor contracts exonerating parties from liability for their conduct. Courts thus strictly construe exculpatory clauses against the benefitted party and will not enforce such agreements if they are ambiguous or release the benefitted party from liability for intentional, willful, or wanton acts. Yet, the parties remain bound by clear and unambiguous language evincing an intent to extinguish liability. While the language of this release is broad, it unambiguously evinces an intent to exonerate NDAD from liability for Reed's injuries. The consequences of dehydration and the allegation of

continued

13.2

REED V. UNIVERSITY OF NORTH DAKOTA, *continued*
589 N.W.2D 880 (N.D. 1999)

improper emergency medical care at the race site fell within the plain meaning of Reed's assumption of all responsibility for injuries incurred as a direct or indirect result of his participation in the race and his agreement not to hold NDAD responsible for any claims. Put differently, a court would render meaningless the plain language of this release if a court construed the language as not exonerating NDAD from responsibility for the injuries incurred by Reed as a result of his participation in this race. Hence, the release, since it clearly and unambiguously evinces an intent to exonerate NDAD from such liability, was valid. Reed further contended that the release is against public policy, because he lacked the bargaining power to negotiate or alter its terms. In considering whether a release is against public policy, other courts generally have considered: (1) the disparity of bargaining power between the parties in terms of the compulsion to sign the agreement and a lack of ability to negotiate the elimination of the clause and (2) the types of services provided by the party seeking exoneration, including whether they are public or essential services. Here, any perceived mandatory requirement for Reed to participate in this race involved his relationship with the UND hockey program rather than with NDAD. Although NDAD may have refused to allow Reed to run in the race if he

had failed to sign the registration form, it had not subjected him to any economic or other compulsion so as to force him to sign the release. Under these circumstances, Reed's argument that any differences in bargaining power between him and NDAD rendered this release invalid was unpersuasive. The release was not against public policy, and it therefore exonerated NDAD from liability for Reed's claims against the organization.

BUSINESS CONSIDERATIONS In deciding such a case, should a court take into account the fact that the entities being sued here were a public university and a charitable organization? Or is the nature of the organization irrelevant to the issue of the possible imposition of liability?

ETHICAL CONSIDERATIONS Do athletic programs, in their zeal to ensure a winning record, make too many demands on an athlete's out-of-class time? Is it ethical for the university to condition an athlete's receiving a scholarship on such things as his or her participation in charity events over which the university has no supervisory control? Why or why not?

EXCEPTIONS: UPHOLDING ILLEGAL AGREEMENTS

The general rule, as mentioned earlier, holds that an illegal bargain is void, and courts will leave the parties to such agreements where they find themselves as a result of the bargain. Despite this general rule, some situations do exist in which a party may bring a successful suit based on an illegal agreement. Put differently, one usually cannot sue for enforcement of an illegal executory agreement, but in certain circumstances one may sue if the performance called for in the bargain has been rendered.

Parties Not *in Pari Delicto*

When one of the parties is less guilty than the other, the law states that the parties are not *in pari delicto* (they are not equally at fault or equally wrong). This allows the less-guilty person to recover if recovery serves the public interest in some way. For instance, the less-guilty party may belong to the class of persons a regulatory statute was designed to protect. Such results thus focus on the conduct of the less-guilty party rather than on the illegality of the subject matter of the contract. For example, if Joanne works for a photographer who does not have a license as required by a local ordinance, she still can recover the wages due her if she is unaware of her boss's noncompliance. The law terms the illegality here *incidental* or *collateral* to Joanne's bargain.

Repentance

Even if the parties are *in pari delicto*, the law allows recovery by the person who shows repentance by rescinding the illegal bargain before its consummation. For example, assume that a partnership attempts to bribe a state senator to enact favorable legislation. This agreement would be illegal because it harms the public. If one of the partners attempts to rescind the transaction before delivery of the money to the senator, he or she can do so. The law calls this action *repentance*. Courts justify the partner's recovery of the money that he or she earlier directed to the senator because such a result furthers the public interest of deterring illegal schemes.

Partial Illegality

Agreements, as you may recall, may consist of several different promises supported by different considerations. While refusing to enforce those parts of the bargain that are illegal, courts enforce the parts of the bargain that involve legal promises and legal considerations if the courts can sever these legal promises. If, instead, either the illegal promise or the illegal consideration (or both) wholly taints the agreement, courts declare the entire agreement void. The *Standard Register Company* decision and others like it that involve a restrictive covenant may, in certain circumstances, provide good examples of partial illegality. If a court finds the restrictive covenant unreasonable in scope, the judge may, owing to the clause's illegality, sever it from the rest of the agreement. The court, however, ordinarily enforces the remainder of the contract (e.g., the sale of a business), because the balance of this contract is perfectly legal; it is divisible from the illegal portion. In short, after severing the illegal portions, courts will give effect to those provisions that constitute a legal contract.

Exhibit 13.1 on page 348 summarizes the key components of legality as an element of contract formation and enforcement.

THE IMPORTANCE OF FORM

At this point, you should have a good grasp of the requirements for a contract formation: agreement (offer and acceptance), consideration, capacity, reality of consent, and legality. In addition, according to the Statute of Frauds, to be enforceable, certain categories of contracts must be in writing. Contracts to answer for the debt of another if the debtor defaults, contracts involving interests in land, contracts not to be performed within one year from the date of their making, promises of executors and administrators to pay a claim against the estate of the deceased out of their own personal funds, contracts made in consideration of marriage, and contracts involving a sale of goods priced at $500 or more, or the lease of goods for $1,000 or more, represent the classifications of contracts that must be in proper form—that is, in writing—in order for the law to give them effect. The writing in these situations provides evidence that the parties actually did contract about the

E X H I B I T 13.1 | **The Requirement of Legality as an Element of Contract Formation and Enforcement**

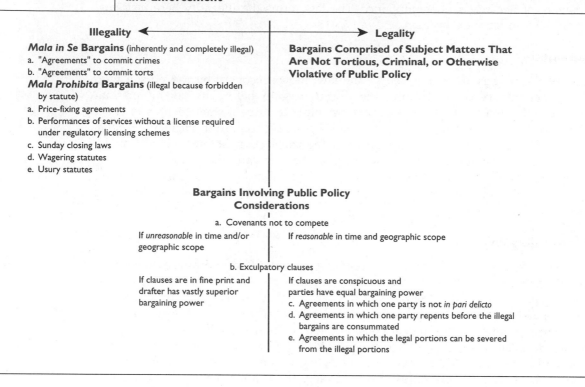

Illegality ◄ ──────────────────────── ► Legality

Mala in Se **Bargains** (inherently and completely illegal)
a. "Agreements" to commit crimes
b. "Agreements" to commit torts

Mala Prohibita **Bargains** (illegal because forbidden by statute)
a. Price-fixing agreements
b. Performances of services without a license required under regulatory licensing schemes
c. Sunday closing laws
d. Wagering statutes
e. Usury statutes

Bargains Comprised of Subject Matters That Are Not Tortious, Criminal, or Otherwise Violative of Public Policy

Bargains Involving Public Policy Considerations
a. Covenants not to compete

If *unreasonable* in time and/or geographic scope | If *reasonable* in time and geographic scope

b. Exculpatory clauses

If clauses are in fine print and drafter has vastly superior bargaining power | If clauses are conspicuous and parties have equal bargaining power
c. Agreements in which one party is not *in pari delicto*
d. Agreements in which one party repents before the illegal bargains are consummated
e. Agreements in which the legal portions can be severed from the illegal portions

---

Perjuries
False statements made under oath during court proceedings.

matters in dispute, and it avoids the **perjuries** traditionally and historically associated with these categories of contracts. In most other situations, the parties are free to contract orally even though it is unwise to do so.

Moreover, once the parties reduce their agreement to writing, judges necessarily are wary of tampering with the contract. For this reason, the parol evidence rule states that oral testimony ordinarily is not admissible to add to, alter, or vary the terms of a written agreement. In certain situations, parol evidence will be admissible to clear up ambiguities. Reference to the trade usages and customs of a particular industry may dispose of these types of ambiguities. Hence, an understanding of the interplay between the Statute of Frauds and the parol evidence rule will represent a useful adjunct to your understanding of contract law.

STATUTE OF FRAUDS

Statute of Frauds
A statute requiring that specified types of contracts be in writing in order to be enforceable.

The historical ancestor of the present-day **Statute of Frauds** was called "An Act for the Prevention of Frauds and Perjuries," passed by the English Parliament in 1677. Because perjury was so widespread in lawsuits involving oral contracts, Parliament decreed that, to be enforceable, certain classes of contracts must be in writing. Thus, the term *Statute of Frauds* is somewhat misleading, because such statutes deal with the requirement of a writing rather than with reality-of-consent situations like fraud. (In the Statute of Frauds, the term *frauds* refers to the wholesale misrepresentations or perjured statements made to early English courts.) Almost every state has a Statute of Frauds modeled on this original statute.

The Statute of Frauds requires that certain types of contracts be in writing before courts will enforce them. Thus, if the subject matter of the contract involves a type of contract enumerated in the Statute of Frauds, the agreement generally cannot be oral but instead must be in writing before a court will give it effect. The Statute of Frauds never is a legal issue unless a valid contract exists; hence, it becomes an issue only after all the stages of contract formation are present.

The Statute of Frauds also is an **affirmative defense,** one used by a person who wants to avoid the enforcement of a contract. A defendant who wishes to utilize this defense must expressly plead it, or it will be waived; if a waiver is found, an oral contract that otherwise would have been unenforceable because of a violation of the Statute of Frauds will be enforced against the defendant. Courts have been somewhat hostile to Statute of Frauds claims because of the injustice such statutes can cause. Consequently, some courts construe these statutes broadly and find various rationales for removing the contract at issue from the coverage of the statute. These interpretations, then, allow the court to give effect to oral contracts that otherwise would not be enforceable.

Affirmative defense
A defense to a cause of action that the defendant must raise.

Types of Contracts Covered

The following sections examine six categories of contracts covered by the Statute of Frauds:

- Contracts to answer for the debt of another if the person so defaults
- Contracts for interests in land
- Contracts not to be performed within one year of the date of their making
- Promises by executors and administrators of estates
- Contracts made in consideration of marriage
- Contracts for the sale of goods priced at $500 or more or the lease of goods for $1,000 or more

Contracts to Answer for the Debt of Another If the Person So Defaults. Ordinarily, oral promises between two persons are perfectly valid and enforceable in court. When Linda orally promises to pay George $200 for a used cash register and he orally promises to sell it to her, a contract exists between the two parties. We call such promises *original* promises because both parties have promised to be *primarily* liable (i.e., liable in all events) if something in the transaction should go awry.

Sometimes people agree to be secondarily liable—that is, only in the event someone else (i.e., the debtor) defaults. Such agreements, called *collateral contracts,* are promises to answer for the debt or default of another. Collateral contracts typically involve three persons: the debtor (the original promisor), the creditor (the promisee), and the third party, who generally is called a **guarantor.** Notice that a collateral contract exhibits definite characteristics:

1. There are three parties (some three-party transactions—**novations,** for example—are not collateral contracts, however).
2. There are two promises, one original (debtor to creditor) and the other collateral (third party to creditor).
3. The second promise is a promise to accept only collateral, or secondary, liability resulting from the default of another.

Since most people would view such collateral promises as somewhat unusual (we generally assume people will be responsible for their own debts but not for another

Guarantor
One who promises to answer for the payment of a debt or the performance of an obligation if the person liable in the first instance fails to make payment or to perform.

Novations
By mutual agreement, substitutions of new contracts in place of preexisting ones, whether between the same parties or with new parties replacing one or more of the original parties.

person's), this provision of the Statute of Frauds requires evidence—through a writing—of this undertaking of possible secondary liability.

The *intent of the parties* determines whether a three-party transaction involves a collateral contract, which must be in writing to be enforceable, or an original contract, which may be enforceable even if oral. For example, if Stein wants his grandson to have a car, he may co-sign the note his grandson has signed with a bank. This is a three-party situation (Stein, his grandson, and the bank), but it is not a collateral contract. Stein and his grandson are joint, original promisors to the bank. The same would be true if Stein had been a **surety** (a concept discussed in Chapter 11). As such, Stein is accepting liability in all events. If the grandson defaults on the car payment, the bank can sue either Stein or his grandson. If, however, Stein wishes to be only secondarily liable and the note is phrased accordingly, the contract is a collateral one. In the event of the grandson's default, the bank must sue the grandson *without success before* it can attempt to hold Stein liable. Note that the intent of the parties is crucial in determining the type of contract—original or collateral—that is involved. By requiring any transaction deemed a collateral contract to be in writing, the bank is protecting itself from a defense based on the Statute of Frauds.

Because courts generally are hostile to the Statute of Frauds, they sometimes allow an exception to the rule that a collateral contract must be in writing to be enforceable. This is called the *leading-object* or *main-purpose* exception: When the third party agrees to be liable chiefly for the purpose of obtaining an economic benefit for him- or herself personally, the second promise, even if oral, will be enforceable. Let us change our earlier example to one in which Stein orally tells the bank he will pay if his grandson defaults. When the grandson fails to pay and the bank sues Stein, Stein will use the Statute of Frauds as his defense: No writing exists, and the contract appears to be a collateral one. If the bank nonetheless can prove that before Stein agreed to be liable, he knew that the institution was about to force the grandson into bankruptcy—which, in turn, meant that Stein might lose sizable loans he had made to his grandson—the bank may be able to show that Stein's "leading object" in making the promise primarily involved preventing economic loss to himself rather than displaying grandfatherly love and generosity. Proving this, the bank can argue that the "main purpose" of Stein's conduct focused on protecting his own economic position vis-à-vis his grandson's impending bankruptcy. Owing to the personal, immediate, pecuniary benefits Stein himself may have realized from the bank's loan, courts will cast aside their usual skepticism concerning such oral promises and impose liability on Stein.

By requiring all promises to be in writing, the wise businessperson or firm avoids such potential legal problems. The following case illustrates a number of these concepts.

Surety
A person who promises to pay or to perform in the event the principal debtor fails to do so.

13.3

GALLAGHER, LANGLAS & GALLAGHER V. BURCO
587 N.W.2D 615 (IOWA APP. 1998)

FACTS Lynn Roose asked that the law firm of Gallagher, Langlas and Gallagher, P.C. (Gallagher) represent her in her dissolution (divorce) action. In August 1994, Attorney Thomas Langlas gave Roose a contract in which he requested a $2,000 retainer fee. Roose never signed or returned the contract. She also did not pay the retainer fee in full. Nonetheless, the firm represented Roose in her lawsuit. On 10 April 1995, the

13.3

GALLAGHER, LANGLAS & GALLAGHER V. BURCO, *continued*

587 N.W.2D 615 (IOWA APP. 1998)

Gallagher attorneys met with Roose and her father, Gaylen Burco, and told Burco about the anticipated child custody trial. The firm contended that, during the meeting, Burco agreed to take responsibility for the remainder of Roose's account; Burco later denied the existence of any such agreement. But at the end of the meeting, Burco gave the firm a check for $1,000 to pay the outstanding balance of $814.92 on Roose's account. Before the trial, when another attorney with the firm contacted Burco requesting an additional retainer to secure the fees to be incurred, Burco told her, "My word as a gentleman should be enough . . . I told Mr. Langlas I would pay and I will pay." When Roose failed to pay her legal fees, in July 1995, the attorneys sent Burco a letter requesting either $5,000 for Roose's legal fees or the signing of a promissory note for that amount. Although neither Roose nor Burco paid the attorney's fees or signed any notes, the firm represented Roose in the July 1995 trial. After the trial, Burco returned the second letter and promissory note with a notation stating he was not responsible for his daughter's attorney's fees. When the firm filed an action against Burco and Roose for the unpaid legal fees, Burco denied the allegations and raised the affirmative defense of the Statute of Frauds.

ISSUES Did the parties' dealings show sufficient definiteness to constitute a valid agreement? Was the agreement unenforceable under the Statute of Frauds?

HOLDINGS Yes to both issues. The agreement constituted a valid contract, but the contract was unenforceable because the collateral promise made by the father was oral.

REASONING The first question involved whether the terms of the communications between Burco and the firm showed sufficient definiteness to form a contract. At the 10 April 1996, meeting, the attorney estimated that Burco daughter's custody trial would cost approximately $1,000 per day. The firm would not guarantee Burco that the trial would last only two or three days. Burco subsequently paid $1,000 towards an existing $814.92 bill, said he would pay for future services, and emphasized that his word was good enough. At the trial, Burco took an active part by testifying and participating in conferences with counsel during recesses. Nonetheless, Burco claimed his guarantee to pay future legal expenses was too vague and

uncertain to form a contract. However, the dealings between the parties were definite. Each party's duties were clear: The attorneys would represent Roose in her custody fight, and Burco would pay her legal fees. These terms are as definite as many attorney-fee agreements and thus are sufficient to prove an oral contract existed. Burco next contended that the Statute of Frauds would bar any evidence of the oral contract. The Statute of Frauds requires that certain contracts be evidenced by some kind of writing before they are enforceable. Among other things, the statute applies to contracts involving a promise to a creditor to answer for the debt, default, or miscarriage of another. In construing its Statute of Frauds, Iowa courts have distinguished between collateral and original promises. Original promises are made when the promise to pay the debt of another arises out of new and original consideration between the newly contracting parties. With an original promise, the guarantor has a personal concern in the debtor's obligation and will achieve a personal benefit out of the debtor's obligation. Put differently, the leading object of the guarantor's promise is to secure some benefit or business advantage for himself or herself. Original promises do not fall within the Statute of Frauds. Collateral promises are made when a promise is made in addition to an already existing contract and the guarantor has no personal concern in the debtor's obligation and fails to gain any benefit from the debtor's obligation. In short, the "main purpose" of the promise must not involve a benefit to the guarantor. Collateral promises fall within the Statute of Frauds. In addition to ascertaining whether the promisor receives a benefit, a court must ascertain the party to whom the credit was extended (the promisor) or the party to whom services were rendered. A court ascertains this intention from the promissory words used, the situation of the parties, and all the surrounding circumstances at the time of the making of the promise. Whether a promise is collateral to an existing contract or creates a primary obligation on the part of the promisor (as in a suretyship) is a question of fact. The trial court had determined that Burco's promise was original rather than collateral "inasmuch as it involved his daughter and grandchild." However, nothing in the record supported this conclusion except the vague notion that the matter affected Burco's family. The evidence showed the benefit to

continued

13.3

GALLAGHER, LANGLAS & GALLAGHER V. BURCO, *continued*

587 N.W.2D 615 (IOWA APP. 1998)

Burco was indirect: If his daughter won custody of his granddaughter, he may have gotten to visit the granddaughter more. But the evidence failed to show this was Burco's primary motivating factor in promising to pay his daughter's debt. Since Burco gained no benefit from his promise, his promise was collateral rather than original. The Statute of Frauds thus applies to Burco's promise and makes the contract unenforceable. Once a court determines the Statute of Frauds applies to a contract, the court must determine if any exceptions apply. One such exception, if proven, is promissory estoppel. The law firm did make a scanty reference to the basic concepts of estoppel during the trial when a firm attorney testified the firm had relied on Burco's "promises" to the firm's "detriment." But Iowa law required the law firm to file a reply to Burco's affirmative defense of the Statute of Frauds if the firm had planned to develop this defense on appeal. The firm's failure to do so constituted a waiver of the contention that promissory estoppel would take Burco's promise outside the coverage of the Statute of Frauds. The Statute of Frauds thus applied, and Burco's oral promise to pay his daughter's debt was unenforceable.

BUSINESS CONSIDERATIONS Should the law firm have taken a "hard-nosed" approach and have refused to represent Roose in the absence of her father's written guarantee of the fees? What are the respective merits and demerits of such an approach?

ETHICAL CONSIDERATIONS Burco's failure to live up to his word exemplifies what some ethicists have identified as the erosion of the worth of a personal oath. Do you agree that formal and informal vows, or promises, do not carry the same depth of commitment they used to reflect? If you do, what are the underlying causes of this phenomenon?

Mortgages
Conditional transfers of property as security for a debt.

Leases
Contracts that grant the right to use and occupy realty.

Easements
Limited rights to use and enjoy the land of another.

Contracts for Interests in Land. Any agreement that involves buying, selling, or transferring interests in land must be in writing to be enforceable. **Mortgages, leases, easements,** and sales agreements about standing timber and buildings attached to the land also should be in writing to satisfy the Statute of Frauds. Thus, if you orally offer to buy someone's house and the seller accepts your offer, this contract will be unenforceable because it does not comply with the Statute of Frauds.

Courts nevertheless will enforce oral contracts for the sale of land if the purchaser has paid part of the purchase price and, with the seller's consent, takes possession of the land and makes valuable improvements on it. This equitable remedy is called the *doctrine of part performance.* For example, assume Green moves onto Berry's land and, with Berry's oral permission, tears down an old garage, repaints the entire house, and rebuilds a barn, all at Green's expense. Before undertaking these actions, Green also has paid $5,000 to Berry. When Berry later tries to claim an absence of any enforceable contract of sale between the two, a court nonetheless can order specific performance of the contract despite noncompliance with the Statute of Frauds. Courts justify such an exception to the requirement of a writing on the ground that the *conduct* of the parties prior to litigation shows the existence of a contract. Courts in such cases conclude that the parties' actions can be explained only by the actuality of such a contract. To avoid the unjust enrichment of the seller, equity also will give remedies in such situations.

Contracts Not to Be Performed Within One Year of the Date of Their Making.
According to the Statute of Frauds, a promise in a contract that cannot be performed within one year from the date of the making of the agreement must be in writing

to be enforceable. To illustrate, an oral promise to haul milk for a dairy producer is invalid under the Statute of Frauds if the milk cannot be hauled in less than one year. This is the case when the parties enter into a contract on 15 December, with the term of the contract stated as running from 1 January to 31 December of the next year. Such a contract is one not to be performed within one year of the date of its making (15 December). Therefore, under the Statute of Frauds, to be enforceable, this agreement must be in writing.

Courts have reacted hostilely to this section of the statute because, when applied, it may harshly affect the parties to the contract. Thus, courts often have limited the coverage of this proviso to situations in which *performance cannot possibly occur within one year's time* (as in our example above). This limitation has led to rather strained results. For example, a bilateral contract in which an employee promises to work for an employer "for the employer's lifetime" in exchange for the employer's promise to pay a monthly salary sounds as if it invariably cannot be performed within one year. Some courts, however, interpret such language to mean that since it is *possible*—though not *probable*—that the employer might die within a year, an oral contract is enforceable despite the Statute of Frauds. Under this approach, if the contract in our earlier example obligated the hauler to transport the milk for "as long as the dairy farmer produces milk," such courts would reason that the dairy farmer possibly could cease operations within one year, thereby making the contract capable of being performed within one year from the date of the making of the contract. Although a remote possibility, the fact that such a contingency could happen makes the oral contract enforceable and this section of the Statute of Frauds inapplicable. Other courts, nevertheless, will adopt the stricter approach and hold that the contracts at issue in both cases must be in writing to be enforceable.

Some jurisdictions allow recovery for oral contracts that fall under this provision of the Statute of Frauds—that is, because they extend for periods longer than one year—when one party to the contract will be able to complete its performance within one year, even though the other party will be unable to do so. Courts also may apply promissory estoppel, which we discussed in Chapter 10, to allow recovery for otherwise unenforceable contracts.

Promises by Executors and Administrators of Estates. Promises by **executors** and **administrators** of estates to pay estate claims out of their own personal funds must be in writing to be enforceable. Since such promises are relatively unusual, the courts require a writing as evidence that the parties actually reached such an agreement.

Executors
The persons named and appointed in a will by the testator to carry out the administration of the estate as established by the will.

Contracts Made in Consideration of Marriage. Like the previous category, unilateral promises to pay money or to transfer property in consideration of a promise to marry are so uncommon that the law will enforce such promises only if they are in writing. If the Benson family promises to pay $20,000 and to transfer the ownership of their condominium in Florida to Pat Lloyd—if Pat promises to marry their child—the Statute of Frauds will require the Bensons' promise to be in writing. By analogy, antenuptial (or prenuptial) agreements, into which couples enter before marriage and which typically spell out the disposition of the marital property should the marriage end in divorce, also ordinarily must be in writing to be enforceable.

Administrators
The persons who have been empowered by an appropriate court to handle the estate of a deceased person.

Contracts for the Sale of Goods Priced at $500 or More or the Lease of Goods for $1,000 or More. In addition to the five common law categories of contracts that need to be in writing to be enforceable under the Statute of Frauds, the Uniform

Commercial Code (UCC) also has several provisions that implicate the Statute of Frauds. The most important of these are UCC Sections 2-201 and 2A-201. Section 2-201 states that contracts for the sale of goods priced at $500 or more are not enforceable unless there is a writing sufficient to indicate that a contract for sale has been made between the parties and the writing is signed by the person against whom enforcement of the contract is sought. Section 2A-201 states that contracts for the leasing of goods calling for total payments of $1,000 or more, excluding payments for options to renew or to buy, are not enforceable unless there is a writing sufficient to indicate that a contract for the lease has been made between the parties and the writing has been signed by the party against whom enforcement is sought. Therefore, according to the Statute of Frauds, a contract for a sale of produce—since the Code would classify produce as goods (i.e., identifiable, movable, personal property)—priced at $500 or more must be in writing. Similarly, a contract for the leasing of a computer—which is also classified as goods under the UCC—with lease payments of $1,000 or more must be in writing. The Code further states that a writing is not insufficient if it omits or incorrectly states a term agreed on, but courts will refuse to enforce the agreement beyond the *quantity* of goods mentioned in such a writing.

Under § 2-201, however, courts will enforce oral contracts if (1) the goods are to be specially manufactured for the buyer and are not suitable for sale to others in the ordinary course of the seller's business; (2) the buyer makes a partial payment or a partial acceptance, although the contract will be enforced only for the portion of goods paid for or accepted; or (3) the party being sued admits in court, or in court documents, that a contract was made for a certain quantity of goods. These same exceptions in addition apply to lease contracts that otherwise would require a writing.

UCC § 2-201 also contains a novel provision that may trap the unaware merchant. A **merchant** who receives a signed written confirmation (e.g., "This is to confirm our sale to you of 2,000 bushels of apples, #2 grade, at $1.25/bushel, delivery Tuesday /s/ Seller") from another merchant and does not object to the confirmation in writing within 10 days is bound to the contract. The policy underlying this result is a familiar one: A valid oral contract on the terms stated must exist if the other party (who, as a merchant, is considered a "pro") does not object to the confirmation. The moral of this section of the UCC is: Answer your mail, merchants!

Writing

As we have seen in other contexts, the writing required to satisfy the Statute of Frauds may be rather negligible; it may take the form of letters, telegrams, receipts, or memoranda. The writing must, at a minimum, identify the parties to the agreement, the subject matter of the agreement, and all material terms and conditions. Several writings may be pieced together as long as they all refer to the same transaction.

Signature

Similarly, anything intended by the parties as a signature will suffice to satisfy the Statute of Frauds. This, of course, would include written signatures, but courts even have held stamped signatures or stationery letterheads to be sufficient. Both parties need not sign the memorandum, as long as the party against whom enforcement is sought, or the party's authorized agent, has signed.

Merchant
A person who deals in goods of this kind, or otherwise, through his or her occupation, holds him- or herself out as having knowledge or skill peculiar to the practice or goods involved in the transaction.

Parol evidence
Oral statements.

Substantive law
The portion of the law that regulates rights, in contrast to law that grants remedies or enforces rights.

Exhibit 13.2 on pages 256 and 257 explains the scope of the Statute of Frauds, the elements required to find coverage, and the exceptions to the general rules.

PAROL EVIDENCE RULE

So far, we have explored some of the concepts and rules concerning the application of the Statute of Frauds. We now turn to another important facet of contract law, the **parol evidence** rule. The law predicates this on the belief that oral evidence should not be admissible to alter, add to, or vary the terms of an integrated, written contract. If the parties appear to have intended the writing as the final expression of their agreement, a court's allowing later oral or written evidence that contradicts that writing will call into question the whole process of reducing one's agreement to writing. The parol evidence rule serves several important purposes. First, it facilitates judicial interpretation by having a single, clear source of proof as to the terms of the agreement between the parties. Second, it emphasizes the importance of writings between the parties. For instance, assume that Larry and Ahmed sign a contract for the sale of a consulting business. They both agree, in writing, that the price of the business is $16,000. If Larry or Ahmed later tries to argue that the price is higher or lower and litigation ensues, the parol evidence rule will preclude oral testimony to this effect. Imagine the havoc a contrary rule would cause. By applying the parol evidence rule, courts therefore uphold the sanctity of totally integrated written contracts.

Because the parol evidence rule is designed to further a policy of protecting writings—those instruments representing the final intentions and terms of the parties—it actually is a rule of **substantive law** rather than a rule of evidence.

EXCEPTIONS TO THE PAROL EVIDENCE RULE

The preceding notwithstanding, courts will disregard the parol evidence rule and will admit parol evidence in certain circumstances. The following sections describe common circumstances in which the parol evidence rule is not applied.

Partially Integrated Contracts

The policy base that underlies the parol evidence rule becomes less compelling in situations in which the contract

13.3 | SALES/ MANUFACTURING

CHECKING THE MAIL

- The Kochanowskis traditionally take a two-week family vacation. Anna is concerned that, if the family takes such a vacation, mail sent to the firm will go unanswered. She suggests that they select an employee to check the mail daily during their absence. Tom does not like the idea of having an employee reading CIT's mail. He asserts that because two weeks is not such a long time, he and Anna can catch up with the mail on their return. They have asked for your advice. What will you tell them? Does the time involved affect your answer?
- The Kochanowskis have recently reviewed and decided to revise the standard form contracts used by the firm. As a part of these revisions, Dan suggests that the firm include a so-called "merger clause" stating that the written contract represents the parties' agreement and that the written terms supersede any previous oral communications. The family members have asked you whether such a merger clause is a good idea for CIT. What advice will you give them on this matter?

BUSINESS CONSIDERATIONS Why is it important for businesspersons to read and react to their mail in a timely manner? Should a business develop a policy that all its written agreements be designed and treated as fully integrated contracts? Why might this be a good policy? What potential drawbacks would such a policy present? **ETHICAL CONSIDERATIONS** Is it ethical to hold a merchant responsible for mail received but unanswered (or even unread), when the same rules do not apply to a nonmerchant? Why does the distinction between merchants and nonmerchants matter? Is it ethical for a salesperson to imply orally that the item he or she is selling is better than it really is, especially if the salesperson knows that the firm uses a fully integrated written contract that tempers the language used in the sales presentation? What ethical issues does such conduct reflect?

E X H I B I T 13.2 | **The Statute of Frauds**

Types of Contracts Covered (and Which Must Be in Writing)	Elements	Exceptions
1. Contracts to answer for the debt of another if the person so defaults	1. There are three parties. 2. There are two promises, one original (debtor to creditor) and the other collateral (third-party guarantor to creditor). 3. The second promise is a promise to accept only secondary liability resulting from the default of another. 4. The intent of the parties determines whether a three-party transaction involves a collateral contract (which must be in writing) or an original contract (which can be oral yet still enforceable).	1. Novations and other three-party transactions are not guaranty contracts but joint, original contracts. 1. The "leading object" or "main purpose" doctrine may apply.
2. Contracts for interests in land	1. The agreement involves buying, selling, or transferring interests in land. 2. Leases, easements, and sale agreements about standing timber and buildings attached to the land also are covered.	1. The doctrine of part performance may take the contract out of the statute.
3. Contracts not to be performed within one year of the date of their making	1. Contracts in which it is impossible to perform the contract completely within one year of the date of the creation of the contract are involved.	1. Courts may circumvent the application of the statute by resorting to the fiction that it is possible (albeit not probable) for the contracts to be performed within one year. 2. Part performance by one party has occurred. 3. Circumstances that justify the application of promissory estoppel exist.

continued

is partially integrated (i.e., the writing is an incomplete statement of the contract). In such cases, although the writing may not be *contradicted* by evidence of earlier terms, it may be *supplemented* by evidence of additional, consistent terms.

Mistake, Fraud, and Other "Reality-of-Consent" Situations

Parol evidence similarly is admissible to show mistake, fraud, duress, and failure of consideration—the kinds of situations covered in Chapter 12. Since the existence of these circumstances casts doubt on the validity of the integrated writing, no overwhelmingly persuasive policy reason to justify the exclusion of contradictory oral statements is present.

Ambiguities and Conditions Precedent

Courts also will allow parol evidence in order to clear up ambiguities and to show that the agreement was not to become binding on the parties until a *condition*

EXHIBIT 13.2 | The Statute of Frauds, continued

Types of Contracts Covered (and Which Must Be in Writing)	Elements	Exceptions
4. Promises by executors and administrators of estates	1. The executors or administrators have promised to pay estate claims out of their own personal funds.	
5. Contracts made in consideration of marriage	1. One person has promised another person to pay a given amount or otherwise to perform a contractual duty in order to induce the person to enter a marriage.	
6. Contracts for the sale of goods priced at $500 or more (UCC § 2-201) or contracts for the lease of goods for $1,000 or more (UCC §2A-201)	1. The contract involves the sale or lease of goods. 2. The price of the goods must be at least $500, or the lease is for at least $1,000. 3. The writing is not insufficient if it omits or incorrectly states an agreed-on term, but the contract will be unenforceable beyond the quantity of goods shown in the writing. 4. The writing must be signed by the person (or by his or her authorized agent or broker) against whom enforcement is sought.	1. Between merchants, a written confirmation sent by one party to another must be objected to by the other within 10 days, or the Statute of Frauds will be satisfied. 2. Oral contracts that are enforceable consist of those involving (a) specially manufactured goods not readily resalable in the ordinary course of the seller's business, (b) goods for which payment has been received, (c) goods for which acceptance has been made, or (d) an admission in a court proceeding by the person against whom enforcement is sought that a contract for sale was made.

precedent (i.e., a certain act or event that must occur before the other party has a duty to perform or before a contract exists) was met, such as reduction of the agreement to writing or approval of the contract by a party's attorney. However, courts may allow evidence about a condition precedent only if this evidence does not contradict the written terms of the contract at issue.

Uniform Commercial Code

Sections 2-202 and 2-208 of the UCC concern the parol evidence rule. Basically, the Code recognizes the rule but then reduces its impact by stating that evidence of course of dealing (the parties' previous conduct), usage of trade (a regularly observed practice in a trade), and course of performance (a contract that contemplates repeated occasions of performance) is admissible. Courts also can admit evidence of consistent, additional terms unless they find that the parties intended the writing as a complete and exclusive statement of the terms of the agreement. Moreover, the Code sets up priorities among these types of evidence: The express terms of the agreement control course of performance, course of dealing, and usage of trade. Evidence relating to course of performance, in turn, controls admissions about course of dealing and usage of trade.

ELECTRONIC COMMUNICATIONS AND THE STATUTE OF FRAUDS

The intersection of technology and contract law principles mentioned in Chapter 10 continues to baffle courts that recently have tried to apply the Statute of Frauds to electronic commerce. To illustrate, assume Mark sends an e-mail in which he offers to buy a computer priced at $1,500 from Joe, and Mark "signs" his name at the bottom of the offer. In response, Joe sends an e-mail in which he accepts the offer, and Joe, too, "signs" his name at the end of his acceptance. Do these "writings" and "signatures" suffice for the purposes of the Statute of Frauds? A 1996 case has construed a fax transmission as "beeps and chirps along a telephone line" rather than as a writing. Under this precedent, then, e-mail, telegram, or fax-generated contracts would be unenforceable under the Statute of Frauds. As one commentator notes, "This ruling freezes technology at the pen." Critics of such conservative judicial stances submit that a more flexible approach will both preserve the evidentiary thrust of the Statute and avoid sacrificing the efficiencies gained from a firm's utilizing the new technologies. Those who advocate this position point out that e-mail–generated digital signatures ordinarily utilize sophisticated encryption technology. With this encryption, it is almost impossible to alter such a signature; accordingly, the signature's authenticity is virtually conclusive.

Assume the losing party has appealed the 1996 case mentioned here, and *you* are the sitting judge. Will *you* uphold this ruling or reverse it? Why?[3]

BUSINESS CONSIDERATIONS Given the unsettled state of the law regarding electronic transmissions, what policies should a firm establish with regard to its use of such technology? How can a firm reap the benefits of cyberspace yet protect its legal rights?

ETHICAL CONSIDERATIONS What general ethical issues inhere in business's increasing use of information technologies? Do these issues differ from those inherent in print-based technologies?

SOURCE: Mark Grossman, *The Connecticut Law Tribune* (27 July 1998), p. 17.

Section 2A-201 of the UCC covers the provisions of the Statute of Frauds concerning contracts for the lease of goods. Section 2A-201 requires a writing when the total payments under the lease contract equal $1,000 or more, excluding any payments for an option to renew the lease or any payments for an option to buy.

SUMMARY

In order for the bargain to be recognized as a valid contract, the law imposes a requirement that the subject matter and purpose of a bargain must be legal. A bargain is illegal if its performance is criminal, tortious, or otherwise opposed to public policy. Some courts distinguish between bargains that violate statutes because they are evil in themselves (*mala in se*) and bargains that are merely forbidden by statute (*mala prohibita*). Many types of bargains (such as price-fixing agreements, bargains in contravention of Sunday closing laws, wagering agreements, and usurious transactions) violate statutes. Performances of services without a license may *click here*

RESOURCES FOR BUSINESS LAW STUDENTS

NAME	RESOURCES	WEB ADDRESSES
Sherman Antitrust Act 15 USC §§ 1–7	The Legal Information Institute (LII) provides a hypertext and searchable version of 15 USC §§ 1–7, popularly known as the Sherman Antitrust Act.	**http://www4.law.cornell.edu/uscode/15/1.html**
Clayton Act 15 USC §§ 12–27	The LII provides a hypertext and searchable version of 15 USC §§ 12–27, popularly known as the Clayton Antitrust Act.	**http://www4.law.cornell.edu/uscode/15/12.html**
Federal Trade Commission Act, 15 USC §§ 41–58	The LII provides a hypertext and searchable version of 15 USC §§ 41–58 popularly known as the Federal Trade Commission Act.	**http://www4.law.cornell.edu/uscode/15/41.html**

make the agreement void if the statute is regulatory. In contrast, if the statute requires licensing as a revenue-enhancing measure, the lack of a license will not void the bargain. When deciding cases, judges today look increasingly to public policy factors. Covenants not to compete (promises to refrain from engaging in the same or a similar business for a period of time in a certain geographic area) and exculpatory clauses (agreements in advance to exonerate another from negligence or other torts), if too restrictive or one-sided, may be struck down on public policy grounds. Some exceptions to the rule that illegal bargains are void exist. These exceptions include agreements in which the parties are not *in pari delicto,* or of equal guilt; agreements in which one party repents before it consummates the illegal bargain; and agreements in which courts can sever the legal portions from the illegal segments.

In accordance with the Statute of Frauds, certain types of contracts must be in writing to be enforceable. These include collateral contracts, contracts for the sale or transfer of interests in land, contracts not to be performed within one year from the date of their making, promises of executors and administrators of estates, promises made in consideration of marriage, and contracts for the sale of goods priced at $500 or more or the lease of goods with payments of $1,000 or more. Nevertheless, very little in the way of a memorandum or signature is necessary to satisfy the Statute of Frauds. The parol evidence rule states that oral evidence is not admissible to alter, add to, or vary the terms of an integrated, written contract. However, the law will not apply the parol evidence rule in some circumstances: partially integrated contracts; agreements involving mistake, duress, fraud, ambiguity, or conditions precedent; or in some commercial contexts.

DISCUSSION QUESTIONS

1. What is the difference between a *mala in se* and a *mala prohibita* bargain?
2. What is an exculpatory clause? Is it always legal? Why or why not?
3. What are *covenants not to compete*? What standards do courts use to judge their legality?
4. Why are wagering and lotteries illegal in various jurisdictions?
5. What is a usurious contract? What kinds of common financing devices would not violate the usury laws?
6. Describe the three most important exceptions to the general rule that an illegal bargain is void.
7. Explain both the historical and the current basis for the Statute of Frauds.
8. What are the most important characteristics of a collateral contract, or a contract to guarantee the debt of another if a person so defaults? Also, explain the exception to the rule that collateral contracts must be in writing.
9. Describe the exceptions to the rule that a contract for a sale of goods priced at $500 or more or the lease of goods with payments of $1,000 or more must be in writing.
10. What is the parol evidence rule? What are the exceptions to it?

CASE PROBLEMS AND WRITING ASSIGNMENTS

1. Bradley Holcom was a licensed real estate agent who arranged the sale of trust deeds for clients looking to invest in loans for the development of real property. John Roes approached Holcom about investing in trust deeds and, from 1991 to 1993, purchased interests in a number of properties through Holcom. In May 1992, Holcom arranged two $179,000 construction loans to Luz Maria Garcia for the development of two properties in Calexico, California. Each loan was reflected by a promissory note secured by one of the two properties, and each note provided for interest at 15 percent (the senior notes). Holcom also personally made two loans, totaling $50,000, to Garcia for the development of the two properties. A second trust deed on the relevant property secured each of the Holcom loans (the junior notes). Less than one month later, at a time when Holcom knew of potential problems with the development of the properties, Holcom sold his interests in the junior notes and the second trust deeds to John Roes for $43,000. When Garcia defaulted on the repayment of the loans, the holders of the senior notes threatened foreclosure. To avoid losing his investment in the properties, Roes paid the interest, costs, and penalties due on the senior notes and ultimately paid them off. He later sued the holders of the senior notes. Specifically, Roes alleged that the senior note holders' violation of California's usury laws entitled him to treble damages for the interest paid under the notes. Would someone other than the debtor—here the holder of a junior encumbrance—have standing to assert a claim under the usury laws? [See *Roes* v. *Wong*, 81 Cal.Rptr.2d 596 (Cal.App. 4 Dist. 1999).]

2. Sysco Corporation (Sysco), a distributor of food and cleaning products, hired Michael Massino, William G. Mitchell, and Scott R. Thomas as marketing associates. Sysco and the three employees came to terms on the essential aspects of their employment—including salary, benefits, bonuses, and territory—left their prior employment, and reported for work with Sysco. At that point, Sysco asked them to sign a restrictive covenant in which they agreed not to disclose Sysco's confidential and proprietary information. The three also agreed that for a one-year period after the termination of their employment with Sysco, they would not "directly or indirectly, on behalf of [themselves] or for any other entity, business or person other than [Sysco], contact, solicit, or sell to any of the customers of [Sysco] with which [they] solicited or had contact while employed by [Sysco]. . . . " After the three went to work for Maines Paper & Food Service, Inc. (Maines) and allegedly solicited the business of some of Sysco's customers in Pennsylvania, Sysco sued to enforce the restrictive covenant each had signed. When the defendants argued that no new consideration supported their signing of the restrictive covenant, Sysco submitted that the "extensive and expensive training program" it had provided to the defendants constituted the required consideration. Would a court find this argument compelling? [See *Sysco Corporation* v. *Maines Paper & Food Service Inc.*, 679 N.Y.S.2d 175 (A.D. 3 Dept. 1998).]

3. Topp Copy Products, Inc. (Topp Copy) entered into a commercial lease for the first floor of a multistoried building. Ernest Singletary was the owner of the building and the landlord on the commercial lease. A toilet in an apartment located above the premises leased by Topp Copy developed a leak, resulting in substantial water damage to Topp Copy's inventory

stored in the leased unit. Alleging negligence, Topp Copy (the lessee) sued Ernest Singletary (the lessor). Singletary, in turn, contended that an exculpatory clause in the parties' lease agreement barred Topp Copy's suit for the water damage caused by the broken plumbing fixture. This clause, in paragraph 19, released Singletary "from any and all liability for damages that may result from the bursting, stoppage and leakage of any water pipe . . . watercloset . . . and drain, and from all liability for any and all damage caused by the water . . . and contents of said water pipes, . . . waterclosets and drains." Topp Copy argued that this exculpatory clause did not apply to its damage because the clause explicitly failed to relieve the landlord of liability for his own negligence and because the clause was ambiguous when read in context with another clause in the agreement. Specifically, Topp Copy asserted that the language of paragraph 15 of the lease—"[a]ll damages or injuries done to the said premises other than those caused by fire and by ordinary wear and tear or by the acts or omission of the landlord shall be repaired by the lessee herein. . . . "—made the exculpatory clause in paragraph 19 of the lease ambiguous. Was that clause enforceable? Did it relieve Singletary of liability for his own negligent conduct? [See *Topp Copy Products, Inc.* v. *Singletary*, 626 A.2d 98 (Pa. 1993).]

4. On 7 April 1980, President Carter severed diplomatic relations with Iran and issued Executive Order 12205. The order proscribed, among other things, "[t]he sale, supply or other transfer, by any person subject to the jurisdiction of the United States, of any items, commodities or products . . . from the United States . . . either to or destined for Iran." In June 1980, National Petrochemical Company of Iran (NPC) sought to purchase supplies of certain urgently needed chemicals for delivery to Iran. Owing to the trade embargoes facing Iran, NPC was not able to procure these chemicals from any of its normal sources. NPC, seeking new sources of supplies, therefore approached numerous new traders and brokers. Consequently, Monnris Enterprises, of Dubai, United Arab Emirates, agreed to serve as an intermediary for NPC's purchase of the chemicals from Rotex, a West German firm. Rotex agreed to make the sale through a Swiss affiliate, Formula S.A. (West Germany was part of the embargo against trade with Iran). The documents involved called for shipment of the chemicals from "any Western European and UAE Ports"; but the chemicals actually were shipped from Houston, Texas, aboard the *Stolt Sheaf*. The original shipping document called for delivery from Texas to Spain, but a subsequent addendum specified Iran as the ultimate destination of

the cargo. War broke out between Iran and Iraq before the *Stolt Sheaf* reached Iran; and Rotex ordered the ship to sail to Taiwan, where Rotex successfully resold the cargo. None of the proceeds from this resale ever reached NPC, although the sale in Taiwan allegedly was made for the account of NPC. NPC sued the *Stolt Sheaf* for negligently and conspiratorially allowing Rotex's sale of the cargo in Taiwan. The *Stolt Sheaf* defended by arguing that NPC, owing to the underlying illegality of the contract, could not recover. Bakhtiari, head of NPC's procurement department, indicated that he knew the bills of lading would not reflect the true destination of the cargo and that he also knew this was done to avoid the effects of the trade embargo. Were the agreements that NPC was attempting to enforce illegal? If so, was NPC nevertheless entitled to recover because it was not *in pari delicto* with those who had intentionally violated the trade embargoes? [See *National Petrochemical Company of Iran* v. *M/T Stolt Sheaf*, 930 F.2d 240 (2d Cir. 1991).]

5. Magnetic Copy Services, Inc. (MCS) is a Colorado corporation that engages in the business of copying magnetic tapes. Seismic Specialists, Inc. (SSI) is a Colorado corporation that, by generating sound waves through a dynamite blast or other vibration equipment, conducts seismic surveys in areas of potential oil and gas exploration. SSI then records sound waves on magnetic tapes, which companies such as MCS duplicate for sale to SSI customers. On 22 October 1986, MCS and SSI signed a contract, prepared by MCS, involving MCS's copying of SSI's field tapes. The contract stated: "SSI agrees to provide MCS 3,000 field tapes to be copied for its clients within one year of this agreement. . . . MCS will pay SSI a commission of $10.00 per tape. . . . " A year after the execution of the contract, SSI had provided only 1,399 tapes to MCS for copying. Nevertheless, SSI continued to provide tapes to MCS for copying during the fall of 1987. As late as this one-year period, several events pertinent to the parties' agreement occurred. For instance, SSI lost one or two of its primary customers, which loss reduced the number of tapes SSI could produce to provide for copying to MCS. In addition, SSI had several hundred tapes copied by companies other than MCS because SSI's customers wanted either a shorter turnaround time on the copying than MCS could provide or wanted a different copying method. Moreover, during this one-year contract period, MCS had cash-flow difficulties, and it sometimes delayed making payments to SSI after it (MCS) had received payment from these customers. At those times, SSI allowed MCS significant flexibility in making its payments. MCS claimed that SSI's failure to produce 3,000 tapes

within one year of the contract constituted a breach of the contract and that SSI therefore was not entitled to its commission on certain tapes, including the last 43 tapes provided before 22 October 1987, the anniversary date of the signing of the contract. Furthermore, MCS argued that it need not pay a commission to SSI for the 538 tapes copied during the months of November and December 1987. At trial, the court allowed SSI's and MCS's employees to testify about the provision specifying that SSI would provide 3,000 tapes to MCS. SSI's employees testified that the reference in the contract to 3,000 tapes constituted a goal, not a guarantee. These employees, however, also testified that SSI always had intended to provide 3,000 tapes but was unable to do so within the year. MCS's employees testified that they had construed SSI's statement as a promise or commitment to provide 3,000 tapes within one year. MCS, moreover, viewed the terms of the contract as clear and unambiguous and thus asserted that the trial court improperly had used parol evidence to vary the terms of the contract. Did the trial court, in admitting parol evidence concerning this contract provision, commit reversible error? [See *Magnetic Copy Services, Inc.* v. *Seismic Specialists, Inc.*, 805 P.2d 1161 (Colo.App. 1990).]

6. **BUSINESS APPLICATION CASE** Albert Vajda, a former manager with Arthur Andersen & Company (Andersen), sued Andersen for damages based on wrongful termination of his employment. Vajda, who had worked at Andersen for over 21 years, claimed that Andersen's employee manual precluded dismissal from employment except for just cause and through procedures that accorded with the company's three-warning policy. Andersen, while contesting the claim that the employee manual had set up enforceable contractual rights, also argued that, in any event, such a contract would be unenforceable under the Statute of Frauds. Discuss the specific provision of the Statute of Frauds on which Andersen had grounded this portion of its contentions and whether a court should agree with Andersen's reasoning. In addition, discuss the steps Andersen could have taken to avoid this litigation. [See *Vajda* v. *Arthur Andersen & Co.*, 624 N.E.2d 1343 (Ill.App. 1 Dist. 1993).]

7. **ETHICAL APPLICATION CASE** Video-Trax, Inc. (VTI) opened a checking account at NCNB National Bank of Florida, Nationsbank, N.A.'s predecessor. As part of the deposit agreement, VTI agreed in writing to pay a flat fee when a check presented to the bank for payment exceeded the collected balance in VTI's account. In addition, the agreement stated that the bank charged interest on overdraft sums to the extent those sums exceeded the balances in VTI's account. The rate of interest charged was the bank's prime rate plus 3 percent and was subject to the maximum rate permissible by law. During the parties' banking relationship, several checks were presented for payment against VTI's account when the account contained insufficient funds to cover the checks. Pursuant to the deposit agreement and the bank's policies, the bank exercised its option to either honor or dishonor any checks. If the bank chose not to honor the check, the bank returned it unpaid. For the duration of the parties' relationship (1992–1997), VTI's account history reflected that, pursuant to this practice, out of a total of 212 checks presented when insufficient funds existed in VTI's account, 92 checks were honored, while 120 checks were returned. The bank calculated the interest charged against the account for overdrafts on the basis of the average daily overdrawn account balance and charged a flat fee of $25–$27 for each overdraft. VTI ultimately sued the bank on the grounds that the $18,000 assessed as periodic charges for interest, when aggregated with the overdraft fees, constituted "interest" in excess of the lawful maximum amount allowed under state usury laws. According to VTI, the $18,000 so assessed on an average overdraft balance of approximately $6,000 represented a total of over 300 percent in interest. The bank refused to refund any of this alleged "excess interest" on the rationale that the "not sufficient fund fee" (NSF) and the overdraft fee (OD) were administrative charges commonly utilized in the banking industry to cover processing charges and to deter depositors from overdrawing their accounts. The bank further maintained that NSF and OD fees do not constitute "interest" within the meaning of the usury provisions of the Bank Act and that VTI would be unable to avoid its contractual obligations by claiming protection under the usury laws. Who had the more persuasive argument here—VTI or the bank? [See *Video Trax, Inc.* v. *Nationsbank, N.A.*, 33 F.Supp. 2d 1041 (S.D.Fla. 1998).]

8. **CRITICAL THINKING CASE** Monica Smith and her husband operated a farm north of Chester, Montana, from 1945 until his death in 1984. After their father's death, Monica's sons, Frank Smith (Frank) and John Smith (Jack) operated the farm as partners for a number of years. Eventually, Jack went on to pursue other occupations, and Frank continued to operate the farm on his own. On Frank's death in 1993, Monica was his only heir. Monica in turn nominated Jack as the personal representative of Frank's estate. During 1993 and part of 1994, Jack operated the Smith farm under a lease from Frank's estate. Unfortunately, frost had

CHAPTER 13 | Legality of Subject Matter and Proper Form of Contracts | 363

damaged the 1993 spring wheat crop, which became marketable only as feed wheat. After harvesting the 1993 crop, Jack placed approximately 21,000 bushels of the feed wheat into storage on the farm. Although the 1993 feed wheat belonged to Monica, Jack was authorized to sell the wheat on her behalf at such times and at such prices as he deemed appropriate. General Mills, Inc. (General Mills) alleged that on 12 August 1994, Jack, acting as an agent on behalf of Monica during the course of a telephone conversation between Jack and the manager of General Mills's Joplin, Montana, grain elevator, entered into a contract for the sale of the feed wheat to the Joplin elevator for a price of $2.55 per bushel. Following this conversation, a written agreement confirming the terms of this contract was prepared and mailed to Jack. Although Jack admitted receiving the contract, he did not execute or return it to the Joplin elevator. Jack later denied the existence of the Joplin contract and ultimately sold the feed wheat to General Mills's Tiber, Montana, grain elevator for $3.00 per bushel under a contract formed on 16 September 1994. The controversy between these parties arose when General Mills withheld $15,000 out of the payment issued to Monica on the Tiber elevator contract. General Mills asserted that owing to Jack's breach of the Joplin elevator contract, General Mills was entitled to offset the difference between the two contracts. In an effort to recover the withheld payment, Monica filed a complaint alleging breach of the Tiber elevator contract. General Mills counterclaimed, asserting that Monica, through her agent, Jack, was in breach of the Joplin elevator contract. To this assertion, Monica pleaded the defense of the Statute of Frauds because Jack had never signed the contract mailed to him by the Joplin elevator. The lower court held that Jack was a merchant for the purposes of Section 2-201(2) of the Uniform Commercial Cost and that the confirmation sent by the Joplin elevator was sufficient to satisfy the Statute of Frauds. Should an appellate court accept the lower court's findings? [See *Smith* v. *General Mills, Inc.*, 968 P.2d 723 (Mont. 1998).]

NOTES

1. *Restatement (Second) of Contracts* (St. Paul, MN: American Law Institute Publishers), p. 178.
2. See *First National Bank of Shreveport* v. *Williams*, 346 So.2d 257, 264 (La.App. 1977).
3. Mark Grossman, "It Might Take More Than Beeps and Chirps to Make a Contract," *The Connecticut Law Tribune* (27 July 1998), p. 17.

14

INTERPRETATION OF THE CONTRACT AND THE RIGHTS AND OBLIGATIONS OF THIRD PERSONS

A G E N D A

The Kochanowskis recognize that CIT will enter into a number of contracts in the near future. They plan to put many of their contracts in writing. They would like to know how much technical language, or "trade talk," they can use in their written agreements and how such language will be interpreted by the courts. They also will need to know how detailed their writings should be. Another concern they have is whether any of their written agreements can be amended or altered orally.

The family knows that third parties have contractual rights in many business situations. For example, they know that a third party's rights are involved each time a customer orders a videophone from CIT and asks to have it sent to a family member as a gift. They also know that third-party rights are involved when supplies are lost or destroyed in the possession of a trucking company. Suppose that a retail distributor who owes CIT $65,000 for inventory that CIT has already delivered to the retailer would like to transfer its current accounts receivable— $40,000 worth—to CIT to discharge the distributor's debt. Should CIT accept this arrangement? What risks would CIT assume? CIT is considering hiring other companies to serve as official repair centers for its videophones. What criteria should be evaluated by CIT before entering into these arrangements with other firms?

These and other questions may arise about the involvement of third parties and the Kochanowskis' written contracts. Be prepared! You never know when one of the Kochanowskis will need your help or advice.

O U T L I N E

JUDICIAL INTERPRETATION

In previous chapters, we stressed the importance of a *meeting of the minds* of the parties to the contract. This phrase highlights one of the essential elements of a contract: The parties must have indicated, by their words or conduct, an intention to agree about some matter. Sometimes the parties do not express their intentions accurately and with complete detail. Because language is not always precise, it may later become apparent that the parties were not binding themselves to identical terms and courses of action. Disputes arise when this variance in expectations is discovered. If the parties cannot resolve these disputes amicably, courts must interpret what the contract "really says."

When the language of the agreement is unclear, *interpretation* is used to determine the meaning of the words and other manifestations of intent that the parties used. It may be difficult to ascertain the parties' intent in order to enforce the contract as the parties intended. Problems arise primarily because words are symbols of expression and can take on a multitude of meanings. Words do not exist in a vacuum. Determining how a certain party intended to use words or actions becomes a factual issue. A court must examine each party's understanding and conduct in the situation; it also must be conscious of how other reasonable persons would have understood these words and actions under similar circumstances. In deciding between the competing views, courts often consider the intentions of the parties through a frame of reference known as the "reasonable person." This perspective allows the court to choose the interpretation that would be most consistent with the expectations of a reasonable person in the same circumstances. Unreasonable expectations will not be protected.

Standards

Certain standards of interpretation have evolved over the years. Probably the most common is the standard of *general usage,* or the meaning that a reasonable person who was aware of all operative uses and who was acquainted with the circumstances involved would attach to the agreement. For example, Suzanne signs an agreement in which she gives $10,000 as a life membership fee for admission to a nursing home. The agreement states that for a trial period of two months, either Suzanne or the nursing home can suspend the agreement. Upon the occurrence of that event, the $10,000 (minus $200 per month) will be returned. What if Suzanne unfortunately dies after one month in the home? Can her estate recover the $9,800, or has the life membership fee been paid irrevocably? A court in a similar case applied general usage; it decided that a reasonable person in Suzanne's position would have understood the provision to mean that until life membership status were obtained, the nursing home should return the money (less the amounts specified) to her estate. The court also asserted that if the nursing home had intended to retain the money in the event of a probationary member's death, it should have expressly stated this fact in the contract. Under different facts, the court might have applied the standard of *limited usage* (the meaning given to language in a particular locale) instead of the standard of general usage.

Rules of Interpretation

To supplement the appropriate standard of interpretation, courts also use *rules of interpretation.* These are also called *rules of construction.* In most states, no one rule is conclusive. Authorities disagree as to the relative importance of these aids to interpretation. You should be aware of the following common rules. Courts should:

1. attempt to give effect to the manifested intentions of the parties.
2. take into account the circumstances surrounding the transaction.
3. examine the contract as a whole to ascertain the intentions of the parties.
4. give ordinary words their ordinary meanings and technical words their technical meanings, unless the circumstances indicate otherwise.
5. favor reasonable constructions over unreasonable alternatives.
6. give effect to the main purpose of the agreement and all its parts, if possible.
7. interpret the contract so specific words or provisions control general ones.
8. give effect to handwritten words over typed words and typed words over printed ones when there is a conflict.
9. construe words most strictly against the party who drafted the agreement.
10. interpret contracts affecting the public interest in favor of the public.

Conduct and Usage of Trade

The *conduct* of the parties often aids in contract interpretation. If the court is in doubt, it will follow the interpretation placed on the agreement by the parties themselves. For example, when one party for years has accepted a grade of wool inferior to the contract specifications, evidence of this conduct will be admissible in determining how to interpret the specifications. Uniform Commercial Code (UCC) § 2-208 incorporates this rule of interpretation. Section 2-208 also addresses the roles of course of performance, course of dealing, and usage of trade in contract construction. To characterize a situation involving judicial interpretation, one should answer the following questions:

1. Do the parties claim competing interpretations?
2. Can general usage resolve the conflict?
3. Can limited usage resolve the conflict?
4. Which rules of interpretation should the court employ?
5. How should the court resolve any conflicts within the rules of interpretation?
6. Is there any conduct of the parties or any "trade usage" that should be considered by the courts in interpreting the contract?

THE PAROL EVIDENCE RULE

Parol evidence rule
When parties have signed a complete, written contract, oral agreements made prior to or at the same time as the writing are not admissible.

Substantive law
The portion of the law that regulates rights, in contrast to law that grants remedies or enforces rights.

As was discussed in the previous chapter, the **parol evidence rule** is an important part of the **substantive law.** Under the parol evidence rule, when the parties to a contract reduce their agreement to a writing with the intent that it embody the full and final expression of their bargain, no other expressions—*written or oral*—made prior to or contemporaneous with the writing are admissible in court. However, there are exceptions to the parol evidence rule, and these exceptions provide an important area of judicial interpretation. One of the important exceptions arises when the parties have a writing that is only a partially integrated contract. When the writing does not provide conclusive proof as to whether the agreement is totally or partially integrated, the court must resolve this issue. Integration will be discussed in the following sections. (In reading the following sections, note that "the parol evidence rule and the problems in interpretation must remain separate if they are to be understood."[1])

Rules of Integration

In general, the more formal and complete the instrument, the more likely a court will conclude that it is a totally integrated agreement. Courts use various tests to determine if the contract is integrated. A common one is the "face-of-instrument" test, where the court examines the "four corners of the writing" to determine if the parties intended the document to be integrated. Other jurisdictions use the "all-relevant-evidence" test, where the court reviews the document and extrinsic evidence to determine if the parties intended an integration. Some writings include clauses called *integration* or *merger* clauses. In these clauses, the parties declare that the writing is the full and final expression of all the terms in the agreement. Courts will then interpret the contract as integrated unless a party can show that the merger clause was induced by fraud or mistake.

Total Integration

A *totally integrated* contract is one that represents the parties' final and complete statement of their agreement. Such a contract can neither be contradicted nor added to by evidence of prior agreements or expressions. The law assumes that the writing supersedes the terms set out earlier in preliminary negotiations.

Partial Integration

If a writing is intended to be the final statement of the parties' agreement but is incomplete, it is a *partially integrated* contract. Such a writing cannot be contradicted by evidence of earlier agreements or expressions, but it can be supplemented by evidence of additional, consistent terms. Perhaps Suzanne and the nursing home orally agreed that her personal physician (rather than the nursing home's) will provide needed medical care. If the parties leave out this provision, the contract represents a partially integrated writing. Since this provision does not appear to contradict the original agreement, some courts may allow the parties to add it later.

Sometimes the proponent of the parol evidence may acknowledge that there is one agreement but may argue that the parties intended to include only certain terms in the written contract. The proponent argues that it was their intent to leave the remaining terms "in parol." Courts may examine whether the subject matter of the parol evidence was mentioned at all in the contract. If it is, this strongly suggests that the writing was intended to cover that provision. The policy base that underlies the parol evidence rule is not *as* compelling in situations in which the contract is partially integrated (i.e., incomplete). In such cases, although the writing may not be contradicted by evidence of earlier terms, it may be supplemented by evidence of additional, consistent terms.

The following example shows how the court may use the rules of integration and the rules of interpretation in resolving a conflict between two parties.

> *John is trying to buy a "fully equipped" car. He enters into a written contract with the dealer for the purchase. The contract specifies that the car will be "fully equipped" upon delivery. When the car is delivered, John notices that it has no air conditioning. He complains to the dealer, insisting that a fully equipped car includes air conditioning. The dealer disagrees, stating that "fully equipped" does not refer to air conditioning. If this dispute cannot be settled by the parties informally, a court may be asked to settle it. If the judge believes the writing was a partial integration, he or she will need to scrutinize the entire transaction, including*

the car salesperson's representations and John's expectations. If instead the court decides the writing was a full integration of the agreement, neither the salesperson's representations nor John's expectations will be considered. However, if the agreement is fully integrated, a judge may apply the standard of limited usage— the meaning of the term as understood locally and in the trade—to see whether a "fully equipped" car ordinarily includes air conditioning.

Note how the court applied the parol evidence rule and the rules of interpretation in the following case. Should the court have allowed an exception to the parol evidence rule in order to interpret the clause as requested?

14.1

BIONGHI V. METROPOLITAN WATER DISTRICT OF SOUTHERN CALIFORNIA
83 CAL.RPTR.2D 388 (C.A. 2ND DIST. 1999)

FACTS Christina Bionghi, d.b.a. Abacus Technical (Abacus), entered into an integrated contract with . . . Metropolitan Water District (MWD). . . . in November of 1993 . . . Under the contract, Abacus would be paid up to $200,000 a year for providing temporary employees for the MWD's Engineering Division. The contract included the provision that "The Agreement may be terminated by [the MWD] . . . 30 days after notice in writing to Consultant [Abacus] of such termination. . . . [MWD's] only obligation in the event of termination shall be payment for services provided by Consultant up to and including the effective date of termination." The contract was amended effective January 1, 1995, to increase the maximum allowable annual fee to $1,250,000. The amendment did not change the termination clause in the original contract.

Both the original and amended contracts included integration clauses. In the original agreement, the clause read "It is understood that no alteration or variation of the terms of this Agreement shall be valid unless made in writing and signed by the parties hereto and that no oral understanding or agreements not incorporated herein shall be binding on any of the parties hereto." The amended agreement included a similar clause . . . [Abacus does not dispute that it received 30 days notice.]

ISSUE Is the contract reasonably susceptible to an interpretation requiring the MWD to have good cause for termination?

HOLDING No. This interpretation is not consistent with the meaning of the language used.

REASONING . . . [W]e conclude that the language used by the parties is not reasonably susceptible to

that interpretation. However, we recognize . . . that the parties may have ascribed such a meaning to the words they used. . . . [T]he extrinsic evidence proffered by Abacus was not admissible here. "The parol evidence rule generally prohibits the introduction of any extrinsic evidence to vary or contradict the terms of an integrated written instrument. It is based upon the premise that the written instrument is the agreement of the parties. Its application involves a two-part analysis: 1) was the writing intended to be an integration, i.e., a complete and final expression of the parties' agreement, precluding any evidence of collateral agreements; and 2) is the agreement susceptible of the meaning contended for by the party offering the evidence? Here, the agreement was integrated. Since there is no dispute about that fact, we turn to the second part of the analysis: is the agreement reasonably susceptible of the meaning contended for by the party offering the evidence? . . . "Although extrinsic evidence is not admissible to add to, detract from, or vary the terms of a written contract, these terms must first be determined before it can be decided whether or not extrinsic evidence is being offered for a prohibited purpose. The fact that the terms of an instrument appear clear to a judge does not preclude the possibility that the parties chose the language of the instrument to express different terms. That possibility is not limited to contracts whose terms have acquired a particular meaning by trade usage, but exists whenever the parties' understanding of the words used may have differed from the judge's understanding. Accordingly, rational interpretation requires at least a preliminary consideration of all credible evidence offered to prove the intention of the parties. Such evidence includes testimony as to the 'circumstances surrounding the making of the

14.1

BIONGHI V. METROPOLITAN WATER DISTRICT OF SOUTHERN CALIFORNIA, *continued*
83 CAL.RPTR.2D 388 (C.A. 2ND DIST. 1999)

agreement . . . including the object, nature and subject matter of the writing . . . ' so that the court can 'place itself in the same situation in which the parties found themselves at the time of contracting.' If the court decides, after considering this evidence, that the language of a contract, in the light of all the circumstances, 'is fairly susceptible of either one of the two interpretations contended for . . . ' extrinsic evidence relevant to prove either of such meanings is admissible." . . .

[I]t calls for a two-step process. First, the court must determine whether the language of the contract is reasonably susceptible to the meanings urged by the parties. In so doing, the court must give consideration to any evidence offered to show that the parties' understanding of words used differed from the common understanding. If the court determines that the contract is reasonably susceptible of the meanings urged, extrinsic evidence relevant to prove the meaning agreed to by the parties is admissible. . . . [T]he termination clause is not on its face reasonably susceptible to meaning that there can be no termination except on good cause. . . . When Abacus's extrinsic evidence is considered as part of this preliminary step, . . . Abacus did not expose any ambiguity, or establish that the words of the contract were reasonably susceptible to the meaning it urged. The evidence offered by Abacus did not concern the "circumstances surrounding the making of the agreement" or allow a court to "place itself in the same situation in which the parties found themselves at the time of contracting." Abacus did not offer evidence concerning either the negotiations which took place before the contract was executed or the drafting process. . . . There was no evidence of the parties' discussion of the meaning of the termination clause as it is found in the contract . . . There was, in sum, no evidence of the situation the parties were in at the time of contracting. . . .

A good cause limit on the right to terminate is a significant contract term. In our view, a contract which provides that it may be terminated on specified notice cannot reasonably be interpreted to require good cause as well as notice for termination, unless extrinsic evidence establishes that the parties used the words in some special sense. Instead, such a contract allows termination with or without good cause. . . . "Testimony of intention which is contrary to a contract's express terms . . . does not give meaning to the contract: rather it seeks to substitute a different meaning." . . . In sum, the contract here was integrated and in unambiguous terms required only notice for termination. . . . [P]arol evidence was not admissible to prove the terms of the contract. . . . [Appellant's petition for review denied by the California Supreme Court, 1999 Cal. LEXIS 4533 (1999).]

BUSINESS CONSIDERATIONS Is it to a business's advantage to require cause to terminate a contract? Who benefits when "cause" is required? Who benefits when "cause" is not required? What should a business do to assure that extrinsic evidence is not introduced into contract disputes? Are "iron-clad" contracts possible?

ETHICAL CONSIDERATIONS When a firm is providing a quality service, is it ethical to terminate them? What ethical duty is owed to suppliers?

ADDITION OF THIRD PARTIES TO THE CONTRACT

A contract affects the legal rights of the parties who directly enter into it. It may also influence the rights of other people. In some situations, these other people are so significant that they have legal rights under the contract and can file a lawsuit to enforce these contractual rights. In some situations, the third person is significant when the contract is initially formed; in others, the third person is added later. This next section discusses what enforceable legal rights, if any, these third persons have.

THIRD-PARTY BENEFICIARY CONTRACTS

Persons and corporations that immediately receive rights in a contract to which they are not a party are called *beneficiaries*. It is really more appropriate to call this kind of beneficiary a *third person* because the additional person is not a party to the contract. However, we shall use the common terminology and refer to this person as a *third party*.

The two people who enter into the contract are commonly called the *promisor* and the *promisee*. The promisor is the party who promises to perform; the promisee is the party to whom that promise is made. Often, in third-party beneficiary contracts, the promise is to deliver goods to or perform a service directly for a third party. For example, Jane is very busy; to save time in shopping for a Father's Day present and mailing it to her father in St. Cloud, Minnesota, she orders a shirt from the Lands' End™ catalog to be gift wrapped and delivered to her father. This arrangement is a third-party beneficiary contract; her father is the third-party beneficiary. A beneficiary does not need to know about the contract for the contract to be valid.

Many businesses rely primarily on these contracts to achieve financial success. Examples include florist shops, singing telegram companies, mail-order companies that send fruit baskets, and life insurance companies.

Because these third parties are called beneficiaries, it is generally assumed that they receive something beneficial and good, but this is not always the case. In most states, the legal requirement for an **intended beneficiary** is that at least one of the contracting parties, usually the promisee, intended to have goods delivered to or services performed for the third party. The third party may not necessarily desire these goods or services. The beneficiary may, in fact, be displeased on receipt of the goods or services. An example is a singing telegram that embarrasses the recipient or is in poor taste.

An Incidental Beneficiary

The most important factor in determining the rights of a third party is whether the third party is an intended or an incidental beneficiary. When at least one of the original parties to the contract *meant* to affect a noncontracting person by establishing the contract, the noncontracting person is an *intended beneficiary*. Intended beneficiaries have legal rights in the contract. If the benefit or action to the noncontracting party was *accidental*, or *not intended*, this party is an *incidental beneficiary*.

For example, suppose an owner of a vacant city lot decides to build a high-rise garage on it. The owner enters into a contract with a builder to construct the garage. The neighboring lot has a high-rise office building on it; consequently, the owner of the office building will benefit financially by the construction of the garage. This person is an incidental beneficiary, because neither the builder nor the lot owner intended to benefit the owner of the office building.

An Intended Beneficiary

An intended beneficiary does not have to be mentioned by name in the contract. It is sufficient for the parties to *clearly intend* to provide the beneficiary with rights under the agreement. In the absence of a clear expression of such an intent, the contracting parties are **presumed** to act solely for themselves. Sometimes the intended

Intended beneficiary
A third-party beneficiary who is intended to receive goods or services.

Presumed
Assumed.

EXHIBIT 14.1 | **Intended Beneficiary**

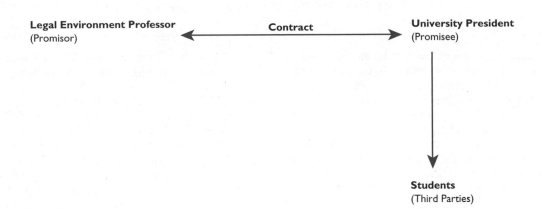

beneficiary may be one person from a group of people for whose benefit the contract was established. Automobile liability insurance, for example, is a contract between an insurance company and an automobile owner, but insurance is also partially for the benefit of drivers and pedestrians who share the road with the **insured**.

Suppose a legal environment professor signs a teaching contract with the university president. Do the students benefit from the employment contract? Of course. Are the students intended or incidental beneficiaries? They are one of the primary reasons for soliciting the faculty member's promise to teach, so the students are intended beneficiaries; they do not need to be listed in the contract. In fact, students may not even be specifically mentioned. However, both the faculty member and the university president know that students are one of the primary reasons for the employment contract. Students would be intended beneficiaries in most states. The legal relationships in this example are diagrammed in Exhibit 14.1.

The distinction between intended and incidental beneficiaries is discussed in the following case.

Insured
Person or entity covered under an insurance policy.

Professional corporation
A corporation providing professional services by licensed professionals.

14.2

IN RE GGM, P.C. V. JENKINS
165 F.3D 1026 (5TH CIR. 1999)

FACTS . . . In December 1988, Zimmermann was extended an offer to join GGM [Gleary, Glast & Middleton, P.C., a law firm]. Upon accepting the offer . . . Zimmermann became a shareholder and director of GGM when he purchased shares in the law firm, which was then a **professional corporation.** At that time, GGM had set the amount of capital contribution required of its shareholders at $50,000. In exchange for this purchase, Zimmermann received shares of stock in the firm. In order to finance this purchase, Zimmermann executed the Note with TCB [Texas

Commerce Bank, N.A.]; he was required by TCB to pledge his shares in GGM as collateral.

In connection with the purchase of shares and the execution of the Note, GGM and TCB executed a Repurchase Agreement . . . the purpose of which was to give additional assurance to TCB that the loan was well-collateralized and to ensure that the shares of stock were not possessed by anyone not a member of the law firm. Under the Repurchase Agreement, GGM agreed to repurchase the shares from TCB in the

continued

14.2

IN RE GGM, P.C. V. JENKINS, *continued*
165 F.3D 1026 (5TH CIR. 1999)

event of Zimmermann's default under the Note upon "receipt of written notice of default in payment of the Note and failure by [Zimmermann] to cure such default within the applicable period set out in the Note."

This Shareholders' Agreement was superseded . . . by a second agreement ("Second Shareholders' Agreement"). The Second Shareholders' Agreement tracked the previous Shareholders' Agreement with respect to GGM's ability to repurchase shares pledged as collateral. The purpose of the Second Shareholders' Agreement was . . . to require the law firm to repurchase the shares upon the occurrence of certain events and to limit the sale of the shares by the shareholders. The Second Shareholders' Agreement also provided that, upon termination of employment, the law firm was obligated to "purchase with its surplus to the extent such surplus is lawfully available" the shareholders' shares. . . . [T]he Second Shareholders' Agreement also expressly provided for the agreement to terminate upon several occurrences, one of which was the dissolution of the law firm. At the time the Second Shareholders' Agreement was executed, Zimmermann, in addition to remaining a Director and Shareholder in GGM, had become its Vice President.

. . . When it became evident to the Board of Directors that GGM was spiraling uncontrollably toward financial collapse, they voted, on May 21, 1992, to dissolve the firm. Although Zimmermann was not present for the vote of dissolution, he participated in and voted for a dissolution plan on June 10, 1992. . . . That same day, GGM began the process of dissolving and winding down its business affairs. On June 14, GGM ceased the practice of law, and Zimmermann's employment with GGM was terminated. On September 11, 1992, an involuntary [bankruptcy] Chapter 11 petition was filed against GGM by its creditors. . . . GGM and TCB sought and obtained approval from the bankruptcy court, in June 1993, for GGM to purchase the shareholder notes, including Zimmermann's Note, which had been in default since March 1993. Shortly thereafter . . . the case was converted to Chapter 7 [bankruptcy], and the Trustee was appointed to represent GGM's estate. . . .

ISSUE Was Zimmermann an intended third-party beneficiary of the Repurchase Agreement between GGM and TCB?

HOLDING No. There was no evidence that Zimmermann was an intended third-party beneficiary.

REASONING . . . Zimmermann waived whatever rights he may have had under the Second Shareholders' Agreement by voting in the affirmative for the Plan of Dissolution in June 1992 because the Second Shareholders' Agreement provided that it would be nullified in the event of the dissolution of the firm. At the time the Second Shareholders' Agreement was executed, Zimmermann was a Vice President, Director, and Shareholder of GGM, and thus clearly knew that the Second Shareholders' Agreement contained the provision which he now challenges. . . . [H]e expressly waived his rights under the Second Shareholders' Agreement to have his shares repurchased when he knowingly voted for a Plan of Dissolution which terminated the prior agreement. . . .

Zimmermann . . . contends that he was a third-party beneficiary to the Repurchase Agreement between GGM and TCB . . . Zimmermann has again overlooked a salient fact: in order to reach the point where the burden of proof is shifted, the party claiming third-party beneficiary status must first demonstrate that (1) it is not privy to the written agreement; (2) the contract was actually made for its benefit; and (3) the contracting parties intended the third party to benefit by it. . . . [T]his burden is a heavy one, . . . but Zimmermann made little to no effort to meet it: he offered his trial testimony and two questionable trial exhibits to establish his status as a third-party beneficiary.

. . . [H]is bald assertions . . . that he was a third-party beneficiary and the fact that GGM obtained shareholders' consent prior to executing the Repurchase Agreement, do not suffice to meet his burden. Indeed, they represent virtually no evidence at all. . . . [W]e do not find that the bankruptcy court's conclusion that Zimmermann's evidence is utterly lacking in merit to be clearly erroneous. . . . [W]e would not reverse because the Trustee presented ample evidence at trial that GGM and TCB did not intend for Zimmermann to be a third-party beneficiary. . . . [W]e affirm the district court's judgment with respect to Zimmermann's argument that he was an intended third-party beneficiary to the Repurchase Agreement. . . .

[W]e agree with the district court that TCB's possession of the stock did not constitute an election to

14.2

IN RE GGM, P.C. V. JENKINS, *continued*
165 F.3D 1026 (5TH CIR. 1999)

retain the shares in satisfaction of Zimmermann's indebtedness. After GGM purchased the Note from TCB, the Trustee elected to sue on the note rather than retaining or selling the collateral. The law allows the Trustee to make such a choice. . . .

BUSINESS CONSIDERATIONS What is the purpose of the GGM and TCB repurchase agreement? Is this

an important business objective? Is there any legal way a shareholder could protect him- or herself from the firm becoming bankrupt?

ETHICAL CONSIDERATION Was Zimmermann's behavior ethical, or was it merely an attempt to obtain funds he would not ordinarily receive during the bankruptcy?

A Donee Beneficiary

The rights of an intended third-party beneficiary in a contract *may* be affected by the type of relationship between the promisee and the third party. If the promisee means to make a gift to the third party, the third party is a *donee beneficiary*. Life insurance policies are excellent examples of third-party beneficiary contracts. If a husband purchases a $100,000 life insurance policy from Prudential Insurance Company of America and names his wife as the beneficiary, she is a donee beneficiary. The husband has no legal obligation to purchase this insurance. (He might be under a legal obligation to purchase life insurance under some marital contracts or divorce decrees, but this is uncommon.) He is, in effect, planning a gift to his wife that will take effect at his death. She is a donee beneficiary. A donee beneficiary example is shown in Exhibit 14.2.

Prudential Insurance Company, the promisor, promises to deliver $100,000 to the promisee's wife if the promisee dies under situations covered by the policy. If Prudential refuses to pay, the wife may sue the company directly as an intended

E X H I B I T   14.2 | **Donee Beneficiary**

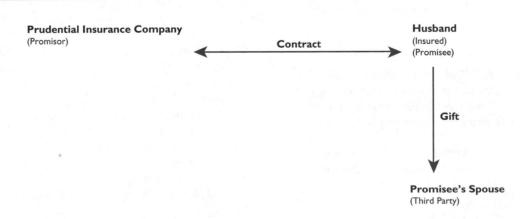

Vested interest
A fixed interest or right to something, even though actual possession may be postponed until later.

third party. Prudential (the promisor) can use the same legal defenses against the wife (the third party) as it can against the husband (the promisee). These defenses might include lack of capacity to enter into a contract, lack of mutual assent, illegality in the contract, mistake in contract formation, fraudulent statements about the promisee's health, an improperly formed contract, or cancellation of the policy. The promisor would not be obligated to make a payment if the cause of death is excluded by the terms of the contract. In addition, the courts usually disallow recovery by the beneficiary if the promisee failed to perform his or her duty under the contract.[2]

According to the law in some states, the donee beneficiary's rights cannot be terminated after the contract is made. However, the promisee can still defeat the rights of the donee beneficiary by not performing his or her (the promisee's) contractual obligations.[3] In other states, the beneficiary's rights are limited to situations in which the beneficiary knows about the contract and has accepted it verbally or by reliance on its terms. If the beneficiary has accepted the contract, the beneficiary has a **vested interest** in it. In these states, a beneficiary with a vested interest must consent before there can be an effective rescission of the contract. This rule applies to both donee and **creditor beneficiaries.** Even so, a donee beneficiary cannot prevent the promisee from taking some action that will defeat the rights of the donee beneficiary; for example, breaching the contract by refusing to pay for the goods or services.

A Creditor Beneficiary

The third party is a *creditor beneficiary* if the promisee owes a legal duty to the third party that is being satisfied by the contract. In a contract between a university president and a professor for teaching services, the third-party beneficiaries are students. The students are creditor beneficiaries. This is true even at state-supported universities where tuition payments only constitute a portion of the cost of offering classes.

Another excellent example involves a life insurance policy. A working couple wishes to purchase a house with a $100,000 mortgage. The bank is willing to lend them $100,000 based on the value of the home and both of their salaries. Since the bank feels that the husband cannot afford the monthly payments without his wife's salary, the bank makes the loan contingent on the purchase of **mortgage insurance** on her life. She agrees to purchase a $100,000 mortgage insurance policy from Metropolitan Life Insurance Company. The bank is a creditor beneficiary. This arrangement is diagrammed in Exhibit 14.3.

If the wife dies during the term of the mortgage, the bank is entitled to sue Metropolitan directly on the insur-

14.1 | MANAGEMENT/ MANUFACTURING

CALL-IMAGE TECHNOLOGY

LIABILITY FOR DAMAGES IN SHIPPING

CIT placed an order for 100 videoscreens from BG, a manufacturer in Palo Alto, California. CIT was a bit concerned because this was the first time it had ordered screens from this supplier, and the videoscreens are the most delicate component of the CIT videophones. BG packed the screens in sturdy cardboard boxes, 20 screens to a box, with foam pellets to cushion them. BG then contracted with Joe's Trucking to deliver the five boxes to CIT. When the boxes were delivered three weeks later, there was substantial damage to three of the boxes and their contents. CIT believes that the screens were in good condition when BG sent them and that the damages occurred during the transportation of the screens. They have asked who is responsible for the damaged goods. What will you tell them?

BUSINESS CONSIDERATIONS What steps could BG have taken to further reduce the risk of loss? How might Joe's Trucking and CIT have reduced the risk of loss? How could/should CIT protect its interests in future situations like this one?

ETHICAL CONSIDERATIONS Do BG and Joe's Trucking owe CIT moral obligations in addition to their legal obligations? Why or why not?

E X H I B I T 14.3 | Creditor Beneficiary

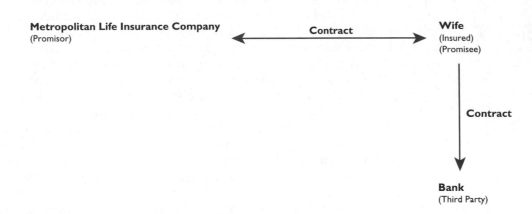

ance contract if Metropolitan refuses to pay. Metropolitan can use any defenses that it had against the wife as defenses against the bank. A third party cannot successfully claim any better rights than those provided in the contract.

If the wife tries to cancel the policy, the bank can successfully sue her; canceling the insurance policy and not replacing it is a breach of the contract. The bank, however, will probably allow the wife to substitute another policy from a different insurance company if the coverage is essentially the same. In practice, if the bank does not trust the wife to make the premium payments, it will require her to make the payments through the bank; then it will be assured that the premium payments are made in a timely manner.

The differences between donee and creditor beneficiaries are not significant. They both have basically the same rights against the promisor. A third party cannot successfully claim any better rights than those provided in the contract. Although many states say that the rights of a creditor beneficiary are directly derived from the promisee, courts usually provide the same type of protection for the donee beneficiary as they do for the creditor beneficiary. The only real differences are their rights against the promisee, and even these differences are becoming less pronounced. The distinction between creditor and donee beneficiaries is excluded from the *Restatement (Second) of Contracts*,[4] which relies solely on the distinction between intended and incidental beneficiaries. The donee/creditor distinction is also beginning to disappear in some states, such as California.[5]

Analysis of Third-Party Beneficiary Contracts

In analyzing a situation involving a potential third party, the following questions should be addressed:

1. Was the additional person involved from the beginning, or was that person added later?
2. Did the promisee intend to benefit the third party, or was it an accident?
3. Was the promisee making a gift to the third party, or was the promisee fulfilling a contract obligation to the third party?

Creditor beneficiary
A third party who is entitled to performance because the promisee has a contractual obligation with him or her.

Mortgage insurance
Insurance that will provide funds to pay the mortgage balance on a home if the insured dies.

DEFINING ASSIGNMENTS AND DELEGATIONS

If the third person becomes involved after the initial contract formation, that person is *not* a third-party beneficiary. Instead, the relationship may be an assignment or a delegation. To understand the distinction between assignments and delegations, remember the distinction between rights and duties. *Contractual rights* are the parts of the contract a person is entitled to *receive.* Examples include delivery of goods, payment for goods, payment for work completed, and discounts for early payment. Payments owed to car dealers, mortgage companies, finance companies, and collection agencies are rights that are commonly assigned.

Contractual duties are the parts of the contract a person is obligated to *give.* Duties include working an eight-hour day, paying 15 percent interest on credit card charges, and providing repair services. A common example is a general contractor who subcontracts certain duties of a construction job such as installing the roof. Rights can be assigned, and duties can be delegated. This may be confusing because judges and lawyers are sometimes careless in their use of terminology; however, duties *cannot* be assigned. A common example is a document that states "I assign all my rights and duties in the 8 April note with Tom Anderson." Despite the language used, the rules of law dealing with delegation always will be applied to duties.

ASSIGNMENTS

Extinguished
Destroyed, wiped out.

An *assignment* occurs when a person transfers a contractual right to someone else. The transferor is called the *assignor,* and the recipient is called the *assignee.* The assignor loses the contractual right when the right is transferred to another party. The assignor's right has been **extinguished,** and now it belongs exclusively to the assignee. The other party to the original contract, the promisor, now has to deliver the promised goods or services to the assignee. The assignee is the only party entitled to them. For example, Mira (a tenant) rents a house from Susan (a landlord). Under the terms of the lease, Mira must pay $400 per month for rent. Susan is in

E X H I B I T   14.4 | **Assignment**

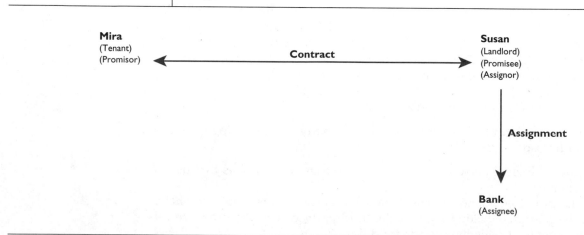

default on a small business loan obtained from the bank and assigns the $400 per month rent payment to the bank. Therefore, Susan (the assignor) has relinquished the legal right to the money—that right now belongs exclusively to the assignee, the bank. This situation is diagrammed in Exhibit 14.4.

Formalities Required for Assignments

Generally, an assignment does not have to follow any particular format. Assignors must use words that indicate an intent to vest a present right in the contract to the assignee. This means that the assignor intends to transfer the right immediately, not at some time in the future. However, this does not mean that the word *assignment* must be used. A writing is not required unless the state Statute of Frauds applies. This includes the Statute of Frauds' provisions in the Uniform Commercial Code as adopted by the individual state. As with other contractual provisions, it is preferable to reduce the assignment to writing. The assignment must contain an adequate description of the rights being assigned.

Consideration, consisting of a bargained-for exchange and a legal detriment (or benefit) for both parties, is not required in order to have a valid assignment. (Consideration is discussed in detail in Chapter 11.) Although the assignee need not give up consideration in exchange for the contract right, consideration is generally present. The existence of consideration affects the legal relationship between the assignor and the assignee—that relationship can be either a contract or a gift. However, the relationship is generally a contract, especially in business settings. In our earlier example, Susan (the landlord) assigns the payments to the bank so that the bank will not sue her or take other action to collect. People in business are not in the habit of making gifts to other businesspeople. A gift assignment occurs, for example, when a sales representative for a computer company assigns the 10 percent Christmas bonus he earns to his eldest daughter for her college education fund.

In the following case, the judge addressed whether a valid assignment exists. Exhibit 14.5 illustrates the relationship of the parties.

E X H I B I T 14.5 | **Assignment in *Cole* v. *Barlar Enterprises, Inc.* Case**

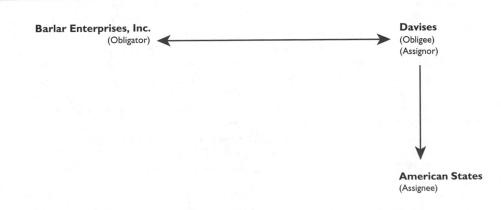

14.3

COLE V. BARLAR ENTERPRISES, INC.

35 F.SUPP.2D 891 (FLA. M.D. TAMPA DIV. 1999)

FACTS . . . This is an . . . action initiated to decide the rights to approximately $30,000 in attorneys' fees and costs. Sometime prior to September 1996, Jeff and Joanne Davis were sued in state court by Barlar Enterprises, Inc. Barlar, a general contractor, was sued for defective construction, and sued, in turn, its subcontractors, two of whom were Jeff and Joanne Davis. Pursuant to an American States insurance policy covering the Davises, American States provided counsel and related costs for the Davises' defense. Upon a finding of non-liability on the part of the Davises, the American States attorneys moved for (and were granted) attorneys' fees and costs. . . . [This dispute is over rights in these fees and costs.]

. . . [O]n October 31, 1996, the Internal Revenue Service sent a Notice of Levy to Barlar, stating that Jeffery Davis owed the Government in excess of $150,000 in delinquent taxes and demanding that Barlar release the approximately $30,000 . . . [Barlar] owed Davis to the Government. Barlar, in turn, filed a Complaint . . . in state court. Barlar's complaint named the Davises and the IRS as defendants, but neglected to name American States or its attorneys. Shortly thereafter, . . the Government removed the case to . . . [federal] Court. . . .

[T]he [American States] insurance policy provision which has sparked the . . . discussion is the following:

If the insured has rights to recover all or part of any payment we have made under this Coverage Part, those rights are transferred to us. The insured must do nothing after loss to impair them. At our request, the insured will bring "suit" or transfer those rights to us and help us enforce them. . . .

ISSUE Whether the funds were assigned to American States at the time the insurance policy was issued and as such were never the property of the Davises for attachment by the IRS.

HOLDING The funds were assigned to American States and were not the property of the Davises.

REASONING The extent to which a taxpayer has "property" or "rights to property" to which a federal tax lien can attach is a state law issue. . . . The Government argues that the funds from the judgment were never effectively assigned to American States on two separate grounds. First, the Government

contends that the insurance policy provision is ambiguous. As binding precedent mandates that ambiguities are construed against the drafter of the contract, the assignment is thus ineffective. The basis for this assertion is that sentences one and three are inconsistent. Upon [review] of the provision, however, the Court finds that no such ambiguity exists. The first sentence is a blanket requirement that any right to recovery of attorneys' fees and costs incurred by American States is transferred to it. The third sentence explains how such a recovery will be accomplished. The Court finds no ambiguity or inconsistency in this language, and accordingly denies the Government's request that the assignment be held ineffective on this ground.

In the alternative to the ambiguity argument, the Government contends that under Florida law, the insurance policy provision does not rise to the level of an assignment, and as such American States has no vested interest in the funds. In support of this assertion, the Government . . . [argues] for the proposition that the language of an assignment must expressly empower the assignee to collect monies directly from any of the assignor's obligors. In addition, the Government cites . . . the following commentary quoted . . . from *Williston on Contracts*: "The distinction is to be drawn between a promise that the promisor will pay out of a particular fund when he collects it and an agreement that the promisee may collect a particular fund, or part of it, and keep it when he has collected [it]."

. . . [T]he Court is not persuaded that the assignment was ineffective. First, the Court notes that in the same section of *Williston on Contracts*, the author also states that "the ultimate criterion is the intention of the assignor to give and the assignee to receive present ownership of the claim." . . . The Court finds . . . that there was an intent to transfer ownership to American States under the insurance provision with the statement that "those rights are transferred to us."

. . . [In a prior case, the] Court cited to the Florida Supreme Court for the proposition that "the true test of an equitable assignment is whether the debtor would be justified in paying the debt to the person claiming as assignee." The Court finds that because American States provided the legal services recovered in the first place, American States would be justified in requiring the losing party to any litigation [to] pay for those costs. . . .

14.3

COLE V. BARLAR ENTERPRISES, INC., *continued*

35 F.SUPP.2D 891 (FLA. M.D. TAMPA DIV. 1999)

The Court [in another case] expressed concern that a taxpayer might make an anticipatory transfer or assignment just prior to the maturing of a contract right in order to avoid a tax lien. This is a valid concern, which this Court also shares. Such a problem, however, is not at issue in the case at bar. When the insurance contract was signed in 1992, no federal tax lien existed, and certainly no law suit arising under the policy for which American States would have to provide legal defense existed. As such, there was no attempt to avoid a tax deficiency.

. . . [T]he Court notes that in the area of assignments, it is a constant concern that income tax be assessed to the person who earns the income, regardless of whether this income has been assigned. . . . In this case, American States earned the right to collect attorneys' fees and costs from the underlying litigation against the Davises by providing successful legal representation, and by pursuing recovery of their costs. To find that the Davises ever "earned" this money or had a right to the money such that a tax lien could attach would not reflect the reality of the situation. The Court finds . . . that under the insurance provision, the . . . money was always the property of American States, and as a result, the federal tax lien against the Davises did not attach. . . .

BUSINESS CONSIDERATIONS What type of insurance did the Davises obtain from American States, and why did they purchase it? What could American States do, if anything, to prevent similar legal problems in the future?

ETHICAL CONSIDERATIONS Is the court justified in its concern about potential income tax evasion? Why or why not?

Notice of the Assignment

Because an assignment extinguishes the assignor's rights and creates rights only for the assignee, one would assume that the person obligated to perform must be informed about the assignment. Surprisingly, this is not a legal requirement; an assignment is perfectly valid even though the person obligated to perform is never informed. An assignee may *want* to give notice to the promisor for a number of reasons, particularly if the assignor is potentially unethical or dishonest.

If the person obligated to perform *has* received notice of the assignment and then pays the assignor or delivers performance to the assignor, the person will still be obligated to pay or deliver performance to the assignee. In many instances, the promisor is not told about the assignment, and the assignor receives the performance and then transfers it to the assignee. Suppose the promisor has not been given notice and delivers performance to the assignor and the assignor does not transfer it to the assignee; then the assignee will be limited to taking action against the assignor. This will be the result even if the assignor has absconded with the funds.

In some cases, assignors have profited by selling the *same* contract right to more than one assignee through mistake, negligence, or fraud. Of course, if the second assignee has notice or knowledge of the prior assignment, that person will receive the assignment *subject* to the rights of the first assignee. In many cases, however, this second assignee lacks notice. The problem is also relatively simple if the first assignment is revocable. The second assignment merely revokes the first.

Dishonest assignors generally disappear with the funds and leave the innocent assignees to resolve their conflicting claims. Three theories are widely used by the courts to resolve these problems. Two of these theories are based on the belief that the first assignee to receive the assignment receives all the rights; the assignor has nothing to assign to later assignees. These theories are collectively called the *American Rule* or the *first-in-time approach*. The *New York Rule* is one version of the first-in-time approach and is applied in some states. If Anita, the promisee, assigns her right to Joel for value on 1 January and then assigns her right to Larry for value on 15 January, Joel will receive the right according to this rule. Under the New York Rule, there are two primary exceptions: (1) if the first assignment is revocable, like an undelivered gift; or (2) if the first assignee fails to obtain documents evidencing the assignment, thus enabling the assignor to "transfer" the rights to a second assignee.

Closely related to the New York Rule is the *Massachusetts Rule*, which is a slightly different first-in-time approach. Under this rule, the first assignee also has priority if the first assignment is not revocable. However, the second assignee will have the priority if the second assignee acquires the assignment in *good faith, for value*, and does any *one* of the following:

1. Obtains payment from the promisor
2. Recovers a judgment against the promisor
3. Obtains the promisor's promise to pay the assignee instead of the assignor, or
4. Receives delivery of tangible evidence representing the claim

See Exhibit 14.6, which describes the first-in-time approach.

Still other states apply the rule that the first assignee to actually give notice to the promisor receives the preferred right. This is called the *first-to-give-notice*

EXHIBIT 14.6 | **Multiple Assignments of the Same Rights: The First-in-Time Approach (American Rule)**

The first assignee takes the rights unless Assignment I is revocable.

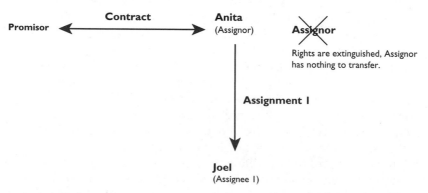

New York Rule
Additional exception: Assignee I fails to obtain documents evidencing Assignment I.

Massachusetts Rule
Assignee 2 will have priority if Assignee 2 obtains the Assignment in good faith, for value, and does one of the following: obtains payment from Promisor, recovers a judgment against Promisor, obtains Promisor's promise to pay, OR receives tangible evidence of the claim.

approach or the *English Rule,* which is followed in California, Florida, and a few other states. In the prior example, if Larry gives notice to the promisor first, he will prevail under the English Rule, provided he takes for value without notice of the prior assignment to Joel. One of the policies underlying this rule is that a prudent assignee, who is about to pay value for the assignment, will check with the person obligated to perform. The promisor, who has notice of earlier assignments, will tell the prospective purchaser, and this information will prevent additional assignments. The advantage of giving notice should be obvious, especially under the English Rule. Exhibit 14.7 illustrates the first-to-give notice approach.

Under all three of these rules of law, the assignor is liable for fraud, and injured parties can collect from the assignor if the assignor can be located with assets. (Similar policy problems arise when multiple security interests are created in the same property or there are multiple transfers of the same property.) However, there is nothing inappropriate if a promisee (assignor) divides up the contract rights and assigns *different* contract rights to different assignees.

Assignable Rights

Assignments have become an important aspect of our business and financial structure. They are useful techniques for marketing goods and increasing cash. A common business practice among retailers is to sell expensive items on time. The retailer assigns the monthly payments to a credit corporation in exchange for cash, then uses the cash to buy more merchandise. A simple example of this practice occurs when a buyer purchases an automobile financed through a car dealership, who then assigns the payments to a credit corporation. Because of the importance of assignments in commercial transactions, courts are generally predisposed to allow assignments. This favorable perspective is obvious in the courts' treatment of contract assignments. Assignments do not require the approval of the promisor. Even when the promisor objects to the assignment in court, the court will still generally allow it.

E X H I B I T 14.7 | **Multiple Assignments of the Same Rights: The First-to-Give Notice Approach (English Rule)**

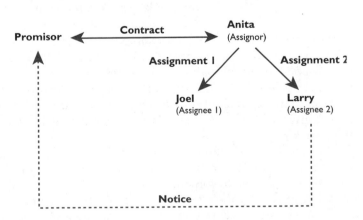

14.2 | FINANCE

ACCEPTING ACCOUNTS RECEIVABLE AS PAYMENT OF DEBT

All Electronics, Inc. (AEI) is one of CIT's major retail distributors in Chicago. AEI has been suffering financial difficulties for over a year and currently owes CIT $65,000 for inventory that it has already received. This $65,000 is 90 days past due, which causes Anna some anxiety. AEI has $40,000 in accounts receivable, most of which are current (not past due). AEI has suggested that it transfer its own accounts receivable to CIT. AEI would prefer to do this to discharge its entire obligation. If this proposal is not acceptable to CIT, then AEI would like to transfer the accounts as partial payment on the obligation. Anna and John have never before accepted another firm's accounts receivable. They ask you for advice. What will you tell them?

BUSINESS CONSIDERATIONS In order to decide if this is a sound business decision, what information should CIT obtain? What are the legal and business consequences of such an arrangement? Why? What would be CIT's position if it accepted the assignments?

ETHICAL CONSIDERATION Evaluate AEI's ethical perspective as it relates to this series of transactions.

To prevent the assignment, the promisor must prove to the court that at least one of the following conditions exists:

1. The assignment will materially change the duty of the promisor.
2. The assignment will materially impair the chance of return performance or reduce its value.
3. The assignment will materially increase the burden or risk imposed by the contract.

Basically, the promisor must convince the court that he or she will be in a substantially worse position if the assignment is allowed. These requirements are discussed in the *Restatement (Second) of Contracts* in § 317(2) (1981) and are also included in § 2-210(2) of the UCC. These provisions are applicable unless the language of the contract provides otherwise or the assignment is forbidden by statute or is against public policy.

When the assignment materially changes the promisor's duty, the promisor must perform a substantially different type or degree of work. Many assignments involve assigning monthly payments. Because this simply requires that the promisor change the address on the payment envelopes, the promisor's duty is not substantially different. As an example of a substantially different duty, Thad (a promisor) agrees to paint the exterior of any one house and makes this promise to Lynda, who owns a 1,000-square-foot single-level house. Lynda assigns the right to Joanne, who owns a 2,500-square-foot two-story house. Thad might convince the court that this assignment materially affects his duty. However, it is unwise for a promisor to enter into a contract that is ambiguous. Generally, a house painter like Thad will provide a bid for a house specifying a particular address.

If the assignment impairs the risk of return performance, it increases the chance that the promisor will not receive consideration from the promisee. For example, Chris wants to have her portrait painted; she locates a talented but struggling artist, John, to paint the portrait for $200. John explains that he needs the money to buy canvas and quality oil paint. Chris agrees to pay him the money on the first of the month, and John is to start the portrait on the fifteenth. Later, however, John wants to assign that payment to his landlord for unpaid rent. Consequently, Chris may convince the court that this assignment will impair her chance of receiving the portrait.

An assignment will not be allowed if it increases the risk or burden of the contract. If John, the artist, tries to assign only $150 of the payment to his landlord, Chris might be able to convince the court that this assignment increases the burden or risk imposed by their contract, because John might purchase inferior materials.

Not all types of assignments are favored. Some types of assignments are considered less desirable and are limited by state law. Common examples are prohibitions or limitations on the assignment of wages. Statutes in Alabama, California, Connecticut, the District of Columbia, Missouri, and Ohio generally prohibit the assignment of future wages. In addition, California, Connecticut, and many other states have special rules that apply to assignments of wages as security for small loans.[6] Recently, assignments of **post-loss** insurance payments also are being scrutinized more closely by the legislature and the courts.

Contract Clauses Restricting Assignments

Another example of court behavior that favors assignments is their interpretation of the language in the original promisor-promisee contract. Even if the contract states that "no assignment shall be made" or that "there shall be no assignment without the prior consent of the promisor," many courts will still allow the assignment. Courts *may* interpret these clauses as promises or covenants not to assign the rights. The assignor is then held legally responsible for making the assignment and must pay the promisor for any loss caused by the assignment. Often the promisor cannot prove any loss in court, so this is a rather hollow right. These clauses can also be interpreted by courts as preventing the transfer of the contract duties. This latter approach is followed by § 2-210(3) of the UCC. If the contracting parties really want to prevent assignments, they must use clauses such as "all assignments shall be void" or "any attempt at assignment shall be null and void." Most courts will interpret this language as actually removing the power to make assignments.

Warranties Implied by the Assignor

An assignor who makes an assignment for value implies that certain things are true about the assigned rights. These implied warranties exist without any action by the assignor. The assignor's knowledge of the warranties is not required. The warranties include (1) the right is a valid legal right and actually exists; (2) there are no valid defenses or limitations to the assigned right that are not specifically stated or apparent; and (3) the assignor will not do anything to defeat or impair the value of the assignment. These warranties need not be expressly stated but, instead, can be implied. If the assignor breaches the warranties, the assignee can successfully sue. The assignor and assignee may expressly agree to limit or exclude warranties.

Rights Created by the Assignment

An assignee obtains the same legal rights in the contract that the assignor had. If the assignee sues the promisor, the promisor generally may use the same defenses

14.3 | MARKETING/ FINANCE

CREATING AUTHORIZED REPAIR CENTERS

Call-Image videophones are sold to consumers with a one-year warranty, which has become the standard in the industry. Currently, consumers must send the videophones back to CIT for any necessary warranty work. Anna and Tom are thinking about identifying certain retailers who are selling CIT videophones in large cities and designating them as "authorized CIT repair centers." John feels this arrangement will improve the marketability of CIT videophones. However, they are concerned about how this might change their relationships with their distributors. They ask you about the legal and business effects of this decision. What do you tell them and why?

BUSINESS CONSIDERATIONS What are the business advantages of such an arrangement? What are the disadvantages? What types of legal arrangements could CIT have with authorized repair centers? What will be CIT's obligations under these arrangements? If you were assisting Amy Chen in drafting these contracts, what provisions would you include and why?

ETHICAL CONSIDERATIONS Is it ethical to require an authorized repair center to also sell CIT products? Why or why not?

Post-loss
Obligations of insurance companies after a covered loss has actually occurred.

against the assignee as were available against the assignor. Examples of these defenses would include fraud in the inducement, duress, undue influence, and breach of contract by the assignor. The promisor will not, however, be able to use every conceivable defense against an assignee.

Waiver of Defenses Clause

A waiver of defenses clause in a contract attempts to give the assignee better legal rights than the assignor had. Often such a clause is part of a standard printed contract prepared by the assignee or assignor and signed by the promisor. Generally the promisor (buyer) is not aware that the contract contains a waiver of defenses clause or does not understand what it means. In the clause, the promisor promises to give up legal defenses in any later lawsuit by the assignee. In other words, the promisor agrees not to exert defenses, such as fraud in the inducement or breach of warranty against any subsequent assignees. Exhibit 14.8 shows the effect on the promisor/assignee relationship of a valid waiver of defenses clause.

If the waiver of defenses clause is effective, it reduces the promisor's bargaining power. For example, if a purchaser buys a product on time and the product is defective, a common reaction is to stop making payments. A waiver of defenses clause means that the buyer must continue to make the payments.

Consumer groups and government agencies have often opposed waiver of defenses clauses because they reduce a consumer's bargaining power. Such a clause is generally enforceable under § 9-206(1) of the UCC, unless there is a different rule under statutes or court decisions for buyers or lessees of consumer goods. Under the UCC, the assignee is subject to the same defenses as a holder in due course of a negotiable instrument. Some states, including Alaska, Missouri, Ohio, and Washington, and the District of Columbia, have statutes that forbid or limit these clauses.[7] The Federal Trade Commission enacted a regulation barring these agreements in contracts by consumers.[8]

E X H I B I T 14.8 | **Comparison of the Contract Rights of the Assignor and the Assignee**

Contract without a Waiver of Defenses Clause

A. Lawsuit by Assignor against Promisor: Promisor can assert defenses; lawsuit against Promisor fails

B. Lawsuit by Assignee against Promisor: Promisor can assert defenses; lawsuit against Promisor fails

Contract with a Waiver of Defenses Clause

A. Lawsuit by Assignor against Promisor: Promisor can assert defenses; lawsuit against Promisor fails

B. Lawsuit by Assignee against Promisor: Promisor has waived the right to assert defenses; since the Promisor has no defenses to assert, the lawsuit against the Promisor is successful

(This figure assumes that the Promisor has a valid defense that can be proved in court.)

DELEGATIONS

Assignments and delegations may occur simultaneously. However, it is easier to understand delegations if they are analyzed as independent transfers. In fact, they are completely separate concepts that can and do occur independently. In a *delegation*, the promisor locates a new promisor to perform the duties under the contract. The original promisor is called the delegator, and the new promisor is called the delegatee. For example, suppose Jeff buys a new automobile from a Hyundai dealer. One of the terms of that contract is a promise by the dealer to provide certain warranty work on the car for three years. Later, Carmen, the mechanic employed by the Hyundai dealer, quits, and the dealer contracts with a garage to do the warranty work. This particular delegation is illustrated in Exhibit 14.9. As with assignments, there may be consideration for the delegation, but it is not necessary. If no consideration exists, the delegation is really a gift from the new promisor to the old promisor.

The purchaser of the car (Jeff) can sue the car dealer who made the promise if the warranty work is not performed. The purchaser can also generally sue the garage for failure to perform. In many states, the purchaser can sue both the dealer (delegator) and the garage (delegatee) at the same time, but the courts will not permit the purchaser to collect twice.

The relationship between the delegator and the delegatee may be that of a contract or of a gift. If a contract relationship is present, the delegator has the right to sue the delegatee for nonperformance. If a gift relationship is present, the court would hold that the delegatee promised to make a gift in the future but failed to deliver it. Generally, promises to make gifts in the future are not enforceable without **promissory estoppel.**

Promissory estoppel
Doctrine used to enforce a gift promise because of the justifiable reliance of the promisee.

Delegations do not occur unless the delegatee assumes the contract duties. This assumption can be either expressly stated or implied. The modern trend in court decisions is to imply the assumption of the duties, especially when there is an assignment and a delegation. Implied assumption of duties is also supported by

E X H I B I T 14.9 | **Delegation**

YOU BE THE JUDGE

ASSIGNMENT OF SOCCER PLAYER'S CONTRACT

Arsenal, a London soccer club, has been attacked for "poaching" young players from other clubs. Arsenal has been criticized for offering £1.6m to the 17-year-old midfielder, Fernando Maceda da Silva (Nano). The Spanish football federation has stated that it could not prevent the transfer of Nano, who plays for the Catalan club's youth team, under a contract with Barcelona, for around 60,000 pesetas (£280) a week. The prevailing view within the Spanish FA is that the Barcelona contract is void because it was signed when Nano was 15; they believe that professional contract terms should not apply before a player's sixteenth birthday. According to the Spanish FA's general secretary, Gerardo Gonzalez, "We cannot go against fundamental rights, which is the freedom for a footballer to play where he wants. However, it is the desire of the Spanish federation that the best Spanish players play in our own country." Barcelona still seems determined to hang on to Nano. Nano has stated, "Arsenal want [sic] me and I am disposed to go there but Barcelona seem determined to do everything to block me going."

Note: These arrangements involve the *assignment* of rights and the *delegation* of duties. If *you* were the judge deciding this case, how would *you* interpret Nano's relationships with Barcelona and Arsenal? Why? How would *you* rule on signing 15- and 17-year-old players?[9]

BUSINESS CONSIDERATIONS Compare the assignment of players in the United States with player transfers in other countries. How are they similar and how are they different? Do they vary depending on the sport? How?

ETHICAL CONSIDERATIONS Is it ethical for a team to transfer a player against his or her will? Is it ethical for a team to prevent the transfer of a player who wishes to move? What rights does a player have to autonomy and freedom of choice? How does this compare to slavery?

SOURCE: Tommy Staniforth, *The Independent* (London) (21 May 1999), Sports, p. 32.

the *Restatement (Second) of Contracts* and the Uniform Commercial Code. An example of this occurs when the parties state that there is an "assignment of the contract" or an "assignment of all my rights under the contract." Such statements are generally interpreted as indicating (1) an assignment, (2) a delegation of the duties by the delegator, and (3) an acceptance of the duties by the delegatee unless there is a clear indication of a contrary intention. This position is followed by the UCC § 2-210(4) and the *Restatement (Second) of Contracts* § 328.

Delegations do not have the favored legal status that assignments do. Courts are more inclined to deny a delegation. If the contract between the promisor and the promisee states that "there shall be no delegations," the courts will prevent delegations. The same is true if the contract requires personal performance. Courts are also more likely to decide that a delegation is unfair to the promisee. Under the UCC § 2-210(1), duties cannot be delegated if the agreement states that there will be no delegation or the promisor has a substantial interest in having the delegator perform the contract. The *Restatement (Second) of Contracts* § 318(2) states that delegations should not be allowed if the promisee has a substantial interest in having the delegator control or perform the acts promised. Consequently, personal service contracts generally cannot be delegated. Section 2-210(3) of the UCC indicates that a contract clause that prohibits the assignment of "the contract" is to be construed as preventing only a delegation of the contract duties to the assignee.

Analysis of Assignments and Delegations

To characterize an assignment or a delegation situation, one should answer the following questions:

1. Was the additional person involved from the beginning or added later?
2. Did the additional person undertake to perform a contract duty or become entitled to a contract right? Or both?
3. Did the language of the original contract prevent this transfer to an additional person?
4. Did the type of rights or duties prevent this transfer to an additional person, because the transfer materially changes the rights or duties of a party?
5. Is this transfer forbidden by state statute?

UNIFORM COMMERCIAL CODE PROVISIONS

When the Uniform Commercial Code is applicable, businesspeople need to review its assignment and delegation provisions. Certain types of assignments are excluded from Article 9 by UCC § 9-104—for example, claims for wages, interests under an insurance policy, claims arising from the commission of a tort, and deposits in banks. Under § 9-201 and § 9-203 of the UCC, provisions of Article 9 may be subordinated to state statutes regulating installment sales to consumers. Section 2-210 of the Code covers assignments and delegations under contracts for the sale of goods. However, some questions concerning assignments are not resolved in either Article 2 or Article 9 of the UCC. (This is only a brief overview of the Code's provisions.)

 click here

RESOURCES FOR BUSINESS LAW STUDENTS

NAME	RESOURCES	WEB ADDRESSES
Preservation of Consumers' Claims and Defenses— 16 C.F.R. 433	The law firm of Arent Fox Kintner Plotkin & Kahn maintains a collection of law resources, including waiver of defense clauses, under the U.S. Code of Federal Regulations (C.F.R.).	**http://www.arentfox.com/al404.html**
Uniform Commercial Code § 2-202	LII provides a hypertext and searchable version of UCC § 2-202, Final Written Expression: Parol or Extrinsic Evidence.	**http://www.law.cornell.edu/ucc/2/2-202.html**
The American Law Institute	The American Law Institute, publisher of *Restatements of the Law*, some Model Codes, and other proposals for law reform, provides press releases, its newsletter, and other publications.	**http://www.ali.org**

Summary

Interpretation is the process of determining the meaning of words and other manifestations of intent that the parties have used in forging their agreement. Certain standards and rules of interpretation have evolved, based on whether the contract is totally integrated or partially integrated. A totally integrated contract represents the parties' final and complete statement of their agreement and cannot be contradicted. Similarly, a partially integrated contract is intended to be the parties' final statement, but it is incomplete. It may be supplemented with consistent, additional terms. The conduct of the parties and usage of trade may aid in contract interpretation. The parol evidence rule states that oral evidence is not admissible to alter, add to, or vary the terms of a totally integrated, written contract. If the contract is not totally integrated, the parol evidence rule is not applicable and the evidence is admissible.

An additional person who is involved in a contract from the beginning may be a third-party beneficiary. If the promisor or promisee meant to affect the third person under the contract, that person will be an intended beneficiary and will have enforceable rights. Intended beneficiaries can file lawsuits to protect their own legal rights. If they sue the promisor, the promisor can use the same defenses that would be valid against the promisee. Creditor beneficiaries can sue a promisee who tries to cancel the contract. Donee beneficiaries generally will not be successful in a suit against the promisee because legally the donee beneficiary did not receive the promised gift.

An additional party who becomes involved after the contract is formed may be an assignee or a delegatee. An assignee receives a contract right from the transferor. An assignment extinguishes the contract right of the assignor and sets up this contract right exclusively in the assignee. The assignee is now entitled to performance under the contract. The assignee does not have to notify the promisor of the assignment. The assignee is better protected if he or she *does* give notice. This is especially important if the assignor makes multiple assignments of the same contract right.

In a delegation, a delegatee assumes the transferor's obligation to perform under the contract. The delegator will still be obligated to perform if the delegatee does not. Generally, courts will respect contract clauses that state that there shall be no delegation.

DISCUSSION QUESTIONS

1. What is the process of contract interpretation?
2. What is the legal difference between a totally integrated contract and a partially integrated contract?
3. The Kochanowskis have recently reviewed the standard form contracts the firm uses, and they have decided to revise some of these contracts. As a part of this revision, Dan suggests that the firm include a so-called merger clause stating that the written contract represents the parties' agreement, and that the written terms supersede any previous oral communications. Is a merger clause a good idea for CIT? Why or why not?
4. How are conduct and usage of trade important in contract interpretation?
5. Legal Hit employees throw cream pies in the face of any target designated by the promisee. If you hired Legal Hit to deliver a cream pie greeting to your boss, what are the legal rights of Legal Hit, you, and your boss?
6. Some states have statutes prohibiting or limiting assignment of wages. What public policies might state legislatures be trying to promote with these statutes?
7. Should waiver of defenses clauses be enforced? What are the advantages and disadvantages of these clauses?
8. Andrew owes Clairise $100. Clairise assigns $25 of this amount to Diane. With knowledge of the assignment, Andrew pays the entire $100 to Clairise. Has Andrew discharged his duty to pay?[10]
9. What are the differences between assignees, delegatees, and third-party beneficiaries? In what ways are they similar?
10. What happens if the assignor assigns the identical contract right to three assignees? Who should recover from whom? Why?

CASE PROBLEMS AND WRITING ASSIGNMENTS

1. Monica Guzman's friend, Barbara Graves, rented a car from AAA Auto Rental (AAA) in Bloomington, Indiana, and listed Guzman as an authorized driver. Guzman telephoned AAA to inform it that she would be driving the rental car to Chicago. At dusk on 8 November 1993, about 25 miles from her destination, the battery light went on in the car. About 10 minutes later, the temperature light came on. Guzman continued to drive the car toward her destination; she passed a couple of exits from the interstate. The car eventually broke down on the interstate. Due to Guzman's failure to stop the car immediately after the warning lights had come on, the car's engine sustained damage from overheating. AAA had the car towed back to Bloomington where substantial repairs to the car's engine—including the resurfacing of the cylinder heads, a valve job, and the replacement of the fan relay switch—were made. The towing and repair bills totaled nearly $1,000. Guzman testified that she had been afraid to pull off the highway. The trial court concluded that Guzman willfully had failed to stop because she was anxious to reach her destination and determined that Guzman had breached the car rental contract when she had failed to return the car in good and safe mechanical condition. The trial court also found Guzman liable for the damages because she had "committed vandalism by the willful infliction of damage to this car by continuing to drive it after knowing it was not operating properly." The court relied on an Indiana statute governing motor vehicle rental companies and their contracts with customers, which permits rental companies to hold renters responsible for "physical damage to the rented vehicle . . . , resulting from vandalism unrelated to the theft of the rented vehicle." The trial court entered judgment in favor of AAA in the amount of $1,437, which represented the sum of the towing and repair bills and AAA's attorneys' fees. Guzman argued that the judgment was incorrect because the car had sustained mechanical, as opposed to physical, damages. She claimed the rental company could recover for mechanical/engine damage only in the event of a collision. Is Guzman's interpretation logical or not? Why? [See *Guzman* v. *AAA Auto Rental*, 654 N.E.2d 838 (Ind.App. 1st Dist. 1995).]

2. A contractual dispute arose between an entertainment financier, Skyvision Entertainment (Skyvision), and creative talent, Tin Whistle, Inc. (Tin Whistle). All parties agreed that the written agreement was partially integrated and was intended as the exclusive embodiment of their agreement with regard to the issues reduced to writing. Tin Whistle relied on paragraph five of the Deal Memorandum, which stated "Skyvision pledges and commits to providing funding and both parties pledge and commit to provide the necessary services to produce and exploit the Series and the Picture." Tin Whistle argued that Skyvision was committed to make the theatrical production, subject only to approval of the screenplay, director, and budget. Skyvision argued that Skyvision was not obligated to make the theatrical production, as Skyvision could

exercise its option not to produce the Picture. Skyvision relied on paragraph 28 of the Deal Memorandum, which states, "Skyvision shall (unless it elects not to produce the Picture) provide funds for development and production of the Picture. . . . " Should parol evidence be admitted? Is there evidence to support Tin Whistle's proposed interpretation? [See *Tin Whistle, Inc.* v. *John Labatt Limited*, 1999 U.S.App. LEXIS 4565 (9th Cir. 1999)[unpublished opinion].]

3. Jeffrey W. Peterson was sitting on the passenger side of his parked truck. The ignition key was in the "off" position. Peterson's shotgun discharged, shooting him in the foot. At the time of the discharge, Peterson apparently was about to alight from his truck to go deer hunting. Peterson filed a claim with his auto insurance company, State Farm Mutual Automobile Insurance Co. State Farm denied Peterson's request for benefits because State Farm determined that his injury had not arisen from "the use or operation of the vehicle." [See "Insurer Must Toe the Line," *The National Law Journal* (14 October 1996), p. A27].

4. W. T. Grant Company (Grant) was a tenant renting commercial property known as No. 41 Main Street, New Milford, Connecticut, from The Gateway Company (Gateway). Under the terms of an approximately 30-year lease, Grant was obligated to keep the premises in good repair. DiNoia was the owner of a shopping center. Grant wanted to vacate the property owned by Gateway and move to the property owned by DiNoia. Grant signed a lease with DiNoia, which provided "in order to induce the tenant, Grant, to execute this lease, landlord, DiNoia, hereby assumes all of tenant's obligations under that certain lease and lease agreement dated June 17, 1954, between The Gateway Company . . . and Tenant Grant . . . [covering] premises known as No. 41 Main Street in the Town of New Milford. . . . " Gateway was not a party to this lease. Did Grant intend to benefit Gateway by entering into the lease provision with DiNoia? [See *The Gateway Company* v. *DiNoia*, 232 Conn. 223 (Conn. 1995).]

5. Colorado has no-fault auto insurance, and Progressive Casualty Ins. Co. (Progressive) issues personal injury protection (PIP) policies under the state statute. The PIP policies include the following clause: "Interest in this policy may not be assigned without our written consent." Parrish Chiropractic Centers, P.C. (Parrish) provides treatment to insureds under these PIP policies. When treatment begins, the insureds are required to sign assignment forms provided by Parrish. This dispute arose when Progressive refused

Parrish's requests for payment and paid the insureds directly. The insureds did not apply the payments to their chiropractic bills. Should the assignments by the insureds to Parrish be permitted? [See *Parrish Chiropractic Centers* v. *Progressive Casualty Ins. Co.*, 874 P.2d 1049 (Colo. 1994).]

6. **BUSINESS APPLICATION CASE** Maurice Quinn owned the controlling interest in two banks. William Carroll, a registered securities dealer, advised Quinn to buy American Home Acceptance Corporation (AHAC) "collateralized mortgage obligations," called bonds throughout the case. Carroll informed Quinn that the bonds would receive an "A" rating from Standard and Poor's, an entity of McGraw-Hill Companies. AHAC contracted for a rating from Standard and Poor's, which initially rated the bonds "A." On behalf of the banks, Quinn purchased the entire bond issue from AHAC. He could not have purchased the bonds for the banks without the "A" rating. About two and a half years later, Standard and Poor's abruptly reduced the rating to "CCC." Bonds rated "CCC" are considered "junk bonds" and are not investment quality. AHAC defaulted on the bonds, causing the banks a large loss. Was Quinn an intended third-party beneficiary of the contract between AHAC and Standard and Poor's? How could Quinn have better protected the banks' interests? Do most investors rely on rating services such as Standard and Poor's? Is such reliance reasonable? [See *Quinn* v. *McGraw-Hill Cos.*, 168 F.3d 331 (7th Cir. 1999).]

7. **ETHICAL APPLICATION CASE** Ron Keller, his brother, and Richard Bleam developed the Tornado lure at the request of Bass Pro Shops. The manufacturing process was developed through Kel-Lure, a company owned by Keller and his brother. Kel-Lure was sold at auction, its assets were purchased by Keller and his brother, and it was reincorporated as Sports Products. Sports Products manufactured the Tornado lures almost exclusively for Bass Pro Shops. In August 1989, the three developers signed a patent assignment on the process for making the Tornado lure in favor of Bass Pro Shops. It read in part that it was made for "good and valuable consideration, the receipt and sufficiency of which are hereby acknowledged." The assignment conformed to 35 U.S.C. 261 (1988), which governs patent assignments. This assignment occurred just before Sports Products moved to Costa Rica and reincorporated as Productos Deportivos, which continued to manufacture the lures. Keller was surprised to learn that he would not become a shareholder in Productos Deportivos, and he terminated his employment with the company in 1990. He

claimed that his brother forced him out of the business. Keller contended that the assignment was not valid because he did not receive consideration and, consequently, he sued. Was the assignment to Bass Pro Shops valid without consideration? What could Ron Keller have done to help ensure that he would have a role in Productos Deportivos? Could he have taken any steps to protect himself? Did Ron Keller's brother treat him ethically? Why or why not? Did Ron Keller have any moral rights? [See *Keller* v. *Bass Pro Shops, Inc.*, 15 F.3d 122, (8th Cir. 1994).]

8. **CRITICAL THINKING CASE** Autumn Massie suffered injuries during her birth at a naval hospital in 1983. The Massies filed a claim with the federal government under the Military Claims Act (MCA), alleging that Autumn's injuries were caused by medical malpractice. In 1986, the government agreed to pay the claim and entered into an agreement (the Agreement), in which the Massies accepted monetary awards in full and final settlement of all claims. These awards included cash payments to the family, a med-ical care trust fund, and the purchase of an annuity. The Agreement states that the annuity "will result in distributions on behalf of the United States" in a certain manner. The Agreement requires the government to purchase the annuity from an "insurance company rated A+ by A. M. Best." The government purchased an annuity from Executive Life Insurance Company; it had an A+ rating at the time of purchase but subsequently went into conservatorship in 1991. In 1993, the insurance company's final bankruptcy rehabilitation plan was approved and the Massies were given the option to participate, which they did. The rehabilitation plan reduced the payments from the annuity significantly. Massie sued, alleging that the government breached the Agreement because the annuity no longer makes payments as the Agreement requires. She argued that the Agreement obligates the government to guarantee the annuity payments. Did the government discharge its obligations the moment it funded the annuity and delegated its duty to Executive Life Insurance Company? [See *Massie* v. *United States*, 166 F.3d 1184 (Fed. Cir. 1999).]

NOTES

1. See John Edward Murray, Jr., *Grismore on Contracts*, Revised Student Edition (The Bobbs-Merrill Company, Inc., Indianapolis, 1965), § 97, p. 152.
2. Walter H. E. Jaeger, ed., *Williston on Contracts*, 3rd ed. (Mount Kisco, NY: Baker Voorhis, 1957), § 395, p. 1066.
3. Ibid., § 396, pp. 1067–1070.
4. *Restatement (Second) of Contracts* § 302 and Introductory Note to Chapter 14 at pp. 438–439.
5. *Allan v. Bekins Archival Service, Inc.*, 154 Cal.Rptr. 458, (Cal. App. 1979), 463 fn 8.
6. *Restatement (Second) of Contracts*, Statutory Note to Chapter 15 at pp. 7–9.
7. *Restatement (Second) of Contracts*, Statutory Note to Chapter 15 at p. 10.
8. 16 C.F.R. § 433.1–.3 (1975, as amended in 1977).
9. Tommy Staniforth, "Football: Arsenal Attacked Over Nano Move," *The Independent* (London) (21 May 1999), Sports, p. 32.
10. *Restatement (Second) of Contracts* § 326, Comment b, Ill. 1.

15

CONTRACTUAL DISCHARGE AND REMEDIES

A G E N D A

The Kochanowskis realize that CIT may, from time to time, have customers who do not pay their bills as these sums come due. The family members therefore want to know what rights they will have in such situations. They also will be ordering component parts that need to be produced to fairly exact standards. They wonder how they can word their contracts so that they will receive parts of the desired specifications—and what they can

do if the suppliers do not meet those specifications. Moreover, they are concerned—both as sellers and as buyers—with the time element in their contracts. How important is the time for performance?

These and other questions are likely to arise during this chapter. Be prepared! You never know when one of the Kochanowskis will ask for your help or advice.

O U T L I N E

TERMINATION OF THE CONTRACT

When parties contract with one another, each party naturally assumes that the other party will faithfully and satisfactorily perform according to the terms of the agreement. Consequently, whenever the parties do what the contract calls for, the law says that they have discharged their duties under the contract. *Discharge* of a contract involves the legally valid termination of a contractual duty. Upon discharge, the parties have fulfilled their agreement; at this time, the parties' duties and obligations to one another end. The law groups the numerous methods for discharging contracts into four main categories: discharge by performance, discharge by agreement of the parties, discharge by operation of law, and discharge by nonperformance. Exhibit 15.1 shows the various methods for discharging a contract and details both the methods of discharge as well as the general rules applied to each method.

E X H I B I T   15.1 | **Methods of Discharging Contracts**

Type of Discharge	General Rules
1. Discharge by performance	1. Completion of the contract on tender of delivery or payment.
a. Complete performance: the parties' exact fulfillment of the terms of the contract.	
b. Substantial performance: less-than-perfect performance that complies with the essential portions of the contract.	1. Applicable only to nonmaterial and nonwillful breaches. 2. The injured party's suit for damages resulting from the minor deviations that have led to substantial (as opposed to complete) performance.
2. Discharge by agreement of the parties	
a. Release: the surrender of a legal claim.	1. Necessitates a writing, consideration, and an immediate relinquishment of rights or claims owed to another.
b. Rescission: the voluntary, mutual surrender and discharge of contractual rights and duties whereby the parties are returned to the original status quo.	1. May be either written or oral (subject to the Statute of Frauds), formal or informal, express or implied.
c. Accord and satisfaction: an agreement whereby the parties decide to accept performance different from that required by their original bargain and the parties' later compliance with this new agreement.	1. Actual agreement and subsequent performance necessary.
d. Novation: a contract that effects an immediate discharge of a previously existing contractual duty, creates a new contractual obligation or duty, and includes as a party to this new agreement one who neither was owed a duty nor obligated to perform in the original contract.	1. Assent of creditor and new obligor required. 2. Different from an accord and satisfaction in that it effects an immediate discharge of an obligation rather than a discharge predicated on a subsequent performance.
3. Discharge by operation of law	
a. Bankruptcy: a court decree/discharge of the debtor's contractual obligations.	1. Revival of the obligation possible if done in compliance with applicable statutory provisions.
b. Statute of limitations: a definite statutory time period during which the plaintiff must commence a lawsuit or be barred forever.	1. Applicable time periods different from state to state.
c. Material alteration of the contract: a serious change in the contract effected by a party to the contract.	1. Must be done intentionally and without the consent of the other party.

---

continued

E X H I B I T   15.1 | **Methods of Discharging Contracts, continued**

Type of Discharge	General Rules
4. Discharge by nonperformance	
a. Impossibility: an unforeseen event or condition that precludes the possibility of the party's performing as promised.	1. Discharge stemming from only objective (as opposed to subjective) impossibility.
	2. Includes such events as the destruction of the contract's subject matter without the fault of either party, supervening illegality, the death or disability of either party whose performance is essential to the performance of the contract, and conduct by one party that makes performance by the other party impossible.
b. Commercial frustration: the destruction of the essential purpose and value of the contract.	1. Destruction of the value of the contract brought about by a supervening event not reasonably anticipated at the contract's formation.
	2. Term *commercially impracticable* used in the UCC.
c. Breach: the nonperformance of the obligations set up by the contract.	
1. Complete (or actual) breach.	1. A party's failure to perform a duty material and essential to the agreement; the other party justified in treating the agreement as at an end.
2. Anticipatory breach: an indication in advance by one of the contracting parties that he or she does not intend to abide by the terms of the contract.	1. Covered by both the common law and the UCC.
d. Conditions: limitations or qualifications placed on a promise.	
1. Express conditions: those in which the parties explicitly or impliedly in fact set out the limitations to which their promises will be subject.	1. Strict compliance with express conditions necessary to avoid a breach.
2. Constructive conditions: those read into the contract or implied in law in order to serve justice.	1. Substantial compliance with constructive conditions necessary to avoid a breach.
3. Condition precedent: performance contingent on the happening of a future event; resultant discharge of both parties stemming from the failure of the condition precedent.	
4. Condition subsequent: the occurrence of a particular event that cuts off all ongoing contractual duties and discharges the obligations of both parties.	

Equitable
Arising from the branch of the legal system designed to provide a remedy where no remedy existed at common law; a system designed to provide fairness when there was no suitable remedy "at law."

Despite the parties' original intentions, the possibility exists that one party will fail to live up to the contractual obligations. As you will learn, such nonperformance constitutes a breach of the contract and entitles the injured party to certain remedies, assuming the injured party does not wish to *waive* (or ignore) the breach. A *remedy* is a cause of action resulting from the breach of a contract. After the occurrence of a breach, remedies attempt to satisfy the parties' expectations as of the time of the contract's formation. Remedies fall into two main categories: those resulting from a court's exercise of its powers "at law" (*legal* remedies) and those arising from a court's use of its powers of equity (**equitable** remedies). Although you have probably always used the term *legal remedies* to encompass both types of relief, in this chapter you will learn to identify the sorts of situations in which it is appropriate for a court to order one kind of relief or the other. You also will become aware that these types of remedies usually are mutually exclusive.

DISCHARGE BY PERFORMANCE

Complete Performance

The simplest, most common, and most satisfactory method of discharge consists of *complete performance.* (Yet, as we will see later in this chapter, rendering complete performance may be easier said than done.) If Johnson has agreed to deliver five carloads of grain, and Kreczewski has promised to pay $2,000 per carload, complete performance will occur when Johnson makes the deliveries to Kreczewski and Kreczewski pays Johnson. The parties' exact fulfillment of the terms of the contract satisfies the intent of their agreement and their reason for contracting. Complete performance also extinguishes all the legal duties and rights that the contract originally set up. Note, too, that performance will be complete if one of the parties *tenders* either the grain or the payment—that is, unconditionally offers to perform his contractual obligation and can so perform. That person will have completely performed the contract even if the other person does not accept the grain or the payment.

As long as Johnson is fulfilling Kreczewski's reasonable expectations under the contract, discharge by complete performance will ensue once the parties have met their respective obligations under the agreement. If during the course of the deliveries, however, Johnson does not live up to the letter of the agreement as to the quality of the grain sent to Kreczewski, Kreczewski should give Johnson prompt notice of these defects and should state formally that he (Kreczewski) expects complete performance. Kreczewski's failure to take such actions may allow Johnson to argue after the fact that Kreczewski has waived his right to expect complete performance.

15.1 | MANUFACTURING/ SALES

ENSURING ACCEPTABLE PERFORMANCE

Anna has recently negotiated a preliminary agreement with a television manufacturer, TeleVision, Inc. (TVI), that calls for TVI to produce the glass screens to be used in Call-Image videophones. Anna realizes that TVI will need to supply screens of very exact specifications; otherwise, these components will not satisfy CIT's production needs. She has asked for your advice as to how to word the final written contract between CIT and TVI so that CIT protects itself and so that the screens will meet CIT's specifications. What advice will you give her?

BUSINESS CONSIDERATIONS Suppose a business is offered a very lucrative contract if it will produce a product to very specific standards. In deciding whether to adopt the offer, what factors should the firm consider? **ETHICAL CONSIDERATIONS** Is it ethical for a person to enter a contract that requires personal satisfaction as to the performance of the other party? What, if anything, would make such a measure unethical?

Substantial Performance

In some circumstances, one party's performance does not mirror precisely the rights and obligations enumerated in the agreement. In such cases, the other party may question whether this degree of performance adequately fulfills the requisites of the contract. The issue raised by such a question involves the legal sufficiency of less-than-complete performance.

The law does not always require exact performance of a contract. Hence, minor deviations from the performance contemplated in the contract may not preclude the discharge of the contract. This type of performance is called *substantial performance.* Construction of a new house in which the contractor still needs to finish the woodwork or touch up the painting in certain rooms—assuming the contractor has completed everything else—probably constitutes substantial performance. A party who has substantially performed may receive the payment to which the parties have agreed. Because substantial performance represents a type of contract breach, since the performance is not perfect and instead is a notch below the parties' reasonable expectations under the contract, the other party can sue for the damages occasioned by substantial, as opposed to complete, performance.

Two criteria must be met before the doctrine of substantial performance is available to discharge the responsibilities of a performing party. First, the breach must not have been material. In other words, the defective performance must not destroy the value or purpose of the contract.[1] Second, the breach must be nonwillful and devoid of bad faith conduct.

Courts usually are more willing to apply the concept of substantial performance to construction contracts than to sales contracts. Why? A disgruntled buyer has a duty to return or to reject a defective computer, whereas a dissatisfied occupier of land necessarily must keep the defective house or garage. The possibility of the unjust enrichment of the landowner in construction situations makes the doctrine of substantial performance more attractive to courts in these circumstances than in most other commercial contexts.

DISCHARGE BY AGREEMENT OF THE PARTIES

The parties themselves can specifically agree to discharge the contract. Provisions to that effect may be part of the original contract between the parties or part of a new contract drafted expressly to discharge the initial agreement.

Release

Release represents a common method of discharging the legal rights that one party has against another. To be valid, a *release* should be in *writing*, should be supported by *consideration*, and should effect an *immediate relinquishment* of rights or claims owed to another. For example, a landowner may sign a release in which he or she agrees, usually in exchange for money, to discharge the builder from the original contractual obligations. Insurance companies commonly execute similar releases that the insured parties must sign before the insurers will pay for the insured parties' injuries.

Rescission

Sometimes the parties may find it advantageous to call off their deal. The law calls this process *rescission.* A contract of rescission is a voluntary, mutual surrender and discharge of contractual rights and duties whereby the law returns the parties to the original status quo. A valid rescission is legally binding. In general, rescission may be either in writing or oral (subject, you will recall, to the Statute of Frauds's requirements under § 2-209 of the UCC; moreover, rescissions of realty contracts often must be written), formal or informal, and express or implied.

The simplest method of rescission involves the termination of executory bilateral contracts. If Johnson and Kreczewski in the earlier example *mutually agree to cancel* their transaction, *express rescission* has occurred. On the other hand, they may subsequently agree that Johnson will deliver seven carloads of grain instead of five. Substituting this later agreement for the old one brings about an *implied rescission* of the earlier agreement. However, problems often ensue if the parties attempt rescission of a unilateral contract (or a bilateral contract where one party has fully executed his or her duties). In these situations, some courts, before they will grant rescission, will infer a promise to pay for the performance rendered or require that consideration be paid to the party who has performed. Courts ordinarily resolve these issues by trying to ascertain the intent of the parties, but, as we have learned, this task often is difficult.

Accord and Satisfaction

The parties may agree to accept performance different from that required by their original bargain (as discussed in Chapter 11 concerning consideration in unliquidated debt situations). The law calls such an agreement an *accord*. When the parties comply with the accord, *satisfaction* occurs, and discharge of the original claim by *accord and satisfaction* (i.e., substituted performance) has resulted. The process of accord and satisfaction requires evidence of assent. Moreover, an accord will not be legally binding unless and until the performance required in the accord (i.e., the satisfaction) is rendered.

Novation

Just as the parties may agree to substituted performances, so they may agree to substituted parties. A *novation* is a contract that effects an immediate discharge of a previously existing contractual obligation, creates a new contractual obligation or duty, and includes as a party to this new agreement one who in the original contract was neither owed a duty nor obligated to perform. A novation, then, is a contract in which a new party is substituted for one of the parties in the previous contract. The novation immediately discharges an obligation, whereas, in contrast, an accord is not executed until performance occurs. As you might expect, both the assent of the person to whom the obligation is owed (usually the creditor) and the assent of the new obligor (the third party) are required for a valid novation. The assent of the previous debtor usually is not required, although that party can, if it wishes, disclaim the benefit of the discharge. The novation, in addition, must be supported by valid consideration.

DISCHARGE BY OPERATION OF LAW

We have seen in other contexts that the law itself can mandate the discharge of certain contracts. As you will learn in Chapter 29, bankruptcy decrees may grant to honest debtors a discharge of contractual obligations by operation of law. Most of the time a creditor will not receive the total owed, and yet the discharge in bankruptcy prevents the creditor from later suing the debtor for nonperformance (usually nonpayment). Most states, however, pursuant to the Bankruptcy Act's provisions, allow the debtor to revive the obligation by a later promise to pay the creditor. This reaffirmation of the debt involves several stringent new requirements under the Bankruptcy Act.

Statutes of limitations in all jurisdictions establish time periods within which, depending on the nature of the claims, litigants must initiate lawsuits. Noncompliance with these statutory time limits may discharge contractual claims by operation of law. For example, one typically must bring claims for breach of common law contracts within six years of the date of the alleged breach. Filing a lawsuit after this time limit makes the claim unenforceable. When the transaction involves a sale of goods, § 2-725 of the UCC states that the injured party ordinarily must file suit within four years of the occurrence of the breach. The underlying claim is discharged by operation of law if the injured party fails to file a lawsuit within this period. These periods of limitations differ from jurisdiction to jurisdiction, so each state's statutes should be checked.

The law also may grant a discharge of any contract that one of the parties to the agreement has materially altered. Before this rule will be applied, it must be shown that the alteration was done intentionally and without the consent of the other party. Thus, if Johnson, without Kreczewski's permission, changes the carload price of the grain on the written contract from $2,000 to $5,000, Kreczewski can obtain a discharge of the contract through operation of law.

DISCHARGE BY NONPERFORMANCE

Under certain circumstances, nonperformance may discharge a contract. Still, as mentioned before, do not expect courts to apply these doctrines in order to save you from a bad bargain.

Impossibility

Until the middle of the last century, courts rejected outright the doctrine of impossibility as a method of discharging contracts. *Impossibility* as a legal concept refers to an unforeseen event or condition that precludes a party's performing as promised. For instance, such events as the destruction of the subject matter of the contract without the fault of either party (Johnson's wheat burns before being loaded), supervening illegality (after the contract's formation, the legislature passes a law making it illegal for trains to carry agricultural products into certain states), or conduct by one party that makes performance by the other party impossible (in carrying out other deals, Kreczewski contracts for every possible car so that Johnson cannot procure the necessary cars for their transaction) generally discharge contracts. These examples denote *objective impossibility* (nonperformance of the contract is unavoidable; *no one* could perform the contract in these circumstances).

Another instance of objective impossibility involves the death or disability of either party to a personal services contract (Johnson hires Pollock to paint his portrait, and Pollock has a debilitating heart attack). This contingency forms an exception to the general rule that a contract will be binding and thus not dischargeable except through performance despite the death or disability of either party, unless the parties have agreed otherwise. The contract will not be discharged, however, if another painter is acceptable to Johnson.

On the other hand, courts have held that circumstances involving subjective impossibility (as opposed to objective impossibility) will not discharge contractual obligations. *Subjective impossibility* consists of nonperformance owing to personal, as contrasted to external, impossibility. In such cases, the contract can be performed, but *this particular person* is unable to fulfill the obligations contemplated in the contract. For this reason, nonperformance owing to insolvency, shortages of materials, strikes, riots, droughts, and price increases ordinarily will not discharge contracts. However, some courts temporarily will suspend the duty to perform until the conditions causing the inability to perform have passed. More liberal courts may even discharge the contract if later performance will place an appreciably greater burden on the one obligated to perform. Given this division of opinion, the parties often will try to protect their rights by including express provisions covering the types of contingencies just described.

Commercial Frustration

Because of the harshness of the general rule that impossibility ordinarily will not discharge the performance called for in a contract, the doctrine of *commercial frustration* (or *frustration of purpose*) has recently emerged as a basis for justifiable nonperformance. Courts will not invoke this doctrine to excuse performance, however, unless the essential purpose and value of the contract have been frustrated. If the parties reasonably could (or should) have foreseen the resultant frustration, courts will hold the nonperforming party to the terms of the bargain. Hence, courts will not utilize this doctrine to release parties from bad bargains. It is important to understand that in these cases performance is possible, but the value of the contract has been frustrated or destroyed by a supervening event that was not reasonably anticipated at the contract's formation. The Uniform Commercial Code uses the term *commercially impracticable* (§ 2-615) in like fashion to excuse nonperformance in cases of severe shortages of raw materials owing to war, embargo, local crop failure, and other similar reasons. Before courts will allow discharge, these factors must have caused a marked increase in price or must have totally precluded the seller from obtaining the supplies necessary for performance.

In the *Chase Precast Corporation* case that follows, the court accepted the doctrine of commercial frustration as a defense.

15.1

CHASE PRECAST CORPORATION V. JOHN J. PAONESSA COMPANY, INC.

566 N.E.2D 603 (MASS. 1991)

FACTS In 1982, the Commonwealth of Massachusetts, through the Department of Public Works, entered into two contracts with the John J. Paonessa Company, Inc. (Paonessa) for resurfacing and improvements to two stretches of Route 128. Part of each contract called for replacing a grass median strip between the north- and southbound lanes with concrete surfacing and precast-concrete median barriers. Paonessa entered into two contracts with Chase Precast Corporation (Chase) under which Chase was to supply, in the aggregate, 25,800 linear feet of concrete median barriers according to the specifications of the department. After this highway construction began in the spring of 1983, the department began receiving protests from angry residents who objected to the use of the concrete median barriers and the removal of the grass median strip. Paonessa and Chase became aware of the protest around 1 June. On 6 June, a group of about 100 citizens filed an action in superior court to stop the installation of the concrete median barriers and other aspects of the work. On 7 June, anticipating modification by the department, Paonessa notified Chase by letter to stop producing concrete barriers for the projects. Upon receipt of the letter the following day, Chase did so. On 17 June, the department and the citizens' group entered into a settlement providing, in part, for the banning of the installation of any additional concrete median barriers. On 23 June, the department deleted the permanent concrete median barriers item from its contracts with Paonessa. Before stopping production on 8 June, Chase had produced approximately one-half of the concrete median barriers called for by its contracts with Paonessa and had delivered most of them to the construction sites. Paonessa paid Chase at the contract price for all that Chase had produced. Although Chase had suffered no out-of-pocket expenses as a result of the cancellation of the remaining portion of the barriers, it sued Paonessa to recover the profits it allegedly had lost owing to the cancellation of the contracts to supply the median barriers. Paonessa defended on the grounds of impossibility and frustration of purpose.

ISSUE Did either the doctrine of impossibility or the doctrine of frustration of purpose serve as a defense to immunize Paonessa from liability?

HOLDING The doctrine of frustration of purpose immunized Paonessa from liability because, at the time of contract formation, the parties had not

continued

15.1

CHASE PRECAST CORPORATION V. JOHN J. PAONESSA COMPANY, INC., *continued*
566 N.E.2D 603 (MASS. 1991)

contemplated the cancellation of the items and thus in the contract had failed to allocate the risk of such cancellation to either party.

REASONING Massachusetts courts have long recognized and applied the doctrine of impossibility as a defense to an action for breach of contract. Under Massachusetts courts' construction of that doctrine,

> where from the nature of the contract it appears that the parties must from the beginning have contemplated the continued existence of some particular specified thing as the foundation of what was to be done, then, in the absence of any warranty that the thing shall exist . . . the parties shall be excused . . . [when] performance becomes impossible from the accidental perishing of the thing without the fault of either party.

Put differently, when an event neither anticipated nor caused by either party, the risk of which was not allocated by the contract, destroys the object or purpose of the contract, thus destroying the value of performance, the parties are excused from further performance.

At least one Massachusetts precedent has called frustration of purpose a companion rule to the doctrine of impossibility. Both doctrines concern the effect of supervening circumstances on the rights and duties of the parties. The difference lies in the effect of the supervening event. Under frustration of purpose, performance remains possible; but the fortuitous event has destroyed the expected value of the performance to the party seeking to be excused. Clearly, frustration of purpose represents a more accurate label for the defense argued in this case than impossibility of performance, since performance was not literally impossible. Paonessa still could have honored its contract to purchase the remaining sections of median barrier, whether or not the department approved their use in the road construction. The principal question in both kinds of cases remains whether an unanticipated circumstance, the risk of which should not fairly be thrown on the promisor, has made performance vitally different from what was reasonably to be expected.

In the present case, Paonessa bore no responsibility for the department's elimination of the median barriers from the projects. Therefore, whether Paonessa can rely on the defense of frustration of purpose turns on whether elimination of the barriers was a risk allocated by the contracts to Paonessa. Simply put, given the commercial circumstances in which the parties dealt, was the contingency that developed one that the parties could reasonably have foreseen as a real possibility that could affect performance? Or, alternatively, was it one of that variety of risks that the parties, by their failure to provide for it explicitly, were tacitly assigning to the promisor? If it was, performance will be required. If it cannot be so considered, performance is excused. This becomes a question for the trier of fact. The purchase order agreements between Chase and Paonessa do not contain a similar provision. Yet this difference in the contracts does not mandate the conclusion that Paonessa assumed the risk of reduction in the quantity of barriers. Chase was aware of the department's power to decrease the quantities of contract items, since Chase had supplied median barriers to the department in the past; and the contractual provision giving the department the power to eliminate items was a standard one. In this case, even if the parties were aware of the department's power to eliminate contract items, the judge could reasonably have concluded that they had not contemplated the cancellation for a major portion of the project of such a widely used item as concrete median barriers and had failed to allocate the risk of such a cancellation. Hence, the doctrine of frustration of purpose would discharge Paonessa's remaining duties to render performance and would immunize it from liability to Chase for lost profits.

BUSINESS CONSIDERATIONS The citizens' group's lawsuit led to Paonessa's canceling the contracts with Chase concerning the median barriers. Should the law allow citizens' protests to interfere with the contractual rights of private parties like Paonessa and Chase? Why or why not? Would the fact that these were state-initiated contracts affect your viewpoint?

ETHICAL CONSIDERATION Paonessa had paid Chase for all the concrete median barriers Chase had produced before the cancellation of the contract occurred. Was Chase's suit for lost profits unethical?

Actual Breach

Breach of contract occurs when one or more of the contracting parties fails to perform the obligations set up by the contract. That degrees of breach exist complicates the issue somewhat. A *complete* or *actual* breach of contract involves the nonperformance of a duty that is so material and essential to the agreement that the other party is justified in treating the agreement as at an end. The Uniform Commercial Code in § 2-703 and § 2-711 embraces this common law principle. Actual breach generally discharges the other party's obligation to perform under the terms of the contract. However, rather than canceling the contract upon breach, the injured (or nonbreaching) party may elect instead to hold the nonperforming party to the contract through various types of remedies, which we will discuss later in this chapter.

Anticipatory Breach

Sometimes one of the contracting parties will indicate in advance, through words or conduct, that he or she does not intend to abide by the terms of the contract. To illustrate, if Johnson unequivocally tells Kreczewski before the time performance is due that he will not send the grain as scheduled, Johnson will have wrongfully repudiated the contract. In legal terms, Johnson's action is called *anticipatory breach,* or *anticipatory repudiation.* In this situation, as in actual breaches, the injured party need not limit its potential responses to discharge of the contract.

The Uniform Commercial Code sanctions a kind of anticipatory repudiation in circumstances less definite than those allowable under the common law. Section 2-609 of the Code states that when reasonable grounds for insecurity arise with respect to one party's performance, the other party may demand adequate assurances of due performance and suspend performance until such assurances are forthcoming. If 30 days pass without reply, the party who has demanded the assurances can deem the contract repudiated. Kreczewski's actual or apparent **insolvency,** for example, may cause Johnson to invoke the provisions of § 2-609. If Kreczewski does not respond within 30 days, Johnson then may treat the contract as repudiated (see § 2-610). The following case involves a situation in which each of the parties to the contract accuses the other of being in breach. Reflect on how the court disposes of these contentions.

15.2 | MANAGEMENT

CALL-IMAGE TECHNOLOGY

DEFENSES TO CONTRACT ENFORCEMENT

One of John's professors mentioned in class last week that a number of subcontractors who encounter difficulties in meeting their contractual obligations often try to use the defenses of impossibility, commercial impracticability, or commercial frustration to escape liability when they fail to satisfy their contracts. Call-Image jobs out much of its work to subcontractors, and John is concerned that these sorts of situations may arise with the firm. He asks you what the firm should do to protect itself. What will you tell him?

BUSINESS CONSIDERATIONS Should a business enter into contracts that it is not sure it can perform and then resort to commercial impracticability as an excuse if it cannot perform as promised? What legal risk is the firm assuming if it uses such an approach to its obligations?

ETHICAL CONSIDERATIONS Is it ethical for a firm to avoid liability by asserting that its promised performance was made impossible or impracticable by some external factor? Is it ethical for a firm to try to collect damages when an external factor made the performance by the other firm impossible or impracticable?

Insolvency
Inability to pay one's debts as they become due.

15.2

IN RE CORNELL & COMPANY, INC.
229 B.R. 97 (BKRTCY.E.D.PA. 1999)

FACTS The debtor, Cornell & Company, Inc. (Cornell), a construction company, had hired a subcontractor to do part of the painting work for a municipal project for which Cornell was the general contractor. The subcontractor later assigned its fee—$975,000—and the subcontract to Delbert L. Smith Company (the defendant). As was customary in the industry, Cornell retained monies to ensure the defendant's completion of the subcontract. The defendant worked for Cornell for three months before the project started to experience difficulties owing in part to the delays associated with the changes in the federal lead-abatement standards. These difficulties, in turn, led to the debtor's filing for bankruptcy. The defendant continued to work on the project once the debtor became current on all the outstanding sums due. However, when the defendant asked for a reduction in the monies retained by the debtor, the debtor refused, owing to its belief that the defendant had not completed enough work on the project to warrant the requested reduction. The parties' relationship continued to deteriorate, and on 13 November 1996, the defendant permanently departed from the project. Even though it contended only two days', work remained, the defendant submitted it could not finish this work because certain tasks that had to precede its work had been left undone. When the defendant refused thereafter to return, the debtor paid an additional $307,000 to another firm to complete the work. In the subsequent bankruptcy proceeding, the defendant filed a claim of $80,374.83 for the unreleased retainage monies on the project. The debtor maintained that the bankruptcy court should deny the claim because the defendant's failure to complete the work had forced the defendant to retain a new subcontractor to finish the work and to incur significant additional costs. These costs, the debtor argued, reflected the fact that the defendant had completed only about 70 percent of the work.

ISSUE Did the defendant's failure to complete its contractual obligations, in conjunction with its abandonment of the project, constitute a material breach of contract that would justify the bankruptcy court's rejection of the defendant's claim against the debtor?

HOLDING Yes. The defendant's unilateral withdrawal from the job site without completing its contractual duties represented a material breach of the contract that excused the non-breaching party from fulfilling its obligations under the contract. Hence, the court was justified in rejecting the claim asserted against the debtor by the defendant.

REASONING The defendant failed to complete a substantial portion of the work in question as mandated by the subcontractor agreements. Despite the parties' respective claims of a 96 percent completion rate (the defendant's estimate) and 70 percent (the debtor's estimate), the evidence revealed that the defendant had completed 86.41 percent of the subcontract work involved. Thus, the defendant's failure to perform any further work on the project evinced the defendant's material breach of its agreement with the debtor, as did the defendant's abandonment of the project. It is well settled that when a party materially breaches a contractual agreement, the non-breaching party is not required to fulfill its duties under the contract. Hence, a party who has materially breached a contract may not complain if the other party refuses to perform its contractual obligations. Since it had breached the contract, the defendant was not entitled either to request or to recover from the debtor the release of the retainage monies. Nor had the defendant proved that it had performed extra work on the project and that the debtor had agreed to compensate the defendant over and above the $975,000 contract price. In rebuttal, the defendant maintained that it was justified in not performing the agreement in question because of the debtor's failure to make certain that other work necessary to be completed prior to the defendant's painting had been done. However, these arguments were unpersuasive. Even after the prerequisite work was completed, the defendant simply refused to return to the job until it had received the retainage monies, which were not yet due to the defendant. One party's delay in making payment where the amount of the work done is disputed or is being negotiated would not, on that basis alone, represent a breach of contract. Rather, a breach would occur where a party unilaterally, as here, leaves a job site without completing its contractual duties. Furthermore, the evidence showed that the debtor was current on its payment obligations to the defendant except for the payment on the retainage, which was not yet due. Therefore, the defendant had no justifiable basis for its continual refusal to perform

IN RE CORNELL & COMPANY, INC., *continued*
229 B.R. 97 (BKRTCY.E.D.PA. 1999)

under the contract. A party who has materially breached a contract may not complain if the other party thereafter refuses to perform. The breaching party has no valid claim against the aggrieved party. Since the defendant had failed to rebut the debtor's evidence of the non-completion of the contract, one must conclude that the claim at issue, based on the defendant's assertion of an entitlement to the contract balance, must be stricken in its entirety.

BUSINESS CONSIDERATIONS What could the parties have done differently to avoid this litigation? Would informal mediation have avoided a lawsuit?

ETHICAL CONSIDERATION Assess the respective ethics of the debtor's refusing to release any of the retainage monies and the defendant's behavior in abandoning the project. Had one party behaved relatively more ethically than the other?

Conditions

The presence of conditions may result in nonperformance that will justify discharge of a contract as well. A *promise* is a vow or a covenant that places on the promisor a duty to do something or to refrain from doing something. A *condition*, in contrast, is an act or event that limits or qualifies a promise. The condition must occur before the promisor has a duty to perform or to refrain from performing.

Courts classify conditions in two ways. The first category emphasizes the *timing* of the qualifying occurrence (the condition) in relation to the promised performance. Three subsets of this category include *conditions precedent, concurrent conditions,* and *conditions subsequent.* The second category stems from the manner in which the conditions arise. Conditions created by law are deemed *constructive* (or *implied*) *conditions.* In contrast, conditions created by the agreement of the parties themselves are called *express conditions.*

Under the first category (timing), an agreement may explicitly state that a certain act or event must occur before the other party has a duty to perform or before a contract results. If so, a *condition precedent* exists. For example, a person may promise (for consideration) to buy a car if the seller can deliver the car within 10 days. A duty to buy the car does not arise unless and until the seller fulfills the condition. Thus, the timing of the condition and any later duty to perform go together.

To be a condition precedent rather than a mere promise, the parties must indicate that the condition is an essential, vital aspect of the transaction. If the buyer in our example later wishes to sue for rescission of the contract or for damages on the ground that the seller has not delivered the car on time, the buyer will have to prove that delivery within 10 days is essential to the transaction. A common condition precedent involves a buyer's signing a contract for the purchase of a new house subject to the sale of the buyer's current residence. The buyer views this provision as an important consideration regarding his or her willingness to enter into the contract.

Concurrent conditions, related to conditions precedent in regard to the timing of the condition and the promised performance, obligate the parties *to perform at the same time.* Concurrent conditions (e.g., the transfer of goods in exchange for payment) underlie most commercial sales.

A *condition subsequent* is any occurrence that the parties have agreed will cut off an existing legal duty. It also may involve a contingency, the happening or

CONFIDENTIALITY AND NONDISPARAGEMENT CLAUSES

In this era of corporate downsizing, severance agreements that contain confidentiality and nondisparagement clauses that prohibit departing employees from saying anything negative about the company to persons who may be suing the company under various state and federal laws have become commonplace. Indeed, severance agreements long have included provisions in which the employee agrees to waive a panoply of claims against a company and to refrain from saying anything negative about the employer to other employees, a competitor, or the media. Simply put, such broadly worded settlement agreements and releases nowadays represent the quid pro quo that employers expect in return for settlement payments. Critics of such agreements have charged that the resultant veil of contractual secrecy unfairly hinders the remaining employees from making informed decisions about such matters as whether they, too, are victims of illegal discrimination. These critics therefore focus on the tension between society's interest in promoting settlements and these agreements' potential suppression of information regarding alleged injuries.

A related issue that can prove vexing to corporations and lead to breach of contract actions derives from so-called golden parachutes, or lucrative severance packages, that a company cobbles together at the last minute during corporate takeovers. To illustrate, during weekend takeover talks with Canada's Potash Corporation of Saskatchewan (PCS), Arcadian Corporation (Arcadian) negotiated severance packages for nine of its highest-ranking executives. The outside counsel who proposed Arcadian's contractual language adopted the terms of a standard employment contract—a common practice even when time is not of the essence. The Arcardian contracts provided that any severance would be tied to all bonuses, profit sharing, and other incentive payments made to company employees after the $1.6 billion takeover. When the plaintiffs argued that this clause included $18 million of long-term incentive payments, PCS rejected such an expansive reading on the rationale that the firm's standard employment agreements reflect the firm's history of emphasizing cash and other types of short-term compensation. Adding to PCS's headaches was the fact that the law of Delaware, the state of Arcadian's incorporation, would govern all disputes and that Delaware precedents discourage courts from

continued

performance of which will defeat a contract already in effect. When a sales contract involving grain storage states that the contract will be of no effect if fire destroys the grain, a condition subsequent exists.

Genuine conditions subsequent are rare. What may sound like a condition subsequent—for example, Acme Insurance will not pay for casualty losses if the premises are unoccupied—will be construed by many courts as a condition precedent. Courts that characterize such a provision as a condition subsequent will interpret the clause as stating that the occurrence of the condition (vacant premises) will cut off an existing legal duty (payment of the casualty loss). Other courts will say that it is a condition precedent (the premises must be kept occupied) that merely sounds like a condition subsequent because of the phrasing. This distinction can be procedurally significant. If it is a condition precedent, the insured has the burden of proof; if it is a condition subsequent, the insurer has the burden of proof. And when the evidence is conflicting, the party who has the burden of proof often loses.

Express conditions (e.g., this sale can be consummated only by payment of cash) are those spelled out by the parties explicitly or impliedly in fact. A *constructive* overturning the plain meaning of a disputed contract term in the absence of a glaring ambiguity. In finding for the plaintiffs, the judge held that the phrase *other incentive payments* encompassed both long-term and short-term incentive pay. The judge also examined the corporate culture of Arcadian, which the judge viewed as showing an emphasis on long-term incentives as a key component of the company's executive compensation strategy. In the judge's opinion, the litigation and the sizable award could be styled as an example of the admonition, "Act in haste; repent at leisure." Executive compensation specialists contend that the creation of complex severance packages in the last minutes of a takeover plague many Fortune 500 companies.

Suppose that a departing employee wanted to talk to the Equal Opportunity Commission (the EEOC) about allegations of discrimination, say sexual harassment, within the firm, and that the former employer was attempting to enforce this sort of clause to prevent such a discussion. If this case were brought before *your* court, how would *you* rule? Would you strike down a settlement agreement that prohibits a departing employee from talking to the EEOC, or would you uphold such a settlement agreement? Furthermore, would you agree that the judge should have upheld the PCA-Arcadian takeover severance package? Why or why not?[2]

BUSINESS CONSIDERATIONS Why would a company want to have a nondisparagement clause in a severance agreement? Why would an employee sign such an agreement? In the takeover context mentioned here, what can a firm do to more fully protect its interests?

ETHICAL CONSIDERATIONS Is it ethical for an employer to ask a departing employee to surrender, upon the termination of the employment, his or her right to free speech in exchange for a settlement package? What sorts of ethical issues does such a contract clause raise? Is it ethical for a hostile takeover target to forge expensive executive severance packages as part of a so-called poison-pill strategy to make the firm less attractive to the raider?

SOURCES: Darryl Van Duch, *The National Law Journal* (28 October 1996), pp. B1, B3; and Darryl Van Duch, *The National Law Journal* (25 January 1999), pp. B1, B3.

---

condition is one not expressed by the parties, but rather read into the contract in order to serve justice (i.e., the condition is implied in law). Differentiating between an express condition implied in fact and a constructive condition can be difficult. For example, a provision regarding place of delivery normally is a condition precedent in a contract involving grain; but if such a condition is lacking, and in the absence of clear intent, a court may imply that the place for delivery is the seller's place of business (see UCC § 2-308).

Nonperformance of an express condition precedent (such as posting a performance bond) causes a failure of the condition that nullifies the other party's duty to perform and discharges the contract. Similarly, the presence of an express condition subsequent (meaning that the occurrence of a particular event cuts off all ongoing contractual duties) discharges the obligations of both parties. For example, the buyer's returning goods before payment is due under the terms of a contract in which the buyer has reserved this right would constitute discharge of the contract. But to avoid a breach of an express condition, courts ordinarily require strict compliance. In contrast, substantial compliance generally avoids a breach of a constructive condition.

It should be noted that a condition may require one party to perform to the satisfaction of the other party. In fact, in certain cases, such as those involving custom tailoring, some courts hold that in order to discharge the contract, the performing party must meet the personal, subjective expectations of the dissatisfied party. Other courts hold that performance is substantial if the performance rendered will satisfy our old friend, a reasonable person. Courts generally will apply this latter test when the parties base performance not on personal tastes or aesthetic preferences (as may be involved in our custom tailoring example), but rather on satisfaction as to merchantability or mechanical utility (as in the purchase of a car).

TYPES OF REMEDIES

Upon breach of contract, in order to satisfy his or her expectations as of the time of contract formation, the injured party can choose among various remedies.

The most common legal remedy sought consists of *damages.* The injured party must *mitigate,* or minimize, these damages; but having fulfilled this legal duty, the injured party at the very least should be able to receive *compensatory damages,* those that will put the party in the same economic position that he or she would have occupied had the other party performed. If the facts permit, the injured party moreover may receive *consequential damages,* those indirect or special damages springing from the effects or aftermath of the breach itself; *punitive damages,* those damages over and above the actual damages that a court may award in order to deter the defendant from future malicious conduct; and *liquidated damages,* those agreed on in advance by the parties in the event that a breach occurs. A court also may award *nominal damages* (a small amount of compensation) for minor, technical contractual breaches that cause no actual losses.

In some situations, money damages will represent inadequate compensation for the loss of the bargain occasioned by the breach. Injured persons in these cases ordinarily resort to *equitable* remedies. These possible modes of relief include *rescission,* the cancellation or termination of the contract through the restoration of the parties to the status quo. Restoration is accomplished by *restitution*—the return of the goods, money, or property involved in the contract or the recovery of the reasonable value of the services rendered. *Specific performance*—that is, the court-ordered enforcement of the contract according to its exact terms—is an alternative type of equitable remedy, as is quasi contract. *Quasi contract,* you may remember, refers to the situation in which a court creates a contract for the parties, despite their wishes and intentions, in order to prevent the unjust enrichment of one party. The remedy available in quasi contract is restitution based, allowing the injured party to recover the reasonable value of the services rendered. *Reformation,* the court's rewriting of a contract in order to remove a mistake and to make the agreement conform to the terms to which the parties originally agreed, and *injunctions,* court-ordered writs directing a person to do or to refrain from doing some specified act, constitute two other equitable remedies.

It has been said that for every legal wrong the law attempts to provide a legal remedy. This chapter explores some of the contractual remedies that are obtainable. Exhibit 15.2 classifies various common types of contractual remedies. It also notes the fact that an injured party may give up the right to receive the performance called for in the contract.

E X H I B I T 15.2	Types of Contractual Remedies

Type of Remedy	Definition
Legal remedies (money damages)	Those damages resulting from a court's exercise of its power "at law."
Compensatory damages	Damages awarded to a nonbreaching party in order to compensate him or her for the actual, foreseeable harm or loss caused by the breach.
Consequential damages	Indirect or special damages springing from the effects or aftermath (i.e., the consequences) of the breach itself; not recoverable unless the breaching party knew, or should have known, at the time of contract formation, of the potential effect of a breach on the nonbreaching party.
Punitive damages	Unusual damages awarded to punish for willful, wanton, malicious harm caused to a nonbreaching party.
Nominal damages	Inconsequential sums that establish that the plaintiff had a cause of action but suffered no measurable pecuniary loss.
Liquidated damages	A provision in a contract that a stated sum of money or property will be paid, or forfeited if previously deposited, if one of the parties fails to perform in accordance with the contract; enforceable unless unreasonable.
Mitigation of damages	Nonbreaching party's duty to reduce the actual losses, if he or she is able to do so.
Equitable remedies	Remedies arising from a court's use of its powers of equity.
Rescission and restitution	The cancellation or abrogation of a contract and the return of the previously rendered consideration or its value; may be mutually agreed to by the parties to a contract or awarded as a remedy by a court.
Specific performance	An order by a court to render a contractually promised performance.
Quasi contract	A court's requiring that one who has received a benefit pay for the benefit conferred so as to prevent the unjust enrichment of the other party.
Reformation	A court's correction of an agreement to conform to the intentions of the parties.
Injunction	An order requiring a person to act or restraining a person from doing some act.
Waiver of breach	A party's relinquishment, repudiation, or surrender of a right that he or she has to seek a remedy for breach of contract.

DAMAGES

When one party breaches a contract, the other party is entitled to payment for lost expectations. The injured party therefore can bring an action for damages. It is not necessary that the injured party have the ability to compute exactly what the damages are, as long as the losses represent the natural and proximate consequences of the breach. In computing damages, courts ask whether the breaching party, as a reasonable person, at the time of contracting should have foreseen that these injuries would result from breach. If the nonperforming party should have foreseen the losses, courts will award damages to the injured party. The amount of damages awarded, of course, will depend heavily on the facts of the case.

Compensatory Damages

The most common type of damages is *compensatory damages,* or those sums of money that will place the injured party in the same economic position that would have been attained had the contract been performed. Such damages also are called *actual damages.* Injured parties may recover only the damages that the parties reasonably can foresee. The 1854 English case *Hadley* v. *Baxendale* enunciated this doctrine, which courts still widely accept as a limitation on the damages recoverable for breach of contract. Under the *Hadley* v. *Baxendale* rule, courts ordinarily will confine compensatory damages awards to those losses naturally arising from the breach, or those the parties may have reasonably contemplated or foreseen, at the time of contract formation, as the probable result of a breach of the contract. Compensatory damages include all damages directly attributable to the loss of the bargain previously agreed on by the parties, including lost profits and any incidental expenses incurred as a result of the breach. In a sale of goods, courts, in formulating the actual damages, usually compute the difference between the contract price and the market price. The same ordinarily is true of land contracts. Thus, if Miranda Construction Company, a developer of real estate for its own particular purposes, orders three bulldozers from Welling Machinery Company and, unfortunately, none of the bulldozers functions properly, Miranda should be able to recover the general or *direct damages* or losses occasioned by the defective equipment. Miranda's costs of repairing the machines constitute one type of direct loss. Alternatively, if Miranda has to buy new bulldozers at higher prices, Miranda will be able to recover the costs associated with obtaining this substitute performance.

Assuming that Miranda's bad luck continues and a seller with whom Miranda has contracted to buy land for investment purposes fails to go through with this realty contract, Miranda can sue the reneging seller for the difference between the price of this piece of land and the one Miranda eventually purchases. Miranda also can sue for such expenses as the additional brokers' fees or commissions involved in obtaining the second parcel of real estate, since these losses flow directly and foreseeably from the seller's breach as well. However, Miranda in both cases must deduct any expenses saved as a result of the breaches.

Consequential Damages

Besides compensatory damages, it also is possible for plaintiffs like Miranda to receive *consequential damages.* Consequential damages are those indirect or special damages springing from the effects or aftermath (i.e., the consequences) of the breach itself. Assume that in addition to the contracts mentioned, Miranda loses a grading contract with the city because the bulldozers will not work and, as a result, also loses several rental contracts from retailers who wished to be part of a mall that Miranda was planning to develop on the real estate it had tried to purchase. Can Miranda sue Welling and the seller for the losses accruing from these special circumstances and not just from the direct breach? To determine liability or the lack thereof, a court will apply the reasonable person test to see whether such lost contracts were a foreseeable result of Welling and the seller's breaches. A judge will not award purely speculative or conjectural damages; but if a court finds that Welling and the seller knew, or should have known, at the time of contract formation, of Miranda's circumstances and the potential effect of their breaches on Miranda, it may award incidental or consequential damages. The Uniform Commercial Code in § 2-715 and § 2-710 also recognizes this doctrine.

Duty to Mitigate

In determining whether to award damages and, if so, how to measure them, courts place on the injured party the duty to *mitigate* (or minimize) these damages if possible. In other words, the injured party must take affirmative steps to prevent the escalation of the losses brought about by the breaching party.

In the bulldozer example, courts will expect Miranda to attempt to procure substitute bulldozers, assuming this is possible without undue risk or expense. If Miranda does not undertake such reasonable steps, its failure to mitigate damages will preclude its receiving consequential damages. Rather, the court will limit its losses to those accruing directly from the breach. But if Miranda can prove that it was impossible to obtain substitute bulldozers, most courts will excuse its failure to mitigate. The duty of mitigation does not require the injured party to go to superhuman lengths. If the risks or expenses in mitigation attempts are unreasonably great, no duty to mitigate arises.

Punitive Damages

In contrast to their willingness to make compensatory and consequential damages available to injured parties, courts generally will not allow the recovery of *punitive damages* in breach of contract situations. Punitive, or exemplary, damages are imposed not to compensate the injured party but to punish the wrongdoer so as to deter future conduct of this sort. The old common law rule was that punitive damages never were appropriate for breaches of contract. Though still rare, some statutes now permit the imposition of punitive damages in contractual situations (such as **treble damages** under the antitrust laws). Furthermore, some courts have been willing to grant punitive damages in situations in which one party has acted willfully. An insurance company that unduly delays paying off legitimate contractual claims against it may be subject to punitive damages in order to discourage this type of conduct. If the circumstances so warrant, consumer transactions also may form the basis for an award of punitive damages.

Treble damages
A statutory remedy that allows the successful plaintiff to recover three times the damages suffered as a result of the injury.

In the past decade, courts have struggled with the issue of whether the due process clause of the Fourteenth Amendment, which requires fundamental fairness, places some outer limits on a jury's otherwise unfettered discretion to award huge punitive damages. Many juries impose punitive damages that far surpass the compensatory damages awarded. The Supreme Court, in *Pacific Mutual Life Insurance Company v. Haslip*, 499 U.S.1 (1991), held that a punitive damages award of more than $800,000 against an insurer whose agent had defrauded an insured was reasonable and did not violate the insurer's due process rights, even though the award exceeded by more than four times the amount of compensatory damages, was more than 200 times the out-of-pocket expenses incurred by the insured, and greatly exceeded the fine that Alabama law imposed for insurance fraud. The Court concluded that the procedural and substantive safeguards imposed by state law (including post-trial procedures that required trial courts to scrutinize all such punitive damages awards) ensured the reasonableness of the amount of punitive damages and the rationality of the award in furthering the purposes of deterrence and punishment. In short, the Court held that such safeguards imposed a sufficiently definite and meaningful constraint on the discretion of state juries to award punitive damages to ensure that such awards were not grossly disproportionate to the severity of the offense and were adequate to protect the due process rights of the persons against whom the juries had assessed the punitive damages.

Five years later, relying on *Haslip,* the Court, in *BMW of North America, Inc.* v. *Gore,* 517 U.S. 559 (1996), for the first time voided a state court's award of punitive damages as unconstitutional under the Fourteenth Amendment's due process clause. The Court held that a $2 million punitive damages award against BMW of North America, Inc. (BMW) for BMW's fraudulent failure to disclose that it had repainted a new $40,000 car, thereby reducing the vehicle's value by $4,000, was "grossly excessive." The jury apparently had arrived at the $4 million punitive damages figure it had awarded (the state supreme court had remitted, that is, lowered, the damages to $2 million) by multiplying the $4,000 compensatory damages award by the 1,000 nationwide instances of BMW's similar nondisclosures of minor repairs. The Court stressed that while Alabama had the right to protect its own citizens through the punishment of firms that engage in deceptive trade practices, such a state would not have the right, by the imposition of a punitive damages award or a legislatively authorized fine, to punish out-of-state activity that was lawful where it had occurred. Hence, the Court viewed this $2 million award as excessive in light of the interest of Alabama consumers and BMW's conduct in Alabama. And while the Court quoted *Haslip* for the proposition that the Court cannot draw a mathematically bright line with regard to when the ratio between the compensatory and the punitive damages awarded would become unconstitutional, the Court concluded that when, as here, the ratio was a breathtaking 500 to 1, any such award must surely "raise a suspicious judicial eyebrow." The Court then held that the grossly excessive award imposed in this case would transcend the constitutional limit. The Court continues to fill in the parameters of this important aspect of law, so watch for new developments in this area.

Liquidated Damages

The parties may agree in advance that, upon breach of contract, a certain sum of money will be paid to the injured party. This remedy is called *liquidated damages.* The amount to which the parties have agreed in advance fully satisfies any liability attendant upon the breach that has occurred. Courts will enforce such provisions if (1) the agreed-on amount is reasonable and not out of proportion to the apparent injury resulting from the breach, and (2) calculation of the resulting damages in advance and with any accuracy will be difficult, if not impossible. In the context of sales contracts, UCC § 2-718 takes a similar approach.

The contractor mentioned earlier, Miranda, may well find itself subject to such a clause. Construction contracts typically have clauses assessing a per-day charge for delays in completing a building on time. Because it is difficult to ascertain the amount of damages that a breach of such a contract will cause, as long as the per-day charge is reasonable, courts generally uphold these clauses.

15.3 | MANAGEMENT

CALL-IMAGE TECHNOLOGY

LIQUIDATED DAMAGES CLAUSES

Amy Chen, CIT's attorney, recently suggested that CIT should begin to include liquidated damages clauses in its contracts with subcontractors. As she pointed out, damages are often difficult to calculate in these cases, and using a liquidated damages clause will eliminate that problem. Dan pointed out that these clauses also could be used to set damages high enough to encourage subcontractors to make *every* effort to perform since the subcontractors will not be able to afford the effects of a breach. The family members have asked for your advice. What will you tell them?

BUSINESS CONSIDERATIONS Why would a business prefer to use a liquidated damages clause instead of trying to compute its actual damages in the event of a breach? What factors should be used in deciding what the total liquidated damages should be?

ETHICAL CONSIDERATIONS Is it ethical to set liquidated damages so high that the other party cannot afford to breach its contract? What ethical issues does such a strategy implicate?

Courts will not enforce *penalties*, however. Penalties consist of amounts unrelated to the possible damages that may occur and usually are excessively large. Such an arbitrary lump sum, even if the parties have agreed to it as satisfaction of a breach, will be void.

Nominal Damages

You have learned that, for most breaches of contract, an action for damages may be possible. However, in certain cases, especially those involving a minor, or technical, breach, the injured party sustains no actual losses or damages. A court nevertheless may award a *small amount of compensation* (say $1) for the breach. This type of remedy is called *nominal damages*. Sometimes a court or jury awards nominal damages because the injured party has not been able to prove the substantial damages that he or she claims to have suffered. Upon proof of a breach, the injured party therefore is entitled only to nominal damages, the token sum that a court will require the defendant to pay as an acknowledgment of the wrongful conduct in which he or she has engaged.

EQUITABLE REMEDIES

When the "at law" remedy of damages is unavailable, indeterminable, or inadequate, courts in the exercise of their powers of equity may award certain remedies. The plaintiff's eligibility to receive such fairness-oriented relief will depend on the absence of bad faith on the plaintiff's part and similar factors. Simply put, a plaintiff will not necessarily receive equitable remedies just because he or she asks for them. When they are available, the most significant types of equitable relief include rescission and restitution, specific performance, quasi contract, reformation, and injunction.

A court's power to award equitable remedies is **discretionary;** hence, courts normally will not give equitable remedies if the injured party has "unclean hands" (i.e., has shown bad faith or dishonesty); if the injured party has unduly delayed bringing the lawsuit; if a **forfeiture** of property will result from the conferring of an equitable decree; if the court itself necessarily will have to supervise the implementation of the remedy granted; or if the remedy at law (ordinarily money damages, as you will recall) is available, determinable, and adequate.

Discretionary
Having the freedom to make certain decisions.

Forfeiture
The loss of a right or privilege as a penalty for certain conduct.

Rescission and Restitution

As you saw earlier in this chapter, the parties may voluntarily agree to rescind, or set aside, their contract before rendering performance. This type of rescission discharges the contract. But rescission also may occur as a result of a material breach of the agreement. Rescission in this context refers to the cancellation or termination of the contract through the restoration of the parties to the status quo. Upon such rescission, the injured party may ask for restitution.

Restitution, or the return of the goods, money, or property involved in the contract or the recovery of the reasonable value of the services rendered, is the legal term that describes the process by which the parties are returned to their original positions at the time of contract formation. In essence, then, restitution relies on quasi-contractual principles rather than on the original agreement, because once rescission has occurred, the original contract no longer exists.

To avoid the unjust enrichment of the breaching party, the law permits restitution by allowing the plaintiff to sue in quasi contract in order to recover. For this reason, in most jurisdictions, one cannot sue for both damages and restitution; damages and restitution constitute *mutually exclusive* remedies. The injured party must *elect* (i.e., choose) to pursue one remedy or the other. If Miranda has paid Welling for the bulldozers, upon Welling's breach, Miranda can treat the contract as at an end (i.e., rescind it) and then recover the money (consideration) already paid to Welling in order to avoid the unjust enrichment of Welling. Or, alternatively, Miranda can sue for damages. The common law *election of remedies* doctrine prevents Miranda from recovering twice.

Note how the judge, in deciding the following case, uses many of these concepts.

15.3

BARKER V. NESS
587 N.W.2D 183 (N.D. 1998)

FACTS Jan M. Ness and Cynthia K. Smith purchased a house that they knew had a water problem in the basement. On 14 July 1993, Ness and Smith sold this home to Karen Barker for $40,000. On 28 March 1996, Barker filed a complaint alleging that Ness and Smith had fraudulently misrepresented the condition of the home as to its structural integrity and the water problems in the basement. In March 1998, after a bench trial, the district court ordered the rescission of the sale of the home. Hence, the district court ordered Barker to restore everything of value received during the ownership of the property to Ness and Smith and to return the property to Ness and Smith. The court also ordered Smith and Ness to pay Barker $33,830.87, a sum arrived at by taking $44,855.87, Barker's total costs relating to the home, and subtracting the $11,025.00 in rental income received by Barker from the house, which sum would be returned to Ness and Smith. On appeal, Barker claimed that the district court had erred in denying her a jury trial and in reducing her restitution by the amount she had received as rental income.

ISSUES Was Barker entitled to a jury trial? Should the district court have deducted the income received on this rental property from the restitution paid to her by the defendants?

HOLDINGS No as to the first question, yes as to the second one. In an equitable proceeding, no absolute right to a trial by jury exists. Because rescission necessitates the restoration of the status quo, Barker had to remit the rent. But this duty meant that the defendants in turn must remit to Barker the value of the use of the money paid to them for the purchase of the house (i.e., the interest earned on the money).

REASONING An individual who has been induced to enter a contract for the purchase of real estate by fraudulent misrepresentation may elect to affirm the contract, in which case he or she retains the property and brings an action for damages. Alternatively, an individual may elect to rescind the contract for fraud and restore everything of value received under the contract. Pursuant to this so-called election of remedies doctrine, a plaintiff must elect between two inconsistent remedies. Although not confined to misrepresentation cases, the doctrine usually applies when a plaintiff has to choose between rescission or damages. Hence, the plaintiff must elect either to sue for damages (affirm the contract) or to rescind the contract (disaffirm the contract) and seek the return of the consideration given. To effect a rescission at law, the plaintiff must give notice to the defendant of the intent to rescind and must make an offer to restore to the defendant what was given in the transaction, unless an exception to the restoration rule applies. The restoration of the status quo as a requirement for rescission at law, though part of a legal action, is nevertheless based on the equitable principle that one who seeks equity must do equity. Therefore, once the trial court renders a formal rescission, it must restore each side to its respective pre-contractual position. In seeking a rescission of the sale of the house, Barker

15.3

BARKER V. NESS, *continued*
587 N.W.2D 183 (N.D. 1998)

proceeded in equity, with other alleged damage claims incidental to and dependent on the claim for rescission. Hence, the district court had not erred when it had refused to grant Barker a jury trial. Barker further argued that the district court had erred when it had reduced her restitution by the value of the rental income she had received while owning the house. The restoration of the status quo as a requirement for rescission at law stems from the aforementioned equitable nature of the action. Accordingly, any offer to restore under this principle should include an offer to remit any rent collected. However, since equity envisions a restoration of both parties to their pre-contractual positions, Ness and Smith were under a concomitant duty to remit to Barker the value of the use of the money paid to them for the purchase of the house.

BUSINESS CONSIDERATIONS How does a person decide whether to sue for damages or for rescission of the contract at issue? On what factors will such a decision hinge?

ETHICAL CONSIDERATION Did Ness and Smith have an ethical duty to disclose, prior to Barker's purchase of the house, the water damage? Fully support whatever position you take.

Specific Performance

Whenever the remedy represented by damages or restitution is inadequate or unjust, the injured party may ask a court to order *specific performance.* In these cases, a court compels the breaching party to perform according to the exact terms of the agreement.

Courts rely on uniqueness as one factor in deciding whether to grant specific performance. Since land by definition is unique, courts ordinarily grant specific performance for breaches of land contracts. For example, should you try to buy a prairie-style home on the river, money damages for breach of that contract are unfulfilling: Money can buy a house similar to the one in the contract, but not that particular house. The inherent uniqueness of real estate therefore may convince a court to order the breaching party to convey the house to you—that is, give you specific performance in order that justice may be done.

The same may be said of contracts involving unique goods or *chattels* (articles of movable personal property). If Bogan breaches a contract to sell a Rembrandt painting, in the absence of fraud or illegality, a court can compel Bogan to convey the painting to the buyer. But when the injured party easily can obtain the personal property or chattels, specific performance is an inappropriate remedy: Money damages will be adequate in these cases. Just as damages and restitution generally are mutually exclusive remedies, so too are damages and specific performance.

Money damages ordinarily will not satisfy the parties in situations involving personal services contracts. If these contracts are at issue, courts are reluctant to force the parties into a relationship in which at least one of the parties will be unhappy. For example, when Reggie Jackson wanted to break his contract with the Oakland A's and play for the Yankees, how could the A's be sure Jackson would give his best efforts if he really wanted to play for the Yankees? For this reason, and because courts are reluctant to force a party into what one party may characterize as involuntary servitude, courts ordinarily do not grant specific performance in contracts that consist of personal services. The A's instead could sue Reggie and the Yankees for money damages once he became a Yankee.

Quasi Contract/Reformation/Injunction

Two concepts covered on several occasions in the contracts section, quasi contract and reformation, bear mentioning again, this time in the context of equitable remedies. *Quasi contract* involves the situation in which a court creates a contract for the parties, despite their wishes and intentions, in order to prevent the unjust enrichment of one party. When the parties have not entered into a contract, but one party knowingly has received a benefit to which he or she is not entitled, an unjust enrichment has occurred. Given the absence of a valid contract, the injured party cannot seek contract-related remedies. In the interests of equity and fairness, however, the injured party may receive a restitution-based remedy, the reasonable value of the services rendered. *Reformation,* on the other hand, concerns a court's rewriting a contract in order to remove a mistake and to make the agreement conform to the terms to which the parties originally agreed. (See the discussion of reformation in Chapter 12.)

An injunction is another type of equitable remedy. An *injunction* is a writ issued by a court of equity ordering a person to do or refrain from doing some specified act. It does not arise often in the context of contracts, however.

LIMITATIONS ON REMEDIES

The parties may attempt in advance to limit the remedies available to the injured party. Chapter 13 discussed such efforts in the context of exculpatory clauses. The UCC also permits the parties to limit remedies. However, if an exclusive remedy as defined in the contract fails in its essential purpose, UCC § 2-719 permits the injured party to seek any remedies available under the Code. This same section, 2-719, also forbids contractual limitations of consequential damages for *personal* injuries resulting from the use of consumer goods. The UCC dubs limitations on these sorts of damages **prima facie unconscionable** but notes that limitations of damages in purely *commercial* settings are not.

Prima facie
At first sight; on its face; something presumed to be true because of its appearance unless disproved by evidence to the contrary.

Unconscionable
Blatantly unfair and one-sided; so unfair as to shock the conscience.

WAIVER OF BREACH

Even though you have spent a great deal of this chapter studying the various remedies available to an injured party when the other party breaches the contract, recall that the beginning of the chapter noted that the injured party may be willing to accept less-than-complete performance. The law terms an injured party's giving up the right to receive the performance set out in the contract a *waiver of breach.* Once a waiver of breach occurs, the waiver in effect eliminates the breach; the performance required under the contract continues as if the breach never happened. In essence, waiver of breach precludes the termination or rescission of the contract; it serves as a method of keeping the contract operative between the parties. As usual, the nonbreaching party later can recover damages for anything that constitutes less-than-complete performance. Thus, if only one of the bulldozers delivered to

RESOURCES FOR BUSINESS LAW STUDENTS

NAME	RESOURCE	WEB ADDRESS
Uniform Commercial Code (UCC)	The Legal Information Institute (LII), maintained by the Cornell Law School, provides a hypertext and searchable version of Articles 1–9 of the Uniform Commercial Code.	**http://www.law.cornell.edu/ucc/ucc.table.html**
The American Law Institute	The American Law Institute, publisher of *Restatements of the Law*, Model Codes, and other proposals for law reform, provides press releases, its newsletter, and other publications.	**http://www.ali.org**

Miranda is slightly defective or if Welling is only slightly late in making what otherwise is a satisfactory delivery, Miranda, in order to receive Welling's performance under the rest of the contract, may choose to waive such breaches.

A waiver of breach ordinarily applies only to the matter waived and not inevitably to the rest of the contract. The same is true of subsequent breaches of the contract: The first waiver normally will not cover additional, later breaches, especially when the later breaches bear no relation to the first one. However, the waiving party may want to stand on his or her rights after the first waiver and indicate unambiguously that he or she will not tolerate future breaches. This action will eliminate the possibility of the breaching party's arguing that the waivers were so numerous and systematic that the breaching party believed less-than-complete performance was acceptable for the duration of the contract. Still, waiver remains a common business response in those circumstances in which the continuation of the contract will further the interests of the injured party.

SUMMARY

Discharge of a contract refers to the legally valid termination of a contractual duty. Performance may be either complete or substantial. Both degrees of performance ordinarily discharge the contract. The parties themselves may agree to discharge the contract. Release, rescission, accord and satisfaction, and novation are examples of this method of discharging contracts. Bankruptcy decrees, the running of statutes of limitations, and material alterations of the contract will justify discharge of a contract by operation of law. In some circumstances, the nonperformance of one of the parties will discharge a contract. Courts that find evidence of the destruction of the subject matter, intervening illegality, or conduct by one party that makes performance by the other party objectively impossible will excuse the resultant nonperformance. This is the doctrine of impossibility. In many other situations, however, impossibility will not justify discharge of the contract. The doctrine of commercial frustration consequently has arisen to mitigate the harshness of the common law's rejection of impossibility as a defense to nonperformance. Breach, whether actual or anticipatory, also may bring about discharge of the contract. The nonoccurrence of express conditions precedent and the occurrence of express conditions subsequent, in addition to constructive conditions, may cause discharge of a contract as well.

Upon one party's breach of a contract, the other party is free to pursue several kinds of remedies unless the injured party waives the breach. Remedies fall into two main categories: legal ("at law") and equitable remedies.

Damages comprise the "at law" remedy. Usually a party sues for compensatory damages, or the amount of money that will place the party in the same economic position that he or she would have enjoyed had the contract been performed. Because the breaching party is liable for the foreseeable consequences of the breach, courts may award these actual losses and may even grant consequential, or special, damages if the facts so warrant. The injured party must mitigate the damages unless doing so will cause unreasonable expense or unreasonable risk. Failure to mitigate will limit the injured party to the recovery of direct losses. Courts impose punitive damages to punish the wrongdoer and to deter future malicious conduct. Some modern courts and statutes reject the old common law rule that punitive damages never can constitute appropriate remedies for breaches of contract. The parties may agree in advance on the sum of money to be paid for breaches of certain types. Such liquidated damages clauses are enforceable unless a court construes them as penalties. If the party sustains no actual damages, nominal damages may be awarded.

When the "at law" remedy of damages is unavailable, indeterminable, or inadequate, courts may order equitable remedies. Rescission and restitution constitute one such remedy and involve the termination of the contract through the restoration of the parties to the status quo. Damages and restitution are mutually exclusive remedies, so the injured party must elect (or choose) one remedy or the other. If either damages or restitution will be inadequate, a court may order specific performance. This is an equitable remedy that compels the breaching party to perform according to the terms of the agreement. Courts usually grant specific performance when the subject matter of the contract is unique, but they are reluctant to grant specific performance in suits involving nonunique goods or personal services contracts. Quasi contract, reformation, and injunctions (writs ordering a person to do or refrain from doing some specified act) represent other types of equitable relief.

The injured party may choose to waive the breach in order to keep the contract going between the parties. Waiver of breach, or the injured party's giving up the right to receive the performance set out in the contract, does not preclude the injured party's seeking recovery for damages resulting from the breach, however.

DISCUSSION QUESTIONS

1. What are the four main methods of contract discharge that the law recognizes?
2. What is *rescission?*
3. Explain fully the doctrine of impossibility and the doctrine of commercial frustration as they relate to contract discharge.
4. What sorts of situations will discharge a contract by operation of law?
5. What is a complete, or material, breach of contract? What are the injured party's options when a complete breach occurs?
6. Name and define the two main types of remedies.
7. Define the *duty of mitigation.*
8. Why does the remedy of restitution differ from an action in damages?
9. Under what circumstances is specific performance an appropriate remedy?
10. What is the legal consequence of waiving a breach of contract?

CASE PROBLEMS AND WRITING ASSIGNMENTS

1. The Evanoskis sued All-Around Travel to recover the monies the couple had paid to the travel agency. Mrs. Evanoski's sudden illness on the day of the scheduled departure for the tour precluded the couple's giving the 72-hour advance notice required under the contract with the travel agency. Was this sudden illness an event the couple could not have foreseen or guarded against so as to invoke the doctrine of impossibility of performance? [See *Evanoski* v. *All-Around Travel,* 682 N.Y. S.2d 342 (Sup. 1998).]

2. In February 1986, Trans World Airlines, Inc. (TWA) entered into an equipment trust agreement with the Connecticut National Bank (CNB). The agreement, commonly known as a sale/leaseback, provided that CNB would purchase 10 aircraft and approximately 96 jet engines from TWA and then would lease them back to TWA until 1 February 1996. In connection with the lease/purchase, CNB received senior secured trust notes, some of which matured on 1 February 1991 and others of which were scheduled to mature on 1 February 1996. The aggregate original principal of these notes amounted to approximately $312 million, with the principal on the 1991 notes being worth $100 million and the balance being covered by the 1996 notes. The agreement stipulated that TWA would pay all the necessary interest and principal on the notes directly to CNB, as trustee, which, in turn, would pay the noteholders, or the trust beneficiaries. TWA also guaranteed payment to the beneficiaries and agreed to indemnify (i.e., to reimburse CNB if CNB suffered a loss attributable to TWA's default) CNB. Finally, the agreement stated that once the lease had expired and TWA had paid off the loss suffered by that party under the notes, the equipment reverted to TWA. TWA met its obligations in a satisfactory fashion until 31 January 1991. At that time, TWA failed to make the required payments of approximately $57 million, $9 million of which represented interest on the 1991 and 1996 notes and the other $48 million of which represented the remaining principal on the then-matured 1991 notes. Consequently, CNB failed to pay the beneficiaries, since the agreement specifically obligated CNB to pay the beneficiaries only to the extent that TWA had paid CNB. CNB then demanded the return of its property and the immediate payment of the approximately $81 million presently due as principal on the 1996 notes. Although the agreement specifically afforded CNB these remedies, TWA failed to make any payments and did not return any of CNB's property. Therefore, on 26 March 1991, CNB filed a lawsuit seeking specific performance of the agreement's default remedies, including the return of the equipment located inside and outside the United States, delivery of various records relating to the property, and a permanent injunction preventing TWA from removing any of the property from the United States. TWA argued that a court's requiring specific performance of the agreement's default provisions would be inappropriate because CNB had a remedy at law. In addition, TWA asserted that requiring it to return the property in light of the tremendous ramifications such an order might have on both TWA and the public at large would be inequitable. Should the court grant CNB's motion for summary judgment and order specific performance of the agreement? [See *Connecticut National Bank* v. *Trans World Airlines, Inc.,* 762 F.Supp. 76 (S.D.N.Y. 1991).]

3. Katherine Lane enrolled her 18-month-old daughter in day care with Kindercare Learning Centers, Inc. (Kindercare). On 9 December 1992, Lane dropped off her daughter at Kindercare's facility at lunchtime. Lane's daughter had been prescribed medication, and Lane filled out an authorization form granting

Kindercare's employees permission to administer the medication to her daughter that day. Just after 5:00 P.M., one of the employees placed the child, who had fallen asleep, in a crib in the infant room. At approximately 6:00 P.M., the employees, apparently unaware that Lane's daughter was still sleeping in the crib, locked the doors of the facility and went home for the day. Shortly thereafter, Lane returned to the facility to pick up her daughter and found the facility locked and unlit. A police officer who responded to Lane's 911 call looked through a window of the facility and saw the child sleeping in the crib. Another officer then broke a window and retrieved the child from the building. The child was upset after the incident but not physically harmed. When Lane went into the facility to retrieve her daughter's belongings, she apparently found the medication authorization form and observed that it had not been initialed to indicate that an employee had given the medication to the child. As a result of the incident, Lane alleged that she had suffered emotional distress. Michigan law allowed the recovery of emotional damages for breach of contracts of a personal nature but not for breaches involving commercial, or pecuniary, contracts. Should Lane prevail on her claim in this case? [See *Lane* v. *Kindercare Learning Centers, Inc.*, 588 N.W.2d 715 (Mich. App. 1998).]

4. On 24 January 1995, Mr. and Mrs. Laurence L. Kesterson and Patrick J. Juhl entered into a loan agreement. The terms of the loan agreement were expressed in a letter drafted by Juhl. According to the agreement, Juhl agreed to lend the Kestersons $145,000 in cash. They in turn agreed to pay Juhl $15,000 as a loan fee and to pay Juhl's attorney $15,000 for the preparation of the loan agreement. As security for the loan, the Kestersons provided Juhl with a trust deed to property in Washington and a mortgage on property in Idaho. The value of the two properties substantially exceeded $145,000. The Kestersons further agreed to pay off the loan within six months. Interest on the outstanding balance accrued at an annual rate of 22 percent. In the event they failed to repay the entire loan within six months, they agreed to pay an "additional loan fee" of 20 percent of the gross sales price of each of the two properties pledged as security for the loan. In the loan agreement, Juhl explained the purpose of that fee as follows: "As I have stated to you, a failure on your part to timely repay the loan will cause me significant financial hardship." The agreement did not specify the nature of the "hardship" that Juhl anticipated. Some evidence indicated that Juhl wanted to have the loan repaid no later than July so that it would be available to him during the building season.

As security for the obligation to pay the 20 percent, the Kestersons agreed to execute warranty deeds conveying the 20 percent interest in each of the two properties to Juhl and to deposit the deeds with Juhl's attorney. The attorney could record the deeds in Juhl's name if the Kestersons failed to repay the loan within the required six months. The Kestersons subsequently deposited the full repayment amount—the $145,000 principal and the $22,000 interest—into an escrow account for Juhl. When the money was not immediately released from escrow—apparently because of a construction lien—Juhl declared the Kestersons to be in breach and recorded the two warranty deeds. Meanwhile, the funds in escrow were released on 15 September 1995. In November 1995, the Kestersons sold the Idaho property for $450,000. They continued to own the Washington property, valued at $60,000. When Juhl subsequently claimed a 20 percent interest in each, for a total of $102,000, the Kestersons sued. They alleged that Juhl had breached the loan agreement by recording the warranty deeds in spite of the fact that they had deposited the full repayment into escrow (i.e., the deposit into escrow constituted full performance). They also sought a declaration that, in any event, they were not obligated to pay the 20 percent "additional loan fee" for untimely repayment, because the fee constituted liquidated damages that amounted to an unlawful penalty. Were the Kestersons correct? [See *Kesterson* v. *Juhl*, 970 P.2d 681 (Or. App. 1998).]

5. Howard Mowers, a self-employed chiropractor, purchased a disability insurance policy from Paul Revere Life Insurance Company (Paul Revere) beginning in July 1989. The policy provided coverage in the event that Mowers became totally disabled with regard to his work. The pertinent contract provision stated: "Total disability means that because of injury or sickness: a. You are unable to perform the important duties of Your Occupation; and b. You are under the regular and personal care of a Physician." The policy also stated that the insured agreed to submit to Independent Medical Exams (IMEs) as often as reasonably required during the pendency of any disability claim. In August 1992, Mowers injured his lower back at work and was forced to reduce his work hours until, eventually, he ceased working entirely. As a consequence, in November 1992, Mowers began receiving disability payments in the amount of $3,760.00 per month. In the fall of 1993, Paul Revere stopped paying the benefits to Mowers, because it required further confirmation of his injuries. At the request of Paul Revere, Mowers submitted to five IMEs by physicians of the company's choosing between 1993 and 1994.

Three of the five examinations explicitly confirmed that he remained totally disabled with regard to his work as a chiropractor. The other two confirmed that Mowers could not lift patients. At that time, Mowers also was under the continuous care of Dr. Gary Witchley. On confirmation of Mowers's continued disability, Paul Revere resumed the payment of the benefits to Mowers. In February 1997, Mowers submitted to a requested sixth IME, performed by Dr. Warren Rinehart. Dr. Rinehart reported that Mowers might be able to resume part-time work if Mowers limited his practice to conducting IMEs and working only with patients who had cervical vertebrae problems. After Dr. Rinehart's report, Paul Revere made arrangements for two functional capacity evaluations (FCEs) for 28 July 1997 and 3 September 1997, so as to determine the extent of Mowers's disability. Mowers did not attend either evaluation. Effective 1 September 1997, the company stopped paying benefits to Mowers. The company based its denial on Dr. Rinehart's opinion that Mowers retained the ability to engage in some aspects of chiropractics. Mowers subsequently filed suit for breach of contract. Paul Revere contended that the court should dismiss the claim because Mowers had failed to perform the condition precedent of submitting to physical examinations as often as reasonably requested by the company. Who had the more persuasive argument here, Paul Revere or Mowers? [See *Mowers* v. *Paul Revere Life Insurance Company*, 27 F.Supp.2d 135 (N.D. N.Y. 1998).]

6. **BUSINESS APPLICATION CASE** In November 1980, Paul L. Gould individually and as president of Paul L. Gould, Inc., entered into a contract with P. A. Argentinis for the construction of a custom-designed house. The agreement incorporated the house plans and specifications prepared for Argentinis by professional architects. The contract contained Gould's various express warranties, including a warranty against water leakage into the premises for one year after closing. The house was to be ready for occupancy by 1 May 1981. At the April 1981 closing, Argentinis gave Gould a purchase money mortgage for the final $50,000 of the total sale price of $334,000. Although a certificate of occupancy had been issued, the Argentinis family was unable to occupy the house as scheduled because 40 to 50 items of construction remained unfinished. The parties thereupon reached a supplemental agreement modifying the terms of the mortgage. The parties agreed to a modified promissory note and mortgage for $43,000 and a cash payment of $3,000, which was to be released upon the completion of those construction items deemed unsatisfactory. The Argentinis family moved into the house in early July

1981, and the cash payment and documents were released to Gould from escrow. Some items due for completion later that month or "within a reasonable period of time" had not yet been performed. Of principal concern to Argentinis were the lack of water pressure in the house and the contaminated well water. In addition, the basement remained vulnerable to flooding during rains. Storm flooding, which occurred within the warranty period, again in June 1982 and twice more in April 1983, caused substantial damage to the personal and real property. Argentinis, within the warranty period, made repeated demands on Gould to rectify the problems of the improperly sited well, the flood-prone basement, and numerous other significant deficiencies. Gould refused to repair the defects unless given an unconditional release concerning all such defects and the right to determine those defects for which he had borne responsibility. Argentinis refused to give this release, refused to make payments on the outstanding debt, and brought suit against Gould for breach of contract and breach of express warranties. When Gould sought to foreclose the $43,000 mortgage, a trial referee ruled that Gould, owing to his failure to substantially complete construction, should not receive the final contract payment. On appeal, Gould claimed that the referee's conclusion that the company had not substantially completed the construction had been against the weight of the evidence. Gould argued that Argentinis's architects had performed inspections as the work progressed and had approved the materials and workmanship. Moreover, Gould submitted, the town building inspector had found that the project met all but one minor code requirement and thus had issued a valid certificate of occupancy. Had Gould substantially performed this contract? What should Argentinis have done differently at the outset so as to ease his burden of proof regarding breach of contract and breach of express warranties? Similarly, what should Gould have done early on to minimize the probabilities that he would face legal liability in this contract? [See *Argentinis* v. *Gould*, 579 A.2d 1078 (Conn.App. 1990), modified at 592 A.2d 378 (Conn. 1991).]

7. **ETHICAL APPLICATION CASE** Warren Kobatake and other nursery owners whose plants were allegedly damaged by Benlate 50DF, a product manufactured by E.I. Dupont de Nemours and Company (DuPont), had settled a products liability case with DuPont. Pursuant to the terms of the settlement agreements, the plaintiffs executed general releases in which they released and discharged DuPont from any and all liabilities relating to the fungicide. The parties further covenanted that the release represented the

parties' complete agreement. Some time afterward, the plaintiffs discovered information that led them to believe that DuPont had acted improperly and fraudulently during the defense of the previous litigation by, among other things, scheming to destroy harmful evidence and presenting perjured testimony. Accordingly, two years after unearthing these facts, the plaintiffs sought to rescind the settlement agreements on the basis of fraud. What factors would a court consider when it rules on this case? Why would a large, well-known firm like DuPont put its reputation on the line and engage in the ethically questionable behavior alleged here? Would a code of ethics have helped to prevent these improprieties? [See *Kobatake* v. *E.I. DuPont de Nemours and Company*, 162 F.3d 619 (11th Cir. 1998).]

8. **CRITICAL THINKING CASE** Riverbend Products, Inc. (Riverbend) processes and sells tomato paste and frozen citrus products. On 14 July 1988, Cliffstar Corporation (Cliffstar) ordered 3.2 million pounds of tomato paste from Riverbend. In the same purchase order, Cliffstar attempted to purchase an option on an additional 500,000 pounds of paste. Delivery of the paste was to be spread over the following year, until 30 June 1989. Riverbend accepted the order in writing on 25 July 1988 but rejected Cliffstar's requested option "due to the uncertainty of the incoming tonnage." Between October and December 1987, Riverbend forecast sales for the 1988 tomato crop of approximately 53 million pounds of tomato paste. By combining firm contracts with spot buys, Riverbend planned to acquire sufficient numbers of raw tomatoes to support its sales forecast. Thereafter, Riverbend received oral and written orders for approximately 78 million pounds of tomato paste. It remained disputed, however, whether Riverbend had accepted these orders and thus had entered into contracts to supply this amount. About the time of the formation of the Cliffstar-Riverbend contract and extending into the early fall, a shortage developed in the tomato crop in Arizona and California. Riverbend's contract growers delivered only 56–58 percent of the 170,000 tons of tomatoes for which Riverbend had contracted. Because of these shortages, Riverbend failed to deliver the 3.2 million pounds of paste to Cliffstar. Instead, Riverbend allocated its available supply among its customers. Riverbend first notified Cliffstar by letter on 27 September 1988 that all contracts were to be reevaluated. Riverbend then notified Cliffstar by letter on 21 November 1988 that Cliffstar would be allocated one million pounds of paste. When Cliffstar demanded its full contract amount, this lawsuit ensued. Riverbend defended its failure to deliver by citing the UCC doctrine of commercial impracticability. Was this a valid defense given the circumstances? Why? Would it be a valid defense under the common law? If it is not, what damages could Cliffstar recover? Explain. [See *Cliffstar Corporation* v. *Riverbend Products, Inc.*, 750 F.Supp. 81 (W.D.N.Y. 1990).]

NOTES

1. A material breach, as we will see in later sections of this chapter, occurs when the performance rendered falls appreciably below the level of performance the parties reasonably expected under the terms of the contract. Such a breach discharges the other party from the contract.

2. Darryl Van Duch, "Keeping Employees Quiet May Exact a Public Price," *The National Law Journal* (28 October 1996), pp. B1, B3; and Darryl Van Duch, "Courts Find Severance Deal Pitfalls," *The National Law Journal* (25 January 1999), pp. B1, B3.

Sales and Leases

The early common law of contracts was inappropriate—if not inadequate—for the commercial society that took form in the Middle Ages. As a result, the law merchant was developed. The sociological and technological advances of the twentieth century made the law merchant as outmoded for this era as the common law had been for the Industrial Revolution. Once again, new rules were developed and codified in the Uniform Commercial Code (UCC), including the sale of goods (Article 2) and the leasing of goods (Article 2A).

Firms involved in international trade also need to be aware of their rights and obligations, but contracts between firms in different nations make such awareness difficult. One potential solution to this problem can be found in the United Nations Convention on Contracts for the International Sale of Goods, the CISG.

The next five chapters discuss how contracts involving the sale or lease of goods are formed; the rules that govern performance, title, and risk of loss; how warranties and liabilities operate in these transactions; what remedies are available for a breach in a sales contract; and how international laws may affect the sales of goods outside the borders of the United States.

16

FORMATION OF THE SALES CONTRACT: CONTRACTS FOR LEASING GOODS

CALL-IMAGE TECHNOLOGY

A G E N D A

The Kochanowskis will enter the electronic communications market as merchants. What added responsibilities will such a status entail? What can or should Tom do differently in his marketing approach because the firm will be treated as a merchant in the industry?

If Tom and Anna are correct, the firm should experience some success soon after entering the market. Should CIT plan to negotiate each sales contract differently, or should Tom and Anna ask Amy Chen to draft a

standard form contract for CIT to use in most Call-Image sales? Should Amy develop a standard purchase order to be used in ordering parts prior to the final construction of a Call-Image videophone? What are the advantages and disadvantages of developing such forms?

These and other questions need to be addressed in covering the material in this chapter. Be prepared! You never know when one of the Kochanowskis will need your help or advice.

O U T L I N E

INTRODUCTION

The common law coverage of contracts provides a good framework for studying agreements between people. As society has progressed and developed in England and in the United States, some elements of the common law have become outdated. When this occurs, the law-making bodies often step in to try to resolve the problems presented by a changing society. One early result of this legislative intervention is the Statute of Frauds (the original statute was enacted by the English Parliament in 1677), which requires that certain types of contracts be in writing in order to be enforceable. Another—and more contemporary—example of legislative intervention to help the law keep pace with society is the Uniform Commercial Code (UCC—the first UCC was adopted in the United States in 1954). The UCC was developed by the National Conference of Commissioners on Uniform State Laws. It is designed to update and modernize the law of commerce in code form and to reflect modern commercial reality.

Under the early common law, contract law developed primarily to reflect the importance of land in the economy of England. The common law treatment of contracts involving the sale of land was quite extensive, whereas the treatment of contracts for the sale of goods was sparse. As a merchant class began to develop in England, the merchants realized that the common law did not adequately treat their contracts or their contractual concerns. As a result, the merchants developed their own law, the **law merchant** (lex mercatoria). Eventually, the law merchant was adopted by parliament as an official part of English law, giving official status to the merchants and their transactions under the law.

This same legal tradition was followed in the United States after its formation. Since the United States had been a part of England, and since the courts in existence were based on English law, it was natural for the United States to follow English laws initially. By the early twentieth century, the law merchant was still in effect, but it was substantially out of date. As a result, the Uniform Sales Act (USA) was enacted to update and modernize the law merchant in the United States. While the USA was significantly more modern than the law merchant, it too was quickly out of date.

The UCC was adopted in 1954 to reflect contemporary commercial practices. The UCC replaced the USA and the NIL (the Uniform Negotiable Instrument Law), among other areas. The Uniform Commercial Code is organized into sections, with each section covering a different aspect of commercial law. For example, the UCC replaced the USA with Article 2, which governs the sale of goods. Other sections of the Code include Article 2A, which deals with the leasing of goods (many modern transactions involve leasing goods rather than buying them); Article 3, which deals with negotiable instruments (checks, a form of negotiable instrument, are often used to pay for goods); Article 4, which deals with banks and customers; Article 4A, which deals with fund transfers; Article 5, which deals with letters of credit (a standard method of payment, especially when the parties are separated geographically); Article 7, which deals with documents of title (often used in sales of goods between merchants); and Article 9, which deals with secured transactions (goods are often used as collateral when goods are sold on credit).

The UCC has been adopted, in whole or in part, in all 50 states. (Louisiana, with its French heritage and its tradition of following the Napoleonic Code, has not adopted all sections of the Code. In particular, it has not adopted Article 2 or Article 2A. South Carolina has not adopted Article 2A. All the other states have

Law merchant
The system of rules, customs, and usages generally recognized and adopted by merchants and traders, and that constituted the law for their transactions.

Money
A legally recognized medium of exchange authorized or adopted by a government.

Investment securities
Bonds, notes, certificates, and other instruments or contracts from which one expects to receive a return primarily from the efforts of others.

Things in action
A personal right; an intangible claim not yet reduced to possession, but recoverable in a suit at law.

Choses in action
A personal right not reduced to possession, but recoverable in a suit at law.

16.1 | MANAGEMENT

CALL-IMAGE TECHNOLOGY

WHAT TYPE OF LAW WILL MOST AFFECT CIT?

The Kochanowskis disagree as to what type of law will be most important in governing their business. Anna has done a great deal of work involving patents over the years, and she has filed for several patents involving the "Call-Image" telephone. She also recognizes that the company's product is likely to be subjected to Federal Communication Commission regulation. As a result, she insists that federal regulation, especially in the areas of patent law and administrative regulations, will be most important. She also feels that recent expansions of international patent law provisions may prove important as the company grows. Tom, recalling his background in marketing, insists that the firm is providing a service, which causes him to believe that traditional common law rules will be the most important in governing the firm. He is cognizant of the fact that the firm is organized under state law, and he thinks that state regulation of business organizations will also prove important to the firm. Dan disagrees with both Anna and Tom. He points out that the Call-Image telephone is a *good* and that the firm will be most involved in *sales* or *leases* of that good, so that Articles 2 and 2A of the UCC are most important to them. The family has asked you to help them settle this dispute. What will you tell them?

BUSINESS CONSIDERATIONS A new business, especially one in a relatively high-tech industry, is likely to be subjected to numerous types of legal and administrative regulations. Is any one type of regulation more important than the others? Should a business try to deduce which areas of law or administrative regulation will most affect it before it begins doing business, or should the firm just seek compliance with *all* areas of the law that affect it?
ETHICAL CONSIDERATIONS Should a business be more concerned with evading regulations, avoiding regulations, or complying with regulations? Explain your reasoning. What ethical issues are raised by efforts to evade regulations? By efforts to avoid regulations?

adopted both articles.) Thus, the coverage and the principles of the Code are applicable nationally, even though the Code itself is state law. This uniformity allows widespread understanding of the rules, and the reasonable expectations that the rules followed in one state are likely to be followed in other states as well.

While the UCC has basically been adopted throughout the United States, it is not applicable internationally unless the parties to an international contract specify that the UCC will control, or unless the contract is entered into in the United States. As international trade increases, the need for a uniform set of legal rules and guidelines will increase. The closest thing to a uniform set of international laws governing such trade that we have at present is the United Nations Convention on Contracts for the International Sale of Goods (CISG). The CISG is similar in many respects to Article 2 of the UCC.

THE SCOPE OF ARTICLE 2

Article 2 of the UCC (Sales) deals with the sale of *goods.* This is a somewhat limited topic when compared to all the types of contracts that a party might enter. However, most of us will enter into more contracts for the sale of goods than any other types of contracts.

To understand the scope of Article 2, we need to know what is covered. Thus, we must begin by defining a sale and then by defining goods. According to § 2-106(1), a *sale* is the passing of title from the seller to the buyer for a price. This is the only definition of a sale in Article 2, but there are several related and similar terms that also need to be examined. For example, the words *contract* and *agreement,* when used in Article 2, refer to either the present or the future sale of goods. *Contract for sale* covers both a present sale and a contract to sell goods in the future. A *present sale* is a sale made at the time the contract is made. *Goods* are defined in § 2-105(1) of the Code. According to that section, *goods* mean "all things that are movable at the time they are identified to the contract." The Code lists several things that are specifically included as goods, such as specially manufactured items, the unborn young of animals, growing crops, and things attached to land, if they are to be separated from the land for their sale. The Code also specifically excludes some things, declaring them *not* to be goods. Examples are **money** when used as a payment for sale, **investment securities,** and **things in action,** such as rights under a contract yet to be performed. (Things in action are also sometimes referred to as **choses in action.**)

In the following case, the court had to decide whether the contract involved a sale of goods, which would allow the case to be resolved in one manner, or the sale of a service, which would allow the case to be resolved in a different manner. Follow the court's reasoning and decide whether you agree with the conclusions the court reached.

16.1

McDANIEL V. BAPTIST MEMORIAL HOSPITAL
469 F.2D 230 (1972)

FACTS Plaintiff-appellant, Kay McDaniel, widow of William Thomas McDaniel, brought suit against defendant Baptist Memorial Hospital for the alleged wrongful death of her husband. . . . It was charged in the complaint that William McDaniel died on February 5, 1970, from serum hepatitis as a consequence of blood transfusions given to him on November 25, 1969, while a patient in the Baptist Memorial Hospital in Memphis, Tennessee. The complaint averred . . . as follows:

2. . . . *the defendant owned, operated, managed, maintained and controlled a certain hospital located in Memphis, Tennessee, wherein it provided, supplied and leased rooms, sold and supplied drugs, blood, medical devices and provided trained, skilled personnel for the needs of patients during their care and treatment in said hospital . . . it also maintained a blood bank, from which it sold and supplied whole blood to patients in the hospital, including the deceased, William Thomas McDaniel . . .*

4. *The defendant, in the rendition of such medical and hospital services and supplies, did supply, sell and transfuse William Thomas McDaniel on November 25, 1969, with approximately 12 pints of blood from its blood bank . . .*

6. *Such blood as was obtained, supplied, sold and transfused by the defendant to the decedent . . . was defective, impure, and contained deleterious contaminants. And was in an unreasonably dangerous condition at the time of the supplying, sale and transfusing of said decedent; that this blood was expected to and did reach the deceased without substantial change in the condition in which it was sold and supplied; that as a direct and proximate result of its use, the said William Thomas McDaniel was caused to and did contract, serum hepatitis as a result of which, the said William Thomas McDaniel died on February 5, 1970; that therefore, the defendant is strictly liable in tort to plaintiff . . .*

ISSUES 1. Is strict liability in tort applicable against a hospital in a case of wrongful death alleged to have been caused by serum hepatitis due to transfusion of contaminated blood even though Tennessee has a statute . . . which exempts hospitals from liability for breach of implied warranty under the state's Uniform Commercial Code? 2. Is the statute . . . unconstitutional?

HOLDING No to both issues, for both statutory and public policy reasons.

REASONING The brief . . . says that appellant relies upon Section 402A of the Restatement of Torts . . . Both the [cited] cases rely on the fact that the supplying of blood constitutes a sale . . . In the last case relied upon by appellant . . . the Court did not decide the question of whether the furnishing of blood constitutes a sale or a service . . . Restatement of the Law considers the matter of strict liability under "Topic 5, Strict Liability," and then goes on to say in Section 402A:

(1) *One who sells any product in a defective condition unreasonably dangerous to the user or consumer or to his property is subject to liability for physical harm thereby caused to the ultimate user or consumer, or to his property, if*
   (a) *the seller is engaged in the business of selling such a product, and*
   (b) *it is expected to and does reach the user or consumer without substantial change in the condition in which it is sold.*
(2) *The rule stated in Subsection (1) applies although*
   (a) *the seller has exercised all possible care in the preparation and sale of his product, and*
   (b) *the user or consumer has not bought the product from or entered into any contractual relationship with the seller.*

From the foregoing, it appears that Restatement, § 402A, imposes "Strict Liability" or "Liability Without

continued

McDANIEL V. BAPTIST MEMORIAL HOSPITAL, *continued*
469 F.2D 230 (1972)

Fault" only upon "One who *sells* any product in a defective condition"; and it is clear that Tennessee in passing its . . . statute, did so deliberately to protect hospitals from "liability without fault." The District Judge's opinion states that the intention of such statute was to "exempt entities such as the defendant Hospital from strict liability in regard to transfusion of blood, blood products, plasma, and other human tissues." . . . No case has been cited to us where "strict liability in tort" has been imposed where the element of a sale is not involved. The District Judge here relied on the Tennessee statute declaring that the transfusion of blood is not a sale. Appellant charges that the relevant statute is unconstitutional. Unless we are, without precedent, ready to make an advance in the doctrine of liability without fault, or declare the Tennessee statute unconstitutional, we must affirm. No doubt the Tennessee Legislature, as were numerous other states, moved to seek to protect its hospitals against liability without fault . . . Because of this situation, many states adopted statutes of the same general tenor as that of Tennessee. The appellee cites some forty-one states which have adopted such a statute . . . We have been cited no case, state or federal, whereby a statute such as the one in question has been declared unconstitutional. The fact that some forty-one states have adopted similar legislation lends weight to the presumption of constitutionality.

Judgment affirmed.

BUSINESS CONSIDERATION Suppose that the legislature decides to repeal its statute protecting hospitals and blood banks from potential liability if or when the hospital or blood bank provides tainted blood to a patient. What sorts of policies or practices would the hospitals or the blood banks need to establish to protect themselves from potentially ruinous liability in this situation?

ETHICAL CONSIDERATIONS Is it ethical for a hospital to avoid liability behind a legislative shield after the hospital provides "tainted" blood to a patient in a transfusion? Might the potential for liability without these legislative shields cause a significant change in how hospitals and blood banks operate, to the detriment of the public?

Statutory enactments that specifically exempt certain transactions from sales law coverage reflect public policy considerations by the legislatures. Hospitals that provide blood, blood products, and human tissues provide a service that is deemed essential to society. By classifying such procedures as "services" rather than "sales," the legislatures of a significant number of states have opted to protect the hospitals, even if some individuals may suffer grievous loss without any recourse as a result.

Transactions under Article 2 must involve two persons. One is the buyer—the person who purchases, or agrees to purchase, the goods. The other person is the seller—the person who provides, or agrees to provide, the goods covered by the contract.

The law of sales is very broad. It covers every sale of goods, whether made by a seller who is a merchant or by one who is a nonmerchant, and whether made to a buyer who is a merchant or to one who is a nonmerchant. Regardless of the status of the parties, Article 2 controls the sale. However, the status of the parties may affect how strictly the sale is regulated by the Code; the key factor here is the status of the parties as merchants or nonmerchants.

A *merchant* is defined as a person who deals in the type of goods involved in the sale, or a person who claims to be (or is recognized as) an **expert** in the type of goods involved in the sale, or a person who employs an expert in the type of goods involved in the sale (§ 2-104). A person who is represented by an agent or a

Expert
A person with a high degree of skill or with a specialized knowledge.

broker or any other intermediary who, by his occupation, holds himself out as an expert is deemed to be a merchant. Any other person is viewed as a nonmerchant.

A merchant is required by the terms of the Code to act in good faith, to cooperate with the other party in the performance of the contract, and to act in a commercially reasonable manner in the performance of the contract. (A "commercially reasonable manner" means that the conduct must comply with the normal fair dealings and practices of the trade.) A nonmerchant is required to act in good faith and cooperate in the performance of the contract. However, a nonmerchant is not required to act in a commercially reasonable manner. Thus, a merchant is held to a higher standard of conduct than is expected of a nonmerchant. Further, merchants are presumed to give an implied warranty of merchantability in their contracts, whereas a nonmerchant does not give such an implied warranty. Obviously, the status of a party as a merchant or as a nonmerchant is an important consideration in determining rights and duties under the sales contract.

FORMING THE CONTRACT

A contract for the sale of goods under Article 2 is formed in basically the same manner as a contract is formed under the rules of common law. A sales contract, however, can be formed with much less formality or rigidity than is required by common law. While the common law requires an exact agreement, a "mirror image" between the offer and the acceptance, the Code recognizes that a contract exists whenever the parties *act* as if they have an agreement. The common law requires that the acceptance has to comply exactly with all the terms of the offer. Any variation is treated as a counteroffer (an attempt to vary the terms of the original offer) rather than as an acceptance. In an effort to reflect commercial reality, the Code will sometimes recognize a contract that would not be considered binding under the common law.

For example, in § 2-204(2), the Code recognizes that a contract exists even though the time of the agreement is uncertain. Further, in § 2-204(3), the Code permits a contract to stand even though some other terms (such as price or quantity) are omitted from the agreement. Under the common law, the omission of any of these terms would negate the existence of a contract. The courts would rule that the attempt to form a contract failed due to the "indefiniteness of the terms." Under the UCC, if the parties intend to have a contract and if remedies can be found in case there is a breach, the mere lack of some terms can be held to be unimportant. A contract will be found to exist, and the missing terms will be supplied under other provisions of the Code.

As in regular common contract law, a contract for the sale of goods needs both an offer and an acceptance. These technical requirements are covered by UCC § 2-206, which states that, unless an offer obviously requires otherwise, it can be accepted in any manner reasonable under the circumstances. Suppose the seller received an offer that included the following clause: "Acceptance must be made by sending a white pigeon carrying your note of acceptance tied to its left leg." Under the common law, a seller could accept this offer only by tying a note to the left leg of a white pigeon. If the message was tied to the right leg or if the pigeon was gray, the seller would be deemed to have made a counteroffer. Under the Code, the seller can accept by complying exactly with the terms of the offer (tying a message to the left leg of a white pigeon); by nearly complying (tying a message to either leg of a pigeon, or using a gray pigeon rather than a white one); or by using any other

Accommodation
Something supplied for a convenience or to satisfy a need.

Seasonably
Timely; something occurring in a prompt or timely manner.

method of accepting that is reasonable under the circumstances. Thus, under some circumstances, the Code even permits the acceptance of an offer by performing rather than by communicating. For example, an offer to buy goods may call for prompt shipment of the goods. Under the common law, the seller could accept this offer only by making a prompt shipment of the goods. However, under the UCC, the seller can accept in any of the following manners:

1. The seller can promptly ship conforming goods to the buyer.
2. The seller can notify the buyer that the goods will be shipped promptly.
3. The seller can promptly ship nonconforming goods to the buyer.

Thus, the UCC permits acceptance in at least three different ways, while the common law only permitted acceptance in one exact manner. However, in the last acceptance under the UCC, the seller would not only have accepted the offer but would also (possibly) have breached the contract that was entered into by shipment-as-acceptance. According to § 2-206(1)(b), a seller who receives an order or other offer, with the offer calling for acceptance by prompt shipment, may ship nonconforming goods as an **accommodation** to the buyer, and the shipment will not be treated as an acceptance of the offer. In order to qualify as an accommodation shipment, however, the seller must **seasonably** notify the buyer that nonconforming goods have been shipped and that the buyer has the option of accepting these (counteroffered) goods or rejecting them and returning them to the seller at the seller's expense. If the seller fails to give the required seasonable notification, the buyer may treat the goods shipped as an acceptance of the offer—and as a breach of the contract, since the goods do not conform to the terms specified in the offer.

The seller who accepts an offer by means of a prompt or current shipment must be careful for another reason. Assume the seller accepts by promptly shipping the goods but does not notify the buyer that the goods have been shipped. If the buyer neither receives the goods nor hears from the seller within a reasonable time, the buyer may treat the offer as lapsed before acceptance. When this happens, the buyer has no duty to pay for the goods when they finally arrive (if they finally arrive). This leaves the seller with unsold goods at some distant point and no contract remedies to fall back on.

16.2 | SALES

CALL-IMAGE TECHNOLOGY

STANDARD FORM SALES CONTRACTS

CIT will be making most of its sales to retailers or wholesalers, parties who will also be recognized as merchants under the provisions of Article 2. Since most of their sales will be similar, Donna has recommended that the firm asks Amy Chen, the family attorney, to prepare a standard form contract that will be easy for the firm to use in filling its orders. Donna envisions a standard form that will contain blanks for the name of the buyer, the quantity of Call-Image telephones being purchased, the price per unit and the total price for the contract, appropriate shipping terms, and any other items that Amy believes should be included. Tom would prefer to have the firm negotiate each contract individually and to wait until a contract is made before setting out the terms in writing. They have asked you for your opinion. What will you tell them?

BUSINESS CONSIDERATIONS What are the drawbacks to preparing a standard form to use as you contract in dealing with other merchants? What are the advantages to using a standard form contract? Should any standard form contract include a reference to industry standards or usages of trade in a "boilerplate" clause?

ETHICAL CONSIDERATION If a business uses a standard form contract, should that form include "fine print" clauses that are advantageous to the firm, or should it avoid using such language? Why?

Standard Form Contracts

Very often both parties to the contract are merchants, and they are transacting business over a substantial distance. When this situation occurs, it is common to have the offer made on a standard form prepared by the offeror and the acceptance made on another standard form, this one prepared by the offeree who is accepting the offer. (A standard form is a preprinted contract form, often with blanks left in certain key places for later completion as the final contract terms are agreed on by the parties.) Use of a standard form contract would normally have negated the contract under the common law, but the Code makes allowance for it. Under § 2-207(1), an acceptance that is made within a reasonable time is effective, even if it includes terms that add to or differ from the terms of the original offer. The only exception is when the acceptance is expressly made subject to an agreement with the new or different terms.

If the purported acceptance includes new or different terms, the Code provides a solution. The new terms are treated as proposed additions to the contract. If the contract is between merchants, the new terms become a part of the contract unless one of the following conditions exists:

1. The offer explicitly limits acceptance to the terms of the offer.
2. The new terms materially alter the contract.
3. The offeror objects to the new terms within a reasonable time.

If the contract is not between merchants, the courts will not normally uphold the new terms unless it can be shown that both parties accepted them. If the offeree proposes different terms, § 2-207(3) controls. This section states that when the parties act as if they have a contract, they have a contract. And if they have writings, the writings will be construed consistently, so that an agreement exists. The written contract will consist of the terms on which the parties agree, as well as the terms included by one party without any objection by the other party. But it will not include any terms that contradict other terms, have been objected to by one of the parties, or materially alter the basic agreement. Exhibit 16.1 shows how a "conflict of forms" problem would be resolved.

E X H I B I T 16.1 | **A "Conflict of Forms" Resolution**

If the Offer Says "..." and	If the Acceptance Says "..."	The Contract Will Say "..."
Include "A"	Nothing about "A" is mentioned	Include "A"
Include "A"	Include "A"	Include "A"
Nothing about "A"	Include "A"	Include "A" (maybe)[a]
Nothing about "A"	Exclude "A"	Exclude "A" (maybe)[b]
Include "A"	Exclude "A"	Nothing on "A" (maybe)[c]
Exclude "A"	Include "A"	Nothing on "A" (maybe)[d]
Exclude "A"	Exclude "A"	Exclude "A"
Exclude "A"	Nothing about "A" is mentioned	Exclude "A"

a. The contract will include "A" unless including "A" will materially alter the duties of the parties, or the offeror objects to the inclusion of "A," or the offer specifically limits acceptance to the offer's original terms.

b. The contract will exclude "A" unless excluding "A" will materially alter the duties of the parties, or the offeror objects to the exclusion of "A", or the offer specifically limits acceptance to the offer's original terms.

c. The contract will not mention "A" unless the exclusion of "A" will materially alter the duties of the parties, or the offeror objects to the exclusion of "A," or the offer specifically limits acceptance to the offer's original terms.

d. The contract will not mention "A" unless the inclusion of "A" will materially alter the duties of the parties, or the offeror objects to the inclusion of "A," or the offer specifically limits acceptance to the offer's original terms.

The following case involved one of these "conflict of forms" controversies. Notice how the court resolved this conflict of forms between these merchants, and compare the court's results with Exhibit 16.1.

16.2

WAUKESHA FOUNDRY, INCORPORATED V. INDUSTRIAL ENGINEERING, INCORPORATED

91 F.3D 1002 (7TH CIR. 1996)

FACTS In 1989, Industrial began to order steel castings from Waukesha Foundry, Inc.... Industrial and Waukesha commenced their relationship and entered into a series of contracts for the sale of metal castings. The typical deal was fairly straightforward. Industrial would telephone Waukesha and place an order for a particular number of castings and then fax a confirming purchase order.... After manufacturing the castings, Waukesha would ship the order to Industrial. It is undisputed that Waukesha enclosed with each order a packing slip and followed each shipment with an invoice. Printed on each packing slip and invoice was a list of terms and conditions of sale, which included the following:

Buyer agrees he has full knowledge of the conditions printed below, and that the same shall be the sole terms and conditions of the agreement between Buyer and Seller and shall be binding if either (1) the goods referred to herein are delivered to and accepted by Buyer, or (2) if Buyer does not within ten days from date of the Seller's acknowledgement deliver to Seller written objection to said conditions of any part thereof.

Paragraph eight of the conditions of sale, entitled "Warranty," reads as follows:

... IT IS EXPRESSLY AGREED THAT NO WARRANTY OF MERCHANTABILITY OR FITNESS FOR USE, NOR ANY OTHER WARRANTY, EXPRESS OR IMPLIED, IS MADE BY THE SELLER HEREUNDER. THE FOREGOING STATES THE SELLER'S ENTIRE AND EXCLUSIVE LIABILITY AND BUYER'S EXCLUSIVE AND SOLE REMEDY FOR ANY CLAIM OF DAMAGES IN CONNECTION WITH THE SALE OF THE PRODUCTS HEREUNDER. SELLER WILL IN NO EVENT BE LIABLE FOR ANY SPECIAL OR CONSEQUENTIAL DAMAGES WHATSOEVER.

Industrial placed sixty orders with Waukesha between 1989 and 1993, and Waukesha claims that it sent Industrial a total of sixty acknowledgement forms, 234 packing slips, and 234 invoices during this four-year period... Neither party has offered a precise assessment of how many defective castings Waukesha delivered to Industrial. It appears that Industrial began to track the incidence of faulty castings and to submit documentation to Waukesha identifying faulty castings and seeking credit sometime in 1992. Both parties agree that according to Industrial's records, 31 percent of the castings inspected between April and December 1992 were defective. The last shipment of castings was delivered sometime around early March 1993.

Waukesha filed a lawsuit against Industrial in Wisconsin state court on May 12, 1993, alleging that Industrial owed it $256,304.99 on outstanding invoices. Industrial removed the case to the Eastern District of Wisconsin on June 7, 1993, and filed a counterclaim on February 18, 1994, alleging that it had suffered cumulative losses of $1.2 million as a result of Waukesha's failure to deliver conforming castings in a breach of the parties' contract. Waukesha filed a motion *in limine* to preclude Industrial from seeking any damages or adducing any evidence based upon its counterclaim ...

ISSUE Did the additional terms included by Waukesha on its acknowledgement forms, packing slips, and invoices become a part of the contract, thus effectively limiting the remedies available to Industrial in the event of any breaches of the contracts?

HOLDING Yes. Waukesha properly proposed these terms as additions to the contracts, and the failure of Industrial to object to the proposed terms made the terms part of the contracts between the parties.

REASONING It is undisputed that Industrial and Waukesha were parties to a series of bilateral contracts for the sale of castings, but certain facts surrounding the formation and modification of these contracts are in dispute. Our attention is focused upon the particulars of the course of dealings between Waukesha and Industrial and the manner in which, if at all, their pattern of conduct may inform our inquiry under the

16.2

WAUKESHA FOUNDRY, INCORPORATED
V. INDUSTRIAL ENGINEERING, INCORPORATED, *continued*
91 F.3D 1002 (7TH CIR. 1996)

UCC. Several provisions of the UCC...provide guidelines for deciding this appeal by illuminating the requirements of contract formation and modification in a course of dealing between merchants.

Primary among the relevant provisions is section 2-207, which governs the addition of proposed terms to an otherwise concluded contract between merchants for the sale of goods. Part of our analysis under that section concerns the parties' course of dealing, and so the provisions of UCC § 1-205 will also figure in our analysis. This section addresses the course of dealing by parties in an ongoing trade relationship and how that course of dealing may inform the precise contours of the actual agreement between the parties. However, the question of whether additional terms become part of a contract is primarily the province of UCC § 2-207 and the gloss we have applied to it in several cases...Industrial and Waukesha reached an agreement for each shipment of castings by virtue of Industrial's placement of an order via the telephone and Waukesha's acceptance of that order...Industrial then faxed a confirming purchase order to Waukesha. There is no need to identify at precisely what point in time each contract of sale between Industrial and Waukesha came into being, for the course of conduct of both parties demonstrates the existence of a series of contracts for the sale of castings...On sixty occasions between 1989 and 1993, Industrial called Waukesha with an order for steel castings. Following each order, Waukesha manufactured and shipped the castings to Industrial. There can be no dispute that this ongoing course of conduct manifested the existence of contracts for the sale of goods between Industrial and Waukesha. The $64,000 (or, in this case, $295,042,17) question is: What terms were part of those contracts? Whatever the truth may be about the acknowledgement forms, it is clear that the parties exchanged writings containing different terms. Industrial faxed a purchase order for each shipment to Waukesha. Waukesha enclosed with every shipment of castings a packing slip that contained the terms and conditions of sale referenced above and followed each shipment with an invoice that also included these terms and conditions. Once the existence of a contract is established, we must refer to UCC § 2-207(2) to determine which, if any, additional terms contained in subsequent written confirmations become part of the agreement...The facts in this case that are undisputed lead to the ineluctable conclusion that Industrial consented to the terms and conditions contained on the more than four hundred packing slips and invoices it received from Waukesha from 1989 to 1993. In fact, undisputed evidence demonstrates that Industrial availed itself of these remedies by returning defective castings for replacement and by requesting equitable credit for its own repairs.... *Pacta sunt servanda*, or, "a deal's a deal."...Industrial Engineering had a deal with Waukesha Foundry, and this deal included the limitation of remedies contained in the hundreds of packing slips and invoices that it received over a four-year period. Under section 2-207 of the UCC, the additional terms contained in these documents became a part of the contracts for the sale of castings and are enforceable. The judgment of the district court is AFFIRMED.

BUSINESS CONSIDERATION What policies or procedures should a business establish to ensure that it does not end up in the same situation Industrial Engineering found itself in this case?

ETHICAL CONSIDERATIONS Is it ethical for a business to include proposed additional terms in its acknowledgement forms, packing slips, and/or invoices? Would it not be more ethical for a firm to negotiate any special terms or limitations it wants to include in the original contract formation?

Firm Offers

Another area that gets special treatment for merchants under the Code is that of firm offers. Under common law, an offer could be freely revoked by the offeror at any time before its acceptance. This right to revoke existed even though the offeror might have "promised" to keep the offer open for some given time period. (If the

Option

A privilege existing in one person, for the giving of consideration, which allows him or her to accept an offer at any time during a specified period.

offeree wanted a guarantee that the offer would remain open, the offeree had to enter into an **option,** giving consideration for the benefit of having a guaranteed time period to decide.) Such a situation makes it very difficult for the offeree to make detailed plans based on the offer.

The Code recognizes that the offeree may have to make plans and explore options before accepting an offer but may still need to be able to rely on the offer being available if and when the decision to accept is reached. The offeree may be harmed if an offer that is supposed to be "open" is revoked. To eliminate this potential problem, the Code guarantees that firm offers cannot be freely revoked before acceptance. Firm offers are only given by merchants. But if a merchant promises in writing to keep an offer open and unmodified for some specified time and signs the writing, a firm offer exists. The offer cannot be revoked by the offeror during the time the offeror agreed to keep the offer open. And if no time was specified, the offer cannot be revoked for a "reasonable time." To place some limit on this, the reasonable time cannot exceed three months.

Statute of Frauds

So far, the discussion has focused on the intent to have a contract and the Code's recognition that a contract exists in such a situation. However, some technical rules still exist that will override intent. One of these involves the Statute of Frauds, which requires that a contract for the sale of goods for $500 or more must be in writing to be enforceable. According to § 2-201 of the Code,

> . . . a contract for the sale of goods for the price of $500 or more is not enforceable by way of action or defense unless there is some writing sufficient to indicate that a contract for sale has been made between the parties and signed by the party against whom enforcement is sought or by his authorized agent or broker. A writing is not insufficient because it omits or incorrectly states a term agreed upon but the contract is not enforceable under this paragraph beyond the quantity of goods shown in such writing.

The Official Comments state that there are only three definite and invariable requirements for the writing:

1. The writing must evidence a contract for the sale of goods;
2. The writing must be "signed," which includes any authentication; and,
3. It must specify a quantity of goods covered by the contract.

An oral agreement that falls within the coverage of the Statute of Frauds is normally unenforceable. However, the Code attempts to recognize modern commercial practices in this area as well. If the parties have any writing (a note, a memorandum, or "other writing") signed by the party being sued, that writing is sufficient to satisfy the statute. (This is the common law rule.) Terms that are omitted or incorrectly stated in the writing will not defeat the proof of the contract's existence. When both parties are merchants, however, a slightly different rule applies. Suppose one merchant sends a written **confirmation** that would be binding on the sender. Under common law rules, the sender would be bound by the writing, but the other party would not be since he or she did not sign it. Under the UCC, the other merchant will also be bound by this written confirmation unless he or she objects to its contents in writing within 10 days after receiving it. This rule forces merchants to read their forms and to cooperate with other merchants.

Confirmation

A written memorandum of the agreement; a notation that provides written evidence that an agreement was made.

E X H I B I T 16.2 | **Bill of Sale**

BILL OF SALE

VEHICLE LICENSE NO OR VESSEL CF NO

	MAKE	BODY TYPE	MODEL	YEAR
VEHICLE OR HULL IDENTIFICATION NO				

FOR MOTOR CYCLE ONLY:

ENGINE NO. _____

For the sum of _____ **Dollars**

($ _____) and/or other valuable consideration in the amount of

$ _____ , the receipt of which is hereby acknowledged, I/we did sell,

transfer and deliver to _____

(BUYER)

ADDRESS	**CITY**	**STATE**	**ZIP CODE**

on the _____ day of _____ 19 _____ my/our right, title
and interest in and to the above described vehicle or vessel.

I/WE certify under penalty of perjury that: (1) I/WE are the lawful owner(s) of the vehicle/vessel and (2) I/WE have the right to sell it, and (3) I/WE guarantee and will defend the title to the vehicle/vessel against the claims and demands of any and all persons arising prior to this date and (4) the vehicle/ vessel is free of all liens and encumbrances.

Signature of seller **X** _____ **Date** _____

ADDRESS	**CITY**	**STATE**	**ZIP CODE**

SOURCE: Courtesy of Bingham Toyota, Clovis, California.

Finally, § 2-201(3) of the Code lists three exceptions to the general provisions of the Statute of Frauds:

1. No writing is needed when the goods are to be specially manufactured for the buyer and are of such a nature that they cannot be resold by the seller in the ordinary course of his or her business, and when the seller has made a substantial start in performing the contract.

2. No writing is needed if the party being sued admits in court or in the legal proceedings that the contract existed.

3. No writing is needed for any portion of the goods already delivered and accepted or already paid for.

Parol evidence rule
A rule stating that when contracts are in writing, only the writing can be used to show the terms of the contract.

When the parties have a written agreement, the **parol evidence rule** applies; that is, the writing is meant to be the final agreement, and the writing cannot be *contradicted* by any oral agreements made at the same time as, or before, the written document. If the writing is intended as a *total integration* of the agreement, the writing is viewed as the entire contract. No additional terms can be introduced. However, even with a total integration, the writing can be *explained* or *supplemented* by additional evidence, including parol (oral) evidence. For example, either party may show that course of dealings, usage of trade, or course of performance gives special meaning to certain terms contained in the writing. If the writing is only deemed to be a partial integration of the contract, evidence can be introduced to show additional terms that are also a part of the contract, even if those terms are not included in the writing. Either party may introduce evidence of additional consistent terms to fill out any apparent gaps in the written agreement.

Course of dealings refers to any prior conduct or contracts between the parties. Prior conduct between the parties sets up a pattern that either party may reasonably expect will be followed in the present setting. *Course of performance* involves repeated performances between the parties in their present contract. If neither party objects to the performance, it is considered appropriate to continue such performance. *Usage of trade* refers to a widely recognized and accepted industry practice. When usage of trade is proven, it is expected to be followed by the parties.

In interpreting a contract, the court will first look to the express language used by the parties. Whenever possible, the court will read the express language of the agreement and then consider the course of performance, any course of dealings, and any usages of trade in a consistent manner. If a consistent interpretation is not possible, however, express terms control any other interpretation. Course of performance controls either course of dealings or usage of trade, and course of dealings controls usage of trade.

Course of dealings and course of performance are normally based on current or prior conduct of the parties with each other. As such, both are readily apparent and difficult to deny. Some trade usage patterns are less obvious, especially since the usage of trade may be applicable to situations in which one (or even both) of the parties are not merchants. For example, in California, it is a standard usage of trade to use a formal bill of sale to transfer an automobile, truck, or boat by contract (see Exhibit 16.2). It is generally the obligation of the parties to acquaint themselves with the usages of trade that apply and to comply with them if necessary.

The following case addresses the issue of usage of trade and also addresses the issue of when and how parol evidence may be introduced, even if the contract is *fully integrated.*

16.3

C-THRU CONTAINER CORPORATION V. MIDLAND MANUFACTURING COMPANY
533 N.W.2D 542 (IOWA 1995)

FACTS C-Thru Container Corporation entered into a contract with Midland Manufacturing Company in March of 1989. In this contract, Midland agreed to purchase bottle-making equipment from C-Thru and to make commercially acceptable bottles for C-Thru. Midland was to pay for the equipment by giving C-Thru a credit against C-Thru's bottle purchases. The contract stated that C-Thru expected to order between

16.3

C-THRU CONTAINER CORPORATION V. MIDLAND MANUFACTURING COMPANY, *continued*
533 N.W.2D 542 (IOWA 1995)

500,000 and 900,000 bottles in 1989. Finally, the contract also provided that if Midland failed to manufacture the bottle, C-Thru could require Midland to pay the entire purchase price plus interest within thirty days.

Midland picked up the equipment as agreed and later sent a notice to C-Thru that it was ready to begin production. C-Thru never ordered any bottles from Midland, but instead purchased its bottles from another supplier at a lower price . . . In 1992, Midland gave C-Thru notice that it was rescinding the 1989 contract based on C-Thru's failure to order any bottles. C-Thru did not respond to this notice. Midland later sent C-Thru notice that it was claiming an artisan's lien for the expenses of moving, rebuilding and repairing the machinery. Midland eventually foreclosed the artisan's lien and sold the machinery.

Approximately one month later, C-Thru notified Midland that Midland had failed to comply with the terms of the contract and that the full purchase price plus interest was due and payable within thirty days. When Midland failed to pay C-Thru the amount requested, C-Thru filed a petition alleging that Midland had breached the contract by being incapable of producing the bottles as agreed to in the contract.

Midland filed a motion for summary judgment. It contended that the contract did not require that it demonstrate an ability to manufacture commercially acceptable bottles as a condition precedent to C-Thru's obligation to place an order. . . . C-Thru resisted Midland's motion. It argued that a material issue of fact existed on whether Midland was unable to manufacture the bottles, thereby excusing C-Thru's failure to place an order. As proof that Midland could not manufacture the bottles, C-Thru pointed to Midland's failure to provide sample bottles. C-Thru relied on deposition testimony that the practice in the bottle-making industry was for the bottle manufacturer to provide sample bottles to verify that it could make commercially acceptable bottles before the purchaser placed any orders.

In ruling on Midland's motion for summary judgment, the trial court found no sample container requirement in the written contract. The court held that the parol evidence rule precluded consideration of any evidence that the practice in the trade was to provide sample bottles before receiving an order. It concluded that no genuine issue of material fact existed and granted Midland summary judgment . . .

ISSUE Should parol evidence of usage of trade be admitted to explain or supplement the written contract between the parties?

HOLDING Yes. Under the UCC parol evidence of usage of trade is admissible to explain or to supplement a written contract even if the contract is fully integrated in the writing.

REASONING Under the common law of Iowa, parol evidence is admissible to shed light on the parties' intentions but it may not be used to modify or add to the contract terms . . . Nevertheless, sale-of-goods contracts, such as the agreement here, are governed by . . . Uniform Commercial Code . . . Section [2-202] contains the applicable UCC parol evidence rule and it states:

> Terms with respect to which the confirmatory memoranda of the parties agree or which are otherwise set forth in a writing intended by the parties as a final expression of their agreement with respect to such terms as are included therein may not be contradicted by evidence of any prior agreement or of a contemporaneous oral agreement but may be explained or supplemented
>
> a. by course of dealing or usage of trade . . . or by course of performance . . . ; and
> b. by evidence of consistent additional terms unless the court finds the writing to have been intended also as a complete and exclusive statement of the terms of the agreement . . .

Thus, unlike the common law, parol evidence may be used to supplement a fully integrated agreement governed by the UCC if the evidence falls within the definition of usage of trade.

The . . . UCC includes the following definition of usage of trade:

> 2. A usage of trade is any practice or method of dealing having such regularity of observance in a place, vocation or trade as to justify an expectation that it will be observed with respect to the transaction in question. The existence and scope of such a usage are to be proved as facts. . . .

continued

16.3

C-THRU CONTAINER CORPORATION V. MIDLAND MANUFACTURING COMPANY, *continued*
533 N.W.2D 542 (IOWA 1995)

Midland does not dispute that a trier of fact could find that the alleged practice in the bottling industry of providing samples to a prospective purchaser is a usage of trade. However, Midland argues usage-of-trade evidence may not be used to add a new term to a contact that is complete and unambiguous.

We first reject Midland's argument that evidence of trade usage is admissible only when the contract is ambiguous. There is no such requirement in [§ 2-202]. Moreover, the official comment to section 2-202 of the Uniform Commercial Code . . . states that this section "definitely rejects" a requirement that the language of the contract be ambiguous as a condition precedent to the admission of trade-usage evidence . . . We also hold that even a "complete" contract may be explained or supplemented by parol evidence of trade usages . . . As the official comment to section 2-202 states, commercial sales contracts "are to be read on the assumption that the course of prior dealings between the parties and the usages of trade were taken for granted when the document was phrased." . . . Therefore, even a completely integrated contract may be supplemented by practices in the industry that do not contradict express terms of the contract . . . The usage-of-trade evidence offered by C-Thru does not contradict any explicit contractual term. It supplements the written agreement which is permitted . . . Taking this evidence in the light most favorable to C-Thru we conclude there exists a genuine issue of fact concerning the performance required of Midland as a prerequisite to C-Thru's obligation to place an order. Therefore summary judgment is not appropriate. We affirm the decision of the court of appeals, reverse the judgment of the district court and remand for further proceedings.

BUSINESS CONSIDERATIONS What should a businessperson do in order to assure himself or herself that any special usages of trade or industry standards are being met in a contract? What might happen to a business when the standards of an industry change, thus creating new usages of trade?

ETHICAL CONSIDERATIONS Is it ethical for a business to negotiate a contract with a new entrant into an industry without mentioning usages of trade or other special circumstances of which the new entrant may not be aware? How should the "experienced" firm act in this situation?

SPECIAL RULES UNDER ARTICLE 2

The basic assumption under Article 2 is that both parties will be acting in good faith, with the seller selling and the buyer buying. And, of course, all is done according to the terms of the contract. If that was all that Article 2 said, the rules of contracts from common law would be more than adequate to cover sales. The true value of the Code's coverage of sales is what it provides if, or when, the contract is defective, incomplete, or unclear in some area.

For example, § 2-302 makes provisions for unconscionable contracts or contract clauses. *Unconscionability* means so unfair or one-sided as to shock the conscience. Unlike the common law, which presumed that equal bargaining power existed, the Code realized that some parties can "force a bargain" on the other party, and such forced bargains may be unconscionable to the party who was forced into the bargain. If the court feels that a contract is unconscionable, it may refuse to enforce it. If the court feels that only a clause of the contract is unconscionable, it normally will enforce all of the contract except the challenged clause.

Open Terms

The Code also recognizes that the parties may intend to have a contract even though the contract may omit some elements. In an effort to give the parties the "benefit of their bargain," the Code allows the omitted terms to be filled in by the court. (Recall from Chapter 13 that the court may complete a contract for the parties, but it will not write or make a contract for the parties.)

What happens when, for example, the parties intend to create a contract but fail to set a price? In such a case, § 2-305 controls. Under this section, the price can be set by either of the parties or by some external factor. If nothing is said about price, the price is a reasonable price at the time of delivery of the goods. If the price is to be set by one of the parties, that party must set the price in good faith. A bad faith price may be treated by the other party as a cancellation of the contract, or the other party may set a reasonable price and perform the contract.

Sometimes the parties set a price and otherwise agree to contract terms but then fail to provide for delivery. Again, the Code provides a method to save the contract and to resolve the problem. Three different delivery sections may be utilized.

First, under § 2-307, the seller can make a complete delivery in one shipment unless the contract allows for several shipments. However, if the seller tenders a partial delivery and the buyer does not object, the seller can continue to make partial shipments until the buyer objects.

Second, § 2-308 covers the place for delivery. If the contract is silent as to the place of delivery, delivery is at the seller's place of business. (Law students often miss this point. At first glance, it seems illogical. In reality, it is very logical. When a person buys a toaster or a can of beans, that person takes delivery at the store—the seller's place of business.) If the seller has no place of business, delivery is at the seller's residence. If the goods are known by both parties to be at some other place, that place is the proper place for the delivery.

E X H I B I T   16.3 | **Open Terms in Sales Contracts**

Open Term	Treatment	Code Section
Price	The buyer or the seller sets the price in *good faith*, of the contract so provides.	2-305(2)
	The price is a *reasonable price* at the time and place of delivery.	2-305(1)
Delivery	If no place for delivery is mentioned, delivery is at the seller's place of business (or the seller's home if the seller has no place of business).	2-308(a)
	If the goods to the contract are identified, and if both parties know the goods are at a place other than the seller's location, delivery is presumed to occur at the location of the goods.	2-308(b)
	If the time for delivery is not mentioned, delivery is to occur within a reasonable time considering the nature of the goods (calendar time) and the nature of the buyer's business (clock time).	2-309
Payment	Payment is expected at the time and place of delivery unless some other payment terms are specified; payment is to be made in any commercially reasonable manner.	2-310, 2-511(1)
	If the seller insists on payment in cash, but did not specify cash payment in the contract, the buyer must be given a reasonable time to procure cash for the payment.	2-511(2)

16.3 | SALES/ MANAGEMENT

CALL-IMAGE TECHNOLOGY

LEASING THE PRODUCT

The firm has recently been contacted by several regional businesses concerning the possibility of leasing a number of Call-Image units directly from the firm rather than purchasing the units from retail outlets. Tom sees a number of benefits to such an agreement but is concerned that these leases could be costly in terms of time and money if any problems develop. Donna believes that these proposed leases could be extremely beneficial, but she is also concerned about potential liabilities in the leasing arrangement. They have asked you what sorts of obligations they would face if they decided to establish a leasing contract with certain commercial firms. They want to know what sorts of warranties would be involved and what other obligations they might face that would be different than their obligations under a sales contract. What will you tell them?

BUSINESS CONSIDERATIONS Should a business consider limiting itself to *only* selling or *only* leasing goods, or should it be willing to both sell and lease its products, as the market desires? What problems might it cause to attempt to do both? What benefits might accrue from a willingness to do both?

ETHICAL CONSIDERATIONS Is it ethical for a business to *refuse* to sell its product to consumers, only allowing them to lease it? Is it ethical for a business to *refuse* to lease its product to consumers, only allowing them to purchase it? What ethical issues would such a policy encompass?

Third, § 2-309 covers the time for delivery. If the contract is silent about when delivery is to occur, delivery is to be within a reasonable time. "Reasonable time" here means reasonable in both clock time and calendar time. The seller is to make delivery during normal business hours (clock time), and the seller is not allowed to delay unduly the number of days before delivery (calendar time).

In addition to these rules, the Code resolves several other potential problems. Under § 2-306, the Code specifically allows requirement contracts and output contracts. In a requirement contract, the seller provides all of a certain good that the buyer needs. In an output contract, the buyer purchases all of a certain good that the seller produces. Both types of contracts were often declared unenforceable at common law since they were too indefinite in terms. Exhibit 16.3 summarizes the treatment of open terms in a sales contract.

Options

The Code also deals with options. If a contract calls for an unspecified product mix, the assortment of goods is at the buyer's option. If the contract is silent as to how the goods are to be shipped, the shipping arrangements are at the seller's option. However, if a party having an option delays unduly, the other party may act. A party may elect to wait until he or she hears what is being done by the other party or may proceed on his or her own. Thus, if the buyer does not notify the seller as to the product mix desired, the seller may delay shipping any goods, and the delay is excused. Or the seller may select his or her own assortment and ship it, providing the act is in good faith. Or the seller may treat the delay as a breach of contract by the buyer and seek remedies for the breach.

Cooperation

As a final and overriding obligation, the parties are required to cooperate with each other in the performance of their duties. Any failure to cooperate or any interference with the performance of the other party can be treated as a breach of contract or as an excuse for a delayed performance.

THE SCOPE OF ARTICLE 2A

When the National Conference of Commissioners on Uniform State Laws decided to codify the coverage of leases, the drafting committee looked for comparable areas for guidance. Eventually they decided that Article 2 of the UCC was most analogous to leases, and they used this article for guidance in their efforts. The coverage of leases was originally embodied in the Uniform Personal Property Leasing Act, which was approved by the National Conference of Commissioners on Uniform State Laws in 1985. It was decided, however, that this coverage would be better suited for inclusion in the UCC, and the Uniform Personal Property Leasing Act was reworked into its present form as Article 2A. In August 1986, the conference approved Article 2A for promulgation as an amendment to the UCC. The Council of the American Law Institute approved and recommended the article in December 1986, and the Permanent Editorial Board of the Uniform Commercial Code approved the article in March 1987. As of July 1999, all of the states except Louisiana and South Carolina had adopted Article 2A.

Article 2A applies to "any transaction, regardless of form, that creates a lease."[1] This broad statement provides coverage for a "consumer lease," a "finance lease," or an "installment lease" contract. As used in this article, *lease* means "a transfer of the right to possession and use of goods for a term in return for consideration, but a sale, including a sale on approval or a sale or return, or retention or creation of a security interest is not a lease. Unless the context clearly indicates otherwise, the term includes a sublease."[2]

Article 2A is intended to provide the same sort of broad coverage to leases, regardless of form, that Article 2 provides for Sales. With the increasing use of leases by both merchants and nonmerchants, such coverage gives a welcome—and necessary—uniformity to this area of the law.

CONTRACTS FOR LEASING GOODS

Much of the coverage from Article 2 was carried into Article 2A, with appropriate changes made to reflect the inherent differences between a sale and a lease. Amendments were also made to Articles 1 and 9 to make these areas consistent with the new coverage of Article 2A. The article is designed to help protect the basic tenets of freedom of contract by permitting the parties to vary certain terms of their lease agreements. At the same time, the parties cannot vary such staples of the UCC as the requirements that the parties act in good faith and in a reasonable manner and that they exercise due diligence and due care.

Article 2A has five parts, as opposed to the seven parts in Article 2. Part 1 contains general provisions. Part 2 covers the formation and construction of lease contracts. Part 3 covers the effect of lease contracts, including enforceability. Part 4 deals with the performance of lease contracts. Part 5 concerns defaults and remedies.

The scope of Article 2A is restricted to leases of goods. It does not include "security leases," which are already provided for in Article 9. Similarly, there is no need for a lessor to file any financing statement or other document in order to protect his or her interest in the leased property. Lessees are entitled to warranty protections similar in scope and coverage to those protections given to buyers of goods under Article 2. Thus, there are both express and implied warranties given to lessees.

Parties to a lease, like parties to a sale, are classified as merchants or nonmerchants. Protections are provided for a lessee in the ordinary course of business, a person who leases goods in the ordinary course of business and in good faith and without knowledge that the lease is a violation of the rights of a third person.

Article 2A recognizes two basic types of leases: consumer leases and finance leases. It also recognizes an "installment lease" contract, with some special

YOU BE THE JUDGE

ARE "SHRINK-WRAP" TERMS PART OF A CONTRACT?

The computer software industry relies heavily on the use of "shrink wrap" license agreements to protect mass-marketed "off-the-shelf" computer software. These "shrink-wrap" licenses are unsigned license agreements that state that the end user/purchaser agrees to the terms of the license by opening the sealed disk package. The typical shrink-wrap license states that the software developer retains title to the software, and that the purchaser has only purchased a *license* to use the program. The shrink-wrap license agreement purports to restrict the rights of the purchaser significantly, while preserving and protecting the rights of the software developer. Often these license agreements are seen by the purchaser for the first time when he or she opens the package at home following the purchase, preparatory to installing the software on his or her computer.

Suppose that a consumer who has purchased a computer software program acted in a manner that was inconsistent with the shrink-wrap agreement, and that the software firm discovered this contrary usage. The software firm has filed suit seeking to recover the software under the terms of the licensing agreement, as specified on the shrink-wrap packaging. The consumer asserts that the contract was a sale of goods under Article 2 of the UCC, and that the shrink-wrap license being asserted by the software firm is not a part of the contract and is, in fact, unconscionable.

Their case has been brought in *your* court. How will *you* decide this controversy?[3]

BUSINESS CONSIDERATIONS Assume that a business wants to include special terms, conditions, or restrictions in the contracts for the sale of its products to the public. What should the business do to ensure, to the greatest possible extent, that these terms, conditions, or restrictions become a part of the contract? Is the use of restrictive language on shrink-wrap packaging an appropriate method for having the terms included?

ETHICAL CONSIDERATIONS Is it ethical for any party to a contract to attempt to hold the other party to terms that were not revealed or communicated at the time and place of the contract formation? What ethical issues are raised by the attempt to add terms after the contract has been entered into by the parties?

SOURCE: Christensen, O'Connor, Johnson & Kindness, http://www.LawInfo.com/law/WA/christensen.

provisions for this type of agreement. A *consumer lease* is one made by a lessor who regularly engages in the business of making leases and that is made to a lessee (excluding an organization) for personal, family, or household usage. In order to qualify as a consumer lease, the total payments called for, excluding renewals or options to buy, may not exceed $25,000. A *finance lease* is one in which the lessor (1) does not select, manufacture, or supply the leased goods; (2) the lessor acquires the goods in connection with the lease; and (3) the lessee either receives a copy of the contract under which the lessor acquired rights to the goods before the lease is signed, or the lessee's approval of the contract under which the lessor acquires rights to the goods is a condition to the effectiveness of the lease contract. An *installment lease* contract is one that authorizes or requires the delivery of goods in separate lots to be separately accepted, even if the contract contains a clause stating that each delivery is to be viewed and treated as a separate lease.

A lease contract may be made in any manner sufficient to show agreement between the parties, including the conduct of the parties. Similarly, a lease contract can be entered into even though some of the terms of the contract are omitted, provided that the parties intended to make a lease and there is a reasonably certain basis for giving appropriate remedies in the event of a breach.

Leases may also be subject to the rules providing for firm offers. A merchant who makes a written offer to lease goods to or from another party in a signed writing is deemed to have made an irrevocable offer when that writing gives assurance that the offer will be held open. The offer may not be revoked for the time stated in the writing. If no time period is stated, the offer is irrevocable for a reasonable time. In no event may the period during which the offer is irrevocable exceed three months. Further, if the offeree is the party who makes the firm offer on a form prepared by the offeree, the offeror must sign the form before the offer is considered "firm" and, therefore, irrevocable.

The Statute of Frauds for leases requires a writing for any lease that calls for total payments, excluding options for renewals or options to buy, of $1,000 or more. If the total payments are less than $1,000, an oral contract is valid and enforceable. Article 2A also recognizes the same three exceptions to the Statute of Frauds as are recognized under Article 2 if there is no writing and the lease has total payments of $1,000 or more (specially manufactured goods, admission in a legal proceeding by the party against whom enforcement is sought, or to the extent the goods have been received and accepted).

ARTICLE 2B—A PROPOSAL ON LICENSING

The increased use of leases rather than sales led to the enactment of Article 2A, which has proved to be an effective tool for regulating leases. As a result, the National Conference of Commissioners on Uniform State Laws has proposed Article 2B—Licenses for Adoption. This article has been proposed due to the increasing use of licensing agreements in contracts, especially with computer software. It is common to find a licensing agreement included on the shrink wrap in which the software is packaged, and a statement that by opening the package the purchaser agrees to the licensing terms. Licensing terms and restrictions are also included in the installation program for many software programs, requiring the installer to agree to the terms or to cancel the installation process. This area could prove interesting in the near future, and we will be keeping an eye on its development and implementation.

SUMMARY

This chapter introduces the law of sales, Article 2 of the Uniform Commercial Code, and the law of leases, Article 2A of the Uniform Commercial Code. It is important to distinguish sales contracts from other types of contracts. Article 2 attempts to deal with "commercial reality" in the sale of goods, whereas common law developed strict and rigid rules for the treatment of contracts. Article 2 also recognizes the difference between a merchant—a person who "specializes" in dealing with a particular type of goods—and a nonmerchant—a "casual dealer" in the goods. The

RESOURCES FOR BUSINESS LAW STUDENTS

NAME	RESOURCES	WEB ADDRESS
Uniform Commercial Code (UCC) Article 2, Sales	The Legal Information Institute (LII), maintained by the Cornell Law School, provides a hypertext and searchable version of Article 2, Sales. LII also maintains links to the UCC as adopted by particular states and to proposed revisions.	**http://www.law.cornell.edu/ucc/2/overview.html**
UCC Article 3, Negotiable Instruments	LII provides a hypertext and searchable version of UCC Article 3, Negotiable Instruments. LII also provides links to Article 3 as enacted by a particular state and to proposed revisions.	**http://www.law.cornell.edu/ucc/3/overview.html**
UCC Article 2A, Leases	LII provides a hypertext and searchable version of UCC Article 2A, Leases. LII also provides links to Article 2A as enacted by a particular state and to proposed revisions.	**http://www.law.cornell.edu/ucc/2A/overview.html**
The National Conference of Commissioners on Uniform State Laws	The National Conference of Commissioners on Uniform State Laws (NCCUSL), the drafters of the UCC, provides drafts and revisions of its uniform and model acts.	**http://www.law.upenn.edu/library/ulc/ulc.htm**
The American Law Institute (ALI)	ALI, publisher of *Restatements of the Law*, Model Codes, and other proposals for law reform, provides press releases, its newsletter, and other publications.	**http://www.ali.org**

Code provides built-in flexibility in the formation of sales contracts. Intent, rather than form, is the key element in sales. Offers and acceptances are likely to be found if the parties act as if they have an agreement. The Code even provides methods to supply missing terms, if it seems appropriate to do so in order to carry out the wishes and intentions of the parties. The Statute of Frauds remains operative under Article 2, but its provisions are less restrictive than they are under common law. Three exceptions to the Statute of Frauds are built into the Code, and the past dealings of the parties may also be taken into consideration in deciding what the parties have agreed to do. Some general obligations are imposed on the parties to prevent or minimize abuses of the less rigid rules of Article 2. The parties are required to act in good faith, they may not act unconscionably, and they must cooperate with each other. Performance options are available to either party if the other party fails to cooperate fully or properly.

Article 2A was enacted because of the growing importance of leases in our society. Many people today lease goods rather than purchase them. Historically, leases were governed by common law, whereas sales of goods have been governed by the UCC since 1954. Despite the similarity between a sale of goods and a lease of goods, there was likely to be a different outcome in a lawsuit. For quite some time, courts have drawn analogies between leases and sales and then applied Article 2 provisions to leases. This will no longer be necessary with the enactment of Article 2A.

Proposed Article 2B, Licensing, provides a nice complement to Articles 2 and 2A. This proposed article should help resolve a number of issues, especially in the area of contracts for computer software, that may not be adequately addressed by Article 2.

DISCUSSION QUESTIONS

1. What does Article 2 of the UCC govern? What does Article 2A of the UCC govern? How is it different from Article 2? How do each of these articles differ from the common law of contracts?

2. The status of "merchant" carries with it certain duties and expectations under the UCC. What are the three separate tests that the UCC uses to determine whether a person in a sales or a leasing contract is a merchant? How are merchants treated differently from nonmerchants under the UCC? Why do you think this difference in treatment exists?

3. What is a *firm offer* under either Article 2 or Article 2A? How is a firm offer treated differently from a similar offer at common law?

4. Generally speaking, how can an offer be accepted under the law of sales? How is this different from the *mirror image* requirement for acceptance at common law? Why does the UCC provide for a different method of acceptance than the common law provides?

5. Assume that a buyer sends the seller a *purchase order,* a form offering to buy a certain quantity of goods. The seller subsequently returns an acknowledgement form accepting the offer. When these two forms are compared, it is discovered that they do not agree on every point. Do the parties have a contract under Article 2? If so, what are its terms? If not, why? Would the same result occur under the provisions of the common law?

6. There are special Statute of Frauds provisions for contracts involving the sale or the leasing of goods under the UCC. According to this provision, when does the Statute of Frauds apply to a sale of goods contract? When does the Statute of Frauds apply to a lease of goods contract? What are the exceptions to the Statute of Frauds under Article 2 on the law of sales? Are there similar exceptions under Article 2A?

7. Assuming that a contract for the sale of goods is governed by the Statute of Frauds, what constitutes a sufficient writing between merchants to satisfy the Statute of Frauds? What special rules apply to writings between merchants under Article 2? If this contract was for the leasing of goods under the Statute of Frauds provisions of Article 2A, would the same requirements be present?

8. If the sales contract is silent as to the place of delivery, where should delivery occur? If the sales contract is silent as to when delivery is to occur, when should delivery be tendered? Explain fully.

9. In interpreting a written sales contract, the court will permit merchants to use parol evidence to establish course of dealings, course of performance, and usage of trade. What do each of these terms mean, and what is the hierarchy among them if there is a conflict between them? Why should merchants be able to use these areas to explain or supplement a written contract?

10. Article 2A distinguishes between a *consumer lease* and a *finance lease.* What is the difference between these two types of leases, and why are they distinguished from one another under Article 2A?

CASE PROBLEMS AND WRITING ASSIGNMENTS

1. Weimer leased and operated a farm from Brugger/Western Ag (hereafter Western Ag). In 1987, Weimer met with McQueen, the manager of Western Ag, to discuss Weimer's proposal for a new lease agreement on the farm. One of the terms of this discussion called for Western Ag to repair the farm's irrigation system, which had fallen into a state of dysfunction. McQueen stated that the new terms looked good, but that they could not be approved until Brugger reviewed them. One week later, Weimer called McQueen and informed him that Weimer could no longer operate the farm unless the irrigation system was repaired. Weimer alleged that McQueen approved the repairs at that point and promised that Western Ag would pay for them. Weimer contacted Tri-Circle about providing labor and materials for the repair of the

irrigation system on the farm, asking Tri-Circle to set up an account separate from Weimer's personal account, to which material and labor expended on specified components of the irrigation system would be charged to Western Ag. Tri-Circle was to send bills to Weimer, who would verify their accuracy before submitting them to Western Ag. By June 1987, Tri-Circle had charged $9,769.33 to the Western Ag account and had sent the bills to Weimer. Weimer, in turn, had forwarded these bills to Western Ag. On 30 June 1987, Western Ag paid the entire balance by check. Subsequent charges totaling $11,540.71 were billed to the Western Ag account in 1987, with the bills sent to Weimer. Weimer testified that he forwarded these bills to Western Ag as before. However, Tri-Circle received no further payments nor had any communications with Western Ag. In December 1987, Tri-Circle sent a letter to Western Ag demanding payment, and in January 1988, Tri-Circle's attorney sent a letter demanding payment for the services billed to the account. Western Ag asserted that the January letter was the first notice it received of any bills for work on the irrigation system and denied any knowledge of the arrangement between Weimer and Tri-Circle. Western Ag denied liability, claiming that Weimer had no authority to set up the account. Tri-Circle then sued Western Ag and Weimer to recover the account balance plus service charges and attorney's fees. [If this was a sales contract between merchants, the finance charges and attorney's fees could be charged.] Was Weimer an authorized agent for Western Ag in this situation? Was the contract between Tri-Circle and Western Ag a contract for the sale of goods between "merchants" so that the finance and service charges were properly assessed? [See *Tri-Circle, Inc.* v. *Brugger Corp.*, 829 P.2d 540 (Idaho App. 1992).]

2. S&B and Tree Top had done business together numerous times over the years, with each transaction being more or less similar and each involving the same type of contract. S&B would order dehydrated apple powder from Tree Top and would use the powder in making strawberry and blueberry "toastettes," which it would then sell to Nabisco. On 27 April, S&B telephoned Tree Top and ordered 40,000 pounds of the apple powder. At that time, S&B informed Tree Top that, as usual, the sale was subject to an S&B purchase order. However, no copy of the purchase order was ever sent to Tree Top. Soon after, Tree Top sent a written confirmation form to S&B. This confirmation form included an arbitration clause in bold print on its face. S&B did not object to this confirmation form, nor had it objected to the confirmation form in any previous

dealings. S&B subsequently filed suit against Tree Top, asserting that the powder was so full of apple stems and splinters that it clogged S&B's equipment, constituting a breach of contract. Tree Top filed a motion to stay the proceedings pending arbitration as provided for in the confirmation form. Should this case be removed to arbitration, or should it be resolved in court? Explain. [See *Schulze and Burch Biscuit Co.* v. *Tree Top, Inc.*, 831 F.2d 709 (7th Cir. 1987).]

3. Bunge Corp. was a major purchaser of corn. Bunge signed three contracts with Toppert, each calling for the delivery of 10,000 bushels of corn to Bunge. Bunge was to pay for each contract as it was performed. Before the first three contracts were performed, Bunge offered Toppert a fourth contract with the same terms as the original contracts, but Toppert did not accept this offer. Toppert delivered the corn for the first contract and began delivery on the second. At that time, Bunge announced that it would not pay for the first contract. Bunge's sole reason for refusing to pay was that it wanted to force Toppert and Toppert's family to sign additional contracts at the same terms. Is this a valid reason not to pay? Explain fully. [See *Toppert* v. *Bunge Corp.*, 377 N.E.2d 324 (Ill. 1978).]

4. City University of New York (CUNY) solicited "firm" bids for the sale of a used IBM computer system. Finalco submitted the highest bid, and CUNY officially awarded the sale of the computer to Finalco. During the bidding process, the parties discussed the need for signing a formal written document as evidence of the contract; however, no written contract was ever prepared. Finalco decided to withdraw its offer to purchase the computer, stating that its prospective lessee for the system had decided not to proceed with the lease, so Finalco no longer had a reason to purchase the computer system. CUNY made repeated demands for performance by Finalco, to no avail. Finally, CUNY sold the system to a substitute buyer for substantially less money. CUNY then sued Finalco for the difference between the price received from the substitute buyer and the bid Finalco had submitted. Finalco denied liability, claiming that no binding contract was ever entered. Was a written contract necessary in this case before an agreement existed? Had Finalco made a firm offer to CUNY in submitting its bid to purchase the computer system? [See *City University of New York* v. *Finalco, Inc.*, 514 N.Y.S.2d 244 (A.D.I. Dept. 1987).]

5. Smith-Scharff was a distributor of paper products. One of its customers was P. N. Hirsch, which

purchased paper bags imprinted with the P. N. Hirsch logo from Smith-Scharff. The two companies had been doing business almost continuously since 1947. Smith-Scharff kept a supply of Hirsch paper bags in stock so that purchase orders could be filled in a timely manner. Hirsch was aware of this practice and kept Smith-Scharff up to date on its (Hirsch's) business forecasts. When P. N. Hirsch was liquidated and its stores sold to Dollar General, the president of Smith-Scharff promptly called the president of P. N. Hirsch, seeking assurances that the bags Smith-Scharff had in stock would be purchased. He was told that Hirsch would honor all of its commitments. Subsequently, Smith-Scharff sent Hirsch a bill for $65,000, representing the amount of all Hirsch bags in stock. Over the next six months, Hirsch ordered and paid for $45,000 worth of bags, leaving Smith-Scharff with an inventory of just over $20,000 in Hirsch bags. When no additional orders from Hirsch were forthcoming, Smith-Scharff sued for the $20,000 balance. Was there an enforceable contract between Smith-Scharff and P. N. Hirsch for the sale of these bags? If so, what were the terms of the contract? [See *Smith-Scharff Paper Co. v. P. N. Hirsch & Co. Stores, Inc.*, 754 S.W.2d 928 (Mo.App. 1988).]

6. **BUSINESS APPLICATION CASE** Jo-Ann, a corporation formed under the laws of Iceland, solicited Alfin, a New Jersey corporation, for permission to sell Glycel products (a line of beauty care products) in Iceland. Jo-Ann also asked for information about other Alfin products. Alfin sent samples of the Glycel products to Jo-Ann, and Jo-Ann then contacted Alfin by telex, stating in part: "We are very excited to be the exclusive distributors for these products in Iceland. We have not received any prices yet. Please send us your net prices on each item as soon as possible." Alfin replied with its own telex, stating prices in terms of a percentage of American retail, and asking for opening orders for the products as soon as convenient. At no time did the parties agree as to: (1) the duration of the agreement, (2) the quantity of products to be purchased, (3) the timing of payments, (4) inventory levels, or (5) the method for termination. Several months later, a representative of Alfin met with Jo-Ann's representatives. Following this meeting, he recommended that Alfin not deal with Jo-Ann, but rather seek another exclusive distributor in Iceland. Alfin eventually agreed to terms with another Iceland firm, GASA, and Jo-Ann sued for breach of contract. Alfin denied that a contract existed between the parties. Did the parties have an agreement under the UCC, or was the alleged agreement void due to its vagueness

and indefiniteness? [See *Jo-Ann, Inc. v. Alfin Fragrances, Inc.*, 731 F.Supp. 149 (D. N.J. 1989).]

7. **ETHICAL APPLICATION CASE** Clearwater Constructors was one of the bidders for the city of Austin's expansion of the Walnut Creek wastewater treatment facility. WesTech Engineering submitted a bid for certain equipment to Clearwater. Clearwater used the WesTech bid in preparing its own bid on the project. Clearwater was awarded the general contract and notified WesTech that its (WesTech's) bid had been accepted by Clearwater. A Clearwater purchase agreement was sent to WesTech in December. WesTech signed the agreement and returned it with an attached letter. The attached letter indicated that the purchase agreement contained different terms from the original WesTech proposal and that WesTech intended for the terms of its original proposal to be "made a part of the [purchase] agreement." Clearwater subsequently signed the purchase agreement. As work progressed on the project, the city's engineering firm decided that the WesTech equipment did not meet the particular specifications for the job as set out in the city's contract. Despite efforts to resolve this disagreement, the engineers refused to approve the WesTech equipment, and Clearwater eventually informed WesTech (1) that it was seeking another source for the equipment, and (2) that it planned to hold WesTech liable for any increased procurement costs. Clearwater eventually purchased the equipment elsewhere, but at a much higher cost. Clearwater sued WesTech for the difference in cost ($123,495). WesTech argued that its agreement with Clearwater was governed by the original bid proposal, as specified by its letter attached to the purchase agreement, which would preclude the liability sought by Clearwater. Was the contract between the parties governed by the WesTech letter, or was it governed by both the purchase agreement and the letter? Is it ethical for a firm to attempt to modify or change the terms of a contract by proposing additional terms in its response to an offer? [See *WesTech Engineering, Inc. v. Clearwater Constructors, Inc.*, 835 S.W.2d 190 (Tex.App.-Austin 1992).]

8. **CRITICAL THINKING CASE** In May 1986, defendant Weyher/Livsey Constructors, Inc., leased a crane from plaintiff Essex Crane Rental Corp. for a minimum term of one year. On 26 January 1987, a cable that supported the boom of the crane failed, causing the death of a Weyher/Livsey employee and property damage. Essex was sued, along with others, for damages arising from the death of the Weyher/

Livsey employee. Essex brought this suit against Weyher/Livsey, seeking a declaration of rights and duties regarding (1) indemnity for the death of the Weyher/Livsey employee, (2) Weyher/Livsey's duty to obtain insurance covering Essex, and (3) Weyher/Livsey's duty to maintain and repair the damaged crane. Weyher/Livsey counterclaimed on seven theories: (1) failure to provide a crane serviceable for twelve months, (2) breach of an implied warranty of fitness for a particular purpose, (3) breach of an implied warranty of merchantability, (4) restitution of lease overpayments, (5) breach of express contract terms and warranties, (6) negligent failure to inspect and maintain the crane, and (7) strict product liability. At the root of most of the issues in this case is the determination of which document, if any, embodies the agreement between the parties. Weyher/Livsey contends that the controlling document is one of two purchase orders Weyher/Livsey prepared. Essex claims that its form lease agreement controls. Weyher/Livsey did not sign the lease agreement, and Essex claims that it never agreed to either of the alleged purchase orders. Essex began transporting the crane to the Weyher/Livsey job site in May 1986 and forwarded the lease agreement to Weyher/Livsey. The lease agreement was never signed by Weyher/Livsey. After using the crane for about two weeks, Weyher/Livsey sent a letter to Essex advising it that Weyher/Livsey would not sign the lease agreement and stating that the terms of the agreement were contained in purchase order number 3039-PO2400. [It is not controverted that Essex never received this purchase order.] Weyher/Livsey refused to pay the agreed rent, alleging that its policy prohibited any payments without a signed purchase order. After Weyher/Livsey had used the crane for about two months, purchase order number 3039-R00100 was forwarded to Essex. This purchase order had been signed by a Weyher/Livsey agent and by an Essex agent. The Essex agent's signature, however, included the notation "subject to our lease #03190." When the cause of action arose, Essex argued that the case should be decided under the common law of contracts since the contract was a lease and not a sale. Weyher/Livsey argued for the application of Article 2 of the UCC, alleging that the crane had been sold to them. [This cause of action arose prior to the adoption of Article 2A in Idaho.] Was this contract a contract for the sale of goods or a contract for the leasing of goods? Knowing that the case arose prior to the adoption of Article 2A, if the contract is for the leasing of goods, should this case be decided under the provisions of the UCC or under the provisions of the common law? If the court decided that evidence of either course of dealings or course of performance would be admissible, had the parties established a course of performance or a course of dealings that would resolve the liability issues between the parties? [See *Essex Crane Rental* v. *Weyher/Livsey Constructors*, 713 F. Supp. 1350 (D. Idaho 1989).]

Notes

1. § 2A-102.
2. § 2A-103(j).
3. "Enforceability of Shrink-Wrap Licenses," Christensen, O'Connor, Johnson & Kindness. (1995), http://www.LawInfo.com/law/WA/christensen.

C H A P T E R

17

PERFORMANCE, TITLE, AND RISK OF LOSS

A G E N D A

Once Call-Image catches on and demand for the video-phone grows, what type of delivery terms should CIT seek in its contracts? How much inventory should be stored, and how should this storage be arranged? What sort of payment terms can CIT give its customers? Should the goods be paid for on delivery, or should credit be extended for some time period?

Furthermore, there are a number of problems the family will need to resolve as they begin selling their product. The Kochanowskis are offering a new product, and CIT is not (yet) a household name. How should Tom plan CIT's entry into the market? Will the Call-Image videophone be sold to wholesalers and/or retailers, or will it be marketed directly to consumers? If the target market involves merchants, should Call-Image be sold by traditional sale of goods contracts, or should the product be sold through a "sale or return" arrangement? Be prepared! You never know when one of the Kochanowskis will need your help or advice.

O U T L I N E

PERFORMANCE OF A SALES CONTRACT

General Obligations

The performance of a sales contract seems very simple and straightforward. The seller delivers the goods to the buyer, who accepts the goods and pays for them. In practice, this is very often what occurs. However, the exceptions to this simple and straightforward process provide a myriad of possibilities that need to be explored and explained if a businessperson expects to protect his or her interests in this area. The performance obligations must be examined, as must the intervening rights of the parties. The topics of *title* (who owns the goods at any particular point in time) and *risk of loss* (who is financially and legally responsible for any loss, damage, or destruction of the goods during performance) also must be examined. Finally, attention must be paid to two other areas: standard shipping terms and special problems.

The parties to a sales contract are required by the Uniform Commercial Code (UCC) to act in good faith. In addition, any merchant who is a party to a sales contract is obligated to act in a commercially reasonable manner. These two standards are broad enough that they could adequately regulate the basic sales contract. The drafters of the Code decided, however, that more specific provisions were needed to supplement these rules and standards.

The most basic and obvious obligation is spelled out in § 2-301. Under that section, the seller is to transfer and deliver conforming goods to the buyer. The buyer is then to accept and pay for the goods so delivered. Both parties are to perform in accordance with the terms of the contract.

Conforming goods are goods that are within the description of the goods as set out in the contract. Payment by the buyer will normally be made at the time and place of delivery and will be made in money. However, § 2-304 permits payment in money, goods, realty, or "other." The manner of payment, whatever the form, will normally be spelled out in the contract.

The Code presumes that both parties will be acting in good faith, with the seller selling and the buyer buying. And, of course, everything is being done according to the terms of the contract. If that was all that Article 2 said, the rules of contracts from common law would be more than adequate to cover sales. The true value of the Code's coverage of sales is what it provides if, or when, the contract is defective, incomplete, or unclear in some area.

Cooperation

As a final and overriding obligation, the parties are required to cooperate with one another in the performance of their respective duties. Any failure to cooperate or any interference with the performance of the other party can be treated as a breach of contract or as an excuse for a delayed performance.

SELLER'S DUTIES

Tender
An offer to perform; an offer to satisfy an obligation.

The seller in a contract for the sale of goods has a very simple basic duty: The seller is to **tender** *delivery* of conforming goods according to the terms of the contract. The parties can agree to make delivery in any manner they desire. If they do not agree, or if they simply fail to consider how delivery is to occur, the Uniform

Commercial Code covers the topic for them. Section 2-503 explains tender of delivery. The seller has properly tendered delivery by putting and holding conforming goods at the buyer's disposition and then notifying the buyer that the goods are available. Normally, the contract will tell the seller when and where to make the goods "available." When it does not, the seller must make his or her tender at a reasonable time and place, and the buyer must provide facilities suitable for receiving the goods. This all sounds technical and confusing, but in practice delivery is fairly simple. There are five possible ways delivery can occur:

1. The buyer personally takes the goods from the seller.
2. The seller personally takes the goods to the buyer.
3. The seller ships the goods to the buyer by means of a **common carrier.**
4. The goods are in the hands of a third person **(bailee),** and no documents of title are involved.
5. The goods are in the hands of a third person (bailee), and the seller is to deliver some **document of title** to the buyer.

If the seller properly tenders delivery under any of these situations and the goods are conforming, the seller has performed his or her duty under the contract.

Tender entitles the seller to have the buyer accept the goods and entitles the seller to receive payment for the goods. If the buyer and seller make the delivery personally and directly (possibilities 1 and 2), proper tender is obvious. The seller will provide properly packaged goods to the buyer. The buyer will accept the goods and pay for them. Very neat and very simple. If the goods are in the hands of a third person, referred to as a bailee, delivery becomes somewhat more complicated. The seller in these cases must either provide the buyer with a **negotiable** document of title covering the goods (possibility 5) or get some acknowledgment from the bailee that the goods now belong to the buyer (possibility 4). If the buyer objects to anything less than a negotiable document of title, the seller must provide a negotiable document in order to prove that a proper tender of delivery was made. The UCC treats the topic of documents of title in Article 7. This article, "Warehouse Receipts, Bills of Lading, and Other Documents of Title," specifies the rights and duties of all relevant parties in the handling of documents of title, whether those documents are negotiable or nonnegotiable. In addition to the coverage of a document of title by Parts 1 and 2 (for a warehouse receipt) or Parts 1 and 3 (for a bill of lading), both Parts 4 and 5 of this article deal with warehouse receipts and bills of lading if the document of title is negotiable. In order to reduce the amount of statutory coverage involved, and to avoid the problems of determining whether there has been "due negotiation" of the document making the holder a "holder by due negotiation" (a favored position under the law), most commercial **warehousemen** and common carriers simply issue nonnegotiable documents of title to protect themselves. Exhibit 17.1 on page 450 shows the first page of such a document. Exhibit 17.2 on page 451 shows the provisions listed on the back of the same document. Note provision 11(a) and 11(b) at the bottom of Exhibit 17.2. These two areas limit and control how a seller of stored goods may tender delivery to a buyer.

None of the methods of delivery that have been described is very troublesome. The problems in understanding delivery normally arise when a common carrier enters the picture (possibility 3). Now the seller must give the goods to the common carrier, who must transport the goods to the buyer, and the buyer must accept the transported goods and make payment for them. As one might expect, the more

Common carrier
A company in the business of transporting goods or people for a fee and holding itself out as serving the general public.

Bailee
One to whom goods are delivered with the understanding that they will be returned at a future time.

Document of title
Written evidence of ownership or of rights to something.

Negotiable
A document that is transferable either by endorsement and delivery or by delivery alone.

Warehousemen
Persons engaged in the business of receiving and storing the goods of others for a fee.

EXHIBIT 17.1 | **A Nonnegotiable Warehouse Receipt (Front)**

Warehouse Receipt

Non-Negotiable

Lot No. ....

WAREHOUSE RULES
PLEASE READ

Present this Warehouse receipt and a written order when any goods are to be withdrawn.

Reasonable notice is required for access to or delivery of goods.

Access to goods by appointment only.

A labor charge will be made for handling of and access to goods in the Warehouse.

This Warehouse Receipt must be returned when all goods enumerated in the Schedule are to be withdrawn.

A platform charge will be made when goods are delivered to outside truckmen.

The final settlement of this account must be made in CASH, at this office. No checks will be accepted upon withdrawal of goods unless certified.

SOURCE: Courtesy of Clinton Transfer and Storage, Inc., Blacksburg, Virginia.

E X H I B I T 17.2 | **A Nonnegotiable Warehouse Receipt (Back)**

TERMS AND CONDITIONS

1. **OWNERSHIP OF PROPERTY:** The customer has represented and warranted to the company that he is the legal owner or in lawful possession of the property and has the legal right and authority to contract for services for all of the property tendered, upon provisions, limitations, terms and conditions herein set forth and that there are no existing liens, mortgages or encumbrances on said property. If there be any litigation as a result of the breach of this clause, customer agrees to pay all charges that may be due together with such costs and expenses including attorneys fees which this company may reasonably incur or become liable to pay in connection therewith and this company shall have a lien on said property for all charges that may be due them as well as for such costs and expenses.

2. **PAYMENT:** (a) It is agreed that the company shall have a general lien upon any and all property deposited with it or hereafter deposited with it. All goods deposited upon which storage and all other charges are not paid when due, will be sold at public auction to pay said accrued charges and expenses of the sale, after due notice to the depositor, and publication of the time and place of said sale, according to law.

   (b) The company shall have a further lien for all monies advanced to any third parties for account of the depositor.

   (c) Accounts are due and payable monthly in advance. Interest will be charged on all accounts unpaid for a period of three months after they become due. All charges must be paid in cash, money order, or certified check before the delivery or transfer of goods deposited under this contract and no transfer will be recognized unless entered on the books of the company.

3. **LIABILITY OF THE COMPANY:** (a) The company when transporting to or from the warehouse for permanent storage acts as a private carrier only, reserving the right to refuse any order for transporting and in no event is a common carrier.

   (b) This contract is accepted subject to delays or damages caused by war, insurrection, labor troubles, strikes, Acts of God or the public enemy, riots, the elements, street traffic, elevator service or other causes beyond the control of the company.

   (c) The company is not responsible for any fragile articles injured or broken, unless packed by its employees and unpacked by them at the time of delivery. The company will not be responsible for mechanical or electrical functioning of any article such as but not limited to, pianos, radios, phonographs, television sets, clocks, barometers, mechanical refrigerators or air conditioners or other instruments or appliances whether or not such articles are packed or unpacked by the company.

   (d) No liability of any kind shall attach to this company for any damage caused to the goods by inherent vice, moths, vermin or other insects, rust, fire, water, changes of temperature, fumigation or deterioration.

   (e) Unless a greater valuation is stated herein, the depositor or owner declared that the value in case of loss or damage arising out of storage, transportation, packing, unpacking, fumigation, cleaning or handling of the goods and the liability of the company for any cause for which it may be liable for each or any piece or package and the contents thereof does not exceed and is limited to 60¢ per lb. per article, or for the entire contents of the entire storage lot does not exceed and is limited to $2,000, upon which declared or agreed value the rates are based, the depositor or owner having been given the opportunity to declare a higher valuation without limitation in case of loss or damage from any cause which would make the company liable and to pay the higher rate based thereon.

   (f) In no event shall the company be responsible for loss or damage to documents, stamps, securities, specie or jewelry or other articles of high and unusual value unless a special agreement in writing is made between the customer and the company with respect to such articles.

4. **MINIMUM PERIOD FOR STORAGE:** On storage accounts three months storage will be charged for any fraction of the first three months period. Thereafter one months storage rate will be charged for thirty days or less.

5. **TERMINATION OF STORAGE:** The company reserves the right to terminate storage of the goods at any time by giving the depositor 30 days written notice of its intention to do so and unless the depositor removes such goods within that period the company is hereby empowered to have the same removed at the cost and expense of the depositor. And upon so doing the company shall be relieved of any liability with respect to such goods therefore or thereafter incurred.

6. **ADDRESS AND CHANGE:** It is agreed that the address of the depositor of goods for storage is as given on the front side of this contract and shall be relied upon by the company as the address of the depositor until change of address is given in writing by the company and acknowledged in writing by the company and notice of any change of address will not be valid or binding upon the company if given or acknowledged in any other manner.

7. **FILING OF CLAIM-NOTICE:** (a) As a condition precedent to recovery, claim must be in writing, supported by a paid freight bill and filed with the company within sixty (60) days after delivery of the goods. No action may be maintained by the depositor against the company either by suit or arbitration to recover for claimed loss or damage, unless commenced within twelve (12) months next after the date of delivery by the company.

   (b) The company shall have the right to inspect and repair alleged damaged articles.

8. **CORRECTION OF ERRORS:** The depositor agrees that unless notice is given in writing to the company within ten days after the receipt of the inventory list accompanying the warehouse receipt and made a part thereof including any exceptions noted thereon as to the condition of the property when received for storage, the inventory list shall be deemed to be correct and complete.

9. **ARBITRATION:** Any controversy or claim arising out of or relating to this contract, the breach thereof, or the goods affected thereby, whether such claims be found in tort or contract shall be settled by arbitration law of the Company's State and under the rules of the American Arbitration Association, provided however, that upon any such arbitration the arbitrator or arbitrators may not vary or modify any of the foregoing provisions.

10. **AGREEMENT:** The contract represents the entire agreement between the parties hereto and cannot be modified except in writing and shall be deemed to apply to all the property whether household goods or goods of any other nature or description which the company may now or any time in the future store, pack, transport or ship for the owner's account.

11. **GENERAL CONDITIONS:** (a) If goods cannot be delivered in the ordinary way by stairs or elevator, the owner agrees to pay an additional charge for hoisting or lowering or other necessary labor to affect delivery. Customer shall arrange in advance for all necessary elevator and other services and any charges for same shall be met by the customer. Customer agrees to pay the hourly charge in this contract for waiting time caused by lack of sufficient elevator service.

    (b) Packing or moving charges do not include the taking or putting up of curtains, mirrors, fixtures, pictures, electric or other fittings, or the relaying of floor coverings of similar services but if such services are ordered a charge will be made therefor.

SOURCE: Courtesy of Clinton Transfer and Storage, Inc., Blacksburg, Virginia.

Carriage
The transportation of goods or people from one location to another.

parties involved in a transaction, the more likely that problems and confusion will enter the picture.

The seller must provide for reasonable **carriage** of the goods, taking into account the nature of the goods, the need for speed, and any other factors that will affect delivery. The seller must then obtain and deliver to the buyer any necessary documents concerning the carriage, and the seller must promptly notify the buyer of the shipment. Again, all these steps seem obvious, and none should cause any undue problems or hardships. The problems arise when the parties use technical and/or legal terms without understanding their meaning. This area generally involves the use of standard shipping terms, a topic discussed later in this chapter. (We will also compare and contrast the standard shipping terms used in the United States under the UCC with the standard shipping terms used in international sales of goods, *Incoterms,* in Chapter 20.)

Exhibit 17.3 illustrates one type of contract a seller may have to use in order to send the goods by means of a common carrier.

INTERVENING RIGHTS

Once the seller's single duty has been performed, the focus of the sales contract shifts. Even though the seller has performed, it is not yet time for the buyer to perform. First, the buyer has an intervening right, the right to inspect the goods. If this inspection results in a discovery of some nonconformity, the seller may have a right to cure the defective performance to avoid a breach. Only after these intervening rights have been exercised or waived does the duty of the buyer to perform arise.

Inspection

The right of the buyer to inspect the goods is covered in § 2-513. This section empowers the buyer to inspect the goods in any reasonable manner and at any reasonable time and place. This includes inspection after the goods arrive at their destination, if the seller ships the goods. The buyer bears the expense of inspection. This serves two functions: (1) It encourages the buyer to use a more reasonable method of inspection (since the buyer must pay for it), and (2) it eliminates "phantom" inspections, with the expenses billed to the other person. If the inspection reveals that the goods do not conform to the contract, the buyer is entitled to recover the expenses of the inspection from the seller, along with any other damages the buyer may be entitled to recover.

There are two circumstances in which the buyer is required to pay for the goods before being allowed to inspect them. If the contract calls for payment against documents or if it is COD, inspection before payment is not allowed. However, such a preinspection payment is not treated as an acceptance under the Code.

In contrast, if the right to inspect the goods before payment exists, a preinspection payment is treated as an acceptance. If the buyer fails to inspect, or refuses to inspect, or inspects poorly, the buyer may waive some rights. Any defects that should be noticed or discovered by a reasonable inspection may not be raised, argued, or relied on after an unreasonable inspection. The one exception is when the seller promises to correct, or cure, the problem and then fails to do so. In other words, unless the defect is hidden (so that a reasonable inspection would not reveal it), the buyer must "speak now or forever hold his peace."

EXHIBIT 17.3 | A Nonnegotiable Bill of Lading (Back)

Contract Terms and Conditions

Sec. 1. (a) The carrier or party in possession of any of the property herein described shall be liable as at common law for any loss thereof or damage thereto, except as hereinafter provided.

(b) No carrier or party in possession of all or any of the property herein described shall be liable for any loss thereof or damage thereto or delay caused by the act of God, the public enemy, the acts of public authority, quarantine, riots, strikes, perils of navigation, the act or default of the shipper or owner, the nature of the property or defect or inherent vice therein. Except in case of negligence of the carrier or party in possession, no carrier or party in possession of all or any of the property herein described shall be liable for the loss or damage thereto or responsible for its condition, operation or functioning, whether or not such property or any part of it is packed, unpacked, or packed and unpacked by the shipper or its agent or the carrier or its agent. Except in case of negligence of the carrier or party in possession, no carrier or party in possession of all or any of the property herein described shall be liable for damage to or loss of contents of pieces of furniture, crates, bundles, cartons, boxes, barrels or other containers unless such contents are open for the carrier's inspection and then only for such articles as are specifically listed by the shipper and receipted for by the carrier or its agent.

(c) Except in case of negligence of the carrier or party in possession, the carrier or party in possession of any of the property herein described shall not be liable for delay caused by highway obstruction, or faulty or impassable highway, or lack of capacity of any highway, bridge, or ferry, or caused by breakdown or mechanical defect of vehicles or equipment.

(d) Except in case of negligence of the carrier or party in possession the carrier or party in possession shall not be liable for loss, damage, or delay occurring while the property is stopped and held or stored in transit upon request of the shipper, owner, or party entitled to make such request, whether such request was made before or after the carrier comes into possession of the property.

(e) In case of quarantine the property may be discharged at the risk and expense of the owners into quarantine depot or elsewhere, as required by quarantine regulations, or authorities, and in such case, carrier's responsibility shall cease when the property is so discharged, or property may be returned by carrier at owner's expense to shipping point earning charges both ways. Quarantine expenses of whatever nature or kind upon or in respect to property shall be borne by the owners of the property or be a lien thereon. The carrier shall not be liable for loss or damage occasioned by fumigation or disinfection or other acts done or required by quarantine regulations or authorities even though the same may have been done by carrier's officers, agents, or employees, nor for detention, loss, or damage of any kind occasioned by quarantine or the enforcement thereof. No carrier shall be liable, except in case of negligence, for any mistake or inaccuracy in any information furnished by the carrier, its agents, or officers, as to quarantine laws or regulations. The shipper shall hold the carriers harmless from any expense they may incur, or damages they may be required to pay, by reason of the introduction of the property covered by this contract into any place against the quarantine laws or regulations in effect at such place.

Sec. 2. (a) No carrier is bound to transport said property by any particular schedule, vehicle, train or vessel or otherwise than with reasonable dispatch. Every carrier shall have the right in case of physical necessity to forward said property by any carrier or route between the point of shipment and the point of destination. In all cases not prohibited by law, where a lower value than actual value has been represented in writing by the shipper or has been agreed upon in writing as the released value of the property as determined by the classification or tariffs upon which the rate is based, such lower value shall be the maximum amount to be recovered, whether or not such loss or damage occurs from negligence.

(b) As a condition precedent to recovery, claims must be filed in writing with the receiving or delivering carrier, or carrier issuing this bill of lading, or carrier in possession of the property when the loss, damage, injury or delay occurred, within nine months after delivery of the property (or in case of export traffic, within nine months after delivery at port of export) or, in case of failure to make delivery, then within nine months after a reasonable time, for delivery has elapsed; and suits shall be instituted against any carrier only within two years and one day from the day when notice in writing is given by the carrier to the claimant that the carrier has disallowed the claim or any part or parts thereof specified in the notice. Where claims are not filed or suits are not instituted thereon in accordance with the foregoing provisions, no carrier hereunder shall be liable, and such claims will not be paid.

(c) Any carrier or party liable on account of loss or damage to any of said property shall have the full benefit of any insurance that may have been effected upon or on account of said property so far as this shall not avoid the policies or contracts of insurance; provided that the carrier reimburse the claimant for the premium paid thereon.

Sec. 3. Except where such service is required as the result of carrier's negligence, all property shall be subject to necessary cooperage, packing and repacking at owner's cost.

Sec. 4. (a) Property not received by the party entitled to receive it within the free time (if any) allowed by tariffs lawfully on file (such free time to be computed as therein provided) after notice of the arrival of the property at destination or at the port of export (if intended for export) has been duly sent or given, and after placement of the property for delivery at destination, or at the time tender of delivery of the property to the party entitled to receive it or at the address given for delivery has been made, may be kept in vehicle, warehouse or place of business of the carrier, subject to the tariff charge for storage and to carrier's responsibility as warehouseman, only, or at the option of the carrier, may be removed to and stored in a warehouse at the point of delivery or at other available points, at the cost of the owner, and there held without liability on the part of the carrier, and subject to a lien for all transportation and other lawful charges, including a reasonable charge for storage. In the event the consignee can not be found at the address given for delivery, then in that event, notice of the placing of such goods in warehouse shall be left at the address given for delivery and mailed to any other address given on the bill of lading for notification, showing the warehouse in which such property has been placed, subject to the provisions of this paragraph.

(b) Where nonperishable property which has been transported to destination hereunder is refused by consignee or the party entitled to receive it upon tender of delivery or said consignee or party entitled to receive it fails to receive it or claim within 15 days after notice of arrival of the property at destination shall have been duly sent or given, the carrier may sell the same at public auction to the highest bidder, at such place as may be designated by the carrier; provided, that the carrier shall have first mailed, sent, or given to the consignor notice that the property has been refused or remains unclaimed, as the case may be, and that it will be subject to sale under the terms of the bill of lading if disposition be not arranged for, and shall have published notice containing a description of the property, the name of the party to whom consigned, and the time and place of sale, once a week for two successive weeks, in a newspaper of general circulation at the place of sale or nearest place where such newspaper is published; provided, that 30 days shall have elapsed before publication of notice of sale after said notice that the property was refused or remains unclaimed was mailed, sent, or given.

(c) Where perishable property which has been transported hereunder to destination is refused by consignee or party entitled to receive it, or consignee or party entitled to receive it shall fail to receive it promptly, the carrier may, in its discretion, to prevent deterioration or further deterioration, sell the same to the best advantage at private or public sale: provided, that if there be time for service of notification to the consignor or owner of the refusal of the property or the failure to receive it and request for disposition of the property, such notification shall be given, in such manner as the exercise of due diligence requires, before the property is sold.

(d) Where the procedure provided for in the two paragraphs last preceding is not possible, it is agreed that nothing contained in said paragraphs shall be construed to abridge the right of the carrier at its option to sell the property under such circumstances and in such manner as may be authorized by law.

(e) The proceeds of any sale made under this section shall be applied by the carrier to the payment of advances, tariff charges, packing, storage, and any other lawful charges and the expense of notice, advertisement, sale, and other necessary expense and of caring for and maintaining the property, if proper care of the same requires special expense; and should there be a balance, it shall be paid to the owner of the property sold hereunder.

(f) Where the carrier is directed to load property from (or render any services at) a place or places at which the consignor or his agent is not present, the property shall be at the risk of the owner before loading.

Where the carrier is directed to unload or deliver property (or render any services) at the place or places at which the consignee or its agent is not present, the property shall be at the risk of the owner after unloading or delivery.

Sec. 5. No Carrier hereunder will carry or be liable in any way for any documents, specie, or for any articles of extraordinary value not specifically rated in the published classifications or tariffs unless a special agreement to do so and a stipulated value of the articles are endorsed hereon.

Sec. 6. Explosives or dangerous goods will not be accepted for shipment. Every party whether principal or agent shipping such goods shall be liable for and indemnify the carrier against all loss or damage caused by such goods and carrier will not be liable for safe delivery of the shipment.

Sec. 7. The owner or consignee shall pay the advances, tariff charges, packing and storage, if any, and all other lawful charges accruing on said property: but, except in those instances where it may lawfully be authorized to do so, no carrier shall deliver or relinquish possession at destination of the property covered by this bill of lading until all tariff rates and charges thereon have been paid. The consignor shall be liable for the advances, tariff charges, packing, storage and all other lawful charges, except that if the consignor stipulates, by signature, in the space provided for that purpose on the face of this bill of lading that the carrier shall not make delivery without requiring payment of such charges and the carrier, contrary to such stipulation, shall make delivery without requiring such payment, the consignor (except as hereinafter provided) shall not be liable for such charges; Provided, that, where the carrier has been instructed by the shipper or consignor to deliver said property to a consignee other than the shipper or consignor, such consignee shall not be legally liable for transportation charges in respect of the transportation of said property (beyond those billed against him at the time of delivery for which he is otherwise liable) which may be found to be due after the property has been delivered to him, if the consignee (a) is an agent only and has no beneficial title in said property, and, (b) prior to delivery of said property has notified the delivering carrier in writing of the fact of such agency and absence of beneficial title, and, in the case of a shipment reconsigned or diverted to a point other than that specified in the original bill of lading, has also notified the delivering carrier in writing of the name and address of the beneficial owner of said property; and in such cases the shipper or consignor, or in the case of a shipment so reconsigned or diverted, the beneficial owner, shall be liable for such additional charges. If the consignee has given to the carrier erroneous information as to who the beneficial owner is, such consignee shall himself be liable for such additional charges. Nothing herein shall limit the right of the carrier to require at time of shipment, the prepayment of the charges. If upon inspection it is ascertained that the articles shipped are not those described in this bill of lading, the advances or tariff charges must be paid upon the articles actually shipped.

Sec. 8. If this bill of lading is issued on the order of the shipper, or his agent, in exchange or in substitution for another bill of lading, the shipper's signature to the prior bill of lading as to the statement of value or otherwise, or election for common law or bill of lading liability, in or in connection with such prior bill of lading shall be considered a part of this bill of lading as fully as if the same were written or made in or in connection with this bill of lading.

Sec. 9. Any alteration, addition or erasure in this bill of lading which shall be made without the special notation hereon of the agent of the carrier issuing this bill of lading shall be without effect and this bill of lading shall be enforceable according to its original tenor.

SOURCE: Courtesy of Clinton Transfer and Storage, Inc., Blackburg, Virginia.

The following case involves the issues of timely inspection, proper rejection, and risk of loss. Note how the court addresses each issue in turn before rendering its final decision.

GRAAFF V. BAKKER BROS. OF IDAHO, INC.
934 P.2D 1228 (WASH.APP. DIV. 3 1997)

FACTS In 1988, Bakker Brothers of Idaho, Inc., agreed to buy Charles E. Graaff's 1989 onion seed crop. Their contract required an 85 percent germination rate. Mr. Graaff harvested the onion seed in September 1989. On October 7, 1989, the seed was received by Bakker. On October 11, Bakker began processing Mr. Graaff's seed . . . At various points in the process, Bakker tested samples for germination. Before processing, the germination rate was 84 percent. After processing, germination rates fell to 69 percent and 67 percent on two separate samples. Because of the low germination rates, Bakker had the seed tested at several independent laboratories. That testing took place in January, February, and April 1990 and produced germination rates ranging from 51 percent to 80 percent.

In January 1990, Bakker told Mr. Graaff that the seed had failed the contract germination requirements and was unmarketable. Bakker said it would not pay Mr. Graaff for the seed unless it found a buyer. It could not find a buyer. On August 14, 1990, Bakker told Mr. Graaff to pick up his seed.

In 1994 Mr. Graaff sued Bakker. Both parties moved for summary judgment. The trial court granted Bakker's motion and dismissed Mr. Graaff's complaint. Mr. Graaff appealed.

ISSUES Does a factual issue remain about when the germination rate should be measured—before or after processing? Did Bakker timely inspect and effectively reject the seed? Did Bakker accept the seed because its acts were inconsistent with Mr. Graaff's ownership?

HOLDINGS The germination rate was to be tested after processing. Bakker did inspect and reject in a timely manner. Bakker did not act in a manner that was inconsistent with the ownership of Graaff.

REASONING We review a motion for summary judgment de novo and engage in the same inquiry as the trial court . . . We consider facts in the light most favorable to the non-moving party. And we will affirm the grant of a summary judgment only when no material facts are in dispute and the moving party is entitled to judgment as a matter of law . . . Mr. Graaff first contends that material issues of fact remain about the contract germination rate. He argues that the germination rate should be tested before processing. The contract here requires an 85 percent germination rate but is silent on whether that is before or after processing. It simply says that Bakker can reject the crop if the germination rate is less than 85 percent . . . Extrinsic evidence is admissible to establish trade usage to give particular meaning to the terms of an agreement . . . Here, Chris Jancik, executive vice president and manager of Bakker, testified . . . that germination tests taken after the seed has been washed and cleaned is the procedure followed in the seed industry for determining if seed is acceptable. His representation of the trade practice is uncontradicted. And we therefore accept it as fact . . . Mr. Graaff next argues that application of trade usage here effectively nullifies the contract's risk of loss provision. He claims that since the contract required him to "deliver all seed F.O.B. as directed" he transported the seed at his own risk and upon delivery to Bakker the risk of loss passed to Bakker . . . "Where a tender of delivery of goods so fails to conform to the contract as to give a right of rejection the risk of loss remains on the seller until cure or acceptance." . . . "[T]he seller by his individual action cannot shift the risk of loss to the buyer unless his action conforms with all the conditions resting on him under the contract." . . . Therefore, even if we assume that the contract's use of F.O.B. passed the risk of loss, the term only became operative when Mr. Graaff tendered conforming goods . . . The post-germination rate of Mr. Graaff's onion seed was below the contract's requirements. The goods were, therefore, nonconforming . . . Mr. Graaff next claims that Bakker did not timely or effectively reject the nonconforming goods. A buyer has a right before acceptance to inspect delivered goods at any reasonable place and in any reasonable manner . . . The reasonableness is again a question of trade usage, past practices between the parties, and the other circumstances of the case . . . Bakker completed washing and drying the seed around November 28, 1989.

17.1

GRAAFF V. BAKKER BROS. OF IDAHO, INC., *continued*

934 P.2D 1228 (WASH.APP. DIV. 3 1997)

Bakker's germination tests were completed [by] . . . February 6, 1990. Independent tests requested by Bakker were completed [between] January 6 [and] April 16, 1990. A germination test takes at least 15 days. The trade practice is to perform the test after processing. Bakker *inspected* the seed in a reasonable time and manner. Once it determined that the seed was nonconforming, Bakker must then reject the seed within a reasonable time and give seasonable notice to Mr. Graaff . . . The timeliness of Bakker's rejection depends on the timeliness of its inspection . . . Here, Mr. Graaff talked with Bakker in January 1990. Based on those conversations, Mr. Graaff understood that because of the seed's low germination rate, Bakker would not purchase the seed unless it could find a buyer. This is an adequate and seasonable notice of *rejection* . . . Mr. Graaff finally claims that even if Bakker's notice of rejection was timely, Bakker subsequently accepted the goods by trying to sell the seeds . . . A merchant buyer is under a duty after rejection of goods in its possession or control to follow any reasonable instructions received from the seller . . . Without such instructions, the merchant buyer must make a reasonable effort to sell the goods for the seller's account if the goods are perishable or threaten to quickly decline in value . . . A buyer's good faith effort to sell is not an acceptance . . . We affirm the trial court's grant of summary judgment in favor of Bakker.

BUSINESS CONSIDERATIONS Should a business have a policy regarding when and how it will inspect goods that it purchases? How important is a proper and adequate inspection in protecting the rights of the buyer?

ETHICAL CONSIDERATIONS Is it ethical for a business to continue inspecting goods and processing them when an initial inspection reveals that the goods do not conform to the contract? When a nonconformity is discovered during inspection, what ethical obligations arise for the buyer?

Cure

Often the buyer will discover, on inspection, that the goods do not conform exactly to the description in the contract. When this happens, the buyer must make a decision. Either (1) the nonconformity is minor, or of little or no consequence, in which case the buyer will normally accept the goods despite the nonconformity; or (2) the goods are too different from those described in the contract to be acceptable. When this happens, the buyer must promptly notify the seller, specifying in detail the problems with the goods that result in nonconformity. If the time for performance has not yet expired, the Code gives the seller a chance to avoid being held in breach. The seller may cure the defect in the goods, putting the goods into conformity with the contract. However, the cure must be completed within the time period in which the original contract was to be performed. No extension of time is permitted without the buyer's permission.

Occasionally, a seller ships nonconforming goods and reasonably expects the buyer to accept them despite the nonconformity. Such an expectation may be realistically based on typical past dealings between the parties, prior performances between the parties, or industry standards. In such a case, if the buyer decides to stand by the literal terms of the contract and refuses to accept the nonconforming goods and so informs the seller, the UCC gives the seller a right to cure even if the time for performance is past. If the seller informs the buyer of an intention to cure the defect, the seller is given a reasonable time to cure by substituting conforming goods so that the seller's performance is in compliance with the contract. The following example addresses this issue.

A merchant seller and a merchant buyer have done business together over several previous contracts, each of which involved the sale of a particular component part the seller uses in its manufacturing process. Each of these previous contracts called for the seller to deliver the component part Brand A. On at least one prior occasion, the seller did not have an adequate supply of Brand A to satisfy the contract, so the seller substituted Brand B (a competing brand with similar characteristics and price), and the buyer accepted the substituted component without objection. In the current contract, the seller once again had an inadequate supply of Brand A and decided to fill the contract by shipping Brand B instead. When the delivery was tendered, the buyer rejected the goods because the component was not Brand A, as called for in the contract. Since the seller reasonably believed that the substitution would be acceptable (based on their prior dealings), the seller will have a reasonable time to ship conforming goods in order to satisfy the contract. If this had been the first time the seller had shipped substitute parts, there would not be a reasonable belief that they would be accepted (unless such a belief was based on industry standards), and there would not be an extension of time to allow the seller to perform.

While a seller who reasonably believes that the substitute goods will be accepted is given an extension of time to satisfy the contract, the seller will not be given unlimited time or opportunity to cure the defect. This has often been a problem in automobile cases.

BUYER'S DUTIES

The buyer's duties with respect to the sales contract arise after the seller's duties have been completed and the intervening rights of the parties have been exercised, if these intervening rights in fact exist in the contract. Since the buyer is not required to inspect the goods, a failure to inspect operates as a waiver, and the buyer's duty to perform arises. If the buyer inspects and discovers a defect, the seller may have a right to cure. If the seller does in fact cure, the duty of the buyer arises. The buyer has a duty to accept the goods and pay for them.

Acceptance

When delivery of the goods is tendered, the buyer has three options:

1. He or she can accept the entire shipment, without regard to the conformity of the goods.
2. He or she can reject the entire shipment, without regard to the conformity of the goods.
3. He or she can accept some of the goods and reject the rest of the shipment.

If the buyer accepts the entire shipment, the seller may view the contract as properly performed and is entitled to payment for the goods as called for in the contract. If the buyer rejects the entire shipment, either the seller is in breach for tendering delivery of nonconforming goods or the buyer is in breach for rejecting a proper tender of delivery. One of the parties will be entitled to damages due to the breach of the contract by the other party. If the buyer decides to accept some of the goods and reject the rest, there is a limitation imposed by the Code. The buyer must accept all conforming goods and may then also accept as many nonconforming goods as he or she desires. This means that the seller breached the contract, at least in part, and that the buyer will be entitled to some remedies.

Obviously, the decision of the buyer to accept—or reject—the goods is of paramount importance. The UCC states that the buyer accepts the goods, and thus is obligated to pay for them, in a number of ways. After having had a reasonable time to inspect the goods, the buyer is deemed to have accepted them in one of the following ways:

1. By signifying that the goods conform to the contract.
2. By signifying that the goods do not conform, but that they will be retained and accepted despite the nonconformity.
3. By failing to make a proper rejection of the goods if they are nonconforming.
4. By doing anything that is not consistent with the seller's ownership of the goods. (Since the buyer is attempting to reject the goods, he or she must treat the goods as if they still belong to the seller. Any conduct by the buyer that is not consistent with this hypothetical ownership of the seller is taken as proof that the buyer owned the goods, and had therefore accepted them!)

As mentioned earlier, acceptance obligates the buyer to pay for the goods at the contract price. It also prevents rejection of the accepted goods unless the defect was hidden or the seller promised to cure the defect and then failed to do so. Also, the acceptance of any part of a commercial unit is treated as an acceptance of the entire commercial unit.

Payment

Once the seller tenders delivery and the buyer accepts (or fails to reject properly), the buyer has a duty to tender payment. Likewise, in the case of a COD contract or a payment against documents, the buyer has a duty to tender payment. The buyer is allowed to tender payment in any manner that is normal in the ordinary course of business, typically by check or draft. A seller who is not satisfied with this can demand cash. But in so doing, the seller must allow the buyer a reasonable extension of time to obtain cash. This would normally be viewed as at least one banking day. Once the buyer tenders payment, the normal contract for the sale of goods is fully performed. Each of the parties received what it wanted, and nothing further is required. However, some contracts present special problems, some of which will be discussed later in the chapter.

In the following case, the court had to interpret the terms of a contract before it could determine the duty of the buyer in the contract.

17.2

MALNOVE INCORPORATED OF NEBRASKA V. HEARTHSIDE BAKING CO., INC.

944 F.SUPP. 657 (N.D.ILL. 1996)

FACTS The parties entered into a contract for the manufacture and sale by Malnove of 250,000 Family Favorite boxes pursuant to Maurice Lenell purchase order No. 30658 dated October 29, 1993 . . . , and

Malnove acknowledgement No. 16860 dated November 4, 1993 . . . Pursuant to this contract, Malnove manufactured and delivered all 250,000 of the Family

continued

17.2

MALNOVE INCORPORATED OF NEBRASKA V. HEARTHSIDE BAKING CO., INC., continued
944 F.SUPP. 657 (N.D.ILL. 1996)

Favorite boxes. Maurice Lenell has paid for all of the Family Favorite boxes except for the final shipment of 30,000 boxes . . . Maurice Lenell seeks to justify its refusal to pay for the final shipment by claiming that the purchase price included purchase of the dies and printing plates used in the production of the Family Favorite boxes . . . Maurice Lenell claims that in the negotiations leading up to the issuance of its purchase order, Malnove advised Maurice Lenell that the price quotes include "all printing plates and cutting dies necessary to duplicate these cartons." . . .

On October 29, 1993, [Malnove and Maurice Lenell] finalize[d] negotiations for the pinwheel cookie boxes. [Maurice Lenell] ordered 500,000 boxes at a price of $122.31 per thousand. [Maurice Lenell] selected the volume of boxes and understood that in reliance upon Maurice Lenell's order, Malnove would proceed to order all of the polyboard it would need to manufacture the boxes . . . On October 29, 1993, Maurice Lenell issued its purchase order No. 30659 for 500,000 pinwheel boxes . . . On November 10, 1993, Malnove issued its acknowledgement No. 16880 for the pinwheel cookie boxes and therein stated that the "Price is based on inventory shipping 90 days from date of completion. At 90 days, inventory will be billed, and will be shipped 30 days after billing." . . . On or about March 9, 1994, [Maurice Lenell] returned a fax from [Malnove] approving the final issue regarding the pinwheel cookie carton and authorizing production to begin . . . This document and the prior course of dealing constitute an agreement with respect to the terms and conditions contained on the reverse side of the acknowledgement and approval of the order for all 500,000 pinwheel boxes. Shortly thereafter, Malnove manufactured all 500,000 pinwheel cookie boxes and delivered the first truckload of 144,000 boxes to Maurice Lenell on or about March 28, 1994 . . . Malnove stored the remaining boxes while awaiting further release from Maurice Lenell . . . Maurice Lenell did not inform Malnove as to when it intended to take further delivery. From time to time between April, 1994 and April, 1995 [Malnove] requested that [Maurice Lenell] take further delivery of the pinwheel boxes . . . The only response . . . was that Maurice Lenell would take delivery of the boxes when they wanted them and they did not want them yet . . . Malnove filed suit against Maurice Lenell, seeking payment of the bal-

ance due under the Family Favorite contract, and also seeking enforcement of the Pinwheel Cookie contract.

ISSUES Did the Family Favorite contract include the printing plates and dies used to produce the Family Favorite cartons? Was Maurice Lenell obligated to take delivery of the balance of the Pinwheel Cookie boxes it had ordered within a reasonable time after being notified that the boxes were ready for shipment?

HOLDINGS No, the contract did not include any rights to the printing plates and dies for the Family Favorite boxes. Yes, Maurice Lenell was obligated to take delivery of the balance of the Pinwheel Cookie boxes within a reasonable time after being informed that the boxes were ready for shipment.

REASONING "The Family Favorite Claim." . . . In the industry, there are two basic ways to charge for printing plates and dies: first, as a separate extra charge or second, to amortize the cost over the price of the production run. In neither event is it customary for the purchaser to receive the printing plates and dies. The Court finds that the purchase order did not contemplate or expressly include the purchase by Maurice Lenell of the printing plates and dies . . . In fact, in none of the prior dealings between the parties did Maurice Lenell ever receive the printing plates and dies. Although the final shipment of the Family Favorite boxes was made in January, 1995, Maurice Lenell did not ask for the printing plates and dies until after suit was filed. Maurice Lenell was not justified in withholding payment for the final shipment of Family Favorite boxes. The acknowledgement form agreed to by the parties provides that Maurice Lenell is liable for a finance charge of 1½% per month on all past due invoices and all expenses and fees, including reasonable attorneys' fees, for collection of past due amounts . . . "The Pinwheel Cookie Claim" . . . The understanding under the parties' contract and in the industry is that Maurice Lenell was obligated to take delivery of all 500,000 cookie boxes within a reasonable period of time . . . The Court finds that a reasonable period of time for Maurice Lenell to take delivery was no later than December 31, 1994, approximately nine months after the initial shipment. . . . Maurice Lenell shall have thirty (30) days from the date of judgment to advise Malnove what it wants

17.2

MALNOVE INCORPORATED OF NEBRASKA V. HEARTHSIDE BAKING CO., INC., *continued*
944 F.SUPP. 657 (N.D.ILL. 1996)

done with the remaining pinwheel boxes and Maurice Lenell shall assume responsibility for the storage charges if it elects not to have the remaining boxes delivered to its plant. . . . Maurice Lenell cannot reasonably expect Malnove to have all the boxes available and then refuse to advise Malnove of a reasonable delivery schedule . . . Maurice Lenell was aware of Malnove's standard terms and conditions contained on the reverse side of Malnove's acknowledgement form and it accepted those terms and conditions in its dealings with Malnove. Maurice Lenell breached its agreement with Malnove by failing to accept delivery of the remaining pinwheel boxes by December 31, 1994 . . . Judgment is entered in favor of plaintiff Malnove and against defendant Maurice Lenell in the amount of . . . $70,921.58 plus court costs and reasonable attorneys' fees . . .

BUSINESS CONSIDERATIONS The breaches of each of these contracts occurred at the end of 1994/ beginning of 1995. Should a business that has multiple contracts with another firm be concerned when the contracts are due to be performed, or at least completed, at approximately the same time? Should the business include any language in the contracts attempting to address issues such as the ones in this case?

ETHICAL CONSIDERATIONS Is it ethical for a business to delay its performance of a contract duty because it has erred in its projections for one of its products and the duty has become overly burdensome for the business?

TITLE TO GOODS

When the term *title* is used, it refers to legal ownership. The legal owner of goods is said to have title. When goods are sold, title passes from the seller to the buyer. Title is an important concept, although its importance is tempered somewhat by the Code's provisions concerning risk of loss.

Historic Importance

Under common law, title was of paramount importance. Nearly all aspects of the contract hinged on title and its location. Risk of loss was placed on the party holding title. The outcome of many lawsuits depended on who had title, so the courts spent a great deal of time and energy on this issue. In some respects, it is not as important today as it was in the past, at least under Article 2 of the UCC.

Modern Rule

The UCC specifically states that all the rights, duties, and remedies of any party apply without regard to title unless title is specifically required. However, in recognition of the importance of title, some provisions have been made to help in locating title in the sale of goods. Under the Code, title passes from the seller to the buyer when the seller completes performance of delivery. Thus, the type of delivery contract becomes important in determining which party has title. If a common carrier is used and the delivery contract is a shipment contract, title passes to the buyer at the time and place of shipment. If a common carrier is used and the contract is a destination contract, title passes to the buyer when delivery is tendered at the destination. These rules apply even though the seller may claim to have

ONE MAN'S JUNK . . .

The city of Roanoke, Virginia, recently adopted a law aimed at removing junked or abandoned vehicles from the yards of city residents if the vehicle is in "plain view." (An earlier law prohibited junked cars being left on city streets.) If a vehicle is located in a yard in plain view, and if that vehicle is junked or abandoned (i.e., it has flat tires, a dead engine, shattered windows, or an expired registration sticker or license plates), the vehicle is "tagged" and the car's owner then has 10 days either to correct the problem with the car or to shield it from plain view. If neither thing is done within the 10 days, the city sends a warning letter by certified mail to the owner warning that the vehicle will be towed within the next 10 days if it is not either fixed, moved, or shielded. If this warning is ignored, the vehicle is towed. The towing company then notifies the vehicle's registered owner that the vehicle will be sold in 10 days unless the owner reclaims it and pays the towing and storage fees.

Suppose that a car is towed as a result of this city ordinance and is then sold to a buyer 10 days after the towing company sends notice to the registered owner of the car. Following this sale, the holder of the certificate of title comes forward and files suit against the buyer, the towing company, and the city, seeking recovery of the automobile. The holder of the certificate of title alleges that he still owns the vehicle and demands its return. The city asserts that the car was abandoned; the towing company alleges that it was allowed to sell the car under the provisions of the city ordinance; the buyer alleges that she purchased the car and is entitled to possession.

The case has been brought before *your* court. How will *you* decide who has title to the car in this case? Explain *your* reasoning.[1]

BUSINESS CONSIDERATIONS What issues should be of concern to a business that procures and sells goods acquired through governmental enactments such as this ordinance? Should such a business have liability insurance to protect itself from potential lawsuits filed by "displaced" owners? Should an insurer be willing to provide insurance for such a business activity?

ETHICAL CONSIDERATIONS Is it ethical for the towing firm to tow these "junked" or "abandoned" vehicles without charge to the city, planning to receive compensation either from the owner who reclaims his or her car, or from the proceeds of the sale of unclaimed vehicles? Is it ethical for the city to allow the towing firm to operate in this manner with the city's support and backing?

SOURCE: *Roanoke Times* (24 May 1999), p. C-1.

"reserved title." The Code states that a reservation of title is, in reality, only the reservation of a security interest.

In some sales contracts, the goods are not to be delivered physically. Again, the Code specifies how title is to pass. If the goods are not to be moved and the seller is to deliver a document of title, title passes when and where the document is given to the buyer. If no documents are to be delivered, title passes at the time and place the contract is made. Of course, under any set of circumstances, title cannot pass unless the goods are in existence and identified to the contract. The existence of the goods presents no problem: Either the goods exist or they do not exist. However, identification can present a problem. Goods are identified to a contract when they are shipped, marked, or otherwise designated by the seller as the goods that will satisfy the contract. (Determining what qualifies as "otherwise designated" is a question of fact.)

Occasionally, title will pass from the buyer back to the seller. If the buyer rejects the goods or refuses to accept, receive, or retain them, title **revests** in the seller. This is true even if the buyer is acting improperly by refusing the goods. Likewise, if the buyer properly revokes an acceptance, title revests in the seller.

The location of title is still important in the area of creditor rights. A creditor of one of the parties may be able to attach any goods that belong to that party. Thus, creditors are very anxious to know where title lies. This also helps explain the UCC's treatment of consignments. The Code is very careful in spelling out the rights of each party when creditors are involved. Section 2-402 deals with the rights of creditors of the seller when goods are sold. The rights of an **unsecured creditor** of the seller are limited by the rights of the buyer to recover the goods once the goods are identified to the contract. In a legal tug-of-war between the buyer and a creditor of the seller, the buyer normally will win if the goods have been identified as the goods covered by the sales contract.

Revests
Vests again; is acquired a second time.

Unsecured creditor
A general creditor; a creditor whose claim is not secured by collateral.

Fraudulent Retention

Another problem arises when, as sometimes happens, the seller "sells" goods but retains possession. In such a case, the seller's creditors can treat the sale as void *if* the retention by the seller is fraudulent under state law. Historically, the seller's only defense was to show that he or she was a merchant who retained the goods in good faith in the ordinary course of business, and then only if the goods were retained only for a commercially reasonable time. Thus, a seller who holds identified goods in "layaway" would have a valid defense to a fraudulent retention charge. But a seller who holds the goods without a valid reason could be in trouble. The following hypothetical case illustrates a fraudulent retention by the seller.

> *John, a blacksmith deeply in debt, feared his creditors would sue him and take his equipment to pay the debts. To prevent this, he "sold" his equipment to Lil, who let John retain possession of "her" equipment. When John's creditors tried to attach the equipment to satisfy the debts, John denied he owned it. He produced the bill of sale as proof.*

The sale in this example would be fraudulent since John retained the goods after the sale in bad faith. The creditors thus could treat the sale as void and attach the equipment.

Different states treat the issue of fraudulent retention differently. Three possible rules exist for a state to follow. In some states, a fraudulent retention by the seller is treated as a conclusive presumption of fraud; if a seller sells goods and then retains possession of them for any reason other than a commercial one, the seller is deemed guilty of fraud. Other states view a retention of the goods by the seller after the sale as *prima facie* proof of fraud; the seller is presumed to be guilty of fraud unless the seller is able to show good cause for the retention. In other states, the retention of the goods by the seller is viewed merely as one bit of evidence, to be viewed together with all the other evidence, in determining whether a fraud has occurred.

The enactment of Article 2A, Leases, has further complicated this issue. Article 2A specifically recognizes the validity of a sale and leaseback arrangement, provided that the buyer in the sale portion of the deals acts in good faith and gives value for the goods purchased. Sale and leaseback arrangements have become very popular in a number of industries, especially construction, and the increase has presented numerous problems with the former attitude toward sellers who retained possession of the goods following the sale. The specific authorization of this sort of dealing under Article 2A should reduce the problems and help clarify this area of law.

Entrustment

As a general rule, any person who sells goods can transfer to the buyer only those rights that are equal to or less than the rights the seller possesses in those goods. Thus, the person who has *valid* title (i.e., the owner of the goods) can sell them and pass valid title to the buyer. A person who has *void* title (i.e., a thief) has no true title to the goods and passes void title to the buyer. The true owner of the goods may legally reclaim the goods from the person who bought them from the thief, if and when the true owner discovers the location of the goods.

However, a special exception to this general rule exists under Article 2. A person who has *voidable* title nonetheless may legally transfer rights that are better than he or she possesses in the goods. A person with voidable title may legally pass full and valid title to a buyer if that buyer is a good-faith purchaser for value. For example, a person who acquires goods through fraud or misrepresentation has voidable title to those goods. The person who was defrauded or who was the victim of the misrepresentation may avoid the transaction and recover title to the goods if this avoidance occurs while the defrauding or misrepresenting party still has possession of the goods. However, if the defrauding or misrepresenting party sells the goods before any attempt to avoid the transaction occurs, the buyer may have full and valid title to the goods.

Entrustment
The delivery of goods to a merchant who regularly deals in goods of the type delivered.

The issue of **entrustment** addresses these problems regarding voidable title and the passage of valid title. An entrustment occurs when there is "any delivery and acquiescence in retention of possession regardless of any conditions expressed between the parties to the delivery or acquiescence and regardless of whether the procurement of the entrusting or the possessor's disposition of the goods has been such as to be larcenous under the criminal law" [UCC 2-403(3)]. Commonly, an entrustment involves a situation in which possession of the goods is given to a merchant who regularly deals in goods of that kind (often for repairs). The entruster, the person who delivers possession of the goods to the merchant, gives the merchant voidable title and thus the legal power to transfer all of the entruster's rights to a buyer who in the ordinary course of business purchases the entrusted goods from the merchant. Thus, an owner who takes his or her goods to a merchant for repairs entrusts those goods to the merchant. If the merchant happens to sell the entrusted goods to a customer in the ordinary course of business, and if the customer acted in good faith, the customer takes valid title to the goods. Of course, the entruster does have rights and remedies against the merchant to whom the goods were entrusted. If the entrustment involves a party who obtains the goods but who is not a merchant in goods of that kind, the entrusted party can transfer good title to any good-faith purchaser for value. The following two examples show the difference between an entrustment to a merchant and an entrustment to a nonmerchant.

Betty took her watch to Roger's Jewelry to have it repaired. Roger's sells new and used watches in its normal business dealings. If a customer comes into the store and "purchases" Betty's watch, that customer will own the watch. Betty's only recourse will be to sue Roger's for her loss. By entrusting the watch to Roger's, she gave Roger's the legal power to transfer good title to any buyer in the ordinary course of business who purchases the watch from Roger's.

Roger took his watch to Betty's Radio Shop to have it repaired. Although Betty's does not deal in watches, Betty sometimes repairs watches for her friends, and she agrees to do this for Roger. If a customer comes into Betty's and purchases Roger's watch, Roger may be able to recover the watch from the customer. Since Betty does not deal in watches, the transaction with Roger was not an entrustment to a merchant. However, if the person who bought the watch bought it as a good-faith purchaser for value, the buyer would still acquire good title due to the entrustment of the watch to Betty by Roger.

The following entrustment case hinged on the status of the seller of the goods. The court was forced to determine whether the seller was a merchant, in which case the buyers would prevail, or a nonmerchant, in which case the entrusting parties would recover the goods. Similar reasoning is likely to be followed by other courts facing the question of whether a party in a transaction is a merchant.

17.3

PRENGER V. BAKER
542 N.W.2D 805 (IOWA 1995)

FACTS In approximately 1988, Ron Rasmus entered into the business of buying, selling, and raising exotic animals, including ostriches. In 1988, defendant Gene Baker began purchasing ostriches and other flightless birds (known as ratites) for investment purposes. For some time previously, Baker, a livestock farmer, had been boarding his extra swine at Rasmus' farm. According to their agreement, Baker could place and remove swine at will, and Rasmus was paid out of the profits when the swine were sold. Because this agreement had proven beneficial, Baker chose to enter into an agreement for a similar arrangement to board ostriches. . . . Between the years 1990 and 1993, Baker purchased what eventually became two adult breeding pairs of ostriches.

On January 12, 1992, Gene Baker sold one of the breeding pairs to his father, Don Baker, for $25,000. Don Baker also chose to leave the birds in the care of Rasmus under the agreement.

On June 18, 1993, Mike Pickard, acting on behalf of Missouri Ratite Center, Inc. (MRC), purchased for MRC the two adult breeding pair from Rasmus for $75,000. Pickard then proceeded to sell one pair to Gary Prenger for $37,500. Both Prenger and MRC left the ostriches with Rasmus. . . .

On September 10, 1993, Gary Baker removed several animals from the Rasmus farm and transported them to his farm. These included . . . the breeding pair purchased by the Prengers, the male purchased by MRC (by Pickard), and several juvenile ostriches. The female of the pair claimed by Pickard (MRC) was not found at this time . . . The female of the Prenger pair later died in January, 1994 . . . while at Baker's farm.

On December 22, 1993, Gary and Carol Prenger filed an action in replevin against Gene Baker alleging he wrongfully retained possession of the birds and requesting return of the birds as well as damages for the value of any birds destroyed or disposed of by Baker. MRC also filed an action in replevin against Baker seeking possession of their pair or the sum of $37,500 in the alternative.

Gene Baker answered, alleging that the birds at issue were owned by Donald Baker and himself and they were entitled to possession.

ISSUES Was Rasmus a merchant in ostriches? Were the birds in question entrusted to Rasmus, so that his subsequent sale to the buyers conveyed good title to the buyers?

continued

17.3

PRENGER V. BAKER, *continued*

542 N.W.2D 805 (IOWA 1995)

HOLDINGS Yes, to both issues.

REASONING This case is controlled by . . . the Iowa adoption of the Uniform Commercial Code. . . . The determination of whether a party to a transaction is a merchant is a question of fact . . . Additionally, the inquiry is of necessity highly dependent on the factual setting of the transaction in question. Consequently, whether a person is a merchant is to be determined according to the circumstances of each case . . . The requirement that the party "deals in goods of that kind" is generally interpreted to mean one who is engaged in regularly selling goods of the kind at issue . . . The Code defines good faith as "honesty in fact in the conduct or transaction concerned." . . . This definition has been universally interpreted to require a wholly subjective test examining what the party actually believed at the time of the transaction . . . The purpose of the good faith purchaser doctrine is to "promote commerce by reducing transaction costs"; it allows the consumer to safely purchase goods without conducting an extensive investigation of the conduct and rights of every previous possessor through the product's chain of distribution . . .

Upon examination of the records and findings of fact made by the district court, it is clear the court's finding the plaintiffs Gary and Carol Prenger and MRC have established the elements of entrustment is supported by substantial evidence. Initially, it is undisputed that the birds in issue here were delivered to Ron Rasmus by Gene Baker to be boarded at the Rasmus farm. Although the parties dispute Rasmus' status as a "merchant" under the U.C.C., the trial court's finding Rasmus is a merchant is supported by substantial evidence and sound legal principles. Whether Rasmus, a farmer, is a merchant within the meaning of the U.C.C. is clearly a question of fact dependent upon the attending circumstances . . . In Iowa this court has examined whether a farmer deals routinely in the type of goods sold, as well as whether he holds himself out as having particular skills or knowledge of the goods . . . In this case, the evidence presented clearly established Rasmus bought and sold exotic animals (including ostriches) on his own and on behalf of Gene Baker. The evidence presented established Rasmus had been in the business of raising and selling exotic animals for at least six years. Thus, the trial court's finding Rasmus was a merchant

under the U.C.C. is clearly supported by substantial evidence.

The third element, that the entrusted merchant must make a sale of the goods, is also clearly established by the evidence. There is no dispute whatsoever that Ron Rasmus sold two of the ostrich pairs to MRC for the sum of $75,000. Thus, the question then becomes whether MRC was a "buyer in the ordinary course of business," thus resulting in MRC acquiring the birds free of any outstanding title of Gene Baker, the true owner . . . The determination of whether a party is a buyer in the ordinary course of business is a question of fact . . . In order to be a buyer in the ordinary course of business, one must act in good faith with no knowledge or notice of any adverse title or ownership claims . . . This knowledge is measured at the time of the transaction at issue, the sale from Rasmus to MRC; it matters not whether the plaintiffs learned of Baker's claims at a later time . . . In this case, neither Prenger nor MRC had any knowledge of Gene Baker's interest in the birds at the time of their purchases. Therefore, they certainly qualify as buyers in the ordinary course of business and take free of any claims of Baker's. Because the trial court's findings that the elements of entrustment were established by the plaintiffs are supported by substantial evidence, the court's order establishing absolute ownership of the "Prenger male" in Gary and Carol Prenger, and the "Pickard male" in MRC is affirmed.

BUSINESS CONSIDERATIONS If a businessperson stores goods with some other party, there is a possibility that the storage will be viewed as an "entrustment." How can the businessperson protect his or her rights in this situation? Should the business have a policy outlining the procedures to be followed prior to storing or otherwise "entrusting" goods to other parties?

ETHICAL CONSIDERATIONS Is it ethical for a person who bought goods in the ordinary course of business to keep those goods despite any asserted claims by the "true" owner who entrusted the goods to a merchant, who, in turn, sold the goods to the buyer? What ethical issues are raised by situations such as this?

Insurable Interest

Insurable interest refers to the right to purchase insurance on goods to protect one's property rights and interests in the goods. The buyer gains an insurable interest when existing goods are identified to the contract, even if the goods are nonconforming. If the goods are not identified, the buyer gains an insurable interest once identification occurs. Likewise, if the goods are not yet in existence, the buyer gains an insurable interest as soon as the goods come into existence.

The seller has an insurable interest in the goods for as long as he or she retains title to or any security interest in the goods; and either party has an insurable interest if that party also has a risk of loss. Notice that title is not necessary for an insurable interest to exist.

Exhibit 17.4 on page 466 outlines the circumstances in which title and risk of loss are transferred from the seller to the buyer in the different types of sales contracts we have discussed. We will take up the subject of risk of loss in the next section.

RISK OF LOSS

Risk of loss refers to the financial responsibility between the parties if the goods are lost, damaged, or destroyed before the buyer has accepted them. Notice that the term refers to the relationship between the buyer and the seller. It does not refer to the possibility that an independent carrier of the goods may be liable. Nor does it refer to the possible liability of any insurer of the goods or of their delivery. The allocation of risk of loss often depends on the method of performance.

A buyer who has risk of loss must pay the seller for the goods if the goods were properly shipped. This situation arises most commonly in a shipment contract: If the seller shipped conforming goods, but during the journey the goods were damaged, destroyed, or lost, the buyer is liable and must perform the contract as agreed. Of course, the buyer may have recourse against the carrier or against an insurer for the loss, but such recourse involves a separate contract or relationship and does not affect the buyer's liability to the seller.

If the contract involved is a destination contract, the seller bears the risk of loss. In this situation, any lost, damaged, or destroyed goods are the responsibility of the seller. The seller will be required to ship more goods or to make up the loss to the buyer in some other manner. And the seller will then have to proceed against the carrier or the insurer for any remedies that may be available.

WHO TAKES THE LOSS?

CIT made a relatively large sale to a new customer recently. Initially, the family was delighted. The sale was significant, and their new customer, an electronic retail store, had the potential to become a major outlet for the Call-Image videophone. However, the delight turned to concern in short order. As per the contract, CIT shipped the units to the customer via Federal Parcel Service, with terms of FOB the customer's warehouse. When the goods were tendered for delivery, the only employee on duty at the customer's warehouse refused to sign for the goods or to accept delivery unless the FPS driver would unload the goods and place them in the receiving area. The driver refused to do so. As a result, the employee refused to sign for the goods. Finally, the FPS driver departed, taking the goods with him back to the FPS shipping center. Tom received a call from the customer, who explained what had happened, and he and Tom agreed that the goods should be brought back to the warehouse as soon as it was practical to do so. However, when Tom then called FPS, he was informed that the goods had been lost or stolen from the warehouse. CIT cannot fill the customer's order at this point in time, and the customer insists that he will sue for breach of contract unless he has the goods he ordered by the end of the week. Tom has asked you what the responsibility of the customer, FPS, and CIT is in this situation. He is particularly interested in the potential liability of CIT under these circumstances. What will you tell him?

BUSINESS CONSIDERATION What should a company do to ensure that goods properly tendered at its warehouse are handled correctly, protecting the interests of the buyer, the seller, and the carrier?

ETHICAL CONSIDERATION Is it ethical for a buyer to threaten to sue the seller for breach of contract when the buyer is the party who contributed the most to the breach by failing to accept a proper tender of delivery?

E X H I B I T 17.4 | **The Movement of Title and Risk of Loss**

Form of Delivery	Circumstances in Which Title Passes to Buyer, § 2-401	Circumstances in Which Risk of Loss Shifts to Buyer, § 2-509
Delivery by carrier		
• with a shipment contract	At the time and place of shipment	When carrier received goods
• with a destination contract	Upon tender of delivery	When delivery is tendered at the destination
Delivery by warehouseman		
• via negotiable document of title	Upon delivery of documents to the buyer	When buyer receives the document
• via nonnegotiable document of title	Upon delivery of documents to the buyer	After the buyer has a reasonable time to notify the bailee
• with no document of title	At the time and place of the contract	Upon the bailee's acknowledgment of the buyer's rights to the goods
Personal delivery		
• by merchant seller	At the time and place of the contract	Upon delivery of the goods to the buyer
• by nonmerchant seller	At the time and place of the contract	Upon tender of delivery of the goods

In contracts that do not involve the use of an independent carrier, the risk of loss will frequently depend on how adequately the parties have performed. Several possibilities are explored next.

Breach of Contract

If the seller breaches the contract by sending nonconforming goods, risk of loss remains with the seller until either the seller cures the defect or the buyer accepts the goods despite the nonconformity. In order for this provision to apply, the goods must be so nonconforming that the buyer may properly reject the tender of delivery. Sometimes the buyer accepts the goods that the seller sends but later finds them to be nonconforming. When this occurs, the buyer often has the right to revoke acceptance. When accepting the goods, the buyer assumes risk of loss. When the nonconformity is discovered and the acceptance is revoked, what happens? The buyer retains risk of loss, but only to the extent of his or her insurance coverage. Any loss in excess of the insurance rests on the seller.

Repudiation
Rejection of an offered or available right or privilege, or of a duty or relation.

Sometimes the buyer breaches a contract, usually by **repudiation,** after the goods are identified but before they are delivered. In such a case, risk of loss has not yet shifted from the seller to the buyer. As a result, the risk still rests on the seller. However, since the buyer is in breach, any loss in excess of the seller's insurance coverage rests on the buyer. Of course, the buyer will face this possible loss only for a commercially reasonable time.

No Breach of Contract

If the contract is not breached, risk of loss is much more technical. It is difficult to determine where risk of loss resides until the entire contract is reviewed. The UCC recognizes four distinct contract possibilities to allocate risk of loss when the contract has not been breached. In addition, the parties can agree by contract to allocate the risk.

The first situation arises in a contract whereby the seller sends the goods by means of a carrier. If the goods are sent by means of a shipment contract, risk of loss passes to the buyer when the goods are delivered to the carrier. This is true even if the seller reserves rights in the goods pending payment. In contrast, the seller may enter into a destination contract with the carrier. Risk of loss then does not pass to the buyer until the goods are properly tendered at the point of destination. Once the goods are made available to the buyer, the buyer has risk of loss.

The second situation arises when the goods are in the hands of a bailee and they are not to be physically delivered. When the bailee is holding the goods, the contract must be very carefully analyzed. The contract may call for the seller to deliver a negotiable document of title to the buyer. If so, risk of loss passes when the buyer receives the document from the seller. If the seller is not to use a negotiable document of title but does use a nonnegotiable document, risk of loss passes only after the buyer has a reasonable opportunity to present the document to the bailee. And sometimes no document at all is used. In such cases, risk of loss passes to the buyer only after the bailee acknowledges the rights of the buyer in the goods.

The third situation arises when the goods are in the possession of the seller and a carrier is not to be used. Under these circumstances, the status of the seller is the key. If the seller is a merchant, risk of loss does not pass to the buyer until the buyer takes possession of the goods. If the seller is not a merchant, risk of loss passes on tender of delivery to the buyer. The following two examples show how risk of loss varies with the status of the seller.

Joan is a used-car dealer. She enters a contract with Bob to sell him a car. She tells Bob that the keys are in the car and to go pick it up at any time. Before Bob gets there, the car is destroyed by a fire. Since Joan is a merchant, she still has risk of loss. She will have to provide Bob with another car or refund his money.

Jack is not a car dealer of any sort. He enters a contract to sell his car to Marie. He tells her that the keys are in the car and she can pick it up at any time. This is a tender of delivery. Before Marie gets the car, it is destroyed by a fire. She must bear the loss since Jack was a nonmerchant.

The fourth set of circumstances applies to a sale on approval. Here risk of loss remains with the seller until the buyer accepts the goods by approval of the sale. Of course, the various ways the buyer can accept should be kept in mind.

Finally, the parties can agree to allocate risk of loss in any way they wish. Risk of loss can be divided in any manner the parties feel is proper. Such an agreement must be very explicit, or the Code provisions just discussed will be applied.

STANDARD SHIPPING TERMS

Every shipping contract must take one of two positions: It is either a shipment contract or a destination contract. In a shipment contract, once the seller makes a proper contract for the carriage of the goods and surrenders them to the care of the carrier, the goods belong to the buyer. The buyer has title and risk of loss. The seller has performed his or her part of the contract. In contrast, in a destination contract, the seller retains title and all risk of loss until the carrier gets the goods to the buyer or wherever the goods are supposed to go under the contract. The seller has not performed until the goods reach their destination.

Under § 2-303, the parties can agree to allocate or share the risk of loss during transit. This sort of arrangement seems to be the exception rather than the rule, however. Most parties seem to ignore the problem of loss during shipment until a loss occurs. And, at that point, it is too late to begin negotiating about what to do if one occurs. Because of this normal oversight, and because so many shipments use standard terms, the UCC allocates risk of loss when the parties to a contract use any of these standard shipping terms. If the parties do not designate how loss is to be allocated, and if the contract does not specify whether it is a shipment contract or a destination contract, the law presumes that the contract is a shipment contract. Thus, once the seller properly transfers the goods to the carrier and makes arrangements for the transportation of the goods, the title and the risk of loss pass to the buyer.

FOB

FOB means "free on board." A seller frequently quotes a price for the goods to the buyer "FOB." This quoted price represents the total cost to the buyer for the goods (including any transportation or loading expenses incurred) at the place named as the FOB point. The buyer is responsible for any costs incurred beyond the FOB point named in the contract. Free on board may be either a shipment contract term or a destination contract term, depending on the place named. If the contract terms are FOB and the named place is the place of shipment (the seller's location), the contract is a shipment contract. Once the seller has the goods loaded by the carrier, the seller has performed fully. If the contract terms are FOB and the named place is the destination (the buyer's location), the contract is a destination contract. The seller has not performed until the goods arrive at the final point, and thus the seller faces the risk of damages during transit.

FAS

FAS means "free along side" and is a standard shipping term for seagoing transportation. This term is normally followed by the name of a vessel and the name of a port. When a seller quotes the price to the buyer "FAS," the seller is telling the buyer that this is the total cost of the goods, including any expenses incurred, to get the goods to the named location. Again, the buyer is responsible for any costs incurred (loading, transportation, insurance, and so on) beyond the FAS point named in the contract. The seller is required only to get the goods to the named vessel and port. Having done so, the seller has performed. The buyer then has all the risks of loading, transporting, and unloading the goods. The buyer is responsible from the dock of shipment to the buyer's location. There is a recent trend to treat FAS as a seagoing FOB term, with the term being either a shipment contract or a destination contract, depending on the named port. This current usage is gradually replacing the more traditional and more correct treatment of FAS as a shipment contract term, with *ex-ship* being the more traditional and more correct term for a destination contract.

Ex-Ship

The term *ex-ship* always involves a destination contract. The seller quotes the buyer an "ex-ship" price, which means the price the buyer is to pay to receive tender of the goods from the named ship at the named dock. Like FAS, ex-ship indicates that the transportation is by sea. However, now the seller is responsible for getting the goods both to the named vessel and port and unloaded from the vessel. Here the seller shoulders the risks of loading, transportation, and unloading the goods. Until the goods reach the destination dock, they are the seller's responsibility.

CIF and C & F

CIF means cost, insurance, freight. *C & F* means cost and freight. When either of these terms is used, the seller quotes a lump-sum price to the buyer. That single price will include the cost of the goods, the freight to get the goods to the buyer, and possibly the cost of the insurance to cover the goods during the carriage. Both terms are deemed to be shipment contracts, with the buyer assuming all the risks associated with the transportation. Under both terms, the seller pays the carrier for the transportation and then includes these freight charges as part of the price quoted to the buyer. The buyer repays the seller for the expenses of the carriage.

No Arrival, No Sale

Under a *no arrival, no sale* contract, the seller faces the risk of loss if the goods are damaged or destroyed during transit. However, even if the goods are damaged or destroyed, the seller may not be responsible to the buyer to perform the contract. If it can be shown that the seller shipped conforming goods and did not cause the loss or damage, the seller is released from the duty to perform. If the goods shipped were not conforming or if the seller caused the loss, however, the seller is still obligated to ship conforming goods.

COD

COD means collect on delivery. COD is a destination contract with a special feature: The buyer is required to pay for the goods on tender by the carrier but is not permitted to inspect the goods until payment has been made. If the buyer is unable or unwilling to pay on tender, the goods are returned to the seller, and the buyer is likely to be sued and found liable for breach of contract.

CALL-IMAGE TECHNOLOGY

METHODS OF SELLING

CIT is having some difficulty gaining adequate shelf space in a number of retail outlets, and this is causing Tom some concern. Lindsay is interested in music, and she knows that many musical instruments are sold by stores that carry a wide range of brand names and cover a large price range. She asked the manager of one such store how he manages to carry so many brands at such diverse prices and was told that many of the instruments were on consignment. She has suggested to the family that they might want to offer a consignment arrangement to the retail store in order to acquire shelf space. John would prefer to use some other method of selling, perhaps a sale or return or a sale on approval. Anna asks what you recommend they do. What will you tell her? What benefits might CIT realize by using a consignment arrangement? What drawbacks might be encountered?

BUSINESS CONSIDERATIONS A firm trying to break into an established industry might have to decide between trying to gain a market share through price competition or using a nonstandard marketing method, such as a sale or return arrangement. What are the benefits to using sale or return rather than reduced price to gain market recognition and share? What are the potential drawbacks to this approach?

ETHICAL CONSIDERATION The rights of the creditors of a retail merchant are different in regard to the merchant's inventory if the merchant has goods through a consignment or a sale or return. If the merchant carries inventory under both bases, what are the ethical obligations of that merchant to provide its creditors with adequate information regarding the inventory?

SPECIAL PROBLEMS

The commercial world is crowded with businesses trying to get, or trying to keep, "a foot in the door"; or just looking for a new gimmick that will provide an edge. As a result, some special forms of business dealings have arisen. The UCC has attempted to deal with two of these special areas: sale on approval and sale or return. Both these forms of business dealings resemble yet another: consignments. The Code deals with these special areas in §§ 2-326 and 2-327.

Sale on Approval

A *sale on approval* exists if the buyer "purchases" goods primarily for personal use with the understanding that the goods can be returned, even if they conform to the contract. The buyer is given a reasonable time to examine, inspect, and try the goods at the seller's risk. Neither title nor risk of loss passes to the buyer until and unless the buyer accepts the goods. The seller retains both title and risk of loss during the buyer's "approval" period even though the buyer has possession of the goods. The buyer is deemed to have accepted the goods if one of the following occurs:

1. The buyer signifies acceptance.
2. The buyer does not return the goods.
3. The buyer subjects the goods to unreasonable usage.

The following example involves a contract for sale on approval.

Sam "purchases" a new lawn mower with a 30-day "free home trial." He uses the mower six times in three weeks, cutting his lawn and in no way abusing the product. After the third week, Sam returns the mower and refuses to pay the purchase price. Since this was a sale on approval and Sam never approved, he is not responsible for payment.

Sale or Return

A *sale or return* exists if the buyer "purchases" goods primarily for resale with the understanding that the unsold goods may be returned to the seller even if they conform to the contract. In this situation, both title and risk of loss lie with the goods. Goods stolen from the buyer cannot be returned, so they are "sold" to the buyer. The seller must be paid for them. The following example indicates how the purpose of a sale or return differs from the purpose of a sale on approval.

Sam "purchases" some automobile stereo systems from Smooth Sounds, Inc., on a sale-or-return contract. Sam displays one of the stereos in his service station. If a customer wants an auto stereo system, Sam will sell it and install it. Sam can return any unsold units to Smooth Sounds for a refund or for credit on future goods. However, a thief breaks into Sam's station and steals the stereos. Sam must pay Smooth Sounds for the stereos since he cannot return them.

Consignment

In a *consignment*, the owner of the goods allows a consignee to display and sell the goods for the owner/consignor. The UCC treats such an arrangement as a sale or return unless one of the following occurs:

1. The consignor ensures that signs are posted specifying that the goods on display are consigned goods.
2. The consignor proves that the creditors of the consignee were generally aware of the consignments.
3. The consignor complies with the rules for secured transactions under Article 9 of the UCC.

Obviously, the Code has limited, if not eliminated, consignment in the modern business world. Most such arrangements today are treated merely as sale-or-return contracts.

Auctions

Auctions receive special mention in § 2-328. In an auction, the auctioneer, on behalf of the seller, sells the goods to the highest bidder. The auctioneer does not normally give the same warranties to a buyer that other sellers of goods give. A sale at auction is not complete until the auctioneer accepts a bid. Even then, if a bid is made while the auctioneer is in the process of **knocking down,** he or she may elect to reopen bidding. The goods at an auction are presumed to be put up "with reserve." An auction will be deemed "without reserve" only if, by its terms, it is specifically and expressly stated to be "without reserve." With reserve means that the auctioneer may declare all the bids to be too low and may refuse to accept any bids or to make any sale. In contrast, if the auction is without reserve, the highest bid made must be accepted and a sale made.

What if the seller enters a bid, directly or indirectly, in an effort to drive up the bidding? The winning bidder in such a case may choose to renounce his or her bidding and to avoid the sale or may elect to take the goods at the last good-faith bid before the seller entered the bidding.

LEASES

Like Article 2, Article 2A is not overly concerned with the concept of title. Article 2A specifically separates title and possession. It states that the provisions governing leases apply whether the lessor or a third party has title to the leased goods, and whether the lessor, the lessee, or a third party has possession of the leased goods.

Risk of loss with respect to the leased goods varies depending on the type of lease involved. In a finance lease, risk of loss passes to the lessee under the provisions of § 2A-219. If the lease is other than a finance lease, risk of loss is retained by the lessor. If the leased goods are in the hands of a bailee *and* risk of loss is to

17.3 | MANAGEMENT

LEASE ARRANGEMENTS FOR CALL-IMAGE

A regional corporation has expressed interest in acquiring Call-Image telephones for each of its offices in the region, a total of 200 units. However, this firm does not want to purchase the equipment, proposing instead that they enter into a lease arrangement with CIT. Anna thinks that the firm should make the contract, believing that the exposure to customers of the other firm will help increase sales. Tom is concerned that such an arrangement will present more problems for the firms than benefits. They have asked you for your advice. What will you tell them? If the firm does enter into the lease arrangement, who will face risk of loss for any damages to the equipment? Might this be a significant factor in making the decision whether to enter the contract?

BUSINESS CONSIDERATIONS What burdens does a business face in leasing its equipment that it would not face in selling the equipment? What benefits accrue to a firm through a lease that might not accrue through a sale? **ETHICAL CONSIDERATIONS** Assume that a large business is about to make a contract with a small supplier and that both parties know this contract will make or break the small firm. Should the business use its size to "persuade" a small supplier to make a lease rather than a sale when the small supplier would prefer to sell goods than to lease them? Should the business use its size to "persuade" a small supplier to sell it goods when the small supplier would prefer to lease them?

Knocking down
The acceptance of a bid by an auctioneer, signified by the falling of the gavel after the announcement that the goods are "Going, going, gone."

RESOURCES FOR BUSINESS LAW STUDENTS

NAME	RESOURCES	WEB ADDRESS
Uniform Commercial Code (UCC) Article 2, Sales	The Legal Information Institute (LII), maintained by the Cornell Law School, provides a hypertext and searchable version of the UCC's Article 2, Sales. LII also provides links to Article 2 as enacted by states and to proposed revisions.	http://www.law.cornell.edu/ucc/2/overview.html
UCC Article 2A, Leases	LII provides a hypertext and searchable version of the UCC's Article 2A, Leases. LII also provides links to Article 2A as enacted by states and to proposed revisions.	http://www.law.cornell.edu/ucc/2A/overview.html
UCC Article 7, Warehouse Receipts, Bills of Lading, and Other Documents of Title	LII provides a hypertext and searchable version of the UCC's Article 7, Warehouse Receipts, Bills of Lading, and Other Documents of Title. LII also provides links to Article 7 as enacted by a particular state and to proposed revisions.	http://www.law.cornell.edu/ucc/7/overview.html

pass to the lessee, rules similar to those under Article 2 are followed in allocating risk of loss:

- If the goods are in the possession of a bailee and delivery is to occur without movement of the goods, risk of loss passes to the lessee on the bailee's acknowledgment of the lessee's right to possession of the goods. (Since there is not a sale, there will not be a document of title involved in such a situation.)
- If the goods are to be delivered to the lessee by a carrier, the carriage contract is presumed to be a shipment contract, passing risk of loss to the lessee when the goods are duly delivered to the carrier. If a destination contract is specified, risk of loss passes to the lessee when the goods are duly tendered at the destination.
- If the goods are to be delivered to the lessee by the lessor, passage of risk of loss depends on the status of the lessor. If the lessor (or the supplier, in the case of a finance lease) is a merchant, risk of loss passes to the lessee when the goods are actually delivered to the lessee. If the lessor is not a merchant, risk of loss passes to the lessee on tender of delivery.

SUMMARY

In this chapter, we examine the concept and importance of title to goods. Under the UCC, title passes at any time the parties agree. If the parties do not agree, title passes when the seller completes his or her performance. Title can revest in the seller if the buyer refuses to accept the goods, rejects them, or revokes the acceptance. The primary area in which title is important today is that of creditor rights.

In the performance of a sales contract, each party has some duty or duties to perform, and each has some rights that may be asserted. The seller is to tender delivery of conforming goods as per the contract. The buyer is to accept and pay for the goods so tendered. The buyer normally has the right to inspect the goods before accepting or paying. If the inspection discloses any defects, the seller frequently has the right to cure, or correct, the defect in the goods or in the performance.

The concept of risk of loss is much more important under the Code than it is under common law. Risk of loss refers to the party—buyer or seller—who must bear the burden of lost, damaged, or destroyed goods when the loss occurs during the performance stage of the contract. Risk of loss is allocated in a similar manner in both a sale of goods and in the leasing of goods under a finance lease. In a non-finance lease, risk of loss remains with the lessor throughout the lease.

The parties to a sale often use standard shipping terms. These terms have been defined by the UCC as forming either a shipment contract or a destination contract. In a shipment contract, the buyer bears the risks of loss or damage during transportation. In a destination contract, the seller bears the risks of loss or damage during transportation.

Some special problems have developed from modern business practices. Before the adoption of the UCC, consignments were frequently used to sell goods. Today, consignments have virtually been replaced by sale-on-approval and sale-or-return contracts. Each of these areas is specifically treated under Article 2. Special treatment is also provided for consignments and for auctions under Article 2.

Article 2A separates title and possession and allocates risk of loss to the parties based on the type of lease contract involved. In a finance lease, risk of loss passes to the lessee in the same manner as risk of loss passes to the buyer in a sales contract. For example, if a carrier is involved, the passage of risk of loss is determined by whether the delivery is a shipment contract or a destination contract. If the lease is other than a finance lease, risk of loss remains with the lessor and does not pass to the lessee.

DISCUSSION QUESTIONS

1. According to the UCC, what constitutes a proper *tender of delivery* by the seller in a sales contract? Does the type of delivery called for in the contract determine what is required of the seller in order to have a proper "tender"?

2. What is the legal effect of a *shipment* contract as compared with that of a *destination* contract when the seller hires a common carrier to deliver the goods to the buyer? How can a party tell if the delivery terms involve a shipment contract or a destination contract?

3. Suppose that goods are to be *consigned* to a merchant for sale. What would the owner/consignor need to show in order to establish that the goods in the hands of the merchant were consigned goods rather than goods that had been sold under a sale-or-return

(or other sales) contract? Why might the owner/consignor want or need to establish that a consignment exists?

4. Biltless Mfg. sends goods to Smart Set Co. under a "no arrival, no sale" contract. After the goods are sent but before they arrive, Biltless learns that it can double its profit by selling the goods to another buyer in another market. Assume that Biltless is able to recover the goods from the carrier before the goods are tendered to Smart Set. What rights can Smart Set assert against Biltless in this situation? Explain.

5. Chen, a merchant, sends Roy some goods under a contract. Roy is to receive the goods by 18 December. On 12 December, Roy receives nonconforming goods from Chen, and Roy promptly calls Chen to inform

her of the nonconformity. What are Chen's rights and duties under these circumstances? What can Chen do to avoid being sued for breach of the contract?

6. Under Article 2 of the Uniform Commercial Code, when does title pass from the seller to the buyer? When does risk of loss pass from the seller to the buyer? Under Article 2A, when does risk of loss pass from the lessor or supplier to the lessee?

7. Ralph operates a repair shop in the local community. While Ralph repairs all sorts of things, he does not sell anything on a regular basis. Harvey takes his watch to Ralph's Repair Shop and asks Ralph to fix it. After the watch is repaired, but before Harvey returns to pay for the repairs, one of Ralph's employees innocently sells Harvey's watch to another customer. The customer buys the watch in good faith, with no knowledge or notice of Harvey's rights or claims on the watch. Who has title to the watch? What should Harvey do in this situation?

8. Marge, a merchant, sold goods to Dennis, receiving payment in full at the time the contract was made. Dennis is to pick up the goods from Marge's store later in the day. When Dennis arrives to pick up the goods, he discovers that they were damaged when they were removed from the showroom floor and taken to the loading dock. Marge insists that, since Dennis has already paid for the goods, he owns them, and he is

therefore responsible for the loss due to the damage. Is Marge correct or not? Explain your reasoning.

9. George sold some goods to Dana but retained possession of them. Several of George's creditors discover the location of the goods, and they attempt to attach these goods to cover the debts George owes them. These creditors allege that the sale to Dana is void as to the creditors since George retained possession of the goods after the sale. George and Dana both insist that the transaction is perfectly valid and that the creditors should not be able to assert any rights to the goods. What must George and/or Dana prove in order to avoid the claims of George's creditors? Has the enactment of Article 2A changed the potential rights of George and Dana?

10. A lessor entered into a 12-month lease contract with a lessee. The goods leased were to be delivered by a common carrier. The contract between the lessor carrier called for a COD delivery. The lessee was to pay the entire lease price plus the delivery fees on tender of delivery by the carrier. When the carrier tendered delivery, the lessee paid the amount owed, unloaded the goods, and inspected them. On inspection, it was determined that the goods had been damaged during shipment. Between the lessor and the lessee, who has risk of loss in this situation? What factor(s) are key in deciding this case?

CASE PROBLEMS AND WRITING ASSIGNMENTS

1. In an attempt to feather their nest, as it were, the Doners decided to invest in the burgeoning, albeit risky, ostrich breeding and production industry. Ostriches are promoted as an alternative food source and, coupled with the demand for their feathers and leather, are completely consumable. The potential rewards of the investment are great: Mr. Doner stated that the hen he purchased from the Snapps for $3,000 was worth at least $20,000 three years later, although she had yet to lay a fertile egg. The risks of the business include ostrich infertility and mortality.

The appellants purchased a "trio" of ostrich chicks by oral agreement from the appellees in 1990 for $9,000. In breeders' parlance, a "trio" means two hens and one male. One male may mate with as many as three hens. The appellants' bid to build a nest egg suffered a bad break in early 1991, when they discovered that their "trio" consisted of two males and one hen. Mr. Doner testified that his first knowledge of the error came when the darker features and feathers of the males appeared. Mr. Snapp testified that it can be difficult to determine an ostrich's sex, and that he had advised Mr. Doner to have the birds' sex confirmed within 90 days of the sale. Mr. Doner denied that he

had been so counseled. There also was disputed testimony as to whether the appellees agreed to exchange a hen for one of the males on learning of the alleged breach. In any event, no agreement was reached between the parties. Rather than bury their heads in the sand, the appellants traded both of their male ostriches in 1992, one to a Michigan breeder for another male of equal value and the other to an Indiana supplier for two female chicks. Since ostrich hens do not mature sexually for three years, the younger hens have not been bred. The hen purchased from the appellants has not produced any offspring. The record indicates that the appellants also acquired another hen, now of breeding age, from the Michigan breeder. This particular hen has produced offspring.

The appellants filed suit against appellees for breach of contract on 15 June 1993. The appellants requested compensatory damages of $15,000 plus lost profits. The appellees filed a motion for summary judgment, asserting that appellants had not raised a genuine issue of material fact on the issue of liability, specifically that the appellants had suffered damage from the alleged breach. The trial judge granted appellees' motion, and the appellants appealed. Did the buyers establish that they had suffered any damages in this case? [See *Doner* v. *Snapp*, 649 N.E.2d 42 (OhioApp. 1994).]

2. In July, the Stephensons purchased a modular home from Frazier. The contract price of $22,500 included the installation of a septic system and the construction of a foundation for the home, both on property owned by the Stephensons. During the installation of the modular home, the Stephensons complained to Frazier about a number of alleged defects in the home and in the foundation that was being constructed. The Stephensons also asserted that the foundation was being built improperly. Frazier replied that the foundation was "100 percent" and that, if they did not like the work, they could take him to court. At that point, the Stephensons ordered Frazier and his crew off of their property and told them the property was "off limits" to them. The Stephensons then notified Frazier that they intended to rescind the contract. Were the Stephensons entitled to rescind the contract and recover their purchase price? Explain. [See *Stephenson* v. *Frazier*, 399 N.E.2d 794 (Ind.App. 1980).]

3. Raveis is a real estate company that sought computerized capacity to provide efficient interconnections between its multiple offices and the various banks with which it dealt. Latham & Assoc., aware of Raveis's needs and of its reliance on Latham's expertise to satisfy these needs, undertook to provide two computer systems that would meet those needs. (Latham misrepresented the extent of its expertise in creating functioning computer systems in order to persuade Raveis to enter into the contracts.)

   The parties entered into two contracts for the delivery of computer systems. The first contract, dated 15 October 1982, called for Latham to deliver hardware and software for a so-called real estate system. Raveis made all scheduled payments under this contract. The second contract, dated 25 March 1984, called for Latham to develop and install a second computer system, the so-called mortgage system. Because of dissatisfaction with the performance of the software tendered under both contracts, Raveis did not fully pay license fees or software support charges for the mortgage system.

   Latham sued to recover the amounts unpaid on the mortgage system; Raveis counterclaimed to recover the payments it had made and the damages it had incurred with respect to the software on both systems. Raveis contended that the software it received did not conform to the express warranties given by Latham in the sale and that it had properly rejected the software in a reasonable and timely manner. Raveis presented no expert testimony in support of its claims that the software did not conform to the warranties allegedly given by Latham. Despite the lack of any expert testimony, the trial court ruled for Raveis, awarding damages of $81,500, and Latham appealed. Latham's appeal focused on (1) the lack of expert testimony at trial; (2) the fact that Raveis delayed too long in attempting to reject the computer systems, thus "accepting" due to an improper rejection of the goods; and (3) the fact that there were no express warranties given to Raveis in the contract. Did Raveis have to present expert testimony in order to establish the breach of any express warranties? Did Raveis reject the goods in a timely and reasonable manner? Was Raveis entitled to damages, or was it restricted to the recovery of monies paid? [See *Latham & Assocs.* v. *Raveis Real Estate*, 589 A.2d 337 (Conn. 1991).]

4. In March 1975, Nahim Amar B., a resident of Mexico, entered into a contract with Karinol, an exporting company operating out of Miami. The terms of the contract, contained in a one-page invoice written in Spanish, called for Amar to purchase 64 electronic watches for $6,006. A notation at the bottom of the contract read: "Please send the merchandise in cardboard boxes duly strapped with metal bands via air parcel post to Chetumal. Documents to Banco de Commercio de Quintana Roo, S.A." There were no provisions in the contract specifically allocating the risk of loss while the goods were in the possession of the carrier, nor were any standard shipping terms used. The evidence established that on 11 April 1975 Karinol properly packaged and shipped the watches to Belize, Central America, to an agent of Amar. The cartons arrived in Belize on 15 April and were stored in the air freight cargo room. On 2 May, Amar's agent opened the boxes and discovered that there were no watches in the boxes. Mr. Pestana, as the representative of Amar (who died in the interim), sued Karinol and its insurer, alleging that the watches were lost or stolen while under the care and control of Karinol and while Karinol had risk of loss. Karinol filed a cross-complaint alleging that Amar had risk of loss and that Karinol was thus not liable. Which party had risk of loss in this case? Why? [*See Pestana* v. *Karinol Corp.*, 367 So.2d 1096 (Fla.App. 1979)].

5. Kingston 1686 House is a restaurant in Kingston, New Hampshire. Law Warehouse stores wine for the state of New Hampshire. B.S.P. is a common carrier. Kingston House ordered 40 cases of wine from Law Warehouse, asking that a carrier be used to deliver the wine. Law Warehouse, in turn, hired B.S.P. as a carrier. B.S.P. attempted to deliver the wine the following Monday, a day on which the restaurant was normally

closed. The only employee on the premises that Monday was an elderly vice president of the restaurant. The driver informed this employee that he would need help in unloading the wine. The employee refused to help, and B.S.P. had the wine returned to its warehouse for storage. Thereafter, B.S.P. refused to deliver the wine unless the restaurant agreed to pay the original delivery charges, storage charges, and a redelivery charge. The restaurant refused to pay any charges beyond the original delivery charges and sued B.S.P. for conversion. B.S.P. countered that it had made a proper tender of delivery, delivery had been refused, and it was entitled to all of the charges for which it sought payment. Should the attempted delivery of goods by a carrier to a consignee at a time when the consignee's business is normally closed be considered a proper tender of delivery? Should the carrier be allowed to refuse to deliver the goods until the consignee paid extra delivery and storage charges? [See *Kingston 1686 House, Inc. v. B.S.P. Transportation, Inc.,* 427 A.2d 9 (N.H. 1981).]

6. **BUSINESS APPLICATION CASE** In 1989, Michael Heinrich wished to buy a particular model new Ford pickup truck. James Wilson held himself out as a dealer/broker, licensed to buy and sell vehicles. Heinrich retained Wilson to make the purchase but did not direct Wilson to any particular automobile dealer. Unbeknownst to Heinrich, Wilson had lost his Washington vehicle dealer license the previous year.

Wilson negotiated with Titus-Will for the purchase of a Ford pickup truck with Heinrich's desired options. Titus-Will had been involved in hundreds of transactions with Wilson over the years and also was unaware that Wilson was no longer licensed to act as a vehicle dealer.

Heinrich made two initial payments to Wilson: an $1,800 down payment and a $3,000 payment when Titus-Will ordered the truck. Wilson gave Heinrich a receipt using a "Used Car Wholesale Purchase Order" that displayed Wilson's alleged vehicle dealer license number. Wilson then ordered the truck from Titus-Will, using his own check to make a $7,000 down payment. The purchase order indicated that the truck was being sold to Wilson. "Dealer" was written in the space on the form for tax. Wilson told the Titus-Will salesman handling the sale that he was ordering the truck for resale.

On 13 October 1989, Wilson told Heinrich that the truck was ready for delivery. Heinrich paid Wilson $15,549.55 as final payment, including tax and license fees. Wilson gave Heinrich a copy of the purchase order and of an options checklist with corresponding prices. These documents indicated that Wilson was buying the truck from Titus-Will. The

Titus-Will salesman had signed off on the options list; Wilson marked it "paid in full" and signed it after Heinrich paid him. On the same day, at Wilson's behest, Heinrich signed a Washington application for motor vehicle title.

Wilson agreed to deliver the truck to Heinrich at Titus-Will on Saturday, 21 October 1989. He arranged with a Titus-Will salesman to deliver a check on the morning of 21 October to a clerk in the Titus-Will office and, in return, to receive the truck keys and paperwork. The clerk accepted Wilson's check for $11,288, postdated to Monday, 23 October 1989, and delivered to Wilson a packet containing the keys to the truck, the owner's manual, an odometer disclosure statement, and a warranty card. The odometer statement . . . showed Wilson as the transferor. Titus-Will did not fill out the warranty card with the name and address of the purchaser because the sale appeared to be dealer to dealer, with the warranty to benefit the ultimate purchaser.

Titus-Will retained the manufacturer's certificate of origin. The certificate of origin is apparently a "pre-title" document used to obtain state title documents when a car is sold to a nondealer. Titus-Will, believing this to be a dealer-to-dealer transaction, planned to give the certificate to Wilson when his check cleared.

Wilson immediately taped Heinrich's application for title in the rear window of the truck that was parked on the Titus-Will lot. When Heinrich arrived, Wilson gave him the keys and the documents and Heinrich drove off.

Wilson's check did not clear. Titus-Will demanded return of the truck. On 6 November, Wilson picked up the truck from Heinrich, telling him he would have Titus-Will make certain repairs under the warranty. Wilson returned the truck to Titus-Will.

On 9 November 1989, Wilson admitted to Heinrich that he did not have funds to cover the check to Titus-Will and that Titus-Will would not release the truck without payment. Heinrich sued Titus-Will and Wilson, seeking replevin of the truck and damages of his loss of use. Heinrich obtained a default judgment against Wilson. He also won title to the truck and $3,500 in damages in his trial against Titus-Will, who appealed. Did Titus-Will entrust the truck to Wilson, giving him voidable title and permitting him to pass valid title to Heinrich, a buyer in the ordinary course of business? From a business perspective, what should Titus-Will have done to protect itself? [See *Heinrich v. Titus-Will Sales, Inc.,* 868 P.2d 169 (Wash. App. 1994).]

7. **ETHICAL APPLICATION CASE** The Bernings owned a Chevrolet van that was in good condition

and had only been driven 40,000 miles. In 1988, the Bernings discovered that the van had water in the oil and would not start. They had it towed to Drumwright, a mechanic, for repairs. Drumwright told them that he would need to remove the engine to determine the problem. He then gave them three alternatives: rebuild the engine at a cost of $1,200; have Drumwright work on the engine at an hourly rate, without a price estimate; or have a secondhand engine installed. He also informed them that he had a secondhand engine "with good compression" that he could install for about $800. The Bernings elected to go with the secondhand engine. Five weeks later, the engine was installed, but there were a few problems: The engine that was installed was not a van engine and did not fit properly in the van; in order to check the engine oil, the firewall, radio, and other equipment had to be removed; the engine tended to overheat and to consume about one quart of oil every 50 miles; and the engine frequently stopped and would not restart. The Bernings then took the van to another mechanic, where they purchased a newly rebuilt engine and a new manifold for $2,000. They then sued Drumwright for his alleged "grossly incompetent auto repair," seeking to revoke their acceptance of the engine and to recover their costs for his work. Drumwright claimed that he had not been paid for his labor, nor had he been paid for the engine. He sought the return of the engine, rental for the miles the secondhand engine had been used to propel the van, and payment for his labor.

Did the Bernings rightfully revoke their acceptance of the engine provided by Drumwright? Did Drumwright have a right to cure the alleged defects in the engine, a right that was denied him by the buyers? Is it ethical for a merchant to attempt to collect for "rental" or usage from a buyer who has rejected the goods or revoked his or her acceptance if those goods were used prior to the discovery of the alleged defects that led to the rejection/revocation? [See *Berning* v. *Drumwright*, 832 P.2d 1138 (Idaho App. 1992).]

8. **CRITICAL THINKING CASE** H. Sand & Co. accepted a subcontract from Carlin-Atlas Joint Venture to install the heating and air conditioning in the reconstruction and expansion of the New York Port Authority Bus Terminal in Manhattan. On 6 June 1977, Sand ordered four chillers from Airtemp Corp., to be used in the air conditioning system that Sand was installing. All four chillers were shipped to Sand by Associated Rigging and Hauling, the agent of Sand. The shipments were made between January and March 1978. One of the chillers (chiller #4) was not tested prior to shipping, allegedly because Airtemp was in the process of relocating its testing facility at the time this chiller was ready for transportation. In November 1978, chiller #4 was sent to the new Airtemp testing center for a test run. This was authorized and paid for by Airtemp. After testing the chiller, Airtemp shipped it back to Associated Rigging and Hauling in January 1979. Sand installed the four chillers in the renovated building as per its contract with Carlin-Atlas.

The chillers were started up for the first time in mid-1980. Sand states that, shortly after being started, the chillers exhibited defects. Airtemp was contacted regarding these problems, but Airtemp refused to perform any repair work without additional payment. As a result, Sand made the repairs itself and withheld $10,000 of the purchase price. The Port Authority officially accepted the equipment on 23 May 1981. On 16 December 1982, Sand sued Airtemp's parent corporation, Fedders, in the Supreme Court of New York County for damages arising from the defects in the chillers. The parties agreed to dismiss the action without prejudice to allow Sand to bring its suit in federal court, and further stipulated that the action be deemed to have commenced on 16 December 1982 for statute-of-limitations purposes. After Sand brought its suit in federal court, Airtemp asserted the statute of limitations as a bar to the case and filed a counterclaim for the withheld $10,000.

After a number of other legal maneuverings, including a claim by the Port Authority of New York against Carlin-Atlas for $650,000 for expenses incurred due to the defective chillers, Airtemp filed a motion for summary judgment. The district court granted the motion and dismissed Sand's action as time-barred under the New York Uniform Commercial Code. Sand appealed from this order. When did tender of delivery of the chillers occur? (If the chillers were tendered between January and March 1978, the action would be barred by the statute of limitations. If tender of delivery was made in January 1979, the suit was filed within the statutory time limit.) What factors should the court examine in reaching its conclusion in this matter? [See *H. Sand & Co., Inc.* v. *Airtemp Corp.*, 934 F.2d 450 (2d Cir. 1991).]

NOTE

1. "Roanoke's Cleanup of Clunkers Rolls Right Along," *Roanoke Times* (24 May 1999), p. C-1.

18

WARRANTIES AND PRODUCT LIABILITY

A G E N D A

While most consumers likely will be pleased with Call-Image, some customers will encounter problems. The family, therefore, must establish a warranty strategy for Call-Image. Should the firm attempt to exclude as many warranty provisions as possible, or should it offer wide warranty protections? Assuming that warranties will be given, should the firm offer a full or a limited warranty under the Magnuson-Moss Act? What should be printed on the box used to package the Call-Image videophone? What warranty information should be packaged with the product?

These and other questions may arise in covering the material in this chapter. Be prepared! You never know when one of the Kochanowskis will need your help or advice.

O U T L I N E

INTRODUCTION

A *warranty* is defined as "a promise that a proposition of fact is true."[1] Since a warranty involves a promise, it becomes a part of the contract. This is especially important in the sale of goods. Warranty protection is very often the best protection that a buyer can have in a sale. There are two types of warranties in sales: **express** and **implied.** (There are also **statutory** warranty provisions, but these tend to be informational rather than coverage based.) The fact that one type of warranty is present does not mean that the other type is absent. In fact, both types will frequently be present in one contract.

At common law, the courts presume that the parties to a contract have equal bargaining power. The courts also strongly believe in "freedom of contract." Thus, they are reluctant to interfere in the contractual relationship. Historically, the rule of caveat emptor—let the buyer beware—was regularly followed. As the commercial world matured, the relative positions of the parties to a sales contract began to change. Businesses grew larger, and the location of the business became more likely to be removed from the location of the individual buyer. The parties became less likely to have equal bargaining power. It was also less likely that the seller of the goods had also manufactured them. The courts and legislatures began to seek means of protecting consumers. Implied warranties (and statutory warranty provisions) and product liability provided those means. The consumer has thus now become so protected that many people feel the modern rule of commerce is caveat venditor—let the seller beware!

Express
Actually stated; communicated from one party to another.

Implied
Presumed to be present under the circumstances; tacit.

Statutory
Created by statute; imposed by law.

EXPRESS WARRANTIES

An *express warranty* can only be given by the seller; it is not present until such time as the seller gives it. However, once given, such a warranty is said by the UCC to be a part of "the basis of the bargain." Section 2-313 mentions three different ways in which the seller creates an express warranty.

1. Any affirmation of a fact or a promise that relates to the goods creates an express warranty that the goods will match the fact or the promise.
2. Any description of the goods creates an express warranty that the goods will match the description.
3. Any sample or model of the goods creates an express warranty that the goods will conform to the sample or the model.

Any of these three methods creates an express warranty if it is a part of "the basis of the bargain." It is not necessary for the seller to use words such as *warrant* or *guarantee.* It is not even necessary for the seller to *intend* to create an express warranty. All that is necessary is that the seller employ one of these methods in a manner that causes the buyer to reasonably believe that a warranty covering the goods has been given.

The Uniform Sales Act, which preceded the UCC, required the buyer to show reliance before an express warranty was found. The UCC seems to have removed the requirement of proving reliance. Instead, reliance appears to be presumed. The rule under the Code is that the seller must disprove the existence of an express warranty. In other words, if the buyer can prove the seller affirmed a fact, described the goods, or used a model or a sample, an express warranty is presumed. To disprove the existence of the warranty, the seller must show proof that the conduct

18.1 | MARKETING/ SALES

CALL-IMAGE TECHNOLOGY

ADVERTISING CALL-IMAGE

Tom wants to advertise the Call-Image videophones extensively on television, preferably with the ads showing the product in use. Dan and John agree with Tom in principle, but they suggest that the ads should be enhanced somewhat to show the product in the best possible light. They have suggested using a larger viewing screen on the unit used in the commercial, so that the images being transmitted are more striking, and they have also suggested that the images should be enhanced if possible. Anna objects to this. She believes that any ads should show only what the product is currently capable of performing. She has, however, agreed to defer to the family in this decision. Tom recognizes the marketing strength of the suggestion by Dan and John, but he also respects Anna's insights and integrity. He has asked you what the firm should do in this situation. What advice will you give?

BUSINESS CONSIDERATIONS Visual ads can be very effective, especially with the technological devices available today. Computer enhancements can place famous people in contemporary settings, and "morphing" can allow the advertiser to transform products from or to something else. While such ads can be effective, they can also be misleading. How much care should an advertiser take to ensure that an ad does not create express warranties that the advertiser will then have to honor? What should the advertiser tell the advertising agency in an effort to protect the advertiser's interests?

ETHICAL CONSIDERATION Many fast-food video commercials use mock-ups of the food being advertised because the lights and the time that a commercial can require often cause the food being advertised to become dry and visually unappetizing. From an ethical perspective, should these commercials include some disclaiming language informing the viewers that the "food" in the commercial is not an actual product? Explain.

described by the buyer was not the basis of the bargain. If such proof cannot be shown, the express warranty is included in the contract.

Express warranties focus on facts. Mere opinions of the seller are not taken to be warranties. The seller is also allowed a certain amount of puffing. However, there is often a fine line between opinion and fact, and the seller should be extremely careful. If a statement is **quantifiable,** it is likely to be treated as a fact. If the statement is **relative,** it normally will be treated as an opinion. Thus, the statement "this car gets 30 miles per gallon" likely would be treated as a warranty. But the statement "this is a good car" likely would not be a warranty. The problem lies with comments that fall between these two extremes.

Exhibit 18.1 illustrates the difficulty faced by the court in deciding whether something is a matter of fact or a matter of opinion. There is a great deal of gray area between things that are obvious facts and those that are obviously opinion, and the court has the task of deciding whether something within this gray area is a fact or an opinion.

If a statement that falls between an obvious fact and an obvious opinion was made by the seller, the court must decide how to interpret this statement in terms of warranty protections. To do so, the court must weigh the relative knowledge of the parties, the reliance (if any) the buyer placed on the seller, the likelihood that the seller was aware of any reliance, and any other pertinent facts that influence the balancing of interests of the two parties. Thus, if the seller conveyed an impression that seemed to be based on facts to the buyer, the court may decide that there was an assertion of facts and therefore may find that an express warranty exists, despite the intent of the seller.

The seller also needs to be careful in advertising. Advertisements that claim certain characteristics for a product may also be treated by the courts as affirmations of fact and thus as express warranties. The following example shows how an advertisement may be viewed by the court in an express warranty case.

A television advertisement for the Pick Pen Company, manufacturers of disposable ballpoint pens, shows a couple on a picnic. The couple removes a can of fruit juice from the picnic hamper, only to discover that they forgot to bring a can opener. One of them reaches into a pocket, removes a Pick Pen, and uses the uncapped pen to punch a hole in the top of the can. The couple smiles, the camera pulls back, and a voice solemnly intones, "Pick Pens! For 79¢, it's not just a great writing instrument."

A customer who has seen this commercial decides to use his or her Pick Pen to open a can. Unfortunately for the customer—and for the Pick Pen Company— the pen shatters and plastic shards enter the customer's wrist and hand, causing serious injury to the customer during this attempted use. A good argument could be made that the commercial had created a belief in the mind of the customer that this use was expressly warranted by the commercial. If, however, the Pick Pen Company used a disclaimer in the commercial—normally by scrolling script across the bottom of the screen—the courts might be less likely to find that the commercial created an express warranty.

Finally, the Code considers the timing of the statement or conduct from the buyer's perspective. Under § 2-209(1), a modification of a sales contract is valid without *consideration*. This means that the seller can create an express warranty before the contract is formed (through sales talk, negotiations, or even commercials); while forming the contract (in the language used in the agreement or in oral commitments made while forming the writing); or even after the contract is formed (through continued reassurances to the buyer that he or she has made a "good deal"). As a result, sellers should remember two things:

1. If they know a fact, they should state it honestly.
2. If they do not know a fact, they should not speculate! It is too easy to give an express warranty without realizing it.

Wat Henry Pontiac Co. v. *Bradley*[2] is one of the landmark cases in express warranty law. In 1944, Mrs. Bradley went to the Wat Henry Pontiac Company to purchase a used car. Mrs. Bradley asked many questions, and the seller assured her that the car in question was in good condition. When Mrs. Bradley stated that she had to drive to Camp Shelby, Mississippi, with her seven-month-old child to see her husband, the salesman allegedly said: "This is a car I can recommend" and "It is in A-1 shape." However, Mrs. Bradley was not allowed to take a "test drive" in the car, allegedly because of wartime gas rationing. Eventually, Mrs. Bradley bought the car and drove it home. Several days later, after she set out for Camp Shelby, the car broke down and required extensive repairs. Mrs. Bradley sued for breach of express warranties concerning the car. The sales manager testified that he gave no warranties in the sale and that he had explained to Mrs. Bradley at the time of the sale that there were no warranties covering the car. The court disagreed! The court pointed out that Mrs. Bradley was not generally knowledgeable concerning automobiles, and she was ignorant of all of the facts concerning this car in this case.

Quantifiable
Capable of exact statement; measurable, normally in numbers.

Relative
Not capable of exact statement or measurable; comparative.

E X H I B I T   18.1 | **Finding an Express Warranty**

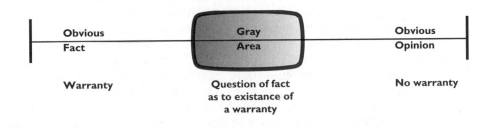

The defects in the car were hidden, and the buyer was denied the opportunity to take a test drive during which the defects might have been discovered. The seller was an expert in automobiles. He repeatedly reassured her as to the quality of the car (albeit in general and nonquantifiable terms) throughout the sale. His statements concerning the condition of the car, when viewed with her inability to personally examine the car prior to the sale, created express warranties and not mere opinion. Many of the principles of express warranty law now included in the Code seem to be based, at least indirectly, on the court's language from this case.

IMPLIED WARRANTIES

As pointed out in the preceding section, express warranties are a part of the contract. They are not present until given by the seller. The court will not find an express warranty unless it is created by the seller as a part of the "basis of the bargain." Thus, a careful seller will not give many—if any—express warranties until—and unless—so desired.

In contrast, implied warranties are imposed by operation of law (subject to certain limitations involving the status of the seller). If the circumstances are correct for the imposition of implied warranties, these warranties will automatically be present in the contract unless they are voluntarily surrendered by the buyer or properly excluded by the seller.

The UCC recognizes four types of implied warranties: the warranty of title, the warranty against infringement, the warranty of merchantability, and the warranty of fitness for a particular purpose. Some, all, or none of these warranties may be present in any given sales contract, depending on the circumstances surrounding the transaction and on the status of the seller of the goods.

Warranty of Title

Every contract for the sale of goods carries a *warranty of title* by the seller unless such a warranty is excluded by specific language warning the buyer that title is not guaranteed or unless the sale is made under circumstances that put the buyer on notice that title is not guaranteed. Absent one of these two conditions, a warranty of title exists to protect the buyer. A warranty of title ensures the buyer of the following:

1. The transfer of the goods by the seller is proper.
2. The buyer is receiving good title.
3. The goods are free of hidden security interests, encumbrances, or liens.

In other words, the buyer is assured that no one may assert a hidden claim to the goods that is superior to the claim of the buyer.

Section 2-312 of the UCC specifies that every seller of goods gives an implied warranty of title unless the contract contains specific language that the warranty is being excluded or the circumstances of the sale are such that the buyer should realize that the seller does not warrant title. Thus, a merchant who is entrusted with goods gives a warranty of title if the merchant sells these goods to a good-faith purchaser. If the merchant has *voidable* title to the entrusted goods, the buyer receives good title, and there is no breach of the warranty. However, if the goods entrusted to the merchant have been stolen, the person who purchases them from the merchant would receive *void* title, and the merchant would be liable for breach of the implied warranty of title.

Warranty Against Infringement

The implied *warranty against infringement* is unique in that it can be given by either the buyer or the seller, although it is normally given by the seller. (None of the other implied warranties can be given by the buyer.) The infringement protected against is the rightful claim of any third person concerning the goods.

Patent infringement is probably the most common type of problem dealt with under this warranty, but another area that is becoming increasingly important is copyright infringement. Videotapes, audiotapes, and computer software normally are copyrighted, and all are easy to copy without a great deal of equipment, expertise, or expense. Experts estimate that pirated copies of copyright-protected materials cost each of these industries a tremendous amount of money, possibly even billions of dollars per year. As a result, more attention is being paid to the protection and enforcement of copyrights. As this trend continues, an increase in the number of cases involving the warranty against infringement will likely occur. (Proposed Article 2B, Licenses, also deals with this area to a significant extent, further emphasizing the increasing importance of the topic of infringement.)

In order for a seller to give this warranty, the seller must be a merchant who regularly deals in the type of goods involved. A buyer who gives the warranty against infringement need not be a merchant. Any buyer who furnishes specifications to the seller in order to have the seller specially manufacture the described goods warrants against infringement if the seller complies with the specifications.

Warranty of Merchantability

Probably the most commonly breached, and the most commonly asserted, implied warranty is the *warranty of merchantability*. A warranty of merchantability is given whenever a merchant of goods, including a merchant of food or drink, makes a sale. It is a very broad warranty, designed to assure buyers that the goods they purchase from a merchant will be suitable for the normal and intended use of goods of that kind. Failure to satisfy any of the following six criteria means that the goods are not merchantable and that the warranty has been breached.

1. The goods must be able to pass without objection in the trade, under the description in the contract.
2. If the goods are **fungible,** they must be of fair average quality within the description.
3. The goods must be suitable for their ordinary purpose and use.
4. The goods must be of even kind, quality, and quantity.
5. The goods must be adequately contained, packaged, and labeled as required under the agreement.
6. The goods must conform to the promises and facts, if any, contained on the label.

Fungible
Virtually identical and interchangeable; not different from other goods of the same description.

Merchant sellers have been found liable for breaching this warranty because of such things as bobby pins in soft-drink containers, worms in canned peas, a decomposing mouse in a soda bottle, and a hair dye that caused the buyer's hair to fall out.

Because many merchantability cases involve disputes over food and drink, the courts have developed special tests to determine merchantability in these cases. These tests are the *foreign–natural test* and the *reasonable expectations test*. Under the foreign–natural test, "foreign" objects found in the food constitute a breach of warranty, whereas "natural" objects found in the food do not. Thus, a chicken bone found in a chicken salad sandwich does not involve a breach since chicken bones are "natural" to chicken. But a cherry pit found in a chicken salad sandwich is "foreign" and thus establishes a breach. Under the reasonable expectations test, the court attempts to establish what a reasonable person expects to find in the food. A reasonable person does not expect to find a "foreign" object in the food, so any foreign object found constitutes a breach. However, a reasonable person may not expect to find a "natural" object in the food either, so that finding such a natural object can also constitute a breach. Thus, a chicken bone in a chicken salad sandwich might show a breach if it is unreasonable to expect to find a bone in such a sandwich. The reasonable expectations in any given case is a question of fact.

One such case, *Webster* v. *Blue Ship Tea Room*,[3] is considered a classic in the law. The case involved a woman (Webster) who ingested a fish bone while eating a bowl of fish chowder in a Boston restaurant. The bone became lodged in her throat, and she required surgery to remove it. The court recognized that Webster was a native New Englander and that she had ordered a seafood dish in a waterfront restaurant in Boston. The court's opinion then treated her presumed knowledge of the preparation of fish chowder, along with a relatively detailed history of fish chowder as a New England dietary staple. The court concluded that a reasonable person eating fish chowder in a New England restaurant would reasonably expect to find fish bones in the chowder, so that the chowder was, in fact, merchantable. This

YOU BE THE JUDGE

SOMETIMES YOU FEEL LIKE A NUT . . .

Thomas Coffer purchased a jar of mixed nuts packaged by Standard Brands. While eating the nuts, Coffer bit down on an unshelled filbert nut, damaging a tooth. Coffer had dental work done to repair the damaged tooth and then filed suit against Standard Brands for breach of the warranty of merchantability. He alleges that he was using the product—the nuts—in their ordinary purpose and that the presence of an unshelled nut among the shelled nuts in the jar constituted a breach of warranty. Standard Brands denied liability. The defense asserted that the state Agriculture Board's regulations and the peanut industry allow a small amount of unshelled nuts to be included with shelled nuts without rendering the package of shelled nuts inedible or adulterated. The defense also pointed out that a nut shell is a natural ingredient in nuts and that a reasonable person would expect to find some shells in a jar of "shelled nuts."

This case has been brought before *your* court. How will *you* decide the case?[4]

BUSINESS CONSIDERATIONS Should Standard Brands have included a warning on the package that some nut shells are to be expected in the contents of the can? Should the ingredients listed on the label include the possible presence of nut shells in the package?

ETHICAL CONSIDERATIONS Is it ethical for a consumer to sue a merchant when the consumer is injured by a natural ingredient found in the product? Is it ethical to expect the producer to make its product 100 percent safe for normal consumers using the product in its normal and intended manner?

SOURCE: *West's Encyclopedia of American Law* (1998). West Legal Directory, http://www.lawoffice.com/.

opinion illustrates one approach a court might take in deciding a merchantability-of-food case.

Merchants who provide services do not give the implied warranty of merchantability. A number of cases involving tainted blood have been decided, with the courts tending to view the provision of blood by a hospital as a "service" rather than a "sale," thus negating any claim that the tainted blood provided to the patient constituted a breach of the warranty of merchantability. Other states have specifically excluded warranty protections in the provision of blood, blood products, and other human tissue.

The following case involved the issue of whether a restaurant was providing "goods" or "services" to its patrons. Study the opinion of the court and then decide if you agree with the results reached.

18.1

KOSTER V. SCOTCH ASSOCIATES
640 A.2D 1225 (N.J.SUPER.L. 1993)

FACTS All of the plaintiffs suffered food poisoning from salmonella entertidis (hereinafter salmonella) after having dined at the defendant's restaurant on five separate days in May 1990. The plaintiffs were all served different foods and there is no direct evidence that any particular food was the cause of the food poisoning. There is some indication, however, that the raw eggs in the caesar salad may have been the source of the salmonella. The plaintiffs contend that the defendant is strictly liable. The defendant responds that principles of strict liability are inapplicable to food served in a restaurant. It also argues that it cannot be liable to the plaintiffs for the harm caused to them because the source of the salmonella was the raw eggs which had been purchased from the third-party defendant and which the restaurant was unable to detect . . .

ISSUES Is a restaurant selling goods? Does the implied warranty of merchantability attach to meals served in a restaurant? Is a restaurant strictly liable for serving adulterated food?

HOLDINGS Yes, to all three questions.

REASONING There are three basic reasons for concluding that the defendant restaurant is strictly liable to the plaintiff: the Uniform Commercial Code . . . ; the [New Jersey] Adulterated Food Statute . . . ; and the [New Jersey] Products Liability Statute . . . In 1927, New Jersey's highest court decided that food served in a restaurant constituted a service rather than a sale and that therefore the warranty of merchantability did not apply . . . The view expressed . . . was a minority one. The majority took the position that the furnishing of food at a restaurant constituted a sale and that therefore the implied warranty of merchantability applied. The minority view was severely criticized by legal authorities. The Connecticut–New Jersey rule has been severely criticized as not only being unrealistic and not in harmony with modern business conditions and methods of serving food, but as being based to some extent upon "a humane solicitude for the plight of that legendary person, the poor boardinghouse keeper, who might be financially ruined by the fortuitous appearance in food furnished a patron of matter in which the processes of decay have good too far . . . " [This] case remained good law until 1963, when the Uniform Commercial Code's implied warranty of merchantability provision was amended to include the serving of food . . . After the adoption of the amendment and a year before it took effect, the Supreme Court . . . held that the ruling . . . should not be applied to food eaten in a cafeteria. The court strongly suggested that [the case] was no longer the law, but declined to extend its rulings to restaurants generally . . . The issue must be met in this case. There is simply no room for dispute with regard to the applicability of the UCC. The service of food in a restaurant is a sale. And a restaurant which sells the food to its customers warrants that the food will not be foul. The sale of food in a restaurant therefore fits perfectly within the UCC definition of the implied warranty of merchantability. The restaurant is thus strictly liable to the plaintiffs.

continued

18.1

KOSTER V. SCOTCH ASSOCIATES, *continued*
640 A.2D 1225 (N.J.SUPER.L. 1993)

The buying, selling and distribution of food to the public is a highly regulated field. New Jersey's Food and Drug Act . . . sets forth the standards and guidelines governing the sale and distribution of food . . . " No person shall distribute or sell, . . . any food, . . . which under any of the provisions of this subtitle is adulterated . . . The statute imposes penalties for its violation . . . but is silent regarding civil liability. Although no recent New Jersey cases have addressed the question of whether a breach of the Adulterated Food Statute imposes civil liability, cases in other jurisdictions with similar statutes have concluded that civil liability should be imposed for a violation of the statute . . . The New Jersey Food and Drug Act clearly incorporates common law principles safeguarding consumers against unwholesome foods. Therefore, a violation of the statute is, in itself, an act of negligence. The defendant restaurant has violated the statute. It is therefore liable.

The third basis for the imposition of liability is the products liability statute . . . The statute provides: "'Product liability action' means any claim or action brought by a claimant for harm caused by a product, irrespective of the theory underlying the claim, except actions of harm caused by breach of any express warranty." . . . The sale of food is the sale of a product . . . The statute also provides that: "A manufacturer or seller of a product shall be liable in a product liability action only if the claimant proves by a preponderance of the evidence that the product causing the harm was not reasonably fit, suitable or safe for its intended purpose . . . " The defendant restaurant served the plaintiffs food which was not reasonably fit, suitable or safe and which caused them harm. It is therefore liable under the Products Liability Statute . . .

BUSINESS CONSIDERATIONS What steps can—and should—a business that sells food and beverages to its customers take to minimize its risk of breaching the warranty of merchantability? Should a restaurant attempt to deny liability by arguing that its customers "assumed the risk" of food poisoning by going to a restaurant?

ETHICAL CONSIDERATIONS From an ethical perspective, should a business that serves food and drink accept responsibility for any harm suffered by its customers from ingesting the food or drink? Is there an ethical duty on the customer to exercise some degree of care in such a setting?

Warranty of Fitness for a Particular Purpose

Any seller, whether a merchant or a nonmerchant, may give the implied warranty of fitness for a *particular* purpose (remember that the warranty of merchantability refers to fitness for a *normal* purpose). In order for this warranty to come into existence, all of the following conditions must be present:

1. The seller must know that the buyer is contemplating a particular use for the goods.
2. The seller must know that the buyer is relying on the seller's skill, judgment, or knowledge in selecting the proper goods for the purpose.
3. The buyer must not restrict the seller's range of choices to a particular brand or price range or otherwise limit the scope of the seller's expert judgment.

WARRANTY EXCLUSIONS

The seller can modify or exclude warranties. The simplest way to exclude an express warranty is not to give one. If the seller is careful, no express warranties will exist. Sometimes a seller will create an express warranty orally but will attempt to exclude any express warranties in writing. In this case, the court will turn to UCC § 2-316(1). The court will take the warranty and the exclusion as consistent with one another if possible; otherwise, the warranty will override the exclusion. Excluding or modifying implied warranties is not so easy. To exclude or modify a warranty of merchantability, either orally or in writing, the word *merchantability* must be used. If the exclusion is written, the exclusion must be **conspicuous.** To exclude or modify a warranty of fitness for a particular purpose, the exclusion must be written, and it must be conspicuous; no oral exclusions of fitness are allowed. Under § 2-316(3), it is possible to exclude all implied warranties of quality (which normally do not exclude title or infringement protections) under three sets of circumstances:

Conspicuous
Easy to see or perceive; obvious.

1. Language such as "as is" or "with all faults" must be used properly so that the buyer is duly informed that no implied warranties are given.
2. If the buyer has thoroughly examined the goods or has refused to examine them before the sale, no implied warranty is given for defects that the examination should have revealed.
3. Under course of dealings, course of performance, or usage of trade, implied warranties are not given as a matter of common practice.

The following case deals with the issue of warranty disclaimers. Both the manufacturer and the retailer included language intended to disclaim liability in their documentation and/or contracts. Decide whether you agree with the court's decision.

18.2

TRANSPORT CORPORATION OF AMERICA, INC. V. INTERNATIONAL BUSINESS MACHINES CORPORATION, INC.

30 F.3D 953 (8TH CIR. 1994)

FACTS In 1989 TCA decided to update its computer system, which is used to process incoming orders, issue dispatching assignments and store all distribution records. The information entered into the computer system is stored onto a backup system at 2:00 A.M. every day. TCA entered into an agreement to purchase an IBM computer system from ICC for $541,313.38. TCA subsequently executed a lease agreement which assigned IBM Credit Corporation its right to purchase the IBM equipment from ICC, but TCA retained possession and use of the computer system. The computer system was installed at TCA's offices . . . on December 29, 1989. On December 19, 1990, almost a year later, the computer system went down and one of the disk drives revealed an error code. TCA properly contacted IBM, and IBM dispatched a service person. Although TCA requested a replacement disk drive, the error code indicated that the service procedure was not to replace any components but to analyze the disk drive. TCA had restarted the computer system and did not want to shut it down for the IBM service procedure. IBM informed TCA that replacement was not necessary under the limited warranty of repair or replace, and agreed to return on December 22, 1990, to analyze the disk drive. On December 21, 1990, the same disk drive completely failed, resulting in the computer system being inoperable until December 22, 1990. TCA alleges that the cumulative downtime for the

continued

18.2

TRANSPORT CORPORATION OF AMERICA, INC.
V. INTERNATIONAL BUSINESS MACHINES CORPORATION, INC., *continued*
30 F.3D 953 (8TH CIR. 1994)

computer system as a result of the disk drive failure was 33.91 hours. This includes the time to replace the disk drive, reload the electronic backup data and manually reenter data which had been entered between 2:00 A.M. and the time the system failed. TCA alleges that it incurred a business interruption loss in the amount of $473,079.46 . . . TCA . . . brought this action against IBM and ICC . . . based on the failure of the disk drive purchased through IBM and ICC, alleging strict liability, negligence, breach of implied warranty, and breach of express warranty . . . IBM and ICC moved for summary judgment on all counts. The district court granted the motion in favor of IBM and ICC on all counts. The district court applied Minnesota law and held that the economic loss doctrine barred TCA's tort claims, the terms of IBM's remarketer agreement with ICC "passed through" to TCA, IBM effectively disclaimed implied warranties, the remedy of repair or replace in IBM's express warranty did not fail of its essential purpose, and ICC's disclaimer of liability for consequential damages was not unconscionable. This appeal followed.

ISSUES Did the economic loss doctrine bar TCA's tort claim? Did IBM effectively disclaim implied warranties as to TCA? Was ICC's disclaimer of liability for consequential damages unconscionable?

HOLDINGS Yes, the economic loss doctrine barred TCA's tort claim. Yes, IBM effectively disclaimed the implied warranties. No, the disclaimer of liability for consequential damages was not unconscionable.

REASONING TCA argues that under Minnesota law, tort claims are not barred by the economic loss doctrine if two conditions are met: there is damage to other property and the parties are not "merchants in goods of the kind." Because TCA is not a merchant in computer systems and the loss of data due to the failed disk drive constitutes damage to other property, TCA argues that the district court erred in holding claims for negligence and strict liability are barred. IBM argues that TCA did not suffer damage to other property because the disk drive was integrated into the computer system. IBM also argues that the risk of failure of the disk drive . . . was reasonably contemplated by TCA. Thus, IBM argues that the Uniform

Commercial Code . . . as adopted in Minnesota controls the remedy in a transaction between sophisticated parties. The economic loss doctrine in Minnesota bars recover under the tort theories of negligence or strict liability for economic losses that arise out of commercial transactions, except those involving personal injury or damage to other property . . . TCA is not a dealer in computers and thus not a merchant in goods of the kind. Therefore, the transaction between TCA and IBM and ICC was not a commercial transaction for purposes of the economic loss doctrine. However, we hold that the economic loss doctrine does apply here because TCA did not experience damage to other property within the meaning of the doctrine. Under Minnesota law, "where a defect in a component part damaged the product into which that component part was incorporated, economic losses to the product as a whole were not losses to 'other property.'" . . . Thus, damage to other components integrated into a single unit are not considered damage to other property for purposes of the economic loss doctrine . . . Furthermore, TCA was aware of the risk of computer system failure and possible loss of data . . . [T]he Court of Appeals of Minnesota held that "tort claims [are] allowed only in limited situations where the nature of the defect or damage is other than that which could ordinarily be contemplated by the parties to a commercial transaction." . . . The fact that TCA backed up the disk drive at 2:00 A.M. every day objectively demonstrates that TCA realized the risk of its failure . . .

TCA next argues that because it was not a party to the negotiations between ICC and IBM, it is not bound by the terms of the remarketer agreement, including IBM's disclaimer of implied warranties. . . . The UCC as adopted in Minnesota has a privity provision that operates to extend all warranties, express or implied, to third parties who may reasonably be expected to use the warranted goods. . . . The seller can disclaim implied warranties . . . Disclaimers of implied warranties are extended to third party purchasers by operation of law . . . The remarketer agreement between IBM and ICC included a disclaimer of "ALL OTHER WARRANTIES, EXPRESS OR IMPLIED, INCLUDING, BUT NOT LIMITED TO, THE IMPLIED WARRANTIES OF MERCHANTABILITY AND FITNESS FOR A PARTICULAR PURPOSE." As

18.2

TRANSPORT CORPORATION OF AMERICA, INC.
V. INTERNATIONAL BUSINESS MACHINES CORPORATION, INC., *continued*
30 F.3D 953 (8TH CIR. 1994)

the district court correctly noted, this language complies with the requirements of . . . § . . . 2-316(2) (that is, it was in writing, conspicuous and mentioned merchantability) and thus effectively disclaimed all implied warranties . . .

TCA next argues that ICC's disclaimer for consequential damages fails of its essential purpose. A seller may limit or exclude consequential damages unless the limitation is unconscionable . . . The UCC encourages negotiated agreements in commercial transactions, including warranties and limitations . . . In the agreement between ICC and TCA, TCA expressly agreed to an ICC disclaimer that stated in part "IN NO EVENT SHALL ICC BE LIABLE FOR ANY INDIRECT, SPECIAL OR CONSEQUENTIAL DAMAGES SUCH AS LOSSES OF ANTICIPATED PROFIT OR OTHER ECONOMIC LOSS IN CONNECTION WITH . . . THIS AGREEMENT." We agree with the district court that the disclaimer of consequential

damages was not unconscionable and that the damages claimed by TCA . . . were consequential damages . . . Accordingly, the judgment of the district court is affirmed.

BUSINESS CONSIDERATIONS Should a business that is making a substantial investment in equipment have a policy of negotiating with the supplier to ensure that it receives adequate warranty protections in the contract? Should the purchasing firm have a policy against entering into such contracts without adequate warranty coverage?

ETHICAL CONSIDERATION Is it ethical for a major supplier of goods to include "boilerplate" language in its sales and lease contracts limiting or excluding its warranty coverage for the products it is distributing?

SCOPE OF WARRANTY PROTECTION

If warranties do exist, the next question is, whom do they protect? At common law, the answer is simple but unsatisfactory. Since the warranty is a part of the contract, it extends only to a party to the contract. Thus, the buyer is covered, but no one else is protected. The UCC has changed this. Section 2-318 contains the following three alternative provisions, and each state has selected one of the alternatives:

1. Warranties extend to any member of the buyer's family or household or any guest in the buyer's home if it is reasonable to expect that person to use or consume the goods.
2. Warranties extend to any natural person (human being) who could reasonably be expected to use or consume the goods.
3. Warranties extend to any person (remember, a corporation is a legal person) who could reasonably be expected to use or consume the goods.

The seller may not exclude or modify the extension of the warranties to those third-party beneficiaries.

STATUTORY WARRANTY PROVISIONS

Before 1975, consumers faced certain problems in the area of warranty law: many manufacturers disclaimed warranty protection, leaving the consumer with little or no protection; and most manufacturers put the warranty terms inside a sealed

18.2 | SALES

WARRANTIES

The professor in John's legal environment of business course recently explained warranty law, its scope, the potential for liability, and the methods for disclaiming or excluding warranties. After the class discussion, John became concerned that the family was not giving enough consideration to its potential warranty liability, which could be very costly to the family business. Accordingly, he is urging the family to carefully consider its policies regarding warranties. John is in favor of excluding any and all warranties that they can possibly exclude from their sales, and he also favors listing the warranty on the packaging, specifying that the product is covered by a "Limited Warranty." Donna is concerned that, by excluding or limiting the warranties, CIT will cause potential customers to doubt the quality and reliability of the product, thus hurting sales. They have asked you what they should do in this area. What will you tell them?

BUSINESS CONSIDERATIONS A firm produces a product that it sells to both consumers and merchants. The Magnuson-Moss Act requires disclosure of warranty information prior to the sale, if the buyer is a consumer, but not if the buyer is a merchant. Should the firm put the warranty information on the product package, thus giving the same warranties to all customers, or should it use one type of packaging, with warranty information, for consumer sales and a second type, without such information, for commercial sales?

ETHICAL CONSIDERATION A company decided to use its excellent warranty coverage as a selling device. In order to emphasize its warranty coverage, the firm's advertising carries the message that the firm offers "a FULL four-year limited warranty." Although this ad is technically honest, it misleads many consumers who assume the emphasis on the word *full* means that they are getting a full warranty. In fact, they are getting a full four years of warranty coverage, with a limited warranty in effect for that time. Is such an ad ethical?

package, so the consumer did not even know what warranty provisions were being offered until after the sale was completed. The warranty terms inside the package frequently were in the form of a warranty card. The instructions told the buyer to complete the card and return it to the manufacturer in order to obtain his or her warranties. In fact, these cards often specified that the buyer was agreeing to accept the express warranties the manufacturer was offering as the exclusive warranties in the contract. By completing and returning the card, the buyer was surrendering any implied warranties that he or she possessed in exchange for a very restricted (frequently 60- or 90-day) express warranty coverage proposed by the merchant.

As a result of these problems, the Magnuson-Moss Act–Consumer Product Warranty Act was passed and took effect in 1975. This law covers any consumer good manufactured after 3 January 1975. The manufacturer must provide the consumer with presale *warranty information.* The manufacturer also should set up informal settlement procedures to benefit the consumer. The manufacturer does not have to give any express warranties under the statute. However, according to the law, a manufacturer who does give an express warranty must designate it as either full or limited. To qualify as a full warranty, the warranty must meet at least four requirements:

1. It must warrant that defects in the goods will be remedied within a reasonable time.
2. It must conspicuously display any exclusions or limitations of consequential damages.
3. Any implied warranty must not be limited in time.
4. It must warrant that if the seller's attempts to remedy defects in the goods fail, the consumer will be allowed to select either a refund or a replacement.

Any warranty that is not full is limited. In a limited warranty, implied warranties may be limited to a reasonable time, frequently the same time as the express warranties given in the contract by the seller. There also may be limits on when the buyer can select a refund or a replacement.

Note that Magnuson-Moss does *not* provide warranty protection. All that this law requires is for the manufacturer or seller who deals in consumer goods to *inform* the consumer of his or her warranty protections. The Magnuson-Moss Act–Consumer Product Warranty Act is a *disclosure law,* designed to ensure that consumers are made aware of the warranty protections available with different products so that they can make an informed and intelligent choice between products based on all of the available information, including warranty coverage.

PRODUCT LIABILITY

While a great deal of energy and emphasis is placed on warranty law and warranty protections, this is not the only area in which buyers and consumers are protected from injuries caused by goods they have purchased and/or are using. Because they are a part of the contract, warranty protections are obvious to the buyer and the seller. Less obvious to the buyer, and to many sellers, are the other sources of remedies to which the buyer may be entitled. These other remedies may well be broader, they often last longer, and they frequently lead to larger judgments for injured parties. Sellers, in particular, need to be aware of the potential liability they face for injuries caused by the goods they sell beyond the liabilities imposed under warranty law.

Assume that a person is injured while using goods he or she has purchased and decides to seek remedies for the injury suffered. The first alternative many people consider is a breach of warranty claim. However, in many cases the warranty protections do not extend to the injury suffered, or the warranty protections have expired. When such a situation occurs, the injured party is not necessarily left without remedies. Although warranty protections are lacking, potential remedies may still be available under tort law. The injured party may be able to assert *negligence* against the manufacturer or may even be able to establish *strict tort liability* against the manufacturer or the seller of the goods.

Negligence

At common law, negligence can be used in only two circumstances: The buyer can argue breach of duties established by the **privity of contract** between the parties; or the buyer can argue that the goods are **innately dangerous,** so that privity of contract is not necessary in order to establish the liability of the seller or the manufacturer.

An injured party trying to establish that the tort of negligence occurred has to show the requisite elements of negligence: duty, breach of duty, harm, and **proximate cause.** Duty, the first element, is often the most difficult to establish. The injured party has to show that he or she is in privity of contract with the negligent party in order to establish that the seller owes a duty to the buyer. If there is privity, the contractual relationship establishes a duty by the seller to provide reasonably safe goods. The buyer next has to establish that the duty is breached, normally by showing that the goods provided are not reasonably safe for their intended use. The injured party then

18.3 | MANAGEMENT

CALL-IMAGE TECHNOLOGY

WARNING NOTICES FOR CALL-IMAGE

There has been some concern expressed by family members about the potential problem presented by product liability lawsuits, especially against smaller businesses. For example, there is some concern about the effect of radiation from prolonged exposure to certain electronic displays (computer monitors, televisions, and so on). Julio is concerned that, although there is currently no evidence that the CIT display causes harm to users, there could be some basis for claims later. He feels that the firm should take affirmative steps, placing a warning label on the monitor urging users to be certain that they maintain "a safe distance" from the screen during use. Donna disagrees with Julio. She feels that such a label would discourage some people from buying the product while encouraging others to file suit. While she agrees that the firm should give warnings to their customers of any dangers the family *knows* might exist, she is not sure how such warnings should be given to protect the firm without unduly alarming customers. They have asked you for your thoughts on this topic. What will you tell them?

BUSINESS CONSIDERATION Should a business include warnings on its products concerning any potential risk the firm can think of in an effort to protect its customers from harm while simultaneously protecting itself from lawsuits, or should it only give warnings for obvious misuses of the goods?

ETHICAL CONSIDERATIONS What is the ethical obligation of a company to warn potential customers of dangers in those areas where the firm knows that a number of customers are likely to misuse a product? Does such a warning plant the idea of the misuse in the minds of some customers, possibly placing them at risk in areas where they would not have been at risk without the warning?

Privity of contract
Direct contractual relationship with another party.

Innately dangerous
Dangerous as an existing characteristic; dangerous from the beginning.

Proximate cause
An act that naturally and foreseeably leads to harm or injury to another.

has to show that he or she was injured while using the goods and that the injury was proximately caused by the seller's breach of duty. This presents a relatively difficult task for the buyer. Even if the buyer can establish that the goods are not reasonably safe, that an injury did occur, and that there is a proximate causative link between the defect and the injury, establishing a duty owed by the manufacturer to the buyer is difficult. In most instances, the injured party is in contact only with an innocent intermediate party and not with the negligent manufacturer. The manufacturer would argue that it only owes a duty to its buyer, the intermediate party. The intermediate party would assert that it has not breached any duty owed to the injured party. The lack of privity thus negates the duty element, effectively removing the possibility of suing the manufacturer for negligence.

Historically, an injured user who was able to argue that the goods were innately dangerous had an easier time establishing his or her case if the innate danger of the goods could be shown. If the goods were found to be imminently or inherently dangerous, privity was not required. However, establishing the imminent or inherent danger of the product is more difficult. A product is deemed to be imminently dangerous if it is reasonably certain to threaten death or severe bodily harm as produced and/or sold. An item is considered to be inherently dangerous if it is dangerous by its nature. Imminent danger is most commonly found in negligent production; inherent danger is most commonly found in negligent use.

The difficulty of establishing either of these bases for proving that the manufacturer is liable for injuries serves as an effective shield from product liability at common law. However, times change, and so has the law's approach to product liability. In 1916, U.S. courts effectively laid the privity defense to rest in product liability cases. In the landmark case of *MacPherson* v. *Buick Motor Co.*,[5] the owner of a Buick automobile was injured when the wooden spoke wheel of his automobile broke while he was driving the car. MacPherson sued Buick for his injuries. Buick denied liability for two reasons. It had not produced the wheel but rather had purchased it from a supplier; so if liability attached to the defect in the wheel, the supplier should be the liable party. Buick also claimed lack of privity in that MacPherson had purchased his car from a dealer, not from the Buick Motor Company. The court rejected both arguments made by Buick, allowing the injured plaintiff to recover damages from Buick despite a lack of privity. Other courts quickly adopted the *MacPherson* rule, and, as a result, privity of contract is seldom asserted as a negligence defense today.

Strict Liability in Tort

The other basis for recovery frequently asserted by an injured party is *strict liability in tort* (also referred to frequently as *strict liability* or *strict tort liability*). Strict liability in tort appears to be a public policy area. It is possible for a manufacturer to disclaim warranty provisions, leaving a purchaser without the protections envisioned by warranty law. Similarly, an injured consumer may not be able to establish the necessary elements for a successful negligence suit. Nonetheless, there seems to be a general feeling that an injured consumer should be able to recover from *someone,* and the manufacturer is seen as the best available source for recovery. Not only is the manufacturer normally better able to absorb the loss than the injured consumer, but the manufacturer is also in a position to pass the cost on to society in the form of higher prices for the goods.

The basis for this theory of recovery is found in *Restatement (Second) of Torts*, § 402A. Section 402A is widely followed by the courts of the United States. The section states:

(1) *One who sells any product in a defective condition unreasonably dangerous to the user or consumer or to his property is subject to liability for physical harm thereby caused to the ultimate user or consumer, or to his property, if*
    (a) *the seller is engaged in the business of selling such a product, and*
    (b) *it is expected to and does reach the user or consumer without substantial change in the condition in which it is sold.*
(2) *The rule stated in subsection (1) applies although*
    (a) *the seller has exercised all possible care in the preparation and sale of his product, and*
    (b) *the user or consumer has not bought the product from or entered into any contractual relation with the seller.*

Note that this provision applies only to a merchant, that the merchant must sell a "defective" product that is "unreasonably" dangerous to the consumer, and that the product must reach the consumer without any substantial change in its condition. If these three criteria are satisfied, and if the consumer is injured using the product, the manufacturer can be held liable even though it used all possible care in the production of the product and even though there is no allegation of negligence.

This basis for liability imposes a substantial potential burden on the manufacturer. The "defective condition unreasonably dangerous to the user or consumer" referred to in part 1 is often measured at the time the injury occurs and not at the time the product was produced. Thus, a manufacturer who produces a product with a long useful life may face liability in the future, due to technological advances in the industry after production of the product but before the product is removed from service. The manufacturer can be found liable under this section for defects in design, defects in construction, or for failing to warn the consumer of a known danger commonly faced when using the product. This is one of the reasons for the warning on the blade platform on power lawn mowers ("Keep hands and feet from under mower while in operation"), the warning label on the power cords of electric hair driers ("Keep away from water—Danger"), and other labels or tags on consumer goods. This also could be an argument for planned obsolescence of products. A product whose useful life is supposed to end before too many technological advances can be made is less likely to lead to liability for the manufacturer.

The following case involves a claim for damages based on negligence, strict product liability, and breach of warranty. The court's opinion dealt only with the issue of preemption by federal regulation, but it raises some interesting points.

18.3

ZIMMERMAN V. VOLKSWAGEN OF AMERICA, INC.
920 P.2D 67 (IDAHO 1996)

FACTS On March 24, 1989, Dorothy Zimmerman was driving her 1987 Volkswagen Golf east on Franklin Road. While in the process of making a left turn . . . Dorothy was struck by a pickup truck which was traveling westbound on Franklin Road. Dorothy was alert and oriented but complained of left knee pain to the emergency medical technician responding to the

continued

18.3

ZIMMERMAN V. VOLKSWAGEN OF AMERICA, INC., *continued*
920 P.2D 67 (IDAHO 1996)

accident. Dorothy was then transported to St. Alphonsus Hospital where she spoke with Dr. Austin Cushman. Dorothy told Dr. Cushman that she did not recall striking anything within the automobile during the accident and thought that she was relatively uninjured although she did note some pain above her waist on the right side. Shortly after speaking with Dr. Cushman, Dorothy became unresponsive and later died from what Dr. Cushman concluded was an internal hemorrhage caused by a liver laceration. In Dr. Cushman's opinion, Dorothy's liver was torn from the inside outward when the restraint system in Dorothy's car caused her body to rapidly decelerate immediately after the collision and the entire force of that deceleration was imparted to her abdomen by the seat belt. The Zimmermans' complaint alleged causes of action against Volkswagen for strict products liability, negligence, and breach of warranty and including a claim for hedonic damages. The district court dismissed the Zimmermans' claim for hedonic damages pursuant to Volkswagen's motion and the breach of warranty claim was dismissed by stipulation. The court subsequently granted Volkswagen's motion for summary judgment finding that the Zimmermans' claims against Volkswagen were both expressly and impliedly preempted by applicable provisions of the National Traffic and Motor Vehicle Safety Act . . . The district court also ordered that Volkswagen be awarded certain of its costs.

ISSUE Did the National Traffic and Motor Vehicle Safety Act preempt state law coverage of strict products liability and negligence in this case?

HOLDING Yes. The federal regulations preempted the state coverage.

REASONING The manufacturer of a motor vehicle is under a duty to design and manufacture its products so as to eliminate unreasonable risks of foreseeable injuries that may occur if the vehicle is involved in a collision or other impact . . . Strict liability in tort is imposed on the manufacturer for its failure to produce a crashworthy vehicle . . . In "second collision" cases the injured occupant of the automobile bears the burden of presenting sufficient evidence that the vehicle was defective and that the defect enhanced or intensified the injuries sustained in the accident . . . The restraint system used in Dorothy's Golf,

identified by its acronym VWRA, is a "passive" system requiring no action on the part of the occupant to actuate it. The VWRA system consists, for the most part, of a shoulder belt which is anchored to the seat on the inboard side and to the door on the outboard side and included a padded knee bar under the dash and a specially designed seat to minimize submarining. There is no lap belt and, when the door closes, the shoulder belt is automatically positioned across the occupant's chest. The VWRA system was designed to comply with Federal Motor Vehicle Safety Standard 208 . . . , a regulation promulgated by the National Highway Traffic Safety Administration (NHTSA), an agency within the Department of Transportation, under the auspices of the Safety Act. This regulation specified motor vehicle performance requirements for the protection of vehicle occupants in crashes and allowed car manufacturers the choice of selecting one of three options for satisfying the federal performance standards, i.e., either complete passive protection, passive restraints, or lap and shoulder belt protection systems with seat belt warnings . . . The VWRA was designed to comply with the second options . . . In their complaint the Zimmermans do not allege that the VWRA failed to operate as it was designed to during the accident and they concede that the VWRA fully complied with the performance standards set forth in FMVSS 208. The only defect in the VWRA the Zimmermans could definitively point to was Volkswagen's failure to also include a lap belt. In determining whether Volkswagen can be held liable for not including a lap belt in Dorothy's Golf, a threshold issue is whether that particular claim is preempted by the Safety Act. The Safety Act provides that the NHTSA shall promulgate safety standards that manufacturers are required to incorporate into their products . . . Section 1392 also mandates uniformity in the development of safety standards through the Safety Act's express exemption provision:

> *Whenever a Federal motor vehicle safety standard established under this subchapter is in effect, no State or political subdivision of a State shall have any authority either to establish, or to continue in effect, with respect to any motor vehicle or item of motor vehicle equipment any safety standard applicable to the same aspect of performance of such vehicle or item of equipment which is not identical to the Federal standard . . .*

18.3

ZIMMERMAN V. VOLKSWAGEN OF AMERICA, INC., *continued*
920 P.2D 67 (IDAHO 1996)

It is well settled that any state law which conflicts with federal law is "without effect" as provided under the Supremacy Clause of the United States Constitution . . . In some cases, state law is expressly preempted by the language of a federal statute . . . As the Zimmermans have conceded, the VWRA fully complied with the performance requirements of FMSS 208. The issue then is whether Volkswagen can be held liable for selecting one of the options clearly available under the regulations promulgated by the NHTSA which do not require a lap belt . . . In this action there exists a federal standard that directly addresses the performance requirements of automobile restraint systems to protect vehicle occupants during crashes. Hence, we . . . hold, instead, that the claims against Volkswagen for failure to include a lap belt with the VWRA are preempted by the express provisions of the Safety Act . . . Thus, although there is certainly substantial evidence to show that the VWRA was the actual cause of Dorothy's injuries, that fact alone does not automatically indicate liability on Volkswagen's part.

> [S]trict liability is not absolute liability because a manufacturer is not an insurer or guarantor that no one will be injured in using his product. The manufacturer is under a duty to produce a product which is free from unreasonable dangerous conditions . . .

Even in strict liability cases, then, the plaintiff must first proffer evidence of a defect in a product before liability against the manufacturer can be found and the only defect in the VWRA that the Zimmermans . . . can point to is the system's failure to include a lap belt. As we have discussed . . . this claim is expressly preempted by the provisions of the Safety Act and, for that reason, the district court's grant of Volkswagen's motion for summary judgment is affirmed.

BUSINESS CONSIDERATIONS Should a manufacturer merely ensure that it produces its goods so that the goods comply with any applicable safety standards, or should the manufacture go beyond those standards? What benefits might accrue from exceeding the standards?

ETHICAL CONSIDERATIONS Is it ethical for a manufacturer to simply meet established safety standards even if the manufacturer knows that the standards are deficient? Is there an ethical duty to produce goods that are as safe as practical, even if that entails exceeding established standards and guidelines?

LEASES

Article 2A provides many of the same types of protections to lessees that Article 2 provides to buyers. Thus, when goods are leased, the lessee receives certain warranties, which are either the same as, or at least analogous to, the warranties given to the buyer in a sale of goods. There are some differences in a few of the warranties, but these differences are due to the difference in the reason the contract is entered. As you can see, these differences are more in style or terminology than in the types of coverage provided. The lessee receives express warranties on the same basis as a buyer of goods does. Express warranties are created when the lessor makes any affirmation of fact or promise that relates to the character, quality, or nature of the goods. These express warranties become part of the basis of the bargain. The lessor also provides express warranties based on descriptions of the goods or by providing any sample or model of the goods being leased. Article 2A of the UCC specifically excludes any statements as to the value of the goods, as well as any statement purporting to be merely the lessor's opinion or commendation of the goods, from attaining the status of an express warranty.

RESOURCES FOR BUSINESS LAW STUDENTS

NAME	RESOURCES	WEB ADDRESS
Uniform Commercial Code (UCC) Article 2, Sales	The Legal Information Institute (LII), maintained by the Cornell Law School, provides a hypertext and searchable version of Article 2, Sales. LII also maintains links to the UCC as adopted by particular states and to proposed revisions.	**http://www.law.cornell.edu/ucc/2/overview.html**
UCC Article 3, Negotiable Instruments	LII provides a hypertext and searchable version of UCC Article 3, Negotiable Instruments. LII also maintains links to Article 3 as adopted by particular states and to proposed revisions.	**http://www.law.cornell.edu/ucc/3/overview.html**
Magnuson-Moss Warranty Act— 15 USC §§ 2301–2312	LII provides a hypertext version of 15 USC §§ 2301–2312, popularly known as the Magnuson-Moss Warranty Act.	**http://www4.law.cornell.edu/uscode/15/ch50.html**
UCC Article 2A, Leases	LII provides a hypertext and searchable version of the UCC Article 2A, Leases. LII also provides links to Article 2A as enacted by particular states and to proposed revisions.	**http://www.law.cornell.edu/ucc/2A/overview.html**

Lessees also receive four implied warranties in their lease contracts. These implied warranties are: the warranty against interference, the warranty against infringement, the warranty of merchantability, and the warranty of fitness for a particular purpose. The warranty against interference is similar to the warranty of title under Article 2. It warrants that, during the term of the lease, no person holds a claim to or interest in the goods that will interfere with the lessee's use and enjoyment of the goods. The other three implied warranties are the same for lessees as they are for buyers. Warranties under Article 2A can be excluded in the same manner as they are excludable under Article 2.

Product liability claims are also available against the lessor or the manufacturer in a lease agreement. The same sorts of claims would be asserted, and the same defenses would be available.

SUMMARY

Warranty law and product liability are two major areas of consumer protection—a subject that has been receiving an increasing amount of attention for some years. Warranty protection comes in two broad forms: express warranties, which are given by the seller; and implied warranties, which are imposed by law. There are also statutory warranty provisions, which are primarily concerned with disclosures to consumer-purchasers. Warranties are considered a part of the contract covering the sale of goods. Warranties may be excluded by the seller or surrendered by the buyer. The method of exclusion depends on the type of warranty involved.

Generally speaking, warranties extend to parties other than the buyer of the product, provided that these other parties are foreseeable users or consumers of the product. Each state has adopted one of three alternatives for the extension of warranty protections beyond the buyer of the goods.

The Magnuson-Moss Warranty Act provides statutory coverage in the warranty area. Magnuson-Moss provides for disclosure of the warranty protections extended to purchasers of consumer goods. It does not provide substantive protections for the purchasers, but it does provide a method for making consumer purchasers aware of what sorts of warranty protections are provided in the contract.

Under product liability, the manufacturer or the seller may be held liable because of negligence in making, designing, or packaging the product. The manufacturer also may be held strictly liable, despite any lack of due care. This is true if the product, in its normal use, is imminently or inherently dangerous.

Leases also carry protections for the lessee in the area of warranty law. Lessees can receive express warranties when the lessor creates a belief in the mind of the lessee as to the character, quality, or nature of the goods being leased. Lessees also enjoy the protection of four implied warranties. These warranties are analogous to the implied warranties of Article 2.

DISCUSSION QUESTIONS

1. According to Article 2 of the UCC, what is necessary before a seller is deemed to give a buyer express warranties in a sales contract? What is necessary to give a lessee express warranties in a lease contract under Article 2A?

2. What does a seller warrant to the buyer in the implied warranty of title? What does the lessor warrant to the lessee in the implied warranty against interference?

3. When does a buyer of goods receive an implied warranty of merchantability? When does the lessee of goods receive an implied warranty of merchantability? What assurances does the buyer or lessee receive with this warranty?

4. What is the purpose of the Magnuson-Moss Act– Consumer Warranty Act? What is the difference between a full warranty and a limited warranty under the Magnuson-Moss Act?

5. What are the requirements that must be satisfied before a seller will be found liable for strict tort liability under § 402A of the *Restatement (Second) of Torts?*

6. Laura purchased a tool from Acme Corporation, a merchant. The tool was sold "as is—with no warranties of any kind, either express or implied." Laura was aware of this limitation at the time she purchased the tool. The tool Laura had purchased from Acme had, in fact, been stolen from Owen. Owen was able to trace the tool to Laura, and he was able to reclaim the tool from Laura. Laura is now seeking damages from Acme, alleging that Acme breached the warranty of title in the sale. Acme denies any liability, asserting that the sale "as is" protects it from liability. How should this case be decided?

7. Mildred was planning a dinner party for several of her friends. In preparation for the dinner, she purchased several pounds of seafood from the local grocer. Mildred followed the recipe for her seafood dish and prepared an entrée that looked and smelled wonderful. Unfortunately, the seafood was tainted, and all of Mildred's dinner guests suffered gastrointestinal distress following the meal. Several of the guests and Mildred are considering filing suit against the grocer, alleging that the seafood was not merchantable. The grocer admits that he may be liable to Mildred but denies any warranty liability to any of the guests. Is the grocer liable to the guests for breach of the warranty of merchantability?

8. Bob is buying a stereo from Earl. Bob asks Earl about the distortion figures for the stereo. Earl does not know the correct answer, but he does not want Bob to realize his lack of knowledge. What will happen if Earl answers, and his answer is incorrect? How should Earl answer?

9. Warren leased an industrial vacuum sweeper for his business. The vacuum sweeper was advertised as a "wet-dry" vacuum, meaning that it could safely vacuum up either wet or dry objects. However, when Warren was using the vacuum sweeper to vacuum some water that had been spilled on the floor of his business, he suffered a serious electrical shock. He filed suit against the vacuum sweeper manufacturer

and the business from whom he leased the item, alleging breach of express warranties. Both deny liability on two bases: that they did not give any express warranty on the product; and that even if they gave warranties to *purchasers* of the vacuum, they did not give warranties to *lessees* of the product. How should this case be resolved?

CASE PROBLEMS AND WRITING ASSIGNMENTS

1. Klages was employed as a night auditor at Conley's Motel. While working, Klages was the victim of an armed robbery at the motel. In order to protect himself in the event of another robbery, Klages purchased a mace pen from General Ordnance. The pen was advertised as a device that would cause "instantaneous incapacitation" of an attacker. The pen was also advertised to be as effective as a gun without the permanent injury from using a gun. Shortly after purchasing the pen, Klages was again held up by an armed robber. He squirted the robber with the mace, hitting him in the face with the mace discharge. The robber was not instantaneously incapacitated, however, and he shot Klages in the head. As a result of the gunshot wound, Klages lost all sight in his right eye. Klages has sued the manufacturer of the mace pen for misrepresentation. What should be the result in this case? [See *Klages* v. *General Ordnance Equipment Corp.*, 367 A.2d 304 (Pa. 1976).]

2. In February 1985, plaintiff (Gordon), a Richmond County automobile dealer, for $3,420 bought what was represented to be a 1977 Cadillac automobile at an automobile auction conducted by the defendant (Northwest Auto Auctions, Inc.). He received an executed document on the defendant's printed form entitled "Bill of Sale and Title Warranty," which carried the notation that it was issued at Northwest Auto Auction and stated:

   "THIS SALE IS SOLELY A TRANSACTION BETWEEN THE BUYING AND SELLING DEALERS." Inter alia, the document identified plaintiff as purchaser and Archie's Auto Sales of Rock Hill, South Carolina, as seller, and stated that:

   The seller covenants with the purchaser that he is the true and lawful owner of the said described automobile; that the same is free and clear from all incumbrances; that he has good right and full power to sell the same as aforesaid; and that he will warrant and defend the same against the lawful claims and demands of all persons whosoever. The purchaser agrees that he has examined the above vehicle and accepts it in its present condition.

10. Rayex sold sunglasses advertised as safe for baseball. A high school athlete was using the baseball sunglasses when he misplayed a fly ball. The ball hit the glasses and they shattered, blinding the athlete in one eye. It was subsequently discovered that the lenses of the sunglasses were unreasonably thin and not impact resistant. How should the athlete argue to establish strict tort liability?

   We, NORTHWEST AUTO AUCTION of Charlotte, N.C., guarantee title to the above car to be free and clear of all liens and encumbrances at the time of execution of this instrument. . . .

   In the transaction, the plaintiff paid the defendant auction company the sale price of $3,420 plus a $20 buyer's fee and received the car and purported title to it. Several months later, after plaintiff had cleaned up the car and sold it for $3,900, the North Carolina Department of Motor Vehicles discovered that it was a 1976 Cadillac that had been stolen in Atlanta in 1984 and returned it to its true owner; and the plaintiff gave its customer another car of equal value. Gordon sued Northwest Auto Auction for breach of the warranty of title. The trial court ruled for the auction company, ruling that the guarantee that "title to be free and clear of all encumbrances" was not a warranty of title. According to the judge, the fact that the automobile was stolen was neither a lien nor an encumbrance on the title. Gordon appealed this ruling. Did the language of the contract in question state that the title was free of liens and encumbrances, or that the automobile was free of liens and encumbrances? [See *Gordon* v. *Northwest Auto Auction, Inc.*, 387 S.E.2d 227 (N.C.App. 1990).]

3. Nicholas Marinelli was driving a 1973 Volkswagen Thing, a convertible utility vehicle with a detachable hardtop roof. He testified that he was returning to the Marinelli residence after giving driving lessons to his sister when he saw an animal approaching from the right side. He further testified that he steered to the right, tried to slow and/or stop by using his brakes, which were defective and did not work, and then applied his emergency brake in an effort to avoid hitting the animal; but this caused the vehicle to skid, and it flipped over. All three passengers (Nicholas, his sister, and her boyfriend) were thrown from the vehicle in the accident. Nicholas suffered minor injuries. His sister and her boyfriend were killed. The three passengers were not wearing their seatbelts at the time of the accident. Nicholas knew that his brakes were defective, but this was not the basis for the lawsuit against

Volkswagen. The parents of the deceased passengers each filed wrongful death actions against Volkswagen, alleging negligence and strict liability by the defendant in the design and construction of the vehicle. Volkswagen denied liability, asserting (among other things) that the decedents were contributorily negligent, that they had assumed the risk by failing to use their seatbelts, and that the driver was guilty of product misuse. Volkswagen also objected to the admission of "crashworthiness" testimony, alleging that the proper test was the Alabama Extended Manufacturers' Liability Doctrine.

Was Volkswagen negligent and/or strictly liable for this crash due to a defective design of the product that made it unreasonably dangerous in its normal and intended use? [See *Volkswagen of America, Inc.* v. *Marinelli*, (628 So.2d 378 (Ala. 1993).]

4. Camacho purchased a new motorcycle from Honda. Some time later, he was involved in an accident while riding his motorcycle, causing serious injuries to both of his legs. As a result, Camacho and his wife sued Honda, seeking recovery for the injuries and also for loss of consortium. The basis of the lawsuit was strict liability, but there were no allegations of any problems or defects in the motorcycle that in any way contributed to the accident. Rather, the Camachos argued that Honda failed to adequately warn them of the dangers of riding a motorcycle at the time of the sale. Honda denied any liability. How should this case be resolved? Should there be any ethical issues raised in this situation concerning any of the parties involved in filing or arguing this case? [See *Camacho* v. *Honda Motor Co., Ltd.*, 701 P.2d 628 (Colo.App. 1985).]

5. Craig Cover received a patent from the U.S. Patent Office for a lighting fixture system having a batt of thermal insulation to protect the wiring from heat produced by the bulb. Cover then entered into an exclusive license arrangement with Pacor to commercialize the patent. Thereafter, Pacor began to supply multilayered batts of insulation to Sea Gull, which designated these insulation units as parts number 6254 and 6255. Pacor did *not* mark the insulation units with the patent number as required by law. Pacor sold these units to Sea Gull until 1993. Beginning in 1988, Sea Gull also ordered parts number 6254 and 6255 from Hydramatic. Sea Gull provided Hydramatic with drawings and specifications for the parts, and Hydramatic produced and delivered the parts to Sea Gull. When Cover discovered that Sea Gull was purchasing his patented lighting system from someone other than the exclusive license holder (Pacor), he filed suit against both the buyer (Sea Gull) and the

producer (Hydramatic) of the allegedly infringing items. Eventually, Cover reached out-of-court settlements with both Sea Gull and Hydramatic. Hydramatic then sued Sea Gull, alleging that Sea Gull had breached the warranty against infringements by providing specifications for specially manufactured goods that infringed a valid patent. Sea Gull denied liability, alleging that it neither knew that the design was for a patented product nor that it had any notice of the patent in question. Sea Gull also claimed that the federal patent law preempted the enforceability of the UCC, so that Hydramatic should be precluded from seeking recovery. How should this case be resolved? Is the preemption argument asserted by Sea Gull persuasive? [See *Cover* v. *Hydramatic Packing Co., Inc.*, 83 F.3d 1390 (Fed. Cir. 1996).]

6. **BUSINESS APPLICATION CASE** Weaver purchased a modified F450 Ford truck from Dan Jones Ford in Florence, Alabama. Weaver paid $5,100 down, financing the balance of $27,949 through Ford Motor Credit Company. The truck was sold with an extended coverage plan, providing coverage for up to 24 months or 100,000 miles. Since Weaver planned to lease the truck as an independent hauler, with himself as driver, he requested Dan Jones Ford to make certain modifications to the truck, including extending the truck frame to accommodate a "sleeper unit" and the addition of a "fifth wheel" to allow the truck to tow a trailer. Dan Jones Ford hired McFall to perform the modification. Weaver took delivery of the truck in Lonoke, Arkansas, where the sleeper unit had been installed. During the drive back to his home in South Carolina, Weaver noticed that the truck was making a loud noise. He had the truck examined by a Ford dealer and was informed that the driveshaft had not been properly aligned during the extension of the frame of the truck. He was also informed that the necessary repairs would not be covered under warranty because the problem was caused by a modification of the truck, and modifications were not covered by the warranties. Dan Jones Ford paid for the repairs, in exchange for Weaver's signing of a "Full and Final Release" surrendering any other rights against Dan Jones Ford for problems with the truck. Weaver continued to have trouble with the truck, much to his chagrin. Finally, Weaver filed suit against Dan Jones Ford, Ford Motor Company, and McFall Welding, alleging breach of contract, breach of express and implied warranties, negligence, fraud, and violation of the Magnuson-Moss Warranty–Federal Trade Commission Improvement Act. Each of the defendants filed a motion for summary judgment based on the "Full and Final Release" Weaver had signed. Resolve this case,

addressing the following issues: Was the release valid against Weaver? Was the truck a consumer good, so that the alleged violation of the Magnuson-Moss Act was valid? Did Weaver have a valid claim against any of the defendants? Also, decide whether a business should have any policies or procedures in place to address a situation where a customer wants to have a product modified or customized for his or her use. [See *Weaver* v. *Dan Jones Ford, Inc.*, 679 So.2d 1106 (Ala.Civ.App. 1996).]

7. **ETHICAL APPLICATION CASE** Thomas purchased a mobile home from Countryside of Hastings, Inc. The purchase agreement included a provision that the mobile home would be delivered and set up on a basement foundation and that it would include such extras as a dishwasher, a disposal, patio doors, and a septic tank. The agreement also provided that Countryside would install an upflow furnace in the basement. The mobile home was delivered and set up as per the contract in 1979. In 1985, Thomas filed suit against Countryside, alleging that the upflow furnace had been improperly installed in that the furnace was not properly connected to a chimney or otherwise vented to the outside. Thomas claimed that the improper installation caused damage to the mobile home and also caused personal injury to him from the inhalation of carbon monoxide. Countryside asserted that the stated cause of action involved an alleged breach of contract and that the statute of limitations for such a cause of action requires the filing of a claim within four years of the breach. Since it had been more than five years since the contract had been performed, the court ruled that Thomas's cause of action was barred by the expiration of the statutory period. Thomas appealed, arguing that his claim was based in tort law for strict product liability rather than in contract law. Under this theory, since Thomas did not discover the alleged improper installation until December of 1984, he filed the lawsuit in a timely manner. Should the court dismiss the case under the statute of limitations for breach of contract or should it allow the case to proceed on its merits under the tort theory of product liability? Why? Is it ethical for an allegedly negligent installer to avoid liability in a situation such as this based purely on the expiration of the

statute of limitations? [See *Thomas* v. *Countryside of Hastings, Inc.*, 524 N.W.2d 311 (Neb. 1994).]

8. **CRITICAL THINKING CASE** Dr. Homsy, a former DuPont research engineer, invented Proplast—a semisoft, porous, spongy material—while doing prosthetic research at Methodist Hospital in Houston, Texas, in 1968. Proplast was produced by combining Teflon, carbon, solvents, and other ingredients. Homsy founded Vitek in 1969 to manufacture and distribute his Proplast prosthetic devices while he continued his research at Methodist Hospital. Vitek patented Proplast in 1976. One of the devices Vitek sold was the Proplast Interpositional Implant designed to correct temporomandibular joint disorders (TMJ). When Homsy first attempted to purchase Teflon from DuPont, he was warned by DuPont that Teflon was an "industrial material" that was "not made for medical use." The FDA authorized the sale of Proplast TMJ implants in 1983. Rynders had Proplast implants surgically placed in her jaw by oral surgeons in 1985 to correct her TMJ disorder. The Proplast implants were removed in 1988, at the recommendation of Rynders's oral surgeon, because she continued to suffer from TMJ problems. Upon removal, the oral surgeon observed that the implants had fractured and that the bony surfaces of Rynders's TMJ had eroded since the implant procedure. Rynders sued DuPont, alleging products liability, breach of the implied warranties of merchantability and fitness for a particular purpose, strict liability, and negligence. DuPont denied liability. It pointed out the disclaimers and warnings that were sent to Dr. Homsy and to Vitek regarding the inappropriateness of using Teflon in medical procedures. However, Rynders argues that DuPont knew Vitek was using the Teflon for medical purposes and continued to provide Vitek with the Teflon that Vitek ordered. She asserts that DuPont had a duty not to sell the product to Vitek if DuPont knew that Vitek was using the product improperly. How should the court resolve this case? What is the best argument in support of DuPont? In support of Rynders? Which do you find more persuasive? [See *Rynders* v. *E.I. DuPont, DeNemours & Co.*, 21 F.3d 835 (8th Cir. 1994).]

NOTES

1. *Black's Law Dictionary*, 6th ed. (St. Paul, MN: The West Publishing Co., 1990), p. 1586.
2. 210 P.2d 348 (Supp. Ct. Okla. 1949).
3. 198 N.E.2d 309 (1964).
4. "Implied Warranty of Merchantability." *West's Encyclopedia of American Law* (1998). West Legal Directory, http://www.lawoffice.com/.
5. 217 N.Y., 382 (1916).

19

REMEDIES

CALL-IMAGE TECHNOLOGY

A G E N D A

Although the Kochanowskis have devoted a great deal of time and effort to making the best possible product, they realize that some of the units they sell will be defective and that a customer who purchases such a defective unit may well sue them for damages. They also realize that, no matter how carefully they select the people or firms with whom they do business, there will probably be times when contracts are breached. They are concerned about the types of remedies they may have to honor and the types of remedies they may have to seek, and they are likely to ask for your advice in these areas. Be prepared! You never know when one of the Kochanowskis will need your help or advice.

O U T L I N E

THE REASON FOR REMEDIES

The overwhelming majority of sales contracts are performed by the parties as expected. The seller tenders conforming goods to the buyer at the time and place of delivery. The buyer then inspects the goods, accepts them, and pays the seller the price agreed to in the contract. Of course, not every tender is letter-perfect; but when the tender of delivery is flawed, the seller normally cures the defect. Again, the parties are left with their bargain as agreed.

In some cases, however, the tender is never made or it is made in so insubstantial a manner that it is treated as a breach of contract. Furthermore, some sellers refuse to cure a defective performance or lack the time to do so, and some buyers refuse to pay the agreed price or are unable to do so. Under these circumstances, the other party must look to **remedies** to minimize the effect of the breach.

This chapter examines remedies first from the seller's viewpoint and then from the buyer's. In either case, certain remedies will be available at some times and other remedies will be available at other times. The last part of the chapter explores some technical rules that affect how and when remedies may be sought or established.

Remedies
Methods for enforcing rights or preventing the violation of rights.

SELLER'S REMEDIES

If the buyer wrongfully **rejects** the goods, refuses to pay for the goods, or otherwise breaches the contract, the seller is entitled to remedies. The remedies available to the seller depend on when the buyer breaches. The seller has six possible remedies if the breach occurs before acceptance. If the breach happens after acceptance, the seller has two possible remedies. Exhibit 19.1 summarizes the types of preacceptance and postacceptance remedies available to the seller. Each of these is discussed in turn.

Rejects
Refuses to accept something when it is offered.

E X H I B I T   19.1 | **Seller's Remedies**

Preacceptance Remedies *Prior to Buyer accepting*

1. Withhold delivery of goods still in the seller's possession.
2. Stop delivery of goods in transit to the buyer. *after buyer accepts goods*
3. Sue for the contract, which includes the right to identify goods to the contract and the right to complete work in process.
4. Resell any goods (or raw materials or work in process).
5. Sue for damages suffered due to the breach, whether based on the resale or based on lost profits.
6. Cancel any future performance obligations.

Postacceptance Remedies

1. Sue for the amount still due under the contract.
2. Reclaim the goods (provided that the buyer is insolvent and the seller asserts the claim within 10 days of delivery *or* that the buyer made a written misrepresentation of solvency, which waives the 10-day limit).

Preacceptance Remedies of the Seller

If the buyer breaches the contract before accepting the goods, the seller may seek up to six different remedies. The seller does not have to choose just one possible remedy: As many of the six can be used as are needed in the particular case.

The first possible remedy is to *withhold delivery* of the goods. The seller does not have to deliver or to continue delivering goods to a buyer who is not willing to perform the contract properly. In addition, if the seller discovers that the buyer is insolvent, the seller may withhold delivery unless the buyer pays in cash all prior charges and the cost of the current shipment.

The second possible seller's remedy is a little more complicated. It is known as *stoppage of delivery in transit.* To use this remedy, the goods must be in the possession of a third person—a **carrier** or a bailee. If the seller discovers that the buyer is insolvent, the seller may stop delivery of any goods in the possession of a third person. If the buyer breaches the contract, the seller may also be able to stop the delivery; however, before the seller can stop delivery because of a breach, the delivery must be of a planeload, carload, truckload, or larger shipment. The seller also must make provisions to protect the carrier or the bailee before a stoppage is permitted. The seller must notify the carrier or bailee in enough time to reasonably allow a stoppage and must indemnify that carrier or bailee for any charges or damages suffered because of the stoppage.

Carrier
A third party hired to deliver the goods from the seller to the buyer.

The third remedy allows the seller to *sue for the contract.* This remedy does provide a potential burden to the seller, however. If or when the buyer pays the contract price, the seller must tender delivery of the goods. Thus, a seller who sues for the contract must be prepared to perform the contract upon the buyer's performance.

The fourth seller's remedy gives the seller the right to *resell* those goods that are still in the seller's possession. A seller who does resell the goods, and who does so in good faith in a commercially reasonable manner, may also be able to collect damages from the buyer. The seller may elect to resell in a public sale or in a private sale and may resell the entire lot of goods as a unit or make the resale by individual units. All the seller has to do is establish that the resale was conducted in a commercially reasonable fashion. This means that the method, time, place, and terms all must be shown to be reasonable. The seller must also give the breaching buyer notice of the sale, if possible. Normally, the issue of reasonableness will be raised in a private sale, but if he or she is given notice, the buyer has little opportunity to defeat the resale. In a public resale, reasonableness is well defined. Except for recognized futures, the resale can be made only on identified goods. It must occur at a normal place for a public sale unless the goods are perishable. The breaching buyer must be given notice of the time and place of the resale. Notice must be given as to where the goods are located so prospective bidders can inspect them. If the seller fails to meet any of these criteria, the resale is not commercially reasonable, and therefore the seller cannot recover any damages. If the seller resells the goods for more than the contract price, an interesting situation arises. If the buyer breached, the seller may keep the excess. If the buyer rightfully rejected the goods, the seller may still keep the excess, but now the excess is defined as anything above the buyer's security interest.

The fifth option available to the seller is to *sue the buyer, either for damages or for lost profits.* If the seller has not yet completed the goods or has not yet identified the goods to the contract, the seller normally will be content to sue for damages. In such a situation, damages are determined by taking the difference between the contract price and the market price at the time and place of breach, adding any incidental damages incurred, and then subtracting any expenses avoided. The seller may discover that the damages computed in this manner do not put him or her in as good a position as performance of the contract would have. If so, the seller may instead elect to sue for lost profits. The seller will show the profits that full performance would have netted and sue for this amount plus the recovery of any expenses reasonably incurred due to the breach. The seller may decide to resell the goods and then to sue for any losses or damages not recovered in the resale. If so, the damages are figured by deducting the resale price from the original contract price, adding **consequential damages** incurred due to the buyer's breach, and then subtracting any expenses saved by not having to deliver the goods to the original buyer.

Consequential damages
Damages or losses that occur as a result of the initial wrong but that are not direct and immediate.

Remedies 3, 4, and 5 allow the seller to exercise some discretion in the treatment of unidentified goods. If the buyer breaches the contract, the seller may identify goods to the contract that were unidentified before the breach, thus helping establish damages. Also, the seller may decide either to complete goods that were incomplete or to stop production and resell the goods for scrap. Either of these options may be used, provided that the seller is exercising reasonable business judgment.

The seller's final preacceptance remedy is the right to *cancel.* On giving notice to the buyer, the seller can cancel all future performance due to the buyer under the contract. Cancellation does not discharge the buyer or hinder the seller in collecting or enforcing any other rights or remedies resulting from the breach; it merely terminates the duties of the seller under the contract due to the breach by the buyer.

The following case involves a seller's preacceptance remedies. In reading the case, ask yourself: Did the seller act properly under the circumstances? Could—or should—the seller have used some remedy other than resale in this situation?

19.1

FIRWOOD MANUFACTURING COMPANY, INC. V. GENERAL TIRE, INC.

96 F.3D 163 (6TH CIR. 1996)

FACTS This dispute arises from a contract between Firwood and General Tire in which General Tire allegedly agreed to purchase fifty-five model 1225 post-cure inflators (PCIs), thirty-thousand dollar machines used by General Tire in its manufacturing process. Following lengthy negotiations between representatives from each company, on October 9, Firwood transmitted [an] offer letter [stating that the price agreed upon was based on a minimum purchase of fifty-five PCIs during 1990, and that if General Tire purchased less than fifty-five units the price would be adjusted for each unit. Firwood also asked for a letter of intent showing anticipated purchase dates for the CPI units] . . . On October 10, General Tire issued two written purchase orders to Firwood in which it revised prior orders to reflect the new price of $31,216 per PCI—the price level available for purchases of a

minimum of fifty-five units—and encouraged Firwood to have all fifty-five PCIs available for delivery . . . Firwood began ordering parts for the PCIs . . . By April 1990 General Tire had purchased twenty-two PCIs from Firwood under the contract. General Tire closed its Barrie plant soon thereafter. On April 11, 1990, Firwood wrote General Tire to remind it of its obligation to purchase fifty-five PCIs. Firwood informed General Tire that the thirty-three remaining PCIs were in the following stages of production: eight units, 100 percent complete; five units, 95 percent complete; and twenty units, 65 percent complete. After learning that General Tire did not intend to complete the purchase of the remaining thirty-five PCIs at issue in this dispute, Firwood began looking for alternative buyers. Firwood contacted every major tire company in the United States. General Tire also

FIRWOOD MANUFACTURING COMPANY, INC. V. GENERAL TIRE, INC., *continued*
96 F.3D 163 (6TH CIR. 1996)

sought alternative buyers for the PCIs. After three years of searching for alternative buyers, during which it sold a few machines, Firwood was ultimately able to sell the balance of the thirty-three PCIs intended for General Tire, but at a price below that called for in the contract with General Tire. While looking for buyers, Firwood filled some of its ongoing orders for spare parts with parts that already had been installed in the thirty-three PCIs intended for General Tire. Although the PCIs themselves were specially made for General Tire, the parts taken from the General Tire PCIs and sold as spare parts were fungible parts regularly sold in Firwood's spare parts business. [Eventually Firwood sued General Tire for breach of contract. The district court entered a judgment in favor of Firwood for damages plus interest, and General Tire appealed.]

ISSUES Could the seller substitute fungible goods for the goods identified to the contract at the time of the breach for resale purposes? Is a lapse of three years between the time of the breach and the time of the resale of the goods a resale within a "commercially reasonable time"?

HOLDINGS Yes, the seller can substitute fungible goods for resale purposes. Yes, the resale in this case was made within a "commercially reasonable time" despite the lapse of three years between the breach and the resale.

REASONING General Tire . . . argues that the District Court erred in denying its motion for judgment as a matter of law when Firwood did not prove its damages under [§ 2-706] . . . That section allows sellers to receive the difference between contract price and resale price, plus incidental expenses, when a buyer breaches:

(1) *Under the conditions stated in [§ 2-703] on seller's remedies, the seller may resell the goods concerned or the undelivered balance thereof. Where the resale is made in good faith and in a commercially reasonable manner the seller may recover the difference between the resale price and the contract price, together with any incidental damages allowed under the provisions of this article . . .*

(2) *. . . Sale may be as a unit or in parcels and at any time and place and on any terms but every aspect of the sale including the method, manner, time, place and terms must be commercially reasonable . . .*

General Tire argues that Firwood cannot recover under [§ 2-706] because it did not comply with this section's requirements. General Tire argues that Firwood did not reasonably identify the goods under the contract because the thirty-three PCIs ultimately sold contained parts not originally included in the machines at the time of the breach. There is also a question whether the resale was commercially reasonable where twenty-nine of the thirty-three machines were sold three years after the breach. We must first decide whether a seller may substitute fungible goods for those identified to the contract at the time of the breach. Here, identical parts were used to replace parts that had been sold in the interim. On this question, we find persuasive the reasoning of those courts that allow sellers to substitute fungible goods for purposes of resale so long as the goods truly are fungible and the resale itself is commercially reasonable . . . The resold model 1225 post-cure inflators remained reasonably identified to the contract. Thus Firwood is not barred from recovery simply because the PCIs it ultimately sold contained parts different than those at the time General Tire breached. The parts were fungible, and the PCIs into which they were placed were essentially the same PCIs specially made for General Tire . . . Noting that § 2-706 is designed to provide the seller the difference between market value and the contract price, and that resale is designed to determine market price, . . . timely resale was particularly important in cases involving substituted goods . . . We must decide whether Firwood's resale of PCIs may not serve as the basis of the damage award because three years after a breach is not commercially reasonable. There is significant support for the view that three years is unreasonable . . . Nevertheless, . . . sellers ought not to be precluded from recovering damages in every case in which resale does not occur immediately: "If no reasonable market existed at [the] time, no doubt a delay may be proper and a subsequent sale may furnish the best test, though confessedly not a perfectly exact one, of the

continued

FIRWOOD MANUFACTURING COMPANY, INC. V. GENERAL TIRE, INC., *continued*
96 F.3D 163 (6TH CIR. 1996)

seller's damages." . . . "What is such a reasonable time depends upon the nature of the goods, the condition of the market and other circumstances of the case: its length cannot be measured by any legal yardstick or divided into degrees." Even though there was a three-year delay between breach and resale here, we cannot say that the jury was required to find that the resale was commercially unreasonable. At the time of the breach, there was no market for PCIs, machines costing over thirty-thousand that have a very specialized use. Moreover, Firwood made a continuing good faith effort to locate other purchasers. While a three-year delay is suboptimal, we are mindful that the U.C.C. remedies are to be liberally construed to ensure that the aggrieved party is "put in as good a position as if the other party had fully performed . . . " Accordingly, we hold that the District Court did not err when

it denied General Tire's motion for judgment as a matter of law . . .

BUSINESS CONSIDERATIONS How much effort should a seller make in seeking buyers to whom it can resell specially ordered goods? What factors should a seller consider in ensuring that any resales it makes are commercially reasonable?

ETHICAL CONSIDERATION The buyer in this case ordered specially manufactured goods and then breached the contract. At that point, was it ethical for the buyer to object to the manner or the time in which the seller was able to resell these specialized goods?

Postacceptance Remedies of the Seller

Once the goods have been accepted by the buyer and the buyer has breached the contract, the seller may seek either or both of two remedies.

The first of these remedies is by far the more common. The seller may *sue the buyer for the price of the goods.* Since the buyer has accepted, the buyer's duty to pay is established. Thus, winning the case is almost a certainty. Many buyers who do not pay, however, are unable to pay. They are insolvent. In such a situation, winning the case is a Pyrrhic victory—the winner suffers nearly as much as the loser.

If the buyer has accepted goods and is insolvent, the seller will possibly seek the second available postacceptance remedy: *reclaiming the goods.* To do so, the seller must prove that the following two conditions have been satisfied:

1. The buyer received the goods on credit while insolvent.
2. The seller demanded the return of the goods within 10 days of delivery to the buyer.

This remedy is obviously of limited value, since many businesses operate on credit terms providing for payment after 30 days (or longer) and the seller has only 10 days in which to act. But there is one exception: If the buyer misrepresented his or her solvency in writing to the seller within three months before delivery, the 10-day limit does not apply. In practice, many sellers extend credit in conjunction with a security interest (as provided for in Article 9 of the UCC) to protect themselves from the drawbacks presented by the "reclaim the goods" postacceptance remedy. Otherwise, if the seller discovers that the buyer is unable to pay after the goods have been accepted, the seller may find him- or herself with little hope of ever collecting the full contract price.

It is possible, at least in theory, for a seller to use all eight potential remedies in a single contract upon a breach by the buyer. In order to use all eight possible remedies, the circumstances would have to be unusual (to say the least), and the conduct of the buyer would have to fit within certain guidelines. Although such a confluence of circumstances is highly unlikely, it could happen, as is shown in the following example.

Tara entered into a contract with Jaime that called for Jaime to produce and deliver 1,000 video games to Tara each month for the next 12 months. Tara was to make payments for each shipment within 30 days of receipt. Jaime did not ordinarily allow deferred or delayed payment, but Tara had provided a written financial statement that presented a picture of a very profitable business. (As it turned out, the financial statement was fraudulent; Tara was, in fact, insolvent at the time of the contract.) Jaime purchased sufficient raw materials to produce 8 months' worth of goods and began the manufacturing process. The performance of the contract can be summarized as follows:

1. The first two monthly shipments were sent to Tara.
2. The third monthly shipment had been turned over to a common carrier for delivery.
3. The fourth monthly shipment was ready for pickup by the common carrier when Jaime learned that Tara was insolvent.
4. The goods for monthly shipments 5 through 8 were, at that time, in various stages of "work in process."
5. The balance of the raw materials to complete the contract had been ordered by Jaime.

Jaime decided to seek any and all remedies that might be available under Article 2. Jaime first looked at the preacceptance remedies. He decided to withhold delivery of the fourth shipment to the carrier and to notify the carrier to stop the goods that were already in transit (the third shipment). The goods in shipments 3 and 4 had been identified to the contract, as was the work in process. Jaime decided to stop the work in process and to sell the partially completed goods for scrap. He also decided to resell the completed goods that were stopped in transit and the goods withheld from delivery. Jaime also called Tara and canceled all future performance on the contract due to Tara's insolvency. Jaime sued for damages on shipments 3 through 8 and for lost profits on shipments 9 through 12. Jaime then decided to exercise the postacceptance remedies. He reclaimed all the unsold goods still in Tara's possession from shipments 1 and 2 and sued for the amount due under the contract for all goods that Tara had disposed of before Jaime was able to assert his right to reclaim the goods from Tara.

19.1 | SALES/FINANCE

SHOULD CIT USE CREDIT SALES TO INCREASE MARKET SHARE?

Tom would like to see the firm get off to a quick start by making a large number of sales early in the firm's existence. If the firm is successful in this, it may gain a significant "brand loyalty," as well as being recognized as *the* innovator in the industry. He believes that the best way to do this is by selling the units on credit to a number of retail outlets. Donna and Julio are concerned about the cash flow of the firm and would prefer to have the early sales be made for cash or, at the very worst, to have a short payment term. They both feel that 30 days is about as much credit as the firm should extend. Anna agrees, to some extent, with Tom, but she is worried about what will happen if any of the stores to whom CIT extends credit defaults or goes bankrupt. Tom does not think this is a problem since, he says, CIT could just go in and repossess any of the units the store has not yet paid for. Dan is not sure that the firm will be allowed to "just go in and repossess" any units. The family asks what you think. What advice will you give them?

BUSINESS CONSIDERATIONS A new company in an industry may have trouble getting its product into stores unless it is willing to take some chances, including making credit sales. What should a company do to maximize its protection if it decides to sell goods on credit? Are the Article 2 postacceptance remedies adequate for the firm's protection?

ETHICAL CONSIDERATIONS Suppose that a credit customer is having a temporary cash flow problem but will probably be able to meet its debt obligation to your company in the near future. Should your company play "hardball" and demand payment when due, be "caring creditors" who allow the debtor a bit of leeway, or take a position somewhere between these extremes? How can the position you choose be justified ethically?

BUYER'S REMEDIES

The buyer also has a range of possible remedies. Like the seller, the buyer's remedy options depend on the timing of the breach. The buyer has six preacceptance and three postacceptance remedies available. These remedies are summarized in Exhibit 19.2. We will discuss each of them in turn.

Preacceptance Remedies of the Buyer

Before the buyer accepts, the seller may breach by nondelivery or by delivery of nonconforming goods. Under either circumstance, the buyer may elect any or all of the following remedies.

The buyer's first remedy is to *sue for damages*. The buyer is allowed to recover the excess of market price over contract price at the time of breach and at the place of delivery. Any additional damages are added to this amount. The amount is then reduced by any expenses the buyer saved because of the breach.

The second remedy available to the buyer is that of *cover*. The buyer covers by buying substitute goods from another source within a reasonable time of the breach. If the goods obtained through cover cost more than the contract price, the buyer can collect the excess costs from the breaching seller, plus other expenses incurred in effecting cover.

The third remedy is available if the goods cannot be obtained by cover. The buyer may seek **specific performance** or **replevin.** If the goods are unique, the court may order specific performance, and the seller will have to deliver the goods in accordance with the contract. If the goods are not unique but are unavailable from other sources at the time, replevin is available. Once the buyer shows an inability to cover, the court will order replevin.

Specific performance
A court order that the breaching party perform the contract as agreed; the object of the contract must be unique.

Replevin
Similar to specific performance, but the object of the contract is not unique; it must be currently unavailable.

Substantially impair
Make worth a great deal less, seriously harm or injure, or reduce in value.

E X H I B I T 19.2 | **Buyer's Remedies**

Preacceptance Remedies

1. Sue for damages for breach of the contract.

2. Cover, and sue for damages resulting from the cost of covering.

3. Seek specific performance (unique goods) or replevin (common goods, temporary short supply in the market).

4. Claim any identified goods still in the seller's possession, provided the seller has become insolvent within 10 days of receiving payment from the buyer.

5. Resell any nonconforming goods shipped by the seller.

6. Cancel any future duties under the contract.

Postacceptance Remedies

1. Revoke the acceptance (if the hidden defect substantially impairs the value of the contract) and then seek any appropriate preacceptance remedies.

2. Sue for damages due to the nonconformity of the goods shipped.

3. Recoup by deducting the damages suffered from the total contract price still owed to the seller (the buyer must notify the seller before using recoupment).

The fourth remedy is probably rare in actual practice. If the seller has identified the goods to the contract, and if the buyer has paid some or all of the contract price, and if the seller becomes insolvent within 10 days of receipt of the payment, the buyer can *claim the identified goods.* The likelihood of this chain of events occurring is not very high, but, if it does occur, the buyer is protected.

The fifth remedy available to the buyer frequently baffles and amazes students: Under appropriate circumstances, the buyer may *resell the goods.* (Students frequently ask: "How can someone resell goods that were never accepted and thus never sold in the first place?") This remedy becomes available when the seller ships nonconforming goods to the buyer. On receipt of the nonconforming goods, the buyer must notify the seller of the nonconformity. Furthermore, if the buyer is a merchant, the buyer must request instructions from the seller as to disposal of the goods. If no instructions are given (or if the seller asks the buyer to resell the goods on the seller's behalf), the buyer must attempt to resell the goods for the seller. The resale must be reasonable under the circumstances. A buyer who does resell the goods will be allowed to deduct an appropriate amount from the sale amount for expenses and commissions and may then apply the balance of the sale proceeds to the damages resulting from the breach. Any excess must be returned to the seller.

The final preacceptance remedy available to the buyer is the right to *cancel.* On discovery of a breach by the seller, the buyer may notify the seller that all future obligations of the buyer are canceled. Cancellation will not affect any other rights or remedies of the buyer under contract.

Postacceptance Remedies of the Buyer

Once the buyer has accepted the goods, the focus shifts. A buyer who accepts cannot reject the goods, since accepting and rejecting are mutually exclusive. However, the buyer may be able to *revoke the acceptance.* Revocation is permitted only if the following criteria are met:

1. The defect must have been hidden; or the seller must have promised to cure the defect, but no cure occurred.
2. The defect must **substantially impair** the value of the contract.

While a hidden defect is not necessarily rare, a hidden defect that also substantially impairs the value of the contract may well be rare. If something is so wrong with the goods that the buyer's rights are substantially harmed, that problem would seem to be one that a reasonable

19.2 | MANUFACTURING/ MANAGEMENT

ADDRESSING DELIVERY PROBLEMS WITH A SUPPLIER

One of the firms that supplies component parts to CIT has recently been troubled by labor problems. Its employees were out on strike for several weeks, and the company has virtually exhausted its inventory of component parts. The strike ended last week, and the president of the company called Dan to let him know that the company planned to be back up to full production very shortly. Since the strike depleted their inventory, however, they might be a few days late with their next shipment to CIT. Dan reported this to the family and asked what they planned to do. Dan would prefer to cancel the contract with this supplier, buy the components from another source, and sue for any damages incurred due to the change and/or the delays that CIT is facing. Anna would prefer to take a wait-and-see position, giving the component-supplying firm time to get its production back up to normal. She believes that a little patience and cooperation with the supplier now will "pay dividends" in the long run. Tom is worried that the delay in receiving component parts may put CIT behind its production schedule, but he is unsure of the best alternative for the firm. He asks you what you think they should do. What advice will you give him?

BUSINESS CONSIDERATIONS Does the fact that one or more remedies are available mean that a business should *use* those remedies? Should a business base its decisions on the fact that remedies are available, or should it view remedies as a last resort after all else has failed?

ETHICAL CONSIDERATIONS Is it a better business practice to work problems out in an equitable manner, or to hold the other person to the literal terms of the bargain? Is it a better ethical practice to work problems out in an equitable manner, or to hold the other person to the literal terms of the bargain?

inspection should reveal. A substantially impairing defect that is not cured when cure is promised is probably more common.

If the buyer properly revokes acceptance, the buyer is treated as if he or she rejected the initial delivery, and the buyer is then permitted to assert any or all of the available preacceptance remedies that apply to the case.

The buyer may accept the goods and later discover a defect or other breach that is not sufficient to permit a revocation. When this happens, the buyer will select the second possible remedy: *suing the seller for damages.* Damages are likely to be measured by comparing the value of the goods as delivered with the value that the buyer would have received if the goods that were delivered had conformed to the contract. Damages can also be established as the expense the buyer incurs in having the defects in the goods repaired by a third person.

The third remedy available to the buyer allows him or her to deduct damages from the price: *recoupment.* Normally, this third remedy will be used together with the second. The buyer must notify the seller that the buyer intends to deduct damages caused by the seller's breach from the contract price still owed to the seller for the contract. If the seller agrees, the matter is concluded. If the seller disagrees, he or she will need to either negotiate with the buyer to reach an agreement or sue the buyer for any alleged underpayment of the balance due on the contract.

MODIFICATIONS

The parties to the contract are allowed to tailor their remedies to fit their particular contract and their particular circumstances. For example, the parties may, by expressly including it in the contract, provide for remedies in addition to those provided by the Uniform Commercial Code. Or they may provide for remedies in lieu of those provided by the Code. Or they may place a limit on the remedies that may be used. If the parties so desire, they can select one remedy that is to be used as the exclusive remedy for their particular contract. (When an exclusive remedy is selected, it must be followed unless circumstances change so that the remedy no longer adequately covers the damages.)

Consequential damages may be excluded or limited by the parties in the contract. Such an agreement will be enforced unless the court finds it to be unconscionable. The parties may also provide for liquidated damages if the provision is reasonable, the difficulty of setting the loss is substantial, and establishing actual loss would be inconvenient, if not impossible. Of course, if the amount designated as liquidated damages is found unreasonable or unconscionable or is deemed to be a penalty, the clause is void.

Sometimes the seller justifiably withholds delivery from the buyer when the buyer has paid part of the contract price. In such a case, the buyer, even though in breach, can recover any payments made in excess of any liquidated damages called for in the contract or, if there is no liquidated damages amount, the lesser of 20 percent of the total contract value or $500.

SPECIAL PROBLEMS

In determining when remedies may be obtained and what remedies to seek, several special problems may arise. The court may be asked to determine whether a breach has occurred or whether the contractual performance was excused. If there

YOU BE THE JUDGE

SHOULD A MANUFACTURER BE LIABLE FOR THE ACTIONS OF A CUSTOMER?

Alex Hardy was driving his Chevrolet S-10 Blazer when he was involved in a one-vehicle accident. Hardy was thrown from the vehicle, allegedly because the door latch failed, and he suffered serious and permanent injuries as a result of the accident. Hardy was paralyzed from the waist down. During the trial, Hardy admitted that he had been drinking beer immediately before he began his fateful drive. He also admitted that he was not wearing a seat belt at the time of the accident. Finally, he admitted that he had fallen asleep at the wheel of his vehicle while driving and was asleep at the time of the accident. However, Hardy also asserted that none of these factors was involved in the crash or the subsequent injuries. According to Hardy's theory, the axle of the truck broke, causing the crash. As a result of the crash, the vehicle rolled over, the door latch failed, and Hardy was thrown from the truck. A jury awarded Hardy $50 million in compensatory damages and an additional $100 million in punitive damages.

General Motors has appealed this case to *your* court. How will *you* rule on this appeal?[1]

BUSINESS CONSIDERATION This case was decided in Alabama, a state which has had numerous very large jury verdicts of late. Should a business that operates in multiple states consider *not* doing business in Alabama—or any other "pro-plaintiff" state—due to the fear of potentially crippling jury awards of damages?

ETHICAL CONSIDERATIONS Is it ethical for a plaintiff who admittedly had been drinking and who admittedly fell asleep at the wheel while driving to sue the manufacturer of the vehicle for injuries suffered in a subsequent accident? Is it ethical for a jury to award a huge verdict to a plaintiff simply because the defendant has "deep pockets" and can afford to pay the award?

SOURCE: *The Detroit News* (5 June 1996).

---

has been a breach, the courts may need to determine when it occurred. There may be a problem with the expectations of the parties or a question as to whether a party is capable of performing as scheduled. And sometimes there is just a special circumstance involved that requires special treatment.

(Anticipatory) Repudiation

Occasionally, one of the parties to a contract will repudiate his or her obligations before performance is due. If such a repudiation will substantially reduce the value expected to be received by the other party, the other party may choose one of three courses of conduct:

1. He or she may await performance for a commercially reasonable time despite the repudiation.
2. The nonrepudiating party may treat the repudiation as an immediate breach and seek any available remedies.
3. The nonrepudiating party may suspend his or her own performance under the contract until there is a resolution of the problem.

A repudiating party is allowed to retract the repudiation at any time up to and including the date performance is due, if the other party permits a retraction. No retraction is allowed if the nonrepudiating party has canceled the contract or has materially changed his or her position in reliance on the repudiation. A retraction reestablishes the contract rights and duties of each party.

Excused Performance

Sometimes a seller may be forced into a delay in making delivery, may not be able to make delivery, or may have to make only a partial delivery. Normally, this would be treated as a breach. Some of these situations fall into the area of excused performance, however, and hence are not treated as a breach. Performance is excused, in whole or in part, if performance has become impracticable because of the occurrence of some event whose nonoccurrence was a basic assumption of the contract. Also, performance is excused if the seller's delay or lack of performance is based on compliance with a governmental order or regulation.

If the seller has an excuse for less than full performance, he or she must notify the buyer seasonably. If performance will be reduced but not eliminated, the seller is allowed to allocate deliveries among customers in a reasonable manner. On receiving notice of a planned allocation due to some excuse, the buyer must elect whether to terminate the contract or to modify it. Modifying it means accepting the partial delivery as a substitute performance. A failure to modify within 30 days will be treated as a termination.

In the following case, the seller argued that its performance should have been excused, thus negating the availability of "cover" as the preacceptance remedy the buyer was trying to use. See if you agree with the arguments the seller raised in its case.

19.2

CONAGRA, INC. V. BARTLETT PARTNERSHIP
540 N.W.2D 333 (NEB. 1995)

FACTS ConAgra, through its grain trading division, Peavey, operates grain elevators in various Nebraska locations and a grain merchandising office in Kearney, Nebraska. During 1992, ConAgra bought and sold in excess of 500,000,000 bushels of corn. The partnership conducts a farming operation, and consists of Roger Race, the managing partner and an experienced farmer, and three other farmers. In the summer of 1992, the partnership had approximately 2,800 acres planted in corn near Bartlett, Nebraska. In previous years, this acreage had yielded approximately 130 bushels per acre. Based on this, Race testified that he expected the total yield for 1992 to be approximately 360,000 bushels. The land farmed by the partnership was in the Sandhills and consisted of marginal soil. Because of the soil, more water, fertilizer, and care than normal were required to secure a good crop. In 1992, the partnership undertook an extensive manure-spreading operation to improve the soil. To keep costs down, the partnership started a practice of hauling corn to ConAgra's elevator in Grand Island and then on the way back hauling manure from Hastings to the land the partnership farmed. Race testified that this unusual arrangement prompted the partnership's interest in selling its corn to ConAgra, a fact known to ConAgra. On or about June 10, 1992, the partnership entered into a series of four contracts for the sale by the partnership and purchase by ConAgra of 300,000 bushels of corn. The first contract called for the delivery of 100,000 bushels of corn sometime in December 1992; the second for the delivery of 70,000 bushels of corn in January 1993; the third for the delivery of 65,000 bushels of corn in February 1993; and the fourth for the delivery of 65,000 bushels of corn in March 1993. Each contract left the price to be determined by the partnership at 20 cents below the

19.2

CONAGRA, INC. V. BARTLETT PARTNERSHIP, *continued*

540 N.W.2D 333 (NEB. 1995)

daily price of corn on the Chicago Board of Trade. The partnership had the right, up until the time of delivery, to pick the day on which the corn would be priced. On August 13, 1992, the partnership's crop was severely damaged by a hailstorm. Race called ConAgra on August 17 or 18 to report the hail damage . . . About a month later, on September 23, 1992, Race called the plant manager and informed him that the salvage value would be close to 70,000 bushels, but to be on the safe side he would like to lock in, or price out, 60,000 bushels. Race testified that at this time he did not understand that there may have been some damages to pay if the partnership could not fulfill its contracts. Later, on November 10, 1992, ConAgra placed a conference call to Race in an attempt to negotiate a settlement of the corn contract . . . After Race discussed the situation with his partners, the partnership decided that it would "try and buy a little corn. To start to fill these contracts," and the partnership eventually purchased 60,000 bushels of "wet" corn to dry in its facilities and deliver to ConAgra. Although it had priced out a total of 130,000 bushels of corn, the partnership delivered only 108,503.04 bushels, 100,000 bushels in fulfillment of the first contract and the remainder on the second contract. This left the partnership 61,496.96 bushels short of the corn it had priced out on the second contract and 130,000 bushels short of the corn it had contracted to sell in the third and fourth contracts . . . On February 18, 1993, ConAgra bought corn on the market to cover the partnership's unfilled obligations under the contracts at a claimed loss of $11,689.88. ConAgra then sued the partnership to recover its losses due to the breach of contract by the partnership.

ISSUES Was the partnership excused from its performance obligation due to the destruction of its crops in the hailstorm? Is ConAgra entitled to recover its claimed losses based on the cost of cover?

HOLDINGS No. The destruction of the crop did not excuse the partnership's duty to perform. Yes, but not the full amount allegedly lost.

REASONING In urging that its performance was excused, the partnership relies on . . . UCC §§ 2-613 and 2-615 . . . Section 2-613 governs casualty to identified goods and provides in relevant part:

Where the contract requires for its performance goods identified when the contract is made, and the goods suffer casualty without fault of either party before the risk of loss passes to the buyer . . . then . . .
(b) if the loss is partial . . . the buyer may nevertheless demand inspection and at his option either treat the contract as avoided or accept the goods with due allowance . . . or the deficiency in quantity but without further right against the seller.

Section 2-615 governs excuse by failure of presupposed conditions and reads in relevant part:
(a) Delay in delivery or nondelivery in whole or in part by a seller . . . is not a breach of his duty under a contract for sale if performance as agreed has been made impracticable by the occurrence of a contingency the nonoccurrence of which was a basic assumption on which the contract was made . . .

[W]e must determine whether the partnership is correct in asserting that the contracts in question contemplated that the corn to be delivered was to be grown on the partnership's land. In making that determination, we are bound by the longstanding principle of Nebraska contract law that a contract which is written in clear and unambiguous language is not subject to interpretation or construction; rather, the intent of the parties must be determined from the contents of the contract and the contract enforced according to its terms . . . The three contracts at issue are identical standardized form contracts which on their face state that the partnership will deliver a given number of bushels of corn to ConAgra within specified timeframes . . . Except for provisions which pertain to the quality of the grain to be delivered, there were no other conditions or specifications as to the grain included in the contracts. The contracts also contained an integration clause which provided that the "[c]ontract is intended by the parties as a final expression of their agreement and is intended also as a complete and exclusive statement of the terms and conditions of their agreement." The contract did not identify the grain in any way other than by kind and amount. Nor did the contract make any reference to corn grown or to be grown by the partnership on any identified acreage. The only limitation the contracts

continued

19.2

CONAGRA, INC. V. BARTLETT PARTNERSHIP, *continued*

540 N.W.2D 333 (NEB. 1995)

placed on the source of the corn was that it be grown in the continental United States. The only conclusion that can be drawn from the language of the contracts is that they contemplated that the partnership could fulfill its contractual obligations by acquiring corn from any place or source so long as the corn was grown within the continental United States. Thus, it cannot be said the contracts at issue are ambiguous. They therefore are not subject to interpretation or construction and must be enforced according to their terms . . . Accordingly, the district court did not err by overruling the partnership's motion for directed verdict . . . Since the record supports none of the assignments of error, the judgment of the district court must be, and hereby is, affirmed.

BUSINESS CONSIDERATIONS What could the partnership have done at the contract formation stage in order to protect itself from the sort of position in which it found itself? Is it an advisable business practice to draft contracts that try to cover as many contingencies or problems as the parties can imagine? Why?

ETHICAL CONSIDERATIONS Was it ethical for ConAgra to hold the partnership to the literal terms of their contracts after the hailstorm destroyed such a significant portion of the partnership's crop? Would ConAgra be breaching a duty to any other interested parties if it had excused the partnership's duty to perform in this case?

Adequate Assurances

When the parties enter a contract for the sale of goods, each expects to receive the benefit of the bargain made. If, before performance is due, either party feels insecure in expecting performance, the insecure party may demand assurances of performance. The insecure party must make a written demand for assurance that performance will be tendered when due. Until the assurances are given, the requesting party may suspend performance. If no assurance is given within 30 days of request, it is treated as repudiation of the contract.

The following case involved an "adequate assurances" issue. The case also involves the breaching of two contracts, the right of one party to cancel the performance of its obligations under the contracts, and a question as to how damages should be determined.

19.3

SMYERS V. QUARTZ WORKS CORP.

880 F.SUPP. 1425 (D.KAN. 1995)

FACTS Michael Smyers operates Engineered Specialty Products ("ESP"). On September 21, 1992, Quartz Works offered to purchase two welders from ESP at a total price of $88,825. At the time of its offer, Quartz Works also sent ESP a check for $66,618.75, representing a seventy-five percent down payment toward the total. Upon receiving Quartz Works' order, ESP sent back a counteroffer reflecting price adjust-

ments for some of the related parts and a total purchase price of $89,125 for the welders. The invoice that ESP sent back to Quartz Works credited the payment Quartz Works had made and indicated that the total amount due was now $22,506.25. The ESP invoice also included two additional terms. The first read "75% DOWN, 25% BEFORE SHIPMENT." The second provided that, if ESP were not timely paid, a

19.3

SMYERS V. QUARTZ WORKS CORP., *continued*

880 F.SUPP. 1425 (D.KAN. 1995)

service charge of 1.5% per month would be applied to the balance due . . . On November 11, 1992, defendant sent another purchase order to ESP. This one was for two single-diffraction goniometers, with accompanying software, and a proposed purchase price of $96,359.80. By its invoice of November 16, 1992, ESP agreed with the proposed price, but again added terms to which Quartz Works apparently did not object. The invoice . . . included the following payment terms: "⅓ DOWN, 90% BEFORE END OF '92, BAL. N/10 [within 10 days after shipment]." It reflected receipt of the one-third payment of $32,199.90 and indicated that the balance due was $64,239.90 . . . The parties agree that when the ninety percent payment was not received by the end of 1992, ESP raised the total price of the goniometers to $99,340, and changed the payment terms to one-third down and two-thirds before shipment of the goniometers. The goniometers were not shipped until October 1, 1993 . . . During [a] September 22 meeting, the parties agreed to modify the payment terms of both the welder contract and the goniometer contract. Instead of requiring final payment prior to shipment, as the contracts had originally done, final payment was to be made upon proof of shipment to defendant. The parties agreed that plaintiff would send a copy of the bills of lading to defendant by facsimile on the day of each shipment, and defendant would send payment by Federal Express that same day for arrival the following day. On September 29, 1993, plaintiff had the welders crated and placed them with Yellow Freight Systems . . . for shipment and delivery to defendant. Although Quartz Works received the welders, subsequently sent them to Mongolia, and received payment for them from its customer, Quartz Work has not paid ESP the $22,506.25 which it acknowledges is due under the welder contract. At this point, for various reasons, Smyers became anxious about whether he would be paid for the goniometers he was about to ship. [Quartz Works] had failed to pay for the welders and had also failed to respond to his messages. In addition, Smyers perceived cash flow problems [with Quartz Works] . . . and mistrust between ESP and Quartz Works had grown throughout the course of their relationship. Finally, because the welders and goniometers were destined for Mongolia, Smyers feared that his recourse in the event of nonpayment would be severely limited. Plaintiff

nonetheless felt obligated to ship the goniometers on October 1, 1992, as agreed. Instead of shipping the goniometers to Quartz Works . . . however, [he] shipped them to ESP as addressee . . . Again, he immediately sent a copy of the bill of lading to the defendant by facsimile . . . Plaintiff continued to demand payment for both the welders and the goniometers; defendant continued to ignore plaintiff's telephone and facsimile messages. The parties had reached an impasse. [Eventually Smyers sued Quartz Works for breach of contract. Quartz Works countersued, alleging that ESP had breached, forcing Quartz Works to "cover" by purchasing goniometers from another source, for a much higher price.]

ISSUES Did ESP have a right to request assurances from Quartz Works concerning its ability to pay for the goniometers? Did ESP make a proper written request for assurances?

HOLDINGS Yes, ESP had reasonable grounds to request assurance from Quartz Works. Yes, the facsimile sent to Quartz Works was a proper written request for assurances.

REASONING Under Kansas law, a party to a contract who becomes reasonably insecure of the other party's ability to fulfill its obligations under the contract may demand assurance of due performance . . . [§ 2-609]. If assurance is not received in a reasonable time, the party demanding such assurance may suspend performance . . . In order to suspend performance of his obligations under the goniometer contract pursuant to this section, plaintiff must (1) have reasonable grounds for insecurity regarding defendant's performance under the contract; (2) demand in writing adequate assurance of defendant's future performance; and (3) not receive such assurance from defendant . . . By October 1, 1993, plaintiff had reasonable grounds for insecurity under the goniometer contract. As mentioned before, plaintiff had been concerned about cash flow problems throughout 1993, and he feared that such problems might affect Quartz Works' ability to pay ESP. In addition, both parties testified that relations between them had sharply deteriorated over time. Most importantly, Quartz Works had not complied with its contractual obligations to pay ESP

continued

SMYERS V. QUARTZ WORKS CORP., *continued*
880 F.SUPP. 1425 (D.KAN. 1995)

for the welders upon proof of shipment. [Quartz Works] had not only failed to offer any explanation for [its] failure to pay, but [it] had even failed to return facsimile and telephones messages from ESP in the days following delivery of the welders. In view of this conduct, Mr. Smyers reasonably feared he would not be paid for the welders, and he was reasonably reluctant to relinquish control over the goniometers, as he had over the welders, because of his concern that once the equipment was shipped to Mongolia, any recourse for ESP in the event of Quartz Works' nonpayment would be severely limited. On September 30, 1993, plaintiff made written demand for assurance of defendant's performance . . . Furthermore, what constitutes adequate assurance is subject to the same evaluation of factual conditions as what constitutes reasonable grounds for insecurity . . . Under certain circumstances, even a demand for payment of earlier accounts due may be construed as a demand for adequate assurance under the Code . . . Under the facts presented here, the Court finds that Mr. Smyers' written demand for payment of the amount due on the welders contract constituted written demand for assurances of defendant's due performance under the goniometers contract. Not only did [Quartz Works] fail to pay for the welders or otherwise respond to Mr. Smyers' repeated attempts to contact him, the record does not reflect any communication at all from

Quartz Works to ESP until October 6, 1993—a week after the welders payment was due . . . In light of all the circumstances, the Court finds that, pursuant to [§ 2-609], Mr. Smyers was justified in suspending performance of his obligations under the goniometers contract as of October 1, 1993. The Court further finds that, by continuing to fail to pay for the welders or to provide other assurances, Quartz Works repudiated the goniometer contract . . . Finally, since the Court has determined that Quartz Works repudiated the goniometer contract by failing to provide adequate assurance upon ESP's reasonable request, defendant's claim for the cover damages it sustained in replacing the undelivered ESP goniometers is denied. . . .

BUSINESS CONSIDERATIONS When should a business seek adequate assurances from the other party to a contract? What sort of "assurances" should a business give when the other party requests them?

ETHICAL CONSIDERATIONS What ethical implications are raised by the adequate assurances rule? When is it ethical—and when is it unethical—to request adequate assurances in a contract?

Duty to Particularize

When the buyer rightfully rejects goods, he or she must do so properly. If the goods are rejected owing to a curable defect, the buyer may reject only by stating exactly what the defect is. A failure to do so will preclude the use of that defect to prove breach in court. And if the buyer cannot prove breach, the seller will be deemed to have performed properly. Thus, a failure to particularize can result in the buyer's being required to pay for nonconforming goods or in other liability to the seller.

STATUTE OF LIMITATIONS

Any lawsuit for breach of a sales contract must be started within four years of the breach, unless the contract itself sets a shorter time period. (The time period cannot be less than one year.) The fact that a breach is not discovered when it occurs is not material. The time limitation begins at breach, not at discovery. This reemphasizes the need for a buyer to inspect goods carefully and completely in order to protect his or her interests.

LEASES

Article 2A provides for remedies in the event a lease contract is breached. As under Article 2, the remedies available depend to a significant extent on when the breach occurs. A brief synopsis of the remedies is set out below.

Lessor's Remedies

If a lessee wrongfully rejects goods tendered under the lease, wrongfully revokes acceptance, fails to make payments when due, or repudiates the lease, the lessor may do any of the following:

1. Cancel the lease contract
2. Proceed respecting goods not identified to the lease contract
3. Withhold delivery of the goods and take possession of goods previously delivered
4. Stop delivery of the goods by any bailee
5. Dispose of the goods and recover damages, or retain the goods and recover damages, or, in a property case, recover rent

If a lessee is otherwise in default, the lessor may exercise the rights and remedies provided in the lease, as well as those listed in Article 2A.

Lessee's Remedies

If a lessor fails to deliver goods in conformity with the lease contract or repudiates the lease contract, or the lessee rightfully rejects the goods or justifiably revokes acceptance of the goods, then the lessee may do any of the following:

1. Cancel the lease contract
2. Recover as much of the rent and security as has been paid; but in the case of an installment lease contract, the recovery is that which is just under the circumstances
3. Cover and recover damages as to all goods affected, whether or not they have been identified to the lease contract, or recover damages for nondelivery

19.3 | SALES/ MANAGEMENT

HANDLING COMPLAINTS FROM RETAILERS

One of the retail outlets that purchased a number of Call-Image videophones has been very difficult to please. The sales manager of the store recently wrote a letter to the firm in which he alleged that the videophones were "unacceptable as delivered" and demanded that CIT send a truck to pick up the shipment. Tom immediately called the sales manager to find out why the units were "unacceptable as delivered," but he could not get any more concrete information from the sales manager as to what the alleged problem was. Dan and Anna want to rent a truck and go recover the units. They are willing to accept the fact that this one store does not want to carry the product, cancel their contract with this customer, and go on. Lindsay and John believe that the sales manager is acting improperly, and they want the firm to refuse to go get the units or to cancel the contract. They would prefer to demand payment from the store and to sue, if need be. They have asked for your opinion. What advice will you give them?

BUSINESS CONSIDERATIONS What are the contractual rights of a merchant who is notified by one of its customers that a product delivered under a contract is unacceptable as delivered? Does it make any difference whether the customer is a merchant or a nonmerchant? What sort of policy should a firm have to handle situations such as this?

ETHICAL CONSIDERATIONS Some retail establishments have a "money-back guarantee," under which they allow customers to return merchandise for a refund with "no questions asked." Suppose that an employee of the store knows that a customer has purchased a product with the intention of only using it one time and then returning it. Could that employee refuse to give the customer a refund on ethical grounds? How should such a situation be handled, from an ethical perspective?

RESOURCES FOR BUSINESS LAW STUDENTS

NAME	RESOURCES	WEB ADDRESS
Uniform Commercial Code (UCC) Articles 7, Warehouse Receipts, Bills of Lading, and other Documents of Title	The Legal Information Institute (LII), maintained by the Cornell Law School, provides a hypertext and searchable version of Article 7, Warehouse Receipts, Bills of Lading, and other Documents of Title. LII also maintains links to Article 7 as adopted by particular states and to proposed revisions.	**http://www.law.cornell.edu/ucc/7/overview.html**
UCC Article 2A, Leases	LII provides a hypertext and searchable version of the UCC Article 2A, Leases. LII also provides links to Article 2A as enacted by particular states and to proposed revisions.	**http://www.law.cornell.edu/ucc/2A/overview.html**

If the lessor fails to deliver the goods or repudiates the contract, the lessee may also take one of the following actions:

1. Recover any goods that have been identified to the contract
2. Obtain specific performance or replevin

If the lessor is otherwise in default under a lease contract, the lessee may exercise the rights and remedies provided in the lease contract and/or those included in Article 2A.

SUMMARY

Although most sales contracts are fully performed and the performance is normally satisfactory, sometimes a nonperformance occurs. When nonperformance is found, the innocent party usually seeks remedies for breach of contract.

When the buyer fails to perform, the seller will seek remedies. The available remedies depend on when the buyer breached. If the buyer breached before acceptance, the seller will seek one or more of six preacceptance remedies. If the buyer accepts the goods and then breaches, the seller will seek one or both of two postacceptance remedies. By the same token, if the seller breaches, the buyer will seek remedies. Again, the buyer's available remedies will depend on when the seller breached. If the seller breached before the buyer accepted the goods, the buyer may seek one or more of six preacceptance remedies. If the seller breaches after the buyer accepts, the buyer has up to three available postacceptance remedies.

Occasionally, a nonperformance turns out not to be a breach. It may involve a special problem that excuses performance or affects the rights of the innocent party. Great care must be exercised by both parties in these special problem areas.

Leases are also normally performed properly by both parties. Again, however, sometimes breaches occur. When they do, the breaching party is held liable for those damages that the nonbreaching party suffers. Article 2A lists specific remedies that are available and also specifically states that the parties are entitled to those damages called for in the lease contract as well as any of the remedies listed in the article. These Code remedies are very similar in nature and application to the remedies provided by Article 2.

DISCUSSION QUESTIONS

1. What remedies can a seller seek if the buyer breaches a sales contract before accepting the goods? Are these remedies mutually exclusive?
2. What are the seller's two potential postacceptance remedies, and when may the seller utilize either or both of them?
3. What are the three possible postacceptance remedies available to the buyer, and when may the buyer utilize each of them? Are these remedies mutually exclusive?
4. What is an *anticipatory repudiation,* and how does it affect contracts formed under the law of sales? Does a repudiation have the same meaning and impact under the law of leases?
5. What is an *adequate assurance,* and when does a party to a sales contract have the right to request such an assurance? What is required in order to maker a proper request for an adequate assurance?
6. Ace Manufacturing agreed to produce and sell some goods to Sampson. The contract called for 10 shipments of 25 units each. After satisfactorily completing 5 shipments, Ace sent the sixth shipment. Order 7 was then "in process." Sampson wrongfully rejected shipment 6. Ace decided to complete the work on order 7 and to sue Sampson for the contract price on shipments 6 and 7 and for lost profits on the remaining 3 shipments. Sampson argued that Ace could not complete order 7 at his (Sampson's) expense. Who is correct? Explain.
7. Tom shipped goods to Martin via Allied Parcel Service. After the goods were shipped, Tom discovered that Martin was insolvent. What can Tom do in this situation to prevent Martin from receiving the goods? What obligation does Tom have to Allied? Suppose

that Tom discovered that Martin had repudiated the contract. Would Tom have the same rights in that situation?
8. Roberto, the seller, was in possession of goods that Suzanne had wrongfully rejected. Roberto sold the goods to Brenda for one-half the contract price without telling anyone about the sale. Can Roberto collect the unpaid balance of the contract price from Suzanne? Does Suzanne have a claim against Roberto for damages even though Suzanne had initially breached the contract? Explain.
9. Bob and Sam entered into a contract that called for Sam to deliver goods to Bob and for Bob to pay $1,500 for them. Bob gave Sam a $500 deposit on the goods. During the contract period, Sam discovered that Bob was insolvent and decided to withhold delivery of the goods to him. While Bob admits that he is in breach, he also asserts that he is entitled to restitution for his deposit on the goods. Is Bob entitled to restitution, and, if so, how much can he recover from Sam? Explain.
10. Martha entered into a contract with Amy that called for Amy to manufacture and deliver goods to Martha, with delivery to occur in six months. Three months later, Martha phoned Amy and repudiated the contract. At the time, Martha thought she could obtain the goods from another source at a substantially lower price. When Martha realized that her repudiation would operate as a breach, she immediately called Amy, apologized for her conduct, and attempted to retract her repudiation. What are Amy's rights in this case? What are Martha's rights in this case?

CASE PROBLEMS AND WRITING ASSIGNMENTS

1. Conveying Techniques manufactures and fabricates conveying and material-processing equipment. Lakewood Pipe processes and sells steel pipe for the oil industry and for agricultural irrigation. In 1979, Conveying sold Lakewood a manual hydrostatic testing system. In 1984, Conveying gave Lakewood a written proposal for the construction and installation

of an automatic system. The two corporate presidents met soon thereafter, and Conveying demonstrated a prototype automatic system. According to Conveying's president (Lee), the president of Lakewood (Tybus) orally agreed to buy the system for $240,000. Tybus denied that he agreed, orally or otherwise. Conveying began construction of the automatic system in late 1984. In December 1984, Lee wrote to Lakewood, summarizing his understanding of the agreement and reminding Lakewood that all of its outstanding accounts receivable must be paid before the system would be installed. [Lee noted that the system had been delayed because Lakewood failed to pay, and he was concerned that Lakewood would not pay for the system prior to installation.] In February 1985, Lakewood informed Conveying that it was not in the market for the automatic system. In March, Conveying billed Lakewood for $80,000, determined by taking 30 percent of the contract price as "cancellation charges" on the contract. Did Lakewood breach a contract with Conveying in this case? If so, were the damages properly computed by Conveying? [See *Lakewood Pipe of Texas, Inc.* v. *Conveying Techniques, Inc.*, 814 S.W.2d 553 (Tex.App. Houston [1stDist.] 1991).]

2. On 19 and 22 February 1985, Ethyl Corporation delivered 6,000 gallons of gasoline additive in a railroad tank car, together with twelve 55-gallon drums of an antioxidant, to Pester's refinery in Kansas. Ethyl invoiced Pester for almost $127,000 for this credit sale. On 25 February 1985, Pester filed for protection under Chapter 11 of the Bankruptcy Code. On 27 February 1985, Pester received a written demand from Ethyl, which was seeking to reclaim the chemicals. Although the chemicals were still on hand at the refinery and were still identifiable, Pester refused to return them to Ethyl. [The chemicals were also subject to the perfected security interests of various of Pester's creditors, and these creditors had claims in excess of the value of Pester's assets.] While Ethyl's claim was still pending, the bankruptcy court approved Pester's reorganization plan, declared that reclamation creditors were an impaired creditor class, and allowed these creditors the option of settling or continuing their reclamation efforts. Only Ethyl continued its reclamation efforts. Pester objected to this ruling. Does a seller who is otherwise entitled to reclaim accepted goods retain the right to reclaim the goods in the face of superior competing claims by secured creditors of the buyer? [See *In Re Pester Refining Co.*, 964 F.2d 842 (8th Cir. 1992).]

3. Banque Arabe et Internationale d'Investissement (BAII) financed an agreement involving the buying and selling of petroleum. Will Petroleum was a small oil trading company that specialized in "blending." Will would purchase unfinished oil, add a component to boost octane, and then sell the oil to petroleum companies. In order to finance its operations, Will borrowed money from various banks, including BAII.

When Will sold the oil after blending, the buyer would send a check to BAII, which would credit its account to repay Will's loan and then credit Will's account with the balance of the check, reflecting Will's profit on the deal. BAII had been involved in more than 50 such transactions between Will and UPG over the years. Will and UPG entered another such agreement in December 1985, with BAII providing the financing. However, UPG became concerned that Will would be unable to perform as agreed and requested assurances from Will as to its ability to meet its obligations. When Will did not provide the necessary assurances, UPG covered by purchasing its oil needs from another firm. As a result, BAII never received payment from UPG as expected. Will Petroleum filed for bankruptcy in February 1986 and assigned its rights under the contracts to BAII. When UPG refused to honor the contracts assigned to BAII, BAII sold the oil to other buyers for approximately $5.5 million less than the agreement between Will and UPG specified. BAII then filed suit against UPG for the difference. Did UPG breach its contract with Will, providing the assignee under that contract with rights against UPG? Explain your answer. [See *BAII Banking Corp.* v. *UPG, Inc.*, 985 F.2d 685 (2d Cir. 1993).]

4. Trinidad is a Colorado corporation that owns and operates an elevator in Imperial, Nebraska. Elmo Frosh is an individual engaged in the business of farming. On or about 26 April 1988, Frosh entered into a written contract with Trinidad whereby Trinidad agreed to buy and Frosh agreed to sell 1,875 hundredweight of dried, edible navy beans, which were to be delivered to Trinidad at Imperial upon completion of the harvest of the 1988 crop. The written contract entered into by the parties on 26 April, at paragraph 7, provided for two options with respect to payment to Frosh. Option 1 provided for payment of $16.25 per hundredweight on 15 January 1989, and option 2 provided for 50 percent payment at $16 per hundredweight upon the completion of the harvest and for 50 percent payment at $16 per hundredweight on 1 December 1988. Option 1 would be accepted if the grower wished to defer income for tax purposes, and option 2 would be used if the grower wished immediate payment. Buffington, who had been employed with Trinidad for only one month when he prepared the Frosh agreement, inadvertently filled out both payment options. The error was first noticed by James Peterson, a commodity trader, when the contract was received in Trinidad's Denver office. Peterson contacted the Imperial office and asked that someone ascertain which option Frosh intended to exercise so that Trinidad's accounting department could process

the contract. Peterson spoke with Roberta Frosh, Trinidad's secretary at the Imperial elevator, and alerted her to the problem. Roberta Frosh had been the bookkeeper and secretary at the Imperial offices for 10 years. She was also the wife of Elmo Frosh. Buffington testified that Roberta Frosh alerted him to the error and told him to prepare a second page, limiting the payment provision to option 2. Buffington testified that he gave the second page to Roberta Frosh to obtain Elmo's signature. Roberta Frosh admitted that she knew about the second page of the contract but denied that anyone from Trinidad had requested that she obtain Elmo's signature. Elmo Frosh never signed a contract with only one payment option. He insisted that the contract was void since no payment option was ever agreed on and sent a letter to that effect to the Denver offices on 8 September. Harvest was completed in mid-October; no beans were delivered as promised in the contract. Because of drought conditions, the price of navy beans rose during the 1988 growing season from $16 per hundredweight in April to $32 per hundredweight in late August–early September and to $36 per hundredweight in late September, when Trinidad purchased beans from other sources. Trinidad sued Frosh for damages. The court instructed the jury that a contract existed and how to compute damages. The jury returned a verdict for Frosh, and Trinidad filed a motion for a judgment n.o.v., which was overruled. Trinidad then appealed. What was the proper measure of damages in this contract between the parties? [See *Trinidad Bean and Elevator Company* v. *Frosh*, 494 N.W.2d 347 (Neb.App. 1992).]

5. The Bowens' home had a Carrier heating and cooling system consisting of four exterior and four interior units. They decided to upgrade their system with equipment having a "12 seer rating" or higher to increase the efficiency of the heating and cooling of the house. In furtherance of this goal, they solicited bids from a number of local firms. Foust Plumbing and Heating's bid was accepted. The bid called for Foust to install a new heat pump system and specified that the seller was to install "four RHEEM 3½ ton heat pump systems with a seer rating of 12." The contract also called for the Bowens to pay $8,159 upon completion of the installation. Shortly after the installation was completed, a compressor went out. Foust removed the defective compressor and ordered a replacement. A few months later, a second compressor went out. Again, Foust removed the defective compressor and ordered a replacement. In October, the Bowens discovered that the new system would not produce any heat. Foust replaced the four interior units, submitting a bill to the Bowens for $1,400 for the work. Despite Foust's best efforts, however, the unit still produced no heat. At this point Foust told the family that the problem was in their breaker system. An electrician was hired to replace the breaker system in the house at a cost of approximately $200. After the breakers were replaced, there was still no heat from the new system. Finally, the Bowens had a second heat and air specialist inspect their system. This second specialist informed the family that the system "did not have a 12 seer rating." The following spring, the Bowens hired Ray Buffington, a Carrier dealer, to replace their system. Buffington removed the Rheems units (which are not compatible with Carrier units) and replaced them with larger Carrier equipment, bringing the system up to the 12 seer rating originally sought. The bill for this work was more than $15,000. The Bowens are now suing to revoke their acceptance of the goods provided by Foust and to recover the money paid to Foust under the contract. Foust objects, insisting that too much time has elapsed for the family to revoke its acceptance, and denys any liability to them. How should this case be resolved? [See *Bowen* v. *Foust*, 925 S.W.2d 211 (Mo.App.S.D. 1996).]

6. **BUSINESS APPLICATION CASE** Star Grain had been a licensed Iowa grain dealer but lost its license on 1 July 1988 when its principal officers and owners were indicted by an Illinois grand jury for defrauding customers and defaulting on certain checks. The defendants in this case were all farmers who had, prior to 1 July 1988, entered into contracts with Star Grain calling for them to deliver various amounts of grain in October and November 1988. When Star Grain had its license suspended, it sought relief under Chapter 11 of the Bankruptcy Code. The defendants objected to Star Grain's attempt to have the bankruptcy court enforce their contracts with Star Grain as debtor-in-possession. On 7 October 1988, Star Grain assigned its contracts with the defendants to Duffe Grain, a licensed grain dealer. Duffe then contacted all of the parties with whom Star Grain had futures contracts, informing them of the assignment and providing information on when and where delivery was to be tendered. All of the farmers except the three defendants ultimately delivered their grain to Duffe as per the assignment. The three defendants eventually sold their grain elsewhere, Duffe reassigned their contracts to Star Grain, and Star Grain sued each for breach of contract. Did the letter from Duffe to the farmers constitute proper notice of a change in delivery to be binding on the farmers? Did the farmers properly demand adequate assurances that the contracts would

be performed, as required by the UCC? Should a merchant, who is expected to act in good faith in a commercially reasonable manner, act in this fashion in performing his contracts? [See *S & S, Inc.* v. *Meyer*, 478 N.W.2d 857 (IowaApp. 1991).]

7. **ETHICAL APPLICATION CASE** Burberrys had an agreement with Abraham Zion Corp. under which Zion was to manufacture 30,000 Burberry raincoats for Burberrys. Burberrys raincoats are of a unique design and style, and their trademarks are registered in the United States. Burberrys provided the distinctive material, patterns, styles, data, labels, tags, and documents necessary for making the raincoats; and 22,000 of the raincoats were produced by Zion. Then a dispute arose between the parties, and their relationship ceased. Burberrys now alleges that Zion plans to produce the remaining 8,000 raincoats and sell them to After Six. Burberrys sued, seeking an injunction *pendente lite* (preliminary injunction pending the suit) to prevent the manufacture and/or sale of the remaining 8,000 raincoats. Should Zion be allowed to complete manufacture of the remaining goods called for under the contract and then resell them as a seller's pre-acceptance remedy? What ethical considerations enter into your resolution of this case? [See *Burberrys (Wholesale) Ltd.* v. *After Six, Inc.*, 471 N.Y.S.2d 235 (Sup. 1984).]

8. **CRITICAL THINKING CASE** On 17 September 1987, Ance and Alice Page purchased a new van from the Treadwell Ford automobile dealership, trading in their old car and financing the remainder of the van's $24,500 purchase price through Treadwell. At the time of the purchase, the Pages received warranties from Ford Motor Company, which had manufactured the basic vehicle, and the Zimmer Corporation, which had installed various modifications transforming the vehicle into a conversion van. Treadwell, however, disclaimed all express or implied warranties. Soon after their purchase, the Pages discovered numerous problems with the van, finding a steady stream of leaks around the van's windshield and top and around its side and back doors. There was water damage to the interior. The Pages also discovered that, among other things, the motors controlling the passenger- and driver-side windows malfunctioned, rubber sealing around the back door had come loose, wall panels and a cabinet were broken, the television set and the interior lights would not work at the same time, the stereo speakers often did not work, molding around the television set was loose, the van rattled badly, the paint on the roof had faded, the gas gauge and the cruise control did not work, the front end was misaligned, and the van used three to five quarts of oil per month. On a regular basis the Pages began taking the van for repairs by Treadwell, the authorized agent for warranty work, traveling some 80 miles round trip with another vehicle to drive home each time. Eventually, many of the defects were repaired, but a number were not, with Treadwell indicating that there were certain problems that could not be corrected. The Pages attempted and failed to receive satisfaction through numerous letters and telephone conversations with Treadwell and Ford. In late 1987, the Pages gave notice to Treadwell of their desire to revoke acceptance of their purchase. Treadwell, however, refused to recognize the Pages' attempt at revocation. On 21 February 1989, the Pages filed suit against Treadwell, Ford, and Zimmer. The jury returned verdicts in favor of Ford and Zimmer but found that the requisite elements of the revocation claim had been met. The court then permitted the revocation and assessed $7,500 in damages against Treadwell. The Pages and Treadwell appealed. Were the Pages entitled to revoke their acceptance after 10 months without a showing of fraud or breach of warranty by the seller? If they were entitled to revoke, were they also entitled to any damages in this case? What arguments can you present in support of the Pages? In support of Treadwell? Which arguments do you think are more persuasive? [See *Page* v. *Dobbs Mobile Bay, Inc.*, 599 So.2d 38 (Ala.Civ.App. 1992).]

NOTE

1. "Tort ReformAdvocates Condemn GM Jury Award." *The Detroit News* (5 June 1996).

20

INTERNATIONAL SALE OF GOODS

A G E N D A

Suppose that CIT solves its initial problems and achieves success locally and regionally. How can the firm place the invention in the international market? What statute(s) will regulate the sale of Call-Image internationally? When will the sales be governed by the UCC? The CISG?

These and other questions will arise during our discussion of sales contracts. Be prepared! You never know when one of the Kochanowskis will need your help or advice.

O U T L I N E

Introduction
The United Nations Convention on Contracts
   for the International Sale of Goods
Obligations Under the CISG
Remedies Under the CISG
ISO 9000
Ethical Issues in the International Sale of Goods

Standard Shipping Terms in International Trade
   (Incoterms)
Proposed International Coverage
Pricing and Payment
Summary
Discussion Questions
Case Problems and Writing Assignments

INTRODUCTION

Business is rapidly "going global," with international trade increasing each year. A significant portion of international trade involves the sale of goods, with the balance comprised of services. Whether goods or services are involved, the trade entails contracts between the parties. Most of these contracts will be performed with few, if any, problems—at least legally. However, some of these contracts will not be performed at all or will not be performed satisfactorily, and legal issues will arise due to the inadequate performance. These legal issues may well present legal problems beyond the "mere" problem of the alleged breach of contract.

There are substantially more than 100 separate nations today, each with its own (somewhat) unique legal system. Familiarity with each of these legal systems would be impractical at best. Yet a person who does business with a person in another nation may be subject to the laws of that other nation in a contract action.

To reduce the complexity somewhat, there are a few overriding legal theories that provide the basis for most—if not all—of the legal systems in the world. A number of countries base their legal systems on a common law tradition in which the law is provided by court cases and statutes used in combination. Legislation is enacted by the government, but that legislation is subject to interpretation by the courts. In addition, areas that are not specifically covered by legislation are interpreted by the courts, and the gaps in the law are filled by court opinions. Common law originated in England and is the basis for the legal systems in Australia, Canada, England, the United States, and a number of other nations that are—or were—closely allied with England in the past.

A second basis for law is found in civil law nations. A civil law nation bases its law and its legal theory on the codes of the nation. The legislation is meant to provide exclusive coverage of a topic. Judicial interpretation is not a major factor in civil law nations, and the courts are not concerned with precedents from prior judicial opinions. Most of Europe follows the civil law tradition, with their systems based on the Napoleonic Code.

Islamic law forms a third basis for law. Islamic law is based on the religious beliefs and doctrines of Islam. Many Middle Eastern nations base their legal systems on Islamic law, and this legal theory has influenced the development of legal systems in a number of developing nations.

A significant part of Eastern Europe and Asia is still influenced by communist or socialist philosophies. These philosophies form an important component of the legal systems in some nations.

In addition, there are many different languages used in the world. Communication between people who speak different languages can make international trade more difficult than national trade between people who share a common language and a culture. Recall the *Frigaliment Importing Co.* case from Chapter 3. The simple word *chicken* caused serious legal problems in that case. As technological advances are made, translation problems and misunderstandings are likely to increase. As the *Frigaliment* case indicates, the potential for confusion or misunderstanding as to what meaning is in effect in a given contract is present with any international sales contract.

Determining which laws are in effect and need to be followed also fosters potential confusion or misunderstanding to a much greater extent in international trade than in domestic trade. This potential for confusion, in turn, has had a negative impact on the growth and development of international trade. Something new was needed to reflect the increasingly international nature of business as the twentieth century progressed. This "something new" became the United Nations Convention on Contracts for the International Sale of Goods, the CISG.

THE UNITED NATIONS CONVENTION ON CONTRACTS FOR THE INTERNATIONAL SALE OF GOODS

The CISG was drafted at the behest of the United Nations to provide for international sales what Article 2 of the Uniform Commercial Code (UCC) provides in the United States for domestic sales, a uniform set of rules governing sales contracts. There had been earlier attempts to provide regulations for international sales, most notably the efforts arising from the international diplomatic conference in The Hague in 1964. In fact, beginning in 1930, the International Institute for the Unification of Private Law (UNIDROIT) began work on a uniform law regulating the international sale of goods. Following World War II, the draft prepared by UNIDROIT was submitted to the diplomatic conference at The Hague. This conference drafted two conventions, one dealing with the international sale of goods (ULIS) and one dealing with the formation of contracts for the international sale of goods (ULF). Both conventions eventually were ratified by several nations, and each went into effect in 1972. However, neither ever received widespread acceptance, being limited almost exclusively to European ratifiers.

Even before either of these conventions went into effect, the United Nations instituted the Conference on International Trade (UNCITRAL) in 1968, charging this conference with the task of unifying the international law governing sales. To help ensure broader acceptance of its actions, the conference was composed of representatives from numerous countries, with broad diversity in the legal traditions and the economic status of the represented states. Initially, UNCITRAL tried to modify ULIS to make it more widely acceptable. However, this effort soon proved hopeless, and UNCITRAL began work on two new conventions to replace the ULIS and the ULF.

Meeting once a year, UNCITRAL took nine years to prepare draft conventions dealing with the international sale of goods and with the formation of international sales contracts. These two drafts were combined into one draft **convention** in 1978, and that combined convention was submitted to an official diplomatic convention convened in Vienna in 1980 by the United Nations General Assembly.

Convention
An agreement between nations; a treaty.

The final language of the CISG was approved at the Vienna Conference in 1980. Sixty-two nations participated in the Vienna Conference, and these nations helped in the drafting of the convention. By having such broad participation (one commentator characterized the participants as 22 Western nations, 11 socialist nations, and 29 third-world nations[1]), the convention provides compromise standards that should eventually prove acceptable to most of the world. There were 20 signatory nations, including the United States. (The U.S. Senate unanimously ratified the CISG in 1986.) The CISG became effective 1 January 1988 for all of the ratifying nations.

As of 1 March 2000, the UN Treaty Section reports that 59 nations have signed and/or ratified the convention. These nations are listed in Exhibit 20.1.[2]

Domestically, there are numerous legal traditions that various nations follow, and there are various levels of economic development among the member nations of the United Nations. Both of these differences present problems in deriving a uniform set of laws to govern the international sale of goods. Common law nations, such as England, the United States, and the numerous nations that are—or have

E X H I B I T 20.1 | CISG Signatory Nations

Nation	Ratification Date	Signature Date	Nation	Ratification Date	Signature Date
Argentina	19 July 1983		Lesotho	18 June 1981	18 June 1981
Australia	17 March 1988		Lithuania	18 January 1995	
Austria	29 December 1987	11 April 1980	Luxembourg	30 January 1997	
Belarus	9 October 1989		Mauritania	20 August 1999	
Belgium	31 October 1996		Mexico	29 December 1987	
Bosnia and Herzegovina	12 January 1994		Mongolia	31 December 1997	
Bulgaria	9 July 1990		Netherlands	11 December 1990	29 May 1981
Burundi	4 September 1998		New Zealand	22 September 1994	
Canada	23 April 1991		Norway	20 July 1988	26 May 1981
Chile	7 February 1990	11 April 1980	Peru	25 March 1999	
China	11 December 1986	30 September 1981	Poland		28 September 1981
Croatia	8 June 1998		Republic of Moldavia	13 October 1994	
Cuba	2 November 1994		Romania	22 May 1991	
Czech Republic[a]	5 March 1990	1 September 1981	Russian Federation[b]	16 August 1990	
Denmark	14 February 1989	26 May 1981	Singapore		11 April 1980
Ecuador	27 January 1992		Slovakia	28 May 1993	
Egypt	6 December 1982		Slovenia	7 January 1994	
Estonia	20 September 1993		Spain	24 July 1990	
Finland	15 December 1987	26 May 1981	Sweden	15 December 1987	26 May 1981
France	6 August 1982	27 August 1981	Switzerland	21 February 1990	
Georgia	16 August 1994		Syrian Arab Republic	19 October 1982	
Germany	21 December 1989	26 May 1981	Uganda	12 February 1992	
Ghana		11 April 1980	Ukraine	3 January 1990	
Greece	12 January 1998		United States of America	11 December 1986	31 August 1981
Guinea	23 January 1991				
Hungary	16 June 1983	11 April 1980	Uruguay	25 January 1999	
Iraq	5 March 1990		Uzbekistan	27 November 1996	
Italy	11 December 1986	30 September 1981	Venezuela		28 September 1981
Kyrgyzstan	11 May 1999		Yugoslavia[c]	27 March 1985	11 April 1980
Latvia	31 July 1997		Zambia	6 June 1986	

a. Slovakia, by succession, 28 May 1993; Czech Republic, by succession, 30 September 1993.
b. Estonia, by accession, 20 September 1993.
c. Slovenia, by succession, 7 January 1994; Bosnia and Herzegovina, by succession, 12 January 1994.

been—heavily influenced by England, traditionally follow a less rigid system in forming and performing sales contracts. Civil law nations, including most of Europe except for England, follow a more rigid system in which statutes provide the entire framework of the sales contract. Nations that follow Islamic law, including most of the Middle East, have different expectations regarding contract law. Socialist nations prefer much more controlled terms and allow much less flexibility in forming contracts, establishing prices, and dealing with remedies. Industrialized nations have different expectations than developing—or "third-world"—nations. All of these differences have made the creation and ratification of the CISG very difficult.

Despite these differences, and despite the difficulties, a convention was agreed on and ratified by 44 (now up to 54) nations. This convention holds out the hope for a truly uniform international law governing the sale of goods. In the interim, the CISG may provide the controlling law for international sale-of-goods contracts under two different sets of circumstances:

1. The contract for the sale of goods is made between firms from different countries, if both countries have ratified the convention.
2. The contract for the sale of goods designates that the law of a particular country will be the applicable law governing the contract, provided that the country whose laws will be applicable has ratified the convention.

OBLIGATIONS UNDER THE CISG

The CISG provides the framework for the international sale of goods in much the same way that Article 2 of the UCC provides the framework for the domestic sale of goods in the United States. However, students should avoid drawing too strict a comparison between the UCC and the CISG. Not all the subjects covered by the UCC are also covered by the CISG, nor does the CISG extend to as many sales as does Article 2. For example, the CISG does not apply to the sale of goods intended for personal or household use unless the seller neither knew or should have known that the goods were being purchased for personal or household use.[3] By contrast, Article 2 does apply to such purchases by a consumer, even providing warranty protection to the consumer in many such situations.

There are some other significant differences between the UCC and the CISG, and some of these differences may prove troublesome for U.S. businesses (as well as businesses from other common law nations) new to the international

EXPANDING SALES INTO THE INTERNATIONAL MARKETPLACE

Amy Chen represents the firm in its legal matters. She has expressed some concerns about the firm's recent interest in expanding its sales into the international marketplace. As Amy points out, she has no experience in international law and has little knowledge of, and no experience with, the CISG. She is quite comfortable with the UCC, and she is very comfortable representing the firm in court as long as the case involves U.S. law. Tom wonders if there is any way for the firm to conduct business internationally without having its contracts subject to the provisions of the CISG. He would also like to know whether the CISG is more "seller-friendly" than Articles 2 or 2A of the UCC. He would like to know what options are available for the firm and has asked you for advice. What will you tell him?

BUSINESS CONSIDERATIONS When a firm enters into a contract with a business located in another country, should the firm include dispute resolution as part of the contract? For example, should the contract include a choice of applicable law and/or a designation as to which nation's courts will hear disputes? Should provisions be made for some alternative dispute-resolution method, such as arbitration?

ETHICAL CONSIDERATIONS Is it ethical to designate a nation's courts and/or laws as the sole means for resolving disputes in an international sale-of-goods contract? Does this provide the party who selects the courts and/or laws with an unfair "home-court advantage," to the detriment of the other firm? How should this issue be resolved in a manner that is fair and equitable to all parties?

marketplace. For example, under common law, in order to have a contract there must be (1) an offer, (2) an acceptance, and (3) consideration. The CISG does not mention "consideration"—a basic element of contract formation in common law countries. Instead, the CISG view is that, since consideration is part of the formation of the contract, it relates to the "validity" of the contract. Validity-of-the-contract issues are to be determined by applicable national law, not by the CISG.

Another formation-of-the-contract issue involves acceptance. Unlike consideration, which is a matter to be resolved under applicable national law, the CISG does address the issue of acceptance. Under common law, an acceptance is effective when sent by the offeree (the "mailbox rule"), placing the risk of misdelivery or nondelivery on the offeror. Under civil law, an acceptance is not effective until it is received by the offeror, placing the risk of misdelivery or nondelivery on the offeree. These two positions are diametrically opposed. This means that in a civil law nation, an offer can be revoked by the offeror at any time prior to his or her receipt of an acceptance. In a common law nation, the offer cannot be revoked once an acceptance has been sent by the offeree.

In Article 18(2), the CISG states that an acceptance is effective when it reaches the offeror—the civil law rule. However, it also states, in Article 16(1), that an offer may not be revoked after an acceptance has been sent (even though it may not yet have been received)—a variation on the common law rule. Finally, Article 18(3) says that an acceptance is effective as soon as the offeree shows acceptance by beginning to perform—another concession to common law traditions.

Another difference involves the need for a written agreement for some contracts. Many U.S. firms are used to the applicability of the Statute of Frauds, requiring that a contract for the sale of goods (subject to numerous exceptions) must be in writing if the contract is for $500 or more. These parties may be shocked to learn that the CISG specifically states that oral contracts for the sale of goods are enforceable.[4] Since there is no need for any writing, U.S. firms may believe that they are still in the negotiations (prewriting) stage while their non-U.S. counterparts (especially if those counterparts are from civil law nations) will believe that an oral agreement has been reached and will be expecting performance. If the CISG is the statute governing the sale, a contract will exist, and the U.S. firm will have to perform despite the lack of a writing.

In the following case, the court had to decide whether it should allow parol evidence in a case governed by the CISG. The court also had to address an allegation of breach of contract in the performance of the agreement. Follow the reasoning of the court, and then decide whether you think the same results would occur under the UCC.

20.1

MITCHELL AIRCRAFT SPARES, INC. V. EUROPEAN AIRCRAFT SERVICE AB
23 F.SUPP.2D 915 (N.D.ILL. 1998)

FACTS Mitchell Aircraft Spares, Inc. filed suit against defendant European Aircraft Service AB ("EAS") . . . asserting claims for breach of contract and breach of warranty. Mitchell acts as a speculator and broker in the market for surplus commercial aircraft parts. Greg

Fletcher . . . is a vice president and part owner of Mitchell . . . EAS buys parts from companies in Western Europe and the United States and sells these parts to airlines, overhaul ships, brokers, and companies like itself. Leif Hedberg . . . is a vice president and

MITCHELL AIRCRAFT SPARES, INC. V. EUROPEAN AIRCRAFT SERVICE AB, *continued*
23 F.SUPP.2D 915 (N.D.ILL. 1998)

part owner of EAS. Hedberg's main responsibilities at EAS are purchasing and sales . . . The dispute between these parties arises from an agreement between the parties that EAS would sell certain aircraft parts, specifically integrated drive generators ("IDGs"), to Mitchell. An IDG is an aircraft part used on L-1011 aircraft and is composed of two parts: a constant speed drive or transmission and a generator. In June of 1996, EAS had three IDGs available for purchase. EAS listed these IDGs on the Inventory Locator Database ("ILD"), which is an international database that contains listings of surplus aircraft parts available for purchase. The parties dispute exactly how EAS listed these parts: Mitchell claims that EAS listed the parts as part number 729640 IDGs; EAS claims that it listed the parts with two or three alternative part numbers, one of which was 729640 . . . On or about June 30, 1996, Fletcher contacted Hedberg about the three IDGs that EAS had listed on the ILD. One of Fletcher's sub-specialities within the Mitchell organization is buying and selling L-1011 IDGs . . . Fletcher asked Hedberg about the availability, the condition, and the price of the three IDGs and about how soon EAS could ship the parts. Hedberg told Fletcher that EAS had three IDGs for the L-1011 available and that they were in "as removed" condition . . . Fletcher and Hedberg then began negotiations over the IDGs . . . Hedberg sent Fletcher a fax dated July 3, 1996. In the fax, Hedberg listed the information off of the data plates on the three IDGs . . . The July 3 fax did not expressly state that the IDGs were part number 729640; rather the fax gave the part numbers for the generators and transmissions that went together to form the IDG . . . Fletcher determined from the information contained in the July 3 fax that the parts available for sale were part number 729640 . . . Fletcher and Hedberg agreed upon a price of $50,000 per IDG. Mitchell then issued a purchase order for the IDGs. The purchase order describes the IDGs as part number 729640 . . . EAS then prepared an invoice which describes the parts as "729640 IDG." The invoice also references Mitchell's purchase order. EAS also provided Mitchell with a "Material Certification Form," which describes the parts as 720460 IDGs and references Mitchell's purchase order. EAS then shipped the IDGs to Mitchell. Mitchell forwarded the IDGs . . . for overhaul . . . [At this point Mitchell learned that the IDGs in question

were part number 708524 rather than 729640.] Mitchell claims to have suffered damages in the amount of $120,000 as a result of having received IDGs that were part number 708524 instead of part number 729640. Unable to resolve the dispute, Mitchell filed suit for breach of contract and breach of warranty . . . [Each party filed a motion for summary judgment.]

ISSUES What specific goods did EAS agree to sell to Mitchell? Can the court consider parol evidence in deciding this dispute under the provisions of the CISG?

HOLDINGS There were unresolved issues of material fact that needed to be resolved at a trial before a determination could be made regarding what specific goods were to be sold. Yes, parol evidence can be admitted in deciding a case under the CISG.

REASONING Before analyzing the evidence submitted by the parties, the court must determine whether it can consider parol evidence in deciding the parties' dispute. Mitchell argues that the court cannot because the contract, i.e., the purchase order, is clear and unambiguous. EAS argues that the court can because the contract is patently ambiguous. Neither Mitchell nor EAS addressed whether parol evidence is admissible under the relevant provisions of the CISG. This court was unable to find any case from the Seventh Circuit or a district court in the Seventh Circuit which has addressed the issue . . . This is not surprising because "there is virtually no case law under the Convention." . . . Thus, the issue of whether the court can consider parol evidence in a contract dispute governed by the CISG is an issue of first impression for this court . . . Accordingly, the court finds that it must consider any evidence concerning any negotiations, agreements, or statements made prior to the issuance of the purchase order in this case in determining whether the parties contracted for EAS to sell Mitchell three IDGs part number 729640 or, alternatively, to sell Mitchell the three IDGs that EAS had available for purchase. One might argue that Illinois law, not the CISG, governs the parol evidence issue in this case because the parol evidence rule is a rule of contract formation, and . . . Illinois law governs contract

continued

20.1

MITCHELL AIRCRAFT SPARES, INC. V. EUROPEAN AIRCRAFT SERVICE AB, *continued*
23 F.SUPP.2D 915 (N.D.ILL. 1998)

formation issues in this case . . . However, the issue of parol evidence is addressed in article 8 of the CISG, which is in Part I of the CISG . . . Neither Sweden nor the United States declared that it would not be bound by Part I of the CISG . . . Thus, the court finds that the CISG, not Illinois law, governs the parol evidence issue in this contract dispute. Assuming that Illinois law would govern the parol evidence issue, however, parol evidence would still be admissible in this case. In Illinois, parol evidence is admissible when the contract is ambiguous . . . Whether an ambiguity exists is a question of law for the court to decide . . . In this case, the purchase order is ambiguous . . . Because the contract contains such an ambiguity, Illinois law allows the court to consider parol evidence in interpreting the contract. Having determined that the CISG requires the court to consider the contract along with any evidence concerning any negotiations, agreements, or statements made prior to the issuance of the purchase order in this case, the court must now determine whether there is a genuine issue of fact as to whether the parties contracted for EAS to sell Mitchell three IDGs having part number 729640 or, alternatively, to sell Mitchell the three IDGs that EAS had available for purchase. . . . Based on the . . . evidence, the court finds that there is a genuine issue

of material fact which precludes summary judgment. There is evidence that the parties contracted for EAS to sell IDGs part number 729640. There is also evidence that the parties contracted for EAS to sell Mitchell the IDGs that EAS had available for purchase. Accordingly, neither party is entitled to summary judgment on this issue . . .

BUSINESS CONSIDERATIONS What steps should a business take to ensure that its contractual agreement is reduced to a writing, and that the terms of that writing are clear and unambiguous, especially when dealing with a business from another country? How might Mitchell have acted in this case to better protect his interests?

ETHICAL CONSIDERATIONS Is it ethical for a buyer to sue a seller for breach of contract in a situation where it appears that both parties were mistaken as to the nature or quality of the goods in question? Is it ethical for a seller to deny specific knowledge in an effort to possibly avoid potential liability if the goods turn out to be nonconforming?

U.S. sellers expect their buyers to inspect the goods tendered for delivery and to give specific reasons for any rejection. A failure to properly reject is deemed to be an acceptance of the goods as tendered, making the buyer liable for the purchase price. Under the CISG, a buyer may not rely on any lack of conformity as a reason to reject the goods unless notice of the nonconformity is given to the seller within a reasonable time. This sounds like the UCC rule, but there is a difference—the CISG states that there is a time limit of two years for the giving of notice, unless the contract includes an agreement setting a different time.[5] To further confuse U.S. firms, even if the buyer fails to give the required notice, Article 44 of the CISG allows the buyer to "reduce the price . . . or claim damages, except for the loss of profit, if he has a reasonable excuse for his failure to give the required notice."[6]

Common law nations treat offers as freely revocable at any time prior to acceptance, unless the offeree has an option or unless the parties are governed by the UCC and a merchant has made a firm offer. Civil law countries generally treat an offer that states a time limit as irrevocable. Thus, there is a basic difference between common law and civil law in this area. The CISG generally adopts the common law approach, making the offer freely revocable at any time prior to acceptance. However, there are, based on civil law, two important exceptions:

1. The offer is irrevocable where the offer states that an acceptance must be made within a stated time.
2. The offer is irrevocable if it was reasonable for the offeree to rely on the offer remaining open, and the offeree did, in fact, rely on the offer remaining open.[7]

Thus, an offer that says the offeree has 20 days to accept is deemed to be irrevocable for the 20-day period even though the offer does not take the form of a firm offer as provided for in the UCC. In addition, the CISG applies a **promissory estoppel**-like exception when the facts of the case make it appear that the offeree relied on the fact that the offer would remain open and will be harmed if the offer is not held open for the time indicated in the offer. (Note that the CISG does not require the offeror to reasonably expect the offeree to reply, to his or her detriment, as the common law would.)

The following case is the first instance where a U.S. court decided a case based on the CISG principles. Think of the similarities between the decision the court reached in applying the CISG and the decision the court would have reached under Article 2 of the UCC.

Promissory estoppel
A legal doctrine that prohibits a promisor from denying that a promise was made due to the justifiable reliance of the promisee that the promise will be kept.

20.2

FILANTO, S.P.A. V. CHILEWICH INT'L CORP.
789 F.SUPP. 1229 (S.D.N.Y. 1992)

FACTS This case is a striking example of how a lawsuit involving a relatively straightforward international commercial transaction can raise an array of complex questions. . . . Plaintiff Filanto is an Italian corporation engaged in the manufacture and sale of footwear. Defendant Chilewich is an export–import firm incorporated in the state of New York. . . . On 28 February 1989, Chilewich's agent in the United Kingdom signed a contract with Raznoexport, the Soviet Foreign Economic Association, which obligated it to supply footwear to Raznoexport. Section 10 of this contract—the "Russian Contract"—is an arbitration clause, which reads in pertinent part as follows:

All disputes or differences which may arise out of or in connection with the present Contract are to be settled, jurisdiction of ordinary courts being excluded, by the Arbitration at the USSR Chamber of Commerce and Industry, Moscow, in accordance with the Regulations of the said Arbitration. [sic]

The first exchange of correspondence between the parties to this lawsuit is a letter dated 27 July 1989 from . . . Chilewich to . . . Filanto, as part of the negotiations to fulfill the Russian Contract. This letter states as follows:

Attached please find our contract to cover our purchases from you. Same is governed by the conditions which are enumerated in the standard contract in

effect with the Soviet buyers [the Russian Contract], copy of which is also enclosed.

Following an exchange of correspondence, Filanto accepted the contract with Chilewich, but attempted to exclude the arbitration provision found in the Russian Contract, and which was also included in the original communication to Filanto from Chilewich. . . . The next document in this case, and the focal point of the parties' dispute regarding whether an arbitration agreement exists, is a Memorandum Agreement dated 13 March 1990. This Agreement . . . is a standard merchant's memo prepared by Chilewich for signature by both parties confirming that Filanto will deliver 100,000 pairs of boots to Chilewich at the Italian/Yugoslav border on 15 September 1990, with the balance of 150,000 pairs to be delivered on 1 November 1990. . . . This Memorandum includes the following provision:

It is understood between Buyer and Seller that [the Russian Contract] is hereby incorporated in this contract as far as practicable, and specifically that any arbitration shall be in accordance with that Contract.

Chilewich signed this Memorandum and sent it to Filanto. Filanto at that time did not sign or return the document. . . . Then, on 7 August 1990, Filanto returned the Memorandum Agreement, sued on here,

continued

20.2

FILANTO, S.P.A. V. CHILEWICH INT'L CORP., *continued*
789 F.SUPP. 1229 (S.D.N.Y. 1992)

that Chilewich had signed and sent to it in March; although Filanto had signed it, Filanto had also appended a cover letter purporting to exclude the arbitration provisions. . . .

It appears that the parties performed as agreed on 15 September 1990, but that problems arose with the scheduled 1 November 1990 performance. According to the complaint, what ultimately happened was that Chilewich bought and paid for 60,000 pairs of boots in January 1991, but never purchased the 90,000 pairs of boots that comprise the balance of Chilewich's original order. It is Chilewich's failure to do so that forms the basis of this lawsuit, commenced by Filanto on 14 May 1991.

ISSUES Did the contract require that the parties submit any claims to arbitration, or had Filanto excluded arbitration? If arbitration was to be used, where was the arbitration to occur?

HOLDINGS The parties were bound to submit their claims to arbitration. The proper place for the arbitration was in Moscow, as per the contract terms.

REASONING There is in the record one document that post-dates the filing of the Complaint: a letter from Filanto to Chilewich dated 21 June 1991. The letter is in response to claims by Chilewich that some of the boots that had been supplied by Filanto were defective. The letter expressly relies on a section of the Russian Contract which Filanto had earlier purported to exclude—Section 9 regarding claims procedures. . . . This letter must be regarded as an admission in law by Filanto, the party to be charged. A litigant may not blow hot and cold in a lawsuit. The letter of 21 June 1991 clearly shows that when Filanto thought it desirable to do so, it recognized that it was bound by the incorporation by reference of portions of the Russian Contract. . . . This position is entirely inconsistent with the position which Filanto had earlier professed, and is inconsistent with its present position. Consistent with the position of the defendant in this action, Filanto admits that the other relevant clauses of the Russian Contract were incorporated by agreement of the parties, and made a part of the bargain. Of necessity, this must include the agreement to arbitrate in Moscow. . . .

As plaintiff correctly notes, the "general principles of contract law" relevant to this action, do *not* include the Uniform Commercial Code; rather, the "federal law of contracts" to be applied in this case is found in the United Nations Convention on Contracts for the International Sale of Goods. . . . Although there is as yet virtually no U.S. case law interpreting the Sale of Goods Convention . . . it may safely be predicted that this will change: absent a choice-of-law provision, and with certain exclusions not here relevant, the Convention governs all contracts between parties with places of business in different nations, so long as both nations are signatories to the Convention. . . . Since the contract alleged in this case was most certainly formed, if at all, after 1 January 1988, and since both the United States and Italy are signatories of the Convention, the Court will interpret the [contract] in light of, and with reference to, the substantive international law of contracts embodied in the Sale of Goods Convention. . . . Chilewich signed the Memorandum Agreement and forwarded it to Filanto; Filanto signed the Memorandum and returned it to Chilewich. . . . The chosen forum in this case does have a reasonable relation to the contract at issue, as the ultimate purchasers of the boots was a Russian concern and the Russian Contract was incorporated by reference into Filanto's Memorandum Agreement with Chilewich. Furthermore, though conditions in the Republic of Russia are unsettled, they continue to improve and there is no reason to believe that the Chamber of Commerce in Moscow cannot provide fair and impartial justice to these litigants.

BUSINESS CONSIDERATIONS Why might two businesses, each from a different nation, want to have any conflicts submitted to arbitration in a third nation? Why might two businesses prefer to submit a case to arbitration rather than taking it to court?

ETHICAL CONSIDERATION Is it ethical to agree to submit a claim to arbitration, and then to file a lawsuit attempting to either avoid the arbitration option or to change the location in which the case will be arbitrated?

Obligations of the Seller

Chapter II of the CISG covers the obligations of the seller of goods under the convention, and Chapter III covers the obligations of the buyer. These chapters include remedies for breach of the contract among the obligations, which reflects the basic implication of the convention that a contract for the sale of goods is expected to be performed by both parties to the contract.

The obligations of the seller under the CISG can be found in Articles 30 through 44 of the convention; these articles are broken down into three sections. The first section is general, calling for the seller to deliver goods, turn over any relevant documents, and surrender any property in the goods as provided in the contract. The second section deals with the conformity of the goods and with any claims by third parties. The third section deals with remedies that are available upon breach by the seller (see "Remedies Under the CISG").

Section I. Articles 31 through 34 describe the obligations of the seller in a contract under the CISG. Under the provisions of Article 31, if the seller is not specifically obligated to deliver the goods at a particular place, then he or she is expected to follow these guidelines:

1. If the contract involves carriage of the goods, the seller is to hand over the goods to the first carrier for transmission to the buyer.
2. If the goods are not to be carried, the seller is to place the goods at the buyer's disposition either where the goods are known by both parties to be located or at the seller's place of business.

Article 32 deals with contracts involving carriage of the goods by independent carrier. It specifies that the seller must notify the buyer of the consignment of the goods to the carrier, must make the reasonable and necessary contracts for carriage of the goods, and must either procure insurance on the goods or give the buyer sufficient information regarding the goods and the carriage to permit the buyer to procure insurance.

Articles 33 and 34 deal with the proper time for delivery and with the handing over of any necessary documents relating to the goods as a part of the performance duty.

Section II. Made up of Articles 35 through 44, Section II deals with conformity of the goods and possible claims by third parties. This section specifies that the goods must be fit for their normal and intended purpose, fit for any particular purpose of which the seller was aware at the time of the contract, and are properly packaged in order to be deemed conforming. Conformity is measured at the time when the risk of loss passes to the buyer, although the seller may cure any nonconformity if the goods are delivered prior to the delivery date as set out in the contract. The buyer is expected to examine the goods as promptly as practical and to notify the seller of any nonconformity in a timely manner, or the buyer loses his or her right to object to any nonconformity in the goods delivered. This section was hotly debated at the conference, and a compromise was reached on this topic. The buyer is given special rights here in that the buyer has up to two years to assert that the goods contain a hidden defect. In addition, a buyer who fails to give timely notice of a defect can still deduct the "value" of the defect from the contract price, provided that the buyer has a "reasonable excuse" for a failure to give timely notice.[8]

The seller is also expected to deliver goods to the buyer that are free of any rights or claims of any third parties, and the seller can be held liable to the buyer and to the third party for any violations of this obligation.

Obligations of the Buyer

Chapter III of the CISG covers the obligations of the buyer under the contract, which consists of the duty to accept the goods and to pay for them. This chapter is also broken down into three sections. Section I, comprised of Articles 54 through 59, discusses the duty of the buyer with respect to payment of the contract price for the goods. Section II, which consists solely of Article 60, explains taking delivery. Section III, made up of Articles 61 through 65, discusses remedies upon a breach by the buyer (description follows).

Section I. This section specifies the payment obligation of the buyer under a number of different sets of circumstances. If the contract is silent as to payment, the buyer is to pay the price generally charged for such goods at the time and place of the conclusion of the contract. If the price is to be based on weight and the method for determining weight is not specified, it is presumed to be net weight. If no place for payment is specified, the buyer is to pay the seller at the seller's place of business or at the place where any documents are handed over, if payment is to be "against documents." In addition, unless the contract specifies a different time, the buyer is to pay for the goods when the goods or the documents are made available by the seller.

Section II. Article 60 is the only article included in this section. This article specifies that the buyer is to take delivery by doing all the acts that are necessary and could reasonably be expected in order to allow the seller to deliver the goods, and in actually taking delivery of the goods.

E X H I B I T   20.2 | **Buyer's Remedies**

1. The buyer may require the seller to perform, unless the buyer has chosen another remedy that is inconsistent with performance by the seller. Additionally, the buyer may require the seller to deliver conforming substitute goods or to cure any nonconformity, if the seller has delivered nonconforming goods.

2. The buyer may set an additional time for the seller to perform, provided that the seller is notified. During this additional time, the buyer will be precluded from seeking other remedies.

3. The buyer can declare the contract avoided if the seller does not deliver the goods within the time permitted under the contract (including any additional time allowed) or within a reasonable time after learning that the seller has breached the agreement.

4. If the seller delivers nonconforming goods, the buyer may reduce the price paid so that payment reflects the actual value of the performance.

5. If the seller tenders delivery prior to the agreed delivery date, the buyer may accept or refuse the delivery; if the seller tenders delivery of a larger shipment than called for in the contract, the buyer may accept any or all of the excess quantity, paying for any accepted goods at the contract rate.

REMEDIES UNDER THE CISG

Remedies for Breach by the Seller

Section III of Chapter II specifies remedies that are available to the buyer upon a breach of the sales contract by the seller. In addition, Articles 74 through 77 provide damages that may be available to either the buyer or the seller upon a breach by the other party. The CISG also specifically states that a party is not deprived of any rights to claim damages if that party seeks other remedies under the convention as well. If the seller fails to deliver conforming goods or fails to meet any other aspect of the agreement, the buyer may seek any or all of the appropriate remedies from the alternatives shown in Exhibit 20.2.

Remedies for Breach by the Buyer

Section III of Chapter III specifies the remedies that are available to the seller upon a breach of the sales contract by the buyer. Again, Articles 74 through 77 provide damages that may be available as well. Recall also that the CISG specifically states that a party is not deprived of any rights to claim damages if that party seeks other remedies under the convention as well. If the buyer fails to accept delivery of the goods or fails to pay for the goods as agreed, the seller may seek any or all of the appropriate remedies from the alternatives shown in Exhibit 20.3.

Damages

Section II of Chapter IV specifies damages that may be available to either party under the convention following a breach of the contract by the other party. These damages may be available even if other remedies are also sought by the non-breaching party.

The basic measure of damages under the CISG is "a sum equal to the loss, including loss of profit, suffered by the other party as a consequence of the breach. Such damages cannot exceed the loss which the party in breach foresaw or ought to have foreseen at the time of the conclusion of the contract."

E X H I B I T 20.3 | **Seller's Remedies**

1. The seller may require the buyer to pay the contract price, to take delivery, or to perform any other obligations, unless he or she has resorted to any other remedies that are inconsistent with this remedy.

2. The seller may fix an additional reasonable period of time during which the buyer can perform, provided that the buyer is notified of this extension. During this additional time period, the seller cannot seek any other remedies.

3. The seller can declare the contract avoided as to any unperformed portion of the contract.

4. If the contract calls for the buyer to specify any form, measurement, or other feature of the goods and he or she fails to do so, the seller may supply such specifications, if he or she does so within a reasonable time.

If the contract is avoided and the buyer then purchases replacement goods, the buyer is entitled to the difference between the price of the replacement goods and the original contract price, plus any other damages computed under the prior damage provisions. If the contract is avoided and the seller then resells the goods, the seller is entitled to the difference between the resale price and the original contract price, plus any other damages computed under the prior damage provisions.

If the contract is avoided and there is a current price for the goods covered by the contract, the nonbreaching party can recover the difference between the current price and the contract price, plus any other damages allowed under Article 74, without the need to purchase (by the buyer) or resell (by the seller). In any case, the party seeking damages must take any and all reasonable steps to mitigate damages, or the other party can use the failure to mitigate as grounds for reducing the damages assessed to the level that would have been attained with mitigation.

The following case involves the assessment of damages when the seller breaches a contract under the CISG. Several subsequent cases have cited this opinion in deciding what damages can be collected upon breach by the seller.

20.3

DELCHI CARRIER SPA V. ROTOREX CORPORATION
71 F.3D 1024 (2ND CIR. 1995)

FACTS In January 1988, Rotorex agreed to sell 10,800 compressors to Delchi for use in Delchi's "Ariele" line of portable air conditioners. Prior to executing the contract, Rotorex sent Delchi a sample compressor and accompanying written performance specifications. The compressors were scheduled to be delivered in three shipments before May 15, 1988. Rotorex sent the first shipment by sea on March 26. Delchi paid for this shipment, which arrived at its Italian factory on April 20, by letter of credit. Rotorex sent a second shipment of compressors on or about May 9. Delchi also remitted payment for this shipment by letter of credit. While the second shipment was en route, Delchi discovered that the first lot of compressors did not conform to the sample model and accompanying specifications. On May 13, after a Rotorex representative visited the Delchi factory in Italy, Delchi informed Rotorex that 93 percent of the compressors were rejected in quality control checks because they had lower cooling capacity and consumed more power than the sample model and specifications. After several unsuccessful attempts to cure the defects in the compressors, Delchi asked Rotorex to supply new compressors conforming to the original sample and specifications. Rotorex refused, claiming that the performance specifications were "inadvertently communicated" to Delchi. In a faxed letter dated May 23, 1988, Delchi cancelled the contract. Although it was able to expedite a previously planned order or suitable compressors from Sanyo, another supplier, Delchi was unable to obtain in a timely fashion substitute compressors from other sources and thus suffered a loss in its sales volume of Arieles during the 1988 selling season. Delchi filed the instant action under the United Nations Convention on Contracts for the International Sale of Goods . . . for breach of contract and failure to deliver conforming goods . . . After three years of discovery and a bench trial on the issue of damages, Judge Munson . . . held Rotorex liable to Delchi for $1,248,331.87 . . . On appeal Rotorex argues that it did not breach the agreement, that Delchi is not entitled to lost profits because it maintained inventory levels in excess of the maximum number of possible lost sales, that the calculation of the number of lost sales was improper, and that the district court improperly excluded fixed costs and depreciation from the manufacturing cost in calculating lost profits . . .

ISSUES Did Rotorex breach the agreement? Is Delchi entitled to lost profits? How should the damages for lost profits be calculated?

HOLDINGS Yes, Rotorex breached the contract. Yes, Delchi is entitled to lost profits. The damages for lost profits are to be calculated under the broad provisions of the CISG.

REASONING The district court held, and the parties agree, that the instant matter is governed by the CISG . . . , a self-executing agreement between the

20.3

DELCHI CARRIER SPA V. ROTOREX CORPORATION, *continued*
71 F.3D 1024 (2ND CIR. 1995)

United States and other signatories, including Italy. Because there is virtually no case law under the Convention, we look to its language and to "the general principles" upon which it is based . . . The Convention directs that its interpretation be informed by its "international character and . . . the need to promote uniformity in its application and the observance of good faith in international trade." . . . We first address the liability issue . . . Under the CISG, "[t]he seller must deliver goods which are of the quantity, quality and description required by the contract," and "the goods do not conform with the contract unless they . . . [p]ossess the qualities of goods which the seller has held out to the buyer as a sample or model." . . . The CISG further states that "[t]he seller is liable in accordance with the contract and this Convention for any lack of conformity." . . . [The court] held that "there is no question that [Rotorex's] compressors did not conform to the terms of the contract between the parties" . . . We agree. The agreement between Delchi and Rotorex was based upon a sample compressor supplied by Rotorex and upon written specifications regarding cooling capacity and power consumption . . . There was thus no genuine issue of material regarding liability, and summary judgment was proper . . . Under the CISG, if the breach is "fundamental" the buyer may either require delivery of substitute goods, . . . or declare the contract void, . . . and seek damages . . . In granting summary judgment, the district court held that "[t]here appears to be no question that [Delchi] did not substantially receive that which [it] was entitled to expect" and that "any reasonable person could foresee that shipping non-conforming goods to a buyer would result in the buyer not receiving that which it expected and was entitled to receive." Because the cooling power and energy consumption of an air conditioner compressor are important determinants of the product's value, the district court's conclusion that Rotorex was liable for a fundamental breach of contract under the Convention was proper. We turn now to the district court's award of damages . . . A reviewing court must defer to the trial judge's findings of fact unless they are clearly erroneous . . . Rotorex contends . . . that the district court improperly awarded lost profits for unfilled orders from Delchi affiliates in Europe and from sales agents

within Italy. We disagree. The CISG requires that damages be limited by the familiar principle of foreseeability . . . However, it was objectively foreseeable that Delchi would take orders for Ariele sales based on the number of compressors it had ordered and expected to have ready for the season. The district court was entitled to rely upon the documents and testimony regarding these lost sales and was well within its authority in deciding which orders were proven with sufficient certainty. Rotorex also challenges the district court's exclusion of fixed costs and depreciation from the manufacturing cost used to calculate lost profits. . . . The CISG does not explicitly state whether only variable expenses, or both fixed and variable expenses, should be subtracted from sales revenues in calculating lost profits. However, courts generally do not include fixed costs in the calculation of lost profits . . . That is, of course, because the fixed costs would have been encountered whether or not the breach occurred. In the absence of a specific provision in the CISG for calculating lost profits, the district court was correct to use the standard formula employed by most American courts and to deduct only variable costs from sales revenue to arrive at a figure for lost profits . . . The Convention provides that a contract plaintiff may collect damages to compensate for the full loss. This includes, but is not limited to, lost profits, subject only to the familiar limitation that the breaching party must have foreseen, or should have foreseen, the loss as a probable consequence . . . We affirm the award of damages . . . [and] We remand for further proceedings in accord with this opinion.

BUSINESS CONSIDERATIONS What obligations are assumed by a seller who provides a sample and/or written specifications concerning the character or quality of goods in a contract under the CISG? How does this compare to the obligations of a seller in a similar situation under Article 2 of the UCC?

ETHICAL CONSIDERATIONS Is it ethical for a firm that has provided written specifications regarding goods it is selling to argue that the writing was "inadvertently" provided to the buyer? What ethical issues are raised by the assertion of such a defense?

The international sale and movement of goods should continue to expand over the foreseeable future. This means that the CISG will become increasingly important to the U.S. domestic business environment in the future, although it will not replace the UCC in its importance. Business will need to be aware of the differences between the CISG in international agreements and the UCC domestically, because conduct that is merely a preliminary negotiation under the UCC may well be a binding contract under the convention.

ISO 9000

The CISG is not the only major international agreement involving business and the sale of goods. Numerous free-trade zones have been established in the recent past, greatly affecting trade both within and outside of these zones. (See Chapter 3 for a brief discussion of free-trade zones.) A number of other initiatives that will have an impact on international trade have also been adopted or proposed. It appears that international business will be a focal point for uniform law for the foreseeable future.

Product quality and quality control are topics that have attracted a substantial amount of attention in the global marketplace. The concerns with these topics led to the promulgation and eventual adoption of an international quality-control standard, ISO 9000.

The International Standards Organization (ISO) is an international agency headquartered in Geneva, Switzerland. The ISO was established to develop uniform international standards in certain specified areas. The ISO is comprised of representatives from the national standards organizations of a number of countries; they have joined their efforts in an attempt to create certain uniform international standards. The first major success was in the area of quality control—ISO 9000.

ISO 9000 is not a standard. Rather, it is a mechanism providing a comprehensive review process and guidelines. By following this review process and the guidelines, companies can ensure that their products comply with the quality standards established for their industry. ISO 9000 is a set of five international standards concerning quality management and quality assurance in the production process. Firms that decide to participate in the program register with the national standards body and acquire an ISO number. As the number of registered firms increases, the importance of participation also increases. Many firms that are active in international trade require ISO 9000 participation as a condition to entering a contract. Quality standards may have a significant impact on international sales over the next few years.

ETHICAL ISSUES IN THE INTERNATIONAL SALE OF GOODS

Some U.S. commentators have argued that business operates under a game theory of ethics and that honesty and good faith cannot reasonably be expected in such a situation. To these commentators, the purpose of business is to generate profits, and so long as those profits are generated in a manner that does not break the law, the business has not acted unethically. These people also feel that business is an amoral institution so that normal societal mores do not—and cannot—apply.

Contemporary social values in the United States do not reflect this approach, nor does the UCC. Our society expects—and demands—more from business than a mere showing of net profits. The "bottom line" is not a justification for acting in an improper manner. For example, the Uniform Commercial Code mandates that all parties to a sales contract are to act in good faith and to cooperate with one another. In addition, the Code requires all merchants in a sales contract to act in a commercially reasonable manner.

Although business ethics is not discussed per se in the CISG, good faith is. The issue of "good faith" provides an interesting example of the problem of ethics in an international setting. Common law nations tend to require good faith in the performance and the enforcement of contracts. Civil law nations expand the good-faith requirement, requiring good faith in the negotiation of a contract, as well as in its performance, enforcement, and interpretation. Since the convention did not determine a uniform meaning for good faith, and since there was strong disagreement as to the scope of good faith if it were to be included, a compromise was reached. Article 7(1) of the CISG requires that the convention must be interpreted in a manner that observes good faith in international trade. This compromise reinforces the difficulty of determining what conduct is deemed ethical in various cultures.

The common law nations were vehemently opposed to including a good-faith requirement in the formation of the contract, a standard practice in civil law nations. The civil law nations were concerned that common law nations do not require good faith in the formation of a contract, although they do require good faith in the performance of the contract. The representative from France expressed a fear that including good faith as a requirement would lead to divergent and arbitrary interpretations by national courts, negating uniformity in applying the CISG.

Concerns with the CISG were also expressed along the lines that separate developed—or industrialized—nations from developing nations, a "north/south" division. The developing nations (frequently joined by the socialist nations) feared they would be placed at a disadvantage by the nature of the goods they sell, as opposed to the goods they import. Generally speaking, developing nations export raw materials and agricultural products; they import finished goods and technological equipment. The compromises reached in this area reflect a recognition of economic differences that mandated a legal—and an ethical—difference in treatment. Included in these compromises were the extended time given for a buyer to discover hidden defects and the ability of the buyer to deduct the "value" of a defect even if there was not a timely notice of the defect, provided that the buyer has a "reasonable excuse" for not giving timely notice. Given the lack of technological expertise, the difficulty of transportation, and the other problems faced by so-called third-world nations, the compromises reached reflect a concern that they be assured of fair treatment in their dealings with industrialized nations.

STANDARD SHIPPING TERMS IN INTERNATIONAL TRADE (INCOTERMS)

When goods are sold in international trade, they do not just magically appear at their ultimate destination. They must be transported, frequently by third parties—common carriers. This transportation is governed to a significant extent by the use of standard shipping terms. Just as the UCC provides for the interpretation of standard shipping terms within the United States, there are provisions for standard shipping terms in international trade. However, these provisions are not found in the CISG.

In 1936, the International Chamber of Commerce first developed the "International Rules for the Interpretation of Trade Terms," which provides for one uniform meaning for international commercial terms, or *Incoterms.* These Incoterms became widely known and followed and are encouraged by trade councils, courts, and international experts. The International Chamber of Commerce has amended the general provisions of these Incoterms a number of times, most recently in 1990. These "Incoterms 1990" have no automatic legal standing and are only applied if the parties agree to accept them and so state in their contract. Because there are terms (i.e., FOB) that are used as Incoterms and are also used in the UCC, the parties should also ensure that their contract designates the applicable source of the term. For example, the contract should say "FOB (Incoterms 1990)" if the parties want the Incoterm interpretation of FOB to control in the contract. It is also important for businesses that do not customarily use Incoterms to be very careful in using them. Many American firms use FOB as a matter of course. If these firms are using Incoterms, they probably mean to use the term "FCA" in order to provide the same responsibility as "FOB" provides under the UCC.

There are four broad categories of Incoterms, with each category placing different burdens and responsibilities on the buyer and the seller. These categories are designated by letters—"E" terms, "F" terms, "C" terms, and "D" terms.

"E" Terms

There is only one "E" term, EXW, which stands for "ex-works." Under this term, the seller fulfills its obligation when the goods are made available to the buyer at the seller's premises. The seller is not responsible for loading the goods or for clearing the goods for export. The buyer bears all risks and responsibilities. The "E" term represents the minimum obligation the seller can face.

"F" Terms

"F" terms require the seller to hand over the designated goods to a nominated carrier free of any risk or expense to the buyer. There are three basic "F" terms.

The first is FCA, which means *free carrier.* To satisfy this term, the seller must hand over goods to a named carrier, cleared for export, at the named location. The name of the location will follow the term, as in "FCA London."

The second is FAS, which means *free along side.* The seller must place goods alongside a named vessel at a named port with all fees and risks covered to that point. The buyer assumes responsibility and risk once the goods reach the docks alongside the named vessel.

The final "F" term is FOB, which means *free on board.* As an Incoterm, FOB transfers risk and responsibility to the buyer as soon as the goods "pass over the ship's rail" at the named destination port. The seller must clear the goods for export under this term, which is only used for sea or inland waterway transportation internationally.

"C" Terms

"C" terms imply that the seller must bear certain costs under the contract. There are four "C" terms.

The first is CFR, which stands for *cost and freight,* and is normally followed by a named location such as Lisbon. The seller must clear the goods for export and bears all risks until the goods pass over the ship's rail at the port of shipment. CFR is only used for sea or inland waterway transportation.

The second is CIF, which is the same as CFR except that the seller must also insure the goods during the carriage. The insurance to be carried need only be a minimum (contract price plus 10 percent) unless the agreement sets a different rate.

The third is CPT, which means *carriage paid to* (named location). The seller makes arrangements for shipping the goods to a named location, pays the freight or carriage charges, and delivers the goods to the carrier. At that point, the risk transfers to the buyer.

The final "C" term is CIP, which means *cost and insurance paid to* (named location). The seller has the same obligations as under CPT, plus the obligation to procure insurance (again at minimum coverage) to protect the buyer's potential risk of loss.

"D" Terms

The final type of Incoterm is the "D" term, which refers to a named destination; the duty of the seller depends on the particular "D" term used.

The first "D" term is DAF, which means *delivered at frontier.* The seller must make the goods available and clear them for export at a named place, but prior to the clearing of customs at the next country. This term is most common with overland transportation of the goods, normally by rail or by truck.

The second term is DES, which means *delivered ex-ship* at some named port. The seller must make the goods available to the buyer on board the ship, prior to clearing the goods for import, at the named port. This is a seagoing transportation term.

A similar term, again used with seagoing transportation, is DEQ, which means *delivery ex-quay.* The seller in a DEQ contract is to place the goods on the quay (dock) cleared for importation before the risk passes to the buyer.

DDU, which stands for *delivered duty unpaid,* may be used for any type of transportation. The seller is to get the goods to a named destination with all fees paid except for import fees and costs, which are to be borne by the buyer.

A similar term, again valid with any type of transport, is DDP, which means *delivered duty paid.* With this term, the seller is to get the goods to the named destination with all costs paid, including import duties and taxes, and cleared for importation.

Exhibit 20.4 on page 542 compares the standard shipping terms used under Article 2 of the UCC and the Incoterms developed by the International Chamber of Commerce. Note that in several cases the *terms* are the same, but their *meanings* are different. Businesspersons need to exercise care in their international contracts to be certain that the delivery term used carries the meaning intended.

20.2 | INTERNATIONAL BUSINESS/SALES

CONCERNS IN AN INTERNATIONAL SALE

CIT was recently contacted by a firm in Brussels, Belgium. The firm wants to purchase 300 CIT units, with an option for another 300 units if the initial order sells as well as this firm expects. The family wants to make the sale, but they are concerned about a number of items. First, they would like to know what law will govern the contract if a dispute arises. Second, they want to know what standard shipping term they should use so that the buyer has risk of loss during transit. Finally, they want to know if there are any other aspects they should be concerned about in this proposed contract. They have asked for your advice. What will you tell them?

BUSINESS CONSIDERATIONS The standard shipping term most commonly used in the United States when the seller wants to pass risk of loss to the buyer is FOB (seller's location). Should an American seller use the same term in an international sale? Does the type of carrier make a difference in selecting the proper term for an international sale?

ETHICAL CONSIDERATIONS Is it ethical for the seller to insist that the buyer bear the risk of loss during transit? Would it be more ethical for the parties to expressly agree to share risk of loss during transit? What problems might such an agreement cause?

E X H I B I T   20.4 | **A Comparison of Standard Shipping: UCC and Incoterms**

UCC Term	Meaning	Incoterm	Meaning
C&F	**Cost and Freight** Seller quotes buyer a price for the goods plus freight. Buyer has risk of loss.	CFR	**Cost and Freight** Seller clears goods for export and bears all risks until the goods pass over the ship's rails. Used for water transport.
CIF	**Cost, Insurance, Freight** Same as C&F, plus seller procures insurance in the buyer's name.	CIF	**Cost, Insurance, Freight** Same as CFR, plus seller insures the goods during transport.
		CPT	**Carriage Paid** Seller makes arrangements to ship the goods to a named destination, pays the freight, and delivers the goods to the carrier. Buyer takes risk when carrier acquires goods.
		CIP	**Cost and Insurance Paid** Same as CPT, plus the seller procures insurance to cover the buyer's risk.
		DAF	**Delivered At Frontier** Seller makes goods available and cleared for export at a named location, but prior to clearance of customs. Normally used for overland transport.
Ex-Ship	**Ex-Ship** Seller makes goods available on the dock beside a ship at a named port. Used with water transport. Seller has all risk until the goods reach the dock.	DES	**Delivered Ex-Ship** Seller makes goods available on board a ship, prior to clearance for import. Used with water transport.
		DEQ	**Delivered Ex-Quay** Seller places goods on the quay (dock) cleared for import before risk shifts to the buyer. Used with water transport.
		DDU	**Delivered Duty Unpaid** Seller gets goods to a named destination with all fees paid except for import duties. Used with any transport.
		DDP	**Delivered Duty Paid** Same as DDU, except the seller has also paid import duties, taxes, and fees.
		EXW	**Ex-Works** Seller makes goods available to the buyer at the seller's premises. Buyer is responsible for all risks upon tender of delivery.
		FCA	**Free Carrier** Seller transfers goods to a named carrier, cleared for export.
FAS	**Free Along Side** Seller gets the goods to a named vessel at a named port, with all fees paid to that point. Buyer has risk during loading. Only used with water transport.	FAS	**Free Along Side** Seller gets the goods to a named vessel at a named port, with all fees paid to that point. Buyer has risk during loading. Only used with water transport.
FOB	**Free On Board** Seller quotes a price for goods, with all fees paid, to the location named. Buyer has risk from that point. Used with all forms of transport.	FOB	**Free On Board** Seller is responsible for getting the goods "over the rail" of a named vessel at a named port and cleared for export. Only used with water transport.
COD	**Collect On Delivery** Buyer is to pay for the goods upon tender at the buyer's location. Can more be used with any form of transport.		
No Arrival-No Sale	Seller has risk during transport but is excused from additional obligations if the goods are lost or destroyed during carriage.		

OIL AND WATER DON'T MIX

In 1987, an Italian seller and a Swiss buyer concluded a contract for the sale of raw oil. The contract contained an FOB clause as well as an express reference to standard terms used in the oil industry. After loading the oil onto the tanker ship, the buyer discovered that during loading operations the oil had been contaminated with water. As a result, the buyer sued the seller to recover damages, alleging that the seller had risk of loss during loading.

The buyer argues that the CISG and the Incoterm FOB require the seller to bear the risk of loss in this case. According to the buyer, the seller is responsible and bears risk of loss until the goods have been loaded into the ship's tanks. Since the contamination of the oil occurred during loading operations, the buyer alleges that the seller has risk of loss. The seller asserts that it has performed its obligation when the loading begins and that the buyer has the risk of loss during the loading operation.

This case has been brought in *your* court. How will *you* decide this case, using the CISG and Incoterms as your guiding legal principles?[9]

BUSINESS CONSIDERATIONS Should a business regularly dealing in the international markets include a choice of law clause, or at least a negation of any laws it does not want applied, in its standard form contracts? Should the firm have a policy of defining any terms and clauses to avoid possible confusion?

ETHICAL CONSIDERATIONS Is it ethical for a business to "opt out" of the coverage of the CISG in its contracts or to attempt to "opt in" to the coverage of the UCC? From an ethical perspective, how might this affect the other party, especially if the other party is foreign?

SOURCE: Unilex Database, http://www.cnr.it/CRDCS/.

PROPOSED INTERNATIONAL COVERAGE

United Nations Convention on International Bills of Exchange and Promissory Notes

The CISG has already been fairly successful, establishing a widely adopted uniform coverage of contracts for the international sale of goods. Following this success, the United Nations was encouraged to continue to propose conventions designed to regulate various aspects of international business. In late 1988, the United Nations General Assembly approved the Convention on International Bills of Exchange and Promissory Notes. This convention, which is now available for ratification by any member nations, has two primary purposes:

1. To create a new type of international negotiable instrument, an international bill of exchange, which will be the standard negotiable instrument for payments in international trade.
2. To provide the same sort of uniform treatment for international negotiable instruments as is provided for interstate transactions in the United States by Article 3 of the UCC.

This convention needs to be studied so that international businesspeople can be ready to comply with its terms if or when it acquires widespread ratification.

20.3 | INTERNATIONAL BUSINESS/SALES

LETTERS OF CREDIT

The firm recently received an order from a prospective customer in Europe who is interested in placing an initial order for 500 Call-Image units, provided that acceptable terms can be worked out. This buyer has offered to pay for the videophones with a letter of credit payable at the Kochanowskis' bank. The family has never done business with a letter of credit before, and they are unsure how to proceed. They ask you whether they should accept the letter of credit as a means for receiving payment or if they should use a method for payment more familiar to them. What advice will you give them?

BUSINESS CONSIDERATIONS Letters of credit are a fairly common payment method for long-distance business transactions, especially internationally. Should a newly organized business consider having a policy on letters of credit in advance, or wait until the need arises before developing a policy? What protections are afforded by a letter of credit that might not be available under other methods for arranging payment when goods are sold internationally?

ETHICAL CONSIDERATIONS What ethical concerns might a company have about using a letter of credit, making payments on the basis of documents that are examined by a banker rather than on the basis of an inspection of the goods by the buyer? How can these concerns be alleviated?

United Nations Convention on Independent Guarantees and Stand-by Letters of Credit

This convention is intended to provide uniformity in the use of guarantees and letters of credit in the international marketplace. It is somewhat analogous to Article 5 of the UCC, Letters of Credit. The convention went into effect 1 January 2000. As of 1 March 2000, seven nations, including the United States, have signed the convention, although only five of these nations have agreed to begin following its provisions on the effective date. (The United States has not yet agreed to adhere to the convention on the effective date.)

United Nations Convention on the Recognition and Enforcement of Foreign Arbitral Awards

In a reflection of the increasing importance of alternate dispute resolution, 121 nations have ratified the 1958 convention providing for judicial recognition of awards granted in foreign arbitration proceedings. This convention allows a business that prevails in an arbitration award in one nation to then enforce that award in the national court of the losing party—or in any other courts that have jurisdiction over the losing party.

PRICING AND PAYMENT

Value-added taxes are likely to be used with greater frequency in the future; this may affect intracompany transfers and result in tax assessments even though no money changes hands in the transaction. Firms will have to pay a tax on the "value added" to the goods they receive while those goods were in the hands of the transferor, even if that transferor is a subsidiary of the transferee. This could lead to accounting problems and/or some "creative" bookkeeping, and it could discourage moving manufacturing or processing facilities to other nations. Value-added taxes may also affect the pricing decisions of firms involved in international trade.

Many international transactions call for payment by means of a letter of credit, a document issued by the buyer and sent to the seller. The seller presents the letter of credit to the bank—together with the required documentary evidence that the seller has the goods and is ready to ship them—and receives payment for the goods. By using a letter of credit, numerous worries are removed or alleviated. The seller receives a document providing for payment before the goods are shipped, easing the seller's concerns about receiving payment for goods to be shipped to another nation. The buyer knows that no payments will be made unless the bank is assured that the seller is ready, willing, and able to ship the goods called for in the contract.

RESOURCES FOR BUSINESS LAW STUDENTS

NAME	RESOURCES	WEB ADDRESS
Pace University School of Law Institute of International Commercial Law (IICL)	Pace University School of Law's IICL provides the full text of the United Nations Convention on Contracts for the International Sale of Goods (CISG), as well as legislative history, cases, commentaries, and a bibliography.	**http://www.cisg.law.pace.edu/**
United Nations Commission on International Trade Law (UNCITRAL)	UNCITRAL, drafter of the CISG, provides background information, texts and recent documents, case law, and the current status of conventions and model laws.	**http://www.un.or.at/uncitral/index.html**
ISO Online	ISO, drafter of international standards guidelines, such as the ISO 9000 and ISO 14000, provides more on the structure of the organization, as well as a catalog of publications.	**http://www.iso.ch/**
International Chamber of Commerce (ICC) World Business Organization	The ICC, developer of the International Rules for the Interpretation of Trade Terms (Incoterms), provides current news, publications, and information on the ICC International Court of Arbitration.	**http://www.iccwbo.org/**
International Centre for Commercial Law	The International Centre for Commercial Law offers current updates on European commercial law, as well as listings for commercial law firms in over 40 European countries.	**http://www.link.org/**

Letters of credit are regulated, at least in the United States, by UCP 500, the Uniform Customs and Practices for Documentary Credit, enacted on 1 January 1994.

Business is becoming truly global, which ultimately should result in a lessening of cultural isolation and increased awareness of the needs, demands, and expectations of the people of other nations. This, in turn, will increase the access to these other nations and—at least under economic theory—should result in the growth of the world economy as each nation strives to maximize its relative competitive advantage and, in so doing, increase its sales and its purchases in the global marketplace.

SUMMARY

Work on an international law of sales began in 1930, prior to World War II, when the International Institute for the Unification of Private Law tried to develop uniform coverage in this area. The initial work was submitted to an international conference at The Hague following World War II and resulted in the creation of two conventions, one dealing with the formation of sales contracts and one dealing with the performance of sales contracts. Unfortunately, neither convention had been widely adopted. The United Nations created an International Conference on International Trade and charged it with creating an international law governing sales. This led to the United Nations Convention on the International Sale of Goods (CISG), which was approved at the Vienna Conference in 1980 and became effective 1 January 1988 for all ratifying nations.

The CISG was created by compromises among the various factions that make up the United Nations. There were disagreements among common law, civil law, and Islamic law nations; between developed and developing nations; and between capitalist and socialist nations. Despite these differences, a convention was created and has been ratified or adopted by 59 nations as of March 2000. The CISG covers formation-of-contracts issues, seller obligations and rights, buyer obligations and rights, and remedies for both sellers and buyers. Ratifying nations have the option of not ratifying all sections of the CISG, but most have opted to follow the entire convention.

The International Standards Organization, a standards agency headquartered in Geneva, has developed guidelines for firms in an effort to establish international standards for quality and for environmental protection. ISO 9000 deals with quality issues. ISO 14000 deals with environmental issues.

The International Chamber of Commerce developed the "International Rules for the Interpretation of Trade Terms," which provides uniform meanings for these Incoterms. Incoterms are broken down into four broad categories, with each category imposing different burdens and responsibilities on the parties to contracts when they use standard shipping terms. The categories are "E" terms, "F" terms, "C" terms, and "D" terms.

The United Nations General Assembly has approved a new convention dealing with International Bills of Exchange and Promissory Notes. This convention is intended to provide a new type of negotiable instrument for use in international trade, and also to provide for a uniform international treatment of negotiable instruments. As international trade grows, U.S. businesses need to be familiar with the CISG and with Incoterms; these will become as important to them as their knowledge of the UCC and its provisions for standard shipping terms.

There is also a voluntary regulatory aspect to international trade, found in the ISO provisions. ISO 9000 provides voluntary standards for quality in production. The ISO 9000 standards provide incentives and methods for businesses to seek "continuous improvement" in quality control. Membership in the ISO movement is growing in most of the industrial world.

The International Chamber of Commerce promulgated international commercial terms (Incoterms) that are used in shipping goods internationally. Several of these terms are similar to the terms provided under the UCC, but their meanings are different.

There are a number of other pending conventions that may have an impact on international trade as well. The only thing preventing their impact is a lack of signatory nations, but that may change over the next several years. This is an area that bears watching.

DISCUSSION QUESTIONS

1. What is a United Nations "convention"? Where does such a convention fall within the hierarchy of laws in the United States, presuming that the United States has joined in the convention?

2. What is the primary difference between a "common law" nation and a "civil law" nation? How do the courts of each type of nation view previous court opinions? How did this difference affect the development of the CISG?

3. When is an acceptance considered valid under the provisions of the CISG? How does this compare to the time when an acceptance becomes valid under the UCC?

4. Which contracts for the sale of goods must be in writing under the CISG? How does this compare to contracts that must be in writing under the UCC?

5. Suppose a seller makes an oral offer to a buyer and promises that the offer will remain open for three weeks. Can the seller revoke this offer before the three weeks have elapsed under the CISG? How does this compare to the ability of an offeror to revoke an oral offer or promise under the UCC?

6. How long does a buyer of goods have to inspect the goods and to inform the seller of any nonconformities under the CISG? How does this compare to the time for inspection and notification under the UCC?

7. What must a buyer do to properly take delivery of goods under a contract governed by the CISG? Does the buyer have similar duties under the UCC?

8. When can a buyer require the seller to deliver goods when the seller breaches due to nondelivery under the CISG? How does this compare to the specific performance or replevin remedy available under the UCC?

9. What options are available to a buyer under the CISG when the seller tenders delivery of nonconforming goods? What options are available to a buyer in similar circumstances under the UCC?

10. When does the CISG require good faith in the contract? When does the UCC require good faith in the contract?

CASE PROBLEMS AND WRITING ASSIGNMENTS

1. Florence Beef agreed to buy four loads of Australian boneless beef from Cunningham. The contract stated that the beef was to be "85% chemically lean." When the beef was tendered for delivery, Florence rejected the goods, claiming that the beef did not meet the requirements specified in the contract. Florence based its rejection on the fact that the beef was not "visually lean," although this test was not a recognized scientific standard for judging the meat. Cunningham claimed that the rejection was based on the declining price for beef just before the shipping date. How should the court resolve this case? Why? [See *A. J. Cunningham Packing Corp.* v. *The Florence Beef Co.*, 785 F.2d 348 (1st Cir. 1986).]

2. A South African agent of Tarbert sold 2,000 metric tons of Kenyan red haricot beans warehoused in Rotterdam, Holland, to Cometals. The contract specified that the seller had to supply a certificate of origin for the goods, stating that the goods originated within the European Community (EC) even though both parties were aware that it was impossible to honestly provide such a certificate. The beans were to be "sound, loyal and merchantable, max. 1 pct impurities, free from live and practically free from dead weevils," and the quality would be certified by an independent surveyor. Cometals subsequently inspected the beans in the warehouse and informed Tarbert that the goods were extensively damaged by weevils, so Cometals rejected the goods. Tarbert sued Cometals for breach of contract, alleging that the goods conformed to the contract so that the rejection was improper. Cometals denied it had breached and also asserted that the contract was void because the certificate of origin could only be obtained through fraud or forgery. Was Tarbert entitled to damages for the alleged breach of contract by Cometals? How does the fact that both parties knew that the required certification could not honestly be provided affect the analysis of this case? [See *Tarbert Trading, Ltd.* v. *Cometals, Inc.*, 663 F.Supp. 561 (S.D.N.Y. 1987).]

3. The U.S. Customs Service imposes certain duties on goods imported into the United States. In 1984, the United States amended the law governing customs duties, permitting "drawback" (a refund of customs duties) for the exportation of merchandise that was not the same merchandise originally imported and on which import duties had been paid. Guess? Inc. produces and sells cotton denim clothing. Many of its products are exported from the United States for sale in other nations. All items exported by Guess? are manufactured in the United States and bear the label "Made in the U.S.A." Many of the items sold in the

United States are made in other nations and then imported into the United States for sale. Guess? argued that the imported clothing and the exported clothing were fungible so that it was entitled to "drawbacks" for the goods it exported. The U.S. Customs Service asserted that the items were not fungible since the labeling of the products was different. How should this case be resolved by the U.S. Court of International Trade? Why? [See *Guess? Incorporated* v. *United States*, 752 F.Supp. 463 (CIT 1990).]

4. Mebco Bank, a Swiss firm, did a substantial amount of business with Refco F/X Associates, mostly in the area of foreign currency exchanges and dealings. Mebco encountered financial difficulties and was being liquidated under the insolvency laws of Switzerland. One of Mebco's creditors at the time of the liquidation proceeding was Refco. Fearing that it would not recover the debt owed it by Mebco, Refco attached the Mebco bank accounts in New York. Under Swiss law, funds "in account" are considered part of the debtor's estate. Refco argued that the funds "in account" were, in reality, goods, since the transactions underlying the debt were foreign currency exchanges. If the funds were goods, Refco prevails under the provisions of Article 2 of the UCC. However, if the funds were not goods, the Swiss liquidator prevails. How should this case be resolved? Why? [See *In re Koreag, Controle et Revision, S.A.*, 961 F.2d 341 (2nd Cir. 1992).]

5. Gestetner was the U.S. distributor of a line of office equipment, including stencil duplicators (mimeograph machines). Case was experimenting with stencil duplicators in an effort to develop a method for producing full-color heat transfers to garments. Case discovered that, with some minor modifications, the Gestetner stencil duplicators were suitable for this heat-transfer process. Case contacted Gestetner to see if Gestetner would be willing to modify its stencil duplicators and then sell them to Case. Gestetner agreed and began to sell the machines to Case. Several months later, problems arose. Case was allegedly in arrears on its account, and Gestetner refused to make any additional shipments until Case brought its account up to date. Case denied liability, asserting that a number of the machines had been defective and could not be sold. Gestetner filed suit for breach of contract. Case filed a motion to dismiss the suit due to the lack of any writing, asserting the Statute of Frauds as an affirmative defense. (The parties never entered into any written agreement in this case.) How would this case be resolved under the UCC? Would a different result occur under the CISG? Explain your answer(s).

[See *Gestetner Corp.* v. *Case Equipment Co.*, 815 F.2d 806 (1st Cir. 1987).]

6. **BUSINESS APPLICATION CASE** Intershoe, Inc., a shoe importer, uses various foreign currencies in its business, including the Italian lira. It frequently entered into foreign currency futures transactions with various banks, including Bankers Trust Company. On 13 March 1985, Intershoe telephoned Bankers Trust and entered into several foreign currency transactions, including one for a futures transaction involving lire. Bankers Trust sent a confirmation of these transactions to Intershoe on 13 March 1985, including a confirmation that the bank had purchased from Intershoe 537,750,000 Italian lire, and that the bank had sold 250,000 U.S. dollars to Intershoe. The treasurer for Intershoe signed this confirmation and returned it to the bank on 18 March 1985. In a letter dated 11 October 1985, the bank notified Intershoe that it was awaiting instructions as to Intershoe's delivery of the lire. Intershoe responded by a letter dated 25 October 1985 that the transaction was a mistake and that it would not go through with the deal. Subsequently, on 19 December 1985, Intershoe filed suit against Bankers Trust, alleging that Intershoe had suffered a loss of $55,019.85 from Bankers Trust's failure to deliver the lire as per the contract. Bankers Trust counterclaimed for its damages under the same contract. Was Intershoe permitted to introduce parol evidence to contradict the contract as represented by the confirmation prepared by Bankers Trust and signed by the treasurer of Intershoe? Would the result of this case be different under the UCC than it would be under the CISG? Explain. What implications might a different result have for businesses involved in international business? [See *Intershoe, Inc.* v. *Bankers Trust Co.*, 571 N.E.2d 641 (N.Y. 1991).]

7. **ETHICAL APPLICATION CASE** Monte Carlo, a New York corporation, contracted with Daewoo, a South Korean corporation, to purchase 2,400 dozen men's shirts, to be manufactured to Monte Carlo's specifications and to bear its label. Daewoo manufactured the shirts, but when the shirts were delivered, the documents were delayed by one day. As a result of this delay, Monte Carlo alleged that the shirts were not available in time for Christmas sales, and it rejected the shipment. Daewoo then sold the shirts to Daewoo International, which, in turn, sold them to numerous discount retailers. The resold shirts contained the Monte Carlo label, and Daewoo International did not have permission to sell the shirts with the labels intact. Monte Carlo sued both Daewoo and Daewoo International for breach of contract and for

trademark infringement. Both defendants denied liability.

Did Daewoo infringe the trademark of Monte Carlo by reselling these shirts to the discount retailers? What ethical issues are raised in this case? [See *Monte Carlo Shirt, Inc.* v. *Daewoo Int'l (America) Corp.,* 707 F.2d 1054 (9th Cir. 1983).]

8. **CRITICAL THINKING CASE** MCC is a Florida business engaged in the retail sale of tiles. Ceramica Nuova is an Italian corporation engaged in the manufacture of ceramic tiles. In 1990, MCC and Ceramic Nuova negotiated an oral agreement for the sale of tiles (MCC used an interpreter since its representative did not speak Italian). Following this negotiation, the terms agreed on were entered on a standard, preprinted order form used by Ceramica Nuova, and representatives of each firm signed the form. MCC alleges that the parties also entered into an oral "requirements" contract in 1991, under which Ceramica Nuova agreed to supply MCC with high-grade ceramic tile at specific discount prices so long as MCC purchased a specified minimum quantity of this tile. MCC completed several order forms requesting tile deliveries pursuant to this second agreement. Ceramica Nuova failed to satisfy orders placed under the second contract in April, May, and August of 1991, and MCC filed suit for breach of contract. Ceramica Nuova denied any obligation, asserting that MCC had defaulted on payments for previous shipments, thus relieving Ceramica Nuova of any further duty to deliver tiles. Ceramica Nuova based its argument on the terms contained on the back side of the standard preprinted form first signed by MCC. These terms, printed in Italian, included a clause allowing Ceramica Nuova to cancel or suspend performance on any contract between the parties if the buyer defaults on payment on any of their contracts. MCC argues that, under the CISG, the subjective intent of the parties is controlling, and that the parties did not intend to be bound by the terms and conditions on the reverse side of the standard form prepared by Ceramica Nuova. MCC also presented oral evidence in support of this position. If the oral evidence is admissible, MCC is entitled to a trial on the merits, with the opportunity to establish the terms of the contract developed during the oral negotiations. If the oral evidence is not admissible, Ceramica Nuova is entitled to a summary judgment based on the terms and conditions contained in the written form. Must a court consider parol evidence in a contract dispute governed by the CISG? How should the "subjective intent" of the parties be determined in a contract under the CISG? Would the same result occur if the case were to be decided under Article 2 of the UCC? [See *MCC-Marble Ceramic Center, Inc.* v. *Ceramica Nuova D'Agostino, S.P.A.,* 144 F.3d 1384 (11th Cir. 1998).]

NOTES

1. Alejandro M. Garro, "Reconciliation of Legal Traditions in the U.N. Convention on Contracts for the International Sales of Goods," *The International Lawyer* 23 (Summer 1989), p. 443, at 444.
2. United Nations, Treaty Section, March 1994.
3. United Nations, Convention on Contracts for the International Sales of Goods, Article 2.
4. Ibid., Article 11.
5. Ibid., Article 39.
6. Ibid., Article 50.
7. Ibid., Article 16.
8. Ibid., Article 44.
9. "The Italian Case Law on CISG." Unilex Database. http://www.cnr.it/CRDCS/.

NEGOTIABLES

"Negotiables" take many forms. Negotiable instruments consist of checks, notes, drafts, and certificates of deposit. All of these forms are governed by Article 3 of the Uniform Commercial Code (UCC). "Negotiables" can also take the form of negotiable documents of title. Documents of title are governed by Article 7 of the UCC.

In general, negotiable instruments are short-term instruments that arise out of commercial transactions. Millions of such instruments are signed each day, not only because they are a safe and convenient means of doing business but also because they are acceptable in the commercial world as credit instruments and/or as substitutes for money. Documents of title are not as widely used, but they also have an important place in our commercial law.

This part of the text explains how and why negotiables are widely used and accepted in the modern commercial world. In addition, the topics of electronic funds transfers and bank–customer relations will be discussed.

P A R T

5

21

INTRODUCTION TO NEGOTIABLES:
UCC ARTICLE 3 AND ARTICLE 7

CALL-IMAGE TECHNOLOGY

A G E N D A

In establishing CIT, the Kochanowskis may need to obtain loans. CIT will also need a checking account to pay its bills. What legal issues are associated with these processes?

CIT will have customers who wish to pay by personal check. These checks create a risk, albeit small, for CIT. Should CIT, because of the risk, refuse to accept payment by personal check? As CIT grows, the company will need to deal with an increasingly large geographic market

area. This entails sales to distant buyers. To avoid the problem of dishonored checks and/or the need to travel to remote locations to seek remedies, CIT may want to consider alternative payment forms. Should CIT use sight drafts? Should it use some other form of draft? Should CIT use letters of credit? Be prepared! You never know when one of the Kochanowskis will need your help or advice.

O U T L I N E

HISTORIC OVERVIEW

An industrial or a commercial society needs some form of negotiable documents or negotiable instruments in order to function efficiently. When goods are transported or stored, some document is needed to reflect their transportation or their storage. When goods are sold and paid for, some instrument is needed to reflect the payment while providing some safety for the parties involved, since sending cash payment is somewhat risky.

Negotiable instruments of various types have been present in nearly every society that has developed a substantial commercial system. Instruments very similar to the contemporary promissory note date back to about 2100 B.C. The merchants of Europe were using negotiable documents and instruments on a broad scale by the thirteenth century. In fact, the use of drafts was so widespread that a substantial portion of the law merchant was devoted to the proper treatment of these instruments.

Negotiable instruments had become so pervasive by the late nineteenth century that the English Parliament began to enact special statutes to govern their use. Following the example of the English Parliament, the National Conference of Commissioners on Uniform State Laws drafted the Uniform Negotiable Instruments Law (NIL) for the United States in 1896. Each of these statutes merely attempted to cover the common law rules that had been developed over the years. The NIL was designed to unify and codify the rules and laws of each jurisdiction regarding all negotiable commercial documents. However, the breadth of the topical coverage made the NIL unwieldy and difficult to apply to the commercial world of the twentieth century.

The Uniform Commercial Code (UCC; also referred to as the Code) was written to comply more readily with the demands of the modern business world. The topical coverage contained in the NIL was updated, divided into different articles, and included in the UCC. The Code has been adopted by every state in the union except Louisiana, and Louisiana has adopted some portions, including Articles 3 and 4, which deal with negotiable instruments and with bank–customer relations. Changes in banking law and the increased use of instruments that were not covered by the original Article 3 (i.e., "share drafts" issued by credit unions) led to the 1990 revision of Article 3, Negotiable Instruments, and Article 4, Bank Deposits and Collections, to more accurately reflect modern practices and usage of instruments. As of May 1999, the revised Articles 3 and 4 have been adopted in 47 states and the District of Columbia (New York, Rhode Island, and South Carolina have not yet adopted the revised version). As a result, our coverage here will only discuss revised Article 3, which will henceforth be referred to simply as Article 3. (Some of the cases included in Chapters 20 to 24 are based on Article 3 before the revision, but the same results would follow under the revised version of the article.)

The UCC has standardized and clarified the rules of negotiable instruments while retaining most of the traditional rules and views of the topic. This codification of negotiable instruments is located in Article 3 of the Code. The UCC has also standardized and clarified the rules governing documents of title. Both warehouse receipts and bills of lading are covered in Article 7 of the Code. Article 7 retains many of the traditional rules and views of documents of title, while also codifying the contemporary use of these documents in the U.S. legal system. Each of these articles will be discussed in some detail in the remainder of this chapter.

THE SCOPE OF ARTICLE 3

Article 3 of the Uniform Commercial Code covers negotiable instruments. A *negotiable instrument* is a written promise or order to pay money to the order of a named person or to bearer. (Prior to its revision, Article 3 covered "commercial paper".) Although Article 3 provides most of the coverage of negotiable instruments, there are also provisions in other articles of the UCC that affect negotiable instruments. For example, a number of definitions from Article 1 apply in Article 3. Article 4, Bank Deposits and Collections, and Article 9, Secured Transactions, also affect the coverage of negotiable instruments. In fact, Article 3 specifies that its (Article 3's) provisions are "subject to" the coverage in Articles 4 and 9. The scope of Article 3 is somewhat narrow, being restricted solely to negotiable instruments, as defined in § 3-104. Further, Section 3-102(a) states that Article 3 does not apply to money, to payment orders governed by Article 4A, or to securities governed by Article 8. Thus, one finds that Article 3 covers negotiable instruments but not other types of commercial or negotiable documents, and that two other articles of the Code may supplement, complement, or override the provisions of Article 3. To fall within the coverage of Article 3, an instrument must qualify as a "negotiable instrument." If an instrument does not qualify, it is likely to be governed by common law provisions, primarily in the area of contract law.

Section 3-104 defines a negotiable instrument and imposes a number of limitations and rules on this definition. Part (a) of the section provides that a negotiable instrument is:

> *an unconditional promise or order to pay a fixed amount of money, with or without interest or other charges described in the promise or order, if it:*
> 1) *is payable to bearer or order . . .;*
> 2) *is payable on demand or at a definite time . . .; and*
> 3) *does not state any other undertaking or instruction by the person promising or ordering payment to do any act in addition to the payment of money . . .*

Part (a) goes on to add that the promise or order may contain

> i) *an undertaking or power to give, maintain, or protect collateral to secure payment,*
> ii) *an authorization or power to the holder to confess judgment or realize on or dispose of collateral, or*
> iii) *a waiver of the benefit of any law intended for the advantage or protection of an obligor.*

Part (c) of Section 3-104 then states that any instrument that meets these criteria and falls within the definition of a check is a negotiable instrument and a check. Part (d) limits this provision somewhat, stating that any instrument other than a check that satisfies these criteria is a negotiable instrument unless:

> *A promise or order other than a check is not an instrument if, at the time it is issued or first comes into possession of a **holder,** it contains a conspicuous statement, however expressed, to the effect that the promise or order is not negotiable or is not an instrument governed by this article.*

Holder
A person who receives possession of a negotiable instrument by means of a negotiation.

This means that a person who issues a check must abide by the provisions of Article 3, but a person who issues any other type of instrument that appears to be negotiable may opt out of Article 3's coverage by placing a conspicuous term on the face of the instrument excluding it from treatment as a negotiable instrument.

The following case dealt with the issue of whether a document was a negotiable instrument under § 3-104. It also addressed a few other issues that will arise in subsequent chapters. Note how the court analyzed the facts in determining negotiability.

21.1

UNIVERSAL PREMIUM ASSURANCE CORPORATION V. YORK BANK AND TRUST COMPANY

69 F.3D 695 (3RD CIR. 1995)

FACTS Universal Premium Acceptance Corporation . . . provides financing to policyholders to pay their insurance premiums. In the fall of 1991, Walter Talbot of the W. Talbot Insurance Agency in Lancaster, Pennsylvania, requested Universal to provide financing for his customers who needed funds to pay premiums on policies issued by the Great American Insurance Company. Universal accepted Talbot's proposal and sent him the necessary documents, including blank drafts. The face of each instrument contained Universal's name and address in the top left corner, and a large UPAC logo in the top center. Below UPAC's address was printed "PAY AND DEPOSIT ONLY TO THE CREDIT OF: _____ INSURANCE CO." with a space for the amount. On the lower right side of the instrument were blanks for the policyholder's name, the insurance agency name, and a line for 'SIGNATURE OF PRODUCER OF RECORD/ BROKER/AGENT." In the lower right hand corner beneath the signature line appear the name and address of the Landmark Bank. The back of each instrument contained pre-printed language: "Acceptance of this draft acknowledges Universal Premium Acceptance Corporation's interest in the unearned or return premium(s) and that we have issued a policy(ies) to the named applicant (insured) in the amount of the premium indicated." Between September 1991 and July 1992, Talbot signed drafts for more than $1 million in favor of Great American, but did not deliver them to the insurance company. Instead, he arranged for his confederate to forge the indorsement of Great American and deposit the drafts in an account they opened at defendant York Bank under the name of "Small Businessman's Service Corporation." York deposited the drafts without securing the indorsement of Small Businessman's Service Corporation and transmitted them to Landmark . . ., Universal's bank in St. Louis. As part of the scheme, Talbot and his associate set up a dummy "Great American Insurance Company" office in Lancaster and furnished its address and telephone number to Universal. To verify that Great American had issued a policy, Universal

would contact that office. After assurances from Talbot's cohorts there that the transaction was in order, Universal would then authorize Landmark to pay the draft. After the fraud was discovered, Talbot was convicted and imprisoned. Universal recovered part of its loss from Talbot and then filed suit in its own behalf and as assignee of Landmark against York. The complaints asserted claims under Articles 3 and 4 of the Uniform Commercial Code as enacted in Pennsylvania . . . as well as for negligence and conversion. The district court granted summary judgment for York . . . Universal has appealed, contending that the limiting language as to the payee of the drafts did not permit York to deposit them in the Small Businesssman's account, that the fictitious payee provision does not apply, and that the negligence claim should not have been resolved in York's favor.

ISSUES Were the drafts negotiable instruments under Article 3? Did the blank indorsements convert the drafts to negotiable bearer instruments? Is York protected from liability by the fictitious payee rule?

HOLDINGS No, to all three issues. The drafts were not negotiable instruments; the blank indorsements did not convert the drafts to negotiable bearer instruments; the fictitious payee rule does not apply to nonnegotiable instruments.

REASONING One of the requirements for negotiability under . . . § 3-104(a)(3) is that an instrument must be "payable to order or to bearer." How the parties regard or characterize the instrument is immaterial. "The negotiability of an instrument cannot be established by waiver . . . [W]here the statute requires certain elements, it is not for private persons to dispense with or waive them." . . . The drafts here did not meet the terms of § 3-104. In some circumstances instruments that are not payable "to order" or "to bearer" may nevertheless be within the scope of Article 3 of the Code except that there can be no holder in due

continued

21.1

UNIVERSAL PREMIUM ASSURANCE CORPORATION
V. YORK BANK AND TRUST COMPANY, *continued*

69 F.3D 695 (3RD CIR. 1995)

course of such an item . . . § 3-805 provides that Article 3 "applies to any instrument whose terms do not preclude transfer and which is otherwise negotiable within this division but which is not payable to order or to bearer . . ." The commentary to section 3-805 cites as a typical example an item that reads "Pay John Doe" without the words "to the order of." . . . Such instruments have been termed "technically non-negotiable" because they meet all requirements as to form except they are not payable to order or to bearer . . . The language on the drafts, "PAY AND DEPOSIT ONLY TO THE CREDIT OF: Great American Insurance Company" goes beyond a mere technicality. Not only did these drafts lack "to the order of," they contained specific instructions—"deposit only to the credit of." Implicit in such language is a warning of non-negotiability . . . The drafts demonstrate that they were not meant to be freely transferable, but were to be "deposited" and "only" to the credit of the insurance company. "Deposited" implies that the instruments were to have a limited use and a short transactional life. "Only" can be understood to modify "deposited" or the payee, but in either instance, the language is quite restrictive. The terms on the face of the item were meant to preclude transfer . . . We hold, therefore, that the drafts were not "otherwise negotiable" within the scope of section 3-805. As an alternative method of finding negotiability, York argues that even if not originally negotiable, the indorsements in blank by "Great American" converted the drafts into "bearer," negotiable instruments. We reject that premise . . . § 3-204(b) provides that a blank indorsement on a negotiable instrument transforms it into a bearer instrument, but that section has no application to a non-negotiable item. An item which is non-negotiable in its inception remains so. Mere indorsement of such a draft does not change its character. As one court remarked, to sanction any other result would enable an indorser to change the rights and liabilities of the prior parties in a most material fashion . . . We conclude, therefore, that the drafts did not become bearer or negotiable instruments by virtue of the forged blank indorsements of the Great American Insurance Company. The general rule is a bank that pays off a forged indorsement is liable to the drawer . . . § 3-405(a) (the fictitious payee exception) provides that an indorsement by any person in the

name of the designated payee is effective if the drawer intends the payee to have no interest in the instrument. That provision is intended to protect banks that cash instruments with such forged indorsements and is based on the assumption that as between the bank and the drawer, the latter is in a better position to prevent the loss. We have held that section 3-205 should be interpreted broadly enough to carry out its purpose . . . § 3-405 is not applicable here because it speaks only to negotiable instruments. Although Article 3 of the Uniform Commercial Code is sometimes applied by analogy to non-negotiable instruments, in that situation as well, the same cautious approach to section 3-405 should be used . . . [T]he direction on the drafts here to "pay and deposit only to the credit of Great American" was explicit. The action of York Bank in permitting the deposit of the drafts in the Small Businessman's Service Corporation instead of Great American's account created quite a different situation than cashing the check of a fictitious payee. The face of the drafts raised a red flag and was enough to put York on notice that something was amiss in the Talbot group's dealings with it. We are not persuaded that the fictitious payee exception should be carried over to the non-negotiable instrument in this case. Our conclusions that the drafts are non-negotiable and that the fictitious payee exemption is not applicable undermine the basic premises upon which the district court based its decision. Consequently, the case must be remanded to the district court for further proceedings during which the parties may develop their contentions consistent with appropriate legal principles . . .

BUSINESS CONSIDERATIONS Why would a business provide blank drafts that are preprinted with instruction as to how and where the drafts should be deposited? How do such instructions protect the interest of the business that provides the preprinted drafts?

ETHICAL CONSIDERATIONS Did Universal act ethically in suing York Bank for the money it could not recover from Talbot? Did York Bank act ethically in attempting to deny liability on a questionable legal basis?

USES OF NEGOTIABLE INSTRUMENTS

Negotiable instruments are widely used in our economy. They are used as a substitute for money. They are used for convenience. They are used as credit instruments. They are used to pay bills, to buy things, and to borrow. Some of the most important uses of each type are set out in the following sections.

Check Usage

The most commonly used type of negotiable instrument is a check. Many people use checks rather than cash for daily purchases. Checks are regularly written to the supermarket for groceries, to the utility companies to pay bills, to the landlord to pay the rent, and to the bank to make loan payments. In addition, many working people receive their salaries or wages in periodic paychecks from their employers.

Checks are widely used because they are easily written, easily carried, and widely accepted. Carrying and using checks is safer than carrying and using cash. If a person loses a blank, unsigned check, no harm is done. All that was lost was a piece of paper. If a person loses cash, the money is gone. The bank will not take an unsigned check, but it will take lost money. Great care should be taken with checks, particularly signed ones. A signed check, otherwise blank, is nearly as good as cash. Anyone finding such a check can complete the blanks and possibly receive cash for it as completed, to the detriment of the depositor/"drawer."

The revision to Article 3 recognizes a number of specialized drafts as "checks" within the coverage of Section 3-104. All of these specialized checks have the primary use of serving as a substitute for money. However, they also have some aspect that distinguishes them from "regular" checks. For example, a *cashier's check* is a check drawn *by* a bank *against* that same bank and then issued to the person who purchased it. Cashier's checks are commonly used by a purchaser who wants to guarantee payment to the payee. (The payee knows that there are sufficient funds on deposit since the bank is holding those funds already and also knows that the cashier's check cannot have payment stopped.)

These are *preaccepted* checks (acceptance is discussed in chapter 24), which ensure the payee that he or she will be paid upon presentment. A *teller's check* is similar to a cashier's check, being drawn by one bank against another bank. Again, the act of issuing the teller's check shows *preacceptance*, ensuring the payee that he or she will be paid upon proper presentment. A *traveler's check* is a special type of check used by people who are away from home and want the security of having checks that will be accepted. A traveler's check is signed once by the drawer upon purchase, but it requires a second signing by that same drawer (a countersigning) before it can be negotiated. The payee knows that a bank is holding the funds used to purchase the traveler's check, so there is no danger of insufficient funds; and the payee can compare the countersignature to the "authenticating" original signature, minimizing the risk of a forgery. A *credit union check* (formerly called a *share draft*) is simply a check drawn against a credit union. As banks become more and more specialized, many individuals are turning to credit unions to handle their personal banking needs simply because the credit union specializes in individual accounts, and the fees imposed are normally substantially less.

Draft Usage

Businesses often use drafts to pay for merchandise ordered, especially when the buyer and the seller are in different states. Drafts may be payable "at sight" (i.e., on demand), or they may be "time drafts" (i.e., they are payable at a future date). Often, a seller of goods will send a draft to the buyer for acceptance. If the buyer accepts, he or she has agreed to pay any holder who makes proper **presentment.** Such a draft is called a *trade* **acceptance.**

With the recent liberalization of federal and state banking laws and regulations, a number of changes have occurred in the area of negotiable instruments. One of these changes has been in the area of drafts. Today, some financial institutions offer accounts similar to the checking accounts offered by banks and savings and loan institutions. These drafting accounts offer the same privileges for these depositors as are available to depositors of banks. Technically, however, these are not checking accounts; there are some minor differences.

Promissory Note Usage

Promissory notes are most often used as instruments of credit. They also are used as evidence to show a preexisting debt. Any time a customer borrows money from a bank, the borrower must sign a promissory note; this signed note proves the existence of the debt, the amount owed, the manner of repayment, and any other terms important to the loan agreement. Notes are so widely used that special types of notes have developed. Real estate loans normally involve a mortgage note. Automobile loans usually involve an installment note. Many banks also use a device called a *commercial loan note* or a *signature note* for short-term unsecured loans (loans made without collateral).

Certificate of Deposit Usage

A *certificate of deposit* (CD) is an instrument issued by a bank evidencing a debt owed to a depositor. These instruments commonly call for the bank to pay to a proper presenter the amount deposited plus interest at a stated future date. Although regularly thought of as a type of special savings account, CDs are really credit instruments. They recognize money "borrowed" by the bank from its depositor.

FUNCTIONS AND FORMS OF NEGOTIABLE INSTRUMENTS

Negotiable instruments have two major functions: They are designed to serve as a substitute for money, and they are designed to serve as credit instruments. In satisfying either use, they carry certain contract rights, certain property rights, and some special rights due exclusively to

21.1 | FINANCE

CALL-IMAGE TECHNOLOGY

COMAKERS FOR COMPANY LOANS

When the family first formed CIT, they needed to borrow money from their bank. The bank's lending officer was more than willing to make the loan, but *not* if the borrower was going to be CIT. She insisted that Tom and Anna had to be comakers of the note along with Call-Image before she was willing to make the loan. Since they needed the money—and they viewed the family and the business as an entity—they agreed to be comakers of the note along with CIT. They recently were discussing their various loans, and this issue arose again. They ask you if the bank treated them fairly or was acting properly in requiring them to sign as comakers. What will you tell them?

BUSINESS CONSIDERATIONS It is very common in a number of business classes to discuss the advantages and disadvantages of the various forms a business may take. Limited liability is often mentioned as an advantage of a corporation. However, when a corporation is newly formed, it has no credit history and no "track record" of being profitable. What should a potential creditor insist on when considering the extension of credit to a newly formed corporation? Why?

ETHICAL CONSIDERATIONS Is it ethical for an entrepreneur to form a corporation or a limited liability partnership or a limited liability corporation to avoid potential liability if his or her entrepreneurial skills do not flourish and the business enterprise fails? How can this be justified—or criticized—from an ethical perspective?

their nature as negotiable instruments. Every negotiable instrument is presumed to be a contract, but not every contract is a negotiable instrument. The difference between a contract and a negotiable instrument is one of form. To be negotiable, an instrument must be (1) current in trade and (2) payable in money. These criteria are obviously too broad and too vague to be of much practical significance. Accordingly, Article 3 has more fully defined the requirements that an instrument must meet in order to be negotiable.

As mentioned earlier, UCC § 3-104 defines the various types of negotiable instruments. These definitions include the following, by subsection of 3-104:

- (e) lists the only forms a negotiable instrument may take:

  An instrument is a "note" if it is a promise and it is a "draft" if it is an order. If an instrument falls within the definition of both "note" and "draft," a person entitled to enforce the instrument may treat it as either.

- (f) defines a "check":

  "Check" means (i) a draft, other than a documentary draft, payable on demand and drawn on a bank or (ii) a cashier's check or teller's check. An instrument may be a check even though it is described on its face by another term, such as "money order."

- (g) defines a "Cashier's check":

  "Cashier's check" means a draft with respect to which a drawer and drawee are the same bank or branches of the same bank.

- (h) defines a "Teller's check":

  "Teller's check" means a draft drawn by a bank (i) on another bank, or (ii) payable at or through a bank.

- (i) defines a "Traveler's check":

  "Traveler's check" means an instrument that (i) is payable on demand, (ii) is drawn on or payable at or through a bank, (iii) is designated by the term "traveler's check" or by a substantially similar term, and (iv) requires, as a condition to payment, a countersignature by a person whose specimen signature appears on the instrument.

- (j) defines a "Certificate of deposit":

  "Certificate of deposit" means an instrument containing an acknowledgment by a bank that a sum of money has been received by the bank and a promise by the bank to repay the sum of money. A certificate of deposit is a note of the bank.

Drafts, including checks, are one form of negotiable instrument. These instruments are paper containing an order, and they are commonly known as *order paper*. Notes, including certificates of deposit, are the other form of negotiable instrument. These instruments are paper containing a promise, and they are commonly known as *promise paper*. Order paper is most commonly used as a substitute for money. Promise paper is most commonly used as a credit instrument, providing proof that credit has been extended and showing evidence of the terms of payment for that credit.

Presentment
A demand by a holder for the maker or the drawee of a negotiable instrument to accept and/or pay the instrument.

Acceptance
The agreement by the maker or the drawee to accept and/or pay a negotiable instrument upon presentment.

Promissory note
A written promise to pay a sum certain in money without conditions, either at a preset time in the future or "on demand."

PAPER CONTAINING AN ORDER ("THREE-PARTY" PAPER)

The distinctive features of paper containing an order (order paper), or three-party paper, are that each instrument contains an *order* to pay money and that at least *three parties* are necessary to fill the legal roles involved. The order element will be pointed out in the following sections, while the rules governing this class of negotiable instrument will be explained later. The three parties involved on order paper are: the *drawer,* the *drawee,* and the *payee.* As noted, this class consists of drafts, including checks in the various forms that checks can take.

Drafts

Draft

An order for a third person to pay a sum certain in money without conditions, either at a preset time in the future or "on demand."

A **draft** is an instrument in which one party, the drawer, issues an instrument to a second party, the payee. The draft is accepted by the payee as a substitute for money. The payee expects to receive money at some time from the third party, the drawee. The reason the payee expects to receive money from the drawee is contained in the basic form of the instrument. As will be pointed out, the drawer issues an order to the drawee to pay a sum of money. This order, coupled with the three roles involved, distinguishes drafts from promise paper. The components of a draft are shown in Exhibit 21.1.

Checks

The most common type of order paper is a check. A check is a special type of draft. Like a draft, a check necessitates the involvement of three parties, but there are two differences. A check is, by definition, a demand instrument; in contrast, a draft may

E X H I B I T   21.1 | A Bank Draft

UNITED VIRGINIA BANK

42764

(6)

DATE ———————— 19———

(1) (2)
PAY TO THE
ORDER OF

(3)

$ (4)

(5)

DOLLARS

(7)

TELLER

MANUFACTURERS HANOVER TRUST COMPANY (8)
NEW YORK, NEW YORK

VOID VOID VOID VOID VOID VOID VOID

AUTHORIZED
SIGNATURE

"042764" '0210'"0030' :0144 7""36834"'

(1) The order. (2) Words of negotiability. (3) The payee. (4) The amount, in numbers. (5) The amount, in words. (6) The date of issue. (7) The drawer's signature. (8) The drawee.

SOURCE: Courtesy of Crestar Bank (formerly United Virginia Bank), Radford, Virginia.

be a demand instrument or a time instrument. Furthermore, a check must be drawn on a bank or payable at or through a bank; in contrast, anyone may be the drawee on a draft. Article 3 now specifically includes cashier's checks, teller's checks, traveler's checks, and checks drawn against credit unions within the definition of "checks" to better reflect contemporary usage of that term. Exhibit 21.2 shows the various elements of a check.

In the case of both a check and a draft, the drawee is obligated to the drawer. This obligation is normally a debt or contractual obligation owed to the drawer by the drawee. When the drawer orders the drawee to pay, the drawer is directing the drawee as to how the debt or contractual obligation should be discharged or partially discharged. The order to the drawee to pay, coupled with the obligation to pay, assures the payee that payment will (normally) be made by the drawee at the appropriate time.

The Order. All drafts (including checks) contain an order. The drawer orders the drawee to pay the instrument. The language used is not a request. The drawer does not "ask," or "hope," or even "expect" the drawee to pay. The drawer demands that payment be made. If you look at Exhibit 21.1 or Exhibit 21.2, you will see that the drawer tells the drawee to "Pay to the order of (Payee)." It should also be noted that the *order* is the word *pay*; the phrase "to the order of" is not the order. This phrase is a term of negotiability; its meaning will be explained later, when negotiability is discussed.

The Drawer. The person who draws an order instrument, who gives the order to the drawee, and who issues the instrument to the payee is known as the drawer. This person originates the check or the draft. The drawer does not pay the payee

E X H I B I T   21.2 | **A Check**

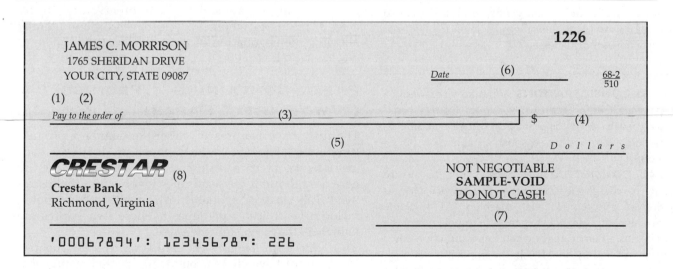

(1) The order. (2) Words of negotiability. (3) The payee. (4) The amount, in numbers. (5) The amount, in words. (6) The date of issue. (7) The drawer's signature. (8) The drawee.

SOURCE: Courtesy of Crestar Bank (formerly United Virginia Bank), Radford, Virginia.

21.2 | FINANCE

SHOULD CIT PLACE ITS ACCOUNT IN A CREDIT UNION?

Dan has his personal checking account with a credit union, and he is very pleased with the service he receives. He is strongly urging the family to place the CIT account with the credit union. Tom and Anna have dealt with a local bank for several years, and they are also generally pleased with the service and treatment they receive with their bank. They believe that their bank can provide the necessary services for the firm, and they would have both their personal and their business accounts together in one bank. Julio disagrees with Dan and with Tom and Anna. Julio believes the family and the business will be better served by having a commercial account with a commercial bank. He thinks that having the account with the credit union would definitely be a bad idea, and that having the account in the same bank as Tom and Anna's personal account would not be as advantageous as using a commercial bank. The family asks what you would recommend to them. What advice will you give them? (Before answering, you might want to contact a local bank and a local credit union for information, suggestions, and guidance.)

BUSINESS CONSIDERATIONS What services would a business want and/or reasonably expect from a bank? How are these services different from those that an individual would want and/or reasonably expect on his or her account?

ETHICAL CONSIDERATION Many banks today are beginning to charge customers fees and service charges for using an automated teller machine (ATM). Some banks are also imposing fees when a customer enters the bank and uses a human teller when the transaction could have been handled by an ATM. Is the imposition of a fee or a service charge for normal and expected banking services ethical?

directly. The drawee is expected to pay the payee or the holder, upon proper presentment. That is why the drawer gives the drawee the order. The drawer expects the order to be obeyed because of a prior agreement or relationship between the drawer and the drawee. If the order is obeyed, the drawee pays the payee or holder, and both the drawer and the drawee have performed.

The Drawee. The drawee is the party to whom the order on the draft is directed. The drawee is told by the drawer to "*Pay* to the order of" the payee. It is the drawee who is expected to make payment to the presenting party. The drawee, however, has no duty to the payee or to the holder to pay, despite the order. The only duty the drawee has is a duty owed to the drawer. The duty of the drawee is to accept the instrument. Before acceptance, there is only the prospect that the drawee will pay when the time for payment arrives. Once the drawee accepts, he or she has a contractual obligation to pay the presenter. This relationship is shown in Exhibit 21.3.

The Payee. The payee is the person to whom the instrument is originally issued. The payee may be specifically designated, as in "Pay to the order of Jane Doe"; the payee may be an office or title, as in "Pay to the order of Treasurer of Truro County"; or the particular payee may be unspecified, as in "Pay to the order of bearer." The payee may decide to seek payment personally, or the payee may decide to further negotiate the instrument. The words "to the order of" allow the payee to order the drawee to make payment to some other party. (*To the order of* means to whomever the payee orders, literally allowing the negotiation of the instrument.)

PAPER CONTAINING A PROMISE ("TWO-PARTY" PAPER)

The distinctive features of paper containing a promise (promise paper), or two-party paper, are that each such instrument contains a *promise*, and that only *two parties* are necessary to fulfill the legal roles involved on the instrument. This class of negotiable instruments involves notes, including certificates of deposit. These two parties are known as the *maker* and the *payee*.

The term *two-party* is confusing to many people. Many stores have signs prominently posted stating that they do not accept "two-party checks." These so-called two-party checks are, in reality, checks that have been negotiated by the payee to a later holder. The store does

E X H I B I T   21.3 | **The Parties on Order Paper**

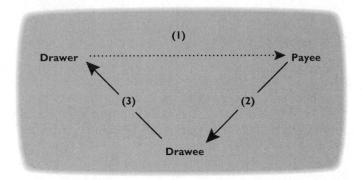

(1) The drawer issues the order instrument to the payee. The instrument contains an order directed to the drawee.

(2) The payee (or an endorsee or holder) presents the order instrument to the drawee in order to collect. The drawee is expected to obey the order directed to it by the drawer.

(3) Assuming that the drawee obeyed the order, the drawer is charged (or his or her account is debited) for the amount of the order instrument.

YOU BE THE JUDGE

IS A GUARANTEE A NEGOTIABLE INSTRUMENT?

LA Partners executed a number of promissory notes. Mondolfo and Chudy signed each of the notes so executed by LA Partners as *coguarantors*. When LA Partners defaulted on one of the notes, Mondolfo paid his obligation on the note to the payee. Shortly thereafter, Mondolfo purchased the defaulted note from the payee and sued Chudy for the entire balance of the note, plus accrued interest. Mondolfo argued that by purchasing the note he had become a holder and was therefore entitled to recover the full amount of the note from Chudy as guarantor. Chudy objected. While admitting his liability for half of the note as guarantor, he argued that he should not be held liable for the entire amount of the note to his coguarantor.

This case has been brought before *your* court. How will *you* decide this case?[1]

BUSINESS CONSIDERATIONS Why would a lender want a guarantor on a promissory note when it already has the unconditional promise of the maker that the note will be repaid? Why would an individual serve as a guarantor on a note issued by a business?

ETHICAL CONSIDERATION Is it ethical for a party who agrees to serve as coguarantor to attempt to avoid his or her liability by buying the instrument and then suing the other guarantors, alleging that he or she has become a holder through purchase of the instrument?

SOURCE: *Commercial Lending Litigation News* (6 March 1998), LRP Publications, http://www.lexis-nexis.com/.

not want to accept a check unless it receives it directly from the drawer. But there is no such legal creature as a check that is "two-party paper." The promise element of promise paper will be pointed out in the following sections, and the rules governing this class of negotiable instrument will be explained later.

(Promissory) Notes

The promissory note is the oldest known form of negotiable instrument. It is normally used as a credit instrument, executed either at the time credit is extended or as evidence of a preexisting debt not yet repaid.

In a note, one party (the maker) promises to pay the other party (the payee) a sum of money at some future time. The promise may call for a lump-sum payment, or it may call for installment payments over time. The note may specify the payment of interest in addition to the principal; it may have the interest included in the principal; or it may be interest free. The note may recite details about collateral. Despite any or all of these possibilities, the basic form is constant. Such an instrument is shown in Exhibit 21.4.

The following case involved an interesting approach to the enforcement of a "promissory note" and emphasizes the importance of being certain that one's instruments are indeed negotiable.

E X H I B I T   21.4 | **A Promissory Note**

FEDERAL BANK

PROMISSORY NOTE

Loan No.

Borrower(s)
Name(s) _____ and _____
            first   middle   last   first   middle   last

Address
(1)   (2)   (3)   (2)
Borrower (jointly and severally if more than one) promises to pay to Federal Savings Bank ("Lender"), or order, in U.S. money, at its office in San Diego, California, or elsewhere Lender designates, principal and interest on unpaid principal from the date advanced until paid, in amount, annual rate and consecutive monthly installments as follows:

Principal $ (4)   Annual Interest Rate   %

Installments $ on the same day of month beginning

Minimum Interest $ 100.00

Interest will be computed on the basis of a 12 month year and 30 day month. The date of payment, whether early or late, will be disregarded for purposes of allocating the payment between principal and interest: each payment will be treated for this purpose as though made on its due date.

continued

EXHIBIT 21.4 | **A Promissory Note, continued**

PREPAYMENT: Full or partial prepayment may be made without penalty except Borrower will pay any minimum interest amount specified. Borrower will tell Lender in writing that Borrower is making a prepayment. Lender will use all prepayments to reduce the principal subject to its right to first apply payments received to any past due interest or other charges. Partial prepayments will not delay the due dates nor change the amount of monthly payments unless Lender agrees in writing to those delays or changes. Full prepayment may be made at any time. Lender may require that partial prepayment be made on the same day as monthly payments are due. Lender may also require that the amount of any partial prepayment be equal to the amount of principal that would have been part of the next one or more monthly payments.

LATE CHARGE: Borrower will pay a late charge of 5% of each installment not paid within 15 days of its due date, or $5.00, whichever is greater.

DEFAULT AND ACCELERATION: If Borrower fails to timely pay any installment when due or to perform any provision contained in any document securing this Note, Lender may, at Lender's option, declare all sums owed hereunder immediately due and payable. Borrower will pay all reasonable expenses and attorney's fees of Lender in any action relating to Borrower's obligations.

SELLER, IF ANY: Borrower intends to use some or all of the loan proceeds to pay _____ , as Seller, amounts due Seller under a contract between Seller and Borrower, dated _____ , Borrower represents that a true and correct copy of the contract has been furnished to Lender and that it contains the entire agreement between Seller and Borrower. The following notice applies only to the named Seller, if any, and to the proceeds hereof paid to said Seller under the described contract.

NOTICE: ANY HOLDER OF THIS CONSUMER CREDIT CONTRACT IS SUBJECT TO ALL CLAIMS AND DEFENSES WHICH THE DEBTOR COULD ASSER   AGAINST THE SELLER OF GOODS OR SERVICES OBTAINED WITH THE PROCEEDS HEREOF. RECOVER   HEREUNDER BY THE DEBTOR SHALL NOT EXCEED AMOUNTS PAID BY THE DEBTOR HEREUNDER.

NON-WAIVER: By accepting payment after its due date or after notice of default, Lender will not waive its right to prompt payment when due of other sums, or to declare a default, or to proceed with any remedy it has. Without affecting the liability of anyone else, Lender may release anyone liable, may change payment terms, and add, alter, substitute, or release security.

❏ This Note is secured by a Security Agreement.
❏ This Note is unsecured.

BEFORE SIGNING ORIGINAL, WE RECEIVED AND READ A COMPLETED COPY HEREOF.

(5)

Borrower's Signature	Date	Borrower's Signature	Date
Borrower's Signature	Date	Borrower's Signature	Date

C-1-424 (REV 6/83)   *(Sign Original Only)*

Courtesy of Great American Federal Savings Bank of San Diego and Fresno, California. (1) The promise. (2) Words of negotiability. (3) The payee. (4) The amount borrowed. (5) The signature of the maker.

21.2

ALMOND V. RHYNE
424 S.E.2D 231 (N.C.APP. 1993)

FACTS On 1 May 1984, Rhyne executed an agreement whereby Rhyne agreed to purchase fifty (50) shares of stock in A & H Millworks, Inc., from Jesse Almond (the deceased). In addition, this agreement gave Rhyne an option to purchase an additional fifty (50) shares of stock. To secure the purchase price of $35,000, Rhyne also executed a document entitled "Promissory Note and Security Agreement."

In either June or September of 1988, after the deceased was diagnosed with cancer, Rhyne visited the deceased. During this visit, Rhyne obtained possession of the promissory note and a stock certificate representing the original fifty (50) shares of stock. Only Rhyne and the decedent were present during this time.

Margaret Almond filed suit on 9 April 1990 to collect the balance owing on the promissory note. No payment has been made on the promissory note since 10 May 1988. On 12 September 1991 the trial court granted Almond's motion for summary judgment for the balance due on the note plus interest.

ISSUE Did Almond deliver the "promissory note" to Rhyne with the intent to cancel the note and discharge the debt?

HOLDING No. Rhyne failed to present admissible evidence sufficient to persuade the court of any intent to discharge the obligation.

REASONING Rhyne argued that his possession of the note and the stock certificate was evidence that Almond intended to cancel the note and discharge the debt as a matter of law. In support of his argument, Rhyne quoted the UCC, § 3-605 [§ 3-604 under the revised Article 3], Discharge by Cancellation or Renunciation. However, the court rejected this argument, stating that the UCC did not govern this case since the "promissory note" was not negotiable under Article 3. The note in question contained language stating that "the terms of the May 1984 Agreement are incorporated herein by reference as though fully written herein." Because of this language, the instrument is conditional, and therefore not a negotiable instrument. Thus, § 3-605 was inapplicable, and the case had to be resolved under common law.

Under the laws of this state, a debtor's obligation under a note can be discharged when the note is surrendered to the debtor and there is ample evidence that the party surrendering the note intended to discharge the debtor. Here, the operation of Rule 601 (c) (Deadman's Statute) precludes evidence that the deceased intended to discharge defendant's obligation.

Several jurisdictions have recognized that surrender of a note to the debtor will discharge the debtor's obligation if it is done with the intent to discharge. . . . Also, other authorities recognize that surrender of an instrument must be accompanied by an intent to discharge the debtor's obligation. . . . We find the approach advocated by these authorities is well-reasoned and applicable to the present situation. Accordingly, having reviewed defendant's pleadings, depositions, and affidavits, and since he has presented no admissible evidence in regards to the deceased's intent when surrendering the documents, we cannot say, as a matter of law, that the debt has been extinguished.

Defendant further contends that at a minimum, surrender of the note created a presumption of discharge. We first observe that cancellation or discharge of an obligation is an affirmative defense and defendant, as payor, bears the burden of proving a valid discharge. Since defendant must prove not only surrender of the note but also an intent to discharge the debt on the part of the deceased, we cannot say that a finding of one element raises a presumption that the other exists. Accordingly, defendant's argument has no merit.

BUSINESS CONSIDERATIONS What precautions should an individual take when dealing with a terminally ill person in an investment setting? What should Rhyne have done in his circumstances to prove that Jesse Almond intended to cancel the note and release Rhyne from liability?

ETHICAL CONSIDERATIONS The maker of a $35,000 note acquires possession of [it] and a certificate for stock that the note was purportedly issued to purchase. Both the note and the stock certificate are acquired from a terminally ill person. The maker then claims that the payee canceled the note and delivered the stock as an "accord and satisfaction." How credible is the witness in this situation? What ethical issues does such testimony raise? Does the "Deadman Statute" seem to provide an adequate solution to this problem?

Certificates of Deposit

A certificate of deposit (or a CD, as it is frequently called) is a special type of note issued by a bank as an acknowledgment of money received, with a promise to repay the money at some future date. Many people think of a CD as a "time savings account," in contrast to a passbook savings account. In reality, though, a CD is not a savings account at all. It is most commonly a time deposit of money with a bank.

A CD normally pays higher interest than a savings account, with the interest varying according to the amount of time the certificate is to run. Most certificates run for some multiple of six months, and they are available in some multiple of $1,000. However, a number of banks offer CDs for shorter time periods such as 90 days. Some banks are beginning to offer CDs for multiples of $100. One type of CD is shown in Exhibit 21.5. Today, many banks offer some variation of a "saver's certificate," which is nonnegotiable, rather than a negotiable certificate of deposit. It appears that the CD is becoming extinct, although some CDs still exist. However, the widespread replacement of CDs with other forms of certificates makes this an area of primarily historic interest.

The Promise. *Promise paper* is so called because it contains a promise. The maker of the instrument *promises* to pay an amount of money to the payee or to a holder. The instrument does not say that the maker "might" pay, or will "probably" pay, or will "agree" to pay. The instrument says that the maker *promises* to pay an amount of money to the payee or to the order of the payee.

E X H I B I T   21.5 | **A Certificate of Deposit**

	INTEREST RATE % PER ANNUM	**INTEREST AMOUNT**	**MATURITY DATE**	**TOTAL AMOUNT PAYABLE**

(1) The date of issue. (2) The amount of the "deposit," in words. (3) The amount of the "deposit," in numbers. (4) The payee. (5) The maturity date. (6) The amount to be paid. (7) The signature of the maker.

SOURCE: Courtesy of Great American Federal Savings Bank (formerly San Diego Federal) of San Diego and Fresno, California.

The Maker. The duties performed by the drawer and the drawee on order paper are effectively combined in promise paper: Both duties fall to the maker. The maker makes the promise—"I promise to pay to the order of (the payee)"; the maker issues the instrument to the payee; and the maker pays the instrument upon proper presentment. However, there is one important difference from order paper. While the drawee is not obligated to any holder until acceptance, the maker is liable to a holder from the date of original issue. This obligation is shown in Exhibit 21.6.

The Payee. As in order paper, the *payee* is the party to whom the instrument is originally issued. Again, the payee may be specifically designated by name, or designated by title or office, or unspecified. The payee on promise paper is the person to whom the promise is made by the maker. By contrast, the payee on order paper is the person to whom the drawee is directed (ordered) to make payment.

THE SCOPE OF ARTICLE 7

The UCC treats the topic of documents of title in Article 7. This article, entitled "Warehouse Receipts, Bills of Lading, and Other Documents of Title," specifies the rights and the duties of all relevant parties in the handling of documents of title, whether those documents are negotiable or nonnegotiable. Part 2 of Article 7 deals with warehouse receipts; Part 3 deals with bills of lading; Part 5 deals with the negotiation and transfer of a document of title.

FUNCTIONS AND FORMS OF DOCUMENTS OF TITLE

The essential function of a *document of title* is to reflect the rights of the owner when the goods are turned over to the custody and care of a bailee, whether for storage or for carriage. A secondary function of a document of title, especially if the document is negotiable, is to enable the owner to transfer title to the goods without having to reclaim possession of the goods in order to make the sale. The owner can negotiate the document of title, and in so doing the owner also transfers title to the goods to the person receiving the negotiation. The importance of the negotiability of a document of title is shown in the following case.

E X H I B I T   21.6 | **The Parties on Promise Paper**

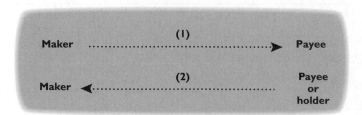

(1) The maker issues the promise paper to the payee, promising to pay the payee (or a subsequent holder) upon presentment.

(2) The payee (or a subsequent holder) presents the promise paper to the maker, expecting to receive payment as per the promise.

21.3

BANK OF NEW YORK V. AMOCO OIL CO.

831 F.SUPP. 254 (S.D.N.Y. 1993) [AFF'D 35 F.3D 643 (2ND CIR. 1994)]

FACTS Amoco uses platinum to prepare catalysts that are used in reactors at Amoco's six refineries around the country. These catalysts accelerate the refining process in the manufacture of gasoline. During the refining process, some platinum is lost—between 2,000 and 4,000 ounces each year. Although Amoco owns 280,000 ounces of platinum, it must occasionally lease platinum from other sources. Sloss, who was Amoco's Senior Supply Negotiator until 1992, testified that he leased from metal trading companies that delivered platinum to Amoco's catalyst manufacturers. A particular shipment of platinum, once it is used to prepare catalysts for use in the refining process, can no longer be traced. . . . When leasing, Amoco would issue a holding certificate to the precious metal company from whom the platinum had been obtained. . . .

DBL Trading leased metals to companies such as Amoco in order to improve profitability on its precious metals inventory. Metal was also used as collateral by DBL Trading in lending transactions with various banks, including Bank of New York (BNY). . . . The amount of the loans made available by BNY were limited to 95% of the daily value of the pledged collateral. BNY would receive a telex from the depository where the collateral was being held, a warehouse receipt, or a holding certificate. The banks' rights in the collateral were reflected in a General Loan and Security Agreement between BNY and DBL Trading, which had been signed in 1982. . . . Three of the four holding certificates at issue in this litigation were accepted by BNY in December of 1989. They conform to previous certificates that BNY had accepted. . . . The fourth certificate is identical in wording to the other three, but is dated 2 January 1990. . . . On 13 February 1990, DBL Trading defaulted on an overnight loan that it had obtained from BNY. BNY immediately began liquidating collateral; after an exchange of communications discussed in detail below, Amoco returned platinum to BNY. It did not do so, however, until 4 April 1990, after this action had been brought. Sloss instructed UOP, Inc., a platinum reclaimer that held platinum in a pool account for Amoco, to transfer 22,230 troy ounces of platinum from Amoco's account to BNY's account. BNY sued Amoco for conversion, alleging that Amoco had refused to turn over the platinum upon the bank's proper demand based on its possession of the holding certificates.

ISSUE Were the holding certificates negotiable documents of title under Article 7, granting the bank the right to immediate transfer upon demand?

HOLDING Yes. The holding certificates fell within Article 7's definition of a negotiable document of title, which gave the bank the right to an immediate transfer of the platinum upon demand.

REASONING BNY bases its conversion claim on the alleged superior rights that it had to the platinum under Article 7 of the UCC. If the holding certificates were negotiable documents of title that DBL Trading duly negotiated to BNY, then BNY obtained title to the platinum, and Amoco was under an obligation to "hold or deliver the goods according to the terms of the document free of any defense or claim by [it] except those arising under the terms of the document." The holding certificates come under the purview of Article 7 only if they fall within the definition of a document of title. The UCC states that the following are documents of title: Bill of lading, dock warrant, dock receipt, warehouse receipt or order for the delivery of goods and also any other document which in the regular course of business or financing is treated as adequately evidencing that the person in possession of it is entitled to receive, hold and dispose of the document and the goods it covers. . . . BNY contends that [the documents] fall within the broad language describing "other documents" that constitute documents of title, and the court agrees. . . . The court finds that BNY did treat the holding certificates as "adequately evidencing that [BNY] is entitled to receive, hold and dispose of the document and the goods it covers." Moreover, industry practice was to accept holding certificates as well, at least in some circumstances, as documents of title. Notwithstanding Amoco's objections, . . . the holding certificates here did constitute documents of title and fall within the purview of Article 7. . . .

In order to be negotiable, a document of title must state "by its terms [that] the goods are to be delivered to bearer or to the order of a named person." Although the holding certificates did not literally comply with [the Code's requirements for negotiability], they represented title to the goods on their face, stating that their are no liens or encumbrances and

continued

21.3

BANK OF NEW YORK V. AMOCO OIL CO., *continued*
831 F.SUPP. 254 (S.D.N.Y. 1993) [AFF'D 35 F.3D 643 (2ND CIR. 1994)]

that the metal was being held for DBL Trading's account or order. They were signed by Amoco's representative, and stated that the goods would be delivered when the certificates were properly endorsed. . . .

The court finds that the holding certificates issued by Amoco constituted negotiable documents of title that were duly negotiated to BNY by DBL Trading. Plaintiff is to be awarded $550,000, as the agreed-on limit, and prejudgment interest thereupon from 4 April 1990.

BUSINESS CONSIDERATION Amoco's representatives had a very lackadaisical attitude in this case. The Senior Supply Negotiator testified that he did not pay too much attention to the language of the holding certificates, and he merely drew a line diagonally across the face of the certificates when they were redeemed. What sort of policies and practices should a business have in place when it is dealing with negotiable documents of title representing goods of substantial value?

ETHICAL CONSIDERATIONS Amoco testified that the individual sources of the platinum were no longer distinguishable once the platinum was used in one of the catalysts. When is it ethical for a firm to commingle fungible goods it is leasing? What precautions should the lessee take to protect the interests of the lessor?

Warehouse Receipts

A *warehouse receipt* is a document issued by a person who takes goods for storage. There is no particular form that a warehouse receipt needs to take, but most will contain at least the following provisions:

1. The location of the warehouse
2. The date the receipt for the goods is issued
3. The number of the receipt (receipts are numbered consecutively)
4. A statement as to whether the stored goods will be delivered to the bailor (nonnegotiable) or either to the bearer or to a named person or that person's order (negotiable)
5. The fees and expenses for the storage (unless the goods are stored in a **field warehousing** arrangement)
6. A description of the goods or the packages stored
7. The signature of the warehouseman or his or her agent

The warehouseman assumes a duty to exercise due care in the handling of the goods and a duty to deliver the goods as agreed in the receipt at the close of the storage period.

The warehouseman assumes liability for any damages to the goods stored with him or her if the damages are caused by a failure to exercise reasonable care. The warehouseman also acquires a warehouseman's lien on the goods for the storage and transportation charges, insurance, and expenses reasonably necessary to preserve the goods.

Field warehousing
A method of perfection in a secured transaction in which the creditor takes "possession" of a portion of the debtor's storage area.

Consignor
A person who ships goods to another party.

Consignee
A person to whom goods are shipped by another party.

Issuer
One who officially distributes an item or document.

Bills of Lading

A *bill of lading* is issued by a carrier who is taking possession and custody of the goods for the purpose of transporting them, normally from a seller to a buyer. The person who arranges the transportation is the **consignor;** the person to whom the goods are to be delivered is the **consignee;** the carrier is the **issuer** of the bill of lading. The bill must adequately describe the goods covered by the bill and must designate whether the goods were consigned to a particular consignee (nonnegotiable) or to a named consignee or order or to the consignee or bearer (negotiable). The carrier is liable for any misdescription or irregularity unless the document is properly qualified by words such as "contents of package unknown," "shipper's weight and count," or comparable language. Even then, the alleged qualification may not be sufficient to protect the carrier.

SUMMARY

"Negotiables" are an important part of the modern commercial world. Negotiable documents cover goods that are placed in the hands of a bailee, either for storage or for transportation. Negotiable instruments are used as a substitute for money or as a credit instrument. Both are governed by the UCC.

Article 3 of the Uniform Commercial Code involves negotiable instruments. These negotiable instruments are "current in trade" and are payable in money. There are two major classes of negotiable instruments, and each major class contains two types of instruments. The first class, paper containing an order ("order paper"), is comprised of checks and drafts. Checks and drafts are used primarily as a substitute for money. There are three legal roles involved on "order paper": the drawer, who "draws" (drafts) the instrument and issues the order; the payee, to whom the instrument is issued; and the drawee, the party who is ordered to pay the instrument upon presentment.

The second class of negotiable instruments, paper containing a promise ("promise paper"), is comprised of promissory notes and certificates of deposit. Promise paper is used principally as a credit instrument. There are two legal roles involved on promise paper: the maker, who makes the promise to pay and who issues the instrument; and the payee, to whom the instrument is issued.

The recent revision to Article 3 has greatly expanded the concept of "checks," making the article more closely reflect contemporary business practices. The revision also removed some of the older, more technical aspects of negotiable instrument law.

CALL-IMAGE TECHNOLOGY

21.3 | FINANCING/ SALES

NEGOTIABLE BILLS OF LADING

A wholesaler in the next state has inquired about purchasing several hundred Call-Image units. She thought the price quoted to her was fair, and she was very pleased with the prospective delivery date the firm offered. She asked if it would be possible to have the goods shipped to her by common carrier with a negotiable bill of lading and to have payment terms of "2/10, net 60." Dan and Tom each expressed concern about the use of a negotiable bill of lading when payment will not be made for up to two months. They are willing to *either* use a negotiable bill of lading *or* give credit terms, but with a nonnegotiable bill of lading. However, they are unsure if they have fully analyzed the situation. They have asked you what you think of this proposal. What will you tell them?

BUSINESS CONSIDERATION The granting of some sort of payment terms is fairly common in business. The use of a negotiable bill of lading is fairly common in business. What possible concerns should a business have with using/granting both to a distant firm the first time they do business together?

ETHICAL CONSIDERATIONS Documents of title are much less strictly interpreted than are negotiable instruments. Among other things, the issue of whether the document is negotiable is often subject to interpretation. Does this "lax" attitude present any potential ethical problems or concerns for a shipper? For the carrier? Explain.

RESOURCES FOR BUSINESS LAW STUDENTS

NAME	RESOURCES	WEB ADDRESS
Uniform Commercial Code (UCC) Article 3, Negotiable Instruments	LII, maintained by the Cornell Law School, provides a hypertext and searchable version of UCC Article 3, Negotiable Instruments. LII also maintains links to Article 3 as adopted by particular states and to proposed revisions.	**http://www.law.cornell.edu/ucc/3/overview.html**
UCC Article 7, Warehouse Receipts, Bills of Lading, and Other Documents of Title	LII provides a hypertext and searchable version of UCC Article 7, Warehouse Receipts, Bills of Lading, and Other Documents of Title.	**http://www.law.cornell.edu/ucc/7/overview.html**
Legal Information Institute (LII) —Negotiable Instruments Law	LII provides an overview of negotiable instruments law, federal and state statutes and regulations, and federal and state court decisions.	**http://www.law.cornell.edu/topics/negotiable.html**
The National Conference of Commissioners on Uniform State Laws (NCCUSL)	NCCUSL, the drafters of the UCC, provides drafts and revisions of its uniform and model acts.	**http://www.law.upenn.edu/bll/ulc/ulc_frame.htm**

Documents of title, including negotiable documents, are governed by Article 7 of the UCC. The two primary types of documents of title are warehouse receipts, issued by a bailee who accepts goods for storage, and bills of lading, issued by a carrier who accepts possession of goods for transportation. However, Article 7 is much more flexible than Article 3. Any other document that in the regular course of business or financing is treated as a document of title is recognized as falling within the coverage of Article 7.

DISCUSSION QUESTIONS

1. Who is expected to make payment on negotiable instruments that are designated as "order paper"? Who is expected to make payment on negotiable instruments that are designated as "promise paper"? Why are different parties expected to pay on these different instruments?

2. What characteristics distinguish a check from other types of drafts? What characteristics distinguish a promissory note from a certificate of deposit?

3. A check or a draft contains a specific type of communication from the drawer to the drawee. What form does this communication take? Why does this communication obligate the drawee to pay the instrument issued by the drawer?

4. Who may serve as a drawee on a check? Who may serve as a drawee on a draft? Is the difference as to who may serve as drawee significant?

5. What duty or duties is/are performed by the "maker" on promise paper? What do we call the party or parties who perform comparable duties on order paper?

6. What are the two major functions of negotiable instruments? Which function is most likely to be involved with the use of a draft or a check? Which

function is most likely to be involved with the use of a note or a certificate of deposit?

7. How does Article 3 define a "check"? Why is this definition important in negotiable instrument law?

8. What is a document of title under the provisions of Article 7? How is a negotiable document of title different from a nonnegotiable document of title?

9. When do the parties to a contract use a warehouse receipt? When do the parties to a contract use a bill of lading? Why do the parties need two different documents of title?

10. What sort of limitation or qualification can a carrier use on a bill of lading to protect itself from liability if the goods delivered are mislabeled or improperly identified? Is it ethical for a carrier to use such language, effectively shielding itself from liability for damages to the goods carried?

CASE PROBLEMS AND WRITING ASSIGNMENTS

1. Goss obtained a loan from Trinity Savings, signing a promissory note that called for interest to be adjusted in conjunction with the interest rates on U.S. Treasury Securities. Eventually, a dispute arose between Goss and Trinity, and Goss sued to cancel the note and to recover the excess interest charges that he alleged to have paid. Is the instrument here a negotiable instrument, so that the case should be resolved under Article 3 of the UCC, or is the instrument nonnegotiable, so that the case should be resolved under common law? (Assume that the revised version of Article 3 is in effect in the jurisdiction in reaching your decision.) Explain. [See *Goss* v. *Trinity Savings & Loan Ass'n,* 813 P.2d 492 (Okla. 1991).]

2. Westway Coffee, a New York firm, placed an order for 1,710 cartons of instant coffee with Dominium, S.A. of São Paulo, Brazil. Dominium agreed to the sale and acquired six containers from Netumar, the owner of the *M.V. Netuno,* in which to ship the coffee. These containers were delivered to Dominium, where they were loaded with the coffee under the supervision of the Brazilian Coffee Institute, the government agency in charge of coffee exports. The institute certified that each container was loaded with 285 cartons of instant coffee, and then sealed and padlocked the containers. The containers were shipped to the Eud Marco warehouse at Netumar's direction, weighed, and stored for 10 days. The containers were then taken to the ship and loaded for carriage to New York. The bills of lading for the containers included the legends "STC" (said to contain), "SLAC" (shipper's load and count), and "Contents of packages are shipper's declaration." When the goods arrived in New York, two of the containers were short of the quantity of coffee expected, with a total shortage of 419 cartons ($138,000 value). Westway sued the carrier for the shortage, and the carrier denied liability.

Did the carrier show "due care" in its handling of the goods? Should the carrier be held liable for the shortage in the goods shipped to the consignee in New York? What ethical issues are raised by this case? [See *Westway Coffee Corp.* v. *M.V. Netuno,* 528 F.Supp. 113 (S.D.N.Y. 1981).]

3. Haygood Contracting, Inc., entered into a contract that called for Haygood to provide paving for a real estate subdivision. The subdivision was being developed by CFI, whose president was Crolley. The initial contract specified a price of $29,500 for the work, and was in written form on a standardized form prepared and signed by Crolley. During the course of performing the contract, it became obvious that some additional work would need to be done, so Haygood prepared a handwritten estimate of $7,275 for this additional work. Crolley initialed the estimate, approving the work. However, below Crolley's initials there appeared two additional charges: one for $500 for "equipment time" and the other for $7,560 for "extra stone." Subsequently, both CFI and Crolley refused to pay for the work, and Haygood sued both CFI and Crolley. Haygood argued that Crolley had approved the charges when he initialed the estimate. Crolley denied that he approved the additional expenses and also denied that he was liable for any of the amount since he signed as a representative of CFI and not as an individual. Under Article 3, Crolley would not be liable since he signed a document containing the name of the principal (CFI), and his signature was in a representative capacity. Under common law principles, Crolley and CFI would both face potential liability, although Haygood would have to elect which party to sue. How should this case be decided? Explain your reasoning. [See *Crolley* v. *Haygood Contracting, Inc.,* 411 S.E.2d 907 (Ga.App. 1991).]

4. The Department of Transportation awarded a contract to Ted's Sheds, Inc., for several metal buildings to be used at various service plazas on the Florida Turnpike. Ted's Sheds provided a Ft. Lauderdale address during the bidding process. When the buildings were delivered, the State received an invoice from Ted's Sheds listing its address as Bonita Springs, Florida. The State approved the invoices for payment, and, on 5 February 1987, the comptroller issued a warrant for $16,932 payable to the order of Ted's Sheds and sent it to the Ft. Lauderdale address listed on the original bid. On 12 February 1987, Ted's Shed of Broward, Inc., presented the original warrant to Seminole National Bank. The warrant was endorsed "Ted's Sheds of Broward, Inc.," and was credited to that account by the bank. Sometime thereafter, the agents of Ted's Sheds, Inc., in Bonita Springs stated that they had not received the warrant and requested a duplicate warrant.

It was then discovered that there were two Ted's Sheds, one in Ft. Lauderdale known as "Ted's Sheds of Broward, Inc.," and one in Bonita Springs, known as "Ted's Sheds, Inc." These separate legal entities shared common corporate officers. On 19 February 1987, the comptroller placed a stop payment order on the original warrant, issued a duplicate warrant to Ted's Sheds, and mailed it to Ted's Sheds, Inc., in Bonita Springs. Subsequently, the Federal Reserve Bank of Miami returned the original warrant to the bank indicating that payment had been stopped by the state treasurer.

The bank initiated this action some 14 months after the original warrant was returned. In the intervening time, Ted's Sheds of Broward, Inc., was involuntarily dissolved. The bank argued that it had no knowledge of the stop payment order and asserted that it was a "holder in due course" entitled to reimbursement by the State of Florida on the theory that state warrants are negotiable instruments. The State maintained that state warrants are not negotiable instruments under the UCC, and thus the bank was not entitled to repayment of these funds. The trial court entered summary judgment for the bank, and the State appealed. Are state warrants negotiable instruments under Article 3 of the UCC? Is a holder of a state warrant entitled to prejudgment interest on the amount of the warrant? [See *State* v. *Family Bank of Hallandale*, 623 So.2d 474 (Fla. 1993).]

5. The case stems from the activities of Richard Caliento, an accountant. He prepared tax returns for various clients. To satisfy their tax liability, the clients issued checks payable to various State taxing entities and gave them to Caliento. Between 1977 and 1979, he forged indorsements on these checks, deposited them in his own account with defendant, and subsequently withdrew the proceeds. In November 1980—shortly after the scheme was uncovered—Caliento died when the plane he was piloting crashed. The State never received the checks. In 1983, after learning of these events, the State commenced this action seeking to recover the aggregate amount of the checks.

The Supreme Court denied defendant's motion to dismiss the complaint and its subsequent motion for summary judgment, concluding that the payee's possession of the checks was not essential to its action against the depository bank. On appeal, the Appellate Division reversed and dismissed the complaint. It held that requiring "delivery, either actual or constructive, [as] an indispensable prerequisite for" a conversion action . . . is consistent with the view of most authorities and supported by practical considerations. In the absence of actual or constructive possession of a check, does the payee have rights against the drawee for honoring a forged indorsement of the payee? Explain and justify your answer. [See *State* v. *Barclay's Bank of New York, N.A.*, 563 N.E.2d 11 (N.Y. 1990).]

6. **BUSINESS APPLICATION CASE** On 16 October 1989, Harris Trust and Savings Bank sold to Siena Publishers the book inventory and accounts receivables of Bookthrift Marketing following a foreclosure on Bookthrift by the bank. Siena agreed to pay $2,250,000 for the assets on an "as is, where is" basis. The sale was financed by the bank, as evidenced by a demand note signed by the president of Siena dated 19 October 1989. In this demand note, Siena promised to pay to the bank on demand the sum of $2,250,000, representing the purchase price of the Bookthrift assets. Siena also agreed to grant the bank a purchase money security interest in all of Siena's accounts receivable, general intangibles, inventory, and equipment. The bank properly perfected its security interest, filing its UCC-1 with the appropriate offices during November 1989. At some time prior to 31 August 1989, Metro Services, Inc., had provided fulfillment and warehousing services for Bookthrift. (Fulfillment services include the receipt and unloading of books from delivering carriers, storage of the books, picking, counting, packing, loading, and shipping the books, and so forth.) Metro was also indebted to Harris Trust and Savings Bank, and Metro also defaulted on its loans. The bank arranged for NCI to purchase Metro's assets. This sale was consummated on 31 August 1989, with the bank receiving full

payment for Metro's debt and NCI purchasing all of Metro's assets except accounts receivables. (This means that NCI did not receive the fulfillment services contract claims against Bookthrift, and thus against Siena.) On 29 August 1990, NCI and Siena entered into a fulfillment services agreement. On 18 March 1992, Siena filed for relief under the Bankruptcy Act. At that time Siena was in default on its fulfillment services agreement with NCI and was unable to pay the note from Harris Bank. Both Harris Bank and NCI claimed priority on the assets of Siena. The bank argued that it had a valid perfected security interest. NCI argued that it had a valid possessory warehouseman's lien and that this lien had priority over the bank's security interest. Did the fulfillment services agreement give NCI a warehouse receipt on the assets of Siena? Explain. Which party, the bank or NCI, should have priority in this case? Why? Should NCI have adopted a policy to help protect its interests when it entered into a fulfillment services agreement? [See *In Re Siena Publishers Associates*, 149 B.R. 359 (S.D.N.Y. 1993).]

7. **ETHICAL APPLICATION CASE** Lassen is an experienced construction lender. It is his practice before entering into a loan agreement to conduct an independent analysis of the financial condition of the borrower. He conducted such an analysis before making the loans in this case. Lassen had a continuing business relationship with Kopfmann Homes, Inc., a builder in the Minneapolis area. Between 1985 and 1990, Lassen made a number of loans to Kopfmann through an account Lassen had with First Bank. In 1986, on the basis of Lassen's recommendation, Kopfmann opened its own account with First Bank. In early 1990, Lassen entered into two loan agreements with Kopfmann. The contracts called for Kopfmann to construct two homes. Each loan was secured by a mortgage. Later that year, Lassen purchased five cashier's checks (totaling nearly $170,000) from First Bank and delivered these checks to Kopfmann. Each of the checks was jointly payable to Kopfmann and Chicago Title Insurance Company. Kopfmann presented each of these checks to First Bank without the indorsement of the title company. First Bank accepted each of the checks, depositing the proceeds into Kopfmann's account. Subsequently, Kopfmann defaulted on the two loans from Lassen. Kopfmann also failed to pay the subcontractors on the two construction jobs. Lassen then sued First Bank, alleging breach of contract, conversion, and fraud. Lassen argued that the bank had a duty to ensure that all required indorsements were present on the checks before accept-

ing them. The bank denied liability to Lassen, asserting that he was not a party to the contracts since the checks in question were cashier's checks, with the bank as both drawer and drawee. Did the bank breach its contracts with Lassen, who purchased the cashier's checks, by not obtaining the indorsements of both joint payees on the checks prior to accepting them? Was it ethical for the bank to deny any obligation to Lassen, the purchaser of the cashier's checks, for its failure to require the indorsements of both joint payees? What more could Lassen have done to protect his interests? [See *Lassen* v. *First Bank Eden Prairie*, 514 N.W.2d 831 (Minn.App. 1994).]

8. **CRITICAL THINKING CASE** On 1 January 1983, Nestor borrowed $36,000 from Tucker County Bank, using a $10,000 certificate of deposit as part of his collateral to secure the loan. In February 1984, Tucker County Bank went into receivership, and the FDIC was appointed as its receiver. On 4 February 1984, CNB entered into an agreement with the FDIC to purchase certain loans and deposit items that were owned by Tucker County Bank. Among the items CNB purchased was the CD Nestor had assigned to the bank as collateral. The CD file contained only a copy of the CD. Nothing appeared on the CD or in the file that made any reference to Nestor's loan. CNB was not informed by the FDIC that the CD was impaired by an assignment as collateral for Nestor's loan. In July 1985, Nestor informed CNB that he wanted to cash in his CD. He also claimed that he had lost the original document. He did not mention to CNB that the CD was assigned as collateral for his loan. Nestor completed an Indemnification Bond for Lost Documents form for CNB and was subsequently paid the value of the CD by the bank.

On 15 September 1987, Cadle purchased a number of items from the FDIC, including Nestor's loan. The loan file on Nestor that Cadle purchased contained the original CD and the related documents showing that the CD had been assigned as collateral for the loan. At some point during 1988, Cadle contacted CNB requesting payment for the CD. CNB informed Cadle that the CD had already been redeemed and retired by Nestor in 1985. Cadle then sued CNB, seeking recovery of the face amount of the CD, plus accrued interest. Cadle argued that CNB should not have allowed redemption of the CD without acquiring the original instrument. He also argued that the security interest he purchased predated CNB's acquisition of its interest and should therefore have priority. CNB argued that it had purchased the items in good faith in the ordinary course of business and that it had no notice or knowledge of any claims against the CD. The circuit court determined that the CD in question was *not* negotiable under the provisions of Article 3, but that it *was* an instrument under the provisions of Article 9. The court then ruled in favor of CNB, and

Cadle appealed. How should the court have resolved this case? Does the fact that the CD was deemed non-negotiable affect the court's decision? What should CNB have done when Nestor claimed that he had lost the original document? [See *Cadle Company* v. *Citizens National Bank*, 490 S.E.2d 334 (W.Va. 1997).]

NOTE

1. "Guarantees Are Not Negotiable Instruments Governed by the UCC."*Commercial Lending Litigation News* (6 March 1998), LRP Publications http://www.lexis-nexis.com.

NEGOTIABILITY

A G E N D A

The Kochanowskis will be receiving most of their payments in the form of instruments issued by their customers. They will need to know if these instruments are negotiable, and therefore governed by Article 3, or non-negotiable, and therefore governed under the provisions of other areas of law, including the common law. They will also be issuing a number of instruments to purchase supplies, pay bills, and generally operate the business. They need to be certain that the instruments they issue are negotiable.

They will be shipping finished goods by means of common carriers, and they will be receiving shipments of component parts by means of common carriers, so they will need to be familiar with documents of title, especially bills of lading. Since they are relatively new to operating their own business, they are quite likely to have a number of questions for you. Be prepared! You never know when one of the Kochanowskis will need your help or advice.

FORMAL REQUIREMENTS FOR NEGOTIABILITY: ARTICLE 3

Negotiable instruments have a special place in business law. Every negotiable instrument is a contract and carries with it the rights that a person would enjoy under contract law. As you remember from contract law, a person possessing rights under a contract can *assign* those rights to another person. The person who assigns his or her rights—the assignor—is expected to give notice to the party who will be conferring the benefits—the obligor—that an assignment has been made, and the assignor will identify the person to whom the rights were transferred—the assignee. You should also remember that the assignee takes the rights assigned under the contract subject to any and every defense the obligor could assert against the assignor. These two things, taking the benefits subject to any defenses and the need for the assignor to give notice, make assignments a less-than-popular method for transferring benefits under a contract.

A negotiable instrument is also a contract. In fact, a negotiable instrument is a *formal* contract, one of the few formal contracts still in use in the U.S. legal system. Since it is a contract, the benefits called for in the instrument can be assigned, the same as the benefits under other types of contracts can be assigned. But, as we just discussed, assignments are not a very good method for ensuring that the assignee will receive the benefits the assignor is trying to transfer. Unless there is more to it than that, negotiable instruments would just be a specialized type of contract with no particular benefits beyond those of other contracts. However, under certain circumstances, the *holder* (think of the holder as roughly analogous to an assignee for now) of a negotiable instrument is permitted to collect the money (receive the benefits under the contract), *despite* any defenses the maker or drawer can assert. This is the primary reason that negotiable instrument law is so important! A person having the right to enforce a "mere" contract through an assignment would not have this same benefit. The holder of a negotiable instrument has all of the rights of an assignee under contract law, *plus* any additional rights conferred on him or her by Article 3 of the Uniform Commercial Code (UCC). Not only that, but the instrument, if correctly made or drawn, will move easily through the commercial world as a substitute for money and/or as a credit instrument.

The benefits derived from holding a negotiable instrument should already be obvious. However, the law is very jealous of these benefits. To carry the benefits of negotiability, an instrument must meet all the formal requirements of negotiability. It is not enough for it to meet "some" of the requirements, or even for it to meet "most" of the requirements. It must meet each and every one of the requirements in order to fall within the coverage of Article 3. Any missing element removes the instrument from Article 3 and places it under the coverage of common law contracts. The requirements for negotiability are set out in § 3-104 (a) of the UCC:

Section 3-104. Negotiable Instrument.

 (a) Except as provided in subsections (c) and (d), "negotiable instrument" means an unconditional promise or order to pay a fixed amount of money, with or without interest or other charges described in the promise or order, if it:
   (1) is payable to bearer or to order at the time it is issued or first comes into possession of a holder;
   (2) is payable on demand or at a definite time; and,

    (3) does not state any other undertaking or instruction by the person prom-
    ising or ordering payment to do any act in addition to the payment of
    money, but the promise or order may contain (i) an undertaking or power
    to give, maintain, or protect collateral to secure payment; (ii) an author-
    ization or power to the holder to confess judgment or realize on or dis-
    pose of collateral; or (iii) a waiver of the benefit of any law intended for
    the advantage or protection of an obligor.

Two other important definitions must also be reviewed before the discussion of *negotiability* can commence:

Section 3-103. Definitions.
  (a) In this Article:
    (6) "Order" means a written instruction to pay money signed by the
    person giving the instruction. The instruction may be addressed to
    any person, including the person giving the instruction, or to one or more
    persons jointly or in the alternative but not in succession. An authori-
    zation to pay is not an order unless the person authorized to pay is also
    instructed to pay. [Emphasis added]
    (9) "Promise" means a written undertaking to pay money signed by the per-
    son undertaking to pay. An acknowledgment of an obligation by the
    obligor is not a promise unless the obligor also undertakes to pay the obli-
    gation. [Emphasis added]

Thus, to qualify as a negotiable instrument, the instrument in question must:

1. be written; *and*
2. be signed by the maker (promise paper) or by the drawer (order paper); *and*
3. contain an unconditional promise or order to pay a fixed amount of money and no other instruction or undertaking by the person who promises or orders payment; *and*
4. be payable on demand or at a definite time; *and*
5. be payable to order or to bearer.

These elements are shown in Exhibit 22.1 on page 582. Notice that every element must be present. The absence of any element negates negotiability. This does not make the paper worthless, but it is no longer negotiable under the law; this means that no holder would have the protections afforded by the UCC. The person holding the paper would only have his or her (potential) contract rights under other areas of law, including the common law.

It should be emphasized that negotiability has *nothing* to do with validity or enforceability. If an instrument is negotiable, this merely means that the instrument is governed by the provisions of Article 3. The enforceability of the instrument or the collection of money called for in the instrument has nothing to do with whether the instrument is negotiable. We will examine each of these elements of negotiability in the sections following the next case. While this case involved a check, a negotiable instrument, it was decided under other areas of law. The court was faced with a "validity" issue in this case. Note that the negotiability of the check was not questioned, merely its enforceability.

22.1

CREEKMORE V. CREEKMORE

485 S.E.2D 68 (N.C.APP. 1997)

FACTS This case arises from a dispute between a brother and a sister over the interpretation of their mother's last will and testament . . . Plaintiff, James H. Creekmore, Jr., and defendant, Judith Carolyn Creekmore, are the only children of the testatrix, Ruby Lamm Creekmore. During her final illness, testatrix executed a last will and testament (hereinafter the "will"). The will disposed of testatrix's assets including real property, personal effects and shares of a closely held corporation denominated in the will as "Lamm Development Corporation," also known as Lamm Development Co. of Wilson, Inc." (hereinafter "LDC"). LDC was a corporation organized by the Lamm and Creekmore families to hold certain real property in Wilson, North Carolina. Until her death, testatrix was an officer and stockholder of the corporation . . . Pursuant to the terms of the will, defendant Judith Creekmore received fifty percent of testatrix's stock in a life estate . . . and plaintiff and defendant each received twenty-five percent of the stock in fee . . . On 6 February 1994, prior to her death, testatrix gave a check for $10,000 to defendant. According to defendant's affidavit, testatrix asked defendant not to deposit the check until after 1 March 1994 because she did not want the check to appear in her February bank statements to which plaintiff had access . . . On 15 November 1994 plaintiff, James H. Creekmore, Jr., filed a complaint seeking a declaratory judgment to construe testatrix's will . . . In its final declaration on 28 December 1995, the court incorporated its prior declarations and made declarations as to the following issue . . . the estate of Ruby Lamm Creekmore has an obligation for payment to Judith Creekmore of the $10,000 check dated 7 February 1994 . . . Plaintiff appeals from judgements filed . . . 28 December 1995.

ISSUE Was the delivery to Judith Creekmore by her mother of a $10,000 check a completed *inter vivos* gift?

HOLDING No. The gift could not be completed until the bank accepted and cashed the check.

REASONING Plaintiff's . . . argument is that the trial court erred in entering declaratory judgment that the estate is indebted to defendant for the $10,000 check made by testatrix because the check was an *inter vivos* gift to take effect in the future and was therefore void. We hold that the trial court erred in holding that the $10,000 check was a valid *inter vivos* gift. North Carolina recognizes two types of valid gifts, *inter vivos* gifts and gifts *causa mortis*. "In all cases of gifts, whether inter vivos or causa mortis, there must be a delivery to complete the gift. And, in North Carolina, the law of delivery is the same for gifts inter vivos and causa mortis.

"However, '[t]he chief distinguishing characteristics between a gift *inter vivos* and one *causa mortis* are that the former is absolute and takes effect *in praesenti*, while the other is revocable and takes effect *in futuro*.'" . . . In the present case, we hold that the check in the amount of $10,000 is neither a valid *inter vivos* gift, nor a valid gift *causa mortis*. The critical issue for this Court, which is one of first impression, is whether a gift in the form of a bank check must be accepted and honored by the drawee bank prior to the death of the donor in order to be effective. The courts of this state have not answered this question, but the majority rule elsewhere is that a donor's own check drawn on a personal checking account is not, prior to acceptance or payment by the bank, the subject of a valid gift either *inter vivos* or *causa mortis* . . . The Uniform Commercial Code makes apparent that transfer of a check does not operate as an assignment of money on deposit. "A check or other draft does not operate as an assignment of funds in the hands of the drawee available for its payment, and the drawee is not liable on the instrument until the drawee accepts it." . . . Thus,

> [b]ecause the check does not operate as an assignment of funds, mere delivery of a check does not place the gift beyond the donor's power of revocation and the check simply becomes an unenforceable promise to make a gift . . .
>
> . . . Until the check is paid, the donor retains [dominion and control] over the funds and the gift is incomplete; the donor could stop payment or write another check for the funds payable to a third person, or the donor may die, thus revoking the donor-drawer's command to the drawee bank to pay the money . . .

Therefore, because defendant did not cash the check before testatrix's death, the $10,000 was never delivered from testatrix to defendant and the attempted gift was incomplete . . . We reverse the judgment of the trial court regarding the attempted *inter vivos* gift and remand for entry of an order modifying the declaratory judgment to reflect that the estate is not

22.1

CREEKMORE V. CREEKMORE, *continued*
485 S.E.2D 68 (N.C.APP. 1997)

indebted to defendant Judith Creekmore in the amount of $10,000. [The issues that did not involve the check were not included in this case brief since they did not involve the topics being covered in this section of the book.]

BUSINESS CONSIDERATIONS The check in question in this case was issued as a gift, and the gift was negated by the death of the drawer prior to the payee's cashing of the check. Would a similar result occur if the drawer issued the check to pay for goods that had been delivered, only to have the drawer die before the payee cashed the check? What effect on the use of checks would such a rule have in the business environment?

ETHICAL CONSIDERATIONS Family "squabbles" in estate distribution situations are often ugly. Is it ethical for one heir to seek to set aside a gift or bequest left to another heir? Does the fact that a significant part of the estate in this case involved a family-owned business make such challenges more or less ethical?

Writing Requirement

Commercial paper represents an intangible right, the right to collect money at some time. However, to satisfy the requirements of Article 3, the proof of this right must be tangible. The simplest way to prove that the right exists is to put it in writing, as defined in § 1-201(46), which states that: "'written' or 'writing' includes printing, typewriting, or any other intentional reduction to tangible form."

For many people, the type of negotiable instrument most frequently encountered is a check. Most checks are in a standard form, preprinted on paper, with magnetic ink to designate the drawee bank and the drawer's account number. Similarly, many drafts are preprinted, in standard form, on paper, with magnetic ink encoding; most certificates of deposit (CDs) are preprinted on paper, with magnetic ink encoding; and many notes are preprinted in a form readily adaptable to the needs of the lender/preparer. These preprinted, standardized forms are familiar; they contain blanks at all the appropriate places to streamline their completion; and they are preencoded with magnetic ink to make computerized processing readily available. However, such convenience is just that—a convenience, but it is not a necessity.

Commercial paper is equally valid when prepared by handwriting on a scratch pad, or on a blank sheet of paper, or on virtually any other relatively permanent thing. For example, several years ago, on a television series entitled *Love American Style,* a couple was marooned on a desert island. The only thing they had for entertainment was a deck of cards. According to the plot, they spent their time playing gin. When they were rescued, the young woman had won $1 million. As evidence, she had a check . . . written on her stomach! Despite the comedic implications, such a check would (theoretically) be valid.

In another (possibly apocryphal) example, a disgruntled taxpayer completed his tax return on 15 April. When he mailed his return, he included a check for the taxes due and a note. The note said: "You've been trying to get it for years, and you've finally succeeded. Here's the shirt off my back." The note was pinned to his check, which was written on his undershirt. However, the joke was on him. The IRS cashed it!

Although the definition of a "writing" was not changed with the revision to Article 3, the Official Comments to the revised article do reflect a change of sorts. According to the Official Comments, in order to qualify as a writing, the "reduction to tangible form" must be on something capable of being readily transferred and easily borne by the payee or holder. Even though no cases have been seen on

E X H I B I T   22.1 | **The Elements of Negotiability**

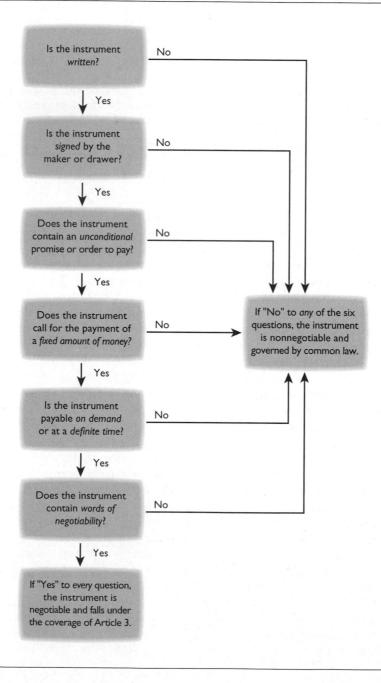

this topic yet, it appears that at least one of the examples above would run afoul of the Official Comments to Revised Article 3 and might not qualify as a writing under the revisions. (*Hint:* It would not involve the disgruntled taxpayer.)

Signature Requirement

On a check or a draft, an order is given by the drawer. On a note or a CD, a promise is given by the maker. Given the widespread use of preprinted forms as negotiable instruments, some protection is needed from fraud or trickery. The UCC tries to minimize the potential for fakery by requiring a signature by the maker or the drawer. Most people think of a signature as a manual subscription, an autograph. Although a manual subscription is, obviously, a signature, it is not the only possible type of signature.

A corporation, being an inanimate object, cannot sign its own name. Yet corporations need to "sign" negotiable instruments, particularly checks. The instruments can, of course, be signed by agents of the corporation. But even this is impractical. Some corporations issue thousands of checks each month. An "authorized signer" could spend an entire career "autographing" checks for the corporation.

Fortunately, the UCC solved this problem. The solution is found in § 1-201(39), which states that: "'signed' includes any symbol executed or adopted by a party with present intention to authenticate a writing." Thus, a corporation can use a stamp to sign checks. Likewise, a negotiable instrument can be signed by affixing an X, or a thumbprint, or any other intentionally affixed symbol. (A number of banks are now requiring a thumbprint along with the indorsement before accepting checks drawn against the bank when the presenter does not have an account with the bank. This is not a "signing" as defined by the Code, but merely a protective device for the bank.)

There are practical problems with unusual types of signatures, but these problems deal more with the acceptability than with the negotiability of the instrument. An unusual signature may be so strange that people will be hesitant to accept it or the instrument containing it. The unusual signature also must be proved by the person trying to claim the instrument.

It makes no difference where the instrument is signed. Although it is normal to sign in the lower right-hand corner of the face of the instrument, the signature can be anywhere. For example, in a note beginning "I, Mary Smith, promise to pay," Mary Smith's signature following the word "I" would be sufficient.

22.1 | FINANCE/ MANAGEMENT

CALL-IMAGE TECHNOLOGY

SIGNING COMPANY CHECKS

It has been agreed that CIT checks will need the signatures of two officers (Tom, Anna, and Dan are currently the only officers, and each will be authorized to sign checks) and that the monthly statements will be reconciled by Donna or Julio. Initially the firm does not expect to be issuing many checks, so the signing function should not take too much time. However, if the company grows as expected, the signing of checks could become a time-intensive activity.

Lindsay thinks the firm should investigate alternate methods for writing and signing checks. The family has asked you what you think. Should the firm plan to write checks manually, or should they obtain a software package, such as Quicken, to prepare checks and simultaneously update the check register? Should the firm use some sort of stamp or imprinting device for signing the checks? What advice will you give them?

BUSINESS CONSIDERATIONS There have been myriad instances in which a business has lost substantial sums of money because the firm had poor internal auditing practices and/or controls, especially with the company's checking account. What sort of safeguards should a firm have in place to minimize the risk of employee malfeasance with business checks? What policies should the business adopt to provide it with the greatest possible protections?

ETHICAL CONSIDERATIONS People have been known to "play games" with their checks, especially when paying bills. Is it ethical to "play the float" by writing checks before deposits are made in the hope (or expectation) that a deposit will be made in time to cover the checks? Is it ethical to send out unsigned checks to creditors so that the check arrives in a timely manner but then must be returned for a signature before it can be sent to the bank?

Unconditional Promise or Order Requirement

Negotiable instruments are designed to move easily through the commercial world. To serve effectively as a substitute for money, a negotiable instrument must be freely transferable. It also needs to be in a form that people can accept. These needs are met by the requirement that the promise made, or the order given, be unconditional. A person taking possession of a negotiable instrument wants to know that payment can reasonably be expected under *every* circumstance. A prospective holder would not be eager to accept an instrument that says payment might be made or will be made only if something happens. The holder wants an unconditional promise that the money will be paid.

The Code has gone to great lengths to define "unconditional." Section 3-106 lists the requirements that must be met to make the promise or order conditional. These requirements will be set out here, with a brief explanation inserted between each of the four subsections of the Code section. According to this Code section:

> (a) Except as provided in this section [3-106], for the purposes of [negotiable instruments], a promise or order is unconditional unless it states (i) an express condition to payment, (ii) that the promise or order is subject to or governed by another writing, or (iii) that rights or obligations with respect to the promise or order are stated in another writing. A reference to another writing does not of itself make the promise or order conditional.

There appears to be a presumption that every promise or order is unconditional *unless* a condition is obvious from reading the instrument. For example, if an instrument says "payment to be made *only if* [statement of condition] that instrument would contain an express condition and would not be negotiable." Similarly, if an instrument contained a clause stating that the payment of the instrument is *governed by* a separate document or writing, the instrument would be conditional and, therefore, nonnegotiable. However, if the instrument merely refers to another writing, there is no conditional attached to payment, and negotiability would not be affected by the reference. Thus, a notation that the instrument is issued as "Payment for Invoice #67542" would not be conditional and would not affect negotiability.

> (b) A promise or order is not made conditional (i) by a reference to another writing for a statement of rights with respect to collateral, prepayment, or acceleration, or (ii) because payment is limited to resort to a particular source of funds.

This subsection makes a significant change in the law of negotiable instruments, again emphasizing the effort to remove conditions from written promises or orders unless they are very explicit. Before the revision to Article 3, the "particular fund" doctrine made an instrument conditional, hence negating negotiability, any time the instrument required payment from a particular fund, *unless* the drawer or maker was a governmental entity. Many students have wondered why a check drawn against their account was not drawn against a "particular fund." The (technically accurate) explanation that the check was *not* drawn against the student's deposited funds, but rather against any or all of the funds in the bank, with the student's account being merely a bookkeeping notation, seemed to be an evasive answer at best, and begged the question at worst. This particular rule was confusing at best, and its demise was long overdue.

> (c) If a promise or order requires, as a condition to payment, a countersignature by a person whose specimen signature appears on the promise or order, the condition does not make the promise or order conditional. If the person whose

specimen signature appears on an instrument fails to countersign the instru-
ment, the failure to countersign is a defense to the obligation of the issuer, but
the failure does not prevent a transferee of the instrument from becoming a
holder of the instrument.

This subsection appears to be intended specifically to permit the inclusion of
traveler's checks within the revised coverage of Article 3.

(d) *If a promise or order at the time it is issued or first comes into possession of a*
holder contains a statement, required by applicable statutory or administrative
law, to the effect that the rights of a holder or transferee are subject to claims
or defenses that the issuer could assert against the original payee, the promise
or order is not thereby made conditional . . . ; but if the promise or order is an
instrument, there cannot be a holder in due course on the instrument.

This subsection reflects the Code's recognition of the "Federal Trade Commission Holder in Due Course Rule" as it affects consumer credit transactions
(explained in the next chapter), while also recognizing that other statutory or
regulatory enactments may also occur in the future. By addressing this issue in general terms, the Code greatly simplifies the task facing courts that would otherwise
have to interpret the effect of these enactments on (1) whether they created a condition and (2) whether it would be possible to attain holder in due course (HDC)
status under the enactment.

In determining whether an instrument is conditional, the courts have frequently
relied on the so-called *four-corner rule.* The four-corner rule requires that every necessary bit of information to determine rights on an instrument must be contained
within its four corners; that is, the information must be found on the face of the
instrument itself. If the holder must look to some source of information other than
the instrument in order to determine rights, the instrument is conditional, and
therefore it is not negotiable. (The four-corner rule also applies to the "time of payment" and, to a lesser extent, the "fixed amount of money" requirement.)

Fixed Amount of Money Requirement

A holder of a negotiable instrument must know how much money is to be received
when the instrument is paid. The amount is commonly specified exactly, which
makes the determination simple, but this is not necessary to satisfy the fixed
amount of money requirement. Article 3 does not address this requirement to any
significant degree, except for a statement in § 1-201(24) defining money and in
§ 3-107 explaining how to handle an instrument that is payable in foreign money.
According to these sections:

1-201. General Definitions.
(24) *"Money" means a medium of exchange authorized or adopted by a domestic*
or foreign government and includes a monetary unit of account established by
intergovernmental organization or by agreement between two or more
nations . . .

3-107. Instrument Payable in Foreign Money.
Unless the instrument otherwise provides, an instrument that states that it is
payable in foreign money may be paid in the foreign money or in an equivalent
amount in dollars calculated by using the current bank-offered spot rate at the place
of payment for the purchase of dollars on the day on which the instrument is paid.

22.2 | FINANCE

NEGOTIABILITY AND PROMISSORY NOTES

The firm has been buying circuit boards from one supplier from the beginning of its operations. This supplier has been very supportive of the CIT enterprise, willingly extending credit to the firm from the start. Tom recently called the supplier to discuss placing a large order, asking that the firm be given credit terms. Because of the size of the order, the supplier sent a promissory note to the firm. The note included a statement that interest would be at "the normal rate" between the firms. Donna, recalling her business law class of a few years ago, stated that this interest term made the note nonnegotiable. John, who is currently enrolled in a legal environment class, says that the law has been changed so that this clause will not affect negotiability. Dan opines that it really doesn't matter whether the note is negotiable or nonnegotiable; the firm will still owe the money. The family once again turns to you for advice. They want to know if the note is negotiable and also whether the negotiability of the note matters. What will you tell them?

BUSINESS CONSIDERATIONS The revisions to Article 3 greatly expanded the permissible language regarding interest while allowing an instrument to retain negotiability. Is this change better or worse for businesses that *make* notes in the course of their operations? Are firms better served if their notes are governed under Article 3 or under common law? Is the negotiability of a note more important to the maker of a note, the payee of the note, or potential holders of the note?

ETHICAL CONSIDERATIONS What ethical considerations arise when a maker inserts a condition into a promissory note, negating negotiability? How important should a condition be before a firm inserts that condition into a note as a method of restricting or limiting its payment obligation?

Historically, to meet the requirement that the instrument calls for the payment of a fixed amount of money, the total amount to be paid must be calculable from the face of the instrument. This requirement once again raised the four-corner rule. All the necessary information for the calculation of the amount to be paid had to be on the instrument, even if the calculation has not yet been done. This requirement no longer applies under the new standards, at least with regard to interest.

Many instruments call for the payment of interest as well as the payment of the principal. The old rules regarding interest were somewhat confusing and substantially out of date. As a result, the rules for the treatment of interest have been changed significantly. The provisions for interest are set out in § 3-112. An instrument is presumed to be issued without interest unless interest is specifically called for in the instrument. However, if interest is called for in the instrument, the interest will run from the date of the instrument. The significant change in the treatment of interest is found in § 3-112(b), which states:

> *Interest may be stated in an instrument as a fixed or variable rate or rates. The amount or rate of interest may be stated or described in the instrument in any manner and may require reference to information not contained in the instrument. If an instrument provides for interest, but the amount cannot be ascertained from the description, interest is payable at the judgment rate in effect at the place of payment of the instrument and at the time interest first accrues.*

This means that an instrument can call for the payment of interest at a variable rate—for example, "the prime rate"—and still satisfy the fixed amount of money requirement. As far as interest is concerned, the four-corner rule is not applicable.

Determinable Time Requirement

A holder wants to know not only how much money will be paid (fixed amount in money) but also *when* payment can be expected. The question of when will depend on the terms of the instrument, but in order to be negotiable the instrument must be payable either on demand or at a definite time. This element of negotiability is discussed in § 3-108 of Article 3. This section provides that:

> (a) A promise or order is "payable on demand" if it (i) states that it is payable on demand or at sight, or otherwise indicates that it is payable at the will of the holder; or does not state any time for payment.

(b) *A promise or order is "payable at a definite time" if it is payable on elapse of a definite period of time after sight or acceptance or at a fixed date or dates or at a time or times readily ascertainable at the time the promise or order is issued, subject to rights of (i) prepayment, (ii) acceleration, (iii) extension at the option of the holder, or (iv) extension to a further definite time at the option of the maker or acceptor or automatically upon or after a specified act or event.*

(c) *If an instrument, payable at a fixed date, is also payable upon demand made before the fixed date, the instrument is payable on demand until the fixed date and, if demand for payment is not made before that date, becomes payable at a definite time on the fixed date.*

The payee or holder must be able to tell when the instrument is payable by looking at the face of the instrument. Unless the instrument specifies that it is to be paid at some future date (payable at a definite time), it is payable on demand. An instrument is payable on demand when payment is to be made on sight, or at presentment, or when no time for payment is stated. Any form of instrument may be payable on demand, but promise paper (notes and CDs) normally is not payable on demand. A check must be payable on demand, by definition. A draft other than a check may be payable on demand, or it may be payable at a definite time.

An instrument is payable at a definite time if, by its terms, it is payable at a time that can be determined from its face. This definite time frequently will be some stated future date such as "24 September 20XX." Or it may be at some time after a stated date such as "90 days after 3 March 20XX." Either of these dates would be definite even if some provision were made for accelerating the payment date. They also would be definite with a provision for extending the time if the holder has the option of extension, or even if the maker or acceptor has the option of extending the time. However, in this last situation, the extension must be a predetermined definite period, not to exceed the original term.

The UCC also stipulates that payment is at a definite time if payment is a stated period after sight (i.e., after presentment). Thus, an instrument calling for payment "60 days after sight" is payable at a definite time. Although the holder must act (present the instrument to the drawee to establish the date of sight), once the act is done, the date for payment is definite.

However, one must be careful in this area. Payment is not at a definite time if it is to occur only upon an act or

22.3 | FINANCE

SPECIAL CHECKS FOR INVENTORY PURCHASES

John is concerned that the firm will, on occasion, pay for component parts by check only to discover that the parts are nonconforming to the contract. He reasons that if this happens the firm will have spent the funds already but will not yet have the parts it needs. As a result, he has suggested that the firm order special checks for its inventory purchases and that these checks should contain a line instructing the bank not to honor the checks until CIT informs the bank that the parts the check is to pay for have been deemed acceptable by the firm. Donna thinks that this could cause some problems with the bank and with the suppliers. Tom thinks that the firm might want to consider using sight drafts, especially with large orders, as a means of preventing payment before determining if the goods are acceptable to the firm. But he isn't sure that this is the proper use of a sight draft. They have asked you for your advice. What will you tell them?

BUSINESS CONSIDERATIONS Many businesses order goods or parts, pay for them by check shortly after they are received, and then do not use or sell them until some time later. It is quite likely that at least some of these goods or parts will be nonconforming. Is there any way the firm can restrict payment of the checks issued to pay for their orders until the goods are determined to conform to the contract? What alternatives are available to the firm?

ETHICAL CONSIDERATIONS Should a business allow the person responsible for receiving inventory orders to issue the checks to pay for the inventory, or should the checks be written by some other person within the organization? What ethical and practical considerations affected your answer the most?

occurrence that is of uncertain date. For example, an instrument payable "30 days after Uncle Charlie dies" is probably not negotiable, since the holder would have to go outside the instrument to determine the time of occurrence before the time to pay the instrument could be set. (The language of the revised article that a definite time exists if the time(s) are "readily ascertainable at the time the promise or order is issued" may change this area. We will have to wait for judicial interpretations to see how broadly or how narrowly this provision will now be construed.)

Words of Negotiability Requirement

To be negotiable, even if every other element is present, an instrument must contain words of negotiability. The words of negotiability are "Pay to the order of (name of payee)" or "Pay to bearer." The reason these words are so important is

---

YOU BE THE JUDGE

FAMILY FEUDS OVER NOTES

Thomas J. Stafford was a farmer in Chesterfield County. He had two children: a daughter, June S. Zink, and a son, Thomas L. Stafford. He also developed a residential subdivision on a parcel of land that he owned. He built four houses in the subdivision, each on a separate sub-divided lot, and sold each of the four houses. In each instance Stafford took back a purchase money note from the purchaser, with the note secured by a deed of trust. Each of the four notes was payable to the order of Thomas Stafford, and each was indorsed by Stafford as follows: "Pay to the order of Thomas J. Stafford or June S. Zink, or the survivor." Proceeds from the notes were deposited into a "collection account" with a local bank. The account was maintained in the name of "Thomas J. Stafford and June S. Zink, as joint tenants with right of survivorship." Thomas J. Stafford died, and his son insisted that the four purchase money notes and the balance in the "collection account" properly belonged in the estate, to be distributed according to the will of the deceased. June Zink argued that the notes and the balance of the "collection account" properly belonged to her, as survivor, in accord with the indorsements on the notes and the provision that the account named her as one of the "joint tenants with right of survivorship." The daughter also asserts that the notes were negotiated to her, as evidenced by the indorsements on each, giving her rights. The son argues that the notes were not negotiated—or even transferred—to June Zink, and that the various writings were merely a failed attempt to create a gift.

This case has been brought before *your* court. How will *you* decide?[1]

BUSINESS CONSIDERATIONS What should a person who operates an unincorporated business do to ensure that the assets of the business—or even the business entity—are preserved in the event of his or her death? How could the notes in this case have been written to ensure that the daughter had rights in the notes *ab initio*?

ETHICAL CONSIDERATIONS It is not uncommon to have survivors argue over the estate of a decedent. Is it ethical for the survivors to do so? From an ethical perspective, is it more ethical for the proceeds of the four notes in question in this case to be included in the estate or to pass directly to the daughter outside the estate?

SOURCE: *Zink v. Stafford, Lawyers Weekly* (18 January 1999), http://www.lawyersweekly.com/.

that the law reads them as authorizing the free transfer of the instrument. Failing to use one of these terms is a denial of free transferability and therefore a denial of negotiability.

If an instrument that is otherwise negotiable calls for payment by stating "Pay to Pete Jones" (rather than "Pay to the order of Pete Jones"), it is not negotiable. By its terms, only Pete Jones is authorized to receive payment; he cannot transfer payment by negotiation (although he may be able to *assign* his right to receive payment under contract law). However, an indorsement that says "Pay to Pete Jones" would not affect negotiability. Indorsements cannot negate negotiability once it exists. To be payable "to order," the terms of the instrument must state that it is payable to the order or assigns of a specified individual or to a specified individual or to the individual's order. The designated individual may be a person, as in "Pay to Paula Lopez or order"; an office, as in "Pay to the order of the Treasurer of Washington County"; an estate or trust, as in "Pay to the order of the Johnson Estate"; or an unincorporated association, as in "Pay to the XYZ Partnership or order." An instrument payable to order requires an indorsement to be further negotiated.

If no particular individual is designated, the instrument must be payable to bearer to be negotiable. An instrument is payable to bearer when, by its terms, it is payable to bearer or to the order of bearer; or to "cash" or the order of "cash"; or to a named person or bearer, as in "Pay to Joe Jakes or bearer" or "Pay to the order of Joe Jakes or bearer" (§ 3-111). An instrument is also considered payable to bearer if no payee is stated. No indorsement is legally needed to negotiate an instrument payable to bearer, although most holders will request (or demand) an indorsement for added protection.

The following case involves "words of negotiability" and how they may restrict the rights of a bank to make payment on an instrument, even if that instrument is not negotiable. (This case was decided under the old Article 3. Follow the court's reasoning, and then decide whether you think the same results would be reached under the revised Article 3.)

22.2

GALATIA COMMUNITY STATE BANK V. KINDY
821 S.W.2D 765 (ARK. 1991)

FACTS Kindy agreed to purchase four diesel engines from Hicks, with Hicks agreeing to deliver the engines to Kindy. The purchase price was $13,000. Kindy agreed to wire transfer $6,500 and to pay the remainder by check. The check was not to be cashed until the engines had been delivered. Kindy wrote and mailed a post-dated check to Hicks in June of 1989. This check had two different amounts on its face: $6,500 in numbers on the number line, and $5,500 imprinted with a check imprinting machine on the line where words normally appear. Kindy stated that he had intentionally put two amounts on the check, reasoning that the bank would call him to find out which amount was to be paid, allowing him to tell the bank whether to honor the check (if the engines had been delivered) or to dishonor the check (if the engines had not been delivered). Hicks presented the check to the Galatia Bank 10 June 1989, and the bank honored the check for $5,500. A bank employee altered the amount in the normal "number" location, changing the "6" in $6,500 to a "5" so that the amounts in each area were in agreement. The check was subsequently presented to the drawee bank, which refused it. Galatia sued Kindy for the amount of the check. Kindy denied liability, asserting

continued

22.2

GALATIA COMMUNITY STATE BANK V. KINDY, *continued*
821 S.W.2D 765 (ARK. 1991)

that he had a defense (nondelivery) and that the bank was a mere holder.

ISSUES Was Galatia Bank a holder in due course and thus entitled to recover from Kindy on the check? Do imprinted numbers, located where the words are normally located, take precedence over figures placed where the figures are normally placed on a check?

HOLDINGS Yes, Galatia was an HDC on the check. Yes, the imprinted numbers in the word location should take precedence over the figures in the figure location.

REASONING The bank employee did not make a "fraudulent and material" alteration of the check. Rather, the alteration by the employee was done in good faith and with no intent to harm anyone. The alteration was done to place the amounts in harmony and to make the controlling amount the amount reflected on the check. Words take precedence over numbers because words are harder to alter than numbers. A person uses a check imprinting machine because its imprint is more difficult to alter than words are. Thus, the purposes of the UCC are best served by considering an amount imprinted by a

check writing machine to be "words," at least for the purpose of resolving an ambiguity between that amount and an amount entered on the line usually used to express the amount in figures. Since the imprinted amount is in "words" and the figures are in numbers, and since "words" take precedence over numbers, the imprinted amount is the amount to be used in resolving the ambiguity.

[Section 3-110(c)(2) of the revised Article would give the same result if the case were tried under the current version of Article 3.]

BUSINESS CONSIDERATION Suppose that your business receives a check from a customer, and that the check has different amounts in words and in numbers. What should you do? Why?

ETHICAL CONSIDERATIONS Should a bank employee take it upon him- or herself to "correct" a mistake made by a customer in drafting a check? Is it ethical for a bank employee to change negotiable instruments issued by its customers, even if it does so in good faith?

CONSTRUCTION AND INTERPRETATION: ARTICLE 3

Article 3 takes a very short-and-simple approach to construction and interpretation. Basically, Section 3-114, which covers contradictory terms, provides the coverage in this area. According to this section: "If an instrument contains contradictory terms, typewritten terms prevail over printed terms, handwritten terms prevail over both, and words prevail over numbers." Despite its brevity, this is an area that is likely to have litigation that will provide additional guidelines as to how courts plan to interpret ambiguities. Judicial decisions will provide the parameters for this area, possibly beyond the simple language of the statutory coverage.

REQUIREMENTS FOR NEGOTIABILITY: ARTICLE 7

Where Article 3 is very strict in determining the negotiability of commercial paper, Article 7 is much more relaxed in determining whether a document of title is negotiable. Section 7-104 states that a document of title is negotiable if:

1. By its terms the goods are to be delivered to bearer or to the order of a named person.
2. Where recognized in international trade, if it runs to a named person or assigns.

Every other document of title is deemed to be nonnegotiable. In fact, a bill of lading that is consigned to a named person is not made negotiable by a provision that specifies that the goods are only to be delivered against an order signed by a named person. Obviously, Article 7 is more concerned with the rights of the parties to the goods than with the rights of the parties in the documents covering the goods.

Whether the document of title is negotiable or nonnegotiable, the bailee has a duty of care. If the bailee fails to exercise due care and the goods are damaged or destroyed, the bailee is liable. The following case involves this scenario.

22.3

FLEETGUARD, INC. V. DIXIE BOX AND CRATING COMPANY
445 S.E.2D 459 (S.C.APP. 1994)

FACTS Fleetguard, located in Tennessee, is a manufacturer of filter paper. Dixie Box, located in Charleston, packages merchandise cargo for transportation, mostly for export. Fleetguard entered into an agreement with Dixie Box to package nine rolls of its filter paper in a moisture proof barrier for international shipment to China. Dixie Box received the paper from Fleetguard in July, 1986, and placed it in its warehouse. In August, 1986, prior to the packaging and shipment of the paper, a fire occurred at the Dixie Box facility. Fleetguard's paper was damaged by smoke and water and has no salvage value. Fleetguard brought this bailment action to recover the value of the paper. The circuit court held Dixie Box failed to rebut a presumption of negligence in its care of Fleetguard's paper and awarded Fleetguard $21,012.87, the value of the paper. On appeal, Dixie Box's sole argument is that it used reasonable care in storing Fleetguard's paper.

ISSUES Did Dixie Box use reasonable care in storing Fleetguard's paper?

HOLDINGS No. Dixie Box failed to establish that it had used reasonable care, or to rebut the presumption that it was negligent in its care of the paper.

REASONING Fleetguard made out a prima facie case by showing that it delivered the paper to Dixie Box in good condition and that Dixie Box returned the paper in a damaged condition. The burden then shifted to Dixie Box to prove that it exercised ordinary care in the storage and safe keeping of the paper . . .

Whether Dixie Box exercised ordinary care was a question of fact, in this case, for the circuit judge sitting without a jury . . . Because this was an action at law, tried without a jury, this Court will not disturb the circuit court's finding on this issue if there is any evidence to support it . . . To show that it had exercised reasonable care to prevent loss from fire, Dixie Box introduced evidence that it equipped the warehouse with fire extinguishers. The warehouse had no night watchman or guard. Moreover, a Dixie Box employee testified that although the warehouse had a burglar alarm, he was "not sure it included fire." There is no other evidence that the warehouse was equipped with a fire alarm system or any other fire safety device. We find the evidence supports the circuit court's finding that Dixie Box failed to rebut the presumption that it was negligent in the case of Fleetwood's [sic] paper. Affirmed.

BUSINESS CONSIDERATIONS Why is there a presumption of negligence when a bailee, whether a warehouseman or a common carrier, returns goods in a damaged condition at the end of the bailment? Is such a presumption fair to a business involved in handling goods in a bailment setting?

ETHICAL CONSIDERATION Is it ethical to presume that a bailee is negligent when bailed goods are returned or delivered in worse condition than they were in when they were delivered to the bailee?

RESOURCES FOR BUSINESS LAW STUDENTS

NAME	RESOURCES	WEB ADDRESS
Uniform Commercial Code (UCC), Article 3, Negotiable Instruments	The Legal Information Institute (LII), maintained by the Cornell Law School, provides a hypertext and searchable version of UCC, Article 3, Negotiable Instruments. LII has links to Article 3 as adopted by particular states and to proposed revisions.	**http://www.law.cornell.edu/ucc/3/overview.html**
UCC, Article 7, Warehouse Receipts, Bills of Lading, and Other Documents of Title	LII provides a hypertext and searchable version of UCC, Article 7, Warehouse Receipts, Bills of Lading and Other Documents of Title.	**http://www.law.cornell.edu/ucc/7/overview.html**

Even though Article 7 is more concerned with rights in the goods, there are certain rights to be gained if the document of title is negotiable, especially if the party qualifies as a holder by due negotiation. In addition, a holder by due negotiation can exist only if the document of title is negotiable. (This topic will be covered in more detail in Chapter 23.)

SUMMARY

This chapter examines the technical requirements for negotiability of an instrument under Article 3. The first requirement is that the instrument be written or reduced to tangible form. Next, the instrument must be signed by the maker or the drawer. The promise (for notes or CDs) or the order (for checks or drafts) must be unconditional. The instrument must call for the payment of a fixed amount in money— a recognized governmental currency. In addition, the time of payment must be determinable from the face of the instrument, or it must be payable on demand. Finally, the instrument must contain "words of negotiability." This means that it must be payable "to order" or "to bearer."

In case the instrument contains ambiguities, the Code provides a method of interpretation. Handwriting takes precedence over typing and over printing. Typing takes precedence over printing. Words take precedence over numbers if the words make sense. If the words do not make sense, the numbers control.

Article 7 of the UCC governs documents of title. Documents of title may be negotiable or nonnegotiable. The requirements for negotiable documents under Article 7 are much less stringent than the requirements under Article 3. Article 7 is more concerned with the goods than it is with the documents covering the goods, but it does provide some special protections if the document is negotiable and the holder qualifies as a holder by due negotiation.

DISCUSSION QUESTIONS

1. What is meant by *signing* under Article 3 of the UCC? Why is this requirement so important in determining whether an instrument is negotiable?
2. In order to qualify as a negotiable instrument, the promise or the order must be "written." How does the UCC define *written,* and how is that definition modified for negotiable instruments? What has been added to this definition by the "Official Comments" to the Code, and what impact does this have on the definition of *written?*
3. What is meant by a *fixed amount of money* under Article 3 of the UCC? How does the Code define *fixed amount?* What is meant by *money?*
4. Why is an instrument that is payable "30 days after sight" payable at a determinable time, but an instrument payable "30 days after my anniversary" not payable at a determinable time? How is the date of "sight" determined?
5. The courts have consistently held that an "IOU is not a negotiable instrument." Below is a typical IOU. Why would such an instrument be deemed nonnegotiable? Be specific.

Betty,

IOU $350.

Jane Doe

6. A promissory note was issued by Larry to Darryl. The note had the following terms included in the body of the instrument:

Interest to be paid at 14 percent per annum. [This term was preprinted on the promissory note form.] Interest at 14.5 percent per annum. [This term was typewritten above the preprinted term.] Plus interest. [This term was handwritten in the margin and initialed by both Larry and Darryl.]

How will interest be computed on this note, and why will that method for computing interest be used?

7. Marvella issued what appeared to be a time draft payable to the order of Herman. The terms of the instrument called for payment "90 days after our marriage." Marvella and Herman were married on 4 January of this year. Subsequently, they got a divorce on 15 March. Herman presented the instrument to the drawee 90 days after the wedding date, demanding payment. The drawee refused to pay, and Herman has sued Marvella on the instrument. Will this case be resolved under the provisions of Article 3, or will it be resolved under the provisions of common law? Why?
8. What is required by Article 7 in order for a document of title to be deemed negotiable? Is this more or less rigorous than the requirements for negotiability under Article 3? Why is there a difference in the requirements of negotiability under the two articles?
9. A bill of lading called for the delivery of the goods to Acme, Inc. It went on to specify that delivery was only to take place on receipt of a written order signed by Mr. Aziz. Is this document of title negotiable? Explain.
10. An international shipment of goods is being made. The bill of lading states that the goods are consigned to "Mr. Smythe-Harrington of London, England, or to his assigns." What information would be required to determine whether this bill of lading is negotiable? Explain.

CASE PROBLEMS AND WRITING ASSIGNMENTS

1. The Campbells issued a note payable to the order of Strand. The note called for payment of $12,500 plus interest, and was issued to purchase shares in a limited partnership that Strand was allegedly forming. Strand subsequently endorsed the note and delivered it to the Centerre Bank for value. Strand never completed the formation of the limited partnership, so the Campbells never acquired their anticipated interest in the venture. Since no limited partnership was formed, the Campbells defaulted on the note. Centerre Bank sued the Campbells for the note, and the Campbells asserted two defenses that they felt excused their default: There was a failure of consideration because the limited partnership was never

formed; and a clause in the note stated that interest could vary with changes in the interest rate the banks charged to Strand, which made the instrument nonnegotiable. How should the court treat the two defenses raised by the Campbells? Does it make any difference in which order the defenses are addressed? Explain your answer. [See *Centerre Bank of Branson* v. *Campbell,* 744 S.W.2d 490 (Mo.App. 1988).]

2. Williams (d.b.a. Howard R. Williams, Inc.) invested with Prasad (d.b.a. P.S. Investment Co.) from time to time. In December 1980, Prasad assigned to Williams a promissory note for $75,000, payable in unconditional payments of $991.14 per month. On 11 April

1983, R & D Development issued a $200,000 promissory note payable to the order of Prasad. In August 1983, Williams assigned the $75,000 note to Prasad in exchange for a partial interest in the $200,000 note from R & D. This assignment was governed by a written document, which specified that Prasad had the right to reacquire the partial interest in the $200,000 note from Williams by issuing another promissory note, which would pay Williams $991.14 per month. On 30 December 1984, Prasad issued a note to Williams in order to reacquire this partial interest. This new note stated that "payments under this note will be paid on and when payments are received from the [R & D] note." R & D filed for bankruptcy in 1987 and stopped making payments at that time. Accordingly, Prasad stopped making payments to Williams at that time. Williams sued Prasad to collect the accrued payments and the balance of the note. Was the note from Prasad to Williams a negotiable instrument, allowing Williams to collect despite the bankruptcy of R & D? [See *Williams* v. *P.S. Investment Co., Inc.*, 401 S.E.2d 79 (N.C.App. 1991).]

3. The Oaks Apartments Joint Venture and its five partners executed a promissory note payable to the order of Meridian Service Corporation, a wholly owned subsidiary of Meridian Savings Association. The note read, in pertinent part:

    > FOR VALUE RECEIVED, THE OAKS APART-MENTS JOINT VENTURE, *a Texas Joint Venture . . . promises to pay to the order of* MERIDIAN SERVICE CORPORATION, *a Texas Corporation . . . the sum of TWO MILLION AND NO/100 DOLLARS ($2,000,000.00) or so much thereof as may be advanced in accordance with the terms of a certain Loan Agreement executed on even date herewith, with interest thereon at the rate provided below.*

    The five partners also executed an unconditional personal guaranty of the note, obligating each partner for 20 percent of the total debt. The Oaks Apartments was subsequently sold to Veigel, who assumed the loan obligation in 1985. Veigel then entered into an agreement with Meridian which modified the time and manner of payment. Veigel subsequently defaulted on the note, and Meridian began attempting to collect from Veigel, the partnership, and each of the partners in 1986. In 1987, Meridian foreclosed on the apartment complex and sold it, leaving a deficit of $755,249.06 on the note. Meridian then sued to recover this deficit. (Resolution Trust replaced Meridian as conservator when Meridian failed.) Resolution Trust argued that it was an HDC of the note and the guaranty, not subject to any defenses. The

partners objected, alleging that the note was not negotiable, so RTC could not be an HDC. Was the note originally signed by Oaks Apartments a negotiable instrument? Is it ethical to try to avoid liability by denying that a note issued by the defendant is negotiable? [See *Resolution Trust Corp.* v. *Oaks Apartments Joint Venture*, 966 F.2d 995 (5th Cir. 1992).]

4. Tate contacted Action Moving & Storage to ship his household belongings from his home in Charlotte, North Carolina, to Monrovia, Liberia. Action inspected the items and gave Tate a written estimate, quoting a price of $4,281.60 to package, store, and then ship the items. Tate accepted the price offered and paid Action $1,000 down with the balance to be paid prior to shipment. (The contract also stated that if the goods were left in Action's possession for six months, they became the property of Action.) On 26 March 1984, Action loaded the goods. On 29 March 1984, Tate left for Liberia. At that point, Action stored the goods since it had not been paid the balance due. Tate wrote to Action on 26 September asking for the final weight of the shipment, enclosed a check for $3,800, and asked for information as to when he could expect to receive his goods. Receiving no answer, Tate again wrote to Action on 24 October 1984. In this letter he instructed Action to deduct $2,708.20 from the $4,800 he had paid for its charges and expenses, send the balance to Tate, and Tate would arrange for another carrier to pick up and deliver the goods. Action ignored the directions, continued to hold the $4,800, and informed Tate that he owed an additional $3,652.24. When Tate did not reply, Action sold the goods at a public sale. (Because there were no documents from the sale, Action's president stated that he believed that Action entered the only bid, $1, for the goods.) Tate sued Action for breach of contract, unfair trade practices, and conversion. Action denied liability. Was there a warehouse receipt issued by Action, requiring it to meet the warehouseman's duties imposed by Article 7? [See *Tate* v. *Action Moving & Storage, Inc.*, 383 S.E.2d 229 (N.C.App. 1989).]

5. Butler Manufacturing and a number of other firms stored goods with Americold Corporation. Americold operated an underground warehouse, storing goods in a limestone cave that was originally formed during a mining operation. A fire broke out in the warehouse on 28 December 1991, causing substantial losses and/or damages to the stored goods. Many of the plaintiffs stored business records with Americold. Each firm that stored such business records executed and signed a standard Records Storage Contract.

These Records Storage Contracts contained an exculpatory clause excusing Americold from any claims against it for ordinary negligence, and another clause purporting to limit the total amount of damages that can be collected from Americold regardless of the cause of action. Americold argues that the exculpatory clauses should be given full force and effect because the contracts were fairly bargained for, and agreed to, by the parties. They add that there was no unconscionable disparity of bargaining power and that the limitations are an acceptable allocation of risk. Butler and the other plaintiffs argue that the exculpatory clauses violate public policy and also violate the duty of care imposed by § 7-204 of the UCC. They urge the court to negate these clauses and to allow them to recover their damages. How should the court resolve this case? What argument, if any, can be made for upholding the exculpatory clauses in the contract? What arguments, if any, can be made for ignoring the exculpatory clauses? [See *Butler Manufacturing Co. v. Americold Corporation*, 835 F.Supp. 1274 (D.Kan. 1993).]

6. **BUSINESS APPLICATION CASE** In 1981, Whistler Village Partnership executed nine promissory notes, each in the original amount of $44,595, payable to Alpine Federal Savings & Loan in connection with Whistler's purchase of nine units of Phase II of the Whistler Village Townhomes in Steamboat Springs, Colorado. Each of the notes was secured by a deed of trust covering one of the nine units. In 1982, Burns and McEncroe purchased the nine condominiums and assumed the loans, executing assumption agreements, which released the original borrowers from liability on the notes. After a disagreement about the management of the property, Burns conveyed his interest in the property to McEncroe by deed dated 11 May 1983. In 1987, Burns and McEncroe executed loan modification agreements, which reduced the interest rates on the loans. Burns and McEncroe defaulted on the notes in 1988, and Alpine began foreclosure proceedings. Alpine obtained an Order Authorizing Sale from the district court in Colorado, and on 11 April 1989, the Public Trustee conducted a foreclosure sale. Alpine purchased the nine units at the sale. Burns did not exercise his right of redemption provided under Colorado law. . . . Alpine later sold the units to third parties, and it instituted this litigation to recover alleged deficiencies on the notes. After Alpine was declared insolvent, Resolution Trust Corporation (RTC) was appointed receiver. The RTC, as receiver, was substituted on each case. . . . After trial in September 1991, the jury returned a verdict in favor of Burns. . . . Over 15 months later, the trial court granted the RTC's motion for judgment notwithstanding the verdict (JNOV). On 15 March 1993, it entered deficiency judgments against Burns in the amount of $44,038.68 and $62,208.68 in the two suits and awarded attorney's fees to the RTC. Were the notes in question negotiable instruments? If so, did RTC qualify as a holder in due course on the notes? Alpine sent the notice of its intent to accelerate the loan to the wrong address, allegedly failing to provide Burns with notice of its intent. What precautions should a business take to ensure that, when it gives notice of a problem under a contract, that notice is properly sent, including having it sent to the right person at the right address? [See *Burns v. Resolution Trust Corp.*, 880 S.W.2d 149 (Tex.App.–Houston [14th Dist.] 1994).]

7. **ETHICAL APPLICATION CASE** O'Mara, a West Virginia corporation with its principal place of business in Steubenville, Ohio, operated 15 Bonanza restaurants. O'Mara hired GSD, an accounting firm, to manage its accounting and other financial matters. Included in GSD's services were the computation of O'Mara's weekly federal withholding taxes, preparation of checks for deposit of these taxes, and reconciliation of bank statements. Smith was the sole owner of GSD and also owned 20 percent of O'Mara. Thompson was the comptroller for both O'Mara and GSD. Smith encountered financial difficulties beginning in 1979, and Smith and Thompson devised a plan whereby Smith would embezzle O'Mara's withholding taxes. This scheme involved endorsing the withholding checks, which were payable to the order of the Heritage Bank, as follows:

Pay to the order of The First National Bank & Trust Company in Steubenville, Ohio FOR DEPOSIT ONLY GAIL SMITH DEVELOPMENT #009-215, W. Gail Smith.

Heritage Bank accepted each of these checks with this indorsement and without question. When O'Mara discovered what had happened, it sued Heritage Bank (along with two other banks similarly involved) to recover the funds. The banks denied liability, asserting that the checks as issued were "bearer" instruments, not "order" instruments. Were these checks "bearer paper" so that Heritage Bank acted properly in accepting them? What ethical issues are raised by the conduct of Smith and Thompson? Was it ethical for the bank to attempt to deny liability by arguing that these instruments were "bearer paper"? [See *O'Mara Enterprises, Inc. v. People's Bank of Weirton*, 420 S.E.2d 727 (W.Va. 1992).]

8. **CRITICAL THINKING CASE** On 13 October 1975, Wachovia Bank issued a $20,000 certificate of deposit to "Timmy S. Holloway, Jr., by Rountree Crisp, Sr., Agent." At the time, Timmy was a six-year-old minor. Crisp died on 5 April 1978. At Crisp's death, the certificate of deposit in Timmy's name with Crisp as agent was found in Crisp's safe deposit box. . . . As to the certificate of deposit in Timmy's name, on 11 April 1980 Wachovia paid to Marcia Coleman, Timmy's mother, and Louise Crisp, Crisp's widow and Timmy's grandmother, the sum of $26,294.92, purportedly the proceeds then due on the certificate of deposit, upon an indorsement reading "Timothy S. Holloway, Jr., by Estate of George R. Crisp, Sr., Marcia Coleman, Adminx." On the same date and on a second occasion, Coleman rolled over the proceeds of the certificate of deposit into new certificates. . . . On 23 October 1981, Coleman presented the [most recent] certificate to Wachovia for payment. Wachovia paid the certificate with a check in the amount of $26,294.92 payable to "Timmy S. Holloway, Jr., by Marcia Coleman." Coleman stated that she did not remember what she did with the $26,294.92 proceeds of the 23 October 1981 check. At this time, Timmy was still a minor. No court had appointed Coleman as Timmy's guardian with authority to receive the funds for him. In June 1986, Coleman was appointed Timmy's guardian for purposes of holding real property inherited by Timmy from his grandmother. . . . Timmy attained his majority on 5 September 1987. Shortly before his eighteenth birthday, Timmy's relationship with his mother had deteriorated to the point that he had moved away from her house and to an aunt's house. In the summer of 1988, Timmy was in need of money, and his aunt told him about the certificate of deposit left by his grandfather. . . . On 12 May 1989, Timmy brought this action against Wachovia seeking to recover the original value of the certificate ($20,000) plus interest. Both parties moved for summary judgment. The trial court denied Timmy's motion and granted Wachovia's motion. The Court of Appeals affirmed. . . . On 4 March 1992, [the court] allowed plaintiff's petition for discretionary review. On appeal, the parties agree that no triable issue of fact exists; neither party has disputed that the case is appropriate for summary judgment. Did the bank breach its contract with Crisp when it paid the certificate to Coleman? In this case, the bank paid the certificate of deposit upon presentment and demand for payment from the administratrix of the estate of Crisp and the mother of the named payee. What more should the bank have done to ascertain the right of Timmy's mother to act as his "legal guardian" in the handling of this nonnegotiable certificate of deposit? [See *Holloway* v. *Wachovia Bank & Trust Co., N.A.*, 423 S.E.2d 752 (N.C. 1992).]

NOTE

1. *Zink* v. *Stafford, Lawyers Weekly* (18 January 1999), http://www.lawyersweekly.com/.

23

NEGOTIATION AND HOLDERS IN DUE COURSE/ HOLDERS BY DUE NEGOTIATION

A G E N D A

CIT will be receiving a number of checks from their customers. How should these checks be indorsed? Does the type of indorsement *really* make a difference? Suppose that some of the checks are dishonored by the bank. What rights will the firm be able to assert on those checks? Should the firm take any special steps or plan any special precautions for handling the checks they receive? Be prepared! You never know when one of the Kochanowskis will ask for your help or advice.

O U T L I N E

TRANSFER

Negotiable instruments are intended to "flow" through the commercial world. In order to "flow," the instrument needs to be *transferred* from person to person. The form these transfers take determines the rights that can be asserted by each person gaining possession of the negotiable instrument.

The Uniform Commercial Code (UCC) defines a *transfer* as a delivery by any person other than the issuer for the purpose of giving the person receiving the instrument the right to enforce the instrument. A transfer, whether by negotiation or not, confers on the transferee the rights possessed by the transferor, including the rights of a holder in due course (HDC) if the transferor has those rights. Thus, as was discussed in the previous chapter, a transfer of a negotiable instrument is treated like an assignment of a contract right. The transferee receives any and all rights of the transferor. However, this is, in effect, the same as an assignment. As was discussed earlier, this is not an ideal position, and if negotiable instruments could only be transferred—treated the same as an assignment—they would not be as readily acceptable as they are in the modern commercial world.

Nonetheless, the transfer of a negotiable instrument does give the transferee some rights in the instrument, although these rights may be fewer than the rights that a holder or a holder in due course possesses, as the following case shows.

23.1

BREMEN BANK AND TRUST COMPANY OF ST. LOUIS V. MUSKOPF
817 S.W.2D 602 (MO.APP. 1991)

FACTS On November 30, 1984 . . . Ferguson . . . executed and delivered to . . . Muskopf: (1) a promissory note in the principal amount of $230,000.00; and (2) their deed of trust on certain real property . . . to secure payment of the note. The deed of trust named . . . Donovan as trustee and Muskopf as beneficiary . . . In December 1985, Muskopf applied and was approved for a loan with Bremen . . . Muskopf executed and delivered a revolving credit note, payable to Bremen in the amount of $80,000.00, the full amount of which was drawn down by January 9, 1986. As security for this loan, Muskopf gave his personal guaranty and a written assignment of the Ferguson note and deed of trust. Muskopf delivered the note and deed of trust to Bremen, and it has retained physical possession since that time. Muskopf did not endorse the back of the note. Moreover, Bremen did not record the assignment of the note and deed of trust until May 15, 1989. Bremen also did not file a statutory request for notice of foreclosure sale as it was permitted to do . . . The Fergusons defaulted on the note in July 1987. Muskopf subsequently contacted a St. Louis law firm regarding foreclosure of the note and deed of trust . . . On October 7, 1987, the decision was made to proceed with foreclosure, but Bremen was not consulted . . . [The law firm] was unable to contact the trustee . . . Donovan, and was told by Muskopf that Donovan was unable to act . . . In reliance on Muskopf's verbal instructions, [the law firm] prepared a document for Muskopf's signature, to remove Donovan as trustee and appoint Campbell [an associate with the firm] successor trustee . . . Campbell performed all the statutorily required steps in preparation of the foreclosure sale . . . The letter report made no mention of Bremen's interest in the property as it was still unrecorded . . . Consequently, no notice of the sale was sent directly to Bremen . . . Bremen had neither knowledge of the appointment of Campbell as successor trustee nor knowledge that a foreclosure sale had taken place until December 1988 or January 1989 when Muskopf filed for bankruptcy. The foreclosure sale was held on November 6, 1987. Muskopf was the highest bidder . . . On November 15, 1987, Campbell prepared a trustee's deed (under foreclosure) in favor of Muskopf. The Fergusons were notified of the results of the foreclosure sale by letter dated November 25, 1987. Subsequently, on November 1, 1989, the Fergusons gave a quit claim deed to the property to one of the subsequent purchasers. Under date of May 11, 1988, Muskopf . . . conveyed the property to . . . Hoffman . . . by general warranty deed . . . Muskopf's second note to Bremen

BREMEN BANK AND TRUST COMPANY OF ST. LOUIS V. MUSKOPF, *continued*
817 S.W.2D 602 (MO.APP. 1991)

remains unpaid, with a balance owing of $74,600.00. Muskopf filed for relief under Chapter 13 of the United States Bankruptcy Code in January 1989. A modification of the automatic stay in bankruptcy was granted by the bankruptcy court to allow Bremen to pursue this action . . . The trial court held that the foreclosure sale was void because the verbal appointment of the successor trustee was ineffective since the appointment of a trustee is a conveyance of an interest in the title to real estate. It further found, however, that, since no party objected, Bremen was not prejudiced by the failure to properly appoint the successor trustee. The subsequent written appointment, therefore, ratified the sale. The trial court also found that Bremen had no standing to object to the foreclosure sale because its interest was not publicly recorded. From this judgment, Bremen appeals.

ISSUE Was Bremen a holder of the original note and deed of trust, so that the foreclosure sale was not valid without its permission?

HOLDING No. The promissory note from the Fergusons was payable to the order of a named person. As such it required an endorsement and delivery to be negotiated.

REASONING . . . Bremen seeks to set aside the foreclosure sale because: (1) it was held without its consent; and (2) it was the holder of the note and deed of trust. We must, therefore, first determine if Bremen is the holder of the indebtedness. If so, then Muskopf was not authorized to appoint Campbell or to direct the foreclosure sale, making it void. Thus, no title could pass . . . A holder is a person who is in possession of a document of title or an instrument or an investment security drawn, issued or endorsed to him or to his order or to bearer or in blank . . . An instrument means a negotiable instrument . . . To be a negotiable instrument, the writing must: (1) be signed by the maker or drawer; (2) contain an unconditional promise to pay a sum certain in money; (3) contain no other promise, order or obligation; (4) be payable on demand or at a definite time; and (5) be payable to order or bearer . . . The promissory note that Muskopf assigned to Bremen is a negotiable instrument. It bears the signatures of O. Dean Ferguson and Vickie L. Ferguson. They promise to pay $230,000.00, plus interest at a rate of 11% per annum pursuant to

a schedule. The note is made payable to the order of . . . Muskopf. The note contains no other promise besides the promise to pay the money. Negotiation is the transfer of an instrument in such form that the transferee becomes a holder. If the instrument is payable to order, as it is here, it is negotiated by delivery with any necessary endorsement . . . An endorsement must be written by, or on behalf of, the holder and on the instrument or on paper so firmly affixed thereto as to become a part thereof . . . Here, Muskopf's assignment was not attached to the note at all. It, therefore, did not effectively negotiate the instrument in such a way that Bremen became a holder of the note . . . Negotiation . . . was not effected and Bremen did not automatically become a holder of the note. While Bremen is not a holder of the note because it lacked effective negotiation, Bremen is a transferee pursuant to the assignment. The transfer of an instrument vests in the transferee such rights as the transferor has therein, but only to the extent of the interest transferred . . . We must determine the extent of the interest Muskopf transferred to Bremen . . . Here, Muskopf executed the assignment of the note and deed of trust for the purpose of pledging collateral security on his revolving credit note with Bremen. The face amount of the note pledged was $230,000.00, although the obligation to Bremen totalled only $80,000.00. We find . . . that this constituted a partial assignment. The revolving credit note was significantly overcollateralized and the Ferguson note was not endorsed. The evidence supports the conclusion that Muskopf did not intend to assign his total interest in the Ferguson note. Going one step further, Bremen was apparently aware of this intention since it failed to record its interest. We, therefore, find that Muskopf did not transfer his "status" and he could request the foreclosure sale and appoint a successor trustee . . . Since Bremen failed to record its interest, it is precluded by the foreclosure sale, for it is established by long-standing authority that a purchaser is charged with constructive notice of all recorded instruments lying within the chain of title, but an instrument outside the chain of title imparts no notice . . . The effect of the recording statutes is that subsequent bona fide purchasers of realty with no actual notice of an unrecorded interest in that realty take free of that unrecorded interest . . . The trial court's judgment is affirmed, as modified.

continued

23.1

BREMEN BANK AND TRUST COMPANY OF ST. LOUIS V. MUSKOPF, *continued*
817 S.W.2D 602 (MO.APP. 1991)

BUSINESS CONSIDERATIONS The borrower in this case transferred his rights in the note to the bank when he delivered the note to the bank. However, he never indorsed the note, so that the note was never negotiated. Should a lender have a policy established to ensure that it only receives notes used as collateral through a negotiation? How important is it for the transferee to be a holder rather than a mere assignee?

ETHICAL CONSIDERATIONS Is it ethical for a borrower who has made a partial assignment of his rights in collateral to dispose of that collateral without the permission of the lender/assignee? What should the borrower do in this situation to ensure that he or she is acting ethically?

NEGOTIATION

Obviously, something more is needed to protect the possessor of the commercial paper and to facilitate the free flow of commercial paper through commercial channels. That "something more" is provided by the UCC, and it is known as negotiation. Section 3-201(a) defines a *negotiation* as "a transfer of possession, whether voluntary or involuntary, of an instrument by a person other than the issuer to a person who becomes a holder thereby." Section 3-201(b) adds that: "Except for negotiation by a remitter, if an instrument is payable to an identified person, negotiation requires transfer of possession of the instrument and its indorsement by the holder. If an instrument is payable to bearer, it may be negotiated by transfer of possession alone."

For example, a check that says "Pay to the order of Ollie Oliver" must be indorsed by Ollie Oliver before it can be negotiated. If Ollie simply transfers possession of the check to another person without indorsing it, the transfer would be an assignment. The terms imposed by the drawer—pay to the order of Ollie Oliver—require that Ollie *prove* he is transferring his rights. His indorsement provides that proof.

In contrast, a check that says "Pay to the order of bearer" does not need to be indorsed to be negotiated. Transfer of possession alone is enough to show negotiation. The terms imposed by the drawer at the time of issue—pay to the order of bearer—tell the drawee that anyone in possession is entitled to payment.

If the instrument requires an indorsement, the indorsement must be written on the instrument itself or on an *allonge*—a paper so firmly affixed to the instrument as to become a part of the instrument. Also, to be a negotiation, the indorsement must transfer the entire instrument or the entire unpaid balance. Any attempt to transfer less than the entire balance of the instrument is treated as a partial assignment, not as a negotiation.

INDORSEMENTS

Section 3-204 defines an indorsement. According to the Code, *indorsement* means "a signature, other than that of a signer as maker, drawer, or acceptor, that alone or accompanied by other words is made on an instrument for the purpose of

(i) negotiating the instrument, (ii) restricting payment of the instrument, or (iii) incurring indorser's liability on the instrument." This section goes on to add that "regardless of the intent of the signer, a signature and its accompanying words is an indorsement unless the accompanying words, terms of the instrument, or other circumstances unambiguously indicate that the signature was made for a purpose other than indorsement."

This means that a signature on a negotiable instrument is *presumed* to be an indorsement unless some other purpose is unambiguously shown as the purpose for the signature's placement on the instrument. There are two reasons that this is important. First, any instrument payable "to order" requires an indorsement before it can be further negotiated. Second, and perhaps more important, each and every indorsement is a separate contract added to the contract that the instrument itself represents, and to any other indorsement contracts already present on the instrument. Indorsers are assuming contractual liability to the person to whom they transfer the instrument and to every subsequent holder or transferee of that instrument. For this reason, many people will not accept the negotiation of a bearer instrument unless the holder indorses it. Even though bearer paper may legally be negotiated by delivery alone, the transferee usually demands the added security of an indorsement, thereby adding the indorsement contract and its rights to the rights represented by the instrument itself.

There are two reasons for indorsing an instrument. One reason is to affect negotiation. The other is to affect liability. The indorsements that affect negotiation will tell the holder (1) that another indorsement is needed to negotiate the instrument further (a special indorsement); (2) that no further indorsements are needed in order to negotiate the instrument further (a blank indorsement); or (3) that the instrument has been restricted to some special channel of commerce such as banking (a restrictive indorsement). The indorsements that affect liability either (1) admit and/or agree to honor the contract of indorsement (an *unqualified indorsement*) or (2) expressly deny any liability on the indorsement contract (a *qualified indorsement*). Every indorsement must affect negotiation as well as liability. Thus, each indorsement must fit one of the categories in the matrix shown in Exhibit 23.1.

E X H I B I T   23.1 | **The Indorsement Matrix**

	Unqualified	Qualified
Special	(1) Designates the next holder, so an additional indorsement is required; does not deny liability for the indorsement contract.	(2) Designates the next holder, so an additional indorsement is required; denies contract liability for the indorsement.
Blank	(3) Does not designate the next holder, making the instrument "bearer paper"; does not deny liability for the indorsement contract.	(4) Does not designate the next holder, making the instrument "bearer paper"; denies contract liability for the indorsement.
Restrictive	(5) Attempts to restrict or limit future negotiation of the instrument, as in "for deposit only"; does not deny liability for the indorsement contract.	(6) Attempts to restrict or limit future negotiation of the instrument, as in "for deposit only"; denies contract liability for the indorsement.

23.1 | FINANCE

DEPOSITING COMPANY CHECKS

John is responsible for depositing checks the company receives into the firm's account. He has been stamping the backs of the checks on the day they are received, using a rubber stamp that reads "Call-Image Technology." The checks are then placed in his "out" basket until he makes his weekly trip to the bank. Lindsay complained to the family that, in her opinion, John was not being careful enough with the checks. Tom and Anna agree. They ask you to talk with John to help him develop a better procedure for handling the checks. What advise and method of indorsing the checks will you recommend, and why?

BUSINESS CONSIDERATIONS How should a business handle checks to minimize its risk of losing funds through embezzlement or theft and maximize its cash position? What sort of indorsement should the stamp have?

ETHICAL CONSIDERATIONS Is it ethical for a firm to have checks indorsed in blank and sitting on a desk? Should the firm share at least part of the blame if it handles checks in this manner and suffers losses as a result?

Notice that each category is numbered. We will use these numbers to refer back to the matrix as we discuss some examples of the various types of indorsements. Throughout the examples, we will be using the check shown in Exhibit 23.2.

Special Indorsements

A *special indorsement* specifies the party to whom the instrument is to be paid or to whose order it is to be paid. This means that a special indorsement makes (or leaves) the instrument payable "to order." Even if the instrument was issued as bearer paper, a special indorsement will make it payable "to order." The party specified will have to indorse it before it can be negotiated further. Exhibit 23.3 shows an example of a special indorsement.

Blank Indorsements

A *blank indorsement* does not specify the party to whom the instrument is to be paid. The normal form of a blank indorsement is a mere signature by the holder. Such an indorsement makes the instrument bearer paper. As such, it is negotiable by transfer of possession alone, without any need for further indorsements. In Exhibit 23.4, a blank indorsement has been added to the previous special indorsement. Note that at this point the check has every indorsement that is necessary for negotiation. Should the check now be lost or stolen, the finder or the thief could effectively negotiate it. To protect against such an occurrence, § 3-205(c) empowers the holder to

---

E X H I B I T   23.2 | **The Check as Issued**

Robert Drawer		**3728**
210 Elm Street	July 4,	19 XX
Anytown, USA		

Pay to the order of ___ Sam Shovel ___ $ __1,000.00__

___One Thousand and XX/100_____ dollars

Last National Bank
Bigtown, USA

Memo _____ *Robert Drawer*

11 000000011 01 123456789

E X H I B I T 23.3 | **A Special Indorsement**

Pay to Charlie Chenn

Sam Shovel }(1)

E X H I B I T 23.4 | **A Blank Indorsement**

Pay to Charlie Chenn }(1)

Sam Shovel

Charlie Chenn }(3)

convert a blank indorsement into a special indorsement by writing, above the signature of the indorser, words identifying the person to whom the instrument is now made payable. This is shown in Exhibit 23.5 on page 604. Here a holder added the words "Pay to Mata Harry, or order" above Charlie Chenn's indorsement. This phrase could have been added by Charlie Chenn when he negotiated the check to Mata Harry. More likely, Mata Harry added the phrase after she received the check from Charlie Chenn. By adding the phrase, she has protected herself against losing the check or having it stolen.

Convert
Change

Restrictive Indorsements

A *restrictive indorsement* purports to prohibit any further negotiation of the instrument, contains a condition restricting any further negotiation, contains words that indicate it is to be deposited or collected, such as "for deposit," "for collection," or "pay any bank," or it has some other restriction specified as to its use. Because restrictive indorsements could be somewhat confusing at times, the revision to Article 3 paid special attention to this area. The new rules governing restrictive indorsements are found in § 3-206, which provides:

(a) *An indorsement limiting payment to a particular person or otherwise prohibiting further transfer or negotiation of the instrument is not effective to prevent further transfer or negotiation of the instrument.*

E X H I B I T   23.5 | Conversion of a Blank Indorsement to a Special Indorsement

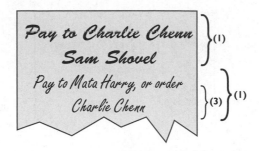

(b) *An indorsement stating a condition to the right of the indorsee to receive pay-ment does not affect the right of the indorsee to enforce the instrument. A per-son paying the instrument or taking it for value or collection may disregard the condition, and the rights and liabilities of that person are not affected by whether the condition has been fulfilled.*

(c) *If an instrument bears a indorsement . . . using the words "for deposit," "for collection," or other words indicating a purpose of having the instrument col-lected by a bank for the indorser or for a particular amount, the following rules apply:*

(1) *A person, other than a bank, who purchases the instrument when so in-dorsed converts the instrument unless the amount paid for the instrument is received by the indorser or applied consistently with the indorsement.*

(2) *A depositary bank that purchases the instrument or takes it for collection when so indorsed converts the instrument unless the amount paid by the bank with respect to the instrument is received by the indorser or applied consistently with the indorsement.*

(3) *A payor bank that is also the depositary bank or that takes the instrument for immediate payment over the counter from a person other than a collect-ing bank converts the instrument unless the proceeds of the instrument are received by the indorser or applied consistently with the indorsement.*

Thus, under the new rules, a restrictive indorsement that purports to restrict payment or negotiation may be disregarded by the indorsee, with no effect on the rights or liabilities of the indorsee. However, a restrictive indorsement that restricts the instrument to banking channels ("for deposit" or "for collection") is a valid restriction, and any person who subsequently deals with that instrument without ensuring that the funds are applied consistently with the indorsement is deemed guilty of *conversion.* This seems to imply that only those restrictive indorsements that restrict the instrument to banking have any meaning or effect, but that the ones that do restrict the instrument to banking have a very serious and substantial effect.

Restrictive indorsements can be confusing at times. Remember that negotiabil-ity is determined by the information contained on the face of the instrument, and that indorsements are normally placed on the back of the instrument. Once an instru-ment as issued satisfies all the tests of negotiability, the instrument is deemed to be negotiable, and no indorsement can remove its negotiable status.

Exhibit 23.6, item (5) shows a restrictive indorsement.

E X H I B I T 23.6 | A Restrictive Indorsement

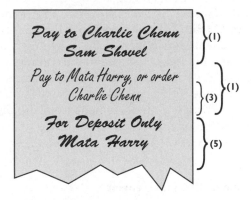

Pay to Charlie Chenn
Sam Shovel } (1)

Pay to Mata Harry, or order
Charlie Chenn } (3) } (1)

For Deposit Only
Mata Harry } (5)

It should be noted that each of these sample indorsements refers to the unqualified indorsement column of the matrix set out in Exhibit 23.1. The reason for this is contained in UCC § 3-415, Obligation of Indorser, which provides:

(a) . . . *If an instrument is dishonored, an indorser is obliged to pay the amount due on the instrument (i) according to the terms of the instrument at the time it was indorsed; or (ii) if the indorser indorsed an incomplete instrument, according to its terms when completed [presuming that the completion was authorized]. The obligation of the indorser is owed to a person entitled to enforce the instrument or to a subsequent indorser who paid the instrument under this section.*

(b) *If an indorsement states that it is made "without recourse" or otherwise disclaims liability of the indorser, the indorser is not liable under subsection (a) to pay the instrument.*

Under this section, an indorsement is presumed to be unqualified. To be qualified, the indorsement must contain specific words of qualification. An unqualified indorsement carries with it a contractual commitment to pay the amount due on the instrument if there is a dishonor. The indorser is committed to the *indorsee* (the person to whom the instrument is transferred by indorsement) or to any later holder if the instrument is dishonored and proper notice of the dishonor is given. The normal order of payment among the indorsers is the reverse of the order in which they indorsed the instrument. Thus, on a dishonored check that had four indorsers, indorser four would collect from indorser three, who in turn would collect

23.2 | FINANCE

QUALIFIED INDORSEMENT

One of the firm's customers recently sent a check to CIT as a payment on its account. The check had been drawn payable to the order of the customer, and the customer then indorsed it over to CIT with a qualified special indorsement. Upon seeing this indorsement, Dan became concerned that the check may be dishonored upon presentment, and he thinks that John should return the check to the customer and demand one of his checks for the balance due. John does not believe there is any cause for concern, but he has agreed that they need to find out for certain. They have asked you for advice. What will you tell them?

BUSINESS CONSIDERATIONS Should a firm have a policy of always using a qualified indorsement? Should a firm have a policy of never using a qualified indorsement? Why? **ETHICAL CONSIDERATIONS** Would it be ethical to adopt a company policy of never accepting a qualified indorsement on the theory that the indorsement would not have been qualified unless there was a problem with the instrument?

from indorser two, who in turn would collect from indorser one. (This is known as the *secondary chain of liability*, and will be discussed in detail in the next chapter.)

A qualified indorsement is one that denies contract liability. The indorser includes words such as *without recourse* in the indorsement. These words have the legal effect of telling later holders that the qualifying indorser will not repay them if the instrument is dishonored. By accepting a qualified indorsement in a negotiation, the later holders also agree to the contract terms of the qualified indorsement. In Exhibit 23.7, each of the earlier indorsements is shown as unqualified; in Exhibit 23.8, the same indorsements are shown as qualified. Note the specific language necessary to change an indorsement from the presumed unqualified indorsement to a qualified indorsement.

E X H I B I T 23.7 | **An Unqualified Indorsement**

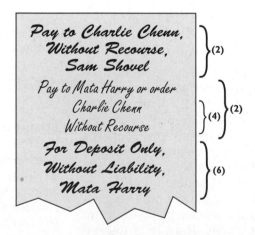

E X H I B I T 23.8 | **A Qualified Indorsement**

HOLDER

At the beginning of this chapter, we examined the transfer of negotiable instruments. It was pointed out that a transfer leaves the transferee in the role of an assignee. It also was stated that a negotiation leaves the transferee in the role of a holder. The role of a holder is important in negotiable instruments. A holder takes an instrument by *negotiation*, giving the holder all of the rights that his or her transferor possessed. However, a holder also acquires personal rights above and beyond those conferred by the transfer. Thus a holder can have better rights than the person from whom the holder received the negotiation. A holder normally acquires *contractual* rights against several parties involved with the instrument. A holder also normally acquires *warranty* rights against some parties involved with the instrument. Also, being a holder is an essential element before the party can become a holder in due course, perhaps the most favored position in the law of negotiable instruments.

A *holder* is a person in possession of a negotiable instrument drawn, issued, or indorsed to him or her, to his or her order, to bearer, or in blank. Thus, the holder either receives the original issue from the maker or drawer or receives a negotiation through indorsement and/or delivery. A holder has the right to transfer, negotiate, discharge, or enforce the instrument in the holder's own name. However, a holder is subject to any defenses on the instrument that a maker or drawer can assert.

HOLDER IN DUE COURSE

To overcome even one of the defenses on the instrument that may be available to the maker or drawer, the holder needs to acquire holder in due course status. Great care needs to be exercised here. The burden of proof for establishing HDC status lies with the person claiming the status. A holder must prove that he or she is a holder in due course; such status is not presumed. A holder or an assignee is subject to any defense that the drawer or maker can assert. A holder in due course is subject only to *some* defenses of the maker or drawer. The holder in due course prevails over most available defenses.

In § 3-302, the Code defines a holder in due course as the holder of an instrument, if:

> (2) the holder took the instrument (i) for value, (ii) in good faith, (iii) without notice that the instrument is overdue or has been dishonored or that there is an uncured default with respect to payment of another instrument as part of the same series, (iv) without notice that the instrument contains an unauthorized signature or has been altered, (v) without notice of any claim to the instrument, and (vi) without notice that any party has a defense or claim in recoupment against the instrument.

The issues of value and good faith are relatively simple to establish. However, the various notice issues can be difficult to prove at times. Each of these three elements of holder in due course status is discussed in the following sections.

For Value

Under Article 3, *value* is more than consideration. Section 3-303 sets out five methods of giving value for an instrument. Notice that each method involves actual performance by the holder, not just a commitment to perform in the future.

YOU BE THE JUDGE

CAN A MONEY ORDER BE A NEGOTIABLE INSTRUMENT?

Two individuals brought American Express money orders, made payable to their order, to Chuckie's, a check-cashing business in Philadelphia. Chuckie's cashed the money orders, but when they were presented to the American Express Bank by Chuckie's, the American Express Bank refused payment, stating that the money orders were stolen. Chuckie's then filed suit against the payees and the American Express Bank in an effort to collect the face amounts of the money orders. Chuckie's alleges that it is a holder in due course, and thus should be able to enforce the instruments against American Express since American Express only had personal defenses on the money orders. American Express Bank denied that the money orders were negotiable instruments. They based this assertion on language preprinted on the back of the money orders. This language stated that a money order would not be paid "if it has been altered or stolen or if an indorsement is missing or forged." Chuckie's argued that the language on the back of the money orders has no bearing on whether the instrument is negotiable.

This case has been brought before *your* court. How will *you* decide the case?[1]

BUSINESS CONSIDERATIONS Should a bank be able to include language preprinted on the back of its instruments that negates negotiability, thus defeating any attempts by holders to qualify as HDCs? Should a check-cashing business have any special policies in place to protect its interests when it accepts an instrument?

ETHICAL CONSIDERATIONS Is it ethical for a bank to include preprinted language on the back of its checks that allegedly denies the negotiability of the instruments? What ethical issues are raised by a bank that tries to eliminate negotiability on the instruments on which it serves as the drawee?

SOURCES: *Legal Communications, Ltd., Pennsylvania Law Weekly* (14 September 1998): 15; *Academic Universe* (14 September 1998), http://www.lexis-nexis.com.

1. The first method involves an instrument issued or transferred for a promise of performance, to the extent the promise has been performed.
2. The second method arises when the transferee acquires a security interest or other lien in the instrument, other than a lien obtained in a judicial proceeding.
3. Third, the instrument is issued or transferred as payment of, or as security for, an antecedent claim against any person, whether or not the claim is due.
4. Fourth, the instrument is issued or transferred in exchange for another negotiable instrument.
5. Fifth, the instrument is issued or transferred in exchange for an irrevocable obligation to a third person by the person taking the instrument.

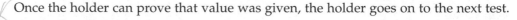 Once the holder can prove that value was given, the holder goes on to the next test.

In Good Faith

The next requirement is that the holder take the instrument in good faith. *Good faith* is defined as "honesty in fact in the transaction." This requirement is actually measured by a negative test. The holder acted with good faith if bad faith is not present. Traditionally, in order to show a lack of good faith, it had to be proved that the holder either had actual knowledge of a defect in the instrument or had ignored facts that would have shown the defect. Usually, all the holder needed to do was to allege that he or she had acted with/in good faith. The burden of proof then shifted to the maker or drawer. It is up to the maker or drawer to prove bad faith, or actual knowledge of some defect, by the holder. (This test was referred to by one court as the "white heart, empty head" test because of the presumption that the parties acted with good faith absent some showing of knowledge or gross negligence.) Very few cases involved bad faith. The revision to Article 3 and the courts' interpretation of this revised article have changed this area significantly. Article 3 now provides in § 3-103(a)(4) that "'good faith' means honesty in fact and the observance of reasonable commercial standards of fair dealing." (Prior to this revision, HDC status could be limited under § 3-305, which allowed a party who had "dealt with" a holder in due course to assert defenses against the HDC *despite* his or her HDC status. This limitation was deemed confusing and was excluded from the revised Article 3.) With this new definition of "good faith," the courts require the holder to show that he or she has "observed reasonable commercial standards" in order to establish that he or she has acted with good faith in the transaction. This new standard is likely to make "good faith" a much more meaningful test in cases in which HDC status is alleged.

The following case addresses the issue of good faith. Note how the court treats good faith, and then decide whether you believe the holder observed reasonable commercial standards and was thus entitled to HDC status and protection.

23.2

NEW BEDFORD INSTITUTION FOR SAVINGS V. C. L. GILDROY
634 N.E.2D 920 (MASS.APP.CT. 1994)

FACTS In the summer of 1987, C. L. Gildroy, a Harvard M.B.A. . . . with many years of experience in banking, real estate, and venture capital operations, was a co-owner of the Hyannis Regency Hotel with Robert F. Welch, Stephen C. Jones, and another. Welch and Jones were at the time also owners of the Taunton Regency Hotel, then under construction, in which Gildroy had no interest. In order to secure funds to complete construction of the Taunton Regency, Welch approached the Taunton Savings Bank (TSB) for a $200,000 loan. Welch represented to TSB that he, Jones, and Gildroy were owners of the Taunton hotel. That representation was false as to Gildroy . . . Ultimately TSB approved the loan and prepared a promissory note for the signatures of Welch, Jones, and Gildroy. Rather than following TSB's normal procedure of conducting loan closings with all borrowers present to execute the documents, the responsible TSB officer . . . allowed Welch to take the note out of the bank in order to obtain the signatures of Jones and Gildroy. Welch presented the TSB note to Gildroy in a stack of documents that Welch advised Gildroy were necessary to sign in connection with applications for refinancing the outstanding construction loan for the Hyannis hotel. Without reading the note—which was titled in capital letters, "Taunton Savings Bank Commercial Loan Note and Disclosure $200,000.00" and bore the words, immediately above the signature lines, "If this note is signed by more than one person . . . their liabilities hereunder shall be joint and several"—Gildroy affixed his signature under those of Welch and Jones. In accordance with Welch's instructions, TSB, after receiving the fully executed note from Welch, deposited the $200,000 loan proceeds into Taunton Regency's checking account at TSB. TSB was not aware of Welch's machinations or the circumstances that led to Gildroy's signing the note. Gildroy was not aware of the loan negotiations, the loan, or Welch's deception. Welch and Jones made required monthly interest payments to TSB on the note for about a year. TSB was then acquired by

continued

NEW BEDFORD INSTITUTION FOR SAVINGS V. C. L. GILDROY, *continued*

634 N.E.2D 920 (MASS.APP.CT. 1994)

the plaintiff, New Bedford Institution for Savings (NBIS) . . . Shortly thereafter, payments on the note stopped, and the loan went into default. Gildroy had never been contacted by either TSB or NBIS regarding the loan until the default occurred and NBIS demanded payment. Upon the failure of any of the comakers to remove the default, NBIS commenced this action against them to enforce their joint and several liabilities. While Welch and Jones defaulted, Gildroy defended vigorously, asserting defenses of fraud and want of consideration flowing to him . . . [T]he judge . . . ruled for Gildroy, holding that neither TSB (because it was the note payee) nor NBIS (because it acquired the note as part of a "bulk transaction") . . . qualified as a holder in due course . . . Based upon that ruling, the judge deemed Gildroy's lack of consideration to be available against NBIS, as one not a holder in due course . . . under ordinary contract principles . . .

ISSUE Was TSB and/or NBIS a holder in due course on the note?

HOLDING Yes, TSB was a holder in due course on the note, and NBIS acquired the rights of TSB, including the rights of an HDC, when it acquired TSB.

REASONING The judge's understanding that an original payee of a note cannot be a holder in due course is belied by a consistent line of Massachusetts authorities to the contrary, both before promulgation of the UCC . . . and since . . . The UCC itself so states plainly . . . Whether TSB, as payee, in fact qualifies as a holder in due course in the instant circumstances depends upon whether it satisfies the requirements that it was a holder of an instrument taken for value, in good faith, and without notice of any defenses against it . . . TSB was undoubtedly a holder of the $200,000 note . . . ("a person who is in possession of . . . an instrument . . . drawn, issued, or indorsed to him or his order . . . "). The payee of an instrument in its possession is always a holder . . . TSB took the note for value when it deposited the $200,000 loan proceeds into the Taunton Regency's checking account in return for the note, which constituted its performance of the agreed consideration . . . As to good faith, the judge expressly found that TSB was "not aware of how the note was signed" and "[a]t the

time of the approval of the loan, TSB had no way of knowing whether . . . Gildroy's signature was genuine." These unchallenged findings are supported by the evidence and are sufficient to constitute the subjective "honesty in fact" test for good faith in Massachusetts . . . [In footnote 6 the court then refers to the 1990 revision of Article 3, which expands the definition of "good faith" to include "the observance of reasonable commercial standards in fair dealing" as well as "honesty in fact." The court stated that the absence of such qualifying language is additional support for the judge's rejection of Gildroy's . . . defense.] Finally, TSB had no "notice" of any defenses available to Gildroy to avoid his obligation on the note, in the sense of having reason to know of it from all the facts and circumstances of which it was aware at the time . . . Despite the judge's findings that TSB did not follow its usual procedures on this particular loan transaction . . . those irregularities were not deemed sufficient to constitute negligence on TSB's part. Further, a holder has no duty to inquire unless "the circumstances reveal a deliberate desire by the holder to evade knowledge of claims made by the maker." . . . No such deliberately cultivated ignorance emerges or can be gleaned from the record before us . . . However unorthodox TSB's handling of this loan may have been relative to its regular usages, no evidence was introduced, nor argument made, demonstrating any deviation by TSB from an applicable standard of care or from reasonable banking practices in similar loan transactions . . . The circumstances of the loan, albeit unusual, were not sufficient to put TSB on notice of Gildroy's defense of fraud . . . Since TSB was a holder in due course, NBIS as its transferee acquired the rights of a holder in due course by virtue of its succession to all of TSB's interest . . . As earlier noted, TSB gave value for the note when it paid the loan proceeds into an account available to Welch and Jones—an indisputable detriment to TSB that legally satisfied the consideration requirement . . . At least two of the comakers, Welch and Jones, undoubtedly received direct benefit from TSB's performance by drawing out the proceeds of the loan. As the document Gildroy signed plainly stated, the liability was joint and several . . . The fact that one of the joint and several obligors did not personally receive any benefit from the transaction is immaterial; consideration enjoyed by any one of the co-obligors is

23.2

NEW BEDFORD INSTITUTION FOR SAVINGS V. C. L. GILDROY, *continued*

634 N.E.2D 920 (MASS.APP.CT. 1994)

sufficient to support the promissory note . . . For the foregoing reasons, we vacate the judgment below and remand the case to the Superior Court for a determination of NBIS's damages and further proceedings not inconsistent with this opinion. *So ordered.*

BUSINESS CONSIDERATIONS Would the court have decided this case differently under the new standards defining "good faith"? Should a business that regularly deals in negotiable instruments—especially notes—establish a policy and then follow it to help

ensure that it is able to establish its "good faith" in similar cases?

ETHICAL CONSIDERATIONS Without regard to whether it acted in good faith, was it ethical for the bank to vary its normal practice by allowing a prospective borrower to take the unsigned note from the bank, and then to accept the note—with all signatures—without question and without actually witnessing the signings? What should the bank have done in this situation to ensure that it acted in an ethical manner?

Without Notice of Defenses or Defects

The final requirement to establish holder in due course status is that the holder take the instrument without notice of any defenses or defects on the instrument. *Notice is present if a reasonable person would know that there was a defense or a defect,* or if a reasonable person would be suspicious and would make further inquiry before accepting the instrument. Article 3 no longer lists the specific facts that constitute notice or the specific facts that do not constitute notice, leaving this area open for judicial interpretation to a much greater extent. There are the four provisions of § 3-302 detailing the requirement for acquiring holder in due course status to provide some guidance. The Code now provides only that notice must be received at a time and in a manner that give a reasonable opportunity to act on it.

In § 3-304, overdue instruments are defined. According to this section, an instrument payable on demand becomes overdue at the earliest of the following times:

(1) *on the day after the day demand for payment is duly made;*

(2) *if the instrument is a check, 90 days after its date; or*

(3) *if the instrument is not a check, when the instrument has been outstanding for a period of time after its date which is unreasonably long under the circumstances of the particular case in light of the nature of the instrument and usage of the trade.*

With respect to an instrument payable at a definite time, the following rules apply:

(1) *if the principal is payable in installments and a due date has not been accelerated, the instrument becomes overdue upon default under the instrument for nonpayment of an installment, and the instrument remains overdue until the default is cured;*

(2) *if the principal is not payable in installments and the due date has not been accelerated, the instrument becomes overdue on the day after the due date;*

(3) *if a due date with respect to principal has been accelerated, the instrument becomes overdue on the date after the accelerated due date.*

Facts That Are Considered Notice. Although the specific provisions contained in the original Article 3 are not included in revised Article 3, some of the things that have traditionally served as notice of a defect or a defense affecting an instrument are set out here. A purchaser of a negotiable instrument has notice of a defect if the instrument is incomplete in some material respect. Thus, a missing signature or a missing amount would be notice. So would a missing date on a time instrument. But a missing date on a demand instrument, such as a check, is not notice since it is not material. It is not material because a demand instrument is payable at issue, and, even if it is not dated, it has been issued. The simple fact of its existence proves that it has been issued. Notice of a defect also exists if the instrument is visibly altered or bears visible evidence of a forgery. Notice exists if the instrument is irregular on its face. This means that an erasure of an obligation of a party or of an amount is notice of a defect. A holder who takes an instrument stamped "NSF" (not sufficient funds), or "Payment Stopped," or "Paid" would have notice of a defense or defect on the instrument. It has been presented, and it has been dishonored or paid. The holder knows this by looking at the face of the instrument. Taking an overdue instrument is also considered notice.

Facts That Are Not Considered Notice. Again, traditional interpretations of Article 3 have shown that the following facts, standing alone, are not notice of a defense or defect on the instrument, even if the holder has knowledge of the fact:

1. The instrument was antedated or postdated.
2. The instrument was issued or negotiated for an executory promise, unless the holder has notice of defenses to the promise.
3. Any party has signed as an accommodation party.
4. A formerly incomplete instrument was completed.
5. Any person negotiating the instrument is or was a fiduciary.
6. There was a default on an interest payment on the instrument.

In addition, it is not treated as notice if any party has filed or recorded a document, if the holder would otherwise qualify as an HDC. In addition, before notice is effective, it must be received in a time and a manner that give a reasonable opportunity to act on the information. Notice must be received before the holder receives the instrument. Once the holder has received the instrument, later notice is irrelevant.

EFFECT OF HOLDER IN DUE COURSE STATUS

The status of holder in due course is a preferred legal position. The HDC takes an instrument free of personal defenses. Although the holder in due course is subject to real defenses, he or she will be able to enforce the instrument against any other defense or defect. This position is far superior to that of a mere holder or an assignee. A holder or an assignee is subject to any and every defense or defect in the instrument, real or personal. A mere holder, an assignee, or a transferee takes possession of a negotiable instrument subject to every available defense. In contrast, an HDC takes the instrument subject only to *real* defenses. The HDC is not subject to *personal* (sometimes referred to as *limited*) defenses.

A personal defense is one that affects the agreement for which the instrument was issued. It does not affect the validity of the instrument. The validity of the instrument is not in question; it is acknowledged to be valid. The underlying agreement is the point of contention. A real defense, on the other hand, questions the legal validity of the instrument.

Personal Defenses

The most common types of personal defenses are those available on a simple contract. The most common of these contract defenses are failure of consideration, fraud, duress, and breach of warranty. In addition, the holder frequently may be faced with the personal defenses of nondelivery, theft, payment, or any other cancellation.

Most of the simple contract defenses were covered in Part 3 and need no further review here. However, fraud does need some added coverage because negotiable instrument law recognizes two types of fraud. One type, fraud in the inducement, is a personal defense. The other type, fraud in the execution, is a real defense. *Fraud in the inducement* is a personal defense because the fraud committed is a fraud related to the agreement. The maker or drawer intentionally and knowingly issues a negotiable instrument to the payee. However, this issue is made to support an underlying agreement, and the agreement is based on fraudulent representations. The underlying contract is voidable because of the fraud, but the instrument is valid, subject only to a personal defense. (Fraud in the execution is discussed in the following section.)

Of the other personal defenses not based on simple contract defenses, only one will be covered here. Nondelivery of the instrument needs special treatment. To issue an instrument, the maker or drawer must deliver the instrument to the payee or to an authorized representative of the payee. If the payee gains possession of the instrument without the knowledge or consent of the maker or drawer, the defense of nondelivery is available against a mere holder. Another type of nondelivery occurs when the maker or drawer gives the payee possession, but with a condition attached before delivery is effective. The condition may be that the payee perform some act, which is then not performed. Technically, delivery never occurred because the condition was never satisfied, and the defense of nondelivery can be raised as a personal defense.

Real Defenses

A *real defense*, sometimes referred to as a *universal defense*, challenges the *validity* of the instrument itself. If a real defense can be established, the negotiable instrument is voided by operation of law, and no one can enforce the instrument. Thus, even an HDC will lose to a real defense. It should be kept in mind that if a maker or drawer alleges a real defense, the maker or drawer must establish the defense as real. A failure to do so will normally still leave a valid personal defense, but such a defense will not prevail against a holder in due course. Section 3-305(a)(1) of the UCC lists the four defenses that are valid against an HDC. These defenses are covered in the following sections. There are two additional *potential* real defenses, found in § 3-403 and § 3-407, that are also discussed here.

Infancy. The first real defense is infancy (or minority), but only "to the extent that it is a defense to a simple contract." *Infancy* refers to the period before a person attains majority status and gains complete contractual capacity. Thus, anyone who is not yet 18 years of age is still, legally, an infant, or a minor. To determine whether infancy is a real defense, state law must be examined. If the statutes or cases in the state where the instrument is issued allow infancy to be asserted as a defense to the underlying contract, the infancy also may be raised as a real defense on the instrument. Even if state law does not give such a broad defense, it is still useful as a personal defense; however, a holder in due course can override that defense.

Duress, Lack of Legal Capacity, or Illegality. The second real defense is *"duress,* lack of legal capacity, or illegality of the transactions which, under other law, nullifies the obligation." Again, the relevant state law will be controlling. If the state statutes or prior cases void the transaction, the instrument also is voided. If not, the defense is merely personal in nature. An example would be the issuance of a check to pay a gambling debt. If gambling agreements are illegal in the state, a defense exists on the instrument, but it is probably only a personal defense. However, if the check contains a notation that it is meant as payment for a gambling debt, the defense becomes real. The instrument itself now reflects the illegality.

Other types of illegality that might affect a negotiable instrument, and hence operate as a real defense on the instrument, include *usury,* agreements that violate public policy, and attempting to do business in a state when not licensed to do so.

Fraud. The third real defense is "fraud that induced the obligor to sign the instrument with neither knowledge nor reasonable opportunity to learn of its character or its essential terms." In this defense, the maker or drawer must prove two things: (1) lack of knowledge of the instrument signed and (2) no reasonable opportunity to discover the nature or terms of the instrument. To establish this defense, the maker or drawer must prove that discovering the nature of the signed instrument was not reasonable at the time of signing. Such proof will be virtually impossible unless the signing person is either illiterate or is involved in a strange set of circumstances. The following hypothetical case illustrates such a setting:

> *Freddy Hornet, a famous rock musician, was signing autographs outside a theater after a performance. Sonya Smith, among others, shoved a paper in front of Freddy for him to sign. However, the paper she shoved was a promissory note, payable to her order, for $50,000. Freddy signed it without reading it, and Sonya left the theater area. An HDC later sued Freddy to collect the money called for in the note. If Freddy can prove these facts, he may have a real defense and will not have to pay the note.*

Discharge in Insolvency. The fourth real defense is a "discharge of the obligor in insolvency proceedings." This area basically refers to a discharge in bankruptcy proceedings. Bankruptcy is a federally guaranteed privilege, and federal law prevails over conflicting state law. The federal bankruptcy law discharges the enforceability of the instrument, creating a statutory real defense on the instrument.

Forgery. Section 3-403 of the Code treats a forgery—or any unauthorized signature—as ineffective against anyone except the person who signed. Thus, a forgery of the signature of the drawer or a draft or the maker of a note is ineffective against the person whose signature was forged. However, if the drawer or maker *ratifies* the signature, the signature becomes authorized, and thus effective against that person. In addition, if the drawer or maker contributed to the forgery, the defense is "reduced" to a personal defense; it is no longer valid against a holder in due course.

Material Alteration. Section 3-407 provides that an unauthorized material alteration is a real defense to the *extent of the alteration.* An HDC can still enforce the instrument as issued but would have to seek recovery for the altered terms from the person who altered the instrument without authorization. Again, if the drawer or maker *contributed* to the alteration, the defense becomes merely personal and is not effective against a holder in due course.

Section 3-406 provides the standards for determining whether an unauthorized signature or an unauthorized alteration becomes merely a personal defense. According to this section, "a person whose failure to exercise reasonable care substantially contributes to an alteration of an instrument or to the making of a forged signature on an instrument is precluding from asserting the alteration or the forgery against a person who, in good faith, pays the instrument or takes it for value or for collection."

In addition to the real defenses, a maker or drawer can avoid liability on an instrument against an HDC under two other circumstances. One circumstance may afford total avoidance: Section 3-403 states that an unauthorized signature is wholly inoperative against the person whose name is signed unless that person ratifies the signing or is not allowed to deny its validity. Thus, a forgery is a possible defense against even a holder in due course. The other circumstance may afford partial avoidance: Section 4-407 states that if an instrument is materially altered through no fault of the maker or drawer, an HDC may enforce it as originally issued (the alteration is a real defense to the extent altered). If the alteration is due to the fault of the maker or drawer, the defense is merely personal and cannot be asserted against a holder in due course.

STATUTORY LIMITATIONS

The protected status given to holders in due course makes abuses possible. If a payee obtains an instrument by wrongful means and then negotiates it to an HDC, the maker or drawer will nearly always be obliged to pay the instrument. As will be seen in the next chapter, the maker or drawer can sue the payee to recover the money paid. However, the payee must be found to be sued, and the finding may not be easy. If the payee and the HDC are working together, the maker or drawer is easily taken, usually with no chance of recovering.

Because of this potential, the Federal Trade Commission (FTC) passed a regulation in 1976 designed to protect consumers. This regulation modifies the holder in due course rules in some circumstances. If a consumer credit transaction is involved, the instrument used must contain the following notice, printed prominently:

> ANY HOLDER OF THIS CONSUMER CREDIT CONTRACT IS SUBJECT TO ALL CLAIMS AND DEFENSES WHICH THE DEBTOR COULD ASSERT AGAINST THE SELLER OF GOODS OR SERVICES OBTAINED HERETO OR WITH THE PROCEEDS HEREOF. RECOVERY HEREUNDER BY THE DEBTOR SHALL NOT EXCEED AMOUNTS PAID BY THE DEBTOR HEREUNDER.

The effect of the rule is to make even an HDC subject to any defenses available against the payee, which is a tremendous protection for the consumer. This rule may have a great impact on the use of consumer credit contracts in the future.

23.3 | FINANCE/ SALES

CONSUMER CREDIT TRANSACTIONS

CIT is considering the viability of making direct sales to consumers on a mail-order basis. As part of this plan, they are considering financing the sales by means of a short-term consumer note. Dan points out that such notes must have the Federal Trade Commission holder in due course notice or the firm will be deemed to have committed an unfair trade practice. He is concerned that if the firm uses two different note forms, it may inadvertently use the wrong form, causing problems for them in their collections. He has asked you what the firm should do. What advice will you give him?

BUSINESS CONSIDERATIONS What should a business do in order to ensure that it complies with the law on consumer credit transactions without extending special treatment to nonconsumer creditors? How important is the FTC/HDC provision on the note if the firm does not sell the note after the loan is made?

ETHICAL CONSIDERATION Is it ethical to refuse to extend credit to consumers in order to avoid special consumer protection statutes, even if credit sales are a major source of revenue with nonconsumer customers?

If the notice is present in a consumer credit transaction, any holder of the instrument has agreed by the terms of the instrument to remain subject to any defenses of the maker or drawer. This means that a consumer could avoid payment to any HDC in possession of the instrument if the consumer could avoid payment to the payee. This is true even if the notice is included in a credit contract with a nonconsumer, as is pointed out in *Jefferson Bank & Trust Co. v. Stamatiou*, 384 So.2d 388 (La. 1980). In that case, Stamatiou purchased a truck from Key Dodge, signing a note that was subsequently assigned to Jefferson Bank & Trust. Although Stamatiou was purchasing the truck for a commercial purpose, the note that Stamatiou signed included the FTC/HDC limitation. (Apparently, the sales manager at the dealership used the consumer loan form by mistake.) When the truck broke down, Stamatiou rescinded the contract and ceased making payments on the loan. The bank sued, alleging that it was entitled to recover on the note due to its status as an HDC. Stamatiou raised the FTC restriction on the protections afforded to an HDC and denied liability, and the court agreed with his argument. While the protection was *intended* for consumer credit transactions, it *could* be used in a commercial loan, and would be given full force and effect when it was. Since the clause was in the note, Stamatiou was allowed to assert his personal defense against the bank despite its HDC status, and was therefore not obligated to pay the note. (This case is still viewed as the definitive case in this area. The new restriction on HDC status included in the revision to Article 3 is based, at least in part, on this opinion.)

If the notice is not included in a consumer credit transaction, an unfair trade practice is involved. The consumer can file suit against any holders who are deemed to have committed an unfair trade practice for all damages involved.

HOLDER BY DUE NEGOTIATION

Delivered
Intentional transfer of physical possession of some thing or right to another person.

When a negotiable warehouse receipt is issued calling for delivery of the goods to the order of a named individual, or to bearer, the document is negotiable. As such, it can be negotiated by indorsement and delivery (if the goods are to be **delivered** "to order") or by delivery alone (if the goods are to be delivered "to bearer"). When a document is negotiated to a person who purchases the instrument in good faith and the purchaser takes the document without notice of any defense against or claim to the goods or the document, the instrument has been duly negotiated. This makes the recipient of the document a holder by due negotiation (HDN), a preferred and protected status in the area of documents of title.

A holder by due negotiation is assured of the following rights:

1. Title to the document
2. Title to the goods the document represents
3. All rights accruing under the laws of agency or estoppel, including the right to goods delivered to the bailee after the document was issued
4. The direct obligation of the issuer of the document to hold or to deliver the goods according to the terms of the document and free of any claims or defenses of the issuer except those specified in the document or specified in Article 7

In contrast, if the document is not negotiable or was not negotiated despite its negotiability, the recipient only acquires the rights and the title the transferor possesses or has the authority to convey. Further, if the document is nonnegotiable, the rights of the recipient may be defeated by any claims or defenses that arise after the transfer but before the bailee receives notice of the transfer.

The following case involved a holder by due negotiation, and the rights of the HDN in a case involving a bankrupt company, its secured creditors, and the holder of the negotiable document of title.

23.3

BLUEBONNET WAREHOUSE COOPERATIVE V. BANKERS TRUST COMPANY

89 F.3D 292 (6TH CIR. 1996)

FACTS All of the states adopted the Uniform Warehouse Receipts Act shortly after it was promulgated. As with many of the uniform acts, however, by the late 1930s it was already outdated. Thus, in the 1940s, the National Conference of Commissioners on Uniform State Laws began drafting the Uniform Commercial Code to replace these laws, enacted decades earlier . . . Adopted by forty-nine states within ten years of disseminating its first draft, the U.C.C. has been hailed as "the most spectacular success story in the history of American law." . . . Unfortunately, in practice, Article Seven of the Code, dealing with documents of title and warehouse receipts specifically, was not successfully followed in this case. Under the Uniform Commercial Code, a warehouse has a possessory lien against the goods covered by a warehouse receipt for storage charges . . . Against a person to whom a negotiable warehouse receipt is duly negotiated, the warehouseman's lien is limited to reasonable storage charges where none are specified on the receipt . . . The Code provides that a person claiming cotton covered by a warehouse receipt must satisfy the warehouseman's lien when the warehouse so requests . . . Further, both the Code and federal Warehouse Act provide that a warehouse is not required to release a bail of cotton until applicable charges relating to that bale have been paid . . . However, the warehouse's lien is possessory; once the cotton is released, the warehouse loses its lien . . . Admittedly, that is precisely what happened here. The Julien Company *was* one of the world's largest cotton merchants, buying and selling around two million bales each year. The Julien Company stored its cotton in several warehouses, including the ones before this court. Bankers Trust, among others, financed Julien Company's cotton merchandising business; it served as collateral custodian for all of Julien Company's warehouse receipts. In turn, L & S Cotton Systems, Inc., served as Bankers Trust's collateral sub-custodian. In order to perfect its security interest in the Julien Company's warehouse receipts, Bankers Trust, through L & S Cotton Systems, took possession of the receipts . . . Bankers Trust insists that by so doing, it could exercise dominion and control over the receipts, but did not become the owner of the receipts or the underlying cotton. Bankers Trust asserts that it is not itself a cotton merchant, was not a customer of the warehouses, and never directly paid any of the warehouses for Julien Company's storage charges. Each warehouse involved in this case stored

continued

23.3

BLUEBONNET WAREHOUSE COOPERATIVE V. BANKERS TRUST COMPANY, *continued*
89 F.3D 292 (6TH CIR. 1996)

the Julien Company's cotton and issued negotiable warehouse receipts representing the individual bales of cotton stored. Most of these receipts contain language stating that "[u]pon surrender of this receipt and the payment of all liens due the warehouse, said cotton will be delivered to the bearer." Most of them also mention the tariffs as specifying charges. Many of the tariffs, in turn, state that whoever surrenders the receipts will be liable for the storage charges. But, none of the warehouses sent its tariffs to Bankers Trust or its collateral sub-custodian, L & S Cotton Systems. Each warehouse did, however, release and ship the Julien Company's cotton, upon the Julien Company's request and direction, without first being paid by the Julien Company for the accrued storage charges. Because Bankers Trust had possession of the receipts, the Julien Company sent a tag list identifying the cotton and shipping document to L & S Cotton Systems, who forwarded these along with the receipts to the warehouses. Despite having the legal right to refuse to ship the cotton until their storage charges were paid, the warehouses waived their lien rights by releasing the cotton and invoicing the Julien Company for the charges. In January 1990, Bankers Trust and two other creditors had the Julien Company placed involuntarily in bankruptcy. At the time, the warehouses had unpaid invoices from the Julien Company dating back six months and totaling over one million dollars; no one ever contacted Bankers Trust or L & S Cotton Systems to request payment. Twenty-one of the warehouses involved here were also plaintiffs in adversary proceedings filed in the Julien Company's bankruptcy. They sought to establish a general lien against cotton still in their possession for payment of the same storage charges at issue here; they claim that the Julien Company owned the cotton, contracted for its storage, and consequently owed the accrued charges. The warehouses' claims were unsuccessful in the bankruptcy proceedings . . . On May 24, 1991, while the bankruptcy proceedings were still pending, the warehouses initiated this action in the district court claiming that Bankers Trust owed the storage charges. The warehouse argued that because Bankers Trust surrendered the warehouse receipts for shipment of the cotton, it owed the storage charges under a theory of either express or implied contract . . . the district court disagreed . . .

ISSUE Was there a contract—either express or implied—between the warehouses and Bankers Trust or from L & S Cotton Systems?

HOLDING No, there was no contract between the warehouses and either Bankers Trust or L & S Cotton Systems.

REASONING To begin, Bankers Trust did become the owner of both the warehouse receipts and the underlying cotton when it took possession of the receipts to perfect its security interest. All of the warehouse receipts purchased by the Julien Company were made to "bearer." As such, they were all negotiable bearer documents of title, . . . and were negotiated by delivery alone . . . Delivery means simply the "voluntary transfer of possession." . . . Further, as documents of title, if Bankers Trust is a holder to whom the warehouse receipts were "duly negotiated," it acquired both title to the documents and title to the goods . . . A negotiable warehouse receipt is duly negotiated when it is negotiated to a holder who purchases it in good faith, without notice, and for value . . . There is no allegation that Bankers Trust took possession of the receipts without good faith or with notice. Bankers Trust's pre-existing claim constitutes value; possessing the receipts as security for previously extended credit is also in the regular course of business . . . Thus the receipts were duly negotiated. Because the warehouse receipts were bearer documents, Bankers Trust owned the cotton when it took possession of them. As the title-holder, Bankers Trust was subject to the warehouseman's lien. Although to do so may have breached its agreement with the Julien Company, Bankers Trust had the legal right to surrender the receipts to the warehouses at any time and demand the cotton . . . The question then becomes whether the warehouse receipts and tariffs may also establish a contract between the warehouses and Bankers Trust. The U.C.C. provides that, unless displaced by a specific provision, principles of law and equity shall supplement the Code . . . Where bailors and third parties owe storage charges, "the warehouseman has ordinary contract rights to payment enforceable in the courts by action . . . such contract rights to payment may be secured by a specific lien . . . Of course, if for some reason the warehouseman's lien . . . is lost or is ineffective, the warehouseman may still assert his

23.3

BLUEBONNET WAREHOUSE COOPERATIVE V. BANKERS TRUST COMPANY, *continued*
89 F.3D 292 (6TH CIR. 1996)

contract rights." . . . Thus the warehouse receipt may constitute a contract separate and apart from the warehouseman's lien. Loss of the lien, therefore, does not necessarily mean that a warehouse loses the right to compensation for services rendered . . . Therefore, if a separate contract for payment exists, it may still be enforced despite waiving the lien. The fact that a contract may exist based on the terms of the warehouse receipts and tariffs does not end our inquiry. Were a contract to exist, for a subsequent holder of the warehouse receipts to become bound by its terms, he must assume the duties and liabilities of that contract. When a contract is assigned, there is a presumption that all rights under the contract are assigned and duties delegated . . . An assignment as security, such as was done here when the Julien Company pledged its warehouse receipts as collateral, "does not ordinarily delegate performance to the secured party, and the secured party does not assume the assignor's duties." . . . Indeed, there is no indication in the record that Bankers Trust ever intended to assume the Julien Company's duty to pay the cotton storage charges. The very purpose of the assign-

ment—to perfect a security interest—goes against such a presumption . . . The Uniform Commercial Code intended that warehouses retain possession of stored goods until the warehouses' lien is satisfied and gives them the legal right to do so. Unfortunately, the warehouses in this case did not enforce their liens. Moreover, they did not even release the cotton on condition of payment by a third party, Bankers Trust . . . Bankers Trust is therefore not legally obligated to pay the warehouses storage charges. Judgment AFFIRMED.

BUSINESS CONSIDERATIONS How could the warehouses have protected themselves in this situation? What should they have insisted on before releasing the cotton?

ETHICAL CONSIDERATION Was it ethical of the warehouses to sue the bank for the unpaid storage fees when it became obvious they would not be able to recover from the Julien Company?

RESOURCES FOR BUSINESS LAW STUDENTS

NAME	RESOURCES	WEB ADDRESS
Uniform Commercial Code (UCC), Article 3, Negotiable Instruments	The Legal Information Institute (LII), maintained by the Cornell Law School, provides a hypertext and searchable version of UCC, Article 3, Negotiable Instruments. LII has links to Article 3 as adopted by particular states and to proposed revisions.	**http://www.law.cornell.edu/ucc/3/overview.html**
Uniform Commercial Code, Article 7, Warehouse Receipts, Bills of Lading and Other Documents of Title	LII provides a hypertext and searchable version of UCC, Article 7, Warehouse Receipts, Bills of Lading, and Other Documents of Title.	**http://www.law.cornell.edu/ucc/7/overview.html**

SUMMARY

A negotiable instrument can be transferred in a number of ways. One way is by issue, the original transfer from the maker or the drawer. Once issued, it can be further transferred by assignment or by negotiation. An assignment gives the assignee no special rights or protections. In contrast, a negotiation may confer some individual rights on the recipient. When a negotiation occurs, the transferee becomes a holder.

Most negotiations involve the use of an indorsement. Indorsements may affect further negotiation, and they may affect liability of the parties. Special, blank, and restrictive indorsements affect negotiations. Qualified and unqualified indorsements affect liability.

Once a negotiation occurs, the holder has the opportunity to achieve the most favored status in commercial paper: He or she may become a holder in due course. An HDC is a holder who takes an instrument in good faith, for value, and without notice of any defenses or defects on the instrument. A holder in due course can defeat a personal defense. A real defense will defeat a holder in due course.

The Federal Trade Commission enacted a special rule in 1976 to protect consumers. The rule denies any protection against any defenses, even for an HDC, on a consumer credit instrument.

Article 7 provides for special protections in handling negotiable documents of title. A person who acquires a negotiable document of title who purchases the document in good faith without notice of any defenses or defects qualifies as a holder by due negotiation. This status confers benefits beyond the benefits acquired in the document itself.

DISCUSSION QUESTIONS

1. Is the distinction between a mere transfer and a negotiation important in determining the rights of a party in possession of a negotiable instrument? Why might this distinction matter to the party in possession of the instrument?

2. How can a holder indorse an instrument to minimize his or her potential secondary liability on the instrument in the event of a dishonor upon presentment? What, if anything, will such an indorsement tell the indorsee?

3. Amita issued Carol a check payable to the order of Carol. Carol sold the check to Lynn but neglected to indorse it at the time of the sale. At that point, what legal status would Lynn possess? What duty, if any, would Carol owe to Lynn? Would Carol have any different duties or obligations if she had given the check to Lynn as a gift, again without any indorsement?

4. Terry issued a check to Phil. Phil indorsed the check and delivered it to Irene. The name on the payee line of the check had originally read "Ben," but Terry had crossed out Ben's name and replaced it with Phil's name. To show what he had done, Terry initialed the change on the payee line. Under these circumstances, can Irene qualify as a holder in due course on the check? Explain your reasoning.

5. Ann is in possession of a check that Dan issued to her. She would like to mail the check to her bank to be deposited to her checking account. How should she indorse the check to give herself the maximum possible legal protection, and why does such an indorsement give her this maximum protection?

6. Lloyd had a promissory note originally issued by Brandy. However, Lloyd is afraid Brandy might default on the note when it comes due. Jim is willing to buy the note from Lloyd. Is there a way for Lloyd to indorse the note to minimize his potential loss if Brandy dishonors the note upon maturity? What should Lloyd do in this case?

7. Charles had a note issued by David. Charles discovered that David was about to go through a bankruptcy, so he negotiated the note to Richard. Richard qualified as a holder in due course. David filed for bankruptcy, and Richard sued David to collect on the note. What are Richard's rights against David? Why?

Denise issued the following check to Bill:

```
                                    3 October 20XX
Denise Jones
1881 Freemont Ln.
Enfield, CT                         $20.00

Pay to the order of _____Bill_____


_____Twenty and no/00_____ dollars

                                  Denise Jones
```

Bill adds the number 2 before the "20.00" and adds the words Two Hundred before the "Twenty." He then negotiates the check to Sarah, an HDC. Sarah presented the check to the bank, but it was dishon-ored due to nonsufficient funds. Sarah is suing Denise to recover on the check. How much will Denise have to pay Sarah, and why?

9. John's Television Sales and Service offered credit terms to its customers who desired credit. To obtain credit, the customer signed a promissory note for the amount of the credit, and after the customer took the television, John sold the signed note to his bank. The notes John provided did not contain the FTC consumer credit language. If a customer has a personal defense on his or her purchase from John, may the customer raise that defense against the bank as well? Why? Might the customer have a claim against John's Television Sales and Service in this situation?

10. What rights are acquired by a holder by due negotiation, and how are these rights superior to the rights of a person who merely possesses a nonnegotiable document of title?

CASE PROBLEMS AND WRITING ASSIGNMENTS

1. On 30 November 1979, Ms. Minix executed a promissory note payable to the order of First Federal Savings and Loan Association. The note called for monthly payments, and it was secured by a mortgage on property located in Pulaski County. On 27 April 1987, Ms. Minix married Larry Tackett, and they executed a second mortgage on the property to Mr. and Mrs. Charles Tackett. By December 1987, Ms. Tackett was in default on the loan from First Federal, which had changed its name to First Savings of Arkansas in 1983; the S&L filed a foreclosure suit on the note and mortgage. The Charles Tacketts were notified of the suit, and they subsequently filed a cross-complaint to foreclose their second mortgage. During the pendency of the suit, First Federal became insolvent and was placed under conservatorship, with the Resolution Trust Company (RTC) appointed as receiver. RTC sold most of the assets of First Federal, including the mortgage note from Ms. Tackett. First Savings of Arkansas purchased the note and requested permission to be substituted as the plaintiff in the lawsuit. Ms. Tackett objected to this substitution, alleging that there was no evidence of a proper assignment or indorsement of the note to First Savings.

    Did First Savings have the right to prosecute this suit without evidence of a negotiation of the note to it? [See *Tackett* v. *First Savings of Arkansas,* 810 S.W.2d 927 (Ark. 1991).]

2. The Aiklens issued a note payable to the order of Schulingkamp in the amount of $10,500, and dated 15 November 1984. The note was given to the payee in conjunction with an offer to purchase real estate. The payee had not accepted the offer by 21 December 1984, at which time the Aiklens sent a telegram withdrawing their offer. On 28 December 1984, Schulingkamp notified the Aiklens that she was accepting the original offer. When Schulingkamp sought to collect the note, the Aiklens refused to pay. Schulingkamp sued, alleging that she had given value for the note and that she was entitled to collect. Had Schulingkamp given value for the note in this case? Explain. [See *Schulingkamp* v. *Aiklen,* 534 So.2d 1327 (La.App. 4th Cir. 1988).]

3. Gilliam loaned Westhampton $345,200. As security for this loan, Westhampton assigned three deed of trust notes to Gilliam. These deed of trust notes were apparently issued by White. White refused to pay the notes when they came due, and Gilliam filed suit to collect the notes. Gilliam asserted that he was a holder in due course on the notes and was, therefore, entitled to receive payment even if White had a defense. White asserted that either he never executed the notes or that, if he executed them, the execution was the result of fraud and constituted a real defense against enforcement of the notes. According to White, the only document he was aware of signing was purported to be a "disclosure statement." White did admit that he had not read the "disclosure statement" very carefully but that he did not know that the papers he was signing were, in fact, deed of trust notes.

    How should the court resolve this case? How much influence would White's experience—or lack of same—in real estate loans and financing have on your decision? Assume that White had substantial experience in real estate transactions. What should he have done to protect his interests in a situation like this? [See *White* v. *Gilliam*, 419 S.E.2d 247 (Va. 1992).]

4. Doyle borrowed money from Trinity Savings & Loan, signing a promissory note that included an adjustable interest rate. The interest rate typed on the appropriate blank on the loan form provided for interest in the amount of 11.375% per annum. After Doyle signed the note, Trinity "whited out" the interest rate, typed in a new interest rate of 15.875% per annum, and appended what were purportedly Doyle's initials to the change. Trinity subsequently sold the note to the Federal National Mortgage Association (FNMA). When the note came due, Doyle refused to pay. He cited the material alteration as a defense to his obligation to Trinity and asserted that the FNMA could not qualify as a holder in due course because the note contained an obvious alteration.

   How should this case be decided? What ethical issues are raised when any negotiable instrument has some essential element "whited out," new terms inserted, and initials appended? [See *Doyle* v. *Resolution Trust Corp.*, 999 F.2d 469 (10th Cir. 1993).]

5. The plaintiff in this adversary proceeding lost over $4 million when an unscrupulous aluminum broker set up phony transactions, diverted aluminum from the plaintiff's intended customers, and failed to pay for goods delivered. The plaintiff now claims that the carrier of the aluminum and the warehouse in which it was stored should be held liable for the loss based on their failure to honor the original bills of lading.

   Met-Al produces ingots from aluminum scrap. Metal Brokers International, Inc. (MBI) brokers aluminum, matching producers with purchasers and facilitating their transactions. Distribution Express, Inc. (DEI) and Hansen Storage Company, respectively, are a trucking company and warehouse owned by the same family. Green, the president of MBI, convinced Met-Al that he was an authorized broker for Emerson Electronics and General Electric (GE) when, in fact, it was not true. As a result, he convinced Met-Al to ship substantial quantities of aluminum to these two companies. After the aluminum left Met-Al's place of business, ostensibly for Emerson and GE, it was cross-docked at Hansen's warehouse. Once the aluminum arrived at Hansen's, Green persuaded DEI to change the original bills of lading issued to Met-Al. Once the bills were changed, MBI diverted the aluminum to other buyers, using the proceeds from

these sales to pay Met-Al. Met-Al believed that it was receiving payments from Emerson or GE, albeit on terms of extended credit. Before the scheme collapsed, MBI had transferred in excess of $13 million of aluminum but had paid Met-Al only slightly more than $8 million. MBI began contracting with DEI to transport the aluminum from Met-Al's place of business to Hansen Storage, a warehouse in which DEI leased storage space, in May 1992. In a typical transaction MBI would notify the DEI drivers about the aluminum waiting at Met-Al's facility. The drivers would proceed to Met-Al's loading dock and announce that they were there for Emerson's aluminum. The aluminum would be loaded onto the trucks, and DEI would issue a bill of lading naming Met-Al as the shipper. Met-Al printed out packing slips to record each shipment, attached them to the bills of lading, and gave them to DEI's truckers. After issuing the bills of lading, DEI would transport its cargo to Hansen, where it leased space, and unload it in its cross-docking area. Once the cargo was in the warehouse, MBI would order DEI to issue another bill of lading, which changed the name and address of the consignee. DEI, as MBI's client, would always comply, even though the new bills of lading were inconsistent with the old ones. In this manner, the aluminum was diverted from the original consignees in St. Louis or Fort Wayne and sold to third parties pursuant to Green's orders. When Met-Al discovered what Green was doing, it suspended any further sales to "Emerson" or to "GE" made through Green and/or MBI. Met-Al was unable to meet its creditors' obligations, filed for bankruptcy in August 1992, and it is currently reorganizing under Chapter 11 of the Bankruptcy Code. MBI was forced into involuntary bankruptcy by its creditors, and a federal indictment has been issued against . . . Green. Met-Al sued DEI and Hansen to recover its losses under Green's scam. Was DEI guilty of conversion due to its conduct in changing the original bills of lading? What sorts of policies and practices should a business have to ensure that it is, in fact, dealing with an authorized representative of some purported third person? [See *Met-Al, Inc.* v. *Hansen Storage Co.*, 828 F.Supp. 1369 (E.D.Wisc. 1993).]

6. **BUSINESS APPLICATION CASE** Michigan Insurance Repair Co. (Michigan) entered into a joint venture with Ultimate Construction for the purpose of doing fire damage repair work. One of the jobs they were to perform was on property owned by Booth and the Madias Brothers, and insured by Allstate. Michigan claimed that it advanced funds to Ultimate to pay for the repairs on this property and that

Ultimate promised to have any checks received from Allstate reflect the rights of Michigan to a share of the proceeds. Eventually, Allstate issued a check for $28,964.94 in payment for the work. The check as issued was payable to the order of "Nella and Chutry Booth and Ultimate Construction and Madias Bros., Inc. and Levin & Levin." On the back of the check were the following indorsements (from top to bottom):

For Deposit Only to Acct. #0051255-04
Ultimate Construction Co., Randy Bidlofsky
C. L. Booth, Chutry Booth
Madias Brothers, Inc. (by Nick Madias, President)
Levin & Levin
Pay to the Order of Manufacturers National Bank
*   of Detroit,*
For Deposit Only, Ultimate Insurance Repair or
*   Construction*

Michigan sued the bank for the amount of the check, claiming that the first indorsement was a restrictive indorsement for deposit to its account, and asserting that the bank violated its duty as imposed by this restrictive indorsement when it deposited the check to the Ultimate account. Was the bank obligated to honor the first restrictive indorsement on this check? Revised Article 3 takes a much harsher attitude toward restrictive indorsements than the prior law. Banks will be much more hesitant to ignore a restrictive indorsement under the revisions. What should a business do to protect itself when it receives a check that has been endorsed restrictively? [See *Michigan Insurance Repair Co., Inc. v. Manufacturers Nat'l Bank of Detroit,* 487 N.W.2d 517 (Mich.App. 1992).]

7. **ETHICAL CONSIDERATION CASE** An Admaster employee prepared a number of Admaster checks payable to the order of Merrill Lynch, signed the checks without authorization, and deposited the checks in the employee's account with Merrill Lynch. The Admaster employee then used the funds so deposited for his personal transactions with Merrill Lynch. Eventually, Admaster learned that its employee had embezzled these funds, and Admaster sued Merrill Lynch to recover the funds taken by the employee. Did Merrill Lynch qualify as a holder in due course on these checks, or did Merrill Lynch have notice of the unauthorized signature, thus negating its HDC status? Should Merrill Lynch have been suspicious of the checks it received from the Admaster employee? Should a business that handles investments and receives large amounts of money be more aware of the likelihood of thefts and embezzlements? Does an investment firm have a higher ethical duty in handling the funds of customers than other types of businesses? [See *Admaster, Inc. v. Merrill Lynch, Pierce, Fenner, & Smith, Inc.,* 583 N.Y.S.2d 408 (A.D. 1 Dept. 1992).]

8. **CRITICAL THINKING CASE** In August 1990, Laminaciones agreed to purchase certain steel processing machinery called a "slitting line" from Delta. Delta asked AITF, a trade finance company specializing in international transactions, to finance the transaction. By the terms of the contract, Delta was to deliver and install the machinery, and Laminaciones was to pay Delta 15 percent of the contract price within 60 days, and to pay the balance in 10 semiannual installments dating from the shipment date, plus interest at 12 percent per annum. As evidence of the debt, Laminaciones was to issue 10 promissory notes to Delta, with Altos Hornos co-signing as guarantor. The notes were to be payable at intervals commencing six months from the date of Delta's shipment of the equipment. Laminaciones agreed to deliver the notes to a U.S. bank. The notes were to be signed but with their maturity dates left blank, and with irrevocable instructions for the notes' completion and their delivery to Delta "against shipping documents for the equipment." AITF agreed to buy the notes from Delta. AITF furnished standard form promissory notes to Laminaciones, with a copy of the contract attached to one of the notes. Laminaciones and Altos Hornos sent a letter back to AITF "confirm[ing] that nothing in the commercial contract impairs the negotiability of the financial obligation." The letter also stated an agreement to be governed by the state law of New York in the event of any disagreement. The signed but undated notes were delivered to Banco Bilbao in New York in February 1991. In April, Delta presented a bill of lading to Banco Bilbao indicating that the slitting line machine had been shipped. Banco Bilbao then dated the notes and delivered them to Delta. Delta immediately indorsed the notes and sold them to AITF for $3,081,438.68. However, Delta had not, in fact, delivered all of the equipment called for by the contract. As a result, Laminaciones canceled the contract in March 1992 and refused to pay the second (or any of the subsequent eight) notes. As a result, AITF demanded payment from Altos Hornos on the dishonored notes. Altos Hornos also refused to pay the notes as they matured. AITF then sued both Laminaciones and Altos Hornos on the notes. Both defendants denied liability due to the alleged breach of contract by Delta. AITF, however, asserted that it was entitled to recovery due to its status as an HDC on the notes. To this argument, both defendants asserted that the notes were not negotiable since they were not dated at

the time they were shipped to the bank, and that, even if the notes were negotiable, AITF could not be a holder in due course because it had dealt with the parties during the negotiations, thus losing the benefits of HDC protection under UCC § 3-305. (New York has not adopted the revised Article 3, so that § 3-305 is still available as a hindrance to some HDCs.) How should the court resolve this case? If the case were tried in another state, one that *has* ratified the revised Article 3, would the same result occur? Explain your reasoning completely. [See *A.I. Trade Finance, Inc.* v. *Laminaciones de Lesaca, S.A.*, 41 F.3d 830 (2d Cir. 1994).]

NOTE

1. "Digests of Recent Opinions: Supreme Court." *Legal Communications, Ltd., Pennsylvania Law Weekly* (14 September 1998), p. 15; "Negotiable Instruments* Money Order* Conditional Language* Holder in Due Course." *Academic Universe* (14 September 1998), http://www.lexis-nexis.com.

24

LIABILITY AND DISCHARGE

AGENDA

CIT is likely to receive a few "bad" checks in the course of its business, and the family will need to know what CIT's rights are in those situations. They will also be granting the bank rights in some of their assets as collateral on several loans. What happens to their collateral if the bank decides to sell the loan? If business goes well, the firm may want to pay off some of its loans early. What are its rights if these loans are paid before their due dates? These are just some of the questions that may arise in this chapter. Be prepared! You never know when one of the Kochanowskis will ask for your help or advice.

OUTLINE

BASIC CONCEPTS

Negotiable instruments are used as a substitute for money. However, at some point, the holder of the instrument is going to want the money for which the instrument has been substituted. Normally, this desire will lead to a *presentment* to the maker or drawee. In most cases, the maker or drawee then will pay the money as called for by the instrument, the instrument will be canceled, and its commercial life will terminate. Unfortunately, such a series of events does not happen every time. Some makers or drawees refuse to pay the presented instrument—they **dishonor** it. When this occurs, the issue of secondary liability arises. Some holders inadvertently fail to make a proper presentment. When this occurs, the issue of discharge arises. These possibilities are shown in Exhibit 24.1. You may want to refer back to this exhibit as you move through this chapter, keeping the roles and responsibilities of the various parties in mind.

Dishonor
A refusal to accept or to pay a negotiable instrument upon proper presentment.

THE CHAINS OF LIABILITY

The term *liability*, when used with negotiable instruments, refers to an obligation to pay the negotiable instrument involved. There are several possible types of liability in commercial paper. The obligation to pay may be based either on *primary* liability or on *secondary* liability. The liability also may be based on contract principles, warranty principles, or the admissions of one of the parties.

Primary Liability

Every negotiable instrument has a primary party, and every negotiable instrument has secondary parties. The primary party is the party who is expected to pay the instrument upon proper presentment. The secondary parties are the parties who face conditional liability if or when the primary party refuses to pay the instrument upon proper presentment.

E X H I B I T 24.1 | **The Movement of a Negotiable Instrument**

Issue ----> Negotiation(s) ----> Presentment <----> Acceptance & Payment (Primary Liability Accepted)

Dishonor; Secondary Liability Claims Arise

Issue	The initial negotiation of an instrument. Normal delivery is to the payee, although it also may be delivered to a remitter.
Negotiation(s)	The transfer of an instrument by indorsement and delivery or by delivery alone, in which the transferee becomes a holder.
Presentment	Demand made to the primary party for the acceptance and/or payment of the instrument.
Acceptance	Commitment by the primary party to pay the instrument as presented.
Dishonor	Refusal by the primary party to accept the instrument; activates secondary liability of the prior parties on the instrument.
Payment	

The *maker* of a note is the primary party on that note. It is the maker to whom the holder will look for payment, and it is the maker who is normally expected to pay the note on its due date. Similarly, the *drawee* is the primary party on a check or a draft. It is the drawee to whom the holder will first look for payment of the order instrument, and it is the drawee who is normally expected to pay the order instrument, either on demand or on its due date.

A substantial difference exists between the position of the primary party on a note and that of a primary party on a check or a draft. On a note, the maker is primarily liable as soon as the note is issued. This is because the primary party, the maker, is also the person who gives the promise to pay. The maker is in a contractual relationship with the payee from the time he or she issues the instrument. By contrast, the drawee is normally not primarily liable on a check or a draft until a holder presents the instrument and the drawee accepts the instrument as presented. (This is not true if the instrument is a cashier's check, certified check, or teller's check.)

The reason the drawee is not normally liable on an order instrument upon issue is that there are usually *two* contractual relationships involved in order paper: the first contract is the contract between the drawer and the payee, the reason for the issuance of the instrument; the second contract is between the drawer and the drawee, the reason the drawee is expected to obey the drawer's order upon proper presentment. No contractual relationship exists between the drawee and the payee on the negotiable instrument issued by the drawer unless or until the drawee *accepts* the instrument, thereby agreeing to honor the order given by the drawer. Thus, a note has a commitment of primary liability from the time of its issue (the maker is legally obligated to the payee or any subsequent holders), but a check or a draft has a mere expectation that primary liability will exist at a future time. (The drawee has not yet made a commitment to the payee or any subsequent holders; its commitment is to the drawer.)

On most negotiable instruments the primary party does, in fact, pay the instrument, honoring the primary liability of the instrument. Occasionally, however, the primary party does not honor his or her primary liability. When this happens, the holder of the dishonored instrument may seek recovery from one of the secondary parties on that instrument.

Secondary Liability

The *drawer* of a check or a draft as well as the *payee* and any *indorsers* of any negotiable instrument are secondary parties on that instrument. Secondary parties face potential **secondary liability** on the instrument. A secondary party agrees, by acting either as the drawer, the payee, or as an indorser, to pay the instrument if certain conditions are met. Remember, though, that secondary liability is *conditional* liability. The secondary parties can only be held liable if the conditions are satisfied or if the secondary party waives the need for the conditions to be met. To hold a secondary party liable on his or her contract (represented by the indorsement or signing of the instrument), a person holding the instrument must prove all three of the following actions:

1. Presentment of the instrument was properly made.
2. The primary party dishonored the instrument upon proper presentment.
3. Notice of the dishonor was properly given to the secondary party.

Secondary liability
Conditional responsibility; liability following denial of primary liability.

It should also be recalled that there are two types of potential secondary liability: contractual liability and warranty liability. Any indorsement that is unqualified (indorsements are presumed to be unqualified) gives a contract to the indorsee and to every subsequent holder that, upon proper presentment and dishonor, the indorser will "buy" the instrument back. However, indorsers who use a qualified indorsement deny this contractual liability. Nonetheless, they, too, face potential secondary liability based on the warranties they give upon transfer and/or presentment. (This warranty liability will be discussed later in the chapter.)

ESTABLISHING LIABILITY

Presentment

Presentment is a demand for acceptance or for payment of a negotiable instrument. The demand is made to the maker, the drawee, or the acceptor of the instrument by the presenter. The rules governing presentment have been changed somewhat in revised Article 3 to more accurately reflect the treatment of negotiable instruments today. The current rule regarding presentment is found in § 3-501. This section is set out below, with a brief explanation of each subsection immediately following that subsection.

> *Section 3-501. Presentment.*
> *"Presentment" means a demand made by or on behalf of a person entitled to enforce an instrument (i) to pay the instrument made to the drawee or a party obliged to pay the instrument or, in the case of a note or accepted draft payable at a bank, to the bank, or (ii) to accept a draft made to the drawee.*

(The holder *demands* payment and/or acceptance from the drawee of order paper or the maker of promise paper. If the instrument is a note payable at a bank or is an accepted draft, the holder demands payment from the bank.)

> *(b) The following rules are subject to Article 4, agreement of the parties, and clearing-house rules and the like:*
> *(1) Presentment may be made at the place of payment of the instrument and must be made at the place of payment if the instrument is payable at a bank in the United States; may be made by any commercially reasonable means, including an oral, written, or electronic communication; is effective when received by the person to whom presentment is made; and is effective if made to any two or more makers, acceptors, drawees, or other payees.*

(The holder is to make presentment at the proper place. This means at the place of payment of the instrument. If the place of payment is a U.S. bank, presentment *must* be made at that bank. Presentment may be made in any reasonable manner and is deemed effective when the presentment is received by the primary party.)

> *(2) Upon demand of the person to whom presentment is made, the person making presentment must (i) exhibit the instrument; (ii) give reasonable identification and, if presentment is made on behalf of another person, reasonable evidence of authority to do so, and . . . sign a receipt on the instrument for any payment made or surrender the instrument if full payment is made.*

(The presenting party must satisfy the reasonable demands or requests of the primary party in order to establish the rights of the presenting party. This includes showing the instrument, showing proof of identity, and signing a receipt for any payments made on the instrument.)

The Code also says that an instrument is not dishonored if the party to whom presentment is made returns the instrument due to the lack of any necessary indorsements, nor is it dishonored if the primary party requires the presenter to comply with the terms of the agreement, the instrument, or any applicable rules of law. Further, as a concession to banks, if presentment is made after the close of business for the day (presuming that the cutoff for the business day is no earlier than 2:00 P.M.), the party to whom presentment is made may treat presentment as occurring on the next business day. (Prior law required that presentment be made through a **clearinghouse** or at a place specified in the instrument. It did not permit presentment by either oral or electronic communication.)

If the presentment is made through the mail, presentment occurs when the mail is received. (This places the danger of postal delay on the presenting party.) If the presentment is to be made at a specified place and if the person who is to receive it is not there at the proper time, presentment is excused. This makes the drawee or the maker responsible for being at the proper place at the proper time. It also removes a possible worry from the presenting party—that the drawee or the maker will be absent when presentment is due and will then deny that a presentment was ever made to that drawee or maker. If a note is payable at a bank in the United States or a draft is to be accepted at such a bank, the note or draft must be presented at that bank.

The rules of presentment are very important because presentment must be properly made before a dishonor can be shown. Dishonor also must be shown before any secondary party (except the drawer) can be held on his or her liability. The only exception to this rule is if presentment is excused.

The rules that govern presentment are fairly straightforward. The holder must make presentment within a reasonable time, or the presentment is improper. The reasonable time concept has two components: The time must be reasonable in both a clock sense (time of day) and a calendar sense (day of the week). In every case, presentment must be made at a reasonable time of day—that is, during normal working hours. An alleged presentment made at a bank or business address at 3:00 A.M. would be improper and would not be effective to prove a dishonor. Article 3 as revised has no time requirements for presentment, leaving the determination of whether presentment was made in a timely manner for interpretation based on the terms of the instrument and on other provisions of the Code.

Instruments that are payable at a definite time must be presented on or before the due date in order to establish that proper presentment was made. Demand instruments are treated differently. The holder of a check must present the check to the drawee bank within 90 days of its date or its issue, whichever is later, to hold the drawer liable on that check. A delay beyond this 90-day period will not excuse the drawer from liability on the underlying obligation, but it *will* excuse the drawer (and any secondary parties) from liability on that particular check. The drawer may be forced to redeem the check by paying cash or by issuing a new negotiable instrument to replace the original check. (The prior requirement that a check had to be presented within seven days of an indorsement in order to hold the indorser liable for the indorsement contract is no longer included in Article 3.

Clearinghouse
An association of banks and financial institutions that "clears" items between banks.

Thus, it appears that the indorsement contract now extends from the time of indorsement until presentment or until 90 days from the date of the check or from the issue of the check, whichever is later.)

Once presentment is made, the focus shifts to the maker, drawee, or acceptor. If the presentment is made for acceptance alone (as when a presenter asks a bank to certify a check), the drawee (the bank in this example) has until the close of business the next business day to accept the instrument. (If the holder agrees—in good faith—another business day may be granted to the drawee to decide whether to accept the instrument.) If the presentment is made for acceptance and payment (or for payment alone, if acceptance occurred previously), payment must be made before the close of the business day on which the presentment was made. (Some short delay in paying the instrument is permitted if the drawee, acceptor, or maker needs to investigate whether payment would be proper.) Any delay beyond these time limits is treated as a dishonor of the instrument presented.

Persons receiving a presentment do have some protection. They can require some proof from the presenter of the presenter's right to have the check; requesting this proof is not treated as a dishonor. They can require the presenter to show them the instrument. They can demand reasonable identification of the presenter. They can require a showing of authority to make the presentment. They can demand the surrender of the instrument upon payment in full. If the presenter fails or refuses to comply with any of these requests, the presentment is considered improper. However, the presenter is allowed a reasonable time to comply with any of the requests.

Acceptance

When the drawee decides to accept an instrument, he or she must sign it. By signing the draft or check, the drawee agrees to honor the instrument as presented. This act of acceptance fixes the primary liability of the drawee. (*Remember:* An order instrument has no primary liability until it has been accepted by the drawee.)

The acceptance can be made even if the instrument is incomplete, but it must be made for the instrument as presented. Suppose the drawee tries to change the terms of the draft in the acceptance. The presenter can treat this as a dishonor or can agree to the changed terms. However, if this draft-varying acceptance is agreed to by the presenter, the drawer and every indorser are discharged from secondary liability.

Dishonor

An instrument is dishonored when proper presentment is made and acceptance or payment is refused. A dishonor also occurs when presentment is excused and the instrument is not accepted or paid. (Under UCC § 3-501(b)(3)(i), the return of an instrument for lack of a proper indorsement is not a dishonor.) The failure of the primary party to accept the instrument within the proper time is also a dishonor. A check returned because of insufficient funds or because of a stop-payment order is dishonored. A refusal by the primary party to accept the instrument is a dishonor, subject to the limitations in § 3-501(b)(3). Dishonor is a denial of primary liability, and it activates the secondary liability of indorsers and of the drawer (see Exhibit 24.2). Remember that, before dishonor, the secondary parties faced only potential secondary liability. The act of dishonor may, and usually will, move this liability from potential to actual.

EXHIBIT 24.2 | **The Chains of Liability on Commercial Paper**

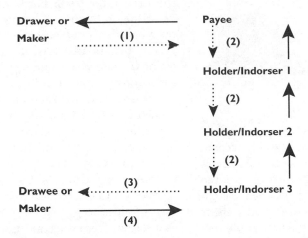

The (potential) primary liability moves in a clockwise manner, following the dashed lines: (1) is the issue, (2) is a negotiation, and (3) is a presentment. If the drawee or maker accepts the instrument, it is paid and discharged. If the drawee or maker dishonors the instrument on presentment (4), secondary liability is activated. Secondary liability moves counterclockwise, following the solid lines. (The number of holder/indorsers may be larger or smaller than the number shown in this exhibit.)

Notice

The holder of a dishonored instrument has an obligation to give *notice* to prior parties in order to establish their secondary liability. The notice may be given to any or all persons who may be secondarily liable on the instrument, and it may be given by any person who has received notice. Thus, if the presenter/holder gives notice of dishonor to Indorser 2, Indorser 2 may then give notice to Indorser 1, and so on. The notice may be given in any commercially reasonable manner, including an oral, a written, or an electronic communication. It may be given in any terms or in any form, as long as it reasonably identifies the instrument and states that it has been dishonored or has not been paid or accepted.

The UCC is primarily concerned with the rights of the holder of a dishonored instrument. Allowance is made for an error in the description of the instrument in the notice. A misdescription will not affect the validity of the notice unless it misleads the person being notified. The notice must be given in a timely manner. Again, there has been a significant change in the time limit for notice under the revised Article 3. This new provision is found in § 3-503, which provides that:

> (c) Subject to Section 3-504(c), with respect to an instrument taken for collection by a collecting bank, notice of dishonor must be given (i) by the bank before midnight of the next banking day following the banking day on which the bank receives notice of dishonor of the instrument, or (ii) by any other person within 30 days following the day on which the person receives notice of dishonor. With respect to any other instrument, notice of dishonor must be given within 30 days following the date on which dishonor occurs.

Section 3-504(c) excuses giving notice of the dishonor within these time limits, *if* the delay is caused by circumstances beyond the control of the person giving notice,

24.1 | FINANCE

DISHONORED CHECKS

One of the checks received as a payment on an account from a CIT customer was returned by the bank for insufficient funds. As is his usual practice, Dan has redeposited the check twice, and both times it was returned dishonored. This is the first time the firm has received a check that the bank did not honor on either the first or the second time it was deposited. Dan recently heard Donna saying something about the need to give notice of a dishonor within three days in order to preserve your rights on a dishonored instrument against prior parties. Dan is now concerned that, by redepositing the check, he has waived the firm's right to collect from the drawer, and that the amount of the check has been lost. He asks you for advice. What will you tell him?

BUSINESS CONSIDERATIONS There are a number of businesses that will hold a dishonored check for a short time and then "rerun" the check through the bank in the hope that the drawer has made a deposit and that the check will be honored the second time through banking channels. Is this a good practice or a bad practice? Why? Should the business give the customer who wrote the check notice that the check has been dishonored but that the firm plans to "rerun" it soon?

ETHICAL CONSIDERATIONS Most banks impose a service charge on their customers for every check presented against the customer's account and dishonored. Is it ethical to present a check more than once, thus potentially increasing the service charges imposed on the customer by the bank, and to have the business also impose a service charge as the payee for a check that is dishonored? When does submission of a check stop being good business and start being an attempt to punish the drawer for writing a bad check?

and *if* that person acts with reasonable diligence once the reason for the delay is removed. (Prior to the revision, the time limit for a bank was the same—its **midnight deadline** on the next banking day. However, other parties only had three days after they learned of the dishonor to give notice, or they lost their secondary liability contract claim. The new rules are obviously much more favorable for secondary parties.)

It is normal for each party to give notice to the party who transferred the instrument to him or her. However, sometimes this transferor cannot be found or, when found, cannot pay. For that reason, a holder should give notice to every prior party who can be located. This increases the chances that the holder eventually will recover on the dishonored instrument.

A failure to give proper or timely notice will operate as a release from the conditional secondary liability for all the secondary parties except the drawer, unless the need to give notice is either excused or the need to receive notice is waived. Failure to give notice, or giving improper notice, may release other secondary parties, but it does not release the drawer or maker.

Frequently, the duty to make presentment or to give notice is waived or excused. When these situations arise, § 3-504 of the Code governs the situation. Under subsection (a), a delay in making presentment is excused if *any* of the following are true:

1. The person entitled to make presentment cannot with reasonable diligence make presentment.
2. The maker or acceptor has repudiated an obligation to pay the instrument, or has died, or is involved in an insolvency proceeding.
3. The terms of the instrument state that presentment is not necessary in order to enforce the obligation of the indorsers or the drawer.
4. The drawer or indorser whose obligation is being enforced has waived presentment or otherwise has no reason to expect or right to require that the instrument be paid or accepted.
5. The drawer instructed the drawee not to pay or accept the instrument or accept the draft, or the drawee was not obligated to the drawer to pay the draft.

Under subsection (b), notice of dishonor is excused if *any* of the following are true:

1. By the terms of the instrument, notice is not necessary to enforce the obligation of a party to pay the instrument.
2. The party whose obligation is being enforced waived notice of dishonor.
3. Presentment was waived, which also constitutes a waiver of notice.

Midnight deadline
Midnight of the next business day after the day on which an item is received.

LIABILITY

A negotiable instrument is a contract with special treatment under the law. One recognition of contract law principles is found in UCC § 3-401. This section states that "a person is not liable on an instrument unless (i) the person signed the instrument, or (ii) the person is represented by an agent or representative who signed the

---

YOU BE THE JUDGE

SHOULD DURESS PROTECT A DRAWER?

James Ruth and Alfonso Frangipane were coworkers. While they worked together, Frangipane encountered serious financial difficulties. Several of the other workers at the plant, including Ruth, loaned Frangipane money. Some time later, Frangipane retired from his employment. at the time of his retirement, Frangipane was entitled to approximately $10,000 in severance pay. Frangipane's employer, who was aware of the loans the coworkers had made to Frangipane and of the fact that these loans had not been repaid, threatened to withhold Frangipane's severance pay unless Frangipane repaid each of his coworkers the amounts they had loaned to him. Frangipane then wrote checks payable to the order of each of the coworkers for the amount owed to each of them and delivered these checks to his employer. The employer then gave Frangipane his severance pay. Soon thereafter, the employer gave each of the coworkers the checks that Frangipane had written to satisfy the debts. Ruth received a check for $2,800, drawn and signed by Frangipane, that contained no restrictive clauses or conditions as to payment. Ruth indorsed the check and deposited it into his bank account. The check was returned by the bank for "insufficient funds." Ruth proceeded to sue Frangipane for the check amount. Frangipane denied any liability, alleging that his employer had forced him to draw the instrument and that this duress operated as a real defense, protecting Frangipane from any liability on the check.

This case has been brought in *your* court. How will *you* decide?[1]

BUSINESS CONSIDERATIONS Should an employer—or a supervisor—become so intimately involved with his or her employees that he or she is aware of the personal and financial concerns or relationships of the employees? Does such involvement by the employer or supervisor represent an invasion of the privacy of the employees?

ETHICAL CONSIDERATIONS Is it ethical for a supervisor to threaten to withhold a benefit from an employee unless that employee honors an obligation owed to a coworker? Is it ethical for an employer or supervisor to become this involved in the personal, nonprofessional affairs of the employees?

SOURCE: *New York Law Journal*, (19 January 1999), New York Law Publishing Company, http://www.lexis-nexis.com.

24.2 | FINANCE

SEEKING RECOVERY FOR A BAD CHECK

Last week, one of the checks received by CIT and deposited into the business account was returned by the bank, stamped "Account Closed" across the face of the check. The check was originally issued by James Smitts, payable to the order of Helen Rudzinski. Ms. Rudzinski, a customer of the firm, had indorsed the check "Pay to CIT, Helen Rudzinski" and had forwarded it to the firm as payment in full for the Call-Image videophone she had ordered. Dan has asked you what the firm can do to recover the amount of this check, and from whom he should seek recovery. He also wants to know if the firm should refuse to accept indorsed checks payable to the order of someone other than CIT in the future. What advice will you give him?

BUSINESS CONSIDERATIONS Many businesses have a policy of not accepting what they call "two-party checks," checks that were drawn to the order to a payee who now wants to indorse the check over to the business. What reasons might a business have for this policy? Do the protections afforded by Article 3 make such a policy unnecessary?

ETHICAL CONSIDERATION Is there an ethical issue raised when a person indorses a check over to a creditor rather than depositing it into his or her own account and then writing a check to the creditor?

instrument and the signature is binding on the represented person . . . " However, once such a signature is found, the signing—or represented—party faces potential liability. The type of liability depends on the capacity in which it was signed. Again, the Code helps. As was pointed out earlier, § 3-204 states that every signature is presumed to be an indorsement unless the instrument clearly indicates some other capacity.

It is important to remember that there are two types of contracts involved with negotiable instruments. The first type of contract is represented by the instrument itself. The maker of promise paper and the acceptor of order paper give a contract. Each agrees to pay the instrument according to the terms of the instrument at the time of his or her engagement, or as completed if it was incomplete. The drawer of order paper promises to pay any holder or any indorser the amount of the instrument if it is dishonored. The second type of contract is the contract encompassed in the indorsement.

Indorsement Liability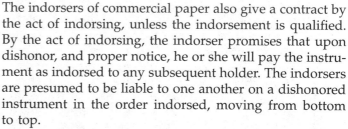

The indorsers of commercial paper also give a contract by the act of indorsing, unless the indorsement is qualified. By the act of indorsing, the indorser promises that upon dishonor, and proper notice, he or she will pay the instrument as indorsed to any subsequent holder. The indorsers are presumed to be liable to one another on a dishonored instrument in the order indorsed, moving from bottom to top.

Two other parties may be involved in contractual liability on commercial paper: the accommodation party and the guarantor. Each of these parties has special potential contract liability. An *accommodation party* is a person who signs an instrument to "lend his name," or his credit, to another party. He signs as a favor, usually without getting anything out of the transaction. The accommodation party is liable to subsequent parties in the capacity in which he signed. If required to pay because of his secondary liability, he is entitled to recover from the party for whom he signed as an accommodator. A person signing an instrument is presumed to be an accommodation party, and there is notice to all subsequent holders that the instrument was signed for accommodation, if the signature is an *anomalous* indorsement (any indorsement made by a person who is not a holder of the instrument is considered anomalous), or if the signature is accompanied by words indicating that the indorser is acting as a surety or as a guarantor with respect to the obligations of another party to the instrument.

In the following case, a party relied on her status as an accommodation party in her attempt to avoid liability on trust deed notes. Notice how the court treated this defense and how her status as an accommodation party was evaluated.

24.1

COMMERCIAL MORTGAGE AND FINANCE COMPANY
V. AMERICAN NATIONAL BANK AND TRUST COMPANY OF CHICAGO
624 N.E.2D 933 (ILL.APP. 2 DIV. 1993)

FACTS On August 8, 1980, plaintiff sent a commitment for a construction loan to shareholders [of Ledgewood Development Corporation]. Hamlett, as president of Ledgewood, and George Zannis, as then-president of plaintiff, signed the document, which provided for a $200,000 loan secured by a trust deed on the Timbers, undeveloped real estate. The commitment letter stated:

Signature of Corporate President and Secretary (including Corporate seal) will be required. Also the Secretary's Certificate and copy of the resolution of the Board of Directors authorizing such loan. Personal guarantees will also be required of Mr. & Mrs. McCaslin and Mr. & Mrs. Hamlett.

The minutes of a special meeting of the board of directors of Ledgewood, on September 29, 1980, stated that the board of directors resolved that the president and secretary of Ledgewood were authorized to mortgage the property to plaintiff for $200,000 for one year, and their officers were further authorized to execute all necessary notes and other documents to effect the loan . . . The trust deed was signed by Hamlett and Mansfield as president and secretary, respectively, of Ledgewood. Five trust deed notes were signed by Hamlett and Mansfield in their corporate capacities and by them and Clara Hamlett and Frank McCaslin as individuals. The notes . . . were due September 30, 1981. A check drawn on plaintiff's account, dated September 30, 1980, was made payable to Ledgewood . . . A contract for the sale of the property, dated September 3, 1981, lists the seller as . . . "Bill Hamlett and Clara Hamlett and Jan Mansfield"; however, the deed conveying the property to Lehman is a corporation warranty deed which lists the grantor as Ledgewood, and it is signed by Hamlett and Mansfield in their corporate capacities. On September 8, 1981, plaintiff sent a letter to Lehman acknowledging his intent to buy the Timbers from Ledgewood. The letter provided that plaintiff waived the right to enforce the acceleration clause in the trust deed in the event of a sale of the property. The letter further stated, "[t]his waiver does not release the original signers of the Trust Deed Notes in the event of default." The letter also provided for an extension of the loan to September 30, 1982. It was accepted by Lehman. Lehman signed a personal guaranty on

September 11, 1981. That guaranty states that Lehman was guaranteeing the credit given to Ledgewood. On September 30, Ledgewood and the shareholders executed an extension agreement with plaintiff and Lehman. This agreement represented that Frank McCaslin and Mansfield had divorced and Frank McCaslin quitclaimed his interest in the property to Mansfield. Plaintiff released Frank McCaslin from further obligations under the notes and accepted Lehman's guaranty. Plaintiff agreed to an extension of time for payment of the notes . . . ; final payment for the balance of the debt was due September 30, 1982; and all other provisions of the notes remained in effect. Eight more extension agreements were signed by Lehman and plaintiff. Each agreement provided for a one-year extension. The last agreement extended the date of payment to September 30, 1990. Only the agreement executed September 20, 1981, mentioned Ledgewood or the shareholders. In 1984, Lehman submitted to plaintiff his personal financial statement for the purpose of obtaining an extension on the loan. Apparently, Lehman died on April 16, 1990, and, on June 26, 1990, plaintiff filed a claim against Lehman's estate for the principal sum and $5,500 interest due on June 30, 1990. Plaintiff filed the foreclosure complaint on November 5, 1990. . . . The court found that Mansfield was not an accommodation maker but a comaker because the loan was for construction on property owned by her and the other shareholders . . . Because Mansfield was a comaker, she was not released by any subsequent extensions . . . The court therefore ordered that judgment be entered against Mansfield . . . Mansfield timely appealed.

ISSUE Did Mansfield sign the trust deed notes as a comaker or as an accommodation party?

HOLDING Mansfield signed as an accommodation party.

REASONING Mansfield . . . contends that the court erred in finding that she executed the trust deed notes as a comaker rather than as an accommodation party under section 3-419 of the Uniform Commercial Code . . . This distinction is critical because, under section 3-605(c) of the Code, an extension of the due date

continued

24.1

COMMERCIAL MORTGAGE AND FINANCE COMPANY
V. AMERICAN NATIONAL BANK AND TRUST COMPANY OF CHICAGO, *continued*
624 N.E.2D 933 (ILL.APP. 2 DIV. 1993)

of the obligation discharges an accommodation party "to the extent the . . . accommodation party proves that the extension caused loss to the . . . accommodation party with respect to the right of recourse." . . . Under section 3-606, which applies here . . . an accommodation party is released from liability on a note when it is extended without his consent or without an express reservation of rights by the holder . . . Under section 3-419, an accommodation party is one who signs an instrument "for the purpose of incurring liability on the instrument without being a direct beneficiary of the value given for the instrument." . . . Under these standards, the evidence does not support the trial court's findings that Mansfield was not an accommodation party. There is no evidence to support the court's finding that Mansfield negotiated the loan or that Ledgewood was a "paper corporation." The loan was made to the corporation, and plaintiff required a resolution from Ledgewood's board of directors approving the mortgage. There is no evidence that Mansfield received any of the $200,000 loan proceeds, but, rather, she testified that the money was deposited in Ledgewood's account and it was used to improve the real estate. The trial court's finding that Mansfield directly received the proceeds from the sale of the property to Lehman also is unsupported by the record because it fails to consider that the sale included other parcels not owned by Ledgewood. Moreover, Mansfield's participation in that sale has no effect on whether she was an accommodation party to the note because once a signer's status has been established, it is not subject to change . . . Plaintiff . . . asserts that . . . the court correctly found that Mansfield was a comaker. Plaintiff's and the trial court's reliance . . . is misplaced . . . Here, . . . the promissory note did not purport to make the shareholders principals, and, in fact, the commitment letter and the August 21, 1981, letter from plaintiff establish that the parties intended the shareholders to be guarantors . . . According to the evidence presented,

Ledgewood owned the property, and the loan was made to Ledgewood. Mansfield deposited funds from the loan into Ledgewood's account, and she received none of the loan proceeds directly. Ledgewood followed all the corporate formalities, including having its board of directors adopt a resolution authorizing the mortgage. Mansfield signed all of the documents in her capacity as secretary of the corporation, and she also signed some of the documents in an individual capacity. There is no evidence in the record from which the court could pierce the corporate veil to find the shareholders and the corporation were not separate entities. The documentary evidence shows that the parties intended the individual shareholders to be accommodation makers . . . We conclude that the trial court's findings were against the manifest weight of the evidence, and we hold that Mansfield was merely an accommodation party. As Mansfield did not consent to the extension of the loan, her obligation was discharged . . . The judgment of the trial court is reversed.

BUSINESS CONSIDERATIONS The officers in this case were asked by the lender to sign the corporation's note as guarantors. Should the officers exercise any special care in signing such notes? Why might the method of signing, or the capacity in which the signing occurs, matter to the officers? Why might it matter to the lender?

ETHICAL CONSIDERATIONS The lender in this case agreed to the sale of the property to Lehman and appeared to agree to substitute Lehman for the original parties. Was it ethical for the lender to go after one of the original parties after Lehman died and his estate did not repay the loan? What could the lender have done to permit it to proceed against Mansfield, and to do so from an ethical position?

If the signature of a party on an instrument is accompanied by words indicating unambiguously that he or she is guaranteeing collection, rather than guaranteeing the payment of the obligation of another party to the instrument, that party is endorsing as a *guarantor*. Revised Article 3 has reduced the obligation of a guarantor somewhat. A guarantor is obliged to pay the amount due on the instrument to any person entitled to enforce the instrument, but only if one of the following conditions is met:

1. An execution of judgment against the party whose obligation was guaranteed has been returned unsatisfied.
2. The party whose obligation was guaranteed is insolvent or involved in an insolvency proceeding.
3. The party whose obligation was guaranteed cannot be served with process.
4. It is otherwise apparent that payment cannot be obtained from the party whose obligation was guaranteed.

Warranty Liability

In addition to the basic contract liabilities just discussed, persons who present or transfer negotiable instruments make certain warranties. These warranties also carry with them the possibility of liabilities, and warranty liabilities cannot be disclaimed as easily as contract liabilities. An indorser may deny contract liability by the use of a qualified indorsement, but warranty liability is still present even if the indorsement is qualified, unless the qualified indorsement also specifically excludes warranties. An indorser could qualify the indorsement so that warranties are also excluded, even though endorsing with such a qualification to later holders makes the indorsement highly unusual. The indorser who would use such an indorsement would be well protected, but the instrument would be very difficult to transfer since few subsequent holders would be willing to accept such a negotiation.

The warranties involved in negotiable instruments are set out in § 3-416 and § 3-417 of the UCC. Section 3-416 provides for *transfer* warranties, while § 3-417 provides for *presentment* warranties. Any person who transfers an instrument for consideration gives transfer warranties to his or her transferee. In addition, if the transfer is by indorsement, the transferee gives the transfer warranties to every subsequent transferee. Notice that the instrument does not need to be negotiated, and the transferee does not have to give value in order to have transfer warranties arise.

The transfer warranties provide protection to the transferee(s) in the following five areas:

1. The warrantor (transferor) is a person entitled to enforce the instrument.
2. All signatures on the instrument are authentic and authorized.
3. The instrument has not been materially altered.
4. The instrument is not subject to a defense or claim in recoupment of any party that can be asserted against the warrantor.
5. The warrantor has no knowledge of any insolvency proceedings commenced with respect to the maker or acceptor or, in the case of an unaccepted draft, the drawer.

Transfer warranties cannot be disclaimed on checks. Notice of any breach of the transfer warranties must be given to the warrantor within 30 days after the claimant has reason to know of the breach of warranty in order to have maximum protection. After 30 days, the liability of the warrantor is reduced by any amount the warrantor can show was lost due to the delay.

If an unaccepted draft is presented to the drawee for payment or acceptance and the drawee pays or accepts the draft, the person making presentment and *any previous transferees* of the draft give presentment warranties to the drawee. The presentment warranties provide the following three protections to the drawee:

1. The warrantor is, or was, at the time the warrantor transferred the draft, a person entitled to enforce the draft or authorized to obtain payment or acceptance of the draft on behalf of a person entitled to enforce the draft.
2. The draft has not been altered.
3. The warrantor has no knowledge that the signature of the drawer is unauthorized.

Not On Test

Again, these warranties cannot be disclaimed on a check, and again notice of a claim for breach of the warranty must be given within 30 days of the time the drawee has reason to know of the breach. Any losses suffered by the warrantor as a result of a delay beyond the 30 days reduces the liability of the warrantor.

The following case involves presentment warranties. The instrument involved is a cashier's check. Follow the court's reasoning, and then decide whether you think the court resolved the case correctly.

24.2

COMERICA BANK V. MICHIGAN NATIONAL BANK
536 N.W.2D 298 (MICH.APP. 1995)

FACTS On November 1, 1987, four individuals formed a partnership, South Central Investing Associates [SCI], for the purpose of "purchasing, developing and/or operating income producing property and related ventures." Approximately ten months later, the partners incorporated SCI Professional Associates, Inc. In 1988, plaintiff extended South Central a $100,000 line of credit that was secured by the personal guarantees of the partners. In July 1989, plaintiff increased the line of credit to $150,000 and subsequently issued a cashier's check for $149,850, listing "South Central Investment Associates" as the payee. In return, South Central executed a promissory note to plaintiff. The intended purpose of this unsecured loan was for the purchase of an apartment building. The purchase agreement, however, clearly reflected that SCI was the buyer. The cashier's check was endorsed "SCI Prof. Assoc., Inc." and deposited in SCI's account with defendant. Plaintiff's account with the Federal Reserve Bank was debited for the amount of the check. South Central eventually failed to pay the promissory note when it matured in November 1989; nevertheless, plaintiff renewed the note on two subsequent occasions. On March 9, 1990, SCI assumed the loan by executing a promissory note in the amount of $150,000 and securing the note by two parcels of real estate that were owned by SCI. A few months later, two partners were arrested and charged with obtaining money under false pretenses. SCI subsequently failed to pay the note when it matured.

Rather than foreclosing on the mortgage, plaintiff informed defendant on May 17, 1991, that defendant had improperly accepted and processed the cashier's check, because the check was improperly endorsed. Defendant refused to reimburse plaintiff the proceeds of the check. Plaintiff then filed the instant action on the basis that defendant was strictly liable for accepting an improperly endorsed check for deposit under Article Four of the UCC. Defendant . . . claimed that it was not responsible because the proceeds of the cashier's check were received by the intended payee, South Central. The trial court . . . granted plaintiff's motion for summary disposition, holding that defendant was liable because the check had not been endorsed by South Central.

ISSUE Did Michigan National Bank breach the presentment warranties on the cashier's check by accepting an improperly endorsed check?

HOLDING Technically, yes. However, since the proceeds of the check reached the intended payee, there was no liability despite the technical breach of the presentment warranty.

REASONING Defendant's liability was predicated on UCC 4-207(1) . . . which provided in relevant part:

Each customer or collecting bank who obtains payment or acceptance of an item and each prior

24.2

COMERICA BANK V. MICHIGAN NATIONAL BANK, *continued*
536 N.W.2D 298 (MICH.APP. 1995)

customer and collecting bank warrants to the payor bank or other payor who in good faith pays or accepts that time that

(a) he has good title to the item or is authorized to obtain payment or acceptance on behalf of one who has good title.

Pursuant to this "presentment warranty" . . . the collecting bank warrants to the drawee bank that there are no forged or improper endorsements. If the bank breaches this warranty by presenting a check with an improper endorsement to the drawee bank for payment, then it is liable to the drawee bank for the amount of the check. Defendant does not dispute that it breached the presentment warranty by accepting for deposit the cashier's check that was not endorsed by South Central. However, defendant contends that it should not be held liable, because South Central, the intended payee, received the proceeds of the check. This issue is one of first impression in this jurisdiction. However, some jurisdictions have held that a bank may escape liability for honoring a check on a faulty or improper endorsement, if the bank can prove that the intended payee received the proceeds of the check . . . This defense is grounded on two basic principles. First, it is aimed at preventing a drawer from being unjustly enriched by recovering for an improperly paid check where the proceeds of the check in fact were received by the payee. It is also justified where a bank's improper payment is not a cause of the drawer's injury flowing from the transaction . . . Finding these decisions sound and persuasive, we hold that the intended-payee defense is available to a bank in defending an action for breach of its presentment warranties. We now turn to the case at hand to determine whether the defendant has established the defense. While it is true that South Central never endorsed the check and deposited the funds in its own account, it is undisputed that South Central received the check. The South Central partners, who were also incorporators of SCI, directed the funds into SCI's account by endorsing the check with the corporation's name. Regardless of whether South Central literally endorsed the check and placed the funds in its own account or another account, South Central obviously intended to transfer the proceeds to SCI in order to purchase the apartment complex. Indeed, plaintiff reviewed the purchase agreement. Therefore, plaintiff's argument that it never intended for anyone but South Central to receive the proceeds of the loan is irrelevant for purposes of applying the intended-payee rule to the facts of this case. As a matter of policy, our decision further advances the intent behind the presentment warranty. In general, the drawee bank will seek reimbursement from the collecting bank under the presentment warranty when the drawee bank has recredited the amount of the check to the drawer's account. A drawee bank is strictly liable to the drawer for the amount of the improper payment where it pays a check over a forged or improper endorsement of a payee under UCC 3-417(1)(a) . . . Naturally, this process begins once the payee has informed the drawer that it never received the check . . . In this case, South Central never informed plaintiff, who was both the drawer and drawee of the cashier's check, that it never received the funds. Instead, plaintiff is utilizing the presentment warranty to recoup its loss for making a bad loan. Accordingly, we find that defendant is not liable for breaching its presentment warranty where it has sufficiently established the intended-payee defense . . . Reversed and remanded for entry of a judgment in favor of defendant.

BUSINESS CONSIDERATIONS It is not uncommon for the drawer of a check to misspell the name of the payee, or to make some other, similar error in drafting the check. Should a business have a policy regarding how it endorses checks to ensure that the endorsement on the check matches the name of the payee on the face of the instrument? What should a business do in this situation?

ETHICAL CONSIDERATIONS Was it ethical for Comerica Bank to seek recovery for the amount of the check from Michigan National Bank when the intended payees of the check had received the funds? Was the court's decision in this case based more on ethical or legal reasoning?

24.3 | FINANCE

FORGED SIGNATURES

CIT recently received a check as payment for a new video-phone system recently. Dan was concerned when the check was received because he thought there was something unusual about the signature. Despite his misgivings, however, he passed the check on to John, who deposited it to the business account in normal fashion. The check was returned by the bank with the notation that the signature of the drawer was a forgery. Dan and John want to know if they have done anything wrong, or if the firm faces any possible liability in this case. They also want to know if the firm can recover the amount of the check, and, if so, from whom they should seek recovery. What will you tell them?

BUSINESS CONSIDERATIONS Many firms use a stamp as their means of "signing" checks. What should the firm do to minimize the risk that someone who is not authorized to issue checks for the firm will manage to acquire some business checks and the stamp and then proceed to "sign" and issue any number of checks without authorization from the firm? If this does happen to a business, would these types of forgeries qualify as real defenses, or would they be mere personal defenses?

ETHICAL CONSIDERATIONS How should a business handle a situation in which the signature on a check looks suspicious to the business? What ethical issues are raised by presenting a check on which the signature raises questions?

The new provisions of Article 3 have removed presentment warranty protections from promise paper, have removed the added protections that were formerly available with a qualified indorsement, and have added a time limit within which the person claiming damages based on a breach of warranty must give notice in order to have maximum protection.

Exhibit 24.3 summarizes the order of liability on a negotiable instrument.

SPECIAL PROBLEMS

As was pointed out earlier, a person's signature or the signature of a person authorized to represent him or her must appear on an instrument before that person can be held liable on the instrument. Thus, a forgery or an unauthorized signature is normally of no legal effect. However, an unauthorized signature can be ratified by the named person, and it then becomes fully effective. There are also some special rules in effect for situations involving *imposters* and for situations involving *fictitious payees.* These two similar areas each requires attention.

An *imposter* is a person who pretends to be the person to whom an instrument is payable in order to induce the issuer of the instrument to issue the instrument to the imposter. Situations involving imposters arise when there is a legitimate reason for issuing the instrument and the person named as payee has a legitimate claim to the instrument, but the issuer is tricked into issuing the instrument to a person claiming to be the payee. A *fictitious payee* is a person who obtains an instrument that either (1) is made payable to the order of a legitimate person, but one who has no legitimate claim to the particular instrument; or (2) is made payable to a nonexistent person, a "fictitious" payee.

Section 3-404 provides the coverage for these two topics. According to subsection (a) of that section, when an imposter acquires a negotiable instrument, "an indorsement of the instrument by any person in the name of the payee is effective as the indorsement of the payee in favor of a person who, in good faith, pays the instrument or takes it for value or for collection." Subsection (b) applies when a fictitious payee acquires the instrument until the instrument is negotiated by a special indorsement. Under this subsection: "(1) any person in possession of the instrument is its holder; and (2) an indorsement by any person in the name of the payee stated in the instrument is effective as the indorsement of the payee in favor of a person who, in good faith, pays the instrument or takes it for value or for collection." However, the provisions of each of these subsections is limited to some extent. If the person who pays the instrument or takes it for value or

E X H I B I T 24.3 | **Liability on a Negotiable Instrument**

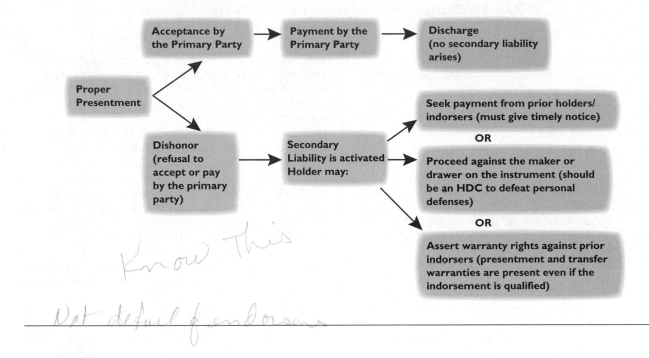

Know This

Not defaul of endorsers

collection does not exercise ordinary care in acquiring the instrument, and if the failure to exercise ordinary care substantially contributes to the loss resulting from paying the instrument, the person suffering that loss can recover the portion of the loss suffered because ordinary care was not exercised.

The following hypothetical cases illustrate these two special problem areas.

Fred stole a radio from Herb. Fred then approached Thelma, told her that he was Herb, and offered to sell the radio to her. Thelma wrote a check payable to the order of Herb to pay for the radio. Under the impostor rule, Fred may effectively indorse the check by writing Herb's name, UCC § 3-403 on unauthorized signatures notwithstanding.

Steve works for Acme. Part of his job is preparing checks to be used in paying bills and then taking those checks to Mr. Burton to be signed for the company. Steve slipped a check payable to Hall and Associates in among the other checks for Mr. Burton to sign. In fact, no money was owed to Hall and Associates. If Steve later removes the phony check and indorses it "Hall and Associates," the indorsement is valid under the fictitious-payee rule, UCC § 3-403 notwithstanding.

In the following case, the court was faced with an interesting set of facts. A company employee had cashed 206 fraudulent checks, and the company was seeking recovery of a significant amount of money. The court had to deal with possible imposter, fictitious payee, and warranty issues. (Note that the Texas courts refer to fraudulent indorsements by employees as the "padded payroll" rule, an interesting name for the phenomenon.)

24.3

TEXAS STADIUM CORPORATION V. SAVINGS OF AMERICA
933 S.W.2D 616 (TEX.APP.-DALLAS 5TH DIST 1996)

FACTS Texas Stadium Corporation ("TSC") . . . is the lessee of Texas Stadium in Irving, Texas. Candace Pratt worked as an accounts payable clerk for TSC from late 1988 until August 1993. As part of her job, Pratt prepared TSC checks, which were later signed by authorized officers of TSC. While employed at TSC, Pratt embezzled money from TSC. As part of her embezzlement scheme, Pratt established a d/b/a account at SOA in the name of Candace A. Pratt d/b/a AAA Lawn Maintenance Service and Repair ("AAA"). To effect her embezzlement scheme, Pratt would prepare a check for an actual vendor, and after having the check signed by an authorized officer of TSC, Pratt would alter the check by either changing the payee name to a version of the AAA name or by adding the AAA name above the original payee name. Pratt also used other methods to embezzle money from TSC. One such method was to prepare a TSC check in a version of the AAA name and then deposit it into her account once it was signed. Once Pratt obtained the appropriate signatures and deposited the checks in her d/b/a account, SOA then forwarded the checks to TSC's bank, and the checks were paid in due course. In all, Pratt deposited 206 checks in her account, totalling $1,060,052.10. After discovering Pratt's scheme, TSC filed suit against Pratt and SOA to recover the money Pratt embezzled. TSC alleged causes of action against Pratt and SOA for negligence, conversion, money had and received, and breach of warranty. In July 1994, SOA moved for summary judgment on all of TSC's claims . . . After hearing the evidence and arguments of counsel, the trial judge granted summary judgment in favor of SOA without specifying the basis for his ruling. TSC and Pratt then entered into an agreed judgment. TSC appeals the summary judgment granted in favor of SOA.

ISSUES Was Savings of America liable to TSC on the checks under any of the theories advanced by TSC in its complaint? Did the "padded payroll" rule protect SOA in this case?

HOLDINGS No. SOA was not liable to TSC. Yes, the "padded payroll" rule protected SOA from the claims of TSC.

REASONING . . . TSC contends the trial judge erred in granting summary judgment because fact issues exist on the applicability of the final payment rule.

TSC specifically contends that fact issues exist on whether SOA (1) was a holder in due course and (2) acted in good faith in accepting the checks. On the record before us, we cannot agree. Under the final payment rule, payment or acceptance of any instrument is final if made in favor of (1) a holder in due course *or* (2) a person who has acted in good faith changed his position in reliance on the payment . . . The final payment rule only becomes operative once an item is finally paid. Final payment occurs when a payor bank pays the item or settles for the item and the time frame for revoking has expired . . . According to TSC, SOA had actual knowledge that the indorsements were not proper, and SOA could therefore not have acted in good faith. We cannot agree with TSC's contentions. "'Good faith' means honesty in fact in the conduct or transaction concerned." . . . Lack of good faith requires actual knowledge of the wrongdoing, not merely notice of suspicious facts . . . Here, the . . . evidence showed SOA had no actual knowledge of Pratt's embezzlement. Thus, the trial judge properly concluded that SOA acted in good faith for purposes of the final payment rule as a matter of law. It is undisputed that SOA changed its position by crediting all of the checks deposited by Pratt and that the payor bank had paid all of the checks. Thus, the final payment rule bars TSC's recovery on its common law cause of action. Because this is an independent ground for application of the final payment rule, we do not address TSC's argument that the trial judge erred in concluding that SOA was a holder in due course . . . TSC contends the trial judge erred in granting summary judgment because fact issues exist on TSC's causes of action for negligence, conversion, and money had and received. We disagree. As noted above, when the final payment rule applies, common law causes of action for negligence, conversion, and money had and received are barred . . . TSC contends the trial judge erred in concluding that Texas law would not allow TSC to bring a direct action for breach of warranty against SOA as collecting bank. Under this point, TSC argues that a drawer is an "other payor" within the meaning of section 4.207 and, thus, that a drawer, like TSC, can sue a collecting bank for breach of warranty. SOA counters that the UCC was intentionally structured so that a drawer sues its drawee bank and the drawee bank, in turn, sues the collecting bank. Thus, it concludes, TSC is prohibited from suing it directly for breach of

TEXAS STADIUM CORPORATION V. SAVINGS OF AMERICA, *continued*
933 S.W.2D 616 (TEX.APP.-DALLAS 5TH DIST 1996)

warranty. The issue of whether a drawer can maintain a direct cause of action against a collecting bank for breach of UCC warranties appears to be a question of first impression in this State . . . [W]e conclude TSC cannot assert a direct action against SOA as collecting bank . . . The UCC was intentionally structured so that a drawer could sue only its drawee bank and the drawee bank, in turn, could sue the collecting bank . . . For these reasons, we conclude that TSC is not an "other payor" within the meaning of section 4.207 and, thus, that TSC cannot bring a direct action against SOA for breach of the presentment warranties . . . TSC contends the trial judge erred in granting summary judgment because facts exist on SOA's intended payee defense. Specifically, TSC contends that section 3.405(a)(3) of the Texas UCC, commonly known as the padded payroll rule, does not apply to the facts of this case, and the trial judge erred in concluding otherwise. We disagree. Under the padded payroll rule, an indorsement by any person in the name of a named payee is effective if an agent or employee of the maker or drawer has supplied the maker with the name of the payee intending the latter to have no such interest . . . Comment four to section 3.405 (a)(3) indicates that the purpose behind the rule is to place the loss resulting from a faithless employee on the employer as a risk of its business. The reason for allocating the loss on the employer is two-fold. First, the employer is normally in a better

position to prevent such forgeries by reasonable care in the selection and supervision of its employees. Second, the employer is normally in a better position to cover any potential losses with fidelity insurance and the cost of such insurance is more appropriately an expense of the employer's business . . . Applying section 3.405 even where slight discrepancies between the named payee and the indorsement exist furthers the policy of the section to place the risk of loss for a faithless employee on the employer . . . Accordingly, we reject TSC's argument that the rule does not apply because the indorsements were not in the named payee's name . . . We affirm the trial court's opinion.

BUSINESS CONSIDERATIONS Should a business have some sort of policy or some system of controls to prevent embezzlement schemes like this from harming the enterprise? What could/should TSC have done differently in this case?

ETHICAL CONSIDERATIONS Under the provisions of UCC §§ 3-404 and 3-405, TSC will not be able to recover from either the drawee or the collecting bank. Is this result ethical? What ethical principles justify placing the entire loss on the drawer unless the embezzler can make restitution?

DISCHARGE

Know

The term *discharge* means to remove liability or potential liability on a negotiable instrument. A **discharge** can take place in a number of ways. Some methods discharge all the parties, and others discharge only a few. The most important and most common types of discharge are explained in the following sections.

Discharge
Release from obligation or liability.

Payment

The most common type of discharge is the payment or other satisfaction of the instrument. In the vast majority of cases, the primary party pays the instrument on presentment and cancels it (or otherwise marks it as paid). If this were not so, negotiable instruments would not be so readily accepted in the commercial world. There are only two exceptions to payment operating as a discharge. A payment will not operate as a discharge when it is made in bad faith to a thief or to a person holding through (receiving the instrument from) or after (receiving the instrument from a party who received it from) a thief. Also, it will not operate as a discharge if the paying party makes a payment that violates a restrictive indorsement. (*Note:* An intermediary bank or a nondepository bank may be discharged even though it ignores the restrictive indorsement, provided it acts in good faith.) In these examples, the bad faith of the payer does not remove liability. The *proper party*, the person who should have received payment, is still entitled to payment, and the liability of the wrongfully paying party remains.

Tender of Payment

If a party tenders payment in full to a holder when an instrument is due, or later, and the holder refuses the payment, a discharge occurs. The party tendering payment is discharged to a limited extent. No additional interest can be added to the instrument after the date of the tender, nor can any other costs or attorney's fees be added to the instrument. Any other parties on the instrument (indorsers, drawers, and the like) are totally discharged if, to collect on the instrument, they could theoretically have sued the party who made the tender of payment.

Cancellation and Renunciation

A holder may discharge a party by canceling that party's signature on the instrument or by canceling the instrument itself. Cancellation may be shown either by striking out a portion, such as one signature, or by striking out the entire instrument. It can also be shown by destroying or mutilating a signature or the entire instrument. To be effective, the cancellation must be done intentionally.

Renunciation operates as a discharge whenever the holder delivers a written and signed statement to the discharged party that renounces (gives up) any rights against that person. Such a discharge is good against the renouncing party but not against any later holders, unless they were aware of the renunciation.

Impairment

Under the UCC section on impairment, a holder may elect to release some party from liability on the instrument. Or a holder may decide to release some collateral that is being used to secure payment of the instrument. However, in so doing, the holder also will discharge some or even all of the secondary parties on the instrument. When the holder releases a particular prior party, the holder also releases any other prior party who might have had recourse against the originally released party. In addition, when a holder releases collateral, the holder releases every prior party, since each prior party might have had recourse against the collateral. There are only two exceptions to these rules:

1. If a prior party agrees to the release of another party or to a release of the collateral, this prior party is not discharged by the release.
2. If the holder expressly reserves rights against a party, that party is not released or discharged. However, the releases by the holder are also not effective as far as the nondischarged party is concerned. In other words, the party who was expressly not discharged does not have any change in his or her position.

RESOURCES FOR BUSINESS LAW STUDENTS

NAME	RESOURCES	WEB ADDRESS
Uniform Commercial Code (UCC) § 1-207	The Legal Information Institute (LII), maintained by the Cornell Law School, provides a hypertext and searchable version of § 1-207, Performance or Acceptance Under Reservation of Rights.	**http://www.law.cornell.edu/ucc/1/1-207.html**
UCC, Article 3, Negotiable Instruments	LII provides a hypertext and searchable version of UCC, Article 3, Negotiable Instruments. LII has links to Article 3 as adopted by particular states and to proposed revisions.	**http://www.law.cornell.edu/ucc/3/overview.html**
UCC, Article 7, Warehouse Receipts, Bills of Lading, and Other Documents of Title	LII provides a hypertext and searchable version of UCC, Article 7, Warehouse Receipts, Bills of Lading, and Other Documents of Title.	**http://www.law.cornell.edu/ucc/7/overview.html**

Other Discharges

If a party is a former holder of an instrument and later reacquires it, a partial discharge occurs. Any person who held the note between the two holdings of the reacquiring party is discharged from liability to the reacquiring party. Also, if the reacquiring party strikes out the indorsements of the intervening persons, that party is totally discharged on the instrument. For example, if George holds a note, indorses it to Betty, and then buys it back from Betty, Betty is discharged from liability to George.

A fraudulent material alteration also acts as a discharge. If the alteration is fraudulent and material, any party who does not consent to the alteration is totally discharged from liability under most circumstances. A holder in due course may still enforce the instrument as it was originally issued, even though it has been materially altered.

Finally, an undue delay in making presentment operates as a discharge for all prior indorsers. An undue delay in giving notice of a dishonor will also operate as a discharge of all prior indorsers and may even discharge a drawer or maker.

SUMMARY

As formal contracts, negotiable instruments carry certain contract responsibilities and liabilities. The maker of promise paper has primary liability on the instrument from its issue date. The drawee of order paper faces potential primary liability. However, once the drawee accepts the instrument, the drawee has primary liability. If the primary liability is denied or refused, every prior holder is secondarily liable. In addition, the drawer of order paper is secondarily liable on a dishonored instrument.

For the holder to enforce the primary liability of the instrument, proper presentment must be made to the maker or drawee. At that point, the primary party will either accept the instrument or dishonor it. If dishonor occurs, the holder will give notice to prior parties to establish their secondary liability.

Negotiable instruments carry both contract liability and warranty liability. The warranty liability may be transfer warranty liability or presentment warranty liability. Transfer warranties exist on all negotiable instruments that are transferred for consideration. Presentment warranties only apply to order paper that is presented to the drawee for acceptance or payment.

The final stage for most instruments is discharge. Discharge can be, and normally is, based on payment or satisfaction. Some discharges are partial, discharging either a portion of the liability or a few of the parties. Tender of payment is a partial discharge. Cancellation, renunciation, and impairment are all discharges of some of the secondary parties.

DISCUSSION QUESTIONS

1. What is meant by *primary liability* under Article 3, and when does it exist on a negotiable instrument? What is meant by *secondary liability* under Article 3, and when does it exist on a negotiable instrument? Is it possible for a party to be both primarily and secondarily liable on the same instrument at the same time?

2. In order to show proper presentment, what must the presenting party establish? What are the rights of the primary party when a presentment is made?

3. There are five transfer warranties involved with negotiable instruments. Who gives transfer warranties, and to whom are they given?

4. What is an *impairment* as it relates to discharge of liability on a negotiable instrument? Why is a discharge granted to some of the parties on an instrument when an impairment occurs?

5. What are the presentment warranties associated with negotiable instruments? Who receives the benefit of these warranties? Who gives these warranties?

6. Who or what is an *imposter* under Article 3? Who or what is a *fictitious payee* under Article 3? How is an indorsement by an imposter or by a fictitious payee treated?

7. Presume that a holder makes proper presentment of a negotiable instrument and that the instrument is dishonored upon presentment. The holder now has three options. What are the three options available to the holder of an instrument that has been dishonored after proper presentment? Under what circumstances should the holder pursue each—or all—of the options available? Explain your reasoning.

8. When a person indorses a check, that person gives an additional contract to the indorsee. How long is that indorsement contract valid? What must the indorsee (or a subsequent transferee) do in order to hold the indorser of the check to the indorsement contract?

9. Amy transferred a note to Jim by delivery alone. At the time of the transfer, the maker of the note was involved in an insolvency proceeding. Because of the insolvency proceeding, Jim was unable to collect the note from the maker. What are Jim's rights against Amy? Would it alter his rights if Amy had indorsed and delivered the note to him initially? Why?

10. Joe issued an interest-bearing demand note to Jane. Jane negotiated the note to Larry. Larry, in turn, negotiated it to Tom. Joe offered to pay Tom, but Tom refused the payment. What effect does Tom's refusal to accept the tender of payment have on the potential secondary liability of each of the other parties who have negotiated the note?

CASE PROBLEMS AND WRITING ASSIGNMENTS

1. Myles and Theresa Bryant issued a promissory note payable to the order of Thomas, with monthly install-ments to begin 1 April 1989. The note stated that pay-ment in full was due if the note were to become two months past due. In November 1989, Thomas sued Myles Bryant for the full amount of the note, alleging that no payments had ever been made. Bryant denied liability, asserting that he and his wife had separated earlier and that he never received any consideration for the note. He also alleged that Thomas was guilty of fraud in procuring the note and that Thomas had failed to meet several conditions orally agreed to with regard to the note. Would a failure by Thomas to sat-isfy the conditions to which he agreed when he ac-cepted the note preclude his ability to recover on the note? Would this same failure to satisfy conditions af-fect a third person taking the note by negotiation from Thomas? Explain your reasoning. [See *Thomas* v. *Bryant,* 597 So.2d 1065 (La.App. 2d Cir. 1992).]

2. Erb was a financial consultant at Shearson Lehman in Provo, Utah, rising to the rank of vice president by 1987. In 1987, Erb was contacted by Matthews, the controller for WordPerfect Corporation and its sister firm, Utah Softcopy, concerning the establishment of several accounts for the firms and for the principals of WordPerfect. Erb established the three accounts and assumed responsibility for managing all three. Shortly thereafter, Matthews delivered a check to Erb for $460,150.23. The check was payable to the order of ABP Investments and was to be used for the Word-Perfect principals. At the time, there was no "ABP In-vestments" account with Shearson, although the WordPerfect principals did business elsewhere under this name. Matthews offered to replace the check with another, payable to the name on the account used at Shearson. However, Erb assured Matthews that there would be no problem with the check as drawn. Erb then opened an account at Shearson in the name ABP Investments and forged the signature of one of the principals. Over the next 11 months, Erb procured and negotiated 37 checks drawn by Shearson Lehman and payable to the order of ABP Investments. The checks, totaling $504,295.30, were all deposited to Erb's personal account at Wasatch Bank, with forged indorsements for ABP Investments. None of the checks contained Erb's indorsement. Eventually, an audit of Erb's handling of the various WordPerfect ac-counts revealed the extent of his misappropriations. Shearson settled with WordPerfect for $1,208,903, and then sued Wasatch Bank for negligence, breach of warranty, and conversion. Wasatch denied liability.

Is a depository bank liable to the drawer of a check when the drawer's faithless employee induces the drawer to issue checks, fraudulently indorses them in the name of the specified payee, and absconds with the funds? What ethical considera-tions are raised by the facts in this case? [See *Shear-son Lehman Brothers, Inc.* v. *Wasatch Bank,* 788 F.Supp. 1184 (D.Utah 1992).]

3. Vincent and Mary Jane Catania were married. They resided on property owned by Vincent's mother and secured by a mortgage. Vincent and Mary Jane were to pay the mortgage and the real estate taxes, but title was to remain in the name of Vincent's mother. In 1977, the mother conveyed title to the property to Joseph Catania, Vincent's brother, without his knowl-edge or consent. (He did not learn of his title to the land until some time after 1980, when he received a tax notice from the town of Enfield.) Vincent and Mary Jane divorced in 1980. The divorce decree called for Vincent to pay the mortgage, insurance, and taxes on the property until their youngest child reached the age of 18. The decree also contained certain conditions calling for the sale of the property and the division of the proceeds between Vincent and Mary Jane. In 1982, Vincent arranged for a second mortgage on the prop-erty, and Joseph—the owner of record of the prop-erty—also signed the loan agreement. Eventually, Vincent defaulted on the mortgage, and Mary Jane paid the bank, receiving an assignment of the mort-gage in exchange. Since Vincent had procured relief through bankruptcy, Mary Jane sued Joseph on the note. Joseph asserted that he was merely an accom-modation party on the mortgage and was not liable to Mary Jane. Was Joseph an accommodation on the note, or was he a comaker on the note? After deciding this case, ask yourself "Why would a person indorse a note as an accommodation party?" [See *Catania* v. *Catania,* 601 A.2d 543 (Conn.App. 1992).]

4. Roberta Ward married Lee Adams in 1951. In 1967, Adams executed a general power of attorney autho-rizing his wife to sign his name and to transact busi-ness on his behalf. In 1981, the parties divorced, with Adams awarded life insurance policies on his life as his separate property in the divorce decree. In May 1981, Ward received two checks from the insurance company—one a dividend, the other representing a portion of the cash surrender value of the policy. Since the 1967 power of attorney was still valid, Ward signed both checks for Adams. She then signed both checks for Burt (her second husband) and deposited

them in Burt's account. In 1983, Adams filed an affidavit of forgery and recovered the amount of both checks from the depository bank, PSNB. PSNB then sued Burt for breach of warranty, alleging that the signatures on the checks were not valid or authorized. Burt denied liability. Were the signatures of Adams's name by Ward on the checks valid or authorized? What should Adams have done differently in this case to better protect his interests? [See *Puget Sound Nat'l Bank* v. *Burt*, 786 P.2d 300 (Wash.App. 1990).]

5. Edward Bauerband (Bauerband) and his wife (Michelle Bauerband) had been customers of Minster State Bank, an Ohio bank, for many years prior to the events in this case. Bauerband applied for a loan from Minster purportedly for himself and his wife. The loan officer knew both Bauerband and his wife. Minster mailed loan documents to Bauerband in Massachusetts, including a promissory note to be executed by Bauerband and his wife. Bauerband forged his wife's name on these documents. The signed note acknowledged falsely that Michelle had received a copy of the note. On return of these documents, Minster issued a bank customer's check payable to the order of both Bauerband and his wife and mailed it to their home in Massachusetts. Bauerband endorsed the check for himself, forged his wife's name on the check, and deposited the check into a business account that he maintained at BayBank Middlesex. Bauerband's wife had no knowledge of the loan transaction, the note, or the check.

    Minster claims that BayBank violated the warranty provisions of [the Code]. . . . In response, BayBank urges that Bauerband was an imposter, which exculpates BayBank under the provisions of [the Code]. . . . Apart from the "imposter" statute, in the face of Bauerband's forgery of his wife's name on the check, BayBank would be liable for warranting to Minster that "all signatures are genuine or authorized" under [the Code].

    The trial court ruled on a motion for summary judgment that Bauerband was an imposter and ordered judgment for BayBank. Minster requested a report to the Appellate Division of the District Court Department, which affirmed the judge's ruling and dismissed the report. Minster appealed, and the case was transferred to the Supreme Court on its own motion. Did the forged indorsement by Bauerband of his wife's name make him an imposter within the sweep of Article 3? What legal significance is there to the question of whether Bauerband "qualifies" as an imposter under Article 3? After resolving the case, ask yourself why the court seemed to have so much difficulty deciding if Bauerband was an imposter?

Does it seem like the court was more concerned (tacitly) with determining which bank was more responsible for Bauerband's acquisition of the money than it was with whether Bauerband was truly an imposter? [See *Minster State Bank* v. *Baybank Middlesex*, 611 N.E.2d 200 (Mass. 1993).]

6. **BUSINESS APPLICATION CASE** Elias had a bank account with First Florida Bank. On 13 August 1986, he wrote a $10,000 check payable to National Computer Consultants, Inc. National Computer indorsed the check and deposited it in its account with Union Bank. Union Bank posted the check to National Computer's account on Thursday, 14 August. Union Bank presented the check to First Florida on the following day at the local clearinghouse. There, Union Bank was credited $10,000, and First Florida was debited $10,000. The clearinghouse forwarded the check to First Florida. On 14 August, Elias gave a verbal stop-payment order to First Florida. Under statutory provisions, First Florida had until midnight Monday, 18 August, to notify Union Bank of its intention to dishonor this check. As a result, First Florida took steps on Monday, 18 August, to return the check to Union Bank via the clearinghouse. Unfortunately, First Florida misrouted the check when it returned the item to the clearinghouse by addressing it to the wrong bank. That bank received the misrouted check and returned it to First Florida through the clearinghouse on 20 August. First Florida did not return the check to the clearinghouse for Union Bank until 21 August. In addition to returning the check, First Florida tried to give Union Bank notice of the dishonor. In August 1986, First Florida was a member of a service offered by Security Pacific to give notice of dishonor on checks over $2,500. Security Pacific provided notice through a computer system to banks participating in its service. It telephonically informed nonmember banks of dishonored checks. Union Bank was not a member of the Security Pacific system. First Florida did not request Security Pacific to give notice of dishonor to Union Bank until 5:54 P.M. on 18 August 1986. Security Pacific gave that notice by telephone at 11:40 A.M. on 19 August 1986. The trial court ruled for First Florida, stating that a "rule of reasonableness" should control, and that First Florida had acted reasonably. Union Bank appealed. Did First Florida give proper notice of dishonor to Union Bank by its midnight deadline? Why should a bank have to adhere to a "midnight deadline" when nonbanks have 30 days to give notice of a dishonor? What public policy reasons might exist for imposing such high standards and requirements on a bank in the area of returned and dishonored checks? Is it ethical to argue for a "rule of reasonableness" when

one's own negligence was the reason for failing to meet a statutory deadline? [See *First Union Nat'l Bank of Florida* v. *First Florida Bank, N.A.*, 616 So.2d 1168 (Fla.App. 2d Dist. 1993).]

7. **ETHICAL APPLICATION CASE** Pauline Pagani was an employee of Maryland Industrial Finishing Company, Inc. (MIFCO) from 13 April 1989 through 23 February 1990. In June 1989, Pagani began embezzling funds by depositing some of MIFCO's checks into her own account at Citizens Bank of Maryland, rather than into MIFCO's account at Citizens. She continued this practice until February 1990, when Brenda Alexander discovered the embezzlement. MIFCO later sued Citizens to recover the funds that were deposited into Pagani's personal account. MIFCO alleged, among other things, that Citizens converted the checks under the UCC and that Citizens was negligent. At trial, Brenda Alexander testified that MIFCO is a small company with seven employees and that it has had an account with Citizens since 1976. Alexander also testified that she instructed Pagani that when MIFCO received a check from a customer, she should retrieve the invoice from the file, mark it paid, and write on it the check information, and to then place the invoice in the "paid" file. Pagani also was instructed to indorse the check by stamping the back with two stamps—one with the name and address of MIFCO and the other containing the words "For deposit only." Pagani was then directed to deposit the indorsed checks into MIFCO's account at Citizens Bank and to file a copy of the deposit slip in MIFCO's files. Were the indorsements made by Pagani "unauthorized" since she did not make the indorsements restrictive, as she had been instructed to do? Was the bank liable under conversion, negligence, or breach of warranty theories? What ethical issues are raised by the facts in this case? How might the parties have acted differently if they were more concerned with ethics than with law? [See *Citizens Bank of Maryland* v. *Maryland Industrial Finishing Co., Inc.*, 659 A.2d 313 (Md.App. 1995).]

8. **CRITICAL THINKING CASE** France bought a used tractor, which he financed with a loan from Ford Motor Credit Company. The purchase price of the tractor was $10,035. France paid $2,000 down, financing the balance. The total payments called for, including finance charges, was $9,845,76, to be paid in 47 monthly payments. The installment note that France signed gave him permission to prepay the full obligation without penalty. On two different occasions, France tried to prepay the balance due, without success. On both occasions, errors in the encoding of the checks he had drawn and issued resulted in payment of less than the balance due. Prior to the first payment due date, France decided to pay off the loan. He contacted Ford Motor Credit and was told that the payoff figure was $8,506.19. France then wrote a check for that amount and forwarded it to Mellon Financial Services, as directed by the Ford Motor Credit office. Unfortunately, the check was encoded for the amount $506.19, and that amount was credited toward France's debt and debited to his checking account. When this encoding error was discovered, France drew a second check, in the amount of $8,000, and sent it to the Mellon Financial Services office to pay off the loan. The check included the following words stamped on the face of the check:

"AMOUNT GUARANTEED TO BE" immediately followed by the handwritten figure $8,000.

Again the check was misencoded, this time for $8, which amount was applied to the France debt and debited to France's checking account. France made no further payments, and Ford Motor Credit initiated a replevin action against France, seeking recovery of the tractor. France objects to the claim asserted by Ford Motor Credit. He alleges that Ford Motor Credit was negligent in the handling of the two checks, and that he (France) has met his contractual obligations on the loan, and that any claims Ford Motor Credit has should be asserted against Mellon Financial Services rather than France. How should this case be resolved? What legal and ethical issues are raised by these facts? What business practices and policies should Mellon Financial and/or Ford Motor Credit have instituted to avoid these sorts of problems? [See *France* v. *Ford Motor Credit Company*, 913 S.W.2d 770 (Ark. 1996).]

NOTE

1. "Check Is Tendered Under Duress, Given Threat of Withheld Severance Pay." *New York Law Journal*, (19 January 1999), New York Publishing Company, http://www.lexis-nexis.com.

25

BANK–CUSTOMER RELATIONS/ ELECTRONIC FUNDS TRANSFERS

CALL-IMAGE TECHNOLOGY

A G E N D A

The Kochanowskis will need to open a checking account for the firm, and they will need to know what sort of account they should get and what sort of financial institution they should deal with. Various family members also need checking accounts, and they will need to know the same things on an individual basis. Most of the banks in their community offer ATM cards. Should they get an ATM card, a debit card, both, or neither? What are their rights and responsibilities when dealing with banks? You may be asked these and other questions during the coverage of this chapter. Be prepared! You never know when one of the Kochanowskis will ask for your help or advice.

O U T L I N E

Basic Concepts
The Customer: Rights and Duties
The Bank: Rights and Duties
Special Problems

Funds Transfers
Summary
Discussion Questions
Case Problems and Writing Assignments

BASIC CONCEPTS

In the United States today, nearly every business organization has a checking account. In addition, many, if not most, of the adults in this country also have checking accounts. Many workers receive their pay by check. Checking account information is normally required on credit and loan applications, and increasingly, is asked for on job applications. Millions of checks move through the economic system each day. Yet few people actually understand the checking system they are using.

A new customer walking into a bank follows the signs that lead to the "New Accounts" desk. Upon sitting down at this desk, the novice depositor is inundated with seemingly trivial information and details. Several different types of accounts—interest-plus checking, free checking, ready-reserve checking, and so on—are briefly mentioned in passing; multiple colors and styles of checks are displayed; a "signature card" is handed to the customer with instructions to "sign at the X"; a deposit ticket is prepared; and a deposit is made in the customer's name in a new account. Before really knowing what has happened, the new customer is back on the street, the proud possessor of a personal checking account. More likely than not, the customer has no idea of what all this means legally.

By signing a signature card, the customer has entered a multirole legal relationship with the bank. The signature card represents a contract with the bank that the customer accepts on signing the card, even though he or she probably is unaware of any of its terms or conditions. In addition, the customer is now governed by Article 4 of the Uniform Commercial Code (UCC), which governs Bank Deposits and Collections. Article 4 was revised, together with Article 3, in 1990. As of May 1999, 47 states and the District of Columbia have adopted the revised versions of both articles (New York, Rhode Island, and South Carolina still follow the earlier versions of both articles). The customer has entered into an agency relationship and has agreed to a debtor–creditor relationship as well.

The contract that the customer entered into is relatively simple. It covers things like service charges that can be imposed by the bank for various services, minimum balance requirements for the customer's account, and technical terms and conditions. Likewise, the coverage afforded by Article 4 of the Code is fairly simple; basically, it spells out the mandatory rights and duties of each of the parties. These will be dealt with later in this chapter.

The agency portion of the agreement is a complete surprise to most depositors. To put it simply, the bank is the agent, and the depositor is the principal. An agent is required to obey any lawful orders of the principal that deal with the agency. This explains, in part, the language used on a check. The depositor (principal) is ordering the bank (agent) to "Pay to the order of" someone. The check does not say, "Please pay" or "I would appreciate it if you would pay." It says, "PAY!" This language is an order, and the order is usually lawful. Therefore, the bank must obey that order or face possible liability to the depositor for the disobedience.

The final relationship is variable. Normally, the customer will have a positive balance in the checking account. As a result, the customer is a creditor of the bank, and the bank is a debtor of the customer. Occasionally, the bank will pay an **overdraft** on the customer's account. When this happens, the customer has a negative balance in the account, and the roles reverse. Now the bank is a creditor of the customer, and the customer is a debtor to the bank.

Overdraft
A check or draft written by the drawer for an amount in excess of the amount on account, and accepted by the drawee.

25.1 | FINANCE

CIT OPENS A CHECKING ACCOUNT

CIT will be receiving money from a number of sources and will be expending money to a number of other sources. The firm will need some way to handle this inflow and outflow of money. Since the firm does not want to deal exclusively in cash, and since purchasing money orders for every expenditure is expensive and time-consuming, CIT will need to open a checking account for the business. Tom and Anna are not sure what sort of checking account they should open or what sort of financial institution they should prefer, if any. They have asked for your advice. What will you tell them?

BUSINESS CONSIDERATION Banks offer a number of different types of checking accounts. A firm that "shops" carefully is likely to be able to find an account that is ideal for the particular needs of that business. What sort of things should be considered in seeking a checking account for a newly formed business?

ETHICAL CONSIDERATIONS An old adage states that ignorance of the law is "no excuse." Does this adage—presuming that it is still true—justify the failure of many banks to fully inform new customers of the rights and responsibilities of both parties to a checking account? Should banks make more of an effort to convey all information to their new customers, or should the banks rely on the customers to read the brochures and learn what they need to know on their own?

THE CUSTOMER: RIGHTS AND DUTIES

The first and main duty of a customer is to act with due care and diligence. Whether writing a check, inspecting a monthly statement, or indorsing a check, or whether making a deposit or cashing a check, the customer is required to act in a careful and reasonable manner. If customers remember that it is their money being handled, and that carelessness could cause them to lose that money, they are more likely to be careful.

Customers have several rights they may exercise. They may stop payment on a previously issued check, and they may collect damages from the bank if the bank errs in the handling of the account to the customer's financial detriment. But before they can exercise these rights, customers must show that they have acted properly and/or that the bank has acted improperly. For example, suppose that Louis issues a check to pay for some merchandise. The merchant presents the check to the bank for payment, and the bank dishonors the check. Louis is now likely to have some problems with the merchant. He may have to pay the merchant a "handling fee" or a "service charge" for the returned check. He may face a lawsuit filed by the merchant to collect the amount of the check plus costs and interest. In many states, a person may face a criminal charge for passing "hot" (bad) checks. But what if the dishonor was due to an error by the bank, not to any carelessness or wrongdoing on Louis's part? Louis will still have to settle his own problems with the merchant, but the criminal action will be dropped. And Louis will be able to proceed against the bank for recovery of the damages he might have suffered in this ordeal.

According to UCC § 4-402, the bank is liable to its customer for any damages proximately caused by a wrongful dishonor of the customer's check, although damages are limited to actual damages proved by the customer. The damages expressly covered in the section include the following:

1. Damages due to an arrest
2. Damages due to a prosecution
3. Any other consequential damages that can actually be proved

From this language, it sounds as if the customer will end up in a reasonably good position: The customer will recover the "handling fees," the interest, and any other costs paid to the merchant; the customer will recover any damages related to the arrest; and the bank will end up taking all the losses on this case. In seeking damages from the bank, however, the customer must prove that the bank's conduct was the proximate cause of the losses suffered by the customer. Such proof is often difficult. If the bank can show that the customer contributed to the loss, the bank probably will owe nothing, and the customer will collect nothing. The following hypothetical case represents the type of problem that might prevent the customer's victory.

> *Bob had a balance of $120.15 in his checking account. He made a deposit of $900 on Friday, using a blank deposit slip provided by the bank. When completing the deposit slip, Bob accidentally wrote his account number incorrectly. The following Tuesday, Bob wrote a $500 check to Sam's Stereo to purchase a CD player. Sam's took the check to the bank on Wednesday, and the bank returned it unpaid due to insufficient funds. Sam's assessed Bob a $10 service charge and demanded that Bob "repurchase" the check, along with a 10 percent "collection fee." Sam's also filed criminal charges against Bob for the "hot check," and Bob was arrested. Bob paid $100 bail to get out of jail after his arrest, and he paid Sam's the $560 in cash to get the proceedings dropped. If Bob now sues the bank, he may learn a shocking lesson. Bob's negligence may have caused the loss, so the bank will not be liable. If Bob had used his own personalized, pre-encoded deposit slips, he probably would have won. Since he did not, he will possibly lose.*

Sometimes the customer not only recovers for the damages proximately caused, but also recovers **exemplary damages** when it is determined that the bank wrongfully handled the customer's account and did so either with malice or with reckless disregard for the rights of its depositor. The following case involves just such a situation—an embezzlement, a "hold" placed on the customer's account, and several dishonored checks.

Exemplary damages
Punitive damages; damages imposed in a case to punish the defendant.

25.1

BESHARA V. SOUTHERN NATIONAL BANK
928 P.2D 280 (OKL. 1996)

FACTS In the early 1980's, the appellant, Robert J. Beshara . . . met Betty J. Mitchell . . . as assistant cashier with the appellee, Southern National Bank . . . in Tulsa, Oklahoma. Shortly thereafter, Beshara and Mitchell began a social relationship. In August of 1986, Beshara opened a checking account with Southern National. As a matter of convenience, Beshara had Mitchell conduct virtually all of his banking business by having her make deposits to and withdrawals from his checking account at the Bank. However, a few days after he opened his checking account with Southern National, Mitchell, without Beshara's authorization or his knowledge, changed the address on his account to her home address in Sand Springs and added her name as an authorized signer on the account. Subsequently, she began embezzling money from the account. When Beshara's monthly statements were mailed to Mitchell's residence, she altered them so that they would conform with his actual

transactions in the account and she sent him the false statements. Mitchell periodically embezzled money from Beshara's checking account until late December of 1988, when another employee of Southern National, while conducting a routine internal audit, discovered a large transfer of money from Beshara's account into another account. On January 9, 1989, with Beshara's checking account showing a balance of $32,425.37, Southern National placed a hold on the account to conduct an internal audit to determine the correct account balance . . . On March 29, 1989, Beshara's attorney wrote the Bank, demanding that this checking account be released from the hold and that the proper account balance be restored. The Bank insisted that it had not completed its audit. In April of 1989, Beshara informed the Bank that he needed some of his money to pay his income taxes which were due. The Bank offered to loan Beshara the

continued

BESHARA V. SOUTHERN NATIONAL BANK, *continued*

928 P.2D 280 (OKL. 1996)

money to pay his taxes but Beshara refused the offer. Five months after Southern National first placed its hold on Beshara's checking account, Beshara wrote two checks against the account. . . . Southern National refused to honor the checks, marked them "refer to maker," and returned them to their respective payees. On August 10, 1989, Southern National mailed a proof of loss claim to its insurance company requesting reimbursement under a fidelity bond for the losses it suffered as a result of Mitchell's embezzlement . . . Hartford issued Southern National three checks [for a total of $200,897.64] for reimbursement of its losses as a result of Mitchell's embezzlements . . . nearly two years before it finally restored the funds in Beshara's account. Beshara sued the Bank on August 17, 1989. Seeking actual and punitive damages, Beshara asserted that the Bank acted in bad faith, wrongfully refused to honor the checks he wrote, and converted his money . . . The trial court granted summary judgment in favor of the Bank, and Beshara appealed.

ISSUE Was the Bank guilty of wrongfully dishonoring the checks Beshara wrote?

HOLDINGS The jury should have been allowed to decide whether the Bank did wrongfully dishonor the checks, and also whether its conduct was so egregious as to constitute the tort of conversion.

REASONING From the outset we note that Beshara does not appear to dispute that the Bank was at least initially justified, as a result of Mitchell's embezzlement, in placing a temporary hold on, or freezing the funds in, the checking account, to investigate Mitchell's actions in his and other accounts and to determine the proper balance of his account. Rather, the gravamen of his allegation is 1) that the Bank placed a hold on the account in January of 1989, and after he made repeated demands to have his account restored, it dishonored the checks he wrote in early May of 1989; and 2) even if the Bank was justified in refusing to honor the checks, at some point in time it determined from its investigation that the account should have had a balance of approximately $104,000, yet the Bank would not restore his account . . . Beshara argues that the Bank's failure to pay the checks he wrote in May of 1989, was wrongful dishonor and that the trial court erred when it granted the Bank's demurrer to his evidence and dismissed

his wrongful dishonor claim. The Bank counters that the trial court did not err because: 1) the evidence established that the Bank was justified in placing a hold on Beshara's account; and 2) Beshara failed to prove any evidence of damages . . . § 4-402 of the Uniform Commercial Code relates to a bank's liability to its customer for wrongful dishonor. . . . A dishonor is wrongful if done in an unjustified, unfair, or wrong manner which is contrary to justice. Wrongful dishonor excludes any permitted or justified dishonor . . . Here . . . Beshara alleged that the Bank wrongfully, willfully, and maliciously refused to honor the checks he wrote in May of 1989, and that he suffered damages which included monetary loss, loss of use of his money, embarrassment, humiliation, and emotional distress. At trial, Beshara presented evidence showing that: 1) at the time the account was frozen he had a balance of $32,425.37; 2) he informed the Bank that his actual balance should have been approximately $104,000; 3) he needed money to pay his income taxes which were due in April of 1989; 4) he had to sell a coin collection at approximately $8,300 below value in order to pay the income taxes; 5) 90 days was a commercially reasonable length of time in which the Bank should have completed its investigation to determine the amount of funds which actually belonged in the account; and 6) he was embarrassed and humiliated and he suffered emotional distress as a result of the length of the hold on his account . . . Whether the Bank withheld Beshara's funds for a commercially reasonable length of time, whether it willfully or intentionally dishonored the checks, or whether any damages were proximately caused by the dishonor is a question of fact for the jury. Consequently, the trial court erred in refusing to submit the wrongful dishonor claim to the jury . . . The relationship between a bank and its depositor is generally considered contractual. Improper refusal to make the funds available would generally be considered a contractual breach of the Bank's obligation to pay Beshara his money. Under the common law each contract carries an implicit and mutual covenant to act towards each other in good faith. Likewise, under the Uniform Commercial Code . . . § 1-203, commercial transactions carry an obligation of good faith in their performance and enforcement. Consequently, the determinative issue raised by the parties' contentions is whether, under the facts presented, a breach of the implied covenant of good faith and fair

25.1

BESHARA V. SOUTHERN NATIONAL BANK, *continued*
928 P.2D 280 (OKL. 1996)

dealing may give rise to an action in tort . . . We found that if the factual situation warranted, an action for a breach of contract may also give rise to a tort action for a breach of the implied covenant of good faith and fair dealing. Beshara alleges that the Bank's actions in withholding the funds in his account were intentional, malicious, and in reckless and wanton disregard. In viewing these allegations as well as all the inferences and conclusions drawn from the alleged facts, we find that Beshara should have been allowed the opportunity to proceed on his allegations for tortious breach of the duty of good faith and fair dealing. Accordingly, the trial court erred in refusing to allow Beshara to proceed on this alternative theory of recovery. . . .

BUSINESS CONSIDERATIONS Should a financial institution have a policy of notifying its customers whenever there is a change to the customer's signature card or a change of address for mailings regarding the account? Should a customer regularly check to make certain that his or her signature card has not been changed?

ETHICAL CONSIDERATIONS The bank in this case received its settlement from its insurance company but refused to release Beshara's funds for two years. What ethical issues are raised by this conduct? From a purely ethical perspective, what should the bank have done in this situation?

The customer also has a right to issue stop-payment orders to the bank. If done properly, the bank must obey this order to stop payment, or it will face liability to the customer for any damages caused by disobeying the order. To be effective and to be properly made, the order must be given to the bank in a reasonable manner. In other words, the bank must receive a complete description of the check (number, payee, amount, date, reason) with enough "lead time" to allow the bank to react to the order. A minimum of a few hours is normally required, but it may take as long as a full banking day to get the word out to the bank's various branch offices.

The customer can give either an oral or a written stop-payment order. A stop-payment order is good for six months, but it lapses after 14 days if the original order was oral and was not confirmed in writing within that 14-day period. A written order can be renewed for additional six-month periods. Of course, every renewal will entail another service charge.

If the customer properly gives the bank a stop-payment order, and the bank pays the check despite the order, the customer may be able to collect damages from the bank. To do so, the customer will have to prove that he or she suffered damages because the check was paid. To prove this, he or she will have to show that the presenter could not have collected from him or her (the customer) if payment had been stopped by the bank as the customer ordered. If the presenter could have enforced the check against the customer (drawer), then the customer will not be able to collect any damages from the bank for paying the check despite the stop-payment order. If payment is stopped by the bank, the drawer may be sued by the holder in an effort to recover his or her money.

In the following case, a payee bank sued a drawer bank for wrongful dishonor of a cashier's check. Although not technically involving a stop-payment order, some of the principles from stop-payment orders as they relate to cashier's checks were applied by the court in reaching its decision.

25.2

BANK ONE, MERRILLVILLE, N.A. V. NORTHERN TRUST BANK/DUPAGE

775 F.SUPP. 266 (N.D.ILL. 1991)

FACTS On or before 7 June 1990, Sakoff wrote a check for $98,581.40 (the Sakoff check) on its account at Northern, payable to the order of Zaragoza. Zaragoza deposited the Sakoff check in its account at Bank One on 7 June 1990. Bank One sent the Sakoff check to Northern for payment. On 13 June 1990, it was returned to Bank One, because the funds in Sakoff's account were insufficient to cover the amount of the Sakoff check.

Dykstra, a Bank One employee, telephoned Northern upon receiving the returned Sakoff check on 13 June, and was told that Sakoff's account did contain sufficient funds to cover the check. On the same day, Dykstra drove to Northern's offices and exchanged the Sakoff check for a Northern cashier's check for $98,581.40. When Bank One sent the cashier's check through the Federal Reserve Bank to Northern for payment, however, Northern refused to honor the check.

The reasons for Northern's refusal to pay relate to another check (the Zaragoza check), drawn on Zaragoza's account at Bank One, for $103,200, which Zaragoza presumably transferred to Sakoff at about the same time Zaragoza received the Sakoff check for $98,581.40. At some point before 12 June 1990, Sakoff deposited Zaragoza's check into Sakoff's account at Northern. Northern then sent the Zaragoza check to Bank One for collection. Bank One received the check on 12 June but, on 13 June, issued notice to Northern, through the Federal Reserve Bank, that it was dishonoring the Zaragoza check, because of insufficient funds in Zaragoza's account. This notice did not reach Northern until after Dykstra had obtained the cashier's check. As a result of Bank One's rejection of the Sakoff check, the funds in Sakoff's account were insufficient to cover the Sakoff check for which Northern had issued its cashier's check.

ISSUE Could Northern dishonor the cashier's check that it had issued to Bank One?

HOLDING No. A bank cannot dishonor a cashier's check it has issued, even if the cashier's check is obtained by fraud.

REASONING According to Bank One, Illinois law forbids a bank from dishonoring its cashier's checks for any reason. On the basis of this understanding of the law, Bank One contends that it is entitled to summary judgment, since any arguments Northern might raise are immaterial to the issue of wrongful dishonor. In response, Northern asserts bad faith on the part of Bank One. Northern contends that when Dykstra drove to Northern to obtain the cashier's check, he was aware that his bank was in the process of dishonoring the Zaragoza check. According to Northern, Bank One feared that its dishonor of the Zaragoza check would result in there being insufficient funds to cover the Sakoff check. This fear allegedly prompted Dykstra to hurry to Northern in order to obtain a cashier's check before Northern received notice of Bank One's dishonor. Northern contends that bad faith such as that alleged justifies a refusal to honor a cashier's check, and that the factual issue of Bank One's bad faith precludes summary judgment.

Although the Illinois [Uniform Commercial] Code does not specifically address the subject of a bank's cashier's checks, the Illinois Appellate Court interpreted the Code's application to this issue. . . . The court employed a line of analysis under the Code which led it to indorse "a rule which prohibits a bank from refusing to honor its cashier's checks." Characterizing the bank's issuance of a cashier's check as acceptance of the item, the court applied Section 4-303, which provides that a stop order on a check is ineffective after acceptance.

In the face of . . . case law which holds that a bank has no right to dishonor its cashier's check, but must instead assert its reason for nonpayment as part of its own action to recover the funds, Northern essentially argues for a "bad faith" or "fraud" exception to the general principle. Northern reasons that, while Illinois courts have held that failure of consideration is no excuse for dishonoring a cashier's check, they have never ruled that the procurer's bad faith does not provide a defense.

As previously discussed, Illinois courts view an issued cashier's check as accepted . . . and as the equivalent of cash. . . . As a consequence of the application of Illinois law to the subject of cashier's checks, Northern . . . can raise no excuse "whether or not effective under other rules of law" justifying its refusal to pay. The proper context for Northern's arguments regarding Bank One's alleged bad faith is its counterclaim rather than as a defense to Bank

25.2

BANK ONE, MERRILLVILLE, N.A. V. NORTHERN TRUST BANK/DUPAGE, *continued*

775 F.SUPP. 266 (N.D.ILL. 1991)

One's action for wrongful dishonor. Unfortunately for Northern in this case, its claim concerning the underlying transaction is not yet ripe for judgment.

Northern must therefore honor its cashier's check and seek to recover the funds in the hands of Bank One, just as it would have to do if it had paid cash. Under Illinois law, Northern assumed the risk of having to pursue litigation to recover improperly paid funds when it issued the cashier's check. [The Illinois court and Northern cited several New York cases which held that a bank could issue a stop-payment order on a cashier's check if that cashier's check was obtained by fraud. The Illinois court, however, applied the majority rule to the case.]

BUSINESS CONSIDERATIONS Suppose that a business is entering into a contract with a distant buyer, and that this is the first contract between the two parties. Should the seller insist on being paid by means of a cashier's check, teller's check, or certified check? Why would this matter to the seller? Why would it matter to the buyer?

ETHICAL CONSIDERATIONS Presuming Northern's allegations are all true, did Dykstra and Bank One act unethically by having Northern issue a cashier's check before notifying Northern that the Zaragoza check was being dishonored by Bank One? Does the exchange of large checks between Zaragoza and Sakoff raise any ethical issues?

The bank periodically must send statements to its customers. One of the changes under revised Article 4 involves the requirements for what the bank must provide in the statement sent to the customer. The prior law required the bank to send the actual canceled checks and other items to the customer for the customer's examination and reconciliation. The revised rules allow the bank to "either return or make available to the customer the items paid or provide information in the statement of account sufficient to allow the customer reasonably to identify the items paid. The statement of account provides sufficient information if the item is described by item number, amount, and date of presentment." This change does increase the burden on the bank to some extent since the bank now must retain the actual items or maintain the capacity to produce legible copies of the items for at least seven years. It also increases the burden on the customer, and to a much greater extent. The customer now must reconcile the statement, verify signature, and notice alterations, all without actually seeing the canceled items. This means the customer must keep adequate and accurate records, especially his or her check register, or face the probability that he or she will not notice any unauthorized signings or material alterations in a timely manner.

The customer has a duty to examine and to reconcile the statements of account received from the bank with reasonable promptness and must notify the bank of any unauthorized signings or alterations promptly in order to retain his or her maximum rights. A failure to act with reasonable promptness may well result in a waiver of the customer's rights in favor of the bank. The bank satisfies its duty to provide a statement to the customer by mailing it or by holding it available for the customer, if the customer so requests. The customer satisfies his or her duty by promptly and carefully examining and balancing the statement when it is received. By failing to make a reasonably prompt investigation and/or failing to notify the

25.2 | FINANCE/ MANAGEMENT

RECONCILING BANK STATEMENTS

Donna and Julio normally reconcile the firm's bank statements within a day or two of receipt. However, when the next statement arrives, both Donna and Julio will be out of town. They are scheduled to attend a professional conference in Orlando, and they plan to spend an additional week sightseeing while they are there. Dan is concerned that their absence will cause an undue delay in reconciling the statement, but he does not want to interfere with their plans if there is no cause for concern. He asks your advice. What will you tell him?

BUSINESS CONSIDERATIONS Reconciling bank statements is not always enjoyable. How should a business view this task? Should statements be reconciled immediately? Should they balance "to the penny," or is close good enough? Who should have the responsibility for this job?

ETHICAL CONSIDERATIONS Suppose the bank has made an error on a statement of account, posting a $19 check as $91. Should the customer tell the bank, or keep the $72 "profit" from this transaction? Would your answer be different if the error was made the other way? If so, how can this be reconciled ethically? When does an error become significant enough that the bank should be notified of it?

bank promptly of any errors or inconsistencies in the statement, the customer will lose the right to assert against the bank:

1. Any unauthorized customer signatures
2. Any material alterations of any of the checks
3. Any other unauthorized signatures or alterations made by the same person, provided that the customer had a reasonable time to examine the statement and to notify the bank of any problems or irregularities

The revision to Article 4 did extend the time period somewhat. Now the "reasonable time" available to the customer may not exceed 30 calendar days. (Under the previous rules, the customer only had 14 days to reconcile the statement and to give notice to the bank.)

To complete the statement inspection duty, the customer must report any unauthorized signatures and/or any material alterations within one year of the statement date or lose the right to raise these issues. If the customer notifies the bank within 30 days of receiving the statement, he or she gets all the money back on the unauthorized signatures, and the alteration amounts back on the alterations. If notice is given to the bank after 30 days but within one year, the customer recovers the amount of the first signature or the first alteration by each signer or alterer, and the customer puts the bank on notice for any future signings or alterations. However, the customer cannot recover on any of the checks containing forgeries or alterations received by the bank between the first one and the date of notice. If notice is over one year after the statement date, the customer cannot recover anything from the bank.

THE BANK: RIGHTS AND DUTIES

Since the bank is the agent of the customer, it must obey any lawful orders of the customer. This duty to obey gives the bank a very important right: It can charge to the customer's account any item that is properly payable from the customer's account. The bank can pay the check even if payment creates an overdraft. The bank can also pay a check that was incomplete when issued and then completed by some later holder. The bank may even know that a holder completed the check and still pay it as completed. The only exception is when the bank has notice that the completion was improper or was done in bad faith.

In accordance with the rules that govern timely presentment, the bank may refuse to honor any **stale checks.** A *stale check* is one that is more than six months old and has not been certified. If the bank dishonors a stale check, it is not liable

Stale checks
Checks that a bank may dishonor due to their age (over six months old) without regard to the drawer's account balance.

to the customer for any damages. Alternatively, the bank may, at its option, honor a stale check. Again, the bank will not be liable for any damages suffered by the customer if it honors the check in good faith. It should be remembered that a written stop payment is good for six months, the period after which a check becomes stale. Suppose a customer issues a written stop-payment order. Six months elapse without the check ever being presented, and the customer does not renew the stop-payment order. The payee now presents the check to the bank. The check is stale. A stop-payment order had been in effect on that check. The bank honors the check. If the bank can prove it acted in good faith, it will face no liability for its payment of the stale check that the customer once tried to stop.

Under normal agency rules, if the principal dies or becomes incompetent, the agency terminates by operation of law. After this termination, if the agent continues to perform its agency duties, the agent becomes personally liable, and the principal has no liability. This rule would be impractical with negotiable instruments, so the UCC expressly changed it. As applied to the bank–customer relationship, agencies do not automatically end at the instant of the principal's death or incompetence. Under § 4-405(1), the bank is fully authorized to perform its banking functions on the account of a customer who has died or has become incompetent until the bank knows of the occurrence and has had adequate time to react to the news. Even if the bank knows of the customer's death, its power to act is not terminated. Section 4-405(2) permits the bank to continue to honor checks drawn on the account for 10 days after the date the bank learns of a customer's death unless a stop-payment is placed on the account by an interested party.

Sometimes banks make mistakes. A bank may honor an instrument that had a stop-payment order covering it, or it may do something else that allows the customer to recover damages from the bank. When this happens, the bank has some protection: It is entitled to subrogation. *Subrogation* means that the bank is given the rights that some other parties could have raised if the bank had not made improper payment. UCC § 4-407 gives the bank three different sets of rights to assert through subrogation:

1. The rights of a holder in due course against the maker or drawer
2. The rights of the payee or any other holder against the maker or drawer
3. The rights of the drawer or maker against the payee or any other holders

Thus, the bank holds the rights of both sides and of every interested party. From this buffet of rights, the bank can select the set of rights that gives it the greatest likelihood of winning the case.

The bank has the right to enforce the terms of its contract with the customer. Among other things, this right allows the bank to impose certain service charges and fees against many of its customers each month. The bank may be able to collect a specific amount every month, it may be able to collect a specific amount in any month the customer's account balance falls below a certain amount, or it may be able to charge a specific amount for every check written by the customer. The bank will impose a service charge for handling a stop-payment order. Likewise, it may charge a customer when it pays an overdraft or when it dishonors a check, if honoring it would have created an overdraft. These service charges are specified in the contract the customer agreed to when the signature card was signed.

The duties of the bank are simple. The bank is required to honor the terms and conditions of its contract. It is required to obey the rules of agency and to act in good faith in a commercially reasonable manner.

SPECIAL PROBLEMS

Two areas deserve further mention: certified checks and unauthorized signatures.

Certified Checks

A *certified check* is one that has already been accepted by the drawee bank. In other words, the bank has assumed primary liability and agreed to pay the check upon a later presentment. Certification can be done at the request of the drawer or of any holder. A refusal by the bank to certify the check is not a dishonor. How does certification occur? Either the drawer or a holder presents the check to the bank and requests certification. If the bank agrees to certify, it follows certain steps. First, it charges the account of the customer and credits its own "Certified Check Account." Thus, the money is held by the bank in the bank's own account, and the customer has already "paid" the amount of the check. Second, the bank punches a hole in the encoded account number of the check to ensure that the check will not be paid a second time on a later presentment. Third, a stamp is made on the face of the check, and the terms of the certification are written into the stamped form.

If the drawer seeks and receives the certification, he or she remains secondarily liable until final payment. However, if a holder seeks and receives the certification, the drawer and all prior indorsers are discharged from liability.

Unauthorized Signatures

Under UCC § 1-201(43), an *unauthorized signature* is one made without any authority, express or implied, and it includes a forgery. An unauthorized signature is wholly inoperative against the person whose name was signed unless that person later ratifies the signing. Normally it cannot be used to impose liability on the purported signer. However, in some circumstances, an unauthorized and unratified signature is still binding on the purported signer. According to § 3-406, if a person contributes to the unauthorized signing through negligence, he or she will be held liable to any good-faith holder of the instrument.

Many businesses "sign" checks by means of a stamp. The business may leave the stamp and its checks in a place where they are easily reached by a nonauthorized person (most likely a thief). Such conduct on the part of the business is negligent, and the negligence may lead to the unauthorized "signing." In such circumstances, the business may not later assert the defense that the signing was unauthorized if the holder is a holder in good faith. Notice that the holder does not have to be a holder in due course; the fact that the holder is in good faith is sufficient. The negligence of the wronged party is the key: The wronged party must be negligent, and the negligence must cause the loss. Otherwise, the unauthorized signature cannot be used against the person whose name was signed.

FUNDS TRANSFERS

Changes in banking laws, the growth of international business, and technology have affected the banking industry to a significant extent over the last quarter of the twentieth century. The savings and loan industry crisis of the 1980s led to numerous changes in banking regulations. International trade frequently requires that large amounts of money be transferred quickly from one nation to another. Technology has reduced the need for personnel and has made automated banking much simpler. Each of these changes has moved banking ahead, while many of the banking regulations have lagged behind. However, the distance between banking practice and banking regulation is narrowing.

Electronic Funds Transfers

Recent technological advances have provided banking with a new method of doing business and with a new type of service. This new method of doing business is the electronic funds transfer (EFT), which allows for computerization of checking accounts and for theoretically faster, more accurate banking transactions.

Electronic fund transfers are regulated by the Electronic Funds Transfer Act (15 U.S.C. 1693), which became effective in 1980. This statute provides the basic legal framework for EFTs, granting extensive authority to the Board of Governors of the Federal Reserve System. In addition, various agencies are granted enforcement power,[1] with special enforcement power given to the Federal Trade Commission for any areas not specifically reserved to the specialized authority of other named agencies. This method of financial dealing eventually may make the current checking or drafting account obsolete, or nearly so, due to the delays and expenses of handling checks or drafts when compared to electronic banking.

The purpose of the Electronic Funds Transfer Act is "to provide a basic framework establishing rights, liabilities, and responsibilities of participants in electronic fund transfer systems."[2] The primary objective of the statute is the provision of individual consumer rights in electronic funds transfers.

The act defines an electronic funds transfer as "any transfer of funds, other than a transaction originated by check, draft, or similar paper instrument, which is initiated through an electronic terminal, telephonic instrument, or computer or magnetic tape so as to order, instruct, or authorize a financial institution to debit or credit an account."[3] It also requires any financial institution providing EFTs to its customers to provide those customers with periodic statements for each account that the customer may access through the use of an EFT. These periodic statements must be provided at least monthly for each monthly cycle in which an EFT occurred, or every three months, whichever is more frequent.[4]

There are four methods for electronically transferring funds recognized by the act: POS transactions; ATM transactions; telephonic transactions; and preauthorized transactions, whether deposits or withdrawals.

Point of Sale (POS) Transactions. The first method is the point-of-sale (POS) transaction, involving the use of a POS terminal and a "debit" card. In a POS transaction, the customer presents the merchant with a debit card, the merchant imprints the card and has the customer sign, and the funds are transferred from the customer's account to the merchant's account. The transaction is similar in format to the use of a credit card, but there should be no delay in receiving the money from the sale for the merchant. Unfortunately, the use of a POS transaction is often no faster or safer for the merchant than the use of a check. In most parts of the country, the POS transaction must be processed through a clearinghouse in the same manner as a check, making the transfer of funds to the merchant no faster than it would be with a check. In addition, the cost is slightly higher for a POS transaction than for a check when a clearinghouse is involved.

Debit/ATM Cards. A second, and more familiar, method is the use of automated teller machine (ATM) transfers. The bank customer inserts his or her card in the

25.3 | FINANCE

CALL-IMAGE TECHNOLOGY

FUNDS TRANSFERS

The firm is currently concluding negotiations for a very large sale with a retail store that has locations throughout the Southwest. The resulting contract should be for an amount in the high six figures. Tom is willing to let the retailer pay for the order by check. Anna would prefer that the customer sends either a cashier's check or a certified check. Dan has pointed out to the family that, given the "time value" of money, the sooner they receive the funds the better they will be. He thinks that the firm should insist on a wire transfer of the funds as soon as the goods are received by the retailer. The family agrees that the time value of money is important, and they like Dan's idea, but they want more information before they make a final decision. They have asked you for advice. What will you tell them?

BUSINESS CONSIDERATIONS What benefits accrue to a seller who receives payment by wire transfer? What disadvantages are felt by the buyer who pays by wire transfer? When should a business insist that it be paid by wire transfer rather than by negotiable instrument?

ETHICAL CONSIDERATIONS Is it ethical to ask a buyer to pay for goods by wire transfer upon receipt? Should the buyer be given some sort of discount since the seller will be receiving his or her funds so quickly, as compared to when the funds would be available if the buyer sent a negotiable instrument?

machine, enters his or her personal identification number (PIN), and selects a transaction. The customer can make a deposit, a withdrawal, a transfer from one account to another, a payment, or a number of other banking transactions.

Telephonic Transactions. If the bank is a participant in a network, the customer may be able to authorize payments to predetermined accounts by phone. Here, the customer calls the bank and, using the buttons on a touch-tone phone, can designate preselected "payees" who will be paid an amount determined by punching in the amount of the "electronic check" so that the funds are automatically transferred.

Preauthorized Transactions. Finally, there are preauthorized automatic payments and preauthorized direct deposits. In both cases, regular amounts are deducted from, or added to, the customer's account balance on designated dates to ensure that payment (or credit) is received without any worries about forgetting to send in the check or drive to the bank to make the deposit.

Rights and Duties with EFTs

In general, a consumer who uses EFTs has the same types of rights and duties as a consumer who has a checking or drafting account with a financial institution. For example, a customer can place a stop-payment order on a preauthorized payment by notifying the bank orally or in writing at least three days prior to the date for preauthorized payment. A consumer can recover damages from a financial institution for failure to make EFT payments as instructed, provided the consumer has sufficient funds on deposit.

Numerous protections also exist for the consumer who is using EFTs. For example, consumer liability is limited in case of unauthorized use of an account, provided the consumer gives proper and timely notice to the bank. A consumer is expected to give the bank "proper and timely" notice of the loss or theft of his or her card or other means of access to his or her account in order to minimize liability. If the consumer gives such "proper and timely" notice, the consumer's liability is limited to the lesser of the amount of money or value accessed wrongfully or $50. "Proper and timely" notice is generally defined as notice given within two business days after the consumer learns of the loss or theft. If the consumer gives notice, but the notice is not "proper and timely," his or her liability is still somewhat limited under the statute. In this case, liability is the lesser of $500 or the amount of unauthorized electronic funds transfers that occur between the time when the consumer should

WHO IS LIABLE WHEN A BANK DELAYS MAKING A FUNDS TRANSFER?

MRF Resources, Ltd. maintained a checking account with Merchant's Bank, as did Galit Diamond, Inc. On 20 May 1993, the bank certified a check drawn by MRF, payable to Galit Diamond in the amount of $58,958. Upon receipt of the check, Galit presented it to Merchants for payment, and the bank posted the funds to Galit's account on that same day. Shortly thereafter, MRF's president informed Merchants that the certified check was forged. As a result, the bank placed a hold on Galit's account. Meanwhile, on 1 June Galit presented Merchants with a funds transfer application accompanied by a check drawn on its Merchants account in the amount of $30,030. The check was intended to cover a funds transfer for $30,000 and the bank's fee for that service. The application directed a credit to the Israeli bank account of Ilan Gertler, the supplier of approximately 60 percent of Galit's diamond inventory. Without rejecting the application or informing Galit that a hold had been placed on its account, Merchants held on to the funds transfer application and check. Gertler eventually received the funds, but a week later than expected. Because the late transfer tainted Galit's creditworthiness, Gertler severed its business relationship with Galit, greatly damaging Galit's ability to conduct its business profitably. Galit alleged that Merchants Bank was liable in damages for wrongfully freezing its account and claimed that Merchants' handling of the certified check violated various provisions of Article 3 of the Uniform Commercial Code, giving rise to liability under Article 4. Merchant's Bank denied any liability. According to Merchant's Bank, the transaction was governed completely by Article 4A, and Article 4A does not make allowance for consequential damages. Galit denied that Article 4A provides exclusive coverage, pointing out that the problem arose from the handling of a cashier's check, and thus must be decided under all three articles—3, 4, and 4A.

This case has been brought in *your* court. How will *you* decide this case?[5]

BUSINESS CONSIDERATION When a business uses a wire transfer, it is normally because the money needs to be transferred immediately. Should a business insist on some sort of receipt or verification that the funds were wired and received when it uses a wire transfer?

ETHICAL CONSIDERATIONS Should the bank have notified Galit that it had placed a hold on the account pending resolution of the questions concerning the cashier's check? Was it ethical for the bank to freeze the account without notifying Galit?

SOURCE: *New York Law Journal,* (20 October 1997), New York Law Publishing Company, http://www.lexis-nexis.com.

have given notice (two business days after discovery) and the date on which notice was actually given. The bank has the burden of proof to establish either that the use was in fact authorized or that the customer did not give proper and/or timely notice.

As the public becomes more familiar and more comfortable with EFTs, the use of this form of money management will grow and develop. As that happens, the use of checks will begin to decline. The decline will be gradual at first, but over the next few decades we may do virtually all our banking electronically.

Article 4A: Funds Transfers

Bank customers have long had a need for a particular type of funds transfer, the *wire transfer*. However, this type of funds transfer has not been uniformly regulated until very recently. Now the UCC has developed Article 4A to provide uniform coverage in the area of funds transfers within the United States. As of July 1998, Article 4A had been adopted by all 50 states and the District of Columbia.

Funds transfers are commonly used to provide a rapid movement of funds from one account to another without the use of a traditional negotiable instrument. A *funds transfer* is defined in § 4A-104 as:

> *The series of transactions, beginning with the originator's payment order, made for the purpose of making payment to the beneficiary of the order. The term includes any payment order issued by the originator's bank or an intermediary bank intended to carry out the originator's payment order. A funds transfer is completed by acceptance by the beneficiary's bank of a payment order for the benefit of the beneficiary of the originator's payment order.*

Note that the funds transfer is defined as a *series* of transactions. The person who is transferring the funds—the *originator*—places the funds transfer order with his or her bank. This bank—the *originator bank*—then transfers the funds to the next bank—an *intermediary bank*—in line. This intermediary bank, in turn, will transfer the funds to the next bank, until, ultimately, the funds reach the *beneficiary bank*. Once the funds reach the beneficiary bank, they are credited to the account of the beneficiary, completing the funds transfer. Each transaction is deemed to be only between the two parties directly involved. Thus, the transfer between the originating bank and the first intermediary bank is a transaction between them, and the originator has no rights against the intermediary bank if something goes awry. The originator can only assert his or her claims against the originator bank based on its alleged wrongdoings.

Section 4A-302 provides guidance for receiving banks in carrying out the funds transfer. If the sender of the funds transfer order specifies how the funds transfer is to be carried out, the receiving bank must follow these specifications. If no specifications are provided, the receiving bank is allowed to use any means that are reasonable under the circumstances, including first-class mail, if such a method is appropriate under the circumstances.

The following case deals in some detail with a number of these issues. This opinion provides one of the best illustrations of how funds transfers are intended to work and the potential risks inherent in using this method of payment.

25.3

GRAIN TRADERS, INC. V. CITIBANK, N.A.
960 F.SUPP. 784 (S.D.N.Y. 1997)

FACTS On December 22, 1994, Grain Traders initiated a funds transfer . . . to effectuate the payment of $310,000 to . . . Kraemer . . . The Funds Transfer was designed to move money from Grain Traders to Kraemer in one day. The payment order [was] issued by Grain Traders to its bank, Banco de Credito Nacional ("BCN") . . . [T]he funds transfer was to proceed as follows: (1) Grain Traders's account at BCN was to be debited $310,000; (2) the $310,000 was then to be "transferred" to Banque De Credit Et Investissement Ltd.'s ("BCI") at Citibank by way of a debit to BCN's Citibank account and a corresponding credit in that

GRAIN TRADERS, INC. V. CITIBANK, N.A., *continued*
960 F.SUPP. 784 (S.D.N.Y. 1997)

amount to BCI's Citibank account; (3) the $310,000 was in turn to be "transferred" from BCI to Banco Extrader, S.A. ("Extrader") by way of an unspecified transaction between BCI and Extrader; and (4) the $310,000 was finally to be transferred to Kraemer by way of a credit to his account at Extrader. After the payment order was issued by Grain Traders to BCN, the Funds Transfer initially proceeded as expected. BCN's account at Citibank was debited $310,000 and BCI's account at Citibank was credited $310,000. At the same time, BCN sent instructions to Citibank, directing Citibank to instruct BCI to instruct Extrader to credit $310,000 to Kraemer . . . Citibank in turn sent instructions to BCI on the same day, notifying BCI that Citibank had credited its account with $310,000 and instructing BCI to instruct Extrader to credit this amount to Kraemer . . . Either just before or just after BCI's account at Citibank was credited with the $310,000, however, the BCI account was placed by Citibank on "hold for funds" status . . . The "hold for funds" status, which was put into place because BCI's account with Citibank was overdrawn by more than $12 million, preventing BCI from making any further withdrawals from the account . . . Kraemer apparently never received a credit to his Extrader account for the $310,000. Kraemer's affidavit, submitted by Grain Traders, states that on December 28, 1994, just six days after the attempted Funds Transfer, the government of Argentina ordered Extrader to suspend payments and that Extrader became insolvent "[s]ome-time later." . . . Likewise, BCI, a Bahamian bank, ceased making payments in January 1995; it was closed by supervisory authorities in the Bahamas on July 31, 1995 . . . Grain Traders commenced this cause of action against Citibank in November 1995 . . .

ISSUE Was Citibank liable to Grain Traders for the failure of the funds transfer?

HOLDING No. Citibank carried out its obligation under the funds transfer order, but, even if it had not, it would not be liable to Grain Traders because it never dealt with Grain Traders.

REASONING Funds transfers, also commonly referred to as wire transfers, are a specialized "method of payment in which the person making the payment (the 'originator') directly transmits an instruction to a bank," generally through electronic means, "to make payment to the person receiving payment (the 'beneficiary') or to instruct some other bank to make payment to the beneficiary." . . . A funds transfer consists of one or more payment orders each instructing the next party in line as to the steps it must follow to carry out the funds transfer . . . Hence, funds are "transferred" through a series of debits and credits to a series of bank accounts. . . . In the present case, Grain Traders was the originator of a funds transfer intended to pay $310,000 to Kraemer, the beneficiary. Grain Traders requested a series of payments order that would "transfer" the funds from its bank—BCN—through two "intermediary" banks—Citibank and BCI—and finally into Kraemer's account at his bank—Extrader. Grain Traders asserts that Citibank did not carry out the Funds Transfer as directed and instead improperly used the funds it received as a set-off against debt owed to Citibank by BCI . . . Grain Traders claims that it is entitled to a refund of the $310,000 from Citibank under the "money back guarantee" of § 4-A-402. . . . Grain Traders argues that its obligation to pay BCN, and BCN's obligation to pay Citibank, was excused because the Funds Transfer was not completed. Grain Traders therefore asserts that it is entitled to a refund of its payment—pursuant to § 4-A-402—from Citibank. Citibank, however, argues that Grain Traders has sued the wrong party . . . Citibank claims that § 4-A-402 only allows a party to a funds transfer to obtain a refund from the next party or bank in line. Hence, Grain Traders may only seek a refund—if at all—from BCN . . . I agree with Citibank's interpretation of § 4-A-402. First, the plain language of § 4-A-402 and other provisions of Article 4-A make it clear that a party to a funds transfer is only entitled to a refund from the specific party to which it made payment. Article 4-A treats a funds transfer as a series of individual transactions, each of which involve two parties dealing directly with each other. This notion is embodied in the very definition of a "funds transfer" as set forth in § 4-A-104(1) . . . Thus, Article 4-A approaches each funds transfer not as a single payment order, but rather as a series of transactions each of which involves only the parties to the individual payment order. After establishing this structure, Article 4-A proceeds to define the rights and duties of each bank involved in a funds transfer.

continued

25.3

GRAIN TRADERS, INC. V. CITIBANK, N.A., *continued*
960 F.SUPP. 784 (S.D.N.Y. 1997)

First, § 4-A-402(3) states that the bank that sent the payment order must pay the bank that received the payment order when the payment order is accepted . . . Thus, the obligation of payment runs only from the sender bank—the bank that sent the payment order—to the bank that received the payment order . . . This subsection further provides that the sending bank's obligation to pay the receiving bank is excused if the funds transfer is not completed . . . Then, § 4-A-402(4) provides that when a sending bank that is not required to pay—because the funds transfer has not been completed—has already paid, the sending bank is entitled to a "refund" from the receiving bank . . . Thus, these sections do not create an obligation to pay or refund a payment with respect to all the parties to a fund transfer, but instead only create an obligation between the sending bank and the receiving bank pursuant to each individual payment order making up the funds transfer. . . . Thus, the plain language of § 4-A-402 makes it clear that a right of refund lies only with respect to parties to a specific payment order and not as to all the parties to a funds transfer. . . . Article 4-A's drafters intended the "money-back guarantee" to apply only as between the parties to a payment order and not the parties to a funds transfer as a whole. Applied to the facts of this case, the originator—Grain Traders— would be entitled to a refund under § 4-A-402(4) from its bank, BCN, but not from Citibank . . . For the foregoing reasons, Grain Traders's motion for summary judgment is denied and Citibank's cross-motion for summary judgment is granted. Accordingly, the Clerk of the Court shall enter judgment in favor of Citibank dismissing the complaint with prejudice and costs.

BUSINESS CONSIDERATIONS What benefits does a business get by paying an obligation through the use of a funds transfer? Are these benefits sufficient to justify using a funds transfer rather than a negotiable instrument? Why might the beneficiary prefer a funds transfer to a negotiable instrument?

ETHICAL CONSIDERATIONS Is it ethical for a person who originates a funds transfer to expect the intermediary banks to provide a "money-back guarantee" when the fee for the funds transfer is so (relatively) low? What would happen to the cost of funds transfers if every bank involved faced potential liability to every party involved?

Finally, § 4A-108 specifically excludes coverage by Article 4A in any area already governed by the Electronic Funds Transfer Act, as that act may be amended from time to time. Thus, the UCC will provide state coverage for funds transfers but will defer to federal regulation of EFTs.

SUMMARY

The most frequently used negotiable instrument is the check. As a result, special attention must be paid to the bank-customer relationship. When a customer opens a checking account, a multirole relationship is created. The bank and the customer have a contract, they are involved in an agency, they have a debtor–creditor relationship, and they are controlled by Article 4 of the UCC.

Customers have a duty to exercise due care in their dealings with their accounts. They are required to inspect their statements carefully and promptly for any irregularities, alterations, or unauthorized signings. They also may issue stop-payment orders to the bank. Since the bank is the agent of its customers, it is obligated to obey such orders.

RESOURCES FOR BUSINESS LAW STUDENTS

NAME	RESOURCES	WEB ADDRESS
Uniform Commercial Code (UCC), Article 4, Bank Deposits and Collections	The Legal Information Institute (LII), maintained by the Cornell Law School, provides a hypertext and searchable version of UCC Article 4, Bank Deposits and Collections. LII also maintains links to Article 4 as adopted by particular states and to proposed revisions.	**http://www.law.cornell.edu/ucc/4/overview.html**
Electronic Funds Transfer Act— 15 USC § 1693	LII provides a hypertext and searchable version of 15 USC § 1693, popularly known as the Electronic Funds Transfer Act.	**http://www.law.cornell.edu/uscode/15/78dd-2.html**
Uniform Commercial Code Article 4A, Funds Transfer	LII provides a hypertext and searchable version of Article 4A, Funds Transfer.	**http://www.law.cornell.edu/ucc/4A/overview.html**

The bank is required to abide by the terms of its contract with the customer. It must pay properly drawn checks if the customer has sufficient funds, and it must act in good faith.

Certified checks and unauthorized signatures can present special problems. A certified check is one that has been accepted by the bank and then circulated through the normal channels of commerce. Unauthorized signings are sometimes caused by the negligence of the customer; in such a case, the bank is not liable for honoring the unauthorized signing.

Credit unions have become actively involved in the business of providing accounts to customers. Credit union checking accounts have become a common alternative to the traditional checking accounts offered by banks. The credit unions tend to have lower minimum balance requirements and lower fees and charges for their credit union members who elect to open checking accounts.

Funds transfers are the "wave of the future" for banking and for businesses. There are two major areas of funds transfers: electronic funds transfers, governed by the Electronic Funds Transfer Act; and funds (wire) transfers, governed by Article 4A of the UCC. By using the capacity and the speed of computers and by eliminating the paper required for traditional checking accounts, funds can be moved more quickly, more accurately, and more efficiently than is possible with checking accounts. This developmental area will continue to grow and to spread over the next several years.

DISCUSSION QUESTIONS

1. Where do the terms and conditions of the contract between the bank and the customer originate? How many different sources are likely to affect this contract?

2. What is a *stop-payment order*? Why must a bank obey a customer's order to "stop payment" on a check? What should a stop-payment order include? Can a bank customer issue a stop-payment order on a preauthorized payment—an EFT—periodically charged to the customer's account?

3. What is the bank customer's duty with respect to the bank statement sent to the customer each month? How has the customer's duty changed under revised Article 4? What should the customer do to maximize his or her protection in meeting this duty? Explain.

4. How does the duty and authority of a bank as an agent for the customer differ from the duty and authority of an agent in other circumstances when the principal dies or becomes incompetent? Why do you think this difference exists?

5. What is the bank's liability to a customer when the bank wrongfully dishonors one of the customer's instruments? What limitations are imposed on this liability?

6. Denise made a deposit at her bank on a personalized deposit slip provided by the bank. Despite the fact that she used a personalized deposit slip, her deposit was mistakenly credited to the account of another customer. She wrote a check that would have been good if the deposit had been properly credited to her account but was not good without the deposit. As a result, the check was dishonored due to insufficient funds. What are her rights in this situation? Would your answer differ if the deposit was made on a blank deposit slip provided in the bank lobby? Why?

7. James received his bank statement on 1 August. He examined the statement and discovered a forgery on 14 August. He notified the bank of the forgery on 3 September. A second forgery by the same person had been presented to the bank and honored by the bank on 2 September. What are James's rights against the bank on the second forged check? Explain fully. Would James have better rights if he had informed the bank of the forgery on 15 August? Why?

8. Bob issued a check to Carl. Carl negotiated it to Dave. Dave negotiated it to Edna. Edna went to the bank seeking certification of the check. The bank refused to certify the check for Edna. Has the bank dishonored the check? What are Edna's rights against each of the parties? Why?

9. What is an *electronic funds transfer*? What current methods can a customer use to transfer funds electronically? What advantages, if any, are provided by EFTs over payment by negotiable instrument?

10. What is a *wire transfer*? How are wire transfers regulated under current U.S. law?

CASE PROBLEMS AND WRITING ASSIGNMENTS

1. Brown was the bookkeeper for Reynolds Lumber. Part of Brown's job involved the depositing of checks received by the company into the corporate account. The checks were all indorsed "For Deposit Only." However, the bank permitted the customers to make a "Less Cash" notation on the deposit slip and receive a portion of the check total back in cash. Over the years between 1962 and 1974, Brown expropriated $75,000 by use of the "Less Cash" notation on the deposit slips she took to the bank. When these expropriations were discovered, Reynolds Lumber sued the bank to recover the funds that Brown had embezzled. According to Reynolds Lumber, the bank had no authority to permit the bookkeeper to take cash back on checks indorsed "For Deposit Only," so the bank had breached its duty to the customer by allowing this practice. The bank countered that it allowed all its customers this right and that it was a standard banking practice. Which side had the more persuasive argument? Who should have prevailed in this case? [See *J.W. Reynolds Lumber Co.* v. *Smackover State Bank*, 836 S.W.2d 853 (Ark. 1992).]

2. The checking account that Saboya maintained with Banco Santander reflected a zero balance on 18 November 1985, when Saboya simultaneously deposited $100 cash and a counterfeit cashier's check for $26,250. Two days later, Sainz presented a check in the amount of $16,100, payable to Sainz and drawn by Saboya. Sainz was informed that the check was good and could be cashed, but Sainz requested a cashier's check instead. Sainz was then given a cashier's check by Banco Santander in exchange for the check drawn by Saboya. Sainz deposited the cashier's check in the Banco Guipuzcoano, in Spain, receiving credit for 2,558,870 pesetas. On the same day, Sainz used the proceeds of the cashier's check and some other funds to purchase a 4 million peseta certificate of deposit.

When Banco Santander learned that the cashier's check deposited by Saboya was counterfeit, it stopped payment on the cashier's check it had issued to Sainz. As a result, Banco Guipuzcoano canceled the CD it had issued to Sainz, seized the original amount of the cashier's check (2,558,870 pesetas) from Sainz, and issued a new certificate of deposit for the 1,441,130 peseta difference. Sainz then sued Banco Santander for the losses he suffered due to the alleged wrongful dishonor of the cashier's check he had purchased from the bank. Who should prevail in this case? If Sainz prevails, should he be entitled to compensatory and consequential damages? [See *Sainz Gonzalez* v. *Banco de Santander-Puerto Rico*, 932 F.2d 999 (1st Cir. 1991).]

3. On 10 April 1989, Spedley Securities, an Australian firm, instructed Security Pacific International Bank by telex to wire $1,974,267.97 into the account of Banque Worms, a French bank, at the New York office of BankAmerica. The transfer was a mistake, which Spedley realized several hours later. As a result, Spedley telexed instructions to Security Pacific to stop the initial transfer and instead to make the payment to National Westminster Bank (NatWest). At the time Security Pacific received the telexes, Spedley had a balance of $84,500 remaining with Security Pacific, although sufficient funds for the transfer were received later that morning. Security Pacific mistakenly disregarded the cancellation of the transfer to Banque Worms and made the transfer later, on 10 April. Banque Worms was notified of the transfer through the Clearing House Interbank Payment System (CHIPS). The wire transfer to NatWest was also made, creating an overdraft in the Spedley account. Security Pacific realized that it had made an error, and it contacted BankAmerica to have the funds returned to Security Pacific. BankAmerica agreed to return the funds, but only if Security Pacific would furnish a Council on International Banking, Inc., indemnity. The indemnity was furnished, and BankAmerica returned the funds the following day. However, Banque Worms refused to consent to having its account debited to reflect the return of the funds, and BankAmerica called on Security Pacific to perform as per its indemnity. Security Pacific was unable to cover the indemnity because Spedley had entered into involuntary liquidation. Banque Worms sued BankAmerica to recover the amount of the wire transfer, BankAmerica instituted a third-party action against Security Pacific for return of the funds, and Security Pacific counterclaimed against Banque Worms seeking a declaration that Banque Worms was not entitled to the funds in question. Was Banque Worms able to show either discharge for value or detrimental reliance so that it was entitled to keep the funds transferred initially? [See *Banque Worms* v. *BankAmerica Int'l*, 570 N.E.2d 189 (N.Y. 1991).]

4. Robert Lietzman and his wife Carolyn were the owners of the O-Bar-O ranch, where they lived. The Lietzmans planned to develop some of their land and formed the O-Bar-O Property Development Company for this reason. Heckman, a business associate of Robert Lietzman, was hired by the O-Bar-O ranch to manage the property development deal. Heckman was the only person whose signature appeared on the signature card of the O-Bar-O Property Development Company. When Robert Lietzman died, Heckman wrote checks transferring the funds on deposit in the O-Bar-O Property Development account to one of his other accounts. Carolyn Lietzman objected to this transfer, arguing that the funds on deposit belonged to her and to her husband and also alleging that the bank had a fiduciary duty to the Lietzmans not to allow the transfer of the funds. She and the representative of her husband's estate sued the bank to recover the funds so transferred, and the bank denied liability. Did the bank owe a duty to Ms. Lietzman on this account, notwithstanding the fact that neither her name nor her husband's name appeared on the account in question? What business reasons exist for allowing a bank to continue to honor checks drawn by one of its customers following the bank's notice of the death of the customer? Does it make more sense, from a business perspective, to allow the bank to continue to honor such checks or to force the bank to dishonor any checks on the death of a customer? [See *Lietzman* v. *Ruidoso State Bank*, 827 P.2d 1294 (N.M. 1992).]

5. In November 1981, Marc Gardner, the president of the plaintiff corporation, M.G. Sales, Inc., made out two checks on its account at Chemical Bank. The checks were both in the amount of $6,000 and were payable to, signed, and indorsed by Gardner. Gardner did not remember whether or not he dated the checks. Apparently, he lost both checks. Consequently, on 16 November 1981, he went to defendant Chemical Bank and obtained two stop-payment orders, which gave 10 November 1981 as the date of the checks. The stop-payment orders were by their terms valid for a period of six months. Gardner did not obtain renewals of the stop-payment orders. In January and February 1983, Leon Fried, the third-party defendant, deposited the checks in his account at another branch of Chemical Bank, and Chemical paid the proceeds of the checks to him. Plaintiff commenced this action against Chemical Bank, one of its officers, and the bank tellers who accepted the checks. The first two causes of action allege that Chemical Bank violated the stop-payment orders, in derogation of its fiduciary obligation, and failed to comply with the Uniform Commercial Code and the applicable banking laws and rules. . . . The IAS court denied various motions by the parties seeking summary judgment. It found that Gardner signed and indorsed the undated checks, then lost them, and failed to renew the stop-payment order. It found,

further, that the fact that the checks were torn and tattered, and that the date on one of them appeared to be altered, did not . . . impair the acceptability of an otherwise valid check. However, the court concluded that there was a question of fact, the allegation that the bank did not accept double-indorsed checks for deposit. Did the bank act improperly in failing to stop payment on the two checks? Did the bank act in good faith, and consistently with its commercial practices, in accepting the two checks indorsed by Fried? The checks deposited by Fried in this case were described as "torn and tattered," and the date on at least one of the checks appeared to have been altered. Should any business—particularly a bank—accept such checks without taking some positive steps to verify the checks with the drawer? [See *M.G. Sales, Inc.* v. *Chemical Bank*, 554 N.Y.S.2d 863 (App.Div. 1 Dept. 1990).]

6. **BUSINESS APPLICATION CASE** Waco Airmotive was established in 1976, chiefly to repair aircraft components. By 1979, its main areas of operations were maintenance on airframes, flight instruction, and fuel sales. In 1979, Waco Airmotive obtained a $295,000 SBA loan from American Bank. Waco Airmotive also obtained other loans from American in 1979. These other loans were eventually combined into a single note for $18,036, due 22 May 1980. On 8 July 1980, Waco Airmotive paid the accrued interest and renewed the smaller note. The terms of the renewal allowed the bank to declare all of the company's notes due under certain specified conditions and also provided for a waiver of notice or demand for payment prior to such an acceleration. At the time of the renewal, the bank knew that Waco Airmotive was several hundred dollars overdrawn on its checking account and also knew that the firm was seven months delinquent on its SBA loan payments, totaling $24,584. On 22 July 1980, the bank offset Waco Airmotive's checking account balance of $31,752.68 to pay the entire balance of the 8 July note, with the balance of the account being applied to the SBA loan delinquency. This led to the dishonoring of more than $15,000 in checks written by Waco Airmotive. The checking balance was subsequently applied totally to the SBA loan, and American reinstated the smaller loan balance. In December, Waco Airmotive gave the bank a new note covering the balance from the 8 July note. The bank eventually sued Waco Airmotive on the December note, and Waco Airmotive counterclaimed against the bank for wrongful offset and for malicious conduct by the bank. Did the bank act improperly when it offset the checking account balance of the depositor to cover the loan delinquencies? Was the conduct of the bank malicious toward its customer, and did that entitle the customer to exemplary damages? Banks very commonly retain a right of setoff with a customer's checking account when that customer also has a loan with the bank. How should such a right be negotiated in the loan agreement so that the interests of both parties are adequately protected? [See *American Bank of Waco* v. *Waco Airmotive, Inc.*, 818 S.W.2d 163 (Tex.App.-Waco 1991).]

7. **ETHICAL APPLICATION CASE** Maria Johnson was a depositor at Republic National Bank. In March 1989, she opened a checking account with the bank by depositing $59,000. From May through July she made a series of cash withdrawals from her account at the bank, eventually depleting the account balance. Unbeknownst to the bank, during this same time period, Ms. Johnson's landlord was attempting to have the Department of Health and Rehabilitative Services take action to determine her competency. No action was accomplished during that period, but Ms. Johnson was adjudged incompetent by reason of organic mental syndrome in September 1989. She was 76 years of age at the time of the hearing. The guardian who was appointed for Ms. Johnson attempted to locate the money she had withdrawn but was unable to ascertain what had happened to it. The guardian then filed suit against the bank to recover the money, alleging that there were "red flags" that should have alerted the bank to the condition of its customer, and that the bank should have taken steps to protect Ms. Johnson. Does a bank have an obligation—legally or ethically—to "protect" its customers even though those customers have not been declared incompetent at the time of the transactions in question? Discuss. [See *Republic Nat'l Bank of Miami* v. *Johnson*, 622 So.2d 1015 (Fla.App. 3rd Dist. 1993).]

8. **CRITICAL THINKING CASE** Duchow's Marine, Inc., financed its inventory of boats with a loan from General Electric Capital Corporation (GECC), which took a security interest in the boats and the proceeds from their sale. The security interest was perfected under Wisconsin law. Duchow's Marine and its owner Roger Duchow (collectively Duchow) promised to deposit proceeds into an account from which they could be disbursed only on GECC's signature. The name on this account at Central Bank was "Duchow Marine, Inc. GE Escrow Account." Following the parties' convention, the court called this the blocked account. Duchow maintained a separate account at Central Bank for revenues from other sources; the court called this the regular account. In November 1990, Duchow sold a yacht to Gray Eagle, Inc., and directed the customer to remit $215,370 of

the purchase price to the regular account. By issuing this instruction, Duchow set out to defraud GECC.

Gray Eagle instructed its bank to make a wire transfer, giving it the number of Duchow's regular account. Gray Eagle's bank, which we call the "originator's bank" following the convention of . . . Article 4A, asked Banker's Bank of Madison, Wisconsin, to make the transfer on its behalf. The originator's bank performed correctly. As an intermediary bank, Banker's Bank should have relayed the payment order exactly. It didn't. Banker's Bank made the transfer by crediting Central Bank's account at Banker's Bank, but it bobtailed the instructions. Banker's Bank told Central Bank (which the UCC calls the "beneficiary's bank") that the credit was for Duchow's benefit. That's all: The payment order omitted account identification. A clerk at Central Bank routed the funds to the first account she found bearing Duchow's name: the blocked account. This credit was made on 23 November 1990. Entirely by chance, Duchow's fraudulent scheme had been foiled. But not for long. Duchow, thinking the funds were in the regular account, promptly wrote a check in an effort to spirit them away. The check appeared on the overdrawn-accounts list of 29 November. When contacted, Roger Duchow asserted that the money belonged in the regular account. Central Bank inquired of Banker's Bank, which on 30 November relayed the full payment order, including the number of Duchow's regular account. Without notifying GECC, Central Bank then reversed the credit to the blocked account, credited Duchow's regular account, and paid the check. When it discovered what had happened, GECC filed this diversity action seeking to hold Central Bank liable for conversion of its funds. Central Bank impleaded Duchow, but no one believed that he or his firm was good for the money; Duchow had not participated in this case. The parties agreed that Wisconsin supplied the applicable law. Did Central Bank convert funds that properly should have been subject to the control of GECC? What steps should a beneficiary's bank take in a wire transfer when there is a report that the funds were erroneously credited to the wrong account, and that report is more than one week after the funds were originally received by the beneficiary's bank? Is it fair to let the intermediary bank off the hook when its error (failing to relay the entire wire transfer order) was a significant factor in the resulting misallocation of the funds? Should there be some allocation of the loss to the intermediary on ethical grounds? [See *General Electric Capital Corporation* v. *Central Bank,* 49 F.3d 280 (7th Cir. 1995).]

NOTES

1. § 1693 (a).
2. § 1693 (b).
3. § 1693 (a)(6).
4. § 1693 (d)(c).

5. "Diamond Dealer Denied Consequential Damages Allegedly Sustained When Bank Delayed Execution of Funds Transfer," *New York Law Journal*, New York Law Publishing Company (20 October 1997), http://www.lexis-nexis.com.

Debtor–Creditor Relations

The use of credit is integral to the U.S. economy. People purchase homes on credit; they purchase automobiles on credit; and they purchase major appliances on credit. In addition, businesses use credit to obtain equipment and inventory.

Secured transactions are used to protect creditors by affording a hedge against losses if or when the debtor defaults. Secured transactions give the creditor access to collateral so as to minimize potential losses when the debtor fails to repay in a timely manner the credit extended to the debtor. The law of secured transactions establishes priorities among creditor claims and sets out a structured method for enforcing the rights of competing creditors in the collateral of the debtor.

Other types of credit are also widely used, especially by consumers. Collateralized loans, signature loans, and credit card transactions represent common forms of consumer credit transactions. There are a number of laws designed to provide consumer protection in credit transactions, while also furnishing guidance for the creditors who deal in these areas.

Bankruptcy law protects debtors who encounter financial problems beyond their control or their ability to repay. Put differently, the law of bankruptcy provides for a fresh start for honest debtors. This section examines the law of secured transactions and bankruptcy.

26

SECURED TRANSACTIONS:
SECURITY INTERESTS AND PERFECTION

A G E N D A

In order to expand the business and to take advantage of the opportunities that consequently arise, the Kochanowskis at times will need to borrow money. They therefore need to know how they can borrow money on the most favorable terms available and what sorts of collateral they can use to obtain those terms. They also want to know what granting a security interest in assets they own means to them and to their other creditors.

Furthermore, it is likely that some customers will want to finance CIT videophones when they purchase the merchandise. How can CIT best protect its interests in this property when it grants credit to these customers?

These and similar questions will arise as you study this chapter. Be prepared! You never know when one of the Kochanowskis will need your help or advice.

O U T L I N E

CREDIT FINANCING AND ARTICLE 9

Credit is an extremely important aspect of current American business practices. Without it, many successful firms might never have gotten started. Yet the person who extends credit (the creditor) undertakes the risk that the person to whom he or she has given credit (the debtor) will not be able to repay the debt in full. Understandably, the creditor wishes to be protected against such losses before they occur. The Uniform Commercial Code's methods of creating protection for the creditor form the basis of this chapter's discussion.

We already have seen that a commercial transaction in one of its simplest forms often involves a sale of goods in which the buyer pays cash. Alternatively, the buyer may use a check or draft to pay for all (or a portion of) the goods. In this chapter, we examine a third method of completing a commercial transaction: The buyer gives the owner of the goods a *security interest.* The portion of the Uniform Commercial Code that deals with these matters is Article 9, Secured Transactions; Sales of **Accounts** and **Chattel Paper.**

Despite the availability of several methods of structuring a commercial transaction, use of secured transactions is very common in business today; hence, an understanding of Article 9 is crucial. To illustrate, assume that Bart Brown wishes to buy a meat freezer and a cash register for his new restaurant business. He may pay for part of the sale in cash and receive possession of the items in exchange for giving the seller of the goods a security interest in this equipment. Such a security interest secures (or ensures) payment by the buyer so that if Bart does not pay the seller, the latter can repossess the goods. Thus, a secured transaction allows buyers to receive goods sooner than if they had been forced to pay cash and, at the same time, permits sellers to protect themselves by retaining the right of repossession in the event of a buyer's nonpayment. As we shall see, to ensure that they will have first rights to the equipment in the event of Bart's **default,** sellers must comply with several additional Article 9 rules relating to perfection and priorities. These concepts are developed further in this chapter and in Chapter 27.

Using the terminology adopted by the Code, the seller is characterized as the *secured party* ("a lender, seller, or other person in whose favor there is a security interest, including a person to whom accounts or chattel paper have been sold").[1] Bart, of course, is the *debtor* ("the person who owes payment or other performance of the obligation secured, whether or not he owns or has rights in the collateral, and includes the seller of accounts or chattel paper").[2] Bart and the seller presumably have entered into a *security agreement* ("the agreement which creates or provides for a security interest").[3] The freezer and cash register constitute *collateral* ("the property subject to a security interest").[4] Article 9's application is very broad: It may cover relatively simple business transactions like the one we have described, or it may extend to highly complex forms of business financing, such as accounts receivable financing.[5]

The 1972 Official Text of Article 9 differs substantially from the 1962 official text. Most states have adopted the 1972 version, but since some states still follow the 1962 rules, you should check to see which version applies in your jurisdiction. Though Chapters 26 and 27 use the 1972 Official Text of Article 9, you also should be aware that the American Law Institute and the National Conference of Commissioners on Uniform State Laws in 1998 and 1999 finished their far-reaching revisions of Article 9. Among other things, this newest version of Article 9 (now called "Secured Transactions") expands the scope of property available for secured

Accounts
Rights to payments for goods sold or leased or for services rendered that are not evidenced by an Instrument or chattel paper.

Chattel paper
A writing that evidences both a monetary obligation and a security interest in specific goods.

Default
A failure to do what should be done, especially in the performance of a contractual obligation, without legal excuse or justification for the nonperformance.

transactions. For example, the revision permits creditors to create original security interests in deposit accounts and in software that is embedded in goods. Moreover, revised Article 9 has eliminated the need for the multiple filings required by the 1962 and 1972 versions of the Code. Instead, under the revision, creditors will file in the state where the debtor is located. Other than fixture filings, the creditor need only file centrally, not locally. This change replaces the earlier mixed system of centralized and local filings. This new provision also clarifies the place for filing if the debtor is an international entity or individual. Again, the drafters' intent focuses on facilitating such credit arrangements. Revised Article 9 in addition permits electronic filings and thereby makes the filing process more medium-neutral. The revision furthermore revamps many of the current rules on priorities when competing creditors assert claims as to certain classes of collateral. The American Law Institute and the National Conference of Commissioners on Uniform State Laws hope that by 1 July 2001, each state's legislature will have adopted this newest version of Article 9. Given this unsettled state of the law, you should make special efforts to stay abreast of the status of Article 9 in your state.

Part of the richness of Article 9 stems from its unified approach to secured financing. Before the UCC was drafted, a wide variety of security devices existed; they had arisen rather haphazardly as a result of 100 years' worth of common law and statutory developments in response to perceived security financing needs. These devices—known by such strange names as "pledges," "chattel mortgages," "conditional sales," "trust receipts," and "factor's liens"—were very technical. Hence, a seller who mistakenly had chosen the wrong device, or who had failed to comply with the ticklish requirements of a particular device, later might find that he or she had no valid security interest. Moreover, these devices remained limited in scope; they could not reach **general intangibles,** such as television or motion picture rights or the goodwill of a business or service, which most people today would recognize as important sources of commercial collateral. Finally, these devices placed great emphasis on who had held title during the course of the parties' dealings.

The Code's creation of a *single* device, the Article 9 security interest, was welcome indeed. Article 9's rejection of the older devices—distinctions based on form (and concepts of title)[6] —has led to a simplified structure. This format more accurately reflects the wide variety of present-day secured financing transactions and allows for commercial recognition of new forms of financing without requiring state legislatures to pass new statutes or change old ones. This chapter focuses on some of the provisions of Article 9 that illustrate the Code's breadth and flexibility.

> **General intangibles**
> Personal property other than goods, accounts, chattel paper, instruments, documents, or money; for example, goodwill, literary rights, patents, or copyrights.

SCOPE OF ARTICLE 9

In general, § 9-102 of Article 9:

> applies (a) to any transaction (regardless of its form) which is intended to create a security interest in personal property or fixtures including goods, documents, instruments, general intangibles, chattel paper or accounts and also (b) to any sale of accounts or chattel paper.

By a *security interest*, Article 9 means "an interest in personal property or fixtures which secures payment or performance of an obligation."[7] The personal property or collateral that will be subject to a security interest takes many forms. Moreover, the Code categorizes collateral according to either (1) the *nature* of the collateral or (2) its *use*. Thus, *documents* (warehouse receipts, bills of lading, and other documents of title); *instruments* (drafts, certificates of deposit, stocks, and bonds); *proceeds* (whatever is received upon the sale, exchange, collection, or other disposition of collateral or proceeds); and the three kinds of collateral defined earlier—*accounts*, *chattel paper*, and *general intangibles*—represent the types of collateral the Code classifies primarily on the basis of their *nature*.

Goods, the most common type of collateral, are categorized on the basis of their *use* by the *debtor*. According to the Code, *goods* include all things that are movable at the time the security interest attaches or that are fixtures.[8] *Consumer goods* consist of those goods used or bought for use primarily for personal, family, or household purposes. Thus, a debtor may give a security interest in his or her furniture or car to a secured party. *Equipment* includes goods used or bought for use primarily in business. Bart's freezer and cash register are equipment collateral, as a truck would be for the electric company. Farm products also constitute a type of goods. The Code defines *farm products* as crops, livestock, or supplies used or produced in farming operations. Interestingly, then, a farmer may give a security interest in wheat, corn, cows, or even milk, since the Code covers the products of crops or livestock in their unmanufactured states as well.[9] *Inventory*, defined as goods held by a person for sale or lease or raw materials used or consumed in a business, is another type of goods. Inventory differs from consumer goods and equipment because inventory is held for sale rather than use.[10] Such things as coal or the packaging for goods are inventory, as is a dealer's supply of cars or a merchant's supply of tires, paint, clothing, or toys. The last type of goods that the Code delineates is *fixtures*. Goods are fixtures when they become so related to particular real estate that an interest in them arises under real estate law.[11] To illustrate, furnaces and central air-conditioning units are fixtures.

These differences in definition within the Code make these classes of goods *mutually exclusive*. In other words, the same property cannot at the same time and to the same person be both equipment and inventory. In borderline cases—for example, a social worker's car or a farmer's pickup—the principal use to which the debtor has put the property determines the type of collateral involved.[12] Because the Code's rules regarding perfection, priorities, and default often turn on the type of collateral involved (as we shall see in Chapter 27), it is important to know which category of collateral is present in a given transaction.

Whatever the kind of collateral that is subject to the security interest, the Code drafters apparently meant Article 9 to apply to all *consensual* security interests in personal property and fixtures as well as to certain sales of accounts and chattel paper (often called *assignments*).[13] In our earlier example, we can say that Bart Brown and the seller of the meat freezer and the cash register each has consented to enter into this commercial transaction. Since personal property is involved (the freezer and register are goods), Bart has agreed to let the seller retain an interest in the goods until Bart pays for them (a method of ensuring the performance of Bart's obligations); and the seller, in turn, has agreed to give the goods to Bart now (even though the seller has not received the total price for them) in exchange for the right to repossess the freezer and register if Bart fails to pay. This transaction therefore fulfills all the requirements of an enforceable security interest.

Given the need for consent between the parties, Article 9 accordingly does not apply to a security interest that arises by **operation of law** rather than through the agreement of the parties. Examples of such situations include a **mechanic's lien** on

Operation of law
Certain automatic results that must occur following certain actions or facts because of established legal principles and not as the result of any voluntary choice by the parties involved.

Mechanic's lien
Given to certain builders, artisans, and providers of material, a statutory protection that grants a lien on the building and the land improved by such persons.

26.1 | MANAGEMENT/ FINANCE

SOURCES OF FINANCING

Tom and Anna would like to borrow money for the operation of the business, but they would prefer not to use their personal assets as security for any credit they receive. They ask you what assets CIT has that might be useful as collateral for any loans they seek. What will you tell them?

BUSINESS CONSIDERATIONS How can businesspersons who are starting a closely held business acquire financing without using their personal assets as collateral? Is it a good idea for the owner/managers of small businesses to have their personal and professional assets closely entwined in the business venture?

ETHICAL CONSIDERATIONS Is it ethical for a lender to insist that the owners of a start-up business use their personal assets as security for loans extended to the business? What ethical principles does this situation involve?

Bart's restaurant that an unpaid contractor obtains as a result of renovating Bart's place of business. The lien represents the money Bart owes for the labor and materials involved in the remodeling of the restaurant. Since Bart and the contractor have not agreed in advance that the contractor will have an interest in Bart's restaurant, this is a nonconsensual arrangement that arises as a consequence of the parties' *status* (the contractor is a creditor who now is using the restaurant as security for the debt that Bart owes) rather than as a result of *mutual consent.* It therefore is not an Article 9 security interest.

This result also stems from the fact that Article 9 in general does not apply to real property or real estate. Instead, as mentioned, it applies only to security interests in *personal property.* Hence, Article 9 has no bearing on land mortgages or on landlords' liens. And although it specifically includes within its scope the old methods of creating security interests (e.g., pledges, chattel mortgages, and factor's liens),[14] Article 9 specifically exempts from its coverage security interests that are subject to any federal statute and certain other categories of transactions, including wage and salary claims and claims resulting from court judgments.[15]

In some cases, a transaction, although covered by Article 9, also may be subject to any local statutes governing usury, retail installment sales, and the like (e.g., the Uniform Consumer Credit Code). In those situations, in the event of a conflict, the provisions of any such statute, and not Article 9, are controlling.[16]

One test a person can use in deciding whether Article 9 applies is to ask whether the transaction is *intended* to have effect as security. If the answer is *yes,* Article 9 probably covers the transaction.

SECURITY INTEREST

As we have just noted, Article 9 broadly defines the term *security interest* as an interest in personal property or fixtures that secures payment or performance of an obligation. One of the advantages of the Code derives from the flexibility of such a sweeping definition. In fact, courts have had few problems concerning how to recognize a security interest. Despite this seeming simplicity of definition, one area— that of leases "intended as security" in contrast to "true" leases—has caused businesspeople and courts some difficulties.

The Code states definitively that Article 9 applies to "a lease intended as security."[17] It also notes that the facts of each case determine whether a lease is intended as security and that the inclusion of an option to purchase does not in and of itself make the lease one intended for security. On the other hand, a provision that upon the expiration of the lease, the person who is leasing (called the *lessee*) becomes the owner, or has the option of buying the property for very little money, makes the lease one intended as security.[18] In this latter situation, the transaction more closely resembles an installment sales contract, especially when, as is often the case, the "rental" payments equal the selling price of the property subject to the "lease." In such circumstances, the *lessor* (the person leasing the personal property to another) actually is a secured party who is using the monthly leasing payments as monthly installments on a conditional sales agreement. This transaction *is* subject to the Code's provisions because it is a lease intended as security, not a true lease.

Why is this an important distinction anyway? The answer will become clear when we discuss the process of perfection. If such a lease is intended as security, it will be subject to Article 9's filing requirements. A true lease will not require an Article 9 filing because Article 9 in general is inapplicable to situations in which one merely pays for the right to use the goods for a specified period of time without ever becoming the owner of the leased property. Debtors in Article 9 transactions are trying to buy the property that is the object of the security interest. At the same time, secured parties are retaining an interest in the property until this transfer of ownership is accomplished by the debtor's paying all that is owed. In a true lease, the parties never contemplate such an eventual transfer of ownership.

Thus, if we change the facts of our earlier hypothetical case and have Bart lease the freezer and cash register, assuming this is a true lease, Article 9 does not govern the transaction. If the owner of the freezer and register in effect is retaining *title* to the goods to ensure that Bart will pay for them, however, we have a *lease intended as security,* and the parties must follow Article 9's rules. As we shall see later, this means that if Bart becomes bankrupt, the **trustee in bankruptcy** will be able to get the equipment because the law will deem Bart the owner of the equipment. He in essence has been paying for the items on an installment sales basis, even though the parties have called the transaction a lease. By failing to file, the original owner of the equipment has not perfected his or her interest in the equipment and will be unable to repossess the equipment (or any other type of collateral). Since the law in these circumstances treats the bankruptcy trustee as a **lien creditor,** the trustee will have superior rights to those of our unperfected original owner.

The next decision involves a bankruptcy case in which the judge grappled with many of these very issues. Note the care with which the court applied the various factors suggesting the absence—or presence—of a lease intended as security.

Trustee in bankruptcy
The person appointed by the bankruptcy court to act as trustee of the debtor's property for the benefit and protection of the creditors.

Lien creditor
One whose debt is secured by a claim on specific property.

26.1

IN RE ARCHITECTURAL MILLWORK OF VIRGINIA, INC.
226 B.R. 551 (BKRTCY.W.D.VA. 1998)

FACTS The debtor, Architectural Millwork of Virginia, Inc., filed a Chapter 11 bankruptcy petition on 25 March 1998. Prior to the filing date, Associates Leasing, Inc. (Associates) and the debtor on 16 May 1996 entered into a truck lease agreement, providing for the lease of a 1995 Freightliner vehicle (the Freightliner agreement). Then, on 2 August 1996, River Ridge Supply (RRS) and the debtor entered into a conditional sales contract regarding a Komatsu forklift (the Komatsu agreement). Contemporaneous with the execution of the Komatsu agreement, RRS assigned to Associates all RRS's rights under the agreement. The Komatsu agreement gave the debtor the option to purchase the forklift for one dollar after the debtor had made all the scheduled payments. The Freightliner agreement, in contrast, permitted the debtor to purchase the truck at the end of the "lease" period at the price that represented the residual value of the truck. When the debtor filed its Chapter 11 petition,

continued

26.1

IN RE ARCHITECTURAL MILLWORK OF VIRGINIA, INC., *continued*
226 B.R. 551 (BKRTCY.W.D.VA. 1998)

the question before the court centered on whether the equipment leases were "true" leases or disguised "security agreements."

ISSUE Were the leases in question "true" leases and thus subject to the bankruptcy laws, or were the leases intended as security and hence covered under Virginia's Commercial Code?

HOLDING The Komatsu agreement was a lease intended as security that fell under the coverage of Virginia's Commercial Code, not the federal bankruptcy laws. However, the Freightliner agreement involved a true lease that, according to the bankruptcy laws, the debtor either must assume or reject.

REASONING This case turns on whether, under the Bankruptcy Code, the agreements in question are true leases or, in fact, security agreements. Courts make such determinations by reference to state law. Of particular importance to this case, then, is the first paragraph of Virginia Code § 8.1-201(37), which reads as follows:

> (37) 1. "Security interest" means an interest in personal property or fixtures which secures payment or performance of an obligation. . . . Whether a lease is intended as security is to be determined by the facts of each case; however, (a) the inclusion of an option to purchase does not of itself make the lease one intended for security, and (b) an agreement that upon compliance with the terms of the lease the lessee shall become or has the option to become the owner of the property for no additional consideration or for a nominal consideration does make the lease one intended for security *(emphasis supplied).*

Although the statute requires a court to examine the facts of each case, the plain language of the statute creates a security interest in property as a matter of law if the parties' contract allows the lessee, upon compliance with the terms of the lease, to become the owner of the leased property for nominal or no additional consideration. Applying this rule to the two agreements involved in this case would produce mixed results. The Komatsu agreement clearly provided for the option to purchase the forklift for one dollar after the completion of all scheduled payments. Consequently, this transaction was, in fact, a security

agreement under the Bankruptcy Code. While the Freightliner agreement would present more interpretive difficulties, a court must deem significant the fact that the final adjustment clause gave the debtor the option to purchase the equipment at the end of the lease at the price set by the residual value, $9,625.00. Indeed, Associates's own representative testified that Associates would release the title to the debtor, without the need for an actual public or private sale, if the debtor offered the residual value at the conclusion of the lease term. The court's accepting Associates's characterization of the final adjustment clause as an option to purchase, however, would represent only the initial step in the process of determining whether the Freightliner agreement was a disguised security agreement and not a true lease. The following provisions of Virginia Code § 8.1-201(37) help to resolve this question:

> 2. *Whether a transaction creates a lease or security interest is determined by the facts of each case; however, a transaction creates a security interest if the consideration the lessee is to pay the lessor for the right to possession and use of the goods is an obligation for the term of the lease not subject to termination by the lessee, and:*
> (a) *The original term of the lease is equal to or greater than the remaining economic life of the goods;*
> (b) *The lessee is bound to renew the lease for the remaining economic life of the goods or is bound to become the owner of the goods;*
> (c) *The lessee has an option to renew the lease for the remaining economic life of the goods for no additional consideration or nominal additional consideration upon compliance with the lease agreement; or*
> (d) *The lessee has an option to become the owner of the goods for no additional consideration or nominal additional consideration upon compliance with the lease agreement.*

As conceded by the debtor, the relevant portions of this statute are found in the main body of paragraph two and in subsection (d). Under this analysis, if (1) the debtor is unable to avoid paying Associates the value of the payments due under the lease, and (2) upon compliance with the lease terms, the debtor can become the owner of the Freightliner for nominal

26.1

IN RE ARCHITECTURAL MILLWORK OF VIRGINIA, INC., *continued*
226 B.R. 551 (BKRTCY.W.D.VA. 1998)

or no consideration, then the transaction creates a security interest. The first of these two conditions exists in this case. While the debtor can terminate the lease early, it cannot avoid or terminate the obligation to pay Associates the value of the consideration due under the Freightliner agreement. Having satisfied the first condition of paragraph two, a court must ascertain whether any of the four criteria detailed in subsections (a) through (d) also exists. If so, then the Freightliner agreement is not a true lease. Associates contended that one cannot characterize the residual value purchase price of $9,625.00 as nominal consideration under subsection (d). The price of $9,625.00 clearly would not qualify as such, particularly in light of the agreement's capitalized cost of only $38,500.00. Furthermore, the testimony of both parties indicated that, at the time of the execution of the agreement, this $9,625.00 residual value was a fair estimate of the vehicle's value at the conclusion of the lease period. Consequently, it was not clear from the evidence whether the parties expected the debtor to recognize much, if any, equity in the vehicle or whether the only economically sensible course for the debtor would involve exercising the option to purchase the vehicle. For example, it makes sense that a lessee would provide insurance on the property while in possession of it under a lease; and it seems perfectly reasonable for a lessee to agree to undertake some of the risks of loss or damage while the lessee enjoys the possession and use of the property. The same holds true for taxes and maintenance. Hence, the court would view such factors as whether the vehicle can be purchased for nominal consideration and the anticipated amount of the lessee's equity in the vehicle as the most important criteria. As to the latter criteria, the final adjustment clause of paragraph 8 of the Freightliner agreement indicated that the debtor in this case theoretically could build up equity in the vehicle if its value could be maintained over the lease term at an amount higher than the $9,625.00 option price. Yet the evidence showed that the parties had expected little, if any, equity actually to accrue for the benefit of the debtor in this transaction. Moreover, the $9,625.00 residual value was a fair estimate, at the time of the execution of the agreement, of the vehicle's anticipated value at the conclusion of the lease payments. This "fact," in conjunction with an application of the first criterion, would lead to the conclusion that the resulting option price of $9,625.00 did not constitute nominal consideration. Thus, the Freightliner agreement constituted a true lease under the bankruptcy laws, but the Komatsu agreement involved a lease intended as security under Virginia's Commercial Code.

BUSINESS CONSIDERATIONS Why would a seller prefer to characterize a lease as a true lease rather than as a lease intended as security? Why would competing creditors prefer to characterize a lease as a lease intended as security rather than as a true lease?

ETHICAL CONSIDERATION Has a seller who recognizes the legal distinctions between a true lease and a lease intended as security acted unethically toward the lessee/debtor if the seller couches the arrangement as a true lease but asks for monthly payments that in effect mean the lessee will pay twice the fair market value of the item leased?

CREATION AND ENFORCEABILITY OF THE SECURITY INTEREST

A security interest is of negligible value unless it is valid and enforceable. It therefore behooves the owner of the freezer and the register in our earlier hypothetical case to attain the status of a *secured creditor* (or secured party). In this way, if Bart, the debtor, later cannot or will not pay for the equipment, the secured party will be able to repossess the goods and, if perfected, enjoy priority over the claims that other third parties, such as the bankruptcy trustee, may assert regarding the property.

However, before the secured party has an enforceable security interest in the collateral, the security interest must attach.[19] *Attachment* is the process by which the secured party and the debtor create the security interest and thereby confer on the secured party certain enforceable rights to the collateral vis-à-vis the debtor. Attachment does not give the secured party rights necessarily superior to those obtained by other creditors (an additional step called *perfection* is necessary to accomplish this). Nevertheless, as the first step in the creation and enforceability of a security interest, attachment remains extremely important.

According to the UCC, attachment occurs when a prospective secured party does all of the following:

1. Enters into a *security agreement* whereby the prospective secured party and the debtor agree that a security interest will attach
2. Possesses a security agreement signed by the debtor or, alternatively, pursuant to agreement, retains possession of the collateral
3. Ascertains that the debtor has rights in the collateral
4. Gives value

The omission of any of the requirements just listed invalidates the security interest. Such an argument underlies the *In re CFLC, Inc.* case.

26.2

IN RE CFLC, INC.
166 F.3D 1012 (9TH CIR. 1999)

FACTS In August 1991, Expeditors International of Washington, Inc. (Expeditors) began providing transportation-related services for CFLC, Inc., formerly known as Everex Systems, Inc. (Everex). These services included freight forwarding, ocean shipping, and customs brokerage. For 17 months prior to Everex's filing its bankruptcy petition, Expeditors handled Everex's export and import shipments and thus was in continuous possession, either directly or through its agents, of Everex's goods. Expeditors billed Everex on Expeditors's regular invoices, which were issued contemporaneously with receipt of the shipments. From August 1991 until January 1993, Expeditors sent approximately 330 invoices that contained fine print on the reverse side entitled "Terms and Conditions of Service." The language of the fifteenth paragraph therein stated:

15. *General Lien on Any Property. The Company shall have a general lien on any and all property (and documents relating thereto) of the Customer, in its possession, custody or control or en route, for all claims for charges, expenses or advances incurred by the company in connection with any shipments of the Customer and if such claim remains unsatisfied for thirty (30)*

days after demand for its payment is made, the Company may sell at public auction or private sale . . . the goods, wares and/or merchandise, or so much thereof as may be necessary to satisfy such lien. . . .

Everex never signed these invoices or any agreement with Expeditors regarding the printed invoice terms. Moreover, the parties neither discussed nor expressly bargained over Section 15 of the invoice or any other provision on the reverse side of the invoice. Furthermore, Everex failed to object to the invoice terms prior to its bankruptcy; and Expeditors did not attempt to enforce Section 15 until 29 October 1992. At that time, Expeditors notified an Everex employee that Expeditors would be asserting its lien on the Everex goods in its possession until Everex made payments on the outstanding invoices. Prior to the filing of the bankruptcy petition, the parties continued their normal business operations. At the time of Everex's bankruptcy filing, Expeditors thus was in possession of Everex property valued at $81,402. Expeditors claimed that Everex owed a balance of almost $43,000 for the past-due invoices and that Expeditors held a security interest in the Everex property because the invoices amounted to a security agreement. Hence,

26.2

IN RE CFLC, INC., *continued*
166 F.3D 1012 (9TH CIR. 1999)

expeditors subsequently filed a complaint in which it asked the bankruptcy court to determine the validity, priority, and extent of the claimed lien.

ISSUE Did Expeditors's pre-printed invoice terms create an Article 9 security interest in Everex's property, either explicitly or through a course of dealing analysis?

HOLDING No. The invoices themselves did not amount to an agreement for a security interest. Furthermore, Expeditors's repeated delivery of the invoice terms did not constitute a course of dealing; the absence of any security agreement that could be supplemented by such evidence would preclude such a conclusion.

REASONING Expeditors argued that its pre-printed invoices created an enforceable Article 9 security interest in Everex's property in either of two ways: (1) Receipt of Expeditors's invoices without objection by Everex had created an agreement that contained the security interest, or (2) the invoices had established a basis for course of dealing analysis that a court in turn could use to supplement the terms of the contract, thereby including a security interest. Section 9203 of the California Commercial Code outlines three requirements for the attachment and enforceability of a security interest: the secured party's possession of the collateral pursuant to an agreement, value given by the secured party, and the debtor's having rights in the collateral. No magic words are necessary to create or provide for a security interest so long as the minimum formal requirements of the Code are met. Although the UCC does not specifically state that an intention to create a security agreement is an element necessary to create a valid security agreement, the law clearly requires an intention to do so. Put differently, the intent to create a security interest must appear on the face of a written document executed by the debtor. Although Expeditors outwardly appeared to have met the three requirements delineated in the UCC, the transactions lacked the requisite intent to create a security interest. Everex executed no documents manifesting its intention to give Expeditors a security interest. Rather, the terms for a security interest appeared only on the creditor's forms. The parties stipulated that they neither had discussed these terms

nor had Everex ever signed the invoices or any other agreement containing these terms. The invoices alone were insufficient to form a security interest because a creditor's pre-printed agreements would fail to create a security interest if the debtor never intended the collateral to be used for this purpose. Expeditors argued that case law supports its contention that Everex's failure to object to the invoice terms would constitute a tacit approval of the creation of a security agreement. Yet, unlike the parties in the precedent cited, Expeditors and Everex never discussed the terms on the invoices and also failed to reach any agreement regarding a security interest. Expeditors possessed Everex's property because Expeditors was providing freight forwarding services, not because Expeditors was securing Everex's obligation through a general lien. Hence, the requirement that both parties demonstrate an intent to create a security interest was absent here. Thus, the pre-printed invoice terms did not create a security interest. Nor could the course of dealing analysis suggested by Expeditors provide evidence of the claimed security interest. The UCC defines course of dealing as "a sequence of previous conduct between the parties to a particular transaction which is fairly to be regarded as establishing a common basis of understanding for interpreting their expressions and other conduct." An inference of the parties' common knowledge or understanding that is based on a prior course of dealing is a question of fact. Course of dealing analysis requires a determination of whether an indication of the common knowledge and understanding of the parties exists. Course of dealing evidence therefore may supplement the agreement by providing evidence of the parties' intentions, but it cannot be used to create an agreement. In short, course of dealing usually refers to the parties' previous dealings that provide evidence of the parties' previous agreement on a specific issue that the parties now dispute. Course of dealing analysis therefore is not proper in a situation in which the only action taken consists of the repeated delivery of a particular invoice by one of the parties. While the circuits disagree as to the advisability of using course of dealing to "fill the void" as to certain contractual issues, the sounder approach here, where the addition of a general lien would do more than "fill the void," would involve refusing to add such terms to the contract without the mutual

continued

26.2

IN RE CFLC, INC., *continued*

166 F.3D 1012 (9TH CIR. 1999)

agreement of the parties. Therefore, in this case it was not proper to use course of dealing analysis to establish a security interest. In sum, no Article 9 security interest was created, since the mere sending of preprinted invoices was insufficient either to establish the mutual intent necessary to create a security interest or to require the application of course of dealing analysis. The bankruptcy appellate panel's ruling that Expeditors had failed to create an Article 9 security interest therefore should be affirmed.

BUSINESS CONSIDERATION Armed with hindsight, what should Expeditors have done differently?

ETHICAL CONSIDERATION Everex had outstanding sums due and owing to Expeditors for a period of many months. Is a debtor's use of the bankruptcy laws unethical vis-à-vis the debtor's creditors, especially if the creditor has been patient regarding the debtor's arrearages?

Pledge

A debtor's delivery of collateral to a creditor, who will possess the collateral until the debt is paid.

Note that the *In re CFLC, Inc.* case centered in part on whether the creditor's having possession of the goods indicated the existence of a security interest. The court held that unless the creditor had both physically retained the goods used as collateral in the transaction and had done so pursuant to an agreement between the parties, attachment had not occurred. On the other hand, a transaction involving a simple **pledge** of a coin collection in which, by agreement, the owner of the collection insists on keeping it until the debtor pays for it ordinarily will be enforceable because, in these circumstances, attachment will have occurred. In most cases, however, as in the situation involving Bart, the debtor will not agree to the secured party's retaining possession of the collateral (without his meat freezer on site, Bart will have few customers!). Thus, in lieu of possession and evidence of an oral security agreement, a *signed security agreement* will be necessary to make the security interest valid.

To comply with the Code,[20] this latter type of security agreement must:

1. be in writing
2. create or provide for a security interest
3. reasonably identify the collateral
4. be signed by the debtor

Although these requirements appear straightforward, a great deal of litigation has resulted from a creditor's failure to use forms that include this minimal information or from a failure to fill out these forms correctly. A security agreement may contain many other terms as well, such as the amount of the indebtedness and the terms of payment; liability in the event of risk of loss or damage to the collateral; a requirement of insurance on and the maintenance and repair of the collateral; a warranty by the debtor that he or she owns the collateral free from liens or security interests; a statement of the debtor's rights (if any) regarding removal of the collateral to another location; and a description of events that constitute default by the debtor. The security agreement in Exhibit 26.1 includes some of these terms.

A security agreement also may extend the security interest of the secured party to all collateral of the kind that is the subject of the agreement and that the debtor may acquire *after* entering into this agreement. Thus, if Bart, subsequent to entering into a security agreement with the seller of the freezer, obtains an industrial-

E X H I B I T   26.1 | **Security Agreement Form**

SECURITY AGREEMENT USED WITH
LOAN ON
GOODS, FIXTURES, OR EQUIPMENT

_____ , 20 _____

_____
(NAME)

_____
(NO. AND STREET)   (CITY)   (COUNTY)   (STATE)

(Hereinafter called "Debtor") hereby grants to KeyBank National Association, South Bend, Indiana (Hereinafter called "Bank"), a security interest in the following property together with all tools, accessories, parts, equipment and accessions now attached to or which may hereafter at any time be placed or added to the property; also any replacements of such property herein described (hereinafter called "Collateral"):

_____

_____

_____

_____

The security interest granted hereby is to secure payment and performance of the liabilities and obligations of DEBTOR to Bank of every kind and description, direct or indirect, absolute or contingent, due or to become due, now existing or hereafter arising (hereinafter called Obligations").

Debtor hereby warrants and covenants:

1. The collateral is being acquired for the following primary uses: _____ personal, or family use, _____ business use, or _____ farming operations.

2. The Collateral _____ will _____ will not be acquired with the proceeds of the loan provided for in this Agreement. (In the event the Collateral will be acquired with the proceeds of the loan, the Bank may disburse such proceeds to the seller of the Collateral.)

3. In the event the Collateral will be attached to real estate, the description of such real estate and the known owner of record of such real estate are set forth hereafter. If the Collateral is attached to such real estate prior to the perfection of the security interest granted herein, the Debtor will, on demand, furnish the Bank with a disclaimer or disclaimers executed by persons having an interest in such real estate. Real estate described:

_____

_____

_____

4. The Collateral will be kept at the address of the Debtor set out below, which in the case of a business is the address of the principal office of such business within this state. Debtor will not remove the Collateral from the state without the prior written consent of the Bank. If the Collateral is being acquired for farming use and the Debtor is not a resident of Indiana, the Collateral will be kept at the address set forth in the description of the Collateral. Debtor will immediately give written notice to the Bank of any change of address and in the case of a business any change in its principal place of business and if the Collateral consists of equipment normally

E X H I B I T   26.1 | **Security Agreement Form, continued**

used in more than one state, any use of the Collateral in any jurisdiction other than a state in which the Debtor shall have previously advised the Bank such Collateral will be used.

5. Debtor has, or will acquire, full and clear title to the Collateral and except for the security interest granted herein, will at all times keep the Collateral free from any adverse lien, security interest or encumbrance.

6. No financing statement covering all or any portion of the Collateral is on file in any public office.

7. Debtor authorizes the Bank at the expense of the Debtor to execute and file on its behalf a financing statement or statements in those public offices deemed necessary by the Bank to protect its security interest in the Collateral. Debtor will deliver or cause to be delivered to the Bank any certificates of title to the Collateral with the security interest of the Bank noted thereon.

8. Debtor will not sell or offer to sell or otherwise transfer the Collateral or any interest therein without the prior written consent of the Bank.

9. Debtor will at all times keep the Collateral insured against loss, damage, theft and other risks in such amounts, under such policies and with such companies as shall be satisfactory to the Bank, which policies shall provide that any loss thereunder shall be payable to the Bank as its interest may appear and the Bank may apply the proceeds of the insurance against the outstanding indebtedness of the Debtor, regardless of whether all or any portion of such indebtedness is due or owing. All policies of insurance so required shall be placed in the possession of the Bank.

Upon failure of the Debtor to procure such insurance or to remove any encumbrance upon the Collateral or if such insurance is cancelled, the indebtedness secured hereby shall become immediately due and payable at the option of the Bank, without notice or demand, or the Bank may procure such insurance or remove any encumbrance on the Collateral and the amount so paid by the Bank shall be immediately repayable and shall be added to and become a part of the indebtedness secured hereby and shall bear interest at the same note rate as the indebtedness secured hereby until paid.

10. Debtor will keep the Collateral in good order and repair and will not waste or destroy the Collateral or any portion thereof. Debtor will not use the Collateral in violation of any statute or ordinance or any policy of insurance thereon and the Bank may examine and inspect such Collateral at any reasonable time or times wherever located.

11. Debtor will pay promptly when due all taxes and assessments upon the Collateral or for its use or operation.

12. The occurrence of any one of the following events shall constitute default under this Security Agreement: (a) nonpayment when due of any installment of the indebtedness hereby secured or failure to perform any agreement contained herein; (b) any statement, representation, or warranty at any time furnished the Bank is untrue in any material respect as of the date made; (c) Debtor becomes insolvent or unable to pay debts as they mature; (d) entry of judgment against the Debtor; (e) loss, theft, substantial damage, destruction, sale or encumbrance to or of all or any portion of the Collateral, or the making of any levy, seizure or attachment, thereof, or thereon; (f) death of the Debtor who is a natural person or of any partner of the Debtor which is a partnership; (g) dissolution, merger or consolidation or transfer of a substantial portion of the property of the

E X H I B I T 26.1 | **Security Agreement Form, continued**

Debtor which is a corporation or partnership; or (h) the Bank deems itself insecure for any other reason whatsoever.

When an event of default shall be existing, the note or notes and any other liabilities may at the option of the Bank and without notice or demand be declared and thereupon immediately shall become due and payable and the Bank may exercise from time to time any rights and remedies of a secured party under the Uniform Commercial Code or other applicable law. Debtor agrees in the event of default to make the Collateral available to the Bank at a place acceptable to the Bank which is convenient to the Debtor. If any notification or disposition of all or any portion of the Collateral is required by law, such notification shall be deemed reasonable and properly given if mailed at least ten (10) days prior to such disposition, postage prepaid to the Debtor at its latest address appearing on the records of the Bank. Expenses of retaking, holding, repairing, preparing for sale and selling shall include the Bank's reasonable attorneys' fees and expenses. Any proceeds of the disposition of the Collateral will be applied by the Bank to the payment of expenses of retaking, holding, repairing, preparing for sale and selling the Collateral, including reasonable attorneys' fees and legal expenses and any balance of such proceeds will be applied by the Bank to the payment of the indebtedness then owing the Bank.

No delay on the part of the Bank in the exercise of any right or remedy shall operate as a waiver thereof, and no single or partial exercise by the Bank of any right or remedy shall preclude other or further exercise thereof or the exercise of any other right or remedy. If more than one party shall execute this Agreement, the term "Debtor" shall mean all parties signing this Agreement and each of them, and such parties shall be jointly and severally obligated hereunder. The neuter pronoun, when used herein, shall include the masculine and the feminine and also the plural. If this agreement is not dated when executed by the Debtor, the Bank is authorized, without notice to the Debtor, to date this Agreement.

This Agreement has been delivered at South Bend, Indiana, and shall be construed in accordance with the laws of the State of Indiana. Wherever possible each provision of this Agreement shall be interpreted in such manner as to be effective and valid under applicable law, but if any provision of this Agreement shall be prohibited by or invalid under applicable law, such provision shall be ineffective to the extent of such prohibition or invalidity, without invalidating the remainder of such provision or the remaining provisions of this Agreement.

This Agreement shall be binding upon the heirs, administrators and executors of the Debtor and the rights and privileges of the Bank hereunder so insured to the benefit of its successors and assigns.

Address: _____

_____   _____

Courtesy of KeyBank, National Association, South Bend, Indiana.

26.2 | SALES/ MANAGEMENT

SHOULD CIT SELL OR LEASE CALL-IMAGE?

Assume that CIT agrees to provide 100 Call-Image video-phones to a local telemarketing firm and that CIT is willing to provide the merchandise on credit. Tom is willing to lease the units to the telemarketing firm. Dan, however, insists that the units should be sold and that CIT should retain a security interest in them. Tom and Dan have asked for your advice. What will you tell them?

BUSINESS CONSIDERATIONS If a business leases equipment to a customer, should the lessor comply with the Article 9 filing requirement even though the transaction is a lease? Why or why not? If a business sells equipment to a customer on credit, what broad language should the seller include in the security agreement so as to maximize its protection?

ETHICAL CONSIDERATION Is it ethical for a creditor who is entering into a secured transaction to use an after-acquired property clause, thus increasing its collateral to substantially more than the total debt secured? Why or why not?

grade bread-making machine, inclusion of an *after-acquired property clause* in the original security agreement means that the seller also may get the bread-making machine if Bart ultimately fails to pay for the freezer and the cash register. Or, alternatively, assume Bart is a seller of stereos and that he gives a security interest to a creditor who has provided him with an inventory of stereos. Every time Bart sells one of the original stereos and uses the money from this sale to purchase another stereo to replenish his inventory, the creditor's security interest in the original inventory of stereos leaves the first stereo, affixes to the proceeds, follows the proceeds through Bart's bank account, and affixes to the stereo purchased to restock the inventory. Such after-acquired property clauses are common in secured transactions.

The need for evidence of the parties' intentions forms the basis for requiring such information on the security agreement. If the parties have spelled out their respective rights and duties in advance, fewer disputes over the terms of the agreement and over the property that represents the collateral for the obligation secured should ensue.

PERFECTION

Thus far, we have focused primarily on the relationship between the creditor and the debtor and how the creditor, by becoming a secured party, may protect his or her interest in the collateral. Yet, in that earlier discussion, we noted that the processes leading to the creation and enforceability of a secured interest only give the secured party rights greater than those of the debtor; they do not necessarily confer on the secured party superior rights to the collateral vis-à-vis other creditors and the bankruptcy trustee.

Now we turn to a discussion of how secured parties can protect themselves against such third parties who also may be claiming rights in the collateral. In other words, how can the seller/secured party in our earlier example protect the freezer and register from Bart's other business creditors (e.g., produce suppliers) if Bart's financial situation deteriorates to the point that either the other creditors or—if Bart is on the verge of insolvency—the trustee in bankruptcy is trying to get all of Bart's equipment so as to satisfy Bart's creditors' claims against him?

Perfection is the process by which secured parties protect their collateral from the clutches of later creditors who also have given value when the debtor has used these same pieces of equipment as collateral for loans from them. The date of perfection, in turn, represents the date from which the law measures priorities whenever competing claims among other perfected creditors exist. The topic of priorities among secured parties is addressed in Chapter 27.

In general, perfection occurs in one of three ways: by the creditor's filing a financing statement, by the creditor's taking possession of the collateral, or by the creditor's refraining from doing anything beyond attachment. This last type is called *automatic perfection* (or perfection by attachment), and it is the method that sellers of high-volume, relatively inexpensive items like televisions or compact disk players ordinarily choose. Rather than file a financing statement or take possession of the collateral, such creditors instead rely solely on their security agreement with the debtor as the means for perfecting their interests in the collateral.

The policy underlying the first two methods involves giving public notice of the existence of the security interest. To deserve the status of a perfected secured creditor, the would-be secured party ought to undertake some affirmative action (either filing or possessing) that will give anyone looking for a security interest in the collateral notice of the secured party's claim. In the third situation, the nature of the collateral makes the costs of providing public notice arguably higher than the benefits one gains from filing; therefore, the Code does not place any affirmative duties on the secured creditor in these situations beyond attachment. Exhibit 26.2 summarizes the methods of perfecting a security interest in various types of collateral.

E X H I B I T 26.2 | Methods of Perfecting a Security Interest

Type of Collateral	Perfection Method (Generally)
Consumer goods (excluding motor vehicles and fixtures)	Automatic (if a purchase money security interest) Possession Filing
Equipment	Filing Possession
Farm products	Filing Possession
Inventory (including motor vehicles)	Filing Possession
Fixtures	Filing Automatic (if a purchase money security interest) Possession (in theory)
Proceeds	Filing Automatic (if security interest in original collateral perfected)
Documents (negotiable)	Filing Possession Automatic (for 21 days)
Instruments	Filing Possession Automatic (for 21 days)
Chattel paper	Filing Possession
Accounts	Filing Automatic (in some instances)
General intangibles	Filing
Letters of credit	Possession
Motor vehicles	Filing Compliance with state certificate of title statutes
Aircraft, copyrights, and the like	Filing (under applicable federal statutes, not under the UCC)

Filing

Whether filing is necessary in order to perfect a security interest depends on the type of collateral involved. If the collateral consists of accounts or general intangibles, filing ordinarily is the only method of perfection.[21] For goods (including fixtures), chattel paper, and negotiable documents, the secured party may file but is not obligated to do so. Because of their negotiability, interests in money, instruments, and **letters of credit** never can be perfected by filing (possession is the usual method).[22]

Letters of credit
Agreements made at the request of a customer that, upon another party's compliance with the conditions specified in the documents, the bank will honor drafts or other demands for payment.

If filing is necessary, § 9-403 of the UCC states that the presentation of a financing statement and the required fees to the appropriate state or local filing officer and that officer's acceptance of the statement constitute filing. Hence, the device that the Code uses to give notice of the security interest is a *financing statement*. An alternative method of filing, which is not discussed in detail here, involves registering the security interest according to the requirements of statutes other than the UCC, such as state acts covering the certification of title for automobiles, trailers, mobile homes, and boats.

According to § 9-402, to be legally effective, a financing statement must contain certain information: the names of the debtor and secured party; their addresses; a statement indicating the types, or describing the items, of collateral; and the signature of the debtor. Exhibit 26.3 represents a typical financing statement form. The filing of such a document allows third parties to obtain information about the security interest from either the secured party or the debtor. Thus, if Bart wants credit from a wholesaler and the latter wants to take a security interest in Bart's equipment, the wholesaler—before extending credit—will check the public records for financing statements so as to see which of Bart's equipment already is subject to security interests held by other creditors. This information will help the wholesaler make its decision about whether to actually extend credit to Bart.

This question arises repeatedly: Does a copy of the security agreement, if filed, constitute the legal equivalent of a financing statement? The Code notes that filing the security agreement will constitute an effective filing if it contains the information required for a financing statement and if the debtor has signed it.[23] But because the description of the collateral in the security agreement serves to create enforceable rights in the collateral for the secured party, it necessarily must be more detailed than the information set out in the financing statement, which only provides public notice of a claimed interest in the collateral. Given these differing rationales, it probably is wise not to treat security agreements and financing statements interchangeably for filing purposes.

On the other hand, a financing statement that substantially complies with the Code's requirements will be effective even though it contains *minor* errors that are not seriously misleading.[24] This provision of the Code is indicative of one policy of Article 9, which is to simplify the filing requirements and "to discourage the fanatical and impossibly refined reading of such statutory requirements in which courts have occasionally indulged themselves."[25] Nevertheless, failure to provide an address, an omission that seems rather negligible, may preclude perfection of the security interest.

The financing statement ordinarily will be effective if it contains enough information to cause the party searching the records to look further; this so-called inquiry notice will enable that party to discover the perfected security interest. In

[handwritten annotations: "1st perfector Gives Notice I have a Interest in that Collateral Thing"]

E X H I B I T   26.3 | **Financing Statement Form**

UNIFORM COMMERCIAL CODE INSTRUCTIONS	STATE OF INDIANA FINANCING STATEMENT	FORM UCC-1 BANKERS SYSTEMS, INC., ST. CLOUD, MINN.

1. Please type this form. Fold only along perforation for mailing.
2. Remove Secured Party and Debtor copies and send other three copies with interleaved carbon paper to the filing officer. Enclose filing fee of $2.00 (plus $.50 if collateral is or is to become a fixture).
3. When filing is to be with more than one office, Form UCC-2 may be placed over this set to avoid double typing.
4. If the space provided for any item(s) is inadequate, the item(s) may be continued on additional sheets, preferably 5" × 8" or sizes convenient to secured party in case of long schedules, indentures, etc. Only one sheet is required. Extra names of debtors may be continued below box "1" in space for description of property.
5. If the collateral is crops or goods which are or are to become fixtures, describe the goods and also the real estate with the name of the record owner if he is other than the debtor.
6. Persons filing a security agreement (as distinguished from a financing statement) are urged to complete this form with or without signature and send with security agreement. An extra charge of $2.00 is imposed for an irregular form.
7. If collateral is goods which are or are to become fixtures, use Form UCC-1a over this Form to avoid double typing, and enclose regular fee plus $.50.
8. The filing officer will return the third page of this Form as an acknowledgment. Secured party at a later time may use third page as a Termination Statement by dating and signing the termination legend on that page.

This Financing Statement is presented to Filing Officer for filing pursuant to the UCC:

1 Debtor(s) (Last Name First) and Address(es)	2 Secured Party(ies) and Address(es)	3 Maturity Date (if any):
	KeyBank National Association 202 South Michigan Street South Bend, Indiana 46601	For Filing Officer (Date, Time, Number, and Filing Office)

4 This financing statement covers the following types (or items) of property (also describe realty where collateral is crops or fixtures):

Assignee of Secured Party	This statement is filed without the debtor's signature to perfect a security interest in collateral check ☒ if so ☐ under a security agreement signed by debtor authorizing secured party to file this statement, or ☐ already subject to a security interest in another jurisdiction when it was brought into this state, or ☐ which is proceeds of the following described original collateral which was perfected.

Check ☒ if covered: ☐ Proceeds of Collateral are also covered.   ☐ Products of Collateral are also covered. No. of additional Sheets presented:

Filed with: ☐ Secretary of State   ☐ Recorder of _____ County

KeyBank National Association

By: _____   By: _____
    Signature(s) of Debtor(s)   Signature(s) of Secured Party(ies)

(1) Filing Officer Copy–Alphabetical   Approved by:
    FORM UCC–1 INDIANA UNIFORM COMMERCIAL CODE

                                              Secretary of State

Courtesy of KeyBank, National Association, South Bend, Indiana.

---

the following case, the court followed this rule of thumb in holding that the defect in the financing statement was not so seriously misleading as to invalidate the creditor's attempted perfection of the security interest.

26.3

IN RE ENVIRONMENTAL ASPECS, INC.

235 B.R. 378 (E.D. N.C. 1999)

FACTS SouthTrust Bank, National Association (SouthTrust) extended a line of credit to Environmental Aspecs, Inc. (EAI), Environmental Aspecs of North Carolina's (EAI of NC's) parent corporation, in June 1994. EAI executed a note and a security agreement evidencing that loan, and SouthTrust perfected its security interest by filing in the appropriate statewide and local office financing statements listing EAI as the debtor. Throughout 1995 and 1996, the bank, based on invoices submitted by those companies, advanced funds to EAI and its subsidiary corporations. Typically, SouthTrust would credit funds received from EAI of NC against the outstanding balance of SouthTrust's loans to EAI. Although SouthTrust apparently knew of the existence of EAI of NC, SouthTrust at that time neither required EAI of NC to execute a security agreement, nor did SouthTrust file financing statements to perfect its interest in property owned by EAI of NC or any other subsidiary. When EAI defaulted on its SouthTrust loans, EAI and its subsidiary corporations executed a 31 October 1997 agreement in which the subsidiaries agreed to be responsible for the obligations of the 1996 loan. Therefore, in November 1997, SouthTrust filed financing statements listing EAI and EAI of NC, among others, as debtors. Meanwhile, back in September 1996, approximately 11 months before SouthTrust filed these financing statements naming EAI of NC as a debtor, EAI of NC had executed a security agreement in favor of Advanced Analytics Laboratories, Inc. (AAL). On 27 and 31 December 1996, AAL filed financing statements with the appropriate state-wide and local offices. When asked to identify the debtor on the financing statements, AAL named EAI—the same legal entity listed as the debtor on SouthTrust's 1994 financing statements. Both the description boxes on the financing statements, located immediately below the debtor's name, and the debtor's signature lines on the statements contained the words, "See Exhibit A attached for description and debtor's signature" and "See Exhibit A attached." The security agreements that were attached to the financing statements as Exhibit A and filed with the appropriate offices, both in the introductory paragraphs and on the signature pages, noted that the debtor was EAI of NC. The agreements also were signed by Dennis L. Mast as President of EAI of NC. In April 1998, EAI and EAI of NC filed for bankruptcy under Chapter 11; and

AAL subsequently filed a motion to determine the priority of the security interests held by SouthTrust. In granting summary judgment for AAL, the bankruptcy court concluded that AAL had perfected its security interest in the assets of EAI of NC in December of 1996, 11 months before SouthTrust had perfected an interest in those assets in November 1997.

ISSUE Was the financing statement in which AAL had erroneously listed the debtor as EAI but attached to which financing statement were security agreements that correctly noted the debtor as EAI of NC sufficient to protect AAL's security interest?

HOLDING Yes. The reference to the attachment in AAL's financing statement and the security agreements filed with the financing statement precluded a finding that the error was so seriously misleading as to invalidate AAL's security interest.

REASONING The formal requisites for the enforceability of a nonpossessory security interest, i.e., a security agreement, are a writing that creates or provides for the interest, the debtor's signature, and a description of the collateral or kinds of collateral. If two or more creditors obtain security interests in the same collateral, their interests may conflict. Under North Carolina's Commercial Code "conflicting security interests rank according to priority in time of filing or perfection. Priority dates from the time a filing is first made covering the collateral or the time the security interest is first perfected, whichever is earlier. . . . " A security interest "is perfected when it has attached and when all the applicable steps required for perfection have been taken . . . If such steps are taken before the security interest attaches, it is perfected at the time it attaches." Moreover, a security interest attaches when the debtor has signed a security agreement that contains a description of the collateral, value has been given, and the debtor has rights in the collateral. While "attachment" relates to the creation and enforceability of a security interest between the parties to the transaction, "perfection" is an additional step that makes the security interest effective against third parties. One of the applicable steps required for perfection is the filing of a financing statement that identifies the debtor, covers the collateral at issue, and contains the debtor's signature.

26.3

IN RE ENVIRONMENTAL ASPECS, INC., *continued*
235 B.R. 378 (E.D. N.C. 1999)

Because filing is a necessary element of perfection, the priority provisions of North Carolina's Commercial Code essentially create a rule in which the first creditor to file a sufficient financing statement has priority. North Carolina's is essentially a system of notice filing pursuant to which the notice provided by a financing statement indicates merely that the secured party who has filed may have a security interest in the collateral described. The Uniform Commercial Code contemplates further inquiry beyond the financing statement, as the financing statement's purpose merely is to alert the third party to the need for further investigation, rather than to provide a comprehensive data bank as to the details of prior security arrangements. . . . The fact that the financing statement is not intended to be all-informative is borne out by the fact that the statement must contain the address of the secured party from which one searching the records can obtain information concerning the security interest. The foregoing rules are pertinent to two of the issues in the present case: 1) the allegedly misleading nature of AAL's 1996 financing statements and 2) the adequacy of SouthTrust's 1994 financing statements concerning EAI of NC. SouthTrust claimed that it had acquired a security interest in the assets of EAI of NC in 1994, but its 1994 financing statements identified only EAI as the debtor and listed only EAI's assets as collateral for that loan. AAL responded that it had acquired a security interest in the assets of EAI of NC, but the financing statements it had filed in 1996 identified the debtor as EAI in some places and as EAI of NC in others. As the bankruptcy court concluded, SouthTrust in 1994 had obtained a security interest only in the assets of EAI, while AAL had perfected a security interest in the assets of EAI of NC in 1996. Although the financing statement identified the debtor as EAI in two places, the attached security agreement, clearly referenced on the financing statement itself as an "attachment," identified EAI of NC as the debtor, contained the signature of the president of EAI of NC, and accurately described the collateral at issue. Moreover, a copy of the security agreement, in and of itself, is sufficient as a financing statement if it contains the requisite information and is signed by the debtor. In any event, as set forth in North Carolina's Commercial Code, "[a] financing statement substantially complying with the requirements of this section is effective even though it contains minor errors which are not seriously misleading." Unquestionably, the financing statement and security agreement filed by AAL would put any potential creditors of EAI of NC on notice of AAL's lien against EAI of NC's assets. The bankruptcy court's conclusion, as a matter of law, that the omission of the words "of North Carolina" in two spaces on the otherwise informative and adequate financing statement, which was attached to a valid security agreement, did not render the financing statement "seriously misleading" was correct. The fact that AAL's negligent omission of the words "of North Carolina" resulted in the naming of an independent legal entity, EAI, does not change the result in this case, given the context in which the mistake was made and the clarifying papers filed with the financing statement. Furthermore, a court should not create a rule pursuant to which an error would be misleading per se where the error happened to result in the naming of another legal entity as the debtor. Rather, a court must base the determination either on whether an error is seriously misleading or a review of the nature of the error and the context in which the error is made. The reference to the attachment on AAL's financing statement and the security agreement filed with AAL's financing statement preclude a determination that AAL's error was seriously misleading in this case.

BUSINESS CONSIDERATION As an aftermath of this litigation, what office procedures should SouthTrust and AAL put in place so as to minimize the probabilities of such litigation in the future?

ETHICAL CONSIDERATION If the court could have applied an ethical—as opposed to a legal—perspective here, would the court have reached a contrary result? Why or why not?

Numerous courts have held that the creditor's filing of a financing statement that lists the debtor's trade or business name rather than its legal name constitutes an insufficient filing to perfect a security interest under § 9-402. Because the law differs among the various jurisdictions on this point, the creditor's precision in filing the appropriate information often determines whether the courts deem the security interest at issue perfected or unperfected. Despite the holding of *In re Environmental Aspecs, Inc.*, then, a prudent creditor will show a sense of meticulousness and attention to detail as to all filings.

Sometimes a creditor files a financing statement even before the security agreement is completed or a security interest attaches,[26] but filing before attachment does not constitute perfection.[27] Without attachment at some later time, no perfection ever occurs.

The Code's flexibility nowhere is more apparent than in its handling of the *proper place for filing* the financing statement. The Code does not take a stand on whether filings should be local or statewide, an issue that had caused a great many pre-Code problems. Instead, in § 9-401(1), the UCC provides three different options that depend on the type of collateral involved, thus allowing the respective states to choose the method they believe is most conducive to giving notice of claims.

A financing statement generally is effective for a period of five years from the date of filing, after which the security interest lapses (or becomes unperfected) unless the secured party files a *continuation statement* before this lapse.[28] The secured party may file such a statement within six months prior to the expiration of the financing statement. The secured party must sign the continuation statement, identify the original statement by file number, and also state that the original statement still remains in effect.[29] The filing of a continuation statement prolongs the effectiveness of the original financing statement for five years, and the Code does not limit the number of such statements a secured party can file.

Assuming that the secured party neither has released all or part of the collateral described in the financing statements[30] nor assigned its security interest to another,[31] the Code imposes certain additional duties on the secured party. For example, the secured party must comply within two weeks whenever the debtor *requests a statement of account or a list of collateral* from the secured party. (Presumably, the debtor will request such information because of a lack of certainty about the total amount owed.) Failure to comply may make the secured party liable for losses to the debtor caused by the noncompliance and, in rare cases, even may cost the secured party its security interest. This will be true regarding any security interests reflected in the lists written up by the debtor should any persons be misled by the secured party's failure to comply (as, for instance, by failing to correct the list).[32] On the other hand, the Code, by limiting the debtor to one such list or statement every six months, protects the secured party from burdensome requests. The secured party can charge $10 for each additional request within this time period.[33]

Once no outstanding obligations remain under the financing statement, the Code sets out a procedure that may require the secured party to file a *termination statement* noting the discharge of the obligations and/or the termination of the financing agreement. Where consumer goods are concerned, the Code places an affirmative duty on the secured party to file a termination statement within one month or within 10 days following written demand by the debtor once the debtor has completely paid for the goods. In all other cases, however, the secured party need not file a termination statement unless the debtor requests such a filing.[34] But when compliance is necessary, the Code subjects noncomplying secured parties to certain penalties. Termination statements, which refer to the appropriate financing statement by file number, clear the public records so that the presence of old, irrelevant financing statements will not leave a would-be creditor with an unrealistic picture of a credit applicant's creditworthiness and reliability.

Possession

As mentioned earlier, the secured party's possession of the collateral is the method used for perfecting the security interest.[35] Historically, when financing arrangements were more primitive, possession of the personal property was the surest sign of ownership; hence, perfection by possession evolved as the most popular method. Even today, secured parties ordinarily must perfect security interests in letters of credit, money, and instruments in this manner and may perfect goods, negotiable documents, or chattel paper in this fashion as well. For instance, a bank may require a debtor to give it possession of the debtor's stocks and bonds as collateral for securing a loan. In such circumstances, the secured creditor has accepted a pledge of these instruments as collateral.

As we discuss in more detail later, the type of collateral involved is relevant in determining whether perfection can occur by possession. If the creditor's possession of collateral (and the debtor's resultant lack of possession) is to put other parties on public notice as to the existence of a claimed security interest, the collateral must be tangible; that is, one must be able to see, touch, or move it. All the types of collateral perfectible by possession share this attribute. On the other hand, contract rights, accounts that constitute a significant portion of the debtor's business, and general intangibles merely represent rights and have no physical embodiment. Thus, one never can perfect these categories of personal property by possession; filing is necessary.

Automatic Perfection

Automatic perfection is the method ordinarily used for perfecting purchase money security interests in consumer goods.[36] In these situations, as mentioned earlier, perfection occurs upon attachment alone. A look at the nature of these transactions shows why filing is unnecessary. The Code defines a *purchase money security interest* as one retained by the seller of the collateral to secure all or part of its price or taken by a person who by making advances or incurring an obligation gives value to enable the debtor to acquire rights in the collateral.[37]

Typically, a seller retains a purchase money security interest in the collateral, whether it is a stove, refrigerator, washing machine, or compact disk player. This means that the seller usually sells to the buyer, on an installment basis, goods that the buyer will use for personal purposes. The seller, in turn, retains a security interest in the consumer goods—for instance, the compact disk player—to secure the unpaid purchase price. If the buyer misses any installment payments, the seller can repossess the collateral. The secured party's purchase money security interest is perfectible the moment the transaction has occurred because a written security agreement signed by the debtor exists; the secured party has given value; and the debtor has rights in the collateral (i.e., attachment has occurred). All this has happened (thanks to the modern wonder of "form contracts") a short time before the debtor, with the compact disk player in hand, walks out of the store.

Given the type of collateral involved (consumer goods) and the frequency with which such transactions occur, the UCC has followed pre-Code law in eliminating

WHO HAS A PERFECTED INTEREST IN THE COLLATERAL?

Bank of the West (BOW) and ITT Commercial Finance Corporation (ITT) are commercial lenders. Over the course of several years, both BOW and ITT had lent money to the same debtor, a fledgling microcomputer dealership that had operated initially as a sole proprietorship run by Carlos Chacon and doing business under the trade name "Compucentro USA." BOW had purchased loans made to the sole proprietorship in August 1988 and February 1990, respectively. Financing statements perfecting BOW's security interests in a broad class of current and after-acquired property under the names "Carlos Chacon d/b/a/ Compucentro USA" and "Carlos R. Chacon and Lorena Chacon d/b/a Compucentro USA" had been filed. On 26 November 1990, Carlos Chacon incorporated the sole proprietorship under the name "Compu-Centro, USA, Inc." On 12 December 1990, using the letterhead of the sole proprietorship bearing the name "Compucentro USA," Chacon informed BOW of the incorporation. On 28 January 1991, BOW filed notices of assignment. These assignment notices did not reflect the debtor's recent incorporation. Rather, they listed the debtor's name as "Chacon, Carlos d/b/a/ Compucentro, USA" and "Carlos R. Chacon and Lorena Chacon d/b/a/ Compucentro USA," respectively. BOW also independently extended financing to the new corporation and on 18 January 1991 filed a new financing statement covering a broad class of current and after-acquired property and specifying the name of the debtor as "Compucentro, USA, Inc." This filing left out the hyphen in the incorporation's legal name. On 14 October 1991, ITT filed a financing statement covering a broad class of current and after-acquired property and specifying the name of the debtor as "Compu-Centro, USA, Inc." In the course of conducting a credit review of the corporation, ITT learned that Compu-Centro, USA, Inc. had existed before its November 1990 incorporation with a different name and business structure and that a $68,000 liability to BOW was outstanding. ITT did not investigate further; and, on 18 October 1991, ITT obtained an official search of the Secretary of State's records concerning the name "Compu-Centro, USA, Inc." ITT's filing was the sole filing reflected on the search report. In the course of its business, Compu-Centro, USA, Inc. entered into a contract with the federal government to supply a medical center with computers. Neither ITT nor BOW provided Compu-Centro, USA, Inc. with the funding used to obtain these computers. Compu-Centro, USA, Inc. thereafter established an account at BOW in which the firm deposited only the proceeds. In 1993, by a check drawn on the BOW account, Compu-Centro, USA, Inc. paid BOW $300,000 out of the $1.3 million received as proceeds of the government contract. The purpose of the payment was to satisfy, in part, the outstanding balance on the debt owed to BOW. At the time of the payment, Compu-Centro, USA, Inc. was in default on its obligation to ITT in the amount of $117,795.14. Consequently, on 7 March 1994, ITT filed an action seeking a declaratory judgment regarding the priority of its security interest in the collateral of Compu-Centro, USA, Inc., and alleging that BOW had converted the proceeds of the government contract.

This case has been brought in *your* court. How will *you* resolve this controversy?[38]

BUSINESS CONSIDERATION What should BOW do to ensure that it holds a validly perfected security interest in the proceeds from the government account?

ETHICAL CONSIDERATION Is it ethical for a later secured creditor to try to overturn an earlier security interest merely on the basis of a technical error in the filing of the interest by the prior creditor?

SOURCES: *U.C.C. Bulletin* (May 1999), at 6, 7; also see *ITT Commercial Finance Corporation v. Bank of the West,* 166 F.3d 295 (5th Cir. 1999).

the filing requirement for these types of commercial deals. It makes little sense to require a merchant to pay the filing fees and other administrative costs associated with filing for every $100 item sold. Moreover, in such situations, few benefits result from filing, since consumer goods— already low in price and also prone to rapid deterioration—are not the types of property that later secured parties will want as collateral anyway. Therefore, the public notice to such creditors afforded by filing has little value and will only clutter the filing offices' records. The same rationale underlies the availability of automatic perfection as a method for perfecting certain transfers of accounts, documents, and instruments as well.

RELATED TOPICS

Two other topics deserve consideration before we leave the issues covered in this chapter: multistate transactions and proceeds.

Multistate Transactions

A related aspect of perfection involves the problem of collateral, such as equipment, that the debtor can move across state or county lines. For example, a debtor in Indiana may take threshing equipment subject to an Indiana security interest to Illinois or Iowa and keep this equipment in the new state for several months (i.e., until the harvesting season ends). The Code's rules for such situations, expressed in § 9-103, are very complex. In general, the Code says that, with respect to ordinary goods, the secured party should perfect its interest by filing (or by some other method) in the state where the collateral is originally located. Upon the debtor's removal of the collateral, the secured party should file in the new jurisdiction.

If a purchase money security interest is involved and both parties at the time of the creation of the security interest understand that the debtor will move the collateral to another jurisdiction, the law of the new jurisdiction controls perfection for 30 days after the debtor receives possession, assuming the collateral is moved in that time. To avoid losing priority of perfection, the secured party ought to file in both jurisdictions. If collateral previously has been perfected in one jurisdiction and then is moved to another, it remains perfected for its period of original perfection or for four months, whichever period expires first. Thus, the secured party should file in the new jurisdiction before this four-month period expires.

The removal of motor vehicles from one jurisdiction to another is covered by state certificate of title laws and by the Code.[39] Because these laws are very complicated, a wise secured creditor, in order to do everything possible to retain a perfected security interest in them, will keep abreast of the debtor's removal of these

26.3 | FINANCE

CALL-IMAGE TECHNOLOGY

MOVING COLLATERAL

CIT has enjoyed quite a bit of success selling the videophones in California, and the firm has decided to establish a major warehouse facility in California so as to provide better service to CIT's West Coast customers. The firm already has arranged a lease of warehouse space, and CIT plans to send several of the firm's trucks and several thousand completed videophones to the new warehouse. Lindsay and John believe that CIT should not do this without CIT's bank's permission, since the trucks and the videophones are collateral for CIT's line of credit with the bank. Tom and Dan do not think that the bank will object to this plan. They are seeking your advice, however, before they finalize the decision. What will you tell them?

BUSINESS CONSIDERATIONS Should a debtor in a secured transaction adhere to a policy of informing the creditor any time that the removal of the collateral from the jurisdiction occurs? Why or why not? What can the creditor in this situation do to maximize its protections in the event that the collateral is removed from the jurisdiction without notice?

ETHICAL CONSIDERATIONS Is it ethical for a debtor to remove collateral from the jurisdiction without notifying the creditor? Is it ethical for the creditor to demand notice from the debtor in advance before the debtor can move the collateral?

RESOURCES FOR BUSINESS LAW STUDENTS

NAME	RESOURCES	WEB ADDRESS
Uniform Commercial Code (UCC) Article 9, Secured Transactions; Sales of Accounts and Chattel Paper	The Legal Information Institute (LII), maintained by the Cornell Law School, provides a hypertext and searchable version of UCC Article 9, Secured Transactions; Sales of Accounts and Chattel Paper. LII also maintains links to Article 9 as adopted by particular states and to proposed revisions.	http://www.law.cornell.edu/ucc/9/overview.html
The National Conference of Commissioners on Uniform State Laws (NCCUSL)	NCCUSL, the drafter of the UCC, provides drafts and revisions of its uniform and model acts.	http://www.law.upenn.edu/bll/ulc/ulc_frame.htm

vehicles. Generally speaking, if the new jurisdiction is a non–certificate of title state, a secured party will need to reperfect (usually by filing) within four months of the collateral's removal to the new jurisdiction. If, in contrast, the jurisdiction to which the debtor has removed the motor vehicle requires perfection by notation of the security interest on the vehicle's title, in this situation reperfection will not occur by filing in the new jurisdiction but rather by the secured party's noting its interest on the motor vehicle's certificate of title. In such circumstances, the secured party may have longer than four months in which to reperfect, since reperfection will be necessary only when the debtor, in order to receive valid registration papers in the new state, requests the surrender of the vehicle's title. At that time, the prudent secured party will note its interest again on the new certificate of title and thus remain perfected.

Proceeds

The final point we should make about security interests and perfection is that the Code allows a secured party's interest to reach the proceeds of the debtor's disposition of the collateral.[40] In other words, the secured party has a "lien" (similar to that which we discussed in the context of multistate transactions) that "floats" over the collateral and includes as "proceeds" whatever is received on the sale, exchange, collection, or other disposition of the collateral.[41] If Bart sells the freezer and the cash register to another person, the secured party's interest in the collateral will extend even to the cash proceeds realized from this sale. Thus, the issue of proceeds, and the Code's treatment of it, implicates not only perfection rules but also priority rules (especially when, as is often the case, the trustee in bankruptcy is involved as well).

SUMMARY

A secured transaction ensures payment by the buyer: If the buyer does not pay the seller, the seller's security interest will allow the seller to repossess the property. A secured transaction consists of a secured party, a debtor, a security agreement, and collateral. The Code categorizes collateral according to its nature or its use. One type of collateral is goods; the different classes of goods are mutually exclusive. Collateral also may consist of documents, instruments, letters of credit, proceeds, accounts, chattel paper, and general intangibles. Article 9 applies to consensual security interests in personal property or fixtures but not to those arising by operation of law. It covers leases meant as security but not "true" leases. Attachment is the process by which the secured party creates an enforceable security interest in the collateral. A signed security agreement, in conjunction with the occurrence of other events, provides evidence that attachment has occurred. Perfection refers to the method by which secured parties protect themselves against later creditors of the debtor. Perfection can take place in one of three ways: (1) by the creditor's filing a valid financing statement, (2) by the creditor's having possession of the collateral, and (3) by automatic perfection. The method of perfection that the secured party should use often depends on the type of collateral involved. If filing is the applicable method, the creditor must use a legally effective financing statement. The Code's rules regarding multistate transactions are very complex, but, in order to ensure continuation of perfection, the secured party should check them whenever the debtor moves the collateral from one jurisdiction to another. The secured party, if he or she has met certain requirements under the Code, generally can reach the proceeds of the debtor's later disposition of the collateral.

DISCUSSION QUESTIONS *Answer Questions*

1. What is a *secured transaction?*
2. Define a *security interest.*
3. Name and define the various types of property that the Code recognizes as collateral.
4. If Will does not pay Carla, the mechanic who fixes his car, and she obtains a judgment against him, does Carla have an Article 9 security interest in Will's car? Why or why not?
5. What is the difference between a true lease and a lease intended as security?
6. What is *attachment,* and what are the requirements for it?

7. Provide the criteria necessary for a valid security agreement.
8. Define *perfection,* and discuss in detail the three methods by which perfection occurs.
9. What kinds of defects cause a financing statement to be ineffective?
10. What problems can arise if Debbie Dunn has given her bank a security interest in bulldozers and she subsequently moves the bulldozers from Indiana to Michigan?

CASE PROBLEMS AND WRITING ASSIGNMENTS

1. On about 20 August 1986, John J. and Clara Lockovich purchased a 22-foot 1986 Chapparel Villian III boat from the Greene County Yacht Club (club) for $32,500. The Lockoviches (the debtors) paid $6,000 to the club and executed a security agreement/lien contract that set forth the purchase and finance terms. In the contract, the Lockoviches granted a security interest in the boat to the holder of the contract. When Gallatin National Bank (Gallatin) paid the club $26,757.14 on the Lockoviches' behalf, the club assigned the contract to Gallatin. Gallatin then filed financing statements in the appropriate Greene County office and with the secretary of the Commonwealth of Pennsyl-

vania. Greene County was the county in which Gallatin was located, but the Lockoviches resided in Allegheny County. The filing of the financing statements therefore was ineffective to perfect the security interest in the boat. The Lockoviches, by failing to remit payments as required, subsequently defaulted under the terms of the security agreement they had signed with Gallatin. Before Gallatin could take action, the Lockoviches filed for relief under Chapter 11 of the Bankruptcy Code. Gallatin then sought, pursuant to the security agreement, to enforce its rights. On 2 October 1989, the bankruptcy court, in denying Gallatin's motion, held that because Gallatin had failed to perfect its security interest in the boat by filing, it was an unsecured creditor. Pursuant to the bankruptcy laws, as a holder of an unperfected security interest, Gallatin's right to the boat remained inferior to that of the debtor-in-possession, a hypothetical lienholder. To perfect its purchase money security interest in the boat, would Gallatin need to file a financing statement? [See *In re Lockovich*, 124 B.R. 660 (W.D.Pa. 1991).]

2. On or about 11 October 1997, Grieb Printing Company, the debtor, executed a lease of equipment with Bayer Financial Services (Bayer). The lease was for 48 months, had a monthly payment of $4,108.71, and gave the debtor the option to purchase the equipment at the end of the lease for one dollar. The lease, which was executed by the debtor's CEO, granted Bayer a security interest in the equipment and authorized Bayer or its agents to sign and execute on the lessee's behalf any and all necessary documents to effect any filings, including the filing of any such financing or continuation statements without further authorization. On 6 October 1997, Bayer filed a financing statement on the equipment. Pursuant to the lease agreement, Bayer signed the financing statement on behalf of the debtor as the debtor's "attorney-in-fact." Before doing so, Bayer did not request that the debtor sign the lease. Bayer then properly filed the financing statement. Approximately five months after obtaining the equipment, the debtor filed a Chapter 7 bankruptcy petition. When the bankruptcy trustee moved to sell the equipment in which Bayer claimed an interest, the trustee argued that Bayer's interest in the collateral was unperfected. The trustee based its contention on the Kentucky statutory provision that makes invalid any filing of a financing statement not signed by an individual authorized to sign on behalf of the corporate debtor. Was the signature that Bayer, the creditor, had placed on the financing statement for the debtor valid under Kentucky law and thus sufficient to protect the creditor's security interest? [See *In re Grieb Printing Company*, 230 B.R. 539 (Bkrtcy.W.D.Ky. 1999).]

3. In 1993, Kenneth W. Gibson, an employee of United Airlines, obtained a Visa card from the airline's credit union. Gibson did not give the credit union any collateral to secure this extension of credit at the time of the issuance of the Visa card. The interest rate for charges always had been 12.96 percent per annum. In 1996, the Gibsons (Kenneth and his wife, Ramona) borrowed approximately $23,000 from the credit union. In connection with the 1996 loan, the Gibsons executed a loan and security agreement that provided

that the balance due to the credit union would accrue interest at the rate of 8.9 percent per annum. Pursuant to the terms of the 1996 agreement, the Gibsons gave the credit union a security interest in collateral consisting of two cars and Mr. Gibson's shares in the credit union. The back of the 1996 loan and security agreement set out a series of preprinted terms and conditions. One of these—the so-called dragnet clause—purported to make the collateral security for any debt owed by either of the Gibsons to the credit union as well as for the 1996 loan obligation. The Gibsons later contended that no one representing the credit union pointed this language out to them in 1996. The 1996 loan and security agreement also contained a preprinted provision (a "choice of law" clause) stating that the agreement "shall be governed by and construed in accordance with the laws of the State of Illinois." When the Gibsons, who resided in California, ultimately filed a petition for an adjustment of debts under Chapter 13 of the Bankruptcy Code, Mr. Gibson owed the credit union $4,846.06 on the Visa card; and the Gibsons owed the credit union $14,759.97 on the 1996 loan obligation. The value of the collateral was sufficient to cover both obligations. The credit union filed two proofs of claim in the Chapter 13 case, one for the Visa card debt and one for the 1996 loan obligation. Originally, only the 1996 loan claim had been described as secured; the Visa claim had been described as unsecured. However, shortly thereafter, the credit union, in an amended claim, asserted secured status for the Visa claim as well. The Gibsons characterized the dragnet clause as unenforceable and the Visa claim as unsecured. How should a court dispose of this case? [See *In re Gibson*, 234 B.R. 776 (Bkrtcy.N.D.Cal. 1999).]

4. Filtercorp, Inc. (Filtercorp) was a Washington corporation that developed and distributed carbonated pads used in the food service industry to filter cooking oils. Beginning in November 1991, the company took out a series of loans from Henry Paulman, an individual salesperson, to help fund further development and meet large orders. The loans were short term, ranging from two to three months, and memorialized by promissory notes drafted by Paulman's attorney. The final note—the subject of the litigation between the parties—was a three-month note, executed on 30 June 1992 and due 30 September 1992. This note stated:

> This note is secured by 75,000 shares of Filter Corp. [sic] stock owned by Robin Bernard, the accounts receivable and inventory of Filter Corp. [sic] (See UCC-1 filing and attached inventory listing.) and John Gardner personally.

The parties never executed a separate security agreement. However, Paulman perfected his security interest by filing a financing statement on 5 October 1992. The financing statement identified the collateral as (1) accounts receivable and (2) materials inventory. Despite the note's reference to an inventory listing, none was ever attached to the note or the financing statement. Whether the parties intended to secure after-acquired inventory or accounts receivable with the June 1992 note thus was unclear. In the course of the subsequent litigation, the parties presented conflicting versions of their intent. Paulman claimed that he and Filtercorp had understood the security interest to attach to future rather than presently held inventory and accounts receivable so as not to interfere with the company's ability to raise additional capital. For this reason, he said he had not attached the inventory listing. In contrast, Robin Bernard, the president of Filtercorp, stated that in light of the short, three-month term of the loan, he had not contemplated an ongoing security interest. When Paulman initiated a suit in early October 1992 to enforce the June 1992 note, Filtercorp defaulted on it. In November 1995, Paulman obtained a judgment of $710,572.81 against Filtercorp. In December 1992, while the state court litigation was pending, Filtercorp became the general partner in a limited partnership named Filtercorp Partners Limited Partnership (Filtercorp LP), in which several limited partners had invested approximately $1.7 million. Filtercorp thereupon transferred all its operating assets to Filtercorp LP, the effect of which transaction was to leave its interest in the limited partnership as its only significant asset. In early 1995, Filtercorp LP borrowed a total of approximately $355,000 from Gateway Venture Lenders III, Charles Brickman, and Donald Eskes (collectively Gateway Lenders), all of whom either had been limited partners of Filtercorp LP or "insiders" for other reasons. Filtercorp LP obtained the last loans on 24 February 1995, at which time it issued promissory notes for all the amounts borrowed and backdated each note according to its respective loan date. At the same time, Filtercorp LP granted Gateway Lenders a blanket security interest in all Filtercorp LP's assets, specifically including after-acquired property. Gateway Lenders filed a corresponding financing statement on 1 March 1995. When Paulman began his efforts to collect the judgment, Filtercorp filed a Chapter 11 bankruptcy petition and asked the court to approve the sale of its assets to Gateway Lenders. The proposed sale had a provision designed to deal with the competing lien claims of Gateway Lenders and Paulman. When Paulman objected to this motion, the court held that Paulman had no security interest in any of Filtercorp's assets. The court concluded that none of Paulman's liens had attached to the after-acquired property or to the accounts receivable because of the absence of any express language granting such an interest. The court also found that it could not determine the intent of the parties when they had signed the note because of the lack of any evidentiary support for the conflicting declarations of Paulman and Filtercorp, Inc.'s president. The court ultimately ruled that Gateway Lenders's security interest was valid and first in priority. On appeal, Paulman framed the issue as whether, under Washington law, a security agreement that grants an interest in "inventory" or "accounts receivable," without more, presumptively includes after-acquired inventory or accounts receivable or whether, to secure after-acquired property, an express after-acquired property clause is required. How should the appellate court decide this issue? [See *In re Filtercorp, Inc.*, 163 F.3d 570 (9th Cir. 1998).]

5. Trans Canada Credit Corporation, Ltd. (Trans Canada), a Canadian corporation, lent money to DiCicco and secured its interest in the loan proceeds with a chattel mortgage. By the terms of the chattel mortgage, Trans Canada could take immediate possession of the vehicle DiCicco purchased upon either DiCicco's removal of the vehicle from Canada or DiCicco's sale or transfer of the vehicle. DiCicco later removed the vehicle from Canada and obtained a Pennsylvania certificate of title on or about 14 April 1987. The certificate of title did not have an indorsement indicating Trans Canada's lien as an encumbrance on the vehicle, but it did bear a notation indicating that the vehicle was an out-of-state vehicle. On 16 May 1987, DiCicco sold the secured vehicle to Richard Kosack, an automobile broker and dealer. Kosack subsequently resold the vehicle at an interstate auto auction. In January 1988, Trans Canada took steps to perfect its security interest under Pennsylvania law. The applicable Pennsylvania statute allows the perfection of a security interest in Pennsylvania before or after the expiration of a four-month period within which an out-of-state lien might otherwise be perfected under the laws of the jurisdiction where the motor vehicle had been located when the secured interest had attached. Thus, Trans Canada subsequently characterized this filing in January 1988 as a "reperfection" of the security interest. Trans Canada, after making several unsuccessful demands on Richard Kosack, d.b.a. Family Motors, filed this lawsuit for $4,875, the uncontested fair market value of the automobile at the time Kosack had resold it at the auto

auction. A nonjury trial resulted in a verdict in favor of Kosack. Upon consideration of various post-trial motions, the trial court, owing to its belief that Trans Canada, as a validly perfected creditor, had enjoyed priority regarding the sold automobile, granted a judgment *non obstante veredicto* (judgment n.o.v.) in favor of Trans Canada. Did the perfection of Trans Canada's security interest in Canada cover the removal of the automobile to Pennsylvania and thus give Trans Canada priority regarding the automobile? [See *Trans Canada Credit Corp., Ltd.* v. *Kosack*, 590 A.2d 1295 (Pa.Super. 1991).]

6. **BUSINESS APPLICATION CASE** Bud Brandenburg, a cattle order buyer, financed his purchases through a number of sources, including Louis Welte and Heritage Bank (Heritage). With Welte's authorization, in the normal course of business, Bud would buy cattle by writing a check (drawn on Welte's Heritage account) to the seller. Bud then would sell the cattle to a third party and use the money to repay Welte. In return for the use of Welte's money, Bud paid a commission or interest. Bud's spouse, Margery, owned Western Cattle, Inc. (Western), a cattle-buying corporation. Margery had an agreement with Continental Grain Company (Continental) wherein Continental would lend money on cattle delivered to the Fall River Feedlot in Hot Springs, South Dakota. Continental would charge Margery for feed, the interest on the loan, and other costs. In October 1991, Margery individually signed a security agreement with Continental and in 1994 a financing statement for livestock she had placed "on feed" at the Fall River Feedlot during 1994. The security agreement contained an after-acquired property clause. Generally, Continental would lend money by sending a check to either Margery or Western when a load of cattle arrived. Continental fed the cattle until they were ready and then sold them, usually to a packer. At that point, Continental would pay off its loan and its bill for feed and costs and forward any profits to Margery's personal bank account. In April 1994, Bud bought 650 heifers through Shasta Livestock Auction Yard's (Shasta's) video auction. Bud branded these cattle with a hoofprint on the right rib. Shasta gave Bud a receipt that indicated that Bud was the buyer of the cattle, and Bud presented two checks to pay for the cattle. One check, written by Western and signed by Margery, was returned for nonsufficient funds. Welte, or his bank, Heritage, stopped payment on the other check, which Bud had written on Welte's account. Before the checks cleared the bank, however, the cattle were shipped to Continental's Fall River Feedlot. A California brand inspection certification identified

Bud as the shipper of the cattle. Moreover, a South Dakota brand inspector's tally identified Bud as the "owner of the brand." Bud told Continental to place the cattle on its feedlot for Margery. Based on several years of past dealings, on 2 May 1994, Continental mailed Western a loan check for $252,437.17. After Shasta discovered that the checks had not cleared the banks, its employees called the Fall River Feedlot and requested the return of the cattle. Claiming it had a security interest from Margery, Continental refused to do so. From February to April 1994, Bud, using Welte's account, had bought a number of cattle without first obtaining a buyer. Bud had sent these cattle to the Fall River Feedlot; he had put them in Margery's name; and Fall River had issued advances on the equity. Bud had taken the advances but, instead of paying Welte, had squandered the money on commodity market speculations. Because of Bud's misuse of Welte's account, Welte ultimately owed Heritage over $700,000.00. On 18 May 1994, Continental filed a lawsuit in which it requested a determination that would deem its security interest in the 1,500 cattle being held for the Brandenburgs as valid and enforceable. Continental also requested that its security interest be given priority over the security interests of Shasta, Welte, and Heritage. On 15 June 1994, Shasta counterclaimed for rescission of its contract with Bud and moved for a determination that Margery had never owned any interest in the livestock owing to her lack of control over the cattle. Had Margery enjoyed sufficient rights in the collateral for Continental's security interest to have attached? Shasta had continued to deal with Bud even after it had had notice of dishonored checks totaling about $573,000 (although Bud ultimately had made most of the "bounced" checks good). Welte also had begun doing business with Bud and had given Bud signature authority on Welte's account prior to Welte's conducting any background check on Bud. Should a business have policies in place for determining the initial creditworthiness of a debtor and when to curtail any further extensions of credit? If so, in making such determinations, what factors might a business employ? [See *Continental Grain Company* v. *Brandenburg*, 587 N.W.2d 196 (S.D. 1998).]

7. **ETHICAL APPLICATION CASE** Gregory Westfall, a resident of Missouri, purchased a Kenworth tractor-trailer truck from Rush Truck Centers of Texas, Inc. (Rush). In order to finance the purchase of the Kenworth, Westfall signed a security agreement in favor of Rush, which firm in that selfsame security agreement assigned its interest to Associates Commercial Corporation (Associates). The security agreement contained Associates's logo in the upper left hand

corner of the first page, and the legend "ORIGINAL FOR ASSOCIATES" appeared at the bottom of each of the five pages in the security agreement. The security agreement stated that Westfall would keep the Kenworth at P.O. Box 367, Mountain Grove, Missouri, or in Oklahoma. Westfall testified at the bankruptcy hearing that the Rush salesperson offered Westfall the option of titling the Kenworth in Texas or Missouri. Westfall stated that he was already aware that he would have to pay Missouri sales taxes if he titled the Kenworth in Missouri. After Westfall indicated that he wanted to title the Kenworth in Oklahoma, the salesperson referred him to Pro-Cert, Inc., a titling company in Oklahoma. Pro-Cert subsequently prepared an Oklahoma lien entry form that identified the collateral as the Kenworth, gave the name and address of the secured party, set out the name and address of the debtor (with a fictitious address in Oklahoma), and showed the assignee as Associates Commercial Corp. in Irving, Texas. Westfall immediately removed the Kenworth to his home state, Missouri, and never operated the Kenworth in Oklahoma. And neither Associates nor Rush ever perfected their respective liens in Missouri. Missouri law recognizes vehicle liens that are perfected in another state. Hence, a Missouri resident can purchase a vehicle in another state, and the lender or seller can perfect its lien under the laws of its state before the vehicle is moved to Missouri. Thus, if the buyer brings the vehicle to Missouri and never registers it (e.g., to avoid sales taxes), the creditor still has a valid lien. Put differently, Missouri statutes recognize a lien that was valid in the state in which the vehicle was located at the time of perfection. Westfall ultimately defaulted on the loan and returned the Kenworth to Rush some time before he filed a Chapter 7 bankruptcy petition on 16 April 1998. During the bankruptcy proceedings, Associates pointed to the statute stating that, as to goods issued under a certificate of title, perfection is governed by the law of the jurisdiction "issuing the certificate until four months after the goods are removed from that jurisdiction and thereafter until the goods are registered in another jurisdiction." Associates also claimed that no other creditor would suffer any harm if Missouri recognized the lien, since the only title available for the Kenworth clearly noted Associates's lien. Was Associates a secured creditor that thus had priority over the bankruptcy trustee's lien, or was Associates a general unsecured creditor whose rights were subordinate to those of the trustee? An employee of Rush, Associates's successor in interest

and to whose rights Associates therefore had succeeded, had submitted to Oklahoma officials the documentation showing a false address for Westfall in Oklahoma. Rush's employee did this so as to help Westfall avoid paying Missouri sales taxes. Was the court's ascribing Rush's employee's conduct to Associates fair in these circumstances? Would it be unethical for an owner to title a vehicle in one jurisdiction if the owner lives in another jurisdiction in which he or she would pay higher sales taxes on the vehicle? [See *In re Westfall,* 227 B.R. 734 (Bkrtcy. W.D.Mo. 1998).]

8. **CRITICAL THINKING CASE** On 18 June 1993 and 24 July 1994, Cheqnet Systems, Inc. (the debtor) signed promissory notes with Citizens First Bank of Fordyce. Prior to filing a petition under Chapter 7 of the Bankruptcy Code, the debtor engaged in the business of check collection. Specifically, the debtor would contract with merchants and promise to pursue the recovery of returned and uncollected checks. The debtor then would remit a portion of any such checks recovered to the merchants. The notes the debtor had signed with the bank granted the bank "a . . . security interest in the property described in the documents executed in connection with the note as well as other property designated as security for the loan now or in the future. Assignment of Contract with Walmart Stores, Inc., and Second Mortgage on Commercial Building More Particularly Described on Mortgage Dated 6-18-93." Other documents, including the mortgage but not including the financing statement the bank later referenced in its motion for summary judgment, were executed with the notes. It was not until nearly three years after the signing of the first note that the debtor and the bank, in April 1996, executed and filed with the appropriate state and local offices a UCC-1 financing statement that listed other collateral. During the Chapter 7 proceedings, the trustee alleged that the bank would not enjoy a perfected security interest in the property of the estate because the security documents failed to reference properly the collateral. The bank, in turn, moved for a summary judgment on the grounds that, as a matter of law, it had perfected its security interest in the debtor's accounts and contract rights as of the date of the filing of the bankruptcy petition. Should the judge grant the bank's summary judgment and thus endorse the bank's argument that its bank's security interest had attached? [See *In re Cheqnet Systems, Inc.,* 227 B.R. 166 (Bkrtcy.E.D.Ark. 1998).]

NOTES

1. Uniform Commercial Code § 9-105(m).
2. Ibid., § 9-105(d). This section further states that "[w]here the debtor and the owner of the collateral are not the same person, the term 'debtor' means the owner of the collateral in any provision of the Article dealing with the collateral, the obligor in any provision dealing with the obligation, and may include both where the context so requires. . . . "
3. Ibid., § 9-105(1).
4. Ibid., § 9-105(c). Collateral also includes accounts and chattel paper that have been sold.
5. Ibid., § 9-106.
6. Section 9-202 makes the concept of title—that is, whether the secured party or the debtor has title to the collateral—immaterial under the Code.
7. Uniform Commercial Code § 1-201(37).
8. Ibid., § 9-105(h). Goods also may include such things as standing timber, growing crops, and the unborn young of animals.
9. Ibid., § 9-109(1)–(3).
10. Ibid., § 9-109(4), Official Comment 3.
11. Ibid., § 9-313(1)(a).
12. Ibid., § 9-109, Official Comment 2.
13. Ibid., § 9-104(c).
14. Ibid., § 9-102(2).
15. Ibid., § 9-104.
16. Ibid., §§ 9-201, 9-203(4).
17. Ibid., § 9-102(2).
18. Ibid., § 1-201(37).
19. Ibid., § 9-203.
20. Ibid., §§ 9-203(1), 9-110.
21. Ibid., §§ 9-302, 9-401.
22. Ibid., § 9-304(l).
23. Ibid., § 9-402(l).
24. Ibid., § 9-402(8).
25. Ibid., § 9-402, Official Comment 9.
26. Ibid., § 9-402(1).
27. Ibid., § 9-303(1).
28. Ibid., § 9-403(2),(3).
29. Ibid.
30. Ibid., § 9-406.
31. Ibid., § 9-405(2).
32. Ibid., § 9-208(2).
33. Ibid., § 9-208(3).
34. Ibid., § 9-404(1).
35. Ibid., § 9-305.
36. Uniform Commercial Code § 9-302(1)(d).
37. Ibid., § 9-107.
38. "Prior Financing Statements Became Seriously Misleading upon Debtor's Incorporation," *U.C.C. Bulletin* (May 1999), at 6, 7; also see *ITT Commercial Finance Corporation* v. *Bank of the West*, 166 F. 3d 295 (5th Cir. 1999).
39. Ibid., §§ 9-103(1)(a), (2); 9-302(3)(b), (4).
40. Ibid., § 9-204.
41. Ibid., § 9-306.

CHAPTER

27

SECURED TRANSACTIONS: PRIORITIES AND DEFAULT

A G E N D A

In order to help CIT grow and prosper, the Kochanowskis at times will have to borrow money. They therefore want to know whether they can use any assets as collateral for more than one loan and what effect this arrangement may have on their creditors. They also will sell a number of Call-Image videophones on credit, and they will be desirous of attaining the best possible security interests in those videophones. To maximize their protections, what methods of perfection can the Kochanowskis use? What rights can they assert against competing creditors?

CIT's creditors presumably will use some of CIT's equipment, most of its inventory, and its patents as collateral. The Kochanowskis want to know what actions the

firm's creditors can take against the collateral, the firm, and the family members in the event that CIT cannot pay its bills as these debts come due. In addition, the firm hopes to sell and lease a significant number of videophones. Some of these sales will be made on an installment basis, and the family plans to retain a security interest in the videophones as collateral for these extensions of credit. The family accordingly will need to understand what rights CIT will have against any customers who default on their obligations to the firm.

These and other questions are likely to arise during your study of this chapter. Be prepared! You never know when one of the Kochanowskis will need your help or advice.

O U T L I N E

THE CODE AND COMPETING CLAIMS FOR THE SAME COLLATERAL

In Chapter 26, we examined the processes of attachment and perfection, the methods by which secured parties protect their respective interests in the collateral against the debtor and against later creditors of the debtor, especially the trustee in bankruptcy, who occupies the status of a lien creditor under the bankruptcy laws. As we discussed, the date of perfection becomes particularly significant when, as sometimes is the case, upon the debtor's default, several secured parties claim a perfected security interest in the same collateral. The Uniform Commercial Code's (UCC's) system for deciding which competing claim is superior—that is, which claim has *priority*—represents a primary focus of this chapter.

PRIORITIES

A secured party's priority over other creditors takes on enormous practical importance. The one catastrophe every creditor fears most is the bankruptcy of the debtor. The reason is simple: In the event of bankruptcy, each creditor runs the risk of receiving only a few cents on every dollar loaned to the debtor. Yet, as we have previously seen, a creditor who attains the status of a perfected secured party can maximize the chances of recovering the money owed. This status gives the creditor first claim to the collateral and thus the best chance (generally by selling the collateral) of realizing most, if not all, of the debt. A perfected secured party, then, will have priority over general (or unsecured) creditors and lien creditors, including the trustee in bankruptcy. After the secured party has disposed of the collateral, any money in excess of that owed to the secured party may be applied to the claims of these other creditors. In many instances, however, no money remains to satisfy these latter claims. Thus, we cannot overemphasize the importance of becoming a secured party. Exhibit 27.1 illustrates the attachment and the perfection of a security interest. It also examines the order of priorities in the event of a conflict among the creditors seeking to enforce their rights in the same collateral.

CONFLICTING INTERESTS IN THE SAME COLLATERAL

Given the advantages attendant on being a secured party, most creditors strive to achieve this status. This fact, in turn, leads to the possibility that several secured parties will claim a security interest in the same collateral. How, then, can we determine who among this class of favored parties has priority? Or, in other words, who has "first dibs" on the collateral?

The UCC's rules on priorities, set out in § 9-312, are difficult to unravel and understand. In general, the Code validates a *first-in-time, first-in-right approach* whereby those who have perfected their claims first have priority. For example, if two competing security interests have been perfected by filing, the first to be filed has priority, whether the security interest attached before or after filing.[1] For this reason, it makes sense for a creditor/lender to file a financing statement covering the transaction even *before* all the requirements for attachment have been met, because the date of filing will control who has priority in the collateral. Thus, the time of attachment often takes on less importance than the time of perfection (here, by filing), even though there can be no perfection without attachment.

EXHIBIT 27.1 | **Anatomy of a Security Interest: Attachment, Perfection, and Priorities**

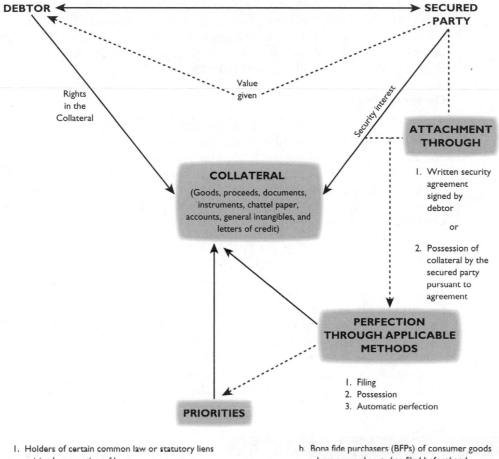

1. Holders of certain common law or statutory liens arising by operation of law.
2. Among perfected secured parties in the same collateral, first in time to file or otherwise perfect. Yet such priorities may be overridden by
   a. Purchase money security interests in which applicable U.C.C. rules have been followed.

b. Bona fide purchasers (BFPs) of consumer goods where secured party has filed beforehand and where BFPs have given value and are ignorant of the security interest.
   c. Buyers in the ordinary course of business.
3. Lien creditors (including trustees in bankruptcy).
4. Unperfected secured parties.
5. General creditors (i.e., sellers on account).

For example, suppose that on 10 December 1999, Third Bank files a financing statement covering CIT's inventory, and Fourth Bank files such a statement on the same inventory on 1 February 2000. Third Bank will have priority over Fourth Bank, even though Fourth Bank may have given value first and thus have attached its interest before Third Bank did. However, note that neither Third Bank nor Fourth Bank can have a perfected interest until attachment occurs. Put differently, Third Bank's earlier filing gives it a superior interest in the inventory under the UCC's first-to-file rules. Because the Code determines priorities from the time of filing— if all secured parties have filed—a would-be secured party should file as early as possible.

The Code's drafters have justified this "race to the recording office" as a necessary protection of the public filing system. In the drafters' view, Fourth Bank, though it has attached its interest first, cannot complain, because before taking its security interest, it could have checked the public records and thus have learned of Third Bank's claimed interest. According to the drafters, lenders like Third Bank who plan to make a series of subsequent advances and who have filed first should be able to make those later advances without having, as a condition of protection, to check each time for filings *later* than theirs.[2]

Order of Perfection

As we learned in Chapter 26, filing represents one of three alternative methods of perfection. With purchase money security interests in consumer goods, for instance, one may rely on automatic perfection; or one may perfect by taking possession of the collateral. In all such cases (that is, where none of the parties has filed), the first to perfect takes priority.

Order of Attachment

If for some reason none of the parties has perfected its security interest, the first interest to attach enjoys priority. Relying on attachment alone as a vehicle for attaining priority, however, generally makes little sense because an *unperfected* secured creditor will not enjoy a preferred status in bankruptcy proceedings. Simply stated, to gain priority over other secured parties and over the trustee in bankruptcy, it is imperative to file as soon as possible if filing is an acceptable mode for perfecting a security interest in the type of collateral involved or, if filing is not appropriate, to perfect one's interest as soon as possible in the appropriate manner.

A priority dispute involving radio station broadcast licenses forms the basis of the next case. Note how the court decided the issues before it.

27.1

MLQ INVESTORS, L.P.
V. PACIFIC QUADRACASTING, INC.
146 F.3D 746 (9TH CIR. 1998), CERT. DENIED, 525 U.S. 1121 (1999)

FACTS In late 1988, the corporate owners of several radio stations entered into a loan agreement with MLQ Investors, L.P.'s (MLQ's) predecessor in interest. The loan documents purported to create a security interest in the station owners' intangible personal property, including all Federal Communication Commission (FCC) broadcast licenses, to the extent permitted by law. In the event of default, the lender was authorized to obtain a court judgment enabling it to sell the collateral and to apply the proceeds to the outstanding debt. Between 1988 and 1994, the station owners defaulted on the loans and failed to pay taxes to the Internal Revenue Service (IRS). MLQ's predecessor in interest had perfected its security interest under the loan documents in December 1988 and January 1989, and subsequently had filed continuation statements. The IRS's first tax lien on the station owners' property arose in 1991. The station owners' debt to MLQ ultimately exceeded the combined value of the owners' assets; hence, in 1994, MLQ filed suit against the station owners and two guarantors for breach of contract, foreclosure of the security interest, and breach of guarantees. MLQ also sought the appointment of a receiver and injunctive relief. In May 1994, after the district court had appointed a receiver, the parties stipulated that the proceeds were to be distributed in accordance with the bankruptcy laws. In late November 1994, the district court entered

27.2

MLQ INVESTORS, L.P.
V. PACIFIC QUADRACASTING, INC., *continued*
146 F.3D 746 (9TH CIR. 1998), CERT. DENIED, 525 U.S. 1121 (1999)

orders authorizing the receiver (assuming the receiver could secure FCC approval for the transfer of the broadcast licenses) to sell all the assets of the radio stations at a private sale and to disburse the sales proceeds to MLQ. One of the guarantors, Walter A. Heusser, appealed this decision on the grounds that a creditor could not obtain a valid security interest in an FCC broadcasting license and consequently would be unable to perfect this interest under the UCC.

ISSUES Could a creditor perfect a security interest in an FCC broadcasting license? If so, would the creditor's security interest have priority over IRS tax liens filed on the debtor's property?

HOLDINGS Yes, to both issues. A creditor could obtain a security interest in the proceeds of the sale of an FCC license, and such an interest would constitute a "general intangible" the creditor could perfect prior to the sale of the license. Because MLQ had perfected its security interest in the debtor's general intangibles before the IRS had filed its tax liens, MLQ's interest would prevail.

Reasoning Heusser argued that a debtor cannot create a voluntary security interest in an FCC broadcasting license because doing so would be inconsistent with federal laws that limit the transfer of such licenses. However, this argument directly contravenes a bankruptcy decision that held that a creditor may perfect a security interest in a debtor's FCC broadcasting license to the extent that the creditor seeks to protect its interest in the proceeds of the debtor's license. In reaching this result, the bankruptcy court recognized a "public/private" distinction between a licensee's right to transfer its license (a "public" right between the FCC and the licensee, which right is governed by the FCC) and the licensee's right to receive remuneration for a transfer (a "private" right between two parties). In other words, according to this precedent, the FCC may prohibit security interests in licenses themselves because the creation of such an interest could result in a foreclosure and a transfer of the license without FCC approval. Such FCC approval is necessary to regulate the airwaves in the public interest. On the other hand, a security interest in the

proceeds of a license, when such a security interest fails to grant the creditor any power or control over the license itself or the segment of the broadcast spectrum it represents, implicates no such public interest. The district court in the present case followed the reasoning of this and other precedents when it determined that MLQ had perfected a security interest in the proceeds of the sale of the FCC broadcasting licenses. Notwithstanding these authorities, Heusser submitted that even if MLQ had attained a security interest in the proceeds from the sale of the licenses, this interest did not arise, and therefore one would be unable to perfect the interest, until the licenses were sold. As a result, Heusser maintained, MLQ's security interest was junior to the IRS tax liens created prior to the sale of the licenses. Granted, the aforementioned precedents make it clear that license holders have no property rights in the actual broadcast frequencies themselves as against the federal government. However, these decisions stand for the proposition that licensees do have a proprietary right in the proceeds from a sale of a license and may grant a security interest in those proceeds. Since the licensee has rights and interests in the license proceeds (including a limited right to pledge those proceeds as collateral), the proceeds constitute general intangibles that are subject to perfection prior to sale. Indeed, a contrary outcome would mean that the distinction between private and public interests in FCC license proceeds would have no meaning; and these private interests would be devoid of value. A security interest in proceeds that a creditor could not perfect until after the foreclosure and sale of the license would, in almost every circumstance, be pre-empted by IRS liens and the claims of other creditors. The fact that in the present case the actual dollar proceeds from the sale of the licenses were generated only after the sale—and thus after the tax lien filing as well—was immaterial, since nearly all forms of security must be reduced to cash before they pay off the debt secured thereby. Here, MLQ had entered into a security agreement with the debtor prior to the dates on which the IRS had filed notices of tax liens on the debtor's property. MLQ also had filed the financing statements necessary to perfect the interest prior to the IRS's filing of notices of its tax liens. In the absence of a

continued

27.1

MLQ INVESTORS, L.P.
V. PACIFIC QUADRACASTING, INC., *continued*
146 F.3D 746 (9TH CIR. 1998), CERT. DENIED, 525 U.S. 1121 (1999)

provision to the contrary, priority for purposes of federal law is governed by the common-law principle that "the first in time is the first in right." Thus, MLQ's interest would have priority.

BUSINESS CONSIDERATION Revised Article 9 makes restrictions on assignments of security interests in certain permits, licenses, and franchises generally ineffective (although the section does not override federal law to the contrary). This provision presumably

will enhance the ability of certain debtors to obtain credit. Why would lenders consider such intellectual property desirable as collateral?

ETHICAL CONSIDERATIONS In this case, the owners of the broadcasting station failed to pay their income taxes when due. Muster arguments for and against the proposition that the current U.S. income tax system unethically benefits certain interests at the expense of others. If you agree that inequities do result, are these differentials justifiable from a utilitarianistic perspective?fact

EXCEPTIONS

We now turn our attention to some very important exceptions to the general rules of priority. The first of these concerns a purchase money security interest that is held by a purchase money secured party.

Purchase Money Security Interests

For reasons that soon will be clear, a purchase money secured party enjoys priority over interests that precede his or her interest in time, provided the party complies with certain provisions of the Code. In other words, a purchase money security interest contradicts our previously described first-to-file-or-to-perfect rules on priorities. An analysis of the types of commercial situations that involve purchase money security interests and purchase money secured parties will explain why the Code sanctions a special status for these interests.

As we learned in Chapter 26, a security interest is a purchase money security interest to the extent that it is "(a) taken or retained by the seller of the collateral to secure all or part of its price; or (b) taken by a person who by making advances or incurring an obligation gives value to enable the debtor to acquire rights in or the use of collateral if such value is in fact so used."[3] As should be apparent from this definition, purchase money secured parties typically are sellers or lenders who, by their extensions of credit, permit the debtor to acquire rights in the collateral. But not all sellers or lenders qualify for purchase money secured party status. Let us reexamine our earlier example involving Third Bank and CIT so as to understand how purchase money secured parties differ from other secured parties.

This time we will assume that Third Bank has agreed to finance CIT's inventory. As CIT's inventory financier, Third Bank agrees to give CIT a *line of credit* on which CIT can draw at irregular intervals and from which the bank can issue *future advances* of funds to CIT if CIT needs them. To protect itself, Third Bank creates and perfects a security interest in all of CIT's present and after-acquired property and all proceeds thereof. In such situations, Third Bank has a so-called *floating lien* over

CIT's inventory, since the lien covers the items of inventory as they stand on the shelf and even "floats" over other inventory and property that CIT acquires through subsequent advances or loans from Third Bank. Third Bank's lien also covers the *proceeds* of any items that CIT sells. Generally speaking, Third Bank will compel CIT to maintain a certain ratio of inventory and will gauge CIT's repayment of the loans and the bank's later advances with reference to this ratio. Typically, Third Bank will ask CIT to promise to refrain from *double financing*, or using this same inventory as collateral for a subsequent loan from another creditor, say Fourth Bank.

Third Bank's reasons for protecting its security interest in the inventory are understandable: The bank knows that, should CIT become bankrupt, the bank will need to have priority if it hopes to realize any money from its extension of credit. Hence, on the one hand, the law wants to protect secured parties like Third Bank so that they will be willing to extend credit to businesspeople or firms like CIT. One way to accomplish this policy objective is to give such lenders priority if they are the first to file or to perfect.

On the other hand, it seems unfair for Third Bank to have the ability to restrict unduly CIT's access to credit. Potential subsequent creditors may see Third Bank's previously filed financing statement on the inventory and may refuse to extend CIT credit because of Third Bank's seeming priority based on its compliance with the first-to-file-or-to-perfect rules. Where will the firm obtain credit if, for some reason, Third Bank refuses to give CIT additional loans or advances?

The UCC, by giving priority to purchase money security interests, attempts to balance both CIT's and Third Bank's interests. In other words, if Fourth Bank advances money (say $10,000) to enable CIT to acquire additional inventory, Fourth Bank has priority over Third Bank to the extent of the value given—here, $10,000—because the law characterizes Fourth Bank in these circumstances as a purchase money secured party; that is, the money advanced by Fourth Bank relates directly to CIT's acquisition of specific, identifiable collateral. (Third Bank, as the inventory financier and the holder of after-acquired property and future advances clauses, is a non-purchase money secured party here.) To earn this priority, however, Fourth Bank has to fulfill certain requirements, depending on the type of collateral involved.

If the collateral consists of inventory, Fourth Bank enjoys priority over Third Bank's conflicting security interest in the same inventory (and in identifiable cash proceeds) received on or before the delivery of the inventory to a buyer (here, CIT). This is true provided that the purchase money security interest has been perfected by filing at the time the debtor receives possession of the inventory and the purchase money secured party notifies *in writing* any persons who previously have filed financing statements covering inventory of the same types that it (the purchase money secured party) has or expects to acquire a purchase money security interest in the inventory of the debtor. The purchase money secured party also must describe the inventory by item or type. To acquire priority over Third Bank, Fourth Bank must meet these requirements.[4]

To those who see this "super priority" for purchase money secured parties as unfair to inventory financiers like Third Bank, the drafters of the Code offer the following policy justifications. The notification procedures required by the Code will tip off Third Bank that CIT is double financing. At this point, if it believes itself vulnerable, Third Bank may curtail future advances to CIT. And, assuming that the security agreement so provides and that it (the bank) gives notice, it may argue that such double financing constitutes a condition of default and may demand payment from CIT. Third Bank thus has ways of protecting itself if it so desires, and in the meantime CIT has acquired new avenues of credit. Third Bank also has the added protection of knowing that it still will have priority with regard to the inventory if Fourth Bank does not comply with the Code's requirements.

If the security interest covers noninventory collateral (such as equipment or consumer goods), Fourth Bank, as a purchase money secured party, has priority over Third Bank, as a holder of a conflicting security interest in the same collateral or its proceeds, if the purchase money security interest is perfected at the time the debtor receives possession of the collateral or within 10 days thereafter.[5] Hence, it is clear that the type of collateral involved dictates what a creditor must do to achieve purchase money secured party status.

Why is less required (a 10-day grace period for filing and no need to give notice to holders of previously filed security interests) of one who wishes to attain priority in noninventory collateral? Apparently, the drafters of the Code believed that arrangements for periodic advances against incoming property are unusual outside the inventory field; thus, they did not think there was a need to notify noninventory secured parties because, in fact, only in rare instances would such a previous financier even exist. Simply put, equipment and consumer goods usually are not valuable enough for several creditors to have taken security interests in them. To illustrate, if CIT buys a new lathe for use in cutting out the housing for the Call-Image videophones, the lathe is equipment because CIT uses it in its business. If Fourth Bank lends CIT the money to buy the lathe, the bank becomes a purchase money secured party if the bank files a financing statement within 10 days of CIT's receipt of the lathe. Fourth Bank enjoys priority over Third Bank, despite a lack of notice to the latter, even if Third Bank has filed a financing statement indicating an interest in "all inventory, equipment, and after-acquired property of Call-Image Technology, Inc." If Fourth Bank does not file within 10 days, Third Bank, under the usual first-to-file-or-to-perfect rules, has a priority claim to the lathe.

If there are two or more competing purchase money security interests in the same type of collateral, the Code, in determining priority in this situation, applies the usual first-to-file-or-to-perfect rules. Thus, the purchase money secured party who files first has superior rights.

The case that follows illustrates how a court can dispose of lawsuits involving assertions of purchase money security interests.

27.2

GENERAL ELECTRIC CAPITAL COMMERCIAL AUTOMOTIVE FINANCE, INC. V. SPARTAN MOTORS, LTD.

675 N.Y.S.2D 626 (A.D. 2 DEPT. 1998)

FACTS On 28 September 1983, a predecessor of General Electric Capital Commercial Automotive Finance, Inc. (GECC) entered into an inventory security agreement with Spartan Motors, Ltd. (Spartan) in connection with Spartan's "floor plan" financing of the dealership's inventory. Pursuant to that agreement, GECC acquired a blanket lien (otherwise known as a "dragnet" lien) on Spartan's inventory so as to secure a debt in excess of $1,000,000. The agreement defined inventory as "[a]ll inventory, of whatever kind or nature, wherever located, now owned or hereafter acquired . . . and all proceeds thereof (whether in the form of cash, instruments, chattel paper, general intangibles, accounts or otherwise)." This security agreement was duly filed in the appropriate state and local offices. On 19 July 1991, Spartan signed a new wholesale security agreement with General Motors Acceptance Corporation (GMAC), in which GMAC agreed to finance—or "floor-plan"—Spartan's inventory. Under this security agreement, GMAC would

27.2

GENERAL ELECTRIC CAPITAL COMMERCIAL AUTOMOTIVE FINANCE, INC. V. SPARTAN MOTORS, LTD., *continued*

675 N.Y.S.2D 626 (A.D. 2 DEPT. 1998)

pay the manufacturers and distributors for each vehicle; Spartan would repay GMAC once a vehicle was sold; and GMAC would have a security interest in the vehicles and the proceeds of the sales thereof. GMAC's security agreement was duly filed. In addition, the following certified letter dated 17 July 1991, officially notified GECC of GMAC's competing security interest in Spartan's inventory:

> This is to notify you that General Motors Acceptance Corporation holds or expects to acquire purchase money security interests in inventory collateral which will from time to time hereafter be delivered to Spartan Motors Ltd. of Poughkeepsie, New York, and in the proceeds thereof. Such inventory collateral consists, or will consist, of the types of collateral described in a financing statement, a true copy of which is annexed hereto and made a part hereof.

On 7 May 1992, Spartan paid $121,500 of its own money to acquire a 1992 600 SEL Mercedes-Benz. Six days later, on 13 May 1992, GMAC reimbursed Spartan; and the vehicle was placed on GMAC's floor plan. On 7 July 1992, Spartan paid $120,000 of its own money to acquire a second 1992 600 SEL Mercedes. Two days later, on 9 July 1992, GMAC reimbursed Spartan for that amount and placed the second vehicle on its floor plan. A few months later, on or about 2 October 1992, GECC, seeking $1,180,999.98 in money then due to GECC under its agreement with Spartan, as well as a determination of who had priority in the two unsold Mercedes-Benzes, commenced this action against Spartan. Soon thereafter, Spartan filed a bankruptcy petition and ceased doing business. Among the assets appropriated and sold by GMAC were the two Mercedes-Benz automobiles, which were auctioned for $194,500. GECC subsequently claimed that, by so doing, GMAC had converted the two vehicles in violation of GECC's antecedent security interest.

ISSUE Did GMAC's agreement with Spartan create a purchase money security interest that would give GMAC priority over GECC's blanket lien, even though GMAC had not advanced funds to Spartan until after the dealership had purchased vehicles on its own?

HOLDING Yes. Because GMAC was "obligated" to give value to enable Spartan to acquire rights in the

two Mercedes-Benzes and the purchase and loan transactions were only days apart, Spartan's purchases and GMAC's reimbursements were sufficiently "closely allied" to have given GMAC a purchase money security interest in the vehicles in question.

REASONING A perfected purchase money security interest provides an exception to the general first-in-time, first-in-right rule of conflicting security interests. Thus, a perfected purchase money security interest in inventory has priority over a conflicting prior security interest in the same inventory if the purported purchase money security interest fits within the Uniform Commercial Code definition and hence qualifies for the exception. Uniform Commercial Code § 9-107 defines a "purchase money security interest" as a security interest:

> (a) taken or retained by the seller of the collateral to secure all or part of its price; or
>
> (b) taken by a person who by making advances or incurring an obligation gives value to enable the debtor to acquire rights in or the use of collateral if such value is in fact so used.

This case, then, presents the question of whether GMAC's reimbursement to Spartan after it had acquired the two Mercedes-Benz vehicles would qualify as an "advance" or "obligation" that had enabled Spartan to purchase the cars, such that GMAC had acquired a purchase money security interest in the vehicles. The arguments *against* finding a purchase money security interest under these circumstances are basically twofold: First, of the few courts to construe Uniform Commercial Code § 9-107(b), many have shown a decided reluctance to hold that a purchase money security interest has been created where, as here, title to and possession of the merchandise have passed to the debtor *before* the advance of the loan. Second, the literal wording of the agreement between GMAC and Spartan appears to accord GMAC purchase money secured status only when the finance company paid Spartan's "manufacturer, distributor or other seller" directly. Nothing in GMAC's contract with Spartan appears to contemplate any obligation on the part of the financier to "reimburse" the auto dealership for funds that the latter already expended

continued

27.2

GENERAL ELECTRIC CAPITAL COMMERCIAL AUTOMOTIVE FINANCE, INC. V. SPARTAN MOTORS, LTD., *continued*

675 N.Y.S.2D 626 (A.D. 2 DEPT. 1998)

to purchase merchandise. In determining whether a security interest exists, a court must focus on the intent of the parties. Thus, an examination of the language used and of the conditions and circumstances confronting the parties when they made the contract becomes the best means for determining that intent. Here, then, a court must determine whether the availability of the loan was a factor in the parties' negotiating the sale and/or whether the lender was committed at the time of the sale to advance the amount required to pay for the items purchased. An application of these principles to the present case indicates that GMAC's reimbursements to Spartan following its two Mercedes-Benz purchases were only six and two days apart, respectively. Moreover, GECC does not dispute GMAC's contention that a post-purchase reimbursement arrangement was common in the trade, as well as routine in Spartan's course of dealing with GMAC and its other financiers, in some circumstances. In the language of Uniform Commercial Code § 9-107(b), the evidence shows that GMAC was committed to give value to enable the car dealership to acquire rights in the collateral. Furthermore, the value so extended was intended to and in fact did enable Spartan to acquire the two Mercedes-Benzes, since without GMAC's backing Spartan could not have afforded to purchase these expensive vehicles. Accordingly, the literal requirements of Uniform Commercial Code § 9-107(b) are satisfied, notwithstanding the inverted purchase-loan chronology. GMAC's election on some occasions to fund Spartan's floor-planning by reimbursing the car dealership for Spartan's purchases was not inconsistent with GMAC's decision on other occasions to accomplish the same goal by following the strict wording of the contract and pre-paying the supplier directly. Whether viewed as a differing course of performance or a course of dealing, the first of these two methods

of financing remains entirely compatible with the method set out in the agreement. Alternatively, the reimbursement procedure used by GMAC may constitute a post-agreement course of performance that, under UCC 2-208[1], modified the written contract. Accordingly, the lower court erred when it had found that, having financed the two vehicles at issue here by way of reimbursements—"the very opposite of an advance"—GMAC had failed to acquire a purchase money security interest under Uniform Commercial Code 9-107(b). Rather, since GMAC had established 1) that it was "obligated" to give value to enable Spartan to acquire rights in the two Mercedes-Benzes and 2) that the purchase and loan transactions were only days apart, one must conclude that Spartan's purchase and GMAC's subsequent reimbursement were sufficiently "closely allied" to give GMAC a purchase money security interest in the vehicles. Under these circumstances, GMAC was entitled both to the proceeds of the sale of the two contested vehicles and a summary judgment against GECC.

BUSINESS CONSIDERATION Assume you work for GMAC and your boss has asked you to redraft the instruments connected with this case so as to ensure that the firm in the future unquestionably will enjoy the status of a purchase money secured party. Although the staff counsel will write the final draft, what language will you incorporate in this first draft?

ETHICAL CONSIDERATIONS Was Spartan behaving in an unethical fashion when it engaged two "floor plan" financiers? Would your answer differ if you had discovered that Spartan had begun dealing with GMAC because it (Spartan) was behind in its payments to GECC?

Bona Fide Purchasers of Consumer Goods

Besides purchase money secured parties, another class of persons who may have priority over a previously perfected security interest is the *bona fide purchaser* of consumer goods.[6] Recall from Chapter 26 that *consumer goods* are those used or bought for use primarily for personal, family, or household purposes.[7] Thus, this section

Consumer Goods

of the Code limits priority to the purchase of this type of collateral. Examination of this Code provision shows further limitations, since to enjoy priority over a previously perfected security interest, a buyer must be ignorant of the security interest, must pay value, and must use the goods for personal, family, or household purposes.

To illustrate, assume that Henry Smith wishes to sell his refrigerator to Margaret Hernandez. Margaret does not know it; but Handley, the owner of the appliance store where Henry bought the refrigerator, has a perfected security interest in this consumer good. (Handley is relying on automatic perfection—that is, the mere attachment of the security interest.) If Margaret pays value and uses the refrigerator in her home, she will have priority; in other words, should Henry default in his payments, she will retain the refrigerator even if Handley tries to repossess it from her. If Margaret plans to use the refrigerator in her dental office for the purpose of keeping anesthetics cold, however, Handley will win because Margaret does not fit § 9-307(2)'s definition of a bona fide purchaser.

So far, we have been assuming that Handley will rely on automatic perfection, which, as discussed in Chapter 26, is the mode generally preferred by the Handleys of the world because they thereby can avoid the expense and inconvenience of filing. Under § 9-307(2), though, if Handley files a financing statement covering a consumer good before a buyer like Margaret purchases it, Handley, not the bona fide purchaser, will have a priority claim to it. Handley, then, must decide whether the possibility that a refrigerator will be sold to a bona fide purchaser outweighs the inconvenience of filing. If he thinks it does, in order to attain priority, he should file. If not, he can rely on automatic perfection to keep him secure from the claims of everyone except this specialized type of bona fide purchaser.

Buyers in the Ordinary Course of Business

According to § 9-307(1), buyers in the ordinary course of business may have priority over a perfected security interest. To use our earlier example, when Henry Smith buys the refrigerator from Handley's Appliance Store, he is a *buyer in the ordinary course of business.* Anyone who buys goods from a merchant seller in a standard (as opposed to an extraordinary) transaction is a buyer in the ordinary course of business. As such, Henry will take the refrigerator free of a security interest created by his seller (Handley may have given a security interest in his inventory of appliances to Third Bank), even though the security interest is perfected and even if Henry knows of Third Bank's perfected security interest. The policy reasons for such a result are clear: Purchasers will not buy refrigerators or compact disk players or garden tractors out of a seller's stock of trade or inventory if lenders like Third Bank can repossess these items. Therefore, buyers in the

27.1 | FINANCE

SECURITY INTEREST

The firm sold 50 Call-Image videophones on credit to a local retail store. CIT retained a security interest in the videophones and properly perfected its interest by filing in the appropriate office in a timely manner. The Kochanowskis have learned that this retail store is having serious financial problems and may be forced to go out of business. They ask you if they can assert their security interest against the units still in the store's possession and against any customers who have purchased units from the store if the retailer ultimately should default on the contract. What will you tell them?

BUSINESS CONSIDERATIONS What should a business creditor that holds a perfected security interest do if it hears that one of its debtors is having financial difficulties? How can the business creditor protect its interests without jeopardizing the future of the debtor?

ETHICAL CONSIDERATION Assuming that it would be legal to do so, would it be ethical for a secured creditor to seek enforcement of its security interest against buyers in the ordinary course of business who purchased collateral from a retail seller that also was a debtor of the secured creditor?

27.2 | FINANCE

PURCHASE MONEY SECURITY INTEREST

CIT sold two Call-Image videophones to a customer and retained a purchase money security interest in the videophones. The customer defaulted on the debt, and CIT later wanted to enforce its interest in the units. Tom learned that the videophones are in the possession of a repairperson whom the customer had hired to work on the videophones. Tom wants to know what rights, owing to the default of the customer, that CIT has in this situation and whether the firm can insist that the repairperson turn over the videophones. What will you tell him?

BUSINESS CONSIDERATIONS Why might a secured creditor, in order to obtain possession of the collateral itself, want to pay a person who has a possessory lien stemming from repairing the collateral? What can the creditor do if it decides not to redeem the collateral from the possessory lienholder?

ETHICAL CONSIDERATIONS Is there an ethical reason for allowing a possessory lienholder to gain priority over a properly perfected security interest? What ethical considerations justify such a rule?

ordinary course of business—by definition, those who may know of the existence of a perfected security interest in the goods but who buy in good faith and without knowledge that the sale of the goods is in violation of the ownership rights or security interest of a third party—have priority in such competing claims situations.

Although many people use the terms *bona fide purchaser* and *buyer in the ordinary course of business* interchangeably, they are distinct concepts. We more appropriately term a consumer who has bought goods from another consumer in an occasional sale a bona fide purchaser. Buyers in the ordinary course of business, in contrast, are purchasers who are buying from a seller who routinely sells from inventory or otherwise regularly engages in such transactions.

Common Law and Statutory Liens

Under § 9-310 of the UCC, certain liens that arise by operation of law have priority over a perfected security interest in the collateral. For example, if Monty Moore takes his car to Harry's Auto Repair and does not pay Harry, the owner (Harry) will have a common law or statutory lien on the car to the extent of the money owed him for his services or materials. Harry can retain possession of the car; and, in the event of Monty's default, Harry can force Westside Savings and Loan, the secured party for Monty's car, to pay him (Harry) for his repairs before Westside realizes any proceeds from the sale of Monty's car.

Fixtures

As discussed in Chapter 26, Article 9 ordinarily does not cover security interests in real estate. As you may remember, however, in addition to covering personal property, Article 9 also encompasses *fixtures*—goods that have become so related to real estate that an interest in them arises under real estate law. Many factories, schools, and homes have a fixture called a furnace. In most cases, a mortgagee (the party who loaned the money for the purchase of the land) has a security interest in the real property, while a secured party may have retained an interest in the furnace. If the seller of the furnace wishes to repossess the furnace but confronts the mortgagee of the land, who claims the furnace as part of his or her real estate security interest, knock-down, drag-out fights over priority sometimes occur as a result of this dovetailing of real property and personal property interests.

Section 9-313 of the Code sets out rules for settling these problems. According to the Code, a perfected security interest in fixtures has priority over the conflicting interest of an **encumbrancer** or an owner of real estate when (1) the security interest is a purchase money security interest; (2) the security interest is perfected by a fixture filing—that is, filing in the office where real estate mortgages are filed or recorded—before the goods become fixtures (or within 10 days thereafter); and

Encumbrancer
The holder of a claim relating to real or personal property.

(3) the debtor has an interest of record in the real estate or is in possession of it. Thus, if Fire Power Furnace Company sells Earl LePage, the lessee of Port-Hole Pub, a furnace on an installment basis and retains a security interest in the furnace until Earl pays for it, Fire Power will have priority over Earl's lessor (or the mortgagee of the pub) if (1) Fire Power is a purchase money secured party, and (2) it perfects its security interest before the furnace is installed (or within 10 days of that time).[8]

Similarly, a perfected security interest in fixtures will have priority if (1) the fixtures are readily removable factory or office machines or readily removable replacements of domestic appliances that are consumer goods and (2) before the goods become fixtures, the security interest is perfected by any method permitted under Article 9.[9] Therefore, if Don Dunn's garbage disposal disintegrates and he buys one (through a conditional sales contract) from Hosinski's Appliance Store, Hosinski's will have priority over Don's mortgagee (whose mortgage covers not only the real property but also the plumbing and appliances) if Hosinski's perfects its security interest before it installs the disposal in Don's home. As you no doubt recall, perfection of such consumer goods may occur through attachment; thus, Hosinski's will have priority as of the moment Don signs the security agreement.

It may, nevertheless, be in Hosinski's best interests to perfect by resorting to a fixture filing: Such a filing will ensure its priority over subsequent encumbrancers or purchasers whose interests arise after Hosinski's.

When the secured party has priority over all owners and encumbrancers of the real estate, that party, upon the debtor's default, may sever and remove the collateral (such as the furnace) from the real estate. A secured party who elects to do this has a duty to reimburse any encumbrancer or owner of the real estate who is not the debtor for any physical injury caused to the property by the removal. Correspondingly, a person entitled to reimbursement may refuse permission concerning the removal of the fixtures until the secured party gives adequate security for the performance of this obligation.[10]

THE CODE AND DEFAULT

Thus far, we have considered the methods by which a secured party can protect its interest in the collateral. Neither the debtor nor the secured party, however, wants to consider the possibility that the debtor will *default*, or fail to meet the obligations set out in the security agreement. Still, this contingency sometimes occurs.

The default of the debtor represents a bittersweet moment for the secured party. On the one hand, default distresses the secured party because it reveals that the debtor may be unable or unwilling to pay the debt to the secured party. But, on the other hand, the secured party has worked hard to preserve his or her status as one superior to an unsecured lender and as one who, upon the

27.3 | FINANCE

CALL-IMAGE TECHNOLOGY

DEFAULT

Third Bank holds a perfected security interest in some of CIT's inventory, and the perfection is by possession (through a field warehousing arrangement). Third Bank is asserting that CIT has defaulted on its obligations and that it (Third Bank) intends to seek recovery under the provisions of Article 9. Tom and Anna ask you what obligations or liabilities Third Bank may owe to CIT and vice versa in this situation. What will you tell them?

BUSINESS CONSIDERATIONS What factors should a secured creditor consider before it decides whether to seek a recovery under Article 9 or under common law? Why might a business decide to forgo its Article 9 protections and seek a non-Code remedy?

ETHICAL CONSIDERATIONS Do you think it is ethical for a secured creditor to elect *not* to enforce its security interest upon default by the debtor? What impact might such a decision have on the other creditors of the defaulting debtor?

debtor's default, thus has rights to the collateral. In brief, Part 5 of Article 9 of the UCC allows the secured party, upon the debtor's default, to take possession of the collateral and to dispose of it in satisfaction of the secured party's claim. Yet the Code provides the debtor with certain protections once the secured party seeks to enforce its rights in the collateral and makes the secured party liable for any noncompliance with applicable Code provisions.

Interestingly, the Code does not define the term *default*. Basically, the parties decide what events constitute default, and the security agreement embodies these conclusions. Simply put, *default* means whatever the security agreement says it means. Nonpayment by the debtor perhaps constitutes the easiest definition of default. But default clauses often are broad and lengthy (see Exhibit 26.1). Security agreements also typically include *acceleration clauses* by which the secured party demands that all obligations be paid immediately. In the absence of bad faith and unconscionability, courts routinely uphold these clauses whenever the secured party can show that the debtor has defaulted. Upon default, the secured party may resort to various alternative remedies. Using non-Code remedies, the secured party may become a judgment creditor, may **garnish** the debtor's wages, or may **replevy** the goods. Code remedies include strict foreclosure (retention of the collateral in satisfaction of the debt) and resale of the collateral. In § 9-501(1), the UCC further provides that non-Code and Code rights and remedies are cumulative. Yet it is clear that before secured parties can utilize another method against the debtor, they must be unsuccessful in enforcing their rights by the first method. Neither the Code nor case law sanctions an approach whereby a secured creditor may employ non-Code and Code remedies simultaneously against the debtor.

Exhibit 27.2 describes the rights and duties of the parties in a secured transaction upon default.

NON-CODE REMEDIES

The Code says that, upon default, secured parties may seek a court judgment, may **foreclose,** or may otherwise enforce the security agreement by any available judicial procedure.[11] Accordingly, secured parties can use their Code remedies of repossession and resale with the possibility of a deficiency judgment for which the debtor is liable, or they can follow the non-Code remedy of becoming judgment creditors whereby they file suit, obtain a judgment, and have the sheriff use a **writ of execution** to levy on the goods and then sell the goods at a public sale. The proceeds of this sale are paid to the secured party. Another non-Code alternative to levying on the goods involves **garnishment** of a set percentage of the debtor's wages. Although certain advantages accrue from following these non-Code remedies in cases where the value of the collateral has decreased so far that the possibility of reaching assets beyond the collateral will be desirable, most creditors, in practice, elect the tidier and speedier remedies of repossession and resale that the UCC allows.

RIGHT OF REPOSSESSION

Unless already in possession of the collateral, a secured party, upon the debtor's default, has the right to take possession of the collateral. In so doing, that party may employ "self-help" measures; that is, secured parties can repossess the collateral themselves without judicial procedures if they can do so without breaching the

---

Garnish
Receive the debtor's assets that are in the hands of a third party; a remedy given to satisfy a debt owed.

Replevy
Acquire possession of goods unlawfully held by another.

Foreclose
Cut off an existing ownership right in property.

Writ of execution
A court-issued writing that enforces a judgment or decree.

Garnishment
A legal proceeding in which assets of a debtor that are in the hands of a third person are ordered held by the third person or turned over to the creditor in full or partial satisfaction of the debt.

E X H I B I T   27.2 | **Rights and Duties Upon the Debtor's Default**

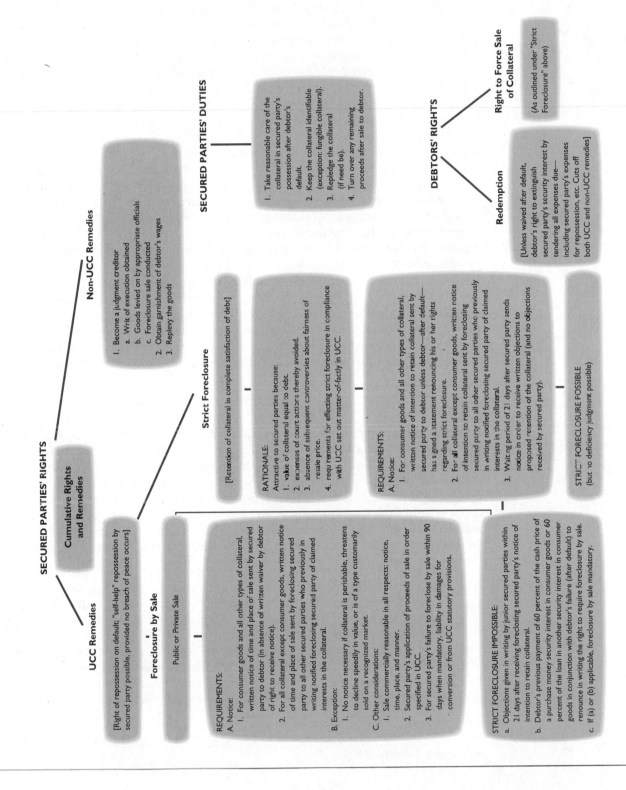

peace.[12] Repossession carries with it inherent dangers, however. Besides risking possible tort liability if the repossession involves a breach of the peace, the secured party also risks UCC liability[13] and the loss of the right to a deficiency judgment.

Needless to say, this aspect of the Code has spawned numerous lawsuits. In general, courts assess such factors as whether the secured party entered the debtor's home or driveway without permission and whether the debtor agreed to the repossession. Although it is difficult to make generalizations in this area, if the creditor repossesses an automobile from a public street and the debtor fails to object to this procedure, most courts will hold that no breach of the peace has occurred. Nevertheless, in recent years, some questions have arisen as to the constitutionality of this "self-help" provision of the Code. Specifically, some have argued that repossession without notice to the debtor may deprive the debtor of due process rights.[14] Statutes authorizing replevin may be subject to the same constitutional argument.

Besides repossession by self-help, if the security agreement so provides, the Code also sanctions the secured party's requiring the debtor to assemble the collateral at a reasonably convenient place to be designated by the secured party.[15] Moreover, when the collateral consists of heavy equipment that makes physical removal burdensome or expensive, the Code permits the secured party to render the equipment unusable and to dispose of the collateral on the debtor's premises, thus eliminating the need for physically removing the collateral.

These rules do not cover accounts and general intangibles, because one cannot possess purely intangible collateral. When the debtor is in default with regard to these types of collateral, the secured party may notify the person who is obligated on the intangibles to make payments directly to the secured party. The secured party also may take control of any UCC proceeds to which he or she is entitled.[16]

STRICT FORECLOSURE

After default and repossession, the secured party may decide to retain the collateral in complete satisfaction of the debt.[17] This remedy, called the secured party's right of strict foreclosure, may be attractive to the secured party for several reasons: (1) The value of the collateral may be approximately equal to the debt; (2) the expenses of court actions are avoided; (3) there can be no subsequent controversies about whether the resale price was fair; and (4) the UCC sets out matter-of-factly the requirements for effecting strict foreclosure. However, to effect strict foreclosure, any secured party must comply with certain requirements, which include the following:

1. The secured party must send written notice of his or her intention to retain the collateral to:
   a. the debtor, unless the debtor after default has signed a statement renouncing his or her right to force a sale of the collateral (in the case of consumer goods, no other notice need be sent);
   b. any other secured parties who in writing have notified the secured party who is foreclosing that they claim an interest in the collateral.
2. After sending notice, the secured party must wait 21 days so as to receive objections in writing concerning this proposed retention of the collateral.[18]

If the secured party receives no such objections, he or she can utilize the remedy of strict foreclosure, but the secured party will thereby give up any claims to a deficiency judgment.

THE PERILS OF SELF-HELP REPOSSESSION

On 25 April 1997, Michael T. Eustler, a motor vehicle repossessor, arrived at the home of Jon Douglas Alexander in Rockbridge County, Virginia, to repossess Alexander's car. Alexander asked if he could remove his "personal property" from inside the car, and Eustler agreed. At the subsequent trial, Alexander testified that a muscular disorder had left him partially disabled for many years. He stated further that the vehicle contained legal documents that pertained to his longstanding (but pending) disability claim, as well as some "tools of his profession." Alexander testified that he related these facts to Eustler and that Eustler agreed to allow the removal of these items. However, according to Alexander, Eustler "jacked up" the vehicle while Alexander was partially seated in the car and demanded that Alexander provide him with the keys. Alexander testified that he went into his house and returned with the keys, which he put on top of the car. Alexander also brought with him an unloaded rifle, which he placed in a flower bed near the vehicle. Alexander stated that because Eustler then approached Alexander in a "belligerent manner," Alexander, out of a fear for his personal safety and his property, retrieved the rifle. At first, Alexander testified, he held the rifle at his side. But when Eustler continued to advance toward Alexander, Alexander raised the rifle to his shoulder and pointed the rifle at Eustler. Eustler's version of the facts differed from Alexander's. Eustler testified that Alexander went into the house and returned with a rifle. Eustler stated that Alexander then opened the left rear door and began to remove items from the back seat. Eustler stated that when he approached the vehicle, Alexander raised the rifle and said, "I could drop you right there." Eustler testified that he immediately returned to his truck, left the premises, and called the police. The police later recovered an unloaded rifle from Alexander's home. Alexander subsequently was convicted of brandishing a weapon. On appeal, he argued that the judge had committed reversible error when the judge had refused to instruct the jury that Virginia precedents recognize brandishing a firearm as lawful resistance to the repossession of personal property.

This appeal has been brought in *your* court. How will *you* decide the issues? Would you agree that a debtor should be able to threaten to use deadly force to stave off a "self-help" repossession?[19]

BUSINESS CONSIDERATIONS What sort of policy should a business creditor establish for dealing with debtors who have fallen behind in their payments? What sort of policy should a business creditor have for using "self-help" in the repossession of collateral? In this case, assuming Alexander actually had a disability, should that fact have had any bearing on the creditor's decision to repossess?

ETHICAL CONSIDERATIONS What is the ethical obligation of a creditor when a debtor falls into arrearages with regard to secured loans? Does the leeway given to secured creditors under the "self-help" provision implicitly condone unethical behavior on their part? If a creditor decides to engage in "self-help" repossessions, does the creditor have an ethical obligation to provide training so that employees will be able to judge more effectively the dangerousness of a given situation? Why or why not?

SOURCE: *Alexander v. Commonwealth of Virginia*, 508 S.E.2d 912 (Va.App. 1999).

In contrast, strict foreclosure is not permissible in certain situations:

1. Whenever the secured party actually receives written objections from those entitled to notification within 21 days, the secured party must sell the collateral.
2. If the collateral consists of consumer goods and the debtor has paid 60 percent of the cash price of a purchase money security interest or 60 percent of the loan in all other security interests in these goods, the secured party must sell the collateral unless the debtor, after default, has renounced in writing the right to require a sale of the collateral.[20]

The policy behind this UCC provision recognizes the debtor's substantial equity in the collateral and the fact that resale may result in a surplus that by right should belong to the debtor. Therefore, in the absence of the debtor's renunciation of the right to demand resale, the secured party cannot retain the collateral. This section also contains penalties for noncompliance. Once the secured party becomes obligated to sell the collateral, failure to do so within 90 days makes the secured party liable in either conversion or damages (under a statutory formula enumerated in the Code).[21]

RESALE OF REPOSSESSED COLLATERAL

The secured party initially may choose to satisfy the debtor's obligation by re-selling, leasing, or otherwise disposing of the collateral.[22] In fact, secured parties use this remedy of *foreclosure by sale* much more frequently than strict foreclosure. The liberality of the Code's provision for resale allows the secured party to realize the highest resale price possible and, at the same time, to reduce the possibility of a *deficiency judgment* (the debtor's liability for the difference between the amount realized at resale and the amount owed to the secured party). In this way, both the secured party and the debtor benefit.

The sale may be either public or private, subject always to the requirement that the method, manner, time, place, and terms of such sale be commercially reasonable.[23] A public sale, or auction, is the more ordinary occurrence, but the Code encourages private sales when, as is often the case, a private sale through commercial channels will increase the chances for a higher resale price.

Notice

Junior secured parties
Any secured parties whose security interests are subordinate to that of the foreclosing secured party.

Secured parties usually must notify debtors of the time and place of any public or private sale. When the collateral consists of nonconsumer goods, foreclosing secured parties in addition must notify any other secured party who has notified them in writing of a claimed interest in the collateral. A secured party who claims an interest must notify the foreclosing secured party before the latter sends notification to the debtor or before the debtor renounces his or her rights. Thus, the burden is on the so-called **junior secured parties** to notify the foreclosing secured party of their interest before a corresponding duty to notify them of sale ever arises. In certain circumstances, the secured party nonetheless may dispense with notification if the collateral is perishable, threatens to decline speedily in value, or is of a type customarily sold on a recognized market.[24] The policy reason for notification stems from a belief that those who have an interest in the collateral—the debtor and junior secured parties—may want to bid on the collateral or send their friends to do so.

A debtor may agree contractually to waive this required notice. Since courts generally enforce the terms set out in security agreements, such waivers ordinarily give secured parties, upon the debtor's default, the right to take possession of the collateral without any notification to the debtor.

Commercially Reasonable Sale

A great deal of litigation has arisen from the Code provision stating that the sale itself must be commercially reasonable. According to the UCC, the fact that the secured party might have obtained a better price at a different time or by a different method in itself does not make the sale commercially unreasonable. Similarly, sales in conformity with the commercial practices of dealers in the type of collateral sold or sales made in the usual manner on recognized markets demonstrate commercial reasonableness as well. Likewise, a court's approval of a sale or the sanctioning of a sale by a creditors' committee makes the sale commercially reasonable.[25] In these cases, the debtor's argument that the resale price is insufficient will not constitute grounds for a court's denying the secured party a deficiency judgment. Moreover, if the secured party has conducted the sale in full compliance with the requirements of § 9-504(3), the law views the sale price as reflecting the true value of the collateral, and courts automatically award any deficiency to the creditor.

But given the secured party's noncompliance with § 9-504(3), courts approach the issue of whether the creditor nonetheless retains the right to a deficiency judgment in three different ways. Some jurisdictions absolutely bar the secured party from recovering the deficiency regardless of whether the noncompliance stems from a failure to give notice or to conduct the sale in a commercially reasonable manner. A second line of cases permits the secured party to recover the deficiency but reduces (or *sets off*) from this amount the debtor's damages, that is, the difference between the *fair market value* (the price obtained if the secured party had sold the collateral in a commercially reasonable way) and the sale price actually realized. The third line of authorities opts for a compromise between the other two views. Under this so-called rebuttable presumption approach, courts will allow the secured party to sue; but these courts impose a presumption that the actual value of the collateral at the time of the wrongful sale equals the amount of indebtedness owed to the secured party. The secured party therefore merits a deficiency judgment only upon the secured party's successfully rebutting this presumption.

Proceeds

The Code even sets out the order for applying the proceeds of the sale.[26] According to the Code, the secured party must apply the proceeds realized from the disposition of the collateral in this order:

1. Payment of the reasonable expenses of retaking and disposing of the collateral, including reasonable attorneys' fees
2. Satisfaction of the debt owed to the secured party
3. Payment of the remaining proceeds to eligible junior secured parties in the same collateral
4. Payment to the debtor of any surplus and corresponding liability on the debtor's part for any deficiency, unless the parties otherwise have agreed

The following case provides an interesting interpretation of the Code's provisions concerning the remedies available to the secured party.

27.3

IN RE GGM, P.C.
165 F.3D 1026 (5TH CIR. 1999)

FACTS In March 1989, Mark J. Zimmermann, an attorney, joined a law firm called GGM, P.C. Pursuant to a shareholders' agreement, Zimmermann financed the capital contribution expected of him by executing, in favor of Texas Commerce Bank, N.A. (TCB), a promissory note for $50,000 and by pledging the GGM shares so purchased as collateral for the note. Two years later, Zimmermann signed a second shareholders' agreement, which, among other things, provided for the firm's repurchasing the shares of a defaulting shareholder and for the firm's terminating the agreement should a dissolution of the firm occur. In June 1992, owing to spiraling financial difficulties, GGM began the process of dissolving and winding down its business affairs. As a consequence, Zimmermann's employment was terminated. In September 1992, GGM's creditors instituted involuntary bankruptcy proceedings against GGM, but in 1993, the case was converted to a Chapter 7 proceeding. The bankruptcy court subsequently approved GGM and TCB's right to purchase the shareholders' notes, including Zimmermann's, which had been in default for several months. When Zimmermann refused the bankruptcy trustee's demand for payment of the note, the trustee sued Zimmermann. At trial, Zimmermann argued that a secured creditor must either retain the collateral or sell it and that because TCB had retained the collateral (here the pledged stock), it had elected to do so in complete satisfaction of the debt. Hence, Zimmermann argued, he was under no obligation to pay the note.

ISSUE Did Article 9 require a creditor to sell or otherwise dispose of the stock pledged as collateral prior to the creditor's maintaining a cause of action to recover a judgment for the balance owed under the terms of a promissory note?

HOLDING No. When a secured creditor elects to refrain from foreclosing on stock and selling it before the creditor sues on a note, the creditor's retention of the stock would not constitute complete satisfaction of the debt.

REASONING Zimmermann predicated his argument concerning TCB's treatment of his collateral on a 1982 Texas precedent, which he submitted stood for the proposition that a secured creditor must either keep its collateral or sell it. Therefore, Zimmermann contended, because TCB had retained the collateral, it had elected to do so in complete satisfaction of its debt. Conceding that this precedent is somewhat confusing on the issue, the appellate court asserted that the lower court had correctly interpreted the precedent in holding that the trustee could have elected to do exactly what he had done: retain the collateral and sue on the debt. The lower court in this case thus had correctly rejected Zimmermann's contention that the sale of the collateral or the retention of the collateral in complete satisfaction of the debt represents the only options available to a creditor. To endorse Zimmermann's reasoning would ignore another provision of the Texas Business and Commerce Code § Section 9.501(a)—which provides that a creditor may "reduce his claim to judgment, foreclose or otherwise enforce the security interest by any available judicial procedure." In this case, the trustee had made no effort to foreclose on the collateral, and, according to TCB's records, the collateral had been returned to Zimmermann in 1994. Consequently, nothing prohibited the trustee from suing on the indebtedness itself. In short, TCB's possession of the stock did not constitute an election to retain the shares in satisfaction of Zimmermann's indebtedness. After GGM's purchase of the note from TCB, the bankruptcy trustee elected to sue on the note rather than retaining or selling the collateral. The law allowed the trustee to make such a choice; and in ruling in favor of the trustee, the lower court had committed no reversible error.

BUSINESS CONSIDERATION The GGM, P.C. shareholders' agreements apparently spelled out the process by which the firm would repurchase the shares of a defaulting shareholder. TCB, the secured creditor, presumably had also provided in its security agreement specific grounds that would constitute default as to the promissory note. What events or contingencies would you expect TCB to have cataloged in the security agreement that covered the pledge of the shares? Explain fully.

ETHICAL CONSIDERATION The court characterized Zimmermann's brief to the court as "a soft-shoe approach" and a "theatrical effort . . . meriting 'two

27.3

IN RE GGM, P.C., *continued*
165 F.3D 1026 (5TH CIR. 1999)

thumbs down.'" The court further noted that Zimmermann had suffused his legal arguments with what the court "generously called myopia." Finally, the court concluded that Zimmermann had "repeatedly mischaracterized . . . the facts and the law of the case," although the court was unsure whether Zimmermann had done so intentionally or carelessly (the court had observed that Zimmermann's brief was replete with egregious grammatical, syntactical, and stylistic errors, including Zimmermann's terming a precedent as "mute" rather than "moot"). Should judges hold a lawyer to higher standards of ethics than they would expect of a layperson? Debate both sides of this issue.

DEBTORS' RIGHTS

Because the debtor has the right to redeem the collateral at any time before the secured party has disposed of it, it is possible that no sale ever will occur. *Redemption* consists of the debtor's tendering payment of all obligations due, including the expenses incurred by the secured party in retaking and preparing the collateral for disposition (usually resale) and in arranging for the resale, and thereby extinguishing the secured party's security interest in the collateral. Such expenses also may encompass attorneys' fees and legal expenses. A debtor who can accomplish redemption before sale or strict foreclosure can retain the collateral. On the other hand, a debtor, after default, may agree to waive the right to redeem.[27] The debtor presumably cannot in the original security agreement waive such rights; rather, default must precede such waivers.

SECURED PARTIES' DUTIES

Besides having to observe the previously mentioned duties regarding disposition of the collateral, secured parties also have the duty of taking reasonable care of the collateral while it is in their possession, either before or after default. They are liable for any losses caused by their failure to meet this obligation, but they do not lose their security interests if such a loss occurs.[28] Unless the parties otherwise have agreed, the secured party can charge to the debtor the payment of reasonable expenses, such as insurance and taxes, incurred in the custody, preservation, or use of the collateral. Moreover, the Code places the risk of accidental loss or damage on the debtor to the extent of any deficiency in insurance coverage. The secured party also may hold as additional security any increase in the value of or any profits (except money) received from the collateral, but the secured party either should turn over any money so received to the debtor or apply it to reduce the secured obligation. There is a duty to keep the collateral identifiable, except for **fungible** collateral that may be commingled. The secured party either may repledge the collateral on terms that do not violate the debtor's right to redeem it or use the collateral (e.g., in an ongoing business, the continued operation of equipment that has been given as security) if this will help preserve it or its value.[29]

Once the secured party defrays the expenses of holding the collateral, as mentioned earlier, the secured party must turn over any remaining proceeds to the

Fungible
Virtually identical; interchangeable; descriptive of things that belong to a class and that are not identifiable individually.

RESOURCES FOR BUSINESS LAW STUDENTS

NAME	RESOURCES	WEB ADDRESS
Uniform Commercial Code (UCC) Article 9, Secured Transactions; Sales of Accounts and Chattel Paper	The Legal Information Institute (LII), maintained by the Cornell Law School, provides a hypertext and searchable version of UCC Article 9, Secured Transactions; Sales of Accounts and Chattel Paper. LII also maintains links to Article 9 as adopted by particular states and to proposed revisions.	**http://www.law.cornell.edu/ucc/9/overview.html**
The National Conference of Commissioners on Uniform State Laws (NCCUSL)	NCCUSL the drafter of the UCC, provides drafts and revisions of its uniform and model acts.	**http://www.law.upenn.edu/bll/ulc/ulc_frame.htm**

debtor. On the other hand, the debtor remains liable for any deficiency—the difference between the available proceeds and the amount of outstanding indebtedness and expenses—unless the parties otherwise have agreed or state law eliminates this obligation.[30]

Debtors sometimes try to argue that the amount received from the sale of the collateral (the usual basis for computing deficiencies or surpluses), if lower than the collateral's market value, makes the sale commercially unreasonable. But courts ordinarily respond unfavorably to such arguments as long as fraud is not present and the secured party has attempted in good faith to attract buyers. Similarly, these arguments generally will not affect the rights of the purchaser at the sale: The purchaser takes the collateral free and clear of such claims if the purchase is made in good faith.[31]

A secured party's failure to comply with the duties regarding disposition of the collateral, however, may subject the secured party to statutory liability under § 9-507 for losses by debtors or junior secured parties and, if consumer goods are involved, to a damages formula that sets up a statutory penalty. As we learned earlier, some courts, as a consequence of creditor noncompliance or misbehavior, also will deny the secured party the right to a deficiency judgment.

SUMMARY

The rules on priorities represent the Code's attempt to decide who, among validly perfected secured parties, has superior rights to the collateral. In general, the Code validates a first-in-time, first-in-right approach. Thus, if competing security interests have been perfected by filing, the first to be filed has priority, whether the security interest attached before or after filing. If neither party has filed, the first party to perfect has priority. And if no one has perfected, the first interest to attach has superior rights to the collateral.

Some exceptions to these priority rules exist. For instance, if a purchase money secured party follows certain Code provisions that make distinctions according to the type of collateral involved, such a party may prevail over earlier, perfected creditors. Similarly, in some situations, bona fide purchasers of consumer goods and buyers in the ordinary course of business may defeat prior perfected interests. Likewise, certain liens that arise by operation of law have priority over perfected security interests in the collateral. Moreover, a secured party holding a security interest in fixtures will defeat a real property claimant if, for example, the secured party follows the requirements of the Code for a "fixture filing" or a filing in an office where real property interests are recorded.

When a debtor defaults, the secured party may pursue either non-Code or Code remedies. Under the Code, the secured party may take possession of the collateral and either retain it in complete satisfaction of the debt (strict foreclosure) or dispose of it by public or private sale (foreclosure by sale). In either case, if the secured party is to escape Code liability, notification of the debtor and perhaps other parties must take place. The secured party's right of strict foreclosure may be limited by the debtor's paying 60 percent of the price of collateral consisting of consumer goods. If a sale is undertaken, the secured party must conduct it in a commercially reasonable manner. Assuming a sale has occurred, the Code also enumerates the order in which the proceeds of a sale should be applied. The debtor's redeeming the collateral prior to foreclosure may cut off the secured party's right to foreclosure by sale or strict foreclosure, however. Whenever the secured party is in possession of the collateral, he or she must take reasonable care of the collateral. Failure to live up to this and other duties subjects the secured party to liability for any losses caused thereby, to possible damages under a statutory formula, and to the possible denial of the right to a deficiency judgment. Debtors ordinarily are liable for any deficiency that remains after the sale or other disposition of the collateral.

DISCUSSION QUESTIONS

1. Why is the issue of priority important?
2. Explain the importance of purchase money secured parties and why they merit priority.
3. List the rules for becoming a purchase money secured party in inventory collateral and in noninventory collateral, respectively.
4. What is a *bona fide purchaser*? Does such a purchaser always have priority? How does this person differ from a *buyer in the ordinary course of business*?
5. Does a secured party have priority over the holder of a common law lien? Explain why or why not.
6. What is *default*? What is *redemption*?
7. What kinds of non-Code remedies can the secured party pursue?

8. Describe fully the UCC's treatment of the right of repossession.
9. Explain the requirements necessary for effecting strict foreclosure. Then set out the situations in which strict foreclosure is not permissible.
10. Discuss the following: (a) the rules relating to foreclosure by sale or resale of the repossessed collateral; (b) the requirements for conducting a sale in a commercially reasonable manner; (c) the order in which the proceeds are applied after a sale; and (d) the secured party's duties of reasonable care of the collateral and the liabilities that may result from a secured party's failure to observe any applicable duties.

CASE PROBLEMS AND WRITING ASSIGNMENTS

1. On 27 April 1992, Darro and Tracy Long purchased a 1980 Ford Escort for $2,795 from Auto Credit, Inc. (Auto Credit). They made a cash down payment of $300 and financed the balance of the purchase price. The terms of the financing required the Longs to pay $38.84 for 84 weeks. The Longs made six timely payments on the vehicle. On 17 June 1992, however, the Longs notified Auto Credit that they intended to make no further payments, and they returned the vehicle to Auto Credit. The car was in virtually the same condition as when the Longs had purchased it, with the exception that they had driven it 3,500 miles. The

balance due for the vehicle at the time was $2,594.02. On 17 June 1992, Auto Credit notified the Longs that if they failed to pay the remainder of the balance within 10 days, the car would be sold at a private sale by the end of June. Auto Credit actually sold the car on 12 August at the Billings Auto Auction for $150. After Auto Credit deducted $229.47, a sum representing its expenses from the sale and finance charges, an additional $79.47 was charged to the Longs' account. Auto Credit subsequently filed a court action to recover a deficiency of $2,934.15. The Longs counterclaimed for damages on the grounds that the sale was commercially unreasonable under UCC § 9-504. In whose favor should the judge rule? [See *Auto Credit, Inc.* v. *Long,* 971 P.2d 1237 (Mont. 1998).]

2. Ford Motor Credit Company (FMCC) hired Badgerland Auto Recovery, Inc. (Badgerland) to repossess a Ford Bronco II from Florence Hollibush, who was behind in her payments and who had had a poor record of making the required payments under her installment contract with FMCC. Badgerland's employee testified that at about midnight on 18 January 1990, he arrived at Hollibush's tavern. Her vehicle was parked in front of the tavern, and the employee hooked the Bronco up to his tow truck. He saw a man looking out of the tavern window at him and entered the tavern to tell the man who he was. He spoke with Hollibush and with William Finn, Hollibush's fiancé. Finn called an attorney and then stated that he would call the sheriff's office. Hollibush observed Finn's conversation and occasionally would say something. Finn told Badgerland's employee, "You are not going to take the Bronco," but, shortly after that, the employee left with Hollibush's automobile. Although Hollibush and Finn's description of the repossession differed considerably from the description given by Badgerland's employee, both testified that Finn had told the employee not to take the automobile. Did the Badgerland employee's subsequent repossession in disregard of the statement not to repossess the car constitute a breach of the peace under § 9-503? Why or why not? [See *Hollibush* v. *Ford Motor Credit Company,* 508 N.W.2d 449 (Wisc.App. 1993).]

3. On 13 December 1997, the debtor, Karen H. Johnson, purchased a new 1998 Honda from College Park Honda (College Park) and received delivery of the car. At that time, several documents, including a retail installment contract and a buyer's order, were executed. Johnson subsequently failed to obtain third-party financing for the purchase of the car. On 24 December 1997, Johnson filed a voluntary Chapter 7 petition in bankruptcy, and, on 2 January 1998, Johnson notified

College Park of that fact. Also on 2 January, College Park and Johnson executed a security agreement and another buyer's order. On 28 January 1998, the debtor again informed College Park that she had filed a bankruptcy petition. On 6 February 1998, College Park repossessed the 1998 Honda. College Park knew that, at the time of the transaction, Johnson lived in the District of Columbia. To perfect a security interest in an automobile under the law of the District of Columbia, the secured party must note its lien on the certificate of title. The bankruptcy trustee ultimately sued College Park to force it to turn over the repossessed car. In these circumstances, what was the status of College Park? Who therefore held superior rights to the car, College Park or the bankruptcy trustee? [See *In re Johnson,* 230 B.R. 466 (Bkrtcy. Dist.Col. 1999).]

4. Biglari Import Export, Inc. (Biglari), the debtor, operates The Ritz Oriental Rug Gallery. In 1986, Biglari borrowed operating capital from the International Bank of Commerce (IBOC) and granted IBOC a lien on its inventory of rugs. Later in the lending relationship, IBOC became concerned about Biglari's business and loan performance and asked that some of the rugs be pledged to the bank. Biglari complied and ultimately delivered 40 rugs into IBOC's possession. IBOC stored the rugs in a storage room in its bank building. The room, though not designed as a collateral storage vault, was the same room in which the bank stored its own records. It had a concrete floor, no windows, and no public access. The room was located toward the rear of the building, on an upper level, and was the only room on that level. A winding stairway led to a vestibule area, which had one door opening out to a fenced courtyard and one door into the employee-only area of the bank. The bank kept this back door locked, and only bank officers had a key to it. According to the witnesses, the rugs were removed from this room on two occasions only, once in July 1988 and again in March 1990. On both occasions, Biglari took out the rugs and brought them back. In March 1990, Biglari removed all 40 rugs so they could be aired out in the sun and mothballed (the standard procedure for maintaining the quality of the rugs). On that occasion, while the bank officer in charge of this loan was on his lunch hour, two Biglari employees picked up the rugs. The employees told bank personnel that the loan officer had approved their coming by to pick up the rugs, and had someone from the bank had let them into the storage room. No one had the employees sign any paperwork relative to checking out the rugs. Three days later, after the mothballing process, two Biglari employees brought the rugs back to the

bank. At that time, no one from the bank checked the bundles to be sure all the 40 rugs were there. The rugs were returned to the storage room, where they remained undisturbed. During an inventory of the rugs taken at the bank in December 1990, the bank came up 10 rugs short. Later, during its bankruptcy proceedings, Biglari argued that the judge should reduce IBOC's secured claim by the value of the 10 rugs because of IBOC's alleged failure to take reasonable care of the collateral in its possession. Had IBOC used reasonable care in the custody and preservation of Biglari's rugs? (See *In re Biglari Import Export, Inc.,* 130 B.R. 43 (Bankr. W.D. Tex. 1991).]

5. SMS Financial, L.L.C. (SMS) sued ABCO Homes, Inc. and H. Eugene and Richard E. Abbott, the makers of a promissory note that SMS had purchased from the Federal Deposit Insurance Corporation (FDIC). The background facts indicated the following: On 17 July 1991, the FDIC had sent to each maker a notice of intent to foreclose on the collateral securing the note. On 17 December 1991, the FDIC had sent a second notice of intent to foreclose on the collateral to H. Eugene Abbott and ABCO. The 17 July 1991 letter demanded that the makers pay such indebtedness in full on or before the 16th day of August 1991. The notice also provided that if the makers failed to pay this sum to the FDIC by such date, the FDIC would exercise its legal rights and remedies to collect such indebtedness, including, but not limited to, foreclosure of the deed of trust and the sale of the property covered thereby in accordance with the terms of the deed of trust. The FDIC subsequently leased the collateral (bowling alley equipment) to Amwest Savings (Amwest) on 21 January 1992, and ultimately sold it to Amwest on 3 September 1992. The Abbotts later argued that the FDIC's failure to provide them with adequate notice of the lease of the collateral made the FDIC's disposition of the collateral commercially unreasonable. Moreover, the Abbotts submitted that the sale violated UCC § 9-504(c) because, in effect, the FDIC had sold the collateral to itself in a private sale, since Amwest, the purchaser of the collateral, was the FDIC's agent at the time of the sale of the equipment. Should the appellate court affirm the lower court's entry of a summary judgment in favor of the Abbotts? [See *SMS Financial, Limited Liability Company* v. *ABCO Homes, Inc.,* 167 F.3d 235 (5th Cir. 1999).]

6. **BUSINESS APPLICATION CASE** On 22 January 1985, pursuant to a written sales contract, Ricardo Andres Ferro purchased from Vergie G. Wright the business and assets of Wright's Studio in Eldon, Missouri. The contract specifically identified the property as the "goodwill of said business, including the right to the exclusive use of the name Wright's Studio, and the telephone listing and the right to continue the use of the same telephone number," and "all of the supplies and equipment of said business which are listed on the schedule which is annexed hereto and designated 'Exhibit A.'" Ferro paid $3,000 cash and signed a promissory note dated 1 February 1985, for the balance of the purchase price in the amount of $7,000. The sales contract stated that the promissory note "shall be secured by a first lien upon the items listed on 'Exhibit A.'" The promissory note provided that it "is secured by a lien on all of the equipment of Wright's Photo Studio in Eldon, Missouri." No financing statements covering this collateral were ever filed. Ferro and Vergie G. Wright also entered into a lease by which Ferro agreed to lease from Wright the building that housed the business of Wright's Studio for a term of five years beginning 1 February 1985. As the owner and operator of Wright's Studio since January 1985, over the next few years Ferro purchased numerous cameras and other photographic equipment to replace the obsolete equipment originally purchased in 1985. Ferro also purchased a computer and software for the maintenance of all his business records. However, after February 1985, Ferro made few of the required payments on the promissory note or rental payments. In late 1997 or early 1998, so as to shore up his personal finances, Ferro worked as a merchant marine in the Gulf of Mexico and, with Wright's permission, left two friends in charge of the studio. Although Ferro paid the rent for the months of January and February 1998 (before he left for the Gulf), from February to September 1998 Ferro made no additional rent payments. As a consequence, on 29 September 1998, Virgie G. Wright and her son, John C. Wright, sent a letter informing Ferro that he was in default under the lease and that the Wrights intended to sell the business—Wright Studio—and all personal property pertaining to the business so as to recoup the $100,000 then due and owing in arrearages. Soon thereafter, the Wrights changed the locks and took control of the business premises and all the business assets of Wright's Studio. When Ferro heard about the lockout, he returned, and a few days later, on 12 November 1998, he filed a bankruptcy petition. Ferro argued that because Vergie G. Wright had failed to secure the promissory note with after-acquired property and had failed to take a security interest in the name of the business and the business's telephone listing, the Wrights had improperly seized the business assets of Wright's Studio—with the exception of the items listed in Exhibit A attached to the sales contract. Ferro

also asserted that the Wrights had failed to properly terminate the lease of the real property prior to the bankruptcy filing. Ferro thus submitted that the lease of the business premises and all the business assets of Wright's Studio seized by the Wrights, except for the items listed in Exhibit A attached to the sales contract, were the property of the bankruptcy estate that the Wrights therefore must surrender. In rebuttal, the Wrights contended that (a) the promissory note contained an after-acquired property clause that would encompass all the business equipment purchased by Ferro subsequent to his purchase of the assets of Wright's Studio, and (b) they had rightfully seized the business assets pursuant to a common law landlord's lien for unpaid rent. The Wrights also asserted that they could lawfully engage in self-help remedies to take control of the real property upon Ferro's failure to pay the arrearages due under the lease and the promissory note. The Wrights claimed that because they had recovered the business assets of Wright's Studio and the real property prior to the bankruptcy filing, such property was not part of the bankruptcy estate, and they consequently could properly refuse to surrender any of the property. Who should win this case, Ferro or the Wrights? What should the Wrights have done differently here? [See *In re Ferro*, 228 B.R. 700 (Bkrtcy.W.D.Mo. 1999).]

7. **ETHICAL APPLICATION CASE** In January 1988, the secured creditor, Kit Car World, Inc., and other corporations owned by Robert and Eileen Tietz, transferred to the debtor, Richard Skolnick, molds, equipment, inventory, and other assets necessary to manufacture and secure replica car kits of a 1953 Corvette. In consideration, the debtor executed a promissory note for $185,000, with the debt secured by all assets related to the replica car kits, including inventory and all after-acquired property. The promissory note and security agreement obligated the debtor to pay $500 on the note each time he collected full payment for a kit and to sell a minimum of 50 car kits the first 15 months and every 12 months thereafter or be deemed in default. The debtor also promised to provide monthly financial reports. In April 1989, the debtor, by failing to make payments when due and to provide the required monthly financial reports, defaulted on the note and the security agreement. The secured creditors then accelerated the balance due under the note and filed suit seeking damages for the unpaid balance and for possession of the property covered by the security agreement. On 2 November 1989, the secured creditors served the debtor with a prejudgment writ of replevin directing seizure of the assets under the security agreement. Among the items seized were

steel frames, fiberglass bodies, molds, and other component parts and inventory used in the assemblage of replica car kits. After the execution of the writ of replevin, the debtor ceased to conduct business. The trial court allowed seven customers of the debtor to file complaints in intervention alleging that they each owned a replica car kit that the secured creditors wrongfully had seized. Although the customers individually had paid the full price for each car kit, the debtor's assets were seized before he could assemble and deliver the kits. In fact, the debtor never had identified any of the goods to the particular contracts in dispute. After a nonjury trial, the trial court entered final judgment in favor of the seven customers for money damages. The court found that the secured creditors had converted the customers' car kits and that, since the car kits constituted consumer goods, the secured creditors had not enjoyed an interest in these car kits pursuant to the after-acquired property clause of the security agreement. On appeal, the secured creditors claimed that, under Florida's Uniform Commercial Code, their interest in the debtor's inventory was superior to any interest claimed by the customers. However, the customers claimed a superior interest as "buyers in the ordinary course of business." If you were the appellate judge, how would you decide this case? If you were to decide this case on ethical—as opposed to legal—grounds, who would win? Why? [See *Kit Car World, Inc.* v. *Skolnick*, 616 So.2d 1051 (Fla.App. 5th Dist. 1993).]

8. **CRITICAL THINKING CASE** In 1980, Color Leasing 3, L.P. (Color Leasing) leased to Consolidated Graphics Corporation (Con-Graph) a Miller printing press worth $360,000. The lease expired on 30 June 1988. Color Leasing executed a bill of sale dated 31 December 1987 for the printing press. On 31 December 1988, Con-Graph executed a promissory note to Color Leasing for $360,000 as well as a security agreement granting Color Leasing "a continuing security interest in all of [Con-Graph's] accounts receivables [sic], contract rights, chattel paper, security agreements, documents, machinery, equipment, fixtures, general intangibles, goods, instruments, inventory, trademarks, patents, license rights and good will whether now owned or hereafter acquired. . . . " Neither the promissory note nor the security agreement made specific reference to the printing press. On 5 January 1989, Color Leasing filed a financing statement reflecting its security interest in the printing press referenced in the bill of sale. Prior to this set of transactions, Old Stone Bank had loaned several million dollars to Con-Graph. The bank had collateralized the loans through a series of security agreements covering Con-Graph's

property, equipment, inventory, and accounts, then existing and after-acquired. The bank had perfected its security interests through blanket filings in 1984, 1986, and 1987. Con-Graph ultimately defaulted on its loans from the bank. Hence, on 14 November 1991, the bank notified Color Leasing, as well as other interested parties, of the bank's plan to seize and sell certain Con-Graph collateral, including the printing press. By a letter dated 18 November 1991, Color Leasing notified the bank of its (Color Leasing's) purported status as a purchase money secured creditor and protested the proposed seizure and sale of the printing press. Nevertheless, the bank subsequently sold the printing press at a private sale. Sometime thereafter, the bank failed and was eventually placed into receivership with the Federal Deposit Insurance Corporation (FDIC). After the FDIC had rejected Color Leasing's claim for damages that the firm allegedly had suffered as a result of the seizure and sale of the printing press, Color Leasing in 1994 filed a lawsuit alleging conversion of the printing press. Color Leasing's cause of action hinged on its claim that it was a non-inventory purchase money secured party that enjoyed priority over the bank, even though the bank had perfected its security interest in after-acquired property long before Color Leasing had become a secured creditor. In support of its claim, Color Leasing maintained that Con-Graph's possession of the printing press had begun on 31 December 1988, the date on which it claimed it had executed the bill of sale, the promissory note, and the security agreement with Con-Graph. (Con-Graph had presented evidence that the 1987 date on the bill of sale was a typographical error.) In rebuttal, the FDIC argued that (a) Color Leasing's security interest had not attached owing to the absence in the security agreement of any specific references to the printing press, and (b) Color Leasing had failed to perfect its security interest at the time the debtor (Con-Graph) had received possession of the collateral or within 10 days thereafter. In short, the FDIC asserted that Con-Graph had become a debtor in possession on 31 December 1987, because of the date on the bill of sale. Color Leasing's final argument was predicated on its belief that, irrespective of when Con-Graph had executed the bill of sale, Con-Graph's possession as debtor had not begun until the execution of the promissory note and the security agreement on 31 December 1988, thereby rendering Color Leasing's 5 January 1989 filing timely. The FDIC countered that possession had begun upon Con-Graph's physical possession of the printing press as lessee or, at the latest, on 31 December 1987, the date that appeared on the bill of sale. Whose argument—Color Leasing's or the FDIC's—would a court find more persuasive? [See *Color Leasing 3, L.P.* v. *FDIC*, 975 F.Supp. 177 (D.R.I. 1997).]

NOTES

1. Uniform Commercial Code § 9-312(5)(a).
2. Ibid., § 9-312, Official Comment 5.
3. Ibid., § 9-107.
4. Ibid., § 9-312(3).
5. Ibid., § 9-312(4).
6. Uniform Commercial Code § 9-307(2).
7. Ibid., § 9-109(1).
8. Ibid., § 9-313(4)(a).
9. Ibid., § 9-313(4)(c).
10. Ibid., § 9-313(8).
11. Uniform Commercial Code § 9-501(1).
12. Ibid., § 9-503.
13. Ibid., § 9-507.
14. *Fuentes* v. *Shevin*, 407 U.S. 67 (1972); *Mitchell* v. *W.T. Grant Co.*, 416 U.S. 600 (1974).
15. Uniform Commercial Code § 9-503.
16. Ibid., § 9-502.
17. Ibid., § 9-505(2).
18. Ibid.
19. *Alexander* v. *Commonwealth of Virginia*, 508 S.E.2d 912 (Va.App. 1999).
20. Ibid., § 9-505(1).
21. Ibid.
22. Ibid., § 9-504.
23. Ibid., § 9-504(3).
24. Ibid.
25. Ibid., § 9-507(2).
26. Ibid., § 9-504(1), (2).
27. Ibid., §§ 9-501(3), 9-506.
28. Ibid., § 9-207(3).
29. Ibid., § 9-207(2).
30. Ibid., § 9-504(2).
31. Ibid., § 9-504(4).

28

OTHER CREDIT TRANSACTIONS

A G E N D A

While the primary concern of the Kochanowskis is the operation—and success—of CIT, they also have other concerns. In many respects, they are a normal family, with all the trials and tribulations that entails. Tom and Anna would like to buy a car for Lindsay, but they doubt that they can pay cash for the type of car they would like to buy. Donna and Julio plan to marry soon, and they would like to live the "American dream," which includes owning their own home—and the obligatory mortgage that goes along with home ownership for most people. Each adult member of the family has at least two credit cards, and each member regularly receives mail offering them new cards with what sound like very attractive terms.

CIT is also planning to open its own store, selling directly to the customer. Tom and Anna expect to be asked for credit terms by a number of customers, and they are interested in the risks—and rewards—of providing "store credit" to some customers.

The family realizes that credit can be a wonderful tool when it is used correctly. They also realize that abusing or misusing credit can cause the individual who does so a great deal of trouble. They will have a number of questions about different types of credit and the legal implications from using each type. Be prepared! You never know when one of the Kochanowskis will need your help or advice.

O U T L I N E

Introduction
Unsecured Credit
Installment Loans
Mortgage Loans
Credit Cards

FTC Consumer Credit Rules
Summary
Discussion Questions
Case Problems and Writing Assignments

INTRODUCTION

The use—and occasional misuse—of credit is an integral part of contemporary American life. Businesses need to obtain credit in making purchases of raw materials in order to produce goods, and they need to grant credit to make the sales of finished goods that allow these businesses to make a return on their investments. Many of these credit transactions take the form of secured transactions, a topic covered in considerable detail in the previous two chapters. However, a significant number of these credit transactions fall outside the coverage of Article 9.

Consumers also use credit. Many consumers use credit to purchase major items, such as homes, automobiles, and major appliances. While the major appliance purchases may well be governed by Article 9, both the home loan and the automobile loan fall outside the provisions of Secured Transactions coverage. Many consumers also use credit to purchase nonmajor items, such as clothing, gasoline, and groceries. A significant number of college students purchase their books and supplies on credit, and they often pay their tuition by means of credit. These transactions also fall beyond the scope of Article 9. In fact, most of these latter transactions do not involve collateral in any sense. These are unsecured credit transactions. These areas will be examined in this section.

UNSECURED CREDIT

In an *unsecured credit* arrangement, the creditor agrees to grant credit to the debtor without the use of any collateral. In such an arrangement, the creditor is relying on the debtor to repay the loan or to honor the debt without the benefit of some form of security in the event the debtor defaults on the obligation. Thus, the creditor will *either* restrict the extension of credit to those debtors who are deemed better credit risks *or* the creditor will charge a significantly higher interest rate for the credit due to the added risk. Unsecured credit may take the form of a *signature loan,* in which the lender agrees to make the loan on the basis of the borrower's signature alone.

Unsecured credit is also found with most public utility accounts (telephone, electricity, water, etc.), bank credit cards (e.g., Visa and MasterCard), and travel and entertainment cards (e.g., American Express, Diners Club, and Carte Blanche). Public utility accounts are regulated by the various state public utility regulatory commissions and by contract law. Credit cards and travel and entertainment cards are discussed in a later section of this chapter. Other types of unsecured credit transactions will be discussed next.

Regulation of unsecured credit transactions is primarily a matter of state law. Federal regulation of these transactions is primarily concerned with ensuring that information is provided to the debtor prior to the creation of the debt and with acceptable methods of collection in the event the debtor defaults on the agreement. Under Title I of the Federal Consumer Credit Protection Act, better known as the Truth in Lending Act (TILA), creditors must provide credit applicants with certain information about the cost of the credit. This information must be provided in a standard format and a standard terminology. The most important of this information is the *APR,* the annualized percentage rate to be charged in the transaction. This figure must be provided in writing, and it must be clear and conspicuous. Failure to do so makes the creditor subject to various penalties and liabilities. (For more detailed coverage of TILA, see Chapter 40.)

28.1 | FINANCE

CALL-IMAGE TECHNOLOGY

PERSONAL LOAN OPTIONS

Tom recently visited the bank where the family has an account, seeking a short-term loan. The loan officer told Tom that the bank was willing to make the loan and then described two options for the loan. The first option, a signature loan, would have a single payment due in six months and would carry an APR of 10.5 percent. The second option, an installment loan, would have 12 monthly payments and an APR of 9.75 percent. The signature loan would not require any collateral, but the installment loan would need some collateral. Tom has asked you which of these loans would be better for him to take. What will you tell him?

BUSINESS CONSIDERATION Although the installment loan has a lower interest rate, Tom will end up paying more money to the bank. Why might a businessperson prefer a lower rate loan/longer term loan when such a loan actually increases the amount to be repaid?

ETHICAL CONSIDERATION Is it ethical for a bank to require collateral for a loan in order to grant a lower rate, when the bank was willing to make the loan to a customer without collateral?

If a debtor defaults on the credit arrangement, the creditor is allowed to use various methods to enforce his or her claim. For example, the "self-help" provisions discussed in the coverage of secured transactions may be available in certain cases. However, with an unsecured credit transaction, the creditor does not have access to such provisions because there is no collateral. The creditor may seek a writ of attachment or a writ of garnishment or may elect to file suit for breach of contract. While these methods are often successful, they are time-consuming and relatively expensive. As a result, many creditors choose to hire a collection agent to collect the unpaid balance. Historically, such debt collection agencies developed a bad reputation. They were known to engage in various types of harassing behavior in their effort to "encourage" the debtor to pay the debt. As a result, the Fair Debt Collection Practices Act was passed. This act only applies to persons who are attempting to collect debts owed to another person, and not to the actual creditor who is acting on his or her own behalf in seeking recovery. However, most creditors also follow the guidelines of the act in the interests of following sound and fair business practices.[1] (The Fair Debt Collection Practices Act is also covered in detail in Chapter 40.)

The federal regulation in this area is effective in providing debtors with information regarding the cost of the credit and in protecting defaulting debtors from some unfair or improper collection practices, but it is not very effective with regard to the terms of the credit agreement. Regulation of the terms and conditions of unsecured credit transactions is left to the states. State regulation in this area includes limits on the interest rates and other finance charges that may be imposed, possible "cooling off" periods for the debtor in some transactions, and other terms and details of the transaction. Each state establishes its own maximum permissible interest rates for various types of loans or credit transactions. If the creditor charges a rate in excess of the state's maximum, the interest is *usurious*. Since *usury* is defined as charging an illegal rate of interest,[2] the contract is tainted with illegality. In some states, the charging of a usurious rate of interest voids the entire contract. In other states, the interest portion is voided due to the illegality, although the debtor still must repay the principal. Some states void the usurious interest, substituting the state interest maximum into the agreement on the theory that the parties only meant to charge the highest legal rate. The following case involves a controversy over usury. Note how the court addresses the issue.

28.1

BEDFORD V. FOX
970 S.W.2D 251 (ARK.1998)

FACTS The Foxes alleged that they entered into an agreement with Color Mate Photo, Inc., on March 18, 1992, to purchase the photography business owned by that corporation. Color Mate Photo, Inc., was owned by Jack Bedford. The name of the corporation was subsequently changed to Jack D. Bedford, Inc. According to the Foxes, Bedford knew that the interest rate charged on two installment promissory notes executed on that date exceeded what is permissible under Article 19, § 13 of the Arkansas Constitution. . . . The Foxes asserted that irrespective of this knowledge, the parties executed the agreement, and the Foxes paid the illegal interest required under the notes. The Foxes asked for a judgment declaring the notes usurious and void as to the unpaid interest plus an award of twice the amount of the interest paid . . . Bedford testified that in November 1991, he and the Foxes agreed that the photography business would be sold for the sum of $350,000 . . . [H]is attorney, David Nixon, prepared the March 18, 1992 "Final Agreement for Sale of Business" as well as the two promissory notes dated that same date, one executed in favor of Color Mate Photo, Inc., now Jack D. Bedford, Inc., in the amount of $245,000, and the other in favor of Jack Bedford in the amount of $30,000. The two notes represented part of the purchase price, which Bedford was financing himself. He testified that the sales agreement stated that it was effective as of November 6, 1991. However, he acknowledged that the promissory notes did not refer to any date other than March 18, 1992, which was the date of their execution by the Foxes. Bedford further explained that prior to March 18, 1992, there had been discussions among the parties about the lawful rate of interest in Arkansas. . . . Bedford testified that he approached the Foxes about raising the principal and lowering the interest rate for the loans because he knew that the 10% interest rate was no longer legal. He maintained that the parties continued with the agreement under the belief that the 10% interest rate had been "locked in" under the preliminary November 6, 1991 sales agreement. Bedford concluded that the reference to the date of November 6, 1991, as the effective date in the March 18, 1992 sales agreement controlled for purposes of the appropriate interest rate under the two promissory notes. . . . Fox testified that he was informed for the first time at closing on March 18, 1992, that Bedford could not legally charge a 10% interest rate under Arkansas's usury laws as of that

date. He stated that Bedford offered to raise the purchase price to $400,000 as a solution and to lower the interest rate. Fox testified that he rejected the offer. He added that he was first told by a third-party banker that the two promissory notes contained an illegal rate of interest in the Fall of 1992, when he attempted to borrow money from McIlroy Bank and Trust to purchase equipment . . . He also admitted that James McCord informed him that the interest rate was illegal on March 18, 1992. Despite this knowledge, Fox stated that he continued making monthly payments on the notes until 1997. Fox further admitted that he calculated as of December 31, 1996, that he owed Bedford $226,841.84 in principal but that he could recover $40,575.36, or twice the amount of the interest that had been paid up to that point, which was $120,286.18. This would have yielded the Foxes a net recovery as of that date in the amount of $13,733.52. A year earlier at the end of 1995, he calculated that they had paid $96,935.98 in interest, which multiplied twice would render a recovery of $193,871.96. At that point, the Foxes still would have owed Bedford and his corporation a net amount of $45,081.63. Therefore, because the Foxes made payments on the notes for an additional year, they went from owing Bedford approximately $45,000 at the end of 1995 to a net recovery of approximately $13,000 at the end of 1996, if they asserted a claim of usury. . . . The trial court entered its order and determined that the interest rate on the two promissory notes was usurious as of March 18, 1992, which was the date the court found to be the date of the contract. The court entered judgment for the Foxes in the amount of $231,009.96 against Jack D. Bedford, Inc., which was twice the amount of interest paid on the $245,000 note, and judgment against Bedford in the amount of $28,286.96, which was twice the amount of interest paid on the $30,000 note. The trial court also determined that the defense of estoppel was not applicable against the Foxes because although all parties knew the 10% interest rate was usurious, the Foxes were not responsible for creating the infirmity. Bedford and Jack D. Bedford, Inc., appeal from the trial court's order.

ISSUES Was the contract usurious? If the contract is usurious, are the Foxes estopped from raising the usury claim?

continued

28.1

BEDFORD V. FOX, *continued*
970 S.W.2D 251 (ARK.1998)

HOLDINGS Yes, the contract was usurious. Yes, the Foxes are estopped from raising the usury claim.

REASONING Even assuming that the agreement was finally struck on March 18, 1992, and, thus, was usurious, we hold that the Foxes were estopped by their actions to raise a usury defense. In order to prove estoppel, the party asserting the defense must prove the following elements: (1) the party to be estopped knew the facts; (2) the party to be estopped intended that the conduct be acted on; (3) the party asserting the estoppel was ignorant of the facts; and (4) the party asserting the estoppel relied on the other's conduct and was injured by that reliance . . . Furthermore, we have said that a debtor may be estopped from asserting the defense of usury when the debtor created the infirmity in the contract in order to take advantage of the creditor . . . We initially focus on the date of March 18, 1992, and have no doubt that Bedford and the Foxes knew that there was a problem with usury on that date and that efforts were being made to correct the problem. Indeed, James Fox testified to that effect. The trial court did find that both parties knew the March 18, 1992 sales agreement was usurious as of that date, but the critical point to our way of thinking is the fact that the March 18, 1992 sales agreement mentions three times that the agreement was effective as of November 6, 1991 . . . Unquestionably, inclusion of this language was driven by a desire to obviate the usury concerns of the parties. Both Bedford and David Nixon testified to that effect and, again, James Fox testified that he knew about the usury problem and efforts to correct it. Where the parties differed in their testimony is that Bedford and Nixon were adamant in their belief that both sides understood the problem had been resolved by fixing the effective date as of November 6, 1991, while James Fox hedged on this point. In applying the law of estoppel to these facts, we believe that all of the elements for establishing estoppel against the Foxes were present. The Foxes knew the March 18, 1992 sales agreement was usurious, as the trial court found. The Foxes intended to purchase Bedford's photography business by signing the March 18, 1992 sales agreement and the two promissory notes, albeit the interest rates for the notes were usurious as of that date. Bedford clearly believed that by making November 6, 1991, the effective date of the agreement, usury was no longer an issue. According to Bedford's attorney at the time, David Nixon, both he and the Foxes' attorney, James McCord, agreed that reference to the effective date of November 6, 1991, cured the problem. And Bedford relied on the Foxes' willingness to close the sales agreement on March 18, 1992, in a belief that the interest rate was not usurious. Indeed, this belief was confirmed over the next five years, as the Foxes continued to make their installment payments. Added to the mix is a hint of subterfuge in that James Fox apparently thought, as evidenced by his usury calculations, that at any time he could rise up, assert usury, and recoup twice the interest paid. He waited until he could net a profit to do this. James Fox's own testimony cements our conclusion that estoppel was a proven defense. The trial court in its ruling from the bench did find that both Bedford and the Foxes knew the March 18, 1992 agreement was usurious. But that finding does not examine the collateral issue of whether Bedford legitimately believed that he had resolved the matter with references to a November 6, 1991 effective date. We hold that the trial court clearly erred in finding that the elements of estoppel were not met by Bedford. We reverse the judgment of the trial court and remand for entry of a judgment consistent with this opinion.

BUSINESS CONSIDERATION Assume that a business is considering accepting a promissory note as payment for goods or services, and that the state has a "floating" interest maximum. The interest rate initially agreed to has now become illegal. What should the business do?

ETHICAL CONSIDERATION Fox obviously realized fairly early in this contract that the interest rate was usurious, and that Arkansas permitted the borrower to recover double the interest paid on a usurious loan. Under these circumstances, was it ethical for Fox to wait until he had paid more interest in order to seek recovery of a larger amount in damages from Bedford?

In some states, there is a single usury provision for all types of credit. However, most states have different usury rates for different types of credit. A closed-end unsecured loan will have one rate; an installment loan with collateral will have another rate; revolving credit arrangements (credit cards) will have still another rate. It is important for a business that extends credit—and an individual who uses credit to make purchases—to be aware of the state rules in this area.

State regulation also extends to other terms and conditions of the credit arrangement. Among the areas of coverage that may be encountered here are the following:

- The Uniform Consumer Credit Code (adopted by 11 states)[3]
- State consumer loan acts
- State home solicitation sales acts
- Negotiable Instrument law (Articles 3 and 4 of the Uniform Commercial Code [UCC])
- Contract law

Again, familiarity with the applicable state statutes will help ensure that both the businessperson who extends credit and the individual who is using credit are acting in the most appropriate manner.

INSTALLMENT LOANS

Installment loans are loans for a fixed time period and with fixed periodic payments. They usually require a monthly payment. While installment loans may be secured or unsecured, most consumer installment loans are secured by some form of collateral. Some of these loans will fall within the coverage of Article 9. For example, if a person purchases a refrigerator on credit and uses the refrigerator as collateral for the loan, the credit arrangement is a purchase money security interest, and Article 9 governs the transaction. However, if a person purchases a car on credit, using the car as collateral for the loan, the transaction falls outside the coverage of Article 9. This transaction will be governed by the state certificate of title rules rather than by Article 9.

Installment loans are subject to many of the same regulatory provisions as are unsecured loans. At the federal level, the lender is still governed by TILA, and the Fair Debt Collection Practices Act still applies to attempts to collect past due accounts by collection agencies. At the state level, the transaction is still covered by Article 3 of the UCC if a promissory note is involved, as is likely. In addition, the Uniform Consumer Credit Code (UCCC) may apply to the transaction, *if* the transaction takes place in one of the 11 states that have adopted the UCCC, and *if* the debtor is a consumer. Since the parties are involved in a contract, the state laws governing contracts also apply. And if the state has a retail installment sales act, or similar legislation, the provisions of that act will also apply to the transaction.

MORTGAGE LOANS

Mortgage loans involve loans in which real estate is used as collateral by the debtor to secure the credit. Mortgage loans are commonly installment loans, but the repayment term tends to be much longer. For example, many mortgage loans have a repayment period of 30 years. By contrast, most installment loans have a repayment term of 5 years or less. Since real estate is used as collateral in a mortgage loan, the interest of the state in regulating the transaction is obvious, and state regulations in this area are substantial. However, there are also some important federal regulations that must be met by the parties, particularly the creditor.

The most important federal regulation is, once again, TILA. Debtors must be made aware of the cost of the credit prior to entering the transaction. Given the length of time involved, and the relative size of the credit involved—mortgages are frequently the largest debt a consumer will assume—the need for full and accurate disclosure is obvious. A second area of coverage at the federal level is the Real Estate Settlement Procedures Act (RESPA), which became effective in 1974. RESPA is also a disclosure act. Home mortgage lenders are required to provide loan applicants with a good-faith estimate of all settlement and closing costs associated with the loan. The lender must also inform the applicant if any of the settlement business is being referred to a company affiliated with the lender. The applicant must be informed of the possibility that the loan will be transferred at some point. If the loan is transferred, both the lender and the new holder of the note must notify the debtor at that time, as well. Finally, the lender must provide the borrower with a list of the actual settlement and closing costs at the time the loan is formally closed.

Most states have a number of statutes that apply to mortgage loans. Included among these statutes are:

- Mortgage lending acts
- Mortgage banker and broker acts
- Secondary mortgage acts
- Home improvement contract acts

State law will also have provisions regarding the warranties that the seller provides to the buyer, statutes governing recording of the deed, and various other aspects. These provisions will be covered in detail in Chapter 43.

28.2 | FINANCE

CALL-IMAGE TECHNOLOGY

CREDIT CARD SOLICITATIONS

Like many other college students, John regularly receives credit card solicitations in the mail. Most of these solicitations inform John that he is "preapproved" for the credit card. The solicitations also state that the card carries a very attractive initial interest rate, such as 2.9 percent. Since John does not yet have a credit card, he is interested in these offers, but he is also somewhat leery. He has heard about "teaser" rates and some other problems that fellow students have encountered with credit card applications. He asks you for your advice regarding these solicitations. What will you tell him?

BUSINESS CONSIDERATION Most college students have minimal income, at best, and yet they regularly receive credit card solicitations from a multitude of credit card issuers. Why would a credit card issuer solicit an application from a person who is probably either unemployed or underemployed, and likely to remain so at least until graduation?

ETHICAL CONSIDERATIONS Is it ethical for a credit card issuer to use a "teaser" rate to procure applications, and then to change the rate at some time in the near future, such as after six months? Is it ethical for a credit card company to change the interest rate the first time a customer is late with his or her payments?

CREDIT CARDS

Credit cards have become ubiquitous in the United States. A significant percentage of the adult population has at least one credit card, and most people may have several. There are three basic types of credit cards: bank cards such as MasterCard, Visa, and Discover; travel and entertainment cards such as American Express, Carte Blanche, and Diners Club; and store or merchant cards such as Sears, J.C. Penney, Exxon, Texaco, and so on. Bank cards and travel and entertainment cards are widely accepted at a variety of locations. By contrast, store or merchant cards are normally accepted only by the stores or merchants who issue the cards. Credit cards involve open-ended credit, and they are often viewed differently from loans for purposes of usury provisions and other state credit coverage. The holder of the card is regarded by the courts as being involved in a "revolving credit" arrangement rather than a loan, and the methods for computing charges and fees are different than the methods used in a "standard" loan. Nonetheless, the number of people who hold credit cards, and the widespread usage of credit cards, has necessitated a great deal of coverage at both the federal and the state levels.

Federal regulation in this area is based, once again, on the Truth in Lending Act. The provisions for credit card protection are found in the Truth in Lending Act Regulations (Regulation Z), Subpart B, which deals with open-ended credit.[4] The credit card issuer must provide a full disclosure of the costs associated with the card, as would be expected under TILA. However, the regulations go much farther.

Section 226.12 (a) prohibits the issuing of unsolicited credit cards. This section states that no credit card may be issued unless it is issued in response to an application from the recipient (the application can be made orally or in writing) or it is a renewal of, or substitution for, a card that has previously been issued and accepted. At this time, there is no prohibition against *solicitation* of applications by the card issuer, but the solicitation may not include the card itself. It is not a defense for the card issuer to send a card that requires a telephone call to an "activation center" before the card can be used. The courts have viewed this as an *issuance*, not as a *solicitation* subject to an oral application (the phone call to the activation center). The following case addressed the issue of whether an unsolicited credit card was issued.

28.2

SWIFT V. FIRST USA BANK
1999 U.S. DIST. LEXIS 8208 (N.D.ILL. 1999)

FACTS This matter is before the Court on a motion to dismiss brought by defendants First USA Bank ("First USA"), First Credit Card Services USA ("First Credit"), and Premiere Communications, Inc. ("Premiere") (collectively "Defendants") . . . Plaintiff Shelley D. Swift filed a class action complaint against Defendants alleging violations of the Truth in Lending Act, 15 U.S.C. § 1642 ("TILA") . . . Swift seeks actual, statutory, and punitive damages, as well as injunctive relief. The complaint contains the following allegations. First USA is a bank which issues credit cards to consumers throughout the United States. First Credit provides marketing services and credit card servicing to credit card issuers such as First USA. Premiere is a telecommunications company that provides telephone services to consumers nationwide. In January 1998, Swift received a credit card solicitation from Defendants in the mail. The cover letter discussed the benefits of the Platinum Connect card ("Connect Card"), which was enclosed with the letter. The letter stated:

Introducing the First USA Platinum Connect card. Whether you decide to use it as a calling card, a

Pre-Approved credit card, or both, you'll receive one free hour of long distance calling. Use your new Platinum Connect card to make all your calls AND purchases. Having one card for both your calling and credit card needs is a great convenience. Because not only is it one card to carry, it is also just one bill to pay every month.

You're Pre-Approved!

Just call 1 (800) 335-2453 to activate your card today. Activating your card is simple, since you're already Pre-Approved. Just call 1 (800) 335-2453 by January 30, 1998, to get your free hour of domestic long distance calling, and if you choose, to take advantage of the credit card and/or calling card features.

The card member agreement further disclosed that Premiere would provide telecommunications services in conjunction with the credit card. Included with the solicitation was a VISA credit card which could be activated by calling an 800 number. Swift had not applied or otherwise requested a credit card from

continued

SWIFT V. FIRST USA BANK, *continued*

1999 U.S. DIST. LEXIS 8208 (N.D.ILL. 1999)

Defendants prior to receiving Defendants' solicitation in the mail, and Swift had never been a customer of Defendants.

ISSUE Was the inclusion of the VISA card with the application solicitation the issuance of an unsolicited credit card?

HOLDING Yes. The card was issued prior to any application by the recipient.

REASONING Section 1642 of TILA provides that "no credit card shall be issued except in response to a request or application therefor." . . . Credit Card is defined as "any card, plate, coupon book or other credit device existing for the purpose of obtaining money, property, labor or service on credit." . . . Regulation Z, drafted by the Federal Reserve Board pursuant to statutory authority, provides that "regardless of the purpose for which the credit card is to be used . . . no credit card shall be issued to any person except (1) In response to an oral or written request or application for the card; or (2) As a renewal of, or substitute for, an accepted credit card." . . . On March 31, 1999, just a week before this Court was originally set to rule on the instant motion, the Federal Reserve Board issued revisions to its Official Commentary to Regulation Z. These revisions explicitly prohibit the activities engaged in by First USA by including among the definition of credit card

> [a] card or device that can be activated upon receipt to access credit, even if the card has a substantive use other than credit. . . . Such a card or device is a credit card notwithstanding the fact that the recipient must first contact the card issuer to access or activate the credit feature. Commentary to Regulation Z, 64 Fed. Reg. 16614 (1999).

. . . The Court ordered supplemental briefing so the parties could have an opportunity to address the effect of these revisions on the present action. . . . This Court need not address whether the revisions should be given retroactive application . . . because, as will be discussed below, First USA's alleged activities were prohibited even under the prior commentary. The prior Federal Reserve Board's Official Staff Commentary on Regulation Z Truth in Lending ("Official FRB Commentary") permitted the issuance of unsolicited devices that are not credit cards:

> 7. *Issuance of non-credit cards. The issuance of an unsolicited device that is not, but may become, a credit card, is not prohibited provided: the device has some substantive purpose other than obtaining credit, such as access to non-credit services offered by the issuer; it cannot be used as a credit card when issued; and a credit capability may be added only on the recipient's request. For example, the card issuer could send a check guarantee card on an unsolicited basis, but could not add a credit feature to that card without the consumer's specific request. The reencoding of a debit card or other existing card that had no credit privileges when issued would be appropriate after the consumer has specifically requested a card with credit privileges. Similarly, the card issuer may add a credit feature, for example, by reprogramming the issuer's computer program or automated teller machines, or by a similar program adjustment.*

Such Official FRB Commentary has the status of a regulation . . . Defendants claim that the mailing of the Connect Card to Swift did not violate the TILA because 1) the solicitation complies with Official FRB Commentary, and 2) an affirmative act—i.e. a request by Swift to add the credit card feature—is required before the card would have any credit card functionality. According to Defendants, consistent with the Official FRB Commentary, the card has two separate substantive purposes other than obtaining credit. First, it is a calling card which can be billed to any credit or debit card. Second, the card has a rewards feature that entitled the consumer to a 10% rebate on all calling card calls. The calling card feature can be activated without activating the credit feature. Additionally, argue the Defendants, the Connect Card has no present credit card functionality because the recipient has to call up to activate the card. The consumer has to dial an 800 number in order for the card to become a credit card. The card may be used as a telephone card without ever adding the credit feature, although a customer would similarly have to activate the calling card feature by dialing the same 800 number. Plaintiff argues that "if something looks like a duck, walks like a duck, and quacks like a duck, then it is a duck . . . Defendants attempt to call their duck a phone." . . . A credit card has already been issued, according to Swift, and the only thing the recipient

28.2

SWIFT V. FIRST USA BANK, *continued*
1999 U.S. DIST. LEXIS 8208 (N.D.ILL. 1999)

must do is activate the card. Issuance and activation are conceptually distinct. Defendants' arguments are wholly unpersuasive. The core of their argument is best described in First USA's reply, which claims that "it is irrelevant whether the call to add the credit feature is considered an application for credit or an acceptance of a pre-approved offer of credit because under the FRB Commentary the key issue is not whether the consumer applied for the credit card or if the credit was extended pursuant to a pre-approved offer, but whether the credit capability is added on the recipient's request." . . . Stripped down to the bones, Defendants argue that so long as the consumer must call to activate the card, TILA § 1642 does not apply. If this Court were to accept Defendants' argument, nothing would be left of § 1642. As experience demonstrates, credit cards sent in the mail must be activated before use. This is true whether the card is on a new (hopefully solicited) account or a replacement card. Semantics aside, Swift alleges that Defendants issued and mailed her a credit card without her request. This would be a violation of TILA. Defen-

dants' arguments regarding the Official FRB Commentary on unsolicited non-credit card devices are insufficient for the same reasons. The Commentary requires that the device cannot be used as a credit card when issued. The Defendants must therefore argue again that the activation phone call is the crucial step to distinguish their Connect Card from a mere unsolicited credit card. For the reasons outlined above, these arguments are unpersuasive.

BUSINESS CONSIDERATIONS Why would a business want to send unsolicited credit cards to potential customers? What benefits might the card issuer be able to realize by sending unsolicited cards?

ETHICAL CONSIDERATIONS Was the conduct of the card issuer in this case ethical? Is it ethical to claim that an inactive credit card sent to a potential customer is not an unsolicited credit card simply because the card is not active?

TILA also limits the liability of cardholders in the event that their cards are used without authorization. If a credit card is lost or stolen, the cardholder faces a maximum liability of $50 for unauthorized use of the card, and the liability is only for use of the card *before* the issuer is notified of the loss or theft. Once the card issuer is notified, the liability of the cardholder ends. However, a different limit applies if the cardholder consents to the use of his or her card by another, only to find out that the other person did not use the card as the cardholder expected. The following case involves this situation.

28.3

MASTERCARD V. TOWN OF NEWPORT
396 N.W.2D 345 (WISC.APP. 1986)

FACTS First Wisconsin National Bank appeals from a judgment for $50 against the Town of Newport. The judgment arises out of purchases exceeding that amount the town clerk charged to a credit card the bank had issued in the town's name.

In 1977 Newport applied to First Wisconsin for a corporate Mastercard account. The town obtained the credit card to enable its clerk to charge fuel for

the town hall, but the application does not state that fact. The application states that Newport:

shall be liable for all credit extended to any person presenting [the] charge card until company delivers . . . written notice that such card has been lost or stolen or returns such card advising . . . in

continued

28.3

MASTERCARD V. TOWN OF NEWPORT, *continued*

396 N.W.2D 345 (WISC.APP. 1986)

writing that the authority of the agent or employee named thereon has been revoked.

The bank opened the account and issued the credit card in the name of "Town of Newport." The town clerk used the card not only for official purposes but also to charge hotel and restaurant expenses and clothing and gift shop purchases for her personal use. The personal purchases were made at unspecified dates from 1980 through April 1983. The town did not notify the bank of any improper or unauthorized use. 15 U.S.C. sec. 1643 provides in relevant part:

(a)(1) A cardholder shall be liable for the unauthorized use of a credit card

only if . . . (B) the liability is not in excess of $50; . . .

15 U.S.C. sec. 1602(o) provides:

The term "unauthorized use," as used in [15 U.S.C. sec. 1643], means a use of a credit card by a person other than the cardholder who does not have actual, implied, or apparent authority for such use and from which the cardholder receives no benefit.

The trial court held that although the town clerk was authorized to possess the card and to use it for business-related purposes, she had no authority to use it for personal purchases. Since the town received no benefit from the personal purchases, the court concluded that the town's liability is limited to $50.

ISSUE Were the purchases in question an "unauthorized use" of the credit card, consequently limiting the town's liability to $50 under 15 U.S.C. sec. 1643(a)?

HOLDING No. From the bank's perspective, these purchases were authorized.

REASONING Because the facts are undisputed, whether the town clerk's purchases constituted an "unauthorized" use within the meaning of 15 U.S.C. sec. 1602(o) is a question of law . . . We decide an issue of law without deference to the conclusion of the trial court . . . The elements of an "unauthorized use," as defined in sec. 15 U.S.C. sec. 602(o), are: (1) the use of a credit card by a person other than the cardholder, (2) the other person does not have actual, implied or apparent authority for such use, and (3) the cardholder receives no benefit from such use. Because the

elements are conjunctively stated, all three must be met. That the first and third elements have been met is uncontested. Reasonable persons can arrive at different understandings of the second element. "[A] use of a credit card by a person other than the cardholder who does not have actual, implied or apparent authority for such use" could refer to authorization for the specific individual purchase or to authorization for use in general. The reference in 15 U.S.C. sec. 1602(o) to "a use" rather than "the use" fails to clarify the definition of unauthorized use. The Truth in Lending regulations, known as Regulation Z, describe "unauthorized use" as "the use by a person, . . . " 12 C.F.R. sec. 226.12(b)(1) . . . Because the statutory definition of "unauthorized use" can be read differently by reasonable persons, it is ambiguous . . . We therefore must employ judicial rules of statutory construction to ascertain the intention of the legislature. We look to the statutory context, subject matter, scope, history and object to be accomplished . . . The statutory context includes provisions regarding loss or theft. 15 U.S.C. sec. 1643(a)(1)(D) and (E) provide that the cardholder is liable for an unauthorized use only if the issuer provided a description of the means by which the cardholder may notify the issuer of loss or theft and if the unauthorized use occurs before the issuer has been notified that an unauthorized use of the credit card has occurred or may occur as the result of "loss, theft, or otherwise." These loss or theft provisions have affected judicial construction of "unauthorized use" in U.S.C. sec. 1602(o). In *Martin* v. *American Express, Inc.* . . . the court concluded that the $50 limitation applies where the card is obtained from the cardholder by loss, theft or wrongdoing. The *Martin* court was "not persuaded that sec. 1643(a) is applicable where a cardholder voluntarily and knowingly allows another to use his card and that person subsequently misuses the card." . . . The *Martin* court said that any other construction would allow a cardholder to defraud the issuer by allowing others to run up large charges on the card and then limit the cardholder's liability to $50 by notifying the issuer. The court held that because the defendant cardholder had authorized another person to charge up to $500 on the holder's credit card, the cardholder was liable for the full $5,300 the other person charged on the card. A similar result was reached in *Cities Service Co.* v. *Pailet* . . . The defendant cardholder gave his credit card to an

28.3

MASTERCARD V. TOWN OF NEWPORT, *continued*
396 N.W.2D 345 (WISC.APP. 1986)

employee of his company for a limited business purpose. The employee used the card for other purposes. Relying on *Martin* v. *American Express, supra,* the *Cities Service* court held that in the absence of evidence that the card was obtained from the cardholder by loss, theft or wrongdoing, the $50 limitation in 15 U.S.C. sec. 1643 was unavailable to him . . . The liability limitation has also been held to be unavailable where the cardholder failed to retake a card from a previously authorized spouse after divorce . . . The legislative history of the statute is consistent with the view that the $50 limitation is intended to apply only if the card has been lost or stolen. The proposed liability limitation amendment which led to the adoption of the relevant statutory language was the subject of a 3-day hearing. The leitmotif of the hearing was that the issuer would bear most of the loss for misused credit cards. The circumstances before us were not specifically addressed. However, the term "unauthorized use" as affecting liability was most often discussed in the context of lost or stolen credit cards. We conclude that when, as here, a credit cardholder authorizes another to use the card for a specific purpose, and the other person uses it for another purpose, such a use is not an "unauthorized use" within the meaning of 15 U.S.C. sec. 1602(o). Because the Town of Newport had authorized its town clerk to use the credit card issued in the name of the town, the $50 liability limitation in 15 U.S.C. sec. 1643(a) is inapplicable. We therefore reverse the judgment and remand for further proceedings consistent with this opinion. By the Court—Judgment reversed and cause remanded for further proceedings consistent with this opinion.

BUSINESS CONSIDERATION A business should take what precautions to prevent unauthorized charges if it gives a company credit card to an employee?

ETHICAL CONSIDERATION The unauthorized use of credit cards could potentially cause problems for a business. Is it ethical for a business to require certain employees to obtain a credit card in their own name and then to reimburse them for job-related expenditures?

Regulation Z also prohibits *offsets* by the card issuer. The card issuer cannot take any action to offset credit card indebtedness by unilaterally asserting a claim on the cardholder's funds on deposit with the issuer of the card. However, if the offset is part of a consensual security agreement between the card issuer and the cardholder, an offset is permissible. Similarly, the card issuer can proceed against funds on deposit on the basis of a judgment obtained against the cardholder, an attachment by the card issuer, or a written plan from the cardholder permitting periodic offsets against a credit card balance.

Other federal regulations that apply to credit card use also exist. The Equal Credit Opportunity Act requires businesses that regularly extend credit as a part of their business to make credit available without discrimination. The Fair Credit Billing Act provides a method for cardholders to challenge any alleged billing errors without liability until the alleged error is investigated. And the Unsolicited Credit Card Act protects the customer from potential liability for misuse of credit cards issued to that person without an application submitted by that person.

State regulation of credit cards tends to be more enabling than restrictive. However, the state usury provisions regarding credit cards still apply. State contract laws are applicable to the credit card relationship between the issuer and the customer. Further, when store or merchant cards are used, there is the possibility that the store or the merchant will retain a security interest in the purchased item, thus making the transaction subject to the provisions of Article 9 of the UCC.

FRAUD ALLEGATIONS AGAINST ADVANTA

Advanta is a leading issuer of standard and gold MasterCard and Visa credit cards, which typically carry no annual fee and a credit limit of about $6,000. Advanta, along with most other credit card issuers, offers low "teaser" rates for a limited period prior to raising its interest rate to a more competitive figure. Historically, the company maintained low charge-off rates because of the strong credit ratings of its customers. In July 1996, the company announced increased earnings over a three-month period of 35 percent over the previous year, and 25 percent growth in earnings over a six-month period. However, in March 1997, the company announced that it expected to report a loss of $20 million, or about $0.44 per share, compared to $41 million in increased earnings for the first quarter of 1996. Advanta attributed the loss to "continuing increases in consumer bankruptcies and charge-offs and lower receivable balances than originally anticipated in the credit card business." The price of Class A stock dropped off from $40.375 per share to $31.875, and Class B stock dropped from $39.6875 to $30.75.

A group of stakeholders have sued, asserting that in an effort to maintain its growth rate, Advanta actually undermined the company's future viability by (1) relaxing its underwriting standards, (2) not repricing its accounts to normal industry standard interest rates, (3) not having the personnel to follow up on delinquent accounts, and (4) extending its investigative period prior to writing off an account because most Chapter 7 bankruptcies result in discharge of all the borrower's debts.

The alleged fraud was based on two factors:

1. In the third quarter of 1996, Advanta had increased its collection period from 30 to 90 days, during which time the company was allowed to further investigate a bankruptcy. Plaintiffs allege the change was simply a way for Advanta to delay reporting the earnings impact of rising charge-off rates.
2. The plaintiffs also alleged that a specific statement issued by Janet Point, Vice President for Investor Relations, was false and misleading. She had informed a news service in September 1996 that Advanta expected to increase its revenues by replacing its introductory teaser rates with the normal rate of 17 percent. However, when the teaser rates expired, the company chose to only raise the rates to 13 to 14 percent to retain the image of being a low-cost provider.

This case has been filed in *your* court. How will *you* decide it?[5]

BUSINESS CONSIDERATIONS Is it an appropriate business decision for the board of directors to allow a lower-than-normal interest rate on credit cards after the "teaser rate" period has expired? Should the board be held liable for losses suffered by the firm when it offers a lower-than-normal rate?

ETHICAL CONSIDERATION Is it ethical for a credit card company to advertise itself as offering low rates, and then to charge the normal rate for the industry after the introductory "teaser rate" has expired?

SOURCE: *Corporate Officers and Directors Liability Litigation Reporter* 13, no. 20, (Andrews Publications, Inc., 1998), p. 11.

FTC Consumer Credit Rules

The Federal Trade Commission has enacted two special *credit practice* rules designed to provide consumer debtors with protections they might not otherwise enjoy under the various other areas of law. The first of these rules is the Federal Trade Commission Holder in Due Course Rule, in effect since 1976. The second is the Federal Trade Commission Credit Practices Rule, in effect since 1985.

The Federal Trade Commission Holder in Due Course rule requires the inclusion in consumer credit contracts of a statement that the debtor retains all rights, claims, and defenses that the consumer could have asserted against the seller, even against holders in due course of the consumer credit instrument. This rule does not apply to real estate transactions or credit card transactions.

The second rule makes it an unfair trade practice for a seller or creditor in a consumer credit transaction to take a contract containing a confession of judgment clause or a waiver of exemptions clause. Nor can the seller or creditor take a contract containing a wage assignment provision or a nonpossessory security interest in household goods or furnishing, except in the form of a purchase money security interest.

This second rule also has a special disclosure requirement when a cosigner is involved in a credit arrangement. The required disclosure statement reads as follows:

> *You are asked to guarantee this debt. Think carefully before you do. If the borrower doesn't pay the debt you will have to. Be sure you can afford to pay if you have to, and that you want to accept this responsibility.*
>
> *You may have to pay up to the full amount of the debt if the borrower does not pay. You may also have to pay late fees or collection costs, which increase this amount. The creditor can collect this debt from you without first trying to collect from the borrower. The creditor can use the same collection methods against you that can be used against the borrower such as suing you, garnishing your wages, etc. If this debt is ever in default that fact becomes a part of your credit record. This notice is not the contract that makes you liable for the debt.*

Failure to include this notice is an unfair trade practice under the provisions of the Federal Trade Commission Act.

TO CO-SIGN OR NOT TO CO-SIGN

One of Dan's fraternity brothers has encountered some financial difficulties since graduating from college, but he has seemingly turned his life—and his fortunes—around recently. In fact, he has developed an idea for a new product that has tremendous potential. Unfortunately, he does not have the funding to turn his idea into reality. He has talked with a number of banks about borrowing the funds he needs, but none of the bankers is willing to make the loan to him without a cosigner. As a result, he approached Dan about cosigning on one or two loans. Realizing that this is a significant risk for Dan, he has also offered Dan a share of the profits from his business if the product is as successful as he expects it to be. Dan would like to help his fraternity brother, but he is concerned about the potential liability to himself if he agrees to co-sign. He has asked you for your advice. What will you tell him?

BUSINESS CONSIDERATION Many businesses have a policy that prohibits the business from cosigning on loans except under extraordinary circumstances. Why might a business have such a policy?

ETHICAL CONSIDERATIONS From an ethical perspective, how should a business view requests to serve as a cosigner on a loan? Which constituent groups are jeopardized by cosignings if the borrower defaults? Which constituent groups might benefit from cosigning a loan?

RESOURCES FOR BUSINESS LAW STUDENTS

NAME	RESOURCES	WEB ADDRESS
Creditalk	Information on budgeting and how to build a good credit history	**http://www.creditalk.com**
Consumer Credit Law	An index to credit laws that protect consumers and provide guidelines for the credit industry	**http://www.law.cornell.edu**
Consumer Information Center	A directory of consumer resources from federal and other agencies	**http://www.pueblo.gsa.gov**
Debt Counselors of America	The nonprofit web resource for getting out of debt. This site offers information about getting out of debt, rebuilding personal credit, and getting finances organized.	**http://www.dca.org**

SUMMARY

While secured transactions form an important part of debtor-creditor relations, they are not the only type of credit transactions involved in this area. This is especially true in the area of consumer credit transactions, where the use of secured transactions under Article 9 tends to be limited to purchase money security interests for furniture and major appliances.

Unsecured credit is fairly common. Many banks grant signature loans to their better customers, and most businesses and consumers rely on unsecured credit for the use of public utilities. The regulation of unsecured credit transactions is primarily a matter of state law. Included in the state regulation is the topic of usury. Every state has a maximum interest rate that can be charged. Excessive interest is deemed usury and is illegal. The federal regulation of unsecured credit is primarily concerned with ensuring that information is provided to the debtor prior to the creation of the debt and with acceptable methods of collection in the event the debtor defaults on the agreement. Title I of the Federal Consumer Credit Protection Act (TILA) requires creditors to provide credit applicants with certain information as to the cost of the credit. This information must be provided in a standard format and in a standard terminology. The most important information that must be given to the applicant is the APR, the annualized percentage rate to be charged in the transaction.

Installment loans are closed-end loans, calling for a fixed periodic payment for a predetermined number of periods, normally a monthly payment. Installment loans may be secured or unsecured, although most consumer installment loans are secured by some form of collateral. Some of these loans will fall within the coverage of Article 9. However, if a person purchases a car on credit, using the car as collateral for the loan, the transaction falls outside the coverage of Article 9, and this transaction will be governed by the state certificate of title rules rather than by Article 9. Installment loans are subject to many of the same regulatory provisions as are unsecured loans. Federal regulation is primarily TILA and the Fair Debt

Collection Practices Act. State coverage includes Article 3 of the UCC, if a promissory note is involved. The Uniform Consumer Credit Code may apply to the transaction. State laws governing contracts will also apply, as will any state statutes governing retail installment sales or similar legislation.

Mortgage loans involve loans in which real estate is used as collateral by the debtor to secure the credit. Mortgage loans are commonly installment loans, but the repayment term tends to be much longer than other types of installment loans. Mortgage loans often have a repayment period of 15, 20, or 30 years. Both federal and state regulations apply to these transactions. The most important federal regulation is, once again, TILA. A second important area of federal coverage is the Real Estate Settlement Procedures Act (RESPA), which is also a disclosure act. Home mortgage lenders are required to provide loan applicants with a good-faith estimate of all settlement and closing costs associated with the loan. Other information that must be disclosed includes referrals to any company affiliated with the lender, and information about possible transfers of the loan to subsequent parties. State coverage in this area includes mortgage lending acts, mortgage banker and broker acts, secondary mortgage acts, and home improvement loan acts.

Credit card coverage is primarily at the federal level, although some state regulation exists. The main source of federal coverage is Regulation Z, the regulations enacted in support of TILA. Among the prohibitions found under Regulation Z are: credit card issuers are prohibited from issuing unsolicited credit cards; credit card holders are only liable for up to $50 from unauthorized usage of the card; and the issuer is prohibited from using offsets to recover credit card payment deficiencies from deposit accounts of the credit cardholder. State law in this area is primarily enabling, although state usury law can have an impact on credit cardholders and issuers.

The Federal Trade Commission has issued two credit practice rules designed to provide some protection and some information to consumer debtors. The first, the FTC holder in due course rule, requires the inclusion of language allowing a consumer debtor to retain and use any defenses against subsequent HDCs on a consumer credit note. The second is a disclosure statement warning cosigners of the potential liability faced by cosigning on a loan or credit application.

DISCUSSION QUESTIONS

1. What is an *unsecured credit transaction?* Why would a creditor extend unsecured credit to a debtor?
2. What is an *installment loan?* Since many installment loans are collateralized, why are they not covered by the provisions of Article 9?
3. What distinguishes a mortgage loan from other types of installment loans? Why is there a different type of coverage for a mortgage loan than for an installment loan taken to purchase an automobile?
4. What are the different types of credit cards? What is the difference in the use and/or terms of each of these types?
5. What information does TILA require a creditor to provide to a debtor prior to the extension of credit? What is the format in which this information must be presented?

6. What is the rule regarding unsolicited credit cards? When can a credit card issuer legally issue a credit card under Regulation Z?
7. What liability does a credit cardholder face if the card is lost or stolen, and the finder or thief charges several hundred dollars of goods and services to the card?
8. What liability does a credit cardholder face if he or she allows a friend to use the card, and that friend charges several hundred dollars of goods and services to the card beyond what the holder authorized?
9. How does the FTC HDC rule provide protection to consumer debtors who sign a consumer credit instrument?
10. How does the FTC rule regarding cosigners provide protection to potential cosigners of credit instruments or agreements?

CASE PROBLEMS AND WRITING ASSIGNMENTS

1. In 1994, Bank of America sent an unsolicited credit card application to Cauffiel at his place of business, Galaxie Corporation. Although Cauffiel is the sole shareholder of Galaxie, the application was addressed to Cauffiel individually. Unbeknownst to Galaxie, Cauffiel, or Bank of America, Galaxie employee, Diadette Mejia, intercepted and completed the application, putting Cauffiel as the primary cardholder and herself as the secondary cardholder. She also changed the billing address to her private residence. In response to the application, Bank of America issued credit cards in the primary name of Cauffiel with Mejia as the secondary cardholder. From October 1994 to February 1996, Mejia made unauthorized purchases and cash advances amounting to more than $116,000 using the credit card. She paid the monthly credit card statements by forging Cauffiel's signature on stolen checks drawn on the bank account of Galaxie. In February 1996, Cauffiel informed Bank of America of Mejia's criminal conduct and arrest, at which time the bank conducted a fraud investigation and closed the account. Cauffiel and Galaxie Corporation sued Bank of America for damages, alleging that the bank was negligent in issuing the credit card to Mejia. The district court granted summary judgment to Bank of America, citing the fact that Galaxie was the only injured party in this case, and determining that Bank of America owed no duty to Galaxie under these facts. Cauffiel and Galaxie Corporation appealed this ruling. Should the court of appeals uphold the district court's determination? [See *Galaxie Corporation* v. *Bank of America, N.A.*, 165 F.3d 27 (6th Cir. 1998).]

2. Glenn LeCompte and his wife, Deborah LeCompte, jointly filed for relief in bankruptcy under Chapter 7 on 13 May 1987. Their complaint under the FCRA against the Credit Bureau of Baton Rouge and Equifax, the two defendants, is that the bankruptcy filing is still present in their credit history. They have attempted to obtain credit by applying to American Bank and Trust Company for a loan and by returning both preapproved credit card applications and unsolicited credit card applications, and have been unable to obtain credit. They state that their bankruptcy attorney and the bankruptcy judge verbally told them that the bankruptcy filing would only remain in their credit histories for a period of seven years. The credit report generated on 16 January 1995 by the Credit Bureau, utilizing the Equifax database, lists the bankruptcy filing, with the same case number, four times. After being notified that it was listed four times, three of the listings were deleted, but the bankruptcy filing of May 1987 is still present on the report. When the LeComptes inquired, via their attorney, as to why this bankruptcy was still listed, counsel for the Credit Bureau first explained that Chapter 7 bankruptcies remained on the credit history for ten years but that Chapter 13 bankruptcies were listed for seven years. A copy of the pamphlet prepared by the Associated Credit Bureaus, Inc., entitled "Consumers, Credit Bureaus and the Fair Credit Reporting Act—an explanation of consumer rights in credit reporting," was sent to the LeComptes. It states, in pertinent part:

   How long does adverse information remain in my file?

   Straight bankruptcies for 10 years, other information for seven years. Suits and judgments can be reported for seven years or until the statute of limitations expires, whichever is longer. Because Chapter 13 filings should reflect an attempt to repay some of the indebtedness, ACB's policy has been to recommend reporting Chapter 13 bankruptcies for seven years, even though they may be legally reported for ten. Paid tax liens, collection accounts, accounts charged to bad debts, may all be reported for seven years.

   The listing of the May 1987 bankruptcy, which they admit they filed, is the only error they allege in their credit report. Further, the only credit denial they attribute to the report is the denial of a loan by the American Bank and Trust Co. The loan denial disclosure statement lists as the reasons the bankruptcy and insufficient down payment. The Credit Bureau report was not provided to American Bank and Trust Co., as there is no indication that it was sent to them and the denial disclosure statement does not show that information from any outside sources was relied on in denying the loan application. Did the Credit Bureau violate the Fair Credit Reporting Act by including the information on the bankruptcy filing? [See *LeCompte* v. *Credit Bureau of Baton Rouge, Inc.*, 1996 U.S. Dist. LEXIS 6791 (E.D.La. 1996).]

3. Fillinger purchased a vehicle from Willowbrook Ford, Inc., under a motor vehicle retail installment contract, which contract was assigned to FMCC. Fillinger also purchased an extended warranty and service contract in the amount of $1,060. In the itemization statement in the installment contract, Willowbrook stated that it paid the $1,060 to FMCC. However, according to Fillinger, Willowbrook actually retained most of the service contract fee, and FMCC had knowledge of this practice. Fillinger has filed suit against Willowbrook Ford and against FMCC, alleging violations of TILA. FMCC filed a motion to dismiss, asking for dismissal

of all claims against it with prejudice. FMCC alleges that assignees of consumer credit notes should not be held liable in situations where the seller did not make a full and complete disclosure, and that FMCC was not aware of the misleading nature of the disclosure statement signed by Fillinger. Should the court dismiss the TILA claim against FMCC, the assignee, for the misleading and inaccurate disclosure provided by Willowbrook Ford? When should an assignee be held liable for the conduct of the assignor? [See *Fillinger* v. *Willowbrook Ford, Inc.,* 1999 U.S.Dist. LEXIS 3629 (N.D.Ill. 1999).]

4. Jerry and Mary Taylor bought a new Hyundai Accent in July 1995, and they bought an extended warranty from the dealer, Quality Hyundai, at the same time. They signed a motor vehicle retail installment contract committing them to pay $12,081 for the car (minus a $900 down payment) and $1,395 for the extended warranty. In conjunction with the sale, Quality gave them a TILA disclosure form that included, under the now-familiar heading "Amounts Paid to Others for You," an entry reporting $1,395 paid to the warranty provider. After the sale, Quality assigned the entire installment contract to Bank One Chicago (although the contract signed by the Taylors designated Bank One Milwaukee as the assignee). The Taylors alleged that the statements indicating that the extended warranty charges were "Amounts Paid to Others for You" were false, in that Quality did not pay the full amount to the warranty provider. The plaintiffs also alleged that the assignee of their installment contract, Bank One, was a sophisticated player in the lending market who must have known that the statements on the TILA forms were false. They therefore sought damages under the TILA, 15 U.S.C. § 1641(a). The district court ruled for the assignee, and the district court also concluded that Quality was not liable under the statute. The Taylors appealed this judgment. How should the appellate court rule in this case? [See *Taylor* v. *Quality Hyundai, Inc.,* 150 F.3d 689 (7th Cir. 1998).]

5. Towers World Airways, Inc., leased a corporate jet and hired Schley to pilot it. The jet was used by Towers for flights that it booked as well as for other charter flights booked by other companies. In February 1988, Towers applied for and received a credit card from PHH Aviation Systems, Inc. Towers gave the credit card to Schley, instructing him that it was only to be used for the purchase of fuel and other airline-related expenses when the jet was being used in connection with Towers flights. Despite these instructions, Schley charged more than $89,000 on the card for charter flights that were not booked by Towers. Towers canceled the card in August 1988 and filed suit seeking a declaratory judgment that it was only liable for $50 on the credit card. According to Towers, the charges by Schley were unauthorized, so that Towers only faced a maximum liability of $50 under the provisions of Regulation Z. PHH disagreed, asserting that Schley was an authorized user of the card and that Towers was liable for all aircraft-related charges made by Schley while the card was in effect. How should this case be resolved? [See *Towers World Airways, Inc.* v. *PHH Aviation Systems, Inc.,* 933 F.2d 174 (2nd Cir. 1991).]

6. **BUSINESS APPLICATION CASE** In November 1987, John Begala entered into a 60-month car loan with PNC. His monthly payment was $442.82. The original loan agreement did not mention the possibility of deferring monthly payments. Between May 1988 and May 1993, Begala received nine unsolicited letters from PNC offering one-month extensions, or deferrals, of his loan, called "payment holidays." One such letter read:

   PNC Bank would like to help you accumulate some extra cash during the vacation season by giving you an opportunity to postpone one loan payment. Here's how it works. The authorization form attached below lists a loan extension fee which is the payment you make now in order to postpone your regular payment. Simply sign the authorization and forward it along with your extension fee payment. Your loan term will automatically be extended by the one payment you're postponing now. That's all there is to it. This offer is good until July 31, 1993, so you can postpone your June or July payment. If you'd like to take advantage of this offer, here's your chance. Remember, just sign and detach the authorization provided below and return it with your extension payment in the enclosed envelope. We must receive your authorization and extension payment prior to your regular payment date in the month during which you wish to postpone a payment.

   The extension authorization form at the bottom of the letter states,

   This is your authorization to extend my installment loan #[_____] one month beyond the present maturity. The extension fee is [_____].

   Begala responded all nine times to the payment holiday offers. The extension fees ranged up to $60 per extension, and over the course of the nine extensions, he paid more than $400 in extension fees. When, in May 1993, Begala attempted to make the final payment on his loan, he discovered that he owed not just a final payment of $442.82, but also approximately

$1,000 in interest that had accumulated as a result of the nine deferrals. Begala filed a complaint against PNC, alleging that the bank had violated its duty under the Truth in Lending Act to disclose the fact that additional finance charges would be assessed due to the payment holidays, as well as the amount of such charges. PNC moved to dismiss the action, contending that it had no duty under TILA to make disclosures regarding the payment holiday program and, therefore, that Begala had failed to state a claim on which relief could be granted. Acting on the defendant's motion, the court dismissed the entire action, finding that because TILA does not create a duty of disclosure when creditors offer payment holidays, Begala had failed to state a claim on which relief could be granted. Begala appealed. The court decided that one argument would be dispositive of the case: whether the statute and regulations implementing TILA create a duty to disclose accurately the interest incurred in payment holidays. How should this issue be decided? Why might a business want to grant its customers "payment holidays" during the life of an installment loan? Is it ethical to grant such "payment holidays" and then to assess additional interest on the lengthened loan? [See *Begala* v. *PNC Bank, Ohio, N.A.*, 163 F.3d 948 (6th Cir. 1998).]

7. **ETHICAL APPLICATION CASE** Defendant American Loan Company, Inc., is a financial institution licensed by the Illinois Department of Financial Institutions. American Loan is in the business of making so called "payday loans"—that is, small, short-term loans—to individuals whom American Loan characterizes as posing a high risk of default. These payday loans are offered to the public at annual interest rates of 261 percent to 521 percent. Because of the extraordinarily high interest rates, these loans are primarily made to individuals to whom more traditional forms of credit are unavailable. On 2 October 1998, Plaintiff Jackson obtained a payday loan from American Loan to be repaid on 15 October 1998. On 12 October 1998, Jackson "renewed" her loan in order to gain more time in which to repay the debt. Upon renewal, Jackson was issued a receipt stating that an "extension fee" had been assessed to her in the amount of $35.00. Subsequently Jackson secured at least two additional payday loans from American Loan and on at least two more occasions "renewed" these loans and received receipts listing "extension fees." Similarly, Plaintiff Davis received multiple payday loans from Defendant and "renewed" these loans. Davis also received receipts listing "extension fees." Jackson sued American Loan for allegedly violating the terms of TILA. According to Jackson, American Loan did not provide adequate disclosure of the finance terms when Jackson "renewed" the "payday loans," and did not properly list the "extension fees" as finance charges, as required by TILA. Is American Loan guilty of violating TILA for either of these alleged offenses? Explain. Was the practice of making "payday loans" or of granting "extensions" at the interest rates charged ethical? [See *Jackson* v. *American Loan Company, Inc.*, 1999 U.S. Dist. LEXIS 9143 (N.D.Ill. 1999).]

8. **CRITICAL THINKING CASE** On several occasions between 1988 and 1992, Draiman used his American Express Platinum Card to purchase airline tickets through the Travel Dimensions travel agency. Draiman provided Travel Dimensions with his Platinum Card number, and when he needed tickets, he would call and place an order. Travel Dimensions would send the tickets to Draiman and the bill to American Express. American Express would then secure payment from Draiman by including the cost of the tickets plus applicable financing charges in its periodic billing statement. On 21 January 1992, Draiman canceled his Platinum Card. Sometime thereafter, Draiman deposited an undisclosed sum of money with Travel Dimensions. On 20 July 1992 Draiman purchased four El Al tickets to Israel at $2,077 each, for a total cost of $8,308. Draiman instructed Travel Dimensions to pay for the El Al tickets by drawing on his deposited funds. Travel Dimensions did not honor that request—instead it charged the amount against the number that it had for Draiman's Platinum Card. American Express knew nothing of Draiman's deposit with, or his instructions to, Travel Dimensions. When American Express received the $8,308 charge from Travel Dimensions, that triggered its reinstatement policy, as set out in these terms in the cardholder agreement:

    If you ask us to cancel your account, but you continue to use the Card, we will consider such use as your request for reinstatement of your account. If we agree to reinstate your account, this Agreement or any amended or new Agreement we send you will govern your reinstated account.

    American Express does not communicate with cardholders to confirm that it is in fact their desire to revive their accounts. In accordance with its written policy, American Express reinstated Draiman's Platinum Card on 26 August 1992 and billed him $8,308. Draiman later actually used the El Al tickets (each of which had his Platinum Card number printed on its face) to travel to Israel. On 15 October 1993, Draiman paid American Express $3,399.98 of the $8,308 total and threatened suit if it tried to collect the $4,908.02 balance, citing purported violations of the Fair Credit

Billing Act, TILA, and other applicable laws. When American Express attempted to collect the debt, the threatened legal action ensued on 11 January 1995 with one twist: Draiman filed not only on his own behalf but also on behalf of a purported class of sim- ilarly aggrieved persons. Did American Express violate the unsolicited credit card provisions of TILA? Was this an unauthorized use of the card, limiting the liability of the cardholder to $50? [See *Draiman* v. *American Express,* 892 F.Supp. 1096 (N.D.Ill. 1995).]

Notes

1. "Summary of Consumer Credit Laws," U.S. Department of Commerce, 1999.
2. *Black's Law Dictionary,* 6th ed. (St. Paul, MN: West Publishing Co., 1990), p. 1545.
3. Colorado, Idaho, Indiana, Iowa, Kansas, Maine, Oklahoma, South Carolina, Utah, Wisconsin, Wyoming.
4. 15 USCS 12 CFR § 226.12.
5. "ED PA Dismisses Fraud Action Against Credit Card Company," *Corporate Officers and Directors Liability Litigation Reporter* 13, n. 20 (Andrews Publishing, Inc., 1998), p. 11.

29

STRAIGHT BANKRUPTCY

A G E N D A

The Kochanowskis have invested virtually everything they own in CIT, and they are very aware of how risky a business venture can be. While they are making every effort to operate their businesses as safely as possible, they recognize the risks inherent in their position. They also realize that they cannot control the business practices of their customers or their suppliers. It is possible that some of CIT's customers may encounter severe financial problems and be forced to resort to bankruptcy.

What legal and financial ramifications will this have on CIT? It is also possible that, despite their best efforts, CIT might encounter financial troubles and face bankruptcy. What remedies and/or relief might be available in bankruptcy? What alternatives does CIT have to a straight bankruptcy?

These are just some of the questions that might arise. Be prepared! You never know when one of the Kochanowskis will ask for your help or advice.

O U T L I N E

HISTORICAL BACKGROUND

When the colonists broke away from England to set up the United States of America, they had a strong desire to avoid the problems they had encountered under the English system of government. The U.S. Constitution and the Bill of Rights were drafted specifically to prevent some of these problems. One such area that the Constitution addresses is the treatment of debtors. Included in this treatment is the area of bankruptcy.

In England, persons unable or unwilling to pay their debts were commonly thrown into debtors' prison. A debtor might remain in prison for years waiting for friends or family to raise the funds necessary to repay the debt, or for the creditors to agree to the debtor's release. Less commonly, the debtor might agree to some form of indentured servitude, working for a preset number of years at little or no salary to repay the debt.

To prevent such treatment of debtors in this country, the founding fathers made provisions in the Constitution to allow "honest debtors" to make a "fresh start" by providing for relief in the form of bankruptcy. Article I, Section 8, of the U.S. Constitution says: "The Congress shall have the Power . . . to establish . . . uniform Laws on the subject of Bankruptcies throughout the United States."

It should be noted that the Constitution only *allows* Congress to establish uniform laws on bankruptcy. There is no constitutional *requirement* that Congress provide bankruptcy laws or relief. Nonetheless, for much of the history of the United States, some form of federal bankruptcy regulation has existed. Specifically, Congress has passed five bankruptcy acts. The first was enacted in 1800. This was followed by the bankruptcy acts of 1841, 1867, 1898, and, most recently, the Bankruptcy Reform Act of 1978, as amended by the Bankruptcy Amendments and Federal Judgeship Act of 1984 and the Bankruptcy Reform Act of 1994.

Although the Constitution seemingly calls for exclusive federal control of this area, the bankruptcy laws tend to coexist with state law in many areas. In fact, state law often is used to define problems or to provide solutions to bankruptcy problems. For example, each state has its own *exemption* provisions, a listing of the assets that an honest debtor can retain following a bankruptcy. There are also federal exemptions that might be available to the debtor. State law determines whether the debtor can choose between the state and the federal exemptions or must choose the state's exemption provisions.

For most of the twentieth century, bankruptcy was governed by the federal Bankruptcy Act, enacted in 1898. This act was quite technical, and many people found it confusing. In 1978, Congress passed a new law, the Bankruptcy Reform Act, which took effect 1 October 1979. The Bankruptcy Reform Act had two major purposes: to provide for fair and equitable treatment of the creditors in the distribution of the debtor's property, and, more important, to give an "honest debtor" a "fresh start." The Reform Act attempted to modernize the bankruptcy coverage, providing treatment for both the debtor and the creditors that was consistent with the credit-intensive, consumer-oriented society of the late twentieth century.

Unfortunately, the Bankruptcy Reform Act had some technical problems that resulted in its being declared unconstitutional. As a result, the Bankruptcy Amendments and Federal Judgeship Act of 1984 was enacted. This act was intended to clarify the jurisdictional authority of the bankruptcy courts and to resolve the constitutional problems discovered in the Bankruptcy Reform Act. At the same time, Congress made the amended bankruptcy coverage more sensitive to the needs of the creditors and made some effort to reduce or eliminate the problem of debtor abuses that had occurred under the former bankruptcy laws. Additional changes were made to the act with the Bankruptcy Reform Act of 1994, again with the aim of balancing protections while ensuring that the basic purpose of bankruptcy was maintained. While far from perfect, the Bankruptcy Reform Act and the accompanying Bankruptcy Amendments and Federal Judgeship Act and the Bankruptcy Reform Act of 1994 are a vast improvement over the 1898 act they replaced. A number of people believe that the Bankruptcy Reform Act of 1994 did not go far enough and that the entire bankruptcy area needs to be substantially revised. (A proposed revision, the Bankruptcy Reform Act of 1999, was being debated in Congress as we went to print. This proposed coverage is set out at the end of the chapter. If enacted, it will constitute a tremendous change in bankruptcy as it is currently viewed in the United States.)

The Bankruptcy Reform Act has (from a business law perspective) three major operative sections, called chapters. These are Chapter 7, Liquidation; Chapter 11, Reorganization; and Chapter 13, Adjustments of Debts of an Individual with Regular Income. A fourth important operative section, Chapter 12, Adjustment of Debts of a Family Farmer with Regular Annual Income, was added under the Bankruptcy Amendments in 1984. (Chapter 12 has expired, but several bills have been introduced in Congress to reactivate Chapter 12, as least in the short term, pending resolution of the proposed Bankruptcy Reform Act of 1999.)

In a Chapter 7 proceeding, the debtor's nonexempt assets are sold, the proceeds are distributed to the creditors, and a discharge is (normally) granted. Under Chapters 11, 12, and 13, the debtor restructures and rearranges finances and (possibly) organization so that the creditors will be paid, hopefully in full, but at least more than in a liquidation proceeding. This chapter examines a "straight bankruptcy" proceeding—that is, a Chapter 7 liquidation. The next chapter looks at other bankruptcy proceedings available under Chapters 11, 12, and 13 and at alternatives to bankruptcy under state law.

THE BANKRUPTCY REFORM ACT

The Bankruptcy Reform Act called for a whole new adjudicative system of bankruptcies. Under the act, each U.S. district court was to contain a separate, adjunct bankruptcy court. These bankruptcy courts were to be staffed by bankruptcy judges, each of whom was to serve a 14-year term, with their salaries to be determined annually by Congress. The bankruptcy judges were to be appointed by the president, subject to approval by the Senate. It was hoped that this new system, which replaced "referees" acting through the district courts, would simplify and speed up bankruptcy proceedings.

The new bankruptcy court/bankruptcy judge system encountered a major roadblock when, on 28 June 1982, the U.S. Supreme Court declared the Bankruptcy Reform Act unconstitutional. The entire area of bankruptcy law was placed in doubt as a result of this ruling. The case that raised the challenge to the Bankruptcy Reform Act involved the Northern Pipeline Company.

Northern Pipeline filed a petition in bankruptcy in January 1980. As a part of its petition, Northern Pipeline sued Marathon Pipe Line Company in the bankruptcy court, alleging that Marathon Pipe Line had breached a contract. (Under the Bankruptcy Reform Act, the bankruptcy court had jurisdiction over all issues relating to the bankruptcy.) Marathon sought dismissal of the suit on the grounds that the bankruptcy courts established by the Bankruptcy Reform Act lacked jurisdiction over the alleged contract action and that the restrictions placed on the appointment of the bankruptcy judges were unconstitutional. The U.S. Supreme Court handed down its opinion in *Northern Pipeline Construction Co.* v. *Marathon Pipe Line Co.*[1] on 28 June 1982. This opinion upheld the position of Marathon Pipe Line, declaring that the Reform Act violated the Constitution in the manner it provided for appointing judges and in the extensive authority given to the bankruptcy judges. This ruling challenged the validity of any further bankruptcy coverage under the Bankruptcy Reform Act.

Congress did nothing to resolve the constitutional problems raised in *Northern Pipeline* for nearly two years. During this period, the bankruptcy courts continued to operate under an "emergency rule" suggested by the Judicial Conference of the United States and accepted by the U.S. courts of appeals.

BANKRUPTCY AMENDMENTS AND FEDERAL JUDGESHIP ACT OF 1984

The Bankruptcy Amendments and Federal Judgeship Act of 1984 went into effect on 10 July 1984. This act addresses the problems presented by the *Northern Pipeline* opinion by restructuring and redefining the bankruptcy court system and its jurisdiction. In addition, it makes a number of substantive changes to the Bankruptcy Reform Act and its coverage.

Under the new law, bankruptcy judges are still appointed for a term of 14 years, and their salary is still established by Congress. However, since the tenure and the salary both are established by statute and are subject to changes by the legislature, the bankruptcy judges are still not Article III judges, the original problem addressed by the court in *Northern Pipeline*. (Article III [federal] judges are appointed "during good behavior," i.e., for life, if the judge so desires. In addition, the compensation of Article III judges "shall not be diminished during their continuance in office."[2]) The appointments are made by the U.S. court of appeals in which the district court is located from a slate of nominees recommended by the judicial councils of each circuit. Only persons who apply to the judicial council for a judgeship may be considered for recommendation by the court of appeals. The judicial council is to submit a list of three nominees for each judgeship. The court of appeals will then either select one of the nominees or reject all of them and request a new submission.

Since these bankruptcy judges are not Article III judges, the bankruptcy courts have only limited jurisdiction under the law. The 1984 Bankruptcy Amendments grant exclusive and original jurisdiction in all bankruptcy matters to the U.S. district court. The district court may then refer any or all such cases to the bankruptcy court for adjudication. After referral to the bankruptcy court, however, the case may be withdrawn by the district court, either on its own motion or on the motion of any party to the proceedings, "for cause shown."

THE BANKRUPTCY REFORM ACT OF 1994

The Bankruptcy Reform Act of 1994 made several substantial changes in the bankruptcy law. It also created a National Bankruptcy Review Commission charged with studying issues and problems related to bankruptcy.

The National Bankruptcy Review Commission was composed of nine members, and it was designed to be as nonpartisan as possible. Three of the members, including the chair of the commission, were appointed by the president. The speaker of the house, the president pro tempore of the Senate, the minority leader of the House, and the minority leader of the Senate each named one member. The chief justice of the Supreme Court named the remaining two members. It had an initial term of two years and seven months, with the initial appointments to be made within 60 days after enactment of the bill. The initial commission's term expired in July 1997. The commission prepared and submitted its report to Congress. One of its strongest recommendations called for some unification of the exemption provisions available to debtors, either by eliminating state "opt-out" provisions, eliminating state exemptions, or putting a limit on exemptions. (The commission ceased to exist on 19 November 1997 [Public Law 103-394], but its recommendations are likely to influence the next revisions or amendments to the bankruptcy code.) There were numerous substantive changes to the Bankruptcy Code included in the Bankruptcy Reform Act of 1994. Among the more important are the following:

- Compensation for trustees is now set at "25 percent of the first $5,000 or less, 10 percent of any amount in excess of $5,000 but not in excess of $50,000, 5 percent on any amount in excess of $50,000 but not in excess of $1,000,000, and reasonable compensation not to exceed 3 percent of such moneys in excess of $1,000,000."[3]
- The debt limits for Chapter 13 debtors is increased from $450,000 to $1,000,000, and the dollar amounts for involuntary petitions, priorities, and exemptions are doubled.[4]
- Future adjustments for these dollar amounts for the future are included in the act on a three-year cycle, beginning 1 April 1998. These adjustments will be based on the Consumer Price Index for All Urban Consumers published by the Department of Labor, rounded to the nearest $25 amount.
- Purchase money security interests are given a 20-day grace period for perfection to reflect the majority state law provisions now in effect, an increase from the 10-day grace period previously allowed.
- Independent sales representatives are classified as employees and are entitled to the same priority status as employees, for purposes of claims against the debtor.
- Limited liability partnerships are treated in bankruptcy as they would be treated in a nonbankruptcy proceeding (limited liability partnerships are discussed in Business Organizations in Chapters 34 to 36), reflecting the growing recognition of this relatively new form of business.
- Debtors who are represented by an attorney may reaffirm debts without the need for a separate reaffirmation hearing as required under the provisions of the original Bankruptcy Reform Act.
- The nondischargeability of "loading up" debts is triggered at $1,000 rather than $500.
- Bankruptcy fraud is now recognized as a crime. This crime involves filing a petition or a document or making a false representation with the intent to devise a scheme to defraud under Chapter 11.
- A streamlined treatment is provided for small businesses (businesses involved in commercial or business activities other than solely real estate and with liquidated debts of $2,000,000 or less) seeking relief under Chapter 11.
- Small business investment companies are not eligible for relief in bankruptcy.

An initial viewing of the Bankruptcy Reform Act of 1994 seemed to provide a balancing of the interests of the debtors and the creditors, providing a more workable structure than the previous coverage. However, in practice, creditors do not seem to be receiving the benefits envisioned in drafting the act. This is one of the leading factors behind the push for a *new* reform act.

STRAIGHT BANKRUPTCY: A CHAPTER 7 LIQUIDATION PROCEEDING

To many people, the term *bankruptcy* means just one thing—a liquidation of the debtor's assets in order for the debtor to obtain a discharge from his or her debts. This form of bankruptcy carries negative connotations to many people. Some view a straight bankruptcy, or a Chapter 7 proceeding, as an admission of failure. Rather than seeing it as a "fresh start" for an "honest debtor," they feel that it is a "cop-out" by a "deadbeat." Times are changing, however. More and more people are beginning to realize that a liquidation is a financial and legal option designed to help a person who has been flooded by debt. The stigma of failure is being removed, and the number of Chapter 7 proceedings increases annually. For example, in 1990, there were 725,484 bankruptcy petitions filed, of which 515,337 were for relief under Chapter 7, and 199,186 were for relief under Chapter 13. By 1996, the number of petitions filed had increased to 1,042,110, of which 712,129 were for relief under Chapter 7, and 316,024 were for relief under Chapter 13.[5] Nonbusiness bankruptcies comprised 91 percent of the petitions in 1990, and 95 percent of the petitions in 1996.[6]

There are two types of Chapter 7 bankruptcies: voluntary and involuntary. *Voluntary* bankruptcies are bankruptcies initiated by the debtor. *Involuntary* bankruptcies are bankruptcies initiated by some combination of creditors of a debtor. The overwhelming majority of bankruptcy petitions are filed voluntarily by the debtor.[7] Any person, firm, or corporation may file a voluntary bankruptcy petition under Chapter 7, with five exceptions:

1. Railroads
2. Government units
3. Banks
4. Savings and loan associations
5. Insurance companies

In addition, any person, firm, or corporation may be subjected to an involuntary petition under Chapter 7, with seven exceptions:

1. Railroads
2. Government units
3. Banks
4. Savings and loan associations
5. Insurance companies
6. Farmers (a *farmer* is defined as an individual who received more than 80 percent of gross income in the prior year from the operation of a farm that he or she owns and operates)
7. Charitable corporations

Filing Fees

The filing fees connected to the various bankruptcy chapters are established by law. For example, a Chapter 7 proceeding has a filing fee of $130 plus a $45 administration fee. For Chapter 11 proceedings, the filing fee is $800. Chapter 13 requires a $130 filing fee plus a $30 administrative fee.

Voluntary Bankruptcy Petition

The debtor who files a voluntary petition does not need to be insolvent. A debtor who desires to eliminate his or her debts can file the petition, consent to the court's jurisdiction, and receive a discharge. In theory, a debtor with $1 million in cash and total debts of $250 can file for bankruptcy. In practice, such an event is extremely unlikely.

The 1984 Bankruptcy Amendments made a major substantive change in this area. Prior to the 1984 act, bankruptcy was viewed as a right of the debtor, and the needs of the debtor or the creditors were not considered by the court. As a result, some creditors alleged that some debtors were abusing the bankruptcy system, using Chapter 7 proceedings to eliminate unsecured debts they could have repaid in full. The law now permits the bankruptcy judge to hold a hearing designed to determine the need of the debtor for the relief being sought. If the judge feels that granting the relief will be a substantial abuse of Chapter 7, the petition can be dismissed.

In addition, the law requires that all debtors be made aware of the alternative provisions of Chapter 13 repayment plans before they are allowed to file a Chapter 7 petition. By so doing, it is hoped that more debtors will elect a repayment plan rather than a liquidation procedure. This will work to the benefit of the creditors and may also help a number of debtors by allowing them to retain more of their assets than they would under a Chapter 7 liquidation.

Involuntary Bankruptcy Petition

Often a debtor will get deeply in debt and try to avoid bankruptcy. When this happens, the creditors may decide to petition the debtor into bankruptcy against his or her will. They do so by initiating an involuntary bankruptcy proceeding.

If a debtor does not fall within one of the groups exempted from involuntary petitions, the debtor is potentially subject to an involuntary petition. The vast majority of debtors in this country do not fit into one of these exceptions. That does not make most debtors subject to an involuntary petition automatically, however. The creditors who file the petition must show that three criteria—one related to the conduct of the debtor, one to the number of creditors of the debtor, and one to the unsecured debt of the debtor—are satisfied before they may file an involuntary petition against the debtor.

Debtor Conduct. The petitioning creditors must establish that the debtor is "guilty" of one of two acts: either the debtor is not paying debts as they become due, or the debtor appointed a receiver or made a general assignment for the benefit of the creditors within the 120 days that preceded the filing of the petition. (Under the latter test, the receiver or assignee must have taken possession of the debtor's property.)

Number of Petitioning Creditors. The petition filed with the court must be signed by the "proper number" of creditors. The proper number of creditors for a particular debtor is determined by the total number of creditors the debtor has. If the debtor has a total of 12 creditors or more, at least 3 creditors must sign the petition. Only 1 creditor must sign the petition if the debtor has fewer than 12 creditors, although more may choose to sign the petition.

Debt Requirement. The creditors who file the petition must have an aggregate claim against the debtor of at least $10,000 that is neither secured nor contingent. This means that a debtor with less than $10,000 in general unsecured debts may not be involuntarily petitioned into bankruptcy. It also explains why more than the minimum number of creditors (from the "number of petitioning creditors" requirement) will often need to sign the petition.

The following example shows one problem that petitioning creditors may face.

Bob has seven creditors. He has made no payments to any of them for four months. He owes Ralph, one of the creditors, $6,000, of which $2,000 is secured by collateral. Ralph wants to file an involuntary petition against Bob. Since Bob is not paying his debts as they come due, the "conduct" requirement is satisfied. Since Ralph has less than 12 creditors, only one of his creditors must sign the petition to satisfy the "number" requirement. However, unless one or more of Bob's other creditors—with a (combined claim) of at least $6,000 in unsecured debt—will join Ralph on a petition, Ralph cannot institute an involuntary petition. His unsecured claim of $4,000 does not satisfy the "debt" requirement.

In this example, Ralph also needs to exercise care prior to filing the petition. If a debtor is involuntarily petitioned into bankruptcy, the debtor may deny that he is

---

YOU BE THE JUDGE

WHEN IS A DEFECTIVE FILING MADE IN BAD FAITH?

Crusader Bank filed an involuntary bankruptcy petition against R & A Business Associates, Inc. R & A objected to the petition, avowing that it had more than 11 qualifying debtors, so that the petition as filed was inadequate. Before the court ruled on the matter, another 9 creditors of R & A filed a motion to join in the petition. R & A objected to their joinder, asserting that a defective petition must be dismissed. R & A also alleged that Crusader Bank had filed the petition in bad faith, thus justifying a dismissal of the petition on the ground of bad faith even if an adequate number of creditors joined in signing the petition. Crusader Bank denied that it filed the petition in bad faith.

This case has been brought in *your* court. How will *you* resolve the issues?[8]

BUSINESS CONSIDERATIONS Should a creditor planning to file an involuntary bankruptcy petition against a debtor have a policy of always seeking at least two other creditors to join in the petition to avoid a challenge for improper filing? What should a creditor do before filing an involuntary bankruptcy petition against a debtor?

ETHICAL CONSIDERATIONS Is it ethical to file an involuntary bankruptcy petition against a debtor, hoping that additional creditors will join the petition if the debtor challenges it? What ethical issues does this raise?

SOURCE: *BCD News and Comment* (6 April 1999), LRP Publications, http://www.lexis-nexis.com/.

bankrupt and request a trial on this issue. A debtor who wins such a trial can collect damages from the creditors who signed the petition. (It is interesting to note that there is supposed to be no stigma attached to a person who seeks a "fresh start" in bankruptcy, yet a person who successfully challenges an involuntary petition is entitled to damages, at least in part, on the basis of defamation.)

THE BANKRUPTCY PROCEEDING

Once a petition is filed, the judge will issue an order for relief (unless the debtor files an answer denying bankruptcy and demands a trial). At this point, the proceeding is in motion, and it will continue until the final orders are entered. Upon entering the order for relief, the judge promptly appoints a trustee from a panel of private trustees. This trustee takes possession of—and legal title to—the debtor's property and begins the administration of the debtor's estate. (At the first creditors' meeting, a new trustee may be selected. If creditors having collective claims of at least 20 percent of the unsecured claims against the debtor request an election, the creditors can select a "permanent" trustee. If no such request is made, the court-appointed trustee serves throughout the proceedings.)

The Trustee

The *trustee* is the key figure in the bankruptcy proceeding. The trustee is the representative of the debtor's estate and will attempt to preserve this estate to protect the interests of the unsecured creditors. The estate that the trustee preserves is made up of all the property the debtor has when the case is begun and any property the debtor acquires within the 180 days following the petition-filing date, reduced by any collateral removed from the estate and by the exempt assets of the debtor. The trustee must gather all of these assets, liquidate them, and generally handle the creditors' claims. The trustee also raises objections to the granting of a discharge if the debtor gives cause to do so. The trustee may be helped by a creditors' committee, a group of at least 3 and at most 11 unsecured creditors who consult with the trustee as needed.

The trustee is responsible for representing the interests of the general unsecured creditors in the bankruptcy petition. While the trustee takes legal title to the debtor's estate, the creditors have equitable title—this means that the trustee possesses the estate for the benefit of the creditors. The trustee's job is difficult and demanding. Under the Bankruptcy Act, both individuals and corporations may serve as trustees, although corporations need to be authorized to perform this function in their corporate charter. In order for an individual to serve as trustee, he or she must be "competent to perform the duties of a trustee." The trustee must also satisfy a residency requirement by residing or having an office in the district where the case is pending or in an adjacent district. Under current bankruptcy law, the U.S. attorney general prescribes qualifications for appointment to a panel of trustees. The U.S. trustee sets up such a panel for the bankruptcy court; the bankruptcy judge appoints the trustee in each bankruptcy case from this panel. The appointment of a trustee is basically a mechanical chore, with the trustees appointed on a rotational basis. This method of appointment has virtually eliminated a common complaint under the prior law—that the trustees were appointed by friendly judges, were too close to the judges in too many instances, and were not always qualified for the role.

Interestingly, the 1994 bankruptcy bill restored the former method for appointing trustees in Chapter 11 proceedings, to an extent. In a Chapter 11 proceeding, any interested party may call for a meeting of the creditors in order to elect a trustee, provided the meeting is called within 30 days of the court's appointment of an operating trustee. There is some expectation that similar provisions will be enacted regarding Chapter 7 trustees in the near future.

Automatic Stay Provision

The filing of a petition in bankruptcy operates as an *automatic stay*, placing any legal actions involving the debtor "on hold." The automatic stay operates to stop lawsuits instituted by the debtor, allowing the trustee the opportunity to settle these cases, bringing any judgment into the bankruptcy estate. The automatic stay also works against creditors who are involved in any legal actions against the debtor. The creditors must suspend any legal actions already commenced and must delay filing any new actions, pending the outcome of the bankruptcy proceedings. Similarly, the creditors may not initiate any repossession actions against the assets of the debtor. This automatic stay provision is designed to ensure that all the creditors are afforded equitable treatment under the bankruptcy proceedings by preventing any one creditor from gaining an advantage through his or her actions at the expense of the other creditors.

The Creditors' Meeting

The court will call for a meeting of the creditors within a reasonable time of the order for relief. The debtor, the trustee, and the creditors—but not the judge—will all attend this meeting. The debtor is expected to provide schedules of anticipated income, assets and their locations, and debts and liabilities at that time, and to submit to an examination by the creditors concerning the debtor's assets, liabilities, and anything else the creditors feel is important. Although the debtor may not like it, it is best to cooperate fully: A refusal to cooperate may result in a denial of discharge. At this first creditors' meeting, the trustee is required to orally advise the debtor as to the possible repercussions from filing for bankruptcy relief and to explain about other bankruptcy chapters that the debtor might want to utilize in lieu of a Chapter 7 liquidation proceeding.

29.1 | FINANCE/ MANUFACTURING

A CIT SUPPLIER FILES FOR CHAPTER 7 BANKRUPTCY

One of the firms that supplies component parts to CIT missed a delivery deadline recently, causing CIT to fall behind in its production schedule. After several phone calls to the supplier, repeated promises to deliver the component, and repeated failures by the supplier to keep these promises or to honor the terms of the contract, CIT decided that it needed to sue the supplier. Accordingly, Amy Chen filed the complaint with the appropriate state court, seeking damages from the supplier for breach of the contract. This morning, Tom received a fax from Amy informing him that the supplier has filed a voluntary petition for relief under Chapter 7 of the Bankruptcy Act. Tom asks you what effect this will have on the lawsuit. What will you tell him?

BUSINESS CONSIDERATIONS Suppose the trustee in bankruptcy offers CIT a settlement to their lawsuit, admitting that the debtor did, in fact, breach and agreeing to pay 50 percent of the amount sought in damages. What should the firm do in this situation? What other alternatives does it have?

ETHICAL CONSIDERATION Assume a business knows it has breached a contract and that it will be held liable for damages in a lawsuit. Assume further that the business is aware of the automatic stay provisions of bankruptcy law. Should the business file a bankruptcy petition in order to halt the lawsuit and then attempt to settle the suit for a substantially lesser amount of money than it would have lost had the case been heard?

The Debtor

The debtor also has certain duties to perform. The debtor must file a relatively detailed series of schedules that are intended to reveal his or her financial position so that (1) the bankruptcy court can properly evaluate the need for relief, and (2) the interests of the various creditors can be protected. The debtor must provide a list of creditors, both secured and unsecured, the address of each creditor, and the amount of debt owed to each. The debtor also must provide a schedule of his or her financial affairs and a listing of all property owned, even if that property will be claimed as an exempt asset. Finally, the debtor must provide a list of current income and expenses. This list may show that the debtor should be in a Chapter 13 repayment plan rather than a Chapter 7 liquidation proceeding. If it does, the court may, on its own motion, dismiss the Chapter 7 proceeding following a hearing and encourage the debtor to refile under Chapter 13. However, the law also carries with it a presumption in favor of the debtor. The debtor is presumed to be entitled to receive the order of relief for whatever chapter was chosen by the debtor. The schedules are prepared by the debtor under oath and signed. Knowingly submitting false information in these schedules is a crime under the bankruptcy law.

The debtor also must cooperate fully with the trustee and surrender all property to the trustee. Finally, the debtor must attend any and all hearings and comply with all orders of the court. If this is done, a discharge will normally result.

Secured Creditors

Once the debtor has selected those assets to be exempted for a "fresh start," the trustee must communicate with the secured creditors concerning their status. Each secured creditor must make a selection. Secured creditors may elect to take their collateral in full satisfaction of their claims; dispose of the collateral and surrender any surplus to the trustee to be included in the bankruptcy estate; dispose of the collateral and participate as unsecured creditors to the extent they are not satisfied by the collateral; or have the trustee dispose of the collateral, paying the secured creditor the proceeds realized (up to the debt amount) and allowing the creditor to participate as an unsecured creditor for any balance owed.

Exemptions

The debtor can exempt some assets from the trustee's liquidation. The exempted assets are intended to provide the foundation for the "fresh start" bankruptcy grants to

---

29.2 | FINANCE

CALL-IMAGE TECHNOLOGY

PERFECTED SECURITY INTEREST

One of CIT's early customers has recently been experiencing financial difficulties. As a result, this firm has not been paying all of its bills as they come due, although the business has been making its regularly scheduled payments to CIT in a generally timely manner. CIT has learned that the unsecured creditors of this business are planning to file an involuntary bankruptcy petition against the business, throwing it into a Chapter 7 proceeding. CIT has a perfected security interest in the Call-Image inventory in the possession of this debtor. Dan asks you what options are available to CIT if the unsecured creditors decide to proceed with the involuntary petition. What will you tell him?

BUSINESS CONSIDERATION Suppose one of the credit customers of a business faces a bankruptcy proceeding. What factors should the business consider when deciding whether to retain its security interest and opt out of the bankruptcy proceeding or to release its security interest and participate in the bankruptcy proceeding as an unsecured general creditor?

ETHICAL CONSIDERATIONS Assume that a secured creditor of a firm undergoing a Chapter 7 bankruptcy has a security interest in the majority of the debtor's nonexempt assets. Is it unethical to retain the security interest, thereby reducing the amount paid to each of the unsecured creditors while maximizing its own recovery when the proceedings are completed? Would it be more ethical to release the security interest, thus increasing the payment to each of the other unsecured creditors but reducing the amount realized by the formerly secured creditor?

those honest debtors who successfully complete the bankruptcy proceeding and receive a discharge. This exemption is, surprisingly, governed to a significant extent by state statutes, which determine what the debtor is allowed to exempt. If state law permits, the debtor may elect to take *either* the state exemptions *or* the federal exemptions. If no such choice is allowed by state law, the debtor must take the state exemptions. Under no circumstances may the debtor take both sets of exemptions.

Thirty-six states have elected the override provision, requiring the debtor to take the state exemptions and prohibiting him or her from using the federal exemptions. In addition, even if the debtor is in one of the 14 states that allow the choice of either the federal or the state exemptions, another limitation has been imposed by the 1984 Bankruptcy Amendments. In a joint filing, both the husband and the wife must select the same exemptions, either state or federal. They no longer will be allowed to select the exemptions individually, allowing one spouse to take the federal exemptions and the other to select the state exemptions.

Certain types of property are exempt under most state statutes. Typically, a debtor who elects (or is required) to take the state exemptions will be able to retain the following types of assets for his or her fresh start:

- Some cash (the amount varies from state to state)
- Residence or homestead
- Clothing
- Tools of the trade
- Insurance
- A cemetery plot
- An automobile (the value varies from state to state, as do the criteria)
- Funds invested in a retirement plan
- Jewelry (the value varies from state to state, although wedding and engagement rings are frequently exempt without regard to value)
- Heirlooms
- Furniture and household items

In addition, the debtor is allowed to exempt some benefits for public policy reasons:

- Veteran's benefits
- Social security benefits
- Unemployment compensation benefits
- Disability benefits
- Alimony

The federal exemptions, as provided for under the Bankruptcy Reform Act, allow the debtor to exempt the following property from the proceeding if state law allows the debtor to select the federal exemptions:

1. The debtor's aggregate interest in real property or personal property that the debtor or a dependent of the debtor uses as a residence, up to $15,000.
2. If the "aggregate interest" in the debtor's residence is less than $15,000, the unused portion of the $15,000 in a joint petition or $7,500 in an individual petition may be used as a "wild card," exempting anything the debtor desires.
3. The debtor's interest in one automobile, up to $2,400.

4. The debtor's interest in household furnishings, household goods, wearing apparel, appliances, books, animals, crops, or musical instruments primarily held for personal use of the debtor, up to $400 in value per item and up to $8,000 aggregate.
5. The debtor's aggregate interest in items of jewelry, up to $1,000.
6. The debtor's aggregate interest in any tools of the debtor's trade, including books, up to $1,500.
7. The debtor's aggregate interest in any other property, up to $800.
8. Any unmatured life insurance policies owned by the debtor.
9. Professionally prescribed health aids.
10. The debtor's right to receive certain benefits, such as social security, veteran's benefits, disability or unemployment benefits, alimony, child support, and some pension or annuity payments.
11. The debtor's right to receive—or property traceable to—any awards under victim's reparation laws, some wrongful death benefits, some life insurance payments, recoveries from bodily injury claims, and payments of the loss of future earnings. (Several of these are limited to the amount that is reasonably necessary to support the debtor and/or any dependents of the debtor. The bodily injury payments are limited to $15,000, excluding pain and suffering.)

The Bankruptcy Reform Act also permits a debtor to convert goods from non-exempt classes to exempt classes before filing the bankruptcy petition. In addition, if there is a lien on, or security interest attached to, otherwise exempt property, the debtor can redeem it—which automatically exempts it—by paying off the lien-holding creditor.

Allowable Claims

Once the permanent trustee has assumed control of the estate and the exempt property has been removed from the estate, the serious business of bankruptcy begins. Those claims of creditors that are allowable must be filed. Only allowable debts may participate in the distribution of the estate. Allowable claims may be filed by the debtor, a creditor, or even the trustee. But they must be filed within six months of the first creditors' meeting.

Nearly every debt that existed before the order for relief will be allowed in the bankruptcy. There are four major exceptions to this statement. Two of these four debts are not allowable:

1. Claims that would be unenforceable against the debtor, such as contracts based on fraud or duress
2. Claims for interest that are figured beyond the petition date, since interest may no longer accrue once a petition is filed

The other two are not fully allowable but are partially allowable:

3. Damages based on a lease violation or termination, to some extent (the landlord can claim a debt only up to the greater of one year's rent or 15 percent of the balance of the lease, with a three-year maximum, plus any unpaid rent already due and payable)
4. Damages based on breach of an employment contract, if those damages exceed one year's compensation, plus unpaid wages due and payable

Recovery of Property

While administering a debtor's estate, a trustee may discover that the debtor committed certain improper actions. A trustee who discovers such conduct is obligated to recover the transferred property for the benefit of the unsecured creditor. These improper acts fall into two major categories: voidable preferences and fraudulent conveyances.

Voidable Preferences. A *voidable preference* is a payment made by a debtor to one or a few creditors at the expense of the other creditors in that particular creditor class. This is not as complicated as it may seem at first glance. A transfer is deemed a preference and therefore voidable if all the following five conditions are met:

1. The transfer benefits a creditor.
2. The transfer covers a preexisting debt.
3. The debtor is insolvent at the time of the transfer. (A debtor is presumed to be insolvent during the 90 days preceding the date of the petition; this presumption is rebuttable by the debtor.)
4. The transfer is made during the 90 days preceding the petition date.
5. The transfer gives the creditor who receives it a greater percentage of the creditor's claim than fellow creditors will receive as a result of the transfer.

A transfer is not deemed a preference if it fits any one of the following tests:

1. The transfer is for a new obligation, as opposed to a preexisting debt.
2. The transfer is made in the ordinary course of business.
3. The transfer involves a purchase-money security interest.
4. The transfer is a payment on a fully secured claim.
5. The transfer is for normal payments made to creditors within 90 days prior to the petition, if the payments total less than $600 per creditor.

The following case addresses the issue of voidable preferences. The bankruptcy that formed the basis for the case was initially filed under Chapter 7, although the ultimate disposition of the case was under Chapter 13. Nevertheless, the resolution of the voidable preference issue is instructive under any chapter of the Bankruptcy Code.

29.1

FINANCIAL SERVICES, INC. V. FINK

522 U.S. 211 (1998)

FACTS Although certain transfers made before the filing of a petition in bankruptcy may be avoided as impermissibly preferential, a trustee may not so displace a security interest for a loan used to acquire the encumbered property if, among other things, the security interest is "perfected on or before 20 days after the debtor receives possession of such property." . . . On August 17, 1994, Diane Beasley purchased a 1994 Ford and gave petitioner, Fidelity Financial Services, Inc., a promissory note for the purchase price, secured by the new car. Twenty-one days later, on September 7, 1994, Fidelity mailed the application necessary to perfect its security interest addressed to the Missouri Department of Revenue . . . Two months after that, Beasley sought relief under Chapter 7 of the Bankruptcy Code. After the proceeding had been converted to one under Chapter 13, respondent, Richard V. Fink, the trustee of Beasley's bankruptcy estate, moved to set aside

continued

29.1

FINANCIAL SERVICES, INC. V. FINK, *continued*
522 U.S. 211 (1998)

Fidelity's security interest. He argued that the lien was a voidable preference, the enabling loan exception being inapposite because Fidelity had failed to perfect its interest within 20 days after Beasley received the car. Fidelity responded that Missouri law treats a lien on a motor vehicle as having been "perfected" on the date of its creation (in this case, within the 20-day period), if the creditor files the necessary documents within 30 days after the debtor takes possession . . . The Bankruptcy Court set aside the lien as a voidable preference, holding that Missouri's relation-back provision could not extend the twenty-day perfection period imposed by § 547(c)(3)(B) . . . Fidelity appealed to the United States District Court for the Western District of Missouri, which affirmed on substantially the same grounds, as did the Court of Appeals for the Eighth Circuit, holding a transfer to be perfected "when the transferee takes the last step required by state law to perfect its security interest." . . . We granted certiorari . . . to resolve a conflict among the Circuits over the question when a transfer is "perfected" under § 547(c)(3)(B) . . .

ISSUE Whether a creditor may invoke this "enabling loan" exception if it performs the acts necessary to perfect its security interest more than 20 days after the debtor receives the property, but within a relation-back or grace period provided by the otherwise applicable state law.

HOLDING No. A transfer of a security interest is "perfected" on the date that the secured party has completed the steps necessary to perfect its interest, so that a creditor may invoke the enabling loan exception only by satisfying state law perfection requirements within the 20-day period provided by the federal statute.

REASONING Without regard to whether Fidelity's lien is a preference under § 547(b), Fink cannot avoid the lien if it falls within the enabling loan exception of § 547(c)(3), one requirement of which is that the transfer of the interest securing the lien be "perfected on or before 20 days after the debtor receives possession." . . . Perfection turns on the definition provided by § 547(e)(1)(B), that "a transfer of . . . property other than real property is perfected when a creditor on a simple contract cannot acquire a judicial lien that is

superior to the interest of the transferee." Like the Courts of Appeals that have adopted its position . . . Fidelity sees in subsection (c)(3)(B) not only a federal guarantee that a creditor will have 20 days to act, but also a reflection of state law that deems perfection within a statutory grace or relation-back period to be perfection as of the creation of the underlying security interest. Under Missouri law, for example, a "lien or encumbrance on a motor vehicle . . . is perfected by the delivery [of specified documents] to the director of revenue," . . . but the date of the lien's perfection is "as of the time of its creation if the delivery of the aforesaid to the director of revenue is completed within thirty days thereafter, otherwise as of the time of the delivery." . . . Thus, Fidelity contends that although it delivered the required documents more than 20 days after Beasley received the car, its lien must be treated as perfected on the day of its creation because it delivered the papers within the 30 days allowed by state law to qualify for the relation-back advantage. If this is sound reasoning, Fidelity's lien was perfected on August 17, 1994, the very day that Beasley drove away in her Ford, and Fidelity may invoke § 547(c)(3)'s enabling loan exception. The assumption that the term "perfected" as used in subsection (c)(3)(B) and defined in subsection (e)(1)(B) may refer to the relation-back date is not to be made so easily, however. It is quite certain, to begin with, that in the relevant context Congress sometimes used the word "perfection" to mean the legal conclusion that for such purposes as calculating priorities perfection of a lien should be treated as if it had occurred on a particular date, and sometimes used it to refer to the acts necessary to support that conclusion. Section 546(b)(1)(A) speaks of state laws that permit "perfection . . . to be effective . . . before the date of perfection." . . . The distinction implicit in speaking of "perfection" antecedent to the "date of perfection" shows that Congress was thinking about the difference between the legal conclusion that may be entailed by applying a relation-back rule and, on the other hand, the acts taken to trigger an application of the rule. Knowing that Congress understood "perfection" in these two different senses, one can see how Fidelity's construction of § 547(e)(1)(B) is a poor fit with the text. Although Fidelity and two Courts of Appeals have thought this provision means that a transfer is perfected as of whatever date an enabling creditor

29.1

FINANCIAL SERVICES, INC. V. FINK, *continued*
522 U.S. 211 (1998)

could claim in a priority fight with a contract creditor armed with a judicial lien, the statute does not speak in such terms. Rather, it says that a transfer is perfected "When" a contract creditor "cannot acquire" a superior lien. "When" and "cannot acquire" are ostensibly straightforward references to time and action in the real world, not tip-offs (like the terms "as if" and "deemed") that the clock is being turned back in some legal universe. A creditor "can" acquire such a lien at any time until the secured party performs the acts sufficient to perfect its interest. Such a lien would, of course, lose its priority if, during the relation-back period, the secured party performed those acts; such a possibility does not mean that a contract creditor "cannot" acquire such a lien, however, but merely that its superiority may be fleeting.

Not until the secured party actually performs the final act that will perfect its interest can other creditors be foreclosed conclusively from obtaining a superior lien. It is only then that they "cannot" acquire such a lien. Thus, the terms of § 547(e)(1)(B) apparently imply that a transfer is "perfected" only when the secured party has done all the acts required to perfect its interest, not at the moment as of which state law may retroactively deem that perfection

effective . . . In light of this history, we see no basis to say that subsequent amendments removing references to state law options had the counterintuitive effect of deferring to such options even beyond what the old law would have done. In short, the text, structure, and history of the preference provisions lead to the understanding that a creditor may invoke the enabling loan exception of § 547(c)(3) only by acting to perfect its security interest within 20 days after the debtor takes possession of its property. Accordingly, we affirm the judgment of the Court of Appeals for the Eighth Circuit. It is so ordered.

BUSINESS CONSIDERATION Should a business that regularly makes secured consumer loans have a policy to ensure that its perfection methods satisfy both state laws and bankruptcy provisions? Why?

ETHICAL CONSIDERATIONS Is it ethical for a creditor to seek a priority under state law that it would not enjoy under bankruptcy law? Is it ethical for bankruptcy law to negate priorities established under state law?

Fraudulent Conveyance. A *fraudulent conveyance* is a transfer by a debtor that involves actual or constructive fraud. Actual fraud is involved if the debtor intended to hinder or delay a creditor in recovering a debt. Such a transfer will occur if the debtor transfers assets to a friend or a relative—or hides assets—to prevent any creditors from foreclosing on the assets. Constructive fraud is involved when the debtor sells an asset for inadequate consideration and as a result of the sale becomes insolvent or if the debtor is already insolvent at the time of the unreasonable sale. It is also deemed constructive fraud to engage in a business that is undercapitalized. Any fraudulent conveyance made during the year preceding the petition may be set aside by the trustee under federal law. In addition, some state statutes permit the avoidance of such conveyances during the preceding two to five years. The trustee uses the time period that most strongly favors the creditors.

Distribution of Assets

Once the trustee has gathered and liquidated all available assets and admitted all allowable claims, the estate is distributed to the creditors. The Bankruptcy Reform Act contains a mandatory priority list of debts. Each class of creditors takes its turn, and no class may receive any payments until all higher-priority classes are paid in

29.3 | FINANCE

CALL-IMAGE TECHNOLOGY

FRAUDULENT CONVEYANCE OR GOOD DEAL?

Thirty days ago, CIT purchased some equipment from a firm that had supplied it with equipment in the past. The firm that sold the equipment to CIT contacted Tom with an extremely good offer for the equipment, and Tom quickly accepted. The family just learned that the firm they purchased the equipment from has been involuntarily petitioned into bankruptcy and that the trustee appointed to handle the bankruptcy is investigating all sales made by the company in the past 90 days. The trustee believes that several of the company's sales were fraudulent conveyances, with the selling price well below fair market value. Tom does not believe that he did anything wrong in accepting the offer to buy the equipment, but he is not sure what evidence the trustee would need in order to establish that a fraudulent conveyance occurred. He has asked you for advice. What will you tell him?

BUSINESS CONSIDERATION Should a business accept an offer that looks "too good to be true" without investigating the reason for it, or should the business just be grateful for the opportunity and try to take advantage of it? Why?

ETHICAL CONSIDERATIONS What ethical issues are raised when a buyer is offered a price that seems unreasonably low? Is it ethical to accept such an offer without investigating the circumstances behind it?

full. All creditors within a given class will be paid on a pro rata basis until either the claims are paid in full or the estate is exhausted.

The highest priority of claims is the expense of handling the estate. All the costs incurred by the trustee in preserving and administering the bankruptcy must be paid first.

The next class of claims involves debts that arise in the ordinary course of business between the date the petition is filed and the date the trustee is appointed.

The third and fourth priorities are interrelated. Priority 3 is wages earned by employees of the debtor during the 90 days preceding the petition, up to a maximum of $4,000 per employee. Priority 4 is unpaid contributions by an employer to employee benefit plans, if they arise during the 180 days before the petition, up to $4,000 per employee. However, these claims are reduced by any claims paid in Priority 3. Thus, the maximum priority for each employee is a total of $4,000. Any claims in excess of this amount go to the bottom of the list.

The fifth priority is given to grain farmers who have a claim against the owner or operator of a grain storage facility and to U.S. fishermen who have a claim against individuals who operate a fish storage or fish-processing facility. In either case, the priority is limited to $4,000 per individual creditor.

The sixth priority is claims by consumers for goods or services paid for but not received. The maximum here is $1,800 per person as a priority, with any surplus claim going to the bottom of the list.

As of 1994, alimony, maintenance agreements or obligations, and child support were granted the next priority, being inserted into the list above obligations owed to the government. This placement reflects the increasing public policy position of "family values" and a desire to help protect spouses or ex-spouses, especially those with children. To further emphasize this change, the payment of alimony, maintenance, or child support is specifically not a voidable preference, nor are such payments subject to the automatic stay provisions of other debts and obligations of the debtor.

The final priority claim is in favor of debts owed to government units. This class consists basically of taxes due during the three years preceding the petition.

After all priority claims are paid, the balance of the estate is used to pay general unsecured creditors. When all unsecured creditors have been paid in full, any monies left are paid to the debtor. Normally, the funds will not cover the general creditor claims, and a pro rata distribution is necessary. This leaves the creditors with less money than they were owed. The debtor must hope for a discharge to make the balance of the claims uncollectible. Exhibit 29.1 summarizes the distribution of proceeds in a Chapter 7 bankruptcy proceeding.

EXHIBIT 29.1 | **Distribution of Proceeds in a Chapter 7 Bankruptcy Proceeding**

Priority 1:   Expenses of the bankruptcy.

If any funds remain,

Priority 2:   Debts arising in the ordinary course of business between the petition date and the date a trustee is appointed (pro rata if necessary).

If any funds remain,

Priority 3:   Wages earned during the 90 days preceding the petition by employees of the debtor but not yet paid, to a maximum of $4,000 per employee (pro rata if necessary).

If any funds remain,

Priority 4:   Fringe benefits earned during the 180 days preceding the petition by employees of the debtor but not yet paid, to a maximum of $4,000 per employee (pro rata if necessary). Priorities 3 and 4 combined cannot exceed $4,000 per employee.

If any funds remain,

Priority 5:   Claims of grain farmers against grain storage facilities, and/or of U.S. fishermen against fish storage or fish-processing facilities, limited to $4,000 per creditor (pro rata if necessary).

If any funds remain,

Priority 6:   Claims by consumers for goods or services paid for but not received, up to $1,800 per consumer (pro rata if necessary).

If any funds remain,

Priority 7:   Claims against the debtor for alimony payments, separate maintenance payments, or child support.

If any funds remain,

Priority 8:   Debts owed to the government, especially for taxes owed for the previous three years.

If any funds remain,

General unsecured creditors: pro rata, together with any excess over the priority claims set out above.

When no funds remain, or when all eight levels have been treated, the court makes a *discharge decision.*

The Discharge Decision

A discharge can be granted only to an individual and only if he or she is an honest debtor. A discharge will be denied if the debtor made a fraudulent conveyance or does not have adequate books and records. In addition, a debtor will be denied a discharge if he or she refuses to cooperate with the court during the proceedings. Furthermore, a discharge will not be granted if a discharge was received during the previous six years. A denial of discharge means that the unpaid portions of any debts continue and are fully enforceable after the proceedings end.

Even if a discharge is granted, some claims are not affected. Under the Bankruptcy Reform Act, certain debts continue to be fully enforceable against the debtor even though the debtor received a discharge. The following 11 major classes of debts are not affected by a discharge:

1. Taxes due to any government unit
2. Loans where the proceeds were used to pay federal taxes
3. Debts that arose because of fraud by the debtor concerning his or her financial condition
4. Claims not listed by the creditors or by the debtor in time for treatment in the proceedings
5. Debts incurred through embezzlement or theft
6. Alimony
7. Child support
8. Liabilities due to malicious torts of the debtor
9. Fines imposed by a government unit
10. Claims that were raised in a previous case in which the debtor did not receive a discharge
11. Student loans, unless the loan is at least five years in arrears

The following case involved a debt based on the fraud of the debtor. While acknowledging the fraud, and the attendant liability faced, the debtor argued that the treble damages attached to the conviction for fraud should be discharged. This Supreme Court's opinion decided the issue, setting a precedent after the circuit courts had divided on the issue.

29.2

COHEN V. DELACRUZ
523 U.S. 213 (1998)

FACTS Petitioner owned several residential properties in and around Hoboken, New Jersey, one of which was subject to a local rent control ordinance. In 1989, the Hoboken Rent Control Administrator determined that petitioner had been charging rents above the levels permitted by the ordinance, and ordered him to refund to the affected tenants, who are respondents in this Court, $31,382.50 in excess rents charged. Petitioner did not comply with the order. Petitioner subsequently filed for relief under Chapter 7 of the Bankruptcy Code, seeking to discharge his debts. The tenants filed an adversary proceeding against petitioner in the Bankruptcy Court, arguing that the debt owed to them arose from rent payments obtained by "actual fraud" and that the debt was therefore nondischargeable under 11 U.S.C. § 523(a)(2)(A). They also sought treble damages and attorney's fees and costs pursuant to the New Jersey Consumer Fraud Act . . . Following a bench trial, the Bankruptcy Court ruled in the tenants' favor . . . The court found that petitioner had committed "actual fraud" . . . and that his conduct amounted to an "unconscionable commercial practice" under the New Jersey Consumer Fraud Act. As a result, the court awarded the tenants treble damages totaling $94,147.50, plus reasonable attorney's fees and costs. Noting that courts had reached conflicting conclusions on whether § 523(a)(2)(A) excepts from discharge punitive damages (such as the treble damages at issue here), the Bankruptcy Court sided with those decisions holding that § 523(a)(2)(A) encompasses all obligations arising out of fraudulent conduct, including both punitive and compensatory damages . . . The District Court affirmed . . . After accepting the finding of the Bankruptcy Court that petitioner had committed fraud under § 523(a)(2)(A) and the New Jersey Consumer Fraud Act, the Court of Appeals turned to whether the treble damages portion of petitioner's liability represents a "debt . . . for money, property, services, or . . . credit, to the extent obtained by . . . actual fraud." . . . The court observed that the term "debt," defined in the Code as a "right to payment," . . . plainly encompasses all liability for fraud, whether in the form of punitive or compensatory damages. And the phrase "to the extent obtained by," the court reasoned, modifies "money, property, services, or . . . credit," and therefore distinguishes not between compensatory and punitive damages awarded for fraud but instead between money or

29.2

COHEN V. DELACRUZ, *continued*
523 U.S. 213 (1998)

property obtained through fraudulent means and money or property obtained through nonfraudulent means . . . Here... the entire award of $94,147.50 (plus attorney's fees and costs) resulted from money obtained through fraud and is therefore nondischargeable . . . We granted certiorari to address the conflict in the lower courts . . . and we now affirm.

ISSUE Whether . . . the Bankruptcy Code bars the discharge of treble damages awarded on account of the debtor's fraudulent acquisition of "money, property, services, or credit," or whether the exception only encompasses the value of the "money, property, services, or credit" the debtor obtains through fraud.

HOLDING That § 523(a)(2)(A) prevents the discharge of all liability arising from fraud, and that an award of treble damages therefore falls within the scope of the exception.

REASONING The Bankruptcy Code has long prohibited debtors from discharging liabilities incurred on account of their fraud, embodying a basic policy animating the Code of affording relief only to an "honest but unfortunate debtor." . . . Section 523(a)(2)(A) continues the tradition, excepting from discharge "any debt . . . for money, property, services, or an extension, renewal, or refinancing of credit, to the extent obtained by . . . false pretenses, a false representation, or actual fraud." The most straightforward reading of § 523(a)(2)(A) is that it prevents discharge of "any debt" respecting "money, property, services, or . . . credit" that the debtor has fraudulently obtained, including treble damages assessed on account of the fraud . . . Moreover, the phrase "to the extent obtained by" . . . does not impose any limitation on the extent to which "any debt" arising from fraud is excepted from discharge. "To the extent obtained by" modifies "money, property, services, or . . . credit"—not "any debt"—so that the exception encompasses "any debt . . . for money, property, services, or . . . credit, to the extent [that the money, property, services, or . . . credit is] obtained by" fraud. Once it is established that specific money or property has been obtained by fraud, however, "any debt" arising therefrom is excepted from discharge. In this case, petitioner received rent payments from respondents for a number of years, of which $31,382.50 was obtained by

fraud. His full liability traceable to that sum—$94,147.50 plus attorney's fees and costs—thus falls within the exception . . . Petitioner submits that § 523(a)(2)(A) excepts from discharge only the portion of the damages award in a fraud action corresponding to the value of the "money, property, services, or . . . credit" the debtor obtained by fraud. The essential premise of petitioner's argument is that a "debt for" money, property, or services obtained by fraud is necessarily limited to the value of the money, property, or services received by the debtor. Petitioner, in this sense, interprets "debt for" . . . to mean "liability on a claim to obtain," i.e., "liability on a claim to obtain the money, property, services, or credit obtained by fraud," thus imposing a restitutionary ceiling on the extent to which a debtor's liability for fraud is nondischargeable. Petitioner's reading of "debt for" . . . however, is at odds with the meaning of the same phrase in parallel provisions . . .When construed in the context of the statute as a whole, then, § 523(a)(2)(A) is best read to prohibit the discharge of any liability arising from a debtor's fraudulent acquisition of money, property, etc., including an award of treble damages for the fraud . . . Limiting the exception to the value of the money or property fraudulently obtained by the debtor could prevent even a compensatory recovery for losses occasioned by fraud . . . As petitioner acknowledges, his gloss . . . would allow the debtor in those situations to discharge any liability for losses caused by his fraud in excess of the amount he initially received, leaving the creditor far short of being made whole. And the portion of a creditor's recovery that exceeds the value of the money, property, etc., fraudulently obtained by the debtor—and that hence would be dischargeable under petitioner's view—might include compensation not only for losses brought about by fraud but also for attorney's fees and costs of suit associated with establishing fraud . . . Those sorts of results would not square with the intent of the fraud exception. As we have observed previously in addressing different issues surrounding the scope of that exception, it is "unlikely that Congress . . . would have favored the interest in giving perpetrators of fraud a fresh start over the interest in protecting victims of fraud." . . . Under New Jersey law, the debt for fraudulently obtaining $31,382.50 in rent payments includes treble damages and attorney's fees and costs, and

continued

29.2

COHEN V. DELACRUZ, *continued*
523 U.S. 213 (1998)

consequently, petitioner's entire debt of $94,147.50 (plus attorney's fees and costs) is nondischargeable in bankruptcy. Accordingly, we affirm the judgment of the Court of Appeals. It is so ordered.

BUSINESS CONSIDERATIONS Might a business enterprise that is facing a conviction for fraud, with a state statute imposing treble damages plus attorney's

fees and costs, look to bankruptcy as a means of avoiding liability for the fraud? Do the provisions preventing such a discharge serve more of a public policy function than a business function?

ETHICAL CONSIDERATION Is it ethical to try to use bankruptcy to obtain a "fresh start" when the primary liability being faced is due to an intentional tort by the debtor?

In addition to these 11 classes of debts, the 1984 Bankruptcy Amendments addressed the problem of debtors who "load up" with debts just prior to filing a petition, expecting to use the bankruptcy proceeding to discharge these recently incurred debts. Under the law, any debtor purchases from one creditor of $1,000 or more in luxury goods or services that are incurred within 40 days of the petition are presumed to be nondischargeable. Similarly, any cash advances of $1,000 or more that are received from one creditor within the 20 days prior to the petition are presumed to be nondischargeable. The debtor will have the burden of proof and will have to convince the court that these debts were not fraudulently incurred with the intent of receiving a discharge in order to have these debts discharged. Notice that a discharge is possible but that the debtor has the burden of proof!

In the following case, a creditor claimed that certain debts of the debtor should be classified as "loading up" debts and should not be discharged. See if you agree with the court's decision as to whether these were, in fact, "loading up" debts.

29.3

IN RE POOR
219 B.R. 332 (BKRTCY.ME.1998)

FACTS Plaintiff, Chase Manhattan Bank USA, N.A. ["Chase"], seeks summary judgment on Count I of its § 523(a)(2) complaint against *pro se* debtor Jeannie Poor. Chase asks that judgment be entered declaring that the obligations created by two transactions— a $3,400.00 balance transfer and a $350.00 credit cash withdrawal—are excepted from Poor's Chapter 7 discharge. It argues that the debts come within § 523(a)(2)(C)'s nondischargeability presumption [as "loading up" debts] and that Poor has not effectively rebutted the presumption in her summary judgment response.

Poor applied to Chase Visa for a credit card in May 1997 . . . The application incorporated a "Chase Visa Balance Transfer Form" inviting Poor to "complete this form today to pay off your outstanding balances at a low fixed APR of just 7.9%. You can transfer one, two, or three balances to your new Chase Visa." . . . Poor accepted the invitation when she applied for a Chase Gold Visa account, requesting the transfer of $3,400.00 of debt from her MBNA MasterCard and $2,600.00 from a Choice Visa account . . . In a letter dated June 9, 1997, Chase notified Poor that it had approved her application and had opened her new

29.3

IN RE POOR, *continued*
219 B.R. 332 (BKRTCY.ME.1998)

Gold Visa account with a $7,300.00 credit limit . . . The missive went on to state: "As you requested, we are transferring the following balances to your new account: Payee MBNA America . . . Amount $3,400.00 Check 5000 Status Balance Transferred . . . " Poor claims to have received her Chase gold card on June 17, 1997 . . . Chase effected the $3,400.00 payment to MBNA by a check . . . and that check "cleared" on June 20, 1997. On that date Chase charged $3,400.00 to Poor's Visa account . . . On June 26, 1997, Poor withdrew $350.00 cash on credit through the Chase account . . . Although Poor's medical records are not properly before me, at oral argument Chase's counsel conceded that Poor was involved in a disabling automobile accident on June 8, 1997, and that the injuries she suffered led to unemployment. Poor and her husband filed a joint Chapter 7 petition on August 19, 1997.

ISSUE Did the balance transfer qualify as a "cash advance," and thus as a "loading up" debt under the provisions of the Bankruptcy Code?

HOLDING The balance transfer was not a "cash advance," and did not constitute a "loading up" debt under the provisions of the Bankruptcy Code.

REASONING For the reasons set forth below, I conclude that the $3,400.00 balance transfer is not a "cash advance" within the meaning of § 523(a)(2)(C). Furthermore, the $350.00 withdrawal, standing alone, does not come under § 523(a)(2)(C) because it does not exceed the statutory presumption's $1,000.00 threshold. Thus, Chase's motion for summary judgment is denied. Chase's summary judgment motion was filed shortly after the pretrial conference, accompanied by a statement of uncontested material facts, a supporting memorandum of law, replete with six exhibits and two affidavits—one from a vice president of Chase and the other from Chase's counsel. Chase's motion comports with pertinent rules governing summary judgment practice . . . Notwithstanding my pretrial conference caution to Poor, a *pro se* litigant, that she would be expected to respond to Chase's motion in accordance with pertinent rules and that she would likely have to prepare and file an affidavit to support her position, her response is inadequate. Her rejoinder, entitled "Defendants [sic] Answer to Complaint," is

but a bundle of unverified assertions and unauthenticated documents. It does not comply with the requirements of Fed. R. Civ. P. 56(e) or Me. D. Ct. R. 56 . . .

Chase has the burden of proving that the § 523(a)(2)(C) presumption applies . . . It can obtain summary judgment only if it demonstrates that the $3,400.00 balance transfer and the $350.00 cash withdrawal qualify as § 523(a)(2)(C) transactions. In relevant part, § 523(a)(2)(C) creates a presumption of nondischargeability for "cash advances aggregating more than $1,000 that are extensions of consumer credit under an open end credit plan obtained by an individual debtor on or within 60 days before the order for relief under this title." § 523(a)(2)(C). If the transactions qualify for the presumption, Chase will prevail, given Poor's failure to respond effectively on the summary judgment record. To trigger the presumption, Chase must prove four elements. (1) The transactions must be "cash advances" within the meaning of the statutory subsection. (2) The debts must qualify as "extensions of consumer credit under an open end credit plan." (3) The aggregate amount of the cash advances borrowed by Poor from Chase within the 60 day period must exceed $1,000. (4) Poor's cash advance(s) must be "obtained" no more than 60 days proceeding [sic] the order for relief. § 523(a)(2)(C). Consistent with longstanding bankruptcy law principles, I will narrowly construe § 523(a)(2)(C)'s exception to discharge, favoring Poor's fresh start . . .

The meaning of "cash advance" for § 523(a)(2)(C) purposes is not crystalline. The Code provides no express definition . . . Given the rapid growth and diversification of financial and credit services, the range of transactions that might be assayed to determine their character as § 523(a)(2)(C) "cash advance[s]" is ever-expanding. Chase asserts that Poor's $3,400.00 balance transfer to MBNA was a cash advance because Chase treats such transfers as cash advances internally and under the terms of its cardholder agreement . . . Such a self-serving characterization is not determinative. My application of subsection (C) to the facts before me pivots on the meaning of the words "cash advance." I embark upon the task of discerning its content wary that examining the words in isolation could potentially disserve or

continued

29.3

IN RE POOR, *continued*
219 B.R. 332 (BKRTCY.ME.1998)

distort the statutory design . . . In short, the legislatively-intended meaning of "cash advance" depends heavily on its context . . . That context is found in the policy and purpose underlying § 523(a)(2)(C)'s enactment. It plainly appears in the subsection's legislative history . . . Poor's transfer of her $3,400.00 credit card balance from MBNA to Chase cannot fairly be characterized as fraudulent or as part of a pre-bankruptcy buying binge. It would pervert the statute's purpose to interpret "cash advance" so expansively as to bring Poor's balance transfer within its scope. The defining characteristics of the transaction witness this conclusion. Poor could not receive cash to spend as she pleased through completing the balance transfer boxes on the Chase application . . .

Moreover, the balance transfer did not result in any increase in Poor's overall debt. A balance transfer—be it accomplished through a form incorporated into the credit application (as it was here), a telephone call, or by use of one of the plethora of "access checks" . . . is, ostensibly, an attempt at debt management. Finally, Poor's balance transfer did not increase her total debt; it did not decrease the potential liquidation distribution to her other creditors . . . Thus, I conclude that Poor's utilization of the balance transfer option offered her by Chase is without the scope of § 523(a)(2)(C)'s presumptive nondischargeability for cash advances. Because the balance transfer does not qualify as a "cash advance" under § 523(a)(2)(C) as a matter of law, Chase is not entitled to summary judgment as to its $3,400.00 claim. Had Chase successfully invoked § 523(a)(2)(C) against the $3,400.00 balance

transfer the June 6, 1997, the $350.00 credit cash withdrawal would be presumptively nondischargeable as a "cash advance" and, therefore, ripe for summary judgment. Chase has advanced a sufficient factual predicate for such a determination and Poor has acknowledged the timing and nature of the transaction. However, as it is the only qualifying cash advance debt owed Chase by Poor it falls below § 523(a)(2)(C)'s $1,000.00 threshold. Therefore, Chase's motion must be denied as to this debt, as well. For the reasons set forth above, Chase's motion for partial summary judgment is DENIED. A separate order will enter forthwith.

BUSINESS CONSIDERATIONS Is it a good business practice for a financial institution to encourage a person with substantial debts to open a new credit account, and then to encourage that person to "transfer" the balance of prior credit accounts to the new account? How could Chase have handled the "transfer" payment in order to show that it was, indeed, a "cash advance"?

ETHICAL CONSIDERATION Is it ethical for a financial institution to encourage a person to transfer accounts, as Poor did here, and then to claim that the funds were a "cash advance" when the debtor suffers an unforeseen injury or illness that forces the debtor into bankruptcy?

Exhibit 29.2 summarizes the steps in a Chapter 7 bankruptcy proceeding.

Finally, even if a discharge is granted, it may be revoked. If the trustee or a creditor requests a revocation of the discharge, the request may be granted. The request must be made within one year of the discharge, and the debtor must have committed some wrongful act, such as fraud, during the proceedings. The possibility of revocation encourages the debtor to remain honest.

On some occasions, a debtor who has been granted a discharge in bankruptcy may decide that he or she wants to repay the creditor despite the discharge. If this is truly the case, the debtor may voluntarily reaffirm the debt and then repay it. However, the requirements for a reaffirmation were substantially increased by the 1984 Bankruptcy Amendments. Prior to the 1984 amendments, a debtor could reaffirm any debts at virtually any time. Too often this led to a debtor reaffirming debts out of a sense of guilt following the discharge and resuming the same sort

E X H I B I T 29.2	**The Steps in a Chapter 7 Bankruptcy Proceeding**

Petition is filed	By the debtor (voluntary), five exceptions exist; by the creditors (involuntary), seven exceptions exist.
Order for relief	Automatic stay on any legal proceedings involving the debtor.
Interim trustee appointed	Takes immediate control of the debtor's estate.
Creditor meeting	Debtor examined, debtor schedules submitted, permanent trustee elected.
Marshaling of assets	Trustee gathers the debtor's estate.
Exemptions taken	Debtor selects exempt assets (federal or state exemptions, if the state law allows such a choice).
Claims allowed	Some claims will not be allowed (interest figured after petition date, wages owed for more than one year in the future, rent due for future periods).
Recovery of assets	Trustee may challenge certain actions of the debtor (voidable preferences and fraudulent conveyances); debtor's insolvency is required.
Distribution of assets	Mandatory provisions (eight priority categories, balance is allocated pro rata).
Discharge decision	Trustee recommends, judge decides.

of financial position as had originally led to the petition. As a result, the 1984 amendments require that any reaffirmations be made in writing and filed with the court. In addition, the written agreement must be filed before the debtor is granted a discharge. If the debtor has an attorney, the attorney must file a declaration that the debtor was fully informed of his or her rights, voluntarily agreed to the reaffirmation, and that the agreement will not impose an undue hardship on the debtor or his or her dependents. If the debtor does not have an attorney, the court must approve the reaffirmation, and the court will not grant approval unless the repayment is in the best interests of the debtor.

THE PROPOSED BANKRUPTCY REFORM ACT OF 1999

Despite these improvements, a number of people continue to complain about the bankruptcy provisions. To many creditors, bankruptcy is considered too easy to use, too readily available, and too often abused by the debtors taking advantage of its provisions. The U.S. Chamber of Commerce—a staunch advocate of bankruptcy reform—provides some interesting data in support of this position. According to the U.S. Chamber of Commerce,[9] in 1997, 1.33 million consumer bankruptcy petitions were filed. These bankruptcies erased $40 billion in consumer debt. They further cite the fact that, according to *Investor's Business Daily*, in 95 percent of all Chapter 7 proceedings, *no* assets are liquidated—meaning that there is virtually *no* money available for the creditors at the conclusion of the proceeding. It is estimated that consumer bankruptcies cost each family in the United States $550 a year in higher costs for credit, goods, and services.[10] As a result, the Bankruptcy Reform

Act of 1999 (previously the Bankruptcy Reform Act of 1997 and the Bankruptcy Reform Act of 1998) has been introduced and has an excellent chance of being passed by Congress.

The proposal would limit the availability of Chapter 7 relief to many debtors. Under the proposed Reform Act, guidelines would be established for a "needs-based" bankruptcy system. These guidelines include a set of formulas that will determine debtor eligibility for bankruptcy relief. Put simply, any debtor who satisfies all of the following criteria would be deemed to have adequate income available to repay his or her creditors and would thus not be eligible for Chapter 7 relief:

1. Current monthly income exceeding 75 percent of the state median family income for a family of equal size (for one earner, income exceeding 75 percent of the state median household income)
2. Projected monthly net income exceeding $50
3. Projected monthly net income sufficient to repay 20 percent or more of unsecured, nonpriority claims during a five-year repayment plan period.

The proposed reform act is intended to determine the amount of financial relief a debtor needs, with the expectation that the debtor will repay what he or she can.

RESOURCES FOR BUSINESS LAW STUDENTS

NAME	RESOURCES	WEB ADDRESS
Legal Information Institute (LII)—Bankruptcy Law Materials	The Legal Information Institute (LII), maintained by the Cornell Law School, provides an overview of bankruptcy law, including the Federal Bankruptcy Code; rules in the Code of Federal Regulations (CFR); state and federal court decisions; and state civil codes.	**http://www.law.cornell.edu/topics/bankruptcy.html**
11 U.S.C. Chapter 7—Liquidation	LII provides a hypertext and searchable version of Chapter 7, Liquidation, of the U.S. Code.	**http://www.law.cornell.edu/uscode/11/ch7.html**
11 U.S.C. Chapter 11—Reorganization	LII provides a hypertext and searchable version of Chapter 11, Reorganization, of the U.S. Code.	**http://www.law.cornell.edu/uscode/11/ch11.html**
11 U.S.C. Chapter 12—Adjustment of Debts of a Family Farmer with Regular Annual Income	LII provides a hypertext and searchable version of Chapter 12, Adjustment of Debts of a Family Farmer with Regular Annual Income.	**http://www.law.cornell.edu/uscode/11/ch12.html**
11 U.S.C. Chapter 13—Adjustment of Debts of an Individual with Regular Income	LII provides a hypertext and searchable version of Chapter 13, Adjustment of Debts of an Individual with Regular Income.	**http://www.law.cornell.edu/uscode/11/ch13.html**
ABI World (American Bankruptcy Institute)	American Bankruptcy Institute provides daily bankruptcy headlines, legislative news, and materials from the National Bankruptcy Review Commission (NBRC).	**http://www.abiworld.org/**

Debtors will be expected to repay all of their secured debts and priority debts over the five-year repayment plan. In addition, debtors may be required to complete a program of financial management training in order to be eligible to receive a discharge.

SUMMARY

Federal law governs the topic of bankruptcy, which is designed to give an honest debtor a fresh start. The Bankruptcy Reform Act, which took effect in October 1979, provided for the establishment of bankruptcy courts as a separate branch of the U.S. district court system. These courts were to be presided over by bankruptcy judges who specialized in handling bankruptcy petitions. Following a constitutional challenge to the bankruptcy courts established by the Bankruptcy Reform Act, the Bankruptcy Amendments and Federal Judgeship Act of 1984 modified these bankruptcy courts and severely restricted the authority of the courts and judges. The Bankruptcy Reform Act of 1994 added a number of additional provisions designed to close loopholes and to further balance the rights of the parties in a bankruptcy proceeding. This act also includes a built-in adapter in an effort to keep the dollar amounts involved in bankruptcy current without the need to amend the Code every few years.

Under Chapter 7 (Liquidation), bankruptcy can be initiated voluntarily by the debtor or involuntarily by the creditors. The debtor initiates the proceedings by filing a voluntary petition. The creditors initiate the proceedings by filing an involuntary petition against the debtor. Five types of "public interest" corporations are prohibited from filing a voluntary petition; any other debtor may file such a petition, even if solvent. Creditors may file an involuntary petition against most debtors, although there are seven classes of debtors who are exempt from an involuntary petition filed against them. Even for those debtors who are legally subject to an involuntary petition, there are safeguards. An involuntary petition can be filed only if the debtor is "guilty" of specified conduct, the proper number of creditors join the petition, and the proper amount of unsecured debts is involved.

Once the petition is filed, a judge appoints a trustee to administer the bankrupt's estate. The trustee is to preserve the estate for the protection of the unsecured creditors. The debtor is allowed some exemptions so that a fresh start is possible. The rest of the estate is available for settling debts. Secured creditors must choose between removing themselves and their collateral from the bankruptcy or surrendering their security interest and participating in the proceedings. Once the exempt property and the collateral securing certain loans are removed, the balance of the estate is liquidated, and the proceeds are applied to the allowable claims of the creditors.

The proceeds are applied first to priority classes set up by the Bankruptcy Reform Act. After all priority classes are paid in full, the remaining proceeds are applied to the claims of the unsecured creditors. The debtor will then seek a discharge. If the debtor has been honest and has cooperated, a discharge will probably be granted. If not, the debts will continue.

There is a proposed Bankruptcy Reform Act of 1999 that, if enacted, will substantially change this area of law. Debtors will be restricted from using Chapter 7 under many circumstances and will be forced to either resort to Chapter 13 and a repayment plan or use nonbankruptcy alternatives to resolve their financial woes.

DISCUSSION QUESTIONS

1. What are the two major purposes of the Bankruptcy Reform Act? What public policy considerations support these two purposes? What public policy considerations oppose them?

2. What are the five classes of debtors who cannot file a *voluntary* petition for a Chapter 7 bankruptcy? What are the seven classes of debtors who cannot be *involuntarily* petitioned into Chapter 7 bankruptcy? What are the public policy considerations for excluding these debtors from a Chapter 7 bankruptcy proceeding?

3. Before a debtor can be involuntarily petitioned into bankruptcy, the petitioning creditors must satisfy three tests. What are these three tests? Why must they be satisfied prior to the imposition of an involuntary bankruptcy proceeding?

4. Ronald is involved in a Chapter 7 bankruptcy. The state in which he lives allows the debtor to select either the federal or the state exemptions. The state exemptions completely exempt the debtor's homestead, one automobile, and personal articles of clothing. However, Ronald does not own a home. What should he do? Would your answer be different if Ronald did own a home? Why?

5. On 1 August of last year, Martha filed a voluntary bankruptcy petition, seeking relief under Chapter 7 of the Bankruptcy Code. Included among the debts she listed on her schedule of assets and liabilities were a $30,000 loan with 18 percent interest per annum from Last Bank and Trust dated 1 June of last year, an employment contract with her housekeeper for the next three years, and a lease on her apartment that runs for five more years. She has not paid her housekeeper for the past two months nor has she paid her rent for the past three months. What portion of each of these debts will be allowable in the bankruptcy proceeding?

6. What does it mean when a debtor *loads up* with debts prior to filing a bankruptcy petition? How does bankruptcy law deal with this problem? Is this treatment an appropriate solution to the problem of debtors who load up with debts in anticipation of bankruptcy?

7. What was the basis for the challenge to the Bankruptcy Reform Act in the *Northern Pipeline* case? Does such a challenge to a statute on procedural grounds make sense from a substantive perspective?

8. Suppose a father gave his daughter a new car when she graduated from college last spring and that the father then filed a petition in bankruptcy seven months after the date of the graduation ceremony. Can the trustee challenge this gift to the daughter as a fraudulent conveyance? If a challenge is made, what will need to be shown in order for the daughter to be allowed to keep the car?

9. What is meant by a *voidable preference* in bankruptcy law? Why is the trustee allowed to recover payments made if those payments fit the definition of a voidable preference?

10. Why are alimony and child support obligations not discharged in a bankruptcy proceeding? Is such a rule good or bad, from a public policy perspective? Do the same justifications apply to not permitting the discharge of taxes or student loans?

CASE PROBLEMS AND WRITING ASSIGNMENTS

1. Stephen and Deborah Cox were married in 1973. Mrs. Cox taught school until 1980, when she quit working after the birth of their first child. Mr. Cox provided the family's sole support thereafter. Over the years of the marriage, Mrs. Cox signed various documents, in which she became the co-owner of at least 14 parcels of real estate, a partner in at least two partnerships, and an officer or director in at least four corporations. Mrs. Cox did not actively participate in any of these ventures, and she did not question Stephen about any of these matters. In September 1984, the Cox family left Oregon for San Francisco to "escape some angry creditors," and then flew on to Hawaii, where they lived as fugitives for several months. On 29 October 1984, an involuntary petition in bankruptcy was filed against Mrs. Cox, and she eventually met with government agents and the trustee in bankruptcy to try to resolve the matter. (Mr. Cox remained a fugitive, and his whereabouts were unknown to the parties.) The trustee in bankruptcy objected to a discharge for Deborah Cox, alleging that she failed to keep proper books and records of her financial dealings, as required by bankruptcy law. She replied that her husband kept the records, so she did not feel a need to duplicate his efforts. Should the court grant Mrs. Cox a discharge in this case if the only objection was her inadequate books and records? Explain. [See *In re Cox*, 904 F.2d 1399 (9th Cir. 1990).]

2. On 13 November 1987, Swicegood filed for relief under Chapter 7 of the U.S. Bankruptcy Code. His debts totaled $861,778.19, with $179,418 of this amount owed to Ginn from a default judgment on promissory notes. In his Statement of Financial Affairs

and Schedule of Assets and Liabilities, Swicegood indicated that his assets totaled $12,700. On 12 February 1988, Ginn filed a complaint in bankruptcy court objecting to the discharge of Swicegood's debts on several grounds not relevant to this appeal. Ginn amended his complaint to add as a ground for objection that Swicegood had omitted from his bankruptcy schedule a Rolex watch, a set of silver flatware, two shares of AT&T stock, golf clubs, and two demitasse sterling silver cups. Swicegood learned from his former wife that she had reviewed his bankruptcy schedules with Ginn's counsel and had informed him that the items were omitted. As a result, Swicegood amended his schedule to include the items he had previously omitted. Did Swicegood intend to defraud his creditors by intentionally omitting certain assets in his schedules? Should he be denied a discharge in this case? What ethical issues are raised by a situation in which the debtor acts in the same manner as Swicegood is alleged to have acted? [See *Swicegood* v. *Ginn*, 924 F.2d 230 (11th Cir. 1991).]

3. Holt purchased a 1988 Ford Aerostar, signing a promissory note and security agreement with Dana Federal Credit Union to finance the purchase. This loan was executed in connection with an open line of credit extended by Dana to Holt on 22 March 1988. On 22 May 1995, Holt filed a voluntary petition for relief under Chapter 7 of the Bankruptcy Code. In his schedule of debts, Holt listed Dana as an unsecured creditor with a claim of $6,012.87. (There were only four other unsecured creditors listed, each with a claim of less than $300.) Dana asserted it was owed $7,926.88. (The Aerostar was not listed among Holt's assets, and the court presumed that the van had either already been repossessed or that it had no value as of the petition date.) Holt proposed to discharge in full his debt to Dana through the Chapter 7 proceeding; Dana objected to the discharge by asserting that Holt had knowingly and fraudulently made numerous false oaths and that the debtor failed to explain the loss of assets that occurred immediately preceding the petition. According to Holt's schedule of assets, he had $7 in cash, $400 in his checking account, and $25 in his savings account on the petition date. However, three days prior to the petition date, Holt had a checking account balance of more than $2,350 and a savings account balance of more than $4,500. Holt also denied depositing any of his severance pay of $9,162 in either his checking or savings accounts, although bank records indicated that he had deposited $4,500 in each of the accounts on the day that he received the severance paycheck. Should the court deny a discharge to a debtor who cannot satisfactorily explain the dissipation of his assets immediately preceding his petition

for relief under the Bankruptcy Code? [See *Matter of Holt*, 190 B.R. 935 (Bkrtcy.N.D.Ala. 1996).]

4. On 6 November 1989, Nadel obtained a judgment against Mayer in the amount of $40,052.62. On 19 December 1989, Nadel recorded the abstract of judgment against real property owned by Mayer located at 1597 Casa Real Lane, San Marcos, California. At the time the judicial lien attached, Mayer used the property as a rental. The property did not become Mayer's principal residence until sometime in July 1992, when he reoccupied the house. On 3 March 1993, Mayer filed for protection under Chapter 7 and claimed an automatic homestead exemption of $100,000 for the property under California law. Mayer claims that he is entitled to the $100,000 exemption because he is older than 55 with a gross annual income of less than $20,000. Nadel timely objected to Mayer's homestead exemption. In the alternative, Nadel claims the homestead exemption amount should be the amount in effect in 1989, when the judgment lien attached, not the amount permitted as of the petition-filing date. Without considering the bankruptcy laws, would the debtor be entitled to the automatic homestead exemption under state law? Does the avoidance provision of the Bankruptcy Code affect the operation of state exemption laws and/or alter the substantive rights they provide? Is the homestead exemption amount fixed at the time a judicial lien attaches or at the time of the bankruptcy petition? [See *In re Mayer*, 156 B.R. 54 (Bkrtcy.S.D.Cal. 1993).]

5. The Governor's Park condominium was created by master deed on 10 July 1986. The Governor's Park Condominium Trust (Trust) was also established in order to represent the organization of condominium owners. On 22 October 1986, Whitten and another person purchased two units that were then rented to tenants. Both units were encumbered by mortgages held by BoWest. Whitten fell into arrears with respect to his common area fee obligations in late 1991 and early 1992, and the Trust attempted, unsuccessfully, to collect rents from Whitten's tenants. Whitten filed a voluntary bankruptcy petition under Chapter 7 on 3 June 1992, stating an intention to surrender both units to BoWest. The Trust was not originally listed as a creditor. However, on 17 July 1992, Whitten amended his schedule to include the Trust's claim for condo fees, which were estimated to be $4,505. Whitten received a discharge, and his case was closed on 10 November 1992, and the condominium units reverted to him at that time. Fifteen months later, BoWest foreclosed its mortgages on both units. At that time, unpaid common area fees for the two units for the period from December 1992 through March 1994

totaled $7,921.17. The Trust collected $2,889 from the mortgagee, leaving an unsecured balance of $5,032.17. On 31 March 1994, the Trust filed suit against Whitten to collect the unpaid postpetition common area fees. Whitten denied liability on the grounds that the debt had been discharged by his bankruptcy. The district court entered judgment for the Trust in the amount of $6,356.37 (including attorney's fees and costs), and Whitten filed a petition to reopen his bankruptcy case to determine whether the debt to the Trust had been discharged. Are the postpetition fees assessed against the debtor discharged by the original bankruptcy proceeding in which Whitten was granted a discharge? [See *In re Whitten*, 192 B.R.10 (Bkrtcy.D.Mass. 1996).]

6. **BUSINESS APPLICATION CASE** Section 547 of the Bankruptcy Code authorizes a trustee to avoid certain property transfers made by a debtor within 90 days before bankruptcy. The Code makes an exception, however, for transfers made in the ordinary course of business. On 17 December 1986, the debtor, ZZZZ Best Co., Inc., borrowed $7 million from Union Bank. On 8 July 1987, the debtor filed a voluntary petition under Chapter 7 of the Bankruptcy Code. During the preceding 90-day period, the debtor had made two interest payments totaling approximately $100,000 and had paid a loan commitment fee of about $2,500 to the bank. After his appointment as trustee of the debtor's estate, Wolas filed a complaint against the bank to recover these payments, pursuant to § 547(b). The bankruptcy court found that the loans had been made "in the ordinary course of business or financial affairs" of both the debtor and the bank, and that both interest payments as well as the payment of the loan commitment fee had been made according to ordinary business terms and in the ordinary course of business. Shortly thereafter, in another case, the court of appeals held that the avoidance of preferential transfers was not available to long-term creditors. The importance of this question of law, coupled with the fact that the Sixth and Ninth Circuits had reached differing opinions, persuaded the court to grant *certiorari*. Can payments made on long-term debts qualify as payments in the ordinary course of business and thus not be treated as voidable preferences? Does the exception to the voidable preference rule for payments made in the ordinary course of business help a struggling business acquire loans in an effort to salvage itself? Why? [See *Union Bank* v. *Wolas*, 502 U.S. 151 (1991).]

7. **ETHICAL APPLICATION CASE** Perez filed a petition for relief under Chapter 7 of the Bankruptcy Act. Hibernia National Bank, one of his creditors, opposed the granting of relief to Perez. On a financial statement dated 31 December 1985, Perez listed the following assets, among others: furnishings with a cash basis of $26,403.06 and a market basis of $21,122; jewelry and furs with a cash basis of $47,883.63 and a market basis of $62,248.72. On a financial statement dated 31 December 1986, these items were not listed, nor were they listed on his schedule of assets in support of his petition for bankruptcy. When asked to explain their absence, Perez stated that the assets belonged to his wife and should not have been included in his 1985 financial statement. The court refused to accept this explanation without evidence in support of it. It would be just as easy to state that the items were erroneously left off the 1986 statement as to state that they were erroneously included on the 1985 statement. Without some evidence, Perez failed to satisfy the court as to why these items should not be included in the bankruptcy estate. During the year prior to the bankruptcy proceeding, Perez received a $290,000 tax refund, which he split equally with his wife. The bankruptcy judge enlarged the pleadings to include this tax refund, even though Hibernia had not listed it. Perez argued that the court acted improperly in enlarging the pleadings in such a manner. Perez filed a petition for relief under Chapter 7 of the Bankruptcy Code. He was denied a discharge for allegedly failing to properly explain the absence of certain items in his bankruptcy schedules that had been included in previous financial statements he had prepared. In addition, the court felt that he had acted in a manner intended to hinder, delay, or defraud his creditors. Perez appealed the findings of the bankruptcy court. Did Perez give a satisfactory explanation for certain items included on his financial statement of 1985 but not included in his bankruptcy schedules in support of his petition? Did Perez's conduct show an intent to hinder, delay, or defraud his creditors? What protections are available to a creditor when it deals with a "dishonest" debtor? Should some sort of penalty be applicable to a debtor who is found to be dishonest after credit has been extended to that debtor? [See *Hibernia National Bank* v. *Perez*, 124 B.R. 704 (E.D.La. 1991).]

8. **CRITICAL THINKING CASE** Swiatek filed a petition seeking relief under Chapter 7 of the Bankruptcy Act on 20 March 1996 and was granted a discharge by the court on 19 July 1996. Prior to the filing of the bankruptcy petition, Pagliaro filed a default judgment against Swiatek and created a lien against Swiatek's real property. Neither party disputes that Pagliaro holds a nonconsensual judicial lien against the property nor that the balance of two mortgages on the property, both senior to the lien of Pagliaro, equals or

exceeds the value of the property. Pagliaro's claim is unsecured and, therefore, not an allowed secured claim. Because of this, Swiatek argues that this lien is void under 11 U.S.C. § 506(d). Section 506 provides, in pertinent part:

a) An allowed claim of a creditor secured by a lien on property in which the estate has an interest . . . is a secured claim to the extent of the value of such creditor's interest in the estate's interest to such property . . . and is an unsecured claim to the extent that the value of such creditor's interest . . . is less than the amount of such allowed claim. Such value shall be determined in light of the purpose of the valuation and of the proposed disposition or use of such property, and in conjunction with any hearing or such disposition or use . . .

d) To the extent that a lien secures a claim against the debtor that is not an allowed secured claim, such lien is void unless—(1) such claim was disallowed only under section 502 (b)(5) or 502 (e) of this title; or (2) such claim is not an allowed secured claim due only to the failure of any entity to file a proof of such claim under section 501 of this title.

The court decided that nothing in the record indicated that (d)(1) or (d)(2) applied in this case, and that, since Pagliaro's claim was not an allowable secured claim, his lien was voidable. Was the judicial lien of Pagliaro an allowed secured claim, thus surviving the discharge in bankruptcy? How might Pagliaro have acted differently in order to strengthen his claim against Swiatek? [See *In re Swiatek* v. *Pagliaro*, 231 B.R. 26 (Bkrtcy.Del. 1999).]

NOTES

1. 458 U.S. 50 (1982).
2. U.S. Constitution, Article III, § 1.
3. Bankruptcy Reform Act of 1994, 11 U.S.C. § 326.
4. Ibid., § 109(e).
5. Administrative Office of the U.S. Courts, Statistical Tables for the Federal Judiciary, http://www.census.gov/statab/.
6. Ibid.
7. Ibid. In 1990, 723,886 of 725,484 were voluntary petitions. In 1996, 1,040,915 of 1,042,110 petitions were voluntary.
8. "Involuntary Petition Was Not Filed in Bad Faith." *BCD News and Comment* (6 April 1999), LRP Publications, http://www.lexis-nexis.com/.
9. "Bankruptcy Reform," *U.S. Chamber of Commerce*, http://www.uschamber.org/policy/bankruptcy (19 March 1999).
10. "Gekas Introduces Bankruptcy Reform Act for 106th Congress," *George W. Gekas, U.S. Congressman, 17th District of Pennsylvania* (24 February 1999).

30

ALTERNATIVES TO STRAIGHT BANKRUPTCY

CALL-IMAGE TECHNOLOGY

AGENDA

The Kochanowskis sell Call-Image videophones to a number of businesses (the CIT technology is *very* popular for business conference calls), many of which are corporations. Although a lot of the sales are made on a cash basis, some customers purchase the units on credit. Tom and Anna are concerned that some of these credit customers may become insolvent and seek relief in bankruptcy. They want to know what can happen to their accounts in a Chapter 11 or a Chapter 13 bankruptcy proceeding. They also are concerned about their alternatives outside of bankruptcy if any customers are unable or unwilling to meet their payment schedules.

These and other questions may arise in the course of this chapter. Be prepared! You never know when one of the Kochanowskis will need your help or advice.

OUTLINE

OTHER BANKRUPTCY PLANS

In the previous chapter, we examined a Chapter 7 liquidation proceeding, commonly referred to as a *straight bankruptcy*. Many people have the mistaken idea that Chapter 7 proceedings are all that the Bankruptcy Reform Act covers. In reality, several other types of proceedings are also available under the Bankruptcy Reform Act. The first sections of this chapter discuss three of the Bankruptcy Reform Act proceedings: a reorganization under Chapter 11, a repayment plan for family farmers under Chapter 12, and a wage earner's repayment plan under Chapter 13. (The provisions for the Chapter 12 proceedings expired 1 October 1998. There are numerous bills pending in Congress to reactivate this chapter.) None of these plans calls for a liquidation of the debtor's assets in order to cover the debts, and under these plans the creditors can reasonably expect to be paid more than would be received under a liquidation proceeding. In fact, many times the creditors will be paid in full by the debtor. In the last sections of the chapter, we discuss alternatives to bankruptcy. These nonbankruptcy alternatives are available under state statutes or through the application of common law principles, in contrast to the federal statutes that provide for bankruptcy. Ironically, a number of these nonbankruptcy alternatives may provide the necessary "action" by the debtor to permit the creditors to file an involuntary petition against the debtor.

REORGANIZATIONS: CHAPTER 11

Chapter 11 bankruptcy proceedings, known as *reorganizations*, are designed to allow the debtor to adjust his or her financial situation, restructuring the business financially in order to save the enterprise. Chapter 11 is used by debtors to avoid liquidations. Although reorganizations are designed primarily for use by corporate debtors, individuals are also allowed to use the reorganization format.

The major advantages of a reorganization are that it allows a business to continue, and it forces creditors who object to go along with the plan despite their objections. In addition, the creditors normally will receive more than they would have in a liquidation under Chapter 7.

Any debtor who can use Chapter 7, except stockbrokers and commodity brokers, can also use Chapter 11. Moreover, railroads, which are prohibited from using Chapter 7, can take advantage of the provisions of Chapter 11. Like a liquidation proceeding, a reorganization may be either voluntary or involuntary. In addition, the same limitations apply here as apply to a liquidation petition (refer to Chapter 29 for a description of how petitions may be initiated).

The Proceedings

Once the petition has been filed, the court will do three things:

1. It will enter an order for relief.
2. It will appoint a trustee, if requested to do so by any interested party.
3. It will appoint creditor committees to represent the creditors. (Equity security holders will be represented by a separate committee.)

Remember that the *automatic stay* provisions also apply in this chapter. When a petition is filed, any legal actions involving the debtor are subject to an automatic stay, freezing the legal proceedings pending resolution of the bankruptcy.

30.1 | FINANCE/ MANAGEMENT

CHAPTER 11 BANKRUPTCY

Mail-Mart, a mail-order retail business, purchased 4,000 Call-Image videophones from CIT on credit. Mail-Mart gave CIT a security interest in all its electronic inventory to secure the credit, and CIT properly perfected its interest prior to delivering the phones. Mail-Mart has filed a petition for relief under Chapter 11 of the Bankruptcy Act and has submitted a reorganization plan to the court. This plan calls for the release of all current security interests on its inventory, thus allowing Mail-Mart to use its inventory as collateral to obtain new financing from a bank. Mail-Mart has also proposed that its payments to the former secured creditors be maintained at the same interest rates, but with an extension in the number of payments to be made to each creditor.

Dan thinks that the plan proposed by Mail-Mart will cost CIT a great deal of money, and he opposes the plan. Tom is also concerned but thinks the firm can handle this situation, provided all the payments still owed are, in fact, made by Mail-Mart. However, the firm would be better served either receiving its scheduled payments or enforcing its security interest. They have asked you how they should proceed. What are CIT's rights in this situation? How should the firm proceed?

BUSINESS CONSIDERATIONS Anytime a business extends credit to a customer, that business assumes the risk of default or bankruptcy affecting the account. What can a business like CIT do to protect itself short of refusing to make credit sales? Why would a business *not* decide to deal strictly on a cash-and-carry basis?

ETHICAL CONSIDERATIONS Suppose that a customer is encountering financial difficulties and facing the possibility of failure. That customer asks for an extension of the time for making its payments. What considerations would cause a creditor to agree to the extension? When should the creditor take a hard-line stance and refuse to vary the payment terms?

The court may appoint a trustee, although the appointment of a trustee is not necessary in Chapter 11. In fact, if no interested party *asks* for the appointment of a trustee, no trustee will be appointed. Instead, the debtor is permitted to retain possession and control of the assets and/or the business (such a debtor is referred to as a *debtor-in-possession*). (The debtor-in-possession is deemed to have the same basic duties as a trustee, including the fiduciary duty owed to the creditors.) The committees appointed by the court will meet with the trustee, if one is appointed, or with the debtor-in-possession, if no trustee is appointed, to discuss the treatment of the proceedings. The committees also will investigate the debtor's finances and financial potential, and they will help prepare a plan for reorganizing the enterprise that will benefit all the interested parties.

In the event that no one asks for the appointment of a trustee, the court may appoint an examiner. The examiner or the trustee will investigate the debtor, the debtor's business activities, and the debtor's business potential. On the basis of this investigation, a recommendation will be made to the court. The recommendation may be a reorganization plan, or it may be a suggestion that the proceedings be transferred from Chapter 11 to Chapter 7 (liquidation) or to Chapter 13 (wage earner plan). The court normally will follow such a recommendation unless a good reason not to do so is presented.

The Plan

The purpose of a reorganization is to develop a plan under which the debtor can avoid liquidation while somehow managing to satisfy the claims of the creditors. Obviously, the right to propose a plan can be very important. If the debtor remains in possession (i.e., no trustee is appointed), only the debtor may propose a plan during the first 120 days after the order for relief. Any interested party (debtor, creditor, stockholder, or trustee) can propose a plan under any of three conditions:

1. If a trustee is appointed, any interested party can propose a plan at any time until a plan is approved by the court.
2. If the debtor fails to propose a plan within the 120-day period, any interested party can propose a plan.
3. If the debtor proposes a plan within 120 days, but it is not accepted by all affected classes of creditors within 180 days of the order for relief, any interested party can propose a plan to the court.

The 1994 Bankruptcy Reform Act includes provisions for a "fast track" reorganization for small-business debtors. This "fast-track" reorganization is covered in § 1121(c). To be eligible for this provision, the business must be a "small business," and it must elect to be considered a "small business." *Small business* is defined in § 101 (51C) as a business with less than $2 million in noncontingent liquidated liabilities. In addition, the business cannot have as its primary activity the owning or managing of real estate. The debtor in a "fast-track" reorganization must file a plan within 100 days, rather than the 120 days granted under a "regular" Chapter 11. All plans must be filed within 160 days, as opposed to the 180 days granted under a "regular" Chapter 11.

For a plan to be confirmed, it must designate all claims by class as well as specify which classes will be impaired and which will not. It also must show how the plan can be implemented successfully. Among the factors that the court will examine in reviewing a plan are the following:

1. Plans to sell any assets
2. Plans to merge, consolidate, or divest
3. Plans to satisfy, or modify, any liens or claims
4. Plans to issue new stock to generate funds

If new stock is to be issued, it must have voting rights. No new nonvoting stock may be issued under a reorganization plan. Each class of creditors that is impaired is allowed to vote on the plan.

According to § 1129, the court can confirm a plan *only if* a number of requirements are met. These include:

1. The plan was proposed in good faith and not by any means forbidden by law;
2. Any payments made or to be made under the plan for services, costs, and expenses in connection with the plan have been approved by, or are subject to approval by, the court;
3. With respect to each impaired class of claims or creditors, the class
   a. has accepted the plan; or
   b. will receive or retain property of a value that is not less than the amount that class or claim would receive or retain if the estate were liquidated under Chapter 7;
4. If a class of claims is impaired, at least one class of claims that is impaired has accepted the plan; and
5. Confirmation of the plan is not likely to be followed by a liquidation.

A class is deemed to have accepted the plan if creditors having at least two-thirds of the dollar amount involved and more than one-half of the total number of creditors vote in favor of the plan. If a creditor class is not impaired by the plan, it does not need to approve the plan. Creditor classes whose claims will be impaired under the plan *must* vote on the plan, and at least one of these impaired classes must approve the plan (§ 1129 (a)(10).) This requirement sounds very straightforward, but even it has an exception, the so-called "cramdown" provisions found in § 1129 (b), which is discussed below.

Despite the vote, no plan can be accepted or rejected by the creditors. The final word is left to the court. The court will hold a hearing on the plan, and the court can confirm or reject it. The court can confirm a plan if it is accepted by at least one class of creditors. If all the creditor classes approve the plan, the court normally will confirm it. Similarly, if all the creditor classes reject the plan, the court normally will reject it. Still, the final word is with the court alone. The vote of the creditor classes simply provides the court with guidance.

Once the court approves a plan, it becomes binding on everyone affected by it. The court also will look at the plan's fairness to each interested group, especially those creditors impaired by the plan. The court also will look at the viability of the plan. Finally, if the court feels the plan will not work or is not fair, it can order the proceedings converted to a Chapter 7 liquidation. This last-ditch power encourages everyone involved to act in good faith, since Chapter 11 usually is better than Chapter 7 for all concerned.

The cramdown provision allows the court to confirm a plan, at the request of the proponent of that plan, notwithstanding *all* of the requirements of § 1129(a), if the plan does not discriminate unfairly, and is fair and equitable, with respect to each class of claims that is impaired by the plan and has not accepted the plan. The following case reflects a recent Supreme Court interpretation of the "cramdown" provisions of the Bankruptcy Code.

30.1

BANK OF AMERICA NATIONAL TRUST AND SAVINGS ASSOCIATION V. 203 NORTH LASALLE STREET PARTNERSHIP

526 U.S. 434 (1999)

FACTS Bank of America National Trust and Savings Association . . . is the major creditor of . . . 203 North LaSalle Street Partnership . . . The Bank lent the Debtor some $93 million, secured by a nonrecourse first mortgage on the Debtor's principal asset, 15 floors of an office building in downtown Chicago. In January 1995, the Debtor defaulted, and the Bank began foreclosure in a state court. In March, the Debtor responded with a voluntary petition for relief under Chapter 11 of the Bankruptcy Code . . . which automatically stayed the foreclosure proceedings . . . The Debtor proceeded to propose a reorganization plan during the 120-day period when it alone had the right to do so . . . The value of the mortgaged property was less than the balance due the Bank, which elected to divide its undersecured claim into secured and unsecured deficiency claims . . . Under the plan, the Debtor separately classified the Bank's secured claim, its unsecured deficiency claim, and unsecured trade debt owed to other creditors . . . So far as we need be concerned here, the Debtor's plan had these further features: (1) The Bank's $54.5 million secured claim would be paid in full between 7 and 10 years after the original 1995 repayment date. (2) The Bank's $38.5 million unsecured deficiency claim would be discharged for an estimated 16% of its present value. (3) The remaining unsecured claims of $90,000, held

by the outside trade creditors, would be paid in full, without interest, on the effective date of the plan. (4) Certain former partners of the Debtor would contribute $6.125 million in new capital over the course of five years (the contribution being worth some $4.1 million in present value), in exchange for the Partnership's entire ownership of the reorganized debtor. The last condition was an exclusive eligibility provision: the old equity holders were the only ones who could contribute new capital. The Bank objected and, being the sole member of an impaired class of creditors, thereby blocked confirmation of the plan on a consensual basis . . . The Debtor, however, took the alternate route to confirmation of a reorganization plan, forthrightly known as the judicial "cramdown" process for imposing a plan on a dissenting class . . . Section 1129(a)(7) provides that if a holder of a claim impaired under a plan of reorganization has not accepted the plan, then such holder must "receive . . . on account of such claim . . . property of a value, as of the effective date of the plan, that is not less than the amount that such holder would so receive . . . if the debtor were liquidated under Chapter 7 . . . on such date." The "best interests" test applies to individual creditors holding impaired claims, even if the class as a whole votes to accept the plan. The absolute priority rule was the basis for the Bank's

BANK OF AMERICA NATIONAL TRUST AND SAVINGS ASSOCIATION V. 203 NORTH LASALLE STREET PARTNERSHIP, *continued*

526 U.S. 434 (1999)

position that the plan could not be confirmed as a cramdown. As the Bank read the rule, the plan was open to objection simply because certain old equity holders in the Debtor Partnership would receive property even though the Bank's unsecured deficiency claim would not be paid in full. The Bankruptcy Court approved the plan nonetheless. . . . The District Court affirmed . . . as did the Court of Appeals . . . We granted certiorari . . . to resolve a Circuit split on the issue..

ISSUE Can a debtor's prebankruptcy equity holder contribute new capital and receive ownership interests in the reorganized entity, despite any objections by a senior class of impaired creditors?

HOLDING No. The old equity holders are disqualified from participating in such a "new value" transaction, which bars a junior interest holder's receipt of any property on account of his prior interest.

REASONING The terms "absolute priority rule" and "new value corollary" (or "exception") are creatures of law antedating the current Bankruptcy Code, and to understand both those terms and the related but inexact language of the Code some history is helpful. The Bankruptcy Act preceding the Code contained no such provision as subsection (b)(2)(B)(ii), its subject having been addressed by two interpretive rules. The first was a specific gloss on the requirement of § 77B . . . that any reorganization plan be "fair and equitable." . . . The reason for such a limitation was the danger inherent in any reorganization plan proposed by a debtor, then and now, that the plan will simply turn out to be too good a deal for the debtor's owners . . . Hence the pre-Code judicial response known as the absolute priority rule, that fairness and equity required that "the creditors . . . be paid before the stockholders could retain [equity interests] for any purpose whatever." . . . The upshot is that this history does nothing to disparage the possibility apparent in the statutory text, that the absolute priority rule now on the books . . . may carry a new value corollary. Although there is no literal reference to "new value" in the phrase "on account of such junior claim," the phrase could arguably carry such an implication in modifying the prohibition against receipt by junior

claimants of any interest under a plan while a senior class of unconsenting creditors goes less than fully paid . . . [U]nder the commonsense rule that a given phrase is meant to carry a given concept in a single statute . . . the better reading of subsection (b)(2)(B)(ii) recognizes that a causal relationship between holding the prior claim or interest and receiving or retaining property is what activates the absolute priority rule . . . Causation between the old equity's holdings and subsequent property substantial enough to disqualify a plan would presumably occur on this view of things whenever old equity's later property would come at a price that failed to provide the greatest possible addition to the bankruptcy estate, and it would always come at a price too low when the equity holders obtained or preserved an ownership interest for less than someone else would have paid. A truly full value transaction, on the other hand, would pose no threat to the bankruptcy estate not posed by any reorganization, provided of course that the contribution be in cash or be realizable money's worth . . . Which of these positions is ultimately entitled to prevail is not to be decided here, however, for even on the latter view the Bank's objection would require rejection of the plan at issue in this case. It is doomed, we can say without necessarily exhausting its flaws, by its provision for vesting equity in the reorganized business in the Debtor's partners without extending an opportunity to anyone else either to compete for that equity or to propose a competing reorganization plan . . . At the moment of the plan's approval the Debtor's partners necessarily enjoyed an exclusive opportunity that was in no economic sense distinguishable from the advantage of the exclusively entitled offeror or option holder . . .

Given that the opportunity is property of some value, the question arises why old equity alone should obtain it, not to mention at no cost whatever. The closest thing to an answer favorable to the Debtor is that the old equity partners would be given the opportunity in the expectation that in taking advantage of it they would add the stated purchase price to the estate . . . Under a plan granting an exclusive right, making no provision for competing bids or competing plans, any determination that the price was top dollar would necessarily be made by a judge

continued

30.1

BANK OF AMERICA NATIONAL TRUST AND SAVINGS ASSOCIATION V. 203 NORTH LASALLE STREET PARTNERSHIP, *continued*

526 U.S. 434 (1999)

in bankruptcy court, whereas the best way to determine value is exposure to a market . . . This is a point of some significance, since it was, after all, one of the Code's innovations to narrow the occasions for courts to make valuation judgments, as shown by its preference for the supramajoritarian class creditor voting scheme in § 1126(c) . . . In the interest of statutory coherence, a like disfavor for decisions untested by competitive choice ought to extend to valuations in administering subsection (b)(2)(B)(ii) when some form of market valuation may be available to test the adequacy of an old equity holder's proposed contribution. . . It is enough to say, assuming a new value corollary, that plans providing junior interest holders with exclusive opportunities free from competition and without benefit of market valuation fall within the prohibition of § 1129(b)(2)(B)(ii). The judgment of

the Court of Appeals is accordingly reversed, and the case is remanded for further proceedings consistent with this opinion. It is so ordered.

BUSINESS CONSIDERATIONS Why would a business want to allow its current equity holders to have "first shot" at the equity in a reorganized business? Would it make more sense, from a business perspective, to allow "bids" for the equity in such a situation?

ETHICAL CONSIDERATION Is it ethical for a business to try to protect its equity holders in a reorganization plan at the possible expense of the creditors of the firm?

Chapter 11 as a Corporate Strategy

Reorganizations have recently taken an interesting twist. A number of corporations, some of which are very large and successful, have availed themselves of Chapter 11 to escape or avoid potentially onerous debts or obligations. Johns-Manville was, at one time, a giant in the asbestos industry. When the effect of asbestos on health became known, Johns-Manville was faced with potential liability to its customers and employees that could have literally reached billions of dollars. Despite the size and success of the firm, such liability would have destroyed it. Rather than await the imposition of such a liability, Johns-Manville went to court seeking a reorganization under Chapter 11. The firm proposed the establishment of a trust fund to be used for victims entitled to compensation due to asbestos-related health problems.[1] The court approved the reorganization plan, and the firm endowed the trust with millions of dollars and continued to operate the business. The firm recently paid its first dividends in several years and has once again assumed its position on the *Fortune* 500 list.

Similar strategies have been used to escape other potentially disastrous liabilities. Several firms have recently used Chapter 11 to avoid burdensome labor contracts. In fact, the use of Chapter 11 to reject a collective bargaining agreement is prevalent enough to have a section of the Bankruptcy Code that addresses this issue. Section 1113, Rejection of Collective Bargaining Agreements, specifies the conditions under which a collective bargaining agreement can be rejected as a part of the debtor's reorganization plan. The court can only approve such a proposal if three conditions are met:

YOU BE THE JUDGE

CLASSIFYING CREDITORS

Bustop Shelters entered into several contracts with Classic. These contracts called for Classic to install 400 shelters at designated bus stops from kits provided by Bustop, to perform periodic maintenance on the installed shelters, and to clean each of the shelters weekly. Bustop and Classic subsequently filed suits against one another, each alleging breach of the contract by the other. Classic prevailed, receiving a damage award in the amount of $440,000. As a result, Bustop filed for relief under Chapter 11, availing itself of the automatic stay provision before Classic could enforce its judgment. Bustop proceeded to submit a reorganization plan under Chapter 11 during its 120-day exclusive period. In this plan, Bustop listed three classes of creditors: Class 1, Citizens Bank, based on a fully secured loan; Class 2, unsecured creditors owed between $201 and $20,000; and Class 3, unsecured creditors owed more than $20,000. (The only creditor in Class 3 was Classic.) The creditors in Classes 1 and 2 approved the plan, while the Class 3 creditor (Classic) rejected it. Bustop is now asking the court to approve the plan despite this rejection by Class 3 under the "cramdown" provisions of the Bankruptcy Code. Classic objects to this request. According to Classic, there should only have been two classes of creditors: Class 1, secured creditors, and Class 2, unsecured creditors. According to Classic, the secured creditors are not impaired by the plan, while the unsecured creditors are impaired. If the unsecured creditors are treated as a single class, this class would have rejected the plan, negating the availability of the "cramdown" provisions.

This case has been brought in *your* court. How will *you* resolve these issues?[2]

BUSINESS CONSIDERATIONS Bustop contracted with Classic to have Classic erect, maintain, and perform weekly cleaning on 400 bus stop shelters. Should Bustop have made such a comprehensive and ongoing contract, or should it have made several different contracts, one for each of the duties involved? Does the likelihood of a breach and/or disagreement increase with the complexity and length of a contract?

ETHICAL CONSIDERATION Is it ethical for a debtor seeking relief under Chapter 11 to "gerrymander" the creditor classes in an effort to isolate the creditors who are most likely to object to the reorganization?

SOURCE: *Bustop Shelters of Louisville v. Classic Homes*, 914 F.2d 810 (6th Cir. 1990).

1. The debtor has made a proposal to the authorized representatives of the employees that provides for any modifications that are necessary to permit the reorganization and that assures that all affected parties are treated fairly and equitably.
2. The authorized representative of the employees has rejected the proposal without good cause.
3. The balance of the equities, in the eyes of the court, clearly favors rejection of the collective bargaining agreement despite the action of the authorized representative of the employees.

The following case shows how one bankruptcy case involving such a labor contract was resolved. Notice how the court attempted to balance the interests of all the parties involved in the plan.

30.2

IN RE JEFLEY, INC.
219 B.R. 88 (BKRTCY.E.D.PENN. 1998)

FACTS Jefley, Inc. ("the Debtor") operates three retail supermarkets . . . It filed the underlying voluntary Chapter 11 bankruptcy case on July 2, 1997. The filing appears to have been prompted by large claims against the Debtor; its owner, Jeffrey Shprintz ("Jeffrey"); and its former owner, Jeffrey's father Earle ("Earle"), by the Internal Revenue Service ("the IRS"). Faced with losses attributed to intensified competition, as well as the burdens imposed by the IRS, the Debtor, during the course of the case took several corrective measures. These included closing its least profitable fourth store, obtaining permission to replace its principal vendor, eliminating consulting fees and stock purchase payments to Earle and Jeffrey's brother, and cutting its administrative staff from seven to four persons. It also negotiated a "pot" plan of reorganization ("the Plan") with the Committee which it filed on January 30, 1998 . . . Under the Plan the Debtor was to remit, for the benefit of unsecured creditors, $100,000 on the effective date and $175,000 annually for the next six years. These payments would result in a recovery between ten (10%) percent and thirty-eight (38%) percent for unsecured creditors, depending on the outcome of objections to certain of the claims. The Motion was filed on January 27, 1998 . . . The Debtor has, for many years, been a party to two collective bargaining agreements with the United Food and Commercial Workers Union. The first, with Local 56, which expired in November 1997, but under which the parties continue to operate, includes 25–28 butchers, wrappers, and sellers of meat and seafood. The other, with Local 1360, which expires on March 20, 1998, includes 110–119 retail clerks. On December 11, 1997, the Debtor advised both Locals that . . . it wished to discuss modifications to numerous terms of the agreements. The Debtor's proposal was based upon its conclusion that its labor costs would have to be reduced by an annual amount of about $720,000, approximately $125,000 and $595,000, respectively, by workers from Locals 56 and 1360, to comply with the terms of the Plan. This proposal contemplated a reduction in the combined salaries of Jeffrey and his wife Joni, who works on a regular but less than full-time basis as an administrator, from $670,000 to $350,000 annually. The modifications proposed included reductions in vacation times, holidays, and personal days; a freeze on employees' pensions and health and welfare contributions; an

increase from 16 hours to 20 hours in the minimum weekly work-time necessary to qualify for health and welfare benefits; reductions of premiums for working on Sundays; and the placement of a cap of $10.00 on cashiers' hourly rates. The last proposal, which caused the most controversy, would have constituted a large savings for the Debtor because, although the Debtor's starting rate of pay, per its union contracts, was only $5.50/hour and the maximum rate after four years was fixed at $9.75/hour, the Debtor retained many employees who had worked for it for many years and received the benefit of across-the-board increases which raised their rates to $14 to $15/hour . . . Local 56 agreed to the proposal, apparently because most of its members were more skilled workers who would be spared the one-third reductions proposed to many of the clerks. Local 1360 did not. . . Local 1360 offered one counter-proposal, on February 4, which contemplated acceptance of many terms involved in the Debtor's proposal, but not the most significant terms, i.e., reductions in Sunday premiums and the proposed caps on hourly rates. The Debtor cashed out Local 1360's counter-proposal as effecting a savings of only $300,000, about half of what was needed . . .

Local 1360 and this court questioned Jeffrey regarding the salaries of him and his wife. He testified that he needed $90,000 net annually to pay his personal share of restitution due as a result of the coupon fraud and $30,000 to send his two children, described as having an attention deficit disorder and reading problems, respectively, to remedial schools. He also indicated that he and Earle are co-owners of realty used by the Debtor for corporate offices. The rent has, however, been reduced to merely cover the mortgage. A sale of this building is contemplated, from which any profits are to be contributed to the Debtor's reorganization. Jeffrey and his family also receive the full use of a 1997 Landcruiser rented by the Debtor for $950 monthly and full health and welfare benefits. The Committee, on its part, expressed an unwillingness to reduce its constituents' dividends as negotiated in the plan . . .

ISSUE Should the Debtor be allowed to reject the collective bargaining agreement in order to effectuate his reorganization plan?

30.2

IN RE JEFLEY, INC., *continued*
219 B.R. 88 (BKRTCY.E.D.PENN. 1998)

HOLDING No. The proposal, as presented, is not "necessary" to the Debtor's reorganization, nor does it treat the union "fairly and equitably."

REASONING At the close of the hearing, we indicated to the parties that we felt that the evidence supported the conclusion that all interests must give a little more. Accepting the $595,000 figure as an accurate statement of the annual dollar reduction in expenses required by the Debtor to survive in Chapter 11, a counter-proposal of Local 1360 which would save only $300,000 was clearly inadequate. It seemed to us that Local 1360's members would have to agree to some further reductions or possibly have their jobs lost in a fatal game of "chicken." However, it also seemed to us that further reductions in the salaries of Jeffrey and his wife and possibly the amount payable to unsecured creditors under the plan were in order as well. These findings would have resulted in our refusal to grant the Motion as it stood, since further compromise on the part of the Debtor's management and creditors appeared necessary. . . .

The procedures of § 1113 appears to have been followed both in letter and spirit by the Debtor and Local 1360. Despite some mild, typical "labor jargon" cross-accusations, both impressed us as proceeding in good faith and with appreciation for the concerns of the other . . . The issue, as we see it, can be boiled down to our deciding whether the Debtor, considering all of the circumstances, has proposed to reduce the union contract benefits only to the extent necessary to achieve equitable treatment of all parties interested in the case . . . It is true that the proposals of the Debtor contain a "snapback" provision, providing that one-third of any excess of profits over projections will be distributed to union employees . . . However, we were convinced that the Debtor and possibly the Committee should be required to give at least a little more in the negotiation process, as well as observing the necessity for movement on the part of Local 1360. The Debtor argued at and after the hearing that Jeffrey and Joni Shprintz cannot reduce their compensation below $350,000 annually, because $120,000 of their net pay of about $225,000 must be devoted to Jeffrey's restitution payments and their children's special education needs. This analysis, which generously assumes that the Debtor should bear the cost of Jeffrey's personal restitution and of his indulgence in very expensive remedial education for children with something less than overwhelming disabilities, still leaves this couple with over $100,000 net annual income, plus the fringe benefit of use of a company vehicle and fully-paid health and welfare benefits . . . For purposes of analysis of the union employees' salaries, the Debtor argues that these employees could not do better at rival supermarkets. Subjecting Jeffrey to the same analysis, we doubt whether there is a substantial market for supermarket executives convicted of coupon fraud. The Committee contends that the percentage return on its dividends under the plan is much less than the percentage of their wages that the union employees are asked to forfeit. However, it seems quite clear that, if the Debtor fails to reach an agreement with Local 1360, a strike or other job actions could ensue which would be fatal to the Debtor's operations and a hope of any recovery by unsecured creditors . . . We cannot find . . . that the changes proposed by the Debtor, at least as presented at the hearing, are/were fair and equitable when the circumstances of union workers are compared to those of non-unionized management employees . . . [W]e find the potential for more sacrifice on the part of management . . . We are disappointed that the agreement between the debtor and Local 1360, which would have apparently proposed a semi-permanent resolution to the parties' differences, was not approved by the Debtor's employees. Both parties may be disappointed that this court is unable to rule on this Motion on the basis of the present record.

BUSINESS CONSIDERATIONS How important is it for a business to keep its employees somewhat satisfied while it plans a reorganization? Should the business assume a "take it or leave it" position, with the implication that the business will liquidate unless the employees go along?

ETHICAL CONSIDERATIONS Is it ethical for a business to propose major reductions in employee compensation while retaining a substantial benefits package for management and the owners in a reorganization? Since the owners are the ones "taking the risk," shouldn't they be well compensated, if possible?

REPAYMENT PLANS FOR FARMERS: CHAPTER 12

Historically, U.S. public policy has provided special protections for farmers. For the most part, this has benefited farmers, but in some instances it has not. One area in which the public policy considerations that urged protection of farmers turned out to be less than ideal was bankruptcy. Under Chapter 7, a farmer cannot be involuntarily petitioned into bankruptcy. While this protects the farmer from an involuntary liquidation, it might leave that farmer unable to forestall creditors who might otherwise have resorted to a bankruptcy proceeding. Admittedly, the farmer can file a voluntary petition, but that will lead to a liquidation—and probably the loss of the farm.

To further complicate the dilemma, farmers who operate large farms are likely to have debts in excess of the ceilings imposed by Chapter 13, which precludes the use of a repayment plan. This left farmers with two options: avoid bankruptcy, using nonbankruptcy alternatives to resolve the financial problems; or make use of Chapter 11, reorganizing the financial condition and position of the operation in an effort to salvage the farm. In many cases, neither alternative was particularly attractive to the debtor–farmer.

As a result, in 1986, Chapter 12, Adjustment of Debts for Family Farmers, was added to the Bankruptcy Code. Chapter 12 seems to be a hybrid chapter, combining elements of Chapters 11 and 13 to produce a specialized, custom-tailored method for granting relief to family farmers.

Under Chapter 12 of the Bankruptcy Code, family farmers who have debts of no more than $1.5 million are allowed to use a special reorganization/repayment plan designed for this one special type of debtor. Chapter 12 allows a family farmer to develop a repayment plan despite a total debt in excess of that allowed under Chapter 13 for other individual debtors and to reorganize the farm and its financial structure to a significant extent in the development of that plan.

This chapter expired on 1 October 1998, although any cases pending at that time continued under its provisions. Numerous proposals to reactive this chapter have been introduced in Congress, but at the time of this writing, this has not yet occurred.

The Proceedings

A family farmer can file a voluntary petition for relief under the provisions of Chapter 12 but cannot be involuntarily petitioned into court. Upon the filing of the petition, the court enters an order for relief, and the automatic stay provision of bankruptcy law takes effect. The petitioning farmer will be allowed to continue to operate the farm as a debtor-in-possession unless there is an objection and a showing of cause for removal of the debtor and the appointment of a trustee. If the debtor remains in possession, the debtor can exercise all powers that would be available to a trustee under a Chapter 11 proceeding.

The Plan

The debtor must either present a plan for the adjustment of debts within 90 days of the petition or must request an extension of time for the preparation of such a plan. The court also can unilaterally extend the time period if it feels that there were circumstances beyond the control of the debtor that made it unduly difficult to meet the 90-day deadline.

The plan must provide for the payment in full in deferred payments of the debts of the farmer. It must also provide for the submission of a portion of the future income of the farmer into the plan for distribution to the creditors. The plan can call for the sale of any or all of the property of the debtor, including farm land and equipment, and such sales are free and clear of any claims of the creditors. Once a plan is submitted, the court will call for a confirmation hearing. This hearing is to occur no later than 45 days after the plan is submitted. Any party with an interest may object to the plan at this hearing, and the court will consider the objections before ruling on the plan. However, if the court feels that the plan conforms to the provisions of Chapter 12, that it has been proposed in good faith, and that it is capable of performance by the debtor, the plan will be approved.

A Chapter 12 proceeding can be converted to a Chapter 7 proceeding at the request of the debtor at any time. In addition, the proceeding can be converted to a Chapter 7 proceeding upon the request of any interested party, provided that the requesting party can present evidence of fraud in connection with the case. Thus, if the farmer commits a fraud in the case and then seeks relief under Chapter 12, his or her creditors can request a removal to Chapter 7, in effect involuntarily petitioning the farmer into a liquidation proceeding.

REPAYMENT PLANS: CHAPTER 13

Chapter 13 of the Bankruptcy Reform Act is designed to allow a debtor with a regular source of income to adjust his or her debts in a manner that (hopefully) will repay all creditors. Chapter 13 plans are available only to individual debtors; they cannot be used by corporations. As a further restriction, they are available only to debtors who have less than $1 million of debt, with a maximum of $750,000 in secured debts and a maximum of $250,000 in unsecured debts. (Prior to the 1994 Bankruptcy Bill, these figures were, respectively, $350,000 and $100,000.) There is also a cost-of-living adjustment (COLA) provision in the 1994 Bankruptcy Bill. The debt ceiling for Chapter 13 proceedings will be adjusted for inflation every three years, thus (hopefully) allowing this relief to keep up with inflation and negating the need for periodic adjustments. The debt ceilings in effect prior to 6 October 1994 made Chapter 13 unavailable to many farmers, which led to the creation of Chapter 12. The increase in consumer debt, coupled with inflation from 1978 through 1994, made the debt ceiling an impediment to the public policy objectives of Chapter 13 proceedings and led to the upward revision on allowable debt and to the inflation adjustment mechanism now in effect.

Debtors who exceed the debt ceiling will have to use Chapter 7, Chapter 11, or some nonbankruptcy alternative. Chapter 13 is only available by means of a voluntary petition. The debtor can seek relief under this option, but the creditors cannot force a debtor to enter a repayment plan. (However, the threat of being forced into Chapter 7 may persuade the debtor that Chapter 13 is in his or her best interests.)

The Proceedings

In many respects, a repayment plan is the simplest bankruptcy proceeding for an individual debtor. The debtor files a voluntary petition seeking relief. The court will issue an order for relief, an automatic stay will take effect, and a trustee will be appointed. The trustee will perform the investigation duties normally followed

CHAPTER 13 BANKRUPTCY

One of John's friends has been working for CIT since the firm first began operations. This friend recently encountered some financial difficulties and asked for an advance on his pay. While the firm has no formal policy regarding advances, the family generally agrees that advances on pay should not be given. However, since the employee is a friend of John's, Tom agreed to advance the young man $3,000. (Donna was opposed to the idea and advised Tom against it in the strongest possible terms.) Several weeks after receiving this advance, the employee filed for relief under Chapter 13 of the Bankruptcy Act. Among the creditors he listed was CIT, listing them for the amount of the advance. He listed total debts of $22,500, all unsecured except for a car loan from his bank. His only assets are his car, his stereo, and his job. He currently takes home $175 per week. In his repayment plan, the employee proposes that he make weekly payments of $37.50 for the next three years. (CIT would receive $5 per week, or a total of $780 under this plan.) The employee is single, and his monthly share for his apartment is $150. Tom has asked you if this repayment plan is likely to be approved by the Bankruptcy Court. What would you tell him? Why?

BUSINESS CONSIDERATIONS Should a business have a formal policy regarding employee salary advances? What can a business do to protect itself from situations such as this if it does, in fact, allow employees to receive advances on their pay?

ETHICAL CONSIDERATIONS Suppose that an employee "takes advantage" of his employer by getting an advance on his or her pay, and then lists that advance as a creditor's claim in bankruptcy. Should the firm retaliate against the employee through a firing or a reassignment? How should the employee be treated following his or her seeming mistreatment of the employer?

under a reorganization, but only if the debtor operates a business. In addition, the trustee will carry out the plan proposed by the debtor, if it is approved by the court.

The Plan

The debtor must file a proposed repayment plan with the court. The plan must provide equal treatment to each creditor claim within any given class of creditors. This does not mean that each class must be treated equally— only that within each class, every creditor must be treated equally. The plan also must make some provisions for clearing up any defaulted debts or defaulted payments on debts. The plan must not call for payments beyond a three-year period, unless the court feels that a longer period is necessary. Even then, the plan must be carried out within five years.

The court will approve the plan if the following conditions are met:

1. The plan appears to be fair to all parties.
2. The plan is in the best interests of the creditors.
3. It appears that the debtor can conform to the plan.
4. The plan proposes to pay at least as much as would have been paid under Chapter 7.

Once approved, the plan is binding on all parties, with or without their consent. At that point, the debtor must turn over to the trustee enough of the debtor's income to make the payments called for under the plan.

If the debtor performs the plan as approved, the court will grant a discharge. The discharge terminates all debts provided for in the plan—if they are dischargeable in a liquidation—that received their full share under the plan. In addition, the court can intercede and grant a discharge during the plan, even though the plan has not been completely carried out. The court will do so only if the following three factors are present:

1. The debtor cannot complete the plan owing to circumstances beyond his or her control.
2. The general (lowest-priority) creditors have received at least as much as they would have received in a liquidation.
3. The court does not feel it is practical to alter the plan.

The likelihood of such a court intervention during the plan is not very high, but the option is there. And, once again, the desire to provide a fresh start for an honest debtor is obvious.

In 1993, the Supreme Court handed down its opinion in *Rake* v. *Wade* [113 S.Ct. 2187 (1993)]. Wade held a long-term promissory note from Rake, with the note secured by a home mortgage. Wade was classified as an "oversecured" mortgagee since the value of the home was significantly higher than the balance owed on the note. The Court allowed Wade to collect interest, both pre- and postpetition, from Rake even though the note was silent on this matter and state law would not have allowed Wade to recover such interest.

Congress did not like the court's opinion in *Rake* v. *Wade*. The Bankruptcy Reform Act of 1994 contains a section intended to overrule the Court's opinion. The 1994 act provides:

> *Interest on Interest. This provision is applicable in Chapter 11, 12 and 13 cases, and provides that if a plan cures a default, the liability for interest is to be determined in accordance with the agreement and nonbankruptcy law. The purpose is to overrule Rake v. Wade . . . , which required the payment of interest on mortgage arrearages when the Chapter 13 debtor attempted to cure the default and reinstate the mortgage even if not contained in the agreement and not required by State law.*[3]

1984 Bankruptcy Amendments

The Bankruptcy Amendments of 1984 have tightened the requirements for a Chapter 13 repayment plan. The new standards also reduce the burden on the courts, since the good faith of the debtor is not an issue. Rather, a more tangible standard than the apparent good faith of the debtor has been substituted.

The more recent law allows any unsecured creditor to block the debtor's proposed repayment plan, but only if the plan does not meet one of two criteria:

1. The plan calls for the payment of 100 percent of the creditor's claim.
2. The plan calls for the debtor to pay 100 percent of all income not necessary to support the debtor's immediate family for at least three years.

Unless the debtor shows that it satisfies one of these two criteria, the Chapter 13 repayment plan will be rejected by the court. The debtor will then have to file a new plan, change over to a Chapter 7 proceeding, or withdraw the petition. Note that these are the *only* criteria available for a creditor to challenge a proposed repayment plan. The creditors do not have a right to "approve" the plan or even vote on it. The following case addresses this issue.

30.3

IN RE FILLION
181 F.3D 859 (7TH CIR. 1999)

FACTS Kenneth W. Bass deeded his farm to his daughter, Marcia Fillion, but Bass retained a limited life interest in the property. Eventually, Bass filed an action in Wisconsin state court to rescind the deed, and Fillion and her husband filed for bankruptcy under Chapter 13 of the Bankruptcy Code . . . The bankruptcy court confirmed the Fillions' Chapter 13 plan and also denied Bass's action for rescission of the deed. The district court affirmed the bankruptcy court on both issues, as do we. In 1959, Bass acquired a 152-acre farm in Dane County, Wisconsin, and has lived there ever since. After working on the farm for many years, Bass began renting out the farm land in

continued

30.3

IN RE FILLION, *continued*
181 F.3D 859 (7TH CIR. 1999)

the 1970's, though he still resided on the farm. Bass's only child, Marcia Fillion, was raised on the farm, but left it in 1980. Over the years, Fillion and her husband, Robin, inquired about purchasing part of the 152-acre farm for building a home. On March 29, 1993, Bass contacted Fillion and arranged to meet her at his attorney's office. At this meeting, Bass proposed that he give the farm to Fillion and her husband, with the conditions that Fillion assume the $18,000 mortgage on the farm and forgive another $5,000 debt her father owed her, and also that Bass retain a life estate in the buildings on the property. Fillion agreed, and a deed specifying these terms was drawn up and signed. Bass claims that at the same meeting, as part of the same transaction, Fillion agreed to support her father for the rest of his life. Fillion disputes this version, claiming that the only conditions to the gift of the farm were included in the deed. In June 1994, more than a year after the gift of the farm, Marcia and Robin Fillion (and their three children) moved onto the farm. Then in September, they moved from a trailer on the farm to the house also occupied by Bass. At this point, the Fillions began paying for the mortgage, taxes, gas and food. Unfortunately for all concerned, the relationship between Bass and the Fillions became acrimonious almost immediately. After about two years of domestic disturbances, Bass filed a civil action in state court seeking to eject the Fillions from the farm and to rescind the deed giving the farm to Marcia Fillion . . . Just days before Bass's motion for partial summary judgment was to be heard by the state court, the Fillions filed a Chapter 13 bankruptcy petition. On the date of the hearing before the state court, the Fillions did not appear, but Bass and the state court were notified of the bankruptcy filing. In violation of the automatic stay imposed by a voluntary bankruptcy filing . . . Bass requested that a default judgment be entered against the Fillions for ejectment. This constituted a continuation of a judicial proceeding against the debtors, and is prohibited by § 362(a)(1). The Fillions filed their Chapter 13 plan in September 1997. This plan proposed to sell part of the farm and to use the proceeds to satisfy the claims of creditors, including Bass. Bass objected to this plan, claiming that the plan was not feasible. Bass also initiated an adversary proceeding in the bankruptcy court on his rescission claim. The bankruptcy court denied the objection to the Chapter 13 plan and granted summary judgment to the Fillions on the rescission claim. Bass appealed both adverse decisions to the district court, which affirmed.

ISSUE Should the court approve a repayment plan over the objection of a creditor of the debtors?

HOLDING Yes, if the plan satisfies the requirements of Chapter 13 it should be approved, notwithstanding any objections by creditors of the debtor.

REASONING We first address Bass's objection to the Fillions' Chapter 13 plan. Confirmation of a Chapter 13 plan requires a substantially different inquiry than needed for a Chapter 11 plan. If a Chapter 13 plan meets the requirements contained in 11 U.S.C. § 1325 . . . then the bankruptcy court must confirm the plan. Creditors do not vote on a Chapter 13 plan . . . Under Chapter 13, if a debtor proposes a plan which complies with 11 U.S.C. § 1325, a creditor has no grounds to object to the plan . . . Our review of this claim is made more difficult by the fact that Bass has neglected to tie his arguments pertaining to his rescission claim to any bankruptcy law involving Chapter 13 plans. We see three plausible objections under 11 U.S.C. § 1325 to confirmation of this Chapter 13 plan: 1) that the plan was not filed in good faith; 2) that the plan proposes the sale of real estate, the ownership of which is disputed; and 3) that the plan is not feasible. The bankruptcy court concluded that because the plan proposes to pay all creditors one hundred percent of the allowed claims (with interest), the plan was filed in good faith. Bass has not challenged this ruling on appeal. Also, a dispute over the ownership of the land is not sufficient to block confirmation of the Chapter 13 plan (or even the actual sale of the property). Section 1303 of the Bankruptcy Code allows Chapter 13 debtors to sell real estate just as a bankruptcy trustee could under 11 U.S.C. § 363(f), and this provision authorizes the trustee to sell real estate which is subject to a bona fide dispute (with the disputed claims to attach to the proceeds of the sale) . . . Thus, the Bankruptcy Code specifically authorizes Chapter 13 debtors to do exactly what the Fillions proposed to do in their Chapter 13 plan. An objection to the plan based on merely the existence of Bass's claim of rescission could not be successful. Bass originally objected to confirmation of the Chapter 13 plan on the grounds of feasibility . . . However, the record developed before the bankruptcy court is void

30.3

IN RE FILLION, *continued*
181 F.3D 859 (7TH CIR. 1999)

of any evidence pertaining to feasibility of the plan per se. The debtors did not testify about their income, debts, and cash flow. But the Chapter 13 trustee and debtors' attorney did comment to the bankruptcy court that if Bass succeeded in his rescission action, the Fillions' plan would not be feasible, and the bankruptcy court apparently accepted this representation. Assuming that feasibility of the plan depends on the Fillions profiting from the sale of at least a portion of the farm, the confirmation of the Chapter 13 plan will depend on whether Bass can succeed in his rescission claim. So we now turn to the merits of Bass's state law rescission claim, brought in an adversary proceeding. Under Wisconsin law, a gift of property from an elderly parent to his or her child in exchange for a promise of support is presumptively improvident and may be rescinded . . . The agreement for support may be verbal, and need not be specific . . . However, the gift and the promise of support must occur at the same time, as part of the same transaction . . . The bankruptcy court concluded that as a factual matter, the deed was not conveyed in exchange for support, in other words, that the "quid pro quo, support for the deeding over the property" was not a part of the transaction. This finding is not clearly erroneous. . .

Thus, the bankruptcy court applied the correct legal standard, by requiring that the support agreement serve as consideration for the conveyance. Bass also argues that there was a mutual mistake in the contract which allows him to rescind the contract . . . Mutual mistakes must concern past or present facts, not unexpected facts that occur after the document is executed . . . Therefore, even if both Bass and Fillion were ignorant of the effect of the granting of a life estate, a mutual mistake of fact did not exist when Bass and Fillion signed the deed. Lastly, Bass contends that Bass and Fillion did not have a meeting of the minds as to the terms of the transaction on March 29, 1993, and therefore, no agreement was made. The bankruptcy court found this not to be the case. It concluded that the agreement reached on March 29, 1993, between Bass and Fillion did not include support . . .

In this case, there was an objective meeting of the minds between Bass and Fillion, as evidenced by the two parties' signatures on the deed. Bass failed to prove an oral contract for support was part of this agreement. Therefore, the contract cannot be rescinded for a lack of assent to the contract. The bankruptcy court applied the correct legal standards, and its fact finding was not clearly erroneous. As the gift of the farm was not in exchange for a promise of support, Wisconsin courts would not construe the promise of support as a condition precedent to the deeding of the property. Of course, this does not mean that Bass has no claim for money damages, and Bass still owns a life interest in the buildings on the farm. The bankruptcy court correctly denied Bass's claim for rescission of the deed, and therefore, the bankruptcy court was also correct to confirm the Fillions' Chapter 13 plan.

AFFIRMED.

BUSINESS CONSIDERATION In this case, Bass alleged that the contract had additional terms that were not included in the writing. Should a businessperson have a policy of ensuring that all terms are included in a writing before signing that writing?

ETHICAL CONSIDERATIONS Is it ethical for a party who agreed to additional terms beyond those included in a writing to deny those terms since they were not included in the written agreement? Is it ethical for a party to claim that additional terms exist when those terms were not included in the written agreement? What ethical issues are raised by facts such as these?

Under the 1978 Bankruptcy Reform Act, debtor payments under a repayment plan did not begin until the plan was confirmed by the court. This gave many debtors a four- to six-month "grace period" in which the debtor retained all of his or her assets but made no payments, to the detriment of the creditors. The 1984 Bankruptcy Amendments call for payments to begin within 30 days of the filing of the plan, subject to confirmation of the plan by the court. The debtor makes these payments to the trustee, who holds the monies paid until confirmation of the plan by the court and then distributes them to the various creditors. If the debtor fails to make payments to the trustee in a timely manner, the plan can be dismissed by the court.

Finally, the 1984 Bankruptcy Amendments provide for the possible modification of the plan after it is confirmed. The trustee, the debtor, or any creditor can petition the court to increase or decrease the debtor's payments whenever the debtor's circumstances or income warrant such a modification. Prior to the 1984 Amendments, decreases were possible, but increases were not permitted.

The four bankruptcy alternatives discussed in this chapter and Chapter 29 are designed to give an honest debtor a fresh start. An individual may use any of the four alternatives. Most businesses can use two of the alternatives. Exhibit 30.1 on pages 801–804 compares these four bankruptcy alternatives.

NONBANKRUPTCY ALTERNATIVES

In many cases, a debtor or creditor will object to undergoing a bankruptcy, perhaps because of a distaste for the stigma of bankruptcy, or for any number of other reasons. But a wish to avoid bankruptcy does not remove the financial problems of the debtor. Often the debtor or creditor will select a nonbankruptcy alternative to allow—or to force—the debtor to "get out from under." Whether such a decision will work depends on a number of factors, including the attitudes of the creditors who did not select or agree to the nonbankruptcy alternative chosen.

Prejudgment Alternatives

The creditors of a troubled debtor frequently will use some prejudgment procedure in an effort either to get paid or to force the debtor into acting before a judicial solution is sought. Three major prejudgment procedures—attachments, garnishments, or receivership—are available to creditors.

Attachment. The first remedy is *attachment.* A creditor can go to the clerk of the court and obtain a writ of attachment on the basis of the creditor's word that the debtor has not satisfied some claim. Usually, the creditor must post a bond to cover any potential liability in case the attachment is not made in good faith. The creditor will then have the sheriff levy on as much of the debtor's estate as is needed to satisfy the claim of the attaching creditor. The sheriff will take control over these assets until the proceedings terminate. Once the attachment occurs, the creditor must proceed to get a judgment against the debtor. If a judgment is obtained, the assets may be sold to cover the judgment unless the debtor pays outright in order to have the assets released. If the creditor fails to get a judgment within some preset time period, the attachment and lien will expire and the attached assets will be returned to the debtor.

Attachments frequently lead to bankruptcy petitions. The creditors who did not seek an attachment can file an involuntary petition, alleging that the attaching creditor has received a preference. If they petition within four months of the attachment, the courts normally will overturn the attachment.

Garnishment. The second major prejudgment remedy is a *garnishment.* (A garnishment can also be used as a postjudgment remedy under some circumstances.) In a garnishment, the targeted assets are in the hands of some third person and not in the hands of the debtor. However, the assets that the third person controls belong to the debtor or are owed to the debtor. For example, a checking account balance belongs to the debtor but is "held" by the bank. The debtor's wages are owed to the debtor but are "held" by the employer.

The creditor will again go to court, this time seeking a writ of garnishment. When the writ is issued, the creditor will officially notify the third person to hold, or retain, the assets pending a judgment. A third person who ignores this notification will become personally liable to the creditor if and when a judgment is entered. Normally, the freezing of the debtor's checking account or paycheck will "encourage" the debtor to resolve the dispute rapidly. Again, if the creditor does not receive cooperation and does not reduce the claim to a judgment within a preset time period, the writ will be dissolved and the garnished assets will be released to the debtor.

Garnishments are provided for under state law. However, federal regulations have been enacted to limit the power of the states to some extent in this area. Title III of the Consumer Credit Protection Act (15. U.S.C. § 601 *et seq.*) restricts the garnishment of wages. Debtors are allowed to retain the *greater* of 75 percent of weekly disposable earnings *or* 30 hours at the federal minimum wage. Thus, a worker who nets $400 per week would be allowed to retain $300 (75 percent of weekly disposable earnings), while a worker who nets $200 per week would be allowed to keep $154.50 (30 times the minimum wage of $5.15). State law limitations on garnishment are followed if the state law provides more protection to the worker/debtor.

Receivership. The third major prejudgment remedy is *receivership.* This is not a favored prejudgment choice today, unless it is initiated by the debtor, because of the ready availability of bankruptcy relief. In a receivership, the court appoints a disinterested third person to manage the affairs of the debtor. This receiver is responsible for preserving the debtor's estate until a judgment is reached. Liens on the property of the debtor continue under a receivership, but the property affected cannot be bothered without permission of the court. Unless the debtor pays the debt or the creditor cancels it, the parties eventually must resolve the case by some other means. This normally is done by the entry of a judgment by the court.

Postjudgment Alternatives

A creditor who wins the case and receives a judgment probably will seek one of three major postjudgment remedies—execution, supplementary proceeding, or garnishment—to satisfy his or her claim.

30.3 | SALES/ MANUFACTURING

CALL-IMAGE TECHNOLOGY

COLLECTING ON UNPAID DEBTS

One of CIT's customers has not yet paid for 100 Call-Image videophones that were delivered to it several months ago. Neither Tom nor Anna wants to sue the firm unless it is absolutely necessary. However, the customer refuses to accept their phone calls or to talk with them concerning the past due bill. Lindsay recently learned that this business is storing quite a large quantity of inventory in a warehouse owned by the family of one of her classmates. She tells you that this inventory is stored in the warehouse and asks you if there is any way for CIT to get possession of the inventory, either to force the business to pay its bill or to sell the inventory to cover the debt owed to CIT. What do you tell her?

BUSINESS CONSIDERATION When a debtor refuses to talk with a creditor concerning the debt, the creditor is forced to take action. What should a debtor do if or when it finds itself unable to make payments as they come due to one or more of its creditors?

ETHICAL CONSIDERATION Suppose that there is a legitimate disagreement as to the amount due on an account between two parties. Suppose, also, that the creditor learns that the debtor's inventory is in the hands of a warehouseman and is therefore susceptible to garnishment. If the creditor garnishes the inventory, the debtor can be forced to agree to pay the amount the creditor asserts is owed, even though the debtor honestly believes that a lesser amount is owed. How should the parties act in this situation? Explain your reasoning.

Execution. The first of these is an *execution.* In an execution, the creditor will attempt to seize and sell as many of the debtor's assets as are needed to cover the judgment. This is done by procuring a writ of execution from the court and then having the sheriff levy on the debtor's assets. After the sheriff levies, the assets seized are appraised, a notice of sale is made, and the goods are sold. (The sale is usually at a public auction, commonly referred to as a *judicial sale.*) The proceeds of the sale or a predetermined percentage of the appraised value, whichever is higher, will be applied to the debts owed to the creditor. (The percentage varies from state to state, since this is a state remedy.)

The debtor is usually allowed to redeem any real property and some personal property within a fixed period after the sale by paying the purchaser the necessary amount. A purchaser also should be aware that only the debtor's interest in the asset has been purchased. There may very well be other liens or claims or other problems to be confronted later. Thus, the selling price usually is fairly low.

Supplementary Proceeding. The second major postjudgment remedy is a *supplementary proceeding.* A supplementary proceeding can be used only if the writ of execution is unsatisfied. In a supplementary proceeding, the creditors attempt to discover any assets of the debtor by examining and questioning any interested parties. If assets are discovered, the creditors can have a receiver appointed to preserve the assets, or they can have the court order a sale of the assets.

Garnishment. The third major postjudgment remedy is a *garnishment.* Garnishments were already discussed as a prejudgment remedy, but there is a slight difference here. Before a judgment is entered, the third person is instructed to hold the assets. After a judgment is entered, the third person is told to turn over the assets to cover the debts owed. If wages are garnished, some amount must be left to allow the debtor to subsist until the debt is paid.

Debtor-Initiated Remedies

Debtors often decide to get out from under on their own by initiating remedies under state law rather than seeking a discharge in bankruptcy. A debtor who so decides usually will choose one of three options—assignment for the benefit of creditors, composition agreement, or extension agreement.

Assignment for the Benefit of Creditors. The first option is an *assignment for the benefit of creditors.* Here the debtor freely and voluntarily transfers property to a third person, in trust, to use in order to pay the creditors. Creditor consent is not needed, and once the transfer is made, the property is beyond the reach of the creditors. Unfortunately for the debtor, such a transfer does not result in an automatic discharge. Not only that, it may result in the filing of a bankruptcy petition by the creditors. To avoid these problems, many debtors prefer to reach a contractual agreement with the creditors. Such an agreement does require creditor consent, but it will also result in discharge. The debtor may seek either a composition, or an extension, or both.

Composition Agreement. In a *composition agreement,* each creditor who is involved agrees to take less money than is owed, if the money is paid immediately, as full satisfaction of the debt. Such an arrangement is a contract between the debtor and the creditors as well as among the creditors. Thus, at least two creditors must join before the composition is valid. Otherwise, it would be invalid because of lack of consideration.

Extension Agreement. In an *extension agreement,* the creditors agree to a longer repayment period in order to receive full payment. Again, the courts view it as a dual contract between the debtor and the creditors and among the creditors.

In either a composition or an extension, the contract among the creditors is based on their acceptance of a change in performance in exchange for an agreement by each not to file suit to collect the original contract. Thus, both a composition and an extension are supported by consideration. Each is a contract, and the court will enforce either as it would enforce any other contract.

E X H I B I T   30.1 | **A Comparison of the Bankruptcy Alternatives**

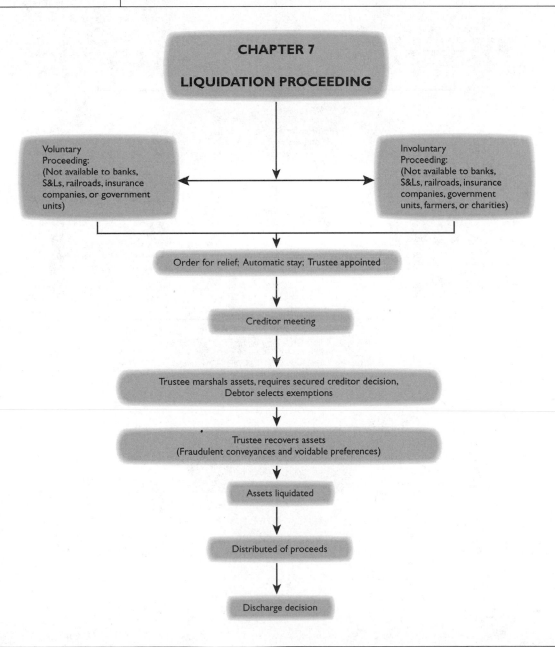

CHAPTER 7

LIQUIDATION PROCEEDING

Voluntary Proceeding: (Not available to banks, S&Ls, railroads, insurance companies, or government units)

Involuntary Proceeding: (Not available to banks, S&Ls, railroads, insurance companies, government units, farmers, or charities)

Order for relief; Automatic stay; Trustee appointed

Creditor meeting

Trustee marshals assets, requires secured creditor decision, Debtor selects exemptions

Trustee recovers assets (Fraudulent conveyances and voidable preferences)

Assets liquidated

Distributed of proceeds

Discharge decision

E X H I B I T   30.1 | **A Comparison of the Bankruptcy Alternatives, continued**

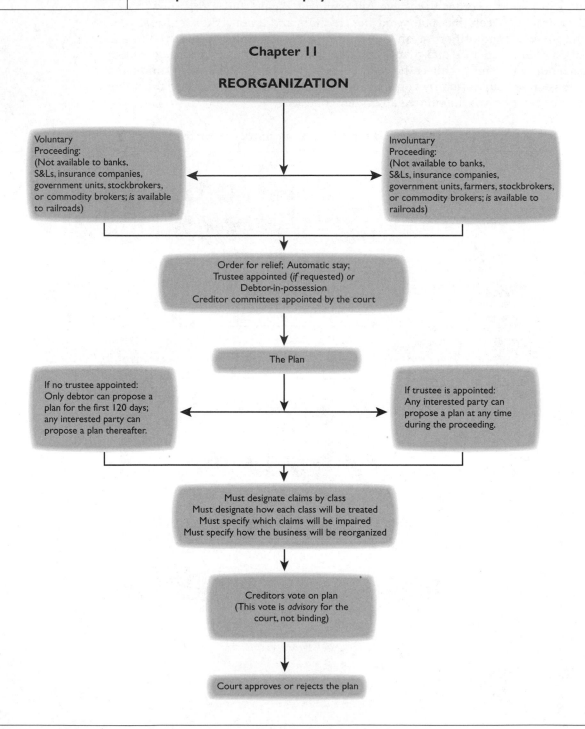

E X H I B I T 30.1 | **A Comparison of the Bankruptcy Alternatives, continued**

CHAPTER 12

DEBT ADJUSTMENT PLAN FOR FAMILY FARMERS

↓

Voluntary petition only

↓

Restricted to family farmers with no more than $1.5 million in debts

↓

Order for relief, Automatic stay
Trustee appointed if requested, *or*
Debtor-in-possession

↓

Farmer must propose plan within 90 days

↓

Court must hold confirmation meeting within 45 days
of submission of the plan

↓

Court reviews plan, accepts or rejects

↓

Debtor may convert to Chapter 7 at any time prior to
completion of the plan upon request; Creditors may
request removal to Chapter 7 "for cause"

E X H I B I T 30.1 | **A Comparison of the Bankruptcy Alternatives, continued**

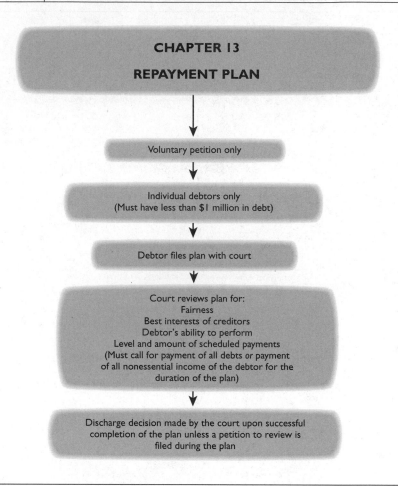

CHAPTER 13

REPAYMENT PLAN

Voluntary petition only

Individual debtors only
(Must have less than $1 million in debt)

Debtor files plan with court

Court reviews plan for:
Fairness
Best interests of creditors
Debtor's ability to perform
Level and amount of scheduled payments
(Must call for payment of all debts *or* payment
of all nonessential income of the debtor for the
duration of the plan)

Discharge decision made by the court upon successful
completion of the plan unless a petition to review is
filed during the plan

RESOURCES FOR BUSINESS LAW STUDENTS

NAME	RESOURCES	WEB ADDRESS
11 U.S.C. Chapter 11—Reorganization	The Legal Information Institute (LII), maintained by Cornell Law School, provides a hypertext and searchable version of Chapter 7, Liquidation, of the U.S. Code.	http://www.law.cornell.edu/uscode/11/ch11.html
11 U.S.C. Chapter 12—Adjustment of Debts of a Family Farmer with Regular Annual Income	LII provides a hypertext and searchable version of Chapter 12, Adjustment of Debts of a Family Farmer with Regular Annual Income.	http://www.law.cornell.edu/uscode/11/ch12.html
11 U.S.C. Chapter 13—Adjustment of Debts of an Individual with Regular Income	LII provides a hypertext and searchable version of Chapter 13, Adjustment of Debts of an Individual with Regular Income.	http://www.law.cornell.edu/uscode/11/ch13.html
Bankruptcy Alternatives	Bankruptcy Alternatives, maintained by Mory Brenner, Attorney at Law, provides questions and answers about alternatives to bankruptcy.	http://www.debtworkout.com/

SUMMARY

An embattled debtor need not always go through liquidation in order to make a fresh start. Other bankruptcy and nonbankruptcy remedies may work equally well.

Under bankruptcy, the debtor may seek a reorganization under Chapter 11 or a repayment plan under Chapter 13. A farmer may seek a repayment plan under Chapter 12. Each of these requires court approval of a plan, and each requires the debtor to propose the plan in good faith. In a reorganization, the debtor adjusts his or her financial position to allow a business to continue. In a repayment plan, the debtor proposes a method of repaying debts over a three- to five-year period. Good faith and fairness are essential in any plans before they will be approved by the courts. Recently, Chapter 11 has been used as a corporate strategy, allowing corporations to escape liabilities or obligations that the firm feels are blatantly unfair or may lead to the demise of the organization.

Some creditors seek nonbankruptcy remedies under state law. The creditor may seek either prejudgment remedies to force the debtor to act or postjudgment remedies in order to collect. Either type of action may result in a bankruptcy proceeding. The debtor also may seek a nonbankruptcy remedy under state law. This normally will involve a contract with the creditors and frequently will result in a bankruptcy proceeding.

DISCUSSION QUESTIONS

1. What role does the examiner play in a reorganization under Chapter 11? How is this different from the role that a trustee plays in a Chapter 11 reorganization? How is the role of the trustee different in Chapter 11 from his or her role in Chapter 7?

2. The 1984 Bankruptcy Amendments provide some specific guidelines for a repayment plan under Chapter 13. What does the court look at in deciding whether to approve a repayment plan under these guidelines? How does this differ from the requirements for a repayment plan under the original Bankruptcy Reform Act? What can a creditor do to challenge a plan under Chapter 13?

3. What can the court do under a repayment plan if, owing to a change in circumstances, the debtor cannot complete the plan as approved by the court? Who may ask the court to intercede and change the repayment plan?

4. What public policy considerations might lead a court to prefer a Chapter 11 reorganization over a Chapter 7 liquidation for a corporation seeking relief in bankruptcy? What considerations will lead the court to order a removal from Chapter 11 to Chapter 7 when a corporation files its petition for reorganization under Chapter 11?

5. Chapter 12 provides relief for individual farmers by allowing them to establish repayment plans. Why did the Bankruptcy Code require a special chapter for farmers when there is already a repayment plan for individual debtors available in Chapter 13 and a reorganization plan available primarily for businesses under Chapter 11?

6. What substantive changes were included in the Bankruptcy Reform Act of 1994? Why do you think Congress felt that these changes were necessary?

7. Why does the law specify that a minimum percentage of appraised value must be applied to debts in an execution, even if the assets sold in the execution bring less at sale than their appraised value? Does this rule reflect more of a public policy concern for the debtor or for the creditor?

8. What are the nonbankruptcy prejudgment alternatives available to a creditor when the debtor cannot or will not make the payments owed to the creditor? What are the nonbankruptcy postjudgment remedies available to the creditor?

9. In a composition agreement, the creditors agree to accept less than the debtor owes and to treat this lesser payment as payment in full. Why is a creditor willing to agree to a composition agreement? Why will a composition agreement occasionally be better for the creditor than a bankruptcy proceeding under Chapter 13?

10. Title III of the Consumer Credit Protection Act imposes limitations on the garnishment of wages. Do these limitations make garnishment a less attractive alternative for creditors? Do these limits seem to reflect a public policy concern for the rights of the debtors at the expense of the creditors?

CASE PROBLEMS AND WRITING ASSIGNMENTS

1. The Internal Revenue Service (IRS) filed liens for employment taxes due but unpaid against Dade Helicopters, Inc., Dade Helicopters Service, Inc., and Tropical Helicopters, Inc. When the taxes remained unpaid, the IRS seized virtually all the assets of three companies—Dade Helicopter Jet Service, Inc., Brickell Investment Corp., and Tropical Helicopter Airways, Inc.—asserting that these companies were "alter-egos" of the taxpayers who were delinquent with their taxes. In fact, despite the similarities in names, these firms were totally separate and distinct from the delinquent taxpayers. Due to these seizures, the three companies were forced to shut down their entire operations immediately, and all three were forced to file for relief under Chapter 11 of the Bankruptcy Code. The debtors petitioned the Bankruptcy Court to order release of the assets in the possession of the IRS and to grant the debtors' costs and attorney's fees. The IRS objected to the award of costs and attorney's fees, although it did not object to the order to release the assets. Should the debtors be granted costs and attorney's fees in this case? Explain your reasoning. [See *In re Brickell Investment Corp.*, 922 F.2d 696 (11th Cir. 1991).]

2. BFP took title to a California home subject to a deed of trust in favor of Imperial Savings Association. After Imperial entered a notice of default because the loan was not being serviced, the home was purchased by Osborne for $433,000 at a properly noticed foreclosure sale. Shortly thereafter, BFP filed for bankruptcy relief and, acting as a debtor-in-possession, filed a complaint to set aside the sale to Osborne as a fraudulent conveyance, claiming that the home was worth more than $725,000 when sold, and thus not exchanged for "reasonably equivalent value" as required by the Bankruptcy Code. Does the consideration received in a noncollusive, regularly conducted, nonjudicial foreclosure sale amount to "reasonably equivalent value" as a matter of law? Explain your answer. [See *BFP v. Resolution Trust Corp.*, 511 U.S. 531(1994).]

3. On 30 November 1988, Francisco Pacana filed a petition seeking relief under Chapter 13 of the Bankruptcy Code. At the same time, he filed a repayment plan with the court. His schedules showed a total unsecured debt of $34,500, which included a $13,900 debt to his ex-wife for child support arrearages. Pacana's plan classified the debt to his ex-wife as a "priority" and provided for payment to her but did not state the timing or the amount of the payments she was to receive. The overall plan called for payment of 14 percent to unsecured creditors, which would include the child support arrearages owed to Ms. Pacana-Siler. The court approved the plan without modification on 13 February 1989. On that date, there was outstanding an unresolved application filed by Ms. Pacana-Siler on 20 January 1989 seeking relief from the automatic stay in order to allow her to enforce the child support debt. The court held a hearing on the application on 3 March 1989 and granted her relief from the stay.

The court ordered that:

to the extent that in addition to what is paid to [Ms. Pacana-Siler] on her priority claim in the Chapter 13 she may collect an additional $250 per month from the debtor to be applied against the arrearages. This additional $250 may be collected upon immediately by agreement with or by levy upon the debtor's wages or other monies due him.

Mr. Pacana appealed, arguing that this order rendered his plan infeasible, because he could not afford to carry out his plan and pay an additional $250 to his ex-wife. He also argued that his plan implied that he intended to pay his ex-wife 100 percent of her claim since he had designated her as a "priority claimant." Can the court grant relief from the automatic stay provisions in a bankruptcy proceeding to provide for collection by a priority creditor? [See *In re Pacana*, 125 B.R. 19 (9th Cir. BAP 1991).]

4. SRJ Enterprises, Inc. (SRJ) owned and operated a Nissan automobile dealership. NBD Park Ridge Bank (NBD) financed SRJ's new vehicle inventory with a loan of approximately $1,400,000 in March 1991. NBD took and perfected a security interest that purportedly covered all the debtor's assets. As additional security, the president of SRJ guaranteed the loan. Later, SRJ borrowed an additional $900,000 from Success National Bank. Success claims to hold a perfected lien on assets of SRJ already subject to NBD's lien. The NBD loan agreement required that SRJ receive and hold all its inventory, and the proceeds from its inventory sales, in trust. NBD also required SRJ to keep a separate account of each item of inventory, to segregate the sales proceeds held in trust, and to pay these proceeds to NBD. Using the jargon of the automobile financing industry, NBD provided "floor planning" financing and employed a "trust receipt" repayment device. According to Success, however, NBD failed to enforce its agreement with SRJ, and as a result SRJ withheld approximately $600,000 of trust proceeds from NBD. Success argues that NBD allowed SRJ to become "out of trust" in an effort to salvage the loan and the business relationship between SRJ and NBD.

At the date of the bankruptcy petition, SRJ owed NBD more than $1,400,000, an amount that Success argues would have been less had NBD enforced its loan agreement with SRJ. SRJ, as debtor-in-possession, sold its assets and franchise rights free and clear of all liens for an amount less than $1,400,000. To the extent they were valid, the lien rights of NBD and of Success attached to the proceeds of this sale. In connection with the sale NBD filed an adversary proceeding against SRJ and Success to determine the validity and the priority of NBD's liens. SRJ and Success filed counterclaims against NBD. (SRJ subsequently dropped its counterclaim.) In its counterclaim, Success alleged that NBD had received a voidable preference and sought to recover the property transferred preferentially. Success also sought to subordinate the claims of NBD. NBD objected to the motion by Success and filed its own motion to dismiss the counterclaim of Success due to Success's lack of standing. Did Success have standing to challenge the alleged preferential transfers from SRJ to NBD, to the detriment of Success? What steps should Success have taken as a junior secured creditor to protect its interests in this situation? What should Success have done differently in an effort to protect itself from a bankruptcy by SRJ? [See *In re SRJ Enterprises, Inc.*, 151 B.R. 189 (Bkrtcy.N.D.Ill. 1993).]

5. The Platas filed a petition for relief under Chapter 12 of the Bankruptcy Code in 1987. They submitted a plan early the following year, which was confirmed by the court. Under the terms of the plan, $29,000 was to be paid during 1988 to the trustee, who would then distribute this money to the creditors. When it became apparent during 1988 that the crops for the year would not generate sufficient income to meet the payment required under the plan, the Platas converted their case from Chapter 12 to Chapter 7. At the time of the conversion, the trustee held $14,000 that had not been distributed. Upon conversion to Chapter 7, the Platas claimed $8,300 of those undistributed dollars as exempt assets under the provisions of the Code. The trustee objected to the return of this money to the debtors. Did the creditors obtain a vested right in the proceeds paid to the trustee prior to distribution? [See *In re Plata*, 958 F.2d 918 (9th Cir. 1992).]

6. **BUSINESS APPLICATION CASE** AppleTree Markets, Inc., filed a petition for relief under Chapter 11 of the Bankruptcy Act. As part of its reorganization plan, AppleTree proposed rejecting the collective bargaining agreement (CBA) it had with the United Food and Commercial Workers (UFCW) Local Unions. AppleTree argues that the UFCW participated in the drafting of AppleTree's First Amended Disclosure Statement in connection with its Second Amended Plan of Reorganization under Chapter 11. According to AppleTree, the disclosure statement was premised in part on the benefits that the bankruptcy estate would receive from the rejection of the collective bargaining agreements. The Bankruptcy Court approved the plan on 29 September 1992. Because the UFCW did not appeal the plan, it became final and nonappealable in October 1992. The collective bargaining agreements expired by their own terms early in 1993. The UFCW then appealed the decision of the Bankruptcy Court to reject the collective bargaining agreement. AppleTree argues that the appeal by the UFCW is moot because the substantial consummation of the plan has so changed the circumstances as to render appellate relief both ineffective and inequitable to the parties to the plan. Should the UFCW be allowed to appeal the Bankruptcy Court's rejection of the collective bargaining agreement after the debtor's reorganization plan, including the rejection of the collective bargaining agreement, has been approved and implemented? When a business proposes a reorganization plan that includes rejection of a collective bargaining agreement, should management show its willingness to make sacrifices in its salary and benefits package before asking the court to allow the firm to reject the collective bargaining agreement? How much should management have to sacrifice before it can properly ask nonmanagement workers to make sacrifices to save the firm? [See *In re Appletree Markets, Inc.,* 155 B.R. 431 (S.D.Tex. 1993).]

7. **ETHICAL APPLICATION CASE** Pioneer filed for relief under Chapter 11 of the Bankruptcy Code. Brunswick Associates, one of Pioneer's unsecured creditors, failed to file its proof of claim by the deadline—the bar date—established by the Bankruptcy Court and included in the Notice of Meeting of Creditors sent to an official of Brunswick. Four weeks after the bar date, Brunswick asked the court for permission to file its proof of claim. The Bankruptcy Code permits late filings where the creditor's failure to comply with the deadline was the result of excusable neglect. The court refused the request, ruling that a late filing will only be permitted if the failure to meet the deadline is due to circumstances beyond the reasonable control of the creditor. Should the creditor be allowed to file its proof of claim after the bar date if the failure to meet the deadline was due to a simple oversight, or excusable neglect, or should the creditor be barred from filing unless it can show that its failure to meet the deadline was due to circumstances beyond its reasonable control? What ethical arguments can be made to support each of these criteria? [See *Pioneer Inv. Services* v. *Brunswick Associates,* 507 U.S. 380 (1993).]

8. **CRITICAL THINKING CASE** Toibb filed a voluntary petition for relief under Chapter 7 of the Bankruptcy Code. The Schedule of Assets and Liabilities accompanying this petition disclosed that Toibb had no secured debts, a disputed federal tax claim of $11,000, and various other unsecured debts totaling $170,605. He only listed two nonexempt assets: 24 percent of the stock of Independence Electric Corporation (IEC) and a possible claim against his former business associates. The schedule stated that the value of each of these assets was unknown. During the course of the Chapter 7 proceedings, the trustee informed the creditors that IEC had offered to purchase Toibb's shares in the firm for $25,000. When Toibb discovered that the stock had such a substantial value, he decided to avoid liquidation by converting to a Chapter 11 proceeding. The Bankruptcy Court initially approved his petition, and Toibb filed his reorganization plan. At that point, the court dismissed his petition, finding that he did not qualify for relief under Chapter 11 because he was not engaged in an ongoing business. Toibb appealed.

   Was Toibb entitled to seek relief under Chapter 11 of the Bankruptcy Code despite the fact that he was not engaged in operating an ongoing business? Is it fair to allow a debtor to select the bankruptcy chapter under which he or she will seek relief? Can an argument be made that it is more ethical to allow the creditors to make this decision? [See *Toibb* v. *Radloff,* 501 U.S. 157 (1991).]

NOTES

1. See, for example, "Reshaping Corporate America," *Management Accountant* 71(9) (March 1990), p. 21; "Court Reverses Own Ruling: Negotiations Over Revised Manville Payout Plan to Continue," *Business Insurance* 27(21) (May 1993), p. 2; or Kevin J. Delaney, *Strategic Bankruptcy* (Berkeley: University of California Press, 1992).

2. *Bustop Shelters of Louisville* v. *Classic Homes,* 914 F.2d 810 (6th Cir. 1998).

3. H.R. 5116 § 306.

Agency

One of our fondest dreams is to have the ability to be in more than one place at the same time. Obviously, this is a physical impossibility. Fortunately, the law has found a way to do legally what cannot be done physically. By using an agent, a person can legally be in more than one place at a time.

An agent is a person empowered to "be you" within the scope of the agency. Whatever the agent hears, you "heard." Whatever the agent says, you "said." Whatever an agent does, you "did." In other words, you are legally responsible for your agent's conduct—within the scope of the agency.

A businessperson derives obvious benefits from "being" in many places at the same time; however, if the agent does not act properly, many problems may arise. Part 7 explores these benefits and problems of agency.

31

THE CREATION AND TERMINATION OF AN AGENCY

CALL-IMAGE TECHNOLOGY

A G E N D A

As CIT grows, the Kochanowskis will need to hire more and more workers. As a consequence, Anna and Tom need to fully understand the duties and responsibilities associated with the relationship between the employer and employee, as well as their relationships with the public at large. What types of work relationships are possible?

CIT does not make its own deliveries to retailers. What is the relationship of CIT to the people who drive the trucks and make the deliveries to the retailers? CIT is considering hiring other companies to serve as authorized repair centers for the videophones. What

constraints should be evaluated by CIT before entering into these arrangements with other firms?

Tom is concerned that salespersons hired to sell Call-Image videophones will copy the technology and start their own competing businesses. Is this a valid concern? How can CIT protect itself from competition by former workers?

These and other questions will arise during our discussion of agency law. Be prepared! You never know when one of the Kochanowskis will need your help or advice.

O U T L I N E

AGENCY LAW AND AGENCY RELATIONSHIPS

Agency law concerns the relationships between workers and the people who hire workers. It includes their duties and responsibilities both to each other and to the public at large. No one can really avoid agency law; almost everyone at some time works as an employee or hires an employee. Moreover, agency relationships arise in both business and nonbusiness situations—for example, when a person returns books to the university library for a friend.

Most agency relationships do not require litigation because they function smoothly. To resolve the legal problems that do arise, one must look to agency law, contract law, and tort law. In most of these subject areas, the court will place significant reliance on state law. Much of the law of agency has been studied by the American Law Institute (ALI) and is discussed in its publication *Restatement (Second) of Agency*. *Restatements* are treatises that summarize detailed recommendations of what the law should be on a particular subject. Although *Restatements* are not legislature- or court-made law, they become part of the legal **precedents** when courts rely on them and incorporate them into court decisions. (See Chapter 1 for a more detailed discussion of precedents.) The three agency chapters in this book rely on the *Restatement (Second) of Agency*.

Precedents
Prior court cases that control the decision in court.

You should note that the position of your state may vary from that in the *Restatement (Second) of Agency*. This *Restatement* explains some key terms:

1. *Agency is the fiduciary relation which results from the manifestation of consent by one person to another that the other shall act on his [sic] behalf and subject to his control, and consent by the other so to act.*
2. *The one for whom action is to be taken is the principal.*
3. *The one who is to act is the agent.*[1]

An *agency relationship* is consensual in nature. It is based on the concept that the parties mutually agree that (1) the agent will act on behalf of the principal and (2) the agent will be subject to the principal's direction and control. The agreement can be expressed or implied. In addition, the parties must be competent to act as principal and agent.

Analysis of Agency Relationships

To analyze a situation involving an agency relationship, ask these questions:

1. Was the dispute between the principal and the agent?
2. Was an agency formed voluntarily by the principal and the agent, or is there some other relationship?
3. Did the parties have the capacity to perform their roles as the principal and the agent?
4. What authority did the principal vest in the agent?
5. Did the agent enter into a contract or commit a tort?

RESTRICTIONS ON CREATING AN AGENCY RELATIONSHIP

Agency law affects a broad range of situations, from a small partnership with two partners to a corporation with thousands of employees, and from a 16-year-old babysitter to a highly skilled developer of computer peripherals. In fact, everything a corporation does, it does through agents. There are few restrictions on who can form agency relationships and what can be done through them. One restriction is that the agreement must require the agent to perform acts that are legal in order to form a *lawful* agency relationship. An agreement to distribute "crank," for example, would not be a lawful agency relationship.

Capacity to Be a Principal

With the exception of minors and incompetents, any person can appoint an agent. It is generally true that any person having capacity to *contract* has capacity to employ a servant agent or a nonservant agent. (The distinction between these two agents is that a principal has more control over the actions of the former than over those of the latter.) Since agency is a consensual relationship, the principal must have capacity to confer a legally operative consent.[2]

Some states have determined that a minor lacks capacity to be a principal. In other states, a minor has the capacity to enter into an agency relationship, but the agency relationship is voidable. The *Restatement (Second) of Agency*, § 20, takes the second position. In this second group of states, the agreements entered into by the minor's agent will also be voidable to the same extent that the minor's own contracts will be voidable. The key to understanding this concept is to remember that the contract is really entered into by the principal.

Capacity to Be an Agent

Generally, anyone can be an agent. Strange as it seems, even persons who do not have the capacity to act for themselves—for example, minors or insane persons—can act as agents for someone else. It is the capacity of the *principal*, not that of the agent, that controls. Obviously, however, principals should exercise care to appoint agents who are able to make sound decisions.

Duties an Agent Can Perform

A principal "appoints" an agent to deal with the public. Generally, an agent can be assigned to do almost any legal task. There are, however, some nondelegable duties such as the following:

1. An employer's duty to provide safe working conditions[3]
2. A person's duty under some contract terms
3. A landlord's duty to tenants
4. A **common carrier**'s duty to passengers
5. A person's duty under a license issued to that person
6. The duty of a person engaged in inherently dangerous work to take adequate precautions to avoid harm

Common carrier
A company in the business of transporting people or goods for a fee and serving the general public.

Other nondelegable duties are defined by various state statutes. These may consist of many different types of duties. If the duty is nondelegable and the principal attempts to delegate it to someone else, the principal will be personally liable if the task is not properly completed. *Nondelegable duties* really means that the *tasks* can be delegated, but the responsibility for their proper completion cannot.

A person who hires another to engage in ultrahazardous physical activities is liable for any injury that results. This rule applies whether the person hired is a servant or an **independent contractor.**

Independent contractor
A person hired to perform a task but not subject to the specific control of the hiring party.

TYPES OF AGENCY RELATIONSHIPS

General and Special Agents

The distinction between general and special agents is a matter of degree. A *special agent* is employed to complete one transaction or a simple series of transactions. The relationship covers a relatively limited period and is not continuous. A *general agent* is hired to conduct a series of transactions over time. The amount of **discretion** the agent has is immaterial in making the distinction between general and special agents, as is the expertise of the agent.

Discretion
The right to use one's own judgment in selecting between alternatives.

In deciding whether an agent is a general agent or a special agent, courts should examine all of the following factors:

1. The number of acts that will need to be completed to achieve the authorized result
2. The number of people who will need to be dealt with before achieving the desired result
3. The length of time that will be necessary to achieve the desired result[4]

The manager of an electronics store is a general agent. In contrast, a person who delivers a package to a customer of the store on a one-time basis is a special agent. Categorizing an agent who is between these two extremes can be difficult. As Exhibit 31.1 shows, a continuum of relationships exists between these roles.

Gratuitous Agents

Payment is not necessary in a principal–agent relationship. If a person volunteers services without an agreement or an expectation of payment, that person may still be an agent. The requirements for a *gratuitous agency* are that one person volunteered to help another and that the person being served accepted this assistance.

E X H I B I T   31.1 | **Distinction Between Special Agents and General Agents**

Relevant factors:	Special Agent	General Agent
Frequency of acts	Few acts or simple series of acts	Many acts or long series of acts
Number of people who will be contacted	Few people	Many people
Length of service	Short period of time	Longer period of time
Irrelevant factors:		
Discretion granted to agent		
Expertise of agent		

The exact number of people contacted and length of time are subject to interpretation by the court. This line constitutes a continuum and not discrete categories.

31.1 | MANAGEMENT

ARE FAMILY MEMBERS AGENTS OF CIT?

John is concerned that various family members may be viewed as agents of CIT and that their conduct could be financially detrimental to the firm. Dan contends that there is virtually no danger of this happening and that John is overreacting. According to Dan, only adults can be agents, so Lindsay and John cannot represent the firm. In addition, Dan says that agents must be full-time employees of the firm, so Donna and Julio are excluded as potential agents. According to Dan, this only leaves Tom, Anna, Dan, and those full-time employees hired by the firm as possible agents of CIT. John asks you if Dan's analysis is correct. What will you tell him?

BUSINESS CONSIDERATIONS What are the business implications of people representing themselves as working for or on behalf of a firm? When does the firm have a legal obligation for the actions of these people? What are the public relations implications of denying that an alleged agent was working on behalf of the firm?

ETHICAL CONSIDERATIONS What ethical obligations does CIT owe to its agents? To members of the public who deal in good faith with agents of CIT?

For example, Sylvia offers to help Joel with his yard work. While she is pruning a tree, she carelessly saws off a limb, which falls on a car belonging to Joel's neighbor. The courts *can* find that Sylvia works for Joel and that Joel is liable for the damage Sylvia causes. Another example is if Bryn is not feeling well the morning her legal environment homework is due. Allison, a sorority sister, is in the same class. Bryn asks Allison to deliver the paper for her. Allison arrives to class late, and the instructor deducts late points from both Bryn's paper and Allison's paper. Bryn will be held responsible for Allison's acts.

SERVANTS AND INDEPENDENT CONTRACTORS

Most workers are either servants or independent contractors. The distinction among the terms *agent, servant,* and *independent contractor* is confusing, partly because authors and judges apply differing definitions to these terms and partly because common usage differs from legal usage. This text uses the definitions of the *Restatement (Second) of Agency.* Using legal definitions, servants and employees are generally synonymous.[5] We usually use the term *servant* to describe someone who is subject to the control of his or her *master.*

Servants

A *master* is a special type of principal who has the right to tell his or her worker both what to do and how to do it. The worker then is included in a special class of workers called *servants or employees.* (The more modern term is *employee.*) A servant is one who works physically for the hiring party. A master (employer) has a right to control how the task is accomplished by the servant (employee). The actual exercise of this control is not necessary; it is sufficient that the master has the *right* to control. Thus, interns in hospitals, airline pilots, sales clerks, and officers of corporations are commonly servants.

The distinction between servants and independent contractors is important, because a principal is rarely liable for the unauthorized *physical* acts of an independent contractor. Principals sometimes label a worker as an independent contractor in an attempt to escape liability, but the courts will look behind the designation and make a judgment about the true nature of the relationship. The distinction between servants and independent contractors is also important in determining rights and benefits under a number of statutes, including unemployment insurance laws, workers' compensation laws, income taxation, the Employment Retirement Income Security Act of 1974 (ERISA), employment discrimination, and bankruptcy exemptions.

EXHIBIT 31.2 | **Distinction Between Servants and Independent Contractors**

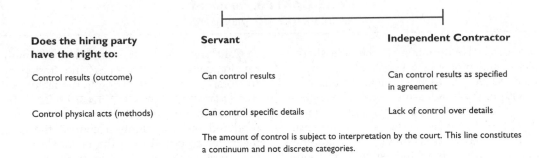

Does the hiring party have the right to:	Servant	Independent Contractor
Control results (outcome)	Can control results	Can control results as specified in agreement
Control physical acts (methods)	Can control specific details	Lack of control over details

The amount of control is subject to interpretation by the court. This line constitutes a continuum and not discrete categories.

The distinction between an independent contractor and a servant is represented in Exhibit 31.2. Remember that this distinction is material only when there is a question about who is responsible for the physical acts of the worker. When the worker has entered into a contract for his or her employer, it is irrelevant whether the worker is a servant or an independent contractor.

Independent Contractors

An *independent contractor* is hired to complete a task for someone else. The physical acts of the independent contractor are not controlled or subject to the control of the hiring party. Instead, the independent contractor relies on his or her own expertise to determine the best way to complete the job. Anyone who contracts to do physical work for another does so as either a servant or an independent contractor. Courts look at many factors in distinguishing between the two.

In addition to considering the *right* to control, courts commonly consider the following factors:

1. Whether the worker hires assistants
2. What the method of payment is; for example, by the number of hours worked or by the job completed
3. Who supplies the tools and equipment to be used
4. Whether the worker is engaged in a distinct occupation or independent business, and how long the relationship is intended to last

The court examined the working relationship of entertainer Nell Carter to her subchapter S corporation in the following case.

31.1

IN RE CARTER
1999 U.S. APP. LEXIS 18647 (9TH CIR. 1999)

FACTS . . . Nell Carter filed for personal bankruptcy under Chapter 7. In her bankruptcy schedules she claimed that a check for $43,260.58 received from her subchapter S corporation constituted employee earn-

ings under California Civil Procedure Code (C.C.P.) § 706.011 and was therefore exempt from inclusion in the bankruptcy estate under C.C.P. § 704.070(b). . . .

continued

31.1

IN RE CARTER, *continued*

1999 U.S. APP. LEXIS 18647 (9TH CIR. 1999)

Carter, a professional entertainer, is the sole share-holder, director, and officer of a subchapter S corporation named Krynicki, Inc. Krynicki enters into agreements with nightclubs, casinos, and other establishments at which Carter entertains, and Carter is then paid by Krynicki for her services. . . . On April 25, 1995, Carter filed [bankruptcy] . . . claiming $39,000 as an exemption from the estate, corresponding to the estimated amount of money from the check remaining in her bank account at the time of the filing. . . . The trustee objected to the claimed exemption. Because California has opted out of the federal scheme of exemptions under 11 USC § 522(d), Carter's right to the exemption is determined under California law. . . . § 706.011 provides: . . .

(c) "Employee" means a public officer and any individual who performs services subject to the right of the employer to control both what shall be done and how it shall be done.

ISSUE Was Carter an "employee" under § 706.011?

HOLDING Yes. Carter was an employee under the statutory definition.

REASONING . . . For Carter to be entitled to an exemption under § 706.011, she must show both that she was an "employee" of Krynicki and that the check for $43,260.58 was payment of "earnings" within the meaning of that provision. . . . The distinction between an employee or an independent contractor is made in many areas of the law, including income taxation, Employment Retirement Income Security Act of 1974 (ERISA), workers' compensation, and employment discrimination . . . Indeed, whenever a federal statute uses the term "employee" and "contains no other provision that either gives specific guidance to the meaning of the term 'employee' or suggests that the common law definition is inappropriate, we must presume that Congress intended to incorporate traditional principles of agency law." California has also recognized that "much 20th-century legislation for the protection of 'employees' has adopted the 'independent contractor' distinction as an express or implied limitation on coverage." When a distinction between "employees" and "independent contractors" becomes relevant, both federal and state law provide multiple-factor tests that distinguish one from the other.

California follows the traditional common law distinction between "employees" and "independent contractors," generally referring to the factors set forth in the *Restatement (Second) of Agency* § 220. The "principal test" is "whether the person to whom service is rendered has the right to control the manner and means of accomplishing the result desired." California courts have developed multiple factors indicative of "control," including: (1) whether the person performing services is engaged in a distinct occupation or business; (2) the kind of occupation, with reference to whether, in the locality, the work is usually done under the direction of the principal or by a specialist without supervision; (3) the skill required in the particular occupation; (4) whether the principal or the worker supplies the instrumentalities, tools, and the place of work for the person doing the work; (5) the length of time for which the services are to be performed; (6) the method of payment, whether by the time or by the job, (7) whether or not the work is a part of the regular business of the principal; and (8) whether or not the parties believe they are creating the relationship of employer-employee. . . . Reflecting on a trend in applying these factors, the California Supreme Court has noted that "the modern tendency is to find employment when the work being done is an integral part of the regular business of the employer, and when the worker, relative to the employer, does not furnish an independent business or professional service."

Using a short-hand version of the standard test, C.C.P. § 706.011 defines an "employee" as "any individual who performs services subject to the right of the employer to control both what shall be done and how it shall be done." We believe that under this definition it is enough that Carter was subject to the "right" of the corporation to control her performance. A test requiring actual control would not be well-designed for a person, like Carter, who claims to be an employee but who is also the sole shareholder of a subchapter S corporation. Because the would-be employee is also the sole shareholder, she is not controlled by the corporation in the same way as a person who is an employee (but not the sole shareholder) of a subchapter S corporation, or who is an employee of a non-subchapter S corporation. . . . California law does not insist on actual control. Under California law, "it is the right to control, not the exercise of the

31.1

IN RE CARTER, *continued*
1999 U.S. APP. LEXIS 18647 (9TH CIR. 1999)

right, which bears on the status of the work arrangement." [Many professionals are in a similar situation—doctors, lawyers, accountants—and they are ordinarily considered employees of their respective corporations, even if they are the sole shareholder. This court, applying the federal common law test of "employee" status, does not consider them independent contractors of their own corporations. . . .]

. . . [I]t is clear that Carter is an employee of Krynicki within the meaning of § 706.011. That section requires that the individual performing services be "subject to the right of the employer to control both what shall be done and how it shall be done," and includes a "corporation" within the definition of employer without distinguishing among types of corporations. Among other things, Carter's performance engagements were made through Krynicki, which had the legal right to specify the services she performed and to control the manner in which she performed them; Carter was paid by Krynicki rather than by the establishments at which she performed; and expenses connected with Carter's performances, including payments to her agent, personal manager,

and musicians, and payments for all professional equipment, were all paid by Krynicki rather than Carter. . . . Carter is an employee because she is subject to the right of control by her corporation, even though in real terms she is . . . [not controlled.] . . . For purposes of § 706.011, the proper focus is on the relationship between Krynicki and Carter. . . .

We . . . reverse and remand for a determination of whether Carter's April 3 check represented "earnings" under C.C.P. § 706.011.

BUSINESS CONSIDERATIONS What special operating or planning concerns should be addressed by closely held corporations? To what extent is Carter really under the control of Krynicki?

ETHICAL CONSIDERATION Is it ethical for a person who is about to file bankruptcy to pay him- or herself earnings or to make other transfers to protect assets?

Independent contractors may be agents, but that is not a necessary condition for being an independent contractor. This is shown in Exhibit 31.3 on page 818. If the independent contractor does not represent the hiring party or act for the hiring party in relation to third parties, the independent contractor is not the hiring party's agent. For example, a nonagent independent contractor who is building a house on an owner's lot cannot bind the owner to a contract. In these situations, the independent contractor does not owe the hiring party any **fiduciary duties.** A *fiduciary* is a person who owes a special duty of good faith and loyalty due to his or her status. Fiduciary relationships include attorney–client, priest–confessor, husband–wife, and agent–principal. Ordinary business transactions, such as contracts, do *not* create fiduciary relationships. Special relationships, such as agency relationships where the agent will represent the principal in contract negotiations, compel the exercise of utmost fairness and good faith by the agent. Agents *do* have fiduciary duties to their principals.

Independent contractors who are agents (1) have fiduciary duties and (2) can bind their principals to contracts. For example, attorneys owe their clients fiduciary duties when they negotiate settlements and then agree to them on the clients' behalf. On the other hand, attorneys are not the clients' servants. Legal clients have no control over when their attorneys come to work in the morning or when they leave work at the end of the day. These relationships are represented in Exhibit 31.4 on page 819.

Fiduciary duty
The legal duty to exercise the highest degree of loyalty and good faith in handling the affairs of the person to whom the duty is owed.

E X H I B I T   31.3 | **Independent Contractors May Also Be Agents**

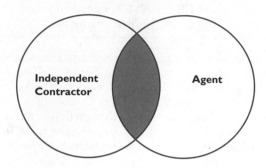

The shaded area indicates independent contractors who are also agents.

When legal questions concern fiduciary duties or contracts, the worker will simply be identified as an agent, rather than applying the cumbersome term *independent contractor agent*.

Responsibility for Independent Contractors

Contract Liability. Principals who engage independent contractors as agents will be liable on the contract *if* the contract was authorized. Authorization is discussed in detail in Chapter 32. This liability complies with the general rule for agents.

Tort Liability. The independent contractor who is injured while working generally cannot recover from the hiring party. Employees of the independent contractor, however, have been permitted to recover from the independent contractor. Liability for injured workers is explored in Case 31.2, *Hutchings* v. *Chevron U.S.A., Inc.*

In addition, a person who hires an independent contractor is not usually responsible to third parties for the independent contractor's physical wrongdoings. Courts do make exceptions. However, these exceptions vary greatly from state to state. Some of the most common exceptions include:

1. The hiring party reserves the right to supervise or control the work
2. The hiring party actually directs the independent contractor to do something careless or wrong
3. The hiring party observes the independent contractor do something wrong and does not stop it
4. The hiring party does not adequately supervise the independent contractor
5. The hiring party is careless in selecting the independent contractor
6. The independent contractor is hired to commit a crime
7. The independent contractor is hired to engage in ultrahazardous activities

In many states, the trend has been to increase the number of situations in which the hiring party can be held liable. For example, in some of these states the courts have reduced the standard from ultrahazardous to merely hazardous activities. The independent contractor is also liable for his or her own wrongdoings.

E X H I B I T 31.4 | **Is the Independent Contractor an Agent?**

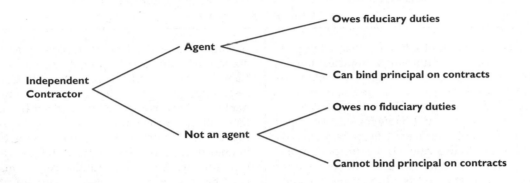

In the next case, an employee of the independent contractor is suing Chevron, who hired the independent contractor. Chevron has asked for a summary judgment in its favor.

31.2

HUTCHINGS V. CHEVRON U.S.A., INC.
1999 U.S. DIST. LEXIS 2079 (E.D. LA. 1999)

FACTS . . . On April 6, 1997, Hutchings, a pipe fitter/rigger, was assigned to work on board the vessel M/V CANDY LADY in order to assist with off-loading groceries and equipment from the boat to the Chevron West Delta 117 fixed platform location in the Gulf of Mexico. A relief crew of three men was being lowered in a personnel basket from the platform to the vessel by a crane located on Chevron's platform. The personnel basket fell and struck Hutchings, pinning him to the deck and allegedly causing him severe injuries. According to Hutchings, he was unable to grab the personnel basket . . . in an attempt to stabilize it . . . (as did his co-worker) because there was only one tag line attached to the basket. Hutchings was an employee of Danos & Curole Marine Contractors, Inc. ("Danos"), an independent contractor of Chevron, at the time of the accident. Danos and Chevron had signed a contract whereby Danos would provide various services for Chevron at the site, including platform repairs and revisions. Also involved in the work were two other independent contractors: Liberty Services, Inc. . . . , which provided crane operations, and the M/V CANDY LADY, . . . which provided offshore vessel services.

ISSUE Could Chevron legally be held liable for Hutchings' injuries?

HOLDING Yes. Chevron could be held liable if it reserved control.

REASONING Summary judgment should be granted only where "the pleadings, depositions, answers . . . and admissions . . . , together with the affidavits . . . show that there is no genuine issue as to any material fact and that the moving party is entitled to a judgment as a matter of law." The party moving for summary judgment bears the initial responsibility . . . [for] identifying those portions of the record which it believes demonstrate the absence of a genuine issue of material fact. . . . [Then] [t]he nonmoving party must come forward with "specific facts showing that there is a genuine issue for trial." . . .

The Outer Continental Shelf Lands Act mandates that when disputes arise involving fixed structures erected on the outer Continental Shelf, applicable laws of the adjacent state will be applied to the extent not inconsistent with other federal laws and regulations. Louisiana law . . . applies to this case.

continued

31.2

HUTCHINGS V. CHEVRON U.S.A., INC., *continued*
1999 U.S. DIST. LEXIS 2079 (E.D. LA. 1999)

Hutchings has alleged that Chevron was negligent and is . . . liable for Hutchings' injuries under Louisiana Civil Code . . . due to Chevron's failure to provide Hutchings with a safe work environment and failure to take precautions for Hutchings' safety.

Generally, a principal is not liable for the negligent acts of an independent contractor. Courts have carved out two exceptions to this rule: (1) a principal can be held liable for the acts of its independent contractors if the work to be performed is ultrahazardous; and (2) a principal can be held liable for the acts of its independent contractors if the principal reserves the right to supervise or control the work. Off-loading procedures are not considered an ultrahazardous activity [based on precedents]. The first exception to the rule . . . then, does not apply to this case.

In considering whether the second exception applies, the court looks both to the contract signed by Chevron and Danos, and to the testimony of the on-site employees. The Chevron-Danos contract expressly provided that Danos would perform its work as an "independent contractor and not as an employee" of Chevron. It also expressly stated that Danos "shall be responsible for the safe performance of the work, and shall assure that the work is performed in accordance with safe practices, and shall implement and maintain at all times safe procedures" to protect its personnel. The contract makes no provision whereby Chevron could retain operational control . . . ; however, it also does not state that Chevron did not retain operational control over the work. In cases where contracts expressly state that the principal is to "direct the results to be accomplished" by the contractor, but that the principal does not have "the right to control the manner in which the details of the work would be performed," courts are likely to find that the principal relinquished operation control to the contractor. . . . Here, then, while Danos took on contractual responsibility for safety, the contract is ambiguous with regard to whether Chevron relinquished control over the day-to-day operations of the work to Danos.

Likewise, the testimony of the on-site employees creates several questions of material fact regarding whether Chevron relinquished operational control. Chevron's company man, . . . "Danny" Ragus, insists that he did not have any right to instruct, control, or manage any of the Danos employees as to how to accomplish the work under the contract. . . . Ragus . . . may not have been the only Chevron representative present the day of the accident. An accident report was completed by a Quent B. Gilbert, who lists himself on the report as "Chevron Representative Preparing Report." In addition, Hutchings, the injured party, has stated that . . . Ragus was the person from whom he generally received instructions, and that a Chevron representative was supervising the Danos employees on the day of Hutchings' alleged injury. Finally, Mr. William J. Welch, Jr., the crane operator responsible for lowering the personnel basket which allegedly injured Hutchings, stated under oath that he reported to the Chevron supervisor. In short, there are several questions of material fact arising from both the contract itself and the testimony of the on-site witnesses regarding operational control.

Even if a jury ultimately finds that Chevron relinquished operational control to Danos and the other independent contractors, Chevron could still be found at least partially liable for Hutchings' injures [sic] if Chevron committed its own acts of negligence. Here, Hutchings has alleged that Chevron was negligent in providing a defective personnel basket, as the basket did not have enough tag lines for each participating person. As the personnel basket was an appurtenance of the platform owned by Chevron, Hutchings alleges, Chevron is liable for the damage caused by the defective condition. If, at trial, the jury determines that the basket was within the control of Chevron, was defective, and caused Hutchings' injures [sic], Chevron could be held liable for Hutchings' injuries under a general theory of negligence.

BUSINESS CONSIDERATIONS How could Chevron and Danos improve safety for workers? How could Chevron have structured the relationship with Danos to reduce liability?

ETHICAL CONSIDERATIONS Do Chevron and Danos owe a duty to care for the workers at the site? Is this moral duty limited to their own workers?

A PLEA UNANSWERED: CALLING THE CONTROL TOWER

John F. Kennedy, Jr.'s private aircraft, a single-engine Piper Saratoga, went down in the Atlantic Ocean on 16 July 1999. He was flying to Martha's Vineyard to attend a wedding. His wife and sister-in-law were also in the plane. The Coast Guard began its search a number of hours after the plane was overdue. Survival experts say that most human beings can endure only 12 to 18 hours of immersion in 68 degree water, the temperature of the water at the presumed impact area. It was later discovered that the plane crashed into the Atlantic Ocean and the occupants were killed. The night of the crash, Adam Budd, a 21-year-old ramp attendant at the airport on Martha's Vineyard, called the Federal Aviation Administration (FAA) Control Center in Bridgeport, Connecticut, about 10:05 P.M. to report the plane was missing. A tape of the call indicates that Budd identified himself as being with airport operations, and he asked for information about the missing plane. According to Budd, the unnamed FAA flight service representative was either not inclined to take the call seriously or did not seem too interested in being of assistance. Budd asked if FAA could track the plane and gave two identification numbers for it. Budd added, "Actually, Kennedy Jr.'s on board. He's uh, they wanna know, uh, where he is." The FAA representative said, "Well, we don't give this information out to people over the phone." Budd replied, "OK, well, if it's too much trouble, it's . . . Take it easy." Then Budd hang up. The agent who took the call justified his actions by saying that the call came in, but the person who called (Budd) did not seem very concerned, so a search was not begun at that time. The FAA representative did not ask Budd whether the flight was overdue. Budd did not use the word *overdue*, which is a key phrase in the precise language of aviation. The representative's attitude has been justified because Budd did not use key phrases or sound very concerned. A FAA spokesperson indicated that there wasn't a sense of urgency in Budd's voice. The search began about four hours later after a friend of the Kennedys phoned the Coast Guard about the plane. (Starting the search earlier may or may not have improved the chances that the occupants would have been found alive.) One argument for not giving out information on the phone is that the caller may have been a journalist trying to get pictures or a story. Who is responsible for Budd and the FAA representative's actions? Are these people agents, servants, or independent contractors? If they are agents, are they special agents or general agents?

If a suit was filed in *your* court, how would *you* rule?[6]

BUSINESS CONSIDERATIONS How could the situation have been handled better? If you were responsible for the Martha's Vineyard airport or the FAA, what changes in training or procedures might you initiate and why? What other industries or professions have specialized, precise language? Who is responsible when the specialized language is not used?

ETHICAL CONSIDERATION Who is morally blameworthy in this situation?

SOURCES: Erica Noonan, *The Fresno Bee* (19 July 1999), pp. A1, A14; David Usborne, *The Independent* (London) (21 July 1999), p. 2; Matthew Brelis, *The Boston Globe* (21 July 1999), p. A12; Jack Sullivan, *The Boston Herald* (21 July 1999), p. 12.

DUTIES OF THE AGENT TO THE PRINCIPAL

The agent must protect the interests of the principal, as the duties discussed in the following sections show. Some of the duties overlap. In fact, when an agent breaches one duty, most likely others will be breached as well.

Duty of Good Faith

The *duty of good faith* is also called the *fiduciary duty,* and the rule is that every agent owes the principal the obligation of faithful service. The most common violations of this duty include concealing essential facts that are relevant to the agency, obtaining secret profits, and self-dealing. Suppose the principal is looking for a parcel of agricultural land, and the agent locates a suitable parcel. The agent arranges for its sale to the principal without first informing the principal that the agent owns a one-third interest in the parcel. In this case, the agent has violated his or her fiduciary duty to the principal.

Duty of Loyalty

An agent has a duty to be loyal to the principal and to protect the principal's best interests. Thus, an agent must not compete with the principal, work for someone who is competing with the principal, or act to further the agent's own interests. An agent may not use his or her agency position for personal benefits at the expense of the principal. Such self-dealings involve a breach of the *duty of loyalty.* The following example shows a variation on a common problem many businesses must confront—employee conversion of firm assets.

> *André works in the marketing division of a large company. One of his responsibilities is to purchase supplies for the division. He tells Katie, the division chief, that the division has 3½-inch computer diskettes no one is using. André indicates that this is not a problem because he will take them home.*
>
> *Allowing André to take the diskettes home will be a breach of fiduciary duties and a poor business practice. He will be setting a bad example for the other employees and he will be unlikely to search for alternatives that would be more beneficial to the division and the company. There are a number of options available to the division: trade the diskettes for supplies with the other divisions, return the diskettes to the vendor (seller) for a credit, or keep the diskettes for future use. Perhaps the employees who use this size diskette already have a supply at their workstations and they will come to the supply room when their supply runs out.*
>
> *If André is permitted to take unused supplies home, this might encourage him to order supplies that he wanted at home with the hope that he would be able to use them himself. Katie should resolve this conflict of interest as soon as possible.*

Duty to Obey All Lawful Instructions

Agents must follow all *lawful* instructions as long as doing so does not subject them to an unreasonable risk of injury. This is true even if agents think the instructions are capricious or unwise. Agents need not follow instructions that are outside the course and scope of the agency relationship. They must repay their principals for damages suffered because they failed to follow instructions that are in the course and scope of their employment.

Duty to Act with Reasonable Care

An agent has a duty to act as a *reasonably careful* agent would under the same circumstances. Again, if the agent fails to live up to this obligation and it causes the principal a loss, the agent will be obliged to reimburse the principal.

Duty to Segregate Funds

The agent has a duty to keep personal funds separate from the principal's funds. If the agent wrongfully uses the principal's funds to purchase something, the court can impose a **trust** and treat the situation as though the purchase were originally made for the benefit of the principal. Such a trust—that is, a trust imposed by a court for the purpose of preventing unjust enrichment—is called a *constructive trust.* Constructive trusts are discussed in Chapter 46.

Trust
An arrangement in which legal title, indicated on the deed or other evidence of ownership, is separated from the equitable or beneficial ownership.

Duty to Account for Funds

An agent has a duty to account for money received. This is really a combined function of delivery of the funds and record keeping. The funds usually must be delivered to the principal (or an authorized third party). If the money was received while the agent was *not* in the course and scope of the employment, the agent has a duty to return the proceeds to the third party. Compare the agent's duty in each of the two examples that follow for an illustration of how this duty is applied.

> *Kamal is a sales representative for Finch, Inc. He takes a potential client to dinner to discuss possible orders the client might place with Finch. The client, impressed with the presentation Kamal makes during the meal, places an order for $10,000 worth of goods, writing a check as payment in full for the goods ordered. Although Kamal is technically "off the clock," this sale would be considered to have occurred in the course and scope of Kamal's employment, and he would be expected to account to Finch for the proceeds from the sale.*

> *Bhudi is also a sales representative for Finch, Inc., but he is not authorized to accept payments for goods he sells for the principal. He takes his wife to dinner to celebrate their anniversary. While they are eating, a client of Finch recognizes Bhudi as an employee of Finch. The client approaches Bhudi's table and hands Bhudi a check for $10,000 as payment for goods ordered from Finch the previous week. Bhudi is technically "off the clock," and he is not authorized to receive payments for his principal. In this situation, Bhudi would be expected to return the check to the client and explain that the check should be sent directly to Finch, the principal.*

Duty to Give Notice

The *duty to give notice* requires that an agent will inform the principal about material facts that are discovered within the scope of the agent's employment. For example, if a tenant gives an apartment manager notice that the tenant will move out at the end of the month, it is

THE RISKS OF HIRING SALESPEOPLE

CIT needs to expand its geographic market area in order to succeed as an entity. To do so, the firm will need to make sales in other regions. Neither Tom nor Anna wants to spend the necessary time away from home, nor do they want to send any of their children out for such extended periods of time. However, they are also hesitant to hire sales representatives for the Call-Image product line. Among other things, they fear that such representatives may copy the product and start a competing firm based on the customers the salespeople have cultivated. Dan does not feel that this is a valid concern. He believes there are protections available to the firm but is not sure that he is fully informed. He has asked for your input about the potential problem. What will you tell the family?

BUSINESS CONSIDERATIONS What policies should a firm establish to maximize its protection in the event an agent violates his or her duty? What are the legal rights of a principal whose agent attempts to utilize technological information obtained in the course of employment for the personal benefit of that agent?
ETHICAL CONSIDERATIONS What are the ethical implications of acting as a sales agent for a firm that produces a highly technical product? What ethical principles would preclude an agent from attempting to establish a business in competition with his or her former principal based on either the knowledge or the customers he or she developed as an agent?

31.3 | MANAGEMENT

PROTECTING AGAINST WORKPLACE VIOLENCE

John has become very concerned about workplace violence. This topic has been discussed in several of his classes as one of the fastest-growing problem areas in the 2000s. One example cited in class involved a manager who fired an employee for using drugs while on the job. The dismissed employee became verbally abusive, and he had to be physically removed from the workplace. At that point he went home to get his hunting rifle, returned to the plant with the rifle, and proceeded to shoot the manager and four of his former coworkers.

Although John is unsure about exactly how to best protect the family members at work, he believes they should at least keep a gun in the office suite for protection. He asks you for any suggestions you have. What will you tell him?

BUSINESS CONSIDERATIONS Workplace violence is not just a legal problem. It also has serious business implications. What policies should a business establish to protect its employees and its business operation from workplace violence? Should a business establish policies for some sort of intervention and/or counseling prior to the dismissal of an employee?

ETHICAL CONSIDERATIONS What should a firm do, from an ethical perspective, before it fires an employee? Is having a gun in the office area an ethical solution to the potential threat of violence in the workplace?

---

assumed that the manager will inform the owner. In fact, the principal may be bound by this notice even though the agent failed to inform the principal. It is said that the notice is "imputed" to the principal.

DUTIES OF THE PRINCIPAL TO THE AGENT

Many of the duties of the principal may be specified in the contract between the principal and the agent. In general, the principal has the following obligations to the agent:

1. To pay the agent per the agreement
2. To maintain proper accounts so that compensation and reimbursement will be correct
3. To provide the agent with the means to do the job
4. To continue the employment for the time period specified in the agreement

With the exception of gratuitous agents, agents are entitled to be paid under the terms of their agreements with the principal. Some types of agents are entitled to compensation under special arrangements such as commission sales. These unique situations are usually mentioned in the written contract. For example, in some states, real estate agents are entitled to their commissions if they find a buyer who is ready, willing, and able to buy the parcel. This is true even if the transfer does not occur because of destruction of the building, the buyer's inability to obtain a loan, or some other circumstance. Some states follow a different rule, whereby a sale must close before a commission is earned.

In addition, if the worker is a servant, his or her master has an obligation to provide the servant with a reasonably safe place to work and safe equipment to use. This obligation is based on common law *and* state and federal safety statutes, such as the federal Occupational Safety and Health Act (OSHA). Under OSHA, the secretary of labor *may* pass regulations permitting workers to refuse to work under hazardous conditions.[7] A master also owes a servant an obligation to compensate him or her for injuries under state workers' compensation laws. Workers' compensation laws are discussed in Chapters 33 and 42.

TERMINATION OF THE AGENCY RELATIONSHIP

Agreement of the Parties

An agency relationship is governed in the first instance by the agreement between the principal and the agent. Commonly the contract will be established for a set period. For example, if a real estate agent has a listing to sell a house according to certain terms, one of the terms may specify the period for which the contract is going to run, say 90 days; that agreement, therefore, will terminate at the end of 90 days.

The parties can consent to amend the agency agreement, to terminate the agency relationship early, or to extend it. For example, if the house we just referred to is not sold within 90 days, the owner and agent may specifically extend the agency agreement for another 60 days.

If the parties consent to the continuation of the agency relationship beyond the period originally stated, this consent may be implied as a renewal of the original contract for the same period and under the same conditions. This is true only if they have not specifically altered the terms and conditions of the original agreement.

Agency at Will

If the agency agreement does not specify a set date, a set period, or a set occurrence that will terminate it, the relationship is an *agency at will*. This is also called the *employment-at-will doctrine*. Either party can terminate the relationship by giving notice to the other. The principal or agent does not need cause or justification to terminate the relationship. This is consistent with the theory that agency is a voluntary relationship between the parties. Traditionally, it was perceived that the two parties were relatively equal in their bargaining position and that, consequently, this rule was fair.

The traditional concept of an agency at will is being eroded rapidly. In addition, courts are recognizing various theories for recovery by the discharged agent. Utilization of these theories of recovery vary depending on the situation and state law.[8] Three common examples follow:

1. The courts are recognizing a breach of employment contract, that is, an express or implied agreement that the employment will not be terminated *or* will not be terminated without following a specific set of procedures. For example, union–management contracts called *collective bargaining agreements* contain express agreements that prevent the dismissal of union employees without a showing of cause and the following of specific procedures. Implied contracts often are based on procedures, policies in personnel manuals, and advertisements for workers.

2. Courts are also recognizing a tort of bad-faith discharge, where the employee has a right of continued employment and has developed a relationship of trust, reliance, and dependency on the employer. It is based on an implicit understanding between the agent and principal that they will deal honestly and fairly with each other. Bad faith is usually evidenced by fraud, malice, or oppression. This is sometimes considered a breach of a covenant of good faith and fair dealing.

3. Some states are holding an employer liable for a tortious discharge if the termination violates public policy. This is based on the theory that employees should not have to forfeit their positions because they acted in a manner that supports some *important* public policy. This basis is commonly used to protect whistle-blowers, for example, employees who report safety violations to OSHA or violations of environmental protection laws to EPA. Many federal and state statutes now have antiretaliation provisions that principals cannot

retaliate against agents who complain to agencies, file reports, or testify against them. For example, public policy provisions are used to protect employees who testify in court about criminal activity.

Most states recognize implied agreements and public policy exceptions. A few recognize the tort of bad-faith discharge. States may not recognize any of these theories, or they may recognize some combination of them. Most of the court cases involve servants instead of independent contractors. Companies should maintain careful records documenting the reasons a worker is discharged, even if an agency at will is involved. Companies are particularly likely to have difficulty when they terminate a worker after a number of years of successful employment including frequent promotions and commendations for the worker. The courts generally use the terms *employer* and *employee* when discussing both agency at will and wrongful discharge.

Other public policy prohibitions exist on firing agents at will. If the agent was fired on the basis of gender, race, religion, or national origin, or some other violation of civil rights, the courts may decide that the principal cannot terminate the relationship. Notice that wrongful discharge has been used to prevent employers from firing employees, but employees in employment-at-will relationships are still free to quit at any time and for any reason. (Wrongful discharge is discussed more fully in Chapters 2 and 42.) In the following case, the court addressed the rights of an agent at will.

31.3

HADDLE V. GARRISON
119 S.CT. 489 (1998)

FACTS . . . Michael A. Haddle, an at-will employee, alleges that respondents conspired to have him fired from his job in retaliation for obeying a federal grand jury subpoena and to deter him from testifying at a federal criminal trial. We hold that such interference with at-will employment may give rise to a claim for damages under the Civil Rights Act of 1871 . . .

According to petitioner's complaint, a federal grand jury indictment in March 1995 charged petitioner's employer, Healthmaster, Inc., and respondents Jeanette Garrison and Dennis Kelly, officers of Healthmaster, with Medicare fraud. Petitioner cooperated with the federal agents in the investigation that preceded the indictment. He also appeared to testify before the grand jury pursuant to a subpoena, but did not testify due to the press of time. Petitioner was also expected to appear as a witness in the criminal trial resulting from the indictment. Although Garrison and Kelly were barred by the Bankruptcy Court from participating in the affairs of Healthmaster, they conspired with G. Peter Molloy, Jr., one of the remaining officers of Healthmaster, to bring about petitioner's termination. They did this both to intimidate petitioner and to retaliate against him for his attendance at the federal-court proceedings.

Petitioner sued for damages in the United States District Court for the Southern District of Georgia, asserting a federal claim under 42 U.S.C. § 1985(2) and various state-law claims. Petitioner stated two grounds for relief under § 1985(2): one for conspiracy to deter him from testifying in the upcoming criminal trial and one for conspiracy to retaliate against him for attending the grand jury proceedings. As § 1985 demands, he also alleged that he had been "injured in his person or property" by the acts of respondents in violation of § 1985(2) and that he was entitled to recover his damages occasioned by such injury against respondents jointly and severally. . . .

ISSUE Can petitioner state a claim for damages by alleging that a conspiracy proscribed by § 1985(2) induced his employer to terminate his at-will employment?

31.3

HADDLE V. GARRISON, *continued*
119 S.CT. 489 (1998)

HOLDING Yes. Haddle can state a valid claim based on a conspiracy proscribed by § 1985(2).

REASONING Because petitioner conceded that he was an at-will employee, the District Court granted the motion [to dismiss] . . . The Eleventh Circuit's rule . . . conflicts with the holdings of the First and Ninth Circuits. We therefore granted certiorari, to decide whether petitioner was "injured in his property or person" when respondents induced his employer to terminate petitioner's at-will employment as part of a conspiracy prohibited by § 1985(2).

Section 1985(2), in relevant part, proscribes conspiracies to "deter, by force, intimidation, or threat, any party or witness in any court of the United States from attending such court, or from testifying to any matter pending therein, freely, fully, and truthfully, or to injure such party or witness in his person or property on account of his having so attended or testified." . . . We must, of course, assume that the facts as alleged in petitioner's complaint are true and that respondents engaged in a conspiracy prohibited by § 1985(2). . . .

We disagree with the Eleventh Circuit's conclusion that petitioner must suffer an injury to a "constitutionally protected property interest" to state a claim for damages under § 1985(2). Nothing in the language or purpose of the proscriptions in the first clause of § 1985(2), nor in its attendant remedial provisions, establishes such a requirement. The gist of the wrong at which § 1985(2) is directed is not deprivation of property, but intimidation or retaliation against witnesses in federal-court proceedings. The terms "injured in his person or property" define the harm that the victim may suffer as a result of the conspiracy to intimidate or retaliate. Thus, the fact that employment at will is not "property" for purposes of the Due Process Clause, does not mean that loss of at-will employment may not "injure . . . in his person or property" for purposes of § 1985(2).

We hold that the sort of harm alleged by petitioner here—essentially third-party interference with at-will employment relationships—states a claim for relief under § 1985(2). Such harm has long been a compensable injury under tort law, and we see no reason to ignore this tradition in this case. . . .

This Court also recognized in [a prior case] . . .

"The fact that the employment is at the will of the parties, respectively, does not make it one at the will of others. The employee has manifest interest in the freedom of the employer to exercise his judgment without illegal interference or compulsion and, by the weight of authority, the unjustified interference of third persons is actionable although the employment is at will."

The kind of interference with at-will employment relations alleged here is merely a species of the traditional torts of intentional interference with contractual relations and intentional interference with prospective contractual relations. This protection against third-party interference with at-will employment relations is still afforded by state law today. For example, the State of Georgia, where the acts underlying the complaint in this case took place, provides a cause of action against third parties for wrongful interference with employment relations. . . . Thus, to the extent that the terms "injured in his person or property" in § 1985 refer to principles of tort law . . . we find ample support for our holding that the harm occasioned by the conspiracy here may give rise to a claim for damages under § 1985(2). The judgment of the Court of Appeals is reversed, and the case is remanded for further proceedings consistent with this opinion.

BUSINESS CONSIDERATIONS How can a business avoid the problems caused by a fraud investigation? How could it avoid the problems caused by the firing of Haddle?

ETHICAL CONSIDERATIONS Analyze the ethics of Healthmaster *if* it did engage in Medicare fraud. Was Haddle a whistle-blower? Analyze Haddle's ethics.

Fulfillment of the Agency Purpose

Logically, an agency relationship terminates when the purpose for which it was created has been fulfilled. It does not make sense to continue the relationship beyond that point.

Revocation

Principals can *revoke* or terminate the authority of their agents to act on their behalf. They should directly notify their agents of the termination. The notice that the agency relationship is being terminated, moreover, should be clear and unequivocal. Indirect notice will *sometimes* be sufficient—for example, hiring a second agent to complete all the duties of the first agent. Due to the agent's obligation to obey, the principal can terminate the agency at any time. This is true even though there was an agreement that the agency relationship would continue longer. Even a statement in the agreement that the agency cannot be terminated does not affect the principal's ability to terminate it. Although the principal may have the *ability* to terminate the agency, he or she may not have the legal *right* to do so; in such a case, the agency can be terminated, but the principal may be liable for damages if this termination is a breach of contract.

Renunciation

Renunciation occurs when the agent notifies the principal that he or she will no longer serve as an agent. In other words, the agent resigns. Since an agency relationship is voluntary, an agent can renounce. However, the agent may be liable to the principal if the renunciation is a breach of their contract.

Operation of Law

In the legal system, *operation of law* "expresses the manner in which rights, and sometimes liabilities, devolve upon a person by the mere application to the particular transaction of the established rules of law, without the act or co-operation of the party. . . . "[9]

There are some occurrences that automatically terminate an agency relationship without any additional action. These include:

1. When the agent dies
2. When either party becomes insane
3. When the principal becomes bankrupt
4. When the agent becomes bankrupt, if the bankruptcy affects the agency
5. When the agency cannot possibly be performed (e.g., when the subject matter of the agency is destroyed)
6. When an unusual and unanticipated change in circumstances occurs that destroys the purpose of the agency relationship
7. When a change in law makes completion of the agency relationship illegal

The traditional rule is that the death of the principal also terminates the agency relationship immediately. Because this rule can cause hardship, many states modified their laws to take a more liberal approach. Under this more liberal rule, the death of the principal does not immediately terminate the agency relationship *if* immediate termination will cause a hardship.

When the relationship is terminated by the operation of law, usually it is unnecessary to give notice to the other party or to the public at large. This rule is discretionary, and a court may decide to require notice if its absence causes a great hardship.

Importance of Notice

When an agent or a principal terminates the agency relationship early, the agent or principal has a duty to notify the other party so that the other party does not waste effort on a relationship that no longer exists. If the principal revokes the agency relationship and does not notify the agent, the principal is obligated to indemnify the agent for liabilities that the agent incurs in the proper performance of his or her duties.[10]

It may be crucial to notify third parties even if it is not legally required, such as in termination by operation of law. The agent may find it advantageous to provide notice, but the principal will find notice even more important. If the principal fails to notify a third party, the third party can transfer money, such as a rent payment, to the agent with the expectation that the agent will forward the funds to the principal. Remember that the agent ordinarily has a duty to do so. If the agent is unhappy with the termination, the agent may unlawfully abscond with the money.

The notice can take various forms. The preferred method is to personally notify the third person by mail, e-mail, electronically transmitted facsimile copy, telephone, or telegram. Personal notice is generally required for all third parties who have had dealings with the agent. The names, addresses, and telephone numbers of these customers are usually in the company data banks or the agent's files. The advantage of using e-mail or an electronically transmitted facsimile copy is that it is fast, and there is written proof of the notification. Notice should be given promptly, since one of its purposes is to prevent losses caused by a disgruntled agent who feels that the termination is unjust.

In addition, the law accepts notice by publication (also called *constructive notice*). Usually, such notice is published in the legal notices in the newspaper. This is the only type of notice that is practical for members of the public who are aware of the agency but who have not had previous dealings with the agent.

The principal will be protected if the third party actually knows that the agency relationship has been terminated, even if the third party did not receive notice from the principal (i.e., the third party may have heard about the termination from the agent or from someone else).

Breach of Agency Agreement

Generally, the principal has the *power* to terminate the agency, even if he or she does not have the right. If the principal wrongfully revokes the agent's authority, the agent can sue for breach of express or implied contract. Many principal–agent contracts contain provisions for arbitrating disputes between them. Arbitration is discussed in Chapter 6. If there is an anticipatory breach and the principal notifies the agent in advance of the breach, the agent can sue the principal immediately for the anticipated damages. The agent, at his or her election, may decide to wait until after the contract period and then sue for actual damages. In either case, the agent has an obligation to *mitigate damages* or to keep them as low as possible by searching for another similar position with another principal in the same locality. Mitigating damages are discussed more fully in Chapter 15.

RESOURCES FOR BUSINESS LAW STUDENTS

NAME	RESOURCES	WEB ADDRESS
American Law Institute (ALI)	ALI, publisher of *Restatements of the Law*, Model Codes, and other proposals for law reform, provides press releases, its newsletter, and other publications.	**http://www.ali.org**
Independent Contractor Report	The *Independent Contractor Report*, a monthly newsletter, has materials on employment tax cases, rulings, and other issues for users of independent contractors.	**http://www.webcom.com/ic_rep**
DB Basics, Inc., Company Policy Manual	DB Basics, Inc., a software development company, maintains its employee handbook on-line.	**http://www.dbbasics.com/Web_Employment_Manual.html**

AGENCY COUPLED WITH AN OBLIGATION

Most agency relationships are formed for the benefit of the principal, but some are formed for the protection and benefit of the agent. The latter most commonly occur when the agent has loaned money to the principal, and the principal is securing the loan with collateral.

The mere statement in a contract that an agency is irrevocable will not make it true. Courts analyze the facts to make sure the agent has an *interest* in the collateral itself. Many of these legal disputes arise because the principal wishes to terminate the agency relationship and the agent wishes to prevent the termination. In an agency coupled with an obligation, the agent does have an interest.

> *Suppose Paula needs $50,000 for an investment. Since the banks will not lend her the money, she decides to borrow the cash from Angela for two years. Angela insists on having collateral, so Paula gives Angela the right to sell her building if Paula does not repay the loan within two years. Angela is entitled to take her $50,000 and her expenses out of the sale, but she has to give the rest of the money to Paula. In this situation, Paula, the principal, has an obligation to repay the $50,000 to her agent, Angela. Angela can, if necessary, sell the property to obtain payment.*

Although a principal cannot terminate such an arrangement at will, the death of a party or a bankruptcy that affects the agency can terminate it.

SUMMARY

Agency relationships center on the agreement between a principal and an agent that the agent will act for the benefit of the principal. The principal must have the capacity to consent to the relationship. The agent need not have contractual capacity. Most agents are compensated. An agent who is not entitled to compensation is called a gratuitous agent.

In analyzing the legal rights of the parties, one must determine whether the worker is a servant or an independent contractor. An independent contractor is hired to complete a job. The hiring party does not direct how the independent contractor does the task. In contrast, a master can exert a great deal of control over a servant and how the servant performs assigned duties. Because the master can control the servant, the master is more likely to be held financially responsible for the servant's physical acts.

An agent has a duty to act in good faith, to act loyally, to obey all lawful instructions, to act with reasonable care, to segregate funds, to account for all funds, and to give notice.

An agency relationship may terminate at a specified time agreed to by the parties, at the will of the parties, or after the purpose of the agency has been fulfilled. It can be revoked or renounced by one of the parties or terminated by operation of law. Even in an agent at will situation, the employer can be successfully sued for breach of an expressed or implied employment contract, bad-faith discharge, or tortious discharge in violation of public policy.

A principal generally has the power to terminate an agency relationship even if the termination is wrongful. The principal does not have the power to terminate an agency coupled with an obligation without the agent's consent.

DISCUSSION QUESTIONS

1. Jesse purchased a new home through Gary, his realtor. The house needed a lot of work, so Jesse arranged for Joyce to paint the interior, for Harry to repair the furnace, for his own daughters to plant grass in the backyard, and for Martha to clean the interior. Based on normal hiring relationships, who are agents, servants, or independent contractors, and why? Are the agents special agents or general agents, and why?

2. Juan hired Jack to deliver one cord of pine wood for the fireplace in the house Juan rented. Jack usually just dumped the wood in the driveway—a practice known as a driveway delivery. However, this time he decided to help Juan stack the wood in the garage. Juan was standing in the garage as Jack backed the truck into position. However, Jack backed the truck too far, damaging both the truck and the garage wall. Is Jack a servant or an independent contractor? Who is liable to the injured third party (the landlord), and why? Who would have been liable if the truck had injured Juan? Why?

3. Kurt went to Lake Tahoe for a week's vacation. Before he left, his friend Karen gave him $5 to bet on a particular football game while he was there. Kurt, however, forgot to place the bet. If he had placed the bet, Karen would have won $15,000. What rights does Karen have? If Karen's team had lost, what rights would she have had? Would it make a difference if Kurt was going to be compensated by Karen for placing the bet?

4. Ron works for Acme Grocery Store. One day while Ron was unloading produce from a truck Jimmy stopped by to talk to him. Jimmy got in the truck and, while handing the boxes to Ron, carelessly dropped a box on a person walking down the alley. Who is responsible for the injury, and why? Is it relevant that Jimmy is not being paid? If so, why?

5. Peter hired Andy to purchase some goods for him on the open market. While Andy was obtaining prices from vendors, Ted offered Andy a $100 rebate if Andy purchased the goods from Ted; Andy did and kept the $100 for himself. What are the rights of the parties? Why?

6. Elaine worked as a travel agent for Travel Enterprises, Inc. As an incentive, a cruise ship line offered travel agents one free passage on a cruise for every 25 paying passengers they book on the line. The cruise ship line felt that this practice was good public relations. Elaine earned two free passages. Who is entitled to these passages, and why? Should Elaine's customers be concerned about this practice? Why or why not?

7. After nine years of marriage, Jill and Jon decided to get a divorce. Their neighbor Charlie, who is an attorney, agreed to do the legal work for both parties and handle the property settlement. Are there any problems with this arrangement? Why or why not?

8. Brad called Marty, his stockbroker, to tell him that Ellen, Brad's friend, wanted to purchase some stock from Marty. Brad directed Marty to charge the

purchases against the brokerage account of Brad and his wife, Sue. What is Marty's responsibility to Brad and his wife? What advice will you give Marty?

9. Steve managed a 200-unit apartment complex. The owners want to convert the apartments to condominiums. The city council planned a hearing on the issue. Instead of sending the notice to the owners, the council sent the notice to Steve. What are the rights and obligations of the parties? Why?

10. Sarah signed a written contract stating that her agency relationship will last for four years and that she will have the irrevocable right to take orders from parents for children's educational software for her principal. In an attempt to downsize and economize, however, her principal fired her. What rights does Sarah have?

CASE PROBLEMS AND WRITING ASSIGNMENTS

1. José Torres was a self-employed gardener doing business as José Torres Gardening Service from 1980 to 1988. He performed weekly gardening services at a number of homes in Torrance, California, including the home of Michael and Ona Reardon. In 1988, the Reardons began discussing the possibility of having Torres trim a 65- to 70-foot tree in their front yard. An agreement was reached in mid-June that Torres would trim the tree for $350. David Boice, the Reardons' neighbor, was present during the final discussion. Boice indicated that he was concerned about a large branch of the tree that overhung his house. He feared that the branch would fall onto his roof. Torres and one helper arrived at 11:00 A.M. on 20 June to do the job. The Reardons were not at home. Boice was at home working in his garage-workshop, and he reminded Torres about the branch. Periodically, Boice came out to watch the progress. He mentioned that Torres was not using safety lines, and Torres responded that he did not need them. Torres used a chain saw to cut the larger branches. When Torres was ready to cut the branch that overhung Boice's house, Boice came out to hold a rope tied to the branch. He was going to pull on it so the branch would not fall on his roof. Torres was wearing a safety belt, but it was not attached to the tree. He did not have enough line to reach a branch that could support his weight. Torres claims that Boice pulled on "Boice's rope" when Torres did not expect it, causing Torres to lose control of the chain saw and fall. Torres became a paraplegic due to the fall and sued the Reardons. Was Torres a servant of the Reardons and, therefore, entitled to workers' compensation? [See *Torres* v. *Reardon*, 5 Cal.Rptr.2d 52 (Cal.App. 2 Dist. 1992).]

2. Industry specialists contend that employees playing games on company computers creates significant costs for businesses. A 1993 survey of 1,000 corporations by a software company found that workers spend an average of 5.1 hours a week doing non-job-related tasks on their company computers. This includes playing games. It is estimated that this costs the nation $10 billion annually in lost productivity. Governor George Allen of Virginia has ordered that games be *deleted* from *all* state-owned computers, including those of university faculty members. To quote an administrative memo, "[T]ime spent by employees playing such games should be considered an improper use of taxpayer funds." The ban, which eliminates playing games during breaks and lunch time, is raising questions among Virginia employees. Assume you are a high-level corporate manager. What approach would you take and why? What are the advantages of this approach? Is Virginia taking an ethical approach to this problem? Why or why not? If an individual feels that playing games is acceptable, is it moral for that individual to play? Why or why not? If you were a judge ruling on this case, how would you rule? [See Rajiv Chandrasekaran, "No More Games for Virginia Employees," *The Fresno Bee* (10 January 1995), p. D10.]

3. Harold Frankel incorporated as a one-person corporation in order to obtain some pension benefits under the federal tax code. He then entered into a contract with Bally, Inc., to serve as a sales representative. When Bally terminated the arrangement, Frankel, age 61, filed a suit against Bally under the federal Age Discrimination in Employment Act (Act). Only employees are covered by the Act. Can a person who incorporates himself be an employee under the Act? [See *Frankel* v. *Bally, Inc.,* 987 F.2d 86 (2nd Cir. 1993).]

4. Jeffrey Paul Russell was an employee of Uniq'wood. As such, he received health-care coverage provided by Uniq'wood, pursuant to a group health insurance contract issued by Blue Cross. Uniq'wood was specified as the group agent. One of its duties was to notify employees of changes in their coverage. Uniq'wood notified Blue Cross to terminate Russell's coverage and notified Russell that it had been canceled. Does Blue Cross owe Russell a fiduciary duty? Why or why not? [See *Russell* v. *Uniq'wood Furniture Galleries, Inc.,* 1994 U.S.Dist. LEXIS 9620 (S.D.Ala., S.Div., 1994).]

5. Robert T. Darden was an insurance "agent" who worked for Nationwide Mutual Insurance Co. Under their written contract, Darden was enrolled in a Nationwide "insurance agents retirement plan," which provided that Darden would forfeit his retirement benefits if he sold insurance for a competitor within one year of retirement and within 25 miles from his prior business location. Darden began selling for a competitor, and Nationwide implemented the forfeiture provision. Darden sued under the federal Employee Retirement Income Security Act of 1974 (ERISA). Only employees have rights under ERISA. Was Darden an employee or an independent contractor when he worked for Nationwide? Was the Nationwide "insurance agents retirement plan" subject to ERISA? [See *Nationwide Mutual Insurance Co.* v. *Darden*, 503 U.S. 318 (1992).]

6. **BUSINESS APPLICATION CASE** From 1953 to July 1967, George Geary worked as a sales representative for United States Steel Corporation (USS). Geary, an agent at will, sold tubular products to the oil and gas industry. USS designed a new product for use under high pressure. Geary believed that this new product had not been adequately tested and posed a serious danger to users. He voiced his concerns to his supervisors and was told to sell the product. He then contacted the vice president in charge of the product to get action. The product was withdrawn from the market. Geary was fired. Under the circumstances, was Geary entitled to protection from being discharged? Should he be protected from being fired? Analyze this case. Based on your analysis, how could USS have better handled the situation? [See *Geary* v. *United States Steel Corporation*, 319 A.2d 174 (Pa. 1974).]

7. **ETHICAL APPLICATION CASE** Robert Jones worked for Western States operating heavy equipment. When the equipment broke down, he was assigned a position in the cyanide leach pit. Previ-ously Jones had attended one of his employer's safety courses, where he had learned about the dangers of absorption of cyanide and the need to avoid contact with open wounds. Since Jones had an open wound from surgery, he asked to be assigned an alternate position. He was then fired for insubordination. Was Jones wrongfully discharged? Why or why not? Analyze the ethical perspective of Western States. Compare this case to *Geary* v. *U.S. Steel Corp.*, 319 A.2d 174 (Pa. 1974), Case Problem and Writing Assignment 6. [See *Western States Minerals Corp.* v. *Jones*, 819 P.2d 206 (Nev. 1991).]

8. **CRITICAL THINKING CASE** Five-year-old Valerie Lakey was playing in a wading pool in North Carolina when she was trapped by suction from water being pumped through the drain in the bottom of the pool. The drain cover, manufactured by Sta-Rite Industries, Inc., was not properly screwed into place. Her parents sued a number of entities in her behalf. The claim against Sta-Rite was based on theories of defective design and failure to warn. Sta-Rite selected an attorney to represent it in pretrial matters and at trial. Sta-Rite had insurance policies including a $2 million general liability policy issued by National Fire Insurance Co. and an excess policy issued by Zurich Re (U.K.) Ltd. with a limit of $20 million. Zurich hired its own attorney, Mark Kreger, who participated in pretrial discussions with Sta-Rite regarding settlement strategy. The jury rendered a compensatory damage verdict in favor of plaintiffs in the amount of $25 million. The parties then settled prior to the punitive damage portion of the trial. Sta-Rite then filed suit against Zurich claiming that Zurich owed it a fiduciary duty of good faith that Zurich breached by refusing to pay its policy limits of $20 million in response to a settlement offer. Was Zurich an agent of Sta-Rite who owed Sta-Rite a duty of good faith? [See *Sta-Rite Industries, Inc.* v. *Zurich Re (U.K.) Ltd.*, 178 F.3d 883 (7th Cir. 1999).]

NOTES

1. *Restatement (Second) of Agency* (Philadelphia: American Law Institute, 1958), § 1.
2. Ibid., § 20, Comment b.
3. Ibid., § 492, Comment a.
4. Ibid., § 3, Comment a.
5. Exceptions occur in areas of unemployment compensation and workers' compensation statutes. These statutes often require that the worker is being paid.

6. Erica Noonan, "Hope of Survivors Runs Out," *The Fresno Bee* (19 July 1999), pp. A1, A14; David Usborne, "Kennedy Alarm Delayed for Hours After Control Tower Was Ignored," *The Independent* (London) (21 July 1999), p. 2; Matthew Brelis, "Some Defend Handling of First Call on Flight Delay; The Kennedy Plain Crash/FAA Procedures," *The Boston Globe* (21 July 1999), p. A12; Jack Sullivan, "Tragedy at Sea,

NTSB to Review Tape of Initial Call About JFK's Plane," *The Boston Herald* (21 July 1999), p. 12.

7. *Whirlpool Corp.* v. *Marshall*, 445 U.S. 1 (1980).

8. On 8 August 1991, the National Conference of Commissioners on Uniform State Laws approved the Model Employment Termination Act 2 (Proposed Official Draft, 1991), commonly called META, which addresses these issues. To date, no states have adopted this model act. (Information on the current status of adoptions of Uniform State Laws provided during a telephone conversation with Katie Robinson, Communications Officer, NCCUSL, 23 February 2000.)

9. *Black's Law Dictionary,* 6th ed. (St. Paul, MN: West Publishing Co., 1990), p. 1092.

10. Harold Gill Reuschlein and William A. Gregory, *Hornbook on the Law of Agency and Partnership,* 2nd ed. (St. Paul, MN: West Publishing Co., 1990), § 89(b), pp. 151–152.

CHAPTER

32

LIABILITY FOR CONTRACTS

CALL-IMAGE TECHNOLOGY

A G E N D A

CIT will use agents in the conduct of its business. Knowing this, the family needs to decide whether CIT should be a disclosed, an undisclosed, or a partially disclosed principal. They also need to decide what authority CIT should expressly grant to its agents, what additional authority these agents will have, and whether there is some means of limiting the authority of the agents.

Tom is concerned that salespersons will negotiate contracts with buyers and distributors that Tom and Anna have not authorized and find unacceptable. What can Tom do to alleviate this concern? In general, what steps should CIT take with its sales force to reduce the risk of this type of problem? What steps should CIT agents take to minimize their personal liability on contracts they negotiate for CIT? CIT will deal with the agents of suppliers and retailers. In these relationships, CIT will be the third party. What rights will CIT have against these agents and their principals?

These and similar questions arise when agents enter into contracts with third parties. Be prepared! You never know when one of the Kochanowskis will need your help or advice.

O U T L I N E

A Framework for Contractual Liability

Imposing Liability on the Principal

Disclosed Principal

Undisclosed Principal

Partially Disclosed Principal

Analysis of Agent's Contracts with Third Parties

Contract Between the Principal and the Agent

Summary

Discussion Questions

Case Problems and Writing Assignments

A FRAMEWORK FOR CONTRACTUAL LIABILITY

An agent may have many and varied duties, which may include negotiating contracts for the principal. This chapter addresses the liability of the agent, the principal, and the third party for the proper performance of these contracts. Agency law varies from state to state. In applying rules of law, the court often is influenced by the reasonable expectations of the third party, that is, how the third party perceives the situation. The distinction between servants and nonservants is not significant when the agent has entered into a contract; the courts will treat both types of agents the same. The distinction is significant if the agent commits a tort. Because the distinction is irrelevant in contract cases, it is logical to use the term *agent* in this chapter. The primary issue for consideration is whether the principal authorized the agent to enter into the contract. The principal will be classified as a disclosed, an undisclosed, or a partially disclosed principal based on whether the principal's identity is to be revealed to the third party. The status of the principal in this regard is determined when the agent and the third party enter the contract; the legal relationships are fixed at that time.

IMPOSING LIABILITY ON THE PRINCIPAL

Regardless of the principal's classification, the principal will not be liable for every act committed by his or her agent or for every contract signed by the agent. To determine whether the principal should be held liable, the court will examine whether the agent was authorized to enter into this type of contract. Authority can be established in a number of different ways, and often they overlap in a given situation. For the third party to recover a judgment against the principal, all that needs to be shown is that *one* type of authority exists. Authority to act as an agent usually includes authority to act only for the benefit, not the detriment, of the principal. These types of authority are listed in Exhibit 32.1. A full discussion follows.

Express Authority

Express authority occurs when the principal informs the agent that the agent has authority to engage in a specific act or to perform a particular task. Generally, express authority need not be in writing, and in most cases, it is not. For example, a principal may say to her secretary, "Please order more stationery." Courts often strictly construe the words the principal uses when giving the authority. If the principal says to the agent, "Locate premises for another card shop," usually the court will interpret this to mean that the agent is authorized only to *find* the premises and not actually to purchase the store. Therefore, an agent should interpret the instructions narrowly or ask for clarification of the scope of authority.

Ratification Authority

Ratification authority occurs when the agent does something that was unauthorized at the time, and the principal approves it later. It requires approval by the principal after the contract was formed by the agent and after the principal has

E X H I B I T 32.1 | **Rights of a Third Party to Sue a Principal**

Principal ---- (Appointment) -----› Agent

[Agent is the *representative* of the principal. Legally the agent's actions are treated as *if* done by the principal.]

Agent ---- (Interacts) -----› Third Person

[Third person can treat the agent's conduct as equivalent to the principal performing the action, *provided* the agent possesses authority.]

Third Person ------ (Sues) -----› Principal

[The third person can sue the principal for conduct of the agent, provided that the conduct was authorized *or* within the course and scope of employment.]

Types of Authority an Agent may possess:

- Express
- Ratification
- Incidental
- Implied
- Emergency
- Apparent
- Estoppel

knowledge of the material facts. When a principal ratifies a contract, he or she must ratify the whole agreement. The principal cannot elect to ratify parts of the contract and disregard the less advantageous parts.

Furthermore, the principal does not need to communicate the ratification verbally to anyone.[1] Generally, ratification may occur by an express statement or may be implied by the principal's clear indication through his or her conduct of an intent to affirm. An example of implied ratification occurs when the principal retains and uses goods delivered under an agreement *after* learning of the contract and its terms. Another example occurs when a principal initiates a lawsuit to enforce the agreement. The ratification needs to follow the same format required of the original authorization. In a limited number of situations, the ratification will have to be in writing. If the agent/third-party contract must be in writing under the **Statute of Frauds,** then the ratification must be written, too.

Courts have imposed additional limitations on the doctrine of ratification. To apply the doctrine the principal must have been capable of forming a contract when the original contract occurred *and* when it was ratified. The *relation back doctrine* is also applied to ratified contracts. It states that *if* the contract is properly ratified, it is as if it were valid the whole time. Modern courts will not apply this doctrine if it will injure an innocent party who obtains rights in the contract between the time of the original contract formation and the ratification.

Ratification cannot occur if important contract terms are concealed from the principal. Ratification will be effective only if the principal knows all the relevant facts. Also, the agent must have **purported** to act for the principal when the agent entered into the contract. If the agent did not reveal his or her agency capacity or if the agent was working for an undisclosed principal, there can be no ratification.

There is often more than one type of authority present. The court in the following case considered both **apparent authority** and ratification authority.

Statute of Frauds
Statute that requires some contracts to be in writing to be enforceable.

Purported
Gave the impression that authority was present.

Apparent authority
Principal gives the appearance that the agent acts with authority.

32.1

TRUSTEES OF THE AMERICAN FEDERATION OF MUSICIANS AND EMPLOYERS' PENSION FUND V. STEVEN SCOTT ENTERPRISES, INC.

40 F.SUPP. 2D 503 (S.DIST.N.Y. 1999)

FACTS . . . [T]he Trustees of the . . . Musicians and Employers' Pension Fund (the "Pension Fund") bring this suit . . . The Pension Fund is . . . maintained for the purpose of providing retirement and related benefits . . . Steven Scott [the defendant] is a company that employs musicians to perform for its clients at various engagements, . . . such as weddings or bar mitzvahs. Steven Scott has been a signatory to various collective bargaining agreements with Local 802 . . . Under these . . . agreements, Steven Scott is required to make certain contributions to the Pension Fund at specified rates. . . . At the core of [the dispute] . . . are fifteen settlement agreements that defendant entered into with [William] Moriarity, Local 802 President and Pension Fund Trustee . . . The substance of each agreement includes the following terms: (1) that Steven Scott agrees to pay a certain sum of money to the Pension Fund for certain employees . . . ; (2) that the agreement is in full settlement of all monetary claims against Steven Scott through a specified date; (3) that the agreement binds Local 802, the Pension Fund, and Steven Scott; and (4) that each party, including Moriarity, "acknowledges, represents, and warrants that they are authorized to enter into, execute, deliver, perform, and implement the agreement." In addition, each agreement contains a ratification clause . . . Each agreement is signed by two parties: Joseph Mileti, an officer and duly authorized agent for Steven Scott, and Moriarity. . . .

Steven Scott tendered each of the fifteen settlement checks, accompanied by a three-page settlement agreement and a list of employee names and contribution amounts, to Local 802, who then forwarded the agreements and checks to the Pension Fund. The checks were processed by Pension Fund clerical workers who were in charge of processing all contributions . . . Employers . . . routinely sent their checks and employee lists . . . to Local 802 . . . [E]ach check was accompanied by a settlement agreement, which unequivocally stated that the check was in full settlement of all obligations owed by Steven Scott . . . The Pension Fund admitted that it received a settlement agreement along with each of the fifteen checks. It is also undisputed that all fifteen settlement checks were cashed by the Pension Fund.

As a Pension Fund Trustee and Local 802 President, Moriarity was authorized to collect Pension Fund contributions from employers. However, Moriarity was not authorized to unilaterally enter into settlement agreements that were in full satisfaction of any owing debts to the Pension Fund. Under the terms of the Trust Agreement . . . , only the Board of Trustees of the Pension Fund has the authority to enter into such agreements or delegate such authority to two or more Trustees . . . [T]he Pension Fund acknowledges that Steven Scott was not mailed a copy of the Trust Agreement until June 1995, and thus could not have known of the Board's exclusive authority to enter into such agreements prior to executing a majority of [the] settlement agreements at issue. . . . [T]he Pension Fund has not alleged any facts to show that Steven Scott had any reason to know of the Board's exclusive authority in such matters. . . .

ISSUE Is the Pension Fund bound by these agreements?

HOLDING Yes. Moriarity had apparent authority to enter into the first thirteen agreements. The Pension Fund ratified all the agreements.

REASONING Since Steven Scott relies on matters outside the face of the complaint . . . , the court must treat it as a motion for summary judgment . . . The court may only grant summary judgment when "no rational jury could find in favor of the non-moving party."

. . . Steven Scott bases its arguments on the principles of . . . apparent authority. . . . [T]he court concludes that the Pension Fund's acts of continually cashing all fifteen settlement checks while failing to repudiate Moriarity's unauthorized actions after receiving notice of at least seven settlement agreements created the appearance of authority that Steven Scott reasonably relied on. ("An agent has apparent authority when conduct by the principal leads a third party to believe that the agent has authorization to act on behalf of the principal.") A principal is estopped from denying the apparent authority of its agent when it remains "silent when he had the opportunity of speaking and when he knew or ought to have known that his silence would be relied upon, and that action would be taken . . . which his statement of truth would prevent. . . . " [T]he Pension Fund's

32.1

TRUSTEES OF THE AMERICAN FEDERATION OF MUSICIANS AND EMPLOYERS' PENSION FUND V. STEVEN SCOTT ENTERPRISES, INC., *continued*

40 F.SUPP. 2D 503 (S.DIST.N.Y. 1999)

silence may be construed as an affirmation of Moriarity's exercise of apparent authority. . . . Steven Scott's reliance on Moriarity's exercise of apparent authority was no longer reasonable after June 1995, the date in which it received notice of the actual scope of Moriarity's agency as outlined in the Pension Fund's Trust Agreement. . . . [A]ny reasonable fact-finder would conclude that Moriarity was acting with apparent authority when he negotiated the first thirteen settlement agreements that are binding on the Pension Fund.

Steven Scott relies on the alternative grounds of ratification . . . "Ratification of the acts of an agent only occurs where the principal has full knowledge of all material facts and takes some action to affirm the agent's actions." Affirmance . . . may be inferred from "knowledge of the principal coupled with a failure to timely repudiate, where the party seeking a finding of ratification has in some way relied upon the principal's silence. . . . " . . . [K]nowledge of the settlement agreements is inferred from the undisputed fact that seven settlement agreements were found within plaintiffs' possession. . . . [T]he Pension Fund admitted to having received copies of all fifteen settlement agreements . . . [T]he Pension Fund was on constructive notice of all settlement agreements within its possession. . . . Once the Pension Fund had knowledge of the settlement agreements, its failure to repudiate Moriarity's actions constituted ratification of the agreements. The Pension Fund cannot now complain that it failed to read or inquire into the meaning of this clause simply because its clerical workers did not notice the settlement agreements or chose not to read the agreements. . . . Perhaps the clerical workers should have routed the settlement agreements and checks to a supervisor . . . [T]he Pension Fund acted unreasonably . . . [A] reasonable fact finder could only conclude that the Pension Fund had full knowledge of all material terms of the settlement agreements and ratified the agreements by cashing the checks according to provisions of the ratification clause that was readily apparent in each settlement agreement. . . . Steven Scott's motion for summary judgment is granted . . .

BUSINESS CONSIDERATIONS What could a business, union, or pension fund do to reduce the risk that agents will exceed their authority? What processes would reduce the application of apparent and ratification authority?

ETHICAL CONSIDERATIONS Was it ethical for Moriarity to exceed his authority without informing Steven Scott? Was it ethical for the Pension Fund to complain when they had received the advantages of the settlement agreements?

Incidental Authority

In most cases, the principal does not discuss the grant of power in detail, if at all. Generally, the agent is given a brief explanation of his or her authority, or he or she is given an objective. This brief grant of express authority includes the power to do all acts that are incidental to the specific authority that is discussed. *Incidental authority* reasonably and necessarily arises in order to enable the agent to complete his or her assigned duties. Suppose an agent is provided with merchandise that is to be sold door to door. The agent will reasonably and necessarily have incidental authority to deliver the merchandise and to collect the purchase price. Incidental authority is also referred to as *incidental powers*.

Implied Authority

Implied authority is based on the agent's position *or* on past dealings between the agent and the third party. One type of implied authority arises when an agent is given a title and a position. It is implied that the agent can enter into the same types of contracts that people with this title normally can. A vice president of sales and marketing, for example, will have implied authority to purchase advertising in newspapers and on radio and to contract with an advertising agency for a new ad campaign. Why? The agent will have this authority because *most* vice presidents of sales and marketing have such authority. In other words, it is customary. When the principal confers the title on the agent, the agent acquires the implied power that accompanies it.

In the alternative, implied authority may exist because of a series of similar dealings in the past between the agent and the third party. If the principal did not object to the past transactions, it is assumed that the principal authorized the earlier contracts and that this type of transaction is within the agent's power. For example, if a secretary customarily orders office supplies for a business on a monthly basis, the secretary has implied authority to continue to order office supplies in this manner.

Implied authority may exceed actual expressed authority. The third party can recover a judgment in court on the basis of this implied authority if (1) the third party reasonably *believed* that the agent had some particular authority, and (2) the third party was unaware that the authority was lacking. Both elements are required.

Emergency Authority

Emergency authority is inherent in all agency relationships. It need not be expressed. It provides the agent with authority to respond to emergencies, even though the principal and agent never discussed the type of emergency or how to respond to it. Suppose the owner of a jewelry shop leaves his manager in charge and goes out for supper. While the owner is absent, a fire starts in the stockroom. In an effort to contain the fire, the manager rushes to the hardware store next door and buys four fire extinguishers on credit. The principal—the owner—must pay for the fire extinguishers because the manager had emergency authority to purchase them.

Emergency authority will be found when all the following circumstances exist:

1. An emergency or unexpected situation occurs that requires prompt action.
2. The principal cannot be reached in sufficient time for a response or advice.
3. The action taken by the agent is reasonable in the situation, and it is expected to benefit the principal.

Apparent Authority

Apparent authority occurs when the principal creates the appearance that an agency exists or that the agent has broader powers than he or she actually has. Here, the representation of authority is made to the third party rather than to the agent.[2] Apparent authority is based on the conduct of the principal; the conduct must cause a reasonable third party to believe that a particular person has authority to act as the principal's agent. An agent with apparent authority may or may not have actual authority.

Apparent authority may be created by intentional or careless acts of the principal and reasonable reliance by the third party. Obviously, if the third party knows the agent lacks this authority, the reliance will not be reasonable.

In some cases, apparent authority exists even though there is no real agent. The person acting in the agent's role may be considered a *purported agent* (i.e., one who claims to be an agent). Sometimes this purported agent is an agent who has been terminated, and sometimes the person never was an agent. For example, suppose a company fires a sales representative but neglects to collect its samples, displays, and order forms from the representative. The ex-representative then takes a number of customer orders and disappears with the cash deposits. The company will have to return the deposits or credit them to the customers' orders, because the ex-representative still has apparent authority to take orders. To help prevent this situation, the company should require the ex-representative to return all its sales materials.

When an agency relationship is terminated, a principal should take certain steps to terminate apparent authority. The principal should inform the agent that the relationship is terminated, call or send notices to people who have dealt with that agent, and sometimes advertise in newspapers and trade journals that the relationship has ended. The principal should collect all identification tags, samples, displays, order forms, and any other materials that can be used as evidence of the agency relationship. These items are *indicia* of the agency relationship.

Sometimes the purported agent never was employed by the principal, and yet the principal's conduct may cause him or her to be liable for the "agent's" actions. For example, a department store may not require its clerks to wear identifying jackets, vests, or even name tags. Suppose a customer selects some merchandise and walks toward a cash register. In place of a cashier, another customer steps behind the cash register, rings up the sale, puts the merchandise in the bag, and pockets the payment. In this case, the store cannot charge the customer again for the merchandise; it is bound by the acts of the purported agent.

Before applying apparent authority, some courts require that (1) the principal's actions give rise to a reasonable belief in the agent's authority and (2) there be detrimental reliance on the part of the third party.[3] A number of factors need to be considered: The existence of apparent authority is a factual issue to be determined in each case.

A third party must act reasonably, or the court will not apply the concept of apparent authority. The third party must take into consideration the facts and circumstances surrounding the transaction and the type of action involved. Sometimes, based on the information available, the third party must investigate further before reasonably relying on apparent authority.

Apparent authority may be used to hold a principal liable on contracts entered into by the agent. It *ordinarily* will not be used to make a principal accountable for physical harm caused by the agent through negligence, assault, trespass, and similar torts.

The court grappled with whether the attorney had apparent authority in the following case.

32.2

FARRIS V. J.C. PENNEY COMPANY, INC.
176 F.3D 706 (3RD CIR. 1999)

FACTS . . . On April 15, 1995, Margaret Farris was injured in a fall at the J.C. Penney store in downtown Philadelphia. She alleges that her injuries were sustained when she was restrained by Penney's employees and falsely accused of shoplifting. Farris and her

continued

32.2

FARRIS V. J.C. PENNEY COMPANY, INC., *continued*

176 F.3D 706 (3RD CIR. 1999)

husband . . . hired attorney Timothy Booker to represent them in connection with the incident, agreeing to pay him a 40% contingent fee. . . .

A trial . . . began before the judge and jury on September 24, 1996. At about noon on the second day of trial, settlement discussions began. Booker and the Farrises met with the trial judge alone. The judge then met with attorney Renee Berger, counsel for J.C. Penney. Later that day, in a meeting with both Booker and Berger, the judge asked Berger if J.C. Penney would authorize her to settle the case for $20,000. After receiving assurance from the judge that $20,000 would indeed settle the matter, Berger secured the necessary authority and communicated that fact to Booker. Ms. Berger then saw Booker enter a witness room with Mrs. Farris where the two remained for about five minutes. At some later point Booker informed Berger that the $20,000 settlement offer had been accepted. In fact, neither of the Farrises authorized Booker to accept the offer. To the contrary, Margaret Farris had told Booker that she did not want the case to be settled until her medical treatment was complete. Nonetheless, the $20,000 settlement figure was communicated to the judge. . . . The entire in-court proceeding with respect to the settlement lasted approximately three minutes and the District Court later found that Mrs. Farris either did not hear or did not understand what was happening until after the jury had been dismissed. Following discharge of the jury, the Farrises left the courtroom with Booker. Crying, Margaret Farris asked Booker, "Why did you do this to me?" Mrs. Farris testified that Booker's response was, "One day you'll thank me." Within minutes of this exchange, Margaret Farris re-entered the courtroom where Ms. Berger stood conferring with a number of the jurors. Mrs. Farris told Ms. Berger that she had never authorized Booker to settle the case.

. . . [T]he trial judge entered an order dismissing the case . . . Because the Farrises declined to sign the release, the settlement check was never issued. Booker sought to have the settlement proceeds disbursed without a signed release but Berger refused. . . . Richard P. Abraham, Esq., replaced Booker as counsel for the Farrises. . . . [A] hearing was held on the motion to enforce the settlement. . . .

ISSUE Would Pennsylvania courts enforce a settlement based on apparent authority of the attorney?

HOLDING Probably. However, Pennsylvania courts would not apply apparent authority under these circumstances.

REASONING The Pennsylvania Supreme Court has never invoked the doctrine of apparent authority to enforce a settlement entered into by an attorney who lacks actual authority to settle . . . "[W]e believe that the Pennsylvania Supreme Court might allow implied, actual or apparent authority to suffice in an appropriate case." . . . Our discussions of apparent authority in the context of Pennsylvania law and the law generally have emphasized that whether the doctrine applies depends upon the client's conduct. . . . We again stressed the fact-dependent nature of the doctrine of apparent authority . . . We then considered the applicability of apparent authority, writing that "there is no consensus" on the doctrine but finding that its applicability represents "the better rule":

> *Enforcing settlement agreements on the basis of apparent authority is consistent with the principles of agency law, the policies favoring settlements generally, and the notions of fairness to the parties in the adjudicatory process.*

In finding that apparent authority could be invoked to validate a settlement we emphasized that the "crucial question in ascertaining whether apparent authority has been created is whether the principal has made representations concerning the agent's authority to the third party." . . .

The . . . [precedents], taken together, establish that in order for the doctrine of apparent authority to apply, the facts must show that the plaintiffs (principals) communicated directly with defense counsel, making representations that would lead defense counsel to believe that the plaintiffs' attorney had authority to settle the case. . . . The Farrises in-court conduct is the linchpin of this case. Normally in-court silence during the reading or entry of a settlement would be a powerful indicator that the particular settlement terms were authorized. The unique facts of this case, however, negate the evidentiary force of the Farrises' silence. . . . Moreover, had J.C. Penney construed Farrises' silence as a manifestation of authority, it was immediately disabused of that notion. As soon as the proceedings were concluded, Mrs. Farris

32.2

FARRIS V. J.C. PENNEY COMPANY, INC., *continued*
176 F.3D 706 (3RD CIR. 1999)

expressed her surprise with and opposition to the settlement both to her own attorney and to counsel for J.C. Penney. [Had there been any manifestation of authority sufficient to support the doctrine of apparent authority, that manifestation was promptly repudiated. The general rule is that a principal may promptly repudiate an agent's acts . . .] J.C. Penney was on notice immediately that the settlement was not authorized and has never paid any amount to anyone as a result of the settlement. . . . This conclusion is consistent with our own case law and the law of Pennsylvania. . . . This is not the "typical" case where a client has acted to create an ambiguity with respect to the attorney's authority, where she has delayed in asserting the lack of authority, or where it is clear that the real motive for challenging a settlement involves a change of heart regarding the substance of the settlement.

BUSINESS CONSIDERATIONS How can parties protect themselves from attorneys entering into settlement agreements without authority? What techniques can generally be used to prevent unauthorized acts of agents?

ETHICAL CONSIDERATIONS Was Booker's agreement to settle ethical? Is it relevant that Booker allegedly said, "One day you'll thank me"?

Authority by Estoppel

Authority by estoppel prevents a principal who has misled a third party from denying the agent's authority. This is also called *ostensible authority.* It occurs when the principal *allows* the purported agent to pass him- or herself off as an agent and does not take steps to prevent the purported agent's representation.

Estoppel authority may occur by itself or in conjunction with other types of authority. When there is only estoppel authority and no other authority, it will be used solely for the protection of the third party. It will not constitute the basis of a successful lawsuit by the principal against the third party. It creates rights for the third party and liabilities for the principal. It protects the third party and allows the third party reimbursement for injuries. As with other doctrines of agency law, the courts are weighing the respective rights of two relatively innocent people—the third party and the principal. The purported agent can be sued for **fraud,** but generally that person cannot be located or has insufficient funds to cover the resulting losses.

Fraud
The intentional misrepresentation of a material fact.

Authority by estoppel is illustrated in Exhibit 32.2 on page 844 and in the example that follows.

Roy was walking to class one Wednesday when he passed Grace and David, who were standing next to Roy's car. He overheard Grace pointing out all the car's features to David. It was evident that Grace was trying to sell the car to David on Roy's behalf. Roy thought this amusing and did not stop to explain the truth. He went to class instead. He later learned that David made a $200 down payment on the car and that Grace disappeared with the money.

In a lawsuit between David and Roy, David will prevail. The court can apply agency by estoppel and decide that Roy is estopped (prevented) from denying that Grace was his agent. Roy knew that Grace was pretending to be Roy's agent, and

32.1 | SALES/ MANAGEMENT

HONORING SALES AGENTS' CONTRACTS

CIT appointed several sales agents. Each agent was assigned a territory, and each was provided with an "order book" containing standard order forms. These order forms contain the list price for Call-Image videophones, including any quantity discounts that can be given. One of the sales agents called on a large retail outlet in another state. The retailer expressed an interest in buying a large number of the Call-Image videophones, but only if CIT would give the retailer an additional 10 percent discount above the quantity discount normally given by CIT. The sales agent agreed to these terms and completed the order form, including an indication of the additional 10 percent discount. Once the form was completed and signed by the sales agent and the store's representative, a copy was faxed to CIT. When Tom received the copy of the order, he was livid. He knows that the additional discount will take virtually all the profit from the sale, but he fears that the firm is bound by the signed order. He asks you whether CIT must honor this contract. What will you tell him?

BUSINESS CONSIDERATIONS What can a firm do to protect itself from overly zealous sales agents? Should it have a policy in place for handling situations such as this, or should each case be handled on an individual basis? How should the business communicate with the buyer in this sort of situation in order to (1) avoid the contract, and (2) retain the buyer as a customer?

ETHICAL CONSIDERATIONS Is it ethical for a firm to refuse to honor a commitment made by one of its agents, even if the agent exceeded his or her authority? Is it ethical for a buyer to utilize its size to force special concessions from a sales agent beyond those normally granted by the firm?

Roy easily could have denied this. Roy's failure to speak helped to cause David's loss. The court will protect David from a loss by allowing him to recover.

*Note that Grace would also be liable to David if she could be located. She would be liable under fraud and breach of **warranty of authority.***

Imputing the Agent's Knowledge to the Principal

In addition to being liable for contracts entered into by an agent, a principal may be legally responsible for information known to the agent but not actually known by the principal. This concept is called *imputing knowledge.* Because an agent has a duty to inform the principal about important facts that relate to the agency, it will be assumed that the agent has performed this duty. (This duty was discussed in Chapter 31.) If the agent fails to perform this duty and the failure causes a loss, the principal—not the third party—should suffer the loss. Courts justify this result because the principal selected the agent, placed the agent in a position of authority, and had (legal) control over the agent.

The agent's knowledge is not always imputed to the principal. Before a principal will be bound by knowledge received by the agent, generally the agent must have actual or apparent authority to receive this type of knowledge. In addition, the information received by the agent must relate to the subject matter of the agency. For example, if the principal owns a real estate firm, a movie theater, and a hardware store, and the agent works in the hardware store, knowledge that the agent obtains about the real estate firm will not be imputed to the principal. The knowledge must be within the scope of the agency.

E X H I B I T 32.2 | **Authority by Estoppel**

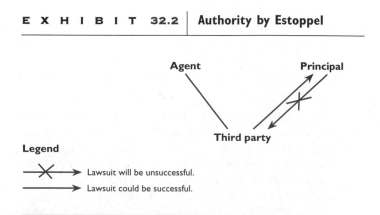

Legend

✗→ Lawsuit will be unsuccessful.

→ Lawsuit could be successful.

DISCLOSED PRINCIPAL

When an agent clearly discloses that he or she is representing a principal and identifies the principal, the principal is *disclosed.* In these situations, the principal may be bound to the contract by any of the types of authority that have been discussed. Exhibit 32.3 illustrates a disclosed principal.

Liability of the Agent

Normally, when an agent indicates that he or she is entering into a contract on behalf of the disclosed principal, the agent will not be liable for the contract. It is clearly understood that the third party should look to the principal alone for performance. As with most legal rules, there are exceptions. For example, if the agent fails to represent his or her capacity as such, the agent will be personally bound. The agent also will be bound if he or she intends to be bound. For example, the agent may say, "You can rely on me," or "You have my word on it." Why would an agent want to be liable on the principal's contract? Why would an agent want to undertake additional liability? An agent might do this if it is necessary to make a sale. The prospective buyer may be unsure about the principal and his or her reputation or financial backing. Perhaps the prospect has a long working relationship with the agent, so the agent's guarantee of performance persuades the prospect. The agent does not have valid grounds to complain if he or she is accepted at his or her word. The third party generally will prefer to sue the principal on the contract instead of the agent since the principal often has more assets.

The third party, then, has legal rights against both the agent and the disclosed principal. This does not mean that the third party can collect twice. The third party is limited to one reimbursement. The traditional approach also required the third party to make an *election* to sue either the agent *or* the principal. Obviously, an important factor in this decision is who has the funds to pay a judgment. If the third party sues the principal and loses, he or she will be barred from then suing the agent. The reverse is also true. The more modern approach permits the third

Warranty of authority
Implied warranties that the agent is an agent for the principal and is permitted to act in this manner.

E X H I B I T 32.3 | **Disclosed Principal**

Dan Kochanowski
Sales Agent for
Call-Image Technology (CIT)
9876 Appian Way
Maineville, Ohio 44444
513-555-8375

32.2 | SALES/ MANAGEMENT

NEGATING THE WARRANTY OF AUTHORITY

When one of the firm's sales agents was discussing the Call-Image videophones with a potential customer, the customer expressed interest in the product. However, the customer refused to place an order unless CIT would provide an "extended maintenance agreement," agreeing to repair or replace any units that malfunctioned within a three-year period. The agent told the customer that he didn't have authority to provide such a commitment. However, the customer insisted that the agent commit to the extended maintenance agreement immediately or there would be no sale. Despite his misgivings, the agent wrote the order, including a three-year extended maintenance agreement. After leaving the customer's office, the agent called Dan and told him what had happened. Dan has asked you what the legal implications of this situation are. What will you tell him?

BUSINESS CONSIDERATIONS How can an agent handle a situation in which a customer makes demands that the agent believes would require the agent to exceed his or her authority? Is an agent legally liable to the customer if the agent knowingly exceeds the authority granted by the principal?

ETHICAL CONSIDERATIONS Does an agent have an ethical obligation to disclose to the third person any conduct that exceeds the authority given to the agent? Does the agent have an ethical obligation to inform the principal if or when the agent exceeds his or her authority?

party to sue both the principal and the agent *together.* However, either defendant can require the third party to make an election prior to judgment.

Warranty of Authority

Whenever an agent of a disclosed principal enters into a contract, the agent makes all of the following implied warranties. These warranties are not stated by the agent; they are implied by the situation.

1. The disclosed principal exists and is competent.
2. The agent is an agent for the principal.
3. The agent is authorized to enter into this type of contract for the principal.

The third party can sue the agent to recover for losses that are caused by the breach of warranty of authority. Perhaps the third party has losses because he or she did not receive the goods that are covered by the contract. Further, suppose the principal is not responsible for the losses because the agent is not authorized to enter into this type of contract. The third party will choose to sue the agent.

If the agent fears that he or she does not have the authority to enter into this type of contract, the agent may be concerned about the warranties of authority. He or she would be wise, then, to negate the warranties. This can be accomplished by stating that there is no warranty or by specifically stating to the third party the limitations on the agent's actual authority. The latter condition is illustrated in the following example.

Rhoda hires Beth as an agent and tells her to locate a parcel of agricultural real estate. Beth locates a parcel that meets Rhoda's specifications. Edele, the owner of the parcel, wants Beth to sign the purchase contract, but Beth is not sure whether she has authority to sign. If she fully and truthfully discloses the situation surrounding her authority, Beth will negate the implied warranty of authority. If Edele still wishes to sign the contract with Beth, he will assume the responsibility and the loss if the contract is not authorized. Edele would be relying on his own judgment.

The agent may be liable for fraud if the agent intentionally misrepresents his or her authority. Exhibit 32.4 illustrates the agent's liability.

Liability of the Third Party

Lawsuit by the Principal. When a principal has been disclosed from the beginning, the third party realizes, or should realize, that the principal has an interest in the contract. The principal can successfully sue the third party on the contract if the agent was authorized to enter into this type of contract for the principal. In other words, the third party will be liable if there is express, implied, incidental, emergency, apparent, or ratification authority. The third party will not be liable if the only type of authority is estoppel authority.

Lawsuit by the Agent. Normally, the agent has no right to sue the third party on a contract. An agent *may* successfully sue the third party if the agent can show that he or she has an interest in the contract. The most common type of interest is one in which the agent is entitled to a commission on a sale. For example, a real estate broker (the agent) enters into a contract on behalf of a homeowner (the principal). The agent is entitled to a 6 percent commission payable from the proceeds of the sale. If the buyer (the third party) breaches the contract, the agent can sue to recover the lost commission. (In this type of case, the principal may decide that it is not worth suing, but the agent may feel that it is.)

An agent may successfully sue the third party when the agent intends to be bound. This rule is based on equitable principles. If the agent is liable to the third party, the third party should be liable to the agent, too. In some cases, a principal may transfer to the agent the right to file the lawsuit. In these cases, also, the agent can sue on the contract. These relationships are illustrated in Exhibit 32.5.

E X H I B I T   32.4 | **Rights of a Third Party to Sue an Agent of a Disclosed Principal**

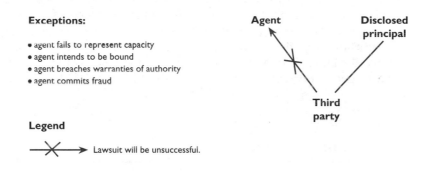

Exceptions:

- agent fails to represent capacity
- agent intends to be bound
- agent breaches warranties of authority
- agent commits fraud

Legend

Lawsuit will be unsuccessful.

E X H I B I T   32.5 | **Rights of an Agent of a Disclosed Principal to Sue a Third Party**

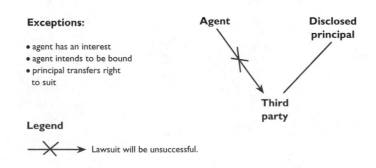

Exceptions:

- agent has an interest
- agent intends to be bound
- principal transfers right to suit

Legend

Lawsuit will be unsuccessful.

UNDISCLOSED PRINCIPAL

An *undisclosed* principal is one whose existence and identity are unknown to the third party. There are many valid reasons why a principal might want to be undisclosed—to be able to negotiate a deal, to negotiate a better deal, or to conceal an investment in a project or a donation to a charity.

There may be situations where the third party would have refused to contract with the principal. If the agent and principal agree that the principal should remain undisclosed for the purpose of defrauding the third party, the third party can have the contract set aside by proving fraud in the court. Exhibit 32.6 illustrates an undisclosed principal.

Liability of the Agent

When the principal is completely undisclosed, the third party believes that he or she is contracting with the agent and that the agent is dealing for him- or herself. Based on the third party's knowledge, that assumption is rational. If there is a default on the contract, the third party can sue the agent. As far as the third party is concerned, at the time of contracting there are only two parties to the contract: the third party and the agent.

Liability of the Principal

If the third party later discovers the identity of the principal, he or she can sue the principal. The principal will be held liable if the agent was authorized to enter into this type of contract for the principal. As mentioned before, traditionally the third party must make an *election* to sue either the agent *or* the principal. There is one important exception, however: if the third party sues the agent and loses *before* discovering the principal. In that case, the third party is not considered to have made an election and will be permitted to sue the principal later.

E X H I B I T 32.6 | **Undisclosed Principal**

Personal Communications for the 21st Century

Dan Kochanowski
9876 Appian Way
Maineville, Ohio 44444
513-555-8375

Liability of the Third Party

The third party may not be the one who suffers damages because of a breach of contract but may, in fact, be the one who committed the breach. Since the third party thought he or she was liable to the agent, it is reasonable to allow the agent to sue the third party. The law allows this action.

Under some circumstances, the undisclosed principal may, in his or her own name, also be able to sue the third party. There are some limitations, however. Generally, the principal can file a lawsuit by him- or herself only if the contract is **assignable.** (See Chapter 14 for a discussion of assignable contracts.) If it is assignable, the third party will not be harmed by either an assignment or a lawsuit by the principal. Since the agent can assign the contract to anyone else, the principal should be able to enforce the contract rights. Either way, the third party will be in the same position. This relationship is shown in Exhibit 32.7. The third party will have to pay any damages only once.

The principal may not be able to sue in his or her own name because the contract is not assignable, or the principal may still wish to keep his or her identity secret. Then the principal can arrange for the agent to file the lawsuit in the agent's name.

Assignable
Legally capable of being transferred from one person to another.

PARTIALLY DISCLOSED PRINCIPAL

A *partially disclosed* principal is one whose existence is known to the third party but whose identity is not. In other words, the agency is disclosed, but the principal is undisclosed. An example is Jorge Lopez's signing a contract as "Jorge Lopez, agent." The rules that are applied to partially disclosed principals are similar to those applied to undisclosed principals. The principal may be sued if the contract is breached, and the suit will be successful if the principal authorized the actions of the agent. Once again, the third party must make an election whether to sue the principal or the agent. If the principal suffers damages, he or she can sue the third party. The contract need not be assignable, because the third party knew that another party in interest was involved. Exhibit 32.8 on page 850 illustrates a partially disclosed principal.

E X H I B I T 32.7 | **Rights of an Undisclosed Principal**

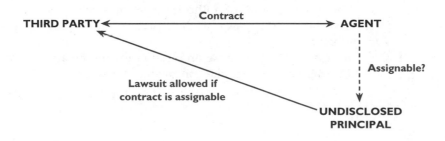

EXHIBIT 32.8 | **Partially Disclosed Principal**

Dan Kochanowski
Sales Agent
9876 Appian Way
Maineville, Ohio 44444
513-555-8375

The general rule is that when an agent is working for a partially disclosed principal, the agent will be personally liable for the contract. The third party is probably relying on the agent's reputation and credit. It is unlikely that the third party is relying on the reputation and credit of the unrevealed principal. An exception arises if the contracting parties agree that the agent will not be held liable. For example, this agreement may occur if the agent indicates that he or she will not be bound and the third party does not object to this limitation.

ANALYSIS OF AGENT'S CONTRACTS WITH THIRD PARTIES

To characterize a contract situation involving any type of principal, one should answer the following questions:

1. Was the person acting as an agent for the hiring party?
2. Did the agent enter a contract on behalf of the hiring party or make contractual promises?
3. Was the agent acting within the scope of his or her contractual authority? What type or types of authority were present?
4. Was the hiring party a disclosed, undisclosed, or partially disclosed principal?
5. Did the third party make an election to sue the agent or principal?
6. Is the agent liable for the contractual promises?

CONTRACT BETWEEN THE PRINCIPAL AND THE AGENT

The Need for a Writing

The agency relationship is consensual in nature. It actually will be a contract if the principal and agent both give up consideration, which is generally the case. As with other contracts, the Statute of Frauds may apply and require written evidence of the contract. The provisions of the Statute of Frauds that are most likely to be applicable are those relating to contracts that cannot possibly be performed within one year and contracts involving the sale of real estate. Even if the Statute of Frauds does not apply, it is wise to write out the contractual provisions.

The *equal dignities rule* also requires that some agency agreements be in writing. This rule states that the agent/principal contract deserves (requires) the same dignity as the agent/third-party contract, as shown in Exhibit 32.9: If contract A must be written, then contract B must be written. For example, if the agent is hired to locate and purchase goods costing more than $500, the UCC Statute of Frauds requires that the agent/third-party contract be in writing, so the principal/agent contract must also be in writing.

Covenants Not to Compete

Some employment contracts contain *covenants* (promises) that the agent will not work for a competing firm. The contract may provide that (1) the agent will not moonlight with the competition, or (2) the agent will not compete with the principal after this employment relationship is terminated. Some contracts contain both prohibitions. The second provision is usually applicable if the agent either quits or is fired.

Competing legal considerations arise in disputes about these covenants. On the one hand, the agent agrees not to compete. Perhaps the agent desperately wants the position and feels that he or she will not be hired unless he or she signs the covenant. The agent may not have equal bargaining power with the principal. Generally, parties *are* bound by their contract provisions. On the other hand, it may be a hardship on the agent to unduly restrict his or her ability to locate another position. In addition, it will be detrimental to society if people are not allowed to seek

---

E X H I B I T 32.9 | **Equal Dignities Rule**

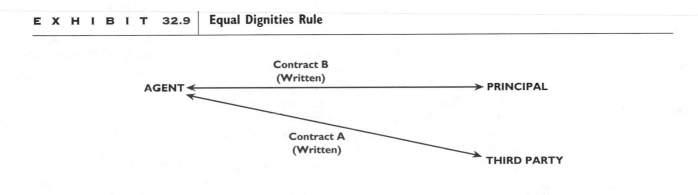

POTENTIAL LOSS OF CLIENTS

BDO is a national accounting firm with 40 offices throughout the United States. Jeffrey Hirshberg began employment in BDO's Buffalo office in 1984, when the accounting firm he had been working for was merged into BDO. In 1989, Hirshberg was promoted to the position of manager. As a condition of receiving the promotion, Hirshberg was required to sign a "Manager's Agreement." In Paragraph "SIXTH," Hirshberg expressly acknowledged that a fiduciary relationship existed between him and the firm by reason of his having received various disclosures that would give him an advantage in attracting BDO clients. Hirshberg agreed that if, within 18 months following the termination of his employment, he served any former client of BDO's Buffalo office, he would compensate BDO "for the loss and damages suffered" in an amount equal to one and one-half times the fees BDO had charged that client over the last fiscal year of the client's patronage. Hirshberg resigned from BDO in October 1993. BDO submitted a list of 100 former clients of its Buffalo office, allegedly lost to Hirshberg, who were billed a total of $138,000 in the year defendant left the firm's practice. Hirshberg denied serving some of the clients; claimed that a substantial number of them were personal clients he had brought to the firm through his own outside contacts; and asserted that with respect to some clients, he had not been the primary BDO representative servicing the account. Is the "reimbursement clause" requiring Hirshberg to compensate BDO for serving any client of the firm's Buffalo office a valid and enforceable restrictive covenant?

If Hirshberg filed his suit in *your* court, how would *you* rule?[4]

BUSINESS CONSIDERATIONS How could BDO improve its protection from accountants who leave its employment? What documentation would assist BDO in proving its case and the appropriate amount of damages?

ETHICAL CONSIDERATIONS Is it ethical for Hirshberg to compete with BDO in violation of the Manager's Agreement? Is it ethical for BDO to restrict Hirshberg's ability to practice his profession?

SOURCE: *BDO Seidman v. Hirshberg,* 712 N.E.2d 1220 (C.A.N.Y. 1999).

the occupations for which they are most highly qualified. For these reasons, courts scrutinize covenants not to compete to determine whether the covenant is legal. As a rule, courts do not favor covenants not to compete. The covenant will be illegal if the court concludes that it is against public policy.

To determine whether the covenant is against public policy, the court will examine its reasonableness. The court will look at the situation surrounding the employment to see whether the principal has a legitimate interest in preventing the competition.

Covenants not to compete are also prevalent in contracts in which the owner of a business sells the business to a buyer and the buyer obtains a promise that the previous owner will not compete with him or her. In such cases, the buyer has an interest in not having competition from the seller. Generally, the buyer pays a larger purchase price so that the seller will sell the **goodwill** of the business *and* sign a

Goodwill
The good name and reputation of a business and the resulting ability to attract customers.

covenant not to compete with the buyer. Courts are more inclined to enforce covenants not to compete in these situations.

Additional requirements exist for a valid covenant not to compete. The time and area specifications of the covenant must be reasonable. What is reasonable, moreover, depends on the type of employment. Covenants containing time periods of two to five years are generally acceptable to the courts. The limitation is really the time period during which the agent is able to draw contacts away from the principal or the time period in which these contacts still have value.

The covenant also must be reasonable in the area or distance specified. Another way to consider this is to ask the following question: How far will customers or clients travel to do business with the agent? The answer depends on the field of the agent's expertise. For example, a patient might travel halfway across the country to see a world-famous heart transplant specialist, but many patients will not even go across town to see a general practitioner.

If the principal has a legitimate business interest and the covenant is reasonable, the principal can sue the breaching agent or former agent for an injunction or contract damages. However, a principal may structure a covenant not to compete that is too broad. The courts apply one of two approaches in such cases. In the first, the court declares the covenant void and ignores it. The agent then can do whatever he or she wishes with impunity. A less common approach is for the court to reform (modify) the contract to make its restrictions reasonable.

Courts may examine the following criteria in determining whether to enforce a covenant not to compete in an *employment* contract:

1. Is the restraint reasonable in the amount of protection it affords the principal, or is it excessive?
2. Is the restraint unreasonable because it is unduly harsh on the agent?
3. If the agent works for a competitor, will that threaten irreparable injury to the principal?
4. Is the agency relationship of a unique and unusual type?

Some state statutes hold that a principal cannot prevent an ordinary employee from engaging in competition once the employment is over.[5]

A covenant not to compete usually is not required in order to prevent an agent from divulging trade secrets or customer lists after the employment is terminated. Under common law, this behavior is a violation of the agent's duty of loyalty. (The duty of loyalty is discussed in Chapter 31.)

The following case addressed the enforceability of a covenant not to compete.

32.3 | MANUFACTURING/ MANAGEMENT

CREATING EMPLOYMENT CONTRACTS TO PROTECT TECHNOLOGY

CIT has been more successful than anticipated, and it is producing videophones at nearly full capacity. In order to keep up with demand, the firm will need to expand its production capacity, including the hiring of new employees. There also have been several suggestions for improvements in the product from a number of customers, and the family would like to hire some engineers to help implement these suggested changes. However, the family is concerned that some of the new employees might reveal (or "borrow") the technology the firm has developed, to the detriment of CIT. They ask you what protections they have or could build into their employment contracts to help protect them. What advice will you give them?

BUSINESS CONSIDERATIONS How can a firm prevent employees from revealing confidential business information or technology? What practical protections are available to a firm that is trying to protect a trade secret? **ETHICAL CONSIDERATIONS** Is it ethical for an employee to utilize information gained in a previous position to benefit a competitor of the former employer? Is it ethical to restrict a former employee from using knowledge or information gained in a job when that knowledge or information makes the former employee a more productive or valuable individual? How can these competing interests be balanced?

32.3

TICOR TITLE INSURANCE CO. V. COHEN
173 F.3D 63 (2ND CIR. 1999)

FACTS . . . Title insurance insures the buyer of real property, or a lender secured by real property, against defects in the legal title to the property . . . This kind of insurance is almost always purchased when real estate is conveyed. . . . [Kenneth] Cohen was employed by Ticor as a title insurance salesman. . . . Cohen began working for Ticor in 1981, shortly after graduating from college, as a sales account manager and within six years was a senior vice president in charge of several major accounts. . . . His clients have consisted almost exclusively of real estate attorneys in large New York law firms. . . .

Ticor and Cohen, both represented by counsel, entered into an Employment Contract on October 1, 1995. There were extensive negotiations over its terms, including the covenant not to compete . . . [Cohen] was made one of the highest paid Ticor sales representatives, being guaranteed during the term of the Employment Contract annual compensation of $600,000, consisting of a base salary of $200,000 plus commissions. His total compensation in 1997 exceeded $1.1 million. In addition to compensation, defendant received expense account reimbursements that by 1997 exceeded $150,000 per year . . . His fringe benefits went far beyond those provided other Ticor sales representatives whose expense reimbursements are generally limited to $30,000 per year. . . .

On April 20, 1998 TitleServ, a direct competitor of Ticor, offered to employ Cohen. . . . TitleServ agreed to indemnify Cohen by paying him a salary during the six-month period (i.e., the 180 days hiatus from employment) in the event that the covenant not to compete was enforced. . . . He admits to speaking with 20 Ticor customers about TitleServ before submitting his letter of resignation, and telling each of them that he was considering leaving Ticor and joining a competitor firm. Cohen maintains that this was an effort on his part to learn more information about TitleServ, including its ability to service the New York market and the opportunity he was being offered. . . . Cohen insists he never discussed transferring any business from Ticor to TitleServ, nor did he discuss any specific deals. However, this assertion is undermined by defendant's deposition testimony concerning conversations with Martin Polevoy of the Bachner Tally law firm, in which he admits he directly solicited Polevoy's business for TitleServ and, . . . eventually secured a promise that Polevoy would follow him by taking his firm's insurance business to TitleServ. . . .

ISSUES Is the covenant not to compete valid? Should the court enforce the covenant with an injunction?

HOLDINGS Yes, the covenant not to compete is valid. Yes, the court will grant an injunction to enforce this covenant.

REASONING . . . An award of an injunction is not something a plaintiff is entitled to as a matter of right . . . An injunction should be granted when the intervention of a court of equity is essential to protect a party's property rights against injuries that would otherwise be irremediable. . . . [I]t would be very difficult to calculate monetary damages that would successfully redress the loss of a relationship with a client that would produce an indeterminate amount of business in years to come. . . . In fact, the employment contract . . . concedes that in the event of Cohen's breach of the post-employment competition provision, Ticor shall be entitled to injunctive relief, because it would cause irreparable injury. . . .

The issue of whether a restrictive covenant not to compete is enforceable . . . depends in the first place upon whether the covenant is reasonable in time and geographic area. . . . [C]ourts must weigh the need to protect the employer's legitimate business interests against the employee's concern regarding the possible loss of livelihood, a result strongly disfavored by public policy in New York. . . . An employer will sometimes believe its clientele is a form of property that belongs to it and any new business a salesperson drums up is for its benefit because this is what the salesperson was hired and paid to do. The employee believes . . . that the duty to preserve customer relationships ceases when employment ends and the employee's freedom to use contacts he or she developed may not be impaired by restraints that inhibit competition and an employee's ability to earn a living. The . . . potential problem is whether a customer will come to value the salesperson more than the employer's product. When the product is not that much different from those available from competitors, such a customer is ripe to abandon the employer and follow the employee should he go to work for a competitor. That scenario fits the circumstances revealed

32.3

TICOR TITLE INSURANCE CO. V. COHEN, *continued*
173 F.3D 63 (2ND CIR. 1999)

by the present record. The way to deal with these conflicting interests is by contract, which is what the parties before us purported to do . . .

New York law subjects a non-compete covenant by an employee to "an overriding limitation of reasonableness" which hinges on the facts of each case. . . . [E]nforcement will be granted to the extent necessary (1) to prevent an employee's solicitation or disclosure of trade secrets, (2) to prevent an employee's release of confidential information regarding the employer's customers, or (3) in those cases where the employee's services to the employer are deemed special or unique. . . . [W]e are satisfied that the reasonableness test was met because the duration of the covenant was relatively short (six months) and the scope was not geographically overbroad. . . . [H]e argues that the services he provided to Ticor were not sufficiently unique to justify injunctive relief. . . . Services that are not simply of value to the employer, but that may also truly be said to be special, unique or extraordinary may entitle an employer to injunctive relief. An injunction may be used to bar such person from working elsewhere. If the unique services of such employee are available to a competitor, the employer obviously suffers irreparable harm.

Unique services have been found in various categories of employment where the services are dependent on an employee's special talents, such categories include musicians, professional athletes, actors and the like. . . . [I]t is not necessary that the employee should be the only "star" of his employer, or that the business will grind to a halt if the employee leaves. Hence . . . in determining uniqueness the inquiry now focuses more on the employee's relationship to the employer's business than on the individual person of the employee. . . . [A]ll of Cohen's clients came to him during his time at Ticor, and were developed, in part, at Ticor's expense. . . . [A]bout half of Cohen's clients he . . . inherited from other departing Ticor salesmen. Cohen maintained these relationships . . . by the use of the substantial entertainment expense account provided by Ticor. . . .

BUSINESS CONSIDERATIONS What should a business do to protect its customers and trade secrets from employees who decide to leave? What techniques offer the most protection?

ETHICAL CONSIDERATION Was it ethical for Cohen to solicit his former clients on behalf of Title-Serv before or after his employment with Ticor terminated?

SUMMARY

A disclosed principal is one whose identity and existence are known to the third party. A partially disclosed principal is one whose existence is known but whose identity is not. When the principal is undisclosed, the third party thinks he or she is dealing only with the agent. The agent will be bound on the contract because the third party believes that the agent is a party to the contract. The type of principal affects the rights and obligations of the agent, the principal, and the third party.

When the principal has been disclosed, the principal can sue and be sued on the contract if there is express, implied, incidental, emergency, apparent, or ratification authority. These types of authority often overlap. If only authority by estoppel exists, it will be applied to protect a third party but not to protect the principal. Information received by the agent within the course and scope of the job generally will be imputed to the principal. Usually, the agent of a disclosed principal will not be bound on the contract itself, but the agent may be responsible for breach of warranty of authority. The third party will be liable to the principal on the contract and to the agent if the agent has an interest or intends to be bound. In

RESOURCES FOR BUSINESS LAW STUDENTS

NAME	RESOURCES	WEB ADDRESS
"Getting Around Barriers to Non-Compete Pacts"	"Getting Around Barriers to Non-Compete Pacts," by James A. Diboise and David J. Berger and originally published in *The National Law Journal*, discusses whether courts will consider trade secret confidentiality as covenants not to compete.	http://wsgrgate.wsgr.com/library/libFileshtm.asp?file=barriers.htm
"Non-Compete Agreements"	"Non-Compete Agreements," by Mindy G. Farber and published in *Women Today*, discusses the merits of having an attorney review any covenant not to compete before signing.	http://www.womenconnect.com/
The Patent Examiner	The Patent Examiner, maintained by the firm of Arent, Fox, Kintner, Plotkin, and Kahn, discusses the basic issues surrounding patent protection and the formation of employment contracts.	http://www.arentfox.com/quickguide/businesslines/intlprop/patentexaminer/newsalerts/corpusurviv/corpsurviv.html

situations of undisclosed or partially disclosed principals, the agent generally will be held liable.

The agency agreement must be in writing, *if* this is required by either the Statute of Frauds or the equal dignities rule. Covenants not to compete may be valid if the principal has a legitimate interest in preventing the competition, provided that the limitation is reasonable in the length of time and the area specified.

DISCUSSION QUESTIONS

1. Sally, a secretary, often orders office supplies, such as photocopy paper, tablets, and pens, for her employer. One day, Sally orders a personal computer from the same company and has it delivered to her home. Sally has the bill sent to her employer. Based on the information provided, does Sally have authority to do this? Why or why not? What additional information would be helpful? Why?

2. What is the difference between *implied authority* and *implied ratification*?

3. Besides collecting samples, displays, and order forms, what else should a principal do to terminate the apparent authority of an agent?

4. Bonnie buys a house through Angie, who is a real estate agent. Before the sale is completed, Angie recommends that they have an appliance inspector examine the house. Angie makes the arrangements. Joe, the inspector, says that all the major appliances are in proper working order. Bonnie completes the sale and is now living in the house. Joe, however, has not been paid yet. Who is obligated to pay Joe? Why?

5. What is a *partially disclosed principal?* How might partial disclosure occur?

6. How do the rights and liabilities of an agent for a partially disclosed principal differ from those of an agent for an undisclosed principal?

7. Carmo farms 200 acres planted with grape vines. His neighbor has an additional 100 acres planted with grapes, which are for sale. Since Carmo and his neighbor have been feuding for 12 years, the neighbor will not sell the land to Carmo. Therefore, Carmo hires Rose to act as his agent without revealing his identity.

Rose buys the land and starts to transfer it to Carmo. Upon discovering this, the neighbor tries to stop the transfer. What are the legal rights of the parties in this situation?

8. Why are warranties of authority applicable only when there is a disclosed principal?

9. Lisa has charges on her telephone bill that she does not understand. The bill states that billing inquiries should be made by calling (800) 555-0106. She calls the number and speaks with Janet. Janet says that she will remove the charges, but this does not occur. Is Lisa entitled to have them removed? Do you think Janet had authority for her statement? Why or why not?

10. Is it reasonable for a fast-food chain to require all new employees to sign an agreement that they will not work for another fast-food restaurant for six months after leaving the chain? Is it legal? Can an ex-employee legally reveal the recipe for a chain's special blend of 11 herbs and spices? Why or why not?

CASE PROBLEMS AND WRITING ASSIGNMENTS

1. Jason Weimer leased and operated a farm owned by Brugger Corporation. When a new lease was negotiated in 1987, Grant McQueen, a manager for Brugger, agreed Brugger would pay for some necessary repairs to the irrigation system. Weimer negotiated with Tri-Circle to make the repairs. Weimer indicated that he had authority from Brugger to arrange for this work. Tri-Circle was directed to set up a separate billing for Brugger for this work and to send the bill to Weimer. When Weimer received the first bill for $9,769, he verified the amount and forwarded the bill to Brugger. Brugger sent Tri-Circle a check for this amount. A second billing for $11,540 was sent to Weimer, approved by him, and forwarded to Brugger. This second bill was not paid, and Tri-Circle sued. Who is liable for this second bill and why? [See *Tri-Circle, Inc.* v. *Brugger Corp.*, 829 P.2d 540 (IdahoApp. 1992).]

2. Dale Morrow was planning a business trip to Honduras in a private plane and wanted flight insurance. He discussed the matter with Terri Bennett, who was the attendant at the insurance counter in the airport and who sold insurance from a number of different companies. Bennett selected an insurance policy for Morrow and completed the application. In the space provided for flight information, Bennett wrote "private air." The printed policy stated that it covered only travel on an aircraft operated by a scheduled air carrier. It also stated that the insurance agent could not vary the terms of the policy. Morrow died when the private plane crashed. Did Bennett have implied or apparent authority to issue insurance coverage to Morrow? Why or why not? [See *Travelers Ins. Co.* v. *Morrow*, 645 F.2d 41 (10th Cir. 1981).]

3. LDDS markets its long-distance service to potential customers through an in-house sales force and through independent contractors. In 1992, Net-Tel signed a representation agreement ("LDDS/Net-Tel Agreement") to operate as an independent contractor with LDDS. LDDS held no management control over Net-Tel, which was explicitly prohibited from using LDDS's trade name or service marks without written approval from LDDS. Integrated, a small business concern managed by Erwin Aguayo and Robert Post, expressed interest in signing an agreement with Net-Tel. Michael Clifford, a representative of Net-Tel, told Aguayo that he had express authority to act on LDDS's behalf. Integrated never verified this with LDDS. Integrated and Net-Tel entered into the Master Corporate Distributor Agreement (MCD Agreement). Under this agreement, Integrated agreed to develop and implement a plan to market LDDS's long-distance service. The MCD Agreement was signed only by representatives of Net-Tel and Integrated, but it incorrectly represented that "Net-Tel was the agent of LDDS" and that "LDDS had authorized Net-Tel to enter into independent distributor agreements with third parties." Neither Net-Tel nor Integrated notified LDDS of the MCD Agreement's existence.

Aguayo met with an LDDS official on 16 November 1993. Most of the meeting consisted of Aguayo's verbal effort to solicit LDDS's participation in Integrated's proposed marketing scheme. The MCD Agreement was not mentioned, and LDDS remained unaware that it existed at the time. George Hampton informed Aguayo that LDDS had attempted such a program in the past and that it had failed. Hampton then wished Aguayo the best of luck in the event that he pursued the program "exclusively" with Net-Tel but declined to obligate LDDS in any way. Integrated then sent a copy of the plan to Net-Tel, but not to LDDS. The plan was administered exclusively between Integrated and Net-Tel. Integrated forwarded a copy of the MCD Agreement to LDDS on 7 April 1994, which was the first time LDDS was made aware of its existence. On the same day, Hampton advised Clifford that Net-Tel was not authorized to use LDDS's name in the MCD Agreement, or any other agreement, without LDDS's written permission. Did Net-Tel have authority to act for LDDS? Is LDDS liable on the MCD Agreement? [See *Integrated Consulting Services, Inc.* v. *LDDS Communications, Inc.,* 1999 U.S. App. LEXIS 7255 (4th Cir. 1999) (Unpublished Opinion).]

4. Partners in a California law firm agreed that partners who withdrew from the firm would forfeit their withdrawal benefits under the partnership agreement *if* they competed with the firm. Assuming that the provision specified a reasonable length of time and geographic area, should the provision be upheld? Why or why not? [See *Howard* v. *Babcock,* 863 P.2d 150 (Cal. 1993).]

5. Continental sued Eugene Grovijohn and his new employer, Amoco Chemicals, to enforce a covenant not to compete. Grovijohn was a plant manager in the plastic bottle division of Continental. He was never employed there as an engineer or technician. Grovijohn had agreed not to disclose, "directly or indirectly," or "use outside of Continental organization during or after [his] employment, any confidential information" without Continental's consent. Amoco hired Grovijohn as a plant manager. There was no evidence that Grovijohn intended to reveal confidential information or that Amoco intended to use confidential information. Should Amoco be prevented from employing Grovijohn in this capacity? Why or why not? Continental has many employees who are exposed to confidential information. What should Continental have done to better protect itself? [See *Continental Group, Inc.* v. *Amoco Chemicals Corp.,* 614 F.2d 351 (3rd Cir.1980).]

6. **BUSINESS APPLICATION CASE** Leonard Taylor, a district manager for Pargas, Inc., diverted checks into his personal account at Rapides Bank. The payee on these checks was his employer. He endorsed the checks with a rubber stamp that had Pargas's name and address on it. Rapides Bank never obtained a corporate resolution authorizing Taylor to endorse the checks. There was no authorization for Taylor to deposit these checks to his personal account. Should Rapides Bank or Pargas suffer the loss? Why? What business practices should Pargas and Rapides Bank establish to prevent this type of problem in the future? [See *Pargas, Inc.* v. *Estate of Taylor,* 416 So.2d 1358 (La.App. 1982).]

7. **ETHICAL APPLICATION CASE** At the suggestion of Robert Petrich, a real estate broker, Mary Chapple decided to build a movie theater on an unimproved lot that she owned and to rent the theater to Dan Rodriques. When the construction bids were in, Chapple felt the lowest bid was still too high, and she asked Petrich to negotiate with Big Bear (the lowest bidder) to obtain a lower price. Big Bear prepared a list of modifications and presented them at a meeting attended by Petrich, Rodriques, and the architect. Those present at the meeting agreed to reduce the capacity of the air conditioner from 20 tons to 8 tons. Chapple was not informed of this agreement. She signed a written contract to have Big Bear construct a movie theater and to install a 20-ton-capacity air conditioning unit. Rodriques signed an addendum to the contract calling for a reduction to an 8-ton air conditioner. No one asked Chapple to sign the addendum. An 8-ton unit was used. Can Chapple successfully sue for breach of contract, or did someone, acting as her agent, authorize the change of plans? What type of authority did the agent have? Should knowledge about this change be imputed to Chapple? Discuss the ethical perspective of Petrich, Rodriques, and the architect. [See *Chapple* v. *Big Bear Super Market No. 3,* 167 Cal.Rptr. 103 (Cal.App. 1980).]

8. **CRITICAL THINKING CASE** Rodney Munroe worked as a salesperson for Holiday Food, a company that sold and delivered frozen foods. Munroe never examined or used the customer list that the company made available to its sales staff. His supervisor provided him with the names and addresses of contacts, which he kept in a personal notebook. During his employment with Holiday Food, Munroe expressly refused to sign a covenant not to compete. When he left to start a competing frozen-food business, Munroe took his notebook with him and started to call on his old contacts. Did Munroe violate his duties to Holiday Food when he solicited orders from his old customers? [See *Holiday Food Co., Inc.* v. *Munroe,* 426 A.2d 814 (Conn.Super. 1981).]

NOTES

1. *Restatement (Second) of Agency* (Philadelphia: American Law Institute, 1958), § 97.
2. Warren A. Seavey, *Handbook of the Law of Agency* (St. Paul, MN: West Publishing Co., 1964), § 8D, p. 19.
3. *General Overseas Films, Ltd.* v. *Robin International, Inc.,* 542 F.Supp. 684 (S.D.N.Y. 1982), p.688, fn. 2.
4. *BDO Seidman* v. *Hirshberg,* 712 N.E.2d 1220 (C.A.N.Y. 1999).
5. See, for example, California Business and Professions Code § 16600.

33

LIABILITY FOR TORTS AND CRIMES

A G E N D A

CIT hires a number of delivery people to deliver Call-Image units to retailers. Is CIT liable for the tortious conduct of these delivery people when they are acting for CIT? What financial risk is involved with hiring delivery people, and how can CIT best minimize this risk?

Tom and Anna have given all the family members sweatshirts with the Call-Image videophone and company logo printed on the back. Lindsay likes to wear her sweatshirt during her high school field hockey practices. One day, while wearing her shirt, Lindsay gets into a fight with a teammate and hits the player with her stick. The other girl suffers moderately serious injury. Can the parents of the injured player successfully sue CIT for damages, saying that Lindsay is advertising for CIT and, as a result, this makes her conduct "job related"?

What duties does CIT owe its employees? What if an employee is injured at work? These and related questions will arise during our discussion of agency law. Be prepared! You never know when one of the Kochanow-skis will need your help or advice.

O U T L I N E

SERVANT'S LIABILITY

Servants engage in physical activities or labor on behalf of the master. These activities bring the servant into close contact with the general public. When the servant is careless or overly aggressive, there is a good chance that members of the public will be injured. This chapter discusses the servant's and the master's responsibility to the public for these types of injuries. These relationships can occur in business and nonbusiness settings.

Vicarious liability
Legal responsibility for the wrong committed by another person.

Vicarious liability for torts involves different policy considerations from those surrounding an agent's ability to bind the principal in business dealings with third persons. In contract matters, there is generally a conscious desire to interact with the public and a conscious decision to enter into business arrangements with the public by means of the agent. In most tort situations, however, neither the master nor the servant desires that the tort occur. But once the tort has occurred, someone has to suffer the financial burden, even if that someone is the innocent victim. Who should pay? The master? The servant? Or the third person?

The general rule of tort law is that everyone is liable for his or her own torts. Furthermore, this general rule is followed in agency law. Since the servant committed the tort, the servant is liable for the harm that occurs. The fact that the servant is working for the master at the time of the tort does not alter the general rule. Refer to Chapter 7 for a more complete discussion of specific torts.

MASTER'S LIABILITY: RESPONDEAT SUPERIOR

When the servant commits a tort that harms a third person, the servant will be responsible for the harm. However, in agency law, some circumstances exist in which the master is also held liable for the torts committed by the servant. Notice that in these situations the *master* is being held liable for the conduct of the *servant*. Since the servant is also liable for the tortious conduct, the liability is said to be *joint and several*. This means that either party may be held liable individually (several liability) or that both parties may be held liable (joint liability).

The theory under which masters are held liable for the torts of their servants even though the masters are not personally at fault is known as *respondeat superior*. Literally, it means "let the master answer." It is also referred to as a "deep-pockets" theory, based on the belief that the master's pockets are deeper (i.e., they hold more money) than those of the servant. The law generally involves an attempt to balance competing interests, which is clearly seen in the application of the *respondeat superior* doctrine. For example, if a victim has suffered $175,000 in injuries from an automobile accident caused by the negligence of a servant, and the servant has a total net worth of only $50,000, the servant cannot fully compensate the victim. However, if the master is a multimillion-dollar corporation, the master can fully compensate the victim. In these circumstances, the court must evaluate all the facts and determine whether *respondeat superior* should be applied in this particular case. This chapter generally uses the traditional terms *master* and *servant* because *respondeat superior* is limited to master–servant relationships.

Respondeat superior has been justified on numerous grounds in court opinions and in legal treatises. The justifications for holding the master liable for wrongful acts of the servant include the following:

1. The master will be more careful in choosing servants in order to avoid liability.
2. The master will be more careful in supervising servants in order to avoid liability.
3. The liability for servants is a cost of conducting business.
4. The master is the person benefiting from the servant's actions.
5. The master can purchase liability insurance.
6. The person with the power to control the conduct should be the person to bear financial responsibility.
7. The master can better afford the costs, especially when compared to an innocent third person who is injured by the servant's conduct.

Respondeat superior is not based on the idea that the master did anything wrong. Rather, it involves a special application of the doctrine of **strict liability.** Simply put, the master hired the servant; the servant did something wrong; the master should pay. Courts often apply a "but for" test in deciding whether to assign liability to the master. "But for" the existence of the master–servant relationship, no harm would have resulted. In other words, someone should pay, and the master is best able to pay and afford the loss; therefore, the master must pay. *Respondeat superior* does require a *wrongful act* by a servant for which the master can be held liable, and a legally defensible reason for imposing liability on the master for that wrongful act. It is not enough that the servant committed a wrongful act and that a third person was injured by it. The wrongful act must be one over which the master can be held legally responsible. It must be an act the master should legally have controlled.

The principal's *right to control* is really what distinguishes servants from nonservants. A principal who has the right to control may be called a *master,* and the worker may be called a *servant. Respondeat superior* applies only to servants. It does not apply to nonservants because the principal lacks control and, thus, is not a master.

Respondeat superior does not make the master an insurer for every act of the servant. The master is only liable for those actions that are within the *course* and *scope* of the employment. Therefore, the issue in most cases based on *respondeat superior* involves a decision as to whether the servant was acting within the course and scope of his or her employment when the tort was committed. To resolve this question, it is important to know the servant's duties, working hours, state of mind, assigned location, and the master's right to control the worker. It is also important to know whether the servant has deviated from his or her route and/or routine, whether the servant has any history of similar sorts of conduct, and any other factors that might show that the conduct was an extreme deviation from what the master should reasonably have expected. It is immaterial if the master fails to exert actual control over how the worker completes the tasks as long as the master has the right to use this control. *Respondeat superior* has been criticized by "masters" on the grounds that it is unconstitutional, but the U.S. Supreme Court recently affirmed that *respondeat superior* is not fundamentally unfair or unconstitutional.[1] In most jurisdictions there seems to be a trend toward increasing the master's liability, even for serious wrongs such as rape.

Factors Listed in the *Restatement of Agency*

The *Restatement (Second) of Agency* indicates the factors that should affect the determination of whether a servant is within the scope of his or her employment. The factors include the following:

Strict liability
Liability for an action simply because it occurred and caused damage, and not because it is the fault of the person who must pay.

General Statement

(1) *Conduct of a servant is within the scope of employment if, but only if:*

   (a) *it is of the kind he is employed to perform;*

   (b) *it occurs substantially within the authorized time and space limits;*

   (c) *it is actuated, at least in part, by a purpose to serve the master; and*

   (d) *if force is intentionally used by the servant against another, the use of force is not unexpectable by the master. . . .* [2]

(2) *In determining whether or not the conduct, although not authorized, is nevertheless so similar to or incidental to the conduct authorized as to be within the scope of employment, the following matters of fact are to be considered:*

   (a) *whether or not the act is one commonly done by such servants;*

   (b) *the time, place, and purpose of the act;*

   (c) *the previous relations between the master and the servant;*

   (d) *the extent to which the business of the master is apportioned between different servants;*

   (e) *whether or not the act is outside the enterprise of the master or, if within the enterprise, has not been entrusted to any servant;*

   (f) *whether or not the master has reason to expect that such an act will be done;*

   (g) *the similarity in quality of the act done to the act authorized;*

   (h) *whether or not the instrumentality by which the harm is done has been furnished by the master to the servant;*

   (i) *the extent of departure from the normal method of accomplishing an authorized result; and*

   (j) *whether or not the act is seriously criminal.*[3]

In many cases, certain factors may indicate that the servant is within the scope of employment, and other factors may indicate the contrary. For example, the master furnishes the truck (the instrumentality), but he or she has no reason to suspect that the servant will drive under the influence of alcohol (engage in this conduct). No one factor controls this decision; the judge or jury weighs all the factors involved to reach a decision. Since the triers of fact exercise a lot of discretion in these cases, fact situations that seem very similar may result in different decisions by different courts. In the following case, the Virginia Supreme Court addressed the jury instruction on *respondeat superior*.

33.1

GIANT OF MARYLAND, INC. V. ENGER
515 S.E.2D 111 (VA. 1999)

FACTS . . . The plaintiff [Charlotte H. Enger] went to the defendant's store to purchase some groceries. She proceeded to the store's produce section to select some bananas. While the plaintiff was in the store, Kenneth M. Brown, the store's manager, saw a piece of celery that had fallen on the floor in the produce area, and he directed [Geo] Asfaw, a produce clerk, to pick up the celery. Asfaw refused to do so, walked toward Brown, stood within an inch of Brown's face,

and stated: "You don't know who I am. I'm the devil. I'm going to burn you." Brown stepped back, and he "motioned" to Julio Rivera, a store employee, "to come over . . . to witness what [Asfaw] had said . . . "

Rivera approached Asfaw from behind, touched him on the shoulder, and said, "hey, man." Asfaw pushed Rivera and assaulted him with karate kicks and punches. As Asfaw was attacking Rivera, Asfaw's foot almost hit the plaintiff in her face. She testified:

33.1

GIANT OF MARYLAND, INC. V. ENGER, *continued*
515 S.E.2D 111 (VA. 1999)

"I walked to the bananas and picked up two bananas and started to turn and put them in the basket. . . . When all of a sudden a man's foot and leg . . . that's all I saw was this foot and leg come kicking right in front of my face with great force. It was such a shock . . . I could even feel it as it just missed me."

After Asfaw finished attacking Rivera, Asfaw decided to leave the store, and he began to walk toward the door. While leaving, he began to remove a name tag that was affixed to a red jacket that store employees were required to wear. The plaintiff testified: "And I thought, well, he's going to try to leave. And I said [to Asfaw], where are you going? What is your name? Why are you taking—and he just looked at me. And I said, why are you taking off your name tag? And then he slugged me, just power. Just reached around and I went flying across the floor." Asfaw attacked the plaintiff by delivering a "karate type of blow" to her chest. As a result of the impact from the blow, the plaintiff sustained injuries to her foot and ankle.

At trial, the trial court granted the following jury instruction over the defendant's objection:

An act is within the scope of employment if it is incidental to the employer's business and is done to further the employer's interest. If an employee departs so far from his duties that his acts are no longer for his employer's benefit, then his acts are not within the scope of his employment. However, if the tortious act of the employee arose out of an activity which was within the employee's scope of employment or within the ordinary course of business, then that act may be considered to be within the scope of employment.

[The jury verdict in favor of Ms. Enger was $137,000.]

ISSUE Did the circuit court err in instructing the jury on the doctrine of *respondeat superior?*

HOLDING Yes. The jury instruction was incorrect.

REASONING The defendant argues that the last sentence of this instruction is an incorrect statement of law because it attempts to make the employer liable for any tort committed while "at work," even though the employee's acts may have been committed outside the scope of employment. Responding, the plaintiff argues that the challenged jury instruction is a correct statement of law and that the trial court did not err by granting it. We disagree with the plaintiff.

Initially, we observe that pursuant to the doctrine of *respondeat superior,* an employer is liable for the tortious acts of its employee if that employee was performing the employer's business and acting within the scope of the employment when the tortious acts were committed. Even though the doctrine of *respondeat superior* is firmly established in Virginia, difficulties often arise in the application of the doctrine to particular facts. Generally, the inferences to be drawn from the established facts are within the province of a jury.

In [precedents], we established the following test to determine whether an employee acted within the scope of his employment:

The test of the liability of the master for the tortious act of the servant, is not whether the tortious act itself is a transaction within the ordinary course of the business of the master, or within the scope of the servant's authority, but whether the service itself, in which the tortious act was done, was within the ordinary course of such business or within the scope of such authority.

We have consistently applied this test in our jurisprudence. A comparison of our established test with the challenged jury instruction compels us to conclude that the jury instruction is erroneous. Under our . . . test, an employer is responsible for an employee's tortious act if that act was within the scope of the duties of the employment and in the execution of the service for which the employee was engaged. The challenged jury instruction differs from the test that we have consistently applied because the instruction allows the jury to find the employer liable for any tort committed during the employee's employment, even if the service that the employee was performing when he committed the tortious acts was not within the ordinary course of the employer's business or not within the scope of the employee's authority.

We reject the plaintiff's contention that the defendant's objection to the instruction is merely a matter of "an elevation of style over substance."

Rather, the jury instruction requires that the jury impose a different test than the test this Court has

continued

33.1

GIANT OF MARYLAND, INC. V. ENGER, *continued*
515 S.E.2D 111 (VA. 1999)

consistently approved. Accordingly, we will reverse the judgment of the circuit court, and we will remand the case for a new trial. . . .

BUSINESS CONSIDERATIONS Should a business establish procedures for handling aggressive employees or employees who have lost control? What

policies might a business establish? How can a company provide a safe environment for its customers? Should Enger have intervened in the dispute? Why or why not?

ETHICAL CONSIDERATION Was it ethical for Enger to intervene in the fight and then complain when she was injured?

33.1 | MANAGEMENT

LIABILITY FOR DRIVERS MAKING DELIVERIES

As CIT's business has expanded, the firm has begun to hire drivers to make deliveries of the product to customers, especially retail outlets. John recently read an article in the local newspaper about a case in which the driver of a delivery van was at fault in an accident. The local court entered a judgment against the employer of the driver for $1.5 million. John is concerned that a similar case would destroy CIT. John has asked you if there is any way for the firm to avoid liability while still hiring drivers to make deliveries for the firm. What will you tell him?

BUSINESS CONSIDERATIONS How can a business minimize its potential financial risk when one of its employees is guilty of negligence? What policies should a business initiate to provide the best possible protection when hiring drivers who will be driving company-owned vehicles?
ETHICAL CONSIDERATION Would it be ethical for a firm to state that its delivery personnel are independent contractors and to require all of its drivers to drive the drivers' personal vehicles and provide proof of adequate insurance coverage?

Time and Place of Occurrence

Two of the factors that courts analyze in determining the course and scope of employment are the time and place of the act[4]—whether the tort occurred on the work premises and whether it occurred during work hours. Asfaw was clearly on the work premises and during his work hours in Case 33.1.

Failure to Follow Instructions

A master can be held liable for a servant's acts even though the master instructed the servant not to perform a specific act or commit torts. The disobedience of the servant does not necessarily exempt the master from liability. Otherwise a master could avoid all liability by simply instructing servants not to commit any torts during the course of employment.

Failure to Act

A master can also be held liable under *respondeat superior* when the servant fails to act as directed, as shown in the following example.

> *A railroad switch operator is supposed to throw a switch on the track at the same time every day. One day, he carelessly fails to do so, a train derails as a result, and passengers on the train are injured. The master (the railroad) is liable for the servant's negligence in failing to act as instructed.*

Respondeat superior does not decrease the servant's liability for wrongdoing, but it makes an additional party, the master, also liable. In many legal situations multiple parties are jointly and severally liable for the occurrence.

Identifying the Master

Another problem that may arise is deciding *who* the master is. Who controls the manner in which the servant will do the work? The master, or employer, is the one who not only can order the work done but also can order how it will be done. In the following case, the court addressed the issue of which entity employed Dr. Adkins.

Assault
A threat to touch someone in an undesired manner.

Workers' compensation
Payments to injured workers based on the provisions in the state workers' compensation statute.

33.2

ADKINS V. FUREY
2 S.W.3D 346 (TX.APP. 4 DIST. SAN ANTONIO 1999)

FACTS . . . Christina Furey, an operating room technician . . . was assisting Dr. [William Bradford] Adkins with a cesarean delivery. After closing the incision, Furey alleges, Dr. Adkins pressed the surgical staple gun to Furey's shoulder and shot a staple into her arm. The gun was unsterile, the staple penetrated her skin and tissue and had to be removed with a Kelly clamp. The incident occurred at Medical Center Hospital, n/k/a [sic] University Hospital. Furey was employed by the Bexar County Hospital District. At the time, Dr. Adkins was a second-year resident in obstetrics and gynecology at the University of Texas Health Science Center (UTHSC) . . .

ISSUES Did Dr. Adkins perform the cesarean procedure as an employee of UTHSC, which is a state entity entitled to sovereign immunity, or as an employee of the Bexar County Hospital District (the District)? Were Dr. Adkins's acts in the course of employment?

HOLDINGS Both questions should be determined by a jury.

REASONING When reviewing a ruling on a motion for summary judgment, . . . the movant has the burden of showing that there is no genuine issue of material fact and that he is entitled to judgment as a matter of law. In deciding whether there is a disputed material fact . . . , the evidence favorable to the nonmovant will be taken as true . . . To conclude that Adkins is entitled to summary judgment under the sovereign immunity umbrella requires affirmative responses to three questions: (1) Whether Dr. Adkins was an employee of UTHSC? (2) If so, whether his actions fall within the course and scope of his duties? and (3) Whether § 101.106 of the [Texas] Tort Claims Act applies to an employee that commits an assault?[5]

Appellant admits that the District served as his paymaster but that UTHSC had control over him. Under the Texas Tort Claims Act, "employee" is defined as: a person, including an officer or agent, who is in the paid service of a governmental unit by competent authority, but does not include an independent contractor, or a person who performs tasks the details of which the governmental unit does not have the legal right to control. . . . [T]he alleged employee must be under the control and direction of the alleged employer. This does not resolve the issue, however, as the statutory definition would seem to require control and paid employment to invoke the Tort Claims Act's waiver of immunity.

A Graduate Medical Training Agreement governs the medial [sic] training and employment in question. It is signed by Dr. Adkins, John A. Guest as president and chief executive officer of the District, and by a Dr. Forland on behalf of . . . [the] Dean of the Medical School for UTHSC. The agreement provides that the District does not have a legal right to control the medical resident's tasks performed at the District's hospital. However, the agreement also provides that the District pays the resident an annual stipend and provides such employee benefits as leave time, insurance, **workers' compensation,** and parking privileges. The agreement also requires the resident to become familiar with and abide by the House Staff Manual, the bylaws of the medical-dental staff, and the policies, rules and regulations of the District.

Jack Park, an attorney who has been employed by UTHSC for nearly 30 years, is the Executive Director for Legal Affairs and Technology Licensing at UTHSC. On the issue of control, his . . . affidavit stated that according to the agreement and as a matter of implementation and practice, the [UTHSC] . . . controls the details of the work preformed [sic] by the House Staff Physicians, like Dr. . . . Adkins. The

continued

33.2

ADKINS V. FUREY, continued
2 S.W.3D 346 (TX.APP. 4 DIST. SAN ANTONIO 1999)

UTHSC recruits, sponsors, trains and makes the decisions as to whether the House Staff Physicians remain in the program. Schedules, rotations, and the details of the practice of medicine are made under the direction of faculty. . . . The District does not assume any right to control the tasks of the House Staff Physicians under the Graduate Medical Training Agreement. . . . [E]very physician who has University Hospital privileges and who, therefore, might be in a position to exercise some control over a medical resident, was also a faculty member of the Health Science Center. There are no non-faculty doctors, or outside doctors, at the Hospital. All physicians in private practice who have been granted privileges at University Hospital have been granted nonpaid faculty status. Nevertheless, . . . all physicians, including medical residents like Dr. Adkins, were under some control of the . . . District. . . . [Parks] opined that providing benefits of worker's compensation insurance and withholding federal taxes also demonstrated evidence of employment by the District. In fact, UTHSC provided worker's compensation benefits to all employees except the House Staff Physicians or medical residents. . . . Park was not aware of any UTHSC documents that list Adkins as its employee and he sent a letter to opposing counsel stating that "the incident referred to in your letter does not involve any University employee nor did it occur in any facility owned or operated by the University."

Dr. John A. Guest, president and chief executive officer for the District, testified . . . that the department heads at UTHSC direct the training activities of the residents, including the medical care to be given, and that none of these activities are controlled by the District. He also stated that the District does assume the right to control activities of residents "to the extent they may engage in behavior that would be outside our rules and regulations, yes." Such conduct was also regulated by UTHSC. He also understood

that the resident doctor "is working for both organizations." They are "being funded by the Bexar County Hospital District. They are under the supervision of the Health Science Center. . . . And the control of the Health Science Center." He also stated that liability coverage is provided by UTHSC and funding is provided by the District. They work under the faculty of the medical school.

. . . Guest testified: "I'm not sure that I see any specific language [in the agreement] as to who the house staff physician works for." "I didn't say anything about his employment. I said as a graduate trainee, he would be under [UTHSC] supervision. . . . I don't know whether he's an employee of the UT Health Science Center." . . . Park stated . . . that . . . Adkins, "while in the operating room performing a cesarean surgery, was performing his duties and tasks" under the agreement. Park also testified . . . that shooting someone with a staple gun would not be in furtherance of the employer's business or an accomplishment of the objective for which the employee was employed. Dr. Guest agreed, "shooting a staple gun at someone is outside the scope of Adkins's employment and in violation of policies, rules, and regulations under the agreement." . . .

BUSINESS CONSIDERATIONS What could a hospital or other organization do to reduce the likelihood that an employee will injure someone with their equipment? What is the role of policies and rules in preventing problems for an organization?

ETHICAL CONSIDERATIONS Was Adkins's behavior ethical? Is "horseplay" in an employment setting inherently unethical, or does the ethical nature of the conduct depend on the results that may arise due to the horseplay?

When analyzing a complicated fact pattern such as the one in Case 33.2, drawing a diagram of the relationships is helpful. Exhibit 33.1 provides an example.

Identifying the master is also complex in cases of borrowed servants. In these cases, who is the master? Is it the lending master, the borrowing master, or both? Again, the important factors are the course of the employment and the ability to control the servant. Consider the following example:

EXHIBIT 33.1	Legal Relationships in Adkins v. Furey

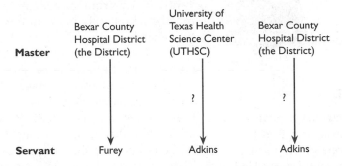

Location of Incident: University Hospital

	Bexar County Hospital District (the District)	University of Texas Health Science Center (UTHSC)	Bexar County Hospital District (the District)
Master			
	↓	? ↓	? ↓
Servant	Furey	Adkins	Adkins

Jamal works for Computer, Inc., which is having its office remodeled by Interiors Redone. Since the contractors doing the work are understaffed, Jamal's supervisor tells Jamal to help them. In this situation, Computer, Inc., is referred to as the gen-eral master and Interiors Redone as Jamal's special master. (The meanings of general master and special master here are similar to those used to define general and special agents in Chapter 31.) Jamal is classified as a borrowed servant. After painting the walls in the main lobby, Jamal negligently fails to put up Wet Paint signs. A customer brushes against the wall and ruins her clothes. Who is Jamal's master at the time of his negligent act?

Some courts will decide that both Computer, Inc., and Interiors Redone are liable. Jamal was subject to the control of both, and his actions benefited both. Other courts will conclude that Interiors Redone is liable because Jamal was working pri-marily for Interiors Redone at the time of the negligence. Still other courts will hold Computer, Inc., liable because ultimately Jamal was subject to its control and it sup-plied his paycheck. To avoid the uncertainties caused by borrowed servants, pru-dent employers enter into agreements about which master will be liable and/or obtain liability insurance for the servants' acts.

A closely related problem occurs when one servant appoints another servant (a subservant) to complete his or her tasks. Under *respondeat superior,* who is respon-sible for the torts of the subservant? If the servant had authority to appoint the sub-servant, the master will be held liable for the subservant. However, if the servant lacked authority, generally the servant will be liable as the "master" under *respon-deat superior.* The primary justification for this rule is that the servant is the one with the right to control the subservant.

Crimes and Intentional Torts

Courts are more reluctant to hold a master liable under *respondeat superior* for inten-tional wrongs such as assault and **battery** than they are for negligence on the part of the servant. In fact, some courts still follow the traditional rule that a master is not responsible for the intentional acts of his or her servant. The modern view, how-ever, is that a master is liable if the servant advanced the master's interests or the servant believed that his or her conduct was advancing the master's interests.

Battery
Unauthorized touching of another person without legal justification or that person's consent.

33.2 | MANAGEMENT

CALL-IMAGE TECHNOLOGY

IS LINDSAY A SERVANT OF CIT?

One of Lindsay's extracurricular activities is playing field hockey for her school team. She was at a field hockey practice last week when she and one of her teammates had an altercation. The other girl pushed Lindsay, Lindsay pushed the other girl back, and tempers flared out of control. In the heat of anger, Lindsay hit the other girl with her stick, causing a moderately serious injury that required stitches to close the cut caused by the edge of Lindsay's stick. During that practice, Lindsay had been wearing a sweatshirt with the CIT logo imprinted on its back. The parents of the other girl are now threatening to sue the firm for damages. They base their claim on the fact that, in their opinion, Lindsay was acting as a servant for CIT when she was wearing the sweatshirt with the CIT logo, thus making her conduct "job related." Tom and Anna have asked you whether the family should be concerned about this claim. What advice will you give them?

BUSINESS CONSIDERATIONS Should a business expect to be held liable whenever any person acts negligently or in a tortious manner while wearing a shirt (or other item of apparel) that advertises the firm? Should it matter if the person wearing the logo is related to a manager of the "advertised" firm?

ETHICAL CONSIDERATIONS Is it ethical for the plaintiff in a tort case to sue the wealthiest potential defendant, regardless of the defendant's degree of fault? Is it ethical for a business to derive the benefits of "free advertising" when people wear its logo on their apparel and yet for the business to deny liability when those same people act in a tortious manner?

Consequently, masters can be held liable under *respondeat superior* for intentional torts such as slander, libel, invasion of privacy, and assault and battery. Cases 33.1 and 33.2 are both examples of batteries committed by servants. Many criminal acts are also torts, and the master may be held civilly liable under *respondeat superior* for the financial losses suffered by the victim of the servant's criminal act. *Respondeat superior* is not used to impose criminal liability on the master.

Courts will hold a master liable for some of a servant's serious wrongdoings, but not for others. The question is often one of degree. How serious was the tort or crime? Should the master have expected it? Is there much variance between the assigned tasks and the wrongdoing? There seems to be a trend toward increasing liability for masters. In these cases, the courts frequently examine the underlying policies for *respondeat superior*.

DIRECT LIABILITY OF THE PRINCIPAL

The agent must be a servant before *respondeat superior* will be applied. However, principals may be held directly responsible for some of the wrongs committed by their agents, even if the agents are not servants. For example, the principal is liable if the principal *instructed* the agent to commit the wrong, did not properly supervise the agent, ratified or approved the agent's tort, or was negligent in the selection of the agent.

Criminal law may also apply to a principal when an agent commits a crime. For example, a principal can be criminally liable based on his or her own fault. If a principal directs or encourages an agent to engage in criminal activity, the principal will probably be held personally liable for such acts as **conspiracy, solicitation,** or **accessory to the crime.** In addition, some criminal statutes create liability for the principal even though the principal does not intend to violate the statute or does not know of the illegal act or condition. For example, state liquor laws often specify that tavern or restaurant owners are liable if minors are served alcohol in their bars. In most states, this is true whether or not the owner approves of such action or even knows that it has occurred. Other examples include statutes that prohibit the sale of impure food or beverages no matter who is at fault. The purpose of these statutes is to assure that principals take every possible precaution to ensure that such activities do not occur in their establishments and by imposing liability on them if these statutes are violated.

INDEMNIFICATION

When a master pays a third person under *respondeat superior* for injuries caused by the servant's unauthorized acts, the master is entitled to *indemnification* (the right to be repaid) from the servant. Unlike most other theories, *respondeat superior* is not based on the fault of the master; it only creates legal liability for the master. The master should be entitled to recover from the person who caused the loss—the servant—so the law permits reimbursement. As a practical matter, the master generally will have insurance to cover the payment. Furthermore, the servant normally will not have sufficient funds to make the payment. If the servant is still employed by the master, the master may be able to withhold part of the reimbursement from each paycheck until the master is completely repaid. Continuing to employ the servant, however, may increase the likelihood that the master will be liable for any similar wrongs by the servant in the future.

Sometimes an agent may be entitled to indemnification from the principal if the agent paid the third person who was injured by the agent's tort. It will depend on the particular facts of the case. Such cases are based on either contract law or the law of restitution.[6] Courts are influenced by what they believe to be just, considering the business and the nature of the particular relationship.[7] Under the *Restatement (Second) of Agency,* an agent is entitled to indemnification if he or she, at the direction of the principal, commits an act that constitutes a tort but that the agent believes is not tortious.[8] In other words, the agent must act in good faith. Obviously, if an agent completes a task that he or she knows to be illegal or tortious, the agent is not entitled to indemnification.[9]

Exhibit 33.2 illustrates the relationships among the primary parties when the servant commits a tort. The servant's right to indemnification is questionable because the courts require that the servant follow the master's instructions in good faith before receiving indemnification. The master's *right* to indemnification is established by law. The master's ability to collect, however, is questionable because, realistically, many servants cannot afford to reimburse the master.

Conspiracy
An unlawful situation in which two or more people plan to engage in criminal behavior.

Solicitation
A situation in which one person convinces another to engage in a criminal activity.

Accessory to the crime
A situation in which one person assists another in the commission of a crime, without being the primary actor.

E X H I B I T   33.2 | **Liability for Tortious Injury to a Third Person**

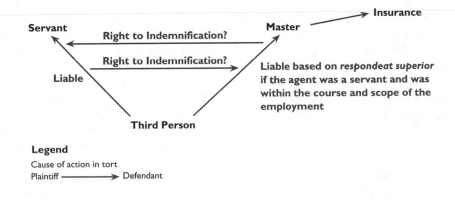

33.3 | MANAGEMENT/ SALES

COMPANY-OWNED AUTOMOBILES

Dan recently read about a person who was arrested for solicitation of a prostitute. The person had his car impounded by the police and sold at auction under state law. Dan has also heard of people who were arrested and convicted for having narcotics in their cars and who had their cars impounded by the police and sold at auction. He is quite concerned because CIT is now employing several sales agents who have been provided with company-owned cars. He asks you whether the police could impound and auction off a CIT-owned automobile if one of the sales agents was arrested for one of these crimes? Could the police seize a CIT vehicle under any other circumstances? What will you tell him?

BUSINESS CONSIDERATIONS What can a business do to minimize its risk when it provides employees with company-owned automobiles? If a company car should happen to be impounded and sold by the police in such a situation, what rights could the company assert, and against whom could it assert those rights?

ETHICAL CONSIDERATIONS Suppose that a husband and wife are co-owners of an automobile, and that the husband is arrested for solicitation of a prostitute while driving that automobile. Under the local law, the police are allowed to take the automobile after his conviction and sell it at auction since it was used in the commission of a crime. Is it ethical for the government to take property used in the commission of this sort of crime and sell it without regard to who co-owns it? Should a company owner be treated in a different manner? Why?

ANALYSIS OF A SERVANT'S TORTS

To characterize a tort situation, one should answer the following questions:

1. Was the person acting as a servant for the hiring party?
2. Did the servant commit a tort?
3. Was the servant acting within the course and scope of the job?
4. Is the master entitled to indemnification from the servant? Is the servant entitled to indemnification from the master?

Remember that the servant is ultimately the one who is liable for the tort, unless he or she is entitled to indemnification from the master. The master may also be liable in his or her own right.

INJURY ON THE JOB

Courts generally use the terms *employer* and *employee* when discussing injuries on the job. Consequently, the same terminology is used here. An employer has a duty to provide employees with a reasonably safe place to work and reasonably safe equipment to use at work. Both the place and equipment should be appropriate to the nature of the employment. For example, some places, such as classrooms, are relatively safe. Other places, like submarines and drilling platforms, are dangerous. If the workplace is not safe, the employer should warn employees about unsafe conditions that the employees may not discover even if they are reasonably careful.[10]

Although courts *sometimes* apply similar rules to employees and independent contractors, there are distinct differences in their legal relationships. Depending on the situation, courts have allowed independent contractors to recover for injuries sustained on the job.[11]

Under the common law, if an employee is hurt at work, the employer can utilize a number of defenses to avoid an obligation to the employee. Negligence by the employee and the employee's assumption of the risk are two such defenses. For example, the employee might have been driving a truck too fast for icy road conditions, or the employee might not have been wearing safety goggles provided by the employer. Assumption of the risk, contributory negligence, and its modern counterpart—comparative negligence—are discussed in detail in Chapter 7.

At common law, the *fellow employee doctrine* also acts to bar recovery by the employee. Traditionally, this concept was called the *fellow servant doctrine*. More recent court cases and treatises call it the fellow employee doctrine. Under this

ACCIDENTAL DEATH

Owen Hart was a 33-year-old wrestler with the World Wrestling Federation (WWF). He wrestled under the name "Blue Blazer." He was fatally injured at a pay-for-view event called "Over the Edge," sponsored by WWF. He was being lowered from the ceiling into the ring by a guy wire when the mishap occurred. He fell about 50 feet, hitting his head. The exact cause of the accident is under investigation. Theories include that he was never properly connected to the harness; the harness malfunctioned; the harness may have caught on the feathers of Hart's costume; or Hart may have released it too soon. Hart was not trained as a stuntman. Thousands of fans in the arena watched the event. Many of them initially thought that it was gag. Robert McCome, a 15-year-old spectator, said, "We thought it was a doll at first. We thought they were just playing with us. We were really shocked when we found out that it was no joke."

Vince McHahon, WWF owner, has vowed that this particular stunt will not be repeated by any WWF performer. He has not ruled out other dangerous stunts. "In its quest for higher ratings and its competition with WCW, the WWF has 'raised the bar' with more dangerous stunts."[12] A memorial to Owen Hart was taped by WWF. Was Owen Hart a servant or an independent contractor? Assume Hart's administrator brought a suit based on tort or the workers' compensation statute.

If this case were brought in *your* court, how would *you* rule?[13]

BUSINESS CONSIDERATIONS How does a death or serious injury impact the entertainment industry? Does it encourage or discourage attendance at future events? Who is responsible—customers, individual companies, or the industry itself? Was the memorial a genuine act of concern for Owen Hart and his family or merely an attempt at damage control? The death was not televised. Is that a prudent business decision? After Hart's fall, the show continued. The other performers were unaware that Hart had been killed by the fall. Is it true that "the show must go on"?

ETHICAL CONSIDERATIONS Is it ethical to ask employees to perform dangerous stunts for the purpose of notoriety, ratings, and selling tickets? Are these performers being respected as individuals, or are they being used merely as a means to greater profit?

SOURCES: M. L. Curly, *The Detroit News* (28 May 1999), Sports, p. F2. Kia Shant'e Breaux, *The Fresno Bee* (24 May 1999), p. A8; Nova Pierson, *The Toronto Sun* (24 May 1999), Sports, p. 5.

theory, an employee cannot recover damages for work-related injuries if the damages are caused by another employee of the same employer. Like assumption of the risk, this doctrine acts as a complete bar to recovery. This rule is applicable to many worksite accidents. Most of the time, when an employee is injured on the job, the injury is caused not by the employer but by another employee at the job site. One justification suggested for this doctrine is that the employer is often remote from the worksite. The employee, on the other hand, is likely to know of hazards at work and to know of careless fellow employees. Another justification used to support the doctrine is that an employee "assumes the risk" of being injured by coworkers. The existence of the fellow employee doctrine encouraged the spread of state workers' compensation statutes.

In some cases, the injured employee will be covered by the workers' compensation statute. In some states, however, particular types of workers are not covered under the workers' compensation statutes. For example, in New Mexico, farm and ranch workers are not covered under the state statute.

These statutes may seem to be the opposite extreme of the fellow employee doctrine. They are not based on the fault of the employer, and the employer's negligence need not be shown in court. The worker only needs to show that his or her injury was caused in the course and scope of the job. In many states, the policies underlying these statutes are to "provide prompt and limited compensation benefits for job-related injuries and to facilitate the employee's speedy return to employment without regard to fault."[14] In other words, these statutes are intended to be "economic insurance" for workers. These statutes exist in most states and provide for a fixed schedule of compensation for listed injuries. Moreover, workers can easily determine how much they are entitled to receive. Therefore, this procedure allows for the quick settlement of claims and discourages many lawsuits. When a workers' compensation statute is applied, the statute generally provides the exclusive remedy for the worker. In other words, legal action against the employer based on common law theories is prohibited.

State statutes vary in format. Some states have organized a fund to which the employers contribute and from which injured employees collect. Some states allow employers to purchase insurance or to establish their own funds. In most states, the employee is allowed to recover even if he or she was negligent in causing the injury, assumed the risk, or was injured by a fellow employee. The injured employee generally receives compensation according to a schedule of payments, depending on the type of disability and how long the employee is unable to work.

Workers' compensation statutes vary in the following respects:

1. Some cover only major industrial occupations.
2. Some exclude small shops with few employees.
3. Some exclude injuries caused intentionally by the employer or other workers.

Because of the variations, it is imperative to examine the particular statute at issue.

If the workers' compensation statute does not apply, generally the employee will be permitted to sue based on common law theories. (Workers' compensation is also discussed in Chapter 42.) Workers' compensation statutes are generally the exclusive remedy, and the worker cannot sue under other theories. The court in the following case explored an exception to the Kentucky workers' compensation statute.

33.3

BRIERLY V. ALUSUISSE FLEXIBLE PACKAGING, INC.
184 F.3D 527 (6TH CIR. 1999)

FACTS . . . [Paul] Brierly was a co-op student attending Shelby County Vocational School and was working with Alusuisse under the supervision of David Ellison . . . Alusuisse manufactures materials for packaging and labeling foods and pharmaceutical medicines. The printing press components . . . gradually develop a buildup . . . , and the workers eliminate the buildup by disassembling the components and running them through a "large-parts washing machine." The washing machine was similar to a dishwasher, but the solvent cleaning solutions used had low flash points and were highly flammable.

33.3

BRIERLY V. ALUSUISSE FLEXIBLE PACKAGING, INC., *continued*
184 F.3D 527 (6TH CIR. 1999)

. . . On Friday, . . . —three days before the accident—the seal on the main pump of the parts washing machine broke, allowing the flammable solvent solution to leak . . . The employee . . . shut the washer down . . . The district court found that the following precautions were taken to minimize the possibility that the removal of the pump would generate sparks and . . . create a fire hazard:

(1) the electricity to the machine was locked out and tagged out; (2) the washing machine and solvent supply reservoir were drained of solvent; (3) the pit below the washer was ventilated with a compressed air hose over the course of the entire weekend to purge any accumulated fumes from underneath the machine; (4) the washing machine door was left open Friday evening so that the interior of the machine could be aired out over the weekend; (5) and a special floor-level ventilation system was left running during the weekend to help purge the room of fumes.

Before the . . . welding . . . , Alusuisse took additional safety measures: "(1) water was placed in the pit below the machine so as to prevent sparks from igniting any dried solvent residue left behind from the leaking pump; and (2) welding blankets were placed on and around the filter basket housing and parts washing machine." . . . [M]aintenance lead-man Reinhold Ritzi decided that he would do the welding because he had more experience . . . Ellison and [Gary] Wordlow gave their final approval for the welding. Wordlow, Ellison, and Ritzi apparently believed that the parts washing room had been monitored with the "LEL" meter, a device which is used to measure the "lowest explosive limit" of solvent vapor in an area before a flammable source is introduced. . . . [I]t was discovered that the LEL meter had not been used. Each of the men involved stated that they had assumed that one of the others had obtained the readings. A "fire watch" crew was assembled . . . Wordlow and other maintenance crew members—including Brierly—stood by with fire extinguishers watching for stray sparks that could ignite a fire. Brierly, the least experienced member of the crew, was almost 12 feet away from the welding site, further away than any of the other crew members. . . . [A] spark ignited undetected residual solvent fumes inside the parts washing machine, causing an explosion. The explosion blew off the steel door . . . of the parts washing machine, and the door struck Brierly, resulting in his death. Wordlow, Ritzi, and one other worker also suffered injuries . . .

Several state and local administrative agencies investigated the explosion . . . The Kentucky Labor Cabinet issued a citation to Alusuisse and assessed a $24,500 civil penalty based on the insufficiency of the precautions taken the day of the accident . . . [T]he grand jury indicted Alusuisse for reckless homicide . . . The indictment alleged that Alusuisse "committed the offense of reckless homicide when it recklessly caused the death of Paul D. Brierly by failing to perceive the substantial and unjustifiable risk of explosion which constituted a gross deviation from the standard of care that a reasonable person would observe in the situation as it then existed." . . .

ISSUE Can Brierly's administrator proceed with a tort action against Alusuisse and Ellison?

HOLDING No. The administrator cannot proceed with a tort action. The exclusive remedy is under the workers' compensation statute.

REASONING . . . The district court granted the defendants' motions for summary judgment on the basis of the exclusive-remedy provision of the Kentucky Workers' Compensation Act . . . The plaintiff . . . argues that this case falls within the "deliberate intention" exception to the exclusivity of remedies established by the Act. Kentucky Revised Statute 342.610(4) provides that an employee or his dependents can file a civil action against his employer if "the injury or death results to the employee through the deliberate intention of his employer to produce such injury or death." Based on the facts . . . before us, we cannot agree.

The plaintiff contends that Alusuisse's intent to kill Brierly can be inferred from the circumstances surrounding his death. But, . . . "the statutory standard . . . requires more than implied intent; it requires 'deliberate intention.'" . . . We conclude that the district court, relying on controlling state law, correctly concluded that the plaintiff's allegations are insufficient to meet the specific or deliberate intent exception . . . The defendants took many precautions, albeit clearly not enough . . . As the district court noted,

continued

33.3

BRIERLY V. ALUSUISSE FLEXIBLE PACKAGING, INC., *continued*
184 F.3D 527 (6TH CIR. 1999)

. . . if Brierly's death was intended, an explosion such as this seems like a strange, clumsy, and unreliable way to carry it out. . . . It seems far fetched that Alusuisse would decide to kill Brierly by creating a spark with a welding rod so as to set off an explosion in an adjacent machine which would then blow off a sealed 350-pound steel door that would strike and kill Brierly.

In light of the Kentucky Supreme Court precedent interpreting the phrase "deliberate intention," we conclude that the plaintiff did not present evidence to the district court from which a reasonable jury could conclude that Alusuisse deliberately intended to cause Brierly's death. Even if Alusuisse's actions were reckless or wanton, which may be a fair characterization, there is no indication or reasonable inference that the company intended to injure or kill Brierly. Accord-

ingly, the Kentucky Workers' Compensation Act provides the exclusive remedy for Brierly's death.

Likewise, the Kentucky Worker's [sic] Compensation Act provides the exclusive remedy against a fellow employee whose actions cause him injury or death [except where it is caused by the willful and unprovoked physical aggression of such employee]. . . .

BUSINESS CONSIDERATIONS When an enterprise must use dangerous materials, what can it do to protect employees and property? What additional safety precautions would be beneficial in this situation?

ETHICAL CONSIDERATIONS What moral duty does an employer owe to its employees? Did Brierly's school owe him any moral duties?

RESOURCES FOR BUSINESS LAW STUDENTS

NAME	RESOURCES	WEB ADDRESS
EFF Legal Issues and Policy: Cyberspace and the Law Archive	The Electronic Frontier Foundation, a non-profit civil liberties organization, provides articles and links to information regarding the use of technology and workplace privacy.	http://www.eff.org/pub/Legal/
Legal Information Institute (LII)—Workers' Compensation Law Materials	LII, maintained by the Cornell Law School, provides an overview of and resources addressing workers' compensation law.	http://wwwsecure.law.cornell.edu/topics/workers_compensation.html

SUMMARY

A servant is liable for his or her own tortious and criminal acts. The fact that the servant was working at the time is immaterial. The fact that the master may also be liable to the third party is irrelevant as well.

A master may be liable for the acts of his or her servants. Much of this liability is based on the doctrine of *respondeat superior*. A master is liable for the torts committed by a servant if the servant was acting within the course and scope of the employment. The courts have discussed many policy reasons for enforcing *respondeat superior*. These include: encouraging masters to be careful in selecting servants; encouraging masters to be careful in supervising servants; servants are a necessary expense of conducting business; the master is benefiting from the servant's acts; the master can purchase liability insurance; the master has control; and the master can better afford these costs.

Numerous factors are used in analyzing what activity is "within the course and scope of the employment." There is no formula, however. Courts look at the factors and determine if *respondeat superior* should be applied. Even when a court holds a master liable to the third party under *respondeat superior*, this does not mean that the master necessarily will bear the ultimate loss. The master generally will be entitled to indemnification from the servant, although such indemnification may not be practical. The master may also have purchased insurance for this risk. In rare cases, the master may owe the servant the duty to reimburse the servant for compensation he or she paid to third parties.

A principal may also be held directly liable if he or she commits a tort or a crime; this liability is not based on *respondeat superior*. It includes situations in which a principal is negligent in selecting an agent or directs an agent to commit a crime or a tort.

The employer owes the employee various duties, such as the duty to compensate the employee according to the terms of the agreement. These duties were discussed in Chapter 31. As discussed in this chapter, the employer has a duty to provide a reasonably safe place to work. At a minimum, this includes furnishing appropriate tools and equipment, adherence to safety regulations, and proper supervision. Injuries to employees on the job are normally covered by workers' compensation statutes. State statutes vary as to who is covered, the amount of compensation, and how the payment is funded.

DISCUSSION QUESTIONS

1. David hires Annabelle as a housekeeper. Her main duties are to remain in the house and clean, prepare meals, and do the laundry. One afternoon, Annabelle receives a call from One-Day Drycleaners. David's suit is ready to be picked up. Annabelle decides to go and get the suit in her car. On the way home, she runs a red light and hits Julie's car. The police officer at the scene says that Annabelle's intoxication is the main cause of the accident. Annabelle had a few drinks with her lunch. David knew that Annabelle had a drinking problem when he hired her and that she is trying to stop drinking. Who is responsible for the damage to Julie's car, and why?

2. Cindy has just started working as an accountant for Big Six Accounting Firm. On her first audit, Cindy's supervisor sends her to get the coffee and doughnuts every morning. One morning, on the way to get the doughnuts, Cindy does not notice that the traffic has stopped in front of her, and she collides with Claudia's car. Who is responsible for the damage to Claudia's car, and why?

3. Consuelo prepares a joint tax return for Sammy and Lenora Johnson during her first year at Big Six Accounting Firm. However, she does not prepare the return correctly, and the IRS assesses $4,000 more in taxes and penalties. What rights do the Johnsons have? Why?

4. After class in the afternoon, Jim has a job delivering floral arrangements for Flowers by Flo. Flo often instructs Jim not to give his friends rides in the truck when he makes deliveries. One day, Jim sees Nanci, a classmate, waiting for the bus. He is going toward her home, so he gives her a ride. On the way, Jim carelessly drives off the side of the road, and Nanci is injured. Who is liable to Nanci for her injuries, and why?

5. Sylvia works as Bill's secretary at Waincoat, Inc. Bill forgot to buy his wife a birthday present, so he sends Sylvia out to buy a gift at lunch. While Sylvia is looking in the discount store for a present, she carelessly runs into another customer with her shopping cart. Who is liable for the injuries to the other customer, and why?

6. Saul works for Central Cable Co. as an installer for cable television in residential areas. The company needs water to repave the street after the cable is installed. Without permission, Saul uses water from Rosemary's tap. When Rosemary arrives home from work and sees this, she is furious. Her water bill is based on usage, and Saul has been using her water all day. Who is liable to Rosemary, and why?

7. Jeff makes deliveries for Superior Meat Packing Company. On Wednesday, he complains to the company mechanic that his truck is not braking correctly. The mechanic says he will check it out immediately. On Thursday afternoon, the brakes fail, and Jeff is unable to stop the truck. He collides with a telephone pole and suffers neck and back injuries. Who is liable? Why?

8. Neal is stationed on the aircraft carrier USS Archer. One night in August, the carrier is having night maneuvers so the pilots and crew can practice night takeoffs and landings. During these maneuvers, one of the planes crashes on the deck, injuring a number of people and killing Neal. The investigation reveals that some of the crew were suffering from fatigue and some were under the influence of narcotics. Can Neal's wife and children recover? From whom and why?

9. Beatrice owns three car dealerships—Toyota, Chevrolet, and Honda—that are located at the major intersection of College Avenue and Main Street. The Chevrolet dealership is located north of College Avenue, which it faces. The Honda and Toyota dealerships are located on the south of College Avenue and face Main Street. Beatrice's sales force is authorized to sell vehicles at any of the dealerships. Salespeople and clients often jaywalk across College Avenue, as do repair people. If potential clients are hit by a car traveling on College Avenue, who would be liable and why? If Beatrice's servants are injured while jaywalking, who would be liable? Why?

10. Joe's Pizza Parlor advertises that their pizza will arrive at the customer's home hot and tasty within 30 minutes. Their television and radio commercials promise customers that if the pizza does not arrive within 30 minutes of ordering, it will be free. The delivery area is limited to a 20-mile radius from Joe's. The drivers have the primary responsibility for timely delivery. If a driver delivers more than one late pizza a week, he or she must pay for the pizza from his or her paycheck. Drivers are responsible for late delivery, even when the kitchen is busy. During busy periods, like Monday night football games, the pizzas are sometimes boxed 20 minutes after the placement of the order. Drivers compensate by driving fast to comply with the guarantee. Under the work contract, drivers supply their own vehicle and their own automobile insurance. Who is responsible if one of Joe's drivers has an accident? Why? What changes in policy could be implemented to reduce the likelihood of an accident?

CASE PROBLEMS AND WRITING ASSIGNMENTS

1. Elizabeth Paraiso was employed as a fitness instructor at a health spa. She received a telephone call from the spa manager, who asked her to go to a supermarket on her way to work to get a birthday cake. They were giving the assistant manager a birthday party. Paraiso left for work early and drove five blocks out of her way to get the cake at a supermarket. While driving back toward her usual route, she reached over to protect the cake so that it would not slide off the car seat. She lost control of her car and struck William Sussman, who was sitting on the bench at the bus stop. Should Sussman be permitted to collect from Paraiso's employer under *respondeat superior*? Why or why not? [See *Sussman* v. *Florida East Coast Properties, Inc.*, 557 So.2d 74 (Fla.App. 1990).]

2. A car driven by Walter Appling, a lawyer employed by Richman and Garrett, collided with the car in which Michael and Georgette Wank were riding. Appling had gone to lunch with a representative of one of the firm's clients and a number of other business contacts. At the lunch, Appling had consumed several alcoholic drinks. Between 3:30 and 4:00 that afternoon, Appling called the office and spoke to one of the partners to inform him that Appling would not be coming back to the office. The partner advised

Appling to stay where he was and someone would come to get him. Appling rejected that suggestion and drove himself in his own automobile. The accident occurred between 6:30 and 6:45 P.M. Appling does not remember where he was going at the time of the accident. There was evidence at the time of trial that Appling had had another accident earlier that afternoon in the parking lot of another restaurant. Is the law firm liable for the alleged negligent driving of Appling? Why? [See *Wank* v. *Richman and Garrett*, 211 Cal.Rptr. 919 (Cal.App. 1985).]

3. Sergeant Schroyer was on duty as a field supervisor at about 2:30 A.M. in Los Angeles. He was responsible for supervising and training police officers who were patrolling the streets. He was wearing his uniform and driving a marked police car by himself. He stopped a vehicle Mary was operating; there were no passengers in her vehicle. He administered a field sobriety test to Mary. She had difficulty performing the specified tasks. She began to cry and asked him not to take her to jail. Schroyer ordered her into his patrol car and then drove her to her home. He said she owed him a "payment" for not arresting her, and he began to rape her. She stopped screaming and struggling with him when he threatened to take her to jail. Should the City of Los Angeles be held responsible for Sergeant Schroyer's acts under *respondeat superior?* [See *Mary M.* v. *City of Los Angeles*, 814 P.2d 1341 (Cal. 1991).]

4. Dusty Lewis, 18, was arrested after a resident of the Dakota Woods apartments called police and claimed that Lewis had raped her. Lewis had been assigned the 8 P.M. to 3 A.M. shift, patrolling the apartment complex. Lewis was arrested early Monday during his first shift at work. Lewis was hired as a security guard that Saturday by Guard Express in Fresno and given a temporary card until appropriate background checks cleared and the state could issue a license. Lewis had a misdemeanor conviction as a juvenile driving without a license. Department spokesman Jay Van Rein said, "If you have a misdemeanor or felony conviction, you can't use a temporary card at all. If he had a misdemeanor conviction, then it was illegal for him to have that card." The victim and her boyfriend and child lived in the apartment complex. Lewis contended that he was a friend of the boyfriend and that he visited the woman during his lunch break and used her phone. He contended that he did not assault her. Eddie Rodriguez, general manager of Guard Express in Fresno, stood by Lewis. He said that Lewis knew the victim for several years. Rodriguez also said that he had been in the guard business for six years, knew about the misdemeanor conviction, and believed that issuing the temporary card was correct.

Rodriguez contended that he used sound judgment in hiring Lewis. Assume that Lewis did assault the victim. Who should be civilly liable for the assault—Lewis, Rodriguez, Guard Express, and/or Dakota Woods apartments? Why? [See Matthew Kreamer, "Guard's Permit at Issue," *The Fresno Bee* (18 August 1999), pp. A1, A10.]

5. The University of California Board of Regents decided to sue doctors who ran a fertility clinic at the University of California (UC) Irvine campus. The University agreed to pay more than $16.7 million to infertile couples who tried to obtain help at the Center for Reproductive Health. The work was primarily done at fertility clinics in Orange and San Diego counties from 1986 to 1995. Drs. Ricardo Asch and Jose Balmaceda allegedly took women's eggs without consent and used them to create children for other infertile patients. Dr. Asch said the university settled 106 patient claims to make him look bad. The university was still trying to settle the last seven claims. The doctors denied wrongdoing; however, they fled the country in 1995 when they were indicted by a federal grand jury on charges of mail fraud and conspiracy to defraud patients of their genetic material.

Cornell University also filed a legal action against the regents, UC Irvine, and the doctors for Cornell's share of any damages awarded to two former patients whose embryos were used at Cornell without the patients' consent. Should the regents and UC Irvine be entitled to reimbursement from the doctors involved? Why or why not? Should Cornell University be entitled to reimbursement from the regents, UC Irvine, and/or the doctors? Why or why not? [See "UC Board Sues Doctors, Fertility Specialists Cost the University System Over $16.7M.," *The Fresno Bee* (18 July 1999), p. A13.]

6. **BUSINESS APPLICATION CASE** Maria Marino drove a cab for Yellow Cab. One day, she parked her cab at the taxicab stand outside the Sundance Hotel and Casino in Las Vegas. She was the first cab in line; she would get the next fare. She was standing next to her cab talking to another taxi driver. James Edwards was the driver of the third cab, owned by Desert Cab. While seated in his cab, James began to verbally harass Maria. Maria approached James's cab, to find out why he was yelling at her. James jumped out of the cab and grabbed Maria, choked her, and threw her in front of his cab. An observer pulled them apart and walked Maria back to her cab. Maria missed work due to her injuries. Should Desert Cab be liable for James's acts under *respondeat superior?* Why or why not? [See *Desert Cab, Inc.* v. *Marino*, 823 P.2d 898 (Nev. 1992).]

7. **ETHICAL APPLICATION CASE** On 15 January 1992, host Johnny Carson said on the *Tonight Show* that Mr. Blackwell called Mother Teresa a "nerdy nun." The fashion critic known as Mr. Blackwell has become famous by bashing celebrities in his annual 10 worst-dressed-women list. Johnny said, "Did you see what he said about Mother Teresa? 'Miss nerdy nun is a fashion no-no.' Come on now, that's just too much. That's right, that's Mr. Blackwell, that's the guy I'm talking about." Mr. Blackwell filed an $11 million lawsuit against Johnny Carson and NBC. According to the suit, "Mr. Blackwell did not make any statement about Mother Teresa." Mr. Blackwell "holds Mother Teresa in high regard and has never maligned her or her saintly work." How should this case against Johnny Carson and NBC be decided, and why? What ethical issues are raised by this fact situation? Mother Teresa has since died. Are the ethical issues more significant since Mother Teresa's death? [See "Mr. Blackwell Isn't Amused, Johnny Sued," *The Fresno Bee* (19 March 1992), p. A2.]

8. **CRITICAL THINKING CASE** Fred Remillard operated 12 McDonald's franchises in western New York state. Two of his employees, Michael Huffcut and Rose Hasset, who worked at separate restaurants 60 miles apart, had an affair. When they were not able to meet, they left "lovey-dovey" messages for each other on their voice mail boxes at work. It was alleged that Remillard listened to the messages, tape-recorded them, and even played them back to Michael's wife, Lisa Huffcut. The affair ended, and the Huffcuts reconciled. They sued McDonald's Corporation and Fred Remillard for $1 million each. They claimed their rights to privacy were violated and that they suffered from intentionally inflicted emotional distress, embarrassment, loss of reputation, and loss of income. In deciding this case, consider the following questions: What right to privacy should employees have in this context, and would nonemployees have a greater right to privacy? Should voice mail recordings be protected by privacy considerations? What arguments can employers make that they should be able to monitor and record messages on company voice mail systems and electronic mail systems? Was Fred Remillard's behavior reasonable in this situation? [See Ben Dubbin, "Voice Mail Love Affair Turns Privacy Issue Public," *The Fresno Bee* (23 January 1995), p. A6.]

NOTES

1. *Pacific Mut. Life Ins. Co.* v. *Haslip,* 111 S.Ct. 1032 (1991).
2. *Restatement (Second) of Agency* (Philadelphia: American Law Institute, 1958), § 228(1).
3. Ibid., § 229(2).
4. Ibid., § 229(2)(b).
5. The Texas Tort Claims Act waives Texas's sovereign immunity for the torts specified. It does not apply to claims "arising out of assault . . . or any other intentional tort." TEX. CIV. PRAC. & REM. CODE § 101.057(2).
6. Warren A. Seavey, *Handbook of the Law of Agency* (St. Paul, MN: West Publishing Co., 1964), § 168, p. 265.
7. *Restatement (Second) of Agency* § 438(2)(b).
8. Ibid., § 439(c) and Comment on Clause (c).
9. Harold Gill Reuschlein and William A. Gregory, *Hornbook on the Law of Agency and Partnership,* 2nd ed. (St. Paul, MN: West Publishing Co., 1990), § 89(B), pp. 151–152.
10. *Restatement (Second) of Agency* § 492.
11. *Rodney* v. *U.S.,* 77-4028 (9th Cir. 1980); *Cioll* v. *Bechtel Corp.,* No. 733794 (San Francisco City Super.Ct., 23 April 1981).
12. M. L. Curley, "Pro Wrestling: McMahon: Stunts Like Hart's Won't Be Repeated," *The Detroit News* (28 May 1999), Sports, p. F2.
13. Ibid., see also Kia Shant'e Breaux, "Wrestler Hart Dies in Plunge at Arena," *The Fresno Bee* (24 May 1999), p. A8; Nova Pierson, "Wrestler Falls to Death: WWF Star Owen Hart Killed in Ring Accident," *The Toronto Sun* (24 May 1999), Sports, p. 5.
14. *Sussman* v. *Florida East Coast Properties,* 557 So.2d 74 (Fla.App. 3 Dist. 1990), at p. 75.

BUSINESS ORGANIZATIONS

Should the entrepreneur "go it alone" in a proprietorship? If so, the entrepreneur will have both absolute authority and total responsibility. Should a partnership be formed? For many businesses, the simplicity of a partnership makes it an ideal form, but the entrepreneur should be aware that a partnership entails the sharing of management powers and duties. Should a corporation be formed? The corporate form offers a number of advantages, including limited personal liability and the ability to franchise, but corporations are subject to heavy federal regulation and taxation.

This part compares and contrasts these three main forms of business—proprietorship, partnership, and corporation—by showing the legal steps taken in their formation, operation, and termination. In addition, this part discusses several variations of these forms, such as limited liability partnerships and corporations. Finally, franchising and securities regulation are addressed.

34

FORMATION OF A BUSINESS

A G E N D A

Anna and Tom realize they have created a product, Call-Image videophones, that will have broad public appeal. Hence, they need to consider what form of business—proprietorship, partnership, or corporation—is best for producing, marketing, and distributing this product. Should the firm incorporate and "go public," selling stock to investors to help acquire badly needed capital? Would such a sale open the possibility that the Kochanowskis may lose control of the business to an outsider? Is there a business form that will allow for outside investment without the fear that investors might take control of management?

These and other questions will arise as you read this chapter. Be prepared! You never know when one of the Kochanowskis will need your help or advice.

O U T L I N E

Historic Overview of Partnerships
Partnerships Defined
Partnership Property
The Partnership Agreement
Limited Liability Partnerships
Taxation of Partnerships
Historic Overview of Corporations
Corporate Nature
Formation of a Corporation
De Jure Versus de Facto Corporations

Corporate Powers
Ultra Vires Acts
Taxation of Corporations
Disregarding the Corporate Entity
Limited Liability Companies
Other Types of Business Organizations
Summary
Discussion Questions
Case Problems and Writing Assignments

HISTORIC OVERVIEW OF PARTNERSHIPS

The partnership form of business organization is very old. It can be traced back to ancient Babylon, and perhaps came into existence even earlier. It was widely used by the Romans during the height of the Roman Empire. In fact, Roman merchants introduced the partnership throughout Europe as they conducted trade with the peoples conquered by the Roman legions. England was one of the nations that "discovered" the Roman partnership. Later, English common law modified this form of organization somewhat and utilized it in the development of the British Empire, including the colonies in North America that later became the United States.

The United States followed the English common law of partnerships for quite some time. Partnership law in the United States, however, has now been codified. Much of the codification has occurred under the leadership of the National Conference of Commissioners on Uniform State Laws (NCCUSL) who prepares uniform acts and encourages state legislatures to adopt them. The controlling law today is found in the Uniform Partnership Act (UPA)[1] or the Revised Uniform Partnership Act (RUPA)[2] for general partnerships.[3] The UPA (1914) was adopted by every state except Louisiana. In 1997, the NCCUSL amended RUPA. Although the UPA is still the majority rule, an increasing number of states are enacting RUPA with the 1997 amendments.[4] As partnership law continues to evolve, there are a number of significant changes. The revisions include limited liability for partners in registered limited liability partnerships. RUPA has moved away from viewing the partnership as an aggregate of the partners to viewing it as a separate entity. This is called an *entity approach* and is expressly stated in § 201. Consequently the partnership can sue and be sued in the partnership name.[5] Under RUPA partnership property is owned in the partnership name. A partner has his or her partnership interest, but is not a co-owner of specific partnership property.[6] RUPA has also changed some of the dissolution rules. A dissolution is no longer required every time a partner leaves.[7] Generally, a partnership can buy the interest of the partner who leaves. "Partnerships based upon aggregate theory are simply more fragile than partnerships based upon entity theory."[8] RUPA also permits, but does not require, the filing of statements when the partnership is formed, dissolved, merged with another partnership, or there are limitations on partnership authority.[9]

Rules for **limited partnerships** are codified in either the Uniform Limited Partnership Act (ULPA) or the Revised Uniform Limited Partnership Act (RULPA).[10] In 1976, the NCCUSL approved RULPA. The NCCUSL amended RULPA in 1985.[11] Some form of RULPA has been adopted by every state except Louisiana and Vermont. The ULPA is followed only in Vermont; consequently, it has little effect. Louisiana does not follow either act.[12]

Partnerships are formed for a variety of reasons. Many **professionals,** for example, enter partnerships because they are not allowed to incorporate under some state laws. Some people enter partnerships to avoid the technical steps and expense required to form a **corporation.** And some people form partnerships because it seems appropriate, without giving the matter serious consideration.

A partnership has many of the best features of the other major types of business organizations—**proprietorships,** limited partnerships, and corporations—but also some of the worst features. A partnership is relatively easy to form, and the formation is normally informal—as is the case with a proprietorship. Like a corporation, a partnership may have a wider financial base than a proprietorship. And like a corporation, the partnership has more expertise from which to draw.

Limited partnership
A partnership where some partners' liability is limited to their contribution.

Professional
In the sense used here, a member of a "learned profession," such as a doctor, a lawyer, or an accountant.

Corporation
An artificial person or legal entity created by or under the authority of a state or nation, composed of a group of persons known as stockholders or shareholders.

Proprietorship
A business with legal rights or exclusive title vested in one individual; a solely owned business.

A partnership is not perpetual, however, as a corporation may be. A partnership will dissolve eventually. Also, the partners face unlimited liability for business-related conduct, as does a proprietor. Shareholders in a corporation, in contrast, have limited liability.

No one form of business organization is perfect. Each has some advantages that the others lack; and each has some drawbacks the others avoid. The decision to choose a type of business organization should never be made lightly or automatically. All "pros" and "cons" for each available alternative should be weighed carefully before a decision is made. A comparison of the various business organizations appears in Exhibit 34.1 on pages 886–887.

PARTNERSHIPS DEFINED

Uniform Partnership Act

Section 6(1) of the Uniform Partnership Act defines a partnership. According to this section, a partnership has five characteristics. It is

1. An association
2. Of two or more persons
3. To carry on a business
4. As co-owners
5. For profit.

The 16 words in the definition are deceptively simple. In fact, a tremendous amount of interpretation often is involved in fitting an organization into the definition of a partnership. To illustrate the potential problem, we will discuss the terms in the order listed.

An Association. The courts have consistently held that a partnership must be entered voluntarily; that is, no one can be forced to be a partner against his or her will. Thus, *an association* has been interpreted as being "a voluntarily entered association." Being realistic, the courts also realize that people occasionally disagree. The test for voluntariness is the willingness to associate at the time of *creation* of the relationship. Later disagreements will not automatically destroy the partnership. Thus, *an association* means a mutual and unanimous assent to be partners jointly and severally at the time of the agreement.

Of Two or More Persons. *Persons* here is interpreted broadly. It means persons in the biological sense, or persons in the legal sense, or persons in any other sense—in other words, two or more identifiable entities that elect to associate. Thus, each partner may be a human being, a corporation, a partnership, or even a **joint venture.**

To Carry on a Business. The third element of the definition has two separate segments. First, it must be determined whether there is a business. A *business* is defined as any trade, occupation, or profession, so most·associations meet this test. Next, it must be determined whether the business is being carried on. *Carrying on* implies some *continuity.* A business must be fairly permanent and lasting in order to be carried on. If a business appears to be short-term, it is quite possible that the court will rule that no partnership exists. If the other elements of a partnership are present, however, the short-term business may qualify as a **joint venture** instead.

As Co-Owners. The fourth element is probably the most important and the most confusing. Co-ownership does not refer to a sharing of title on the assets used in the business. Instead, it refers to a sharing of ownership of the *business itself.* The business is an **intangible asset.** A business often uses assets of a tangible nature, but it need not own any tangible assets. For example, several accountants may enter a partnership. The partnership owns a business that provides services, and services are intangible. The accountants may lease an office; they may rent furniture; they may not own a single tangible asset, and yet they co-own a business. How, then, is one to know if people involved in a business are co-owners? The simplest way is to look at the agreement the people made when the business began. If the agreement states that they are partners, or co-owners, of the business, they are co-owners of the business. But all too often the agreement is ambiguous, unclear, or oral. In such a situation, the agreement is of no help in resolving the co-ownership question. Then the courts must look beyond the agreement.

The courts normally will look at how the parties treat **profits.** If the parties share profits, or net returns, there is *prima facie* evidence that a partnership exists—that is, the partnership is presumed to exist unless disproved by evidence to the contrary. The sharing of profits creates a **rebuttable presumption** that a partnership was formed. The burden then shifts to the parties to *disprove,* or to rebut, the presumption.

The UPA recognizes five rebuttals.[13] If one of the parties can prove that profits were shared for one of the reasons listed below, no partnership exists. If such proof is not made, the sharing of profits establishes that a partnership did exist. The rebuttal is valid if profits are shared for one of the following purposes:

1. As payment of a debt, by installments or otherwise (a promissory note or a judgment note should be produced as evidence)
2. As payment of wages to an employee or of rent to a landlord
3. As payment of an annuity to the representatives of a deceased partner
4. As payment of interest on a loan (again, some document probably will be necessary)
5. As payment of consideration in the sale of goodwill or other property, whether by installment payments or otherwise

For Profit. The fifth and final element of the definition of a partnership is probably the easiest to show. A partnership must operate *for profit.* To be specific, all that is needed is a *profit motive.* If the business was created to generate profits and to return these profits to the owners of the business, this test for the existence of a partnership is satisfied. Thus, nonprofit associations cannot, by definition, be partnerships. However, an unprofitable business can be a partnership, provided that profits are the goal of the business. In short, the court is looking at the motive of the organization, not the financial bottom line.

In the following case, the court analyzed whether the parties had formed a partnership. The court is using the California statute based on UPA (1914). In California, RUPA (1994) became effective 1 January 1999.

Joint venture
A commercial or maritime enterprise undertaken by several persons jointly; an association of two or more persons to carry out a single business enterprise for profit.

Intangible asset
Property that cannot be touched or felt.

Profits
The gain made in the enterprise, after deducting the costs incurred for labor, materials, rents, and all other expenses.

Rebuttable presumption
A legal assumption that will be followed until a stronger proof or presumption is presented.

34.1

HOLMES V. LERNER
88 CAL.RPTR.2D 130 (CA. APP. 1ST DIST. DIV. 1, 1999)

FACTS . . . [Patricia] Holmes and [Sandra Kruger] Lerner[14] became friends. . . . At Lerner's mansion outside of London, . . . Holmes . . . developed her own [nail] color. . . . On July 31, 1995, the two women returned from England and stayed at Lerner's West Hollywood condominium. . . . Lerner and Holmes worked with the colors in a nail kit to try to recreate the purple color Holmes had made in England. . . . Holmes . . . said that she wanted to call the purple color she had made "Plague." . . . The two women . . . decided that "Urban Decay" was a good name for their concept. Lerner said to Holmes: "This seems like a good [thing], it's something that we both like, and isn't out there. Do you think we should start a company?" Holmes responded: "Yes, I think it's a great idea." Lerner told Holmes that they would have to do market research, determine how to have the polishes produced, and that there were many things they would have to do. . . . They did not separate out which tasks each of them would do, but planned to do it all together. Lerner went to the telephone and called David Soward, the general partner of & Capital, and her business consultant. Holmes heard her say "Please check Urban, for the name, Urban Decay, to see if it's available and if it is, get it for us." Holmes knew that Lerner did not joke about business, and was certain . . . that Lerner was serious about the new business. The telephone call to secure the trademark for Urban Decay confirmed in Holmes' mind that they were forming a business based on the concepts they had originated in England and at the kitchen table that day. Holmes knew that she would be taking the risk of sharing in losses as well as potential success, but the two friends did not discuss the details at that time. Although neither of the two women had any experience in the cosmetics business, they began work on their idea immediately. . . . Holmes and Lerner discussed their plans for the company, and agreed that they would attempt to build it up and then sell it. . . .

[The participants attended meetings which they call board meetings.] . . . They discussed financing, and Soward reluctantly agreed to commit $500,000 towards the project. Urban Decay was financed entirely by & Capital, the venture capital partnership composed of Soward as general partner, and Lerner and her husband as the only limited partners. . . . [. . . Holmes was spending four to five days a week at the warehouse.] Holmes was reimbursed for mileage, but received no pay for her work. . . . [Holmes inquired about her role in Urban Decay a number of times. When it became obvious that they were excluding her, she initiated this lawsuit.]

ISSUE Did Holmes and Lerner form a partnership?

HOLDING Yes. The jury verdict for Holmes was supported by substantial evidence.

REASONING . . . [W]e determine that an express agreement to divide profits is not a prerequisite to prove the existence of a partnership. We also determine that the oral partnership agreement between Lerner and Holmes was sufficiently definite to allow enforcement. . . . Holmes testified that she and Lerner did not discuss sharing profits of the business during the July 31, "kitchen table" conversation. . . . The applicable version of the UPA [UPA (1914)]. . . . defines a partnership as: "an association of two or more persons to carry on as co-owners a business for profit." . . . The UPA . . . provides that in determining whether a partnership exists, "the receipt by a person of a share of the profits of a business is prima facie evidence that he is a partner. . . . ." This . . . indicates that the Legislature intends profit sharing to be evidence of a partnership, rather than a required element of the definition of a partnership. . . . The presence or absence of any of the various elements set forth in section 15007, including sharing of profits and losses, is not necessarily dispositive. . . . [T]he rules to establish the existence of a partnership in section 15007 should be viewed in the light of the crucial factor of the intent of the parties revealed in the terms of their agreement, conduct, and the surrounding circumstances when determining whether a partnership exists. The UPA provides for the situation in which the partners have not expressly stated an agreement regarding sharing of profits. Section 15018 provides in relevant part: "The rights and duties of the partners in relation to the partnership shall be determined, subject to any agreement between them, by the following rules: (a) Each partner shall . . . share equally in the profits and surplus remaining after all liabilities, including those to partners, are satisfied." . . . The definition in section 15006 provides that the association with the intent to carry on a business for profit is the essential requirement for a partnership. . . . The trial court . . . refused to add additional elements to the statutory

34.1

HOLMES V. LERNER, *continued*
88 CAL.RPTR.2D 130 (CA. APP. 1ST DIST. DIV. 1, 1999)

definition and properly instructed the jury in the language of section 15006. . . . The actual sharing of profits (with exceptions which do not apply here) is prima facie evidence, which is to be considered, in light of any other evidence, when determining if a partnership exists. In this case, there were no profits to share at the time Holmes was expelled from the business, so the evidentiary provision of section 15007, subdivision (4) is not applicable. According to section 15006, parties who expressly agree to associate as co-owners with the intent to carry on a business for profit, have established a partnership. Once the elements of that definition are established, other provisions of the UPA and the conduct of the parties supply the details of the agreement. Certainly implicit in the Holmes-Lerner agreement to operate Urban Decay together was an understanding to share in profits and losses as any business owners would. The evidence supported the jury's implicit finding that Holmes birthed an idea which was incubated jointly by Lerner and Holmes, from which they intended to profit once it was fully matured in their company. . . .

Holmes produced substantial evidence of an agreement as well as evidence of actions of the parties in conformance with their agreement. "Parties are far less liable to have been mistaken as to the intention of their contract during the period while harmonious and practical construction reflects that intention, than they are when subsequent differences have impelled them to resort to law." . . . [T]here is nothing unusual about a partnership in which one party supplies an idea, which the other party brings into a substantive form. . . . The agreement here . . . was that Holmes and Lerner would start a cosmetics company based on the unusual colors developed by Holmes, identified by the Urban theme and the exotic names. The additional terms were filled in as the two women immediately began work on the multitude of details necessary to bring their idea to fruition. The fact that Holmes worked for almost a year, without expectation of pay, is further confirmation of the agreement. Lerner and Soward never objected to her work, her participation in board meetings and decision making, or her exercise of authority over the retail warehouse operation. . . . [Later] Holmes . . . was frozen out of the business altogether. . . .

BUSINESS CONSIDERATIONS How could Holmes have better protected her interests? When a person originates an idea, how can he or she protect the idea from investors, suppliers, and partners?

ETHICAL CONSIDERATION How would you analyze Lerner and Soward's ethics?

Note that under the provisions of RUPA (1994), the sharing of profits is recharacterized as an evidentiary presumption, rather than *prima facie* evidence.[15]

Limited Partnership

A limited partnership can be created by two or more persons, as long as there is at least one **limited partner** and at least one general partner. With the exception of classifying the partners, a limited partnership has the same characteristics as a general partnership set up under the UPA. A limited partnership is more formal than a general partnership, however. In order to set up a limited partnership, the partners must sign and swear to a written certificate that details all the important elements of the partnership agreement. This certificate must be filed with the correct public official, as specified in the statutes of the state where the limited partnership is created.

A limited partner is so called because the limited partners have *limited liability*. In other words, a limited partner is not personally liable for any obligations of the partnership. However, there is a price to pay for this protection: A limited partner

Limited partner
A limited-partnership member who furnishes certain funds to the partnership and whose liability is restricted to the funds provided.

E X H I B I T   34.1 | **A Comparison of Different Types of Business Organizations**

	Proprietorship	Partnership	Limited Partnership[a]
Creation	Proprietor opens the business, subject to state and local licensing laws, and so on.	Partners enter into an agreement, either orally or in writing; no formalities are required.	Partners enter into a partnership agreement and file a written form designating the limited partners and the general partners.
Termination	Proprietor closes the business; death, insanity, or bankruptcy of the owner also terminates the business.	Partners agree to dissolve the partnership; death, bankruptcy, or withdrawal of any partner also dissolves the partnership. The terms of the agreement or a court order may dissolve the partnership. Liquidation of the assets after a dissolution winds up the business.	Partners follow same procedure as for a partnership, but with a difference in the order of distributing assets in case of a dissolution and liquidation of the business.
Taxation[b]	All business profits are taxed as regular income of the owner; there are no federal income taxes on the business, per se.	The business must file a federal tax return, but it is for information only. The income of the business is taxed as regular income to the partners.	The same tax procedure is followed as for a regular, general partnership.
Liability	Proprietor has unlimited personal liability. First, business assets will be used, and then the personal assets of the owner.	Partners have unlimited personal liability. First, business assets will be used, and then the personal assets of the partners. The partners are jointly and severally liable for the debts.	General partners have unlimited personal liability. First, business assets will be used, and then the personal assets of the general partners. The general partners are jointly and severally liable for the debts. Limited partners are only liable to the extent of their contribution.
Advantages	Simplicity of creation; complete ownership and control of the firm.	Informality of creation; greater potential for expertise and capital in management (because there is more than one manager).	Somewhat greater flexibility than a general partnership; increased opportunities to raise capital.
Disadvantages	Limited capital; limited expertise; limited existence (when the owner dies, the business terminates).	Limited existence; lack of flexibility; potential liability.	Some rigidity in ownership and decision making; personal liability of general partners; limited existence.

a. This applies to limited partnerships under the Revised Uniform Limited Partnership Act.
b. There may be significant tax consequences of changing from one business form to another.
c. This may also be an advantage.

EXHIBIT 34.1 | **A Comparison of Different Types of Business Organizations, continued**

Limited Liability Partnership	Corporation	Limited Liability Company
Partners enter into a partnership agreement and the partnership files a copy or some other notice with the state.	Parties prepare and file *formal* legal documents known as articles of incorporation with the state of incorporation; they must comply with any relevant state or federal security statutes or regulations.	LLCs may be formed by two or more members, who enter into an agreement. Generally LLCs must file articles of organization with the state government.
Partners follow same procedure as for a general partnership.	Parties close the business, liquidate all business assets, surrender the corporate charter, and distribute the assets as per state law; termination may also be due to state action revoking the charter.	Statute and/or agreement will probably limit the term of the LLC: State laws vary on whether the association can be renewed for an additional period.
The same tax procedure is followed as for a regular, general partnership.	A normal corporation is treated as a separate taxable entity and pays taxes on its profits. Any dividends are also taxed to the stockholders. This is called "double taxation." A Subchapter S corporation, regulated by the IRS, is taxed as if it were a general partnership despite its corporate status. A Subchapter S corporation is treated differently only for federal tax purposes. States may also tax them as partnerships.	LLC is taxed as a partnership or a corporation depending on its characteristics and tax law. Characteristics are determined by the agreement and the state statute. The LLC may have different taxation for state and federal purposes.
Partner is liable without limit for his/her own wrongs and wrongs of people the partner directly supervises; the partner's liability is limited to the partner's contribution for the wrongs of others.	Stockholders are *not* personally liable for debts of the corporation, so there is limited liability. Stockholders may lose their investment in the corporation if it fails.	All members are liable for association debts only to the extent of their capital contribution(s).
Limited liability except for a partner's own wrongs and the wrongs of people the partner directly supervises.	Longevity—potential for perpetual existence; potentially unlimited access to capital and to expertise; freely transferable ownership; limited personal liability of the owners.	Limited liability for all the members.
Unlimited liability for partner's own wrongs; only permitted in some states.	"Double taxation" (except for Subchapter S corporation); much more federal regulation; considerably more state regulation; formality and rigidity of the organization.	LLCs cannot be formed in all states. LLC statutes vary greatly from state to state. Professionals may not be permitted to form an LLC, depending on the state. There may be limitations on the transferability of shares.[c] Selling interests in an LLC may be subject to state and federal securities regulations. There is uncertainty about how the LLC and its members will be taxed. LLCs may have a limited term of existence.[c]

34.1 | FINANCE/ MANAGEMENT

CALL-IMAGE TECHNOLOGY

OBTAINING NECESSARY CAPITAL

Tom and Anna Kochanowski believe that the firm needs a large infusion of capital in order to succeed. They have suggested that the firm incorporate and "go public" by offering stock for sale. Tom and Anna believe that the family can incorporate, sell 45 percent of the stock, and acquire enough funds to establish the business financially. Dan is opposed to the idea of selling any stock. He feels that such a sale opens up the possibility that an "outsider" could—by purchasing stock in the future—take control of the business away from the family. As an alternative, Dan mentions that he has heard about some type of partnership that might be used to raise money without surrendering any control. Tom and Anna ask you if you know what type of partnership Dan is talking about. What do you tell them? What alternatives might exist for the Kochanowskis that will allow them to raise capital and at the same time retain control of the firm? What will you advise them to do?

BUSINESS CONSIDERATION What factors should a firm consider in evaluating methods to obtain capital?
ETHICAL CONSIDERATIONS Is it ethical to sell interests in CIT solely to obtain funds and not provide the purchasers with any control in the firm? Is this using investors solely as a means to CIT's ends?

is precluded from management of the business. A limited partner who takes part in management loses the limited status[16] and may be treated as a general partner, subject to unlimited personal liability—but only in dealings with third persons who actually know of the limited partner's participation in the management of the business. Limited partners who act as agents or employees of a general partner or of the firm or who advise the general partners about business are not considered to be involved in management. The partnership agreement *may* grant voting rights to limited partners under RULPA.[17] RULPA specifically addresses the type of acts that alone will not be considered control or management.[18]

A limited partnership must be set up in accordance with the controlling state laws governing limited partnerships—either the Uniform Limited Partnership Act, which is followed in Vermont, or the Revised Uniform Limited Partnership Act, which is followed in all the other states, except Louisiana. Louisiana follows its own statutes. Although most of the topical coverage is essentially the same, there are some technical differences between the ULPA and the RULPA. Under the RULPA, for example, the certificate of agreement forming the limited partnership must be filed with the secretary of state for the state in which the limited partnership is formed. The revised act calls for profits and losses to be shared on the basis of capital contributions unless the agreement specifies some other distribution. The distribution of assets upon termination of the entity and the liquidation of its assets is treated differently under the revised act than under the ULPA. One of the interesting aspects of the RULPA is § 1105, which specifies that any cases not provided for in the revised act are to be governed by the provisions of the ULPA. Our discussion will center on the RULPA, since it has been adopted by 48 states. Any parties who plan to establish a limited partnership, however, need to check the applicable statute for the state of origin.

Throughout this chapter and Chapters 35 and 36, we will discuss the majority rule contained in the RULPA.

PARTNERSHIP PROPERTY

Although no partnership is *required* to own property, most partnerships do, in fact, own some property. Even if the partnership chooses not to own property, it must have access to possession and use of some physical assets. And this access and use may lead to ownership, at least under the UPA and in the eyes of the court.

Section 8 of the UPA defines partnership property for general partnerships. Under this section, the following kinds of property are deemed to be *partnership property* (property owned by the partnership rather than the partners as individuals):

1. All property originally contributed to the partnership as a partner's capital contribution(s)
2. All property acquired on account of the partnership
3. All property acquired with partnership funds, unless a contrary intention is shown
4. Any interest in real property that is acquired in the partnership name
5. Any conveyance to a partnership in the partnership name, unless a contrary intention is shown

If an individual partner wants to retain personal ownership but allow the partnership to use property, he or she should be extremely cautious. Unless the intention is made obvious, the property the partner thought he or she still owned may legally belong to the partnership. (The reason this is so important is discussed in detail in Chapter 36, which covers dissolution.)

THE PARTNERSHIP AGREEMENT

A partnership is created by agreement of the partners. The agreement is a contract. This contract may be oral, unless it falls within the Statute of Frauds. In other words, no formality is required in setting up a general partnership. (Note, however, the formal requirements for creating a limited partnership, which we have already discussed.) Under RUPA, the partnership agreement is primary, and can include written, oral, or implied agreements. For the most part, the agreement takes priority over RUPA: that is, RUPA will provide terms for the partners only if they failed to specify the terms themselves.[19]

A reasonably prudent, cautious person is expected to take great care in negotiating the basic partnership agreement and then reducing the agreement to written form. Yet all too often a partnership is begun with little or no detailed negotiation, as illustrated in Case 34.1. And even if the parties are very careful, situations may arise that were never considered and, therefore, are not covered by the agreement. To minimize the harm such situations can create, the UPA imposes certain rules, which apply unless the agreement provides otherwise, and specifies certain areas that the agreement must cover.

Imposed Rules

Unless the agreement between the parties states otherwise, the following rules are imposed by operation of law:

1. Each partner is entitled to an equal voice in the management of the business. (Limited partners are obviously exceptions to this rule.)
2. Each partner is entitled to an equal share of profits, without regard to capital contributions. (The RULPA takes the opposite approach for limited partnerships.)
3. Each partner is expected to share any losses suffered by the business in the same proportion as profits are to be shared.
4. The books of the partnership are to be kept at the central office of the business. (RUPA considers access to the partnership books so important that the partnership agreement cannot waive a partner's right of access.[20])

In addition, some rules are imposed and must be followed by the *general* partners, no matter what the agreement says. Any attempt to modify these rules in the agreement is contrary to public policy, so any modification will be deemed void. Some of the rules are:

1. Each partner is deemed to be an agent for the partnership and for each partner, as long as the partner is acting in a business-related matter.
2. Each partner is personally liable, without limit, for torts or contracts for which the partnership has insufficient assets to cover the debt or liability.
3. Each partner is expected to devote service to the partnership only and not to any competing business ventures.

Express Terms

In addition to those terms imposed by law, the partnership agreement should cover some other areas. For instance, the agreement should designate the name of the business. This name cannot be deceptively similar to the name of any other company or business, and it cannot mislead the public as to the nature of the business. (If a limited partnership is involved, the name should reflect that fact.)

The agreement should cover the duration of the business—how long the partnership will last. Such an understanding in the beginning can avoid serious disagreements later. It also should cover the purpose of the business. Understanding the business's functions not only makes it easier to operate the business but also helps to avoid any controversies later.

Finally, the agreement should discuss in detail how, or if, a partner can withdraw from the business. In this area, the rights of a withdrawing partner should be very carefully spelled out so that no one, including a court, will misconstrue the agreement's terms.

Of course, any other items the partners feel should be included can be discussed, agreed on, and included. In fact, the more detailed the original agreement, the better. A carefully drawn, well-thought-out agreement will always benefit honest partners.

LIMITED LIABILITY PARTNERSHIPS

A relatively new form of business organization, limited liability partnerships (LLPs), has attracted great attention. LLPs are currently permitted only in some states; however, the numbers are growing rapidly—both of states permitting this form of business and of enterprises adopting this form once it is permitted. Many enterprises that were general partnerships are becoming LLPs. Examples include Coopers & Lybrand, Ernst & Young, and Price Waterhouse.[21] Sometimes the enabling legislation is passed as amendments to the state's partnership act or as part of the state's limited liability company act. The 1997 amendments to RUPA expressly provide for limited liability partnerships.[22]

The advantage of an LLP over a general partnership is, as the name implies, the limit on the liability of the partners. In an LLP, a partner's personal assets are protected from liability claims against the partnership. Generally, the protection is from liability arising from negligence, wrongful acts, or misconduct committed in the ordinary course of business by any *other* partner, employee, agent, or representative. The exception to this is liability created by the partner him- or herself. In other words, a partner has unlimited liability for his or her own wrongdoings and limited liability for the wrongdoings of others. Generally, the statutes broadly

THREE ACCOUNTING FIRMS NOW LIMITED LIABILITY PARTNERSHIPS

Coopers & Lybrand, Ernst & Young, and Price Waterhouse have changed the form of their enterprise to that of a limited liability partnership (LLP). Arthur Andersen & Co. and Deloitte & Touche intend to file for LLP status shortly. KPMG Peat Marwick is also considering making the switch. These recent changes occurred because New York amended its law during the summer of 1994: It now permits accounting firms to form LLPs.

Assume that the change in the form of these firms has been challenged in *your* court due to its potential impact on parties who may sue these firms at a later date. How will *you* address these issues, and how will *you* resolve the case?[23]

BUSINESS CONSIDERATIONS Why is this new form of business so popular with the Big Six accounting firms? Will it be this popular with smaller firms? What should a business consider before deciding to adopt this form of organization?

ETHICAL CONSIDERATIONS Is it ethical for an existing business to change its structure so that its owners face less potential liability? Would it be ethical to deny a firm the right to change to a form approved by the legislature because of potential future claims?

SOURCE: *The Wall Street Journal* (2 August 1994), p. A8.

interpret the partner's own wrongs to include the wrongs of persons under that partner's direct supervision and control. As in other general partnerships, the partners are jointly liable for contracts and jointly and severally liable for the normal business debts of the partnership.

The RUPA amendments require an election to become a limited liability partnership. The partnership must register with the state. In addition, it must identify itself as an LLP to those with whom it does business. The registration and identification requirements provide clear notice of the limited liability status. Creditors will evaluate creditworthiness accordingly.[24]

Under the 1997 RUPA amendments, LLPs are treated as partnerships in all respects.[25] Some states have not adopted the 1997 amendments and may treat an LLP differently in some respects. Some states will not permit professionals to use LLPs. Other states permit professionals to form LLPs, but may require the professional LLPs to purchase liability insurance. For example, South Carolina requires professional LLPs to carry a minimum of $100,000 of insurance.

TAXATION OF PARTNERSHIPS

For taxation purposes, the partnership form of business is neither an advantage nor a disadvantage. Basically, the partnership is not taxed, but the individual partners are taxed on the receipts of the firm. Why? Federal income tax rules and regulations do not recognize the partnership as a taxable entity. The firm must file an annual federal tax return, but the return is for information purposes only. Each partner is taxed on his or her share of the firm's profits for the year, whether these profits are distributed to the partners or not. Each partner is also taxed on the capital gains—or may take the deductions for capital losses—the firm experiences during the tax year.

Many states also treat the partnership as a mere conduit for the transfer of income to the partners. In these states, the partnership is not taxed, but the partners are taxed on the firm's income whether it is distributed or retained by the firm for reinvestment or expansion.

HISTORIC OVERVIEW OF CORPORATIONS

No exact moment of recorded history pinpoints the existence of the first corporation. But some evidence suggests that people recognized the concept of corporate personality to some extent as early as the time of Hammurabi (about 1750 B.C.). Certainly by Roman times, vestiges of corporateness had appeared through imperial **fiat.** From its very origins, then, the concept of corporateness depended on legislative grant. Canon law, borrowing from the Romans, distinguished between the *corporation sole* (composed of a single person, usually a high-ranking church officeholder) and the *corporation aggregate* (composed of several persons). The *fiction theory*—that a corporation is an artificial legal person separate from its shareholders—probably developed from the papacy's desire to accommodate priests who had taken vows of poverty forbidding them to hold property. Since controlling the activities and finances of these clergymen was very lucrative, the church (the corporation) devised ways to allow church officers to own property. This separation of the artificial person from the natural person associated with it spawned the modern view that the corporation, not the shareholders, owns the corporate property and that shareholders ordinarily are not liable for debts incurred by the corporation. The development of the law merchant, the forerunner of modern commercial law, mirrored these and similar views of corporateness.

By the seventeenth century, English monarchs had tightened control over corporations, which were deemed to exist by virtue of *concessionary grants* of power from the state. Not surprisingly, the concession theory was part of the common law heritage that remained with American colonists after they gained independence from Britain. At first, Americans viewed corporations with suspicion because several well-known, unsavory schemes had been perpetrated through use of the corporate form. But such suspicions gradually relaxed as the advantages of corporations, such as the potential to raise capital, became apparent. As the corporate form developed, however, each state jealously guarded its power over these artificial creatures. This careful regulation of corporations, augmented now by federal securities statutes, remains an essential characteristic of the law of corporations.

CORPORATE NATURE

We define a *corporation* as an artificial person created under the statutes of a state or nation, organized for the purpose set out in the application for corporate existence. A corporation is an invisible, intangible, artificial person. Therefore, because it is considered a person, the corporation ordinarily enjoys most of the rights that

Fiat
An order issued by legal authority.

natural (flesh-and-blood) persons possess. For example, it is a citizen and a resident of the state in which it has been incorporated. Thus, under the Fourth Amendment, it cannot be the object of unreasonable searches or seizures. Similarly, under the Fourteenth Amendment, it must be afforded its rights of due process and equal protection. In addition, a corporation assumes the nationality of either the nationality and/or the residence of the persons controlling it (called the *aggregate test*), or the nation in which it was incorporated or where it has its principal place of business (dubbed the *entity test*).

Advantages of the Corporate Form

The popularity of the corporation as a business form results from its comparative advantages over other types of business organizations. These advantages include:

1. *Insulation from liability.* Corporate debts are the responsibility of the corporation. The shareholders' liability ordinarily is limited to the amount of their investment; creditors of the corporation normally cannot reach the shareholders' personal assets to pay for corporate debts.
2. *Centralization of management functions.* Centralizing the management functions in a small group of persons possessing management expertise avoids some of the friction that may plague partnerships.
3. *Continuity of existence.* The corporation continues to exist in the eyes of the law even after the deaths of the officers, directors, or shareholders, or the withdrawal of their shares. This potential for perpetual existence provides stability. A corporation exists in perpetuity unless a specific length of time is stated in its articles of incorporation.
4. *Free transferability of shares.* This creates opportunities for access to outside capital (as well as allowing investors to sell their interests without the need for unanimous approval or the dissolution of the firm).

These attributes unquestionably convince many large and small businesses to employ the corporate form. In a given situation, however, another form may better suit the business's needs. This is a decision that requires careful thought and the advice of knowledgeable experts, such as a lawyer, accountant, or investment adviser. There are also distinct disadvantages that may result from choosing the corporate form.

FORMATION OF A CORPORATION

The process of forming a corporation involves complicated issues that demand the attention of well-versed professionals. One of these considerations consists of choosing the most desirable type of corporation for the particular circumstances.

Types of Corporations

The *public-issue private corporation* is the best-known type of private corporation. We are all familiar with American Telephone & Telegraph (AT&T), General Motors (GM), International Business Machines (IBM), General Electric (GE), and other large public-issue corporations. The central advantage of public-issue corporations is their access to capital in the form of new shares. The shareholder, however, has very little say in the management of such giant concerns.

For this reason, there is another type of private corporation, the *close corporation*. This form limits the management of the firm to a select few shareholders and restricts the transferability of shares in order to consolidate control. Close corporations allow a firm to enjoy many of the advantages of the corporate form (such as favorable tax treatment) without giving up the day-to-day control more commonly associated with sole proprietorships or general partnerships. An inherent disadvantage of close corporations, on the other hand, stems from a lack of free transferability of shares; these shares are often not as liquid or saleable as those of public-issue corporations.

Private corporations may also include *professional corporations,* those organized for conducting a particular occupation or profession. Doctors, lawyers, dentists, and accountants may find it advantageous financially (because of tax and pension benefits, for example) to form such corporations. Most states have special statutes regulating professional corporations. Typically, these statutes limit share ownership in such corporations to duly licensed professional persons. Despite the limited liability offered by the corporate form, under these statutes the professional is ordinarily personally liable for his or her own malpractice or similar torts as well as for any such acts performed by others who are under the professional's supervision.

A city is an example of a *public* or *municipal corporation.* We often call some public utilities *quasi-public corporations* because they are private corporations that, nevertheless, furnish public services such as electricity, gas, or water.

Corporations are generally for-profit. But *nonprofit corporations,* or those organized for charitable purposes, also exist. Special statutes in some jurisdictions regulate educational institutions, charities, private hospitals, fraternal orders, religious organizations, and other types of nonprofit corporations.

Promoters

Despite the negative connotation of the word, promoters may be vital to the formation of the corporation, practically speaking. Although the law does not require the services of promoters as a precondition to incorporating, *promoters* begin the process of forming a corporation by procuring subscribers for the stock or by taking other affirmative steps toward incorporating. Thus, promoters facilitate the creation of the corporation by bringing interested parties together and by encouraging the venture until the corporation is formed. We can also label promoters *preincorporators.*

Novation
In this context, a new contract that replaces the prior contract and substitutes the corporation for the promoter. It releases the promoter from his or her liability.

Ratification
Accepting an act that was unauthorized when committed and becoming bound to that act upon its acceptance.

Promoters' activities raise a host of legal issues. Since the promoter is working on behalf of an entity not yet created, questions arise as to who is liable on contracts made on the corporation's behalf before its inception: the promoter or the corporation? The general rule is that the promoter will be liable for goods and services rendered to him or her before the corporation's formation. However, the corporation may become liable for the promoter's contracts (and possibly torts) after formation by **novation,** or by adoption or **ratification** of the promoter's contracts. In most cases, this liability is joint and the promoter remains personally liable. The promoter's liability *will* be eliminated if there is a novation or an express release of liability.

The possibility of double-dealing is inherent in the process of promotion. For this reason, the law treats promoters as owing fiduciary duties to the corporation. Therefore, the promoter must act in good faith, deal fairly, and make full disclosure to the corporation. The liability of promoters as fiduciaries is not as pervasive a problem today as in the past because of the disclosures mandated by the Securities Act of 1933. In a few cases, however, the promoter has had to give back to the corporation secret profits, embezzled funds, and other damages. Therefore, anyone desiring to act as a promoter should seek professional advice beforehand.

Articles of Incorporation

The document that signals the official existence of the corporation is the *articles of incorporation*. State statutes prescribe the contents of the articles. Typically the articles include:

1. The name of the corporation
2. Its purpose
3. Its duration
4. The location of its principal office or **registered agent** (also called *resident agent*)
5. Its powers, its capital structure (i.e., the number of shares and minimum **stated capital**)
6. Its directors and their names (these people are usually the incorporators)
7. The signatures of the incorporators (in most jurisdictions they do not have to be shareholders)

Once the incorporators file the articles with the appropriate state official (ordinarily, the secretary of state) and pay all the required filing fees, the state issues a formal *certificate of incorporation,* or license.

Registered agent
Person designated by a corporation to receive service of process within the state.

Stated capital
The amount of consideration received by the corporation for all shares of the corporation.

Corporate Charter/Certificate of Incorporation

In most states, corporate existence begins with the issuance of the certificate of incorporation by the secretary of state in the state of incorporation. After it issues such a certificate, the state normally will not interfere with this grant of power. Unless the corporation's conduct poses a definite and serious danger to the welfare of the state's citizens (e.g., by engaging in wholesale fraud), the state will honor the certificate and allow the corporation to conduct its usual business without impediment. Exhibit 34.2 on page 896 represents a typical certificate of incorporation.

Organizational Meeting

In some jurisdictions, official corporate existence begins not on the issuance of the certificate of incorporation, but after the first organizational meeting of the corporation. The organizational meeting is important because it is during the meeting that (1) bylaws are adopted, (2) the preincorporation agreements are approved, and (3) officers are elected.

Bylaws

Bylaws are the rules and regulations adopted by a corporation for the purpose of self-regulation, especially of day-to-day matters not covered by other documents. These ordinarily are not filed in a public place as the articles of incorporation are. Rather, they constitute the corporation's internal rules for the governance of its own

E X H I B I T   34.2 | **Certificate of Incorporation**

STATE OF INDIANA
OFFICE OF THE SECRETARY OF STATE

CERTIFICATE OF INCORPORATION

OF

. . . ., INC. . . . .

. . . .

    I, EDWIN J. SIMCOX, *Secretary of State of Indiana, hereby certify that Articles of Incorporation of the above Corporation, in the form prescribed by my office, prepared and signed in duplicate by the incorporator(s), and acknowledged and verified by the same, have been presented to me at my office accompanied by the fees prescribed by law; that I have found such Articles conform to law; that I have endorsed my approval upon the duplicate copies of such Articles; that all fees have been paid as required by law; that one copy of such Articles has been filed in my office; and that the remaining copy of such Articles bearing the endorsement of my approval and filing has been returned by me to the incorporator(s) or his(their) representatives; all as prescribed by the provisions of the*

INDIANA GENERAL CORPORATION ACT . . . .

. . . ., *as amended.*

NOW, THEREFORE, *I hereby issue to such Corporation this Certificate of Incorporation, and further certify that its corporate existence has begun.*

In Witness Whereof, I have hereunto set

my hand and affixed the seal of the State

of Indiana, at the City of Indianapolis,

this. . . . .*day of*

. . . ., *20*. . . . .

. . . .
EDWIN J. SIMCOX, *Secretary of State*

By. . . . .
                                            Deputy

SOURCE: Courtesy of Douglas D. Germann, Sr., Attorney-at-Law, Mishawaka, Indiana.

affairs. They must, however, be consistent with the jurisdiction's corporate statute and the corporation's articles. Bylaws typically cover the location of the corporation's offices and records; describe the meetings of the shareholders and the directors; set out the powers and duties of the board of directors, officers, and executive committee; establish the capitalization of the corporation; and establish the methods for conducting the corporation's business, such as execution of contracts, signatures on deeds, and notices of meetings.

DE JURE VERSUS DE FACTO CORPORATIONS

As we have seen, it is relatively easy to obtain corporate status if one carefully follows the required statutory procedures. Nevertheless, because it is not a perfect world, it is still necessary to examine the consequences of failure to comply with such statutory requirements. *Defective incorporation,* as this concept is called, may be a matter of degree. If the defect in formation (or non-compliance with the incorporation statute) is slight, the law characterizes the corporation as *de jure* (valid by law). The general rule is that where substantial compliance with all steps necessary for incorporation has occurred, the resultant entity is a de jure corporation. If an address is wrong in a provision mandating an address or a relatively insignificant provision has been overlooked, courts will not invalidate corporate status. Such minor flaws ordinarily will not cause the loss of de jure status.

Sometimes, however, the defect involved is so serious that the law cannot consider the corporation as de jure. Corporateness and all its attributes may still be retained, however, if certain conditions are met: (1) A law under which the business could have been incorporated exists; (2) there was a good-faith effort to comply with the statute; and (3) there was some use or exercise of corporate powers. Such entities are called *de facto* corporations (corporations in fact, if not in law). Only the state can attack the existence of a de facto corporation. Hence, if the state does not bring an action to dissolve its certificate (or its charter), the firm will enjoy all the powers and privileges that exist in the corporate form.

This result is probably fair. Even if the defects in compliance are serious, if both the entity and third parties have previously dealt with each other in the belief that corporateness exists, fulfilling the expectations of the parties seems justifiable. Yet the law should scrutinize the parties' nonfulfillment of statutory dictates in order to avoid the frustration of legislative intent. In recent years, statutory provisions have increasingly reflected the view that the issuance of a certificate of incorporation will create a presumption that the corporation has been validly formed (i.e., it has attained de jure status) except in

CALL-IMAGE TECHNOLOGY

34.2 | MANAGEMENT

DE JURE VERSUS DE FACTO CORPORATIONS

Tom and Anna Kochanowski have just about decided that the benefits of incorporating CIT outweigh the disadvantages of the corporate form. They are unsure, however, about the legal steps involved in incorporation and ask your advice as to what CIT must do to incorporate. What will you advise them to do?

BUSINESS CONSIDERATION What advice and guidelines can you suggest to an enterprise to ensure that it forms a de jure corporation rather than a de facto corporation?

ETHICAL CONSIDERATIONS Is it ethical to grant a business that does not comply fully with the state's incorporation statute the benefits of limited liability and perpetual existence? Would it be more ethical, due to some minor flaw in formation of the enterprise, to treat the stockholders as partners? If the creditor or supplier believed it was a de jure corporation when it dealt with the business, is it ethical for the creditor or supplier to complain about the status after the fact?

actions brought by the state. If the state has taken no action and has issued no certificate, the presumption is that corporate status is as yet unrealized. In this case, third parties can hold individual shareholders personally liable. These developments have greatly eroded the importance of the de facto doctrine, but some courts have continued to make distinctions between de jure and de facto corporations. It is, therefore, important to understand both the historical backdrop and the modern trends in this area of the law.

CORPORATE POWERS

The articles of incorporation may set forth the powers of the corporation. Such provisions actually may be redundant because state statutes normally specify what corporations can permissibly do. These express powers include the ability to conduct business, to exist perpetually (unless the articles define a shorter period or the state dissolves the corporation), to sue and be sued, to use the corporate name or seal, and to make bylaws. In addition, corporations possess implied powers to do everything reasonably necessary for the conduct of the business. Typical implied powers consist of holding or transferring property, acquiring stock from other corporations, borrowing money, executing commercial paper, issuing bonds, effecting loans, reacquiring the corporation's own shares, and contributing to charity. Statutes may enumerate these and other implied powers.

ULTRA VIRES ACTS

As noted earlier, the powers of corporations were more heavily circumscribed years ago than they are today. Since the strict application of the concession theory had held that corporate status was a privilege (in contrast to a right), acts outside the legal boundaries for the corporation were ultra vires and therefore void. *Ultra vires* means beyond the scope or legal power of a corporation as established by the corporation's charter or by state statute. When sued, corporations could use ultra vires as a defense to enforcement of a contract. With the advent of implied powers, the consequent relaxation of the concession theory, and a widening of permissible corporate purposes, a corporation's use of this doctrine for avoidance of contractual duties has become largely outmoded. Thus, the modern trend is to curtail application of the ultra vires doctrine as a defense by the corporation and in general to uphold the validity of actions taken by the corporation unless the action is a public wrong or forbidden by statute. Sometimes, however, the result depends on whether the transaction is executory (to be performed) or executed (performed).

State statutes have abolished the *defense* of ultra vires in most jurisdictions. The statutes usually continue to permit suits only in three situations:

Injunctive actions
Lawsuits asking a court of equity to order a person to do or to refrain from doing some specified act.

1. Shareholder **injunctive actions** against the corporation
2. Shareholder suits on behalf of the corporation to recover damages caused by an impermissible act
3. Proceedings by the state to dissolve the corporation because of repeated violations of applicable law

For practical purposes, these situations constitute the only areas that remain for application of the ultra vires doctrine.

TAXATION OF CORPORATIONS

The tax treatment of corporations stems from the law's recognition of corporations as separate entities for federal income tax purposes. This is a disadvantage of the corporate form. The corporation pays taxes on all its income as earned; and this income, when distributed to shareholders in the form of dividends, produces taxable income for the shareholders. This structure in effect brings about so-called "double taxation." Moreover, because corporate losses are not passed on to the shareholders, shareholders do not receive the tax advantages that otherwise accompany such losses.

The creation of what the Internal Revenue Code terms an *S corporation* (regular corporations are dubbed *C corporations*) may offset these tax drawbacks and, thereby, provide tax relief. Subchapter S of the Internal Revenue Code permits certain corporations to avoid corporate income taxes and, at the same time, to pass operating losses on to their shareholders. In this sense, federal tax laws covering S corporations are analogous to the laws covering partnerships, but S corporations are uniquely corporate at the same time. Attaining S corporation status involves an elective procedure and the necessity for strict compliance with statutory requirements.

Federal tax laws limit eligibility for Subchapter S election to domestic small-business corporations having 35 or fewer shareholders (individuals, estates, and certain trusts qualify as shareholders, but partnerships, corporations, and nonqualifying trusts do not) and only one class of stock issued and outstanding. Moreover, the presence of even one nonresident-alien shareholder or passive investment income in excess of statutory limitations makes the corporation ineligible for S status. In order to make a proper election, all shareholders must consent to the election, and the filing must be timely and proper. Once an election occurs, renewals are unnecessary; S status remains in effect as long as none of the events that can trigger loss of the status occurs.

DISREGARDING THE CORPORATE ENTITY

We have seen that the law sometimes will recognize corporateness when incorporation has been defective. Now we will examine situations that call for disregarding the corporate entity even when compliance with the incorporation statute has occurred.

The usual rule is that the shareholders in a corporation enjoy limited liability. Because the corporation is a separate entity from the shareholders, the law normally will not be interested in who owns or runs the corporation. Sometimes, though, it will be necessary to *pierce the corporate veil* in order to serve justice. In other words, the law will ignore the shield that keeps the corporation and its shareholders' identities separate. For example, the corporate veil will be "pierced" when the corporate form is being used to defraud others or for similar illegitimate purposes. Courts may pierce the corporate veil to place liability on the shareholder who is using the corporate form without permission. Courts examine the facts closely to see if a particular situation justifies disregard of corporateness. Put another way, if the corporation is a mere "shell" or "instrumentality," or in reality is the "alter ego" of the shareholder, courts can use their powers of equity to impose liability on the controlling shareholders.

The law may impose personal liability on a shareholder, despite the fact that these are corporate liabilities. Examples include: (1) if the shareholder is the sole shareholder in an association that is so thinly capitalized initially that it cannot reasonably meet its obligations; or (2) if the shareholder is draining off the corporation's assets for his or her own personal use. If the shareholder instead can reasonably meet his or her personal obligations and does not drain off corporate assets, he or she will achieve limited liability. In this case, there will be no personal liability. This is not to say that "one-person" corporations are always candidates for disregarding corporate entity—quite the contrary. The usual rule is that the law will not disregard corporateness if there has been no domination by the shareholder for an improper purpose (such as fraud or evasion of obligations) with resultant injury to the corporation, third parties, or the public at large. Courts will uphold corporateness as long as the controlling shareholder keeps corporate affairs and transactions separate from personal transactions; adequately capitalizes the business initially and forgoes the draining off of corporate assets; incorporates for legitimate reasons (tax savings, limitation of liability, and so on); and directs the policies of the corporation toward its own interests, not personal ones. These same principles, in general, apply to situations involving parent/subsidiary (i.e., affiliated) companies, which also poses problems of whether corporateness should be retained or disregarded. Case 34.2 involved a parent/subsidiary situation. Exhibit 34.3 illustrates these points.

E X H I B I T 34.3 | **Piercing the Corporate Veil**

CORPORATE VEIL
[Represents limitation of liability of corporate shareholders
for corporate debts to the shareholders' investment
(i.e., shares of stock) in corporation]

Corporate Creditors → Corporate Assets →

Stockholders of corporation and their personal assets

Factors for a Court's Disregarding the Corporate Entity:

1. Corporation mere "alter ego" of shareholder(s).
2. Nonseparation of corporation and personal affairs (i.e., nonobservance of corporation formalities and/or commingling of shareholders' personal assets with corporate assets.)
3. Inadequate initial financing of corporation.
4. "Draining"/"milking" the corporation (or subsidiary) for shareholders' (or parent corporation's) sake.
5. Policies of corporation dominated by desire to serve shareholders' interests, not corporation's.
6. Use of corporate form for fraud or other illegitimate purposes or reasons resulting in injury to the corporation, third parties, or the public.

Stockholders' (or parent corporation's) personal assets reached by corporate creditors owing to court's piercing of corporate veil

Note how the U.S. Supreme Court compared the concepts of piercing the corporate veil with direct liability under the Comprehensive Environmental Response, Compensation, and Liability Act of 1980 (CERCLA) in the following case.

34.2

UNITED STATES V. BESTFOODS
524 U.S. 51 (1998)

FACTS The United States brought this action for the costs of cleaning up industrial waste generated by a chemical plant . . . under . . . [CERCLA]. . . . Ott Chemical Co. (Ott I) began manufacturing chemicals at a plant near Muskegon, Michigan, and its intentional and unintentional dumping of hazardous substances significantly polluted the soil and ground water . . . CPC International Inc.[26] incorporated a wholly owned subsidiary to buy Ott I's assets in exchange for CPC stock. The new company, also dubbed Ott Chemical Co. (Ott II), continued chemical manufacturing . . . and continued to pollute its surroundings. CPC kept the managers of Ott I . . . on board as officers of Ott II. . . . [S]everal . . . Ott II officers and directors were also given positions at CPC, and they performed duties for both corporations. . . .

By 1981, the federal Environmental Protection Agency had undertaken to see the site cleaned up, and its . . . plan called for expenditures well into the tens of millions of dollars. . . . [T]he United States filed this action . . . (By that time, Ott I and Ott II were defunct.) . . . [T]he parties stipulated that the Muskegon plant was a "facility" within the meaning of . . . [CERCLA], that hazardous substances had been released at the facility, and that the United States had incurred reimbursable . . . costs to clean up the site. . . . We granted certiorari to resolve a conflict among the Circuits over the extent to which parent corporations may be held liable under CERCLA for operating facilities ostensibly under the control of their subsidiaries. . . .

ISSUE May a parent corporation be held liable for a polluting facility owned or operated by the subsidiary?

HOLDING No, a parent corporation will not be liable unless the corporate veil may be pierced. However, a corporate parent that actively participated in, and exercised control over, the operations of the facility itself may also be held directly liable under CERCLA as an operator of the facility.

REASONING It is a general principle of corporate law . . . that a parent corporation (so-called because of control through ownership of another corporation's stock) is not liable for the acts of its subsidiaries. . . . Thus . . . "the exercise of the 'control' which stock ownership gives to the stockholders . . . will not create liability beyond the assets of the subsidiary. That 'control' includes the election of directors, the making of by-laws . . . and the doing of all other acts incident to the legal status of stockholders. Nor will a duplication of some or all of the directors or executive officers be fatal." . . . [T]here is an equally fundamental principle of corporate law, . . . that the corporate veil may be pierced and the shareholder held liable for the corporation's conduct when, . . . the corporate form would otherwise be misused to accomplish certain wrongful purposes . . . on the shareholder's behalf. . . . Nothing in CERCLA purports to rewrite this well-settled rule. . . .

CERCLA liability may turn on operation as well as ownership, and nothing in the statute's terms bars a parent corporation from direct liability for its own actions in operating a facility owned by its subsidiary. . . . In such instances, the parent is directly liable for its own actions. . . . [W]hereas the rules of veil-piercing limit derivative liability for the actions of another corporation, CERCLA's "operator" provision is concerned primarily with direct liability for one's own actions. . . . It is this direct liability that is properly . . . at issue here. Under the . . . language of the statute, any person who operates a polluting facility is directly liable for the costs of cleaning up the pollution. This is so regardless of whether that person is the facility's owner, the owner's parent corporation or business partner . . . [T]he difficulty comes in defining actions sufficient to constitute direct parental "operation." . . . To sharpen the definition for purposes of CERCLA . . . , an operator must manage, direct, or conduct operations specifically related to pollution, that is, operations having to do with the leakage or disposal of hazardous waste, or decisions about compliance with environmental regulations. . . . "The

continued

34.2

UNITED STATES V. BESTFOODS, *continued*

524 U.S. 51 (1998)

question is not whether the parent operates the *subsidiary,* but rather whether it operates the *facility,* and that operation is evidenced by participation in the activities of the facility. . . . Control of the subsidiary, if extensive enough, gives rise to indirect liability under piercing doctrine, not direct liability under the statutory language." . . . The analysis should . . . have rested on the relationship between CPC and the Muskegon facility itself. . . . "[I]t is entirely appropriate for directors of a parent corporation to serve as directors of its subsidiary, and that fact alone may not serve to expose the parent corporation to liability for its subsidiary's acts." . . . [D]irectors and officers holding positions with a parent and its subsidiary can and do "change hats" to represent the two corporations separately, despite their common ownership. . . . The Government would have to show that, despite the . . . presumption to the contrary, the officers and directors were acting in their capacities as CPC officers and directors, and not as Ott II officers and directors, when they committed those acts. . . . [T]he statute . . . must be read to contemplate "operation" as including the exercise of direction over the facility's activities. . . . Yet another possibility . . . is that an agent of the parent with no hat to wear but the parent's hat might manage or direct activities at the facility.

. . . [T]he acts of direct operation that give rise to parental liability must necessarily be distinguished from the interference that stems from the normal relationship between parent and subsidiary. Again norms of corporate behavior . . . are crucial reference points. . . . "Activities that involve the facility but which are consistent with the parent's investor status, such as monitoring of the subsidiary's performance, supervision of the subsidiary's finance and capital budget decisions, and articulation of general policies and procedures, should not give rise to direct liability." The critical question is whether, in degree and detail, actions directed to the facility by an agent of the parent alone are eccentric under accepted norms of parental oversight of a subsidiary's facility. There is . . . some evidence that CPC engaged in just this type and degree of activity at the Muskegon plant. . . . G. R. D. Williams worked only for CPC . . . and thus, his actions were of necessity taken only on behalf of CPC. . . . " He "actively participated in and exerted control over a variety of Ott II environmental matters," and he "issued directives. . . . " We think that these findings are enough to raise an issue of CPC's operation of the facility through Williams's actions . . . .

BUSINESS CONSIDERATION What should a business do to avoid responsibility for a wholly owned subsidiary?

ETHICAL CONSIDERATION Should CPC be responsible for the expenses since it benefited from Ott's activities?

LIMITED LIABILITY COMPANIES

Limited liability companies (LLCs) and limited liability partnerships are hybrid forms of business organizations. The state enabling statute that allows LLPs is often the same state statute that authorizes LLCs. In addition to the usual concerns about whether the enterprise will be financially successful, additional uncertainties arise with the LLC form of business organization. There are concerns about both federal and state tax structures. Will the LLC be taxed in the manner expected and desired by the investor? The conclusion depends on the state statute, the articles of organization, and any Revenue Rulings or private letter rulings of the Internal Revenue Service (IRS). In general, businesspeople need to remember that state statutes vary and what is true of New York LLCs may not be true of Florida LLCs. Some states allow for much flexibility while others are more restrictive.

History of Limited Liability Companies

The first LLC statute was enacted in Wyoming in 1977. After enacting the statute, however, a number of questions arose about the federal income tax treatment of an LLC and how sister states would treat Wyoming LLCs. Florida adopted the next LLC statute in 1982, primarily to attract foreign capital to the state.[27] Colorado and Kansas followed in 1990. Now approximately 40 states have adopted LLC acts, 10 of these in 1993.[28] In addition, some states recognize out-of-state LLCs or permit registration of foreign LLCs.[29] For example, the California Franchise Tax Board recognizes out-of-state LLCs, and Mississippi allows the registration of foreign LLCs.

The purpose of limited liability companies is to provide limited liability for all investors, who are called members. (Limited liability connotes that investors may lose their investments in the enterprise, but not their personal assets.) No need exists for a general partner. LLCs have an advantage over limited partnerships in this regard: A limited partnership must have at least one general partner who is personally liable for the partnership's debts. With an LLC, each member's liability is limited to his or her capital investment. Many state statutes require LLCs to file articles of organization with the state similar to the articles of incorporation filed by corporations. There are generally no limitations on who may become a member of an LLC, as opposed to Subchapter S corporations, which have a number of restrictions on who may be a shareholder.

LLCs are based on state statutes, so the provisions vary from state to state. Generally, the statutes dictate the following characteristics:

1. The LLC must be formed by two or more members.
2. The LLC must have a stated term of duration not to exceed 30 years.
3. All members of the LLC must have limited liability to the extent of their invested capital plus any additional capital contribution contractually promised by the members.
4. The LLC members' shares are not freely transferable. (Due to this requirement, LLCs are not appropriate where a large number of investors are anticipated.)
5. The central management must be elected by the members.

The statutes also require that the entity indicate in its name that it is an LLC. Most states require the use of "limited liability company," "limited company," "L.L.C.," or "L.C." in the title.

Most states require the following information in the LLC's articles of organization:

1. Name
2. Duration
3. Purpose
4. Address of the initial registered office and the name of the initial registered agent at that address
5. Statement that the LLC is to be managed by a manager or managers or a statement that it will be managed by the members
6. Name and address of each initial manager or managers, if applicable, or each initial member
7. Name and address of each organizer (Organizers serve the role of promoters in LLCs.)

The articles of organization must be filed with the state. Often the filing fee is less for articles of organization than it is for articles of incorporation. For example, Texas charges $300 to file articles of incorporation, but only $200 for articles of organization.[30]

Taxation of Limited Liability Companies

LLCs are not automatically treated as partnerships. Federal tax law is not controlled by the label the parties attach to the enterprise. Rather, the IRS examines whether the enterprise has the characteristics of a corporation or not. Section 301.7701-1(b) of the IRS Procedure and Administration Regulations divides organizations into categories for purposes of taxation; these categories include corporations, partnerships, and trusts.

34.3 | FINANCE

CALL-IMAGE TECHNOLOGY

LIMITED LIABILITY WITHOUT DOUBLE TAXATION

Tom and Anna Kochanowski have decided to incorporate CIT in order to take advantage of the protections of limited liability that incorporation provides, among other reasons. John, however, is concerned that the firm will face "double taxation" if it incorporates. He knows that other methods of organization exist whereby CIT can gain limited liability but not be subject to double taxation. He is unsure what those methods are, however, or how CIT could organize under one of them. John asks you what methods are available for organizing the business with limited liability for the family but without double taxation. What will you tell him?

BUSINESS CONSIDERATIONS What factors need to be considered by a group of people before they decide on the appropriate form of business organization? Is there a single best form for businesses?

ETHICAL CONSIDERATIONS What is the ethical duty of a business in regard to the tax code? Is it ethical to select a particular form of organization to avoid or reduce taxation?

Under the federal tax law, there is no question that an LLC is an association, which is a nontechnical term. An association must bear a resemblance to a corporation in order to be taxed as a corporation under federal tax law.[31] The law then prescribes the characteristics of a corporation; it must have the following:

1. Associates
2. An intent to conduct a business for profit and to divide those profits
3. Continuity of life
4. Centralization of management functions
5. Liability for business debts limited to business assets
6. Free transferability of investors' interests[32]

The IRS Regulations (in § 301.7701-2(a)(2)) provide that characteristics common to both corporations and partnerships are not material in making the distinction. Since the first two characteristics exist in all business organizations, attention focuses on the latter four. "[I]f an unincorporated organization possesses more corporate characteristics than noncorporate characteristics, it constitutes an association taxable as a corporation."[33]

The exact interpretation is left to the courts, the Department of the Treasury, and the IRS. In determining the characteristics of the LLC, reliance is placed on the LLC's articles of organization and the applicable state's statute. Generally, most members hope that the LLC has the income pass-through characteristics of partnerships. However, the desire for partnership tax treatment may not be universal. Individual and corporate tax rates are progressive at the federal level and under most state laws. In some instances, less taxation is owed if the entity is taxed at the corporate rates. This is especially true if the entity is retaining net profits and not distributing them. This aspect of tax planning should not be overlooked.

Obviously, states are not empowered to enact federal tax laws. It is likely that the IRS and the courts will decide that partnership taxation is appropriate if the LLC lacks two of the following: continuity of life, centralized management, and/or transferability of shares. Always remember that an LLC will not automatically qualify for partnership taxation.

Flexibility and Variance

LLC statutes vary from state to state. One characteristic on which LLC statutes vary is whether professional services associations can form an LLC.[34] Many states will not permit an LLC to continue in perpetuity as a corporation can. Most LLC statutes or the LLC articles greatly restrict the transferability of shares.[35] Some states, including Idaho, Missouri, Arkansas, North Carolina, Colorado, and Texas,[36] allow one person to form an LLC.[37] Another unresolved issue is whether the selling of LLC interests falls under the applicable state and/or federal securities laws. The Securities and Exchange Commission's position appears to be that LLCs consisting of a large number of members are required to file under the 1933 and 1934 securities statutes. One factor in the determination is whether the members actually manage the enterprise or whether the entity uses centralized managers. A corporation can become a member in many states, which differs from a Subchapter S corporation. It has also been suggested that members in an LLC can distribute profits and losses in different proportions than the membership interests. For example, four members with a 25 percent interest each could agree to give one member 50 percent of the profits and losses.[38]

The NCCUSL has drafted a Uniform Limited Liability Company Act, which was approved by the Commissioners on 4 August 1994.[39] In addition, there is a Prototype Limited Liability Company Act issued by a committee of the American Bar Association Section on Business Law. Most states have already enacted their own particular version of an LLC-enabling statute.[40] However, uniform legislation may be slowly adopted by the states.

The court in the following case analyzed the characteristics of a Delaware LLC.

34.3

EXCHANGE POINT LLC
V. UNITED STATES SECURITIES AND EXCHANGE COMMISSION
1999 U.S. DIST. LEXIS 8766 (S.DIST.N.Y. 1999)

FACTS Exchange Point LLC ("Exchange Point" or "Movant") moves the Court to quash or modify a subpoena issued by the Securities and Exchange Commission ("SEC") on First Union National Bank ("First Union") with respect to Exchange Point's bank account. . . . Exchange Point is a single member limited liability company organized under Delaware law. Alon Moussaief is the sole owner and president of Exchange Point. Exchange Point . . . operates as a conduit firm in . . . check cashing for Israeli clients. . . . [A] person in Israel will cash a check at one of Exchange Point's Israeli affiliate's offices, and the Israeli affiliate will forward the check to Exchange Point's U.S. office. The check will then be cleared by means of Exchange Point's bank account at First Union. Exchange Point also has engaged in wire transfers for customers. . . . The SEC's investigation involves allegations that certain entities may have manipulated the prices of certain securities in a scheme to defraud investors. The SEC has information that certain funds may have been wired through Exchange Point's account at First Union. . . . [T]he SEC has issued a subpoena duces tecum (the "Subpoena") on First Union. . . .

continued

34.3

EXCHANGE POINT LLC
V. UNITED STATES SECURITIES AND EXCHANGE COMMISSION, *continued*

1999 U.S. DIST. LEXIS 8766 (S.DIST.N.Y. 1999)

ISSUE Is Movant a "person" under the RFPA [Right to Financial Privacy Act of 1978] with standing to object to the Subpoena?

HOLDING No. Movant, as a limited liability company, is not a person as defined by the RFPA and does not have standing to object.

REASONING A "customer" of a financial institution may object to a government subpoena of bank records to that institution under . . . RFPA. A "customer" is defined under . . . RFPA as "any person or authorized representative of that person who utilized or is utilizing any service of a financial institution." A "person" is defined in . . . RFPA as "an individual or a partnership of five or fewer individuals." . . . An LLC under Delaware law is similar to a limited partnership:

> *The Delaware Limited Liability Company Act (Act) . . . is modeled on Delaware's . . . limited partnership statute. Rather than having general partners and limited partners as a limited partnership does . . . , the owners of a Delaware LLC are designated as members. The management of an LLC may be vested in its members or in a manager or managers selected by the members or in a combination of members and managers. A manager of an LLC need not be a member. A member is treated under the Act in many ways similar to the way a limited partner is treated under the limited partnership statute. A manager of an LLC, to the extent one is selected, is treated similarly under the Act as a general partner is treated under the limited partnership statute, except that a manager does not have general liability. . . .*

Additionally, a member of an LLC is not subject to the same risks that he or she may become liable for the company's debt:

> *A significant advantage of an LLC as an alternative form of business entity is that the members and managers have limited liability to third parties. The Act provides that the debts, obligations and liabilities of a Delaware LLC, whether arising in contract, tort or otherwise, shall be solely the debts, obligations and liabilities of the Delaware LLC as an entity. . . . [T]he Act provides that no member or manager shall be obligated personally for any debt, obligation or liability of a Delaware LLC solely [by reason of] being a member or acting as a manager. In contrast to a limited partner in a limited partnership, the limitation on the liability of a member is not jeopardized, in fact or in theory, when the member participates in the management or control of the business of a Delaware LLC.*

Both parties agree that whether Exchange Point has standing under the RFPA is an issue of first impression. . . . [A] "person" who may qualify as a customer under the RFPA is defined as "an individual or a partnership of five or fewer individuals." Because a sole proprietorship is basically a "partnership of one," courts have considered it a person under the RFPA and a sole proprietorship . . . has been found to have standing to challenge a government subpoena of financial records. Similarly, courts have found that a limited partnership, under . . . RFPA . . . is included under the term "partnership" and is entitled to standing if it has fewer than 5 partners. A corporation . . . is "unambiguously" not included in the definition of a person under the RFPA and is not entitled to challenge a subpoena or seek reimbursement under the statute. Nor are the protections of the RFPA available to a partnership with one or more corporate partners; a trust; or an employee benefit plan. . . . Because the RFPA's definition of person is not ambiguous, the Court must apply its plain, ordinary meaning. "A definition which declares what a term means excludes any meaning that is not stated." . . . Here, a limited liability company is plainly not covered by the plain meaning of the words "individual or a partnership of less than five individuals." . . . [T]he Court notes a key difference between an LLC and all of the entities that have been held to be persons under the RFPA: an LLC need not have any member or manager that is liable for the debts of the company, even in the case of a wholly owned LLC with only one member-manager. . . . Exchange Point is much more similar to a wholly owned corporation with one shareholder than a partnership or sole proprietorship. . . . [As stated by a Delaware superior court:]

> *Although the statute treats an LLC as a partnership for federal income tax purposes, an LLC is largely a creature of contract . . . An LLC . . . constitutes a separate legal entity . . . [and] the interest of*

34.3

EXCHANGE POINT LLC
V. UNITED STATES SECURITIES AND EXCHANGE COMMISSION, *continued*
1999 U.S. DIST. LEXIS 8766 (S.DIST.N.Y. 1999)

a member in the LLC is analogous to shareholders of a corporation. A member usually contributes personal property and has no interest in specific assets owned by the LLC . . . [A] member or manager of an LLC cannot be held liable for the company's debts or obligations above his or her contribution to the company. . . . The Court finds these aspects of the LLC constitute a distinct, but artificial entity under Delaware law.

"The primary purpose of the [RFPA] is to protect the privacy rights of individuals and small partnerships." . . .

BUSINESS CONSIDERATIONS Is client privacy important in Exchange Point's type of business? In what types of business is client privacy important? Should Exchange Point protect client privacy even when the client(s) may have violated the law?

ETHICAL CONSIDERATIONS Is it ethical for Exchange Point to try to protect clients who may have violated the law? Is the manipulation of stock prices unethical or just illegal?

OTHER TYPES OF BUSINESS ORGANIZATIONS

Three other types of business organizations exist that are very similar to partnerships, yet qualify as their own business forms: partnerships by estoppel, joint ventures, and **mining partnerships.**

Partnerships by Estoppel

Technically, no partnership can exist without an agreement. A third person who is dealing with someone who *claims* to be a partner but is not, however, may be able to proceed against the partnership and/or the alleged partner. Such a situation may lead to a partnership by **estoppel.** To use estoppel, three facts must be shown:

1. Someone who is not a partner was held out to be a partner by the firm.
2. The third person justifiably relied on the holding out.
3. The person will be harmed if no liability is imposed.

> **Mining partnership**
> An association of several owners of a mine for cooperation in working the mine.

> **Estoppel**
> A legal bar or impediment that prevents a person from claiming or denying certain facts as a result of his or her previous conduct.

Joint Ventures

A *joint venture* has all the characteristics of a partnership except one. It is not set up to "carry on a business." A joint venture, by definition, is established to carry out a limited number of transactions, very commonly a single deal. As soon as that deal (or those transactions) is completed, the joint venture terminates. Why is this form important? The agency power in a joint venture is limited; thus, a member of the venture is less likely to be held responsible for the conduct of the other members of the venture. Also, the death of a joint venturer does not automatically dissolve the joint venture. In all other respects, partnership law is applicable.

Mining Partnerships

A *mining partnership* is a uniquely American creation. It is a partnership, but it has special characteristics not found in a nonmining partnership. In a regular

RESOURCES FOR BUSINESS LAW STUDENTS

NAME	RESOURCES	WEB ADDRESS
U.S. Small Business Administration (SBA)	The SBA provides information and materials, such as forms, software, and publications, to help start, finance, and expand a business.	**http://www.sba.gov/**
Internal Revenue Service (IRS)	The IRS and its publication the *Digital Daily* provide tax advice and information on a variety of issues, including business formation issues.	**http://www.irs.ustreas.gov/**
Code of Hammurabi	The Yale Law School maintains a hypertext version of the legal code of Hammurabi.	**http://www.yale.edu/lawweb/avalon/hamframe.htm**
National Conference of Commissioners on Uniform State Laws (NCCUSL).	The NCCUSL provides summaries of uniform acts, states of adoption, drafting projects, topics under discussion, and information about the organization and its history.	**http://www.nccusl.org**
University of Pennsylvania	The University of Pennsylvania Law School maintains the NCCUSL archives. Its web site provides the full text of uniform acts and model acts.	**http://www.law.upenn.edu/bll/ulc/ulc_frame.htm**

partnership, a partner cannot sell his or her interest or leave the interest to his or her heirs in a will. In a mining partnership, however, the selling of an interest or the bequeathing of an interest by will is permitted.

One theory about how this special treatment evolved is that during the California gold rush, after partners discovered gold, one partner would suddenly and "mysteriously" have a fatal accident that left the mine to the surviving partner. In an effort to extend the life span of successful miners, mining partnership laws were developed. The death of a partner merely brought another partner, the deceased partner's heir, into the business. Thus, no advantage was gained by the death of a partner.

SUMMARY

Every business enterprise must have an organizational form, choosing among a proprietorship, a partnership, a limited partnership, an LLP, an LLC, and a corporate form. Partnerships fall between the two extremes of organizational form—that is, proprietorships and corporations. A partnership has the advantages of being easily formed and of having multiple contributors, whose different opinions and expertise are always available. A partnership also has the disadvantages of somewhat limited existence and unlimited personal liability for each general partner. A partnership is defined in the Uniform Partnership Act as an association of two or more persons carrying on a business as co-owners for profit. This definition requires that the partners voluntarily agree to enter the business and that the business be somewhat permanent in nature. Co-ownership is the key element of the definition. This element is so important that a sharing of profits by the people involved creates a presumption of co-ownership, which, in turn, creates a presumption that a partnership exists.

A limited partnership is similar to a regular, or general, partnership with two major exceptions: There must be at least one limited partner who may not participate in the management of the business, and somewhat formal documents must be prepared and correctly filed in order to establish the limited partnership. A general partner is also required.

A limited liability partnership is a relatively new development. In this type of partnership, a partner is personally liable for his or her own wrongs and for the wrongs of people he or she supervises. A partner will not be personally liable for the wrongs of other partners.

A corporation is an artificial entity created by the state and endowed with certain powers by the state. The historical development of corporations illustrates an acceptance of the "entity" theory of corporations—that is, that the corporation is an entity separate and distinct from its shareholders. As a business form, corporations have the advantages of limited liability, centralization of management functions, continuity of existence, free transferability of shares, and sometimes favorable tax treatment. There are various types of for-profit corporations: public-issue private corporations, close corporations, professional corporations, public corporations, and quasi-public corporations. Nonprofit corporations exist in all jurisdictions as well.

The filing of the articles of incorporation signals the corporation's official beginning, but some jurisdictions require the issuance of a certificate of incorporation or an organizational meeting before the corporation can attain corporate status. In general, corporate status will not be lost if substantial compliance with incorporation statutes occurs; courts will view the entity as a de jure (legal) corporation. Courts will even grant de facto (in fact, but not in law) corporations corporate status on the fulfillment of certain requirements. In some jurisdictions, the issuance of a certificate of incorporation by the state eliminates the need to resort to the de facto doctrine. This development actually represents the modern trend: to presume de jure status in such circumstances, except in actions brought by the state.

Corporations enjoy certain express and implied powers. Years ago, courts held that corporations were not responsible for ultra vires acts (those beyond the power of the corporation), but the law now limits the application of this doctrine to a few specialized situations.

At times, courts will disregard corporate status even when complete compliance with the state statute has taken place. "Piercing the corporate veil" in order to impose personal liability on a shareholder will occur when the corporation becomes the means for furthering illegitimate ends.

Limited liability corporations (LLCs) have a number of advantages over the older forms of business. The LLC can be a hybrid of the generally favorable features of partnerships and corporations. Whether it is successful will depend on the provisions of the state statute, the articles of organization, and the federal and state tax codes. Generally, the formation of the LLC is an attempt to provide for tax consequences, including both income and active losses, only in the hands of the ultimate recipient, and to insulate personal assets from the LLC's debts. Many state statutes restrict the transferability of LLC shares and limit the life of the organization.

Extreme care must be used in establishing an LLC. Members must conform to the applicable state statute. Many states seem to follow the federal tax rules for determining tax treatment, which look to the entity's characteristics, while some have not specifically addressed the issue. For federal tax purposes, it is important to structure the LLC so that it complies with the IRS Regulations and Revenue Rulings.

There are three additional forms of business operation. The first is *partnership by estoppel*, where there is no partnership agreement, but the parties act as if there were an agreement, to the detriment of some third party. The other two types of organizations are joint ventures and mining partnerships. Both have special rules that separate them from ordinary general partnerships.

DISCUSSION QUESTIONS

1. Bob, Carol, and Ted set up a partnership. Later, Bob and Ted want to bring in Alice as a fourth partner. Carol, however, objects to allowing Alice to enter. A vote is taken, and Alice receives two votes of approval and one of disapproval. Will Alice be admitted as a fourth partner? Explain your answer.
2. Ed, Tim, and Dennis have a business concept they are sure will succeed if they can establish it properly. Unfortunately, they are short of capital and cannot afford to begin the business without financial support. Marge is willing to put up the necessary capital, but she is unwilling to face the liability of a general partner. Therefore, Marge agrees to be a limited partner in the business. What must the parties do to establish a limited partnership under the RULPA?
3. Larry and Darrin form a partnership. Darrin contributes $10,000. Larry lets the partnership use an office building he owns, rent free. Three years later, the business dissolves. Darrin claims the building is partnership property. Larry claims he still owns the building personally. Who is correct, and why?
4. Sam and Ruth enter a partnership, but Sam does not want Ruth to be his agent or to participate in managing the business. What should he do to see that his wishes are carried out?

5. Mohamed and Eliza are partners. In order to get a loan, they tell the bank that Denise is also a partner. Relying on Denise's credit, the bank makes the loan. Mohamed and Eliza default, and the bank sues Denise. What must the bank prove in order to hold Denise liable for the loan?
6. Name five advantages of corporations as business associations.
7. How does a *de jure* corporation differ from a *de facto* corporation? What requirements are necessary for a corporation to acquire de facto status?
8. Jesse, José, and Esmeralda want to form a limited liability company that will be taxed as a partnership. What type of taxation do they desire? What provisions should they include in their articles of organization to help assure taxation as a partnership?
9. Assume that Tom and Anna Kochanowksi have decided to incorporate CIT to protect their personal assets. What must they do to avoid having the corporate veil pierced? What advice and guidelines can you provide them?
10. Discuss the express and implied powers of corporations. What is the *ultra vires doctrine,* and what are the circumstances in which it may be applied?

CASE PROBLEMS AND WRITING ASSIGNMENTS

1. Three sisters, Louise W. Veal, LaWanda W. Davis, and Lynn W. Martin, agreed to purchase and operate a farm together. The sisters had other jobs, so they did not operate the farm themselves. None of them lived on the farm. The sisters agreed to split the profits from the farm. There is no partnership agreement. Did the three sisters form a partnership? Why or why not? [See *In re LLL Farms*, 111 B.R. 1016 (Bankr. M.D. Ga. 1990).]

2. Robert Edward Pitman was a limited partner in Ramsey Homebuilders. Michael C. Ramsey was the sole

general partner; however, he had a poor credit history. Consequently, Ramsey was unable to borrow the money or obtain the credit needed to sustain the partnership's business. Pitman secured a partnership account with Flanagan Lumber Company through Flanagan's credit manager. When the partnership failed to pay its debts, Flanagan sued Pitman. Pitman claimed that he was a limited partner and was not liable for partnership debts. Should Pitman be held liable? Why or why not? [See *Pitman* v. *Flanagan Lumber Co.,* 567 So.2d 1335 (Ala. 1990).]

3. Lincoln M. Polan formed a corporation entitled Industrial Realty Company. Polan was the sole shareholder. The state issued a certificate of incorporation. However, the corporation never held an organizational meeting; no officers were elected; no stocks were issued; and no payments were made to the corporation for stock. The corporation failed to observe other corporate formalities as well. Polan, acting for the corporation, signed a lease for commercial space in a building controlled by Kinney Shoe Corp. The first rental payment was made by Polan from his personal funds. No further rental payments were made. Kinney obtained a court judgment against the corporation for $66,400 in unpaid rent. When the corporation did not pay, Kinney filed suit against Polan individually. Should the court pierce the corporate veil? Why or why not? [See *Kinney Shoe Corp.* v. *Polan*, 939 F.2d 209 (4th Cir. 1991).]

4. Civil penalties of $90,350 were assessed against WRW Corporation (WRW) for violating safety standards under the Federal Mine Safety and Health Act. The violations had resulted in the deaths of two miners. WRW then liquidated its assets and went out of business. Roger Richardson, Noah Woolum, and William Woolum were the sole shareholders, officers, and directors of WRW. The three were later indicted and convicted of willful violations under the act and were sentenced to prison and paid criminal fines. The United States brought a lawsuit against WRW and the three men to recover the civil penalties previously assessed. Should the corporate veil be pierced and the three individuals be held liable for the civil penalty? Why or why not? [See *United States* v. *WRW Corporation*, 986 F.2d 138 (6th Cir. 1993).]

5. More than a decade after initiating action, Robert Evans, a subcontractor, on 9 August 1978 won a judgment of $124,176.45 against Multicon Construction Corporation (MCC). By that time, MCC, an Ohio corporation, had ceased doing business in Massachusetts and, if it existed at all, was an empty shell. Evans, therefore, sought alternative sources of recovery by invoking Rule 69 of the Massachusetts Rules of Civil Procedure, which makes available postjudgment discovery and equips the court with "all the traditional flexibility of a court of equity," including enforcement of orders of the court against persons who may not originally have been parties. Under Rule 69, Evans argued that MCC had been a sham corporation functioning as a front for John W. Kessler and Peter H. Edwards, the individuals who had organized MCC. Evans claimed that the factors typically utilized in piercing the corporate veil justified a court's holding Edwards and Kessler personally liable for the judg-

ment that Evans had won against MCC. Should a court pierce the corporate veil to hold the officers of MCC personally liable? [See *Evans* v. *Multicon Construction Corporation*, 574 N.E.2d 395 (Mass.App. 1991).]

6. **BUSINESS APPLICATION CASE** Samuel Shaw took a Delta flight to Salt Lake City and then connected with a SkyWest flight from Salt Lake City to Elko, Nevada. The SkyWest flight crashed just before landing in Elko, seriously injuring Shaw. Shaw sued Delta, claiming that Delta was SkyWest's partner. Delta had a contract with SkyWest, under which Delta served as SkyWest's ticketing and marketing agent. Was there a partnership between Delta and SkyWest? Why or why not? What could Delta do to avoid these claims in the future? [See *Shaw* v. *Delta Airlines, Inc.*, 798 F.Supp. 1453 (D.Nev. 1992).]

7. **ETHICAL APPLICATION CASE** McElfish was the president and a primary stockholder of Gags Enterprises, Inc. Gags owned the Sandspur Bar in Melbourne, Florida. The bar had a studio apartment attached to the back, which was occupied at various times by McElfish, who acted as the bar's manager. As he had done on other occasions, McElfish invited Schroeder to go with him to a party at another lounge in Melbourne to assist him in entertaining business clients. After the party, they returned to the apartment at the Sandspur. An argument arose between them that resulted in McElfish's inflicting numerous personal injuries on Schroeder. McElfish explained that he had been trying to remove Schroeder from the premises because she was rowdy and intoxicated and that he had wanted to lock up the bar for the evening. Should Gags be liable for the $31,500 in compensatory damages and $30,000 in punitive damages awarded by the jury to Schroeder? Why? What ethical issues are raised by this lawsuit? Explain. [See *Kent Ins. Co.* v. *Schroeder*, 469 So.2d 209 (Fla.App. 1985).]

8. **CRITICAL THINKING CASE** Petrogradsky, a Russian bank, sued a New York bank for a $66,749.45 balance standing to its credit. In 1917, as a result of the Bolshevik Revolution, the Russian bank's assets had been confiscated and its stock canceled. On this basis, the New York bank argued that the Russian bank, as a corporation, had been dissolved and no longer was a juristic (legal) person. Therefore, the New York bank had refused to pay the credit balance. Had the Russian bank ceased to exist as a legal person? [See *Petrogradsky Mejdunarodny Kommerchesky Bank* v. *National City Bank of New York*, 170 N.E. 479 (N.Y. 1930), Cert. Den. 282 U.S. 878 (1930).]

NOTES

1. Officially, this is the UPA (1914).
2. The NCCUSL made the Revised Uniform Partnership Act available in 1992. It is not officially called the Revised Uniform Partnership Act or RUPA; officially, it is the Uniform Partnership Act or UPA (1992). Unofficially, it is called RUPA, even by the NCCUSL. We will use the standard nomenclature and call it RUPA. It was further amended by the commissioners in 1993 and 1994; in 1994, they released UPA (1994), which is basically the 1992 version with the 1993 and 1994 amendments.
3. The following states have adopted the RUPA (1992) (1994): Connecticut, Florida, West Virginia, and Wyoming. See "A Few Facts About the Uniform Partnership Act (1994)(1997)," NCCUSL web site, http://www.nccusl.org/uniformact_factsheets/uniforma-cts-fs-upa9497.htm.
4. Ibid. The following states have adopted the RUPA with the 1997 amendments: Alabama, Arizona, Arkansas, California, Colorado, District of Columbia, Hawaii, Idaho, Iowa, Kansas, Maryland, Minnesota, Montana, Nebraska, New Mexico, North Dakota, Oklahoma, Oregon, Puerto Rico, U.S. Virgin Islands, Vermont, Virginia, and Washington.
5. See "Revised Uniform Partnership Act Reflects Modern Business Practices, 28 Jurisdictions Have Now Updated Venerable 80-Year-Old Partnership Law," NCCUSL web site, http://www.nccusl.org/pressreleases/pr1-00-5.htm.
6. See "Uniform Partnership Act (1994)," NCCUSL web site, http://www.nccusl.org/uniformact_summaries/uniformacts-s-upa1994.htm.
7. See "Revised Uniform Partnership Act Reflects Modern Business Practices, 28 Jurisdictions Have Now Updated Venerable 80-Year-Old Partnership Law," NCCUSL web site, http://www.nccusl.org/pressreleases/pr1-00-5.htm.
8. See "Uniform Partnership Act (1994)," NCCUSL web site, http://www.nccusl.org/uniformact_summaries/uniformacts-s-upa1994.htm.
9. Ibid.
10. The following states have adopted the ULPA (1976): California, Connecticut, Maryland, Michigan, Montana, Missouri, Nebraska, New Jersey, South Carolina, Washington, and Wyoming. See "A Few Facts About The Uniform Limited Partnership Act," NCCUSL web site, http://www.nccusl.org/uniformact_fact-sheets/uniformacts-fs-ulpa.htm.
11. Ibid. The following states have adopted ULPA with the 1985 amendments: Alabama, Alaska, Arizona, Arkansas, Colorado, Delaware, District of Columbia, Florida, Georgia, Hawaii, Idaho, Illinois, Indiana, Iowa, Kansas, Kentucky, Maine, Massachusetts, Minnesota, Mississippi, Nevada, New Hampshire, New Mexico, New York, North Carolina, North Dakota, Ohio, Oklahoma, Oregon, Pennsylvania, Rhode Island, South Dakota, Tennessee, Texas, U.S. Virgin Islands, Utah, Vermont, Virginia, West Virginia, and Wisconsin.
12. Ibid.
13. Uniform Partnership Act § 7(4).
14. Sandra Lerner is a successful entrepreneur and an experienced businessperson. She and her husband were the original founders of Cisco Systems. She received a substantial amount of money when she sold her interest in Cisco, which she invested in a venture capital limited partnership called "& Capital Partners."
15. RUPA § 16202, subd. (c)(3).
16. Uniform Partnership Act § 303.
17. See "Revised Uniform Limited Partnership Act, A Summary," NCCUSL web site, http://www.nccusl.org/uniformact_summaries/uniformacts-s-llpt97attupa1994.htm.
18. Ibid.
19. See NCCUSL web site, "Revised Uniform Partnership Act Reflects Modern Business Practices, 28 Jurisdictions Have Now Updated Venerable 80-year-old Partnership Law," http://www.nccusl.org/pressreleases/pr1-00-5.htm.
20. See "Uniform Partnership Act (1994)," NCCUSL web site, http://www.nccusl.org/uniformact_summaries/uniformacts-s-upa1994.htm.
21. "Three Accounting Firms Now Limited Partnerships," *The Wall Street Journal* (2 August 1994), p. A8.
22. See "A Few Facts About the Uniform Partnership Act (1994)(1997)," NCCUSL web site, http://www.nccusl.org/uniformact_factsheets/uniformacts-fs-upa9497.htm. The following states have adopted the RUPA with the 1997 amendments: Alabama, Arizona, Arkansas, California, Colorado, District of Columbia, Hawaii, Idaho, Iowa, Kansas, Maryland, Minnesota, Montana, Nebraska, New Mexico, North Dakota, Oklahoma, Oregon, Puerto Rico, U.S. Virgin Islands, Vermont, Virginia, and Washington.
23. Ibid.
24. Ibid.
25. "Three Accounting Firms Now Limited Partnerships," *The Wall Street Journal* (2 August 1994), p. A8.
26. CPC has recently changed its name to Bestfoods. The court uses the name CPC throughout the opinion.
27. Carol J. Miller and Radie Bunn, "Limited Liability Companies—A Taxing Alternative." Paper presented at the annual meeting of the Academy of Legal Studies in Business, 11 August 1994.
28. G. Kent Renegar and David Kunz, "The Growth of the Limited Liability Company: Is It Warranted?" Paper

presented at the annual meeting of the Academy of Legal Studies in Business, 11 August 1994 and published in the *Proceedings of the Meeting*.

29. Ibid. The authors provide an interesting analysis of the number of LLC filings.

30. Diane M. Baldwin and Frances B. Whiteside, *Introduction to Business Organizations* (Dallas, TX: Pearson Publications), p. 112.

31. An association is broadly defined under the Internal Revenue Code. It includes any organization formed to transact specified affairs or to seek some objective. It has a representative individual or group that makes decisions for the whole, and it does not terminate with a change of membership (I.R.S. Regs. 39.3797-2).

32. Treas. Reg. § 301.7701-2(a)(1)—301.7701-4.

33. Rev. Rul. 88-76, 1988-2 C.B. 360, 1988 IRB LEXIS 3773, *4.

34. California specifically forbids LLCs from providing professional services, Cal. Corp. Code § 17000 (1996). An earlier draft, however, allowed professional limited liability companies in Chapter 9. The Uniform Limited Liability Company Act, drafted by the NCCUSL, expressly permits professional LLCs (in § 101(3)).

35. Transferability of shares is also greatly restricted in Subchapter S corporations. The Internal Revenue Code limits who may own stock in a Subchapter S corporation. The corporation, desiring to maintain Subchapter S status, will generally also have ownership restrictions, because all shareholders must agree to be treated as a Subchapter S corporation.

36. Miller and Bunn, "Limited Liability Companies."

37. Renegar and Kunz, "The Growth of the Limited Liability Company."

38. Fred S. Steingold, *The Legal Guide for Starting and Running A Small Business* (Berkeley, CA: Nolo Press 1992), p. 1/20.

39. The Uniform Limited Liability Company Act has been adopted by Alabama, Hawaii, Illinois, Montana, South Carolina, South Dakota, U.S. Virgin Islands, Vermont, and West Virginia. Information on the current status of adoptions of Uniform State Laws was provided by Katie Robinson, Public Affairs Coordinator, NCCUSL, during a telephone conversation on 20 October 1999.

40. For an analysis of the three general forms for LLCs, see Miller and Bunn, "Limited Liability Companies."

35

OPERATION OF A BUSINESS ORGANIZATION

CALL-IMAGE TECHNOLOGY

A G E N D A

The Kochanowskis are still unsure what form of business they should select for CIT. If they choose to form a partnership, who would have authority and responsibility for decisions? How much—if any—ownership should they give to their children? If they decide to incorporate, how should the corporation be structured? Obviously, it will be a for-profit enterprise, but should it be publicly owned or closely held? Should the children be given stock and titles, and, if so, what will this mean to and for them legally? If Tom and Anna decide to incorporate the business, what legal steps must they follow in managing and operating the firm? How do these steps compare to those followed in a proprietorship or a partnership? Can they be compelled to distribute profits, or can they retain the firm's earnings to help it grow?

These and other questions will arise as you read this chapter. Be prepared! You never know when one of the Kochanowskis will need your help or advice.

O U T L I N E

Operation of a Partnership
Rights of the Partners
Duties of the Partners
Rights of Third Persons Who Deal
  with Partnerships
Operation of a Corporation
Rights of the Shareholders of a Corporation

Liabilities of Shareholders
Rights and Duties of the Managers
  of a Corporation
Summary
Discussion Questions
Case Problems and Writing Assignments

OPERATION OF A PARTNERSHIP

A partner has certain rights by virtue of his or her status as a partner. These rights *may* be limited or defined by the partnership agreement, the type of partnership formed, and any statutory restrictions. If there is no agreement to limit the rights, each partner is a manager for the enterprise, an agent for every other partner, and a principal of every other partner. As a result, all the regular rules of agency apply. Each partner is a fiduciary of the other partners. When a partner deals with some third party, the firm is bound by the conduct if it was actually or apparently authorized.

RIGHTS OF THE PARTNERS

A person who enters a partnership acquires certain rights. Some of these rights are gained through the agreement, and some are gained through the terms of the Uniform Partnership Act (UPA).[1] This book cannot cover all the rights that the partners might include in the agreement, but it can examine those rights imposed by operation of law. The text will emphasize the UPA since it is still the majority rule.

Management *Know*

By virtue of his or her status as a partner, each partner is entitled to an equal voice in management. In conducting the ordinary business of the partnership, a majority vote controls. In order to conduct any extraordinary business, a unanimous vote is required.[2] A matter is considered extraordinary if it changes the basic nature or the basic risk of the business.

While the UPA requires that each partner be given an equal voice in managing the business, the partners are allowed to agree on the definition of *equal*. Such an agreement can be beneficial to a dynamic business. If the partnership is forced to conduct its business by majority vote, opportunities may be lost because a vote cannot occur quickly enough.

To avoid this problem, many partnership agreements *define* the management voice of each partner. Remember that the agreement must include such a definition to be valid. For instance, a partnership composed of A, B, C, and D might provide the following management divisions:

1. A is in charge of purchasing.
2. B is in charge of marketing.
3. C is in charge of accounting and personnel.
4. D is in charge of paper clips and office neatness.
5. Any other areas are governed by a vote.

Under such an agreement, B can make marketing decisions immediately, without needing to meet with the

35.1 | FINANCE/ MANAGEMENT

LIABILITY IN A GENERAL PARTNERSHIP

Assume that CIT is continuing to operate as a general partnership. Tom, a partner, signed a contract with a marketing consulting firm to develop a new marketing plan at a cost of $20,000. He entered this contract without consulting with the other partners in the firm, believing that the consultants he was hiring would provide a better opportunity for CIT to establish its niche in the industry. Unfortunately, when the plan is implemented, it is a disaster. Dan thinks that his father should have consulted with the family before signing the contract and asks you whether CIT and/or the other partners are liable for this contract action. What will you tell him? What is Tom's personal liability in this situation to the consulting firm and/or CIT?

BUSINESS CONSIDERATION Assume that a partnership does not want an individual partner to unilaterally enter into specialized service contracts for the firm. What should the partnership do to prevent such conduct?
ETHICAL CONSIDERATIONS Suppose that an individual partner *does* enter into a contract without consulting with his or her partners. Is it ethical for the firm to refuse to honor the contract because it was not discussed by the partners? Why or why not?

partners to vote on the issue. Likewise, A can decide matters concerning purchasing; C can make personnel decisions; and D can dust the furniture without first consulting the other partners. Absent such an agreement, each partner has a truly equal voice in management, with decisions made by majority vote.

Reimbursement

Each partner is entitled to repayment by the partnership for any money spent to further the interests of the partnership. In addition, each partner is entitled to interest on the advances or payments made, unless the agreement says otherwise. Each partner is also entitled to a return of his or her **capital contribution** at the close of the partnership, provided enough money is present to repay each partner after all liabilities have been satisfied.[3]

Capital contribution
Money or assets invested by the business owners for commencing and/or promoting an enterprise.

Profits and Losses

Unless the agreement states otherwise, each partner is entitled to an equal share of the profits of the business. The profits are not automatically divided in the same percentage as capital was contributed, nor are they automatically divided in any other unequal manner. This is the only remuneration to which any partner is always entitled.[4] No partner is automatically permitted to draw a salary from the business even if that partner devotes extra time to running the business. However, the agreement can be worded in such a manner that a partner receives a salary from the business, with the remaining profits then divided in some predetermined manner. Any salary provision for partners must be expressly set out in the agreement. Losses are divided among the partners in the same ratio as profits are shared.

Books and Records

Each partner is entitled to free access to the books and records of the business. This includes the right to inspect the records and to copy them as the partner sees fit. Similarly, each partner is expected to give, and entitled to receive, detailed information on any matter that affects the partnership.[5]

Partnership Property

Under the UPA, each partner is a co-owner of partnership property with the other partners. The ownership is defined as **tenancy in partnership.**[6] This tenancy entitles the partner to possess the property for partnership purposes but not to possess it for nonpartnership purposes. If all the partners agree to a nonpartnership usage, however, such a usage is allowed. This tenancy also carries with it a right of survivorship. This means that if a partner dies, the other *partners* own the property. It is *not* inherited by the heirs of the deceased partner if any other partners are still surviving. Thus, the last surviving partner will own the partnership property individually. The heirs of the last partner may not possess the property except for partnership purposes.

Tenancy in partnership
A special form of ownership of property, found only in partnerships, that gives each partner an equal right to possess and to use partnership assets for partnership purposes and that carries a right of survivorship.

The Revised Uniform Partnership Act (RUPA) has moved away from viewing the partnership as an aggregate of the partners to viewing it as a separate entity.[7] RUPA states simply that since a partnership is a separate entity, its property belongs to it and not to the partners.[8] A partner has his or her partnership interest, but is not a co-owner of specific partnership property.[9]

Right to an Account

Any partner is entitled to a formal *account*—that is, a statement or record of business transactions or dealings—if he or she feels mistreated in the partnership.[10] Specifically, any partner who is excluded from the business or from use of business properties is entitled to an account. And the UPA provides for an account in any other circumstances that render it just and reasonable. In effect, any time an internal argument or disagreement arises about the business operation, the courts will say an account is just and reasonable.

Each partner is a fiduciary for every other partner and is expected to account to the other partners and to the partnership for any benefits received or any profits derived without the knowledge and consent of the other partners.[11]

DUTIES OF THE PARTNERS

Agency Duties

Each partner is an *agent* of the partnership and of every other partner. Thus, any conduct by a partner that is *apparently* authorized is binding on the partnership. And because each partner is *personally* liable for partnership debts, such an act makes each partner at least *potentially* personally liable.

This obviously creates a potential financial hazard to the partners. To reduce somewhat the danger that a reckless partner can present, the UPA restricts some agency power. Under § 9(3), there is no apparent authority to do any of five specific acts unless *unanimously approved*. These five acts are as follows:

1. Making an **assignment for the benefit of creditors** by transferring partnership property to a trust for the creditors of the business
2. Selling or otherwise disposing of the **goodwill** of the business
3. Performing any act that makes it impossible to carry on the business
4. Confessing a judgment against the partnership (In this situation, *confessing a judgment* is an acknowledgment in court that the partnership is legally to blame. Standard form contracts may provide that the party contracting with the partnership has authority to confess judgment against it.)
5. Submitting a partnership claim or liability to an **arbitrator**

Notice the scope of these acts. The first three frustrate business, and the last two remove the partners' rights to their "day in court." With these five exceptions, any other act of a partner within the scope of apparent authority is binding.

For example, a partner may sell and convey real property owned in the partnership name.[12] The conveyance may be made in the business name *or in the name of the partner*. In either case, the conveyance is valid, even if unauthorized, if the grantee has passed title on to an innocent third party in a subsequent sale. If the grantee is still in possession of the property, the other partners can recover the property, provided the sale was not authorized.

Also, if a partner makes an **admission** about partnership affairs, and the admission is within the partner's authority, the partnership is bound.[13] The firm must honor the admission and uphold it if it was within the admitting partner's authority, even if it harms the business.

Since each partner is an agent, *notice* given to any partner on a partnership matter is as valid as notice given to each of the partners.[14] This is simply the

Assignment for the benefit of creditors
An assignment in trust made by debtors for the payment of their debts.

Goodwill
An intangible asset based on a firm's good reputation.

Arbitrator
An independent person chosen by the parties or appointed by statute and to whom the issues are submitted for settlement outside of court.

Admission
A statement acknowledging the truth of an allegation, and accepted in court as evidence against the party making the admission.

application of basic agency law to a partnership/agency situation. Similarly, knowledge gained, or *remembered,* while one is a partner is imputed to each partner.

If a partner acts, or fails to act, within the course and scope of the business, and the act or omission causes harm to a third person, each partner is as liable to the third person as the partner who committed the tort.[15] The partners face joint and several liability. In other words, they can be sued together or separately for the harm. Thus, the injured party might be harmed by partner A but sue only partners B and C and win the suit. In such a case, B and C must pay for the harm caused by A even though A was not named as a defendant. Again, this is merely an application of agency law principles to the partnership setting.

Likewise, if a partner *misapplies* money or property of a third person that is in the possession of the partnership, the partnership is liable. All the partners, or each of them, may need to answer for the breach of trust of one partner.[16] Again, the liability is joint and several.

Obviously, being a partner *may* be hazardous to your financial health. Even if you are a careful, cautious person, you face potential financial liability, maybe even disaster, from the conduct of your partners. What rights do you have that protect you? What rights are available for the protection of any partner from the excesses of another member of the partnership?

One such right protects the other partners and the partnership from an individual creditor of a partner. For example, assume that Ali, Bill, and Cindi are partners. The business is very profitable, and Bill and Cindi are solvent. However, Ali is in deep financial trouble. Several of Ali's creditors sue him to collect their claims. They win the suit, only to discover that Ali cannot pay the judgment from his personal assets. Can these creditors foreclose on Ali's share of the partnership assets? No. All the creditors can do is get a **charging order** from a court.[17] Under a charging order, the debtor/partner's *profits* are paid to the creditors until the claims are fully paid. Thus, the partnership can continue, and Bill and Cindi are protected. Only Ali, the debtor, suffers.

On the other hand, suppose that the partnership is in financial difficulty but that some of the partners are solvent. Can the partnership's creditors proceed directly against the individual partners, bypassing or ignoring the assets of the firm? No. The creditors of the firm must first proceed against the assets of the firm.

Charging order
A court order permitting a creditor to receive profits from the operation of a business; especially common in partnership situations.

Fiduciary Duties

Another protection given to the partners is the legal status assigned to each partner. Each member of a partnership is a *fiduciary* of the other partners and of the business itself.[18] The fiduciary position carries with it certain responsibilities and certain duties. Each partner is required to account for, and to surrender to the firm, any profits derived from the business or from the use of business assets. No partner is allowed to have a conflict of interest with the partnership. And each partner is entitled to indemnification from a partner who causes a loss or liability from misconduct in the course and scope of employment. RUPA (1994) explicitly addresses the fiduciary duties of partners to each other, including the obligations of loyalty, due care, and good faith.[19]

In *Henkels & McCoy, Inc.* v. *Adochio,* the court discussed whether the general partner's decision to distribute funds was correct. Exhibit 35.1 on page 921 illustrates the business entities in Chestnut Woods Partnership.

35.1

HENKELS & MCCOY, INC. V. ADOCHIO
138 F.3D 491 (3RD CIR. 1998)

FACTS . . . Cedar Ridge, as general contractor for Chestnut Woods, entered into a written subcontract with Henkels & McCoy, Inc. (Henkels), . . . to have it furnish the labor, materials, and equipment for the installation of the storm and sanitary sewer systems for the project. Cedar Ridge agreed to pay Henkels a fixed-price of $300,270 under the contract. Henkels completed the installation of the storm and sewer systems but Chestnut Woods defaulted in making the payments due under the contract. . . . Henkels filed . . . [suit] against Cedar Ridge and Red Hawk. . . . The court entered a . . . judgment which was not satisfied. . . . Henkels then filed suit against G&A in its capacity as a general partner of Red Hawk and obtained a . . . judgment. . . . Efforts to obtain payment on this judgment . . . proved fruitless . . . Henkels . . . brought . . . . suit against the . . . limited partners of Red Hawk. . . .

The Red Hawk partnership, consisting of 20 (1 deceased) limited partners and one corporate general partner, G&A, was formed in 1986. Pursuant to their partnership agreement, the Partners contributed . . . capital which ultimately they allocated to two distinct partnership projects, Timber Knolls and Chestnut Woods. In 1987, Red Hawk and Cedar Ridge entered into a joint venture agreement forming the Chestnut Woods Partnership, with both Red Hawk and Cedar Ridge as general partners. Under the joint venture agreement, Red Hawk would provide the capital funds for the project and Cedar Ridge would provide the general management. . . . Cedar Ridge agreed to act as both the managing partner and the general contractor of the . . . project. . . . Cedar Ridge had the right to incur liabilities on behalf of the partnership in connection with the partnership's reasonable and legitimate business, borrow money in the name of the partnership, and incur reasonable and legitimate expenses related to . . . Chestnut Woods. . . .

Red Hawk and Cedar Ridge entered into a second and distinct joint venture agreement to form the Timber Knolls partnership. . . . Red Hawk contributed $2.3 million . . . and Cedar Ridge again agreed to act as both the managing partner and the general contractor of the project. . . . [T]he Timber Knolls project never commenced operations. . . . [The funds contributed to Timber Knolls were returned to Red Hawk, which then returned the funds to its limited partners.]

ISSUE Are the limited partners obligated to return capital contributions distributed to them in violation of their partnership agreement?

HOLDING Yes. The limited partners must return the distributions.

REASONING . . . [W]e confine our analysis to the relevant sections of the partnership agreement in conjunction with Section 42:2A-46(b) [of New Jersey's statute] which, in its entirety, reads as follows: "b. If a limited partner has received the return of any part of his contribution in violation of the partnership agreement or this chapter, he is liable to the limited partnership for a period of six years thereafter for the amount of the contribution wrongfully returned." . . . Section 12(a) of the Red Hawk partnership agreement specifically provided that cash receipts be used for the establishment of reasonable reserves (for creditors) before such receipts be distributed to the Partners. . . .

The contract, signed only by Henkels and Cedar Ridge, . . . states that Henkels shall invoice and be paid by Cedar Ridge, and provides that the Chestnut Woods property shall not serve as security for payment or be subjected to liens. . . . [The] fundamental principles of agency and partnership law . . . largely control the outcome of this case. . . . [W]hen Cedar Ridge signed the contract with Henkels as General Contractor, it simultaneously also was acting as a partner in the joint venture pursuant to its express authority to "act as the . . . GENERAL CONTRACTOR" as provided in the Chestnut Woods partnership/joint venture agreement. Second, it is elementary that "every partner is an agent of the partnership for the purpose of its business, and the act of every partner . . . binds the partnership, unless the partner so acting has in fact no authority to act for the partnership in the particular matter." This principle holds true even when, as here, the principal is undisclosed and the agent signs the contract in his individual capacity for the benefit of the partnership. But when a third party creditor ascertains an agency relationship, it may hold the partnership as principal liable (and ultimately the individual partners) even though the creditor was unaware of the agency relationship at the time that he extended the credit to the agent. . . . [I]t is undisputed that Red Hawk was a partner with Cedar Ridge in the Chestnut Woods Partnership, that Cedar Ridge had

continued

35.1

HENKELS & MCCOY, INC. V. ADOCHIO, *continued*
138 F.3D 491 (3RD CIR. 1998)

actual authority to enter into the contract with Henkels, that the sewer systems were being installed for the benefit of the Chestnut Woods Partnership, and that Cedar Ridge was entitled to reimbursement from Chestnut Woods for all monies paid by Cedar Ridge to Henkels. . . .

[M]any New Jersey statutes define creditor very broadly to include "the holder of any claim, of whatever character, . . . whether secured or unsecured, matured or unmatured, liquidated or unliquidated, absolute or contingent." . . . [T]he contract between Henkels and Cedar Ridge was entered into on December 29, 1988. Thus Henkels and Cedar Ridge had definite obligations to each other under the contract over a week prior to the first distribution by the general partner to the Red Hawk limited partners. . . . G&A made the bulk of the distributions after Henkels had commenced work and was incurring costs and expenses in fulfilling its commitments under the contract. . . . Henkels was not only a creditor of Cedar Ridge, but of Chestnut Woods, and thus Red Hawk and its partners. . . .

Under the New Jersey ULPL, partners are only jointly liable for contract obligations of the partnership, and . . . a contract creditor of the partnership must first exhaust the partnership's assets before it can pursue the assets of the individual partners. . . . Henkels qualified as a creditor of Red Hawk at the time the distributions were made. . . . [P]ursuant to Section 12(a) of the Red Hawk limited

partnership agreement governing the distribution of all cash receipts, the Red Hawk general partner was required to establish reasonable reserves from the cash received on the Timber Knolls promissory notes to meet its ongoing liability before distributing such cash to the individual limited partners. . . . [W]e do not need to expressly define reasonable reserves . . . because it is unnecessary to the disposition of this appeal. . . . [U]nder any standard and using any definition of reasonable reserves, the Red Hawk general partner's failure to establish any reserves in the face of the fixed obligation and imminent payments due under the contract with Henkels and the operations of the Chestnut Woods development was callous and not reasonable. . . .

BUSINESS CONSIDERATIONS What would constitute adequate reserves for a partnership developing residential property? How could a general partner develop guidelines for establishing adequate reserves?

ETHICAL CONSIDERATIONS Was it ethical for the general partner of Red Hawk to pay the funds to the general and limited partners maintaining a very small reserve? Why or why not? Is there a conflict of interest between the Chestnut Woods Partnership and the failed Timber Knolls Partnership? Why?

RIGHTS OF THIRD PERSONS WHO DEAL WITH PARTNERSHIPS

When partners are dealing internally, each is aware of the rights and duties of the other partner(s). Each general partner should know the terms of the basic agreement and the limits of his or her authority. A third person who deals with the partnership, however, lacks this advantage. Any nonpartner who deals with the firm must rely on *appearances*. As a result, a third person who deals with the partnership may be given certain rights by the court that are specifically denied by the basic partnership agreement.

Contracts

As noted earlier, each partner is an agent of the partnership. Thus, if a partner negotiates a contract on behalf of the partnership, that partner is negotiating as an agent.

EXHIBIT 35.1 | **Legal Relationships in Henkels & McCoy, Inc., v. Adochio**

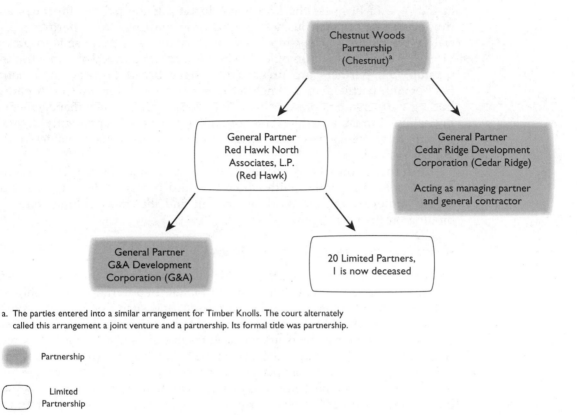

a. The parties entered into a similar arrangement for Timber Knolls. The court alternately called this arrangement a joint venture and a partnership. Its formal title was partnership.

Partnership

Limited Partnership

Corporation

From agency law, we know that if the agent has the *apparent authority* to perform an act, the principal is bound by the act. The same rule applies here. If the partner has the apparent authority to enter the contract, the partnership is bound to honor it.

In many instances, the partner has the actual authority to enter the contract. If so, the partnership is obviously bound, and the partner who negotiated the contract is no more liable than the other partners.

In some cases, the partner has the apparent authority to enter the contract but lacks the actual authority. (Recall, for example, the division of duties discussed earlier in this chapter.) Under these circumstances, the partnership must still honor the contract with the third person. But the partner who negotiated the contract will be liable to the partnership for any losses that arise because the partner exceeded his or her authority.

In still other cases, the partner does not have even apparent authority; if a contract is negotiated, the negotiating partner is personally obligated to perform, but the firm is *not* liable on the agreement.

When the court examines these agreements, the apparent authority of the partner is of overriding importance. To assist in making this decision, courts often look at the type of business the firm is conducting. If the partnership buys and sells products as its primary business purpose, the court views the partnership (unofficially) as a *trading* partnership. If the primary business purpose is to provide services, the court views it (unofficially) as a *nontrading* partnership. In a trading partnership, the partners are presumed to have broad powers. In a nontrading partnership, partners are deemed to have much narrower powers. A partner in a trading partnership is presumably authorized to perform *any* management-related duties. In contrast, a partner in a nontrading business is apparently authorized to do only those things reasonably necessary to further the main business purpose of the partnership.

A third person who is dealing with a partnership for the first time needs to exercise care. The partner with whom the third person is dealing may exceed his or her authority, and the third person will find that the resulting contract is not binding on the partnership.

Borrowing in the Partnership Name

Perhaps the most important area in which the court applies the trading-versus-nontrading distinction is in the borrowing of money. In a trading partnership, the firm sells inventory. Inventory must be purchased, and such purchases require money. Thus, a partner has the apparent authority to borrow money in the firm's name.

In a nontrading partnership, the need for money is less obvious. As a result, the courts are less apt to impose liability on the firm for a loan that was made to a single partner even though that partner borrowed the money in the partnership name.

The court in the next case was dealing with liability on a real estate mortgage. Exhibit 35.2 on page 925 helps illustrate the legal relationships of the parties in this case.

35.2

COTTAGES OF HASTINGS, LTD. V. MURPHY
1999 NEB.APP. LEXIS 176 (NEB.CT.APP. 1999)

FACTS Cottages is a Nebraska limited partnership organized for the purpose of constructing; developing; acquiring; and holding for investment . . . an approximately 120-unit, low-income, multifamily residential development in Hastings, Nebraska. . . . Cottages' certificate of limited partnership was filed in the Nebraska Secretary of State's office on October 13, 1993, and identified one general partner, CILE Corporation (hereinafter CILE). The president and sole shareholder of CILE was Charles Cooper. Cottages' limited partnership agreement . . . identified several limited partners. . . . [W]e are concerned with only one limited partner, Cottage Lifestyles, Inc. (hereinafter CLI). The sole shareholders and directors of CLI were John Arkell, president, and John Ahern, vice president.

On October 27, 1993, title to the certain real property was conveyed by the city . . . to Cottages and filed with the . . . register of deeds. . . . On December 8, 1993, CLI and [David and Phyllis Murphy] signed an agreement which recited that the Murphys agreed to loan $100,000 to CLI pursuant to the terms of a promissory note in the amount of $110,000 ($100,000 loan principal and $10,000 interest). The promissory note, which was executed on this same date, was signed by Arkell as follows: "Cottages of Hastings, Ltd., By John W. Arkell, Gen. Ptnr., Pres. Of Cottages Lifestyles, Inc." The note specifically provided that it was secured by a mortgage covering the subject property. . . . Arkell also signed a mortgage upon the subject property in favor of the Murphys and on behalf

35.2

COTTAGES OF HASTINGS, LTD. V. MURPHY, *continued*

1999 NEB.APP. LEXIS 176 (NEB.CT.APP. 1999)

of Cottages in the same manner as he endorsed the promissory note. . . . [T]he Murphys delivered a draft for $100,000 to Arkell which was payable to "David M. Murphy or Cottages of Hastings, LTD." This draft was endorsed by "David M. Murphy" and "Cottages of Hastings by John Arkell its Partner." The Murphy mortgage was filed of record with the . . . register of deeds on December 27. On May 19, 1994, CILE withdrew as general partner of Cottages, and CLI was substituted as general partner. . . . [O]n June 14, CLI withdrew as general partner of Cottages and was succeeded by Hastings Development Corporation . . . (hereinafter HDC). . . .

On February 1, 1995, all of CLI's interest in Cottages was sold to Paramount Financial Group, Inc. (hereinafter Paramount). Paragraph 3 of the . . . agreement between CLI and Paramount provided that "CLI, and also John Ahern and John Arkell, individually hereby agree to release . . . and discharge Paramount . . . from and for: . . . (iii) any duties and obligations they may have incurred solely for the benefit of CLI, Arkell or Ahern relating to . . . each of the Listed Partnerships . . . " [These partnerships included Cottages.] . . . [S]chedule 3 of the . . . agreement included a schedule of liens and debts which listed the $110,000 Murphy mortgage. . . .

ISSUES Did Arkell have apparent or ostensible authority to bind Cottages? Did the Murphys fail to exercise due diligence to determine the extent of CLI's authority to execute the promissory note and mortgage? Did one or more of the general partners of Cottages ratify the promissory note and mortgage?

HOLDINGS No, Arkell did not have authority. Yes, the Murphys failed to exercise due diligence. No, there was no ratification.

REASONING A quiet title action sounds in equity. In an appeal of an equitable action, an appellate court tries factual questions de novo on the record and reaches a conclusion independent of the findings of the trial court. . . . [W]here credible evidence is in conflict on a material issue of fact, the appellate court considers and may give weight to the fact that the trial judge heard and observed the witnesses and accepted one version of the facts rather than another.

. . . The legal rules applicable to agency relationships also apply to partnerships. "Apparent authority is the power which enables a person to affect the legal relations of another with third persons, professedly as agent for the other, from and in accordance with the other's manifestation to such third persons . . . " "Apparent or ostensible authority to act as an agent may be conferred if the alleged principal affirmatively, intentionally, or by lack of ordinary care causes third persons to act upon the apparent agency." However, apparent authority for which a principal may be liable must be traceable to the principal and cannot be established by the acts, declarations, or conduct of an agent. Whether an act is within the scope of an agent's apparent authority is a factual question to be determined from all the circumstances. The record is clear that when the promissory note and mortgage were executed on December 8, 1993, the sole general partner of Cottages was CILE. This information was a matter of public record which the Murphys could have ascertained by checking with the office of the Nebraska Secretary of State. The Murphys failed to exercise due diligence to determine the extent of CLI's authority to execute the note and mortgage. Had the Murphys exercised due diligence, they would have discovered that CLI was not the general partner of Cottages and did not have the authority to execute the note and mortgage. Thus, the Murphys are held charged with constructive knowledge of this information. . . . [E]ven though Arkell believed that he had authority to execute the mortgage, this belief was not enough to bind Cottages by virtue of Arkell's apparent authority. . . . Arkell did not have the apparent or ostensible authority to bind Cottages to the mortgage on the subject property, and the Murphys failed to exercise due diligence in determining the extent of CLI's authority to execute the promissory note and mortgage.

. . . Ratification is the acceptance of a previously unauthorized contract and takes effect from the [time of the] making of such a contract. Ratification of an agent's unauthorized acts may be made by overt action or inferred from silence and inaction. . . . [R]etention of benefits secured by an unauthorized act of an agent with knowledge of the source of such benefits and the means by which they were obtained is a ratification of the agent's act. . . . [T]he promissory note and mortgage were never Cottages' liabilities to

continued

35.2

COTTAGES OF HASTINGS, LTD. V. MURPHY, *continued*
1999 NEB.APP. LEXIS 176 (NEB.CT.APP. 1999)

ratify. By the terms of the note, the Murphys loaned $100,000 to CLI, not to Cottages. The debt to the Murphys was always carried on CLI's books, not Cottages' books. Further, there is no evidence in the record to establish that Cottages obtained any benefit from the $100,000 loaned by the Murphys. . . . [W]e simply cannot tell what this money was used for. Consequently, the Murphys' loan was made to CLI and was a liability of CLI, the record does not reflect that Cottages obtained any benefit from the loan, and thus, no ratification took place when CLI became general partner

of Cottages. . . . [W]e have conducted a de novo review of the record and find no evidence that the Murphy mortgage was ratified by Cottages. . . .

BUSINESS CONSIDERATIONS What would a prudent lender do in the Murphys' position? Why?

ETHICAL CONSIDERATIONS What is CLI's moral obligation to the Murphys? Why?

Torts and Crimes

Tortfeasor
A wrongdoer; one who commits a tort.

Again, remember that each partner is an agent for every other partner. Under agency law, when a *tort* is committed by an agent, the agent is liable as the **tortfeasor.** And the principal may also be liable, jointly and severally, with the agent, under the theory of *respondeat superior.* If the injured person can establish that the partner was performing in "the course and scope of employment," the firm and each of the partners are liable for the tort. For example, assume Mary, Ned, and Oscar are partners. Ned is driving to a business meeting to represent the firm in some negotiations. On the way to the meeting, Ned runs a stop sign and hits Sam. Since Ned was on a job-related errand, all three partners are liable to Sam, as is the partnership itself.

If the tort is willful and malicious, however, the firm is normally not liable. From our previous example, assume Oscar is driving to a business meeting to represent the firm. On the way, Oscar sees Tom crossing the street. Oscar is still angry at Tom for an insult from long ago. Oscar accelerates the car and *intentionally* runs over Tom. Since the tort was willful and malicious, neither Mary nor Ned nor the firm is liable to Tom.

However, if the willful and malicious tort is one that furthers any business interests of the firm, the other partners may be liable. If the intentional tort is not related to the business purpose, the other partners can still be held liable, provided that they assent to or ratify the conduct. Otherwise, the other partners face no liability for intentional torts.

Aid and abet
To help, assist, or facilitate the commission of a crime; to promote the accomplishment of a crime.

If a partner commits a crime, what liability do the noncriminal partners face? For most crimes, the other partners are not liable. Most crimes require a specific criminal intent. To be convicted of such a crime, a person must commit it or **aid and abet** in its commission. Unless evidence of involvement is shown, only the partner who committed the crime will be liable. However, some crimes can be committed *without* a specific criminal intent. Such crimes are normally *regulatory* in nature; in other words, they involve violations of administrative areas rather than violations in traditional criminal areas. If one of these crimes is committed, all the partners are criminally liable.

E X H I B I T 35.2 | Legal Relationships in Cottages of Hastings, Ltd. v. Murphy

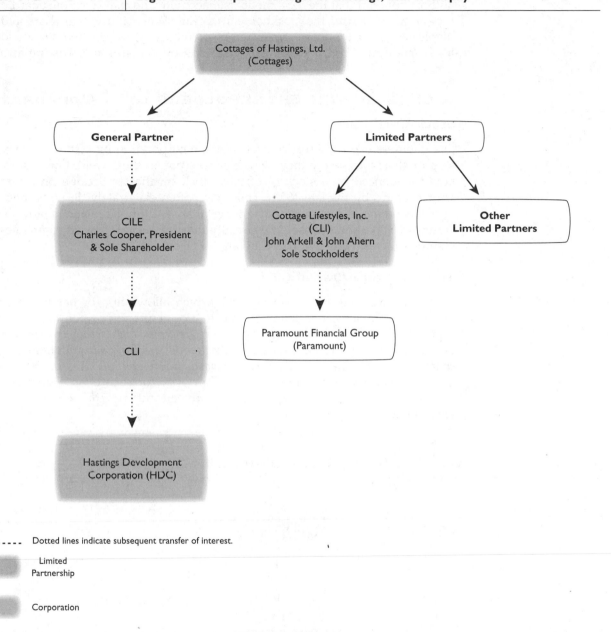

Dotted lines indicate subsequent transfer of interest.

Limited Partnership

Corporation

OPERATION OF A CORPORATION

The officers and the board of directors bear the responsibilities for both the day-to-day operations and the overall policies of a corporation. The management of the entity is centralized. The managers are ultimately answerable to the shareholders, the owners. Stock certificates signify the ownership interests of the shareholders. Shareholders exert only indirect control, generally through the election of directors.

Exhibit 35.3 shows the legal relationship between the three primary groups. Some authors contend that the legal model is inaccurate and that often the board of directors actually control the stockholders instead. When individual shareholders are displeased with the management or performance of a firm, the shareholders are likely to do the "Wall Street walk" by selling their shares and walking away.

RIGHTS OF THE SHAREHOLDERS OF A CORPORATION

Stock Certificates

Shareholders exert indirect control over the corporation by virtue of their ownership of shares; the more they own, the more power they wield. Ownership is generally evidenced by a stock certificate. Stock certificates became prevalent in the United States by the late 1800s. They were often elaborately designed and played a role as financial document, advertising pitch, and public relations ploy. The stock certificate is becoming obsolete especially in large publicly traded companies. Ownership is increasingly evidenced by an "electronic book entry."[20]

Types of Stock Owned

A shareholder may own *common stock*, which allows him or her to receive dividends, to vote on corporate issues, and to receive property upon the corporation's liquidation. Or the shareholder may own *preferred stock*, which, as its name suggests, confers priority with regard to dividends, voting, or liquidation rights. Furthermore, within the preferred stock classification, several classes, or series, may exist that set out different gradations of priority for each class. Under most state statutes, the articles of incorporation must spell out the preferences; such preferences generally will not be implied.

E X H I B I T   35.3 | **Legal Model of Corporate Governance**

The most common preference right involves priority with regard to *dividends* (cash, property, or other shares that the board of directors declares as payment to shareholders). For example, preferred stockholders may receive dividends paid at a specified rate (e.g., 7 percent) before any other classes of stock receive dividends. If any dividends remain after payment to the various classes of preferred stockholders, preferred shareholders often have *participation rights;* that is, they can take part in this further distribution of dividends rather than have their dividend rights restricted to the preferred stock dividend. In addition to dividend and participation rights, preferred shareholders receive corporate assets before any other stockholder does if the corporation is liquidated. After the debts of the corporation are paid, preferred shareholders are the first to receive the **par value** of their stocks (plus any outstanding dividends); common stockholders receive corporate assets only if sufficient assets remain to pay their stocks' par values. If there are any additional assets after payment to the common stockholders, the preferred and common shareholders normally share this balance in proportion to the shares that each holds individually. Preferred shareholders also may enjoy *conversion rights* (the option to change preferred stock into common stock or corporate bonds) and/or *redemption rights* (the enforced repurchase of shares by the corporation in certain authorized circumstances). These features are summarized in Exhibit 35.4.

Par value
The face value assigned to a stock and printed on the stock certificate.

Shareholders' Meetings

Notice. In general, shareholders' meetings may not occur unless the corporation has sent written notice of the meeting to all shareholders of record. Statutory and bylaw provisions often spell out the procedures for giving notice. Such notice ordinarily contains the time, date, and place of the meeting, as well as a statement of the purpose of the meeting. Most statutes require at least ten days' notice before a meeting can legitimately be conducted, but shareholders can expressly waive this requirement in writing before or after the meeting, or they can impliedly waive it by not protesting the lack of notice.

E X H I B I T   35.4 | Stock Characteristics

Type of Stock	Characteristics
Common	Basic shares issued by a corporation; they generally have a lower priority for dividends and distribution of assets upon dissolution
Preferred	Shares that include special rights to dividends and/or distribution of assets upon dissolution
Cumulative Preferred	Shares that include the right to a specified dividend; any unpaid dividends owed to these shareholders must be paid before dividends can be paid on the common stock
Convertible Preferred	Shares that include the shareholder's right to convert them into another type of stock; generally they are convertible into common stock or corporate bonds
Redeemable Preferred	Shares that the corporation can repurchase according to the terms of the redemption agreement

Quorum. Shareholder meetings cannot take place in the absence of a quorum. State statutes and corporate bylaws or articles usually state the percentage of *outstanding shares,* or shares entitled to vote, that constitutes a quorum. A majority of such votes is usually necessary, yet the Model Business Corporation Act sanctions articles that set the quorum requirement at a mere one-third of all outstanding shares.[21] *Dissident shareholders* (those who disagree with the actions of management) may prevent a quorum by not attending meetings. The law remains unsettled as to whether a subsequent walkout of dissident shareholders, once a quorum is present, invalidates the meeting.

Election and Removal of Directors. One of the foremost powers held by shareholders is their capacity to elect and remove directors. Although the articles of incorporation usually designate the people who are to serve as the initial directors, these directors may serve only until the first annual meeting. At that time, the shareholders may elect some (or all) of them to the board of directors. If vacancies occur on the board because of deaths or resignations, the shareholders normally vote to fill these vacancies. The articles of incorporation or bylaws, however, may permit the directors to fill these posts. Directors usually serve staggered terms. This means that only a certain proportion of directors (e.g., one-third) will be up for reelection at any given meeting. Such staggered terms ensure continuity of leadership on the board. In recent years, there has been a trend toward adding **outsiders** to the board of directors.

Shareholders have *inherent power* (i.e., power regardless of the articles or bylaws) to remove a director for cause. Previous cases have upheld the exercise of such rights when directors have engaged in embezzlement or other misconduct, failed to live up to their duties to the corporation, or undertaken unauthorized acts. The director, of course, may appeal his or her removal to a court of law. Statutes, articles of incorporation, and bylaws may also allow removal without cause.

Amendment of the Bylaws. Bylaws are provisions intended to regulate the corporation and its management. To be valid, bylaws must comply with state incorporation statutes and the articles of incorporation. Shareholders retain inherent power to amend (or repeal) bylaws. State law generally mandates the proportion of outstanding shares needed to approve an amendment.

Voting. The voting rights exercised by shareholders at meetings allow them *indirect control* of the corporation and the board of directors. All shareholders of record as of the date of the shareholders' meeting ordinarily appear on the voting list and can vote. Shareholders can either be present at the meeting and vote in person, or they can assign their voting rights to others, who then vote their shares for them by **proxy.** (*Proxy* can be used to designate both the person or the document used to appoint someone to act in a representative capacity as a proxy.) If a distant shareholder in a public-issue corporation does not want to participate personally in the meeting, he or she can sign a document called a proxy, which gives the named individual authority to act as his or her agent. Exhibit 35.5 shows a proxy.

Whoever controls large blocs of proxies in a public-issue corporation may, in effect, dictate the outcome of the election. For this reason, management (and sometimes dissident stockholders) in such corporations may solicit proxy votes in order to consolidate voting power. Not surprisingly, then, vicious proxy fights have occurred at various times in U.S. corporate history. Because of these high stakes and the accompanying possibilities for abuse, federal law now ensures that proxy

Outsiders
Directors who are not shareholders or officers.

Proxy
A person appointed and designated to act for another, especially at a public meeting.

E X H I B I T   35.5 | **Proxy**

_____, a California Corporation.

The undersigned, as record holder of the shares of stock of _____,
described above, revokes any previous proxies and appoints _____
as the undersigned's proxy to attend the special shareholders' meeting on
_____, and any adjournment of that meeting.

The proxy holder is entitled to cast a total number of votes equal to, but not exceeding
_____ which the undersigned would be entitled to cast if the undersigned were personally present.

The undersigned authorizes the undersigned's proxy holder to vote and otherwise represent the undersigned with regards to any business that may come before this meeting in
the same manner and with the same effect as if the undersigned were personally present.

THIS PROXY MAY BE REVOKED AT ANY TIME IN WRITING.

Dated: _____, 20 _____.

SOURCE: Courtesy of Robyn Esraelian, Richardson, Jones and Esraelian, Attorneys-at-Law, Fresno, California.

solicitations are carried out fairly. Within the corporation, impartial parties called
inspectors, judges, or tellers oversee the election to ensure fairness (see Chapter 38).

In most corporate matters, a shareholder can cast one vote for each share held.
This is called _straight voting_. Unless the voting involves an extraordinary corporate
matter (e.g., dissolution, merger, amendment of the articles of incorporation, or sale
of substantially all the assets), the decision made by a majority generally controls.
Thus, votes of more than 50 percent for any ordinary corporate matter usually bind
the corporation. In extraordinary matters, statutes may require a higher proportion
(for example, two-thirds) of votes for the action taken to be legally binding.

To offset shareholders who own large blocs of votes and who may therefore be
able to control appreciably the outcomes of elections, most state statutes today
either permit or require _cumulative voting_. Cumulative voting applies only to the
election of directors and is a method for ensuring some minority representation on
the board.

The following example illustrates the difference between straight and cumulative voting. Assume that at the annual shareholders' meeting, three directors will
be elected from a field of six candidates—U, V, W, X, Y, and Z. Under straight voting, shareholder A, who owns 100 shares, can cast 100 votes for each of three directors, say U, V, and W. If, instead, cumulative voting is used, A can cast 300 votes
for U or can divide 300 votes among any three candidates in any proportion he
or she wishes (e.g., 150 for U, 100 for V, and 50 for Y). In this fashion, A's votes
accumulate—hence, the term _cumulative voting_. The ability of a minority shareholder to have an impact on the election of directors thus becomes more formidable under cumulative voting than under straight voting.

To dilute any advantage that the minority might gain through cumulative voting, management may stagger the terms of directors, reduce or enlarge the size of the board, or remove directors elected by the minority. To counter such steps, lawmakers in many jurisdictions have passed statutory provisions that protect cumulative voting rights by making such steps illegal or by using statutorily enacted formulas that safeguard the beneficial effects of cumulative voting.

Voting trusts, like proxies and cumulative voting, represent devices used to consolidate votes for control. A shareholder can create a voting trust by transferring to **trustees** the shares he or she owns. Once the shareholder has entered into such a trust, the shareholder has no right to vote the shares until the trust terminates. The trustees issue a *voting trust certificate* to the shareholder to indicate that the shareholder retains all rights incidental to share ownership except voting. In contrast to proxies, which are generally revocable, voting trusts are normally irrevocable. State statutes, however, usually limit the duration of voting trusts to a specified time period, such as ten years (with possible extensions).

Pooling agreements are similar to voting trusts. In such agreements, shareholders agree to vote the shares each owns in a specified way. Both voting trusts and pooling agreements remain valid and enforceable as long as they do not, in effect, preempt the directors' managerial functions. This could happen if the shareholders

Trustees
Persons in whom a power is vested under an express or implied agreement in order to exercise the power for the benefit of another.

Institutional shareholders
A purchaser of shares acting for an institution, such as a pension fund, trust fund, mutual fund, insurance company, or bank.

YOU BE THE JUDGE

TROUBLE AT ADM

Archer Daniels Midland (ADM) is an agribusiness giant and global producer of goods such as corn syrup, vegetable oil, and ethanol. Its slogan is "supermarket to the world." ADM was besieged by a group of irate **institutional shareholders** at its annual stockholders' meeting in October 1996. Just prior to the meeting, it had pled guilty to federal charges that it had fixed prices of lysine and citric acid.[22] It had agreed to pay a $100 million criminal fine. In addition, it owed $90 million in related civil settlements. Many of the institutional shareholders blamed the company's troubles on the unusually close relationship between ADM's management and its board of directors. Of the 17-person board of directors, 10 were current or former executives of ADM or relatives of Dwayne Andreas, the CEO. A number of the other directors were loyal to Andreas. The shareholders felt that the board failed to adequately oversee the company's operations due to the lack of independence. The institutional shareholders proposed a number of changes including that a majority of the directors should be outsiders; Andreas should resign; and there should be secret shareholder voting. The proposals failed.

The shareholders have filed suit in *your* court. How will *you* decide this case?[23]

BUSINESS CONSIDERATIONS What type of corporate structure improves a corporation's performance? What type of structure reduces the likelihood of criminal behavior? Who should pay the criminal fine?

ETHICAL CONSIDERATION Is price fixing unethical?

SOURCES: *The New York Times* (16 November 1997), pp. B1, B10; *Chicago Tribune* (18 April 1997), Business Section, p. 1; *Business Week* (18 November 1996), p. 82; *Washington Post* (1 November 1996), p. F3; and *The New York Times* (15 October 1996), pp. A1, C3.

who enter into these arrangements are also directors. For example, it is legal for the shareholders to agree through voting trusts or pooling agreements to vote for director A at the annual meeting's election of directors (even if director A is also one of the shareholders who enters into the arrangement). If the shareholders' agreements involve their pledging to bring about the dismissal of the current chief executive officer (CEO) of the corporation, however, voting trusts or pooling arrangements to this effect normally will be unenforceable. Why? Selection of officers is ordinarily a function of the directors.

Shareholders of close corporations probably utilize voting trusts and pooling arrangements more than their counterparts in publicly held corporations. Modern statutes recognize that close corporations are more similar to partnerships than are most other corporate entities. Consequently, some states will enforce agreements that treat shareholders as if they were directors, when all the shareholders are parties to the agreement. Such statutory developments illustrate the law's ability to change whenever reality dictates such modifications.

Dividends

Most shareholders buy shares in for-profit, public-issue corporations primarily to receive dividends. Such shareholders normally are less concerned about the control functions than about the financial aspects of their shares—namely, dividends. Thus far, we have spoken of a *right* to receive dividends, but that constitutes a very loose use of the term. Actually, there is no absolute right to receive dividends. The power to declare dividends resides with the board of directors. In the absence of demonstrated bad faith on the directors' part, shareholders cannot compel the directors to declare dividends. The directors alone decide, first, *if* dividends will be distributed. If so, they also determine the timing, type, and amount of the dividends.

Of course, shareholders hope to receive the financial profits represented by dividends. *Cash dividends* are the most common type, but dividends may also take the form of *property* or *stocks*.

If cash dividends are involved, the directors must make certain that the dividends will be paid from a *lawful source*. In general, statutes limit the sources of dividends to *current net profits* (those earned in the preceding accounting period) or *earned surplus* (the sum of the net profits retained by the corporation during all previous years of existence). Any declaration of dividends that will impair the corporation's *original capital structure* (the number of shares originally issued times their stated value) is illegal and may subject the directors and shareholders to personal liability. Similarly, payment of dividends during the corporation's insolvency or any payment that will bring about insolvency or financial difficulties is illegal. Exhibit 35.6 on page 932 illustrates the decision-making process in declaring dividends.

As noted earlier, preferred stockholders enjoy priority with regard to the distribution of dividends. They are also protected by the rules that limit the source of dividends because directors normally cannot declare dividends if the declaration will thereby jeopardize the **liquidation preferences** of the preferred shareholders. Once a dividend is lawfully declared, preferred stockholders receive their dividends first. Common stockholders receive dividends only if adequate funds remain after the preferred stockholders have been paid. Sometimes, preferred stockholders have *participating* preferred stock. This means they not only receive their original dividend but also share (or participate) with the common stockholders in any dividends that are paid after the preferred stockholders have received their original dividends.

Liquidation preferences
Priorities given to creditors and owners when the enterprise is terminated and the assets are distributed.

E X H I B I T   35.6 | **The Decision to Issue Dividends: A Flowchart**

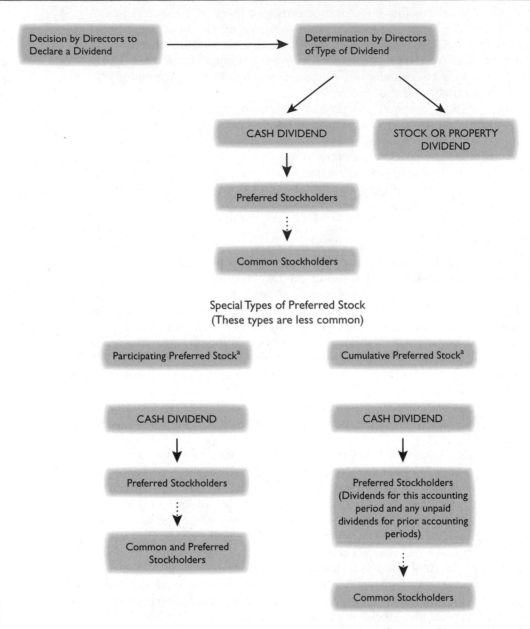

- - - - - Stockholders receive dividends only if sufficient funds remain.

a. Preferred stock can be both participating and cumulative.

In other words, participating preferred stockholders may be able to dip into the dividend fund twice. Usually, however, preferred stock is nonparticipating.

There is another complexity in declaring preferred dividends. Preferred dividends may be *cumulative*, which means that the sum (or accumulation) of all preferred dividends that were not paid in a given year must be paid before common shareholders receive any dividends. In contrast, in *noncumulative* preferred dividends, the preferred stockholder receives only the dividend preferences for the *current accounting period,* and the common stockholders then receive their dividends should any funds remain. Under this type of preference, the preferred shareholders lose all dividends for any years in which the directors have chosen not to declare a dividend.

Preemptive Stock Rights

Sometimes it is necessary for a corporation to increase its capital by issuing new shares. Since this is an extraordinary matter involving amendment of the articles of incorporation (the original number of shares and their par value will change with this new capitalization), shareholders must vote on the issuance of these new shares. A shareholder's interest in this matter extends beyond voting rights. For example, assume Bonnie owns 10 shares of Samp Corporation. Samp's original capitalization involved 100 shares sold at $100 each ($10,000 stated capital). At that time, Bonnie owned 10 percent of Samp Corporation (10 shares/100 total shares). If Samp issues another 100 shares as a result of the amending of the articles, Bonnie then will own 5 percent of the corporation (10 shares/200 total shares). As a result of this new capitalization, her voting power will decrease proportionately, and so will her right to receive a higher amount of dividends and a higher proportion of corporate assets in the event of liquidation.

Early on, common law courts, realizing the inherent unfairness of this sequence of events, began to protect the Bonnies of the corporate world by a doctrine called *preemptive rights.* These courts promoted the notion that the right of first refusal is inherent in stock ownership; hence, before the corporation can sell to anyone else, it must offer to sell to Bonnie the number of shares that will maintain her proportionate interest. Bonnie, in effect, can preempt the rights of other would-be purchasers of the stock because she can purchase before they have the chance to do so. Nevertheless, once the corporation notifies Bonnie of her preemptive rights, she has a limited time to exercise them. If she does not take advantage of the offer, she waives her rights of preemption.

Preemptive rights normally apply only to shares issued for cash and not to shares issued in exchange for property (such as a commercial building), or services (such as shares issued to lure a CEO to Samp), or to shares issued as share dividends, or to treasury stock (stock originally issued but subsequently reacquired by the corporation). In this last situation, there is no new issue and, hence, no reduction in Bonnie's proportionate interest in Samp Corporation. In the two prior situations, preemptive rights may cripple the corporation's financing efforts and obstruct the corporation's legitimate, profit-maximizing activities, such as acquiring property and recruiting top-flight executives. Because of the possible frustration of these worthwhile aims, courts and statutes alike deny Bonnie's preemptive rights, despite the dilution of her proportional ownership interests. In addition, judicial and statutory treatment of Bonnie's preemptive rights might be different if Samp is a publicly held (as opposed to a close) corporation.

Inspection of Corporate Books and Records

The rights of shareholders to inspect corporate records arise from both common law doctrines and express statutory provisions. In general, shareholders have access to such corporate materials as stockholder lists; minutes of shareholders' meetings;

board or officers' meetings; financial records, such as books of account or other periodic summaries; and business documents, including tax returns, contracts, and office correspondence or memoranda.

At common law, inspection rights were qualified (rather than absolute) because shareholders needed to demonstrate that the reason for inspection involved a "proper purpose"; that is, the motivation for the inspection related to his or her status as a shareholder. Requests that seek shareholder lists to communicate with shareholders about corporate matters or attempt to examine corporate financial records to determine the value of shares, the propriety of dividends, or possible mismanagement ordinarily qualify as proper purposes. On the other hand, shareholder requests that ask for information to learn trade secrets for the benefit of the corporation's competitors or to bring *strike suits* (those without any real merit) in order to impede the management of the corporation normally will constitute improper purposes. Assuming the inspection is for a proper purpose, the shareholder generally can employ attorneys, accountants, and other personnel to aid in examining records, making copies or summaries, and the like.

Most statutes similarly require a showing of proper purpose, but once the shareholder has alleged a proper purpose, the burden of proof shifts to the corporation to show an improper purpose on the shareholder's part. Sometimes statutes change the burden of proof or the party who has the burden, depending on the type of record being requested. Statutes may also restrict inspection rights only to certain shareholders (e.g., those who have held their shares for at least six months or who own at least 5 percent of the outstanding shares). These statutory restrictions, however, do not eliminate the shareholder's common law inspection rights. But, as previously mentioned, the shareholder, not the corporation, has the burden of proving proper purpose under these common law doctrines.

Federal securities law and state statutes that mandate annual disclosure of profits and losses, officer compensation, and so on have made inspection rights somewhat less important. The information made available to the shareholder under these statutes encompasses the type of information that shareholders in the past could obtain only by exercising their rights of inspection.

Transfer of Shares

As discussed earlier, ownership of share (stock) certificates signifies ownership of a portion of the corporate entity. Thus, these shares are the shareholder's property. Shareholders, like other owners of property, generally can transfer their shares to someone else (by gift or sale). A transfer of shares generally occurs through endorsement and delivery of the stock certificate in conjunction with a surrender of the certificate for subsequent reissue to the new owner by the corporation's secretary or, in a large corporation, by its transfer agent. Stock exchange rules regulate the conduct of transfer agents, who are professionals who help the corporate secretary with the myriad details attendant on large-scale transfers of stocks. Transfers of stock in these situations, including the cumbersomeness of actual physical transfers of stock certificates, cause numerous administrative headaches. As a result, present-day techniques, such as a brokerage firm's holding title to stock through bookkeeping entries rather than actual transfers of certificates, will likely lead to the abolition of stock certificates and their replacement by computer printouts.

Generally, the right to transfer stock remains unfettered. Restrictions placed on the stock itself, however, may limit this right of transferability. Such restrictions commonly occur in close corporations. It is easy to understand why these restrictions may be advisable. We have already discussed the fact that close corporations are like partnerships in that the controlling shareholders actively take part in the day-to-day management of the corporation. Consequently, shareholders in close corporations often attempt to preserve their control over the affairs of the corporation through voting trusts and pooling arrangements. Such attempts at consolidation of power will be meaningless without restrictions on the stock's transferability.

Courts try to balance the legitimate interests of the shareholders in limiting the corporation to a few congenial shareholders and the right of a shareholder to transfer his or her property. In our legal system, this right of **alienation** is considered to be inherent in the ownership of property. A *right of first refusal,* where the shareholder who wishes to sell must first offer his or her shares to the corporation or to the other shareholders, is enforceable as a valid restriction on transfer because it is a reasonable restraint on alienation. The restriction must be conspicuously placed on the stock certificate to be valid. A common restriction is "future sale or disposition of these shares shall take place in accordance with the shareholder agreement that controls them; and sale of them cannot take place until the holder of them offers them to the corporation or to each other shareholder, on the same terms." In contrast, a restriction that states that "these shares are nontransferable" will probably be unreasonable and, therefore, unenforceable.

Alienation
The transfer of ownership to another.

A conspicuous notice is meant to protect any subsequent purchaser of the shares by informing him or her of the restricted nature of the stock. If this notice of restriction on transfer is missing, the purchaser will not have to abide by the restriction unless he or she otherwise has notice of it. If the restriction is reasonable and appears on the face of the stock certificate, however, the corporation can refuse to transfer the shares to the purchaser. The purchaser's remedy involves forcing the seller to return the money paid to the seller for the shares.

If the transfer satisfies all legal requirements, including the applicable provisions of Article 8 of the UCC and state securities laws, the purchaser (transferee) pays the price asked and the shareholder (transferor) then endorses and delivers the stock to the purchaser. The corporation, when notified, must register the transfer and change corporate records to denote the new ownership in order to guarantee the new owner the rights incidental to stock ownership in the corporation.

LIABILITIES OF SHAREHOLDERS

As we learned in Chapter 34, one of the most significant advantages of the corporate form of business is the limited liability afforded to shareholders. In other words, the shareholders risk only their investment. Except for situations in which courts can disregard the corporate entity, shareholders normally do not become personally liable for corporate debts. In this section, we will look at some other circumstances that may cause liability for a shareholder.

Watered Stock

At the time of the formation of the corporation, the articles of incorporation spell out the *capital structure* of the corporation. In brief, the money to operate the corporation initially results from the issuance of securities to investors. The authorization for such securities ordinarily occurs early in the process of the corporation's formation, probably by board action at the organizational meeting.

The consideration that the corporation receives for these shares constitutes the stated capital of the corporation. The board of directors establishes a fixed value of each share of such capital stock (e.g., $10 per share). This is called *par value stock*. The corporation may also issue no-par value stock, which has no fixed value but may be sold at whatever price the directors deem reasonable (called *stated value*). No-par value shares permit a corporation to issue stock in return for assets that currently are worth little but have the possibility of high, though speculative, returns (e.g., technology patents).

If no statutory provisions to the contrary exist, the corporation may issue shares in exchange for any lawful consideration, including cash received, property received, or services actually rendered. Just as the board of directors generally sets the price of the shares, it also normally fixes the value of the property received or services rendered. As long as the board makes these decisions in good faith and in the absence of fraud, courts will not impose legal liability on the directors for these decisions.

However, the shareholder who receives shares of a corporation that are issued as fully paid when, in fact, the full par value has not been paid by the purchaser owns *watered stock*. The shareholder is personally liable for the deficiency, that is, "the water." For example, if a shareholder pays $8 per share and the par value or stated value is $10 per share, the shareholder is liable to the corporation for $2 per share.

Watered-stock problems normally arise in situations in which services have been rendered in exchange for stock. For example, assume CIT incorporates and issues $4,000 worth of its shares to Ted in exchange for his design of a videophone circuit board. The circuit board is later found to be worth $2,000. Ted will be liable for $2,000 worth of watered stock. Usually Ted's liability is to the corporation, but some states will allow corporate creditors to impose liability on Ted if CIT becomes insolvent and unable to meet its obligations as they come due. A later purchaser from Ted normally will not be liable for watered stock, however, because the rule regarding watered stock applies only to initial corporate issuances and purchases of stock, rather than to later transfers of the stock.

The use of no-par value stock and the impact of federal and state securities regulation have greatly reduced the incidence of suits alleging liability for watered stock. Still, shareholders should be aware of this legal doctrine.

Stock Subscriptions

Stock subscriptions are agreements by investors ("subscribers") to purchase shares in a corporation. The law views a subscription as an offer, and most state statutes make subscriptions irrevocable for a certain period unless the subscription itself provides otherwise. A subscriber may enter into such agreements either before or after the corporation's formation. If the stock subscription occurs before the corporation's formation (usually as a result of promoters' activities), some states treat the subscription as an offer that is automatically accepted by the corporation upon its formation, creating a valid contract. Other states, however, require formal acceptance of the subscription/offer before a valid contract between the subscriber and the corporation arises.

Because an accepted stock subscription constitutes a contract, various types of liabilities arise on the breach of the subscription contract. Thus, the corporation can sue the subscriber for the subscription price if the subscriber refuses to pay the agreed price. In some cases, creditors of a corporation that has become insolvent may force the subscriber to pay the amount owed on the subscription. By the same token, the subscriber can sue the corporation if the corporation refuses to issue the shares that are the object of the subscription. As in the case of watered stock, securities laws have reduced the incidence of shareholder liability for stock subscriptions.

Illegal Dividends

We noted earlier that cash dividends must be paid from a lawful source. Any declaration of dividends that will impair the original capital structure of the corporation is illegal and may subject both the directors and the shareholders to personal liability. Shareholders who receive an illegal dividend are absolutely liable for its return if the corporation is insolvent at the time the dividend is paid. In such cases, the corporation's creditors can sue the shareholders directly for the amount of the illegal dividend. If the corporation is solvent when an illegal distribution takes place and remains solvent even after it, however, only shareholders who knew the dividend was illegal (e.g., from an improper source) must repay the dividend to the corporation. Innocent shareholders can retain the dividends. Directors who have been held liable for distributing illegal dividends can force shareholders who knew of the illegal dividends to pay the amounts received back to the directors. The shareholders and directors thus share liability in such circumstances.

Dissolution

Dissolution signals the legal termination of the corporation's existence. It may occur *voluntarily* (by actions of the incorporators or shareholders) or *involuntarily* (by court actions initiated by the state or a shareholder). It is important to note that majority (or controlling) shareholders may incur liability if the purpose of the dissolution is to freeze out minority stockholders and to strip them of rights or profits they would otherwise enjoy. The basis of this liability is that controlling shareholders owe fiduciary duties to minority shareholders. Generally speaking, controlling shareholders must exert control for the benefit of all shareholders, not just for themselves. Dissolutions that prejudice minority shareholders' interests while greatly enhancing majority shareholders' interests may subject the latter to personal liability if minority shareholders sue.

RIGHTS AND DUTIES OF THE MANAGERS OF A CORPORATION

Board of Directors

The right to manage the affairs of the corporation falls squarely on the board of directors. Although shareholders, the ultimate owners of the corporation, retain the power to elect and remove directors, this prerogative does not give shareholders a direct voice in management. Nor can shareholders compel the board to take any action. The directors are not agents of the shareholders; they owe loyalty primarily to the corporation. As we discussed, however, different rules may apply if the corporation is a close corporation.

Number and Qualifications. The articles of incorporation usually name the initial directors. Older statutes required at least three directors, but the modern trend—due, no doubt, in part to the increased numbers of close corporations—is to permit as few as one or two directors. To avoid deadlocks, the articles or bylaws usually authorize an uneven number of directors.

Unless otherwise provided in the relevant statutes, articles, or bylaws, directors need not be either shareholders in the corporation or residents of the state where the corporation has its principal place of business. Where such qualifications are required, the election of unqualified persons is voidable, not void. In other words, until the corporation employs proper proceedings to displace the unqualified directors, the law considers them *de facto directors* (i.e., directors in fact if not in law). Consequently, most of their acts as directors are effective, and de facto directors must live up to the same corporate duties and standards as do qualified directors. Directors generally have the right to appoint interim replacements on the board when vacancies arise owing to the death, resignation, or incapacity of a director.

Term of Office. Directors serve for the time specified in state statutes, unless the articles or bylaws limit the term to a shorter period. Directors usually serve for one year unless the corporation has set up a *classified board* (a board divided into classes of directors with staggered election dates). Directors continue to hold office until the shareholders elect their successors and the latter take office. Thus, sitting directors do not automatically drop off the board at the end of their terms.

Sometimes shareholders remove directors before their terms on the board end. Shareholders may remove directors for cause, which was the only basis for removal at common law. Modern statutes relax this standard by permitting a majority of shareholders to remove directors at any time during their terms without cause. In those jurisdictions that require cumulative voting, however, directors cannot be removed if the number of votes cast against the removal would have been sufficient to elect those directors to the board. In most jurisdictions, directors who have been removed can seek court review of such dismissals to determine if the proper procedures were followed.

Meetings. Traditionally, the board could validly exercise its powers only when acting collectively, not individually. The law emphasized the value of decision making arrived at through collective debate, deliberation, and judgment. For this reason, statutes set out rules permitting the board to act only when it was formally convened. Moreover, directors traditionally had to be present to vote (they could not vote by proxy or send substitutes to deliberate for them). Directors could vote only at a duly announced and formalized meeting.

Today, most modern statutes dispense with the formalities previously required of directors' meetings. Thus, even though the bylaws usually fix the times for regular or special board meetings, statutes today allow meetings to occur even without prior notice. To be a valid meeting, however, either before or after the meeting, each absent director—in writing—must waive the right to prior notice, consent to the meeting, or approve the minutes of the meeting.

Similarly, some states even allow the board to act without a meeting, assuming the articles or bylaws permit informal action, as long as all directors consent and file their consents in the corporate minute book. In fact, telephone conference calls suffice in several states. Given this decided trend toward informality, the board can hold its meetings anywhere unless the articles or bylaws declare otherwise. Meetings outside the corporation's state of incorporation or principal place of business are, in general, perfectly legal.

Unless the articles or bylaws set a higher or lower percentage, a simple majority of the directors ordinarily constitutes a quorum. Actions taken by a quorum of directors are binding on the corporation. Yet two questions may arise in any discussion about quorums. First, can directors who intentionally miss a meeting to prevent a quorum later question the validity of the action taken at the meeting? Since different cases have produced different results, you should check the law in your particular jurisdiction. Second, can directors count toward the quorum (or vote) if the board will be voting on matters in which they are personally interested? Modern statutes generally allow directors to participate as long as there has been compliance with statutory provisions meant to ensure fairness to the corporation (such as disclosure of the interest). If there is no such statute, the case results vary from jurisdiction to jurisdiction. Some cases have allowed interested directors to be counted; other cases have not.

Directors usually cannot agree in advance about how they will vote on corporate matters. Such a formal agreement is not binding because it is void on public policy grounds; directors owe fiduciary duties to the corporation and must be free to exercise their judgment in a totally unrestricted fashion. Such agreements may be valid, however, among directors in a close corporation if all the shareholders/directors agree to the plan.

Delegation of Duties. Most statutes authorize the board of directors to delegate managerial authority to officers and executive (or other) committees. Such delegations of duties ensure the smooth running of the day-to-day affairs of the corporation and promote efficiency by utilizing the expertise of the various committee members (as in a salary committee).

If no statutory provisions specifically allow the delegation of duties, courts will interpret any attempts at delegation very strictly. Moreover, if the delegation becomes too broad and pervasive, such actions will probably be void because it is too great a relinquishment of the board's management functions. Similarly, attempts to place control of the corporation in fewer persons than the entire board of directors will be illegal (even in close corporations), because the corporation deserves the best efforts of all its directors, who, in turn, owe fiduciary duties to the corporation. Delegation of authority to persons outside the directorial ranks (except for officers), such as arbitrators or management consultants, therefore, becomes extremely difficult to justify legally.

Compensation. In times past, the corporation had no duty to compensate directors for their services. Older cases ruled that directors were not to be paid for their services unless the articles or bylaws authorized the compensation before the directors had rendered the services. Even under these precedents, however, directors could receive payment for extraordinary services taken at the board's request (i.e., recruitment of executive officers), despite the lack of a prearranged, specific agreement. The payment is based on quasi-contractual grounds. Today, although many corporations still pay their directors little or no compensation for their services, an increasing number of corporations do pay rather hefty sums. Since directors often are not substantial shareholders and are subject to ever-expanding duties and potential liability, compensation seems more justifiable.

The directors normally determine the salaries of the officers of the corporation. Possible conflict-of-interest concerns may arise when directors also serve as officers because, in effect, the directors will be participating in setting their own salaries. As noted earlier in the discussion of quorum requirements, statutes may empower interested directors to vote on these issues as long as disclosure of the interest has been made and the transaction is otherwise fair to the corporation. The board can hire officers to serve for periods longer than the board's tenure as long as the period involved is reasonable in length. Likewise, the amount of compensation paid to officers also must be reasonable. Otherwise, the compensation package (fixed salary, bonuses, share options, profit sharing, annuities, deferred-compensation plans, etc.) may be attacked as a "waste" of corporate assets. Directors may be held liable for this waste.

Corporate salaries in the millions of dollars are not uncommon today. Moreover, it has become a relatively common strategy for the board to give *golden parachutes*—hefty, guaranteed salary packages—to their CEOs when the corporation is the target of a hostile takeover attempt. Since the acquirer will be obligated to pay these inflated salaries after the acquisition, golden parachutes become a strategy for fending off a takeover attempt. Golden parachutes, which allow officers to receive money for doing no work after their severance from the corporation, raise controversial questions about possible conflicts of interest and waste of corporate assets.

Liabilities. State corporation statutes, common law doctrines, and federal securities and antitrust laws may impose liability on a director for noncompliance with the duties or requirements set out in those doctrines and statutes. Directors, by the very nature of their positions, make numerous decisions, collectively and individually. Increasingly, the performance of these duties subjects directors to possible personal liability, either individually or with the other members of the board who have approved or engaged in the forbidden conduct. Directors must use great caution in order to avoid liability in the form of civil damages or criminal fines.

Although not always the case, today it is legal—indeed, common—for corporations to *indemnify* (pay back or reimburse) their directors for liabilities accruing from their corporate positions. Through indemnification, directors receive money from the corporation for the losses and expenses incurred by them from litigation brought against them personally for actions undertaken on behalf of the corporation in their corporate capacities. Statutes may limit the right of indemnification in certain circumstances. For instance, indemnification may be unavailable for criminal fines when directors have engaged in unlawful activities that they knew at the time were illegal. Statutes often empower corporations to purchase liability insurance for their directors, officers, and other employees to cover nonindemnifiable liabilities. These policies are commonly called *D and O liability insurance* (directors and officers' liability and reimbursement policies). Exhibit 35.7 summarizes the management responsibilities in a corporation.

Other Rights. Because directors alone have the right to declare dividends, they (as well as the shareholders) may be personally liable for improper dividends.

Directors, like shareholders, may enter into agreements about how they will vote as directors. But if such agreements unduly hamper the board's managerial functions, the agreements will be void on public policy grounds. These agreements ordinarily will be valid, however, in close corporations in which all the shareholders/directors have assented to the terms.

The rights of directors to inspect corporate records are even more compelling than shareholders' rights. Why? Access to corporate records is essential if directors are to discharge their fiduciary duties and decision-making functions. Unlike shareholders' rights, many states characterize the directors' right of inspection as absolute. Yet this right is likely to be lost if directors abuse the right by using it for an improper purpose that damages the corporation, such as misappropriation of trade secrets or confidential trade information.

EXHIBIT 35.7 | **Management of the Corporation**

Directors   **Officers**

Duties/Responsibilities

1. Management of corporation and setting of overall policies.
2. Delegation of managerial authority to officers and executives.
3. Selection and/or possible removal of officers.
4. Determination of officers' salaries.
5. Obligation to exercise independent, disinterested judgment.

Duties/Responsibilities

1. Oversight of day-to-day operations of the firm.
2. Execution of policies established by board of directors.
3. Fulfillment of agents' applicable duties.

Liability

1. Failure to abide by applicable fiduciary duties.
2. Failure to comply with securities laws.
3. Indemnification and/or insurance may be available to offset personal liability.

Rights

1. Actions by a quorum of directors generally binding on corporation.
2. Appointment of interim replacements on board when vacancies arise.
3. Declaration of dividends.
4. Inspection of corporate records.
5. Court review of removal in certain situations.

Rights

1. Authority to bind corporation in certain situations owing to agency law.
2. Compensation.
3. Court review of removal in certain situations.

FIDUCIARY DUTIES

Diligence

Obliges managers to perform their duties with due care; i.e., in a non-negligent fashion.

Loyalty

Obliges managers to show undivided loyalty to corporation; i.e., to place corporate interests above their own personal interests.

Obedience

Obliges managers to avoid illegal and/or *ultra vires* acts.

Business Judgment Rule (BJR)

Rule that exonerates managers from personal liability, if the managers' decision was made in good faith and without clear and gross negligence.

Situations Giving Rise to Potential Breach

Conflicts of Interest

Personal interests of managers at odds with corporation's interest; necessitates full disclosure to corporation of conflicts.

Corporate Opportunities

Managers' diversion to themselves of deals or potential deals that in fairness and justice belong to the corporation.

Freeze-outs of Minority Shareholders

Actions by managers that prejudice minority shareholders' rights; e.g., changing liquidation preferences to benefit controlling shareholders at expense of minority shareholders.

Officers

The selection or removal of officers represents an important managerial function of the board of directors. While directors are responsible for the overall policies of the corporation, officers conduct the day-to-day operations of the firm and execute the policies established by the board. These lines of authority are well established in American law. The directors should manage, and the officers should carry out the management goals delegated to them by the directors.

Qualifications. Officers are agents of the corporation and, therefore, must fulfill the fiduciary duties placed on agents. Statutes often name the officers that a corporation must have, and usually either these statutes or the corporate bylaws spell out the respective officers' authority. Typical officers include president, vice president, secretary, and treasurer (or comptroller). The top executive may also be called the chairman of the board, the chief executive officer, or the general manager. The same person ordinarily can serve as more than one officer, but some statutes prohibit the same person from serving as both president and secretary.

Term of Office. The board ordinarily appoints the officers, who serve at the will of the directors. Some modern statutes, on the other hand, allow the shareholders to elect the officers. Either the board or the president can appoint junior or senior officers.

Officers usually serve at the pleasure of the board because the board in most jurisdictions can remove officers with or without cause, even when the officer has a valid employment contract. But after removal without cause, the corporation may be liable in damages to the former officer for breach of the employment contract. As we shall see later in this chapter, the directors normally escape personal liability if they have removed the officer in accordance with the *business judgment rule;* that is, they have exercised due care while making corporate decisions. In rare instances, the state, the courts, or the shareholders can remove officers. These instances nearly always involve a removal with cause.

Compensation. In earlier times, officers, like directors, traditionally served without pay because they usually were shareholders who expected their investment in the corporation to multiply by virtue of their work on the corporation's behalf. Thus, there was no need to supplement these corporate profits with a salary. Today, since neither officers nor directors are required to be shareholders, the corporation usually pays the officers a prearranged, fixed salary (recall in this context the possibility of golden parachutes as well). In addition, the corporation commonly adds to this salary, profit-sharing plans, bonuses, share options, deferred-compensation plans, pensions, annuities, and other fringe benefits like healthcare and expense accounts. Such compensation packages often turn out to be substantial indeed.

Compensation, to be lawful, should be reasonable and not represent waste of corporate assets. If waste is present, both directors and officers may be liable to the corporation for this waste. Courts have even ordered officers to return amounts deemed excessive compensation to the corporation.

Agency Law. Because officers are agents of the corporation, they have authority to bind the corporation. To help with this section, you should review the material on agency in Chapters 31 through 33. Generally, an officer's authority may be either express, implied, or apparent. The definitions used by courts in the corporate area may vary slightly from those used with other agencies.

Express authority derives from state statutes, the articles, or the bylaws. Any of these three sources may spell out the duties, responsibilities, and authority of the respective officers, although the bylaws are the most common source. Under express authority, the corporation has determined the boundaries within which the officer shall act on behalf of the corporation.

Implied authority, on the other hand, also known as *inherent authority,* derives from the virtue of the office or title of the person. Presidents have inherent authority to direct corporate meetings and to act on behalf of the corporation with regard to transactions occurring in the ordinary and regular course of business. For example, a president normally has authority to hire real estate brokers for the purpose of selling corporate property. Yet the president cannot validly sell or mortgage corporate assets without the approval of the board (and sometimes that of the shareholders). The president can have authority, however, to bind the corporation to sales or services contracts arising in the usual course of business; for instance, the president of a grain elevator can authorize purchases of wheat from local farmers. Courts sometimes uphold expansions of authority for presidents who are CEOs or general managers.

Vice presidents normally possess no authority by virtue of their office. Similarly, neither the treasurer nor the secretary can normally bind the corporation. The law ordinarily limits them to fairly ministerial intracorporate functions. Some jurisdictions, however, do give the treasurer authority to write, accept, indorse, and negotiate corporate checks and promissory notes.

Corporate officers may have *apparent authority* to bind the corporation. Apparent authority arises when the corporation, by its actions, indicates to a third party that an officer or agent is empowered to engage in certain transactions on behalf of the corporation. For example, if the corporation has customarily allowed its president to buy property on the corporation's behalf without prior board approval, he or she has apparent authority to bind the corporation to such a real estate transaction. The corporation cannot later allege lack of actual authority as a defense to consummation of the sale.

Likewise, the seller of the property may use the theory of estoppel to counter a defense of lack of actual authority. Estoppel may be used when the third party has been damaged because of the third party's good faith in and reasonable reliance on the corporation's creation of circumstances that appear to clothe the officer with apparent authority. In fact, estoppel may bind the corporation to transactions that result from unauthorized acts of the officer.

Subsequent *ratification* (approval) of previously unauthorized acts will also bind the corporation. Even if the president had no authority to buy real estate, a later board resolution that approves the purchase constitutes a ratification and binds the corporation to the completion of the transaction.

Liabilities. Officers who attempt to contract on behalf of the corporation without authority to do so may be personally liable to the other contracting party. Similarly, nondisclosure of the fact that the officer is acting on behalf of the corporation, even when the officer's actions are authorized, will lead to the personal liability of the officer. Officers who commit torts may be personally liable to the injured party, although the corporation may also be liable for torts committed by the officer during the scope of his or her employment under the doctrine of *respondeat superior.* Thus, a bank president who converts funds to his or her own use may be liable to the depositor, as may the bank under *respondeat superior.*

Fiduciary Duties Owed to the Corporation

Directors, officers, and controlling shareholders owe duties to the corporation and sometimes to shareholders and creditors. These are called fiduciary duties because the directors, officers, and controlling shareholders occupy a position of trust and good faith with regard to the corporation and other constituencies. Generally speaking, these obligations fall into three broad categories: the duty of obedience, the duty of diligence (or due care), and the duty of loyalty. These duties may arise from statute, but more often they issue from case law.

Obedience. Directors, officers, controlling shareholders, and other corporate managers must restrict their actions and those of the corporation to lawful pursuits. Any action taken beyond the scope of the corporation's power is an illegal, *ultra vires* act. By definition, violation of a positive rule of law or statute constitutes an illegal act. Any such actions by managers violate the duty of obedience and may subject them to personal liability.

Diligence. Because corporate managers act on behalf of the corporation, they are obligated to perform their duties with the amount of diligence or due care that a reasonably prudent person would exercise in the conduct of his or her own personal affairs in the same or similar circumstances. You probably notice the familiar ring of this language. We discussed this kind of standard when we addressed negligence (see Chapter 7). Basically, the duty of due care obliges a corporate manager to perform his or her duties in a nonnegligent fashion. Note that the law does not expect a director, officer, or controlling shareholder to be perfect or all-knowing. Honest errors of judgment will not lead to liability for breach of the duty of diligence. If liability were imposed in such situations, who would ever consent to be a director or officer?

Instead, the law excuses the conduct if the manager has made the error in good faith and without being clearly and grossly negligent. This is the *business judgment rule*. A jury must decide whether the manager's decision satisfies the business judgment rule or is grossly negligent and, hence, unacceptable. A manager who fails to attend corporate meetings or pays no attention to corporate affairs and is consequently ill-prepared may incur liability for breach of the duty of diligence or due care. Similarly, failure to fire an obviously unworthy employee, failure to obtain casualty insurance, failure to heed warning signs suggesting illegal conduct (such as embezzlement), or reliance on unreasonable statements by attorneys or accountants may lead to liability.

Nonetheless, the manager will incur liability only for such losses as his or her own negligent conduct causes. Consequently, if a director formally dissents about a matter that is later held to be negligent, that director will avoid liability. If the director does not dissent, it is usually no defense that the director was a figurehead

---

35.2 | FINANCE/ MANAGEMENT

CALL-IMAGE TECHNOLOGY

AVOIDING LIABILITY

Tom, as you recall, contracted for a unique marketing plan that he fully expected would be a great success. Unfortunately, the plan was a disaster, and the firm lost a significant amount of money on it. While the firm will weather this financial storm, the setback made Tom consider what might have happened if the firm was publicly owned. He is afraid that such a result in a publicly held firm might have resulted in his dismissal and/or liability for the losses. Tom has asked you what liabilities he would have faced if CIT had been publicly owned at the time he made the decision to contract for the marketing plan. What will you tell him?

BUSINESS CONSIDERATIONS What must a manager be able to show in order to avoid liability for a decision gone bad? Is this a difficult defense to establish? Why or why not?

ETHICAL CONSIDERATIONS What ethical duties do managers owe to the firm and/or the shareholders? To whom do managers owe the greatest duty?

or served without pay, but a manager's reasonable reliance on expert reports, such as those by accountants or attorneys, usually exonerates the manager from liability unless violations of securities acts are involved.

The court in the following case addressed the application of the business judgment rule.

35.3

SOLOMON V. ARMSTRONG
1999 DEL. CH. LEXIS 62 (CT. OF CHANCERY DELAWARE NEW CASTLE 1999)

FACTS . . . On June 7, 1996, General Motors Corporation ("GM"), a Delaware corporation, effected a split-off of its wholly-owned subsidiary, Electronic Data Systems Holding Corporation ("EDS"). The terms of the transaction provided for: 1) an exchange of GM Class E shares for EDS shares on a one-to-one basis; 2) new information technology service agreements . . . between GM and EDS; and 3) a $500 million lump sum cash transfer payment from EDS to GM. Before the split-off, . . . GM had three classes of common stock: GM 1-2/3 common stock, GM Class E common stock, and GM Class H common stock. The latter two classes of stock, so-called tracking stocks, derived their value from the GM operations to which they were tied. While dividends payable to holders of GM 1-2/3 common stock were based on GM's total income, dividends payable to holders of Class E common stock were tied to EDS's income, and dividends payable to holders of Class H common stock were based upon the income of GM's wholly-owned subsidiary, GM Hughes Electronics Corp. The certificate of incorporation and bylaws provided for a formulaic system to ensure a proper accounting of earnings attributable to each stock. . . . On August 7, 1995, GM announced that it planned to pursue a split-off of EDS to holders of GM Class E common stock. GM determined that it would only consummate a transaction that was tax-free and that would not trigger the Exchange Rate.[24] Under GM bylaws, a sub-committee of GM directors, the Capital Stock Committee (or the "Committee") was charged with charting a course for the split-off. The purported aim of the Committee was to structure a process that would protect the interests of all of GM's various classes of shareholders. . . . [T]he Committee put together two management teams, one consisting of GM officers . . . , and the other consisting of EDS officers . . . , which were charged with negotiating the terms and conditions of the split-off. . . . The GM team was authorized to use the assistance of GM's treasurer's office staff and legal staff, and also engaged outside counsel . . . , and . . .

financial advisor. . . . The EDS team was responsible for negotiating the terms of the transaction from the perspective of the holders of GM Class E common stock. The EDS team was authorized to use its own financial and legal staffs, and also engaged outside counsel . . . [and] financial advisors. . . . [Plaintiffs also note: "In connection with the Split-Off, [financial advisors] . . . were to receive a fee in the total amount of $7.5 million, $6.5 million of which was contingent upon consummation of the Split-Off. . . . "] Negotiations commenced between the teams on various issues . . . [T]he Capital Stock Committee suggested that the GM board promulgate a series of directives. . . . On March 22, 1996, the GM and EDS teams recommended to the Capital Stock Committee the terms of the split-off. . . . On March 31, 1996, the GM board approved the split-off, subject to the approval of a majority of the holders of each of: 1) the GM 1-2/3 common stock, voting separately as a class; 2) the GM Class E common stock, voting separately as a class; and 3) all classes of GM common stock, voting together. The GM board . . . agreed to recommend to the GM shareholders the terms of the split-off. . . . [Shareholders approved the split-off.]

ISSUES Did the board violate the business judgment rule? Was the shareholder vote coerced or based on false statements?

HOLDINGS No. No. The board followed an acceptable procedure in the split-off.

REASONING Most corporations that go through fundamental corporate governance changes can protect their decisions by perfecting a fair process. . . . Directors must often resolve conflicts among classes of stock, and the fact that a majority of the directors own more of one class than another does not necessarily implicate the directors' good faith or loyalty. . . . No basis exists for assuming wrongdoing on the banks'

continued

35.3

SOLOMON V. ARMSTRONG, *continued*

1999 DEL. CH. LEXIS 62 (CT. OF CHANCERY DELAWARE NEW CASTLE 1999)

part [and, by implication, the board's part] without allegations of an actual manifestation of bias in favor of GM through the investment banks' manipulation of financial information. . . . [B]oth the form and the substance of the transaction in this case is radically different from a parent-subsidiary freeze-out merger or any other transaction with a controlling shareholder. The certificate of incorporation protected shareholders' interests in the form of contractual limitations on the board's power—primarily through the combination of veto power and the Exchange Rate. The Capital Stock Committee provided independent oversight for the resolution of conflicting interests. . . . Together, these circumstances compel me to reject the notion that the Court should conceptualize the split-off transaction as akin to a minority freeze-out. That conceptualization could too easily deprive the board of business judgment protection in a situation where the business judgment rule's presumptions seem appropriate.

. . . There are two legally relevant questions that guide the Court's analysis as to whether the board acted in all of the various classes' best interests. First, was the process for allocating value reasonably aimed at providing a fair result to all shareholders taken together and each and every class of shareholders taken separately? Second, even to the extent that aspects of the process may have been flawed, were all shareholders sufficiently informed about the details of the process and empowered to make an independent decision on the substantive terms of the transaction? If either question is answered in the affirmative the business judgment rule's presumptions must remain in effect. . . . Thus, the question is whether plaintiffs have alleged facts from which it might be inferred that the directors or their agents did not follow the certificate's provisions: 1) in good faith; 2) employing a rational (i.e., non-arbitrary) basis for making the

allocation; 3) on a reasonably informed basis (i.e., with due care); or 4) in the shareholders' interests, as opposed to the directors' or anyone else's personal profit or betterment (i.e., that they acted with due loyalty). If no basis exists for such an inference, then the business judgment rule should protect the board's allocation determination. I conclude that plaintiffs have failed to make the necessary showing. . . . In most respects, the GM board and the Capital Stock Committee went about this task in the right way: 1) the negotiations persisted for quite some time; 2) the two teams seemed to come close to impasse before the GM board stepped in; 3) all of the relevant groups retained highly reputable legal counsel; and 4) disclosure of the events surrounding the transaction appears to have been thorough. . . .

[S]o long as the shareholder vote to approve or disapprove the transaction was made on a fully-informed, non-coerced basis, that vote operates . . . as an independent foundation for the application of the business judgment rule. Of course, plaintiffs may defeat the business judgment rule's presumptions . . . by alleging materially false or misleading statements in the disclosure statements on which the vote was predicated. . . . When dealing with ratification and disclosure issues, courts inquire as to the type and quality of information in shareholders' hands prior to the vote. . . . I dismiss all of plaintiffs' claims relating to disclosure violations. . . .

BUSINESS CONSIDERATION What should a corporation do when it wants to split off a subsidiary?

ETHICAL CONSIDERATION What would constitute fair procedures for a stock "split-off"?

Loyalty. Because directors, officers, and controlling shareholders enjoy positions of trust with the corporation, they must act in good faith and with loyalty toward the corporation and its shareholders. The undivided loyalty expected of fiduciaries means that managers must place the interests of the corporation above their own personal interests. Sometimes these corporate interests and personal interests collide, and it becomes necessary to resort to applicable statutes and case law. Usually such "collisions" involve (1) corporate opportunities or (2) conflicts of interest.

Knoe

The *corporate opportunity doctrine* forbids directors, officers, and controlling shareholders from diverting to themselves business deals or potential deals that in fairness or in justice belong to the corporation. For the sake of simplicity, we will call these persons "managers." Personal gains at the expense of the corporation represent a breach of the managers' fiduciary duties. A corporate opportunity is commonly found (1) if the manager discovers the opportunity in his or her capacity as director, and (2) it is reasonably foreseeable that the corporation will be interested in the opportunity because it relates closely to the corporation's line of business. For example, if Wanda is a director in a real estate development corporation (Real Property Corporation) and Ray offers to sell property to Wanda because he knows she is a director of Real Property, Wanda should not buy the property for herself. To do so will violate her duty of loyalty. If the corporation might reasonably be interested in the land for its corporate development program, Wanda must disclose this opportunity to the corporation. Once she has given the corporation this right of first refusal, Wanda ordinarily can purchase the property if the corporation refuses the opportunity or is financially unable to implement the purchase.

If Wanda breaches the duty of loyalty and purchases the land for herself, corporate remedies will include damages (the profits Wanda makes as a result of the purchase and subsequent sale) or the imposition of a **constructive trust** (a court will treat Wanda as a trustee who is holding the property for the benefit of the corporation). A court then can force Wanda to convey the property to Real Property Corporation and/or to pay Real Property any profits she realized on the transaction.

The most common example of a possible conflict of interest occurs when a director, officer, or controlling shareholder personally contracts with the corporation. For example, suppose Wanda is willing to sell a piece of her own property to the corporation. Because of her personal interests, she will undoubtedly hope to make as much money as possible on the transaction. Yet her position as a director of Real Property obligates her to accept as low a price as possible in order to benefit the company. Wanda obviously faces a difficult dilemma. Most states will allow the transaction (1) if Wanda makes a full disclosure of her interest to the board of directors of Real Property before the board begins its deliberations on the proposed contract, and (2) if the resultant contract is fair and reasonable to the corporation. If Wanda does not fully disclose her interest or if the terms of the contract are unfair or unreasonable, however, the contract will be voidable by the corporation.

An additional concern in these situations stems from whether Wanda (who is called an *interested* director) should be allowed to vote on the contract. At common law, Wanda could not vote—or even be counted toward the quorum— at the meeting where the matter was to be discussed. Although modern statutes (and articles or bylaws) vary, in

Constructive trust
A trust imposed by law to prevent the unjust enrichment of the person in possession of the property (the purported owner).

35.3 | FINANCE

SUBCHAPTER S CORPORATIONS

The Kochanowskis have decided either to incorporate CIT as a Subchapter S corporation or to remain a general partnership. They are concerned, however, about the need to satisfy several of the more burdensome and/or time-consuming aspects of corporate existence. They need to know what requirements they will face as a Subchapter S corporation in such matters as annual meetings, distribution of authority, tax returns, and rights of shareholders. They also need to know how these requirements might vary if they were just to remain a partnership. What advice will you give them?

BUSINESS CONSIDERATIONS What business criteria are important in making the decision to adopt any particular form of business organization? What personal factors should a businessperson consider?

ETHICAL CONSIDERATIONS Will the businesspersons have different ethical duties if they operate the business as a partnership as compared to a corporation? Why or why not?

RESOURCES FOR BUSINESS LAW STUDENTS

NAME	RESOURCES	WEB ADDRESS
American Success Institute	American Success Institute promises a "free business education on the web," providing tips on operating small businesses.	**http://www.success.org/**
EDUCAUSE, Inc., articles of incorporation	Educom, a not-for-profit corporation specializing in education information, maintains its articles of incorporation, bylaws, trustees' terms of office, and trustees' names and addresses, online.	**http://www.educause.edu/coninfo/cearticles.html**
Limited liability companies	Attorney Steven E. Davidson provides basic information on limited liability companies, including a state-by-state comparison chart.	**http://www.llcweb.com/**

general, Wanda can vote and be counted toward the quorum if, as noted earlier, she discloses her interest and if the resultant contract is fair to the corporation.

As previously discussed, the duty of loyalty also prohibits directors, officers, or controlling shareholders from prejudicing minority shareholders' rights by freezing out minority shareholders through such actions as forcing dissolution of the corporation or modifying the distribution of assets if the firm is liquidated.

In the context of corporate takeovers, allegations of breach of fiduciary duties commonly arise. As the sophistication of both the "raider" and the target corporation has increased, directors of the latter have responded creatively to mount a host of defensive moves meant to blunt the would-be acquiring firm's appetite for the target corporation. The development of exotic (but apt) terms such as **greenmail** and **poison pill** to describe these thrusts and countermeasures masks the more important issue of whether the law will approve of these deterrent efforts.

Greenmail
The process by which a firm threatens a corporate takeover by buying a significant portion of a corporation's stock and then selling it back to the corporation at a premium when the corporation's directors and executives, fearing for their positions, agree to buy out the firm.

Poison pill
Any strategy adopted by the directors of a target firm in order to decrease the firm's attractiveness to an acquiring firm during an attempted hostile takeover.

SUMMARY

Each partner has certain rights in the business by virtue of his or her status as a partner. These rights may be limited or defined by the agreement. If no agreement exists, each partner has an equal voice in management, a right to an equal share of profits or losses, equal access to books and records of the firm, and an equal right to use partnership property for partnership purposes. Each one also has a right to be reimbursed for expenditures and a right to an account.

Each partner is an agent for every other partner and is a principal of every other partner. As a result, all the rules of agency apply. Each partner is a fiduciary of the other partners. When a partner deals with some third party, the firm is bound by the conduct if it was apparently or actually authorized. Agency principles also apply to the torts of a partner. If the tort is in the course and scope of employment, the partners are jointly and severally liable. If it is beyond the scope of employment, only the tortfeasor is liable, unless the other partners ratify the conduct. Any liability for crimes committed by a partner is not imposed on the non-acting partners unless they ratify the conduct.

Ownership of corporate shares carries with it certain rights. The types of rights shareholders enjoy may vary depending on the type of stock involved. Ownership of common stock permits the shareholder to receive dividends (without priority) and to vote on corporate issues. In contrast, ownership of preferred stock confers priority as to dividends, voting, and/or liquidation rights. In addition, preferred stock may have participation rights, conversion rights, and/or redemption rights.

Shareholders' meetings provide the vehicle by which both common and preferred stockholders exercise their most significant control over the corporation. Corporate bylaws usually require an annual meeting (primarily for election of directors) and may authorize special meetings in appropriate circumstances. Such meetings ordinarily cannot legally occur in the absence of either prior notice or a quorum. One of the shareholders' foremost powers involves the election and removal of directors. Shareholders have inherent power to remove a director for cause and may have power to remove a director without cause. Shareholders may also amend or repeal bylaws.

Shareholders can cast their votes either in person or by proxy. For most corporate matters, straight voting is used. However, for the election of directors, many state statutes either permit or require cumulative voting. Cumulative voting protects the interests of minority shareholders but may be countered by such strategies as staggered terms for directors. Other devices used to consolidate voting power include voting trusts and pooling arrangements. These devices are especially useful in close corporations.

Dividends represent financial returns on shareholders' investments. Yet shareholders cannot compel directors to declare dividends; the directors alone have this power. The board also must make certain that dividends, if declared, have been paid from a lawful source. Dividends may be cumulative or noncumulative.

When a corporation increases its capital by issuing new shares, shareholder approval is necessary. To protect a shareholder's proportionate interest in the corporation when recapitalization occurs, the doctrine of preemptive rights is ordinarily applicable.

Shareholders' rights to inspect corporate records arise from both common law doctrines and express statutory provisions. Ordinarily, if a shareholder can demonstrate a proper purpose for requesting access to the records, the shareholder will be able to examine certain corporate documents.

Shareholders may be liable to the corporation or creditors for watered stock, and a subscriber may be liable to the corporation or to creditors if the subscriber breaches a stock subscription. Declaration and distribution of illegal dividends may subject both directors and shareholders to personal liability. Controlling shareholders also may incur liability if the purpose of the corporation's dissolution is to freeze out minority stockholders and to strip these stockholders of rights or profits they would otherwise enjoy.

The right to manage the corporation falls squarely on the board of directors. Shareholders cannot compel directors to take any action, because the directors are not the agents of the shareholders but, rather, owe loyalty primarily to the corporation. The modern trend is to lower the number of directors and to lessen the traditionally stringent rules concerning directors' qualifications. Directors generally can appoint replacements on the board when vacancies arise due to death, resignation, or incapacity.

Most statutes authorize the board of directors to delegate managerial authority to officers and executive committees. Broad delegations of authority to persons outside the directorial ranks are usually invalid.

Directors may or may not receive compensation from the corporation. The directors normally determine officers' compensation. Such compensation packages are usually legal if reasonable in amount. Otherwise, a shareholder can attack the compensation as a waste of corporate assets.

Performance of directorial duties may lead to personal liability for directors. Occasionally, the corporation will indemnify the directors for liabilities accruing from their corporate positions. Directors have the right to declare dividends, enter into agreements, and inspect corporate records.

Officers are agents of the corporation and, thus, have the fiduciary duties placed on agents. The board ordinarily appoints the officers, who serve at the will of the directors. Officers may bind the corporation by express, implied, or apparent authority. But the unauthorized acts of officers may make them personally liable to the other contracting party.

Directors, officers, and controlling shareholders owe fiduciary duties to the corporation. Broadly speaking, these duties fall into three categories: the duty of obedience, the duty of diligence (or due care), and the duty of loyalty. The duty of obedience forbids *ultra vires* acts. The business judgment rule constitutes a defense to liability for violation of the duty of diligence. Under this rule, the manager will not be liable if he or she makes an erroneous decision in good faith and without clear and gross negligence. The duty of loyalty, among other things, precludes directors, officers, and controlling shareholders from usurping corporate opportunities or prejudicing the corporation due to undisclosed conflicts of interest.

DISCUSSION QUESTIONS

1. Tim and Ed are partners. Tim, however, is tired of the business and sells it to Eugenia. Ed objects to the sale and sues to have it declared void. Eugenia claims Tim has the apparent authority to sell. How should the court rule, and why?

2. Manpal and Barbara are partners. Barbara calls a customer and says the firm will not be able to deliver certain goods on time. The customer immediately sues for anticipatory breach. Manpal objects to the suit, saying the customer has no grounds to expect a breach. Do you agree? Explain.

3. April, Jim, and Dan are partners in a retail business. Dan borrows $10,000 from the bank to "buy more goods." The loan is made in the partnership name. Dan, however, takes the money to Las Vegas and loses it all at the roulette table. If the bank sues April and Jim on the loan, what should be the result? Explain.

4. Explain what the following have to do with shareholders' meetings: (a) proxies, (b) straight voting, (c) cumulative voting, (d) voting trusts, and (e) pooling agreements.

5. Explain how a shareholder secures the right to inspect corporate documents.

6. How can shareholder liability arise for watered stock, stock subscriptions, illegal dividends, and dissolution?

7. What are the limitations on directors' delegations of authority to officers and corporate committees?

8. Briefly enumerate the rights and liabilities of directors. How do officers' rights and liabilities differ from those of directors?

9. In what ways can corporate managers prevent charges of conflicts of interest from being levied against them?

10. Judge Benjamin Cardozo wrote, "Many forms of conduct permissible in a workaday world, for those acting at arm's length, are forbidden to those bound by fiduciary ties. A . . . [fiduciary] is held to something stricter than the morals of the market place. Not honesty alone, but the punctilio of an honor the most sensitive, is the standard of behavior. As to this there has developed a tradition that is unbending and inveterate." Is his description of fiduciary duty helpful? Why or why not? How do you define *fiduciary duty*? [See *Meinhard* v. *Salmon*, 164 N.E. 545 (N.Y. 1928).]

CASE PROBLEMS AND WRITING ASSIGNMENTS

1. Bill Hodge entered into a contract with Rex Voeller to purchase land owned by a partnership. Voeller was the managing general partner of the partnership, which owned and operated a drive-in movie theater. Voeller signed the contract in the partnership's name and on behalf of the partnership and his partners. One of the partners objected to the sale, and the deed was not transferred to Hodge. Hodge has sued for specific performance of the contract. How will the court resolve this case? What factors will the court examine in reaching its decision? [See *Hodge* v. *Garrett*, 614 P.2d 420 (1980).]

2. Kaneco was a limited partnership involved in the oil and gas industry. Kaneco hired Winterhawk, Ltd. to operate its business, agreeing to pay a management and administration fee based on a percentage of drilling and completion costs. In order to acquire funding for its projects, Kaneco obtained a loan from the bank, secured with letters of credit. The loan proceeds were paid directly to Winterhawk by deposits to its general checking account, as per Kaneco's instruction. Winterhawk's president, Robert Fullop, apparently misappropriated substantial amounts of the loan proceeds, and Kaneco was placed in a poor financial position. Eventually, Kaneco had difficulty making its payments on the loan, and the bank informed the general partners that the loan was being called since the loan balance exceeded the value of the letters of credit. Kaneco sought an injunction to prevent the bank from calling the loan or calling the letters of credit. Kaneco argued that the general partners were not jointly and severally liable for the loan balance. How should the court resolve this case? Why? [See *Kaneco Oil & Gas, Ltd., II* v. *University Nat'l Bank*, 732 P.2d 247 (Colo.App. 1986).]

3. At the opening of the 2 November 1989 annual meeting of the Center for Communications and Development/KMOJ Radio (CCD/KMOJ), a nonprofit corporation, the president of the board of directors announced the suspension of the right to vote of 2 directors. Several directors protested the suspension as a violation of the bylaws. When the president refused to reconsider this matter, 7 of the 13 directors left the meeting. The seventh departing director requested that the record of the meeting reflect that she had not been part of the decision and that she had "challenged the quorum of those remaining." The president continued the meeting, and the board added four new directors and reelected the president for another term. The 7 directors who had left the meeting brought a lawsuit to enjoin the president and new directors from acting on behalf of the corporation until a procedurally correct annual meeting could be held. They also sought a temporary injunction to prohibit the president from decreasing community programming on the radio station or significantly altering the station's operations or policies. Minnesota corporate statutes provided for enactment of bylaws "for the purpose of administering and regulating the affairs of the corporation" as long as the bylaws were "not inconsistent with law or the articles of incorporation." Section 5.5 of CCD/KMOJ's bylaws stated: "Once established, a quorum remains established until the adjournment of the meeting or until a member calls for a quorum count and one is found lacking." The trial court granted summary judgment against the departing directors. Was the case against the directors so clear that a trial was unnecessary? Why or why not? [See *Johnson* v. *Edwards*, 467 N.W.2d 333 (Minn.App. 1991).]

4. Southwest Breeders, Inc., an Oklahoma corporation, had offered to sell shares of its stock to Jack Agosta. At the time, Southwest Breeders' articles of incorporation allowed the corporation, through its officers and directors, to issue no more than 50,000 shares of its stock at $1 per share. On 31 March 1986, Agosta purchased 15,000 shares of the stock. Agosta later discovered that the officers and directors had, on 27 December 1985, issued to themselves 1,370,000 shares at below par value, clearly in excess of the amount allowed by the articles of incorporation. Southwest Breeders subsequently filed an amendment of its articles of incorporation with the secretary of state that authorized it to increase the number of shares of its stock from 50,000 to 50,000,000. Agosta filed suit to rescind his contract, seeking $6,000 in damages for his purchase of the overissued stock. Agosta then filed a motion for summary judgment, which the trial court sustained on the ground that the sale of the overissued stock to Agosta constituted a sale of nonexistent stock for which the officers and directors remained personally liable. On appeal, Southwest Breeders alleged that the trial court had erred in characterizing the sale of stock to Agosta as unauthorized and, therefore, void. How should the appellate court rule? [See *Agosta* v. *Southwest Breeders, Inc.*, 810 P.2d 377 (Okla.App. 1991).]

5. Eugene Doemling incorporated Specialty Plastics, Inc. (Specialty) in 1975 to manufacture and sell plastic containers to another business he owned, Imaging Systems Corp. Doemling was the sole shareholder of Specialty and served on its board of directors. When Specialty declared bankruptcy in December

1982, Doemling was serving as its president. In early 1981, Doemling personally purchased a B75 and a B100 blow molder and related equipment and leased both machines to Specialty. During the lease term, Specialty was responsible for the equipment's installation, maintenance, and repair. In June 1982, Doemling personally purchased a Uniloy 300 blow molder and related equipment and leased it to Specialty. Doemling purchased all of this equipment in his personal capacity; Specialty's board of directors had approved none of the leases. In December 1982, Doemling unilaterally terminated Specialty's leases on the B100 blow molder and the Uniloy 300 blow molder. He sold the B100 molder to a third party for $65,000 and the Uniloy 300 for $72,500. These sales resulted in substantial personal profits ($38,000) for Doemling. On 1 May 1984, Doemling unilaterally terminated Specialty's remaining lease on the B75 blow molder. He sold the B75 to a third party for $85,000 and, thus, realized an additional profit of $50,500. During the course of the three leases, Specialty had paid Doemling a total of $24,300 in rental payments. Specialty also had expended an additional $23,331 for the installation, maintenance, and repair of the three blow molders and related equipment. When Specialty filed for bankruptcy under Chapter 11, the bankruptcy court concluded that Doemling had usurped a corporate opportunity that had properly belonged to Specialty. It, therefore, ordered Doemling to give up any profits he had made through this opportunity and to pay Specialty all the money he had received in rent; all the profits he had realized as a result of the sale of the three blow molders; and all the money Specialty had spent for the installation, repair, and maintenance of the machines. The bankruptcy court further found that Doemling's actions with regard to the purchase and leasing of these machines constituted *defalcation* (misconduct, moral dereliction) and, therefore, held that Doemling's obligation to repay these monies was nondischargeable in bankruptcy. Should the appellate court uphold the bankruptcy court's decision? Why? [See *Committee of Unsecured Creditors of Specialty Plastics, Inc.* v. *Doemling*, 127 B.R. 945 (W.D.Pa. 1991), 952 F.2d. 1391 (3rd Cir. 1991).]

6. **BUSINESS APPLICATION CASE** Charles Zwick served as Southeast Banking Corp.'s chairman and CEO. He was ousted from his $500,000 a year job in January 1991 and signed a severance agreement of $1.25 million, consisting of monthly payments of $41,667 spread over two-and-a-half years. Although once the leading corporate lender in Florida, Southeast's banks were failing. Due to pressure from regulatory entities, such as the comptroller of the currency,

and from shareholders, Southeast stopped paying Zwick the agreed-upon sum after only a few months. Zwick then sued Southeast for breach of contract. The comptroller of the currency argued that regulators acted within their lawful powers by cracking down on golden parachutes extended to departing executives at failing banks. Zwick's attorney, however, maintained that regulators, in these circumstances, unlawfully interfered with valid and legal contracts when they brought pressure to bear on Southeast to cease payments under the severance arrangement. Why might a business decide to provide golden parachutes to its key executives? How does such a decision affect the duty of the board of directors to its other constituents? [See Joann S. Lublin, "Firms Rethink Lucrative Severance Pacts for Top Executives as Criticism Swells," *Wall Street Journal* (11 November 1991), p. B1.]

7. **ETHICAL APPLICATION CASE** Danny Hill was an officer and general manager of Southeastern Floor Covering Co., Inc. (Southeastern), which completed ceiling and floor-covering work for general contractors. Southeastern often subcontracted its asbestos-removal work to Southern Interiors. Southeastern bid on construction work on the Chata project. Hill arranged with Southern Interiors for it to bid on the Chata project directly without involving Southeastern. Southern Interiors was awarded the bid, and Hill earned $90,000 according to their arrangement. When Southeastern discovered the arrangement, it sued Hill. Should Southeastern be awarded the $90,000 payment Hill received? What ethical issues are raised? [See *Hill* v. *Southeastern Floor Covering Co., Inc.*, 596 So.2d 874 (Miss. 1992).]

8. **CRITICAL THINKING CASE** Thomas Scanlon had been employed by Steel Suppliers, Inc., a company engaged in warehousing and distributing structural steel, for 30 years. He had served as president and a director. On 21 November 1984, Steelvest, Inc., a corporation owned by William Lucas, purchased the assets of Steel Suppliers for approximately $5 million. After this purchase, Steelvest continued Steel Suppliers, as a separate, unincorporated division under the same name. At Lucas's request, Scanlon agreed to stay on as president and general manager of Steel Suppliers. He also subsequently became a director of Steelvest and a member of its executive committee. Scanlon's employment with Steel Suppliers continued for 11 months after the purchase by Steelvest. During these 11 months, Scanlon began to formulate a plan to start and incorporate his own steel business, which would compete directly with Steelvest. Toward this end, he sought the advice of counsel, contacted

potential investors, and sought financing. He disclosed none of these activities to any representative of Steelvest. Furthermore, he recruited two CEOs of major clients of Steelvest to invest in his new company. Scanlon resigned from his employment with Steel Suppliers and Steelvest on 15 October 1985. One day prior to this, on 14 October, Scanlon had completed most of the necessary arrangements for setting up his new business, including the signing of documents for the purchase of property to be used as the site for the business. Immediately after Scanlon's resignation from Steelvest, he, along with the other investors,

incorporated Scansteel Service Center, Inc., which began actual operations soon thereafter. Nine office and supervisory employees of Steelvest resigned to take employment with Scansteel. On 2 June 1986, Steelvest instituted this action against Scansteel and Scanlon, alleging a breach of fiduciary duties by Scanlon and a conspiracy on the part of the investors and the bank that had provided the financing for the formation of Scansteel. Did Scanlon breach his fiduciary duties to Steelvest by planning and organizing a directly competitive business? [See *Steelvest, Inc.* v. *Scansteel Service Center, Inc.*, 807 S.W.2d 476 (Ky. 1991).]

NOTES

1. Uniform Partnership Act (UPA) refers to the 1914 act drafted by the National Conference of Commissioners on Uniform State Laws (NCCUSL). The UPA is the rule in about half the jurisdictions today.
2. Uniform Partnership Act § 18(h).
3. Ibid., § 18(a), (b), (c).
4. Ibid., § 18(f).
5. Ibid., §§ 19 and 20.
6. Ibid., § 25.
7. The following states have adopted the RUPA with the 1997 amendments: Alabama, Arizona, Arkansas, California, Colorado, District of Columbia, Hawaii, Idaho, Iowa, Kansas, Maryland, Minnesota, Montana, Nebraska, New Mexico, North Dakota, Oklahoma, Oregon, Puerto Rico, U.S. Virgin Islands, Vermont, Virginia, and Washington. "A Few Facts About the Uniform Partnership Act (1994)(1997)," NCCUSL web site, http://www.nccusl.org/uniformact_factsheets/uniformacts-fs-upa9497.htm.
8. Revised Uniform Partnership Act, § 203.
9. "Uniform Partnership Act (1994)," NCCUSL web site, http://www.nccusl.org/uniformact_summaries/uniformacts-s-upa1994.htm.
10. Uniform Partnership Act § 22.
11. Ibid., § 21.
12. Ibid., § 10.
13. Ibid., § 11.
14. Ibid., § 12.
15. Ibid., § 13.
16. Ibid., § 14.
17. Ibid., § 28.
18. Ibid., § 21.
19. "A Few Facts About the Uniform Partnership Act (1994)(1997)," NCCUSL web site, http://www.nccusl.org/uniformact_factsheets/uniformacts-fs-upa9497.htm.
20. "The Art of the Market" (book excerpt), *Fortune* (27 September 1999), pp. 230–239. Book excerpt from Bob Tamarkin and Les Krantz, with commentary by George LeBarre, *The Art of the Market* (New York: Tabori & Chang, 1999).
21. The Model Business Corporation Act (1969) began as a drafting effort in 1943 by the American Bar Association's Section on Corporation, Banking, and Business Law; its intent was to modernize corporate law and to achieve greater uniformity among jurisdictions by creating a statute that balances the interests of the state, the corporation, the shareholders, and management. Most of the states follow either the older Model Business Corporation Act or the 1984 version, the Revised Model Business Corporation Act.
22. For more information about the price-fixing scandal, see Ronald Henkoff, "Behind the ADM Scandal: Betrayal," *Fortune* (3 February 1997), pp. 82–87, and Mark Whitacre's interview with Ronald Henkoff, "I Thought I Was Going to Be a Hero," *Fortune* (3 February 1997), pp. 87–91.
23. "The Tale of the Secret Tapes," *The New York Times* (16 November 1997), pp. B1, B10; "ADM's New CEO: Allen Andreas," *Chicago Tribune* (18 April 1997), Business Section, p. 1; "It Isn't Dwayne's World Anymore," *Business Week* (18 November 1996), p. 82; "Andreas Creates Executive Team," *Washington Post* (1 November 1996), p. F3; and "Archer Daniels Midland Agrees to Big Fine for Price Fixing," *The New York Times* (15 October 1996), pp. A1, C3.

    Postcript: ADM did change its governance process. Andreas would now share power as part of a four-person executive committee. Four managers stepped down from the board, several others were replaced, and two executives who were implicated in the price-fixing scandal left the company, including Andreas's son and heir apparent. In April 1997, Andreas, age 79, finally retired as CEO: He retained the title of chairman of the board. He was succeeded by his nephew, G. Allen Andreas, as CEO.
24. Under the Exchange Rate, Class E shareholders had a right to redeem their shares.

36

BUSINESS TERMINATIONS
AND OTHER EXTRAORDINARY EVENTS

A G E N D A

CIT may be a big success in developing and marketing Call-Image. On the other hand, the enterprise may fail miserably. If the firm is a success, it is likely that a large corporation may wish to acquire CIT. The Kochanowskis do not wish to give up ownership of the company, and they would resist any takeover efforts. If the other firm persists in its efforts to acquire CIT, how can the Kochanowskis prevent a takeover? What legal or ethical restrictions may limit its actions? If the enterprise is a failure, the Kochanowskis are afraid that they will lose everything they have acquired over the years. How can they protect their assets while providing adequate support to the firm to give it a chance to succeed?

These and other questions will arise as you read this chapter. Be prepared! You never know when one of the Kochanowskis will need your help or advice.

O U T L I N E

Termination of a Sole Proprietorship
Partnership Termination
Partnership Dissolution
Continuation of the Partnership Business
Winding Up the Partnership
Changes in Corporate Structure
Liquidation of the Corporation

Dissolution of the Corporation
Corporate Merger and Consolidation
Sale of Substantially All the Assets
Stock Acquisition
Summary
Discussion Questions
Case Problems and Writing Assignments

TERMINATION OF A SOLE PROPRIETORSHIP

The termination of a sole proprietorship is a relatively simple matter. The owner simply pays the business debts and thereby acquires the remaining assets. As an alternative, the owner might sell the business to someone else. Care must be used to assure that business liabilities are handled correctly, however. Often, but not always, this is an obligation undertaken by the buyer.

PARTNERSHIP TERMINATION

The ending of a partnership differs from what most people expect. The partnership may end while the business enterprise continues; if so, a dissolution occurs. Or the partnership and the business enterprise may both end. If so, a dissolution and a **winding up** occur. These variations in the termination of a partnership are the focus of this section.

Winding up
Paying the accounts and liquidating the assets of a business for the purpose of making distributions and dissolving the concern.

PARTNERSHIP DISSOLUTION

Technically, a *dissolution* is "the change in the relation of the partners caused by any partner ceasing to be associated in the carrying on as distinguished from the winding up of the business."[1] This means that anytime a partner leaves the business, the partnership is dissolved. The change in the relations of the partners changes the partnership.

The fact that a partner leaves the business does not mean that the *business* must cease to exist. The remaining partners may continue the business, or they may need to terminate it. What they may or may not do depends on the method and manner of dissolution.

Section 31 of the Uniform Partnership Act (UPA) lists several different causes of dissolution. (Note that references in this chapter to the UPA are to the UPA (1914), which is still the majority rule.) Any of these events will cause a dissolution of the partnership, but they may not require a winding up of the business. We shall examine these causes of dissolution next.

Without Violation of the Agreement

A dissolution may be caused by the terms of the partnership agreement. For example, the time period established in the agreement may expire, or the original purpose of the partnership may be fulfilled. If a partnership was established to operate for two years, and two years have elapsed, the partnership is dissolved. If a partnership was established to sell 100 parcels of land, and all the land has been sold, the partnership is dissolved. Of course, a new agreement may be made to extend the time or to modify the purpose, if the partners so desire.

If the agreement does not specify a particular time period or a particular, limited purpose, a partner may simply decide to quit. Unless the agreement denies this right to withdraw, such a decision operates as a dissolution without violation of the agreement.

All the partners may decide to terminate the partnership. If so, the partnership is dissolved without violating the agreement. This is true even if a definite time period was specified and that time has not yet expired. And it is true even *if* a particular purpose was declared and the purpose has not yet been achieved.

Finally, a partnership is dissolved without violation of the agreement if any partner is expelled from the partnership by the other partners, *provided* that the expulsion is permitted by the agreement. Thus, if Xavier, Yvonne, and Stella vote to remove Antwoine from the firm, and the agreement permits such a vote, the partnership is dissolved without violation of the agreement.

Normally, a dissolution that does not violate the agreement will lead to a winding up *unless* the agreement itself provides for a continuation of the business. If the agreement does not specify that a continuation is permitted, the partner who causes the dissolution may demand that a winding up take place. Such a demand must be obeyed, even though it normally will harm the remaining partners who may wish to continue the business. Thus, every partnership agreement should contain some provisions for continuing the business. (Of course, an *expelled* partner cannot demand a winding up of the business if the expulsion was done in good faith by the other partners.)

In Violation of the Agreement

No one can be forced to be a partner against his or her will. Thus, any partner has the *power* to withdraw from any partnership at any time, but may not have the *right* to do so. Thus, a withdrawing partner may violate the terms of the partnership agreement by withdrawing. If so, the remaining partners may continue the business if they desire, even though the partnership has been (technically) dissolved. The partner who withdrew in violation of the agreement has no right to demand or require a winding up.

Similarly, the partner who withdraws in violation of the agreement does not have the right to demand that the business be continued. Once a partner withdraws in violation of the agreement, the remaining innocent partners may decide to do whatever they believe is most appropriate—the options belong to the remaining partners.

By Operation of Law

A partnership may also be dissolved by operation of law, if any one of the following three events occurs:

1. Something happens that makes it unlawful for the business to continue or for the partners to continue the business. (Thus, a law that prohibits anyone from selling elephant tusks will terminate a partnership in the tusk-selling business. And a partnership that loses its import license will be dissolved even though importing itself is still legal.)
2. A partner dies.
3. A partner or the partnership becomes bankrupt.

By Court Order

The final method for dissolving a partnership is by court order. As explained in § 32 of the UPA, a court will order a dissolution only if *asked* to do so. The person who wants to dissolve the partnership must petition the court; the court will not go searching for partnerships that should be dissolved.

Most commonly, the petitioning person is one of the partners or a representative of one of the partners. Even if a petition is filed, dissolution is not automatic.

The court must have *grounds* to grant the request. The following grounds will justify a dissolution by court decree:

1. Insanity of any partner
2. Incapacity, other than insanity, of a partner that prevents that partner from performing the contractual duties called for in the agreement
3. Misconduct by any partner that makes continued operation of the business difficult
4. Intentional or repeated breach of the agreement by a partner, or any behavior that makes the continuation of the business impossible or impractical
5. Evidence that the business can be continued only at a loss with no prospect of a profit turnaround in the near future
6. Any other circumstances that, in the court's opinion, justify dissolution as the equitable response

Note that insanity does *not* automatically dissolve the partnership; a petition must be filed seeking dissolution. If the remaining partners wish to continue the business with an insane partner, they have the right to do so.

It is also possible that some person may purchase the interest of a partner and then decide to seek a court-ordered dissolution.[2] Such a court order may be granted only if one of two sets of circumstances can be proven:

1. The agreement had a specific term or a particular purpose that has been fulfilled or satisfied.
2. The partnership was a partnership **at will** at the time of the purchase.

At will
Having no specific date or circumstance to bring about a dissolution.

In the following case the court reviewed whether a dissolution was improper under the Revised Uniform Limited Partnership Act (RULPA).

36.1

HORIZON/CMS HEALTHCARE CORPORATION
V. SOUTHERN OAKS HEALTH CARE, INC.

732 SO. 2D 1156 (FLORIDA APP. 5TH DIST. 1999)

FACTS Horizon/CMS Healthcare (hereinafter "Horizon") appeals the final judgment in favor of Southern Oaks Health Care, Inc. (hereinafter "Southern Oaks"). . . . Horizon is a large, publicly traded provider of both nursing home facilities and management for nursing home facilities. It wanted to expand into Osceola County. . . . Southern Oaks was already operating in Osceola County. . . . Horizon and Southern Oaks decided to form a partnership to own the proposed . . . facility, . . . and agreed that Horizon would manage both the Southern Oaks facility and the new Royal Oaks facility. . . . Southern Oaks and Horizon entered into several partnership and management contracts in 1993. In 1996, Southern Oaks filed suit alleging numerous defaults and breaches of the twenty-year agreements. . . . [T]he court ordered that the partnerships be dissolved, finding that "the parties to the various agreements . . . are now incapable of continuing to operate in business together" and that because it was dissolving the partnerships, "there is no entitlement to future damages. . . . "

The pertinent contracts provided in section 7.3 "Causes of Dissolution":

> . . . [T]he Partnership shall be dissolved in the event that: (a) the Partners mutually agree to terminate the Partnership; (b) the Partnership ceases to maintain any interest (which term shall include, but not be limited to, a security interest) in the Facility; (c) the Partnership, by its terms as set forth in this Agreement, is terminated; (d) upon thirty (30) days prior

continued

36.1

HORIZON/CMS HEALTHCARE CORPORATION V. SOUTHERN OAKS HEALTH CARE, INC., continued

732 SO. 2D 1156 (FLORIDA APP. 5TH DIST. 1999)

written notice to the other Partner, either Partner elects to dissolve the Partnership on account of an Irreconcilable Difference which arises and cannot, after good faith efforts, be resolved; . . . (g) pursuant to a court decree; or (h) on the date specified in Section 2.4.

The term "irreconcilable difference" used in the above quote is defined in the contracts as:

[A] reasonable and good faith difference of opinion between the Partners where either (i) the existence of the difference of opinion has a material and adverse impact on the conduct of the Partnerships' Business, or (ii) such difference is as to (x) the quality of services which is or should be provided at the long-term care facilities owned by the Partnership, (y) the adoption of a budget for a future fiscal year, or (z) any matter requiring unanimous approval of the Partners under the terms of this Agreement. . . .

ISSUE Did Horizon wrongfully cause the dissolution of the partnership?

HOLDING No. The dissolution was proper under the partners' contracts and Florida law. Southern Oaks is not entitled to reimbursement for lost profits in the future.

REASONING [In 1995, Florida enacted the Revised Uniform Partnership Act (RUPA), effective January 1, 1996 for general partnerships formed on or after that date. However, RUPA applies retroactively to all general partnerships, whenever they were initially formed, beginning January 1, 1998. The prior partnership law, the Uniform Partnership Act, was repealed effective January 1, 1998.]

. . . [T]he trial court's finding that the parties are incapable of continuing to operate in business together is a finding of "irreconcilable differences," a permissible reason for dissolving the partnerships under the express terms of the partnership agreements. Thus, dissolution was not "wrongful," assuming there can be "wrongful" dissolutions, and Southern Oaks was not entitled to damages for lost future profits. Additionally, the partnership contracts also permit dissolution by "judicial decree." Although neither party cites this provision, it appears that pur-

suant thereto, the parties agreed that dissolution would be proper if done by a trial court for whatever reason the court found sufficient to warrant dissolution. Second, even assuming the partnership was dissolved for a reason not provided for in the partnership agreements, damages were properly denied. Under RUPA, it is clear that wrongful dissociation triggers liability for lost future profits. ("A partner who wrongfully dissociates is liable to the partnership and to the other partners for damages caused by the dissociation. The liability is in addition to any other obligation of the partner to the partnership or to the other partners."). However, RUPA does not contain a similar provision for dissolution; RUPA does not refer to the dissolutions as rightful or wrongful. [RUPA] Section 620.8801, "Events causing dissolution and winding up of partnership business," outlines the events causing dissolution without any provision for liability for damages. Under subsection 620.8801(5), the statute recognizes judicial dissolution:

A partnership is dissolved, and its business must be wound up, only upon the occurrence of any of the following events:
(5) On application by a partner, a judicial determination that:
(a) The economic purpose of the partnership is likely to be unreasonably frustrated;
(b) Another partner has engaged in conduct relating to the partnership business which makes it not reasonably practicable to carry on the business in partnership with such partner; or
(c) It is not otherwise reasonably practicable to carry on the partnership business in conformity with the partnership agreement; . . .

Paragraph (5)(c) provides the basis for the trial court's dissolution in this case. While "reasonably practicable" is not defined in RUPA, the term is broad enough to encompass the inability of partners to continue working together, which is what the court found. . . . RUPA brought significant changes to partnership law, among which was the adoption of the term "dissociation." Although the term is undefined in RUPA, dissociation appears to have taken the place of "dissolution" as that word was used pre-RUPA. "Dissolution" under RUPA has a different meaning,

36.1

HORIZON/CMS HEALTHCARE CORPORATION V. SOUTHERN OAKS HEALTH CARE, INC., *continued*
732 SO. 2D 1156 (FLORIDA APP. 5TH DIST. 1999)

although the term is undefined in RUPA. It follows that the pre-RUPA cases providing for future damages upon wrongful dissolution are no longer applicable to a partnership dissolution. In other words a "wrongful dissolution" referred to in the pre-RUPA case law is now, under RUPA, known as "wrongful dissociation." Simply stated, under section 620.8602, only when a partner dissociates and the dissociation is wrongful can the remaining partners sue for damages. . . . The trial court ordered dissolution of the partnership, not the dissociation of Horizon for wrongful conduct. There no longer appears to be "wrongful" dissolution—either dissolution is provided for by contract or

statute or the dissolution was improper and the dissolution order should be reversed. . . .

BUSINESS CONSIDERATIONS How can a business prepare for the "retroactive" application of the law? What should partners say about dissolution or dissociation in their partnership agreement?

ETHICAL CONSIDERATIONS Did Horizon behave unethically? Why?

CONTINUATION OF THE PARTNERSHIP BUSINESS

Once a dissolution occurs, an important decision must be made. Will the business terminate through a winding up, or will the business continue? In most cases, an ongoing business is more valuable than the assets that make up the business; the sum is greater than its parts. Thus, the remaining partners normally want to continue operating the business if they can possibly do so. This may not be satisfactory to a withdrawing partner, however. For this reason, the partners should consider the problem of a continuation when they draw up the original agreement, and they should make provisions for the problem at that time.

The remaining partners have the *right* to elect to continue the business under any one of the following circumstances:

1. The withdrawing partner withdraws in violation of the agreement.
2. The withdrawing partner consents to the continuation when he or she could have demanded a termination and winding up.
3. The agreement permits a continuation following a dissolution.

Unless one of these circumstances occurs, a dissolution will be followed by a winding up.

Withdrawing Partners

Anytime the business is continued following a withdrawal, the continuing partners have a duty to the withdrawing partner. The withdrawing partner must be both indemnified (i.e., secured against anticipated losses) and bought out. The purpose of the indemnification is to protect the withdrawing partner from any claims of creditors of the partnership. The withdrawing partner is still liable for any debts owed that arose during membership in the partnership and association with the business. Without an indemnification agreement, a withdrawing partner might be tempted to force a winding up in order to minimize potential liability. But the indemnification agreement is assurance that the continuing partners will repay any losses the withdrawing partner may suffer on account of partnership obligations.

Withdrawing partners are also entitled to payment for their interest in the business, including any undistributed profits, at the time of withdrawal. However, if a withdrawal is in violation of the partnership agreement, the continuing partners may first deduct *damages,* based on breach of contract theories. The amount of these damages should adequately cover the harm caused by the breach.

The continuing partners may pay former partners in a lump sum and settle the matter. If they do not, or cannot, make a lump-sum payment, the withdrawing partners are allowed to elect how payment will be made. They can either: (1) receive interest on the unpaid portion until they receive payment in full; or (2) elect to receive a portion of profits that corresponds to their unpaid portion of their share until they are paid in full. This election must be made at the time of withdrawal, however, and once made, it cannot be changed unless the continuing partners agree to the change.

Entering Partners

Occasionally, a new partner is brought into the business. When this happens, a continuation obviously occurs. No one wants to enter a business in order to see it go through a winding up. The continuation is treated slightly differently, however, when a new partner enters the firm. As a partner, the new entrant is liable for the debts of the partnership. But existing creditors did not rely on the new partner's credit when they decided to extend credit. As a result, it seems unfair to impose unlimited liability on the new partner. UPA § 41(7) resolves this problem by specifying that the new partner is liable to preexisting creditors only up to the amount of his or her capital contribution. In other words, an entering partner has limited liability to preexisting creditors but faces unlimited personal liability with respect to future creditors.

WINDING UP THE PARTNERSHIP

Winding up is the termination of the business enterprise. In winding up, one must **marshal** and **liquidate** the assets of the business and then distribute the proceeds of this process to the proper parties.

General Partnerships

The priority for distributing the proceeds is set out in the UPA § 40. The first priority is the claims owed to creditors who are not partners. If the proceeds are sufficient to pay this class entirely, they will be so paid. Any surplus carries over to the next priority class. Any deficit will cause two things to happen: (1) a pro rata distribution of the proceeds within the class; and (2) a collection of the balance from the personal assets of the partners, jointly and severally.

The second priority in receiving the proceeds is claims owed to the partners as *creditors* of the business. Again, any surplus will be applied to the next priority class, and any deficit will be made up from the personal assets of the partners. Note that a partner who wishes to be treated as a creditor of the firm will need to present clear and convincing evidence of the debt. It is normally presumed that any monies advanced to the firm were advanced as a capital contribution, not as a loan. The

Marshal
To arrange assets or claims in such a way as to secure the proper application of the assets to the claims.

Liquidate
To settle with creditors and debtors and apportion any remaining assets.

court probably will demand some written proof, such as a promissory note, that the funds were meant as a loan. Without such proof, the partner is likely to find that what he or she viewed as a loan was, in the eyes of the court, a capital contribution.

The third priority is the return of the capital contributions of the partners. Any surplus will be carried over to the fourth and final priority. Any deficit will be allocated among the partners pro rata.

The fourth and final priority category is profits. Any monies left over after all the other classes have been satisfied will be distributed as profits, according to the terms of the partnership agreement. There can be no deficit here.

Creditors of the partnership have first claim on any partnership assets. If the partnership is actually in bankruptcy, the Bankruptcy Reform Act of 1978 § 723 provides that partnership creditors can recover from the individual partners at the same time as the individual creditors of the partners.

If an individual partner cannot pay his or her creditors, the creditors of the individual partner can claim against that partner's partnership interest. However, these creditor claims are limited by the UPA § 28. Usually, if the partnership is solvent, the creditors of the individual partner will be given a **charging order** by the court. This charging order allows the business to continue to operate and minimizes the amount of disruption to the partnership, while providing some recovery for the creditor.

Charging order
A court order permitting a creditor to receive profits from the operation of a business; especially common in partnership situations.

The three examples that follow illustrate how the various interested parties may be treated in a dissolution of a partnership and a winding up of the business. In each example, there are three partners—Jerrod, Carmen, and Eric—whose net worths are shown in the first example. In addition, each partner has made the capital contributions specified, and Jerrod has made a loan to the firm. Notice the effect the different asset positions of the partners have on the partners individually.

Partners	Personal Assets	Personal Liabilities	Net Worth
Carmen	$ 80,000	$ 40,000	$ 40,000
Eric	40,000	100,000	(60,000)
Jerrod	100,000	20,000	80,000

Each partner has already contributed $50,000 to the partnership; moreover, profits and losses are to be shared equally. Jerrod has already loaned the firm $30,000 (there is a signed promissory note for this loan).

Example 1

Further assume that the partnership has $200,000 in proceeds and $290,000 in liabilities to regular creditors, plus the $30,000 owed to Jerrod.

Step 1. Partnership proceeds are distributed to regular creditors (priority 1), leaving a deficit of $90,000.

Step 2. Each partner owes an additional $30,000 to priority 1 creditors. However, Eric has no money, and so Jerrod and Carmen must pay the full $90,000 between them (Jerrod will pay $50,000 and Carmen will pay $40,000) and hold claims against Eric (Jerrod for $20,000 and Carmen for $10,000). Both Carmen and Eric are now insolvent.

Step 3. Under priority 2, Jerrod, Carmen, and Eric each owe Jerrod $10,000. Jerrod "pays" himself, and Carmen and Eric each owe Jerrod $10,000.

Consequently Jerrod had a net worth of $80,000, which has decreased to $30,000 plus $40,000 in debts owed by Carmen and Eric. Carmen had a net worth of $40,000, which has decreased to ($10,000), including the amount that Carmen owes Jerrod. Carmen also has a claim of $10,000 against Eric. Eric had a net worth of ($60,000), which has technically decreased to ($100,000).

Example 2

Assume instead that the partnership has $309,000 in proceeds and $300,000 in liabilities to regular creditors, plus the $30,000 owed to Jerrod.

Step 1. The priority 1 debts are paid in full, and the $9,000 surplus is carried over.

Step 2. Priority 2 debts are paid until the money runs out. Thus, Jerrod receives the $9,000 carried over from priority 1 and is still owed $21,000. Jerrod "pays" himself $7,000; Carmen pays Jerrod $7,000; Eric owes $7,000. Eric is insolvent, and Jerrod probably will not collect from Eric.

Consequently, Jerrod had a net worth of $80,000, which has increased to $96,000 plus a $7,000 debt owed by Eric. Carmen had a net worth of $40,000, which has decreased to $33,000. Eric had a net worth of ($60,000), which has technically decreased to ($67,000).

Example 3

Assume instead that the partnership has $500,000 in proceeds, $200,000 in liabilities to regular creditors, and the $30,000 owed to Jerrod.

Step 1. Priority 1 debts are paid in full, leaving a surplus of $300,000.

Step 2. Priority 2 debts are paid in full (Jerrod gets his $30,000), leaving a $270,000 surplus.

Step 3. Priority 3 is next. Each partner receives a full return of his or her capital contribution, leaving a surplus of $120,000.

Step 4. The final priority is satisfied; the $120,000 is distributed as profits, with $40,000 going to each of the partners.

In addition, the partners will also be paid in full in this case. Jerrod receives:

$$
\begin{array}{ll}
\$\ 30,000 & \text{loan payment} \\
50,000 & \text{return of capital} \\
40,000 & \text{profits} \\
\underline{80,000} & \text{prior net worth} \\
\$200,000 & \text{new net worth}
\end{array}
$$

Carmen and Eric each receive:

$$
\begin{array}{ll}
\$\ 50,000 & \text{return of capital} \\
\underline{\$\ 40,000} & \text{profits} \\
\$\ 90,000 & \text{distribution}
\end{array}
$$

Consequently, Carmen had a net worth of $40,000, which has increased to $130,000. Eric had a net worth of ($60,000), which has increased to $30,000.

Limited Partnerships

The distribution of assets in a limited partnership is substantially different from that in a normal, general partnership under the UPA. The ULPA and the RULPA differ in their treatment of distributions, and we will discuss the latter since the vast majority of states follow it. The Revised Act calls for distribution in the following order:

1. Claims of nonpartner creditors and claims of partners as creditors
2. Any amounts owed to former partners prior to their withdrawal from the firm
3. Return of capital contributions of all partners
4. The remainder distributed as profits to all of the partners

The two examples that follow illustrate how various interested parties may be treated in a dissolution of a limited partnership and a winding up of the business under the RULPA. In each example, there are two general partners—Alice and Bob—and two limited partners—Chuck and Diane. The financial positions and contributions of each of the four are set out in the first example.

Partners	Personal Assets	Personal Liabilities	Net Worth
Alice	$150,000	$ 75,000	$ 75,000
Bob	375,000	135,000	240,000
Chuck	100,000	150,000	(50,000)
Diane	200,000	185,000	15,000

Each partner has already contributed $75,000 to the firm. The general partners are to receive 30 percent of the profits each, and the limited partners are to receive 20 percent of the profits each. Chuck has already loaned the firm an additional $50,000 and has a signed promissory note.

Example 1

Further assume the partnership has $400,000 in proceeds and $500,000 in liabilities to nonpartner creditors. Under the RULPA, the distribution is as follows:

Step 1. Claims of creditors, both partner and nonpartner, are first priority. Here, the $400,000 in proceeds are allocated to the $550,000 in debt owed to nonpartners and to Chuck. These debtors are paid at the rate of approximately 73 percent each, which is calculated by dividing $400,000 by $550,000. The balance of $150,000 in debt is owed by the general partners individually. Since Alice and Bob have the funds, they share this liability equally.

Step 2. Amounts owed to former partners are paid next; however, there are no former partners in this example.

Step 3. Capital contributions of all partners are returned. Since the firm has no money left, the general partners are personally liable for this $300,000 ($75,000 times 4) claim. Bob "pays" himself, and he pays Chuck and Diane $75,000 each. Alice "pays" herself and owes Bob $75,000 for her share of the payments to Chuck and Diane.

Step 4. Remaining funds are distributed as profits; however, no funds remain in this example.

Example 2

Assume instead that the partnership has $500,000 in proceeds and $100,000 in liabilities to nonpartner creditors. Under the RULPA, the distribution is as follows:

Step 1. Claims of creditors, both partner and nonpartner, are satisfied first. The entire $150,000 owed is paid, leaving $350,000.

Step 2. Any amounts owed to former partners are paid; however, there are none in this example.

Step 3. Capital contributions of all partners are returned. The entire $300,000 is paid, leaving a balance of $50,000.

Step 4. The balance is distributed as profits. Each general partner gets $15,000 (30 percent each), and each limited partner gets $10,000 (20 percent each).

CHANGES IN CORPORATE STRUCTURE

In Chapter 35, we briefly touched on the subject of dissolution when we discussed shareholders' rights in the event of the liquidation of the corporation. So far, though, we have paid scant attention to fundamental changes in the corporate structure that may endanger the rights of shareholders and creditors. We will now focus on actions bringing about some of these fundamental changes—dissolution, merger and consolidation, sale of substantially all the corporate assets, and stock acquisition. Exhibit 36.1 illustrates these four major changes in corporate structure.

LIQUIDATION OF THE CORPORATION

The process of *liquidation* consists of the winding up of the affairs of a business in order to go out of business, that is, the marshaling of assets and their subsequent conversion to cash in order to pay the claims of creditors. During this winding up, the corporation pays all debts and creditors from the corporate assets and then distributes any remaining assets to the shareholders. The process of dissolution, which denotes the end of the corporation's legal existence, may immediately precede or follow liquidation. Although the terms *dissolution* and *liquidation* are often used together, they are not synonymous.

Throughout the liquidation period, the corporation has all the rights and powers reasonably necessary to effect liquidation. Moreover, during this period, the corporation can sue and be sued. Under most statutes, the board of directors continues the management of the corporation unless a court has ordered the dissolution and liquidation. In the latter case, the court may appoint a **receiver** to oversee the

Receiver
An unbiased person appointed by a court to receive, preserve, and manage the funds and property of a party.

E X H I B I T 36.1 | **Fundamental Changes in Corporate Structure**

MERGER OR CONSOLIDATION

Rationales:
- Economies of scale
- Knowledge (i.e., acquisition of "know-how")
- Diversification
- Securing of competitive advantages
- Tax savings
- Utilization of assets
- Preservation of management prerogatives

Formalities:
- Both boards' adoption of merger plan
- Both corporations' shareholder approval (usually 2/3 of outstanding shares or more needed) unless short-form merger involved
- Filing of plan with state
- Issuance of certificate of merger
- Provision of appraisal rights to dissenting shareholders and compliance with statutory procedures covering such rights, including:
  (a) Dissenting shareholders' written notice of objection to merger
  (b) Dissenting shareholders' written demand on corporation for fair value/fair market value of shares
  (c) On failure to agree, either corporation or dissenting shareholders petition court for an appraisal proceeding

Effect:
- Assets, rights, and liabilities of acquired firm assumed by surviving firm by operation of law
- Dissolution of acquired firm

SALE OF SUBSTANTIALLY ALL THE ASSETS

Formalities:
- Simpler than merger procedures
- Approval only by seller's shareholders (i.e., approval of buyer's shareholders unnecessary)
- Provision of appraisal rights to seller's dissenting shareholders and compliance with applicable statutory procedures
- Compliance with statutory provisions protecting creditors' rights
- These formalities not applicable to sale, in the regular course of business, of substantially all the assets created by the corporation

Effect:
- Liabilities of seller ordinarily not assumed by purchaser by operation of law

STOCK ACQUISITION

Formalities:
- Simpler than procedures for merger or sale of substantially all the assets
- Compliance with all applicable state statutes and federal securities laws
- Neither board action nor shareholder approval by either corporation needed; necessary only for shareholders of target firm to decide to sell to would-be acquirer or refrain from selling
- Transactions may be deemed de facto mergers and set aside by courts

DISSOLUTION

Voluntary **(Initiated by shareholders)**	**Involuntary** **(Initiated by shareholders** **or other entities)**
Formalities:	**Types:**
- Board recommendation	- At request of state, owing to
- Shareholder approval (usually 2/3 of outstanding shares or more needed)	(a) Securities fraud; or (b) Noncompliance with state statutory procedures (e.g., failure to pay taxes or file annual reports)
- Filing of notice to creditors	- At request of shareholders, owing to
- Filing of certificate of dissolution	(a) Mismanagement; or
- Liquidation of corporation either before or after dissolution	(b) Deadlock among directors or controlling shareholders so serious as to warrant dissolution
	- At request of creditors, owing to the need to preserve creditors' rights

liquidation. If the directors unlawfully continue the business of the corporation after dissolution and beyond the time reasonably necessary to wind up the corporation's affairs, they may become personally liable for the corporation's debts. Directors and controlling shareholders should exercise caution during the liquidation process.

State statutes normally protect creditors during liquidation because the creditors have rights superior to those of the stockholders in liquidations. The statutes require the corporation to notify creditors of dissolution and liquidation so that these creditors can file their claims against the corporation during this time period. A creditor who receives notice but does not file a claim may lose the right to sue later on this claim. Creditors who keep this right may recoup from shareholders any distributions of corporate assets that have occurred before payment of creditors' claims. To protect creditors, the law characterizes the illegal distributions as held "in trust" for the benefit of the creditors. The directors also may incur liability for distributions illegally declared up to the amount of claims that remain unpaid.

After the corporation has satisfied its debts to its creditors, the shareholders ordinarily receive the proportion of the remaining net assets represented by their respective share ownership. As discussed earlier, however, the articles of incorporation may set out one or more classes of shares as entitled to liquidation preferences over another class or classes of shares. For instance, preferred stockholders usually receive their shares of the net assets before holders of common stock do. (Note, however, that preferred shareholders *never* receive payment before creditors do.) But if the preferred shareholders do not enjoy liquidation preferences, they will participate with the common shareholders on a share-for-share basis. Sometimes the articles give the preferred shareholders both liquidation preferences and participation rights with the common shareholders. Because cash is the usual method for satisfying liquidation preferences, the corporation may need to sell its assets to raise the amount required to take care of these preferences. Under most statutes, the corporation can distribute property instead of cash in satisfying liquidation preferences, but it will be illegal to favor some shareholders through grants of property (as when a corporation gives controlling shareholders valuable patents or trademarks) while doling out cash to minority shareholders.

DISSOLUTION OF THE CORPORATION

Dissolution involves termination of the corporation as a *legal entity*, or juristic person. The term *dissolution* is not synonymous with *liquidation*, which refers to the winding up or termination of the corporation's business or affairs. Corporate existence remains impervious to most events, including such unusual occurrences as bankruptcy or the cessation of business activities. Dissolution, then, because it represents an extraordinary circumstance, or an organic change in corporate structure, must occur formally in order to have legal effect. Dissolutions are of two types: voluntary and involuntary.

Voluntary Dissolution

As we learned in Chapter 34, corporations theoretically can exist perpetually. On the other hand, a corporation's articles may limit the period of corporate life to, say, 10 years. Alternatively, the incorporators may decide at some point to end the corporation's existence, even though the articles specify the perpetual duration of the corporation. In both cases, such *voluntary* dissolutions must be carried out through formal procedures.

Statutes ordinarily set out the requirements for these nonjudicial, voluntary dissolutions. Typically, these statutes mandate (1) board action recommending dissolution, (2) shareholder voting to approve the dissolution (usually by the holders of two-thirds of the outstanding shares), and/or (3) filing of a notice to creditors prior to dissolution.

On compliance with these and any other necessary procedures, a certificate of dissolution is filed with the secretary of state or other designated state officer. At this time, the dissolution is legally effective. Remember, though, that liquidation may follow or precede dissolution, so it is possible that some limited corporate activity may occur after dissolution. In voluntary liquidation, the shareholders share proportionately—subject, of course, to any liquidation preferences—in the net assets of the corporation that remain after satisfaction of creditors' claims. As discussed in earlier chapters, courts prohibit dissolutions that freeze out minority shareholders, especially if a controlling shareholder initiated the dissolution. Also, be aware that the rules regarding dissolutions may vary when a close corporation, instead of a publicly held corporation, is involved.

Involuntary Dissolution

Occasionally, the state, the shareholders, or the corporation's creditors may request the dissolution of the corporation because of wrongdoing or prejudice to shareholders or creditors. Such judicial proceedings are *involuntary* because the corporation itself is not asking for dissolution. Involuntary dissolutions by their very nature occur less frequently than voluntary ones.

Dissolution at the Request of the State. Because the corporation is a creation of the state, the state retains the power to rescind the certificate of a corporation whose actions present a clear danger to the public. For instance, the state may ask for involuntary dissolution of a corporation that has engaged in systematic securities fraud. More often, however, grounds for involuntary dissolution involve noncompliance with state requirements, such as failure to pay taxes or to file annual reports.

Rather than seek dissolution, the state may seek suspension of the corporation. *Suspension* works as a deprivation of the corporation's right to conduct its business and certain other powers, but is not as drastic or as permanent a remedy as dissolution. When the firm again complies with the corporate statutes, the state can order a reinstatement of the corporation.

Dissolution at the Request of Shareholders. Shareholders can petition the courts for dissolution of the corporation. Statutes generally authorize shareholder actions based on freeze-outs (or oppression) of minority shareholders' interests, allegations of corporate waste of assets, and other examples of corporate mismanagement. Courts sometimes order dissolutions in similar circumstances even in the absence of express statutory provisions. Deadlock among directors or shareholders constitutes an additional ground for involuntary dissolution. For example, courts intervene when a shareholder shows that the deadlock among directors or controlling shareholders has so paralyzed the corporation that it can no longer conduct its business advantageously.

As a less severe alternative, some state statutes permit the appointment of a provisional (or temporary) director who breaks the deadlock and thus allows the corporation to continue functioning. Statutes also may allow holders of a majority of the outstanding shares to purchase the shares owned by the shareholders who are requesting dissolution. Statutes may contain provisions setting out a minimum number of shareholders (i.e., one-third of the corporate shareholders) who must join in the petition for involuntary dissolution before it can be presented to a court.

In contrast to these potential actions, shareholders in close corporations frequently agree in advance that upon the occurrence of a certain event, such as deadlock, each shareholder will be able to request dissolution. Courts ordinarily enforce such agreements.

Dissolution at the Request of Creditors. The theory of corporate personality normally prevents creditors from compelling the involuntary dissolution of the corporation. But in order to protect creditors' rights during dissolution and liquidation, statutes require prior notice to creditors. Statutes also allow the appointment of a receiver who takes over the corporation's business and conducts it for the benefit of the creditors. In some circumstances, creditors can petition for the involuntary bankruptcy of the corporation to preserve their rights. Neither the appointment of a receiver nor the institution of involuntary bankruptcy proceedings results in the dissolution of the corporation, however. As we have seen, formal statutory procedures spell out the necessary steps for effecting this fundamental change in corporate structure. Courts are reluctant to force dissolution and generally do so only if they have no other alternative.

CORPORATE MERGER AND CONSOLIDATION

Like dissolutions, mergers and consolidations bring about fundamental, or organic, changes in the corporation's structure. Dissolution is also related to these two concepts because dissolution of a corporation (or corporations) occurs automatically when either a merger or a consolidation occurs, and the procedures for carrying out a merger or consolidation are similar to dissolution procedures.

Technically, a merger differs from a consolidation. In a *merger,* one corporation (called the *acquirer* or *acquiring firm*) purchases another firm (called the *acquired* or *disappearing firm*) and absorbs it into itself. This new entity is called the *survivor corporation;* the acquired firm no longer exists.

A *consolidation* is similar, except that in a consolidation two or more existing corporations combine to form a wholly new corporate entity. Since most statutes treat the procedures for mergers and consolidations as if the two were identical transactions, this part of our discussion focuses only on mergers. But, as noted, they are analytically different ways of bringing about major changes in corporate structure.

Rationales for Merger

For various reasons, the last three decades have witnessed a phenomenal upsurge in the number of mergers. We will review some of the more common motivations for this.

Economies of Scale. *Economies of scale* refer to reductions in per-unit costs resulting from larger plant size. A merger may permit a firm to achieve economies of scale and thus to compete much more efficiently: The larger the firm, the easier it is for the firm to receive discounts on sales and advertising and thereby to achieve lower costs. Accumulation of resources resulting from merged firms also facilitates access to financing. Two beer producers that merge generally present a more attractive credit risk for lending institutions than a wine business operating from someone's basement. Bigness may also spawn more research and development (R&D). A merged firm, for example, ordinarily is able to allocate more funds to R&D activities. The capital in the struggling wine business, in contrast, typically goes for electricity, rent, and other overhead costs. The vintner may want to invest in research on capping methods or grape hybrids, but economies of scale make such research and development much more feasible in large firms. Mergers can cut costs by allowing the new firm to reduce the amount of workers. Mergers between manufacturers and customers (called *vertical mergers*) may lessen transaction costs, also bringing about economies of scale.

As you will learn in Chapter 39, a firm can use economies of scale to drive out smaller, less efficient firms because of the dominance it may achieve due to its size and wealth ("deep pockets"). Antitrust laws generally protect the competitive environment from any retaliatory, abusive conduct in which large firms may engage. In the absence of antitrust concerns, mergers to effect economies of scale are legal and customary.

Knowledge. Often a larger company will merge with a smaller company because the latter possesses valuable technological information or know-how. An established computer firm, for example, may find a merger with a software firm valuable if the software firm has made technological breakthroughs deemed valuable by the computer firm. Thinking back to economies of scale, it may well be cheaper for the computer firm to purchase the software firm and its patents, trademarks, and trade secrets than to expend the R&D funds necessary to create similar software. Furthermore, the merged firm may be able to retain the staff of the smaller firm and thereby realize further future gains from these persons' collective expertise and inventive or creative capacities.

Diversification. The 1970s marked a large increase in the number of mergers undertaken for the purpose of diversification. Many firms jumped into areas previously unrelated to their principal lines of business through **conglomerate mergers.** Diversification minimizes the risks that are inherent in a firm's restricting itself to one industry and the risks caused by economic cycles (e.g., tobacco companies acquired food producing companies). It permits a company to gain access to new technologies, markets, skills, and workers. For instance, a traditional retailer may acquire an e-commerce firm. Critics of diversification have argued that diversification dilutes capital markets by making it easier for a diversified company to hide its actual profits and losses. These critics maintain that lending institutions' abilities to assess

36.1 | FINANCE/ MANAGEMENT

SHOULD CIT DIVERSIFY?

During a field trip with her high school class, Lindsay saw a for-sale sign on a local fast-food restaurant. Lindsay has suggested that CIT might want to purchase this business to provide a steady source of cash until CIT establishes its reputation and builds a regular market. She feels that the restaurant does a steady business and that the funds generated from this enterprise should carry the firm for the first year or two. The other members of the Kochanowski family, however, are unsure about this suggestion and ask for your opinion. What legal complications might arise if CIT tries to expand into the operation of a fast-food restaurant?

BUSINESS CONSIDERATIONS What are the advantages and disadvantages of diversification by a newly formed business? What information should a firm acquire in order to make an informed decision in this instance? **ETHICAL CONSIDERATIONS** Does a business have any duties to expand or not expand when an opportunity presents itself? Do these duties vary depending on the business form of the enterprise, i.e., limited liability company, corporation, partnership, sole proprietorship?

Conglomerate mergers
Mergers between non-competing firms in different industries.

TELECOMMUNICATIONS MERGERS

On 5 October 1999, it was announced that MCI/WorldCom agreed to buy Sprint for $115 billion. These firms are number 2 and 3 in the U.S. long-distance industry. According to some sources, the combined MCI Worldcom/Sprint will have 30 percent of the market. The Federal Communications Commission (FCC) has not yet approved this deal; however, it rarely interferes in telecom acquisitions.

Tele-Trend tracks consumer telecommunications spending and behavior. According to Tele-Trend, the 1999 merger of SBC and Ameritech, Inc. will create the second-largest U.S. residential communications company based on dollar market share. MCI/WorldCom's acquisition of Sprint will create the fourth-largest firm. AT&T, which recently acquired TCI, will continue as number 1. Third place will be the new combination of Bell Atlantic and GTE. Together these four new firms will have more than 70 percent of the market. (Tele-Trend collects data from actual household bills.)

The global market is also consolidating rapidly. Deutsche Telekom has tried to expand. Its bid to acquire Telecom Italia failed in May 1999. It also tried to buy Sprint, an effort that failed on 5 October 1999 when it was announced that Sprint would be acquired by MCI/WorldCom Inc. Deutsche Telekom is having difficulty competing even in Europe. The German government owns a 66 percent stake in Deutsche Telekom. This currently protects it from a hostile takeover. However, governmental officials are hinting that the government will begin to sell off its interest in mid-2000. Deutsche Telekom already acquired a British mobile phone company, One-2-One, for top dollar. Some analysts contend that Deutsche Telekom paid too much. The German government's interests in the firm may have caused difficulty in its bids to acquire other companies such as Telecom Italia. It currently has a 10 percent interest in Sprint. European Union regulators are pressuring Deutsche Telekom to sell off part of its mobile-phone network.

Assume that a group of shareholders object to the MCI/WorldCom-Sprint purchase, and they have filed suit in your court to prevent it. How will *you* decide this case? What factors will *you* consider?[3]

BUSINESS CONSIDERATIONS Should the FCC approve this merger? Should Sprint shareholders accept the offer? Is it beneficial to them? What additional information would be helpful? Is the merger beneficial to consumers?

ETHICAL CONSIDERATIONS What ethical considerations are raised by takeover bids? Are there different ethical considerations with hostile takeovers compared to relatively friendly takeovers?

SOURCES: *Business Week International Editions* (25 October 1999), International Business; Germany, p. 26; *PR Newswire* (21 October 1999), Financial News; and *Investor's Business Daily* (14 October 1999), p. A8.

creditworthiness are impaired by corporate diversification resulting from mergers. This concern, coupled with some experts' fears about the implications of the excessive concentrations of economic power represented by diversified companies, argue for limiting conglomerate mergers. At this time, governmental regulators are not enforcing a strict policy against conglomerate mergers. (Antitrust enforcement policies often change with the political, social, and economic climate of the country.)

Even without regulatory concerns, a company should limit its mergers to firms that are similar in culture and related to its core competencies. Recently there have been concerns about the acquisitions by Amazon[4] and Medtronic.[5]

Competition. Inherent in much of what we have discussed so far is an underlying desire to control, if not curtail, competition. One firm clearly does not want to be at the mercy of another firm in times of scarcity. Therefore, a merger between a supplier of aluminum and a fabricator of aluminum, for instance, seems a viable strategy for reducing some of the supply-side uncertainties. Naturally, though, antitrust concerns may also lurk in mergers designed to control the competitive process, so regulator caution is warranted. A merger with a competitor may permit the new firm to raise its prices.

One example of such a problem involved the planned merger between Microsoft and Intuit in 1996. When the proposed merger was announced, the Justice Department objected on the grounds that competition in the software market would be harmed. Eventually, Microsoft withdrew its offer rather than enter a prolonged and expensive legal battle over the competitive effect of the proposed merger.

Other Rationales. Other rationales for mergers include tax savings, utilization of cash-rich assets to infuse businesses that need such assets for expansion and growth, and preservation of rights of management. Critics of the last rationale have argued that many mergers occur because of the egos of important management officials who want to become the executive officers of even bigger companies. Such "power trips," these critics assert, lead to the possible sacrifice of shareholders' interests, personnel displacement, and the uprooting of smaller corporations from the local community of which they were an integral part. The previously mentioned controversies over hostile takeovers, "golden parachutes," "poison pills," and defensive mergers (i.e., mergers in which corporation A merges with corporation C to avoid A's being taken over by corporation B) often surface in such criticisms as well.

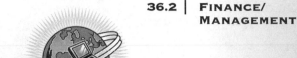

36.2 | FINANCE/ MANAGEMENT

HOW TO DISCOURAGE A TAKEOVER

CIT has had success in developing and marketing the Call-Image videophone. The videophones have been featured in articles in business journals and in the news. As a result of this success and the publicity, Person-to-Person, a long-distance telephone service, wishes to acquire CIT. The Kochanowskis have a family meeting (which you attend) and decide they are not ready to sell the firm. They ask for your advice about resisting this takeover attempt. (Assume that CIT is a regular, or Subchapter C, corporation.) What can the Kochanowskis legally do to discourage or prevent a takeover? What legal limitations may restrict their options? Why is this problem less likely with a Subchapter S corporation?

BUSINESS CONSIDERATIONS From a practical perspective, what can a business do to discourage or prevent a takeover? Which techniques are most effective? Why?

ETHICAL CONSIDERATIONS From an ethical perspective, what can a business do to discourage or prevent a takeover? What ethical limitations may restrict their options?

Procedure

Board of Directors. Whatever the rationale for the merger, once the firms have decided to merge, state statutes set out the steps that must be followed in bringing about the merger. Such statutes generally require that each corporation's board of directors adopt a merger plan that includes (1) the names of each corporation and the surviving corporation, (2) the appropriate terms and conditions of the merger, (3) the method for converting the acquired firm's securities into the securities of the acquiring firm (stock for cash, stock for stock, and the like), and (4) any amendments

**36.3 | FINANCE/
MANAGEMENT**

MERGERS AND ACQUISITIONS

A business that provides a key component for the production of Call-Image videophones is experiencing financial difficulties. If this firm fails, CIT will need to find another source for this component, probably at a substantially higher cost per unit. The owner of the business has proposed either selling his firm to CIT or merging with CIT. If CIT buys the firm, it will need to expend a substantial amount of cash. If CIT agrees to merge, the seller of the component part wants 20 percent of the common stock in CIT. The Kochanowskis have asked your advice as to their best course of conduct. What do you recommend?

BUSINESS CONSIDERATIONS Should a business have a policy regarding potential mergers, or should it analyze and decide on each opportunity separately as it arises? **ETHICAL CONSIDERATIONS** What duties does a business owe to its supplier in a situation like the one confronting CIT? What duties does it owe to its owners and other constituents?

Market value
The current price the stock will sell for on a stock exchange.

Fair market value
The current price for selling an asset between informed willing buyers and informed willing sellers.

to the articles of the acquiring corporation that have resulted from the merger. Thorny problems can arise from these procedures.

Shareholders. After each of the boards of directors has adopted a merger plan, the shareholders of both corporations ordinarily must approve the merger. As with dissolutions, normally the holders of two-thirds of the outstanding shares must approve this fundamental change, although in a few states, approval by a bare majority of the holders of the outstanding stock suffices.

In some states, statutory provisions dispense with the necessity for shareholder approval in *short-form mergers* (those involving a merger between a subsidiary and a parent company that owns 90 to 100 percent of the subsidiary's stock). Because the parent's ownership interest is so high, a vote of approval is a mere formality; requiring such a vote thus makes little practical sense.

Once all the required steps have been followed, the directors file the plan with the appropriate state office. After the state approves this plan, the surviving corporation receives a certificate of merger and can begin conducting business.

Effect of Merger

Once the state issues the certificate of merger, the acquired corporation ceases to exist; only one corporation survives. The survivor takes on all the assets, rights, and liabilities of the disappearing (acquired) corporation by operation of law. This means, among other things, that creditors of the acquired corporation are now the creditors of the survivor corporation. Similarly, pending damages suits (such as products liability cases) against the acquired corporation, if successful, will be paid by the survivor corporation.

Appraisal Rights

Thus far, we have discussed the positive qualities of a merger from the point of view of those who want it. In any given merger, however, persons will object to, or dissent from, the merger. Many people believe it is unfair to require someone to become a shareholder in a new corporation that may be totally different from the one in which he or she originally invested. Therefore, statutes in most states give dissenting shareholders appraisal rights. *Appraisal rights* allow dissenters to sell their shares back to the corporation for the cash equivalent of the **market value** or **fair market value** of the shares. In this way, a dissenting shareholder can avoid becoming a shareholder in the survivor corporation and still protect his or her original investment.

To be eligible for appraisal rights, a shareholder ordinarily must follow a set statutory procedure. The respective state statutes vary regarding the steps with which a dissenting shareholder must comply. However, in general such statutes require the following steps:

1. The dissenter must send a written notice of his or her objection to the merger before the meeting at which the merger will be considered.
2. The shareholder must make a written demand on the corporation for the fair value of the shares after the merger has been approved.
3. The corporation must then make a written offer to purchase at a price it believes represents the fair value (or the fair market value) of the shares.
4. If the corporation and the dissenting shareholder disagree about the fair value of the shares, either party may petition a court to determine the fair value of the shares in an appraisal proceeding.

Valuation of shares is quite complicated and requires a sophisticated understanding of valuation issues. This task becomes somewhat easier if the stock is traded on the New York, American, Tokyo, or other active stock exchanges; in such cases, a court will place great importance on the market price of the stock when assigning a fair value to it. Otherwise, a court usually will arrive at its valuation determination by weighing a number of factors, including market price, investment value, net asset value, and dividends.

Some jurisdictions deny appraisal rights for certain types of mergers (e.g., shareholders of the parent company in a short-form merger may have no appraisal rights) and certain types of corporations (those with stock listed on a national securities exchange or those with more than 2,000 shareholders). Since appraisal rights generally represent the exclusive remedy for a dissenting shareholder who opposes a merger, the shareholder must use vigilance in complying with the strict statutory provisions and short time periods involved.

In determining the value of shares in an appraisal proceeding, a court retains broad discretionary powers. In the following case, the Delaware Supreme Court reviewed the appraisal of the *Court of Chancery* (a court of equity).

36.2

M.P.M. ENTERPRISES, INC. V. GILBERT
731 A.2D 790 (DELA. SUPREME CT. 1999)

FACTS . . . Jeffrey D. Gilbert instituted a statutory appraisal action as the sole dissenting stockholder of . . . M.P.M. Enterprises, Inc. (MPM), following MPM's merger into a subsidiary of Cookson Group, PLC (Cookson). . . . Prior to the merger, MPM was a Delaware corporation, headquartered in Franklin, Massachusetts. It was engaged in the design, manufacture and distribution of screen printers. Business was very good in the 1980s and early 1990s. . . . In March 1995, MPM and Cookson signed an Agreement of Merger. . . . On May 2, 1995, the parties consummated the merger. Gilbert owned 600 shares of MPM's common stock and 200 shares of MPM's preferred stock, giving him an ownership stake in MPM of 7.273%. . . . Under the terms of the merger, Gilbert would have received $4.56 million. . . . Apparently believing that these sums did not reflect MPM's going concern value at the date of the merger, Gilbert chose to exercise his statutory appraisal right . . . and filed an action. . . .

MPM presented expert testimony concerning MPM's going concern value at the date of the merger from William A. Lundquist. . . . Gilbert presented expert testimony from Kenneth W. McGraw. . . . As is often the case . . . , these experts came up with widely divergent appraisal values. Lundquist . . . placed MPM's going concern value at $81.7 million. . . . McGraw . . . plac[ed] MPM's going concern value at $357.1 million. Lundquist arrived at his appraisal

continued

36.2

M.P.M. ENTERPRISES, INC. V. GILBERT, *continued*
731 A.2D 790 (DELA. SUPREME CT. 1999)

value through two separate discounted cash flow ("DCF") analyses. . . . He constructed both a "sell-side" DCF (representing the transaction from MPM's point of view) and a "buy-side" DCF (representing the transaction from a buyer's point of view). . . . Lundquist compared the values derived from the buy-side analysis to the terms of the merger, as well as two earlier offers for equity interests in MPM from Dover Technologies and TA Associates, Inc. (the "prior offers"). . . . He also concluded . . . that MPM's equity value at the time of the merger was $90.5 million. . . . McGraw performed two analyses: a DCF analysis and a comparative public companies analysis. McGraw took the values from each of these approaches, weighted them equally, and arrived at a fair market value for MPM's equity at the date of the merger of $357.1 million. In evaluating the various approaches, the Court of Chancery settled on a DCF analysis as the best method for discerning MPM's going concern value at the date of the merger. . . .

ISSUE Did the Court of Chancery commit legal error or abuse its discretion by applying an appraisal analysis that accorded no weight to the terms of the merger giving rise to the appraisal action or to the terms of two prior offers for equity stakes in the subject corporation?

HOLDING No. The Court of Chancery did not commit legal error or abuse its discretion in its choice and application of appraisal methods.

REASONING We review the findings of the trial court in a statutory appraisal proceeding with a high level of deference. In such cases, "the discretion to weigh the evidence belongs to the Court of Chancery with our review one of abuse of that discretion." . . .

[T]he Court of Chancery did not err in its decision regarding the admissibility of the terms of the merger and of the prior offers. It did admit all of these offers into evidence. . . . Therefore, the inquiry must shift to whether the Court abused its discretion in refusing to give any weight to the terms of the merger and of the prior offers in its appraisal of Gilbert's shares. Section 262(h) requires the trial court to "appraise the shares, determining their fair value exclusive of any element of value arising from the accomplishment or expectation of the merger or consolidation." Fair value, as used in § 262(h), is more properly described as the value of the company to the stockholder as a going concern, rather than its value to a third party as an acquisition. We have long recognized that failure to value a company as a going concern may result in an understatement of fair value. . . . [Precedents] acknowledged the Court's discretion to use "any techniques or methods which are generally considered acceptable in the financial community and otherwise admissible in court, subject to our interpretation of 8 Del. C. § 262(h)." Assuming the variables applied by the trial court are proper, a DCF analysis is one such technique or method of determining going concern value. . . . The initial determination by the Court of Chancery of the variables . . . in the DCF analysis was a well-reasoned use of discretion. The Court certainly acted as an independent appraiser of MPM, using its judgment to discern which facets of the experts' competing analyses correctly set forth the assumptions necessary for a proper DCF analysis. The only question remaining is whether the Court abused its discretion in refusing to compare the figures derived from this properly-applied DCF analysis to the merger value and the valuations implicit in the prior offers. Values derived in the open market through arms-length negotiations offer better indicia of reliability than the interested party transactions that are often the subject of appraisals under § 262. But the trial court, in its discretion, need not accord any weight to such values when unsupported by evidence that they represent the going concern value of the company at the effective date of the merger or consolidation. . . . [S]ection 262(h) explicitly states that the trial court "shall appraise the shares, determining their fair value exclusive of any element of value arising from the accomplishment or expectation of the merger or consolidation. . . . " Under section 262, the fairness of the price on the open market is not the overriding consideration. Instead section 262(h) requires that the Court of Chancery discern the going concern value of the company irrespective of the synergies involved in a merger. A fair merger price in the context of a breach of fiduciary duty claim will not always be a fair value in the context of determining going concern value. . . . A merger price resulting from arms-length negotiations where there are no claims of collusion is a very strong indication of fair value. But in an appraisal action, that merger price

36.2

M.P.M. ENTERPRISES, INC. V. GILBERT, *continued*
731 A.2D 790 (DELA. SUPREME CT. 1999)

must be accompanied by evidence tending to show that it represents the going concern value of the company rather than just the value of the company to one specific buyer. . . . MPM failed to present this additional evidence. . . . This led the Court of Chancery to decide that these values were of only marginal relevance, if any. . . . [T]his determination was not an abuse of discretion.

BUSINESS CONSIDERATIONS What factors should a shareholder consider in deciding whether to assert appraisal rights? Why would the firm be opposed to the exercise of appraisal rights?

ETHICAL CONSIDERATIONS Were any ethical duties breached in this case? Why?

SALE OF SUBSTANTIALLY ALL THE ASSETS

Rather than acquiring another firm through a merger, a corporation can instead buy all, or substantially all, of another firm's assets. For example, a shipping company may buy the ships of a rival company as an alternative to merging with it. This method of acquisition is procedurally much simpler than a merger. Approval by the shareholders of the acquired firm ordinarily is necessary, but approval by the acquiring firm's shareholders is not. Even then, a *sale of substantially all the assets* made in the regular course of the corporation's business (as when a corporation is formed to build a tanker, and the tanker is then sold to an oil company) would not normally require shareholder approval. Shareholder approval thus becomes necessary only in the event of a fundamental change in the corporate structure (i.e., the disposal of operating assets in order to terminate the business activities of the corporation). Most states provide appraisal rights for dissenting shareholders in these circumstances as well. In addition, the statutes governing sales of substantially all the assets contain various methods of protecting creditors. In a merger, the acquiring firm takes on all the liabilities of the acquired firm by operation of law; but because this is not ordinarily the case when all or substantially all the assets are sold, corporate statutory provisions, the provisions on bulk transfers in UCC Article 6, and decisional law have been developed to give creditors remedies if such sales prejudice their rights.

In the following case, Allied Products Corporation bought most of White Farm's assets from bankruptcy. The court analyzed Allied's liability for injury allegedly caused by White Farm.

36.3

SORENSON V. ALLIED PRODUCTS CORPORATION
706 N.E.2D 1097 (CT.APP. INDIANA, 3RD DIST. 1999)

FACTS Sorenson was employed as a mechanic by Fowler Oliver Sales, Inc. (Fowler) from 1964–1971 and 1977–1993, where he replaced worn out brake assemblies and clutch disks containing asbestos. The

[parts] . . . were used in Oliver brand and White Farm Equipment Company (White Farm) brand tractors and combines. The Oliver brand name was

continued

36.3

SORENSON V. ALLIED PRODUCTS CORPORATION, *continued*

706 N.E.2D 1097 (CT.APP. INDIANA, 3RD DIST. 1999)

discontinued sometime after Oliver was purchased by White Farm. . . . Fowler was a White Farm dealership of new equipment . . . , but continued to provide service and maintenance on the discontinued Oliver product line as well as the White Farm product line. In 1985, White Farm was placed in involuntary bankruptcy by its creditors. On October 9, 1985, Allied entered into an Asset Purchase Agreement (Agreement) with White Farm to purchase White Farm assets related to the manufacturing of tractors, planters and tillage equipment. The Agreement provided that Allied would purchase . . . assets. . . . Allied agreed to issue and deliver to White Farm 340,000 shares of a new series of preferred stock. The Agreement specifically provided that:

> *Allied shall not assume or in any way become liable for, any claims, liabilities or obligations or [sic] any kind or nature, whether accrued, absolute, contingent or otherwise, or whether due or to become due or otherwise arising out of the events or transactions of facts which shall have occurred prior to the final closing date except as expressly assumed by Allied . . .*

On October 31, 1985, the bankruptcy court ruled that White Farm was authorized to immediately consummate the acquisition agreement with Allied and that the reorganization assets shall immediately be transferred to Allied free and clear of all liens, claims and encumbrances. On November 11, 1987, the bankruptcy court confirmed a plan of reorganization. . . . In 1986, Allied entered into new dealer contracts with a number of White Farm dealers, including Fowler. Allied also began selling replacement brakes and clutches to dealers of old Oliver and White Farm brand tractors and combines.

Sorenson became sick in late 1993 and died on April 24, 1994 of mesothelioma from asbestos exposure. The doctor that diagnosed Sorenson with mesothelioma stated that the latency period for the effects of asbestos exposure is thirty to fifty years. . . . [H]e concluded that Sorenson must have been exposed to asbestos prior to 1986, when Allied attained White Farm's assets. Sandra [Sorenson, widow and Administratrix of his estate] brought a claim against Allied alleging that Allied supplied the brakes and clutches that Sorenson inspected, serviced and repaired. . . .

ISSUE Can Allied be held liable as a successor of White Farm's liability?

HOLDING No. There are no grounds for successor liability in this case.

REASONING . . . The present claim is a . . . tort that does not deal in any way with the bankruptcy sale. . . . [T]he bankruptcy court has neither the power to discharge Sorenson's claim nor the power to enjoin a successor liability claim because this is a successor liability tort claim having nothing to do with White Farm's bankruptcy.

. . . Sandra claims that the transaction between Allied and White Farm amounted to a de facto merger. We disagree. Where one corporation purchases the assets of another, the buyer does not assume the debts and liabilities of the seller. Generally recognized exceptions to this rule include (1) an implied or express agreement to assume the obligation; (2) a fraudulent sale of assets done for the purpose of escaping liability; (3) a purchase that is a de facto consolidation or merger; or (4) instances where the purchase is a mere continuation of the seller. . . . [A] successor's liability, under these exceptions, takes place only when the predecessor corporation no longer exists, such as when a corporation dissolves or liquidates in bankruptcy. Sandra argues that the facts of this case meet the third or fourth exception. . . . In [court case], the Illinois Court of Appeals applied Indiana law and stated the criteria for establishing a de facto merger as: (1) continuity of ownership; (2) continuity of management, personnel, and physical operation; (3) cessation of ordinary business and dissolution of the predecessor as soon as practically and legally possible; and (4) assumption by the successor of the liabilities ordinarily necessary for the uninterrupted continuation of the business of the predecessor. The 7th Circuit found that a major factor in support of a finding of de facto merger is a transfer of stock as consideration, stating that "the question of whether cash or stock is given in consideration for the assets is really a question of ownership." The continuity of ownership factor raises the issue of whether shareholders of the predecessor corporation become shareholders of the successor corporation at the time the assets were sold. It is undisputed that the Agreement provided that Allied was to issue transfer stock to White Farm in exchange for the assets. However, the Agreement and the bankruptcy court only allowed that stock to be distributed to White Farm's secured creditors. Thus, White Farm's shareholders

36.3

SORENSON V. ALLIED PRODUCTS CORPORATION, *continued*
706 N.E.2D 1097 (CT.APP. INDIANA, 3RD DIST. 1999)

never held any stock in Allied. Since the White Farm shareholders never had possession of the Allied shares, they never possessed the authority to participate fully in the management function of Allied. . . . [T]he White Farm shareholders never exerted ownership over Allied. Another factor in determining the existence of a de facto merger is the continuity of management, personnel, and physical location. It is clear that Allied did not hire any of White Farm's directors or officers and, . . . there was no continuity of upper-tier management. . . . Additionally, the White Farm shareholders never dissolved that corporation. . . . [T]wo entities remain in the marketplace because White Farm did not cease operations and dissolve as soon as possible. Allied also cannot be said to have assumed White Farm's normal ongoing business liabilities. Allied terminated White Farm's dealer contracts and labor agreements. . . . Allied did not purchase an ongoing business with a sales force and business contracts. In fact, Allied hired less than 30% of White Farm's employees. . . .

The test for a mere continuation of the seller's business is not the continuation of the business operation, but rather the continuation of the corporate entity. An indication that the corporate entity has been continued is a common identity of stock, directors, and stockholders and the existence of only one corporation at the completion of the transfer. . . . White Farm's shareholders never dissolved the corporation so two corporations remained at the completion of the transfer. . . . Allied's purchase of White Farm did not qualify as a mere continuation of the seller's business. . . .

BUSINESS CONSIDERATIONS Could Allied have better protected its interests? If so, how?

ETHICAL CONSIDERATIONS Was it ethical for Sandra Sorenson to attempt to hold Allied liable? Why?

STOCK ACQUISITION

An alternative method for acquiring the business of another corporation involves stock acquisitions. Instead of buying substantially all the assets of a corporation, the acquiring corporation's directors may decide to buy the stock of the acquired corporation. Because the acquisition implicates only the latter corporation's individual shareholders, who can decide for themselves whether to sell at the price offered for the stock, the directors of the acquired corporation have no right to approve or disapprove the stock acquisition. Similarly, no requirements usually exist for shareholder approval or appraisal rights. However, federal securities laws may apply to such corporate takeovers, as we will see in Chapter 38.

Because sales of substantially all the assets and stock acquisitions may have the ultimate effect of mergers, some companies have characterized their acquisitions in one of these fashions in order to avoid the strict statutory procedures required of mergers. Transactions that take the *form* of sales of assets or stocks but nevertheless have the effect of mergers are called *de facto mergers*. Sandra Sorenson raised this issue in Case 36.3. Because shareholders and creditors can be injured through de facto mergers, courts in jurisdictions that recognize the doctrine can set the transactions aside and require compliance with the relevant merger statutes (shareholder approval, appraisal rights, and so on).

RESOURCES FOR BUSINESS LAW STUDENTS

NAME	RESOURCES	WEB ADDRESS
General Business Forms	The 'Lectric Law Library's™ business forms include a variety of sample partnership and corporation documents.	**http://www.lectlaw.com/formb.htm**
U.S. Chamber of Commerce	U.S. Chamber of Commerce provides news, information, services, and products to assist small-business owners.	**http://www.uschamber.org/**
Law Journal EXTRA! (LJX!)— Corporate Law	LJX!, sponsored by the New York Law Publishing Company, provides daily corporate law news, case law, and legal analysis.	**http://www.ljx.com/practice/corporate/index.html**
CNNfn: The Financial Network	CNNfn, Turner Broadcasting's financial news complement to CNN, provides reports on mergers and takeovers. CNNfn is interactive, allowing visitors to "ask the experts" or respond to the day's programs.	**http://www.cnnfn.com/**

SUMMARY

When a partnership undergoes a change in the relationship among the partners, a dissolution occurs. Thus, a withdrawal by any partner is a dissolution, whether the agreement allows such conduct or not. Likewise, a dissolution will occur when the purpose of the partnership agreement has been carried out or when its time has expired. A dissolution will happen by operation of law if a partner dies; if any partner goes bankrupt; or if the purpose becomes illegal, or the partners cannot legally continue in the business. A dissolution can also be ordered by the court. When a dissolution occurs because a partner withdraws, the remaining partners may be allowed to continue the business. If they do, the withdrawing partner must be bought out and indemnified.

Often the partnership must be wound up if a dissolution occurs. In a winding up, the assets of the firm are marshaled and liquidated, and the proceeds are distributed according to law. In a general partnership under the UPA, the proceeds must be used first to pay debts that the partners owe to nonpartner creditors. Next, the creditors who are also partners must be paid. After that, the partners recover their capital contributions. Anything left is distributed as profits.

The process of liquidation (or winding up) of a corporation occurs when it pays all debts and creditors from the corporate assets and then distributes any remaining assets to the shareholders. Directors may incur personal liability if they continue the business of the corporation beyond the time reasonably necessary to wind up the corporation's affairs. Creditors who have preserved their claims against the corporation can recoup from shareholders any assets that were distributed prior to the payment of creditors. Directors may also incur liability for the remaining unpaid claims. After creditors' claims have been satisfied, the shareholders normally receive the proportion of the remaining net assets represented by their respective share ownership, subject to any liquidation preferences that the corporation has authorized.

Dissolution of a corporation involves the termination of the corporation as a legal person. It is not synonymous with the term liquidation, which refers to the winding up of the corporation's business. Dissolutions may be either voluntary or involuntary. Statutes set out the formal requirements for a voluntary dissolution. Typically, a voluntary dissolution involves board action, shareholder approval, and notice to creditors. Upon voluntary dissolution, the shareholders share proportionately in the net assets of the corporation that remain after satisfaction of creditors' claims. Involuntary dissolutions—those effected by judicial proceedings—occur less frequently than voluntary dissolutions.

The state can rescind or suspend the corporation's certificate when the corporation's actions present a clear danger to the public. Upon compliance with corporate statutes, the state often orders the corporation's reinstatement. Shareholders also can petition the courts for dissolution of the corporation. Statutes sometimes limit the conditions under which shareholders can petition for involuntary dissolution. Creditors normally cannot compel involuntary dissolution of the corporation. Neither the appointment of a receiver nor the institution of involuntary bankruptcy proceedings results in the dissolution of the corporation.

Mergers and consolidations can bring about fundamental changes in the corporation's structure. Technically, mergers and consolidations differ, because in a merger one firm absorbs another, whereas in a consolidation both firms combine to produce a wholly new entity. The upsurge in mergers stems from a desire to effect economies of scale, to gain technical knowledge, to diversify, to control competition, and to avoid taxes. The negative aspects of mergers include the possible sacrifice of shareholders' interests, personnel displacement, and the uprooting of firms from the local community. State statutes set out the procedures necessary for bringing about a merger. The directors ordinarily adopt a merger plan, which the shareholders of both firms must approve. Shareholder approval is not necessary in short-form mergers. After the state approves the filed merger plan, the surviving corporation receives a certificate of merger and can begin conducting business. At this time, the acquired corporation ceases to exist. The surviving corporation takes on all the assets, rights, and liabilities of the transferor (i.e., acquired) corporation by operation of law.

Most state statutes permit appraisal rights for stockholders who object to the merger. Appraisal rights allow dissenters to sell their shares back to the corporation for cash equal to the shares' fair market value. To be eligible for appraisal rights, shareholders usually must follow a set statutory procedure. If the corporation and dissenting shareholders cannot agree about the fair market value of the shares, either party may petition a court to determine their value in an appraisal proceeding.

Rather than merging, a corporation instead can buy all or substantially all the assets of another firm. This method of acquisition entails far fewer procedures than a merger. Nevertheless, most statutes in this area try to protect creditors' rights when such sales take place. Stock acquisitions are also simpler than mergers but may be subject to federal securities laws.

Care must be taken to avoid de facto mergers (e.g., transactions taking either the form of a sale of substantially all the assets or a stock acquisition but nevertheless having the effect of a merger). Because noncompliance with merger statutes can prejudice the rights of shareholders and creditors, courts may set such sales aside and order compliance with the procedures mandated by the merger statute.

DISCUSSION QUESTIONS

1. Julio Rodriguez, Donna Kochanowski's fiancé, is an equal partner in an accountancy partnership with Justin Franz and Alex Sophorn. However, Julio and Donna wish to establish their own accountancy partnership after their marriage. Julio is unsure of his obligations to his current partners and their obligations to him. He also wants to continue to provide accounting advice and tax return preparation to some of his present clients even after he has established an office with Donna. What legal rights and obligations does Julio have? What should Julio do and why?

2. Abner, Bert, and Lois are partners in a bakery. Abner, however, suffers a nervous breakdown and is placed in a mental institution. Abner's wife demands his share of the business, alleging that his insanity has dissolved the partnership. Discuss her allegation.

3. Scott is in a partnership, but is also heavily in debt. One of his creditors has gone to court and obtained a charging order against Scott's share of the business. Under what circumstances can this creditor seek a court-ordered dissolution of the business?

4. Maria entered an existing partnership as a new partner in 1995. She contributed $20,000 at that time. By 1997, her share had grown to $50,000. How much can creditors who had claims predating Maria's entry into the firm collect from Maria's share of the business? From her personal assets?

5. Given the following figures, work out the final financial position of each of the partners (net worth, cash, amounts owed, amounts receivable) following a winding up of their general partnership business:

	Bill	Charles	Larry	BCL Partnership
Assets	$70,000	$50,000	$50,000	$200,000
Liabilities	20,000	45,000	85,000	190,000
Capital contribution	50,000	25,000	25,000	
Profits	50%	25%	25%	

6. Given the following figures, work out the final financial position of each of the partners (net worth, cash, amounts owed, amounts receivable) following a winding up of their business under the RULPA.

	Beth (General Partners)	Cheryl (General Partners)	Linda (Limited Partner)	B & C (The Firm)
Assets	$67,500	$123,250	$ 87,900	$350,000
Liabilities	24,000	101,000	86,400	200,000
Capital contribution	50,000	50,000	100,000	
Loans to firm	0	5,000	7,000	
Share of profit	35%	35%	30%	

7. Who can bring about an involuntary corporate dissolution, and how is this done?

8. In 1999, Mattel Inc. acquired the Learning Company for $3.8 billion. Five months after the merger, Mattel announced that due to problems at the Learning Company, it would have a $50 million to $100 million third-quarter after-tax loss. "A Mattel spokesman said that the company had done due diligence on the Learning Company and that its problems came as a big surprise." However, analysts say that the problems at the Learning Company were well known for years prior to the merger. What constitutes due diligence for the managers at the acquiring company? What can an investor do to protect him- or herself?[6]

9. Explain the meaning and importance of *appraisal rights.*

10. Why in a given case will a sale of substantially all the corporate assets be preferable to a merger?

CASE PROBLEMS AND WRITING ASSIGNMENTS

1. Junior Lewis Nestle and Eric Ellis formed a partnership, Red Rocks Meat and Deli, which they operated from a building leased from Wester & Co. In 1978, Nestle withdrew from the business, selling his interest to John Herline. Ellis and Herline agreed that Nestle should be released from any and all liabilities of the firm. Subsequently, Herline also withdrew, and Ellis continued the business as a proprietorship. In 1980, Ellis and Wester renegotiated the lease, giving the firm additional space and increasing the total rent due under the lease agreement. When Ellis fell behind in his rent payments under the new lease, Wester filed suit against Nestle, arguing that he was liable for the lease jointly and severally with Ellis due to their partnership. Nestle denied that he was liable for the rent because he had withdrawn from the firm two years earlier. How should the court resolve this case? What factors will be decisive? Why? [See *Wester & Co. v. Nestle*, 669 P.2d 1046 (Colo.App. 1983).]

2. C. L. Barnhouse Co. was a limited partnership with two general partners and three limited partners. One of the limited partners was a trust created by Dorothy Kilpatrick and represented by the trustee, Kilpatrick's son. The Kilpatrick trust stated that, on the death of Kilpatrick, the trust was to terminate and all trust assets were to be distributed to the beneficiaries. The partnership agreement provided that the partnership was to terminate on the death of any of the partners, limited or general. It also specified that, on the termination of the partnership, the capital contributions of each partner were to be returned, and then all other assets were to be distributed as per the agreement. Kilpatrick died, and the general partners notified the limited partners that Kilpatrick's death terminated the limited partnership. The trustee argued that the death of Kilpatrick did not terminate the limited partnership. Did the death of Kilpatrick, which terminated her trust, serve to dissolve the limited partnership as well? Why? [See *Porter* v. *Barnhouse*, 354 N.W.2d 227 (Iowa 1984).]

3. Clyde and Graydon Bohn formed a partnership to operate a farm. The partnership agreement included a buy-out provision that was to be based on "the capital amount" of the partnership. Clyde died, and Graydon offered the estate $135,000 to buy out the interest of Clyde. The estate refused the offer, asserting that the buy-out price should be one-half the fair market value of the partnership. The net fair market value of the farm as of the date of Clyde's death was $1,500,000. An accountant testified that the phrase used in the partnership agreement, "the capital amount," has no known definition in the accounting profession. What should the court decide is the proper amount to be paid in order to allow Graydon Bohn to buy out the interest of his deceased partner and continue to operate the business? Why? [See *Bohn* v. *Bohn Implement Co.*, 325 N.W.2d 281 (N.D. 1982).]

4. Roberta Hesek, the surviving spouse of David Hesek, a shareholder in 245 South Main Street, Inc., petitioned the court for judicial dissolution of the corporation. The remaining shareholders, in turn, sought a court order compelling Roberta to resell her husband's shares pursuant to a stock-redemption agreement her husband had executed in 1973. The corporation's shareholders had entered into agreements in 1970 and 1973 providing for the redemption of corporate stock on the death of a shareholder. Accordingly, on the death of Roberta's husband, the corporation had given timely notice of its intent to redeem the husband's shares of stock and had tendered the agreed-on price. In these circumstances, did

Roberta, as the surviving spouse of a shareholder, have standing to petition for judicial dissolution of the corporation? Why or why not? [See *Hesek* v. *245 South Main Street, Inc.*, 566 N.Y.S.2d 127 (1991).]

5. The officers of Glen Alden Corp. entered into a reorganization agreement with the officers of List Industries Corp. Glen Alden was a coal company, and List was a more diversified company owning interests in textiles, theaters, real estate, and gas and oil. Glen Alden's shareholders approved the transaction. As a result of the reorganization agreement, Glen Alden acquired most of the assets and all the liabilities of List, and List was dissolved. Stephen Farris, a shareholder in Glen Alden, sought an injunction against the reorganization, stating that it was actually a merger and that it had not given appraisal rights to dissenting shareholders. Glen Alden argued that the transaction was a purchase of corporate assets with respect to which shareholders had no rights of dissent or appraisal. Was the transaction a purchase of assets or a de facto merger? [See *Farris* v. *Glen Alden Corporation*, 143 A.2d 25 (Pa. 1958).]

6. **BUSINESS APPLICATION CASE** Don Tyson, chairman of Tyson Foods, met with Jim Keeler, the president of WLR Foods. They discussed Tyson's acquiring WLR. Keeler presented Tyson's offer to WLR's board of directors, which rejected the offer. Tyson made a tender offer to acquire WLR stock for $30 per share—the market price was only $19.25. The WLR board met on 28 January 1994 to obtain legal and investment advice. The board met again on 4 February 1994 and rejected Tyson's tender offer. At that time the board approved lucrative severance packages for some of the officers and employees. They adopted a *poison pill* that would issue shares to existing shareholders if the tender offer was successful. The purpose of the poison pill was to make the tender offer less attractive to Tyson and to dilute Tyson's interest in WLR if the tender offer was successful. Did the WLR board behave properly? Why did they consult with their advisers on 28 January 1994? WLR is a Virginia corporation, and Virginia has an antitakeover statute. Is the Virginia statute or federal law controlling in this situation? Why? [See *WLR Foods, Inc.* v. *Tyson Foods, Inc.*, 869 F.Supp. 419 (W.D.Va. 1994); 65 F.3d 1172 (4th Cir. 1995).]

7. **ETHICAL APPLICATION CASE** Minority shareholders, including Phil Neal, challenged an appraisal, pursuant to Delaware statutes, of approximately 120,000 shares of the stock of Alabama By-Products Corporation (ABC). Following a short-form merger

between ABC and Drummond Holding Corporation, effective 13 August 1985, Drummond absorbed ABC. The ABC minority shareholders were cashed out, pursuant to the merger, and received $75.60 per share. That consideration reflected the $75.00 per share paid to ABC shareholders pursuant to a tender offer less than six months earlier, plus a $0.60 quarterly dividend omitted in 1985. After a six-day trial, the court of chancery (also called the court of equity) concluded that the fair value of ABC stock on 13 August 1985 was $180.67 per share and that Neal and the other minority shareholders were entitled to that amount plus interest. ABC, however, contended that the court of chancery committed an error of law when determining value in a statutory appraisal proceeding. Was it proper for the court of chancery to consider the majority shareholders' wrongdoing when determining the value of the dissenting shareholders' stock in a statutory appraisal hearing? [See *Alabama By-Products Corporation* v. *Neal*, 588 A.2d 255 (Del. 1991).]

8. **CRITICAL THINKING CASE** Cadbury Schweppes PLC, a London group, and Dr Pepper–Seven-Up Cos., Inc., are competitors in the soft-drink market. Cadbury offered to purchase all the shares of Dr Pepper that it did not currently own, which was about 75 percent of the company. After an 18-month negotiation period, Cadbury increased its initial offer to a cash price of $33 per share. (A few days prior to the offer, the closing price of Dr Pepper on the New York Stock Exchange was $30.50.) Dr Pepper shareholders were urged to accept the offer.

After Cadbury had acquired about one-quarter of Dr Pepper, Dr Pepper began taking steps to make a takeover more difficult. During the negotiation, John Albers, Dr Pepper chairman, kept forcing the price up until the price seemed about right. Observers noted that Dr Pepper got about all it could from Cadbury. Cadbury was to finance the deal by a variety of techniques, including asking shareholders to accept extra stock in lieu of cash dividends, borrowing funds, and offering preferred stock for purchase. Cadbury also was to assume Dr Pepper's $828.4 million debt.

According to the deal, Cadbury would be entitled to sell Dr Pepper worldwide; however, it would receive only the U.S. rights to sell Seven-Up brands. (Pepsi owns the international rights to Seven-Up brands.) As Cadbury's group finance director, David Kappler, stated, "What we are really buying is brands." Cadbury expected to assume third place in the U.S. soft drink market with this acquisition.

Should Dr Pepper shareholders accept the offer? Is it beneficial to them? Is it beneficial to Cadbury and/or Cadbury's shareholders? What ethical considerations are raised by takeover bids? Are there different ethical considerations with hostile takeovers compared to relatively friendly takeovers? [See Dirk Beveridge, "Cadbury Hits on Right Bid for Dr Pepper," *The Fresno Bee* (27 January 1995), p. C1.]

NOTES

1. Uniform Partnership Act § 29.
2. Ibid., §§ 27 and 28.
3. Gail Edmondson, with Jack Ewing, Stephen Baker, and Bill Echikson, "Time is Running Out," *Business Week International Editions* (25 October 1999), International Business; Germany, p. 26; "1999's Mergers Create New 'Top Four' Telecommunications Companies, Says Tele-Trend Report," *PR Newswire* (21 October 1999), Financial News; and "MCIWorldCom/Sprint Deal Would Link the No. 2 and No. 3 Players. Is This Anti-Competitive?" *Investor's Business Daily* (14 October 1999), p. A8.
4. Katrina Brooker, "Amazon vs. Everybody," *Fortune* (8 November 1999), pp. 120–129.
5. Bethany McLean, "How Smart is Medtronic Really?" *Fortune* (25 October 1999), pp. 173–180.
6. Gretchen Morgenson, "Market Watch: On the Acquisitions Road, Stay Alert to the Hazards," *The New York Times* Late Edition-Final (10 October 1999), § 3, p. 1.

37

FRANCHISING

A G E N D A

A friend has informed the Kochanowskis that they should consider franchising CIT. Such a distributional system could give the firm access to new financing and allow it to expand its market. CIT would like to know what establishing a franchising system for the production and sale of Call-Image videophones would involve. CIT also would find it helpful to obtain information concerning the potential risks and/or benefits that franchising might provide.

These and other questions are likely to arise in the course of this chapter. Be prepared! You never know when one of the Kochanowskis will need your help or advice.

THE SIGNIFICANCE OF FRANCHISING AS A BUSINESS METHOD

Although franchising began in the United States over a century ago when breweries licensed beer gardens as a means of distributing their products, franchising did not become recognized as a distinct method of doing business until after World War II.[1] Since then, and especially in the last 20 years, franchising has significantly helped the United States achieve its position as the world's largest market.

Presently, more than 2,000 U.S. companies encompassing over 40 different economic sectors use the franchise method for distributing their goods or services both domestically and internationally.[2] The types of businesses that use franchise systems include the following: automobile dealerships; gas stations; restaurants; convenience stores; soft-drink bottlers; nonfood merchandising businesses (such as drug, electronics, cosmetics, and home furnishings companies); travel agencies; hotels, motels, and campgrounds; automobile and truck rental services; printing and copying services; tax preparation firms; real estate businesses; accounting firms; cleaning services; lawn and garden services; laundry services; equipment rental businesses; early childhood education and daycare centers; and beauty salons. Overall, franchising has developed into an important and popular method of marketing and distribution. This chapter examines why this phenomenon has occurred.

DEFINITION

No universally accepted definition of the word *franchise* exists. The following definition, taken from the Washington Franchise Investment Protection Act, § 19.100.010(4), is typical:

> (a) *An agreement, express or implied, oral or written, by which: (i) A person is granted the right to engage in the business of offering, selling, or distributing goods or services under a marketing plan prescribed or suggested in substantial part by the grantor or its affiliate; (ii) The operation of the business is substantially associated with a trademark, service mark, trade name, advertising, or other commercial symbol designating, owned by, or licensed by the grantor or its affiliate; and (iii) The person pays, agrees to pay, or is required to pay, directly or indirectly, a franchise fee.*

Service marks
Distinctive symbols designating the services offered by a particular business or individual.

Trademarks
Distinctive marks or symbols used to identify a particular company as the source of its products.

Logotypes
Identifying symbols.

Service marks, trademarks, and **logotypes** are symbols that identify the origin of goods and services. The person or firm that grants a franchise to another is called the *franchisor*. The person receiving the franchise is known as the *franchisee*. Franchises, or retail businesses involving sales of products or services to consumers, fall into three general categories:

1. *Trade name franchising,* in which the franchisee purchases the right to be identified with the franchisor's trade name (e.g., True Value Hardware) but does not distribute particular products exclusively under the franchisor's name.
2. *Product distributorships,* in which a manufacturer/franchisor licenses a franchisee to sell its product either exclusively or with other products via a limited distribution network. The franchisee often has the exclusive right to sell the product in a designated area or territory. Examples of such franchises include automobiles (e.g., Chevrolet), gasoline products (e.g., Shell or Citgo), and soft drinks (e.g., Pepsi Cola).

3. *Pure franchises* (also called *business format franchises*), in which a franchisee operates a business under the franchisor's trade name and is identified as a member of a select group of persons who deal in this particular business format. In exchange for the franchise, the franchisee ordinarily must follow a standardized or prescribed format as to the methods of operation and may be subject to the franchisor's control with regard to the materials used in making the product, site selection, the design of the facility, the hours of the business, the qualifications of personnel, and the like. Fast-food restaurants, hotels, and car rental agencies often conduct business in this type of franchise.[3]

As a result of the closings of gas stations and automobile and truck dealerships, the overall number of product distributorships has decreased since 1972.[4] In contrast to this decrease in distributorships, pure franchises have increased in number. Large franchisors (those with 1,000 or more units each) should continue to dominate this category of franchising; most of these large franchisors engage either in restaurant businesses or in the retailing of automotive products and services.[5]

BENEFITS OF FRANCHISING

Whatever form the particular franchise takes, the advantages of a franchise system as a method of doing business make it attractive to both potential franchisees and franchisors. The benefits to franchisees include the following:

1. The opportunity to start a business despite limited capital and experience
2. The goodwill that results from marketing a nationally known, high-quality trademark or service mark, which not only benefits the individual franchisees but also raises customer acceptance throughout the system
3. The availability of the franchisor's business expertise in such areas as inventory control, warehousing, advertising, market research, and product innovation
4. An assured supply of materials, the use of bulk buying techniques, and access to training and supervision

The benefits to franchisors include:

1. The franchisee's investment of capital
2. The goodwill and other advantages flowing from the franchisee's entrepreneurial abilities, including the enhanced value of the trademark or service mark
3. The availability of an assured distribution network, which brings about economies of scale in labor costs, produces a more certain demand curve, and reduces wide fluctuations in sales
4. A larger asset base, which makes the franchisor better able to secure credit, enhance profits, avoid financial risks, attract the best talent, lobby for favorable legislation, and defray litigation costs[6]

Simply put, the franchisor and the franchisee are able to accomplish more together than they can through individual effort. In an era of increasing vertical integration, some observers view franchising as the last bastion for the independent businessperson. Franchising provides independent businesspersons with the means of opening and operating their own businesses, and it allows small businesses to compete with mammoth corporations. In addition, franchising fosters the expansion of an established product or service. It also may bring about the rescue of an otherwise failing business.

By lowering barriers to entry, franchising as a type of business system furthers many of the antitrust policies you will learn about in Chapter 39. It thus provides social and economic benefits to the public at large as well as to individual consumers. On the other hand, the franchisor's often extensive control over the franchisee's conduct of the business, together with other aspects of the franchisor/franchisee relationship, has spawned complicated legal questions. The remainder of this chapter considers some of these issues.

Exhibit 37.1 catalogs more fully both the advantages and disadvantages of franchising from the franchisees' and the franchisors' respective points of view.

37.1 | MANAGEMENT

CALL-IMAGE TECHNOLOGY

FRANCHISING CIT

During a recent family dinner, Donna suggested that Tom and Anna should consider franchising CIT. Donna stated that, by franchising, CIT could rapidly expand into a number of states that the firm would be unable to reach for quite some time under its current operating system. If Tom and Anna subsequently ask you for your advice concerning the benefits and the risks of franchising, what would you tell them?

BUSINESS CONSIDERATIONS Why might a relatively small but dynamic business want to consider franchising? Why might this same firm prefer to avoid franchising or otherwise permitting outsiders to have access to its products or ideas?

ETHICAL CONSIDERATION Is it ethical for a franchisor to be able to control the conduct of its franchisees as completely as many franchisors do? Explain your reasoning.

FRANCHISING COMPARED WITH OTHER BUSINESS RELATIONSHIPS

A franchise generally involves a form of marketing or distribution in which one party grants to another the right or privilege to do business in a specified manner in a particular place over a certain period of time. It sometimes has been difficult to distinguish franchising from other types of business relationships. The distinction nonetheless may be legally important, since in recent years virtually every state has passed laws dealing specifically with franchising; and the Federal Trade Commission (FTC) has established regulations covering franchising. Until trouble develops, the two parties may view the holder of the right to do business in a prescribed manner as an independent contractor. But when the grantor terminates its business relationship with the holder, the latter party, in order to fall under the protection of such statutes, may try to characterize the relationship as a franchise. Even before the relationship between the two parties sours, governmental agencies tend to see the relationship as one of employment, not of independent contracting. If the holder of the privilege is an employee or agent rather than an independent contractor, the law requires the grantor to pay withholding and social security taxes, federal minimum wages, and workers' compensation. In addition, in such circumstances, the grantor may be subject to the provisions of other labor laws and private antitrust suits.

It is especially difficult to classify the relationship if the holder of the privilege is a distributor. As we already have noted, a distributor may be a franchisee. Yet, depending on the details surrounding the distributor's relationship with its supplier, it also is possible that a distributor instead is an employee, a **consignee,** or an independent contractor. As you might expect, courts, in making such

Consignee
A person to whom goods are shipped for sale and who generally can return all unsold goods to the consignor.

E X H I B I T 37.1 | **Franchising: Advantages and Disadvantages**

For Franchisees

Advantages

- Quicker start-up time
- Initial and ongoing management training and support
- The goodwill that results from marketing a nationally known, high-quality trademark or service mark, which raises customer acceptance
- Standardized quality of goods and services
- Access to national advertising programs
- Possible, but often limited, financial support from the franchisor
- Proven products and business formats
- Benefits resulting from the franchisor's experience
- Centralized buying power—potentially leading to lower costs
- Advice as to site selection
- Territorial protection
- Increased likelihood of success compared to other business formats

Disadvantages

- Costliness (e.g., required franchise fees and royalties, the latter of which may be payable even if the firm fails to make a profit)
- Limited scope for creativity and independence owing to the franchisor's strict control over operating standards and procedures (i.e., "assistance" becoming control)
- Requirements to buy supplies, equipment, etc. from the franchisor, or suppliers approved by the franchisor
- Limitations on product lines
- Market saturation, with the franchisor allowing many franchises in the same area
- Training programs that promise more than they deliver
- Restrictions on growth stemming from a defined sales territory
- Burdensome paperwork/accountability

For Franchisors

Advantages

- A relatively quick way to grow with limited capital
- Ability to grow without the cost and inconvenience of identifying and developing key managers internally
- Potential for gaining a share of a regional or national market relatively quickly
- Franchisees' investment of capital
- Increased income from franchisees through fees and ongoing royalty payments
- Goodwill and other advantages flowing from the franchisees' entrepreneurial abilities, including the enhanced value of the trademark or service mark
- The availability of an assured distribution network, which brings about economies of scale in labor costs, produces a more certain demand curve, and reduces wide fluctuations in sales
- A larger asset base, which makes the franchisor better able to secure credit, enhance profits, reduce financial risks, attract the best talent, lobby for favorable legislation, and defray litigation costs

Disadvantages

- Actions of one franchisee can reflect badly on the entire franchise
- Monitoring and policing of franchisees
- Conflicts with franchisees who want to do things differently
- Laws protecting franchisees from terminations

SOURCES: Norman Scarborough and Thomas Zimmerer, *Effective Small Business Management*, 6th ed. (New Jersey: Prentice-Hall, 2000), pp. 104–114; Harold Brown, *Franchising—Realities and Remedies*, 2nd ed. (New York: Law Journal Press, 1978), pp. 6–12.

Cooperatives
Groups of individuals, commonly laborers or farmers, who unite in a common enterprise and share the profits proportionately.

Concessionaires
Operators of refreshment centers.

Cartage
The act of carrying by truck, usually within a city; hauling by truck.

determinations, delve deeply into the particular facts at issue (most notably, evidence of the grantor's degree of control over the distributor).

Still, the law is fairly well settled with regard to certain issues: Ordinarily not deemed franchises are **cooperatives, concessionaires,** joint ventures, general partnerships (although a partnership can act either as a franchisor or a franchisee), and sales agencies. In addition, as you will learn in Chapter 38, a franchise agreement usually does not amount to a security under federal or state law because the distributors/franchisees invest their own efforts in the franchise and do not expect to obtain benefits solely from the efforts of others. In other words, the typical franchising arrangement lacks the "passive investment" component generally associated with certain types of securities.

In the following case, the court had to decide whether the business relationship at issue involved a franchise arrangement.

37.1

EAST WIND EXPRESS, INC. V. AIRBORNE FREIGHT CORPORATION
974 P.2D 369 (WASH.APP.DIV. 2 1999)

FACTS Airborne Freight Corporation (Airborne) conducts a nationwide delivery service for packages from the pick-up point to the packages' ultimate destination. Airborne receives packages at one of several stations located around the country; and from there the packages go to Wilmington, Ohio, for sorting and routing to the ultimate destination station. Once at the destination station, either an Airborne employee or an independent contractor under a **cartage** contract with Airborne delivers the packages. By sending a letter, including a sample contract, to potential cartage contractors within a given geographic area, Airborne invites bids for pick-up and delivery service. Beginning in 1990, East Wind Corporation (East Wind) held a cartage contract with Airborne. Pursuant to a new contract signed in 1993, East Wind was to provide pick-up, transport, and delivery of shipments between Airborne's customers and Airborne's facilities in northern Oregon. The customer contacted Airborne, at which time Airborne generated the pick-up information and relayed it to an East Wind driver. While delivering packages that recently had arrived from Airborne's sorting facility, East Wind would pick up the package from the customer and deliver it to the Airborne facility. Airborne billed the customer and was responsible for the package from pick-up to the ultimate destination. East Wind could not receive any portion of any charges made by Airborne to its shippers. Rather, Airborne paid East Wind based on the average number of packages East Wind carried per day. The 1993 contract further provided that "usage of the Airborne trademarks or [trade name] on vehi-

cle(s) and driver uniforms shall constitute an advertising service, the compensation for which is included in the agreed to rates reflected in SCHEDULE A of this Agreement." East Wind chose to put the Airborne logo on its trucks; its drivers wore Airborne uniforms; and East Wind was required to maintain the trucks, uniforms, and logos according to standards established by Airborne. When the relationship between East Wind and Airborne subsequently deteriorated, Airborne terminated the contract. East Wind thereupon sued Airborne for alleged violations of Washington's franchise act. In its summary judgment motion, Airborne asserted that, as a matter of law, the contract between East Wind and Airborne did not constitute a franchise and that Airborne therefore could properly terminate its relationship with East Wind at will.

ISSUE Was East Wind a franchisee entitled to the protections of Washington's franchise act?

HOLDING No. East Wind was an independent contractor hired by Airborne to pick up and deliver Airborne's customers' packages. Since East Wind refrained from marketing, selling, or distributing Airborne's services to Airborne's customers, East Wind was not a franchisee.

REASONING The Washington state legislature enacted the Washington Franchise Investment Protection Act (FIPA) so as to curb franchisor sales abuses and unfair competitive practices. The FIPA defines

37.1

EAST WIND EXPRESS, INC. V. AIRBORNE FREIGHT CORPORATION, *continued*

974 P.2D 369 (WASH.APP.DIV. 2 1999)

franchising, regulates the sales of franchises through registration and disclosure requirements, and provides a "franchisee bill of rights." Registration and disclosure prevent fraud in franchise sales, and the "bill of rights" ameliorates the non-negotiable nature of the franchisor–franchisee relationship. According to the applicable statute, a franchise is

(a) *An agreement, express or implied, oral or written, by which: (i) A person is granted the right to engage in the business of offering, selling, or distributing goods or services under a marketing plan prescribed or suggested in substantial part by the grantor or its affiliate; (ii) The operation of the business is substantially associated with a trademark, service mark, trade name, advertising, or other commercial symbol designating, owned by, or licensed by the grantor or its affiliate; and (iii) The person pays, agrees to pay, or is required to pay, directly or indirectly, a franchise fee.*

To establish that it is a franchisee, East Wind therefore must demonstrate that: (1) Airborne granted it the right to offer, sell, or distribute goods or services under a marketing plan substantially provided by Airborne; (2) the operation of East Wind's business was substantially associated with Airborne's trademark; and (3) it paid Airborne a franchise fee. The evidence showed that Airborne's service consisted of package deliveries, a service it markets and sells directly to customers. Granted, East Wind delivered and picked up some of Airborne's packages; but East Wind did not market or sell this service to individual customers. Rather, the customer called Airborne, which then noted the shipment in its computer sys-

tem. Thereupon, the East Wind dispatcher, working from an Airborne-provided computer terminal, radioed an East Wind driver and coordinated East Wind's pickup and delivery of Airborne's shipments for Airborne's customers. In short, Airborne sold the service to its customers; and East Wind provided delivery of the packages. Hence, as the evidence indicated, Airborne did not grant to East Wind the right to offer, to sell, or to distribute any goods or services under a marketing scheme substantially provided by Airborne. Therefore, East Wind was not Airborne's franchisee. Simply put, East Wind merely provided transportation services to the customers who ship goods with Airborne. Accordingly, East Wind did not have a franchise relationship with Airborne. East Wind consequently could not avail itself of the benefits of FIPA, and Airborne properly could terminate East Wind's cartage contract at will.

BUSINESS CONSIDERATION Assume the CEOs of East Wind and Airborne have asked you to prepare a memo in which you explain how the respective companies could have avoided the litigation in which they found themselves embroiled. What ideas would you stress most heavily?

ETHICAL CONSIDERATIONS The contract between these parties apparently did not characterize their relationship. Given the absence of such language, was East Wind's assertion that it fell under the protection of the state's franchise laws ethical? Did either party, ethically speaking, have the right to stake out the moral high ground?

SETTING UP THE FRANCHISING RELATIONSHIP

To recruit franchisees, franchisors usually advertise in such periodicals as *Inc., Entrepreneur,* and so on. The franchisor typically sends "franchise kits" to those who answer the advertisements. Ordinarily, this franchise kit points out in glowing terms the potential for success in this particular business. To the uninitiated layperson or the businessperson with little previous experience and limited capital—those who may be most inclined to enter a franchising arrangement—the franchisor's promotional documents, market studies, and statistics seem highly persuasive. Even at the outset, then, the franchisee relies heavily on the franchisor for guidance. But, as we will see, the pervasiveness of the franchisor's control often leads to subsequent legal difficulties.

Although many variables are involved, the details of a franchising arrangement usually follow a set pattern. Once the parties have established initial contact and have decided to enter into a franchising relationship, first, the parties typically sign a detailed agreement. In this agreement, the franchisor grants to the franchisee the right to use the mark or standardized product or service in exchange for a franchise fee. The franchisor then uses its real estate expertise to designate a specific franchise location, designs and arranges for the standardized construction of the facility, and installs fixtures and equipment therein. In exchange for an advertising fee (usually a percentage of gross sales) paid by the franchisee, the franchisor intensively advertises the product. In addition, the franchisor creates training programs, prepares training manuals, and sets out stringent guidelines—even for the hiring of personnel, the personnel's dress and grooming standards, and the like—for the day-to-day operation of the business.

Royalty fee
Payment made in exchange for the granting of a right or a license.

Once the franchise becomes operative, the franchisee must follow the procedures delineated in the franchisor's confidential operating manual or risk termination of the franchise. This manual usually mandates strict accounting procedures and authorizes the franchisor to inspect the books and records at any time. The franchisee customarily pays to the franchisor a set **royalty fee** (usually based on a certain percentage of the gross sales) on a monthly or semimonthly basis. The franchise agreement normally obligates the franchisee to secure liability insurance to protect the franchisee and franchisor against casualty losses and tort suits. Usually, the franchisee has the responsibility of meeting state requirements regarding workers' compensation as well.

The last two areas customarily covered in the franchise agreement—quality control and termination—pose most of the potential legal problems. It is easy to understand the franchisor's desire for quality control: Only by maintaining uniform standards of quality and appearance can the franchisor preserve its reputation and foster the public's acceptance of its product. For this reason, franchisors typically obligate the franchisee to buy products and supplies from them at set prices or from suppliers who can meet the franchisors' exacting specifications and standards.

Forcing franchisees to buy only from their own franchisors without any other possible sources probably constitutes antitrust violations—a topic we shall discuss later in this chapter. As the law currently stands, the same is true if the franchisor sets resale prices for the franchisee; nevertheless, within the law, the franchisor can suggest resale prices. Critics of franchising have argued that, practically speaking, the franchisee will have a difficult, if not impossible, time finding a supplier who will meet the franchisor's specifications, with the result that under the guise of quality control franchisees often must pay inflated prices for supplies.

The termination provisions of a franchising agreement also constitute legal pitfalls for the unwary. The franchise agreement ordinarily sets out the duration of the franchise (say 10 years) and usually contains provisions for renewals after this time period has passed. As part of the covenants, or promises, made about the term of the agreement, the franchisee usually agrees to a covenant not to compete for a set time period after the termination of the franchise. The conditions of default, such as a franchisee's insolvency or failure to pay monthly or semimonthly fees when due, that lead to termination are reproduced in the franchise agreement. In these and other "for cause" situations, the agreement normally calls for the franchisor to give the franchisee time (e.g., 10 days) to cure these instances of default. Most agreements provide for notice of termination, and the existing state laws on franchising generally set out a required notice period (say 90 days) before the franchisor can effect a termination.

When prospective franchisees lack business acumen, they are likely to accept without question the 30- to 50-page agreement that the franchisor typically offers. This disparity in bargaining power has led to the passage of state and federal laws and the promulgation of administrative regulations designed to protect franchisees when they enter their agreements (through mandated disclosures) and upon termination (through notice provisions). By closely scrutinizing franchise agreements, courts, too, increasingly have tried to protect franchisees.

Most litigation involving franchises has centered on the termination provisions in the franchising agreement. Because termination can leave the franchisee with little to show after years of effort and expense, courts, whenever possible, try to find a basis of relief so the franchisee is not without a remedy. However, courts will not force franchisors to stick with obviously inept franchisees.

DECISIONAL LAW AND STATUTES AFFECTING FRANCHISING

Courts have been sensitive to the issue of damages in the franchising context. This is particularly true in circumstances involving terminations, because upon termination the franchisee may be left with nothing. Termination provisions, especially when coupled with transferability terms that allow the franchisor to reject potential buyers, may clothe the franchisor with an inordinate amount of power vis-à-vis the franchisee.

37.2 | MANAGEMENT

POTENTIAL PROBLEMS WITH FRANCHISING

Anna seems to be convinced that franchising CIT is an excellent idea and that the firm should move with all due speed to establish franchises in the neighboring states. Dan and John are both hesitant to proceed without further investigation. They ask you what potential problems CIT might encounter in establishing franchises, especially from an agency and a liability perspective. What will you tell them?

BUSINESS CONSIDERATIONS If it establishes franchises, what steps should a business take to ensure that the law will not view the franchisees as the employees or agents of the franchisor? Why should a firm take such steps?

ETHICAL CONSIDERATIONS Is it ethical to use franchising to expand a business venture while simultaneously trying to avoid the traditional liability areas businesses face as they expand? How does franchising affect the ethical duties a business owes to its constituents?

In shaping relief, as we have seen, courts can turn to common law, their own powers of equity, and/or applicable statutes. Some of the statutes mentioned earlier were designed by their drafters to correct perceived abuses and overreaching by franchisors; indeed, few regulations pertain to the conduct of franchisees. Clearly, such statutes have improved the bargaining position of franchisees, but some critics have argued that they also make franchise systems more rigid and encourage litigation. Some state legislatures have passed special laws to protect automobile dealers from excessive competition. These statutes typically require that a franchisor who wishes to establish a new dealership or to relocate an existing one must give notice to established automobile dealers and to the state motor vehicle regulatory agency. This notice provision allows established dealers to object to the granting of any additional dealership licenses and thereby to protect their economic stakes in a particular territory. In *New Motor Vehicle Board of California* v. *Orrin W. Fox Co.,*[7] the Supreme Court upheld a California statute of this type even though

Fox had argued that the statute violated antitrust laws and was unconstitutional on grounds of due process.

On the federal level, the Automobile Dealers' Franchise Act, also known as the Automobile Dealers' Day in Court Act (15 U.S.C. § 1221), in a similar fashion allows a terminated dealer to bring a federal court action seeking retention of the franchise if the dealer can prove that the franchisor has conducted the termination in bad faith and coercively. The federal Petroleum Marketing Practices Act (15 U.S.C. § 2801) protects motor fuel distributors and dealers from arbitrary terminations as well. However, even with these statutes, courts have allowed franchisors to terminate franchisees for such reasons as misconduct or, alternatively, failure to meet sales quotas, to observe quality standards, to maintain appropriate investment levels, and the like. Nevertheless, the presence of these laws helps ensure that the bargaining power between franchisors and franchisees will be more commensurate and balanced. The following case illustrates these points.

37.2

COFFEE V. GENERAL MOTORS ACCEPTANCE CORPORATION
5 F.SUPP. 2D 1365 (S.D.GA. 1998)

FACTS LMC Motors, Inc. (LMC), which operated a General Motors (GM) dealership in Eastman, Georgia, and General Motors Acceptance Corporation (GMAC) were involved in an inventory financing arrangement. L. Mitchell Coffee, Jr. (Coffee) was the president and sole shareholder of LMC. Under the "floor plan" financing arrangement at issue here, the lender (GMAC) provided a line of credit to the dealership (LMC), which the dealership would use to finance the purchase of vehicles from the manufacturer (GM). Pursuant to the agreement covering this inventory financing arrangement, GMAC extended a $1.5 million line of credit to LMC, the purpose of which was to permit LMC to finance up to eighty vehicles. GMAC, however, frequently adjusted the number of vehicles it would finance—and hence the amount it would advance on LMC's behalf—based on a sixty-day supply of vehicles. According to GMAC, this "sixty-day-supply" rule is standard company policy and also constitutes an accepted guideline within the automobile industry. GMAC also periodically adjusted LMC's credit limit based on LMC's sales rates and other financial criteria, such as liquidity and capitalization. GMAC admitted that, under these policies, it had "suspended" LMC's line of credit on two different occasions: once from February to September 1990, and again from March to July 1993. According to GMAC, the company initiated the 1990 suspension at Coffee's request after GMAC's discovery that LMC had $650,000 in previously undisclosed, off-balance sheet debts. According to Coffee, however, GMAC

refused to "reinstate" the line of credit until Coffee had made an additional $100,000 capital contribution to LMC. The 1993 suspension, on the other hand, was initiated by GMAC because a check from LMC to GMAC had been returned for insufficient funds. GMAC therefore conditioned reinstatement of the credit line on satisfaction of several financial criteria, including an additional capital contribution by Coffee. On 5 April 1994, GMAC advised LMC that it (GMAC) intended to terminate the inventory financing arrangement and that GMAC would make a formal demand for payment in ninety days. On 5 July 1994, GMAC demanded payment of the principal amount outstanding on the line of credit, plus the accrued interest on that amount. To shore up LMC's finances, at about the same time, Coffee entered into negotiations with two individuals—Frank Andrews and Woody Butts—regarding their potential investment in LMC. Andrews, Butts, and Coffee subsequently formed ABC Motors in July 1994; and ABC Motors in turn executed an asset purchase agreement with LMC. GMAC thereafter provided floor plan financing to ABC Motors. Although LMC timely paid all amounts owed to GMAC under the terms of the agreement, LMC incurred substantial operating losses during its existence. Coffee alleged that GMAC's repeated and unjustified reductions in LMC's credit limit and GMAC's consequent refusal to finance the purchase of new vehicles at certain critical times had precipitated these losses. GMAC, on the other hand, attributed LMC's losses to poor management and

37.2

COFFEE V. GENERAL MOTORS ACCEPTANCE CORPORATION, *continued*

5 F.SUPP. 2D 1365 (S.D.GA. 1998)

further claimed that it was justified—and in fact authorized under the agreement—in adjusting LMC's credit limit and in terminating the financing relationship. In 1996, Coffee sued GMAC for having allegedly breached its contract with LMC and for having violated the Automobile Dealers' Day in Court Act. GMAC thereupon moved for a summary judgment.

ISSUES Had GMAC, by adjusting LMC's credit limit, breached GMAC's contract with LMC? Had GMAC acted with "good faith" as required under the Automobile Dealers' Day in Court Act?

HOLDINGS As to both issues, maybe yes, maybe no. The existence of genuine issues of fact as to both claims made the award of a summary judgment inappropriate at this time.

REASONING The court noted that the loan agreement between LMC and GM had provided that GMAC would extend to LMC a $1,500,000 line of credit, subject to certain terms and conditions. Moreover, in paragraph 3 of this document, the parties had agreed that GMAC could,

> at its option, terminate the line of credit and refuse to advance funds hereunder upon the occurrence of any of the following: [1] a default by LMC in the payment or performance of any obligation hereunder or under any other agreement entered into with GMAC; [2] the institution of a proceeding in bankruptcy, receivership or insolvency by or against LMC or its property; [3] an assignment by LMC for the benefit of creditors; [4] cancellation of LMC's General Motors franchise; [5] the filing of a notice of any tax lien against any of LMC's property; [6] a misrepresentation by LMC for the purpose of obtaining credit or an extension of credit; [7] a refusal by LMC, upon request by GMAC, to furnish financial information to GMAC at reasonable intervals or to permit GMAC to examine LMC's books and records, etc. . . .

The line of credit so extended was to be used exclusively for the purposes of acquiring personal property to be placed in LMC's inventory. Coffee contended that this contract obligated GMAC to finance up to $1.5 million worth of vehicles and that GMAC could refuse to advance funds or terminate the line of credit only on the occurrence of one of the events enumerated in paragraph 3 of the loan agreement. GMAC, on the other hand, submitted that it was not unconditionally obligated to advance $1.5 million on behalf of LMC. Indeed, GMAC asserted that it was entitled to summary judgment on the breach of contract claim because nothing in the relevant documents required it to advance the full amount of LMC's line of credit. Yet, under the express terms of the written agreement, GMAC had extended a line of credit to LMC in the amount of $1.5 million. Hence, GMAC did not have authority under the agreement to adjust the line of credit based on the number of vehicles financed or on any other criteria. If GMAC had wished to retain discretion over the lending decision, it easily could have inserted language to that effect in the form contract. Nevertheless, it would be premature to grant summary judgment in favor of Coffee on this issue, as a modification of the agreement may have occurred owing to GMAC's authority to terminate the agreement at any time. Therefore, GMAC argued, the parties had modified their original agreement; and GMAC consequently was not liable for breach. Because a genuine issue of fact existed as to whether one of the contingencies that would allow GMAC to terminate the line of credit had actually occurred, summary judgment was not appropriate on the breach of contract claim. The same held true for the claim predicated on an alleged violation of the Automobile Dealers' Day in Court Act (ADDCA). The ADDCA, a remedial statute enacted to redress the economic imbalance and unequal bargaining power between large automobile manufacturers and local dealerships, protects dealers from unfair termination and other retaliatory and coercive practices. The statute permits an "automobile dealer" to bring suit against an "automobile manufacturer" for "the failure of said automobile manufacturer . . . to act in good faith in performing or complying with any of the terms of the franchise, or in terminating, canceling, or not renewing the franchise with said dealer." GMAC first claimed that Coffee lacked standing to sue in his individual capacity under the ADDCA because he is not an "automobile dealer" within the meaning of the Act. However, as the various agreements between LMC and GM indicate, Coffee was essential to the dealership's operations. Moreover, because of Coffee's personally guaranteeing LMC's indebtedness to

continued

COFFEE V. GENERAL MOTORS ACCEPTANCE CORPORATION, *continued*
5 F.SUPP. 2D 1365 (S.D.GA. 1998)

GMAC and his intertwining his personal wealth with the dealership's financial affairs, Coffee had standing to assert a claim under the ADDCA. GMAC next argued that it was entitled to summary judgment on the ADDCA claim because Coffee could not show that GMAC had failed to act in good faith. GMAC pointed to the evidence to the effect that GMAC had had legitimate concerns about LMC's performance and that GMAC had treated LMC in the manner GMAC treated all financially troubled dealerships. Other evidence, though, showed that GMAC had acted in a coercive and intimidating manner in its dealings with LMC and Coffee. Also, it was undisputed that Coffee and LMC had timely met all financial obligations under their agreements with GMAC. At this stage in the litigation, it therefore remained unclear whether GMAC had acted with the requisite bad faith. Accordingly, GMAC's motion for summary judgment would be denied.

BUSINESS CONSIDERATIONS Given the existence of state franchise laws, do franchisors need the protections offered by such federal laws as the Automobile Dealers' Day in Court Act? Do such acts tip the balance too far in favor of franchisees? Do these enactments represent an unwarranted intrusion by federal law into areas traditionally regulated by the states?

ETHICAL CONSIDERATION Evaluate both GMAC's and LMC's actions from the perspective of the Golden Rule. Did one party behave better, ethically speaking, than the other?

The FTC has promulgated a trade regulation rule on franchise disclosure meant to satisfy the same aims that underlie the Automobile Dealers' Day in Court Act and the Petroleum Marketing Practices Act. This 1979 rule, and state laws that mandate similar disclosure provisions, have helped to do away with the abuses associated with the sale of franchises. Continuing investigations of the franchise industry under the power to prohibit deceptive and unfair trade practices granted to the FTC by the Federal Trade Commission Act should effectively reinforce these other regulatory measures.

Furthermore, antitrust laws, such as the Sherman Antitrust Act and the Clayton Act, may apply to various aspects of the franchising relationship. We learned earlier that, as a condition of using their trademark or service mark, franchisors often attempt to impose on franchisees territorial restrictions and restrictions on supplies or prices that may run afoul of the antitrust laws. Consumer protection statutes also may affect the franchising relationship: Franchises that extend credit on installments or through charge accounts may be subject to various truth-in-lending statutes. In addition to its requirement of good faith, the UCC's warranty provisions and its section on unconscionability may be applicable to franchising. Since the law on franchising at this time appears to be unsettled yet proliferating, a thoughtful examination of such laws by franchisors and franchisees alike seems warranted.

The following case involved alleged violations of federal antitrust laws.

37.3

QUEEN CITY PIZZA, INC. V. DOMINO'S PIZZA, INC.
129 F.3D 724 (3RD CIR. 1997), CERT. DENIED, SUB NOM., BAUGHANS, INC. V. DOMINO'S PIZZA, INC., 523 U.S. 1059 (1998)

FACTS Domino's Pizza, Inc. is a fast-food service company that sells pizza through a national network of over 4,200 stores. Domino's is the second largest pizza company in the United States, with revenues in excess of $1.8 billion per year. A franchisee joins the Domino's system by executing a standard franchise agreement with Domino's. Pursuant to the franchise agreement, the franchisee receives the right to sell pizza under the "Domino's" name and format. In return, Domino's receives franchise fees and royalties. The essence of a successful nationwide fast-food chain is product uniformity and consistency. For these reasons, section 12.2 of Domino's standard franchise agreement requires that all pizza ingredients, beverages, and packaging materials used by a Domino's franchisee conform to the standards set by Domino's; that Domino's may, in its "sole discretion require that ingredients, supplies and materials used in the preparation, packaging, and delivery of pizza be purchased exclusively from [it] or from approved suppliers or distributors;" and that Domino's impose reasonable limitations on the number of approved suppliers or distributors of any product." Under this standard franchise agreement, Domino's sells approximately 90 percent of the $500 million in ingredients and supplies used by Domino's franchisees. These sales, worth some $450 million per year, form a significant part of Domino's profits. Franchisees purchase only 10 percent of their ingredients and supplies from outside sources. With the exception of fresh dough, Domino's does not manufacture the products it sells to franchisees. Instead, it purchases these products from approved suppliers and then resells them to the franchisees at a markup. The plaintiffs in this case consisted of eleven Domino's franchisees and the International Franchise Advisory Council, Inc. (IFAC), a Michigan corporation made up of approximately 40 percent of the Domino's franchisees in the United States and aimed at promoting the franchisees' common interests. The plaintiffs contended that Domino's had a monopoly in "the $500 million aftermarket [of] sales of supplies to Domino's franchisees" and used its monopoly power to unreasonably restrain trade, limit competition, and extract supra-competitive profits. To support their claims, the plaintiffs alleged that: (1) when they attempted to lower costs by making fresh pizza dough on site, Domino's increased the processing fees and altered the quality standards and inspection practices for store-produced dough, thereby eliminating all the potential savings and financial incentives for the plaintiffs to make their own dough; (2) Domino's prohibited stores that produced dough from selling this dough to other franchisees, even though the dough-producing stores were willing to sell dough at a price 25 percent to 40 percent below Domino's price; (3) Domino's blocked IFAC's attempts to buy less expensive ingredients and supplies from other sources in that Domino's intentionally issued ingredient and supply specifications so vague that potential suppliers could not provide would-be purchasers with meaningful price quotations; and (4) Domino's refused to sell fresh dough to franchisees unless the franchisees purchased other ingredients and supplies from Domino's. As a result of these and other alleged practices, the plaintiffs maintained that each franchisee store now pays between $3,000 and $10,000 more per year for ingredients and supplies than it would in a competitive market—costs that in turn are passed on to consumers. When the lower court dismissed all the antitrust claims, owing to the plaintiffs' failure to allege a relevant market, the plaintiffs appealed.

ISSUES Did the ingredients, supplies, and materials used by and in the operation of pizza franchise stores qualify as a relevant market for purposes of the franchisees' monopolization and attempted monopolization claims against the franchisor? Did the franchisor-approved dough that the franchise agreement required franchisees to use qualify as a separate market for the franchisees' claim that the franchisor had unlawfully tied the sale of such dough to the franchisees' purchase of other ingredients and supplies?

HOLDINGS No as to both issues. The plaintiffs' claims would fail because the proposed relevant market—ingredients and supplies (including dough)—was not a relevant market for antitrust purposes under either Section Two or Section One of the Sherman Act. The relevant market would include all reasonably interchangeable products. Hence, the plaintiffs' claim that contractual restraints could render otherwise identical products non-interchangeable for the purposes of the definition of the relevant market must fail.

continued

37.3

QUEEN CITY PIZZA, INC. V. DOMINO'S PIZZA, INC., *continued*

129 F.3D 724 (3RD CIR. 1997), CERT. DENIED, SUB NOM., BAUGHANS, INC. V. DOMINO'S PIZZA, INC., 523 U.S. 1059 (1998)

REASONING The plaintiffs alleged that Domino's willfully acquired and maintained a monopoly in the market for ingredients, supplies, materials, and distribution services used in the operation of Domino's stores, in violation of Section Two of the Sherman Act. The offense of monopoly under Section Two of the Sherman Act has two elements: (1) the possession of monopoly power in the relevant market and (2) the willful acquisition or maintenance of that power as distinguished from growth or development as a consequence of a superior product, business acumen, or historic accident. The outer boundaries of a relevant market are determined by the concept of reasonable interchangeability of use. When assessing reasonable interchangeability, a court may consider such factors as price, use, qualities, and cross-elasticity of demand between the product itself and the substitutes for it. As to the latter factor, a price increase of a good within a relevant product market would tend to create a greater demand for other like goods in that market. Here, the dough, tomato sauce, and paper cups that meet Domino's standards and that are used by Domino's stores are interchangeable with the dough, sauce, and cups available from other suppliers and used by other pizza companies. Thus, a court cannot restrict the relevant market, which is defined to include all reasonably interchangeable products, solely to those products currently approved by Domino's for use by Domino's franchisees. For that reason, the plaintiffs' proposed relevant market is invalid. Nor is section 12.2 of Domino's standard franchising agreement, whereby Domino's franchisees can use only Domino's-approved products, sufficient by itself to create a relevant market in approved products. When determining whether a product is interchangeable for the purposes of defining a relevant market, a court looks not to the contractual restraints assumed by a particular plaintiff, but to the uses to which consumers put the product. Thus, the relevant inquiry here is not whether a Domino's franchisee might reasonably use both approved or non-approved products interchangeably without triggering liability for breach of contract, but whether pizza makers in general might use such products interchangeably. Clearly, they could. Were a court to adopt the plaintiffs' position that contractual restraints render otherwise identical products non-interchangeable for purposes of the definition of the relevant market, the existence of any exclusive dealing arrangement, output or requirements contract, or franchise tying agreement in itself would support a claim for violation of the antitrust laws. Courts and legal commentators have long recognized that franchise tying contracts that require the franchisee to purchase inputs such as ingredients and supplies from the franchisor are an essential and important aspect of the franchise form of business organization. Among other things, such tying contracts reduce agency costs and prevent franchisees from free riding—offering products of substandard quality insufficient to maintain the reputational value of the franchise product while benefiting from the quality control efforts of other actors in the franchise system. Franchising is a bedrock of the American economy. More than one-third of all dollars spent in retailing transactions in the United States are paid to franchise outlets. A court therefore must reject any suggestion that the antitrust laws were designed to erect a serious barrier to this form of business organization. Here, the plaintiffs' acceptance of a franchise package that included purchase requirements and contractual restrictions is consistent with the existence of a competitive market in which franchises are valued, in part, according to the terms of the proposed franchise agreement and the availability of alternative franchise opportunities. If they had viewed the contractual restrictions in section 12.2 of the general franchise agreement as overly burdensome or risky, the plaintiffs could have purchased a different form of restaurant or made some alternative investment. They chose not to do so. Unlike the plaintiffs in the landmark *Kodak Co. v. Image Technical Services, Inc.* case, the plaintiffs here must purchase products of Domino's not because of Domino's power over a unique product, but because they are bound by contract to do so. If Domino's acted unreasonably when, under the franchise agreement, it restricted plaintiffs' ability to purchase supplies from other sources, the plaintiffs' remedy, if any, lies in contract, not antitrust, law. The plaintiffs' allegation that Domino's had imposed an unlawful tying arrangement in violation of Section One of the Sherman Act when Domino's had required its franchisees to buy ingredients and supplies from them as a condition of obtaining Domino's fresh dough would fail for the same reasons. In a tying arrangement, the seller sells one item, known as the tying product, on the condition that the buyer also

QUEEN CITY PIZZA, INC. V. DOMINO'S PIZZA, INC., *continued*
129 F.3D 724 (3RD CIR. 1997), CERT. DENIED, SUB NOM., BAUGHANS, INC. V. DOMINO'S PIZZA, INC., 523 U.S. 1059 (1998)

purchases another item, known as the tied product. The antitrust concern over tying arrangements is limited to those situations in which the seller can exploit its power in the market for the tying product to force buyers to purchase the tied product when they otherwise would not, thereby restraining competition in the tied product market. Even if a seller has obtained a monopoly in the tying product legitimately (as through a patent), courts have seen the expansion of that power to other product markets as illegitimate and suppressive of competition. The first inquiry in any Section One tying case is whether the defendant has sufficient market power over the tying product, which inquiry requires a finding that two separate product markets exist and a determination of precisely what the tying and tied products markets are. Here, the plaintiffs claimed that Domino's had used its power in the purported market for Domino's-approved dough to force the plaintiffs to buy unwanted ingredients and supplies from Domino's. This claim would fail because the proposed tying market—the market in Domino's-approved dough—is not a relevant market for antitrust purposes owing to Domino's dough's reasonable interchangeability with other brands of pizza dough. True, a Domino's franchisee must use this approved dough or face a suit for breach of contract. But the particular contractual restraints assumed by a plaintiff are not sufficient by themselves to render interchangeable commodities non-interchangeable for purposes of the definition of the relevant market. If Domino's had had market power in the overall market for pizza dough and had forced plaintiffs to purchase other unwanted ingredients so as to obtain dough, the plaintiffs might have shown a valid tying claim. But where the defendant's "power" to "force" the plaintiffs to purchase the alleged tying product stemmed not from the market, but from the plaintiffs' contractual agreement to purchase the tying product, no claim would lie. For that reason, the plaintiffs' claim as to this issue was properly dismissed.

BUSINESS CONSIDERATIONS Did the court reject too quickly the argument that consumers would absorb, in higher prices for pizzas, the markups Domino's realized on its sales of fresh dough (and other items) to its franchisees? Or was the court correct in holding that Domino's—to ensure quality control—could alter the inspection practices and quality standards for dough-producing stores, even though in so doing, Domino's in effect thereby eliminated the financial incentives such stores otherwise would have realized?

ETHICAL CONSIDERATION Had the court decided this case on ethical as opposed to legal grounds, would the result have been different? Why or why not?

CHALLENGES TO FRANCHISING REGULATORY STATUTES

Some franchisors have bridled at the passage of such franchising statutes because they view these laws as serious limitations on their freedom to contract and manage their businesses. Consequently, franchisors have raised constitutional arguments against these laws. The parts of the Constitution relied on in these challenges include the following:

1. *Impairment of the obligation of contracts.* The Constitution prohibits a state from passing a law that makes substantive changes in contractual rights.
2. *Due process.* The Fourteenth Amendment bans vague, standardless laws.
3. *Federal supremacy.* Article VI of the Constitution makes federal law the supreme law of the land. Thus, a state franchising law that conflicts with a

37.3 | MANAGEMENT

QUALITY CONTROL OVER FRANCHISES

The Kochanowskis have decided to franchise CIT, and they plan to offer franchises to investors in each of the neighboring states. They are concerned, however, with quality control and the preservation of the image and the name the firm has established. They ask for your advice as to how they can make provisions for these issues in the franchise agreement. What will you tell them?

BUSINESS CONSIDERATIONS Why might a franchisor want to control the materials used by the franchisees in operating their franchises? How much freedom should the franchisor grant to the franchisees, and how much control should the franchisor exercise for the sake of company image and consistency?

ETHICAL CONSIDERATIONS Is it ethical for a franchisor to require the franchisee to purchase materials and supplies from the franchisor? Would it be more ethical for the franchisor to allow the franchisee to act as he or she desires, but to make termination of the franchise easier if the franchisee fails to meet certain quality standards?

federal law (say the Lanham Act's regulation of trademarks or the Federal Arbitration Act) will be unconstitutional.

4. *Interstate commerce.* Article I, § 8 of the Constitution prohibits the states from placing undue burdens on interstate commerce.

THE FRANCHISING ENVIRONMENT

Industry Statistics

Industry promotional literature and trade groups such as the International Franchise Association (IFA) for decades have touted franchising as a particularly robust and viable method of conducting business. While no one disputes the high level of general interest in franchising—governmental reports note that franchises account for approximately 34 percent of all retail sales in the United States—these reports and other academic studies of the franchising environment dispute the accuracy of the data that, for instance, indicate low failure rates for franchises.[8] The methodologies employed by the industry advocates for franchising and the resultant flawed data sound a cautionary note for the would-be franchisor. Since independent empirical research has questioned what these glowing numbers really mean, the wise potential entrepreneur who finds him- or herself drawn to franchising will view these statistics with some skepticism.[9]

INTERNATIONAL MARKETS

These imperfect industry data have not stanched the expansion of U.S. franchises abroad. Indeed, government studies suggest that U.S. franchisors will continue to pierce international markets, despite the numerous problems inherent in complying with the local laws of other nations. Canada remains the most important market for U.S. franchisors. As recent statistics show, Canada represented about one-third of all U.S. international outlets; Japan constituted the second-largest foreign outlet; and Australia ranked third. Interestingly, in a similar fashion, Canada, Mexico, Japan, the United Kingdom, and the continental European countries are setting up an increasing number of franchises in the United States. The international ramifications of franchising thus should become even more significant as the growth of communication and transportation systems continues to narrow the gap among consumer preferences around the world and as the advantages of franchising become more apparent to the U.S.'s international neighbors. This is a development that promises to be well worth watching.

WHO OWNS THESE ADVERTISING DOLLARS: THE DEALERS OR GM?

For years, General Motors Corp. (GM) assessed a certain percentage of each car sold and used these monies for the company's national advertising campaign. And for years, GM "rebated" the $500 million in advertising assessments it had collected from its dealers so that the dealers could use the funds for local advertisements on television and radio, as well as in the dealers' hometown newspapers. In December 1998, however, GM informed its dealers that it was eliminating this "rebate program." Instead, GM's hand-picked regional advertising executives would retain and then spend the assessments. This change in policy particularly angered some Illinois and Indiana dealerships that had used the rebated sums for establishing local marketing approaches that had resulted in a substantially larger market share than that enjoyed by the company nationally. Hence, the Illinois and Indiana groups brought class-action suits against GM under their respective state franchising statutes. The Indiana suit also alleged that GM had engaged in criminal conversion of "their" (i.e., the dealers') advertising monies. GM responded with a countersuit against the Illinois dealers for conspiring to foil the company's legitimate business plans by paying the group's attorney's fees with advertising assessments allegedly owed to GM (the Indiana group had not used these assessments for attorney's fees).

The factual backdrop for the dispute originated in the 1960s and 1970s, when GM encouraged many Illinois and Indiana dealerships to form associations called "dealer marketing groups" (DMGs) and to advertise GM products locally. Initially, such dealers funded this advertising through voluntary assessments paid to their associations. Subsequently—and apparently at the dealers' request—GM agreed to collect the assessments (the aforementioned 1 percent of the manufacturer's suggested retail price [MSRP]) from the dealers and to "remit" the monies to the DMGs. GM always accounted for these monies as a separate liability account (i.e., as the dealers' funds). In the 1980s, encouraged by the success of the Midwestern dealers' marketing approach, GM established new company-wide advertising programs based on it. GM thereupon began referring to these new programs as "dealer marketing initiative programs" and to the dealers' 1 percent payment as the "GM Marketing Adjustment," a sum subsequently added as a line item to the cost of a GM auto. For years, the company continued to remit this money to the dealers and their various associations, regardless of who technically "owned" it. But when GM announced this radical change in its marketing approach, the Illinois and Indiana groups balked.

The issue apparently boils down to who owns those advertising dollars. If a judge decides that the advertising assessments belong to the GM dealers, then the dealers probably will recover damages under the state automobile franchise acts. If the judge concludes that the assessments belong to GM, then the company presumably can do whatever it desires with the funds. According to GM's attorneys, when GM expanded the Chicago area incentive program to the national level, tied the local dealer assessment to 1 percent of the MSRP, and made this sum a line item on a GM auto's invoice, GM had made the 1 percent part of the sale price of each car. The GM attorneys further claim that, under the typical GM franchise agreement, any such sales proceeds belong to GM—not the dealers, who generally receive only commissions and other financial incentives. And, therefore, if the GM dealers do not own the local market assessments, then the dealers will be unable to recharacterize what GM attorneys call a new "marketing strategy" as a disguised dealer-funded "advertising campaign" that violates state law. The attorneys for the class action plaintiffs concede that GM has drafted the franchise agreements to give GM a good deal of latitude with regard to such revenue-sharing disputes.

continued

However, these attorneys argue, the agreements more closely resemble contracts of adhesion (or so-called "take-it-or-leave-it" contracts) than true franchise agreements like those found in the fast-food restaurant business.

This case is being heard in *your* court. Given these arguments, how will *you* decide the case?[10]

BUSINESS CONSIDERATIONS Why would a national or international business want to allow local franchises to have their own local advertising campaigns? Why would regional franchises prefer to have their own advertising campaign, rather than relying on the ads run by the franchisor for the national market?

ETHICAL CONSIDERATIONS Is it ethical for the franchisor to specify how or where the franchisees may advertise? Is it ethical for a franchisee to devise its own advertising approach separate and distinct from the ads run by the franchisor?

SOURCE: Darryl Van Duch, *The National Law Journal* (16 August 1999), pp. A-1, A-8.

RESOURCES FOR BUSINESS LAW STUDENTS

NAME	RESOURCES	WEB ADDRESS
Franchising Online	The American Bar Association's (ABA's) forum on franchising, a Forum Committee of the ABA, provides publications and information on laws affecting franchising.	**http://www.abanet.org/forums/franchising/home.html**
FranInfo	FranInfo provides tips and materials on buying a franchise or making a business into a franchise. FranInfo also provides a detailed directory of franchises.	**http://www.frannet.com/**
Federal Trade Commission (FTC) Act, 15 U.S.C. § 41–58	The Legal Information Institute provides a hypertext and searchable version of 15 U.S.C. § 41–58, popularly known as the Federal Trade Commission Act.	**http://www4.law.cornell.edu/uscode/15/41.html**
FTC	The FTC provides information on proposed franchising rules, as well as news and press releases, speeches and articles, and facts for consumers and businesses.	**http://www.ftc.gov/**

SUMMARY

Franchising has become a significant method of doing business both in the United States and abroad. A franchise is an agreement in which one person pays a fee in exchange for a license to use a trademark, service mark, or logotype while engaging in the distribution of goods or services. The person or firm granting the franchise is called the franchisor; the person receiving the franchise is known as the franchisee. Franchises fall into three general categories: trade name franchising, product distributorships, and pure (or business format) franchises. For both franchisees and franchisors, the advantages of franchising make it an attractive method of doing business. Courts have had some problems in distinguishing franchise relationships from other types of business relationships, such as independent contracting. Yet such a distinction may be important under state and federal franchising laws, tax laws, labor laws, and antitrust laws. Some areas of the law are settled: Cooperatives, concessionaires, joint ventures, general partnerships, and sales agencies generally are not deemed the legal equivalent of a franchise. A franchise is not considered a security, either.

To ensure product uniformity and to protect the goodwill associated with its trademark or service mark, the franchisor strictly controls the franchise relationship. Two areas ordinarily covered in the franchise agreement—quality control and termination—pose the most numerous legal problems. State and federal laws may cover these two aspects of the agreement, and a wise franchisor should take care not to run afoul of these laws by pressing for unreasonable provisions or terms. Special industry laws at both the federal and state levels also may protect franchisees. The Federal Trade Commission's franchise disclosure regulations, antitrust laws, consumer protection statutes, and the Uniform Commercial Code constitute further bases for controlling abusive behavior by franchisors. Franchisors have challenged such statutes on constitutional grounds, sometimes successfully.

In the last few years, academicians and other experts have questioned the accuracy of industry-generated franchising data. Hence, the would-be franchisee should treat these data with caution. No one doubts that franchising will continue to play an important role in domestic retail sales, however. Similarly, the international aspects of franchising should continue to gain in significance in the coming decades as more sophisticated communication and transportation systems allow for the global dissemination of goods and services.

DISCUSSION QUESTIONS

1. Name eight different types of businesses that use franchising as their distributional method. Then list and describe the two main classifications of franchises.
2. Define the term *franchise*.
3. Describe four benefits of franchising for the franchisee and franchisor, respectively.
4. For what purposes does the law make distinctions between franchising and other types of business relationships such as independent contracting?
5. Briefly explain the steps involved in setting up a franchising arrangement, and describe what areas the franchising agreement normally covers.
6. Discuss why quality-control and termination clauses are important to franchisors and how these same provisions nevertheless pose legal pitfalls for franchisors.
7. Enumerate the types of statutes that franchisees can use to curb the power of franchisors.
8. What four constitutional bases have franchisors used to challenge franchising statutes?
9. Why should a would-be franchisee be cautious in approaching industry-generated data concerning franchising?
10. Name the three most important international markets for U.S. franchisors.

CASE PROBLEMS AND WRITING ASSIGNMENTS

1. White Hen Pantry (WHP) is a franchisor of convenience stores. WHP entered into a franchise agreement with Wayne Whitacre for a convenience store to be operated in Valparaiso, Indiana. Christel Helmchen was a clerk in WHP's Valparaiso store. In the early morning of 14 November 1990, Christel was abducted from the store, raped, and murdered. Christel's parents later brought suit against WHP on the grounds that WHP had been negligent in failing to provide adequate security at the store. The franchise agreement contained a video system policy that mandated the types and location of equipment should a franchisee choose to use video surveillance. However, WHP neither required nor forbade video surveillance. At trial, WHP's director of loss prevention testified that security measures are solely the province of the franchisee. In support of this testimony, he noted that WHP does not conduct store inspections for security. In rebuttal, the Helmchens relied on correspondence in which the director of loss prevention had discussed WHP's video surveillance policy. Apparently, this letter was in response to inquiries from franchisees. While the letter did not recommend video surveillance as an effective crime deterrent, it did provide certain mandates in the event a franchisee chose to employ video surveillance. Another letter addressed prevention strategies when a franchisee or its employees faced an armed robbery situation. A third letter offered methods to reduce the risks associated with theft and robbery. The Helmchens, in addition, pointed to the operation manual that also set out useful techniques that one could employ if confronted with an armed robbery. Assume that, in this jurisdiction, the franchisor owes no general duty to provide a secure workplace for the employees of its franchisees. Nonetheless, a duty may arise depending on the extent of control a franchisor has over the operations of the franchise. Had the Helmchens provided the proof necessary to support the existence of such a duty on the part of WHP? [See *Helmchen* v. *White Hen Pantry, Inc.*, 685 N.E.2d 180 (Ind.App. 1997).]

2. Jim White Agency (JWA), d/b/a Jim White Nissan, was a licensed automobile dealership in Toledo, Ohio. JWA was in the business of selling and servicing Nissan motor vehicles under a franchise agreement with Nissan Motor Corporation in U.S.A. [sic] (Nissan). That agreement provided, in pertinent part:

   Dealer shall not move, relocate, or change the usage of the Dealership Location or any of the Dealership Facilities, or substantially modify any of the Dealership Facilities, nor shall Dealer or any person named in the Final Article of this Agreement directly or indirectly establish or operate any other locations or facilities for the sale or servicing of Nissan Products or for the conduct of any other of the Dealership Operations contemplated by this Agreement, without the prior written consent of Seller.

   The JWA dealership was on "automobile row," an area in Toledo in which 17 other dealerships were located. In 1992, JWA sought, and was granted, approval to relocate the Nissan dealership next to a Toyota dealership—a move of approximately 50 yards. In the early 1990s, JWA began to experience significant sales decreases and, thus, in 1992, sought a buyer for the dealership. After receiving several offers, JWA entered into a verbal agreement with Jim Yark. Nissan had tentatively approved the sale to Yark when JWA announced that instead of selling the dealership, it would combine—or "dual"—the Nissan dealership with a Chevrolet dealership it owned and which was located several miles from "automobile row." To that end, in 1994, JWA requested permission to move the Nissan dealership to the Chevrolet location. Michael Clubb, a Dealer Operations Manager for Nissan for the region where JWA was located, became the primary intermediary between Nissan and JWA. After learning of JWA's desire to "dual" the Nissan and Chevrolet dealerships, Clubb sent JWA a letter indicating Nissan's opposition to JWA's relocation. These reasons included: (1) marketing reports that indicated that "automobile row" was the best location for selling Nissan cars; (2) JWA's financial problems that had resulted from poor management practices rather than location; and (3) the "planning volume" figures (i.e., the numbers showing the sales potential for any given market) that indicated that a nondualed dealership was in Nissan's best interests. Thereafter, JWA accused Nissan of bad faith in refusing to allow JWA to move the dealership and threatened legal action. JWA in addition sent a letter requesting approval of the deal to Clubb's superior. When the Nissan regional headquarters decided to deny this request for relocation, JWA sued Nissan for allegedly violating the "good faith" requirement of the Ohio Dealers Act provision that states: "Notwithstanding the terms, provisions, or conditions of any agreement, franchise, or waiver, no franchisor shall: (A) In acting or purporting to act under the terms, provisions, or conditions of a franchise or in terminating, canceling, or failing to renew a franchise, fail to act in good faith." To determine if Nissan had acted in bad faith, the trier of fact would have to ascertain whether Nissan's actions were "commercially unjustifiable." The lower court had framed the issue as whether it should find the franchisor liable for failure to act in good faith where the franchisor has done no more than insist on enforcing its contract rights to the detriment of its franchisee. If you were the appellate court, how would you answer this issue in this case? [See *Jim White Agency* v. *Nissan Motor Corporation in U.S.A.*, 126 F.3d 832 (6th Cir. 1997).]

3. Northeast Express Regional Airlines, Inc. (NERA) and Precision Valley Aviation, Inc. (PVA) were two regional, commuter airlines with principal operations in the state of Maine. In 1989, Northwest Airlines, Inc. (Northwest) was seeking to strengthen its presence in New England by expanding its jet capacity in Boston, Massachusetts. To further that goal, on 2 May 1989, Northwest entered into an Airline Service Agreement (ASA) with PVA and on 5 January 1990, it entered into a similar agreement with NERA. Both ASAs were amended by various letter agreements that provided PVA and NERA with additional compensation. Both ASAs expired by their own terms on 1 December 1994. Pursuant to the terms of these ASAs, both PVA and NERA identified their respective commuter airlines as a "Northwest Airlink" and flew under Northwest's designation code, colors, and logo. These ASAs provided that Northwest would pay NERA and PVA for each passenger flown and ticketed on a Northwest flight based on a "straight-rate prorate" formula. Both NERA and PVA gave Northwest letters of credit as security for a $2 million advance made by Northwest at the inception of the parties' relationship. Both agreements contained an integration clause stating that the ASAs constituted the full agreement between the parties and could be modified only by a duly executed subsequent writing. Additionally, the ASAs stated that the agreements were to be governed by the laws of the State of Minnesota. NERA and PVA, while operating under the ASAs, requested continual financial accommodations from Northwest, concessions that Northwest often granted and evidenced by a written amendment to the ASAs. On 25 May 1994, Northwest sent written notice of default to PVA and NERA and provided each with notice that the ASAs would terminate in six months. On 28 May 1994, NERA and PVA filed voluntary petitions for relief under Chapter 11 of the Bankruptcy Code. In the ensuing bankruptcy litigation, NERA and PVA claimed they were franchisees under the Minnesota Franchise Act. Using the facts of this case and the principles discussed in this chapter, evaluate NERA and PVA's claims. [See *In re Northeast Express Regional Airlines, Inc.*, 228 B.R. 53 (Bkrtcy.D.Me. 1998).]

4. Lithuanian Commerce Corporation (LCC) had served as the exclusive Lithuanian distributor of L'eggs pantyhose for Sara Lee Hosiery (Sara Lee), the manufacturer of L'eggs pantyhose. LCC alleged that, while it was Sara Lee's exclusive Lithuanian distributor, Sara Lee donated a large number of pantyhose to areas neighboring Lithuania. LCC claimed that this action created a black market for pantyhose in Lithuania and hampered LCC's sales of L'eggs pantyhose. After LCC complained about Sara Lee's so-called "dumping" of pantyhose in the Baltic, the two parties reached a settlement in which Sara Lee provided LCC with a large number of Mexican-made pantyhose at no cost. LCC alleged that the Mexican pantyhose Sara Lee provided pursuant to this latter agreement were defective or, at the very least, significantly different from the American versions of the L'eggs styles of pantyhose LCC had previously received from Sara Lee. LCC claimed that, as a result of the poor quality of these Mexican-made pantyhose, LCC's business suffered both in terms of the lost profits it should have realized had the pantyhose been of standard quality and in the loss of customer goodwill that LCC had experienced. In response, Sara Lee submitted that LCC had examined samples of the pantyhose and, therefore, that LCC had had full knowledge of the nature and quality of the Mexican-made pantyhose. Further, Sara Lee asserted counterclaims that alleged that LCC and its principals, Algis Vasys and Laima Zajanckauskiene, had made false claims in their advertisements for L'eggs pantyhose by stating that L'eggs pantyhose have medicinal and therapeutic value and that LCC had failed to pay invoices due to Sara Lee. LCC received mail at its New Jersey office, and Mr. Vasys conducted one business meeting there with the CEO of another international company to investigate the possibility of establishing a distributorship arrangement between LCC and that international firm. Mr. Vasys also testified that he had used the New Jersey office to store the Mexican-made pantyhose that he had received from Sara Lee. Vasys moreover testified that the LCC office is a house that he repeatedly used for personal use, such as sleeping, and for storing office supplies. Vasys testified further that LCC is not authorized to sell pantyhose in New Jersey or anywhere in the United States. Rather, all LCC's sales take place in Lithuania, Latvia, Estonia, and Kaliningrad. LCC subsequently sued Sara Lee for damages based on breach of warranty and for violations of the New Jersey Franchise Practices Act (NJFPA). Sara Lee argued that LCC had failed to present sufficient evidence on which a jury could reasonably assess damages. Sara Lee further argued that LCC was not a franchisee because the NJFPA applies

only to an arrangement, the performance of which contemplates or requires the franchisee to establish or maintain a place of business within the State of New Jersey. Thus, according to Sara Lee, a franchise would exist under the NJFPA only if: (1) a "community of interest" between the franchisor and the franchisee were present; (2) the franchisor granted a "license" to the franchisee; and (3) the parties contemplated that the franchisee would maintain a "place of business" in New Jersey. For which company should the judge rule, LCC or Sara Lee? [See *Lithuanian Commerce Corporation, Ltd.* v. *Sara Lee Hosiery*, 23 F.Supp. 2d 509 (D. N.J. 1998).]

5. The Mitsubishi keiretsu (the traditional Japanese form of conglomerate) is a well-known manufacturer of heavy equipment, including forklift trucks. In June 1985, To-Am Equipment Co., Inc. (To-Am) entered into a dealership agreement for these forklifts with a company affiliated with Mitsubishi, Machinery Distribution, Inc. (MDI). In 1992, MDI became part of a new entity, MCFA, which assumed MDI's role in the contract. Since 1973, To-Am had been servicing, renting, and repairing forklifts in South Chicago. Over the years it also had sold a number of different brands of forklifts, including those made by Clark, Yale, and Hyster, although prior to its contract with MCFA it had sold only used forklifts. Before allowing To-Am to become a Mitsubishi dealer, MCFA required To-Am to relocate to a larger showroom. To-Am complied and moved to Frankfort, Illinois. During the years it served as a Mitsubishi dealer, To-Am continued to handle used forklifts manufactured by Mitsubishi's competitors—in other words, the dealership did not require exclusivity on To-Am's part. On the other hand, the agreement conferred on To-Am an exclusive Area of Primary Responsibility (APR), consisting of four Illinois counties and one county in Indiana, in which MCFA did not have and agreed to refrain from creating a competing dealership. Under the 1985 contract, To-Am was required to participate in Mitsubishi's warranty program. This meant, among other things, that To-Am had to maintain trained personnel and provide prompt warranty and nonwarranty service on all Mitsubishi products within its APR. To comply with these requirements, To-Am participated in all of MCFA's training programs, apparently for the most part at To-Am's own expense. Article III, paragraph 14 of the agreement expressly required To-Am to "maintain an adequate supply of current [MCFA] sales and service publications." To-Am did so by keeping a master set of manuals in its parts department, a second set in its service department, and additional manuals in its mobile service vehicles (a necessity in this business). MCFA had provided one set of these manuals in 1985 when To-Am became a distributor; but thereafter To-Am had to order additional manuals for the other locations where it kept manuals, for updating, and for replacing obsolescent manuals. MCFA invoiced To-Am for these additional manuals, and over the years To-Am paid more than $1,600 for them. At trial, MCFA argued that it had updated To-Am's manuals with all new releases free of charge and that it viewed one full set (which it claimed to have supplied to To-Am) as an "adequate supply." Other evidence, however, indicated that MCFA dealers, including To-Am, did not receive free updates and that one set was inadequate for a dealer of To-Am's size. In February 1994, MCFA notified To-Am that, in accordance with Article XI, paragraph 1 of the agreement, which permitted either party to terminate upon 60 days' written notice "or as required by law," MCFA was terminating the dealership agreement effective 2 April 1994. This step was a blow to To-Am's business, even though after MCFA's action To-Am continued to service, repair, lease, and rent Mitsubishi forklift trucks and continued to service and repair other brands of forklift trucks. The reason was simple: Mitsubishi forklifts were the only new vehicles that To-Am had been selling. Even though new truck sales are themselves relatively low profit generators for dealers, such sales can create substantial downstream business, ranging from trade-ins that could be resold as used equipment or carried as rental equipment, to service and parts sales. While dealer profit margins on new equipment sales might be as low as 3 percent, the margins on these downstream business opportunities ranged from 30 to 50 percent. Thus, the loss of To-Am's line of new trucks had ripple effects on its business extending far beyond the immediate lost sales. In 1995, To-Am sued MCFA for violations of the Illinois Franchise Disclosure Act (owing to the allegedly wrongful termination of To-Am's franchise without good cause) and for breach of contract by MCFA (for MCFA's failure to repurchase To-Am's inventory following this termination). In rebuttal, MCFA contended that To-Am had failed to pay a sufficient franchise fee as defined by the Franchise Disclosure Act (which requires a payment in excess of $500) and thus could not be considered a franchisee. If you were the judge, how would you decide this case? [See *To-Am Equipment Co., Inc.* v. *Mitsubishi Caterpillar Forklift America, Inc.*, 152 F.3d 658 (7th Cir. 1998).]

6. **BUSINESS APPLICATION CASE** In 1976, Katherine Apostoleres became the sole shareholder of Minerva, Inc., which owned the rights to a Dunkin' Donuts of

America, Inc. (Dunkin') franchise in Brandon, Florida. In 1978, Apostoleres became the sole shareholder of Rosebud, Inc., which owned the rights to a Dunkin' Donuts franchise in Temple Terrace, Florida. Apostoleres and her family (the franchisees) operated both stores. In early 1982, Dunkin' offered to all its franchisees the right to renew the term of the franchisees' existing franchise agreements for an additional 10 years at a fixed cost of $5,000 each. In return, Dunkin' required the franchise owners to participate in a program to abide by advertising decisions favored by at least two-thirds of the local franchise owners in a given television market. Apostoleres refused to accept the offer because she did not want to be bound by the "two-thirds" clause. In August 1982, Dunkin' employees audited Apostoleres's Temple Terrace and Brandon stores and during this audit employed the "yield-and-usage" method, which, by taking the weights of a small number of donuts and extrapolating how many donuts should have been produced based on those weights, projects a store's gross sales. The franchisees' agreements with Dunkin' did not authorize Dunkin' to conduct an audit based on such methodology. In late 1982, the audits revealed that reported sales generally agreed with the sales run through the cash registers, bank deposits, and tax returns for the audited period; however, the yield-and-usage analysis indicated an underreporting of gross sales at both stores. The franchisees denied such underreporting and asserted that the yield-and-usage analysis provided inherently unreliable results. In September 1985, Dunkin' again audited the two stores. The audit of the Temple Terrace store disclosed no underreporting, but the audit of the Brandon store reflected an underreporting of gross sales based on the yield-and-usage analysis. This audit also detected a substantial difference between the total sales rung into the registers at the Brandon store and the total sales actually reported to Dunkin'. In a 17 June 1986 letter, Dunkin' gave the franchisees notice of immediate termination of the franchises. Despite the notice of termination and the ensuing litigation, the franchisees continued to operate profitably the two stores as Dunkin' franchises. When Dunkin' sued for damages accruing from the allegedly unreported sales, the franchisees counterclaimed that Dunkin' had breached the obligations of good faith and fair dealing implied in the franchise agreements. The franchisees argued that Dunkin's predicating the audit on Mrs. Apostoleres's refusal to subscribe to the franchise renewal option offered by Dunkin' and Dunkin's failure to disclose in the franchise agreement the yield-and-usage test as a measure for enforcing its contractual rights evinced the company's lack of good faith. Would you agree with the franchisees' assertions? Why or why not? [See *Dunkin' Donuts of America, Inc.* v. *Minerva, Inc.*, 956 F.2d 1566 (11th Cir. 1992).]

7. **ETHICAL APPLICATION CASE** Roger L. Pung and M&M Chevrolet, Inc. (M&M) entered into an agreement to purchase the assets of Archie Oldsmobile/ AMC, Inc. Because both parties were franchisees of General Motors Corporation (GMC), the agreement was expressly conditioned on approval by GMA. When GMC declined to give its approval, the plaintiffs sued GMC under the Michigan Dealer Act (MDA). The MDA separately defines "new motor vehicle dealer" and "proposed new motor vehicle dealer." However, the statute gives standing to sue only to new motor vehicle dealers and not to proposed new motor vehicle dealers. Moreover, the MDA makes manufacturers liable only for the damages suffered by a new motor vehicle dealer. When GMC challenged M&M's right to sue under the MDA, M&M claimed it had standing under the statute as a prospective dealership purchaser, inasmuch as it already was a GMC dealer under an unrelated dealership agreement. Whose argument was more compelling, GMC's or M&M's? Was the legislature's decision to grant protection to existing dealerships but not prospective new dealers unethical? Explain. [See *Pung* v. *General Motors Corporation*, 573 N.W.2d 80 (Mich.App. 1997).]

8. **CRITICAL THINKING CASE** Lois H. and Howard L. Gruver and E. Patrick Halpin purchased new Midas International Corporation (Midas) muffler shop franchises in 1983 and 1984, respectively. Midas previously had done market studies indicating that both franchisees' franchise locations would be unprofitable. However, Midas represented to both franchisees that its studies had indicated that the franchises would be profitable. The franchises nonetheless lost money. The franchise agreements gave the franchisees the right to terminate the franchises upon 30 days' notice. Upon termination, however, accrued liabilities remained; and Midas was entitled to the prompt repayment of all money due. Midas could require that the franchisees sell all Midas parts in their inventory back to Midas, with the right to set off the repurchase price against the money due from the franchisees. The franchisees individually approached Midas concerning terminating their franchises. In the Gruvers' case, Midas did not draw up a termination agreement until three-and-one-half months later. In the meantime, Midas refused to extend further credit to the Gruvers and required them to pay cash for all items purchased from the company.

In Halpin's case, Midas also cut off credit, but Midas drew up a termination agreement within approximately one month. After brief discussions with their lawyers, the franchisees executed the termination agreements, which provided that Midas would buy back the Gruver franchise for $95,160.60 and the Halpin franchise for $87,756.15. Midas also agreed to employ Halpin as a manager at another muffler shop. Under the termination agreements, all the money that the franchisees received, however, would be paid back to Midas to satisfy their debts or would be paid to a bank to release liens on the property that Midas owned. The agreements further provided that the franchisees would release all the claims they had against Midas. The Gruvers at that point knew that, as to Midas, they had potentially successful fraud claims arising out of their purchases of the Midas franchises. Halpin did not have specific evidence to support such claims at that time, although he suspected that evidence supporting some such claims existed and, prior to signing his termination agreement, had discussed with his attorney the viability of such claims. Both the Gruvers and Halpin subsequently sued Midas for fraud, breach of contract, and related claims stemming from their purchases of the Midas franchises. Midas moved for summary judgment on the ground that the franchisees in their termination agreements had released these claims. The franchisees claimed that the termination agreements were invalid because they had entered into the agreements under economic duress, defined as: (1) wrongful acts or threats, (2) financial distress caused by those acts, and (3) the absence of any reasonable alternative to the terms presented by the wrongdoer. How should the appellate court rule in this case? [See *Gruver* v. *Midas International Corporation*, 925 F.2d 280 (9th Cir. 1991).]

NOTES

1. Harold Brown, *Franchising—Realities and Remedies*, 2nd ed. (New York: Law Journal Press, 1978), p. 1; Norman Scarborough and Thomas Zimmerer, *Effective Small Business Management*, 6th ed. (Englewood Cliffs, NJ: Prentice-Hall, 2000), pp. 104–114.
2. International Franchise Association Educational Foundation, Inc., and Horwath International, *Franchising in the Economy 1988–1990* (Washington, DC: 1990), p. 13.
3. Scarborough and Zimmerer, *Effective Small Business Management*, p. 103.
4. International Franchise Association, *Franchising in the Economy 1988–1990*, p. 94.
5. Ibid., p. 13.
6. Brown, *Franchising*, pp. 6–12; Scarborough and Zimmerer, *Effective Small Business Management*, pp. 104–114.
7. 439 U.S. 96 (1978).
8. Timothy Bates, *Survival Patterns Among Newcomers to Franchising*, 13 Journal of Business Venturing 113, at 116 (1998). See also J. Howard Beales III and Timothy J. Muris, *The Foundations of Franchise Regulation: Issues and Evidence*, 2 Journal of Corporate Finance 157–197 (1995).
9. Bates, *Survival Patterns*, at 116–118.
10. Darryl Van Duch, "Big Risk for GM in Ad Suit," *The National Law Journal* (16 August 1999), pp. A-1, A-8.

38

SECURITIES REGULATION

CALL-IMAGE TECHNOLOGY

A G E N D A

The Kochanowskis have incorporated CIT, and they are now considering taking the firm public in order to raise money for needed expansion and growth. They therefore will consider issuing stock, bonds, and debentures to the public. They also will need to know how these offerings may affect their liability and what they moreover must do in order to satisfy the federal securities laws. Furthermore, they will need to know how they can comply with the applicable state security regulations. In addition, the firm is considering an expansion into the international marketplace. If this occurs, the family members are likely to have questions about the Foreign Corrupt Practices Act and its impact on their dealings.

These and other questions may arise as you study this chapter. Be prepared! You never know when one of the Kochanowskis will need your help or advice.

O U T L I N E

Federal Laws
State Regulation
The Foreign Corrupt Practices Act

Summary
Discussion Questions
Case Problems and Writing Assignments

FEDERAL LAWS

In Chapters 33 and 34, we briefly examined some provisions of the 1933 and 1934 Securities Acts. It is not possible in one chapter to discuss fully the complex interplay of federal and state securities laws, but we will attempt to understand the broad outlines of this complicated area of the regulation of business.

Securities regulation has come to be known as "federal corporate law." This label in large measure stems from the interplay of the extensive federal laws and the rules set forth by the Securities and Exchange Commission (SEC), the federal agency charged with primary responsibility for the enforcement and administration of the federal laws covering securities, public utility holding companies, trust indentures, investment companies, and investment advisers. The SEC consists of five members appointed by the president for five-year terms. To ensure impartiality, securities law requires that no more than three of the commissioners be members of the same political party. The SEC and its staff generally have enjoyed a first-rate reputation among securities professionals.

Uncollateralized
Having no underlying security to guarantee performance.

The Securities Act of 1933

The Securities Act of 1933 (the '33 Act) defines a *security* as "any note, stock, treasury stock, bond, debenture, evidence of indebtedness, . . . or participation in any profit-sharing agreement, . . . investment contract, . . . fractional undivided interest in oil, gas, or other mineral rights, or, in general, any interest or instrument commonly known as a 'security.'" The Supreme Court in *Gould* v. *Ruefenacht*, 471 U.S. 701 (1985), held that where an instrument bears the label "stock" and possesses all the characteristics typically associated with stock, the instrument is a "security"; in such cases, a court need not look beyond the character of the instrument to the economic substance of the transaction.

But in other situations in which the instrument bears no such label, courts oftentimes must construe what the statutory term *investment contract* means. Subsequent case decisions interpreting this phrase have made it clear that, in this sense, a security involves (1) an investment of money (2) in a common enterprise (3) whereby the investor has no managerial functions but instead expects to profit solely from the entrepreneurial or managerial efforts of others. For this reason, court determinations of what constitutes a security based on this so-called "economic reality" test have been broad and far reaching. Courts have construed investments in condominiums, citrus groves, and cattle, when others have been employed to manage such assets, as securities subject to the federal securities laws.

The '33 Act basically is a disclosure statute meant to protect the unsophisticated investing public. By requiring the registration of most securities when they initially are offered and by enforcing various antifraud provisions, the '33 Act ensures such protection.

In *Reves* v. *Ernst & Young*, the Supreme Court in its threshold analysis needed to decide whether certain promissory notes constituted securities under federal law. If so, the '34 Act's antifraud provisions were applicable. Note the detailed analysis the Court, in reaching its conclusion, followed.

38.1

REVES V. ERNST & YOUNG
494 U.S. 56 (1990)

FACTS The Farmers Co-operative of Arkansas and Oklahoma (the Co-Op) is an agricultural cooperative that, at the time relevant here, had approximately 23,000 members. In order to raise money to support its general business operations, the Co-Op sold promissory notes payable on demand by the holder. Although the notes were **uncollateralized** and uninsured, they paid a variable rate of interest that the Co-Op adjusted monthly so as to keep the rate higher than the rate paid by local financial institutions. The Co-Op, marketing the scheme as an "Investment Program," advertised the notes as safe, secure investments. Despite these assurances, in 1984, the Co-Op filed for bankruptcy. At the time of the filing, over 1,600 people held notes worth a total of $10 million. Reves and others, a class of holders of the notes, filed suit against Arthur Young & Co. (Arthur Young), Ernst & Young's predecessor, the firm that had audited the Co-Op's financial statements. Alleging violations of the '34 Act's antifraud provisions and Arkansas's security laws, Reves asserted that in order to inflate the assets and net worth of the Co-Op, Arthur Young, in its audit, had intentionally failed to follow generally accepted accounting principles. Reves maintained that if Arthur Young had properly treated the assets in the audits, he (Reves) would not have purchased the demand notes because the Co-Op's insolvency would have been apparent. At trial, Reves and the others prevailed on both their federal and state law claims and received a $6.1 million judgment. Arthur Young appealed on the grounds that the demand notes did not constitute "securities" under either federal law or Arkansas law and that the statutes' antifraud provisions therefore were inapplicable. Agreeing with Arthur Young on both the state and federal issues, a panel of the Eighth Circuit Court of Appeals reversed.

ISSUE Were the notes issued by the Co-Op "securities" within the meaning of the '34 Act?

HOLDING Yes. The demand notes issued by the Co-Op fell under the "note" category of instruments that are "securities."

REASONING Section 3(a)(10) of the '34 Act, the starting point for analysis, states, as does the '33 Act, that

the term "security" means any note, stock, treasury stock, bond, debenture, certificate of interest or participation in any profit-sharing agreement or in any oil, gas, or other mineral royalty or lease, any collateral-trust certificate, preorganization certificate or subscription, transferable share, investment contract, voting-trust certificate, certificate of deposit . . . or in general, any instrument commonly known as a "security," or any certificate of interest or participation in, temporary or interim certificate for, receipt for, or warrant or right to subscribe to or purchase, any of the foregoing; but shall not include currency or any note, draft, bill of exchange, or banker's acceptance which has a maturity at the time of issuance of not exceeding nine months. . . .

Congress, in enacting the securities laws, meant to regulate investments, in whatever form they are made and by whatever name they are called. A commitment to an examination of the economic realities of a transaction does not necessarily entail a case-by-case analysis of every instrument, however.

Some instruments obviously fall within the class Congress intended to regulate because they by their nature are investments. For example, in *Landreth Timber Co. v. Landreth*, 471 U.S. 681 (1985), the Supreme Court held that an instrument bearing the name "stock" that, among other things, is negotiable, offers the possibility of capital appreciation, and carries the right to dividends contingent on the profits of a business enterprise plainly is within the class of instruments Congress intended the securities laws to cover. *Landreth Timber* does not signify a lack of concern with economic reality; rather, it signals a recognition that stock, as a practical matter, always is an investment if it has the economic characteristics traditionally associated with stock. Unlike "stock," the term "note" " . . . encompasses instruments with widely varying characteristics, depending on whether issued in a consumer context, as commercial paper, or in some other investment context." Thus, notes are not securities per se but must be defined using the "family resemblance" test. Under that test, a note is presumed to be a security unless it bears a strong resemblance, determined by a court's examining four specified factors, to one of a judicially crafted list of categories of instruments that are not securities.

continued

38.1

REVES V. ERNST & YOUNG, *continued*
494 U.S. 56 (1990)

Applying this approach, one can conclude that the notes at issue here constitute "securities." Given the facts of this case, an examination of the four relevant factors provides few reasons to treat the notes as non-securities: (1) The Co-Op sold them to raise capital, and purchasers bought them to earn a profit in the form of interest, so that the notes most naturally are conceived of as investments in a business enterprise; (2) there was "common trading" of the notes, which were offered and sold to a broad segment of the public; (3) the public reasonably perceived from the advertisements that the notes were investments; and (4) the application of the securities acts was necessary, since the notes were uncollateralized and uninsured and would escape federal regulation entirely if a court held the acts inapplicable.

BUSINESS CONSIDERATIONS The Court determined that Arthur Young's auditors had not followed generally accepted accounting principles when they had audited the Co-Op's financial statements. Should the firm fire the staff members responsible for these audits? How could a firm minimize the risk that it would face such litigation?

ETHICAL CONSIDERATION Should educational institutions and firms be expected to instill a sense of ethics into students and employees, respectively, or is the development of an admirable ethical perspective solely an individualized, personal endeavor?

Securities exchanges
Organized secondary markets in which investors buy and sell securities at central locations.

Procedures. Section 5 is the heart of the '33 Act. It provides that any security that is not exempt must be registered with the SEC before a firm can sell it through the mails or through any facility of interstate commerce, such as **securities exchanges.** All U.S. issuers now are required to utilize EDGAR, the SEC's electronic data-gathering system, when the firms engage in any initial public offering (IPO). The corporation issuing the security must file a *registration statement* with the SEC and provide investors and would-be investors with a *prospectus*—a document presented by a corporation or its agents, which document announces the issuance of corporate securities, states the nature of the securities and the financial status of the issuing firm, and asks the general public to purchase the securities covered. The registration statement contains detailed information about the plan for offering and distributing the security, the names and salaries of managers and others who control the corporation, a description of the security, and information about the issuer and its business, including detailed financial reports. The prospectus must contain similar information in summary form.

The underlying purpose of both the registration statement and the prospectus is the protection of the unsophisticated investor. These documents purport to inform a prospective investor of everything he or she should know before a purchase of a security occurs. Some critics argue, however, that the SEC requires so much information that an unsophisticated investor can make little sense of the myriad details that appear in the registration statement and the prospectus. These commentators believe that the SEC's "overregulation" actually has undercut the worthy purposes of the '33 Act.

Underwriters
Persons or institutions that, by agreeing to sell securities to the public and to buy those not sold, ensure the sale of corporate securities.

Although the '33 Act prohibits all offers to buy or sell prior to the filing of a registration statement, some activities can take place before this filing. For example, the issuer (the corporation selling the stock) typically enlists the services of third parties, such as **underwriters,** who agree to help the issuer finance the stock offering. During this prefiling period, then, the issuer can enter into preliminary negotiations with such underwriters. Next, during the registration process's so-called "waiting period," the SEC has 20 days in which to examine the registration statement. If the registration statement is complete and accurate, it becomes effective at the end of this 20-day waiting period.

During this period, the issuer or underwriter can accept oral purchase orders. But the SEC limits written advertisements to "tombstone ads," so designated because they are boxed in the shape of a tombstone, and written information to preliminary "red herring" prospectuses, so dubbed because of the red lettering on them, to the effect that a registration statement has been filed but is not yet effective.

After the registration statement becomes effective but before any sale can occur—this is the so-called "posteffective period"—the issuer or underwriter must provide virtually every would-be investor with a prospectus (the so-called "statutory prospectus") that sets out the information required by the statute. The issuer must make sure the information contained in the prospectus remains accurate during the posteffective period as well; otherwise, the sale of the securities will not be legal. These rules reinforce the '33 Act's "truth-in-securities" policies.

Exemptions. The '33 Act exempts from the registration and prospectus requirements discussed above certain *classes of securities*. Note, however, that there are no exemptions from the antifraud provisions, which we will examine in the next section of this chapter. The exempted classes include securities issued by federal and state governments and banks; short-term commercial paper; issues by nonprofit organizations; issues by savings and loan associations subject to state or federal regulation; issues by common carriers subject to the jurisdiction of the Surface Transportation Board; certain qualifying employee pension plans; insurance policies and certain annuities subject to regulation by state and federal authorities; and intrastate issues of securities.

In addition, the '33 Act exempts certain *transactions:* private offerings (those that do not involve public offerings of securities, as is the usual case); transactions by persons other than issuers, underwriters, or dealers; certain brokers' and dealers' transactions; and small public issues (defined generally as transactions up to $5 million and that involve sales only to "accredited investors"). As the latter exemption shows, SEC rules oftentimes may limit the issuers who qualify, the aggregate offering price, the number and qualifications of investors, the manner in which the issuer conducts the offering, the resale of the shares, and the like. In short, the SEC has established prerequisites and complex rules that firms must follow if they hope to secure an exemption from the registration process for this and certain other transactions.

For instance, in one famous case, Ralston Purina Co. (Ralston Purina) had sold nearly $2 million of unregistered stock to its "key employees." The "key employees" who had purchased the stock included shop and dock foremen, stenographers, copywriters, clerical assistants, and veterinarians. Because it had made offers to only a few of its employees, Ralston Purina construed its actions as falling under the "private offering" exemption. Asserting that the aim of the '33 Act is to protect investors by promoting full disclosure of the information thought necessary for informed investment decisions, the Supreme Court concluded that Ralston Purina had not shown that the employees involved here had enjoyed access to the kind of information that registration would disclose. Thus, the Court held that this attempted private offering (or "private placement") was not a bona fide exempt transaction and that registration under the 1933 Act should have occurred.[1]

Antifraud Provisions. In addition to registration requirements, the '33 Act contains several antifraud provisions. Section 12 prohibits oral or written misstatements of material facts or omissions of material facts necessary to keep the statements from being misleading in the circumstances in which they were made. Section 17 is a general antifraud provision that makes it unlawful for any person to use the mails or interstate commerce to employ any device or scheme that will defraud another person or to engage in any transaction, practice, or course of business that defrauds or deceives the purchaser. Basically, § 17 makes illegal any form of fraud, untrue statement of a material fact, or omission of a material fact involving the sale of any securities in interstate commerce or through the mail.

Section 27A of the 1995 Private Securities Litigation Reform Act (PSLRA) redefines when liability exists for certain misleading "forward-looking" statements. The PSLRA represents the most sweeping and comprehensive reform of the nation's securities laws in the last two decades. Designed to reassert legislative control over securities fraud litigation, the PSLRA sets out specific procedural and substantive rules with regard to these and other sections of the '33 Act. To encourage corporate executives to offer investors more meaningful information, § 27A, the so-called "safe harbor" provision, exempts from liability filed registration documents containing certain types of forward-looking statements (including projections of revenues, income, earnings per share, and company plans or objectives relating to certain products or services) by certain issuers and underwriters. (Significantly, this safe harbor is not applicable to IPOs.) To fall within the available safe harbor, a forward-looking statement (either oral or written) should be accompanied by meaningful cautionary statements identifying important factors that would cause actual results to differ materially from those projected in the forward-looking statements. Registration statements consisting of traditional "boilerplate" language in which the issuer's purported cautionary statements mention "lack of demand," "an increase in competition," and so on, presumably would not suffice. But information relating to the issuer's business that discusses the possible loss of a major customer or a serious glitch in the development of technology for a product in the proto-type stage would fulfill the statutory requirements for a "meaningful cautionary statement."

38.1 | FINANCE/ MANAGEMENT

ISSUING STOCK IN CIT

Tom and Anna want to issue stock in CIT. To generate funds for the expansion of the firm, they believe that, if successful, this IPO will result in a huge inflow of cash for the firm. However, they also know that the firm's IPO is likely to be subject to regulation under the Securities Act of 1933. They ask you what they will need to do so as to qualify for an exemption from registration under the '33 Act or, in the alternative, what they will need to do to comply with the registration requirements. What advice will you give them?

BUSINESS CONSIDERATIONS Why might a business prefer a potentially smaller inflow of funds if this meant that the firm qualified for an exemption from registering under the '33 Act? What factors should a firm consider in deciding whether the registration requirements justify a larger public offering?

ETHICAL CONSIDERATIONS Is it ethical for a firm to tailor its securities offerings so as to avoid registration of the securities under the '33 Act? Are the directors of a business acting ethically toward their constituents if they fail to consider a security-issuing plan that legally avoids registration?

Besides providing encouragement for executives to offer investors more meaningful information, other central aims of the PSLRA include the discouragement of class action suits brought for frivolous—or purely entrepreneurial—reasons (so-called "strike suits") and the preservation of such suits in situations in which shareholders in fact have been the victims of securities fraud. The act accomplishes these goals by codifying stringent pleading requirements for certain private actions under the '34 Act (but not the '33 Act) and by awarding sanctions (e.g., costs and attorney's fees) for a party's failing to fulfill these pleading requirements. Given the PSLRA's complexities as well as those that generally inhere in the issuance of securities, anyone who contemplates issuing securities should seek the counsel of professionals who specialize in the securities field.

Liabilities and Remedies. The potential liabilities spawned by the '33 Act also constitute a significant reason for seeking competent advice. Section 11 imposes civil liability for any registration statement that contains untrue statements of a material fact or omissions of material facts that would make the registration statement misleading in the circumstances in which a purchaser buys the securities. Such a purchaser can receive as damages an amount not exceeding the price paid for the securities.

Section 11 places liability on every person who signed the registration statement; on every person who was a director or was identified in the registration statement as about to become a director; on every accountant, engineer, appraiser, or any other professional expert whose statement or report appears in the registration statement; and on every underwriter. By showing that they acted with "due diligence," all such persons, except the issuer, may escape liability.

This statutory defense of "due diligence" varies as to the type of defendant involved and whether the misrepresentations or omissions are found in the "expertised" or "nonexpertised" portions of the registration statement. The defense generally is available to anyone who, after reasonable investigation, had reasonable grounds to believe, and did believe, that the registration statement was accurate and did not omit material facts that either were required or necessary to make the statement not misleading.

A landmark, pre-PSLRA case, *Escott* v. *BarChris Construction Corp.*,[2] illustrates many of these concepts. Suing under § 11 of the '33 Act, the purchasers of certain securities of BarChris Construction Corporation (BarChris) alleged that the registration statement filed with the SEC concerning this stock had contained materially false statements and material omissions. The defendants included the persons who had signed the registration statement (primarily directors and officers), the underwriters (investment bankers), and Peat, Marwick, Mitchell & Co. (BarChris's auditors). The court framed the issues as whether the registration statement had included materially false statements and material omissions and, if so, whether the defendants had successfully shown the statutory defense—that is, that they had acted with due diligence. The court concluded that the registration statement had included materially false statements and material omissions. Moreover, the court determined that only the outside directors had been able to sustain even a part of their due diligence defense (and they could show due diligence only with respect to the expertised portion of the registration statement). The court emphasized that a material fact is a fact that, had it been correctly stated or disclosed, would have deterred the average prudent investor from purchasing the securities in question. Therefore, BarChris's overstatement of its sales and gross profits and its understatement of its liabilities in 1961 constituted material facts. But the prospectus statements about BarChris's status in December 1960 consisted of rather minor and hence nonmaterial errors. On the other hand, the prospectus's 1961 balance sheet had contained material errors. Nonetheless, although the due diligence statutory defense had been available to all the defendants except the issuer, BarChris, none of the inside directors and officers had sustained the due diligence defense with respect to either the expertised (i.e., the financial reports prepared by accountants) or the unexpertised portions of the registration statement. The outside directors similarly had not sustained their due diligence defense as to the unexpertised part of the registration statement, primarily because they had neither familiarized themselves with its contents nor questioned its major points. On the other hand, the outside directors, because of their confidence in the auditors, Peat, Marwick, Mitchell & Co., had shown due diligence regarding the expertised portion of the statement. Like the inside directors and officers, the underwriters and the auditors had failed to establish the due diligence defense with respect to either portion of the registration statement.

In this context, note that the PSLRA changes § 11's longstanding joint and several liability rules, in which each defendant potentially was liable for all the damages awarded to the plaintiff, to a standard that embraces proportionate liability. The PSLRA grounds this change on the rationale that the imposition of joint and several liability in the past had led to the plaintiff's joining "deep pocket" defendants (lawyers, accountants, underwriters, and directors) in the lawsuit, even though these persons bore little responsibility for the plaintiff's injuries.

These defendants often felt overwhelming pressures to settle—even if the suits were meritless—so as to avoid the enormous damage awards recoverable by plaintiffs in huge class action suits. Hence, the PSLRA adopts a "fair share" rule approach to liability in general and applies this rule in specific to outside directors who have refrained from "knowingly" violating the securities laws. These outside directors ordinarily will be liable only for the portion of damages attributable to their percentage of responsibility. In enacting this legislation, Congress hoped to give qualified persons an incentive to sit on the boards of start-up and high-technology companies without these persons becoming apprehensive about their possible exposure to grossly disproportionate liability. It is important to note that the PSLRA applies solely to the allocation of damages; the PSLRA otherwise preserves the plaintiff's Section 11 claims against all other defendants as well as the rights of contribution and settlement set out in the '33 Act. Nor does the PSLRA change the state-of-mind requirements of § 12 and § 17; reckless conduct, for example, would not violate the '33 Act.

Additionally, § 12 exacts civil liability from any person who sells securities through the mails or in interstate commerce by means of a prospectus or oral communication that includes misrepresentations or omissions of necessary material facts. Such persons can avoid liability if they can show that they did not know, and in the exercise of reasonable care could not have known, about the untruths or omissions. The injured party can sue only the person who actually sold the security but can rescind the sale and recover the price paid for the security. The PSLRA amends § 12 to allow a defendant to escape liability if he or she can prove that any depreciation in the value of the security resulted from factors unrelated to the alleged misstatement or omission (e.g., from a general market decline). Thus, purchasers suing under the '33 Act's civil liability provision must prove that the alleged misstatements or omissions actually *caused* their losses. In *Gustafson* v. *Alloyd, Inc.*,[3] the Supreme Court held that § 12 claims can arise only from initial stock offerings and not from a private sale agreement. The Court reasoned that such a contract is not held out to the public as a prospectus, that is, the document that solicits the public to acquire securities. Hence, the Court held, under the plain meaning of the statute—as reinforced in § 10—a "prospectus" must set out the information contained in the registration statement required in public offerings. Because a private contract indisputably does not have to specify the information enumerated in a registration statement, the Court rejected the argument that the contract in question was tantamount to a prospectus. In addition to § 12's civil liabilities, § 17's antifraud provisions may be used as a basis for criminal liability. Moreover, § 24 sets up criminal sanctions for willful violations of the '33 Act.

38.2

IN RE NATIONSMART CORPORATION SECURITIES LITIGATION
130 F.3D 309 (8TH CIR. 1997), CERT. DENIED, 524 U.S. 927 (1998)

FACTS NationsMart Corporation (NationsMart) was formed in 1992 with the goal of applying the low-price, one-stop shopping concept, made successful by Wal-Mart and Kmart "supercenters," to the dry-cleaning, laundry, and shoe-repair markets. On 22 December 1993, NationsMart commenced an initial public offering (IPO) of two million units at $7.00 per unit. The prospectus stated that NationsMart expected to use the net proceeds of the IPO to fund the 51 existing NationsMart stores, as well as to open 108 new stores by November 1994 and 600 new stores by 1998. The prospectus contained detailed financial data about NationsMart, a discussion and analysis of the company's financial situation, and its strategy for future growth. The prospectus acknowledged that NationsMart had previously experienced financial losses but stated that NationsMart's management believed that, based on a "financial model," projected income from existing stores, in conjunction with the proceeds of the public offering, would "significantly improve the capital resources of the Company. . . . "
Another section of the prospectus included some of the risks investors faced in buying the offered units, such as NationsMart's limited operating history and the absence of a prior market for its shares; its dependence on leases from Wal-Mart, Kmart, and other "host retailers;" and its need for additional financing in the future. The prospectus also cautioned that NationsMart's financial model reflected "only the best judgment of management" and was subject to conditions beyond the company's control. On 14 July 1994, NationsMart announced that it was experiencing slower-than-expected growth and that it would open 35 to 45 fewer stores than the prospectus had anticipated. NationsMart also disclosed that it had settled a "whistleblower" lawsuit with a former executive who had sued NationsMart after her discharge in March 1994. Following these announcements, NationsMart's common stock fell to $1.875 and continued to decline until mid-1995, when the stock was delisted. A 1994 class action filed against NationsMart and its underwriters alleged, among other things, violations of Sections 11 and 12 of the '33 Act. The

plaintiffs claimed that the defendants had made false statements in and had omitted material information from the prospectus, specifically, that the defendants had known that the company would not be able to implement the business plan outlined in the prospectus with the proceeds of the offering. The plaintiffs also submitted that, in the months before the effective date of the public offering, the defendants had failed to disclose that the favorable trends described in the prospectus were not likely to materialize; that the costs to operate existing NationsMart stores and to open new stores were rising; and that corporate overhead was increasing. The district court dismissed the § 11 claim owing to the plaintiffs' failure under Federal Rule of Civil Procedure 9(b) to meet the requirement that one plead "the circumstances constituting fraud or mistake" with particularity. The plaintiffs subsequently appealed this part of the court's ruling.

ISSUE Did Rule 9(b)'s particularity requirement apply to claims under § 11 of the '33 Act?

HOLDING No. The particularity requirement of Rule 9(b) was inapplicable to such claims because proof of fraud or mistake is not a prerequisite to establishing liability under Section 11 of the '33 Act.

REASONING Section 11 imposes civil liability on all persons who prepare and sign materially misleading registration statements. A registration statement is materially misleading if it contains an untrue statement of material fact or if it omits a material fact necessary to prevent the statement from being misleading. Any person who purchases a registered security is entitled to sue under this section. To establish a prima facie § 11 claim, plaintiffs need show only that they bought the security and that there was a material misstatement or omission. Scienter is not required for establishing liability under this section. As the Supreme Court in *Herman & MacLean* . . . stated, the liability of the issuer of a materially misleading registration statement is "virtually absolute, even for

continued

IN RE NATIONSMART CORPORATION SECURITIES LITIGATION, *continued*
130 F.3D 309 (8TH CIR. 1997), CERT. DENIED, 524 U.S. 927 (1998)

innocent misstatements." Persons besides the issuer who face liability under § 11—e.g., anyone who signed the registration statement, such as officers, directors, and underwriters—must prove that, after reasonable investigation, they had reasonable grounds to believe that the statement was not materially misleading. The plaintiffs made clear that they did not allege in the context of their § 11 claim that the defendants had engaged in fraudulent or intentional conduct. The allegations of innocent or negligent misrepresentation, which are at the heart of a § 11 claim, were sufficient. Granted, other circuit courts of appeals have sometimes applied Rule 9(b) to claims brought under §§ 11 and 12(2) of the Securities Act of 1933; but § 11 does not require proof of fraud for recovery. Given the broad scope of liability under § 11 and the liberal pleading requirements of Federal Rule 8(a), these allegations therefore are sufficient to state a claim. Consequently, the district court should not have dismissed the complaint under Rule 12(b)(6). The district court also based its dismissal of part of the plaintiffs' § 11 claim on the "safe harbor" provision of SEC Rule 175, which protects "forward-looking statements" made in documents filed with the SEC. Under this regulation, a "forward-looking statement" can include statements of management's future plans and objectives, as well as statements of future economic performance contained in management's discussion and analysis of financial conditions. Hence, material misstatements in a registration statement may be protected from § 11 liability if they are forward-looking. Many of the statements in the prospectus were indeed forward-looking (e.g., NationsMart's projections that it would open 108 new stores by 1994 and 600 new stores by 1998; that the proceeds from the public offering would be sufficient to cover the plans for expansion; and that Nations-Mart's history of operating losses would give way to future growth). However, forward-looking statements fall outside the protection of Rule 175 if they are not generally believed, if they lack a reasonable basis, or if the speaker knows of undisclosed facts that seriously undermine the accuracy of the statement. The NationsMart prospectus had contained numerous

statements that "bespoke caution" and warned investors of the financial risks associated with buying stock in NationsMart. Cautionary statements that can defeat a plaintiff's claim that the offering materials were materially misleading under the federal securities law, though, cannot be general risk warnings or mere boilerplate; the statements must be detailed and specific. Here, many statements in the "Risk Factors" section—such as the warning that "there can be no assurance that any of the Company's Centers or that the Company as a whole will generate income from operations or provide cash from operating activities in the future"—failed to provide the sort of detail that would "bespeak caution" to a potential investor. In addition, the bespeaks-caution doctrine would not immunize the defendants from liability under § 11 if they had omitted material information from the offering materials. The plaintiffs alleged that Nations-Mart's management had failed to disclose specific facts indicating that its judgment was flawed. If taken as true, these allegations would call into question whether management was in fact exercising its "best judgment" in formulating the company's financial model, as it claimed in the prospectus. Because of the inadequate and nonspecific warnings of short-term risks and because of the plaintiffs' allegations that the defendants had omitted material information from the prospectus, the bespeaks-caution doctrine could not, simply as a matter of pleading, defeat the plaintiffs' § 11 claim. . . .

BUSINESS CONSIDERATION Should a firm put in place specific policies aimed at ensuring that the statements made in the prospectus and the registration statement fall within the "safe harbor" rule, or should the firm evaluate all such statements on a case-by-case basis? Explain your reasoning.

ETHICAL CONSIDERATION If you were to consider the "safe harbor" rule and the "bespeaks-caution" doctrine from an ethical (as opposed to a legal) perspective, would you support these concepts? Why?

The Securities Exchange Act of 1934

Whereas the 1933 Act deals with the initial issuance of securities, the Securities Exchange Act of 1934 (the '34 Act) regulates the secondary distribution of securities. As such, the '34 Act's jurisdiction extends to the registration and distribution of securities through national stock exchanges, national securities associations, brokers, and dealers. The '34 Act also covers proxy solicitations of registered securities, regulates tender offers, limits insider trading, forbids short-swing profits, and in general tries to eliminate fraud and manipulative conduct with respect to the sale or purchase of securities. Thus, in many ways the '33 and '34 Acts are similar and supplement each other. But the reach of the '34 Act, with its supervision of national exchanges and over-the-counter sales of securities, is even broader than that of the '33 Act.

Registration and Reporting. The '34 Act requires any issuer who trades securities on a national stock exchange to register with the SEC. In addition, any firm engaged in interstate commerce with total assets of over $5 million and at least 500 shareholders must comply with the registration provisions of § 12. For violations of § 12, the SEC can revoke or suspend the registration of the security involved.

Like the '33 Act, the '34 Act tries to ensure that the investing public will have sufficient information about publicly traded securities when these investors make their decisions about whether to buy stocks. Hence, the '34 Act mandates certain disclosures by firms covered by the act when the securities are listed with national exchanges or traded over the counter. Basically, these obligatory disclosures include detailed registration statements similar to the information required under the '33 Act as well as annual and quarterly reports. SEC Forms 8-A, 8-K, 10-K, and 10-Q, which companies use for compiling this information, are complex and contain substantial numbers of facts and figures relating to the companies' businesses. Other SEC provisions impose liability on the company for damages resulting from an investor's reliance on misleading statements contained in any such documents.

Proxy Solicitations. A *proxy* is an assignment by the shareholder of the right to vote the shares held by the shareholder. Since proxies become a device for consolidating corporate power and control, one cannot underestimate their importance both to management and to those "dissident" shareholders who wish to oust the present management. Because of the high stakes involved for both competing factions, it is vitally important that the information provided to shareholders be accurate. If shareholders receive misleading information, they will make their decision regarding who should be given their proxies—management or dissidents—in ignorance of the true facts. To prevent such abuses, § 14 of the '34 Act makes it illegal for a company registered under § 12 to solicit proxies in a manner that violates the SEC rules and regulations that protect the investing public. Section 14 also sets out rules mandating disclosure of pertinent information to shareholders at corporate meetings even when no solicitation of proxies will occur.

The disclosure required of proxy solicitations includes a proxy statement, which contains detailed information, and a proxy form, on which the shareholder can note his or her approval or disapproval of each proposal that will be decided at the corporation's meeting. Before either the corporation or the dissidents send proxies to shareholders, the SEC must approve the statement and the form. These preliminary proxies must be filed with the SEC at least 10 days before they are sent to shareholders. If the meeting involves the election of directors, any proxy statement also must include an annual report detailing, among other things, the financial aspects of the company (including a graph that analyzes the company's performance) and the company's executive compensation plans and arrangements (including "golden parachutes"). Similarly, as mentioned earlier, any proxy contest requires full disclosure of all pertinent facts regarding the matters under consideration, such as the identity of all participants in the proxy contest and the reasons for the proxy solicitation.

Section 14 furthermore authorizes the inclusion of shareholder proposals of no more than 500 words in any management-backed proxy solicitation. This SEC rule allows any eligible shareholder to express an opinion regarding the recommendations management has made without incurring the significant costs involved in an independent proxy solicitation. This dimension of § 14 thus attempts to preserve the balance of power between management and the insurgents so as to safeguard the democratic aspects of the corporation.

As you probably have surmised, management usually opposes the inclusion of such proposals. SEC rules authorize the exclusion of proposals that are not "proper subjects" for action by shareholders, proposals that center on personal claims or grievances, proposals that are not significantly related to the corporation's business or are beyond the corporation's power to effectuate (e.g., proposals that primarily promote economic, political, racial, religious, or social causes), and proposals that are substantially similar to a proposal submitted but not approved within the past five years. In disputes over whether the corporation can exclude the proposal, the SEC normally decides who is correct. Management bears the burden of proof regarding why it properly excluded the proposal. Shareholder proposals have dealt with management compensation, company policies allegedly leading to discrimination or pollution, and even opposition to the Vietnam War. Shareholder proposals, however, usually are unsuccessful.

The corporation ordinarily pays for the expenses incurred in proxy contests if either management or the insurgents win. The law is unsettled as to whether the corporation should pay the costs of a contest if management loses, but the trend is to make the corporation (not the managers themselves) pay even in those circumstances.

Liability for misleading proxy statements or those that omit a material fact necessary to make the statement true and not misleading is absolute. Any person who sells or buys securities in reliance on such statements can recover from the corporation.

Tender Offers. In addition to regulating proxies, since 1968 the Williams Act, codified in § 13 and § 14, also has regulated tender offers or takeover bids, whether hostile or friendly, wherein one publicly held corporation (the "tender offeror") attempts to acquire control of another publicly held company (the "target"). Section 14, in conjunction with § 13, sets forth filing and registration requirements for any person who becomes the owner of more than 5 percent of any class of securities registered under § 12. In general, these provisions force the offeror to provide the target company's shareholders with the names of the offerors and their interests, the purpose of the takeover, the method of disposing of the target firm's stocks and assets, and so forth. Additionally, any statements the management of the target firm makes in opposition to the merger also must be filed with the SEC. Provisions for liability under this aspect of the '34 Act are similar to those instituted for violations of the proxy rules.

Insider Trading. Directors, officers, and controlling shareholders may violate the federal securities laws if they engage in "insider trading." We noted that the '34 Act makes such activities illegal and sets out possibilities of far-ranging liability. Section 10(b) of the '34 Act makes unlawful any manipulative or deceptive device used through the mails or in interstate commerce in connection with the purchase or sale of any security. By providing for liability for any fraudulent or deceitful activity that involves misleading material facts or omissions of material facts that would make a statement misleading in the circumstances in which it was made, SEC Rule 10(b)-5 augments § 10(b).

When material inside information is involved, the insider *either* must publicly disclose the information so as to ensure that the investing public that does not have access to the information will remain free from prejudice *or* must abstain from trading in the securities.

Nevertheless, it is difficult to judge when information is important enough to be considered "material." *Basic Incorporated* v. *Levinson*,[4] a Supreme Court case involving the company's public statements concerning the possibility of a merger, provides guidelines in this important area. In the *Basic* decision, the Court reiterated that the standard of materiality set forth in *TSC Industries, Inc.* v. *Northway* will govern future § 10(b) and Rule 10(b)-5 cases. In short, materiality depends on the significance the reasonable investor would place on the withheld or misrepresented information. If, as noted in the *TSC Industries, Inc.* v. *Northway, Inc.* case, there is a substantial likelihood that the disclosure of the omitted fact would have been viewed as significant by a reasonable investor, the information is material. Hence, the Court identified no valid justification for artificially excluding from the definition of materiality information concerning merger discussions, which otherwise would be considered significant to the trading decision of a reasonable investor, merely because the parties (or their representatives) had failed to reach an agreement-in-principle as to price and structure. The Court noted that the lower courts in this case had accepted a presumption, created by the fraud-on-the-market theory and subject to rebuttal by Basic, that persons who had traded Basic shares had done so in reliance on the integrity of the price set by the market; but that because of Basic's material misrepresentations, that price had been fraudulently depressed. Requiring plaintiffs to show a speculative state of facts—that is, how they would have acted if omitted material information had been disclosed or if the misrepresentations had not been made—would place an unnecessarily unrealistic evidentiary burden on the Rule 10(b)-5 plaintiff who had traded on an impersonal market. Because most publicly available information is reflected in the market price, the Court stressed, an investor's reliance on any public material misrepresentations, therefore, may be presumed for purposes of a Rule 10(b)-5 action. Nevertheless, any showing that severs the link between the alleged misrepresentation and either the price received (or paid) by the plaintiffs, or their decision to trade at a fair market price, will be legally sufficient to rebut the presumption of reliance. According to the Court, materiality in the merger context thus depends on the probability that the transaction will be consummated and its significance to the issuer of the securities. Simply put, materiality depends on the facts and must be determined on a case-by-case basis. Courts may apply a presumption of reliance supported by the fraud-on-the-market theory; that presumption, however, is rebuttable.

Although § 10(b) does not expressly provide for civil liability, it, as a broad antifraud provision, applies to any manipulative or deceptive device used in connection with any purchase or sale of any security by any person; there are no exemptions from coverage. Similarly, Rule 10(b)-5 has been applied to the activities of corporate insiders—directors, officers, controlling shareholders, employees, lawyers, accountants, bankers, consultants, and anyone else who has access to material inside information that may affect the price of the stock. Prior to 1980, persons considered insiders included even those who purchased or sold stock based on tips provided directly or indirectly by directors, officers, and the like. For example, the SEC considered a barber who overheard a director's discussion of an upcoming business trip and bought stock based on this market information an insider as well. But the *Chiarella* v. *United States*[5] case has cast some doubt on whether such remote "tippees" should be liable.

Chiarella was a printer who worked for a firm that printed takeover bids. Although the identities of the firms had been left blank, Chiarella—using the information contained in the documents he was preparing for printing—was able to deduce the names of the target companies. Without disclosing his knowledge, Chiarella purchased stock in the target companies and sold the stock when the takeover attempts became public knowledge. Chiarella thereby gained $30,000 in 14 months. The SEC indicted him on 17 counts of violating § 10(b) and Rule 10(b)-5 of the '34 Act.

However, the Supreme Court held that neither Section 10(b) nor Rule 10(b)-5 would apply to Chiarella. According to the Court, he was not a corporate insider, a fiduciary, or a tippee. Rather, he was a complete stranger who had dealt with the sellers only through impersonal market transactions. The Court therefore believed that affirming Chiarella's conviction would recognize a general duty between all participants in market transactions to forgo actions based on material, nonpublic information. In the Court's opinion, the imposition of such a broad duty, departing as it would from the established doctrine that duty arises from a specific relationship between two parties, would be ill advised.

According to the *Chiarella* case, then, the mere possession of inside information does not create a legal duty owed to faceless market participants. The Supreme Court's decision in *Dirks* v. *Securities and Exchange Commission*,[6] by emphasizing the basic principle that only some persons, under some circumstances, will be barred from trading while they are in possession of material, nonpublic information, appears to reinforce *Chiarella*'s holding.

In 1973, Raymond Dirks was an officer of a New York broker/dealer firm that specialized in providing investment analyses of insurance company securities to institutional investors. On 6 March, Ronald Secrist, a former officer of Equity Funding of America (Equity Funding), told Dirks that the assets of Equity Funding, a diversified corporation primarily engaged in selling life insurance and mutual funds, had been vastly overstated as the result of fraudulent corporate practices. Stressing that various regulatory agencies had failed to act on similar charges made by Equity Funding employees, Secrist urged Dirks to verify the fraud and to disclose it publicly. Although neither Dirks nor his firm owned or traded any Equity Funding stock, some of Equity Funding's clients and investors ultimately sold their holdings in Equity Funding as a result of information that Dirks had shared with them during his investigation. The SEC also subsequently investigated Dirks's involvement and found that his repeating of confidential corporate information had violated securities rules. However, since he had played an important role in bringing Equity Funding's massive fraud to light, the SEC merely **censured** him.

The Supreme Court found that Dirks, as a tippee of material nonpublic information received from the insiders of a corporation with which Dirks was unaffili-

Censured
Formally reprimanded for specific conduct.

ated, in these circumstances had no duty to abstain from the use of such inside information. The Court based its holding on the following grounds: The tippers had been motivated by a desire to expose fraud rather than from a desire either to receive personal benefits or to bestow valuable information on him so that he could derive monetary benefits from what they had told him.

Hence, in the absence of personal gain to the insider, there was no breach of duty to the stockholders. Similarly, in the absence of such a breach by the insider, there could be no derivative breach by someone like Dirks. In short, tippees in Dirks's position would inherit no duty to disclose or abstain until a breach of the insider's fiduciary duty had occurred. Dirks's conduct, therefore, had not violated the antifraud provisions of the '33 or '34 Acts.

The *Chiarella* and *Dirks* cases thus appear to limit significantly the concept of who an "insider" is for § 10(b) purposes. According to *Chiarella*, "outsiders"—those who are not in positions of trust or confidence within the companies involved in the litigation—can escape the duty to abstain from trading on nonpublic material information, unless they are actual tippees of insiders. Reinforcing *Chiarella, Dirks* holds that tippees of insiders who have divulged material inside information out of motives other than personal gain may avoid liability as well. Because the tippees' potential liability derives from the insiders' fiduciary duties to the corporation, the absence of any breach of those duties by the insiders leads to a finding of no breach on the tippees' part, either.

For years after these decisions, the SEC continued to prosecute the outsiders and their tippees on the theory that outsiders' misappropriation of nonpublic material information works a fraud on the securities markets or constitutes fraud as to the outsiders' employers, owing to the outsiders' breach of a fiduciary duty or similar relationship of trust and confidence. As such, the SEC reasoned, this fraudulent conduct violates the securities laws' insider-trading prohibitions. In 1997, in *U.S.* v. *O'Hagan*, the Supreme Court finally resolved the split in the federal circuit courts of appeals that had developed as to the legal validity of this so-called "misappropriation" (or "fraud-on-the-market") theory. Note how in this case the Court disposed of several significant securities law issues.

38.3

U.S. V. O'HAGAN
521 U.S. 642 (1997)

FACTS James Herman O'Hagan was a partner in the law firm of Dorsey & Whitney, which Grand Metropolitan PLC (Grand Met), had retained as local counsel to represent Grand Met regarding a potential tender offer for the common stock of the Pillsbury Company (Pillsbury). Both Grand Met and Dorsey & Whitney took precautions to protect the confidentiality of Grand Met's tender offer plans. O'Hagan in fact did no work on the Grand Met representation. Less than a month after Dorsey & Whitney had withdrawn from representing Grand Met, Grand Met publicly announced its tender offer for Pillsbury stock. While Dorsey & Whitney was still representing Grand Met,

O'Hagan began purchasing call options for Pillsbury stock. When Grand Met announced its tender offer, O'Hagan sold his Pillsbury call options and common stock at a profit of more than $4.3 million. After investigating O'Hagan's transactions, the Securities and Exchange Commission (SEC) alleged that O'Hagan had defrauded his law firm and its client, Grand Met, by using for his own trading purposes material, nonpublic information regarding Grand Met's planned tender offer. A conversation between O'Hagan and the Dorsey & Whitney partner heading the firm's Grand Met representation constituted the nonpublic
continued

38.3

U.S. V. O'HAGAN, *continued*
521 U.S. 642 (1997)

information O'Hagan allegedly had misappropriated from the firm. O'Hagan was charged with 37 different federal violations. After his conviction and his being sentenced to a 41-month term of imprisonment, the Court of Appeals for the Eighth Circuit reversed all of O'Hagan's convictions. Liability under § 10(b) and Rule 10b-5, the Eighth Circuit held, may not be grounded on the "misappropriation theory" of securities fraud on which the prosecution had relied. This court also held that Rule 14e-3(a)—which prohibits trading while in possession of material, nonpublic information relating to a tender offer—exceeds the SEC's § 14(e) rulemaking authority because the rule contains no breach of fiduciary duty requirement. The Eighth Circuit further concluded that O'Hagan's mail fraud and money laundering convictions, resting as they did on violations of the securities laws, could not stand once the reversal of the securities fraud convictions had occurred.

ISSUES Was O'Hagan, a person who had traded in securities for personal profit, using confidential information misappropriated in breach of a fiduciary duty to the source of the information, guilty of violating § 10(b) and Rule 10b-5? Had the Commission exceeded its rulemaking authority by adopting Rule 14e-3(a), which proscribes trading on undisclosed information in the tender offer setting, even in the absence of a duty to disclose?

HOLDINGS Yes as to the first issue, no as to the second. This misappropriation is a proper subject of a § 10(b) charge because such misappropriation meets the statutory requirement that there be "deceptive" conduct "in connection with" a securities transaction. Rule 14e-3(a) qualifies under § 14(e) as a "means reasonably designed to prevent" fraudulent trading on material, nonpublic information in the tender offer context. Rule 14e-3(a)'s "disclose or abstain from trading" command serves to prevent the type of misappropriation charged against O'Hagan and therefore is a proper exercise of the SEC's prophylactic power under § 14(e).

REASONING Section 10(b) of the '34 Act proscribes (1) using any deceptive device (2) in connection with the purchase or sale of securities, in contravention of rules prescribed by the SEC. Under the "traditional" or "classical theory" of insider trading liability, § 10(b)

and Rule 10b-5 are violated when a corporate insider trades in the securities of his or her corporation on the basis of material, nonpublic information. Trading on such information qualifies as a "deceptive device" under § 10(b), because "a relationship of trust and confidence [exists] between the shareholders of a corporation and those insiders who have obtained confidential information by reason of their position with that corporation." *Chiarella* v. *United States* . . . That relationship "gives rise to a duty to disclose or to abstain from trading because of the necessity of preventing a corporate insider from . . . taking unfair advantage of uninformed stockholders. The classical theory applies not only to officers, directors, and other permanent insiders of a corporation, but also to attorneys, accountants, consultants, and others who temporarily become fiduciaries of a corporation. See *Dirks* v. *SEC* . . . The "misappropriation theory" holds that a person commits fraud "in connection with" a securities transaction, and thereby violates § 10(b) and Rule 10b-5, when he or she misappropriates confidential information for securities trading purposes, in breach of a duty owed to the source of the information. Under this theory, a fiduciary's undisclosed, self-serving use of a principal's information to purchase or sell securities, in breach of a duty of loyalty and confidentiality, defrauds the principal of the exclusive use of that information. In lieu of premising liability on a fiduciary relationship between a company insider and a purchaser or seller of the company's stock, the misappropriation theory bases liability on a fiduciary-turned-trader's deception of those who entrusted him or her with access to confidential information. The two theories therefore are complementary, each addressing efforts to capitalize on nonpublic information through the purchase or sale of securities.

In this case, the indictment alleged that O'Hagan, in breach of a duty of trust and confidence he owed to his law firm, Dorsey & Whitney, and to its client, Grand Met, had traded on the basis of nonpublic information regarding Grand Met's planned tender offer for Pillsbury common stock. The Government was correct in submitting that such misappropriation, as just defined, satisfies § 10(b)'s requirement that chargeable conduct involve a "deceptive device or contrivance" used "in connection with" the purchase or sale of securities. First, misappropriators, that is, fiduciaries who pretend loyalty to the principal while secretly converting the principal's information for

38.3

U.S. V. O'HAGAN, *continued*
521 U.S. 642 (1997)

personal gain, "dupe" or defraud the principal. Still, because the deception essential to the misappropriation theory involves feigning fidelity to the source of information, if the fiduciary discloses to the source that he or she plans to trade on the nonpublic information, there is no "deceptive device" and thus an absence of a § 10(b) violation—although the fiduciary-turned-trader may remain liable under state law for breach of the duty of loyalty. The § 10(b) requirement that the misappropriator's deceptive use of information be "in connection with the purchase or sale of [a] security" is satisfied because the fiduciary's fraud is consummated when, without disclosure to his principal, he or she uses the information to purchase or sell securities. The securities transaction and the breach of duty thus coincide. The theory is also well-tuned to an animating purpose of the Exchange Act: to insure honest securities markets and thereby promote investor confidence. In sum, considering the inhibiting impact on market participation of trading on misappropriated information and the congressional purposes underlying § 10(b), it makes scant sense to hold a lawyer like O'Hagan a § 10(b) violator if he works for a law firm representing the target of a tender offer, but not if he works for a law firm representing the bidder. Although the Eighth Circuit construed *Chiarella*, *Dirks*, and *Central Bank* as foreclosing the application of the misappropriation theory to situations like O'Hagan's, the misappropriation theory is both consistent with the '34 Act and these precedents. Hence, in holding that the misappropriation theory was inconsistent with § 10(b) and Rule 10b-5, the Eighth Circuit had erred.

The Eighth Circuit also was wrong in concluding that the SEC had exceeded its rulemaking authority under § 14e-3(a) without requiring a showing that the trading at issue entailed a breach of fiduciary duty. As the *U.S.* v. *Chestman* . . . case notes, one violates Rule 14e-3(a) if he or she trades on the basis of material nonpublic information concerning a pending tender offer that he or she knows or has reason to know has been acquired "directly or indirectly" from an insider of the offeror or issuer, or someone working on their behalf. Rule 14e-3(a) is a disclosure provision. It creates a duty in those traders who fall within its ambit to abstain or disclose, without regard to whether the trader owes a pre-existing fiduciary duty to respect the confidentiality of the information. Rule 14e-3(a)'s "disclose or abstain from trading" command, as applied to this case, is a "means reasonably designed to prevent" fraudulent trading on material, nonpublic information in the tender offer context. Therefore, insofar as it serves to prevent the type of misappropriation charged against O'Hagan, Rule 14e-3(a) is a proper exercise of the Commission's prophylactic power under § 14(e).

BUSINESS CONSIDERATIONS Assume your CEO has asked you to summarize the present state of the law regarding insider trading and to put on a training session for the benefit of your colleagues. What concepts will you stress? Why?

ETHICAL CONSIDERATIONS What ethical considerations did O'Hagan's conduct raise? To forestall this kind of conduct, should a firm promulgate an ethics code? If so, what points should this code emphasize?

Short-Swing Profits. Section 16(b) also is aimed at gains by corporate insiders. This provision of the '34 Act requires everyone who is directly or indirectly the owner of more than 10 percent of any security registered under § 12 or who is a director or officer in a so-called § 12 corporation to make periodic filings with the SEC. In these SEC filings, they must disclose the number of shares owned and any changes in the amount of shares held.

This section, designed to prevent unfair use of information obtained by virtue of an inside position in the corporation, forces insiders to **disgorge,** or return to the corporation, any profits they realize from the purchase or sale of any security that takes place in any time period of less than six months—that is, *short-swing profits.*

Disgorge
Give up ill-gotten or illicit gains.

Section 16(b) is inapplicable to any transaction in which the beneficial owner was not an owner at both the time of purchasing and the time of selling; on the other hand, directors and officers face liability if they held their positions at the time either of sale or of purchase. Interestingly, though, § 16(b) covers transactions that fit the enumerated criteria even when the transactions were not actually based on inside information. In essence, then, it is a preventative section. Thus, if director Wallis sells stock in Continuing Corp. for $5,000 and five months later buys an equal number of shares for $3,000, Wallis will have to pay back to the corporation the $2,000 in profits so realized.

Note that in a merger case involving § 16(b), *Gollust* v. *Mendell*,[7] the Supreme Court held that a plaintiff who had properly instituted a § 16(b) action as the owner of a security of the issuer had standing to continue to prosecute the action even after a merger involving the issuer had resulted in exchanging the stockholder's interest in the issuer for stock in the issuer's new corporate parent.

Liabilities and Remedies. The '34 Act creates a private right of action for those who have dealt in securities on the basis of misleading registration statements (liability pursuant to §§ 12 and 18), tender offers (§ 13), and proxy solicitations (§ 14). Under § 16(b), the corporation or a shareholder suing in a derivative action for the benefit of the corporation may recover short-swing profits realized by officers, directors, and shareholders controlling at least 10 percent of the securities involved. Private actions under § 10(b) and Rule 10(b)-5, the catch-all antifraud provision, may be brought by any purchasers or sellers of any securities against any person who has engaged in fraudulent conduct, including a corporation that has bought or sold its own shares. Recall in this context that the PSLRA of 1995 preserves the state-of-mind requirements set out in the '34 Act and interpreted in subsequent Supreme Court and other court holdings.

The early § 10(b) cases had expansively imposed liability under § 10(b) and Rule 10(b)-5. However, in *Ernst & Ernst* v. *Hochfelder*, 425 U.S. 185 (1976), *reh'g. denied*, 425 U.S. 986 (1976), the Supreme Court limited the reach of § 10(b) in that the Court required a private person to prove that the securities law violator intended to deceive, manipulate, or defraud the injured party. After *Hochfelder*, proof of negligent conduct alone will not constitute a violation of § 10(b). Similarly, *Santa Fe Industries, Inc.* v. *Green*, 430 U.S. 462 (1977), which held that the term *fraud* in § 10(b) and Rule 10(b)-5 would not cover management's breach of fiduciary duties in connection with a securities transaction, signals somewhat of a retreat from the Court's prior, expansive view of possible liability under § 10(b).

Yet the SEC's ability (under the Insider Trading Sanctions Act of 1984) to penalize insider traders up to three times the amount of the profit gained or the loss avoided as a result of the unlawful purchase or sale suggests the availability of potent remedies aimed at discouraging securities laws' violations. Such penalties are payable to the U.S. Treasury; private parties cannot seek relief based on this act. This act also increases the criminal penalties that can be levied against individual violators from $10,000 to $100,000.

In addition, the Insider Trading and Securities Fraud Enforcement Act of 1988, which creates an express private right of action in favor of any market participants who traded contemporaneously with those who violated the '34 Act or SEC rules by trading while in possession of material, nonpublic information, supplements all other existing express and implied remedies and does not limit either the SEC or the Attorney General's authority to assess penalties for illegal use of material, nonpublic information. However, the 1988 legislation limits the damages one can receive in such private actions to the profits gained or losses avoided by the illegal trading (less any disgorgement ordered in an SEC action brought under the 1984 Act). The 1988 Act also allows private individuals who provide information that leads to the imposition of penalties to receive a bounty of up to 10 percent of any penalty.

Although the 1988 legislation considerably bolsters the remedies provided under the 1984 Act, Congress in 1988—as it had done in 1984 as well—declined to expand the definition of what constitutes illegal insider trading under the misappropriation theory to include trading by anyone who merely is in possession of material, nonpublic information. Some legislators rejected the "possession" test as unduly broad, and others thought the law should prohibit only the improper use of such information. In short, Congress in the 1988 amendments ultimately declined to add any express definition of insider trading to the '34 Act.

Nonetheless, the legislative history of the 1988 Act reflects a clear endorsement of the misappropriation theory as articulated by lower federal courts and as approved subsequently by the Supreme Court in *O'Hagan*. Indeed, both the 1984 and the 1988 Acts seem to represent a congressional backlash directed at the perceived leniency of the Supreme Court's holdings in the *Chiarella* and *Dirks* cases.

Those who advocate more potent remedies for violations of the securities laws and who disagree with the *Chiarella* and *Dirks* holdings recently were dealt a harsh blow by the Supreme Court—see *Central Bank of Denver* v. *First Interstate Bank of Denver, NA*.[8] By further limiting the scope of the implied remedies available to litigants under the '34 Act, this case built on these earlier precedents. Prior to 1994, plaintiffs often sued not only the person who had violated a specific provision of the securities acts but also those who had "aided and abetted" the wrongdoer. By bringing "aiding" and "abetting" cases under § 10(b) and Rule 10(b)-5, a plaintiff could expand the number of persons from whom he or she could seek damages (several courts had held that "aiders" and "abettors," along with the primary violator, were jointly and severally liable). Simply put, the plaintiff was assured of a "deep pocket" because the plaintiff could recover from the most solvent defendant. Alternatively, the court, by requiring each defendant to contribute to the overall monetary award granted to the successful plaintiff, could distribute the damages among all the defendants. Because the '34 Act was silent as to a defendant's potential liability for aiding and abetting and as to the right of contribution, it was only a matter of time before the issue reached the Supreme Court.

In *Central Bank*, the Court concluded that Congress never intended to impose secondary liability under § 10(b) and that the '34 Act consequently does not reach those who aid and abet but instead prohibits only the making of a material misstatement (or omission) or the commission of a manipulative act. However, the Court refrained from holding that secondary actors (like accountants) are always free from liability under the act. Rather, such secondary actors may be held liable as primary actors if the plaintiff can prove all the requirements for primary liability, including a material misstatement (or omission) on which a purchaser or seller of securities has relied. The federal courts presently are split over the threshold required for a secondary actor's conduct to constitute primary liability. Some, under the so-called bright line test, will find primary liability only if the defendant makes a material misstatement or omission. Other courts, though, predicate liability on the "substantial participation" of the defendant. At some point, the Supreme Court presumably will provide a definitive answer to such questions.

38.2 | FINANCE/ MANAGEMENT

INSIDER TRADING RULES UNDER THE '34 ACT

CIT stock is being sold on a national exchange, which sales subject the firm to regulation under the '34 Act. The initial public reaction to the firm and its prospects has been good, and the stock has had steady increases in its market price. CIT is currently negotiating with a small technology firm that has invented a new video-imaging process. This new process will greatly increase the sharpness of the images shown on the Call-Image videophones. No one outside the immediate family is aware of these negotiations. Dan, Donna, and Amy want to purchase a significant number of CIT shares before the news "leaks out" about the negotiations. However, they are concerned that if they do so, they will be guilty of insider trading. They ask you what they should do to avoid liability under the '34 Act in this situation. What will you tell them?

BUSINESS CONSIDERATIONS What should the officers, directors, and controlling shareholders of a firm whose stock is publicly traded be concerned about when they trade in their firm's securities? What can the firm do to minimize its potential liability when an insider trading scandal erupts?

ETHICAL CONSIDERATIONS Is it ethical for an insider to trade in securities when he or she has information that is not yet available to the general public? Is it ethical to prevent people from using the knowledge or information they have acquired through their jobs from making a profit based on that knowledge or information?

Interestingly, in enacting the PSLRA, Congress refused to give an express private right of action for aiding and abetting; hence, the *Central Bank* ruling survives the PSLRA. The 1995 Act, however, does give the SEC enforcement authority to bring actions against aiders and abettors.

Recall that the PSLRA sets out a "fair share" rule of proportionate liability for those who have engaged in "non-knowing" violations. Joint liability will befall only those who knowingly violate the securities law. As in the '33 Act, the plaintiffs who sue for damages will have to prove that the alleged misstatements actually caused their losses. The PSLRA further requires the calculation of damages based on the mean trading price of the stock (i.e., the average daily trading price of the stock determined as of the close of the market each day during the 90-day period after the dissemination of any information that corrects the misleading statement or omission).

Experts have posited that the PSLRA will have a dramatic impact on private actions brought under Rule 10(b)-5. Since the representations that form the basis of such actions often involve forward-looking statements, the "safe harbor" rule probably will lessen the incidence of such actions. Presumably, the PSLRA's pleading rules that require that scienter be pleaded with particularity in lawsuits involving the '34 Act (as opposed to the '33 Act) similarly will dampen the ardor of class action lawyers and plaintiffs who used to rush to the courthouse to file class action suits whenever a major company announced a sharp decline in the company's stock. The legal developments spawned by this newest securities law therefore bear watching.

Besides the remedies allowable under the '33 and '34 Acts, the Supreme Court's opinion in *Sedima S.P.R.L. v. Imrex Co., Inc.,*[9] which apparently allowed securities cases to be brought under the Racketeer Influenced and Corrupt Organizations Act (RICO), for a time represented a significant remedial vehicle as well. To illustrate, some commentators argued that then-Drexel, Burnham, Lambert, Inc.'s much-ballyhooed decision to plead guilty to six criminal counts and to pay a record-breaking $650 million in fines and restitution for securities violations stemmed from its desire to avoid further indictments under RICO. However, the PSLRA brings to an end this chapter in the history of securities litigation. By removing fraud as a predicate act for the purposes of a private civil action based on RICO except in certain rare instances, the PSLRA has turned this past remedy for securities violations into little more than a legal artifact.

Yet since the late 1980s, the Supreme Court has validated, under the provisions of the Federal Arbitration Act, arbitration of both RICO and securities act claims. In a related vein, then, in *First Options of Chicago, Inc.* v. *Kaplan*,[10] the Supreme Court recently held that whenever it is clear that the opposing sides have agreed to submit the question to arbitration, a court should defer to the arbitrator's decision. In all other circumstances, federal courts have wide latitude to review the arbitrator's determination and to come to an independent conclusion regarding this issue. In giving courts authority to "second-guess" arbitrators on this procedural issue, the Supreme Court disappointed securities industry organizations that had urged the Court to restrict such judicial authority so as to make the arbitration process more streamlined and speedier. Nonetheless, particularly with regard to disputes between investors and their brokers, arbitration represents an increasingly significant possible remedy for investors. Some securities experts, though, have raised questions concerning the legal validity of mandatory arbitration of disputes between securities firms and their employees, especially those involving charges of employment discrimination or harassment. The developments in this area therefore bear watching.

Securities and Exchange Commission Actions

The '34 Act empowers the SEC to conduct investigations of possible violations of the securities laws. Many times such investigations lead to censure or, alternatively, culminate in a consent decree signed by the alleged wrongdoer in exchange for less stringent sanctions. But the SEC also can order an administrative hearing conducted by an administrative law judge to determine if penalties are in order with respect to any security, person, or firm registered with the SEC. As mentioned earlier, revocation of registration or suspension of the distribution of the security (or the activities of the person or firm) are two of the enforcement powers that the SEC possesses. The SEC itself may review the hearing officer's decision and, if necessary, modify the sanctions originally levied. A party adversely affected by a final SEC order can seek review of such an order in a federal circuit court of appeals.

Besides administrative proceedings, the SEC can, on a "proper showing" of a reasonable likelihood of further violations, bring court actions to enjoin violations of the securities laws. The SEC also can refer cases to the Justice Department, which then mounts criminal actions against willful violators of securities laws and rules. A crackdown on Wall Street insider-trading abuses in recent years led to successful criminal cases against well-known traders such as Ivan Boesky, Dennis Levine, and Michael Milken.

STATE REGULATION

Because the assorted federal statutes preserve the states' power to regulate securities activities, any transactions involving securities may be subject to state law as well as federal law. Such state laws, often called "blue sky" laws, though varied, normally include three types of provisions: (1) antifraud stipulations, (2) registration requirements for brokers and dealers, and (3) registration prerequisites for the sale and purchase of securities. With respect to the last, three methods of securities registration ordinarily exist: notification (a streamlined method for securities with a stable earnings record), qualification (a formalized program similar to the procedures mandated by the '33 Act), and coordination (a regimen that directs the issuer to file with the state a copy of the prospectus filed with the SEC under the '33 Act). State laws frequently exempt from registration the same classes of securities exempted from the '33 Act and additionally often exempt stocks listed on the major stock exchanges. Exempted transactions customarily include private placements, or limited offerings, and isolated nonissuer transactions. State laws generally provide for sanctions and liabilities similar to those imposed under federal law, but the small securities staffs in most states make the possibility of civil liability a more potent deterrent for violations.

In 1956, the National Conference of Commissioners on Uniform State Laws drafted a Uniform Securities Act meant for adoption by the states. This attempt at uniformity for resolving securities questions among the various states has not been wholly successful, however.

Before we leave the issue of state regulation of securities, you should know that in 1996 the Supreme Court—in *Matsushita Electric Industrial Co., Ltd.* v. *Epstein*[11]— interpreted the full-faith-and-credit clause of the U.S. Constitution as meaning that federal courts must give class action settlement judgments in a state court the same preclusive effect that the settlement would have in the state court, notwithstanding the fact that the settlement at issue had released claims under the '33 Act (over which the state court had no jurisdiction) and claims under the '34 Act were then pending on appeal in a separate action in the federal courts. Among other reasons, this case is interesting because it involved the very type of class action that had galvanized Congress into enacting the PSLRA. Moreover, this case may put a premium on being the first to file, whether in state court or federal court, a tactic the PSLRA had hoped to thwart, at least in the federal courts. The future resolution of these issues warrants your consideration as well.

THE FOREIGN CORRUPT PRACTICES ACT

One additional topic merits your attention. On 19 December 1977, then-President Jimmy Carter signed into law the Foreign Corrupt Practices Act (FCPA). The FCPA resulted from post-Watergate congressional hearings about questionable payments made to foreign officials by hundreds of U.S. firms, including Exxon, Northrop Corporation, Lockheed Aircraft Company, Gulf Oil, and GTE Corp. Testimony revealed that, in order to land sizable contracts for themselves, companies had given foreign officials large payments, or bribes. In their defense, these U.S. firms argued that foreign officials often demanded such payments as a condition of doing business and that without such "grease" payments, or sums paid to facilitate transactions by minor governmental functionaries, bureaucratic red tape would have brought business dealings to a complete halt.

Congressional investigators found that such questionable payments often took the form of secret slush funds, dubious transfers of funds or assets between subsidiaries and parent companies, improper invoicing methods (e.g., false payments for goods or services that never were received), and bookkeeping practices designed to camouflage improper payments or procedures. Indeed, these corrupt practices by U.S. corporations even included payments to engineer the overthrow of foreign governments hostile to U.S. business interests and bribes to foreign officials to keep competitors out of certain countries. To compound the improprieties, these same firms often deducted such so-called business expenses from their tax returns.

Since accounting irregularities, including secret funds and falsified or inadequate books, formed the vehicle by which firms most often had effected these questionable payments and bribes, Congress, by enacting the FCPA, attempted to put an end to these practices. Containing both antibribery provisions and accounting

NEW RULES CONCERNING ARBITRATION IN THE SECURITIES INDUSTRY

For years, the National Association of Securities Dealers (NASD) required all securities industry personnel to sign standard Form U-4, which obligated securities industry employees to arbitrate any dispute, claim, or controversy that might arise between the employee, the firm, a customer, or any other person. Most securities firms made the signing of Form U-4 a condition of employment. As of 1 January 1999, NASD rules specifically exempt statutory discrimination and harassment claims from such required arbitration. This SEC-approved rule change does not require securities firms to drop their mandatory arbitration programs. Rather, the rule change merely takes NASD out of the business of dictating that there must be mandatory arbitration clauses in securities industry employees' contracts. The new rule moreover does not prevent brokerage firms from including such arbitration requirements in individual employees' contracts. Nonetheless, employees now can sue their employers in court, unless the employees have entered into a private mandatory arbitration agreement. For those workers who must sign such arbitration agreements, NASD's rules would: (1) require securities industry employers to give a disclosure statement to each employee whenever that employee is asked to sign a new or amended Form U-4. That disclosure statement would state that the employee is agreeing to mandatory arbitration of any nondiscrimination employment-related claims and explain that the employee's engaging in mandatory arbitration means that he or she is giving up the right to sue a member, customers, or another employee in court; (2) permit only "public" arbitrators—those not extensively involved in the securities industry—to hear discrimination claims. The parties, however, could agree to waive any of these qualifications after a dispute arose; (3) allow arbitrators to award discrimination claimants any relief that would be available in court, including reasonable attorney's fees; and (4) provide options for employers to avoid bifurcating, or splitting, discrimination and nondiscrimination employment claims between the courts and arbitration. Allowing statutory discrimination claims to be filed in court could lead to bifurcation of cases, with the discrimination claims proceeding in court while the other employment claims would be arbitrated. These new rules provide that if the parties agree to resolve all their claims in court, the parties would not have to arbitrate the related nondiscrimination claims. Even if an employee has filed his or her related claims in arbitration, the proposal would allow employers several opportunities in the course of the dispute to file a motion to combine those claims with the discrimination litigation.

Assume that a securities industry firm has asked for an injunction to prevent NASD from enforcing these rules. Assume, too, that a securities industry employee has filed a lawsuit claiming that Form U-4 constitutes an unconscionable contract of adhesion.

How would *you* dispose of these matters if they came before *your* court?[12]

BUSINESS CONSIDERATIONS What advantages derive from the securities industries' requiring mandatory arbitration of all disputes? What drawbacks inhere in this policy?

ETHICAL CONSIDERATIONS Is it ethical for securities firms to require employees to sign Form U-4 as a condition of employment? Is it ethical for an employee to sign the form and then to argue subsequently that the agreement is not binding in certain circumstances?

SOURCES: 67 *U.S.L.W.* 2747–2748 (15 June 1999); 67 *U.S.L.W.* 1543 (16 March 1999).

standards, the FCPA itself amends §§ 13(a) and 13(b)-2 of the Securities Exchange Act of 1934. The FCPA's antibribery sections provide criminal penalties for actions taken by issuers (i.e., firms subject to the '34 Act) or any domestic concern (even those not subject to the '34 Act) when an officer, director, employee, agent, or stockholder acting on behalf of such businesses corruptly uses the mail or any instrumentality of interstate commerce either to offer or actually to pay money (or anything of value) to foreign officials for the purpose of influencing foreign officials to assist the firm "in obtaining or retaining business for or with, or directing business to, any person."[13] In addition, it is unlawful under the FCPA to offer or to give payments or gifts for similar purposes to any foreign political party (or officials or candidates thereof) or to any person who the U.S. concern knows will transmit the payment or thing of value to any of the classes of persons specifically prohibited from receiving such bribes.[14]

Gifts or payments that are lawful under the written laws and regulations of the foreign country involved or that constitute bona fide reasonable expenditures (such as travel or lodging) incurred by such persons during the performance of a contract with the foreign government do not fall within the FCPA's proscriptions. Moreover, these antibribery provisions do not extend to payments made to these classes of persons when the payments' purpose is to expedite or facilitate the performance of "routine governmental action." Hence, "grease" payments to obtain permits or licenses to do business in the foreign country, visas, work orders, phone service, police protection, or inspections are legal as long as the employee receiving them is not a person known as someone who is acting as a conduit for governmental officials to whom the FCPA forbids corrupt payments or gifts.

However, decisions by foreign officials to award or continue business with a particular party are not included in the definition of routine governmental action.[15] Purely commercial bribery of corporate officials who lack governmental connections and who do not act as conduits for governmental officials thus appears to be legal, but business records, in order to comply with the FCPA's accounting standards described below, should reflect such payments. Recent amendments to the FCPA empower the Attorney General, after consultation with the SEC and others, to issue guidelines describing specific types of conduct that satisfy the strictures of the act and, when requested by firms, to issue opinions as to whether certain specified prospective conduct by these firms conforms with the act. Once promulgated, these regulations and advisory opinions should greatly facilitate U.S. firms' attempts to comply with the FCPA.

Although all individuals and domestic concerns (whether these latter be corporations, partnerships, sole proprietorships, or any other sort of association) are subject to the FCPA antibribery provisions, only issuers subject to the SEC's jurisdiction must comply with the FCPA's accounting standards. These record-keeping standards require issuers to do the following:

(A) make and keep books, records, and accounts, which, in reasonable detail, accurately and fairly reflect the transactions and dispositions of the assets of the issuer; and

(B) devise and maintain a system of internal accounting controls sufficient to provide reasonable assurances that—

    (i) transactions are executed in accordance with management's general or specific authorization;

(ii) *transactions are recorded as necessary (i) to permit preparation of financial statements in conformity with generally accepted accounting principles or any other criteria applicable to such statements, and (ii) to maintain accountability for assets;*

(iii) *access to assets is permitted only in accordance with management's general or specific authorization; and*

(iv) *the recorded accountability for assets is compared with the existing assets at reasonable intervals and appropriate action is taken with respect to any differences.*[16]

Because they largely eliminate the possibility of secret slush funds for bribing foreign officials, these provisions are beneficial. Yet the statute gives no specific guidelines for setting up a particular internal control system. Rather, it leaves the choice of the particular system to the individual firm. The statute's vagueness therefore has created confusion on the part of some businesspeople as to what type of record-keeping system will suffice. Given the FCPA's criminal penalties for knowingly failing to comply, this is not an idle worry.

Further compounding such apprehensions is the SEC's promulgation of far-ranging regulations designed to promote the reliability of the information requested in the FCPA's record-keeping provisions. These regulations prohibit both the falsification of accounting records and misleading statements made by an issuer's directors or officers to auditors or accountants during the preparation of required documents and reports.

The FCPA's imposition of criminal penalties—setting corporate fines of a maximum of $2 million for violations and a maximum of five years' imprisonment and/or $100,000 in fines for willful violations by corporate individuals—and individual civil penalties not to exceed $10,000 should adequately deter U.S. corporations and corporate personnel engaged in international business from undertaking such illegal activities. Adding further strength to these criminal penalties is the FCPA's prohibition of a corporation's indemnification of its employees against liability under this act.[17] Other remedies available under the '34 Act, such as injunctions, also may be used in the enforcement of the FCPA by the Justice Department and the SEC, which share enforcement responsibilities under it.

Critics of the FCPA argue that its provisions and resultant regulations have greatly increased both U.S. firms' costs of doing business and the enforcement agencies' costs, all of which negatively affect the public. On

38.3 | MANAGEMENT/ INTERNATIONAL BUSINESS

SHOULD CIT ADOPT BRIBERY AS A CORPORATE STRATEGY?

The Kochanowskis are investigating the possibility of selling the firm's products internationally. John thinks he recalls learning in one of his management classes that bribery of governmental officials as a way of procuring business is a common occurrence in many countries. John therefore advocates following that old adage, "When in Rome, do as the Romans do." He consequently supports giving CIT's sales personnel a "slush fund" that the staff can use for bribing the appropriate officials in whichever country they target for obtaining sales. The rest of the family suggests that John immediately undertake a close reading of the FCPA. What will the FCPA teach John about the advisability of embracing bribery as a corporate strategy?

BUSINESS CONSIDERATIONS In recent years, the International Chamber of Commerce has added anti-bribery provisions to its organizational rules, as has the General Assembly of the United Nations. The Organization for Economic Cooperation and Development similarly has advocated that its member states criminalize the bribery of foreign officials. What policies should a business institute to ensure compliance with the provisions of the FCPA and these other organizations' rules? Do you believe that the FCPA hampers the ability of U.S. firms to compete in a global market?

ETHICAL CONSIDERATIONS Does the FCPA improve the ethical conduct of U.S. firms? Does the FCPA represent a type of "cultural imperialism" in which the United States expects the rest of the world to accede to its view of what is—or is not—ethical?

RESOURCES FOR BUSINESS LAW STUDENTS

NAME	RESOURCES	WEB ADDRESS
Securities and Exchange Commission (SEC)	The SEC provides information about federal securities laws and investor protection in the securities market.	http://www.sec.gov/
Electronic Data Gathering (EDGAR)	EDGAR is a searchable database of corporate information maintained by the SEC.	http://www.sec.gov/
Securities Act of 1933	The University of Cincinnati's Center for Corporate Law maintains the Securities Act of 1933.	http://www.law.uc.edu/CCL/33Act/
Securities Exchange Act of 1934	The University of Cincinnati's Center for Corporate Law maintains the Securities Exchange Act of 1934.	http://www.law.uc.edu/CCL/34Act/
Foreign Corrupt Practices Act—15 U.S.C. § 78dd-2	The Legal Information Institute, maintained by the Cornell Law School, provides a hypertext and searchable version of 15 U.S.C. § 78dd-2, popularly known as the Foreign Corrupt Practices Act.	http://www4.law.cornell.edu/uscode/15/78dd-2.html

the other hand, such laws and supplementary regulations carry the attendant advantages of heightened investor information and fewer scandals involving U.S. bribery of foreign officials.

Since the FCPA is of relatively recent vintage, case law interpreting it is sparse. Plus, because of the legal, social, and ethical issues it represents, the FCPA promises to remain a controversial law.

SUMMARY

The Securities Act of 1933 and the Securities Exchange Act of 1934 extensively regulate securities. In essence, a security involves instruments labeled as stock and that possess all the characteristics typically associated with stock, as well as an investment in an enterprise whereby the investor has no managerial functions but instead expects to profit solely from the efforts of others. The '33 Act basically is a disclosure statute meant to protect the unsophisticated investing public. In furtherance of this purpose, the act requires, on the initial distribution of stock, the issuer's filing of a detailed registration statement with the SEC and the furnishing of a prospectus to virtually all potential investors. Until the registration statement becomes effective, selling and promotional activities remain limited. The '33 Act exempts certain classes of securities from its registration and prospectus requirements: securities issued by federal and state banks, short-term commercial paper, issues by nonprofit organizations, issues by savings and loan associations subject to state or federal regulation, issues by common carriers subject to the jurisdiction of the Surface Transportation Board, certain qualifying employee pension plans, insurance policies and certain annuities subject to regulation by state and federal authorities, and intrastate issues of securities.

The '33 Act, in addition, exempts certain transactions, such as private offerings. The '33 Act also contains several antifraud provisions. Civil liability may attend violations of the '33 Act. One section places liability on everyone who signed the registration statement, was named as a director, contributed an expert opinion to the statement, or underwrote the issue. All such persons, except the issuer, may escape liability if they can show they acted with "due diligence." Other sections of the '33 Act establish civil and criminal liability.

The '34 Act regulates the secondary distribution of securities. Its reach therefore is even broader than that of the '33 Act. The '34 Act covers proxy solicitations and tender offers, limits insider trading, forbids short-swing profits, and in general tries to eliminate fraud and manipulative conduct with respect to the sale or purchase of securities. According to the '34 Act, any issuer who trades securities on a national stock exchange must register with the SEC. Like the '33 Act, the '34 Act mandates certain disclosures by the firms that it covers when the securities are listed with national stock exchanges or traded over the counter. Regulation of proxy solicitations is an important facet of the '34 Act. In order to further the democratic aspects of corporations, the '34 Act authorizes the inclusion—in management proxy solicitations—of shareholder proposals that involve "proper subjects." Liability for misleading proxy statements is absolute, as is liability for misleading statements made during tender offers or takeover bids. The '34 Act also prohibits insider trading because of the injury to the investing public that otherwise may ensue. When material inside information is involved, the insider either must publicly disclose the information or refrain from trading in the securities. Under the '34 Act's section on short-swing profits, directors, officers, and beneficial shareholders in certain corporations must refrain from buying or selling securities within a six-month period. Possible liability under the '34 Act is far reaching, despite the existence of some Supreme Court decisions suggesting less expansive impositions of liability. A recent securities enactment, the Private Securities Litigation Reform Act of 1995, limits class action suits to situations in which shareholders in fact have been the victims of securities fraud and discourages suits brought for frivolous—or entrepreneurial—purposes. This statute's adoption of a proportionate approach to liability for damages represents Congress's attempt to attract high-quality professionals to the boards of directors of start-up companies.

The Securities and Exchange Commission can conduct administrative hearings with respect to securities violations and can seek injunctions to stop continuing violations. State securities laws (i.e., "blue sky" laws) usually set up antifraud provisions and registration requirements for brokers and dealers and for the sale of securities. Since 1977, the Foreign Corrupt Practices Act has forbidden U.S. businesses from making payments to foreign officials for the purpose of obtaining foreign business. Noncompliance with the FCPA's antibribery provisions and record-keeping standards may subject individuals or corporations to civil or criminal penalties.

DISCUSSION QUESTIONS

1. What, essentially, is a *security*?
2. Explain the primary purposes of the Securities Act of 1933 and the Securities Exchange Act of 1934.
3. List the types of information the '33 Act requires a registration statement to include.
4. What are "tombstone ads" and "red herring" prospectuses?
5. List the '33 Act's exempt classes of securities and transactions.
6. Explain what a *proxy* is, and describe the SEC rules surrounding proxy solicitations.

7. What are the '34 Act's provisions regarding insider trading?
8. Discuss the laws regarding short-swing profits and why the '34 Act prohibits these profits.
9. Enumerate the liabilities and remedies possible under both the '33 and '34 Acts (include the PSLRA of 1995's amendments as well).
10. Explain the enforcement powers held by the SEC and how state regulation of securities differs from federal regulation.

CASE PROBLEMS AND WRITING ASSIGNMENTS

1. After California had deregulated its utility industry in 1997, Scott J. Levine and his wife, Sabrina Levine, formed Friendly Power Company LLC (FPC-LLC). A few months later, they formed Friendly Power Company, Inc. (FPL-Inc.), as well as Friendly Power Franchise Company (FPC-Franchise). FPC-LLC became a utility company licensed to operate in California, while FPC-Franchise was incorporated in Colorado. All three companies are located in Miami Lakes, Florida. Under a so-called franchise agreement, FPC-Franchise signed a contract with FPC-Inc. pursuant to which agreement FPC-Franchise had the authority to enter into exclusive licenses with franchise operators who in turn would convert residential customers to Friendly Power. Under this agreement, FPC-Franchise would give FPC-Inc. 90 percent of the monies generated from the sales of these franchises. The franchise agreement that FPC-Franchise in turn signed with its "franchisees" contained the following provisions: FPC-Franchise would pay two dollars for every household that a franchise converted to Friendly Power. Each franchise was assigned a protected geographical territory, and each was required to achieve and maintain a 5 percent market share of the electric power customers in its protected territory within five years from the date of its franchise agreement. Ultimately, FPC-Franchise sold 17 franchises priced between $200,000 and $600,000 each. Several of these franchisees consisted of telemarketing operations aimed at attracting investors who would buy partnership units in various franchises. According to the franchise agreements, 40 percent of the investors' funds would go to Friendly Power as payment for the purchase price of the franchises. An additional 40 percent of the investors' funds would go to the telemarketing operations as payment for these services. The remaining 20 percent of the investors' monies would be held for future working capital once the franchise's

escrowed funds had been exceeded. At that point, the investors would be entitled to 50 percent of Friendly Power's net profits on sales to residential customers in the franchise territory. However, FPC-Franchise early on notified the investors that they likely would not see a profit for quite some time after their initial investment. In the meantime, the franchise agreement permitted Friendly Power to use the investors' funds as capital for its business of providing electrical power to commercial customers in the state of California. Each Friendly Power franchise consisted of between 50 and 94 partners. Each investor in addition signed a participation agreement, which mandated that each investor be involved in the day-to-day operations of the franchise and actively participate in one or more of the management committees responsible for overseeing and conducting the franchise. Friendly Power began providing electricity to its customers on 1 May 1998. By 17 July 1998, FPC-Franchise had released only the San Francisco franchise's escrow fund. In contrast, by this time, Friendly Power had received $2.4 million from 308 investors. On 17 July 1998, when the SEC froze all of Friendly Power's assets, Friendly Power no longer could buy power. With its funds frozen and its credit terminated, Friendly Power on 8 August 1998 notified the California Energy Commission that it would no longer be able to provide power to its customers, and all the customers reverted to their respective previous utility providers. The SEC subsequently alleged that the Levines and Friendly Power had offered unregistered securities for sale in violation of the '33 Act. Were the "franchises" at issue here securities? [See *SEC* v. *Friendly Power Company LLC,* 49 F.Supp. 2d 1363 (S.D.Fla. 1999).]

2. On 1 July 1987, Sercenco, S.A. (Sercenco) and General Electric Technical Services Company, Inc. (GE) entered into a service sales representative agreement

(the contract), pursuant to which GE designated Sercenco as GE's authorized service sales representative for Peru for the period 1 July 1987 through 30 June 1990. Among other things, the contract contained provisions forbidding violations of antibribery laws such as the Foreign Corrupt Practices Act (FCPA) and requiring compliance with GE's written policy against bribing foreign officials to procure sales. In 1991, Sercenco was the sole service sales representative in Peru for several of GE's subsidiaries and was a party to four other contracts with GE, one of which concerned services in Peru and one of which related to services in Venezuela. Each of those contracts contained similar antibribery provisions. Sercenco's problems with GE arose out of events relating to a four-year equipment maintenance agreement that Sercenco had entered into in April 1988 (the 1988 agreement) with Electricidad del Peru, S.A. (ElectroPeru), a government-owned electric utility company located in Peru. Sercenco alleged that in 1990, an ElectroPeru employee acting on behalf of Luis Ampuero Salas (Ampuero), the prospective general manager of ElectroPeru, solicited a $200,000 bribe. After Sercenco refused to pay, Sercenco was approached again by the same employee and was warned that, if it did not reconsider its position, it would face problems with the new administration of ElectroPeru. Sercenco again refused to comply with the demand, and ElectroPeru allegedly retaliated by claiming that Sercenco had overbilled ElectroPeru. As a result, over $1 million in invoiced payables to Sercenco were held back while ElectroPeru's auditors reviewed all of Sercenco's dealings with ElectroPeru. After a lengthy dispute over the alleged overbilling, in December 1990, ElectroPeru agreed in writing to reduce its claims from over $1 million to about $25,000. However, notwithstanding the signed settlement agreement, Ampuero managed to block the payment of Sercenco's invoices. In the spring of 1991, in order to increase the pressure on Sercenco, Ampuero allegedly began to lodge fabricated complaints to GE about the quality of service that Sercenco was providing to ElectroPeru. Sercenco and GE conducted numerous telephone conversations and meetings from the spring of 1991 to August 1991 to discuss these complaints. Sercenco informed GE of the demand to pay a bribe to Ampuero and of the great financial pressure Ampuero was exerting on Sercenco by blocking the payment of Sercenco's invoices. Sercenco reiterated that it had done nothing wrong, that Ampuero had demanded a bribe, and that he was merely trying to pressure Sercenco by making untrue allegations about Sercenco to GE. GE repeatedly instructed Sercenco to "resolve" the problem without involving GE. Sercenco claimed that

GE thereby had communicated to Sercenco, in so many words, that Sercenco had better acquiesce to Ampuero's demand for payment in order to preserve ElectroPeru as a customer of GE products. After corresponding with Ampuero, GE then issued to Sercenco a letter that instructed Sercenco to terminate any commercial activity on behalf of GE with ElectroPeru, unless and until the ongoing dispute between ElectroPeru and Sercenco had been "satisfactorily resolved." Sercenco interpreted this correspondence as a statement that it would have to pay the bribe that Ampuero had demanded if it wanted to retain its position as GE's service sales representative and thus the ElectroPeru account. Once GE had advised Ampuero of the suspension of the Sercenco-ElectroPeru contract, Ampuero distributed copies of this letter to many governmental entities that were clients or potential clients of Sercenco. Finally, on 7 January 1992, GE sent a letter to Sercenco indicating that GE had decided not to renew the contract that had expired by its own terms on 31 December 1991, as well as four other agreements. Sercenco's pleas for reconsideration fell on deaf ears; GE at that point replaced Sercenco as its service sales representative in Peru, with an affiliate of Sumitomo. Sercenco alleged that GE had selected Sumitomo because GE knew that Sumitomo, a Japanese company not subject to the provisions of the FCPA, had a history of paying bribes to officials of government-owned or government-controlled companies in exchange for contracts and would continue doing so. Ultimately, Sercenco commenced a suit against ElectroPeru for all sums due under the 1988 agreement and was granted a $9 million recovery by Peruvian courts. Sercenco also filed suit against GE. Specifically, Sercenco claimed that GE's actions in furtherance of GE's scheme to increase the sales of GE products through bribery, extortion, unlawful and/or fraudulent procurement practices, and other fraudulent and unlawful means were violations of the FCPA, the RICO Act, and the federal mail and wire fraud statutes. Although the FCPA sets out no explicit private right of action, Sercenco argued that the courts should construe the FCPA so as to provide an implied private right of action for a sales representative that has been subjected to coercion and extortion by a manufacturer's pressuring it to commit violations of the FCPA. Should the court interpret the FCPA in this fashion, or should it limit Sercenco's remedies to state law claims such as breach of contract, fraud, and unfair competition? [See *J.S. Service Center Corporation* v. *General Electric Technical Services Company, Inc.*, 937 F.Supp. 216 (S.D. N.Y. 1996).]

3. Alan Carr, a Canadian, owned Europe and Overseas Commodity Traders, S.A. (EOC), a venture capital company incorporated in Panama. EOC had an account with the London branch of Banque Paribas, a French bank. In October 1993, Carr was visiting England. On October 7, John Arida, an account manager at Paribas's London office, informed Carr that a substantial amount of cash had accumulated in EOC's account. Arida thereupon offered to recommend an attractive investment opportunity for the money. Carr said he expressed interest in the proposal but explained that he was preparing to leave for Florida on the 9th and thus would be happy to hear more after his arrival in Florida. In a series of telephone conversations that began on 14 October, Carr and Arida resumed their discussion of EOC's investment in the Paribas Global Bond Futures Fund (the Fund). Carr subsequently alleged that Arida had misled him by conveying the following inaccurate information: (a) that the Fund was overseen by Paribas's proprietary trading desk; (b) that the investors' capital in the Fund was traded along with Paribas's own capital; and (c) that the Fund traded securities based primarily on technical as opposed to fundamental considerations. In reliance on these statements, Carr claimed that he, while in Florida, ordered $1,800,000 in purchases for EOC. Arida claimed that Carr was in England when Carr ordered the first purchase of Fund shares. However, the documents Arida offered in support of this allegation were inconclusive. Carr thereafter sued Paribas for, among other things, violations of the '33 Act owing to the sale of unregistered securities. Under SEC regulations and securities law precedents, U.S. courts would have jurisdiction over the transactions involved here if the conduct at issue would have the effect of creating a market for such unregistered securities in the United States. Did the securities sold to EOC fall under the registration requirements of the '33 Act and thus give the court subject matter jurisdiction over the sales to EOC? Explain. [See *Europe and Overseas Commodity Traders, S.A.* v. *Banque Paribas London,* 147 F.3d 118 (2d Cir. 1998), *cert. denied,* 525 U.S. 1139 (1999).]

4. Valence Technology, Inc. (Valence) was founded in 1989 to develop new battery technology. In May 1992, after announcing that it was developing a new solid electrolyte rechargeable battery, Valence raised $33 million in an IPO. Valence advertised its batteries as having an extended life cycle compared to conventional rechargeable batteries. Valence announced that it was focusing in particular on applying this technology to the commercial manufacture of batteries for use in cellular telephones and laptop computers.

After Valence had raised $82.8 million in a second IPO, in December 1992, Valence announced the conclusion of a $100 million contract with Motorola, which was to begin using Valence's batteries in its cellular telephones in 1994. On 15 February 1993, *Forbes* magazine published an article about Valence entitled "Story Stock." The article claimed that while "the folks at Valence can put on a good show" in demonstrating prototypes of their battery, the investment community remained largely ignorant to "what is really energizing this stock . . . insiders unloading shares for a price hundreds of times what they paid, an underwriting firm . . . [that helps] them do that, and journalists who . . . take at face value the boastful pronouncements of the company's publicity department." According to the article, although Valence's battery "works beautifully in the lab," "the world doesn't know" whether it will "last" or if it can be "made cheaply." The article took particular aim at Carl Berg, Valence's largest shareholder. It noted his participation in two other Silicon Valley enterprises through which he had made large profits even though the companies themselves had suffered financially. According to the article," . . . outside investors may do poorly, but Berg usually gets his money out." Valence and its officers made several public pronouncements in response to the *Forbes* article. Lev Dawson, then the CEO of Valence, sent to *Forbes* a letter (that Valence later distributed to shareholders) describing the article as "inaccurate." The press follow-up to the *Forbes* article was modest. The *San Francisco Chronicle* published a story on 27 February 1993, reiterating the *Forbes* article's claim that "there was no reliable evidence that the batteries will work as advertised." *Bloomberg Business News,* in contrast, in a 17 February 1993 wire story entitled "Valence Chairman Calls Forbes Article 'Inaccurate,'" reported Dawson's response to the *Forbes* article. Later press coverage resumed its largely positive tone: September 1993 stories in the *Dow Jones Wire Service* and *The Wall Street Journal* reported Valence's announcement that it would deliver the batteries for the Motorola contract in the coming year. Neither story mentioned the *Forbes* article. The week after the publication of the *Forbes* article, Valence's stock dropped from about $15.00 per share to $12.50 per share. Two days later, on 25 February, it rose back to $15.00 and by 28 September had reached $20.00. In December 1993, Valence completed its third public offering, raising $51.5 million. On 3 May 1994, Valence announced that it was unable to meet Motorola's specifications and that it would not be delivering batteries under that contract as planned. On that day, Valence's stock dropped from $9.50 to $5.25. On 9 August 1994, when Valence announced that it was abandoning its new battery technology, its stock dropped to $3.375. When James L. Berry and other investors sued Valence for securities fraud under § 10(b) and Rule 10(b)-5, the defendants claimed that the statute of limitations would bar the plaintiffs' claims. Specifically, the defendants maintained that the *Forbes* article had placed the plaintiffs on "inquiry notice" of the possibility of fraud more than one year before they had sued. Did the *Forbes* article raise sufficient suspicion of fraud to cause a reasonable investor to investigate the matter further and thus trigger the running of the one-year limitations' period? Explain fully. [See *Berry* v. *Valence Technology, Inc.*, 175 F.3d 699 (9th Cir. 1999) *cert. denied*, 120 S.Ct. 528 (1999).]

5. Keith Loeb's wife, Susan, was the niece of the president and controlling shareholder of the target corporation. The government presented evidence that Susan's mother, Shirley Witkin (the sister of the target's president), had told Susan of the impending favorable sale of the target but had added that Susan should tell no one except her husband. The next day, Susan told Loeb of the sale and admonished him not to tell anyone because "it could possibly ruin the sale." Loeb testified that he telephoned broker Robert Chestman the next day and told Chestman that he (Loeb) "had some definite, some accurate information" that the target was being sold at a "substantially higher" price than the market value of its stock. That day, Chestman purchased shares of the target for himself and for Loeb. A jury later convicted Chestman of 10 counts of fraudulent trading in connection with the tender offer in violation of Rule 14(e)-3(a), 10 counts of securities fraud in violation of '34 Act Rule 10(b)-5, and other offenses. The government based its Rule 10(b)-5 case against Chestman on the misappropriation theory, which holds that one who misappropriates nonpublic information in breach of a fiduciary duty and trades on that information to his or her own advantage violates § 10(b) and Rule 10(b)-5. Chestman, challenging his convictions for fraudulent trading in connection with a tender offer, claimed that the SEC had exceeded its rulemaking authority under § 14(e) when it had adopted Rule 14(e)-3 in its present form. Specifically, Chestman asserted that the rule improperly imposes liability in three ways: (1) in the absence of either a duty to disclose or a fiduciary duty; (2) for trading while in the possession of material nonpublic information, whether or not such information is used in effecting the transaction; and (3) on the basis of a "quasi-negligence standard." Was Rule 14(e)-3(a), which bars trading on the basis of material nonpublic information concerning a tender offer that the trader knows or has reason to know has been acquired from an insider of the offeror or issuer or the insider's agent, within the Securities and Exchange Commission's rulemaking authority under §§ 14(e) and 23(a)(1) of the '34 Act, even though the rule dispenses with the common law fraud element of breach of fiduciary duty? [See *United States* v. *Chestman*, 947 F.2d 551 (2nd Cir. 1991), *cert. denied*, 503 U.S. 1004 (1992).]

6. **BUSINESS APPLICATION CASE** Lynn Sinay, David Rosenberg, and Aline Halye purchased Lamson & Sessions Company (Lamson) common stock. In their complaints, the plaintiffs alleged securities fraud pursuant to § 10(b) of the '34 Act and Rule 10(b)-5. The plaintiffs did not assert that fraud had been committed individually upon them because they had relied on statements by defendants when they had purchased their shares. Instead, they contended that Lamson and the other defendants had engaged in a course of conduct that artificially had inflated the common stock's market price (i.e., the plaintiffs asserted a "fraud-on-the-market" theory). Following several November 1986 acquisitions, Lamson's earnings had increased dramatically. On 24 October 1988, Lamson publicly had disclosed that its performance during the first three quarters had been "gratifying," although it was experiencing a "normal seasonal decline" in its commercial and residential markets that would last "into the first quarter of 1989." On 23 December 1988, Lamson had reported that it was having a "tremendous year." On 21 February 1989, Lamson had stated that it was pleased with the 1988 results and that it planned to continue to develop its position in the domestic and worldwide transportation markets. In an April 1989 interview with the *Dow Jones Wire Service*, John B. Schulze, a Lamson officer, had noted that Lamson "does not quarrel with analysts' earnings estimates for 1989 in the area of $1.50 to $1.60. . . . " Schulze further had asserted that Lamson was "counting on new products to offset a weaker construction market for 1989." Notwithstanding these positive forecasts, Lamson's financial condition began to erode in 1989. Owing to prolonged higher interest rates, the construction market failed to rebound after the winter slowdown. Moreover, Lamson experienced severe labor problems at its Midland plant. The plaintiffs claimed that the defendants knew or should have known that the construction market's decline would be long term and that a major and devastating strike would occur. Therefore, according to the plaintiffs, the defendants, by failing to issue sufficiently cautionary statements concerning Lamson's future, deceived the market. Should a court hold the

defendants liable for securities violations based on a corporate officer's statements of honestly held views derived from information currently before the corporation? Why? Assume that your boss at Lamson has asked you to draft a policy that will govern future public statements by corporate personnel. Based on the facts of this case and what you have derived from the *Basic Incorporated* case, as well as the PSLRA of 1995 if the latter were applicable, how would you respond? [See *Sinay* v. *Lamson & Sessions Company,* 948 F.2d 1037 (6th Cir. 1991).]

7. **ETHICAL APPLICATION CASE** Life Partners, Inc. (LPI) arranges transactions relating to viatical settlements and performs certain post-transactional administrative services. A *viatical settlement* is an investment contract pursuant to which an investor acquires an interest in the life insurance policy of a terminally ill person—typically an AIDS patient—at a discount of 20 to 40 percent, depending on the particular insured's life expectancy. When the insured dies, the investor receives the insurance benefits. The investor's profit is the difference between the discounted purchase price paid to the insured and the death benefits collected from the insurer, less transaction costs, premiums paid, and other administrative expenses. LPI sells fractional interests in insurance policies to retail investors, who may pay as little as $650 and buy as little as 3 percent of the benefits of a policy. In order to reach its customers, LPI uses some 500 commissioned "licensees," mostly independent financial planners. For its efforts, LPI's net compensation is roughly 10 percent of the purchase price after the payment of referral and other fees. Brian Pardo, LPI's chairman, claimed that LPI was by far the largest of about 60 firms serving the rapidly growing market for viatical settlements; in 1994, the company accounted for more than half of the industry's estimated annual revenues of $300 million. In 1995, the SEC sued LPI. Specifically, the SEC contended that the fractional interests marketed by LPI are securities and that LPI had violated the '33 and '34 Acts by selling the viatical settlements without first complying with the registration and other requirements of those acts. In rebuttal, LPI argued that (1) viatical settlements are exempt from the securities laws because they are insurance contracts within the meaning of the McCarran-Ferguson Act; and (2) the fractional interests sold by LPI are not in any event securities

within the meaning of the '33 and '34 Acts. Who had the stronger argument, LPI or the SEC? Would you characterize LPI's activities—investing in the life insurance policies of terminally ill persons—as an example of admirable ethics? Why? [See *SEC* v. *Life Partners, Inc.,* 87 F.3d 536 (D.C.Cir. 1996).]

8. **CRITICAL THINKING CASE** Steven G. Cooperman and five other purchasers of the common stock of Individual, Inc. (Individual) sued Individual, its board of directors, and the underwriters who had participated in Individual's March 1996 IPO. The plaintiffs claimed that the defendants had made materially false and misleading statements and had omitted material facts in connection with the registration statement and prospectus for the IPO. Specifically, the plaintiffs alleged that the defendants had failed to disclose that, at the time the IPO became effective, a conflict existed between Yosi Amram—the director, founder, chief executive officer, and president of Individual—and a majority of the board of directors about the strategic direction the company should take. In 1989, Yosi Amram had founded the company, a provider of electronic customized information services, and was largely responsible for the firm's rapid growth. According to the plaintiffs, Amram believed that the company should grow and expand through rapid, often costly, acquisitions of new businesses. The majority of the board, however, believed that Individual should grow through building its core business by, among other things, expanding the subscriber base, extending its information base and providers, and enhancing its knowledge processing systems. The prospectus did not disclose the existence of any disagreement between Amram and the majority of the board. Instead, the prospectus stated that the company's future objective was to maintain growth through the development of Individual's existing core business. The plaintiffs further maintained that, owing to this conflict, Amram ultimately had left Individual and thereby had caused a sharp decline in the company's stock. Hence, the plaintiffs alleged that the defendants' failure to disclose the conflict between Amram and the majority of the board at the time of the IPO constituted an omission of a material fact in violation of Section 11 of the '33 Act. Should the court rule in favor of Cooperman and the other plaintiffs? [See *Cooperman* v. *Individual, Inc.,* 171 F.3d 43 (1st Cir. 1999).]

NOTES

1. *Securities and Exchange Commission* v. *Ralston Purina Co.*, 346 U.S. 119 (1953).
2. 283 F.Supp. 643 (S.D. N.Y. 1968).
3. 513 U.S. 561 (1995).
4. 485 U.S. 224 (1988).
5. 445 U.S. 222 (1980).
6. 463 U.S. 646 (1983).
7. 501 U.S. 115 (1991).
8. 511 U.S. 164 (1994).
9. 473 U.S. 479 (1985).
10. 514 U.S. 938 (1995).
11. 516 U.S. 367 (1996).
12. "NASD Proposes Changes to Rules for Arbitrating Employment Disputes," 67 *U.S.L.W.* 2747–2748 (15 June 1999); "Employment Discrimination—Arbitration," 67 *U.S.L.W.* 1543 (16 March 1999).
13. 15 U.S.C. § 78(dd-1), (dd-2).
14. Ibid.
15. Ibid.
16. Ibid., § 78(m).
17. Ibid., § 78(ff).

GOVERNMENT REGULATION OF BUSINESS

Government regulation of business is a controversial area. There are people who believe that such regulation is an inappropriate exercise of the government's power and that the nation would be better served by a return to a laissez–faire economy. Other people believe that the government does not go far enough in regulating business and that the nation would be better served by a government more actively involved in the regulation and operation of business.

However, for better or for worse, government regulation of business is a fact. The government regulates competition through the Sherman, Clayton, Robinson–Patman, and Federal Trade Commission acts. Its also provides protection of consumers through various consumer credit and product safety acts. The government also regulates business in order to provide environmental protection through the NEPA, the EPA, and a myriad of environmental statutes. The government also regulates business by providing guidelines and standards dealing with labor and employment.

Government regulation of business is closely related to the social contract theory discussed in Chapter 2. It is also an area that creates controversy concerning whether business should be proactive or reactive as it meets its social and legal obligations and expectations. Throughout the rest of this section of the text, consider the social contract theory and the benefits and burdens of being either proactive or reactive.

39

ANTITRUST LAW

CALL-IMAGE TECHNOLOGY

A G E N D A

The Kochanowskis have developed a "one-of-a-kind" product, and that puts them in a position to potentially dominate the market. Such market dominance is both good and bad. It may provide the opportunity for large profits, and it may lead to charges of violating various antitrust laws. The family will need to be aware of the scope of the Sherman Act, the Clayton Act, and the Federal Trade Commission Act. They will also need to be aware of various "unfair trade practices." This is all new territory for them, and they may have a significant number of questions.

Be prepared! You never know when one of the Kochanowskis will need your help or advice.

O U T L I N E

THE BASIS OF REGULATORY REFORM

For the first 114 years of U.S. history, business had a fairly free field in which to work. There was little federal regulation and little effective state regulation. The courts and the federal government took a "hands-off" attitude toward business. In such an environment, Cornelius Vanderbilt, buccaneering railroad tycoon of the 1800s, was able to crow, "What do I care about the law? Hain't I got the power?"

The tide began to turn in the late 1800s as the public tired of the irresponsible behavior of some of the so-called *robber barons.* The press began to call for reforms and for public protection from "big business." Finally, in 1890, a beachhead was established. The assault on business had begun with the passage of the Sherman Act. Government regulation of business was to become a major factor in the management of commercial affairs. All the regulations that affect business today, all the government inputs and interventions that confront the modern businessperson, can be traced back to the cornerstone of business regulation. The law that changed U.S. business so dramatically, the Sherman Antitrust Act, began the era of government regulation. Government regulation was subsequently bolstered with the passage of the Clayton Act and the Federal Trade Commission Act, both in 1914, and again with the Robinson–Patman Act, an amendment to § 2 of the Clayton Act, which was passed in 1936. Each of these statutes will be examined in detail over the balance of this chapter.

THE SHERMAN ACT

Congress passed the Sherman Antitrust Act in 1890. The purpose of the act was to preserve the economic ideal of a pure-competition economy. To reach this ideal, the Sherman Act prohibits combinations that restrain trade, and it prohibits attempts to monopolize any area of commerce. Violations of the act can result in fines, imprisonment, injunctive relief, and civil damages.

Section 1: Contracts, Combinations, or Conspiracies in Restraint of Trade

The Sherman Act is a fairly short statute, but its few words cover a great number of actions. Section 1 states:

> Every contract, combination in the form of trust or otherwise, or conspiracy, in restraint of trade or commerce among the several States, or with foreign nations, is hereby declared to be illegal. Every person who shall make any contract or engage in any combination or conspiracy hereby declared to be illegal shall be deemed guilty of a felony.[1]

Violations of § 1 require a *contract,* a *combination,* or a *conspiracy.* Each of these three requires two or more persons acting in concert in some manner that restrains trade or commerce among the states or with a foreign nation before a violation can be found. Thus, § 1 requires two or more persons acting together before a violation can be found. One person cannot be guilty of a § 1 violation, since one person is acting alone, by definition.

As originally enacted, § 1 presented problems to the courts. Because nearly every contract can, at least in theory, be viewed as a restraint of trade, the prohibition against contracts "in restraint of trade" seemed too broad. In fact, if this section were to be interpreted literally, virtually all business dealings that affect interstate commerce (including foreign trade) could, theoretically, be prohibited by § 1 of the Sherman Act. For example, a customer in State X who contracts to buy some item from seller A in State Y normally will not buy the same type of item from any of the competitors of seller A, whether those sellers are located in State X, State Y, or some other state or nation. As a result, the courts initially interpreted the Sherman Act very narrowly. The courts were willing to rule against combinations or conspiracies "in restraint of trade," but had a more difficult time ruling against contracts. For example, the courts *did* rule that some union activities were combinations or conspiracies in restraint of trade, and thus were violative of § 1 of the Sherman Act. However, these rulings tended to promote—rather than hinder—the "big business" of the era. Obviously, interpretations of this sort worked in such a way that the objective of the act was virtually negated. The courts needed some method for evaluating contracts that allegedly restrained trade "among the states," and they found that method in the "rule of reason."

The Rule of Reason. Eventually, the Supreme Court found a method for evaluating contracts that allegedly restrain trade among the several states in violation of § 1 of the Sherman Act. *Standard Oil Co. of New Jersey* v. *United States*[2] introduced the rule of reason to the Supreme Court. According to this "rule," the Sherman Act did *not* prohibit every contract, combination, or conspiracy in restraint of trade among the several states. Rather, the act only prohibits those contracts, combinations, or conspiracies that *unreasonably* restrain trade among the several states. If the contract, combination, or conspiracy is *reasonable* under the circumstances, the conduct is not in violation of the law. Although the Court determined in this case that the conduct by Standard Oil of New Jersey was unreasonable, the Court did accept, in theory, this defense. Thus was born the "rule of reason" defense to charges of violations of § 1 of the Sherman Act.

Both the rule of reason and the economic theory of competition seemed to be invoked by the Court in a recent case.[3] Sears, Roebuck and Company applied for membership with Visa, USA, the association of credit card issuers who offer the Visa card in the United States. The association denied the application by Sears, and Sears filed suit against Visa, USA, alleging that the credit card association was combining or conspiring illegally in an effort to prevent Sears from issuing Visa cards. The Court found that the harm to competition would be greater if the association admitted Sears than it would be if Sears was prevented from joining the association. According to the Court, the credit card industry was better served by having Visa, MasterCard, American Express, Diners/Carte Blanche, and Discover (issued by and through Sears). Competition was keen, and the market was highly competitive. Admitting Sears would reduce the number of competitors and would seriously harm banks that issue Visa in head-to-head competition with Sears for the potential Visa customers in the market. According to the Court, the association acted in a reasonable manner under the circumstances.

Once it was established, the "rule-of-reason" defense provided business with an opportunity that it lost no time in using to its best advantage. Given a sufficient amount of time to prepare a defense, almost any business can show that its conduct was "reasonable" under the circumstances. Because of the results that the rule of reason produced, the courts had to reevaluate their approach. The amended approach retained the rule of reason but added a new category: The courts declared some conduct to be so lacking in social value as to be an automatic violation of § 1. These actions, called *per se violations*, tend to contradict directly the economic model of pure competition.

Per se Violations. As noted in the preceding section, the courts restricted the availability of the rule-of-reason defense for alleged Sherman Act violations by the imposition of per se violations. The acts that are deemed to be per se violations are acts that are inherently contradictory to the economic theory of pure competition. If a firm is found guilty of a per se violation, it is not permitted to defend its conduct; it will be found guilty of a violation of the Sherman Act by definition.

Historically, the per se violations under the Sherman Act, § 1, were as follows:

1. Horizontal price fixing (agreements on price among competitors)
2. Vertical price fixing (agreements on price among suppliers and customers)
3. Horizontal market divisions (agreements among competitors as to who can sell in which region)
4. Group boycotts (agreements among competitors not to sell to a particular buyer or not to buy from a particular seller)

Clearly, few businesses would be careless (or stupid) enough actually to overtly agree to such conduct. As a result, the courts have had to infer such agreements from the conduct of the parties. For example, in the area of price fixing, if the courts find that the parties have acted in a manner that amounts to conscious parallelism, a violation is likely to be found. Conscious parallelism, by itself, is not conclusive proof of a violation of § 1. However, it is to be weighed—and weighed heavily— by the courts in determining whether a § 1 violation is present. Generally, conscious parallelism coupled with some other fact, however slight, is sufficient to support a jury verdict of price fixing in violation of § 1. But if the conduct of the firms amounts only to price leadership, no violation is present. How can anyone distinguish conscious parallelism from price leadership? There is no answer to this problem; it poses a Gordian knot for the court every time it is raised.

The two hypothetical cases that follow show the problem of deciding whether conduct is permitted or prohibited.

Alpha, Beta, and Gamma are concrete producers in Minnesota, Iowa, and Wisconsin, respectively. All three must compete with Omega, a concrete producer with plants in all three states. Alpha, Beta, and Gamma agree that each company will sell only in its home state so that each can reduce expenses and thus compete more effectively with Omega. Before the agreement, each of the small companies had 10 percent of the market, and Omega had 70 percent. After the agreement, each of the small companies had 17 percent, and Omega had 49 percent. Despite this apparent increase in competition, the conduct of Alpha, Beta, and Gamma is a per se violation of § 1 of the Sherman Act because it is a horizontal market division.

Al, Bob, and Charlie are cement salesmen in Michigan, Ohio, and Indiana, respectively. They all work for Oscar Concrete, a cement producer with plants in all three states. Oscar tells them that Al is to sell cement only in Michigan, Bob is to sell only in Ohio, and Charlie is to sell only in Indiana. While this is obviously a horizontal market division, since only one firm is involved, it is not a violation of § 1 of the Sherman Act.

"Quick Look" Analysis. The courts have recently added a third method for evaluating allegations that certain conduct violates § 1 of the Sherman Act. This method, the *"quick look"* analysis, allows the defendant firms an opportunity to rebut the presumption that certain conduct is automatically anticompetitive. If the court agrees with the rebuttal evidence of the defendant firms, the court removes the conduct from the per se category and applies a rule-of-reason analysis.

Under the traditional approach, the per se rule absolutely prohibits certain conduct, denying the firms accused of violating the act the opportunity to show that there is a business justification for the conduct. By contrast, the rule of reason allows the accused firms an opportunity to present a business justification, and thus to avoid being held in violation of the statute. When a quick look analysis is applied, the courts allow the firms charged with traditional per se violations to present a business justification. The "quick look," gives these firms the opportunity to show that there *is* a business justification for their conduct, and that they should not be found in violation of the law.

In 1967, the Court ruled that non-price vertical restrictions imposed by a supplier on its customers was a per se illegal market division.[4] The following year, the Court ruled that a maximum resale price-fixing arrangement was also illegal per se.[5] However, by 1979, the Court had begun to restrict the application of the per se doctrine, beginning to apply the quick look analysis to certain types of cases. In *Broadcast Music, Inc.* v. *CBS, Inc.*[6] the Court upheld the right of an association of music copyright holders to establish a common price for the "blanket license" of their compositions. In rejecting the challenge by CBS, the Court stated that, in determining whether to apply the rule of reason or the per se rules, the Court should decide "whether the practice facially appears to be one that would always or almost always tend to restrict competition and decrease output" or is "one designed to increase economic efficiency and render markets more, rather than less, competitive." This formulation provides the framework for the quick look analysis.

To date, the quick look has been limited in its application to some vertical restraints and some cooperative pricing agreements. Thus, while horizontal price-fixing, horizontal market divisions, and group boycotts still are viewed as per se violations, vertical market divisions and maximum price arrangements have been evaluated under the quick look provisions. In addition, some tying arrangements are now being evaluated under a quick look analysis. (This expansion did not bode well for Microsoft in its antitrust battle with the Justice Department, although the Microsoft case had not been completely resolved as we went to print.) The businesses charged with violations of § 1 of the Sherman Act are allowed the opportunity to rebut the presumption of anticompetitive effect in these cases. If they are successful, the case is decided under the rule of reason. If they are not, the conduct is found to be a violation of § 1 of the Sherman Act.

The following case is a recent Supreme Court application of the quick look test. In deciding this case, the Court overturned a prior decision that utilized the per se doctrine. See if you agree with the result the Court reached in this case.

39.1

STATE OIL COMPANY V. KHAN
522 U.S. 3 (1997)

FACTS Barkat U. Khan . . . entered into an agreement with petitioner, State Oil Company, to lease and operate a gas station and convenience store owned by State Oil. The agreement provided that respondents would obtain the station's gasoline supply from State Oil at a price equal to a suggested retail price set by State Oil, less a margin of 3.25 cents per gallon. Under the agreement, respondents could charge any amount for gasoline sold to the station's customers, but if the price charged was higher than State Oil's suggested retail price, the excess was to be rebated to State Oil. Respondents could sell gasoline for less than State Oil's suggested retail price, but any such decrease would reduce their 3.25 cents-per-gallon margin. About a year after respondents began operating the gas station, they fell behind in lease payments. State Oil then gave notice of its intent to terminate the agreement and commenced a state court proceeding to evict respondents. At State Oil's request, the state court appointed a receiver to operate the gas station. The receiver operated the station for several months without being subject to the price restraints in respondents' agreement with State Oil. According to respondents, the receiver obtained an overall profit margin in excess of 3.25 cents per gallon by lowering the price of regular-grade gasoline and raising the price of premium grades. Respondents sued State Oil . . . alleging in part that State Oil had engaged in price fixing in violation of § 1 of the Sherman Act by preventing respondents from raising or lowering retail gas prices. According to the complaint, but for the agreement with State Oil, respondents could have charged different prices based on the grades of gasoline, in the same way that the receiver had, thereby achieving increased sales and profits. State Oil responded that the agreement did not actually prevent respondents from setting gasoline prices, and that, in substance, respondents did not allege a violation of antitrust laws by their claim that State Oil's suggested retail price was not optimal. The District Court found that the allegations in the complaint did not state a *per se* violation of the Sherman Act because they did not establish the sort of "manifestly anticompetitive implications or pernicious effect on competition" that would justify *per se* prohibition of State Oil's conduct . . . The District Court held that respondents had not shown that a difference in gasoline pricing would have increased the station's sales; nor had they shown that State Oil had market power or that its pricing provisions affected competition in a relevant market . . . Accordingly, the District Court entered summary judgment for State Oil . . . The Court of Appeals for the Seventh Circuit reversed . . . The court first noted that the agreement between respondents and State Oil did indeed fix maximum gasoline prices by making it "worthless" for respondents to exceed the suggested retail prices . . . After reviewing legal and economic aspects of price fixing, the court concluded that State Oil's pricing scheme was a *per se* antitrust violation under *Albrecht* v. *Herald Co.* . . . Although the Court of Appeals characterized *Albrecht* as "unsound when decided" and "inconsistent with later decisions" of this Court, it felt constrained to follow that decision . . . the court found that respondents could have suffered antitrust injury from not being able to adjust gasoline prices. We granted certiorari to consider . . . whether State Oil's conduct constitutes a *per se* violation of the Sherman Act . . .

ISSUE Is vertical maximum price fixing a *per se* violation of § 1 of the Sherman Act, as held in *Albrecht* v. *Herald Co.*?

HOLDING No. Albrecht should be overruled, and vertical maximum price fixing should be evaluated under the rule of reason.

REASONING Although the Sherman Act prohibits every agreement "in restraint of trade," this Court has long recognized that Congress intended to outlaw only unreasonable restraints . . . As a consequence, most antitrust claims are analyzed under a "rule of reason," according to which the finder of fact must decide whether the questioned practice imposes an unreasonable restraint on competition, taking into account a variety of factors, including specific information about the relevant business, its condition before and after the restraint was imposed, and the restraint's history, nature, and effect . . . Some types of restraints, however, have such predictable and pernicious anticompetitive effect, and such limited potential for procompetitive benefit, that they are deemed unlawful *per se* . . . *Per se* treatment is appropriate "once experience with a particular kind of restraint enables the Court to predict with confidence that the rule of reason will condemn it." . . . Thus, we have expressed reluctance to adopt *per se* rules with regard

continued

39.1

STATE OIL COMPANY V. KHAN, *continued*
522 U.S. 3 (1997)

to "restraints imposed in the context of business relationships where the economic impact of certain practices is not immediately obvious." . . . *Albrecht* involved a newspaper publisher who had granted exclusive territories to independent carriers subject to their adherence to a maximum price on resale of the newspapers to the public . . . the Court concluded that it was *per se* unlawful for the publisher to fix the maximum resale price of its newspapers . . . *Albrecht* was animated in part by the fear that vertical maximum price fixing could allow suppliers to discriminate against certain dealers, restrict the services that dealers could afford to offer customers, or disguise minimum price fixing schemes. . . . The Court rejected the notion . . . that, because the newspaper publisher "granted exclusive territories, a price ceiling was necessary to protect the public from price gouging by dealers who had monopoly power in their own territories." . . . We recognize that the *Albrecht* decision presented a number of theoretical justifications for a *per se* rule against vertical maximum price fixing. But criticism of those premises abounds. . . . Not only are the potential injuries cited in *Albrecht* less serious than the Court imagined, the *per se* rule established therein could in fact exacerbate problems related to the unrestrained exercise of market power by monopolist-dealers. Indeed, both courts and antitrust scholars have noted that *Albrecht*'s rule may actually harm consumers and manufacturers. . . . After reconsidering *Albrecht*'s rationale and the substantial criticism the decision has received, however, we conclude that there is insufficient economic justification for *per se* invalidation of vertical maximum price fixing. . . . [T]here remains the question whether *Albrecht* deserves continuing respect under the doctrine of *stare decisis*. The Court of Appeals was correct in applying that principle despite disagreement with *Albrecht*, for it is this Court's prerogative alone to overrule one of its precedents. We approach the reconsideration of decisions of this Court with the utmost caution. *Stare decisis* reflects "a policy judgment that 'in most matters it is more important that the applicable rule of law be settled than that it be settled right.'" . . . This Court has expressed its reluctance to overrule decisions involving statutory interpretation . . . and has acknowledged that *stare decisis* concerns are at their acme in cases involving

property and contract rights . . . Both of those concerns are arguably relevant in this case. But *"stare decisis* is not an inexorable command." . . . In the area of antitrust law, there is a competing interest, well-represented in this Court's decisions, in recognizing and adapting to changed circumstances and the lessons of accumulated experience. Thus, the general presumption that legislative changes should be left to Congress has less force with respect to the Sherman Act in light of the accepted view that Congress "expected the courts to give shape to the statute's broad mandate by drawing on common-law tradition." . . . As we have explained, the term "restraint of trade," as used in § 1, also "invokes the common law itself, and not merely the static content that the common law had assigned to the term in 1890." . . . Accordingly, this Court has reconsidered its decisions construing the Sherman Act when the theoretical underpinnings of those decisions are called into serious question . . . Now that we confront *Albrecht* directly, we find its conceptual foundations gravely weakened. In overruling *Albrecht*, we of course do not hold that all vertical maximum price fixing is *per se* lawful. Instead, vertical maximum price fixing, like the majority of commercial arrangements subject to the antitrust laws, should be evaluated under the rule of reason.

BUSINESS CONSIDERATIONS Does the development of the quick look analysis favor businesses that are seeking to expand their market power or control at the expense of public policy considerations favoring a competitive economy? Should a business be willing to take a chance in previously prohibited areas of conduct in the hope that the quick look analysis will expand to other *per se* areas?

ETHICAL CONSIDERATIONS Is it more ethical for the courts to follow precedents, which provide the guidelines under which businesses have been operating for quite some time, or to change the interpretation of certain areas, eliminating some traditional *per se* violations? What ethical issues are raised by a decision in which the court abandons a traditional interpretation of a traditional legal area?

Section 2: Monopolizing and Attempts to Monopolize

Section 2 of the Sherman Act is nearly as brief as § 1 and is equally as broad. Section 2 makes the following provision:

> Every person who shall monopolize, or attempt to monopolize, or combine or conspire with any other person or persons, to monopolize any part of the trade or commerce among the several States, or with foreign nations, shall be deemed guilty of a misdemeanor.

Note that § 2 can be violated either by one person acting alone or by multiple parties acting in concert. In contrast, § 1 can be violated only by multiple parties acting together. (To avoid confusion, remember that it takes two people to violate § 1, while it takes only one person to violate § 2.)

Many people have the mistaken idea that monopolies are prohibited by § 2. In fact, no law prohibits having monopoly power. The prohibition in § 2 is against monopolizing, that is, seeking a monopoly or attempting to keep a monopoly once one is attained. Either act is monopolizing and is illegal under § 2. Having a monopoly, however, is not illegal.

If a firm is found to dominate an industry, it may also be found to possess monopoly power. As a rule of thumb, control of 70 percent or more of the *relevant market* is deemed to be monopoly power. However, defining the relevant market may be difficult. In determining the relevant market, the courts must determine the relevant *geographic* market—where the product is sold—and the relevant *product* market—what is being sold or provided by the seller. In so doing, the courts examine the *product* produced by the challenged firm, *substitute* goods produced by other firms, and the elasticity of demand between the challenged product and the substitutes. If the courts find that the product in question controls 70 percent or more of this relevant market, the challenged firm possesses monopoly power under the courts' interpretation of § 2 of the Sherman Act. If the firm possesses less than 70 percent of the relevant market, it lacks monopoly power under § 2 of the Sherman Act.

United States v. E. I. DuPont de Nemours and Co.[7] is a landmark in U.S. antitrust law involving relevant product market. DuPont acquired the exclusive U.S. right to produce cellophane from the French patent holder of the process. By 1947, duPont had acquired 75 percent of the cellophane market in the United States, which led the Justice Department to file charges against duPont for violating § 2 of the Sherman Act. At trial, duPont admitted that it controlled the market for *cellophane* but denied that it controlled the relevant product market. According to duPont, the relevant product market was for *flexible wrapping materials,* including aluminum foil, wax paper, saran wrap, and various other materials. In this broader market, duPont only had a 20 percent market share. The court agreed with duPont's argument, establishing a precedent for the determination of relevant product market.

When a dominant position in the relevant product market is present, there is a presumption that § 2 was, or is, violated. However, a number of defenses exist to rebut this presumption. The dominant firm may argue that it is not attempting to retain its power, or that it acquired its position legally, or that its position was "thrust upon" it. Any of these defenses is sufficient to prevent a § 2 prosecution.

The next hypothetical case shows how the defense can be applied:

> Ralph developed a new product, Kleenzall, which does what other soaps or cleansers do, except that it does it better and is cheaper. Kleenzall is good for washing dishes,

39.1 | SALES/ MANAGEMENT

CALL-IMAGE TECHNOLOGY

DOES CIT HAVE A MONOPOLY?

The growth of Call-Image has been beyond the wildest dreams of CIT. Videophones currently comprise 20 percent of the domestic telephone market, and CIT controls more than 92 percent of the videophone market. Unfortunately, Amy has recently learned that the firm will be investigated by the Justice Department, which believes that CIT violated § 2 of the Sherman Act in gaining its dominant position. The family does not understand how the firm can be viewed as a monopoly when they control less than 20 percent of the market, and they also don't understand why the Justice Department thinks they have improperly gained their share of the market. They have asked you to explain this, and then to tell them what you think they should do. What advice will you give them?

BUSINESS CONSIDERATIONS Is there any problem with a business gaining a dominant position in its market? Should a business aim for a lesser degree of control to avoid potential problems under the Sherman Act, or should it maximize its potential, dealing with the Sherman Act problems if or when they arise?

ETHICAL CONSIDERATIONS Section 2 of the Sherman Act prohibits monopolizing, and a *virtual-monopoly* position is defined by the courts as controlling 70 percent or more of the relevant product market. Economic theory states that a monopoly exists when an industry only contains one firm. Is it ethical for the courts to define a virtual-monopoly position differently than economic theory defines monopoly position, when the purpose of the Sherman Act is to provide for industrial conduct that is more in line with economic competition?

clothes, floors, walls, and even hair. Kleenzall is such a good product that Ralph has 95 percent of every cleanser and soap market. The major soap producers sue Ralph for monopolizing the industry in violation of the Sherman Act, § 2. The court, however, finds that Ralph is not guilty. He did nothing wrong in acquiring his market share. Rather, this monopoly was "thrust upon" him by sheer efficiency. However, if Ralph subsequently takes steps to prevent other firms from entering the cleanser market or acts in any manner that seems to be precluding or preventing competition, he may be found guilty of monopolizing. Possessing his monopoly power is legal, but attempting to retain it is illegal!

Remedies

When a Sherman Act violation is shown, both criminal and civil remedies are available. An individual can be fined up to $100,000 and can receive up to three years in prison; a corporation that is convicted can be fined up to $1 million. Also, an injunction can be issued against the prohibited conduct. As a final disincentive, any harmed parties can recover treble damages plus attorney's fees. This means an injured firm can take its damages, multiply them by three, and then add attorney's fees. In at least one case, damages assessed exceeded $200 million. Needless to say, such damages strongly discourage prohibited conduct.

THE CLAYTON ACT

By 1914, Congress realized that the Sherman Act alone was not sufficient to solve the major business problems of the country. The Sherman Act was remedial in nature: If a problem existed, the act could be used to help correct the problem. Unfortunately, it is possible (if not probable) that by the time the "remedy" is sought, the injured party has suffered irreparable harm or has ceased to exist as a business entity. Nothing, however, was available to prevent a problem from developing. In an effort to correct this regulatory deficiency, Congress decided to enact some preventative legislation. The result was the Clayton Act, which was designed to nip problems "in their incipiency." The Clayton Act has four major provisions, each addressing a different potential problem.

Section 2: Price Discrimination

The first regulating section of the Clayton Act, § 2, prohibits price discrimination. The original § 2 made it illegal for a *seller* to discriminate in price between different purchasers unless the price difference could be justified by a difference in costs. This provision soon placed a number of sellers in a terrible bind. Major purchasers often demanded special prices from sellers. If the sellers refused, they lost the business; if they agreed, they violated the law. This placed some sellers in an untenable position, while shielding the buyers—who often initiated the price discrimination—from liability, since the law only applied to the seller. As a result, § 2 was amended in 1936 when the Robinson–Patman Act became law. Under this act, *buyers* were prohibited from knowingly accepting a discriminatory price. In addition, the act prohibited buyers from knowingly accepting indirect benefits such as dummy brokerage fees and promotional kickbacks. And, of course, sellers were still prohibited from granting discriminatory prices to their customers absent a cost differential justifying the price.

The mere fact that a different price is granted to different buyers is not enough to assure a conviction for price discrimination. In fact, a number of potential defenses exist.

1. The person accused of price discrimination can defend against the charge by showing that he or she is meeting, but not beating, the price being offered by a competitor.
2. The accused can also defend by showing that the lower price is being offered because of obsolescence, seasonal variations, or damage to the goods being sold.
3. The accused can also show that the price differential is based on legitimate cost savings based on quantity discounts, and that such discounts are generally available to any other customers who place orders of sufficient size.

FTC v. *Standard Oil Co. (of Indiana)*,[8] a landmark opinion, involved an allegation of price discrimination and a defense of meeting—but not beating—the competition. Standard Oil was selling gasoline to four large "jobbers" in the Detroit area at a lower price than it was selling gasoline to numerous smaller competitors in the same market. Standard showed that its lower price for the "jobbers" was only to meet—and not to beat—the price of a competitor, thus allowing Standard to retain its customers. The court accepted this defense, finding that Standard Oil was not guilty of price discrimination.

The Robinson–Patman Act also changed the standards needed to show a violation. Under the original § 2, it was necessary to show that general competition had been harmed, but under the Robinson–Patman Act, it is sufficient to prosecute on a showing that a competitor was injured. The following example illustrates this point:

> Bill's Bathtub Boutique is the largest customer of Paula's Porcelain Palace. Bill's biggest competitor is Dan's Discount Tub Store. Bill tells Paula that unless she gives him a 10 percent price reduction, he will take his business elsewhere. If Paula gives this price reduction to Bill but not to Dan, both Bill and Paula will be in violation of the Robinson–Patman Act.

In a recent Puerto Rico case,[9] an interesting Robinson–Patman issue was raised. Caribe BMW purchased new automobiles directly from the manufacturer. Caribe's competitors in the market purchased their new BMWs from a wholly owned subsidiary of the manufacturer and were able to purchase at a lower price than that offered to Caribe. The court ruled that a manufacturer and its wholly owned

39.2 | MANAGEMENT/ MANUFACTURING

TYING PRODUCTS

A regional manufacturer of answering machines has approached CIT with what it considers a "can't miss" deal. The manufacturer wants to produce an answering machine that has video- as well as audiotape capabilities and that can only be used with Call-Image videophones. According to the president of this company, each firm can use the success of the other firm to gain a larger market share in their respective industries. Although the idea is intriguing, the family is afraid there may be some legal implication they have overlooked. They ask you what you think of the idea. What advice will you give them?

BUSINESS CONSIDERATIONS What potential problems could arise under the various antitrust laws from tying your product to the products of another firm? Could this be considered an attempt by each firm to monopolize its respective industry? Is this more or less of a problem than would be faced if a firm tied one of its products to another of its products?

ETHICAL CONSIDERATIONS In the United States, basically, a firm must act and then await results if it is considering conduct that may or may not violate antitrust provisions. In the European Union, firms can ask for a "negative clearance," seeking advance permission to do something that eventually may be determined to violate the Union's rules of competition. Is it more ethical to be allowed to seek advance permission, or to act and then wait to see if the government will challenge the conduct? Why?

subsidiary are a single entity for purposes of applying the Robinson–Patman Act so that there was a discriminatory pricing practice in effect, entitling Caribe to remedies for violation of the act.

Section 3: Exclusive Dealings and Tying Arrangements

The second major prohibition under the Clayton Act is found in § 3. This section bans exclusive-dealing contracts and tying arrangements when their "effect may be to substantially lessen competition or tend to create a monopoly." Notice again the preventive intent of the act: Actual harm need not be shown, merely the *likelihood* that harm will eventually occur.

In an *exclusive-dealing contract*, one party requires the other party to deal with him, and him alone. For example, the seller tells the buyer that unless the buyer buys only from the seller, and not from the seller's competitors, the seller will not deal with the buyer. For such a demand to be effective, the seller must be in a very powerful market position.

In a *tying arrangement*, one party—usually the seller—refuses to sell one product unless the buyer also takes a second product or service from the seller. For example, a manufacturer of cosmetics might refuse to sell a facial moisturizer unless the buyer agrees to purchase the manufacturer's soap. Usually for this sort of arrangement to work, the seller needs a highly valued, unique product to which he or she can "tie" a commonly available product. As a defense to a charge that such an arrangement lessens competition or creates a monopoly, the seller may attempt to show that the tied product is tied for quality-control reasons. To do so, the seller must prove that no competitors produce a competing product that works adequately with the controlled product.

The Supreme Court has ruled that a "not insubstantial" amount of commerce must be affected in order to have an illegal tying arrangement.[10] The Ninth Circuit went even further, ruling that there is no requirement for multiple purchasers in order to have an illegal tying arrangement,[11] so long as the effect on commerce is not insubstantial. The amount involved was approximately $100,000 per year for an indeterminate number of years, and the Court ruled that such an amount was sufficiently substantial to allow the trial to proceed even though only one firm was precluded from the market due to the tying arrangement. This could, potentially, open up a number of claims for damages due to tying arrangements by firms that believed there had to be multiple purchasers affected before Section 3 of the Clayton Act was applicable.

YOU BE THE JUDGE

IT'S ABOUT TO BE A SMALLER (INTERNET) WORLD

The Walt Disney Company recently announced plans to merge with Infoseek, one of the earliest Internet firms, in an effort to consolidate all of its online operations into a single enterprise. The merger will provide Disney with a large and powerful Internet outlet, go.com, designed to compete with such other Internet portals as Yahoo.com and AOL.com. Disney and Infoseek are already operating go.com jointly, and have been doing so for the past year. When the merger plans were announced, Disney stock edged slightly higher, while Infoseek shares declined in value by nearly 11 percent.

Assume that a group of Infoseek shareholders have decided to challenge this proposed merger and have filed suit in *your* court. Their lawsuit alleges that the merger violates § 7 of the Clayton Act. How will *you* rule in this case?[12]

BUSINESS CONSIDERATIONS Why would a business that is already involved in a joint operation with another firm want to merge with that other firm? Why would the target firm or its shareholders possibly object to the proposed merger? Does this sort of merger signal the potential beginning of a concentration trend in the Internet portal market?

ETHICAL CONSIDERATIONS Is it ethical for a large operation such as Disney to enter into a joint venture with a smaller firm and then to decide to take over the smaller firm via merger a short time later? From an ethical perspective, should such a merger be prohibited unless initiated by the smaller firm?

SOURCE: *The Roanoke Times* (13 July 1999), p. A7.

Section 7: Antimerger Provisions

The third major section of the Clayton Act, § 7, concerns mergers. As originally written, the only prohibited type of merger was one in which the stock of another firm was acquired with the effect "substantially to lessen competition, or [to] tend to create a monopoly." This prohibition was so narrow that it was rather easily evaded by merging firms.

To broaden the scope of the law, Congress amended § 7 in 1950 by passing the Cellar–Kefauver Act. The amended § 7 prohibits the acquisition of stock or assets of another firm that may tend to have a negative effect on any line of commerce. As a result, firms are now subject to § 7 in almost any type of merger—horizontal, vertical, or conglomerate. A horizontal merger is one between competing firms; a vertical merger is one between a firm and one of its major suppliers or customers; a conglomerate merger is one between firms in two noncompetitive industries.

Not all mergers are prohibited by § 7. The government must establish that if the merger is allowed, the result "may be to substantially lessen competition" in an industry. For example, as a challenge to a merger, the government might argue that a "concentration trend" has been established or that one of the firms was a "potential entrant" into one of the industries affected by the merger. The government would thus argue that the industry after the proposed merger was less competitive than the industry prior to the proposed merger. The burden then shifts to the defendants to justify the proposed merger by showing that the effect is not a likely substantial lessening of competition. For example, the merging firms might raise the "failing-company" doctrine, showing that without the merger one of the firms would have gone out of business. If one of the firms would have gone out of business anyway, the same number of firms remains in the industry following the merger as would have existed without the merger, and jobs were saved with the firm that would otherwise have ceased to exist. The following example illustrates the failing-company doctrine.

> *Fred's Stereo is in severe financial difficulty. Irv's Interstate Sound Store, the largest stereo dealer in the region, buys Fred's. Under the failing-company doctrine, if Fred's would have gone bankrupt, the merger with Irv's is probably permissible. (Of course, such a merger would be less likely to be challenged if the firm taking over Fred's had not been the largest competitor in the region. In such a case, the merged firms would be better able to compete with Irv's, the largest firm, and might be able to show that competition would be enhanced with the merger even if Fred's was not about to go out of business.)*

The following case involved a challenge to a proposed merger by one of the competitors of one of the merging firms *despite* the approval of the merger by the Department of Justice.

39.2

ALLIEDSIGNAL, INC. V. B.F. GOODRICH CO.
1999 U.S. APP. LEXIS 13993 (7TH CIR. 1999)

FACTS An aircraft landing system is composed of three component parts: the landing gear, the wheels and brakes (sold together as a package), and the brake control system. The industry is currently dominated by a few large firms. AlliedSignal manufactures wheels and brakes. B.F. Goodrich manufactures landing gear and wheels and brakes. Coltec manufactures landing gear through its subsidiary Menasco Aerospace, Ltd. The only other major player in this industry is a French company which manufactures landing gear under the name Messier-Dowty, and wheels and brakes under the name Messier-Bugatti. AlliedSignal and Coltec currently operate under a Strategic Alliance Agreement ("SAA") which provides for cooperation between AlliedSignal and Coltec in the preparation of joint bids on landing systems. Their principal competitor in these bids is B.F. Goodrich, which generally pairs its wheels and brakes with its own landing gear. The proposed merger between B.F. Goodrich and Coltec would bring Coltec's aircraft landing gear division under the control of B.F. Goodrich and result in a single large domestic manufacturer of aircraft landing gear . . . AlliedSignal alleges several harms resulting from the proposed merger. First, in preparing joint bids and the integrated landing systems which result,

AlliedSignal and Coltec have shared confidential proprietary information. AlliedSignal is concerned that B.F. Goodrich would have access to this information once Coltec is under B.F. Goodrich's control. In its capacity as a landing gear purchaser, AlliedSignal alleges that B.F. Goodrich could use its market power to charge it uncompetitive prices for landing gear. Last, AlliedSignal fears that B.F. Goodrich could leverage its dominant post-merger position in domestic landing gear production to favor B.F. Goodrich's own wheels and brakes over those of AlliedSignal in the formation of integrated landing systems. Crane Co., Eldec Corp. and Hydro-Aire, Inc. . . . are sellers of component parts for landing gear systems to both Coltec and B.F. Goodrich. They join AlliedSignal's Clayton Act claim out of a concern that the merger will allow B.F. Goodrich monopoly buying power (monopsony) for their goods. Neither the Federal Trade Commission nor the Department of Defense (which reviewed the merger because of the parties' status as defense contractors) has objected to the merger. . . . As explored more fully below, AlliedSignal claims antitrust injury in part from an increase in the price of landing gear it purchases as a landing systems integrator. The SAA, though it does provide for shared information and

39.2

ALLIEDSIGNAL, INC. V. B.F. GOODRICH CO., *continued*
1999 U.S. APP. LEXIS 13993 (7TH CIR. 1999)

cooperation, does not regulate the price Coltec may charge for its landing gear. Therefore, B.F. Goodrich-Coltec could fully comply with the SAA and still cause AlliedSignal antitrust injury by charging uncompetitive prices. . . . To show some likelihood of success on the merits of its Section 7 claim, AlliedSignal had to demonstrate (1) that the effect of the merger had some likelihood of substantially lessening competition or tending to create a monopoly . . . and (2) that AlliedSignal had some likelihood of being within the class of plaintiffs with standing to assert the likely antitrust injuries . . . The district court found that AlliedSignal had made the requisite showing of likely anticompetitive effects and found two possible bases for AlliedSignal's antitrust standing. After concluding that AlliedSignal would suffer irreparable injury in the absence of a preliminary injunction and then balancing the relative harms to the respective parties along with the public interest, the district court concluded that a preliminary injunction was warranted. As noted above, we review the district court's decision for an abuse of discretion.

ISSUE Did the proposed merger between B.F. Goodrich, Coltec Industries, and Menasco Aerospace, Ltd. violate § 7 of the Clayton Act?

HOLDING There was an adequate showing of potential anticompetitive harm to permit the court to affirm a preliminary injunction staying the proposed merger, pending a bench trial on the merits regarding the merger.

REASONING Section 7 of the Clayton Act prohibits mergers the effect of which "may be to substantially lessen competition, or to tend to create a monopoly." . . . AlliedSignal defines three product markets in which the B.F. Goodrich-Coltec merger may lessen competition: (1) the worldwide market for wide body landing gear; (2) the worldwide market for narrow body landing gear; and (3) the worldwide market for military landing gear. AlliedSignal observes that the merger would reduce the worldwide number of firms that design and manufacture landing gear for each of these three markets from three to two and that after the merger, B.F. Goodrich-Coltec would control approximately 64% of the worldwide market for landing gear for wide-body jets, 44% of the worldwide market for narrow-body jets, and 59% of the world-

wide market for landing gear for U.S. military jets . . . Based on this evidence, the district court found that AlliedSignal had made a sufficient showing of a likely Section 7 violation to warrant a preliminary injunction. B.F. Goodrich raises two objections to the district court's finding that the merger would likely have anticompetitive effects. First, B.F. Goodrich argues that although B.F. Goodrich-Coltec might possess market power in landing gear, the airplane manufacturers will continue to possess overwhelming buying power and will be able to squelch any monopoly rents B.F. Goodrich attempts to extract. Second, B.F. Goodrich relies on the failure of either the FTC or the Department of Defense to object to the merger as evidence that post-merger competition in the landing gear market will remain robust. Neither of these objections convinces us that the district court abused its discretion in concluding that AlliedSignal had shown a sufficient likelihood of a Section 7 violation . . . Courts do not generally defer to an agency's decision not to challenge a merger . . . To the contrary, federal regulators will not necessarily challenge every potentially troublesome merger, which is why Congress made private enforcement "an integral part of the congressional plan for protecting competition," . . . The district court did not abuse its discretion in concluding that the failure of the FTC or DOD to object to the merger does not bar AlliedSignal's private enforcement action. Having concluded that the district court did not abuse its discretion in finding a sufficient likelihood of a Section 7 violation, we turn to AlliedSignal's antitrust standing. Section 4 of the Clayton Act sets forth the group of persons who may maintain private damages actions under the antitrust law. . . . [I]t is well-settled that "Congress did not intend the antitrust laws to provide a remedy in damages for all injuries that might conceivably be traced to an anti-trust violation." . . . The doctrine of antitrust standing therefore limits the class of plaintiffs under § 4 to those who can show "a direct link between the antitrust violation and the antitrust injury." . . . The Supreme Court has identified several factors to be considered in determining whether a plaintiff is the proper party to bring a private action under the antitrust laws: (1) the causal connection between the antitrust violation and the plaintiff's injury; (2) the nature of the plaintiff's injury and the relationship between the plaintiff's injury and the type of activity

continued

39.2

ALLIEDSIGNAL, INC. V. B.F. GOODRICH CO., *continued*
1999 U.S. APP. LEXIS 13993 (7TH CIR. 1999)

sought to be redressed under the antitrust laws; and (3) the speculative nature of the plaintiff's claim for damages and the potential for duplicative recovery or complex apportionment of damages . . . Given the early procedural stage of this case and the necessarily tentative nature of the district court's conclusions, we do not believe that the district judge abused his discretion in concluding that AlliedSignal has some likelihood of showing antitrust standing. B.F. Goodrich argues that a preliminary injunction should not have issued because it has promised to hold separate the landing gear division of Coltec from B.F. Goodrich's landing gear facility until at least the end of August 1999 and hence any harm to AlliedSignal and the Crane Plaintiffs resulting from the merger would not be irreparable. On the basis of this record, we cannot definitively determine that the proposed separation between Coltec's landing gear division and the remainder of Coltec would adequately preserve the status quo pending a trial on the merits of the antitrust claim. In addition, if the merger were consummated with the Coltec landing gear division held

separate, this might unduly prejudice the scope of a possible remedy should the merger ultimately be found to violate Section 7. The district court did not abuse its discretion in finding a sufficient likelihood of irreparable harm. The district court's grant of a preliminary injunction is AFFIRMED. The case is REMANDED for further proceedings consistent with this opinion.

BUSINESS CONSIDERATIONS Why would a business want to merge with one of its largest competitors? Why might a business be hesitant to merge with one of its largest competitors?

ETHICAL CONSIDERATIONS How does a proposed merger affect each of the four constituent groups of a business? If some of the constituent groups will benefit from a proposed merger but others will be harmed, what should the firm do from an ethical perspective?

Section 8: Interlocking Directorates

The final substantive section of the Clayton Act is § 8. This section prohibits *interlocking directorates*. In other words, no one may sit on the boards of directors of two or more competing corporations if either of the firms has capital and surplus in excess of $1 million and if a merger between them violates any antitrust law.

THE FEDERAL TRADE COMMISSION ACT

The year 1914 was a very busy one for antitrust regulation. Congress passed not only the Clayton Act but also the Federal Trade Commission Act. The Federal Trade Commission Act did two important things:

1. It created the Federal Trade Commission (FTC) to enforce antitrust laws, especially the Clayton Act.
2. In § 5, it provided a broad area of prohibitions to close loopholes left by other statutes.

Section 5 of the act prohibits "unfair methods of competition" and "unfair and deceptive trade practices." This broad language permits the FTC to regulate conduct that technically might be beyond the reach of the other, more specific antitrust statutes. The area of unfair and deceptive trade practices was intentionally made broad and somewhat vague to grant the FTC the leeway to proceed against any commercial practices that seem to be unfair or deceptive under the circumstances. If the statute is specific, businesspeople will find methods to circumvent it, methods that may be unfair or deceptive but within the technical limits of the law. The strength of the law has been its breadth, as well as the willingness of the FTC to attack practices that had been followed for many years.

To further strengthen the FTC position, a violation can be found without proof of any actual deception. A mere showing that there is a "fair possibility" that the public will be deceived is sufficient to establish that the conduct is unfair and deceptive. In addition, if a representation made by a company is ambiguous, with one honest meaning and one deceptive meaning, the FTC will treat it as deceptive and as a material aspect of the transaction so that remedies are available.

If the FTC opposes a business practice as unfair or deceptive, it issues a cease-and-desist order. The business must stop the challenged conduct or face a fine for disobeying the order. The fine is $5,000 per violation. This may sound small, but realize that each day the order is ignored constitutes a separate violation. Thus, ignoring the order for one week costs $35,000 in fines; for a month, $150,000 in fines; and so on.

In recent years, the FTC has become particularly concerned about two business practices: deceptive advertising and bait-and-switch advertising. In an effort to force truth in advertising, the FTC has been carefully studying the commercials run by corporations and, in many cases in which the advertising was deemed especially misleading, ordering corrective advertising.

The following case involves an FTC attack on "misleading advertising," and the Court's rejection of the quick look analysis in favor of a more detailed rule-of-reason analysis for the facts.

39.3

CALIFORNIA DENTAL ASSOCIATION V. FEDERAL TRADE COMMISSION
526 U.S. 756 (1999)

FACTS The CDA is a voluntary nonprofit association of local dental societies to which some 19,000 dentists belong, including about three-quarters of those practicing in the State . . . The dentists who belong to the CDA through these associations agree to abide by a Code of Ethics (Code) including the following § 10:

Although any dentist may advertise, no dentist shall advertise or solicit patients in any form of communication in a manner that is false or misleading in any material respect. In order to properly serve the public, dentists should represent themselves in a manner that contributes to the esteem of the public. Dentists should not misrepresent their training and competence in any way that would be false or misleading in any material respect. . . .

The CDA has issued a number of advisory opinions interpreting this section, and through separate advertising guidelines intended to help members comply with the Code and with state law the CDA has advised its dentists of disclosures they must make under state law when engaging in discount advertising. Responsibility for enforcing the Code rests in the first instance with the local dental societies, to which applicants for CDA membership must submit copies of their own advertisements and those of their employers or referral services to assure compliance with the Code. The local societies also actively seek information about potential Code violations by applicants or CDA members. Applicants who refuse to withdraw or revise objectionable advertisements may be denied membership; and members who, after a hearing, remain similarly recalcitrant are subject to censure, suspension, or expulsion from the CDA . . . The Commission brought a complaint against the CDA, alleging that it applied its guidelines so as to restrict truthful, nondeceptive advertising, and so violated § 5 of the FTC Act . . . The complaint alleged that the CDA had unreasonably restricted two types of advertising:

continued

39.3

CALIFORNIA DENTAL ASSOCIATION V. FEDERAL TRADE COMMISSION, *continued*
526 U.S. 756 (1999)

price advertising, particularly discounted fees, and advertising relating to the quality of dental services . . . An Administrative Law Judge (ALJ) held the Commission to have jurisdiction over the CDA . . . He found that, although there had been no proof that the CDA exerted market power, no such proof was required to establish an antitrust violation under *In re Mass. Bd. of Registration in Optometry* . . . since the CDA had unreasonably prevented members and potential members from using truthful, nondeceptive advertising, all to the detriment of both dentists and consumers of dental services. He accordingly found a violation of § 5 of the FTC Act . . . The Commission adopted the factual findings of the ALJ except for his conclusion that the CDA lacked market power . . . The Commission treated the CDA's restrictions on discount advertising as illegal per se . . . In the alternative, the Commission held the price advertising (as well as the nonprice) restrictions to be violations of the Sherman and FTC Acts under an abbreviated rule-of-reason analysis . . . The Court of Appeals for the Ninth Circuit affirmed, sustaining the Commission's assertion of jurisdiction over the CDA and its ultimate conclusion on the merits . . . We granted certiorari to resolve conflicts among the Circuits on the Commission's jurisdiction over a nonprofit professional association and the occasions for abbreviated rule-of-reason analysis . . .

ISSUES Does the jurisdiction of the FTC extend to the California Dental Association (CDA), a nonprofit professional association? Does a "quick look" analysis suffice to justify finding that certain advertising restrictions adopted by the CDA violated the antitrust laws?

HOLDINGS Yes, the Commission's jurisdiction under the Federal Trade Commission Act extends to an association that provides substantial economic benefit to its for-profit members. No. Since any anticompetitive effects of given restraints are far from intuitively obvious, the rule of reason demands a more thorough enquiry into the consequences of those restraints than the Court of Appeals performed.

REASONING The FTC Act gives the Commission authority over "persons, partnerships, or corporations," . . . and defines "corporation" to include "any company . . . or association, incorporated or unincorporated, without shares of capital or capital stock or certificates of interest, except partnerships, which is organized to carry on business for its own profit or that of its members," . . . the Commission has long held that some circumstances give it jurisdiction over an entity that seeks no profit for itself. . . . The FTC Act is at pains to include not only an entity "organized to carry on business for its own profit," . . . but also one that carries on business for the profit "of its members," . . . Nonprofit entities organized on behalf of for-profit members have the same capacity and derivatively, at least, the same incentives as for-profit organizations to engage in unfair methods of competition or unfair and deceptive acts. It may even be possible that a nonprofit entity up to no good would have certain advantages, not only over a for-profit member but over a for-profit membership organization as well; it would enjoy the screen of superficial disinterest while devoting itself to serving the interests of its members without concern for doing more than breaking even . . . In a market for professional services, in which advertising is relatively rare and the comparability of service packages not easily established, the difficulty for customers or potential competitors to get and verify information about the price and availability of services magnifies the dangers to competition associated with misleading advertising. What is more, the quality of professional services tends to resist either calibration or monitoring by individual patients or clients, partly because of the specialized knowledge required to evaluate the ser-vices, and partly because of the difficulty in determining whether, and the degree to which, an outcome is attributable to the quality of services (like a poor job of tooth-filling) or to something else (like a very tough walnut) . . . Patients' attachments to particular professionals, the rationality of which is difficult to assess, complicate the picture even further . . . The existence of such significant challenges to informed decision making by the customer for professional services immediately suggests that advertising restrictions arguably protecting patients from misleading or irrelevant advertising call for more than cursory treatment as obviously comparable to classic horizontal agreements to limit output or price competition . . . The question is not whether the universe of possible advertisements has been limited (as assuredly it has), but whether the limitation on advertisements obviously tends to limit

39.3

CALIFORNIA DENTAL ASSOCIATION V. FEDERAL TRADE COMMISSION, *continued*
526 U.S. 756 (1999)

the total delivery of dental services . . . Although the Court of Appeals acknowledged the CDA's view that "claims about quality are inherently unverifiable and therefore misleading," . . . it responded that this concern "does not justify banning all quality claims without regard to whether they are, in fact, false or misleading," . . . As a result, the court said, "the restriction is a sufficiently naked restraint on output to justify quick look analysis." . . . As the circumstances here demonstrate, there is generally no categorical line to be drawn between restraints that give rise to an intuitively obvious inference of anticompetitive effect and those that call for more detailed treatment. What is required, rather, is an enquiry meet for the case, looking to the circumstances, details, and logic of a restraint. The object is to see whether the experience of the market has been so clear, or necessarily will be, that a confident conclusion about the principal tendency of a restriction will follow from a quick (or at least quicker) look, in place of a more sedulous one. And of course what we see may vary over time, if rule-of-reason analyses in case after case reach identical conclusions. For now, at least, a less quick look was required for the initial assessment of the ten-

dency of these professional advertising restrictions. Because the Court of Appeals did not scrutinize the assumption of relative anticompetitive tendencies, we vacate the judgment and remand the case for a fuller consideration of the issue. It is so ordered.

BUSINESS CONSIDERATIONS Advertising can be very beneficial to a firm or an industry if done well. It might also be harmful to a firm or an industry if done poorly. What sort of policy should a firm or an industry have for deciding how to advertise? Should an industry group be permitted to limit the advertising content of the individual members of the industry?

ETHICAL CONSIDERATIONS Is it ethical for an industry group to restrict the right of individual members of the industry in their advertising? Is it ethical for an industry group to advertise on behalf of its members, giving them a potential advantage over nonmembers in the same industry?

Bait-and-switch advertising involves advertising a product at an especially enticing price to get the customer into the store (the *bait*) and then talking the customer into buying a more expensive model (the *switch*) because the advertised model is sold out or has some alleged defect. An advertiser who refuses to show the advertised item to the customer or who has insufficient quantities on hand to satisfy reasonable customer demand is engaging in an unfair trade practice in violation of § 5 of the FTC Act.

UNFAIR TRADE PRACTICES

Some common law unfair trade practices, such as palming off goods and violating trade secrets, also deserve mention. *Palming off* involves advertising, designing, or selling goods as if they were the goods of another. The person who is palming off goods is fraudulently taking advantage of the goodwill and brand loyalty of the imitated producer. This practice also frequently involves patent, copyright, or trademark infringements.

Trade secrets are special processes, formulas, and the like that are guarded and treated confidentially by the holder of the trade secret. Employees of a firm that has trade secrets must not betray their loyalty to the firm by revealing the trade

39.3 | MANAGEMENT/ MARKETING

SHOULD A MANUFACTURER POLICE ITS RETAIL CUSTOMERS?

World-Mart, one of CIT's largest customers, recently placed an order for a large number of the top-of-the-line Call-Image units. In the same order, World-Mart ordered a very small number of the standard unit model. World-Mart has been advertising a sale on the standard model at a significant saving to the retail customers. Given the discrepancy in the quantities ordered, Tom is afraid that World-Mart is involved in a bait-and-switch practice, advertising a sale on units it does not have enough inventory to cover. He is also concerned that, if this is true, CIT could receive some bad publicity when the practice comes to light. He has asked you what he should do in this situation. What advice will you give him?

BUSINESS CONSIDERATIONS Is a manufacturer responsible for the conduct of its customers when that conduct involves potential violations of antitrust law? What responsibility should a manufacturer have for the conduct of its customers after the sale is completed?

ETHICAL CONSIDERATIONS Is it ethical for a manufacturer to deal with a customer if the manufacturer believes that customer is violating the law or public policy and is using the products of the manufacturer in this illegal conduct? Does the manufacturer have an ethical duty to report the suspected improper conduct to a government agency?

secrets to others. To do so is a tort, and the employee can be held liable for any damages suffered by the employer. In addition, the firm or person who receives the information is guilty of appropriating the trade secret, and use of the secret can be stopped by injunction; the recipient of the information will also be liable for damages suffered by the trade secret holder. As we just mentioned, palming off frequently involves the infringement of a patent, a copyright, or a trademark. These three areas, along with a few others, such as service marks and trade names, are protected by federal statutes.

A *patent* is a federally created and protected monopoly power given to inventors. If a person invents something that is new, useful, and not obvious to a person of ordinary skill in the industry, the inventor is entitled to a patent. In exchange for making the method of production public, the patent grants the inventor an exclusive right to use, make, or sell the product for 20 years. If anyone violates this exclusive right, the patent holder can file an infringement suit. If the court upholds the patent, the infringer will be enjoined from further production and will be liable for damages to the holder of the patent.

A *copyright*, protected by the Copyright Office of the Library of Congress, is the protection given to writers, artists, and composers. The creator of a book, song, work of art, or similar item has the exclusive right to the profits from the creation for the life of the creator plus 50 years. Any infringement can result in an infringement action in federal court, with injunctive relief and damages being awarded to the holder of the copyright.

A *trademark* is a mark or symbol used to identify a particular brand name or product. Copying the trademark of a competitor or using a symbol deceptively similar to that of a competitor is a violation of the Lanham Act of 1946, and the violator is subject to an injunction and the imposition of damages.

EXEMPTIONS

Some conduct appears to violate various antitrust laws, and yet the actor is never challenged for the conduct. Many people are confused by this lack of action, questioning why that party is allowed to do something when others are not allowed to do the same thing. The reason is probably that the particular party belongs to a group specifically exempted from antitrust coverage.

Labor unions are exempt from the provisions of the Sherman Act by the Norris–LaGuardia Act, passed in 1932. They are also exempt from the Clayton Act by § 6 of the Clayton Act. The exemption applies only to "labor disputes" and normal union activities.

RESOURCES FOR BUSINESS LAW STUDENTS

NAME	RESOURCES	WEB ADDRESS
Sherman Antitrust Act—15 U.S.C. §§ 1–7	Legal Information Institute (LII) provides a hypertext and searchable version of 15 U.S.C. §§ 1–7, popularly known as the Sherman Antitrust Act.	**http://www4.law.cornell.edu/uscode/15/1.html**
Clayton Act—15 U.S.C. §§ 12–25	LII provides a hypertext and searchable version of 15 U.S.C. §§ 12–25, popularly known as the Clayton Antitrust Act.	**http://www4.law.cornell.edu/uscode/15/12.html**
Robinson–Patman Act— 15 U.S.C. § 13	LII provides a hypertext and searchable version of 15 U.S.C. § 13, popularly known as the Robinson–Patman Act.	**http://www4.law.cornell.edu/uscode/15/13.html**
U.S. Department of Justice, Antitrust Division	The Antitrust Division of the U.S. Department of Justice provides press releases, speeches and congressional testimony, antitrust guidelines, court cases, and international agreements and documents.	**http://www.usdoj.gov/atr/atr.htm**
U.S. Federal Trade Commission (FTC)	The FTC provides news and press releases, speeches and articles, and facts for consumers and businesses.	**http://www.ftc.gov/**

Farm cooperatives are also exempt from antitrust coverage so long as they are engaged in the sale of farm produce. (A number of other exemptions exist, but they have little impact on business law.)

SUMMARY

Since 1890, the federal government has regulated business to ensure competition. This legislative effort is referred to as antitrust law. The cornerstone of antitrust law is the Sherman Act, which prohibits joint conduct that unreasonably restricts competition or attempts to monopolize any area of commerce. Some conduct is considered so lacking in social value that it constitutes a per se violation. Other questionable conduct is measured under the rule of reason. Recently a third test, the quick look analysis, has been developed. This allows a defendant firm to rebut the presumption of harm to competition with some of the traditional per se violations. If the rebuttal is found persuasive by the court, the case is decided under the rule of reason. In any case, if a violation is found, the injured parties are entitled to recover treble damages from the violators.

The Sherman Act, however, did not suffice in preventing many violations. The Sherman Act is remedial in nature, only applying to a situation *after* harm—often irreparable—has occurred. As a result, Congress enacted some preventative legislation, laws designed to *prevent* economic or competitive harm before it caused irreparable injury. One of these statutes is the Clayton Act, which prohibits price discrimination (by means of the Robinson–Patman Act), exclusive-dealing contracts and tying arrangements, a number of mergers (by means of the Cellar–Kefauver Act), and interlocking directorates. The purpose of the Clayton Act is to stop anti-competitive conduct "in its incipiency." In order to do this, the government can attack conduct within the regulated areas if the effect of such conduct may be to substantially lessen competition in any line of trade or commerce. Notice that the government does not have to prove that competition *will* be harmed; it merely must show that competition is *likely* to be harmed. This provides a powerful tool to the government in its antitrust campaigns.

As a means of protecting competition, Congress passed the Federal Trade Commission Act. This act has two major aspects: It created the Federal Trade Commission to act as a watchdog in the antitrust area, and it prohibits unfair and deceptive trade practices. There are numerous other unfair trade practice areas as well, but most of these are regulated under state law.

DISCUSSION QUESTIONS

1. Section 1 of the Sherman Act is intended to protect competition by prohibiting restraints on trade. In order to apply this section, the court frequently uses the so-called rule of reason. What is the rule of reason, and how does it affect § 1 of the Sherman Act?

2. The courts have decided that a number of actions are likely to be so anticompetitive that the conduct cannot be defended under the rule-of-reason analysis. These actions have been deemed per se violations of § 1 of the Sherman Act. What are the traditional per se violations? What public policy or economic theory considerations justify treating these actions as violations per se?

3. Recently, the Supreme Court has recognized an exception to the per se violation standards. This exception involves a *quick look* analysis in which the defendant firms can rebut the presumption that the challenged conduct is a violation of § 1 per se. Does this quick look analysis reflect a better public policy approach to enforcing the Sherman Act than the strict per se interpretation it is supplanting, at least in some areas of antitrust analysis?

4. What is *conscious parallelism,* and how does it relate to § 1 of the Sherman Act? What is *price leadership,* and how does it relate to § 1 of the Sherman Act? How can a person distinguish conscious parallelism from price leadership?

5. Can a firm totally dominate an industry and not be guilty of monopolizing in violation of § 2 of the Sherman Act? Can a firm be found guilty of monopolizing an industry if it only controls three-quarters of the relevant market?

6. Section 2 of the Clayton Act prohibits price discrimination; however, it has been found to be less effective than originally expected. As a result, the Robinson–Patman Act was passed to supplement the provisions of § 2 of the Clayton Act. What are the major prohibitions that the Robinson–Patman Act added to § 2 of the Clayton Act?

7. What is the major difference in philosophy between the coverage of the Sherman Act and the coverage of the Clayton Act and the Federal Trade Commission Act? Which philosophy is more effective in protecting competition?

8. What is *bait-and-switch* advertising or selling, and why is such conduct treated as an unfair trade practice under the provisions of the Federal Trade Commission Act? What must a firm show to avoid prosecution if it is accused of bait-and-switch advertising?

9. Samantha is a major shirt manufacturer. She sells shirts at one price but gives a quantity discount on orders of 5,000 shirts or more. Only two of Samantha's customers, out of 600 total customers, can take advantage of this quantity discount. Is Samantha in violation of any antitrust laws? Explain your reasoning.

10. Archaic Airlines advertises that it "gets you there ON TIME more often than any other airline." In fact, Archaic has a very bad record as to arriving on time, with over half of its flights arriving more than 30 minutes late. What might the FTC do to Archaic in regard to this advertising campaign?

CASE PROBLEMS AND WRITING ASSIGNMENTS

1. Prior to 1988, Nissan advertising was conducted on two distinct levels: national advertising that was developed, placed, and paid for by Nissan; and local advertising that was obtained and paid for by individual Nissan dealerships. The Baltimore-area Nissan dealers used Faulkner, a local advertising firm, to prepare their advertising. Because of the size and importance of the Nissan account, Faulkner worked exclusively on Nissan advertising. In May 1988, Nissan announced a new "local-market advertising" plan that was to take effect 1 October 1988. Under the plan, Nissan was going to increase the wholesale price of its products in order to pay for increased advertising that was to be developed by Nissan and its ad agency. This new advertising was for both national and local use. At the same time, Nissan discontinued its prior habit of providing contributions to local dealers to develop and pay for their advertising campaigns. As a result, the Baltimore Nissan dealers stopped using Faulkner for their advertising, effectively eliminating Faulkner's business. Faulkner has sued Nissan, alleging that this arrangement is an illegal tying contract. How will the court resolve this case? What factors will the court examine in reaching its decision? [See *Faulkner Advertising Associates, Inc.* v. *Nissan Motor Corp.*, 905 F.2d 769 (4th Cir. 1990).]

2. The commercial printing industry in the United States has two major methods for printing: gravure and web offset. Gravure (or rotogravure) printing has nine commercial printing companies in this country. Two of the nine firms, R. R. Donnelley and Sons Co. and the Meredith Corporation, reached an agreement in which Donnelley would take over all the commercial printing operations of Meredith. The FTC objected to the agreement, alleging that the effect would be to substantially lessen competition in a line of commerce, commercial printing. Donnelley and Meredith defended the agreement, arguing that limiting the line of commerce to gravure printing is unrealistic and distorts the overall effect on the industry of the proposed takeover. Gravure printing only represents 16 percent of all commercial printing in the country. If the takeover is allowed to stand, Donnelley would be the number-one gravure commercial printer in the country but would still possess only 8 percent of the total commercial printing industry market. Is the FTC definition of the relevant line of commerce appropriate in this case, or has the FTC defined the line of commerce too narrowly? Discuss fully. [See *FTC* v. *R. R. Donnelley & Sons Co.*, 1990 U.S. Dist. Lexis 18992 (1990).]

3. Falls City Industries, Inc. is a regional brewer of Falls City beer. This beer is sold primarily in Kentucky and Indiana. From 1972 to 1978, Falls City sold its beer to Vanco, its only wholesale distributor in Vanderburgh County, Indiana, at a higher price than it sold to its only wholesale distributor in Henderson County, Kentucky. These two counties form a single metropolitan district that extends across the state line separating the two counties. Indiana law requires that all brewers who sell beer in Indiana must sell that beer to all Indiana wholesalers at the same price. The state law also prohibits Indiana wholesalers from selling beer to out-of-state retailers and prohibits Indiana retailers from purchasing beer from out-of-state wholesalers.

   Vanco filed suit against Falls City for price discrimination in violation of § 2 of the Clayton Act as amended by the Robinson–Patman Act. Falls City insisted that it did not discriminate in that it charged all Indiana wholesalers the same price. How should this case be resolved? What is the likely business impact on beer retailers in the two counties if the different prices are upheld by the court? [See *Falls City Industries, Inc.* v. *Vanco Beverage, Inc.*, 460 U.S. 428 (1983).]

4. The Detroit Auto Dealers Association (DADA) is a trade association in Detroit to which most of the automobile dealers in the Detroit area belong. In 1960, DADA voted to close dealer showrooms on several weekday evenings. In 1973, DADA voted to close dealer showrooms on Saturdays. As a result of these two votes, automobile dealer showrooms in Detroit were virtually all closed at the same times, effectively precluding shopping for new cars during those hours. The Federal Trade Commission viewed this conduct as a restraint of trade and initiated an administrative action against DADA and its members, alleging a violation of the Sherman Act. According to the FTC, the members of DADA had conspired or combined to set uniform hours for having the showrooms open in restraint of trade. How should this case be resolved? [See *Detroit Auto Dealers Association, Inc.* v. *FTC*, 955 F.2d 457 (6th Cir. 1992).]

5. In 1958, Von's Grocery was the third-largest grocery store chain in the Los Angeles geographic market, while Shopping Bag Food Stores was the sixth largest. By 1960, the combined sales of these two stores was 7.5 percent of the $2.5 billion in retail grocery sales for Los Angeles. Over the previous decade, both stores had grown rapidly: Von's had nearly doubled its number of stores, and its sales had increased fourfold;

Shopping Bag had more than doubled its number of stores, and its sales had increased sevenfold; Von's had doubled its market share, with Shopping Bag tripling its share. When the two stores merged in 1960, the resulting chain was the second largest in the L.A. market, with sales of over $172 million per year. From the date of the merger through 1963, the number of single stores in the area decreased from 5,365 to 3,590. In that same period, the number of chains with at least two stores increased from 96 to 150. Despite this trend, the district court rejected the government's argument that there was a concentration trend in the industry and upheld the merger of Von's and Shopping Bag. The government appealed that ruling to the Supreme Court. Did the merger between Von's and Shopping Bag violate § 7 of the Clayton Act as amended by Cellar–Kefauver? [See *United States* v. *Von's Grocery Co.*, 384 U.S. 270 (1966).]

6. **BUSINESS APPLICATION CASE** Discon, Inc. sold "removal services"—the removal of obsolete telephone equipment—through Materiel Enterprises Company, a subsidiary of NYNEX Corporation, for the use of New York Telephone Company, another subsidiary of NYNEX. Materiel Enterprises began to purchase "removal services" from AT&T Technologies rather than Discon, and Discon filed suit, alleging that the arrangement between AT&T, Materiel Enterprises, and NYNEX violated the Sherman Act. According to Discon, Materiel Enterprises paid AT&T more than Discon had charged for the same services. Materiel Enterprises then passed these higher costs on to New York Telephone, which, in turn, passed the higher costs on to consumers. (This was permitted by the New York regulatory agency, which characterized the costs as approved service charges.) Discon also alleged that Materiel Enterprises received a year-end "rebate" from AT&T Technologies, and then shared this "rebate" with NYNEX. According to its complaint, Discon alleged that this conduct amounted to a prohibited group boycott which had, in effect, driven Discon out of business. Does this conduct amount to a prohibited group boycott? Would the argument put forward by Discon be stronger if the firms were not interrelated? [See *NYNEX Corp. et al.* v. *Discon, Inc.*, 525 U.S. 128 (1998).]

7. **ETHICAL APPLICATION CASE** Warner-Lambert is the producer of Listerine mouthwash. Listerine has been produced, without a change in the formula, since 1879. From its inception in 1879 to 1972, Listerine was represented in advertising as a beneficial treatment for colds, cold symptoms, and sore throats. In 1972, the Federal Trade Commission issued a cease-and-desist order prohibiting such advertising claims in the future. In addition, the FTC ordered Warner-Lambert to run corrective advertising to remove any lasting impressions implanted with the public that Listerine was an effective cold and sore throat medicine. Warner-Lambert agreed to stop running the challenged ads, but objected to running the corrective ads. Can the FTC require a company to run corrective advertising to remedy the alleged harm done by prior misleading or deceptive advertising? Is it ethical for a business to make claims in its advertising without knowing that it can substantiate any claims the ads make? [See *Warner-Lambert Co.* v. *FTC*, 562 F.2d 749 (D.D.Cir. 1977).]

8. **CRITICAL THINKING CASE** The National Collegiate Athletic Association (NCAA), an association of major colleges, voted to restrict the number of television appearances permitted by the football teams of member schools. The NCAA also reached an agreement with the broadcast networks that guaranteed each member school a minimum price for broadcast rights to the games of each school televised by the networks. The Board of Regents of the University of Oklahoma challenged this restriction on the number of games any school was permitted to have televised, alleging that this was an illegal restriction in violation of the Sherman Act. The NCAA defended its action, alleging that such a horizontal restriction was necessary in order to guarantee that the product—televised college football games—was to remain available. How should the court resolve this case? Should these allegations be deemed as per se violations, if proven, or should they be subjected to a quick look analysis? [See *National Collegiate Athletic Association* v. *Board of Regents of the University of Oklahoma*, 468 U.S. 85 (1984).]

NOTES

1. 15 U.S.C. § 1.
2. 221 U.S. 1 (1911).
3. *SCFC ILC, Inc.* v. *Visa, USA, Inc.* 36 F.3d 958 (10th Cir. 1994).
4. *United States* v. *Arnold, Schwinn & Co.,* 388 U.S. 365 (1967).
5. *Albrecht* v. *Herald Co.,* 390 U.S. 145 (1968).
6. 441 U.S. 1 (1979).
7. 351 U.S. 377 (1956).
8. 355 U.S. 396 (1958).
9. *Caribe BMW, Inc.* v. *Bayerische Werke Aktiengesellschaft,* 19 F.3d 745 (1st Cir. 1994).
10. *Jefferson Parish Hospital District #2* v. *Hyde,* 466 U.S. 2 (1984).
11. *Datagate, Inc.* v. *Hewlett-Packard Co.,* 60 F.3d 1421 (9th Cir. 1995).
12. "Disney Takes Over Infoseek," *The Roanoke Times* (13 July 1999), p. A7.

C H A P T E R

40

CONSUMER PROTECTION

A G E N D A

CIT plans to sell Call-Image videophones to customers both directly and indirectly. For direct sales, the firm is considering extending credit to some customers. The Kochanowskis would like to know the consumer protection statutes with which the family members will need to comply if they do extend credit to these customers. Tom and Anna also want to know what information they can expect to receive if they seek a credit report on prospective employees. Because a significant number of CIT's customers will be consumers, Tom and Anna are concerned about consumer product safety as well. Should CIT be apprehensive, or should the firm not worry about the federal government's Consumer Product Safety Commission's possible jurisdiction over CIT's videophones?

These and other questions are likely to arise as you study this chapter. Be prepared! You never know when one of the Kochanowskis will need your help or advice.

INTRODUCTION

For many years, state laws regulated consumer credit activities. But the lack of uniformity among such laws, coupled with the increasing need to protect consumers from fraudulent practices, erroneous information found in credit reports, discrimination in the extension of credit, and harassing debt-collection practices, has led to the enactment of numerous federal laws. Product safety also remains a significant issue for the vast majority of the American public. In this chapter, we consider the most noteworthy of these consumer protection laws.[1]

CONSUMER CREDIT

Consumer credit has become a gargantuan business in the United States and increasingly draws the attention of federal lawmakers and regulators. On a given day, we in the United States purchase 500,000 appliances, 40,000 motor vehicles, and 15,000 homes on credit.[2] The ubiquity of such credit transactions in turn has led to a giant industry involving the sale of credit reports by credit bureaus. To generate the two million such reports that are sold every working day, credit bureaus retain information on 90 percent of the adults in our country—some 170 million people.[3]

THE CONSUMER CREDIT PROTECTION ACT

Title I of the Consumer Credit Protection Act of 1968, more commonly known as the Truth in Lending Act (TILA), represents the landmark modern consumer protection law. After its enactment, other federal legislation followed.

TILA, in essence, is a disclosure statute designed to force creditors to inform consumers, via a standardized form and terminology, of the actual costs of credit. This information enables consumers to make more informed decisions about credit. Indeed, to comply with TILA, creditors, prior to the consummation of any credit transaction, must provide every consumer with a separate disclosure statement that satisfies the dictates of both TILA and the Federal Reserve Board (FRB), which enforces TILA. Failure to comply with TILA's disclosure provisions subjects the creditor to various civil, criminal, and statutory liabilities.

Although primarily a disclosure statute, TILA also regulates transactions in which a consumer uses his or her home as collateral for a loan (i.e., for home equity or home improvement loans), with the exception of transactions involving the purchase or initial construction of a home. For situations covered by the statute, TILA allows a three-day cooling-off period, during which the consumer may decide to rescind (i.e., cancel) the loan. Congress apparently wanted to allow the consumer the opportunity to reconsider any transaction that may encumber the consumer's title to his or her home. The power of rescission potentially lasts for three years from the consummation of the transaction or the sale of the property, whichever occurs first.[4]

Upon its initial enactment, TILA resulted in a great deal of litigation that benefited consumers, much to the chagrin of the lending industry. Largely in response to lobbying efforts by lenders, Congress in 1980 enacted the Truth in Lending Simplification and Reform Act, which the FRB subsequently labeled the "new" truth-in-lending act. Designed avowedly to simplify the disclosures mandated by the

1968 act (which, according to the FRB, resulted in consumer confusion owing to the detail required), the 1980 act makes creditor compliance easier. But experts debate whether providing consumers with less information actually furthers the law's overriding purpose of enhancing consumers' ability to shop meaningfully for credit. Litigation under the new act nonetheless has decreased dramatically. In response to litigation stemming from the part of TILA that deals with home equity loans, Congress in 1995 amended that portion of TILA so as to give lenders some relief from the numerous class action suits that in the mid-1990s had sought the remedy of rescission for the entire class. Hence, these amendments, among other things, provide retroactive and prospective relief from liability for certain types of creditor finance charges.

Regulation Z promulgated by the FRB summarizes the scope of TILA. Therefore, one always should read the statute in conjunction with this regulation. In general, Regulation Z covers persons who regularly offer or extend credit to consumers who seek to use the credit for personal, family, or household purposes and the transaction is subject to a finance charge or, by written agreement, is payable in four or more installments. In the initial disclosure statement, the creditor in a clear and conspicuous manner must provide detailed information in a meaningful sequence to the consumer concerning finance charges (including interest, time differential charges, service charges, points, loan fees, appraisal fees, and certain insurance premiums), any other charges, the creditor's retention of a security interest, and a statement of billing rights that respectively outlines the consumer's rights and the creditor's responsibilities.

In addition, creditors must furnish the consumer with periodic statements that disclose various items: the previous balance, credits, the amount of the finance charge, the annual percentage rate charged, the closing date of the billing cycle, the new balance, the address to be used for notice of billing errors, and so on. The creditor also must promptly credit consumer payments and refund credit balances. A consumer must notify a creditor in writing of an alleged billing error within 60 days of the creditor's transmitting the bill to the consumer. TILA and Regulation Z tell the consumer exactly how to satisfy these notification procedures. Within 30 days after receiving notification from the consumer, the creditor must acknowledge in writing the disputed bill or item. And no later than 90 days after receipt of the consumer's notice, the creditor either must correct the disputed bill or, alternatively, explain in writing why the creditor believes the account is correct and supply copies of documented evidence of the consumer's indebtedness.

A creditor who complies with these provisions has no further obligations to the consumer, even if the consumer continues to make substantially the same allegations regarding the alleged error. Until the dispute is settled, however, the creditor may not do the following: try to collect the cost of the disputed item; close or restrict the consumer's account during the controversy, although the creditor can apply the disputed amount to the consumer's credit limit; or make or threaten to make an adverse report that the consumer is in arrears or that his or her bill is delinquent because of nonpayment of the disputed amount. Any creditor who fails to comply with these provisions forfeits the amount in dispute, plus any finance charges, provided the amount does not exceed $50.

These requirements cover "open-ended" credit transactions, such as those accomplished pursuant to credit cards (Visa, MasterCard, American Express, etc.) or department store revolving charge accounts. If you check a credit card bill, you will notice that it sets out the information required under Regulation Z.

Regulation Z (as well as TILA) also applies to "closed-end" credit transactions, such as consumer loans from finance companies; credit purchases of cars, major appliances, and furniture; and real estate purchases. Different disclosure rules exist for closed-end transactions. In addition, both TILA (through the Consumer Leasing Act) and Regulation M regulate consumer leases of greater than four months' duration (rent-to-own transactions, which are terminable without penalty during the first four months not covered). This portion of TILA covers only leases of personal property (as opposed to real estate) and does not apply to leases where the total contractual obligation exceeds $25,000. Persons who lease automobiles, for example, are protected by the required lease disclosures and the remedies available under this part of TILA.

Other provisions of TILA prohibit the issuance of a credit card except in response to an oral or written request or application and limit the liability of the cardholder to $50 in cases of unauthorized use of the card if the cardholder notifies the creditor of an unauthorized use because of the loss or theft of the card. In some circumstances, a person who knowingly and fraudulently uses or traffics in counterfeit access devices (i.e., credit cards, plates, codes, account numbers, or any means of account access) and during a one-year period obtains $1,000 in value as a result of this conduct, is subject to a maximum fine of not more than the greater of $100,000 or twice the value obtained by the offense, or imprisonment of not more than 10 years (or both).

Remedies sought by individuals for creditors' violations of TILA include actual damages and statutory damages of twice the finance charges (but not less than $100 or more than $1,000). Class actions for actual damages as well as statutory damages of an amount equal to the lesser of $500,000 or 1 percent of the creditors' net worth also are possible. Awards of attorney's fees to successful litigants are available under the statute, too. Criminal penalties for each willful and knowing failure to make the proper disclosures required by the act include fines of not more than $5,000 and/or one year's imprisonment. Several agencies—the FRB and the Federal Trade Commission (FTC), for example—have responsibility for the administrative enforcement of TILA. Defenses to liability include the expiration of the one-year statute of limitations (for disclosure violations), creditor bona fide clerical errors, and the creditor's timely correction of an error.

Turner v. *E-Z Check Cashing of Cookeville, TN, Inc.* illustrates many of these concepts.

40.1

TURNER V. E-Z CHECK CASHING OF COOKEVILLE, TN, INC.

35 F.SUPP.2D 1042 (M.D.TENN. 1999)

FACTS Turner is a forty-seven-year-old woman with an eighth-grade education. E-Z Check Cashing (EZ) is co-owned and managed by Ricky Edwards. Edwards operates four check-cashing businesses, three of which also perform pawn broking services. The "check-cashing" transactions conducted by EZ differ from the usual "check-cashing" transactions at a bank. EZ's business consists of "deferred present-ment" transactions in which a customer writes a check to EZ in an amount that includes (1) a principal amount the customer receives immediately in cash, plus (2) an additional "service fee" to be collected at least thirty days later. At the end of the thirty-day period, the customer may (1) repay the principal amount and service fee and retrieve the *continued*

40.1

TURNER V. E-Z CHECK CASHING OF COOKEVILLE, TN, INC., *continued*
35 F.SUPP.2D 1042 (M.D.TENN. 1999)

uncashed check, (2) pay only the service fee and write a new check for the principal amount and service fee, or (3) allow the business to deposit the original check. A "Good Faith Estimate of Settlement Charges" is appended to the agreement. In this document, EZ describes the transaction as a loan. Before agreeing to "cash a check" for a customer, EZ investigates (at a cost of 45 cents per check) the customer's check-writing history through two national databases and requires the customer to provide references. If a customer has no outstanding bad checks and otherwise is deemed acceptable, EZ will "cash" the check. This means that EZ will advance the customer cash in the amount of the principal portion of the check and hold the check for thirty days. Turner's series of transactions with EZ began on 2 July 1996, when she borrowed $300.00. Pursuant to this "check-cashing" agreement, Turner wrote a check to EZ for $405.00, which included the $300.00 cash advancement to Turner, plus $105.00 in service fees. At the end of thirty days, Turner either could pay EZ $105.00 in cash and provide another check in the amount of $405.00 (to be held for the next thirty days) or do nothing, at which time EZ would deposit the original $405.00 check, in settlement of the principal amount of the cash advanced originally and the associated charges. On 31 July, the due date, Turner chose to pay a service charge of $105.00 and to defer payment on the principal ($300.00) for an additional thirty days. Through these transactions, Turner paid EZ $840.00 over an eight-month period. Finally, on 4 April 1997, Turner failed to pay the $105.00 service fee; and EZ deposited her $405.00 check. When that check was dishonored because of the closure of her bank account, Edwards, in a letter dated 11 April 1997, threatened Turner with criminal prosecution unless she reimbursed EZ for the amount of the returned check ($405.00), plus a check recovery fee of ten percent of the check amount ($81.00). In May 1997, Turner filed a Chapter 7 bankruptcy petition; and on 19 June 1997, she filed a lawsuit alleging violations of TILA and Regulation Z by EZ. Turner claimed that EZ had failed: (1) to provide the disclosures required by TILA and Regulation Z; (2) to make the required disclosures conspicuously in writing; (3) to properly disclose the finance charges; and (4) to state accurately the annual percentage rate (APR), all of which omissions allegedly violated TILA and Regulation Z.

ISSUES Did TILA cover a deferred presentment check cashing transaction? Did the creditor's disclosures violate TILA?

HOLDINGS Yes as to both issues. The deferred presentment check cashing business was a "creditor" for the purposes of TILA. The finance charges should have reflected an APR of 400 percent rather than the 24 percent listed on the form. This error, coupled with EZ's various other failures to comply with TILA's requirements, made EZ liable to Turner.

REASONING TILA is a comprehensive regulatory scheme intended to deter the predatory extension of credit that can disrupt the national economy and increase the personal bankruptcy rate. Its provisions are intended to aid the unsophisticated consumer in determining the total costs of financing. One of its primary mechanisms for accomplishing this is the requirement of "a meaningful disclosure of credit terms so that the consumer will be able to compare more readily the various credit terms available to him or her and avoid the uninformed use of credit, and to protect the consumer against inaccurate and unfair credit billing and credit card practices." Because TILA is a remedial act designed to protect consumers, courts construe it liberally in favor of consumers. Courts thus focus on the substance, not the form, of credit-extending transactions. Before deciding whether EZ had violated TILA's disclosure provisions as Turner had alleged, the court first must determine whether check-cashing businesses are subject to TILA's requirements. Courts that have addressed the issue have held, without exception, that deferred presentment transactions are extensions of "credit" under TILA and its regulations. As one such court noted, deferred presentment transactions are "nothing more than interest[-]bearing loans . . . It is hard to imagine how charges for exchanging money today for more money at a later date could be classified as anything but interest on a loan." Moreover, since the essence of EZ's business is to earn a profit from engaging in a check-cashing deferred presentment scheme with the public, which activities involve extensions of credit, EZ is a "creditor" within the meaning of TILA. To fall within TILA, any deferred presentment transactions must be considered "consumer transactions." Thus, the creditor must advance money as a loan to a natural person; and it must loan the money for personal, family, or

40.1

TURNER V. E-Z CHECK CASHING OF COOKEVILLE, TN, INC., *continued*
35 F.SUPP.2D 1042 (M.D.TENN. 1999)

household purposes, rather than for business or commercial purposes. Certainly it would not be reasonable to assume the $300.00 she had borrowed from EZ, in light of her other liabilities, would have been sufficient to start or continue a commercial enterprise. Furthermore, EZ's disclosure statement says on its face it is a "Truth-in-Lending Disclosure Statement." Under these facts and circumstances, Turner clearly sought a loan for personal purposes as defined by TILA; hence, this transaction was a "consumer" credit transaction under the Act. Having concluded that the parties and transactions here are subject to TILA and therefore to Regulation Z, the court next must address the question of whether Turner is entitled to summary judgment on the issue of EZ's alleged TILA violations. TILA and the regulations of the Federal Reserve require creditors, before they extend credit, to provide borrowers with certain information. Additionally, TILA specifies that this prerequisite information be "conspicuously segregated from all other terms, data, or information provided in connection with a transaction, including any computations or itemizations." The information that a creditor must segregate includes: the "amount financed"; the "finance charge"; the finance charge expressed as an APR (if it exceeds a statutory minimum); the "total of payments," consisting of the sum of the amount financed and the finance charge; the number, amount, and due dates or period of payments required to repay the total; in a sale of property or services, the "total sale price"; and the like. An examination of EZ's disclosure form, particularly the "total of payments" section, indicates that EZ attempted to comply with TILA. Here, the amount financed was stated as $300.00 and the amount of the finance charge as $6.00. However, EZ listed the "total of payments" as $405.00, a difference of $99.00. The $99.00 difference, which clearly is not the principal (here $300), therefore, can only be a "finance charge." Accordingly, the actual APR EZ charged Turner was in excess of 400 percent. And failure to disclose an APR of 400 percent constitutes a TILA violation. Furthermore, EZ failed to disclose: the number, the amount, and the due dates of required payments, and many other

required items. Failure to make these disclosures also is a violation of TILA. The foregoing facts moreover show EZ's violation of Regulation Z, which provides that information required to be disclosed by the creditor shall be disclosed "clearly and conspicuously" and that the terms "annual percentage rate" and "finance charge" be disclosed more conspicuously than other information, except for the information that related to the creditor's identity. However, EZ's disclosure document, in listing the terms "annual percentage rate" and "finance charge," uses the same type size, font, and boldness as it does in listing other terms, data, and information; thus, these terms are no more conspicuous than the others. As a result, EZ thereby violated TILA. Furthermore, EZ's disclosure stated the finance charge as $6.00. Yet, the actual finance charge imposed, calculated in the manner specified by TILA, was $105.00 per month, or $1,260.00 per year. EZ did not disclose the finance charge as required by TILA and therefore violated the act. Finally, the amount financed and the finance charge at issue here required EZ to disclose an APR. Although EZ had stated an APR, EZ gave this rate as 24 percent rather than the accurate rate of 400.2 percent. This incorrect statement violated TILA. Consequently, owing to the foregoing reasons, Turner's motion for a summary judgment would be granted.

BUSINESS CONSIDERATIONS What should EZ have done to make certain its cash-checking documents complied with TILA and Regulation Z? Should firms that extend consumer credit provide its employees with training sessions and legal seminars on such subjects as consumer credit? In making such decisions, what factors should a firm consider?

ETHICAL CONSIDERATIONS Do businesses like EZ unethically prey on disadvantaged members of society? Does utilitarianism (or any other ethical theory) provide an ethical justification for such business activities?

THE FAIR CREDIT REPORTING ACT

Banks and other lenders, would-be secured creditors (discussed in Chapters 26 and 27), landlords, insurance companies, department stores, and employers often seek information about consumers. Moreover, as we have noted, credit transactions pervade domestic (and international) life. Virtually everyone in our country has a credit card. Therefore, each credit card use becomes part of the credit history of the user. Credit-reporting agencies (or bureaus) in turn summarize this information into credit (or consumer) reports and sell these reports to lenders, landlords, insurers, retailers, and employers. Credit-reporting agencies may be either local or national in scope.

Given the statistics cited earlier, one readily understands the importance of credit bureaus to the U.S. economy. Credit bureaus continually update the information they hold regarding consumers—by some estimates, a total of two billion pieces of information concerning private consumer transactions and two million pieces of public record information (i.e., bankruptcies, tax liens, foreclosures, court judgments, etc.) are reported each month.[5] Even though credit-reporting services both facilitate a given consumer's access to various avenues of credit and speed up credit transactions, the centralization of these vast stores of information covering virtually the entire adult population has spawned concerns about the accuracy of the information and the adequacy of the safeguards employed by these agencies to protect the privacy of individual consumers. Indeed, studies have shown that one-half of all credit reports contain erroneous information;[6] and a litany of consumer complaints chronicles the denials of credit based on false information and the difficulties inherent in correcting such records.

Because of these abuses, Congress in 1970 passed the Fair Credit Reporting Act (FCRA) as a part of the Consumer Credit Protection Act. Congress enacted the FCRA to require consumer-reporting agencies to adopt reasonable procedures for meeting the needs of commerce for consumer credit, personnel, insurance, and other information in a manner that is fair and equitable to the consumer and ensures the confidentiality, accuracy, relevancy, and proper use of such information. It applies, then, to all persons or entities that collect information concerning a consumer's creditworthiness, credit standing, credit capacity, character, general reputation, personal characteristics, or mode of living when third parties use this information either to deny or to increase the amount charged for credit or insurance used primarily for personal, family, or household purposes.

In addition, the FCRA applies whenever such information is used for the purposes of employment, governmental benefits or licenses, insurance underwriting, or other legitimate business transactions. Credit reports and licenses issued for any other reasons require a court order or the permission of the consumer.

Interestingly, the FCRA does not apply to all such credit reports but only to those compiled by any entity that *regularly* engages in the practice of disseminating or evaluating consumer credit or other information concerning consumers for the purpose of furnishing consumer reports to third parties. Thus, the act covers credit reports generated by credit bureaus, whose reports ordinarily set out only financial information about the consumer in question—bank accounts, charge accounts and other indebtedness, creditworthiness, marital status, occupation, income, and perhaps some nonfinancial information. The act also covers credit-reporting bureaus whose reports focus not so much on credit information of the type compiled by credit bureaus but rather involve more personal information typically gathered through interviews with neighbors, colleagues, and the like. In short, whether the report centers respectively on financial matters or investigatory matters pursuant to a prospective employment or landlord/tenant relationship, both types of credit reports raise significant privacy issues.

In placing obligations on third-party users of credit information and those credit agencies or bureaus that report information about consumers, the FCRA attempts to protect such consumers from invasion of privacy and breach of confidentiality. It expressly obligates every consumer-reporting agency to maintain reasonable procedures designed to avoid violations of the act. Among other things, this obligation means that such agencies must report only accurate and up-to-date information and report these data only to those persons or entities eligible to receive the information.

Congress in enacting this legislation unfortunately set out no test for ensuring the relevancy of the information. Thus, while agencies must report information that is accurate, complete, and up to date, consumers have little recourse against credit bureaus and credit-reporting bureaus that report irrelevant information (e.g., political beliefs or lifestyle issues) that arguably encroaches on the subject's privacy. Moreover, although the FCRA mandates that those who furnish information to credit bureaus must provide correct information, the consumer has no direct right of redress against the furnisher of the inaccurate information. However, the act does set out procedures by which the consumer can dispute the accuracy of the information furnished. In this fashion, the act broadens the protection available to the consumer.

Besides setting out limitations on consumer-reporting agencies and furnishers of information, the FCRA places on both reporting agencies and users certain obligations regarding the proper disclosure of the information compiled. The limitations on the uses of such information discussed earlier (employment, governmental benefits or licenses, insurance underwriting, or any other legitimate business purpose) fulfill this goal, and the act requires that every consumer-reporting agency undertake reasonable procedures to verify that the users of the information furnished avail themselves of the report for only these purposes. Reasonable procedures include prospective users' identifying themselves and certifying the purpose for which they are seeking the information. Prospective users also must certify that they will use the information only for this—and no other—purpose.

Users of consumer reports similarly must satisfy certain statutory obligations. For example, users of investigative consumer reports must notify the consumer in advance of the preparation of the report that he or she may be the subject of an investigation concerning his or her character, general reputation, personal characteristics, and mode of living. Other provisions allow for the purging of dated and inaccurate information in such investigative reports. Likewise, recent amendments to the FCRA spell out the obligations of any employers who use consumer reports. Among other things, the employers must obtain the consumer's written authorization before the employer seeks a consumer report for employment purposes. Similarly, the consumer must consent to the furnishing of any report that contains medical information about the consumer. Other consumer protections include prohibitions on the inclusion of certain items of stale information (e.g., civil suits, civil judgments, and records of arrests that antedate the report by more than seven years). Moreover, whenever a user of a consumer report denies credit, insurance, or employment or charges a higher rate for credit or insurance and bases the denial or increase wholly or in part on the information contained in a credit report, the user must advise the consumer of the adverse action and supply the name and address of the reporting agency that compiled the report. Adverse actions involving only denial of credit or an increased charge for the extension of credit pursuant to information obtained from persons other than a consumer-reporting agency obligate the user, upon request, to disclose to the consumer the nature (but not the source) of the information. In this latter situation, the user also must inform the consumer of his or her statutory right to learn of the information that caused the adverse decision.

Consumers' rights, then, in addition to the FCRA's prohibition on the use of inaccurate and outdated information, include notification of an agency's reliance on adverse information contained in consumer reports. Moreover, by statute the consumer enjoys limited access to any files concerning him or her and the right in certain circumstances to correct erroneous information. The information that the consumer can receive from a consumer credit-reporting agency includes the nature and substance of all information in its files concerning the consumer, the sources of information (except for the sources of information compiled pursuant to investigative reports), and the recipients of any consumer reports that the agency has furnished concerning the consumer for employment purposes within the last two years or for any purpose within the one-year period preceding the request.

Note that under the FCRA the consumer cannot actually see his or her file. But once the consumer receives the information, he or she can dispute the completeness or accuracy of any information contained in the file. When the consumer directly conveys to the reporting agency such questions, the agency within 30 days must investigate the information disputed by the consumer unless the agency has reasonable grounds to believe the consumer's claim is frivolous or irrelevant. If the agency's reinvestigation fails to resolve the dispute, the consumer can file a statement that sets forth the nature of the dispute. Unless it has reasonable grounds to believe the statement is frivolous or irrelevant, the agency must clearly note in any subsequent consumer report containing the disputed information that the consumer disputes the information and provide either the consumer's statement or a clear and accurate codification or summary thereof. At the request of the consumer, the agency must send a similar notice to any users that the consumer can identify as having received within the last two years a report concerning employment or having received within the last six months a report for any purpose. The statute expressly mandates that the agency clearly and conspicuously disclose to the consumer his or her right to make such a request.

The FCRA sets out civil remedies for violations of the act. For willful failure to comply with the act, suits for compensatory or punitive damages are possible; for

40.1 | MANAGEMENT

CALL-IMAGE TECHNOLOGY

CREDIT-REPORTING AGENCIES

CIT recently has fired one of its employees. Following this firing, a credit-reporting agency has contacted the firm and has asked questions about the former employee. Fearing possible liability for the firm under the Fair Credit Reporting Act if the information reported by the firm turns out to be inaccurate or if the agency misuses the information, Dan believes that CIT should not answer the questions. Tom does not see these reservations as legitimate concerns. Rather, he thinks that CIT should provide the information, especially since CIT uses this credit-reporting agency when CIT seeks information concerning prospective employees. Dan and Tom ask your opinion on this matter. What will you advise them?

BUSINESS CONSIDERATIONS Should a business establish a policy for providing information concerning employees—or former employees—to credit-reporting agencies? What factors would affect the formation of such a policy?

ETHICAL CONSIDERATIONS Is it ethical for a former employer to provide information about a former employee to a credit-reporting agency? How can the employer, from an ethical perspective, relate the employment performance of a person to the latter's credit-worthiness?

violations stemming from negligent noncompliance, an injured consumer can recover only compensatory damages. In addition, for either type of violation, the injured party who successfully sues can recover court costs and attorney's fees.

The FCRA prohibits court actions brought for defamation, invasion of privacy, or negligence with respect to the reporting of information, unless the suit involves false information furnished with malice or with a willful intent to injure the consumer. Any person who under false pretenses knowingly and willfully obtains information concerning a consumer faces fines and/or two years' imprisonment.

The Federal Trade Commission (FTC), discussed in Chapter 39, functions as the principal enforcement agency for violations of the FCRA, because the law views violations of the act as unfair or deceptive trade practices. As such, the FTC can order various administrative remedies (such as cease-and-desist orders) against consumer-reporting agencies, users, or other persons not regulated by other federal agencies (such as the Federal Reserve Board) that themselves have enforcement authority when credit-reporting agencies' and users' activities fall within these agencies' regulatory purview.

In *Stevenson v. TRW, Inc.*, the judge addressed many of these principles.

40.2

STEVENSON V. TRW, INC.

987 F.2D 288 (5TH CIR. 1993)

FACTS TRW, Inc. (TRW) is one of the nation's largest credit-reporting agencies. John M. Stevenson is a 78-year-old real estate and securities investor. In late 1988, Stevenson began receiving numerous phone calls from bill collectors regarding arrearages in accounts that were not his. In August 1989, Stevenson wrote TRW and obtained a copy of his credit report dated 6 September 1989. On that credit report, the statement "See Reverse Side for Explanation" was printed in red, boldface type and appeared on the bottom, right-hand portion of each page. The boilerplate notice on the reverse side had four paragraphs, the latter of which stated that Stevenson could request that TRW send a corrected report to any of the creditors Stevenson listed on the four blank lines that followed paragraph four. The other paragraphs were printed in red, boldface type; but the fourth paragraph used black, regular-size type. Stevenson discovered many errors in the 6 September report. Some accounts belonged to another John Stevenson living in Arlington, Texas; and some appeared to belong to his estranged son, John Stevenson, Jr. In all, Stevenson disputed approximately sixteen accounts, seven inquiries, and much of the identifying information. Stevenson called TRW to register his complaint and then, on 6 October 1989, wrote TRW's president and CEO and requested the correction of his (Stevenson's) credit report. Stevenson's letter worked its way to TRW's customer relations department by

20 October 1989; and on 1 November 1989, that office began its reinvestigation by sending consumer dispute verification forms (CDVs) to the subscribers that had reported the disputed accounts. The CDVs ask subscribers to check whether the information about a consumer matches the information in TRW's credit report. Subscribers who receive CDVs typically have 20 to 25 working days to respond. If a subscriber fails to respond or indicates that TRW's account information is incorrect, TRW deletes the disputed pieces of information. Stevenson understood from TRW that the entire process should take from three to six weeks. As a result of its initial investigation, by 30 November 1989, TRW had removed several of the disputed accounts from the report. TRW also realized that Stevenson's estranged son, by using Stevenson's social security number, apparently had fraudulently obtained some of the disputed accounts. This information led TRW in December 1989 to add a warning statement advising subscribers that Stevenson's identifying information had been used without his consent to obtain credit. By 9 February 1990, TRW claimed that it had removed all the disputed accounts containing "negative" credit information. Inaccurate information, however, either continued to appear on Stevenson's reports or was reentered after TRW had deleted it. As a consequence, Stevenson, filing suit in Texas state court, alleged both common law libel and

continued

40.2

STEVENSON V. TRW, INC., *continued*
987 F.2D 288 (5TH CIR. 1993)

violation of the Fair Credit Reporting Act (FCRA). TRW removed the case to federal court, where, in a bench trial, the judge found in favor of Stevenson on both counts. The judge awarded $1 in nominal damages on the libel claim, $30,000 in actual damages for mental anguish, $20,700 in attorney's fees, and $100,000 in punitive damages.

ISSUE Did TRW, by failing to delete promptly inaccurate or unverifiable entries on Stevenson's credit record and by failing to provide Stevenson clear and conspicuous notice of his rights, negligently and willfully violate the FCRA?

HOLDING Yes and no. TRW, by taking an unreasonably long time to reinvestigate Stevenson's dispute and by failing to delete promptly the information found to be inaccurate or unverifiable, had negligently violated the FCRA. TRW, by failing to disclose clearly and conspicuously to Stevenson his right to have corrected copies of his credit report sent to his creditors, also had negligently violated the act. The district court, however, had erred in finding that TRW's violations were willful. Hence, the findings of negligence, the award of $30,000 in actual damages based on the finding of mental anguish, and the award of $20,700 in attorney's fees were affirmed; but the findings of willfulness and the punitive damages award were reversed.

REASONING Congress enacted the FCRA to guard against consumer-reporting agencies' use of inaccurate or arbitrary information when they evaluate an individual for credit, insurance, or employment. Congress further required that consumer-reporting agencies "follow reasonable procedures to assure the maximum possible accuracy of the information concerning the individual about whom" a credit report relates. [The trial court had found that TRW had done so.] A consumer-reporting agency that negligently fails to comply with the FCRA's requirements is liable for actual damages, costs, and reasonable attorney's fees. Willful noncompliance renders a consumer-reporting agency additionally liable for punitive damages. Moreover, consumers have the right to see their credit information and to dispute the accuracy or completeness of their credit reports. When it receives a complaint, a consumer-reporting agency must reinvestigate the disputed information "within a

reasonable period of time" and "promptly delete" credit information it finds to be inaccurate or unverifiable. According to the FTC, "[a]lthough consumer reporting agencies are able to reinvestigate most disputes within 30 days, a 'reasonable time' for a particular reinvestigation may be shorter or longer depending on the circumstances of the dispute." TRW contends that 10 weeks was a reasonable time to complete its reinvestigation of Stevenson's complicated dispute, especially since his claim involved fraudulently obtained inaccurate accounts. The record, however, contains evidence from which the district court could find that TRW had not deleted unverifiable or inaccurate information promptly. First, TRW did not complete its reinvestigation until 9 February 1990, although TRW's subscribers were supposed to return the CDVs by 4 December 1989. Second, the FCRA requires prompt deletion if the disputed information is inaccurate or unverifiable. Stevenson had disputed incorrect accounts listed with one business, but those accounts appeared on his credit report as late as 22 March 1991. A firm's allowing inaccurate information back onto a credit report after the firm has deleted the information because it is inaccurate is negligent. Additionally, in spite of the complexity of Stevenson's dispute, TRW contacted the subscribers only through the CDVs rather than by calling the subscribers. In short, TRW's claims concerning the complexities associated with Stevenson's case do not excuse its negligent failure to meet the "prompt deletion" requirement, particularly since the statute places the burden of reinvestigation squarely on TRW. The FCRA authorizes the awarding of actual damages, punitive damages, and reasonable attorney's fees when the reporting agency willfully fails to comply with any of the FCRA's requirements. To be found in willful noncompliance, a defendant must have "knowingly and intentionally committed an act in conscious disregard for the rights of others." Given the lack of any conscious intention to thwart Stevenson's right to have inaccurate information removed promptly from his report, the district court's finding of willful noncompliance was clearly erroneous. But the district court had not erred in finding that TRW, by sending Stevenson the same boilerplate form it sends everyone, had negligently violated the notice requirement of the FCRA. However, because the notice appears in a paragraph on dispute resolution procedures and is visible, TRW had not knowingly

40.2

STEVENSON V. TRW, INC., *continued*
987 F.2D 288 (5TH CIR. 1993)

and intentionally obscured the notice in conscious disregard of consumers' rights. The finding of willful noncompliance and the award of punitive damages therefore would be reversed.

BUSINESS CONSIDERATION How should TRW revamp both the reinvestigation procedures and the

boilerplate form letter that were in issue in this case so as to avoid the types of problems TRW had encountered?

ETHICAL CONSIDERATIONS Had the court based its decision concerning TRW's conduct on ethics rather than the law, would the court's decision have been different? What ethical concerns did the conduct of TRW raise?

THE EQUAL CREDIT OPPORTUNITY ACT

When Congress first passed the Equal Credit Opportunity Act (ECOA) in 1974, it prohibited only discrimination based on sex or marital status whenever creditors extend credit. Congress at that time was responding to evidence showing that creditors more often denied credit to single women than to single men and that married, divorced, and widowed women could not get credit in their own names. Instead, these women had to obtain credit in their husbands' names.

To broaden the protections available to low-income consumers so as to enable them to have access to credit commensurate with the credit opportunities enjoyed by more affluent consumers, Congress in 1976 amended the statute to prohibit, in addition, discrimination based on race, religion, national origin, age (provided an applicant has the capacity to contract), receipt of public assistance benefits, and the good-faith exercise of rights under the Consumer Credit Protection Act (i.e., TILA). Although part of TILA, ECOA covers more than consumer credit transactions. In short, ECOA covers any creditor who deals with any applicant in any aspect of a credit transaction.

Federal Reserve Board (FRB) Regulation B (extensively revised in 1985), the implementing regulation for ECOA, broadly defines a credit transaction as involving every aspect of an applicant's dealings with a creditor regarding an application for credit or an existing extension of credit, including but not limited to information requirements; investigation procedures; standards of creditworthiness; terms of credit; the furnishing of credit information, revocation, alteration, or termination of credit; and collection procedures. ECOA and Regulation B exempt certain transactions, such as those made pursuant to special-purpose credit programs designed to benefit an economically disadvantaged class of persons, from coverage. Partial exemptions also exist for public utility services credit transactions (i.e., public utilities can ask questions about an applicant's marital status) and incidental consumer credit transactions, such as those involving physicians, hospitals, and so on.

Since creditors generally evaluate applicants' creditworthiness as a precondition of extending credit, Regulation B sets out the rules that creditors must follow in making such evaluations and the forms that creditors can use to ensure that they do not discriminate on any of the prohibited bases while they undertake these evaluations. In addition, ECOA requires creditors to give notice to applicants of any actions taken by the creditors concerning the applicants' requests for credit.

Creditor actions typically take three forms: approval of the application, extension of credit under different terms than those requested, or an adverse action (e.g., denial of the application). Regulation B then prescribes a notification regime specifically tailored to the type of action taken. Exhibit 40.1 represents a communication that generally will satisfy these notification requirements. Creditors typically must send such a notification within 30 days of receiving a completed application.

Remedies under ECOA include actual damages and/or punitive damages, to a maximum of $10,000 for individual actions or a maximum of $500,000 (or 1 percent of the creditor's net worth—whichever is greater) for class actions. Equitable relief, attorney's fees, and costs also may be granted. A two-year statute of limitations generally applies. The usual administrative remedies are available as well. The enforcement agencies in addition can ask the U.S. Attorney General to institute civil

---

E X H I B I T 40.1 | **Form C-2—Sample Notice of Action Taken and Statement of Reasons**

Dear Applicant:

Thank you for your recent application. Your request for [a loan/a credit card/an increase in your credit limit] was carefully considered, and we regret that we are unable to approve your application at this time, for the following reason(s):

YOUR INCOME:
_____ is below our minimum requirement.
_____ is insufficient to sustain payments on the amount of credit requested.
_____ could not be verified.

YOUR EMPLOYMENT:
_____ is not of sufficient length to qualify.
_____ could not be verified.

YOUR CREDIT HISTORY:
_____ of making payments on time was not satisfactory.
_____ could not be verified.

YOUR APPLICATION:
_____ lacks a sufficient number of credit references.
_____ lacks acceptable types of credit references.
_____ reveals that current obligations are excessive in relation to income.

OTHER: _____

The consumer reporting agency contacted that provided information that influences our decision in whole or in part was [the name, address, and telephone number of the reporting agency]. The reporting agency is unable to supply specific reasons why we have denied credit to you. You do, however, have a right under the Fair Credit Reporting Act to know the information contained in your credit file. Any questions regarding such information should be directed to [the consumer reporting agency].

If you have any questions regarding this letter, you should contact us at [creditor's name, address, and telephone number].

NOTICE: The federal Equal Credit Opportunity Act prohibits creditors from discriminating against credit applicants on the basis of race, color, religion, national origin, sex, martial status, age (provided the applicant has the capacity to enter into a binding contract); because all or part of the applicant's income derives from any public assistance program; or because the applicant has in good faith exercised any right under the Consumer Credit Protection Act. The federal agency that administers compliance with this law concerning this creditor is [the name and address as specified by the appropriate agency listed in Appendix A].

SOURCE: 12 Code of Federal Regulations § 202 (App.C) (1999).

actions against any creditor who has engaged in a pattern or practice of denying or discouraging credit applicants in violation of the act.

THE FAIR DEBT COLLECTION PRACTICES ACT

No Harrassment

As Title V of the Consumer Credit Protection Act (TILA), Congress in 1977 passed the Fair Debt Collection Practices Act (FDCPA). This part of TILA regulates the activities of those who collect bills owed to others (including attorneys who regularly engage in consumer debt-collection activity, even when the activity consists of litigation).[7] The act specifically exempts from its coverage the activities of secured parties, process servers, and federal or state employees who are attempting to collect debts pursuant to the performance of their official duties.

Congress intended the law to eliminate abusive, deceptive, and unfair debt-collection practices and thereby to protect consumers. The act thus limits the manner in which a debt collector can communicate with the debtor. For example, the statute expressly prohibits, without the consumer's consent, any communications made at an unusual or inconvenient time, that is, before 8:00 A.M. and after 9:00 P.M. local time at the debtor's location. The debt collector, moreover, cannot communicate with the debtor at the debtor's place of employment if the debt collector knows or has reason to know that the debtor's employer prohibits the consumer from receiving such communications. In addition, in most circumstances, if the debt collector knows an attorney represents the consumer with respect to the debt, the debt collector can contact only the attorney, not the debtor. A debt collector typically cannot communicate with third parties (e.g., the debtor's neighbors, coworkers, or friends) concerning the collection of the debt, either. Prior to 1996, debt collectors had to disclose in all communications that the purpose of the communication (whether oral or written) involved the collection of a debt and that the debt collector would use any information so received for that purpose. Since 1996, the debt collector need disclose the previously required information only in its initial communication (whether oral or written) with the debtor. Pursuant to this recent amendment, the debt collector, as to all subsequent communications, must disclose only that the communication is from a debt collector.

The statute also permits the cessation of further communication with the debtor if he or she in writing notifies the debt collector that he or she refuses to pay the debt and wishes all communications to stop. At that point, the debt collector can advise the consumer only of the termination of further efforts to collect the debt or of the debt collector's intention to invoke any available remedies.

Similarly, debt collectors must refrain from unfair or unconscionable means of debt collection. For example, the debt collector is prohibited from accepting post-dated checks, making collect phone calls to debtors, or adding amounts—interest, fees, or expenses—not expressly allowed by the underlying debt agreement or by state law.

So that the debtor can dispute the debt if he or she has grounds to do so, the act requires the bill collector to send the debtor a written verification of the debt. The debtor then has 30 days in which he or she in writing must dispute the debt; otherwise, the debt collector can assume the validity of the debt.

The FTC has primary enforcement responsibilities under the FDCPA. Civil remedies of actual damages plus additional statutory damages, not to exceed $1,000, that the court can set are possible in individual suits. In class actions, $1,000 per person may be awarded, but the total damages so awarded cannot exceed the lesser of $500,000 or 1 percent of the debt collector's net worth.

Under a separate statute, a criminal penalty of $1,000 or a sentence of one year's imprisonment, or both, may be imposed on anyone who, during the course of debt-collection efforts, uses the words *federal, national,* or *the United States* to convey the false impression that the communication originates from, or in any way represents, the United States or any of its agencies or instrumentalities. Successful litigants may recover costs and attorney's fees as well.

Consider these principles as you analyze *Veillard* v. *Mednick.*

40.3

VEILLARD V. MEDNICK
24 F.SUPP.2D 863 (N.D.ILL. 1998)

FACTS Doctors Service Bureau, Inc. (DSBI) has been a licensed collection agent in Illinois since 1989. Richard Mednick, an attorney licensed in Illinois, is listed as an attorney in the telephone book, *Sullivan's Law Directory*, and directory assistance. Mednick employs non-attorneys to collect debts. Patrick Veillard is a resident of New York who became indebted to Nations Credit Commercial Corporation (Nations) through the use of a credit card. Nations sent Veillard's debt to DSBI, which in turn retained Mednick to collect the money. Mednick's office then sent Veillard an unsigned collection letter, dated 6 October 1997, seeking to obtain the money owed to Nations. The letterhead used in the letter was from "RICHARD M. MEDNICK AND ASSOCIATES," but the letter itself did not explicitly mention that Mednick and Associates is a law firm or that Mednick is an attorney. The body of the letter stated:

DEAR PATRICK VEILLARD:

Your seriously past-due account has been placed with us for collection.

Unless you notify this office within 30 days after receiving this notice that you dispute the validity of the debt or any portion thereof, this office will assume this debt is valid. If you notify this office in writing within 30 days from receiving this notice, this office will obtain verification of the debt or obtain a copy of a judgment and mail you a copy of such judgment or verification. If you request this office in writing within 30 days after receiving this notice, this office will provide you with the name and address of the original creditor, if different from the current creditor.

Your best interest will be served by resolving this matter as soon as possible as our client shows this obligation to be due immediately.

Yours truly,
J. Dancer
for Richard M. Mednick
Debt Collector

THIS IS AN ATTEMPT TO COLLECT A DEBT. ANY INFORMATION OBTAINED WILL BE USED FOR THAT PURPOSE.

40.3

VEILLARD V. MEDNICK, *continued*
24 F.SUPP.2D 863 (N.D.ILL. 1998)

Veillard claimed that Mednick and DSBI had violated the FDCPA because the letter created the false impression that the communication had originated with Mednick, a lawyer who was not actually involved in the collection of the debt. According to Veillard, by using letterhead that suggests the letter is from a law firm, Mednick and DSBI were being deceptive in violation of the Act. Veillard also submitted that the letter overshadows and contradicts the validation notice requirement. Specifically, Veillard contended, the statement "Your best interest will be served by resolving this matter as soon as possible as our client shows this obligation to be due immediately" is likely to induce the debtor to pay within the validation period so as to avoid legal action.

ISSUE Did the dunning letter at issue here violate the FDCPA?

HOLDING Yes. A dunning letter written on a law firm's letterhead could have led an unsophisticated consumer to be deceived or misled into thinking an attorney was involved in the matter. Moreover, the statement urging the debtor to pay the debt as soon as possible overshadowed the notification that the debtor had 30 days in which to challenge the validity of the debt owed and thus was another violation of the FDCPA.

REASONING Congress enacted the FDCPA in 1977 "to eliminate abusive debt collection practices by debt collectors." To this end, the act sets certain standards for debt collectors' communications with debtors. Among them is a requirement that debt collectors advise debtors of their (the debtors') rights to dispute the debt and demand verification. The FDCPA also bans false and misleading statements in collection letters and prohibits a debt collector's collecting a debt through "unfair or unconscionable fees beyond the amount in arrears." The law evaluates communications from debt collectors "through the eyes of the unsophisticated consumer." This standard presumes a level of sophistication that "is low, close to the bottom of the sophistication meter" and thereby "protects the consumer who is 'uninformed, naive, or trusting.'" Still, the standard "admits an objective element of reasonableness," which "protects debt collectors from

liability for unrealistic or peculiar interpretations of collection letters." Veillard claimed that Mednick and DSBI had violated several provisions of the FDCPA, including Section 1692e, which states that a debt collector "may not use any false, deceptive, or misleading representation...with the collection of any debt." Likewise, section 1692e(3) prohibits any "false representation or implication that any individual is an attorney or that any communication is from an attorney." Debt collectors also violate § 1692e(10) when they use "any false representation or deceptive means to collect...any debt." To comply with the strictures of the FDCPA, an attorney sending dunning letters must be directly and personally involved in the debt collection. The use of an attorney's letterhead and his or her signature on collection letters could give consumers the false impression that the letters represent communications from an attorney. Moreover, as one court has noted,

> an unsophisticated consumer [who gets] a letter from an "attorney," knows the price of poker has just gone up. And that clearly is the reason why the dunning campaign escalates from the collection agency, which might not strike fear in the heart of the consumer, to the attorney, who is better positioned to get the debtor's knees knocking.

Hence, some courts hold that using the term "attorney" in the absence of an attorney's actually working on the file is confusing as a matter of law. Although the letter here is unsigned, it comes from "J. Dancer for Richard M. Mednick." And even though the letter refers to Dancer as a debt collector, the letter, by stating that Dancer wrote the letter on behalf of Mednick, could lead an unsophisticated debtor to conclude that Mednick had supervised the file. Thus, the question is whether an unsophisticated debtor would be misled into believing that Mednick is a lawyer. Mednick and DSBI claimed that, because the word "attorney" is absent from the letter, only a very sophisticated and extremely suspicious consumer would investigate whether Mednick has a law license. In addition, they argued that because other professionals such as architects, engineers, and realtors use "and associates," an unsophisticated consumer could not reasonably

continued

40.3

VEILLARD V. MEDNICK, *continued*
24 F.SUPP.2D 863 (N.D.ILL. 1998)

believe the letter had come from a law firm. However, a person nowadays does not need to have a *Sullivan's Directory* or other legal publication to determine that Richard Mednick and Associates is a law firm. The unsophisticated consumer need only request a telephone number from directory assistance to determine this fact. In addition, it would be unusual for a nonlawyer, using the connotation "and Associates," to be involved in the business of collecting debts. The circumstances surrounding the disputed letter thus could lead an unsophisticated consumer to believe that Richard Mednick and Associates is a law firm prepared to take legal action on the debt. Accordingly, Mednick and DSBI had violated various provisions of the FDCPA. Moreover, to ensure that consumers have a fair chance to dispute and demand verification of their debts, § 1692g of the FDCPA requires debt collectors to send debtors a "validation notice." A validation notice must explain that the debtor has 30 days to dispute the validity of all or a portion of the debt. If the debtor disputes the debt, the collector must cease collection efforts until it sends information verifying the debt. If the debtor does not dispute the debt, the collector may assume it is valid. A validation notice that explains the debtor's right to contest a debt nevertheless violates § 1692g if the notice is somehow overshadowed or otherwise contradicted by accompanying or subsequent messages. Veillard claimed that the letter's 30-day notification information conflicts with the sentence "Your best interest will be served by resolving this matter as soon as possible as our client shows this obligation to be due immediately," and creates confusion in violation of § 1692g. The confusion here is that Mednick does not explain what will happen if Veillard disputes the validity of the debt. Mednick could have cleared up the confusion by stating: "If you should dispute this debt, we will discontinue collection efforts immediately until we verify that the debt is accurate." While some courts have exempted from liability a statement like "your immediate attention to this matter is in your best interest," Mednick's letter, in contrast, ended with the unequivocal comment "our client shows this obligation to be due immediately." Hence, Mednick's resembles other letters in which courts have found violations of § 1692g. Accordingly, Veillard's motion for a summary judgment would be granted.

BUSINESS CONSIDERATIONS Why would rational, profit-maximizing firms conduct themselves as Mednick and DSBI did here? How should firms facing this type of situation transact business?

ETHICAL CONSIDERATIONS Was the conduct of the defendants ethical? How should debt-collection firms, from an ethical perspective, act?

THE UNIFORM CONSUMER CREDIT CODE

Designed to replace state laws governing consumer credit, the Uniform Consumer Credit Code (UCCC) resulted from the drafting efforts of the National Conference of Commissioners on Uniform State Laws and was meant to make consistent the widely varying state laws concerning installment sales and loans, revolving charge accounts, home solicitation sales, home improvement loans, and truth-in-lending. Simply put, its drafters wished to do for consumer law what the Uniform Commercial Code had done for commercial law.

First promulgated in 1969 and later revised in 1974, the UCCC has failed to gain wide acceptance. To date, only seven states have enacted it, and many of them have chosen to replace the UCCC's provisions with their own. Still, it represents an additional statutory attempt to benefit consumers.

YOU BE THE JUDGE

THE USE OF CREDIT CARDS FOR ONLINE GAMBLING

A Marin County, California, woman who lost $70,000 while gambling online with 12 credit cards sued MasterCard, Visa, and the banks that had issued the credit cards. She argued that because gambling is illegal in California, the credit card companies never should have authorized her charges. She claimed that the credit card companies in effect are aiding and abetting illegal Internet gambling and making a lot of money from these activities. In a related vein, a Minneapolis attorney recently filed a class action lawsuit alleging that credit card firms' fomenting such illegal online gambling amounts to racketeering and precludes the companies from collecting on the debts (state laws oftentimes make the collection of gambling debts unenforceable). The operators of online gambling web sites argued that the absence of laws specifically outlawing Internet gambling—only three states explicitly ban Internet gambling, although many prosecutors construe a federal law banning interstate sports betting over the telephone and state laws banning gambling in general as providing a basis for prohibiting online gambling—makes such betting legal. For the 300 web sites that offer such gambling, business is booming, with revenues expected to exceed $2.3 billion in 2001.

Assume *you* are the judge who must decide these cases. In whose favor will *you* rule? Why?[8]

BUSINESS CONSIDERATIONS Should a business that provides products or services that involve potentially addictive and damaging behavior take steps to protect its customers from the potentially injurious consequences of the customers' conduct becoming addictive? What responsibility does the business have to the customer or to society for the harm resulting from addictive behavior "aided and abetted" by the goods or services provided by the company to the consumers?

ETHICAL CONSIDERATION Is it ethical for a consumer credit-granting business, especially credit card companies, to provide a means (i.e., credit) for its customers to participate in addictive behavior, even if such activities (i.e., the provision of credit) are legal?

SOURCE: Tom Lowery, *USA Today* (17 August 1999), p. B1.

THE CONSUMER PRODUCT SAFETY ACT

The Consumer Product Safety Act of 1972 established the Consumer Product Safety Commission (CPSC). An independent federal regulatory agency, the CPSC consists of five members appointed by the president with the advice and consent of the Senate. The CPSC has authority over a great number of consumer products, but products expressly excluded from the commission's jurisdiction include tobacco and tobacco products, motor vehicles, pesticides covered under FIFRA (a statute discussed in Chapter 41), firearms and ammunition, food, and cosmetics.

To help protect the public from injuries from consumer products, the commission can do the following: set and enforce safety standards; ban hazardous products; collect information on consumer-related injuries; administratively order firms to report publicly defects that could create substantial hazards; force firms to take corrective action (repair, replacement, or refund) with regard to substantially hazardous consumer products in commerce; seek court orders for recalls of

40.3 | FINANCE/ MANAGEMENT

CALL-IMAGE TECHNOLOGY

CREDIT COLLECTION

Several of CIT's credit customers have fallen behind in making their credit payments; a few have even defaulted. All efforts by the firm to collect these amounts have failed, and Tom and Dan think that the firm should hire a collection agency to recover the firm's money. Anna, preferring a low-key approach to collection, wants the firm to write to these customers and remind them of their obligation to repay the debts. The family members all agree that they would like to recover the funds, but they remain unsure of the legal implications of various collection efforts. They ask you what they should do. What will you advise them?

BUSINESS CONSIDERATIONS Why would a business be willing to hire a debt-collection agency to recover past-due accounts? What factors should a business consider before it takes such a step?

ETHICAL CONSIDERATIONS Is it ethical for a business to turn its debt collections over to an independent third party who was not involved in the extension of credit? Is it ethical for a firm to accept collections that the debt-collection agency may have acquired in an unethical manner?

imminently hazardous products; conduct research on consumer products; and engage in outreach educational programs for consumers, industry, and local government.

Products banned by the CPSC include certain all-terrain vehicles, unstable refuse bins, lawn darts, tris (a chemical flame-retardant found in children's apparel), products containing asbestos, and paint containing lead. Products subject to CPSC standards include matchbooks, automatic garage door openers, bicycles, cribs, rattles, disposable lighters, toys with small parts, and the like.

SUMMARY

Various federal and state statutes protect consumers' rights. The Consumer Credit Protection Act of 1968, better known as the Truth in Lending Act (TILA), mandates the disclosure (via a standardized form and terminology) of the actual costs of credit so as to enable consumers to make more informed decisions about credit. Failure to comply with the act's disclosure provisions (or with its implementing regulation, Regulation Z) subjects the creditor to various civil, criminal, and statutory liabilities. The Fair Credit Reporting Act of 1970 requires consumer-reporting agencies to adopt reasonable procedures for guaranteeing the accuracy of information disseminated in credit reports. The act also limits the uses that one can make of such information. Consumers enjoy a variety of rights under the statute, including notification of an agency's reliance on adverse information and mechanisms for disputing the accuracy of information contained in files. Civil, criminal, and administrative remedies are available under the act. The Equal Credit Opportunity Act of 1974 (ECOA) prohibits discrimination based on sex, marital status, race, religion, national origin, age (provided the applicant has the capacity to contract), receipt of public assistance benefits, and the good-faith exercise of rights under TILA. Regulation B extensively implements ECOA by, among other things, setting out the rules that creditors must follow when they evaluate the creditworthiness of any applicant and when they provide notification to the consumer of the action taken. The remedies available for violations of ECOA resemble those granted under TILA. The Fair Debt Collection Practices Act of 1974 (FDCPA) regulates the activities of debt collectors. Congress intended the law to eliminate abusive, deceptive, and unfair debt-collection practices and thereby to protect consumers. The act limits the manner in which the debt collector can communicate with the debtor and limits the third parties whom the debt collector can contact about the debt. Remedial awards are similar to those granted under other statutes, but the Federal Trade Commission has primary enforcement responsibilities under the FDCPA. The Uniform Consumer Credit Code represents yet another statute—this time at the state level—that protects

RESOURCES FOR BUSINESS LAW STUDENTS

NAME	RESOURCES	WEB ADDRESS
Consumer Credit Protection Act—15 USC § 1601	The Legal Information Institute (LII), maintained by the Cornell Law School, provides a hypertext and searchable version of 15 USC § 1601, the Consumer Credit Protection Act, better known as the Truth in Lending Act.	**http://www4.law.cornell.edu/uscode/15/1601.html**
Federal Reserve Board Regulations	The Federal Reserve Board provides summaries of its regulations, including Regulations B and Z.	**http://www.bog.frb.fed.us/frregs.htm**
U.S. Consumer Product Safety Commission	The U.S. Consumer Product Safety Commission provides consumer news and information, as well as notices on recalls and business contracts.	**http://www.cpsc.gov/**
The Consumer Law Page	The Consumer Law Page, maintained by The Alexander Law Firm, provides articles, brochures, and reference materials.	**http://consumerlawpage.com/**

consumers. The Consumer Product Safety Act established the Consumer Product Safety Commission (CPSC). The CPSC regulates hazardous products and can even ban those that pose imminent hazards to the public.

DISCUSSION QUESTIONS

1. Explain the disclosures a creditor typically must make to the consumer under the Truth in Lending Act (TILA).
2. Describe the remedies available for creditors' violation of the Truth in Lending Act (TILA).
3. Explain in detail the coverage of the Fair Credit Reporting Act (FCRA).
4. Delineate the civil remedies that are permitted—and prohibited—by the FCRA.
5. Explain what Regulation B of the Equal Credit Opportunity Act (ECOA) requires of creditors for compliance.
6. Outline the general requirements of the Fair Debt Collection Practices Act (FDCPA).
7. Set out the civil and criminal penalties that can result from violations of the FDCPA.
8. Explain the underlying purposes of the Uniform Consumer Credit Code (UCCC).
9. Describe in detail the powers enjoyed by the Consumer Product Safety Commission (CPSC).
10. Mention some of the products subject to the standards set by the Consumer Product Safety Commission and some of the products it has banned.

CASE PROBLEMS AND WRITING ASSIGNMENTS

1. In June 1992, Ocie M. Williams applied for a rural housing assistance loan through the Farmers Home Administration (FHA). Prior to issuing Williams a loan, the FHA requested a credit report from the Credit Bureau of Clanton (Credit Bureau). The Credit Bureau is a consumer-reporting agency within the terms of the Fair Credit Reporting Act (FCRA). The report prepared by the Credit Bureau disclosed two

public record items: (1) an April 1990 mortgage foreclosure notice published in a local paper against Williams by Colonial Bank, which foreclosure had resulted in the sale of the property to another party; and (2) a materialmen's lien filed in April 1990 by William E. Knight in the amount of $14,720. The report indicated that the lien had been paid in June 1990. Upon receiving the credit report, the FHA determined that Williams was not eligible for a loan because of his credit history. When Williams learned of this decision, he approached the Credit Bureau and asked it to reinvestigate the two public record items that had appeared on his credit report. Although Williams acknowledged that a mortgage foreclosure on his property had occurred, he maintained that it should not have been included in his credit report because the bank had effected an improper foreclosure. Similarly, he contended that Knight had lacked any basis for filing the materialmen's lien and that the lien should not have appeared on the credit report, even though the credit report also revealed that the lien had been satisfied. Williams thus admitted that the credit report had accurately reflected the contents of the public records; nonetheless, he requested a reinvestigation. When the Credit Bureau did not follow up on Williams's request, he filed suit under the FCRA. In these circumstances, had the Credit Bureau violated the act? Why or why not? [See *Williams* v. *Colonial Bank*, 826 F.Supp. 415 (M.D.Ala. 1993).]

2. Linda Weill, an elementary school art teacher, developed a type of finger paint consisting of colored foam dispensed from a self-pressurized canister that she named "Rainbow Foam Paint." Rainbow Foam Paint basically is shaving cream colored with pre-mixed food coloring and is intended for use by children ages three and older. Weill obtained a U.S. patent for her product in 1986 and formed a company, X-Tra Art, Inc., to distribute the product. Rainbow Foam Paint has been on the market since 1986 and is, according to Weill, purchased primarily by teachers for use in the classroom. The product also is marketed as a children's bath product. On 3 April 1987, the California Department of Health Services approved the product "for purchase by schools for use by children in kindergarten and grades 1–6." Although the product contains hazardous hydrocarbon propellants, such as isobutane and propane, the material safety data sheet provided by the manufacturer indicates that Rainbow Foam Paint, like other aerosol shaving creams containing hydrocarbon propellants, is classified as nonflammable. In 1990, Consumers Union, publisher of *Consumer Reports* magazine, mentioned in its

children's magazine *Zillions* that Rainbow Foam Paint was a possible hazard because of flammability. The magazine stated that Rainbow Foam Paint could "catch fire if used near a flame . . . if not shaken" and thus was a dangerous toy that needed a "big, bold" warning, which it lacked. Weill contacted Consumers Union concerning the article and demanded an immediate retraction. She received a letter from Consumers Union dated 12 December 1990, which stated that the report in *Zillions* had been inaccurate and that Consumers Union intended "to retract it in the next issue" of the magazine since Consumers Union had concluded that "the momentary flash [it] observed . . . presents no hazard." Shortly afterward, Weill nonetheless notified Consumers Union that she intended to sue it for money damages despite the retraction. Thereafter, Consumers Union, in a letter to Weill on 31 December 1990 stated that it would not print a retraction of the *Zillions* report and that the Consumers Union was referring the matter to the Consumer Product Safety Commission (CPSC), as Consumers Union believed the product violated the Federal Hazardous Substances Act (FHSA). On 2 January 1991, the CPSC collected 14 cans of Rainbow Foam Paint from an X-Tra Art, Inc., officer. On 9 January 1991, the CPSC extensively tested the product in the upright, sideways, and upside-down positions, under the method prescribed in the applicable regulations. Following these tests, the CPSC determined that Rainbow Foam Paint canisters were flammable when placed in the upside-down position and might cause substantial personal injury with reasonably foreseeable use. Therefore, the CPSC concluded that Rainbow Foam Paint was a "banned hazardous substance" under the FHSA. The CPSC thereupon requested that Weill stop distributing the product and indicated that she could be fined up to $1,250,000 if she failed to do so. When Weill refused to cease the distribution of the paint, the CPSC notified the U.S. attorney's office, which initiated a seizure order. After protracted litigation, the district court, granting summary judgment for Weill and X-Tra Art, Inc. (the claimants), ruled that Rainbow Foam Paint was not a banned hazardous substance within the meaning of the FHSA because it came within the exemption for adequately labeled art materials. The court rejected the contention that the product should be classified as a toy because it was sold in toy stores. With respect to the argument that warning labels on the product were inadequate because the product was targeted at children too young to read the warning labels, the court stated that, "it must be concluded that the label on Rainbow Foam Paint . . . adequately warns adults who would potentially supervise the use of the product with children." The district court therefore concluded that "Congress may have decided to rely on the premise that [any] danger is alleviated, as a child's access to the product would only be through an adult." Had the CPSC properly classified Rainbow Foam Paint as a hazardous substance under the Consumer Product Safety Act? [See *U.S.* v. *Articles of Banned Hazardous Substances,* 34 F.3d 91 (2d Cir. 1994).]

3. On 19 October 1987, John Venesio Graciano, Jr., completed a credit application by which he sought to borrow $6,300 from East Cambridge Savings Bank to purchase an automobile. Graciano listed another person's social security number as his and indicated that he worked for New England Tea & Coffee in Malden, Massachusetts. On 27 October 1987, the bank verified Graciano's employment at New England Tea & Coffee and approved his application. Unbeknownst to the bank, Graciano was using someone else's social security number—and that someone else had a very similar name—John Victor Graziano, Jr., the plaintiff in this case. The plaintiff and Graciano had different addresses, different places of employment, and different dates of birth. And, of course, the plaintiff and Graciano had different, albeit similar, names. The bank nonetheless failed to ascertain the true identity and social security number of its loan applicant, Graciano. On 30 October 1987, Graciano signed a promissory note for $4,500 and was given a bank draft in that amount, payable to him and the dealer from whom he was purchasing the automobile. After Graciano failed to make any payments on the note, on 30 June 1988, the matter was referred to the bank's attorney for collection. The attorney sought and, on 14 February 1989, recovered for the bank a judgment against Graciano in the amount of $6,315.64. Prior to and after this judgment, the bank requested consumer reports on Graciano on at least three occasions: 18 July 1988, 11 February 1992, and 25 November 1992. The bank made each request so that the bank could obtain information as to the whereabouts of Graciano and thereby facilitate the bank's efforts to collect its judgment. By entering into the computer system the social security number Graciano falsely had provided to the bank—that is, the plaintiff's social security number—the bank thereafter requested the first report on Graciano. The bank received two reports, one for Graciano and one for the plaintiff. The bank requested the second and third reports after it already knew or should have known that two individuals with similar names were using the same social security number.

The plaintiff claimed that he never had requested any credit or taken a loan from the bank. Nor, he asserted, had he ever been a customer of the bank. On 10 December 1992, the plaintiff received a letter from an attorney for the bank, which letter informed the plaintiff that, as he currently owed the bank $8,589.27, the plaintiff should contact the attorney for the purpose of working out an agreeable payment plan. The letter was addressed to the plaintiff's correct address, but the name on the letter was "John V. Graciano." Before being contacted by the bank's attorney, the plaintiff had been aware that someone had been misusing his social security number for employment purposes. Indeed, on 12 March 1991, the plaintiff had advised the Social Security Administration that his number was being misused. Bringing suit against the bank, the plaintiff subsequently claimed that the bank's actions of requesting credit reports—pursuant to its collection efforts—represented a violation of the FCRA because the bank had willfully obtained the plaintiff's consumer reports under false pretenses. Should the court accept the plaintiff's contentions? [See *Graziano* v. *TRW, Inc.,* 877 F.Supp. 53 (D.Mass. 1995).]

4. Citicorp Retail Services, Inc. (CRSI) had retained Great Lakes Collection Bureau (Great Lakes) to provide debt-collection services. CRSI's contract with Great Lakes stated that Great Lakes must have CRSI's prior written authorization before Great Lakes attempted to collect on any referred account or implied in any communication to a referred account that CRSI would sue the debtor. In an attempt to collect the $483.43 that Diane W. Bentley owed CRSI, Great Lakes sent her two computer-generated letters (i.e., dunning letters) dated 30 November 1990 and 18 December 1990. The 30 November 1990 dunning letter included the following language:

Your creditor is now taking the necessary steps to recover the outstanding amount of $483.43. They have instructed us to proceed with whatever legal means necessary to enforce collection. This is an attempt to collect and any information obtained will be used for that purpose.

Great Lakes programs its computer to generate this form letter whenever the agency receives a new account. The 18 December follow-up letter stated in relevant part:

This office has been unable to contact you by telephone, therefore your delinquent account has been referred to my desk where a decision must be made as to what direction must be taken to enforce collection. Were our client to retain legal counsel in your area, and it was determined that suit should be filed against you, it could result in a judgment. Such judgment might, depending upon the law in your state, include not only the amount of your indebtedness, but the amount of any statutory costs, legal interest, and where applicable, reasonable attorney's fees.

Again, depending upon the law in your state, if such judgment were not thereupon satisfied, it might be collected by attachment of an execution upon your real and personal property.

Garnishment may also be an available remedy to satisfy an unsatisfied judgment, if applicable in the state in which you reside.

We therefore suggest you call our office immediately toll free at [this number] to discuss payment arrangements or mail payment in full in the enclosed envelope.

No legal action has been or is now being taken against you.

In fact, CRSI had not actually authorized Great Lakes "to proceed with whatever legal means is necessary to enforce collection" as represented in the first letter. And, despite its representations to the contrary in the second letter, Great Lakes had failed to telephone Bentley prior to 18 December and had not referred her account to anyone's desk for a decision regarding her account. Moreover, even in cases where its advice is solicited, Great Lakes recommends legal proceedings to its clients only for approximately 1 percent of the collection accounts referred to it. Did the Great Lakes letter violate the Fair Debt Collection Practices Act's prohibition against the use of any false, deceptive, or misleading representation or means in connection with the collection of a debt? [See *Bentley* v. *Great Lakes Collection Bureau*, 6 F.3d 60 (2d Cir. 1993)].

5. Teresa and Randy Barney brought a class action against Holzer Clinic, Ltd. (the Clinic). The Barneys alleged that the Clinic's refusals to schedule appointments for and its cancellation of the appointments of Medicaid recipients violated the Equal Credit Opportunity Act (ECOA). The Barneys claimed that the Clinic's refusal to schedule an appointment because of a person's status as a Medicaid recipient is a denial of credit because, if an appointment had been scheduled, the Medicaid recipient could receive the benefit of the Clinic's credit policy. The Barneys therefore sought to recover damages for the emotional harm they allegedly had suffered because of the Clinic's acts. Would the denial of medical services to persons who receive Medicaid benefits constitute actionable discrimination under ECOA? [See *Barney* v. *Holzer Clinic, Ltd.*, 902 F.Supp. 139 (S.D.Ohio 1995).]

6. **BUSINESS APPLICATION CASE** Based on her own creditworthiness, Linda J. Pierce obtained a Citibank Chase Visa account with defendant Citibank (South Dakota), N.A. Her husband, Michael Pierce, maintained several accounts with defendant Citicorp Credit Services, Inc. (Citicorp). Citicorp is a corporate affiliate of Citibank. When Citicorp notified Michael Pierce by letter on 11 January 1991 that, owing to his delinquent Citibank bankcard account, Citicorp had closed all his accounts, Citicorp included the account number of Linda Pierce among the numbers of the accounts closed. Linda Pierce, who lived with her husband, did not receive notice of the closing of her account; and her name was left off of the notice sent to Michael Pierce. Linda Pierce thereafter continued to receive regular statements on her account and continued to make payments on that account until 15 May 1991, when she learned from a customer service representative of Citibank that the account had been closed. In that telephone conversation, the customer service representative informed Linda Pierce that she could not use her card until the accounts of Michael Pierce were brought current because her account was linked with those of her husband. On 18 July 1991, Linda Pierce sent a registered letter to Citibank and requested a written response within 10 days as to why the bank had not renewed her account. On 11 September 1991, Citibank renewed her account; reinstated her credit privileges; and, in a letter dated 11 September 1991, informed her that Citicorp appreciated the efforts she had made to return her account to good standing. Linda Pierce thereafter used the account until she filed a petition in bankruptcy on 13 May 1992. Linda Pierce subsequently claimed that Citicorp, and Citibank acting as an agent for Citicorp, by failing to provide her with written notice of the closure or suspension of her charge account, had violated ECOA. Citicorp and Citibank contended that, despite the absence of a written notification's being sent to Linda Pierce, she was not entitled to relief because (1) her claim would be barred by the statute of limitations; (2) by receiving actual notice of the cancellation, she had waived her right to written notice; and (3) Citibank's failure to notify her in writing would constitute an inadvertent error permissible under ECOA. Who had the stronger arguments? Why? What intrafirm policies should the banks institute so as to avoid similar litigation in the future? [See *Pierce* v. *Citibank (South Dakota), N.A.*, 843 F.Supp. 646 (D.Or. 1994).]

7. **ETHICAL APPLICATION CASE** In February 1988, PHH Aviation Systems, Inc. (PHH) issued a credit card to Towers World Airways, Inc. (Towers) to

purchase fuel and other aircraft-related goods and ser-vices for a corporate jet leased by Towers from PHH. World Jet Corporation (World Jet), a subsidiary of United Air Fleet, was responsible for maintaining the aircraft. An officer of Towers designated Fred Jay Schley, an employee of World Jet, as the chief pilot of the leased jet and gave him permission to make purchases with the PHH credit card at least in connection with noncharter flights that were used exclusively by Tower's executives. Notwithstanding United Air Fleet's agreement to pay the cost of fuel on chartered flights, which provided service for other clients, Schley (prior to the cancellation of the card in August 1988) used the credit card to charge $89,025.87 to Towers in connection with such flights. When Towers sought a declaratory judgment that would absolve it of any liability for any charges incurred in connection with chartered flights, the district court denied Towers's petition for declaratory relief and entered judgment for PHH for the full amount in dispute ($89,025.87). The district court held Towers liable for the $89,025.87, pursuant to the terms of the credit agreement between Towers and PHH, which provided that "[the] Aircraft Operator shall be responsible for all purchases made with a Card from the date of its issuance until the Aircraft Operator reports that a card is lost, stolen, misplaced or canceled by calling PHH." The district court held that the Truth in Lending Act (TILA), which limits a cardholder's liability for "unauthorized" uses, was inapplicable to charges incurred by one to whom the cardholder has "voluntarily and knowingly allow[ed]" access for another limited purpose. On appeal, Towers conceded liability but contended that summary judgment had been improperly granted on the question of whether the TILA limits its liability to $50. Was Schley's use of the card to incur $89,025.87 in connection with chartered flights unauthorized within the meaning of the TILA provision that limits a cardholder's liability? If the court had based its decision on ethics, would the result differ? [See *Towers World Airways, Inc.* v. *PHH Aviation Systems, Inc.*, 933 F.2d 174 (2d Cir. 1991).]

8. **CRITICAL THINKING CASE** On several occasions between 1988 and 1992, Nachson Draiman used his American Express Platinum Card when he purchased airline tickets through the Travel Dimensions travel agency. Draiman provided Travel Dimensions with his Platinum Card number, and when he needed tickets, he would call and place an order. Travel Dimensions in turn would send the tickets to Draiman and the bill to American Express Travel Related Service Company (American Express). By including the cost

of the tickets plus applicable financing charges in its periodic billing statement, American Express then would secure payment from Draiman. On 21 January 1992, Draiman canceled his Platinum Card. Sometime thereafter, Draiman deposited an undisclosed sum of money with Travel Dimensions. On 20 July 1992, Draiman purchased four El Al tickets to Israel for a total cost of $8,308. Draiman instructed Travel Dimensions to pay for the El Al tickets by drawing on his deposited funds. Travel Dimensions did not honor that request—instead it charged the amount against the number that it had for Draiman's Platinum Card. American Express of course knew nothing of Draiman's deposit with, or his instructions to, Travel Dimensions. When American Express received the $8,308 charge from Travel Dimensions, that triggered American Express's reinstatement policy, as set out in these terms in the cardholder agreement:

> If you ask us to cancel your account, but you continue to use the Card, we will consider such use as your request for reinstatement of your account. If we agree to reinstate your account, this Agreement or any amended or new Agreement we send you will govern your reinstated account.

American Express does not communicate with cardholders to confirm that it is in fact their desire to revive their accounts. In accordance with its written policy, then, American Express reinstated Draiman's Platinum Card on 26 August 1992, and billed him $8,308. Draiman later actually used the El Al tickets (each of which had his Platinum Card number printed on its face) to travel to Israel. On 15 October 1993, Draiman paid American Express $3,399.98 of the $8,308 total and threatened suit if it tried to collect the $4,908.02 balance. When American Express attempted to collect the debt, Draiman, citing purported violations of the Fair Credit Billing Act, TILA, and other applicable laws, on 11 January 1995, brought the threatened legal action with one twist: Draiman filed not only on his own behalf but also on behalf of a purported class of similarly aggrieved persons. Draiman grounded his lawsuit on two different theories: (1) that American Express, by resuscitating his canceled Platinum Card without his permission, had issued an unsolicited credit card in violation of TILA; and (2) that, owing to Travel Dimensions's unauthorized use of his Platinum Card, he would be entitled to the $50 limitation on liability afforded by TILA in certain circumstances. How should the court rule on Draiman's contentions? [See *Draiman* v. *American Express Travel Related Services Co.*, 892 F.Supp. 1096 (N.D.Ill. 1995).]

NOTES

1. See, for example, Jonathan Sheldon, ed., *Fair Credit Reporting Act*, 3rd ed. (Boston: National Consumer Law Center, 1994). This and other National Consumer Law Center publications, such as Ernest L. Sarason, ed., *Truth in Lending* (1986); Gerry Azzata, ed., *Equal Credit Opportunity Act* (1988); and the annual cumulative supplements to these works provide more detailed information on consumer law, as does Gene A. Marsh, *Consumer Protection Law in a Nutshell* (St. Paul, MN: West Publishing Group, 1999) and Howard J. Alperin and Ronald F. Chase, *Consumer Law: Sales Practices and Credit Regulation* (Minneapolis: West Publishing Co., 1986).

2. Jonathan Sheldon, ed., *Fair Credit Reporting Act*, 3rd ed. (Boston: National Consumer Law Center, 1994), p. 31.

3. Ibid.

4. *Beach* v. *Ocwen Federal Bank*, 523 U.S. 410 (1998).

5. Sheldon, *Fair Credit Reporting Act*, p. 32.

6. Ibid.

7. *Heintz* v. *Jenkins*, 514 U.S. 291, 299 (1995).

8. Tom Lowery, "Debtors Take Credit Cards to Task for Allowing Bets," *USA Today* (17 August 1999), p. B1.

41

ENVIRONMENTAL PROTECTION

A G E N D A

CIT will manufacture its videophone units at several factories in the United States. The firm wants to make its factories as similar as possible but has concerns about the differing state environmental protection standards that will force the company to adapt location-specific responses to such laws. The family members want each community to view CIT as a "good neighbor." Accordingly, they want to know what they must do to meet this objective. In particular, they seek a corporate strategy that will ensure that the firm refrains from polluting these respective communities in any fashion. As CIT opens new facilities, the family members in addition want to ensure that the firm meets or exceeds federal expectations. What sorts of environmentally friendly technologies should they install in their facilities?

These and other questions are likely to arise as you study this chapter. Be prepared! You never know when one of the Kochanowskis will need your help or advice.

INTRODUCTION

Environmental law constitutes an extremely complex, pervasive, and controversial area of the law. Acronym laden and comprised of highly technical statutes and regulations, environmental law poses genuine challenges to students and legal practitioners alike. Hence, in this chapter we will highlight only some of the most important principles.[1]

During the heyday of environmental protection efforts in the 1970s, the United States distinguished itself by taking the first steps aimed at halting the destruction of our planet's biodiversity. It did so largely through statutory engraftments onto common law **nuisance** principles. Nuisance laws prohibit interference with the rights of others; however, though providing the framework for modern-day statutory environmental law, such laws proved inadequate to solve the sheer magnitude of the problems these laws must address.

Nuisance
Unlawful use of one's own property so as to injure the rights of another.

THE ENVIRONMENTAL PROTECTION AGENCY

Congress instead chose to opt for a statutory approach that leaves enforcement largely to an administrative agency called the Environmental Protection Agency (EPA), itself established by executive order in 1970. In general, the EPA has the power to enforce environmental laws, adopt regulations, conduct research on pollution, and assist other governmental entities concerned with the environment. To enforce federal environmental laws, the EPA can subject suspected violators to administrative orders and civil penalties and can refer criminal matters to the Department of Justice as well.

The laws Congress passes and the EPA enforces consider the economic aspects of environmental law; take a technological approach to environmental concerns; mandate risk assessment in the implementation of these laws; and use the imposition of liability, sometimes even strict liability, as a hammer to ensure compliance. Early legislation required compliance primarily by business and industry, especially the chemical industry. In the last 15 years, however, small businesses and state and local governments increasingly have borne the burden of the compliance costs associated with environmental issues.

Hence, the virtual absence of any legislative enactments in the 1990s may indicate the increasing politicization of this area of the law. In general, what seems a simple (and valid) argument—take all steps necessary to save the environment—is complicated by the staggering costs involved. In 1999, for example, the EPA budgeted nearly $7.8 billion for its numerous programs and initiatives.[2] Moreover, EPA figures (which many critics argue may be underestimated by as much as a multiple of 30) place the costs to local taxpayers for environmental compliance in the year 2000 at over $32 billion (in 1986 dollars), an estimate that does not take into account the costs imposed on businesses and consumers.[3] Another recent article estimates that compliance with all governmental regulations in 1995, including environmental laws, cost U.S. businesses $600 billion (calculated in 1991 dollars).[4] Critics of such environmental regulations question whether the benefits derived from compliance outweigh these gargantuan costs; they suggest the money spent on complying with environmental mandates might be better spent on education, medical research, and the like.[5] Pro-environmentalists, however, argue that we have no choice but to protect the environment. Simply put, it is the only one we have—if we ruin it, we cannot replenish or replace it.

THE NATIONAL ENVIRONMENTAL POLICY ACT

The National Environmental Policy Act of 1969 (NEPA) became effective when then-President Nixon signed it into law in 1970. Congress enacted NEPA as a means of furthering a national policy to encourage a productive and harmonious relationship between people and the environment. Congress also viewed NEPA as a vehicle for promoting efforts to eliminate environmental damage and thereby enhance the health and welfare of the citizenry.

In short, § 101 of NEPA declares that it is the federal government's continuing responsibility, in cooperation with state and local governments and other concerned private and public organizations, to use all practicable means, consistent with other essential national policy considerations, to attain the broadest range of beneficial uses of the environment (including the preservation of healthy and aesthetically and culturally pleasing surroundings) while at the same time avoiding the degradation of the environment, risks to health and safety, and other undesirable or unintended consequences. In fulfilling this purpose, NEPA directs that, to the fullest extent possible, all agencies of the federal government live up to these environmental responsibilities.

Environmental Impact Statement

NEPA effectuates this goal primarily by requiring virtually all federal agencies to prepare a detailed *environmental impact statement* (EIS) whenever the agency proposes legislation, recommends any actions, or undertakes any activities that may affect the environment. Among other things, an EIS must:

- Describe the anticipated impact that the proposed action will have on the environment
- Describe any unavoidable adverse consequences of the action or activity
- Examine the possible alternative methods of achieving the desired goals
- Distinguish between long-term and short-term environmental effects
- Describe the irreversible and irretrievable commitments of resources that will occur if the proposed action is implemented

The statute requires wide dissemination of EISs in draft form to other federal, state, and local agencies; the president; and the Council on Environmental Quality (i.e., the CEQ, the importance of which is discussed in the next section).

Given the substantial data gathering necessary for successful compliance with the prerequisites of an EIS, many agencies have tried to exempt themselves from having to prepare this statement. However, numerous court decisions since 1970 indicate that the following criteria show a need for an EIS: (1) a proposed federal action (2) that is "major" and (3) that has a significant impact on the environment. Courts have made the definitional thresholds for points 1 and 2 law; hence, if a federal agency has control over the proposed action (no matter how small the undertaking, or even if it is regional in scope), coupled with a substantial commitment of resources, the EIS requirement applies. Similarly, court decisions under point 3 have not limited interpretations of the term *environment* solely to the natural environment (lakes, rivers, wetlands, wilderness areas, beaches, and so forth). The broad goals of the act (e.g., the preservation of aesthetically and culturally pleasing surroundings, including the historical aspects of our national heritage) support the view that projects covered by NEPA involve more than just proposals that have an impact on various natural habitats. On the other hand, Congress clearly did not intend to require an EIS for every conceivable federal project, even though all such proposed activities in some fashion affect the quality of life of the citizenry.

Hence, considerable litigation has centered around the content of the EIS. CEQ regulations set out detailed requirements that cover the preparation of an EIS. The agency first makes an *environmental assessment* (an EA) of the need for an EIS. An interdisciplinary, interagency evaluation of the need for the proposed action; the likely environmental effects of the proposed action; the alternatives to the proposed action; and the agency, interest group, and public comments received concerning the proposal all factor into the EA as well.

Unless the agency makes a *finding of no significant impact* (i.e., a FONSI), the agency, by determining the scope—or subject matter—of the EIS, begins the preparation of the EIS. Court and agency decisions have held that agencies cannot avoid the application of NEPA by breaking up long-term projects—for example, highway, flood control, and hydroelectric projects that cover wide areas—into segments that separately seem to show an absence of environmental risks even though the overall project does. The EIS must adequately discuss the consequences of each alternative, including the alternative that the agency take "no action" on a given problem.

In deciding whether to include a given alternative, courts use a *rule-of-reason* test that gauges whether a reasonable person would view the alternative as sufficiently significant to merit an extended discussion. The EIS need not mention implausible or purely speculative alternatives. Besides the scope of the EIS, the timing of the EIS also has spawned litigation. Agencies contemplating any action that has environmental repercussions must make sure that the preparation of the EIS occurs sufficiently in advance of the commencement of the project in question so that the EIS makes an important, practical contribution to the decision-making process rather than serving merely as a rationalization or justification for decisions already made by the agency.

Robertson v. *Methow Valley Citizens Council*,[6] a landmark case construing NEPA, held that NEPA does not require federal agencies to include in each EIS either a fully developed plan detailing the steps the agency would take so as to mitigate adverse environmental impacts or a worst-case analysis. Rather, according to the Supreme Court, the statutory requirement that a federal agency contemplating a major action prepare such an EIS ensures that the agency, in reaching its decision, will have available, and will carefully consider, detailed information concerning significant environmental impacts. Simply by focusing the agency's attention on the environmental consequences of a proposed project, NEPA ensures that important effects will not be overlooked or underestimated only to be discovered after resources have been committed. According to the Court, publication of an EIS, both in draft and final form, also gives the public the assurance that the agency in its decision-making process indeed has considered environmental concerns and, perhaps more significantly, provides a springboard for public comment. The EIS moreover serves the function of offering those governmental bodies that regulate development of the environment adequate notice of the expected consequences and the opportunity to plan and implement corrective measures in a timely manner. In the Court's view, the sweeping policy goals announced in NEPA thus are realized through a set of "action-forcing" procedures that require that agencies take a "hard look" at the environmental consequences and that provide for broad dissemination of relevant environmental information. This "hard look," however, need not include the formulation and adoption of a complete mitigation plan, the Court emphasized.

It would be inconsistent with NEPA's reliance on procedural mechanisms—as opposed to substantive, result-based standards—to demand the presence of a fully developed plan that will mitigate environmental harm before an agency can act. Simply put, the Court explained, it now is well settled that NEPA by itself does not mandate particular results but simply prescribes the necessary process. If the adverse environmental effects of the proposed action are adequately identified and evaluated, the agency is not constrained by NEPA from deciding that other values outweigh the environmental costs.

Council on Environmental Quality

The responsibility for ensuring the success of the EIS process falls to the Council on Environmental Quality (CEQ). Established by NEPA as an advisory council to the president, the CEQ develops regulations covering EISs and otherwise plays a leading role in developing and recommending to the president national policies that will foster and promote the improvement of the environmental quality of the nation. The CEQ assists and advises the president in the preparation of the Environmental Quality Report, which the president by law submits annually to Congress. By statute, the three-member CEQ can maintain a staff to help keep it abreast of developing environmental issues. Although the EPA represents the primary enforcement agency for federal environmental laws, courts give great deference to the CEQ's guidelines and regulations.

Amendments to NEPA in the late 1970s set up a nine-member Science Advisory Board to provide scientific information to the administrator of the EPA (the head of the agency) and various other congressional bodies that address scientific and technical issues affecting the environment. These amendments also give to the EPA administrator the task of coordinating environmental research, development, demonstration, and educational programs so as to minimize unnecessary duplication of programs, projects, and research facilities. Centralizing these responsibilities within the EPA and its staff facilitates the achievement of both NEPA's mandates and the broader environmental objectives and challenges facing the nation.

AIR POLLUTION

The impurities, dirt, and contaminants that a variety of sources emit into the air generally fall into five different classes. The first class is *carbon monoxide*—a colorless, odorless, poisonous gas produced by burning fossil fuels. Discharges from car engines represent the largest source of carbon monoxide. The second class is *particulates*—liquid or solid substances produced by facilities using stationary fuel combustion and other industrial processes. Sources ranging from factories to home furnaces emit such particles. The third class is *sulfur oxides*—corrosive, poisonous gases caused by use of sulfurous fuels. Electrical utility power plants and industrial plants emit most sulfur oxides. The fourth class is *nitrogen oxides*—gases produced by the very hot burning of fuel. These derive from stationary combustion plants, such as steel mills, and transportation vehicles such as trains, trucks, and buses. Once emitted into the atmosphere, sulfur oxides combine with nitrogen oxides to form "acid rain." Finally, the fifth class—*hydrocarbons*—consists of particulates derived from unburned and wasted fuel. Unlike carbon monoxide, hydrocarbons in and of themselves are nontoxic. However, when hydrocarbons combine in the atmosphere with nitrogen oxides, complex secondary pollution—known as *smog*—often results. Smog causes respiratory difficulties, eye and lung irritation, damage to trees and other vegetation, offensive odors, and haze.

However, it is nearly impossible to gauge with precision the so-called "threshold" or "safe" levels and/or "dangerous" levels of air pollution. Regulators therefore are relegated to setting exposure levels that kick in only when demonstrable adverse effects already have occurred. As a result, risk management continues to be a problematic issue in this area of environmental law.

As we shall see, the Clean Air Act (CAA) and its amendments reflect this and other complexities: the ever-expanding recognition of the health risks associated with pollution, rapidly changing technologies, a veritable explosion of scientific data relating to air pollution, and industry resistance to policymakers' attempts to redress this problem.

The Clean Air Act

The Clean Air Act represents an oft-amended, lengthy (the statute itself is approximately 300 pages long), technical, complex, and comprehensive approach to combating air pollution. Efforts to regulate air pollution actually began in the 1950s when Congress supplied technical and financial assistance to the states to help control interstate pollution in some circumstances.

The first federal CAA, enacted in 1963, concentrated on controlling emissions from stationary industrial sources (the so-called "tall-stack" types of facilities). Only four years later, Congress, in the Air Quality Act of 1967, saw the need to pass amendments that address the problem of mobile air emissions from sources such as cars and trucks. The 1967 amendments established atmospheric areas as well as air quality control regions and called for the development of state plans to implement these **ambient** air standards. Under these early enactments, each state retained primary responsibility for ensuring the air quality within its own borders.

Ambient
Pertaining to the surrounding atmosphere or the environment.

The 1970 Amendments

To achieve national air quality standards as well, the 1970 amendments, by establishing timetables for meeting state goals, appreciably strengthened the federal role in combating air pollution. Under these provisions, the administrator of the EPA is responsible for establishing *national ambient air quality standards* (NAAQSs) for air pollutants that reasonably would be anticipated to endanger the public health or welfare.

The 1970 amendments directed the administrator to establish two kinds of standards: (1) primary standards that, in the judgment of the administrator and allowing for an adequate margin of safety, are necessary in order to protect the public health; and (2) secondary standards that, in the judgment of the administrator, are necessary to protect the public welfare—crops, livestock, buildings, and the like—from any known or anticipated adverse effects associated with the presence of such air pollutants in the ambient air.

These amendments also require each state, after reasonable notice and public hearings, within nine months of the promulgation of any NAAQSs to submit to the EPA a *state implementation plan* (SIP) setting out how the state proposes to implement and maintain that standard within its *air quality control regions* (AQCRs). Before the EPA administrator can approve it, the SIP must provide for the establishment and operation of procedures necessary to monitor and control ambient air quality as well as for a program providing for the enforcement of emissions regulations. Any SIP must allow for the attainment of primary standards "as expeditiously as practicable" but in no case later than three years from the date the administrator approves the plan. The state must attain secondary standards within a "reasonable time." Once approved, a SIP has the force of both federal and state law.

The EPA administrator originally promulgated NAAQSs for particulates, sulfur dioxide, carbon monoxide, nitrogen oxide, ozone, and hydrocarbons. In 1978, the EPA administrator also added lead, which can cause retardation and brain damage in children, to this list and in 1983 revoked the hydrocarbon standard.

The 1977 Amendments

Congress realized that the achievement of its national air quality objectives would necessitate strict timetables aimed at forcing cleanup actions on the part of industry and government. Hence, the 1970 amendments contemplated prompt action. But by 1977, it had become clear that the original timetables were too optimistic. The 1977 Clean Air Act amendments therefore allowed delays in compliance in certain situations. By 1977, Congress also recognized that achievement of the nation's air quality objectives must encompass not only existing stationary sources and motor vehicles but also new stationary sources, new motor vehicles, and hazardous pollutants (such as asbestos, mercury, and vinyl chloride) produced by either existing or new sources. In addition, in 1977, Congress characterized this new undertaking as a federal responsibility; thus, Congress directed the EPA to establish such nationally uniform emission standards.

The 1990 Amendments

The 1990 amendments retain the basic strategies of the 1970 and 1977 amendments but also set new compliance dates for many of the deadlines established under the 1977 amendments that had come and gone.

Title I of these amendments, by mandating overall reductions of emissions within six years, attacks urban air pollution—particularly ozone concentrations.

Title II, by strengthening tailpipe emission standards for all cars and trucks and forcing manufacturers to design a certain number of clean-fuel cars each year, tackles mobile sources of emissions.

Title III requires the EPA to set permissible emission standards for some 190 toxic pollutants. In setting these standards, the administrator must consider the costs associated with achieving that standard, as well as the substances' health and environmental impacts.

Title IV for the first time sets up timetables aimed specifically at limiting emissions of nitrogen oxide and sulfur dioxide, the chief components of acid rain, by the year 2000. Focusing on the major emitting facilities, phase one of this title forces these facilities to achieve sulfur emissions of 2.5 pounds per million BTUs by 1995. Phase two, which must be achieved by the year 2000, cuts the allowable emissions to 1.2 pounds per million BTUs. Interestingly, this title contains economic incentives that allow complying facilities to "bank" or transfer emissions credits so as to use reductions of a given magnitude at one site to justify an increase in emissions levels at another site. As we shall see in the *Chevron U.S.A. Inc.* v. *Natural Resources Defense Council, Inc.*, case on page 1099, although some litigation has arisen over the mechanics of this trading, it does represent an economic-incentives approach to pollution control (similar to the Clean Water Act's permit process that we shall discuss later) that many environmental economists over the years have championed.

Title V sets up a permit system aimed at controlling emissions by major point sources—buildings, structures, facilities, or installations that emit air pollution. This portion of the amendment gives the EPA and state agencies that control air pollution the authority to regulate atmospheric discharges that may damage the general welfare or health and safety of the citizenry. Although industry groups have criticized the permit system as an unnecessary regulatory impediment to private enterprise, this system highlights the fact that Congress views atmospheric emissions as intrusions on publicly held and environmentally essential ecological systems, rather than as absolute rights, and thus regulable by the appropriate agencies.

Title VI for the first time regulates (and provides for the eventual phaseout of) various chlorofluorocarbons, hydrochlorofluorocarbons, and carbon tetrachlorides that bring about the depletion of the ozone layer. In this fashion, Title VI mirrors Title IV's provisions concerning acid rain.

Title VII strengthens the act's civil and criminal investigation, record-keeping, and enforcement provisions. These new provisions allow the EPA to impose penalties in a more expeditious fashion and permit citizens' suits that address allegedly unreasonable EPA delays in enforcement and repeated violations by emitters.

The remaining titles set out various miscellaneous provisions, including the institution of a program to monitor and improve air quality standards along the United States–Mexico border, the establishment of an interagency task force to conduct research on air quality, and the retraining of workers laid off or terminated as a consequence of a firm's complying with the Clean Air Act.

Enforcement mechanisms under the Clean Air Act include administrative penalties (not to exceed $25,000 per day per violation), orders issued by the administrator of the EPA, and criminal actions brought by the U.S. Attorney General, including fines of $1,000,000 for each violation and/or imprisonment of up to 15 years in cases where one knowingly releases hazardous air pollutants into the ambient air. In setting civil penalties, the administrator or the courts may take into account the size of the business, the economic impact of the penalty on the business, the violator's full compliance history and good-faith efforts to comply, the duration and seriousness of the violation, and so forth. Those mounting successful citizens' suits may receive attorney's fees and recoup their court costs as well.

According to a 1996 EPA report, the concentrations of five major air pollutants—carbon monoxide, lead, nitrogen dioxide, particulate matter, and sulfur dioxide—declined by an average of about 7 percent in 1995, with the latter pollutant decreasing by 17 percent.[7] The levels of ozone, however, increased by 4 percent, although the overall trend for the last 10 years indicates a reduction in this pollutant.[8] The report also notes that air quality data over the last 25 years show an emissions decline among these six pollutants of about 29 percent, while gross domestic product increased by about 99 percent during the same period.[9] The EPA interprets these data as indicative of the fact that the United States can reduce air pollution without sacrificing economic growth. On the other hand, a report authored by certain environmental groups in August 1999 noted that more states had exceeded the ozone levels in 1999 than in 1998 and that many of the nation's most popular summer vacation spots had ozone levels that rivaled (and sometimes exceeded) those from nearby urban areas. Although the heat wave of 1999 undoubtedly affected these air pollution levels, they are a source of concern.[10]

To ameliorate such problems, the EPA in 1999 budgeted $507 million to reduce air pollution, including $65 million to develop the states' monitoring of fine particulates, for which the agency had announced specific standards in 1997.

Chevron U.S.A. Inc. v. *Natural Resources Defense Council, Inc.*, a landmark case, addressed the Clean Air Act.

41.1

CHEVRON U.S.A. INC. V. NATURAL RESOURCES DEFENSE COUNCIL, INC.

467 U.S. 837 (1984)

FACTS The Clean Air Act Amendments of 1977 impose certain requirements on states that have not achieved the national air quality standards established by the Environmental Protection Agency (EPA) pursuant to earlier legislation, including the requirement that such "nonattainment" states establish a permit program regulating "new or modified major stationary sources" of air pollution. Generally, a permit may not be issued for such sources unless stringent conditions are met. EPA regulations promulgated in 1981 to implement the permit requirement allow a state to adopt a plantwide definition of the term "stationary source," under which an existing plant that contains several pollution-emitting devices may install or modify one piece of equipment without meeting the permit conditions if the alteration will not increase the total emissions from the plant, thus allowing a state to treat all the pollution-emitting devices within the same industrial grouping as though they were encased within a single "bubble." The Natural Resources Defense Council, Inc., filed a petition for review in the court of appeals, which set aside the regulations embodying the "bubble concept" as contrary to law. Although recognizing that the amended Clean Air Act does not explicitly define what Congress envisioned as a stationary source to which the permit program should apply and that the legislative history had failed to address the issue, the court concluded that, in view of the purpose of the nonattainment program to improve rather than merely maintain air quality, a plantwide definition was inappropriate.

ISSUE Was the EPA's plantwide definition a permissible construction of the statutory term "stationary source"?

HOLDING Yes. The legislative history indicated that the EPA should have broad discretion as to the implementation of the policies of the 1977 amendments.

Moreover, the plantwide definition was fully consistent with the policy of allowing reasonable economic growth; and the EPA had advanced a reasonable explanation for its conclusion that the regulations serve environmental objectives as well.

REASONING The question presented by this and other cases is whether the EPA's decision to allow states to treat all the pollution-emitting devices within the same industrial grouping as though they were encased within a single "bubble" is based on a reasonable construction of the statutory term "stationary source." With regard to judicial review of an agency's construction of the statute that it administers, if Congress has not directly spoken to the precise question at issue, the question for the court is whether the agency's answer represents a permissible construction of the statute. An examination of the legislation and its history supports the conclusion of the court of appeals that Congress did not have a specific intention as to the applicability of the "bubble concept" in these cases. To the extent any congressional "intent" can be discerned from the statutory language, it would appear that the listing of overlapping, illustrative terms was intended to enlarge, rather than to confine, the scope of the EPA's power to regulate particular sources and thus effectuate the policies of the Clean Air Act. Similarly, the legislative history is consistent with the view that the EPA, in implementing the policies of the 1977 amendments, should have broad discretion. The plantwide definition is fully consistent with the policy of allowing reasonable economic growth, and the EPA has advanced a reasonable explanation for its conclusion that the regulations serve environmental objectives as well. Policy arguments concerning the bubble concept should be addressed to legislators or administrators, not to judges. The EPA's interpretation of the statute here represents a reasonable accommodation of manifestly

continued

41.1

CHEVRON U.S.A. INC. V. NATURAL RESOURCES DEFENSE COUNCIL, INC., continued

467 U.S. 837 (1984)

---

competing interests and is entitled to deference. Hence, the decision of the court of appeals to set aside the regulations embodying the bubble concept as contrary to law was erroneous.

BUSINESS CONSIDERATIONS Some commentators have submitted that the "economic-incentives" approach in this case represents the most feasible way

to balance the compliance costs incurred by businesses and the protection of the environment. Should businesses follow the economic-incentives approach, or is there a better approach for these firms to follow?

ETHICAL CONSIDERATIONS Does a purely ethical approach to air pollution mandate adherence to a "zero-tolerance" policy? Is it ethical for society to be expected to pay for the "spillover" costs of pollution not borne by the polluter?

WATER POLLUTION

The Clean Water Act

The Clean Water Act (CWA), like the Clean Air Act, exemplifies the complexities involved in regulating a resource that affects virtually every sphere of human activity. Both also exemplify the so-called "technology-forcing" approach to environmental law.

Passed in 1972 as the Federal Water Pollution Control Amendments (the FWPCA), when Congress amended this act in 1977, Congress changed the name of the act to the Clean Water Act. Both the FWPCA and the CWA owe doctrinal debts to several earlier federal forays into water pollution control, including the Rivers and Harbors Act of 1899, the Water Pollution Control Act of 1948 (and its 1956 amendments), the Water Quality Act of 1965, and the 1970 Water Quality Improvements Act.

Congress in the CWA set as the primary aim of this legislation the restoration and maintenance of the chemical, physical, and biological integrity of the nation's waters as well as national goals for the achievement of this objective. These goals include, within certain timetables, the elimination of discharges of pollutants into navigable rivers; the elimination of the discharge of toxic pollutants in toxic amounts; water quality sufficient to protect fish, shellfish, and wildlife and to provide recreation in and on the water; federal assistance for the construction of publicly owned waste treatment works; the development and implementation of (1) areawide waste treatment management planning procedures designed to control pollutants at their sources in each state and (2) programs to control point and nonpoint sources of pollution; and research efforts aimed at developing the technology necessary to eliminate the discharge of pollutants into the nation's navigable waters, the waters of the continental shelf, and the oceans.

Under the CWA, the federal role over water policy takes precedence over the states' role, since the administrator of the EPA, in cooperation with the appropriate federal and state agencies, has the responsibility for developing comprehensive programs for preventing, reducing, and eliminating water pollution. For example, the CWA prohibits discharges into navigable waters unless one has a permit to do so. Subsequent EPA regulations and court decisions under the commerce clause make it clear that the term *water* encompasses all waters used in foreign or interstate commerce: rivers, territorial seas, wetlands, interstate lakes, streams, and ponds. The states, by enforcing the federally mandated standards in a manner much like that previously discussed under the Clean Air Act, augment this extensive federal regime. Each state must submit a plan describing how it intends to implement water quality standards applicable to interstate waters and to meet the **effluent** limitation guidelines promulgated by the EPA administrator.

Effluent
Pertaining to an outflow of materials or an emanation.

The CWA targets two areas for pollution control and regulation: point sources, such as pipes, ditches, channels, wells, animal feeding operations, or floating vessels that emit water pollutants; and nonpoint sources, such as farms and other agricultural activities, forest lands, mining, and forestry. Congress and the EPA view effluent limitations and ambient water control standards, in conjunction with a permit program, as a technology-based means of eliminating most pollution from point sources. The onus is on the polluter to choose abatement procedures—even costly ones—designed to eliminate water pollution at the source of its discharge. However, Congress and the EPA see technology as having fewer beneficial effects on pollution from nonpoint sources.

Although this view is debatable, the fact that Congress makes distinctions in this fashion has brought about significant legal implications: Point sources must comply with the applicable effluent limitations and must obtain—and satisfy—any and all relevant permits. Nonpoint sources remain exempt from both requirements, although they do have to comply with applicable state management programs.

The CWA attempts, on a case-by-case basis, to resolve questions about whether the point source designation applies to a given polluter. But the CWA itself sets out three mechanisms for regulating discharges from point sources: *effluent limitations* (ELs), *water quality standards* (WQSs), and pollution discharge permits issued pursuant to the *national pollutant discharge elimination system* (NPDES) *permit program*.

Effluent Limitations. The first of these, ELs, involves industry-specific restrictions on the number of pounds of a given pollutant that a given point source can discharge per day or per week into navigable waters. The CWA mandates the use of technology to reduce the quantities, rates, and concentrations of the chemical and biological effluent released from point sources and has as its ultimate goal the complete eradication of such industrial pollutants. The allowable ELs depend on the industrial processes utilized in a given industry, the available technology, and cost factors.

Water Quality Standards. In contrast to ELs, WQSs derive from the designated uses of the navigable waters involved (e.g., fish and wildlife propagation, recreation, agriculture, or industry), as well as their use and value for navigation. The CWA gives the EPA authority to oversee the states' development of minimum ambient standards for particular lakes, rivers, and streams. Then, once a state achieves its desired water standards, the state must comply with EPA-mandated antidegradation standards that ensure the state's continued maintenance of these desired WQSs.

Prior to 1972, pursuant to the FWPCA, federal water pollution control efforts centered on these state WQSs plans and had as their goal the elimination of pollutant discharges into all navigable bodies of water by 1985. Enforcement remained problematic, however, because authorities could not act on a given discharge until the pollution had lowered the quality of the affected water below the water's specified ambient level. Enforcement also faltered when multiple polluters had discharged effluent into the same body of water, since it was hard to prove the contribution each had made to lowering the specified ambient levels of the entire body of water.

The 1972 amendments illustrate Congress's intent to use ELs as the main supplement to the ambient water standards and, therefore, as the primary weapon for controlling point source–generated pollution. These amendments reserve the application of WQSs to those situations wherein compliance with the applicable ELs nevertheless may interfere with the maintenance of water quality in certain areas.

National Pollutant Discharge Elimination System. The NPDES program, however, by forcing each point-source polluter to obtain a permit, forms the linchpin of these federal antipollution efforts. In brief, the NPDES program dictates, as prerequisites for obtaining a permit, that a given point source (other than publicly owned wastewater works), by using within a certain time frame (but no later than 1977) the "best practicable control technology available" (BPT) as defined by the EPA administrator, comply with the ELs. Point sources that discharge nonconventional pollutants, such as ammonia, chlorine, or iron, are subject to a phased-in timetable and the standards of "best available control technology economically achievable" (BAT) by 1983. The ELs for conventional pollutants, such as suspended solids like oil or grease and fecal coliform, must achieve the standard known as "best conventional control technology" (BCT). For discharges of heat from point sources, the 1972 amendments allow a unique variance system designed to ensure the elimination of pollution and the propagation of a balanced, indigenous population of shellfish, fish, and wildlife. These amendments also establish "pretreatment standards" that industrial facilities that discharge into municipal wastewater treatment systems must meet so as to preclude these facilities' evading the NPDES permit program and discharging effluent directly into city sewers. Publicly owned treatment works (POTWs)—that is, municipal wastewater treatment facilities—by 1977 must meet the secondary treatment standards or the even more stringent ELs needed to ensure WQSs. Both BPT and BAT allow those setting the ELs to take into account cost considerations when they compute the degree of effluent reduction attainable under either standard, although BAT standards to a lesser degree take cost into account.

In short, the 1972 amendments leave enforcement primarily to the states but allow a variety of federal enforcement mechanisms as well. In permitting citizens to bring lawsuits to enforce the ELs set out in state or federal permits or to enforce EPA orders, the 1972 amendments appreciably strengthened the FWPCA.

Just as Congress had amended the Clean Air Act in 1977, so too it amended the FWPCA that same year. As mentioned earlier, besides renaming the FWPCA the Clean Water Act, the 1977 amendments authorize the EPA to grant some extensions of the 1977 BPT deadlines on a case-by-case basis. The 1977 amendments also apply the BCT standard to conventional pollutants and therefore replace the BAT standard for all pollutants except toxic and nonconventional ones.

The 1977 amendments reflect an especially stringent approach to toxic pollutants, that is, those that, if ingested, inhaled, or assimilated, can cause death, disease, cancer, physical deformity, behavioral abnormality, or genetic mutation. The CWA requires the administrator of the EPA to publish a list of toxic pollutants, including asbestos, arsenic, copper, cyanide, lead, mercury, polychlorinated biphenyls (PCBs), and vinyl chloride, and, by 1 July 1984, to establish industry-specific ELs that reflect the BAT. Under applicable law, the administrator can even establish a zero tolerance for certain ELs if the EPA deems such actions necessary

CHAPTER 41 | Environmental Protection | 1103

to provide an ample margin of safety or to attain the applicable WQSs. Moreover, the cost-benefit analysis that the EPA can consider in establishing ELs for conventional pollutants is not available to the agency when it sets ELs reflecting the BAT for toxic and nonconventional pollutants.

In the Water Quality Act of 1987, Congress amended the CWA so as to extend the compliance deadlines for toxic pollutants to 1989 and for some secondary treatment plants to 1988. These amendments also tried to maintain WQSs by requiring the states to identify the navigable bodies of waters within the state that, without additional action to control nonpoint sources of pollution (e.g., runoffs from agricultural or urban uses), cannot reasonably be expected to attain or maintain applicable WQSs. The states then must set up a management program and schedules for implementing the best management practices to control pollution emanating from nonpoint sources to the navigable waters within the state and to improve the quality of such waters.

The NPDES, then, represents the vehicle by which the EPA—or the state—can issue permits to any discharger of any pollutant on the condition that the individual discharger agree to abide by all ELs and other pollution standards within a certain time period. Those denied an NPDES permit by the EPA can seek court review in a U.S. circuit court of appeals, as can those who have been the object of the EPA's veto of any application permit issued under a state program. Variances under the NPDES-permit program are possible for those facilities that show that they fundamentally differed with respect to the factors considered by the administrator when he or she established the ELs applicable to those facilities and that the alternative requirement (variance) will not result in a non-water quality environmental impact markedly more adverse than the impact considered by the EPA administrator in establishing the national ELs at issue.

In response to the oil spill caused by the wreck of the Exxon *Valdez* in 1989, Congress passed the Oil Pollution Act of 1990. Although it amends the CWA, the act is modeled after CERCLA, a statute we will discuss shortly, in that it sets up a comprehensive system for removing oil spills caused by vessels or offshore facilities and a trust-fund system approach for paying for the costs and damages from all such spills.

Negligent violations of the CWA can subject violators to a maximum fine of $25,000 per day of violation and/or one year's imprisonment. Knowing violations increase the possible fines to a maximum of $50,000 per day of violation and/or three years' imprisonment. With some exemptions, an individual who knowingly violates the CWA and thereby endangers another shall, upon conviction, face fines of not more than $250,000 and/or 15 years' imprisonment. Organizations convicted

41.1 | MANUFACTURING/ MANAGEMENT

MINIMIZING LIABILITY FOR TOXIC SMOKE

One of the CIT manufacturing facilities has been spewing a great deal of smoke recently, thus causing some concern among the family members that the location may be in violation of the Clean Air Act. An industrial engineer has analyzed the location and reported that the smoke consists of asbestos, vinyl chloride, and various other particulates that represent by-products of the production process for Call-Image units. The family members want to take steps to reduce the pollution emanating from the plant and thereby avoid any potential liability for violating environmental statutes. They ask you what they should do in this situation. What advice will you give them?

BUSINESS CONSIDERATIONS Should a business spend more money at the time of plant construction in order to be "ahead of the game" in pollution control and reduction, or should it be satisfied with meeting current environmental standards, even though it knows that these standards may change in the future? What factors would influence such a decision?

ETHICAL CONSIDERATIONS Is it ethical for a business to do less than the law requires in the area of environmental protection if the business in so doing is meeting the existing legal requirements and industry standards? Is it ethical for a business, in order to be more environmentally protective, to exceed legal requirements and industry standards—at a cost to the shareholders?

41.2 | MANUFACTURING/ MANAGEMENT

CALL-IMAGE TECHNOLOGY

MINIMIZING LIABILITY FOR WATER POLLUTION

The Kochanowskis have just learned that one of their facilities is discharging effluents into the local drainage system and that this system flows into the community's primary water reservoir. The effluents from this particular facility contain contaminant concentrations that frequently exceed the standards set for the community. The family members wish to avoid any legal problems or liabilities and also to ensure that they refrain from harming the community. They ask you what they should do. What will you tell them?

BUSINESS CONSIDERATIONS Should a business attempt to work with local government officials to reduce pollution, or should it "go it alone" in an effort to act in the most efficient manner possible? Why might working with the local government be advisable? Why might such an approach be unhelpful?

ETHICAL CONSIDERATIONS Is it more ethical for a firm to reveal that it has been polluting but is taking steps to stop, or to attempt to hide past pollution while working to reduce or eliminate pollution in the future? Explain your response.

Aquifers
Water-bearing strata of permeable rock, sand, or gravel.

of such violations may face fines of $1,000,000. The administrator of the EPA can set civil fines of $25,000 per day of violation but in setting these fines can take into consideration the factors mentioned in the Clean Air Act's civil enforcement provisions. Administrative penalties vary, depending on the type of violation, and range from a maximum of $10,000 per violation and a maximum aggregate amount ranging from $25,000 to $125,000. The citizens' suit provisions and awards are similar to those set out in the Clean Air Act.

In 1999, the Clinton administration dedicated $645 million to its "Clean Water Action Plan," whereby the EPA will spearhead a far-reaching new initiative to clean up U.S. rivers, lakes, and coastal waters. Among other things, this program increases the grants given to states for the implementation of water quality improvement projects and places a high priority on efforts aimed at restoring and protecting the national wetlands.

The Safe Drinking Water Act

As an adjunct to the Clean Water Act, the Safe Drinking Water Act (SDWA), enacted in 1974 and amended in 1986, regulates water supplied by public water systems to home taps. The passage of this legislation stems from congressional awareness of the contaminants that have seeped into groundwater supplies and **aquifers** and that have caused cancer and other serious diseases and organ damage. The more than 200 reported instances of illnesses caused by waterborne microorganisms and parasites—including an earlier outbreak involving the water supply in Milwaukee, Wisconsin, and more recent ones in Washington County, New York, and Clark County, Washington—underscore the seriousness of this problem. As a consequence, the EPA has reiterated publicly the two SDWA rules that address microbial contamination such as the *E. Coli* illnesses linked to these outbreaks.[11]

Under the SDWA, the EPA must promulgate national primary drinking water regulations (NPDWRs) that in turn set maximum contaminant levels (MCLs) or, alternatively, require specific treatment techniques designed to reduce contaminants to acceptable levels. By using the most economically and technologically feasible treatment techniques available, public water supply operators must try to meet these MCL standards or goals (where no adverse effects on health occur). Variances from these NPDWRs are possible under certain circumstances. The 1986 amendments require the EPA to take more aggressive action to establish standards for 83 specific contaminants, to promulgate a national priority list of known contaminants, and to establish MCL goals and NPDWRs for at least 25 of the contaminants on this list. The 1996 amendments, among other things, for the first time develop a risk-based method to identify drinking water contaminants that could pose a threat to human health.

The 1996 amendments, in addition, require the EPA to publish, by 6 February 1998, a list of contaminants that are known or anticipated to occur in public water systems and may require regulation. An additional list of such contaminants must be published every five years thereafter. Moreover, the newly amended law requires the EPA to determine every five years whether to regulate at least five of the listed contaminants. Under these new amendments, the EPA, when identifying these contaminants, must take into account their danger to sensitive populations such as infants, children, pregnant women, the elderly, and people with illnesses. In its identification method, the EPA will consider factors such as the potential adverse health effects, information on concentrations in drinking water supplies, human exposure via drinking water and other sources, and data uncertainty. This approach will be used to identify and classify contaminants that are not currently regulated and to reevaluate already regulated contaminants. Because microbial contaminants pose unique challenges, the EPA will use a similar but separate approach for their identification. As of 1999, the SDWA regulated about 83 contaminants.[12] As of 1 January 2000, the EPA requires large systems—those that serve over 10,000 people—to monitor their systems for 12 contaminants that the EPA anticipates will occur, as well as for the targeted 36 unregulated contaminants for which the EPA has established approved test methods.[13] The EPA estimates the cost of such monitoring programs at nearly $40 million over the five-year period, 2000–2004.[14]

States may have primary enforcement responsibilities under the SDWA if the states have adopted drinking water regulations no less stringent than the national standards and if they have implemented adequate monitoring, inspection, recordkeeping, and enforcement procedures. If the EPA has primary responsibility, the enforcement provisions of the act resemble those under the Resource Conservation and Recovery Act (RCRA), discussed later in this chapter.

NOISE POLLUTION

The Noise Control Act of 1972

Probably because noise seems less noxious to us than filthy water or sulfurous-smelling air, Congress did not address the issue of noise until 1972 when it passed the federal Noise Control Act. Prior to that time, litigants seeking remedies to limit the increasingly higher decibel levels caused by post-World War II urbanization and mechanization relied on common law nuisance theories.

Compared to many of the other statutes discussed in this chapter, this act is simple and straightforward. Recognizing the noise generated by transportation vehicles and equipment, machinery, and appliances as a growing danger to the health and welfare of U.S. citizens—particularly those residing in urban areas—Congress placed the primary responsibility for controlling such noise on state and local governments. However, Congress expressly noted that federal oversight and action are necessary for noise sources in commerce when control of such sources will require uniform national treatment. Hence, the statute preempts the states' regulation of emissions standards for major noise sources such as construction equipment, transportation equipment, motors or engines, and electrical equipment. For these sources, the EPA must promulgate regulations that are necessary to protect the public health and welfare with an adequate margin of safety. The EPA also has the power to fashion regulations for any nonmajor product for which noise emissions standards are feasible and requisite to protect the public health and welfare.

To coordinate federal noise control policies, this legislation furthermore empowers the EPA to file status reports concerning all federal agencies' noise research and noise control programs, to enforce the labeling of products (including imported ones) as to the level of noise emitted by the products, and to prohibit the removal of noise control devices.

The 1978 amendments, called the Quiet Communities Act, reinforce the significant role that state and local governments play in noise control. The amendments provide federal financial and technical assistance aimed at facilitating state and local research related to noise control and developing noise abatement plans. Similar to the remedies we have seen in other statutes, civil and criminal penalties are possible for violations of the Noise Control Act, as are citizens' suits.

LAND CONSERVATION AND POLLUTION

Public domain
Lands that are open to public use.

The protection and preservation of land constitute the most obvious areas of federal environmental regulation. As early as the presidency of Theodore Roosevelt, concern for protecting the environment and preserving America's natural resources surfaced in the United States. The **public domain**—that is, land owned and/or controlled by the federal government—today comprises nearly 677 million acres. Hence, federally controlled land, national parks, and wildlife refuges occupy about as much land as the subcontinent of India does. In addition to the federal regulation and control of federal lands, a number of federal statutes regulate private land. The following sections discuss some of the most significant of these regulations.

The Toxic Substances Control Act

The Toxic Substances Control Act (TSCA) passed by Congress in 1976 represents the first statutory enactment that comprehensively addresses toxic chemicals and their impact on health and the environment. Congress passed this law for three reasons: (1) to develop data detailing the effect of chemical substances and mixtures on health and the environment by those who manufacture and process such chemicals (i.e., industry); (2) to provide adequate governmental authority to regulate chemicals that present an unreasonable risk of injury to health or the environment and to take steps with regard to those chemicals that are imminent hazards; and (3) to ensure the exercise of this governmental authority in such a fashion as to avoid impediments or unnecessary economic barriers to technological innovation while at the same time to fulfill the primary purpose of the TSCA—the avoidance of unreasonable risk of injury to health or the environment.

Like the NEPA, then, it focuses on risk assessment. But note that the TSCA, by giving authority to the EPA to regulate chemicals even before they come onto the market, screens pollutants before (not after, as most other statutes do) those pollutants expose humans and the environment to these substances' effects. The TSCA also permits the government to consider the sum total of the health and environmental hazards caused by a given chemical or mixture.

Despite these lofty purposes, the legislative history of the TSCA shows that Congress chose not to seek a risk-free environment. Granted, Congress requires the administrator of the EPA, after he or she receives notice of the proposed manufacture of any new substances, to subject these chemical substances and mixtures to testing and thereby ensure the development of test data by manufacturers. The

TSCA similarly mandates premanufacture notifications for such substances and the regulation of the postmanufacturing distribution of the chemicals.

Yet Congress, by requiring the EPA to test and regulate only those chemicals that pose an "unreasonable risk" of injury to health or the environment, has given the EPA a great deal of discretion, including the consideration of the relative costs of the various test protocols and methodologies that firms, in order to perform the required testing, may need to utilize. In actual practice, the EPA has taken a lax view toward the stringency it will require of companies that provide test data. Similarly, although the EPA can choose among several options, including prohibiting the manufacturing, processing, or distributing of any substance that poses an unreasonable risk, the statute directs the EPA, in arriving at its decision, to use the least burdensome requirements. As a consequence, the EPA has stopped the manufacture and/or distribution of only a minuscule number of chemical substances.

Nevertheless, the statute authorizes the EPA to regulate *imminent hazards*—those that present imminent and unreasonable risks of widespread injury to health or the environment—through emergency judicial relief leading to an injunction and/or seizure of the chemicals or substances. A special section of the TSCA sets out a timetable for phasing out the manufacture of PCBs. Other provisions allow for civil and criminal penalties and carry over the citizens' lawsuit provisions set out in other acts.

The Federal Insecticide, Fungicide, and Rodenticide Act

Given the importance of agriculture in our country's history, it is no surprise that Congress passed a federal Insecticide Act in 1910. Surprisingly, this act was aimed at protecting farmers from becoming victims of unsavory and fraudulent marketing practices rather than at protecting the environment.

In 1947, owing to the proliferation of pesticides and insecticides, Congress responded to those newly emerging, but as yet embryonic, environmental concerns when it passed the Federal Insecticide, Fungicide, and Rodenticide Act (FIFRA). This early version of FIFRA mandated the registration of "economic poisons [pesticides] involved in interstate commerce and the inclusion of labels, warnings, and instructions on such pesticides." The 1962 publication of Rachel Carson's *Silent Spring*, which cataloged the environmental risks and dangers created by pesticides, insecticides, and herbicides, in conjunction with litigation based on the use and sale of DDT, prodded Congress into action.

In 1970, the newly established EPA became responsible for the enforcement of FIFRA, and in 1972, Congress passed the Federal Environmental Pesticide Control Act (FEPCA). The FEPCA, in amending FIFRA, changes FIFRA's focus from labeling to concerns for the environment. Under FIFRA as amended, all persons who distribute or sell pesticides must register them with the EPA. The EPA will register a pesticide if the administrator determines that the pesticide, when used in accordance with widespread and common practice, will not generally cause unreasonable adverse effects on the environment. The EPA can register any approved pesticide for general use, restricted use (e.g., by exterminators), or both. The EPA subsequently can cancel the registration of any pesticide that fails to live up to this standard and can suspend a registration whenever such action is necessary to prevent an imminent hazard.

Although, like NEPA and the TSCA, FIFRA is at heart a risk-assessment statute, the 1975 and 1978 amendments make it clear that in determining "unreasonable adverse effects on the environment," the EPA must take into account the benefits, as well as the costs, associated with the use of the pesticide. It is possible, then, for the EPA to register an economically beneficial pesticide even though it might pose harm to health or the environment.

FIFRA sets out several types of unlawful acts, all of which, in general, involve the sale of unregistered or mislabeled pesticides. It also authorizes "stop sale" and/or seizure orders by the EPA. Furthermore, civil and criminal penalties are available under the act.

Despite the fact that applicants must provide data in support of any application, the EPA has been able to assure the safety of only a handful of the 50,000 pesticides currently on the market. Similarly, the EPA has canceled or suspended the registration of only a few pesticides—for example, DDT, kepone, and chlordane. In part to appease the critics who had advocated amendments to the FIFRA that would address these issues, Congress enacted the Food Quality Protection Act of 1996 (FQPA). FQPA mandates more stringent health standards for the EPA's pesticide reviews so as to ensure the wholesomeness of the American food supply and in particular to protect children from the health threats posed by pesticide residues. Through these processes, the EPA will remove harmful pesticides from the market or restrict the uses of each pesticide and thereby minimize dietary exposure to such potentially toxic substances. The 1999 EPA budget accordingly provided $636 million to be used for the implementation of FQPA.

The Resource Conservation and Recovery Act

Another act passed in 1976, the Resource Conservation and Recovery Act (RCRA), is a broader statute than the TSCA and FIFRA. The RCRA encompasses all types of waste, including hazardous and toxic waste and waste generated by households across the country. The predecessors of the RCRA include the Solid Waste Disposal Act of 1965 and the Resource Recovery Act of 1970. The RCRA, a more comprehensive statute, stemmed from congressional awareness of the environmental problems posed by the generation and disposal of wastes of all types.

Although oftentimes referred to as solid waste, waste actually takes the form of liquids, gases, sludges, and semisolids as well. All of us undoubtedly recognize the complexities associated with the disposal of the billions of tons of household waste generated annually. At some point, virtually everything we buy ends up in a landfill or at some other type of disposal site. The pollution control efforts that we already have studied—emissions and wastewater sludge, for example— ironically also create waste. Moreover, the characteristics of such waste have changed over the years. The toxic substances considered earlier add yet another dimension to the waste disposal calculus. In short, we presently are paying the price for decades of dumping solid waste on land. We also are running out of room for land-based disposal sites; few communities, owing to fears of groundwater contamination, want to accept other states' waste (as the litigation discussed in Chapter 5 demonstrates).

The RCRA indicates Congress's understanding that it may no longer view waste disposal as a purely state or local problem. Rather, Congress sees waste disposal as national in scope and concern and, therefore, worthy of federal assistance in the development and application of new and improved methods of waste reduction and disposal practices as well as potential new energy sources. By virtue of its being yet another technology-forcing statute, the RCRA therefore gives the EPA the power to regulate nonhazardous solid waste and to oversee the management and disposal of hazardous waste.

With regard to nonhazardous solid waste, the RCRA provides federal technical and financial assistance to states that voluntarily develop environmentally sound methods of solid waste disposal, including recycling. These state management plans, which resemble the SIPs discussed under the Clean Air Act, must follow EPA guidelines and, among other things, protect ground and surface water from contamination brought on by **leachings** and runoffs. Any approved state plan must distinguish between sanitary landfills and open dumps, the latter of which must be closed or upgraded so as to eliminate health hazards and minimize potential health hazards.

By making lawful only dumping into a solid waste facility that complies with the EPA's criteria for a sanitary landfill, Congress apparently intends to abolish open dumping, even in states that do not develop a state solid waste management program. The RCRA also obligates the EPA to publish the names of all the open dump sites in the United States. This public list presumably will spur states to take action to eliminate the environmental and health hazards associated with these sites and also provides the impetus for citizens' suits.

The EPA's powers to regulate hazardous waste under the RCRA far exceed its powers over nonhazardous solid waste. Adopting what one court has called "cradle-to-grave" regulation, the EPA sets out stringent standards covering those who own or operate treatment, storage, or disposal facilities (TSDFs). Such persons or entities must obtain permits issued by the EPA or the states authorized to issue such permits. The RCRA mandates that the EPA identify and list hazardous waste (i.e., solid waste that, among other things, can cause or significantly contribute to an increase in serious irreversible illness or pose a substantial present or potential threat to the environment) on the basis of several criteria: toxicity, persistence, degradability in its nature, potential for accumulation in tissue, and other related factors such as flammability or corrosiveness. (Interestingly, the RCRA excludes nuclear waste from its coverage.) EPA regulations thus list certain chemicals, each identified by so called EPA hazardous waste numbers.

The EPA, aided by the permit, record-keeping, labeling, container usage, and report provisions of the RCRA, relies on a **manifest** system to track hazardous waste from the cradle to the grave and to ensure that everyone from the generator of the waste, through the transporter, and to the operator of the disposal facility meets and maintains the applicable federal regulatory standards. Since the 1984 amendments to the RCRA, even small generators of hazardous waste must supply this extensive documentation. By setting minimal technological requirements (e.g., the provision of two or more liners and a leachate collection system) and groundwater monitoring for both new and existing sanitary landfills, these amendments also phase out the land disposal of hazardous wastes, in particular. In addition, the 1984 amendments broadly regulate leaking underground storage tanks and, like CERCLA (discussed next), set up a federal trust to remediate leaks under certain circumstances. In 1989, Congress initiated in certain northeastern and midwestern states a demonstration program for tracking the disposal of medical waste products.

Like the Clean Air Act and the Clean Water Act, the permit system established under the RCRA provides the EPA with broad enforcement powers. Civil and criminal penalties are available for violations of the RCRA, as are citizens' suits. Furthermore, under the RCRA, the EPA can seek injunctive relief if the handling,

Leachings
Oozing of water that contains soil, sediments, chemicals, and other impurities.

Manifest
A list or invoice.

transport, storage, or disposal of solid or hazardous waste presents an imminent and substantial endangerment to health or the environment. The 1984 RCRA amendments extend the coverage of this provision even to past or present generators, transporters, or operators who have contributed or are contributing to an activity that presents such an imminent danger. Subsequent court decisions have construed this as a strict liability provision akin to its counterpart in CERCLA.

The Comprehensive Environmental Response, Compensation, and Liability Act

The Comprehensive Environmental Response, Compensation, and Liability Act (CERCLA), perhaps better known as the "Superfund," was passed in 1980. In this enactment, Congress meant to fill in the gaps left by the TSCA and the RCRA, neither of which had regulated hazardous waste disposal sites, as the infamous Love Canal disaster unfortunately all too aptly demonstrated.

The CERCLA authorizes the administrator of the EPA to regulate "hazardous substances," including those deemed toxic or hazardous under the CWA, the TSCA, or the RCRA, which, when released into the environment, may present substantial danger to the public health or welfare or the environment. The act specifically excludes petroleum and natural gas from the definition of hazardous substances.

Any owner or operator of a vessel or offshore or onshore facility engaged in the storage, treatment, or disposal of hazardous waste must notify the EPA of any release of hazardous materials. This notification aids the EPA's implementation of a national contingency plan (NCP), which, under the CERCLA, establishes the procedures and standards for responding to releases of hazardous substances, pollutants, and contaminants and for setting priorities dealing with such substances. The act moreover gives the U.S. president authority to undertake any response (including short-term emergency removal and long-term remedial actions) consistent with the NCP and which action the president deems necessary to protect the public health or welfare or the environment. The CERCLA also gives the government the injunctive or administrative authority to compel private parties to take steps to abate all imminent and substantial endangerment to the public health or welfare or the environment caused by the actual or threatened release of hazardous substances from a facility.

The CERCLA furthermore imposes liability for all costs of removal or remedial action incurred by federal or state governments that are not inconsistent with the NCP; for all other necessary costs of any response incurred by any other person when such costs are consistent with the NCP; and damages to, or loss of natural resources resulting from, the release of hazardous substances.

Recent court decisions have construed this part of the CERCLA as a strict liability standard that can result in joint and several liability among responsible generators, owners, operators, transporters, and so on, up to $50,000,000 in toto. For releases or threats of releases caused by willful misconduct or willful negligence, this limitation on liability does not apply. The statute itself sets out defenses to liability for releases or threats of releases caused by acts of God, acts of war, or by an act or omission of a third party who was not an agent or employee (e.g., a third party's leachate runoffs). Innocent landowners also escape liability, but the burden of proof necessary to sustain this defense makes it virtually unusable.

In the following case, the Supreme Court provided some definitive guidance on the issue of who could face liability for hazardous waste in situations involving parent-subsidiary corporations.

41.2

UNITED STATES V. BESTFOODS
524 U.S. 51 (1998)

FACTS In 1957, Ott Chemical Co. (Ott I) began manufacturing chemicals at a plant near Muskegon, Michigan. The firm's intentional and unintentional dumping of hazardous substances significantly polluted the soil and ground water at the site. In 1965, CPC International Inc. (CPC) incorporated a wholly owned subsidiary to buy Ott I's assets in exchange for CPC stock. The new company, also dubbed Ott Chemical Co. (Ott II), continued its chemical manufacturing operations and further polluted the surroundings. CPC retained the managers of Ott I, including its founder, president, and principal shareholder, Arnold Ott, as officers of Ott II. Arnold Ott and several other Ott II officers and directors also were given positions at CPC, and they performed duties for both corporations. In 1972, CPC sold Ott II to Story Chemical Company (Story), which operated the Muskegon plant until its bankruptcy in 1977. Shortly thereafter, the Michigan Department of Natural Resources (MDNR) found the land littered with thousands of leaking and even exploding drums of waste, and the soil and water saturated with noxious chemicals. The MDNR subsequently sought a buyer for the property who would be willing to contribute toward its cleanup; and after extensive negotiations, the Story bankruptcy trustee in 1977 transferred the site to Aerojet-General Corp. (Aerojet). To purchase the property, Aerojet created a wholly owned California subsidiary, Cordova Chemical Company (Cordova/California), and Cordova/California in turn created a wholly owned Michigan subsidiary, Cordova Chemical Company of Michigan (Cordova/Michigan), which manufactured chemicals at the site until 1986. By 1981, the federal EPA had undertaken to see the site cleaned up, and its long-term remedial plan called for expenditures well into the tens of millions of dollars. To recover some of that money, in 1989, the United States filed this action under § 107 of the CERCLA and named five defendants as responsible parties: CPC (which later changed its name to Bestfoods), Aerojet, Cordova/California, Cordova/Michigan, and Arnold Ott. (By that time, Ott I and Ott II were defunct.) At the trial in the district court, the primary issue centered on whether CPC and Aerojet, as the parent companies of Ott II and the Cordova companies, had "owned or operated" the facility within the meaning of § 107(a)(2).

ISSUE Could parent corporations face liability under the CERCLA for operating facilities ostensibly controlled by their subsidiaries?

HOLDING Yes. When (but only when) the corporate veil may be pierced, a parent corporation may be charged with derivative CERCLA liability for its subsidiary's actions in operating a polluting facility. Put differently, a corporate parent that actively participates in, and exercises control over, the operations of its subsidiary's facility may be held directly liable in its own right under § 107(a)(2) as an operator of the facility. Derivative liability aside, CERCLA does not bar a parent corporation from direct liability for its own actions. Under the plain language of § 107(a)(2), any person who operates a polluting facility is directly liable for the costs of cleaning up the pollution, and this is so even if that person is the parent corporation of the facility's owner.

REASONING A deeply ingrained principle of corporate law holds that a parent corporation (so-called because of control through ownership of another corporation's stock) is not liable for the acts of its subsidiaries. Although this respect for corporate distinctions when the subsidiary is a polluter has been severely criticized in the literature, nothing in the CERCLA purports to reject this bedrock principle; and against this venerable common-law backdrop, the congressional silence is audible. But there is an equally fundamental principle of corporate law, applicable to the parent-subsidiary relationship as well as generally, that a court may pierce the corporate veil and hold the shareholder liable for the corporation's conduct when, among other things, the corporate form would otherwise be misused to accomplish certain wrongful purposes, most notably fraud, on the shareholder's behalf. Nothing in the CERCLA purports to rewrite this well-settled rule, either. The court of appeals was therefore correct in concluding that when (but only when) the corporate veil may be pierced, a parent corporation may be charged with derivative CERCLA liability for its subsidiary's actions. Under the plain language of the statute, any person who operates a polluting facility is directly liable for the costs of cleaning up the pollution. This is so regardless of whether that person is the facility's

continued

41.2

UNITED STATES V. BESTFOODS, *continued*

524 U.S. 51 (1998)

owner, the owner's parent corporation or business partner, or even a saboteur who sneaks into the facility at night to discharge the facility's poisons out of malice. The difficulty, though, comes in defining actions sufficient to constitute direct parental "operation." In the organizational sense more obviously intended by the CERCLA, an operator is simply someone who directs the workings of, manages, or conducts the affairs of a facility. To sharpen the definition for purposes of the CERCLA's concern with environmental contamination, an operator must manage, direct, or conduct operations specifically related to pollution, that is, operations having to do with the leakage or disposal of hazardous waste, or make decisions about compliance with environmental regulations. Hence, the court of appeals correctly rejected the district court's analysis of direct liability and the district court's premising of liability on little more than CPC's ownership of Ott II, CPC's majority control of Ott II's board of directors, and CPC's placing its officials in key management positions at Ott II. In imposing direct liability on these grounds, the district court failed to recognize that it is entirely appropriate for directors of a parent corporation to serve as directors of its subsidiary. In sum, the district court's automatic attribution of the actions of dual officers and directors to the corporate parent, erroneously, even if unintentionally, treated the CERCLA as though it had displaced or fundamentally altered common law standards of limited liability. The court of appeals therefore was correct in holding that a participation-and-control test looking to the parent's supervision over the subsidiary, especially one that assumes that dual officers always act on behalf of the parent, cannot be used to identify the operation of a facility that will result in direct parental liability. Nonetheless, a return to the ordinary meaning of the word "operate" in the organizational sense will indicate why the Sixth Circuit erred when it confined its examples of direct parental operation to exclusive or joint ventures and declined to find at least the possibility of direct operation by CPC in this case. For example, a dual officer or director might depart so far from the norms of parental influence exercised through dual office holding as to serve the parent, even when ostensibly acting on behalf of the subsidiary in operating the facility. In this regard, norms of corporate behavior (undisturbed by any CERCLA provision) become crucial reference points for a court's distinguishing between the acts of direct operation that give rise to parental liability and the interference that stems from the normal relationship between parent and subsidiary. For instance, activities that involve the facility but which are consistent with the parent's investor status, such as the monitoring of the subsidiary's performance, the supervision of the subsidiary's finance and capital budget decisions, and the articulation of general policies and procedures, should not give rise to direct liability. The critical question is whether, in degree and detail, actions directed to the facility by an agent of the parent alone are unusual under accepted norms of parental oversight of a subsidiary's facility. There is, in fact, some evidence that CPC engaged in just this type and degree of activity at the Muskegon plant. As the district court's opinion notes, G.R.D. Williams, who worked only for CPC, "actively participated in and exerted control over a variety of Ott II environmental matters," and he "issued directives regarding Ott II's responses to regulatory inquiries. . . . " These findings raise an issue of CPC's operation of the facility through Williams's actions, the extent of which is an issue vigorously disputed by each of the parties. On remand, then, the district court must use the theory of direct operation set out here, for a reevaluation of Williams's role, and of the role of any other CPC agent who might be said to have had a part in operating the Muskegon facility.

BUSINESS CONSIDERATIONS Assume the CEO has asked you to study the *Bestfoods* case and to supply her with a draft policy that, when enacted, will govern the firm's relationship with its subsidiaries as to environmental matters. In preparing this draft, you will need to identify both the opportunities the Court's holding provides to the parent corporation for avoiding liability as well as the threats of vicarious or direct liability that might be imposed on the parent. What points will you include in this document?

ETHICAL CONSIDERATIONS Would the Supreme Court have arrived at a different decision if it had grounded its conclusions in ethics rather than the law? What ethical factors might have influenced the Court's decision?

To finance governmental cleanups and remedial actions in those situations in which the government cannot identify or find the parties responsible for the damage, the CERCLA establishes a Hazardous Substance Superfund. The Superfund Amendments and Reauthorization Act of 1986 (SARA), an incredibly complex statute, among other things increases the fund from the $1.6 billion originally enacted to $8.5 billion through 1991. Various excise taxes on petroleum and chemical feedstocks, appropriations from general revenues, and the costs recovered from responsible parties furnish the monies for the Superfund. In 1999, the EPA budgeted $2.1 billion for the Superfund, a 40 percent increase over 1998 funding levels. These increases are part of the Clinton administration's commitment to clean up two-thirds of the nation's worst toxic waste dumps by 2001.

To implement a cleanup plan, the EPA, using a scientific model, must place the site on the national priorities list of waste sites that present the greatest danger to the public health or welfare. When the EPA decides remedial action is appropriate for a given site, all "potentially responsible parties" (PRPs)—present and past owners or operators, including, since the passage of SARA, state and local governments, generators, and transporters—are notified.

If no defenses are available to the PRPs, the EPA, through feasibility studies, begins to negotiate with these parties in order to arrive at a settlement of the total costs. Since liability is joint and several, the PRPs usually find it advisable to allocate financial responsibility among themselves and to present their settlement agreement to the EPA for its approval. Special statutory provisions cover settlements, which generally take the form of a consent decree or an administrative order setting forth the terms of the settlement.

Exhibit 41.1 on page 1114 summarizes the environmental acts and statutes—enacted from 1895 through 1996—discussed in this chapter.

WILDLIFE CONSERVATION

The Endangered Species Act

The Endangered Species Act of 1973 (ESA) in § 7 states that each federal agency, in consultation with the secretary of the interior, must ensure that no agency action is likely to jeopardize the continued existence of an endangered or threatened species or result in the destruction or adverse modification of any critical habitat of such species. Congress enacted the ESA, the world's first attempt to protect wildlife in a comprehensive manner so as to prevent the extinction of various animals and plants. Indeed, according to scientific estimates, the world loses approximately 100 species per day.[15]

Since 1973, the ESA has helped bring about the stabilization or the improvement of the conditions of 270 threatened or endangered species, including the U.S.'s national symbol, the bald eagle.[16] But the impact of the ESA reaches beyond the borders of the United States because its prohibitions concerning the international trading of wildlife and its protection of the American habitats of migrating birds implicate international interests as well.

The national commitment to protecting species and their habitats invokes more than mere sentimentality or altruism—fully 40 percent of all ingredients in prescription medicines (including digitalis and penicillin) derive from plants, animals, and microorganisms.[17] The loss of a species therefore may involve the loss of the medicinal capacity to save thousands of lives.

E X H I B I T   41.1 | **Representative Environmental Statutes (1895–1996)**

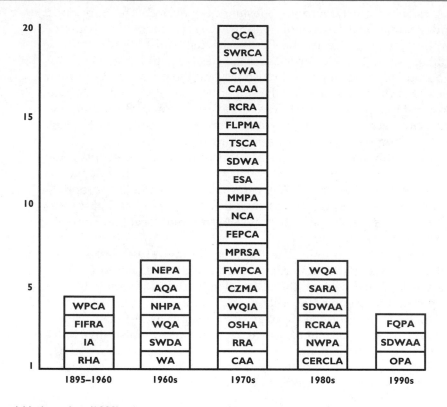

RHA	Rivers and Harbors Act (1899)
IA	Insecticide Act (1910)
FIFRA	Federal Insecticide, Fungicide, and Rodenticide Act (1947)
WPCA	Water Pollution Control Act (1948)
WA	Wilderness Act (1964)
SWDA	Solid Waste Disposal Act (1965)
WQA	Water Quality Act (1965)
NHPA	National Historic Preservation Act (1966)
AQA	Air Quality Act (1967)
NEPA	National Environmental Policy Act (1969)
CAA	Clean Air Act (1970)
RRA	Resource Recovery Act (1970)
OSHA	Occupational Safety and Health Act (1970)
WQIA	Water Quality Improvements Act (1970)
CZMA	Coastal Zone Management Act (1970)
FWPCA	Federal Water Pollution Control Act (1972)
MPRSA	Marine Protection, Research and Sanctuaries Act (1972)
FEPCA	Federal Environmental Pesticide Control Act (1972)
NCA	Noise Control Act (1972)
MMPA	Marine Mammal Protection Act (1972)

ESA	Endangered Species Act (1973)
SDWA	Safe Drinking Water Act (1974)
TSCA	Toxic Substances Control Act (1976)
FLPMA	Federal Land policy and Management Act (1976)
RCRA	Resource Conservation and Recovery Act (1976)
CAAA	Clean Air Act Amendments (1977)
CWA	Clean Water Act (1977)
SWRCA	Soil and Water Resources Conservation Act (1977)
QCA	Quiet Communities Act (1978)
CERCLA	Comprehensive Environmental Response, Compensation, and Liability Act (1980)
NWPA	Nuclear Waste Policy Act (1982)
RCRAA	Resource Conservation and Recovery Act Amendments (1984)
SDWAA	Safe Drinking Water Act Amendments (1986)
SARA	Superfund Amendments and Reorganization Act (1986)
WQA	Water Quality Act (1987)
OPA	Oil Pollution Act (1990)
SDWAA	Safe Drinking Water Act Amendments (1996)
FQPA	Food Quality Protection Act (1996)

The provisions of the ESA that preserve genetic diversity help ensure blight- and disease-resistant plants.[18] The harm to wildlife represented by pesticides mirrors the preservation of healthy ecosystems mandated by the Clean Air Act and other statutes discussed in this chapter—clearly a vital national (and international) interest. In 1995, for example, recreational activities in the United States related to wildlife (hunting, fishing, hiking, and so on) totaled $50 billion.[19] Similarly, commercial and recreational fishing resulted in over 100,000 jobs.[20] The declining fish stocks in our nation's navigable waters, lakes, oceans, and contiguous waters and the attendant loss of gainful employment illustrate the economic dimensions of wildlife protection.

Celebrated cases under the ESA wherein dam or road construction projects were halted to protect the habitat of fish or butterflies, for example, have led to public controversies of great magnitude. *Babbitt* v. *Sweet Home Chapter of Communities for a Great Oregon* represents a recent landmark decision in this regard. Note, too, how the Supreme Court, in disposing of this case, relied on the *Chevron U.S.A. Inc.* v. *National Resources Defense Council, Inc.*, decision as a leading precedent.

41.3

BABBITT
V. SWEET HOME CHAPTER OF COMMUNITIES FOR A GREAT OREGON
515 U.S. 687 (1995)

FACTS The Endangered Species Act of 1973 (ESA) makes it unlawful for any person to "take" endangered or threatened species and defines "take" to mean to "harass, harm, pursue," "wound," or "kill." In the regulations relating to the ESA, the Secretary of the Interior further defines harm to include "significant habitat modification or degradation where it actually kills or injures wildlife." Sweet Home Chapter of Communities for a Great Oregon (Sweet Home) includes small landowners, logging companies, and families dependent on the forest products industries in the Pacific Northwest and the Southeast, as well as organizations that represent these groups' interests. Sweet Home, challenging the statutory validity of the regulation defining "harm," sued Bruce Babbitt, the Secretary of the Interior (Secretary). Sweet Home's complaint for a declaratory judgment challenged the regulation on its face, specifically that the application of the regulation to the red-cockaded woodpecker, an endangered species, and the northern spotted owl, a threatened species, had economically injured its constituent groups. The district court upheld the Secretary's definition, but the court of appeals reversed.

ISSUE In defining "harm" to include habitat modification, had the Secretary reasonably construed Congress's intent?

HOLDING Yes. The Secretary's definition of "harm" rested on a permissible construction of the ESA.

REASONING Section 9(a)(1) of the ESA provides the following protection for endangered species:

Except as provided in § 1535(g)(2) and § 1539 of this title, with respect to any endangered species of fish or wildlife listed pursuant to § 1533 of this title it is unlawful for any person subject to the jurisdiction of the United States to . . . (B) take any such species within the United States or the territorial sea of the United States.—16 U.S.C. § 1538(a)(1)

Section 3(19) of the act defines the statutory term "take":

The term "take" means to harass, harm, pursue, hunt, shoot, wound, kill, trap, capture, or collect, or to attempt to engage in any such conduct. —16 U.S.C. § 1532(19)

The act does not further define the terms it uses to define "take." The Interior Department regulations that implement the statute, however define the statutory term "harm":

"Harm" in the definition of "take" in the Act means an act which actually kills or injures wildlife. Such
continued

41.3

BABBITT
V. SWEET HOME CHAPTER OF COMMUNITIES FOR A GREAT OREGON, *continued*
515 U.S. 687 (1995)

act may include significant habitat modification or degradation where it actually kills or injures wildlife by significantly impairing essential behavioral patterns, including breeding, feeding, or sheltering.
—50 CFR § 17.3 (1994)

This regulation has been in place since 1975.

Sweet Home advanced three arguments to support its submission that Congress had not intended the word "take" in § 9 to include habitat modification, as the Secretary's "harm" regulation provides. First, Sweet Home correctly noted that language in the Senate's original version of the ESA would have defined "take" to include "destruction, modification, or curtailment of [the] habitat or range" of fish or wildlife, but the Senate had deleted that language from the bill before enacting it. Second, Sweet Home argued that Congress had intended the act's express authorization for the federal government to buy private land in order to prevent habitat degradation in § 5 to constitute the exclusive check against habitat modification on private property. Third, because the Senate had added the term "harm" to the definition of "take" in a floor amendment without debate, Sweet Home claimed that the Court should not interpret the term so expansively as to include habitat modification. Because this case was decided on motions for summary judgment, the Court may appropriately make certain factual assumptions when it frames the legal issue.

First, the Court assumes Sweet Home has no desire to harm either the red-cockaded woodpecker or the spotted owl; the organization merely wishes to continue logging activities that would be entirely proper if not prohibited by the ESA. On the other hand, the Court assumes, for the sake of argument, that those activities will have the effect, even though unintended, of detrimentally changing the natural habitat of both listed species and that, as a consequence, members of those species will be killed or injured. Under Sweet Home's view of the law, the Secretary's only means of forestalling that grave result—even when the actor knows it is certain to occur—is to use his § 5 authority to purchase the lands on which the survival of the species depends. The Secretary, on the other hand, submits that the § 9 prohibition on takings, which Congress defined to include "harm,"

places on Sweet Home (and other groups) a duty to avoid the harm that such a habitat alteration will cause the birds unless such groups, pursuant to § 10, first obtain a permit. The text of the act provides three reasons for concluding that the Secretary's interpretation is reasonable. First, an ordinary understanding of the word "harm" supports it. The dictionary definition of the verb form of harm is "to cause hurt or damage to: injure" [*Webster's Third New International Dictionary* 1034 (1966)]. In the context of the ESA, that definition naturally encompasses habitat modification that results in actual injury or death to members of an endangered or threatened species. Sweet Home argues that the Secretary should have limited the purview of "harm" to direct applications of force against protected species, but the dictionary definition does not include the word "directly" or suggest in any way that only direct or willful action that leads to injury constitutes "harm."

Second, the broad purpose of the ESA supports the Secretary's decision to extend protection against activities that cause the precise harms Congress enacted the statute to avoid. Whereas predecessor statutes enacted in 1966 and 1969 had not contained any sweeping prohibition against the taking of endangered species except on federal lands, the 1973 act applied to all land in the United States and to its territorial seas. As stated in § 2 of the act, among its central purposes is "to provide a means whereby the ecosystems upon which endangered species and threatened species depend may be conserved . . . "— 16 U.S.C. § 1531(b). Congress's intent to provide comprehensive protection for endangered and threatened species therefore supports the permissibility of the Secretary's "harm" regulation.

Third, the fact that in 1982 Congress authorized the Secretary to issue permits for takings that § 9(a)(1)(B) otherwise would prohibit—"if such taking is incidental to, and not the purpose of, the carrying out of an otherwise lawful activity"—strongly suggests that Congress understood § 9 to prohibit indirect as well as deliberate takings. No one could seriously request an "incidental" take permit to avert § 9 liability for direct, deliberate action against a member of an endangered or threatened species. Moreover, the Court can refrain from deciding whether the statutory definition of "take" compels the Secretary's

41.3

BABBITT
V. SWEET HOME CHAPTER OF COMMUNITIES FOR A GREAT OREGON, *continued*
515 U.S. 687 (1995)

interpretation of "harm," because the Court's conclusions that Congress did not unambiguously manifest its intent to adopt Sweet Home's view and that the Secretary's interpretation is reasonable suffice to decide this case . . . see generally *Chevron U.S.A. Inc., v. Natural Resources Defense Council, Inc.,* 467 U.S. 837 (1984).

When it enacted the ESA, Congress delegated broad administrative and interpretive power to the Secretary. The task of defining and listing endangered and threatened species, of fashioning appropriate standards for issuing permits under § 10 for takings that would otherwise violate § 9, and of properly interpreting a term such as "harm" requires an expertise that exceeds the normal province of Congress. When Congress has entrusted the Secretary with broad discretion, the Court is especially reluctant to substitute its views of wise policy for his (see *Chevron,* 467 U.S., at 865–866). In this case, that reluctance accords with the Court's conclusion, based on the text, structure, and legislative history of the ESA, that the Secretary reasonably construed the intent of

Congress when he defined harm to include "significant habitat modification or degradation that actually kills or injures wildlife." The judgment of the court of appeals therefore is reversed.

BUSINESS CONSIDERATIONS The Court in this case also notes that the ESA "encompasses a vast range of economic and social endeavors and enterprises" that the law must address through "case-by-case resolution and adjudication." Identify these economic and social interests, and explain where a business should strike the balance between these competing causes.

ETHICAL CONSIDERATIONS Does the application of ethics require a "zero-tolerance" policy when economic activity may affect endangered or threatened species? How much harm to endangered or threatened species can be permitted before the conduct in question becomes unethical?

Some noted jurists have submitted that courts deciding environmental cases should accord standing to the trees, animals, and so forth involved in the litigation. Yet, as some recent cases show,[21] the constitutional requirement of a litigant's having a case or controversy before the litigant will have standing to bring a lawsuit represents a formidable procedural obstacle to environmental interest groups seeking to block further development of land (e.g., logging on U.S. Forest Service land). The doctrine of ripeness, which holds that the facts of a case must have developed sufficiently to permit the trier of fact to make an intelligent and useful decision, similarly constitutes another procedural stumbling block that thwarts such pro-environmentalists' efforts to challenge agency land and resource management plans.[22] Whether the Supreme Court continues to be receptive to disposing of such cases on these procedural grounds warrants our continued attention.

ENFORCEMENT AND REMEDIES

In the last few years, the EPA has aggressively enforced environmental laws. During fiscal year 1998, the EPA brought a total of 2,782 enforcement actions, the second-highest combined total in the agency's history.[23] These referrals included 677 criminal and civil cases that netted over $180 million in penalties and fines.[24] Cost recovery actions at Superfund sites and commitments made by responsible

41.3 | MANAGEMENT/ FINANCE

CALL-IMAGE TECHNOLOGY

POTENTIALLY RESPONSIBLE PARTIES

Given the robustness of the sales of Call-Image, the Kochanowskis are contemplating an expansion of their manufacturing facilities. Tom has learned of a site that seems advantageous, in that it is in close proximity to the family's present facility and the major interstate highway that runs nearby. When Tom mentions this parcel of land, Anna reminds him that years ago a plastics plant was located there. She wonders whether the owners of that plant properly disposed of the vinyl chloride, phosgene gas, and other toxic chemicals used in the manufacture of plastics. Hence, she expresses some apprehensions about buying the property without checking out these issues. Brushing aside Anna's reservations, Tom wants to move forward quickly. Just as he is about to make an offer on the real estate, he has second thoughts and calls you. How will you respond to Tom's summary of Anna's concerns?

BUSINESS CONSIDERATIONS When a firm decides to purchase property, why should it concern itself with the possibility of earlier pollution on the site? Explain why such environmental issues should rank high or low on the firm's priorities as it contemplates the acquisition of a given piece of real estate.

ETHICAL CONSIDERATIONS Is it ethical for a firm to ignore the possibility that a parcel of land is polluted and thus take a "wait-and-see" attitude regarding this possibility? Or will an ethically minded firm be more proactive in such circumstances?

parties pursuant to Superfund cleanups annually return substantial amounts of money to governmental coffers as well. Simply put, enforcement of environmental laws is "big business."

INTERNATIONAL ASPECTS

Environmental regulation is on the rise not only in the United States but around the world as well. While some European countries—Germany and the Netherlands, for example—have traditionally undertaken regulatory efforts that rival those of the United States, in many other countries environmental laws are nonexistent or at best embryonic. The environmental contamination and degradation found in post-Communist Eastern European countries, besides providing telling examples of what results from lax environmental standards, have discouraged much-needed privatization and foreign investments.

Realizing the need for environmental oversight and modeling its efforts on U.S. legislation, the European Union (EU) has adopted the Eco-audit Management and Audit Scheme (EMAS) Regulation that mandates environmental registers at each plant to catalog pollution emissions, land contamination, and the like; public disclosure of such environmental statements; and external verification of the company's environmental management system. Recently enacted environmental laws covering products now regulate product features (such as shape and recyclability), labeling, packaging, hazardous chemicals, and waste (its generation, transboundary shipment, etc.).[25] These laws also ban certain products such as asbestos, heavy metals, and vinyl chloride.

Such efforts are a harbinger of the future, since South American and Asian nations of necessity soon will recognize the need to enact environmental laws as well. Closer to home, the passage of the North American Free Trade Agreement (NAFTA), about which you learned in Chapter 3, also shows sensitivity to environmental concerns. A subsequent environmental side agreement between the United States and Mexico attempts to address the degradation of the environment along the U.S.–Mexican border. In 1999, EPA budgeted $396 million for reducing the transboundary threats to human health and shared ecosystems (especially along the U.S.–Mexico border). Part of these funds will be used to implement the Montreal Protocol on Substances That Deplete the Ozone Layer, a treaty to which the United States is a signatory nation. Pursuant to this treaty, the EPA will establish and enforce rules aimed at controlling the production and emission of ozone-depleting compounds and at identifying safer alternatives that curtail ozone depletion. Moreover, the trade talks occurring during the

YOU BE THE JUDGE

A COLLISION OF RIGHTS

President Clinton on 5 August 1999 signed an executive order that sets a one-year moratorium on public access to certain chemical safety information that, pursuant to the Clean Air Act (CAA), chemical facilities must submit to the EPA. Under § 112(r) of the CAA, facilities that process or store threshold levels of nearly 130 different hazardous or toxic chemicals must submit risk management plans (RMPs) that, among other things, include an off-site consequences analysis (OCA) for each facility. Such OCA information includes the reporting of facilities' worst-case projections for deaths, injuries, and property damage that could occur in the event of the accidental release of any of the chemicals regulated under Section 112(r). The EPA, which began implementing § 112(r) in 1996, originally intended to make all the data and information set out in these RMPs available to the public, in the interests of communities' right-to-know. In furtherance of these right-to-know policies, the EPA presumed the availability of such information on the Internet as well. However, the FBI and the Department of Justice, in addition to state and local emergency response and security personnel and their professional organizations, subsequently voiced concerns in congressional testimony and in other venues that the ready availability of OCA information would make the facilities reporting under § 112(r) ready targets for terrorists. Adding further complexity to this concern was the fact that, under the CAA, the EPA lacks authority to deny access to this information. Owing to the deadline facing the EPA represented by Freedom of Information Act (FOIA) requests for such data, Congress and the Clinton administration thus had to make a decision about whether to restrict—temporarily or permanently—general public access to such OCA information, whether on the Internet or in any other form. Although it imposes criminal penalties for unauthorized disclosure of OCA information, the new law does allow access to OCA information by state and local emergency response and law enforcement personnel. Other officials designated by the EPA will have access to such information as well. Lastly, the law requires a General Accounting Office three-year study that will examine the threat of criminal activities at large chemical facilities. Critics of the law, among other things, argue that full disclosure of accident scenarios is necessary to overcome EPA institutional complacency, to encourage safer technologies, and to honor the public's right to know. Assume that someone has challenged the constitutionality of this law.

The case has been brought before *your* court. How will *you* go about balancing the public's right to know with the public safety policies and business policies that the statute raises?[26]

BUSINESS CONSIDERATIONS Is it in the best interests of a business that deals in hazardous chemicals for that business to disclose the potential risks should an accident occur or to withhold such information? Would businesses that manufacture or store dangerous chemicals be more likely to favor or to oppose the moratorium on access to this information?

ETHICAL CONSIDERATIONS Is it ethical for a business to withhold information about the potential risk that its activities present to the community in which the business is located? Is it ethical for a firm to withhold such information from its investors? Is it ethical for the government to impose a moratorium on the release of such information?

SOURCE: 30 *Environmental Reporter* 747 (The Bureau of National Affairs, Inc.: Washington, DC), 1999.

RESOURCES FOR BUSINESS LAW STUDENTS

NAME	RESOURCES	WEB ADDRESS
U.S. Environmental Protection Agency (EPA)	The EPA provides educational materials, regulations, publications, news, and text for the National Environmental Policy Act of 1969.	**http://www.epa.gov/**
Council on Environmental Quality (CEQ)	The CEQ provides, among other services, NEPANet (National Environmental Policy Act), which includes environmental impact statements (EISs) and a library of environmental resources.	**http://www.whitehouse.gov/CEQ/**

Uruguay Round of the General Agreement on Tariffs and Trade (GATT), also discussed in Chapter 3, involve environmental issues, as does the Kyoto Protocol. This latter initiative requires industrialized countries to reduce, by 2008–2012, their combined greenhouse gas emissions by at least 5.2 percent compared to 1990 levels. This protocol will take effect once 55 countries have ratified it. Although 73 countries have signed it, only three countries had completed the ratification process as of 1999.

In a further augmentation of the U.S.'s role in combating environmental degradation, then-President Clinton, through a 1999 executive order, decreed that the United States must factor environmental considerations into the development of its trade negotiating objectives. Consequently, certain U.S.-negotiated agreements— including comprehensive multilateral trade rounds, bilateral or plurilateral free trade agreements, and major new trade liberalization agreements in national resource sectors—will require an environmental review as to the agreements' environmental impacts in the United States and, when appropriate, the transboundary impacts as well. The primary responsibility for conducting such reviews lies with the U.S. trade representative.

SUMMARY

Environmental law involves complicated issues and highly technical statutes. The National Environmental Policy Act of 1969 mandates that virtually all federal agencies prepare detailed EISs whenever any agency undertakes any activities that may affect the environment.

The Clean Air Act, enacted in 1963 and amended subsequently, takes a technology-forcing approach to air pollution. It directs the EPA to establish national ambient air quality standards and state implementation plans that set out how the state proposes to implement and maintain those standards within its air quality regions. The 1990 amendments attack urban air pollution brought on by motor vehicle emissions, toxic pollutants, and acid rain. Among other things, beyond controlling emissions from mobile sources, these amendments set up a permit process aimed at minimizing emissions from major point sources. Civil, criminal, and administrative actions (including citizens' suits) are possible for violations of the act.

The Clean Water Act, so named in 1977 after having been enacted under a different name in 1972, sets out an extensive, joint federal and state comprehensive program for preventing, reducing, and eliminating water pollution. The CWA does so by regulating both point and nonpoint sources. The three mechanisms used to regulate discharges from point sources include effluent limitations, water quality standards, and the national pollutant discharge elimination system's permit program. States also must comply with EPA-mandated antidegradation standards designed to ensure the maintenance of desirable water quality standards. The CWA sets out a timetable and the technological standards to be used for permit holders' compliance with the act. The act takes an especially stringent approach to toxic pollutants such as asbestos, mercury, lead, PCBs, and so forth. The penalties imposed for violations of the CWA resemble those set out in the Clean Air Act.

The Safe Drinking Water Act of 1974 regulates the water supplied by public water systems to home taps. This act uses EPA-issued national primary drinking water regulations that have as their goal the reduction of contaminant levels in drinking water. States may have primary enforcement responsibilities under the SDWA if they have adopted drinking water regulations no less stringent than the national standards and if they have implemented adequate monitoring, inspection, record-keeping, and enforcement procedures.

The Noise Control Act of 1972 leaves to the federal government control over noise sources that require national uniformity of treatment or protection of the public health and welfare with an adequate margin of safety. Otherwise, the primary responsibility for controlling noise lies with state and local governments. The remedies granted for violations of this act resemble those permitted under the previous acts.

The Toxic Substances Control Act of 1976, by giving authority to the EPA to regulate chemicals before they come onto the market, screens pollutants before humans and the environment are exposed to these substances' effects. Yet the EPA's laxness regarding the stringency it will require of companies that provide test data, coupled with the congressional mandate requiring the testing and regulation only of chemicals that pose an "unreasonable risk" of injury to health or the environment, has undercut the statute's worthy goals. Besides the civil and criminal penalties set out in other acts, the TSCA, through emergency judicial relief leading to an injunction or seizure of the chemicals at issue, authorizes the EPA to regulate "imminent hazards."

The Federal Insecticide, Fungicide, and Rodenticide Act of 1947 mandates the registration of all insecticides and pesticides with the EPA. The EPA will register only those products that, when used in accordance with widespread and common practice, will not generally cause adverse effects on the environment. The EPA subsequently can cancel the registration of any pesticide that fails to live up to this standard and can suspend a registration whenever such is necessary to prevent an imminent hazard. Recent amendments to the FIFRA—specifically, the Food Quality Protection Act of 1996—set out stringent standards aimed at ensuring the wholesomeness of the American food supply and protecting children from the health threats posed by pesticide residues. Civil and criminal penalties, as well as EPA "stop sale" or seizure orders, are available under the FIFRA.

The Resource Conservation and Recovery Act of 1976 requires the EPA to regulate nonhazardous solid waste, typically through approved state management plans. The EPA's "cradle-to-grave" regulation of hazardous waste involves a permit/manifest system that covers those who own or operate treatment, storage, or disposal facilities. Under the RCRA, the EPA enjoys broad enforcement powers. Anyone involved in the handling, transport, storage, or disposal of solid or hazardous waste that presents an immediate and substantial endangerment to health or the environment faces the imposition of strict liability.

The Comprehensive Environmental Response, Compensation, and Liability Act (or "Superfund"), by regulating hazardous waste disposal sites, fills in the gaps left by the RCRA and the TSCA. Pursuant to the National Contingency Plan, CERCLA authorizes cleanups of hazardous waste sites and makes generators, owners, operators, and transporters of hazardous wastes strictly liable for such response costs. CERCLA also establishes a "Superfund" to finance cleanups whenever the government cannot identify the parties responsible for the damage. The Superfund Amendments and Reauthorization Act of 1986 has increased the money allocated to the Superfund.

The Endangered Species Act of 1973, by protecting the critical habitats of wildlife, attempts to conserve endangered or threatened species of plants and animals. Celebrated cases under the ESA wherein dam or road construction projects were halted to protect the habitat of fish or butterflies, for example, have led to public controversies of great magnitude. International efforts to improve the environment in this and other nations are on the rise and therefore bear watching.

DISCUSSION QUESTIONS

1. Describe fully when an agency needs to prepare an environmental impact statement (EIS) and the general prerequisites of an EIS.
2. Explain in detail the manner in which the Clean Air Act addresses the problem of air pollution.
3. Explain the following three Clean Water Act mechanisms and their importance to the fulfillment of the act's dictates: effluent limitations, water quality standards, and the national pollutant discharge elimination system's permit program.
4. How does the Safe Drinking Water Act differ from the Clean Water Act?
5. How has Congress allocated the responsibility for noise control among the federal government and state and local governments?
6. Explain Congress's threefold purpose in enacting the Toxic Substances Control Act.
7. How does the Federal Insecticide, Fungicide, and Rodenticide Act differ from the TSCA?
8. How do the Resource Conservation and Recovery Act and the Comprehensive Environmental Response, Compensation, and Liability Act, respectively, regulate waste?
9. Explain some of the more significant economic aspects of the Endangered Species Act.
10. Describe some of the international aspects of environmental law.

CASE PROBLEMS AND WRITING ASSIGNMENTS

1. The City of Tacoma, Washington, and a local utility district wanted to build a hydroelectric plant on the Dosewallips River in Washington State. The Washington Department of Ecology, the state environmental agency, conditioned the permit for the project on the maintenance of minimum stream flows that would sufficiently protect salmon and steelhead runs, since the state had designated the river as a fish habitat. In justification of its action, the agency noted that § 303 of the Clean Water Act (CWA) requires each state, subject to federal approval, to institute comprehensive standards establishing the designated uses of the navigable waters involved and the water quality criteria for such waters based on such uses. Under EPA regulations, the standards also must include an antidegradation policy that will maintain existing

instream water uses and the level of water quality necessary to protect those uses. Section 401 of the CWA requires states to provide a water quality certification before a federal license or permit can be issued for any activity that may result in a discharge into intrastate navigable waters. The certification must "set forth any effluent limitations and other limitations . . . necessary to assure that any applicant" will comply with various provisions of the act and "any other appropriate" state law requirement. Under Washington's comprehensive water quality standards, characteristic uses of the river's classification include fish migration, rearing, and spawning. The city and the local utility district argued that the state could impose only water quality limitations specifically tied to a "discharge," but the agency submitted that, pursuant to § 401, it had the power to condition the grant of the permit on the maintenance of minimum stream flows. Who had the stronger arguments here—the state agency or those who wanted to build the dam? Why? [See *PUD No. 1 of Jefferson County and City of Tacoma* v. *Washington Department of Ecology,* 511 U.S. 700 (1994).]

2. The Oregon Public Utility Commission (Commission) promulgated a rule stating that (1) trains were not required to sound whistles at grade crossings "equipped with operating automatic gates, flashing lights, and audible protective devices;" (2) the Commission was empowered to prohibit whistle sounding at such crossings; and (3) railroads were to provide written notification of such prohibitions to their employees. In 1988, the City of Eugene, Oregon, petitioned the Commission to prohibit whistle sounding by Southern Pacific Transportation Company (Southern Pacific) trains. The Commission then issued an order that banned train whistles at certain crossings in the city between 10 P.M. and 6 A.M. On 13 September 1991, the Commission, having found that the prohibition of routine train whistles in Eugene during nighttime hours would significantly increase the risk of accidents, rescinded this order. Southern Pacific, a California-based railroad that operates freight trains in Oregon and many other states, contended that the federal Noise Control Act (NCA) of 1972, by directing the establishment of standards for railroad noise emissions, preempts the Oregon state law. Under a provision labeled "state and local standards and controls," the NCA sets forth two provisions pertaining to its preemption of state laws:

   [A]fter the effective date of a regulation under this section applicable to noise emissions resulting from the operation of any equipment or facility of a surface carrier engaged in interstate commerce by railroad, no State . . . may adopt or enforce any standard applicable to noise emissions resulting from the operation of the . . . equipment . . . unless such standard is identical to a standard . . . prescribed by any regulation under this section.

   In addition, another provision states:

   [N]othing in this section shall diminish or enhance the rights of any State . . . to establish . . . controls on levels of environmental noise . . . if the Administrator . . . determines that such . . . control . . . is necessitated by special local conditions and is not in conflict with regulations promulgated under this section.

   The Commission maintained that no EPA regulation covering locomotive whistles exists and that the EPA has decided that state and local authorities are best suited to regulate acoustic warning devices such as train whistles. Was this case moot? If not, did the NCA preempt the Oregon regulations regarding the sounding of train whistles? Why? [See *Southern Pacific Transportation Co.* v. *Public Utility Commission of the State of Oregon,* 9 F.3d 807 (9th Cir. 1993).]

3. Owen Electric Steel Company of South Carolina, Inc. (Owen) is engaged in the production of steel. In the course of production, "slag" floats to the surface of the molten metal and is removed. A third-party contractor continuously processes slag at the Owen plant in Cayce, South Carolina. After curing (lying on bare soil for six months), the slag becomes amenable for the construction industry's use as a road base material or for other commercial purposes. As an operator of a facility that treats, stores, or disposes of hazardous wastes (TSDF) under the RCRA, Owen must apply for and obtain an EPA permit for the facility. The permit the EPA had mailed to Owen identified the Cayce site's slag processing area (SPA) as a solid waste management unit (SWMU). But Owen claimed that its slag did not constitute "solid waste" under the RCRA (i.e., "other discarded material") because the slag ultimately is recycled and used in roadbeds. The EPA countered that, because the slag lies dormant and exposed on the ground for six months before such use, it is "discarded" even if it is later "picked up" and used in another capacity. Whose reasoning was more persuasive, Owen's or the EPA's? Why? [See *Owen Electric Steel Company of South Carolina, Inc.* v. *Browner,* 37 F.3d 146 (4th Cir. 1994).]

4. KFC Western, Inc. (KFC) owns and operates a Kentucky Fried Chicken restaurant on a parcel of property in Los Angeles. In 1988, KFC discovered during the course of a construction project that the property was contaminated with petroleum. The County of Los

Angeles Department of Health Services ordered KFC to attend to the problem, and KFC spent $211,000 removing and disposing of the oil-tainted soil. Three years later, KFC, bringing this suit under the citizen-suit provision of the Resource Conservation Recovery Act (RCRA), sought to recover these cleanup costs from Alan and Margaret Meghrig. KFC claimed that the contaminated soil was a "solid waste" covered by the RCRA, that it had previously posed an "imminent and substantial endangerment to health or the environment," and that the Meghrigs were responsible for the "equitable restitution" of KFC's cleanup costs under the RCRA because, as prior owners of the property, they had contributed to the waste's "past or present handling, storage, treatment, transportation, or disposal." The district court held that the provision of the RCRA at issue neither permits the recovery of past cleanup costs nor does the RCRA authorize a cause of action for the remediation of toxic wastes that fail to pose an "imminent and substantial endangerment to health or the environment" at the time a suit is filed. The district court thus dismissed KFC's complaint. The court of appeals for the Ninth Circuit reversed and found that a district court would have authority under the RCRA to award restitution of past cleanup costs and that a private party could proceed with a suit under the RCRA if the waste at issue presented an "imminent and substantial endangerment" at the time it was cleaned up. Was the court of appeals's determination correct? [See *Meghrig* v. *KFC Western, Inc.*, 516 U.S. 479 (1996).]

5. In the late evening of 3 January 1992, or the early morning of 4 January 1992, a number of containers loaded with drums of arsenic trioxide were lost overboard from the vessel *M/V Santa Clara I* during a severe storm in the Atlantic Ocean off the coast of New Jersey. The loss of the drums overboard resulted in a response by the United States, led by the U.S. Coast Guard (Coast Guard) with the support of the U.S. Environmental Protection Agency (EPA), pursuant to the exercise of their apparent authority under § 104 of the Comprehensive Environmental Response, Compensation, and Liability Act (CERCLA) to respond to a release or a substantial threat of a release of a hazardous substance into the environment. On 20 February 1992, the Coast Guard issued an administrative order to the owner and operator of the *M/V Santa Clara I*. This order, directing the owner and operator to search for, locate, recover, and dispose of the containers and drums of arsenic trioxide, was issued pursuant to the Coast Guard's authority under § 106 of the CERCLA and Section 311(c) of the Clean Water

Act. Although the owner and operator of the ship objected to the government's risk assessment of the arsenic trioxide [sic] to the ocean environment, they conducted the mission of locating and recovering the arsenic trioxide drums. Through the concerted efforts of the United States and the owner and operator of the ship, the Coast Guard was able to locate the position of the drums more than 30 miles offshore and under 120 to 130 feet of water. The United States thereafter sued, pursuant to § 107(a) of the CERCLA, to recover the costs incurred by the government in responding to the loss of the arsenic trioxide from the *M/V Santa Clara I*. Upon the institution of this litigation, the owner and operator filed a counterclaim seeking reimbursement of the costs incurred when they had complied with the administrative cleanup order. Should the court allow this counterclaim? [See *U.S.* v. *M/V Santa Clara I*, 819 F.Supp. 507 (D.S.C. 1993).]

6. **BUSINESS APPLICATION CASE** Section 307(b)(1) of the Clean Air Act provides that petitions to review "nationally applicable regulations" issued by the EPA under the act are reviewable only in the U.S. Court of Appeals for the District of Columbia (D.C.) Circuit, while petitions to review "locally or regionally applicable" actions by the agency are reviewable only in the regional courts of appeals. Designed to reduce the amount of acid rain, the regulations create, effective in the year 2000, a national system of tradable pollution permits. Each permit—allowance is the term used in the regulations—authorizes an electrical utility to emit a ton of sulfur dioxide per year from a specified generating plant owned by the utility. A utility, of course, may have more than one allowance; in fact, the average is several thousand. The regulations use a variety of formulas to determine, on the basis of generating capacity, type of fuel, and other factors, how many allowances each of the nation's 2,200-plus electrical generating plants will be allocated; a table in the regulations sets forth these allocations. The total number of allowances may not exceed 8.95 million; and as the nation's electrical utilities emit more than 8.95 million tons of sulfur dioxide a year, the new program will reduce the total emissions of this pollutant. A novel feature of the program authorizes a utility that can reduce its emissions at very low cost to sell one or more of its allowances to a utility that will incur a much higher cost to reduce its emissions. The program thus helps minimize the costs associated with limiting emissions. Madison Gas and Electric Company (Madison) challenged the allocation of the sulfur-dioxide emission allowances for its Wisconsin electrical generating plants. Madison argued that the

allowances are based on an incorrect determination of Madison's generating capacity, one of the factors that governs how many allowances each plant will receive. The EPA argued that, despite the local incidence of the determination, Madison could challenge the EPA's decision only in the D.C. Circuit because the determination is part of the national acid rain program. The EPA further noted that if courts around the country began giving utilities more allowances, the 8.95 million ceiling might be pierced. Had Madison filed its lawsuit in the correct court? Why? Does the tradable pollution permit system at issue here represent a workable compromise between protecting business from exorbitant compliance costs and protecting the environment, or does the balance represented by this permit system tip too far in one direction? Explain. [See *Madison Gas and Electric Company* v. *U.S. Environmental Protection Agency,* 4 F.3d 529 (7th Cir. 1993).]

7. **ETHICAL APPLICATION CASE** The Clean Water Act (CWA) provides for two sets of water quality measures: effluent limitations, which are promulgated by the Environmental Protection Agency (EPA), and water quality standards, which are promulgated by the states. The CWA generally prohibits the discharge of effluent into a navigable body of water unless the point source obtains a national pollution discharge elimination system (NPDES) permit from a state with an EPA-approved permit program or from the EPA itself. A Fayetteville, Arkansas, sewage treatment plant received an EPA-issued permit authorizing it to discharge effluent into a stream that ultimately reaches the Illinois River upstream from the Oklahoma border. The State of Oklahoma and other Oklahoma parties, appearing before the EPA to challenge the permit, alleged, among other things, that the discharge violated Oklahoma water quality standards, which allow no degradation of water quality in the upper Illinois River. The EPA's chief judicial officer, remanding the initial affirmance of the permit by the administrative law judge (ALJ), ruled that the act requires an NPDES permit to impose any effluent limitations necessary to comply with applicable state water quality standards and that those standards would be violated only if the record shows by a preponderance of the evidence that the discharge would cause an actual detectable violation of Oklahoma's water quality standards. After making detailed findings of fact, the ALJ concluded that Fayetteville had satisfied the chief judicial officer's standard. Reversing, the court of appeals ruled that the CWA does not allow a permit to be issued where a proposed source

would discharge effluent that would contribute to conditions currently constituting a violation of applicable water quality standards. It determined that the Illinois River already was degraded, that the Fayetteville effluent would reach the river in Oklahoma, and that the effluent would contribute to the river's deterioration even though it would not detectably affect the river's water quality. Did the EPA's finding that discharges from the new source would not cause a detectable violation of Oklahoma's water quality standards satisfy the EPA's duty to protect the interests of the downstream state? If the court had decided this case on either utilitarianistic principles or on the Golden Rule, would the result have differed? [See *Arkansas* v. *EPA,* 503 U.S. 91 (1992).]

8. **CRITICAL THINKING CASE** The Endangered Species Act of 1973 (ESA) requires the secretary of the interior to specify animal species that are "threatened" or "endangered" and designate their "critical habitat." The ESA also requires federal agencies to ensure that any action they authorize, fund, or carry out is not likely to jeopardize a listed species or adversely modify its critical habitat. If an agency determines that a proposed action may adversely affect such a species, it must formally consult with the Fish and Wildlife Service (Service), which in turn must provide the agency with a written statement (the Biological Opinion) explaining how the proposed action will affect the species or its habitat. If the Service concludes that such an action will result in jeopardy or adverse habitat modification, the Biological Opinion must outline any "reasonable and prudent alternatives" that the Service believes will avoid that consequence. If the Biological Opinion concludes that no jeopardy or adverse habitat modification will result, or if it offers reasonable and prudent alternatives, the Service must issue a written statement (known as the "Incidental Take Statement") specifying the terms and conditions under which an agency may take the species.

The Klamath Project, one of the oldest federal reclamation schemes, consists of a series of lakes, rivers, dams, and irrigation canals in northern California and southern Oregon. The project was undertaken by the secretary of the interior pursuant to the Reclamation Act of 1902 and is administered by the Bureau of Reclamation (Bureau), which is under the Secretary's jurisdiction. In 1992, the Bureau notified the Service that operation of the project might affect the Lost River sucker and shortnose sucker species of fish that had been listed as endangered in 1988. After formal consultation with the Bureau, the Service issued a Biological Opinion that concluded that the "long-term operation of the Klamath Project was likely to jeopardize the continued existence of the Lost River and shortnose suckers." The Biological Opinion identified "reasonable and prudent alternatives" the Service believed would avoid jeopardy, which alternatives included the maintenance of minimum water levels on the Clear Lake and Gerber reservoirs. The Bureau later notified the Service that it intended to operate the project in compliance with the Biological Opinion. The petitioners—two Oregon irrigation districts that receive Klamath Project water and the operators of two ranches within those districts—subsequently filed a lawsuit against the director and regional director of the Service and the secretary of the interior. The complaint asserted that there is an absence of any scientifically or commercially available evidence indicating that the populations of endangered suckers in the Clear Lake and Gerber reservoirs have declined, are declining, or will decline as a result of the Bureau's operation of the Klamath Project and that there is an absence of any commercially or scientifically available evidence indicating that the restrictions on lake levels imposed in the Biological Opinion will have any beneficial effect on the populations of suckers in the Clear Lake and Gerber reservoirs. The complaint further stated that petitioners' uses of the reservoirs and related waterways for recreational, aesthetic, and commercial purposes, as well as for their primary sources of irrigation water, will be "irreparably damaged" by the actions taken by the Service. In essence, the petitioners claimed a competing interest in the water that the Biological Opinion declares necessary for the preservation of the suckers. The district court, dismissing the complaint for lack of jurisdiction, concluded that the petitioners lacked standing because their "recreational, aesthetic, and commercial interests . . . do not fall within the zone of interests sought to be protected by the ESA." Affirming, the court of appeals for the Ninth Circuit held that the "zone of interests" test limits the class of persons who may obtain judicial review under the citizen-suit provision of the ESA and that "only plaintiffs who allege an interest in the preservation of endangered species fall within the zone of interests protected by the ESA." At the Supreme Court, the petitioners thus raised two questions: first, whether the standing rule known as the "zone of interests" test applies to claims brought under the citizen-suit provision of the ESA; and second, if so, whether the petitioners have standing under that test notwithstanding the fact that the interests they seek to vindicate are economic rather than environmental. How should the Court rule in this case? Why? [See *Bennett* v. *Spear,* 520 U.S. 154 (1997).]

NOTES

1. John Henry Davidson and Orlando E. Delogu, *Federal Environmental Regulation,* 2 vols. (Salem, NH: Butterworth Legal Publishers, 1994); Roger W. Findley and Daniel A. Farber, *Environmental Law in a Nutshell,* 4th ed. (Minneapolis: West Publishing Co., 1996); and William H. Rodgers, Jr., *Handbook on Environmental Law,* 2d ed. (Minneapolis: West Publishing Co., 1994) provide more detailed and comprehensive information concerning environmental law.
2. This, and all other information and figures relating to 1999, can be found at the United States Environmental Protection Agency web site, http://www.epa.gov/.
3. Thomas DiLorenzo, "Federal Regulations: Environmentalism's Achilles Heel," *USA Today Magazine* (September 1994), p. 48.
4. Linda Grant, "Shutting Down the Regulatory Machine," *U.S. News & World Report* (13 February 1995), p. 70.
5. Ibid.
6. 490 U.S. 332 (1989).
7. "Concentrations of Five Major Air Pollutants Drop by Average 7 Percent But Ozone Up 4 Percent," 27 *Environmental Reporter* 1803 (The Bureau of National Affairs, Inc.: Washington, DC), 1996.
8. Ibid.
9. Ibid.
10. "Ozone Levels Worse in 1999 Than in 1998, with Vacation Spots Hit Hard, Report Says," 30 *Environmental Reporter* 742–743 (The Bureau of National Affairs, Inc.: Washington, DC), 1999.
11. "Federal Rules in Place to Protect against E. Coli Outbreaks," 30 *Environmental Reporter* 983 (The Bureau of National Affairs, Inc.: Washington, DC), 1999.
12. "Up to 30 Unregulated Contaminants to Be Monitored Under Final EPA Rule," 30 *Environmental Reporter* 983 (Bureau of National Affairs, Inc.: Washington, DC), 1999.
13. Ibid.

14. Ibid.

15. Tim Eichenberg and Robert Irvin, "Congress Takes Aim at Endangered Species Act," *The National Law Journal* (13 February 1995), p. A21.

16. Ibid.

17. Ibid., pp. A21, A22.

18. Ibid., p. A22.

19. Ibid.

20. Ibid.

21. See, e.g., *Ohio Forestry Association* v. *Sierra Club,* 523 U.S. 726 (1998) and *Steel Co.* v. *Citizens for a Better Environment,* 523 U.S. 83 (1998).

22. Ibid.

23. "Agency Reports Progress in 1998 Actions, Says Conclusions Unaffected by Data Errors," 30 *Environmental Reporter* 525 (The Bureau of National Affairs, Inc.: Washington, DC), 1999.

24. Ibid.

25. Turner Y. Smith, Jr., "Environmental Regulation on the Rise Worldwide," *The National Law Journal* (19 September 1994), pp. C15 , C16.

26. "Clinton Signs Bill Limiting Public Access to Chemical Accident Information," 30 *Environmental Reporter* 747 (The Bureau of National Affairs, Inc.: Washington, DC), 1999.

42

LABOR AND FAIR EMPLOYMENT PRACTICES

A G E N D A

As CIT grows and prospers, it will hire more employees. The firm therefore will need to ensure that it complies with all applicable federal and state laws regulating labor. CIT also may have to deal with one or more unions. The firm must be certain that it uses fair employment practices and thus avoids any improper discrimination in its hiring and promotion practices. In this regard, the firm must take steps to protect against sexual harassment, and it must provide a reasonably safe work environment.

The firm in addition will have concerns about social security, workers' compensation, and unemployment insurance. Each of these areas requires careful attention to detail and strict compliance with the applicable laws and regulations.

These and other issues are likely to arise during your study of this chapter. Be prepared! You never know when one of the Kochanowskis will need your help or advice.

O U T L I N E

INTRODUCTION

Labor law and fair employment practices law provide the framework under which workers—particularly unions—operate and under which employees are regulated and protected. Labor law applies to the relationship between management and workers. Among other things, this aspect of the law defines unfair labor practices and unfair management practices. Fair employment practices law deals with employer rights and responsibilities that help to guarantee the equitable treatment of all the employees within the organization. Most of these protections consist of federal regulations, although important state laws exist as well. Exhibit 42.1 provides an overview of the most significant statutes relating to labor and fair employment practices law. We will discuss these statutes as we progress through the material in this chapter.

LABOR

Federal Statutes

Unions are a fact of life in the United States today, but this was not always so. Violence and bloody battles between employers and prounion workers marked the rise of unionism in this country. The courts, moreover, were as hostile as most employers to unions. In fact, in the 1800s and early 1900s, both state and federal courts viewed workers' concerted activities (strikes, **picketing,** and the like) as common law criminal conspiracies, tortious interference with contract, or antitrust violations. Although Congress had passed the Clayton Act in 1914 in part to shield unions from liability under the antitrust laws, subsequent Supreme Court decisions had narrowed this newly won statutory protection.

Picketing
Union activity in which persons stand near a place of work affected by an organizational drive or a strike so as to influence workers regarding union causes.

Norris-LaGuardia Act (1932). Responding to these developments, Congress passed the Norris-LaGuardia Act in 1932. This act immunized certain activities—peaceful refusals to work, **boycotts,** and picketing, for example—from federal court action. The act barred the issuance of federal injunctions in the context of labor disputes as well as the institution of *yellow dog* contracts (i.e., promises to refrain from union membership as a condition of employment). It thus allowed employees to organize and to engage in collective bargaining free from court or employer intervention, as long as the concerted activity did not involve **wildcat strikes,** violence, sabotage, trespass, and the like.

Boycotts
Concerted refusals to deal with firms so as to disrupt their business.

Wildcat strikes
Unauthorized withholdings of services or labor during the term of a contract.

The Norris-LaGuardia Act signaled a policy aimed at keeping the courts out of the labor field. Free from regulation, then, employees and employers, by using the economic weapons appropriate to each side, fought for their respective goals. The unions used strikes, picketing, and boycotts; and the employers used discharges of employees.

The Wagner Act (1935). In 1935, Congress passed the Wagner Act, also called the National Labor Relations Act. This legislation heralded the beginning of an *affirmative*—as opposed to a neutral—approach to labor organizations. In § 7 of the Wagner Act, Congress approved the right of employees to organize themselves and "to form, join, or assist labor organizations, to bargain collectively through representatives of their own choosing, and to engage in concerted activities for the purpose of collective bargaining or other mutual aid or protection." The right to refrain from engaging in concerted activities is protected as well. Buttressing § 7 is § 8,

E X H I B I T   42.1 | **Representative Statutes Affecting Employment**

NRLA	Wagner Act (National Labor Relations Act) [1935]	Allows employees to organize and to engage in collective bargaining; enumerates employer unfair labor practices; establishes the National Labor Relations Board (NLRB).
LMRA	Taft-Hartley Act (Labor Management Relations Act) [1947]	Prohibits unfair labor practices by unions; separates the NLRB's functions; empowers courts to grant various civil and criminal remedies; creates the Federal Mediation and Conciliation Service.
LMRDA	Landrum-Griffin Act (Labor Management Reporting and Disclosure Act) [1959]	Requires extensive reporting of unions' financial affairs; allows civil and criminal sanctions for union officers' financial wrongdoings; mandates democratic procedures in the conduct of union elections and meetings.
	Title VII of the Civil Rights Act [1964]	Prohibits discrimination in the terms, conditions, and privileges of employment on the basis of race, color, religion, sex, or national origin.
EPA	Equal Pay Act [1963]	Prohibits discrimination in wages on the basis of sex.
ADEA	Age Discrimination in Employment Act [1967]	Protects certain workers (in general, age 40 or older) from discrimination in employment based on age.
	Rehabilitation Act [1973]	Directs federal contractors to take affirmative action with regard to "otherwise qualified" handicapped individuals.
PDA	Pregnancy Discrimination Act [1978]	Protects workers from pregnancy-related discrimination.
	Immigration Reform and Control Act [1986]	Prohibits immigration-related discrimination based on national origin or citizenship status.
ADA	Americans with Disabilities Act [1990]	Protects disabled workers from employment discrimination.
	Civil Rights Act [1991]	Amends earlier statutes so as to broaden the scope of protections afforded under antidiscrimination law; prohibits "race norming" of employment tests; in some circumstances, allows compensatory and punitive damage awards and jury trials.
FMLA	Family and Medical Leave Act [1993]	Mandates that eligible employees receive up to 12 weeks of leave during any 12-month period for certain family- or medically related events.
OSH Act	Occupational Safety and Health Act [1970]	Mandates safe and healthful workplace conditions.
SSA	Social Security Act [1935]	Provides federal benefits to the aged, the disabled, and other "fully insured" workers.
FUTA	Federal Unemployment Tax Act [1954]	Provides (through a coordinated federal and state effort) economic security for temporarily unemployed workers.
	State Workers' Compensation Statutes	Provide financial benefits to reimburse workers for workplace-related injury or death.

which enumerates employer **unfair labor practices,** such as coercion of or retaliation against employees who exercise their § 7 rights, domination of unions by employers, discrimination in employment (e.g., hiring and firing) designed to discourage union activities, and refusals by employers to bargain collectively and in good faith with employee representatives (i.e., with unions). Section 9 sets out the process by which the employees in the appropriate bargaining unit can conduct secret elections for choosing their representative in the collective bargaining process. The Wagner Act also established a new administrative agency, the National Labor Relations Board (NLRB), to oversee such elections and also to investigate and remedy unfair labor practices. Section 10 permits the appropriate federal circuit court of appeals to review any NLRB order. A 1937 case, *NLRB v. Jones & Laughlin Steel Corp.,* upheld the constitutionality of the Wagner Act.[1]

The Taft-Hartley Act (1947). After the passage of the Wagner Act, unions grew appreciably in size and influence. As a result, the power balance between employees and employers became so prounion that, in 1947, Congress passed legislation meant to counter the perceived excesses of the NLRB and pervasive court deference to its orders. The Taft-Hartley Act, also called the Labor Management Relations Act (LMRA), attempted to curb union excesses. It amended § 8 of the Wagner Act to prohibit certain unfair labor practices by unions, including engaging in **secondary boycotts,** forcing an employer to discriminate against employees on the basis of their union affiliation or lack of it, refusing to bargain in good faith, requiring an employer to pay for services not actually performed by an employee *(featherbedding),* and **recognitional picketing.** Congress also amended § 7 to allow employees to refrain from joining a union and participating in its collective activities.

In addition, the Taft-Hartley Act, by separating the NLRB's functions, cut back the authority of the board. The Office of General Counsel took on the prosecution of the board's unfair labor practices cases, leaving to the five-person board the decision-making (or *adjudicatory*) function. This reconfiguration significantly changed the nature of the NLRB, which had served simultaneously as both prosecutor and decision maker under the Wagner Act.

The Taft-Hartley Act also empowered courts of appeals to set aside NLRB findings concerning unfair labor practices cases, authorized district courts to issue labor injunctions requested by the NLRB for the purpose of stopping unfair labor practices, set out the possibility of fines and imprisonment for anyone resisting NLRB orders, and provided for civil remedies for private parties damaged by secondary boycotts or various union activities.

Other sections protect the employer's right of free speech (by refusing to characterize as unfair labor practices an employer's expressions of its opinions about unionism when they contain no threats of reprisal), preserve the employees' rights to engage in peaceful **informational picketing,** and prohibit *closed shop* agreements (contracts that obligate the employer to hire and retain only union members). *Union shop* clauses (provisions that require an employee, after being hired, to join a union in order to retain his or her job) are legal. The Taft-Hartley Act also created a Federal Mediation and Conciliation Service for settling disputes between labor and management. To foster conciliation efforts further, the act established a cooling-off period that the parties must observe in certain circumstances before strikes can occur. It also preserved the power of states, under their right-to-work laws, to invalidate other union devices designed to consolidate the unions' hold on workers.

A recent case construing the Taft-Hartley Act follows.

Unfair labor practices
Employment or union activities that are prohibited by law as injurious to labor policies.

Secondary boycotts
Union activities meant to pressure parties not involved in the labor dispute and to influence the affected employer.

Recognitional picketing
Prohibited picketing in which a union attempts to force recognition of a union different from the currently certified bargaining representative.

Informational picketing
Picketing for the purpose of truthfully advising the public that an employer does not employ members of, or have a contract with, a labor organization.

42.1

WRIGHT V. UNIVERSAL MARITIME SERVICE CORPORATION
525 U.S. 70 (1998)

FACTS In 1970, Caesar Wright was a member of Local 1422 of the International Longshoremen's Association, AFL-CIO (Union), which uses a hiring hall to supply workers to several stevedore companies represented by the South Carolina Stevedores Association (SCSA). Clause 15(B) of the collective bargaining agreement (CBA) between the Union and the SCSA provides that matters under dispute which cannot be promptly settled between the local and an individual employer within five days shall be subject to arbitration. Clause 15(F) of the CBA provides that the agreement covers all matters affecting wages, hours, and other terms and conditions of employment and that employers will not be required to negotiate on any other matters. . . . On 18 February 1992, while working for Stevens Shipping and Terminal Company (Stevens), Wright injured his right heel and his back. Wright thereafter sought compensation from Stevens for permanent disability, ultimately settled the claim for $250,000 and $10,000 in attorney's fees, and received Social Security disability benefits. After Wright had obtained a written note from his doctor approving such activity, between 2 January and 11 January Wright worked for four stevedoring companies, none of which complained about his performance. When, however, the stevedoring companies realized that Wright had previously settled a claim for permanent disability, they informed the Union that they would not accept Wright for employment, because a person certified as permanently disabled (which they regarded Wright to be) is unqualified to perform longshore work under the CBA. The Union responded that the employers had misconstrued the CBA, suggested that the Americans with Disabilities Act (ADA) entitled Wright to return to work if he could perform his duties, and asserted that refusing Wright employment would constitute a "**lockout**" in violation of the CBA. When Wright found out that the stevedoring companies would no longer accept him for employment, he contacted the Union. Wright claimed that instead of suggesting the filing of a grievance, the Union told him to file a claim under the ADA. In January 1996, Wright did so. The district court dismissed the case without prejudice because Wright had failed to pursue the grievance procedure provided by the CBA. The United States Court of Appeals for the Fourth Circuit affirmed the lower court's decision.

ISSUE Did the CBA's general arbitration clause require Wright to use these arbitration procedures for alleged violations of the Americans with Disabilities Act?

HOLDING No. Wright's ADA claim is not subject to the presumption of arbitrability the Supreme Court has found in § 301 of the Labor Management Relations Act. That presumption derives from its underlying rationale, i.e., that arbitrators are in a better position than courts to interpret the terms of a CBA. The dispute here ultimately concerns not the application or interpretation of any CBA, but the meaning of a federal statute, the ADA. Although an ordinary textual analysis of a CBA may show that matters beyond the interpretation and application of contract terms are subject to arbitration, they will not be presumed to be so. Moreover, in order for a union to waive employees' rights to a federal judicial forum for statutory antidiscrimination claims, the agreement to arbitrate such claims must be clear and unmistakable rather than embodied in a general arbitration clause, which is the case here.

REASONING The Fourth Circuit's conclusion that the general arbitration provision in the CBA governing Wright's employment was sufficiently broad to encompass a statutory claim arising under the ADA and that such a provision was enforceable brings into question two lines of Supreme Court precedents. The first is represented by *Alexander* v. *Gardner-Denver Co.*, which held that an employee does not forfeit his or her right to a judicial forum for a claimed discriminatory discharge in violation of Title VII of the Civil Rights Act of 1964, if "he [or she] first pursues his [or her] grievance to final arbitration under the nondiscrimination clause of a collective-bargaining agreement." In rejecting the argument that the doctrine of election of remedies barred the Title VII lawsuit, the Court reasoned that a grievance is designed to vindicate a "contractual right" under a CBA, while a lawsuit under Title VII asserts "independent statutory rights accorded by Congress." The statutory cause of action would not be waived by the union's agreement to the arbitration provision of the CBA, since prospective waivers of an employee's rights under Title VII are null and void. The second line of cases implicated here, *Gilmer* v. *Interstate/Johnson Lane Corp.*, held that

42.1

WRIGHT V. UNIVERSAL MARITIME SERVICE CORPORATION, *continued*
525 U.S. 70 (1998)

a claim brought under the Age Discrimination in Employment Act of 1967 (ADEA) could be subject to compulsory arbitration pursuant to an arbitration provision in a securities registration form. In concluding that statutory claims may be the subject of an arbitration agreement, the Court relied on the federal policy favoring arbitration embodied in the Federal Arbitration Act (FAA). Some tension between these two lines of cases obviously exists. Although *Gardner-Denver* and *Gilmer* are relevant for various purposes to the case at hand, the defendants rely upon the presumption of arbitrability the Supreme Court has found in § 301 of the Labor Management Relations Act (LMRA). Under this presumption, a court should refrain from denying an order to arbitrate the particular grievance unless the arbitration clause in the CBA is clearly not susceptible of an interpretation that covers the asserted dispute. The cause of action Wright asserts arises not out of contract, but out of the ADA (a federal statute), and is distinct from any right conferred by the CBA. Although the defendants had argued that Wright is not qualified for his position as the CBA requires, even if that were true, he would still prevail if the refusal to hire violated the ADA. Moreover, as Supreme Court precedents indicate, any CBA requirement to arbitrate a statutory claim must be particularly clear. The same standard applies to a union-negotiated waiver of employees' statutory right to a judicial forum for claims of employment discrimination. Although that is not a substantive right, and whether *Gardner-Denver*'s seemingly absolute prohibition of union waivers of employees' federal forum rights survives *Gilmer, Gardner-Denver* at least stands for the proposition that the right to a federal judicial forum is of sufficient importance to be protected against a less-than-explicit union waiver in a CBA. The CBA in this case does not meet that standard. Its arbitration clause is very general, providing for arbitration of "matters under dispute"— which could be understood to mean matters in dispute under the contract. And the remainder of the contract contains no explicit incorporation of statutory antidiscrimination requirements. Likewise, even though Clause 17 of the CBA states that "it is the intention and purpose of all parties hereto that no provision or part of this Agreement shall be violative of any Federal or State Law," that is not the same as making compliance with the ADA a contractual commitment that would be subject to the arbitration clause. Hence, the CBA in this case does not contain a clear and unmistakable waiver of the covered employees' rights to a judicial forum for federal claims of employment discrimination. Thus, the Court does not need to reach the question of whether such a waiver would be enforceable. The judgment of the Fourth Circuit is vacated, and the case is remanded for further proceedings consistent with this opinion.

BUSINESS CONSIDERATIONS What could the employers and the union, respectively, have done differently in this case? If you were the CEO of the stevedoring companies that had presumed Wright was permanently disabled, would you have questioned this stance?

ETHICAL CONSIDERATIONS Is it ethical for a company to require as part of its CBA that an employee arbitrate claims of discrimination? Do the disputes and contractual rights that a worker ordinarily would expect to take to arbitration differ from such claims? Did the union act ethically vis-à-vis Wright? Explain your reasoning.

The Landrum-Griffin Act (1959). By the 1950s, Congress had unearthed substantial corruption among union leadership. Union members had been prejudiced by officers' plundering of union treasuries and by these officers' often tyrannical treatment of the rank-and-file members.

In 1959, Congress responded with the Landrum-Griffin Act, also called the Labor Management Reporting and Disclosure Act (LMRDA). As this latter title suggests, the act requires extensive reporting of financial affairs; allows civil and criminal sanctions for financial wrongdoings by union officers; and, by providing a "bill

Lockout
A plant closing or any other refusal by an employer to furnish work to employees during labor disputes.

Look over

of rights" for union members regarding elections and meetings, mandates democratic procedures in the conduct of union affairs. In addition, the Landrum-Griffin Act amended portions of the Taft-Hartley Act to outlaw *hot cargo* clauses (provisions in contracts requiring the employer to cease doing business with nonunion companies).

Taken together, these acts cover almost all employers and employees, excluding federal, state, and local government employers and employees; employers covered under the Railway Labor Act; agricultural workers; domestic workers; independent contractors; and most supervisors. Even though government workers are not covered, they can organize themselves under the authority of Executive Order 11491, entitled Labor–Management Relations in the Federal Service, promulgated in 1969. In addition, about two-thirds of the states have enacted laws permitting collective bargaining in the public sector for state and municipal employees. Such executive orders and statutes ordinarily forbid strikes by public employees (such as police officers and firefighters), but such strikes nevertheless have occurred in recent years. The arrival of collective bargaining in the public sector is fairly new, but it promises to have significant implications for the future as our economy becomes more service oriented and the number of government employees proliferates.

Further Issues. Although we cannot describe fully the pervasive regulation of labor embodied in the Wagner, Taft-Hartley, and Landrum-Griffin acts, we will highlight a few of the more important issues.

Questions invariably arise when employees select their bargaining representative. The Wagner Act sets forth the procedures that must be followed during this process. Briefly, these procedures include, upon a required showing of employee interest, the union's petitioning for an election that will lead to its recognition as the exclusive bargaining representative of the employees. The NLRB decides whether the election has been conducted validly and, if so, certifies the union as the exclusive bargaining agent.

The employer, who ordinarily resists the election/representation process, may attempt to "decertify" the union. The employer typically argues that the employees do not constitute an appropriate bargaining unit (i.e., the employees have different duties, skills, or responsibilities) or that the union has engaged in unfair labor practices. The NLRB initially adjudicates such complaints, but the circuit courts of appeals can review final NLRB orders. In many cases, the employer prevails.

Not to be outdone, unions usually have alleged unfair labor practices by employers during the certification process. Consequently, these affairs often become real donnybrooks of contradictory allegations because each side is fighting for the economic power signified by union representation or the lack of such representation.

The certification process may raise property issues as well, because organizers ordinarily wish to distribute union literature to employees in firms where they hope ultimately to hold a certification election. The right to engage in protected activity mandated by the Wagner Act thus clashes with the employer's property rights and the efficient conduct of its business. Board decisions generally invalidate the soliciting of employees and the distributing of literature during working hours and in working areas as long as such restrictions do not unduly interfere with the free exercise of employee rights guaranteed by the Wagner Act. As mentioned earlier, during this process, it is likewise permissible for the employer to state its views about unionism unless these statements convey a threat against prounion employees or promise a benefit to anti-union employees.

Once the bargaining representative has been empowered, the Wagner Act requires *good-faith bargaining* by both the employer and the union. This, of course, is a nebulous term; in essence, it mandates both sides' meeting and discussing certain issues with as much objectivity as possible. The duty to bargain in good faith does not absolutely presume agreement between the parties. Under this duty, an employer cannot bypass the union to deal directly with the employees.

The Wagner Act requires good-faith bargaining over "wages, hours, and other terms and conditions of employment." Basically, then, the duty to bargain covers only those topics that have a direct impact on the employees' job security. Decisions that are not essentially related to conditions of employment but rather are managerial decisions "which lie at the core of entrepreneurial control"[2] fail to suffice as mandatory bargaining subjects. Pay differentials for different shifts, piecework and incentive plans, transfers, fringe benefits, and severance pay are mandatory subjects. Courts have had more trouble classifying bonuses and meals provided by the employer. Managerial decisions to terminate the company's business or to shut down a plant are ordinarily *permissive,* or nonmandatory, subjects. An employer, however, might be forced to bargain about the *effects* of such decisions, such as **severance pay,** that impinge on the conditions of employment.

Although the labor laws view collective bargaining as the parties' meeting, asserting their positions, stating their objections to the other party's position, and disclosing the information necessary for each side to arrive at an informed decision, both sides permissibly can use economic weapons outside the bargaining room. Hence, employee strikes or work stoppages and employer lockouts do not in themselves violate the duty to bargain in good faith. An employer's unilateral granting of a wage increase without notice to the union during the process of negotiations does constitute bad-faith bargaining, however. On the other hand, such unilateral changes made after bargaining has reached an impasse are legal.

The NLRB can require either side who has refused, directly or indirectly, to bargain in good faith to begin bargaining and to cease and desist from any unfair labor practice that has accompanied the bad-faith bargaining. The board also can use such powers for ending violations of any of the employer or union unfair labor practices that have occurred outside the bargaining context.

NLRB orders are not self-enforcing, however; they become law only when imposed by a federal circuit court of appeals. Because litigation is time-consuming,

42.1 | MANAGEMENT

UNIONS

CIT has been wildly successful, and the firm has increased its workforce significantly. One of the newly hired workers, a strong union advocate, has started discussing the possibility of forming a union at CIT. Several of the employees, reasoning that a strong bargaining representative will help them, seem to favor forming a union. Others, including a number of the original employees, oppose the formation of a union. They believe that the Kochanowskis have treated the workers fairly and that a union will set up an "us versus them" mentality that will not be in the long-term interests of the firm or the employees. Tom is concerned that such discussions will divide the loyalty of the workers and thereby harm the firm. He asks you what he can legally do to prevent the formation of a union and what he must legally do if the employees decide to proceed. What will you tell him?

BUSINESS CONSIDERATIONS What should a business do if it learns that its employees are considering petitioning the NLRB for a union-certification election? Should the business take steps to discourage the formation of a union, or should the business wait until after the vote to choose a course of conduct?

ETHICAL CONSIDERATION Is it ethical for a business to take affirmative steps to thwart union-organizing activities if the management of the firm honestly believes that the introduction of a union will have harmful long-term effects on the business?

Severance pay
Wages paid upon the termination of one's job.

these limitations on the NLRB's enforcement powers sometimes make policing the actions of maverick employers or unions difficult. Board hearings and resultant orders, if resisted, bring on court scrutiny. If the court affirms the NLRB order, the court issues an injunction. In the meantime, however, the allegedly unfair labor practices may have continued and may have successfully stifled the employer or employee interests at issue.

State Law

The supremacy clause of the Constitution empowers Congress to pass laws, such as the federal labor laws, that will preempt the states' regulation of labor. Supreme Court decisions construing the labor laws (which are silent on the issue of preemption) have held that federal preemption powers are broad. Because of the NLRB's expertise and a desire for uniformity of case results, federal laws ordinarily will oust the states' jurisdiction in activities that arguably are protected or prohibited by federal labor statutes.

Matters that only peripherally affect the federal statutory scheme or matters that are of deep local concern may constitute legitimate state interests that state law (and courts) therefore may regulate. The law in this area is unsettled and the cases controversial; generally, however, state courts can adjudicate lawsuits involving damages from violence or other criminal or tortious activity, retaliatory discharges, and those causes of action covering all employers and employees exempted under federal statutes.

EMPLOYMENT

Fair Employment Practices Laws

Besides this extensive federal and state regulation of labor, several federal and state statutes designed to ensure equal employment opportunity for persons historically foreclosed from the workplace have come into existence since 1964.

Civil Rights Act of 1964. Foremost among these laws is the Civil Rights Act of 1964. Title VII of that statute prohibits discrimination in employment on the basis of race, color, religion, sex, or national origin. Under Title VII, an employer cannot lawfully make decisions to hire; discharge; compensate; or establish the terms, conditions, or privileges of employment for any employee based on the categories just enumerated.

In addition, an employer cannot segregate, limit, or classify employees or applicants for employment in discriminatory ways. Moreover, a union cannot discriminate against or refuse to refer for employment or apprenticeship programs any individual because of race, color, religion, sex, or national origin. And employment agencies cannot discriminate with respect to referrals for jobs or use advertisements indicating a discriminatory preference or limitation.

Furthermore, none of the three groups—employers, unions, or employment agencies—can discriminate against any individual because the individual has opposed unlawful employment practices. An employer that relegates blacks to manual labor jobs, or an employment agency or labor organization that refers only white males for executive jobs or only women for nursing or secretarial jobs, is in violation of Title VII.

Title VII's coverage, in general, extends to employers in interstate commerce that have on their weekly payrolls at least 15 full- or part-time employees[3] for at

least 20 weeks per year, to any national or international labor organizations that consist of at least 15 members or that operate a hiring hall, and to employment agencies that regularly procure employees for employers or work opportunities for potential employees. Because of amendments added in 1972, Title VII currently covers most federal, state, and local governmental and educational employees as well.

Title VII authorized the creation of the Equal Employment Opportunity Commission (EEOC), a bipartisan, five-member group appointed by the president. The EEOC presently serves as the enforcement agency for Title VII, the Pregnancy Discrimination Act of 1978, the Equal Pay Act of 1963, the Age Discrimination in Employment Act of 1967, the Rehabilitation Act of 1973, the Americans with Disabilities Act of 1990, the Civil Rights Act of 1991, and other statutes. The EEOC also can bring lawsuits relating to broad patterns and practices of discrimination. Complaints by individual grievants, or charges filed by the EEOC or state fair employment or human rights commissions may trigger the EEOC's jurisdiction.

The jurisdictional requirements for successful suits under Title VII are complex. In brief, a charge must be filed within 180 days or 300 days after the alleged discrimination has occurred, the latter time period being applicable in *deferral* states (those that have their own fair employment practices commissions). In deferral states, the local commission has exclusive jurisdiction for 60 days, at which point the EEOC has concurrent jurisdiction over the charge.

If the EEOC has retained jurisdiction for at least 180 days and has decided no reasonable cause exists to file an action on behalf of the grievant, the EEOC may issue a right-to-sue letter to the grievant. Within 90 days of receiving the right-to-sue letter, the grievant must file suit in the appropriate district court or, generally speaking, lose the right to sue. Under its National Enforcement Plan, the EEOC can certify that it will be unable to investigate the claim in 180 days and immediately issue a right-to-sue letter. Besides the EEOC's resultant cost savings, this plan has resulted in dramatic increases in the number of lawsuits filed in the federal courts.

Moreover, because the process is grievant oriented and because judges do not expect laypersons to write complaints that resemble legal briefs, courts give grievants considerable leeway in describing and recognizing when discrimination arguably has happened. In addition, the conciliation orientation of the process makes it possible to clear up the grievance before litigation becomes necessary. Still, remember that procedural pitfalls dot this entire area of the law.

Substantive pitfalls also may snare the unaware employer, since many employment practices that seem neutral actually may lead to discrimination. For instance, in the early 1970s, several cases involving testing procedures and mandatory high school diplomas arose. These cases show that selection criteria that seem outwardly neutral may foreclose blacks and other protected persons from jobs merely because statistically fewer blacks than whites are graduated from high school. Selection criteria that require a certain score on an aptitude test or a high school diploma may, as a landmark case notes, "operate as 'built-in' headwinds for minority groups and [may be] unrelated to measuring job capability . . . [Title VII] proscribes not only overt discrimination but also practices that are fair in form, but discriminatory in operation. The touchstone is business necessity. If an employment practice which operates to exclude [minorities] cannot be shown to be related to job performance, the practice is prohibited."[4]

Any job requirement that prevents a disproportionate number of blacks or other minorities from securing employment or promotion has a *disparate impact* (i.e., an unequal effect) on minorities and may be illegal. The employer then has the burden of proving that the requirement is job related. The EEOC has issued guidelines for selecting employees, but these guidelines do not have the force of law. Nonetheless, if courts so wish, they may give these EEOC guidelines considerable deference.

Besides facing liability stemming from disparate impact, employers also may be liable for the *disparate treatment* of their employees. Such cases ordinarily arise when an employer allows whites or males to break rules without punishment but institutes penalties if blacks or women break the same rules. A 1976 case, *McDonald* v. *Santa Fe Trail Transportation Co.,* also held that whites can sue for racial discrimination when they receive disparate treatment.[5] In this case, the employer had accused two whites and one black of misappropriating a shipment of antifreeze. The company fired both white employees but retained the black worker. The Supreme Court concluded that Title VII prohibits all forms of racial discrimination, including **reverse discrimination** of this type.

Reverse discrimination
Claims by whites that they have been subjected to adverse employment decisions because of their race and the application of employment discrimination statutes designed to protect minorities.

The allegations of reverse discrimination that spring from another source—affirmative action plans—pose some of the most controversial issues in the area of fair employment practices involving race. Title VII places on the employer the duty to maintain a racially balanced workforce. Yet if the employer takes affirmative steps—slotting certain apprenticeship openings for blacks, for example—to bring about such a racial balance, these actions may adversely affect the white incumbents who wish to take part in these training programs. Two diametrically opposed policies clash here: the interests of the minority candidate who in the past has been disadvantaged because of race and of the white incumbent worker who has taken no part in this discrimination but who now, because the employer is seeking to bring about equality of opportunity for black workers, must lose employment opportunities.

In these situations, whites occasionally have brought suits alleging reverse discrimination. A famous 1978 case, *Regents of the University of California* v. *Bakke,*[6] involved a white student who alleged that the University of California at Davis, by rejecting his application for medical school and admitting 16 minority students with credentials inferior to his, had discriminated against him on the basis of his race, in violation of the Fourteenth Amendment. The Supreme Court, in a very complex opinion, held that university quota systems that absolutely prefer minority candidates (the university had reserved 16 spots out of 100 for minorities) are illegal but that a university in its admissions process may take race into account.

The issue of reverse discrimination becomes even thornier in the private sector, where employers may face charges by the EEOC if they do not aggressively engage in affirmative action and may face suits by white workers alleging reverse discrimination if they do.

In *United Steelworkers of America* v. *Weber,*[7] the Supreme Court addressed this particular issue. In this case, the United Steelworkers of America and Kaiser Aluminum & Chemical Corporation (Kaiser) had entered into a master collective-bargaining agreement covering 15 Kaiser plants. The agreement included an affirmative action plan aimed at eliminating racial imbalances in Kaiser's workforce. This plan reserved for black employees 50 percent of the openings in Kaiser training programs until Kaiser's percentage of skilled black craftworkers equaled the percentage of blacks in the local labor force. Brian Weber, a white worker who had accrued more seniority than some of the black workers selected for the training program, was rejected as a trainee. Weber sued, alleging that Kaiser's affirmative action plan constituted reverse discrimination against white workers and, because of Kaiser's use of race in the selection of apprentices for training programs, violated

Title VII's ban on discrimination. The Supreme Court held that a private, voluntary, race-conscious affirmative action plan, such as at issue here, did not violate Title VII's prohibition against racial discrimination. In the Court's view, one of the purposes of Title VII involves opening up job opportunities traditionally closed to blacks; thus, Kaiser's self-evaluation efforts to eliminate its racially imbalanced workforce were appropriate. Moreover, because the Kaiser plan opened up opportunities for blacks without unnecessarily trammeling the interests of white workers, its affirmative action plan was legal. But the Supreme Court's holding in *Adarand Constructors, Inc.* v. *Peña,* a public sector case decided on constitutional grounds (and discussed in Chapter 5), may spawn court challenges to such race-conscious affirmative action plans.[8] Future legal developments therefore warrant your attention.

Besides racial discrimination, Title VII also prohibits religious discrimination. Sincere religious beliefs (or the lack thereof) are protected under Title VII. Typically, cases arise when a job shift necessitates work on the day the employee considers his or her Sabbath. If a person's religion forbids work on Fridays after sundown, for instance, Title VII mandates that the employer make a "reasonable accommodation" to the employee's beliefs unless to do so would pose an "undue hardship" on the conduct of the business.

The 1977 case, *Trans World Airlines, Inc.* v. *Hardison,*[9] however, by holding that an employer does not have to undertake an accommodation that requires more than a minimal expense or that violates a collective-bargaining agreement, has severely undercut the guarantees represented by Title VII. Furthermore, under other provisions of Title VII, educational institutions may make religion a **bona fide occupational qualification** (BFOQ). The University of Notre Dame, for example, can hire only Roman Catholic professors if it so wishes.

Bona fide occupational qualifications also may constitute a limited defense to charges of sex discrimination. For example, it is not a violation of Title VII for a movie director to cast only women in women's roles. Issues implicating the ban on sex discrimination include stereotypes about the ability to perform a job (such as an employer who thinks only men can be telephone "linemen" and only women can be telephone directory assistants), height/weight requirements that are not job related (women usually are smaller than men), and so-called "sex-plus" cases. In the last, the employer adds a selection criterion for women that is not added for men (such as when women with pre-school-aged children are not hired but men who have such children are).

By imposing liability on employers for sexual advances or requests for sexual favors made by the employers' agents and supervisory employees (so-called "quid pro quo" sexual harassment) and for sexual misconduct that creates an intimidating, hostile, or offensive working environment for women (so-called "hostile environment" harassment), recent Title VII cases have protected women from sexual harassment in the workplace. In doing so, the latter line of cases has relied on *Meritor* v. *Vinson,*[10] the landmark Supreme Court case that held that an employer could face liability for harassment that created a hostile or offensive working environment, even though the plaintiff had suffered no "tangible" losses of an "economic character." Yet, based on its belief that the lower courts had not sufficiently fleshed out the facts, the *Meritor* Court declined to issue a definitive ruling on employer liability. While the Court called for the application of agency principles to the issue of an employer's liability for a supervisor's conduct, the Court elaborated very little beyond this statement. Since *Meritor,* the various courts of appeals, as well as

Bona fide occupational qualification (BFOQ) A defense to charges of discrimination based on religion, sex, or national origin but not to charges of racial discrimination; a situation in which one of these categories is essential to the performance of the job.

Constructive discharge
A termination of employment that results from an employer's making the employee's working conditions so intolerable that the employee feels compelled to leave.

employers have struggled with the issue of how to apply agency principles in determining whether an employer would be liable for the conduct of its supervisors in situations involving sexual harassment. *Burlington Industries, Inc.* v. *Ellerth*, the case that follows, answers this important question.

42.2

BURLINGTON INDUSTRIES, INC. V. ELLERTH
524 U.S. 742 (1998)

FACTS Kimberly Ellerth quit her job after 15 months as a salesperson in one of Burlington Industries's (Burlington's) many divisions, allegedly because she had been subjected to constant sexual harassment by one of her supervisors, Ted Slowik. Burlington did not view Slowik, a mid-level manager who had authority to hire and promote employees, subject to higher approval, as a policy-maker. Against a background of repeated boorish and offensive remarks and gestures allegedly made by Slowik, Ellerth emphasized three incidents in which one could construe Slowik's comments as threats to deny her tangible job benefits. For instance, on one occasion, while on a business trip, Slowik allegedly made remarks about Ellerth's breasts. When she gave him no encouragement, Slowik allegedly told her to "loosen up" and warned her that he could make her "life very hard or very easy at Burlington." Ellerth refused all of Slowik's advances, yet suffered no tangible retaliation and was, in fact, promoted once. Despite her knowledge that Burlington had a policy against sexual harassment, Ellerth never informed anyone in authority about Slowik's conduct. In filing this lawsuit, Ellerth alleged Burlington had engaged in sexual harassment and had forced her **constructive discharge** in violation of Title VII of the Civil Rights Act of 1964. The district court granted Burlington a summary judgment. Reversing the district court, the Seventh Circuit produced a decision consisting of eight separate opinions and no consensus as to a controlling rationale.

ISSUE Under Title VII of the Civil Rights Act of 1964, could an employee who refuses the unwelcome and threatening sexual advances of a supervisor, yet suffers no adverse, tangible job consequences, recover against the employer without showing the employer is negligent or otherwise at fault for the supervisor's actions?

HOLDING Yes. An employer may be held liable for a supervisor's harassing acts even if the employer was not aware of them. But the employer may assert an affirmative defense under which an employer may escape liability when no adverse job action has been taken against the employee. To prove this defense, the employer must show that it (the employer) took reasonable care to prevent and quickly redress any harassment and that the plaintiff unreasonably failed to make use of employer remedies or otherwise to avoid harm.

REASONING When a plaintiff proves that a tangible employment action resulted from a refusal to submit to a supervisor's sexual demands, he or she establishes that the employment decision itself constitutes a change in the terms and conditions of employment and thus becomes actionable under Title VII. Because Ellerth's claim involves only unfulfilled threats, it should be categorized as a hostile work environment claim that requires a showing of severe or pervasive conduct. The question to be decided here turns on whether an employer has vicarious liability when a supervisor creates a hostile work environment by making explicit threats to alter a subordinate's terms or conditions of employment, based on sex, but does not fulfill the threat. Because Title VII defines "employer" to include "agents," Congress in express terms has directed federal courts to interpret Title VII based on agency principles. As *Meritor* v. *Vinson* acknowledged, the *Restatement (Second) of Agency* (1957) (hereinafter *Restatement*) is a useful beginning point for a discussion of general agency principles. Section 219(1) of the *Restatement* sets out the central principle of agency law that a master is subject to liability for the intentional torts and negligence committed by his or her servants while acting in the scope of their employment. While some early decisions absolved employers of liability for the intentional torts of their employees, the law now imposes liability where the employee's purpose, however misguided, is wholly or in part to further the master's business even if the employer has forbidden the conduct. As the much-cited § 219(2) of the *Restatement* notes, although a supervisor's sexual harassment is

42.2

BURLINGTON INDUSTRIES, INC. V. ELLERTH, *continued*
524 U.S. 742 (1998)

outside the scope of employment because the conduct was for personal motives, an employer is negligent with respect to sexual harassment if it knew or should have known about the conduct and failed to stop it. Negligence thus sets a minimum standard for employer liability under Title VII; but Ellerth seeks to invoke the more stringent standard of **vicarious liability.** *Restatement* 219(2)(d) concerns vicarious liability for intentional torts committed by an employee when the employee "was aided in accomplishing the tort by the existence of the agency relation" (the aided in the agency relation standard). The aided in the agency relation standard, therefore, requires the existence of something more than the employment relationship itself. When a supervisor makes a tangible employment decision concerning a subordinate, there is assurance that, in the absence of the agency relationship, the injury could not have been inflicted. Moreover, a tangible employment action in most cases inflicts direct economic harm. Tangible employment actions also are the means by which the supervisor brings the official power of the enterprise to bear on subordinates: The decision in most cases is documented in official company records; and the decision may be subject to review by higher level supervisors. For these reasons, a tangible employment action taken by the supervisor becomes for Title VII purposes the act of the employer. Whatever the exact contours of the aided in the agency relation standard, its requirements will always be met when a supervisor takes a tangible employment action against a subordinate. In that instance, it would be implausible to interpret agency principles to allow an employer to escape liability. Whether the agency relation aids in the commission of supervisor harassment that does not culminate in a tangible employment action is less obvious. On the one hand, a supervisor's power and authority invest his or her harassing conduct with a particular threatening character; and, in this sense, a supervisor always is aided by the agency relation. On the other hand, the acts of harassment a supervisor might commit might be identical to the acts a co-employee would commit; and [neither the EEOC nor any court has endorsed vicarious liability in such circumstances]. Hence, an accommodation of agency principles for harm caused by the misuse of supervisory authority with Title VII's equally basic policies of encouraging forethought by employers and eliminating the need for objecting employees to take action leads to the following conclusion: An employer is subject to vicarious liability to a victimized employee for an actionable hostile environment created by a supervisor with immediate (or successively higher) authority over the employee. When no tangible employment action is taken, a defendant employer may raise an affirmative defense to liability or damages, subject to proof by a preponderance of the evidence. The defense consists of two necessary elements: (a) that the employer exercised reasonable care to prevent and correct promptly any sexually harassing behavior and (b) that the plaintiff employee unreasonably failed to take advantage of any preventive or corrective opportunities provided by the employer or to avoid harm otherwise. While proof that an employer had promulgated an anti-harassment policy with complaint procedures is not necessary in every instance as a matter of law, the need for a stated policy suitable to the employment circumstances may appropriately be addressed in any case when the parties litigate the first element of the defense. And while proof that an employee failed to fulfill the corresponding obligation of reasonable care to avoid harm is not limited to showing any unreasonable failure to use any complaint procedure provided by the employer, a demonstration of such failure will normally suffice to satisfy the employer's burden under the second element of the defense. No affirmative defense is available, however, when the supervisor's harassment culminates in a tangible employment action, such as discharge, demotion, or undesirable reassignment.

BUSINESS CONSIDERATIONS Assume your employer has asked you to draft a policy that takes into account the *Ellerth* holding. What will you identify as the main provisions of this policy? Why?

ETHICAL CONSIDERATIONS Argue for or against the following proposition: A company's tolerating a work environment rife with sexual innuendos and insults is just as unethical as a company's tolerating a work environment rife with racial or ethnic slurs.

Vicarious liability
The liability that an employer or principal faces owing to an employee's wrongful acts committed in the scope of the employment or agency.

Faragher v. *City of Boca Raton*,[11] a companion case decided the same day, involved allegations of hostile environment sexual discrimination. Faragher, a female lifeguard, and a coworker alleged that during five years of employment, one supervisor touched them inappropriately on a number of occasions; and another made offensive comments and gestures. According to the district court's undisputed findings, the harassment was pervasive and severe enough to be actionable, and the supervisors in question had unlimited authority over the lifeguards. The district court also found that the city had failed to disseminate among the beach employees its policy against sexual harassment, had failed to keep track of supervisors, and had provided no assurance that employees could bypass the harassing supervisors when employees made complaints. Under these circumstances, the Supreme Court concluded, the city would not be able to mount a successful affirmative defense of the type enunciated in *Ellerth*. Hence, the Court found the city vicariously liable for its supervisory employees' sexual harassment of the two women, since the Court could not find that the city had exercised reasonable care to prevent the supervisors' harassing conduct.

Although most cases have involved harassment of women by men, men who face harassment from women supervisors have standing to sue under Title VII as well. Moreover, in yet another recent case, the Supreme Court in *Oncale* v. *Sundowner Offshore Services, Inc.*[12] held that workplace sexual harassment is actionable under Title VII when the offender and the victim are the same sex. Joseph Oncale, a male, worked as a roustabout on an oil platform in the Gulf of Mexico. He alleged that his male coworkers forcibly subjected him to sexually humiliating actions, physically assaulted him in a sexual manner, and threatened to rape him. Although the lower courts had held that same-sex sexual harassment is never actionable under Title VII, the Court declared that "nothing in Title VII necessarily bars a claim of discrimination 'because of . . . sex' merely because the plaintiff and the defendant (or the person charged with acting on behalf of the defendant) are of the same sex."[13] Moreover, to support an inference of discrimination based on sex, the Court explained, the harassing conduct need not be motivated by sexual desire. The Court also rejected the employer's contention that the Court's recognizing same-sex harassment claims would make Title VII "a general civility code" for the workplace.[14] Rather, the Court stressed, common sense, coupled with an appropriate sensitivity to the social context in which the conduct occurred (e.g., a football coach's swatting a player on the buttocks as the player runs onto the field would not be the equivalent of similar conduct by the coach if the behavior were directed at the coach's secretary [be the secretary male or female]) would "enable courts and juries to distinguish between simple teasing or roughhousing among members of the same sex, and conduct which a reasonable person in the plaintiff's position would find severely hostile or abusive."[15]

Employers thus face potentially large recoveries if they fail to take corrective actions to end sexual harassment once they know, or should have known, that it had occurred. Wise employers should establish and then vigorously enforce anti–sexual harassment policies. To illustrate, in 1994, a female secretary in one of the largest law firms in the country won a $3.5 million judgment against the firm and the partner who allegedly had harassed numerous women over a 14-year period. More recently, in 1999, Ford Motor Company agreed to pay $7.5 million in damages and millions more in training costs as part of its settlement of an EEOC-initiated sexual discrimination complaint brought on behalf of female workers in two Chicago area plants. This settlement follows the 1998 one involving Mitsubishi

Motor Manufacturing Company's record-breaking $34 million agreement to settle a similar case at its plant in Normal, Illinois.

The Pregnancy Discrimination Act of 1978, passed by Congress as an amendment to Title VII, dictates that an employer treat pregnancy in the same fashion as any other disability. To do otherwise constitutes actionable sex discrimination. *International Union UAW* v. *Johnson Controls, Inc.*[16] illustrates an interesting gloss on the Pregnancy Discrimination Act (PDA).

Johnson Controls, Inc.'s (Johnson Controls's) battery-manufacturing process used lead, occupational exposure to which entails health risks, including the risk of harm to a fetus carried by a female employee. After eight of its employees had become pregnant while maintaining blood lead levels exceeding that noted by the Occupational Safety and Health Administration (OSHA) as critical for a worker planning to have a family, Johnson Controls announced a policy barring all women, except those whose infertility could be medically documented, from jobs involving actual or potential lead exposure exceeding the OSHA standard. The International Union UAW (the UAW), a group including employees affected by the company's fetal-protection policy, filed a class action in the district court and claimed that the policy constituted sex discrimination violative of Title VII of the Civil Rights Act of 1964. The district court granted summary judgment for Johnson Controls, and the court of appeals affirmed. The question before the Supreme Court focused on whether Johnson Controls's sex-specific fetal-protection policy, in which the company had excluded fertile female employees from certain jobs because of its concern for the health of the fetuses the women might conceive, violated Title VII's ban on sex discrimination. According to the Court, by excluding women with childbearing capacity from lead-exposed jobs, Johnson Controls's policy created a facial classification based on gender and explicitly discriminated against women on the basis of their sex under Title VII. Moreover, in using the words "capable of bearing children" as the criterion for exclusion, the policy explicitly classified on the basis of potential for pregnancy, which classification, under the PDA, constitutes explicit sex discrimination. According to the Court, the bias in Johnson Controls's policy was obvious: The company gives fertile men, but not fertile women, a choice as to whether they wish to risk their reproductive health for a particular job. Johnson Controls's fetal-protection policy therefore explicitly discriminated against women on the basis of their sex. In the Court's view, the PDA, in which Congress expressly provided that, for purposes of Title VII, discrimination "on the basis of sex" includes discrimination "because of or on the basis of pregnancy, childbirth, or related medical conditions" also bolstered this conclusion. In other words, for all Title VII purposes, discrimination

42.2 | MANAGEMENT

CALL-IMAGE TECHNOLOGY

HIRING REQUIREMENTS

From its inception, CIT has had a policy of refusing to hire any full-time nonfamily applicants who have failed at least to graduate from high school. Tom and Anna have included this requirement in the firm's hiring manual because they believe that any high-tech firm—and CIT is high-tech—needs a well-educated workforce if it is to succeed. John recently has noticed this provision in the personnel manual, and he is concerned that this requirement makes CIT vulnerable to lawsuits claiming that the firm is guilty of racial discrimination in its hiring practices. He asks you what he should do in this situation. What advice will you give him? Why?

BUSINESS CONSIDERATIONS Should a business have a policy for any situation in which it decides to change the requirements an applicant must meet so as to be considered for a position? What factors should any such policy include? Could a firm's changing its job descriptions or hiring qualifications lead to any possible legal vulnerabilities?

ETHICAL CONSIDERATIONS Would it be ethical for a business to establish higher job requirements for a given position than are absolutely necessary to perform the described job? What ethical concerns would such a job description raise? What should a company do to act ethically, as well as legally, in this situation?

based on a woman's pregnancy is, on its face, discrimination because of her sex. Johnson Controls's use of the words "capable of bearing children" illustrated that it explicitly had classified on the basis of potential for pregnancy. Moreover, the Court stressed, the beneficence of an employer's purpose does not undermine the conclusion that an explicit, gender-based policy is sex discrimination. Nevertheless, under § 703(e)(1) of Title VII, an employer may discriminate on the basis of "religion, sex, or national origin in those certain instances where religion, sex, or national origin is a bona fide occupational qualification reasonably necessary to the normal operation of that particular business or enterprise." And while Johnson Controls argued that its fetal-protection policy falls within the so-called third-party safety exception to the BFOQ, Supreme Court cases have stressed that discrimination on the basis of sex because of safety concerns is allowed only in narrow circumstances. In the present case, the unconceived fetuses of Johnson Controls's female employees, however, were neither customers nor third parties whose safety is essential to the business of battery manufacturing. No one can disregard the possibility of injury to future children. Yet the BFOQ is not so broad that it transforms this deep social concern into an essential aspect of battery making. Consequently, the employer must direct its concerns about a woman's ability to perform her job safely and efficiently to these aspects of the woman's job-related activities that fall within the "essence" of the particular business. Johnson Controls's professed moral and ethical concerns about the welfare of the next generation would not suffice to establish a BFOQ of female sterility. Decisions about the welfare of future children, the Court concluded, must be left to the parents who conceive, bear, support, and raise them rather than to the employers who hire those parents.

In addition to prohibiting various types of sex discrimination, Title VII's ban on national origin discrimination similarly prevents harassment in the form of ethnic slurs based on the country in which one was born or the country from which one's ancestors came. Repeated ethnic jokes and other derogatory statements directed at one's ethnic origins in a given case may constitute national origin discrimination.

National origin discrimination often takes the form of "covert discrimination." To illustrate, any height/weight requirements may foreclose Spanish-surnamed Americans from employment opportunities, as may language difficulties or accents. If an employer fails to hire a worker on the basis of such criteria, the employer must prove that the criteria are job related.

Narrow BFOQs may exist in national origin cases. It is legal to hire a French person to be a French chef, for example. It also is legal to refuse to hire non-American citizens (because the prohibition against national origin discrimination in

42.3 | MANAGEMENT

CALL-IMAGE TECHNOLOGY

HARASSMENT POLICY

CIT employs several drivers, who operate company trucks delivering Call-Image videophones to customers. Each driver is assigned a particular truck. Sam, one of the drivers, took a personal leave day, so another driver was assigned the truck Sam normally drives. At the end of the day, the other driver informed Tom that Sam had taped several "girlie" pictures to the dashboard of the delivery truck and that the driver found the pictures sexist and insulting. Tom apologized to this driver and promised to look into the situation. Tom later sought your advice as to what liability arising from these circumstances CIT could face. What would you tell him?

BUSINESS CONSIDERATIONS Should a business establish a strong policy addressing discrimination and harassment before any complaints arise, or should the firm wait until there is a problem and then address that particular problem? If the business decides to become proactive, what sorts of conduct should its policy cover?
ETHICAL CONSIDERATIONS Is it ethical for a business to prohibit the free speech of some of its employees if other employees find such speech offensive? How can an employer protect the freedoms and rights of each employee and simultaneously protect all employees from discrimination and harassment?

Title VII does not include citizenship)[17] unless the discrimination in favor of citizens has the purpose or effect of discrimination on the basis of national origin. The protected categories under Title VII do not include **alienage** in and of itself. Likewise, it is not a violation of Title VII for an employer to refuse to hire persons who are unable to obtain security clearances because they have relatives in countries that are on unfriendly terms with the United States.

Alienage
The status of being a foreign-born resident who has not yet become a naturalized citizen.

Immigration Reform and Control Act of 1986. Providing yet another protection against national origin discrimination, the Immigration Reform and Control Act of 1986, although principally aimed at stemming the flow of illegal aliens into the United States, out of fairness also bans immigration-related discrimination based on national origin or citizenship status. This act therefore prohibits an employer's turning away job applicants because they appear to be aliens or noncitizens. Besides being narrower in scope than Title VII (the 1986 act covers only hiring, recruitment of workers for a fee, and discharges), Title VII also preempts this act whenever Title VII applies to the conduct in question. The 1986 act's legislative history makes it clear that Congress did not intend it to expand the rights granted under Title VII.

Equal Pay Act of 1963. In addition to Title VII, several other federal statutes protect various classes of persons. The Equal Pay Act of 1963 prohibits discrimination in wages on the basis of sex. Therefore, men and women performing work in the same establishment under similar working conditions must receive the same rate of pay if the work requires equal skill, equal effort, and equal responsibility. Different wages may be paid if the employer bases the differential on seniority, merit, piecework, or any factor other than sex (e.g., participation in training programs).

The Age Discrimination in Employment Act of 1967. The Age Discrimination in Employment Act of 1967 (the ADEA), in general, protects workers aged 40 or older from adverse employment decisions based on age. BFOQs based on safety or human and economic risks—age 55 retirement for police officers, for instance—may be upheld, as may differentiation in age based on a bona fide seniority system and discharges or disciplinary actions undertaken for good cause. The Supreme Court recently held that a plaintiff who alleges discrimination under the ADEA does not have to show, as part of his or her *prima facie* case, that the employer replaced the plaintiff with a worker under age 40 (*O'Connor* v. *Consolidated Coin Caterers Corporation.*[18] According to the Court, the fact that one person in the protected class has lost out to another person in the protected class is irrelevant, so long as the plaintiff can show that he or she has lost out because of his or her age.

Another recent case, *Oubre* v. *Entergy Operations, Inc.,*[19] held that a release of all claims against her employer that the employee had signed as a part of a termination agreement would not bar the employee's subsequent lawsuit based on the ADEA. The Supreme Court based its holding on the employer's noncompliance with the Older Workers Benefit Protection Act (OWBPA) passed by Congress in 1996 as an amendment to the ADEA. Specifically, the Court held that, under the OWBPA, Oubre's waiver had not been knowing and voluntary because the waiver had failed to comply with the requirements of the statute. Specifically, this attempted waiver was flawed in that it had not given Oubre sufficient time to consider her options; it had failed to provide her with a seven days' period in which to change her mind; and it had omitted any specific references to ADEA claims. Hence, the Court concluded, the waiver was ineffective and thus would not bar her bringing a subsequent ADEA action, despite her failure to return the monies she had received for signing the release. Owing to this holding, a prudent employer will take steps to ensure the firm's strict compliance with OWBPA whenever the firm provides terminated employees with an agreement that includes a waiver of age-related claims.

The Rehabilitation Act of 1973. The Rehabilitation Act of 1973 directs federal contractors to take affirmative action with respect to "otherwise qualified" handicapped individuals. A handicapped individual includes any person who "has a physical or mental impairment which substantially limits one or more of such person's major life functions, has a record of such impairment, or is regarded as having such an impairment." Federal contractors must make "reasonable accommodation" to such persons' impairments unless to do so would pose an "undue hardship" on the operation of their programs.

The Americans with Disabilities Act of 1990. The Americans with Disabilities Act of 1990 (ADA) seeks to redress discrimination against individuals with disabilities and to guarantee such individuals equal access to public services (including public accommodations and transportation), public services operated by private entities, and telecommunications relay services, to name a few.

Title I, which prohibits employment discrimination, adopts the Rehabilitation Act of 1973's definition of handicap but uses the more up-to-date term *disability*. The ADA, in requiring an employer to provide "reasonable accommodation to the known physical or mental limitations" of a person with a disability unless such accommodation "would impose an undue hardship on the operation of the business" of the covered entity, obviously continues to borrow heavily from the 1973 act. Reasonable accommodation under the ADA includes such actions as making existing facilities accessible to and usable by persons with disabilities, restructuring jobs, and providing part-time or modified work schedules.

However, the act does not require the employer to implement any job accommodation if the employer can demonstrate that the accommodation would impose an "undue hardship" on the operation of the business. The ADA defines *undue hardship* as an action requiring "significant difficulty or expense" with reference to the following factors: (1) the nature and cost of the accommodation; (2) the size, type, and financial resources of the specific facility where the accommodation would have to be made; (3) the size, type, and financial resources of the covered employer; and (4) the covered employer's type of operation, including the composition, structure, and functions of its workforce and the geographic separateness and administrative or fiscal relationship between the specific facility and the covered employer.

The legislative history indicates that the "significant difficulty or expense" standard encompasses any "action that is unduly costly, extensive, substantial, disruptive, or that will fundamentally alter the nature of the program." Significant, too, is the fact that in defining "undue hardship," Congress rejected all attempts to put a cap on the level of difficulty or expense that would constitute an "undue hardship," including an amendment to create a presumption that the cost of any accommodation exceeding 10 percent of the annual salary of the position in question constitutes an "undue hardship."

The employment discrimination provisions under Title I cover employers that have on their weekly payrolls 15 or more full- or part-time employees for each working day in each of 20 or more calendar weeks in the current or preceding calendar year. Hence, the ADA's provisions apply to an estimated 3.9 million business establishments and 666,000 employers. Like the Civil Rights Act of 1964, the ADA covers employers, employment agencies, labor organizations, and joint labor/management committees, but exempts religious entities. Thus, the ADA's coverage goes beyond that of the Rehabilitation Act of 1973, which applies only to employers doing business with the federal government. The ADA in addition expressly protects employees or applicants who have completed (or who are participating in) a drug rehabilitation program and no longer are engaging in the use of illegal drugs. Without fear of violating the ADA, employers can, however, impose sanctions against employees who currently are using illegal drugs and may hold such employees (and/or employees who are alcoholics) to the same performance and conduct standards to which it holds other employees, even if the unsatisfactory performance or behavior is related to the employees' drug use or alcoholism. The ADA also protects from discrimination persons who have acquired immunodeficiency syndrome (AIDS) or who are HIV-positive. Indeed, in *Bragdon* v. *Abbott*,[20] the Supreme Court's first pronouncement on the ADA, the Court held that an individual infected with the human immunodeficiency virus (HIV) could invoke the protections of the ADA, even if the virus that causes AIDS is in its asymptomatic phase. The Court, however, stopped short of characterizing HIV infection as a per se disability under the ADA.[21] The Court instead remanded the case for an assessment of whether the plaintiff-patient's HIV infection posed a significant threat to the health and safety of others so as to justify the defendant-dentist's refusal to treat the plaintiff in his office.[22]

At the congressional hearings for the ADA, experts testified that it potentially would cover about 43 million Americans and that its enactment therefore might cause a flood of litigation. Indeed, the EEOC itself predicted that complainants would file between 12,000 and 15,000 charges during the first year the statute took effect—a prediction borne out by the number of actual filings.[23] Since that first year, over 107,000 ADA-related charges have been filed with the agency.[24] As with any comparatively new legislation, the overall impact of the ADA remains unclear. In addition to the costs associated with the hiring process and those resulting from the predicted increases in litigation under the act, the expenses of converting existing facilities to make them accessible to individuals with disabilities obviously concern many employers, particularly small firms. Yet data from a pre-ADA survey of federal contractors showed that the compliance costs/workplace changes incurred under the Rehabilitation Act of 1973 for half of the companies amounted to zero dollars and for 30 percent of the companies less than $500. In only 8 percent of the cases did the changes cost more than $2,000.

Various federal circuit courts had struggled with the ADA issue that is the focus of the following case. Note how the Supreme Court disposed of the conflicting holdings that had developed in the circuit courts of appeals.[25]

42.3

SUTTON V. UNITED AIR LINES, INC.

527 U.S. 471 (1999)

FACTS Karen Sutton and Kimberly Hinton, severely myopic twin sisters, have uncorrected visual acuity of 20/200 or worse. However, with corrective measures, both function identically to individuals without similar impairments. They applied to United Airlines, Inc. (United), a major commercial airline carrier, for employment as commercial airline pilots but were

continued

42.3

SUTTON V. UNITED AIR LINES, INC., *continued*
527 U.S. 471 (1999)

rejected because they did not meet United's minimum requirement of uncorrected visual acuity of 20/100 or better. Consequently, they filed suit under the ADA, which prohibits covered employers from discriminating against individuals on the basis of their disabilities. The district court held that the plaintiffs were not actually disabled because they could fully correct their visual impairments and that United had refrained from regarding them as disabled. Instead, the court concluded, United regarded them as unable to satisfy the requirements of a particular job—global airline pilot. Employing similar logic, the Tenth Circuit Court of Appeals affirmed the district court's decision.

ISSUE Should the determination of whether one is disabled within the meaning of the ADA be determined with reference to measures that mitigate the individual's impairment, including, in this instance, eyeglasses and contact lenses?

HOLDING Yes. If a person is taking measures to correct for, or mitigate, a physical or mental impairment, the effects of those measures—both positive and negative—must be taken into account when one judges whether that person is "substantially limited" in a major life activity and thus "disabled" under the act.

REASONING The ADA prohibits discrimination by covered entities, including private employers, against qualified individuals with a disability. The act identifies a "qualified individual with a disability" as "an individual with a disability who, with or without reasonable accommodation, can perform the essential functions of the employment position that such individual holds or desires." In turn, a "disability" is defined as:

   (A) *a physical or mental impairment that substantially limits one or more of the major life activities of such individual;*
   (B) *a record of such an impairment; or*
   (C) *being regarded as having such an impairment.*

Accordingly, to fall within the statutory definition of disability, one must have an actual disability (subsection (A)), have a record of a disability (subsection (B)), or be regarded as having one (subsection (C)). The first question thus centers on whether the plaintiffs

stated a claim under subsection (A) of the disability definition, that is, whether they alleged that they possess a physical impairment that substantially limits them in one or more major life activities. Because the plaintiffs claimed that with corrective measures their vision "is 20/20 or better," they are not actually disabled within the meaning of the Act if the "disability" determination is made with reference to these measures. Consequently, with respect to subsection (A) of the disability definition, the plaintiffs maintained that whether an impairment is substantially limiting should be determined without regard to corrective measures. They argued that, because the ADA does not directly address the question at hand, the Court should defer to the [EEOC and Department of Justice] interpretations of the statute. These guidelines specifically direct that the determination of whether an individual is substantially limited in a major life activity be made without regard to mitigating measures. United, in turn, submitted that the Court should not defer to the agency guidelines because they conflict with the plain meaning of the ADA [and thus are unreasonable]. Here, United is correct that the approach adopted by the agency guidelines—that persons are to be evaluated in their hypothetical uncorrected state—is an impermissible interpretation of the ADA. With regard to the act as a whole, it is apparent that if a person is taking measures to correct for, or mitigate, a physical or mental impairment, the effects of those measures—both positive and negative—must be taken into account when one judges whether that person is "substantially limited" in a major life activity and thus "disabled" under the act. Three separate provisions of the ADA, read in concert, lead to this conclusion. First, the act defines a "disability" as "a physical or mental impairment that *substantially limits* one or more of the major life activities" of an individual. Because the phrase "substantially limits" appears in the act in the present indicative verb form, a court must read the language as requiring that a person, in order to demonstrate a disability, be presently—not potentially or hypothetically—substantially limited. To be sure, a person whose physical or mental impairment is corrected by mitigating measures still has an impairment; but once corrected, the impairment does not "substantially limit" a major life activity. Second, the agency guidelines' directive that persons be judged in their

42.3

SUTTON V. UNITED AIR LINES, INC., *continued*
527 U.S. 471 (1999)

uncorrected or unmitigated state runs directly counter to the individualized inquiry mandated by the ADA. The agency approach instead would often require courts and employers to speculate about a person's condition and would, in many cases, force them to make a disability determination based on general information about how an uncorrected impairment usually affects an individual, rather than on the individual's actual condition. Finally, and critically, findings enacted as part of the ADA require the conclusion that Congress did not intend to bring under the statute's protection all those whose uncorrected conditions amount to disabilities. Congress found that "some 43,000,000 Americans have one or more physical or mental disabilities, and this number is increasing as the population as a whole is growing older." This figure is inconsistent with the definition of disability pressed by the plaintiffs. Had Congress intended to include all persons with corrected physical limitations among those covered by the act, Congress undoubtedly would have cited in its findings a much higher number of disabled persons. Applying this reading of the act to the case at hand, it is clear that the court of appeals correctly resolved the issue of disability in United's favor. With corrective measures, the plaintiffs' visual acuity is 20/20; and they function identically to individuals without a similar impairment. Accordingly, because disability under the Act is to be determined with reference to corrective measures, the courts below were correct in holding that the plaintiffs had not stated a claim that they are substantially limited in any major life activity. However, the inquiry does not end here. Under subsection (C), individuals who are "regarded as" having a disability are disabled within the meaning of the ADA as well. There are two apparent ways in which individuals may fall within this statutory definition: (1) a covered entity mistakenly believes that a person has a physical impairment that substantially limits one or more major life activities, or (2) a covered entity mistakenly believes that an actual, nonlimiting impairment substantially limits one or more major life activities. These misperceptions often "result from

stereotypic assumptions not truly indicative of . . . individual ability." Assuming without deciding that working is a major life activity and that the EEOC regulations interpreting the term "substantially limits" are reasonable, the plaintiffs failed to allege adequately that United regards their poor eyesight as an impairment that substantially limits them in the major life activity of working. They alleged only that United regards their poor vision as precluding them from holding positions as global airline pilots. Because the position of global airline pilot is a single job, this allegation did not support the claim that United regards Sutton and Hinton as having a *substantially limiting* impairment. Indeed, a number of other positions utilizing the plaintiffs' skills, such as regional pilot and pilot instructor to name a few, were available to them. Even under the EEOC's Interpretative Guidance, to which the plaintiffs argued the Court should show deference, "an individual who cannot be a commercial airline pilot because of a minor vision impairment, but who can be a commercial airline co-pilot or a pilot for a courier service, would not be substantially limited in the major life activity of working." Because the plaintiffs did not allege, and were unable to demonstrate, that United's requirement reflects a belief that the plaintiffs' vision substantially limits them, the decision of the court of appeals affirming the dismissal of the plaintiffs' claim that they are regarded as disabled must be affirmed.

BUSINESS CONSIDERATIONS How does an employer balance the policy of hiring workers with disabilities and public safety (or other similar concerns)? Since the employer must undertake an individualized determination of when a disability exists, what factors should be considered in such an assessment?

ETHICAL CONSIDERATIONS Whose position here is ethically more admirable in the context of determining the existence of a disability: the Supreme Court or the EEOC's? Support your reasoning.

Civil Rights Act of 1991. Congress enacted the Civil Rights Act of 1991 after a two-year struggle. Interestingly, Congress in part passed this act to overturn a series of 1989 and 1991 Supreme Court cases that had significantly eroded the rights of complainants alleging employment discrimination. Thus, the act reflected Congress's displeasure with the present Court's judicial attitude toward civil rights cases. The act, in its amendments of Title VII, therefore reaffirms the holdings of such cases as *Griggs v. Duke Power Co.*[26] The new act's amendments to § 1981 of the Civil Rights Act of 1866 also specify that this statute covers all forms of racial discrimination in employment (including racial harassment).

Besides these procomplainant provisions, the act in addition mandates the impartial use of tests and thus prohibits "race norming" of employment tests. In other words, employers must record and report actual scores and will be unable to modify scores, use different cutoff scores, or otherwise adjust the results of employment-related tests on the basis of race, color, religion, sex, or national origin even if employers have taken these actions so as to assure minority inclusion in the applicant pool. In a similar vein, the act effects no changes in the law regarding what constitutes lawful affirmative action and/or illegal reverse discrimination. It also restricts challenges to court-ordered consent decrees by individuals who had a reasonable opportunity to object to such decrees or whose interests were adequately represented by another party.

The act does broaden the scope of federal antidiscrimination law. It makes clear that Americans employed abroad by U.S.-owned or U.S.-controlled firms can avail themselves of the protection of Title VII, the ADA, and the ADEA, unless compliance with these laws will constitute a violation of the host country's laws. The act moreover extends coverage of the antidiscrimination laws to congressional employees and executive-branch political appointees and sets up discrete internal mechanisms for addressing such claims.

The act furthermore broadens the categories of victims who can seek compensatory and punitive damages based on intentional discrimination, although it provides for caps of $50,000 to $300,000 (depending on the size of the employer's workforce) for discrimination based on the complainant's disability, sex, or religion. Any complainant eligible for compensatory or punitive damages may request a jury trial as well. The act also allows successful complainants to recover expert witness fees in addition to attorney's fees.

Other amendments deal with the availability of interest payments for delayed awards, extensions of filing deadlines for lawsuits brought against the government, notification by the EEOC to the complainant when the EEOC dismisses charges under the ADEA, and a longer statute of limitations's period for a claimant who brings an action under the ADEA. The act obligates the EEOC to establish a Technical Assistance Training Institute for entities covered by the laws the EEOC enforces. In addition, the act mandates an EEOC outreach/education program for individuals who historically have been the object of employment discrimination. Title II of the act, the Glass Ceiling Act of 1991, sets up a commission to study why impediments to the advancement of women and minorities exist and to make recommendations for eliminating such barriers. Businesses that show substantial efforts to advance such groups to management and decision-making positions in business are eligible to receive national awards recognizing their efforts.[27]

Given the novelty of this landmark legislation, subsequent court decisions will serve to answer the various questions spawned by the act. In 1994, the Supreme Court, in *Landgraf v. USI Film Products*,[28] answered one such question—whether the

1991 act applies retroactively to Title VII cases pending on appeal at the time of the 1991 act's enactment—by ruling that it does not. Even more significantly, a 1999 Supreme Court case—*Kolstad* v. *American Dental Association*[29]—held that courts may award punitive damages in Title VII cases without a showing of "egregious" misconduct in addition to proof of the employer's state of mind. Although punitive damages had been available under Title VII since the passage of the Civil Rights Act of 1991, the lower courts had set out a variety of standards for imposing such damages against employers that violate the statute. In resolving the split in the circuit courts of appeals as to the standard of conduct needed for an employer to face liability for punitive damages, the Court stressed that the 1991 act limits compensatory and punitive damages awards to cases of intentional discrimination (as opposed to cases relying on the "disparate impact" theory of discrimination) and further conditions the availability of punitive damages on a showing that the defendant engaged in a discriminatory practice "with malice or with reckless indifference to the federally protected rights of an aggrieved individual."[30] Hence, according to the Court, an award of punitive damages is predicated on the defendant's state of mind and does not require—as the court of appeals erroneously had held— a showing of egregious or outrageous discrimination independent of the employer's state of mind. Citing the *Ellerth* case, the Court held that, with regard to punitive damages, an employer may not be held vicariously liable for the discriminatory employment decisions of managerial agents where these decisions are contrary to the employer's good-faith efforts to comply with Title VII.[31]

Family and Medical Leave Act of 1993. The first major piece of legislation passed under the Clinton Administration was the Family and Medical Leave Act of 1993 (FMLA). Regulations promulgated by the Department of Labor obligate certain employers of 50 or more persons to do the following: formulate a family leave policy, revise employee handbooks and policy manuals so that they are consistent with such a policy, alter any inconsistent policies, and prepare for the paperwork required under the act.

Divided into 6 titles and 26 sections, the FMLA covers public employers of any size and private employers that have on their weekly payrolls 50 or more employees during each of 20 or more calendar workweeks in the current or preceding calendar year. Employees eligible to take leave under the act must have worked for the employer for at least 12 months and for at least 1,250 hours in the 12 months immediately preceding the commencement of any leave taken under the act. Employees who work at job facilities that employ fewer than 50 persons remain ineligible for FMLA leave unless the employer has 50 or more employees working within a 75-mile radius of any worksite. Part-time employees count, but laid-off employees do not.

Section 102 of the FMLA provides generally that "an eligible employee shall be entitled to a total of 12 work weeks of leave during any 12-month period" for the following family-related events: (1) the birth of a child; (2) the placement of a child with the employee for adoption or foster care; (3) the care of a seriously ill spouse, child, or parent; and (4) a serious health condition of the employee that makes him or her unable to perform any of the essential functions of his or her job.

The FMLA does not require the employer to pay for any leave taken under the act. However, eligible employees can use any accrued vacation or personal leave for FMLA purposes. Similarly, an eligible employee may elect to use any paid leave—sick, family, or disability leave—in accordance with the terms of the employer's leave policies. In fact, the employer can require employees to exhaust all "banked" personal, sick, and vacation leave as part of the 12 weeks' leave. In such cases, though, the FMLA prohibits employers from imposing more stringent conditions on leave taken under the act than the employers would require under their own leave plans. The act moreover obligates employers to reinstate an employee who has availed him- or herself of FMLA leave to the employee's former position or to one that involves "substantially equivalent skill, effort, responsibility, and authority."

Interestingly, the FMLA exempts the highest-paid 10 percent of salaried employees within the aforementioned 75-mile radius from the right to reinstatement after they have taken a leave. In short, the FMLA allows an employer to refuse restoration of employment to these "key employees" if an employer can show that "substantial and grievous" economic injury would occur if the key employees were restored to their respective original positions. The regulations never set forth a precise test for calculating the level of hardship that an employer must sustain before it can deny reinstatement (or restoration) to key employees, however.

Once the employer has determined that a given worker is a key employee, the employer, upon the key employee's request for leave, must notify the employee in writing of this determination. The employer's failure to comply with the specific notification requirements delineated in the regulations will cause the forfeiture of its rights to deny reinstatement (or restoration). Furthermore, the employer cannot require an employee to "requalify" for such benefits as life or disability insurance or profit-sharing plans once the worker completes his or her FMLA leave.

Although the act itself does not specifically define the term *family*, the regulations do and apparently contemplate coverage of a wide spectrum of persons beyond the traditional family unit. The regulations define *spouse* as a husband or wife recognized as such for purposes of marriage under state law (including common law marriages in jurisdictions that recognize these relationships). Partners in same-sex "marriages" presumably do not qualify for benefits and protection under the FMLA. The parental relationship described in the act can be either biological or one that is *in loco parentis;* but parents "in law" are not included. *Son* or *daughter* means a biological, adopted, or foster child, stepchild, legal ward, or child of a person standing *in loco parentis* and who either is under age 18 or 18 and older and incapable of self-care owing to mental or physical disability. The regulations define a person who is *in loco parentis* as including anyone with day-to-day responsibilities to care for and financially support a child. A biological or legal relationship specifically is not required under the regulations.

The act also defines a *serious health condition* as "an illness, injury, impairment, or physical or mental condition that involves inpatient care in a hospital, hospice, or residential facility or continuing treatment by a health care provider." According to the regulations, a serious health condition is one that requires either an overnight stay in a hospital; a period of incapacity requiring an absence from work of more than three days and that involves continuing treatment by a health care provider; or continuing treatment for a chronic or long-term health condition that, if left untreated, likely will result in a period of incapacity for more than three days. Prenatal care and care administered for a long-term or chronic condition that is incurable (e.g., Alzheimer's disease) and for which condition the person is not receiving active treatment by a healthcare provider are included as well.

Given this broad threshold for eligibility, many businesspeople fear that the FMLA will be susceptible to abuse by employees who show tendencies toward chronic, unjustified absenteeism. The medical certification requirements set out under the act, however, do provide a hedge against employee abuse of the FMLA's provisions. According to the act, the employer may require the employee to produce medical documentation as to the need for medical leave in many circumstances. The healthcare providers who give such certifications ordinarily furnish specific information about the medical facts underlying the condition that has triggered the need for a leave, the commencement date, and the probable duration of the leave. In strictly circumscribing the information an employer can obtain from a certifying healthcare professional, the act, among other things, prohibits the employer from requesting additional information from such a provider. Rather, if an employer doubts the validity of the certificate produced by the employee, the employer can, at its own expense, require a second opinion by a healthcare provider of its choice, so long as the doctor is not "employed on a regular basis by the employer."

The act also allows employees to take *intermittent leave*, that is, "leave taken in separate blocks of time due to a single illness or injury, rather than for one continuous period of time, and may include leave of periods from an hour or more to several weeks." Intermittent leave can include leave taken for medical appointments, chemotherapy, and the like. (The regulations require the employee to give notice to the employer of the need for intermittent leave, but the regulations are more lenient regarding notification for unforeseeable leave.) Employees instead may opt for a *reduced leave* schedule, which the regulations define as a reduction in an employee's usual number of working hours per week or per day.

Intermittent or reduced leave taken for the purpose of caring for a family member or for a serious health condition of the employee requires only the fulfillment of the applicable certification standards; it is not necessary for the employee to obtain the employer's permission in advance. The employer and employee must agree to any intermittent or reduced leave that the employee takes for the birth or adoption of a child, however.

The act allows an employer to require an employee who has requested intermittent or reduced leave to transfer to another position. The transfer must be temporary, and the new position must reflect equivalent pay and benefits (if not equivalent duties). Employers also have the right, consistent with the leave being taken, to transfer an employee to a part-time position. These transfer provisions give the employer some leeway to place the affected employee in a position that more easily accommodates recurrent and unpredictable absences.

The act requires the employer to post notices regarding the FMLA at the worksite. Failure to do this subjects the employer to fines of up to $100 per offense. Furthermore, if the employer has reduced its policies to writing, information concerning the FMLA and its entitlements must be included in all employee handbooks. In the absence of such written policies, the employer must provide written guidance as to an employee's rights and obligations under the FMLA whenever an employee requests leave under the act.

Like other federal fair employment practices laws, the FMLA contains antidiscrimination/antiretaliation provisions. Violations of these provisions may result in civil lawsuits, liquidated damages, or administrative remedies.

Other Protections. The Vietnam Era Veterans' Readjustment Assistance Act of 1974, various executive orders, and the Civil Rights Acts of 1866 and 1871 form alternative bases for guaranteeing equal access to the workplace. State law often augments this extensive federal scheme as well.

Occupational Safety and Health Act

Congress passed the Occupational Safety and Health Act (the OSH Act) in 1970. This act attempts to assure safe and healthful workplace conditions for working men and women. The act does so by authorizing enforcement of the standards developed under the act—through the Occupational Safety and Health Administration (OSHA); by assisting and encouraging the states' efforts to assure safe and healthful working conditions; and by providing for research, information, education, and training in the field of occupational safety and health, through the National Institute for Occupational Safety and Health (NIOSH).

The act covers most employers and employees, including agricultural employees, nonprofit organizations, and professionals (such as doctors, lawyers, accountants, and brokers). In fact, the act reaches almost any employer that employs at least one worker and whose business in any way affects interstate commerce. Atomic energy workers, however, are exempted.

Because personal illnesses and injuries arising from the workplace produce significant burdens in terms of lost production, lost wages, medical expenses, and disability payments, Congress designed an act meant to highlight the existence of such factors and to provide standards for preventing future illnesses, injuries, and losses. To this end, the OSH Act sets out methods by which employers can reduce workplace hazards and foster attention to safety. The act further authorizes the secretary of labor to set mandatory occupational safety and health standards for businesses covered under the act and to create an Occupational Safety and Health Review Commission for hearing appeals from OSHA citations and penalties. In *Martin* v. *Occupational Safety and Health Review Commission*,[32] the Supreme Court held that when this "split enforcement" structure (i.e., the secretary's powers of enforcement and rule making versus the commission's adjudicatory powers) leads to reasonable but conflicting interpretations of an ambiguous OSHA regulation promulgated by the secretary of labor, courts should defer to the secretary's interpretations.

To help ensure that no employee suffers diminished health, functional capacity, or life expectancy as a result of work experiences, OSHA requires each employer to furnish to its employees a safe and healthful workplace, one that is free from "recognized hazards" that may cause or are likely to cause death or serious physical harm to employees. An example of a recognized hazard might include excessive toxic substances in the air.

OSHA allows inspectors to enter the workplace to inspect for compliance with regulations. Upon an employer's refusal to admit the inspector, OSHA regulations now require a warrant. The refusal in and of itself does not constitute probable cause for the issuance of the warrant. But the standards for demonstrating the need for the warrant are relatively easy to meet and ordinarily do not impede OSHA's functions very much. Employers normally do not have advance knowledge of an inspector's arrival. By writing to the secretary of labor, employees may request an inspection if they believe a violation that threatens physical harm exists.

Inspections typically involve a tour through the business and an examination of each work area for compliance with OSHA standards. After the inspector has informed the employer of the reason for the inspection, the inspector will give the employer a copy of the complaint (if one is involved) or the reason for the inspection if it results from an agency general administrative plan. When an employee has initiated the complaint, OSHA by request will withhold the employee's name. An employer representative and an employee-selected representative generally accompany the inspector on this walk-around tour. The inspector may order the immediate correction of some violations, such as blocked aisles, locked fire exits, or unsanitary conditions. The inspector additionally reviews the records OSHA requires the employer to maintain, including records of deaths, injuries, illnesses, and employee exposure to toxic substances. After the inspection, the inspector and employer engage in a closing conference, during which they discuss probable violations and methods for eliminating these violations. The inspector then files his or her report with the commission.

Citations and proposed penalties may be issued to the employer, and a copy of these will be sent to the complaining party, if there is one. Normally, no citation is issued if a violation of a standard or rule lacks an immediate or direct relationship to safety or health, although a notice of a minimal violation (without a proposed penalty) may be sent to the employer even in these situations. OSHA requires the prominent posting of citations in the workplace.

Penalties, when imposed, are severe: fines of up to $70,000 for each violation may be levied for willful or repeated violations. An employer also will be fined up to $7,000 for each serious violation—one in which there is a "substantial probability" that the consequences of an accident resulting from the violation will be death or serious harm. Employers can defend by showing they did not, and could not with the exercise of "reasonable diligence," know about the condition or hazard. For even nonserious violations (such as a failure to paint steps and banisters or to post citations), fines of up to $7,000 are possible. Prison terms are possible in the event of willful violations that cause an employee's death. The OSHA Commission assesses these penalties in light of the size of the employer's business, the seriousness of the violation, the presence or absence of employer good faith, and the past history of violations.

An employer that wishes to contest any penalties can resort to the procedures established by the commission. In general, these require an investigation and a decision by an administrative law judge. The commission, in turn, has the power to review this decision. An employer that still disagrees with the decision can appeal to the appropriate federal circuit court of appeals for review, as can the secretary of labor if he or she disagrees with the commission's decision.

Upon proof of inability to comply because of the unavailability of materials, equipment, or personnel to effect the changes within the required time, employers may request temporary exemptions from OSHA standards. Permanent exemptions may be granted when the employer's method of protecting employees is as effective as that required by the standard. Needless to say, such exemptions are not granted retroactively.

Other provisions of OSHA protect employees from discrimination or discharge based on filing a complaint, testifying about violations, or exercising any rights guaranteed by the act. The act prohibits employees from stopping work or walking off the job because of "potential unsafe conditions at the workplace" unless the employee, through performance of the assigned work, would subject "himself [or herself] to serious injury or death from a hazardous condition at the workplace."

In *Whirlpool Corp.* v. *Marshall*,[33] the Supreme Court held that the secretary of labor has the authority to promulgate a regulation allowing workers to refuse to perform in hazardous situations. According to the Court, the promulgation of the regulation was a valid exercise of the authority granted the secretary of labor under the Occupational Safety and Health Act, especially given the act's fundamental purpose of preventing occupational deaths and serious injuries.

Social Security

The Social Security Act, first enacted in 1935 as part of President Franklin D. Roosevelt's New Deal policies, has spawned numerous controversies. Current debate about social security centers on fears that the system will become bankrupt and on proposed plans to allay this possibility.

By *social security*, most people mean the federal old-age, survivors', and disability insurance benefits plan. Broad in scope, social security benefits today are payable to workers, their dependents, and their survivors. Through the Supplemental Security Income (SSI) program administered by the Department of Health and Human Services, the federal social security system also makes payments to the blind, the disabled, and the aged who are in need of these benefits. The states also can supplement this pervasive federal scheme if they so choose.

In general, federal social security benefits are computed on the worker's earning records. A *fully insured* worker is one who has worked at least 40 quarters (10 years). To use 2000 as an example, such workers will earn one-quarter of coverage for each $780 in earnings, whether wages, farm wages, or income from self-employment, up to a maximum of four quarters. Fully insured workers who receive retirement benefits include retired workers, 62 years and older; their spouses, or divorced spouses, 62 and older; spouses of any age who care for a child entitled to benefits; and children or grandchildren under 18 (or 19 if a student) or of any age if disabled before age 22. Additionally, survivors' benefits go to certain classes of fully insured workers, as do disability benefits for qualified workers.

Be aware, however, that computing social security benefits involves complicated arithmetical formulas noting the worker's age; date of retirement, disability, or death; and yearly earnings history. Cost-of-living escalators tied to the **consumer price index** in certain circumstances may raise benefits as well. Disability benefits—those granted to a worker who has been disabled at least five months—are computed in a similar manner, subject to some limitations for younger disabled workers.

Additionally, for eligibility, the worker must prove that he or she no longer can engage in substantial gainful employment. The disability must be expected to last at least 12 months or to result in death. Finally, the worker, if near retirement age, must have sufficient quarters of coverage to be considered fully insured and must have worked at least 20 of the last 40 quarters before the disability began. Blind persons and some younger workers who become disabled face less stringent eligibility requirements. Receipt of benefits paid under workers' compensation or other federal, state, or local disability plans may lessen the amount of benefits received from social security.

Monthly payments made to a retired or disabled worker's family or to the survivors of an insured worker are equal to a certain percentage (usually 50 or 75 percent) of the worker's benefits. For example, if a worker were entitled to $379 per month in benefits, the worker's wife or divorced wife who was married to the worker for at least 10 years and is not now married will receive $189.50 or $284.25 in monthly benefits. The act limits the amount one family can receive in total benefits. Similarly, benefits for a nondisabled child who no longer is attending high school normally end at age 18. Lump-sum death benefits to eligible persons cannot exceed $255. Social security coverage extends to most types of employment and self-employment. Among those excluded, however, are employees of the federal government and railroad workers.

Consumer price index
Measurement of how the price of a group of consumer goods changes between two time periods.

Those who have been denied benefits may utilize certain administrative steps to appeal an SSA decision. Usually, such persons file a request for reconsideration within 60 days of the date of the initial determination. The agency then conducts a thorough and independent review of the evidence. After this reconsideration, a person who remains adversely affected can file for a hearing or review by an administrative law judge (ALJ). After the hearing, the ALJ issues a written decision that in understandable language sets out his or her findings of fact. All parties receive copies of this decision. The decision is binding unless appealed to the Appeals Council of the SSA or to a federal district court.

The Federal Insurance Contribution Act (FICA) taxes paid by employees and employers on wages earned by workers not only fund social security retirement benefits but also help provide qualified persons with hospital insurance. Called *Medicare,* this protection normally is available to persons 65 years and older and to some disabled persons under 65. Medicare (Part A) covers doctors' services, hospital care, some nursing home care, certain home health services, and hospice care. In 2000, the tax rate paid was 7.65 percent on a maximum of $72,600 in employee wages. The Medicare tax rate for that amount of wages is 1.45 percent. In 1993, Congress removed the maximum base amount (formerly $135,000); hence, for 1994 and thereafter, the employer must match the employee's portion. Aside from such costs, the record keeping burdens involved with compliance under the Social Security Act also irk many employers.

In addition to receiving Medicare Part A, qualified persons can pay for a government-subsidized plan called Medicare Part B that will cover medical services beyond hospitalization, such as doctors' services and related medical expenses involving outpatient and rehabilitation costs, ambulance services, lab tests, and the like. In order to fill in the gaps in healthcare protection left by the Medicare program, some persons also purchase Medicare supplemental insurance ("Medigap" insurance) from insurance companies. Another program, Medicaid, provides broad medical assistance to "categorically needy" individuals.

Unemployment Insurance

In addition to retirement, disability, and Medicare benefits, social security covers unemployment insurance through the Federal Unemployment Tax Act (FUTA). Unemployment insurance represents a coordinated federal and state effort to provide economic security for temporarily unemployed workers. The funds used in the unemployment insurance system come from taxes, or "contributions," paid predominantly by employers. In a few states, employees also pay these taxes. Those contributing pay federal taxes, which the government uses to administer the federal/state program, as well as state taxes, which the state uses to finance the payment of weekly benefits to unemployed workers.

Various credits allowed under federal law significantly reduce the amount of taxes paid in federal contributions. Essentially, computation of the taxes is based on a specified percentage of wages paid by the employer/employees. *Wages* include anything paid as compensation for employment and thus may consist of salaries, fees, bonuses, and commissions. Since 1983, the amount of wages subject to federal taxes for unemployment compensation is at most $7,000 for each employee per calendar year. In 1999, the FUTA applied at a rate of 6.2 percent on the first $7,000 of covered wages paid during the year to each employee. The federal government allows a credit for FUTA sums paid to the state, however. State contribution rates

YOU BE THE JUDGE

SHOULD THE EEOC PROTECT UNDOCUMENTED WORKERS?

In what most commentators view as a controversial, as well as a major, policy turnaround, the Equal Employment Opportunity Commission (EEOC) has issued enforcement guidance entitled "Remedies Available to Undocumented Workers under Federal Employment Discrimination Laws." Meant as a deterrent to abusive employer conduct directed at illegal immigrants because employers view such workers as defenseless and devoid of civil rights, the new guidance would allow the EEOC to seek, with a few exceptions, backpay for such workers, damages, and attorney's fees. Reversing its earlier policy that the agency had only limited responsibilities for workers illegally in the country, the EEOC has taken the position that undocumented workers' vulnerability to abuse and exploitation by employers means that the agency must take steps to ensure that workplace civil rights apply to all employees. The EEOC, however, will not seek reinstatement of workers who, even if they have been the victims of discrimination, are working in this country illegally. On the other hand, the EEOC ordinarily does not turn over undocumented workers' names to the U.S. Immigration and Naturalization Service. According to the chairwoman of the EEOC, Ida L. Castro, "[A]ny time an employee is able to breach [the] civil rights requirements for a group of workers such as undocumented workers, without the deterrence of economic or legal penalties, discrimination is free to flourish." Castro states flatly that the EEOC "will not tolerate such blatant abuse and, in conformity with federal employment discrimination and immigration laws, will fully pursue all remedies available under the law without apology." Critics of the EEOC's new stance construe it as sanctioning the conduct of people who break the law willingly and knowingly and thereby bring about reduced wages for all American workers. These critics also posit that the EEOC—rather than offering additional protections for undocumented workers—should increase its investigations of immigrant-dominated firms that hire their own immigrants and then prosecute those firms for employment discrimination against other Americans. The EEOC disputes the contention that the agency's new policy will undermine the government's efforts to curtail the flow of undocumented workers to the U.S. and to root out the employers who hire these workers. In the EEOC's view, its present stance in the long run will bolster compliance with the law by doing away with employer incentives to hire undocumented workers, who in the past would have refrained from complaining because of the lack of any entity with which to lodge their complaints.

This case has been brought before *your* court. As the judge who must dispose of this legal challenge, how would *you* strike an appropriate balance between the competing immigration law and fair employment practices law policies implicated by the EEOC's position?[34]

BUSINESS CONSIDERATIONS Should a business have a hiring policy that gives preference to citizens of the nation where the employment will occur? Should an employer give preference to employees from the same nation as the domicile of the employer?

ETHICAL CONSIDERATIONS Is it ethical to hire immigrants simply because the employer can hire them for less pay than domestic workers would require? Is it ethical to refuse to hire immigrants despite the fact that they may be willing to work for less than domestic workers would?

SOURCE: Stephen Franklin, *Chicago Tribune* (26 October 1999), Section 1, p. 1; Stephen Franklin, *Chicago Tribune* (2 November 1999), Section 3, pp. 1, 4; Ida L. Castro, *Chicago Tribune* (3 November 1999), Section 1, p. 28.

may vary, but most have set a standard rate (such as 5.4 percent). Hence, the amount to be paid to the Internal Revenue Service (IRS) could be as low as 0.8 percent (6.2 percent − 5.4 percent).

State rates, almost without exception, utilize "experience rating" or "merit rating" systems whereby the rate employers pay reflects each individual employer's experience with unemployment. Under such systems, employers whose workers suffer the most involuntary unemployment pay higher rates than employers whose workers suffer less unemployment. Since the aim of unemployment compensation involves the achievement of regular employment and the prevention of unemployment, such systems provide incentives to employers to keep their workforces intact and thereby to perpetuate the goals of these laws.

State provisions regarding the criteria for eligibility and the amount of benefits vary greatly. For instance, in different jurisdictions, unemployment compensation may not be available to employees discharged for cause, to those who quit their jobs without cause, or to those who refuse to seek or accept a job for which they are qualified.

Workers' Compensation

Workers' compensation statutes are not the same as unemployment statutes, although both concern the welfare of workers. Workers' compensation laws in the various states attempt to reimburse workers for injuries or death arising within the employment context. *Compensation* in this area therefore does not refer to wages or salaries but rather to the money paid by the employer to indemnify the worker for employment-related injury or death. The employer usually self-insures; buys insurance; or, as discussed earlier, pays money into a state insurance fund at a "merit" or "experience" rate reflective of the employer's actual incidence of employee injuries. By utilizing administrative proceedings in front of a workers' compensation board, injured workers then receive compensation for their injuries in the form of medical care and disability benefits, the latter often based on a specific statutory scale (such as 60 percent of average weekly wages up to $100 in average weekly wages for 26 weeks).

Workers' compensation acts thus impose *strict liability* on the employer for injuries to employees during the scope of their employment. These laws first arose out of lawmakers' concern for employees injured as a result of increased industrial mechanization, but these acts serve other functions as well. For instance, through such statutes, employees can receive compensation without engaging in costly litigation; and the employer, by passing these costs on to consumers, can recoup the costs of workers' compensation. Both sides benefit, because the employee receives reimbursement for the injuries suffered and the employer's liability to the employee usually ends there; that is, the statutes ordinarily prohibit the employee from suing the employer in a court of law. Such acts, then, are grounded in public policy concerns.

The classes of employees covered by such acts depend on the particular statute involved. Agricultural, domestic, or casual laborers often are not covered because the right to compensation ordinarily depends on the nature of the work performed, the regularity of such work, and/or the status of the worker (i.e., whether, at the time of the injury, the worker was working as an independent contractor for someone else).

To be covered, an employee ordinarily must be a worker—that is, a person who performs manual labor or similar duties. For this reason, workers' compensation statutes presumably do not cover directors, officers, or stockholders. Yet under the dual capacity doctrine, such persons can receive compensation if, when they suffer injury, they are performing the ordinary duties of the business. For example, a general manager of a tree-pruning service who is injured while pruning trees will be able to recover. If the general manager instead were working as an independent contractor (not for the corporation), he or she normally would be ineligible to receive workers' compensation.

Typically, however, just about any employment-related injury or disease makes the covered employee eligible for workers' compensation. For this reason, even a negligent employee usually can recover for injuries suffered while he or she was in the employment relationship. Contrast this statutory result with what would occur at common law: The employer could use the employee's contributory negligence as a complete bar to recovery.

Recent decisions allow recoveries for occupational diseases such as asbestosis, for work-related stress, and even for injuries suffered before or after working hours. Although workers' compensation takes the place of an employee's suing the employer for the injuries suffered, employees still can file product liability suits against manufacturers or suppliers and also can sue any fellow employees who cause their injuries.

RESOURCES FOR BUSINESS LAW STUDENTS

NAME	RESOURCES	WEB ADDRESS
National Labor Relations Board	The National Labor Relations Board provides speeches, publications, Board decisions, and other materials.	http://www.nlrb.gov/
Americans with Disabilities Act (ADA) Document Center	The ADA Document Center provides the full text for the ADA, regulations, guidelines, and other documents.	http://janweb.icdi.wvu.edu/kinder/
Family and Medical Leave Act (FMLA) of 1993	The Department of Labor provides the full text for the FMLA, fact sheets, compliance guides, and regulations.	http://www.dol.gov/dol/esa/
Equal Employment Opportunity Commission (EEOC)	The EEOC provides publications and media releases, fact sheets, and information on the laws enforced by the commission.	http://www.eeoc.gov/
Occupational Safety and Health Administration (OSHA)	OSHA, part of the Department of Labor, provides publications and media releases, program information, software, and data.	http://www.osha.gov/index.html
Social Security Administration (SSA)	The SSA maintains publications, legal information, forms, and other facts.	http://www.ssa.gov/

SUMMARY

The Wagner, Taft-Hartley, and Landrum-Griffin Acts set out a pervasive federal scheme for the regulation of labor. This blueprint of federal labor law broadly regulates employees' rights to organize and to engage in concerted activities in furtherance of their objectives. Both employees and employers are protected from unfair labor practices. The National Labor Relations Board retains jurisdiction over labor disputes, oversees elections, arbitrates disputes about the duty to bargain, and almost wholly preempts the states' jurisdiction over labor matters, except for criminal violations or torts, retaliatory discharges, and the like.

A host of federal statutes extensively regulates fair employment practices. Title VII of the Civil Rights Act of 1964 prohibits employers, labor organizations, or employment agencies from engaging in employment discrimination based on race, color, religion, sex, or national origin. The Equal Employment Opportunity Commission enforces many of these federal laws and sets out the complex procedures with which a grievant must comply. Employment criteria that have a disparate impact on minorities are illegal unless the employer can show that the criteria are job related. Employers also may be liable for the disparate treatment of their employees. The issue of reverse discrimination remains controversial in the Title VII context. Limited defenses based on BFOQs are available for the protected categories of religion, sex, and national origin; a BFOQ never can be based on race, however. The Immigration Reform and Control Act of 1986, the Equal Pay Act of 1963, the Age Discrimination in Employment Act of 1967, the Rehabilitation Act of 1973, the Americans with Disabilities Act of 1990, the Civil Rights Act of 1991, the Family and Medical Leave Act of 1993, and other federal statutes protect qualified individuals against employment discrimination. State law often supplements this comprehensive federal scheme.

The Occupational Safety and Health Act attempts to ensure safe and healthful working conditions for American workers. Inspections of the workplace provide a mechanism for realizing this statutory goal. Warrantless inspections conducted after the owner refuses entry to the inspector are illegal. Workers, in contrast, legally can walk off the job if performance of the work assignment can lead to serious injury or death.

Federal and state social security benefits aid workers, the disabled, the blind, and the aged. Computations of benefits are complex. Those who have been denied benefits may utilize certain administrative steps to appeal such agency decisions.

Unemployment insurance is designed to provide economic security for temporarily unemployed workers. The contributions paid into the insurance fund stem from a specified percentage of wages paid by the employer or employee. State taxable wage bases may differ from the federal figure, and state provisions regarding the criteria for eligibility and the amount of benefits vary greatly.

State workers' compensation statutes attempt to reimburse workers for injuries or death resulting from the employment relationship. In return, such statutes generally prohibit the employee from suing the employer in a court of law. The classes of employees covered in such acts depend on the particular statute involved; but eligible employees may recover for occupational diseases, injuries resulting from the employee's own negligence, and injuries sustained before or after working hours. Workers' compensation statutes ordinarily do not preclude an employee's maintaining either a product liability suit against a manufacturer or a suit against a fellow employee who caused the injuries at issue.

DISCUSSION QUESTIONS

1. List a few of the rights guaranteed and the practices prohibited by the Wagner, Taft-Hartley, and Landrum-Griffin Acts.
2. Describe a few of the issues and enforcement problems involved in the collective-bargaining process.
3. Explain the boundaries of state regulation of labor.
4. What are the protected classes of employees under Title VII?
5. Define and describe the two methods by which an employee can show liability for discrimination on the basis of the protected categories set out in Title VII.
6. Why is the issue of reverse discrimination such a difficult problem?
7. Define the term *bona fide occupational qualification*.
8. Name other statutes that guarantee fair employment, and explain how these more recent statutes build on earlier fair employment practices statutes.
9. Describe a typical OSHA inspection.
10. Name the classes of persons eligible for social security, unemployment insurance, and workers' compensation.

CASE PROBLEMS AND WRITING ASSIGNMENTS

1. Under Pennsylvania's Workers' Compensation Act, once an employer becomes liable for an employee's work-related injury—because liability either is uncontested or is no longer at issue—the employer or its insurer must pay for all "reasonable" and "necessary" medical treatment. To ensure that only medical expenses meeting these criteria are paid, and in an attempt to control costs, Pennsylvania amended its workers' compensation system. These amendments provided that a self-insured employer or private insurer may withhold payment for disputed treatment pending an independent "utilization review," as to which, among other things, the insurer files a one-page request for review with the State Workers' Compensation Bureau (Bureau). The Bureau in turn forwards the request to a "utilization review organization" (URO) of private healthcare providers, and the URO determines whether the treatment is reasonable or necessary. The plaintiffs—employees and employee representatives—subsequently filed this suit under 42 U.S.C. § 1983 against various Pennsylvania officials, a self-insured public school district, and a number of private workers' compensation insurers. The plaintiffs alleged that, in withholding benefits without predeprivation notice and an opportunity to be heard, the state and the private defendants, acting "under color of state law," had deprived the plaintiffs of property in violation of due process. The district court dismissed the private insurers from the suit on the ground that they are not "state actors." This court also later dismissed the state officials and school district on the ground that the act does not violate due process. Disagreeing as to both issues, the Third Circuit held that a private insurer's decision to suspend payment under the act constitutes state action. This court, emphasizing the parties' assumption that employees have a protected property interest in workers' compensation medical benefits, held that due process requires that payments of medical bills not be withheld until the employees have had an opportunity to submit their view in writing to the URO as to the reasonableness and necessity of the disputed treatment. Did this comprehensive state regulation of workers' compensation convert private insurance companies' actions into state action sufficient to trigger the due process clause of the Fourteenth Amendment? Did the injured workers have a constitutionally protected property interest in receiving payments for medical bills prior to the completion of a "utilization review" evaluation of the treatment plan? [See *American Manufacturers Mutual Insurance Co. v. Sullivan*, 526 U.S. 40 (1999).]

2. The National Labor Relations Board's (the Board's) general counsel had issued a complaint alleging that Health Care & Retirement Corporation of America (Health Care), the owner and operator of the Heartland Nursing Home (Heartland) in Urbana, Ohio, had committed unfair labor practices when it disciplined four licensed practical nurses. At Heartland, the director of nursing has overall responsibility for the nursing department. An assistant director of nursing, between 9 and 11 staff nurses (including both registered nurses and the 4 licensed practical nurses involved in this case), and between 50 and 55 nurses' aides also work at Heartland. The staff nurses, who are the senior-ranking employees on duty after 5 P.M. during the week and at all times on weekends—approximately 75 percent of the time—have a responsibility to ensure adequate staffing, make daily work assignments, monitor the aides' work to ensure proper performance, counsel and discipline aides, resolve aides' problems and grievances, evaluate aides' performances, and, finally, report to management. In

light of these varied activities, Health Care contended that the four nurses involved in this case were supervisors and thus not protected under the Labor Management Relations Act (LMRA). Disagreeing, the administrative law judge (ALJ) concluded that the nurses were not supervisors. The ALJ stated that the nurses' supervisory work did not "equate to responsibly directing the aides in the interest of the employer." The Board stated only that "[t]he judge found, and we agree, that the staff nurses are employees within the meaning of the Act." The U.S. Court of Appeals for the Sixth Circuit reversed, because it had decided in earlier cases that the Board's test for determining the supervisory status of nurses was inconsistent with the statute. Hence, the Sixth Circuit held that the four licensed practical nurses involved in this case were supervisors. Was the Board's test for determining if nurses are supervisors rational and consistent with the statutory definition of supervisors under the LMRA? [See *NLRB* v. *Health Care & Retirement Corporation of America*, 511 U.S. 571 (1994).]

3. Lechmere, Inc. (Lechmere) owned and operated a retail store located in a shopping plaza in a large metropolitan area. Lechmere also was part owner of the plaza's parking lot, which was separated from a public highway by a 46-foot-wide grassy strip, almost all of which was public property. In a campaign to organize Lechmere employees, nonemployee union organizers placed handbills on the windshields of cars parked in the employees' part of the parking lot. After Lechmere had denied the organizers access to the lot, they distributed handbills and picketed from the grassy strip. In addition, they were able to contact directly 20 percent of the employees. The union, filing an unfair labor practice charge with the National Labor Relations Board (the Board), alleged that Lechmere, by barring the organizers from its property, had violated the NLRA. An administrative law judge, ruling in the union's favor, recommended that the Board order Lechmere to cease and desist from barring the organizers from the parking lot. The Board affirmed, and the court of appeals enforced the Board's order. The Supreme Court granted Lechmere's petition for *certiorari*. Had Lechmere, by barring nonemployee union organizers from its property, committed an unfair labor practice? [See *Lechmere, Inc.* v. *NLRB*, 502 U.S. 527 (1992).]

4. Teresa Harris worked as a manager at Forklift Systems, Inc. (Forklift), an equipment rental company, from April 1985 until October 1987. Charles Hardy was Forklift's president. Throughout Harris's time at Forklift, Hardy frequently insulted her because of her gender and often made her the target of unwanted sexual innuendos. Hardy told Harris on several occasions, in the presence of other employees, "You're a woman, what do you know" and "We need a man as the rental manager"; at least once, he told her she was "a dumb a__ woman." Again, in front of others, he suggested that the two of them "go to the Holiday Inn to negotiate [Harris's] raise." Hardy occasionally asked Harris and other female employees to retrieve coins from his front pants pocket. He also threw objects on the ground in front of Harris and other women and asked them to pick up the objects. In addition, he made sexual innuendos about Harris's and other women's clothing. In mid-August 1987, Harris complained to Hardy about his conduct. Hardy, saying he was surprised that Harris was offended, claimed he was only joking and apologized. He also promised he would stop; and based on this assurance, Harris stayed on the job. But in early September, Hardy began anew. While Harris was arranging a deal with one of Forklift's customers, he asked her, again in front of other employees, "What did you do, promise the guy . . . some [sex] Saturday night?" On 1 October, Harris collected her paycheck and quit. Claiming that Hardy's conduct had created an abusive work environment for her because of her gender, Harris subsequently sued Forklift. The U.S. District Court for the Middle District of Tennessee found this to be "a close case" but held that Hardy's conduct had not created an abusive environment. The court found that some of Hardy's comments offended Harris, and would offend the reasonable woman, but that the remarks were not so severe as to be expected to seriously affect Harris's psychological well-being. Nor, the court concluded, had Hardy created a working environment so poisoned as to be intimidating or injurious to Harris. In focusing on the employee's psychological well-being, the district court was following Sixth Circuit precedents. In a brief, unpublished decision, the U.S. Court of Appeals for the Sixth Circuit affirmed. To be actionable as "abusive work environment" sexual harassment, must the defendant's conduct seriously affect the plaintiff's psychological well-being or lead the plaintiff to suffer injury? [See *Harris* v. *Forklift Systems, Inc.*, 510 U.S. 17 (1993).]

5. Approximately two months before a vote on unionization, the employer, Wiljef Transportation, Inc. (Wiljef), read to its employees a corporate bylaw stating: "Section 2—Corporate Dissolution. Wiljef Transportation, Inc., hereby expresses as a matter of corporate policy that operations will cease and the corporation will be dissolved in the event of [the] unionization of its employees. As hereby authorized

by the Board of Directors, this bylaw may be announced to the employees of Wiljef Transportation, Inc. at any time deemed appropriate by the Board.' The firm had adopted the bylaw in 1979, and the announcement occurred in 1988. In the ensuing union representation election, the employees rejected unionization. Supreme Court precedents, in addressing the tension between an employer's right to announce the probable consequences of unionization and the employees' right to organize without threat of retaliation, had made the following points. On the one hand, the employer's right to communicate its views to its employees is firmly established in the First Amendment and is recognized in § 8(c) of the NLRA, which provides that "the expressing of any views, argument, or opinion . . . shall not constitute or be evidence of an unfair labor practice . . . if such expression contains no threat of reprisal or force or promise of benefit." On the other hand, the exceptions to the freedom of expression recognized in § 8(c) reflect the right of employees to associate free of coercion by the employer. By declaring that it is an unfair labor practice to interfere with, restrain, or coerce employees who are exercising their right to organize in unions, § 8(a)(1) of the NLRA codifies that right. The difficulty in attempting to reconcile these two rights lies in determining when speech becomes essentially coercive rather than factually informative or predictive so as to fall outside the protection of the First Amendment and thus violate the NLRA. The issue in this case centered on whether the announcement of the bylaw constituted a "permitted prediction" of the plant's closure or a "proscribed threat." The NLRB had held that the announcement represented a threat in violation of § 8(a)(1) of the NLRA, and Wiljef had appealed to the Court of Appeals for the Seventh Circuit. How should that court rule in this case? [See *Wiljef Transp., Inc.* v. *NLRB,* 946 F.2d 1308 (7th Cir. 1991).]

6. **BUSINESS APPLICATION CASE** Before beginning a truckdriver's job with Albertsons, Inc. (Albertsons), Hollie Kirkingburg was examined to see if he met the Department of Transportation's (DOT's) basic vision standards for commercial truckdrivers. These standards require corrected distant visual acuity of at least 20/40 in each eye and distant binocular acuity of at least 20/40. Although he has amblyopia, an uncorrectable condition that leaves him with 20/200 vision in his left eye and thus effectively with monocular vision, the doctor erroneously certified that Kirkingburg had met the DOT standards. When Kirkingburg's vision was correctly assessed at a 1992 physical, he was told that he had to get a waiver of the DOT standards under a waiver program begun

that year. Albertsons, however, fired him for failing to meet the basic DOT vision standards and refused to rehire him after his receipt of a waiver. Claiming that firing him violated the Americans with Disabilities Act of 1990 (ADA), Kirkingburg sued Albertsons. In granting summary judgment for Albertsons, the district court found that Kirkingburg was unqualified without an accommodation because he had failed to meet the basic DOT standards and the waiver program had made no alterations to those standards. The Ninth Circuit reversed, finding that Kirkingburg had established a disability under the act by demonstrating that the manner in which he sees differed significantly from the manner in which most people see; that although the ADA allowed Albertsons to rely on government regulations in setting a job-related vision standard, Albertsons could not use compliance with the DOT regulations to justify its requirement because the waiver program was a legitimate part of the DOT's regulatory scheme; and that although Albertsons could set a vision standard different from the DOT's, the firm had to justify its independent standard and would be unable to do so in the circumstances of this case. Under the ADA, must an employer who requires as a job qualification that an employee meet an otherwise applicable federal safety regulation justify enforcing the regulation solely because its standard may be waived in an individual case? [See *Albertsons, Inc.,* v. *Kirkingburg,* 527 U.S. 555 (1999).]

7. **ETHICAL APPLICATION CASE** Michael Manso worked as a casual dockworker at ABF Freight System, Inc.'s (ABF's) trucking terminal in Albuquerque, New Mexico, from the summer of 1987 to August 1989. He was fired three times. The first time, in June 1988, Manso was one of 12 employees discharged in a dispute over a contractual provision relating to so-called preferential casual dockworkers (i.e., those workers "on call" who could be discharged if they failed to be available for work two times). The grievance Manso's union filed eventually secured his reinstatement; Manso also filed an unfair labor practice charge against ABF over the incident. Manso's return to work was short-lived. Three supervisors—warning him of likely retaliation from top management—alerted him, for example, to the perception that ABF was "gunning" for him and that "the higher echelon was after [him]." Within six weeks, ABF discharged Manso for a second time on pretextual grounds—ostensibly for failing to respond to a call to work made under a stringent verification procedure ABF recently had imposed on preferential casuals. Once again, a grievance panel ordered Manso reinstated.

Manso's third discharge came less than two months later. On 11 August 1989, Manso arrived four minutes late for the 5 A.M. shift. At the time, ABF had no policy regarding lateness. After Manso was late to work, however, ABF decided to discharge preferential casuals—though not other employees—who were late twice without good cause. Six days later, Manso triggered the policy's first application when he arrived at work nearly an hour late for the same shift. Manso had telephoned at 5:25 A.M. to explain that he was having car trouble on the highway and repeated that excuse when he arrived. ABF conducted a prompt investigation; ascertained that he had been lying; and, pursuant to its new policy on lateness, fired him for tardiness. Manso thereupon filed a second unfair labor practice charge. In the hearing before the administrative law judge (ALJ), the ALJ credited most of Manso's testimony about the events surrounding his dismissals but expressly concluded that Manso had lied about the car trouble's making him late to work. Accordingly, although deciding that ABF illegally had discharged Manso owing to Manso's being a party to the earlier union grievance, the ALJ denied Manso relief for the third discharge based on the ALJ's finding that ABF had dismissed Manso for cause. The National Labor Relations Board (the Board) affirmed the ALJ's finding that Manso's second discharge was unlawful but reversed with respect to the third discharge. Acknowledging that Manso had lied to his employer and that ABF presumably could have discharged him for that dishonesty, the Board nevertheless emphasized that ABF in fact had not discharged him for lying and that the ALJ's conclusion to the contrary was "a plainly erroneous factual statement of [ABF]'s asserted reasons." Instead, Manso's lie had "established only that he did not have a legitimate excuse for the [17 August] lateness." The Board, focusing primarily on ABF's retroactive application of its lateness policy to include Manso's first time late to work, held that ABF had "seized upon" Manso's tardiness "as a pretext to discharge him again and for the

same unlawful reasons it [had] discharged him on [19 June]." The Board therefore ordered ABF to reinstate Manso with back pay. The court of appeals enforced the Board's order. Would an ALJ's finding that the employee had purposely testified falsely during the administrative hearing result in the employee's forfeiting the remedies of reinstatement and back pay? If the Court had decided this case on ethical grounds, would the result differ? [See *ABF Freight System, Inc.* v. *NLRB,* 510 U.S. 317 (1994).]

8. **CRITICAL THINKING CASE** After suffering a stroke and losing her job, Carolyn Cleveland sought and obtained Social Security Disability Insurance (SSDI) benefits owing to her claim that she was unable to work because of her disability. The week before her SSDI award, she filed suit under the Americans with Disabilities Act of 1990 (ADA), contending that her former employer, Policy Management Systems Corporation (PMSC), had discriminated against her owing to her disability. In granting PMSC's summary judgment, the district court concluded that Cleveland's claim that she was totally disabled for SSDI purposes estopped her (i.e., prevented her from asserting a given claim) from proving an essential element of her ADA claim, namely, that she could "perform the essential functions" of her job, at least with "reasonable . . . accommodation." The Fifth Circuit affirmed, holding that the application for or receipt of SSDI benefits creates a rebuttable presumption that a recipient is estopped from pursuing an ADA claim and that Cleveland had failed to rebut the presumption. Would an individual who applies for or receives Social Security disability benefits be automatically barred from simultaneously pursuing an action alleging discrimination on the basis of disability under the ADA? Would the law erect a strong presumption against the recipient's success under the ADA? [See *Cleveland* v. *Policy Management Systems Corporation,* 526 U.S. 795 (1999).]

NOTES

1. See 301 U.S. 1 (1937).
2. *Fibreboard Paper Products Corp.* v. *NLRB,* 379 U.S. 203, 223 (1964).
3. *Walters* v. *Metropolitan Educational Enterprises, Inc.,* 519 U.S. 202 (1997).
4. *Griggs* v. *Duke Power Co.,* 401 U.S. 424, 431–432 (1971).
5. 427 U.S. 273 (1976).
6. 438 U.S. 265 (1978).
7. 443 U.S. 193 (1979), *reh'g denied,* 444 U.S. 889 (1979).

8. 515 U.S. 200 (1995).
9. 432 U.S. 63 (1977).
10. 477 U.S. 57 (1986).
11. 524 U.S. 775 (1998).
12. 523 U.S. 75 (1998).
13. Ibid. at 79.
14. Ibid. at 80.
15. Ibid. at 81–82.
16. 499 U.S. 187 (1991).

17. *Espinoza* v. *Farah Mfg. Co., Inc.*, 414 U.S. 86 (1973).
18. 519 U.S. 1040 (1996).
19. 522 U.S. 422 (1999).
20. 524 U.S. 624 (1998).
21. Ibid. at 641–642.
22. Ibid. at 655.
23. "Americans with Disabilities Act of 1990 (ADA) Changes," U.S. Equal Opportunity Commission web site. (12 January 2000), http://www.eeoc.gov/stats/ada.html.
24. Ibid.
25. *Murphy* v. *United Parcel Service, Inc.*, 527 U.S. 516 (1999) (the question of whether hypertension is a disability must be addressed without consideration of mitigating measures).
26. 401 U.S. 424 (1971)
27. See *BNA Employee Relations Weekly* (Special Supplement: Civil Rights Act of 1991) (11 November 1991), pp. S1–S6.
28. 511 U.S. 244 (1994).
29. 527 U.S. 526 (1999).
30. Ibid. at 2122.
31. Ibid. at 2129.
32. 499 U.S. 144 (1991).
33. 445 U.S. 1 (1980).
34. Stephen Franklin, "EEOC Seeks to Protect Undocumented; Policy Change Aims to Prevent Abuses," *Chicago Tribune* (26 October 1999), Section 1, p. 1; Stephen Franklin, "EEOC Tries to Clarify New Policy," *Chicago Tribune* (2 November 1999), Section 3, pp. 1, 4; Ida L. Castro, "Protecting Workers from Discrimination," *Chicago Tribune* (3 November 1999), Section 1, p. 28.

PROPERTY PROTECTION

In the United States, property ownership is one of our most fundamental rights. Preserving the right to pursue and maintain property was a primary concern of our founders; this is evident in the Constitution, especially in the search-and-seizure limits of the Fourth Amendment and the due process clause of the Fifth Amendment. The Constitution balances the right to own property with the need for government to maintain order and promote the good of society, however. Hence, the government has the right of *eminent domain,* or the right to take private lands if they are necessary for public use. Balancing the rights of businesses and individuals with the needs of government is a pressing issue in today's society.

Part 10 examines how local, state, and federal laws treat property and property rights, as well as the manner in which property is transferred. This part addresses real property and personal property. Moreover, this part examines an increasingly significant type of property—intellectual property—and how the law attempts to address the new challenges that technology poses for business.

P A R T

10

43

REAL PROPERTY AND JOINT OWNERSHIP

A G E N D A

A number of property issues will arise as CIT conducts business. For example, Anna and Tom will need to buy real property to construct manufacturing plants and to lease buildings for warehouse space. What issues are important as Tom and Anna engage in these undertakings? What type of deed would CIT prefer? Why? The Kochanowskis have a barn on land they own, and they would like to renovate it into a warehouse. If the land is not zoned for commercial use, can the Kochanowskis lawfully do this? What problems may arise from such a venture?

Tom and Anna plan to purchase some land on which to build a vacation home. They want to be sure that if something happens to one of them, the property will automatically pass to the surviving spouse. What is the best way to arrange this? Why?

Assume a CIT debtor is a joint owner in an apartment complex—can CIT attach the debtor's interest and force a sale? What issues would affect CIT's rights? Be prepared! You never know when one of the Kochanowskis will need your help or advice.

PROPERTY RIGHTS

There are two distinctly different meanings for *property*. First, the term means an object that is subject to ownership, a valuable asset. Second, it means a group of rights and interests that are protected by the law, commonly called "a bundle of rights." A multitude of rights are associated with property ownership. Ownership entitles a person to use the property personally, to give someone else the use of it, to rent it to someone else, or to use it to secure a loan. The owner may sell the property, make improvements to it, or abandon it. Courts commonly note that this "bundle of rights" includes the rights to enjoyment and use, to economically exploit the land based on present and potential uses, and to exclude others.

Ownership of real property normally entitles the owner to continued use and enjoyment of the property in its present condition. For example, suppose you owned a house with a beautiful view of the mountains. If someone purchased an adjacent lot and started constructing a three-story house that would block your view, you could sue for an injunction to protect your view. Such a lawsuit would succeed in some states.[1] Many states also recognize that property owners have the right of support from adjoining lands; the right to use bodies of water adjacent to the property; limited rights to the airspace above it; the right to things growing on it; the right to things attached to it; and the right to things, like minerals, below its surface. However, owners or prior owners may have transferred these rights. Many communities now recognize and protect the right to have sun fall on existing solar collectors.

REAL PROPERTY DEFINED

Definition of Real Property

This chapter deals with *real property* or, as it is commonly called, *real estate*. Significant differences exist between real and personal property. Real property is land and things that are permanently attached to the land, including buildings, roadways, and storage structures. Property that is permanently attached to buildings is also considered real property and is called a *fixture*. Personal property consists of everything else capable of being owned.

Definition of a Fixture

A *fixture* is property that at one time was movable and independent of real estate but became attached to it. Examples are water heaters, central air-conditioning units, furnaces, built-in ovens, installed dishwashers, bathroom sinks, and copper pipes for plumbing. A builder who is constructing a house will buy a water heater, take it to the construction site, and permanently attach it to the plumbing lines and the gas or electric lines. After the personal property has been attached, it becomes a fixture.

In determining whether an item is a fixture as opposed to personal property, courts will look at the reasonable expectations and understandings of most people. For instance, most people are shocked if they buy a house and, when they move in, discover that the sellers removed the handles on the kitchen cabinets and the plates over the light switches. The same buyers, however, expect the sellers to remove the tables, chairs, and other furniture. Ceiling lights are fixtures, while table lamps are household goods. Plants in a flower bed are real property; plants in pots are personal property. Wall-to-wall carpeting is real property; area rugs are personal property. Refrigerators, mirrors, and paintings are generally personal property but may be real property if they are an integral part of the building.

In making this determination, courts also consider how much damage would occur if the property in question were removed.

The Nature of Plants

Another issue concerns plants: Are they real property (real estate) or personal property? Real estate includes plants that are growing on the land, such as fruit and shade trees, tomatoes, strawberries, artichokes, and trees that are being grown for timber. If a farmer sells land with crops still growing on it, the farmer is clearly selling real estate.

Sometimes a farmer or another landowner may sell the plants but keep the land. In this case, did the landowner sell real or personal property? The **common law** rule is that if the plants were still growing when the **title** passed to the buyer, the sale was of real estate. If the title passed after the plants were severed from the land, the sale was of personal property. This rule is difficult to apply because in many instances the buyer and seller never discuss when title should pass.

Since the common law rule was difficult to apply, the Uniform Commercial Code (UCC) now uses a different test for the situation where the owner is selling the plants but retaining the land. The UCC test is generally much easier to apply. Under it, the determining factor is *who* is going to remove the plants or trees. If the *buyer* is going to remove them, the buyer has purchased real property. If the seller is going to remove them, the sale is of personal property. After defining the difference between real and personal property, the UCC generally is not concerned with real estate, although some sections of the UCC discuss crops and fixtures. A few states still follow the common law rule, and some states use their own rules.

State Governance

Property laws vary from state to state. The laws of a state where the real property is located govern the land, regardless of the residence of the owner. For example, if you live in Wyoming but own land in Florida, Florida law governs your transactions with respect to the Florida real property.

Federal Regulation

Title III of the Americans with Disabilities Act (ADA) regulates property that is open to the public. These properties are commonly called *public accommodations* and include motels, hotels, restaurants, movie theaters, and retail stores. Under the act, newly constructed public accommodations must be designed to accommodate handicapped individuals. Architects and builders must comply with regulations established by the U.S. attorney general. Generally, new structures must be designed and built to be readily accessible to and usable by individuals with disabilities unless it is structurally impossible. When existing structures are being renovated, the areas being renovated must be made accessible too. The act itself does not specify the types of accommodations necessary. Court decisions and the U.S. attorney's regulations have begun to provide guidance in interpreting the statute. Critics of the statute claim that the act is ambiguous as to what handicaps must be accommodated and what accommodations are required. Under the statute,

Common law
A body of law that has developed from prior case decisions, customs, and usage.

Title
Legal ownership of property; also, evidence of ownership.

disabled Americans can initiate private litigation or the Justice Department can bring litigation. In addition to damages, violators may be subject to civil penalties of up to $50,000 for the first violation and up to $100,000 for subsequent violations. Note that the ADA also includes employment provisions that are administered by the EEOC.[2] The ADA is discussed in greater detail in Chapter 42.

ACQUISITION OF REAL PROPERTY

Ownership of land and things growing on the land is a society-based concept. The idea that individuals can own land, trees, and plants is prevalent in European countries and the United States; however, it is not universal. A notable exception is found in Native American cultures.

Original Occupancy

Original occupancy (original entry) occurs when the government allows the private ownership of land that was previously owned by the government. In the United States, title may have been acquired by grant from either the U.S. government or other countries that colonized here. Original occupancy may be accomplished under an outright grant to specific people or families, or it may have occurred under homestead entry laws. *Homestead entry laws* are laws that allowed settlers to claim public lands by entering the land, filing an application with the government, and paying any required fees. Homesteading was a popular way to settle large amounts of land during pioneer days in the United States, but it is not generally available today.

Voluntary Transfer by the Owner

The owner of real property may sell, trade, or give title to another by executing (signing) a deed. The recipient can be a private individual, business entity, or government body. In any of these cases, the transfer of title occurs by the execution and delivery of a written deed of conveyance. A *deed* is the type of title evidence that is used for real estate, and it indicates who owns the land. A written document is required by the Statute of Frauds. This document must adequately describe the property that is being transferred. Documents that transfer important interests in real estate must also be in writing (e.g., a *mortgage,* which is a loan of money secured by real estate).

A deed describes the land being transferred and generally includes the following items:

1. The names of the grantor(s) (transferor) and the grantee(s) (transferee)
2. The amount of consideration, if any, that was paid by the grantee
3. A statement that the grantor intended to make the transfer (commonly called *words of conveyance*)
4. An adequate description of the property (The street address by itself will not be sufficient; usually this description contains information provided by a private or government survey.)
5. A list and description of any ownership rights that are not included in the conveyance (such as mineral rights, oil rights, or **easements**)
6. The quantity of the estate conveyed

Easements
Rights to the access and use of someone else's real estate.

7. Any covenants or warranties from the grantor or grantee (Some covenants or warranties may be implied under state law; others may be expressed in the deed, such as that the grantee can never permit alcohol to be sold on the premises. Usually the deed specifies that these *covenants,* or promises, are binding on the grantee and his or her heirs and legal transferees.)
8. The signature of the grantor or grantors

Types of Deeds. A *warranty deed* contains a number of implied covenants made by the grantor to the effect that a good and marketable title is being conveyed. All the following covenants are included:

1. Covenant of title (The grantor owns the estate or interest that he or she is purporting to convey.)
2. Covenant of right to convey (The grantor has the power, authority, and right to transfer this interest in the property.)
3. Covenant against encumbrances (There are no encumbrances on the property except for those listed on the deed; encumbrances include easements, mortgages, and similar restrictions on ownership.)
4. Covenant of quiet enjoyment (The grantor promises that the grantee's possession or enjoyment of the property will not be disturbed by another person with a lawful claim of title.)
5. Covenant to defend (The grantor promises to defend the grantee against any lawful or reasonable claims of a third party against the title of the grantee. This usually includes providing a legal defense in court, if necessary.)

A *grant deed* contains fewer promises than a warranty deed. Basically, it includes only a covenant that the grantor has not conveyed this property interest to anyone else. The grantor also promises that all the encumbrances are listed on the deed.

With a *quitclaim deed,* the grantor makes no promises about his or her interest in the property. The grantor simply releases to the grantee any interest in the property that he or she *may* possess.

Delivery of the Deed. To complete a transfer of real property, the grantor *must* deliver the deed to the grantee or have it delivered to the grantee by a third person. The delivery establishes the grantor's intention to transfer the property.

Instead of handing the deed directly to the grantee, the grantor may use a third person to make the transfer. Sometimes, as in a real estate sales transaction, it may be important to use an impartial third party to assist in the transfer and to protect both the buyer and seller. This third party has the obligation of supervising the transfer, including such activities as collecting the deed, collecting the funds, checking that past utility bills, liens, and tax bills have been paid, prorating real estate taxes, prorating interest payments if a mortgage is being assumed, and assuring that the parties have fulfilled any conditions, such as repairs and inspections of the premises. This procedure is called an **escrow** and is a common method of transferring property in some states. The person who supervises this type of delivery may be an attorney, an *escrow officer* (an employee of a bank or escrow company who oversees the escrow transaction), or another agent.

Escrow
Process of preparing for the exchange of real estate, deed, and money. It is managed by a third party.

Intestate succession statute
Statute that determines who will receive assets if a decedent does not have a valid will disposing of them.

Recording of the Deed. Recording is accomplished by filing the deed with the proper authority, usually the county clerk or county recorder. The recorder files the deed or a copy of it in a deed book. Deed books usually are arranged in chronological order. The recorder also enters information about the transfer in an index, which is normally organized by the names of the grantors and grantees or by the location of the property. The index simplifies the task of locating information about a particular parcel. The recording gives the whole world "notice" of the transfer to this grantee. Recording is not a legal prerequisite to the transfer, but it does establish the grantee's interest in the property, and in many states recorded deeds have precedence over unrecorded deeds.

Transfer by Will or Intestate Succession

A person can arrange to transfer real property by provisions in a valid will. If a person does not have a valid will, the property will pass by the **intestate succession statute** of the state where the property is located. This statute will determine who inherits the property if a valid will does not exist. (Wills and intestate succession are discussed in detail in Chapter 46.)

PROTECTION OF REAL PROPERTY

Real property is subject to loss by operation of law; it can also be lost due to actions of the government, of another person, or of nature. This loss is generally involuntary on the part of the owner. To prevent it, the owner should be alert to these potential problems.

Involuntary Transfers by Operation of Law

An owner who is in default on a mortgage or trust deed may lose the property. The lender may institute foreclosure proceedings and take possession of the real estate. The lender must follow the appropriate state laws. Usually, the property will be sold at a foreclosure sale.

In most states, if the owner has not paid a court judgment, the judgment creditor may ask the court for a writ of execution. Following the applicable state procedures, the sheriff will attach the property and sell it at a judgment sale. (Under state law, some property, both real and personal, may be exempt from attachment under a judgment sale.)

If the owner has not paid people who supplied labor or materials for the premises, these suppliers may also be able to force a sale under state law. These workers may have mechanic's liens for the value of the supplies or services rendered to improve the property. Even if they do not force a sale of the real property, generally they can prevent a voluntary sale by the owner unless they are paid from the proceeds.

43.1 | MANAGEMENT/ FINANCE

PROTECTION AGAINST CLAIMS ASSERTED BY MATERIAL PROVIDERS

Tom and Anna decided to have the furnace inspected at the CIT plant before the cold weather began. Immediately following the inspection, the service person informed them that they had a cracked heat exchanger and that the unit must be shut off until it is repaired. Since the system would have to be idled anyway, the Kochanowskis decided to replace the furnace with a new energy-efficient unit installed by Cool Air, Inc., a licensed heating-and-cooling contractor that sells, installs, and services furnaces and air-conditioning units. Dan has expressed some concern about having the work done by Cool Air, because he believes that this will give Cool Air a claim against the firm and its assets if there are any problems in making payments. However, he recognizes the need for heat in the plant during the winter months. Dan asks you how CIT can be protected against claims asserted by suppliers. What will you tell him?

BUSINESS CONSIDERATIONS Should an installer in this situation insist on having the family members serve as cosigners on the contract as protection against any possible default by the firm? Should the family members be concerned if they are asked to serve as cosigners on the contract?

ETHICAL CONSIDERATIONS Suppose that the service person knew that the current furnace could be repaired but that it would not last very long even with repairs. Should he or she try to talk the customers into purchasing a new furnace in order to protect their long-term interests, or should he or she make the repairs (a short-term solution) knowing that a new furnace will be needed soon? How should this sort of issue be handled from an ethical perspective?

Remand
The return of a case to the lower court for additional hearings.

Postdeprivation
After a deprivation or taking away.

Facially
On its face, apparent.

Involuntary Transfers by Government Action

Government bodies have the right to take private lands if they are necessary for public use. This is called the right of *eminent domain.* Under this doctrine, the government must have a legitimate public use for the land and must pay the owner a reasonable amount for it.

A different type of taking occurs when the government enacts land-use laws. Zoning and planning laws restrict how property may be used. They may prevent certain types of structures from being built on the property; for example, some areas may be limited to single-family residences. Or certain industries may not be permitted to operate plants in particular areas because of the air pollution these plants would cause. Sometimes these ordinances restrict the number and placement of establishments that sell alcohol (e.g., bars are not allowed within one-quarter mile of public schools). In order to be valid, zoning and planning laws must be based on a compelling government interest, and the restrictions must be reasonable.

The constitutionality of zoning laws was addressed in the landmark U.S. Supreme Court case *Lucas* v. *South Carolina Coastal Council,* 112 S.Ct. 2886 (1992), and the cases that have followed it. (See Case Problem and Writing Assignment # 2.) In the following case, the Supreme Court addressed whether a landowner who is denied a development permit is entitled to have a jury trial.

43.1

CITY OF MONTEREY V. DEL MONTE DUNES AT MONTEREY, LTD.
119 S.CT. 1624 (1999)

FACTS This case began with attempts by . . . Del Monte Dunes . . . to develop a parcel of land within . . . the city of Monterey. The city, in a series of repeated rejections, denied proposals to develop the property. . . . The property . . . was a 37.6 acre oceanfront parcel . . . zoned for multifamily residential use. . . . The parcel had been used . . . by an oil company . . . [that] had introduced nonnative ice plant . . . [The ice plant encroached on buckwheat, the habitat of an endangered butterfly.] . . . [T]he landowners submitted an application to develop the property. . . . Although the zoning requirements permitted the development of . . . more than 1,000 units for the entire parcel, the landowners' proposal was limited to 344 . . . units. . . . [T]he city's planning commission denied the application but stated that a proposal for 264 units would receive favorable consideration. . . . [T]he landowners submitted a revised proposal for 264 units. . . . [T]he planning commission again denied the application . . . saying a plan for 224 units would be received with favor. The landowners . . . prepared a proposal for 224 units, which . . . the planning commission denied. . . . The landowners appealed to the city council, which . . . referred the project back to the commission, with instructions to consider a proposal

for 190 units. The landowners . . . reduced the scope of their . . . proposal. . . . [T]he planning commission rejected the landowners' proposal. . . . The council again overruled the commission, finding the proposal conceptually satisfactory and in conformance with . . . previous decisions. . . . The council then approved one of the site plans. . . . [Landowners'] final plan . . . was designed, in accordance with the city's demands, to provide the public with a beach, a buffer zone between the development and the adjoining state park, and view corridors so the buildings would not be visible to motorists on the nearby highway; the proposal also called for restoring and preserving as much of the sand dune structure and buckwheat habitat as possible. . . . [T]he planning commission . . . denied the development plan. . . . [T]he city council [also] denied the final plan, . . . declining to specify measures the landowners could take to satisfy the concerns raised by the council. . . . The council did not base its decision on the landowners' failure to meet any of the specific conditions earlier prescribed by the city. . . .

After five years, five formal decisions, and 19 different site plans, . . . Del Monte Dunes decided the city would not permit development of the property under any circumstances. Del Monte Dunes commenced suit

43.1

CITY OF MONTEREY V. DEL MONTE DUNES AT MONTEREY, LTD., *continued*
119 S.CT. 1624 (1999)

against the city . . . under 42 U.S.C. § 1983. . . . The District Court dismissed the claims. . . . The Court of Appeals reversed. . . . On **remand,** the District Court [submitted some] . . . claims to a jury . . . The jury delivered a general verdict for Del Monte Dunes on its takings claim . . . and [made] a damages award of $1.45 million. . . . The Court of Appeals affirmed. . . . We granted certiorari. . . .

ISSUE Was this matter properly submitted to the jury?

HOLDING Yes. It was properly submitted to the jury.

REASONING . . . As the city . . . proposed the essence of the instructions given to the jury, it cannot now contend that the instructions did not provide an accurate statement of the law. . . . [W]e note that the trial court's instructions are consistent with our previous general discussions of regulatory takings liability. . . . [T]he jury was instructed to consider whether the city's denial of the final proposal was reasonably related to a legitimate public purpose. . . . [T]he jury was instructed . . . that the various purposes asserted by the city were legitimate public interests. . . . [T]he question submitted to the jury . . . was confined to whether . . . the city's particular decision to deny Del Monte Dunes' final development proposal was reasonably related to the city's . . . justifications. . . .

We next address whether it was proper for the District Court to submit the question of liability on Del Monte Dunes' regulatory takings claim to the jury. . . . [T]he answer depends on whether Del Monte Dunes had a statutory or constitutional right to a jury trial. . . . Section 1983 authorizes a party who has been deprived of a federal right under the color of state law to seek relief through "an action at law, suit in equity, or other proper proceeding for redress." . . . Our settled understanding of § 1983 and the Seventh Amendment . . . compel the conclusion that a suit for legal relief brought under the statute is an action at law. Here Del Monte Dunes sought legal relief. . . . [A]t the time of the city's actions, the State of California did not provide a compensatory remedy for temporary regulatory takings. . . . Had the city paid for the property or had an adequate **postdeprivation** remedy been available, Del Monte Dunes would have suffered no constitutional injury from the taking alone. . . . Damages for a constitutional violation are a legal remedy. . . . [J]ust compensation is, like ordinary money damages, a compensatory remedy. . . . ("The Fifth Amendment does not proscribe the taking of property; it proscribes taking without just compensation"). Even when the government takes property without initiating condemnation proceedings, there is no constitutional violation "'unless or until the state fails to provide an adequate post-deprivation remedy for the property loss.'" . . . [W]e conclude the cause of action sounds in tort. . . .

Although this Court has decided many regulatory takings cases, none of our decisions has addressed the proper allocation of liability determinations between judge and jury. . . . [W]e have held that whether a regulation of property goes so far that "there must be an exercise of eminent domain and compensation to sustain the act . . . depends upon the particular facts." . . . [W]e hold that the issue [of] whether a landowner has been deprived of all economically viable use of his property is a predominantly factual question. . . . [W]e hold that it was proper to submit this narrow, factbound question to the jury. . . . A federal court . . . cannot entertain a takings claim under § 1983 unless or until the complaining landowner has been denied an adequate postdeprivation remedy. Even the State of California, where this suit arose, now provides a **facially** adequate procedure for obtaining just compensation for temporary takings such as this one. . . . [T]he disputed questions were whether the government had denied a constitutional right in acting outside the bounds of its authority, and, if so, the extent of any resulting damages. These were questions for the jury. . . .

BUSINESS CONSIDERATION What can a business do to avoid some of the problems faced by this developer?

ETHICAL CONSIDERATIONS Can the city's refusal to approve the construction be justified on an act utilitarian basis that it provided the greatest good for the greatest number? Why or why not? What about Monterey's decision not to take the property by eminent domain and pay compensation? Was this decision just?

Private Restrictions on Land Use

Land use regulation
Laws that regulate the possession, ownership, and use of real property.

Generally, an owner can use property as he or she wishes. Sometimes the government uses **land use regulation** to limit the uses. In addition, *restrictive covenants* limit how land may be used. These are private agreements between landowners on the use of the property and may take the form of building restrictions or *covenants, conditions, and restrictions (CC&Rs)*. These are the techniques used by condominiums and planned developments to control the building on and use of the lots. Restrictive covenants may be enforced by private lawsuits *if* they are lawful. Formerly, restrictive covenants were used to enforce racial segregation. The covenant would state that no owner could sell his or her property to a nonwhite person. The U.S. Supreme Court declared that restrictive covenants based on race are illegal in the landmark decision of *Shelley* v. *Kraemer.*[3]

43.2 | MANAGEMENT

ZONING RESTRICTIONS

The Kochanowskis have a large barn on their residential property. This barn has been vacant for quite some time, and Dan thinks that, with minor renovations, it will make an excellent warehouse from which to ship Call-Image videophones. Anna points out that the property is not zoned for commercial activities and that such a use might be criminal without the proper zoning. Dan thinks that since Call-Image is a family-owned and operated business, such restrictions do not apply. Anna and Dan seek your advice. What will you tell them?

BUSINESS CONSIDERATIONS What are the advantages and disadvantages of renovating the barn into a CIT warehouse? What factors should a family business consider in making this sort of decision? Would different factors enter into the decision for a publicly owned corporation?

ETHICAL CONSIDERATIONS Among the factors that might affect any decisions on this issue are: Will there be an increase in traffic and/or noise in the neighborhood? How will such a use affect the neighbors? What ethical obligations exist for CIT under these circumstances?

Adverse Possession

Adverse possession occurs when an individual tries to take title and possession of real estate from the owner. A person who has physical possession of real property has better legal rights to that property than anyone else, except for the true owner and people who claim possession through the true owner. If the possession is of an adverse nature and it continues for a sufficient length of time, the adverse possessor may actually take ownership from the true owner.

For possession to be adverse, it must be actual, open, and notorious. *Actual* possession means that the adverse possessor is actually on the land and is using the real estate in a reasonable manner for that type of land—as a residence, a farm, a ranch, or a business office. It is not sufficient that the adverse possessor state that he or she is using the land; actual use is required.

For possession to be *open,* it must be obvious that the adverse possessor is on the property. It will not be sufficient if the person stays out of sight during the day and walks around the property only at night. Openness is required in order to reasonably put the owner and the rest of the world on notice that the adverse possessor is using the property.

Finally, for possession to be *notorious,* it must be adverse or hostile to the true owner. Generally, people who occupy or use the property with the owner's permission, such as co-owners and renters, cannot be adverse possessors.

The required holding period varies from state to state and is specified by state statute. The period may range from 5 to 30 years. Entry under color of title may affect the holding period. Entering under *color of title* means that the holder thought that he or she had a legal right to take possession of the real property and had title to it. For example, a person with a defective deed would enter under color of title. Some states specify a shorter holding period if the holder entered under color of title and/or if the holder paid real estate taxes. In some states, the payment of real estate taxes is a necessary requirement for adverse possession; in some others, color of title is required. The possession must be continuous for the specified time period. However, the adverse possessor may leave the property for short periods to go to work, to classes, or on a brief vacation. He or she may not leave the property for an extended period of time.

The policy behind the doctrine of adverse possession is to encourage the use of land, a very valuable resource. The doctrine tends to encourage the use of land by someone else, if the owner is not using it. As the old adage says, possession may be nine-tenths of the law. This doctrine applies only to privately owned real property, however; government land may not be taken by adverse possession.

If the owner is not able to use or rent the property, he or she should periodically check to make sure that no one is using it. If it is being used without permission, the owner should take prompt legal steps to remove the occupant.

In the following case, the appellate court considered whether the plaintiffs acquired the land on which they built their home by adverse possession. Note the elements required for adverse possession in New York.

Fee interest
Broadest form of real estate ownership; an absolute interest in which the owner is entitled to the entire property and can transfer it during life and at death. Also called a *fee* or a *fee simple*.

Quiet title
Proceeding to establish that the petitioner is the owner of property.

RPAPL
Abbreviation for New York statute on real estate entitled Real Property Actions and Proceedings Law.

43.2

GUARDINO V. COLANGELO
691 N.Y.S.2D 664 (SUP.CT. N.Y., APP. DIV., 3RD DEPT., 1999)

FACTS . . . [I]n 1974 the original grantor, Albert Christiana, filed in the Columbia County Clerk's Office a map of a four-lot subdivision. . . . In 1975 he conveyed by deed one of the parcels to plaintiffs: a 0.76-acre lot set forth on the filed map as Parcel "K" which included an easement over a proposed 50-foot wide private roadway leading to the public highway. . . . The deed specifically refers to the filed map on which the four lots, the private roadway and a cul-de-sac, located at the interior end of the roadway, are depicted. Thereafter, Christiana, without the aid of a surveyor, had a cul-de-sac created in a location somewhat different from, but in proximity to, that depicted on the filed map. To this day, a narrow driveway connects the disputed area with the public highway. In 1977 plaintiffs, also without the aid of a surveyor and relying on the misplaced cul-de-sac, erected a house on what they believed was their property; the house was actually built . . . within a portion of the mapped cul-de-sac, entirely outside their property. . . .

Christiana and his successors . . . conveyed the remaining three lots in the subdivision. . . . [T]he deeds to these three lots conveyed a **fee interest** in the private roadway as tenants in common where, by contrast, plaintiffs' deed had conveyed only an easement over that roadway. From 1977 to 1993, none of the other lot owners attempted to use any portion of the

mapped cul-de-sac, nor did they object to the location of plaintiffs' house. In 1993 plaintiffs had their property surveyed, revealing their encroachment. Shortly thereafter, with full knowledge of plaintiffs' encroachment, defendant RMF Partners purchased Parcel "O" from Christiana's successor, as an undeveloped 1.70-acre lot which borders the mapped cul-de-sac within which plaintiff's house has stood since 1977.

In 1994 plaintiffs commenced the instant action to **quiet title** with respect to the area of their encroachment based on adverse possession. RMF answered and asserted a counterclaim . . . [After the commencement of this action, the other two lot owners . . . deeded their interest in the disputed area to plaintiffs.] . . . Supreme Court determined that plaintiffs had, by adverse possession, acquired "the land upon which their residence and immediate improvements . . . are located." . . . [New York calls its general jurisdiction trial court the Supreme Court.]

ISSUE Did the plaintiffs acquire title by adverse possession to the property on which they built their house in 1977?

HOLDING Yes. The case is remanded to the trial court for a more accurate description of the property that is possessed by adverse possession.

continued

GUARDINO V. COLANGELO, *continued*
691 N.Y.S.2D 664 (SUP.CT. N.Y., APP. DIV., 3RD DEPT., 1999)

REASONING It is well settled that to prevail on a claim to title by adverse possession, it is the possessor's burden "to establish that the character of the possession is 'hostile and under a claim of right, actual, open and notorious, exclusive and continuous' for the statutory period of 10 years." Here, the record reveals that in 1977 plaintiffs built their house on property which was later acquired . . . by RMF in common with the owners of the two remaining lots. Clearly, the erection of a building constitutes an "open and notorious" use of the disputed area. Moreover, "hostility may be found even though the possession occurred inadvertently or by mistake." Our review of the record supports Supreme Court's conclusion that plaintiffs satisfied their burden and were entitled to judgment declaring that they are the owners of the disputed area by adverse possession.

We find incorrect RMF's assertion that plaintiffs were tenants in common with RMF and the other lot owners and, thus, plaintiffs were required to adversely possess the disputed area for 20 years rather than 10 years. RMF relies on the common-law rule that "where parties hold property as tenants in common, **RPAPL** 541 creates a statutory presumption which the adverse claimant must overcome . . . that a possessory tenant in common holds the property for the benefit of the other co-tenant(s). . . . However, plaintiffs are not tenants in common with RMF or the others. . . . The plain language of the relevant deeds demonstrates . . . that the deed to plaintiffs, unlike the deeds conveying the other three lots in the subdivision, conveys only an easement and not a fee interest in the disputed area. Accordingly, RPAPL 541 does not extend the 10-year period with respect to plaintiffs' adverse possession claim. Moreover, even if plaintiffs were co-tenants, the RPAPL 541 presumption ceases "immediately upon an ouster by one tenant of the other." . . . In our view, plaintiffs' erection of a house and improvements within the disputed area was so open, public and unequivocal that it clearly constituted ouster, rendering inapplicable the additional 10-year period.

. . . RMF's (and its predecessors') failure to assert legal title despite plaintiffs' unequivocal acts of hostility through the statutory period is deemed acquiescence by RMF in plaintiffs' adverse possession. . . . [A] fee owner faced with such an open, hostile and adverse exercise of ownership to his property must assert his rights or will be presumed to have acquiesced to the encroachment under settled principles of adverse possession. Further, RMF's assertion that—in addition to fee title—it also has an easement in the roadway based upon the filed map is unpersuasive. While a conveyance which refers to a subdivision map showing an abutting street gives rise to a presumption that an implied easement . . . will also pass with the grant, the determinative factor in whether an easement by implication is created is "the intention of the parties at the time of the conveyance." . . . [T]he language in the conveyance to RMF reflects an intent to convey an interest superior to an easement, i.e., a fee ownership. . . . In our view, Supreme Court correctly concluded that, despite plaintiffs' adversely acquired encroachment, RMF still has access to Parcel "O" over that portion of the 120-foot diameter mapped cul-de-sac on which plaintiffs have not encroached. Therefore, RMF's assertion of an easement by necessity on and across the disputed area is also unavailing.

Although Supreme Court properly concluded that plaintiffs acquired title by adverse possession to the area of their encroachment, Supreme Court's description of the precise area adversely possessed is inadequate. In furtherance of the marketability of the title to the parcels in question, a more clear description of the parameters of the land acquired by plaintiffs by adverse possession is imperative. . . . [T]his matter will be remitted to Supreme Court for a determination . . . of the exact description of the area awarded to plaintiffs, giving due regard to its conclusion that RMF has ample space . . . to enter and exit its lot. . . .

BUSINESS CONSIDERATIONS What could a business do to avoid becoming an adverse possessor? Why would a business wish to avoid using adverse possession? What could a business do to avoid having its property acquired by adverse possession?

ETHICAL CONSIDERATIONS Is it ethical for RMF to acquire the lot with knowledge of the encroachment, and then complain about it? Who is morally responsible in this situation and why?

Easements

In some situations, a person may be entitled to use the land of another in a particular manner. This right is called an *easement.* An easement is not a right to *own* the property, but the right to *use* it in a particular manner. An easement may belong to a particular person, or it may run with the land. The latter means that the easement belongs to the owner of a particular parcel of land, called the *dominant parcel.* The parcel that is subject to the easement is the *servient parcel.* In *Guardino* v. *Colangelo* (Case 43.2) the plaintiff had an easement over the private roadway. This easement ran with the land.

An easement may be an *express* easement; that is, it was stated by the person who created the easement. Or it can be created by *prescription,* which is much like adverse possession: A person starts to use the servient parcel openly, and, after the state's statutory period, he or she will be entitled to continue the use. Easements also are created by *contract,* when an owner of property sells someone a right to use it. For example, an owner may sell an easement to an oil company to come onto the property to drill exploratory oil wells. An easement can also be created by *necessity.* The most common example of necessity occurs when an owner divides a parcel and deeds a **landlocked** portion to someone else: The only method of access is across the servient estate. A requirement for an easement by necessity is that both parcels were originally one large parcel.

Landlocked
Surrounded by land owned by others.

Easements can also be created by *implication.* This can occur when a parcel is divided, and the owner of the dominant parcel needs to use the servient parcel. However, the proof of need is not required to be as great as it is for an easement by necessity. For example, suppose an owner of a parcel of land decides to sell the northeast corner of the parcel. The owner had previously run a sewer system from this northeast corner to the main sewer line through the rest of the parcel. The buyer can reasonably expect to use the same sewer line when he or she owns the northeast corner. It would be *possible* to run a new sewer line to the northeast corner, but it was implied that the new owner could use the existing one.

The manner and type of use are restricted by the easement. A person who exceeds the amount of use that is permitted under the easement will lose the easement, and his or her rights will be extinguished.

RENTAL OF REAL PROPERTY

Types of Tenancies

The owner of real property may decide to allow another person to use the property. If the owner is willing to exchange temporary possession of the property for money or other consideration, there is a rental agreement. Most students are tenants because they live in a university dormitory, an apartment near campus, or rent a house with others.

Tenancies are governed by the rules of both contract law and real estate law. Several basic types of tenancies exist, which are based on the length of the rental period. These include tenancies for a fixed term, periodic tenancies, tenancies at will, and tenancies at sufferance.

A *tenancy for a fixed term* is a tenancy for a set period of time; the beginning and ending dates are established. Generally, the Statute of Frauds requires a written lease if the tenancy is for one year or longer. Such tenancies automatically end at the set time. (Some states have set a maximum allowable term for a tenancy for a fixed term.) If the tenant has not vacated the premises by the end of the lease period, the landlord can explicitly execute a new lease with the tenant or can elect to treat the tenant's actions as an implicit renewal of the lease for another term of the same length. However, an implicit renewal cannot exceed one year due to the Statute of Frauds.

A *periodic tenancy* starts at a specific time and continues for successive periods until terminated. It may be established to run from year to year, month to month, week to week, or some similar period. The beginning date is specified, but the ending date is not. Either party may terminate it after proper notice. The lease normally specifies how much notice is necessary and to whom it should be addressed.

A *tenancy at will* can be terminated any time at the desire of *either* the landlord or the tenant.

A *tenancy at sufferance* is one in which the tenant entered into possession properly and with the landlord's permission but wrongfully remained in possession after the period of the tenancy.

Rights and Duties of Tenants

The tenant rents the right to exclusive possession and control of the premises, which means that the tenant is the only one entitled to be in possession. Generally, the lease specifies that the property can only be used for a particular, stated purpose. Some leases specify that the property can only be used for lawful purposes.

At common law, the landlord is not entitled to enter the premises. The landlord often obtains permission from the tenant to enter the premises either on an ad hoc basis or because such a right is reserved in the lease. Even at common law, the landlord has the right to enter the premises in case of an emergency.

If the tenant is a business, it may need to install trade fixtures, such as neon signs, commercial refrigeration units, and industrial ovens. If a tenant attaches trade fixtures to the property, the tenant is allowed to remove them before the end of the lease. But if the removal causes any damage, the tenant must repair it. Even though the common law provides for trade fixtures, it is advisable for the parties to address them in the written lease. For clarity, the specific trade fixtures can even be listed in the lease. The parties' memories may not be accurate after a long-term lease, for example, 20 or 30 years.

Under a normal lease, the landlord is required to make sure the property is in good condition for the purposes specified in the lease and must maintain the property in good condition. Tenants do not have an obligation to make major improvements or repairs. However, a tenant may contractually agree to make certain modifications or improvements. For example, in exchange for an exceptionally low rent, a tenant might agree to remodel a property at his or her own expense. In such a case, it is wise to specify who will pay for these improvements and who will get the benefit of them at the end of the lease.

Warranty of Habitability. Some states have held that an implied warranty of habitability exists in residential housing leases. That is, the landlord impliedly promises that the premises will be fit for living—for example, that the heating system will work, that there will be running water, and that there will be indoor plumbing. When the courts recognize this warranty, the tenant can use a breach of warranty as a basis for terminating a lease, as a means of reducing the rent, or as a defense for nonpayment of the rent.

Constructive Eviction. Most states recognize an implied covenant that the owner will protect the tenant's right to quiet enjoyment (use) of the premises. *Constructive eviction* occurs when the owner does not protect this interest of the tenant and allows a material interference with the tenant's enjoyment of the premises. Suppose, for example, that you rent an apartment and your neighbor's habit of playing drums in the middle of the night is interfering with your sleep. Although your neighbor's behavior is in violation of the lease, the landlord will not enforce the lease provisions. The landlord's behavior constitutes constructive eviction, and you can move out without any further liability to pay rent. However, if you do not take some action promptly, the court may decide that you waived your right to complain about the noise.

Assignment and Subleases. The transfer of the tenant's entire interest in the lease is an *assignment.* If the tenant transfers only part of his or her interest and retains the balance, the transfer is a *sublease.* (Note that this terminology is slightly different from that in Chapter 14.) Ordinarily, assignments and subleases are allowed unless the lease specifically provides that they are not. Most leases do prohibit assignments and subleases without the prior written approval of the landlord.

Rights and Duties of Landlords

Landlords have the right to retake possession of their property at the end of the lease. In most rental situations, the landlord expressly reserves the right to terminate the lease if the tenant breaches any promises contained in it, including the promise to adequately care for the property.

Rent. Rent is the compensation that the landlord receives in exchange for granting the tenant the right to use the landlord's property. Most leases require the tenant to pay the rent in advance. Many landlords require that tenants pay the first and last month's rent in advance, which provides added protection for the landlord. If the tenant is behind in paying the rent, it usually takes a number of weeks to force the tenant to leave the premises. If the tenant has not paid the rent, the landlord has a number of available options. The landlord can sue for the rent that has not been paid or can start procedures to have the tenant evicted (removed) from the premises. In some states, the landlord has a lien on the tenant's personal belongings that are on the premises. This allows a form of self-help called a *lockout:* The landlord locks the tenant out of the premises while all the tenant's personal property is inside. For example, North Carolina law allows a landlord to gain possession of the property by peaceable means, including lockouts.[4]

43.3 | MANAGEMENT/ MANUFACTURING

CALL-IMAGE TECHNOLOGY

LONG- OR SHORT-TERM LEASE?

CIT wants to rent a new plant in order to expand its production and shipping capacities. The firm has located a parcel that is ideal for its needs: It has good access, adequate space, and a reasonable rent. CIT prefers a relatively long-term lease, due in part to the renovations CIT will need to make to the leased property. The landlord, however, is only willing to sign a five-year lease. He is willing to insert a clause stating that the lease will be renewable for additional periods of five years each, subject to certain conditions. Because the landlord is not willing to meet the terms proposed by CIT, Tom and Anna ask you whether the firm should sign the lease. What advice will you give them? What additional information would be helpful?

BUSINESS CONSIDERATIONS What terms should be included in the lease in order to protect CIT's rights? What concerns should the Kochanowskis have with regard to the renovations? How should they protect themselves and their interests?

ETHICAL CONSIDERATIONS Suppose a prospective tenant explains planned renovations for a rental property during the negotiations. The landlord recognizes that the building will be worth a great deal more in rent with the renovations and decides to negotiate a shorter lease term than was originally anticipated. Does such conduct raise any ethical concerns? Why? How should such a situation be treated from an ethical perspective?

States generally select one of the following approaches to determine the amount of self-help allowed to a landlord who is entitled to possession of the premises:

1. A landlord can use necessary and reasonable self-help.
2. A landlord must rely only on the remedies provided by the courts.
3. A landlord can gain possession by *peaceable* means.

Damage by the Tenant. The landlord has the right to reimbursement from the tenant for any damage caused by the tenant. For example, if Rudy, a tenant, negligently fills his waterbed, and it leaks and causes substantial damage to the premises, Rudy is liable for the damage. Tenants are also responsible for any damage caused to the premises by their guests. This right to collect for damages exists at common law and is usually stated in the lease. The tenant is responsible for damage caused negligently or intentionally but not for *ordinary wear and tear*—the deterioration that occurs through ordinary usage.

Security Deposits. For protection, the landlord will usually collect a security deposit. This money is to be used after the tenant has vacated the premises to repair any damage negligently or intentionally caused by the tenant. It is not to be used to clean the premises or to repair normal wear and tear. As such, a security deposit generally cannot be used to repaint walls that have become dirty through normal use. It can be used to replace doors in which holes have been punched, however. Any money that remains should be returned to the tenant within a reasonable period after the tenancy terminates. Some states have statutes that establish when the landlord must return the security deposit.

Forcible Entry and Detainer
A summary proceeding to recover possession of premises unlawfully or forcibly detained.

Pro se
Prepared by an individual appearing in his or her own behalf without hiring an attorney.

Duty to Protect a Tenant and His or Her Guests. Landlords generally have the same responsibility to their tenants' guests as they do to the tenants themselves. The landlord does not warrant that the premises are safe but does have the duty to warn the tenant of *latent defects*—defects that are not immediately obvious and of which the tenant may not be aware. This duty of the landlord extends only to latent defects that the landlord knew or should have known existed.

Rights After Abandonment by a Tenant. If the tenant wrongfully abandons the premises during the term of the lease, the landlord has various options. The landlord can make a good-faith effort to find a suitable tenant, but if one cannot be found, the landlord can leave the premises vacant and collect the rent from the tenant who abandoned the premises. The tenant is legally obligated to pay the rent, and the landlord can obtain a court judgment for the payment. Practically, the landlord will be able to collect *if* the tenant can be located and is solvent. If the landlord is able to rerent the premises, he or she is technically renting the premises on the tenant's behalf. If a lower rent is obtained, the original tenant is liable for the difference.

As an alternative, the landlord can repossess the premises and rerent them on his or her own behalf. The original tenant who abandoned the premises is relieved of any liability for additional rent. If the landlord is able to rerent the premises for more money, the landlord will benefit. There may be a factual issue whether the rerenting is for the landlord's or the tenant's behalf.

The following case arose out of a landlord's attempt to evict a tenant.

43.3

WRIGHT V. BOGS MANAGEMENT, INC.

1999 U.S. DIST. LEXIS 7747 (N.DIST.ILL., E.DIV. 1999)

FACTS . . . Marvin Wright . . . filed this action . . . against Bogs Management, Inc., Robert Bogs, and Phyllis Bogs . . . and the Village of Lansing and the Lansing Police Department ("Village") . . . In 1997, Marvin Wright was living at an apartment in Lansing, Illinois that had been leased to his brother-in-law, Reginald Washington. . . . Due to non-payment of rent, Bogs served Wright with a 5-Day Notice on June 14, 1997. On July 23, 1997, Bogs served Wright and Washington with a Summons and Complaint in **Forcible Entry and Detainer** seeking possession of the property and rent money. On July 24, 1997 a judgment was entered in favor of Wright and Washington . . . due to a defective 5-Day Notice given by Bogs. Immediately following the judgment, Bogs served another 5-Day Notice. . . . Wright alleges that, later that same day, Phyllis Bogs [cursed him, using vulgar language and several racial slurs directed toward him]. When Wright threatened to sue Bogs for her remarks, she [tried to have him arrested for assault.] . . . Upon arriving at the apartment complex, the police informed Bogs that Wright's threat to sue did not constitute an assault . . .

On July 31, 1997, the Bogs filed another Complaint in Forcible Entry and Detainer seeking possession and money damages. [That case was continued until August 22, 1997.] . . . On August 15, 1997, Phyllis Bogs posted notices barring Wright from the apartment complex. . . . The Bogs then called the Lansing Police Department and informed the . . . officers that Wright was a "trespasser." Wright alleges that he informed the officers that there was a Forcible Entry and Detainer action pending. . . . Wright also claims that . . . one police officer told him that Ms. Bogs carries a lot of political weight in the Village and "damn near owns just about everything in Lansing." . . . August 16, 1997, Wright went to the Lansing Police Department where he again explained to the Lieutenant that the forcible entry and detainer case was scheduled for August 22, 1997. The Lieutenant told Wright: "Those laws don't mean anything to me. You would have to let the court decide that matter." . . . August 17, 1997 Wright went back to the Lansing Police Department where he spoke with the Captain. The Captain told Wright that he was aware of the circumstances, but that there was nothing he could do and that . . . Ms. Bogs "carries a lot of weight in the Village of Lansing, and that the Lansing Police Department is not going to go against Phyllis Bogs." . . . On August 19, 1997, Wright complains that the Lansing Police Department and the Bogs conspired to have him arrested and charged with "criminal trespass to real property." Wright was detained for approximately three hours and then released after posting bond. . . . [H]e was acquitted of . . . "criminal trespass to real property" . . .

ISSUE Should Wright's claims of illegal lockout and intentional infliction of emotional distress be dismissed?

HOLDING No. Wright is permitted to amend the illegal lockout complaint.

REASONING . . . In reviewing a motion to dismiss, the court must take all well-pleaded factual allegations as true and draw all reasonable inferences . . . in the light most favorable to the non-moving party. . . . When a **pro se** complaint is involved, as in this case, the court must . . . "' . . . construe pro se pleadings liberally.' . . . to give a pro se plaintiff a break when, although he stumbles on a technicality, his pleading is . . . understandable."

. . . Wright alleges . . . "Illegal Lockout." . . . Although Wright contends that he suffered damages because he was not permitted to obtain his belongings from the Bogs' apartment building, he identifies no specific cause of action . . . for his alleged injury. The court found no case law suggesting that a cause of action exists for an "illegal lockout." Yet, a review of the facts included in the complaint indicate [sic] that Wright may have a state law claim for common law constructive eviction or forcible entry under Illinois' Forcible Entry and Detainer Act. . . . The court grants Plaintiff Wright leave to amend his complaint. . . .

Wright claims that Bogs Defendants are liable for intentional infliction of emotional distress [IIED]. . . . In Illinois, for a plaintiff to sustain a cause of action for IIED, (1) the conduct involved must be truly extreme and outrageous, (2) the actor must either intend that his conduct inflict severe emotional distress, or know that there is at least a high probability that his conduct will cause severe emotional distress, and (3) the conduct must in fact cause severe emotional distress. " . . . [A]n objective standard based on all the facts and circumstances of the particular case

continued

43.3

WRIGHT V. BOGS MANAGEMENT, INC., *continued*

1999 U.S. DIST. LEXIS 7747 (N.DIST.ILL., E.DIV. 1999)

is employed." A review of the case law . . . suggests that Wright does have a claim for IIED. Although "the threshold for extreme and outrageous conduct is high," plaintiff has alleged facts that bear out his claim of extreme and outrageous conduct. Wright charges that "defendants' treatment of plaintiff constitutes extreme and outrageous conduct which exceeds all bounds usually tolerated by a decent society." While Wright does not point to any specific conduct by defendants, he describes their actions throughout the complaint. Wright alleges that the Bogs Defendants, his landlords, (1) conspired with the police to have him falsely arrested; (2) illegally locked him out of his home and prevented him from retrieving his possessions; (3) caused the Sheriff's department to place his belongings on the street; and (4) converted a number of his belongings for their own use. . . . Wright claims that Phyllis Bogs verbally abused and threatened him. . . . Courts have held that "a cause of action for intentional infliction of emotional distress may arise from abuse by defendant of position or relation, such as landlord-tenant, which gives him actual or apparent authority to adversely affect plaintiff's interest; yet, existence of such relationship, standing alone, does not relieve plaintiff of [the] burden of proving [the] extreme and outrageous nature of defendant's conduct." . . . If it is true that defendants' [sic] conspired to have Wright falsely arrested, for no other reason than that they wanted him off their property, such conduct would qualify as extreme and outrageous conduct. The defendants' use

of their clout to convince the police to arrest Wright serves as undeniable evidence of an extreme abuse of power. Wright has also satisfied his burden under the second prong of the test. . . . [T]he Bogs Defendants' actions manifest an intent to do more than merely protect their interests . . . [as] landlords. . . . Phyllis Boggs' verbally abusive threats suggest that racial animus, rather than monetary concerns, motivated her actions to have Wright arrested. . . . [A] reasonable person could infer the Bogs Defendants' intent to cause severe emotional distress from their calls for Wright's arrest. . . . Wright alleged that he has suffered great mental pain and embarrassment as a result of defendants' actions. . . . [H]e claims he has been unable to work and earn an adequate living since his dispute with the Bogs Defendants. . . . Wright has alleged all of the essential elements of an intentional infliction of emotional distress claim. . . .

BUSINESS CONSIDERATIONS How could the Bogs Defendants have handled this matter in a better way? If you were their advisor while this issue was developing, what would your advice be? If you were to advise Wright, what would you tell him?

ETHICAL CONSIDERATIONS Is it ethical for a tenant to remain on the rental property knowing that the rent is overdue? Did Phyllis Bogs behave in an ethical manner?

Legislative Trends

Landlord and tenant laws are undergoing change. Two federal statutes address discrimination in housing—the Civil Rights Act of 1866 and the Civil Rights Act of 1968. The 1968 Fair Housing Act, which is contained in the latter Civil Rights Act, is the basis for most of the recent litigation and is the more comprehensive of the two acts. As originally passed, it prohibits discrimination based on race, color, religion, or national origin. Discrimination based on sex was added in 1974, and discrimination based on familial status was included in 1988.

Familial status includes having children under 18 years of age. The 1988 amendment also increased the amount of protection by providing three methods for enforcement: (1) the Department of Housing and Urban Development can initiate a lawsuit in federal court or before an administrative law judge, *if* all the parties agree; (2) the person subjected to the discrimination can file a suit in either state or federal court, and the court may award actual damages, punitive damages, or equitable relief; or (3) the U.S. attorney general can file a suit if a pattern or practice of discrimination exists. As with most statutes, there are exceptions. For example, single-family units owned by a private investor with less than four houses *may* be exempt from the act as a whole, and housing solely for the elderly (over 62 years of age) is exempt from the age discrimination provisions.

Some states are very protective of tenants' rights. Other states are more protective of the landlord. Recent examples of protenant legislation include laws that require the payment of interest on security deposits or prevent retaliatory eviction. *Retaliatory eviction* occurs when a landlord evicts a tenant who has filed complaints about violations of law, including building- or health-code violations. To recover for retaliatory eviction, generally, the tenant must prove *all* of the following elements:

1. The tenant's complaint was bona fide, reasonable, and serious in nature.
2. The tenant did not create the problem him- or herself.
3. The complaint was filed before the landlord began the eviction proceedings.
4. The primary reason the landlord began the eviction proceedings was to retaliate against the tenant for filing the complaint.

In some states, retaliatory eviction has been prohibited by court decisions and not legislative statutes.

Some states and/or cities have rent control statutes that prohibit landlords from raising the rent. Although rent control is intended to protect tenants, many economists argue that it is ineffective. They say that it actually creates a shortage of rental housing, because investors choose other investments that provide a higher rate of return. Also, landlords may not provide necessary repairs. After unsatisfactory results, rent controls are being abolished in some areas. Massachusetts voters abolished them in 1994. The California legislature enacted a statute, effective in 1999, allowing landlords to raise the rents on vacant apartments even where there are local rent controls.[5]

JOINT OWNERSHIP OF PROPERTY

Joint ownership exists when two or more people have concurrent title to property; that is, they own the property at the same time. There are five forms of joint ownership: tenancy in common, joint tenancy with rights of survivorship, tenancy by the entireties, community property, and partnership property. (Chapter 34 discusses partnership property; it is not covered in this chapter.) Generally, these forms of joint ownership can exist with personal property as well as with real property. Most of these forms can be created voluntarily by the tenants, or they can be created by someone else for the tenants.

A legal characteristic of most forms of joint ownership is that each of the co-owners (the tenants) has an undivided right to use the whole property. Thus, the parcel described on the deed is not divided equally among the tenants; instead, each of them has the right to use all the property. If a dispute arises about the use of the property that the tenants are unable to resolve among themselves, they can file their complaint with the court. The primary remedies available to resolve such a dispute are (1) to sell the property and divide the proceeds or (2) to divide the property equitably and give each tenant a separate parcel. Either of these is considered an action for partition. Note that because the usable value of adjoining

RENT CONTROL IN SANTA MONICA

Santa Monica, California, may have the toughest rent control law in the United States. Santa Monica is currently governed by members of a political party called Santa Monicans for Renters' Rights (SMRR—pronounced "smur.") Rents there average about $552 a month. By one estimate, this is 30 percent below market value. When Santa Monica created its rent control program, it was aware that rent control might encourage landlords to "economize" on maintenance or convert properties to other uses such as condos. To maintain its rent control program, the local rent control board has 250 pages of regulation, a staff of 50, and an annual budget of $4.2 million.

John Rodriguez, a barber and owner of three small apartment buildings, says "They're using our money to give to other people without any proof whatsoever that those people are in need." Until 1986, landlords could not even go out of business. A California law has been enacted that permits landlords, even in Santa Monica, to go out of business.

In 1990, Santa Monica landlord Phyllis Anderson paid each of her tenants $3,500 to vacate their apartments. She still is unable to convert her six-unit apartment building to another use. If she sold her building to someone else, the purchaser would be restricted by the same rules.

Suppose a group of landlords challenges this law in *your* court. How will *you* rule in this case?[6]

BUSINESS CONSIDERATIONS Would you consider investing in rental property in a community where there is rent control? Why or why not? What would you do if you were the owner when rent control was initiated?

ETHICAL CONSIDERATIONS Should the government regulate and control how owners use their real property? What ethical issues are raised by such regulation?

SOURCE: *Fortune*, (5 August 1996), pp. 24, 26.

parcels may differ, the separate segments may differ in size and shape. Exhibit 43.1 summarizes joint ownership of property. Since property rights are governed by state law, there may be some variance from state to state.

Tenancy in Common

A *tenancy in common* occurs when two or more people own the same property. Each tenant has an undivided right to use the whole property. Usually, a tenancy in common is indicated by words like "Bennett and McCormick, as tenants in common" on the deed or other evidence of title. If the deed simply says "Bennett and McCormick," most courts will presume that they are tenants in common.

There is no legal limit on the number of tenants in a tenancy in common. Practically speaking, however, if there are too many tenants, conflicts will probably arise among them regarding the use of the property. Each tenant may sell, assign, or give away his or her interest. A tenant may also will away the interest in a valid will. If the tenant has no valid will, then the interest in the tenancy will pass to his or her heirs under the state intestate succession statute. (Chapter 46 discusses wills and intestate succession in greater detail.) A creditor of an individual tenant can attach his or her interest in the tenancy in common.

EXHIBIT 43.1 | **Comparison of Forms of Joint Ownership**

Remember that because property rights are governed by state law, a wide variation may exist from state to state.

	Tenancy in Common	Joint Tenancy with Rights of Survivorship	Tenancy by the Entireties	Community Property
Requirements for Creation				
Requires equal ownership interests		●	★	★
Restricted to married couples			★	★
Limited to two people			★	★
Restricted to human beings		✓	★	★
Applicable to both real and personal property	★	✓	✓	★
Rights of One Tenant Acting Alone to Transfer or Encumber His or Her Share Without the Consent of the Others				
May use the whole property (undivided right to the whole)	★	★	★	★
May be transferred by will	★			★
May not be transferred by will		★	★	
Will pass to surviving tenants at death, if there is no valid will[b]		★	★	✓[a]
Will pass to intestate heirs at death, if there is no valid will	★			✓[a]
May be sold during life	★[c]	✓		✓ ●
May be mortgaged or assigned during life	★[c]	✓		✓
May be transferred by gift during life	★[c]	✓		
May be attached by a creditor of a tenant	★	★		

a. Most community property states have different intestate succession provisions for the passage of separate property and community property. The community property commonly passes to the surviving spouse if there is no valid will provision covering this property.

b. In some type of tenancies, courts would say the interest "remains" with the surviving cotenants instead of "passing" to them.

c. Generally, a tenant in common will have this power. However, in many states, if the tenancy in common is between spouses and consists of real estate, the signature of the second spouse will be required.

★ The trait applies to the specific form of joint ownership.

✓ This is true in most states.

● This is true in many situations.

Tenants in common do not have to have equal interests in the property. For example, if there are four tenants in common, one may have a one-half interest, one may have a one-quarter interest, and the other two may have a one-eighth interest each.

Joint Tenancy with Rights of Survivorship

A *joint tenancy with rights of survivorship* occurs when two or more people own property together. Again, there is no legal maximum number of tenants. However, the practical question remains: How many cotenants can get along with one another? As in a tenancy in common, each tenant has an undivided right to use the whole property. Generally, each tenant has an equal interest in the property. Joint tenancies differ from tenancies in common in that when one tenant dies, his or her interest passes to the remaining cotenants. The survivors continue to hold an undivided interest in the whole property. Generally, a will does not have any effect on a joint tenancy with rights of survivorship. (There is a movement in the U.S. legal community that advocates changing state laws regarding the ability to will joint tenancies and insurance policies. A few courts are devising theories to this effect.) The interest in the cotenancy property will pass from one tenant to another immediately on death by operation of law. Eventually, the tenant who outlives the others will own the complete interest. In most states, corporations are not allowed to be joint tenants because corporations do not die.

Because of the survivorship feature, joint tenancies often are used as substitutes for wills. Given the potential for disputes during life, however, this practice may be unwise. In addition, in most states if a joint tenant wrongfully causes the death of another joint tenant, he or she will not be allowed to benefit and will be prevented from taking the **decedent**'s interest.

Decedent
A person who has died.

Joint tenancies may be divided during a court action for partition. In most states, a joint tenant can sell, make a gift of, or assign his or her interest during his or her life. A creditor of the joint tenant can attach the interest. A transferee of the joint tenant will take the interest as a tenant in common. A transferee includes a purchaser, a donee, an assignee, or a creditor who obtained rights through an attachment procedure. The transferee does not receive the survivorship rights of a joint tenant because the other joint tenants never agreed to share the risk of survivorship with the transferee.

Tenancy by the Entireties

In a *tenancy by the entireties,* two tenants, who must be husband and wife, share the property. Each tenant is a joint owner in the whole property. This type of ownership has a survivorship feature. If one spouse dies, the survivor receives the whole property. Unlike joint tenants with rights of survivorship, many states allow a tenant who wrongfully caused the death of his or her spouse (cotenant) to benefit and to take title to the whole. Generally, only creditors of the family unit can attach entireties property. One spouse normally cannot unilaterally dispose of his or her interest, unless the parties obtain a legal separation or a divorce. The tenants can, however, agree to sever the tenancy. A valid will does not affect distribution of entireties property. Tenancies by the entireties are not recognized in all states; for example, **community property states** do not have tenancies by the entireties.

Community property states
States in which married couples generally create community property.

Community Property

Community property is recognized in eight states—Arizona, California, Idaho, Louisiana, Nevada, New Mexico, Texas, and Washington—as well as the Commonwealth of Puerto Rico. This discussion emphasizes the general features of community property laws, which vary from state to state. Louisiana community property law is most dissimilar, because it is based on Louisiana's French heritage. The community property laws in the other states are based predominantly on Spanish civil law.[7] Remember, too, that community property laws are also evolving.

Community property is a form of co-ownership that can occur only between husband and wife. It is based on the concept that financially the marriage is a partnership. One-half of most of the property that is acquired or accumulated during marriage belongs to each spouse. Technically, this assumes that one-half of each asset belongs to the husband and one-half belongs to the wife. Thus, most states require that both the husband and the wife sign any deeds to transfer real property. In most states, this requirement does not extend to personal property. In fact, the names of both spouses do not have to appear on the community property or on any title evidence to the property. For example, although a paycheck may bear the name of only one spouse, it is nonetheless community property and, as such, belongs to both spouses. The primary source of community property for most couples is wages and earnings.

A couple begins to form community property once they are married. In most situations, they stop forming community property once they establish separate residences. In a divorce proceeding, the community property usually is divided.

This is not meant to imply that a married couple will have only community property. Each may own property separately, just as in **separate property states.** Separate property normally includes the following:

> **Separate property states**
> States in which married couples cannot create community property.

1. Property owned by either spouse before their marriage
2. Property given to *one* spouse by gift, by will, or by intestate succession
3. Property that is acquired with separate property funds

In addition, in some states—California, for example—income, rents, or profits earned from separate property are also separate property; in other states—Idaho, Texas, and Louisiana—this income is community property if received during the marriage. In Louisiana, a husband or wife can file a declaration that this income should be separate property instead of community property. All property other than that previously mentioned is usually community property.

For most purposes, a husband and wife can contractually agree to split their community property into two shares of separate property. However, if they are careless and mix their respective separate properties and/or community properties, it may all become community property. If the property becomes so mixed that it cannot be separated into community and separate property, the courts say that it is hopelessly commingled and treat all of it as community property.

Community property does not have a survivorship feature. A spouse can will his or her share of the community property to someone else. If the decedent does not have a valid will, most intestate succession statutes provide that the property will pass to the surviving spouse.

The National Conference of Commissioners on Uniform State Laws (NCCUSL) adopted the Uniform Marital Property Act.[8] When it is enacted by a state legislature, it modifies the property rights of married couples and makes the state more like a community property state. Wisconsin adopted the act in 1983.[9] Initially, a number of other states introduced the bill; however, none has adopted it.[10]

Distinguishing Among the Forms of Joint Ownership

The words used on the deed or other title evidence are controlling as to whether the tenants are tenants in common, joint tenants with rights of survivorship, or tenants by the entireties. If the language on the deed is not clear, under state law there will be a presumption as to the form of joint ownership. If the tenants are husband and wife, most states will presume that the property is community property or entireties property. If the state recognizes neither form of ownership, it will presume a joint tenancy with the right of survivorship. If the tenants are not related to each other by marriage, most states will presume that they are tenants in common.

Transfer on Death Ownership

Transfer on death or pay on death ownership should be distinguished from forms of joint ownership. When an owner opens a bank account, purchases securities, or acquires other assets, he or she may designate the form of ownership as transfer or pay on death. Transfer on death (TOD) is used for investment securities. Pay on death (POD) is generally used for bank accounts. The NCCUSL has drafted a Uniform Transfer on Death Securities Registration Act that has been adopted in 46 states.[11] With this type of ownership, the recipient does not have an interest in the asset during the owner's life. The recipient cannot withdraw the assets or mortgage them. The recipient only is entitled to the assets at the owner's death, if the owner has not changed the title evidence to indicate a new recipient. These forms of ownership are relatively new. However, they are becoming popular as substitutes for wills. Transfer on death ownership is also discussed in Chapter 46.

RESOURCES FOR BUSINESS LAW STUDENTS

NAME	RESOURCES	WEB ADDRESS
U.S. Department of Housing and Urban Development (HUD)	HUD provides information on real property and planning issues for both consumers and businesses, as well as information on the Fair Housing Act and the Civil Rights Acts.	**http://www.hud.gov/**
Legal Information Institute (LII)—Land Use Law Materials	LII, maintained by the Cornell Law School, provides an overview of land use law, links to statutes, federal and state judicial court decisions, and other materials.	**http://www.law.cornell.edu/topics/land_use.html**
TenantNet	TenantNet, an informal network of tenants and tenant leaders in New York, provides news, information, and resources on landlord-tenant law.	**http://tenant.net/**

SUMMARY

Property ownership includes title to the property and the right to control possession of the property. Real property consists of land and objects that are built on the land, growing on the land, and/or permanently attached to the land. A fixture is property that was personal in nature before it was permanently attached to a building.

Real property can be acquired by a grant from the government or by transfer from the owner. An owner may trade, sell, give, or will the property or leave it to another person by intestate succession. Lifetime transfers will be described in a deed; the deed will be delivered to the grantee; and, in most cases, the deed will be recorded. Although not legally required, recording protects the grantee and the public.

An owner may lose title to or use of the property. This loss can be caused by unpaid debts, by government restrictions on the use of the land, or by eminent domain. An owner may also lose his or her interest by the adverse possession of another person. Easements can restrict the owner's use of the property.

An owner can enter into a rental agreement called a lease. Under a lease, a tenant is entitled to the exclusive possession of the owner's real estate. The lease is the contract that will govern many terms of the landlord-tenant relationship. Under modern law, the landlord must repair the premises. A tenant who negligently or intentionally damages the property is liable for the cost of those repairs. The landlord can require a security deposit in order to assure that there are funds for making such repairs. The tenant is justified in leaving the premises when there is constructive eviction. A landlord can evict a tenant if the tenant fails to pay the rent. Commercial leases may contain different provisions than the leases of houses or apartments.

Two or more people, called cotenants, can own an interest in the same piece of property at the same time. They may be tenants in common, in which case each tenant owns an undivided right in the whole parcel and there are no survivorship rights. Or they may be joint tenants with rights of survivorship. Such tenants can dispose of their interests during life; at death, their interest will pass to the remaining cotenants by operation of law. Tenants in a tenancy by the entireties must be husband and wife. In community property states, a husband and wife can create community property. Most of the assets that they acquire during their marriage will be community property. The form of ownership is relevant to a business entity that may desire to purchase the asset from one or more tenants, or the business entity may be a creditor that wishes to attach the tenancy property. Joint ownership provides rights immediately; transfer on death or pay on death ownership provides rights to the recipient only after the owner has died.

DISCUSSION QUESTIONS

1. After Al's mother and father died, Al, who is responsible for their estate, decides to sell their home. After locating buyers for the property and entering into a sales contract with them, Al removes the petunias, his father's prize-winning roses, and a load of topsoil that is on the flower beds. The buyers are unhappy about this. Who has the right to these items? Why?

2. Describe the typical provisions included in a deed.

3. Kim moves onto a piece of real estate in California. He begins to use the property in an open, actual, and notorious manner and continues to do so for five years. He also pays the real estate taxes on this parcel. The applicable holding period is five years. Who owns this parcel? Why? Is it material that Nancy, the original owner, also paid real estate taxes? What are the legal rights of the parties? Why?

4. Jack and Rosie are neighbors. In 1970, Rosie built a fence around her property. However, she did not have the boundary surveyed, and the fence was built four feet into Jack's property. Who owns this four-foot strip of land now? Why?

5. Why is it difficult for a lessee (tenant) to be successful as an adverse possessor?

6. Carmen is a tenant who has complained to the health inspector about a rodent infestation in her apartment complex. Should the court protect Carmen from eviction? Why or why not?

7. Suppose that a business wishes to rent premises to use as a sports bar in a shopping mall. What provisions might the business want to include in the lease? Why?

8. Why might a person want to establish a joint tenancy with rights of survivorship with another person who is not a relative?

9. How is community property made or acquired in a community property state?

10. Why might a person prefer to establish a tenancy in common instead of a joint tenancy with rights of survivorship?

CASE PROBLEMS AND WRITING ASSIGNMENTS

1. Private citizens wanted to enter the common areas of a multibusiness office complex to make antiabortion statements. The protestors carried signs and placards and shouted at prospective patients of Cherry Hill Women's Center, one of the ten tenants on the property. These protestors did not have the permission of the owner of the property. Does the landowner have the right to keep the protestors off the property? Why or why not? [See *Brown* v. *Davis*, 495 A.2d 900 (N.J.Super. 1984).]

2. In the late 1970s, David H. Lucas and others were involved in extensive residential development on the Isle of Palms, a barrier island east of Charleston, South Carolina. In 1986, Lucas paid $975,000 for two residential lots for his personal investment, intending to build single-family homes on the lots. At the time, the lots were zoned for single-family residential use, and there were no other restrictions on them. In 1988, the state legislature passed the Beachfront Management Act, based on an official report that the beaches named in the act were seriously eroding. The act directed the South Carolina Coastal Council to establish a baseline and permanently prohibited the building of *any* inhabitable structures between the baseline and the ocean. The legislature concluded that the area was not stabilized, and setback lines were required to protect people and property from storms, high tides, and beach erosion. No exceptions were allowed under the act. When the baseline was established, Lucas's lots were between the baseline and the ocean, thereby preventing Lucas from building any inhabitable structures on either of his parcels. Did the state take Lucas's property in violation of the Fifth Amendment of the Constitution, which prohibits the taking of property without due process of law? Must the state pay Lucas for the lots because the act deprived him of all economically viable use of the property? [See *Lucas* v. *South Carolina Coastal Council*, 112 S.Ct. 2886 (1992).]

3. This dispute is between neighbors who live in adjoining subdivisions. "The parcel in dispute is where the backyards of Robert and Rusty Silacci and Richard and Janet Abramson converge. Toro Creek runs through the Silacci property. It is the section across Toro Creek and next to Abramson's property that is the portion in dispute." The parcel is about 1,600 square feet in size. David Scott, who previously owned the Abramsons' parcel, placed a three-foot-high picket fence completely around the parcel in question. At the time, the land actually belonged to Carlton. Carlton had given permission to Scott and his other neighbors to take flood-control measures beside Toro Creek. Carlton sold his property, and eventually it was owned and developed into Toro Hills Estates. Monterey County required the developer, Chamberlain Group, to grant a scenic easement along Toro Creek where there are trails used by hikers and

those on horseback. The developer promised that it would not build any structures or gardens that would affect this easement. The developer sold a lot to Bob Franscioni in 1989. "A month after the sale, Chamberlain wrote Abramson to say that his rear fence was encroaching on Franscioni's lot. Chamberlain offered to relocate the fence to the correct boundary line. Abramson replied that he believed he was entitled to keep the property located inside of his fence. Later in 1989 Abramson wrote Franscioni suggesting that Franscioni grant him an easement. Franscioni, who had no use for the disputed parcel, talked to Abramson about it and gave him oral permission to use the land. Abramson testified at trial, however, that he did not believe he needed Franscioni's permission, and that he would have continued to use the land without it." Nothing further happened until 1991, when Dinna Silacci purchased the lot from Franscioni. She offered to rent the property to Abramson for $50 per year. She also recorded a consent to use the property "to stop adverse use by Abramson." Abramson did not respond to the offer to lease the property, so she informed him that her son would remove the fence. Dinna Silacci then transferred the property to her son, Robert Silacci, who initiated this lawsuit. Do the Abramsons have the right to continue to use this enclosed yard based on a prescriptive easement? [See *Silacci* v. *Abramson*, 53 Cal.Rptr.2d 37 (Cal.App. 1996).]

4. The Shaughnesseys purchased a tract of land in 1954. They subdivided 12 acres into lots and retained 4 acres for themselves. In 1967, the Witts purchased the lot next to the one the Shaughnesseys kept. The Witts built a house on this lot and began living there. In 1968, the Witts cleared an area of land that ran along their property. They built a swimming pool, a deck, a playground, a dog run, and a fence along the property line. Neither owner realized that the Witts had encroached 40 feet onto the Shaughnesseys' property. In 1988, the Shaughnesseys sold their 4-acre lot to the Millers. When a survey showed the encroachment, the Millers demanded that the Witts stop using the property. When the Witts refused, the Millers sued to establish their ownership rights in the property. This is called a suit to quiet title. Who is entitled to the strip of land? Why? [See *Witt* v. *Miller*, 845 S.W.2d 665 (Mo.App. 1993).]

5. The landlord owned a 36-unit apartment complex. George Becker, one of its tenants, slipped and fell against his glass shower door and broke his arm. The shower doors were made of untempered glass. The glass doors were installed before the landlord purchased the premises, and it did not know that the doors were made of untempered glass. One of the witnesses testified that tempered glass and untempered glass look the same except for the small identification mark in one corner. It was agreed that, had the shower door been made of tempered glass, the extent of the injury would have been reduced. Should the landlord be liable for latent defects in rental units if the defects existed when the tenant leased the premises? Why? [See *Becker* v. *IRM Corp.*, 698 P.2d 116 (Cal. 1985).]

6. **BUSINESS APPLICATION CASE** Golden West Baseball Co. (club) owns the California Angels baseball team. In 1964, the club was anxious to relocate the Angels from Dodger Stadium, which had been their home stadium. The club wanted their own stadium and also felt that the terraced parking at Dodger Stadium was not suitable. In negotiations with Anaheim's mayor, the club said that it would need about 150 acres, a stadium with approximately 45,000 seats, parking for 12,000 automobiles, and adequate ingress and egress from the property. The club entered into an agreement with the city of Anaheim (city) to have a stadium built and then to use the stadium and parking facilities on game days. The agreement was for a 35-year term with a 30-year renewal option. Numerous draft agreements were exchanged before the final draft. The agreement provided that Anaheim would provide all facilities and equipment, including the parking areas on game days. The city also wished to lease the facilities for other purposes to assist in defraying the costs of construction. The agreement provided that the areas not needed would remain under the city's exclusive control. The contract stated that the city may use the area "except to the extent occupied by the stadium, and to the extent necessary to provide the minimum parking for stadium use." Negotiations began in 1977 to move the Los Angeles Rams (football team) to the Anaheim Stadium. The city entered into an agreement to build an office complex at the site of the stadium, as part of that negotiation and as an inducement to the Rams to move. The club wanted to prevent the construction. One of its main concerns was whether there would be adequate parking on game days. Is the club's agreement to use the stadium property a lease? Should the club have foreseen this problem? How could the club have protected its interests? [See *Golden West Baseball Co.* v. *City of Anaheim*, 31 Cal.Rptr.2d 378 (Cal.App. 1994).]

7. **ETHICAL APPLICATION CASE** In March 1994, Neil Fisher purchased a novel home in Coconut Grove, Florida, for $310,000. Built in 1967, the house is surrounded by dense trees and has a mature oak tree that

grows through a roofed area in the back yard called the "outdoor living room." Fisher wants to remove the tree which he claims has grown too large for its location. He contends that the tree is ruining the brick floor around it and is causing cracks in the house foundation. However, there is a county law that provides that homeowners can be fined as much as $25,000 for removing a specimen oak tree more than 18 inches in diameter without a permit. The law applies even if the tree is on the homeowner's lot. This tree exceeds 18 inches in diameter. Fisher's request for a permit has been denied by government officials. The attitude of the local residents can be summarized by these statements. "This is like the Rio Grande or the Amazon . . . You have to put your foot down somewhere to maintain your neighborhood," said Michael Goldstein of the Coconut Grove Council. Ted Stahl, cochairman of the council, stated, "There has been too much slaughtering of trees that have been here for years and years . . . This tree is a part of the land." Should Fisher be permitted to remove the tree on his lot? Why or why not? Is this county law ethical? Why or why not? [See Charles Struse, "Man Can't Remove Oak in Own Home," *The Fresno Bee* (29 May 1994), p. D7.]

8. **CRITICAL THINKING CASE** Gertrude and Herbert Potthoff were unable to agree on a property settlement in their divorce. They maintained one basic bank account, but only Herbert could withdraw monies. They deposited funds from Herbert's medical practice, loan proceeds, proceeds from the sale of stock, stock dividends, interest income, and proceeds from the sale of Gertrude's separate property into the account. From it they paid the expenses of the medical practice, living expenses, costs of investments, and costs of real estate. Before the Potthoffs' marriage, Herbert purchased property on which he built the Palm Grove Shopping Center with his separate funds. He also spent considerable time and effort making it a successful investment. Is the bank account community property? Is the Palm Grove Shopping Center separate property? [See *Potthoff* v. *Potthoff*, 627 P.2d 708 (C.A.Ariz. 1981).]

NOTES

1. This is not always true. In the classic case of *Fontainebleau Hotel Corp.* v. *Forty-Five Twenty-Five, Inc.*, 114 So.2d 367 (Fla. 1959), the court held that there were no rights to sunlight or view.
2. Laura M. Litvan, "The Disabilities Law: Avoid the Pitfalls," *Nation's Business* (January 1994), pp. 25–27.
3. 334 U.S. 1 (1948).
4. See *Spinks* v. *Taylor*, 278 S.E.2d 501 (N.C. 1981).
5. "Slow Death for Rent Control," *Fortune* (5 August 1996), pp. 24, 26.
6. Ibid.
7. For an excellent discussion of the historical basis for community property law in each state, see W. S. McClanahan, *Community Property Law in the United States* (Lawyers Cooperative and Bancroft-Whitney, 1982), chs. 1–3. For an interesting discussion of the origins of community property in Europe and its adoption in other countries, see William Q. DeFuniak and Michael J. Vaughn, *Principles of Community Property*, 2nd ed. (Tucson, AZ: University of Arizona Press, 1971), ch. II.
8. For a copy of the act as adopted by the NCCUSL, see 9A Uniform Laws Annotated (U.L.A.) 97 (1987) and pocket parts.
9. See Wisconsin 1983, Act 186, Effective 1-1-86, W.S.A. 766.001 to 766.97.
10. Information on the current status of adoptions of Uniform State Laws provided by Katie Robinson, Public Affairs Coordinator, NCCUSL, during a telephone conversation on 20 March 2000.
11. The Uniform TOD Security Registration Act has been adopted by Alabama, Alaska, Arizona, Arkansas, California, Colorado, Connecticut, Delaware, Florida, Georgia, Hawaii, Idaho, Illinois, Indiana, Iowa, Kansas, Kentucky, Maine, Maryland, Massachusetts, Michigan, Minnesota, Mississippi, Missouri, Montana, Nebraska, Nevada, New Hampshire, New Jersey, New Mexico, North Dakota, Ohio, Oklahoma, Oregon, Pennsylvania, Rhode Island, South Carolina, South Dakota, Tennessee, Utah, Vermont, Virginia, Washington, West Virginia, Wisconsin, and Wyoming. "Transfer on Death Security Registration: An Answer to the Woes of Joint Ownership of Securities," NCCUSL web site, http://www.nccusl.org/pressreleases/pr1-00-1.htm.

44

PERSONAL PROPERTY AND BAILMENTS

A G E N D A

In addition to owning real property, as discussed in Chapter 43, CIT owns personal property. For example, CIT owns the rights to produce and sell its Call-Image interactive videophone. How can the Kochanowski family protect this asset? What type of property is it? What are the rights and obligations that accompany ownership? How can CIT best protect its property?

CIT was interviewing a number of applicants for positions in its factory. After all of the applicants left, Dan noticed two umbrellas in the waiting room. What should Dan do with them? Does CIT have any sort of claim on the umbrellas? If so, what is the basis for its claim?

CIT leases equipment from an electronics firm. Tom Kochanowski is concerned that CIT may be liable for any damages to the equipment and, consequently, feels that this equipment should be insured by CIT during the lease period. Dan disagrees, arguing that, in leases of industrial equipment, the party leasing the equipment assumes the risk relating to damages. Who is correct? Why? When CIT rents extra delivery trucks, what are the legal rights of the lessor and CIT?

Be prepared! You never know when one of the Kochanowskis will need your help or advice.

O U T L I N E

Ownership of Property
Acquisition of Personal Property
Protection of Personal Property
Bailments of Personal Property

Summary
Discussion Questions
Case Problems and Writing Assignments

OWNERSHIP OF PROPERTY

Classifications of Property

The concepts of property rights and joint ownership discussed in Chapter 43 apply to personal property as well. As noted in that chapter, real estate is land and everything constructed on or otherwise permanently attached to the land or to any of the buildings. All property that is not classified as real property is personal property.

Personal property is divided into two categories: tangible and intangible. *Tangible* personal property is property that is movable and can be felt, tasted, or seen. It has texture, color, size, a temperature, and similar characteristics. Examples of tangible personal property include textbooks, pens, briefcases, calculators, computers, cell phones, and pagers.

Intangible personal property cannot be reduced to physical possession; it cannot be held in a person's hand. It may, however, be reduced to legal possession and is often very valuable. Intangible personal possessions include things such as stock ownership, patent rights, copyrights, accounts receivable, and corporate goodwill. A physical thing may just represent *rights.* A good example of this is money—without a government willing and able to stand behind its money, money is just metal or colored paper. Another example of a tangible representation is a patent. The right to use an invention or process is intangible; however, a patent holder applies to the U.S. government and if the application is approved, he or she receives a document from the patent office and a patent number. The valuable right is the right to use and sell the invention. The government paperwork evidences that right. The distinction between tangible and intangible personal property is not significant in most contexts and does not control the parties' legal relationships.

The traditional label for a piece of personal property is a *chattel.* Chattels are divided into chattels real, chattels personal, and chattels personal in action. A *chattel real* involves an interest in land, but the chattel *itself* is personal—for example, a leasehold or other legal right to use land. The owner of the chattel real does not own the land but does have valuable legal rights. *Chattels personal* are tangible, movable personal property such as desks, chairs, chalk, and overhead projectors. A *chattel personal in action,* also called a *chose in action,* is the right to file a lawsuit or to bring legal action.

Components of Ownership

The three components of ownership that are important with respect to real property are also important with respect to personal property. These components are ownership, possession, and title. *Ownership* includes all the rights related to the ownership of property. *Possession* includes the right to control the property by having it in one's custody or by directing who shall have custody of it. The concept of *title* includes both the current legal ownership of the property and the method of its acquisition. Title also refers to the written evidence of ownership that appears on a certificate of title for property, such as a "pink slip" for an automobile or a stock certificate.

ACQUISITION OF PERSONAL PROPERTY

Original Possession

Original possession occurs when the owner is the first person to possess the property. In other words, the owner created the ownership rather than receiving it by transfer from another person. One way to obtain ownership by original possession is to create the property through physical or mental labor; an artist, for example, acquires ownership through original possession by creating a painting or a sculpture.

Another way to obtain ownership by original possession is to take something that has never been owned before and reduce it to possession, as when someone pans for gold in a wilderness area and takes possession of any nuggets found. When a person creates property, there is usually no dispute about who actually owns it. Disputes do arise, however, when people are hunting or trapping wild animals. For example, suppose that a group of hunters is about to trap a fox when a farmer spots the fox near some chicken coops and shoots it. A dispute may then ensue about who owns the fox. A court would decide that the farmer owned the fox and its pelt because the hunters did not reduce the fox to their possession. The farmer took control over it first.[1] Today, state statutes may declare that the state is the owner of wild animals, unless the animal was hunted or trapped in accordance with state hunting statutes.

Voluntary Transfers of Possession

Individuals can also acquire real and personal property by having it transferred to them voluntarily by the previous owner. The transfer can occur by purchase, gift, gift *causa mortis*, inheritance, or intestate succession.

Purchases. The most common way to acquire property owned by another is to *purchase* it. When property is sold by the previous owner, there is an exchange of consideration: The buyer gives up one form of property, often money, and the seller gives up another form of property. Sometimes the parties *barter,* or exchange goods or services for the property. Bartering is becoming increasingly popular for goods; organizations even exist to assist businesses in locating other businesses with which to barter.

Gifts. A person can also obtain ownership of property through a *gift.* The person who transfers the property is called the *donor,* and the person who receives the property is called the *donee.* Three requirements must be satisfied for a valid transfer by gift.

First, the donor (the previous owner) must *intend* to make a present gift—that is, to transfer the property without receiving full and fair consideration. This includes the intent to pass title to the donee now—for example, if the donor says, "I want you to have this." However, if the owner says, "I want you to have this next Sunday," it is not a present transfer. Consequently, it is not a valid gift. In most gift situations, the donor is freely giving up the property without receiving any consideration at all. Sometimes it is difficult to determine whether the intent of the donor was to make a gift or, alternatively, to sell or to lend the property. This is particularly true if the donor has died or if the donor and the donee have had a disagreement. However, if the transfer is to be treated as a valid gift, it must be shown that the donor's intent was to make a gift.

The second requirement for a valid gift is that the donor *deliver* the gift property to the donee. When the donor hands the gift to the recipient, *actual delivery* occurs. Sometimes actual delivery is not practical because of the situation of the parties or the type of property being transferred. Consequently, courts permit *constructive delivery.* For example, if Roberto, a hospitalized man, has some antique coins in his safe deposit box and wants to give them to his son, Fernando, he can give Fernando the keys and a note that will allow him access to the box, thereby effecting constructive delivery of the gift property.

The third requirement for a valid gift is *acceptance* by the donee. The donee must be willing to take the property from the donor. In most cases, this is not an issue. However, a donee may refuse to accept a gift if the donee feels it will "obligate" him or her to the donor, as when a sales agent making a bid for a contract offers the purchasing agent a two-week vacation in Hawaii. Sometimes a donee may refuse a gift because the gift property has little use or value to the donee or creates legal liabilities for the donee. For instance, a donee might refuse a gift of real estate if it is substandard tenement housing that has many building code violations.

Transfer tax
Tax on the ability to transfer assets.

A transfer by gift may be subject to a **transfer tax** such as a gift tax. If so, usually the donor must pay the tax. Most state and federal gift taxes also apply when the transfer is for less than full and adequate consideration, including when the donor receives nominal consideration. *Nominal consideration* occurs when the consideration is very small in proportion to the value of the property. For example, if a donor transfers a diamond ring worth $700,000 to a donee for $5, the value of the gift will be treated as the fair market value of the ring ($700,000) less the $5 that was paid for it. Any gift tax is figured on this amount ($699,995), and the donor is obligated to pay the tax. The gift is *not* subject to income tax when it is received by the donee.

If the donor intends to make a gift, delivers the property, and the donee accepts it, the transfer is a valid gift. Once transfer of a gift has been completed, it generally cannot be revoked. The power of the donor to revoke the gift and reacquire the property is considered inconsistent with surrendering control of the property. The donor cannot legally take the property back from the donee, no matter how much the donor wants or needs to have it returned. In most cases, a completed gift, also called an *executed gift,* is final. However, the gift can be set aside or revoked if the donee engaged in **fraud, duress,** or **undue influence** that resulted in the making of the gift.

Fraud
Use of a false statement of material fact to obtain a gift or contract.

Duress
Wrongful use of force to obtain a gift or contract.

Undue influence
Wrongful use of trust and confidence to obtain a gift or contract.

There are a few cases where a gift may be revocable. Conditions that make a gift revocable *may* be stated by words or inferred from the circumstances. Justice may require the creation of a condition even though the donor had no condition in mind.[2] A number of states consider engagement rings to be conditional gifts. Courts reason that an engagement ring is given as a pledge or symbol of the promise to marry. It is given subject to the implied condition that if the marriage does not take place either because of death, a disability recognized by the law, breach of the promise by the donee, or mutual consent, the gift shall be returned.[3] It only becomes the absolute property of the donee if the marriage takes place. When the marriage does not occur due to the fault of the donor, courts take one of two primary approaches to engagement rings, the fault rule or the no-fault rule. The majority of states are using the fault rule. Under the fault rule, the donee must return the ring if it is her fault that the marriage does not occur; the donee can keep the ring if it is the donor's fault. However, an increasing number of jurisdictions are adopting the no-fault rule. Under the no-fault rule, absent an agreement to the contrary, the ring must be returned to the donor regardless of the circumstances surrounding the termination of the engagement.[4]

A promise to make a gift at some time in the future is not binding on the promisor. The promisor can change his or her mind with impunity. An executory promise to make a gift is enforceable in the case of *promissory estoppel,* however.

This equitable doctrine is applied by the courts to avoid injustice. It is based on the concept that the promisor makes a definite promise that he or she expects, or should reasonably expect, will induce the donee to act or refrain from acting based on the promise. The donor will be held to his or her promise to prevent injustice.

Certain types of property require special formalities before the owner can make gifts of them. To transfer a *chose in action* (a right to bring legal action), the transferor must make an assignment of the right. An *assignment* is a formal transfer of a contract right. (Assignments are discussed in detail in Chapter 14.) To transfer **negotiable instruments,** the transferor must make either an assignment or a negotiation. A *negotiation* is an indorsement or notation on the document that it should be paid to a specific person or that it should be paid to the bearer or holder. The *bearer* or *holder* is the person who is in possession of the document.

Gifts fall into three categories: *inter vivos* gifts, testamentary gifts, or gifts *causa mortis. Inter vivos* gifts are made while the transferor is still alive; they are lifetime gifts. *Testamentary gifts* are completed when the owner dies; they are the provisions that a person puts in a will and are commonly called *testamentary transfers.* These transfers do not actually take place until death. Gifts *causa mortis* must meet special requirements about the donor's intention.

Negotiable instruments
Transferable documents used as credit instruments and as substitutes for money. Examples include checks, drafts, promissory notes, and certificates of deposit.

***Gifts* Causa Mortis.** Gifts *causa mortis* occur while the property owner is still alive. The donor is making the gift because he or she expects to die soon. Generally, the donor is contemplating death from a specific cause. The requirements for a gift *causa mortis* are that (1) the donor must intend to make the gift, (2) the gift must be made in contemplation of death, (3) the gift property must be actually or constructively delivered, and (4) the donor must die from the contemplated cause. If the donor does not die from the contemplated cause, the gift will be revoked. In this case, the donor or the donor's estate can reclaim the gift property. Since the donor was motivated, at least in part, by the expectation of death, it is logical that if the donor does not die, he or she should be able to get the property back.

A gift *causa mortis* is a legal concept and is distinct from various tax concepts that require lifetime gifts to be included in the estate for tax purposes.

Inheritances. A person can receive property from the estate of someone who dies. If the person who died has a valid will covering the property, the recipient specified in the will receives the property by inheritance. Like gifts, inheritances may be subject to state and/or federal transfer taxes.

Property Received by Intestate Succession. The property of a person who dies without a valid will is transferred to recipients by intestate succession. The same occurs if property is omitted from an incomplete will. The people who receive this property are specified in the state intestate succession statute. As with other death-time transfers, this transfer may be subject to estate or inheritance taxes. Transfers by wills and intestate succession statutes are discussed in greater detail in Chapter 46.

Involuntary Transfers of Possession

Custody or title of property may be involuntarily transferred by the true owner. Such a situation occurs when there is accession or confusion or when property is lost or mislaid.

Accession. *Accession* occurs when a person takes property that he or she does not own and adds to it. Accession can be interpreted as addition or augmentation. For example, a person takes some lumber and makes it into a dining room table. The question that arises is: Who owns the dining room table? Should it be the person who owned the lumber or the person who worked on the lumber and changed its nature? The court examines a number of factors in making its decision on this question; the most important is whether the worker knew that he or she had no right to the lumber. As with many legal problems, the court weighs the conflicting equities.

Title *normally* remains with the rightful owner of the lumber and is not transferred to the laborer. Depending on the circumstances, the courts may determine that the laborer is an *innocent trespasser* who believes that his or her use of the property is lawful. An innocent trespasser does not acquire title *simply* by adding labor and additional materials. The innocent trespasser *will* acquire title, however, under any one of the following conditions:

1. Because of the work effort, the original property has lost its identity. (The innocent trespasser took iron ore and made it into steel.)
2. A great difference exists in the relative values of the original property and the new property. (The innocent trespasser took a rough diamond and cut and polished it into a beautiful pear shape.)
3. A completely new type of property has been created, and the innocent trespasser has added the major portion of it. (The innocent trespasser placed her notebook on a table in the library. After selecting a couple of references, the trespasser sat down and started to write her research paper. Much later the trespasser discovered that she had sat at the wrong table and used someone else's notebook.)

If the innocent trespasser does acquire title by accession, the trespasser is obligated to pay the rightful owner for the value of the property taken. This value will be based on the worth of the property at the time the trespasser took it. These cases are really exceptions to the general rule that the trespasser usually does not acquire title.

If title to the property stays with the original owner, the innocent trespasser can recover for the value of the services rendered in improving the property. If the owner were allowed to keep these improvements without payment, the owner would have an unjust enrichment, and the innocent trespasser would suffer an unjust loss. The owner is obligated to pay for the reasonable value of the improvements. This is comparable to the theory underlying quasi contracts; however, there are minor differences.

A *willful trespasser*—one who knows he or she has no right to the property— cannot acquire title to the new property. The transfer of title under such conditions would permit willful trespassers to benefit from their wrongdoings and might even encourage them to repeat such an action. A willful trespasser is liable for any damages that he or she caused and will not be entitled to any compensation for improvements made to the property through his or her efforts.

> *Suppose, for example, Marti took some bricks she found in a neighbor's yard. Marti knew she was not entitled to the bricks, but since she thought her neighbor did not want them, she decided to go ahead and use them to build a barbecue. Although heavy, the barbecue is movable, and the neighbor is entitled to have it. Marti is not entitled to any money for her labor in building the barbecue. If the neighbor incurs any financial damages because he was planning to use the bricks in another manner, he can recover the damages from Marti.*

In rare instances, title may pass to the willful trespasser solely because the owner permits it. In other words, the owner does not want the improved property. However, the original owner may collect the value of the improved property from the willful trespasser. In our example, if the neighbor decides that he does not want the barbecue, he may allow the title to pass to Marti by default, and he can collect from Marti the value of the brick barbecue instead of the value of the bricks alone. Such action only occurs at the option of the original owner.

Some legal disputes involve cases in which a third party has purchased the property created by the trespasser. Generally, the dispute is between the original owner and the third-party purchaser. To be protected, the third party must be a bona fide purchaser for value. A *bona fide purchaser for value* is a person who buys property in good faith, for a reasonable value, and without actual or constructive knowledge that there are any problems with the transfer. The bona fide purchaser will have the same rights and liabilities as the trespasser. If the original owner could have recovered the property from the trespasser, he or she can obtain it from the bona fide purchaser. Good-faith purchasers do have the right to remove any additions or improvements that they have personally made if this can be done without harming the property. For example, if the bona fide purchaser added a modem to a computer, the modem could be removed without harming the computer.

Confusion. *Confusion* occurs when the personal, fungible property of two or more people is mixed together and cannot be separated. *Fungible property* includes things such as sand, gravel, wheat, corn, rye, oil, and gasoline, and generally consists of very small particles or grains. When wheat of the same type and quality belonging to two different farmers is mixed together, confusion occurs: The particles of wheat cannot be separated and returned to their respective owners.

Confusion may be caused by the wrongdoing of one of the owners or may occur without any misconduct. Generally, confusion is voluntary and lawful. For example, farmers often store their fungible crops, such as corn, in the same storage bin or silo. If confusion occurs *without misconduct,* the farmers receive an undivided interest in the new confused mass. If the corn in the bin is sold, the farmers divide the proceeds in proportion to the amount they put into the bin. If there are any losses, the farmers divide them proportionately.

If the confusion is caused by *intentional wrongdoing,* different rules apply. If the new mixture is not divisible, title to the whole mass will pass to the innocent party. Therefore, it is to the wrongdoer's benefit to show that the new mass is divisible. If the wrongdoer can prove that the new mass is divisible and that the mixture has at least the same *unit value* (value per ton, pound, gallon, etc.) as the property belonging to the innocent party, the wrongdoer will be entitled to a share of the new mass. The wrongdoer must prove what amount or share belongs to him or her. The court will probably be suspicious of the wrongdoer. The wrongdoer's proof must be clear and convincing.

Lost or Mislaid Property. *Lost property* is property that has been unintentionally lost by the true owner. The owner does not know where the property was lost or where it may be retrieved. A person who finds lost property has good title to the property. The true owner is the only one with better title to the property than the finder. The finder of lost property generally is entitled to keep possession of it unless a statute or ordinance provides that possession should be given to the police.

Mislaid property is property that was intentionally set somewhere by the owner. The manner of placement and the location of the property indicate whether the

WHO OWNS THE LUGGAGE?

There is a 30,000-square-foot facility in Scottsboro, Alabama, nicknamed "The Lost Luggage Capital of the World." "The Unclaimed Baggage Center offers anything from designer clothing to sporting goods, and adds about 7,000 new items a day—2 million a year."[5] All but one of the U.S. airlines send lost luggage here. Airlines give up tracking the owners after 90 days. The store also obtains merchandise from trains, trucks, and ships. Store spokesman Brock Warner says, "Of all lost bags, only .005 comes here, so statistically, it's pretty incredible."[6] The firm sells both the luggage and its contents. The store tries to sell items for 50 to 60 percent less than the retail price, according to Warner. Some of the more expensive items are appraised and then sold for about half the appraised value—for example, a 6-carat diamond ring that was appraised at $50,000 to $60,000. Other valuable items are sold at auction, such as Egyptian artifacts dating to 1567 B.C. and numbered Salvador Dali prints. The store has a concierge to help customers find lodgings or a place to dine. E-commerce has also reached the Unclaimed Baggage Center, and you can now order online at www.unclaimedbaggage.com.

Assume that the owner of luggage finds her luggage and its contents at the Unclaimed Baggage Center. She files suit in *your* court to reclaim them. How will *you* decide this case? Sometimes the owner's name and telephone numbers are clearly marked on the luggage (inside or outside). Would that affect your ruling?[7]

BUSINESS CONSIDERATIONS What procedures would reduce the amount of lost luggage? What does the owner usually do when his or her luggage is lost? What does the airline usually do?

ETHICAL CONSIDERATIONS What is the ethical perspective of the airlines and the Unclaimed Baggage Center? The Center's web site offers advice on how to avoid losing your luggage. Does this influence your assessment of their ethics? What are the airlines' moral responsibilities to their customers?

SOURCES: *The Times-Picayune* (22 April 1999), p. E2; *The Associated Press State & Local Wire* (8 March 1999), PM Cycle; and *The News and Observer* (Raleigh, NC) (13 June 1999), p. H2.

owner merely forgot to pick up the property or lost it. For example, if a student left her calculator on a classroom desk, the calculator would be mislaid, not lost. The owner of mislaid property usually will be able to remember where the property was left and to reclaim it. The finder of mislaid property has good title against everyone except the true owner.

A critical distinction exists between *title to* the property and *possession of* the property. Although the finder of the mislaid property has good title, he or she is not entitled to possession. The owner of the premises where the property is found or the person in charge of the premises is entitled to hold the mislaid property. The reason is that when the true owner remembers where the mislaid property was left, he or she will return to that location to retrieve it. It is logical to leave the personal property on the premises to make it easier for the true owner to reclaim it.

Note that the owner of the premises is entitled to *hold* mislaid property, but not lost property. However, if the finder of the lost or mislaid property was a trespasser on the property, the owner of the premises has title to the personal property that was found.

To increase the likelihood that the true owner will be able to reclaim the property, some state statutes and local ordinances require the finder of lost and/or mislaid property to complete certain steps before becoming the final owner. These statutes generally have two requirements:

1. That a specified type of notice be placed in the newspaper
2. That the property be given to the police to be claimed by the true owner

If the property is not claimed within a stated period, the police will allow the finder to claim it.

Abandoned Property

Sometimes an owner is no longer interested in owning a piece of personal property and may *abandon* it by throwing it away without intending to reclaim it or by relinquishing it to someone else without intending to retake possession. If the property is relinquished to someone else, that person will become the new owner of the property. Generally, this type of transfer will be considered a gift. If the property is thrown away, the person who finds it and reduces it to possession will acquire title. The property will once again be subject to original possession.

In the following case, the federal district court considered whether R.M.S. Titanic, Inc. should be entitled to continue its exclusive salvaging operations. R.M.S. Titanic, Inc. is attempting to gain "original possession" of the Titanic and its contents. As you read the court's opinion, decide whether you believe the property on board the ship has been lost, mislaid, or abandoned. Consider also whether others should be allowed to salvage the property, or whether others should be excluded from salvaging it.

44.1

R.M.S. TITANIC, INC. V. WRECKED AND ABANDONED VESSEL
924 F.SUPP. 714 (E.DIST.VA NORFOLK DIV. 1996)[8]

FACTS . . . RMS Titanic, Inc. (RMST) filed a . . . complaint asking the Court to declare it to be the sole and exclusive owner of any items salvaged from the RMS TITANIC (TITANIC). . . . [N]otice to other potential salvors and interested parties was given via publication. . . . [T]he Court entered an Order on June 7, 1994, conferring salvor-in-possession status of the TITANIC to RMST . . . On February 20, 1996, John A. Joslyn . . . filed a motion . . . asking the Court to rescind its order . . .

RMST . . . has a number of outstanding liens and encumbrances against certain TITANIC artifacts. . . . RMST has a number of outstanding debts. . . . Despite its debt load, RMST remains a financially viable entity. . . . RMST presented evidence that it has a number of exhibition contracts signed or pending. . . .

RMST's marketing partner has organized two cruises to the wreck site . . . to generate income to finance the 1996 salvage operations. . . . IFREMER . . . was recently paid the money owed it from the 1994 expedition. [IFREMER is the French government's oceanographic institute which has provided the salvage vessels, equipment, and technicians . . .] . . . This type of salvage operation is highly speculative and the expedition costs are high. Because RMST does not sell the artifacts it recovers, it is even more difficult to raise money . . .

Since the 1994 expedition, RMST has not visited the site of the wreck. RMST has . . . been involved in a number of onshore activities since that time [including exhibits]. . . . [T]he company recently began sell-
continued

44.1

R.M.S. TITANIC, INC. V. WRECKED AND ABANDONED VESSEL, *continued*
924 F.SUPP. 714 (E.DIST.VA NORFOLK DIV. 1996)

ing the coal retrieved from the vessel to the public. [The coal lumps are not considered artifacts.] . . . RMST has been committed to its role as "caretaker" of the retrieved artifacts. . . . RMST has kept its promise to maintain and preserve the TITANIC artifacts. RMST has planned an expedition for August of 1996. . . . RMST is finalizing an agreement to permit the production of a two-hour documentary detailing this event . . .

ISSUE Should RMST's status as salvor in possession be rescinded?

HOLDING No. RMST is entitled to keep its exclusive possessory rights.

REASONING The underlying purpose of salvage law is the complete salvaging of a distressed vessel. . . . [C]ourts sitting in admiralty have the authority to grant exclusive salvage rights and salvage awards to salvors who "have the intention and the capacity to save the property." . . . [A] salvor can lose his exclusive possessory rights to the wreck if he fails to "exercise due diligence and be reasonably successful in his attempts." . . . [A] salvor must demonstrate that its efforts are "(1) undertaken with due diligence, (2) ongoing, and (3) clothed with some prospect for success" in order for it to maintain its rights. . . . [T]he Court will address each prong of the . . . standard in turn.

The due diligence inquiry—whether RMST has shown a level of salvage activity that is reasonable under the circumstances—focuses primarily on the salvor's past operations. There is no set formula with which to measure the due diligence of a salvor. . . . [T]he Court finds that RMST has satisfied the due diligence prong of the test. This case deals with one of the most famous shipwrecks in history, and . . . the archaeological preservation of the wreck itself as well as the recovered artifacts is of extreme importance to this Court. . . . [T]he TITANIC lies two-and-a-half miles below the ocean surface and the use of a manned submersible is required to reach it. . . . [T]he cost of financing an expedition to the wreck site may be exorbitant and result in a slow recovery of artifacts. . . . [F]ailure of RMST to dive in 1995 does not by itself indicate a lack of diligence on its part. Weather conditions in the North Atlantic Ocean

permit expeditions only within a three month weather window. . . . [T]he salvor has failed to salve for one diving season and is planning an expedition during the next weather window. . . . [S]alvors may be temporarily absent from the wreck site; RMST's temporary absence from the wreck site . . . does not indicate a lack of dominion over the wreck. . . . RMST's salvage activities are reasonable in the circumstances. RMST and its predecessors have organized expeditions in 1987, 1993, and 1994 . . . [T]he Court should compare both the salvor's representations as to its plans and the Court's expectations at the time the salvor was given exclusive rights with its actual accomplishments. . . . [T]he Court used its discretion to grant RMST salvor-in-possession rights because it believed that granting exclusive rights would lead to the actual salvaging of the TITANIC and the use of the recovered artifacts in the public interest and . . . would prevent a destructive "free-for-all" looting of the historical vessel. . . . RMST has been an [sic] guardian of the . . . artifacts: it has recovered thousands of artifacts from the wreck site, has hired a qualified conservator to actively conserve and preserve artifacts, and has organized exhibitions . . .

RMST must next establish that its salvage operations are ongoing. The evaluation of whether a salvor's operations are "ongoing" focuses not only on past operations, but also on present intentions . . . [I]t is clear that RMST's present intention is to continue to salvage the wreck site. RMST has successfully recovered numerous artifacts in the past and has stated its intention to continue to do so. It has a charter agreement with IFREMER to dive in August of this year. . . . RMST's temporary absence from the wreck site in conjunction with its intention to return is not sufficient to support a finding that RMST has abandoned its salvage operations. . . . RMST's on-shore activities . . . also indicate that RMST is still committed to the salvaging of the TITANIC. . . .

RMST must also demonstrate that its efforts are clothed with a prospect of success. RMST and its predecessor in interest have made three successful expeditions to the TITANIC . . . The only real question . . . is whether RMST has the financial capabilities to finance further salvage operations at the site. . . . [A]lthough . . . RMST's financial condition leaves much to be desired, it has a number of sponsors and

44.1

R.M.S. TITANIC, INC. V. WRECKED AND ABANDONED VESSEL, *continued*

924 F.SUPP. 714 (E.DIST.VA NORFOLK DIV. 1996)

backers . . . RMST has the necessary contracts in place to secure both divers and equipment for the 1996 expedition . . . [T]his is a highly speculative business and, because the artifacts are being conserved and preserved for the public welfare rather than sold to the highest bidder, it is more difficult to raise the large sums of money necessary for the expeditions to the wreck site. . . . [T]he Court finds . . . a strong probability for a successful 1996 expedition . . . [T]he Court concludes that RMST should remain the sole salvor in possession of the TITANIC wreck site . . .

BUSINESS CONSIDERATIONS Some speculative ventures offer very large potential returns, but they can also be very expensive. How might a business finance a speculative venture, such as salvaging the TITANIC? How can RMST best protect its interest in the TITANIC wreck site?

ETHICAL CONSIDERATIONS If RMST lacks the necessary finances, is it ethical for it to maintain its "salvor in possession" status? What is RMST's ethical perspective? What is Joslyn's ethical perspective?

PROTECTION OF PERSONAL PROPERTY

If an owner of personal property fails to protect the property adequately, it may be taken by someone else. Sometimes this taking is legal, but often it is not. In either case, the owner will suffer a temporary or permanent loss. To protect against such a loss, the owner should be aware of the means—legal or illegal—by which property may be taken, including conversion, escheat, unclaimed property statute, judicial sale, and mortgage foreclosure or repossession of property. The owner should also note that insurance can be purchased to reduce the risk of some losses.

Conversion

Conversion occurs when one person takes the personal property of the owner. It is unauthorized and unjustified interference, whether permanent or temporary, with the owner's use and control of property. A transitory interference constitutes trespass to personal property rather than conversion. A more lengthy interference—but not necessarily a permanent one—constitutes conversion. Under the theory of conversion, the owner can sue the taker for the return of the property called *replevin* or for money to replace the property. Conversion is the tort equivalent of a number of crimes, including theft, armed robbery, embezzlement, and obtaining property by false pretenses. In a criminal proceeding, the state will protect its interest in having citizens abide by the law. In a civil proceeding, the individual will protect his or her property rights.

Conversion *can* occur when the owner of personal property voluntarily releases the property to another person, who then uses the property in a manner different from that originally authorized. For example, if the owner of an automobile leaves the vehicle with a car dealer for repairs and the dealer uses it as a demonstrator, the dealer is liable if the automobile is damaged while a prospective customer is taking it for a test drive. In a suit for conversion, the owner generally prefers to have the personal property returned and repaired, if necessary. Another option available to the owner under the laws of most states is to force the wrongdoer to keep the personal property and to pay for it. The price will be its value at the time

44.1 | FINANCE/ MANAGEMENT

CALL-IMAGE TECHNOLOGY

DESTRUCTION OF PERSONAL PROPERTY

Donna encountered a fairly serious problem at her CPA office last week. Ray Goodall, one of her clients, came to the office for an appointment to review his new business plan and tax strategy. Ray is a computer consultant who designs software systems for his clients. While waiting for Donna, Ray noticed that the office system was using an old version of a virus scan and protection system he had designed. When the secretary left the room, Ray installed the latest version of his virus scan and protection software on the system. He did this without the knowledge or permission of Donna or the secretary. Although Ray meant no harm, and in fact had only the best of intentions, there was a problem with his new software. During his installation, he erased a substantial portion of Donna's client records, which were on the hard drive. Even though a hard copy of all these records exists, a large portion of them had not yet been saved to zip disks. As a result, Donna will have to pay her secretary overtime in order to re-create the files on the computer. Donna would prefer not to sue one of her clients, but she doesn't know what she can or should do. She asks for your advice. What will you tell her?

BUSINESS CONSIDERATIONS How should a business handle a delicate situation such as the one Donna has with Ray? What should a business do to protect itself from being put into this sort of predicament?

ETHICAL CONSIDERATIONS What ethical obligation does Ray owe to Donna? Is it ethical to require employees to use a password in order to prevent non-employees or unauthorized personnel from gaining access to company computers?

the property was taken. This remedy is granted only at the election of the owner. It is not available at the request of the wrongdoer.

Escheat

When the rightful owner of property cannot be located, the property can *escheat,* or revert, to the state government. The effect of escheat is that the property is given to the government. Usually the property is in a third person's custody, and then possession is transferred to the state. The policy behind this doctrine is that the state is more deserving of the property than anyone else if the true owner cannot be found. Escheat tends to occur when a person dies and the **heirs** or relatives cannot be located. In effect, the state becomes the person's heirs. It also can occur when a person does not keep careful financial records and so forgets about small bank accounts, stocks and bonds, or other assets. Often there is an assumption that the owner has died if the owner does not contact the property holder after a period of time.

Escheat is governed by the appropriate state statute, and the rules vary from state to state. Often, escheated property becomes part of the state's general fund. For a specified period after the escheat, the rightful owner can claim the property from the state. To successfully claim the property, however, the rightful owner will need adequate proof of identity and of a right to the property. Many states have replaced all or part of their escheat laws with unclaimed property statutes, which are discussed in the next section.

Unclaimed Property Statutes

Many states have enacted unclaimed property statutes. Unclaimed property acts differ from escheat statutes. In escheat laws, title passes to the government; in unclaimed property acts, title does not transfer to the government. Unclaimed property acts provide rules about when the property is "unclaimed." The acts proscribe the following steps: (1) the holder is required to report to the state that it has unclaimed property; (2) the holder attempts to formally notify the owner; (3) the property is transferred to the state; and (4) the state once again tries to notify the owner. The state then holds the property for the owner in perpetuity.[9] The advantage of giving custody to the state is to conserve and maintain the property for the owner. Otherwise, the holder with custody of the property may assess fees and deplete the asset.[10] These fees are called *dormancy charges.* Unclaimed property acts generally place restrictions on dormancy charges.[11] The National Conference of Commissioners on Uniform State Laws (NCCUSL) proposed the Uniform Disposition of

Unclaimed Property Act (1954), which was enacted by 32 states.[12] The act was followed by the Uniform Unclaimed Property Act in 1981, which was enacted in 27 states.[13] The most recent act is the Uniform Unclaimed Property Act (1995),[14] which replaces both of the previous statutes.[15] It has been adopted by Arkansas, Kansas, Louisiana, Maine, Michigan, Montana, New Mexico, and West Virginia.[16] It states that "property is unclaimed if, for the applicable period of time . . . the apparent owner has not communicated in writing or by other means reflected in a contemporaneous record prepared by or on behalf of the holder, with the holder concerning the property or the account in which the property is held, and has not otherwise indicated an interest in the property."[17] The act is an attempt to streamline the process of dealing with unclaimed property. The NCCUSL encourages passage of the 1995 act because:

1. The state will be the custodian for unclaimed property and the property becomes available to the state as a source of revenue.[18]
2. The unclaimed property is preserved for the owners. The state is the perpetual custodian until the real owner claims the property.
3. When multiple states claim the same property, the act provides a system of priorities to resolve the conflict.
4. The periods of abandonment have been shortened. Most property will be unclaimed after five years; however, special rules apply to certain types of property.[19]
5. Collection rules and reporting procedures have been improved. Penalties for noncompliance have been increased.
6. The act provides the powers and procedures to assist and encourage interstate cooperation.
7. Uniformity among the states would benefit both the states and the owners.[20]

The federal government has also enacted an unclaimed deposits act, which was amended in 1993. In the following case, the Seventh Circuit addressed the application of the Illinois unclaimed property act.

Heirs
People who actually inherit property from the decedent.

ERISA
Federal statute regulating employee retirement programs.

Preempt
Taken over by the federal government to the exclusion of the state government.

44.2

COMMONWEALTH EDISON COMPANY V. VEGA
174 F.3D 870 (7TH CIR. 1999)[21]

FACTS Commonwealth Edison Company [Com Ed] and its defined-benefit pension plan brought this suit under **ERISA,** against the administrator of the Illinois Uniform Disposition of Unclaimed Property Act, seeking a declaration that ERISA **preempts** the Illinois statute to the extent that the statute regulates such plans. . . . Illinois seeks to apply the Uniform Act to benefits payable under Com Ed's pension plan that are not claimed by a plan beneficiary within five years. When benefits are due to a participant in the plan, the plan writes a check to the participant. Until the participant deposits or cashes the check and the check is paid by the plan through the system for clearing bank transactions, the money due the participants remains in the plan's coffers. It is placed in a separate account as soon as the check is written, but if the check isn't cashed within a year the money is retransferred to the general account and is available to pay other participants. Com Ed does not and could not (without adverse tax consequences) impose a deadline on when the beneficiary may cash his check. It could be five, or ten, or even more than ten years after the check was written. All this time the plan will have the use of the money due the beneficiary. Were the plan to be terminated, the administrator would have a legal duty to search and make provision for missing beneficiaries. But until then, the plan's only duty of search is whatever is

continued

COMMONWEALTH EDISON COMPANY V. VEGA, *continued*
174 F.3D 870 (7TH CIR. 1999)

implicit in the fiduciary obligation that ERISA imposes on plans. The Com Ed plan owes about $125,000 to beneficiaries who have not yet cashed or deposited their checks even though more than five years have passed since the checks were written. The state wants this money. The plan wants to retain it. Com Ed [also] wants the plan to retain it . . . the more money there is in the plan, the less money Com Ed will be required to contribute to it to make sure that the plan has enough to meet its obligations. The parties are . . . fighting over who gets to keep the interest on this money—the plan, and perhaps ultimately Com Ed, or the state.

ISSUE Is Illinois entitled to hold the funds from the uncashed checks?

HOLDING No. Com Ed is entitled to hold the funds as administrator of the retirement plan.

REASONING The Uniform Disposition of Unclaimed Property Act (1954), in force in about a third of the states, requires anyone in possession of intangible property that is unclaimed by its owner for seven years (five under the Illinois version of the Act) to transfer the property to the custody of the state. . . . These are not escheat statutes. The state does not acquire title to the property. It is merely a custodian. The owner can reclaim his property at any time. But not only does the state have the free use of the property unless and until the owner reclaims it; the state is not required to . . . pay any interest to a reclaiming owner. . . . In effect, the property is an interest-free loan to the state—in perpetuity if the owner never shows up to claim it.

ERISA preempts any state regulation that "relates to" an ERISA plan. The Uniform Act, although it does not refer explicitly to ERISA plans, relates to the Com Ed plan directly and substantially. Remember that until the check to the beneficiary is actually presented to the plan for payment through the banking system, and paid, the money due to the beneficiary is an asset of the plan. The state . . . wants to take a chunk of an ERISA plan's assets and put it in the state treasury. After that happens, any beneficiary of the plan who wants his benefits will have to apply to the state for them. The state becomes the plan administrator with respect to those assets. Not only does the state become the custodian of the assets, in violation of ERISA's

provisions regarding plan administration . . . ; it depletes those assets, by taking the interest that accrues on them. If the ERISA plan entitled a beneficiary to interest for the period between when benefits were due him and when he actually collected them, the state would actually be reducing his ERISA benefits. Even if the plan does not provide for interest, as Com Ed's does not, the state would still be reducing the plan's assets. . . . The Act is the device by which the state appropriates those assets [and interest] for itself. It . . . [subjects] the plan to the varying laws of the different states. Participants in the Com Ed plan are scattered over 44 states. Though there are only two basic state-law regimes governing unclaimed property (the two uniform laws), states have tended to custom-tailor whichever uniform law they have chosen to their particular needs. The consequence is numerous variations in the amount of time before the state takes over the money . . . and in the formalities for claiming the money from the state. . . .

The state reinforces this characterization of the operation of the Uniform Act when it argues that its having custody of the unclaimed benefits gives the beneficiaries more secure protection than the retention of custody by the plan would. The State of Illinois has better credit than Commonwealth Edison. And while the pension plan is funded—that is, its assets, which Com Ed cannot touch, are actuarially equivalent to its expected obligations to participants and beneficiaries, and vested benefits under a defined-benefits plan are federally insured, participants and beneficiaries are not completely protected. Actuarial projections are by definition probabilistic . . . So state custody does add a dollop of safety to unclaimed ERISA benefits, though given the State of Illinois's reputation as a late payer, the tiny increment in safety may well be offset by delay in payment and resulting loss in the interest value of the money. In any event, ERISA's preemption clause, and the case law interpreting it, make clear that a state cannot take over the operation of an ERISA plan, no matter how forcefully it argues that it can do a better job than the plan's trustees and administrators. . . .

Escheat laws determine title. If state law vests title to the state in unclaimed benefits, those benefits no longer belong to the beneficiary; they belong to the state. In fact, the state is the beneficiary. . . . This case is different because the state does not claim to have an ownership interest in unclaimed benefits. It

44.2

COMMONWEALTH EDISON COMPANY V. VEGA, *continued*
174 F.3D 870 (7TH CIR. 1999)

doesn't want to step into the shoes of the beneficiary; it wants to step into the plan's shoes. That is precisely what ERISA bars. . . .

BUSINESS CONSIDERATIONS What can a business do to reduce the likelihood that property in its possession will be transferred to the state under

unclaimed property statutes or escheat statutes? Was it advantageous to Commonwealth Edison and the trustees to retain the property? Why or why not?

ETHICAL CONSIDERATIONS What is the ethical perspective of the states' unclaimed property statutes? Is it ethical for the state to claim possession of the beneficiaries' monies?

Judicial Sale

When a person loses a civil lawsuit, the court may order that person to make payment to the other party. This payment is called a *judgment,* and the person entitled to payment is a *judgment creditor.* If the person does not make the required payment, additional action may be necessary. This action commonly consists of an execution of judgment. The person who is entitled to payment procures a writ of execution from the clerk of court's office. With this writ, the sheriff can seize the debtor's property and sell it. This is called a *judicial sale* or a *sheriff's sale.*

After reimbursing the costs of the sheriff's office in seizing this asset, selling it, and executing on it, the remaining money is then given to the judgment creditor to satisfy the judgment. If the receipts exceed the expenses and the judgment, the excess is generally transferred to the property owner. However, the treatment of this excess is governed by state law and by the type of judgment. Notices of judicial sales are often included with other legal notices in the newspaper. A purchaser at a judicial sale buys the rights that the seller (the sheriff) had to sell. The sheriff's office generally does not warrant (promise) that it is entitled to sell the property. In addition, the true owner *may* have a limited period within which he or she may redeem the property, even if it is in the hands of a third-party purchaser. State law governs the amount of money that would be owed to the third party.

Repossession of Property

A lender who wants to protect an interest in a loan may create a security interest in some collateral. If the lender follows the requirements for creating and perfecting a security interest, the lender will have a security interest in the property. Security interests are discussed in detail in Chapters 26 and 27. If the borrower does not repay the loan under the terms of the contract, the lender can repossess (retake) the property. Usually the lender prefers to have cash and, thus, will sell the collateral. If the collateral is real estate, the loan is called a *mortgage,* and taking possession of the property is called a *mortgage foreclosure.* A person who buys repossessed property or foreclosed property buys only the seller's legal interest. The purchaser may lose the property if the foreclosure or repossession was wrongful.

BAILMENTS OF PERSONAL PROPERTY

A *bailment* arises when a person delivers custody of personal property to someone else. The *bailor* is the owner of the property, and the *bailee* is the one who has possession of (but not title to) the property. Whenever an owner allows another person to have custody of the owner's personal property, a bailment exists. It is understood that the bailee is to use the property in a specific way. For example, if the attendants of a parking garage drive a customer's car for any purpose other than parking or safeguarding it, they breach their duty as bailees. It is further understood that the bailee is to return the property at the end of the bailment.

If the bailee is giving up consideration, a contract also exists. If Elizabeth rents a car from Zeta Car Rental Company, a bailment relationship exists. Elizabeth is the bailee, and Zeta Car Rental Company is the bailor. Their relationship will be governed by *both* the rules of bailments and the rules of contracts. However, a contract is not a requirement for a bailment. A bailment can occur gratuitously. All the following elements are necessary for a bailment:

1. The bailor must retain title.
2. The possession of the property must be delivered to the bailee.
3. The bailee must accept possession.
4. The bailee must have possession of the property for a specific purpose and must have temporary control of the property.
5. The parties must intend that the property will be returned to the bailor unless the bailor directs that the property be delivered to another person.

A bailment is not a sale of personal property. A sale involves a transfer of title and requires an exchange of consideration. A permanent change of possession occurs with the sale. It is not always easy to recognize whether a situation is a bailment. A particularly controversial question is whether parking in a garage constitutes a bailment or the rental of a space to park a car. Generally, the question is resolved by examining whether the driver has relinquished control over the car. If the driver retains control of the vehicle by driving into a self-service parking lot, parking the car, locking it, and removing the keys, courts will decide that there was a license of space. At the other extreme, if a person drives to a hotel where an attendant parks the car, keeps the keys, and gives the driver a claim check, there is a bailment. Transfer of possession of the car is essential. However, courts have held that the *keys* do not necessarily have to be surrendered.

Bailee's Duty of Care

Disputes often arise when the property is damaged while in the hands of the bailee. In a lawsuit, the issue concerns whether or not the bailee took proper care of the property. The answer will depend on provisions in local statutes, the language of any bailment contract, and the type of bailment. In the following case, the court discussed the bailor's claim that the bailee was responsible for damage to its property.

44.3

HARTFORD FIRE INSURANCE COMPANY V. B. BARKS & SONS, INC.

1999 U.S. DIST. LEXIS 7733 (E.DIST.PA. 1999)

FACTS . . . Barks is a corporation, which is in the business of freezing and maintaining perishable food items in its refrigerated warehouse for its customers. . . . In the fall of 1996, Ocean Spray . . . stored cranberries . . . in Barks' warehouse. During the 1996 cranberry season, the temperatures inside Barks' warehouse allegedly increased. Ocean Spray . . . subsequently notified Barks of claims for . . . spoilage losses suffered as a result of the alleged elevated temperature inside Barks' warehouse. Barks has sought indemnity from Hartford for the claims of Ocean Spray . . . for food spoilage pursuant to its commercial general liability policy and its commercial inland marine policy. [The claim against Hartford based on the insurance policies is part of this lawsuit.] . . . Hartford employed an investigator, Otis Wright, to examine the Barks warehouse. . . . Wright concluded that the temperature inside Barks' warehouse increased because the heat emitted from the large quantity of cranberries being stored inside the warehouse exceeded the capacity of the refrigeration system.

. . . On July 28, 1998, Ocean Spray filed a cross-claim against Barks, alleging that its cranberries were damaged while being stored at Barks' warehouse during the fall of 1996 because of high temperatures, which were the result of the breakdown or failure of Barks' refrigeration equipment. . . .

ISSUE Is Ocean Spray entitled to summary judgment on its bailment and/or negligence claims?

HOLDING No. Ocean Spray is not entitled to a judgment as a matter of law since there are a number of material facts to be resolved.

REASONING Summary judgment is appropriate "if the pleadings, depositions, answers to interrogatories, and admissions on file, together with the affidavits . . . show that there is no genuine issue as to any material fact and that the moving party is entitled to a judgment as a matter of law." . . . Personal property . . . generally means "all property other than real estate." . . . (Pennsylvania Landlord–Tenant Act defines agricultural crops, whether harvested or growing, as personal property). . . .

Ocean Spray is seeking compensation for spoilage to its cranberries, which were being stored at defendant Barks' warehouse in September of 1996 through June of 1997. Ocean Spray filed a . . . claim against Barks . . . setting forth counts for breach for [sic] bailment agreement and negligence.

Ocean Spray contends that Barks breached its bailment agreement with Ocean Spray as a matter of law and, therefore, judgment should be entered against Barks and in favor of Ocean Spray. Bailment involves "delivery of personalty for the accomplishment of some purpose . . . that after the purpose has been fulfilled, it shall be redelivered to the person who delivered it, otherwise dealt with according to his directions or kept until he re-claims it." A cause of action for breach of a bailment agreement involves a shifting burden of proof. First, Ocean Spray, as bailor, must put forth evidence of a prima facie case: that it delivered personalty to Barks, the bailee; that it made a demand for return of the property; and the bailee failed to return the property, or returned it in damaged condition. Once the prima facie case is met, Barks, the bailee, must come forward with evidence "accounting for the loss." If the bailee fails to do so, it is liable for the loss because it is assumed the bailee failed to exercise reasonable care required by the agreement. If the bailee successfully puts forth "evidence showing that the personalty was lost and the manner in which it was lost, and the evidence does not disclose a lack of due care on his part, then the burden of proof again shifts to the bailor who must prove negligence on the part of the bailee."

Although not clearly spelled out, case law indicates the bailee's burden of "accounting for the loss" encompasses a showing the bailee was not negligent and/or his actions were not the cause of the loss. . . . Accordingly, on Ocean Spray's bailment claim, Barks bears an initial burden of putting forth evidence it was not negligent and/or that it did not cause the damage to Ocean Spray's cranberries. Ocean Spray satisfies the prima facie case. No dispute exists regarding whether Ocean Spray's cranberries were in Barks' care, that Ocean Spray made a demand for their return, and the cranberries were damaged. Also no dispute exists that the cranberries were damaged by elevated temperatures. . . . Barks . . . produced evidence of Ocean Spray's own negligence in causing the spoilage of the cranberries. Evidence shows that

continued

44.3

HARTFORD FIRE INSURANCE COMPANY V. B. BARKS & SONS, INC., *continued*

1999 U.S. DIST. LEXIS 7733 (E.DIST.PA. 1999)

Ocean Spray delivered cranberries to Barks straight from the bog. The cranberries were moist and warm when they arrived on the dock at Barks, two conditions that made it more difficult to bring down the temperature of the cranberries in the freezer. Ocean Spray did not take precautions by shipping its cranberries in refrigerated tractor-trailers.

Ocean Spray has put forth evidence that the refrigeration unit at Barks' warehouse experienced failures during the relevant time. . . . Ocean Spray contends that Barks' negligence caused the elevated temperatures, which resulted in the spoiled cranberries. This issue of comparative negligence of Ocean Spray shifts the burden back to Ocean Spray to demonstrate that it was Barks' negligence, and not Ocean Spray's own negligence, that caused the spoilage of the cranberries. . . . No issue exists as to whether the cranberries were stored at Barks' facility and then spoiled. Many factual disputes exists as to why the cranberries spoiled. Under these circumstances, issues of material fact exist as to whether a bailment was breached. Accordingly, Ocean Spray's motion for partial summary judgment on its breach of bailment . . .claim is denied.

In order to sustain a cause of action in negligence, a plaintiff must show that: (1) defendant owed them a duty of care; (2) defendant breached that duty; (3) a causal link existed between the breach of duty and plaintiff's injury and harm; and (4) damages. Pennsylvania courts hold that the existence of a duty "'is predicated on the relationship existing between the parties at the relevant time.'" . . . [T]he Court cannot find as a matter of law that Barks breached its duty of care to Ocean Spray. Accordingly, Ocean Spray's motion for partial summary judgment on its negligence claim is denied. . . .

BUSINESS CONSIDERATIONS What could the bailor or bailee have done to reduce the likelihood of loss in this case? What could a storage facility do to reduce the amount of claims of loss?

ETHICAL CONSIDERATIONS Would it be ethical for Ocean Spray to deliver wet, warm cranberries to the facility? Why or why not? What is Ocean Spray's ethical perspective?

Classifications of Bailments

Bailments are divided into types based on who benefits from the bailment relationship. The classification affects the bailee's obligation and his or her liability if any damage occurs to the property. This responsibility is summarized in Exhibit 44.1.

Bailor Benefit Bailments. When the bailment is established solely to benefit the bailor, the bailee will be responsible only for gross negligence in caring for the property. An example of a bailor benefit bailment is when the owner leaves a laptop computer with a friend until the owner returns after lunch. What is

E X H I B I T   44.1 | **The Responsibility of the Bailee**

Type of Bailment	Who Will Benefit	The Bailee Will Be Liable for . . .
Bailor benefit	Bailor (owner)	Gross negligence
Mutual benefit	Bailor and bailee	Ordinary negligence
Bailee benefit	Bailee (possessor)	Slight negligence

considered to be negligence in court will depend on the circumstances and the evidence presented.

Mutual Benefit Bailments. When a bailment is established for the benefit of both the bailor and the bailee, a *mutual benefit bailment* exists. Both parties expect to gain from the bailment relationship. In such bailments, the bailee is responsible for ordinary negligence. A mutual benefit bailment occurs, for example, when the owner of a suit takes it to a dry-cleaning establishment. The owner will benefit by having the suit cleaned and pressed. The dry cleaner will benefit because it is going to be paid. The dry cleaner will be responsible if it carelessly cleans the suit in cleaning fluid that is too hot and causes the suit to shrink. *Hartford Fire Insurance Company v. B. Barks & Sons, Inc.* (Case 44.3) involved a mutual benefit bailment.

Bailee Benefit Bailments. When a bailment is established solely for the benefit of the bailee, a *bailee benefit bailment* exists. The bailee will be responsible for slight negligence in caring for the property. When the bailor loans a car to a fraternity brother to drive to a job interview, a bailee benefit bailment occurs.

Limitations on a Bailee's Liability

Some states and localities have statutes or ordinances that provide maximum limits on the liability of the bailee in certain types of bailments.

If the bailment is based on a contract, the terms of the contract may increase or decrease the liability of the bailee. A *quasi-public bailee* offers services to the public. For example, he or she may operate a common carrier, a garage, a hotel, or a public parking lot. A quasi-public bailee generally will not be permitted to limit his or her liability contractually unless specifically permitted to do so by statute. Even when a statute permits a bailee to restrict liability, any limitation on liability must be reasonable.

A private bailee can restrict his or her liability under the terms of the agreement *if* this restriction does not conflict with the real purpose of the contract between the bailee and the bailor. The bailee must inform the bailor of any limitation on the bailee's liability. Most courts hold that a printed ticket stub or a posted notice on the premises does not adequately inform the bailor of the limitations *unless* the bailor's attention is directed to the sign or the ticket stub.

Termination of a Bailment

A bailment terminates at the end of the period that the parties specify or when a specified condition occurs. If

44.2 | MANUFACTURING/ MANAGEMENT

SHOULD CIT PURCHASE INSURANCE ON LEASED PRODUCTION EQUIPMENT?

CIT leases some of its production equipment from a large electronics firm. This equipment is extremely expensive and relatively fragile. Tom is concerned that the firm will be responsible for any damage to it. He feels that CIT should procure insurance to protect the firm from liability in the event the equipment is damaged. Dan, however, insists that the electronics firm is responsible for maintenance and bears the risk of loss for any damage done to the equipment. He asserts that, since the equipment was leased for industrial use, the electronics firm alone is responsible. They ask you which of their positions is correct. What will you tell them?

BUSINESS CONSIDERATIONS The leasing of equipment creates a bailment, but it also entails a contract for the lease of goods, governed by Article 2A of the UCC. Does Article 2A change the common law treatment of bailments in this sort of situation? Does the lessor or the lessee bear the risk of loss if leased equipment is damaged during the lease, presuming that the equipment is being used by the parties in the manner expected?
ETHICAL CONSIDERATIONS From an ethical perspective, and without regard to who is legally responsible for risk of loss, how should CIT behave in this situation? Is it ethical to underinsure a piece of equipment if the insuring party knows that the other party bears the risk of loss legally? Is it ethical to overinsure a piece of equipment in the hope that the insurer will not notice the overinsurance in the event of a loss?

44.3 | MANAGEMENT

DISCLAIMERS TO AVOID LIABILITY

Dan was in Chicago recently to meet with a potential client. He drove his rental car to a downtown parking garage in which the parking attendants park the cars and retain the keys. Dan decided he would not need his overcoat, so he left it on the passenger seat of the car. He handed the attendant the keys to the car, took his claim check, and left for his appointment. When Dan returned later that day to reclaim the car, he discovered that his overcoat was missing. When Dan complained to the attendants, they denied any knowledge of the loss, and they also pointed to the back of the claim check. The back of the ticket contained the following clause: "The management is not responsible for any personal property or electronic devices left in parked cars. The customer assumes any and all risk of loss for items left in the vehicle."

Dan does not believe that the garage should be able to avoid liability in this manner. He asks you for advice. What will you tell him?

BUSINESS CONSIDERATIONS Is it a good business practice for a firm to use exculpatory clauses, especially those placed on the back of "claim checks," in an effort to avoid liability? What could/should the parking garage do to reduce its customers' potential for loss? What could/should the customers do to reduce their potential for loss?

ETHICAL CONSIDERATIONS Is it ethical for a business to include exculpatory clauses on the back of "claim checks"? Is it ethical for a business to attempt to deny liability for the losses suffered by its customers? Is it ethical for the customers to blame the business for losses caused by the carelessness of the customers?

---

the bailment was for an indefinite time, it may be terminated at the will of either the bailor or the bailee. A bailment terminates when the purpose or performance of the bailment has been completed. If either party causes a material breach of the bailment relationship, the victim can terminate the bailment, and the wrongdoer will be liable for any damages he or she caused. The bailment terminates if the bailed property is destroyed or becomes unfit or unsuitable for the purpose of the bailment. Generally, a bailment also terminates by operation of law if death, insanity, or bankruptcy of either party makes performance by the bailee impossible.

Bailee's Duty to Return the Property

A bailee has a general duty to return the bailor's property to the bailor; however, there are exceptions to this rule. The bailee is not liable to the bailor if the property is lost, destroyed, or stolen through no fault of the bailee. The bailee is not liable if the property is taken away by legal process such as an attachment for a sheriff's sale. The bailee is not liable if the property is claimed by someone who has a better legal right to possession than the bailor has.

Sometimes a bailee has a duty to return the property to someone other than the bailor. For example, there may be a duty to "return" the property to a transferee who has bought the property from the bailor. A common business practice involves transferring property to a warehouse or common carrier that has an obligation to hold this property and then transfer it to a purchaser who presents a receipt or bill of lading.

The bailee does not have to return the property if the bailee has a lien on it. Many states have statutes that allow the bailee to keep the property in his or her possession until the bailor pays for the bailment; this is called a *possessory lien*. If the bailor fails to make payment, most statutes permit the bailee to sell the property. A common type of bailee's lien is a mechanic's lien, which arises when services have been performed on personal property. For example, if a garage repairs an automobile and the owner does not have the money to pay for the repairs, the garage can keep the automobile until the owner does pay. In most cases, the bailee loses the lien if the bailee willingly releases the goods to the bailor. An example would be if the bailor came to reclaim the property and the bailee released it without receiving payment. Generally, there is no bailee's lien if the bailor and bailee agree at the beginning that the bailor is going to pay on credit.

RESOURCES FOR BUSINESS LAW STUDENTS

NAME	RESOURCES	WEB ADDRESS
Internal Revenue Service	The Internal Revenue Service, and its publication, the *Digital Daily*, provide tax advice and information on a variety of issues, including personal property issues.	**http://www.irs.ustreas.gov/**
U.S. Internal Revenue Code—26 USC	The Legal Information Institute, maintained by the Cornell Law School, includes the U.S. Internal Revenue Code, 26 USC, in a hypertext and searchable format.	**http://www4.law.cornell.edu/uscode/26/**
Legal Information Institute (LII)—Estate and gift tax law materials	The LII provides an overview of estate and gift tax law, including relevant sections from the U.S. Code and Code of Federal Regulation, court cases, and links.	**http://wwwsecure.law.cornell.edu/topics/estate_gift_tax.html**

SUMMARY

Personal property is classified as tangible or intangible property based on its physical characteristics. Discussions of legal interests in property revolve around ownership rights, title, and possession. Often, one business has title to property, but another business has possession. Title to personal property can be acquired by original possession, by voluntary transfer from the owner to the transferee, or by involuntary transfer from the owner. A transferee of personal property generally will not acquire any better title than the transferor had. This is true even though the transferee thought that the transferor had good title. This limitation on title is especially important in judicial sales, sales of repossessed property, conversion, confusion, and accession.

When property is lost, the owner does not know where the property is. The finder is entitled to lost property; the only one with a superior claim is the true owner. Mislaid property was set down; however, the owner failed to pick it up before he or she left. The finder of mislaid property must leave the personalty with the owner or manager of the premises. The true owner may remember where the property is and return to retrieve it. The owner of the premises is entitled to hold the mislaid property. The finder has good title to the mislaid property; only the true owner has a superior claim.

Ownership of property may escheat to the state when a custodian of property cannot locate the owner. A more modern approach is unclaimed property statutes. Under these statutes, title does not pass to the state; when a custodian cannot locate the owner, possession of the property may pass to the state. The true owner can claim the property at any time by following the state claim procedures.

A bailment occurs when the owner/bailor transfers the possession of personal property to someone else, the bailee. The owner keeps title. After the purpose of the bailment has been completed, generally possession is returned to the owner. Many businesses, such as dry cleaners and repair shops, basically deal in bailment relationships. The bailee's obligation is influenced by any contract between the bailee and the bailor. The bailee's duty of care is affected by whether it is a bailor benefit bailment, a mutual benefit bailment, or a bailee benefit bailment relationship.

DISCUSSION QUESTIONS

1. What are the differences between title and possession?
2. What happens if the donor of a gift *causa mortis* dies but not from the expected cause? Who is likely to complain in such a situation?
3. James takes a piece of rough turquoise stone, polishes it, and sets it in a silver setting in a necklace. James reasonably believes that he found the stone on public land. In reality, he had found it on private land, where the owner had mined it and placed it in a pile for polishing. Who owns the jewelry and why? What are the legal rights of the parties?
4. Is an umbrella on a desk likely to be lost or mislaid property? Why? If the umbrella is on the floor, is it likely to be lost or mislaid property? Why?
5. Ric visits José's Mexican Restaurant for lunch and hangs his coat on the coat rack provided for that purpose. When he leaves, Ric walks out and leaves his coat. Kelly finds it. Who is entitled to title of the coat? Who is entitled to possession of the coat?

6. Twice a year the city of Cedarville has a large trash pickup. At this time, the trash collectors will take non-hazardous waste items they would normally refuse. Charlotte hauls an old washing machine to the curb and adds it to her pile of other debris. Dennis drives by and picks up her washing machine, puts it in his truck, and drives away. Who legally owns the washing machine and why?
7. Define *escheat*. What is its purpose? How do escheat statutes differ from unclaimed property statutes?
8. What are the requirements for a bailment relationship?
9. What legal rights does a bailor have when a bailee has damaged the property or allowed someone else to damage it?
10. CIT is considering purchasing a fleet of cars for key employees. CIT would purchase four vehicles and assign them to employees who could operate them for both business and personal use. What are the advantages and disadvantages of such a plan? Why?

CASE PROBLEMS AND WRITING ASSIGNMENTS

1. Rodger Lindh asked Janis Surman to marry him on 24 August 1993. Janis accepted, and Rodger gave her a diamond engagement ring worth approximately $21,000. Rodger became unsure about the relationship and requested the return of the ring in October 1993. The couple reconciled, and Rodger returned the ring to Janis. Janis wore the ring. She also began to make wedding plans. On 20 March 1994, Rodger unexpectedly told Janis that he no longer loved her, and he broke their engagement. Rodger was unable or unwilling to explain his change of heart. He would not agree to counseling. Rodger asked Janis to return the ring, but she refused. Rodger filed a civil action to recover the ring or its value. Should the court require Janis to return the diamond engagement ring? Is this a conditional gift? Is it subject to Janis's agreement to marry Rodger, or is it subject to the actual marriage itself? [See *Lindh v. Surman*, 702 A.2d 560, (Pa.Super. 1997), Petition for Allowance of Appeal Granted by the Supreme Court at 1998 Pa. LEXIS 1157 (Pa. 1998).]

2. John F. Kennedy, Jr.'s private aircraft, went down in the Atlantic Ocean on 16 July 1999. He was flying to

Martha's Vineyard to attend a wedding. His wife and sister-in-law were also in the plane. Around 19 July 1999, contents of the plane began washing ashore. Who owns these items? If the plane can be located and salvaged, who would own the plane? Why? [See Erica Noonan, "Hope of Survivors Runs Out," *The Fresno Bee* (19 July 1999), pp. A1, A14; David Usborne, "Kennedy Alarm Delayed for Hours After Control Tower Was Ignored," *The Independent* (London), (21 July 1999), p. 2; Matthew Brelis, "Some Defend Handling of First Call on Flight Delay; The Kennedy Plane Crash/FAA Procedures," *The Boston Globe* (21 July 1999), p. A12; Jack Sullivan, "Tragedy at Sea, NTSB to Review Tape of Initial Call About JFK's Plane," *The Boston Herald* (21 July 1999), p. 12.]

3. Joyce Ferrucci was a guest at the Showboat Hotel & Casino in Atlantic City, New Jersey. While a guest at the hotel, she stayed in room 1104. She did not have exclusive possession and control of the room. The defendant's agents, servants, and employees would enter rooms for cleaning, maintenance, noise complaints, and security matters. Ferrucci had the right to

occupy room 1104 for a limited time subject to the rules and procedures of the hotel. When moving past the bed in the room, Ferrucci took approximately four steps before her body twisted and she fell over the corner of the bed. Ferrucci claims the bed was defective and caused her to fall. Ferrucci claims the hotel owner engages in the bailment of products, including furniture and beds in hotel rooms, to guests of their hotel. She contends that the hotel retained title, delivered furniture, including the bed, to Ferrucci for a particular purpose, creating a bailment. Did the hotel create a bailment? Why or why not? [See *Ferrucci* v. *Atlantic City Showboat, Inc.,* 51 F.Supp. 2d 129 (Dist. of Conn. 1999).]

4. Ronald Numbers worked as a taxi driver for Suburban Taxi Corporation. From July 1992 until December 1992, Numbers operated his own cab. In December, the cab needed repairs, so Numbers left it on Suburban's lot for those repairs. Suburban required a $300 deposit before the repairs would be started. Numbers did not deposit this amount. When Numbers noticed his cab had been removed, he was informed that the cab had been moved to improve security. In the interim, Numbers leased a cab from Suburban. The leased cab was damaged the first week in a traffic accident. Suburban asked Numbers to pay $950 into a "damage" account for the repair of the leased taxi; Numbers paid some money into the "damage" account but not the full amount. On 23 March 1993, Numbers requested the return of his own cab. Suburban refused, stating that it would not return Numbers's cab until he paid for the damages to the leased vehicle. Numbers never received possession of his cab. Was Suburban the bailee of Numbers's cab? Why? Was Suburban justified in keeping possession of Numbers's cab? Why? [See *Numbers* v. *Suburban Taxi Corp.,* 1995 Minn.App. LEXIS 727 (Minn.App. 1995) (Unpublished opinion).]

5. William Seebold, president of Eagle Boats, was contacted by *Trailer Boats,* a boating magazine, about doing a feature article on a motorboat manufactured by Eagle and including pictures taken on Grand Lake in Oklahoma. At the time of the inquiry, a boat owned by Hoppies Village Marina (Hoppies) was in the Eagle Boat repair facility undergoing minor paint repairs. This boat was a 1991 Seebold Eagle 265 Limited Edition motorboat with a 1990 Buccaneer Deluxe Tri-Axle trailer. This boat is considered "to be the 'cadillac' of motorboats in its class." Seebold contacted Paul Hopkins, the owner of Hoppies, and Michael Atkinson, its sales manager. Hopkins agreed to loan this boat and trailer to Eagle Boats, Ltd., and William See-

bold, president of Eagle Boats. It was also agreed that the magazine article would include information about the boat, Eagle Boats, Ltd., and Hoppies. Seebold would transport the boat to Oklahoma and then return it to Hoppies using Hoppies's trailer.

The night before the magazine demonstration, Seebold parked the boat, trailer, and Eagle's truck in the parking lot of a motel. They were parked near the roadway across the parking lot from the one dusk-to-dawn light. The trailer did not have a locking device that would lock it onto the truck, which was locked. No one was left to guard the boat, and it was not locked in any manner. Although other boats and trailers were in the parking lot, this was the most expensive boat there. It was also the closest to the road. Both the boat and trailer were stolen between 11:00 P.M. and about 5:00 A.M. Seebold offered evidence that failure to use locks is common in the industry. He testified that at his facility, he simply chains the boats together and locks the chain. He also produced sworn statements by Hopkins and Atkinson that it is common not to use locking devices. Seebold admitted that he could have put a chain around the boat and trailer and locked it to the truck; he did not have a chain with him. Suit was filed by a group of insurance underwriters that had issued a policy on this boat, had paid Hoppies for its losses, and was subrogee of its claim against the defendants. Did the bailee fail to exercise proper care over the bailed property? [See *Institute of London* v. *Eagle Boats, Ltd.,* 918 F.Supp. 297 (E.D.Mo. 1996).]

6. **BUSINESS APPLICATION CASE** On receiving a shipping order, Delta obtained a cargo container from Imparca Lines, a commercial shipper. The cargo container was loaded and sealed by Delta and then delivered into the possession of Imparca by Delta's agent. The container was placed on a vessel chartered by Imparca, and Imparca issued a clean bill of lading. The bill of lading indicated that the carrier, Imparca, discharged its duties when it delivered the container into the custody of government authorities at the named port, as required by the laws of the foreign port. The 20-foot cargo container was placed on the dock in Puerto Cabello in the custody of the Instituto Nacional de Puertos (INP). INP was responsible for the operation of this seaport, including stevedoring, warehousing, receiving, and delivering cargo. The goods subsequently disappeared, and the consignee sought recourse from Imparca. Should the carrier be responsible for the disappearance of the goods? Why? [See *Allstate Ins. Co.* v. *Imparca Lines,* 646 F.2d 166 (5th Cir. 1981).]

7. **ETHICAL APPLICATION CASE** John Moore was treated by Dr. David Golde at the UCLA Medical Center. John had hairy-cell leukemia. Dr. Golde discovered that John's blood contained substances that were valuable in medical research. In October 1967, John's spleen was removed at the recommendation of Dr. Golde. Prior to the surgery, Dr. Golde made arrangements to take portions of John's spleen to a separate research unit. Dr. Golde also arranged to draw John's blood when John visited the UCLA Medical Center. Dr. Golde did not inform John of his plan to conduct research or obtain John's permission. Dr. Golde established a cell line from John's blood, and the Regents of the University of California acquired a patent on the cell line. Dr. Golde arranged for the commercial development of the cell line. As part of the arrangement, Genetics Institute agreed to pay Dr. Golde and the Regents at least $330,000 over three years and to give Dr. Golde 75,000 shares of its stock. Did Dr. Golde and/or the Regents convert John's property? Why? Did Dr. Golde fail to obtain informed consent or violate his fiduciary duty? Why? What should Dr. Golde, the Regents, and Genetics Institute have done? What ethical issues are raised in this case? [See *Moore* v. *The Regents of the University of California*, 793 P.2d 479 (Cal. 1990).]

8. **CRITICAL THINKING CASE** From 1990 through 1992, the Federal Deposit Insurance Corporation (FDIC) was appointed as the receiver for more than 30 banks principally located or doing business in Massachusetts. Massachusetts claimed title to some of the insurance on deposits in these banks under its abandoned property statute, Mass. Gen. L. ch. 200A. It contended that the deposit insurance escheated to the state. The statute indicated that escheat should occur when the named depositors failed to communicate with their banks over an extended period of time. Some of the claims arose before the banks' failures, and some arose thereafter. Should the Massachusetts statute or the federal Unclaimed Deposits Amendments Act of 1993, 107 Stat. 220, govern? Why? [See *Massachusetts* v. *FDIC*, 47 F.3d 456 (1st Cir. 1995).]

NOTES

1. The classic case on this subject is *Pierson* v. *Post*, 3 Cai.R. 175 (N.Y. 1805).
2. See *Lindh* v. *Surman*, 702 A.2d 560 (Pa.Super. 1997), Petition for Allowance of Appeal Granted by the Supreme Court at 1998 Pa. LEXIS 1157 (Pa. 1998).
3. Ibid.
4. Ibid.
5. "North Alabama Store for Who-Knows-What Drawing National Attention," *The Associated Press State & Local Wire* (8 March 1999), PM Cycle.
6. Ibid.
7. "Sightings," *The Times-Picayune* (22 April 1999), p. E2; "Their Loss Could Be Your Find," *The News and Observer* (Raleigh, NC) (13 June 1999), p. H2; Note 5, op. cit.
8. There have been numerous lawsuits since the wreck of the Titanic was discovered. This case is commonly referred to as *Titanic I*. In *Titanic II*, more properly referred to as *R.M.S. Titanic, Inc.* v. *The Wrecked & Abandoned Vessel*, 9 F.Supp. 2d 624 (E.Dist. VA Norfolk Div. 1998), the court dealt with jurisdictional issues that arise since the wreck lies in international waters. That decision was affirmed in part, reversed in part, and remanded in *R.M.S. Titanic, Inc.* v. *Haver*, 171 F.3d 943 (4th Cir. 1999). The appellate court expressed concerns about this court decision that only the salvor-in-possession could view or photograph the wreck.
9. "Uniform Unclaimed Property Act (1995), A Summary," NCCUSL web site, http://www.nccusl.org/ uniformact_summaries/uniformacts-s-uupa 1995.htm.
10. "Why Every State Should Adopt the Uniform Unclaimed Property Act (1995)," NCCUSL web site, http://www.nccusl.org/uniformact_why/ uniformacts-why-uupa.htm.
11. http://www.nccusl.org/uniformact_summaries/ uniformacts-s-uupa1995.htm.
12. http://www.nccusl.org/uniformact_why/ uniformacts-why-uupa.htm.
13. Ibid.
14. "A Few Facts About the Uniform Unclaimed Property Act (1995)," NCCUSL web site, http://www.nccusl. org/uniformact_factsheets/uniformacts-fs-uupa. htm.
15. Ibid.
16. Ibid.
17. http://www.nccusl.org/uniformact_summaries/ uniformacts-s-uupa1995.htm.
18. For example, in 1994 California collected $277 million in unclaimed property; $81 million was subsequently reclaimed.
19. http://www.nccusl.org/uniformact_summaries/ uniformacts-s-uupa1995.htm.
20. http://www.nccusl.org/uniformact_why/ uniformacts-why-uupa.htm.
21. The court also addressed state immunity from suit under the Eleventh Amendment.

45

INTELLECTUAL PROPERTY, COMPUTERS, AND THE LAW

A G E N D A

CIT is a high-tech operation with much of its product development based on patent law. As a result, the family is very concerned about the protections afforded under U.S. patent law and about the effectiveness of a patent in the international arena. The family also has registered the Call-Image name as a trademark, and the firm would like to protect this trademark to the greatest extent possible. One apprehension the Kochanowskis have is that, as the first product in the field, Call-Image may become synonymous with videophones. The family members therefore question what they can do to prevent this contingency from depriving them of their trademarked name. They moreover are worried that someone will steal their ideas and duplicate their product at a lower price.

They consequently want to know how to prevent this misappropriation. These and other questions are likely to arise as you study this chapter.

Be prepared! You never know when one of the Kochanowskis will need your help or advice.

O U T L I N E

INTRODUCTION

In this chapter, we will examine the law's treatment of intellectual property, or the property that comes from the human capacity to create. The body of law that addresses intellectual property derives from a variety of common law, state, and federal statutory and nonstatutory sources. Intellectual property law encompasses several substantive legal areas: copyrights, patents, trademarks, trade secrets, and unfair competition. We will use computers as a special illustration of the importance of intellectual property to U.S. businesses and international competitors.

In the intellectual property arena, several public policies coalesce to serve two goals; these policies (1) ensure incentives to create so as to guarantee a wider array of products and services in the marketplace and (2) promote competition so as to provide public access to intellectual creations. By granting property rights (sometimes even monopolies) to creators, the law serves the first goal; and by limiting the duration of such exclusive rights and/or circumscribing the rights thereby granted so as to maximize the amount of information found in the public domain, the law facilitates the second goal. This area of the law also seeks to protect creators and businesspeople from injurious trade practices.

Through your studying of the material in this chapter, then, you will learn how this hodgepodge of disparate legal doctrines affects business. Also, you will see how the law attempts to reconcile the tension between those who, in order to protect investments or ownership rights in intellectual property, want to restrict others from the free use of this type of property, and those who, in furtherance of free markets, argue for largely unrestricted access to such information and inventions.

COPYRIGHTS

The U.S. Constitution in Article I, Section 8 authorizes Congress "to promote the progress of science and the useful arts." In conferring statutory protection on artistic works created by writers, artists, and composers, Congress as early as 1790 exercised this constitutional power. The most important of the early copyright laws, the Copyright Act of 1909, remained virtually unchanged until January 1978, when the present copyright statute, the Copyright Act of 1976, became effective. In reality, vestiges of the 1909 act remain with us, however, since it still covers works created prior to 1 January 1978. The Berne Convention Implementation Act of 1988, which became effective in March 1989, further amended the 1976 act. Under these 1988 amendments, works published after 1 March 1989 do not need a copyright notice. Hence, one first must ascertain which law governs a given copyrighted work and proceed accordingly.

Section 102 of the Copyright Act of 1976 protects any original works of authorship fixed in any tangible medium of expression now known or later developed, from which they can be perceived, reproduced, or otherwise communicated, either directly or with the aid of a machine or a device. Works of authorship include, but are not limited to, (1) literary works; (2) musical works, including any accompanying music; (3) pantomimes and choreographic works; (4) pictorial, graphic, and sculptural works; (5) motion pictures and other audiovisual works; (6) sound recordings; and (7) architectural works. Hence, copyright laws traditionally have protected *only expressions of ideas,* not the ideas themselves. Procedures, plans, methods, systems, concepts, and principles are not copyrightable, either.

The Copyright Office of the Library of Congress administers copyrights in the United States. Among other things, the Copyright Office registers copyrights; issues certificates of registration; keeps records of copyright registrations, licenses, and assignments; and oversees deposits of copyrighted materials. Unlike the Patent and Trademark Office's stringent and detailed oversight of patents and trademarks (covered later in this chapter), the Copyright Office merely determines whether applications involve copyrightable subject matter and have fulfilled all the registration requirements. In 1997, the Copyright Office registered 569,200 works.[1]

To be copyrightable, the works of authorship listed in § 102 must show originality. Courts have construed this term to involve at the very least minimal creative intellectual activity. Works of authorship moreover must be fixed in tangible form. The notes dancing in a creator's head do not become copyrightable until the songwriter puts the notes and words on paper or records the resultant melody (i.e., the creator fixes the song in a tangible medium of expression). Section 101 of the 1976 act defines a work as "fixed" in a tangible medium of expression when its embodiment in a copy or phono record, by or under the authority of the author, is sufficiently permanent to permit it to be perceived, reproduced, or otherwise communicated for a period of more than transitory duration. This provision also states that fixation can occur simultaneously with transmission; therefore, radio or television broadcasts of live sporting events fall under this copyright protection if recordings or tapes of the events are occurring concurrently with the broadcast.

Courts typically grant more limited copyright protection to useful articles (i.e., pictorial, graphic, or sculptural works). Only if the creator can show aesthetic or conceptual elements separable from the utilitarian aspects of the article will the article become copyrightable. Bicycle racks or wrought iron benches, for example, that began as pieces of sculpture are primarily utilitarian rather than aesthetic objects. Hence, the creators of these items typically cannot register them for copyright protection. This policy furthers the goal of increasing competition between useful goods and thus benefits the public more than a creator's being granted a statutory monopoly over utilitarian goods. In short, in these instances, copying benefits the public more than would insulating the item from competition.

The Copyright Office similarly will not accept applications involving typeface designs or fonts. Copyright law, however, does protect compilations of materials—for example, collective works (such as anthologies or encyclopedias) or directories, catalogs, and automated databases. But if the research involves only labor (a mere reordering or alphabetizing of materials) and very little creativity, courts treat the compilations like nonfiction, factually based works (history books or biographies) and afford little protection under the copyright laws. Derivative works—for example, a motion picture screenplay based on a novel—are copyrightable as well, as long as one has the right to use the original work and the derivative work varies substantially from the original, or the transformation involves substantial artistic skill, judgment, or labor.

The following case, *Feist Publications, Inc.* v. *Rural Telephone Service Co., Inc.* involves the Supreme Court's interpretation of some of these issues.

45.1

FEIST PUBLICATIONS, INC. V. RURAL TELEPHONE SERVICE CO., INC.
499 U.S. 340 (1991

FACTS Rural Telephone Service Company, Inc. (Rural) is a certified public utility providing telephone service to several communities in Kansas. Pursuant to state regulation, Rural publishes a typical telephone directory, consisting of white pages and yellow pages. It obtains data for the directory from subscribers, who must provide their names and addresses to obtain telephone service. Feist Publications, Inc. (Feist) is a publishing company that specializes in area-wide telephone directories covering a much larger geographic range than directories like Rural's. When Rural refused to license its white pages listings to Feist for a directory covering 11 different telephone service areas, Feist extracted the listings it needed from Rural's directory without Rural's consent. Although Feist altered many of Rural's listings, several remained identical to the listings in Rural's white pages. The district court, granting summary judgment to Rural in its copyright infringement suit, held that telephone directories are copyrightable. The court of appeals affirmed this ruling.

ISSUE Were the names, addresses, and telephone numbers that Feist had copied in compiling its telephone directory white pages copyrightable?

HOLDING No. Rural's white pages were not entitled to copyright protection. Hence, Feist's use of them did not constitute copyright infringement.

REASONING Article I, Section 8, Clause 8 of the Constitution mandates originality as a prerequisite for copyright protection. The constitutional requirement necessitates independent creation plus a modicum of creativity. Since facts do not owe their origin to an act of authorship, they are unoriginal and thus uncopyrightable. Although a compilation of facts may possess the requisite originality because the author typically chooses which facts to include, in what order to place them, and how to arrange them so that readers may use them effectively, copyright protection extends only to those components of the work that are original to the author, not to the facts themselves. This fact/expression dichotomy severely limits the scope of protection in fact-based works. The Copyright Act of 1976 and its predecessor, the Copyright Act of 1909, leave no doubt that originality—rather than effort—is the touchstone of copyright protection in directories and other fact-based works. The 1976 Act explains that copyright extends to "original works of authorship" and that there can be no copyright in facts. A compilation is not copyrightable per se but is copyrightable only if its facts have been "selected, coordinated, or arranged in such a way that the resulting work as a whole constitutes an original work of authorship." Thus, the statute envisions that some ways of selecting, coordinating, and arranging data are not sufficiently original to trigger copyright protection. Even a compilation that is copyrightable receives only limited protection, for the copyright does not extend to facts contained in the compilation.

A fundamental axiom of copyright law holds that no one can copyright facts or ideas. Given these propositions, one can see that Rural's white pages do not meet the constitutional or statutory requirements for copyright protection. While Rural has a valid copyright in the directory as a whole because it contains some original material in the yellow pages, there is nothing original in Rural's white pages. The raw data involve only uncopyrightable facts; and the way in which Rural selected, coordinated, and arranged those facts is not original in any way. Rural's selection of listings—subscribers' names, towns, and telephone numbers—therefore lacks the modicum of creativity necessary to transform mere selection into copyrightable expression. Moreover, there is nothing remotely creative about arranging names alphabetically in a white pages directory. It is an age-old practice, firmly rooted in tradition and so commonplace that it has come to be expected as a matter of course. Hence, the names, towns, and telephone numbers copied by Feist neither were original to Rural nor protected by the copyright in Rural's combined white and yellow pages directory. Because Rural's white pages lack the requisite originality, Feist's use of the listings cannot constitute infringement. The judgment of the court of appeals therefore warrants reversal.

BUSINESS CONSIDERATIONS Although the Court in this case reiterates that facts ordinarily are not copyrightable, what business interests was Rural

45.1

FEIST PUBLICATIONS, INC. V. RURAL TELEPHONE SERVICE CO., INC., *continued*
499 U.S. 340 (1991

attempting to protect when it instituted this litigation? Would refraining from suing have constituted a more efficient allocation of the firm's resources?

ETHICAL CONSIDERATIONS Had the Court decided this case solely on ethical grounds, would its holding have favored Rural? Why or why not?

Protection and Infringement

A copyright, in essence, consists of a bundle of exclusive rights that enables the copyright owner—usually the author or one to whom the author has transferred rights—to exploit a work for commercial purposes. These exclusive rights include: (1) reproducing the copyrighted work; (2) preparing derivative works (or adaptations) based on the copyrighted work; (3) distributing copies or phono records of the copyrighted work; (4) performing publicly literary, musical, dramatic, and choreographic works, pantomimes, and motion pictures or audiovisual works; and (5) displaying publicly the works themselves or individual images of the works mentioned in (4) as well as pictorial, graphic, or sculptural works.

Therefore, to prove an infringement of a copyrighted work, the owner typically must show by circumstantial evidence (since the existence of direct evidence would be rare) that the defendant had access to the copyrighted work and that the owner's work shows either striking or substantial similarities to the defendant's. Once the trier of fact determines copying has occurred, a finding of unlawful appropriation will result from the plaintiff's showing substantial similarities between the defendant's work and the plaintiff's.

Under the right of reproduction, the Copyright Act itself allows for certain exceptions; for example, reproductions of nondramatic musical works, such as operas or motion picture sound tracks, subject to compulsory licensing under the act, do not constitute infringements if the user complies with certain conditions, including the payment of royalties to the owner. By the same token, the act exempts from the exclusive rights enjoyed by the copyright holder imitations of sound recordings (when the reproductions go beyond a mere "lifting" of the original expression) and reproductions transmitted by public educational or religious broadcasters under certain conditions. Without violating the copyright laws, one also can reproduce pictures of copyrighted useful art (like the bike rack) or architectural works. In addition, in certain circumstances, libraries can make reproductions of works needed to preserve or secure their collections or archives and of works, subject to some limitations, requested by library users.

The copyright holder's exclusive right to distribute the work differs from the exclusive right to reproduce the work. Under this right of distribution, the copyright owner can control the initial sale or distribution of the work to the public but, except in some situations involving the rentals of records, cannot control any subsequent transfers of the work. Sales of pirated works do not constitute "initial sales," so sellers of pirated works may find themselves subject to an infringement action even if the sellers are unaware that the compact disks, tapes, or records were pirated.

The exclusive right of public performance is subject to various exemptions as well. For example, a bar or restaurant that displays a standard-sized television so that its patrons can watch it free of charge does not infringe the copyright of a program broadcast on the television set. Similarly, pupils can perform copyrighted works in the course of face-to-face teaching activities in the classroom, as opposed to performing the work pursuant to a school play open to the public. Record shops and stores selling televisions, without violating the copyright laws, can also play songs and show public performance as a means of promoting sales.

Compulsory licensing sections in the act apply to cable television systems' secondary transmissions of primary broadcasts, satellite retransmissions, operators of electronic video game arcades, and operation of jukeboxes (even though, under the Berne Convention, jukeboxes are covered under voluntary—as opposed to compulsory—licenses through 1999).

The American Society of Composers, Authors, and Publishers (ASCAP) and Broadcast Music, Inc. (BMI) act as agents for owners of copyrights and issue licenses on behalf of such authors. After securing a license from ASCAP or BMI, a radio or television station can perform any of the works of any authors these societies represent. Each society, in turn, pays the royalties so received to the authors and monitors the stations' compliance with the licenses granted. This system results in greater efficiencies than one that requires each station to negotiate separately with each artist and for each artist individually to police copyright law compliance. The exceptions for the exclusive right to display the work correlate with those just discussed under the right of public performance.

Anyone who violates any of the copyright owner's exclusive rights provided in the statute or who imports copies or phono records into the United States in violation of the statute is an infringer of the copyright or the right of the author, as the case may be. The courts have imposed liability for infringements that are either direct or contributory—that is, those that induce or materially contribute to another person's direct infringement.

Defendants' most common defense against charges of infringement is the "fair use" doctrine. The statute itself states that the fair use of a copyrighted work for purposes of criticism, comment, news reporting, teaching (including multiple copies for classroom use), scholarship, or research is not an infringement of the copyright. The statute then sets out a nonexhaustive list of factors courts shall consider when they determine whether the use made of a work in any particular case is a fair use. These factors include: (1) the purpose and character of the use, including whether such use is of a commercial nature or is for nonprofit educational purposes; (2) the nature of the copyrighted work; (3) the amount and substantiality of the portion used in relation to the copyrighted work as a whole; and (4) the effect of the use on the potential market for or value of the copyrighted work. The statute further states that the fact that a work is unpublished shall not itself bar a finding of fair use if a court, after considering all the above factors, makes such a distinction.

Various professional groups have set out guidelines to ensure that copying done, for example, by libraries and/or by teachers for classroom use, falls either under express statutory exemptions or the fair use doctrine. These efforts underscore the importance of complying with the Copyright Act.

The fair use doctrine sometimes implicates parody, or a work in which one person imitates another's work so as to ridicule the latter. The importance of parody in our country's history has led many courts to protect parodic uses of a copyrighted work, despite the owner's unwillingness to grant a license to the parodist. In *Campbell v. Acuff-Rose Music, Inc.*, the Supreme Court wrangled with these issues.

45.2

CAMPBELL V. ACUFF-ROSE MUSIC, INC.
510 U.S. 569 (1994)

FACTS In 1964, Roy Orbison and William Dees wrote a rock ballad called "Oh, Pretty Woman" and assigned their rights in it to Acuff-Rose Music, Inc. (Acuff-Rose). Acuff-Rose registered the song for copyright protection. A quarter century later, Luther Campbell, a member of the rap music group 2 Live Crew, wrote a song entitled "Pretty Woman." On 5 July 1989, 2 Live Crew's manager informed Acuff-Rose that 2 Live Crew had written a parody of "Oh, Pretty Woman"; that the group would afford all credit for ownership and authorship of the original song to Acuff-Rose, Dees, and Orbison; and that the group would pay a fee for the use it wished to make of the song. Acuff-Rose refused this requested permission. Despite Acuff-Rose's refusal, 2 Live Crew released records, cassette tapes, and compact discs of "Pretty Woman" in a collection of songs entitled "As Clean as They Wanna Be." The albums and compact discs identify the authors of "Pretty Woman" as Orbison and Dees and the publisher as Acuff-Rose. Almost a year later, after the sale of nearly a quarter of a million copies of "As Clean as They Wanna Be," Acuff-Rose sued 2 Live Crew for copyright infringement. Reasoning that the commercial purpose of 2 Live Crew's song was no bar to "fair use"; that 2 Live Crew's version was a parody; that 2 Live Crew had taken only that which was necessary to "conjure up" the original in order to parody it; and that it was extremely unlikely that 2 Live Crew's song would lessen the demand for the original, the district court granted summary judgment for 2 Live Crew. The court of appeals, arguing that the "blatantly commercial purpose" of the 2 Live Crew song prevented this parody from constituting a fair use of a copyrighted work, reversed the lower court's decision.

ISSUE Did 2 Live Crew's commercial parody constitute a fair use of the copyrighted work?

HOLDING Yes. Because the group merely parodied the original song, 2 Live Crew had not infringed on Acuff-Rose's copyright of "Oh, Pretty Woman." Despite its commercial intent, 2 Live Crew, in an effort to satirize the original song, could borrow from "Oh,

Pretty Woman" and in so doing would not contravene the Copyright Act.

REASONING It is uncontested here that, except for a finding of fair use through parody, 2 Live Crew's song would represent an infringement of Acuff-Rose's rights in "Oh, Pretty Woman" under the Copyright Act of 1976. From the infancy of copyright protection, some opportunity for fair use of copyrighted materials has been thought necessary to fulfill copyright's very purpose, "[t]o promote the Progress of Science and useful Arts. . . . " (U.S. Constitution, Article I, Section 8, Clause 8) The Copyright Act of 1976 sets some limitations on these exclusive rights but does not establish any hard-and-fast guidelines for courts to use in a fair-use inquiry. The 1976 act merely states that courts should consider four factors: (1) the purpose and character of the use, including whether such use is of a commercial nature or is for nonprofit educational purposes; (2) the nature of the copyrighted work; (3) the amount and substantiality of the portion used in relation to the copyrighted work as a whole; and (4) the effect of the use on the potential market for or value of the copyrighted work. In short, the fair-use doctrine requires courts to avoid a rigid application of the copyright statute when, on occasion, it would stifle the very creativity the law seeks to foster. Such an inquiry involves a case-by-case approach that considers the four statutory factors together, not in isolation. Under the factor relating to a work's purpose and character, the new work, by adding some sort of new expression, meaning, or message, must transform the original work. Any parody alters the message of the original work on which it is based and, by using the original work, creates a new work that, in part, comments on the original. Although the Court might not assign a high rank to the parodic element here, it is fair to say that one could reasonably perceive 2 Live Crew's song as commenting on the original or criticizing it to some degree. Moreover, the court of appeals erroneously interpreted the Copyright Act of 1976 as indicating that every commercial use of copyrighted material is presumptively unfair.

continued

45.2

CAMPBELL V. ACUFF-ROSE MUSIC, INC., *continued*
510 U.S. 569 (1994)

Yet this represents only one consideration that a court, when looking at the "purpose" and "character" criterion, can take into account. When fair use is raised in defense of parody, the threshold question is whether a parodic character may reasonably be perceived. Regardless of 2 Live Crew's desire to sell records, the group's parody constituted a legitimate use of the original copyrighted work. As for the factor concerning the nature of the work, the Court agreed that Orbison's song fell within the type of material protected under the Copyright Act but concluded that this factor had little bearing on the case. As for the amount of the copyrighted work used, the Court ruled that 2 Live Crew had not drawn too heavily from the original song. Parody's humor, or in any event its comment, necessarily springs from a recognizable allusion to its object through distorted imitation, the Court emphasized. The art lies in the tension between its known original and its parodic twin. This recognition, in turn, derives from the quotation of the original's most distinctive or memorable features, which the parodist can be sure the audience will know. Hence, 2 Live Crew's quotation of the opening riff and first line of the original song was not excessive. Finally, in examining the potential of the 2 Live Crew work on the market for the original song, the Court rejected the appellate court's reliance on *Sony Corp. of America* v. *Universal Studios, Inc.,* a case involving the home copying of television programming. Using the *Sony* case, the appellate court assumed—from an intention to use the work for commercial gain—the likelihood of significant market harm. But no "presumption" or inference of market harm that might find support in *Sony* is applicable to a case involving something beyond mere duplication for commercial purposes. When the second use is transformative, market substitution is at least less certain;

and one may not infer market harm so readily. Indeed, as to parody pure and simple, it is more likely that the new work will not affect the market for the original in a way cognizable under this factor, that is, by acting as a substitute for it. This is so because the parody and the original usually serve different market functions. Moreover, no protectable derivative market for criticism exists, since creators of original works generally will refuse to license parodies or lampoons of their work. Hence, from the evidence presented at trial, one can draw no conclusion about the likely effect of 2 Live Crew's parodic rap song on the market for a nonparodic, rap version of "Oh, Pretty Woman." For this and the other reasons cited, 2 Live Crew's song represented a fair use of copyrighted material under the Copyright Act of 1976. The erroneous conclusion by the court of appeals that the commercial nature of 2 Live Crew's parody of "Oh, Pretty Woman" rendered it a presumptively unfair use therefore merits reversal and remand to the lower court.

BUSINESS CONSIDERATIONS Acuff-Rose presumably thought 2 Live Crew's parody would negatively affect the market for "Oh, Pretty Woman." On what basis did the firm reach this conclusion? Is it possible the parody actually could bring about an appreciation in the value of the original "Oh, Pretty Woman"?

ETHICAL CONSIDERATIONS One of the purposes of parody is to satirize the original. Does "making fun" of the original constitute unethical behavior on the parodist's part? From an ethical perspective, should a parodist be required to obtain permission in advance before producing a parody?

The identity of the owner of a copyright ordinarily poses few problems because the original author usually is the owner. But co-ownership over "joint works" does exist. "Works for hire," or works prepared by an employee within the scope of his or her employment (e.g., architectural drawings), or work specifically commissioned for use as an instructional text (e.g., this textbook) and considered as works for hire belong, respectively, to the employer or to the person who commissions the works. Works prepared by employees of the U.S. government as a part of that person's official duties enjoy no copyright protection; rather, these works fall within the public domain and generally can be copied at will. By putting the transfer (or assignment) in writing and by recording such actions with the Copyright Office, one can transfer ownership of copyrights.

Since the Berne Convention Implementation Act, which took effect on 1 March 1989, it is not necessary, to ensure copyright protection, that an author put the copyright notice, the copyright symbol, the author's name, and the date of the first publication on the work. However, such notice still is necessary for works copyrighted under the 1976 act and published (i.e., released to the public) before 1 March 1989. The 1976 act allows the omission of the required notice in certain limited circumstances, but failure to include the required notice generally results in loss of copyright protection.

Hence, as mentioned earlier, one first must determine which law governs the copyrighted work in question. Registering the work with the Copyright Office remains advisable, however, because registration makes proof of infringement easier in some cases and makes the owner eligible for certain types of damages, court costs, and attorney's fees.

Under the 1976 act, federal copyright commences with the fixation of the work in a copy or phono record for the first time. The duration of a copyright covered by the 1976 act (i.e., works created on or after 1 January 1978) generally is the life of the author plus 70 years. After that time, the law presumes the work has passed into the public domain and therefore is not copyrightable.

Remedies

Civil remedies for infringements include injunctions, the impoundment and destruction of infringing items, and damages. Plaintiffs can choose between actual damages, including the infringer's profits attributable to the infringement if the court, in computing the damages, did not take these into account, or statutory damages ranging from a minimum of $750 to $30,000 for all infringements involved in the action with respect to one work. A court may increase the damages to $150,000 for willful infringements. Similarly, the court may lower the damages to $200 if the infringer can prove it was unaware that its actions constituted an infringement. The court in its discretion can award court costs to either party and may award attorney's fees to either prevailing plaintiffs or prevailing defendants.[2]

Criminal penalties range from a maximum of $10,000 and one year's imprisonment (or both) to a maximum $25,000 and one year's imprisonment (or both) for the first offense involving willful infringement and a maximum of $50,000 and two years' imprisonment (or both) for subsequent offenses.

International Dimensions

As noted earlier, U.S. copyright laws have undergone some changes since the United States became a member of the Berne Convention (the International Union for the Protection of Literary and Artistic Works) in March 1989. The Berne Convention makes national treatment of copyrights the linchpin of the treaty. In other words, each member nation must automatically extend the protection of its laws to the other signatory nations' nationals and to works originally published in a member nation's jurisdiction. The Berne Convention is not self-executing; each member nation therefore must enact implementing legislation.

The United States has taken a minimalist approach to compliance with the Berne Convention; in other words, it has not accepted in toto every provision of the treaty. But since the United States has enacted into law many of the treaty's provisions, it is important to U.S. intellectual property law. Apropos of this, the World Intellectual Property Organization's (WIPO's) December 1996 treaties have updated the Berne Convention to reflect the changes in information technology and to set intellectual property standards for the digital age. These treaties, among other things, have closed some loopholes that had left the U.S. recording industry without copyright protection in the international arena. Specifically, these WIPO treaties require signatory nations to prohibit any circumventions of copy-protection measures for copyrighted works. As a consequence, the WIPO signatories must outlaw the manufacture, import, or sale of any devices used to accomplish such circumventions. The most recent implementation of the 1996 treaties is the Digital Millennium Copyright Act of 1998, a U.S. enactment that furthers the WIPO treaties' objective of resolving disputes concerning liability for the use of copyrighted works on the Internet as well as other copyright problems. For example, one section of the 1998 act identifies the conditions under which an online service provider can avoid liability for the presence of infringing materials that appear on its system. Another provision expands the fair use exemption for libraries and archives. Hence, this recent act, in attempting to adjust copyright law to fit the global challenges represented by the emerging information technologies, disposes of a number of timely issues.

The Universal Copyright Convention (the Convention), administered by the United Nations, represents another international treaty that covers copyrights. Although it imposes fewer substantive requirements on copyrights than does the Berne Convention, some Berne Convention members also have joined the Universal Copyright Convention as a means of establishing relationships concerning copyrights with Convention members who have not signed the Berne Convention.

Recent amendments to GATT (the General Agreement on Tariffs and Trade) expand the protections afforded to copyrighted works, including computer programs. The European Union's (EU's) "Directive on the Legal Protection of Computer Software," slated to cover EU members as of 1 January 1993, represents another promising initiative in the international arena.

45.1 | MANAGEMENT

CALL-IMAGE TECHNOLOGY

COPYRIGHT INFRINGEMENT

John has come up with what he believes is a creative idea for a commercial for Call-Image. He has described it to the rest of the family members, and they also think it could be a very successful ad. In the ad John envisions, an extraterrestrial finds itself marooned on earth and it is trying to "call home" to get one of its fellow extraterrestrials to pick it up. As the extraterrestrial dials, the call goes through, and its mother's face appears on the CIT video screen; the voice of the announcer then describes the pleasure of seeing "distant relatives" when one calls home and uses a Call-Image videophone. The family members ask you if this ad involves any copyright infringement problems. What will you tell them?

BUSINESS CONSIDERATIONS Why do businesses use the voices, names, and likenesses of famous people to sell their products? Are these types of ads less effective if the advertiser casts unknown people to show the use of the product?

ETHICAL CONSIDERATIONS Is it ethical for a business to utilize computer imaging to place famous people who have died into commercials with contemporary stars or contemporary settings? What ethical concerns does the use of the likenesses of deceased celebrities in commercials raise?

Computers

Copyright law also covers computers. Although it was unclear whether computer programs were copyrightable under the 1909 act, the Copyright Office began accepting computer programs for registration as books as early as 1964, despite the misgivings of register officials. At the time of the passage of the 1976 act, the "jury," in the form of the National Commission on New Technological Uses (CONTU), was still out regarding the copyrightability of computer software. However, by adding the phrase "computer program" and certain other provisions exempting the copying of computer programs from the 1976 act's infringement provisions, the Computer Software Copyright Act of 1980 amended the 1976 act. As a result of these amendments, today few doubts remain as to the copyrightability of computer programs, despite the omission of this phrase from the listed categories of proper subject matters for copyright protection.

Under the 1980 amendments, "[a] 'computer program' is a set of statements or instructions to be used directly or indirectly in a computer in order to bring about a certain result." According to the 1980 amendments, computer databases also are copyrightable as "compilations" or "derivative works." Infringements of copyrights—for example, unauthorized copying, distribution, or derivation—do not occur if the owner (i.e., a copyright holder) of a copy of a computer program only makes or authorizes the making of a new copy or adaptation when the copy is an essential step in the utilization of the program in conjunction with a machine (i.e., for use with the owner's computer) or for archival purposes (i.e., for making backup copies in case the original copy is accidentally destroyed). The fair-use doctrine, whereby, for instance, your professor uses computer software for an in-class performance or display, and the right of libraries to reproduce and distribute copyrighted works, including computer software in some circumstances, apparently do not constitute infringements, either. The act presently does not differentiate, for infringement purposes, between human-readable or machine-readable copies; copies of whichever form may constitute infringements unless the copying falls into one of these exemptions.

Yet controversies still abound owing to the fact that the 1976 act continues the long-standing expression/idea dichotomy of copyright law. This duality, that the program as written is protectable but the unique ideas contained in the program are not, of course looms as a significant impediment to software developers who wish to copyright their manuals: It is easy to produce competing products once the ideas underlying the original package become known. Thus, upon the developers' meeting the required statutory criteria, the manuals will be copyrightable, but the formats may not be.

Similarly, the audiovisual display aspects of a video game may be copyrightable, whereas the idea—a crazy character that "munches" everything, for instance—behind the game, or the game per se, ordinarily will be ineligible for copyright protection. The same may be true in general of flowcharts, components of machines, and printed circuit boards that do not have computer programs embedded in them: These normally are not copyrightable. The unsettled state of the law in this area merely complicates developers' problems.

The *Apple Computer, Inc.* v. *Franklin Computer Corporation* case[3] represents an early but significant decision regarding the application of the copyright laws to computer software, particularly computer operating systems. Apple Computer, Inc. (Apple) had filed suit against Franklin Computer Corporation (Franklin) for copyright infringement owing to Franklin's copying of 14 of Apple's **operating system computer programs** for use with Franklin's ACE 100 personal computer.[4] Franklin admitted it had copied Apple's programs and **ROM chips (read-only memory chips)** but argued it had done so because it had not been feasible for Franklin to

Operating system computer programs Collections of systems software programs designed to help someone else program or use a computer and that allow the computer to execute programs and manage programming tasks.

ROM chips (read-only memory chips) Computer chips on which the data and information used to run computer operating systems are affixed; chips that can be "read" by a computer program but generally cannot be changed or altered.

Object code
Translation of source code into lower-level language, consisting of numbers and symbols that the computer converts into electronic impulses (machine language).

Source code
Human-readable version of the program that gives instructions to the computer.

write its own operating system programs.[5] Franklin also asserted that the Apple programs were uncopyrightable subject matter because the **object code** on which the programs had relied was not a "writing"; moreover, according to Franklin, the programs were "processes," "systems," or "methods of operation" unprotected by law.[6] This opinion addressed the important issue of whether the object code, which is not readable by people, is a "writing" within the Copyright Act's coverage and hence copyrightable; or instead, given its normal use, whether the object code is a method of operation or a system, which is uncopyrightable.[7] In holding that Apple's computer programs, whether in **source code** or in object code embedded in ROM chips, constitute "literary works" protected under the Copyright Act of 1976 from unauthorized copying from either their object code or source code version, the court answered a question that had vexed early software developers.[8] For a more recent disposition of a similar issue, see *Lotus Development Corporation* v. *Borland International, Inc.*[9]

Copyright claims represent a fertile area for litigation. Apple Computer, Inc., Microsoft Corporation, and Hewlett-Packard Company recently have litigated the copyrightability of the visual display aspects of computer user interfaces. Given the huge economic stakes and the ever-changing technology involved in such cases, companies presumably will continue this zealous protection of their rights through resort to the courts. These developments therefore bear watching.

PATENTS

The same provision of the Constitution that provides the basis for copyright protection furnishes the grounds for patents. Congress's power to promote the progress of science and the useful arts secures for inventors, rather than authors, the exclusive right to their respective discoveries. Today, most experts lump the terms "useful arts," "inventors," and "discoveries" with patent rights and leave the promotion of science through writings to copyright law.

Since the first patent statute in 1790, the statutory categories of patentable subject matter have consisted of (1) any process (the earlier term was "art," but the term "process" now includes a process, art, or method); (2) machine; (3) manufacture; (4) composition of matter, including certain nonnaturally occurring plants, such as hybrids; and (5) any new and useful improvement thereof. The Supreme Court has held that such utility patents may cover genetically engineered living matter as well. As in copyright law, ideas per se are not patentable. Neither are laws of nature (e.g., "for every action there is an equal and opposite reaction"), mathematical formulas, scientific truths or principles, methods of doing business, and mental processes.

Utility patents last for 20 years from the filing date, after which time the monopoly granted to the patentee (i.e., the holder of the patent) ends. *Design patents* (i.e., patents involving original, ornamental designs for articles of manufacture) last for only 14 years from the date of the grant of the patent. Once either type of patent protection ends, others can make, use, or sell the invention with impunity.

To be patentable, an invention must demonstrate novelty. In other words, prior art must show an absence of anything substantially identical to the claimed invention; the claimed invention therefore must be unanticipated. Public knowledge or use of the invention by others in this country before the application for the patent indicates a lack of novelty. The public use or sale of the invention more than one year prior to the application of the patent thus will result in the denial of a patent.

Just as it is hard to imagine an invention that lacks novelty, so too, it is difficult to imagine as worthy of patent protection an invention that lacks utility. Both the Constitution and the Patent Act of 1952 describe protected discoveries and inventions as "useful" ones. Hence, to deserve protection under the patent laws, the inventor's discovery must provide significant current benefits to society.

Last, an invention must consist of nonobvious subject matter. In other words, if the differences between the subject matter one seeks to patent and prior art are such that the subject matter as a whole will be obvious, at the time the invention is made, to a person having ordinary skill in the art to which the subject matter pertains, the invention does not warrant protection.

These three requirements clearly overlap. The ingenuity that underlies inventions goes beyond the mere carrying forward of an old idea. Yet Thomas Alva Edison, one of our greatest inventors, surely captured another aspect of invention when he noted that it involves 1 percent inspiration and 99 percent perspiration!

By making an application to the U.S. Patent and Trademark Office (PTO), inventors who believe they have met these requirements begin the process of receiving a patent. This application includes a declaration that the applicant first discovered the invention for which he or she solicits the patent; any drawings necessary to explain the patent; detailed descriptions, specifications, and disclosures (including all prior art) of the subject matter the applicant claims as his or her invention; and the required filing fees. The substantive information provided in the specifications should (1) enable any person skilled in the art to make or use the invention after the expiration of the term of the patent and (2) inform the public of the limits of the monopoly asserted by the inventor for the life of the patent.

The Commissioner of Patents and Trademarks will issue a patent if the PTO examiner to whom the Commissioner has given the application approves the application. Applicants who receive rejection notices, usually owing to the examiner's finding prior art or the existence of "double-patenting" (the act prohibits the granting of two patents for the same invention), can appeal to the PTO Board of Patent Appeals and Interferences and then either to the U.S. Court of Appeals for the Federal Circuit or the U.S. District Court for the District of Columbia. Stringent time periods apply to the entire process.

In 1999, the Supreme Court, in *Dickinson* v. *Zurko*,[10] settled a split in the circuit courts of appeals when the Court held that the appropriate standard of review for the Federal Circuit to apply to issues of fact in appeals from the PTO is not the more stringent "clearly erroneous" standard but instead the standard set out in the Administrative Procedure Act (APA). Hence, the Federal Circuit must follow the APA and set aside only those agency factual determinations that the court finds to be arbitrary, capricious, an abuse of discretion, or unsupported by substantial evidence.

The PTO reports that in 1998, it granted a record 163,209 patents, an increase of about 32 percent over 1997's figures.[11] Patents issued to international residents accounted for about 44 percent of such patents.[12] In 1998, residents of California received the most domestically issued patents, about 20 percent of the total issued to U.S. residents.[13]

Protection and Infringement

Given the economic value of patents, this area of the law tends to invite litigation between parties with adverse interests. Holders of patents (i.e., patentees) typically bring patent infringement actions when they believe someone has encroached on or invaded the area covered by the claims the patentee has made concerning the patent. The Patent Act covers direct infringements, indirect infringements, and contributory infringements.

A *direct infringement* involves a party who, without the patent holder's permission, makes, uses, or sells the patented invention in the United States during the term of the patent. For example, Video, Inc. manufactures and sells videophones that directly resemble CIT videophones. In this case, CIT has grounds to bring an action for direct infringement.

The act also covers *indirect infringements.* These may take the form of inducements to infringe, in which another party has directly infringed on the patentee's patent and has actively and knowingly aided and abetted an infringement by a third party. For example, Video, Inc. sells a telephone that, when mixed with other components, infringes on CIT's patent for Call-Image. Video, Inc. then sells the telephones and components to See and Speak, which, following Video, Inc.'s instructions, also manufactures the product. Since Video, Inc. knows that a direct infringement will result from its actions, it has induced See and Speak to infringe on CIT's patent and thereby has committed an indirect infringement.

Finally, the act covers *contributory infringements,* in which another party sells a material component of a patented invention and knows that the component has been specially made or adapted for use in a patented invention and that infringement will occur. For example, Video, Inc. sells a video process specially made for Call-Image (and the process has no substantial, noninfringing use) to See and Speak, and Video, Inc. knows See and Speak will use the process to infringe on the patentee's invention. Video, Inc. is liable as a contributory infringer, while See and Speak becomes liable as a direct infringer once it uses the process.

One can engage in a direct infringement even though totally ignorant of the existence of a patent, since the issuance of a patent serves as constructive notice to the world of the patent's existence. On the other hand, indirect infringements involving inducements or contributory infringements require knowledge on the defendant's part before courts can impose liability.

Persons sued for patent infringement will try to overcome the presumption of validity and prove that the patent is invalid owing to some omitted condition of patentability (e.g., novelty); infringement cannot exist in the absence of a valid patent. Abuse of patent provides another defense to infringement actions. For instance, if a patentee uses the patent as a means of engaging in anticompetitive activities and for the purpose of extending its monopoly beyond that granted by Congress, any infringement action brought by the patentee will be unsuccessful. Activities that violate the antitrust laws, such as illegal tie-ins and other activities discussed in Chapter 39, when used in conjunction with a patent, will lead to a finding of noninfringement. Refusing any and all requests to license the patent does not constitute patent misuse, however.

The Supreme Court in 1996 held that when an infringement action involves the interpretation of a patent claim (i.e., the portion of the patent document that defines the scope of the patentee's rights), such an interpretation is a question of law exclusively within the province of the court; juries are not empowered to engage in such interpretive activities. However, juries can decide questions of fact, such as whether infringement has occurred.[14]

Remedies

Remedies for actionable patent infringement include damages and equitable relief in the form of injunctions. The statute directs courts to award damages in an amount adequate to compensate the patentee (the holder of the patent) for the infringement (such amounts will include lost profits attributable to the infringement) but in no event less than a reasonable royalty representative of the infringer's use of the invention.

The act also allows courts to impose costs and to award reasonable attorney's fees to the prevailing party in exceptional cases, such as circumstances involving clear fraud and wrongdoing or in circumstances in which the court believes the award of attorney's fees will prevent gross injustice. But given the enormity of the attorney's fees in typical patent cases, courts rarely award such fees.

In either jury or nonjury trials, courts have authority to treble the damages assessed. A court's award of damages denies the infringer its ill-gotten gains and also restores to the patentee the benefits he or she would have derived from the monopoly had the infringing sales not occurred. The Patent Act expressly allows courts to use expert testimony for determining the damages or royalties that would be reasonable under the circumstances.

The 1999 Supreme Court case of *Florida Prepaid Postsecondary Education Expense Board* v. *College Savings Bank*[15] restricted the power of Congress to provide a judicial forum for violations of intellectual property rights. Striking down a 1992 amendment to the patent laws in which Congress had expressly abrogated the states' sovereign immunity from claims of patent infringement, the Supreme Court characterized the 1992 changes as an invalid exercise of power under the Fourteenth Amendment's due process clause. In so holding, the Court noted that the lack of evidence of widespread patent infringement by the states, as well as Congress's failure to consider the adequacy of state remedies for patent infringement, precluded Congress from invoking its powers under the Fourteenth Amendment to eliminate state immunity from patent infringement suits.[16]

International Dimensions

Given the value of patent rights, patent law (like copyright law) now has international dimensions. Prior to the enactment of various international treaties, an inventor had to patent the invention in each foreign jurisdiction and in accordance with the law of that particular nation.

To overcome these inefficiencies and complexities, the Paris Convention for the Protection of Industrial Property, administered by the World Intellectual Property Organization (WIPO), came into existence in 1883. About 140 nations, including the United States, are members of the Paris Convention. Like the Berne Convention, the Paris Convention, by emphasizing the concept of national treatment in which each member can determine the nature and extent of the substantive protections afforded to patents, in a given situation may not fully protect patented inventions. Moreover, the Paris Convention has done little to alleviate the need for separate filings in each signatory nation's jurisdiction, and it has no enforcement mechanisms for policing violations of the convention.

Owing to these shortcomings, the Patent Cooperation Treaty (PCT) became effective in 1978. The PCT's procedures—especially the filing system—allow inventors in the 96 or so nations, including the United States, that have signed the treaty to use one filing for securing patent rights in the jurisdictions represented by the signatory nations. The present GATT (General Agreement on Tariffs and Trade) round and NAFTA (North American Free Trade Agreement), international efforts discussed in Chapter 3, also provide transnational patent protection to inventors. In particular, the recent GATT changes appear to involve reasonable steps that will result in further harmonization of the international treatment of patents.

Computers

Neither the old law nor the significant amendments to the patent laws contemplated the inclusion of computer or program-related inventions within these classifications. As a result, by the 1960s, the PTO and the Court of Customs and Patent Appeals (CCPA) had drawn strict battle lines regarding the patentability of computer programs and other software. The CCPA was for it; the PTO was against it.

Although it was clear that computer programs met the first requirement of patentability—that is, that they potentially arose under one of the four categories of patentable subject matter ("process" or "machine," presumably)—doubts existed as to whether software fulfilled the remaining conditions of patentability. Those arguing for patentability viewed computer systems consisting of both hardware and software either as a process (a method for operating a machine) or as a physical component of the hardware itself and thus protected by the machine requirement, with the program being one element in the overall apparatus. Other authorities, by characterizing software as ideas standing alone, laws of nature, scientific truths or principles, algorithms (mathematical formulas), mental steps, printed matter, functions of a machine, and/or methods of doing business, however, relegated computer software to areas lying outside patent protection. Indeed, for many years that was the fate that befell program-related invention cases, since questions arose as to whether an invention containing as one of its elements a computer program implementing such an algorithm was patentable.

Preempt
Seize upon to the exclusion of others.

Many precedents relied on the so-called preemption test in which the PTO was obliged to examine whether the patent claim on the software would wholly **preempt** the other uses of the algorithm (i.e., calculations, formulas, or equations). If so, the invention fell into one of the categories of nonstatutory subject matter and was unpatentable because the claim merely recited a mathematical algorithm. If, instead, the algorithm was but one of several steps or procedures leading to the transformation of the data into a wholly different state or thing, the invention complied with the statutory subject matter and was patentable.

Compiler program
One that converts a high-level programming language into binary or machine code.

After several cases in the 1970s holding computer-related inventions unpatentable, the Supreme Court in *Diamond* v. *Diehr*[17] applied the preemption test and held that a process for curing synthetic rubber, which includes in several of its steps the use of a mathematical formula and a programmed digital computer, was patentable subject matter. *Diamond* v. *Diehr* involved the question of the patentability of a computer program used as an integral part of a machine. A subsequent CCPA decision, *In re Pardo,*[18] ruled that a **compiler program,** one designed to translate source code to object code, alone may constitute patentable subject matter.

TRADEMARKS

From their inception, trademarks have served as a means by which tradespeople and craftspersons identify goods as their own. Indeed, archaeologists have found centuries-old artifacts bearing such trade symbols. In further recognition of the social and economic dimensions of such marks, the medieval guilds used trademarks as a means of controlling quality and fostering customer goodwill. Statutes as early as the thirteenth century codified these ideas. These early statutory developments sought to prohibit "palming off," or one producer's passing off its goods as the goods of a competitor and, through this "free-riding" on the established customer base and goodwill of a competitor, thus taking away sales from the other.

Present-day trademark law, by protecting against consumer confusion as to the origin of goods, advances this goal. In contrast to patents, no analogous constitutional foundation for the protection of trademarks exists. Rather, as we have seen in earlier chapters, the commerce clause provides the basis for the federal regulation of trademarks. However, both federal and state law protect trademarks.

Over the years, an extensive body of state trademark law had developed in the common law, principally through the state common law relating to unfair competition. The 1946 Lanham Act, the most important federal protection of trademarks, provides a structure by which the enforcement of these common law principles can occur through federal oversight and thereby builds on these common law roots. Just as the Lanham Act allows the registration of various marks, so too, some states have statutory registration provisions. The PTO oversees the federal registration of trademarks. The number of trademarks issued jumped from 24,700 in 1980 to 101,400 in 1996.[19]

Protection and Infringement

The Lanham Act defines a *trademark* as any word, name, symbol, device, or any combination thereof used to identify and distinguish the services of one person from the services of others and to indicate the source of the goods even if the source is unknown. This definition underscores the fact that a trademark always exists pursuant to commercial activity or use and may cover an extensive array of things, including the distinctive features of the product (i.e., "trade dress") such as the product's shape, packaging, its logo or artwork, and so on. All these aspects may be worthy of trademark protection.

Well-known trademarks include Coca-Cola, Pepsi, Tide, Chanel, Mercedes-Benz (and its logo), Kodak, Ralph Lauren, and so forth. *Service marks*—or those that identify and distinguish services rather than products (e.g., McDonald's, United Airlines, or Prudential Insurance); *certification marks,* or those that identify the goods and services of others as having certain characteristics (e.g., the Good Housekeeping seal of approval or the Underwriters' Laboratories seal); and *collective marks,* or those that signify membership in a group and the goods or services produced by the group (e.g., the Wool Council, the Beef Council, etc.)—are protectable under trademark law as well.

To deserve protection, the trademark—whatever its form—must be distinctive. Arbitrary, fanciful, and suggestive terms by definition are distinctive. Calling a brand of gasoline "Mobil" on the one hand seems arbitrary, but this designation also suggests mobility—presumably one of our goals when we put gasoline in our tanks. "Snuggles" as a name for laundry softeners, "Pampers" as a name for disposable diapers, and "Coppertone" as a name for suntan oils clearly meet these tests.

Note that all these marks embody some degree of imaginativeness. Without distinctiveness, identifying the source of the goods and avoiding consumer confusion become decidedly more difficult. Such marks in themselves also serve narrow marketing functions. Purely descriptive marks—adjectives such as "sweet" or "chicken"; geographic designations like "California" or "New York" in reference to wines; and people's surnames like L.L. Bean and Marriott Hotels used as marks— do not qualify as distinctive until they have acquired "secondary meaning." In other words, when the consumer public no longer views the marks as purely descriptive terms but rather as indicative of the source of the goods or products, the marks have become distinctive. In a similar vein, common geometric shapes, flowers, or slogans, for instance, generally lack the required characteristic of distinctiveness and will not merit trademark status unless the owner can demonstrate secondary meaning.

The Lanham Act specifically provides that the PTO Commissioner may accept as *prima facie* evidence of distinctiveness proof that the mark has been in substantially exclusive and continuous use in interstate commerce for five years. Even though one cannot place nondistinctive marks on the Principal Register of trademarks, owners, as a means of protecting against international infringements of the mark, often place such marks on the Lanham Act's Supplemental Register.

Qualitex Co. v. *Jacobson Products Co., Inc.* involved the issue of whether color, standing alone, could constitute a trademark.

45.3

QUALITEX CO. V. JACOBSON PRODUCTS CO., INC.
514 U.S. 159 (1995)

FACTS Qualitex Company (Qualitex) for years has colored the dry cleaning press pads it manufactures with a special shade of green-gold. After Jacobson Products Company, Inc. (Jacobson), a Qualitex rival, began to use a similar shade on its own press pads, Qualitex registered its color as a trademark and added a trademark infringement count to its previously filed lawsuit challenging Jacobson's use of the green-gold color. Qualitex won in the district court, but the Ninth Circuit set aside the judgment on the infringement claim because, in its view, the Lanham Act does not permit registration of color alone as a trademark.

ISSUE Would the Lanham Act permit the registration of a trademark that consists, purely and simply, of a color?

HOLDING Yes. A color sometimes could meet the ordinary legal requirements for a trademark. When it does, no special legal rule would preclude color alone from serving as a trademark.

REASONING The Lanham Act gives a seller or producer the exclusive right to "register" a trademark and to prevent his or her competitors from using that trademark. Both the language of the act and the basic underlying principles of trademark law seem to include color within the universe of things that can qualify as a trademark. The language of the Lanham Act describes that universe in the broadest of terms. It says that trademarks "includ[e] any word, name, symbol, or device, or any combination thereof." Since human beings might use as a "symbol" or "device" almost anything at all that is capable of carrying meaning, this language, read literally, is not restrictive. The Supreme Court and the Patent and Trademark Office decision have authorized for use as a mark a particular shape (of a Coca-Cola bottle), a particular sound (of NBC's three chimes), and even a particular scent (of plumeria blossoms on sewing thread). If a shape, a sound, and a fragrance can act as symbols, so may color. A color also is capable of satisfying the more important part of the statutory definition of a trademark, which requires that a

45.3

QUALITEX CO. V. JACOBSON PRODUCTS CO., INC., *continued*
514 U.S. 159 (1995)

person use or intend to use the mark to identify and distinguish his or her goods, including a unique product, from those manufactured or sold by others and to indicate the source of the goods, even if that source is unknown. Over time, customers may come to treat a particular color on a product or its packaging (say a color that in context seems unusual, such as pink on a firm's industrial bolt) as signifying a brand. And, if so, that color will come to identify and distinguish the goods—that is, to "indicate" their source much in the same way that descriptive words (say "Trim" on nail clippers or "Car-Freshner" on deodorizers), owing to the attainment of a "secondary meaning," can come to indicate a product's origin. Nothing in the basic objectives of trademark law presents any obvious theoretical objection to the use of color alone as a trademark where that color has attained a "secondary meaning" and therefore identifies and distinguishes a particular brand (and thus indicates its "source"). Trademark law thereby encourages the production of quality products and simultaneously discourages those who, by capitalizing on a consumer's inability to evaluate the quality of an item offered for sale, hope to sell inferior products. It is the source-distinguishing ability of a mark—not its ontological status as color, shape, fragrance, word, or sign—that permits it to serve these basic purposes. The "functionality" doctrine of trademark law does not preclude the use of color as a mark, either. This doctrine prevents trademark law, which seeks to promote competition by protecting a firm's reputation, from instead inhibiting legitimate competition by allowing a producer to control a useful product feature. But since color sometimes is unessential to a product's use or purpose and has little effect on cost or quality, the

doctrine of "functionality" will not constitute an absolute bar to the use of color alone as a mark. It appears, then, that color alone, at least sometimes, can meet the basic legal requirements for use as a trademark. It can act as a symbol that distinguishes a firm's goods and identifies their source, without serving any other significant function. Indeed, the district court in this case entered findings (accepted by the Ninth Circuit) showing that Qualitex's green-gold press pad color has met these requirements. The green-gold color acts as a symbol. Having developed a secondary meaning (customers identified the green-gold color as Qualitex's), it identifies the press pads' source. And, the green-gold color serves no other function. Accordingly, unless there is some special reason that convincingly militates against the use of a color alone as a trademark, trademark law will protect Qualitex's use of the green-gold color on its press pads. Hence, the Ninth Circuit, in barring Qualitex's use of color as a trademark, erred. For these reasons, the judgment of the Ninth Circuit must be reversed.

BUSINESS CONSIDERATIONS Has the Court in this case involved itself in so-called "slippery slope" reasoning? In other words, has it failed to take into account the practical business problems spawned by this decision? What are some difficulties businesses might face as they try to abide by this decision?

ETHICAL CONSIDERATIONS Did either Qualitex or Jacobson have a greater claim to the "moral high ground" in this case? Why or why not? What should each firm have done to act more ethically?

Generic terms never can qualify for trademark protection. This result derives from the fact that a generic term—that is, one that merely refers to the group of products or services of which this item is a part—cannot identify the specific source or tradesperson from which the goods originate. Trademark law shows numerous examples of words that have passed into generic usage and thereby have lost their trademark status. Aspirin, calico, cellophane, escalator, linoleum, shredded wheat, thermos, yo-yo, and zipper represent a few such formerly trademarked terms.

A deceptive mark—for example, a personal security service that superimposes its logo over the seal of the United States and thereby falsely gives the impression of a connection with the U.S. presidency—cannot obtain trademark status. Neither can an immoral, scandalous, or offensive mark.

Similarly, the Lanham Act specifically precludes trademark status for marks that disparage any person (living or dead), institution, belief, or national symbol; use without consent the name, portrait, or signature of a living person; use the name, portrait, or signature of a deceased U.S. president during the lifetime of his or her spouse without the spouse's consent; and/or so resemble an already registered mark as to be likely to cause confusion, mistake, or deception.

The law recognizes as the owner of the mark the person or entity that first uses—and then continues to use—the mark in trade and affixes it to goods or services. Under federal law, before one can register the mark on the Lanham Act's Principal Register, one must demonstrate prior use or a bona fide good-faith intent to use the mark in the future in commerce, the affixation requirement, and use of the mark in interstate commerce.

When the PTO receives the application for registration, it undertakes an examination of the mark similar to that conducted with regard to applications for patents. An examiner checks the application for compliance with the statutory prerequisites and makes sure the proposed mark is not confusingly similar to previously registered marks. Once the examiner completes this investigation, assuming he or she approves the mark, the PTO publishes the mark in its *Official Gazette*.

Anyone who believes the registration may damage himself or herself can, within 30 days, file an opposition with the PTO. Once registration has occurred, one, in some cases, can sue for cancellation of the mark. After exhausting all administrative remedies (including appeals to the Trademark Trial and Appeal Board), aggrieved unsuccessful applicants, or those who unsuccessfully allege opposition or cancellation, can sue in either the Court of Appeals for the Federal Circuit or a U.S. district court. Once granted, registration ordinarily lasts for 10 years and is renewable for 10-year periods so long as the mark remains in commercial use. Registration on the Supplemental Register offers fewer protections but, as discussed earlier, may prove advantageous for those who wish to register marks in countries other than the United States.

The law protects the trademark owner from infringement when the infringer's use will likely cause an appreciable number of consumers to be confused about the source of the goods or services. The factors courts have used to determine the "likelihood of confusion" include, but are not limited to, the following: (1) similarities in the two marks' appearance, sound, connotation, meaning, and impression; (2) similarities in the customer base, sales outlets (i.e.,"trade channels"), or the character of the sale ("impulse" versus "nonimpulse" sales); (3) the strength of the mark; (4) evidence of actual confusion; and (5) the number and nature of similar marks on similar or related products and services. As in patent law, one can be guilty of contributory infringement as well.

Defenses to infringement include "fair use." As we have noted earlier, one can use one's surname—even if it is the same as another famous, trademarked name like McDonald's, Campbell's, or Hilton—as long as one's use does not create the likelihood of consumer confusion. Abandonment of the mark, whether actual (i.e., discontinuation of the use of the mark with the intent not to resume usage) or constructive (acts or omissions by the owner that bring about loss of distinctiveness), constitutes a defense to infringement as well. The Lanham Act expressly provides that nonuse of the mark for two consecutive years constitutes *prima facie* evidence of an intent to abandon the mark.

The plaintiff's registration of the mark on the Principal Register gives him or her certain advantages in an infringement action, since registration serves as *prima facie* evidence of the mark's validity and the registrant's exclusive right to use it in connection with the goods or services described in the registration. Ordinarily, then, at least until the mark becomes incontestable, defendants challenging the validity of the mark must prove the registrant's noncompliance with the prerequisites of the Lanham Act (or the common law). Incontestability status derives from the registrant's continuous use of the mark in interstate commerce for five consecutive years, the absence of any decision adverse to the registrant's claim of ownership or any pending proceeding, and the registrant's filing an affidavit to this effect with the Commissioner of the PTO.

Attainment of incontestability status gives the registrant of the mark a decided edge. For example, loss of an incontestable mark can occur only through cancellation of the mark; in certain limited, statutorily enumerated circumstances; or through the challenger's showing one of the statutorily enumerated defenses to incontestability. Such defenses, among others, include proof that the mark is generic; registration or incontestability has been obtained fraudulently; the registrant has abandoned the mark; the mark falls within the aforementioned categories prohibited as a deceptive mark; that the mark is functional; or the use of the mark constitutes a violation of the antitrust laws. Moreover, in the context of descriptive products or services, incontestability, in effect, substitutes for proof of secondary meaning. Hence, even though the registrant of a generic mark can never use incontestability to protect the mark, owing to this presumption of secondary meaning, the registrant of a merely descriptive mark can avail himself or herself of the protection represented by the incontestability doctrine. On the other hand, one can assert fair use and certain equitable defenses against even an incontestable mark.

Remedies

The Lanham Act sets out certain statutory remedies for trademark infringement, including the equitable remedies of an injunction or an accounting to recover the profits the defendant unfairly has garnered from the infringing use. In addition, the plaintiff may recover actual damages, and the court in its discretion can treble these damages if the circumstances (e.g., willfulness or bad faith on the infringer's part) so dictate. The court similarly can adjust the amount recovered for lost profits to a figure the court considers "just." The court can award court costs and in exceptional cases may award reasonable attorney's fees to the prevailing party. Special rules apply to counterfeit marks. Treble damages, attorney's fees, and prejudgment interest awards usually result from the use of such marks.

45.2 | MANAGEMENT

TRADEMARK INFRINGEMENT

A new competitor in the videophone market has recently unveiled its new logo, which is very similar to the trademark CIT has been using since its inception. Dan wants the family to file a trademark infringement suit against this firm. John and Lindsay, expressing concern, point out that CIT does not have a particularly distinctive name or symbol and that the firm's name is used as an adjective for virtually all videophones. They fear that CIT may have lost its right to protect its trademark. The family members ask for your advice. What will you tell them?

BUSINESS CONSIDERATIONS How can a business protect its trademark so that the trademark does not become a generic term for the product it is intended to promote? Should a business consider changing its logo periodically so as to make the logo appear "fresh" and "new" to the public?

ETHICAL CONSIDERATIONS What ethical concerns derive from a firm's apparent copying of the logo of a more successful rival? Is a firm that attempts to prevent any competitors from using a trademarked logo even remotely similar to its own behaving in an ethically admirable fashion?

In a companion case to the patent law holding mentioned earlier, the Supreme Court, in *College Savings Bank* v. *Prepaid Postsecondary Education Expense Board*,[20] held that Congress had overstepped its constitutional powers when it had amended the Lanham Act in 1992 to abrogate states' immunity from false advertising suits filed in federal court. According to the Court, the protection against false advertising set out in § 43(a) of the Lanham Act does not implicate property rights protected by the due process clause. Consequently, Congress could not rely on its remedial powers under the Fourteenth Amendment to abrogate state sovereign immunity.

International Dimensions

The Paris Convention mentioned earlier in our discussion of patent law applies to trademarks. The "national treatment" rationale of the Paris Convention affords to trademark holders from member nations the same protection a nation grants to its own nationals—no more and no less. Under this rationale, one can register a trademark in another member nation either by complying specifically with that nation's requirements or by registering the mark in one's home country. Member nations then cannot refuse to register any such marks unless the mark is confusingly similar to a preexisting mark; or it is nondistinctive, immoral, deceptive, or uses the insignia of a member nation without that nation's consent. The requirements of U.S. trademark law (e.g., use in trade and commerce as a prerequisite to registration and the cancellation provisions of U.S. law) decidedly limit the usefulness of the Paris Convention (and, for that matter, the Madrid Protocol) to many international applicants. Therefore, U.S. businesses have welcomed the protections codified in the Trademark Law Treaty of 1994, to which the U.S. became a signatory in 1998. Aimed at simplifying and making uniform domestic trademark and service mark registration processes in its member nations, the 1994 treaty supplants the former regime for protecting marks, in which the mark owner had to comply with a patchwork of highly technical procedural requirements in individual countries. The standardization offered by this new convention thus removes many of the impediments to the international registration of marks that heretofore had plagued mark owners. In this sense, the Trademark Law Treaty has greatly changed the landscape of trademark and service mark registration in the international arena.

TRADE SECRETS

Protection

Trade secrecy law provides an alternative method for protecting intellectual property, and a firm therefore can use it to protect "know-how" or other information that gives the firm a differential competitive advantage over its competitors who either are unaware of or do not use the information. We already have seen some of the limitations on the protection of software under copyright law, in that only the written expression of the software and not the ideas embodied in it are protectable, and under patent law, in that strict compliance with statutory requirements is necessary for patentability.

However, various state and common law doctrines, such as trade secrets, unfair competition, and misappropriation, may apply to certain aspects of software—including know-how, information, and ideas—and thus encompass concepts too nebulous for copyright or patent protection. These doctrines may cover computer hardware as well. According to the *Restatement (First) of Torts*, § 757(b), a trade secret may include:

> [a]ny formula, pattern, device or compilation of information which is used in one's business, and which gives [one] an opportunity to obtain an advantage over competitors who do not know or use it. The subject matter of a trade secret must be secret . . . so that, except by the use of improper means, there would be difficulty in acquiring the information.

In determining whether given information is a trade secret, courts generally consider:

1. The extent to which the information is known outside the owner's business
2. The extent to which the information is known by employees and others involved in the business
3. The extent of measures taken by the owner to guard the secrecy of the information
4. The value of the information to the owner and to its competitors
5. The amount of effort or money expended by the owner in developing the information
6. The ease or difficulty with which others could properly acquire or duplicate the information

To qualify as a trade secret, the know-how, manufacturing processes, customer lists, or other proprietary information must be used continuously in the business. In addition, the business, by ensuring the physical security of the information, limiting disclosure only to those who actually need the information in order to complete their jobs, and putting those who have access to the information on notice that the firm expects them to retain it in confidence, must guard the secrecy of the information. For example, CIT may require employees to sign confidentiality agreements and restrictive covenants, review papers that employees will present publicly, conduct exit interviews with departing employees, and so on. One need only take reasonable precautions—as opposed to those deriving from herculean efforts or gargantuan costs—to guard and/or prevent access to the proprietary information.

Common knowledge is not protectable under trade secrecy law because such knowledge presumably is of little value to the owner of the information. Similarly, if through reverse engineering one can easily acquire or duplicate the information, it may not qualify as a trade secret.

Liability

Courts ground liability for misappropriation of a trade secret on two principal theories: (1) breach of contractual or confidential relations (note the way in which courts often blur the distinction between contract and tort law) and (2) acquisition of the information through improper means. Under the first line of reasoning, courts will prohibit persons in an agency (including employment) and/or a fiduciary relationship from disclosing or using information acquired in the course of employment. As we saw in Chapter 13, sometimes an employee expressly promises not to compete with the employer for a given period of time in a given geographical area if the employee leaves this particular job. In the absence of such an express contract, courts generally will not imply such a restrictive covenant. But in some circumstances—for example, where a third party learns of confidential information from the employee—

the law *will* imply a confidential relationship between the third party and the owner of the trade secret. In such circumstances, the third party's disclosure or use of the information will represent actionable misappropriation.

The law also imposes liability for impropriety in the methods used to acquire the trade secret. The law will not countenance conduct that falls below generally accepted standards of commercial morality. If a competitor of CIT induces the firm's key engineer to disclose proprietary information, the competitor will have acquired the information through improper means. Liability similarly will result from the acquisition of information through bribery; commercial espionage; or other illegal conduct such as fraud, theft, and trespass. However, as we discussed earlier, information obtained through reverse engineering, independent discovery, or the owner's failure to take reasonable and inexpensive precautions probably does not involve improper means and thus represents a lawful acquisition of information.

45.3 | MANAGEMENT

PATENT OR TRADE SECRET?

The Kochanowskis have invested a great deal of time, energy, and money in the development of the Call-Image videophone; and they want to derive as much protection for their invention as the law allows. Tom believes they will receive the greatest protection by applying for patents on the product and then for additional patents on each development as they improve the product. Anna prefers to treat their process as a trade secret and not make the information publicly available. They ask for your advice. What will you tell them?

BUSINESS CONSIDERATIONS What factors should an inventor, in deciding to seek a patent, consider? What drawbacks argue against one's seeking a patent?

ETHICAL CONSIDERATIONS Is it ethical for a firm to copy a patented item and then hope that it can prevail in any litigation that results from the patent holder's suing the firm? Is it ethical for a firm to attempt to enforce questionable patents and to use the expense of litigation as a means of preventing competitors from making the product?

Remedies

Remedies for misappropriation of a trade secret include injunctions and actions for damages. Such damages may include the plaintiff's lost profits, the profits made by the defendant, or the royalty amount a reasonable person would have agreed to pay. State criminal laws may apply to misappropriations of trade secrets as well.

On the federal level, the Economic Espionage Act of 1996 (EEA) seeks to punish a broad spectrum of activity that interferes with an owner's proprietary rights in commercial trade secrets. In establishing a comprehensive and systemic approach to trade-secret theft and economic espionage, the EEA facilitates investigations and prosecutions by federal authorities. In enacting the EEA, Congress apparently was responding to the losses—estimated at $1.5 billion in 1995[21] alone—resulting from competitors' activities (e.g., the "raiding" of employees) and misappropriations by foreign enterprises. Hence, the substantive provisions of the EEA address "economic espionage," including activities in behalf of foreign instrumentalities, and "theft of trade secrets" resulting from certain domestic commercial endeavors. Prohibited activities include misappropriating, concealing, procuring by fraud or deception, possessing, altering or destroying, copying, downloading-uploading, or conveying trade secrets without permission.

The EEA thus seeks to proscribe "traditional" acts of misappropriation (i.e., when conversion removes protectable information from the owner's control), as well as "nontraditional" methods—when "the original property never leaves the control of the rightful owner, but the unauthorized duplication or misappropriation effectively destroys the value of what is left with the rightful owners."[22] The sanctions that can be levied against those who engage in such prohibited activities include fines, imprisonment, and criminal forfeiture. Organizations acting in concert with or on behalf of foreign instrumentalities may be fined no more than $10 million. Other organizations may be fined no more than $5 million. Individuals acting in concert with or on behalf of foreign instrumentalities may be fined no more than $500,000 or imprisoned no more than 15 years, or both.[23] Other individuals also may be fined and imprisoned up to 10 years (or both). The criminal forfeiture provision permits the seizure and forfeiture of the property used to facilitate the misappropriation or impermissible possession of a trade secret. The EEA in such provisions thus mirrors the broad seizure powers enjoyed by the government under antidrug enforcement criminal statutes.[24] Try to keep abreast of the developments that stem from this relatively new statute.

Computers

The owner of software who wishes to use trade secret protection may find it advantageous, since trade secret protection avoids the public registration required to devise and enforce rights under the patent and copyright laws. However, because maintaining the secrecy of the proprietary information in question may be difficult and because lack of secrecy constitutes one of the primary defenses to a charge of trade secret misappropriation, the owner of the trade secret should implement various mechanisms to ensure secrecy.

Actions that employers can take to protect trade secrets about software (or hardware) include the creation of nondisclosure, noncompetition, and confidentiality agreements with employees. Employers also should limit physical access to areas where the development of **proprietary** software is taking place as well as to storage areas. All software and documents containing trade secrets should bear proprietary labels, and the software should use **encrypted code** so that only those who have the key for unscrambling it can make the program intelligible. Finally, employers should provide constant reminders to employees about secrecy obligations and conduct exit interviews with departing employees regarding the information the company considers proprietary.

The licensing of software, in order to preserve secrecy, mandates special steps by the owner of the software. Besides restricting disclosures by the licensee, the licensor/owner should limit the rights the licensee retains in the software by virtue of the license, prohibit copying except for use or archival purposes, formulate special coding techniques to identify misappropriated software, distribute the software in object code as opposed to source code, and stipulate that the breach of any confidentiality provision will result in the immediate termination of the licensing agreement.

As we have seen, it is easier for a court to discern a relationship between the owner of the trade secret and the person or entity using or disclosing the trade secret than it is for a court to ascribe property concepts to the trade secret. Why? It is difficult to determine where general information, which is unprotectable, leaves off and proprietary information in the form of the trade secret, which is protectable, begins. Courts often derive these relationships impliedly from the parties' status as employer/employee, vendor/buyer, and the like. However, the parties cannot enjoy a confidential relationship unless a protectable trade secret first exists. Once

Proprietary
Characterized by private, exclusive ownership.

Encrypted code
Code typed in one set of symbols and interpreted by the machine as another; used for security.

it does, though, the trade secret may last perpetually until the owner loses the differential advantage it affords.

As we learned earlier, the loss of a protectable trade secret may occur through another party's independent discovery of the secret or any other legitimate means, such as reverse engineering or the public dissemination of the knowledge underlying the trade secret through either a failure to keep the information secret or flaws in the methods the owner has employed to ensure secrecy. Mass distribution of software copies to those with whom the software owner has a confidential relationship generally does not eliminate trade-secret protection as long as the owner otherwise has taken precautions to preserve secrecy.

UNFAIR COMPETITION

Our system of law allows, in the name of "competition," rather freewheeling activities. However, courts will give remedies to those injured by activities such as the solicitation of a former employer's customers or employees, the competition between an employee and his or her employer while the employee still works for the employer, wrongful terminations by the employer, and the "palming off" of one's goods as those of another.

Protection and Remedies

The common law and statutory restrictions on "unfair competition" often form the legal bases on which aggrieved persons in these circumstances sue. Misappropriation, another basis for relief, derives from the common law principles of unfair competition and often becomes a "catch-all" theory used in situations in which patent, copyright, and trade secret law do not cover the aspect of the business in dispute. One note of caution is in order, however. The Supreme Court in several decisions has held that federal law will preempt such state causes of action if they interfere with federal policies.[25]

Palming off, or conduct in which a competitor—by deceptively "palming off" (or "passing off") his or her goods or services as originating from the other firm— tries to divert another firm's patronage or business to itself, represents the oldest theory of unfair competition. The common law recognized the unfairness of one firm's "free-riding" on the effort, investment, and goodwill of another and thus granted injunctions and/or damages to those injured by such palming off.

Since such activities often involved the wrongdoer's misrepresenting or copying the plaintiff's trademark or trade dress, the Lanham Act, in outlawing trademark infringement, basically "federalizes" these common law theories, although it changes them in certain significant ways. Indeed, § 43(a) of the Lanham Act also provides protection to commercial people even in the absence of federal trademark registration; hence, it has carved out broad civil remedies for commercial activities that affect interstate commerce.

Section 43(a) creates three different types of "unfair competition" claims: (1) "palming off" (or "passing off") claims under which the act prohibits any person's falsely designating the origin of particular goods or services if these false designations are likely to cause confusion, mistake, or deception with regard to this person's affiliation or connection to another person's goods, services, or commercial activities; (2) false advertising claims; and (3) product disparagement-type claims (i.e., derogatory, false, injurious statements about a competitor's product, service, or title). To recover under § 43(a), the plaintiff must show that the defendant's activities affected interstate commerce; the defendant made material, false, misleading, or deceptive statements or designations that led to a likelihood of confusion among consumers; and actual injury or the likelihood of it to the plaintiff.

While consumers ordinarily have no standing to sue (only injured competitors do), § 43(a), by allowing injunctive relief upon the plaintiff's showing a likelihood of damage, indirectly protects consumers' interests; the plaintiff need not show the defendant's actual diversion of patronage or trade. A showing of such a loss of business will be necessary if the plaintiff seeks money damages, however. Otherwise, the remedies ordinarily available for infringement of trademarks apply to § 43(a) claims.

The Federal Trade Commission (FTC), discussed in Chapter 39, has jurisdiction over "unfair or deceptive acts or practices in or affecting commerce." The FTC's enforcement mechanisms, particularly the wide latitude the FTC has in fashioning cease-and-desist orders, represents yet another avenue for protecting the owners of intellectual property from unfair trade practices. In the international arena, the Paris Convention protects its signatories against unfair trade practices.

Antidilution Statutes. In recent years, the legal system has begun to recognize that competitive injury can result even if the parties are not competitors and even if there is an absence of confusion as to the source of the goods. In other words, the law in some circumstances will protect one who owns strong, distinctive, well-known marks from another's use of an identical or similar mark if such use is likely to tarnish, degrade, or dilute the distinctive power of the mark. Simply put, the states that have enacted these so-called "antidilution" statutes recognize that even nonconfusing uses of identical or similar marks over time may gradually erode the distinctive value of the mark, as well as advertising and other public promotional efforts the mark owner has undertaken to promote product goodwill and to capture, as well as retain, a robust market share.

In granting relief, state courts, as well as federal courts under their diversity jurisdiction, have utilized the dilution doctrine. As we learned in Chapter 5, the law protects truthful, nondeceptive commercial speech. Hence, like the *2 Live Crew* case we studied under copyright law, some cases brought under the dilution theory implicate aspects of the First Amendment, particularly if the defendant's use involves parody.

Celebrated dilution cases have included Pillsbury's seeking to enjoin a company's portraying and marketing Pillsbury's trade figures, "Poppie Fresh" and "Poppin' Fresh," in obscene sexual positions; General Electric's seeking to enjoin an underwear company's using an electric light bulb on its underwear named "Genital Electric"; and Coca-Cola's seeking to enjoin a poster captioned "Enjoy Cocaine" in script similar to that used in the Coca-Cola trademark. These cases illustrate the tension between the owner's desire to protect its mark from tarnishment and the value our society from its inception has placed on parody. Note, too, that only owners of distinctive marks can sue under such statutes, since only they have marks capable of suffering dilution or erosion.

The Federal Trademark Dilution Act of 1995 adds to rather than replaces state antidilution statutes. This act codifies as federal law the principle that no one can undertake a diluting use of a famous mark even in circumstances in which there is

HOW MUCH OF PROFESSOR ARTHUR MILLER DOES HARVARD UNIVERSITY OWN?

The pioneer in making law accessible to the public via television—Professor Arthur Miller—finds himself embroiled in a dispute worthy of discussion on the law-related public television series he originated. In 1998, Professor Miller, one of Harvard University's most recognizable faculty members, agreed to make 11 videotaped lectures for a course on civil procedure for Concord University School of Law (Concord). Concord is an online, degree-granting institution created by the Washington Post Company's Kaplan Educational Centers. According to Professor Miller, these Internet lectures are remarkably similar in format to what he did when he originated "Miller's Court" in 1979. At that time, he says, television represented the next frontier for teaching law to the masses. Now, he claims, the Web is the frontier teaching venue. Harvard, of course, disagrees and draws distinctions between the Internet lectures at issue here and educational television programs. Harvard notes, for example, that Concord is a school of 170 students, each of whom pays $4,200 per year in tuition and fees. Harvard also points to its existing policies that prohibit faculty members from teaching for another educational institution unless the faculty member first obtains the dean's permission. Professor Miller concedes that he failed to obtain the law school dean's permission but argues these conflict-of-interest rules are inapplicable to him anyway because he is not teaching at Concord. Miller stresses that he never meets, interacts, or exchanges e-mail with any of the Concord students. Concord professors also respond to any questions generated by the videotaped materials and grade all class materials and tests. Yet those who disagree with Miller emphasize the inequities of a student's getting a Harvard course on the Internet at a price much less than the $30,000 in annual tuition Harvard students pay. According to these critics, the university provides the basic intellectual capital that comprises a given course. As a law school colleague of Miller's has stated: "Concord's program is like watching television. Concord wants Arthur because they want to associate Concord with Harvard. It's a dilution of the Harvard name." Miller scoffs at such criticisms by noting that he has been doing videotaped and audiotaped lectures of his courses for 25 years and sees the Concord venture as nothing different. This legal imbroglio stems largely from the profits that professors and universities can derive from capitalizing on the Internet's educational opportunities. Several well-respected universities—including Duke and Stanford—offer online graduate degrees. Accordingly, Harvard's law school recently amended its conflict-of-interest rules to cover the activities of any faculty member who wants to serve as a teacher, researcher, or salaried consultant to an Internet-based university.

One can imagine Professor Miller's framing his own situation in this way: "A Harvard professor wants to give an online course at a smaller school. . . . Who owns his teaching: the professor or the university? Can two institutions offer his lectures at the same time?"

Assume Harvard places this intellectual property dispute before *your* court. How will *you* dispose of this case? Why?[26]

BUSINESS CONSIDERATION Should Harvard take a hard-line approach in this case, or would a less stringent approach be more advisable?

ETHICAL CONSIDERATIONS Evaluate, respectively, the ethics of Professor Miller, Harvard, and Concord. Is any of these parties entitled to stake out the moral high ground? Why or why not?

SOURCE: *The Wall Street Journal* (22 November 1999), pp. A1, A10.

an absence of the likelihood of customer confusion as to the source of the goods. This statute, then, apparently has ushered in a new era of federal trademark protection, an era that potentially will greatly expand the safeguards afforded to famous, strong, distinctive marks. Be alert for the legal developments that will result from this congressional enactment.

THE SEMICONDUCTOR CHIP PROTECTION ACT OF 1984

Congress's enactment of the Semiconductor Chip Protection Act of 1984 as an amendment to the copyright laws affords developers of integrated circuits a 10-year monopoly over their resultant semiconductor chips. Although it contains ideas common to copyright, patent, and trade secret law, this act creates a new class of intellectual property law.

Congress directed the legislation at both domestic and international chip pirates who in the past had merely taken chips apart, reconstructed the circuit design on the chip (known as the mask), and then made copies of the original chip. Obviously, as long as copyright law did not protect semiconductor chips (they were deemed utilitarian/useful articles and hence uncopyrightable even though the circuit diagrams might be), the incentive for pirates to reap profits by copying while at the same time avoiding the mammoth costs associated with developing the chips clearly existed. By prohibiting reverse engineering that has as its end purpose the copying of the chip, the act eliminates this result but, by allowing reverse engineering leading to the creation of a new chip, preserves current law.

Protection and Remedies

The act itself protects only mask works, or the layouts of the integrated circuits that appear on the chips; it does not protect the semiconductor chips themselves; any other product that performs the function of chips, such as circuit boards; or works embodied in mask works, such as computer programs. Indeed, not all mask works are protected, either. For instance, if the mask work is not "fixed" in a semiconductor chip, as is the case of information merely stored on diskettes, or if the mask work embodies designs that are commonplace and unoriginal, the act is inapplicable. The duration of the protection is 10 years from the time of registration or the first commercial exploitation of the mask work, whichever occurs first. The process of registration contains special procedures for protecting proprietary information.

The same remedies generally available under the copyright laws relating to infringement—injunctions, damages, attorney's fees, and import exclusion and seizure—apply in this context, except that criminal sanctions are unavailable. Some provisions of the act protect the mask works of nonpirating foreign companies under certain circumstances as well.

Although interpretive questions undoubtedly will arise as the first cases begin to appear under this act, note that this statute, at the time of its enactment, represented the first federal intellectual property law in over 100 years.

RESOURCES FOR BUSINESS LAW STUDENTS

NAME	RESOURCES	WEB ADDRESS
Patent and Trademark Office (PTO)	The Patent and Trademark Office allows for patent searches; as well, it provides forms, legal materials, and the PTO museum.	**http://www.uspto.gov/**
World Intellectual Property Organization (WIPO)	The World Intellectual Property Organization maintains the Berne Convention, the Paris Convention WIPO Copyright Treaty, and the WIPO Performances and Phonograms Treaty, among other resources.	**http://www.wipo.org/eng/general/copyrght/bern.htm**
Copyright Office, Library of Congress	The Copyright Office provides publications and extensive information on copyright topics, including the basics of copyright law.	**http://lcweb.loc.gov/copyright/**
Lanham Act	The Legal Information Institute (LII), maintained by the Cornell Law School, provides a hypertext and searchable version of the Lanham Act (the Trademark Act of 1946).	**http://wwwsecure.law.cornell.edu/lanham/lanham.table.html**

SUMMARY

Intellectual property encompasses several substantive areas of the law: copyrights, patents, trademarks, trade secrets, and unfair competition. Computers constitute an especially apt illustration of the significance of intellectual property both in the United States and in the international arena. Intellectual property law strives to serve two oftentimes competing goals: ensuring incentives to create a wider array of products and services in the marketplace while at the same time, by providing public access to intellectual creations, promoting competition. The law serves the first goal when the law grants property rights (sometimes even monopolies) to creators and the second when the law limits the duration of such exclusive rights and/or circumscribes the rights thus granted so as to maximize the amount of information found in the public domain. This area of the law also seeks to safeguard creators and businesspeople from injurious trade practices.

The copyright laws protect any original works of authorship. To be copyrightable, works of authorship must show originality; and the works must be fixed in a tangible medium of expression. Ideas are not copyrightable. A copyright in essence consists of a bundle of exclusive rights that enables the copyright owner—usually the author or one to whom the author has transferred rights—to exploit a work for commercial purposes. To ensure copyright protection, one must ascertain the governing law: the 1909 Copyright Act, the 1976 Copyright Act, or the Berne Convention. Violations of any of the copyright owner's exclusive rights constitute infringement. The courts have imposed liability for both direct and contributory infringement. The most common defense against charges of infringement is the "fair use" doctrine. Civil remedies for infringement include injunctions, the impoundment and destruction of infringing items, and damages. Criminal penalties also are available.

The Patent Act of 1952 grants to inventors the exclusive right to their respective discoveries that consist of patentable subject matter. The Supreme Court has held that such utility patents may cover genetically engineered living matter as well. As in copyright law, ideas per se are not patentable. Utility patents last for 20 years from the filing date, while design patents last for only 14 years from the date of the grant of the patent, after which time the monopoly granted to the patentee ends. At that point, others can make, use, or sell the invention with impunity. To be patentable, an invention must demonstrate novelty, utility, and nonobviousness. Obtaining a patent involves detailed disclosures to the Patent and Trademark Office. Infringements may be either direct, indirect (e.g., inducements to infringe), or contributory ones. Persons sued for patent infringement may claim lack of patentability or patent misuse as a defense. Remedies for infringement include injunctive relief as well as damages.

Over the years, an extensive body of state trademark law has developed in the common law, principally through the state common law relating to unfair competition. By providing a structure by which the enforcement of these common principles can occur through federal oversight, the 1946 Lanham Act—the most important federal protection of trademarks—builds on these common law roots. The Lanham Act defines a trademark as any word, name, symbol, device, or any combination thereof used to identify and distinguish the services of one person from the services of others and to indicate the source of the goods, even if the source is unknown. This definition underscores the fact that a trademark always exists pursuant to commercial activity or use and may cover an extensive array of things, including the distinctive features of the product (i.e., "trade dress") such as the product's shape, its packaging, its logo or artwork, and so on. To deserve protection, the trademark—whatever its form—must be distinctive; generic terms never can qualify for trademark protection. Purely descriptive marks do not qualify as distinctive until they have acquired "secondary meaning."

Under federal law, before one can register the mark on the Lanham Act's Principal Register, one must demonstrate prior use, the affixation requirement, and the use of the mark in interstate commerce. Obtaining a trademark involves registration with the PTO; certain parties can file oppositions to the registration or sue for cancellation of the mark. The law protects the trademark owner from infringements that will result in a likelihood of confusion concerning the source of the goods. Defenses to a cause of action based on infringement include "fair use" and abandonment of the mark. Registration of the mark on the Principal Register gives the owner certain advantages in an infringement action, as does the mark's becoming incontestable. Under the Lanham Act, an owner may resort to certain equitable and at law remedies.

Trade secret law protects proprietary information that gives the owner a differential advantage over his or her competitors. To merit protection, the information must be secret and used continuously in the business. The law does not protect as trade secrets either common knowledge or information easily acquired from reverse engineering. Misappropriation can occur through breach of contractual or confidential relations or the use of improper means to acquire the secret. Remedies include injunctions and damages actions. State and federal criminal laws may apply to such misappropriations as well.

In "federalizing" common and state law unfair competition claims, the Lanham Act allows recovery on three bases: (1) "palming off," (2) false advertising, and (3) product disparagement. State and federal "antidilution" laws also protect one who owns a strong, distinctive, well-known mark from another's use of an identical or similar mark if such use is likely to tarnish, degrade, or dilute the distinctive power of the mark. As we have seen in other contexts, parody may constitute a defense to actions brought under this theory.

The Federal Trade Commission also has authority to protect the owners of intellectual property from unfair trade practices. Several international treaties regulate intellectual property as well.

DISCUSSION QUESTIONS

1. What does the law require before it will grant copyright protection?
2. What factors constitute "fair use" under the Copyright Act?
3. What does the law mandate before it will grant patent protection?
4. What is a *trademark,* and what does the law require before it will grant trademark protection?
5. What factors will a court use to determine a "likelihood of confusion" under trademark law?
6. What advantages derive from the registration of a trademark on the Lanham Act's Principal Register?

7. What must one do to protect information as a trade secret? In determining whether information constitutes a trade secret, what factors can a court consider?
8. Name and define the theories on which courts ground liability for misappropriation of a trade secret.
9. Explain in detail how the Lanham Act protects against unfair competition.
10. Explain fully the international protections accorded to various types of intellectual property.

CASE PROBLEMS AND WRITING ASSIGNMENTS

1. On 19 April 1982, Wayne Pfaff filed an application for a patent on a computer chip socket. Section 102(b) of the Patent Act of 1952 provides that no person is entitled to patent an "invention" that has been "on sale" more than one year before filing a patent application. Therefore, 19 April 1981, would constitute the critical date for purposes of the so-called "on-sale" bar of Section 102(b); if the one-year period had begun to run before that date, Pfaff would lose his right to patent his invention. Pfaff commenced work on the socket in November 1980, when representatives of Texas Instruments asked him to develop a new device for mounting and removing semiconductor chip carriers. In response to this request, he prepared detailed engineering drawings that described the design, the dimensions, and the materials to be used in making the socket. Pfaff sent those drawings to a manufacturer in February or March 1981. Prior to 17 March, Pfaff showed a sketch of his concept to representatives of Texas Instruments. On 8 April 1981, they provided Pfaff with a written confirmation of a previously placed oral purchase order for 30,100 of his new sockets for a total price of $91,155. In accordance with his normal practice, Pfaff did not make and test a prototype of the new device before he offered to sell the invention in commercial quantities. The manufacturer took several months to develop the customized tooling necessary to produce the device, so Pfaff did not fill the order until July 1981. The evidence therefore indicated that Pfaff first reduced his invention to practice (i.e., he fully assembled the invention and used it) in the summer of 1981. The socket achieved substantial commercial success before Patent No. 4,491,377 (the '377 patent) was issued to Pfaff on 1 January 1985. After the issuance of the patent, Pfaff brought an infringement action against Wells Electronics, Inc. (Wells), the manufacturer of a competing socket. Wells prevailed when a court found no infringement had occurred. After Wells began to market a modified device, Pfaff brought this suit, alleging that the modifications infringed six of the claims in the '377 patent. The district court held that two of those claims were invalid because they had been anticipated in the prior art. Nevertheless, the court concluded that four other claims were valid and that various models of Wells's sockets had infringed upon three of these claims. The district court rejected Wells's § 102(b) defense because Pfaff had filed the application for the '377 patent less than a year after he had reduced the invention to practice. The court of appeals reversed, finding all six claims invalid. Four of the claims described the socket that Pfaff had sold to Texas Instruments prior to

8 April 1981. Because that device had been offered for sale on a commercial basis more than one year before the patent application was filed on 19 April 1982, the appeals court concluded that those claims were invalid under § 102(b). That conclusion rested on the court's view that as long as the invention was "substantially complete at the time of sale," the one-year period would begin to run, even though the invention had not yet been reduced to practice. Did the commercial marketing of a newly invented product mark the beginning of the one-year period even though the invention had not yet been reduced to practice? [See *Pfaff* v. *Wells Electronics, Inc.*, 525 U.S. 55 (1998), *reh'g denied*, 525 U.S. 1094 (1999).]

2. L'anza Research International, Inc. (L'anza), is a California corporation engaged in the business of manufacturing and selling shampoos, conditioners, and other hair care products. L'anza has copyrighted the labels that are affixed to those products. In the United States, L'anza sells exclusively to domestic distributors who have agreed to resell within limited geographic areas and then only to authorized retailers such as barber shops, beauty salons, and professional hair care colleges. L'anza's adoption of this distributional system stems from its belief that the American public is generally unwilling to pay the price charged for high-quality products, such as L'anza's products, when they are sold along with the less expensive, lower-quality products generally carried by supermarkets and drug stores. L'anza promotes the domestic sales of its products with extensive advertising in various trade magazines and at the point of sale, as well as by providing special training to authorized retailers. L'anza also sells its products in foreign markets. In those markets, however, it does not engage in comparable advertising or promotion; its prices to foreign distributors are 35 to 40 percent lower than the prices charged to domestic distributors. In 1992 and 1993, L'anza's distributor in the United Kingdom arranged the sale of three shipments to a distributor in Malta; each shipment contained several tons of L'anza products with copyrighted labels affixed. Although some facts remained unclear, it was undisputed that the goods were manufactured by L'anza and first sold by L'anza to a foreign purchaser. It also was undisputed that the goods found their way back to the United States without the permission of L'anza and were sold in California by unauthorized retailers who had purchased them at discounted prices from Quality King Distributors, Inc. (Quality King). Apparently, Quality King bought all three shipments from the Malta distributor, imported them, and then resold them to retailers who were not in L'anza's authorized

chain of distribution. After determining the source of the unauthorized sales, L'anza brought suit against Quality King and several other defendants. The complaint alleged that the importation and subsequent distribution of those products bearing copyrighted labels violated L'anza's exclusive rights under the copyright laws to reproduce and distribute the copyrighted material in the United States. To rebut L'anza's claim, Quality King asserted the "first sale" doctrine as a defense. The "first sale" doctrine means that the exclusive right of the copyright holder to sell the copyrighted article applies only to the first sale of the work. After a lawful first sale, any subsequent purchaser is the owner and can sell the item. To counter Quality King's claim, L'anza submitted that § 602, which gives copyright owners the right to prohibit the unauthorized importation of copies, would be meaningless if the court permitted Quality King to use the "first sale" doctrine as a defense. The district court subsequently rejected Quality King's defense based on the "first sale" doctrine and entered summary judgment in favor of L'anza. Who had the more persuasive argument: L'anza or Quality King? [See *Quality King Distributors, Inc.* v. *L'anza Research International, Inc.*, 523 U.S. 135 (1998).]

3. Signature Financial Group, Inc. (Signature) is the assignee of the '056 patent entitled "Data Processing System for Hub and Spoke Financial Services Configuration." The PTO issued the '056 patent to Signature on 9 March 1993. The '056 patent is generally directed to a data processing system (the system) for implementing an investment structure developed for use in Signature's business as an administrator and accounting agent for mutual funds. In essence, the system, identified as Hub and Spoke®, facilitates a structure whereby mutual funds (Spokes) pool their assets in an investment portfolio (Hub) organized as a partnership. This investment configuration provides the administrator of a mutual fund with the advantageous combination of economies of scale in administering investments coupled with the tax advantages of a partnership. State Street Bank & Trust. Co. (State Street) and Signature both act as custodians and accounting agents for multitiered partnership fund financial services. State Street negotiated with Signature for a license to use the patented data processing system described and claimed in the '056 patent. This patented invention relates generally to a system that allows an administrator to monitor and record the financial information flow and make all calculations necessary for maintaining a partner fund financial services configuration. In particular, this system provides means for a daily allocation of assets for

two or more Spokes that are invested in the same Hub. The system determines the percentage share each Spoke maintains in the Hub, while taking into consideration daily changes both in the value of the Hub's investment securities and in the concomitant amount of each Spoke's assets. In determining these daily changes, the system also allows for the allocation among the Spokes of the Hub's daily income, expenses, and net realized and unrealized gain or loss, as well as the calculation of each day's total investments based on the concept of a book capital account. The determination of a true asset value of each Spoke and an accurate calculation of allocation ratios between or among the Spokes thereby result. The system additionally tracks all the relevant data determined on a daily basis for the Hub and each Spoke, so that aggregate year-end income, expenses, and capital gain or loss can be determined for accounting and for tax purposes for the Hub and, as a result, for each publicly traded Spoke. Any firm using the system must quickly and accurately perform these calculations because each Spoke sells shares to the public, and the price of those shares is substantially based on the Spoke's percentage interest in the portfolio. Indeed, in some instances, a mutual fund administrator must calculate the value of the shares to the nearest penny within as little as an hour and a half after the market closes. Given the complexity of the calculations, a computer or equivalent device is a virtual necessity to perform the task. The '056 patent application claimed that the Hub and Spoke® system was a machine and thus constituted patentable subject matter. The Supreme Court has identified three categories of subject matter that are unpatentable, namely "laws of nature, natural phenomena, and abstract ideas." Specifically, the Court has held that mathematical algorithms are not patentable subject matter to the extent that they are merely abstract ideas. From a practical standpoint, this means that to be patentable, an algorithm must be applied in a "useful" way. Courts also have refused patentability to so-called "business methods" as well. Was the '056 patent invalid because it consists of nonstatutory subject matter, specifically either a mathematical algorithm or a business method? [See *State Street Bank & Trust Co.* v. *Signature Financial Group, Inc.*, 149 F.3d 1368 (Fed. Cir. 1998), *cert. denied*, 525 U.S. 1093 (1999).]

4. West Publishing Company and West Publishing Corporation (collectively West) create and publish printed compilations of federal and state judicial opinions. In doing so, West employs a particular arrangement of information, in which it designates the parties, the court, and the date of the decision; selects and arranges information about attorneys and subsequent procedural developments; and selects parallel and alternative citations. Matthew Bender & Company, Inc. (Matthew Bender) manufactures and markets compilations of judicial opinions stored on compact disc-read only memory (CD-ROM) discs, in which opinions Matthew Bender embeds (or intends to embed) citations that show the page location of the particular text in West's printed version of the opinions (the so-called "star pagination" feature). Bender sought a judgment declaring that such star pagination would not infringe West's copyrights in West's compilations of judicial opinions. After the district court found in favor of Matthew Bender, West appealed. West contended that the use of star pagination allows a user of Matthew Bender's CD-ROM discs (by inputting a series of commands) to "perceive" West's copyright-protected arrangements of cases in West's case reports and that Matthew Bender's products (when star pagination is added) constitute unlawful copies of West's arrangements. Using the *Feist* case, evaluate whether Matthew Bender had infringed West's copyright. [See *Matthew Bender & Co.* v. *West Publishing Company*, 158 F.3d 693 (2d Cir. 1998), *cert. denied*, 526 U.S. 1154 (1999).]

5. The primary asset of the bankruptcy estate of Cybernetic Services, Inc. (the debtor) is a patent for a data recorder designed to capture data from a video signal regardless of the horizontal line in which the data are located. Matsco, Inc. (Matsco) and Matsco Financial Corporation (Financial) filed a motion requesting relief from the automatic stay order that prevents a creditor's foreclosing on any assets of the debtor. Matsco and Financial had undertaken all the steps necessary to have a blanket security interest in all of the debtor's assets, including "general intangibles." The parties agreed that this security interest covered the patent. A UCC-1 financing statement covering general intangibles was properly prepared, executed by the debtor, and timely filed with the Secretary of State of the State of California. However, Matsco and Financial did not file either the financing statement or any other document with the federal Patent and Trademark Office (PTO). The Chapter 7 trustee asserted that Matsco and Financial should be denied relief from the stay because they lacked a perfected security interest in the patent. The trustee argued that, in order to perfect a security interest in the patent, a creditor must make the appropriate filing with the PTO. The bankruptcy court disagreed and concluded that Article 9 of the Uniform Commercial Code (UCC), as adopted by California, rather than the Patent Act, would govern the perfection of a security

interest in a patent. When the bankruptcy court granted Matsco and Financial relief from the automatic stay, the trustee appealed. Had the bankruptcy court erred in ruling that filing a UCC financing statement with the California Secretary of State rather than with the PTO would perfect Matsco and Financial's security interest in the patent? [See *Moldo* v. *Matsco, Inc. (In re Cybernetic Services, Inc.)*, 239 B.R. 917 (9th Cir. 1999).]

6. **BUSINESS APPLICATION CASE** Deere & Company (Deere) is the world's largest supplier of agricultural equipment. For over 100 years, Deere has used a deer design as a trademark for identifying its products and services. Deere owns numerous trademark registrations for different versions of the Deere logo. Although these versions vary slightly, all depict a static, two-dimensional silhouette of a leaping male deer in profile. The Deere logo is a widely recognizable and valuable business asset. MTD Products, Inc. (MTD), an Ohio company, manufactures and sells lawn tractors. In 1993, W. B. Doner & Company (Doner), MTD's advertising agency, decided to create and produce a commercial that would use the Deere logo, without Deere's authorization, for the purpose of comparing Deere's line of lawn tractors to MTD's "Yard-Man" tractor. The intent was to identify Deere as the market leader and convey the message that the Yard-Man was of comparable quality but less costly than a Deere. Doner altered the Deere logo in several respects. For example, the deer in the MTD logo was somewhat differently proportioned than the deer in the Deere logo. The MTD logo also lacked the name "John Deere." More significantly, the deer in the commercial logo was animated and assumed various poses. For instance, the deer, as a two-dimensional cartoon, ran in apparent fear as it was pursued by the Yard-Man lawn tractor and a barking dog. MTD submitted the commercial to ABC, NBC, and CBS for clearance prior to airing, together with substantiation of the various claims made regarding the Yard-Man lawn tractor's quality and cost relative to the corresponding Deere model. Each network ultimately approved the commercial. The commercial ran from the week of 7 March 1994 through the week of 23 May 1994.

Filing a complaint seeking a preliminary injunction and a temporary restraining order, Deere alleged subsequent violations of the New York antidilution statute and § 43(a) of the Lanham Act, as well as common law claims of unfair competition and unjust enrichment. Following a hearing, the district court denied Deere's application for a temporary restraining order but ultimately found that Deere had demonstrated a likelihood of prevailing on its dilution claim and hence granted preliminary injunctive relief limited to activities within New York. The court later concluded that Deere had not shown a likelihood of success on the merits of its Lanham Act claim. On appeal, MTD argued that the antidilution statute does not prohibit a trademark's commercial uses that fail to confuse consumers or to result in a loss of the trademark's ability to identify a single manufacturer, or to tarnish the trademark's positive connotations. In its cross-appeal, Deere contended that the court should not have limited injunctive relief to New York state. How should the appellate court decide this case? Can an upstart firm ever compete effectively with a well-known firm if the jurisdiction in question has an antidilution statute? Should the parodic nature of the ad immunize MTD from liability? Justify your responses. [See *Deere & Company* v. *MTD Products, Inc.*, 41 F.3d 39 (2d Cir. 1994).]

7. **ETHICAL APPLICATION CASE** Mavety Media Group, Ltd. (Mavety) published *Black Tail*, an adult entertainment magazine featuring photographs of both naked and scantily clad African-American women. On 7 June 1990, Mavety filed a PTO application seeking federal registration of its trademark "Black Tail," based on Mavety's bona fide intention to use the mark in connection with goods identified as "magazines." In accordance with the regulation governing the filing of an amendment to allege the first use of the mark, Mavety provided published issues of *Black Tail*. The examiner ultimately refused registration because the mark consisted of or comprised immoral or scandalous matter. The examiner expressly relied on a dictionary reference defining "tail" as "sexual intercourse—usu. considered vulgar." On 15 August 1991, Mavety, responding to the examiner's decision, contended that a substantial composite of the population would not interpret the mark to be a reference to sexual intercourse but rather as a reference to "the rear end," a meaning not usually considered vulgar. Mavety supported its contention with the magazine specimens of record that depicted the use of the mark—for example, on the magazine cover above a photograph of a woman displaying her derriere. Mavety also provided newspaper articles showing that many consumers would interpret "Black Tail" as connoting the full evening dress worn by men at formal occasions and thus the quality, class, and experience of an expensive lifestyle, consistent with the familiar genre of adult entertainment magazines such as *Playboy* and *Penthouse*. In addition, Mavety argued that the federal trademark register contains numerous

marks consisting of words with nonsexual primary meanings that nonetheless have sexual connotations. When the Trademark Trial and Appeal Board (TTAB) of the PTO affirmed the examiner's refusal to register Mavety's mark, Mavety instituted a lawsuit in the Court of Appeals for the Federal Circuit. How should that court rule in this case? Had the court decided this case on ethical (as opposed to legal) grounds, would your answer have differed? Explain fully. [See *In re Mavety Media Group, Ltd.*, 33 F.3d 1367 (Fed. Cir. 1994).]

8. **CRITICAL THINKING CASE** Service Merchandise Company, Inc. (Service Merchandise) opened its first store in Nashville, Tennessee, in 1960 and registered its service mark with the U.S. Patent and Trademark Office (PTO) for the first time in 1977. The firm now owns and operates approximately 304 "Service Merchandise" retail stores across the country, with 37 stores in Texas and seven stores in the Houston area. Service Jewelry Stores, Inc. (Service Jewelry) is a Texas corporation that owns and operates two jewelry stores in Houston, Texas. Service Merchandise sells a variety of goods, but, by virtually always displaying featured jewelry items in the first several pages of any advertisements, it particularly emphasizes its selection of jewelry. Service Jewelry concentrates solely on jewelry sales and service. It devotes approximately 60 percent of its business to jewelry service or repair and the rest to the retail sale of jewelry; Service Jewelry custom-makes 90 percent of the jewelry it sells. Both Service Merchandise and Service Jewelry's marks begin with the word "Service" in red script letters that are larger than the words following in nonscript letters. Service Jewelry follows the word "Service" with the phrase "Jewelry Store" instead of "Merchandise." The evidence also showed that customers have asked Service Merchandise about its "new store" (which inquiries referred to Service Jewelry's store), and postal authorities have delivered mail intended for Service Jewelry to Service Merchandise. In its suit for trademark infringement, Service Merchandise also asserted the incontestability of the mark. What arguments would you expect Service Jewelry to make in its own behalf, and how should a court rule in this case? [See *Service Merchandise Company v. Service Jewelry Stores, Inc.*, 737 F.Supp. 983 (S.D. Texas 1990).]

NOTES

1. *Statistical Abstract of the United States,* U.S. Department of Commerce, Bureau of the Census (118th ed.) (Washington, DC: 1998), p. 557.
2. *Fogerty* v. *Fantasy, Inc.*, 510 U.S. 517 (1994).
3. 714 F.2d 1240 (3d Cir. 1983), *cert. dismissed,* 464 U.S. 1033 (1984).
4. Ibid. at 1244.
5. Ibid. at 1245.
6. Ibid. at 1250.
7. Ibid. at 1240–1241.
8. Ibid. at 1249.
9. 49 F.3d 807 (1st Cir. 1995), *affirmed,* 516 U.S. 233 (1996).
10. 527 U.S. 150 (1999).
11. 57 *Patent, Trademark & Copyright Journal* 347 (25 February 1999).
12. Ibid.
13. Ibid.
14. *Markman* v. *Westview Instruments, Inc.*, 517 U.S. 370, 371 (1996).
15. 527 U.S. 627 (1999).
16. Ibid.
17. 450 U.S. 175 (1981).
18. 684 F.2d 912 (CCPA 1982).
19. *Statistical Abstract of the United States,* U.S. Department of Commerce, Bureau of the Census (118th ed.) (Washington, DC: 1998), p. 557.
20. 527 U.S. 666 (1999).
21. Greenlee, "Spies Like Them: How to Protect Your Company from Industrial Spies," 78 *Management Accounting* 31 (December 1996).
22. Chaim A. Levin, "Trade-Secret Thieves Face Fines, Prosecution," *The National Law Journal* (27 January 1997), p. C13.
23. Ibid.
24. Ibid., p. C12.
25. *Sears, Roebuck & Co.* v. *Stiffel Co.*, 376 U.S. 225 (1964); *Compco Corporation* v. *Day-Brite Lighting, Inc.*, 376 U.S. 234 (1964); *Bonito Boats, Inc.* v. *Thunder Craft Boats, Inc.*, 489 U.S. 141 (1989).
26. Amy Dochser Marcus, "Why Harvard Law Wants to Rein in One of Its Star Professors," *The Wall Street Journal* (22 November 1999), pp. A1, A10.

46

WILLS, ESTATES, AND TRUSTS

A G E N D A

Like many small-business owners, Tom and Anna Kochanowski are concerned about protecting their family in the event that either of them should become incapacitated or die. How should Tom and Anna write their wills to ensure that CIT continues to operate and provide income and security following the death of either—or both—of them? With a small business, continuity is important. They don't want CIT to stop operating for a significant period of time if anything should happen to either of them. Tom and Anna also want to provide for their children. Tom has read the book *How to Avoid Probate!* by Norman F. Dacey. As a result, he would like to avoid probate in the administration of his estate. What are the advantages and disadvantages of avoiding probate in Tom's estate? How can Tom and Anna control medical and financial decisions if they become extremely ill and/or incompetent? How can they transfer CIT to family members? What restrictions would be appropriate? Would a trust be proper? Who could serve as the trustee? Who should be appointed Lindsay's guardian?

These and other questions will be raised in this chapter. Be prepared! You never know when one of the Kochanowskis will need your help or advice.

O U T L I N E

The Transfer of an Estate
Wills
Requirements for a Valid Will
Testamentary Dispositions and Restrictions
Intestate Succession
Probate and Estate Administration
Avoiding Probate
Transfer Taxes
Retirement Plans
Durable Powers of Attorney and Living Wills

Trusts Defined
Express Trusts
Advantages of Trusts
Disadvantages of Trusts
Selection of Trustees and Executors
Duties of Trustees and Executors
Implied Trusts
Summary
Discussion Questions
Case Problems and Writing Assignments

THE TRANSFER OF AN ESTATE

Almost everyone has an estate, no matter how modest it might be. It may consist only of compact disks, a television, and a 10-speed bike; conversely, it may consist of some office buildings, rental houses, sizable money market accounts, and shares in Call-Image Technologies. This chapter deals with critical planning decisions—what happens to an estate when someone dies—and addresses techniques for transferring an estate to family members and friends. The discussion is general because the rules vary significantly from state to state.

Under the U.S. Constitution, property transfers, including wills, are governed by state law. The **probate codes** in the states vary greatly. The *Uniform Probate Code* is a statute drafted by the National Conference of Commissioners on Uniform State Laws (NCCUSL) for adoption by the states as their probate code. Its purposes are to unify state laws and respond to complaints that probate procedures are too complicated, costly, and time consuming. It was first introduced in 1966 and has undergone revision since then. The following states have adopted all or almost all of the *Uniform Probate Code:* Alaska, Arizona, Colorado, Hawaii, Idaho, Maine, Michigan, Minnesota, Montana, Nebraska, New Jersey, New Mexico, North Dakota, Pennsylvania, South Carolina, South Dakota, Utah, and Wisconsin. The District of Columbia, the U.S. Virgin Islands, and all the other states, except Louisiana, have adopted some sections of the code. Some of these states have adopted whole sections or articles of the code.[1] This chapter discusses many of the widely adopted sections.

WILLS

In a will, a person indicates who should inherit his or her property at death. The law that controls the validity of a person's will is the law of his or her **domicile.** A will provides an opportunity to name a guardian for any minor children the person may have. In fact, a will is the only way parents can specify who will raise a minor child if they both die. If parents do not use this technique for naming a guardian, the court will appoint one, and the court may not choose the best person. For example, grandparents may no longer be physically or emotionally capable of raising a young child. Because the court is not likely to be aware of these problems, the court may appoint the grandparents as guardians. The parents (and the courts) have the option of dividing the guardian's duties and appointing someone to care for the child's physical needs while appointing someone else to care for his or her financial needs and manage the inheritance. This option is valuable if one person is not competent in caring for *both* the child and the finances, but would be very competent in caring for one of them.

A will is also the place to name a **personal representative** for the estate. The personal representative nominated in the will is generally the one appointed by the court, if he or she is able to serve. The judge will appoint an alternate if the nominee is dead, disabled, or incompetent. The will should also contain a **residuary clause** for all the property that is not specifically mentioned elsewhere in the will. (It is not advisable to include burial instructions in a will because often the will is not located and read until after the funeral. Such instructions should be written as a separate document, with copies distributed to the personal representative, close family members, and the attorney.)

Some changes in family relationships affect the validity of a will. Children who are born after a will is executed (signed) receive a share of the estate as *after-born*

Probate codes
State statutes that deal with the estates of incompetents and people who have died with or without a valid will.

Domicile
One's permanent home and principal residence. It is the place to which a person will return after traveling.

Personal representative
A person who manages the financial affairs of another or an estate.

Residuary clause
A clause that disposes of the remainder (the residual) of an estate.

children. After-born children generally are entitled to their **intestate share.** If a marriage occurs after a will has been executed, the new spouse also will take a share of the estate. A divorce may change an existing will, too. In most states, a divorce with a property settlement will revoke gifts willed to the ex-spouse; however, a few states, including California, still require a revocation by the **testator** or **testatrix.** (In this chapter, we will use the term *testator* to refer to a man or a woman.)

To make changes in a will, it is not necessary to write a completely new document. The testator can simply make the desired changes in a **codicil.** The codicil also acts to confirm the unchanged will provisions. Care should be taken to assure that the will and the codicil read together will make sense. To be valid, a codicil must satisfy the same requirements as a will.

The testator may destroy the effect of a will by making a new will and stating in it that the old will is revoked. This is commonly called a *revocation clause.* If the new will does not specifically revoke the old will, the courts in some states will try to interpret the two wills together. In such a case, the new will revokes the older will only to the extent that they contain contradictory or inconsistent provisions. A testator also can cancel an old will by physically destroying the signed original, with the intention of revoking it.

Wills can be categorized by the manner in which they are formed. Generally, wills can be *formal, holographic,* or *nuncupative.* Wills also can be categorized by the types of dispositions they contain.

Formal Wills

The most common type of will is called a *formal,* or attested, will. It is generally drafted by an attorney and printed by the attorney's staff. A will prepared by a competent attorney is more likely to achieve the desired results than one prepared by a layperson. Familiarity with the terminology of wills is important because the words used in the will often have a special significance that differs from their ordinary meaning. In addition, each state has its own technical requirements.

A will *can* be a very lengthy document, and it must be executed in strict compliance with the procedures specified in the state statute. Generally, the testator must sign the will at the end of the document in the presence of at least two witnesses. The testator *must* ask these two individuals to act as witnesses to the will. The witnesses must be disinterested persons; that is, they must have no interest in any of the property passing under the will or by intestate succession. The primary purposes of witnesses are to swear that the signatures are valid and to swear that the testator was lucid and seemed competent. In most states, the will also must be dated.

California, Maine, and Wisconsin have a special type of formal will called a *statutory will.* This will is so named because it has been approved by the state legislature, and the language used in the will is specified in the state probate statute. Printing companies in the state can print form wills using the approved language. A form will is sold to an individual testator who fills in the appropriate names and executes the will. Despite its title, a statutory will is a formal will, and consequently it must be witnessed by two disinterested witnesses.

Holographic Wills

Holographic wills (called *olographic wills* in some states) are required to be written, signed, and usually dated in the testator's own handwriting. Although not universally accepted, they are allowed in a number of states, including Alaska,

Intestate share
Portion of the estate that a person is entitled to inherit if there is no valid will.

Testator
A man who makes a will.

Testatrix
A woman who makes a will.

Codicil
A separate written document that modifies an existing will.

Arizona, Arkansas, California, Idaho, Kentucky, Louisiana, Mississippi, Montana, Nevada, New Jersey, North Carolina, North Dakota, Oklahoma, Pennsylvania, South Dakota, Tennessee, Texas, Utah, Virginia, West Virginia, and Wyoming. Holographic wills also are allowed under the Uniform Probate Code § 2-503.

A testator who writes a holographic will runs the risk of not expressing his or her intentions properly and not complying with the technical requirements. The testator may be unaware of and hence unable to take advantage of techniques to reduce costs and taxes. An attorney or an accountant with tax expertise may be able to make recommendations that will greatly reduce the taxes.

Most of the states that allow holographic wills require that they be dated. They do not, however, have to be witnessed. Traditionally, holographic wills have to be written completely in the testator's hand with *no* printed or typed matter. Recently, some courts and legislatures have become more lenient about accepting printed matter on a holographic will. For example, the California legislature enacted a statutory change requiring only that the signature and the material provisions be in the testator's handwriting.[2] Also, a court may accept the will if the printed matter is not an integral part of the will. Many of the states that allow holographic wills require that the will be kept with the important papers of the **decedent.** The purpose of this requirement is to assist in establishing the testator's intent to make a will and ascertaining that the document was important to him or her.

Decedent
A person who has died.

Nuncupative Wills

Nuncupative, or oral, wills are permitted in a number of states under limited circumstances. Usually, nuncupative wills can be used only to dispose of personal property; this is true in Kansas, Nebraska, Virginia, and Washington. Georgia, however, allows real property to pass in this manner. Some states place a limit on the value of the property transferred by a nuncupative will. The Uniform Probate Code makes no provision for nuncupative wills, and many states do not permit them.

Nuncupative wills also are restricted to certain situations. Generally, an oral will is valid (1) if it is made by a civilian who anticipates death from an injury received the same day, or (2) if it is made by a soldier in the field or a sailor on a ship who is in peril or in fear of death. Because of the dangers inherent in military service and duty at sea, some states recognize a separate category of wills called *soldiers' and sailors' wills* (also sometimes called *soldiers' and seamen's wills*). These states may exempt soldiers and sailors from the usual requirements for oral or written wills.[3]

A nuncupative will must be heard by two or three disinterested witnesses, at least one of whom must have been asked by the decedent to act as a witness. This requirement is helpful in distinguishing between nuncupative wills and oral instructions to change a written will or a plan to change a will. Many statutes require that the nuncupative will be written down within 30 days and/or *probated* (i.e., established in probate court as genuine and valid) within six months from the time it was spoken.

Matching Wills

Wills also can be categorized by the types of dispositions they contain. For example, married couples or business partners may have matching provisions in their wills. Matching wills are appropriate when the testators have identical testamentary objectives. For this reason, they are also called *reciprocal wills*. These wills may be mutual, joint, or contractual.

Mutual wills are separate wills in which the testators, usually a husband and wife, have matching provisions in their respective wills. For example, the separate will of each spouse might provide for "the transfer of my assets to my spouse. If my spouse does not survive me, then my assets shall be divided equally among my children."

In *joint wills*, two people sign the same document as their last will and testament. Usually, the dispositive provisions are the same. Joint wills are not recommended. Many state courts have difficulty analyzing the legal relationship between the two signers. The difficulty normally arises after the first person dies and the second person wants to change the will. The issue is whether the second person can modify the will or is contractually obligated to leave it unchanged. This conflict may cause court trials and appeals. As is the case with any lengthy trial and appeal, a large amount of the estate may be expended in trying to resolve the legal rights of the parties.

In *contractual wills*, people enter into a valid contract in which one or more of them promise to make certain dispositions in their wills. This agreement must meet the usual requirements for a valid contract, including consideration and the absence of fraud and **undue influence.** This arrangement lacks flexibility, but it may be desirable in some situations. If it is desirable, it is preferable to make a separate agreement to avoid the interpretive problems of joint wills.

Undue influence
Wrongful use of influence to get a person to write certain provisions in a will.

REQUIREMENTS FOR A VALID WILL

The requirements for a valid will vary from state to state and apply to formal, holographic, and nuncupative wills. A person must be an adult at the time the will is executed in order for it to be valid. The modern rule is that anyone 18 or older can execute a valid will. Eighteen is the age used in the Uniform Probate Code and the Model Execution of Wills Act. The Model Act, written by the NCCUSL, is intended as an example for states to follow in drafting their own laws. All states have now adopted the age of 18, with the following exceptions: Alabama (age 19), Louisiana (age 16), and Wyoming (age 19).[4]

A testator also must have **testamentary capacity.** Often, wills contain the declaration, "I, Jane Doe, being of sound mind and body. . . . " This statement is *not* necessary. In addition, a person need not be physically healthy to write or sign a valid will. However, *actual* testamentary capacity is required at the time the will is signed. Actual testamentary capacity is narrowly defined by the courts. The common requirements are that the person understands the nature and extent of his or her assets, knows who his or her close relatives are, and understands the purpose of a will.[5] In many states, even a prior adjudication of incompetency will not automatically invalidate a will on the grounds of insanity. If a decedent is suspected of having been incompetent when he or she executed the will, some relatives probably will contest the will. One of the purposes of having disinterested witnesses is so that they will be able to testify about the testator's competency.

The court in the following case discussed whether the testatrix was competent to revoke a prior will and make a new one. Note that some states, like Georgia, *permit* the testator to file his or her will with the probate court while he or she is still alive.

Testamentary capacity
Sufficient mental capability or sanity to execute a valid will.

MURCHISON V. SMITH

508 S.E.2D 641 (GA. 1998)

FACTS . . . The elderly Ms. [Annie Bell] Smith was diagnosed with terminal lung cancer in December 1994. On January 31, 1995, she executed a will leaving the bulk of her estate to her brother-in-law, Caesar Smith and his wife Lois Smith, who were assisting Ms. Smith and providing her with care. The will also named Caesar Smith as sole executor. . . .

Ms. Smith executed another will on March 10, 1995, while she was hospitalized. Ms. Smith's cousin, Dorothy Davis-Murchison, a college professor, had been coming to town to visit Ms. Smith since learning of her terminal illness, and Murchison was at the hospital at the time of the execution of the March will. This will made some specific bequests to friends and family members, including an invalid brother, but left the bulk of the estate to Murchison. It provided a specific bequest to Murchison as well as naming her the residuary beneficiary. In the event that Murchison failed to survive the testatrix, the property was to go to Murchison's daughter. Murchison's name was also handwritten into a space provided for the recipient of any remaining balances on all bank accounts; the name "Lois Smith" had been written in the space but was lined through and initialed "A.B.S." There was also a handwritten provision, again apparently initialed by the testatrix, appointing Murchison as executor. The will bore Murchison's own initials on a change in a bequest to Ms. Smith's brother. The will made no mention of Caesar Smith or any provision for him or for his wife Lois; Ms. Smith later commented to Lois that Murchison had "rewritten her will" and that Lois was not mentioned.

Ms. Smith was released from the hospital, and on March 20, 1995, Murchison accompanied her to the probate court, where Ms. Smith's January will was on file. Ms. Smith was on oxygen and appeared to be clad in a nightgown or robe. Murchison did most of the talking. Ms. Smith's January will was withdrawn and a will dated March 10, 1995, was filed. . . . The probate judge, who in his capacity as private counsel had drafted the January will, told Ms. Smith that he wanted to make a copy of the January will before she withdrew it. Murchison cautioned Ms. Smith to write "cancelled" or "revoked" on the January will. Ms. Smith wrote "revoked" across the January will, or it was written by the judge or Murchison at Smith's direction, and the judge made a copy of it. Murchison took photographs of Ms. Smith's actions in the probate court. . . .

Ms. Smith died April 16, 1995. The original January will was not found after her death; Murchison maintained that Ms. Smith had torn it up. Caesar Smith petitioned to probate the copy of the January will. Murchison petitioned to probate the March will . . . The probate court issued an order declaring that the January will was revoked . . . A de novo appeal to the superior court followed. After a two-day trial, a jury determined that the January will was not revoked, and the superior court entered judgment accordingly. . . .

ISSUE Was Ms. Smith's January will validly revoked?

HOLDING No. The jury verdict in favor of the January will stands.

REASONING . . . [F]ormer OCGA § 53-3-6 [Georgia Probate Code] provides that if a will is lost during the testator's lifetime, destroyed without the consent of the testator during the testator's lifetime, or lost or destroyed subsequent to the death of the testator, a copy of the will, clearly proved to be such by the subscribing witnesses and other evidence, may be admitted to probate in lieu of the original. In such cases, the presumption is that the will was revoked by the testator, but the presumption may be rebutted by clear and convincing proof. Whether the presumption of revocation is overcome by clear and convincing proof is "determined by the trier of fact, and in reviewing the verdict, 'the evidence must be accepted which is most favorable to the party in whose favor the verdict was rendered.' The presumption of revocation may be rebutted by circumstantial as well as direct evidence, including declarations of the testatrix."

Evidence of the testatrix's diminished mental capacity is . . . relevant to the issues of **duress** and Murchison's exercise of undue influence . . . [T]he amount of influence which may dominate a mind impaired by age or disease may be decidedly less than that required to control a strong mind. It is not essential to establish testamentary incapacity by someone who was present when the will was signed or who saw the testator the day the will was executed. A party can demonstrate that the testator lacked testamentary capacity at the time of a will's execution by showing the testator's state of mind within a reasonable period of time both before and after the events

46.1

MURCHISON V. SMITH, *continued*
508 S.E.2D 641 (GA. 1998)

in question. . . . [A] court must allow the issue of testamentary capacity to go to the jury when there is a genuine conflict in the evidence regarding the testator's state of mind.

Caesar Smith introduced testimony that Ms. Smith's health and mental state had been deteriorating since her cancer treatments began in late January or early February 1995. Witnesses described her as depressed, very irritable, fearful, "not too clear," and that sometimes she "just rambled," and her mind had begun to waver. A physician inquired if she was "senile" because of her responses. In March 1995, Ms. Smith was said to be crying constantly, unclear in thought, "speaking out in different tones of voices," hallucinating at times, and susceptible to any suggestion. A witness testified that on March 19, 1995, . . . Ms. Smith's state of mind was "in and out, going and coming." There was also testimony that Murchison had Ms. Smith sign or initial a document on April 13, 1995, three days before Ms. Smith died, while Smith was hospitalized, on constant pain medication, and "about dead" and "out of it."

This testimony . . . created a genuine conflict in the evidence regarding the state of Ms. Smith's mind at the time she executed the March will and caused "revoked" to be scrawled across the January will. . . . [I]nferences could be drawn by the jury establishing a lack of the requisite mental capacity, and consequently, the lack of intent to revoke the January will. . . . [T]he jury was authorized to find that the statutory presumption of revocation was rebutted by clear and convincing evidence. . . . Because there was sufficient evidence to support a finding of Ms. Smith's lack of testamentary capacity, and . . . lack of intent to revoke the January will, there is no need to address the sufficiency of the evidence with regard to the allegations of duress and . . . undue influence.

BUSINESS CONSIDERATIONS What should a court or business do when dealing with people who may be incompetent? Why?

ETHICAL CONSIDERATIONS What are the probate judge's moral duties since he participated in the preparation of the January will? Why? Discuss Murchison's ethics.

A recent technique developed to assist with proof of competence and volition is a *self-proved (self-proving) will.* This special type of formal will is accepted under the Uniform Probate Code. The purpose of a self-proved will is to reduce the amount of proof necessary when the testator dies and the will is offered for **probate.**[6] This is achieved by preparing and attaching sworn **affidavits** to the will when it is signed. The sworn affidavit states that the will is signed in compliance with the law. (In some states, the self-proved will must be signed by the testator and the witnesses before a notary public or other officer authorized to administer oaths.) The affidavits may include an optional statement that the witnesses believe that the testator is of sound mind and is acting of his or her own volition and without undue influence. Generally, then, the witnesses are not needed when the will is actually submitted for probate unless someone contests the will.

As noted earlier, formal and holographic wills must be signed by the testator. Many states require that a proper signature appear at the end of the document.

Duress
Wrongful use of force to get a person to write certain provisions in a will.

Probate
The procedure for verifying that a will is authentic and should be implemented.

Affidavit
Written statement made under oath.

TESTAMENTARY DISPOSITIONS AND RESTRICTIONS

A person has quite a bit of freedom in the dispositions that he or she may make in a will. These provisions are very important to the testator, and the court generally will give effect to them. But a person's ability to make testamentary dispositions has limits. Restrictions vary from state to state, but we will discuss some of the common restrictions. One concerns willing too large a portion of the estate to charity to the detriment of the family. These prohibitions are called *mortmain*, or fear of death, statutes, and they operate to restrict the types and amounts of charitable gifts.

Another widely prohibited disposition is a **trust** that is established for too long a period of time. The allowable length of time is specified in the rule against perpetuities, which is discussed briefly in the section of this chapter on private trusts.

In addition, most states do not allow the testator to will money to pets. Animals are not legal beneficiaries under wills or trusts. However, some states do allow the testator to establish an **honorary trust** for the benefit of the animal. Where permitted, the testator is restricted in the amount that may be placed in an honorary trust. The trust is limited to an amount of assets that is not excessive with respect to the animal's reasonable needs.

Will provisions can be set aside if they are against public policy. Examples include provisions that encourage beneficiaries to get divorced or that separate children from their parents. Obviously, a person cannot will away someone else's property (e.g., the spouse's half of the **community property**) or property that passes by operation of law, as in a joint tenancy with rights of survivorship.

If a testator suspects that someone will want to contest the will, a *no-contest clause* may be inserted in it. Basically, such a clause indicates that if a person contests the validity of the will in court, that person will not inherit any assets from the estate. The no-contest clause is used as a threat by the testator, and in that sense it may be effective; however, many states do not enforce no-contest clauses or they make exceptions to them. Regardless of a state's approach to no-contest clauses, if the person is successful in having the will declared invalid, that person can inherit. In other words, the no-contest clause will be invalid along with the rest of the will. Depending on the circumstances, the person may inherit under a prior will or under the state intestate succession statute.

Contrary to popular belief, a person is not required to leave assets to family members and other relatives. In **common law states,** there is an exception to this rule for a spouse: A widow or widower who is not willed at least a statutory minimum amount often can *elect against the will* (i.e., choose to take a preset minimum percentage of the estate rather than the amount provided by the will). Other family members may be excluded, but a testator should mention them and the fact that they are being excluded. This is often accomplished by leaving them a nominal amount, such as $5 or $10. If the testator fails to do this, the omitted family members can claim that they were *pretermitted* (forgotten) **heirs.** Courts generally will award intestate shares to pretermitted heirs on the grounds that the omission was a mistake. In addition, the omission of a close family member can indicate that the testator was mentally incompetent.

Actual heirs may receive their shares under different theories or
In writing a will, a testator may select between per capita (per head)
(per line) distribution of assets. In *per capita* distribution, each bene
described group receives an equal share, no matter how many gene
she is below the decedent. For example, in a gift to the decedent's
grandchildren, each one would receive an equal share. This is true w
the grandchild's parent is alive. In contrast, in a *per stirpes* distributio

Trust
An arrangement in which one person or business holds property and invests it for another.

Honorary trust
An arrangement that does not meet trust requirements and thus is not enforceable, although it may be carried out voluntarily.

Community property
A special form of joint ownership between husband and wife permitted in certain states called community property states.

Common law states
States in which married couples cannot create community property.

Heirs
Persons who actually inherit property from the decedent.

dent's children and grandchildren, each child of the decedent receives an equal share. If any child has already died, his or her children would equally divide that child's share. If a child is still alive, his or her offspring would not directly receive any assets. This is also called taking by **right of representation.** Exhibit 46.1 illustrates the distinction between a per stirpes and a per capita gift made to children and grandchildren.

The Uniform Probate Code introduced a new type of distribution called *per capita at each generation:* it is also called *per capita with representation.* For this method of distribution, the shares are determined at the first generation at which there are *any* living **issue.** This generation might be children, grandchildren, or even great-grandchildren. Once the shares are established for each line, then the issue of any deceased line members divide that line member's share. As you might assume, per capita at each generation distribution is really a hybrid between regular per stirpes and per capita distributions. Strict per stirpes distribution, by contrast, always divides the shares at the first generational level below the decedent, even though no one at that level is still alive. Exhibit 46.2 on page 1264 illustrates the difference between per capita at each generation and strict per stirpes distributions. Most states use the per capita at each generation rule in their **intestate statutes.** If a will or trust does not provide a clear indication about which approach should be used, the courts look to the intestacy statutes of that state. Consequently, most states will use a per-capita-at-each-generation approach if the will or trust is ambiguous. A person writing a will or trust can select which of these three methods he or she prefers and can include a clear statement to that effect. Individuals will have different ideas about which method is most fair.

Right of representation
Right of children to inherit in their parent's place, if the parent is deceased.

Issue
Lineal descendents, such as children, grandchildren, and great-grandchildren.

Intestate statutes
State statutes that specify who receives property when the decedent does not leave a valid will.

E X H I B I T   46.1 | **Testamentary Distributions to Surviving Children and Grandchildren**

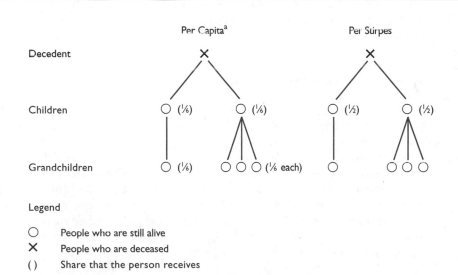

Legend

○   People who are still alive
✕   People who are deceased
( )   Share that the person receives

a. This distribution assumes that the testator provided for per capita distribution to "my children and grandchildren."

E X H I B I T 46.2 | **Testamentary Distributions to Surviving Children and Grandchildren**

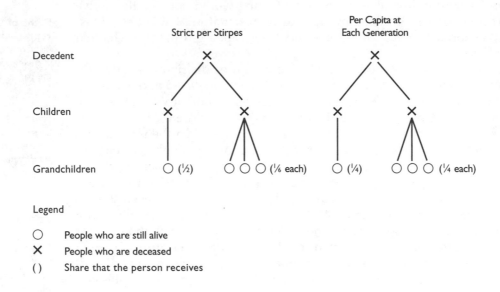

Legend

O   People who are still alive
X   People who are deceased
( ) Share that the person receives

Wills can be set aside (ignored) by the court if they were signed because of fraud in the inducement, fraud in the execution, duress, or undue influence. These concepts are used in wills cases in much the same manner as they are used in contract situations.

A person also might wish to make a gift of his or her organs at death. The person must comply with the state laws concerning organ donations. Most states have adopted the Revised Uniform Anatomical Gift Act (1987) to make it easier to obtain organs.[7]

INTESTATE SUCCESSION

For various reasons, people often fail to sign or to execute a valid will. States provide for the transfer of the assets of these people by the state intestate succession statute. People who die without a valid will are said to have died *intestate*. Sometimes, especially with holographic wills, people fail to provide for the disposition of *all* their assets. In a properly drafted will, such disposition is assured by the use of a residuary clause that states: "I leave all the rest and residue of my estate to. . . " Any assets *not* covered by the will provisions pass by intestate succession.

The intestacy statutes vary from state to state. Passage of personal property is governed by the intestate law of the decedent's domicile. Real property is governed by the intestate law where the property is located. Some states have different provisions for the passage of personal property and the passage of real property within the state's control.

Community property states provide for different chains of distribution for community property and separate property. As mentioned in Chapter 43, community property is a form of joint ownership between husband and wife. In states that allow this form of joint ownership, most property that is acquired during marriage is owned one-half by the husband and one-half by the wife.

Generally, legislators enact a statute to dispose of property in the manner they think most people would desire. For example, under the Uniform Probate Code, if the decedent leaves a surviving spouse but no surviving issue or parent(s), the surviving spouse takes all the intestate property.[8] If there are surviving issue who are issue of both the decedent and the surviving spouse, the spouse takes the first $50,000 plus one-half the balance of the estate. The issue would share the rest by per capita at each generation.[9]

These intestate provisions are applicable to separate property states and to separate property in community property states under the Uniform Probate Code. Exhibit 46.3 summarizes the Uniform Probate Code intestate succession provisions for separate property.

PROBATE AND ESTATE ADMINISTRATION

Probate hearings are a series of hearings in probate court in which the judge makes sure that the estate is being properly administered. The judge will conduct a hearing if any **interested party** contests the validity of the will. For example, an interested party may complain that the testator lacked capacity to make a will; the

Interested party
A party with an interest in the estate, such as a beneficiary, heir, or creditor.

E X H I B I T   46.3 | **Intestate Succession Under the Uniform Probate Code[a]**

Survivors	Spouse's Share	Remainder of Estate to Others
Spouse (if there is no issue or parent of decedent)	100%	Not applicable
Spouse and issue, all of whom are also issue of the surviving spouse	First $50,000, plus ½ the balance	To the issue, if they are of the same degree of kinship, equally[b]
Spouse and issue, one or more of whom are not issue of the surviving spouse	½ to the spouse	To the issue, if they are of the same degree of kinship, equally[b]
Spouse and parent(s) (if there is no surviving issue)	First $50,000, plus ½ the balance	To parent or parents equally
Issue of decedent (if there is no surviving spouse)	Not applicable	To the issue, if they are of the same degree of kinship, equally[b]
Parent(s) (if there is no surviving spouse or issue)	Not applicable	To parent or parents equally
Issue of parents (if there is no surviving spouse, issue, or parents)	Not applicable	To the issue of the parents or either parent by representation[b]
Grandparents and issue of grandparents (if there is no surviving spouse, issue, parents, or issue of a parent)	Not applicable	½ to paternal grandparent(s) or to their issue[b] if they are both deceased; ½ to maternal grandparents(s) or to their issue[b] if they are both deceased; if there is no grandparent or issue on one side, that share goes to the other side

a. This is a representation of the Uniform Probate Code §§ 2-101–103. It does not reflect the alternative provisions for community property states.

b. These transfers are made per capita at each generation.

46.1 | MANAGEMENT/ PERSONAL LAW

CALL-IMAGE TECHNOLOGY

PROVIDING FOR THE FAMILY AND CIT

Tom and Anna are both in excellent health, and the continued success and growth of the firm seemingly assures them a comfortable life and a good retirement. Nonetheless, they are concerned about what would happen to their children—and to the firm—if some tragedy were to befall them. They would like to provide for their children (with a minimum tax burden) if anything should happen to them. They also would like to make certain that the firm remains a family-owned enterprise. They have asked you for advice as to what they can or should do to ensure that their wishes are carried out. What advice will you give them?

BUSINESS CONSIDERATIONS What might Tom and Anna do to assure that CIT continues to operate as a family-owned business to provide income and security for their family? Would they be better served by establishing a trust or by making other provisions in their wills?
ETHICAL CONSIDERATIONS Suppose a person decides to write a will and must decide whether to select distribution of the estate per capita, per stirpes, or per capita at each generation. What ethical issues should be considered in making such a decision? Is it ethical to use either a will or a trust in an effort to delay or avoid taxes?

Surcharged
Assessed a fee by the court for failure to follow fiduciary duties.

testator was subject to undue influence, duress, or fraud; or the will was not executed in compliance with state law. The judge confirms whether the will is valid and was properly executed under state law. Even after the judge has accepted the validity of the will, this judicial order can be revoked if it is shown that the will was fraudulently offered for probate.

If the decedent had a valid will that named a representative, that person will be called an *executor*. A court-appointed representative will be called an *administrator*. (Some localities still use the more traditional terminology of calling male representatives executors or administrators, and female representatives executrixes or administratrixes.) The administrator will be appointed following any guidelines provided in the state probate code. Some states require that an executor or an administrator reside in the same state as the decedent. There usually is a minimum age of 18.

The concept of administering an estate is relatively simple. The judge supervises the personal representative of the estate in the completion of his or her duties. The personal representative must advertise in newspapers of general circulation in order to locate the creditors of the deceased. Some states may require personal notice to creditors if the personal representative knows their identity. If a creditor does not file a claim against the estate in a timely manner, the claim will be barred. The representative will also collect the assets of the decedent, collect money owed to the decedent, pay the lawful debts owed by the decedent, pay the necessary expenses of estate administration, and pay any state and/or federal taxes. It is often necessary to sell assets to make these disbursements. The remaining assets are then distributed to the proper beneficiaries. A court generally will oversee this procedure through probate hearings.

The personal representatives are responsible for the proper administration and probate of the estate. The personal representative has fiduciary duties to the lawful beneficiaries of the estate. They also must make sure that the duties mentioned in this section are properly completed. Personal representatives have a significant responsibility for which they receive a fee. They can be **surcharged** from personal funds if they violate their duties by failing to perform as required or by performing incorrectly. Some common examples of wrongdoing include failure to pay taxes, failure to probate the will, failure to sell assets that are declining in value, failure to minimize taxes, failure to sell assets at a fair price, self-dealing, such as selling estate or trust assets to oneself or to a friend, and fraud. In the following case, the court reviewed an executor's sale of estate assets.

46.2

MARTIN V. KARLEBACH

86 CAL.RPTR. 2D 37 (C.A. CA, 2ND DIST., DIV. 4, 1999)
PETITION FOR REVIEW DENIED BY THE CALIFORNIA SUPREME COURT, 1999 CAL. LEXIS 6924 (CA. 1999)

FACTS . . . Patrick M. Martin . . . challenges the probate court's denial of his petition to vacate a sale of estate property by respondent Alice M. Karlebach (hereafter Karlebach), executor of the estate of Rose Gennett Martin . . . (hereafter Rose), who was Karlebach's mother and Martin's grandmother . . . At the time of her death, Rose owned 35 of the 80 outstanding shares in Refrigeration Supplies Distributors, Inc. (hereafter RSD), a family business . . . Karlebach, who is Martin's aunt, is an officer, director, and shareholder in RSD. Rose's will made Martin a beneficiary of one-sixth of her residuary estate. The will also nominated Karlebach to be executor . . . To pay estate taxes, Karlebach decided to sell a portion of the estate's RSD shares to RSD. RSD and Karlebach hired Cronkite & Roda, an independent professional appraiser, to place a value on the shares. In September 1995, Cronkite & Roda told Karlebach and RSD that the 35 RSD shares were worth $9.7 million, or approximately $277,142.86 per share, on the date of Rose's death. Following a vote of RSD's board of directors, RSD redeemed 22.5 shares for $6.235 million in November 1995 . . .

[T]he . . . Internal Revenue Service (hereafter IRS) began an audit of the estate. On March 19, 1997, Martin filed his objections . . . alleging . . . that Karlebach had secured the probate court's approval of the first . . . account . . . without informing the court that she had a conflict of interest with respect to the sale of the shares. . . . [T]he IRS told Karlebach that it disputed the redemption value of the shares. . . . On December 10, 1997, Martin filed a petition to vacate the sale of the shares. The petition contended that the sale was voidable at his request because Karlebach, as executor, had breached her duty under Probate Code section 9880 et seq., not to purchase estate property indirectly without his consent. On May 29, 1998, the probate court filed an order denying Martin's request to void the sale of the shares. . . .

ISSUE Should the court grant Martin's request to set aside the sale of the shares?

HOLDING Yes. The sale should be set aside.

REASONING . . . "An executor is an officer of the court and occupies a fiduciary relation toward all parties having an interest in the estate. Executors occupy trust relations toward the legatees, and are bound to the utmost good faith in their transactions with the beneficiary. . . An executor also bears a 'duty to disclose all the facts . . . and to refrain from taking an unfair advantage of [the legatees]." Section 9880 et seq., establish the duties of executors and other personal representatives with respect to purchases of estate property. Section 9880 provides that "except as provided in this chapter," an executor may neither "(a) Purchase any property of the estate . . . , directly or indirectly," nor "(b) Be interested in any such purchase." This statute is a codification of the principle that executors may not deal with themselves, or place themselves in a position antagonistic to the estate's beneficiaries. Transactions in violation of section 9880 are not void—only voidable. They are "voidable only at the instance of those interested in the estate."

However, section 9883 permits an executor to petition the probate court for an order allowing the executor to purchase estate property in two sets of circumstances, which are stated in sections 9881 and 9882. The probate court may approve such a sale when (1) the executor files written consents from all known heirs and devisees, and shows that the sale is to the estate's advantage, or (2) the decedent's will authorizes the sale. Finally, sections 9884 and 9885 provide that, subject to conditions not relevant here, an executor may buy estate property pursuant to a written contract executed while the decedent was alive or pursuant to an option given in the decedent's will.

. . . Karlebach is an officer and director of RSD, and she personally owns as many as 5 RSD shares, which, when conjoined with the 35 shares in Rose's estate, gave Karlebach control of up to 50 percent of the outstanding shares in RSD prior to the redemption. She played an important role in determining the redemption price of the shares, and . . . the redemption of 22.5 outstanding shares would have significantly enhanced the relative amount of control that she exercised in virtue of her own shares. The record . . . discloses that Karlebach exercised positions of control over the estate and RSD, that she played a key role in arranging the sale of the RSD shares, and that the redemption personally benefited her through her holdings in RSD.

continued

46.2

MARTIN V. KARLEBACH, *continued*
86 CAL.RPTR. 2D 37 (C.A. CA, 2ND DIST., DIV. 4, 1999)
PETITION FOR REVIEW DENIED BY THE CALIFORNIA SUPREME COURT, 1999 CAL. LEXIS 6924 (CA. 1999)

The key issue . . . is whether the probate court erred in denying Martin's request to void the sale of the shares . . . Here, . . . the probate court apparently found that Karlebach's intentions or good faith did not warrant voiding the underlying sale. Nonetheless, Karlebach arranged for a self-interested purchase of estate property without Martin's consent, and thus, . . . he was entitled to have the sale of shares voided at his request. . . . Karlebach . . . contends that the probate court was authorized to approve the sale of shares because she did not purchase the shares within the meaning of section 9880, subdivision (a), and she merely had an interest in the sale of the shares within the meaning of section 9880, subdivision (b). . . .

First, California courts have repeatedly indicated that sales of estate property in which an executor purchases the property or has an interest in the sale are voidable at the request of the beneficiaries. Second, in view of Karlebach's role as director, officer, and shareholder in RSD, she is properly viewed as having indirectly purchased the shares, within the meaning of section 9880, subdivision (a). . . . "It is apparent that the object was not to declare who might or might not

become a purchaser of the property of the estate; but it was to prevent the property from being sold at a price less than its true value, which might be the case if the administrator, either directly or indirectly, prevented competition among the bidders, by entering into the market, either personally or by his agents, or if, with a view of purchasing, he was tempted to undervalue the property in his proceedings respecting the sale."

. . . Karlebach's conduct in arranging to have RSD redeem the shares fell under the proscription against indirect . . . competition found in section 9880, subdivision (a) . . . We . . . conclude that the trial court erred in denying Martin's request to void the sale of the shares. . . .

BUSINESS CONSIDERATION When is it advisable to grant an executor or trustee power to purchase estate or trust assets?

ETHICAL CONSIDERATION   Discuss Karlebach's ethics.

In many jurisdictions, the judge can reduce the commissions paid to the personal representative and the fees paid to the attorney and accountant if they are excessive. Executors, administrators, and, in many states, attorneys usually are paid based on a percentage of the value of the assets in the estate. In some states, maximum fees are established in the probate code.

AVOIDING PROBATE

Often, people believe that it is wise to avoid probate. Examples of property that is not subject to probate include entireties property, joint tenancy with rights of survivorship, and life insurance paid to a named beneficiary. (Refer to Exhibit 43.1 on page 1187 for an explanation of the survivorship feature of forms of joint ownership.) New forms of ownership are being originated that also avoid probate, for example, pay-on-death ownership. When the owner dies, the survivor becomes the next owner. The survivor does not have an interest during the owner's life; consequently, that person cannot access the funds, and the owner does not require the other person's signature. It is currently available for bank accounts, some government securities, and some states permit pay-on-death registration for securities. The

Uniform Transfer on Death Security Registration Act permits investment securities to be held in pay-on-death form, which the act calls Transfer on Death or TOD. Most states have enacted the Uniform Act.[10] If, during life, a person places assets into a trust with named beneficiaries, these assets will not be probated. Another option of the property owner is to enter into a valid contract that provides, in part, for the passage of property at the owner's death. All these arrangements may serve as substitutes for a valid will and, depending on state law, may escape the technical requirements of the state statute of wills. However, even assets that are not subject to probate may still be subject to an **estate tax** and/or an **inheritance tax.** A valid will may be advisable even when an owner is trying to avoid probate. The owner may acquire property later that will not avoid probate, such as paychecks and inheritances from other decedents.

Avoiding probate of an estate may reduce the amount of time necessary for the administration of that estate. In the case of joint tenancies with rights of survivorship, one owner will have immediate access to these assets at the other owner's death, although some states restrict this immediate access for bank accounts and safe deposit boxes. An important consideration for some people is the additional privacy afforded by avoiding probate. Probate, like most court proceedings, is part of the public record; anyone who is so inclined can read the will and the inventory of assets. Costs usually are assessed in the probate of an estate; some, such as fees for filing court documents, are nominal. The amount of some fees may be based on the amount and value of probate assets; avoiding probate or reducing the amount of probate assets eliminates or reduces these costs. Probate costs increase markedly when lawsuits arise concerning the validity of the will, its interpretation, or asset distribution. These *will contests* reduce the amount of assets to be distributed to the beneficiaries. Sometimes these contests are caused by poorly drafted wills or holographic wills. Probate costs and taxes may increase significantly if a person dies intestate or without prudent estate planning.

Avoiding probate has some disadvantages. The extent to which these concerns are disadvantageous will depend on the people involved and the method used to avoid probate. Some of the techniques—for example, establishing and operating out of a trust—require additional paperwork and attention to detail. Avoiding probate also may create a higher inheritance or estate tax liability on the decedent's estate or on the estates of other family members. In probate, the creditors of the decedent are located and paid, and the estate is discharged of all further obligation to them. Without probate, there is no discharge from potential creditors' claims. In addition, the purpose of probate is to protect lawful beneficiaries and creditors. This may be particularly important when beneficiaries are not knowledgeable or are confused. The court can intervene to protect them from unscrupulous people. Unfortunately, this purpose is not always served effectively under some state probate codes and procedures.

Thus, it is not always advantageous to avoid probate. As with any estate-planning decision, consideration must be given to the individuals and the assets involved. One factor that is often overlooked is that an asset's status as a probate or nonprobate asset does *not* avoid estate or inheritance taxation on it.

Legislative sympathy exists for reducing some of the procedures involved in probate. Texas and Washington began permitting executors to perform at least some functions without court supervision. This is called *independent administration,* as distinguished from the more traditional *supervised administration.* In Texas, the testator may indicate that the executor is an *independent executor.* When this occurs, the

Estate tax
A tax assessed on the total net (taxable) value of the estate.

Inheritance tax
A tax assessed on transfers of estate assets at the owner's death. The rates vary depending on the owner's relationship to the recipient.

executor conducts all duties outside the court, except for probating the will, filing an inventory, appraisal of assets, and list of claims against the estate. The Washington provision is similar and is implemented if the testator executes a *nonintervention will.*

The Uniform Probate Code has followed and expanded these examples. Under the Uniform Probate Code, all administrations are unsupervised unless the personal representative or any interested party requests a court ruling to the contrary.[11] Supervised administration, however, is still the majority rule.

The Uniform Probate Code also includes provisions for informal probate with simplified procedures in many situations. A number of states have declined to adopt simplified procedures on the grounds that they do not provide adequate protection from abuses by dishonest and/or incompetent personal representatives.

TRANSFER TAXES

Federal Transfer Taxes

The federal government taxes the owner when he or she exercises the right to transfer property. This may take the form of gift taxes if the owner transfers the asset during lifetime. If the transfer is effective on death, a federal estate tax may be due. Estate taxes treat the entire estate as one unit, subject to certain exclusions, deductions, and credits. See Exhibits 46.4 through 46.6 for a simplified explanation of

---

EXHIBIT 46.4 | Overview of the Federal Estate Tax

Gross Estate

 Deduct: Claims, debts, and allowable taxes
 Administration and funeral expenses

Adjusted Gross Estate

 Deduct: Marital deduction
 Charitable deduction

Taxable Estate

 Add: Adjusted taxable gifts[a]

Base Amount for Estate Tax

 Calculate tentative estate tax on the base amount using the Unified Tax Rate Schedule in Exhibit 46.5.
 Deduct: Gift tax payable on adjusted taxable gifts[a]
 Unified Credit for Gift and Estate Taxes from Exhibit 46.6
 Credit for state death taxes paid (Maximum permitted per IRS table)[b]

Net Federal Estate Tax

---

a. The federal sytem is a unified system where prior taxable gifts influence the estate tax rates. Consequently, the adjusted taxable gifts are added into the tax base. The gift tax payable is deducted later in the calculation.

b. In states with independent death taxes, the state estate or inheritance taxes may be much greater than the credit for state death taxes. States that do not assess estate or inheritance taxes generally impose a tax equal to the amount of the credit on those estates that are subject to federal estate taxes. The estate will have to pay this amount to either the state or federal government. This is generally called a state "pickup tax."

E X H I B I T 46.5 | Unified Tax Rate Schedule

Gross estate taxes are calculated on the estate tax base. Find the appropriate line in the table below. Subtract the amount in column A from the base amount. Multiply the difference by the amount in column D. This is the tax on the excess. Add the tax on the excess to the tax amount from column C.

A Taxable Amount Over	B Taxable Amount Not Over	C Tax on Amount in Column A	D Rate of Tax on Excess Over Amount in Column A (Percent)
0	10,000	0	18
10,000	20,000	1,800	20
20,000	40,000	3,800	22
40,000	60,000	8,200	24
60,000	80,000	13,000	26
80,000	100,000	18,200	28
100,000	150,000	23,800	30
150,000	250,000	38,800	32
250,000	500,000	70,800	34
500,000	750,000	155,800	37
750,000	1,000,000	248,300	39
1,000,000	1,250,000	345,800	41
1,250,000	1,500,000	448,300	43
1,500,000	2,000,000	555,800	45
2,000,000	2,500,000	780,800	49
2,500,000	3,000,000	1,025,800	53
3,000,000	—	1,290,800	55

federal transfer taxes. These exhibits are intended to illustrate federal estate taxes. The exhibits do not use the technical terms. The Taxpayer Relief Act of 1997 increased the Unified Credit over the next couple of years; consequently, more estate assets can transfer without taxes. The increases are illustrated in Exhibit 46.6 on page 1272. Federal transfer tax rates are progressive, as are federal income taxes. The federal transfer tax system consists of an estate tax, a gift tax, and a generation-skipping transfer tax. The generation-skipping transfer tax is discussed in the "Disadvantages of Trusts" section of this chapter. The system attempts to detect and tax all transfers.

State Transfer Taxes

A few states have gift taxes.[12] States may also have either estate taxes[13] or inheritance taxes.[14] In inheritance taxes, each recipient's share or inheritance is taxed

E X H I B I T 46.6 | **Unified Credit for Gift and Estate Taxes**

Decedents Dying in	Unified Credit	Gross Estate Plus Adjusted Taxable Gifts Exceeds[a]
2000 & 2001	$220,550	$675,000
2002 & 2003	$229,800	$700,000
2004	$287,300	$850,000
2005	$326,300	$950,000
2006 and after	$345,800	$1,000,000

a. This column indicates the amount of gross estate and lifetime taxable gifts together that can be transferred before the estate will be subject to federal estate taxes.

separately. Inheritance taxes are generally based on the recipient's relationship to the decedent and the value of the assets received. The trend seems to be to abolish state inheritance and estate taxes. Most states will impose a "pickup tax" equal to the amount of the credit for state death taxes on the federal estate tax return.[15]

RETIREMENT PLANS

People are living longer. With increased longevity come increased concerns about income during retirement. Retirement plans are very complex and have both income tax and transfer tax consequences for the family. There are also significant financial and tax effects for the employer. For many people, their pension or retirement plans may be one of their largest assets.

Some plans are employer plans. One type is a *defined-benefit plan,* where the employer promises to pay the retiree a set benefit based on a percentage of the employee's average earnings and the number of years worked under the plan. The funds for the employees are pooled together; however, the employer keeps separate records on the amount each employee earns. Payments may be made monthly beginning with retirement, or there may be a lump-sum payment at retirement. The retiree may have a choice, or the plan may require one type of payment. The type of payment will have tax consequences. These plans are common for people employed by the military, many unions, and many large companies.

A *defined-contribution plan* is an employer plan where the employer promises to contribute a certain amount to the plan each year. The contribution is generally a percentage of the worker's earnings. Each employee has a separate account. The money is invested. When an employee retires, the amount the employee receives is based on the amount contributed plus the earnings. At retirement, payments may be periodic or by a lump sum. Again the type of payment will affect taxation.

DURABLE POWERS OF ATTORNEY AND LIVING WILLS

Durable powers of attorney can be used to make future financial or medical decisions. A person may create a durable power, if the maker is concerned that he or she may become unavailable, incapacitated, or incompetent. The maker executes a formal document appointing another person to make decisions for the maker. If the appointment is solely for decisions about medical treatment, it is called a *durable power of attorney for health care*. In the following case, the court addressed the validity of a power of attorney that was to become effective when the maker became incompetent. Note how the court compared this power of attorney to ordinary agency relationships. A legal durable power of attorney is "durable" because it does not terminate when the maker becomes incompetent.

Constructive trust
Equitable remedy where the court imposes a trust to prevent unjust enrichment.

46.3

COMERICA BANK–TEXAS
V. TEXAS COMMERCE BANK NATIONAL ASSOCIATION
2 S.W.3D 723 (C.A. TEXAS, 6TH DIST. TEXARKANA, 1999)

FACTS . . . On September 23, 1986, Gayl Hall Bradfield signed an instrument entitled "General Power of Attorney" naming Robert N. Virden as her attorney-in-fact. The General Power of Attorney provided in relevant part:

> Notwithstanding the other provisions of this general power of attorney, the rights, power and authority of my attorney shall commence only upon my disability as hereinafter defined and shall remain in full force thereafter until said disability is terminated. This general power of attorney shall not terminate on my disability or incompetency. Disability shall be defined as a substantial impairment of my ability to care for my property by reason of age, illness, infirmity, mental weakness, intemperance and/or addiction to drugs.

On January 11, 1991, Bradfield established the Gayl Hall Bradfield Trust. [Comerica Bank was the trustee of this trust.] The trust contained certain assets held for the benefit of Bradfield. The trust provided that on Bradfield's death, the assets be distributed to identified institutions and individuals. In 1993, Bradfield amended the trust to add additional assets. On August 19, 1991, Bradfield made a holographic will, which named Texas Commerce Bank as executor of her estate. . . . Texas Commerce Bank became Chase Bank of Texas. . . . In 1995, Bradfield became incapacitated. After her incapacity, Virden, acting as Bradfield's attorney-in-fact, transferred to the trust certain assets held by Bradfield, individually, and assets payable to Bradfield, individually. Bradfield died on January 12, 1997. Chase filed suit against Comerica . . . to impose a **constructive trust** on the assets Virden transferred to the trust. . . .

ISSUE Was the instrument granting Virden power of attorney valid?

HOLDING Yes. The power of attorney was valid; it continued to be valid during in the period of Bradfield's incompetency.

REASONING A power of attorney is a written instrument by which one person, the principal, appoints another person, the attorney-in-fact, as agent and confers on the attorney-in-fact the authority to perform specified acts on behalf of the principal. . . . [T]he [Texas] Legislature enacted Section 36A of the Probate Code allowing durable powers of attorney. . . . This section . . . authorizes a power of attorney to remain in force in the event the principal becomes incapacitated. Section 36A does not expressly provide that a power of attorney may become effective only in the event the principal becomes incapacitated. In 1993, the Texas Legislature passed the Durable Power of Attorney Act, authorizing a springing durable power of attorney.[16] The Code now provides that a power of attorney may contain a provision that "this power of attorney is not affected by subsequent disability or incapacity of the principal," or "this power of attorney becomes effective on the disability or incapacity

continued

46.3

COMERICA BANK–TEXAS
V. TEXAS COMMERCE BANK NATIONAL ASSOCIATION, *continued*
2 S.W.3D 723 (C.A. TEXAS, 6TH DIST. TEXARKANA, 1999)

of the principal."

Historically, an agency authority called power of attorney existed only when the principal was capable of acting on his or her own behalf. At common law, an agency relationship, including one created by power of attorney, terminated upon the incapacity of the principal. . . . [T]he reason given for not allowing the power of attorney to continue to exist was because the statutes provided for the appointment of a guardian when a person did not have the capacity to handle his own estate. In turn, when a person died, the executor or administrator of the estate was designated by the Probate Code to handle the affairs of the estate. These provisions in the law precluded the continuation of the authority of an agent after disability or death.

The passage of Section 36A . . . allowed for the first time a power of attorney to be recognized and legally effected even during the disability of the principal. This altered significantly the previous law that had required that an insane or incompetent person was to have a guardian under the supervision of the court. This statutory provision left no question that if the proper language was contained in a power of attorney, the power of attorney could continue during the disability pursuant to the terms of agency authority specifically granted by the principal. Because there had been no case in point and because the language in the statute speaks in terms of the power not terminating on disability, the later clarification that it can take effect upon disability removed any doubt on that question. . . .

In the present case, however, this Court should apply the standard of construction to the power of attorney that would comport with legality and would presume the parties intended to obey the law. There is language in the general power of attorney in this case that suggests that its authorization is being made before the disability . . . The instrument in question had the legal effect at the time of the signing of creating a general power of attorney to commence in the future. This would be no different from a power of attorney that was to begin when the principal left for Europe, when the principal purchased a new business, or some similar future event. The difference is the authorization of the agency was triggered by a future event other than the disability of the principal. . . .

There is no contention that Gayl Bradfield was not competent at the time she executed the power of attorney. . . . [T]he spirit of the law . . . was to permit powers of attorney to continue to exist if that was the intent of the principal. This designation of a power of attorney existed prior to the disability and was signed by the principal prior to the disability, and the legal effect of this instrument did not terminate upon the disability even though the rights, power, and authority under the power of attorney did not commence until the disability began. . . .

BUSINESS CONSIDERATION What safeguards should a business use when dealing with people with power of attorney?

ETHICAL CONSIDERATIONS Was it ethical for Virden to put Bradfield's assets into her trust? Who should pay the costs of this litigation? Is this litigation ethical if the costs are being paid from Bradfield's assets?

People often include a *living will* as part of their estate plan. This document does not dispose of assets at the owner's death. It explains how the individual feels about the administration of certain medical treatments, especially life-prolonging treatment, when the patient is very ill and recovery is doubtful. The document often states that the living will requests should be honored "if there is no reasonable expectation of recovery." This is often subject to medical interpretation, and the medical experts may not agree on this issue. Living wills are popular because of recent developments in medical research that allow a patient to live even though there is little hope of recovery. Problems arise when a patient is physically incapable of making and/or communicating his or her desires about potential medical treatments. Living wills are legal in most states, but compliance with the state statute, of course, is critical.

TRUSTS DEFINED

A *trust* is a fiduciary relationship where specific property is transferred to the care of a trustee, or manager. Trusts may be voluntary arrangements created by the property owner, or they may be legal arrangements imposed by the courts or implied by the law in order to reach a fair result. In a trust, legal title and equitable ownership rights are split between two or more people. One person has the legal right to the asset; another person has the beneficial right to the use and enjoyment of the asset. The American Law Institute has drafted the *Restatement of the Law of Trusts (III),* which is a treatise of trust law and includes recommendations on many aspects of trusts. The Restatement itself is not a statute; however, when a court relies on a section, it becomes part of the precedents of the state.

EXPRESS TRUSTS

Trusts that are created voluntarily by the owner of the property are called *express trusts.* (Trusts that are created by operation of law are discussed in the section of this chapter on implied trusts.) The owner transfers real or personal property to a trustee for the benefit of a named person. During the period of the trust, the trustee manages the property and pays the income to the people specified in the **trust deed.** If the trust is to take effect during the owner's life, it is called an *inter vivos* (lifetime or living) trust. If it is to take effect at death, it is called a *testamentary trust.* Testamentary trusts are usually included as part of the will and do not have a separate trust deed. They must comply with the state's statute of wills.

> **Trust deed**
> A legal document that specifies the recipients of a trust, their interests, and how the trust should be managed; also called a deed of trust.

Generally, at least three people are needed for an express trust: a creator, a trustee, and one or more beneficiaries. A creator also may be called a *settlor* or a *trustor.* The creator is the one who establishes the trust and is usually the person who puts assets into the trust. The *trustee,* who may be a person or a business entity, is in charge of managing the assets. *Corpus, res,* or *principal* are the names used for the assets. The *beneficiaries* are the recipients. Depending on the trust instrument, the beneficiaries may receive the income from the assets, the assets themselves, or both. The Uniform Principal and Income Act of 1997 provides procedures on how to separate principal and income in estates and trusts.[17] Once assets are placed in the trust (or estate), the distinction may be quite complex and includes issues of whether principal or income should be used to pay expenses and taxes. The act updates two prior Uniform Acts to conform with modern trust investment practices. Consideration is not required to establish a trust.

To be valid, a trust must meet a few requirements. The intention or purpose of the creator must be expressed—for example, by stating that "this trust is established for my children's college educations." In many cases, though, the courts have concluded that the intention of the creator may be inferred from his or her actions if this intention is not stated. Creators commonly establish trusts for one of these purposes: to provide for more than one beneficiary, to protect beneficiaries from themselves and from overreaching by others, and to legally reduce taxes.

46.2 | PERSONAL LAW/ MANAGEMENT

CALL-IMAGE TECHNOLOGY

PROTECTING AGAINST FINANCIAL HARDSHIPS

Anna's mother suffered from Alzheimer's disease for three years prior to her death. One of Tom's cousins was seriously injured in an industrial accident and spent several years on life-support before dying. As a result, both Anna and Tom have observed the suffering and financial hardships that a family endures in such a situation. Both are determined to do everything in their power to protect their family from this sort of ordeal. They have each asked you for advice on methods for dealing with these sorts of situations. What advice will you give them?

BUSINESS CONSIDERATIONS What can a closely held firm do to protect itself and its constituents in the event a primary policy maker of the firm suffers from a debilitating disease or injury? Should a business have a policy or procedure in place in the event such a situation arises? What if the person is unaware that he or she has become incompetent, such as may occur with Alzheimer's disease or some types of senility?

ETHICAL CONSIDERATIONS Suppose a person establishes a durable power of attorney for healthcare issues. What criteria should the "attorney" use in making decisions? Should the "attorney" only be concerned with the wishes of the "maker," or should the desires of the other family members also be considered?

Under the Statute of Frauds, most trust deeds must be in writing because they cannot possibly be performed within one year. Even if a writing were not required by the Statute of Frauds, it would be foolish to have oral trust provisions. Many potential legal problems do not arise until after the creator has died. Trusts generally contain lengthy and complex provisions about what the trustee can and cannot do; these certainly should be reduced to writing.

A trust may terminate when its purpose is completed or when its term is over. Under some circumstances, the trust may terminate by mutual agreement of all the beneficiaries or when it becomes uneconomical. Depending on the trust deed, the power to terminate the trust may rest with the trustee, the creator, or someone else. When the trust is terminated, the trust assets are transferred to the specified **remainder beneficiaries.**

A *revocable trust* is one that can be revoked or canceled by the creator. In rare instances, the creator may give this power to another individual. This trust usually becomes permanent and irrevocable at the death of the creator. On the other hand, an *irrevocable trust* is one that may not be terminated during the specified term of the trust. Once the assets are placed in trust, they must remain there for the term of the trust under the conditions specified in the trust deed.

Whether a trust is revocable or irrevocable depends on the trust document. It is always wise to specify this aspect of the trust; otherwise, the trust will be governed by state law. In most states, the trust will be irrevocable unless the creator has stated a contrary intention in the trust deed. In a minority of states, including California, it will be presumed to be revocable unless a contrary intention is expressed.

There are various categories of express trusts, based on the clauses contained in the trust deed. A specific trust may contain provisions in more than one of these categories. This sampling of trust provisions indicates the variety that is possible with trusts.

Private Trusts

Remainder beneficiaries
Persons with an interest in what remains in the trust corpus after use by the income beneficiaries.

A *private trust* is one that is not created for the general public good. The beneficiaries of this type of trust are individual citizens and not society as a whole. A private trust is limited by the time period specified in the *rule against perpetuities.* The rule against perpetuities is really a common law rule that prohibits the remote vesting of trust or property interests. It requires that an interest vest within the time limit set by the rule. The rule does not apply to interests that are already vested—that is, nonforfeitable—even if the beneficiary will not receive the vested interest until far into the future. The distinction between interests that are vested and those that are not is subtle. This illustration should help. If a trustee had tickets to a concert in three months, beneficiaries with vested interests would be assured that they are entitled to a ticket, even though the concert is in the future. Beneficiaries without vested interests do not know yet whether they will receive a ticket.

Section 1 of the Uniform Statutory Rule Against Perpetuities, drafted by the NCCUSL, states the general rule as "A nonvested property interest is invalid unless: (1) when the interest is created, it is certain to vest or terminate no later than 21 years after the death of an individual then alive; or (2) the interest either vests or terminates within 90 years after its creation." The "individual" must be an individual who is related to the trust or its creator; it is not just *any* individual. The Uniform Statutory Rule Against Perpetuities with 1990 Amendments has been adopted in about half the states.[18]

Charitable Trusts

A *charitable trust* is one in which money is given to a charity for a public purpose. A qualified charity for tax purposes is a corporation organized for religious, charitable, scientific, literary, or educational purposes, including the encouragement of art and the prevention of cruelty to children or animals. Charities also include the United States or any state or political subdivision or any veterans' organization or its departments or posts.[19] Transfers to charities, either outright or in trust, may pass tax free. However, the strict requirements of the Internal Revenue Service must be met. In addition, the charitable organization must qualify under state and federal rules. An organization that qualifies for federal tax purposes may not qualify for state tax purposes. The opposite is also true. California, for example, requires that the organization be a California charity or a national charity that is going to use the assets in California. To qualify for favorable tax treatment under federal law, a trust with charitable and noncharitable beneficiaries must meet the stringent requirements imposed by the 1969 Tax Reform Act. In most states, charitable trusts are excluded from the *rule against perpetuities.*

If the original charitable purpose cannot be fulfilled, a court of equity may apply the *cy-pres* doctrine. The application of this doctrine means that the court will try to follow the transferor's intention as closely as possible. This is usually accomplished by substituting another charitable beneficiary with a similar purpose for the charity initially specified. Before a substitution can occur, it must be shown that the original charity no longer exists or that the original terms no longer apply.

Cy-pres doctrine
Doctrine permitting the court to modify the trust in order to follow the creator's charitable intention as closely as possible.

Additional Types of Express Trusts

A trust that will accumulate income is called an *accumulation trust.* The trustee will not disburse the income to or for the use of the **income beneficiaries** or remainder beneficiaries. The earnings will be reinvested in the trust for the period of time specified. Most states restrict the length of time that a private trust can accumulate income to the identical time period prescribed by the *rule against perpetuities.*

Income beneficiaries
Persons with an income interest in a trust.

A *sprinkling trust* is one that gives the trustee the power to determine which income beneficiaries should receive income each year and how much they should receive. A prudent creator should provide the trustee with some standards to use in making this decision. Income that is not distributed in any particular year is added to the corpus, as in an accumulation trust.

As the name implies, a *spendthrift trust* is established when one or more of the beneficiaries are spendthrifts and need to be protected from their own imprudent spending habits. They are permitted in most, but not all, states. This type of trust also may be used if the beneficiary is unduly subject to manipulation and/or control by family members and friends. Generally, the beneficiary (1) cannot anticipate the receipt of income or corpus from a spendthrift trust, (2) cannot assign it to creditors or borrow against it, and (3) will not necessarily receive all the income earned in any one year. Income will be paid to the beneficiary only when actually necessary. The trustee often will pay it directly to the creditor for services ordered by the trustee. Under some circumstances, creditors *may* be able to attach the trust assets.

A *discretionary trust* allows the trustee to pay or not to pay the income or principal at his or her discretion. It is commonly used in states that either do not allow or greatly restrict spendthrift trusts. In these situations, the creator generally names an affectionate family member as an alternate beneficiary, and, when the primary beneficiary has difficulties with creditors, the trustee makes the distributions to the alternate. It is hoped that the alternate will feel a moral obligation to care for the primary beneficiary.

ADVANTAGES OF TRUSTS

One of the advantages of trusts over other methods of transferring assets is the flexibility that trusts permit. With an outright gift, the gift property belongs to the beneficiary. If that transfer turns out to be inappropriate, generally the transferor cannot change it. With gifts in trust, the trustee maintains control over the assets for a specified period of time under the instructions in the trust deed. For example, a trust can be established for one's children so that each will receive a third of his or her share of the corpus when he or she reaches 25, 30, and 35.

Another aspect of this flexibility is that funding a trust can occur over a period of time. A trust deed can be written to permit the creator to add assets to the trust later. In fact, the trust deed can be written so that other people can add assets to the creator's trust. Moreover, trust income can be paid out to the income beneficiaries equally, based on percentages, or based on need. Beneficiaries can receive the income in a lump sum at the end of the trust or annually, quarterly, monthly, or as needed.

DISADVANTAGES OF TRUSTS

The flexibility of trusts can be an advantage; by the same token, lack of flexibility can be a disadvantage. If a trust is irrevocable and an emergency arises or circumstances change, the trustee generally will be constrained by the trust deed. If the creator did not anticipate this occurrence in the document, the trustee may not be able to modify his or her actions to fit the situation. Another disadvantage of trusts is fees. Rarely is a trustee willing to undertake the responsibility of being a trustee without receiving a fee.

Trusts also may increase the amount of taxes that must be paid, depending on the nature and terms of the trust. Under the tax codes, trusts are taxed in complex ways. Before establishing a trust, one should determine (1) who will pay income tax on its income, (2) who will have the advantage of any income tax deductions, (3) whether the trust will be subject to gift taxes, (4) whether the trust will be subject to estate and/or inheritance taxes when the creator or a beneficiary dies, and (5) whether the trust will be subject to any generation-skipping transfer taxes. A *generation-skipping transfer tax* is a tax imposed on some trust (and nontrust) transfers to a recipient who is two or more generations younger than the donor. For example, a man who makes a gift to his granddaughter rather than to his daughter makes a generation-skipping transfer. All the tax considerations listed here are complex, with varying tax rates, deductions, exclusions, exemptions, and credits.

SELECTION OF TRUSTEES AND EXECUTORS

Because trustees and executors have broad powers and broad discretion, it is important to select them wisely. Successor trustees and executors also may be named in a trust or a will in case the first person named is unable or unwilling to serve as the personal representative. If a decedent does not have a valid will naming a suitable executor, the probate court will appoint an administrator for the estate. In such a case, the owner of the assets will have no say in the selection. Trustees or guardians may be appointed to invest and protect the estates of the people who are mentally incompetent. Administrators, executors, and trustees may be referred to as *fiduciaries*, since each one has a fiduciary duty to protect the rights of the creator and the beneficiaries.

The legal requirements for serving as a fiduciary are very simple. In most states, the fiduciary must be 18 years of age or older. Some states also require that the fiduciary be a resident of the state. It generally simplifies transactions if the fiduciary does reside in the state.

A common consideration in selecting a fiduciary is whether to select a *corporate fiduciary*, such as the trust department of a bank, or an *individual fiduciary*, such as a family member or a friend. A corporate fiduciary usually does not die or dissolve, often has the expertise needed to do a competent job, and does not need to be bonded for the faithful performance of its duties. Although corporate trustees may last forever, individual trust officers do not. Often, a creator or testator will select a bank because of past dealings with a particular trust officer. Remember, however, that the trust officer may leave or die. Moreover, some corporate trust departments do not earn a very good rate of return on the assets that they invest. The same may be true, though, for any individual trustee. Corporate trustees will require a fee, but they may be willing to negotiate and handle the trust for a smaller fee. Many states have statutes that prescribe the maximum fees.

Individual trustees may be willing to serve without fees. They also may have more knowledge about the business and family members than corporate trustees have. In addition, they may be personally concerned for the well-being of the beneficiaries. They may, however, be biased toward certain beneficiaries. In fact, they may be so closely involved with the family that they will be subject to overreaching by family members.

46.3 | PERSONAL LAW/ MANAGEMENT

CREATING A TRUST

Tom and Anna would like to create a trust to provide for the education and support of John and Lindsay until each child reaches the age of 25. They have asked you what they should include in the proposed trust instrument and also what pitfalls or problems they should seek to avoid in creating the trust. What will you tell them?

BUSINESS CONSIDERATIONS Would it be wise to appoint a business associate as the trustee of a trust established to provide for one's children? How much latitude should a trustee be given in administering a trust such as the one proposed by Tom and Anna?

ETHICAL CONSIDERATIONS Is it prudent or ethical to appoint a family member or close family friend as trustee? What ethical issues would such an appointment raise? What advantages might such a person have as the trustee?

A decision to choose a corporate trustee may be affected by the selection of individuals available to serve in that capacity. A trustee should be honest, mature, competent, impartial, and knowledgeable and should have the ability and time to make sound business decisions. Obviously, the final selection of any personal representative should depend on the facts and circumstances of each case.

DUTIES OF TRUSTEES AND EXECUTORS

The trustee has two primary duties in relation to the property in his or her care. First, the trustee is supposed to preserve and protect the trust corpus. This includes identifying, protecting, and safeguarding the assets. The other primary function of the trustee is to make the assets productive. In other words, the trustee is supposed to invest and manage the assets to produce income for the beneficiaries. This task must be accomplished without violating the trustee's other duties.

The trustee has some other, more specific duties. They include an obligation to follow the terms of the trust and a duty of care that must be exercised in administering someone else's property. The rule, as stated by a majority of courts, is that a trustee must exercise the degree of *care, skill, and prudence* that a reasonably prudent businessperson would exercise in dealing with his or her own property. This standard is applied whether the person actually possesses the necessary skill and knowledge. A majority of the states have enacted the Uniform Prudent Investor Act (1994) to provide guidance to trustees.[20] The act takes a portfolio approach to the trust assets, where the court reviews the portfolio as a whole. Under the prior law, a trustee who lost money on any one investment could be sued, even if the trust assets as a whole had a substantial increase in value. The current approach is consistent with the concept of a well-rounded portfolio of investments, common in financial planning today. The act also makes fundamental changes in the way trustees invest, gives trustees broader choices in making investments, and yet still holds them to a strict standard of care.

The trustee also has a duty of loyalty. There are, in reality, two aspects of this duty. One is an obligation not to take advantage of situations involving conflicts of interest. In many instances, the trustee has an obligation to avoid even potential conflicts of interest. Obviously, then, a trustee should not personally enter into a transaction with the trust. Such a transaction usually is a breach of fiduciary duty and consequently is voidable and can be set aside. The other aspect of the duty of loyalty is to be as impartial as possible among the beneficiaries. Impartiality is not always possible because there is a natural conflict between the income beneficiaries and the remainder beneficiaries. (Remainder beneficiaries are also called *principal* beneficiaries or *corpus* beneficiaries.) The Uniform Principal and Income Act of 1997 provides guidance on what is income and what is corpus.

As stated by Justice Putnam of the Supreme Court in the classic decision *Harvard College* v. *Amory*,[21] "All that can be required of a trustee . . . is that he shall conduct himself faithfully and exercise sound discretion. He is to observe how men of prudence, discretion, and intelligence manage their own affairs, not in regard to speculation, but in regard to the permanent disposition of their funds, considering the probable income, as well as the probable safety of the capital to be invested."

It is commonly stated that a trustee has a duty not to delegate, but this is really just a cautionary note. Not every act of trust administration must be completed by the trustee personally. A trustee may delegate to others the performance of any act

ACCUSED MURDERER'S RIGHT TO FAMILY ASSETS AND TO SERVE AS TRUSTEE

Dana Ewell's father, mother, and sister were murdered in their home on 19 April 1992, Easter weekend. Dana is accused of hiring Joel P. Radovich, his former college roommate, to murder his family in order to split their $8 million estate. The prosecutor has asked for the death penalty against both men. Both defendants have pleaded not guilty.

After the murders, Dana was made the trustee of the affairs of Glee Mitchell, his 90-year-old maternal grandmother. Investigators contend that he spent about $93,000 of estate funds for the care of Glee Mitchell, who resides in a Turlock convalescent home. Initially, he withdrew funds from Mitchell's accounts at the rate of about $1,000 a month for his own use. The rate of withdrawal increased, and, prior to his arrest, he withdrew funds at the rate of about $10,000 a month. Meanwhile, he wrote many checks from the trust account, including checks for more than $15,000 to a Fresno law firm, checks for $5,500 in flying lessons for Radovich, checks for almost $40,000 for his girlfriend Monica Zent, and checks for $2,500 to Neiman Marcus. Checks were also written to the Fresno County Library and the RD Fund for the Blind and for car detailing, doctors, pest control, utility bills, cleaning, and magazine subscriptions. Reports indicate that Dana spent over $160,000 on himself and his friends. He even incurred fees for excessive activity on some of Mitchell's accounts. Spokespersons for Dana indicate that Mitchell was always generous with family members and that Mitchell encouraged Dana to spend even more money on himself.

If Dana's conduct was challenged in *your* court, how would *you* rule?[22]

BUSINESS CONSIDERATIONS Does a business or charity have an obligation to scrutinize the source of checks received to determine if the check is drawn on a trust account? Is this an overwhelming burden to place on businesses or charities? Why or why not?

ETHICAL CONSIDERATIONS Is it ethical for a law firm to accept checks drawn on the trust account for services rendered to Dana Ewell as an individual? Is it ethical for Dana's friends to accept gifts from trust assets?

SOURCES: Jerry Bier, *The Fresno Bee* (26 January 1996), pp. B1, B3; Tom Kertscher, *The Fresno Bee* (19 June 1995 and 7 April 1995), pp. A1, A14.

or the exercise of any power when it is consistent with the trustee's general duty of care owed to the beneficiaries. In other words, the trustee may employ agents when a reasonably prudent owner of the same type of property with similar objectives would employ agents. The Uniform Prudent Investor Act (1994) authorizes trustees to utilize portfolio managers and investment advisers. In addition, the trustee must exercise due care in selecting and supervising agents.

The trustee must be careful in selecting trust investments. This generally includes a duty to diversify the types of investments. The statutes in many states list or define what investments a trustee may make. These are often called *legal investments.* A creator, however, may grant a trustee the specific power to invest in nonlegal investments. Such a provision gives the trustee broader investment power, but it does not remove the general obligation to invest wisely. Obviously, this duty does not imply that the trustee guarantees that all investments will increase in value or that no money will be lost. Generally, trustees limit themselves to conservative investments. The standard test of whether a trustee has fulfilled this obligation is whether other prudent investors, *at that time,* would have chosen other, better investments; the judgment should not be made in hindsight. The trustee may be surcharged for unwise investment decisions and must pay personally for any losses caused by negligent decisions. Under the common law, the trustee could not offset profits on other investments against these losses.

The trustee has a duty to maintain clear and accurate records regarding the administration of the trust. This obligation, called the *duty to account,* includes recording the location and type of assets and the receipt and expenditure of income. In some jurisdictions, the trustee must file periodic accountings with the court. In others, it is sufficient for the trustee to account to the trust beneficiaries.

The trustee must not mix his or her personal funds with trust funds, a situation known as *commingling of assets.* The trustee may not borrow money or mortgage trust property unless that power was expressly provided in the trust document. The trustee *will* have the incidental authority to carry out ordinary duties.

The executor's duties parallel those of a trustee. They both have fiduciary duties to the beneficiaries. The executor is responsible for filing estate and inheritance tax returns, paying the applicable taxes, and filing accounts with the probate court. The executor should try to complete the estate work and distribute the remaining assets quickly and prudently. This will help prevent a loss in the value of assets.

IMPLIED TRUSTS

Express trusts are voluntarily and intentionally created by the owner of the assets. Implied trusts, on the other hand, are created by operation of law. They are either implied by the law or imposed by the courts. Implied trusts may arise in the context of an express trust, but that is not a legal requirement.

Resulting Trusts

A *resulting trust* is based on the owner's presumed intention and occurs when the owner of property disposes of the property but the disposition is not complete. The owner fails to make a complete, effective disposition of all his or her equitable interests. (A disposition will be considered complete if the state rules of trust interpretation determine who receives the interests.) A portion of the owner's interest reverts to the owner or the owner's heirs. A resulting trust will occur only if the owner is acting in good faith. This type of trust most commonly occurs under any one of the following circumstances:

1. The owner does not state who should acquire a beneficial interest, such as a remainder interest; for example, the owner transfers a vacation home to a cousin for 10 years.
2. The owner does not state what should happen under certain unanticipated situations; for example, a child dies before his or her parents.
3. The express trust is not enforceable because it is not in the proper form; for example, the owner fails to name the beneficiaries.
4. The express trust fails completely or in part, because it is illegal, impractical, *or* impossible or because a beneficiary refuses an interest in the trust; for example, a charitable purpose becomes impractical and the court finds *cy-pres* inapplicable.

A resulting trust also may occur when a person purchases real property with his or her own money and puts the title in the name of another person. The law presumes that the purchaser intends that the recipient hold the property as "trustee" for the purchaser. This is often called a *purchase money resulting trust*. The presumption may be rebutted by evidence that the purchaser has a different intention. In many states, the courts will presume that the purchaser intends a gift, *if* the purchaser and transferee are closely related.

Constructive Trusts

A *constructive trust* is actually an equitable remedy. It arises by operation of law and serves to redress a wrong or to prevent an unjust enrichment. A court of equity imposes this trust when a person gains legal title to property but has an equitable duty to transfer the property to someone else. The following are some examples of how this trust can occur:

1. A person takes title as a trustee, but the trust is not enforceable; for example, a trustee receives assets under an oral trust that is unenforceable under the Statute of Frauds. To allow the trustee to keep the property would create unjust enrichment.
2. A person obtains property by breaching a fiduciary duty; for example, an employee embezzles company funds.

 click here

RESOURCES FOR BUSINESS LAW STUDENTS

NAME	RESOURCES	WEB ADDRESS
Legal Information Institute (LII)—Estates and Trusts Law Materials	LII, maintained by the Cornell Law School, provides an overview of estates and trust law, including relevant sections from the U.S. Code and Code of Federal Regulation, court cases, the Uniform Probate Code, and links.	**http://wwwsecure.law.cornell.edu/topics/estates_trusts. html**
American Bar Association's Section of Real Property, Probate and Trust Law	The Real Property, Probate and Trust Law Section, with more than 30,000 members, publishes the scholarly journal "Real Property, Probate and Trust Law Journal," and the practical bimonthly magazine "Probate & Property."	**http://www.abanet.org/rppt/home.html**
National Conference of Commissioners on Uniform State Laws	It contains press releases, questions and answers about selected uniform acts including information about which states have adopted the act and why the act should be adopted.	**http://www.nccusl.org**

3. A person is either guilty of a wrong *or* would receive unjust enrichment. Depending on state law, the person may be guilty of fraud, conversion, theft, duress, or murder of the transferor. Some situations may involve mistake. For example, the transferor may own two lots and sell one lot to the transferee, but the deed mistakenly mentions both lots. The court will impose a constructive trust on the second lot for the benefit of the transferor.

Constructive trusts are not limited to these situations. As with other equitable remedies, constructive trusts are created to correct unfair results.

SUMMARY

A will states how a person would like to have property pass at his or her death. This property includes business assets, such as patents, copyrights, and ownership interests in business enterprises. For a will to be valid, a person must intend it to be his or her will. The person must have testamentary capacity. The will must conform to the state's statutory requirements. Some legal documents, such as trusts and deeds for property, can act as substitutes for will provisions. In the absence of a valid will, the property passes by intestate succession, which is controlled by state law. A formal will is drafted by an attorney, the state legislature (with statutory wills), or the testator. This is the most common type of will. It must be signed by the testator and witnessed by two disinterested witnesses. Self-proved wills can permit the probate of the will without locating the witnesses. Some states also permit nuncupative (oral) wills and holographic (handwritten) wills.

Most estates are subject to probate proceedings. During the hearings, the probate court oversees the proper administration of the estate by the personal representative. The representative must pay debts, collect assets, pay taxes, and distribute assets to the beneficiaries.

Living wills explain the individual's desires concerning medical treatment, if the maker is unable to speak for him- or herself. Durable powers of attorney allow the maker to designate a person to make medical decisions for him or her. These documents are especially important to healthcare providers.

An express trust is an arrangement whereby the owner of assets voluntarily places the legal ownership in a trustee and the equitable ownership in one or more beneficiaries. Creators are motivated to establish trusts for many purposes, including the following: to protect beneficiaries from themselves and creditors, to free beneficiaries from the responsibilities of asset management, to split an asset or estate among multiple beneficiaries, to test a pattern of transfers before finalizing it, to save taxes, and to increase flexibility. The trustee is obligated to manage the trust assets prudently. Trustees are often business entities. Trusts can be flexible and established to accommodate numerous situations. However, they may be expensive because of trustee's fees and added tax burdens. Care must be utilized in selecting an appropriate trustee, because a trustee has broad discretion in managing the trust. The trustee must exercise due care in selecting investments for the trust. He or she may be surcharged for making careless decisions or violating his or her fiduciary duties.

DISCUSSION QUESTIONS

1. What problems may occur if a person chooses to write a holographic will? What advantages might there be to this?

2. Brian has inherited a million dollars from his parents' estate. Brian, who has an extremely low IQ, wants to have his attorney write a will leaving his estate to his gardener and excluding his nieces and nephews. Can such a will be valid? If so, under what circumstances?

3. Mary Ann is writing a new will. She is quite displeased with her sister. She intends to include the following statement in her will, "To my sister, Rosa, I leave nothing. She has lied and cheated and will never amount to anything." Mary Ann asks for your advice. What would you recommend and why?

4. Rachael bequeaths the remainder of her estate "to Bank of America in trust to pay all the income to Bill for life, and on Bill's death to transfer the remainder to Bill's issue who are still alive." Bill dies without having any issue. The will has no provision controlling this situation. What will happen? Why?

5. What will be the intestate distribution under the Uniform Probate Code when a husband dies survived by his wife and his mother?

6. Distinguish strict per stirpes distributions from per capita at each generation distributions. When will the shares be the same? When will they be different?

7. What are the differences between estate taxes and inheritance taxes?

8. How do defined-benefit plans and defined-contribution plans differ?

9. What are the advantages and disadvantages of living wills?

10. Executors and trustees may be asked to serve without fees. Why might they be reluctant to do so? Under what circumstances might they be willing to do so?

CASE PROBLEMS AND WRITING ASSIGNMENTS

1. Diana Krueger died on 3 May 1992. Her heirs were her four nephews—Fred, William, Rhinhold, and Daniel Bieber. Krueger executed two wills during her life—a holographic will on 8 January 1979 and a formal, attested will prepared by an attorney on 9 March 1990. The 1990 will contained a clause expressly revoking all previous wills, including the holographic will. The original, signed copy of the 1990 will was not located after Krueger's death. Fred Bieber testified that he and his wife took Krueger home from the hospital on the 14th or 15th of March 1990. While there, Krueger asked Fred to get a box from a closet. Krueger opened the box and took out an envelope that contained the 1979 holographic will. Krueger read the will word for word to Fred. One of the gifts provided that her "Books and Diploma" go to her niece Doris. Krueger crossed out the name of Doris, who had died, and asked Fred to write in "Fred Bieber['s] daughters." Fred did so. Should the holographic will be accepted as valid? [See *In re Estate of Krueger*, 529 N.W.2d 151 (N.D. 1995).]

2. Clara Hicks resided in a nursing home at the time she executed a will in 1977. She was 87 at that time. The will was read to her at the time of execution, and she indicated her approval of the will provisions leaving a larger share to one particular nephew. That nephew visited her at least once a week and responded to her needs and requests. Dr. Hicks (unrelated), who visited her monthly in the nursing home, testified at trial that he thought that she was competent and that she understood her affairs. Did Clara Hicks have testamentary capacity? Was Clara Hicks subjected to undue influence? Why or why not? [See *Estate of Hicks*, 327 S.E.2d 345 (S.C. 1985).]

3. Mary Eickhold signed a will in 1980. It provided that one-half of her farm should go to her brother and one-half to her sister and the residue of her estate should be divided between them. In 1981, she signed a codicil providing that the residue of her estate should go to four of her nephews. The same codicil directed the executor to sell her farm and to divide the proceeds with the rest of the residue. The attorney, who drafted both documents, testified at trial that Mary understood that her brother and sister would still receive the farm. The attorney could not remember whether he explained to her the effect that a sale of the farm would have on this bequest. Was Mary's brother entitled to one-half of the proceeds from the farm? Why or why not? What ethical implications are raised by this case? [See *Matter of Estate of Eickhold*, 365 N.W.2d 44 (Iowa App. 1985).]

4. Wells Fargo Bank was the trustee of a testamentary trust under Abraham L. Gump's will. The trustee filed its eighth annual accounting, which included a request for $32,689 compensation for the trustee.

However, the trustee was awarded only $10,000 in fees by the probate court. In accordance with the trust deed, the trustee was managing some real estate occupied by a retail store. The retail store underpaid its rent under the formula provided by the lease. The bank negligently accepted the underpayment as full payment of the rent. Did the probate court unduly penalize the negligent trustee? What would be an appropriate penalty for the trustee? [See *Estate of Gump*, 180 Cal.Rptr. 219 (Cal.App. 1982).]

5. Mr. and Mrs. Wiemer entered into a trust agreement, with Havana Bank as trustee, to enable them to purchase and work a farm. As part of the financial arrangement, Northwestern Mutual executed a $70,000 first mortgage on the farm; Havana held the second mortgage. After Mr. Wiemer died, Havana took $8,000 from the trust account and paid itself part of its own second mortgage. Consequently, the trust was unable to make the next payment to Northwestern, and Northwestern foreclosed on the first mortgage. Did the trustee breach its trust duties? [See *Northwestern Mutual Life Insurance Co.* v. *Wiemer*, 421 N.E.2d 1002 (Ill.App. 1981).]

6. **BUSINESS APPLICATION CASE** Harold Colson died in 1968. In his will, which had been written in 1957, he provided for a scholarship fund to be established and administered by the Wesley United Methodist Church Board of Trustees. The fund was to provide one $500 scholarship per year from trust income to a male member of the congregation who was attending Harvard College. The trust corpus was generating $3,200 of income per year, the tuition at Harvard had risen to $2,600 per year, Harvard was admitting women as well as men, and no member of the congregation had ever applied for the scholarship. The trustees requested a modification of the trust under the *cy-pres* doctrine. The family of the creator petitioned for a cancellation of the old trust. How should the court rule and why? [See *Wesley United Methodist Church* v. *Harvard College*, 316 N.E.2d 620 (Mass. 1974).]

7. **ETHICAL APPLICATION CASE** Margarita Savain executed a will on 7 October 1983 (will #1). Savain was admitted to the hospital early in May 1992, and she was apparently dying. One of the medicines administered to her was Demerol, a narcotic painkiller. As a consequence, there was conflicting information about her state of mind while she was on the medication. While in the hospital, she signed another will (will #2). In this will, she left all her property to her

"good friend" and tenant, John Shack. John Shack contacted an attorney on 8 May 1992. The attorney prepared will #2 according to Shack's instructions and delivered it to the hospital the same day. Shack paid for the preparation of the will. The attorney did not know Savain prior to the signing of the will. The signing of will #2 was witnessed by Shack's employer and a hospital nurse, Ms. Melisano, who was instructed to act as a witness by her supervisor. Melisano said that when she arrived in the hospital room, Shack, his employer (who recommended the attorney to Shack), and the attorney were already there. She asked if they had read the will to Savain, and they indicated that they had. It was not read again in her presence. Savain signed the document, and Melisano signed at the request of the attorney. Savain did not make any statements about the document, although the attesting clause said it was her will. The discussion at the time centered around Savain's return to her home and getting food for her.

On 12 May 1992, Savain executed a third instrument (will #3), naming Ecedro Rabsatt as the sole beneficiary of her estate. Rabsatt had been a close friend of Savain's for a long time. Will #3 was drafted by Rita James, a nonlawyer who used to work as a legal secretary. Savain met with James several weeks prior to entering the hospital to outline the will provisions. James was not paid for preparing will #3. The attesting witnesses were Rabsatt's cousin, Randolph Thomas, and James's common law husband, Alvin Canton. Both had a longtime relationship with Rabsatt. Thomas testified that, at the signing, Savain never discussed the fact that the document was her will. He also indicated that Rabsatt, not Savain, asked him to sign the document. Savain died on 24 May 1992. Were wills #2 and/or #3 executed properly? Did John Shack and his employer behave ethically? Did Ecedro Rabsatt and his friends and relatives behave ethically? Did Melisano have a duty to speak out if Savain seemed incompetent or confused? To whom should Melisano communicate her concerns? [See *Rabsatt* v. *Estate of Savain*, 878 F.Supp. 762 (D.V.I., 1995).]

8. **CRITICAL THINKING CASE** At the age of 90, Austin Davis signed a will leaving his estate to his step-great-grandchildren. Ten days later, the testator executed a will naming his next-door neighbor as his sole beneficiary. In this will, he specifically revoked his prior wills. The neighbor did not order the will prepared, but she did drive the testator to the attorney's office. The neighbor lived next door to the testator for 10 years. During the last year or so, the neighbor was

hired to provide meals and general care for the testator. The testator said that his step-great-grandchildren did not care anything about him and that he did not want them to have his money. He also said that he wanted his money to go to someone who helped him.

Was the testator competent to execute a will? Did the neighbor exert undue influence? Explain your answer. [See *Edwards* v. *Vaught*, 681 S.W.2d 322 (Ark. 1984).]

NOTES

1. Information on the current status of adoptions of the Uniform State Laws was provided by Katie Robinson, Public Affairs Coordinator, NCCUSL, during a telephone conversation on 24 March 2000.
2. California Probate Code § 6111(a).
3. 79 *American Jurisprudence 2d, Wills*, §§ 733, 740 (Rochester, NY: Lawyers' Cooperative, 1962); kept current with periodic updates.
4. *The Book of The States*, 1990–91 ed., Vol. 28 (Lexington, KY: The Council of State Governments, 1990), p. 417.
5. 79 *American Jurisprudence 2d, Wills*, §§ 733, 740.
6. See California Probate Code, § 329, for an example of a probate code section permitting self-proving wills.
7. The Revised Uniform Anatomical Gift Act (1987) has been adopted in Arizona, Arkansas, California, Connecticut, Hawaii, Idaho, Indiana, Iowa, Minnesota, Montana, Nevada, New Hampshire, New Mexico, North Dakota, Oregon, Pennsylvania, Rhode Island, Utah, Vermont, Virginia, Washington, and Wisconsin. National Conference of Commissioners on Uniform State Laws web page, "A Few Facts About the Revised Uniform Anatomical Gift Act (1987)," http://www.nccusl.org/uniformact_factsheets/uniformacts-fs-aga87.htm
8. Uniform Probate Code, § 2-102(1).
9. Ibid., §§ 2-102(3), 2-103, and 2-106 as amended in 1990.
10. The Uniform TOD Security Registration Act has been adopted by Alabama, Alaska, Arizona, Arkansas, California, Colorado, Connecticut, Delaware, Florida, Georgia, Hawaii, Idaho, Illinois, Indiana, Iowa, Kansas, Kentucky, Maine, Maryland, Massachusetts, Michigan, Minnesota, Mississippi, Missouri, Montana, Nebraska, Nevada, New Hampshire, New Jersey, New Mexico, North Dakota, Ohio, Oklahoma, Oregon, Pennsylvania, Rhode Island, South Carolina, South Dakota, Tennessee, Utah, Vermont, Virginia, Washington, West Virginia, Wisconsin, and Wyoming. National Conference of Commissioners on Uniform State Laws web page, "Transfer on Death Security Registration: An Answer to the Woes of Joint Ownership of Securities," http://www.nccusl.org/pressreleases/pr1-00-1.htm.
11. Uniform Probate Code § 3-502.
12. The only states that still have a gift tax are Connecticut, Delaware, Louisiana, North Carolina, and Tennessee. Joshua S. Rubenstein and Eileen Caulfield Schwab, "Historic New York Estate and Gift Tax Reform," *New York Law Journal* (20 August 1997), Outside Counsel, p.1 at p. 1.
13. The states that have an independent estate tax are Ohio and Oklahoma. Ibid.
14. The states that have an independent inheritance tax are Delaware, Indiana, Iowa, Kansas, Kentucky, Louisiana, Maryland, Michigan, Nebraska, North Carolina, Pennsylvania, South Dakota, and Tennessee. In Mississippi, Montana, and New Jersey, the death tax is limited to the death tax credit for property passing to spouses and descendents. These states have an inheritance tax for property passing to other people. Ibid.
15. The states that limit their death tax to the federal state death tax credit are Alabama, Alaska, Arizona, Arkansas, California, Colorado, Connecticut, District of Columbia, Florida, Georgia, Hawaii, Idaho, Illinois, Maine, Massachusetts, Minnesota, Mississippi, Missouri, Montana, Nevada, New Hampshire, New Jersey, New Mexico, New York, North Dakota, Oregon, Rhode Island, South Carolina, Texas, Utah, Vermont, Virginia, Washington, West Virginia, Wisconsin, and Wyoming. Ibid.
16. See TEX. PROB. CODE ANN. § 482 (Vernon Supp. 1999).
17. The Uniform Principal and Income Act has been adopted by Arkansas, California, Connecticut, Iowa, North Dakota, Oklahoma, and Virginia. National Conference of Commissioners on Uniform State Laws web page, "A Few Facts About the Uniform Principal and Income Act," http://www.nccusl.org/uniformact_factsheets/uniformacts_fs-upia.htm.
18. The Uniform Statutory Rule Against Perpetuities with 1990 amendments has been adopted in Alaska, Arizona, California, Colorado, Connecticut, Florida, Georgia, Hawaii, Indiana, Kansas, Massachusetts, Michigan, Minnesota, Montana, Nebraska, Nevada,

New Jersey, New Mexico, North Carolina, North Dakota, Oregon, South Carolina, South Dakota, Tennessee, Utah, and West Virginia. National Conference of Commissioners on Uniform State Laws web page, "A Few Facts About the Uniform Statutory Rule Against Perpetuities Act," http://www.nccusl.org/uniformact_factsheets/uniformacts_fs-usrap.htm.

19. Internal Revenue Code § 2055.

20. The Uniform Prudent Investor Act has been adopted by Alaska, Arizona, Arkansas, California, Colorado, Connecticut, District of Columbia, Hawaii, Idaho, Indiana, Iowa, Maine, Massachusetts, Michigan, Minnesota, Missouri, Nebraska, New Hampshire, New Jersey, New Mexico, North Carolina, North Dakota,

Ohio, Oklahoma, Oregon, Pennsylvania, Rhode Island, Utah, Vermont, Virginia, Washington, West Virginia, and Wyoming. National Conference of Commissioners on Uniform State Laws web page, "A Few Facts About the Uniform Prudent Investor Act," http://www.nccusl.org/uniformact_factsheets/uniformacts_fs-upria.htm.

21. 9 Pick. 446, 461 (1830).

22. Jerry Bier, "Third Ewell Judge Ousted," *The Fresno Bee* (26 January 1996), pp. B1, B3; Tom Kertscher, "Ewell Allegedly Misused $160,000," *The Fresno Bee* (19 June 1995), pp. A1, A10; Tom Kertscher, "Ewell Uncles Win Round: Aunt Can't Move Money," *The Fresno Bee* (7 April 1995), pp. A1, A14.

APPENDIX A

THE CONSTITUTION OF THE UNITED STATES

Preamble

We the People of theUnited States,in Order to form a more perfect Union, establish Justice, insure domestic Tranquility, provide for the common defense, promote the general Welfare, and secure the Blessings of Liberty to ourselves and our Posterity, do ordain and establish this Constitution for the United States of America.

Article I

Section 1.   All legislative Powers herein granted shall be vested in a Congress of the United States, which shall consist of a Senate and House of Representatives.

Section 2.   The House of Representatives shall be composed of Members chosen every second Year by the People of the several States, and the Electors in each State shall have the Qualifications requisite for Electors of the most numerous Branch of the State Legislature.

No Person shall be a Representative who shall not have attained to the Age of twenty five Years, and been seven Years a Citizen of the United States, and who shall not, when elected, be an Inhabitant of that State in which he shall be chosen.

Representatives and direct Taxes shall be apportioned among the several States which may be included within this Union, according to their respective Numbers, which shall be determined by adding to the whole Number of free Persons, including those bound to Service for a Term of Years, and excluding Indians not taxed, three fifths of all other Persons. The actual Enumeration shall be made within three Years after the first Meeting of the Congress of the United States, and within every subsequent Term of ten Years, in such Manner as they shall by Law direct. The number of Representatives shall not exceed one for every thirty Thousand, but each State shall have at Least one Representative; and until such enumeration shall be made, the State of New Hampshire shall be entitled to chuse three, Massachusetts eight, Rhode Island and Providence Plantations one, Connecticut five, New-York six, New Jersey four, Pennsylvania eight, Delaware one, Maryland six, Virginia ten, North Carolina five, South Carolina five, and Georgia three.

When vacancies happen in the Representation from any State, the Executive Authority thereof shall issue Writs of Election to fill such vacancies.

The House of Representatives shall chuse their Speaker and other Officers; and shall have the sole Power of Impeachment.

Section 3.   The Senate of the United States shall be composed of two Senators from each State, chosen by the Legislature thereof, for six Years; and each Senator shall have one Vote.

Immediately after they shall be assembled in Consequence of the first Election, they shall be divided as equally as may be into three Classes. The Seats of the Senators of the first Class shall be vacated at the Expiration of the second Year, of the second Class at the Expiration of the fourth Year, and of the third Class at the Expiration of the sixth Year, so that one third may be chosen every second Year; and if Vacancies happen by Resignation or otherwise, during the Recess of the Legislature of any State, the Executive thereof may make temporary Appointments until the next Meeting of the Legislature, which shall then fill such Vacancies.

No Person shall be a Senator who shall not have attained to the Age of thirty Years, and been nine Years a Citizen of the United States, and who shall not, when elected, be an Inhabitant of that State for which he shall be chosen.

The Vice President of the United States shall be President of the Senate, but shall have no Vote, unless they be equally divided.

The Senate shall chuse their other Officers, and also a President pro tempore, in the Absence of the Vice President, or when he shall exercise the Office of President of the United States.

The Senate shall have the sole power to try all Impeachments. When sitting for that Purpose, they shall be an Oath or Affirmation. When the President of the United States is tried, the Chief Justice shall preside: And no Person shall be convicted without the Concurrence of two thirds of the Members present.

Judgment in Cases of Impeachment shall not extend further than to removal from Office, and disqualification to hold and enjoy any Office of honor, Trust or Profit under the United States: but the Party convicted shall nevertheless be liable and subject to Indictment, Trial, Judgment and Punishment, according to Law.

Section 4.   The Times, Places and Manner of holding Elections for Senators and Representatives, shall be prescribed in each State by the Legislature thereof: but the Congress may at any time by Law make or alter such Regulations, except as to the Places of chusing Senators.

The Congress shall assemble at least once in every Year, and such Meeting shall be on the first Monday in December, unless they shall by Law appoint a different Day.

Section 5.   Each House shall be the Judge of the Elections, Returns and Qualifications of its own Members, and a Majority of each shall constitute a Quorum to do Business; but a smaller Number may adjourn from day to day, and may be authorized to compel the Attendance of absent Members, in such Manner, and under such Penalties as each House may provide.

Each House may determine the Rules of its Proceedings, punish its Members for disorderly Behaviour, and, with the Concurrence of two thirds, expel a Member.

Each House shall keep a Journal of its Proceedings, and from time to time publish the same, excepting such Parts as may in their Judgment require Secrecy; and the Yeas and Nays of the Members of either House on any question shall, at the Desire of one fifth of those Present, be entered on the Journal.

Neither House, during the Session of Congress, shall, without the Consent of the other, adjourn for more than three days, nor to any other Place than that in which the two Houses shall be sitting.

Section 6. The Senators and Representatives shall receive a Compensation for their Services, to be ascertained by Law, and paid out of the Treasury of the United States. They shall in all Cases, except Treason, Felony and Breach of the Peace, be privileged from Arrest during their Attendance at the Session of their respective Houses, and in going to and returning from the same; and for any Speech or Debate in either House, they shall not be questioned in any other Place.

No Senator or Representative shall, during the Time for which he was elected, be appointed to any civil Office under the Authority of the United States, which shall have been created, or the Emoluments whereof shall have been encreased during such time; and no Person holding any Office under the United States, shall be a Member of either House during his Continuance in Office.

Section 7. All Bills for raising Revenue shall originate in the House of Representatives; but the Senate may propose or concur with Amendments as on other Bills.

Every Bill which shall have passed the House of Representatives and the Senate, shall, before it become a Law, be presented to the President of the United States; If he approve he shall sign it, but if not he shall return it, with his Objections to that House in which it shall have originated, who shall enter the Objections at large on their Journal, and proceed to reconsider it. If after such Reconsideration two thirds of that House shall agree to pass the Bill, it shall be sent, together with the Objections, to the other House, by which it shall likewise be reconsidered, and if approved by two thirds of that House, it shall become a Law. But in all such Cases the Votes of both Houses shall be determined by Yeas and Nays, and the Names of the Persons voting for and against the Bill shall be entered on the Journal of each House respectively. If any Bill shall not be returned by the President within ten Days (Sundays excepted) after it shall have been presented to him, the Same shall be a Law, in like Manner as if he had signed it, unless the Congress by their Adjournment prevent its Return, in which Case it shall not be a Law.

Every Order, Resolution, or Vote to which the Concurrence of the Senate and House of Representatives may be necessary (except on a question of Adjournment) shall be presented to the President of the United States; and before the Same shall take Effect, shall be approved by him, or being disapproved by him, shall be repassed by two thirds of the Senate and House of Representatives, according to the Rules and Limitations prescribed in the Case of a Bill.

Section 8. The Congress shall have Power to lay and collect Taxes, Duties, Imposts and Excises, to pay the Debts and provide for the common Defence and general Welfare of the United States; but all Duties, Imposts and Excises shall be uniform throughout the United States;

To borrow Money on the credit of the United States;

To regulate Commerce with foreign Nations, and among the several States, and with the Indian Tribes;

To establish an uniform Rule of Naturalization, and uniform Laws on the subject of Bankruptcies throughout the United States;

To coin Money, regulate the Value thereof, and of foreign Coin, and fix the Standard of Weights and Measures;

To provide for the Punishment of counterfeiting the Securities and current Coin of the United States;

To establish Post Offices and post Roads;

To promote the Progress of Science and useful Arts, by securing for limited Times to Authors and Inventors the exclusive Right to their respective Writings and Discoveries;

To constitute Tribunals inferior to the supreme Court;

To define and punish Piracies and Felonies committed on the high Seas, and Offenses against the Law of Nations;

To declare War, grant Letters of Marque and Reprisal, and make Rules concerning Captures on Land and Water;

To raise and support Armies, but no Appropriation of Money to that Use shall be for a longer Term than two Years;

To provide and maintain a Navy;

To make Rules for the Government and Regulation of the land and naval Forces;

To provide for calling forth the Militia to execute the Laws of the Union, suppress Insurrections and repel Invasions;

To provide for organizing, arming, and disciplining, the Militia, and for governing such Part of them as may be employed in the Service of the United States, reserving to the States respectively, the Appointment of the Officers, and the Authority of training the Militia according to the discipline described by Congress;

To exercise exclusive Legislation in all Cases whatsoever, over such District (not exceeding ten Miles square) as may, by Cession of particular States, and the Acceptance of Congress, become the Seat of the Government of the United States, and to exercise like Authority over all Places purchased by the Consent of the Legislature of the State in which the Same shall be, for the Erection of Forts, Magazines, Arsenals, dock-Yards, and other needful Buildings;—And

To make all Laws which shall be necessary and proper for carrying into Execution the foregoing Powers, and all other Powers vested by this Constitution in the Government of the United States, or in any Department or Officer thereof.

Section 9. The Migration or Importation of such Persons as any of the States now existing shall think proper to admit, shall not be prohibited by the Congress prior to the Year one thousand eight hundred and eight, but a Tax or Duty may be imposed on such Importation, not exceeding ten dollars for each Person.

The Privilege of the Writ of Habeas Corpus shall not be suspended, unless when in Cases of Rebellion or Invasion the public Safety may require it.

No Bill of Attainder or ex post facto Law shall be passed.

No Capitation, or other direct, Tax shall be laid, unless in Proportion to the Census or Enumeration herein before directed to be taken.

No Tax or Duty shall be laid on Articles exported from any State.

No Preference shall be given by any Regulation of Commerce or Revenue to the Ports of one State over those of another; nor shall Vessels bound to, or from, one State, be obliged to enter, clear, or pay Duties in another.

No Money shall be drawn from the Treasury, but in Consequence of Appropriations made by Laws; and a regular Statement and Account of the Receipts and Expenditures of all public Money shall be published from time to time.

No Title of Nobility shall be granted by the United States: And no Person holding any Office of Profit or Trust under them, shall, without the Consent of the Congress, accept of any present, Emolument, Office, or Title, of any kind whatever, from any King, Prince, or foreign State.

Section 10. No State shall enter into any Treaty, Alliance, or Confederation; grant Letters of Marque and Reprisal; coin Money; emit Bills of Credit; make any Thing but gold and silver Coin a Tender in Payment of Debts; pass any Bill of Attainder, ex post facto Law, or Law impairing the Obligation of Contracts, or grant any Title of Nobility.

No State shall, without the Consent of the Congress, lay any Imposts or Duties on Imports or Exports, except what may be absolutely necessary for executing its inspection Laws: and the net Produce of all Duties and Imposts, laid by any State on Imports or

Exports, shall be for the Use of the Treasury of the United States; and all such Laws shall be subject to the Revision and Controul of the Congress.

No State shall, without the Consent of Congress, lay any Duty of Tonnage, keep Troops, or Ships of War in time of Peace, enter into any Agreement or Compact with another State, or with a foreign Power, or engage in War, unless actually invaded, or in such imminent Danger as will not admit of delay.

Article II

Section 1. The executive Power shall be vested in a President of the United States of America. He shall hold his Office during the Term of four Years, and, together with the Vice President, chosen for the same Term, be elected, as follows:

Each State shall appoint, in such Manner as the Legislature thereof may direct, a Number of Electors, equal to the whole Number of Senators and Representatives to which the State may be entitled in the Congress: but no Senator or Representative, or Person holding an Office of Trust or Profit under the United States, shall be appointed an Elector.

The Electors shall meet in their respective States, and vote by Ballot for two Persons, of whom one at least shall not be an Inhabitant of the same State with themselves. And they shall make a list of all the Persons voted for, and of the Number of Votes for each; which List they shall sign and certify, and transmit sealed to the Seat of the Government of the United States, directed to the President of the Senate. The President of the Senate shall, in the presence of the Senate and House of Representatives, open all the Certificates, and the Votes shall be counted. The Person having the greatest Number of Votes shall be the President, if such Number be a Majority of the whole Number of Electors appointed; and if there be more than one who have such Majority, and have an equal Number of Votes, then the House of Representatives shall immediately chuse by Ballot one of them for President; and if no Person have a Majority, then from the five highest on the List the said House shall in like Manner chuse the President. But in chusing the President, the Votes shall be taken by States, the Representation from each State having one Vote; A quorum for this Purpose shall consist of a Member or Members from two thirds of the States, and a Majority of all the States shall be necessary to a Choice. In every Case, after the Choice of the President, the Person having the greatest Number of Votes of the Electors shall be the Vice President. But if there should remain two or more who have equal Votes, the Senate shall chuse from them by Ballot the Vice President.

The Congress may determine the Time of Chusing the Electors, and the Day on which they shall give their Votes; which Day shall be the same throughout the United States.

No Person except a natural born Citizen, or a Citizen of the United States, at the time of the Adoption of this Constitution, shall be eligible to the Office of President; neither shall any Person be eligible to that Office who shall not have attained to the Age of thirty five Years, and been fourteen Years a Resident within the United States.

In Case of the Removal of the President from Office, or of his Death, Resignation, or Inability to discharge the Powers and Duties of the said Office, the Same shall devolve on the Vice President, and the Congress may by Law provide for the Case of Removal, Death, Resignation or Inability, both of the President and Vice President, declaring what Officer shall then act as President, and such Officer shall act accordingly, until the Disability be removed, or a President shall be elected.

The President shall, at stated Times, receive for his Services, a Compensation, which shall neither be encreased nor diminished during the Period for which he shall have been elected, and he shall not receive within that Period any other Emolument from the United States, or any of them.

Before he enter on the Execution of his Office, he shall take the following Oath or Affirmation:—"I do solemnly swear (or affirm) that I will faithfully execute the Office of President of the United States, and will to the best of my Ability, preserve, protect and defend the Constitution of the United States."

Section 2. The President shall be Commander in Chief of the Army and Navy of the United States, and of the Militia of the several States, when called into the actual Service of the United States; he may require the Opinion, in writing, of the principal Officer in each of the executive Departments, upon any Subject relating to the Duties of their respective Offices, and he shall have Power to grant Reprieves and Pardons for Offenses against the United States, except in Cases of Impeachment.

He shall have Power, by and with the Advice and Consent of the Senate, to make Treaties, providing two thirds of the Senators present concur; and he shall nominate, and by and with the Advice and Consent of the Senate, shall appoint Ambassadors, other public Ministers and Consuls, Judges of the supreme Court, and all other Officers of the United States, whose Appointments are not herein otherwise provided for, and which shall be established by Law: but the Congress may by Law vest the Appointment of such inferior Officers, as they think proper, in the President alone, in the Courts of Law, or in the Heads of Departments.

The President shall have Power to fill up all Vacancies that may happen during the Recess of the Senate, by granting Commissions which shall expire at the End of their next Session.

Section 3. He shall from time to time give to the Congress Information of the State of the Union, and recommend to their Consideration such Measures as he shall judge necessary and expedient; he may, on extraordinary Occasions, convene both Houses, or either of them, and in Case of Disagreement between them, with Respect to the Time of Adjournment, he may adjourn them to such Time as he shall think proper, he shall receive Ambassadors and other public Ministers; he shall take Care that the Laws be faithfully executed, and shall Commission all the Officers of the United States.

Section 4. The President, Vice President and all civil Officers of the United States, shall be removed from Office on Impeachment for, and Conviction of, Treason, Bribery, or other high Crimes and Misdemeanors.

Article III

Section 1. The judicial Power of the United States, shall be vested in one supreme Court, and in such inferior Courts as the Congress may from time to time ordain and establish. The Judges, both of the supreme and inferior Courts, shall hold their Offices during good Behaviour, and shall, at Times, receive for their Services, a Compensation, which shall not be diminished during their Continuance in Office.

Section 2. The judicial Power shall extend to all Cases, in Law and Equity, arising under this Constitution, the Laws of the United States, and Treaties made, or which shall be made, under their Authority;—to all Cases affecting Ambassadors, other public Ministers and Consuls;—to all Cases of admiralty and maritime Jurisdiction;—to Controversies to which the United States shall be a Party;—to controversies between two or more States;—between a State and Citizens of another State;—between Citizens of different States;—between Citizens of the same State claiming Lands under Grants of different States; and between a State, or the Citizens thereof, and foreign States, Citizens or Subjects.

In all Cases affecting Ambassadors, other public Ministers and Consuls, and those in which a State shall be Party, the supreme Court shall have original Jurisdiction. In all the other Cases before mentioned, the supreme Court shall have appellate Jurisdiction, both as to Law and Fact, with such Exceptions, and under such Regulations as the Congress shall make.

The Trial of all Crimes, except in Cases of Impeachment, shall be by Jury; and such Trial shall be held in the State where the said Crimes shall have been committed; but when not committed within any State, the Trial shall be at such Place or Places as the Congress may by Law have directed.

Section 3. Treason against the United States, shall consist only in levying War against them, or in adhering to their Enemies, giving them Aid and Comfort. No Person shall be convicted of Treason unless on the Testimony of two Witnesses to the same overt Act, or on Confession in open Court.

The Congress shall have Power to declare the Punishment of Treason, but no Attainder of Treason shall work Corruption of Blood, or Forfeiture except during the Life of the Person attainted.

Article IV

Section 1. Full Faith and Credit shall be given in each State to the public Acts, Records, and judicial Proceedings of every other State. And the Congress may by general Laws prescribe the Manner in which such Acts, Records and Proceedings shall be proved, and the Effect thereof.

Section 2. The Citizens of each State shall be entitled to all Privileges and Immunities of Citizens in the several States.

A Person charged in any State with Treason, Felony, or other Crime, who shall flee from Justice, and be found in another State, shall on Demand of the executive Authority of the State from which he fled, be delivered up, to be removed to the State having Jurisdiction of the Crime.

No Person held to Service or Labour in one State, under the Laws thereof, escaping into another, shall, in Consequence of any Law or Regulation therein, be discharged from such Service or Labour, but shall be delivered up on Claim of the Party to whom such Service or Labour may be due.

Section 3. New States may be admitted by the Congress into this Union; but no new State shall be formed or erected within the Jurisdiction of any other State; nor any State be formed by the Junction of two or more States, or Parts of States, without the Consent of the Legislatures of the States concerned as well as the Congress.

The Congress shall have Power to dispose of and make all needful Rules and Regulations respecting the Territory or other Property belonging to the United States; and nothing in this Constitution shall be so construed as to Prejudice any Claims of the United States, or of any particular State.

Section 4. The United States shall guarantee to every State in this Union a Republican Form of Government, and shall protect each of them against Invasion; and on Application of the Legislature, or of the Executive (when the Legislature cannot be convened) against domestic Violence.

Article V

The Congress, whenever two thirds of both Houses shall deem it necessary, shall propose Amendments to this Constitution, or, on the Application of the Legislatures of two thirds of the several States, shall call a Convention for proposing Amendments, which, in either Case, shall be valid to all Intents and Purposes, as Part of this Constitution, when ratified by the Legislatures of three fourths of the several States, or by Conventions in three fourths thereof, as the one or the other Mode of Ratification may be proposed by the Congress; Provided that no Amendment which may be made prior to the Year One thousand eight hundred and eight shall in any Manner affect the first and fourth Clauses in the Ninth Section of the first Article; and that no State, without its Consent, shall be deprived of its equal Suffrage in the Senate.

Article VI

All Debts contracted and Engagements entered into, before the Adoption of this Constitution, shall be as valid against the United States under this Constitution, as under the Confederation.

This Constitution, and the Laws of the United States which shall be made in Pursuance thereof; and all Treaties made, or which shall be made, under the Authority of the United States, shall be the supreme Law of the Land; and the Judges in every State shall be bound thereby, any Thing in the Constitution or Laws of any State to the Contrary notwithstanding.

The Senators and Representatives before mentioned, and the Members of the several State Legislatures, and all executive and judicial Officers, both of the United States and of the Several States, shall be bound by Oath or Affirmation, to support this Constitution; but no religious Test shall ever be required as a Qualification to any Office or public Trust under the United States.

Article VII

The Ratification of the Conventions of nine States, shall be sufficient for the Establishment of this Constitution between the States so ratifying the Same.

Amendment I [1791].

Congress shall make no law respecting an establishment of religion, or prohibiting the free exercise thereof; or abridging the freedom of speech, or the press; or the right of the people peaceably to assemble, and to petition the Government for a redress of grievances.

Amendment II [1791].

A well regulated Militia, being necessary to the security for a free State, the right of the people to keep and bear Arms, shall not be infringed.

Amendment III [1791].

No Soldier shall, in time of peace be quartered in any house, without the consent of the Owner, nor in time of war, but in a manner to be prescribed by law.

Amendment IV [1791].

The right of the people to be secure in their persons, houses, papers, and effects, against unreasonable searches and seizures, shall not be violated, and no Warrants shall issue, but upon probable cause, supported by Oath or Affirmation, and particularly describing the place to be searched, and the persons or things to be seized.

Amendment V [1791].

No person shall be held to answer for a capital, or otherwise infamous crime, unless on a presentment or indictment of a Grand Jury, except in cases arising in the land or naval forces, or in the Militia, when in actual service in time of War or public danger; nor shall any person be subject for the same offense to be twice put in jeopardy of life or limb; nor shall be compelled in any criminal case to be a witness against himself, nor be deprived of life, liberty, or property, without due process of law; nor shall private property be taken for public use, without just compensation.

Amendment VI [1791].

In all criminal prosecutions, the accused shall enjoy the right to a speedy and public trial, by an impartial jury of the State and district wherein the crime shall have been committed, which district shall have been previously ascertained by law, and to be informed of the nature and cause of the accusation; to be confronted with the Witnesses against him; to have compulsory process for obtaining witnesses in his favor, and to have the Assistance of counsel for his defence.

Amendment VII [1791].

In suits at common law, where the value in controversy shall exceed twenty dollars, the right of trial by jury shall be preserved, and no fact tried by a jury, shall be otherwise re-examined in any Court of the United States, than according to the rules of the common law.

Amendment VIII [1791].

Excessive bail shall not be required, no excessive fines imposed, nor cruel and unusual punishments inflicted.

Amendment IX [1791].

The enumeration in the Constitution, of certain rights, shall not be construed to deny or disparage others retained by the people.

Amendment X [1791].

The powers not delegated to the United States by the Constitution, nor prohibited by it to the States, are reserved to the States respectively, or to the people.

Amendment XI [1798].

The judicial power of the United States shall not be construed to extend to any suit in law or equity, commenced or prosecuted against one of the United States by Citizens of another State, or by Citizens or Subjects of any Foreign State.

Amendment XII [1804].

The Electors shall meet in their respective states and vote by ballot for President and Vice-President, one of whom, at least, shall not be an inhabitant of the same state with themselves; they shall name in their ballots the person voted for as President, and in distinct ballots the person voted for as Vice-President, and they shall make distinct lists of all persons voted for as President, and of all persons voted for as Vice-President, and of the number of votes for each, which lists they shall sign and certify, and transmit sealed to the seat of the government of the United States, directed to the President of the Senate;—The President of the Senate shall, in the presence of the Senate and House of Representatives, open all the certificates and the votes shall then be counted;—The person having the greatest number of votes for President, shall be the President, if such number be a majority of the whole number of Electors appointed; and if no person have such majority, then from the persons having the highest numbers not exceeding three on the list of those voted for as President, the House of Representatives shall choose immediately, by ballot, the President. But in choosing the President, the votes shall be taken by states, the representation from each state having one vote; a quorum for this purpose shall consist of a member or members from two-thirds of the states, and a majority of all the states shall be necessary to a choice. And if the House of Representatives shall not choose a President whenever the right of choice shall devolve upon them, before the fourth day of March next following, then the Vice-President shall act as President, as in the case of the death or other constitutional disability of the President. The person having the greatest number of votes as Vice-President, shall be the Vice-President, if such number be a majority of the whole number of Electors appointed, and if no person have a majority, then from the two highest numbers on the list, the Senate shall choose the Vice-President; a quorum for the purpose shall consist of two-thirds of the whole number of Senators, and a majority of the whole number shall be necessary to a choice. But no person constitutionally ineligible to the office of President shall be eligible to that of the Vice-President of the United States.

Amendment XIII [1865].

Section 1. Neither slavery nor involuntary servitude, except as a punishment for crime whereof the party shall have been duly convicted, shall exist within the United States, or any place subject to their jurisdiction.

Section 2. Congress shall have power to enforce this article by appropriate legislation.

Amendment XIV [1868].

Section 1. All persons born or naturalized in the United States, and subject to the jurisdiction thereof, are citizens of the United States and of the State wherein they reside. No State shall make or enforce any law which shall abridge the privileges or immunities of citizens of the United States; nor shall any State deprive any person of life, liberty, or property, without due process of law; nor deny to any person within its jurisdiction the equal protection of the laws.

Section 2. Representatives shall be appointed among the several States according to their respective numbers, counting the whole number of persons in each State, excluding Indians not taxed. But when the right to vote at any election for the choice of electors for President and Vice President of the United States, Representatives in Congress, the Executive and Judicial officers of a State, or the members of the Legislature thereof, is denied to any of the male inhabitants of such State, being twenty-one years of age, and citizens of the United States, or in any way abridged, except for participation in rebellion, or other crime, the basis of representation therein shall be reduced in the proportion which the number of such male citizens shall bear the whole number of male citizens twenty-one years of age in such State.

Section 3. No person shall be a Senator or Representative in Congress, or elector of President and Vice President, or hold any office, civil or military, under the United States, or under any State, who, having previously taken an oath, as a member of Congress, or as an officer of the United States, or as a member of any State legislature, or as an executive or judicial officer of any State, to support the Constitution of the United States, shall have engaged in insurrection or rebellion against the same, or given aid or comfort to the enemies thereof. But Congress may by a vote of two-thirds of each House, remove such disability.

Section 4. The validity of the public debt of the United States, authorized by law, including debts incurred for payment of pensions and bounties for services in suppressing insurrection or rebellion, shall not be questioned. But neither the United States nor any State shall assume or pay any debt or obligation incurred in aid of insurrection or rebellion against the United States, or any claim for the loss or emancipation of any slave; but all such debts, obligations and claims shall be held illegal and void.

Section 5. The Congress shall have power to enforce, by appropriate legislation, the provisions of this article.

Amendment XV [1870].

Section 1. The right of citizens of the United States to vote shall not be denied or abridged by the United States or by any State on account of race, color, or previous condition of servitude.

Section 2. The Congress shall have power to enforce this article by appropriate legislation.

Amendment XVI [1913].

The Congress shall have power to lay and collect taxes on incomes, from whatever source derived, without apportionment among the several States, and without regard to any census or enumeration.

Amendment XVII [1913].

The Senate of the United States shall be composed of two Senators from each State, elected by the people thereof, for six years; and each Senator shall have one vote. The electors in each State shall have the qualifications requisite for electors of the most numerous branch of the State legislatures.

When vacancies happen in the representation of any State in the Senate, the executive authority of each State shall issue writs of election to fill such vacancies; *Provided,* That the legislature of any State may empower the executive thereof to make temporary appointments until the people fill the vacancies by election as the legislature may direct.

This amendment shall not be construed as to affect the election or term of any Senator chosen before it becomes valid as part of the Constitution.

Amendment XVIII [1919].

Section 1. After one year from the ratification of this article the manufacture, sale, or transportation of intoxicating liquors within, the importation thereof into, or the exportation thereof from the United States and all territory subject to the jurisdiction thereof for beverage purposes is hereby prohibited.

Section 2. The Congress and the several States shall have concurrent power to enforce this article by appropriate legislation.

Section 3. This article shall be inoperative unless it shall have been ratified as an amendment to the Constitution by the legislatures of the several States, as provided in the Constitution, within seven years from the date of the submission hereof to the States by the Congress.

Amendment XIX [1920].

The right of citizens of the United States to vote shall not be denied or abridged by the United States or by any State on account of sex.

Congress shall have power to enforce this article by appropriate legislation.

Amendment XX [1933].

Section 1. The terms of the President and Vice President shall end at noon on the 20th day of January, and the terms of Senators and Representatives at noon on the 3d day of January, of the years in which such terms would have ended if this article had not been ratified; and the terms of their successors shall then begin.

Section 2. The Congress shall assemble at least once in every year, and such meeting shall begin at noon on the 3d day of January, unless they shall by law appoint a different day.

Section 3. If, at the time fixed for the beginning of the term of the President, the President elect shall have died, the Vice President elect shall become President. If a President shall not have been chosen before the time fixed for the beginning of his term, or if the President elect shall have failed to qualify, then the Vice President elect shall act as President until a President shall have qualified; and the Congress may by law provide for the case wherein neither a President elect nor a Vice President elect shall have qualified, declaring who shall then act as President, or the manner in which one who is to act shall be selected, and such person shall act accordingly until a President or Vice President shall have qualified.

Section 4. The Congress may by law provide for the case of the death of any of the persons from whom the House of Representatives may choose a President whenever the right of choice shall have devolved upon them, and for the case of the death of any of the persons from whom the Senate may choose a Vice President whenever the right of choice shall have devolved upon them.

Section 5. Sections 1 and 2 shall take effect on the 15th day of October following the ratification of this article.

Section 6. This article shall be inoperative unless it shall have been ratified as an amendment to the Constitution by the legislatures of three-fourths of the several States within seven years from the date of its submission.

Amendment XXI [1933].

Section 1. The eighteenth article of amendment to the Constitution of the United States is hereby repealed.

Section 2. The transportation or importation into any State, Territory, or possession of the United States for delivery or use therein of intoxicating liquors, in violation of the laws thereof, is hereby prohibited.

Section 3. This article shall be inoperative unless it shall have been ratified as an amendment to the Constitution by conventions in the several States, as provided in the Constitution, within seven years from the date of the submission hereof to the States by the Congress.

Amendment XXII [1951].

Section 1. No person shall be elected to the office of the President more than twice, and no person who has held the office of President, or acted as President, for more than two years of a term to which some other person was elected President shall be elected to the office of the President more than once. But this Article shall not apply to any person holding the office of President when this Article was proposed by the Congress, and shall not prevent any person who may be holding the office of President, or acting as President, during the term within which this Article becomes operative from holding the office of President, or acting as President during the remainder of such term.

Section 2. This article shall be inoperative unless it shall have been ratified as an amendment to the Constitution by the legislatures of three-fourths of the several States within seven years from the date of its submission to the States by the Congress.

Amendment XXIII [1961].

Section 1. The District constituting the seat of Government of the United States shall appoint in such manner as the Congress may direct:

A number of electors of President and Vice President equal to the whole number of Senators and Representatives in Congress to which the District would be entitled if it were a State, but in no event more than the least populous State; they shall be in addition to those appointed by the States, but they shall be considered, for the purposes of the election of President and Vice President, to be electors appointed by a State; and they shall meet in the District and perform such duties as provided by the twelfth article of amendment.

Section 2. The Congress shall have power to enforce this article by appropriate legislation.

Amendment XXIV [1964].

Section 1. The right of citizens of the United States to vote in any primary or other election for President or Vice President, for electors for President or Vice President, or for Senator or Representative in Congress, shall not be denied or abridged by the United States or any State by reason of failure to pay any poll tax or other tax.

Section 2. The Congress shall have power to enforce this article by appropriate legislation.

Amendment XXV [1967].

Section 1. In case of the removal of the President from office or of his death or resignation, the Vice President shall become President.

Section 2. Whenever there is a vacancy in the office of the Vice President, the President shall nominate a Vice President who shall take office upon confirmation by a majority vote of both Houses of Congress.

Section 3. Whenever the President transmits to the President pro tempore of the Senate and the Speaker of the House of Representatives his written declaration that he is unable to discharge the powers and duties of his office, and until he transmits to them a written declaration to the contrary, such powers and duties shall be discharged by the Vice President as Acting President.

Section 4. Whenever the Vice President and a majority of either the principal officers of the executive departments or of such other body as Congress may by law provide, transmit to the President pro tempore of the Senate and the Speaker of the House of Representatives their written declaration that the President is unable to discharge the powers and duties of his office, the Vice President shall immediately assume the powers and duties of the office as Acting President.

Thereafter, when the President transmits to the President pro tempore of the Senate and the Speaker of the House of Representatives his written declaration that no inability exists, he shall resume the powers and duties of his office unless the Vice President and a majority of either the principal officers of the executive department or of such other body as Congress may by law provide, transmit within four days to the President pro tempore of the Senate and the Speaker of the House of Representatives their written declaration that the President is unable to discharge the powers and duties of his office. Thereupon Congress shall decide the issue, assembling within forty-eight hours for that purpose if not in session. If the Congress, within twenty-one days after receipt of the latter written declaration, or, if Congress is not in session, within twenty-one days after Congress is required to assemble, determines by two-thirds vote of both Houses that the President is unable to discharge the powers and duties of his office, the Vice President shall continue to discharge the same as Acting President; otherwise, the President shall resume the powers and duties of his office.

Amendment XXVI [1971].

Section 1. The right of citizens of the United States, who are eighteen years of age or older, to vote shall not be denied or abridged by the United States or by any State on account of age.
Section 2. The Congress shall have power to enforce this article by appropriate legislation.

Amendment XXVII [1992].

No law, varying the compensation for the services of the Senators and Representatives, shall take effect, until an election of Representatives shall have intervened.

APPENDIX B

UNIFORM COMMERCIAL CODE

ARTICLE I
General Provisions

■ **PART I** Short Title, Construction, Application and Subject Matter of the Act

§ 1-101. Short Title.

This Act shall be known and may be cited as Uniform Commercial Code.

§ 1-102. Purposes; Rules of Construction; Variation by Agreement.

(1) This Act shall be liberally construed and applied to promote its underlying purposes and policies.

(2) Underlying purposes and policies of this Act are

(a) to simplify, clarify and modernize the law governing commercial transactions;

(b) to permit the continued expansion of commercial practices through custom, usage and agreement of the parties;

(c) to make uniform the law among the various jurisdictions.

(3) The effect of provisions of this Act may be varied by agreement, except as otherwise provided in this Act and except that the obligations of good faith, diligence, reasonableness and care prescribed by this Act may not be disclaimed by agreement but the parties may by agreement determine the standards by which the performance of such obligations is to be measured if such standards are not manifestly unreasonable.

(4) The presence in certain provisions of this Act of the words "unless otherwise agreed" or words of similar import does not imply that the effect of other provisions may not be varied by agreement under subsection (3).

(5) In this Act unless the context otherwise requires

(a) words in the singular number include the plural, and in the plural include the singular;

(b) words of the masculine gender include the feminine and the neuter, and when the sense so indicates words of the neuter gender may refer to any gender.

§ 1-103. Supplementary General Principles of Law Applicable.

Unless displaced by the particular provisions of this Act, the principles of law and equity, including the law merchant and the law relative to capacity to contract, principal and agent, estoppel, fraud, misrepresentation, duress, coercion, mistake, bankruptcy, or other validating or invalidating cause shall supplement its provisions.

§ 1-104. Construction Against Implicit Repeal.

This Act being a general act intended as a unified coverage of its subject matter, no part of it shall be deemed to be impliedly repealed by subsequent legislation if such construction can reasonably be avoided.

§ 1-105. Territorial Application of the Act; Parties' Power to Choose Applicable Law.

(1) Except as provided hereafter in this section, when a transaction bears a reasonable relation to this state and also to another state or nation the parties may agree that the law either of this state or of such other state or nation shall govern their rights and duties. Failing such agreement this Act applies to transactions bearing an appropriate relation to this state.

(2) Where one of the following provisions of this Act specifies the applicable law, that provision governs and a contrary agreement is effective only to the extent permitted by the law (including the conflict of laws rules) so specified:

Rights of creditors against sold goods. Section 2-402.

Applicability of the Article on Leases. Sections 2A-105 and 2A-106.

Applicability of the Article on Bank Deposits and Collections. Section 4-102.

Governing law in the Article on Funds Transfers. Section 4A-507.

[Publisher's Editorial Note: If a state adopts the repealer of Article 6—Bulk Transfers (Alternative A), there should not be any item relating to bulk transfers. If, however, a state adopts Revised Article 6—Bulk Sales (Alternative B), then the item relating to bulk sales should read as follows:]

Bulk sales subject to the Article on Bulk Sales. Section 6-103.

Applicability of the Article on Investment Securities. Section 8-110.

Perfection provisions of the Article on Secured Transactions. Section 9-103.

§ 1-106. Remedies to Be Liberally Administered.

(1) The remedies provided by this Act shall be liberally administered to the end that the aggrieved party may be put in as good a position as if the other party had fully performed but neither consequential or special nor penal damages may be had except as specifically provided in this Act or by other rule of law.

(2) Any right or obligation declared by this Act is enforceable by action unless the provision declaring it specifies a different and limited effect.

§ 1-107. Waiver or Renunciation of Claim or Right After Breach.

Any claim or right arising out of an alleged breach can be discharged in whole or in part without consideration by a written waiver or renunciation signed and delivered by the aggrieved party.

§ 1-108. *Severability.*

If any provision or clause of this Act or application thereof to any person or circumstances is held invalid, such invalidity shall not affect other provisions or applications of the Act which can be given effect without the invalid provision or application, and to this end the provisions of this Act are declared to be severable.

§ 1-109. *Section Captions.*

Section captions are parts of this Act.

■ PART 2 General Definitions and Principles of Interpretation

§ 1-201. *General Definitions.*

Subject to additional definitions contained in the subsequent Articles of this Act which are applicable to specific Articles or Parts thereof, and unless the context otherwise requires, in this Act:

(1) "Action" in the sense of a judicial proceeding includes recoupment, counterclaim, set-off, suit in equity and any other proceedings in which rights are determined.

(2) "Aggrieved party" means a party entitled to resort to a remedy.

(3) "Agreement" means the bargain of the parties in fact as found in their language or by implication from other circumstances including course of dealing or usage of trade or course of performance as provided in this Act (Sections 1-205, 2-208, and 2A-207). Whether an agreement has legal consequences is determined by the provisions of this Act, if applicable; otherwise by the law of contracts (Section 1-103). (Compare "Contract".)

(4) "Bank" means any person engaged in the business of banking.

(5) "Bearer" means the person in possession of an instrument, document of title, or certificated security payable to bearer or indorsed in blank.

(6) "Bill of lading" means a document evidencing the receipt of goods for shipment issued by a person engaged in the business of transporting or forwarding goods, and includes an airbill. "Airbill" means a document serving for air transportation as a bill of lading does for marine or rail transportation, and includes an air consignment note or air waybill.

(7) "Branch" includes a separately incorporated foreign branch of a bank.

(8) "Burden of establishing" a fact means the burden of persuading the triers of fact that the existence of the fact is more probable than its non-existence.

(9) "Buyer in ordinary course of business" means a person who in good faith and without knowledge that the sale to him is in violation of the ownership rights or security interest of a third party in the goods buys in ordinary course from a person in the business of selling goods of that kind but does not include a pawnbroker. All persons who sell minerals or the like (including oil and gas) at wellhead or minehead shall be deemed to be persons in the business of selling goods of that kind. "Buying" may be for cash or by exchange of other property or on secured or unsecured credit and includes receiving goods or documents of title under a pre-existing contract for sale but does not include a transfer in bulk or as security for or in total or partial satisfaction of a money debt.

(10) "Conspicuous": A term or clause is conspicuous when it is so written that a reasonable person against whom it is to operate ought to have noticed it. A printed heading in capitals (as: NON-NEGOTIABLE BILL OF LADING) is conspicuous. Language in the body of a form is "conspicuous" if it is in larger or other contrasting type or color. But in a telegram any stated term is "conspicuous". Whether a term or clause is "conspicuous" or not is for decision by the court.

(11) "Contract" means the total legal obligation which results from the parties' agreement as affected by this Act and any other applicable rules of law. (Compare "Agreement".)

(12) "Creditor" includes a general creditor, a secured creditor, a lien creditor and any representative of creditors, including an assignee for the benefit of creditors, a trustee in bankruptcy, a receiver in equity and an executor or administrator of an insolvent debtor's or assignor's estate.

(13) "Defendant" includes a person in the position of defendant in a cross-action or counterclaim.

(14) "Delivery" with respect to instruments, documents of title, chattel paper, or certificated securities means voluntary transfer of possession.

(15) "Document of title" includes bill of lading, dock warrant, dock receipt, warehouse receipt or order for the delivery of goods, and also any other document which in the regular course of business or financing is treated as adequately evidencing that the person in possession of it is entitled to receive, hold and dispose of the document and the goods it covers. To be a document of title a document must purport to be issued by or addressed to a bailee and purport to cover goods in the bailee's possession which are either identified or are fungible portions of an identified mass.

(16) "Fault" means wrongful act, omission or breach.

(17) "Fungible" with respect to goods or securities means goods or securities of which any unit is, by nature or usage of trade, the equivalent of any other like unit. Goods which are not fungible shall be deemed fungible for the purposes of this Act to the extent that under a particular agreement or document unlike units are treated as equivalents.

(18) "Genuine" means free of forgery or counterfeiting.

(19) "Good faith" means honesty in fact in the conduct or transaction concerned.

(20) "Holder," with respect to a negotiable instrument, means the person in possession if the instrument is payable to bearer or, in the case of an instrument payable to an identified person, if the identified person is in possession. "Holder" with respect to a document of title means the person in possession if the goods are deliverable to bearer or to the order of the person in possession.

(21) To "honor" is to pay or to accept and pay, or where a credit so engages to purchase or discount a draft complying with the terms of the credit.

(22) "Insolvency proceedings" includes any assignment for the benefit of creditors or other proceedings intended to liquidate or rehabilitate the estate of the person involved.

(23) A person is "insolvent" who either has ceased to pay his debts in the ordinary course of business or cannot pay his debts as they become due or is insolvent within the meaning of the federal bankruptcy law.

(24) "Money" means a medium of exchange authorized or adopted by a domestic or foreign government and includes a monetary unit of account established by an intergovernmental organization or by agreement between two or more nations.

(25) A person has "notice" of a fact when

    (a) he has actual knowledge of it; or

    (b) he has received a notice or notification of it; or

    (c) from all the facts and circumstances known to him at the time in question he has reason to know that it exists.

A person "knows" or has "knowledge" of a fact when he has actual knowledge of it. "Discover" or "learn" or a word or phrase of similar import refers to knowledge rather than to reason to know. The time and circumstances under which a notice or notification may cease to be effective are not determined by this Act.

(26) A person "notifies" or "gives" a notice or notification to another by taking such steps as may be reasonably required to inform the other in ordinary course whether or not such other

actually comes to know of it. A person "receives" a notice or notification when

    (a) it comes to his attention; or

    (b) it is duly delivered at the place of business through which the contract was made or at any other place held out by him as the place for receipt of such communications.

(27) Notice, knowledge or a notice or notification received by an organization is effective for a particular transaction from the time when it is brought to the attention of the individual conducting that transaction, and in any event from the time when it would have been brought to his attention if the organization had exercised due diligence. An organization exercises due diligence if it maintains reasonable routines for communicating significant information to the person conducting the transaction and there is reasonable compliance with the routines. Due diligence does not require an individual acting for the organization to communicate information unless such communication is part of his regular duties or unless he has reason to know of the transaction and that the transaction would be materially affected by the information.

(28) "Organization" includes a corporation, government or governmental subdivision or agency, business trust, estate, trust, partnership or association, two or more persons having a joint or common interest, or any other legal or commercial entity.

(29) "Party", as distinct from "third party", means a person who has engaged in a transaction or made an agreement within this Act.

(30) "Person" includes an individual or an organization (See Section 1-102).

(31) "Presumption" or "presumed" means that the trier of fact must find the existence of the fact presumed unless and until evidence is introduced which would support a finding of its non-existence.

(32) "Purchase" includes taking by sale, discount, negotiation, mortgage, pledge, lien, issue or re-issue, gift or any other voluntary transaction creating an interest in property.

(33) "Purchaser" means a person who takes by purchase.

(34) "Remedy" means any remedial right to which an aggrieved party is entitled with or without resort to a tribunal.

(35) "Representative" includes an agent, an officer of a corporation or association, and a trustee, executor or administrator of an estate, or any other person empowered to act for another.

(36) "Rights" includes remedies.

(37) "Security interest" means an interest in personal property or fixtures which secures payment or performance of an obligation. The retention or reservation of title by a seller of goods notwithstanding shipment or delivery to the buyer (Section 2-401) is limited in effect to a reservation of a "security interest". The term also includes any interest of a buyer of accounts or chattel paper which is subject to Article 9. The special property interest of a buyer of goods on identification of those goods to a contract for sale under Section 2-401 is not a "security interest", but a buyer may also acquire a "security interest" by complying with Article 9. Unless a consignment is intended as security, reservation of title thereunder is not a "security interest", but a consignment in any event is subject to the provisions on consignment sales (Section 2-326).

Whether a transaction creates a lease or security interest is determined by the facts of each case; however, a transaction creates a security interest if the consideration the lessee is to pay the lessor for the right to possession and use of the goods is an obligation for the term of the lease not subject to termination by the lessee, and

    (a) the original term of the lease is equal to or greater than the remaining economic life of the goods,

    (b) the lessee is bound to renew the lease for the remaining economic life of the goods or is bound to become the owner of the goods,

    (c) the lessee has an option to renew the lease for the remaining economic life of the goods for no additional consideration or nominal additional consideration upon compliance with the lease agreement, or

    (d) the lessee has an option to become the owner of the goods for no additional consideration or nominal additional consideration upon compliance with the lease agreement.

A transaction does not create a security interest merely because it provides that

    (a) the present value of the consideration the lessee is obligated to pay the lessor for the right to possession and use of the goods is substantially equal to or is greater than the fair market value of the goods at the time the lease is entered into,

    (b) the lessee assumes risk of loss of the goods, or agrees to pay taxes, insurance, filing, recording, or registration fees, or service or maintenance costs with respect to the goods,

    (c) the lessee has an option to renew the lease or to become the owner of the goods,

    (d) the lessee has an option to renew the lease for a fixed rent that is equal to or greater than the reasonably predictable fair market rent for the use of the goods for the term of the renewal at the time the option is to be performed, or

    (e) the lessee has an option to become the owner of the goods for a fixed price that is equal to or greater than the reasonably predictable fair market value of the goods at the time the option is to be performed.

For purposes of this subsection (37):

    (x) Additional consideration is not nominal if (i) when the option to renew the lease is granted to the lessee the rent is stated to be the fair market rent for the use of the goods for the term of the renewal determined at the time the option is to be performed, or (ii) when the option to become the owner of the goods is granted to the lessee the price is stated to be the fair market value of the goods determined at the time the option is to be performed. Additional consideration is nominal if it is less than the lessee's reasonably predictable cost of performing under the lease agreement if the option is not exercised;

    (y) "Reasonably predictable" and "remaining economic life of the goods" are to be determined with reference to the facts and circumstances at the time the transaction is entered into; and

    (z) "Present value" means the amount as of a date certain of one or more sums payable in the future, discounted to the date certain. The discount is determined by the interest rate specified by the parties if the rate is not manifestly unreasonable at the time the transaction is entered into; otherwise, the discount is determined by a commercially reasonable rate that takes into account the facts and circumstances of each case at the time the transaction was entered into.

(38) "Send" in connection with any writing or notice means to deposit in the mail or deliver for transmission by any other usual means of communication with postage or cost of transmission provided for and properly addressed and in the case of an instrument to an address specified thereon or otherwise agreed, or if there be none to any address reasonable under the circumstances. The receipt of any writing or notice within the time at which it would have arrived if properly sent has the effect of a proper sending.

(39) "Signed" includes any symbol executed or adopted by a party with present intention to authenticate a writing.

(40) "Surety" includes guarantor.

(41) "Telegram" includes a message transmitted by radio, teletype, cable, any mechanical method of transmission, or the like.

(42) "Term" means that portion of an agreement which relates to a particular matter.

(43) "Unauthorized" signature means one made without actual, implied, or apparent authority and includes a forgery.

(44) "Value". Except as otherwise provided with respect to negotiable instruments and bank collections (Sections 3-303, 4-210 and 4-211) a person gives "value" for rights if he acquires them

(a) in return for a binding commitment to extend credit or for the extension of immediately available credit whether or not drawn upon and whether or not a charge-back is provided for in the event of difficulties in collection; or

(b) as security for or in total or partial satisfaction of a pre-existing claim; or

(c) by accepting delivery pursuant to a pre-existing contract for purchase; or

(d) generally, in return for any consideration sufficient to support a simple contract.

(45) "Warehouse receipt" means a receipt issued by a person engaged in the business of storing goods for hire.

(46) "Written" or "writing" includes printing, typewriting or any other intentional reduction to tangible form.

§ 1-202. *Prima Facie Evidence by Third Party Documents.*

A document in due form purporting to be a bill of lading, policy or certificate of insurance, official weigher's or inspector's certificate, consular invoice, or any other document authorized or required by the contract to be issued by a third party shall be prima facie evidence of its own authenticity and genuineness and of the facts stated in the document by the third party.

§ 1-203. *Obligation of Good Faith.*

Every contract or duty within this Act imposes an obligation of good faith in its performance or enforcement.

§ 1-204. *Time; Reasonable Time; "Seasonably".*

(1) Whenever this Act requires any action to be taken within a reasonable time, any time which is not manifestly unreasonable may be fixed by agreement.

(2) What is a reasonable time for taking any action depends on the nature, purpose and circumstances of such action.

(3) An action is taken "seasonably" when it is taken at or within the time agreed or if no time is agreed at or within a reasonable time.

§ 1-205. *Course of Dealing and Usage of Trade.*

(1) A course of dealing is a sequence of previous conduct between the parties to a particular transaction which is fairly to be regarded as establishing a common basis of understanding for interpreting their expressions and other conduct.

(2) A usage of trade is any practice or method of dealing having such regularity of observance in a place, vocation or trade as to justify an expectation that it will be observed with respect to the transaction in question. The existence and scope of such a usage are to be proved as facts. If it is established that such a usage is embodied in a written trade code or similar writing the interpretation of the writing is for the court.

(3) A course of dealing between parties and any usage of trade in the vocation or trade in which they are engaged or of which they are or should be aware give particular meaning to and supplement or qualify terms of an agreement.

(4) The express terms of an agreement and an applicable course of dealing or usage of trade shall be construed wherever reasonable as consistent with each other, but when such construction is unreasonable express terms control both course of dealing and usage of trade and course of dealing controls usage of trade.

(5) An applicable usage of trade in the place where any part of performance is to occur shall be used in interpreting the agreement as to that part of the performance.

(6) Evidence of a relevant usage of trade offered by one party is not admissible unless and until he has given the other party such notice as the court finds sufficient to prevent unfair surprise to the latter.

§ 1-206. *Statute of Frauds for Kinds of Personal Property Not Otherwise Covered.*

(1) Except in the cases described in subsection (2) of this section a contract for the sale of personal property is not enforceable by way of action or defense beyond five thousand dollars in amount or value of remedy unless there is some writing which indicates that a contract for sale has been made between the parties at a defined or stated price, reasonably identifies the subject matter, and is signed by the party against whom enforcement is sought or by his authorized agent.

(2) Subsection (1) of this section does not apply to contracts for the sale of goods (Section 2-201) nor of securities (Section 8-113) nor to security agreements (Section 9-203).

§ 1-207. *Performance or Acceptance Under Reservation of Rights.*

A party who with explicit reservation of rights performs or promises performance or assents to performance in a manner demanded or offered by the other party does not thereby prejudice the rights reserved. Such words as "without prejudice", "under protest" or the like are sufficient.

§ 1-208. *Option to Accelerate at Will.*

A term providing that one party or his successor in interest may accelerate payment or performance or require collateral or additional collateral "at will" or "when he deems himself insecure" or in words of similar import shall be construed to mean that he shall have power to do so only if he in good faith believes that the prospect of payment or performance is impaired. The burden of establishing lack of good faith is on the party against whom the power has been exercised.

§ 1-209. *Subordinated Obligations.*

An obligation may be issued as subordinated to payment of another obligation of the person obligated, or a creditor may subordinate his right to payment of an obligation by agreement with either the person obligated or another creditor of the person obligated. Such a subordination does not create a security interest as against either the common debtor or a subordinated creditor. This section shall be construed as declaring the law as it existed prior to the enactment of this section and not as modifying it. Added 1966.

Note: This new section is proposed as an optional provision to make it clear that a subordination agreement does not create a security interest unless so intended.

ARTICLE 2
Sales

■ PART I Short Title, Construction and Subject Matter

§ 2-101. *Short Title.*

This Article shall be known and may be cited as Uniform Commercial Code—Sales.

§ 2-102. *Scope; Certain Security and Other Transactions Excluded From This Article.*

Unless the context otherwise requires, this Article applies to transactions in goods; it does not apply to any transaction which although in the form of an unconditional contract to sell or present sale is intended to operate only as a security transaction nor does this Article impair or repeal any statute regulating sales to consumers, farmers or other specified classes of buyers.

§ 2-103. *Definitions and Index of Definitions.*

    (1)   In this Article unless the context otherwise requires

        (a) "Buyer" means a person who buys or contracts to buy goods.

        (b) "Good faith" in the case of a merchant means honesty in fact and the observance of reasonable commercial standards of fair dealing in the trade.

        (c) "Receipt" of goods means taking physical possession of them.

        (d) "Seller" means a person who sells or contracts to sell goods.

    (2)   Other definitions applying to this Article or to specified Parts thereof, and the sections in which they appear are:

        "Acceptance". Section 2-606.

        "Banker's credit". Section 2-325.

        "Between merchants". Section 2-104.

        "Cancellation". Section 2-106(4).

        "Commercial unit". Section 2-105.

        "Confirmed credit". Section 2-325.

        "Conforming to contract". Section 2-106.

        "Contract for sale". Section 2-106.

        "Cover". Section 2-712.

        "Entrusting". Section 2-403.

        "Financing agency". Section 2-104.

        "Future goods". Section 2-105.

        "Goods". Section 2-105.

        "Identification". Section 2-501.

        "Installment contract". Section 2-612.

        "Letter of Credit". Section 2-325.

        "Lot". Section 2-105.

        "Merchant". Section 2-104.

        "Overseas". Section 2-323.

        "Person in position of seller". Section 2-707.

        "Present sale". Section 2-106.

        "Sale". Section 2-106.

        "Sale on approval". Section 2-326.

        "Sale or return". Section 2-326.

        "Termination". Section 2-106.

    (3)   The following definitions in other Articles apply to this Article:

        "Check". Section 3-104.

        "Consignee". Section 7-102.

        "Consignor". Section 7-102.

        "Consumer goods". Section 9-109.

        "Dishonor". Section 3-502.

        "Draft". Section 3-104.

    (4)   In addition Article 1 contains general definitions and principles of construction and interpretation applicable throughout this Article.

§ 2-104. *Definitions: "Merchant"; "Between Merchants"; "Financing Agency".*

    (1)   "Merchant" means a person who deals in goods of the kind or otherwise by his occupation holds himself out as having knowledge or skill peculiar to the practices or goods involved in the transaction or to whom such knowledge or skill may be attributed by his employment of an agent or broker or other intermediary who by his occupation holds himself out as having such knowledge or skill.

    (2)   "Financing agency" means a bank, finance company or other person who in the ordinary course of business makes advances against goods or documents of title or who by arrangement with either the seller or the buyer intervenes in ordinary course to make or collect payment due or claimed under the contract for sale, as by purchasing or paying the seller's draft or making advances against it or by merely taking it for collection whether or not documents of title accompany the draft. "Financing agency" includes also a bank or other person who similarly intervenes between persons who are in the position of seller and buyer in respect to the goods (Section 2-707).

    (3)   "Between merchants" means in any transaction with respect to which both parties are chargeable with the knowledge or skill of merchants.

§ 2-105. *Definitions: Transferability; "Goods"; "Future" Goods; "Lot"; "Commercial Unit".*

    (1)   "Goods" means all things (including specially manufactured goods) which are movable at the time of identification to the contract for sale other than the money in which the price is to be paid, investment securities (Article 8) and things in action. "Goods" also includes the unborn young of animals and growing crops and other identified things attached to realty as described in the section on goods to be severed from realty (Section 2-107).

    (2)   Goods must be both existing and identified before any interest in them can pass. Goods which are not both existing and identified are "future" goods. A purported present sale of future goods or of any interest therein operates as a contract to sell.

    (3)   There may be a sale of a part interest in existing identified goods.

    (4)   An undivided share in an identified bulk of fungible goods is sufficiently identified to be sold although the quantity of the bulk is not determined. Any agreed proportion of such a bulk or any quantity thereof agreed upon by number, weight or other measure may to the extent of the seller's interest in the bulk be sold to the buyer who then becomes an owner in common.

    (5)   "Lot" means a parcel or a single article which is the subject matter of a separate sale or delivery, whether or not it is sufficient to perform the contract.

    (6)   "Commercial unit" means such a unit of goods as by commercial usage is a single whole for purposes of sale and division of which materially impairs its character or value on the market or in use. A commercial unit may be a single article (as a machine) or a set of articles (as a suite of furniture or an assortment of sizes) or a quantity (as a bale, gross, or carload) or any other unit treated in use or in the relevant market as a single whole.

§ 2-106. *Definitions: "Contract"; "Agreement"; "Contract for Sale"; "Sale"; "Present Sale"; "Conforming" to Contract; "Termination"; "Cancellation".*

    (1)   In this Article unless the context otherwise requires "contract" and "agreement" are limited to those relating to the present or future sale of goods. "Contract for sale" includes both a present sale of goods and a contract to sell goods at a future time. A "sale" consists in the passing of title from the seller to the buyer for a price (Section 2-401). A "present sale" means a sale which is accomplished by the making of the contract.

    (2)   Goods or conduct including any part of a performance are "conforming" or conform to the contract when they are in accordance with the obligations under the contract.

    (3)   "Termination" occurs when either party pursuant to a power created by agreement or law puts an end to the contract otherwise than for its breach. On "termination" all obligations which are still executory on both sides are discharged but any right based on prior breach or performance survives.

    (4)   "Cancellation" occurs when either party puts an end to the contract for breach by the other and its effect is the same as that of "termination" except that the cancelling party also retains

any remedy for breach of the whole contract or any unperformed balance.

§ 2-107. Goods to Be Severed From Realty: Recording.

(1) A contract for the sale of minerals or the like (including oil and gas) or a structure or its materials to be removed from realty is a contract for the sale of goods within this Article if they are to be severed by the seller but until severance a purported present sale thereof which is not effective as a transfer of an interest in land is effective only as a contract to sell.

(2) A contract for the sale apart from the land of growing crops or other things attached to realty and capable of severance without material harm thereto but not described in subsection (1) or of timber to be cut is a contract for the sale of goods within this Article whether the subject matter is to be severed by the buyer or by the seller even though it forms part of the realty at the time of contracting, and the parties can by identification effect a present sale before severance.

(3) The provisions of this section are subject to any third party rights provided by the law relating to realty records, and the contract for sale may be executed and recorded as a document transferring an interest in land and shall then constitute notice to third parties of the buyer's rights under the contract for sale.

■ PART 2 Form, Formation and Readjustment of Contract

§ 2-201. Formal Requirements; Statute of Frauds.

(1) Except as otherwise provided in this section a contract for the sale of goods for the price of $500 or more is not enforceable by way of action or defense unless there is some writing sufficient to indicate that a contract for sale has been made between the parties and signed by the party against whom enforcement is sought or by his authorized agent or broker. A writing is not insufficient because it omits or incorrectly states a term agreed upon but the contract is not enforceable under this paragraph beyond the quantity of goods shown in such writing.

(2) Between merchants if within a reasonable time a writing in confirmation of the contract and sufficient against the sender is received and the party receiving it has reason to know its contents, it satisfies the requirements of subsection (1) against such party unless written notice of objection to its contents is given within ten days after it is received.

(3) A contract which does not satisfy the requirements of subsection (1) but which is valid in other respects is enforceable

(a) if the goods are to be specially manufactured for the buyer and are not suitable for sale to others in the ordinary course of the seller's business and the seller, before notice of repudiation is received and under circumstances which reasonably indicate that the goods are for the buyer, has made either a substantial beginning of their manufacture or commitments for their procurement; or

(b) if the party against whom enforcement is sought admits in his pleading, testimony or otherwise in court that a contract for sale was made, but the contract is not enforceable under this provision beyond the quantity of goods admitted; or

(c) with respect to goods for which payment has been made and accepted or which have been received and accepted (Sec. 2-606).

§ 2-202. Final Written Expression: Parol or Extrinsic Evidence.

Terms with respect to which the confirmatory memoranda of the parties agree or which are otherwise set forth in a writing intended by the parties as a final expression of their agreement with respect to such terms as are included therein may not be contradicted by evidence of any prior agreement or of a contemporaneous oral agreement but may be explained or supplemented

(a) by course of dealing or usage of trade (Section 1-205) or by course of performance (Section 2-208); and

(b) by evidence of consistent additional terms unless the court finds the writing to have been intended also as a complete and exclusive statement of the terms of the agreement.

§ 2-203. Seals Inoperative.

The affixing of a seal to a writing evidencing a contract for sale or an offer to buy or sell goods does not constitute the writing a sealed instrument and the law with respect to sealed instruments does not apply to such a contract or offer.

§ 2-204. Formation in General.

(1) A contract for sale of goods may be made in any manner sufficient to show agreement, including conduct by both parties which recognizes the existence of such a contract.

(2) An agreement sufficient to constitute a contract for sale may be found even though the moment of its making is undetermined.

(3) Even though one or more terms are left open a contract for sale does not fail for indefiniteness if the parties have intended to make a contract and there is a reasonably certain basis for giving an appropriate remedy.

§ 2-205. Firm Offers.

An offer by a merchant to buy or sell goods in a signed writing which by its terms gives assurance that it will be held open is not revocable, for lack of consideration, during the time stated or if no time is stated for reasonable time, but in no event may such period of irrevocability exceed three months; but any such term of assurance on a form supplied by the offeree must be separately signed by the offeror.

§ 2-206. Offer and Acceptance in Formation of Contract.

(1) Unless otherwise unambiguously indicated by the language or circumstances

(a) an offer to make a contract shall be construed as inviting acceptance in any manner and by any medium reasonable in the circumstances;

(b) an order or other offer to buy goods for prompt or current shipment shall be construed as inviting acceptance either by a prompt promise to ship or by the prompt or current shipment of conforming or nonconforming goods, but such a shipment of non-conforming goods does not constitute an acceptance if the seller seasonably notifies the buyer that the shipment is offered only as an accommodation to the buyer.

(2) Where the beginning of a requested performance is a reasonable mode of acceptance an offeror who is not notified of acceptance within a reasonable time may treat the offer as having lapsed before acceptance.

§ 2-207. Additional Terms in Acceptance or Confirmation.

(1) A definite and seasonable expression of acceptance or a written confirmation which is sent within a reasonable time operates as an acceptance even though it states terms additional to or different from those offered or agreed upon, unless acceptance is expressly made conditional on assent to the additional or different terms.

(2) The additional terms are to be construed as proposals for addition to the contract. Between merchants such terms become part of the contract unless:

(a) the offer expressly limits acceptance to the terms of the offer;

(b) they materially alter it; or

(c) notification of objection to them has already been given or is given within a reasonable time after notice of them is received.

(3) Conduct by both parties which recognizes the existence of a contract is sufficient to establish a contract for sale although the writings of the parties do not otherwise establish a contract. In such case the terms of the particular contract consist of those terms on which the writings of the parties agree, together with any supplementary terms incorporated under any other provisions of this Act.

§ 2-208. *Course of Performance or Practical Construction.*

(1) Where the contract for sale involves repeated occasions for performance by either party with knowledge of the nature of the performance and opportunity for objection to it by the other, any course of performance accepted or acquiesced in without objection shall be relevant to determine the meaning of the agreement.

(2) The express terms of the agreement and any such course of performance, as well as any course of dealing and usage of trade, shall be construed whenever reasonable as consistent with each other; but when such construction is unreasonable, express terms shall control course of performance and course of performance shall control both course of dealing and usage of trade (Section 1-205).

(3) Subject to the provisions of the next section on modification and waiver, such course of performance shall be relevant to show a waiver or modification of any term inconsistent with such course of performance.

§ 2-209. *Modification, Rescission and Waiver.*

(1) An agreement modifying a contract within this Article needs no consideration to be binding.

(2) A signed agreement which excludes modification or rescission except by a signed writing cannot be otherwise modified or rescinded, but except as between merchants such a requirement on a form supplied by the merchant must be separately signed by the other party.

(3) The requirements of the statute of frauds section of this Article (Section 2-201) must be satisfied if the contract as modified is within its provisions.

(4) Although an attempt at modification or rescission does not satisfy the requirements of subsection (2) or (3) it can operate as a waiver.

(5) A party who has made a waiver affecting an executory portion of the contract may retract the waiver by reasonable notification received by the other party that strict performance will be required of any term waived, unless the retraction would be unjust in view of a material change of position in reliance on the waiver.

§ 2-210. *Delegation of Performance; Assignment of Rights.*

(1) A party may perform his duty through a delegate unless otherwise agreed or unless the other party has a substantial interest in having his original promisor perform or control the acts required by the contract. No delegation of performance relieves the party delegating of any duty to perform or any liability for breach.

(2) Unless otherwise agreed all rights of either seller or buyer can be assigned except where the assignment would materially change the duty of the other party, or increase materially the burden or risk imposed on him by his contract, or impair materially his chance of obtaining return performance. A right to damages for breach of the whole contract or a right arising out of the assignor's due performance of his entire obligation can be assigned despite agreement otherwise.

(3) Unless the circumstances indicate the contrary a prohibition of assignment of "the contract" is to be construed as barring only the delegation to the assignee of the assignor's performance.

(4) An assignment of "the contract" or of "all my rights under the contract" or an assignment in similar general terms is an assignment of rights and unless the language or the circumstances (as in an assignment for security) indicate the contrary, it is a delegation of performance of the duties of the assignor and its acceptance by the assignee constitutes a promise by him to perform those duties. This promise is enforceable by either the assignor or the other party to the original contract.

(5) The other party may treat any assignment which delegates performance as creating reasonable grounds for insecurity and may without prejudice to his rights against the assignor demand assurances from the assignee (Section 2-609).

■ PART 3 General Obligation and Construction of Contract

§ 2-301. *General Obligations of Parties.*

The obligation of the seller is to transfer and deliver and that of the buyer is to accept and pay in accordance with the contract.

§ 2-302. *Unconscionable Contract or Clause.*

(1) If the court as a matter of law finds the contract or any clause of the contract to have been unconscionable at the time it was made the court may refuse to enforce the contract, or it may enforce the remainder of the contract without the unconscionable clause, or it may so limit the application of any unconscionable clause as to avoid any unconscionable result.

(2) When it is claimed or appears to the court that the contract or any clause thereof may be unconscionable the parties shall be afforded a reasonable opportunity to present evidence as to its commercial setting, purpose and effect to aid the court in making the determination.

§ 2-303. *Allocation or Division of Risks.*

Where this Article allocates a risk or a burden as between the parties "unless otherwise agreed", the agreement may not only shift the allocation, but may also divide the risk or burden.

§ 2-304. *Price Payable in Money, Goods, Realty, or Otherwise.*

(1) The price can be made payable in money or otherwise. If it is payable in whole or in part in goods each party is a seller of the goods which he is to transfer.

(2) Even though all or part of the price is payable in an interest in realty the transfer of the goods and the seller's obligations with reference to them are subject to this Article, but not the transfer of the interest in realty or the transferor's obligations in connection therewith.

§ 2-305. *Open Price Term.*

(1) The parties if they so intend can conclude a contract for sale even though the price is not settled. In such a case the price is a reasonable price at the time for delivery if

(a) nothing is said as to price; or

(b) the price is left to be agreed by the parties and they fail to agree; or

(c) the price is to be fixed in terms of some agreed market or other standard as set or recorded by a third person or agency and it is not so set or recorded.

(2) A price to be fixed by the seller or by the buyer means a price for him to fix in good faith.

(3) When a price left to be fixed otherwise than by agreement of the parties fails to be fixed through fault of one party the

other may at his option treat the contract as cancelled or himself fix a reasonable price.

(4) Where, however, the parties intend not to be bound unless the price be fixed or agreed and it is not fixed or agreed there is no contract. In such a case the buyer must return any goods already received or if unable so to do must pay their reasonable value at the time of delivery and the seller must return any portion of the price paid on account.

§ 2-306. *Output, Requirements and Exclusive Dealings.*

(1) A term which measures the quantity by the output of the seller or the requirements of the buyer means such actual output or requirements as may occur in good faith, except that no quantity unreasonably disproportionate to any stated estimate or in the absence of a stated estimate to any normal or otherwise comparable prior output or requirements may be tendered or demanded.

(2) A lawful agreement by either the seller or the buyer for exclusive dealing in the kind of goods concerned imposes unless otherwise agreed an obligation by the seller to use best efforts to supply the goods and by the buyer to use best efforts to promote their sale.

§ 2-307. *Delivery in Single Lot or Several Lots.*

Unless otherwise agreed all goods called for by a contract for sale must be tendered in a single delivery and payment is due only on such tender but where the circumstances give either party the right to make or demand delivery in lots the price if it can be apportioned may be demanded for each lot.

§ 2-308. *Absence of Specified Place for Delivery.*

Unless otherwise agreed

(a) the place for delivery of goods is the seller's place of business or if he has none his residence; but

(b) in a contract for sale of identified goods which to the knowledge of the parties at the time of contracting are in some other place, that place is the place for their delivery; and

(c) documents of title may be delivered through customary banking channels.

§ 2-309. *Absence of Specific Time Provisions; Notice of Termination.*

(1) The time for shipment or delivery or any other action under a contract if not provided in this Article or agreed upon shall be a reasonable time.

(2) Where the contract provides for successive performances but is indefinite in duration it is valid for a reasonable time but unless otherwise agreed may be terminated at any time by either party.

(3) Termination of a contract by one party except on the happening of an agreed event requires that reasonable notification be received by the other party and an agreement dispensing with notification is invalid if its operation would be unconscionable.

§ 2-310. *Open Time for Payment or Running of Credit; Authority to Ship Under Reservation.*

Unless otherwise agreed

(a) payment is due at the time and place at which the buyer is to receive the goods even though the place of shipment is the place of delivery; and

(b) if the seller is authorized to send the goods he may ship them under reservation, and may tender the documents of title, but the buyer may inspect the goods after their arrival before payment is due unless such inspection is inconsistent with the terms of the contract (Section 2-513); and

(c) if delivery is authorized and made by way of documents of title otherwise than by subsection (b) then payment is due at the time and place at which the buyer is to receive the documents regardless of where the goods are to be received; and

(d) where the seller is required or authorized to ship the goods on credit the credit period runs from the time of shipment but post-dating the invoice or delaying its dispatch will correspondingly delay the starting of the credit period.

§ 2-311. *Options and Cooperation Respecting Performance.*

(1) An agreement for sale which is otherwise sufficiently definite (subsection (3) of Section 2-204) to be a contract is not made invalid by the fact that it leaves particulars of performance to be specified by one of the parties. Any such specification must be made in good faith and within limits set by commercial reasonableness.

(2) Unless otherwise agreed specifications relating to assortment of the goods are at the buyer's option and except as otherwise provided in subsections (1)(c) and (3) of Section 2-319 specifications or arrangements relating to shipment are at the seller's option.

(3) Where such specification would materially affect the other party's performance but is not seasonably made or where one party's cooperation is necessary to the agreed performance of the other but is not seasonably forthcoming, the other party in addition to all other remedies

(a) is excused for any resulting delay in his own performance; and

(b) may also either proceed to perform in any reasonable manner or after the time for a material part of his own performance treat the failure to specify or to cooperate as a breach by failure to deliver or accept the goods.

§ 2-312. *Warranty of Title and Against Infringement; Buyer's Obligation Against Infringement.*

(1) Subject to subsection (2) there is in a contract for sale a warranty by the seller that

(a) the title conveyed shall be good, and its transfer rightful; and

(b) the goods shall be delivered free from any security interest or other lien or encumbrance of which the buyer at the time of contracting has no knowledge.

(2) A warranty under subsection (1) will be excluded or modified only by specific language or by circumstances which give the buyer reason to know that the person selling does not claim title in himself or that he is purporting to sell only such right or title as he or a third person may have.

(3) Unless otherwise agreed a seller who is a merchant regularly dealing in goods of the kind warrants that the goods shall be delivered free of the rightful claim of any third person by way of infringement or the like but a buyer who furnishes specifications to the seller must hold the seller harmless against any such claim which arises out of compliance with the specifications.

§ 2-313. *Express Warranties by Affirmation, Promise, Description, Sample.*

(1) Express warranties by the seller are created as follows:

(a) Any affirmation of fact or promise made by the seller to the buyer which relates to the goods and becomes part of the basis of the bargain creates an express warranty that the goods shall conform to the affirmation or promise.

(b) Any description of the goods which is made part of the basis of the bargain creates an express warranty that the goods shall conform to the description.

(c) Any sample or model which is made part of the basis of the bargain creates an express warranty that the whole of the goods shall conform to the sample or model.

(2) It is not necessary to the creation of an express warranty that the seller use formal words such as "warrant" or "guarantee" or that he have a specific intention to make a warranty, but an affirmation merely of the value of the goods or a statement purporting to be merely the seller's opinion or commendation of the goods does not create a warranty.

§ 2-314. Implied Warranty: Merchantability; Usage of Trade.

(1) Unless excluded or modified (Section 2-316), a warranty that the goods shall be merchantable is implied in a contract for their sale if the seller is a merchant with respect to goods of that kind. Under this section the serving for value of food or drink to be consumed either on the premises or elsewhere is a sale.

(2) Goods to be merchantable must be at least such as

(a) pass without objection in the trade under the contract description; and

(b) in the case of fungible goods, are of fair average quality within the description; and

(c) are fit for the ordinary purpose for which such goods are used; and

(d) run, within the variations permitted by the agreement, of even kind, quality and quantity within each unit and among all units involved; and

(e) are adequately contained, packaged, and labeled as the agreement may require; and

(f) conform to the promises or affirmations of fact made on the container or label if any.

(3) Unless excluded or modified (Section 2-316) other implied warranties may arise from course of dealing or usage of trade.

§ 2-315. Implied Warranty: Fitness for Particular Purpose.

Where the seller at the time of contracting has reason to know any particular purpose for which the goods are required and that the buyer is relying on the seller's skill or judgment to select or furnish suitable goods, there is unless excluded or modified under the next section an implied warranty that the goods shall be fit for such purpose.

§ 2-316. Exclusion or Modification of Warranties.

(1) Words or conduct relevant to the creation of an express warranty and words or conduct tending to negate or limit warranty shall be construed wherever reasonable as consistent with each other, but subject to the provisions of this Article on parol or extrinsic evidence (Section 2-202) negation or limitation is inoperative to the extent that such construction is unreasonable.

(2) Subject to subsection (3), to exclude or modify the implied warranty of merchantability or any part of it the language must mention merchantability and in case of a writing must be conspicuous, and to exclude or modify any implied warranty of fitness the exclusion must be by a writing and conspicuous. Language to exclude all implied warranties of fitness is sufficient if it states, for example, that "There are no warranties which extend beyond the description on the face hereof."

(3) Notwithstanding subsection (2)

(a) unless the circumstances indicate otherwise, all implied warranties are excluded by expressions like "as is", "with all faults" or other language which in common understanding calls the buyer's attention to the exclusion of warranties and makes plain that there is no implied warranty; and

(b) when the buyer before entering into the contract has examined the goods or the sample or model as fully as he desired or has refused to examine the goods there is no implied warranty with regard to defects which an examination ought in the circumstances to have revealed to him; and

(c) an implied warranty can also be excluded or modified by course of dealing or course of performance or usage of trade.

(4) Remedies for breach of warranty can be limited in accordance with the provisions of this Article on liquidation or limitation of damages and on contractual modification of remedy (Sections 2-718 and 2-719).

§ 2-317. Cumulation and Conflict of Warranties Express or Implied.

Warranties whether express or implied shall be construed as consistent with each other and as cumulative, but if such construction is unreasonable the intention of the parties shall determine which warranty is dominant. In ascertaining that intention the following rules apply:

(a) Exact or technical specifications displace an inconsistent sample or model or general language of description.

(b) A sample from an existing bulk displaces inconsistent general language of description.

(c) Express warranties displace inconsistent implied warranties other than an implied warranty of fitness for a particular purpose.

§ 2-318. Third Party Beneficiaries of Warranties Express or Implied.

Note: If this Act is introduced in the Congress of the United States this section should be omitted. (States to select one alternative.)

Alternative A A seller's warranty whether express or implied extends to any natural person who is in the family or household of his buyer or who is a guest in his home if it is reasonable to expect that such person may use, consume or be affected by the goods and who is injured in person by breach of the warranty. The seller may not exclude or limit the operation of this section.

Alternative B A seller's warranty whether express or implied extends to any natural person who may reasonably be expected to use, consume or be affected by the goods and who is injured in person by breach of the warranty. A seller may not exclude or limit the operation of this section.

Alternative C A seller's warranty whether express or implied extends to any person who may reasonably be expected to use, consume or be affected by the goods and who is injured by breach of the warranty. A seller may not exclude or limit the operation of this section with respect to injury to the person of an individual to whom the warranty extends. As amended 1966.

§ 2-319. F.O.B. and F.A.S. Terms.

(1) Unless otherwise agreed the term F.O.B. (which means "free on board") at a named place, even though used only in connection with the stated price, is a delivery term under which

(a) when the term is F.O.B. the place of shipment, the seller must at that place ship the goods in the manner provided in this Article (Section 2-504) and bear the expense and risk of putting them into the possession of the carrier; or

(b) when the term is F.O.B. the place of destination, the seller must at his own expense and risk transport the goods to that place and there tender delivery of them in the manner provided in this Article (Section 2-503);

(c) when under either (a) or (b) the term is also F.O.B. vessel, car or other vehicle, the seller must in addition at his own expense and risk load the goods on board. If the term is F.O.B. vessel the buyer must name the vessel and in an appropriate case the seller must comply with the provisions of this Article on the form of bill of lading (Section 2-323).

(2) Unless otherwise agreed the term F.A.S. vessel (which means "free alongside") at a named port, even though used only in connection with the stated price, is a delivery term under which the seller must

(a) at his own expense and risk deliver the goods alongside the vessel in the manner usual in that port or on a dock designated and provided by the buyer; and

(b) obtain and tender a receipt for the goods in exchange for which the carrier is under a duty to issue a bill of lading.

(3) Unless otherwise agreed in any case falling within subsection (1)(a) or (c) or subsection (2) the buyer must seasonably give any needed instructions for making delivery, including when the term is F.A.S. or F.O.B. the loading berth of the vessel and in an appropriate case its name and sailing date. The seller may treat the failure of needed instructions as a failure of cooperation under this Article (Section 2-311). He may also at his option move the goods in any reasonable manner preparatory to delivery or shipment.

(4) Under the term F.O.B. vessel or F.A.S. unless otherwise agreed the buyer must make payment against tender of the required documents and the seller may not tender nor the buyer demand delivery of the goods in substitution for the documents.

§ 2-320. *C.I.F. and C. & F. Terms.*

(1) The term C.I.F. means that the price includes in a lump sum the cost of the goods and the insurance and freight to the named destination. The term C. & F. or C.F. means that the price so includes cost and freight to the named destination.

(2) Unless otherwise agreed and even though used only in connection with the stated price and destination, the term C.I.F. destination or its equivalent requires the seller at his own expense and risk to

(a) put the goods into the possession of a carrier at the port for shipment and obtain a negotiable bill or bills of lading covering the entire transportation to the named destination; and

(b) load the goods and obtain a receipt from the carrier (which may be contained in the bill of lading) showing that the freight has been paid or provided for; and

(c) obtain a policy or certificate of insurance, including any war risk insurance, of a kind and on terms then current at the port of shipment in the usual amount, in the currency of the contract, shown to cover the same goods covered by the bill of lading and providing for payment of loss to the order of the buyer or for the account of whom it may concern; but the seller may add to the price the amount of premium for any such war risk insurance; and

(d) prepare an invoice of the goods and procure any other documents required to effect shipment or to comply with the contract; and

(e) forward and tender with commercial promptness all the documents in due form and with any indorsement necessary to perfect the buyer's rights.

(3) Unless otherwise agreed the term C. & F. or its equivalent has the same effect and imposes upon the seller the same obligations and risks as a C.I.F. term except the obligation as to insurance.

(4) Under the term C.I.F. or C. & F. unless otherwise agreed the buyer must make payment against tender of the required documents and the seller may not tender nor the buyer demand delivery of the goods in substitution for the documents.

§ 2-321. *C.I.F. or C. & F.: "Net Landed Weights"; "Payment on Arrival"; Warranty of Condition on Arrival.*

Under a contract containing a term C.I.F. or C. & F.

(1) Where the price is based on or is to be adjusted according to "net landed weights", "delivered weights", "out turn" quantity or quality or the like, unless otherwise agreed the seller must reasonably estimate the price. The payment due on tender of the documents called for by the contract is the amount so estimated, but after final adjustment of the price a settlement must be made with commercial promptness.

(2) An agreement described in subsection (1) or any warranty of quality or condition of the goods on arrival places upon the seller the risk of ordinary deterioration, shrinkage and the like in transportation but has no effect on the place or time of identification to the contract for sale or delivery or on the passing of the risk of loss.

(3) Unless otherwise agreed where the contract provides for payment on or after arrival of the goods the seller must before payment allow such preliminary inspection as is feasible; but if the goods are lost delivery of the documents and payment are due when the goods should have arrived.

§ 2-322. *Delivery "Ex-Ship".*

(1) Unless otherwise agreed a term for delivery of goods "ex-ship" (which means from the carrying vessel) or in equivalent language is not restricted to a particular ship and requires delivery from a ship which has reached a place at the named port of destination where goods of the kind are usually discharged.

(2) Under such a term unless otherwise agreed

(a) the seller must discharge all liens arising out of the carriage and furnish the buyer with a direction which puts the carrier under a duty to deliver the goods; and

(b) the risk of loss does not pass to the buyer until the goods leave the ship's tackle or are otherwise properly unloaded.

§ 2-323. *Form of Bill of Lading Required in Overseas Shipment; "Overseas".*

(1) Where the contract contemplates overseas shipment and contains a term C.I.F. or C. & F. or F.O.B. vessel, the seller unless otherwise agreed must obtain a negotiable bill of lading stating that the goods have been loaded on board or, in the case of a term C.I.F. or C. & F., received for shipment.

(2) Where in a case within subsection (1) a bill of lading has been issued in a set of parts, unless otherwise agreed if the documents are not to be sent from abroad the buyer may demand tender of the full set; otherwise only one part of the bill of lading need be tendered. Even if the agreement expressly requires a full set

(a) due tender of a single part is acceptable within the provisions of this Article on cure of improper delivery (subsection (1) of Section 2-508); and

(b) even though the full set is demanded, if the documents are sent from abroad the person tendering an incomplete set may nevertheless require payment upon furnishing an indemnity which the buyer in good faith deems adequate.

(3) A shipment by water or by air or a contract contemplating such shipment is "overseas" insofar as by usage of trade or agreement it is subject to the commercial, financing or shipping practices characteristic of international deep water commerce.

§ 2-324. *"No Arrival, No Sale" Term.*

Under a term "no arrival, no sale" or terms of like meaning, unless otherwise agreed,

(a) the seller must properly ship conforming goods and if they arrive by any means he must tender them on arrival but he assumes no obligation that the goods will arrive unless he has caused the non-arrival; and

(b)   where without fault of the seller the goods are in part lost or have so deteriorated as no longer to conform to the contract or arrive after the contract time, the buyer may proceed as if there had been casualty to identified goods (Section 2-613).

§ 2-325.   *"Letter of Credit" Term; "Confirmed Credit".*

(1)   Failure of the buyer seasonably to furnish an agreed letter of credit is a breach of the contract for sale.

(2)   The delivery to seller of a proper letter of credit suspends the buyer's obligation to pay. If the letter of credit is dishonored, the seller may on seasonable notification to the buyer require payment directly from him.

(3)   Unless otherwise agreed the term "letter of credit" or "banker's credit" in a contract for sale means an irrevocable credit issued by a financing agency of good repute and, where the shipment is overseas, of good international repute. The term "confirmed credit" means that the credit must also carry the direct obligation of such an agency which does business in the seller's financial market.

§ 2-326.   *Sale on Approval and Sale or Return; Consignment Sales and Rights of Creditors.*

(1)   Unless otherwise agreed, if delivered goods may be returned by the buyer even though they conform to the contract, the transaction is

(a)   a "sale on approval" if the goods are delivered primarily for use, and

(b)   a "sale or return" if the goods are delivered primarily for resale.

(2)   Except as provided in subsection (3), goods held on approval are not subject to the claims of the buyer's creditors until acceptance; goods held on sale or return are subject to such claims while in the buyer's possession.

(3)   Where goods are delivered to a person for sale and such person maintains a place of business at which he deals in goods of the kind involved, under a name other than the name of the person making delivery, then with respect to claims of creditors of the person conducting the business the goods are deemed to be on sale or return. The provisions of this subsection are applicable even though an agreement purports to reserve title to the person making delivery until payment or resale or uses such words as "on consignment" or "on memorandum". However, this subsection is not applicable if the person making delivery

(a)   complies with an applicable law providing for a consignor's interest or the like to be evidenced by a sign, or

(b)   establishes that the person conducting the business is generally known by his creditors to be substantially engaged in selling the goods of others, or

(c)   complies with the filing provisions of the Article on Secured Transactions (Article 9).

(4)   Any "or return" term of a contract for sale is to be treated as a separate contract for sale within the statute of frauds section of this Article (Section 2-201) and as contradicting the sale aspect of the contract within the provisions of this Article on parol or extrinsic evidence (Section 2-202).

§ 2-327.   *Special Incidents of Sale on Approval and Sale or Return.*

(1)   Under a sale on approval unless otherwise agreed

(a)   although the goods are identified to the contract the risk of loss and the title do not pass to the buyer until acceptance; and

(b)   use of the goods consistent with the purpose of trial is not acceptance but failure seasonably to notify the seller of election to return the goods is acceptance, and if the goods conform to the contract acceptance of any part is acceptance of the whole; and

(c)   after due notification of election to return, the return is at the seller's risk and expense but a merchant buyer must follow any reasonable instructions.

(2)   Under a sale or return unless otherwise agreed

(a)   the option to return extends to the whole or any commercial unit of the goods while in substantially their original condition, but must be exercised seasonably; and

(b)   the return is at the buyer's risk and expense.

§ 2-328.   *Sale by Auction.*

(1)   In a sale by auction if goods are put up in lots each lot is the subject of a separate sale.

(2)   A sale by auction is complete when the auctioneer so announces by the fall of the hammer or in other customary manner. Where a bid is made while the hammer is falling in acceptance of a prior bid the auctioneer may in his discretion reopen the bidding or declare the goods sold under the bid on which the hammer was falling.

(3)   Such a sale is with reserve unless the goods are in explicit terms put up without reserve. In an auction with reserve the auctioneer may withdraw the goods at any time until he announces completion of the sale. In an auction without reserve, after the auctioneer calls for bids on an article or lot, that article or lot cannot be withdrawn unless no bid is made within a reasonable time. In either case a bidder may retract his bid until the auctioneer's announcement of completion of the sale, but a bidder's retraction does not revive any previous bid.

(4)   If the auctioneer knowingly receives a bid on the seller's behalf or the seller makes or procures such a bid, and notice has not been given that liberty for such bidding is reserved, the buyer may at his option avoid the sale or take the goods at the price of the last good faith bid prior to the completion of the sale. This subsection shall not apply to any bid at a forced sale.

■ PART 4   Title, Creditors and Good Faith Purchasers

§ 2-401.   *Passing of Title; Reservation for Security; Limited Application of This Section.*

Each provision of this Article with regard to the rights, obligations and remedies of the seller, the buyer, purchasers or other third parties applies irrespective of title to the goods except where the provision refers to such title. Insofar as situations are not covered by the other provisions of this Article and matters concerning title became material the following rules apply:

(1)   Title to goods cannot pass under a contract for sale prior to their identification to the contract (Section 2-501), and unless otherwise explicitly agreed the buyer acquires by their identification a special property as limited by this Act.

Any retention or reservation by the seller of the title (property) in goods shipped or delivered to the buyer is limited in effect to a reservation of a security interest. Subject to these provisions and to the provisions of the Article on Secured Transactions (Article 9), title to goods passes from the seller to the buyer in any manner and on any conditions explicitly agreed on by the parties.

(2)   Unless otherwise explicitly agreed title passes to the buyer at the time and place at which the seller completes his performance with reference to the physical delivery of the goods, despite any reservation of a security interest and even though a document of title is to be delivered at a different time or place; and in particular and despite any reservation of a security interest by the bill of lading

(a) if the contract requires or authorizes the seller to send the goods to the buyer but does not require him to deliver them at destination, title passes to the buyer at the time and place of shipment; but

(b) if the contract requires delivery at destination, title passes on tender there.

(3) Unless otherwise explicitly agreed where delivery is to be made without moving the goods,

(a) if the seller is to deliver a document of title, title passes at the time when and the place where he delivers such documents; or

(b) if the goods are at the time of contracting already identified and no documents are to be delivered, title passes at the time and place of contracting.

(4) A rejection or other refusal by the buyer to receive or retain the goods, whether or not justified, or a justified revocation of acceptance revests title to the goods in the seller. Such revesting occurs by operation of law and is not a "sale".

§ 2-402. *Rights of Seller's Creditors Against Sold Goods.*

(1) Except as provided in subsections (2) and (3), rights of unsecured creditors of the seller with respect to goods which have been identified to a contract for sale are subject to the buyer's rights to recover the goods under this Article (Sections 2-502 and 2-716).

(2) A creditor of the seller may treat a sale or an identification of goods to a contract for sale as void if as against him a retention of possession by the seller is fraudulent under any rule of law of the state where the goods are situated, except that retention of possession in good faith and current course of trade by a merchant-seller for a commercially reasonable time after a sale or identification is not fraudulent.

(3) Nothing in this Article shall be deemed to impair the rights of creditors of the seller

(a) under the provisions of the Article on Secured Transactions (Article 9); or

(b) where identification to the contract or delivery is made not in current course of trade but in satisfaction of or as security for a pre-existing claim for money, security or the like and is made under circumstances which under any rule of law of the state where the goods are situated would apart from this Article constitute the transaction a fraudulent transfer or voidable preference.

§ 2-403. *Power to Transfer; Good Faith Purchase of Goods; "Entrusting".*

(1) A purchaser of goods acquires all title which his transferor had or had power to transfer except that a purchaser of a limited interest acquires rights only to the extent of the interest purchased. A person with voidable title has power to transfer a good title to a good faith purchaser for value. When goods have been delivered under a transaction of purchase the purchaser has such power even though

(a) the transferor was deceived as to the identity of the purchaser, or

(b) the delivery was in exchange for a check which is later dishonored, or

(c) it was agreed that the transaction was to be a "cash sale", or

(d) the delivery was procured through fraud punishable as larcenous under the criminal law.

(2) Any entrusting of possession of goods to a merchant who deals in goods of that kind gives him power to transfer all rights of the entruster to a buyer in ordinary course of business.

(3) "Entrusting" includes any delivery and any acquiescence in retention of possession regardless of any condition expressed between the parties to the delivery or acquiescence and regardless of whether the procurement of the entrusting or the possessor's disposition of the goods have been such as to be larcenous under the criminal law.

(4) The rights of other purchasers of goods and of lien creditors are governed by the Articles on Secured Transactions (Article 9), Bulk Transfers (Article 6) and Documents of Title (Article 7).

■ PART 5   Performance

§ 2-501. *Insurable Interest in Goods; Manner of Identification of Goods.*

(1) The buyer obtains a special property and an insurable interest in goods by identification of existing goods as goods to which the contract refers even though the goods so identified are nonconforming and he has an option to return or reject them. Such identification can be made at any time and in any manner explicitly agreed to by the parties. In the absence of explicit agreement identification occurs

(a) when the contract is made if it is for the sale of goods already existing and identified;

(b) if the contract is for the sale of future goods other than those described in paragraph (c), when goods are shipped, marked or otherwise designated by the seller as goods to which the contract refers;

(c) when the crops are planted or otherwise become growing crops or the young are conceived if the contract is for the sale of unborn young to be born within twelve months after contracting or for the sale of crops to be harvested within twelve months or the next normal harvest season after contracting whichever is longer.

(2) The seller retains an insurable interest in goods so long as title to or any security interest in the goods remains in him and where the identification is by the seller alone he may until default or insolvency or notification to the buyer that the identification is final substitute other goods for those identified.

(3) Nothing in this section impairs any insurable interest recognized under any other statute or rule of law.

§ 2-502. *Buyer's Right to Goods on Seller's Insolvency.*

(1) Subject to subsection (2) and even though the goods have not been shipped a buyer who has paid a part or all of the price of goods in which he has a special property under the provisions of the immediately preceding section may on making and keeping good a tender of any unpaid portion of their price recover them from the seller if the seller becomes insolvent within ten days after receipt of the first installment on their price.

(2) If the identification creating his special property has been made by the buyer he acquires the right to recover the goods only if they conform to the contract for sale.

§ 2-503. *Manner of Seller's Tender of Delivery.*

(1) Tender of delivery requires that the seller put and hold conforming goods at the buyer's disposition and give the buyer any notification reasonably necessary to enable him to take delivery. The manner, time and place for tender are determined by the agreement and this Article, and in particular

(a) tender must be at a reasonable hour, and if it is of goods they must be kept available for the period reasonably necessary to enable the buyer to take possession; but

(b) unless otherwise agreed the buyer must furnish facilities reasonably suited to the receipt of the goods.

(2) Where the case is within the next section respecting shipment tender requires that the seller comply with its provisions.

(3) Where the seller is required to deliver at a particular destination tender requires that he comply with subsection

(1) and also in any appropriate case tender documents as described in subsections (4) and (5) of this section.

(4)   Where goods are in the possession of a bailee and are to be delivered without being moved

(a)   tender requires that the seller either tender a negotiable document of title covering such goods or procure acknowledgment by the bailee of the buyer's right to possession of the goods; but

(b)   tender to the buyer of a non-negotiable document of title or of a written direction to the bailee to deliver is sufficient tender unless the buyer seasonably objects, and receipt by the bailee of notification of the buyer's rights fixes those rights as against the bailee and all third persons; but risk of loss of the goods and of any failure by the bailee to honor the non-negotiable document of title or to obey the direction remains on the seller until the buyer has had a reasonable time to present the document or direction, and a refusal by the bailee to honor the document or to obey the direction defeats the tender.

(5)   Where the contract requires the seller to deliver documents

(a)   he must tender all such documents in correct form, except as provided in this Article with respect to bills of lading in a set (subsection (2) of Section 2-323); and

(b)   tender through customary banking channels is sufficient and dishonor of a draft accompanying the documents constitutes non-acceptance or rejection.

§ 2-504.   *Shipment by Seller.*

Where the seller is required or authorized to send the goods to the buyer and the contract does not require him to deliver them at a particular destination, then unless otherwise agreed he must

(a)   put the goods in the possession of such a carrier and make such a contract for their transportation as may be reasonable having regard to the nature of the goods and other circumstances of the case; and

(b)   obtain and promptly deliver or tender in due form any document necessary to enable the buyer to obtain possession of the goods or otherwise required by the agreement or by usage of trade; and

(c)   promptly notify the buyer of the shipment.

Failure to notify the buyer under paragraph (c) or to make a proper contract under paragraph (a) is a ground for rejection only if material delay or loss ensues.

§ 2-505.   *Seller's Shipment Under Reservation.*

(1)   Where the seller has identified goods to the contract by or before shipment:

(a)   his procurement of a negotiable bill of lading to his own order or otherwise reserves in him a security interest in the goods. His procurement of the bill to the order of a financing agency or of the buyer indicates in addition only the seller's expectation of transferring that interest to the person named.

(b)   a non-negotiable bill of lading to himself or his nominee reserves possession of the goods as security but except in a case of conditional delivery (subsection (2) of Section 2-507) a non-negotiable bill of lading naming the buyer as consignee reserves no security interest even though the seller retains possession of the bill of lading.

(2)   When shipment by the seller with reservation of a security interest is in violation of the contract for sale it constitutes an improper contract for transportation within the preceding section but impairs neither the rights given to the buyer by shipment and identification of the goods to the contract nor the seller's powers as a holder of a negotiable document.

§ 2-506.   *Rights of Financing Agency.*

(1)   A financing agency by paying or purchasing for value a draft which relates to a shipment of goods acquires to the extent of the payment or purchase and in addition to its own rights under the draft and any document of title securing it any rights of the shipper in the goods including the right to stop delivery and the shipper's right to have the draft honored by the buyer.

(2)   The right to reimbursement of a financing agency which has in good faith honored or purchased the draft under commitment to or authority from the buyer is not impaired by subsequent discovery of defects with reference to any relevant document which was apparently regular on its face.

§ 2-507.   *Effect of Seller's Tender; Delivery on Condition.*

(1)   Tender of delivery is a condition to the buyer's duty to accept the goods and, unless otherwise agreed, to his duty to pay for them. Tender entitles the seller to acceptance of the goods and to payment according to the contract.

(2)   Where payment is due and demanded on the delivery to the buyer of goods or documents of title, his right as against the seller to retain or dispose of them is conditional upon his making the payment due.

§ 2-508.   *Cure by Seller of Improper Tender or Delivery; Replacement.*

(1)   Where any tender or delivery by the seller is rejected because non-conforming and the time for performance has not yet expired, the seller may seasonably notify the buyer of his intention to cure and may then within the contract time make a conforming delivery.

(2)   Where the buyer rejects a non-conforming tender which the seller had reasonable grounds to believe would be acceptable with or without money allowance the seller may if he seasonably notifies the buyer have a further reasonable time to substitute a conforming tender.

§ 2-509.   *Risk of Loss in the Absence of Breach.*

(1)   Where the contract requires or authorizes the seller to ship the goods by carrier

(a)   if it does not require him to deliver them at a particular destination, the risk of loss passes to the buyer when the goods are duly delivered to the carrier even though the shipment is under reservation (Section 2-505); but

(b)   if it does require him to deliver them at a particular destination and the goods are there duly tendered while in the possession of the carrier, the risk of loss passes to the buyer when the goods are there duly so tendered as to enable the buyer to take delivery.

(2)   Where the goods are held by a bailee to be delivered without being moved, the risk of loss passes to the buyer

(a)   on his receipt of a negotiable document of title covering the goods; or

(b)   on acknowledgment by the bailee of the buyer's right to possession of the goods; or

(c)   after his receipt of a non-negotiable document of title or other written direction to deliver, as provided in subsection (4)(b) of Section 2-503.

(3)   In any case not within subsection (1) or (2), the risk of loss passes to the buyer on his receipt of the goods if the seller is a merchant; otherwise, the risk passes to the buyer on tender of delivery.

(4)   The provisions of this section are subject to contrary agreement of the parties and to the provisions of this Article on sale on approval (Section 2-327) and on effect of breach on risk of loss (Section 2-510).

§ 2-510. *Effect of Breach on Risk of Loss.*

(1)　Where a tender or delivery of goods so fails to conform to the contract as to give a right of rejection the risk of their loss remains on the seller until cure or acceptance.

(2)　Where the buyer rightfully revokes acceptance he may to the extent of any deficiency in his effective insurance coverage treat the risk of loss as having rested on the seller from the beginning.

(3)　Where the buyer as to conforming goods already identified to the contract for sale repudiates or is otherwise in breach before risk of their loss has passed to him, the seller may to the extent of any deficiency in his effective insurance coverage treat the risk of loss as resting on the buyer for a commercially reasonable time.

§ 2-511. *Tender of Payment by Buyer; Payment by Check.*

(1)　Unless otherwise agreed tender of payment is a condition to the seller's duty to tender and complete any delivery.

(2)　Tender of payment is sufficient when made by any means or in any manner current in the ordinary course of business unless the seller demands payment in legal tender and gives any extension of time reasonably necessary to procure it.

(3)　Subject to the provisions of this Act on the effect of an instrument on an obligation (Section 3-310), payment by check is conditional and is defeated as between the parties by dishonor of the check on due presentment.

§ 2-512. *Payment by Buyer Before Inspection.*

(1)　Where the contract requires payment before inspection non-conformity of the goods does not excuse the buyer from so making payment unless

(a)　the non-conformity appears without inspection; or

(b)　despite tender of the required documents the circumstances would justify injunction against honor under the provisions of this Act (Section 5-114).

(2)　Payment pursuant to subsection (1) does not constitute an acceptance of goods or impair the buyer's right to inspect or any of his remedies.

§ 2-513. *Buyer's Right to Inspection of Goods.*

(1)　Unless otherwise agreed and subject to subsection (3), where goods are tendered or delivered or identified to the contract for sale, the buyer has a right before payment or acceptance to inspect them at any reasonable place and time and in any reasonable manner. When the seller is required or authorized to send the goods to the buyer, the inspection may be after their arrival.

(2)　Expenses of inspection must be borne by the buyer but may be recovered from the seller if the goods do not conform and are rejected.

(3)　Unless otherwise agreed and subject to the provisions of this Article on C.I.F. contracts (subsection (3) of Section 2-321), the buyer is not entitled to inspect the goods before payment of the price when the contract provides

(a)　for delivery "C.O.D." or on other like terms; or

(b)　for payment against documents of title, except where such payment is due only after the goods are to become available for inspection.

(4)　A place or method of inspection fixed by the parties is presumed to be exclusive but unless otherwise expressly agreed it does not postpone identification or shift the place for delivery or for passing the risk of loss. If compliance becomes impossible, inspection shall be as provided in this section unless the place or method fixed was clearly intended as an indispensable condition failure of which avoids the contract.

§ 2-514. *When Documents Deliverable on Acceptance; When on Payment.*

Unless otherwise agreed documents against which a draft is drawn are to be delivered to the drawee on acceptance of the draft if it is payable more than three days after presentment; otherwise, only on payment.

§ 2-515. *Preserving Evidence of Goods in Dispute.*

In furtherance of the adjustment of any claim or dispute

(a)　either party on reasonable notification to the other and for the purpose of ascertaining the facts and preserving evidence has the right to inspect, test and sample the goods including such of them as may be in the possession or control of the other; and

(b)　the parties may agree to a third party inspection or survey to determine the conformity or condition of the goods and may agree that the findings shall be binding upon them in any subsequent litigation or adjustment.

■ PART 6　Breach, Repudiation and Excuse

§ 2-601. *Buyer's Rights on Improper Delivery.*

Subject to the provisions of this Article on breach in installment contracts (Section 2-612) and unless otherwise agreed under the sections on contractual limitations of remedy (Sections 2-718 and 2-719), if the goods or the tender of delivery fail in any respect to conform to the contract, the buyer may

(a)　reject the whole; or

(b)　accept the whole; or

(c)　accept any commercial unit or units and reject the rest.

§ 2-602. *Manner and Effect of Rightful Rejection.*

(1)　Rejection of goods must be within a reasonable time after their delivery or tender. It is ineffective unless the buyer seasonably notifies the seller.

(2)　Subject to the provisions of the two following sections on rejected goods (Sections 2-603 and 2-604),

(a)　after rejection any exercise of ownership by the buyer with respect to any commercial unit is wrongful as against the seller; and

(b)　if the buyer has before rejection taken physical possession of goods in which he does not have a security interest under the provisions of this Article (subsection (3) of Section 2-711), he is under a duty after rejection to hold them with reasonable care at the seller's disposition for a time sufficient to permit the seller to remove them; but

(c)　the buyer has no further obligations with regard to goods rightfully rejected.

(3)　The seller's rights with respect to goods wrongfully rejected are governed by the provisions of this Article on seller's remedies in general (Section 2-703).

§ 2-603. *Merchant Buyer's Duties as to Rightfully Rejected Goods.*

(1)　Subject to any security interest in the buyer (subsection (3) of Section 2-711), when the seller has no agent or place of business at the market of rejection a merchant buyer is under a duty after rejection of goods in his possession or control to follow any reasonable instructions received from the seller with respect to the goods and in the absence of such instructions to make reasonable efforts to sell them for the seller's account if they are perishable or threaten to decline in value speedily. Instructions are not reasonable if on demand indemnity for expenses is not forthcoming.

(2)　When the buyer sells goods under subsection (1), he is entitled to reimbursement from the seller or out of the proceeds for reasonable expenses of caring for and selling them, and if the expenses include no selling commission then to such commission as is usual in the trade or if there is none to a reasonable sum not exceeding ten per cent on the gross proceeds.

(3)   In complying with this section the buyer is held only to good faith and good faith conduct hereunder is neither acceptance nor conversion nor the basis of an action for damages.

§ 2-604.   *Buyer's Options as to Salvage of Rightfully Rejected Goods.*

Subject to the provisions of the immediately preceding section on perishables if the seller gives no instructions within a reasonable time after notification of rejection the buyer may store the rejected goods for the seller's account or reship them to him or resell them for the seller's account with reimbursement as provided in the preceding section. Such action is not acceptance or conversion.

§ 2-605.   *Waiver of Buyer's Objections by Failure to Particularize.*

(1)   The buyer's failure to state in connection with rejection a particular defect which is ascertainable by reasonable inspection precludes him from relying on the unstated defect to justify rejection or to establish breach

(a)   where the seller could have cured it if stated seasonably; or

(b)   between merchants when the seller has after rejection made a request in writing for a full and final written statement of all defects on which the buyer proposes to rely.

(2)   Payment against documents made without reservation of rights precludes recovery of the payment for defects apparent on the face of the documents.

§ 2-606.   *What Constitutes Acceptance of Goods.*

(1)   Acceptance of goods occurs when the buyer

(a)   after a reasonable opportunity to inspect the goods signifies to the seller that the goods are conforming or that he will take or retain them in spite of their nonconformity; or

(b)   fails to make an effective rejection (subsection (1) of Section 2-602), but such acceptance does not occur until the buyer has had a reasonable opportunity to inspect them; or

(c)   does any act inconsistent with the seller's ownership; but if such act is wrongful as against the seller it is an acceptance only if ratified by him.

(2)   Acceptance of a part of any commercial unit is acceptance of that entire unit.

§ 2-607.   *Effect of Acceptance; Notice of Breach; Burden of Establishing Breach After Acceptance; Notice of Claim or Litigation to Person Answerable Over.*

(1)   The buyer must pay at the contract rate for any goods accepted.

(2)   Acceptance of goods by the buyer precludes rejection of the goods accepted and if made with knowledge of a non-conformity cannot be revoked because of it unless the acceptance was on the reasonable assumption that the non-conformity would be seasonably cured but acceptance does not of itself impair any other remedy provided by this Article for non-conformity.

(3)   Where a tender has been accepted

(a)   the buyer must within a reasonable time after he discovers or should have discovered any breach notify the seller of breach or be barred from any remedy; and

(b)   if the claim is one for infringement or the like (subsection (3) of Section 2-312) and the buyer is sued as a result of such a breach he must so notify the seller within a reasonable

time after he receives notice of the litigation or be barred from any remedy over for liability established by the litigation.

(4)   The burden is on the buyer to establish any breach with respect to the goods accepted.

(5)   Where the buyer is sued for breach of a warranty or other obligation for which his seller is answerable over

(a)   he may give his seller written notice of the litigation. If the notice states that the seller may come in and defend and that if the seller does not do so he will be bound in any action against him by his buyer by any determination of fact common to the two litigations, then unless the seller after seasonable receipt of the notice does come in and defend he is so bound.

(b)   if the claim is one for infringement or the like (subsection (3) of Section 2-312) the original seller may demand in writing that his buyer turn over to him control of the litigation including settlement or else be barred from any remedy over and if he also agrees to bear all expense and to satisfy any adverse judgment, then unless the buyer after seasonable receipt of the demand does turn over control the buyer is so barred.

(6)   The provisions of subsections (3), (4) and (5) apply to any obligation of a buyer to hold the seller harmless against infringement or the like (subsection (3) of Section 2-312).

§ 2-608.   *Revocation of Acceptance in Whole or in Part.*

(1)   The buyer may revoke his acceptance of a lot or commercial unit whose non-conformity substantially impairs its value to him if he has accepted it

(a)   on the reasonable assumption that its non-conformity would be cured and it has not been seasonably cured; or

(b)   without discovery of such non-conformity if his acceptance was reasonably induced either by the difficulty of discovery before acceptance or by the seller's assurances.

(2)   Revocation of acceptance must occur within a reasonable time after the buyer discovers or should have discovered the ground for it and before any substantial change in condition of the goods which is not caused by their own defects. It is not effective until the buyer notifies the seller of it.

(3)   A buyer who so revokes has the same rights and duties with regard to the goods involved as if he had rejected them.

§ 2-609.   *Right to Adequate Assurance of Performance.*

(1)   A contract for sale imposes an obligation on each party that the other's expectation of receiving due performance will not be impaired. When reasonable grounds for insecurity arise with respect to the performance of either party the other may in writing demand adequate assurance of due performance and until he receives such assurance may if commercially reasonable suspend any performance for which he has not already received the agreed return.

(2)   Between merchants the reasonableness of grounds for insecurity and the adequacy of any assurance offered shall be determined according to commercial standards.

(3)   Acceptance of any improper delivery or payment does not prejudice the aggrieved party's right to demand adequate assurance of future performance.

(4)   After receipt of a justified demand failure to provide within a reasonable time not exceeding thirty days such assurance of due performance as is adequate under the circumstances of the particular case is a repudiation of the contract.

§ 2-610.   *Anticipatory Repudiation.*

When either party repudiates the contract with respect to a performance not yet due the loss of which will substantially impair the value of the contract to the other, the aggrieved party may

(a) for a commercially reasonable time await performance by the repudiating party; or

(b) resort to any remedy for breach (Section 2-703 or Section 2-711), even though he has notified the repudiating party that he would await the latter's performance and has urged retraction; and

(c) in either case suspend his own performance or proceed in accordance with the provisions of this Article on the seller's right to identify goods to the contract notwithstanding breach or to salvage unfinished goods (Section 2-704).

§ 2-611. *Retraction of Anticipatory Repudiation.*

(1) Until the repudiating party's next performance is due he can retract his repudiation unless the aggrieved party has since the repudiation cancelled or materially changed his position or otherwise indicated that he considers the repudiation final.

(2) Retraction may be by any method which clearly indicates to the aggrieved party that the repudiating party intends to perform, but must include any assurance justifiably demanded under the provisions of this Article (Section 2-609).

(3) Retraction reinstates the repudiating party's rights under the contract with due excuse and allowance to the aggrieved party for any delay occasioned by the repudiation.

§ 2-612. *"Installment Contract"; Breach.*

(1) An "installment contract" is one which requires or authorizes the delivery of goods in separate lots to be separately accepted, even though the contract contains a clause "each delivery is a separate contract" or its equivalent.

(2) The buyer may reject any installment which is non-conforming if the non-conformity substantially impairs the value of that installment and cannot be cured or if the non-conformity is a defect in the required documents; but if the non-conformity does not fall within subsection (3) and the seller gives adequate assurance of its cure the buyer must accept that installment.

(3) Whenever non-conformity or default with respect to one or more installments substantially impairs the value of the whole contract there is a breach of the whole. But the aggrieved party reinstates the contract if he accepts a non-conforming installment without seasonably notifying of cancellation or if he brings an action with respect only to past installments or demands performance as to future installments.

§ 2-613. *Casualty to Identified Goods.*

Where the contract requires for its performance goods identified when the contract is made, and the goods suffer casualty without fault of either party before the risk of loss passes to the buyer, or in a proper case under a "no arrival, no sale" term (Section 2-324) then

(a) if the loss is total the contract is avoided; and

(b) if the loss is partial or the goods have so deteriorated as no longer to conform to the contract the buyer may nevertheless demand inspection and at his option either treat the contract as avoided or accept the goods with due allowance from the contract price for the deterioration or the deficiency in quantity but without further right against the seller.

§ 2-614. *Substituted Performance.*

(1) Where without fault of either party the agreed berthing, loading, or unloading facilities fail or an agreed type of carrier becomes unavailable or the agreed manner of delivery otherwise becomes commercially impracticable but a commercially reasonable substitute is available, such substitute performance must be tendered and accepted.

(2) If the agreed means or manner of payment fails because of domestic or foreign governmental regulation, the seller may withhold or stop delivery unless the buyer provides a means or manner of payment which is commercially a substantial equivalent. If delivery has already been taken, payment by the means or in the manner provided by the regulation discharges the buyer's obligation unless the regulation is discriminatory, oppressive or predatory.

§ 2-615. *Excuse by Failure of Presupposed Conditions.*

Except so far as a seller may have assumed a greater obligation and subject to the preceding section on substituted performance:

(a) Delay in delivery or non-delivery in whole or in part by a seller who complies with paragraphs (b) and (c) is not a breach of his duty under a contract for sale if performance as agreed has been made impracticable by the occurrence of a contingency the non-occurrence of which was a basic assumption on which the contract was made or by compliance in good faith with any applicable foreign or domestic governmental regulation or order whether or not it later proves to be invalid.

(b) Where the causes mentioned in paragraph (a) affect only a part of the seller's capacity to perform, he must allocate production and deliveries among his customers but may at his option include regular customers not then under contract as well as his own requirements for further manufacture. He may so allocate in any manner which is fair and reasonable.

(c) The seller must notify the buyer seasonably that there will be delay or non-delivery and, when allocation is required under paragraph (b), of the estimated quota thus made available for the buyer.

§ 2-616. *Procedure on Notice Claiming Excuse.*

(1) Where the buyer receives notification of a material or indefinite delay or an allocation justified under the preceding section he may by written notification to the seller as to any delivery concerned, and where the prospective deficiency substantially impairs the value of the whole contract under the provisions of this Article relating to breach of installment contracts (Section 2-612), then also as to the whole,

(a) terminate and thereby discharge any unexecuted portion of the contract; or

(b) modify the contract by agreeing to take his available quota in substitution.

(2) If after receipt of such notification from the seller the buyer fails so to modify the contract within a reasonable time not exceeding thirty days the contract lapses with respect to any deliveries affected.

(3) The provisions of this section may not be negated by agreement except in so far as the seller has assumed a greater obligation under the preceding section.

■ PART 7 Remedies

§ 2-701. *Remedies for Breach of Collateral Contracts Not Impaired.*

Remedies for breach of any obligation or promise collateral or ancillary to a contract for sale are not impaired by the provisions of this Article.

§ 2-702. *Seller's Remedies on Discovery of Buyer's Insolvency.*

(1) Where the seller discovers the buyer to be insolvent he may refuse delivery except for cash including payment for all

goods theretofore delivered under the contract, and stop delivery under this Article (Section 2-705).

(2) Where the seller discovers that the buyer has received goods on credit while insolvent he may reclaim the goods upon demand made within ten days after the receipt, but if misrepresentation of solvency has been made to the particular seller in writing within three months before delivery the ten day limitation does not apply. Except as provided in this subsection the seller may not base a right to reclaim goods on the buyer's fraudulent or innocent misrepresentation of solvency or of intent to pay.

(3) The seller's right to reclaim under subsection (2) is subject to the rights of a buyer in ordinary course or other good faith purchaser under this Article (Section 2-403). Successful reclamation of goods excludes all other remedies with respect to them.

§ 2-703. *Seller's Remedies in General.*

Where the buyer wrongfully rejects or revokes acceptance of goods or fails to make a payment due on or before delivery or repudiates with respect to a part or the whole, then with respect to any goods directly affected and, if the breach is of the whole contract (Section 2-612), then also with respect to the whole undelivered balance, the aggrieved seller may

(a) withhold delivery of such goods;

(b) stop delivery by any bailee as hereafter provided (Section 2-705);

(c) proceed under the next section respecting goods still unidentified to the contract;

(d) resell and recover damages as hereafter provided (Section 2-706);

(e) recover damages for non-acceptance (Section 2-708) or in a proper case the price (Section 2-709);

(f) cancel.

§ 2-704. *Seller's Right to Identify Goods to the Contract Notwithstanding Breach or to Salvage Unfinished Goods.*

(1) An aggrieved seller under the preceding section may

(a) identify to the contract conforming goods not already identified if at the time he learned of the breach they are in his possession or control;

(b) treat as the subject of resale goods which have demonstrably been intended for the particular contract even though those goods are unfinished.

(2) Where the goods are unfinished an aggrieved seller may in the exercise of reasonable commercial judgment for the purposes of avoiding loss and of effective realization either complete the manufacture and wholly identify the goods to the contract or cease manufacture and resell for scrap or salvage value or proceed in any other reasonable manner.

§ 2-705. *Seller's Stoppage of Delivery in Transit or Otherwise.*

(1) The seller may stop delivery of goods in the possession of a carrier or other bailee when he discovers the buyer to be insolvent (Section 2-702) and may stop delivery of carload, truckload, planeload or larger shipments of express or freight when the buyer repudiates or fails to make a payment due before delivery or if for any other reason the seller has a right to withhold or reclaim the goods.

(2) As against such buyer the seller may stop delivery until

(a) receipt of the goods by the buyer; or

(b) acknowledgment to the buyer by any bailee of the goods except a carrier that the bailee holds the goods for the buyer; or

(c) such acknowledgment to the buyer by a carrier by reshipment or as warehouseman; or

(d) negotiation to the buyer of any negotiable document of title covering the goods.

(3) (a) To stop delivery the seller must so notify as to enable the bailee by reasonable diligence to prevent delivery of the goods.

(b) After such notification the bailee must hold and deliver the goods according to the directions of the seller but the seller is liable to the bailee for any ensuing charges or damages.

(c) If a negotiable document of title has been issued for goods the bailee is not obliged to obey a notification to stop until surrender of the document.

(d) A carrier who has issued a non-negotiable bill of lading is not obliged to obey a notification to stop received from a person other than the consignor.

§ 2-706. *Seller's Resale Including Contract for Resale.*

(1) Under the conditions stated in Section 2-703 on seller's remedies, the seller may resell the goods concerned or the undelivered balance thereof. Where the resale is made in good faith and in a commercially reasonable manner the seller may recover the difference between the resale price and the contract price together with any incidental damages allowed under the provisions of this Article (Section 2-710), but less expenses saved in consequence of the buyer's breach.

(2) Except as otherwise provided in subsection (3) or unless otherwise agreed resale may be at public or private sale including sale by way of one or more contracts to sell or of identification to an existing contract of the seller. Sale may be as a unit or in parcels and at any time and place and on any terms but every aspect of the sale including the method, manner, time, place and terms must be commercially reasonable. The resale must be reasonably identified as referring to the broken contract, but it is not necessary that the goods be in existence or that any or all of them have been identified to the contract before the breach.

(3) Where the resale is at private sale the seller must give the buyer reasonable notification of his intention to resell.

(4) Where the resale is at public sale

(a) only identified goods can be sold except where there is a recognized market for a public sale of futures in goods of the kind; and

(b) it must be made at a usual place or market for public sale if one is reasonably available and except in the case of goods which are perishable or threaten to decline in value speedily the seller must give the buyer reasonable notice of the time and place of the resale; and

(c) if the goods are not to be within the view of those attending the sale the notification of sale must state the place where the goods are located and provide for their reasonable inspection by prospective bidders; and

(d) the seller may buy.

(5) A purchaser who buys in good faith at a resale takes the goods free of any rights of the original buyer even though the seller fails to comply with one or more of the requirements of this section.

(6) The seller is not accountable to the buyer for any profit made on any resale. A person in the position of a seller (Section 2-707) or a buyer who has rightfully rejected or justifiably revoked acceptance must account for any excess over the amount of his security interest, as hereinafter defined (subsection (3) of Section 2-711).

§ 2-707. *"Person in the Position of a Seller".*

(1) A "person in the position of a seller" includes as against a principal an agent who has paid or become responsible for the price of goods on behalf of his principal or anyone who otherwise holds a security interest or other right in goods similar to that of a seller.

(2) A person in the position of a seller may as provided in this Article withhold or stop delivery (Section 2-705) and resell (Section 2-706) and recover incidental damages (Section 2-710).

§ 2-708. Seller's Damages for Non-Acceptance or Repudiation.

(1) Subject to subsection (2) and to the provisions of this Article with respect to proof of market price (Section 2-723), the measure of damages for non-acceptance or repudiation by the buyer is the difference between the market price at the time and place for tender and the unpaid contract price together with any incidental damages provided in this Article (Section 2-710), but less expenses saved in consequence of the buyer's breach.

(2) If the measure of damages provided in subsection (1) is inadequate to put the seller in as good a position as performance would have done then the measure of damages is the profit (including reasonable overhead) which the seller would have made from full performance by the buyer, together with any incidental damages provided in this Article (Section 2-710), due allowance for costs reasonably incurred and due credit for payments or proceeds of resale.

§ 2-709. Action for the Price.

(1) When the buyer fails to pay the price as it becomes due the seller may recover, together with any incidental damages under the next section, the price

(a) of goods accepted or of conforming goods lost or damaged within a commercially reasonable time after risk of their loss has passed to the buyer; and

(b) of goods identified to the contract if the seller is unable after reasonable effort to resell them at a reasonable price or the circumstances reasonably indicate that such effort will be unavailing.

(2) Where the seller sues for the price he must hold for the buyer any goods which have been identified to the contract and are still in his control except that if resale becomes possible he may resell them at any time prior to the collection of the judgment. The net proceeds of any such resale must be credited to the buyer and payment of the judgment entitles him to any goods not resold.

(3) After the buyer has wrongfully rejected or revoked acceptance of the goods or has failed to make a payment due or has repudiated (Section 2-610), a seller who is held not entitled to the price under this section shall nevertheless be awarded damages for non-acceptance under the preceding section.

§ 2-710. Seller's Incidental Damages.

Incidental damages to an aggrieved seller include any commercially reasonable charges, expenses or commissions incurred in stopping delivery, in the transportation, care and custody of goods after the buyer's breach, in connection with return or resale of the goods or otherwise resulting from the breach.

§ 2-711. Buyer's Remedies in General; Buyer's Security Interest in Rejected Goods.

(1) Where the seller fails to make delivery or repudiates or the buyer rightfully rejects or justifiably revokes acceptance then with respect to any goods involved, and with respect to the whole if the breach goes to the whole contract (Section 2-612), the buyer may cancel and whether or not he has done so may in addition to recovering so much of the price as has been paid

(a) "cover" and have damages under the next section as to all the goods affected whether or not they have been identified to the contract; or

(b) recover damages for non-delivery as provided in this Article (Section 2-713).

(2) Where the seller fails to deliver or repudiates the buyer may also

(a) if the goods have been identified recover them as provided in this Article (Section 2-502); or

(b) in a proper case obtain specific performance or replevy the goods as provided in this Article (Section 2-716).

(3) On rightful rejection or justifiable revocation of acceptance a buyer has a security interest in goods in his possession or control for any payments made on their price and any expenses reasonably incurred in their inspection, receipt, transportation, care and custody and may hold such goods and resell them in like manner as an aggrieved seller (Section 2-706).

§ 2-712. "Cover"; Buyer's Procurement of Substitute Goods.

(1) After a breach within the preceding section the buyer may "cover" by making in good faith and without unreasonable delay any reasonable purchase of or contract to purchase goods in substitution for those due from the seller.

(2) The buyer may recover from the seller as damages the difference between the cost of cover and the contract price together with any incidental or consequential damages as hereinafter defined (Section 2-715), but less expenses saved in consequence of the seller's breach.

(3) Failure of the buyer to effect cover within this section does not bar him from any other remedy.

§ 2-713. Buyer's Damages for Non-Delivery or Repudiation.

(1) Subject to provisions of this Article with respect to the proof of market price (Section 2-723), the measure of damages for non-delivery or repudiation by the seller is the difference between the market price at the time when the buyer learned of the breach and the contract price together with any incidental and consequential damages provided in this Article (Section 2-715), but less expenses saved in consequence of the seller's breach.

(2) Market price is to be determined as of the place for tender or, in cases of rejection after arrival or revocation of acceptance, as of the place of arrival.

§ 2-714. Buyer's Damages for Breach in Regard to Accepted Goods.

(1) Where the buyer has accepted goods and given notification (subsection (3) of Section 2-607) he may recover as damages for any non-conformity of tender the loss resulting in the ordinary course of events from the seller's breach as determined in any manner which is reasonable.

(2) The measure of damages for breach of warranty is the difference at the time and place of acceptance between the value of the goods accepted and the value they would have had if they had been as warranted, unless special circumstances show proximate damages of a different amount.

(3) In a proper case any incidental and consequential damages under the next section may be recovered.

§ 2-715. Buyer's Incidental and Consequential Damages.

(1) Incidental damages resulting from the seller's breach include expenses reasonably incurred in inspection, receipt, transportation and care and custody of goods rightfully rejected, any commercially reasonable charges, expenses or commissions in connection with effecting cover and any other reasonable expense incident to the delay or other breach.

(2) Consequential damages resulting from the seller's breach include

(a) any loss resulting from general or particular requirements and needs of which the seller at the time of contracting had reason to know and which could not reasonably be prevented by cover or otherwise; and

(b) injury to person or property proximately resulting from any breach of warranty.

§ 2-716. Buyer's Right to Specific Performance or Replevin.

(1) Specific performance may be decreed where the goods are unique or in other proper circumstances.

(2) The decree for specific performance may include such terms and conditions as to payment of the price, damages, or other relief as the court may deem just.

(3) The buyer has a right of replevin for goods identified to the contract if after reasonable effort he is unable to effect cover for such goods or the circumstances reasonably indicate that such effort will be unavailing or if the goods have been shipped under reservation and satisfaction of the security interest in them has been made or tendered.

§ 2-717. Deduction of Damages From the Price.

The buyer on notifying the seller of his intention to do so may deduct all or any part of the damages resulting from any breach of the contract from any part of the price still due under the same contract.

§ 2-718. Liquidation or Limitation of Damages; Deposits

(1) Damages for breach by either party may be liquidated in the agreement but only at an amount which is reasonable in the light of the anticipated or actual harm caused by the breach, the difficulties of proof of loss, and the inconvenience or nonfeasibility of otherwise obtaining an adequate remedy. A term fixing unreasonably large liquidated damages is void as a penalty.

(2) Where the seller justifiably withholds delivery of goods because of the buyer's breach, the buyer is entitled to restitution of any amount by which the sum of his payments exceeds

(a) the amount to which the seller is entitled by virtue of terms liquidating the seller's damages in accordance with subsection (1), or

(b) in the absence of such terms, twenty per cent of the value of the total performance for which the buyer is obligated under the contract or $500, whichever is smaller.

(3) The buyer's right to restitution under subsection (2) is subject to offset to the extent that the seller establishes

(a) a right to recover damages under the provisions of this Article other than subsection (1), and

(b) the amount or value of any benefits received by the buyer directly or indirectly by reason of the contract.

(4) Where a seller has received payment in goods their reasonable value or the proceeds of their resale shall be treated as payments for the purposes of subsection (2); but if the seller has notice of the buyer's breach before reselling goods received in part performance, his resale is subject to the conditions laid down in this Article on resale by an aggrieved seller (Section 2-706).

§ 2-719. Contractual Modification or Limitation of Remedy.

(1) Subject to the provisions of subsection (2) and (3) of this section and of the preceding section on liquidation and limitation of damages,

(a) the agreement may provide for remedies in addition to or in substitution for those provided in this Article and may limit or alter the measure of damages recoverable under this Article, as by limiting the buyer's remedies to return of the goods and repayment of the price or to repair and replacement of non-conforming goods or parts; and

(b) resort to a remedy as provided is optional unless the remedy is expressly agreed to be exclusive, in which case it is the sole remedy.

(2) Where circumstances cause an exclusive or limited remedy to fail of its essential purpose, remedy may be had as provided in this Act.

(3) Consequential damages may be limited or excluded unless the limitation or exclusion is unconscionable. Limitation of consequential damages for injury to the person in the case of consumer goods is prima facie unconscionable but limitation of damages where the loss is commercial is not.

§ 2-720. Effect of "Cancellation" or "Rescission" on Claims for Antecedent Breach.

Unless the contrary intention clearly appears, expressions of "cancellation" or "rescission" of the contract or the like shall not be construed as a renunciation or discharge of any claim in damages for an antecedent breach.

§ 2-721. Remedies for Fraud.

Remedies for material misrepresentation or fraud include all remedies available under this Article for non-fraudulent breach. Neither rescission or a claim for rescission of the contract for sale nor rejection or return of the goods shall bar or be deemed inconsistent with a claim for damages or other remedy.

§ 2-722. Who Can Sue Third Parties for Injury to Goods.

Where a third party so deals with goods which have been identified to a contract for sale as to cause actionable injury to a party to that contract

(a) a right of action against the third party is in either party to the contract for sale who has title to or a security interest or a special property or an insurable interest in the goods; and if the goods have been destroyed or converted a right of action is also in the party who either bore the risk of loss under the contract for sale or has since the injury assumed that risk as against the other;

(b) if at the time of the injury the party plaintiff did not bear the risk of loss as against the other party to the contract for sale and there is no arrangement between them for disposition of the recovery, his suit or settlement is subject to his own interest, as a fiduciary for the other party to the contract;

(c) either party may with the consent of the other sue for the benefit of whom it may concern.

§ 2-723. Proof of Market Price: Time and Place.

(1) If an action based on anticipatory repudiation comes to trial before the time for performance with respect to some or all of the goods, any damages based on market price (Section 2-708 or Section 2-713) shall be determined according to the price of such goods prevailing at the time when the aggrieved party learned of the repudiation.

(2) If evidence of a price prevailing at the times or places described in this Article is not readily available the price prevailing within any reasonable time before or after the time described or at any other place which in commercial judgment or under usage of trade would serve as a reasonable substitute for the one described may be used, making any proper allowance for the cost of transporting the goods to or from such other place.

(3) Evidence of a relevant price prevailing at a time or place other than the one described in this Article offered by one party is not admissible unless and until he has given the other party such notice as the court finds sufficient to prevent unfair surprise.

§ 2-724. Admissibility of Market Quotations.

Whenever the prevailing price or value of any goods regularly bought and sold in any established commodity market is in issue, reports in official publications or trade journals or in newspapers or periodicals of general circulation published as the reports of such market shall be admissible in evidence. The circumstances of the preparation of such a report may be shown to affect its weight but not its admissibility.

§ 2-725. *Statute of Limitations in Contracts for Sale.*

(1)   An action for breach of any contract for sale must be commenced within four years after the cause of action has accrued. By the original agreement the parties may reduce the period of limitation to not less than one year but may not extend it.

(2)   A cause of action occurs when the breach occurs, regardless of the aggrieved party's lack of knowledge of the breach. A breach of warranty occurs when tender of delivery is made, except that where a warranty explicitly extends to future performance of the goods and discovery of the breach must await the time of such performance the cause of action accrues when the breach is or should have been discovered.

(3)   Where an action commenced within the time limited by subsection (1) is so terminated as to leave available a remedy by another action for the same breach such other action may be commenced after the expiration of the time limited and within six months after the termination of the first action unless the termination resulted from voluntary discontinuance or from dismissal for failure or neglect to prosecute.

(4)   This section does not alter the law on tolling of the statute of limitations nor does it apply to causes of action which have accrued before this Act becomes effective.

ARTICLE 2A
Leases

■ PART I   General Provisions

§ 2A-101. *Short Title.*

This Article shall be known and may be cited as the Uniform Commercial Code—Leases.

§ 2A-102. *Scope.*

This Article applies to any transaction, regardless of form, that creates a lease.

§ 2A-103. *Definitions and Index of Definitions.*

(1)   In this Article unless the context otherwise requires:

(a)   "Buyer in ordinary course of business" means a person who in good faith and without knowledge that the sale to him [or her] is in violation of the ownership rights or security interest or leasehold interest of a third party in the goods buys in ordinary course from a person in the business of selling goods of that kind but does not include a pawnbroker. "Buying" may be for cash or by exchange of other property or on secured or unsecured credit and includes receiving goods or documents of title under a pre-existing contract for sale but does not include a transfer in bulk or as security for or in total or partial satisfaction of a money debt.

(b)   "Cancellation" occurs when either party puts an end to the lease contract for default by the other party.

(c)   "Commercial unit" means such a unit of goods as by commercial usage is a single whole for purposes of lease and division of which materially impairs its character or value on the market or in use. A commercial unit may be a single article, as a machine, or a set of articles, as a suite of furniture or a line of machinery, or a quantity, as a gross or carload, or any other unit treated in use or in the relevant market as a single whole.

(d)   "Conforming" goods or performance under a lease contract means goods or performance that are in accordance with the obligations under the lease contract.

(e)   "Consumer lease" means a lease that a lessor regularly engaged in the business of leasing or selling makes to a lessee who is an individual and who takes under the lease primarily for a personal, family, or household purpose [, if the total payments to be made under the lease contract, excluding payments for options to renew or buy, do not exceed $].

(f)   "Fault" means wrongful act, omission, breach, or default.

(g)   "Finance lease" means a lease with respect to which:

(i)   the lessor does not select, manufacture, or supply the goods;

(ii)   the lessor acquires the goods or the right to possession and use of the goods in connection with the lease; and

(iii)   one of the following occurs:

(A)   the lessee receives a copy of the contract by which the lessor acquired the goods or the right to possession and use of the goods before signing the lease contract;

(B)   the lessee's approval of the contract by which the lessor acquired the goods or the right to possession and use of the goods is a condition to effectiveness of the lease contract;

(C)   the lessee, before signing the lease contract, receives an accurate and complete statement designating the promises and warranties, and any disclaimers of warranties, limitations or modifications of remedies, or liquidated damages, including those of a third party, such as the manufacturer of the goods, provided to the lessor by the person supplying the goods in connection with or as part of the contract by which the lessor acquired the goods or the right to possession and use of the goods; or

(D)   if the lease is not a consumer lease, the lessor, before the lessee signs the lease contract, informs the lessee in writing (a) of the identity of the person supplying the goods to the lessor, unless the lessee has selected that person and directed the lessor to acquire the goods or the right to possession and use of the goods from that person, (b) that the lessee is entitled under this Article to the promises and warranties, including those of any third party, provided to the lessor by the person supplying the goods in connection with or as part of the contract by which the lessor acquired the goods or the right to possession and use of the goods, and (c) that the lessee may communicate with the person supplying the goods to the lessor and receive an accurate and complete statement of those promises and warranties, including any disclaimers and limitations of them or of remedies.

(h)   "Goods" means all things that are movable at the time of identification to the lease contract, or are fixtures (Section 2A-309), but the term does not include money, documents, instruments, accounts, chattel paper, general intangibles, or minerals or the like, including oil and gas, before extraction. The term also includes the unborn young of animals.

(i) "Installment lease contract" means a lease contract that authorizes or requires the delivery of goods in separate lots to be separately accepted, even though the lease contract contains a clause "each delivery is a separate lease" or its equivalent.

(j) "Lease" means a transfer of the right to possession and use of goods for a term in return for consideration, but a sale, including a sale on approval or a sale or return, or retention or creation of a security interest is not a lease. Unless the context clearly indicates otherwise, the term includes a sublease.

(k) "Lease agreement" means the bargain, with respect to the lease, of the lessor and the lessee in fact as found in their language or by implication from other circumstances including course of dealing or usage of trade or course of performance as provided in this Article. Unless the context clearly indicates otherwise, the term includes a sublease agreement.

(l) "Lease contract" means the total legal obligation that results from the lease agreement as affected by this Article and any other applicable rules of law. Unless the context clearly indicates otherwise, the term includes a sublease contract.

(m) "Leasehold interest" means the interest of the lessor or the lessee under a lease contract.

(n) "Lessee" means a person who acquires the right to possession and use of goods under a lease. Unless the context clearly indicates otherwise, the term includes a sublessee.

(o) "Lessee in ordinary course of business" means a person who in good faith and without knowledge that the lease to him [or her] is in violation of the ownership rights or security interest or leasehold interest of a third party in the goods, leases in ordinary course from a person in the business of selling or leasing goods of that kind but does not include a pawnbroker. "Leasing" may be for cash or by exchange of other property or on secured or unsecured credit and includes receiving goods or documents of title under a pre-existing lease contract but does not include a transfer in bulk or as security for or in total or partial satisfaction of a money debt.

(p) "Lessor" means a person who transfers the right to possession and use of goods under a lease. Unless the context clearly indicates otherwise, the term includes a sublessor.

(q) "Lessor's residual interest" means the lessor's interest in the goods after expiration, termination, or cancellation of the lease contract.

(r) "Lien" means a charge against or interest in goods to secure payment of a debt or performance of an obligation, but the term does not include a security interest.

(s) "Lot" means a parcel or a single article that is the subject matter of a separate lease or delivery, whether or not it is sufficient to perform the lease contract.

(t) "Merchant lessee" means a lessee that is a merchant with respect to goods of the kind subject to the lease.

(u) "Present value" means the amount as of a date certain of one or more sums payable in the future, discounted to the date certain. The discount is determined by the interest rate specified by the parties if the rate was not manifestly unreasonable at the time the transaction was entered into; otherwise, the discount is determined by a commercially reasonable rate that takes into account the facts and circumstances of each case at the time the transaction was entered into.

(v) "Purchase" includes taking by sale, lease, mortgage, security interest, pledge, gift, or any other voluntary transaction creating an interest in goods.

(w) "Sublease" means a lease of goods the right to possession and use of which was acquired by the lessor as a lessee under an existing lease.

(x) "Supplier" means a person from whom a lessor buys or leases goods to be leased under a finance lease.

(y) "Supply contract" means a contract under which a lessor buys or leases goods to be leased.

(z) "Termination" occurs when either party pursuant to a power created by agreement or law puts an end to the lease contract otherwise than for default.

(2) Other definitions applying to this Article and the sections in which they appear are:

"Accessions". Section 2A-310(1).
"Construction mortgage". Section 2A-309(1)(d).
"Encumbrance". Section 2A-309(1)(e).
"Fixtures". Section 2A-309(1)(a).
"Fixture filing". Section 2A-309(1)(b).
"Purchase money lease". Section 2A-309(1)(c).

(3) The following definitions in other Articles apply to this Article:

"Account". Section 9-106.
"Between merchants". Section 2-104(3).
"Buyer". Section 2-103(1)(a).
"Chattel paper". Section 9-105(1)(b).
"Consumer goods". Section 9-109(1).
"Document". Section 9-105(1)(f).
"Entrusting". Section 2-403(3).
"General intangibles". Section 9-106.
"Good faith". Section 2-103(1)(b).
"Instrument". Section 9-105(1)(i).
"Merchant". Section 2-104(1).
"Mortgage". Sect 9-105(1)(j).
"Pursuant to commitment". Section 9-105(1)(k).
"Receipt". Section 2-103(1)(c).
"Sale". Section 2-106(1).
"Sale on approval". Section 2-326.
"Sale or return". Section 2-326.
"Seller". Section 2-103(1)(d).

(4) In addition Article 1 contains general definitions and principles of construction and interpretation applicable throughout this Article.

As amended in 1990.

§ 2A-104. Leases Subject to Other Law.

(1) A lease, although subject to this Article, is also subject to any applicable:

(a) certificate of title statute of this State: (list any certificate of title statutes covering automobiles, trailers, mobile homes, boats, farm tractors, and the like);

(b) certificate of title statute of another jurisdiction (Section 2A-105); or

(c) consumer protection statute of this State, or final consumer protection decision of a court of this State existing on the effective date of this Article.

(2) In case of conflict between this Article, other than Sections 2A-105, 2A-304(3), and 2A-305(3), and a statute or decision referred to in subsection (1), the statute or decision controls.

(3) Failure to comply with an applicable law has only the effect specified therein.

As amended in 1990.

§ 2A-105. Territorial Application of Article to Goods Covered by Certificate of Title.

Subject to the provisions of Sections 2A-304(3) and 2A-305(3), with respect to goods covered by a certificate of title issued under a statute of this State or of another jurisdiction, compliance and the effect of compliance or noncompliance with a certificate of title statute are governed by the law (including the conflict of laws rules) of the jurisdiction issuing the certificate until the earlier of (a) surrender of the certificate, or (b) four months after the goods are removed from that jurisdiction and thereafter until a new certificate of title is issued by another jurisdiction.

§ 2A-106. Limitation on Power of Parties to Consumer Lease to Choose Applicable Law and Judicial Forum.

(1) If the law chosen by the parties to a consumer lease is that of a jurisdiction other than a jurisdiction in which the lessee resides at the time the lease agreement becomes enforceable or within 30 days thereafter or in which the goods are to be used, the choice is not enforceable.

(2) If the judicial forum chosen by the parties to a consumer lease is a forum that would not otherwise have jurisdiction over the lessee, the choice is not enforceable.

§ 2A-107. Waiver or Renunciation of Claim or Right After Default.

Any claim or right arising out of an alleged default or breach of warranty may be discharged in whole or in part without consideration by a written waiver or renunciation signed and delivered by the aggrieved party.

§ 2A-108. Unconscionability.

(1) If the court as a matter of law finds a lease contract or any clause of a lease contract to have been unconscionable at the time it was made the court may refuse to enforce the lease contract, or it may enforce the remainder of the lease contract without the unconscionable clause, or it may so limit the application of any unconscionable clause as to avoid any unconscionable result.

(2) With respect to a consumer lease, if the court as a matter of law finds that a lease contract or any clause of a lease contract has been induced by unconscionable conduct or that unconscionable conduct has occurred in the collection of a claim arising from a lease contract, the court may grant appropriate relief.

(3) Before making a finding of unconscionability under subsection (1) or (2), the court, on its own motion or that of a party, shall afford the parties a reasonable opportunity to present evidence as to the setting, purpose, and effect of the lease contract or clause thereof, or of the conduct.

(4) In an action in which the lessee claims unconscionability with respect to a consumer lease:

(a) If the court finds unconscionability under subsection (1) or (2), the court shall award reasonable attorney's fees to the lessee.

(b) If the court does not find unconscionability and the lessee claiming unconscionability has brought or maintained an action he [or she] knew to be groundless, the court shall award reasonable attorney's fees to the party against whom the claim is made.

(c) In determining attorney's fees, the amount of the recovery on behalf of the claimant under subsections (1) and (2) is not controlling.

§ 2A-109. Option to Accelerate at Will.

(1) A term providing that one party or his [or her] successor in interest may accelerate payment or performance or require collateral or additional collateral "at will" or "when he [or she] deems himself [or herself] insecure" or in words of similar import must be construed to mean that he [or she] has power to do so only if he [or she] in good faith believes that the prospect of payment or performance is impaired.

(2) With respect to a consumer lease, the burden of establishing good faith under subsection (1) is on the party who exercised the power; otherwise the burden of establishing lack of good faith is on the party against whom the power has been exercised.

■ PART 2 Formation and Construction of Lease Contract

§ 2A-201. Statute of Frauds.

(1) A lease contract is not enforceable by way of action or defense unless:

(a) the total payments to be made under the lease contract, excluding payments for options to renew or buy, are less than $1,000; or

(b) there is a writing, signed by the party against whom enforcement is sought or by that party's authorized agent, sufficient to indicate that a lease contract has been made between the parties and to describe the goods leased and the lease term.

(2) Any description of leased goods or of the lease term is sufficient and satisfies subsection (1)(b), whether or not it is specific, if it reasonably identifies what is described.

(3) A writing is not insufficient because it omits or incorrectly states a term agreed upon, but the lease contract is not enforceable under subsection (1)(b) beyond the lease term and the quantity of goods shown in the writing.

(4) A lease contract that does not satisfy the requirements of subsection (1), but which is valid in other respects, is enforceable:

(a) if the goods are to be specially manufactured or obtained for the lessee and are not suitable for lease or sale to others in the ordinary course of the lessor's business, and the lessor, before notice of repudiation is received and under circumstances that reasonably indicate that the goods are for the lessee, has made either a substantial beginning of their manufacture or commitments for their procurement;

(b) if the party against whom enforcement is sought admits in that party's pleading, testimony or otherwise in court that a lease contract was made, but the lease contract is not enforceable under this provision beyond the quantity of goods admitted; or

(c) with respect to goods that have been received and accepted by the lessee.

(5) The lease term under a lease contract referred to in subsection (4) is:

(a) if there is a writing signed by the party against whom enforcement is sought or by that party's authorized agent specifying the lease term, the term so specified;

(b) if the party against whom enforcement is sought admits in that party's pleading, testimony, or otherwise in court a lease term, the term so admitted; or

(c) a reasonable lease term.

§ 2A-202. Final Written Expression: Parol or Extrinsic Evidence.

Terms with respect to which the confirmatory memoranda of the parties agree or which are otherwise set forth in a writing intended by the parties as a final expression of their agreement with respect to such terms as are included therein may not be contradicted by evidence of any prior agreement or of a contemporaneous oral agreement but may be explained or supplemented:

(a) by course of dealing or usage of trade or by course of performance; and

(b) by evidence of consistent additional terms unless the court finds the writing to have been intended also as a complete and exclusive statement of the terms of the agreement.

§ 2A-203. Seals Inoperative.

The affixing of a seal to a writing evidencing a lease contract or an offer to enter into a lease contract does not render the writing a sealed instrument and the law with respect to sealed instruments does not apply to the lease contract or offer.

§ 2A-204. Formation in General.

(1) A lease contract may be made in any manner sufficient to show agreement, including conduct by both parties which recognizes the existence of a lease contract.

(2) An agreement sufficient to constitute a lease contract may be found although the moment of its making is undetermined.

(3) Although one or more terms are left open, a lease contract does not fail for indefiniteness if the parties have intended to make a lease contract and there is a reasonably certain basis for giving an appropriate remedy.

§ 2A-205. Firm Offers.

An offer by a merchant to lease goods to or from another person in a signed writing that by its terms gives assurance it will be held open is not revocable, for lack of consideration, during the time stated or, if no time is stated, for a reasonable time, but in no event may the period of irrevocability exceed 3 months. Any such term of assurance on a form supplied by the offeree must be separately signed by the offeror.

§ 2A-206. Offer and Acceptance in Formation of Lease Contract.

(1) Unless otherwise unambiguously indicated by the language or circumstances, an offer to make a lease contract must be construed as inviting acceptance in any manner and by any medium reasonable in the circumstances.

(2) If the beginning of a requested performance is a reasonable mode of acceptance, an offeror who is not notified of acceptance within a reasonable time may treat the offer as having lapsed before acceptance.

§ 2A-207. Course of Performance or Practical Construction.

(1) If a lease contract involves repeated occasions for performance by either party with knowledge of the nature of the performance and opportunity for objection to it by the other, any course of performance accepted or acquiesced in without objection is relevant to determine the meaning of the lease agreement.

(2) The express terms of a lease agreement and any course of performance, as well as any course of dealing and usage of trade, must be construed whenever reasonable as consistent with each other; but if that construction is unreasonable, express terms control course of performance, course of performance controls both course of dealing and usage of trade, and course of dealing controls usage of trade.

(3) Subject to the provisions of Section 2A-208 on modification and waiver, course of performance is relevant to show a waiver or modification of any term inconsistent with the course of performance.

§ 2A-208. Modification, Rescission and Waiver.

(1) An agreement modifying a lease contract needs no consideration to be binding.

(2) A signed lease agreement that excludes modification or rescission except by a signed writing may not be otherwise modified or rescinded, but, except as between merchants, such a requirement on a form supplied by a merchant must be separately signed by the other party.

(3) Although an attempt at modification or rescission does not satisfy the requirements of subsection (2), it may operate as a waiver.

(4) A party who has made a waiver affecting an executory portion of a lease contract may retract the waiver by reasonable notification received by the other party that strict performance will be required of any term waived, unless the retraction would be unjust in view of a material change of position in reliance on the waiver.

§ 2A-209. Lessee Under Finance Lease as Beneficiary of Supply Contract.

(1) The benefit of a supplier's promises to the lessor under the supply contract and of all warranties, whether express or implied, including those of any third party provided in connection with or as part of the supply contract, extends to the lessee to the extent of the lessee's leasehold interest under a finance lease related to the supply contract, but is subject to the terms of the warranty and of the supply contract and all defenses or claims arising therefrom.

(2) The extension of the benefit of a supplier's promises and of warranties to the lessee (Section 2A-209(1)) does not: (i) modify the rights and obligations of the parties to the supply contract, whether arising therefrom or otherwise, or (ii) impose any duty or liability under the supply contract on the lessee.

(3) Any modification or rescission of the supply contract by the supplier and the lessor is effective between the supplier and the lessee unless, before the modification or rescission, the supplier has received notice that the lessee has entered into a finance lease related to the supply contract. If the modification or rescission is effective between the supplier and the lessee, the lessor is deemed to have assumed, in addition to the obligations of the lessor to the lessee under the lease contract, promises of the supplier to the lessor and warranties that were so modified or rescinded as they existed and were available to the lessee before modification or rescission.

(4) In addition to the extension of the benefit of the supplier's promises and of warranties to the lessee under subsection (1), the lessee retains all rights that the lessee may have against the supplier which arise from an agreement between the lessee and the supplier or under other law.

As amended in 1990.

§ 2A-210. Express Warranties.

(1) Express warranties by the lessor are created as follows:

(a) Any affirmation of fact or promise made by the lessor to the lessee which relates to the goods and becomes part of the basis of the bargain creates an express warranty that the goods will conform to the affirmation or promise.

(b) Any description of the goods which is made part of the basis of the bargain creates an express warranty that the goods will conform to the description.

(c) Any sample or model that is made part of the basis of the bargain creates an express warranty that the whole of the goods will conform to the sample or model.

(2) It is not necessary to the creation of an express warranty that the lessor use formal words, such as "warrant" or "guarantee," or that the lessor have a specific intention to make a warranty, but an affirmation merely of the value of the goods or a statement purporting to be merely the lessor's opinion or commendation of the goods does not create a warranty.

§ 2A-211. Warranties Against Interference and Against Infringement; Lessee's Obligation Against Infringement.

(1) There is in a lease contract a warranty that for the lease term no person holds a claim to or interest in the goods that arose from an act or omission of the lessor, other than a claim by way of infringement or the like, which will interfere with the lessee's enjoyment of its leasehold interest.

(2) Except in a finance lease there is in a lease contract by a lessor who is a merchant regularly dealing in goods of the kind a warranty that the goods are delivered free of the rightful claim of any person by way of infringement or the like.

(3) A lessee who furnishes specifications to a lessor or a supplier shall hold the lessor and the supplier harmless against any claim by way of infringement or the like that arises out of compliance with the specifications.

§ 2A-212. Implied Warranty of Merchantability.

(1) Except in a finance lease, a warranty that the goods will be merchantable is implied in a lease contract if the lessor is a merchant with respect to goods of that kind.

(2) Goods to be merchantable must be at least such as

    (a) pass without objection in the trade under the description in the lease agreement;

    (b) in the case of fungible goods, are of fair average quality within the description;

    (c) are fit for the ordinary purposes for which goods of that type are used;

    (d) run, within the variation permitted by the lease agreement, of even kind, quality, and quantity within each unit and among all units involved;

    (e) are adequately contained, packaged, and labeled as the lease agreement may require; and

    (f) conform to any promises or affirmations of fact made on the container or label.

(3) Other implied warranties may arise from course of dealing or usage of trade.

§ 2A-213. Implied Warranty of Fitness for Particular Purpose.

Except in a finance lease, if the lessor at the time the lease contract is made has reason to know of any particular purpose for which the goods are required and that the lessee is relying on the lessor's skill or judgment to select or furnish suitable goods, there is in the lease contract an implied warranty that the goods will be fit for that purpose.

§ 2A-214. Exclusion or Modification of Warranties.

(1) Words or conduct relevant to the creation of an express warranty and words or conduct tending to negate or limit a warranty must be construed wherever reasonable as consistent with each other; but, subject to the provisions of Section 2A-202 on parol or extrinsic evidence, negation or limitation is inoperative to the extent that the construction is unreasonable.

(2) Subject to subsection (3), to exclude or modify the implied warranty of merchantability or any part of it the language must mention "merchantability", be by a writing, and be conspicuous. Subject to subsection (3), to exclude or modify any implied warranty of fitness the exclusion must be by a writing and be conspicuous. Language to exclude all implied warranties of fitness is sufficient if it is in writing, is conspicuous and states, for example, "There is no warranty that the goods will be fit for a particular purpose".

(3) Notwithstanding subsection (2), but subject to subsection (4),

    (a) unless the circumstances indicate otherwise, all implied warranties are excluded by expressions like "as is," or "with all faults," or by other language that in common understanding calls the lessee's attention to the exclusion of warranties and makes plain that there is no implied warranty, if in writing and conspicuous;

    (b) if the lessee before entering into the lease contract has examined the goods or the sample or model as fully as desired or has refused to examine the goods, there is no implied warranty with regard to defects that an examination ought in the circumstances to have revealed; and

    (c) an implied warranty may also be excluded or modified by course of dealing, course of performance, or usage of trade.

(4) To exclude or modify a warranty against interference or against infringement (Section 2A-211) or any part of it, the language must be specific, be by a writing, and be conspicuous, unless the circumstances, including course of performance, course of dealing, or usage of trade, give the lessee reason to know that the goods are being leased subject to a claim or interest of any person.

§ 2A-215. Cumulation and Conflict of Warranties Express or Implied.

Warranties, whether express or implied, must be construed as consistent with each other and as cumulative, but if that construction is unreasonable, the intention of the parties determines which warranty is dominant. In ascertaining that intention the following rules apply:

    (a) Exact or technical specifications displace an inconsistent sample or model or general language of description.

    (b) A sample from an existing bulk displaces inconsistent general language of description.

    (c) Express warranties displace inconsistent implied warranties other than an implied warranty of fitness for a particular purpose.

§ 2A-216. Third-Party Beneficiaries of Express and Implied Warranties.

Alternative A A warranty to or for the benefit of a lessee under this Article, whether express or implied, extends to any natural person who is in the family or household of the lessee or who is a guest in the lessee's home if it is reasonable to expect that such person may use, consume, or be affected by the goods and who is injured in person by breach of the warranty. This section does not displace principles of law and equity that extend a warranty to or for the benefit of a lessee to other persons. The operation of this section may not be excluded, modified, or limited, but an exclusion, modification, or limitation of the warranty, including any with respect to rights and remedies, effective against the lessee is also effective against any beneficiary designated under this section.

Alternative B A warranty to or for the benefit of a lessee under this Article, whether express or implied, extends to any natural person who may reasonably be expected to use, consume, or be affected by the goods and who is injured in person by breach of the warranty. This section does not displace principles of law and equity that extend a warranty to or for the benefit of a lessee to other persons. The operation of this section may not be excluded, modified, or limited, but an exclusion, modification, or limitation of the warranty, including any with respect to rights and remedies, effective against the lessee is also effective against the beneficiary designated under this section.

Alternative C A warranty to or for the benefit of a lessee under this Article, whether express or implied, extends to any person who may reasonably be expected to use, consume, or be affected by the goods and who is injured by breach of the warranty. The operation of this section may not be excluded, modified, or limited with respect to injury to the person of an individual to whom the warranty extends, but an exclusion, modification, or limitation of the warranty, including any with respect to rights and remedies, effective against the lessee is also effective against the beneficiary designated under this section.

§ 2A-217. Identification.

Identification of goods as goods to which a lease contract refers may be made at any time and in any manner explicitly agreed to by the parties. In the absence of explicit agreement, identification occurs:

(a) when the lease contract is made if the lease contract is for a lease of goods that are existing and identified;

(b) when the goods are shipped, marked, or otherwise designated by the lessor as goods to which the lease contract refers, if the lease contract is for a lease of goods that are not existing and identified; or

(c) when the young are conceived, if the lease contract is for a lease of unborn young of animals.

§ 2A-218. Insurance and Proceeds.

(1) A lessee obtains an insurable interest when existing goods are identified to the lease contract even though the goods identified are nonconforming and the lessee has an option to reject them.

(2) If a lessee has an insurable interest only by reason of the lessor's identification of the goods, the lessor, until default or insolvency or notification to the lessee that identification is final, may substitute other goods for those identified.

(3) Notwithstanding a lessee's insurable interest under subsections (1) and (2), the lessor retains an insurable interest until an option to buy has been exercised by the lessee and risk of loss has passed to the lessee.

(4) Nothing in this section impairs any insurable interest recognized under any other statute or rule of law.

(5) The parties by agreement may determine that one or more parties have an obligation to obtain and pay for insurance covering the goods and by agreement may determine the beneficiary of the proceeds of the insurance.

§ 2A-219. Risk of Loss.

(1) Except in the case of a finance lease, risk of loss is retained by the lessor and does not pass to the lessee. In the case of a finance lease, risk of loss passes to the lessee.

(2) Subject to the provisions of this Article on the effect of default on risk of loss (Section 2A-220), if risk of loss is to pass to the lessee and the time of passage is not stated, the following rules apply:

(a) If the lease contract requires or authorizes the goods to be shipped by carrier

(i) and it does not require delivery at a particular destination, the risk of loss passes to the lessee when the goods are duly delivered to the carrier; but

(ii) if it does require delivery at a particular destination and the goods are there duly tendered while in the possession of the carrier, the risk of loss passes to the lessee when the goods are there duly so tendered as to enable the lessee to take delivery.

(b) If the goods are held by a bailee to be delivered without being moved, the risk of loss passes to the lessee on acknowledgment by the bailee of the lessee's right to possession of the goods.

(c) In any case not within subsection (a) or (b), the risk of loss passes to the lessee on the lessee's receipt of the goods if the lessor, or, in the case of a finance lease, the supplier, is a merchant; otherwise the risk passes to the lessee on tender of delivery.

§ 2A-220. Effect of Default on Risk of Loss.

(1) Where risk of loss is to pass to the lessee and the time of passage is not stated:

(a) If a tender or delivery of goods so fails to conform to the lease contract as to give a right of rejection, the risk of their loss remains with the lessor, or, in the case of a finance lease, the supplier, until cure or acceptance.

(b) If the lessee rightfully revokes acceptance, he [or she], to the extent of any deficiency in his [or her] effective insurance coverage, may treat the risk of loss as having remained with the lessor from the beginning.

(2) Whether or not risk of loss is to pass to the lessee, if the lessee as to conforming goods already identified to a lease contract repudiates or is otherwise in default under the lease contract, the lessor, or, in the case of a finance lease, the supplier, to the extent of any deficiency in his [or her] effective insurance coverage may treat the risk of loss as resting on the lessee for a commercially reasonable time.

§ 2A-221. Casualty to Identified Goods.

If a lease contract requires goods identified when the lease contract is made, and the goods suffer casualty without fault of the lessee, the lessor or the supplier before delivery, or the goods suffer casualty before risk of loss passes to the lessee pursuant to the lease agreement or Section 2A-219, then:

(a) if the loss is total, the lease contract is avoided; and

(b) if the loss is partial or the goods have so deteriorated as to no longer conform to the lease contract, the lessee may nevertheless demand inspection and at his [or her] option either treat the lease contract as avoided or, except in a finance lease that is not a consumer lease, accept the goods with due allowance from the rent payable for the balance of the lease term for the deterioration or the deficiency in quantity but without further right against the lessor.

■ PART 3 Effect of Lease Contract

§ 2A-301. Enforceability of Lease Contract.

Except as otherwise provided in this Article, a lease contract is effective and enforceable according to its terms between the parties, against purchasers of the goods and against creditors of the parties.

§ 2A-302. *Title to and Possession of Goods.*

Except as otherwise provided in this Article, each provision of this Article applies whether the lessor or a third party has title to the goods, and whether the lessor, the lessee, or a third party has possession of the goods, notwithstanding any statute or rule of law that possession or the absence of possession is fraudulent.

§ 2A-303. *Alienability of Party's Interest Under Lease Contract or of Lessor's Residual Interest in Goods; Delegation of Performance; Transfer of Rights.*

(1) As used in this section, "creation of a security interest" includes the sale of a lease contract that is subject to Article 9, Secured Transactions, by reason of Section 9-102(1)(b).

(2) Except as provided in subsections (3) and (4), a provision in a lease agreement which (i) prohibits the voluntary or involuntary transfer, including a transfer by sale, sublease, creation or enforcement of a security interest, or attachment, levy, or other judicial process, of an interest of a party under the lease contract or of the lessor's residual interest in the goods, or (ii) makes such a transfer an event of default, gives rise to the rights and remedies provided in subsection (5), but a transfer that is prohibited or is an event of default under the lease agreement is otherwise effective.

(3) A provision in a lease agreement which (i) prohibits the creation or enforcement of a security interest in an interest of a party under the lease contract or in the lessor's residual interest in the goods, or (ii) makes such a transfer an event of default, is not enforceable unless, and then only to the extent that, there is an actual transfer by the lessee of the lessee's right of possession or use of the goods in violation of the provision or an actual delegation of a material performance of either party to the lease contract in violation of the provision. Neither the granting nor the enforcement of a security interest in (i) the lessor's interest under the lease contract or (ii) the lessor's residual interest in the goods is a transfer that materially impairs the prospect of obtaining return performance by, materially changes the duty of, or materially increases the burden or risk imposed on, the lessee within the purview of subsection (5) unless, and then only to the extent that, there is an actual delegation of a material performance of the lessor.

(4) A provision in a lease agreement which (i) prohibits a transfer of a right to damages for default with respect to the whole lease contract or of a right to payment arising out of the transferor's due performance of the transferor's entire obligation, or (ii) makes such a transfer an event of default, is not enforceable, and such a transfer is not a transfer that materially impairs the prospect of obtaining return performance by, materially changes the duty of, or materially increases the burden or risk imposed on, the other party to the lease contract within the purview of subsection (5).

(5) Subject to subsections (3) and (4):

(a) if a transfer is made which is made an event of default under a lease agreement, the party to the lease contract not making the transfer, unless that party waives the default or otherwise agrees, has the rights and remedies described in Section 2A-501(2);

(b) if paragraph (a) is not applicable and if a transfer is made that (i) is prohibited under a lease agreement or (ii) materially impairs the prospect of obtaining return performance by, materially changes the duty of, or materially increases the burden or risk imposed on, the other party to the lease contract, unless the party not making the transfer agrees at any time to the transfer in the lease contract or otherwise, then, except as limited by contract, (i) the transferor is liable to the party not making the transfer for damages caused by the transfer to the extent that the damages could not reasonably be prevented by the party not making the transfer and (ii) a court having jurisdiction may grant other appropriate relief, including cancellation of the lease contract or an injunction against the transfer.

(6) A transfer of "the lease" or of "all my rights under the lease", or a transfer in similar general terms, is a transfer of rights and, unless the language or the circumstances, as in a transfer for security, indicate the contrary, the transfer is a delegation of duties by the transferor to the transferee. Acceptance by the transferee constitutes a promise by the transferee to perform those duties. The promise is enforceable by either the transferor or the other party to the lease contract.

(7) Unless otherwise agreed by the lessor and the lessee, a delegation of performance does not relieve the transferor as against the other party of any duty to perform or of any liability for default.

(8) In a consumer lease, to prohibit the transfer of an interest of a party under the lease contract or to make a transfer an event of default, the language must be specific, by a writing, and conspicuous.

As amended in 1990.

§ 2A-304. *Subsequent Lease of Goods by Lessor.*

(1) Subject to Section 2A-303, a subsequent lessee from a lessor of goods under an existing lease contract obtains, to the extent of the leasehold interest transferred, the leasehold interest in the goods that the lessor had or had power to transfer, and except as provided in subsection (2) and Section 2A-527(4), takes subject to the existing lease contract. A lessor with voidable title has power to transfer a good leasehold interest to a good faith subsequent lessee for value, but only to the extent set forth in the preceding sentence. If goods have been delivered under a transaction of purchase, the lessor has that power even though:

(a) the lessor's transferor was deceived as to the identity of the lessor;

(b) the delivery was in exchange for a check which is later dishonored;

(c) it was agreed that the transaction was to be a "cash sale"; or

(d) the delivery was procured through fraud punishable as larcenous under the criminal law.

(2) A subsequent lessee in the ordinary course of business from a lessor who is a merchant dealing in goods of that kind to whom the goods were entrusted by the existing lessee of that lessor before the interest of the subsequent lessee became enforceable against that lessor obtains, to the extent of the leasehold interest transferred, all of that lessor's and the existing lessee's rights to the goods, and takes free of the existing lease contract.

(3) A subsequent lessee from the lessor of goods that are subject to an existing lease contract and are covered by a certificate of title issued under a statute of this State or of another jurisdiction takes no greater rights than those provided both by this section and by the certificate of title statute.

As amended in 1990.

§ 2A-305. *Sale or Sublease of Goods by Lessee.*

(1) Subject to the provisions of Section 2A-303, a buyer or sublessee from the lessee of goods under an existing lease contract obtains, to the extent of the interest transferred, the leasehold interest in the goods that the lessee had or had power to transfer, and except as provided in subsection (2) and Section 2A-511(4), takes subject to the existing lease contract. A lessee with a voidable leasehold interest has power to transfer a good leasehold interest to a good faith buyer for value or a good faith sublessee for value, but only to the extent set forth in the preceding sentence. When goods have been delivered under a transaction of lease the lessee has that power even though:

(a)   the lessor was deceived as to the identity of the lessee;

(b)   the delivery was in exchange for a check which is later dishonored; or

(c)   the delivery was procured through fraud punishable as larcenous under the criminal law.

(2)   A buyer in the ordinary course of business or a sublessee in the ordinary course of business from a lessee who is a merchant dealing in goods of that kind to whom the goods were entrusted by the lessor obtains, to the extent of the interest transferred, all of the lessor's and lessee's rights to the goods, and takes free of the existing lease contract.

(3)   A buyer or sublessee from the lessee of goods that are subject to an existing lease contract and are covered by a certificate of title issued under a statute of this State or of another jurisdiction takes no greater rights than those provided both by this section and by the certificate of title statute.

§ 2A-306. Priority of Certain Liens Arising by Operation of Law.

If a person in the ordinary course of his [or her] business furnishes services or materials with respect to goods subject to a lease contract, a lien upon those goods in the possession of that person given by statute or rule of law for those materials or services takes priority over any interest of the lessor or lessee under the lease contract or this Article unless the lien is created by statute and the statute provides otherwise or unless the lien is created by rule of law and the rule of law provides otherwise.

§ 2A-307. Priority of Liens Arising by Attachment or Levy on, Security Interests in, and Other Claims to Goods.

(1)   Except as otherwise provided in Section 2A-306, a creditor of a lessee takes subject to the lease contract.

(2)   Except as otherwise provided in subsections (3) and (4) and in Sections 2A-306 and 2A-308, a creditor of a lessor takes subject to the lease contract unless:

(a)   the creditor holds a lien that attached to the goods before the lease contract became enforceable;

(b)   the creditor holds a security interest in the goods and the lessee did not give value and receive delivery of the goods without knowledge of the security interest; or

(c)   the creditor holds a security interest in the goods which was perfected (Section 9-303) before the lease contract became enforceable.

(3)   A lessee in the ordinary course of business takes the leasehold interest free of a security interest in the goods created by the lessor even though the security interest is perfected (Section 9-303) and the lessee knows of its existence.

(4)   A lessee other than a lessee in the ordinary course of business takes the leasehold interest free of a security interest to the extent that it secures future advances made after the secured party acquires knowledge of the lease or more than 45 days after the lease contract becomes enforceable, whichever first occurs, unless the future advances are made pursuant to a commitment entered into without knowledge of the lease and before the expiration of the 45-day period.

As amended in 1990.

§ 2A-308. Special Rights of Creditors.

(1)   A creditor of a lessor in possession of goods subject to a lease contract may treat the lease contract as void if as against the creditor retention of possession by the lessor is fraudulent under any statute or rule of law, but retention of possession in good faith and current course of trade by the lessor for a commercially reasonable time after the lease contract becomes enforceable is not fraudulent.

(2)   Nothing in this Article impairs the rights of creditors of a lessor if the lease contract (a) becomes enforceable, not in current course of trade but in satisfaction of or as security for a pre-existing claim for money, security, or the like, and (b) is made under circumstances which under any statute or rule of law apart from this Article would constitute the transaction a fraudulent transfer or voidable preference.

(3)   A creditor of a seller may treat a sale or an identification of goods to a contract for sale as void if as against the creditor retention of possession by the seller is fraudulent under any statute or rule of law, but retention of possession of the goods pursuant to a lease contract entered into by the seller as lessee and the buyer as lessor in connection with the sale or identification of the goods is not fraudulent if the buyer bought for value and in good faith.

§ 2A-309. Lessor's and Lessee's Rights When Goods Become Fixtures.

(1)   In this section:

(a)   goods are "fixtures" when they become so related to particular real estate that an interest in them arises under real estate law;

(b)   a "fixture filing" is the filing, in the office where a mortgage on the real estate would be filed or recorded, of a financing statement covering goods that are or are to become fixtures and conforming to the requirements of Section 9-402(5);

(c)   a lease is a "purchase money lease" unless the lessee has possession or use of the goods or the right to possession or use of the goods before the lease agreement is enforceable;

(d)   a mortgage is a "construction mortgage" to the extent it secures an obligation incurred for the construction of an improvement on land including the acquisition cost of the land, if the recorded writing so indicates; and

(e)   "encumbrance" includes real estate mortgages and other liens on real estate and all other rights in real estate that are not ownership interests.

(2)   Under this Article a lease may be of goods that are fixtures or may continue in goods that become fixtures, but no lease exists under this Article of ordinary building materials incorporated into an improvement on land.

(3)   This Article does not prevent creation of a lease of fixtures pursuant to real estate law.

(4)   The perfected interest of a lessor of fixtures has priority over a conflicting interest of an encumbrancer or owner of the real estate if:

(a)   the lease is a purchase money lease, the conflicting interest of the encumbrancer or owner arises before the goods become fixtures, the interest of the lessor is perfected by a fixture filing before the goods become fixtures or within ten days thereafter, and the lessee has an interest of record in the real estate or is in possession of the real estate; or

(b)   the interest of the lessor is perfected by a fixture filing before the interest of the encumbrancer or owner is of record, the lessor's interest has priority over any conflicting interest of a predecessor in title of the encumbrancer or owner, and the lessee has an interest of record in the real estate or is in possession of the real estate.

(5)   The interest of a lessor of fixtures, whether or not perfected, has priority over the conflicting interest of an encumbrancer or owner of the real estate if:

(a)   the fixtures are readily removable factory or office machines, readily removable equipment that is not primarily used or leased for use in the operation of the real estate, or readily removable replacements of domestic appliances that are goods subject to a consumer lease, and before the goods become fixtures the lease contract is enforceable; or

(b) the conflicting interest is a lien on the real estate obtained by legal or equitable proceedings after the lease contract is enforceable; or

(c) the encumbrancer or owner has consented in writing to the lease or has disclaimed an interest in the goods as fixtures; or

(d) the lessee has a right to remove the goods as against the encumbrancer or owner. If the lessee's right to remove terminates, the priority of the interest of the lessor continues for a reasonable time.

(6) Notwithstanding subsection (4)(a) but otherwise subject to subsections (4) and (5), the interest of a lessor of fixtures, including the lessor's residual interest, is subordinate to the conflicting interest of an encumbrancer of the real estate under a construction mortgage recorded before the goods become fixtures if the goods become fixtures before the completion of the construction. To the extent given to refinance a construction mortgage, the conflicting interest of an encumbrancer of the real estate under a mortgage has this priority to the same extent as the encumbrancer of the real estate under the construction mortgage.

(7) In cases not within the preceding subsections, priority between the interest of a lessor of fixtures, including the lessor's residual interest, and the conflicting interest of an encumbrancer or owner of the real estate who is not the lessee is determined by the priority rules governing conflicting interests in real estate.

(8) If the interest of a lessor of fixtures, including the lessor's residual interest, has priority over all conflicting interests of all owners and encumbrancers of the real estate, the lessor or the lessee may (i) on default, expiration, termination, or cancellation of the lease agreement but subject to the agreement and this Article, or (ii) if necessary to enforce other rights and remedies of the lessor or lessee under this Article, remove the goods from the real estate, free and clear of all conflicting interests of all owners and encumbrancers of the real estate, but the lessor or lessee must reimburse any encumbrancer or owner of the real estate who is not the lessee and who has not otherwise agreed for the cost of repair of any physical injury, but not for any diminution in value of the real estate caused by the absence of the goods removed or by any necessity of replacing them. A person entitled to reimbursement may refuse permission to remove until the party seeking removal gives adequate security for the performance of this obligation.

(9) Even though the lease agreement does not create a security interest, the interest of a lessor of fixtures, including the lessor's residual interest, is perfected by filing a financing statement as a fixture filing for leased goods that are or are to become fixtures in accordance with the relevant provisions of the Article on Secured Transactions (Article 9).

As amended in 1990.

§ 2A-310. Lessor's and Lessee's Rights When Goods Become Accessions.

(1) Goods are "accessions" when they are installed in or affixed to other goods.

(2) The interest of a lessor or a lessee under a lease contract entered into before the goods became accessions is superior to all interests in the whole except as stated in subsection (4).

(3) The interest of a lessor or a lessee under a lease contract entered into at the time or after the goods became accessions is superior to all subsequently acquired interests in the whole except as stated in subsection (4) but is subordinate to interests in the whole existing at the time the lease contract was made unless the holders of such interests in the whole have in writing consented to the lease or disclaimed an interest in the goods as part of the whole.

(4) The interest of a lessor or a lessee under a lease contract described in subsection (2) or (3) is subordinate to the interest of

(a) a buyer in the ordinary course of business or a lessee in the ordinary course of business of any interest in the whole acquired after the goods became accessions; or

(b) a creditor with a security interest in the whole perfected before the lease contract was made to the extent that the creditor makes subsequent advances without knowledge of the lease contract.

(5) When under subsections (2) or (3) and (4) a lessor or a lessee of accessions holds an interest that is superior to all interests in the whole, the lessor or the lessee may (a) on default, expiration, termination, or cancellation of the lease contract by the other party but subject to the provisions of the lease contract and this Article, or (b) if necessary to enforce his [or her] other rights and remedies under this Article, remove the goods from the whole, free and clear of all interests in the whole, but he [or she] must reimburse any holder of an interest in the whole who is not the lessee and who has not otherwise agreed for the cost of repair of any physical injury but not for any diminution in value of the whole caused by the absence of the goods removed or by any necessity for replacing them. A person entitled to reimbursement may refuse permission to remove until the party seeking removal gives adequate security for the performance of this obligation.

§ 2A-311. Priority Subject to Subordination.

Nothing in this Article prevents subordination by agreement by any person entitled to priority.

As added in 1990.

■ PART 4 Performance of Lease Contract: Repudiated, Substituted and Excused

§ 2A-401. Insecurity: Adequate Assurance of Performance.

(1) A lease contract imposes an obligation on each party that the other's expectation of receiving due performance will not be impaired.

(2) If reasonable grounds for insecurity arise with respect to the performance of either party, the insecure party may demand in writing adequate assurance of due performance. Until the insecure party receives that assurance, if commercially reasonable the insecure party may suspend any performance for which he [or she] has not already received the agreed return.

(3) A repudiation of the lease contract occurs if assurance of due performance adequate under the circumstances of the particular case is not provided to the insecure party within a reasonable time, not to exceed 30 days after receipt of a demand by the other party.

(4) Between merchants, the reasonableness of grounds for insecurity and the adequacy of any assurance offered must be determined according to commercial standards.

(5) Acceptance of any nonconforming delivery or payment does not prejudice the aggrieved party's right to demand adequate assurance of future performance.

§ 2A-402. Anticipatory Repudiation.

If either party repudiates a lease contract with respect to a performance not yet due under the lease contract, the loss of which performance will substantially impair the value of the lease contract to the other, the aggrieved party may:

(a) for a commercially reasonable time, await retraction of repudiation and performance by the repudiating party;

(b) make demand pursuant to Section 2A-401 and await assurance of future performance adequate under the circumstances of the particular case; or

(c) resort to any right or remedy upon default under the lease contract or this Article, even though the aggrieved party has notified the repudiating party that the aggrieved party would await the repudiating party's performance and assurance and has urged retraction. In addition, whether or not the aggrieved party is pursuing one of the foregoing remedies, the aggrieved party may suspend performance or, if the aggrieved party is the lessor, proceed in accordance with the provisions of this Article on the lessor's right to identify goods to the lease contract notwithstanding default or to salvage unfinished goods (Section 2A-524).

§ 2A-403. Retraction of Anticipatory Repudiation.

(1) Until the repudiating party's next performance is due, the repudiating party can retract the repudiation unless, since the repudiation, the aggrieved party has cancelled the lease contract or materially changed the aggrieved party's position or otherwise indicated that the aggrieved party considers the repudiation final.

(2) Retraction may be by any method that clearly indicates to the aggrieved party that the repudiating party intends to perform under the lease contract and includes any assurance demanded under Section 2A-401.

(3) Retraction reinstates a repudiating party's rights under a lease contract with due excuse and allowance to the aggrieved party for any delay occasioned by the repudiation.

§ 2A-404. Substituted Performance.

(1) If without fault of the lessee, the lessor and the supplier, the agreed berthing, loading, or unloading facilities fail or the agreed type of carrier becomes unavailable or the agreed manner of delivery otherwise becomes commercially impracticable, but a commercially reasonable substitute is available, the substitute performance must be tendered and accepted.

(2) If the agreed means or manner of payment fails because of domestic or foreign governmental regulation:

(a) the lessor may withhold or stop delivery or cause the supplier to withhold or stop delivery unless the lessee provides a means or manner of payment that is commercially a substantial equivalent; and

(b) if delivery has already been taken, payment by the means or in the manner provided by the regulation discharges the lessee's obligation unless the regulation is discriminatory, oppressive, or predatory.

§ 2A-405. Excused Performance.

Subject to Section 2A-404 on substituted performance, the following rules apply:

(a) Delay in delivery or nondelivery in whole or in part by a lessor or a supplier who complies with paragraphs (b) and (c) is not a default under the lease contract if performance as agreed has been made impracticable by the occurrence of a contingency the nonoccurrence of which was a basic assumption on which the lease contract was made or by compliance in good faith with any applicable foreign or domestic governmental regulation or order, whether or not the regulation or order later proves to be invalid.

(b) If the causes mentioned in paragraph (a) affect only part of the lessor's or the supplier's capacity to perform, he [or she] shall allocate production and deliveries among his [or her] customers but at his [or her] option may include regular customers not then under contract for sale or lease as well as his [or her] own requirements for further manufacture. He [or she] may so allocate in any manner that is fair and reasonable.

(c) The lessor seasonally shall notify the lessee and in the case of a finance lease the supplier seasonally shall notify the lessor and the lessee, if known, that there will be delay or nondelivery and, if allocation is required under paragraph (b), of the estimated quota thus made available for the lessee.

§ 2A-406. Procedure on Excused Performance.

(1) If the lessee receives notification of a material or indefinite delay or an allocation justified under Section 2A-405, the lessee may by written notification to the lessor as to any goods involved, and with respect to all of the goods if under an installment lease contract the value of the whole lease contract is substantially impaired (Section 2A-510):

(a) terminate the lease contract (Section 2A-505(2)); or

(b) except in a finance lease that is not a consumer lease, modify the lease contract by accepting the available quota in substitution, with due allowance from the rent payable for the balance of the lease term for the deficiency but without further right against the lessor.

(2) If, after receipt of a notification from the lessor under Section 2A-405, the lessee fails so to modify the lease agreement within a reasonable time not exceeding 30 days, the lease contract lapses with respect to any deliveries affected.

§ 2A-407. Irrevocable Promises: Finance Leases.

(1) In the case of a finance lease that is not a consumer lease the lessee's promises under the lease contract become irrevocable and independent upon the lessee's acceptance of the goods.

(2) A promise that has become irrevocable and independent under subsection (1):

(a) is effective and enforceable between the parties, and by or against third parties including assignees of the parties; and

(b) is not subject to cancellation, termination, modification, repudiation, excuse, or substitution without the consent of the party to whom the promise runs.

(3) This section does not affect the validity under any other law of a covenant in any lease contract making the lessee's promises irrevocable and independent upon the lessee's acceptance of the goods.

As amended in 1990.

■ PART 5 Default

A. In General
§ 2A-501. Default: Procedure.

(1) Whether the lessor or the lessee is in default under a lease contract is determined by the lease agreement and this Article.

(2) If the lessor or the lessee is in default under the lease contract, the party seeking enforcement has rights and remedies as provided in this Article and, except as limited by this Article, as provided in the lease agreement.

(3) If the lessor or the lessee is in default under the lease contract, the party seeking enforcement may reduce the party's claim to judgment, or otherwise enforce the lease contract by self-help or any available judicial procedure or nonjudicial procedure, including administrative proceeding, arbitration, or the like, in accordance with this Article.

(4) Except as otherwise provided in Section 1-106(1) or this Article or the lease agreement, the rights and remedies referred to in subsections (2) and (3) are cumulative.

(5) If the lease agreement covers both real property and goods, the party seeking enforcement may proceed under this Part as to the goods, or under other applicable law as to both the real property and the goods in accordance with that party's rights and remedies in respect of the real property, in which case this Part does not apply.

As amended in 1990.

§ 2A-502. Notice After Default.

Except as otherwise provided in this Article or the lease agreement, the lessor or lessee in default under the lease contract is not entitled to notice of default or notice of enforcement from the other party to the lease agreement.

§ 2A-503. Modification or Impairment of Rights and Remedies.

(1) Except as otherwise provided in this Article, the lease agreement may include rights and remedies for default in addition to or in substitution for those provided in this Article and may limit or alter the measure of damages recoverable under this Article.

(2) Resort to a remedy provided under this Article or in the lease agreement is optional unless the remedy is expressly agreed to be exclusive. If circumstances cause an exclusive or limited remedy to fail of its essential purpose, or provision for an exclusive remedy is unconscionable, remedy may be had as provided in this Article.

(3) Consequential damages may be liquidated under Section 2A-504, or may otherwise be limited, altered, or excluded unless the limitation, alteration, or exclusion is unconscionable. Limitation, alteration, or exclusion of consequential damages for injury to the person in the case of consumer goods is prima facie unconscionable but limitation, alteration, or exclusion of damages where the loss is commercial is not prima facie unconscionable.

(4) Rights and remedies on default by the lessor or the lessee with respect to any obligation or promise collateral or ancillary to the lease contract are not impaired by this Article.

As amended in 1990.

§ 2A-504. Liquidation of Damages.

(1) Damages payable by either party for default, or any other act or omission, including indemnity for loss or diminution of anticipated tax benefits or loss or damage to lessor's residual interest, may be liquidated in the lease agreement but only at an amount or by a formula that is reasonable in light of the then anticipated harm caused by the default or other act or omission.

(2) If the lease agreement provides for liquidation of damages, and such provision does not comply with subsection (1), or such provision is an exclusive or limited remedy that circumstances cause to fail of its essential purpose, remedy may be had as provided in this Article.

(3) If the lessor justifiably withholds or stops delivery of goods because of the lessee's default or insolvency (Section 2A-525 or 2A-526), the lessee is entitled to restitution of any amount by which the sum of his [or her] payments exceeds:

(a) the amount to which the lessor is entitled by virtue of terms liquidating the lessor's damages in accordance with subsection (1); or

(b) in the absence of those terms, 20 percent of the then present value of the total rent the lessee was obligated to pay for the balance of the lease term, or, in the case of a consumer lease, the lesser of such amount or $500.

(4) A lessee's right to restitution under subsection (3) is subject to offset to the extent the lessor establishes:

(a) a right to recover damages under the provisions of this Article other than subsection (1); and

(b) the amount or value of any benefits received by the lessee directly or indirectly by reason of the lease contract.

§ 2A-505. Cancellation and Termination and Effect of Cancellation, Termination, Rescission, or Fraud on Rights and Remedies.

(1) On cancellation of the lease contract, all obligations that are still executory on both sides are discharged, but any right based on prior default or performance survives, and the cancelling party also retains any remedy for default of the whole lease contract or any unperformed balance.

(2) On termination of the lease contract, all obligations that are still executory on both sides are discharged but any right based on prior default or performance survives.

(3) Unless the contrary intention clearly appears, expressions of "cancellation," "rescission," or the like of the lease contract may not be construed as a renunciation or discharge of any claim in damages for an antecedent default.

(4) Rights and remedies for material misrepresentation or fraud include all rights and remedies available under this Article for default.

(5) Neither rescission nor a claim for rescission of the lease contract nor rejection or return of the goods may bar or be deemed inconsistent with a claim for damages or other right or remedy.

§ 2A-506. Statute of Limitations.

(1) An action for default under a lease contract, including breach of warranty or indemnity, must be commenced within 4 years after the cause of action accrued. By the original lease contract the parties may reduce the period of limitation to not less than one year.

(2) A cause of action for default accrues when the act or omission on which the default or breach of warranty is based is or should have been discovered by the aggrieved party, or when the default occurs, whichever is later. A cause of action for indemnity accrues when the act or omission on which the claim for indemnity is based is or should have been discovered by the indemnified party, whichever is later.

(3) If an action commenced within the time limited by subsection (1) is so terminated as to leave available a remedy by another action for the same default or breach of warranty or indemnity, the other action may be commenced after the expiration of the time limited and within 6 months after the termination of the first action unless the termination resulted from voluntary discontinuance or from dismissal for failure or neglect to prosecute.

(4) This section does not alter the law on tolling of the statute of limitations nor does it apply to causes of action that have accrued before this Article becomes effective.

§ 2A-507. Proof of Market Rent: Time and Place.

(1) Damages based on market rent (Section 2A-519 or 2A-528) are determined according to the rent for the use of the goods concerned for a lease term identical to the remaining lease term of the original lease agreement and prevailing at the times specified in Sections 2A-519 and 2A-528.

(2) If evidence of rent for the use of the goods concerned for a lease term identical to the remaining lease term of the original lease agreement and prevailing at the times or places described in this Article is not readily available, the rent prevailing within any reasonable time before or after the time described or at any other place or for a different lease term which in commercial judgment or under usage of trade would serve as a reasonable substitute for the one described may be used, making any proper allowance for the difference, including the cost of transporting the goods to or from the other place.

(3) Evidence of a relevant rent prevailing at a time or place or for a lease term other than the one described in this Article offered by one party is not admissible unless and until he [or she] has given the other party notice the court finds sufficient to prevent unfair surprise.

(4) If the prevailing rent or value of any goods regularly leased in any established market is in issue, reports in official publications or trade journals or in newspapers or periodicals of general circulation published as the reports of that market are

admissible in evidence. The circumstances of the preparation of the report may be shown to affect its weight but not its admissibility.

As amended in 1990.

B. Default by Lessor
§ 2A-508. Lessee's Remedies.

(1) If a lessor fails to deliver the goods in conformity to the lease contract (Section 2A-509) or repudiates the lease contract (Section 2A-402), or a lessee rightfully rejects the goods (Section 2A-509) or justifiably revokes acceptance of the goods (Section 2A-517), then with respect to any goods involved, and with respect to all of the goods if under an installment lease contract the value of the whole lease contract is substantially impaired (Section 2A-510), the lessor is in default under the lease contract and the lessee may:

(a) cancel the lease contract (Section 2A-505(1));

(b) recover so much of the rent and security as has been paid and is just under the circumstances;

(c) cover and recover damages as to all goods affected whether or not they have been identified to the lease contract (Sections 2A-518 and 2A-520), or recover damages for nondelivery (Sections 2A-519 and 2A-520);

(d) exercise any other rights or pursue any other remedies provided in the lease contract.

(2) If a lessor fails to deliver the goods in conformity to the lease contract or repudiates the lease contract, the lessee may also:

(a) if the goods have been identified, recover them (Section 2A-522); or

(b) in a proper case, obtain specific performance or replevy the goods (Section 2A-521).

(3) If a lessor is otherwise in default under a lease contract, the lessee may exercise the rights and pursue the remedies provided in the lease contract, which may include a right to cancel the lease, and in Section 2A-519(3).

(4) If a lessor has breached a warranty, whether express or implied, the lessee may recover damages (Section 2A-519(4)).

(5) On rightful rejection or justifiable revocation of acceptance, a lessee has a security interest in goods in the lessee's possession or control for any rent and security that has been paid and any expenses reasonably incurred in their inspection, receipt, transportation, and care and custody and may hold those goods and dispose of them in good faith and in a commercially reasonable manner, subject to Section 2A-527(5).

(6) Subject to the provisions of Section 2A-407, a lessee, on notifying the lessor of the lessee's intention to do so, may deduct all or any part of the damages resulting from any default under the lease contract from any part of the rent still due under the same lease contract.

As amended in 1990.

§ 2A-509. Lessee's Rights on Improper Delivery; Rightful Rejection.

(1) Subject to the provisions of Section 2A-510 on default in installment lease contracts, if the goods or the tender or delivery fail in any respect to conform to the lease contract, the lessee may reject or accept the goods or accept any commercial unit or units and reject the rest of the goods.

(2) Rejection of goods is ineffective unless it is within a reasonable time after tender or delivery of the goods and the lessee seasonably notifies the lessor.

§ 2A-510. Installment Lease Contracts: Rejection and Default.

(1) Under an installment lease contract a lessee may reject any delivery that is nonconforming if the nonconformity substantially impairs the value of that delivery and cannot be cured or the nonconformity is a defect in the required documents; but if the nonconformity does not fall within subsection (2) and the lessor or the supplier gives adequate assurance of its cure, the lessee must accept that delivery.

(2) Whenever nonconformity or default with respect to one or more deliveries substantially impairs the value of the installment lease contract as a whole there is a default with respect to the whole. But, the aggrieved party reinstates the installment lease contract as a whole if the aggrieved party accepts a nonconforming delivery without seasonably notifying of cancellation or brings an action with respect only to past deliveries or demands performance as to future deliveries.

§ 2A-511. Merchant Lessee's Duties as to Rightfully Rejected Goods.

(1) Subject to any security interest of a lessee (Section 2A-508(5)), if a lessor or a supplier has no agent or place of business at the market of rejection, a merchant lessee, after rejection of goods in his [or her] possession or control, shall follow any reasonable instructions received from the lessor or the supplier with respect to the goods. In the absence of those instructions, a merchant lessee shall make reasonable efforts to sell, lease, or otherwise dispose of the goods for the lessor's account if they threaten to decline in value speedily. Instructions are not reasonable if on demand indemnity for expenses is not forthcoming.

(2) If a merchant lessee (subsection (1)) or any other lessee (Section 2A-512) disposes of goods, he [or she] is entitled to reimbursement either from the lessor or the supplier or out of the proceeds for reasonable expenses of caring for and disposing of the goods and, if the expenses include no disposition commission, to such commission as is usual in the trade, or if there is none, to a reasonable sum not exceeding 10 percent of the gross proceeds.

(3) In complying with this section or Section 2A-512, the lessee is held only to good faith. Good faith conduct hereunder is neither acceptance or conversion nor the basis of an action for damages.

(4) A purchaser who purchases in good faith from a lessee pursuant to this section or Section 2A-512 takes the goods free of any rights of the lessor and the supplier even though the lessee fails to comply with one or more of the requirements of this Article.

§ 2A-512. Lessee's Duties as to Rightfully Rejected Goods.

(1) Except as otherwise provided with respect to goods that threaten to decline in value speedily (Section 2A-511) and subject to any security interest of a lessee (Section 2A-508(5)):

(a) the lessee, after rejection of goods in the lessee's possession, shall hold them with reasonable care at the lessor's or the supplier's disposition for a reasonable time after the lessee's seasonable notification of rejection;

(b) if the lessor or the supplier gives no instructions within a reasonable time after notification of rejection, the lessee may store the rejected goods for the lessor's or the supplier's account or ship them to the lessor or the supplier or dispose of them for the lessor's or the supplier's account with reimbursement in the manner provided in Section 2A-511; but

(c) the lessee has no further obligations with regard to goods rightfully rejected.

(2) Action by the lessee pursuant to subsection (1) is not acceptance or conversion.

§ 2A-513. Cure by Lessor of Improper Tender or Delivery; Replacement.

(1) If any tender or delivery by the lessor or the supplier is rejected because nonconforming and the time for performance has not yet expired, the lessor or the supplier may seasonably

notify the lessee of the lessor's or the supplier's intention to cure and may then make a conforming delivery within the time provided in the lease contract.

(2) If the lessee rejects a nonconforming tender that the lessor or the supplier had reasonable grounds to believe would be acceptable with or without money allowance, the lessor or the supplier may have a further reasonable time to substitute a conforming tender if he [or she] seasonably notifies the lessee.

§ 2A-514. Waiver of Lessee's Objections.

(1) In rejecting goods, a lessee's failure to state a particular defect that is ascertainable by reasonable inspection precludes the lessee from relying on the defect to justify rejection or to establish default:

(a) if, stated seasonably, the lessor or the supplier could have cured it (Section 2A-513); or

(b) between merchants if the lessor or the supplier after rejection has made a request in writing for a full and final written statement of all defects on which the lessee proposes to rely.

(2) A lessee's failure to reserve rights when paying rent or other consideration against documents precludes recovery of the payment for defects apparent on the face of the documents.

§ 2A-515. Acceptance of Goods.

(1) Acceptance of goods occurs after the lessee has had a reasonable opportunity to inspect the goods and

(a) the lessee signifies or acts with respect to the goods in a manner that signifies to the lessor or the supplier that the goods are conforming or that the lessee will take or retain them in spite of their nonconformity; or

(b) the lessee fails to make an effective rejection of the goods (Section 2A-509(2)).

(2) Acceptance of a part of any commercial unit is acceptance of that entire unit.

§ 2A-516. Effect of Acceptance of Goods; Notice of Default; Burden of Establishing Default After Acceptance; Notice of Claim or Litigation to Person Answerable Over.

(1) A lessee must pay rent for any goods accepted in accordance with the lease contract, with due allowance for goods rightfully rejected or not delivered.

(2) A lessee's acceptance of goods precludes rejection of the goods accepted. In the case of a finance lease, if made with knowledge of a nonconformity, acceptance cannot be revoked because of it. In any other case, if made with knowledge of a nonconformity, acceptance cannot be revoked because of it unless the acceptance was on the reasonable assumption that the nonconformity would be seasonably cured. Acceptance does not of itself impair any other remedy provided by this Article or the lease agreement for nonconformity.

(3) If a tender has been accepted:

(a) within a reasonable time after the lessee discovers or should have discovered any default, the lessee shall notify the lessor and the supplier, if any, or be barred from any remedy against the party not notified;

(b) except in the case of a consumer lease, within a reasonable time after the lessee receives notice of litigation for infringement or the like (Section 2A-211) the lessee shall notify the lessor or be barred from any remedy over for liability established by the litigation; and

(c) the burden is on the lessee to establish any default.

(4) If a lessee is sued for breach of a warranty or other obligation for which a lessor or a supplier is answerable over the following apply:

(a) The lessee may give the lessor or the supplier, or both, written notice of the litigation. If the notice states that the person notified may come in and defend and that if the person notified does not do so that person will be bound in any action against that person by the lessee by any determination of fact common to the two litigations, then unless the person notified after seasonable receipt of the notice does come in and defend that person is so bound.

(b) The lessor or the supplier may demand in writing that the lessee turn over control of the litigation including settlement if the claim is one for infringement or the like (Section 2A-211) or else be barred from any remedy over. If the demand states that the lessor or the supplier agrees to bear all expense and to satisfy any adverse judgment, then unless the lessee after seasonable receipt of the demand does turn over control the lessee is so barred.

(5) Subsections (3) and (4) apply to any obligation of a lessee to hold the lessor or the supplier harmless against infringement or the like (Section 2A-211).

As amended in 1990.

§ 2A-517. Revocation of Acceptance of Goods.

(1) A lessee may revoke acceptance of a lot or commercial unit whose nonconformity substantially impairs its value to the lessee if the lessee has accepted it:

(a) except in the case of a finance lease, on the reasonable assumption that its nonconformity would be cured and it has not been seasonably cured; or

(b) without discovery of the nonconformity if the lessee's acceptance was reasonably induced either by the lessor's assurances or, except in the case of a finance lease, by the difficulty of discovery before acceptance.

(2) Except in the case of a finance lease that is not a consumer lease, a lessee may revoke acceptance of a lot or commercial unit if the lessor defaults under the lease contract and the default substantially impairs the value of that lot or commercial unit to the lessee.

(3) If the lease agreement so provides, the lessee may revoke acceptance of a lot or commercial unit because of other defaults by the lessor.

(4) Revocation of acceptance must occur within a reasonable time after the lessee discovers or should have discovered the ground for it and before any substantial change in condition of the goods which is not caused by the nonconformity. Revocation is not effective until the lessee notifies the lessor.

(5) A lessee who so revokes has the same rights and duties with regard to the goods involved as if the lessee had rejected them.

As amended in 1990.

§ 2A-518. Cover; Substitute Goods.

(1) After a default by a lessor under the lease contract of the type described in Section 2A-508(1), or, if agreed, after other default by the lessor, the lessee may cover by making any purchase or lease of or contract to purchase or lease goods in substitution for those due from the lessor.

(2) Except as otherwise provided with respect to damages liquidated in the lease agreement (Section 2A-504) or otherwise determined pursuant to agreement of the parties (Sections 1-102(3) and 2A-503), if a lessee's cover is by a lease agreement substantially similar to the original lease agreement and the new lease agreement is made in good faith and in a commercially reasonable manner, the lessee may recover from the lessor as damages (i) the present value, as of the date of the commencement of the term of the new lease agreement, of the rent under the new lease agreement applicable to that period of the new lease term which is comparable to the then remaining term of the original

lease agreement minus the present value as of the same date of the total rent for the then remaining lease term of the original lease agreement, and (ii) any incidental or consequential damages, less expenses saved in consequence of the lessor's default.

(3)   If a lessee's cover is by lease agreement that for any reason does not qualify for treatment under subsection (2), or is by purchase or otherwise, the lessee may recover from the lessor as if the lessee had elected not to cover and Section 2A-519 governs.

As amended in 1990.

§ 2A-519. Lessee's Damages for Non-delivery, Repudiation, Default, and Breach of Warranty in Regard to Accepted Goods.

(1)   Except as otherwise provided with respect to damages liquidated in the lease agreement (Section 2A-504) or otherwise determined pursuant to agreement of the parties (Sections 1-102(3) and 2A-503), if a lessee elects not to cover or a lessee elects to cover and the cover is by lease agreement that for any reason does not qualify for treatment under Section 2A-518(2), or is by purchase or otherwise, the measure of damages for non-delivery or repudiation by the lessor or for rejection or revocation of acceptance by the lessee is the present value, as of the date of the default, of the then market rent minus the present value as of the same date of the original rent, computed for the remaining lease term of the original lease agreement, together with incidental and consequential damages, less expenses saved in consequence of the lessor's default.

(2)   Market rent is to be determined as of the place for tender or, in cases of rejection after arrival or revocation of acceptance, as of the place of arrival.

(3)   Except as otherwise agreed, if the lessee has accepted goods and given notification (Section 2A-516(3)), the measure of damages for non-conforming tender or delivery or other default by a lessor is the loss resulting in the ordinary course of events from the lessor's default as determined in any manner that is reasonable together with incidental and consequential damages, less expenses saved in consequence of the lessor's default.

(4)   Except as otherwise agreed, the measure of damages for breach of warranty is the present value at the time and place of acceptance of the difference between the value of the use of the goods accepted and the value if they had been as warranted for the lease term, unless special circumstances show proximate damages of a different amount, together with incidental and consequential damages, less expenses saved in consequence of the lessor's default or breach of warranty.

As amended in 1990.

§ 2A-520. Lessee's Incidental and Consequential Damages.

(1)   Incidental damages resulting from a lessor's default include expenses reasonably incurred in inspection, receipt, transportation, and care and custody of goods rightfully rejected or goods the acceptance of which is justifiably revoked, any commercially reasonable charges, expenses or commissions in connection with effecting cover, and any other reasonable expense incident to the default.

(2)   Consequential damages resulting from a lessor's default include:

(a)   any loss resulting from general or particular requirements and needs of which the lessor at the time of contracting had reason to know and which could not reasonably be prevented by cover or otherwise; and

(b)   injury to person or property proximately resulting from any breach of warranty.

§ 2A-521. Lessee's Right to Specific Performance or Replevin.

(1)   Specific performance may be decreed if the goods are unique or in other proper circumstances.

(2)   A decree for specific performance may include any terms and conditions as to payment of the rent, damages, or other relief that the court deems just.

(3)   A lessee has a right of replevin, detinue, sequestration, claim and delivery, or the like for goods identified to the lease contract if after reasonable effort the lessee is unable to effect cover for those goods or the circumstances reasonably indicate that the effort will be unavailing.

§ 2A-522. Lessee's Right to Goods on Lessor's Insolvency.

(1)   Subject to subsection (2) and even though the goods have not been shipped, a lessee who has paid a part or all of the rent and security for goods identified to a lease contract (Section 2A-217) on making and keeping good a tender of any unpaid portion of the rent and security due under the lease contract may recover the goods identified from the lessor if the lessor becomes insolvent within 10 days after receipt of the first installment of rent and security.

(2)   A lessee acquires the right to recover goods identified to a lease contract only if they conform to the lease contract.

C.   Default by Lessee
§ 2A-523. Lessor's Remedies.

(1)   If a lessee wrongfully rejects or revokes acceptance of goods or fails to make a payment when due or repudiates with respect to a part or the whole, then, with respect to any goods involved, and with respect to all of the goods if under an installment lease contract the value of the whole lease contract is substantially impaired (Section 2A-510), the lessee is in default under the lease contract and the lessor may:

(a)   cancel the lease contract (Section 2A-505(1));

(b)   proceed respecting goods not identified to the lease contract (Section 2A-524);

(c)   withhold delivery of the goods and take possession of goods previously delivered (Section 2A-525);

(d)   stop delivery of the goods by any bailee (Section 2A-526);

(e)   dispose of the goods and recover damages (Section 2A-527), or retain the goods and recover damages (Section 2A-528), or in a proper case recover rent (Section 2A-529);

(f)   exercise any other rights or pursue any other remedies provided in the lease contract.

(2)   If a lessor does not fully exercise a right or obtain a remedy to which the lessor is entitled under subsection (1), the lessor may recover the loss resulting in the ordinary course of events from the lessee's default as determined in any reasonable manner, together with incidental damages, less expenses saved in consequence of the lessee's default.

(3)   If a lessee is otherwise in default under a lease contract, the lessor may exercise the rights and pursue the remedies provided in the lease contract, which may include a right to cancel the lease. In addition, unless otherwise provided in the lease contract:

(a)   if the default substantially impairs the value of the lease contract to the lessor, the lessor may exercise the rights and pursue the remedies provided in subsections (1) or (2); or

(b)   if the default does not substantially impair the value of the lease contract to the lessor, the lessor may recover as provided in subsection (2).

As amended in 1990.

§ 2A-524. Lessor's Right to Identify Goods to Lease Contract.

(1)   After default by the lessee under the lease contract of the type described in Section 2A-523(1) or 2A-523(3)(a) or, if agreed, after other default by the lessee, the lessor may:

(a)   identify to the lease contract conforming goods not already identified if at the time the lessor learned of the default they were in the lessor's or the supplier's possession or control; and

 (b) dispose of goods (Section 2A-527(1)) that demonstrably have been intended for the particular lease contract even though those goods are unfinished.

(2) If the goods are unfinished, in the exercise of reasonable commercial judgment for the purposes of avoiding loss and of effective realization, an aggrieved lessor or the supplier may either complete manufacture and wholly identify the goods to the lease contract or cease manufacture and lease, sell, or otherwise dispose of the goods for scrap or salvage value or proceed in any other reasonable manner.

As amended in 1990.

§ 2A-525. Lessor's Right to Possession of Goods.

(1) If a lessor discovers the lessee to be insolvent, the lessor may refuse to deliver the goods.

(2) After a default by the lessee under the lease contract of the type described in Section 2A-523(1) or 2A-523(3)(a) or, if agreed, after other default by the lessee, the lessor has the right to take possession of the goods. If the lease contract so provides, the lessor may require the lessee to assemble the goods and make them available to the lessor at a place to be designated by the lessor which is reasonably convenient to both parties. Without removal, the lessor may render unusable any goods employed in trade or business, and may dispose of goods on the lessee's premises (Section 2A-527).

(3) The lessor may proceed under subsection (2) without judicial process if it can be done without breach of the peace or the lessor may proceed by action.

As amended in 1990.

§ 2A-526. Lessor's Stoppage of Delivery in Transit or Otherwise.

(1) A lessor may stop delivery of goods in the possession of a carrier or other bailee if the lessor discovers the lessee to be insolvent and may stop delivery of carload, truckload, planeload, or larger shipments of express or freight if the lessee repudiates or fails to make a payment due before delivery, whether for rent, security or otherwise under the lease contract, or for any other reason the lessor has a right to withhold or take possession of the goods.

(2) In pursuing its remedies under subsection (1), the lessor may stop delivery until

 (a) receipt of the goods by the lessee;

 (b) acknowledgment to the lessee by any bailee of the goods, except a carrier, that the bailee holds the goods for the lessee; or

 (c) such an acknowledgment to the lessee by a carrier via reshipment or as warehouseman.

(3) (a) To stop delivery, a lessor shall so notify as to enable the bailee by reasonable diligence to prevent delivery of the goods.

 (b) After notification, the bailee shall hold and deliver the goods according to the directions of the lessor, but the lessor is liable to the bailee for any ensuing charges or damages.

 (c) A carrier who has issued a nonnegotiable bill of lading is not obliged to obey a notification to stop received from a person other than the consignor.

§ 2A-527. Lessor's Rights to Dispose of Goods.

(1) After a default by a lessee under the lease contract of the type described in Section 2A-523(1) or 2A-523(3)(a) or after the lessor refuses to deliver or takes possession of goods (Section 2A-525 or 2A-526), or, if agreed, after other default by a lessee, the lessor may dispose of the goods concerned or the undelivered balance thereof by lease, sale, or otherwise.

(2) Except as otherwise provided with respect to damages liquidated in the lease agreement (Section 2A-504) or otherwise determined pursuant to agreement of the parties (Sections 1-102(3) and 2A-503), if the disposition is by lease agreement substantially similar to the original lease agreement and the new lease agreement is made in good faith and in a commercially reasonable manner, the lessor may recover from the lessee as damages (i) accrued and unpaid rent as of the date of the commencement of the term of the new lease agreement, (ii) the present value, as of the same date, of the total rent for the then remaining lease term of the original lease agreement minus the present value, as of the same date, of the rent under the new lease agreement applicable to that period of the new lease term which is comparable to the then remaining term of the original lease agreement, and (iii) any incidental damages allowed under Section 2A-530, less expenses saved in consequence of the lessee's default.

(3) If the lessor's disposition is by lease agreement that for any reason does not qualify for treatment under subsection (2), or is by sale or otherwise, the lessor may recover from the lessee as if the lessor had elected not to dispose of the goods and Section 2A-528 governs.

(4) A subsequent buyer or lessee who buys or leases from the lessor in good faith for value as a result of a disposition under this section takes the goods free of the original lease contract and any rights of the original lessee even though the lessor fails to comply with one or more of the requirements of this Article.

(5) The lessor is not accountable to the lessee for any profit made on any disposition. A lessee who has rightfully rejected or justifiably revoked acceptance shall account to the lessor for any excess over the amount of the lessee's security interest (Section 2A-508(5)).

As amended in 1990.

§ 2A-528. Lessor's Damages for Non-acceptance, Failure to Pay, Repudiation, or Other Default.

(1) Except as otherwise provided with respect to damages liquidated in the lease agreement (Section 2A-504) or otherwise determined pursuant to agreement of the parties (Sections 1-102(3) and 2A-503), if a lessor elects to retain the goods or a lessor elects to dispose of the goods and the disposition is by lease agreement that for any reason does not qualify for treatment under Section 2A-527(2), or is by sale or otherwise, the lessor may recover from the lessee as damages for a default of the type described in Section 2A-523(1) or 2A-523(3)(a), or, if agreed, for other default of the lessee, (i) accrued and unpaid rent as of the date of default if the lessee has never taken possession of the goods, or, if the lessee has taken possession of the goods, as of the date the lessor repossesses the goods or an earlier date on which the lessee makes a tender of the goods to the lessor, (ii) the present value as of the date determined under clause (i) of the total rent for the then remaining lease term of the original lease agreement minus the present value as of the same date of the market rent at the place where the goods are located computed for the same lease term, and (iii) any incidental damages allowed under Section 2A-530, less expenses saved in consequence of the lessee's default.

(2) If the measure of damages provided in subsection (1) is inadequate to put a lessor in as good a position as performance would have, the measure of damages is the present value of the profit, including reasonable overhead, the lessor would have made from full performance by the lessee, together with any incidental damages allowed under Section 2A-530, due allowance for costs reasonably incurred and due credit for payments or proceeds of disposition.

As amended in 1990.

§ 2A-529. Lessor's Action for the Rent.

(1) After default by the lessee under the lease contract of the type described in Section 2A-523(1) or 2A-523(3)(a) or, if agreed, after other default by the lessee, if the lessor complies with subsection (2), the lessor may recover from the lessee as damages:

(a) for goods accepted by the lessee and not repossessed by or tendered to the lessor, and for conforming goods lost or damaged within a commercially reasonable time after risk of loss passes to the lessee (Section 2A-219), (i) accrued and unpaid rent as of the date of entry of judgment in favor of the lessor, (ii) the present value as of the same date of the rent for the then remaining lease term of the lease agreement, and (iii) any incidental damages allowed under Section 2A-530, less expenses saved in consequence of the lessee's default; and

(b) for goods identified to the lease contract if the lessor is unable after reasonable effort to dispose of them at a reasonable price or the circumstances reasonably indicate that effort will be unavailing, (i) accrued and unpaid rent as of the date of entry of judgment in favor of the lessor, (ii) the present value as of the same date of the rent for the then remaining lease term of the lease agreement, and (iii) any incidental damages allowed under Section 2A-530, less expenses saved in consequence of the lessee's default.

(2) Except as provided in subsection (3), the lessor shall hold for the lessee for the remaining lease term of the lease agreement any goods that have been identified to the lease contract and are in the lessor's control.

(3) The lessor may dispose of the goods at any time before collection of the judgment for damages obtained pursuant to subsection (1). If the disposition is before the end of the remaining lease term of the lease agreement, the lessor's recovery against the lessee for damages is governed by Section 2A-527 or Section 2A-528, and the lessor will cause an appropriate credit to be provided against a judgment for damages to the extent that the amount of the judgment exceeds the recovery available pursuant to Section 2A-527 or 2A-528.

(4) Payment of the judgment for damages obtained pursuant to subsection (1) entitles the lessee to the use and possession of the goods not then disposed of for the remaining lease term of and in accordance with the lease agreement.

(5) After default by the lessee under the lease contract of the type described in Section 2A-523(1) or Section 2A-523(3)(a) or, if agreed, after other default by the lessee, a lessor who is held not entitled to rent under this section must nevertheless be awarded damages for non-acceptance under Section 2A-527 or Section 2A-528.

As amended in 1990.

§ 2A-530. Lessor's Incidental Damages.

Incidental damages to an aggrieved lessor include any commercially reasonable charges, expenses, or commissions incurred in stopping delivery, in the transportation, care and custody of goods after the lessee's default, in connection with return or disposition of the goods, or otherwise resulting from the default.

§ 2A-531. Standing to Sue Third Parties for Injury to Goods.

(1) If a third party so deals with goods that have been identified to a lease contract as to cause actionable injury to a party to the lease contract (a) the lessor has a right of action against the third party, and (b) the lessee also has a right of action against the third party if the lessee:

(i) has a security interest in the goods;

(ii) has an insurable interest in the goods; or

(iii) bears the risk of loss under the lease contract or has since the injury assumed that risk as against the lessor and the goods have been converted or destroyed.

(2) If at the time of the injury the party plaintiff did not bear the risk of loss as against the other party to the lease contract and there is no arrangement between them for disposition of the recovery, his [or her] suit or settlement, subject to his [or her] own interest, is as a fiduciary for the other party to the lease contract.

(3) Either party with the consent of the other may sue for the benefit of whom it may concern.

§ 2A-532. Lessor's Rights to Residual Interest.

In addition to any other recovery permitted by this Article or other law, the lessor may recover from the lessee an amount that will fully compensate the lessor for any loss of or damage to the lessor's residual interest in the goods caused by the default of the lessee.

As added in 1990.

ARTICLE 3
Negotiable Instruments

■ PART I   General Provisions and Definitions

§ 3-101.   Short Title.

This Article may be cited as Uniform Commercial Code—Negotiable Instruments.

§ 3-102.   Subject Matter.

(a) This Article applies to negotiable instruments. It does not apply to money or to payment orders governed by Article 4A. A negotiable instrument that is also a certificated security under Section 8-102(1)(a) is subject to Article 8 and to this Article.

(b) In the event of conflict between the provisions of this Article and those of Article 4, Article 8, or Article 9, the provisions of Article 4, Article 8 and Article 9 prevail over those of this Article.

(c) Regulations of the Board of Governors of the Federal Reserve System and operating circulars of the Federal Reserve Banks supersede any inconsistent provision of this Article to the extent of the inconsistency.

§ 3-103.   Definitions.

(a) In this Article:

(1) "Acceptor" means a drawee that has accepted a draft.

(2) "Drawee" means a person ordered in a draft to make payment.

(3) "Drawer" means a person that signs a draft as a person ordering payment.

(4) "Good faith" means honesty in fact and the observance of reasonable commercial standards of fair dealing.

(5) "Maker" means a person that signs a note as promisor of payment.

(6) "Order" means a written instruction to pay money signed by the person giving the instruction. The instruction may be addressed to any person, including the person giving the instruction, or to one or more persons jointly or in the alternative but not in succession. An authorization to pay is not an order unless the person authorized to pay is also instructed to pay.

(7) "Ordinary care" in the case of a person engaged in business means observance of reasonable commercial standards, prevailing in the area in which that person is located, with respect to the business in which that person is engaged. In the case of a bank that takes an instrument for processing for collection or payment by automated means, reasonable

commercial standards do not require the bank to examine the instrument if the failure to examine does not violate the bank's prescribed procedures and the bank's procedures do not vary unreasonably from general banking usage not disapproved by this Article or Article 4.

(8) "Party" means party to an instrument.

(9) "Promise" means a written undertaking to pay money signed by the person undertaking to pay. An acknowledgment of an obligation by the obligor is not a promise unless the obligor also undertakes to pay the obligation.

(10) "Prove" with respect to a fact means to meet the burden of establishing the fact (Section 1-201(8)).

(11) "Remitter" means a person that purchases an instrument from its issuer if the instrument is payable to an identified person other than the purchaser.

(b) Other definitions applying to this Article and the sections in which they appear are:

"Acceptance" Section 3-409.
"Accommodated party" Section 3-419.
"Accommodation indorsement" Section 3-205.
"Accommodation party" Section 3-419.
"Alteration" Section 3-407.
"Blank indorsement" Section 3-205.
"Cashier's check" Section 3-104.
"Certificate of deposit" Section 3-104.
"Certified check" Section 3-409.
"Check" Section 3-104.
"Consideration" Section 3-303.
"Draft" Section 3-104.
"Fiduciary" Section 3-307.
"Guarantor" Section 3-417.
"Holder in due course" Section 3-302.
"Incomplete instrument" Section 3-115.
"Indorsement" Section 3-204.
"Indorser" Section 3-204.
"Instrument" Section 3-104.
"Issue" Section 3-105.
"Issuer" Section 3-105.
"Negotiable instrument" Section 3-104.
"Negotiation" Section 3-201.
"Note" Section 3-104.
"Payable at a definite time" Section 3-108.
"Payable on demand" Section 3-108.
"Payable to bearer" Section 3-109.
"Payable to order" Section 3-110.
"Payment" Section 3-603.
"Person entitled to enforce" Section 3-301.
"Presentment" Section 3-501.
"Reacquisition" Section 3-207.
"Represented person" Section 3-307.
"Special indorsement" Section 3-205.
"Teller's check" Section 3-104.
"Traveler's check" Section 3-104.
"Value" Section 3-303.

(c) The following definitions in other Articles apply to this Article:

"Bank" Section 4-105.
"Banking day" Section 4-104.
"Clearing house" Section 4-104.
"Collecting bank" Section 4-105.
"Customer" Section 4-104.
"Depositary bank" Section 4-105.
"Documentary draft" Section 4-104.
"Intermediary bank" Section 4-105.
"Item" Section 4-104.
"Midnight deadline" Section 4-104.
"Payor bank" Section 4-105.
"Suspends payments" Section 4-104.

(d) In addition, Article 1 contains general definitions and principles of construction and interpretation applicable throughout this Article.

§ 3-104. *Negotiable Instrument.*

(a) "Negotiable instrument" means an unconditional promise or order to pay a fixed amount of money, with or without interest or other charges described in the promise or order, if it:

(1) is payable to bearer or to order at the time it is issued or first comes into possession of a holder;

(2) is payable on demand or at a definite time; and

(3) does not state any other undertaking or instruction by the person promising or ordering payment to do any act in addition to the payment of money except that the promise or order may contain (i) an undertaking or power to give, maintain, or protect collateral to secure payment, (ii) an authorization or power to the holder to confess judgment or realize on or dispose of collateral, or (iii) a waiver of the benefit of any law intended for the advantage or protection of any obligor.

(b) "Instrument" means negotiable instrument.

(c) An order that meets all of the requirements of subsection (a) except subparagraph (1) and otherwise falls within the definition of "check" in subsection (f) is a negotiable instrument and a check.

(d) Notwithstanding subsection (a), a promise or order other than a check is not an instrument if, at the time it is issued or first comes into possession of a holder, it contains a conspicuous statement, however expressed, indicating that the writing is not an instrument governed by this Article.

(e) An instrument is a "note" if it is a promise, and is a "draft" if it is an order. If an instrument falls within the definition of both "note" and "draft," the person entitled to enforce the instrument may treat it as either.

(f) "Check" means (i) a draft, other than a documentary draft, payable on demand and drawn on a bank or (ii) a cashier's check or teller's check. An instrument may be a check even though it is described on its face by another term such as "money order."

(g) "Cashier's check" means a draft with respect to which the drawer and drawee are the same bank or branches of the same bank.

(h) "Teller's check" means a draft drawn by a bank (i) on another bank, or (ii) payable at or through a bank.

(i) "Traveler's check" means an instrument that (i) is payable on demand, (ii) is drawn on or payable at or through a bank, (iii) is designated by the term "traveler's check" or by a substantially similar term, and (iv) requires, as a condition to payment, a countersignature by a person whose specimen signature appears on the instrument.

(j) "Certificate of deposit" means an instrument containing an acknowledgment by a bank that a sum of money has been received by the bank, and a promise by the bank to repay the sum of money. A certificate of deposit is a note of the bank.

§ 3-105. *Issue of Instrument.*

(a) "Issue" means the first delivery of an instrument by the maker or drawer, whether to a holder or nonholder, for the purpose of giving rights on the instrument to any person.

(b) An unissued instrument, or an unissued incomplete instrument (Section 3-115) that is completed, is binding on the maker or drawer, but nonissuance is a defense. An instrument that is conditionally issued or is issued for a special purpose is binding on the maker or drawer, but failure of the condition or special purpose to be fulfilled is a defense.

(c) "Issuer" applies to issued and unissued instruments and means any person that signs an instrument as maker or drawer.

§ 3-106. *Unconditional Promise or Order.*

(a) Except as provided in subsections (b) and (c), for the purposes of Section 3-104(a), a promise or order is unconditional unless it states (i) an express condition to payment or (ii) that the promise or order is subject to or governed by another writing, or that rights or obligations with respect to the promise or order are stated in another writing; however, a mere reference to another writing does not make the promise or order conditional.

(b) A promise or order is not made conditional (i) by a reference to another writing for a statement of rights with respect to collateral, prepayment, or acceleration, or (ii) because payment is limited to resort to a particular fund or source.

(c) If a promise or order requires, as a condition to payment, a countersignature by a person whose specimen signature appears on the promise or order, the condition does not make the promise or order conditional for the purposes of Section 3-104(a). If the person whose specimen signature appears on an instrument fails to countersign the instrument, the failure to countersign is a defense to the obligation of the issuer, but the failure does not prevent a transferee of the instrument from becoming a holder of the instrument.

(d) If a promise or order at the time it is issued or first comes into possession of a holder contains a statement, required by applicable statutory or administrative law, to the effect that the rights of a holder or transferee are subject to claims or defenses that the issuer could assert against the original payee, the promise or order is not thereby made conditional for the purposes of Section 3-104(a), but there cannot be a holder in due course of the promise or order.

§ 3-107. *Instrument Payable in Foreign Money.*

Unless the instrument otherwise provides, an instrument that states the amount payable in foreign money may be paid in the foreign money or in an equivalent amount in dollars calculated by using the current bank-offered spot rate at the place of payment for the purchase of dollars on the day on which the instrument is paid.

§ 3-108. *Payable on Demand or at a Definite Time.*

(a) A promise or order is "payable on demand" if (i) it states that it is payable on demand or at sight, or otherwise indicates that it is payable at the will of the holder, or (ii) it does not state any time of payment.

(b) A promise or order is "payable at a definite time" if it is payable on elapse of a definite period of time after sight or acceptance or at a fixed date or dates or at a time or times readily ascertainable at the time the promise or order is issued, subject to rights of (i) prepayment, (ii) acceleration, or (iii) extension at the option of the holder or (iv) extension to a further definite time at the option of the maker or acceptor or automatically upon or after a specified act or event.

(c) If an instrument, payable at a fixed date, is also payable upon demand made before the fixed date, the instrument is payable on demand until the fixed date and, if demand for payment is not made before that date, becomes payable at a definite time on the fixed date.

§ 3-109. *Payable to Bearer or to Order.*

(a) A promise or order is payable to bearer if it:

(1) states that it is payable to bearer or to the order of bearer or otherwise indicates that the person in possession of the promise or order is entitled to payment,

(2) does not state a payee, or

(3) states that it is payable to or to the order of cash or otherwise indicates that it is not payable to an identified person.

(b) A promise or order that is not payable to bearer is payable to order if it is payable (i) to the order of an identified person or (ii) to an identified person or order. A promise or order that is payable to order is payable to the identified person.

(c) An instrument payable to bearer may become payable to an identified person if it is specially indorsed as stated in Section 3-205(a). An instrument payable to an identified person may become payable to bearer if it is indorsed in blank as stated in Section 3-205(b).

§ 3-110. *Identification of Person to Whom Instrument Is Payable.*

(a) A person to whom an instrument is payable is determined by the intent of the person, whether or not authorized, signing as, or in the name or behalf of, the maker or drawer. The instrument is payable to the person intended by the signer even if that person is identified in the instrument by a name or other identification that is not that of the intended person. If more than one person signs in the name or behalf of the maker or drawer and all the signers do not intend the same person as payee, the instrument is payable to any person intended by one or more of the signers.

(b) If the signature of the maker or drawer of an instrument is made by automated means such as a check-writing machine, the payee of the instrument is determined by the intent of the person who supplied the name or identification of the payee, whether or not authorized to do so.

(c) A person to whom an instrument is payable may be identified in any way including by name, identifying number, office, or account number. For the purpose of determining the holder of an instrument, the following rules apply:

(1) If an instrument is payable to an account and the account is identified only by number, the instrument is payable to the person to whom the account is payable. If an instrument is payable to an account identified by number and by the name of a person, the instrument is payable to the named person, whether or not that person is the owner of the account identified by number.

(2) If an instrument is payable to:

(i) a trust, estate, or a person described as trustee or representative of a trust or estate, the instrument is payable to the trustee, the representative, or a successor of either, whether or not the beneficiary or estate is also named;

(ii) a person described as agent or similar representative of a named or identified person, the instrument is payable either to the represented person, the representative, or a successor of the representative;

(iii) a fund or organization that is not a legal entity, the instrument is payable to a representative of the members of the fund or organization; or

(iv) an office or to a person described as holding an office, the instrument is payable to the named person, the incumbent of the office, or a successor to the incumbent.

(d) If an instrument is payable to two or more persons alternatively, it is payable to any of them and may be negotiated, discharged, or enforced by any of them in possession of the instrument. If an instrument is payable to two or more persons not alternatively, it is payable to all of them and may be negotiated, discharged, or enforced only by all of them. If an instrument payable to two or more persons is ambiguous as to whether it is payable to the persons alternatively, the instrument is payable to the persons alternatively.

§ 3-111. *Place of Payment.*

Except as otherwise provided for items in Article 4, an instrument is payable at the place of payment stated in the instrument. If no place of payment is stated, an instrument is payable at the address of the drawee or maker stated in the instrument. If no address is stated, the place of payment is the place of business of the drawee or maker. If a drawee or maker has more than one place of business, the place of payment is any place of business of the drawee or maker chosen by the person entitled to enforce the instrument. If the drawee or maker has no place of business, the place of payment is the residence of the drawee or maker.

§ 3-112. *Interest.*

(a) Unless otherwise provided in the instrument, (i) an instrument is not payable with interest, and (ii) interest on an interest-bearing instrument is payable from the date of the instrument.

(b) Interest may be stated in an instrument as a fixed or variable amount of money or it may be expressed as a fixed or variable rate or rates. The amount or rate of interest may be stated or described in the instrument in any manner and may require reference to information not contained in the instrument. If an instrument provides for interest but the amount of interest payable cannot be ascertained from the description, interest is payable at the judgment rate in effect at the place of payment of the instrument and at the time interest first accrues.

§ 3-113. *Date of Instrument.*

(a) An instrument may be antedated or postdated. The date stated determines the time of payment if the instrument is payable at a fixed period after date. Except as provided in Section 4-401(3), an instrument payable on demand is not payable before the date of the instrument.

(b) If an instrument is undated, its date is the date of its issue or, in the case of an unissued instrument, the date it first comes into possession of a holder.

§ 3-114. *Contradictory Terms of Instrument.*

If an instrument contains contradictory terms, typewritten terms prevail over printed terms, handwritten terms prevail over both, and words prevail over numbers.

§ 3-115. *Incomplete Instrument.*

(a) "Incomplete instrument" means a signed writing, whether or not issued by the signer, the contents of which show at the time of signing that it is incomplete but that the signer intended it to be completed by the addition of words or numbers.

(b) Subject to subsection (c), if an incomplete instrument is an instrument under Section 3-104, it may be enforced (i) according to its terms if it is not completed, or (ii) according to its terms as augmented by completion. If an incomplete instrument is not an instrument under Section 3-104 but, after completion, the requirements of Section 3-104 are met, the instrument may be enforced according to its terms as augmented by completion.

(c) If words or numbers are added to an incomplete instrument without authority of the signer, there is an alteration of the incomplete instrument governed by Section 3-407.

(d) The burden of establishing that words or numbers were added to an incomplete instrument without authority of the signer is on the person asserting the lack of authority.

§ 3-116. *Joint and Several Liability; Contribution.*

(a) Except as otherwise provided in the instrument, two or more persons who have the same liability on an instrument as makers, drawers, acceptors, indorsers who are indorsing joint payees, or anomalous indorsers, are jointly and severally liable in the capacity in which they sign.

(b) Except as provided in Section 3-417(e) or by agreement of the affected parties, a party with joint and several liability that pays the instrument is entitled to receive from any party with the same joint and several liability contribution in accordance with applicable law.

(c) Discharge of one party with joint and several liability by a person entitled to enforce the instrument does not affect the right under subsection (b) of a party with the same joint and several liability to receive contribution from the party discharged.

§ 3-117. *Other Agreements Affecting an Instrument.*

Subject to applicable law regarding exclusion of proof of contemporaneous or prior agreements, the obligation of a party to an instrument to pay the instrument may be modified, supplemented, or nullified by a separate agreement of the obligor and a person entitled to enforce the instrument if the instrument is issued or the obligation is incurred in reliance on the agreement or as part of the same transaction giving rise to the agreement. To the extent an obligation is modified, supplemented, or nullified by an agreement under this section, the agreement is a defense to the obligation.

§ 3-118. *Statute of Limitations.*

(a) Except as provided in subsection (e), an action to enforce the obligation of a party to pay a note payable at a definite time must be commenced within six years after the payment date or dates stated in the note or, if a payment date is accelerated, within six years after the accelerated payment date.

(b) Except as provided in subsection (d) or (e), if demand for payment is made to the maker of a note payable on demand, an action to enforce the obligation of a party to pay the note must be commenced within six years after the demand. If no demand for payment is made to the maker, an action to enforce the note is barred if neither principal nor interest on the note has been paid for a continuous period of 10 years.

(c) Except as provided in subsection (d), an action to enforce the obligation of a party to an unaccepted draft to pay the draft must be commenced within six years after dishonor of the draft or 10 years after the date of the draft, whichever period expires first.

(d) An action to enforce the obligation of the acceptor of a certified check or the issuer of a teller's check, cashier's check, or traveler's check must be commenced within six years after demand for payment is made to the acceptor or issuer, as the case may be.

(e) An action to enforce the obligation of a party to a certificate of deposit to pay the instrument must be commenced within six years after demand for payment is made to the maker, but if the instrument states a maturity date and the maker is not required to pay before that date, the six-year period begins when a demand for payment is in effect and the maturity date has passed.

(f) This subsection applies to an action to enforce the obligation of a party to pay an accepted draft, other than a certified check. If the obligation of the acceptor is payable at a definite time, the action must be commenced within six years after the payment date or dates stated in the draft or acceptance. If the obligation of the acceptor is payable on demand, the action must be commenced within six years after the date of the acceptance.

(g) Unless governed by other law regarding claims for indemnity or contribution, an action (i) for conversion of an instrument, for money had and received, or like action based on conversion, (ii) for breach of warranty, or (iii) to enforce an obligation, duty, or right arising under this Article and not governed by this section must be commenced within three years after the cause of action accrues.

§ 3-119. *Notice of Right to Defend Action.*

In an action for breach of an obligation for which a third person is answerable over pursuant to this Article or Article 4, the defendant may give the third person written notice of the litigation, and the person notified may then give similar notice to any other person who is answerable over. If the notice states (i) that the person notified may come in and defend and (ii) that failure to do so will bind the person notified in an action later brought by the person giving the notice as to any determination of fact common to the two litigations, the person notified is so bound unless after seasonable receipt of the notice the person notified does come in and defend.

■ PART 2 Negotiation, Transfer and Indorsement

§ 3-201. *Negotiation.*

(a) "Negotiation" means a transfer of possession, whether voluntary or involuntary, of an instrument to a person who thereby becomes its holder if possession is obtained from a person other than the issuer of the instrument.

(b) Except for a negotiation by a remitter, if an instrument is payable to an identified person, negotiation requires transfer of possession of the instrument and its indorsement by the holder. If an instrument is payable to bearer, it may be negotiated by transfer of possession alone.

§ 3-202. *Negotiation Subject to Rescission.*

(a) Negotiation is effective even if obtained (i) from an infant, a corporation exceeding its powers, or a person without capacity, or (ii) by fraud, duress, or mistake, or in breach of duty or as part of an illegal transaction.

(b) To the extent permitted by law, negotiation may be rescinded or may be subject to other remedies, but those remedies may not be asserted against a subsequent holder in due course or a person paying the instrument in good faith and without knowledge of facts that are a basis for rescission or other remedy.

§ 3-203. *Rights Acquired by Transfer.*

(a) An instrument is transferred when it is delivered by a person other than its issuer for the purpose of giving to the person receiving delivery the right to enforce the instrument.

(b) Transfer of an instrument, regardless of whether the transfer is a negotiation, vests in the transferee any right of the transferor to enforce the instrument, including any right as a holder in due course, but the transferee cannot acquire rights of a holder in due course by a transfer, directly or indirectly, from a holder in due course if the purchaser engaged in fraud or illegality affecting the instrument.

(c) Unless otherwise agreed, if an instrument is transferred for value and the transferee does not become a holder because of lack of indorsement by the transferor, the transferee has a specifically enforceable right to the unqualified indorsement of the transferor, but negotiation of the instrument does not occur until the indorsement is made.

(d) If a transferor purports to transfer less than the entire instrument, negotiation of the instrument does not occur. The transferee obtains no rights under this Article and has only the rights of a partial assignee.

§ 3-204. *Indorsement.*

(a) "Indorsement" means a signature, other than that of a maker, drawer, or acceptor, that alone or accompanied by other words, is made on an instrument for the purpose of (i) negotiating the instrument, (ii) restricting payment of the instrument, or (iii) incurring indorser's liability on the instrument, but regardless of the intent of the signer, a signature and its accompanying words is an indorsement unless the accompanying words, the terms of the instrument, the place of the signature, or other circumstances unambiguously indicate that the signature was made for a purpose other than indorsement. For the purpose of determining whether a signature is made on an instrument, a paper affixed to the instrument is a part of the instrument.

(b) "Indorser" means a person who makes an indorsement.

(c) For the purpose of determining whether the transferee of an instrument is a holder, an indorsement that transfers a security interest in the instrument is effective as an unqualified indorsement of the instrument.

(d) If an instrument is payable to a holder under a name that is not the name of the holder, indorsement may be made by the holder in the name stated in the instrument or in the holder's name or both, but signature in both names may be required by a person paying or taking the instrument for value or collection.

§ 3-205. *Special Indorsement; Blank Indorsement; Anomalous Indorsement.*

(a) If an indorsement is made by the holder of an instrument, whether payable to an identified person or payable to bearer, and the indorsement identifies a person to whom it makes the instrument payable, it is a "special indorsement." When specially indorsed, an instrument becomes payable to the identified person and may be negotiated only by the indorsement of that person. The principles stated in Section 3-110 apply to special indorsements.

(b) If an indorsement is made by the holder of an instrument and it is not a special indorsement, it is a "blank indorsement." When indorsed in blank, an instrument becomes payable to bearer and may be negotiated by transfer of possession alone until specially indorsed.

(c) The holder may convert a blank indorsement that consists only of a signature into a special indorsement by writing, above the signature of the indorser, words identifying the person to whom the instrument is made payable.

(d) "Anomalous indorsement" means an indorsement made by a person that is not the holder of the instrument. An anomalous indorsement does not affect the manner in which the instrument may be negotiated.

§ 3-206. *Restrictive Indorsement.*

(a) An indorsement limiting payment to a particular person or otherwise prohibiting further transfer or negotiation of the instrument is not effective to prevent further transfer or negotiation of the instrument.

(b) An indorsement stating a condition to the right of the indorsee to receive payment does not affect the right of the indorsee to enforce the instrument. A person paying the instrument or taking it for value or collection may disregard the condition, and the rights and liabilities of that person are not affected by whether the condition has been fulfilled.

(c) The following rules apply to an instrument bearing an indorsement (i) described in Section 4-201(2), or (ii) in blank or to a particular bank using the words "for deposit," "for collection," or other words indicating a purpose of having the instrument collected for the indorser or for a particular account:

(1) A person, other than a bank, that purchases the instrument when so indorsed converts the instrument unless the proceeds of the instrument are received by the indorser or are applied consistently with the indorsement.

(2) A depository bank that purchases the instrument or takes it for collection when so indorsed converts the

instrument unless the proceeds of the instrument are received by the indorser or applied consistently with the indorsement.

(3) A payor bank that is also the depositary bank or that takes the instrument for immediate payment over the counter from a person other than a collecting bank converts the instrument unless the proceeds of the instrument are received by the indorser or applied consistently with the indorsement.

(4) Except as otherwise provided in paragraph (3), a payor bank or intermediary bank may disregard the indorsement and is not liable if the proceeds of the instrument are not received by the indorser or applied consistently with the indorsement.

(d) Except for an indorsement covered by subsection (c), the following rules apply to an instrument bearing an indorsement using words to the effect that payment is to be made to the indorsee as agent, trustee, or other fiduciary for the benefit of the indorser or another person:

(1) Unless there is notice of breach of fiduciary duty as provided in Section 3-307, a person that purchases the instrument from the indorsee or takes the instrument from the indorsee for collection or payment may pay the proceeds of payment or the value given for the instrument to the indorsee without regard to whether the indorsee violates a fiduciary duty to the indorser.

(2) A later transferee of the instrument or person that pays the instrument is neither given notice nor otherwise affected by the restriction in the indorsement unless the transferee or payor knows that the fiduciary dealt with the instrument or its proceeds in breach of fiduciary duty.

(e) Purchase of an instrument bearing an indorsement to which this section applies does not prevent the purchaser from becoming a holder in due course of the instrument unless the purchaser is a converter under subsection (c).

(f) In an action to enforce the obligation of a party to pay the instrument, the obligor has a defense if payment would violate an indorsement to which this section applies and the payment is not permitted by this section.

§ 3-207. Reacquisition.

Reacquisition of an instrument occurs if it is transferred, by negotiation or otherwise, to a former holder. A former holder that reacquires the instrument may cancel indorsements made after the reacquirer first became a holder of the instrument. If the cancellation causes the instrument to be payable to the reacquirer or to bearer, the reacquirer may negotiate the instrument. An indorser whose indorsement is canceled is discharged, and the discharge is effective against any later holder.

■ PART 3 Enforcement of Instruments

§ 3-301. Person Entitled to Enforce Instrument.

"Person entitled to enforce" an instrument means (i) the holder of the instrument, (ii) a nonholder in possession of the instrument who has the rights of a holder, or (iii) a person not in possession of the instrument who is entitled to enforce the instrument pursuant to Section 3-309. A person may be a person entitled to enforce the instrument even though the person is not the owner of the instrument or is in wrongful possession of the instrument.

§ 3-302. Holder in Due Course.

(a) Subject to subsection (c) and Section 3-106(d), "holder in due course" means the holder of an instrument if:

(1) the instrument when issued or negotiated to the holder does not bear such apparent evidence of forgery or alteration or is not otherwise so irregular or incomplete as to call into question its authenticity, and

(2) the holder took the instrument (i) for value, (ii) in good faith, (iii) without notice that the instrument is overdue or has been dishonored or that there is an uncured default with respect to payment of another instrument issued as part of the same series, (iv) without notice that the instrument contains an unauthorized signature or has been altered, (v) without notice of any claim to the instrument stated in Section 3-306, and (vi) without notice that any party to the instrument has any defense or claim in recoupment stated in Section 3-305(a).

(b) Notice of discharge of a party to the instrument, other than discharge in an insolvency proceeding, is not notice of a defense under subsection (a), but discharge is effective against a person who became a holder in due course with notice of the discharge. Public filing or recording of a document does not of itself constitute notice of a defense, claim in recoupment, or claim to the instrument.

(c) Except to the extent a transferor or predecessor in interest has rights as a holder in due course, a person does not acquire rights of a holder in due course of an instrument taken (i) by legal process or by purchase at an execution, bankruptcy, or creditor's sale or similar proceeding, (ii) by purchase as part of a bulk transaction not in ordinary course of business of the transferor, or (iii) as the successor in interest to an estate or other organization.

(d) If, under Section 3-303(a)(1), the promise of performance that is the consideration for an instrument has been partially performed, the holder may assert rights as a holder in due course of the instrument only to the fraction of the amount payable under the instrument equal to the value of the partial performance divided by the value of the promised performance.

(e) If (i) the person entitled to enforce an instrument has only a security interest in the instrument and (ii) the person obliged to pay the instrument has a defense, claim in recoupment or claim to the instrument that may be asserted against the person who granted the security interest, the person entitled to enforce the instrument may assert rights as a holder in due course only to an amount payable under the instrument which, at the time of enforcement of the instrument, does not exceed the amount of the unpaid obligation secured.

(f) To be effective, notice must be received at such time and in such manner as to give a reasonable opportunity to act on it.

(g) This section is subject to any law limiting status as a holder in due course in particular classes of transactions.

§ 3-303. Value and Consideration.

(a) An instrument is issued or transferred for value if:

(1) the instrument is issued or transferred for a promise of performance, to the extent the promise has been performed;

(2) the transferee acquires a security interest or other lien in the instrument other than a lien obtained by judicial proceedings;

(3) the instrument is issued or transferred as payment of, or as security for, an existing obligation of any person, whether or not the obligation is due;

(4) the instrument is issued or transferred in exchange for a negotiable instrument; or

(5) the instrument is issued or transferred in exchange for the incurring of an irrevocable obligation to a third party by the person taking the instrument.

(b) "Consideration" means any consideration sufficient to support a simple contract. The drawer or maker of an instrument has a defense if the instrument is issued without consideration. If an instrument is issued for a promise of performance, the drawer or maker has a defense to the extent performance of the promise is due and the promise has not been performed. If an instrument is issued for value as stated in subsection (a), the instrument is also issued for consideration.

§ 3-304. *Overdue Instrument.*

(a) An instrument payable on demand becomes overdue at the earliest of the following times:

(1) on the day after the day demand for payment is duly made;

(2) if the instrument is a check, 90 days after its date; or

(3) if the instrument is not a check, when the instrument has been outstanding for a period of time after its date which is unreasonably long under the circumstances of the particular case in light of the nature of the instrument and trade usage.

(b) With respect to an instrument payable at a definite time the following rules apply: (1) If the principal is payable in installments and a due date has not been accelerated, the instrument becomes overdue upon default under the instrument for nonpayment of an installment, and the instrument remains overdue until the default is cured. (2) If the principal is not payable in installments and the due date has not been accelerated, the instrument becomes overdue on the day after the due date. (3) If a due date with respect to principal has been accelerated, the instrument becomes overdue on the day after the accelerated due date.

(c) Unless the due date of principal has been accelerated, an instrument does not become overdue if there is default in payment of interest but no default in payment of principal.

§ 3-305. *Defenses and Claims in Recoupment.*

(a) Except as stated in subsection (b), the right to enforce the obligation of a party to pay the instrument is subject to the following:

(1) A defense of the obligor based on (i) infancy of the obligor to the extent it is a defense to a simple contract, (ii) duress, lack of legal capacity, or illegality of the transaction that nullifies the obligation of the obligor, (iii) fraud that induced the obligor to sign the instrument with neither knowledge nor reasonable opportunity to learn of its character or its essential terms, or (iv) discharge of the obligor in insolvency proceedings.

(2) A defense of the obligor stated in another section of this Article or a defense of the obligor that would be available if the person entitled to enforce the instrument were enforcing a right to payment under a simple contract.

(3) A claim in recoupment of the obligor against the original payee of the instrument if the claim arose from the transaction that gave rise to the instrument. The claim of the obligor may be asserted against a transferee of the instrument only to reduce the amount owing on the instrument at the time the action is brought.

(b) The right of a holder in due course to enforce the obligation of a party to pay the instrument is subject to defenses of the obligor stated in subsection (a)(1), but is not subject to defenses of the obligor stated in subsection (a)(2) or claims in recoupment stated in subsection (a)(3) against a person other than the holder.

(c) Except as stated in subsection (d), in an action to enforce the obligation of a party to pay the instrument, the obligor may not assert against the person entitled to enforce the instrument a defense, claim in recoupment, or claim to the instrument (Section 3-306) of another person, but the other person's claim to the instrument may be asserted by the obligor if the other person is joined in the action and personally asserts the claim against the person entitled to enforce the instrument. An obligor is not obliged to pay the

instrument if the person seeking enforcement of the instrument does not have rights of a holder in due course and the obligor proves that the instrument is a lost or stolen instrument.

(d) In an action to enforce the obligation of an accommodation party to pay an instrument, the accommodation party may assert against the person entitled to enforce the instrument any defense or claim in recoupment under subsection (a) that the accommodated party could assert against the person entitled to enforce the instrument, except the defenses of discharge in insolvency proceedings, infancy, or lack of legal capacity.

§ 3-306. *Claims to an Instrument.*

A person taking an instrument, other than a person having rights of a holder in due course, is subject to a claim of a property or possessory right in the instrument or its proceeds, including a claim to rescind a negotiation and to recover the instrument or its proceeds. A person having rights of a holder in due course takes free of the claim to the instrument.

§ 3-307. *Notice of Breach of Fiduciary Duty.*

(a) This section applies if (i) an instrument is taken from a fiduciary for payment or collection or for value, (ii) the taker has knowledge of the fiduciary status of the fiduciary, and (iii) the represented person makes a claim to the instrument or its proceeds on the basis that the transaction of the fiduciary is a breach of fiduciary duty. Notice of breach of fiduciary duty by the fiduciary is notice of the claim of the represented person. "Fiduciary" means an agent, trustee, partner, corporation officer or director, or other representative owing a fiduciary duty with respect to the instrument. "Represented person" means the principal, beneficiary, partnership, corporation, or other person to whom the duty is owed.

(b) If the instrument is payable to the fiduciary, as such, or to the represented person, the taker has notice of the breach of fiduciary duty if the instrument is (i) taken in payment of or as security for a debt known by the taker to be the personal debt of the fiduciary, (ii) taken in a transaction known by the taker to be for the personal benefit of the fiduciary, or (iii) deposited to an account other than an account of the fiduciary, as such, or an account of the represented person.

(c) If the instrument is made or drawn by the fiduciary, as such, payable to the fiduciary personally, the taker does not have notice of the breach of fiduciary duty unless the taker knows of the breach of fiduciary duty.

(d) If the instrument is made or drawn by or on behalf of the represented person to the taker as payee, the taker has notice of the breach of fiduciary duty if the instrument is (i) taken in payment of or as security for a debt known by the taker to be the personal debt of the fiduciary, (ii) taken in a transaction known by the taker to be for the personal benefit of the fiduciary, or (iii) deposited to an account other than an account of the fiduciary, as such, or an account of the represented person.

§ 3-308. *Proof of Signatures and Status as Holder in Due Course.*

(a) In an action with respect to an instrument, the authenticity of, and authority to make, each signature on the instrument is admitted unless specifically denied in the pleadings. If the validity of a signature is denied in the pleadings, the burden of establishing validity is on the person claiming validity, but the signature is presumed to be authentic and authorized unless the action is to enforce the liability of the purported signer and the signer is dead or incompetent at the time of trial of the issue of validity of the signature. If an action to enforce the instrument is brought against a person as the undisclosed principal of a person who signed the instrument as a party to the instrument, the plaintiff has the burden of establishing that the defendant is liable on the instrument as a represented person pursuant to Section 3-402(a).

(b) If the validity of signatures is admitted or proved and there is compliance with subsection (a), a plaintiff producing the instrument is entitled to payment if the plaintiff proves entitlement to enforce the instrument under Section 3-301, unless the defendant proves a defense or claim in recoupment. If a defense or claim in recoupment is proved, the right to payment of the plaintiff is subject to the defense or claim except to the extent the plaintiff proves that the plaintiff has rights of a holder in due course which are not subject to the defense or claim.

§ 3-309.   *Enforcement of Lost, Destroyed, or Stolen Instrument.*

(a) A person not in possession of an instrument is entitled to enforce the instrument if (i) that person was in rightful possession of the instrument and entitled to enforce it when loss of possession occurred, (ii) the loss of possession was not the result of a voluntary transfer by that person or a lawful seizure, and (iii) that person cannot reasonably obtain possession of the instrument because the instrument was destroyed, its whereabouts cannot be determined, or it is in the wrongful possession of an unknown person or a person that cannot be found or is not amenable to service of process.

(b) A person seeking enforcement of an instrument pursuant to subsection (a) must prove the terms of the instrument and the person's right to enforce the instrument. If that proof is made, Section 3-308 applies to the case as though the person seeking enforcement had produced the instrument. The court may not enter judgment in favor of the person seeking enforcement unless it finds that the person required to pay the instrument is adequately protected against loss that might occur by reason of a claim by another person to enforce the instrument. Adequate protection may be provided by any reasonable means.

§ 3-310.   *Effect of Instrument on Obligation for Which Taken.*

(a) Unless otherwise agreed, if a certified check, cashier's check, or teller's check is taken for an obligation, the obligation is discharged to the same extent discharge would result if an amount of money equal to the amount of the instrument were taken in payment of the obligation. Discharge of the obligation does not affect any liability that the obligor may have as an indorser of the instrument.

(b) Unless otherwise agreed and except as provided in subsection (a), if a note or an uncertified check is taken for an obligation, the obligation is suspended to the same extent the obligation would be discharged if an amount of money equal to the amount of the instrument were taken.

(1) In the case of an uncertified check, suspension of the obligation continues until dishonor of the check or until it is paid or certified. Payment or certification of the check results in discharge of the obligation to the extent of the amount of the check.

(2) In the case of a note, suspension of the obligation continues until dishonor of the note or until it is paid. Payment of the note results in discharge of the obligation to the extent of the payment.

(3) If the check or note is dishonored and the obligee of the obligation for which the instrument was taken has possession of the instrument, the obligee may enforce either the instrument or the obligation. In the case of an instrument of a third person which is negotiated to the obligee by the obligor, discharge of the obligor on the instrument also discharges the obligation.

(4) If the person entitled to enforce the instrument taken for an obligation is a person other than the obligee, the obligee may not enforce the obligation to the extent the obligation is suspended. If the obligee is the person entitled to enforce the instrument but no longer has possession of it because it was lost, stolen, or destroyed, the obligation may not be enforced to the extent of the amount payable on the instrument, and to that extent the obligee's rights against the obligor are limited to enforcement of the instrument.

(c) If an instrument other than one described in subsection (a) or (b) is taken for an obligation, the effect is (i) that stated in subsection (a) if the instrument is one on which a bank is liable as maker or acceptor, or (ii) that stated in subsection (b) in any other case.

§ 3-311.   *Accord and Satisfaction by Use of Instrument.*

(a) This section applies if a person against whom a claim is asserted proves that (i) that person in good faith tendered an instrument to the claimant as full satisfaction of the claim, (ii) the amount of the claim was unliquidated or subject to a bona fide dispute, and (iii) the claimant obtained payment of the instrument.

(b) Unless subsection (c) applies, the claim is discharged if the person against whom the claim is asserted proves that the instrument or an accompanying written communication contained a conspicuous statement to the effect that the instrument was tendered as full satisfaction of the claim.

(c) Subject to subsection (d), a claim is not discharged under subsection (b) if the claimant is an organization and proves that within a reasonable time before the tender, the claimant sent a conspicuous statement to the person against whom the claim is asserted that communications concerning disputed debts, including an instrument tendered as full satisfaction of a debt, are to be sent to a designated person, office or place, and the instrument or accompanying communication was not received by that designated person, office, or place.

(d) Notwithstanding subsection (c), a claim is discharged under subsection (b) if the person against whom the claim is asserted proves that within a reasonable time before collection of the instrument was initiated, an agent of the claimant having direct responsibility with respect to the disputed obligation knew that the instrument was tendered in full satisfaction of the claim, or received the instrument and any accompanying written communication.

■ PART 4   Liability of Parties

§ 3-401.   *Signature.*

(a) A person is not liable on an instrument unless (i) the person signed the instrument, or (ii) the person is represented by an agent or representative who signed the instrument and the signature is binding on the represented person under Section 3-402.

(b) A signature may be made (i) manually or by means of a device or machine, and (ii) by the use of any name, including any trade or assumed name, or by any word, mark, or symbol executed or adopted by a person with present intention to authenticate a writing.

§ 3-402.   *Signature by Representative.*

(a) If a person acting, or purporting to act, as a representative signs an instrument by signing either the name of the represented person or the name of the signer, the represented person is bound by the signature to the same extent the represented person would be bound if the signature were on a simple contract. If the represented person is bound, the signature of the representative is the "authorized signature of the represented person" and the represented person is liable on the instrument, whether or not identified in the instrument.

(b)   If a representative signs the name of the representative to an instrument and that signature is an authorized signature of the represented person, the following rules apply:

(1)   If the form of the signature shows unambiguously that the signature is made on behalf of the represented person who is identified in the instrument, the representative is not liable on the instrument.

(2)   Subject to subsection (c), if (i) the form of the signature does not show unambiguously that the signature is made in a representative capacity or (ii) the represented person is not identified in the instrument, the representative is liable on the instrument to a holder in due course that took the instrument without notice that the representative was not intended to be liable on the instrument. With respect to any other person, the representative is liable on the instrument unless the representative proves that the original parties to the instrument did not intend the representative to be liable on the instrument.

(c)   If a representative signs the name of the representative as drawer of a check without indication of the representative status and the check is payable from an account of the represented person who is identified on the check, the signer is not liable on the check if the signature is an authorized signature of the represented person.

§ 3-403.   *Unauthorized Signature.*

(a)   Except as otherwise provided in this Article, an unauthorized signature is ineffective except as the signature of the unauthorized signer in favor of a person who in good faith pays the instrument or takes it for value. An unauthorized signature may be ratified for all purposes of this Article.

(b)   If the signature of more than one person is required to constitute the authorized signature of an organization, the signature of the organization is unauthorized if one of the required signatures is missing.

(c)   The civil or criminal liability of a person who makes an unauthorized signature is not affected by any provision of this Article that makes the unauthorized signature effective for the purposes of this Article.

§ 3-404.   *Impostors; Fictitious Payees.*

(a)   If an impostor by use of the mails or otherwise induces the maker or drawer of an instrument to issue the instrument to the impostor, or to a person acting in concert with the impostor, by impersonating the payee of the instrument or a person authorized to act for the payee, an indorsement of the instrument by any person in the name of the payee is effective as the indorsement of the payee in favor of any person that in good faith pays the instrument or takes it for value or for collection.

(b)   If (i) a person whose intent determines to whom an instrument is payable (Section 3-110(a) or (b)) does not intend the person identified as payee to have any interest in the instrument, or (ii) the person identified as payee of the instrument is a fictitious person, the following rules apply until the instrument is negotiated by special indorsement:

(1)   Any person in possession of the instrument is its holder.

(2)   An indorsement by any person in the name of the payee stated in the instrument is effective as the indorsement of the payee in favor of any person that in good faith pays the instrument or takes it for value or for collection.

(c)   Under subsection (a) or (b) an indorsement is made in the name of a payee if (i) it is made in a name substantially similar to that of the payee or (ii) the instrument, whether or not indorsed, is deposited in a depositary bank to an account in a name substantially similar to that of the payee.

(d)   With respect to an instrument to which subsection (a) or (b) applies, if a person paying the instrument or taking it for value or for collection fails to exercise ordinary care in paying or taking the instrument and that failure substantially contributes to loss resulting from payment of the instrument, the person bearing the loss may recover from the person failing to exercise ordinary care to the extent the failure to exercise ordinary care contributed to the loss.

§ 3-405.   *Employer Responsibility for Fraudulent Indorsement by Employee.*

(a)   This section applies to fraudulent indorsements of instruments with respect to which an employer has entrusted an employee with responsibility as part of the employee's duties. The following definitions apply to this section:

(1)   "Employee" includes, in addition to an employee of an employer, an independent contractor and employee of an independent contractor retained by the employer.

(2)   "Fraudulent indorsement" means (i) in the case of an instrument payable to the employer, a forged indorsement purporting to be that of the employer, or (ii) in the case of an instrument with respect to which the employer is drawer or maker, a forged indorsement purporting to be that of the person identified as payee.

(3)   "Responsibility" with respect to instruments means authority (i) to sign or indorse instruments on behalf of the employer, (ii) to process instruments received by the employer for bookkeeping purposes, for deposit to an account, or for other disposition, (iii) to prepare or process instruments for issue in the name of the employer, (iv) to supply information determining the names or addresses of payees of instruments to be issued in the name of the employer, (v) to control the disposition of instruments to be issued in the name of the employer, or (vi) to otherwise act with respect to instruments in a responsible capacity. "Responsibility" does not include the assignment of duties that merely allow an employee to have access to instruments or blank or incomplete instrument forms that are being stored or transported or are part of incoming or outgoing mail, or similar access.

(b)   For the purpose of determining the rights and liabilities of a person who, in good faith, pays an instrument or takes it for value or for collection, if an employee entrusted with responsibility with respect to the instrument or a person acting in concert with the employee makes a fraudulent indorsement to the instrument, the indorsement is effective as the indorsement of the person to whom the instrument is payable if it is made in the name of that person. If the person paying the instrument or taking it for value or for collection fails to exercise ordinary care in paying or taking the instrument and that failure substantially contributes to loss resulting from the fraud, the person bearing the loss may recover from the person failing to exercise ordinary care to the extent the failure to exercise ordinary care contributed to the loss.

(c)   Under subsection (b) an indorsement is made in the name of the person to whom an instrument is payable if (i) it is made in a name substantially similar to the name of that person or (ii) the instrument, whether or not indorsed, is deposited in a depositary bank to an account in a name substantially similar to the name of that person.

§ 3-406.   *Negligence Contributing to Forged Signature or Alteration of Instrument.*

(a)   A person whose failure to exercise ordinary care substantially contributes to an alteration of an instrument or to the making of a forged signature on an instrument is precluded from asserting the alteration or the forgery against a person that, in good faith, pays the instrument or takes it for value.

(b) If the person asserting the preclusion fails to exercise ordinary care in paying or taking the instrument and that failure substantially contributes to loss, the loss is allocated between the person precluded and the person asserting the preclusion according to the extent to which the failure of each to exercise ordinary care contributed to the loss.

(c) Under subsection (a) the burden of proving failure to exercise ordinary care is on the person asserting the preclusion. Under subsection (b) the burden of proving failure to exercise ordinary care is on the person precluded.

§ 3-407. *Alteration.*

(a) "Alteration" means (i) an unauthorized change in an instrument that purports to modify in any respect the obligation of a party to the instrument, or (ii) an unauthorized addition of words or numbers or other change to an incomplete instrument relating to the obligation of any party to the instrument.

(b) Except as provided in subsection (c), an alteration fraudulently made by the holder discharges any party to whose obligation the alteration applies unless that party assents or is precluded from asserting the alteration. No other alteration discharges any party, and the instrument may be enforced according to its original terms.

(c) If an instrument that has been fraudulently altered is acquired by a person having rights of a holder in due course, it may be enforced by that person according to its original terms. If an incomplete instrument is completed and is then acquired by a person having rights of a holder in due course, it may be enforced by that person as completed, whether or not the completion is a fraudulent alteration.

§ 3-408. *Drawee Not Liable on Unaccepted Draft.*

A check or other draft does not of itself operate as an assignment of funds in the hands of the drawee available for its payment, and the drawee is not liable on the instrument until the drawee accepts it.

§ 3-409. *Acceptance of Draft; Certified Check.*

(a) "Acceptance" means the drawee's signed agreement to pay a draft as presented. It must be written on the draft and may consist of the drawee's signature alone. Acceptance may be made at any time and becomes effective when notification pursuant to instructions is given or the accepted draft is delivered for the purpose of giving rights on the acceptance to any person.

(b) A draft may be accepted although it has not been signed by the drawer, is otherwise incomplete, is overdue, or has been dishonored.

(c) If a draft is payable at a fixed period after sight and the acceptor fails to date the acceptance, the holder may complete the acceptance by supplying a date in good faith.

(d) "Certified check" means a check accepted by the bank on which it is drawn. Acceptance may be made as stated in subsection (a) or by a writing on the check which indicates that the check is certified. The drawee of a check has no obligation to certify the check, and refusal to certify is not dishonor of the check.

§ 3-410. *Acceptance Varying Draft.*

(a) If the terms of a drawee's acceptance vary from the terms of the draft as presented, the holder may refuse the acceptance and treat the draft as dishonored. In that case, the drawee may cancel the acceptance.

(b) The terms of a draft are not varied by an acceptance to pay at a particular bank or place in the United States, unless the acceptance states that the draft is to be paid only at that bank or place.

(c) If the holder assents to an acceptance varying the terms of a draft, the obligation of each drawer and indorser that does not expressly assent to the acceptance is discharged.

§ 3-411. *Refusal to Pay Cashier's Checks, Teller's Checks, and Certified Checks.*

(a) In this section, "obligated bank" means the acceptor of a certified check or the issuer of a cashier's check or teller's check bought from the issuer.

(b) If the obligated bank wrongfully (i) refuses to pay a cashier's check or certified check, (ii) stops payment of a teller's check, or (iii) refuses to pay a dishonored teller's check, the person asserting the right to enforce the check is entitled to compensation for expenses and loss of interest resulting from the nonpayment and may recover consequential damages if the obligated bank refused to pay after receiving notice of particular circumstances giving rise to the damages.

(c) Expenses or consequential damages under subsection (b) are not recoverable if the refusal of the obligated bank to pay occurs because (i) the bank suspends payments, (ii) the obligated bank is asserting a claim or defense of the bank that it has reasonable grounds to believe is available against the person entitled to enforce the instrument, (iii) the obligated bank has a reasonable doubt whether the person demanding payment is the person entitled to enforce the instrument, or (iv) payment is prohibited by law.

§ 3-412. *Obligation of Maker.*

A maker of a note is obliged to pay the note (i) according to its terms at the time it was issued or, if not issued, at the time it first came into possession of a holder, or (ii) if the maker signed an incomplete instrument, according to its terms when completed as stated in Sections 3-115 and 3-407. The obligation is owed to a person entitled to enforce the note or to an indorser that paid the note pursuant to Section 3-415.

§ 3-413. *Obligation of Acceptor.*

(a) An acceptor of a draft is obliged to pay the draft (i) according to its terms at the time it was accepted, even though the acceptance states that the draft is payable "as originally drawn" or equivalent terms, (ii) if the acceptance varies the terms of the draft, according to the terms of the draft as varied, or (iii) if the acceptance is of a draft that is an incomplete instrument, according to its terms when completed as stated in Sections 3-115 and 3-407. The obligation is owed to a person entitled to enforce the draft or to the drawer or an indorser that paid the draft pursuant to Section 3-414 or 3-415.

(b) If the certification of a check or other acceptance of a draft states the amount certified or accepted, the obligation of the acceptor is that amount. If (i) the certification or acceptance does not state an amount, (ii) the instrument is subsequently altered by raising its amount, and (iii) the instrument is then negotiated to a holder in due course, the obligation of the acceptor is the amount of the instrument at the time it was negotiated to the holder in due course.

§ 3-414. *Obligation of Drawer.*

(a) If an unaccepted draft is dishonored, the drawer is obliged to pay the draft (i) according to its terms at the time it was issued or, if not issued, at the time it first came into possession of a holder, or (ii) if the drawer signed an incomplete instrument, according to its terms when completed as stated in Sections 3-115 and 3-407. The obligation is owed to a person entitled to enforce the draft or to an indorser that paid the draft pursuant to Section 3-415.

(b) If a draft is accepted by a bank and the acceptor dishonors the draft, the drawer has no obligation to pay the draft because of the dishonor, regardless of when or by whom acceptance was obtained.

(c)   If a draft is accepted and the acceptor is not a bank, the obligation of the drawer to pay the draft if the draft is dishonored by the acceptor is the same as the obligation of an indorser stated in Section 3-415(a) and (c).

(d)   Words in a draft indicating that the draft is drawn without recourse are effective to disclaim all liability of the drawer to pay the draft if the draft is not a check or a teller's check, but they are not effective to disclaim the obligation stated in subsection (a) if the draft is a check or a teller's check.

(e)   If (i) a check is not presented for payment or given to a depositary bank for collection within 30 days after its date, (ii) the drawee suspends payments after expiration of the 30-day period without paying the check, and (iii) because of the suspension of payments the drawer is deprived of funds maintained with the drawee to cover payment of the check, the drawer to the extent deprived of funds may discharge its obligation to pay the check by assigning to the person entitled to enforce the check the rights of the drawer against the drawee with respect to the funds.

§ 3-415.   Obligation of Indorser.

(a)   Subject to subsections (b), (c) and (d) and to Section 3-419(d), if an instrument is dishonored, an indorser is obliged to pay the amount due on the instrument (i) according to the terms of the instrument at the time it was indorsed, or (ii) if the indorser indorsed an incomplete instrument, according to its terms when completed as stated in Sections 3-115 and 3-407. The obligation of the indorser is owed to a person entitled to enforce the instrument or to a subsequent indorser that paid the instrument pursuant to this section.

(b)   If an indorsement states that it is made "without recourse" or otherwise disclaims liability of the indorser, the indorser is not liable under subsection (a) to pay the instrument.

(c)   If notice of dishonor of an instrument is required by Section 3-503 and notice of dishonor complying with that section is not given to an indorser, the liability of the indorser under subsection (a) is discharged.

(d)   If a draft is accepted by a bank after an indorsement was made and the acceptor dishonors the draft, the indorser is not liable under subsection (a) to pay the instrument.

(e)   If an indorser of a check is liable under subsection (a) and the check is not presented for payment, or given to a depositary bank for collection, within 30 days after the day the indorsement was made, the liability of the indorser under subsection (a) is discharged.

§ 3-416.   Transfer Warranties.

(a)   A person that transfers an instrument for consideration warrants to the transferee and, if the transfer is by indorsement, to any subsequent transferee that:

(1)   the warrantor is a person entitled to enforce the instrument,

(2)   all signatures on the instrument are authentic and authorized,

(3)   the instrument has not been altered,

(4)   the instrument is not subject to a defense or claim in recoupment stated in Section 3-305(a) of any party that can be asserted against the warrantor, and

(5)   the warrantor has no knowledge of any insolvency proceeding commenced with respect to the maker or acceptor or, in the case of an unaccepted draft, the drawer.

(b)   A person to whom the warranties under subsection (a) are made and who took the instrument in good faith may recover from the warrantor as damages for breach of warranty an amount equal to the loss suffered as a result of the breach, but not more than the amount of the instrument plus expenses and loss of interest incurred as a result of the breach.

(c)   The warranties stated in subsection (a) cannot be disclaimed with respect to checks. Unless notice of a claim for breach of warranty is given to the warrantor within 30 days after the claimant has reason to know of the breach and the identity of the warrantor, the warrantor is discharged to the extent of any loss caused by the delay in giving notice of the claim.

(d)   A cause of action for breach of warranty under this section accrues when the claimant has reason to know of the breach.

§ 3-417.   Presentment Warranties.

(a)   If an unaccepted draft is presented to the drawee for payment or acceptance and the drawee pays or accepts the draft, (i) the person obtaining payment or acceptance, at the time of presentment, and (ii) a previous transferor of the draft, at the time of transfer, warrant to the drawee making payment or accepting the draft in good faith that:

(1)   the warrantor is or was, at the time the warrantor transferred the draft, a person entitled to enforce the draft or authorized to obtain payment or acceptance of the draft on behalf of a person entitled to enforce the draft;

(2)   the draft has not been altered; and

(3)   the warrantor has no knowledge that the signature of the purported drawer of the draft is unauthorized.

(b)   A drawee making payment may recover from any warrantor damages for breach of warranty equal to the amount paid by the drawee less the amount the drawee received or is entitled to receive from the drawer because of payment of the draft. In addition the drawee is entitled to compensation for expenses and loss of interest resulting from the breach. The right of the drawee to recover damages under this subsection is not affected by any failure of the drawee to exercise ordinary care in making payment. If the drawee accepts the draft (i) breach of warranty is a defense to the obligation of the acceptor, and (ii) if the acceptor makes payment with respect to the draft, the acceptor is entitled to recover from any warrantor for breach of warranty the amounts stated in the first two sentences of this subsection.

(c)   If a drawee asserts a claim for breach of warranty under subsection (a) based on an unauthorized indorsement of the draft or an alteration of the draft, the warrantor may defend by proving that the indorsement is effective under Section 3-404 or 3-405 or the drawer is precluded under Section 3-406 or 4-406 from asserting against the drawee the unauthorized indorsement or alteration.

(d)   This subsection applies if (i) a dishonored draft is presented for payment to the drawer or an indorser or (ii) any other instrument is presented for payment to a party obliged to pay the instrument, and payment is received. The person obtaining payment and a prior transferor of the instrument warrant to the person making payment in good faith that the warrantor is or was, at the time the warrantor transferred the instrument, a person entitled to enforce the instrument or authorized to obtain payment on behalf of a person entitled to enforce the instrument. The person making payment may recover from any warrantor for breach of warranty an amount equal to the amount paid plus expenses and loss of interest resulting from the breach.

(e)   The warranties stated in subsections (a) and (d) cannot be disclaimed with respect to checks. Unless notice of a claim for breach of warranty is given to the warrantor within 30 days after the claimant has reason to know of the breach and the identity of the warrantor, the warrantor is discharged to the extent of any loss caused by the delay in giving notice of the claim.

(f)   A cause of action for breach of warranty under this section accrues when the claimant has reason to know of the breach.

§ 3-418. *Payment or Acceptance by Mistake.*

(a) Except as provided in subsection (c), if the drawee of a draft pays or accepts the draft and the drawee acted on the mistaken belief that (i) payment of the draft had not been stopped under Section 4-403, (ii) the signature of the purported drawer of the draft was authorized, or (iii) the balance in the drawer's account with the drawee represented available funds, the drawee may recover the amount paid from the person to whom or for whose benefit payment was made or, in the case of acceptance, may revoke the acceptance. Rights of the drawee under this subsection are not affected by failure of the drawee to exercise ordinary care in paying or accepting the draft.

(b) Except as provided in subsection (c), if an instrument has been paid or accepted by mistake and the case is not covered by subsection (a), the person paying or accepting may recover the amount paid or revoke acceptance to the extent allowed by the law governing mistake and restitution.

(c) The remedies provided by subsection (a) or (b) may not be asserted against a person who took the instrument in good faith and for value. This subsection does not limit remedies provided by Section 3-417 for breach of warranty.

§ 3-419. *Instruments Signed for Accommodation.*

(a) If an instrument is issued for value given for the benefit of a party to the instrument ("accommodated party") and another party to the instrument ("accommodation party") signs the instrument for the purpose of incurring liability on the instrument without being a direct beneficiary of the value given for the instrument, the instrument is signed by the accommodation party "for accommodation."

(b) An accommodation party may sign the instrument as maker, drawer, acceptor, or indorser and, subject to subsection (d), is obliged to pay the instrument in the capacity in which the accommodation party signs. The obligation of an accommodation party may be enforced notwithstanding any statute of frauds and regardless of whether the accommodation party receives consideration for the accommodation.

(c) A person signing an instrument is presumed to be an accommodation party and there is notice that the instrument is signed for accommodation if the signature is an anomalous indorsement or is accompanied by words indicating that the signer is acting as surety or guarantor with respect to the obligation of another party to the instrument. Except as provided in Section 3-606, the obligation of an accommodation party to pay the instrument is not affected by the fact that the person enforcing the obligation had notice when the instrument was taken by that person that the accommodation party signed the instrument for accommodation.

(d) If the signature of a party to an instrument is accompanied by words indicating unambiguously that the party is guaranteeing collection rather than payment of the obligation of another party to the instrument, the signer is obliged to pay the amount due on the instrument to a person entitled to enforce the instrument only if (i) execution of judgment against the other party has been returned unsatisfied, (ii) the other party is insolvent or in an insolvency proceeding, (iii) the other party cannot be served with process, or (iv) it is otherwise apparent that payment cannot be obtained from the party whose obligation is guaranteed.

(e) An accommodation party that pays the instrument is entitled to reimbursement from the accommodated party and is entitled to enforce the instrument against the accommodated party. An accommodated party that pays the instrument has no right of recourse against, and is not entitled to contribution from, an accommodation party.

§ 3-420. *Conversion of Instrument.*

(a) The law applicable to conversion of personal property applies to instruments. An instrument is also converted if the instrument lacks an indorsement necessary for negotiation and it is purchased or taken for collection or the drawee takes the instrument and makes payment to a person not entitled to receive payment. An action for conversion of an instrument may not be brought by (i) the maker, drawer, or acceptor of the instrument or (ii) a payee or indorsee who did not receive delivery of the instrument either directly or through delivery to an agent or a co-payee.

(b) In an action under subsection (a), the measure of liability is presumed to be the amount payable on the instrument, but recovery may not exceed the amount of the plaintiff's interest in the instrument.

(c) A representative, other than a depositary bank, that has in good faith dealt with an instrument or its proceeds on behalf of one who was not the person entitled to enforce the instrument is not liable in conversion to that person beyond the amount of any proceeds that it has not paid out.

■ PART 5 Dishonor

§ 3-501. *Presentment.*

(a) "Presentment" means a demand (i) to pay an instrument made to the maker, drawee, or acceptor or, in the case of a note or accepted draft payable at a bank, to the bank, or (ii) to accept a draft made to the drawee, by a person entitled to enforce the instrument.

(b) Subject to Article 4, agreement of the parties, clearing house rules and the like,

(1) presentment may be made at the place of payment of the instrument and must be made at the place of payment if the instrument is payable at a bank in the United States; may be made by any commercially reasonable means, including an oral, written, or electronic communication; is effective when the demand for payment or acceptance is received by the person to whom presentment is made; is effective if made to any one of two or more makers, acceptors, drawees or other payors; and

(2) without dishonoring the instrument, the party to whom presentment is made may (i) treat presentment as occurring on the next business day after the day of presentment if the party to whom presentment is made has established a cut-off hour not earlier than 2 p.m. for the receipt and processing of instruments presented for payment or acceptance and presentment is made after the cut-off hour, (ii) require exhibition of the instrument, (iii) require reasonable identification of the person making presentment and evidence of authority to make it if made on behalf of another person, (iv) require a signed receipt on the instrument for any payment made or surrender of the instrument if full payment is made, (v) return the instrument for lack of a necessary indorsement, or (vi) refuse payment or acceptance for failure of the presentment to comply with the terms of the instrument, an agreement of the parties, or other law or applicable rule.

§ 3-502. *Dishonor.*

(a) Dishonor of a note is governed by the following rules:

(1) If the note is payable on demand, the note is dishonored if presentment is duly made and the note is not paid on the day of presentment.

(2) If the note is not payable on demand and is payable at or through a bank or the terms of the note require presentment, the note is dishonored if presentment is duly made and the note is not paid on the day it becomes payable or the day of presentment, whichever is later.

1342 | Appendix B

(3) If the note is not payable on demand and subparagraph (2) does not apply, the note is dishonored if it is not paid on the day it becomes payable.

(b) Dishonor of an unaccepted draft other than a documentary draft is governed by the following rules:

(1) If a check is presented for payment otherwise than for immediate payment over the counter, the check is dishonored if the payor bank makes timely return of the check or sends timely notice of dishonor or nonpayment under Section 4-301 or 4-302, or becomes accountable for the amount of the check under Section 4-302.

(2) If the draft is payable on demand and subparagraph (1) does not apply, the draft is dishonored if presentment for payment is duly made and the draft is not paid on the day of presentment.

(3) If the draft is payable on a date stated in the draft, the draft is dishonored if (i) presentment for payment is duly made and payment is not made on the day the draft becomes payable or the day of presentment, whichever is later, or (ii) presentment for acceptance is duly made before the day the draft becomes payable and the draft is not accepted on the day of presentment.

(4) If the draft is payable on elapse of a period of time after sight or acceptance, the draft is dishonored if presentment for acceptance is duly made and the draft is not accepted on the day of presentment.

(c) Dishonor of an unaccepted documentary draft occurs according to the rules stated in subparagraphs (2), (3), and (4) of subsection (b) except that payment or acceptance may be delayed without dishonor until no later than the close of the third business day of the drawee following the day on which payment or acceptance is required by those subparagraphs.

(d) Dishonor of an accepted draft is governed by the following rules:

(1) If the draft is payable on demand, the draft is dishonored if presentment for payment is duly made and the draft is not paid on the day of presentment.

(2) If the draft is not payable on demand, the draft is dishonored if presentment for payment is duly made and payment is not made on the day it becomes payable or the day of presentment, whichever is later.

(e) In any case in which presentment is otherwise required for dishonor under this section and presentment is excused under Section 3-504, dishonor occurs without presentment if the instrument is not duly accepted or paid.

(f) If a draft is dishonored because timely acceptance of the draft was not made and the person entitled to demand acceptance consents to a late acceptance, from the time of acceptance the draft is treated as never having been dishonored.

§ 3-503. *Notice of Dishonor.*

(a) The obligation of an indorser stated in Section 3-415(a) and the obligation of a drawer stated in Section 3-414(c) may not be enforced unless (i) the indorser or drawer is given notice of dishonor of the instrument complying with this section or (ii) notice of dishonor is excused under Section 3-504(c).

(b) Notice of dishonor may be given by any person; may be given by any commercially reasonable means including an oral, written, or electronic communication; is sufficient if it reasonably identifies the instrument and indicates that the instrument has been dishonored or has not been paid or accepted. Return of an instrument given to a bank for collection is a sufficient notice of dishonor.

(c) Subject to Section 3-504(d), with respect to an instrument taken for collection by a collecting bank, notice of dishonor must be given (i) by the bank before midnight of the next banking day following the banking day on which the bank receives notice of dishonor of the instrument, and (ii) by any other person within 30 days following the day on which the person receives notice of dishonor. With respect to any other instrument, notice of dishonor must be given within 30 days following the day on which dishonor occurs.

§ 3-504. *Excused Presentment and Notice of Dishonor.*

(a) Presentment for payment or acceptance of an instrument is excused if (i) the person entitled to present the instrument cannot with reasonable diligence make presentment, (ii) the maker or acceptor has repudiated an obligation to pay the instrument or is dead or in insolvency proceedings, (iii) by the terms of the instrument presentment is not necessary to enforce the obligation of indorsers or the drawer, or (iv) the drawer or indorser whose obligation is being enforced waived presentment or otherwise had no reason to expect or right to require that the instrument be paid or accepted.

(b) Presentment for payment or acceptance of a draft is also excused if the drawer instructed the drawee not to pay or accept the draft or the drawee was not obligated to the drawer to pay the draft.

(c) Notice of dishonor is excused if (i) by the terms of the instrument notice of dishonor is not necessary to enforce the obligation of a party to pay the instrument, or (ii) the party whose obligation is being enforced waived notice of dishonor. A waiver of presentment is also a waiver of notice of dishonor.

(d) Delay in giving notice of dishonor is excused if the delay was caused by circumstances beyond the control of the person giving the notice and the person giving the notice exercised reasonable diligence after the cause of the delay ceased to operate.

§ 3-505. *Evidence of Dishonor.*

(a) The following are admissible as evidence and create a presumption of dishonor and of any notice of dishonor stated:

(1) a document regular in form as provided in subsection (b) which purports to be a protest;

(2) a purported stamp or writing of the drawee, payor bank, or presenting bank on or accompanying the instrument stating that acceptance or payment has been refused unless reasons for the refusal are stated and the reasons are not consistent with dishonor;

(3) a book or record of the drawee, payor bank, or collecting bank, kept in the usual course of business which shows dishonor, even if there is no evidence of who made the entry.

(b) A protest is a certificate of dishonor made by a United States consul or vice consul, or a notary public or other person authorized to administer oaths by the law of the place where dishonor occurs. It may be made upon information satisfactory to that person. The protest must identify the instrument and certify either that presentment has been made or, if not made, the reason why it was not made, and that the instrument has been dishonored by nonacceptance or nonpayment. The protest may also certify that notice of dishonor has been given to some or all parties.

■ PART 6 Discharge and Payment

§ 3-601. *Discharge and Effect of Discharge.*

(a) The obligation of a party to pay the instrument is discharged as stated in this Article or by an act or agreement with the party which would discharge an obligation to pay money under a simple contract.

(b) Discharge of the obligation of a party is not effective against a person acquiring rights of a holder in due course of the instrument without notice of the discharge.

© 2000 by The American Law Institute and the National Conference of Commissioners on Uniform State Laws. Reprinted with permission.

§ 3-602. Payment.

(a)   Subject to subsection (b), an instrument is paid to the extent payment is made (i) by or on behalf of a party obliged to pay the instrument, and (ii) to a person entitled to enforce the instrument. To the extent of the payment, the obligation of the party obliged to pay the instrument is discharged even though payment is made with knowledge of a claim to the instrument under Section 3-306 by another person.

(b)   The obligation of a party to pay the instrument is not discharged under subsection (a) if:

(1)   a claim to the instrument under Section 3-306 is enforceable against the party receiving payment and (i) payment is made with knowledge by the payor that payment is prohibited by injunction or similar process of a court of competent jurisdiction, or (ii) in the case of an instrument other than a cashier's check, teller's check, or certified check, the party making payment accepted, from the person having a claim to the instrument, indemnity against loss resulting from refusal to pay the person entitled to enforce the instrument, or

(2)   the person making payment knows that the instrument is a stolen instrument and pays a person that it knows is in wrongful possession of the instrument.

§ 3-603. Tender of Payment.

(a)   If tender of payment of an obligation of a party to an instrument is made to a person entitled to enforce the obligation, the effect of tender is governed by principles of law applicable to tender of payment of an obligation under a simple contract.

(b)   If tender of payment of an obligation to pay the instrument is made to a person entitled to enforce the instrument and the tender is refused, there is discharge, to the extent of the amount of the tender, of the obligation of an indorser or accommodation party having a right of recourse against the obligor making the tender.

(c)   If tender of payment of an amount due on an instrument is made by or on behalf of the obligor to the person entitled to enforce the instrument, the obligation of the obligor to pay interest after the due date on the amount tendered is discharged. If presentment is required with respect to an instrument and the obligor is able and ready to pay on the due date at every place of payment stated in the instrument, the obligor is deemed to have made tender of payment on the due date to the person entitled to enforce the instrument.

§ 3-604. Discharge by Cancellation or Renunciation.

(a)   A person entitled to enforce an instrument may, with or without consideration, discharge the obligation of a party to pay the instrument (i) by an intentional voluntary act such as surrender of the instrument to the party, destruction, mutilation, or cancellation of the instrument, cancellation or striking out of the party's signature, or the addition of words to the instrument indicating discharge, or (ii) by agreeing not to sue or otherwise renouncing rights against the party by a signed writing.

(b)   Cancellation or striking out of an indorsement pursuant to subsection (a) does not affect the status and rights of a party derived from the indorsement.

§ 3-605. Discharge of Indorsers and Accommodation Parties.

(a)   For the purposes of this section, the term "indorser" includes a drawer having the obligation stated in Section 3-414(c).

(b)   Discharge of the obligation of a party to the instrument under Section 3-605 does not discharge the obligation of an indorser or accommodation party having a right of recourse against the discharged party.

(c)   If a person entitled to enforce an instrument agrees, with or without consideration, to a material modification of the obligation of a party to the instrument, including an extension of the due date, there is discharge of the obligation of an indorser or accommodation party having a right of recourse against the person whose obligation is modified to the extent the modification causes loss to the indorser or accommodation party with respect to the right of recourse. The indorser or accommodation party is deemed to have suffered loss as a result of the modification equal to the amount of the right of recourse unless the person enforcing the instrument proves that no loss was caused by the modification or that the loss caused by the modification was less than the amount of the right of recourse.

(d)   If the obligation of a party to an instrument is secured by an interest in collateral and impairment of the value of the interest is caused by a person entitled to enforce the instrument, there is discharge of the obligation of an indorser or accommodation party having a right of recourse against the obligor to the extent of the impairment. The value of an interest in collateral is impaired to the extent (i) the value of the interest is reduced to an amount less than the amount of the right of recourse of the party asserting discharge, or (ii) the reduction in value of the interest causes an increase in the amount by which the amount of the right of recourse exceeds the value of the interest. The burden of proving impairment is on the party asserting discharge.

(e)   If the obligation of a party to an instrument is secured by an interest in collateral not provided by an accommodation party and the value of the interest is impaired by a person entitled to enforce the instrument, the obligation of any party who is jointly and severally liable with respect to the secured obligation is discharged to the extent the impairment causes the party asserting discharge to pay more than that party would have been obliged to pay, taking into account rights of contribution, if impairment had not occurred. If the party asserting discharge is an accommodation party not entitled to discharge under subsection (d), the party is deemed to have a right to contribution based on joint and several liability rather than a right to reimbursement. The burden of proving impairment is on the party asserting discharge.

(f)   Under subsection (d) or (e) causation of impairment includes (i) failure to obtain or maintain perfection or recordation of the interest in collateral, (ii) release of collateral without substitution of collateral of equal value, (iii) failure to perform a duty to preserve the value of collateral owed, under Article 9 or other law, to a debtor or surety or other person secondarily liable, or (iv) failure to comply with applicable law in disposing of collateral.

(g)   An accommodation party is not discharged under subsection (c) or (d) unless the person agreeing to the modification or causing the impairment knows of the accommodation or has notice under Section 3-419(c) that the instrument was signed for accommodation. There is no discharge of any party under subsection (c), (d), or (e) if (i) the party asserting discharge consents to the event or conduct that is the basis of the discharge, or (ii) the instrument or a separate agreement of the party provides for waiver of discharge under this section either specifically or by general language indicating that parties to the instrument waive defenses based on suretyship or impairment of collateral.

ARTICLE 4
Bank Deposits and Collections

■ **PART I**   General Provisions and Definitions

§ 4-101. Short Title.

This Article may be cited as Uniform Commercial Code—Bank Deposits and Collections.

---

§ 4-102. *Applicability.*

(a) To the extent that items within this Article are also within Articles 3 and 8, they are subject to those Articles. If there is conflict, this Article governs Article 3, but Article 8 governs this Article.

(b) The liability of a bank for action or non-action with respect to an item handled by it for purposes of presentment, payment, or collection is governed by the law of the place where the bank is located. In the case of action or non-action by or at a branch or separate office of a bank, its liability is governed by the law of the place where the branch or separate office is located.

§ 4-103. *Variation by Agreement; Measure of Damages; Action Constituting Ordinary Care.*

(a) The effect of the provisions of this Article may be varied by agreement, but the parties to the agreement cannot disclaim a bank's responsibility for its lack of good faith or failure to exercise ordinary care or limit the measure of damages for the lack or failure. However, the parties may determine by agreement the standards by which the bank's responsibility is to be measured if those standards are not manifestly unreasonable.

(b) Federal Reserve regulations and operating circulars, clearing-house rules, and the like have the effect of agreements under subsection (a), whether or not specifically assented to by all parties interested in items handled.

(c) Action or non-action approved by this Article or pursuant to Federal Reserve regulations or operating circulars is the exercise of ordinary care and, in the absence of special instructions, action or non-action consistent with clearing-house rules and the like or with a general banking usage not disapproved by this Article, is prima facie the exercise of ordinary care.

(d) The specification or approval of certain procedures by this Article is not disapproval of other procedures that may be reasonable under the circumstances.

(e) The measure of damages for failure to exercise ordinary care in handling an item is the amount of the item reduced by an amount that could not have been realized by the exercise of ordinary care. If there is also bad faith it includes any other damages the party suffered as a proximate consequence.

§ 4-104. *Definitions and Index of Definitions.*

(a) In this Article, unless the context otherwise requires:

(1) "Account" means any deposit or credit account with a bank, including a demand, time, savings, passbook, share draft, or like account, other than an account evidenced by a certificate of deposit;

(2) "Afternoon" means the period of a day between noon and midnight;

(3) "Banking day" means the part of a day on which a bank is open to the public for carrying on substantially all of its banking functions;

(4) "Clearing house" means an association of banks or other payors regularly clearing items;

(5) "Customer" means a person having an account with a bank or for whom a bank has agreed to collect items, including a bank that maintains an account at another bank;

(6) "Documentary draft" means a draft to be presented for acceptance or payment if specified documents, certificated securities (Section 8-102) or instructions for uncertificated securities (Section 8-102), or other certificates, statements, or the like are to be received by the drawee or other payor before acceptance or payment of the draft;

(7) "Draft" means a draft as defined in Section 3-104 or an item, other than an instrument, that is an order;

(8) "Drawee" means a person ordered in a draft to make payment;

(9) "Item" means an instrument or a promise or order to pay money handled by a bank for collection or payment. The term does not include a payment order governed by Article 4A or a credit or debit card slip;

(10) "Midnight deadline" with respect to a bank is midnight on its next banking day following the banking day on which it receives the relevant item or notice or from which the time for taking action commences to run, whichever is later;

(11) "Settle" means to pay in cash, by clearing-house settlement, in a charge or credit or by remittance, or otherwise as agreed. A settlement may be either provisional or final;

(12) "Suspends payments" with respect to a bank means that it has been closed by order of the supervisory authorities, that a public officer has been appointed to take it over, or that it ceases or refuses to make payments in the ordinary course of business.

(b) Other definitions applying to this Article and the sections in which they appear are:

"Agreement for electronic presentment" Section 4-110.
"Bank" Section 4-105.
"Collecting bank" Section 4-105.
"Depository bank" Section 4-105.
"Intermediary bank" Section 4-105.
"Payor bank" Section 4-105.
"Presenting bank" Section 4-105.
"Presentment notice" Section 4-110.

(c) The following definitions in other Articles apply to this Article:

"Acceptance" Section 3-409.
"Alteration" Section 3-407.
"Cashier's check" Section 3-104.
"Certificate of deposit" Section 3-104.
"Certified check" Section 3-109.
"Check" Section 3-104.
"Good faith" Section 3-103.
"Holder in due course" Section 3-302.
"Instrument" Section 3-104.
"Notice of dishonor" Section 3-503.
"Order" Section 3-103.
"Ordinary care" Section 3-103.
"Person entitled to enforce" Section 3-301.
"Presentment" Section 3-501.
"Promise" Section 3-103.
"Prove" Section 3-103.
"Teller's check" Section 3-104.
"Unauthorized signature" Section 3-403.

(d) In addition, Article 1 contains general definitions and principles of construction and interpretation applicable throughout this Article.

As amended in 1990 and 1994.

§ 4-105. *"Bank"; "Depositary Bank"; "Payor Bank"; "Intermediary Bank"; "Collecting Bank"; "Presenting Bank".*

In this Article:

(1) "Bank" means a person engaged in the business of banking, including a savings bank, savings and loan association, credit union, or trust company;

(2) "Depositary bank" means the first bank to take an item even though it is also the payor bank, unless the item is presented for immediate payment over the counter;

(3) "Payor bank" means a bank that is the drawee of a draft;

(4) "Intermediary bank" means a bank to which an item is transferred in course of collection except the depositary or payor bank;

(5) "Collecting bank" means a bank handling an item for collection except the payor bank;

(6) "Presenting bank" means a bank presenting an item except a payor bank.

§ 4-106. Payable Through or Payable at Bank: Collecting Bank.

(a) If an item states that it is "payable through" a bank identified in the item, (i) the item designates the bank as a collecting bank and does not by itself authorize the bank to pay the item, and (ii) the item may be presented for payment only by or through the bank.

Alternative A

(b) If an item states that it is "payable at" a bank identified in the item, the item is equivalent to a draft drawn on the bank.

Alternative B

(b) If an item states that it is "payable at" a bank identified in the item, (i) the item designates the bank as a collecting bank and does not by itself authorize the bank to pay the item, and (ii) the item may be presented for payment only by or through the bank.

(c) If a draft names a nonbank drawee and it is unclear whether a bank named in the draft is a co-drawee or a collecting bank, the bank is a collecting bank.

§ 4-107. Separate Office of Bank.

A branch or separate office of a bank is a separate bank for the purpose of computing the time within which and determining the place at or to which action may be taken or notices or orders shall be given under this Article and under Article 3.

§ 4-108. Time of Receipt of Items.

(a) For the purpose of allowing time to process items, prove balances, and make the necessary entries on its books to determine its position for the day, a bank may fix an afternoon hour of 2 P.M. or later as a cutoff hour for the handling of money and items and the making of entries on its books.

(b) An item or deposit of money received on any day after a cutoff hour so fixed or after the close of the banking day may be treated as being received at the opening of the next banking day.

§ 4-109. Delays.

(a) Unless otherwise instructed, a collecting bank in a good faith effort to secure payment of a specific item drawn on a payor other than a bank, and with or without the approval of any person involved, may waive, modify, or extend time limits imposed or permitted by this [Act] for a period not exceeding two additional banking days without discharge of drawers or indorsers or liability to its transferor or a prior party.

(b) Delay by a collecting bank or payor bank beyond time limits prescribed or permitted by this [Act] or by instructions is excused if (i) the delay is caused by interruption of communication or computer facilities, suspension of payments by another bank, war, emergency conditions, failure of equipment, or other circumstances beyond the control of the bank, and (ii) the bank exercises such diligence as the circumstances require.

§ 4-110. Electronic Presentment.

(a) "Agreement for electronic presentment" means an agreement, clearing-house rule, or Federal Reserve regulation or operating circular, providing that presentment of an item may be made by transmission of an image of an item or information describing the item ("presentment notice") rather than delivery of the item itself. The agreement may provide for procedures governing retention, presentment, payment, dishonor, and other matters concerning items subject to the agreement.

(b) Presentment of an item pursuant to an agreement for presentment is made when the presentment notice is received.

(c) If presentment is made by presentment notice, a reference to "item" or "check" in this Article means the presentment notice unless the context otherwise indicates.

§ 4-111. Statute of Limitations.

An action to enforce an obligation, duty, or right arising under this Article must be commenced within three years after the [cause of action] accrues.

■ PART 2 Collection of Items: Depositary and Collecting Banks

§ 4-201. Status of Collecting Bank as Agent and Provisional Status of Credits; Applicability of Article; Item Indorsed "Pay Any Bank".

(a) Unless a contrary intent clearly appears and before the time that a settlement given by a collecting bank for an item is or becomes final, the bank, with respect to an item, is an agent or sub-agent of the owner of the item and any settlement given for the item is provisional. This provision applies regardless of the form of indorsement or lack of indorsement and even though credit given for the item is subject to immediate withdrawal as of right or is in fact withdrawn; but the continuance of ownership of an item by its owner and any rights of the owner to proceeds of the item are subject to rights of a collecting bank, such as those resulting from outstanding advances on the item and rights of recoupment or setoff. If an item is handled by banks for purposes of presentment, payment, collection, or return, the relevant provisions of this Article apply even though action of the parties clearly establishes that a particular bank has purchased the item and is the owner of it.

(b) After an item has been indorsed with the words "pay any bank" or the like, only a bank may acquire the rights of a holder until the item has been:

(1) returned to the customer initiating collection; or

(2) specially indorsed by a bank to a person who is not a bank.

§ 4-202. Responsibility for Collection or Return; When Action Timely.

(a) A collecting bank must exercise ordinary care in:

(1) presenting an item or sending it for presentment;

(2) sending notice of dishonor or nonpayment or returning an item other than a documentary draft to the bank's transferor after learning that the item has not been paid or accepted, as the case may be;

(3) settling for an item when the bank receives final settlement; and

(4) notifying its transferor of any loss or delay in transit within a reasonable time after discovery thereof.

(b) A collecting bank exercises ordinary care under subsection (a) by taking proper action before its midnight deadline following receipt of an item, notice, or settlement. Taking proper action within a reasonably longer time may constitute the exercise of ordinary care, but the bank has the burden of establishing timeliness.

(c) Subject to subsection (a)(1), a bank is not liable for the insolvency, neglect, misconduct, mistake, or default of another bank or person or for loss or destruction of an item in the possession of others or in transit.

§ 4-203. *Effect of Instructions.*

Subject to Article 3 concerning conversion of instruments (Section 3-420) and restrictive indorsements (Section 3-206), only a collecting bank's transferor can give instructions that affect the bank or constitute notice to it, and a collecting bank is not liable to prior parties for any action taken pursuant to the instructions or in accordance with any agreement with its transferor.

§ 4-204. *Methods of Sending and Presenting; Sending Directly to Payor Bank.*

(a) A collecting bank shall send items by a reasonably prompt method, taking into consideration relevant instructions, the nature of the item, the number of those items on hand, the cost of collection involved, and the method generally used by it or others to present those items.

(b) A collecting bank may send:

(1) an item directly to the payor bank;

(2) an item to a nonbank payor if authorized by its transferor; and

(3) an item other than documentary drafts to a nonbank payor, if authorized by Federal Reserve regulation or operating circular, clearing-house rule, or the like.

(c) Presentment may be made by a presenting bank at a place where the payor bank or other payor has requested that presentment be made.

§ 4-205. *Depositary Bank Holder of Unindorsed Item.*

If a customer delivers an item to a depositary bank for collection:

(1) the depositary bank becomes a holder of the item at the time it receives the item for collection if the customer at the time of delivery was a holder of the item, whether or not the customer indorses the item, and, if the bank satisfies the other requirements of Section 3-302, it is a holder in due course; and

(2) the depositary bank warrants to collecting banks, the payor bank or other payor, and the drawer that the amount of the item was paid to the customer or deposited to the customer's account.

§ 4-206. *Transfer Between Banks.*

Any agreed method that identifies the transferor bank is sufficient for the item's further transfer to another bank.

§ 4-207. *Transfer Warranties.*

(a) A customer or collecting bank that transfers an item and receives a settlement or other consideration warrants to the transferee and to any subsequent collecting bank that:

(1) the warrantor is a person entitled to enforce the item;

(2) all signatures on the item are authentic and authorized;

(3) the item has not been altered;

(4) the item is not subject to a defense or claim in recoupment (Section 3-305(a)) of any party that can be asserted against the warrantor; and

(5) the warrantor has no knowledge of any insolvency proceeding commenced with respect to the maker or acceptor or, in the case of an unaccepted draft, the drawer.

(b) If an item is dishonored, a customer or collecting bank transferring the item and receiving settlement or other consideration is obliged to pay the amount due on the item (i) according to the terms of the item at the time it was transferred, or (ii) if the transfer was of an incomplete item, according to its terms when completed as stated in Sections 3-115 and 3-407. The obligation of a transferor is owed to the transferee and to any subsequent collecting bank that takes the item in good faith. A transferor cannot disclaim its obligation under this subsection by an indorsement stating that it is made "without recourse" or otherwise disclaiming liability.

(c) A person to whom the warranties under subsection (a) are made and who took the item in good faith may recover from the warrantor as damages for breach of warranty an amount equal to the loss suffered as a result of the breach, but not more than the amount of the item plus expenses and loss of interest incurred as a result of the breach.

(d) The warranties stated in subsection (a) cannot be disclaimed with respect to checks. Unless notice of a claim for breach of warranty is given to the warrantor within 30 days after the claimant has reason to know of the breach and the identity of the warrantor, the warrantor is discharged to the extent of any loss caused by the delay in giving notice of the claim.

(e) A cause of action for breach of warranty under this section accrues when the claimant has reason to know of the breach.

§ 4-208. *Presentment Warranties.*

(a) If an unaccepted draft is presented to the drawee for payment or acceptance and the drawee pays or accepts the draft, (i) the person obtaining payment or acceptance, at the time of presentment, and (ii) a previous transferor of the draft, at the time of transfer, warrant to the drawee that pays or accepts the draft in good faith that:

(1) the warrantor is, or was, at the time the warrantor transferred the draft, a person entitled to enforce the draft or authorized to obtain payment or acceptance of the draft on behalf of a person entitled to enforce the draft;

(2) the draft has not been altered; and

(3) the warrantor has no knowledge that the signature of the purported drawer of the draft is unauthorized.

(b) A drawee making payment may recover from a warrantor damages for breach of warranty equal to the amount paid by the drawee less the amount the drawee received or is entitled to receive from the drawer because of the payment. In addition, the drawee is entitled to compensation for expenses and loss of interest resulting from the breach. The right of the drawee to recover damages under this subsection is not affected by any failure of the drawee to exercise ordinary care in making payment. If the drawee accepts the draft (i) breach of warranty is a defense to the obligation of the acceptor, and (ii) if the acceptor makes payment with respect to the draft, the acceptor is entitled to recover from a warrantor for breach of warranty the amounts stated in this subsection.

(c) If a drawee asserts a claim for breach of warranty under subsection (a) based on an unauthorized indorsement of the draft or an alteration of the draft, the warrantor may defend by proving that the indorsement is effective under Section 3-404 or 3-405 or the drawer is precluded under Section 3-406 or 4-406 from asserting against the drawee the unauthorized indorsement or alteration.

(d) If (i) a dishonored draft is presented for payment to the drawer or an indorser or (ii) any other item is presented for payment to a party obliged to pay the item, and the item is paid, the person obtaining payment and a prior transferor of the item warrant to the person making payment in good faith that the warrantor is, or was, at the time the warrantor transferred the item, a person entitled to enforce the item or authorized to obtain payment on behalf of a person entitled to enforce the item. The person making payment may recover from any warrantor for breach of warranty an amount equal to the amount paid plus expenses and loss of interest resulting from the breach.

(e) The warranties stated in subsections (a) and (d) cannot be disclaimed with respect to checks. Unless notice of a claim for breach of warranty is given to the warrantor within 30 days after the claimant has reason to know of the breach and the identity of the warrantor, the warrantor is discharged to the extent of any loss caused by the delay in giving notice of the claim.

(f)   A cause of action for breach of warranty under this section accrues when the claimant has reason to know of the breach.

§ 4-209.   *Encoding and Retention Warranties.*

(a)   A person who encodes information on or with respect to an item after issue warrants to any subsequent collecting bank and to the payor bank or other payor that the information is correctly encoded. If the customer of a depositary bank encodes, that bank also makes the warranty.

(b)   A person who undertakes to retain an item pursuant to an agreement for electronic presentment warrants to any subsequent collecting bank and to the payor bank or other payor that retention and presentment of the item comply with the agreement. If a customer of a depositary bank undertakes to retain an item, that bank also makes this warranty.

(c)   A person to whom warranties are made under this section and who took the item in good faith may recover from the warrantor as damages for breach of warranty an amount equal to the loss suffered as a result of the breach, plus expenses and loss of interest incurred as a result of the breach.

§ 4-210.   *Security Interest of Collecting Bank in Items, Accompanying Documents and Proceeds.*

(a)   A collecting bank has a security interest in an item and any accompanying documents or the proceeds of either:

(1)   in case of an item deposited in an account, to the extent to which credit given for the item has been withdrawn or applied;

(2)   in case of an item for which it has given credit available for withdrawal as of right, to the extent of the credit given, whether or not the credit is drawn upon or there is a right of charge-back; or

(3)   if it makes an advance on or against the item.

(b)   If credit given for several items received at one time or pursuant to a single agreement is withdrawn or applied in part, the security interest remains upon all the items, any accompanying documents or the proceeds of either. For the purpose of this section, credits first given are first withdrawn.

(c)   Receipt by a collecting bank of a final settlement for an item is a realization on its security interest in the item, accompanying documents, and proceeds. So long as the bank does not receive final settlement for the item or give up possession of the item or accompanying documents for purposes other than collection, the security interest continues to that extent and is subject to Article 9, but:

(1)   no security agreement is necessary to make the security interest enforceable (Section 9-203 (1)(a));

(2)   no filing is required to perfect the security interest; and

(3)   the security interest has priority over conflicting perfected security interests in the item, accompanying documents, or proceeds.

§ 4-211.   *When Bank Gives Value for Purposes of Holder in Due Course.*

For purposes of determining its status as a holder in due course, a bank has given value to the extent it has a security interest in an item, if the bank otherwise complies with the requirements of Section 3-302 on what constitutes a holder in due course.

§ 4-212.   *Presentment by Notice of Item Not Payable by, Through, or at Bank; Liability of Drawer or Indorser.*

(a)   Unless otherwise instructed, a collecting bank may present an item not payable by, through, or at a bank by sending to the party to accept or pay a written notice that the bank holds the item for acceptance or payment. The notice must be sent in time to be received on or before the day when presentment is due and the bank must meet any requirements of the party to accept or pay under Section 3-501 by the close of the bank's next banking day after it knows of the requirement.

(b)   If presentment is made by notice and payment, acceptance, or request for compliance with a requirement under Section 3-501 is not received by the close of business on the day after maturity or, in the case of demand items, by the close of business on the third banking day after notice was sent, the presenting bank may treat the item as dishonored and charge any drawer or indorser by sending it notice of the facts.

§ 4-213.   *Medium and Time of Settlement by Bank.*

(a)   With respect to settlement by a bank, the medium and time of settlement may be prescribed by Federal Reserve regulations or circulars, clearing-house rules, and the like, or agreement. In the absence of such prescription:

(1)   the medium of settlement is cash or credit to an account in a Federal Reserve bank of or specified by the person to receive settlement; and

(2)   the time of settlement, is:

(i)   with respect to tender of settlement by cash, a cashier's check, or teller's check, when the cash or check is sent or delivered;

(ii)   with respect to tender of settlement by credit in an account in a Federal Reserve Bank, when the credit is made;

(iii)   with respect to tender of settlement by a credit or debit to an account in a bank, when the credit or debit is made or, in the case of tender of settlement by authority to charge an account, when the authority is sent or delivered; or

(iv)   with respect to tender of settlement by a funds transfer, when payment is made pursuant to Section 4A-406(a) to the person receiving settlement.

(b)   If the tender of settlement is not by a medium authorized by subsection (a) or the time of settlement is not fixed by subsection (a), no settlement occurs until the tender of settlement is accepted by the person receiving settlement.

(c)   If settlement for an item is made by cashier's check or teller's check and the person receiving settlement, before its midnight deadline:

(1)   presents or forwards the check for collection, settlement is final when the check is finally paid; or

(2)   fails to present or forward the check for collection, settlement is final at the midnight deadline of the person receiving settlement.

(d)   If settlement for an item is made by giving authority to charge the account of the bank giving settlement in the bank receiving settlement, settlement is final when the charge is made by the bank receiving settlement if there are funds available in the account for the amount of the item.

§ 4-214.   *Right of Charge—Back or Refund; Liability of Collecting Bank: Return of Item.*

(a)   If a collecting bank has made provisional settlement with its customer for an item and fails by reason of dishonor, suspension of payments by a bank, or otherwise to receive settlement for the item which is or becomes final, the bank may revoke the settlement given by it, charge back the amount of any credit given for the item to its customer's account, or obtain refund from its customer, whether or not it is able to return the item, if by its midnight deadline or within a longer reasonable time after it learns the facts it returns the item or sends notification of the facts. If the return or notice is delayed beyond the bank's midnight deadline or a longer reasonable time after it learns the facts, the bank may revoke the settlement, charge back the credit, or obtain refund from its customer, but it is liable for any loss resulting from the delay. These rights to revoke, charge back, and obtain refund terminate if and when a settlement for the item received by the bank is or becomes final.

(b)   A collecting bank returns an item when it is sent or delivered to the bank's customer or transferor or pursuant to its instructions.

(c)   A depositary bank that is also the payor may charge back the amount of an item to its customer's account or obtain refund in accordance with the section governing return of an item received by a payor bank for credit on its books (Section 4-301).

(d)   The right to charge back is not affected by:

(1)   previous use of a credit given for the item; or

(2)   failure by any bank to exercise ordinary care with respect to the item, but a bank so failing remains liable.

(e)   A failure to charge back or claim refund does not affect other rights of the bank against the customer or any other party.

(f)   If credit is given in dollars as the equivalent of the value of an item payable in foreign money, the dollar amount of any charge-back or refund must be calculated on the basis of the bank-offered spot rate for the foreign money prevailing on the day when the person entitled to the charge-back or refund learns that it will not receive payment in ordinary course.

As amended in 1990.

§ 4-215.   *Final Payment of Item by Payor Bank; When Provisional Debits and Credits Become Final; When Certain Credits Become Available for Withdrawal.*

(a)   An item is finally paid by a payor bank when the bank has first done any of the following:

(1)   paid the item in cash;

(2)   settled for the item without having a right to revoke the settlement under statute, clearing-house rule, or agreement; or

(3)   made a provisional settlement for the item and failed to revoke the settlement in the time and manner permitted by statute, clearing-house rule, or agreement.

(b)   If provisional settlement for an item does not become final, the item is not finally paid.

(c)   If provisional settlement for an item between the presenting and payor banks is made through a clearing house or by debits or credits in an account between them, then to the extent that provisional debits or credits for the item are entered in accounts between the presenting and payor banks or between the presenting and successive prior collecting banks seriatim, they become final upon final payment of the item by the payor bank.

(d)   If a collecting bank receives a settlement for an item which is or becomes final, the bank is accountable to its customer for the amount of the item and any provisional credit given for the item in an account with its customer becomes final.

(e)   Subject to (i) applicable law stating a time for availability of funds and (ii) any right of the bank to apply the credit to an obligation of the customer, credit given by a bank for an item in a customer's account becomes available for withdrawal as of right:

(1)   if the bank has received a provisional settlement for the item, when the settlement becomes final and the bank has had a reasonable time to receive return of the item and the item has not been received within that time;

(2)   if the bank is both the depositary bank and the payor bank, and the item is finally paid, at the opening of the bank's second banking day following receipt of the item.

(f)   Subject to applicable law stating a time for availability of funds and any right of a bank to apply a deposit to an obligation

of the depositor, a deposit of money becomes available for withdrawal as of right at the opening of the bank's next banking day after receipt of the deposit.

§ 4-216.   *Insolvency and Preference.*

(a)   If an item is in or comes into the possession of a payor or collecting bank that suspends payment and the item has not been finally paid, the item must be returned by the receiver, trustee, or agent in charge of the closed bank to the presenting bank or the closed bank's customer.

(b)   If a payor bank finally pays an item and suspends payments without making a settlement for the item with its customer or the presenting bank which settlement is or becomes final, the owner of the item has a preferred claim against the payor bank.

(c)   If a payor bank gives or a collecting bank gives or receives a provisional settlement for an item and thereafter suspends payments, the suspension does not prevent or interfere with the settlement's becoming final if the finality occurs automatically upon the lapse of certain time or the happening of certain events.

(d)   If a collecting bank receives from subsequent parties settlement for an item, which settlement is or becomes final and the bank suspends payments without making a settlement for the item with its customer which settlement is or becomes final, the owner of the item has a preferred claim against the collecting bank.

■ PART 3   Collection of Items: Payor Banks

§ 4-301.   *Deferred Posting; Recovery of Payment by Return of Items; Time of Dishonor; Return of Items by Payor Bank.*

(a)   If a payor bank settles for a demand item other than a documentary draft presented otherwise than for immediate payment over the counter before midnight of the banking day of receipt, the payor bank may revoke the settlement and recover the settlement if, before it has made final payment and before its midnight deadline, it

(1)   returns the item; or

(2)   sends written notice of dishonor or nonpayment if the item is unavailable for return.

(b)   If a demand item is received by a payor bank for credit on its books, it may return the item or send notice of dishonor and may revoke any credit given or recover the amount thereof withdrawn by its customer, if it acts within the time limit and in the manner specified in subsection (a).

(c)   Unless previous notice of dishonor has been sent, an item is dishonored at the time when for purposes of dishonor it is returned or notice sent in accordance with this section.

(d)   An item is returned:

(1)   as to an item presented through a clearing house, when it is delivered to the presenting or last collecting bank or to the clearing house or is sent or delivered in accordance with clearing-house rules; or

(2)   in all other cases, when it is sent or delivered to the bank's customer or transferor or pursuant to instructions.

§ 4-302.   *Payor Bank's Responsibility for Late Return of Item.*

(a)   If an item is presented to and received by a payor bank, the bank is accountable for the amount of:

(1)   a demand item, other than a documentary draft, whether properly payable or not, if the bank, in any case in which it is not also the depositary bank, retains the item beyond midnight of the banking day of receipt without settling for it or, whether or not it is also the depositary bank, does

not pay or return the item or send notice of dishonor until after its midnight deadline; or

(2) any other properly payable item unless, within the time allowed for acceptance or payment of that item, the bank either accepts or pays the item or returns it and accompanying documents.

(b) The liability of a payor bank to pay an item pursuant to subsection (a) is subject to defenses based on breach of a presentment warranty (Section 4-208) or proof that the person seeking enforcement of the liability presented or transferred the item for the purpose of defrauding the payor bank.

§ 4-303. When Items Subject to Notice, Stop-Payment Order, Legal Process, or Setoff; Order in Which Items May Be Charged or Certified.

(a) Any knowledge, notice, or stop-payment order received by, legal process served upon, or setoff exercised by a payor bank comes too late to terminate, suspend, or modify the bank's right or duty to pay an item or to charge its customer's account for the item if the knowledge, notice, stop-payment order, or legal process is received or served and a reasonable time for the bank to act thereon expires or the setoff is exercised after the earliest of the following:

(1) the bank accepts or certifies the item;

(2) the bank pays the item in cash;

(3) the bank settles for the item without having a right to revoke the settlement under statute, clearing-house rule, or agreement;

(4) the bank becomes accountable for the amount of the item under Section 4-302 dealing with the payor bank's responsibility for late return of items; or

(5) with respect to checks, a cutoff hour no earlier than one hour after the opening of the next banking day after the banking day on which the bank received the check and no later than the close of that next banking day or, if no cutoff hour is fixed, the close of the next banking day after the banking day on which the bank received the check.

(b) Subject to subsection (a), items may be accepted, paid, certified, or charged to the indicated account of its customer in any order.

■ PART 4 Relationship Between Payor Bank and Its Customer

§ 4-401. When Bank May Charge Customer's Account.

(a) A bank may charge against the account of a customer an item that is properly payable from the account even though the charge creates an overdraft. An item is properly payable if it is authorized by the customer and is in accordance with any agreement between the customer and the bank.

(b) A customer is not liable for the amount of an overdraft if the customer neither signed the item nor benefited from the proceeds of the item.

(c) A bank may charge against the account of a customer a check that is otherwise properly payable from the account, even though payment was made before the date of the check, unless the customer has given notice to the bank of the postdating describing the check with reasonable certainty. The notice is effective for the period stated in Section 4-403(b) for stop-payment orders, and must be received at such time and in such manner as to afford the bank a reasonable opportunity to act on it before the bank takes any action with respect to the check described in Section 4-303. If a bank charges against the account of a customer a check before the date stated in the notice of postdating, the bank is liable for damages for the loss resulting from its act. The loss may include damages for dishonor of subsequent items under Section 4-402.

(d) A bank that in good faith makes payment to a holder may charge the indicated account of its customer according to:

(1) the original terms of the altered item; or

(2) the terms of the completed item, even though the bank knows the item has been completed unless the bank has notice that the completion was improper.

§ 4-402. Bank's Liability to Customer for Wrongful Dishonor; Time of Determining Insufficiency of Account.

(a) Except as otherwise provided in this Article, a payor bank wrongfully dishonors an item if it dishonors an item that is properly payable, but a bank may dishonor an item that would create an overdraft unless it has agreed to pay the overdraft.

(b) A payor bank is liable to its customer for damages proximately caused by the wrongful dishonor of an item. Liability is limited to actual damages proved and may include damages for an arrest or prosecution of the customer or other consequential damages. Whether any consequential damages are proximately caused by the wrongful dishonor is a question of fact to be determined in each case.

(c) A payor bank's determination of the customer's account balance on which a decision to dishonor for insufficiency of available funds is based may be made at any time between the time the item is received by the payor bank and the time that the payor bank returns the item or gives notice in lieu of return, and no more than one determination need be made. If, at the election of the payor bank, a subsequent balance determination is made for the purpose of reevaluating the bank's decision to dishonor the item, the account balance at that time is determinative of whether a dishonor for insufficiency of available funds is wrongful.

As amended in 1990.

See Appendix IX for material relating to changes made in text in 1990.

§ 4-403. Customer's Right to Stop Payment; Burden of Proof of Loss.

(a) A customer or any person authorized to draw on the account if there is more than one person may stop payment of any item drawn on the customer's account or close the account by an order to the bank describing the item or account with reasonable certainty received at a time and in a manner that affords the bank a reasonable opportunity to act on it before any action by the bank with respect to the item described in Section 4-303. If the signature of more than one person is required to draw on an account, any of these persons may stop payment or close the account.

(b) A stop-payment order is effective for six months, but it lapses after 14 calendar days if the original order was oral and was not confirmed in writing within that period. A stop-payment order may be renewed for additional six-month periods by a writing given to the bank within a period during which the stop-payment order is effective.

(c) The burden of establishing the fact and amount of loss resulting from the payment of an item contrary to a stop-payment order or order to close an account is on the customer. The loss from payment of an item contrary to a stop-payment order may include damages for dishonor of subsequent items under Section 4-402.

§ 4-404. Bank Not Obliged to Pay Check More Than Six Months Old.

A bank is under no obligation to a customer having a checking account to pay a check, other than a certified check, which is presented more than six months after its date, but it may charge its customer's account for a payment made thereafter in good faith.

§ 4-405. *Death or Incompetence of Customer.*

(a)   A payor or collecting bank's authority to accept, pay, or collect an item or to account for proceeds of its collection, if otherwise effective, is not rendered ineffective by incompetence of a customer of either bank existing at the time the item is issued or its collection is undertaken if the bank does not know of an adjudication of incompetence. Neither death nor incompetence of a customer revokes the authority to accept, pay, collect, or account until the bank knows of the fact of death or of an adjudication of incompetence and has reasonable opportunity to act on it.

(b)   Even with knowledge, a bank may for 10 days after the date of death pay or certify checks drawn on or before that date unless ordered to stop payment by a person claiming an interest in the account.

§ 4-406. *Customer's Duty to Discover and Report Unauthorized Signature or Alteration.*

(a)   A bank that sends or makes available to a customer a statement of account showing payment of items for the account shall either return or make available to the customer the items paid or provide information in the statement of account sufficient to allow the customer reasonably to identify the items paid. The statement of account provides sufficient information if the item is described by item number, amount, and date of payment.

(b)   If the items are not returned to the customer, the person retaining the items shall either retain the items or, if the items are destroyed, maintain the capacity to furnish legible copies of the items until the expiration of seven years after receipt of the items. A customer may request an item from the bank that paid the item, and that bank must provide in a reasonable time either the item or, if the item has been destroyed or is not otherwise obtainable, a legible copy of the item.

(c)   If a bank sends or makes available a statement of account or items pursuant to subsection (a), the customer must exercise reasonable promptness in examining the statement or the items to determine whether any payment was not authorized because of an alteration of an item or because a purported signature by or on behalf of the customer was not authorized. If, based on the statement or items provided, the customer should reasonably have discovered the unauthorized payment, the customer must promptly notify the bank of the relevant facts.

(d)   If the bank proves that the customer failed, with respect to an item, to comply with the duties imposed on the customer by subsection (c), the customer is precluded from asserting against the bank:

(1)   the customer's unauthorized signature or any alteration on the item, if the bank also proves that it suffered a loss by reason of the failure; and

(2)   the customer's unauthorized signature or alteration by the same wrong-doer on any other item paid in good faith by the bank if the payment was made before the bank received notice from the customer of the unauthorized signature or alteration and after the customer had been afforded a reasonable period of time, not exceeding 30 days, in which to examine the item or statement of account and notify the bank.

(e)   If subsection (d) applies and the customer proves that the bank failed to exercise ordinary care in paying the item and that the failure substantially contributed to loss, the loss is allocated between the customer precluded and the bank asserting the preclusion according to the extent to which the failure of the customer to comply with subsection (c) and the failure of the bank to exercise ordinary care contributed to the loss. If the customer proves that the bank did not pay the item in good faith, the preclusion under subsection (d) does not apply.

(f)   Without regard to care or lack of care of either the customer or the bank, a customer who does not within one year after the statement or items are made available to the customer (subsection (a)) discover and report the customer's unauthorized signature on or any alteration on the item is precluded from asserting against the bank the unauthorized signature or alteration. If there is a preclusion under this subsection, the payor bank may not recover for breach or warranty under Section 4-208 with respect to the unauthorized signature or alteration to which the preclusion applies.

§ 4-407. *Payor Bank's Right to Subrogation on Improper Payment.*

If a payor bank has paid an item over the order of the drawer or maker to stop payment, or after an account has been closed, or otherwise under circumstances giving a basis for objection by the drawer or maker, to prevent unjust enrichment and only to the extent necessary to prevent loss to the bank by reason of its payment of the item, the payor bank is subrogated to the rights

(1)   of any holder in due course on the item against the drawer or maker;

(2)   of the payee or any other holder of the item against the drawer or maker either on the item or under the transaction out of which the item arose; and

(3)   of the drawer or maker against the payee or any other holder of the item with respect to the transaction out of which the item arose.

■ PART 5   Collection of Documentary Drafts

§ 4-501. *Handling of Documentary Drafts; Duty to Send for Presentment and to Notify Customer of Dishonor.*

A bank that takes a documentary draft for collection shall present or send the draft and accompanying documents for presentment and, upon learning that the draft has not been paid or accepted in due course, shall seasonably notify its customer of the fact even though it may have discounted or bought the draft or extended credit available for withdrawal as of right.

§ 4-502. *Presentment of "On Arrival" Drafts.*

If a draft or the relevant instructions require presentment "on arrival", "when goods arrive" or the like, the collecting bank need not present until in its judgment a reasonable time for arrival of the goods has expired. Refusal to pay or accept because the goods have not arrived is not dishonor; the bank must notify its transferor of the refusal but need not present the draft again until it is instructed to do so or learns of the arrival of the goods.

§ 4-503. *Responsibility of Presenting Bank for Documents and Goods; Report of Reasons for Dishonor; Referee in Case of Need.*

Unless otherwise instructed and except as provided in Article 5, a bank presenting a documentary draft:

(1)   must deliver the documents to the drawee on acceptance of the draft if it is payable more than three days after presentment; otherwise, only on payment; and

(2)   upon dishonor, either in the case of presentment for acceptance or presentment for payment, may seek and follow instructions from any referee in case of need designated in the draft or, if the presenting bank does not choose to utilize the referee's services, it must use diligence and good faith to ascertain the reason for dishonor, must notify its transferor of the dishonor and of the results of its effort to ascertain the reasons therefor, and must request instructions.

However the presenting bank is under no obligation with respect to goods represented by the documents except to follow any reasonable instructions seasonably received; it has a right to reimbursement for any expense incurred in following instructions and to prepayment of or indemnity for those expenses.

§ 4-504. Privilege of Presenting Bank to Deal With Goods; Security Interest for Expenses.

(a)   A presenting bank that, following the dishonor of a documentary draft, has seasonably requested instructions but does not receive them within a reasonable time may store, sell, or otherwise deal with the goods in any reasonable manner.

(b)   For its reasonable expenses incurred by action under subsection (a) the presenting bank has a lien upon the goods or their proceeds, which may be foreclosed in the same manner as an unpaid seller's lien.

ARTICLE 4A
Funds Transfers

■ PART I   Subject Matter and Definitions

§ 4A-101. Short Title.

This Article may be cited as Uniform Commercial Code—Funds Transfers.

§ 4A-102. Subject Matter.

Except as otherwise provided in Section 4A-108, this Article applies to funds transfers defined in Section 4A-104.

§ 4A-103. Payment Order—Definitions.

(a)   In this Article:

(1)   "Payment order" means an instruction of a sender to a receiving bank, transmitted orally, electronically, or in writing, to pay, or to cause another bank to pay, a fixed or determinable amount of money to a beneficiary if:

(i)   the instruction does not state a condition to payment to the beneficiary other than time of payment,

(ii)   the receiving bank is to be reimbursed by debiting an account of, or otherwise receiving payment from, the sender, and

(iii)   the instruction is transmitted by the sender directly to the receiving bank or to an agent, funds-transfer system, or communication system for transmittal to the receiving bank.

(2)   "Beneficiary" means the person to be paid by the beneficiary's bank.

(3)   "Beneficiary's bank" means the bank identified in a payment order in which an account of the beneficiary is to be credited pursuant to the order or which otherwise is to make payment to the beneficiary if the order does not provide for payment to an account.

(4)   "Receiving bank" means the bank to which the sender's instruction is addressed.

(5)   "Sender" means the person giving the instruction to the receiving bank.

(b)   If an instruction complying with subsection (a)(1) is to make more than one payment to a beneficiary, the instruction is a separate payment order with respect to each payment.

(c)   A payment order is issued when it is sent to the receiving bank.

§ 4A-104. Funds Transfer—Definitions.

In this Article:

(a)   "Funds transfer" means the series of transactions, beginning with the originator's payment order, made for the purpose of making payment to the beneficiary of the order. The term includes any payment order issued by the originator's bank or an intermediary bank intended to carry out the originator's payment order. A funds transfer is completed by acceptance by the beneficiary's bank of a payment order for the benefit of the beneficiary of the originator's payment order.

(b)   "Intermediary bank" means a receiving bank other than the originator's bank or the beneficiary's bank.

(c)   "Originator" means the sender of the first payment order in a funds transfer.

(d)   "Originator's bank" means (i) the receiving bank to which the payment order of the originator is issued if the originator is not a bank, or (ii) the originator if the originator is a bank.

§ 4A-105. Other Definitions.

(a)   In this Article:

(1)   "Authorized account" means a deposit account of a customer in a bank designated by the customer as a source of payment orders issued by the customer to the bank. If a customer does not so designate an account, any account of the customer is an authorized account if payment of a payment order from that account is not inconsistent with a restriction on the use of that account.

(2)   "Bank" means a person engaged in the business of banking and includes a savings bank, savings and loan association, credit union, and trust company. A branch or separate office of a bank is a separate bank for purposes of this Article.

(3)   "Customer" means a person, including a bank, having an account with a bank or from whom a bank has agreed to receive payment orders.

(4)   "Funds-transfer business day" of a receiving bank means the part of a day during which the receiving bank is open for the receipt, processing, and transmittal of payment orders and cancellations and amendments of payment orders.

(5)   "Funds-transfer system" means a wire transfer network, automated clearing house, or other communication system of a clearing house or other association of banks through which a payment order by a bank may be transmitted to the bank to which the order is addressed.

(6)   "Good faith" means honesty in fact and the observance of reasonable commercial standards of fair dealing.

(7)   "Prove" with respect to a fact means to meet the burden of establishing the fact (Section 1-201(8)).

(b)   Other definitions applying to this Article and the sections in which they appear are:

"Acceptance" Section 4A-209
"Beneficiary" Section 4A-103
"Beneficiary's bank" Section 4A-103
"Executed" Section 4A-301
"Execution date" Section 4A-301
"Funds transfer" Section 4A-104
"Funds-transfer system rule" Section 4A-501
"Intermediary bank" Section 4A-104
"Originator" Section 4A-104
"Originator's bank" Section 4A-104
"Payment by beneficiary's bank to beneficiary" Section 4A-405
"Payment by originator to beneficiary" Section 4A-406
"Payment by sender to receiving bank" Section 4A-403
"Payment date" Section 4A-401
"Payment order" Section 4A-103
"Receiving bank" Section 4A-103
"Security procedure" Section 4A-201
"Sender" Section 4A-103

(c)   The following definitions in Article 4 apply to this Article:

"Clearing house" Section 4-104

"Item" Section 4-104

"Suspends payments" Section 4-104

(d)   In addition Article 1 contains general definitions and principles of construction and interpretation applicable throughout this Article.

§ 4A-106. *Time Payment Order Is Received.*

(a)   The time of receipt of a payment order or communication cancelling or amending a payment order is determined by the rules applicable to receipt of a notice stated in Section 1-201(27). A receiving bank may fix a cut-off time or times on a funds-transfer business day for the receipt and processing of payment orders and communications cancelling or amending payment orders. Different cut-off times may apply to payment orders, cancellations, or amendments, or to different categories of payment orders, cancellations, or amendments. A cut-off time may apply to senders generally or different cut-off times may apply to different senders or categories of payment orders. If a payment order or communication cancelling or amending a payment order is received after the close of a funds-transfer business day or after the appropriate cut-off time on a funds-transfer business day, the receiving bank may treat the payment order or communication as received at the opening of the next funds-transfer business day.

(b)   If this Article refers to an execution date or payment date or states a day on which a receiving bank is required to take action, and the date or day does not fall on a funds-transfer business day, the next day that is a funds-transfer business day is treated as the date or day stated, unless the contrary is stated in this Article.

§ 4A-107. *Federal Reserve Regulations and Operating Circulars.*

Regulations of the Board of Governors of the Federal Reserve System and operating circulars of the Federal Reserve Banks supersede any inconsistent provision of this Article to the extent of the inconsistency.

§ 4A-108. *Exclusion of Consumer Transactions Governed by Federal Law.*

This Article does not apply to a funds transfer any part of which is governed by the Electronic Fund Transfer Act of 1978 (Title XX, Public Law 95-630, 92 Stat. 3728, 15 U.S.C. § 1693 et seq.) as amended from time to time.

■ PART 2   Issue and Acceptance of Payment Order

§ 4A-201. *Security Procedure.*

"Security procedure" means a procedure established by agreement of a customer and a receiving bank for the purpose of (i) verifying that a payment order or communication amending or cancelling a payment order is that of the customer, or (ii) detecting error in the transmission or the content of the payment order or communication. A security procedure may require the use of algorithms or other codes, identifying words or numbers, encryption, callback procedures, or similar security devices. Comparison of a signature on a payment order or communication with an authorized specimen signature of the customer is not by itself a security procedure.

§ 4A-202. *Authorized and Verified Payment Orders.*

(a)   A payment order received by the receiving bank is the authorized order of the person identified as sender if that person authorized the order or is otherwise bound by it under the law of agency.

(b)   If a bank and its customer have agreed that the authenticity of payment orders issued to the bank in the name of the customer as sender will be verified pursuant to a security procedure, a payment order received by the receiving bank is effective as the order of the customer, whether or not authorized, if (i) the security procedure is a commercially reasonable method of providing security against unauthorized payment orders, and (ii) the bank proves that it accepted the payment order in good faith and in compliance with the security procedure and any written agreement or instruction of the customer restricting acceptance of payment orders issued in the name of the customer. The bank is not required to follow an instruction that violates a written agreement with the customer or notice of which is not received at a time and in a manner affording the bank a reasonable opportunity to act on it before the payment order is accepted.

(c)   Commercial reasonableness of a security procedure is a question of law to be determined by considering the wishes of the customer expressed to the bank, the circumstances of the customer known to the bank, including the size, type, and frequency of payment orders normally issued by the customer to the bank, alternative security procedures offered to the customer, and security procedures in general use by customers and receiving banks similarly situated. A security procedure is deemed to be commercially reasonable if (i) the security procedure was chosen by the customer after the bank offered, and the customer refused, a security procedure that was commercially reasonable for that customer, and (ii) the customer expressly agreed in writing to be bound by any payment order, whether or not authorized, issued in its name and accepted by the bank in compliance with the security procedure chosen by the customer.

(d)   The term "sender" in this Article includes the customer in whose name a payment order is issued if the order is the authorized order of the customer under subsection (a), or it is effective as the order of the customer under subsection (b).

(e)   This section applies to amendments and cancellations of payment orders to the same extent it applies to payment orders.

(f)   Except as provided in this section and in Section 4A-203(a)(1), rights and obligations arising under this section or Section 4A-203 may not be varied by agreement.

§ 4A-203. *Unenforceability of Certain Verified Payment Orders.*

(a)   If an accepted payment order is not, under Section 4A-202(a), an authorized order of a customer identified as sender, but is effective as an order of the customer pursuant to Section 4A-202(b), the following rules apply:

(1)   By express written agreement, the receiving bank may limit the extent to which it is entitled to enforce or retain payment of the payment order.

(2)   The receiving bank is not entitled to enforce or retain payment of the payment order if the customer proves that the order was not caused, directly or indirectly, by a person (i) entrusted at any time with duties to act for the customer with respect to payment orders or the security procedure, or (ii) who obtained access to transmitting facilities of the customer or who obtained, from a source controlled by the customer and without authority of the receiving bank, information facilitating breach of the security procedure, regardless of how the information was obtained or whether the customer was at fault. Information includes any access device, computer software, or the like.

(b)   This section applies to amendments of payment orders to the same extent it applies to payment orders.

§ 4A-204. *Refund of Payment and Duty of Customer to Report with Respect to Unauthorized Payment Order.*

(a)   If a receiving bank accepts a payment order issued in the name of its customer as sender which is (i) not authorized and not effective as the order of the customer under Section 4A-202, or (ii) not enforceable, in whole or in part, against the customer under Section 4A-203, the bank shall refund any payment of the payment order received from the customer to the extent the bank is not entitled to enforce payment and shall pay interest on the refundable amount calculated from the date the bank received payment to the date of the refund. However, the customer is not entitled to interest from the bank on the amount to be refunded if the customer fails to exercise ordinary care to determine that the order was not authorized by the customer and to notify the bank of the relevant facts within a reasonable time not exceeding 90 days after the date the customer received notification from the bank that the order was accepted or that the customer's account was debited with respect to the order. The bank is not entitled to any recovery from the customer on account of a failure by the customer to give notification as stated in this section.

(b)   Reasonable time under subsection (a) may be fixed by agreement as stated in Section 1-204(1), but the obligation of a receiving bank to refund payment as stated in subsection (a) may not otherwise be varied by agreement.

§ 4A-205. *Erroneous Payment Orders.*

(a)   If an accepted payment order was transmitted pursuant to a security procedure for the detection of error and the payment order (i) erroneously instructed payment to a beneficiary not intended by the sender, (ii) erroneously instructed payment in an amount greater than the amount intended by the sender, or (iii) was an erroneously transmitted duplicate of a payment order previously sent by the sender, the following rules apply:

(1)   If the sender proves that the sender or a person acting on behalf of the sender pursuant to Section 4A-206 complied with the security procedure and that the error would have been detected if the receiving bank had also complied, the sender is not obliged to pay the order to the extent stated in paragraphs (2) and (3).

(2)   If the funds transfer is completed on the basis of an erroneous payment order described in clause (i) or (iii) of subsection (a), the sender is not obliged to pay the order and the receiving bank is entitled to recover from the beneficiary any amount paid to the beneficiary to the extent allowed by the law governing mistake and restitution.

(3)   If the funds transfer is completed on the basis of a payment order described in clause (ii) of subsection (a), the sender is not obliged to pay the order to the extent the amount received by the beneficiary is greater than the amount intended by the sender. In that case, the receiving bank is entitled to recover from the beneficiary the excess amount received to the extent allowed by the law governing mistake and restitution.

(b)   If (i) the sender of an erroneous payment order described in subsection (a) is not obliged to pay all or part of the order, and (ii) the sender receives notification from the receiving bank that the order was accepted by the bank or that the sender's account was debited with respect to the order, the sender has a duty to exercise ordinary care, on the basis of information available to the sender, to discover the error with respect to the order and to advise the bank of the relevant facts within a reasonable time, not exceeding 90 days, after the bank's notification was received by the sender. If the bank proves that the sender failed to perform that duty, the sender is liable to the bank for the loss the bank proves it incurred as a result of the failure, but the liability of the sender may not exceed the amount of the sender's order.

(c)   This section applies to amendments to payment orders to the same extent it applies to payment orders.

§ 4A-206. *Transmission of Payment Order Through Funds-Transfer or Other Communication System.*

(a)   If a payment order addressed to a receiving bank is transmitted to a funds-transfer system or other third-party communication system for transmittal to the bank, the system is deemed to be an agent of the sender for the purpose of transmitting the payment order to the bank. If there is a discrepancy between the terms of the payment order transmitted to the system and the terms of the payment order transmitted by the system to the bank, the terms of the payment order of the sender are those transmitted by the system. This section does not apply to a funds-transfer system of the Federal Reserve Banks.

(b)   This section applies to cancellations and amendments of payment orders to the same extent it applies to payment orders.

§ 4A-207. *Misdescription of Beneficiary.*

(a)   Subject to subsection (b), if, in a payment order received by the beneficiary's bank, the name, bank account number, or other identification of the beneficiary refers to a nonexistent or unidentifiable person or account, no person has rights as a beneficiary of the order and acceptance of the order cannot occur.

(b)   If a payment order received by the beneficiary's bank identifies the beneficiary both by name and by an identifying or bank account number and the name and number identify different persons, the following rules apply:

(1)   Except as otherwise provided in subsection (c), if the beneficiary's bank does not know that the name and number refer to different persons, it may rely on the number as the proper identification of the beneficiary of the order. The beneficiary's bank need not determine whether the name and number refer to the same person.

(2)   If the beneficiary's bank pays the person identified by name or knows that the name and number identify different persons, no person has rights as beneficiary except the person paid by the beneficiary's bank if that person was entitled to receive payment from the originator of the funds transfer. If no person has rights as beneficiary, acceptance of the order cannot occur.

(c)   If (i) a payment order described in subsection (b) is accepted, (ii) the originator's payment order described the beneficiary inconsistently by name and number, and (ii) the beneficiary's bank pays the person identified by number as permitted by subsection (b)(1), the following rules apply:

(1)   If the originator is a bank, the originator is obliged to pay its order.

(2)   If the originator is not a bank and proves that the person identified by number was not entitled to receive payment from the originator, the originator is not obliged to pay its order unless the originator's bank proves that the originator, before acceptance of the originator's order, had notice that payment of a payment order issued by the originator might be made by the beneficiary's bank on the basis of an identifying or bank account number even if it identifies a person different from the named beneficiary. Proof of notice may be made by any admissible evidence. The originator's bank satisfies the burden of proof if it proves that the originator, before the payment order was accepted, signed a writing stating the information to which the notice relates.

(d)   In a case governed by subsection (b)(1), if the beneficiary's bank rightfully pays the person identified by number and that person was not entitled to receive payment from the originator, the amount paid may be recovered from that person to the extent allowed by the law governing mistake and restitution as follows:

(1)   If the originator is obliged to pay its payment order as stated in subsection (c), the originator has the right to recover.

(2)   If the originator is not a bank and is not obliged to pay its payment order, the originator's bank has the right to recover.

§ 4A-208. *Misdescription of Intermediary Bank or Beneficiary's Bank.*

(a)   This subsection applies to a payment order identifying an intermediary bank or the beneficiary's bank only by an identifying number.

(1)   The receiving bank may rely on the number as the proper identification of the intermediary or beneficiary's bank and need not determine whether the number identifies a bank.

(2)   The sender is obliged to compensate the receiving bank for any loss and expenses incurred by the receiving bank as a result of its reliance on the number in executing or attempting to execute the order.

(b)   This subsection applies to a payment order identifying an intermediary bank or the beneficiary's bank both by name and an identifying number if the name and number identify different persons.

(1)   If the sender is a bank, the receiving bank may rely on the number as the proper identification of the intermediary or beneficiary's bank if the receiving bank, when it executes the sender's order, does not know that the name and number identify different persons. The receiving bank need not determine whether the name and number refer to the same person or whether the name refers to a bank. The sender is obliged to compensate the receiving bank for any loss and expenses incurred by the receiving bank as a result of its reliance on the number in executing or attempting to execute the order.

(2)   If the sender is not a bank and the receiving bank proves that the sender, before the payment order was accepted, had notice that the receiving bank might rely on the number as the proper identification of the intermediary or beneficiary's bank even if it identifies a person different from the bank identified by name, the rights and obligations of the sender and the receiving bank are governed by subsection (b)(1), as though the sender were a bank. Proof of notice may be made by any admissible evidence. The receiving bank satisfies the burden of proof if it proves that the sender, before the payment order was accepted, signed a writing stating the information to which the notice relates.

(3)   Regardless of whether the sender is a bank, the receiving bank may rely on the name as the proper identification of the intermediary or beneficiary's bank if the receiving bank, at the time it executes the sender's order, does not know that the name and number identify different persons. The receiving bank need not determine whether the name and number refer to the same person.

(4)   If the receiving bank knows that the name and number identify different persons, reliance on either the name or the number in executing the sender's payment order is a breach of the obligation stated in Section 4A-302(a)(1).

§ 4A-209. *Acceptance of Payment Order.*

(a)   Subject to subsection (d), a receiving bank other than the beneficiary's bank accepts a payment order when it executes the order.

(b)   Subject to subsections (c) and (d), a beneficiary's bank accepts a payment order at the earliest of the following times:

(1)   when the bank (i) pays the beneficiary as stated in Section 4A-405(a) or 4A-405(b), or (ii) notifies the beneficiary of receipt of the order or that the account of the beneficiary has been credited with respect to the order unless the notice indicates that the bank is rejecting the order or that funds with respect to the order may not be withdrawn or used until receipt of payment from the sender of the order;

(2)   when the bank receives payment of the entire amount of the sender's order pursuant to Section 4A-403(a)(1) or 4A-403(a)(2); or

(3)   the opening of the next funds-transfer business day of the bank following the payment date of the order if, at that time, the amount of the sender's order is fully covered by a withdrawable credit balance in an authorized account of the sender or the bank has otherwise received full payment from the sender, unless the order was rejected before that time or is rejected within (i) one hour after that time, or (ii) one hour after the opening of the next business day of the sender following the payment date if that time is later. If notice of rejection is received by the sender after the payment date and the authorized account of the sender does not bear interest, the bank is obliged to pay interest to the sender on the amount of the order for the number of days elapsing after the payment date to the day the sender receives notice or learns that the order was not accepted, counting that day as an elapsed day. If the withdrawable credit balance during that period falls below the amount of the order, the amount of interest payable is reduced accordingly.

(c)   Acceptance of a payment order cannot occur before the order is received by the receiving bank. Acceptance does not occur under subsection (b)(2) or (b)(3) if the beneficiary of the payment order does not have an account with the receiving bank, the account has been closed, or the receiving bank is not permitted by law to receive credits for the beneficiary's account.

(d)   A payment order issued to the originator's bank cannot be accepted until the payment date if the bank is the beneficiary's bank, or the execution date if the bank is not the beneficiary's bank. If the originator's bank executes the originator's payment order before the execution date or pays the beneficiary of the originator's payment order before the payment date and the payment order is subsequently canceled pursuant to Section 4A-211(b), the bank may recover from the beneficiary any payment received to the extent allowed by the law governing mistake and restitution.

§ 4A-210. *Rejection of Payment Order.*

(a)   A payment order is rejected by the receiving bank by a notice of rejection transmitted to the sender orally, electronically, or in writing. A notice of rejection need not use any particular words and is sufficient if it indicates that the receiving bank is rejecting the order or will not execute or pay the order. Rejection is effective when the notice is given if transmission is by a means that is reasonable in the circumstances. If notice of rejection is given by a means that is not reasonable, rejection is effective when the notice is received. If an agreement of the sender and receiving bank establishes the means to be used to reject a payment order, (i) any means complying with the agreement is reasonable and (ii) any means not complying is not reasonable unless no significant delay in receipt of the notice resulted from the use of the noncomplying means.

(b)   This subsection applies if a receiving bank other than the beneficiary's bank fails to execute a payment order despite the existence on the execution date of a withdrawable credit balance in an authorized account of the sender sufficient to cover the order. If the sender does not receive notice of rejection of the order on the execution date and the authorized account of the sender does not bear interest, the bank is obliged to pay interest to the sender on the amount of the order for the number of days elapsing after the execution date to the earlier of the day the order is canceled pursuant to Section 4A-211(d) or the day the sender receives notice or learns that the order was not executed, counting the final day of the period as an elapsed day. If the withdrawable credit balance during that period falls below the amount of the order, the amount of interest is reduced accordingly.

(c) If a receiving bank suspends payments, all unaccepted payment orders issued to it are deemed rejected at the time the bank suspends payments.

(d) Acceptance of a payment order precludes a later rejection of the order. Rejection of a payment order precludes a later acceptance of the order.

§ 4A-211. Cancellation and Amendment of Payment Order.

(a) A communication of the sender of a payment order cancelling or amending the order may be transmitted to the receiving bank orally, electronically, or in writing. If a security procedure is in effect between the sender and the receiving bank, the communication is not effective to cancel or amend the order unless the communication is verified pursuant to the security procedure or the bank agrees to the cancellation or amendment.

(b) Subject to subsection (a), a communication by the sender cancelling or amending a payment order is effective to cancel or amend the order if notice of the communication is received at a time and in a manner affording the receiving bank a reasonable opportunity to act on the communication before the bank accepts the payment order.

(c) After a payment order has been accepted, cancellation or amendment of the order is not effective unless the receiving bank agrees or a funds-transfer system rule allows cancellation or amendment without agreement of the bank.

(1) With respect to a payment order accepted by a receiving bank other than the beneficiary's bank, cancellation or amendment is not effective unless a conforming cancellation or amendment of the payment order issued by the receiving bank is also made.

(2) With respect to a payment order accepted by the beneficiary's bank, cancellation or amendment is not effective unless the order was issued in execution of an unauthorized payment order, or because of a mistake by a sender in the funds transfer which resulted in the issuance of a payment order (i) that is a duplicate of a payment order previously issued by the sender, (ii) that orders payment to a beneficiary not entitled to receive payment from the originator, or (iii) that orders payment in an amount greater than the amount the beneficiary was entitled to receive from the originator. If the payment order is canceled or amended, the beneficiary's bank is entitled to recover from the beneficiary any amount paid to the beneficiary to the extent allowed by the law governing mistake and restitution.

(d) An unaccepted payment order is canceled by operation of law at the close of the fifth funds-transfer business day of the receiving bank after the execution date or payment date of the order.

(e) A canceled payment order cannot be accepted. If an accepted payment order is canceled, the acceptance is nullified and no person has any right or obligation based on the acceptance. Amendment of a payment order is deemed to be cancellation of the original order at the time of amendment and issue of a new payment order in the amended form at the same time.

(f) Unless otherwise provided in an agreement of the parties or in a funds-transfer system rule, if the receiving bank, after accepting a payment order, agrees to cancellation or amendment of the order by the sender or is bound by a funds-transfer system rule allowing cancellation or amendment without the bank's agreement, the sender, whether or not cancellation or amendment is effective, is liable to the bank for any loss and expenses, including reasonable attorney's fees, incurred by the bank as a result of the cancellation or amendment or attempted cancellation or amendment.

(g) A payment order is not revoked by the death or legal incapacity of the sender unless the receiving bank knows of the death or of an adjudication of incapacity by a court of competent jurisdiction and has reasonable opportunity to act before acceptance of the order.

(h) A funds-transfer system rule is not effective to the extent it conflicts with subsection (c)(2).

§ 4A-212. Liability and Duty of Receiving Bank Regarding Unaccepted Payment Order.

If a receiving bank fails to accept a payment order that it is obliged by express agreement to accept, the bank is liable for breach of the agreement to the extent provided in the agreement or in this Article, but does not otherwise have any duty to accept a payment order or, before acceptance, to take any action, or refrain from taking action, with respect to the order except as provided in this Article or by express agreement. Liability based on acceptance arises only when acceptance occurs as stated in Section 4A-209, and liability is limited to that provided in this Article. A receiving bank is not the agent of the sender or beneficiary of the payment order it accepts, or of any other party to the funds transfer, and the bank owes no duty to any party to the funds transfer except as provided in this Article or by express agreement.

■ PART 3 Execution of Sender's Payment Order by Receiving Bank

§ 4A-301. Execution and Execution Date.

(a) A payment order is "executed" by the receiving bank when it issues a payment order intended to carry out the payment order received by the bank. A payment order received by the beneficiary's bank can be accepted but cannot be executed.

(b) "Execution date" of a payment order means the day on which the receiving bank may properly issue a payment order in execution of the sender's order. The execution date may be determined by instruction of the sender but cannot be earlier than the day the order is received and, unless otherwise determined, is the day the order is received. If the sender's instruction states a payment date, the execution date is the payment date or an earlier date on which execution is reasonably necessary to allow payment to the beneficiary on the payment date.

§ 4A-302. Obligations of Receiving Bank in Execution of Payment Order.

(a) Except as provided in subsections (b) through (d), if the receiving bank accepts a payment order pursuant to Section 4A-209(a), the bank has the following obligations in executing the order:

(1) The receiving bank is obliged to issue, on the execution date, a payment order complying with the sender's order and to follow the sender's instructions concerning (i) any intermediary bank or funds-transfer system to be used in carrying out the funds transfer, or (ii) the means by which payment orders are to be transmitted in the funds transfer. If the originator's bank issues a payment order to an intermediary bank, the originator's bank is obliged to instruct the intermediary bank according to the instruction of the originator. An intermediary bank in the funds transfer is similarly bound by an instruction given to it by the sender of the payment order it accepts.

(2) If the sender's instruction states that the funds transfer is to be carried out telephonically or by wire transfer

or otherwise indicates that the funds transfer is to be carried out by the most expeditious means, the receiving bank is obliged to transmit its payment order by the most expeditious available means, and to instruct any intermediary bank accordingly. If a sender's instruction states a payment date, the receiving bank is obliged to transmit its payment order at a time and by means reasonably necessary to allow payment to the beneficiary on the payment date or as soon thereafter as is feasible.

(b)   Unless otherwise instructed, a receiving bank executing a payment order may (i) use any funds-transfer system if use of that system is reasonable in the circumstances, and (ii) issue a payment order to the beneficiary's bank or to an intermediary bank through which a payment order conforming to the sender's order can expeditiously be issued to the beneficiary's bank if the receiving bank exercises ordinary care in the selection of the intermediary bank. A receiving bank is not required to follow an instruction of the sender designating a funds-transfer system to be used in carrying out the funds transfer if the receiving bank, in good faith, determines that it is not feasible to follow the instruction or that following the instruction would unduly delay completion of the funds transfer.

(c)   Unless subsection (a)(2) applies or the receiving bank is otherwise instructed, the bank may execute a payment order by transmitting its payment order by first class mail or by any means reasonable in the circumstances. If the receiving bank is instructed to execute the sender's order by transmitting its payment order by a particular means, the receiving bank may issue its payment order by the means stated or by any means as expeditious as the means stated.

(d)   Unless instructed by the sender, (i) the receiving bank may not obtain payment of its charges for services and expenses in connection with the execution of the sender's order by issuing a payment order in an amount equal to the amount of the sender's order less the amount of the charges, and (ii) may not instruct a subsequent receiving bank to obtain payment of its charges in the same manner.

§ 4A-303. Erroneous Execution of Payment Order.

(a)   A receiving bank that (i) executes the payment order of the sender by issuing a payment order in an amount greater than the amount of the sender's order, or (ii) issues a payment order in execution of the sender's order and then issues a duplicate order, is entitled to payment of the amount of the sender's order under Section 4A-402(c) if that subsection is otherwise satisfied. The bank is entitled to recover from the beneficiary of the erroneous order the excess payment received to the extent allowed by the law governing mistake and restitution.

(b)   A receiving bank that executes the payment order of the sender by issuing a payment order in an amount less than the amount of the sender's order is entitled to payment of the amount of the sender's order under Section 4A-402(c) if (i) that subsection is otherwise satisfied and (ii) the bank corrects its mistake by issuing an additional payment order for the benefit of the beneficiary of the sender's order. If the error is not corrected, the issuer of the erroneous order is entitled to receive or retain payment from the sender of the order it accepted only to the extent of the amount of the erroneous order. This subsection does not apply if the receiving bank executes the sender's payment order by issuing a payment order in an amount less than the amount of the sender's order for the purpose of obtaining payment of its charges for services and expenses pursuant to instruction of the sender.

(c)   If a receiving bank executes the payment order of the sender by issuing a payment order to a beneficiary different from the beneficiary of the sender's order and the funds transfer is completed on the basis of that error, the sender of the payment order that was erroneously executed and all previous senders in the funds transfer are not obliged to pay the payment orders they issued. The issuer of the erroneous order is entitled to recover from the beneficiary of the order the payment received to the extent allowed by the law governing mistake and restitution.

§ 4A-304. Duty of Sender to Report Erroneously Executed Payment Order.

If the sender of a payment order that is erroneously executed as stated in Section 4A-303 receives notification from the receiving bank that the order was executed or that the sender's account was debited with respect to the order, the sender has a duty to exercise ordinary care to determine, on the basis of information available to the sender, that the order was erroneously executed and to notify the bank of the relevant facts within a reasonable time not exceeding 90 days after the notification from the bank was received by the sender. If the sender fails to perform that duty, the bank is not obliged to pay interest on any amount refundable to the sender under Section 4A-402(d) for the period before the bank learns of the execution error. The bank is not entitled to any recovery from the sender on account of a failure by the sender to perform the duty stated in this section.

§ 4A-305. Liability for Late or Improper Execution or Failure to Execute Payment Order.

(a)   If a funds transfer is completed but execution of a payment order by the receiving bank in breach of Section 4A-302 results in delay in payment to the beneficiary, the bank is obliged to pay interest to either the originator or the beneficiary of the funds transfer for the period of delay caused by the improper execution. Except as provided in subsection (c), additional damages are not recoverable.

(b)   If execution of a payment order by a receiving bank in breach of Section 4A-302 results in (i) noncompletion of the funds transfer, (ii) failure to use an intermediary bank designated by the originator, or (iii) issuance of a payment order that does not comply with the terms of the payment order of the originator, the bank is liable to the originator for its expenses in the funds transfer and for incidental expenses and interest losses, to the extent not covered by subsection (a), resulting from the improper execution. Except as provided in subsection (c), additional damages are not recoverable.

(c)   In addition to the amounts payable under subsections (a) and (b), damages, including consequential damages, are recoverable to the extent provided in an express written agreement of the receiving bank.

(d)   If a receiving bank fails to execute a payment order it was obliged by express agreement to execute, the receiving bank is liable to the sender for its expenses in the transaction and for incidental expenses and interest losses resulting from the failure to execute. Additional damages, including consequential damages, are recoverable to the extent provided in an express written agreement of the receiving bank, but are not otherwise recoverable.

(e)   Reasonable attorney's fees are recoverable if demand for compensation under subsection (a) or (b) is made and refused before an action is brought on the claim. If a claim is made for breach of an agreement under subsection (d) and the agreement does not provide for damages, reasonable attorney's fees are recoverable if demand for compensation under subsection (d) is made and refused before an action is brought on the claim.

(f)   Except as stated in this section, the liability of a receiving bank under subsections (a) and (b) may not be varied by agreement.

■ PART 4 Payment

§ 4A-401. Payment Date.

"Payment date" of a payment order means the day on which the amount of the order is payable to the beneficiary by the beneficiary's bank. The payment date may be determined by instruction of the sender but cannot be earlier than the day the order is received by the beneficiary's bank and, unless otherwise determined, is the day the order is received by the beneficiary's bank.

§ 4A-402. Obligation of Sender to Pay Receiving Bank.

(a)   This section is subject to Sections 4A-205 and 4A-207.

(b)   With respect to a payment order issued to the beneficiary's bank, acceptance of the order by the bank obliges the sender to pay the bank the amount of the order, but payment is not due until the payment date of the order.

(c)   This subsection is subject to subsection (e) and to Section 4A-303. With respect to a payment order issued to a receiving bank other than the beneficiary's bank, acceptance of the order by the receiving bank obliges the sender to pay the bank the amount of the sender's order. Payment by the sender is not due until the execution date of the sender's order. The obligation of that sender to pay its payment order is excused if the funds transfer is not completed by acceptance by the beneficiary's bank of a payment order instructing payment to the beneficiary of that sender's payment order.

(d)   If the sender of a payment order pays the order and was not obliged to pay all or part of the amount paid, the bank receiving payment is obliged to refund payment to the extent the sender was not obliged to pay. Except as provided in Sections 4A-204 and 4A-304, interest is payable on the refundable amount from the date of payment.

(e)   If a funds transfer is not completed as stated in subsection (c) and an intermediary bank is obliged to refund payment as stated in subsection (d) but is unable to do so because not permitted by applicable law or because the bank suspends payments, a sender in the funds transfer that executed a payment order in compliance with an instruction, as stated in Section 4A-302(a)(1), to route the funds transfer through that intermediary bank is entitled to receive or retain payment from the sender of the payment order that it accepted. The first sender in the funds transfer that issued an instruction requiring routing through that intermediary bank is subrogated to the right of the bank that paid the intermediary bank to refund as stated in subsection (d).

(f)   The right of the sender of a payment order to be excused from the obligation to pay the order as stated in subsection (c) or to receive refund under subsection (d) may not be varied by agreement.

§ 4A-403. Payment by Sender to Receiving Bank.

(a)   Payment of the sender's obligation under Section 4A-402 to pay the receiving bank occurs as follows:

(1)   If the sender is a bank, payment occurs when the receiving bank receives final settlement of the obligation through a Federal Reserve Bank or through a funds-transfer system.

(2)   If the sender is a bank and the sender (i) credited an account of the receiving bank with the sender, or (ii) caused an account of the receiving bank in another bank to be credited, payment occurs when the credit is withdrawn or, if not withdrawn, at midnight of the day on which the credit is withdrawable and the receiving bank learns of that fact.

(3)   If the receiving bank debits an account of the sender with the receiving bank, payment occurs when the debit is made to the extent the debit is covered by a withdrawable credit balance in the account.

(b)   If the sender and receiving bank are members of a funds-transfer system that nets obligations multilaterally among participants, the receiving bank receives final settlement when settlement is complete in accordance with the rules of the system. The obligation of the sender to pay the amount of a payment order transmitted through the funds-transfer system may be satisfied, to the extent permitted by the rules of the system, by setting off and applying against the sender's obligation the right of the sender to receive payment from the receiving bank of the amount of any other payment order transmitted to the sender by the receiving bank through the funds-transfer system. The aggregate balance of obligations owed by each sender to each receiving bank in the funds-transfer system may be satisfied, to the extent permitted by the rules of the system, by setting off and applying against that balance the aggregate balance of obligations owed to the sender by other members of the system. The aggregate balance is determined after the right of setoff stated in the second sentence of this subsection has been exercised.

(c)   If two banks transmit payment orders to each other under an agreement that settlement of the obligations of each bank to the other under Section 4A-402 will be made at the end of the day or other period, the total amount owed with respect to all orders transmitted by one bank shall be set off against the total amount owed with respect to all orders transmitted by the other bank. To the extent of the setoff, each bank has made payment to the other.

(d)   In a case not covered by subsection (a), the time when payment of the sender's obligation under Section 4A-402(b) or 4A-402(c) occurs is governed by applicable principles of law that determine when an obligation is satisfied.

§ 4A-404. Obligation of Beneficiary's Bank to Pay and Give Notice to Beneficiary.

(a)   Subject to Sections 4A-211(e), 4A-405(d), and 4A-405(e), if a beneficiary's bank accepts a payment order, the bank is obliged to pay the amount of the order to the beneficiary of the order. Payment is due on the payment date of the order, but if acceptance occurs on the payment date after the close of the funds-transfer business day of the bank, payment is due on the next funds-transfer business day. If the bank refuses to pay after demand by the beneficiary and receipt of notice of particular circumstances that will give rise to consequential damages as a result of nonpayment, the beneficiary may recover damages resulting from the refusal to pay to the extent the bank had notice of the damages, unless the bank proves that it did not pay because of a reasonable doubt concerning the right of the beneficiary to payment.

(b)   If a payment order accepted by the beneficiary's bank instructs payment to an account of the beneficiary, the bank is obliged to notify the beneficiary of receipt of the order before midnight of the next funds-transfer business day following the payment date. If the payment order does not instruct payment to an account of the beneficiary, the bank is required to notify the beneficiary only if notice is required by the order. Notice may be given by first class mail or any other means reasonable in the circumstances. If the bank fails to give the required notice, the bank is obliged to pay interest to the beneficiary on the amount of the payment order from the day notice should have been given until the day the beneficiary learned of receipt of the payment order by the bank. No other damages are recoverable. Reasonable attorney's fees are also recoverable if demand for interest is made and refused before an action is brought on the claim.

(c)   The right of a beneficiary to receive payment and damages as stated in subsection (a) may not be varied by agreement or a funds-transfer system rule. The right of a beneficiary to be notified as stated in subsection (b) may be varied by agreement of the beneficiary or by a funds-transfer system rule if the beneficiary is notified of the rule before initiation of the funds transfer.

§ 4A-405. *Payment by Beneficiary's Bank to Beneficiary.*

(a)   If the beneficiary's bank credits an account of the beneficiary of a payment order, payment of the bank's obligation under Section 4A-404(a) occurs when and to the extent (i) the beneficiary is notified of the right to withdraw the credit, (ii) the bank lawfully applies the credit to a debt of the beneficiary, or (iii) funds with respect to the order are otherwise made available to the beneficiary by the bank.

(b)   If the beneficiary's bank does not credit an account of the beneficiary of a payment order, the time when payment of the bank's obligation under Section 4A-404(a) occurs is governed by principles of law that determine when an obligation is satisfied.

(c)   Except as stated in subsections (d) and (e), if the beneficiary's bank pays the beneficiary of a payment order under a condition to payment or agreement of the beneficiary giving the bank the right to recover payment from the beneficiary if the bank does not receive payment of the order, the condition to payment or agreement is not enforceable.

(d)   A funds-transfer system rule may provide that payments made to beneficiaries of funds transfers made through the system are provisional until receipt of payment by the beneficiary's bank of the payment order it accepted. A beneficiary's bank that makes a payment that is provisional under the rule is entitled to refund from the beneficiary if (i) the rule requires that both the beneficiary and the originator be given notice of the provisional nature of the payment before the funds transfer is initiated, (ii) the beneficiary, the beneficiary's bank and the originator's bank agreed to be bound by the rule, and (iii) the beneficiary's bank did not receive payment of the payment order that it accepted. If the beneficiary is obliged to refund payment to the beneficiary's bank, acceptance of the payment order by the beneficiary's bank is nullified and no payment by the origina-tor of the funds transfer to the beneficiary occurs under Section 4A-406.

(e)   This subsection applies to a funds transfer that includes a payment order transmitted over a funds-transfer system that (i) nets obligations multilaterally among participants, and (ii) has in effect a loss-sharing agreement among participants for the purpose of providing funds necessary to complete settlement of the obligations of one or more participants that do not meet their settlement obligations. If the beneficiary's bank in the funds transfer accepts a payment order and the system fails to complete settlement pursuant to its rules with respect to any payment order in the funds transfer, (i) the acceptance by the beneficiary's bank is nullified and no person has any right or obligation based on the acceptance, (ii) the beneficiary's bank is entitled to recover payment from the beneficiary, (iii) no payment by the originator to the beneficiary occurs under Section 4A-406, and (iv) subject to Section 4A-402(e), each sender in the funds transfer is excused from its obligation to pay its payment order under Section 4A-402(c) because the funds transfer has not been completed.

§ 4A-406. *Payment by Originator to Beneficiary; Discharge of Underlying Obligation.*

(a)   Subject to Sections 4A-211(e), 4A-405(d), and 4A-405(e), the originator of a funds transfer pays the beneficiary of the originator's payment order (i) at the time a payment order for the benefit of the beneficiary is accepted by the beneficiary's bank in the funds transfer and (ii) in an amount equal to the amount of the order accepted by the beneficiary's bank, but not more than the amount of the originator's order.

(b)   If payment under subsection (a) is made to satisfy an obligation, the obligation is discharged to the same extent discharge would result from payment to the beneficiary of the same amount in money, unless (i) the payment under subsection (a) was made by a means prohibited by the contract of the beneficiary with respect to the obligation, (ii) the beneficiary, within a reasonable time after receiving notice of receipt of the order by the beneficiary's bank, notified the originator of the beneficiary's refusal of the payment, (iii) funds with respect to the order were not withdrawn by the beneficiary or applied to a debt of the beneficiary, and (iv) the beneficiary would suffer a loss that could reasonably have been avoided if payment had been made by a means complying with the contract. If payment by the originator does not result in discharge under this section, the originator is subrogated to the rights of the beneficiary to receive payment from the beneficiary's bank under Section 4A-404(a).

(c)   For the purpose of determining whether discharge of an obligation occurs under subsection (b), if the beneficiary's bank accepts a payment order in an amount equal to the amount of the originator's payment order less charges of one or more receiving banks in the funds transfer, payment to the beneficiary is deemed to be in the amount of the originator's order unless upon demand by the beneficiary the originator does not pay the beneficiary the amount of the deducted charges.

(d)   Rights of the originator or of the beneficiary of a funds transfer under this section may be varied only by agreement of the originator and the beneficiary.

■ PART 5   Miscellaneous Provisions

§ 4A-501. *Variation by Agreement and Effect of Funds-Transfer System Rule.*

(a)   Except as otherwise provided in this Article, the rights and obligations of a party to a funds transfer may be varied by agreement of the affected party.

(b)   "Funds-transfer system rule" means a rule of an association of banks (i) governing transmission of payment orders by means of a funds-transfer system of the association or rights and obligations with respect to those orders, or (ii) to the extent the rule governs rights and obligations between banks that are parties to a funds transfer in which a Federal Reserve Bank, acting as an intermediary bank, sends a payment order to the beneficiary's bank. Except as otherwise provided in this Article, a funds-transfer system rule governing rights and obligations between participating banks using the system may be effective even if the rule conflicts with this Article and indirectly affects another party to the funds transfer who does not consent to the rule. A funds-transfer system rule may also govern rights and obligations of parties other than participating banks using the system to the extent stated in Sections 4A-404(c), 4A-405(d), and 4A-507(c).

§ 4A-502. *Creditor Process Served on Receiving Bank; Setoff by Beneficiary's Bank.*

(a)   As used in this section, "creditor process" means levy, attachment, garnishment, notice of lien, sequestration, or similar process issued by or on behalf of a creditor or other claimant with respect to an account.

(b)   This subsection applies to creditor process with respect to an authorized account of the sender of a payment order if the creditor process is served on the receiving bank. For the purpose of determining rights with respect to the creditor process, if the receiving bank accepts the payment order the balance in the authorized account is deemed to be reduced by the amount of the payment order to the extent the bank did not otherwise receive payment of the order, unless the creditor process is served at a time and in a manner affording the bank a reasonable opportunity to act on it before the bank accepts the payment order.

(c) If a beneficiary's bank has received a payment order for payment to the beneficiary's account in the bank, the following rules apply:

(1) The bank may credit the beneficiary's account. The amount credited may be set off against an obligation owed by the beneficiary to the bank or may be applied to satisfy creditor process served on the bank with respect to the account.

(2) The bank may credit the beneficiary's account and allow withdrawal of the amount credited unless creditor process with respect to the account is served at a time and in a manner affording the bank a reasonable opportunity to act to prevent withdrawal.

(3) If creditor process with respect to the beneficiary's account has been served and the bank has had a reasonable opportunity to act on it, the bank may not reject the payment order except for a reason unrelated to the service of process.

(d) Creditor process with respect to a payment by the originator to the beneficiary pursuant to a funds transfer may be served only on the beneficiary's bank with respect to the debt owed by that bank to the beneficiary. Any other bank served with the creditor process is not obliged to act with respect to the process.

§ 4A-503. Injunction or Restraining Order With Respect to Funds Transfer.

For proper cause and in compliance with applicable law, a court may restrain (i) a person from issuing a payment order to initiate a funds transfer, (ii) an originator's bank from executing the payment order of the originator, or (iii) the beneficiary's bank from releasing funds to the beneficiary or the beneficiary from withdrawing the funds. A court may not otherwise restrain a person from issuing a payment order, paying or receiving payment of a payment order, or otherwise acting with respect to a funds transfer.

§ 4A-504. Order in Which Items and Payment Orders May Be Charged to Account; Order of Withdrawals From Account.

(a) If a receiving bank has received more than one payment order of the sender or one or more payment orders and other items that are payable from the sender's account, the bank may charge the sender's account with respect to the various orders and items in any sequence.

(b) In determining whether a credit to an account has been withdrawn by the holder of the account or applied to a debt of the holder of the account, credits first made to the account are first withdrawn or applied.

§ 4A-505. Preclusion of Objection to Debit of Customer's Account.

If a receiving bank has received payment from its customer with respect to a payment order issued in the name of the customer as sender and accepted by the bank, and the customer received notification reasonably identifying the order, the customer is precluded from asserting that the bank is not entitled to retain the payment unless the customer notifies the bank of the customer's objection to the payment within one year after the notification was received by the customer.

§ 4A-506. Rate of Interest.

(a) If, under this Article, a receiving bank is obliged to pay interest with respect to a payment order issued to the bank, the amount payable may be determined (i) by agreement of the sender and receiving bank, or (ii) by a funds-transfer system rule if the payment order is transmitted through a funds-transfer system.

(b) If the amount of interest is not determined by an agreement or rule as stated in subsection (a), the amount is calculated by multiplying the applicable Federal Funds rate by the amount on which interest is payable, and then multiplying the product by the number of days for which interest is payable. The applicable Federal Funds rate is the average of the Federal Funds rates published by the Federal Reserve Bank of New York for each of the days for which interest is payable divided by 360. The Federal Funds rate for any day on which a published rate is not available is the same as the published rate for the next preceding day for which there is a published rate. If a receiving bank that accepted a payment order is required to refund payment to the sender of the order because the funds transfer was not completed, but the failure to complete was not due to any fault by the bank, the interest payable is reduced by a percentage equal to the reserve requirement on deposits of the receiving bank.

§ 4A-507. Choice of Law.

(a) The following rules apply unless the affected parties otherwise agree or subsection (c) applies:

(1) The rights and obligations between the sender of a payment order and the receiving bank are governed by the law of the jurisdiction in which the receiving bank is located.

(2) The rights and obligations between the beneficiary's bank and the beneficiary are governed by the law of the jurisdiction in which the beneficiary's bank is located.

(3) The issue of when payment is made pursuant to a funds transfer by the originator to the beneficiary is governed by the law of the jurisdiction in which the beneficiary's bank is located.

(b) If the parties described in each paragraph of subsection (a) have made an agreement selecting the law of a particular jurisdiction to govern rights and obligations between each other, the law of that jurisdiction governs those rights and obligations, whether or not the payment order or the funds transfer bears a reasonable relation to that jurisdiction.

(c) A funds-transfer system rule may select the law of a particular jurisdiction to govern (i) rights and obligations between participating banks with respect to payment orders transmitted or processed through the system, or (ii) the rights and obligations of some or all parties to a funds transfer any part of which is carried out by means of the system. A choice of law made pursuant to clause (i) is binding on participating banks. A choice of law made pursuant to clause (ii) is binding on the originator, other sender, or a receiving bank having notice that the funds-transfer system might be used in the funds transfer and of the choice of law by the system when the originator, other sender, or receiving bank issued or accepted a payment order. The beneficiary of a funds transfer is bound by the choice of law if, when the funds transfer is initiated, the beneficiary has notice that the funds-transfer system might be used in the funds transfer and of the choice of law by the system. The law of a jurisdiction selected pursuant to this subsection may govern, whether or not that law bears a reasonable relation to the matter in issue.

(d) In the event of inconsistency between an agreement under subsection (b) and a choice-of-law rule under subsection (c), the agreement under subsection (b) prevails.

(e) If a funds transfer is made by use of more than one funds-transfer system and there is inconsistency between choice-of-law rules of the systems, the matter in issue is governed by the law of the selected jurisdiction that has the most significant relationship to the matter in issue.

ARTICLE 5
Letters of Credit

§ 5-101. Short Title.

This Article shall be known and may be cited as Uniform Commercial Code—Letters of Credit.

§ 5-102. Scope.

(1)   This Article applies

(a)   to a credit issued by a bank if the credit requires a documentary draft or a documentary demand for payment; and

(b)   to a credit issued by a person other than a bank if the credit requires that the draft or demand for payment be accompanied by a document of title; and

(c)   to a credit issued by a bank or other person if the credit is not within subparagraphs (a) or (b) but conspicuously states that it is a letter of credit or is conspicuously so entitled.

(2)   Unless the engagement meets the requirements of subsection (1), this Article does not apply to engagements to make advances or to honor drafts or demands for payment, to authorities to pay or purchase, to guarantees or to general agreements.

(3)   This Article deals with some but not all of the rules and concepts of letters of credit as such rules or concepts have developed prior to this act or may hereafter develop. The fact that this Article states a rule does not by itself require, imply or negate application of the same or a converse rule to a situation not provided for or to a person not specified by this Article.

§ 5-103. Definitions.

(1)   In this Article unless the context otherwise requires

(a)   "Credit" or "letter of credit" means an engagement by a bank or other person made at the request of a customer and of a kind within the scope of this Article (Section 5-102) that the issuer will honor drafts or other demands for payment upon compliance with the conditions specified in the credit. A credit may be either revocable or irrevocable. The engagement may be either an agreement to honor or a statement that the bank or other person is authorized to honor.

(b)   A "documentary draft" or a "documentary demand for payment" is one honor of which is conditioned upon the presentation of a document or documents. "Document" means any paper including document of title, security, invoice, certificate, notice of default and the like.

(c)   An "issuer" is a bank or other person issuing a credit.

(d)   A "beneficiary" of a credit is a person who is entitled under its terms to draw or demand payment.

(e)   An "advising bank" is a bank which gives notification of the issuance of a credit by another bank.

(f)   A "confirming bank" is a bank which engages either that it will itself honor a credit already issued by another bank or that such a credit will be honored by the issuer or a third bank.

(g)   A "customer" is a buyer or other person who causes an issuer to issue a credit. The term also includes a bank which procures issuance or confirmation on behalf of that bank's customer.

(2)   Other definitions applying to this Article and the sections in which they appear are:

"Notation of Credit". Section 5-108.

"Presenter". Section 5-112(3).

(3)   Definitions in other Articles applying to this Article and the sections in which they appear are:

"Accept" or "Acceptance". Section 3-409.

"Contract for sale". Section 2-106.

"Draft". Section 3-104.

"Holder in due course". Section 3-302.

"Midnight deadline". Section 4-104.

"Security". Section 8-102.

(4)   In addition, Article 1 contains general definitions and principles of construction and interpretation applicable throughout this Article.

§ 5-104. Formal Requirements; Signing.

(1)   Except as otherwise required in subsection (1)(c) of Section 5-102 on scope, no particular form of phrasing is required for a credit. A credit must be in writing and signed by the issuer and a confirmation must be in writing and signed by the confirming bank. A modification of the terms of a credit or confirmation must be signed by the issuer or confirming bank.

(2)   A telegram may be a sufficient signed writing if it identifies its sender by an authorized authentication. The authentication may be in code and the authorized naming of the issuer in an advice of credit is a sufficient signing.

§ 5-105. Consideration.

No consideration is necessary to establish a credit or to enlarge or otherwise modify its terms.

§ 5-106. Time and Effect of Establishment of Credit.

(1)   Unless otherwise agreed a credit is established.

(a)   as regards the customer as soon as a letter of credit is sent to him or the letter of credit or an authorized written advice of its issuance is sent to the beneficiary; and

(b)   as regards the beneficiary when he receives a letter of credit or an authorized written advice of its issuance.

(2)   Unless otherwise agreed once an irrevocable credit is established as regards the customer it can be modified or revoked only with the consent of the customer and once it is established as regards the beneficiary it can be modified or revoked only with his consent.

(3)   Unless otherwise agreed after a revocable credit is established it may be modified or revoked by the issuer without notice to or consent from the customer or beneficiary.

(4)   Notwithstanding any modification or revocation of a revocable credit any person authorized to honor or negotiate under the terms of the original credit is entitled to reimbursement for or honor of any draft or demand for payment duly honored or negotiated before receipt of notice of the modification or revocation and the issuer in turn is entitled to reimbursement from its customer.

§ 5-107. Advice of Credit; Confirmation; Error in Statement of Terms.

(1)   Unless otherwise specified an advising bank by advising a credit issued by another bank does not assume any obligation to honor drafts drawn or demands for payment made under the credit but it does assume obligation for the accuracy of its own statement.

(2)   A confirming bank by confirming a credit becomes directly obligated on the credit to the extent of its confirmation as though it were its issuer and acquires the rights of an issuer.

(3)   Even though an advising bank incorrectly advises the terms of a credit it has been authorized to advise the credit is established as against the issuer to the extent of its original terms.

(4)   Unless otherwise specified the customer bears as against the issuer all risks of transmission and reasonable translation or interpretation of any message relating to a credit.

§ 5-108. "Notation Credit"; Exhaustion of Credit.

(1)   A credit which specifies that any person purchasing or paying drafts drawn or demands for payment made under it must note the amount of the draft or demand on the letter or advice of credit is a "notation credit".

(2)   Under a notation credit

(a)   a person paying the beneficiary or purchasing a draft or demand for payment from him acquires a right to honor only if the appropriate notation is made and by transferring or forwarding for honor the documents under the credit such a person warrants to the issuer that the notation has been made; and

(b)   unless the credit or a signed statement that an appropriate notation has been made accompanies the draft or demand for payment the issuer may delay honor until evidence of notation has been procured which is satisfactory to it but its obligation and that of its customer continue for a reasonable time not exceeding thirty days to obtain such evidence.

(3)   If the credit is not a notation credit

(a)   the issuer may honor complying drafts or demands for payment presented to it in the order in which they are presented and is discharged pro tanto by honor of any such draft or demand;

(b)   as between competing good faith purchasers of complying drafts or demands the person first purchasing has priority over a subsequent purchaser even though the later purchased draft or demand has been first honored.

§ 5-109. Issuer's Obligation to Its Customer.

(1)   An issuer's obligation to its customer includes good faith and observance of any general banking usage but unless otherwise agreed does not include liability or responsibility

(a)   for performance of the underlying contract for sale or other transaction between the customer and the beneficiary; or

(b)   for any act or omission of any person other than itself or its own branch or for loss or destruction of a draft, demand or document in transit or in the possession of others; or

(c)   based on knowledge or lack of knowledge of any usage of any particular trade.

(2)   An issuer must examine documents with care so as to ascertain that on their face they appear to comply with the terms of the credit but unless otherwise agreed assumes no liability or responsibility for the genuineness, falsification or effect of any document which appears on such examination to be regular on its face.

(3)   A non-bank issuer is not bound by any banking usage of which it has no knowledge.

§ 5-110. Availability of Credit in Portions; Presenter's Reservation of Lien or Claim.

(1)   Unless otherwise specified a credit may be used in portions in the discretion of the beneficiary.

(2)   Unless otherwise specified a person by presenting a documentary draft or demand for payment under a credit relinquishes upon its honor all claims to the documents and a person by transferring such draft or demand or causing such presentment authorizes such relinquishment. An explicit reservation of claim makes the draft or demand non-complying.

§ 5-111. Warranties on Transfer and Presentment.

(1)   Unless otherwise agreed the beneficiary by transferring or presenting a documentary draft or demand for payment warrants to all interested parties that the necessary conditions of the credit have been complied with. This is in addition to any warranties arising under Articles 3, 4, 7 and 8.

(2)   Unless otherwise agreed a negotiating, advising, confirming, collecting or issuing bank presenting or transferring a draft or demand for payment under a credit warrants only the matters warranted by a collecting bank under Article 4 and any such bank transferring a document warrants only the matters warranted by an intermediary under Articles 7 and 8.

§ 5-112. Time Allowed for Honor or Rejection; Withholding Honor or Rejection by Consent; "Presenter".

(1)   A bank to which a documentary draft or demand for payment is presented under a credit may without dishonor of the draft, demand or credit

(a)   defer honor until the close of the third banking day following receipt of the documents; and

(b)   further defer honor if the presenter has expressly or impliedly consented thereto.

Failure to honor within the time here specified constitutes dishonor of the draft or demand and of the credit [except as otherwise provided in subsection (4) of Section 5-114 on conditional payment].

Note: The bracketed language in the last sentence of subsection (1) should be included only if the optional provisions of Section 5-114(4) and (5) are included.

(2)   Upon dishonor the bank may unless otherwise instructed fulfill its duty to return the draft or demand and the documents by holding them at the disposal of the presenter and sending him an advice to that effect.

(3)   "Presenter" means any person presenting a draft or demand for payment for honor under a credit even though that person is a confirming bank or other correspondent which is acting under an issuer's authorization.

§ 5-113. Indemnities.

(1)   A bank seeking to obtain (whether for itself or another) honor, negotiation or reimbursement under a credit may give an indemnity to induce such honor, negotiation or reimbursement.

(2)   An indemnity agreement inducing honor, negotiation or reimbursement

(a)   unless otherwise explicitly agreed applies to defects in the documents but not in the goods; and

(b)   unless a longer time is explicitly agreed expires at the end of ten business days following receipt of the documents by the ultimate customer unless notice of objection is sent before such expiration date. The ultimate customer may send notice of objection to the person from whom he received the documents and any bank receiving such notice is under a duty to send notice to its transferor before its midnight deadline.

§ 5-114. Issuer's Duty and Privilege to Honor; Right to Reimbursement.

(1)   An issuer must honor a draft or demand for payment which complies with the terms of the relevant credit regardless of whether the goods or documents conform to the underlying contract for sale or other contract between the customer and the beneficiary. The issuer is not excused from honor of such a draft or demand by reason of an additional general term that all documents must be satisfactory to the issuer, but an issuer may require that specified documents must be satisfactory to it.

(2)   Unless otherwise agreed when documents appear on their face to comply with the terms of a credit but a required document does not in fact conform to the warranties made on negotiation or transfer of a document of title (Section 7-507) or of a certificated security (Section 8-306) or is forged or fraudulent or there is fraud in the transaction:

(a) the issuer must honor the draft or demand for payment if honor is demanded by a negotiating bank or other holder of the draft or demand which has taken the draft or demand under the credit and under circumstances which would make it a holder in due course (Section 3-302) and in an appropriate case would make it a person to whom a document of title has been duly negotiated (Section 7-502) or a bona fide purchaser of a certificated security (Section 8-302); and

(b) in all other cases as against its customer, an issuer acting in good faith may honor the draft or demand for payment despite notification from the customer of fraud, forgery or other defect not apparent on the face of the documents but a court of appropriate jurisdiction may enjoin such honor.

(3) Unless otherwise agreed an issuer which has duly honored a draft or demand for payment is entitled to immediate reimbursement of any payment made under the credit and to be put in effectively available funds not later than the day before maturity of any acceptance made under the credit.

[(4) When a credit provides for payment by the issuer on receipt of notice that the required documents are in the possession of a correspondent or other agent of the issuer

(a) any payment made on receipt of such notice is conditional; and

(b) the issuer may reject documents which do not comply with the credit if it does so within three banking days following its receipt of the documents; and

(c) in the event of such rejection, the issuer is entitled by charge back or otherwise to return of the payment made.]

[(5) In the case covered by subsection (4) failure to reject documents within the time specified in sub-paragraph (b) constitutes acceptance of the documents and makes the payment final in favor of the beneficiary.]

Amended in 1977.

Note: Subsections (4) and (5) are bracketed as optional. If they are included the bracketed language in the last sentence of Section 5-112(1) should also be included.

§ 5-115. Remedy for Improper Dishonor or Anticipatory Repudiation.

(1) When an issuer wrongfully dishonors a draft or demand for payment presented under a credit the person entitled to honor has with respect to any documents the rights of a person in the position of a seller (Section 2-707) and may recover from the issuer the face amount of the draft or demand together with incidental damages under Section 2-710 on seller's incidental damages and interest but less any amount realized by resale or other use or disposition of the subject matter of the transaction. In the event no resale or other utilization is made the documents, goods or other subject matter involved in the transaction must be turned over to the issuer on payment of judgment.

(2) When an issuer wrongfully cancels or otherwise repudiates a credit before presentment of a draft or demand for payment drawn under it the beneficiary has the rights of a seller after anticipatory repudiation by the buyer under Section 2-610 if he learns of the repudiation in time reasonably to avoid procurement of the required documents. Otherwise the beneficiary has an immediate right of action for wrongful dishonor.

§ 5-116. Transfer and Assignment.

(1) The right to draw under a credit can be transferred or assigned only when the credit is expressly designated as transferable or assignable.

(2) Even though the credit specifically states that it is non-transferable or nonassignable the beneficiary may before performance of the conditions of the credit assign his right to proceeds. Such an assignment is an assignment of an account under Article 9 on Secured Transactions and is governed by that Article except that

(a) the assignment is ineffective until the letter of credit or advice of credit is delivered to the assignee which delivery constitutes perfection of the security interest under Article 9; and

(b) the issuer may honor drafts or demands for payment drawn under the credit until it receives a notification of the assignment signed by the beneficiary which reasonably identifies the credit involved in the assignment and contains a request to pay the assignee; and

(c) after what reasonably appears to be such a notification has been received the issuer may without dishonor refuse to accept or pay even to a person otherwise entitled to honor until the letter of credit or advice of credit is exhibited to the issuer.

(3) Except where the beneficiary has effectively assigned his right to draw or his right to proceeds, nothing in this section limits his right to transfer or negotiate drafts or demands drawn under the credit.

§ 5-117. Insolvency of Bank Holding Funds for Documentary Credit.

(1) Where an issuer or an advising or confirming bank or a bank which has for a customer procured issuance of a credit by another bank becomes insolvent before final payment under the credit and the credit is one to which this Article is made applicable by paragraphs (a) or (b) of Section 5-102(1) on scope, the receipt or allocation of funds or collateral to secure or meet obligations under the credit shall have the following results:

(a) to the extent of any funds or collateral turned over after or before the insolvency as indemnity against or specifically for the purpose of payment of drafts or demands for payment drawn under the designated credit, the drafts or demands are entitled to payment in preference over depositors or other general creditors of the issuer or bank; and

(b) on expiration of the credit or surrender of the beneficiary's rights under it unused any person who has given such funds or collateral is similarly entitled to return thereof; and

(c) a charge to a general or current account with a bank if specifically consented to for the purpose of indemnity against or payment of drafts or demands for payment drawn under the designated credit falls under the same rules as if the funds had been drawn out in cash and then turned over with specific instructions.

(2) After honor or reimbursement under this section the customer or other person for whose account the insolvent bank has acted is entitled to receive the documents involved.

ARTICLE 6
Bulk Transfers

§ 6-101. Short Title.

This Article shall be known and may be cited as Uniform Commercial Code—Bulk Transfers.

§ 6-102. "Bulk Transfer"; Transfers of Equipment; Enterprises Subject to This Article; Bulk Transfers Subject to This Article.

(1) A "bulk transfer" is any transfer in bulk and not in the ordinary course of the transferor's business of a major part of the materials, supplies, merchandise or other inventory (Section 9-109) of an enterprise subject to this Article.

(2) A transfer of a substantial part of the equipment (Section 9-109) of such an enterprise is a bulk transfer if it is made in connection with a bulk transfer of inventory, but not otherwise.

(3) The enterprises subject to this Article are all those whose principal business is the sale of merchandise from stock, including those who manufacture what they sell.

(4) Except as limited by the following section all bulk transfers of goods located within this state are subject to this Article.

§ 6-103. *Transfers Excepted From This Article.*

The following transfers are not subject to this Article:

(1) Those made to give security for the performance of an obligation;

(2) General assignments for the benefit of all the creditors of the transferor, and subsequent transfers by the assignee thereunder;

(3) Transfers in settlement or realization of a lien or other security interest;

(4) Sales by executors, administrators, receivers, trustees in bankruptcy, or any public officer under judicial process;

(5) Sales made in the course of judicial or administrative proceedings for the dissolution or reorganization of a corporation and of which notice is sent to the creditors of the corporation pursuant to order of the court or administrative agency;

(6) Transfers to a person maintaining a known place of business in this State who becomes bound to pay the debts of the transferor in full and gives public notice of that fact, and who is solvent after becoming so bound;

(7) A transfer to a new business enterprise organized to take over and continue the business, if public notice of the transaction is given and the new enterprise assumes the debts of the transferor and he receives nothing from the transaction except an interest in the new enterprise junior to the claims of creditors;

(8) Transfers of property which is exempt from execution.

Public notice under subsection (6) or subsection (7) may be given by publishing once a week for two consecutive weeks in a newspaper of general circulation where the transferor had its principal place of business in this state an advertisement including the names and addresses of the transferor and transferee and the effective date of the transfer.

§ 6-104. *Schedule of Property, List of Creditors.*

(1) Except as provided with respect to auction sales (Section 6-108), a bulk transfer subject to this Article is ineffective against any creditor of the transferor unless:

(a) The transferee requires the transferor to furnish a list of his existing creditors prepared as stated in this section; and

(b) The parties prepare a schedule of the property transferred sufficient to identify it; and

(c) The transferee preserves the list and schedule for six months next following the transfer and permits inspection of either or both and copying therefrom at all reasonable hours by any creditor of the transferor, or files the list and schedule in *(a public office to be here identified)*.

(2) The list of creditors must be signed and sworn to or affirmed by the transferor or his agent. It must contain the names and business addresses of all creditors of the transferor, with the amounts when known, and also the names of all persons who are known to the transferor to assert claims against him even though such claims are disputed. If the transferor is the obligor of an outstanding issue of bonds, debentures or the like as to which there is an indenture trustee, the list of creditors need include only the name and address of the indenture trustee and the aggregate outstanding principal amount of the issue.

(3) Responsibility for the completeness and accuracy of the list of creditors rests on the transferor, and the transfer is not rendered ineffective by errors or omissions therein unless the transferee is shown to have had knowledge.

§ 6-105. *Notice to Creditors.*

In addition to the requirements of the preceding section, any bulk transfer subject to this Article except one made by auction sale (Section 6-108) is ineffective against any creditor of the transferor unless at least ten days before he takes possession of the goods or pays for them, whichever happens first, the transferee gives notice of the transfer in the manner and to the persons hereafter provided (Section 6-107).

[§ 6-106. *Application of the Proceeds*]

In addition to the requirements of the two preceding sections:

(1) Upon every bulk transfer subject to this Article for which new consideration becomes payable except those made by sale at auction it is the duty of the transferee to assure that such consideration is applied so far as necessary to pay those debts of the transferor which are either shown on the list furnished by the transferor (Section 6-104) or filed in writing in the place stated in the notice (Section 6-107) within thirty days after the mailing of such notice. This duty of the transferee runs to all the holders of such debts, and may be enforced by any of them for the benefit of all.

(2) If any of said debts are in dispute the necessary sum may be withheld from distribution until the dispute is settled or adjudicated.

(3) If the consideration payable is not enough to pay all of the said debts in full distribution shall be made pro rata.]

Note: This section is bracketed to indicate division of opinion as to whether or not it is a wise provision, and to suggest that this is a point on which State enactments may differ without serious damage to the principal of uniformity. In any State where this section is omitted, the following parts of sections, also bracketed in the text, should also be omitted, namely:
Section 6-107(2)(e).
6-108(3)(c).
6-109(2).
In any State where this section is enacted, these other provisions should be also.

Optional Subsection (4)

[(4) The transferee may within ten days after he takes possession of the goods pay the consideration into the (specify court) in the county where the transferor had its principal place of business in this state and thereafter may discharge his duty under this section by giving notice by registered or certified mail to all the persons to whom the duty runs that the consideration has been paid into that court and that they should file their claims there. On motion of any interested party, the court may order the distribution of the consideration to the persons entitled to it.]

Note: Optional subsection (4) is recommended for those states which do not have a general statute providing for payment of money into court.

§ 6-107. *The Notice.*

(1) The notice to creditors (Section 6-105) shall state:

(a) that a bulk transfer is about to be made; and

(b) the names and business addresses of the transferor and transferee, and all other business names and addresses used by the transferor within three years last past so far as known to the transferee; and

(c) whether or not all the debts of the transferor are to be paid in full as they fall due as a result of the transaction, and if so, the address to which creditors should send their bills.

(2) If the debts of the transferor are not to be paid in full as they fall due or if the transferee is in doubt on that point then the notice shall state further:

(a) the location and general description of the property to be transferred and the estimated total of the transferor's debts;

(b) the address where the schedule of property and list of creditors (Section 6-104) may be inspected;

(c) whether the transfer is to pay existing debts and if so the amount of such debts and to whom owing;

(d) whether the transfer is for new consideration and if so the amount of such consideration and the time and place of payment; [and]

[(e) if for new consideration the time and place where creditors of the transferor are to file their claims.]

(3) The notice in any case shall be delivered personally or sent by registered or certified mail to all the persons shown on the list of creditors furnished by the transferor (Section 6-104) and to all other persons who are known to the transferee to hold or assert claims against the transferor.

§ 6-108. *Auction Sales; "Auctioneer".*

(1) A bulk transfer is subject to this Article even though it is by sale at auction, but only in the manner and with the results stated in this section.

(2) The transferor shall furnish a list of his creditors and assist in the preparation of a schedule of the property to be sold, both prepared as before stated (Section 6-104).

(3) The person or persons other than the transferor who direct, control or are responsible for the auction are collectively called the "auctioneer". The auctioneer shall:

(a) receive and retain the list of creditors and prepare and retain the schedule of property for the period stated in this Article (Section 6-104);

(b) give notice of the auction personally or by registered or certified mail at least ten days before it occurs to all persons shown on the list of creditors and to all other persons who are known to him to hold or assert claims against the transferor; [and]

[(c) assure that the net proceeds of the auction are applied as provided in this Article (Section 6-106).]

(4) Failure of the auctioneer to perform any of these duties does not affect the validity of the sale or the title of the purchasers, but if the auctioneer knows that the auction constitutes a bulk transfer such failure renders the auctioneer liable to the creditors of the transferor as a class for the sums owing to them from the transferor up to but not exceeding the net proceeds of the auction. If the auctioneer consists of several persons their liability is joint and several.

§ 6-109. *What Creditors Protected; [Credit for Payment to Particular Creditors].*

(1) The creditors of the transferor mentioned in this Article are those holding claims based on transactions or events occurring before the bulk transfer, but creditors who become such after notice to creditors is given (Sections 6-105 and 6-107) are not entitled to notice.

[(2) Against the aggregate obligation imposed by the provisions of this Article concerning the application of the proceeds (Section 6-106 and subsection (3)(c) of 6-108) the transferee or auctioneer is entitled to credit for sums paid to particular creditors of the transferor, not exceeding the sums believed in good faith at the time of the payment to be properly payable to such creditors.]

§ 6-110. *Subsequent Transfers.*

When the title of a transferee to property is subject to a defect by reason of his non-compliance with the requirements of this Article, then:

(1) a purchaser of any such property from such transferee who pays no value or who takes with notice of such noncompliance takes subject to such defect, but

(2) a purchaser for value in good faith and without such notice takes free of such defect.

§ 6-111. *Limitation of Actions and Levies.*

No action under this Article shall be brought nor levy made more than six months after the date on which the transferee took possession of the goods unless the transfer has been concealed. If the transfer has been concealed, actions may be brought or levies made within six months after its discovery.

Note to Article 6: Section 6-106 is bracketed to indicate division of opinion as to whether or not it is a wise provision, and to suggest that this is a point on which State enactments may differ without serious damage to the principle of uniformity. In any State where Section 6-106 is not enacted, the following parts of sections, also bracketed in the text, should also be omitted, namely:

Sec. 6-107(2)(e).
6-108(3)(c).
6-109(2).

In any State where Section 6-106 is enacted, these other provisions should be also.

ARTICLE 7
Warehouse Receipts, Bills of Lading and Other Documents of Title

■ PART 1 General

§ 7-101. *Short Title.*

This Article shall be known and may be cited as Uniform Commercial Code—Documents of Title.

§ 7-102. *Definitions and Index of Definitions.*

(1) In this Article, unless the context otherwise requires:

(a) "Bailee" means the person who by a warehouse receipt, bill of lading or other document of title acknowledges possession of goods and contracts to deliver them.

(b) "Consignee" means the person named in a bill to whom or to whose order the bill promises delivery.

(c) "Consignor" means the person named in a bill as the person from whom the goods have been received for shipment.

(d) "Delivery order" means a written order to deliver goods directed to a warehouseman, carrier or other person who in the ordinary course of business issues warehouse receipts or bills of lading.

(e) "Document" means document of title as defined in the general definitions in Article 1 (Section 1-201).

(f) "Goods" means all things which are treated as movable for the purposes of a contract of storage or transportation.

(g) "Issuer" means a bailee who issues a document except that in relation to an unaccepted delivery order it means the person who orders the possessor of goods to deliver. Issuer includes any person for whom an agent or employee purports to act in issuing a document if the agent or employee has real or apparent authority to issue documents, notwithstanding that the issuer received no goods or that the goods were misdescribed or that in any other respect the agent or employee violated his instructions.

(h) "Warehouseman" is a person engaged in the business of storing goods for hire.

(2) Other definitions applying to this Article or to specified Parts thereof, and the sections in which they appear are:

"Duly negotiate". Section 7-501.

"Person entitled under the document". Section 7-403(4).

(3) Definitions in other Articles applying to this Article and the sections in which they appear are:

"Contract for sale". Section 2-106.

"Overseas". Section 2-323.

"Receipt" of goods. Section 2-103.

(4) In addition Article 1 contains general definitions and principles of construction and interpretation applicable throughout this Article.

§ 7-103. Relation of Article to Treaty, Statute, Tariff, Classification or Regulation.

To the extent that any treaty or statute of the United States, regulatory statute of this State or tariff, classification or regulation filed or issued pursuant thereto is applicable, the provisions of this Article are subject thereto.

§ 7-104. Negotiable and Non-Negotiable Warehouse Receipt, Bill of Lading or Other Document of Title.

(1) A warehouse receipt, bill of lading or other document of title is negotiable

(a) if by its terms the goods are to be delivered to bearer or to the order of a named person; or

(b) where recognized in overseas trade, if it runs to a named person or assigns.

(2) Any other document is non-negotiable. A bill of lading in which it is stated that the goods are consigned to a named person is not made negotiable by a provision that the goods are to be delivered only against a written order signed by the same or another named person.

§ 7-105. Construction Against Negative Implication.

The omission from either Part 2 or Part 3 of this Article of a provision corresponding to a provision made in the other Part does not imply that a corresponding rule of law is not applicable.

■ PART 2 Warehouse Receipts: Special Provisions

§ 7-201. Who May Issue a Warehouse Receipt; Storage Under Government Bond.

(1) A warehouse receipt may be issued by any warehouseman.

(2) Where goods including distilled spirits and agricultural commodities are stored under a statute requiring a bond against withdrawal or a license for the issuance of receipts in the nature of warehouse receipts, a receipt issued for the goods has like effect as a warehouse receipt even though issued by a person who is the owner of the goods and is not a warehouseman.

§ 7-202. Form of Warehouse Receipt; Essential Terms; Optional Terms.

(1) A warehouse receipt need not be in any particular form.

(2) Unless a warehouse receipt embodies within its written or printed terms each of the following, the warehouseman is liable for damages caused by the omission to a person injured thereby:

(a) the location of the warehouse where the goods are stored;

(b) the date of issue of the receipt;

(c) the consecutive number of the receipt;

(d) a statement whether the goods received will be delivered to the bearer, to a specified person, or to a specified person or his order;

(e) the rate of storage and handling charges, except that where goods are stored under a field warehousing arrangement a statement of that fact is sufficient on a non-negotiable receipt;

(f) a description of the goods or of the packages containing them;

(g) the signature of the warehouseman, which may be made by his authorized agent;

(h) if the receipt is issued for goods of which the warehouseman is owner, either solely or jointly or in common with others, the fact of such ownership; and

(i) a statement of the amount of advances made and of liabilities incurred for which the warehouseman claims a lien or security interest (Section 7-209). If the precise amount of such advances made or of such liabilities incurred is, at the time of the issue of the receipt, unknown to the warehouseman or to his agent who issues it, a statement of the fact that advances have been made or liabilities incurred and the purpose thereof is sufficient.

(3) A warehouseman may insert in his receipt any other terms which are not contrary to the provisions of this Act and do not impair his obligation of delivery (Section 7-403) or his duty of care (Section 7-204). Any contrary provisions shall be ineffective.

§ 7-203. Liability for Non-Receipt or Misdescription.

A party to or purchaser for value in good faith of a document of title other than a bill of lading relying in either case upon the description therein of the goods may recover from the issuer damages caused by the non-receipt or misdescription of the goods, except to the extent that the document conspicuously indicates that the issuer does not know whether any part or all of the goods in fact were received or conform to the description, as where the description is in terms of marks or labels or kind, quantity or condition, or the receipt or description is qualified by "contents, condition and quality unknown", "said to contain" or the like, if such indication be true, or the party or purchaser otherwise has notice.

§ 7-204. Duty of Care; Contractual Limitation of Warehouseman's Liability.

(1) A warehouseman is liable for damages for loss of or injury to the goods caused by his failure to exercise such care in regard to them as a reasonably careful man would exercise under like circumstances but unless otherwise agreed he is not liable for damages which could not have been avoided by the exercise of such care.

(2) Damages may be limited by a term in the warehouse receipt or storage agreement limiting the amount of liability in case of loss or damage, and setting forth a specific liability per article or item, or value per unit of weight, beyond which the warehouseman shall not be liable; provided, however, that such liability may on written request of the bailor at the time of signing such storage agreement or within a reasonable time after receipt of the warehouse receipt be increased on part or all of the goods thereunder, in which event increased rates may be charged based on such increased valuation, but that no such increase shall be permitted contrary to a lawful limitation of liability contained in the warehouseman's tariff, if any. No such limitation is effective with respect to the warehouseman's liability for conversion to his own use.

(3) Reasonable provisions as to the time and manner of presenting claims and instituting actions based on the bailment may be included in the warehouse receipt or tariff.

(4) This section does not impair or repeal . . .

Note: Insert in subsection (4) a reference to any statute which imposes a higher responsibility upon the warehouseman or invalidates contractual limitations which would be permissible under this Article.

§ 7-205. Title Under Warehouse Receipt Defeated in Certain Cases.

A buyer in the ordinary course of business of fungible goods sold and delivered by a warehouseman who is also in the business of buying and selling such goods takes free of any claim under a warehouse receipt even though it has been duly negotiated.

§ 7-206. Termination of Storage at Warehouseman's Option.

(1) A warehouseman may on notifying the person on whose account the goods are held and any other person known to claim an interest in the goods require payment of any charges and removal of the goods from the warehouse at the termination of the period of storage fixed by the document, or, if no period is fixed, within a stated period not less than thirty days after the notification. If the goods are not removed before the date specified in the notification, the warehouseman may sell them in accordance with the provisions of the section on enforcement of a warehouseman's lien (Section 7-210).

(2) If a warehouseman in good faith believes that the goods are about to deteriorate or decline in value to less than the amount of his lien within the time prescribed in subsection (1) for notification, advertisement and sale, the warehouseman may specify in the notification any reasonable shorter time for removal of the goods and in case the goods are not removed, may sell them at public sale held not less than one week after a single advertisement or posting.

(3) If as a result of a quality or condition of the goods of which the warehouseman had no notice at the time of deposit the goods are a hazard to other property or to the warehouse or to persons, the warehouseman may sell the goods at public or private sale without advertisement on reasonable notification to all persons known to claim an interest in the goods. If the warehouseman after a reasonable effort is unable to sell the goods he may dispose of them in any lawful manner and shall incur no liability by reason of such disposition.

(4) The warehouseman must deliver the goods to any person entitled to them under this Article upon due demand made at any time prior to sale or other disposition under this section.

(5) The warehouseman may satisfy his lien from the proceeds of any sale or disposition under this section but must hold the balance for delivery on the demand of any person to whom he would have been bound to deliver the goods.

§ 7-207. Goods Must Be Kept Separate; Fungible Goods.

(1) Unless the warehouse receipt otherwise provides, a warehouseman must keep separate the goods covered by each receipt so as to permit at all times identification and delivery of those goods except that different lots of fungible goods may be commingled.

(2) Fungible goods so commingled are owned in common by the persons entitled thereto and the warehouseman is severally liable to each owner for that owner's share. Where because of overissue a mass of fungible goods is insufficient to meet all the receipts which the warehouseman has issued against it, the persons entitled include all holders to whom overissued receipts have been duly negotiated.

§ 7-208. Altered Warehouse Receipts.

Where a blank in a negotiable warehouse receipt has been filled in without authority, a purchaser for value and without notice of the want of authority may treat the insertion as authorized. Any other unauthorized alteration leaves any receipt enforceable against the issuer according to its original tenor.

§ 7-209. Lien of Warehouseman.

(1) A warehouseman has a lien against the bailor on the goods covered by a warehouse receipt or on the proceeds thereof in his possession for charges for storage or transportation (including demurrage and terminal charges), insurance, labor, or charges present or future in relation to the goods, and for expenses necessary for preservation of the goods or reasonably incurred in their sale pursuant to law. If the person on whose account the goods are held is liable for like charges or expenses in relation to other goods whenever deposited and it is stated in the receipt that a lien is claimed for charges and expenses in relation to other goods, the warehouseman also has a lien against him for such charges and expenses whether or not the other goods have been delivered by the warehouseman. But against a person to whom a negotiable warehouse receipt is duly negotiated a warehouseman's lien is limited to charges in an amount or at a rate specified on the receipt or if no charges are so specified then to a reasonable charge for storage of the goods covered by the receipt subsequent to the date of the receipt.

(2) The warehouseman may also reserve a security interest against the bailor for a maximum amount specified on the receipt for charges other than those specified in subsection (1), such as for money advanced and interest. Such a security interest is governed by the Article on Secured Transactions (Article 9).

(3) (a) A warehouseman's lien for charges and expenses under subsection (1) or a security interest under subsection (2) is also effective against any person who so entrusted the bailor with possession of the goods that a pledge of them by him to a good faith purchaser for value would have been valid but is not effective against a person as to whom the document confers no right in the goods covered by it under Section 7-503.

(b) A warehouseman's lien on household goods for charges and expenses in relation to the goods under subsection (1) is also effective against all persons if the depositor was a legal possessor of the goods at the time of deposit. "Household goods" means furniture, furnishings and personal effects used by the depositor in a dwelling.

(4) A warehouseman loses his lien on any goods which he voluntarily delivers or which he unjustifiably refuses to deliver.

§ 7-210. Enforcement of Warehouseman's Lien.

(1) Except as provided in subsection (2), a warehouseman's lien may be enforced by public or private sale of the goods in bloc or in parcels, at any time or place and on any terms which are commercially reasonable, after notifying all persons known to claim an interest in the goods. Such notification must include a statement of the amount due, the nature of the proposed sale and the time and place of any public sale. The fact that a better price could have been obtained by a sale at a different time or in a different method from that selected by the warehouseman is not of itself sufficient to establish that the sale was not made in a commercially reasonable manner. If the warehouseman either sells the goods in the usual manner in any recognized market therefor, or if he sells at the price current in such market at the time of his sale, or if he has otherwise sold in conformity with commercially reasonable practices among dealers in the type of goods sold, he has sold in a commercially reasonable manner. A sale of more goods than apparently necessary to be offered to insure satisfaction of the obligation is not commercially reasonable except in cases covered by the preceding sentence.

(2) A warehouseman's lien on goods other than goods stored by a merchant in the course of his business may be enforced only as follows:

(a) All persons known to claim an interest in the goods must be notified.

(b) The notification must be delivered in person or sent by registered or certified letter to the last known address of any person to be notified.

(c) The notification must include an itemized statement of the claim, a description of the goods subject to the lien, a demand for payment within a specified time not less than ten days after receipt of the notification, and a conspicuous statement that unless the claim is paid within the time the goods will be advertised for sale and sold by auction at a specified time and place.

(d) The sale must conform to the terms of the notification.

(e) The sale must be held at the nearest suitable place to that where the goods are held or stored.

(f) After the expiration of the time given in the notification, an advertisement of the sale must be published once a week for two weeks consecutively in a newspaper of general circulation where the sale is to be held. The advertisement must include a description of the goods, the name of the person on whose account they are being held, and the time and place of the sale. The sale must take place at least fifteen days after the first publication. If there is no newspaper of general circulation where the sale is to be held, the advertisement must be posted at least ten days before the sale in not less than six conspicuous places in the neighborhood of the proposed sale.

(3) Before any sale pursuant to this section any person claiming a right in the goods may pay the amount necessary to satisfy the lien and the reasonable expenses incurred under this section. In that event the goods must not be sold, but must be retained by the warehouseman subject to the terms of the receipt and this Article.

(4) The warehouseman may buy at any public sale pursuant to this section.

(5) A purchaser in good faith of goods sold to enforce a warehouseman's lien takes the goods free of any rights of persons against whom the lien was valid, despite noncompliance by the warehouseman with the requirements of this section.

(6) The warehouseman may satisfy his lien from the proceeds of any sale pursuant to this section but must hold the balance, if any, for delivery on demand to any person to whom he would have been bound to deliver the goods.

(7) The rights provided by this section shall be in addition to all other rights allowed by law to a creditor against his debtor.

(8) Where a lien is on goods stored by a merchant in the course of his business the lien may be enforced in accordance with either subsection (1) or (2).

(9) The warehouseman is liable for damages caused by failure to comply with the requirements for sale under this section and in case of willful violation is liable for conversion.

■ PART 3 Bills of Lading: Special Provisions

§ 7-301. *Liability for Non-Receipt or Misdescription; "Said to Contain"; "Shipper's Load and Count"; Improper Handling.*

(1) A consignee of a non-negotiable bill who has given value in good faith or a holder to whom a negotiable bill has been duly negotiated relying in either case upon the description therein of the goods, or upon the date therein shown, may recover from the issuer damages caused by the misdating of the bill or the non-receipt or misdescription of the goods, except to the extent that the document indicates that the issuer does not know whether any part of all of the goods in fact were received or conform to the description, as where the description is in terms of marks or labels or kind, quantity, or condition or the receipt or description is qualified by "contents or condition of contents of packages unknown", "said to contain", "shipper's weight, load and count" or the like, if such indication be true.

(2) When goods are loaded by an issuer who is a common carrier, the issuer must count the packages of goods if package freight and ascertain the kind and quantity if bulk freight. In such cases "shipper's weight, load and count" or other words indicating that the description was made by the shipper are ineffective except as to freight concealed by packages.

(3) When bulk freight is loaded by a shipper who makes available to the issuer adequate facilities for weighing such freight, an issuer who is a common carrier must ascertain the kind and quantity within a reasonable time after receiving the written request of the shipper to do so. In such cases "shipper's weight" or other words of like purport are ineffective.

(4) The issuer may by inserting in the bill the words "shipper's weight, load and count" or other words of like purport indicate that the goods were loaded by the shipper; and if such statement be true the issuer shall not be liable for damages caused by the improper loading. But their omission does not imply liability for such damages.

(5) The shipper shall be deemed to have guaranteed to the issuer the accuracy at the time of shipment of the description, marks, labels, number, kind, quantity, condition and weight, as furnished by him; and the shipper shall indemnify the issuer against damage caused by inaccuracies in such particulars. The right of the issuer to such indemnity shall in no way limit his responsibility and liability under the contract of carriage to any person other than the shipper.

§ 7-302. *Through Bills of Lading and Similar Documents.*

(1) The issuer of a through bill of lading or other document embodying an undertaking to be performed in part by persons acting as its agents or by connecting carriers is liable to anyone entitled to recover on the document for any breach by such other persons or by a connecting carrier of its obligation under the document but to the extent that the bill covers an undertaking to be performed overseas or in territory not contiguous to the continental United States or an undertaking including matters other than transportation this liability may be varied by agreement of the parties.

(2) Where goods covered by a through bill of lading or other document embodying an undertaking to be performed in part by persons other than the issuer are received by any such person, he is subject with respect to his own performance while the goods are in his possession to the obligation of the issuer. His obligation is discharged by delivery of the goods to another such person pursuant to the document, and does not include liability for breach by any other such persons or by the issuer.

(3) The issuer of such through bill of lading or other document shall be entitled to recover from the connecting carrier or such other person in possession of the goods when the breach of the obligation under the document occurred, the amount it may be required to pay to anyone entitled to recover on the document therefor, as may be evidenced by any receipt, judgment, or transcript thereof, and the amount of any expense reasonably incurred by it in defending any action brought by anyone entitled to recover on the document therefor.

§ 7-303. *Diversion; Reconsignment; Change of Instructions.*

(1) Unless the bill of lading otherwise provides, the carrier may deliver the goods to a person or destination other than that stated in the bill or may otherwise dispose of the goods on instructions from.

(a)   the holder of a negotiable bill; or

(b)   the consignor on a non-negotiable bill notwithstanding contrary instructions from the consignee; or

(c)   the consignee on a non-negotiable bill in the absence of contrary instructions from the consignor, if the goods have arrived at the billed destination or if the consignee is in possession of the bill; or

(d)   the consignee on a non-negotiable bill if he is entitled as against the consignor to dispose of them.

(2)   Unless such instructions are noted on a negotiable bill of lading, a person to whom the bill is duly negotiated can hold the bailee according to the original terms.

§ 7-304.   *Bills of Lading in a Set.*

(1)   Except where customary in overseas transportation, a bill of lading must not be issued in a set of parts. The issuer is liable for damages caused by violation of this subsection.

(2)   Where a bill of lading is lawfully drawn in a set of parts, each of which is numbered and expressed to be valid only if the goods have not been delivered against any other part, the whole of the parts constitute one bill.

(3)   Where a bill of lading is lawfully issued in a set of parts and different parts are negotiated to different persons, the title of the holder to whom the first due negotiation is made prevails as to both the document and the goods even though any later holder may have received the goods from the carrier in good faith and discharged the carrier's obligation by surrender of his part.

(4)   Any person who negotiates or transfers a single part of a bill of lading drawn in a set is liable to holders of that part as if it were the whole set.

(5)   The bailee is obliged to deliver in accordance with Part 4 of this Article against the first presented part of a bill of lading lawfully drawn in a set. Such delivery discharges the bailee's obligation on the whole bill.

§ 7-305.   *Destination Bills.*

(1)   Instead of issuing a bill of lading to the consignor at the place of shipment a carrier may at the request of the consignor procure the bill to be issued at destination or at any other place designated in the request.

(2)   Upon request of anyone entitled as against the carrier to control the goods while in transit and on surrender of any outstanding bill of lading or other receipt covering such goods, the issuer may procure a substitute bill to be issued at any place designated in the request.

§ 7-306.   *Altered Bills of Lading.*

An unauthorized alteration or filling in of a blank in a bill of lading leaves the bill enforceable according to its original tenor.

§ 7-307.   *Lien of Carrier.*

(1)   A carrier has a lien on the goods covered by a bill of lading for charges subsequent to the date of its receipt of the goods for storage or transportation (including demurrage and terminal charges) and for expenses necessary for preservation of the goods incident to their transportation or reasonably incurred in their sale pursuant to law. But against a purchaser for value of a negotiable bill of lading a carrier's lien is limited to charges stated in the bill or the applicable tariffs, or if no charges are stated then to a reasonable charge.

(2)   A lien for charges and expenses under subsection (1) on goods which the carrier was required by law to receive for transportation is effective against the consignor or any person entitled to the goods unless the carrier had notice that the consignor lacked authority to subject the goods to such charges and expenses. Any other lien under subsection (1) is effective against the consignor and any person who permitted the bailor to have control or possession of the goods unless the carrier had notice that the bailor lacked such authority.

(3)   A carrier loses his lien on any goods which he voluntarily delivers or which he unjustifiably refuses to deliver.

§ 7-308.   *Enforcement of Carrier's Lien.*

(1)   A carrier's lien may be enforced by public or private sale of the goods, in bloc or in parcels, at any time or place and on any terms which are commercially reasonable, after notifying all persons known to claim an interest in the goods. Such notification must include a statement of the amount due, the nature of the proposed sale and the time and place of any public sale. The fact that a better price could have been obtained by a sale at a different time or in a different method from that selected by the carrier is not of itself sufficient to establish that the sale was not made in a commercially reasonable manner. If the carrier either sells the goods in the usual manner in any recognized market therefor or if he sells at the price current in such market at the time of his sale or if he has otherwise sold in conformity with commercially reasonable practices among dealers in the type of goods sold he has sold in a commercially reasonable manner. A sale of more goods than apparently necessary to be offered to ensure satisfaction of the obligation is not commercially reasonable except in cases covered by the preceding sentence.

(2)   Before any sale pursuant to this section any person claiming a right in the goods may pay the amount necessary to satisfy the lien and the reasonable expenses incurred under this section. In that event the goods must not be sold, but must be retained by the carrier subject to the terms of the bill and this Article.

(3)   The carrier may buy at any public sale pursuant to this section.

(4)   A purchaser in good faith of goods sold to enforce a carrier's lien takes the goods free of any rights of persons against whom the lien was valid, despite noncompliance by the carrier with the requirements of this section.

(5)   The carrier may satisfy his lien from the proceeds of any sale pursuant to this section but must hold the balance, if any, for delivery on demand to any person to whom he would have been bound to deliver the goods.

(6)   The rights provided by this section shall be in addition to all other rights allowed by law to a creditor against his debtor.

(7)   A carrier's lien may be enforced in accordance with either subsection (1) or the procedure set forth in subsection (2) of Section 7-210.

(8)   The carrier is liable for damages caused by failure to comply with the requirements for sale under this section and in case of willful violation is liable for conversion.

§ 7-309.   *Duty of Care; Contractual Limitation of Carrier's Liability.*

(1)   A carrier who issues a bill of lading whether negotiable or non-negotiable must exercise the degree of care in relation to the goods which a reasonably careful man would exercise under like circumstances. This subsection does not repeal or change any law or rule of law which imposes liability upon a common carrier for damages not caused by its negligence.

(2)   Damages may be limited by a provision that the carrier's liability shall not exceed a value stated in the document if the carrier's rates are dependent upon value and the consignor by the carrier's tariff is afforded an opportunity to declare a higher value or a value as lawfully provided in the tariff, or where no tariff is filed he is otherwise advised of such opportunity; but no such limitation is effective with respect to the carrier's liability for conversion to its own use.

(3)   Reasonable provisions as to the time and manner of presenting claims and instituting actions based on the shipment may be included in a bill of lading or tariff.

■ **PART 4   Warehouse Receipts and Bills of Lading: General Obligations**

§ 7-401.   *Irregularities in Issue of Receipt or Bill or Conduct of Issuer.*

The obligations imposed by this Article on an issuer apply to a document of title regardless of the fact that

(a)   the document may not comply with the requirements of this Article or of any other law or regulation regarding its issue, form or content; or

(b)   the issuer may have violated laws regulating the conduct of his business; or

(c)   the goods covered by the document were owned by the bailee at the time the document was issued; or

(d)   the person issuing the document does not come within the definition of warehouseman if it purports to be a warehouse receipt.

§ 7-402.   *Duplicate Receipt or Bill; Overissue.*

Neither a duplicate nor any other document of title purporting to cover goods already represented by an outstanding document of the same issuer confers any right in the goods, except as provided in the case of bills in a set, overissue of documents for fungible goods and substitutes for lost, stolen or destroyed documents. But the issuer is liable for damages caused by his overissue or failure to identify a duplicate document as such by conspicuous notation on its face.

§ 7-403.   *Obligation of Warehouseman or Carrier to Deliver; Excuse.*

(1)   The bailee must deliver the goods to a person entitled under the document who complies with subsections (2) and (3), unless and to the extent that the bailee establishes any of the following:

(a)   delivery of the goods to a person whose receipt was rightful as against the claimant;

(b)   damage to or delay, loss or destruction of the goods for which the bailee is not liable [, but the burden of establishing negligence in such cases is on the person entitled under the document];
Note: The brackets in (1)(b) indicate that State enactments may differ on this point without serious damage to the principle of uniformity.

(c)   previous sale or other disposition of the goods in lawful enforcement of a lien or on warehouseman's lawful termination of storage;

(d)   the exercise by a seller of his right to stop delivery pursuant to the provisions of the Article on Sales (Section 2-705);

(e)   a diversion, reconsignment or other disposition pursuant to the provisions of this Article (Section 7-303) or tariff regulating such right;

(f)   release, satisfaction or any other fact affording a personal defense against the claimant;

(g)   any other lawful excuse.

(2)   A person claiming goods covered by a document of title must satisfy the bailee's lien where the bailee so requests or where the bailee is prohibited by law from delivering the goods until the charges are paid.

(3)   Unless the person claiming is one against whom the document confers no right under Sec. 7-503(1), he must surrender for cancellation or notation of partial deliveries any outstanding negotiable document covering the goods, and the bailee must cancel the document or conspicuously note the partial delivery thereon or be liable to any person to whom the document is duly negotiated.

(4)   "Person entitled under the document" means holder in the case of a negotiable document, or the person to whom delivery is to be made by the terms of or pursuant to written instructions under a non-negotiable document.

§ 7-404.   *No Liability for Good Faith Delivery Pursuant to Receipt or Bill.*

A bailee who in good faith including observance of reasonable commercial standards has received goods and delivered or otherwise disposed of them according to the terms of the document of title or pursuant to this Article is not liable therefor. This rule applies even though the person from whom he received the goods had no authority to procure the document or to dispose of the goods and even though the person to whom he delivered the goods had no authority to receive them.

■ **PART 5   Warehouse Receipts and Bills of Lading: Negotiation and Transfer**

§ 7-501.   *Form of Negotiation and Requirements of "Due Negotiation".*

(1)   A negotiable document of title running to the order of a named person is negotiated by his indorsement and delivery. After his indorsement in blank or to bearer any person can negotiate it by delivery alone.

(2)   (a)   A negotiable document of title is also negotiated by delivery alone when by its original terms it runs to bearer.

(b)   When a document running to the order of a named person is delivered to him the effect is the same as if the document had been negotiated.

(3)   Negotiation of a negotiable document of title after it has been indorsed to a specified person requires indorsement by the special indorsee as well as delivery.

(4)   A negotiable document of title is "duly negotiated" when it is negotiated in the manner stated in this section to a holder who purchases it in good faith without notice of any defense against or claim to it on the part of any person and for value, unless it is established that the negotiation is not in the regular course of business or financing or involves receiving the document in settlement or payment of a money obligation.

(5)   Indorsement of a non-negotiable document neither makes it negotiable nor adds to the transferee's rights.

(6)   The naming in a negotiable bill of a person to be notified of the arrival of the goods does not limit the negotiability of the bill nor constitute notice to a purchaser thereof of any interest of such person in the goods.

§ 7-502.   *Rights Acquired by Due Negotiation.*

(1)   Subject to the following section and to the provisions of Section 7-205 on fungible goods, a holder to whom a negotiable document of title has been duly negotiated acquires thereby:

(a)   title to the document;

(b)   title to the goods;

(c)   all rights accruing under the law of agency or estoppel, including rights to goods delivered to the bailee after the document was issued; and

(d)   the direct obligation of the issuer to hold or deliver the goods according to the terms of the document free of any defense or claim by him except those arising under the terms of the document or under this Article. In the case of a delivery order the bailee's obligation accrues only upon acceptance and the obligation acquired by the holder is that the issuer and any indorser will procure the acceptance of the bailee.

(2) Subject to the following section, title and rights so acquired are not defeated by any stoppage of the goods represented by the document or by surrender of such goods by the bailee, and are not impaired even though the negotiation or any prior negotiation constituted a breach of duty or even though any person has been deprived of possession of the document by misrepresentation, fraud, accident, mistake, duress, loss, theft or conversion, or even though a previous sale or other transfer of the goods or document has been made to a third person.

§ 7-503. Document of Title to Goods Defeated in Certain Cases.

(1) A document of title confers no right in goods against a person who before issuance of the document had a legal interest or a perfected security interest in them and who neither

(a) delivered or entrusted them or any document of title covering them to the bailor or his nominee with actual or apparent authority to ship, store or sell or with power to obtain delivery under this Article (Section 7-403) or with power of disposition under this Act (Sections 2-403 and 9-307) or other statute or rule of law; nor

(b) acquiesced in the procurement by the bailor or his nominee of any document of title.

(2) Title to goods based upon an unaccepted delivery order is subject to the rights of anyone to whom a negotiable warehouse receipt or bill of lading covering the goods has been duly negotiated. Such a title may be defeated under the next section to the same extent as the rights of the issuer or a transferee from the issuer.

(3) Title to goods based upon a bill of lading issued to a freight forwarder is subject to the rights of anyone to whom a bill issued by the freight forwarder is duly negotiated; but delivery by the carrier in accordance with Part 4 of this Article pursuant to its own bill of lading discharges the carrier's obligation to deliver.

§ 7-504. Rights Acquired in the Absence of Due Negotiation; Effect of Diversion; Seller's Stoppage of Delivery.

(1) A transferee of a document, whether negotiable or non-negotiable, to whom the document has been delivered but not duly negotiated, acquires the title and rights which his transferor had or had actual authority to convey.

(2) In the case of a non-negotiable document, until but not after the bailee receives notification of the transfer, the rights of the transferee may be defeated

(a) by those creditors of the transferor who could treat the sale as void under Section 2-402; or

(b) by a buyer from the transferor in ordinary course of business if the bailee has delivered the goods to the buyer or received notification of his rights; or

(c) as against the bailee by good faith dealings of the bailee with the transferor.

(3) A diversion or other change of shipping instructions by the consignor in a non-negotiable bill of lading which causes the bailee not to deliver to the consignee defeats the consignee's title to the goods if they have been delivered to a buyer in ordinary course of business and in any event defeats the consignee's rights against the bailee.

(4) Delivery pursuant to a non-negotiable document may be stopped by a seller under Section 2-705, and subject to the requirement of due notification there provided. A bailee honoring the seller's instructions is entitled to be indemnified by the seller against any resulting loss or expense.

§ 7-505. Indorser Not a Guarantor for Other Parties.

The indorsement of a document of title issued by a bailee does not make the indorser liable for any default by the bailee or by previous indorsers.

§ 7-506. Delivery Without Indorsement: Right to Compel Indorsement.

The transferee of a negotiable document of title has a specifically enforceable right to have his transferor supply any necessary indorsement but the transfer becomes a negotiation only as of the time the indorsement is supplied.

§ 7-507. Warranties on Negotiation or Transfer of Receipt or Bill.

Where a person negotiates or transfers a document of title for value otherwise than as a mere intermediary under the next following section, then unless otherwise agreed he warrants to his immediate purchaser only in addition to any warranty made in selling the goods

(a) that the document is genuine; and

(b) that he has no knowledge of any fact which would impair its validity or worth; and

(c) that his negotiation or transfer is rightful and fully effective with respect to the title to the document and the goods it represents.

§ 7-508. Warranties of Collecting Bank as to Documents.

A collecting bank or other intermediary known to be entrusted with documents on behalf of another or with collection of a draft of other claim against delivery of documents warrants by such delivery of the documents only its own good faith and authority. This rule applies even though the intermediary has purchased or made advances against the claim or draft to be collected.

§ 7-509. Receipt or Bill: When Adequate Compliance With Commercial Contract.

The question whether a document is adequate to fulfill the obligations of a contract for sale or the conditions of a credit is governed by the Articles on Sales (Article 2) and on Letters of Credit (Article 5).

■ PART 6 Warehouse Receipts and Bills of Lading: Miscellaneous Provisions

§ 7-601. Lost and Missing Documents.

(1) If a document has been lost, stolen or destroyed, a court may order delivery of the goods or issuance of a substitute document and the bailee may without liability to any person comply with such order. If the document was negotiable the claimant must post security approved by the court to indemnify any person who may suffer loss as a result of non-surrender of the document. If the document was not negotiable, such security may be required at the discretion of the court. The court may also in its discretion order payment of the bailee's reasonable costs and counsel fees.

(2) A bailee who without court order delivers goods to a person claiming under a missing negotiable document is liable to any person injured thereby, and if the delivery is not in good faith becomes liable for conversion. Delivery in good faith is not conversion if made in accordance with a filed classification or tariff or, where no classification or tariff is filed, if the claimant posts security with the bailee in an amount at least double the value of the goods at the time of posting to indemnify any person injured by the delivery who files a notice of claim within one year after the delivery.

§ 7-602. *Attachment of Goods Covered by a Negotiable Document.*

Except where the document was originally issued upon delivery of the goods by a person who had no power to dispose of them, no lien attaches by virtue of any judicial process to goods in the possession of a bailee for which a negotiable document of title is outstanding unless the document be first surrendered to the bailee or its negotiation enjoined, and the bailee shall not be compelled to deliver the goods pursuant to process until the document is surrendered to him or impounded by the court. One who purchases the document for value without notice of the process or injunction takes free of the lien imposed by judicial process.

§ 7-603. *Conflicting Claims; Interpleader.*

If more than one person claims title or possession of the goods, the bailee is excused from delivery until he has had a reasonable time to ascertain the validity of the adverse claims or to bring an action to compel all claimants to interplead and may compel such interpleader, either in defending an action for non-delivery of the goods, or by original action, whichever is appropriate.

ARTICLE 8
Revised (1994) Investment Securities

■ **PART I   Short Title and General Matters**

§ 8-101. *Short Title.*

This Article may be cited as Uniform Commercial Code— Investment Securities.

§ 8-102. *Definitions.*

(a)   In this Article:

(1)   "Adverse claim" means a claim that a claimant has a property interest in a financial asset and that it is a violation of the rights of the claimant for another person to hold, transfer, or deal with the financial asset.

(2)   "Bearer form," as applied to a certificated security, means a form in which the security is payable to the bearer of the security certificate according to its terms but not by reason of an indorsement.

(3)   "Broker" means a person defined as a broker or dealer under the federal securities laws, but without excluding a bank acting in that capacity.

(4)   "Certificated security" means a security that is represented by a certificate.

(5)   "Clearing corporation" means:

(i)   a person that is registered as a "clearing agency" under the federal securities laws;

(ii)   a federal reserve bank; or

(iii)   any other person that provides clearance or settlement services with respect to financial assets that would require it to register as a clearing agency under the federal securities laws but for an exclusion or exemption from the registration requirement, if its activities as a clearing corporation, including promulgation of rules, are subject to regulation by a federal or state governmental authority.

(6)   "Communicate" means to:

(i)   send a signed writing; or

(ii)   transmit information by any mechanism agreed upon by the persons transmitting and receiving the information.

(7)   "Entitlement holder" means a person identified in the records of a securities intermediary as the person having a security entitlement against the securities intermediary. If a person acquires a security entitlement by virtue of Section 8-501(b)(2) or (3), that person is the entitlement holder.

(8)   "Entitlement order" means a notification communicated to a securities intermediary directing transfer or redemption of a financial asset to which the entitlement holder has a security entitlement.

(9)   "Financial asset," except as otherwise provided in Section 8-103, means:

(i)   a security;

(ii)   an obligation of a person or a share, participation, or other interest in a person or in property or an enterprise of a person, which is, or is of a type, dealt in or traded on financial markets, or which is recognized in any area in which it is issued or dealt in as a medium for investment; or

(iii)   any property that is held by a securities intermediary for another person in a securities account if the securities intermediary has expressly agreed with the other person that the property is to be treated as a financial asset under this Article.

As context requires, the term means either the interest itself or the means by which a person's claim to it is evidenced, including a certificated or uncertificated security, a security certificate, or a security entitlement.

(10)   "Good faith," for purposes of the obligation of good faith in the performance or enforcement of contracts or duties within this Article, means honesty in fact and the observance of reasonable commercial standards of fair dealing.

(11)   "Indorsement" means a signature that alone or accompanied by other words is made on a security certificate in registered form or on a separate document for the purpose of assigning, transferring, or redeeming the security or granting a power to assign, transfer, or redeem it.

(12)   "Instruction" means a notification communicated to the issuer of an uncertificated security which directs that the transfer of the security be registered or that the security be redeemed.

(13)   "Registered form," as applied to a certificated security, means a form in which:

(i)   the security certificate specifies a person entitled to the security; and

(ii)   a transfer of the security may be registered upon books maintained for that purpose by or on behalf of the issuer, or the security certificate so states.

(14)   "Securities intermediary" means:

(i)   a clearing corporation; or

(ii)   a person, including a bank or broker, that in the ordinary course of its business maintains securities accounts for others and is acting in that capacity.

(15)   "Security," except as otherwise provided in Section 8-103, means an obligation of an issuer or a share, participation, or other interest in an issuer or in property or an enterprise of an issuer:

(i)   which is represented by a security certificate in bearer or registered form, or the transfer of which may be registered upon books maintained for that purpose by or on behalf of the issuer;

(ii)   which is one of a class or series or by its terms is divisible into a class or series of shares, participations, interests, or obligations; and

(iii) which:

    (a) is, or is of a type, dealt in or traded on securities exchanges or securities markets; or

    (b) is a medium for investment and by its terms expressly provides that it is a security governed by this Article.

(16) "Security certificate" means a certificate representing a security.

(17) "Security entitlement" means the rights and property interest of an entitlement holder with respect to a financial asset specified in Part 5.

(18) "Uncertificated security" means a security that is not represented by a certificate.

(b) Other definitions applying to this Article and the sections in which they appear are:

Appropriate person Section 8-107

Control Section 8-106

Delivery Section 8-301

Investment company security Section 8-103

Issuer Section 8-201

Overissue Section 8-210

Protected purchaser Section 8-303

Securities account Section 8-501

(c) In addition, Article 1 contains general definitions and principles of construction and interpretation applicable throughout this Article.

(d) The characterization of a person, business, or transaction for purposes of this Article does not determine the characterization of the person, business, or transaction for purposes of any other law, regulation, or rule.

§ 8-103. *Rules for Determining Whether Certain Obligations and Interests Are Securities or Financial Assets.*

(a) A share or similar equity interest issued by a corporation, business trust, joint stock company, or similar entity is a security.

(b) An "investment company security" is a security. "Investment company security" means a share or similar equity interest issued by an entity that is registered as an investment company under the federal investment company laws, an interest in a unit investment trust that is so registered, or a face-amount certificate issued by a face-amount certificate company that is so registered. Investment company security does not include an insurance policy or endowment policy or annuity contract issued by an insurance company.

(c) An interest in a partnership or limited liability company is not a security unless it is dealt in or traded on securities exchanges or in securities markets, its terms expressly provide that it is a security governed by this Article, or it is an investment company security. However, an interest in a partnership or limited liability company is a financial asset if it is held in a securities account.

(d) A writing that is a security certificate is governed by this Article and not by Article 3, even though it also meets the requirements of that Article. However, a negotiable instrument governed by Article 3 is a financial asset if it is held in a securities account.

(e) An option or similar obligation issued by a clearing corporation to its participants is not a security, but is a financial asset.

(f) A commodity contract, as defined in Section 9-115, is not a security or a financial asset

§ 8-104. *Acquisition of Security or Financial Asset or Interest Therein.*

(a) A person acquires a security or an interest therein, under this Article, if:

    (1) the person is a purchaser to whom a security is delivered pursuant to Section 8-301; or

    (2) the person acquires a security entitlement to the security pursuant to Section 8-501.

(b) A person acquires a financial asset, other than a security, or an interest therein, under this Article, if the person acquires a security entitlement to the financial asset.

(c) A person who acquires a security entitlement to a security or other financial asset has the rights specified in Part 5, but is a purchaser of any security, security entitlement, or other financial asset held by the securities intermediary only to the extent provided in Section 8-503.

(d) Unless the context shows that a different meaning is intended, a person who is required by other law, regulation, rule, or agreement to transfer, deliver, present, surrender, exchange, or otherwise put in the possession of another person a security or financial asset satisfies that requirement by causing the other person to acquire an interest in the security or financial asset pursuant to subsection (a) or (b).

§ 8-105. *Notice of Adverse Claim.*

(a) A person has notice of an adverse claim if:

    (1) the person knows of the adverse claim;

    (2) the person is aware of facts sufficient to indicate that there is a significant probability that the adverse claim exists and deliberately avoids information that would establish the existence of the adverse claim; or

    (3) the person has a duty, imposed by statute or regulation, to investigate whether an adverse claim exists, and the investigation so required would establish the existence of the adverse claim.

(b) Having knowledge that a financial asset or interest therein is or has been transferred by a representative imposes no duty of inquiry into the rightfulness of a transaction and is not notice of an adverse claim. However, a person who knows that a representative has transferred a financial asset or interest therein in a transaction that is, or whose proceeds are being used, for the individual benefit of the representative or otherwise in breach of duty has notice of an adverse claim.

(c) An act or event that creates a right to immediate performance of the principal obligation represented by a security certificate or sets a date on or after which the certificate is to be presented or surrendered for redemption or exchange does not itself constitute notice of an adverse claim except in the case of a transfer more than:

    (1) one year after a date set for presentment or surrender for redemption or exchange; or

    (2) six months after a date set for payment of money against presentation or surrender of the certificate, if money was available for payment on that date.

(d) A purchaser of a certificated security has notice of an adverse claim if the security certificate:

    (1) whether in bearer or registered form, has been indorsed "for collection" or "for surrender" or for some other purpose not involving transfer; or

    (2) is in bearer form and has on it an unambiguous statement that it is the property of a person other than the transferor, but the mere writing of a name on the certificate is not such a statement.

(e) Filing of a financing statement under Article 9 is not notice of an adverse claim to a financial asset.

§ 8-106. *Control.*

(a) A purchaser has "control" of a certificated security in bearer form if the certificated security is delivered to the purchaser.

(b)   A purchaser has "control" of a certificated security in registered form if the certificated security is delivered to the purchaser, and:

(1)   the certificate is indorsed to the purchaser or in blank by an effective indorsement; or

(2)   the certificate is registered in the name of the purchaser, upon original issue or registration of transfer by the issuer.

(c)   A purchaser has "control" of an uncertificated security if:

(1)   the uncertificated security is delivered to the purchaser; or

(2)   the issuer has agreed that it will comply with instructions originated by the purchaser without further consent by the registered owner.

(d)   A purchaser has "control" of a security entitlement if:

(1)   the purchaser becomes the entitlement holder; or

(2)   the securities intermediary has agreed that it will comply with entitlement orders originated by the purchaser without further consent by the entitlement holder.

(e)   If an interest in a security entitlement is granted by the entitlement holder to the entitlement holder's own securities intermediary, the securities intermediary has control.

(f)   A purchaser who has satisfied the requirements of subsection (c)(2) or (d)(2) has control even if the registered owner in the case of subsection (c)(2) or the entitlement holder in the case of subsection (d)(2) retains the right to make substitutions for the uncertificated security or security entitlement, to originate instructions or entitlement orders to the issuer or securities intermediary, or otherwise to deal with the uncertificated security or security entitlement.

(g)   An issuer or a securities intermediary may not enter into an agreement of the kind described in subsection (c)(2) or (d)(2) without the consent of the registered owner or entitlement holder, but an issuer or a securities intermediary is not required to enter into such an agreement even though the registered owner or entitlement holder so directs. An issuer or securities intermediary that has entered into such an agreement is not required to confirm the existence of the agreement to another party unless requested to do so by the registered owner or entitlement holder.

§ 8-107.   *Whether Indorsement, Instruction, or Entitlement Order Is Effective.*

(a)   "Appropriate person" means:

(1)   with respect to an indorsement, the person specified by a security certificate or by an effective special indorsement to be entitled to the security;

(2)   with respect to an instruction, the registered owner of an uncertificated security;

(3)   with respect to an entitlement order, the entitlement holder;

(4)   if the person designated in paragraph (1), (2), or (3) is deceased, the designated person's successor taking under other law or the designated person's personal representative acting for the estate of the decedent; or

(5)   if the person designated in paragraph (1), (2), or (3) lacks capacity, the designated person's guardian, conservator, or other similar representative who has power under other law to transfer the security or financial asset.

(b)   An indorsement, instruction, or entitlement order is effective if:

(1)   it is made by the appropriate person;

(2)   it is made by a person who has power under the law of agency to transfer the security or financial asset on behalf of the appropriate person, including, in the case of an instruction or entitlement order, a person who has control under Section 8-106(c)(2) or (d)(2); or

(3)   the appropriate person has ratified it or is otherwise precluded from asserting its ineffectiveness.

(c)   An indorsement, instruction, or entitlement order made by a representative is effective even if:

(1)   the representative has failed to comply with a controlling instrument or with the law of the State having jurisdiction of the representative relationship, including any law requiring the representative to obtain court approval of the transaction; or

(2)   the representative's action in making the indorsement, instruction, or entitlement order or using the proceeds of the transaction is otherwise a breach of duty.

(d)   If a security is registered in the name of or specially indorsed to a person described as a representative, or if a securities account is maintained in the name of a person described as a representative, an indorsement, instruction, or entitlement order made by the person is effective even though the person is no longer serving in the described capacity.

(e)   Effectiveness of an indorsement, instruction, or entitlement order is determined as of the date the indorsement, instruction, or entitlement order is made, and an indorsement, instruction, or entitlement order does not become ineffective by reason of any later change of circumstances.

§ 8-108.   *Warranties in Direct Holding.*

(a)   A person who transfers a certificated security to a purchaser for value warrants to the purchaser, and an indorser, if the transfer is by indorsement, warrants to any subsequent purchaser, that:

(1)   the certificate is genuine and has not been materially altered;

(2)   the transferor or indorser does not know of any fact that might impair the validity of the security;

(3)   there is no adverse claim to the security;

(4)   the transfer does not violate any restriction on transfer;

(5)   if the transfer is by indorsement, the indorsement is made by an appropriate person, or if the indorsement is by an agent, the agent has actual authority to act on behalf of the appropriate person; and

(6)   the transfer is otherwise effective and rightful.

(b)   A person who originates an instruction for registration of transfer of an uncertificated security to a purchaser for value warrants to the purchaser that:

(1)   the instruction is made by an appropriate person, or if the instruction is by an agent, the agent has actual authority to act on behalf of the appropriate person;

(2)   the security is valid;

(3)   there is no adverse claim to the security; and

(4)   at the time the instruction is presented to the issuer:

(i)   the purchaser will be entitled to the registration of transfer;

(ii)   the transfer will be registered by the issuer free from all liens, security interests, restrictions, and claims other than those specified in the instruction;

(iii)   the transfer will not violate any restriction on transfer; and

(iv)   the requested transfer will otherwise be effective and rightful.

(c)   A person who transfers an uncertificated security to a purchaser for value and does not originate an instruction in connection with the transfer warrants that:

(1)   the uncertificated security is valid;

(2)   there is no adverse claim to the security;

(3) the transfer does not violate any restriction on transfer; and

(4) the transfer is otherwise effective and rightful.

(d) A person who indorses a security certificate warrants to the issuer that:

(1) there is no adverse claim to the security; and

(2) the indorsement is effective.

(e) A person who originates an instruction for registration of transfer of an uncertificated security warrants to the issuer that:

(1) the instruction is effective; and

(2) at the time the instruction is presented to the issuer the purchaser will be entitled to the registration of transfer.

(f) A person who presents a certificated security for registration of transfer or for payment or exchange warrants to the issuer that the person is entitled to the registration, payment, or exchange, but a purchaser for value and without notice of adverse claims to whom transfer is registered warrants only that the person has no knowledge of any unauthorized signature in a necessary indorsement.

(g) If a person acts as agent of another in delivering a certificated security to a purchaser, the identity of the principal was known to the person to whom the certificate was delivered, and the certificate delivered by the agent was received by the agent from the principal or received by the agent from another person at the direction of the principal, the person delivering the security certificate warrants only that the delivering person has authority to act for the principal and does not know of any adverse claim to the certificated security.

(h) A secured party who redelivers a security certificate received, or after payment and on order of the debtor delivers the security certificate to another person, makes only the warranties of an agent under subsection (g).

(i) Except as otherwise provided in subsection (g), a broker acting for a customer makes to the issuer and a purchaser the warranties provided in subsections (a) through (f). A broker that delivers a security certificate to its customer, or causes its customer to be registered as the owner of an uncertificated security, makes to the customer the warranties provided in subsection (a) or (b), and has the rights and privileges of a purchaser under this section. The warranties of and in favor of the broker acting as an agent are in addition to applicable warranties given by and in favor of the customer.

§ 8-109. *Warranties in Indirect Holding.*

(a) A person who originates an entitlement order to a securities intermediary warrants to the securities intermediary that:

(1) the entitlement order is made by an appropriate person, or if the entitlement order is by an agent, the agent has actual authority to act on behalf of the appropriate person; and

(2) there is no adverse claim to the security entitlement.

(b) A person who delivers a security certificate to a securities intermediary for credit to a securities account or originates an instruction with respect to an uncertificated security directing that the uncertificated security be credited to a securities account makes to the securities intermediary the warranties specified in Section 8-108(a) or (b).

(c) If a securities intermediary delivers a security certificate to its entitlement holder or causes its entitlement holder to be registered as the owner of an uncertificated security, the securities intermediary makes to the entitlement holder the warranties specified in Section 8-108(a) or (b).

§ 8-110. *Applicability; Choice of Law.*

(a) The local law of the issuer's jurisdiction, as specified in subsection (d), governs:

(1) the validity of a security;

(2) the rights and duties of the issuer with respect to registration of transfer;

(3) the effectiveness of registration of transfer by the issuer;

(4) whether the issuer owes any duties to an adverse claimant to a security; and

(5) whether an adverse claim can be asserted against a person to whom transfer of a certificated or uncertificated security is registered or a person who obtains control of an uncertificated security.

(b) The local law of the securities intermediary's jurisdiction, as specified in subsection (e), governs:

(1) acquisition of a security entitlement from the securities intermediary;

(2) the rights and duties of the securities intermediary and entitlement holder arising out of a security entitlement;

(3) whether the securities intermediary owes any duties to an adverse claimant to a security entitlement; and

(4) whether an adverse claim can be asserted against a person who acquires a security entitlement from the securities intermediary or a person who purchases a security entitlement or interest therein from an entitlement holder.

(c) The local law of the jurisdiction in which a security certificate is located at the time of delivery governs whether an adverse claim can be asserted against a person to whom the security certificate is delivered.

(d) "Issuer's jurisdiction" means the jurisdiction under which the issuer of the security is organized or, if permitted by the law of that jurisdiction, the law of another jurisdiction specified by the issuer. An issuer organized under the law of this State may specify the law of another jurisdiction as the law governing the matters specified in subsection (a)(2) through (5).

(e) The following rules determine a "securities intermediary's jurisdiction" for purposes of this section:

(1) If an agreement between the securities intermediary and its entitlement holder specifies that it is governed by the law of a particular jurisdiction, that jurisdiction is the securities intermediary's jurisdiction.

(2) If an agreement between the securities intermediary and its entitlement holder does not specify the governing law as provided in paragraph (1), but expressly specifies that the securities account is maintained at an office in a particular jurisdiction, that jurisdiction is the securities intermediary's jurisdiction.

(3) If an agreement between the securities intermediary and its entitlement holder does not specify a jurisdiction as provided in paragraph (1) or (2), the securities intermediary's jurisdiction is the jurisdiction in which is located the office identified in an account statement as the office serving the entitlement holder's account.

(4) If an agreement between the securities intermediary and its entitlement holder does not specify a jurisdiction as provided in paragraph (1) or (2) and an account statement does not identify an office serving the entitlement holder's account as provided in paragraph (3), the securities intermediary's jurisdiction is the jurisdiction in which is located the chief executive office of the securities intermediary.

(f) A securities intermediary's jurisdiction is not determined by the physical location of certificates representing financial assets, or by the jurisdiction in which is organized the issuer of the financial asset with respect to which an entitlement holder has a security entitlement, or by the location of facilities for data processing or other record keeping concerning the account.

§ 8-111. Clearing Corporation Rules.

A rule adopted by a clearing corporation governing rights and obligations among the clearing corporation and its participants in the clearing corporation is effective even if the rule conflicts with this [Act] and affects another party who does not consent to the rule.

§ 8-112. Creditor's Legal Process.

(a) The interest of a debtor in a certificated security may be reached by a creditor only by actual seizure of the security certificate by the officer making the attachment or levy, except as otherwise provided in subsection (d). However, a certificated security for which the certificate has been surrendered to the issuer may be reached by a creditor by legal process upon the issuer.

(b) The interest of a debtor in an uncertificated security may be reached by a creditor only by legal process upon the issuer at its chief executive office in the United States, except as otherwise provided in subsection (d).

(c) The interest of a debtor in a security entitlement may be reached by a creditor only by legal process upon the securities intermediary with whom the debtor's securities account is maintained, except as otherwise provided in subsection (d).

(d) The interest of a debtor in a certificated security for which the certificate is in the possession of a secured party, or in an uncertificated security registered in the name of a secured party, or a security entitlement maintained in the name of a secured party, may be reached by a creditor by legal process upon the secured party.

(e) A creditor whose debtor is the owner of a certificated security, uncertificated security, or security entitlement is entitled to aid from a court of competent jurisdiction, by injunction or otherwise, in reaching the certificated security, uncertificated security, or security entitlement or in satisfying the claim by means allowed at law or in equity in regard to property that cannot readily be reached by other legal process.

§ 8-113. Statute of Frauds Inapplicable.

A contract or modification of a contract for the sale or purchase of a security is enforceable whether or not there is a writing signed or record authenticated by a party against whom enforcement is sought, even if the contract or modification is not capable of performance within one year of its making.

§ 8-114. Evidentiary Rules Concerning Certificated Securities.

The following rules apply in an action on a certificated security against the issuer:

(1) Unless specifically denied in the pleadings, each signature on a security certificate or in a necessary indorsement is admitted.

(2) If the effectiveness of a signature is put in issue, the burden of establishing effectiveness is on the party claiming under the signature, but the signature is presumed to be genuine or authorized.

(3) If signatures on a security certificate are admitted or established, production of the certificate entitles a holder to recover on it unless the defendant establishes a defense or a defect going to the validity of the security.

(4) If it is shown that a defense or defect exists, the plaintiff has the burden of establishing that the plaintiff or some person under whom the plaintiff claims is a person against whom the defense or defect cannot be asserted.

§ 8-115. Securities Intermediary and Others Not Liable to Adverse Claimant.

A securities intermediary that has transferred a financial asset pursuant to an effective entitlement order, or a broker or other agent or bailee that has dealt with a financial asset at the direction of its customer or principal, is not liable to a person having an adverse claim to the financial asset, unless the securities intermediary, or broker or other agent or bailee:

(1) took the action after it had been served with an injunction, restraining order, or other legal process enjoining it from doing so, issued by a court of competent jurisdiction, and had a reasonable opportunity to act on the injunction, restraining order, or other legal process; or

(2) acted in collusion with the wrongdoer in violating the rights of the adverse claimant; or

(3) in the case of a security certificate that has been stolen, acted with notice of the adverse claim.

§ 8-116. Securities Intermediary as Purchaser for Value.

A securities intermediary that receives a financial asset and establishes a security entitlement to the financial asset in favor of an entitlement holder is a purchaser for value of the financial asset. A securities intermediary that acquires a security entitlement to a financial asset from another securities intermediary acquires the security entitlement for value if the securities intermediary acquiring the security entitlement establishes a security entitlement to the financial asset in favor of an entitlement holder.

■ PART 2   Issue and Issuer

§ 8-201. Issuer.

(a) With respect to an obligation on or a defense to a security, an "issuer" includes a person that:

(1) places or authorizes the placing of its name on a security certificate, other than as authenticating trustee, registrar, transfer agent, or the like, to evidence a share, participation, or other interest in its property or in an enterprise, or to evidence its duty to perform an obligation represented by the certificate;

(2) creates a share, participation, or other interest in its property or in an enterprise, or undertakes an obligation, that is an uncertificated security;

(3) directly or indirectly creates a fractional interest in its rights or property, if the fractional interest is represented by a security certificate; or

(4) becomes responsible for, or in place of, another person described as an issuer in this section.

(b) With respect to an obligation on or defense to a security, a guarantor is an issuer to the extent of its guaranty, whether or not its obligation is noted on a security certificate.

(c) With respect to a registration of a transfer, issuer means a person on whose behalf transfer books are maintained.

§ 8-202. Issuer's Responsibility and Defenses; Notice of Defect or Defense.

(a) Even against a purchaser for value and without notice, the terms of a certificated security include terms stated on the certificate and terms made part of the security by reference on the certificate to another instrument, indenture, or document or to a constitution, statute, ordinance, rule, regulation, order, or the like, to the extent the terms referred to do not conflict with terms stated on the certificate. A reference under this subsection does not of itself charge a purchaser for value with notice of a defect going to the validity of the security, even if the certificate expressly states that a person accepting it admits notice. The terms of an uncertificated security include those stated in any instrument, indenture, or document or in a constitution, statute, ordinance, rule, regulation, order, or the like, pursuant to which the security is issued.

(b) The following rules apply if an issuer asserts that a security is not valid:

(1)   A security other than one issued by a government or governmental subdivision, agency, or instrumentality, even though issued with a defect going to its validity, is valid in the hands of a purchaser for value and without notice of the particular defect unless the defect involves a violation of a constitutional provision. In that case, the security is valid in the hands of a purchaser for value and without notice of the defect, other than one who takes by original issue.

(2)   Paragraph (1) applies to an issuer that is a government or governmental subdivision, agency, or instrumentality only if there has been substantial compliance with the legal requirements governing the issue or the issuer has received a substantial consideration for the issue as a whole or for the particular security and a stated purpose of the issue is one for which the issuer has power to borrow money or issue the security.

(c)   Except as otherwise provided in Section 8-205, lack of genuineness of a certificated security is a complete defense, even against a purchaser for value and without notice.

(d)   All other defenses of the issuer of a security, including nondelivery and conditional delivery of a certificated security, are ineffective against a purchaser for value who has taken the certificated security without notice of the particular defense.

(e)   This section does not affect the right of a party to cancel a contract for a security "when, as and if issued" or "when distributed" in the event of a material change in the character of the security that is the subject of the contract or in the plan or arrangement pursuant to which the security is to be issued or distributed.

(f)   If a security is held by a securities intermediary against whom an entitlement holder has a security entitlement with respect to the security, the issuer may not assert any defense that the issuer could not assert if the entitlement holder held the security directly.

§ 8-203.   *Staleness as Notice of Defect or Defense.*

After an act or event, other than a call that has been revoked, creating a right to immediate performance of the principal obligation represented by a certificated security or setting a date on or after which the security is to be presented or surrendered for redemption or exchange, a purchaser is charged with notice of any defect in its issue or defense of the issuer, if the act or event:

(1)   requires the payment of money, the delivery of a certificated security, the registration of transfer of an uncertificated security, or any of them on presentation or surrender of the security certificate, the money or security is available on the date set for payment or exchange, and the purchaser takes the security more than one year after that date; or

(2)   is not covered by paragraph (1) and the purchaser takes the security more than two years after the date set for surrender or presentation or the date on which performance became due.

§ 8-204.   *Effect of Issuer's Restriction on Transfer.*

A restriction on transfer of a security imposed by the issuer, even if otherwise lawful, is ineffective against a person without knowledge of the restriction unless:

(1)   the security is certificated and the restriction is noted conspicuously on the security certificate; or

(2)   the security is uncertificated and the registered owner has been notified of the restriction.

§ 8-205.   *Effect of Unauthorized Signature on Security Certificate.*

An unauthorized signature placed on a security certificate before or in the course of issue is ineffective, but the signature is effective in favor of a purchaser for value of the certificated security if the purchaser is without notice of the lack of authority and the signing has been done by:

(1)   an authenticating trustee, registrar, transfer agent, or other person entrusted by the issuer with the signing of the security certificate or of similar security certificates, or the immediate preparation for signing of any of them; or

(2)   an employee of the issuer, or of any of the persons listed in paragraph (1), entrusted with responsible handling of the security certificate.

§ 8-206.   *Completion or Alteration of Security Certificate.*

(a)   If a security certificate contains the signatures necessary to its issue or transfer but is incomplete in any other respect:

(1)   any person may complete it by filling in the blanks as authorized; and

(2)   even if the blanks are incorrectly filled in, the security certificate as completed is enforceable by a purchaser who took it for value and without notice of the incorrectness.

(b)   A complete security certificate that has been improperly altered, even if fraudulently, remains enforceable, but only according to its original terms.

§ 8-207.   *Rights and Duties of Issuer With Respect to Registered Owners.*

(a)   Before due presentment for registration of transfer of a certificated security in registered form or of an instruction requesting registration of transfer of an uncertificated security, the issuer or indenture trustee may treat the registered owner as the person exclusively entitled to vote, receive notifications, and otherwise exercise all the rights and powers of an owner.

(b)   This Article does not affect the liability of the registered owner of a security for a call, assessment, or the like.

§ 8-208.   *Effect of Signature of Authenticating Trustee, Registrar, or Transfer Agent.*

(a)   A person signing a security certificate as authenticating trustee, registrar, transfer agent, or the like, warrants to a purchaser for value of the certificated security, if the purchaser is without notice of a particular defect, that:

(1)   the certificate is genuine;

(2)   the person's own participation in the issue of the security is within the person's capacity and within the scope of the authority received by the person from the issuer; and

(3)   the person has reasonable grounds to believe that the certificated security is in the form and within the amount the issuer is authorized to issue.

(b)   Unless otherwise agreed, a person signing under subsection (a) does not assume responsibility for the validity of the security in other respects.

§ 8-209.   *Issuer's Lien.*

A lien in favor of an issuer upon a certificated security is valid against a purchaser only if the right of the issuer to the lien is noted conspicuously on the security certificate.

§ 8-210.   *Overissue.*

(a)   In this section, "overissue" means the issue of securities in excess of the amount the issuer has corporate power to issue, but an overissue does not occur if appropriate action has cured the overissue.

(b)   Except as otherwise provided in subsections (c) and (d), the provisions of this Article which validate a security or compel its issue or reissue do not apply to the extent that validation, issue, or reissue would result in overissue.

(c)   If an identical security not constituting an overissue is reasonably available for purchase, a person entitled to issue or validation may compel the issuer to purchase the security and deliver it if certificated or register its transfer if uncertificated, against surrender of any security certificate the person holds.

(d) If a security is not reasonably available for purchase, a person entitled to issue or validation may recover from the issuer the price the person or the last purchaser for value paid for it with interest from the date of the person's demand.

■ PART 3 Transfer of Certificated and Uncertificated Securities

§ 8-301. *Delivery.*

(a) Delivery of a certificated security to a purchaser occurs when:

(1) the purchaser acquires possession of the security certificate;

(2) another person, other than a securities intermediary, either acquires possession of the security certificate on behalf of the purchaser or, having previously acquired possession of the certificate, acknowledges that it holds for the purchaser; or

(3) a securities intermediary acting on behalf of the purchaser acquires possession of the security certificate, only if the certificate is in registered form and has been specially indorsed to the purchaser by an effective indorsement.

(b) Delivery of an uncertificated security to a purchaser occurs when:

(1) the issuer registers the purchaser as the registered owner, upon original issue or registration of transfer; or

(2) another person, other than a securities intermediary, either becomes the registered owner of the uncertificated security on behalf of the purchaser or, having previously become the registered owner, acknowledges that it holds for the purchaser.

§ 8-302. *Rights of Purchaser.*

(a) Except as otherwise provided in subsections (b) and (c), upon delivery of a certificated or uncertificated security to a purchaser, the purchaser acquires all rights in the security that the transferor had or had power to transfer.

(b) A purchaser of a limited interest acquires rights only to the extent of the interest purchased.

(c) A purchaser of a certificated security who as a previous holder had notice of an adverse claim does not improve its position by taking from a protected purchaser.

§ 8-303. *Protected Purchaser.*

(a) "Protected purchaser" means a purchaser of a certificated or uncertificated security, or of an interest therein, who:

(1) gives value;

(2) does not have notice of any adverse claim to the security; and

(3) obtains control of the certificated or uncertificated security.

(b) In addition to acquiring the rights of a purchaser, a protected purchaser also acquires its interest in the security free of any adverse claim.

§ 8-304. *Indorsement.*

(a) An indorsement may be in blank or special. An indorsement in blank includes an indorsement to bearer. A special indorsement specifies to whom a security is to be transferred or who has power to transfer it. A holder may convert a blank indorsement to a special indorsement.

(b) An indorsement purporting to be only of part of a security certificate representing units intended by the issuer to be separately transferable is effective to the extent of the indorsement.

(c) An indorsement, whether special or in blank, does not constitute a transfer until delivery of the certificate on which it appears or, if the indorsement is on a separate document, until delivery of both the document and the certificate.

(d) If a security certificate in registered form has been delivered to a purchaser without a necessary indorsement, the purchaser may become a protected purchaser only when the indorsement is supplied. However, against a transferor, a transfer is complete upon delivery and the purchaser has a specifically enforceable right to have any necessary indorsement supplied.

(e) An indorsement of a security certificate in bearer form may give notice of an adverse claim to the certificate, but it does not otherwise affect a right to registration that the holder possesses.

(f) Unless otherwise agreed, a person making an indorsement assumes only the obligations provided in Section 8-108 and not an obligation that the security will be honored by the issuer.

§ 8-305. *Instruction.*

(a) If an instruction has been originated by an appropriate person but is incomplete in any other respect, any person may complete it as authorized and the issuer may rely on it as completed, even though it has been completed incorrectly.

(b) Unless otherwise agreed, a person initiating an instruction assumes only the obligations imposed by Section 8-108 and not an obligation that the security will be honored by the issuer.

§ 8-306. *Effect of Guaranteeing Signature, Indorsement, or Instruction.*

(a) A person who guarantees a signature of an indorser of a security certificate warrants that at the time of signing:

(1) the signature was genuine;

(2) the signer was an appropriate person to indorse, or if the signature is by an agent, the agent had actual authority to act on behalf of the appropriate person; and

(3) the signer had legal capacity to sign.

(b) A person who guarantees a signature of the originator of an instruction warrants that at the time of signing:

(1) the signature was genuine;

(2) the signer was an appropriate person to originate the instruction, or if the signature is by an agent, the agent had actual authority to act on behalf of the appropriate person, if the person specified in the instruction as the registered owner was, in fact, the registered owner, as to which fact the signature guarantor does not make a warranty; and

(3) the signer had legal capacity to sign.

(c) A person who specially guarantees the signature of an originator of an instruction makes the warranties of a signature guarantor under subsection (b) and also warrants that at the time the instruction is presented to the issuer:

(1) the person specified in the instruction as the registered owner of the uncertificated security will be the registered owner; and

(2) the transfer of the uncertificated security requested in the instruction will be registered by the issuer free from all liens, security interests, restrictions, and claims other than those specified in the instruction.

(d) A guarantor under subsections (a) and (b) or a special guarantor under subsection (c) does not otherwise warrant the rightfulness of the transfer.

(e) A person who guarantees an indorsement of a security certificate makes the warranties of a signature guarantor under subsection (a) and also warrants the rightfulness of the transfer in all respects.

(f) A person who guarantees an instruction requesting the transfer of an uncertificated security makes the warranties of a special signature guarantor under subsection (c) and also warrants the rightfulness of the transfer in all respects.

(g) An issuer may not require a special guaranty of signature, a guaranty of indorsement, or a guaranty of instruction as a condition to registration of transfer.

(h) The warranties under this section are made to a person taking or dealing with the security in reliance on the guaranty, and the guarantor is liable to the person for loss resulting from their breach. An indorser or originator of an instruction whose signature, indorsement, or instruction has been guaranteed is liable to a guarantor for any loss suffered by the guarantor as a result of breach of the warranties of the guarantor.

§ 8-307. *Purchaser's Right to Requisites for Registration of Transfer.*

Unless otherwise agreed, the transferor of a security on due demand shall supply the purchaser with proof of authority to transfer or with any other requisite necessary to obtain registration of the transfer of the security, but if the transfer is not for value, a transferor need not comply unless the purchaser pays the necessary expenses. If the transferor fails within a reasonable time to comply with the demand, the purchaser may reject or rescind the transfer.

■ PART 4 Registration

§ 8-401. *Duty of Issuer to Register Transfer.*

(a) If a certificated security in registered form is presented to an issuer with a request to register transfer or an instruction is presented to an issuer with a request to register transfer of an uncertificated security, the issuer shall register the transfer as requested if:

(1) under the terms of the security the person seeking registration of transfer is eligible to have the security registered in its name;

(2) the indorsement or instruction is made by the appropriate person or by an agent who has actual authority to act on behalf of the appropriate person;

(3) reasonable assurance is given that the indorsement or instruction is genuine and authorized (Section 8-402);

(4) any applicable law relating to the collection of taxes has been complied with;

(5) the transfer does not violate any restriction on transfer imposed by the issuer in accordance with Section 8-204;

(6) a demand that the issuer not register transfer has not become effective under Section 8-403, or the issuer has complied with Section 8-403(b) but no legal process or indemnity bond is obtained as provided in Section 8-403(d); and

(7) the transfer is in fact rightful or is to a protected purchaser.

(b) If an issuer is under a duty to register a transfer of a security, the issuer is liable to a person presenting a certificated security or an instruction for registration or to the person's principal for loss resulting from unreasonable delay in registration or failure or refusal to register the transfer.

§ 8-402. *Assurance That Indorsement or Instruction Is Effective.*

(a) An issuer may require the following assurance that each necessary indorsement or each instruction is genuine and authorized:

(1) in all cases, a guaranty of the signature of the person making an indorsement or originating an instruction including, in the case of an instruction, reasonable assurance of identity;

(2) if the indorsement is made or the instruction is originated by an agent, appropriate assurance of actual authority to sign;

(3) if the indorsement is made or the instruction is originated by a fiduciary pursuant to Section 8-107(a)(4) or (a)(5), appropriate evidence of appointment or incumbency;

(4) if there is more than one fiduciary, reasonable assurance that all who are required to sign have done so; and

(5) if the indorsement is made or the instruction is originated by a person not covered by another provision of this subsection, assurance appropriate to the case corresponding as nearly as may be to the provisions of this subsection.

(b) An issuer may elect to require reasonable assurance beyond that specified in this section.

(c) In this section:

(1) "Guaranty of the signature" means a guaranty signed by or on behalf of a person reasonably believed by the issuer to be responsible. An issuer may adopt standards with respect to responsibility if they are not manifestly unreasonable.

(2) "Appropriate evidence of appointment or incumbency" means:

(i) in the case of a fiduciary appointed or qualified by a court, a certificate issued by or under the direction or supervision of the court or an officer thereof and dated within 60 days before the date of presentation for transfer; or

(ii) in any other case, a copy of a document showing the appointment or a certificate issued by or on behalf of a person reasonably believed by an issuer to be responsible or, in the absence of that document or certificate, other evidence the issuer reasonably considers appropriate.

§ 8-403 *Demand That Issuer Not Register Transfer.*

(a) A person who is an appropriate person to make an indorsement or originate an instruction may demand that the issuer not register transfer of a security by communicating to the issuer a notification that identifies the registered owner and the issue of which the security is a part and provides an address for communications directed to the person making the demand. The demand is effective only if it is received by the issuer at a time and in a manner affording the issuer reasonable opportunity to act on it.

(b) If a certificated security in registered form is presented to an issuer with a request to register transfer or an instruction is presented to an issuer with a request to register transfer of an uncertificated security after a demand that the issuer not register transfer has become effective, the issuer shall promptly communicate to (i) the person who initiated the demand at the address provided in the demand and (ii) the person who presented the security for registration of transfer or initiated the instruction requesting registration of transfer a notification stating that:

(1) the certificated security has been presented for registration of transfer or the instruction for registration of transfer of the uncertificated security has been received;

(2) a demand that the issuer not register transfer had previously been received; and

(3) the issuer will withhold registration of transfer for a period of time stated in the notification in order to provide the person who initiated the demand an opportunity to obtain legal process or an indemnity bond.

(c) The period described in subsection (b)(3) may not exceed 30 days after the date of communication of the notification. A shorter period may be specified by the issuer if it is not manifestly unreasonable.

(d) An issuer is not liable to a person who initiated a demand that the issuer not register transfer for any loss the person suffers as a result of registration of a transfer pursuant to an effective indorsement or instruction if the person who initiated the demand does not, within the time stated in the issuer's communication, either:

(1) obtain an appropriate restraining order, injunction, or other process from a court of competent jurisdiction enjoining the issuer from registering the transfer; or

(2) file with the issuer an indemnity bond, sufficient in the issuer's judgment to protect the issuer and any transfer agent, registrar, or other agent of the issuer involved from any loss it or they may suffer by refusing to register the transfer.

(e) This section does not relieve an issuer from liability for registering transfer pursuant to an indorsement or instruction that was not effective.

§ 8-404. Wrongful Registration.

(a) Except as otherwise provided in Section 8-406, an issuer is liable for wrongful registration of transfer if the issuer has registered a transfer of a security to a person not entitled to it, and the transfer was registered:

(1) pursuant to an ineffective indorsement or instruction;

(2) after a demand that the issuer not register transfer became effective under Section 8-403(a) and the issuer did not comply with Section 8-403(b);

(3) after the issuer had been served with an injunction, restraining order, or other legal process enjoining it from registering the transfer, issued by a court of competent jurisdiction, and the issuer had a reasonable opportunity to act on the injunction, restraining order, or other legal process; or

(4) by an issuer acting in collusion with the wrongdoer.

(b) An issuer that is liable for wrongful registration of transfer under subsection (a) on demand shall provide the person entitled to the security with a like certificated or uncertificated security, and any payments or distributions that the person did not receive as a result of the wrongful registration. If an overissue would result, the issuer's liability to provide the person with a like security is governed by Section 8-210.

(c) Except as otherwise provided in subsection (a) or in a law relating to the collection of taxes, an issuer is not liable to an owner or other person suffering loss as a result of the registration of a transfer of a security if registration was made pursuant to an effective indorsement or instruction.

§ 8-405. Replacement of Lost, Destroyed, or Wrongfully Taken Security Certificate.

(a) If an owner of a certificated security, whether in registered or bearer form, claims that the certificate has been lost, destroyed, or wrongfully taken, the issuer shall issue a new certificate if the owner:

(1) so requests before the issuer has notice that the certificate has been acquired by a protected purchaser;

(2) files with the issuer a sufficient indemnity bond; and

(3) satisfies other reasonable requirements imposed by the issuer.

(b) If, after the issue of a new security certificate, a protected purchaser of the original certificate presents it for registration of transfer, the issuer shall register the transfer unless an overissue would result. In that case, the issuer's liability is governed by Section 8-210. In addition to any rights on the indemnity bond, an issuer may recover the new certificate from a person to whom it was issued or any person taking under that person, except a protected purchaser.

§ 8-406. Obligation to Notify Issuer of Lost, Destroyed, or Wrongfully Taken Security Certificate.

If a security certificate has been lost, apparently destroyed, or wrongfully taken, and the owner fails to notify the issuer of that fact within a reasonable time after the owner has notice of it and the issuer registers a transfer of the security before receiving notification, the owner may not assert against the issuer a claim for registering the transfer under Section 8-404 or a claim to a new security certificate under Section 8-405.

§ 8-407. Authenticating Trustee, Transfer Agent, and Registrar.

A person acting as authenticating trustee, transfer agent, registrar, or other agent for an issuer in the registration of a transfer of its securities, in the issue of new security certificates or uncertificated securities, or in the cancellation of surrendered security certificates has the same obligation to the holder or owner of a certificated or uncertificated security with regard to the particular functions performed as the issuer has in regard to those functions.

■ PART 5 Security Entitlements

§ 8-501. Securities Account; Acquisition of Security Entitlement From Securities Intermediary.

(a) "Securities account" means an account to which a financial asset is or may be credited in accordance with an agreement under which the person maintaining the account undertakes to treat the person for whom the account is maintained as entitled to exercise the rights that comprise the financial asset.

(b) Except as otherwise provided in subsections (d) and (e), a person acquires a security entitlement if a securities intermediary:

(1) indicates by book entry that a financial asset has been credited to the person's securities account;

(2) receives a financial asset from the person or acquires a financial asset for the person and, in either case, accepts it for credit to the person's securities account; or

(3) becomes obligated under other law, regulation, or rule to credit a financial asset to the person's securities account.

(c) If a condition of subsection (b) has been met, a person has a security entitlement even though the securities intermediary does not itself hold the financial asset.

(d) If a securities intermediary holds a financial asset for another person, and the financial asset is registered in the name of, payable to the order of, or specially indorsed to the other person, and has not been indorsed to the securities intermediary or in blank, the other person is treated as holding the financial asset directly rather than as having a security entitlement with respect to the financial asset.

(e) Issuance of a security is not establishment of a security entitlement.

§ 8-502. Assertion of Adverse Claim Against Entitlement Holder.

An action based on an adverse claim to a financial asset, whether framed in conversion, replevin, constructive trust, equitable lien, or other theory, may not be asserted against a person who acquires a security entitlement under Section 8-501 for value and without notice of the adverse claim.

§ 8-503. Property Interest of Entitlement Holder in Financial Asset Held by Securities Intermediary.

(a) To the extent necessary for a securities intermediary to satisfy all security entitlements with respect to a particular financial asset, all interests in that financial asset held by the securities intermediary are held by the securities intermediary for the entitlement holders, are not property of the securities intermediary, and are not subject to claims of creditors of the securities intermediary, except as otherwise provided in Section 8-511.

(b) An entitlement holder's property interest with respect to a particular financial asset under subsection (a) is a pro rata property interest in all interests in that financial asset held by the securities intermediary, without regard to the time the entitlement holder acquired the security entitlement or the time the securities intermediary acquired the interest in that financial asset.

(c) An entitlement holder's property interest with respect to a particular financial asset under subsection (a) may be enforced against the securities intermediary only by exercise of the entitlement holder's rights under Sections 8-505 through 8-508.

(d) An entitlement holder's property interest with respect to a particular financial asset under subsection (a) may be enforced against a purchaser of the financial asset or interest therein only if:

(1) insolvency proceedings have been initiated by or against the securities intermediary;

(2) the securities intermediary does not have sufficient interests in the financial asset to satisfy the security entitlements of all of its entitlement holders to that financial asset;

(3) the securities intermediary violated its obligations under Section 8-504 by transferring the financial asset or interest therein to the purchaser; and

(4) the purchaser is not protected under subsection (e).

The trustee or other liquidator, acting on behalf of all entitlement holders having security entitlements with respect to a particular financial asset, may recover the financial asset, or interest therein, from the purchaser. If the trustee or other liquidator elects not to pursue that right, an entitlement holder whose security entitlement remains unsatisfied has the right to recover its interest in the financial asset from the purchaser.

(e) An action based on the entitlement holder's property interest with respect to a particular financial asset under subsection (a), whether framed in conversion, replevin, constructive trust, equitable lien, or other theory, may not be asserted against any purchaser of a financial asset or interest therein who gives value, obtains control, and does not act in collusion with the securities intermediary in violating the securities intermediary's obligations under Section 8-504.

§ 8-504. Duty of Securities Intermediary to Maintain Financial Asset.

(a) A securities intermediary shall promptly obtain and thereafter maintain a financial asset in a quantity corresponding to the aggregate of all security entitlements it has established in favor of its entitlement holders with respect to that financial asset. The securities intermediary may maintain those financial assets directly or through one or more other securities intermediaries.

(b) Except to the extent otherwise agreed by its entitlement holder, a securities intermediary may not grant any security interests in a financial asset it is obligated to maintain pursuant to subsection (a).

(c) A securities intermediary satisfies the duty in subsection (a) if:

(1) the securities intermediary acts with respect to the duty as agreed upon by the entitlement holder and the securities intermediary; or

(2) in the absence of agreement, the securities intermediary exercises due care in accordance with reasonable commercial standards to obtain and maintain the financial asset.

(d) This section does not apply to a clearing corporation that is itself the obligor of an option or similar obligation to which its entitlement holders have security entitlements.

§ 8-505. Duty of Securities Intermediary With Respect to Payments and Distributions.

(a) A securities intermediary shall take action to obtain a payment or distribution made by the issuer of a financial asset. A securities intermediary satisfies the duty if:

(1) the securities intermediary acts with respect to the duty as agreed upon by the entitlement holder and the securities intermediary; or

(2) in the absence of agreement, the securities intermediary exercises due care in accordance with reasonable commercial standards to attempt to obtain the payment or distribution.

(b) A securities intermediary is obligated to its entitlement holder for a payment or distribution made by the issuer of a financial asset if the payment or distribution is received by the securities intermediary.

§ 8-506. Duty of Securities Intermediary to Exercise Rights as Directed by Entitlement Holder.

A securities intermediary shall exercise rights with respect to a financial asset if directed to do so by an entitlement holder. A securities intermediary satisfies the duty if:

(1) the securities intermediary acts with respect to the duty as agreed upon by the entitlement holder and the securities intermediary; or

(2) in the absence of agreement, the securities intermediary either places the entitlement holder in a position to exercise the rights directly or exercises due care in accordance with reasonable commercial standards to follow the direction of the entitlement holder.

§ 8-507. Duty of Securities Intermediary to Comply With Entitlement Order.

(a) A securities intermediary shall comply with an entitlement order if the entitlement order is originated by the appropriate person, the securities intermediary has had reasonable opportunity to assure itself that the entitlement order is genuine and authorized, and the securities intermediary has had reasonable opportunity to comply with the entitlement order. A securities intermediary satisfies the duty if:

(1) the securities intermediary acts with respect to the duty as agreed upon by the entitlement holder and the securities intermediary; or

(2) in the absence of agreement, the securities intermediary exercises due care in accordance with reasonable commercial standards to comply with the entitlement order.

(b) If a securities intermediary transfers a financial asset pursuant to an ineffective entitlement order, the securities intermediary shall reestablish a security entitlement in favor of the person entitled to it, and pay or credit any payments or distributions that the person did not receive as a result of the wrongful transfer. If the securities intermediary does not reestablish a security entitlement, the securities intermediary is liable to the entitlement holder for damages.

§ 8-508. Duty of Securities Intermediary to Change Entitlement Holder's Position to Other Form of Security Holding.

A securities intermediary shall act at the direction of an entitlement holder to change a security entitlement into another available form of holding for which the entitlement holder is eligible, or to cause the financial asset to be transferred to a securities account of the entitlement holder with another securities intermediary. A securities intermediary satisfies the duty if:

(1) the securities intermediary acts as agreed upon by the entitlement holder and the securities intermediary; or

(2) in the absence of agreement, the securities intermediary exercises due care in accordance with reasonable commercial standards to follow the direction of the entitlement holder.

§ 8-509. Specification of Duties of Securities Intermediary by Other Statute or Regulation; Manner of Performance of Duties of Securities Intermediary and Exercise of Rights of Entitlement Holder.

(a) If the substance of a duty imposed upon a securities intermediary by Sections 8-504 through 8-508 is the subject of other statute, regulation, or rule, compliance with that statute, regulation, or rule satisfies the duty.

(b) To the extent that specific standards for the performance of the duties of a securities intermediary or the exercise of the rights of an entitlement holder are not specified by other statute, regulation, or rule or by agreement between the securities intermediary and entitlement holder, the securities intermediary shall perform its duties and the entitlement holder shall exercise its rights in a commercially reasonable manner.

(c) The obligation of a securities intermediary to perform the duties imposed by Sections 8-504 through 8-508 is subject to:

(1) rights of the securities intermediary arising out of a security interest under a security agreement with the entitlement holder or otherwise; and

(2) rights of the securities intermediary under other law, regulation, rule, or agreement to withhold performance of its duties as a result of unfulfilled obligations of the entitlement holder to the securities intermediary.

(d) Sections 8-504 through 8-508 do not require a securities intermediary to take any action that is prohibited by other statute, regulation, or rule.

§ 8-510. Rights of Purchaser of Security Entitlement From Entitlement Holder.

(a) An action based on an adverse claim to a financial asset or security entitlement, whether framed in conversion, replevin, constructive trust, equitable lien, or other theory, may not be asserted against a person who purchases a security entitlement, or an interest therein, from an entitlement holder if the purchaser gives value, does not have notice of the adverse claim, and obtains control.

(b) If an adverse claim could not have been asserted against an entitlement holder under Section 8-502, the adverse claim cannot be asserted against a person who purchases a security entitlement, or an interest therein, from the entitlement holder.

(c) In a case not covered by the priority rules in Article 9, a purchaser for value of a security entitlement, or an interest therein, who obtains control has priority over a purchaser of a security entitlement, or an interest therein, who does not obtain control. Purchasers who have control rank equally, except that a securities intermediary as purchaser has priority over a conflicting purchaser who has control unless otherwise agreed by the securities intermediary.

§ 8-511. Priority Among Security Interests and Entitlement Holders.

(a) Except as otherwise provided in subsections (b) and (c), if a securities intermediary does not have sufficient interests in a particular financial asset to satisfy both its obligations to entitlement holders who have security entitlements to that financial asset and its obligation to a creditor of the securities intermediary who has a security interest in that financial asset, the claims of entitlement holders, other than the creditor, have priority over the claim of the creditor.

(b) A claim of a creditor of a securities intermediary who has a security interest in a financial asset held by a securities intermediary has priority over claims of the securities intermediary's entitlement holders who have security entitlements with respect to that financial asset if the creditor has control over the financial asset.

(c) If a clearing corporation does not have sufficient financial assets to satisfy both its obligations to entitlement holders who have security entitlements with respect to a financial asset and its obligation to a creditor of the clearing corporation who has a security interest in that financial asset, the claim of the creditor has priority over the claims of entitlement holders.

■ **PART 6   Transition Provisions for Revised Article 8**

§ 8-601. Effective Date.
This [Act] takes effect . . .

§ 8-602. Repeals.
This [Act] repeals . . .

§ 8-603. Savings Clause.
(a) This [Act] does not affect an action or proceeding commenced before this [Act] takes effect.

(b) If a security interest in a security is perfected at the date this [Act] takes effect, and the action by which the security interest was perfected would suffice to perfect a security interest under this [Act], no further action is required to continue perfection. If a security interest in a security is perfected at the date this [Act] takes effect but the action by which the security interest was perfected would not suffice to perfect a security interest under this [Act], the security interest remains perfected for a period of four months after the effective date and continues perfected thereafter if appropriate action to perfect under this [Act] is taken within that period. If a security interest is perfected at the date this [Act] takes effect and the security interest can be perfected by filing under this [Act], a financing statement signed by the secured party instead of the debtor may be filed within that period to continue perfection or thereafter to perfect.

ARTICLE 9
Secured Transactions;
Sales of Accounts and Chattel Paper

Note: The adoption of this Article should be accompanied by the repeal of existing statutes dealing with conditional sales, trust receipts, factor's liens where the factor is given a non-possessory lien, chattel mortgages, crop mortgages, mortgages on railroad equipment, assignment of accounts and generally statutes regulating security interests in personal property.

Where the state has a retail installment selling act or small loan act, that legislation should be carefully examined to determine what changes in those acts are needed to conform them to this Article. This Article primarily sets out rules defining rights of a secured party against persons dealing with the debtor; it does not prescribe regulations and controls which may be necessary to curb abuses arising in the small loan business or in the financing of consumer purchases on credit. Accordingly there is no intention to repeal existing regulatory acts in those fields by enactment or re-enactment of Article 9. See Section 9-203(4) and the Note thereto.

■ **PART I** Short Title, Applicability and Definitions

§ 9-101. *Short Title.*

This Article shall be known and may be cited as Uniform Commercial Code—Secured Transactions.

§ 9-102. *Policy and Subject Matter of Article.*

(1) Except as otherwise provided in Section 9-104 on excluded transactions, this Article applies

(a) to any transaction (regardless of its form) which is intended to create a security interest in personal property or fixtures including goods, documents, instruments, general intangibles, chattel paper or accounts; and also

(b) to any sale of accounts or chattel paper.

(2) This Article applies to security interests created by contract including pledge, assignment, chattel mortgage, chattel trust, trust deed, factor's lien, equipment trust, conditional sale, trust receipt, other lien or title retention contract and lease or consignment intended as security. This Article does not apply to statutory liens except as provided in Section 9-310.

(3) The application of this Article to a security interest in a secured obligation is not affected by the fact that the obligation is itself secured by a transaction or interest to which this Article does not apply.

§ 9-103. *Perfection of Security Interest in Multiple State Transactions.*

(1) Documents, instruments and ordinary goods.

(a) This subsection applies to documents and instruments and to goods other than those covered by a certificate of title described in subsection (2), mobile goods described in subsection (3), and minerals described in subsection (5).

(b) Except as otherwise provided in this subsection, perfection and the effect of perfection or non-perfection of a security interest in collateral are governed by the law of the jurisdiction where the collateral is when the last event occurs on which is based the assertion that the security interest is perfected or unperfected.

(c) If the parties to a transaction creating a purchase money security interest in goods in one jurisdiction understand at the time that the security interest attaches that the goods will be kept in another jurisdiction, then the law of the other jurisdiction governs the perfection and the effect of perfection or non-perfection of the security interest from the time it attaches until thirty days after the debtor receives possession of the goods and thereafter if the goods are taken to the other jurisdiction before the end of the thirty-day period.

(d) When collateral is brought into and kept in this state while subject to a security interest perfected under the law of the jurisdiction from which the collateral was removed, the security interest remains perfected, but if action is required by Part 3 of this Article to perfect the security interest,

(i) if the action is not taken before the expiration of the period of perfection in the other jurisdiction or the end of four months after the collateral is brought into this state, whichever period first expires, the security interest becomes unperfected at the end of that period and is thereafter deemed to have been unperfected as against a person who became a purchaser after removal;

(ii) if the action is taken before the expiration of the period specified in subparagraph (i), the security interest continues perfected thereafter;

(iii) for the purpose of priority over a buyer of consumer goods (subsection (2) of Section 9-307), the period of the effectiveness of a filing in the jurisdiction from which the collateral is removed is governed by the rules with respect to perfection in subparagraphs (i) and (ii).

(2) Certificate of title.

(a) This subsection applies to goods covered by a certificate of title issued under a statute of this state or of another jurisdiction under the law of which indication of a security interest on the certificate is required as a condition of perfection.

(b) Except as otherwise provided in this subsection, perfection and the effect of perfection or non-perfection of the security interest are governed by the law (including the conflict of laws rules) of the jurisdiction issuing the certificate until four months after the goods are removed from that jurisdiction and thereafter until the goods are registered in another jurisdiction, but in any event not beyond surrender of the certificate. After the expiration of that period, the goods are not covered by the certificate of title within the meaning of this section.

(c) Except with respect to the rights of a buyer described in the next paragraph, a security interest, perfected in another jurisdiction otherwise than by notation on a certificate of title, in goods brought into this state and thereafter covered by a certificate of title issued by this state is subject to the rules stated in paragraph (d) of subsection (1).

(d) If goods are brought into this state while a security interest therein is perfected in any manner under the law of the jurisdiction from which the goods are removed and a certificate of title is issued by this state and the certificate does not show that the goods are subject to the security interest or that they may be subject to security interests not shown on the certificate, the security interest is subordinate to the rights of a buyer of the goods who is not in the business of selling goods of that kind to the extent that he gives value and receives delivery of the goods after issuance of the certificate and without knowledge of the security interest.

(3) Accounts, general intangibles and mobile goods.

(a) This subsection applies to accounts (other than an account described in subsection (5) on minerals) and general intangibles (other than uncertificated securities) and to goods which are mobile and which are of a type normally used in more than one jurisdiction, such as motor vehicles, trailers, rolling stock, airplanes, shipping containers, road building and construction machinery and commercial harvesting machinery and the like, if the goods are equipment or are inventory leased or held for lease by the debtor to others, and are not covered by a certificate of title described in subsection (2).

(b) The law (including the conflict of laws rules) of the jurisdiction in which the debtor is located governs the perfection and the effect of perfection or non-perfection of the security interest.

(c) If, however, the debtor is located in a jurisdiction which is not a part of the United States, and which does not provide for perfection of the security interest by filing or recording in that jurisdiction, the law of the jurisdiction in the United States in which the debtor has its major executive office in the United States governs the perfection and the effect of perfection or non-perfection of the security interest through filing. In the alternative, if the debtor is located in a jurisdiction which is not a part of the United States or Canada and the collateral is accounts or general intangibles for money due or to become due, the security interest may be perfected by notification to the account debtor. As used in this paragraph, "United States" includes its territories and possessions and the Commonwealth of Puerto Rico.

(d)   A debtor shall be deemed located at his place of business if he has one, at his chief executive office if he has more than one place of business, otherwise at his residence. If, however, the debtor is a foreign air carrier under the Federal Aviation Act of 1958, as amended, it shall be deemed located at the designated office of the agent upon whom service of process may be made on behalf of the foreign air carrier.

(e)   A security interest perfected under the law of the jurisdiction of the location of the debtor is perfected until the expiration of four months after a change of the debtor's location to another jurisdiction, or until perfection would have ceased by the law of the first jurisdiction, whichever period first expires. Unless perfected in the new jurisdiction before the end of that period, it becomes unperfected thereafter and is deemed to have been unperfected as against a person who became a purchaser after the change.

(4)   Chattel paper.

The rules stated for goods in subsection (1) apply to a possessory security interest in chattel paper. The rules stated for accounts in subsection (3) apply to a non-possessory security interest in chattel paper, but the security interest may not be perfected by notification to the account debtor.

(5)   Minerals.

Perfection and the effect of perfection or non-perfection of a security interest which is created by a debtor who has an interest in minerals or the like (including oil and gas) before extraction and which attaches thereto as extracted, or which attaches to an account resulting from the sale thereof at the wellhead or minehead are governed by the law (including the conflict of laws rules) of the jurisdiction wherein the wellhead or minehead is located.

(6)   Uncertificated securities.

The law (including the conflict of laws rules) of the jurisdiction of organization of the issuer governs the perfection and the effect of perfection or non-perfection of a security interest in uncertificated securities.

§ 9-104. *Transactions Excluded From Article.*

This Article does not apply

(a)   to a security interest subject to any statute of the United States, to the extent that such statute governs the rights of parties to and third parties affected by transactions in particular types of property; or

(b)   to a landlord's lien; or

(c)   to a lien given by statute or other rule of law for services or materials except as provided in Section 9-310 on priority of such liens; or

(d)   to a transfer of a claim for wages, salary or other compensation of an employee; or

(e)   to a transfer by a government or governmental subdivision or agency; or

(f)   to a sale of accounts or chattel paper as part of a sale of the business out of which they arose, or an assignment of accounts or chattel paper which is for the purpose of collection only, or a transfer of a right to payment under a contract to an assignee who is also to do the performance under the contract or a transfer of a single account to an assignee in whole or partial satisfaction of a preexisting indebtedness; or

(g)   to a transfer of an interest in or claim in or under any policy of insurance, except as provided with respect to proceeds (Section 9-306) and priorities in proceeds (Section 9-312); or

(h)   to a right represented by a judgment (other than a judgment taken on a right to payment which was collateral); or

(i)   to any right of set-off; or

(j)   except to the extent that provision is made for fixtures in Section 9-313, to the creation or transfer of an interest in or lien on real estate, including a lease or rents thereunder; or

(k)   to a transfer in whole or in part of any claim arising out of tort; or

(l)   to a transfer of an interest in any deposit account (subsection (1) of Section 9-105), except as provided with respect to proceeds (Section 9-306) and priorities in proceeds (Section 9-312).

§ 9-105. *Definitions and Index of Definitions.*

(1)   In this Article unless the context otherwise requires:

(a)   "Account debtor" means the person who is obligated on an account, chattel paper or general intangible;

(b)   "Chattel paper" means a writing or writings which evidence both a monetary obligation and a security interest in or a lease of specific goods, but a charter or other contract involving the use or hire of a vessel is not chattel paper. When a transaction is evidenced both by such a security agreement or a lease and by an instrument or a series of instruments, the group of writings taken together constitutes chattel paper;

(c)   "Collateral" means the property subject to a security interest, and includes accounts and chattel paper which have been sold;

(d)   "Debtor" means the person who owes payment or other performance of the obligation secured, whether or not he owns or has rights in the collateral, and includes the seller of accounts or chattel paper. Where the debtor and the owner of the collateral are not the same person, the term "debtor" means the owner of the collateral in any provision of the Article dealing with the collateral, the obligor in any provision dealing with the obligation, and may include both where the context so requires;

(e)   "Deposit account" means a demand, time, savings, passbook or like account maintained with a bank, savings and loan association, credit union or like organization, other than an account evidenced by a certificate of deposit;

(f)   "Document" means document of title as defined in the general definitions of Article 1 (Section 1-201), and a receipt of the kind described in subsection (2) of Section 7-201;

(g)   "Encumbrance" includes real estate mortgages and other liens on real estate and all other rights in real estate that are not ownership interests;

(h)   "Goods" includes all things which are movable at the time the security interest attaches or which are fixtures (Section 9-313), but does not include money, documents, instruments, accounts, chattel paper, general intangibles, or minerals or the like (including oil and gas) before extraction. "Goods" also includes standing timber which is to be cut and removed under a conveyance or contract for sale, the unborn young of animals, and growing crops;

(i)   "Instrument" means a negotiable instrument (defined in Section 3-104), or a certificated security (defined in Section 8-102) or any other writing which evidences a right to the payment of money and is not itself a security agreement or lease and is of a type which is in ordinary course of business transferred by delivery with any necessary indorsement or assignment;

(j) "Mortgage" means a consensual interest created by a real estate mortgage, a trust deed on real estate, or the like;

(k) An advance is made "pursuant to commitment" if the secured party has bound himself to make it, whether or not a subsequent event of default or other event not within his control has relieved or may relieve him from his obligation;

(l) "Security agreement" means an agreement which creates or provides for a security interest;

(m) "Secured party" means a lender, seller or other person in whose favor there is a security interest, including a person to whom accounts or chattel paper have been sold. When the holders of obligations issued under an indenture of trust, equipment trust agreement or the like are represented by a trustee or other person, the representative is the secured party;

(n) "Transmitting utility" means any person primarily engaged in the railroad, street railway or trolley bus business, the electric or electronics communications transmission business, the transmission of goods by pipeline, or the transmission or the production and transmission of electricity, steam, gas or water, or the provision of sewer service.

(2) Other definitions applying to this Article and the sections in which they appear are:

"Account". Section 9-106.
"Attach". Section 9-203.
"Construction mortgage". Section 9-313(1).
"Consumer goods". Section 9-109(1).
"Equipment". Section 9-109(2).
"Farm products". Section 9-109(3).
"Fixture". Section 9-313(1).
"Fixture filing". Section 9-313(1).
"General intangibles". Section 9-106.
"Inventory". Section 9-109(4).
"Lien creditor". Section 9-301(3).
"Proceeds". Section 9-306(1).
"Purchase money security interest". Section 9-107.
"United States". Section 9-103.

(3) The following definitions in other Articles apply to this Article:

"Check". Section 3-104.
"Contract for sale". Section 2-106.
"Holder in due course". Section 3-302.
"Note". Section 3-104.
"Sale". Section 2-106.

(4) In addition Article 1 contains general definitions and principles of construction and interpretation applicable throughout this Article.

§ 9-106. Definitions: "Account"; "General Intangibles".

"Account" means any right to payment for goods sold or leased or for services rendered which is not evidenced by an instrument or chattel paper, whether or not it has been earned by performance. "General intangibles" means any personal property (including things in action) other than goods, accounts, chattel paper, documents, instruments, and money. All rights to payment earned or unearned under a charter or other contract involving the use or hire of a vessel and all rights incident to the charter or contract are accounts.

§ 9-107. Definitions: "Purchase Money Security Interest".

A security interest is a "purchase money security interest" to the extent that it is

(a) taken or retained by the seller of the collateral to secure all or part of its price; or

(b) taken by a person who by making advances or incurring an obligation gives value to enable the debtor to acquire rights in or the use of collateral if such value is in fact so used.

§ 9-108. When After-Acquired Collateral Not Security for Antecedent Debt.

Where a secured party makes an advance, incurs an obligation, releases a perfected security interest, or otherwise gives new value which is to be secured in whole or in part by after-acquired property his security interest in the after-acquired collateral shall be deemed to be taken for new value and not as security for an antecedent debt if the debtor acquires his rights in such collateral either in the ordinary course of his business or under a contract of purchase made pursuant to the security agreement within a reasonable time after new value is given.

§ 9-109. Classification of Goods; "Consumer Goods"; "Equipment"; "Farm Products"; "Inventory".

Goods are

(1) "consumer goods" if they are used or bought for use primarily for personal, family or household purposes;

(2) "equipment" if they are used or bought for use primarily in business (including farming or a profession) or by a debtor who is a non-profit organization or a governmental subdivision or agency or if the goods are not included in the definitions of inventory, farm products or consumer goods;

(3) "farm products" if they are crops or livestock or supplies used or produced in farming operations or if they are products of crops or livestock in their unmanufactured states (such as ginned cotton, wool-clip, maple syrup, milk and eggs), and if they are in the possession of a debtor engaged in raising, fattening, grazing or other farming operations. If goods are farm products they are neither equipment nor inventory;

(4) "inventory" if they are held by a person who holds them for sale or lease or to be furnished under contracts of service or if he has so furnished them, or if they are raw materials, work in process or materials used or consumed in a business. Inventory of a person is not to be classified as his equipment.

§ 9-110. Sufficiency of Description.

For purposes of this Article any description of personal property or real estate is sufficient whether or not it is specific if it reasonably identifies what is described.

§ 9-111. Applicability of Bulk Transfer Laws.

The creation of a security interest is not a bulk transfer under Article 6 (see Section 6-103).

§ 9-112. Where Collateral Is Not Owned by Debtor.

Unless otherwise agreed, when a secured party knows that collateral is owned by a person who is not the debtor, the owner of the collateral is entitled to receive from the secured party any surplus under Section 9-502(2) or under Section 9-504(1), and is not liable for the debt or for any deficiency after resale, and he has the same right as the debtor.

(a) to receive statements under Section 9-208;

(b) to receive notice of and to object to a secured party's proposal to retain the collateral in satisfaction of the indebtedness under Section 9-505;

(c) to redeem the collateral under Section 9-506;

(d) to obtain injunctive or other relief under Section 9-507(1); and

(e) to recover losses caused to him under Section 9-208(2).

§ 9-113. *Security Interests Arising Under Article on Sales.*

A security interest arising solely under the Article on Sales (Article 2) is subject to the provisions of this Article except that to the extent that and so long as the debtor does not have or does not lawfully obtain possession of the goods

(a) no security agreement is necessary to make the security interest enforceable; and

(b) no filing is required to perfect the security interest; and

(c) the rights of the secured party on default by the debtor are governed by the Article on Sales (Article 2).

§ 9-114. *Consignment.*

(1) A person who delivers goods under a consignment which is not a security interest and who would be required to file under this Article by paragraph (3)(c) of Section 2-326 has priority over a secured party who is or becomes a creditor of the consignee and who would have a perfected security interest in the goods if they were the property of the consignee, and also has priority with respect to identifiable cash proceeds received on or before delivery of the goods to a buyer, if

(a) the consignor complies with the filing provision of the Article on Sales with respect to consignments (paragraph (3)(c) of Section 2-326) before the consignee receives possession of the goods; and

(b) the consignor gives notification in writing to the holder of the security interest if the holder has filed a financing statement covering the same types of goods before the date of the filing made by the consignor; and

(c) the holder of the security interest receives the notification within five years before the consignee receives possession of the goods; and

(d) the notification states that the consignor expects to deliver goods on consignment to the consignee, describing the goods by item or type.

(2) In the case of a consignment which is not a security interest and in which the requirements of the preceding subsection have not been met, a person who delivers goods to another is subordinate to a person who would have a perfected security interest in the goods if they were the property of the debtor.

■ PART 2 Validity of Security Agreement and Rights of Parties Thereto

§ 9-201. *General Validity of Security Agreement.*

Except as otherwise provided by this Act a security agreement is effective according to its terms between the parties, against purchasers of the collateral and against creditors. Nothing in this Article validates any charge or practice illegal under any statute or regulation thereunder governing usury, small loans, retail installment sales, or the like, or extends the application of any such statute or regulation to any transaction not otherwise subject thereto.

§ 9-202. *Title to Collateral Immaterial.*

Each provision of this Article with regard to rights, obligations and remedies applies whether title to collateral is in the secured party or in the debtor.

§ 9-203. *Attachment and Enforceability of Security Interest; Proceeds; Formal Requisites.*

(1) Subject to the provisions of Section 4-210 on the security interest of a collecting bank, Section 8-321 on security interests in securities and Section 9-113 on a security interest arising under the Articles on Sales and Leases, a security interest is not enforceable against the debtor or third parties with respect to the collateral and does not attach unless:

(a) the collateral is in the possession of the secured party pursuant to agreement, or the debtor has signed a security agreement which contains a description of the collateral and in addition, when the security interest covers crops growing or to be grown or timber to be cut, a description of the land concerned;

(b) value has been given; and

(c) the debtor has rights in the collateral.

(2) A security interest attaches when it becomes enforceable against the debtor with respect to the collateral. Attachment occurs as soon as all of the events specified in subsection (1) have taken place unless explicit agreement postpones the time of attaching.

(3) Unless otherwise agreed a security agreement gives the secured party the rights to proceeds provided by Section 9-306.

(4) A transaction, although subject to this Article, is also subject to . . . *, and in the case of conflict between the provisions of this Article and any such statute, the provisions of such statute control. Failure to comply with any applicable statute has only the effect which is specified therein.

*Note: At * in subsection (4) insert reference to any local statute regulating small loans, retail installment sales and the like.*

The foregoing subsection (4) is designed to make it clear that certain transactions, although subject to this Article, must also comply with other applicable legislation.

This Article is designed to regulate all the "security" aspects of transactions within its scope. There is, however, much regulatory legislation, particularly in the consumer field, which supplements this Article and should not be repealed by its enactment. Examples are small loan acts, retail installment selling acts and the like. Such acts may provide for licensing and rate regulation and may prescribe particular forms of contract. Such provisions should remain in force despite the enactment of this Article. On the other hand if a retail installment selling act contains provisions on filing, rights on default, etc., such provisions should be repealed as inconsistent with this Article except that inconsistent provisions as to deficiencies, penalties, etc., in the Uniform Consumer Credit Code and other recent related legislation should remain because those statutes were drafted after the substantial enactment of the Article and with the intention of modifying certain provisions of this Article as to consumer credit.

§ 9-204. *After-Acquired Property; Future Advances.*

(1) Except as provided in subsection (2), a security agreement may provide that any or all obligations covered by the security agreement are to be secured by after-acquired collateral.

(2) No security interest attaches under an after-acquired property clause to consumer goods other than accessions (Section 9-314) when given as additional security unless the debtor acquires rights in them within ten days after the secured party gives value.

(3) Obligations covered by a security agreement may include future advances or other value whether or not the advances or value are given pursuant to commitment (subsection (1) of Section 9-105).

§ 9-205. *Use or Disposition of Collateral Without Accounting Permissible.*

A security interest is not invalid or fraudulent against creditors by reason of liberty in the debtor to use, commingle or dispose of all or part of the collateral (including returned or repossessed goods) or to collect or compromise accounts or chattel paper, or to accept the return of goods or make repossessions, or to use, commingle or dispose of proceeds, or by reason of the failure of the secured party to require the debtor to account for proceeds or replace collateral. This section does not relax the requirements of possession where perfection of a security interest depends upon possession of the collateral by the secured party or by a bailee.

§ 9-206. Agreement Not to Assert Defenses Against Assignee; Modification of Sales Warranties Where Security Agreement Exists.

(1) Subject to any statute or decision which establishes a different rule for buyers or lessees of consumer goods, an agreement by a buyer or lessee that he will not assert against an assignee any claim or defense which he may have against the seller or lessor is enforceable by an assignee who takes his assignment for value, in good faith and without notice of a claim or defense, except as to defenses of a type which may be asserted against a holder in due course of a negotiable instrument under the Article on Negotiable Instruments (Article 3). A buyer who as part of one transaction signs both a negotiable instrument and a security agreement makes such an agreement.

(2) When a seller retains a purchase money security interest in goods the Article on Sales (Article 2) governs the sale and any disclaimer, limitation or modification of the seller's warranties.

§ 9-207. Rights and Duties When Collateral Is in Secured Party's Possession.

(1) A secured party must use reasonable care in the custody and preservation of collateral in his possession. In the case of an instrument or chattel paper reasonable care includes taking necessary steps to preserve rights against prior parties unless otherwise agreed.

(2) Unless otherwise agreed, when collateral is in the secured party's possession

(a) reasonable expenses (including the cost of any insurance and payment of taxes or other charges) incurred in the custody, preservation, use or operation of the collateral are chargeable to the debtor and are secured by the collateral;

(b) the risk of accidental loss or damage is on the debtor to the extent of any deficiency in any effective insurance coverage;

(c) the secured party may hold as additional security any increase or profits (except money) received from the collateral, but money so received, unless remitted to the debtor, shall be applied in reduction of the secured obligation;

(d) the secured party must keep the collateral identifiable but fungible collateral may be commingled;

(e) the secured party may repledge the collateral upon terms which do not impair the debtor's right to redeem it.

(3) A secured party is liable for any loss caused by his failure to meet any obligation imposed by the preceding subsections but does not lose his security interest.

(4) A secured party may use or operate the collateral for the purpose of preserving the collateral or its value or pursuant to the order of a court of appropriate jurisdiction or, except in the case of consumer goods, in the manner and to the extent provided in the security agreement.

§ 9-208. Request for Statement of Account or List of Collateral.

(1) A debtor may sign a statement indicating what he believes to be the aggregate amount of unpaid indebtedness as of a specified date and may send it to the secured party with a request that the statement be approved or corrected and returned to the debtor. When the security agreement or any other record kept by the secured party identifies the collateral a debtor may similarly request the secured party to approve or correct a list of the collateral.

(2) The secured party must comply with such a request within two weeks after receipt by sending a written correction or approval. If the secured party claims a security interest in all of a particular type of collateral owned by the debtor he may indicate that fact in his reply and need not approve or correct an itemized list of such collateral. If the secured party without reasonable excuse fails to comply he is liable for any loss caused to the debtor thereby; and if the debtor has properly included in his request a good faith statement of the obligation or a list of the collateral or both the secured party may claim a security interest only as shown in the statement against persons misled by his failure to comply. If he no longer has an interest in the obligation or collateral at the time the request is received he must disclose the name and address of any successor in interest known to him and he is liable for any loss caused to the debtor as a result of failure to disclose. A successor in interest is not subject to this section until a request is received by him.

(3) A debtor is entitled to such a statement once every six months without charge. The secured party may require payment of a charge not exceeding $10 for each additional statement furnished.

■ PART 3 Rights of Third Parties; Perfected and Unperfected Security Interests; Rules of Priority

§ 9-301. Persons Who Take Priority Over Unperfected Security Interests; Rights of "Lien Creditor".

(1) Except as otherwise provided in subsection (2), an unperfected security interest is subordinate to the rights of

(a) persons entitled to priority under Section 9-312;

(b) a person who becomes a lien creditor before the security interest is perfected;

(c) in the case of goods, instruments, documents, and chattel paper, a person who is not a secured party and who is a transferee in bulk or other buyer not in ordinary course of business or is a buyer of farm products in ordinary course of business, to the extent that he gives value and receives delivery of the collateral without knowledge of the security interest and before it is perfected;

(d) in the case of accounts and general intangibles, a person who is not a secured party and who is a transferee to the extent that he gives value without knowledge of the security interest and before it is perfected.

(2) If the secured party files with respect to a purchase money security interest before or within ten days after the debtor receives possession of the collateral, he takes priority over the rights of a transferee in bulk or of a lien creditor which arise between the time the security interest attaches and the time of filing.

(3) A "lien creditor" means a creditor who has acquired a lien on the property involved by attachment, levy or the like and includes an assignee for benefit of creditors from the time of assignment, and a trustee in bankruptcy from the date of the filing of the petition or a receiver in equity from the time of appointment.

(4) A person who becomes a lien creditor while a security interest is perfected takes subject to the security interest only to the extent that it secures advances made before he becomes a lien creditor or within 45 days thereafter or made without knowledge of the lien or pursuant to a commitment entered into without knowledge of the lien.

§ 9-302. *When Filing Is Required to Perfect Security Interest; Security Interests to Which Filing Provisions of This Article Do Not Apply.*

(1)   A financing statement must be filed to perfect all security interests except the following:

(a)   a security interest in collateral in possession of the secured party under Section 9-305;

(b)   a security interest temporarily perfected in instruments or documents without delivery under Section 9-304 or in proceeds for a 10 day period under Section 9-306;

(c)   a security interest created by an assignment of a beneficial interest in a trust or a decedent's estate;

(d)   a purchase money security interest in consumer goods; but filing is required for a motor vehicle required to be registered; and fixture filing is required for priority over conflicting interests in fixtures to the extent provided in Section 9-313;

(e)   an assignment of accounts which does not alone or in conjunction with other assignments to the same assignee transfer a significant part of the outstanding accounts of the assignor;

(f)   a security interest of a collecting bank (Section 4-210) or in securities (Section 8-321) or arising under the Articles on Sales and Leases (see Section 9-113) or covered in subsection (3) of this section;

(g)   an assignment for the benefit of all the creditors of the transferor, and subsequent transfers by the assignee thereunder.

(2)   If a secured party assigns a perfected security interest, no filing under this Article is required in order to continue the perfected status of the security interest against creditors of and transferees from the original debtor.

(3)   The filing of a financing statement otherwise required by this Article is not necessary or effective to perfect a security interest in property subject to

(a)   a statute or treaty of the United States which provides for a national or international registration or a national or international certificate of title or which specifies a place of filing different from that specified in this Article for filing of the security interest; or

(b)   the following statutes of this state; [list any certificate of title statute covering automobiles, trailers, mobile homes, boats, farm tractors, or the like, and any central filing statute]; but during any period in which collateral is inventory held for sale by a person who is in the business of selling goods of that kind, the filing provisions of this Article (Part 4) apply to a security interest in that collateral created by him as debtor; or

(c)   a certificate of title statute of another jurisdiction under the law of which indication of a security interest on the certificate is required as a condition of perfection (subsection (2) of Section 9-103).

(4)   Compliance with a statute or treaty described in subsection (3) is equivalent to the filing of a financing statement under this Article, and a security interest in property subject to the statute or treaty can be perfected only by compliance therewith except as provided in Section 9-103 on multiple state transactions. Duration and renewal of perfection of a security interest perfected by compliance with the statute or treaty are governed by the provisions of the statute or treaty; in other respects the security interest is subject to this Article.

Amended in 1972 and 1977.

§ 9-303. *When Security Interest Is Perfected; Continuity of Perfection.*

(1)   A security interest is perfected when it has attached and when all of the applicable steps required for perfection have been taken. Such steps are specified in Sections 9-302, 9-304, 9-305 and 9-306. If such steps are taken before the security interest attaches, it is perfected at the time when it attaches.

(2)   If a security interest is originally perfected in any way permitted under this Article and is subsequently perfected in some other way under this Article, without an intermediate period when it was unperfected, the security interest shall be deemed to be perfected continuously for the purposes of this Article.

§ 9-304. *Perfection of Security Interest in Instruments, Documents, and Goods Covered by Documents; Perfection by Permissive Filing; Temporary Perfection Without Filing or Transfer of Possession.*

(1)   A security interest in chattel paper or negotiable documents may be perfected by filing. A security interest in money or instruments (other than certificated securities or instruments which constitute part of chattel paper) can be perfected only by the secured party's taking possession, except as provided in subsections (4) and (5) of this section and subsections (2) and (3) of Section 9-306 on proceeds.

(2)   During the period that goods are in the possession of the issuer of a negotiable document therefor, a security interest in the goods is perfected by perfecting a security interest in the document, and any security interest in the goods otherwise perfected during such period is subject thereto.

(3)   A security interest in goods in the possession of a bailee other than one who has issued a negotiable document therefor is perfected by issuance of a document in the name of the secured party or by the bailee's receipt of notification of the secured party's interest or by filing as to the goods.

(4)   A security interest in instruments (other than certificated securities) or negotiable documents is perfected without filing or the taking of possession for a period of 21 days from the time it attaches to the extent that it arises for new value given under a written security agreement.

(5)   A security interest remains perfected for a period of 21 days without filing where a secured party having a perfected security interest in an instrument (other than a certificated security), a negotiable document or goods in possession of a bailee other than one who has issued a negotiable document therefor

(a)   makes available to the debtor the goods or documents representing the goods for the purpose of ultimate sale or exchange or for the purpose of loading, unloading, storing, shipping, transshipping, manufacturing, processing or otherwise dealing with them in a manner preliminary to their sale or exchange, but priority between conflicting security interests in the goods is subject to subsection (3) of Section 9-312; or

(b)   delivers the instrument to the debtor for the purpose of ultimate sale or exchange or of presentation, collection, renewal or registration of transfer.

(6)   After the 21 day period in subsections (4) and (5) perfection depends upon compliance with applicable provisions of this Article.

§ 9-305. *When Possession by Secured Party Perfects Security Interest Without Filing.*

A security interest in letters of credit and advices of credit (subsection (2)(a) of Section 5-116), goods, instruments (other than certificated securities), money, negotiable documents, or chattel paper may be perfected by the secured party's taking possession of the collateral. If such collateral other than goods covered by a negotiable document is held by a bailee, the secured party is deemed to have possession from the time the bailee receives notification of the secured party's interest. A security interest is perfected by possession from the time possession is taken without a relation back and continues only so long as possession is retained, unless otherwise specified in this Article. The security interest may be otherwise perfected as provided in this Article before or after the period of possession by the secured party.

§ 9-306. *"Proceeds"; Secured Party's Rights on Disposition of Collateral.*

(1) "Proceeds" includes whatever is received upon the sale, exchange, collection or other disposition of collateral or proceeds. Insurance payable by reason of loss or damage to the collateral is proceeds, except to the extent that it is payable to a person other than a party to the security agreement. Money, checks, deposit accounts, and the like are "cash proceeds". All other proceeds are "non-cash proceeds".

(2) Except where this Article otherwise provides, a security interest continues in collateral notwithstanding sale, exchange or other disposition thereof unless the disposition was authorized by the secured party in the security agreement or otherwise, and also continues in any identifiable proceeds including collections received by the debtor.

(3) The security interest in proceeds is a continuously perfected security interest if the interest in the original collateral was perfected but it ceases to be a perfected security interest and becomes unperfected ten days after receipt of the proceeds by the debtor unless

    (a) a filed financing statement covers the original collateral and the proceeds are collateral in which a security interest may be perfected by filing in the office or offices where the financing statement has been filed and, if the proceeds are acquired with cash proceeds, the description of collateral in the financing statement indicates the types of property constituting the proceeds; or

    (b) a filed financing statement covers the original collateral and the proceeds are identifiable cash proceeds; or

    (c) the security interest in the proceeds is perfected before the expiration of the ten day period.

Except as provided in this section, a security interest in proceeds can be perfected only by the methods or under the circumstances permitted in this Article for original collateral of the same type.

(4) In the event of insolvency proceedings instituted by or against a debtor, a secured party with a perfected security interest in proceeds has a perfected security interest only in the following proceeds:

    (a) in identifiable non-cash proceeds and in separate deposit accounts containing only proceeds;

    (b) in identifiable cash proceeds in the form of money which is neither commingled with other money nor deposited in a deposit account prior to the insolvency proceedings;

    (c) in identifiable cash proceeds in the form of checks and the like which are not deposited in a deposit account prior to the insolvency proceedings; and

    (d) in all cash and deposit accounts of the debtor in which proceeds have been commingled with other funds, but the perfected security interest under this paragraph (d) is

        (i) subject to any right to set-off; and

        (ii) limited to an amount not greater than the amount of any cash proceeds received by the debtor within ten days before the institution of the insolvency proceedings less the sum of (I) the payments to the secured party on account of cash proceeds received by the debtor during such period and (II) the cash proceeds received by the debtor during such period to which the secured party is entitled under paragraphs (a) through (c) of this subsection (4).

(5) If a sale of goods results in an account or chattel paper which is transferred by the seller to a secured party, and if the goods are returned to or are repossessed by the seller or the secured party, the following rules determine priorities:

    (a) If the goods were collateral at the time of sale, for an indebtedness of the seller which is still unpaid, the original security interest attaches again to the goods and continues as a perfected security interest if it was perfected at the time when the goods were sold. If the security interest was originally perfected by a filing which is still effective, nothing further is required to continue the perfected status; in any other case, the secured party must take possession of the returned or repossessed goods or must file.

    (b) An unpaid transferee of the chattel paper has a security interest in the goods against the transferor. Such security interest is prior to a security interest asserted under paragraph (a) to the extent that the transferee of the chattel paper was entitled to priority under Section 9-308.

    (c) An unpaid transferee of the account has a security interest in the goods against the transferor. Such security interest is subordinate to a security interest asserted under paragraph (a).

    (d) A security interest of an unpaid transferee asserted under paragraph (b) or (c) must be perfected for protection against creditors of the transferor and purchasers of the returned or repossessed goods.

§ 9-307. *Protection of Buyers of Goods.*

(1) A buyer in ordinary course of business (subsection (9) of Section 1-201) other than a person buying farm products from a person engaged in farming operations takes free of a security interest created by his seller even though the security interest is perfected and even though the buyer knows of its existence.

(2) In the case of consumer goods, a buyer takes free of a security interest even though perfected if he buys without knowledge of the security interest, for value and for his own personal, family or household purposes unless prior to the purchase the secured party has filed a financing statement covering such goods.

(3) A buyer other than a buyer in ordinary course of business (subsection (1) of this section) takes free of a security interest to the extent that it secures future advances made after the secured party acquires knowledge of the purchase, or more than 45 days after the purchase, whichever first occurs, unless made pursuant to a commitment entered into without knowledge of the purchase and before the expiration of the 45 day period.

§ 9-308. *Purchase of Chattel Paper and Instruments.*

A purchaser of chattel paper or an instrument who gives new value and takes possession of it in the ordinary course of his business has priority over a security interest in the chattel paper or instrument

    (a) which is perfected under Section 9-304 (permissive filing and temporary perfection) or under Section 9-306 (perfection as to proceeds) if he acts without knowledge that the specific paper or instrument is subject to a security interest; or

    (b) which is claimed merely as proceeds of inventory subject to a security interest (Section 9-306) even though he knows that the specific paper or instrument is subject to the security interest.

§ 9-309. *Protection of Purchasers of Instruments, Documents and Securities.*

Nothing in this Article limits the rights of a holder in due course of a negotiable instrument (Section 3-302) or a holder to whom a negotiable document of title has been duly negotiated

(Section 7-501) or a bona fide purchaser of a security (Section 8-302) and the holders or purchasers take priority over an earlier security interest even though perfected. Filing under this Article does not constitute notice of the security interest to such holders or purchasers.

§ 9-310. Priority of Certain Liens Arising by Operation of Law.

When a person in the ordinary course of his business furnishes services or materials with respect to goods subject to a security interest, a lien upon goods in the possession of such person given by statute or rule of law for such materials or services takes priority over a perfected security interest unless the lien is statutory and the statute expressly provides otherwise.

§ 9-311. Alienability of Debtor's Rights: Judicial Process.

The debtor's rights in collateral may be voluntarily or involuntarily transferred (by way of sale, creation of a security interest, attachment, levy, garnishment or other judicial process) notwithstanding a provision in the security agreement prohibiting any transfer or making the transfer constitute a default.

§ 9-312. Priorities Among Conflicting Security Interests in the Same Collateral.

(1)   The rules of priority stated in other sections of this Part and in the following sections shall govern when applicable: Section 4-208 with respect to the security interests of collecting banks in items being collected, accompanying documents and proceeds; Section 9-103 on security interests related to other jurisdictions; Section 9-114 on consignments.

(2)   A perfected security interest in crops for new value given to enable the debtor to produce the crops during the production season and given not more than three months before the crops become growing crops by planting or otherwise takes priority over an earlier perfected security interest to the extent that such earlier interest secures obligations due more than six months before the crops become growing crops by planting or otherwise, even though the person giving new value had knowledge of the earlier security interest.

(3)   A perfected purchase money security interest in inventory has priority over a conflicting security interest in the same inventory and also has priority in identifiable cash proceeds received on or before the delivery of the inventory to a buyer if

(a)   the purchase money security interest is perfected at the time the debtor receives possession of the inventory; and

(b)   the purchase money secured party gives notification in writing to the holder of the conflicting security interest if the holder had filed a financing statement covering the same types of inventory (i) before the date of the filing made by the purchase money secured party, or (ii) before the beginning of the 21 day period where the purchase money security interest is temporarily perfected without filing or possession (subsection (5) of Section 9-304); and

(c)   the holder of the conflicting security interest receives the notification within five years before the debtor receives possession of the inventory; and

(d)   the notification states that the person giving the notice has or expects to acquire a purchase money security interest in inventory of the debtor, describing such inventory by item or type.

(4)   A purchase money security interest in collateral other than inventory has priority over a conflicting security interest in the same collateral or its proceeds if the purchase money security interest is perfected at the time the debtor receives possession of the collateral or within ten days thereafter.

(5)   In all cases not governed by other rules stated in this section (including cases of purchase money security interests which do not qualify for the special priorities set forth in subsections (3) and (4) of this section), priority between conflicting security interests in the same collateral shall be determined according to the following rules:

(a)   Conflicting security interests rank according to priority in time of filing or perfection. Priority dates from the time a filing is first made covering the collateral or the time the security interest is first perfected, whichever is earlier, provided that there is no period thereafter when there is neither filing nor perfection.

(b)   So long as conflicting security interests are unperfected, the first to attach has priority.

(6)   For the purposes of subsection (5) a date of filing or perfection as to collateral is also a date of filing or perfection as to proceeds.

(7)   If future advances are made while a security interest is perfected by filing, the taking of possession, or under Section 8-321 on securities, the security interest has the same priority for the purposes of subsection (5) with respect to the future advances as it does with respect to the first advance. If a commitment is made before or while the security interest is so perfected, the security interest has the same priority with respect to advances made pursuant thereto. In other cases a perfected security interest has priority from the date the advance is made.

§ 9-313. Priority of Security Interests in Fixtures.

(1)   In this section and in the provisions of Part 4 of this Article referring to fixture filing, unless the context otherwise requires

(a)   goods are "fixtures" when they become so related to particular real estate that an interest in them arises under real estate law

(b)   a "fixture filing" is the filing in the office where a mortgage on the real estate would be filed or recorded of a financing statement covering goods which are or are to become fixtures and conforming to the requirements of subsection (5) of Section 9-402

(c)   a mortgage is a "construction mortgage" to the extent that it secures an obligation incurred for the construction of an improvement on land including the acquisition cost of the land, if the recorded writing so indicates.

(2)   A security interest under this Article may be created in goods which are fixtures or may continue in goods which become fixtures, but no security interest exists under this Article in ordinary building materials incorporated into an improvement on land.

(3)   This Article does not prevent creation of an encumbrance upon fixtures pursuant to real estate law.

(4)   A perfected security interest in fixtures has priority over the conflicting interest of an encumbrancer or owner of the real estate where

(a)   the security interest is a purchase money security interest, the interest of the encumbrancer or owner arises before the goods become fixtures, the security interest is perfected by a fixture filing before the goods become fixtures or within ten days thereafter, and the debtor has an interest of record in the real estate or is in possession of the real estate; or

(b)   the security interest is perfected by a fixture filing before the interest of the encumbrancer or owner is of record, the security interest has priority over any conflicting interest of a predecessor in title of the encumbrancer or owner, and the debtor has an interest of record in the real estate or is in possession of the real estate; or

(c)   the fixtures are readily removable factory or office machines or readily removable replacements of domestic appliances which are consumer goods, and before the goods become fixtures the security interest is perfected by any method permitted by this Article; or

(d)   the conflicting interest is a lien on the real estate obtained by legal or equitable proceedings after the security interest was perfected by any method permitted by this Article.

(5)   A security interest in fixtures, whether or not perfected, has priority over the conflicting interest of an encumbrancer or owner of the real estate where

(a)   the encumbrancer or owner has consented in writing to the security interest or has disclaimed an interest in the goods as fixtures; or

(b)   the debtor has a right to remove the goods as against the encumbrancer or owner. If the debtor's right terminates, the priority of the security interest continues for a reasonable time.

(6)   Notwithstanding paragraph (a) of subsection (4) but otherwise subject to subsections (4) and (5), a security interest in fixtures is subordinate to a construction mortgage recorded before the goods become fixtures if the goods become fixtures before the completion of the construction. To the extent that it is given to refinance a construction mortgage, a mortgage has this priority to the same extent as the construction mortgage.

(7)   In cases not within the preceding subsections, a security interest in fixtures is subordinate to the conflicting interest of an encumbrancer or owner of the related real estate who is not the debtor.

(8)   When the secured party has priority over all owners and encumbrancers of the real estate, he may, on default, subject to the provisions of Part 5, remove his collateral from the real estate but he must reimburse any encumbrancer or owner of the real estate who is not the debtor and who has not otherwise agreed for the cost of repair of any physical injury, but not for any diminution in value of the real estate caused by the absence of the goods removed or by any necessity of replacing them. A person entitled to reimbursement may refuse permission to remove until the secured party gives adequate security for the performance of this obligation.

§ 9-314.   *Accessions.*

(1)   A security interest in goods which attaches before they are installed in or affixed to other goods takes priority as to the goods installed or affixed (called in this section "accessions") over the claims of all persons to the whole except as stated in subsection (3) and subject to Section 9-315(1).

(2)   A security interest which attaches to goods after they become part of a whole is valid against all persons subsequently acquiring interests in the whole except as stated in subsection (3) but is invalid against any person with an interest in the whole at the time the security interest attaches to the goods who has not in writing consented to the security interest or disclaimed an interest in the goods as part of the whole.

(3)   The security interests described in subsections (1) and (2) do not take priority over

(a)   a subsequent purchaser for value of any interest in the whole; or

(b)   a creditor with a lien on the whole subsequently obtained by judicial proceedings; or

(c)   a creditor with a prior perfected security interest in the whole to the extent that he makes subsequent advances

if the subsequent purchase is made, the lien by judicial proceedings obtained or the subsequent advance under the prior perfected security interest is made or contracted for without knowledge of the security interest and before it is perfected. A purchaser of the whole at a foreclosure sale other than the holder of a perfected security interest purchasing at his own foreclosure sale is a subsequent purchaser within this section.

(4)   When under subsections (1) or (2) and (3) a secured party has an interest in accessions which has priority over the claims of all persons who have interests in the whole, he may on default subject to the provisions of Part 5 remove his collateral from the whole but he must reimburse any encumbrancer or owner of the whole who is not the debtor and who has not otherwise agreed for the cost of repair of any physical injury but not for any diminution in value of the whole caused by the absence of the goods removed or by any necessity for replacing them. A person entitled to reimbursement may refuse permission to remove until the secured party gives adequate security for the performance of this obligation.

§ 9-315.   *Priority When Goods Are Commingled or Processed.*

(1)   If a security interest in goods was perfected and subsequently the goods or a part thereof have become part of a product or mass, the security interest continues in the product or mass if

(a)   the goods are so manufactured, processed, assembled or commingled that their identity is lost in the product or mass; or

(b)   a financing statement covering the original goods also covers the product into which the goods have been manufactured, processed or assembled.

In a case to which paragraph (b) applies, no separate security interest in that part of the original goods which has been manufactured, processed or assembled into the product may be claimed under Section 9-314.

(2)   When under subsection (1) more than one security interest attaches to the product or mass, they rank equally according to the ratio that the cost of the goods to which each interest originally attached bears to the cost of the total product or mass.

§ 9-316.   *Priority Subject to Subordination.*

Nothing in this Article prevents subordination by agreement by any person entitled to priority.

§ 9-317.   *Secured Party Not Obligated on Contract of Debtor.*

The mere existence of a security interest or authority given to the debtor to dispose of or use collateral does not impose contract or tort liability upon the secured party for the debtor's acts or omissions.

§ 9-318.   *Defenses Against Assignee; Modification of Contract After Notification of Assignment; Term Prohibiting Assignment Ineffective; Identification and Proof of Assignment.*

(1)   Unless an account debtor has made an enforceable agreement not to assert defenses or claims arising out of a sale as provided in Section 9-206 the rights of an assignee are subject to

(a)   all the terms of the contract between the account debtor and assignor and any defense or claim arising therefrom; and

(b)   any other defense or claim of the account debtor against the assignor which accrues before the account debtor receives notification of the assignment.

(2)   So far as the right to payment or a part thereof under an assigned contract has not been fully earned by performance, and notwithstanding notification of the assignment, any modification of or substitution for the contract made in good faith and in accordance with reasonable commercial standards is effective

against an assignee unless the account debtor has otherwise agreed but the assignee acquires corresponding rights under the modified or substituted contract. The assignment may provide that such modification or substitution is a breach by the assignor.

(3) The account debtor is authorized to pay the assignor until the account debtor receives notification that the amount due or to become due has been assigned and that payment is to be made to the assignee. A notification which does not reasonably identify the rights assigned is ineffective. If requested by the account debtor, the assignee must seasonably furnish reasonable proof that the assignment has been made and unless he does so the account debtor may pay the assignor.

(4) A term in any contract between an account debtor and an assignor is ineffective if it prohibits assignment of an account or prohibits creation of a security interest in a general intangible for money due or to become due or requires the account debtor's consent to such assignment or security interest.

■ PART 4 Filing

§ 9-401. *Place of Filing; Erroneous Filing; Removal of Collateral.*

First Alternative Subsection (1)

(1) The proper place to file in order to perfect a security interest is as follows:

   (a) when the collateral is timber to be cut or is minerals or the like (including oil and gas) or accounts subject to subsection (5) of Section 9-103, or when the financing statement is filed as a fixture filing (Section 9-313) and the collateral is goods which are or are to become fixtures, then in the office where a mortgage on the real estate would be filed or recorded;

   (b) in all other cases, in the office of the [Secretary of State].

Second Alternative Subsection (1)

(1) The proper place to file in order to perfect a security interest is as follows:

   (a) when the collateral is equipment used in farming operations, or farm products, or accounts or general intangibles arising from or relating to the sale of farm products by a farmer, or consumer goods, then in the office of the _____ in the county of the debtor's residence or if the debtor is not a resident of this state then in the office of the _____ in the county where the goods are kept, and in addition when the collateral is crops growing or to be grown in the office of the _____ in the county where the land is located;

   (b) when the collateral is timber to be cut or is minerals or the like (including oil and gas) or accounts subject to subsection (5) of Section 9-103, or when the financing statement is filed as a fixture filing (Section 9-313) and the collateral is goods which are or are to become fixtures, then in the office where a mortgage on the real estate would be filed or recorded;

   (c) in all other cases, in the office of the [Secretary of State].

Third Alternative Subsection (1)

(1) The proper place to file in order to perfect a security interest is as follows:

   (a) when the collateral is equipment used in farming operations, or farm products, or accounts or general intangibles arising from or relating to the sale of farm products by a farmer, or consumer goods, then in the office of the _____ in the county of the debtor's residence

or if the debtor is not a resident of this state then in the office of the _____ in the county where the goods are kept, and in addition when the collateral is crops growing or to be grown in the office of the _____ in the county where the land is located;

   (b) when the collateral is timber to be cut or is minerals or the like (including oil and gas) or accounts subject to subsection (5) of Section 9-103, or when the financing statement is filed as a fixture filing (Section 9-313) and the collateral is goods which are or are to become fixtures, then in the office where a mortgage on the real estate would be filed or recorded;

   (c) in all other cases, in the office of the [Secretary of State] and in addition, if the debtor has a place of business in only one county of this state, also in the office of _____ of such county, or, if the debtor has no place of business in this state, but resides in the state, also in the office of _____ of the county in which he resides.

Note: One of the three alternatives should be selected as subsection (1).

(2) A filing which is made in good faith in an improper place or not in all of the places required by this section is nevertheless effective with regard to any collateral as to which the filing complied with the requirements of this Article and is also effective with regard to collateral covered by the financing statement against any person who has knowledge of the contents of such financing statement.

(3) A filing which is made in the proper place in this state continues effective even though the debtor's residence or place of business or the location of the collateral or its use, whichever controlled the original filing, is thereafter changed.

Alternative Subsection (3)

[(3) A filing which is made in the proper county continues effective for four months after a change to another county of the debtor's residence or place of business or the location of the collateral, whichever controlled the original filing. It becomes ineffective thereafter unless a copy of the financing statement signed by the secured party is filed in the new county within said period. The security interest may also be perfected in the new county after the expiration of the four-month period; in such case perfection dates from the time of perfection in the new county. A change in the use of the collateral does not impair the effectiveness of the original filing.]

(4) The rules stated in Section 9-103 determine whether filing is necessary in this state.

(5) Notwithstanding the preceding subsections, and subject to subsection (3) of Section 9-302, the proper place to file in order to perfect a security interest in collateral, including fixtures, of a transmitting utility is the office of the [Secretary of State]. This filing constitutes a fixture filing (Section 9-313) as to the collateral described therein which is or is to become fixtures.

(6) For the purposes of this section, the residence of an organization is its place of business if it has one or its chief executive office if it has more than one place of business.

Note: Subsection (6) should be used only if the state chooses the Second or Third Alternative Subsection (1).

§ 9-402. *Formal Requisites of Financing Statement; Amendments; Mortgage as Financing Statement.*

(1) A financing statement is sufficient if it gives the names of the debtor and the secured party, is signed by the debtor, gives an address of the secured party from which information concerning the security interest may be obtained, gives a mailing address of the debtor and contains a statement indicating the types, or

describing the items, of collateral. A financing statement may be filed before a security agreement is made or a security interest otherwise attaches. When the financing statement covers crops growing or to be grown, the statement must also contain a description of the real estate concerned. When the financing statement covers timber to be cut or covers minerals or the like (including oil and gas) or accounts subject to subsection (5) of Section 9-103, or when the financing statement is filed as a fixture filing (Section 9-313) and the collateral is goods which are or are to become fixtures, the statement must also comply with subsection (5). A copy of the security agreement is sufficient as a financing statement if it contains the above information and is signed by the debtor. A carbon, photographic or other reproduction of a security agreement or a financing statement is sufficient as a financing statement if the security agreement so provides or if the original has been filed in this state.

(2)   A financing statement which otherwise complies with subsection (1) is sufficient when it is signed by the secured party instead of the debtor if it is filed to perfect a security interest in

(a)   collateral already subject to a security interest in another jurisdiction when it is brought into this state, or when the debtor's location is changed to this state. Such a financing statement must state that the collateral was brought into this state or that the debtor's location was changed to this state under such circumstances; or

(b)   proceeds under Section 9-306 if the security interest in the original collateral was perfected. Such a financing statement must describe the original collateral; or

(c)   collateral as to which the filing has lapsed; or

(d)   collateral acquired after a change of name, identity or corporate structure of the debtor (subsection (7)).

(3)   A form substantially as follows is sufficient to comply with subsection (1):

Name of debtor (or assignor) _____
Address _____
Name of secured party (or assignee) _____
Address _____

1.   This financing statement covers the following types (or items) of property:
(Describe) _____
2.   (If collateral is crops) The above described crops are growing or are to be grown on:
(Describe Real Estate) _____
3.   (If applicable) The above goods are to become fixtures on*
*Where appropriate substitute either "The above timber is standing on _____ " or "The above minerals or the like (including oil and gas) or accounts will be financed at the wellhead or minehead of the well or mine located on _____ "

Describe Real Estate) _____ and this financing statement is to be filed [for record] in the real estate records. (If the debtor does not have an interest of record) The name of a record owner is _____
4.   (If products of collateral are claimed) Products of the collateral are also covered.
(use

_____
whichever   Signature of Debtor (or Assignor)
is

_____
applicable) Signature of Secured Party (or Assignee)

(4)   A financing statement may be amended by filing a writing signed by both the debtor and the secured party. An amendment does not extend the period of effectiveness of a financing statement. If any amendment adds collateral, it is effective as to the added collateral only from the filing date of the amendment.

In this Article, unless the context otherwise requires, the term "financing statement" means the original financing statement and any amendments.

(5)   A financing statement covering timber to be cut or covering minerals or the like (including oil and gas) or accounts subject to subsection (5) of Section 9-103, or a financing statement filed as a fixture filing (Section 9-313) where the debtor is not a transmitting utility, must show that it covers this type of collateral, must recite that it is to be filed [for record] in the real estate records, and the financing statement must contain a description of the real estate [sufficient if it were contained in a mortgage of the real estate to give constructive notice of the mortgage under the law of this state]. If the debtor does not have an interest of record in the real estate, the financing statement must show the name of a record owner.

(6)   A mortgage is effective as a financing statement filed as a fixture filing from the date of its recording if

(a)   the goods are described in the mortgage by item or type; and

(b)   the goods are or are to become fixtures related to the real estate described in the mortgage; and

(c)   the mortgage complies with the requirements for a financing statement in this section other than a recital that it is to be filed in the real estate records; and

(d)   the mortgage is duly recorded.

No fee with reference to the financing statement is required other than the regular recording and satisfaction fees with respect to the mortgage.

(7)   A financing statement sufficiently shows the name of the debtor if it gives the individual, partnership or corporate name of the debtor, whether or not it adds other trade names or names of partners. Where the debtor so changes his name or in the case of an organization its name, identity or corporate structure that a filed financing statement becomes seriously misleading, the filing is not effective to perfect a security interest in collateral acquired by the debtor more than four months after the change, unless a new appropriate financing statement is filed before the expiration of that time. A filed financing statement remains effective with respect to collateral transferred by the debtor even though the secured party knows of or consents to the transfer.

(8)   A financing statement substantially complying with the requirements of this section is effective even though it contains minor errors which are not seriously misleading.

Note: Language in brackets is optional.

Note: Where the state has any special recording system for real estate other than the usual grantor-grantee index (as, for instance, a tract system or a title registration or Torrens system) local adaptations of subsection (5) and Section 9-403(7) may be necessary. See Mass.Gen.Laws Chapter 106, Section 9-409.

§ 9-403.   *What Constitutes Filing; Duration of Filing; Effect of Lapsed Filing; Duties of Filing Officer.*

(1)   Presentation for filing of a financing statement and tender of the filing fee or acceptance of the statement by the filing officer constitutes filing under this Article.

(2)   Except as provided in subsection (6) a filed financing statement is effective for a period of five years from the date of filing. The effectiveness of a filed financing statement lapses on the expiration of the five year period unless a continuation statement is filed prior to the lapse. If a security interest perfected by filing exists at the time insolvency proceedings are commenced by or against the debtor, the security interest remains perfected until termination of the insolvency proceedings and thereafter for a period of sixty days or until expiration of the five year period, whichever occurs later. Upon lapse the security interest becomes

unperfected, unless it is perfected without filing. If the security interest becomes unperfected upon lapse, it is deemed to have been unperfected as against a person who became a purchaser or lien creditor before lapse.

(3) A continuation statement may be filed by the secured party within six months prior to the expiration of the five year period specified in subsection (2). Any such continuation statement must be signed by the secured party, identify the original statement by file number and state that the original statement is still effective. A continuation statement signed by a person other than the secured party of record must be accompanied by a separate written statement of assignment signed by the secured party of record and complying with subsection (2) of Section 9-405, including payment of the required fee. Upon timely filing of the continuation statement, the effectiveness of the original statement is continued for five years after the last date to which the filing was effective whereupon it lapses in the same manner as provided in subsection (2) unless another continuation statement is filed prior to such lapse. Succeeding continuation statements may be filed in the same manner to continue the effectiveness of the original statement. Unless a statute on disposition of public records provides otherwise, the filing officer may remove a lapsed statement from the files and destroy it immediately if he has retained a microfilm or other photographic record, or in other cases after one year after the lapse. The filing officer shall so arrange matters by physical annexation of financing statements to continuation statements or other related filings, or by other means, that if he physically destroys the financing statements of a period more than five years past, those which have been continued by a continuation statement or which are still effective under subsection (6) shall be retained.

(4) Except as provided in subsection (7) a filing officer shall mark each statement with a file number and with the date and hour of filing and shall hold the statement or a microfilm or other photographic copy thereof for public inspection. In addition the filing officer shall index the statement according to the name of the debtor and shall note in the index the file number and the address of the debtor given in the statement.

(5) The uniform fee for filing and indexing and for stamping a copy furnished by the secured party to show the date and place of filing for an original financing statement or for a continuation statement shall be $_____ if the statement is in the standard form prescribed by the [Secretary of State] and otherwise shall be $_____, plus in each case, if the financing statement is subject to subsection (5) of Section 9-402, $_____. The uniform fee for each name more than one required to be indexed shall be $_____. The secured party may at his option show a trade name for any person and an extra uniform indexing fee of $_____; shall be paid with respect thereto.

(6) If the debtor is a transmitting utility (subsection (5) of Section 9-401) and a filed financing statement so states, it is effective until a termination statement is filed. A real estate mortgage which is effective as a fixture filing under subsection (6) of Section 9-402 remains effective as a fixture filing until the mortgage is released or satisfied of record or its effectiveness otherwise terminates as to the real estate.

(7) When a financing statement covers timber to be cut or covers minerals or the like (including oil and gas) or accounts subject to subsection (5) of Section 9-103, or is filed as a fixture filing, [it shall be filed for record and] the filing officer shall index it under the names of the debtor and any owner of record shown on the financing statement in the same fashion as if they were the mortgagors in a mortgage of the real estate described, and, to the extent that the law of this state provides for indexing of mortgages under the name of the mortgagee, under the name of the secured party as if he were the mortgagee thereunder, or where indexing is by description in the same fashion as if the financing statement were a mortgage of the real estate described.

Note: In states in which writings will not appear in the real estate records and indices unless actually recorded the bracketed language in subsection (7) should be used.

§ 9-404. *Termination Statement.*

(1) If a financing statement covering consumer goods is filed on or after _____, then within one month or within ten days following written demand by the debtor after there is no outstanding secured obligation and no commitment to make advances, incur obligations or otherwise give value, the secured party must file with each filing officer with whom the financing statement was filed, a termination statement to the effect that he no longer claims a security interest under the financing statement, which shall be identified by file number. In other cases whenever there is no outstanding secured obligation and no commitment to make advances, incur obligations or otherwise give value, the secured party must on written demand by the debtor send the debtor, for each filing officer with whom the financing statement was filed, a termination statement to the effect that he no longer claims a security interest under the financing statement, which shall be identified by file number. A termination statement signed by a person other than the secured party of record must be accompanied by a separate written statement of assignment signed by the secured party of record complying with subsection (2) of Section 9-405, including payment of the required fee. If the affected secured party fails to file such a termination statement as required by this subsection, or to send such a termination statement within ten days after proper demand therefor, he shall be liable to the debtor for one hundred dollars, and in addition for any loss caused to the debtor by such failure.

(2) On presentation to the filing officer of such a termination statement he must note it in the index. If he has received the termination statement in duplicate, he shall return one copy of the termination statement to the secured party stamped to show the time of receipt thereof. If the filing officer has a microfilm or other photographic record of the financing statement, and of any related continuation statement, statement of assignment and statement of release, he may remove the originals from the files at any time after receipt of the termination statement, or if he has no such record, he may remove them from the files at any time after one year after receipt of the termination statement.

(3) If the termination statement is in the standard form prescribed by the [Secretary of State], the uniform fee for filing and indexing the termination statement shall be $_____, and otherwise shall be $_____, plus in each case an additional fee of $_____ for each name more than one against which the termination statement is required to be indexed.

Note: The date to be inserted should be the effective date of the revised Article 9.

§ 9-405. *Assignment of Security Interest; Duties of Filing Officer; Fees.*

(1) A financing statement may disclose an assignment of a security interest in the collateral described in the financing statement by indication in the financing statement of the name and address of the assignee or by an assignment itself or a copy thereof on the face or back of the statement. On presentation to the filing officer of such a financing statement the filing officer shall mark the same as provided in Section 9-403(4). The uniform fee for filing, indexing and furnishing filing data for a financing statement so indicating an assignment shall be $_____ if the statement is in the standard form prescribed by the [Secretary of

State] and otherwise shall be $_____, plus in each case an additional fee of $_____ for each name more than one against which the financing statement is required to be indexed.

(2) A secured party may assign of record all or part of his rights under a financing statement by the filing in the place where the original financing statement was filed of a separate written statement of assignment signed by the secured party of record and setting forth the name of the secured party of record and the debtor, the file number and the date of filing of the financing statement and the name and address of the assignee and containing a description of the collateral assigned. A copy of the assignment is sufficient as a separate statement if it complies with the preceding sentence. On presentation to the filing officer of such a separate statement, the filing officer shall mark such separate statement with the date and hour of the filing. He shall note the assignment on the index of the financing statement, or in the case of a fixture filing, or a filing covering timber to be cut, or covering minerals or the like (including oil and gas) or accounts subject to subsection (5) of Section 9-103, he shall index the assignment under the name of the assignor as grantor and, to the extent that the law of this state provides for indexing the assignment of a mortgage under the name of the assignee, he shall index the assignment of the financing statement under the name of the assignee. The uniform fee for filing, indexing and furnishing filing data about such a separate statement of assignment shall be $_____ if the statement is in the standard form prescribed by the [Secretary of State] and otherwise shall be $_____, plus in each case an additional fee of $_____; for each name more than one against which the statement of assignment is required to be indexed. Notwithstanding the provisions of this subsection, an assignment of record of a security interest in a fixture contained in a mortgage effective as a fixture filing (subsection (6) of Section 9-402) may be made only by an assignment of the mortgage in the manner provided by the law of this state other than this Act.

(3) After the disclosure or filing of an assignment under this section, the assignee is the secured party of record.

§ 9-406. Release of Collateral; Duties of Filing Officer; Fees.

A secured party of record may by his signed statement release all or a part of any collateral described in a filed financing statement. The statement of release is sufficient if it contains a description of the collateral being released, the name and address of the debtor, the name and address of the secured party, and the file number of the financing statement. A statement of release signed by a person other than the secured party of record must be accompanied by a separate written statement of assignment signed by the secured party of record and complying with subsection (2) of Section 9-405, including payment of the required fee. Upon presentation of such a statement of release to the filing officer he shall mark the statement with the hour and date of filing and shall note the same upon the margin of the index of the filing of the financing statement. The uniform fee for filing and noting such a statement of release shall be $_____ if the statement is in the standard form prescribed by the [Secretary of State] and otherwise shall be $_____, plus in each case an additional fee of $_____ for each name more than one against which the statement of release is required to be indexed.

[§ 9-407. Information From Filing Officer].

[(1) If the person filing any financing statement, termination statement, statement of assignment, or statement of release, furnishes the filing officer a copy thereof, the filing officer shall upon request note upon the copy the file number and date and hour of the filing of the original and deliver or send the copy to such person.]

[(2) Upon request of any person, the filing officer shall issue his certificate showing whether there is on file on the date and hour stated therein, any presently effective financing statement naming a particular debtor and any statement of assignment thereof and if there is, giving the date and hour of filing of each such statement and the names and addresses of each secured party therein. The uniform fee for such a certificate shall be $_____ if the request for the certificate is in the standard form prescribed by the [Secretary of State] and otherwise shall be $_____. Upon request the filing officer shall furnish a copy of any filed financing statement or statement of assignment for a uniform fee of $_____ per page.]

Note: This section is proposed as an optional provision to require filing officers to furnish certificates. Local law and practices should be consulted with regard to the advisability of adoption.

§ 9-408. Financing Statements Covering Consigned or Leased Goods.

A consignor or lessor of goods may file a financing statement using the terms "consignor," "consignee," "lessor," "lessee" or the like instead of the terms specified in Section 9-402. The provisions of this Part shall apply as appropriate to such a financing statement but its filing shall not of itself be a factor in determining whether or not the consignment or lease is intended as security (Section 1-201(37)). However, if it is determined for other reasons that the consignment or lease is so intended, a security interest of the consignor or lessor which attaches to the consigned or leased goods is perfected by such filing.

■ PART 5 Default

§ 9-501. Default; Procedure When Security Agreement Covers Both Real and Personal Property.

(1) When a debtor is in default under a security agreement, a secured party has the rights and remedies provided in this Part and except as limited by subsection (3) those provided in the security agreement. He may reduce his claim to judgment, foreclose or otherwise enforce the security interest by any available judicial procedure. If the collateral is documents the secured party may proceed either as to the documents or as to the goods covered thereby. A secured party in possession has the rights, remedies and duties provided in Section 9-207. The rights and remedies referred to in this subsection are cumulative.

(2) After default, the debtor has the rights and remedies provided in this Part, those provided in the security agreement and those provided in Section 9-207.

(3) To the extent that they give rights to the debtor and impose duties on the secured party, the rules stated in the subsections referred to below may not be waived or varied except as provided with respect to compulsory disposition of collateral (subsection (3) of Section 9-504 and Section 9-505) and with respect to redemption of collateral (Section 9-506) but the parties may by agreement determine the standards by which the fulfillment of these rights and duties is to be measured if such standards are not manifestly unreasonable:

(a) subsection (2) of Section 9-502 and subsection (2) of Section 9-504 insofar as they require accounting for surplus proceeds of collateral;

(b) subsection (3) of Section 9-504 and subsection (1) of Section 9-505 which deal with disposition of collateral;

(c) subsection (2) of Section 9-505 which deals with acceptance of collateral as discharge of obligation;

(d) Section 9-506 which deals with redemption of collateral; and

(e) subsection (1) of Section 9-507 which deals with the secured party's liability for failure to comply with this Part.

(4) If the security agreement covers both real and personal property, the secured party may proceed under this Part as to the personal property or he may proceed as to both the real and the personal property in accordance with his rights and remedies in respect of the real property in which case the provisions of this Part do not apply.

(5) When a secured party has reduced his claim to judgment the lien of any levy which may be made upon his collateral by virtue of any execution based upon the judgment shall relate back to the date of the perfection of the security interest in such collateral. A judicial sale, pursuant to such execution, is a foreclosure of the security interest by judicial procedure within the meaning of this section, and the secured party may purchase at the sale and thereafter hold the collateral free of any other requirements of this Article.

§ 9-502. Collection Rights of Secured Party.

(1) When so agreed and in any event on default the secured party is entitled to notify an account debtor or the obligor on an instrument to make payment to him whether or not the assignor was theretofore making collections on the collateral, and also to take control of any proceeds to which he is entitled under Section 9-306.

(2) A secured party who by agreement is entitled to charge back uncollected collateral or otherwise to full or limited recourse against the debtor and who undertakes to collect from the account debtors or obligors must proceed in a commercially reasonable manner and may deduct his reasonable expenses of realization from the collections. If the security agreement secures an indebtedness, the secured party must account to the debtor for any surplus, and unless otherwise agreed, the debtor is liable for any deficiency. But, if the underlying transaction was a sale of accounts or chattel paper, the debtor is entitled to any surplus or is liable for any deficiency only if the security agreement so provides.

§ 9-503. Secured Party's Right to Take Possession After Default.

Unless otherwise agreed a secured party has on default the right to take possession of the collateral. In taking possession a secured party may proceed without judicial process if this can be done without breach of the peace or may proceed by action. If the security agreement so provides the secured party may require the debtor to assemble the collateral and make it available to the secured party at a place to be designated by the secured party which is reasonably convenient to both parties. Without removal a secured party may render equipment unusable, and may dispose of collateral on the debtor's premises under Section 9-504.

§ 9-504. Secured Party's Right to Dispose of Collateral After Default; Effect of Disposition.

(1) A secured party after default may sell, lease or otherwise dispose of any or all of the collateral in its then condition or following any commercially reasonable preparation or processing. Any sale of goods is subject to the Article on Sales (Article 2). The proceeds of disposition shall be applied in the order following to

(a) the reasonable expenses of retaking, holding, preparing for sale or lease, selling, leasing and the like and, to the extent provided for in the agreement and not prohibited by law, the reasonable attorneys' fees and legal expenses incurred by the secured party;

(b) the satisfaction of indebtedness secured by the security interest under which the disposition is made;

(c) the satisfaction of indebtedness secured by any subordinate security interest in the collateral if written notification of demand therefor is received before distribution of the proceeds is completed. If requested by the secured party, the holder of a subordinate security interest must seasonably furnish reasonable proof of his interest, and unless he does so, the secured party need not comply with his demand.

(2) If the security interest secures an indebtedness, the secured party must account to the debtor for any surplus, and, unless otherwise agreed, the debtor is liable for any deficiency. But if the underlying transaction was a sale of accounts or chattel paper, the debtor is entitled to any surplus or is liable for any deficiency only if the security agreement so provides.

(3) Disposition of the collateral may be by public or private proceedings and may be made by way of one or more contracts. Sale or other disposition may be as a unit or in parcels and at any time and place and on any terms but every aspect of the disposition including the method, manner, time, place and terms must be commercially reasonable. Unless collateral is perishable or threatens to decline speedily in value or is of a type customarily sold on a recognized market, reasonable notification of the time and place of any public sale or reasonable notification of the time after which any private sale or other intended disposition is to be made shall be sent by the secured party to the debtor, if he has not signed after default a statement renouncing or modifying his right to notification of sale. In the case of consumer goods no other notification need be sent. In other cases notification shall be sent to any other secured party from whom the secured party has received (before sending his notification to the debtor or before the debtor's renunciation of his rights) written notice of a claim of an interest in the collateral. The secured party may buy at any public sale and if the collateral is of a type customarily sold in a recognized market or is of a type which is the subject of widely distributed standard price quotations he may buy at private sale.

(4) When collateral is disposed of by a secured party after default, the disposition transfers to a purchaser for value all of the debtor's rights therein, discharges the security interest under which it is made and any security interest or lien subordinate thereto. The purchaser takes free of all such rights and interests even though the secured party fails to comply with the requirements of this Part or of any judicial proceedings

(a) in the case of a public sale, if the purchaser has no knowledge of any defects in the sale and if he does not buy in collusion with the secured party, other bidders or the person conducting the sale; or

(b) in any other case, if the purchaser acts in good faith.

(5) A person who is liable to a secured party under a guaranty, indorsement, repurchase agreement or the like and who receives a transfer of collateral from the secured party or is subrogated to his rights has thereafter the rights and duties of the secured party. Such a transfer of collateral is not a sale or disposition of the collateral under this Article.

§ 9-505. Compulsory Disposition of Collateral; Acceptance of the Collateral as Discharge of Obligation.

(1) If the debtor has paid sixty per cent of the cash price in the case of a purchase money security interest in consumer goods or sixty per cent of the loan in the case of another security interest in consumer goods, and has not signed after default a statement renouncing or modifying his rights under this Part a secured party who has taken possession of collateral must dispose of it under Section 9-504 and if he fails to do so within ninety days after he takes possession the debtor at his option may recover in conversion or under Section 9-507(1) on secured party's liability.

(2) In any other case involving consumer goods or any other collateral a secured party in possession may, after default, propose

to retain the collateral in satisfaction of the obligation. Written notice of such proposal shall be sent to the debtor if he has not signed after default a statement renouncing or modifying his rights under this subsection. In the case of consumer goods no other notice need be given. In other cases notice shall be sent to any other secured party from whom the secured party has received (before sending his notice to the debtor or before the debtor's renunciation of his rights) written notice of a claim of an interest in the collateral. If the secured party receives objection in writing from a person entitled to receive notification within twenty-one days after the notice was sent, the secured party must dispose of the collateral under Section 9-504. In the absence of such written objection the secured party may retain the collateral in satisfaction of the debtor's obligation.

§ 9-506. *Debtor's Right to Redeem Collateral.*

At any time before the secured party has disposed of collateral or entered into a contract for its disposition under Section 9-504 or before the obligation has been discharged under Section 9-505(2) the debtor or any other secured party may unless otherwise agreed in writing after default redeem the collateral by tendering fulfillment of all obligations secured by the collateral as well as the expenses reasonably incurred by the secured party in retaking, holding and preparing the collateral for disposition, in arranging for the sale, and to the extent provided in the agreement and not prohibited by law, his reasonable attorneys' fees and legal expenses.

§ 9-507. *Secured Party's Liability for Failure to Comply With This Part.*

(1) If it is established that the secured party is not proceeding in accordance with the provisions of this Part disposition may be ordered or restrained on appropriate terms and conditions. If the disposition has occurred the debtor or any person entitled to notification or whose security interest has been made known to the secured party prior to the disposition has a right to recover from the secured party any loss caused by a failure to comply with the provisions of this Part. If the collateral is consumer goods, the debtor has a right to recover in any event an amount not less than the credit service charge plus ten per cent of the principal amount of the debt or the time price differential plus 10 per cent of the cash price.

(2) The fact that a better price could have been obtained by a sale at a different time or in a different method from that selected by the secured party is not of itself sufficient to establish that the sale was not made in a commercially reasonable manner. If the secured party either sells the collateral in the usual manner in any recognized market therefor or if he sells at the price current in such market at the time of his sale or if he has otherwise sold in conformity with reasonable commercial practices among dealers in the type of property sold he has sold in a commercially reasonable manner. The principles stated in the two preceding sentences with respect to sales also apply as may be appropriate to other types of disposition. A disposition which has been approved in any judicial proceeding or by any bona fide creditors' committee or representative of creditors shall conclusively be deemed to be commercially reasonable, but this sentence does not indicate that any such approval must be obtained in any case nor does it indicate that any disposition not so approved is not commercially reasonable.

ARTICLE 10
Effective Date and Repealer

§ 10-101. *Effective Date.*

This Act shall become effective at midnight on December 31st following its enactment. It applies to transactions entered into and events occurring after that date.

§ 10-102. *Specific Repealer; Provision for Transition.*

(1) The following acts and all other acts and parts of acts inconsistent herewith are hereby repealed: (Here should follow the acts to be specifically repealed including the following:

> Uniform Negotiable Instruments Act
> Uniform Warehouse Receipts Act
> Uniform Sales Act
> Uniform Bills of Lading Act
> Uniform Stock Transfer Act
> Uniform Conditional Sales Act
> Uniform Trust Receipts Act
> Also any acts regulating:
> Bank collections
> Bulk sales
> Chattel mortgages
> Conditional sales
> Factor's lien acts
> Farm storage of grain and similar acts
> Assignment of accounts receivable)

(2) Transactions validly entered into before the effective date specified in Section 10-101 and the rights, duties and interests flowing from them remain valid thereafter and may be terminated, completed, consummated or enforced as required or permitted by any statute or other law amended or repealed by this Act as though such repeal or amendment had not occurred.

Note: Subsection (1) should be separately prepared for each state. The foregoing is a list of statutes to be checked.

§ 10-103. *General Repealer.*

Except as provided in the following section, all acts and parts of acts inconsistent with this Act are hereby repealed.

§ 10-104. *Laws Not Repealed.*

(1) The Article on Documents of Title (Article 7) does not repeal or modify any laws prescribing the form or contents of documents of title or the services or facilities to be afforded by bailees, or otherwise regulating bailees' businesses in respects not specifically dealt with herein; but the fact that such laws are violated does not affect the status of a document of title which otherwise complies with the definition of a document of title (Section 1-201).

[(2) This Act does not repeal _____*, cited as the Uniform Act for the Simplification of Fiduciary Security Transfers, and if in any respect there is any inconsistency between that Act and the Article of this Act on investment securities (Article 8) the provisions of the former Act shall control.]

*Note: At * in subsection (2) insert the statutory reference to the Uniform Act for the Simplification of Fiduciary Security Transfers if such Act has previously been enacted. If it has not been enacted, omit subsection (2).*

ARTICLE 11
(Reporters' Draft) Effective Date and Transition Provisions

This material has been numbered Article 11 to distinguish it from Article 10, the transition provision of the 1962 Code, which may still remain in effect in some states to cover transition problems from pre-Code law to the original Uniform Commercial Code. Adaptation may be necessary in particular states. The terms "[old Code]" and "[new Code]" and "[old U.C.C.]" and "[new U.C.C.]" are used herein, and should be suitably changed in each state.

Note: This draft was prepared by the Reporters and has not been passed upon by the Review Committee, the Permanent Editorial Board, the American Law Institute, or the National Conference of Commissioners on Uniform State

---

Laws. It is submitted as a working draft which may be adapted as appropriate in each state.

§ 11-101. *Effective Date.*

This Act shall become effective at 12:01 A.M on , ——————— 19————— .

§ 11-102. *Preservation of Old Transition Provision.*

The provisions of [here insert reference to the original transition provision in the particular state] shall continue to apply to [the new U.C.C.] and for this purpose the [old U.C.C. and new U.C.C.] shall be considered one continuous statute.

§ 11-103. *Transition to [New Code]—General Rule.*

Transactions validly entered into after [effective date of old U.C.C.] and before [effective date of new U.C.C.], and which were subject to the provisions of [old U.C.C.] and which would be subject to this Act as amended if they had been entered into after the effective date of [new U.C.C.] and the rights, duties and interests flowing from such transactions remain valid after the latter date and may be terminated, completed, consummated or enforced as required or permitted by the [new U.C.C.]. Security interests arising out of such transactions which are perfected when [new U.C.C.] becomes effective shall remain perfected until they lapse as provided in [new U.C.C.], and may be continued as permitted by [new U.C.C.], except as stated in Section 11-105.

§ 11-104. *Transition Provision on Change of Requirement of Filing.*

A security interest for the perfection of which filing or the taking of possession was required under [old U.C.C.] and which attached prior to the effective date of [new U.C.C.] but was not perfected shall be deemed perfected on the effective date of [new U.C.C.] if [new U.C.C.] permits perfection without filing or authorizes filing in the office or offices where a prior ineffective filing was made.

§ 11-105. *Transition Provision on Change of Place of Filing.*

(1) A financing statement or continuation statement filed prior to [effective date of new U.C.C.] which shall not have lapsed prior to [the effective date of new U.C.C.] which shall remain effective for the period provided in the [old Code], but not less than five years after the filing.

(2) With respect to any collateral acquired by the debtor subsequent to the effective date of [new U.C.C.], any effective financing statement or continuation statement described in this section shall apply only if the filing or filings are in the office or offices that would be appropriate to perfect the security interests in the new collateral under [new U.C.C.].

(3) The effectiveness of any financing statement or continuation statement filed prior to [effective date of new U.C.C.] may be continued by a continuation statement as permitted by [new U.C.C.], except that if [new U.C.C.] requires a filing in an office where there was no previous financing statement, a new financing statement conforming to Section 11-106 shall be filed in that office.

(4) If the record of a mortgage of real estate would have been effective as a fixture filing of goods described therein if [new U.C.C.] had been in effect on the date of recording the mortgage, the mortgage shall be deemed effective as a fixture filing as to such goods under subsection (6) of Section 9-402 of the [new U.C.C.] on the effective date of [new U.C.C.].

§ 11-106. *Required Refilings.*

(1) If a security interest is perfected or has priority when this Act takes effect as to all persons or as to certain persons without any filing or recording, and if the filing of a financing statement would be required for the perfection or priority of the security interest against those persons under [new U.C.C.], the perfection and priority rights of the security interest continue until 3 years after the effective date of [new U.C.C.]. The perfection will then lapse unless a financing statement is filed as provided in subsection (4) or unless the security interest is perfected otherwise than by filing.

(2) If a security interest is perfected when [new U.C.C.] takes effect under a law other than [U.C.C.] which requires no further filing, refiling or recording to continue its perfection, perfection continues until and will lapse 3 years after [new U.C.C.] takes effect, unless a financing statement is filed as provided in subsection (4) or unless the security interest is perfected otherwise than by filing, or unless under subsection (3) of Section 9-302 the other law continues to govern filing.

(3) If a security interest is perfected by a filing, refiling or recording under a law repealed by this Act which required further filing, refiling or recording to continue its perfection, perfection continues and will lapse on the date provided by the law so repealed for such further filing, refiling, or recording unless a financing statement is filed as provided in subsection (4) or unless the security interest is perfected otherwise than by filing.

(4) A financing statement may be filed within six months before the perfection of a security interest would otherwise lapse. Any such financing statement may be signed by either the debtor or the secured party. It must identify the security agreement, statement or notice (however denominated in any statute or other law repealed or modified by this Act), state the office where and the date when the last filing, refiling or recording, if any, was made with respect thereto, and the filing number, if any, or book and page, if any, of recording and further state that the security agreement, statement or notice, however denominated, in another filing office under the [U.C.C.] or under any statute or other law repealed or modified by this Act is still effective. Section 9-401 and Section 9-103 determine the proper place to file such a financing statement. Except as specified in this subsection, the provisions of Section 9-403(3) for continuation statements apply to such a financing statement.

§ 11-107. *Transition Provisions as to Priorities.*

Except as otherwise provided in [Article 11], [old U.C.C.] shall apply to any questions of priority if the positions of the parties were fixed prior to the effective date of [new U.C.C.]. In other cases questions of priority shall be determined by [new U.C.C.].

§ 11-108. *Presumption that Rule of Law Continues Unchanged.*

Unless a change in law has clearly been made, the provisions of [new U.C.C.] shall be deemed declaratory of the meaning of the [old U.C.C.].

Acceleration clauses Clauses in contracts that advance the date for payment based on the occurrence of a condition or the breach of a duty.

Acceptance The agreement by the maker or the drawee to accept and/or pay a negotiable instrument upon presentment.

Accessory to the crime A situation in which one person assists another in the commission of a crime, without being the primary actor.

Accommodation Something supplied for a convenience or to satisfy a need.

Accounts Rights to payments for goods sold or leased or for services rendered that are not evidenced by an instrument or chattel paper.

Actionable Furnishing legal grounds for an action.

Adduced Given as proof.

Administrators The persons who have been empowered by an appropriate court to handle the estate of a deceased person.

Admission A statement acknowledging the truth of an allegation, and accepted in court as evidence against the party making the admission.

Advisory opinion A formal opinion by a judge, court, or law officer on a question of law but not presented in an actual case.

Affidavit Written statement made under oath.

Affirmative defense A defense to a cause of action that the defendant must raise.

Aid and abet To help, assist, or facilitate the commission of a crime; to promote the accomplishment of a crime.

Alien A person or corporation belonging to another country.

Alienage The status of being a foreign-born resident who has not yet become a naturalized citizen.

Alienation The transfer of ownership to another.

Alternate dispute resolution (ADR) Methods of resolving disputes other than traditional litigation.

Ambient Pertaining to the surrounding atmosphere or the environment.

Ambiguities Uncertainties regarding the meanings of expressions used in contractual agreements.

Amicus brief Court brief filed by individual or group who does not have standing in the dispute.

Amoral Being neither moral nor immoral; lying outside the sphere to which moral judgments apply.

Apparent authority Principal gives the appearance that the agent acts with authority.

Appellate court A court that has the power to review the decisions of lower courts.

Appellee Party who "defends" the decision of the lower court.

Aquifers Water-bearing strata of permeable rock, sand, or gravel.

Arbitration The submission for determination of a disputed matter to private unofficial persons selected in a manner provided by law or agreement, with the substitution of their award or decision for the judgment of a court.

Arbitrator An independent person chosen by the parties or appointed by statute and to whom the issues are submitted for settlement outside of court.

Arraigned Called before a court to enter a plea on an indictment or criminal complaint.

Assault A threat to touch someone in an undesired manner.

Assignable Legally capable of being transferred from one person to another.

Assignment for the benefit of creditors An assignment in trust made by debtors for the payment of their debts.

Attachment Seizure of the defendant's property.

At will Having no specific date or circumstance to bring about a dissolution.

Aural privacy A privacy right for normal conversations; the right to privacy from eavesdropping.

Autonomous The right of the individual to govern him- or herself according to his or her own reason.

Bail The posting of money or property for the release of a person charged with a crime while ensuring his or her presence in the court at future hearings.

Bailee One to whom goods are delivered with the understanding that they will be returned at a future time.

Bankruptcy An area of law designed to give an "honest debtor" a fresh start; the proceedings undertaken against a person or a firm under the bankruptcy laws.

Bar In the legal sense, to prevent or to stop.

Battery Unauthorized touching of another person without legal justification or that person's consent.

Beyond a reasonable doubt The degree of proof required in a criminal trial, which is proof to a moral certainty; there is no other reasonable interpretation.

Bona fide In good faith; honest; without deceit; innocent.

Bona fide occupational qualification (BFOQ) A defense to charges of discrimination based on religion, sex, or national origin but not to charges of racial discrimination; a situation in which one of these categories is essential to the performance of the job.

Bona fide purchaser A person who purchases in good faith, for value, and without notice of any defects or defenses affecting the sale or transaction.

Boycotts Concerted refusals to deal with firms so as to disrupt their business.

Cancellation Any action shown on the face of a contract that indicates an intent to destroy the obligation of the contract.

Capital contribution Money or assets invested by the business owners for commencing and/or promoting an enterprise.

Carriage The transportation of goods or people from one location to another.

Carrier A third party hired to deliver the goods from the seller to the buyer.

Cartage The act of carrying by truck, usually within a city; hauling by truck.

Cases and controversies Claims brought before the court in regular proceedings to protect or enforce rights or to prevent or punish wrongs.

Caucusing Mediation technique in which the mediator meets with each party separately.

Caveat emptor Let the buyer beware.

Censured Formally reprimanded for specific conduct.

Certiorari A writ used by a superior court to direct a lower court to send it the records and proceedings in a case for review.

Charging order A court order permitting a creditor to receive profits from the operation of a business; especially common in partnership situations.

Chattel paper A writing that evidences both a monetary obligation and a security interest in specific goods.

Chattels Articles of personal (as opposed to real) property.

Choses in action A personal right not reduced to possession, but recoverable in a suit at law.

Circumscribe Limit the range of activity associated with something.

Civil rights The rights in the first 10 amendments to the U.S. Constitution (the Bill of Rights) and due process and equal protection under the Fourteenth Amendment.

Class action suit Lawsuit involving a group of plaintiffs or defendants who are substantially in the same position as each other.

Clearinghouse An association of banks and financial institutions that "clears" items between banks.

Codicil A separate written document that modifies an existing will.

Common carrier A company in the business of transporting goods or people for a fee and holding itself out as serving the general public.

Common law Unwritten law, which is based on custom, usage, and court decisions; distinct from statute law, which consists of laws passed by legislatures.

Common law states States in which married couples cannot create community property.

Community property A special form of joint ownership between husband and wife permitted in certain states called community property states.

Community property states States in which married couples generally create community property.

Commutative justice The attempt to give all persons identical treatment based on the assumption that equal treatment is appropriate. Individual differences are not considered.

Compiler program One that converts a high-level programming language into binary or machine code.

Complaint In civil practice, the plaintiff's first pleading. It informs the defendant that he or she is being sued.

Concessionaires Operators of refreshment centers.

Condemnation proceeding Court proceeding to take property for public use or declare property forfeited.

Conditional sales contracts Sales contracts in which the transfer of title is subject to a condition, most commonly the payment of the full purchase price by the buyer.

Confirmation A written memorandum of the agreement; a notation that provides written evidence that an agreement was made.

Conglomerate mergers Mergers between noncompeting firms in different industries.

Consequential damages Damages or losses that occur as a result of the initial wrong but that are not direct and immediate.

Conservator A person appointed by a court to manage the affairs of one who is incompetent.

Consignee A person to whom goods are shipped by another party. Also a person to whom goods are shipped for sale and who generally can return all unsold goods to the consignor.

Consignor A person who ships goods to another party.

Conspicuous Easy to see or perceive; obvious.

Conspiracy An unlawful situation in which two or more people plan to engage in criminal behavior.

Constructive discharge A termination of employment that results from an employer's making the employee's working conditions so intolerable that the employee feels compelled to leave.

Constructive trust A trust imposed by law to prevent the unjust enrichment of the person in possession of the property (the purported owner).

Consumer price index Measurement of the price of a group of consumer goods changes at a particular time.

Contingency fee A fee stipulated to be paid to an attorney only if the case is settled or won, or is based on some other contingency or event.

Contracts of adhesion Contracts in which the terms are not open to negotiation; so-called take-it-or-leave-it contracts.

Convention An agreement between nations; a treaty.

Convert Change

Cooperatives Groups of individuals, commonly laborers or farmers, who unite in a common enterprise and share the profits proportionately.

Corporation An artificial person or legal entity created by or under the authority of a state or nation, composed of a group of persons known as stockholders or shareholders.

Counterclaimed Presented a cause of action in opposition to the plaintiff's.

Court of Common Pleas Title used in some states for trial courts of general jurisdiction.

Creditor beneficiary A third party who is entitled to performance because the promisee has a contractual obligation with him or her.

Criminal forfeiture The government confiscates property as a punishment for criminal activity.

Criminal law The body of law dealing with public wrongs called crimes.

Currency transaction report (CTR) A report businesses must file if a customer brings $10,000 or more in cash to the business.

Cy-pres doctrine Doctrine permitting the court to modify the trust in order to follow the creator's charitable intention as closely as possible.

De novo The court will hear the case or issue anew.

Debit card Card that transfers funds from customer's bank account to merchant's bank account.

Decedent A person who has died.

Default A failure to do what should be done, especially in the performance of a contractual obligation, without legal excuse or justification for the nonperformance.

Defendant A person who answers a lawsuit; the person whose behavior is the subject of the complaint.

Defraud To deprive a person of property or of any interest, estate, or right by fraud, deceit, or artifice.

Delegated Assigned responsibility and/or authority by the person or group normally empowered to exercise the responsibility or authority.

Delivered Intentional transfer of physical possession of some thing or right to another person.

Deposition The process of asking a potential witness questions under oath before a court reporter.

Descriptive theory Theory that describes how things are. It reports what is observed.

Deterrent A danger, difficulty, or other consideration that stops or prevents a person from acting.

Dictum An observation or remark by a judge that is not necessarily involved in the case or essential to its resolution. An aside written by the judge.

Discharge Release from obligation or liability.

Discretion The right to use one's own judgment in selecting between alternatives.

Discretionary Having the freedom to make certain decisions.

Disenfranchised Restricted from enjoying certain constitutional or statutory rights; burdened by systemic prejudice or bigotry.

Disgorge Give up ill-gotten or illicit gains.

Dishonor A refusal to accept or to pay a negotiable instrument upon proper presentment.

Distributive justice The attempt to allocate justice in a way that considers individual differences.

District court Trial court in the federal court system.

Diversity of citizenship The parties are citizens of different states.

Document of title Written evidence of ownership or of rights to something.

Domicile One's permanent home and principal residence. It is the place to which a person will return after traveling.

Double jeopardy A rule of criminal law that states that a person will not be tried in court more than once by the same government for the same criminal offense.

Draft An order for a third person to pay a sum certain in money without conditions, either at a preset time in the future or "on demand."

Draw An arrangement by which an employee receives a predetermined amount each pay period.

Due process The proper exercise of judicial authority as established by general concepts of law and morality.

Duress When one party enters into a contract due to a wrongful threat of force. Wrongful use of force to obtain a gift or contract.

Easements Limited rights to use and enjoy the land of another.

Effluent Pertaining to an outflow of materials or an emanation.

Emancipation Freedom from the control or power of another; release from parental care; or the attainment of legal independence.

Eminent domain A state's or municipality's power to take private property for public use.

Employment at will An employment relationship in which, owing to the absence of any contractual obligation to remain in the relationship, either party can terminate the relationship at any time and for any reason not prohibited by law.

Encrypted code Code typed in one set of symbols and interpreted by the machine as another; used for security.

Encumbrancer The holder of a claim relating to real or personal property.

Entrustment The delivery of goods to a merchant who regularly deals in goods of the type delivered.

Equal protection The assurance that any person before the court will be treated the same as every other person before the court.

Equitable Arising from the branch of the legal system designed to provide a remedy where no remedy existed at common law; a system designed to provide fairness when there was no suitable remedy "at law."

ERISA Federal statute regulating employee retirement programs.

Escrow Process of preparing for the exchange of real estate, deed, and money. It is managed by a third party.

Estate tax A tax assessed on the total net (taxable) value of the estate.

Estoppel A legal bar or impediment that prevents a person from claiming or denying certain facts as a result of his or her previous conduct.

European Union (EU) The EU, formerly called the Common Market, creates a free-trade zone among the member nations of Europe.

Exculpatory clauses Parts of agreements in which a prospective plaintiff agrees in advance not to seek to hold the prospective defendant liable for certain losses for which the prospective defendant otherwise would be liable.

Executors The persons named and appointed in a will by the testator to carry out the administration of the estate as established by the will.

Exemplary damages Punitive damages; damages imposed in a case to punish the defendant.

Expert A person with a high degree of skill or with a specialized knowledge.

Ex post facto **law** A law passed after an occurrence or act, which retrospectively changes the legal consequences of such act.

Express Actually stated; communicated from one party to another.

Extinguished Destroyed, wiped out.

Facial/facially On its face, apparent.

Fact finding A process where an arbitrator investigates a dispute and issues findings of fact and a nonbinding report.

Fair market value The current price for selling an asset between informed willing buyers and informed willing sellers.

Fee interest Broadest form of real estate ownership; an absolute interest in which the owner is entitled to the entire property and can transfer it during life and at death. Also called a fee or a fee simple.

Fiat An order issued by legal authority.

Fiduciary One who holds a special position of trust or confidence and who thereby is expected to act with the utmost good faith and loyalty.

Fiduciary duty The legal duty to exercise the highest degree of loyalty and good faith in handling the affairs of the person to whom the duty is owed.

Field warehousing A method of perfection in a secured transaction in which the creditor takes "possession" of a portion of the debtor's storage area.

First impression Case that is presented to the court for an initial decision; the case presents an entirely novel question of law for the court's decision. It is not governed by any existing precedent.

Forcible Entry and Detainer A summary proceeding to recover possession of premises unlawfully or forcibly detained.

Foreclose Cut off an existing ownership right in property.

Foreign corporation A corporation that had its articles of incorporation approved in another state.

Foreseeability The knowledge or notice that a result is likely to occur if a certain act occurs.

Forfeiture The loss of a right or privilege as a penalty for certain conduct.

Forum The court conducting the trial.

Franchising Special privileges granted by a corporation that allow the franchisee to conduct business under the corporate name of the franchisor.

Fraud The intentional misrepresentation of a material fact. Use of a false statement of material fact to obtain a gift or contract.

Free enterprise The carrying on of free, legitimate business for profit.

Fungible Virtually identical; interchangeable; descriptive of things that belong to a class and that are not identifiable individually.

Gag order Order by judge to be silent about a pending case.

Garnish Receive the debtor's assets that are in the hands of a third party; a remedy given to satisfy a debt owed.

Garnishment A legal proceeding in which assets of a debtor that are in the hands of a third person are ordered held by the third person or turned over to the creditor in full or partial satisfaction of the debt. Procedure to obtain possession of the defendant's property when it is in the custody of another person.

General intangibles Personal property other than goods, accounts, chattel paper, instruments, documents, or money; for example, goodwill, literary rights, patents, or copyrights.

Goodwill An intangible asset based on a firm's good reputation and ability to attract customers.

Goods Movable, identifiable items of personal property.

Grand jury A jury that receives complaints of criminal conduct and returns a bill of indictment if the jury is convinced that a trial should be held.

Greenmail The process by which a firm threatens a corporate takeover by buying a significant portion of a corporation's stock and then selling it back to the corporation at a premium when the corporation's directors and executives, fearing for their positions, agree to buy out the firm.

Guarantor One who promises to answer for the payment of a debt or the performance of an obligation if the person liable in the first instance fails to make payment or to perform.

Guardian A person legally responsible for taking care of another who lacks the legal capacity to do so.

Habeas corpus The name given to a variety of writs issued to bring a party before a court or judge.

Hacker An outsider who gains unauthorized access to a computer or computer network.

Heirs People who actually inherit property from the decedent.

Holder A person who receives possession of a negotiable instrument by means of a negotiation.

Honorary trust An arrangement that does not meet trust requirements and thus is not enforceable, although it may be carried out voluntarily.

Illusory Fallacious; nominal as opposed to substantial; of false appearance.

Impeach To question the truthfulness of a witness by means of some evidence.

Implied Presumed to be present under the circumstances; tacit.

Implied consent A concurrence of wills manifested by signs, actions, or facts, or by inaction or silence, that raises a presumption that agreement has been given.

Income beneficiaries Persons with an income interest in a trust.

Indemnify To reimburse a party for a loss suffered by that party for the benefit of another.

Independent contractor A person hired to perform a task but not subject to the specific control of the hiring party.

Indictment A written accusation of criminal conduct issued to a court by a grand jury.

Informational picketing Picketing for the purpose of truthfully advising the public that an employer does not employ members of, or have a contract with, a labor organization.

Inheritance tax A tax assessed on transfers of estate assets at the owner's death. The rates vary depending on the owner's relationship to the recipient.

Injunction A court order prohibiting a person from doing a certain thing or ordering that some particular thing be done.

Injunctive actions Lawsuits asking a court of equity to order a person to do or to refrain from doing some specified act.

Innately dangerous Dangerous as an existing characteristic; dangerous from the beginning.

In personam jurisdiction Authority over a specific person or corporation within the control of the court.

In rem jurisdiction Authority over property or status within the control of the court.

Insolvency Inability to pay one's debts as they become due.

Institutional shareholders A purchaser of shares acting for an institution, such as a pension fund, trust fund, mutual fund, insurance company, or bank.

Insular Isolated from others.

Insured Person or entity covered under an insurance policy.

Intangible asset Property that cannot be touched or felt.

Intended beneficiary A third-party beneficiary who is intended to receive goods or services.

Interested party A party with an interest in the estate, such as a beneficiary, heir, or creditor.

Interstate Between two or more states; between a point in one state and a point in another state.

Intestate share Portion of the estate that a person is entitled to inherit if there is no valid will.

Intestate statutes State statutes that specify who receives property when the decedent does not leave a valid will.

Intestate succession statute Statute that determines who will receive assets if a decedent does not have a valid will disposing of them.

Intrastate Begun, carried on, and completed wholly within the boundaries of a single state.

Intra vires Acts within the scope of the power of a corporation.

Inverse condemnation An action brought by a property owner against a governmental entity that has the power of eminent domain; the property owner typically seeks just compensation for land taken for public use in situations in which the governmental entity does not intend to initiate eminent domain proceedings.

Investment securities Bonds, notes, certificates, and other instruments or contracts from which one expects to receive a return primarily from the efforts of others.

Invidious Repugnant; discrimination stemming from bigotry or prejudice.

Issue Lineal descendents, such as children, grandchildren, and great-grandchildren.

Issuer One who officially distributes an item or document.

Joint venture A commercial or maritime enterprise undertaken by several persons jointly; an association of two or more persons to carry out a single business enterprise for profit.

Judgment as a matter of law A decision by the court to remove the issue from the jury because there is only one possible answer to the issue.

Judgment debtor A person against whom a judgment has been entered.

Judicial questions Questions that are proper for a court to decide.

Judicial restraint A judicial policy of refusing to hear and decide certain types of cases.

Judicial review The power of the courts to say what the law is.

Junior secured parties Any secured parties whose security interests are subordinate to that of the foreclosing secured party.

Justiciability Capable of a court decision; decidable by a court.

Knocking down The acceptance of a bid by an auctioneer, signified by the falling of the gavel after the announcement that the goods are "Going, going, gone."

Laissez-faire Let (the people) do as they choose; a doctrine opposing governmental interference in economic affairs beyond the minimum necessary for the maintenance of peace and property rights.

Land use regulation Laws that regulate the possession, ownership, and use of real property.

Landlocked Surrounded by land owned by others.

Lapse The expiration or the loss of an opportunity because of the passage of a time limit within which the opportunity had to be exercised.

Law merchant The system of rules, customs, and usages generally recognized and adopted by merchants and traders, and that constituted the law for their transactions.

Leachings Oozing of water that contains soil, sediments, chemicals, and other impurities.

Leases Contracts that grant the right to use and occupy realty.

Lessor Individual or company owner who rents out property.

Letters of credit Agreements made at the request of a customer that, upon another party's compliance with the conditions specified in the documents, the bank will honor drafts or other demands for payment.

Libel Any written or printed statement that tends to expose a person to public ridicule or injures a person's reputation.

License A permission granted by a competent authority to do some act that, without such authorization, would be illegal or a trespass or a tort.

Lien creditor One whose debt is secured by a claim on specific property.

Limited partner A limited-partnership member who furnishes certain funds to the partnership and whose liability is restricted to the funds provided.

Limited partnership A partnership where some partners' liability is limited to their contribution.

Liquidate To settle with creditors and debtors and apportion any remaining assets.

Liquidation preferences Priorities given to creditors and owners when the enterprise is terminated and the assets are distributed.

Lockout A plant closing or any other refusal by an employer to furnish work to employees during labor disputes.

Logotypes Identifying symbols.

Mala *prohibita* Wrong because it is prohibited.

Manifest A list or invoice.

Market value The current price the stock will sell for on a stock exchange.

Marshal To arrange assets or claims in such a way as to secure the proper application of the assets to the claims.

Mechanic's lien Given to certain builders, artisans, and providers of material, a statutory protection that grants a lien on the building and the land improved by such persons.

Mercantile Having to do with business, commerce, or trade.

Merchant A person who regularly deals in goods of this kind, or otherwise, through his or her occupation, holds him- or herself out as having knowledge or skill peculiar to the practice or goods involved in the transaction.

Midnight deadline Midnight of the next business day after the day on which an item is received.

Mining partnership An association of several owners of a mine for cooperation in working the mine.

Money A legally recognized medium of exchange authorized or adopted by a government.

Monopoly The power of a firm to carry on a business or a trade to the exclusion of all competitors.

Moot Abstract; a point not properly submitted to the court for a resolution. A point not capable of resolution.

Moot case A case not properly submitted to a court for resolution because it seeks to determine an abstract question that does not arise upon the existing fact pattern.

Mortgage insurance Insurance that will provide funds to pay the mortgage balance on a home if the insured dies.

Mortgages Conditional transfers of property as security for a debt.

Motion Request to a judge to take certain action. These requests are often in writing.

Mutual assent The parties agree to be bound by exactly the same terms.

Negative clearance Permission given by the EU Commission to a firm(s) to act in a manner that appears to violate EU competition laws.

Negligence Failure to do something a reasonable person would do, or doing something a reasonable and prudent person would not do.

Negligence per se Inherent negligence; negligence without a need for further proof.

Negotiable A document that is transferable either by endorsement and delivery or by delivery alone.

Negotiable instruments Checks, drafts, notes, and certificates of deposit; governed by Article 3 of the UCC, negotiable instruments are used for credit and/or as substitutes for money.

Nolo contendere A plea in a criminal proceeding that has the same effect as a plea of guilty but that cannot be used as evidence of guilt.

North American Free Trade Agreement (NAFTA) The North American Free Trade Agreement is a treaty between the United States, Canada, and Mexico designed to create a free-trade zone within North America.

Novations By mutual agreement, substitutions of new contracts in place of preexisting ones, whether between the same parties or with new parties replacing one or more of the original parties.

Nuisance Unlawful use of one's own property so as to injure the rights of another. Wrongs that arise from the unreasonable or unlawful use of a person's own property.

Object code Translation of source code into lower-level language, consisting of numbers and symbols that the computer converts into electronic impulses (machine language).

Objective Capable of being observed and verified without being distorted by personal feelings and prejudices.

Obviousness of hazard The hazard in the product is obvious, such as a sharp knife.

Oligopoly An economic condition in which a small number of firms dominates a market, but no one firm controls it.

Operating system computer programs Collections of systems software programs designed to help someone else program or use a computer and that allow the computer to execute programs and manage programming tasks.

Operation of law Certain automatic results that must occur following certain actions or facts because of established legal principles and not as the result of any voluntary choice by the parties involved.

Option A privilege existing in one person, for the giving of consideration, which allows him or her to accept an offer at any time during a specified period.

Output contract A contract that calls for the buyer to purchase all the seller's production during the term of the contract.

Outsiders Directors who are not shareholders or officers.

Overdraft A check or draft written by the drawer for an amount in excess of the amount on account, and accepted by the drawee.

Parol evidence Oral statements.

Parol evidence rule A rule stating that when contracts are in writing, only the writing can be used to show the terms of the contract.

Par value The face value assigned to a stock and printed on the stock certificate.

Party Plaintiff or defendant in the lawsuit.

Perjuries False statements made under oath during court proceedings.

Personal property Property that is not real estate.

Personal representative A person who manages the financial affairs of another or an estate.

Petit jurors Ordinary jurors comprising the panel for the trial of a civil or criminal action.

Picketing Union activity in which persons stand near a place of work affected by an organizational drive or a strike so as to influence workers regarding union causes.

Plaintiff A person who files a lawsuit; the person who complains to the court.

Pleadings Statements filed in court specifying the claims of the parties.

Pledge A debtor's delivery of collateral to a creditor, who will possess the collateral until the debt is paid.

Plenary Full; complete; absolute.

Poison pill Any strategy adopted by the directors of a target firm in order to decrease the firm's attractiveness to an acquiring firm during an attempted hostile takeover.

Political questions Questions that would encroach on executive or legislative powers, concerning government, the state, or politics.

Postdeprivation After a deprivation or taking away.

Post-loss Obligations of insurance companies after a covered loss has actually occurred.

Precedents Decided cases that establish legal authority for later cases.

Preempt Seize upon to the exclusion of others. Taken over by the federal government to the exclusion of the state government.

Prejudicial Causing harm, injurious, disadvantageous, or detrimental.

Prepayment clauses Contract clauses that allow the debtor to pay the debt before it is due without penalty.

Prescriptive theory Theory that reports what people should do or what should occur.

Presentment A demand by a holder for the maker or the drawee of a negotiable instrument to accept and/or pay the instrument.

Presumed Assumed.

Preventive law Law designed to prevent harm or wrongdoing before it occurs.

Prima facie At first sight; on its face; something presumed to be true because of its appearance unless disproved by evidence to the contrary.

Privatization The process of going from government ownership of business and other property to private individual ownership.

Privilege A particular benefit or advantage beyond the common advantages of other citizens; an exceptional right, power, franchise, or immunity held by a person, class, or company.

Privity of contract Direct contractual relationship with another party.

Pro se Prepared by an individual appearing in his or her own behalf without hiring an attorney.

Proactive Identifying potential problem areas and participating in resolving them.

Probate The procedure for verifying that a will is authentic and should be implemented.

Probate codes State statutes that deal with the estates of incompetents and people who have died with or without a valid will.

Procedural law The methods of enforcing rights or obtaining redress for the violation of rights.

Professional In the sense used here, a member of a "learned profession," such as a doctor, a lawyer, or an accountant.

Professional corporation A corporation providing professional services by licensed professionals.

Profits The gain made in the enterprise, after deducting the costs incurred for labor, materials, rents, and all other expenses.

Promisee One to whom a promise or commitment has been made.

Promisors Those who make a promise or commitment.

Promissory estoppel A doctrine that prohibits a promisor from denying the making of a promise or from escaping the liability for that promise because of the justifiable reliance of the promisee that the promise would be kept.

Promissory note A written promise to pay a sum certain in money without conditions, either at a preset time in the future or "on demand."

Proprietary Characterized by private, exclusive ownership.

Proprietorship A business with legal rights or exclusive title vested in one individual; a solely owned business.

Prothonotary Title used in some states to designate the chief clerk of courts.

Proximate cause An act that naturally and foreseeably leads to harm or injury to another.

Proxy A person appointed and designated to act for another, especially at a public meeting.

Public domain Lands that are open to public use.

Purported Gave the impression that authority was present.

Quantifiable Capable of exact statement; measurable, normally in numbers.

Quasi *in rem* jurisdiction Authority obtained through property under the control of the court.

Quasi-judicial Partly judicial; empowered to hold hearings but not trials.

Quasi-legislative Partly legislative; empowered to enact rules and regulations but not statutes.

Quiet title Proceeding to establish that the petitioner is the owner of property.

Ratification Accepting an act that was unauthorized when committed and becoming bound to that act upon its acceptance.

Reactive Permitting others to act first and waiting to see what develops.

Real property Real estate and property permanently attached to real estate.

Rebuttable presumption A legal assumption that will be followed until a stronger proof or presumption is presented.

Receiver An unbiased person appointed by a court to receive, preserve, and manage the funds and property of a party.

Recognitional picketing Prohibited picketing in which a union attempts to force recognition of a union different from the currently certified bargaining representative.

Reformation Equitable remedy whereby a court corrects a written instrument in order to remove a mistake and to make the agreement conform to the terms to which the parties originally had agreed.

Registered agent Person designated by a corporation to receive service of process within the state.

Rejection A refusal to accept what is offered.

Rejects Refuses to accept something when it is offered.

Relative Not capable of exact statement or measurable; comparative.

Remainder beneficiaries Persons with an interest in what remains in the trust corpus after use by the income beneficiaries.

Remand The return of a case to the lower court for additional hearings.

Remanded Sent back; sending a case back to the court from which it came for purposes of having some action taken on it there.

Remedies Methods for enforcing rights or preventing the violation of rights.

Removed A request to have the case moved to another court.

Replevin Similar to specific performance, but the object of the contract is not unique; it must be currently unavailable.

Replevy Acquire possession of goods unlawfully held by another.

Repudiation Rejection of an offered or available right or privilege, or of a duty or relation.

Requirements contract A contract in which the seller agrees to provide as much of a product or service as the buyer needs during the contract term.

Res judicata A rule of civil law that states that a person will not be sued more than once by the same party for the same civil wrong.

Residuary clause A clause that disposes of the remainder (the residual) of an estate.

Restitutionary An equitable basis by which the law restores an injured party to the position he or she would have enjoyed had a loss not occurred.

Reverse discrimination Claims by whites that they have been subjected to adverse employment decisions because of their race and the application of employment discrimination statutes designed to protect minorities.

Revests Vests again; is acquired a second time.

Revocation The cancellation, rescission, or annulment of something previously done or offered.

Rhetoric The art or science of using words effectively.

Right of representation Right of children to inherit in their parent's place, if the parent is deceased.

ROM chips (read-only memory chips) Computer chips on which the data and information used to run computer operating systems are affixed; chips that can be "read" by a computer program but generally cannot be changed or altered.

Royalty fee Payment made in exchange for the granting of a right or a license.

RPAPL Abbreviation for New York statute on real estate entitled Real Property Actions and Proceedings Law.

Scienter Guilty knowledge; specifically, one party's prior knowledge of the cause of a subsequent injury to another person.

Seasonably Timely; something occurring in a prompt or timely manner.

Secondary boycotts Union activities meant to pressure parties not involved in the labor dispute and to influence the affected employer.

Secondary liability Conditional responsibility; liability following denial of primary liability.

Secured transactions Credit arrangements, covered by Article 9 of the UCC, in which the creditor retains a security interest in certain assets of the debtor.

Securities exchanges Organized secondary markets in which investors buy and sell securities at central locations.

Security interest Collateral interest taken in the property of another to secure payment of a debt or contract performance.

Separate property states States in which married couples cannot create community property.

Service marks Distinctive symbols designating the services offered by a particular business or individual.

Service of process Delivery of a notice to the person named to inform that person of the nature of the legal dispute.

Severance pay Wages paid upon the termination of one's job.

Shuttle mediation Mediation technique in which the mediator physically separates the parties during the session and then runs messages between them.

Slander Any oral statement that tends to expose a person to public ridicule or injures a person's reputation.

Solicitation A situation in which one person convinces another to engage in a criminal activity.

Source code Human-readable version of the program that gives instructions to the computer.

Sovereign Above or superior to all others; that from which all authority flows.

Specific performance A court order that the breaching party perform the contract as agreed; the object of the contract must be unique.

Stale checks Checks that a bank may dishonor due to their age (over six months old) without regard to the drawer's account balance.

Standing Legal involvement; the right to sue.

Stare decisis To abide by, or adhere to, decided cases; policy of courts to stand by decided cases and not to disturb a settled point of law.

Stated capital The amount of consideration received by the corporation for all shares of the corporation.

Statute of Frauds A statute requiring that specified types of contracts be in writing in order to be enforceable.

Statutory Created by statute; imposed by law.

Strict liability Liability for an action simply because it occurred and caused damage, and not because it is the fault of the person who must pay.

Sua sponte Voluntarily, without prompting or suggestion, of his or her own will or motion.

Subject matter jurisdiction The power of a court to hear certain kinds of legal questions.

Subjective Capable of being observed and verified through individual feelings and emotions.

Subpoena duces tecum A court order to produce evidence at a trial.

Substantially impair Make worth a great deal less, seriously harm or injure, or reduce in value.

Substantive law The portion of law that creates and defines legal rights. It is distinct from the law that defines how laws should be enforced in court.

Suit Lawsuit; the formal legal proceeding used to resolve a legal dispute.

Summons A writ requiring the sheriff to notify the person named that he or she must appear in court to answer a complaint.

Supervening Coming or happening as something additional or unexpected.

Surcharged Assessed a fee by the court for failure to follow fiduciary duties.

Surety A person who promises to pay or to perform in the event the principal debtor fails to do so.

Tenancy in partnership A special form of ownership of property, found only in partnerships, that gives each partner an equal right to possess and to use partnership assets for partnership purposes and that carries a right of survivorship.

Tender An offer to perform; an offer to satisfy an obligation.

Test A case brought to ascertain an important legal principle or right.

Testamentary Pertaining to a will.

Testamentary capacity Sufficient mental capability or sanity to execute a valid will.

Testator A man who makes a will.

Testatrix A woman who makes a will.

Things in action A personal right; an intangible claim not yet reduced to possession, but recoverable in a suit at law.

Time-price differential sales contracts Contracts with a difference in price based on the date of payment, with one price for an immediate payment and another for a payment at a later date.

Title Legal ownership of property; also, evidence of ownership.

Tortfeasor A wrongdoer; one who commits a tort.

Tortious Relating to private or civil wrongs or injuries.

Trademarks Distinctive marks or symbols used to identify a particular company as the source of its products.

Transfer tax Tax on the ability to transfer assets.

Transportation Carrying or conveying from one place to another; the removal of goods or persons from one place to another.

Treble damages A statutory remedy that allows the successful plaintiff to recover three times the damages suffered as a result of the injury.

Trust An arrangement in which legal title, indicated on the deed or other evidence of ownership, is separated from the equitable or beneficial ownership. An arrangement in which one person or business holds property and invests it for another.

Trust deed A legal document that specifies the recipients of a trust, their interests, and how the trust should be managed; also called a deed of trust.

Trustee in bankruptcy The person appointed by the bankruptcy court to act as trustee of the debtor's property for the benefit and protection of the creditors.

Trustees Persons in whom a power is vested under an express or implied agreement in order to exercise the power for the benefit of another.

Ultra vires Acts beyond the scope of the power of a corporation.

Uncollateralized Having no underlying security to guarantee performance.

Unconscionability Condition of being so unreasonably favorable to one party, or so one-sided, as to shock the conscience.

Unconscionable Blatantly unfair and one-sided; so unfair as to shock the conscience.

Underwriters Persons or institutions that, by agreeing to sell securities to the public and to buy those not sold, ensure the sale of corporate securities.

Undue influence Wrongful use of trust and confidence to obtain a gift or contract.

Unfair labor practices Employment or union activities that are prohibited by law as injurious to labor policies.

Uniform Commercial Code (UCC) State statutory provisions covering various aspects of commercial law in the United States.

United Nations Convention on Contracts for the International Sale of Goods (CISG) A treaty developed by the United Nations and intended to provide uniform treatment for contracts involving the international sales of goods.

Unsecured creditor A general creditor; a creditor whose claim is not secured by collateral.

U.S.C. Abbreviation for the United States Code (statutes).

Vested interest A fixed interest or right to something, even though actual possession may be postponed until later.

Vicarious liability Legal responsibility for the wrong committed by another person.

Viruses Computer programs that destroy, damage, rearrange, or replace computer data.

Voir dire The examination of potential jurors to determine their competence to serve on the jury.

Waiver The voluntary surrender of a legal right; the intentional surrender of a right.

Warehousemen Persons engaged in the business of receiving and storing the goods of others for a fee.

Warranties Representations that become part of the contract and that are made by a seller of goods at the time of the sale and that concern the character, quality, or nature of the goods.

Warranty of authority Implied warranties that the agent is an agent for the principal and is permitted to act in this manner.

Wildcat strikes Unauthorized withholdings of services or labor during the term of a contract.

Winding up Paying the accounts and liquidating the assets of a business for the purpose of making distributions and dissolving the concern.

With prejudice A dismissal of a lawsuit that also prohibits reinitiating the lawsuit.

Workers' compensation Payments to injured workers based on the provisions in the state workers' compensation statute.

Writ A writing issued by a court in the form of a letter ordering some designated activity.

Writ of execution A court-issued writing that enforces a judgment or decree.

Wrongful death Unlawful death. It does not necessarily involve a crime.

*This is a landmark case.

*This is a landmark case.

*This is a landmark case.

*This is a landmark case.

*This is a landmark case.

NAME	WEB ADDRESS
Legal Information Institute (LII)—Workers' Compensation Law Materials	http://wwwsecure.law.cornell.edu/topics/workers_compensation.html
Limited liability companies	http://www.llcweb.com/
LRP Publications	http://www.lexis-nexis.com
Magnuson-Moss Warranty Act—15 USC §§ 2301–2312	http://www4.law.cornell.edu/uscode/15/ch50.html
The Multilaterals Project	http://www.fletcher.tufts.edu/
National Conference of Commissioners on Uniform State Laws (NCCUSL)	http://www.nccusl.org
NCCUSL: Transfer on Death Security Registration	http://www.nccusl.org/pressreleases/pr1-00-1.htm
NCCUSL: Revised Uniform Partnership Act	http://www.nccusl.org/pressreleases/pr1-00-5.htm
NCCUSL: Uniform Acts	http://www.nccusl.org/uniformacts.htm
NCCUSL: The Uniform Partnership Act (1994)(1997)	http://www.nccusl.org/uniformact_factsheets/uniformacts-fs-upa9497.htm
NCCUSL: Uniform Partnership Act (1994)	http://www.nccusl.org/uniformact_summaries/uniformacts-s-upa1994.htm
National Fraud Information Center	http://www.fraud.org./
National Labor Relations Board	http://www.nlrb.gov/
The National Registry of Experts (NRE)	http://www.expert-registry.com/
New York Law Publishing Company	http://www.lexis-nexis.com
"Non-Compete Agreements"	http://www.womenconnect.com/
Occupational Safety and Health Administration (OSHA)	http://www.osha.gov/index.html
Oyez Oyez Oyez: A Supreme Court Resource	http://oyez.nwu.edu
Pace University School of Law Institute of International Commercial Law (IICL)	http://www.cisg.law.pace.edu/
The Patent Examiner	http://www.arentfox.com/quickguide/businesslines/intlprop/patentexaminer/newsalerts/corpusurviv/corpsurviv.html
Patent and Trademark Office (PTO)	http://www.uspto.gov/
Preservation of Consumers' Claims and Defenses—16 C.F.R. 433	http://www.arentfox.com/al404.html
Racketeer Influenced and Corrupt Organizations (RICO) Act, 18 U.S.C. § 1961	http://www4.law.cornell.edu/uscode/18/1961.html
Robinson–Patman Act—15 U.S.C. § 13	http://www4.law.cornell.edu/uscode/15/13.html
Securities Act of 1933	http://www.law.uc.edu/CCL/33Act/
Securities and Exchange Commission (SEC)	http://www.sec.gov/
Securities Exchange Act of 1934	http://www.law.uc.edu/CCL/34Act/
Sherman Antitrust Act 15 USC §§ 1–7	http://www4.law.cornell.edu/uscode/15/1.html
Social Security Administration (SSA)	http://www.ssa.gov/
Society of Professionals in Dispute Resolution (SPIDR)	http://www.spidr.org/
StateLaw	http://www.washlaw.edu
Students for Responsible Business (SRB)	http://www.srbnet.org/
TenantNet	http://tenant.net/
Thomas: Legislative Information on the Internet	http://thomas.loc.gov/
Trial Behavior Consulting, Incorporated	http://www.trialbehavior.com